MARKESINIS AND DEAKIN'S TORT LAW

Sixth Edition

BY

SIMON DEAKIN, ANGUS JOHNSTON, AND BASIL MARKESINIS

CLARENDON PRESS · OXFORD

OXFORD
UNIVERSITY PRESS

Great Clarendon Street, Oxford OX2 6DP

Oxford University Press is a department of the University of Oxford.
It furthers the University's objective of excellence in research, scholarship,
and education by publishing worldwide in

Oxford New York

Auckland Cape Town Dar es Salaam Hong Kong Karachi
Kuala Lumpur Madrid Melbourne Mexico City Nairobi
New Delhi Shanghai Taipei Toronto

With offices in

Argentina Austria Brazil Chile Czech Republic France Greece
Guatemala Hungary Italy Japan Poland Portugal Singapore
South Korea Switzerland Thailand Turkey Ukraine Vietnam

Oxford is a registered trade mark of Oxford University Press
in the UK and in certain other countries

Published in the United States
by Oxford University Press Inc., New York

British Library Cataloguing in Publication Data
Data available

Library of Congress Cataloging in Publication Data
Data Available

Typeset by Newgen Imaging Systems (P) Ltd., Chennai, India

Printed and bound in Great Britain by
William Clowes Ltd, Beccles, Suffolk

ISBN 978–0–19–928246–3 (pbk)
ISBN 978–0–19–928657–7 (hbk)

1 3 5 7 9 10 8 6 4 2

PREFACE TO THE SIXTH EDITION

Some time ago a British Prime Minister famously remarked that 'a week in politics is a long time'. If that is true, then four years—the time which has lapsed since the last edition saw the light of day—represents a very considerable time span in the life of Tort Law during which courts and Parliament have both played their parts in making it necessary not just to revise but at times to rewrite large chunks of this book. This, however, does not mean that all the parts of this book have been subjected to the same degree of reconsideration and rewriting; nor, indeed, have they been allocated the same amount of space. For the time may well be approaching when those who teach the subject or write about it should realise that the contours of tort textbooks should be radically revised, so as to omit subjects which though, perhaps, intellectually interesting, occupy only slightly the real world or, conversely, include topics which trespass into areas, such as administrative law and human rights law, which have traditionally been left to other books to examine. The moment for such a major revolution has not yet quite arrived; and since different teachers still like a broad menu from which to make their own choices, we have still attempted to provide a fairly comprehensive treatment of all topics which have, over the years, been brought under the heading of torts or civil wrongs. But one change will be immediately obvious; and it was prompted by the many, friendly and most useful suggestions made (anonymously) to the publisher by the teachers who use this book. Most thus asked us (among other things) to 'cut down' the size of our chapters into smaller, more manageable units in a way that would allow both them and their students to focus quickly on only those topics which were going to be discussed in the classroom. We complied with pleasure; and in retrospect feel embarrassed that we did not notice this need ourselves. We also regret that we do not know their names to thank them individually for the trouble they took to be constructively critical about our book. But we write largely for an audience; and ours has been helpfully critical for over twenty years now, so much so that it is tempting to dedicate this book to them.

Indeed, this is the sixth edition to appear in the space of just over twenty years, largely thanks to the initiative of the then Editor of the Oxford University Press, Mr Adam Hodgkin. Like all editors in such responsible positions he sought advice on the new proposal. The reactions were positive on the contents; but they were also accompanied by the warning 'that there was no room for another textbook on tort'. We are grateful to Adam Hodgkin for allowing his professional experience to decide this issue and gratified that we have proved him right. Our debt to him continues towards all of his successors who have backed the book and the staff of the Press who have in so many ways worked closely to help us make it the success we think it has become.

As a textbook, our work retains as its main ambition the task of presenting the law, in its ever-growing complexity, as accurately and as clearly as we could achieve this. To do this we have consciously sacrificed 'pedantic accuracy' to readability (though the numerous and, at times, long footnotes give some indication of our wish to be as complete and as accurate as we could) in presenting the complex material. At the same time, however, we have strengthened the already existing tendency not only to give our own views on controversial issues as clearly and boldly as we could, but also to try to present the whole area of torts law in the form of recurring and important themes. One—the growing foreign influence, mainly emanating from the two European Courts of Luxembourg and Strasbourg—has already been mentioned and all that one can do is to note how much it is growing in its breadth and depth.

The other theme that runs through this book is the concern we feel at the growing ferocity with which some authors (and judges) are desperately trying to cut down the reach of tort. Our concern at this movement is strongly felt (and strongly voiced) because we note that, at the same time that tort is being 'closed down', the frontiers of the welfare state are being folded back. All this is happening at a time when the increase in the financial differential between those who are rich and those who are not well off is getting bigger and bigger. If that sounds like a political concern one must admit that it is but only to a point. For our aim is not to promote one set of political ideas over another—between us we hold a variety of eclectic opinions and do not share the same views on all matters anyway—but to make sure that victims of accidents are not left totally unprotected because of the ability of academics (and some judges) to manipulate complex notions in the vacuum of a legal laboratory. The book thus displays a marked attachment to an idea best expressed by the current Senior Law Lord—Lord Bingham—that '[i]f [the child/claimant] can make good her complaints (a vital condition, which I forebear constantly to repeat), it would require very potent considerations of public policy, which do not in my view exist here, to override *the rule of public policy which has first claim on the loyalty of the law: that wrongs should be remedied*'.[1]

This intellectual duel that we have with those who believe that the 'default position is no liability' has reached new heights in the area of statutory liability, but not only there. Again, we feel we have to point all this out to our readers. If the result of our philosophy results in provoking thinking and argument, so much the better for that is what education is really all about. And a good Preface in a book is like a good overture to an opera: it should aim to give the reader/listener a foretaste of what is to follow.

There is another reason why we have not tried to hide the impact that politics and politically motivated legislation is having on our subject which, on the face of it, is a so-called 'black letter law' subject and not one overtly linked to politics as, say, constitutional law is. This is because we feel that the students of today are knowledgeable enough to realise that even tort legislation may reflect a political agenda, for instance, an attempt to save money for the National Health Service, without, perhaps, fully working out the economic consequences that such decisions may have on other sectors of the economy such as for instance the insurance industry. Professor Richard Lewis has made this point in an article published in the *Modern Law Review* in 2006 when commenting on the Courts Act 2003 which introduced as of 2005 the possibility of our courts ordering compensation to be paid in the form of periodical payments. An important

[1] Sir Thomas Bingham (as he then was) in *M.* v. *Newham LBC* and *X* v. *Bedfordshire CC* [1994] 2 WLR 554 at 571.

but 'dry' topic such as the law of damages acquires a new and livelier dimension if it is so seen and analysed.

The same, we think, is true of the emerging tort of privacy which our judges still prefer to call breach of confidence and on which they hold widely varying views while also pretending (as the judgments in the House of Lords in the *Campbell* case show) to be reading from the same hymn sheet. Much can be said for keeping up appearances and concealing from the student deep judicial divergences on specific issues. Equally, much can also be said in drawing their attention to these human factors, these differences in outlook and mental disposition, which lead judges—and have always led judges—to decide the same issues differently while remaining loyal to their judicial oath. We have opted to follow, where appropriate, this second approach, in the belief that it will give students a fairer picture of what is happening in the real world and academic colleagues the chance to use our views as a starting-point in order to push students into doing some thinking of their own. Hiding judicial differences, philosophies and even rivalries has thus not been high on our agenda, for our students should realise that these factors, too, may help shape the final judgment.

Books such as these are not written without incurring considerable intellectual debts. We have already acknowledged the help received anonymously by colleagues who use this book as a teaching tool. To the anonymous counsellors one must also add the eponymous ones. To those already thanked in previous editions we now add Professor Mads Andenas of the University of Leicester, Professor Hannes Unberath of the University of Jena (Germany), Dr Colm O'Cinneide of University College London, and Mr John Randall QC. Likewise a deep sense of gratitude is, once again, expressed towards our Texan colleagues Professor David Anderson and Professor David Robertson for updating what have become highly acclaimed and oft-quoted chapters on American law. These are intended to make our (mainly) British readers look at their own system in comparative juxtaposition with that of the United States which is nowadays—arguably—producing some of the most challenging—occasionally also infuriating—new ideas on our subject but is also going through a period of retrenchment compared to where it was some twenty-five years ago. Finally, though Professor—now Judge—Andrew Grubb was unable to join us in this edition because of his joining the Bench, we take the opportunity to thank him again for past contributions and to state the obvious, *viz.*, that the loss to academy is the gain to the Bench.

The book takes into account development in the law up to the end of March 2007. It has also been possible to incorporate references to the decisions of the House of Lords in *OBG Ltd.* v. *Allan*, *Douglas* v. *Hello! Ltd. (No. 3)* and *Mainstream* v. *Young*, which were handed down on 2 May 2007, and *Sempra Metals Ltd.* v *IRC*, handed down on 18 July 2007 (although this decision came too late for us to analyse it in any depth).

Sir Basil Markesinis, QC, FBA
University of Texas at Austin
Simon Deakin, FBA
University of Cambridge
Angus Johnston
University of Cambridge
Vernal Equinox 2007

Books such as these are [illegible] without incurring considerable intellectual debts. We have already acknowledged the help received from [illegible] colleagues who use this book as a teaching tool. To the anonymous [illegible] we [illegible] add those of many more [illegible] to those already listed in previous editions we [illegible] Professor [illegible] of the University of [illegible], Professor [illegible] of the University of [illegible], Dr Colm O'Cinneide of University College London and Mr [illegible] QC [illegible] a deep sense of gratitude [illegible] [illegible] colleagues Professor David Anderson and Professor [illegible] [illegible] [illegible] [illegible] on [illegible] law, there are [illegible] [illegible] [illegible] [illegible] own [illegible] comparative [illegible] with [illegible] [illegible] [illegible] some of the most challenging [illegible] [illegible] subject but [illegible] [illegible] [illegible] [illegible] some twenty [illegible] years. Finally, [illegible] Professor—now Judge—[illegible] unable to join us in this edition because of his [illegible] the opportunity to thank him again for past contributions and [illegible] to the Bench.

Basil Markesinis QC, [illegible]

[illegible]

[illegible]

[illegible] 2007

OUTLINE TABLE OF CONTENTS

Preface to the Sixth Edition v

Abbreviations xxix

Table of United Kingdom Cases xxxix

Table of Cases from Other Jurisdictions lxxvii

Table of United Kingdom Legislation lxxxix

Table of Legislation from Other Jurisdictions xcvii

Table of International Instruments xcix

PART I SETTING THE SCENE

1 INTRODUCTION 3

2 SOME GENERAL WARNINGS FOR THE NOVICE TORT LAWYER 73

PART II THE TORT OF NEGLIGENCE

3 ESTABLISHING LIABILITY IN PRINCIPLE 113

4 OTHER ELEMENTS OF LIABILITY 223

5 AN AMERICAN PERSPECTIVE ON NEGLIGENCE LAW 283

PART III SPECIAL FORMS OF NEGLIGENCE

6 LIABILITY FOR OCCUPIERS AND BUILDERS 341

7 BREACH OF STATUTORY DUTY 377

8 LIABILITY OF PUBLIC AND STATUTORY BODIES 397

PART IV INTERFERENCE WITH THE PERSON

9 INTENTIONAL INTERFERENCE 451

10 MALICIOUS PROSECUTION 475

PART V LAND, CHATTELS AND INTENTIONAL INTERFERENCE WITH ECONOMIC INTERESTS

11 INTERFERENCE WITH CHATTELS 483
12 LAND 495
13 LESSER INTERFERENCE WITH LAND: NUISANCE 509
14 DECEIT 565
15 THE ECONOMIC TORTS 571

PART VI STRICTER FORMS OF LIABILITY

16 THE RULE IN *RYLANDS V. FLETCHER* 607
17 LIABILITY FOR ANIMALS 631
18 EMPLOYER'S LIABILITY 649
19 VICARIOUS LIABILITY 665
20 PRODUCT LIABILITY 703

PART VII PROTECTION OF HUMAN DIGNITY (IN PRIVATE LAW)

21 DEFAMATION AND INJURIOUS FALSEHOOD 753
22 THE PROTECTION OF HUMAN PRIVACY 819
23 DEFAMATION AND PRIVACY: AN AMERICAN PERSPECTVE 865

PART VIII DEFENCES AND REMEDIES

24 DEFENCES 891
25 DAMAGES 939
26 OTHER REMEDIES AND MULTIPLE LIABILITIES 1029

Index 1043

CONTENTS

Preface to the Sixth Edition v
Abbreviations xxix
Table of United Kingdom Cases xxxix
Table of Cases from Other Jurisdictions lxxvii
Table of United Kingdom Legislation lxxxix
Table of Legislation from Other Jurisdictions xcvii
Table of International Instruments xcix

PART I SETTING THE SCENE

1 INTRODUCTION 3
1 Tort at the Crossroads 3
2 Tort and Contract 17
(A) The Division between Contract and Tort 17
(B) The Escape 'Into' Tort Prompted by a Rigidly Conceived Law of Contract 22
(C) The Escape 'Out' of Contract and into the Domain of Tort 27
3 Elements of Wrongdoing and the Role of Policy 30
4 Economic Analysis of Tort Law 36
(A) Some General Remarks 36
(B) The 'Coase Theorem' and the Concept of Transaction Costs 38
(C) Accident Compensation and Internalisation 41
(D) The Theory of the Inherent Efficiency of the Common Law 42
(E) Empirical Studies of the Effects of Tort Law 44
(F) Economic Analysis in the Context of One Tort Case: The *Norsk* Decision 45
(i) The Facts of *Norsk* 45
(ii) The Majority and Concurring Opinions 45
(iii) The Minority 47
5 Functions of Tort 49
6 Fault as the Basis of Tortious Liability 55

7 Alternative Systems of Compensation 58
(A) First Level 62
(B) Second Level 62
(i) Criminal Injuries Compensation Schemes 62
(ii) Compensation Orders 66
(iii) The Motor Insurers' Bureau 68
(iv) Special *Ex Gratia* Payment Schemes 69
(C) Third Level 70

2 SOME GENERAL WARNINGS FOR THE NOVICE TORT LAWYER 73
1 General Comments 73
2 Judicial Mentality and Outlook, and How It Affects Decision-Making 75
3 Academic Interests and Practitioners' Concerns: Close or Far Apart? 82
4 Ivory Tower Neatness v. The Untidiness of the Real World 87
5 Tort's Struggle to Solve Modern Problems with Old Tools 91
6 Tort Law Needs to Be Reformed but Systematic Reform Remains Unlikely 93
7 Are Liability Rules Restricted because the Damages Rules Have Been Left Unreformed or because the Relationship between Liability and Damages Has Been Neglected? 97
8 Tort Law Is, in Practice, Often Inaccessible to the Ordinary Victim 98
9 Human Rights Law Is Set to Influence Tort Law, but this Influence Is Likely to Be Gradual and Indirect 100
10 Miscellaneous Matters 107

PART II THE TORT OF NEGLIGENCE

3 ESTABLISHING LIABILITY IN PRINCIPLE 113
1 The Duty Concept and the Elements of the Tort of Negligence 113
(A) The Conceptual Structure of Negligence 113
(B) The Duty Concept 116
(C) Duty, Foreseeability and Fault 118
(D) Causation and Damage 120
(E) The Utility of Existing Concepts 123

2 Formulating the Duty of Care 125
(A) Before and After *Anns* 125
(B) The Three-Stage Test 127
(C) The Impact of Human Rights Law on the Duty Concept 132
3 Kinds of Damage 138
(A) Physical (Bodily) Harm and Damage to Property 138
(B) Psychiatric Injury and Illness 139
(i) Defining Psychiatric Harm 139
(ii) Primary Victims 140
(iii) Secondary Victims 142
(a) The Claimant Must Not Have Been Abnormally Susceptible to Psychiatric Illness 145
(b) The Psychiatric Harm Must Have Occurred through 'Shock' 145
(c) The Claimant Must Have Been in Physical Proximity to the Accident or its Aftermath 146
(d) The Claimant Must Have Had a Close Personal or Familial Relationship with the Accident Victim 150
(iv) A 'Relational' Duty of Care with Regard to Psychiatric Well-Being 152
(v) Employees 155
(C) 'Pure' Economic Loss 157
(i) Liability for Negligent Misstatements 160
(ii) Negligence in the Performance of a Service 172
(iii) Pure Economic Loss Arising from Defects in Buildings and Products 180
(iv) Relational Economic Loss Arising from Damage to the Property of a Third Party 185
(v) Overlapping and Concurrent Duties in Contract and Tort 189
(vi) Insurance Considerations and Related Aspects of Policy 195
(vii) The Respective Roles of Parliament and the Courts 197
(viii) Economic Loss: A Summary and Conclusion 198
4 The Manner of Infliction 199
(A) Acts and Omissions 199
(i) A Duty to Rescue? 201
(ii) Failure to Warn 203
(iii) Failure to Take Adequate Precautions 204
(B) Liability for the Acts of Third Parties 205
(i) Parents and Children 205
(ii) Custodial Authorities 205
(iii) Landowners 206
(iv) A Wider Principle? 207

5 Parties 208
(A) Protected Defendants 208
(i) Public Bodies 208
(ii) Persons Involved in the Administration of Justice 213
(iii) Other Professionals 215
(iv) Regulatory Bodies 215
(v) The Armed Forces 216
(B) Protected Claimants 217
(i) Injuries Sustained by the Embryo in the Womb 217
(ii) Rescuers 219

4 OTHER ELEMENTS OF LIABILITY 223
1 Breach of Duty: Negligence as Fault 223
(A) The Objective Standard 227
(i) The Standard of the Reasonable Person 227
(ii) Negligence Distinguished from 'Mere Errors' 227
(iii) General or Variable? 229
(B) Professional Standards 232
(C) Weighing the Risk and Gravity of Harm against the Cost of Prevention 235
(i) Risk and Foreseeability of Damage 236
(ii) Assessing the Costs of Prevention 238
(D) Proof of Carelessness 241
2 Causation of Damage 244
(A) The Nature of the Causal Inquiry 244
(B) But-for Causation 249
(i) 'Probabilistic Cause': Questions of Risk and Proof 249
(ii) 'Indeterminate Cause': Cases involving Multiple Defendants 252
(iii) Exposure to Risk as a Basis for Establishing a Causal Link 254
(iv) Supervening or Overtaking Causes 257
(v) Loss of a Chance 261
3 Remoteness of Damage 266
(A) Intervening Acts of Third Parties 266
(B) Act of the Claimant 268
(C) Foreseeability of the Extent of Damage 271
(D) Foreseeability of the Causal Sequence 274
(E) Remoteness and Damage to Property 276
(F) Remoteness and Pure Economic Loss 277
(G) Remoteness of Damage in Contract and Tort 279
4 The Tort of Negligence: A Summary and Conclusion 281

5 AN AMERICAN PERSPECTIVE ON NEGLIGENCE LAW 283
1 Fundamental Differences in Legal Culture 283
2 The Quest for Conceptual Clarity: The Traditional Model 286
3 Recent Efforts to Revise the Traditional Model 290
4 Pure Economic Damage 293
(A) The Pure Economic Loss Problem Viewed Generally 295
(B) Economic Loss Caused by Negligent Harm to a Public Resource 296
(C) Economic Loss Caused by Negligent Injury to the Person or Property of Another 296
(D) Economic Loss Caused by Negligence in the Performance of a Service 297
(E) Economic Loss Caused by Defects in Buildings and Products 298
(F) Postscript: Bright-Line Rules Seldom Stay Bright for Long 300
5 Psychiatric Injury (Nervous Shock) 302
6 Liability for the Crimes and Intentional Harms of Third Parties 307
(A) A Taxonomic Choice 310
(B) The Legal Causation Issue 311
(C) The Nonfeasance Issue 313
(i) Liability Based on Affirmative Negligent Conduct ('Misfeasance') 314
(ii) Liability Based on the Defendant's Failure to Take Reasonable Steps to Alleviate Dangers Created by the Defendant's Prior Conduct 317
(iii) Liability Based on the Defendant's Failure to Carry Through after Volunteering Assistance 319
(iv) Liability Based on a Pre-Existing Special Relationship between the Defendant and *X* 320
(v) Liability Based on a Pre-Existing Relationship between the Defendant and the Victim 322
7 Recurrent Problems of Factual Causation and Damages 323
(A) Factual Causation in General 323
(B) The Market Share Theory 324
(C) 'Probabilistic Causation' and 'Lost Opportunity' Theories 325
(D) Multiple Tortfeasors Generally 327
(E) Joint and Several Liability 329
(i) The Standard Operation of the Doctrine of Joint and Several Liability 329
(ii) Using a 'Joint and Several Liability' Approach to Solve Cause-in-Fact Problems 329
(F) Pre-Existing Conditions and Looming Threats 331
8 Three Postscripts 333
(A) The Relationship between Intentional Torts and Negligence 333
(B) In the Life of the Law There Is Sometimes Progress 334
(C) The Socio-Political Role of Negligence Law 335

PART III SPECIAL FORMS OF NEGLIGENCE

6 LIABILITY FOR OCCUPIERS AND BUILDERS 341
1 Introductory Remarks 341
2 The Occupiers' Liability Acts 1957 and 1984 343
(A) The Scope of the Acts 343
(B) Occupier 344
(C) Lawful Visitor under the 1957 Act 346
(D) Common Duty of Care 351
(E) Liability for Independent Contractors 359
(F) Protected Entrants under the 1984 Act 363
(i) The Development of the Common Law 363
(ii) The Intervention of the Legislator: The 1984 Act 365
(G) Liability of Non-Occupiers: Vendors, Landlords, Builders, Local Authorities 368
(i) Vendors and Landlords 368
(ii) Builders 371
(iii) Local Authorities 374

7 BREACH OF STATUTORY DUTY 377
1 The Nature of the Action 377
2 The Components of Liability 383
(A) The Availability of a Civil Remedy 383
(B) The Scope of the Civil Remedy 389
(C) Causation, Remoteness and Defences 391
(D) A Wider Principle of Civil Liability? 393
(E) Liability for Breach of Obligations arising under European Community Law 395

8 LIABILITY OF PUBLIC AND STATUTORY BODIES 397
1 The Distinctive Nature of the Liability of the Government, Public Authorities and Statutory Bodies 397
(A) Historical Development 397
(B) Reasons for the Distinctive Nature of Governmental Liability 399
2 The Liability of Statutory Bodies in Negligence 405
(A) The Recognition of a Common Law Action 405

(B) A Qualified Protection from Liability? 407
(i) The Statutory Context 412
(a) Statute as the Source of the Private-Law Action 412
(b) Aligning Public-Law and Private-Law Tests for Determining the Legitimate Exercise of Statutory Powers 414
(c) Statute as Framing the Common-Law Duty of Care 415
(ii) Justiciability and Public Policy 418
(a) Weighing Justiciability and Policy: General Considerations 418
(b) Recent Approaches to Justiciability and Policy: Comparing *Phelps* and *East Berkshire* 422
3 Liability for Breach of Statutory Duty 426
4 Public Law as a Source of Liability 426
(A) Damages for *Ultra Vires* Acts? 426
(B) The Tort of Misfeasance in a Public Office 427
5 Public Law as a Source of Immunity 431
(A) Validity of Administrative Action as a Private-Law Defence 431
(B) Procedural Immunity under CPR Part 54 432
6 Crown Proceedings in Tort 434
7 Liability for Breaches of European Community Law 435
8 Liabilities Arising under the Human Rights Act 1998 438
9 Towards a Synthesis of the Law Relating to Governmental Liability? 445

PART IV INTERFERENCE WITH THE PERSON

9 INTENTIONAL INTERFERENCE 451
1 Introduction: The Meaning of Intentional Interference 451
2 Assault 453
3 Battery 454
(A) Contact 454
(B) Defences 455
4 False Imprisonment 462
(A) Confinement 463
(B) Defences 466
(i) Consent 466
(ii) Justification and Necessity 467
5 Residuary Trespass and Harassment: The Tort in *Wilkinson* v. *Downton* and the Protection from Harassment Act 1997 471

10 MALICIOUS PROSECUTION 475

1 The Defendant Initiated a Prosecution 476

2 The Prosecution Failed 477

3 Absence of Reasonable and Probable Cause 478

4 Malice 479

PART V LAND, CHATTELS AND INTENTIONAL INTERFERENCE WITH ECONOMIC INTERESTS

11 INTERFERENCE WITH CHATTELS 483

1 Introduction 483

2 Trespass to Goods 483

3 Conversion 486

4 Negligence 492

12 LAND 495

1 Trespass to Land *Quaere Clausum Fregit* 495

2 Defences 504

13 LESSER INTERFERENCE WITH LAND: NUISANCE 509

1 Definition 509

2 Basis of Liability 509

3 Unreasonable Interference 513

(A) Material Damage to Property 513

(B) Interference with Use or Enjoyment of Land 520

(i) Duration of Interference 522

(ii) Sensitivity 524

(iii) Character of the Neighbourhood 525

(iv) Fault 526

(v) Malice 528

4 Who Can Sue and Who Can Be Sued? 530

(A) Who Can Sue 530

(B) Who Can Be Sued 535

5 Defences 539

6 Remedies 544
(A) Injunction 544
(B) Abatement 548
7 Public Nuisance 550
8 Nuisance and Other Forms of Liability 556
9 Nuisance and Protection of the Environment 559
(A) Efficiency of the Action in Nuisance 559
(B) Statutory Nuisances 562

14 DECEIT 565
1 A False Statement 565
2 A Statement of Existing Fact 566
3 The Defendant's State of Mind 567
4 Causation 568
5 Damage, Damages and Defences 569

15 THE ECONOMIC TORTS 571
1 The Framework of the Economic Torts 571
2 Wrongful Interference with the Claimant's Pre-Existing Right 575
(A) Inducing Breach of Contract 576
(B) Other Forms of Interference with Contract 580
(i) 'Indirect' Interference with Contract 581
(ii) 'Bare' Interference with Contractual Performance 582
(iii) Making a Contract Less Valuable 585
(C) Inducing Breach of Fiduciary Duty 585
(D) Inducing Breach of Statutory Duty 585
3 Interference with the Claimant's Trade or Business by Unlawful Means 586
(A) Intention to Harm the Claimant 586
(B) Unlawful Means 588
(i) Physical Threats 589
(ii) Fraud and Misrepresentation 589
(iii) Breach of Contract and Inducing Breach of Contract 590
(iv) Crime 592
(v) Interference with Statutory Obligations 593
(vi) Other Categories 594
(C) Economic Duress 595
(D) Defences 595

4 Conspiracy 596
(A) Conspiracy to Injure 596
(B) Conspiracy Using Unlawful Means 597
5 The Trade-Dispute Immunity 598
6 The Future of the Economic Torts 602

PART VI STRICTER FORMS OF LIABILITY

16 THE RULE IN *RYLANDS* V. *FLETCHER* 607
1 General Observations 607
2 The Requirements of Liability 611
(A) The Thing Must Be Brought on to the Defendant's Land (i.e. 'Accumulated') 611
(B) Escape 611
3 Controlling Mechanisms 613
(A) 'Non-Natural Use' of Land 614
(B) Foreseeability 617
(C) Defences 618
(i) Statutory Authority 618
(ii) Consent of the Claimant 619
(iii) Act of Third Party 619
(iv) Act of God 620
(v) Default of the Claimant 621
4 Who is Protected and for What? 621
5 *Rylands* v. *Fletcher* and Nuisance 623
6 *Rylands* v. *Fletcher* and the Future of Strict Liability in General 624

17 LIABILITY FOR ANIMALS 631
1 Application of the General Law 631
2 Liability for Straying Livestock 634
3 Liability for 'Dangerous Animals' 636
4 Liability for Non-Dangerous Animals 638
5 Defences 644
6 Remoteness of Damage and Strict Liability 646
7 Liability for Dogs 646

18 EMPLOYER'S LIABILITY 649
1 Introduction 649
2 The Employer's Liability to his Employees 650
(A) Social Security 650
(B) Tort Law Systems 651
(i) Competent Staff 659
(ii) Adequate Materials 659
(iii) Safe Place of Work 660
(iv) Proper System 661
(C) Statutory Duties 662

19 VICARIOUS LIABILITY 665
1 Identifying the 'Employee' and his 'Employer' 666
2 The Employee Must Commit a Tort 677
3 Course of Employment 678
(A) Policy Factors 679
(B) Tests Based on Implied Authority 680
(C) Distinguishing between 'Authorised Acts' and 'Unauthorised Modes' 682
(D) Road-Traffic Cases: Detour, Deviation and Travel to and from Work 685
(E) Intentional Torts and the Test of 'Sufficient Connection' 687
(i) Theft 687
(ii) Deceit 688
(iii) Sexual and Other Assaults 690
(iv) Harassment 692
4 Contribution between Employer and Employee 693
5 Liability for the Torts of Independent Contractors 695
6 The Changing Contours of Employers' Liability: An Epilogue 697
(A) The Gradual and Unsystematic Expansion of the Non-Delegable Duties 697
(B) Extending the Notion of Employee Status 698
(C) Imposing Additional Affirmative Duties on Employers 698
(D) Purposive Extension of the Vicarious Liability Rules 699
(E) Synthesis of the Employer's Vicarious and Personal Duties? 700

20 PRODUCT LIABILITY 703
1 Introduction 703
2 The Evolution of Product Liability Law in England and America 704

(A) The Rejection of the 'Privity of Contract Fallacy' 704
(B) From Negligence to Strict Liability 708
(i) Liability for Breach of Warranty 708
(ii) Strict Liability in Tort 710
(iii) Directive 85/374/EEC and the Consumer Protection Act 1987 714
(iv) Return to Negligence? 719
3 The Causes of Action and Components of Liability 723
(A) The Parties to the Action 723
(B) The 'Products' Covered 730
(C) The Scope and Standard of Responsibility 731
(i) The Concept of Defect 732
(ii) Special Duties: Duty to Warn and Post-Sale Duties 736
(iii) The Producer's Defences 738
(D) Causation and Remoteness 740
(E) The Categories of Recoverable 'Damage' 742
(F) Exclusion and Limitation of Liability 744
(G) Limitation of Actions 745
(H) Choice of Law 746
4 Conclusion 746

PART VII PROTECTION OF HUMAN DIGNITY (IN PRIVATE LAW)

21 DEFAMATION AND INJURIOUS FALSEHOOD 753
1 Defamation: Introduction 753
(A) The Meaning of 'Defamatory' 753
(B) Libel and Slander 756
2 Defamation: Elements of Liability 759
(A) The Allegation Must Be Defamatory 759
(B) The Defamatory Statement Must Refer to the Claimant 766
(C) Publication 772
3 Defences 779
(A) Unintentional Defamation 779
(B) Consent 782
(C) Justification or Truth 783
(D) Fair Comment 785
(i) Public Interest 786
(ii) True Facts 787

(iii) Fairness 788
(iv) Absence of Malice 790
(E) Privilege 790
(i) Absolute Privilege 791
(a) Parliamentary Privilege 791
(b) Judicial Privileges 792
(c) Executive Privileges 794
(ii) Qualified Privilege 794
(a) Matters of Public Interest 795
(b) Matters of Interest to the Publisher 796
(c) Matters of Interest to Others 796
(d) Common Interest 797
(e) Journalistic Privilege: The *Reynolds* Breakthrough 798
(f) Qualified Privilege Is Defeated by Malice 805
4 Defamation: Damages 806
5 Defamation: Mitigation of Damage 811
(A) Apology 811
(B) Claimant's Reputation 811
6 Defamation: Epilogue 813
7 Injurious Falsehoods and Passing Off 816

22 THE PROTECTION OF HUMAN PRIVACY 819
1 Definitional Difficulties and Other Objections to Recognising a Wider Protection of Privacy 820
2 The Protection Afforded by English Law: Casuistry versus Principle 825
3 The Protection Afforded by English Law in the Most Important Types of Cases 833
(A) Intrusions 833
(B) Appropriation of Personality 835
(C) Public Disclosure of True Private Facts 836
(i) The Growth of the Action for Breach of Confidence 836
(ii) What Is Protected? Continuing the Move away from Confidence and towards Privacy 842
(iii) Weakening the Last of the *Coco* Requirements (Detriment) 844
(iv) Information in the Public Domain 845
(v) Public Figures, Public Officials, Public Functions 849
4 Europe: The Brooding Omnipresence in the Sky 852
5 The Reach of the Human Rights Act 1998 855
6 The Development of English Law: Lessons that Will not Be Learnt 859

23 DEFAMATION AND PRIVACY: AN AMERICAN PERSPECTVE 865
1 English and American Defamation Law Compared 865
2 Public Officials 869
3 Public Figures 872
4 Private Plaintiffs 873
5 Truth and Falsity 877
6 Opinion and Rhetoric 878
7 The Law in Practice 880
8 Invasion of Privacy 883

PART VIII DEFENCES AND REMEDIES

24 DEFENCES 891
1 The Role of Defences in the Law of Torts 891
2 Contributory Negligence 892
(A) Causation and Contributory Negligence 892
(B) Claimant's Fault 897
(C) Apportionment 899
(D) Identification 901
(E) The Scope of the Defence and of the Contributory Negligence Act 1945 901
3 Consent 905
(A) Consent as a Defence to Negligence and Strict Liability 906
(i) Consent as Assumption of Risk 906
(ii) The Scope of the Modern Defence 910
(B) Consent as a Defence to Torts of Intentional Interference 914
4 Exclusion and Limitation of Liability 914
(A) The Nature of the Defence 914
(B) The Application of the Unfair Contract Terms Act 1977 915
(C) Extending the Effect of Exemption Clauses to Third Parties 920
5 Illegality 922
6 Necessity 926
7 Inevitable Accident, Act of God 926
8 Authorisation 927

9 Limitation of Action 927
(A) The Accrual of the Cause of Action 928
(B) The Discoverability Tests under the Limitation Act 1980 931
(C) Limitation and Concurrent Duties in Contract and Tort 932
(D) The Disapplication of the Normal Limitation Rules 936
(E) The Effect of Limitation: Procedural or Substantive? 937
(F) Reform of the Law Relating to Limitation of Actions 937

25 DAMAGES 939
Preliminary Observations 939
1 The Notions of Damage and Damages 940
2 Types of Damages 941
(A) General and Special Damages 941
(B) Nominal and Substantial Damages 942
(C) Contemptuous and Aggravated Damages 942
(D) Punitive (or Exemplary) Damages 944
(E) Compensatory Damages 951
3 The Principle of Full Compensation 951
4 The Interrelationship of Tort and Other Compensation Systems 954
(A) Introductory Remarks 954
(B) Benefits not Covered by the Statutory Regime 956
(i) General Observations 956
(ii) Insurance Moneys 957
(iii) Benevolent Donations 960
(iv) Payments Made by Local Authorities 961
(C) Benefits Subject to the Statutory Regime 962
5 Miscellaneous Matters 965
(A) Lump Sums (and Alternative Options): The Theoretical Options 965
(i) Postponed or Split Trials 967
(ii) Interim Damages 968
(iii) Provisional Damages 968
(iv) Structured Settlements 970
(v) Periodic (and Reviewable) Payments 973
(B) Duty to Mitigate 975
(C) Itemisation of Awards 976

6 Pecuniary Losses 978
(A) Medical and Other Expenses up to the Date of the Trial 978
(i) Generally 978
(ii) Loss of Earnings 979
(iii) Past Medical Care 980
(a) Medical Treatment and Therapies 980
(b) House Care Etc. 980
(c) Personal Expenses 983
(d) Travel Costs 983
(e) Aids and Equipment 984
(f) Accommodation 985
(g) Other Possible Headings 985
(B) Prospective Losses 986
(i) Introductory Remarks 986
(ii) The Multiplicand 987
(iii) The Multiplier 987
(iv) Future Loss of Earnings 990
(v) Medical Treatment and Therapies 992
(C) Third Parties Taking Care of Claimant's Needs 994
(D) Reduction of Expectation of Life 998
7 Non-Pecuniary Losses 999
(A) The 'Assessment' Concept of Damages 999
(B) Pain and Suffering 1001
(C) Loss of Amenities 1001
(D) Damages for Bereavement 1004
(E) Loss of Marriage Prospects 1005
(F) Loss of Congenial Employment 1005
(G) Psychiatric Injury 1006
8 Death in Relation to Tort 1006
(A) Survival of Causes of Action 1006
(B) Death as Creating a Cause of Action 1008
(i) Introduction 1008
(ii) Who Brings the Action 1010
(iii) The Assessment of the Award 1015
(iv) Pecuniary Gains and Other Deductions and the Question of Duplication of Damages 1017
9 Damage to Property 1019

26 OTHER REMEDIES AND MULTIPLE LIABILITIES 1029

1 Injunctions 1029

(A) Prohibitory Injunctions 1030

(B) Mandatory Injunctions 1030

(C) *Quia Timet* Injunctions 1031

(D) Interlocutory (or Interim) Injunctions 1031

2 Damages in Lieu of an Injunction 1032

3 Joint and Concurrent Liability 1033

(A) Joint and Concurrent Liability Distinguished 1033

(B) Successive Actions 1033

(C) Contribution and Apportionment 1034

(D) Indemnity 1040

(E) Secondary Civil Liability 1040

Index 1043

ABBREVIATIONS

A & E	Adolphus & Ellis' Queen's Bench Reports
AC	Official Law Reports: Appeal Cases
AD	New York Supreme Court Appellate Division Reports
AD	*Australian Digest*
Ala.	Alabama Reports
Ala.	Sup. Ct. Alabama Supreme Court
ALJR	Australian Law Journal Reports
All ER	All England Law Reports
All ER Rev.	*All England Law Reports Review*
ALR	Australian Law Reports
AMC	American Maritime Cases
Am, Bar Found. Res. J	*American Bar Foundation Research Journal*
Am. J Comp. L	*American Journal of Comparative Law*
Anglo-Am. LR	*Anglo-American Law Review*
Anst.	Anstruther's Exchequer Reports
App. Cas.	Law Reports, Appeal Cases
Ariz. LR	*Arizona Law Review*
ATC	Annotated Tax Cases
Aust. Bus. LR	*Australian Business Law Review*
Aust. LJ	*Australian Law Journal*
B & Ad.	Barnewall & Adolphus's King's Bench Reports
B & Ald.	Barnewall & Alderson's King's Bench Reports
B & C	Barnewall & Cresswell's King's Bench Reports
B & S	Best & Smith's Queen's Bench Reports
BCLR	British Columbia Law Reports
BGH	German Federal Supreme Court
BGH JZ	Decisions of the Bundesgerichtshof of published in the *Juristenzeitung*
BGH NJW	Decisions of the Bundesgerichtshof of published in the *New Juristiche Wochenzeitung*
BGHZ	Entscheidungen des Bundesgerichtshofes in Zivilsachen
BHRC	Butterworths Human Rights Cases
Bing.	Bingham's Common Pleas Reports
Bing NC	Bingham's New Cases, English Common Pleas
BLR	Building Law Reports
BMLR	British Medical Law Reports
Boston ULR	*Boston University Law Review*
Buffalo LJ	*Buffalo Law Journal*

Burr	Burrow's King's Bench Reports tempore Mansfield
BVerfGE	Entscheidungen des Bundesverfassungsgerichts
C & K	Carrington & Kirwan's Nisi Prius Reports
C & P	Carrington & Payne's Nisi Prius Reports
CA	Court of Appeal
Cal. LR	*California Law Review*
Cal. Rptr.	California Reporter
Cal.App.	California Appellate Reports
Camp.	Campbell's Nisi Prius Cases
Can. BR	*Canadian Bar Review*
Can. Sup. Ct.	Canadian Supreme Court
Car & M	Carrington & Marshman's Nisi Prius Reports
Car & P	Carrington & Payne's Nisi Prius Reports
CB	Common Bench Reports
CB (NS)	Common Bench Reports (New Series)
CCLT	Canadian Cases on the Law of Torts
Ch.	Law Reports: Chancery's Division
Ch. App.	Law Reports, Chancery Appeal Cases
Ch. D	Law Reports, Chancery Division (2nd Series)
Chicago-Kent LR	*Chicago-Kent Law Review*
Cl	Current Law
Cl & F	Clark & Finnelly's House of Lords Cases
CLJ	*Cambridge Law Journal*
CLP	*Current Legal Problems*
CLR	Commonwealth Law Reports
CLY	Current Law Yearbook
CM & R	Crompton, Meeson & Roscoe's Exchequer Reports
Col. LR	*Columbia Law Review*
Const. LJ	*Construction Law Journal*
Conv.	*Conveyancer*
Conv. (NS)	*Conveyancer (New Series)*
Cornell LR	*Cornell Law Review*
Cowp.	Cowper's King's Bench Reports
Cox	Cox's Criminal Cases
CP	Law Reports: Common Pleas
CPD	Law Reports, Common Pleas Division
CPLR	Civil Practice Law Reports
CPR	Civil Procedure Rules
Cr. App. R	Criminal Appeal Reports
Cr. M & R	Crompton, Meeson & Roscoe Exchequer Reports
Crim. LR	*Criminal Law Review*
Cro. Jac.	Croke's King's Bench Reports
CS Appeals	Social Security Commissioner Decisions: Child Support Appeals

D & R	Dowling & Ryland's King's Bench Reports
DC Civ.	Circuit Court of the District of Columbia
De G & Sm.	De Gex & Smale's Chancery Reports
De GJ & S	De Gex, Jones & Smith's Chancery Reports
De GM & G	De Gex, Macnaghten & Gex's Reports
Den.	Denison & Pearce's Crown Cases Reserved
Denning LJ	*Denning Law Journal*
DePaul LR	*DePaul Law Review*
Dickinson J Int. Law	*Dickinson Journal of International Law*
DLR	Dominion Law Reports
Dublin University LJ	*Dublin University Law Journal*
Duke LJ	*Duke Law Journal*
E & B	Ellis & Blackburn's Queen's Bench Reports
EAT	Employment Appeal Tnbunal
East	East's Term Reports, King's Bench
ECHR	European Convention on Human Rights
ECJ	European Court of Justice
ECLR	*European Competition Law Review*
ECR	European Court Reports
EctHR	European Court of Human Rights
EG	Estates Gazette
EGCS	Estates Gazette Case Summaries
EGLR	Estates Gazette Law Reports
EHRLR	*European Human Rights Law Review*
EHRR	European Human Rights Reports
El. & Bl.	Ellis & Blackburn's Queen's Bench Reports
ELR	*European Law Review*
EMLR	Entertainment and Media Law Reports
Ent. LR	*Entertainment Law Review*
Env. LR	Environmental Law Reports
Eq.	Law Reports, Equity Cases
ER	English Reports
Eur. Bus. LR	*European Business Law Review*
EWCA Civ.	Court of Appeal of England and Wales, Civil Division
EWCA Crim.	Court of Appeal of England and Wales, Criminal Division
EWHC	High Court (Aministrative Court)
Ex.	Exchequer
Exch.	Exchequer Reports
F	Federal Reporter
F & F	Foster & Finlayson's Nisi Prius Reports

Fam.	Law Reports: Family Division
FCR	Family Court Reporter
Fla.	Florida Reports
FLR	Family Law Reports
Fost.	Foster's Crown Cases
FSR	Fleet Street Reports
Ga.	Georgia Reports
Geo. Wash. LR	*George Washington Law Review*
H & C	Hurl Stone & Coltman's Exchequer Reports
H & N	Hurl Stone & Norman's Exchequer Reports
Hare	Hare's Chancery Reports
Harv. LR	*Harvard Law Review*
Haw.	West's Hawaii Reports
HBL	Henry Blackstone's Reports
HC	House of Commons
HCA	High Court of Australia
HKLRD	Hong Kong Law Reports & Digest
HL	House of Lords
HLC	Clark & Finnelly's House of Lords Reports New Series
HL Debs.	House of Lords Debates
HLR	Housing Law Reports
HRLR	Human Rights Law Reports
Hurl. & C	Hurlstone & Coltman's Exchequer Reports
ICLQ	*International Comparative Law Quarterly*
ICR	Industrial Cases Reports
ILJ	*Industrial Law Journal*
Ill.	Illinois Reports
Ill.LR	*Illinois Law Review*
ILT	Irish Law Times
Ind. Law	*Mazengarb's Industrial Law Bulletin*
Int. Encl. Comp. L	*International Encyclopaedia of Comparative Law*
Iowa LR	*Iowa Law Review*
Ir. Jur.	*Irish Jurist*
IRLR	Industrial Relations Law Reports
Israel L. Rev	*Israel Law Review.*
J Env. Law	*Journal of Environmental Law*
J Law & Econ.	*Journal of Law and Economics*
J Maritime Law & com.	*Journal of Maritime Law and Commerce*
J of Contract Law	*Journal of Contract Law*

J Law Soc.	*Journal of Law and Society*
JBL	*Journal of Business Law*
JEL	*Journal of Environmental Law*
Jo. LS	*Journal of Legal Studies*
JP	Justice Of the Peace Reports
JPIL	*Journal of Personal Injury Litigation*
JR	*Judicial Review*
Jur.	Jurist Reports
KB	Law Reports: King's Bench Division
KCLJ	*Kings College Law Journal*
KIR	Knight's Industrial Reports
L & TR	Landlord and Tenants Reports
La. App.	Louisiana Court of Appeals Reports
La. LR	*Louisiana Law Review*
Law and CP	*Law and Contemporary Problems*
Ld. Raym.	Lord Raymond's King's Bench and Common Pleas Reports
Leg. Stud.	*Legal Studies*
Lev.	Levinz's King's Bench and Common Pleas Reports
Lew. CC	Lewin's Crown Cases Reserved
LGLR	Local Government Law Reports
LGR	Local Government Reports
LIEI	*Legal Issues in European Integration*
LJ	Law Journal
LJ Adm.	Law Journal Reports, Admiralty New Series
LJ Ex.	Law Journal Reports, Exchequer New Series
LJKB	Law Journal Reports, King's Bench New Series
LJNCCR	Law Journal Newspaper County Court Reports
LJPC	Law Journal Reports, Privy Council New Series
LJQB	Law Journal Reports, Queen's Bench New Series
Ll. L Rep.	Lloyd's Law Reports
Lloyd's Rep.	Lloyd's Reports
Lloyd's Rep. Med.	Lloyd's Reports: Medical
LMCLQ	*Lloyd's Maritime and Commercial Law Quarterly*
Lofft.	Lofft's King's Bench Reports
LQR	*Law Quarterly Review*
LR	Law Reports
LR Ir.	Law Reports, Ireland
LRC	Law Reports of the Commonwealth
LSG	*Law Society's Gazette*
LT	Law Times

M & M	Moody & Malkin's Nisi Prius Reports
M & R	Maclean & Robinson's Appeal Cases
M & S	Moore & Scott's Common Pleas Reports
M & W	Meeson & Welsby's Exchequer Reports
Macq.	Macqueen's Scotch Appeal Cases
Malaya LR	*Malaya Law Review*
Man & G	Manning & Granger's Common pleas Reports
Mass.	Massachusetts Reports
Mass. Law	*Massachusetts Law Review*
Mass. App. Div.	Massachusetts Appellate Division Advance Sheets
McGill LJ	*McGill Law Journal*
Md.	Maryland Reports
Md. App.	Maryland Appeal Reports
Med L Rev.	*Medical Law Review*
Med. LR	Medical Law Reports
Media L Rep	Media Law Reports (US)
Metcalf	Metcalf's Massachusetts Reports
Mich. LR	*Michigan Law Review*
Minn. LR	*Minnesota Law Review*
Misc.	New York Miscellaneous Reports
Miss. LJ	*Mississippi Law Journal*
MLR	*Modern Law Review*
Mod. Rep.	Modern Reports
MR	Master of the Rolls
MULR	*Melbourne University Law Review*
NBR	New Brunswick Reports (Canada)
NC	North Carolina Reports
NE	North Eastern Reporter
Neb.	Nebraska Reporter
NH	New Hampshire Reports
NI	Northern Irish Reports
NILQ	*Northern Ireland Legal Quarterly*
NJ	New Jersey Reporter
NJ Sup. Ct. App. Div.	New Jersey Report Supreme Court Appellate Division
NLJ	*New Law Journal*
NM	New Mexico Reporter
NPC	New Practice Cases
NSWLR	New South Wales Law Reports (Australia)
NW	Northwestern Reporter
NWUL Rev.	*Northwestern University Law Review*
NY	New York Reports

NYS	New York Supplement
NYULR	*New York University Law Review*
NZAR	New Zealand Administrative Reports
NZLR	New Zealand Law Reports
NZULR	*New Zealand Universities Law Review*
Ohio App.	Ohio Appellate Reports
OJ	*Official Journal of the EC*
OJLS	*Oxford Journal of Legal Studies*
Okl. St. Ann.	*Oklahoma Statutes Annotated*
Ont.	Ontario Reports (Canada)
Or.	Oregon Reports
Oregon LR	*Oregon Law Review*
Osgoode Hall LJ	*Osgoode Hall Law Journal*
P	Law Reports: Probate
P	Pacific Reporter
P & CR	Property Planning and Compensation Reports
Pa. Law	Laws of Pennsylvania
PIQR	Personal Injuries and Quantum Reports
PL	*Public Law*
PN	*Professional Negligence*
PNLR	Professional Negligence and Liability Reports
QB	Law Reports: Queen's Bench Division
QBD	Queen's Bench Division
Qd R.	Queensland Reports
RPC	Reports of Patent Cases
RSC Ord.	Rules of the Supreme Court, Order
RTR	Road Traffic Reports
RVR	Rating and Valuation Reports
S Cal. LR	*Southern California Law Review*
Salk.	Salkeld's King's Bench Reports
SASR	South Australian State Reports
Sayer	Sayer's King's Bench Reports
SC	Session Cases
SCC	Supreme Court Circular
SCR	Supreme Court Reports (Canada)
SCt.	Supreme Court
SE	South Eastern Reporter
SI	Statutory Instrument

SJ	*Solicitors' Journal*
SJLB	Solicitors' Journal Law Brief
SLR	*Student Law Review*
SLT	Scots Law Times
Smith's LC	Smith's Leading Cases
So.	Southern Reporter
St. Tr.	State Trials
Stan. LR	*Stanford Law Review*
Stark.	Starkie's Nisi Prius Reports
Stra.	Strange's King's Bench Reports
Style	Style's King's Bench Reports
Sup. C. of BC	Supreme Court of British Columbia
Sup. Ct	Supreme Court
SW	South Western Reporter
Swans.	Swanston's Chancery Reports
Syd. LR	*Sydney Law Review*
T & CC	Technology and Construction Court
T & R	Durnford & East's Term Reports, King's Bench
T. Ray	T. Raymond's King's Bench and Common Pleas Reports
Taunt.	Taunton's Common Pleas Reports
TCLR	Trade and Competition Law Reports
Tenn. LR	*Tennessee Law Review*
Term Rep.	Durnford & East's Term Report King's Bench
Tex. App.	White & Willson's Civil Cases, Court of Appeals, Texas
Tex. LR	*Texas Law Review*
TLR	Times Law Reports
Tort and Insurance LJ	*Tort and Insurance Law Journal*
Tort LR	*Tort Law Review*
Tul. LR	*Tulane Law Review*
UBCLR	*University of British Columbia Law Review*
U Chi. LR	*University of Chicago Law Review*
U Cinn. LR	*University of Cincinnati Law Review*
U Fla. LR	*University of Florida Law Review*
U Pa. LR	*University of Pennsylvania Law Review*
UCLA LR	*University of California of Los Angeles Law Review*
UKHL	House of Lords (United Kingdom)
UKHRR	United Kingdom Human Rights Reports
UKPC	Privy Council
UNSWLJ	*University of New South Wales Law Journal*

US App D	United States Court of Appeal Reports
US Sup. Ct	United States: Supreme Court Reports
USC	United States Code
UTLJ	*University of Toronto Law Journal*
UWALR	*University of Western Australia Law Review*
Val. U LR	*Valaparaiso University Law Review*
Vand. LR	*Vanderbilt Law Review*
Vaughan	Vaughan's Common Pleas Reports
Virginia LR	*Virginia Law Review*
VR	Victoria Reports (Australia)
Wash.	Washington Virginia Reports
Wils. KB	Wilson's King's Bench and Commons Pleas Reports
Wis.	Wisconsin Reports
WL	Westlaw Transcripts
WLR	Weekly Law Reports
Wms. Saund.	Saunders' King's Bench Reports
WN	Weekly Notes
WN (NSW)	Weekly Notes (New South Wales)
WWR	Western Weekly Reports (Canada)
Yale LJ	*Yale Law Journal*
YB	Year Books
YEL	*Yearbook of European Law*

TABLE OF UNITED KINGDOM CASES

A (A Child) v. Newham LBC (2001) WL 1612596 (unreported) ... 843

A (Children) (Conjoined Twins: Surgical Separation), Re [2001] Fam 147 ... 457

A v. B and C [2002] WLR 542; [2002] EWCA 337; [2003] QB 195; [2002] 2 All ER 545 ... 832, 841, 842, 846, 849, 850, 851, 883, 885, 1032

A v. Essex CC [2004] 1 WLR 1881 ... 210, 415, 420

A v. Hoare [2006] EWCA Civ 395 ... 929

A v. Leeds Teaching Hospital NHS Trust (Re Organ Retention Group Litigation) [2005] QB 506 ... 486

A v. National Blood Authority [2001] 3 All ER 289; [2002] Lloyd's Rep.Med. 487 ... 730, 734, 736, 740, 748, 973

AB v. South West Water Services Ltd. [1993] 2 WLR 507; [1993] QB 507 ... 943, 944, 945, 946

AB v. Tameside and Glossop Health Authority [1997] 8 Med. LR 91 ... 154

Abbott v. Will Gannon & Smith Ltd. [2005] EWCA Civ 198 ... 930, 935

Abu v. MGN Ltd. [2003] 1 WLR 2201 ... 782

A. C. Billings & Son v. Riden [1958] AC 240 ... 369, 530

Acrow (Automation) Ltd. v. Rex Chainbelt Inc. [1971] 3 All ER 1175 ... 594

AD and OH (a child: by AD his litigation friend) v. Bury MBC [2006] EWCA Civ 1; [2006] 1 WLR 917 ... 96, 105

Adam v. Ward [1917] AC 309 ... 794

Adams v. Bracknell Forest BC [2005] 1 AC 76 ... 931, 936

Adams v. Rhymney Valley DC [2001] PNLR 68 ... 235

Adamson v. Jarvis (1827) 4 Bing. 66; 130 ER 693 ... 1035

Addis v. Crocker [1961] 1 QB 11 ... 792

Admiralty Commissioners v. SS America [1917] AC 38 ... 1007, 1008

Agip (Africa) Ltd. v. Jackson & Co. [1990] Ch. 265 ... 53

Aiken v. Stewart Wrightson Members Agency Ltd. [1995] 1 WLR 1281 ... 172

Air Canada v. Secretary of State for Trade [1983] 2 AC 394 ... 794

Airedale NHS Trust v. Bland [1993] 1 All ER 821; AC 789 ... 455, 456, 457, 458, 459, 460, 461, 462, 914

Airfix Footwear Ltd. v. Cope [1978] ICR 1210 ... 671

AK (Medical Treatment: Consent), Re [2001] FLR 129 ... 456

Akenzua v. Secretary of State for Home Department [2003] 1 WLR 741 ... 428, 429

Al-Fagih v. H. H. Saudi Research & Marketing (UK) (QBD, 28 July 2000, unreported) ... 755

Al-Kandari v. J. R. Brown & Co. [1987] QB 514; [1988] QB 665 ... 153, 174, 214

Alcoa Minerals of Jamaica Inc. v. Broderick [2002] 1 AC 371 ... 277

Alcock v. Chief Constable of South Yorkshire [1991] 3 WLR 1057; [1992] 1 AC 310 ... 117, 119, 139, 140, 143, 144, 146, 147, 148, 149, 150, 151, 153, 155, 156, 207, 303, 744

Alexander v. Arts Council of Wales [2001] 1 WLR 1840 ... 766

Alexander v. Home Office [1988] 1 WLR 968 ... 942, 943

Alexandrou v. Oxford [1993] 4 All ER 328 ... 212, 419

Alfred McAlpine Construction Ltd. v. Panatown Ltd. [2001] 1 AC 518 (HL) ... 26, 27, 175, 176, 369

Aliakmon, The. *see* Leigh and Sillivan Ltd v. The Aliakmon Shipping Co Ltd

Allan v. Bloomsbury HA [1993] 1 All ER 651 ... 218

Allan v. Greater Glasgow Health Board 1998 SLR 580 ... 218

Allason v. Campbell *The Times* 8 May 1996 ... 817

Allason v. Haines [1995] EMLR 143 ... 791

Allen v. Flood [1898] AC 1 ... 571, 572, 573, 576, 579, 583, 590, 591, 595

Allen v. Greenwood [1980] Ch. 119 ... 520

Allen v. Gulf Oil Refining Ltd. [1981] AC 1001 ... 540, 541, 542, 560, 619

Alliance and Leicester Building Society v. Edgestop Ltd. [1994] 2 All ER 38 ... 903

Allied Maples Group Ltd. v. Simmons & Simmons [1995] 1 WLR 1602 ... 263

Allin v. City and Hackney Health Authority [1996] 7 Med. LR 167 ... 155

Allsop v. Church of England Newspaper Ltd. [1972] 2 QB 161 ... 762, 763

Amec Developments Ltd. v. Jury's Hotel Management (UK) Ltd. [2001] 1 EGLR 81 (Ch. D) ... 501, 502
American Cyanamid Co. v. Ethicon Ltd. [1975] AC 396 ... 551, 601, 830, 1031, 1032
American Express Co. v. British Airways Board [1983] 1 WLR 701 ... 382
AMF International v. Magnet Bowling Ltd. [1968] 1 WLR 1028 ... 345, 360, 362, 370
Amiri Flight Authority v. BAE Systems plc [2003] EWCA Civ 1447 ... 185
Ancell v. McDermott [1993] 4 All ER 355 ... 212, 419
Anchor Brewhouse Developments Ltd. v. Berkeley House (Docklands Developments) Ltd. [1987] 2 EGLR 187 ... 496
Anderson v. Oppenheimer (1880) 5 QBD 602 ... 619
Anderson v. Pacific Insurance Co. (1872) LR 7 CP 65 ... 566
Andreae v. Selfridge & Company Ltd. [1938] Ch. 1 (CA) ... 522
Andreou v. Institute of Chartered Accountants of England and Wales [1998] 1 All ER 14 ... 433
Andrews v. Hopkinson [1957] 1 QB 229 ... 725, 727
Andrews v. Initial Cleaning Services Ltd. [2000] ICR 166 (CA) ... 345
Andrews v. Reading Borough Council [2005] EWHC 256; [2006] RVR 56 ... 533
Andrews v. Schooling [1991] 1 WLR 783 ... 370, 373
Andrews v. Secretary of State for Health (2000) 54 BMLR 111 ... 155
Aneco Insurance Underwriting v. Johnson & Higgins [2002] 1 Lloyd's Rep. 157 ... 1023
Anglian Water Services Ltd. v. Crawshaw Robbins Ltd. [2001] BLR 173 ... 521, 523
Anglo-Cyprian Trade Agencies Ltd. v. Paphos Wine Ltd. Industries [1951] 1 All ER 873, 874 ... 942
Annable v. Southern Derbyshire HA (conjoined appeal with Heil v. Rankin) ... 1003
Anns v. Merton London Borough Council [1978] AC 728 ... 26, 45, 46, 59, 96, 122, 123, 125, 126, 127, 128, 131, 168, 175, 180, 181, 182, 198, 203, 210, 369, 372, 374, 378, 398, 400, 407, 408, 409, 410, 416, 933
Anthony v. The Coal Authority [2005] EWHC 1654 (QB) ... 528
Anthony v. Haney and Harding (1832) 8 Bing. 186 ... 503
Anton Piller KG v. Manufacturing Processes Ltd. [1976] Ch. 55 ... 834
Anufrijeva v. Southwark London Borough Council [2004] QB 1124 ... 441, 442
Apley Estates Co. Ltd. v. de Bernales [1947] Ch. 217 ... 1034
Appleby v. UK (2003) 37 EHRR 38 ... 498
Appleton v. Garrett [1996] 5 PIQR P1 ... 942, 943, 944
Archer v. Brown [1985] 1 QB 401 ... 942, 943, 950
Archer v. Williams [2003] EMLR 38 ... 837, 843
Arenson v. Arenson [1977] AC 405 ... 213
Argent v. Minister of Social Security and Another [1968] 1 WLR 1749 ... 669
Argyll v. Argyll [1967] Ch. 302 ... 838, 839
Arkwright v. Newbold (1881) 17 Ch. D 301 ... 565
Armagas Ltd. v. Mundagas SA, The Ocean Frost [1985] 3 WLR 640 ... 689
Armitage v. Johnson [1997] IRLR 162 ... 943
Armory v. Delamirie (1721) 1 Stra. 505; 93 ER 664 ... 486
Armstrong v. Sheppard and Short Ltd. [1959] 1 QB 384 ... 1030
Arscott v. The Coal Authority [2004] EWCA Civ 892; [2005] Env LR 6 ... 528
Arthur J. S. Hall & Co. v. Simons [2000] 3 WLR 543; [2002] 1 AC 615 ... 117, 134, 135, 214
Arthur v. Anker [1996] 2 WLR 602 ... 503, 504, 635
Asghar v. Ahmed (1984) 17 HLR 25 (CA) ... 948
Ashby v. Tolhurst [1937] 2 KB 242 ... 487
Ashby v. White (1703) 1 Smith's LC 253 ... 428
Ashdown v. Samuel Williams & Sons Ltd. [1957] 1 QB 409 ... 190, 357, 660, 915
Asher v. Whitlock (1865) LR 1 QB 1 ... 501
Ashton v. Jennings [1674] 2 Lev. 133; 83 ER 485 ... 454
Ashton v. Turner [1981] QB 137 ... 898, 924
Ashworth Hospital Authority v. MGN [2001] 1 WLR 515 (CA) and [2002] 1 WLR 2033 (HL) ... 800
Askey v. Golden Wine Co. Ltd. [1948] 2 All ER 35 ... 1040
Aspro Travel Ltd. v. Owners Abroad Group plc [1996] 1 WLR 132 ... 765, 769, 775
Associated British Ports v. Transport and General Workers Union [1989] IRLR 399; [1989] IRLR 291; IRLR 305 ... 586, 594, 601, 602
Associated Newspaper Group v. Wade [1979] ICR 664 ... 594
Associated Newspaper Ltd. v. Dingle [1964] AC 371 ... 795

Atkinson v. Newcastle and Gateshead Waterworks Co. (1877) LR 2 Exch. D 441 ... 385, 387, 426
Attia v. British Gas Corp. [1988] QB 304 ... 152, 744
Attorney-General of St Christopher, Nevis and Anguilla v. Reynolds [1980] AC 637 ... 945, 947
Attorney-General v. Corke [1933] Ch. 89 ... 610
Attorney-General v. Cory Brothers & Co. Ltd. [1921] 1 AC 521 ... 619
Attorney-General v. Gastonia Coaches Ltd. [1977] RTR 219 ... 551
Attorney-General v. Guardian Newspapers Ltd. [1987] 1 WLR 1248; [1988] 3 WLR 776 ... 839
Attorney-General v. Guardian Newspapers Ltd. (No. 2) [1990] 1 AC 109 ... 772, 838, 846, 859
Attorney-General v. Nissan [1970] AC 179 ... 927
Attorney-General v. PYA Quarries Ltd. [1957] 2 QB 169 ... 522, 551, 552, 559
Attorney-General of Virgin Islands v. Hartwell [2004] 1 WLR 1273 ... 692
Attorney-General's Reference (No. 6 of 1980) [1981] QB 715 ... 462
Attwood v. Chapman [1914] 3 KB 275 ... 792
Austin v. Commissioner of Police of the Metropolis [2005] EWHC 480; [2005] HRLR 20 ... 463, 464, 468
Austin v. Dowling (1870) LR 5 CP 534 ... 465, 476
Auty v. National Coal Board [1985] 1 All ER 930; [1985] 1 WLR 784 ... 954, 1019

B (A Minor) (Wardship: Sterilisation), Re [1988] AC 199 ... 457
B (Adult: Refusal of Medical Treatment), Re [2002] 2 All ER 449 ... 456
B v. McDonald's Restaurants Ltd. [2002] EWHC 490 ... 353, 733
Baddeley v. Earl Granville (1887) 19 QBD 423 ... 393, 913
Badger v. Ministry of Defence [2005] EWHC 2941 ... 740, 896
Bailey v. Armes [1999] ECGS 21 (CA) ... 345
Baker v. Bolton (1808) 1 Camp. 493; 170 ER 1033 ... 1007, 1008
Baker v. T. E. Hopkins & Son Ltd. [1959] 1 WLR 966 ... 219, 661
Baker v. Willoughby [1970] AC 467 (HL) ... 58, 246, 257, 258, 259, 324, 328, 329, 333
Balfour v. Barty-King [1957] 1 All ER 156; [1957] 1 QB 496 ... 625, 696
Ballantine v. Newalls Insulation Co. Ltd. [2000] PIQR Q327 ... 963
Bamford v. Turnley (1860) 3 B & S 62; 122 ER 25 ... 511
Banbury v. Bank of Montreal [1918] AC 626 ... 567
Bank voor Handel en Scheepvaart NV v. Slatford [1953] 1 QB 248 ... 670
Banque Financière de la Cité SA v. Westgate Insurance Co. [1991] 2 AC 249 ... 131, 165
Banques Bruxelles Lambert case *see* South Australia Asset Management Corp. v. York Montague Ltd. [1997] AC 191
Barber v. Somerset County Council [2004] IRLR 475; [2004] 1 WLR 1089 ... 157, 655
Barclays Bank plc v. Fairclough Building Ltd. [1995] QB 214 ... 904, 905
Barker v. Corus UK Ltd. [2006] 2 AC 572; 2 WLR 1027 ... 121, 247, 255, 256, 257, 1039
Barnes v. Addy (1874) LR 9 Ch 1041
Barnes v. Hampshire CC [1969] 1 WLR 1563 ... 200, 204
Barnes v. Irwell Valley Water Board [1939] 1 KB 21 ... 115, 727
Barnet Group Hospital Management Committee v. Eagle Star Insurance Co. Ltd. [1960] 1 QB 107 ... 980
Barnett v. Chelsea and Kensington Hospital [1969] 1 QB 428 ... 121, 201, 249
Barnett v. Packer [1940] 3 All ER 575 ... 125
Barrett v. Enfield LBC [2001] 2 AC 550 ... 210, 211, 213, 215, 234, 399, 401, 411, 415, 421, 422, 423, 701
Barrett v. Ministry of Defence [1995] 3 All ER 87 ... 201, 203
Barretts & Baird (Wholesale) Ltd. v. Institution of Professional Civil Servants [1987] IRLR 3 ... 586, 600
Barrow v. Bankside Agency Ltd. [1996] 1 WLR 257 ... 965
Bartonshill Coal Co. v. Maguire (1853) 3 Macq. 300 ... 908
Bartonshill Coal Co. v. Reid (1856) 3 Macq. 266 ... 907, 908
Barwick v. English Joint Stock Bank (1867) LR 2 Ex. 259 ... 688
Basébé v. Matthews (1867) LR 2 CP 684 ... 478
Basley v. Clarkson 3 Lev. 37 ... 505
Bass v. Gregory (1890) 25 QBD 481 ... 520
Batty v. Metropolitan Property Realizations Ltd. [1978] QB 554 ... 20, 372
Baxall Securities Ltd. v. Sheard Walshaw Partnership [2001] BLR 36 (QBD) ... 372
Bayley v. The Manchester, Sheffield and Lincolnshire Railway Co. (1873) LR 8 CP 148 ... 683

BBMB Finance (Hong Kong) Ltd. v. Eda Holdings Ltd. [1991] 2 All ER 129 . . . 490
Beard v. London General Omnibus Co. [1900] 2 QB 530 . . . 684
Beaumont v. Greathead (1846) 2 CB 494; 135 ER 1039 . . . 942
Beckham v. MGN Ltd. 28 June 2001 (unreported) . . . 837, 843
Behrens v. Bertram Mills Circus Ltd. [1957] 2 QB 1 . . . 142, 637, 646
Behrens v. Richards [1905] 2 Ch. 614 . . . 546
Bell v. Peter Browne & Co.[1990] 2 QB 495 . . . 932, 935, 936
Bell v. Todd [2002] Lloyd's Rep. Med. 12 . . . 961
Bellefield Computer Services Ltd. v. E. Turner & Sons Ltd. [2000] BLR 97 . . . 183, 372
Bellingham v. Dhillon and Another [1973] 1 QB 304 . . . 976
Benham v. Gambling [1941] AC 157 . . . 1004
Benjamin v. Storr (1874) LR 9 CP 400 . . . 385, 512
Bennet v. Chemical Construction (GB) Ltd. [1971] 1 WLR 1571 . . . 242
Benson v. Biggs Wall & Co. Ltd. [1983] 1 WLR 72 . . . 999
Bent's Brewery Co. Ltd. v. Hogan [1945] 2 All ER 570 . . . 600
Beresford v. Royal Insurance Co. [1938] AC 586 . . . 1010
Berezovsky v. Forbes (No. 1) [1999] EMLR 278 . . . 777
Berkoff v. Burchill [1996] 4 All ER 1008 . . . 756
Bernard v. Attorney-General of Jamaica [2005] IRLR 398 . . . 692
Bernstein v. Skyviews & General Ltd. [1978] QB 479 . . . 496, 834
Berry v. BTC [1962] 1 QB 306 . . . 475
Berry v. Humm [1915] 1 KB 627 . . . 1014
Berryman v. Hounslow LBC [1997] PIQR P83 (CA) . . . 352
Best v. Samuel Fox & Co. Ltd. [1952] AC 716 . . . 143
Bestobell Paints Ltd. v. Gigg (1975) 119 SJ 678 . . . 1032
Beta Construction v. Channel Four Television Co. Ltd. [1990] 1 WLR 104 . . . 814
Bhoomidas v. Port of Singapore Authority [1978] 1 All ER 956 . . . 675
Biddle v. Bond (1865) 6 B & S 225; 122 ER 1179 . . . 490
Bird v. Jones (1845) 7 QB 742 . . . 463
Bird v. King Line Ltd. [1970] 2 Lloyd's Rep. 349 . . . 354, 355
Birkett v. Hayes [1982] 1 WLR 816 . . . 978
Birse Construction Ltd. v. Haite Ltd. (Watson and Others, Third Parties) [1996] 1 WLR 675 . . . 1034
Bishop v. J. A. Starnes & Sons Ltd. [1971] 1 Lloyd's Rep. 162 . . . 356
Bissett v. Wilkinson [1927] AC 177 . . . 566
Blackpool and Fylde Aero Club v. Blackpool BC [1990] 1 WLR 1195 . . . 164
Blackshaw v. Lord [1983] 3 WLR 283; [1984] QB 1 . . . 797, 799, 806
Blair v. Associated Newspapers Ltd., Case no. HQ0001236 (2001) (unreported) . . . 837, 846
Blair and Sumner v. Deakin (1887) 57 LT 522 . . . 543
Blake v. Galloway [2004] 1 WLR 2844 . . . 228, 912, 913
Blake v. The Midland Railway Co. (1852) 18 QB 93; 118 ER 35 . . . 1004, 1015
Blamire v. South Cumbria HA [1993] PIQR Q1 . . . 990, 992
Blamires v. Lancashire & Yorkshire Railway (1873) LR 8 Ex. 283 . . . 379
Bliss v. Hall (1838) 4 Bing. NC 183; 132 ER 758 . . . 542
Blyth v. Birmingham Waterworks Co. (1856) 11 Ex. 781 . . . 223
Bognor Regis District Council v. Campion [1972] 2 QB 169 . . . 771, 816
Bolam v. Friern Hospital Management Committee [1957] 1 WLR 582 . . . 224, 225, 226, 232, 233, 234, 456, 459, 460, 461
Boldack v. East Lindsey DC (1999) 31 HLR 41 (CA) . . . 369, 370
Bolitho v. City and Hackney Health Authority [1998] AC 232 . . . 234, 249
Bolton v. Stone [1951] AC 850 . . . 120, 225, 236, 237, 523
Bone v. Seale [1975] 1 WLR 797 . . . 510, 511
Bonnington Castings Ltd. v. Wardlaw [1956] AC 613 . . . 250
Booth Steamship Co. Ltd. v. Cargo Fleet Iron Co. Ltd. [1916] 2 KB 570 . . . 489
Borders (UK) Ltd. v. Commissioner of Police of the Metropolis [2005] EWCA Civ 197 . . . 491
Bottomley v. Bannister [1932] 1 KB 458 . . . 115, 369, 372
Bourgoin SA v. Ministry of Agriculture, Fisheries and Food [1986] 1 QB 716 . . . 427, 430, 434, 435, 437
Bourhill v. Young [1943] AC 92 . . . 142, 145, 148
Bowater v. Bowley Regis Corporation [1944] KB 476 . . . 912

Bower v. Peate (1876) 1 QBD 321 . . . 537, 607, 696

Boxfoldia Ltd. v. NGA [1988] IRLR 383 . . . 579

Boyce v. Paddington BC [1903] 1 Ch. 109 . . . 385

Boyle v. Kodak Ltd. [1969] 1 WLR 661 . . . 392

Bracewell v. Appleby [1975] Ch. 408 . . . 1033

Bradburn v. Great Western Railway (1874) LR 10 Exch. 1 . . . 957

Bradford v. Robinson Rentals [1967] 1 WLR 337 . . . 273

Bradford Building Society v. Borders [1941] 2 All ER 205, 208 . . . 566

Bradford City Metropolitan Council v. Arora [1991] 2 QB 507 . . . 945

Bradford Corporation v. Pickles [1895] AC 587 . . . 528, 529, 608

Bradford Third Equitable Benefit Building Society v. Borders [1941] 2 All ER 205 . . . 565

Bradford-Smart v. West Sussex CC [2002] EWCA Civ 7; [2002] 1 FCR 425 (CA) . . . 137, 154, 200, 424

Brandt v. Liverpool Brazil and River Plate Steam Navigation Co. [1924] 1 KB 575 . . . 24

Branson v. Bower (No. 2) [2002] 2 WLR 452 . . . 789, 790

BRB (Residuary) Ltd. v. Cully (QBD (T & CC), unreported, 1 Aug. 2001) . . . 495

Breeden v. Lampard (21 Mar. 1985) . . . 639, 640

Brent Walker Group plc v. Time Out Ltd. [1991] 2 QB 772 . . . 787

Brew Bros. Ltd. v. Snax (Ross) Ltd. [1970] 1 QB 612 . . . 538

Bridges v. Harkesworth (1851) 15 Jur. 1079 . . . 485, 487

Briess v. Woolley [1954] AC 333 . . . 566

Brigden v. American Express Bank Ltd. [2000] IRLR 94 . . . 920

Brightman v. Johnson . . . 1002

Brimelow v. Casson [1924] 1 Ch. 302 . . . 580

Brinsmead v. Harrison (1872) LR 7 CP 547 . . . 1033

British Celanese Ltd. v. A. H. Hunt Ltd. [1969] 1 WLR 959 . . . 523, 534, 607, 617

British Columbia Electric Railway v. Loach [1916] 1 AC 719 . . . 893

British Gas v. Stockport Metropolitan Borough Council [2001] Env. LR 44 . . . 614, 615

British Motor Trade Association v. Salvadori [1949] Ch. 556 . . . 577

British Railways Board v. Herrington [1971] 2 QB 107; [1972] AC 877 . . . 342, 351, 364, 366, 367, 371, 515

British Road Services Ltd. v. Arthur Crutchley & Co. Ltd. [1968] 1 All ER 811 . . . 696

British Steel plc v. Customs and Excise Commissioners [1997] 2 All ER 366 . . . 433

British Transport Commission v. Gourley [1956] AC 185 . . . 957, 980, 990

British Waterways Board v. Severn Trent Water [2002] Ch. 25 (CA) . . . 496

British Westinghouse Co. Ltd. v. Underground Electric Railways Co. of London Ltd. [1912] AC 673 . . . 1022

Brittain v. Garner *The Times* 18 Feb. 1989 . . . 991

Brize v. Dickason (1786) 1 Term Rep. 285 . . . 937

Broadway Approvals Ltd. v. Odhams Press [1965] 1 WLR 805 . . . 790, 948

Brook v. Cook (1961) 105 SJ 684 . . . 646

Brooke v. Bool [1928] 2 KB 578 . . . 1033

Brooks v. Commissioner of Police for the Metropolis [2002] EWCA Civ 407 (CA) . . . 213, 412

Brooks v. Commissioner of Police of the Metropolis [2005] 1 WLR 1495 (HL) . . . 133, 213, 419

Broom v. Morgan [1953] 1 QB 597 . . . 665, 678

Broome v. Cassell & Co. Ltd. [1972] AC 1027 . . . 809, 946, 947, 949, 950

Broome v. Perkins [1987] RTR 321 . . . 231

Brown v. Chapman (1848) 6 CB 365; 136 ER 1292 . . . 465

Brown v. Cotterill (1934) 51 TLR 21 . . . 706, 730

Brown v. Edgington (1841) 2 Man. & G 279; 133 ER 751 . . . 708

Brown v. Hawkes [1891] 2 QB 718 . . . 479

Brown v. KMR Services Ltd. [1995] 4 All ER 598 . . . 172

Brown v. Morgan [1953] 1 QB 397 . . . 567

Brown v. Robinson [2004] UKPC 56 . . . 692

Brown v. Stradling (1836) LJPC 295 . . . 477

Browning v. War Office [1963] 1 QB 750 . . . 961

Bruce v. Odhams Press Ltd. [1936] 1 KB 697 . . . 767

Brunsden v. Humphrey (1884) 14 QBD 141 . . . 965

Bryanston Finance Ltd. v. de Vries [1975] QB 703 . . . 796, 797, 798, 1034

Bunker v. Charles Brand & Sons Ltd. [1969] 2 QB 480 . . . 346, 355

Burgess v. Florence Nightingale Hospital for Gentlewomen [1955] 1 QB 349 . . . 1014

Burns v. Edman [1970] 2 QB 541 . . . 990, 1013

Buron v. Denman (1848) 2 Ex. 167 . . . 927

Burris v. Azadani [1995] 1 WLR 1372 . . . 1032

Burton v. De Vere Hotels Ltd. [1996] IRLR 596 ... 681
Burton v. Hughes (1824) 2 Bing. 173; 130 ER 272 ... 485
Burton v. Islington Health Authority [1993] QB 204 ... 117, 217, 218
Business Computers International Ltd. v. Registrar of Companies [1987] 3 All ER 465 ... 214
Butchart v. Home Office [2006] EWCA Civ 239 ... 152, 205
Butterfield v. Forrester (1809) 11 East 60; 103 ER 926 ... 892, 894, 903
Bybrook Barn Garden Centre v. Kent CC [2001] Env. LR 30 ... 515
Byers v. London Borough of Brent QBD ... 1006
Byrne v. Deane [1937] 1 KB 818 ... 754, 755, 773

C (A Minor) (Wardship: Medical Treatment), Re [1990] Fam 26 ... 457
Cabell v. Shelborne Hotel [1939] 2 KB 534 ... 352
Cable and Wireless plc v. Muscat [2006] IRLR 354 ... 676
Cairns v. Visteon Ltd., EAT, Appeal No. UKEAT/0494/06/JOJ ... 676
Cakebread v. Hopping Bros. (Whetstone) Ltd. [1947] KB 641 ... 270, 894
Cala Homes (South) Ltd. v. McAlpine Homes East Ltd. (No. 2) [1996] FSR 36 ... 948
Calder v. H. Kitson Vickers (& Sons) Engineers Ltd. [1988] ICR 232 ... 673
Calveley v. Chief Constable of Merseyside Police [1989] AC 1228; 1 All ER 1025 ... 212, 386
Cambridge Water Co. v. Eastern Counties Leather plc [1994] 2 AC 264; [1994] 2 WLR 53 ... 525, 526, 527, 561, 562, 607, 614, 617, 618, 622, 623, 626, 627, 628, 629
Camden Nominees v. Forcey [1940] Ch. 352 ... 580
Cameron v. Network Rail Infrastructure Ltd. [2007] 1 WLR 163 ... 440
Caminer v. Northern and London Investment Trust Ltd. [1951] AC 88 ... 555
Campbell v. Frisbee [2003] EMLR 76 ... 845
Campbell v. Mirror Group Newspapers Ltd. [2002] EWHC 499; [2002] EMLR 30; [2003] 2 WLR 80; [2003] 1 All ER 224 (CA) (HC) ... 828, 832, 833, 843, 845, 846, 851, 853, 854, 856, 858
Campbell v. Mirror Group Newspapers Ltd. [2004] 2 AC 457 (HL) ... 102, 841, 842, 843, 848, 883, 884
Campbell v. Mirror Group Newspapers Ltd. [2004] 2 WLR 1232 (HL) ... 80, 843, 844, 858
Campbell v. N.I. Housing Executive [1996] 1 BNIL 99 ... 365
Campbell v. Spottiswoode (1863) 3 B & S 769 ... 789
Campbell Davys v. Lloyd [1901] 2 Ch. 518 ... 549
Candler v. Crane, Christmas & Co. [1951] 2 KB 164 ... 162, 166
Cantwell v. Criminal Injuries Compensation Board (2001) SLT 966 ... 959
Caparo Industries plc v. Dickman [1989] QB 653; [1990] 2 AC 605 ... 123, 128, 131, 132, 162, 165, 166, 167, 168, 170, 193, 196, 199, 413, 743
Capital and Counties Bank Ltd. v. G. Henty & Sons (1882) 7 App. Cas. 741 ... 764
Capital and Counties plc v. Hampshire CC [1997] QB 1004 ... 201, 209, 417, 420
Capps v. Miller [1989] 1 WLR 839 ... 897
Carlgarth, The [1927] P 93 ... 349, 505
Carlill v. Carbolic Smoke Ball Co. [1892] 2 QB 484; [1893] 1 QB 256 ... 24, 709, 725
Carmarthenshire County Council v. Lewis [1956] AC 549 ... 201, 205
Carmichael v. National Power plc [1998] IRLR 301 ... 671
Carr-Glynn v. Frearsons [1997] 2 All ER 614; [1998] 4 All ER 225 ... 173, 174, 178
Carslogie Steamship Co. v. Royal Norwegian Government [1952] AC 292 ... 266
Carstairs v. Taylor (1871) LR 6 Ex. 217 ... 619
Cartledge v. E. Jopling & Sons Ltd. [1963] AC 758 ... 929, 930
Carty v. Croydon LBC [2005] 1 WLR 2312 ... 137, 210, 234, 235
Case of Thorns, The (1466) YB 6 Ed. fo. 7 pl. 18 ... 462
Cassell v. Riverside HA [1992] PIQR Q168 ... 992
Cassell & Co. Ltd. v. Broome [1972] AC 1027 ... 753, 806, 809, 1034
Cassidy v. Daily Mirror Newspapers Ltd. [1929] 2 KB 331 ... 753, 761
Cassidy v. Ministry of Health [1951] 2 KB 343 ... 669, 677
Caswell v. Powell Duffryn Associated Collieries Ltd. [1940] AC 152 ... 377, 382, 392, 539, 893, 899
Caswell v. Powell Duffryn Collieries Ltd. [1940] AC 921 ... 903
Catnic Components v. Hill & Smith Ltd. [1983] FSR 512 ... 946
Cattle v. Stockton Waterworks Co. (1875) LR 10 QB 453 ... 188, 577, 621

Cattley v. St John Ambulance Brigade (1990, unreported) ... 228
Cavalier v. Pope [1906] AC 428 ... 114, 369, 370
Cayzer, Irvine & Co. v. Carron Co. (1884) 9 App. Cas. 873 ... 379, 892
CBS Songs Ltd. v. Amstrad Consumer Electronics plc [1986] FSR 159 (CA) ... 1041
CBS Songs Ltd. v. Amstrad Consumer Electronics plc [1988] AC 1013 (HL) ... 574, 1033
Central Railway Co. of Venezuela v. Kisch (1867) LR 2 HL 99 ... 569, 903
Century Insurance Co. Ltd. v. Northern Ireland Road Transport Board [1942] AC 509 ... 683
Chadwick v. British Railways Board [1967] 1 WLR 912 ... 151, 152
Chaplin v. Hicks [1911] 2 KB 786 ... 263
Chapmam v. Pickersgill (1762) 2 Wils. KB 145; 95 ER 734 ... 476
Chapman v. Honig [1963] 2 QB 502 ... 529, 594
Chapman v. Lord Ellesmere [1932] 2 KB 431 ... 782
Chapman v. Oakleigh Animal Products (1970) 8 KIR 1063 ... 659
Chappell v. Somers & Blake [2004] Ch. 19 ... 174
Charing Cross Electricity Supply Co. v. Hydraulic Power Co. [1914] 3 KB 772 ... 526, 613, 619
Charleston v. News Group Newspapers Ltd. [1995] 2 All ER 313 ... 760
Charrington v. Simons & Co. Ltd. [1971] 1 WLR 598 ... 545, 1030
Chatterton v. Gerson [1981] QB 432 ... 456
Chatterton v. Secretary of State for India [1895] 2 QB 189 ... 794
Chaudhry v. Prabhakar [1989] 1 WLR 29 ... 163
Chauhan v. Paul [1998] CLY 3990 (CA) ... 642
Cherry Tree Machine Co. Ltd. and Shell Tankers (UK) Ltd. v. Dawson [2001] PIQR P19 ... 389
Cheshire v. Bailey [1905] 1 KB 237 ... 687
Chester v. Ashfar [2003] QB 356 (CA) ... 456
Chester v. Ashfar [2005] 1 AC 134 (HL) ... 233, 265
Chic Fashions (West Wales) Ltd. v. Jones [1967] 2 QB 299 ... 499
Chipchase v. British Titan Products Co. Ltd. [1956] 1 QB 545 ... 389
Christie v. Davey [1893] 1 Ch. 316 ... 529
Christie v. Leachinsky [1947] AC 573 ... 467
Church of Scientology of California v. Johnson-Smith [1972] 1 QB 522 ... 791
Cinnamond v. British Airways Authority [1980] 1 WLR 582 ... 499
City of London Corp. v. Appleyard [1963] 1 WLR 982 ... 485
Clare v. L. Whittaker & Son (London) Ltd. [1976] ICR 1 ... 346
Clark v. Ardington Electrical Services (No. 2) [2003] QB 36 ... 1023
Clark v. Bowlt [2006] EWCA Civ 978 (2006) 150 SJLB 886 ... 641
Clark v. Bruce Lance [1988] 1 WLR 881 ... 174
Clark v. Oxfordshire Health Authority [1998] IRLR 125 ... 671
Clark v. University of Lincolnshire and Humberside [2000] 1 WLR 1998 ... 403, 434
Clarke v. Rotax Aircraft Equipment Ltd. [1975] 1 WLR 1570 ... 978
Clarke v. Taylor (1836) 2 Bing. NC 654 ... 784
Clay v. A. J. Crump & Sons Ltd. [1964] 1 QB 533 ... 732
Clay v. Pooler [1982] 3 All ER 570 ... 999
Clayton v. Le Roy [1911] 2 KB 1031 ... 488
Clef Aquitaine SARL v. Laporte Materials (Barrow) Ltd. [2001] QB 488 ... 569
Clegg, Parkinson & Co. v. Earby Gas Co. [1896] 1 QB 592 ... 387
Clift v. Welsh Office [1999] 1 WLR 796 (CA) ... 522, 541
Clissold v. Cratchley [1910] 2 KB 244 ... 476
Close v. Steel Company of Wales Ltd. [1962] AC 367 ... 392
Clunis v. Camden and Islington HA [1998] QB 978 ... 388, 924
Cocks v. Thanet DC [1983] 2 AC 286 ... 403, 432, 433
Coco v. A. N. Clark (Engineers) Ltd. (1969) RPC 41 ... 838, 839, 840, 844
Coddington v. International Harvester Co. of Great Britain (1969) 6 KIR 146 ... 659
Coenen v. Payne [1974] 1 WLR 984 ... 968
Cole v. Turner (1704) 6 Mod. Rep. 149; 87 ER 907 ... 454
Colledge v. Bass Mitchells and Butlers Ltd. [1988] ICR 125 ... 956
Collier v. Anglian Water Authority *The Times* 26 Mar. 1983 ... 346
Collingwood v. Home & Colonial Stores Ltd. [1936] 3 All ER 200 ... 615
Collins v. Renison (1754) 1 Sayer 138; 96 ER 830 ... 502
Collins v. Wilcock [1984] 1 WLR 1172 ... 454
Colls v. Home and Colonial Stores Ltd. [1904] AC 179 ... 520

Coltman v. Bibby Tankers Ltd. [1988] AC 276 ... 660
Columbia Picture Industries v. Robinson [1987] Ch. 38, 87D-F ... 947
Colvilles Ltd. v. Devine [1969] 1 WLR 475 ... 243
Colwell v. St Pancras BC [1904] 1 Ch. 707 ... 530
Commissioner for Railways v. F. J. Quinlan [1964] AC 1054 ... 363
Commissioner for Railways v. McDermott [1967] 1 AC 169 ... 344
Condon v. Basi [1985] 1 WLR 866 ... 228, 913
Conerney v. Jacklin [1985] Crim. LR 234 ... 774
Connolly v. Tasker ... 1003
Connor v. Chief Constable of Merseyside Police [2006] EWCA Civ 1549 ... 464, 468, 479
Consolidated Co. v. Curtis [1892] 1 QB 495 ... 487
Constantine v. Imperial Hotels Ltd. [1944] KB 693 ... 942
Conway v. Rimmer [1968] AC 910 ... 794
Conway v. George Wimpey & Co. Ltd. [1951] 2 KB 266 ... 684, 685
Cook v. Alexander [1974] QB 279 ... 795
Cook v. J. L. Kier and Co. [1970] 1 WLR 774 ... 1002
Cookson v. Harewood [1932] 2 KB 478 ... 783
Cookson v. Knowles [1979] AC 556 ... 989, 1017
Cooper v. Firth Brown Ltd. [1963] 1 WLR 418 ... 980, 990
Cooper v. Williams [1963] 2 All ER 282 ... 1011
Cope v. Sharpe (No. 2) [1912] 1 KB 496 ... 505
Cornelius v. De Taranto [2000] EMLR 12; [2003] WLR 80 ... 845
Cornwell v. Myskow [1987] 1 WLR 630 ... 788
Corporation of Manchester v. Farnworth [1930] AC 171 ... 540
Costello v. Chief Constable of Derbyshire [2001] 1 WLR 1437 (CA) ... 487
Cotton v. Derbyshire Dales DC *The Times* 20 June 1994 ... 356
Couch v. Steel (1854) 3 El & Bl. 402 ... 385
Countryside Residential (North Thames) Ltd. v. T (A Child) *The Times* 4 Apr. 2000; [2000] 2 EGLR 59 ... 500
Coupland v. Eagle Bros. Ltd. [1969] 210 EG 581 ... 356
Cowper v. Laidler [1903] 2 Ch. 337 ... 546
Cox v. Glue (1848) 5 CB 533; 136 ER 987 ... 497
Cox v. Hockenhull [2000] 1 WLR 750 ... 1014
Crédit Lyonnais Bank Nederland NV v. Export Credit Guarantee Department [1998] 1 Lloyd's Rep. 19 ... 598
Crédit Lyonnais Bank Nederland NV v. Export Credit Guarantee Department [2000] 1 AC 486 ... 574, 1041
Crehan v. Inntrepreneur Pub Co. (CPC) [2007] ICR 1344 ... 395
Creswell v. Eaton [1991] 1 WLR 1113 ... 1014
Crofter Hand Woven Harris Tweed Co. v. Veitch [1942] AC 435 ... 573, 596, 597, 599
Crossley v. Rawlinson [1982] 1 WLR 369 ... 219
Crown River Cruises Ltd. v. Kimbolton Fireworks Ltd. [1996] 2 Lloyd's Rep. 533 ... 522, 535, 611, 612
Cruise v. Express Newspapers [1999] QB 931 ... 785
Cullen v. Chief Constable of the Royal Ulster Constabulary [2003] 1 WLR 1763 ... 381
Cullen v. Morris (1819) 2 Stark. 577 ... 428
Cummings v. Granger [1977] QB 397 ... 543, 631, 638, 639, 640, 645
Cunard v. Antifyre Ltd. [1933] 1 KB 551 ... 522, 530
Cundy v. Lindsay (1878) 3 App. Cas. 459 ... 487
Cunningham v. Harrison [1973] QB 942 ... 980, 982, 985, 994
Cunningham v. Reading Football Club Ltd. [1992] PIQR P141 ... 352
Cunningham v. Whelan (1917) 521 LT 67 ... 632
Curran v. Northern Ireland Co-Ownership Housing Association Ltd. [1987] AC 718 ... 416
Curtis v. Betts [1990] 1 All ER 769 ... 631, 639, 640
Curwen v. James [1963] 1 WLR 748 ... 1016
Customs & Excise Commissioners v. Barclays Bank plc [2006] 3 WLR 1 (HL) ... 123, 124, 130, 131, 162, 196
Cutler v. McPhail [1962] 2 QB 292 ... 775
Cutler v. Vauxhall Motors Ltd. [1971] 1 QB 418 ... 260
Cutler v. Wandsworth Stadium Ltd. [1949] AC 398 ... 377, 379, 384, 385, 393, 586, 592, 593

D v. East Berkshire Community NHS Trust [2005] 2 AC 373 (HL); [2004] QB 558 (CA) ... 104, 105, 135, 136, 137, 211, 213, 399, 401, 411, 417, 418, 422, 424, 425, 441, 445
D. & F. Estates Ltd. v. Church Commissioners for England [1989] AC 177 ... 89, 169, 182, 184, 372, 698
Daborn v. Bath Tramways Motor Co. [1946] 2 All ER 333 ... 240
Dacas v. Brook Street Bureau (UK) Ltd. [2004] IRLR 368 ... 676

Daiichi v. Stop Huntingdon Animal Cruelty [2004] 1 WLR 1503 . . . 474
Dakhyl v. Labouchere [1908] 2 KB 325 . . . 787
Daly v. General Steam Navigation Co. Ltd. [1981] 1 WLR 120 . . . 981
Daniel v. Ferguson [1981] 2 Ch. 27 . . . 1030
Daniells v. Mendonca (1999) 78 P & CR 401 (CA) . . . 1030
Daniels v. R. White & Sons Ltd. [1938] 4 All ER 258 . . . 707, 731
Dann v. Hamilton [1939] 1 KB 509 . . . 745, 891, 906, 910
Darbishire v. Warran [1963] 1 WLR 1067 . . . 1021
Darby v. National Trust [2001] PIQR P27 (CA) . . . 349, 356
Darley Main Colliery Co. v. Mitchell (1886) 11 App. Cas. 127 929
Darlington BC v. Wiltshier Northern Ltd. [1995] 1 WLR 68 . . . 26, 175
Davey v. Harrow Corp. [1958] 1 QB 60 . . . 513
David v. Abdul Cader [1963] 1 WLR 834 . . . 428
Davidson v. Chief Constable of North Wales and Another [1994] 2 All ER 597 . . . 465, 466
Davie v. New Merton Board Mills Ltd. [1959] AC 604 . . . 657
Davies v. Davies [1975] QB 172 . . . 633
Davies v. Ilieff (Ch. D, unreported, 21 Dec. 2000) . . . 501
Davies v. Mann (1842) 10 M & W 546; 152 ER 588 . . . 893
Davies v. Presbyterian Church of Wales [1986] 1 WLR 323 . . . 666
Davies v. Radcliffe [1990] 1 WLR 821 . . . 128
Davies v. Swan Motor Co. [1949] 2 KB 291 . . . 894, 901
Davies v. Taylor [1974] AC 207 . . . 1014
Davis Contractors Ltd. v. Fareham UDC [1956] AC 686 . . . 223
Davison v. Gent (1857) 1H & N 744; 156 ER 1400 . . . 501
Davy v. Spelthorne BC [1984] AC 262 . . . 427
Dawson & Co. v. Bingley Urban District Council [1911] 2 KB 149 . . . 387
D.C. Thomson & Co. Ltd. v. Deakin [1952] Ch. 646 . . . 577, 581, 583
De Francesco v. Burnum (1890) 43 Ch. D 165 . . . 576
De Jetley Marks v. Lord Greenwood [1936] 1 All ER 863 . . . 580
De La Bere v. Pearson Ltd. 1 KB 280 . . . 23
Dean v. Hogg (1834) 10 Bing. 345; 131 ER 937 . . . 501
Deane v. Ealing LBC [1993] ICR 329 . . . 946
Delaney v. T. P. Smith Ltd. [1946] KB 39 . . . 500
Delaware Mansions Ltd. v. Westminster City Council [2002] 1 AC 321 (HL) . . . 513, 533
Delegal v. Highley (1861) 3 Bing. NC 950; 132 ER 677 . . . 477
Dennis v. Ministry of Defence [2003] EWHC 793 (QB); [2003] Env. LR 34 . . . 522, 533, 535, 539, 547
Dennis v. Ministry of Defence [2003] EWHC 793 (QB); [2034] Env. LR 34 . . . 543
Department of the Environment v. Thomas Bates & Sons [1991] 1 AC 499 . . . 182
Department for Transport, Environment and the Regions v. Mott, MacDonald Ltd. [2006] EWCA Civ 1089; [2006] 1 WLR 3356 . . . 391
Department of Transport v. Williams [1993] TLR 367 . . . 593
Derbyshire County Council v. Times Newspapers Ltd. [1993] 1 All ER 1011; [1993] AC 534 . . . 102, 771, 772, 783, 816
Derry v. Handley (1867) 16 LT 263 . . . 775
Derry v. Peek (1889) 14 App. Cas. 337 . . . 162, 565, 566, 568
Design Progression Ltd. v. Thurloe Properties Ltd. [2005] 1 WLR . . . 946
Despina R, The [1979] AC 685 . . . 965
Dewell v. Sanders (1618) Cro. Jac. 490; 79 ER 419 . . . 551
Dewey v. White (1827) M & M 56; 173 ER 1079 . . . 505
Dews v. National Coal Board [1988] AC 1 . . . 980
Deyong v. Shenburn [1946] KB 227 . . . 125
Dhaliwal v. Personal Representatives of Hunt [1995] 4 PIQR Q56 . . . 978, 979
Dhesi v. Chief Constable of the West Midlands Police *The Times* 9 May 2000 (CA) . . . 644
Diamond v. Bank of London and Montreal Ltd. [1979] QB 333 . . . 567
Dick Bentley Productions Ltd. v. Harold Smith (Motors) Ltd. [1965] 1 WLR 623 . . . 23
Dickinson v. Del Solar [1930] 1 KB 376 . . . 33
Dimbleby & Sons Ltd. v. National Union of Journalists [1984] 1 WLR 427 . . . 583, 584
Dimmock v. Hallett (1866) LR 2 . . . 725
Dimond v. Lovell [2000] 2 WLR 1121; [2002] 1 AC 384 . . . 1023, 1024, 1025
Dimskal Shipping Co. v. International Transport Workers' Federation, The Evia Luck [1991] 4 All ER 871 . . . 595
Dingle v. Associated Newspapers Ltd. [1961] 2 QB 162 . . . 1037

Director of Public Prosecutions v. Jones [1999] 2 AC 240 . . . 497, 498
Dixon's Case *see* R v. Broadcasting Standards Commission *ex parte* British Broadcasting Corporation [2001] QB 885
Dodd Properties (Kent) Ltd. v. Canterbury City Council [1980] 1 All ER 928; [1980] 1 WLR 433 . . . 276, 1021
Dodds v. Dodds [1978] QB 543 . . . 1010
Dodwell v. Burford (1670) 1 Mod. Rep. 24; 86 ER 703 . . . 455
Doe d. Carter v. Barnard (1849) 13 QB 945 . . . 501
Doe d. Johnson v. Baytup (1835) 3 A & E 188; 111 ER 384 . . . 501
Dominion Natural Gas Co. Ltd. v. Collins [1909] AC 640 . . . 114
Donnelly v. Joyce [1974] QB 454 . . . 979, 982, 983, 994, 995, 996, 997
Donoghue v. Folkestone Properties Ltd. [2003] 2 WLR 1138 (CA) . . . 367, 368
Donoghue v. Stevenson [1932] AC 562 . . . 24, 81, 96, 114, 115, 125, 128, 138, 158, 173, 180, 189, 200, 243, 272, 281, 341, 372, 374, 397, 407, 452, 574, 608, 624, 703, 705, 707, 710, 724, 726, 732, 747, 891
Dooley v. Cammell Laird & Co. Ltd. [1951] 1 Lloyds Rep. 271 . . . 155
Dorset Yacht Co. Ltd. v. Home Office [1970] AC 1004 . . . 126, 128, 206, 212, 266, 267, 313, 318, 321, 322, 403, 431
Dott v. Brown [1936] 1 All ER 543 . . . 971
Doughty v. Turner Manufacturing Co. Ltd. [1964] 1 QB 518 . . . 274
Douglas v. Hello! Ltd. (No. 1) [2001] 2 WLR 992; [2001] QB 967 (HC); (No. 2) [2003] EWCA Civ 139 (CA); [2003] EMLR 28 (CA); (No. 3) [2005] EWCA Civ 595 (CA); [2006] QB 125 (CA); [2007] UKHL 21 (HL) . . . 574, 575, 579, 587, 588, 599, 602, 603, 832, 837, 840, 841, 848, 851, 852, 855, 856, 857, 945, 1032
Douglas Valley Finance Co. Ltd. v. S. Hughes (Hirers) Ltd. [1969] 1 QB 738 . . . 488
Dow Jones & Co. v. Gutnick [2002] HCA 56; 194 ALR 433 . . . 882
Downs v. Chappell [1996] 3 All ER 344; [1997] 1 WLR 426 . . . 569
Downsview Nominees Ltd. v. First City Corp. [1993] 3 All ER 937 . . . 131
Doyle v. Olby (Ironmongers) Ltd. [1969] 2 QB 158 . . . 280, 569
DPP v. Jones [1999] 2 AC 240 . . . 495, 551
Drane v. Evangelou [1978] 1 WLR 455 (CA) . . . 944, 948
Draper v. Hodder [1972] 2 QB 556 . . . 632, 643
Drinkwater v. Kimber [1952] 2 QB 281 . . . 1033
Drummond-Jackson v. British Medical Association [1970] 1 WLR 688 . . . 760
Dubai Aluminium Co. Ltd. v. Salaam [2002] UKHL 48, [2003] 2 AC 366 . . . 679, 689, 694, 699
Duchess of Argyll v. Duke of Argyll [1967] Ch. 302 . . . 839
Duck v. Mayeu [1892] 2 QB 511 . . . 1034
Duffy v. Thanet District Council (1984) 134 NLJ 680 . . . 683
Duke v. GEC Reliance Systems Ltd. [1988] AC 618 . . . 395
Dulieu v. White [1901] 2 KB 669 . . . 141
Duller v. South East Lincs Engineers [1981] CLY 585 . . . 990
Duncan v. Findlater (1839) 6 Cl. & F 894; 7 ER 934 . . . 665
Dunlop v. Woollahra Municipal Council [1982] AC 158 . . . 428, 593
Dunlop Pneumatic Tyre Co. Ltd. v. Selfridge & Co. Ltd. [1915] AC 847 . . . 173, 724
Dunn v. Birmingham Land Co. (1872) LR 7 QB 244 . . . 621
Dunster v. Abbott [1954] 1 WLR 58 . . . 343, 350
Duport Steels Ltd. v. Sirs in 1980 [1980] 1 WLR 142 . . . 599
Dutton v. Bognor Regis Urban District Council [1972] 1 QB 373 . . . 94, 127, 138, 369, 370, 372, 627, 1035

E (A Child) v. Townfoot Stables [2004] CLY 169 . . . 640
E. Hobbs (Farms) Ltd. v. The Baxenden Chemical Co. Ltd. [1992] 1 Ll. L Rep. 54 . . . 625, 737
E. Hulton & Co. v. Jones [1910] AC 20 . . . 768
Eagle v. Chambers [2003] EWCA Civ 1108 . . . 901
Earl of Lonsdale v. Nelson (1823) 2 B & C 302; 107 ER 396 . . . 549
Easson v. London & North Eastern Railway Co. [1944] KB 421 . . . 242
East Suffolk Rivers Catchment Board v. Kent [1940] 1 KB 319; [1941] AC 74 . . . 125, 203, 209, 406, 407, 408, 410, 420
East v. Maurer [1991] 2 All ER 737; 1 WLR 461 . . . 280, 569
Eastern and South African Telegraph Co. Ltd. v. Cape Town Cos. Ltd. [1902] AC 381 . . . 524
Eden v. West & Co. [2002] EWCA Civ 991; [2003] PIQR Q2 (CA) . . . 355

Edgington v. Fitzmaurice (1885) 29 Ch. D 459 . . . 566, 569
Edward Wong Finance Co. Ltd. v. Johnson Stokes & Master [1984] AC 296 . . . 235
Edwards v. Railway Executive [1952] AC 737 . . . 348
Edwin Hill & Partners v. First National Finance Corp. [1989] 1 WLR 225 . . . 577, 580
Egerton v. Harding [1975] QB 62 . . . 634
Eglantine Inn Ltd. v. Smith [1948] NI 29 . . . 773
Eiles v. Southwark London Borough Council [2006] EWHC 1411 . . . 534
Electrical, Electronic, Telecommunication and Plumbing Union v. Times Newspapers Ltd. [1980] QB 585 . . . 771
Elguzouli-Daf v. Commissioner of Police of the Metropolis [1995] QB 335 . . . 60, 214, 419, 443
Ellis v. Burton [1975] 1 WLR 386 . . . 455
Ellis v. Home Office [1953] 2 QB 135 . . . 200, 205
Ellis v. The Loftus Iron Co. (1874) LR 10 CP 10 . . . 634
Ellis v. Pasmore [1934] 2 KB 164 . . . 499
Ellis v. Scruttons Maltby Ltd. and Cunard Steamship Co. [1975] 1 Lloyd's Rep. 564 . . . 345
Elsee v. Smith (1822) 1 D & R 97 . . . 476
Elvin and Powell Ltd. v. Pummer Roddis Ltd. (1933) 50 TLR 158 . . . 488
Elwes v. Brigg Gas Co. (1886) 33 Ch. D 562 . . . 485, 497
Emblen v. Myers (1860) 6H & N 54; 158 ER 23 . . . 944
Emeh v. Kensington and Chelsea and Westminster AHA [1985] QB 1012 . . . 178, 218, 269, 976
Emerald Construction Co. Ltd. v. Lowthian [1966] 1 WLR 691 . . . 577
English and Scottish Co-Operative Properties Mortgage and Investment Society Ltd. v. Odhams Press Ltd. [1940] 1 All ER 1 . . . 758
Entick v. Carrington (1765) 2 Wils. KB 275; 19 Howell's St Tr 1029; 95 ER 807 . . . 484, 496, 825, 833
Esso Petroleum Co. Ltd. v. Mardon [1976] QB 801 . . . 20, 23, 163, 918
Eurymedon, The. *see* New Zealand Shipping Co. Ltd. v. AM Satterthwaite and Co. Ltd. (The Eurymedon)
Eustace v. Eyre [1947] LJNCCR 106 . . . 646
Evans v. Glasgow District Council, 1978 SLT 17 . . . 319
Evans v. London Hospital Medical College [1981] 1 WLR 184 . . . 477
Evans v. Pontypridd Roofing Ltd [2001] EWCA Civ 1657 . . . 981
Evans v. Triplex Safety Glass Co. Ltd. [1938] 1 All ER 283 . . . 707, 710, 732
Everett v. Ribbands [1952] 2 QB 191 . . . 476
Exchange Telegraph Co. v. Gregory & Co. [1896] 1 QB 147 . . . 576

F, Re [1990] 2 AC 1 . . . 454, 458, 460, 462, 505, 926
F v. R (1984) 33 SASR 189 . . . 456
Fagan v. Metropolitan Police Commissioner [1969] 1 QB 439 . . . 455
Fairchild v. Glenhaven Funeral Services Ltd. [2002] 1 WLR 1052 (CA) . . . 341
Fairchild v. Glenhaven Funeral Services Ltd. [2003] 1 AC 32; [2002] 3 WLR 89 (HL) . . . 77, 82, 85, 121, 180, 246, 247, 248, 253, 254, 255, 256, 257, 259, 741, 1039, 1040
Fairlie v. Perth and Kinross Healthcare NHS Trust [2004] SLT 400 . . . 425
Fairman v. Perpetual Investment Building Society [1923] AC 74 . . . 342
Falconer v. Aslef [1986] IRLR 331 . . . 584
Fardon v. Harcourt-Rivington (1932) 146 LTR 391 . . . 632
Farmer v. Rash [1969] 1 WLR 160 . . . 1009
Farr v. Butters Bros. & Co. [1932] 2 KB 606 . . . 125, 732
Farrington v. Thomson and Bridgland [1959] VR 286 . . . 428
Fashade v. North Middlesex Hospital NHS Trust [2001] 4 QB 13 . . . 970
Fay v. Prentice (1845) 1 CB 828; 135 ER 769 . . . 557
Fayed v. Al-Tajir [1988] QB 712 . . . 794
Federal Bank of the Middle East v. Hadkinson [2000] 2 All ER 395 . . . 839, 844
Fellowes v. Rother DC [1983] 1 All ER 513 . . . 431, 540
Ferguson v. John Dawson & Partners (Contractors) Ltd. [1976] 1 WLR 1213 . . . 673
Ferguson v. Welsh [1987] 1 WLR 1553 . . . 343, 345, 349, 360, 362
Fielding v. Variety Incorporated [1967] 2 QB 841 . . . 816
Fields v. Davis [1955] CLY 1543 . . . 759
First National Commercial Bank v. Humberts [1995] 2 All ER 673 . . . 935
Fish v. Wilcox and Gwent Health Authority [1994] 5 Med. LR 230 . . . 982
Fisher v. CHT Ltd. (No. 2) [1966] 2 QB 475 . . . 345

Fisher v. Harrods Ltd. [1966] 1 Lloyd's Rep. 500 . . . 726
Fitzgerald v. Ford [1996] PIQR Q72 . . . 982
Fitzgerald v. Lane [1987] QB 781 (CA) . . . 252, 254, 259
Fitzgerald v. Lane [1989] AC 328 (HL) . . . 331, 1037
Fitzjohn v. Mackinder (1861) 9 CB (NS) 505; 142 ER 99 . . . 477
Flack v. Hudson [2001] QB 698 . . . 643
Fletcher v. Autocar and Transporters [1968] 2 QB 322 . . . 1001
Fletcher v. Rylands (1866) LR 1 Ex. 1 265 . . . 452
Fletcher v. Smith (1877) 2 App. Cas. 781 . . . 513
Flint v. Lovell [1935] 1 KB 354 . . . 1004
Flitcroft Case *see* A v. B plc
Flora v. Wakom Ltd [2006] EWCA Civ 1103 . . . 973
Forsikringsaktieselskapet Vesta v. Butcher [1989] AC 852 (CA) . . . 347, 904, 1037
Forster v. Oughtred & Co. [1982] 1 WLR 86 . . . 935, 936
Fortunity, The [1961] 1 WLR 351 . . . 1020
Foster v. Tyne and Wear County Council [1986] 1 All ER 567 . . . 978, 979
Foster v. Warblington UDC [1906] 1 KB 648 . . . 530
Fouldes v. Willoughby (1841) 8M & W 540 . . . 484, 486
Foulger v. Newcomb (1867) LR 2 Ex. 327 . . . 759
Fournier v. Canadian National Railway [1927] AC 167 . . . 965
Fowler v. Lanning [1959] 1 QB 426 . . . 452, 466
Fowley Marine (Emsworth) Ltd. v. Gafford [1967] 2 QB 808 . . . 498
Francis v. Home Office [2006] EWHC 3021 . . . 428
Francome v. Mirror Group Newspapers Ltd. [1984] 1 WLR 892; 2 All ER 408 . . . 825, 838, 839, 850
Franklin v. Giddens [1978] Qd R. 72 . . . 839
Freeman v. Home Office (No. 2) [1984] 1 QB 524 . . . 456
Freeman v. Lockett [2006] EWHC 102 . . . 961
French v. Sussex CC [2004] EWHC 3217 . . . 157
Froggatt v. Chesterfield and North Derbyshire Royal Hospital NHS Trust, QBD, 13 Dec. 2002 . . . 145, 154
Froom v. Butcher [1976] QB 286 . . . 895, 897, 900, 901
Frost v. Chief Constable of South Yorkshire . . . 654
Fuhri v. Jones 1979 CA No. 199 30 Mar. 1979 . . . 1000
Fullam v. Newcastle Chronicle and Journal Ltd. [1977] 1 WLR 651 . . . 763

Gaca v. Pirelli General plc [2004] 1 WLR 2683 . . . 961
Galoo Ltd. (in liquidation) v. Bright Grahame Murray [1994] 1 WLR 1360 . . . 167
Galt v. British Railways Board (1983) 133 NLJ 870 . . . 155
Gammell v. Wilson [1982] AC 27 . . . 999, 1008
Garden Cottage Foods Ltd. v. Milk Marketing Board [1984] AC 130 . . . 395, 586
Gardiner v. Moore [1969] 1 QB 55 . . . 1034
Gardner v. Marsh & Parsons [1997] 3 All ER 871 . . . 976
Gardner v. Moore [1984] AC 548 . . . 1040
Gardner v. Slade (1849) 18 LJQB 334 . . . 800
Garnac Grain Co. Inc. v. H. M. F. Faure and Fairclough Ltd. [1968] AC 1130 . . . 975
Gaskill v. Preston [1981] 3 All ER 427 . . . 956
Gathercole v. Miall (1846) 15 M & W 319; 153 ER 872 . . . 787
Gaylor v. Davies [1924] 2 KB 75 . . . 636
GE Commercial Finance Ltd. v. Gee [2005] EWHC 2056 . . . 567, 568
Geddis v. Bann Reservoir Proprietors (1878) 3 App. Cas. 430 . . . 397, 402, 406, 619
Gee v. Pritchard (1818) 2 Swans 402; 36 ER 670 (privacy) 1029
Geier v. Kujawa, Weston and Warne Bros. Transport [1970] 1 Lloyd's Rep . . . 356
General Cleaning Contractors v. Christmas [1953] AC 180 . . . 354, 660, 661
General Engineering Services Ltd. v. Kingston and Saint Andrew Corp. [1989] 1 WLR 69 . . . 681
Generale Bank Nederland NV v. Export Credit Guarantee Department [1998] 1 Lloyd's Rep. 19 . . . 679, 689
George v. Pinnock [1973] 1 WLR 118 . . . 978
George v. Stagecoach [2003] EWCH 2042 . . . 992
George and Richard, The (1871) LR 3 A & E 466 . . . 1011
George Wimpey & Co. Ltd. v. British Overseas Airways Corporation [1955] AC 169 . . . 1036
Gerhold v. Baker [1918] WN 368 . . . 794
Gerrard v. Crowe [1921] 1 AC 395 . . . 611
GFI Group v. Eaglestone [1994] FSR 535 . . . 1031
Ghani v. Jones [1970] 1 QB 693 . . . 834
Ghannan v. Glasgow Corporation, 1950 SLT 2 . . . 352

Gibbs v. Rea [1998] AC 786 . . . 444, 476, 479
Gilbert v. Stone (1647) Style 72; 82 ER 539 . . . 30
Gilding v. Eyre (1861) 10 CB (NS) 592 . . . 477
Giles v. Thompson [1994] 1 AC 142 . . . 1023, 1025
Giles v. Walker (1890) 24 QBD 656 . . . 611
Gillick v. BBC [1996] EMLR 267 . . . 754
Gillick v. West Norfolk Area Health Authority [1986] AC 112 . . . 457
Gillingham Borough Council v. Medway (Chatham) Dock Company Ltd. [1993] QB 343 . . . 543
Ginty v. Belmont Building Supplies Ltd. [1959] 1 All ER 414 . . . 392, 896
GKR Karate (UK) Ltd. v. Yorkshire Post Ltd. [2001] 1 WLR 2571 . . . 802
Glanville v. Sutton [1928] 1 KB 571 . . . 642
Glasgow Corporation v. Muir [1943] AC 448 . . . 224
Glasgow Corporation v. Taylor [1922] 1 AC 44 . . . 351, 353
Gleghorn v. Oldham (1927) 43 TLR 465 . . . 913
Glen v. Korean Airlines Co. Ltd. [2003] QB 1386 . . . 496
Glen-Mor Fashions Ltd. v. Jaeger Company Shops Ltd. (unreported, transcript on LEXIS), Court of Appeal, 20 Nov. 1991 . . . 164
Glencore International AG v. Metro Trading International Inc. [2001] 1 Lloyd's Rep. 284 (QBD) . . . 489
Glinski v. McIver [1962] AC 726 . . . 478
Glossop v. Heston and Isleworth Local Board (1879) 12 Ch. D 102 (CA) . . . 518
Gloster v. Chief Constable of Greater Manchester Police [2000] PIQR P114 . . . 638, 639, 640
Godfrey v. Demon Internet [1999] 4 All ER 342 . . . 778
Gold v. Essex County Council [1942] 2 KB 293 . . . 669
Gold v. Haringey HA [1988] QB 481 . . . 218
Goldman v. Hargrave [1967] 1 AC 645 . . . 206, 239, 509, 513, 514, 515, 518, 519, 526, 528, 537, 558, 611
Goldsmith v. Bhoyrul [1998] 2 WLR 435 . . . 772
Goldsmith v. Pressdram Ltd. [1977] QB 83 . . . 758
Goldsmith v. Sperrings Ltd. [1977] 1 WLR 478 . . . 777
Goldsoll v. Goldman [1914] 2 Ch. 603 . . . 576
Good Luck, The [1989] 2 Lloyd's Rep. 238 . . . 905
Goodes v. East Sussex CC [2000] 1 WLR 1356; PIQR P148 (HL) . . . 209, 391, 426, 554
Goodwill v. British Pregnancy Advisory Service [1996] 1 WLR 1397 . . . 173, 177, 178, 218
Gorringe v. Calderdale MBC [2004] UKHL 15; [2004] 1 WLR 1057 . . . 79, 209, 210, 391, 399, 402, 403, 554, 850
Gorris v. Scott (1874) LR 9 Exch. 125 . . . 392, 393
Gough v. Chief Constable of the West Midlands [2004] EWCA Civ 206 . . . 487
Gough v. Thorne [1966] 1 WLR 1387 . . . 898
Gould v. McAuliffe [1941] 2 All ER 527 . . . 349
Gouriet v. Union of Post Office Workers [1978] AC 435 . . . 394, 592, 593
Gourock Ropework Co. v. Greenock Corp., 1966 SLT 125 . . . 538
Governors of the Peabody Donation Fund v. Sir Lindsay Parkinson & Co. [1985] AC 210 . . . 59, 128, 181, 210, 398, 416, 426
Gower v. London Borough of Bromley [1999] ELR 356 . . . 137, 154
Graham v. Dodds [1983] 1 WLR 808 . . . 1017
Gran Gelato Ltd. v. Richcliff (Group) Ltd. [1992] 1 All ER 865; [1992] Ch. 560 . . . 175, 902, 905
Grant v. Australian Knitting Mills Ltd. [1936] AC 85 . . . 243, 706, 707, 727, 730, 731, 742
Grant v. Sun Shipping Co. Ltd. [1948] AC 549 . . . 241, 893, 899
Granville v. Sutton [1928] 1 KB 571 . . . 646
Grappelli v. Derek Block (Holdings) Ltd. [1981] 2 All ER 272 . . . 763
Gray v. Jones [1939] 1 All ER 798 . . . 758
Grealis v. Opuni [2003] EWCA Civ 177 . . . 898
Great Central Railway Co. v. Bates [1921] 3 KB 578 . . . 348
Greater Nottingham Co-operative Society v. Cementation Piling and Foundation Ltd. [1989] QB 71 . . . 191
Greatorex v. Greatorex [2000] 1 WLR 1976 . . . 149, 219
Grech v. Odhams Press Ltd. [1958] 2 QB 275 . . . 787
Green v. The Chelsea Waterworks Co. (1894) 70 LT 547 . . . 619
Green v. DB Group Services Ltd. [2006] IRLR 764 . . . 654, 693
Green v. Fibreglass Ltd. [1958] 2 QB 245 . . . 361
Green v. Goddard (1704) 2 Salk. 641; 91 ER 540 . . . 503
Green v. Lord Somerleyton [2003] EWCA Civ 198; [2004] 1 P & CR 33 . . . 514, 516, 528
Greenfield v. Irwin [2001] 1 WLR 1279 . . . 138, 178, 218
Greenlands v. Wilmshurst [1913] 3KB 507 . . . 800

Greenock Corporation v. Caledonian Railways Co. [1917] AC 556 . . . 620, 927
Greenwell v. Prison Commissioners (1951) 101 LJ 486 . . . 409
Greer v. Alstons Engineering Sales and Services Ltd. [2003] UKPC 46 . . . 490
Gregg v. Scott [2005] 2 AC 176 . . . 247, 248, 257, 264, 265
Gregory v. Kelly [1978] RTR 426 . . . 898
Gregory v. Piper (1829) 9 B & C 591 . . . 495, 496
Gregory v. Portsmouth City Council [2000] 1 AC 419 . . . 475, 476
Greig v. Insole [1978] 1 WLR 302 . . . 576, 579
Greystoke Castle, The [1947] AC 265 . . . 187, 188
Grice v. Stourport Tennis Club [1997] CLY 3859 (CA) . . . 345
Griffin v. South West Water Services Ltd. [1995] IRLR 15 . . . 440
Griffiths v. Benn (1911) 27 TLR 346 . . . 816
Grobbelaar v. News Group Newspapers Ltd. [2002] 1 WLR 3024 . . . 765, 803, 815
Gross v. Lewis Hillman Ltd. [1970] Ch. 445 . . . 565
Groves v. Lord Wimborne [1898] 2 QB 402 . . . 382, 386, 652
Gulf Oil (GB) Ltd. v. Page [1987] Ch. 327 . . . 757, 758
Guppys (Bridport) Ltd. v. Brookling and James (1984) 14 HLR 1 (CA) . . . 946, 948
Gwilliam v. North Hertfordshire Hospital NHS Trust [2002] 3 WLR 1425 . . . 361, 362
GWK Ltd. v. Dunlop Rubber Co. Ltd.(1926) 42 TLR 376 . . . 577, 578

H v. Ministry of Defence [1991] 2 QB 103 . . . 977, 978
H. Parsons (Livestock) Ltd. v. Uttley, Ingham & Co. Ltd. [1978] QB 791 . . . 279
H. West & Son Ltd. v. Shephard [1964] AC 326 . . . 1001, 1002
Habinteg Housing Association v. James (1995) 27 HLR 299 . . . 538
Hadley v. Baxendale (1854) 9 Exch. 341 . . . 279, 742
Hadmor Productions Ltd. v. Hamilton [1982] IRLR 102; [1983] 1 AC 191 . . . 581, 591, 600
Hagen v. ICI Chemicals and Polymers Ltd. [2002] IRLR 31 . . . 569
Hale v. Jennings Bros. [1938] 1 All ER 579 . . . 621
Hale v. London Underground [1993] PIQR Q30 . . . 1005, 1006
Haley v. London Electricity Board [1965] AC 778 . . . 238
Halford v. Brookes [1991] 1 WLR 428 . . . 455
Hall v. Brooklands Racing Club [1933] 1 KB 205 . . . 223
Hall v. Woolston Hall Leisure Ltd. [2000] IRLR 578 . . . 671, 673
Halsey v. Esso Petroleum Co. Ltd. [1961] 1 WLR 683 . . . 521, 534, 551, 621
Halsey v. Milton Keynes General NHS Trust [2004] EWCA Civ 576 . . . 258
Hamble Fisheries Ltd. v. L. Gardner & Sons Ltd., The Rebecca Elaine [1999] 2 Lloyd's Rep. 1 . . . 185
Hambrook v. Stokes Bros [1925] 1 KB 141 . . . 146
Hamilton v. Guardian *The Times* 22 July 1995 . . . 791
Hampstead & Suburban Properties Ltd. v. Diomedous [1969] 1 Ch. 248 . . . 530
Hannington v. Mitie Cleaning (South East) Ltd. [2002] EWCA Civ 1847, 26 Nov. 2002 (CA) . . . 354
Hanson v. Waller [1901] 1 QB 390 . . . 680
Harbutt's Plasticine Ltd. v. Wayne Tank and Pump Co. Ltd. [1912] AC 673 . . . 1022
Hardwick v. Hudson [1999] 1 WLR 1770; [1999] 3 All ER 426 . . . 982, 996
Hardy v. Motor Insurers' Bureau [1964] 2 QB 745 . . . 924, 1040
Harrhy v. Thames Trains Ltd. [2003] EWHC 2120 . . . 157
Harris v. Birkenhead Corporation [1975] 1 WLR 379 . . . 346
Harris v. Brights Asphalt Contractors Ltd. [1953] 1 QB 617 . . . 993
Harris v. Empress Motors Ltd [1983] 1 WLR 65 . . . 999
Harris v. Evans [1998] 1 WLR 1285 . . . 210, 215, 216, 419
Harris v. Harris [1973] 1 Lloyd's Rep. 445 (CA) . . . 978
Harris v. James (1876) 45 LJQB 545 . . . 538
Harris v. Lewisham and Guy's Mental Health Trust [2000] 3 All ER 769 . . . 1007
Harris v. Wyre Forest District Council [1988] QB 835 CA; [1990] 1 AC 831 (HL) . . . 168, 169, 359, 916, 917, 918
Harrison v. British Railways Board [1981] 3 All ER 639 . . . 219, 268
Harrison v. Michelin Tyre Co. Ltd. [1985] 1 All ER 918 . . . 659, 678, 682, 683, 685
Harrison v. Southwark and Vauxhall Water Co. [1891] 2 Ch. 409 . . . 522
Hart v. Chief Constable of Kent [1983] RTR 484 . . . 463

Hart v. Griffiths-Jones [1948] 2 All ER 729 ... 1007
Hartley v. Mayoh & Co. [1952] 2 All ER 525; [1954] 1 QB 383 ... 391, 727
Hartman v. South Essex Mental Health and Community Care Trust [2005] IRLR 293; [2005] EWCA Civ 6 ... 157, 655
Hartt v. Newspaper Publishing plc *The Independent* 27 Oct. 1989; CLY 1989 ... 753
Harvey v. O'Dell Ltd. [1958] 2 QB 78 ... 694
Harvey v. Walters (1873) LR 8 CP 162 ... 539
Haseldine v. Daw Ltd. [1941] 2 KB 343 ... 361, 730
Hassall v. Secretary of State for Social Security [1995] 1 WLR 812 ... 963
Hasselblad (GB) Ltd. v. Orbinson [1985] 2 WLR 1 ... 792
Hatton v. Sutherland [2002] EWCA Civ 76 ... 157
Haward v. Fawcetts [2006] 1 WLR 682 ... 932
Hawkins v. Coulsdon and Purley UDC [1954] 1 QB 319 ... 346
Hay v. Hughes [1975] QB 790 ... 1014
Hayden v. Hayden [1992] 1 WLR 986 ... 1018
Hayes v. Dodd [1990] 2 All ER 815 ... 744
Haynes v. Harwood [1935] 1 KB 146 ... 125, 204
Hayward v. Thompson [1982] QB 47 ... 767
Hazell v. British Transport Commission [1958] 1 WLR 169 ... 223
Heasmans v. Clarity Cleaning Co. Ltd. [1987] ICR 949 ... 681
Heath v. Brighton Corporation (1908) 98 LT 718 ... 524
Heaven v. Pender (1883) 11 QBD 503 ... 115, 286, 287, 291, 292, 310
Hebbert v. Thomas (1835) 1 Cr. M & R 861 ... 499
Hebridean Coast, The [1961] AC 545 ... 1022, 1023
Hedley Byrne & Co. Ltd. v. Heller & Partners Ltd. [1964] AC 465 ... 18, 22, 24, 27, 28, 84, 89, 94, 96, 125, 130, 132, 161, 162, 163, 164, 165, 166, 167, 169, 170, 171, 172, 173, 183, 184, 192, 193, 197, 199, 215, 277, 280, 381, 427, 567, 568, 656, 709, 726, 743, 902, 916, 917, 918, 933, 934, 935
Hehir v. Commissioner of Police for the Metropolis [1982] 1 WLR 715 ... 774
Heil v. Rankin [2001] QB 272 ... 1000, 1003
Heilbut, Symons & Co. v. Buckleton [1913] AC 30 ... 708, 726
Hellewell v. Chief Constable of Derbyshire [1995] 1 WLR 804 ... 836, 859
Hemmings v. Stoke Poges Golf Club [1920] 1 KB 720 ... 503
Henderson v. Henry E. Jenkins [1970] AC 282 ... 242
Henderson v. Merrett Syndicates Ltd. [1995] 2 AC 145 ... 18, 20, 29, 172, 192, 199, 215, 277
Henwood v. Harrison (1872) LR 7 CP 606 ... 794
Herbage v. Times Newspapers Ltd. and Others (unreported) ... 830
Herd v. Weardale Steel, Coal and Coke Co. Ltd. [1915] AC 67 ... 467
Herniman v. Smith [1938] AC 305 ... 478
Heron II, The [1969] 1 AC 350 ... 279
Herring v. Boyle (1834) 1 CM & R 377; 149 ER 1126 ... 465
Herrington v. British Railways Board [1972] AC 877 ... 348
Herschtal v. Stewart and Arden Ltd. [1940] 1 KB 155 ... 730, 732
Hevican v. Ruane [1991] 3 All ER 65 ... 140, 146, 147
Hewitt v. Bonvin [1940] 1 KB 188 ... 677
Hewlett v. Crutchley (1813) 5 Taunt. 277; 128 ER 696 ... 478
Hewlett Packard Ltd. v. Murphy [2002] IRLR 4 ... 671
Hickman v. Maisey [1900] 1 QB 752 ... 497, 498
Hicks v. Chief Constable of South Yorkshire [1992] 2 All ER 65 ... 1001
Hicks v. Faulkner (1878) 8 QBD 167 ... 478
Higgs v. Foster (t/a Avaion Coaches) [2004] EWCA Civ 843 ... 368
HIH Casualty and General Insurance Ltd. v. Chase Manhattan Bank Ltd. [2001] 2 Lloyd's Rep. 483 ... 570
Hill v. Chief Constable of South Yorkshire [1990] 1 All ER 1046 ... 468
Hill v. Chief Constable of West Yorkshire [1989] AC 53 (HL); [1988] QB 60 (CA) ... 34, 59, 60, 128, 129, 133, 212, 213, 215, 412, 418, 419, 424, 444, 445
Hill v. James Crowe (Cases) Ltd. [1978] ICR 298 ... 707
Hill v. Tapper (1863) 2H & C 121 ... 500
Hills v. Potter [1984] 1 WLR 641 ... 456
Hilton v. Thomas Burton (Rhodes) Ltd. [1961] 1 WLR 705 ... 686
Hilyer v. St Bartholomew's Hospital [1909] 2 KB 820 ... 669
Hinz v. Berry [1970] 2 QB 40 ... 139, 1001
Hirst and Agu v. Chief Constable of West Yorkshire Police (1987) 85 Cr. App. R 143 ... 497

HL Motorworks (Willesden) Ltd. v. Alwahbi [1977] RTR 276 ... 1023
HM Commissioners of Customs and Excise v. Barclays Bank plc [2006] UKHL 28; [2006] 3 WLR 1 ... 75
Hoare & Co. v. McAlpine [1923] 1 Ch. 167 ... 609
Hobson v. Gledhill [1978] 1 All ER 945 ... 645
Hodge v. Anglo-American Oil Co. (1922) 12 Lloyd's Rep 183 ... 115
Hodgson v. Trapp [1989] AC 807 ... 963, 983
Hoffman v. Sofaer [1982] 1 WLR 1350 ... 965, 1002
Hogg v. Doyle, CA Judgment of 6 Mar. 1991 (unreported) ... 983
Holbeck Hall Hotel v. Scarborough BC [2000] QB 836 (CA) ... 513, 515, 516, 558
Holden v. Chief Constable of Lancashire [1986] 3 All ER 836; [1987] QB 380 (CA) ... 945, 947
Holden v. Express Newspapers Ltd. 7 June 2001 ... 837
Holding and Management (Solitaire) Ltd v. Ideal Homes North West Ltd. [2004] EWHC 2408 ... 182
Hole v. Barlow (1858) 4 CB (NS) 334; 140 ER 1113 ... 511
Hole v. Ross-Skinner [2003] EWCA Civ 774 ... 633, 636
Hollins v. Fowler (1875) LR 7 HL 757 ... 487, 489
Hollywood Silver Fox Farm Ltd. v. Emmett [1936] 2 KB 468 ... 529
Holman v. Johnson (1775) 1 Cowp. 341 ... 923
Holmes v. Ashford [1950] 2 All ER 76 ... 726
Holmes v. Bagge (1853) 1 E & B 782; 118 ER 629 ... 502
Holmes v. Mather (1875) 133 LT 361; (1875) LR 10 Ex. 261 ... 452, 483
Holmes v. Wilson (1839) 10 A & E 503; 113 ER 190 ... 496
Holt v. Payne Skillington (a firm) *The Times* 22 Dec. 1995 ... 29
Holtby v. Brigham & Cowan (Hull) Ltd. [2000] 3 All ER 421 ... 1038, 1039
Home Brewery plc v. William Davis & Co. (Loughborough) Ltd. [1987] 1 All ER 637 ... 513
Home Office v. Dorset Yacht Co. [1970] AC 1004 ... 96, 125, 409
Honeywill & Stein Ltd. v. Larkin Brothers Ltd. [1934] 1 KB 191 ... 668, 696
Hooper v. Rogers [1975] Ch. 43 ... 530, 1032
Hopkins v. Crowe (1836) 4 A & E 774; 111 ER 974 ... 465
Hopwood v. Muirson [1945] KB 313 ... 759
Horbury Building Systems Ltd. v. Hampden Insurance NV [2004] EWCA Civ 418 ... 182
Horley v. Luminar Leisure Ltd. [2006] IRLR 817 ... 676
Horrocks v. Lowe [1975] AC 135 ... 806
Horsford v. Bird [2006] UKPC 3 ... 501, 502
Hotson v. East Berkshire Area Health Authority [1987] AC 750 ... 82, 85, 122, 247, 248, 257, 262, 263, 264
Hounslow LBC v. Jenkins [2004] EWHC 217 (Ch) ... 486
Housecroft v. Burnett [1986] 1 All ER 332 ... 982, 986, 991, 997, 1002
Howard v. Walker [1947] KB 680 ... 125
Howard E. Perry & Co. Ltd. v. British Railways Board [1980] 1 WLR 1375 ... 488
Howard Marine & Dredging Co. v. A. Ogden & Sons (Excavations) Ltd. [1978] QB 574 ... 163, 164
HSBC Rail (UK) Ltd. v. Network Rail Infrastructure Ltd. [2006] 1 All ER 343 (CA); [2006] 1 WLR 643 ... 483, 485
Hsu v. Commissioner of Police of the Metropolis [1997] 2 All ER 762; [1997] 3 WLR 403 ... 944, 947, 977
Hubbard v. Pitt [1976] QB 142 ... 498, 535, 550, 551
Huckle v. Money (1763) 2 Wils. KB 205; 95 ER 768 ... 945
Hudson v. Nicholson (1839) 5M & W 437; 151 ER 185 ... 496
Hudson v. Ridge Manufacturing Co. Ltd. [1957] 2 QB 348 ... 659
Hughes v. Lord Advocate [1963] AC 837 ... 248, 274, 275, 276, 278, 393, 727
Hughes v. McKeown [1965] 1 WLR 963 ... 986
Hughes v. Percival (1883) 8 App. Cas. 443 ... 537, 696
Hulley v. Silversprings Bleaching Co. [1922] 2 Ch. 268 ... 539
Hulton v. Jones [1910] AC 20 ... 779
Humphries v. Cousins (1877) 2 CPD 239 ... 513, 539
Hunt v. Great Northern Railway Co. [1891] 2 QB 189 ... 797
Hunt v. Severs [1994] 2 AC 350; 2 All ER 385 ... 982, 986, 995, 996
Hunt v. The Star Newspaper Co. Ltd. [1908] 2 KB 309 ... 789
Hunt v. Wallis *The Times* 10 May 1991: [1994] PIQR P128 ... 643
Hunter v. British Coal Corporation [1999] QB 140 ... 147

Hunter v. Butler [1996] RTR 396 . . . 990
Hunter v. Canary Wharf Ltd. [1997] 2 WLR 684; AC 655 (CA) . . . 472, 510, 511, 521, 529, 531, 532, 533, 534, 535, 543, 551, 622, 623, 627, 827, 835
Huntley v. Thornton [1957] 1 WLR 321 . . . 597
Hurley v. Dyke [1979] RTR 265 . . . 736
Hurst v. Picture Theatres Corp. [1915] 1 KB 1 . . . 504
Hussain v. Lancaster City Council [2000] QB 1 . . . 536
Hussain v. New Taplow Paper Mills Ltd. [1988] AC 514 . . . 957, 959, 960
Hutchinson v. The York, Newcastle and Berwick Railway Co. (1850) 5 Exch. 343; 155 ER 150 . . . 665, 907
Huth v. Huth [1915] 3 KB 32 . . . 773
Hyde Park Residence v. Yelland [1999] RPC 655 . . . 942

IBA v. EMI Electronics Ltd. (1981) 14 BLR 1 . . . 740
IBL Ltd. v. Coussens [1991] 2 All ER 133 . . . 490
Ichard v. Frangoulis [1977] 1 WLR 556 . . . 10, 1002
ICI Ltd. v. Shatwell [1965] AC 656 . . . 382, 393, 649, 665, 678, 911, 913
Ilford Urban District Council v. Beal [1925] 1 KB 671 . . . 539
Ilkiw v. Samuels [1963] 1 WLR 991 . . . 683, 684
Ilott v. Wilkes (1820) 3 B & Ald. 304 . . . 645
Iman Abouzaid v. Mothercare (UK) Ltd. *The Times* 20 Feb. 2001 . . . 734, 736, 748
Incledon v. Watson (1862) 2 F & F 841; 175 ER 1312 . . . 566
Indermaur v. Dames (1866) LR 1 CP 274 . . . 342, 627
Initial Services v. Putterill [1968] 1 QB 396 . . . 838
Inland Revenue Commissioners v. Rossminster Ltd. [1980] AC 952 . . . 834
Innes v. Wylie [1844] 1 C & K 257 . . . 453
International Factors Ltd. v. Rodriguez [1979] QB 35 . . . 486
Inverugie Investments Ltd. v. Hackett [1995] 1 WLR 713 . . . 501
Investors in Industry Commercial Properties Ltd. v. South Bedfordshire DC [1986] QB 1034 . . . 416
Iqbal v. Whipps Cross University Hospital NHS Trust [2006] EWHC 3111 (QB) . . . 982
Irene's Success, The [1982] QB 481 . . . 186
Iron Trade Mutual Insurance Co. Ltd. v. J. K. Buckenham Ltd [1990] 1 All ER 808 . . . 933, 936
Ironmonger v. Movefield Ltd. [1988] IRLR 461 . . . 671, 676
Irvine v. Talksport Ltd. [2002] 1 WLR 2355; [2002] 2 All ER 414; [2003] EWCA Civ 423, [2003] 2 All ER 881, [2003] EMLR 26 . . . 835, 836
Irving v. The Post Office [1987] IRLR 289 . . . 681
Island Records, *ex parte* [1978] Ch. 122 . . . 387, 394, 395, 592, 1029
Islington London Borough Council v. University College London Hospital NHS Trust 444 [2005] EWCA Civ 596 . . . 198
Iveson v. Moore (1699) 1 Ld. Raym. 486; 91 ER 1224 . . . 553

J (A Minor) (Wardship: Medical Treatment), Re [1991] Fam 33 . . . 457
J. & E. Hall Ltd. v. Barclay [1937] 3 All ER 620 . . . 1020
J. T. Stratford & Son Ltd. v. Lindley [1965] AC 269 . . . 576
Jackson v. Horizon Holidays Ltd. [1975] 1 WLR 1468 . . . 10, 177
Jacobs v. London County Council [1950] AC 361 . . . 554
Jacobs v. Morton (1994) 72 BLR 92 . . . 373
Jaffay and Others v. Society of Lloyds [2002] EWCA Civ 1101; (2002) 146 SJLB 214 (CA) . . . 172
Jaggard v. Sawyer [1995] 1 WLR 269 . . . 546, 1033
Jagger v. News of the World . . . 837
Jameel (Mohamed) and Another v. Wall Street Journal Europe Sprl [2006] 3 WLR 642; [2004] 2 All ER 92 . . . 769, 770, 803, 804, 805
James v. Greenwich LBC, EAT, Appeal No. UKEAT/0006/06/ZT 21 December 2006 . . . 677
James v. Phelps (1840) 11 A & E 483; 113 ER 499 . . . 478
James v. Woodall Duckham Construction Co. Ltd. [1969] 1 WLR 903 . . . 1001
James McNaughton Paper Group Ltd. v. Hicks Anderson & Co. [1991] 2 QB 113 . . . 167
Jameson v. Central Electricity Generating Board [1997] 3 WLR 151; [2000] 2 WLR 141; [2000] AC 455 . . . 1009, 1019, 1034
Jan de Nul (UK) v. AXA Royale Belge SA (formerly NV Royale Belge) [2002] 1 Lloyd's Rep. 583 (CA); [2000] 2 Lloyd's Rep. 700 (QBD) . . . 528, 530, 552, 553, 554

Janvier v. Sweeney [1919] 2 KB 316 ... 471
Jarvis v. Moy Davies & Co. [1936] 1 KB 399 ... 215
Jasperson v. Dominion Tobacco Co. [1923] AC 709 ... 576
Jauffer v. Abkar *The Times* 10 Feb. 1984 ... 230
Jaundrill v. Gillett *The Times* 30 Jan. 1996 ... 631, 633, 638
Jayes v. IMI (Kynoch) Ltd. [1958] ICR 155 ... 896
J.D. Williams & Co. Ltd. v. Michael Hyde & Associates Ltd. [2001] BLR 99; [2000] Lloyd's Rep. PN 823 ... 235
JEB Fasteners Ltd. v. Marks, Bloom & Co. [1983] 1 All ER 583 ... 902
Jefford v. Gee [1970] 2 QB 130 ... 977
Jewish Maternity Home Trustees v. Garfinkle (1926) 95 LJKB 766 ... 499
Jobling v. Associated Dairies Ltd. [1982] AC 794 ... 58, 121, 258, 259, 260, 261, 328, 332, 333
Joe Lee Ltd. v. Damleny [1927] 1 Ch. 300 ... 576
Joel v. Morrison (1834) 6 C & P 501, 503; 172 ER 1338 ... 685
John Lewis & Co. v. Tims [1952] AC 676 ... 467
John Summers & Sons Ltd. v. Frost [1955] AC 740 ... 389, 662
John v. Mirror Group Newspapers Ltd. [1996] All ER 35 (CA); [1996] 3 WLR 593; [1997] QB 586 ... 808, 881, 947, 950
Johnson (t/a Johnson Butchers) v. B.J.W. Property Developments Ltd. [2002] EWHC 1131 (TCC); [2002] 3 All ER 574 ... 537, 558, 622, 624
Johnson v. Emerson & Sparrow (1872) LR 6 Ex. Ch. 329 ... 476
Johnson v. Lindsay & Co. [1891] AC 371 ... 907
Johnstone v. Bloomsbury Area Health Authority [1991] 1 WLR 1314; [1992] 1 QB 333 ... 28, 239, 279, 653, 658, 919
Johnstone v. Pedlar [1921] 2 AC 262 ... 927
Jolley v. Sutton LBC [1998] 1 Lloyd's Rep. 433 (HC, QBD) ... 351
Jolley v. Sutton London Borough Council [2000] 1 WLR 1082 (HL); [1998] 1 WLR 1546 (CA) ... 268, 275, 276, 278
Jones v. Boyce (1816) 1 Starkie 493;171 ER 540 ... 899
Jones v. Chappell (1875) LR 20 Eq. 539 ... 530
Jones v. Department of Employment [1989] QB 1 ... 388, 414
Jones v. The Festiniog Ry. Co. (1868) LR 3 QB 733 ... 621
Jones v. Jones [1916] 2 AC 481 ... 759
Jones v. Jones [1985] QB 704 (CA) ... 985
Jones v. Livox Quarries Ltd. [1952] 2 QB 608 ... 270, 392, 894, 895, 899
Jones v. Manchester Corp. [1952] 2 QB 852 ... 693, 694
Jones v. Pritchard [1908] 1 Ch. 630 ... 539, 549
Jones v. Sherwood [1942] 1 KB 127 ... 453
Jones v. Skelton [1963] 1 WLR 1362 ... 763
Jones v. Stones [1999] 1 WLR 1739 (CA) ... 505
Jones v. Swansea City Council [1990] 1 WLR 54 ... 429, 430
Jones v. Tower Boot Co. Ltd. [1997] ICR 254; [1997] IRLR 168 ... 679, 681
Jones v. Williams (1837) 2 M & W 326; 150 ER 781 ... 499
Jones v. Williams (1843) 11 M & W 176; 152 ER 764 ... 549
Joyce v. Motor Surveys [1948] Ch. 252 ... 816
Joyce v. Sengupta [1993] 1 WLR 337 ... 816
Joyce v. Yeomans [1981] 1 WLR 549 ... 978, 979
J.T. Stratford & Son Ltd. v. Lindley [1965] AC 269 ... 581
Junior Books Ltd. v. Veitchi Co. Ltd. [1983] 1 AC 520 ... 19, 24, 35, 127, 176, 183, 184

K v. JMP Co. Ltd. [1976] QB 85 ... 1015
K v. Secretary of State for the Home Department [2002] EWCA Civ 983 ... 419
Kandalla v. British Airways Board [1981] QB 158 ... 1013
Kapetan Georgis, The [1988] 1 Lloyd's Rep. 352 ... 725
Karagozlou v. Commissioner of Police for the Metropolis [2006] EWCA Civ 1691 ... 428
Kars v. Kars (1996) 141 ALR 37 ... 982
Kassam v. Kampala Aerated Water [1965] 1 WLR 668 ... 1013
Kaye (Gordon) v. Andrew Robertson and Sport Newspapers [1991] FSR 62 ... 53, 827, 828, 833, 855
KD v. Chief Constable of Hampshire [2005] EWHC 2550 ... 454, 474, 694
Keays v. Murdoch Magazines (UK) Ltd. and Another [1991] 1 WLR 1184 ... 760, 764
Keegan v. Chief Constable of Merseyside Police [2003] EWCA Civ 936; [2003] 1 WLR 2187 (CA) ... 444, 479
Keen v. Tayside Contracts Ltd. 2003 SLT 500 ... 156, 157
Kelly v. Sherlock (1866) LR 1 QB 686 ... 942
Kelsen v. Imperial Tobacco Co. Ltd. [1957] 2 QB 334 ... 496, 1030
Kemsley v. Foot [1952] AC 345 ... 788

Kendillon v. Maltby (1842) Car. & M 402 . . . 775
Kennaway v. Thompson [1981] QB 88 . . . 544, 545, 546, 547, 548, 1030
Kent v. Griffiths [2000] 2 WLR 1158 . . . 202, 420
Kent v. Griffiths (No. 2) . . . 1003
Keppel Bus Co. Ltd. v. Sa'ad bin Ahmad [1974] 1 WLR 1082 . . . 680
Kerby v. Redbridge HA [1994] PIQR Q1 . . . 1001
Kerr v. Kennedy [1942] 1 KB 409 . . . 758, 759
Kerrison v. Smith [1897] 2 QB 445 . . . 504
Kerry v. Carter [1969] 1 WLR 1372 . . . 900
Kettelman v. Hansel Properties Ltd. [1987] AC 189 . . . 930
Khashoggi v. IPC Magazines Ltd. [1986] 1 WLR 1412 . . . 785
Khodaparast v. Shad [2000] 1 All ER 545; [2000] 1 WLR 618; [2000] EMLR 265 . . . 817, 944
Khorasandjian v. Bush [1993] QB 727 . . . 471, 472, 531, 534, 827, 835
Kiam v. MGN Ltd. [2003] QB 281 . . . 808
King v. Liverpool CC [1986] 1 WLR 890 . . . 207
King v. Phillips [1953] 1 QB 429 . . . 142
King v. Smith [1995] ICR 339 . . . 661
Kingshott v. Associated Kent Newspapers Ltd. [1991] 1 QB 88 . . . 795
Kirby v. National Coal Board 1958 SC 514 . . . 682
Kirby v. Sadgrove (1797) 3 Anst. 892; 145 ER 1073 . . . 549
Kirby-Harris v. Baxter [1995] EMLR 516 . . . 756
Kirk v. Brent London Borough Council [2005] EWCA Civ. 1701 . . . 534
Kirk v. Gregory (1876) 1 Ex. D 55 . . . 484
Kirkham v. Chief Constable of Greater Manchester [1990] 2 QB 283 . . . 204, 212, 911
Kirklees MBC v. Wickes [1992] 3 WLR 170 . . . 435
Kitchen v. Royal Air Force Association [1958] 2 All ER 241 . . . 263
Kite, The [1933] P 154 . . . 243
Kite v. Napp *The Times* 1 June 1982 . . . 638, 642
Kite v. Nolan [1982] RTR 253 . . . 230
Knapp v. Railway Executive [1949] 2 All ER 508 . . . 390
Knightley v. Johns [1982] 1 WLR 349 . . . 268
Knowles v. Liverpool City Council *The Times* 2 July 1992 . . . 660
Knupffer v. London Express Newspaper Ltd. [1944] AC 116 . . . 768
Kooragang Investments Property Ltd. v. Richardson and Wrench Ltd. [1982] AC 462 . . . 689
Koursk, The [1924] P 140 . . . 1033
KR and Others v. Bryn Alyn Community Holdings Ltd. (In Liquidation) [2003] QB 1441 . . . 929, 936
Kralj v. McGrath [1986] 1 All ER 54 . . . 145, 232, 943, 1001
Kubach v. Hollands [1937] 3 All ER 907 . . . 736
Kuddus v. Chief Constable of Leicestershire Constabulary [2002] 2 AC 122 . . . 945, 946, 947, 948, 949, 951
Kuwait Airways Corp. v. Iraqi Airways Co. (Nos. 4 and 5) [2001] 3 WLR 1117; [2001] 1 Lloyd's Rep. 161 (CA) . . . 490, 491, 1019
Kuwait Airways Corp. v. Iraqi Airways Co. (Nos. 4 and 5) [2002] 2 AC 883 (HL) . . . 247, 486

L v. Pembrokeshire CC [2006] EWHC 1029; [2007] PIQR P1 . . . 425
L v. Reading BC [2001] 1 WLR 1575 . . . 420
Lagan Navigation Co. v. Lambeg Bleaching, Dyeing and Finishing Co. Ltd. [1927] AC 226 . . . 548
Lagden v. O'Connor [2004] 1 AC 1067 . . . 245, 277, 278, 976
Laiqat v. Majid . . . 496
Lake v. King (1668) 1 Wms. Saund. 120; 85 ER 128 . . . 791
Lamb v. Camden London Borough Council [1981] QB 625 . . . 195, 207, 245, 266, 267, 271, 517
Lambert v. Bessey (1681) T. Ray 421 . . . 462
Lambert v. Lewis [1982] AC 225 . . . 725
Lancashire CC v. Municipal Mutual Insurance Ltd. [1996] 3 WLR 493 . . . 945
Lane v. Holloway [1968] 1 QB 379 . . . 462, 904
Lane v. Shire Roofing Company (Oxford) Ltd. [1995] IRLR 493 . . . 666, 672
Langford v. Hebran [2001] EWCA Civ 361; [2001] PIQR Q160 . . . 1006
Langridge v. Levy (1837) 2M & W 519; 150 ER 863 . . . 114, 565, 568, 705
Latham v. R. Johnson & Nephew Ltd. [1913] 1 KB 398 . . . 230, 353
Lather v. Pointer (1826) 5 B & C 547 . . . 676
Latimer v. AEC Ltd. [1953] AC 643 . . . 120, 225, 238, 239, 660
Launchbury v. Morgans [1973] AC 127; [1971] 2 QB 245 . . . 95
Laverton v. Kiapasha (t/a Takeaway Supreme) [2002] EWCA Civ 1656; (2002) 146 SJLB 266; [2002] NPC 145 (CA) . . . 351
Law Debenture Trust Ltd. v. Ural Caspian Oil Corp. [1995] 1 All ER 157 . . . 585

Law Society v. Sephton [2006] UKHL 22 . . . 936
Lawrence v. Pembrokeshire County Council [2006] EWHC 1029 (QB); [2007] PIQR P1 . . . 9, 31, 96, 105
Le Fanu v. Malcolmson (1848) 1 HLC 637, 9 ER 910 . . . 769
Le Lievre v. Gould [1893] 1 QB 491 . . . 115, 128
Lea v. Carrington (1889) 23 QBD 45 . . . 465
Leaf v. International Galleries [1950] 2 KB 86 . . . 731
League against Cruel Sports v. Scott [1985] 2 All ER 489 . . . 632, 6382
Leakey v. National Trust [1980] QB 485 . . . 206, 513, 514, 516, 517, 518, 519, 528, 558, 611
Lee Ting Sang v. Chung Chi-Keung [1990] 2 AC 374 . . . 666, 671, 673
Lee v. Sheard [1956] 1 QB 192 . . . 986
Leeman v. Montagu [1936] 2 All ER 1677 . . . 632
Leigh and Sillivan Ltd. v. The Aliakmon Shipping Co. Ltd. (The Aliakmon) [1986] AC 785 . . . 19, 24, 27, 123, 176, 177, 185, 186, 187, 193, 194, 725, 743
Leigh v. Gladstone (1909) 26 TLR 169 . . . 459
Leitch & Co. v. Leydon [1931] AC 90 . . . 484
Lemmon v. Webb [1894] 3 Ch. 1; [1895] AC 1 . . . 539, 548, 549
Lennon v. Commissioner of Police of the Metropolis [2004] 1 WLR 2594 . . . 163
Leong San Tan 1986 (unreported) . . . 983
Les Editions Nice Versa Inc. v. Aubry [1999] 5 BHRC 437 . . . 846
Letang v. Cooper [1965] 1 QB 232 . . . 452, 466, 483
Lethbridge v. Phillips (1819) 2 Stark. 544; 171 ER 731 . . . 488
Lewis v. Averay [1982] 1 QB 198 . . . 487
Lewis v. Daily Telegraph [1964] AC 234 . . . 753, 760, 761, 762, 763, 769, 770, 783, 810
Lewis v. Deyne [1940] AC 921 . . . 903
Lewis v. Ponsford (1838) 8 Car. & P 687; 173 ER 674 . . . 833
Liberace v. Daily Mirror Newspapers *The Times* 17 and 18 June 1959 . . . 760
Liesbosch Dredger v. SS Edison [1933] AC 449 . . . 245, 276, 277, 278, 976, 1019, 1020
Liesbosch, The. *see* Liesbosch Dredger v. SS Edison [1933] AC 449
Lim Poh Choo v. Camden & Islington Area Health Authority [1980] AC 174; [1979] QB 196 . . . 954, 966, 978, 993, 1001, 1002
Limpus v. London General Omnibus Co. (1862) 1 H & C 526; 158 ER 993 . . . 684
Lincoln v. Daniels [1962] 1 QB 237 . . . 792
Lincoln v. Hayman [1982] 1 WLR 488 . . . 956
Lion Laboratories v. Evans [1984] 2 All ER 417 . . . 838
Lipkin, Gorman v. Karpnale Ltd. [1989] 1 WLR 1340 . . . 903, 905
Lippiatt v. South Gloucestershire CC [2000] QB 51 . . . 536, 537, 610
Lister v. Hesley Hall Ltd. [2002] 1 AC 215 . . . 470, 665, 679, 688, 690, 691, 692, 699, 700
Lister v. Romford Ice and Cold Storage Co. Ltd. [1957] AC 555 . . . 694, 695, 700, 1035, 1040
Litster v. Forth Dry Dock & Engineering Co. Ltd. [1990] 1 AC 456 . . . 728
Liversidge v. Anderson [1942] AC 206 . . . 407
Livingstone v. Rawyards Coal Co. (1880) 5 App. Cas. 25 . . . 951
Llandudno Urban District Council v. Woods [1899] 2 Ch. 705 . . . 546
Llanover, The [1947] P 80 . . . 1020
Lloyd v. Grace, Smith & Co. [1912] AC 716 . . . 688
Lloyde v. West Midlands Gas Board [1971] 1 WLR 749 . . . 242
Lloyds Bank v. Savory [1933] AC 201 . . . 235
Lloyds Bank Ltd. v. The Chartered Bank of India, Australia and China [1929] 1 KB 40 . . . 491
Lloyds Bank and Mellows v. Railway Executive [1952] 1 TLR 1207 . . . 1016
LMS International Ltd. v. Styrene Packaging & Insulation Ltd. [2005] EWHC 2065 (TCC); [2006] BLR 50 . . . 616, 625
Lochgelly Iron and Coal Co. v. M'Mullan [1934] AC 1 . . . 113
Lock v. Ashton (1842) 12 QB 871; 116 ER 1097 . . . 465
Loftus-Brigham v. Ealing London Borough Council [2003] EWCA Civ 1490 . . . 534
London Artists Ltd. v. Littler [1969] 2 QB 375 . . . 786, 787
London Computer Operators Training Ltd. v. BBC [1973] 1 WLR 424 . . . 763
London Corporation, The [1935] P 70 . . . 1020
London Graving Dock Co. v. Horton [1951] AC 737 . . . 355
London Passenger Transport Board v. Upson [1949] AC 155 . . . 241, 377, 899
London and South of England Building Society v. Stone [1983] 1 WLR 1242 . . . 976
Longden v. British Coal Corporation [1998] AC 653; [1998] IRLR 29 . . . 959

Longdon-Griffiths v. Smith [1950] 2 All ER 662 ... 665
Lonrho Ltd. v. Shell Petroleum Co. Ltd. (No. 2) [1982] AC 173 ... 385, 387, 393, 394, 472, 573, 586, 592, 597, 602
Lonrho plc v. Fayed [1990] 2 QB 479 (CA); [1992] 1 AC 448 (HL) ... 574, 590, 597
Lonrho plc v. Tebbit [1991] 4 All ER 973; [1992] 4 All ER 280 ... 421, 427, 431
Lonskier v. B. Goodman Ltd. [1928] 1 KB 421 ... 497
Lord Chesham v. Chesham UDC (1935) 79 SJ 453 ... 539
Loutchansky v. Times Newspapers Ltd. [2001] 3 WLR 404 ... 799
Loutchansky v. Times Newspapers (Nos. 2, 3, 4 and 5) [2002] 2 WLR 640; [2002] EMLR 14 ... 777, 802, 806, 815
Lowery v. Walker [1911] AC 10 ... 348
Lucas-Box v. News Group Newspapers Ltd. [1986] 1 WLR 147 ... 784
Lukowiak v. Unidad Editorial [2001] EMLR 1043 (HC, QBD) ... 784
Lumley v. Gye (1853) 2 El. & Bl. 216; 118 ER 749 ... 576, 579, 580, 581, 582, 587, 1041
Lumley v. Wagner (1852) 1 De GM & G 604; 42 ER 687 ... 576
Lynch v. Knight (1861) 9 HLC 577; 11 ER 854 ... 758
Lyon v. Daily Telegraph [1943] KB 746 ... 790
Lyons, Sons & Co. v. Gulliver [1914] 1 Ch. 631 ... 556

M. Isaacs & Sons Ltd. v. Cook [1925] 2 KB 391 ... 794
M/S Aswan Engineering Establishment Co. Ltd. v. Lupdine Ltd. [1987] 1 WLR 1 ... 743
McAuley v. London Transport Executive [1957] 2 Lloyd's Rep. 500 ... 976
McCafferty v. Metropolitan Police District Receiver [1977] 1 WLR 1073 ... 660, 661
McCall v. Abelesz [1976] QB 585 ... 386
McCamley v. Cammell Laird Shipbuilders [1990] 1 WLR 963 ... 997
McCarey v. Associated Newspapers [1965] 2 QB 86 ... 948
McCartan Turkington Breen (A Firm) v. Times Newspapers Ltd. [2001] 2 AC 277 ... 793
McCoubrey v. Ministry of Defence [2007] EWCA Civ 17 ... 931
McDermid v. Nash Dredging and Reclamation Co. Ltd. [1987] AC 906 ... 661, 697, 698, 700
MacDonald v. Advocate General for Scotland [2003] IRLR 512 ... 681
Macfarlane v. EE Caledonia Ltd. [1994] 2 All ER 1 ... 156, 179, 654
MacFarlane v. Tayside Health Board [2000] 2 AC 59 ... 129, 130, 138, 178, 218, 223, 269
McGeown v. N.I. Housing Executive [1995] 1 AC 233 ... 365
McGhee v. National Coal Board [1973] 1 WLR 1 ... 249, 250, 251, 252, 253, 254, 255, 256, 257, 261
McGinlay v. British Railways Board [1983] 1 WLR 1427 ... 353, 355, 912
McKay v. Essex Health Authority [1982] QB 1166 ... 83, 218
McKenna v. British Aluminium [2002] Env. LR 30 ... 531, 535, 558, 623, 629
McKennitt v. Ash [2006] EWCA Civ 1714; [2007] EMLR 4 ... 851
McKew v. Holland & Hannen & Cubitts (Scotland) Ltd. [1969] 3 All ER 1621 ... 149, 268, 271, 896
Mackintosh v. Mackintosh, 2 M 1357 ... 224, 225
McLoughlin v. O'Brian [1983] 1 AC 410 ... 34, 35, 96, 139, 146, 147, 150, 154, 744
McManus v. Beckham [2002] 1 WLR 2982 ... 776
McMeechan v. Secretary of State for Employment [1995] IRLR 461 ... 666, 673
McMillan v. Singh (1984) 17 HLR 120 (CA) ... 948
McPhail v. Persons, Names Unknown [1973] Ch. 447 ... 502
McPherson v. Daniels (1829) 10 B & C 263, 272; 109 ER 448 ... 783
McQuaker v. Goddard [1940] 1 KB 697 ... 637
Macrae v. Swindells [1954] 1 WLR 597 ... 1022
McTear v. Imperial Tobacco Ltd., 2005 2 SC 1 ... 256, 740
McVittie v. Bolton Corp. [1945] KB 281 ... 520
McWilliams v. Sir William Arrol & Co. Ltd. [1962] 1 WLR 295 ... 249, 382, 391
Maersk Colombo, The [2001] 2 Lloyd's Rep. 275 ... 1020
Mafo v. Adams [1970] 1 QB 548 ... 946, 948
Maguire v. Sefton MBC [2006] 1 WLR 2550 ... 341, 347
Mainstream Properties Ltd. v. Young [2005] EWCA Civ 861 (CA) ... 579
Mainstream Properties Ltd. v. Young [2007] UKHL 21 (HL) ... 574, 575, 579, 588, 599, 602, 603
Majrowski v. Guy's and St. Thomas's NHS Trust [2006] 3 WLR 125; [2006] ICR 1129 ... 470, 474, 692, 693

MAK and another v. Dewsbury Healthcare NHS Trust and another [2005] 2 AC 373 ... 104, 105
Malfroot v. Noxal Ltd. (1935) 51 TLR 551 ... 726
Malone v. Commissioner of Police of the Metropolis (No. 2) [1979] Ch. 344 ... 484, 825, 838
Malone v. Laskey [1907] 2 KB 141 ... 530, 538, 561
Malyon v. Plummer [1964] 1 QB 330 ... 1014
Malz v. Rosen [1966] 1 WLR 1008 ... 476, 478
Manchester Airport plc v. Dutton [2000] QB 133 (CA) ... 500
Mangena v. Wright [1909] 2KB 958 ... 787
Manifest Shipping Co. Ltd. v. Uni-Polaris Shipping Co. Ltd. [2003] 1 AC 469 ... 567
Mansfield v. Weetabix Ltd. [1998] 1 WLR 1263 ... 57, 231
Manson v. Associated Newspapers [1965] 1 WLR 1038 ... 948
Mapp v. News Group Newspapers Ltd. [1998] 2 WLR 260 ... 762, 764
Marc Rich & Co. AG v. Bishop Rock Marine Co. Ltd., The Nicholas H [1996] AC 211 ... 46, 129, 138, 193, 195, 196, 216, 420, 516
Marcic v. Thames Water Utilities Ltd. [2001] 3 All ER 698; [2002] QB 929 (CA); [2003] UKHL 66; [2004] 2 AC 42 ... 440, 441, 513, 517, 518, 519, 520, 528, 537, 618
Marcic v. Thames Water Utilities Ltd. (No. 2) [2002] QB 1003 ... 546
Marcq v. Christie Manson & Woods Ltd. (t/a Christie's) [2002] 4 All ER 1005 (QBD); [2004] QB 286 (CA) ... 487
Mark v. Associated Newspapers (No. 1) [2002] EMLR 38 (CA) ... 784
Market Investigations Ltd. v. Minister of Social Security [1969] 2 QB 173 ... 670, 672
Marr v. London Borough of Lambeth [2006] EWHC 1175 ... 137
Marriott v. East Grinstead Gas and Water Co. [1909] 1 Ch. 70 ... 546
Marshall v. Osmond [1983] QB 1034 ... 228, 231
Martin v. Watson [1996] 1 AC 74 ... 477
Martin d. Tregonwell v. Strachan (1744) 5 Term Rep. 107 n; 101 ER 61 ... 500
Martindale v. Duncan [1973] 1 WLR 574 ... 1021
Martins v. Hotel Mayfair [1976] 2 NSWLR 15 ... 621
Mason v. Levy Auto Parts of England Ltd. [1967] 2 QB 530 ... 617, 625
Mason v. Williams and Williams Ltd. [1955] 1 All ER 808 436 ... 707
Massey v. Crown Life Insurance Co. [1978] 1 WLR 676 ... 673
Masters v. Brent LBC [1978] QB 841 ... 513, 533
Matania v. National Provincial Bank Ltd. [1936] 2 All ER 633 ... 537, 696
Matthews v. Ministry of Defence [2002] 1 WLR 2621 (CA) ... 134
Matthews v. Ministry of Defence [2003] 1 AC 1163 (HL) ... 435
Matthews v. Ministry of Defence [2003] 2 WLR 435 (HL) ... 217
Matthews v. Wicks *The Times* 25 May 1987 ... 635, 636
Mbasogo v. Logo Ltd. (No. 1) [2005] EWHC 2034 ... 453
MCC Proceeds Ltd. v. Lehman Brothers [1998] 4 All ER 675 ... 486
Mead v. Clarke Chapman [1956] 1 WLR 76 ... 1016
Meade v. Haringey LBC [1979] 1 WLR 637; [1979] ICR 494 ... 585, 586, 1041
Mead's v. Belt's Case (1823) 1 Lew. CC 184; 168 ER 1006 ... 453
Meah v. McCreamer (No. 1) [1985] 1 All ER 367 ... 141, 898, 924
Meah v. McCreamer (No. 2) [1986] 1 All ER 943 ... 157, 267
Mediana, The [1900] AC 113 ... 1023
Mee v. Cruikshank (1902) 86 LT 708 ... 470
Meering v. Graham-White Aviation Co. Ltd. (1919) 122 LT 44 ... 465
Mehmet v. Perry [1977] 2 All ER 529 ... 1014
Mehta v. Royal Bank of Scotland [1999] 3 EGLR 153 ... 500
Melville v. Home Office ... 655, 656
Mercury Communications Ltd. v. Director-General of Telecommunications [1996] 1 WLR 48 ... 433
Mercury Communications Ltd. v. Scott-Garner [1974] ICR 74 ... 601
Merest v. Harvey (1814) 5 Taunt. 442; 128 ER 761 ... 833, 944
Merivale v. Carson (1888) 20 QBD 275 ... 788, 790
Merkur Island Shipping Corp. v. Laughton [1983] 2 AC 570 ... 583, 584
Merrett v. Babb [2001] 3 WLR 1 ... 170
Merricks v. Nott-Bower [1965] 1 QB 57 ... 794
Merryweather v. Nixon (1799) 8 TR 186; 101 ER 1337 ... 693, 1034
Mersey Docks and Harbour Board v. Coggins and Griffith (Liverpool) Ltd. [1947] AC 1 ... 674
Mersey Docks and Harbour Board Trustees v. Gibbs (1866) LR 1 HL 93 ... 397, 405, 406

Messenger Newspaper Group Ltd. v. National Graphical Association [1984] IRLR 397 . . . 589, 943, 950
Metall und Rohstoff AG v. Donaldson, Lufkin and Jenrette Inc. [1990] 1 QB 391 . . . 585, 597
Metcalfe v. London Passenger Transport Board [1938] 2 All ER 352 . . . 965
Metropolitan Asylum District Managers v. Hill (1881) 6 App. Cas. 193 . . . 540
Metropolitan Police District Receiver v. Croydon Corp. [1957] 1 QB 154 . . . 960
Metropolitan Properties Ltd. v. Jones [1939] 2 All ER 202 . . . 530
Meux v. Great Eastern Railway Co. [1895] 2 QB 387 . . . 485
M'Gibbon v. M'Curry (1909) 43 ILT 132 . . . 636
Michaels v. Taylor Woodrow Developments Ltd. [2001] Ch. 493 . . . 587, 594, 598
Middlebrook Mushrooms Ltd. v. Transport and General Workers Union [1993] IRLR 232 . . . 439, 582
Middleweek v. Chief Constable of Merseyside (1985) [1992] 1 AC 179 . . . 469
Midgley v. Midgley [1893] 3 Ch. 282 . . . 1041
Midland Bank Trust Co. Ltd. v. Hett, Stubbs & Kemp [1979] Ch. 384 . . . 20, 28, 29, 192, 936
Midwood & Co. Ltd. v. Manchester Corporation [1905] 2 KB 597 . . . 523, 526, 535, 607, 612
Miles v. Forest Rock Granite Co. Ltd. (1918) 34 TLR 500 . . . 621
Miliangos v. George Frank (Textiles) Ltd. [1976] AC 443 . . . 965
Millar v. Bassey [1994] EMLR 44 . . . 577, 578
Millar v. Taylor (1769) 4 Burr 2303 . . . 839
Miller v. Jackson [1977] QB 966 . . . 523, 542, 544, 545, 546, 557, 558, 1029, 1030
Millington v. Duffy (1984) 17 HLR 232 (CA) . . . 948
Mills v. Brooker [1919] 1 KB 555 . . . 549
Mills v. News Group Newspapers Ltd. [2001] EMLR 41 . . . 843
Mills v. Winchester Diocesan Board of Finance [1989] Ch. 428 . . . 414
Milne v. Express Newspapers [2003] 1 WLR 927 . . . 781, 881
Milne v. Telegraph Group [2001] EMLR 30 . . . 810
Mineral Transporter, The [1986] AC 1 . . . 123, 186
Ministry of Defence v. Cannock [1994] IRLR 509 . . . 946
Ministry of Housing and Local Government v. Sharp [1970] 2 QB 223 . . . 171, 427
Mint v. Good [1951] 1 KB 517 . . . 371, 538
Minter v. Priest [1930] AC 558 . . . 792
Miraflores v. George Livanos [1967] 1 AC 826 . . . 1036
Mirant-Asia Pacific v. OAPIL [2004] EWHC 1750 . . . 182
Mirvahedy v. Henley [2003] 2 AC 491; [2003] 2 WLR 882 . . . 631, 638, 639, 640, 641, 642, 643, 644
Mitchell v. Darley Main Colliery Co. (1884) 14 QBD 125 . . . 512
Mitchell v. Jenkins (1835) 5 B & Ad. 588; 110 ER 908 . . . 479
Mitchell v. Laing (1998) SLT 203 . . . 963
Mitchell v. Mulholland (No. 2) [1972] 1 QB 65, 77 . . . 954
Moeliker v. A. Reyrolle & Co. Ltd. [1977] 1 All ER 9; [1977] 1 WLR 132 . . . 978, 979, 992
Mogul Steamship Co. Ltd. v. McGregor, Gow & Co. (1889) LR 23 QBD 598; [1892] AC 25 . . . 571, 572, 594
Mohammed Amin v. Bannerjee [1947] AC 322 . . . 476
Moloney v. Lambeth London Borough Council [1966] 198 EG 895 . . . 353
Monarch Airlines Ltd. v. London Luton Airport Ltd. [1998] 1 Lloyd's Rep. 403 . . . 341
Monk v. Warbey [1935] 1 KB 75 . . . 381, 384, 386
Monsanto plc v. Tilly [2000] Env. LR 313 (CA) . . . 499, 506
Monson v. Tussauds Ltd. (1934) 50 TLR 581 . . . 757
Moore v. DER Ltd. [1971] 1 WLR 1476 . . . 1020, 1023
Moore v. News of the World Ltd. [1972] 1 QB 441 . . . 785
Moorgate Mercantile Co. Ltd. v. Finch and Read [1961] 1 QB 701 . . . 489
Moorgate Mercantile Co. Ltd. v. Twitchings [1977] AC 890 . . . 490
Morales v. Ecclestone [1991] RTR 151 . . . 898
More v. Weaver [1928] 2 KB 520 . . . 792
Morgan v. Fry [1968] QB 710 . . . 580
Morgan v. Lingen (1863) 8 LT 800 . . . 754
Morgan v. Odhams Press Ltd. [1971] 1 WLR 1239 . . . 760, 764, 767, 780
Morgan v. Scoulding [1938] 1 KB 786 . . . 1008
Morgan v. T. Wallis [1974] 1 Lloyd's Rep 165 . . . 976
Morgan Crucible Co. plc v. Hill Samuel & Co. Ltd. [1991] Ch. 295 . . . 167, 170, 196
Morgans v. Launchbury [1971] 2 QB 245 . . . 677

Moriarty v. McCarthy [1978] 1 WLR 155 ... 985, 986, 1005
Morison v. Moat (1851) 8 Hare 241, 68 ER 482 ... 838
Morren v. Swinton and Pendlebury BC [1965] 1 WLR 576 ... 669
Morris v. Beardmore [1980] 2 All ER 753; [1981] AC 446 ... 834, 859
Morris v. C.W. Martin & Sons Ltd. [1966] 1 QB 716 ... 538, 687, 688, 696
Morris v. Ford Motor Co. Ltd. [1973] QB 792 ... 694, 695, 1040
Morris v. Murray [1991] 2 QB 6 ... 910, 911
Morris v. Richards [2003] EWCA Civ 232 ... 976
Mortin v. Shoppee (1828) 3 C & P 373 ... 453
Moss v. Christchurch Rural District Council [1925] 2 KB 750 ... 1020
Motis Exports Ltd. v. Dampskibsselskabet AF 1912 Aktieselskab [1999] 1 Lloyd's Rep. 837 ... 489
Mount Carmel Investments Ltd. v. Peter Thurlow Ltd. [1988] 1 WLR 1978 ... 502
Mowan v. Wandsworth London Borough Council [2001] 3 EGCS 133 ... 536
Muirhead v. Industrial Tank Specialities Ltd. [1986] QB 507 ... 182
Mulcahy v. Ministry of Defence [1996] 2 All ER 758; [1996] QB 732 ... 216, 217, 653
Mulholland & Tedd Ltd. v. Baker [1939] 3 All ER 253 ... 609
Mullin v. Richards [1998] 1 WLR 1304 ... 230
Mulvane v. Joseph (1968) 112 SJ 927 ... 986
Munster v. Lamb (1883) 11 QBD 588 ... 792
Murphy v. Bradford MBC *The Times* 11 Feb. 1991 ... 352
Murphy v. Brentwood District Council [1991] 1 AC 398 ... 26, 27, 28, 29, 45, 46, 89, 108, 117, 122, 123, 127, 131, 160, 168, 169, 170, 171, 175, 176, 180, 181, 182, 183, 184, 185, 192, 195, 197, 198, 199, 207, 210, 282, 284, 372, 373, 374, 378, 398, 400, 410, 416, 427, 706, 725, 742, 743, 916, 921, 933, 934, 935
Murphy v. Culhane [1977] QB 94 ... 462, 543, 904, 924
Murray v. Hibernian Dance Club [1997] PIQR P46 (CA) ... 345
Murray v. Ministry of Defence [1988] 1 WLR 692 ... 465
Murray v. Shuter [1972] 1 Lloyd's Rep. 6 ... 1009
Murray v. Shuter [1976] QB 972 ... 999
Murray, Ash and Kennedy v. Hall (1849) 7 CB 441; 137 ER 175 ... 500
Mutual Life & Assurance Co. v. Evatt [1971] AC 793 ... 163
N. v. Chief Constable of Merseyside Police [2006] EWHC 3041 ... 692
Nabi v. British Leyland (UK) Ltd. [1980] 1 WLR 529 ... 956
Nahhas v. Pier House (Cheyne Walk) Management Ltd. [1984] 270 EG 328 ... 688
Nance v. British Columbia Electric Railway Co. Ltd. [1951] AC 601 ... 897
National Bank of Greece SA v. Pinios Shipping Co. (No. 1) [1989] 3 WLR 185 ... 28
National Coal Board v. England [1954] AC 403 ... 925
National Coal Board v. J. E. Evans & Co. (Cardiff) Ltd. [1951] 2 KB 861 ... 484, 499, 539
National Phonograph Co. Ltd. v. Edison Bell Co. Ltd. [1908] 1 Ch. 335 ... 589
National Sailors' and Firemen's Union of Great Britain and Ireland v. Reed [1926] Ch. 536 ... 601
National Telephone Co. v. Baker [1893] 2 Ch. 186 ... 609
National Union of General and Municipal Workers v. Gillian [1946] KB 81 ... 771
Naylor v. Payling [2004] PIQR P36; [2004] EWCA Civ 560 ... 362, 651
Neal v. Bingle [1998] 2 WLR 57 ... 963
Neath RDC v. Williams [1951] 1 KB 115 ... 611
Nelson v. Nicholson *The Independent* 22 Jan. 2001 ... 495, 1030
Nethermere (St Neots) Ltd. v. Taverna and Gardiner [1984] IRLR 240 ... 671
Nettleship v. Weston [1971] 2 QB 691 ... 224, 226, 230, 231, 906, 910
Network Rail v. Morris [2004] EWCA Civ 172; [2004] Env LR 41 ... 524, 525
New Zealand Shipping Co. Ltd. v. AM Satterthwaite and Co. Ltd. (The Eurymedon) [1975] AC 154 (PC) ... 23, 725, 921
Newcastle-under-Lyme v. Wolstanton Ltd. [1947] Ch. 92 ... 530
Newcomen v. Coulson (1877) 5 Ch. D 133 ... 549
News Group Newspapers Ltd. v. Sogat (82) [1986] IRLR 336 ... 601
Newstead v. London Express Newspaper Ltd. [1940] 1 KB 377 ... 768, 780
Ng Chun Pui v. Lee Chuen Tat [1988] RTR 298 ... 242
NHS Trust A v. M [2001] 2 FLR 367 ... 461
Nicholas H, The. *see* Marc Rich & Co. AG v. Bishop Rock Marine Co. Ltd. [1996] AC 211
Nicholls v. Austin (Leyton) Ltd. [1946] AC 493 ... 434
Nicholls v. Ely Beet Sugar Factory Ltd. (No 1) [1931] 2 Ch. 84 (Ch D) ... 500

Nicholls v. Ely Beet Sugar Factory Ltd. (No 2) [1936] Ch 343 (CA) ... 510
Nichols v. Marsland (1876) 2 Ex. D 1 ... 539, 620, 927
Nimmo v. Alexander Cowan & Sons [1968] AC 107 ... 389, 390, 662
Nitrigin Eireann Teoranta v. Inco Alloys Ltd. [1992] 1 All ER 854 ... 184, 934
Noble v. Harrison [1926] 2 KB 332 ... 514, 555
Nobles v. Schofield, CA Judgment of 14 May 1998 ... 141
Nocton v. Lord Ashburton [1914] AC 932 ... 162
Norman v. Future Publishing [1999] EMLR 325 ... 756
North Glamorgan NHS Trust v. Walters [2002] EWCA Civ 1792 ... 145
Norwich City Council v. Harvey [1989] 1 WLR 828 ... 194, 920, 921
Norwood v. Navan [1981] RTR 457 ... 677
Nottingham Health Authority v. City of Nottingham [1988] 1 WLR 903 ... 1036
Nottingham Patent Brick and Tile Co. v. Butler (1886) 16 QBD 778 ... 165
Nunn v. Parkes & Co. (1924) 59 LJ 806 ... 530
NWL v. Woods [1979] ICR 867 ... 601
Nykredit Mortgage Bank plc v. Edward Erdman Group Ltd. (No. 2) [1997] 1 WLR 1627 ... 902, 1023

Oakley v. Walker (1977) 121 SJ 619 ... 986
OBG Trilogy *see* Douglas v. Hello! Ltd; Mainstream Properties Ltd. v. Young; OBG Ltd. v. Allan
OBG Ltd. v. Allan [2007] UKHL 21 ... 574, 575, 576, 578, 579, 580, 582, 584, 585, 586, 588, 589, 590, 591, 593, 594, 595, 598, 599, 602, 603
O'Connell v. Jackson [1972] 1 QB 270 ... 897
O'Connor v. Waldron [1935] AC 76 ... 792
Offer-Hoare v. Larkstore Ltd. [2005] EWCA 2742 ... 183
O'Grady v. Westminster Scaffolding [1962] 2 Lloyd's Rep. 238 ... 1021
Ogwo v. Taylor [1988] AC 431 ... 219, 343, 355
O'Kelly v. Trusthouse Forte plc [1983] IRLR 369; [1984] QB 90 ... 667, 671
Old Gates Estate Ltd. v. Toplis & Harding & Russell [1939] 3 All ER 209 ... 125
Oliver v. Ashman [1962] 2 QB 210 ... 998, 999
OLL Ltd. v. Secretary of State for Transport [1997] 3 All ER 897 ... 201, 417, 420
Olutu v. Home Office [1997] 1 All ER 385 ... 470
On Demand Information plc (In Administrative Receivership) v. Michael Gerson (Finance) plc [2001] 1 WLR 155 (CA) ... 486
Orange v. Chief Constable of West Yorkshire [2002] QB 347 ... 204, 212
O'Reilly v. Mackman [1983] 2 AC 237 ... 403, 404, 432, 433, 434
O'Reilly v. National Rail and Tramway Appliances Ltd. [1966] 1 All ER 499 ... 659
Organ Retention Group Litigation, In Re, 2004] EWHC 644 ... 154
Orme v. Associated Newspapers Ltd. *The Times* 4 Feb. 1981 ... 769
Ormrod v. Crosville Motor Services Ltd. [1953] 1 WLR 1120 ... 677
Oropesa, The [1943] P 32 ... 268
O'Rourke v. Camden LBC [1998] AC 189 ... 388, 426, 432
Osborn v. Boulter [1930] 2 KB 226 ... 773, 796
O'Shea v. Mirror Group Newspapers [2001] EMLR 40 ... 768
Osman v. Ferguson [1993] 4 All ER 344 ... 63, 133, 212, 421, 443, 444
Otto v. Bolton & Norris [1936] 2 KB 46 ... 372
Owens v. Brimmell [1977] QB 859 ... 898
Owens v. Liverpool Corporation [1939] 1 KB 394 ... 153
Owners of Cargo Lately Laden on Board the Ship or Vessel 'Starsin' v. Owners and/or Demise Charterers of the Ship or Vessel 'Starsin' [2003] UKHL 12 ... 185

P (A Minor), Re (1981) 80 LGR 301 ... 457
P. Perl (Exporters) Ltd. v. Camden London Borough Council [1984] QB 342 ... 207, 267, 517
Pacific Associates Inc. v. Baxter [1990] QB 993 ... 194, 921
Padbury v. Holliday & Greenwood Ltd. (1912) 28 TLR 494 ... 696
Page v. Read (1984) 134 New LJ 723 ... 346
Page v. Sheerness Steel Co. Plc 989
Page v. Smith [1996] AC 155 ... 141, 142, 145, 273
Page Motors Ltd. v. Epsom and Ewell Borough Council (1982) 80 LGR 337 ... 539
Paine v. Colne Valley Electricity Supply Co. Ltd. [1938] 4 All ER 803 ... 732
Palfrey v. GLC [1985] ICR 437 ... 956
Palmer v. Bowman [2000] 1 All ER 22 ... 611
Palmer v. Tees AHA (2000) 2 LGLR 69; [2000] PIQR P1 ... 419

Pamplin v. Express Newspapers (No. 2) [1988] 1 All ER 282 . . . 811
Pankhurst v. White [2006] EWCA Civ 2093 . . . 901
Pannett v. P. McGuiness & Co. Ltd. [1972] 2 QB 599 . . . 348, 365
Pao On v. Lau Yiu Long [1980] AC 614 (PC), The Atlantic Baron [1979] QB 705 . . . 595, 602
Paris v. Stepney Borough Council [1951] AC 367 . . . 225, 238, 658
Parker v. British Airways Board [1982] QB 1004 . . . 485, 487
Parker v. Oloxo Ltd. [1937] 3 All ER 524 . . . 706, 730
Parkinson v. Lyle Shipping Co. Ltd. [1964] 2 Lloyd's Rep. 79 . . . 659
Parkinson v. St James and Seacroft University Hospital NHS Trust [2002] QB 266 . . . 178, 179, 218
Parmiter v. Coupland and Another (1840) 6M & W 105 . . . 753
Parry v. Cleaver [1970] AC 1 . . . 956, 957, 958, 959, 960, 961
Parsons v. BNM Laboratories [1964] 1 QB 95 . . . 956
Parsons (Livestock) Ltd. v. Uttley Ingham & Co. Ltd. [1978] QB 791 . . . 20, 273
Pasley v. Freeman (1789) 3 Term Rep. 51; 100 ER 450 . . . 565
Pass of Ballater, The [1942] P 112 . . . 538, 657
Patel v. W. H. Smith (Eziot) Ltd. [1987] 1 WLR 853 . . . 1031
Payne v. Railway Executive [1952] 1 KB 26 . . . 959
Payne v. Rogers (1749) 2 HBL 350; 126 ER 590 . . . 538
Payton v. Brooks [1974] 1 Lloyd's Rep. 241; RTR 169 . . . 1021
Pearce v. Governors of Mayfield Secondary School [2003] IRLR 512 . . . 681
Pearce v. Secretary of State for Defence [1988] AC 755 . . . 208
Pearson v. Lambeth BC [1950] 2 KB 353 . . . 342
Peek v. Gurney (1873) LR 6 HL 377 . . . 565, 568
Pemberton v. Southwark LBC [2000] 1 WLR 1672 (CA) . . . 500, 530, 532
Pennington v. Brinsop Hall Coal Co. (1877) 5 Ch. D 769 . . . 547
Penny v. Northampton BC (1974) 72 LGR 733 . . . 365
Pepper v. Hart [1993] AC 593 . . . 642
Perec v. Brown (1964) 108 SJ 219 . . . 1015
Performance Cars Ltd. v. Abraham [1961] 1 QB 33 . . . 258, 259
Performing Rights Society Ltd. v. Mitchell and Booker (Palais de Danse) Ltd. [1924] 1 KB 762 . . . 668, 669
Perrett v. Collins [1998] 2 Lloyd's Rep. 255 . . . 129, 420
Perry v. Clissold [1907] AC 73 . . . 501
Perry v. Kendricks Transport Ltd. [1956] 1 WLR 85 . . . 620, 621
Perry v. Sidney Phillips & Son [1982] 1 WLR 1297 . . . 1021
Peruvian Guano Co. Ltd. v. Dreyfus Brothers & Co. [1892] AC 166 . . . 1020
Petch v. Customs and Excise Commissioners [1993] ICR 789 . . . 653, 655
Peter Walker & Sons Ltd. v. Hodgson [1909] 1 KB 239 . . . 790
Phelps v. Hillingdon London Borough Council [1999] 1 WLR 500; [2001] 2 AC 619 . . . 105, 134, 137, 154, 210, 211, 213, 215, 234, 399, 400, 401, 411, 415, 417, 422, 423, 424, 426, 701
Philco Radio and Television Corp. v. Spurling [1949] 2 All ER 882 . . . 268
Phillips v. Britannia Hygienic Laundry Co. [1923] 2 KB 832 . . . 385, 386
Phillips v. Homfray (1883) 24 Ch. D 439 . . . 53
Phillips v. Perry & Dalgety Agriculture Ltd. (unreported, CA), 6 Mar. 1997 . . . 354
Phillips Products v. Hyland [1987] 1 WLR 659 . . . 674, 675, 917
Phipps v. Rochester Corporation [1955] 1 QB 450 . . . 348, 353, 354, 356
Photo Production Ltd. v. Securicor Transport Ltd. [1980] AC 827 . . . 583, 916
Pickering v. Liverpool Daily Post [1991] 4 All ER 622 . . . 380, 382
Pickett v. British Rail Engineering Ltd. [1980] AC 136 . . . 977, 999
Pidduck v. Eastern Scottish Omnibuses Ltd. [1990] 1 WLR 993 . . . 1018
Pigney v. Pointer's Transport Services Ltd. [1957] 1 WLR 1121 . . . 269, 1009, 1010
Pirelli General Cable Works Ltd. v. Oscar Faber & Partners [1983] 2 AC 1 . . . 28, 96, 122, 161, 183, 184, 930, 933, 934, 935
Pitcher v. Martin [1937] 3 All ER 918 . . . 632
Pitts v. Hunt [1991] 1 QB 24 . . . 271, 898, 900, 910, 923, 924, 925
Platform Home Loans Ltd. v. Oyston Shipways Ltd. [1998] Ch 466; [2000] 2 AC 190 . . . 278, 902, 1023
Plato Films v. Speidel [1961] AC 1090 . . . 811, 812
Plumb v. Cobden Flour Mills Co. Ltd. [1914] AC 62 . . . 683

Poland v. Parr & Sons [1927] 1 KB 236 . . . 680
Polemis and Furness, Withy & Co., Re [1921] 3 KB 560 . . . 272, 273, 280, 1009
Pollard v. Photographic Co. (1888) 40 Ch. D 345 . . . 838
Polly Peck v. Trelford [1986] QB 1000 . . . 785
Pontardawe RDC v. Moore-Guyn [1929] 1 Ch. 656 . . . 611
Poole v. HM Treasury [2006] EWHC 2731 . . . 438
Popplewell v. Hodkinson (1869) LR 4 Exch. 248 . . . 529
Port Swettenham Authority v. T. W. Wu & Co. [1979] AC 580 . . . 687
Porteous v. NCB, 1967 SLT 117 (SC) . . . 658
Portsea Island Mutual Co-operative Society Ltd. v. Michael Brashier Associates Ltd. (1990) 6 Const. LJ 63 . . . 192
Portsmouth NHS Trust v. Wyatt [2005] EWCA Civ 1181 . . . 459
Pounder v. London Underground Ltd. [1995] PIQR . . . 1012
Powell v. Fall (1880) 5 QBD 597 . . . 612
Prager v. Times Newspapers Ltd. [1988] 1 WLR 77 . . . 784
Pratt v. British Medical Association [1919] 1 KB 244 . . . 580
Pratt v. Smith 19 Dec. 2002, unreported . . . 1006
Pratt and Goldsmith v. Pratt [1975] VR 378 . . . 146
Precis Ltd. v. William M. Mercer Ltd. [2004] EWCA Civ 114 . . . 194, 922
Prentice v. Hereward Housing Association [2001] 2 All ER (Comm.) 900 . . . 344
Pretty v. DPP [2002] 1 AC 800 . . . 456, 461, 462, 914
Price v. City of Nottingham (Unreported, 1 July 1998) (CA) . . . 368
Pride of Derby and Derbyshire Angling Association Ltd. v. British Celanese Ltd. [1953] Ch. 149 . . . 546, 560, 618, 1030
Pride Valley Foods v. Hall and Partners [2001] EWCA Civ 1001 . . . 895
Priest v. Last [1903] 2 KB 148 . . . 724
Priestley v. Fowler (1837) 3 M & W 1; 150 ER 1030 . . . 652, 907
Prince Albert v. Strange (1848) 2 De G & Sm. 652; 64 ER 293 . . . 838
Pritchard v. J. H. Cobden Ltd. [1987] 2 WLR 627; [1988] Fam 22 . . . 157, 985
Prudential Assurance Co. v. Lorenz (1971) 1 KIR 78 . . . 585
Pullman v. W. Hill & Co. Ltd. [1891] 1 QB 524 . . . 772, 773

Qualcast (Wolverhampton) Ltd. v. Haynes [1959] AC 743 . . . 225
Quartz Hill Consolidated Gold Mining Co. v. Eyre (1883) 11 QBD 674 . . . 476
Quick v. Taff Ely BC [1986] QB 809 . . . 371
Quinland v. Governor of Swaleside Prison [2003] QB 306 . . . 471
Quinn v. Leathem [1901] AC 495 . . . 573, 577, 596

R v. Barnard (1837) 7 C & P 784; 173 ER 342 . . . 565
R v. Beasley (1981) 73 Cr App. R 44 . . . 453
R v. Bishop [1975] QB 274 . . . 754
R v. Bournewood Community and Mental Health NHS Trust *ex parte* L [1999] AC 458 . . . 458, 463
R v. Broadcasting Standards Commission *ex parte* British Broadcasting Corporation [2001] QB 885 . . . 820, 821, 822, 823, 824, 832
R v. Brown [1994] 1 AC 212 . . . 462
R v. Central Independent Television plc [1994] Fam 192 . . . 79, 850
R v. Chesterfield Justices *ex parte* Bramley [2000] QB 576; [2000] 1 All ER 41 . . . 485
R v. Chief Constable of Devon and Cornwall *ex parte* Central Electricity Generating Board [1982] QB 458 . . . 454
R v. Coney (1882) 8 QBD 534 . . . 462
R v. Criminal Injuries Compensation Board *ex parte* Clowes [1977] 1 WLR 1353 . . . 64
R v. Criminal Injuries Compensation Board *ex parte* K [1999] QB 1131 . . . 1018
R v. Criminal Injuries Compensation Board *ex parte* Kent and Milne [1998] PIQR Q98 . . . 65
R v. Criminal Injuries Compensation Board *ex parte* Webb [1987] QB 74 . . . 64
R v. Cross (1812) 3 Camp. 224; 170 ER 1362 . . . 551
R v. Department of Health *ex parte* Source Informatics [2001] QB 424 . . . 843
R v. Deputy Governor of Parkhurst Prison *ex parte* Hague [1992] 1 AC 58 . . . 386, 469, 470
R v. Donovan [1934] 2 KB 498 . . . 462
R v. The Eastern Counties Ry. Co. (1842) 10 M & W 58; 152 ER 380 . . . 631
R v. Foley (1889) 17 Cox 142 (Ir.); 93 ER 379 . . . 485
R v. Governor of Brockhill Prison *ex parte* Evans (No. 2) [2000] 4 All ER 15; [2001] 2 AC 19 . . . 102, 466, 471
R v. Johnson [1997] 1 WLR 367 . . . 552
R v. Jones and Smith [1976] 1 WLR 672 . . . 350

R v. Khan [1997] AC 558 ... 859
R v. Loveridge [2001] EWCA Crim. 973 ... 848
R v. Madden [1975] 1 WLR 1379 ... 550, 552
R v. Miller [1983] 2 AC 161 ... 455
R v. Ministry of Agriculture, Fisheries and Food *ex parte* Hedley Lomas, Case C–5/94; [1996] 3 WLR 787 ... 437
R v. Mitchell [2003] EWCA Crim. 2188; [2004] RTR 14 ... 491
R v. Norbury [1978] Crim. LR 435 ... 552
R v. Norden (1755) Fost. 129 ... 453
R v. Rimmington and Goldstein [2006] 1 AC 459 ... 550, 552, 553
R v. St George (1840) 9 C & P 483 ... 453
R v. Secretary of State for the Home Department *ex parte* Fire Brigades' Union [1995] AC 513 ... 64
R v. Secretary of State for Transport *ex parte* Factortame Ltd. (No. 5) [2000] 1 AC 524 ... 405
R v. Secretary of State for Transport *ex parte* Factortame (No. 5) [2000] 1 AC 524 ... 436
R v. Secretary of State for Transport *ex parte* Factortame (No. 6) [2001] 1 WLR 942; [2001] 1 CMLR 47 ... 943
R v. Secretary of State for Transport *ex parte* Factortame (No. 7) [2001] 1 WLR 942 ... 395, 436
R v. Soul (1980) 70 Cr. App. R 295 ... 550
R v. Thurborn (1849) 1 Den. 387; 169 ER 293 ... 485
R v. Venna [1976] QB 421 ... 453
R v. Wicks [1936] 1 All ER 384 ... 758
R (On the application of Bernard) v. Enfield London Borough Council [2003] HRLR 4 ... 441
R (On the application of Heather) v. Leonard Cheshire Foundation [2002] HRLR 30 ... 440
R. A. Lister & Co. Ltd. v. E. G. Thomson (Shipping) Ltd. and Another (No. 2) [1987] 1 WLR 1614 ... 1035
Radcliffe v. Ribble Motor Services Ltd. [1939] AC 215 ... 908, 909
Radley v. London and North Western Railway (1875) LR 10 Ex. 100 ... 893
Rae v. Mars (UK) Ltd. [1990] 3 EG 80 ... 356
Rahman v. Arearose Ltd. [2001] QB 351 ... 1037, 1038
Rainham Chemical Works v. Belvedere Fish Guano Co. [1921] 2 AC 465 ... 609, 615
Ramsden v. Lee [1992] 2 All ER 204 ... 932
Rance v. Mid-Downs HA [1991] 1 All ER 801 ... 218
Rand v. East Dorset Health Authority [2001] PIQR Q1 ... 963
Rantzen v. Mirror Group Newspapers (1986) Ltd. [1993] 2 WLR 953; [1993] 4 All ER 975 (CA) ... 807, 881
Rapier v. London Tramways Co. [1893] 2 Ch. 588 ... 526
Ratcliff v. McConnell [1999] 1 WLR 670 ... 367, 368
Ratcliffe v. Evans [1892] 2 QB 524 ... 817, 941
Ravenscroft v. Rederiaktiebolaget Transatlantic [1991] 3 All ER 73; [1992] 2 All ER 470 ... 140, 147
Rayson v. South London Tramways Co. [1893] 2 QB 324 ... 475
Rayware Ltd. v. TGWU [1989] IRLR 134 ... 601
RCA Corp. v. Pollard [1983] Ch. 135 ... 387, 585, 593, 602
Re-Source American International Ltd v. Platt Service Ltd [2003] EWHC 1142 (TCC) ... 622
Read v. Coker (1853) 13 CB 850 ... 453
Read v. Croydon Corporation [1938] 4 All ER 631 ... 387
Read v. The Great Eastern Railway Co. (1868) LR 3 QB 555 ... 1009
Read v. J. Lyons & Co. Ltd. [1947] AC 156 ... 611, 612, 613, 615, 621, 625
Reading v. Attorney-General [1951] AC 507 ... 52
Ready Mixed Concrete (South East) Ltd. v. Minister of Pensions and National Insurance [1968] 2 QB 497 ... 672
Rebecca Elaine, The. *see* Hamble Fisheries Ltd. v. L. Gardner & Sons Ltd.
Redgrave v. Hurd (1881) 20 Ch. D 1 ... 902
Redland Bricks Ltd. v. Morris [1970] AC 652 ... 1030, 1031
Redpath v. Belfast and County Down Railway [1947] NI 167 ... 961
Redrow Homes Ltd. v. Bett Brothers plc 1997 SLT 1125 ... 948
Reeman v. Department of Transport [1997] 2 Lloyd's Rep. 648 ... 216
Rees v. Darlington Memorial Hospital NHS Trust [2002] 2 WLR 1483; [2004] 1 AC 309 ... 123, 130, 138, 178, 179, 219
Rees v. Mabco (102) Ltd 1003
Rees v. Morgan [1976] CL ... 633
Reeves v. Commissioner of Police of the Metropolis [1998] 2 WLR 401 (CA) ... 420
Reeves v. Commissioner of Police of the Metropolis [2000] 1 AC 360 (HL) ... 204, 212, 269, 896, 897, 899, 900, 911

Reffell v. Surrey CC [1964] 1 WLR 358 . . . 344
Regan v. Paul Properties DPF No. 1 Ltd. [2006] 3 WLR 1131 . . . 546
Regan v. Williamson [1976] 1 WLR 305 . . . 1014
Reid v. Rush & Tompkins Ltd. [1989] 3 All ER 228; [1990] 1 WLR 212 . . . 28, 191, 656
Revill v. Newberry [1996] 1 All ER 291; 2 WLR 239 . . . 9, 344, 363
Reynolds v. Commissioner of Police of the Metropolis [1985] QB 881 . . . 476
Reynolds v. Kennedy (1784) 1 Wils. KB 232; 95 ER 591 . . . 478
Reynolds v. Times Newspapers [1998] 3 WLR 862 (CA) . . . 942
Reynolds v. Times Newspapers [1999] 4 All ER 609; [2001] 2 AC 127 (HL) . . . 771, 772, 783, 784, 789, 794, 802, 803, 804, 805, 806, 815, 816
Rialas v. Mitchel (1984) 128 SJ 704 CA . . . 979
Rialto, The [1998] 1 Lloyd's Rep. 322 . . . 598
Ribee v. Norrie [2001] PIQR P8 (CA) . . . 535, 622
Richards v. Naum [1967] 1 QB 620 . . . 794
Richardson v. LRC Products Ltd. [2000] PIQR P164 . . . 735
Richardson v. Pitt-Stanley [1995] ICR 303 . . . 651
Richardson v. Redpath, Brown and Co. Ltd. [1944] AC 62 . . . 975
Riches v. Director of Public Prosecutions [1973] 1 WLR 1019 . . . 478
Riches v. News Group Newspapers [1986] QB 256 (CA) . . . 806, 947, 950
Rickards v. Lothian [1913] AC 263 . . . 614, 616, 619, 620
Ricket v. Metropolitan Ry. Co. (1867) LR 2 HL 175 . . . 553
Ricketts v. Thomas Tilling Ltd. [1915] 1 KB 644 . . . 684
Rickless v. United Artists Corporation [1988] QB 40 . . . 387, 394
Riddick v. Thames Board Mills Ltd. [1977] QB 881 . . . 774
Riden v. A. C. Billings & Son Ltd. [1957] 1 QB 46 . . . 343
Rigby v. Chief Constable of Northamptonshire [1985] 1 WLR 1242; [1985] 2 All ER 983 . . . 228, 506, 611, 612, 926
Rimmer v. Liverpool City Council [1985] QB 1 . . . 369
River Wear Commissioners v. Adamson (1977) 2 App. Cas. 743 . . . 452
Riverstone Meat Co. Ltd. v. Lancashire Shipping Co. Ltd. [1961] AC 807 . . . 696
Rivlin v. Bilainkin [1953] 1 QB 485 . . . 791
RK and another v. Oldham NHS Trust and another [2005] 2 AC 373 . . . 104, 105
Roach v. Yates [1953] 1 QB 617 . . . 994
Robb v. Salamis (M & I) Ltd. 2007 SLT 158 . . . 395
Robert Addie & Sons (Collieries) v. Dumbreck [1929] AC 358 . . . 363, 364
Roberts v. Alfred Holt & Co. (1945) 61 TLR 289 . . . 659
Roberts v. Gable [2007] EWCA Civ 721
Roberts v. Ramsbottom [1980] 1 WLR 823 . . . 57, 231
Roberts v. Rose (1865) LR 1 Ex. 82 . . . 549
Robertson v. Ridley [1989] 2 All ER 474 . . . 345
Robertson and Rough v. Forth Bridge Joint Board [1995] IRLR 251 . . . 156, 654
Robinson v. Balmain New Ferry Co. Ltd. [1910] AC 295 . . . 467
Robinson v. Harman (1848) 1 Exch. 850; 154 ER 363 . . . 951
Robinson v. Kilvert (1889) 41 Ch. D 88 . . . 524
Robinson v. Post Office [1974] 1 WLR 1176 . . . 273
Robson v. Hallett [1967] 2 QB 939 . . . 350
Roe v. Ministry of Health [1954] 2 QB 66 . . . 232, 669
Roe v. Sheffield City Council and Others [2003] EWCA Civ 1; [2004] QB 653 . . . 555
Rogers v. Kennay (1846) 9 QB 592 and OBG Ltd. v. Allan [2005] QB 762 . . . 486
Rogers, Sons & Co. v. Lambert & Co. [1891] 1 QB 318 . . . 490
Roles v. Nathan [1963] 1 WLR 1117 . . . 354, 355
Rondel v. Worsley [1969] 1 AC 191 . . . 34, 117, 135, 214, 792
Ronex Properties Ltd. v. John Laing Construction Ltd. [1983] QB 398 . . . 937, 1036
Rookes v. Barnard [1964] AC 1129 . . . 472, 574, 588, 590, 591, 594, 595, 597, 598, 599, 720, 809, 944, 945, 946, 947, 948, 949, 950
Roper v. Johnson (1873) LR 8 CP 167 . . . 975
Rose v. Ford [1937] AC 826 . . . 1004
Rose v. Miles (1815) 4M & S 101; 105 ER 773 . . . 553
Rose v. Plenty [1976] 1 WLR 141 . . . 685
Ross v. Caunters [1980] Ch. 297 . . . 24, 85, 173, 174
Ross v. Fedden (1872) 26 LT 966 . . . 608
Ross v. Hopkinson *The Times* 17 Oct. 1956 . . . 780
Rost v. Edwards [1990] 2 QB 460 . . . 791
Roswell v. Prior (1701) 12 Mod. Rep. 635; 88 ER 1570 . . . 538

Rothwell v. Chemical & Insulating Co. Ltd. [2006] EWCA Civ 27 . . . 142

Rowe v. Kingston-upon-Hull CC [2003] EWCA Civ 1281 . . . 936

Rowley v. London and North Western Ry. Co. (1873) LR 8 Exch. 221 . . . 951

Rowling v. Takaro Properties Ltd. [1988] AC 473 . . . 398, 427

Roy v. Kensington and Chelsea and Westminster Family Practitioner Committee [1992] 1 AC 625 . . . 403, 433

Roy v. Prior [1971] AC 470 . . . 476

Royal Aquarium and Summer and Winter Garden Society Ltd. v. Parkinson [1892] 1 QB 431 . . . 792

Royal Baking Powder Co. v. Wright Crossley & Co. (1901) 18 RPC 95 . . . 817

Royscott Trust Ltd. v. Rogerson [1991] 3 All ER 294 . . . 164, 280, 568, 731

Rubber Improvements Ltd. v. Daily Telegraph *see* Lewis v. Daily Telegraph [1964] AC 234

Rushmer v. Polsue & Alfieri Ltd. [1906] 1 Ch. 234 . . . 525, 561

Rushton v. Turner Brothers Asbestos Co. Ltd. [1960] 1 WLR 96 . . . 896

Russell v. Smith [2003] EWHC 2060 . . . 901

Ruxley Electronics and Construction Ltd. v. Forsyth [1996] AC 344 . . . 511

Ryan v. Liverpool Health Authority [2002] Lloyd's Rep. Med. 23 . . . 961

Ryeford Homes Ltd. v. Sevenoaks District Council (1989) 16 Const. LR 75 . . . 534

Rylands v. Fletcher (1865) 3 H & C 774; 159 ER 737 (Court of Exchequer); (1866) LR 1 Ex. 265 (Court of Exchequer Chamber); (1866) LR 1 265; (1868) LR 3 HL 330 (HL) . . . 81, 96, 158, 498, 518, 523, 532, 535, 539, 561, 607, 608, 609, 610, 611, 612, 613, 615, 616, 617, 618, 619, 620, 621, 622, 623, 624, 625, 626, 627, 628, 629, 903, 913, 927

Rylands v. Fletcher (1866) LR 1 Exch. 265: (1868) LR 3 HL 330 . . . 402, 556, 609, 634, 636, 696

S (Adult: Refusal of Medical Treatment), Re [1992] 3 WLR 806 . . . 217

S, Re [2005] 1 AC 593 . . . 852

S v. Gloucestershire CC [2001] Fam 313 . . . 422

S. & K. Holdings Ltd. v. Throgmorton Publications Ltd. [1972] 1 WLR 1036 . . . 764

SA de Rémorquage à Hélice v. Bennetts [1911] 1 KB 243 . . . 188

Sadgrove v. Hole [1901] 2 KB 1 . . . 773

Safeway Stores v. Tate [2001] QB 1120 . . . 765, 766

Sahib Foods Ltd. (In Liquidation) v. Paskin Kyriakides Sands (A Firm) [2003] EWCA Civ 1832 . . . 895, 897

Saif Ali v. Sydney Mitchell & Co. [1980] AC 198 . . . 214

St George's Healthcare NHS Trust v. S [1998] 3 All ER 673 . . . 459

St Helens Smelting Co. v. Tipping (1865) 11 HLC 642; 11 ER 1483 . . . 510, 523, 525, 532

St Martins Property Construction v. Sir Robert McAlpine Ltd. [1994] 1 AC 85 (HL) . . . 26, 27, 175, 176, 177

Saleslease Ltd. v. Davis [1999] 1 WLR 1644 (CA) . . . 490

Salmon v. Seafarer Restaurants Ltd. [1983] 1 WLR 1264 . . . 355

Salsbury v. Woodland [1970] 1 QB 324 . . . 696

Salter v. UB Frozen and Chilled Foods Ltd. [2003] SLT 1011 . . . 141

Saltman Engineering Co. Ltd. v. Campbell Engineering Co. Ltd. (1948) 65 RPC 203 . . . 838

Sampson v. Hodson-Pressinger [1981] 3 All ER 710 . . . 538, 1033

Samuel Payne v. John Setchell Ltd. [2002] BLR 489 . . . 182

Sandeman Coprimar SA v. Transportes Integrales SL [2003] QB 1270 (CA) . . . 490

Sandhar v. Secretary of State for Transport, Environment and the Regions [2004] EWCA Civ 1440; [2005] 1 WLR 1632 . . . 209, 554

Saunders v. Edwards [1987] 1 WLR 1116 . . . 925, 926

Savage v. Fairclough [2000] Env. LR 183 . . . 528

Savage v. Wallis [1966] 1 Lloyd's Rep. 357 . . . 976

Savand, The [1998] 2 Lloyd's Rep. 97 . . . 277

Savill v. Roberts (1698) 12 Mod. 208; 88 ER 1267 . . . 475

Sayers v. Harlow UDC [1958] 1 WLR 623 . . . 347, 899

Scala Ballroom (Wolverhampton) Ltd. v. Ratcliffe [1958] 1 WLR 1057 . . . 597

Scally v. Southern Health and Social Services Board [1991] 4 All ER 563; [1991] ICR 771; [1992] 1 AC 294 . . . 191, 380, 382, 656

Schering Agrochemicals Ltd. v. Resibel NVSA (Court of Appeal, 26 Nov. 1992; unreported) 905

Schloimovitz v. Clarendon Press *The Times* 6 July 1973 . . . 769

Schneider v. Heath (1813) 3 Camp. 506; 170 ER 1462 . . . 565

Schofield v. Saunders & Taylor Ltd 1003

Schott Kem Ltd. v. Bentley [1991] 1 QB 61 ... 968
Scott Lithgow Ltd. v. GEC Electrical Projects Ltd. 1992 SLT 244 ... 182
Scott v. Associated British Ports (Unreported, 22 Nov. 2000) (CA) ... 367
Scott v. Green & Sons [1969] 1 WLR 301 ... 390
Scott v. London and St Katherine Docks Co. (1865) 3H & C 596 ... 242
Scott v. Sampson (1881) 8 QBD 491 ... 811
Scruttons Ltd. v. Midland Silicones Ltd. [1962] AC 446 ... 173, 921
Searle v. Wallbank [1947] AC 341 ... 633
Seaward v. Paterson [1897] 1 Ch. 545 ... 1041
Secretary of State for Employment v. ASLEF (No. 2) [1972] 2 All ER 949 ... 529
Secretary of State for the Home Department v. Robb [1995] Fam 127 ... 459
Secretary of State for Work and Pensions v. Parliamentary Commissioner for Administration [2007] EWHC 242 (Admin); *The Times* 27 Feb. 2007 ... 404
Sedleigh-Denfield v. O'Callaghan [1940] AC 880 ... 206, 513, 514, 517, 521, 528, 536, 539
Selvanayagam v. University of the West Indies [1983] 1 WLR 585 ... 976
Sempra Metals Ltd. v. Her Majesty's Commissioners of Inland Revenue [2007] UKHL 34 ... 977
Semtex Ltd. v. Gladstone [1954] 1 WLR 945 ... 694
Series 5 Software v. Clarke [1996] 1 All ER 853; [1996] FSR 273 ... 1031
Serville v. Constance [1954] 1 WLR 487 ... 816
Settelen v. Metropolitan Police Commissioner [2004] EWHC 217 ... 487
Shah v. Standard Chartered Bank [1998] 3 WLR 592 ... 784
Shakoor v. Situ [2001] 1 WLR 410 ... 232
Shanklin Pier Ltd. v. Detel Products Ltd. [1951] 2 KB 584 ... 726
Shanson v. Howard [1997] 4 CL 237 ... 756
Sharp v. Avery and Kerwood [1938] 4 All ER 85 ... 138
Sharp v. Highland and Islands Fire Board 2005 SLT 855 ... 228
Shaw v. Wirral HA [1993] 4 Med. LR 275 ... 981
Sheldon v. R. H. M. Outhwaite (Underwriting Agencies) Ltd. [1996] AC 102 ... 936
Shelfer v. City of London Electric Lighting Co. [1895] 1 Ch. 287 ... 546, 547, 562, 1030, 1032
Shelley Films Ltd. v. Rex Features Ltd. [1994] EMLR 134 ... 840, 841
Shendish Manor v. Coleman [2001] EWCA Civ 913 ... 945
Shepherd v. The Post Office *The Times* 15 June 1995 ... 1009
Sheppard v. Glossop Corp. [1921] 3 KB 132 ... 406
Shevill v. Presse Alliance SA [1996] AC 959 ... 769
Shiffman v. Order of St John [1936] 1 All ER 557 ... 621
Shine v. Tower Hamlets London Borough Council [2006] EWCA Civ 85 ... 225
Ship v. Croskill (1870) LR 10 Eq. 73 ... 566
Shoreham UDC v. Dolphin Canadian Proteins Ltd. (1972) 71 LGR 261 ... 547
Short v. J. & W. Henderson Ltd. (1946) 62 TLR 427 ... 668
Sidaway v. Bethlem Royal Hospital [1985] AC 871 ... 226, 233, 234, 456
Silkin v. Beaverbrook Newspapers [1958] 1 WLR 743 ... 789
Sim v. H. J. Heinz Co. Ltd. [1959] 1 WLR 313 ... 829, 835
Sim v. Stretch [1936] 2 All ER 1237 ... 753
Simaan General Contracting Co. v. Pilkington Glass Ltd. (No. 2) [1988] QB 758 ... 127, 182
Simkiss v. Rhondda Borough Council (1983) LGR 461 ... 353, 354
Simmons v. Hoover Ltd. [1977] QB 284 ... 580
Simms v. Leigh Rugby Football Club Ltd. [1969] 2 All ER 923 ... 355, 913
Simms v. Simms [2002] EWHC 2734 (Fam) ... 459
Simpson v. A.I. Dairies Farms Ltd. [2001] NPC 14 ... 355
Simpson v. Savage (1856) 1 CB (NS) 347; 140 ER 143 ... 530
Simpson & Co. v. Thomson (1887) 3 App. Cas. 279 ... 188
Singh v. Gillard [1988] 138 NLJ 144 ... 811, 813
Sirros v. Moore [1975] QB 118 ... 117, 213
Six Carpenters' Case, The ... 499
Skuse v. Granada Television [1996] EMLR 278 ... 753, 760, 767
Slack v. Glenie (unreported, CA, 19 Apr. 2000) ... 355
Slater v. Clay Cross Co. Ltd. [1956] 2 QB 264 ... 355, 912
Slim v. Daily Telegraph Ltd. [1968] 2 QB 157 ... 789
Slipper v. British Broadcasting Corporation [1991] 1 QB 283 ... 775
Smeaton v. Ilford Corporation [1954] Ch. 450 ... 618

Smith v. Ainger *The Times* 5 June 1990 ... 631, 638
Smith v. Austin Lifts Ltd. [1959] 1 WLR 100 ... 660
Smith v. Chadwick (1884) 9 App. Cas. 187 ... 565
Smith v. Charles Baker & Sons [1891] AC 325 ... 652, 891, 907, 909
Smith v. Crossley Bros. Ltd. (1971) 95 ... 659
Smith v. Eric S. Bush [1990] 1 AC 831 ... 89, 132, 163, 168, 169, 170, 196, 197, 199, 359, 916, 917, 918
Smith v. Kenrick (1849) 7 CB 515; 137 ER 205 ... 611
Smith v. Leech, Brain & Co. Ltd. [1962] 2 QB 405 ... 121, 248, 273, 276
Smith v. Linskills [1995] 3 All ER 326 ... 214
Smith v. Littlewoods Organisation Ltd. [1987] 2 WLR 480; [1987] AC 241 ... 34, 118, 119, 129, 199, 200, 202, 206, 207, 225, 238, 239, 267, 308, 318, 319, 322, 517, 558, 698
Smith v. Liverpool CC [2006] EWCA Civ 743 ... 936
Smith v. Lloyds TSB Bank plc [2001] QB 541 (CA) ... 491
Smith v. Manchester Corporation [1974] 17 KIR 1 ... 992
Smith v. Moss [1940] 1 KB 424 ... 678
Smith v. North Metropolitan Tramways Co. (1891) 55 JP 630 ... 680
Smith v. Prendergast *The Times* 18 Oct. 1984 ... 632
Smith v. Scott [1973] Ch. 314 ... 610
Smith v. Stages [1989] AC 928 ... 686
Smith v. Stemler [2001] CLY 2309 ... 943, 944
Smith v. Stone (1647) Style 65; 82 ER 533 ... 30, 499
Smith (Administrator of Cosslett (Contractors) Ltd.) v. Bridgend CC [2001] ... 486
Smith New Court Securities Ltd. v. Scrimgeour Vickers (Asset Management) Ltd. [1997] AC 254 ... 569
Smithies v. NATSOPA [1909] 1 KB 310 ... 577, 580
Smoker v. London Fire and Civil Defence Authority [1991] 2 All ER 449 ... 959, 960
Snook v. Mannion [1982] Crim. LR 601 ... 350
Société Commerciale de Réassurance v. ERAS (International) Ltd. [1992] 2 All ER 82 ... 932, 935
Sole v. W. J. Hallt Ltd. [1973] QB 574 ... 347
Solloway v. Hampshire CC (1981) 79 LGR 449 ... 513
Sorrell v. Smith [1925] AC 700 ... 573, 596
SOS Kinderdorf International v. Bittaye [1996] 1 WLR 987 ... 580, 584
South Australia Asset Management Corp. v. York Montague Ltd. [1996] 3 All ER 365; [1997] AC 191 ... 269, 277, 278, 279, 570, 902, 1023, 1024
South Hetton Coal Co. Ltd. v. North-Eastern News Association Ltd. [1894] 1 QB 133, 139 ... 769, 771, 786, 816
South Portland Cement v. Cooper [1974] AC 623 ... 365
South Staffordshire Water Co. v. Sharman [1896] 2 QB 44 ... 485
South Wales Miners' Federation v. Glamorgan Coal Co. Ltd. [1905] AC 239 ... 580
Southern Water Authority v. Carey [1985] 2 All ER 1077 ... 194, 921
Southport Corp. v. Esso Petroleum Co. Ltd. [1953] 2 All ER 1204 (HC, QBD); [1953] 3 WLR 773 (HC, QBD); [1954] 2 QB 182 (CA); [1956] AC 218 (HL) ... 459, 495, 506, 535, 536, 926, 927
Southport Tramways Co. v. Ganey [1897] 2 QB 66 ... 502
Southwark London Borough Council v. Mills [2001] 1 AC 1 (HL) ... 538
Southwark London Borough Council v. Williams [1971] 1 Ch. 734 ... 505
Sowden v. Lodge [2004] EWCA Civ 1370 ... 961
Sparham-Souter v. Town and Country Developments (Essex) Ltd. [1976] QB 858 ... 930, 935
Sparrow v. Fairey Aviation Co. Ltd. [1964] AC 1019 ... 434
Spartan Steel & Alloys Ltd. v. Martin & Co. (Contractors) Ltd. [1973] QB 27 ... 34, 84, 123, 187, 188, 725
Speight v. Gosnay (1891) 60 LJQB 231 ... 758, 775
Spicer v. Smee [1946] 1 All ER 489 ... 523, 537
Spittle v. Bunney [1988] 1 WLR 847 ... 1014
Spring v. Guardian Assurance plc [1994] 3 All ER 129; [1995] 2 AC 296 ... 88, 171, 172, 656, 783, 797
Springhead Spinning Co. v. Riley (1868) LR 6 Eq. 551 ... 394, 593, 1029
SS Strathfillan v. SS Ikala [1929] AC 196 ... 1022
Stafford v. Conti Commodity Services Ltd. [1981] 1 All ER 691 ... 243
Standard Chartered Bank v. Pakistan National Shipping Corp. [2000] 1 Lloyd's Rep. 218 ... 568, 570
Standard Chartered Bank v. Pakistan National Shipping Corp. (No. 2) [2002] 3 WLR 1547 ... 462, 470, 903, 904
Stanley v. Powell [1891] 1 QB 86 ... 452

Stanley v. Saddique (Mohammed) [1991] 2 WLR 459; [1992] QB 1 ... 1018
Stansbie v. Troman [1948] 2 KB 48 ... 204, 267
Staples v. West Dorset District Council (1995) 93 LGR 536; [1995] PIQR P439 ... 352, 356
Stapley v. Gypsum Mines Ltd. [1953] AC 663 ... 270, 894, 895, 896, 900, 901
Staton v. NCB [1957] 1 WLR 893 ... 682
Staveley Iron & Coal Co. Ltd. v. Jones [1956] AC 627 ... 677, 899
Stearn v. Prentice Brothers [1919] 1 KB 394 ... 512
Steel v. McDonald's Corp. [1999] All ER 384 D ... 769
Steele v. Robert George and Co. Ltd. [1942] AC 497 ... 975
Stennett v. Hancock and Peters [1939] 2 All ER 578 ... 727
Stephens v. Anglian Water Authority [1987] 3 All ER 379 ... 529
Stephens v. Avery and Others [1988] Ch. 449 ... 839
Stephens v. Myers (1830) 4 C & P 349 ... 453
Stern v. Piper [1996] 3 WLR 715 ... 783
Stevedoring & Haulage Services Ltd. v. Fuller [2001] IRLR 627 ... 671
Stevens v. Woodward (1881) 6 QBD 318 ... 620
Stevens v. Yorkhill NHS Trust 2006 SLT 889 ... 154
Stevenson Jordon and Harrison Ltd. v. MacDonald and Evans [1952] 1 TLR 101 ... 670
Stocznia Gdanska SA v. Latvian Shipping Co. [2002] 2 Lloyd's Rep. 436 ... 574, 581, 582, 591
Stoke-on-Trent City Council v. W. & J. Wass Ltd. [1988] 1 WLR 1406 ... 52, 53, 54
Stokes v. Guest, Keen and Nettlefield (Bolts and Nuts) Ltd. [1968] 1 WLR 776 ... 655, 661
Stone v. Taffe [1974] 1 WLR 1575 ... 349, 350, 355
Storey v. Ashton (1869) LR 4 QB 476 ... 686
Stott v. West Yorkshire Road Car Co. Ltd. and Another (Home Bakeries Ltd. and Another, Third Parties) [1971] 2 QB 651 ... 1035
Stovin v. Wise [1996] AC 923 ... 36, 59, 78, 79, 130, 131, 168, 195, 196, 199, 201, 203, 209, 211, 399, 400, 401, 402, 410, 414, 415, 417, 426, 430
Stowell v. The Railway Executive [1949] 2 KB 519 ... 342
Stratford v. Lindley [1965] AC 269 ... 577, 591
Stuart v. Bell [1891] 2 QB 341 ... 797
Sturges v. Bridgman (1879) 11 Ch. D 852 ... 525, 539, 542, 543, 545
Sun Life Assurance Co. of Canada v. W. H. Smith & Sons Ltd. (1934) 150 LT 211 ... 777
Sunbolf v. Alford (1838) 3M & W 248; 150 ER 1135 ... 466, 467
Surtees v. Kingston-upon-Thames BC [1992] 2 FLR 559 ... 200, 230
Surzur Overseas Ltd. v. Koros [1999] 2 Lloyd's Rep. 611 ... 598
Sutcliffe v. Pressdram Ltd. [1991] 1 QB 153 ... 807
Sutradhar v. National Environmental Research Council [2006] UKHL 33 ... 129, 164
Swadling v. Cooper [1931] AC 1 ... 893
Swain v. Buri [1996] PIQR P442 ... 366
Swain v. Pearl [1996] PIQR P442 ... 368
Swaine v. Great Northern Ry. Co. (1846) 4 De GJ & S 211; 46 ER 899 ... 523
Swinney v. Chief Constable of Northumbria Police Force [1997] QB 464 ... 212, 420
Sykes v. Harry [2001] QB 1014 (CA) ... 371

T (Adult: Refusal of Medical Treatment), Re [1992] Fam 95 ... 457
T v. Surrey CC [1994] 4 All ER 577 ... 420
Tadd v. Eastwood [1985] ICR 132 (CA) ... 782, 792
Taff Vale Railway Co. v. Amalgamated Society of Railway Servants [1901] AC 426 ... 598
Taff Vale Railway v. Jenkins [1913] AC 1 ... 1013
Tai Hing Cotton Mill Ltd. v. Liu Chong Hing Bank Ltd. [1986] AC 80 ... 27, 28, 29, 190, 191, 919, 920
Targett v. Torfaen BC [1992] 3 All ER 27 ... 372, 373
Tarleton v. McGawley (1793) Peake NP 270; 170 ER 153 ... 589
Tarry v. Ashston (1876) 1 QBD 314 ... 696
Tate and Lyle v. Greater London Council [1983] 2 AC 509 ... 540
Taylor v. Caldwell (1863) 32 LJQB 164 ... 81
Taylor v. Metropolitan Police Commissioner *The Times* 6 Dec. 1989 ... 66
Taylor v. O'Connor [1971] AC 115 ... 986, 1017
Tear v. Freebody (1858) 4 CB (NS) 228 ... 486
Telnikoff v. Matusevitch [1990] 3 WLR 725; [1992] 2 AC 343 ... 785, 787, 789
Temperton v. Russell [1893] 1 QB 715 ... 576
Tempest v. Snowdon [1952] 1 KB 130 ... 478
Tennant Radiant Heat Ltd. v. Warrington Development Corp. [1988] 11 EG 71 ... 904
Tesco Stores Ltd. v. Pollard [2006] EWCA Civ 393 ... 733, 741
Tesco Stores Ltd. v. Wards Construction (Investment) Ltd. (1995) 76 BLR 94 ... 374

Tetley v. Chitty [1986] 1 All ER 663 . . . 538, 545, 547
Thake v. Maurice [1986] QB 644 . . . 28, 218
Thames Valley Police v. Hepburn [2002] EWCA Civ 1841 . . . 467
Theaker v. Richardson [1962] 1 WLR 151 . . . 773
Theakston v. MGN [2002] EWHC 137; [2002] EMLR 22 . . . 846
Theyer v. Purnell [1918] 2 KB 333 . . . 636
Thomas v. British Rail Board [1976] QB 912 . . . 365
Thomas v. NUM (South Wales Area) [1985] IRLR 136 . . . 601
Thomas v. Quartermaine (1887) 18 QBD 685 . . . 906
Thomas v. Sorrell (1674) Vaughan 330 . . . 505
Thomas Bradbury, Agnew & Co. Ltd. [2002] 2 WLR 452 . . . 790
Thomas Witter Ltd. v. TBP Properties Ltd. [1996] 2 All ER 573 . . . 568
Thompson v. Bridges, 273 SW 529 (1925) . . . 759
Thompson v. Commissioner of Police for the Metropolis [1997] 3 WLR 403; [1998] QB 498 . . . 942, 944, 947, 950, 951, 977
Thompson v. London County Council [1899] 2 QB 840 . . . 1033
Thompson v. Park [1944] KB 408 . . . 504
Thompson v. Price [1973] QB 838 . . . 1016
Thompson v. Smiths Ship Repairers (North Shields) Ltd. [1960] AC 145 . . . 235
Thompson v. Smiths Ship Repairers (North Shields) Ltd. [1984] QB 405; 1 All ER 881 . . . 661
Thompson v. T. Lohan (Plant Hire) Ltd. [1987] 1 WLR 649 . . . 674, 675
Thompstone v. Tameside and Glossop Acute Services NHS Trust [2006] EWHC 2904 QB . . . 973
Thomson v. Cremin [1956] 1 WLR 103 . . . 360
Thomson v. Deakin [1952] Ch. 646 . . . 577
Thornton v. Kirklees Metropolitan Borough Council [1979] 1 WLR 637; [1979] QB 626 . . . 388, 426, 432
Thorpe v. Brumfit (1873) LR 8 Ch. 650 . . . 543
Three Rivers DC v. Bank of England (No. 3) [2000] 2 WLR 1220; [2003] 2 AC 1 . . . 401, 429, 430, 437
Thurman v. Wild (1840) 11 A & E 453; 113 ER 487 . . . 1034
Thurston v. Todd (1966–7) 84 WN Pt. 1 . . . 954
Tigress, The (1863) 32 LJ Adm. 97 . . . 489
Tiline v. White Cross Insurance Association Ltd. [1921] 3 KB 327 . . . 1040
Tillet v. Ward (1882) 10 QBD 17 . . . 636
Tims v. John Lewis & Co. Ltd. [1951] 2 KB 459 . . . 476
Tinsley v. Milligan [1994] 1 AC 340 . . . 924
Tolley v. J. S. Fry & Sons Ltd. [1930] 1 KB 467; [1931] AC 333 . . . 754, 761, 827, 830, 835
Tomlinson v. Congleton BC [2004] 1 AC 46; [2003] 3 WLR 705; [2003] 2 WLR 1120 . . . 344, 350, 352, 367, 368
Toogood v. Spyring [1834] 1 CM & R 181 . . . 794
Topp v. London Country Bus (South West) Ltd. [1993] 1 WLR 976 . . . 205, 267
Torquay Hotel Co. Ltd. v. Cousins [1969] 2 Ch. 106 . . . 577, 581, 583, 584, 586, 588
Towers & Co. Ltd. v. Gray [1961] 2 QB 351 . . . 485
Townend v. Askern Coal and Iron Co. [1934] Ch. 463 . . . 1020
Tozer v. Child (1857) 7 El. & Bl. 377 . . . 428
T.P. and K.M. v. United Kingdom [2001] 2 FLR 246 . . . 133
Transco plc v. Stockport MBC [2004] 2 AC 1 . . . 518, 610, 612, 614, 615, 616, 618, 622, 625, 626
Transco plc v. United Utilities Water Plc [2005] EWHC 2784 (QBD) . . . 484
Tremain v. Pike [1969] 3 WLR 1556 . . . 273
Trevett v. Lee [1955] 1 WLR 113 . . . 539, 555, 903
Trotman v. North Yorkshire CC [1999] LGR 584 . . . 690
Trustees of the Dennis Rye Pension Fund v. Sheffield CC [1997] 4 All ER 747 . . . 433
'Truth' (NZ) Ltd. v. P. N. Holloway [1960] 1 WLR 997 . . . 776
Tuberville v. Savage [1669] 1 Mod. Rep. 3; 86 ER 684 . . . 453
Turner v. Metro-Goldwyn-Mayer Pictures Ltd. [1950] 1 All ER 449 . . . 796
Tutin v. Mary Chipperfield Promotions Ltd. (1980) 130 NLJ 807 . . . 637
Tutton v. A. D. Walter Ltd. [1986] QB 61 . . . 366, 367, 496
Tweddle v. Atkinson (1861) 1 B & S 393 . . . 173
Twine v. Bean's Express Ltd. (1946) 62 TLR 458 . . . 685
UBAF Ltd. v. European American Banking Corp. [1984] QB 713 . . . 567
Udale v. Bloomsbury AHA [1983] 1 WLR 1098 . . . 218
Union Traffic Ltd. v. TGWU [1989] IRLR 127 . . . 601

Union Transport Finance Ltd. v. British Car Auctions Ltd. [1978] 2 All ER 385 ... 486
United States of America and Republic of France v. Dolfus Mieg et Cie SA and Bank of England [1952] AC 582 ... 485
Universe Sentinel, The [1983] 1 AC 366 ... 595
Universe Tankships Inc. of Monrovia v. International Transport Workers' Federation [1983] 1 AC 366 ... 595

Vacwell Engineering Co. Ltd. v. BDH Chemicals Ltd. [1971] 1 QB 88 ... 274, 726, 730, 732
Valentine v. Hyde [1919] 2 Ch. 129 ... 599
Van Colle v. Chief Constable of Hertfordshire Police [2006] EWHC 360 ... 136, 212, 412, 421, 444
Van Oppen v. Trustees of Bedford School [1990] 1 WLR 235 ... 191
Vandepitte v. Preferred Accident Insurance Co. of New York [1933] AC 70 ... 194
Vasey v. Surrey Free Inns (1995) 10 CL 641 ... 679, 681
Vellino v. Chief Constable of Greater Manchester [2001] 1 WLR 218 ... 922, 9221
Venables v. News Group Newspapers [2001] 1 All ER 908 ... 840, 857
Vera Cruz, The (1884) 10 App. Cas. 59 ... 1010
Vernon v. Boseley (No. 1) [1997] 1 All ER 577 ... 140
Viasystems (Tyneside) Ltd. v. Thermal Transfer Northern Ltd. [2005] EWCA Civ 1151 ... 676, 677
Victorian Railway Commissioners v. Coultas (1888) 13 App. Cas. 222 ... 141
Videan v. British Transport Commission [1963] 2 QB 650 ... 363
Vine v. Waltham Forest LBC [2000] 1 WLR 2383 (CA) ... 484
Vizetelly v. Mudie's Select Library Ltd. [1900] 2 QB 170 ... 777, 778
Vodden v. Gayton [2001] PIQR P4 ... 365
Volute, The [1922] 1 AC 129 ... 896
Vose v. Lancashire and Yorkshire Railway Co. (1858) 2 LJ Ex. 249 ... 908

W (A Minor) (Wardship: Medical Treatment), Re [1991] 4 All ER 177 ... 457
W (A Minor) (Wardship: Medical Treatment), Re [1992] 4 All ER 627 ... 457
W v. Edgell [1990] Ch. 59 ... 839
W v. Essex County Council [1999] Fam 90; [2001] 2 AC 592 ... 141, 153
W v. Meah; D v. Meah [1986] 1 All ER 935 ... 943
W. B. Anderson & Sons Ltd. v. Rhodes (Liverpool) Ltd. [1967] 2 All ER 850 ... 567
W. H. Smith & Son v. Clinton (1908) 99 LT 840 ... 1040
Wagon Mound, The (No. 1) [1961] AC 388 ... 142, 247, 248, 271, 272, 273, 274, 278, 279, 280, 525, 569, 646, 741, 1009
Wagon Mound, The (No. 2) [1967] 1 AC 617 ... 237, 238, 274, 554
Wah Tat Bank Ltd. v. Chan [1975] AC 507 ... 1034
Wainwright v. Home Office [2001] EWCA Civ 2081; [2002] 3 WLR 405 (CA) ... 832, 855
Wainwright v. Home Office [2003] UKHL 53; [2004] 2 AC 406 (HL) ... 93, 102, 454, 472, 473, 474, 848, 855, 860
Wakley v. Cooke and Healey (1849) 4 Exch. 511 ... 784
Wales v. Wadham [1977] 1 WLR 199 ... 566
Walford v. Miles [1992] AC 128 ... 164
Walker v. Baird [1892] AC 491 ... 927
Walker v. Brewster (1876) LR 5 Eq. 25 ... 834
Walker v. Great Northern Railway (1891) 28 LR Ir. 69 ... 117
Walker v. Northumberland County Council [1995] 1 All ER 737 ... 157, 653, 654, 655
Walkin v. South Manchester HA [1995] 1 WLR 1543 ... 218, 931
Wallace v. Newton [1982] 1 WLR 375 ... 639
Walter v. Selfe (1851) 4 De G & Sm. 315; 64 ER 849 ... 521
Walton v. Calderdale Healthcare NHS Trust [2005] EWHC 1053 QB ... 961
Wandsworth LBC v. A [2000] 1 WLR 1246 (CA) ... 504
Wandsworth LBC v. Railtrack plc [2002] QB 756 (CA) ... 515, 554, 560
Waple v. Surrey [1998] 1 WLR 860 ... 792
Ward v. Cannock Chase DC [1985] 3 All ER 537 ... 267
Ward v. James [1966] 1 QB 273 ... 977
Ward v. Lewis [1955] 1 WLR 9 ... 775
Ward v. Macauley (1791) 4 Term Rep. 489; 100 ER 1135 ... 488
Ward v. McMaster [1985] IR 29 ... 370
Ward v. Tesco Stores Ltd. [1976] 1 WLR 810 ... 242, 243
Ward v. Weeks (1830) 7 Bing. 211 ... 775
Warner Holidays Ltd. v. Secretary of State for Social Services [1983] ICR 440 ... 672, 673
Warner v. Basildon Development Corp. (1991) 7 Const. LJ 146 ... 198, 374, 935

Warnink v. Townend and Sons [1979] AC 731 ... 817, 829
Warren v. Henlys Ltd. [1948] 2 All ER 935 ... 680
Warren v. Northern General Hospital NHS Trust (conjoined appeal with Heil v. Rankin) ... 1003
Warriner v. Warriner [2002] EWCA Civ 81; [2003] 3 All ER 447 ... 988
Wason v. Walter (1868) LR 4 QB 73 ... 795
Waters v. Commissioner of Police of the Metropolis [2000] IRLR 70 ... 472, 654, 700
Watkin v. Hall (1868) LR 3 QB 396 ... 775
Watkins v. Secretary of State for the Home Department [2006] 2 WLR 807 ... 428
Watson v. British Boxing Board of Control [2001] QB 1134 ... 129, 195, 215, 420, 912
Watson v. Buckley, Osborne, Garret & Co. Ltd. [1940] 1 All ER 174 ... 726, 727
Watson v. Willmott [1990] 3 WLR 1103 ... 1018
Watt v. Hertfordshire County Council [1954] 1 WLR 835 ... 240
Watt v. Jamieson 1954 SC 56 ... 512
Watt v. Longsdon [1930] 1 KB 130 ... 797
Watts v. Lowcur Ltd 698
Watts v. Times Newspapers [1996] 2 WLR 427 ... 798
WB v. H. Bauer Publishing [2002] EMLR 8 ... 839
Webb v. Chief Constable of Merseyside Police [2000] QB 427 ... 487, 926
Webb v. EMO Air Cargo Ltd. (No. 2) [1995] 1 WLR 1454 ... 395
Webb v. Times Publishing Co. Ltd. [1960] 2 QB 535 ... 795
Wednesbury ... 414, 415
Weld-Blundell v. Stephens [1920] AC 956 ... 838
Weldon v. Home Office [1992] 1 AC 58 ... 469, 470
Wells v. Cooper [1958] 2 QB 265 ... 227
Wells v. Wells [1997] 1 WLR 652 (CA) ... 954
Wells v. Wells [1998] 3 WLR 329; [1999] 1 AC 345 (HL) ... 952, 966, 987, 988, 989
Wells (Merstham) Ltd. v. Buckland Sand & Silica Co. Ltd. [1965] 2 QB 170 ... 726
Welsh v. Chief Constable of the Merseyside Police [1993] 1 All ER 692 ... 214, 419
Welton v. North Cornwall DC [1997] 1 WLR 570 ... 215, 419, 420
Wershof v. Metropolitan Police Commissioner [1978] 3 All ER 540 ... 479
West Bromwich Albion FC v. El Safty [2005] EWHC 2866 ... 164
West London Commercial Bank Ltd. v. Kitson (1884) 13 QBD 360 ... 567
West Wiltshire DC v. Garland [1995] Ch. 297 ... 388
Westripp v. Baldock [1939] 1 All ER 279 ... 496
Westwood v. Post Office [1974] AC 1 ... 899
Wheat v. Lacon & Co. Ltd. [1966] 1 QB 335; [1966] AC 552 ... 344, 345, 346, 351
Wheeler v. J. J. Saunders [1995] 2 All ER 697 ... 543
Wheeler v. New Merton Board Mills Ltd. [1933] 2 KB 669 ... 382, 393, 913
White v. Blackmore [1972] 2 QB 651 ... 356, 357, 358, 914
White v. Chief Constable of South Yorkshire Police [1999] 2 AC 455; [1998] 3 WLR 1510 ... 84, 116, 117, 127, 141, 144, 145, 151, 152, 156, 157, 196, 655, 656
White v. Jones [1995] 2 AC 207 ... 18, 24, 26, 80, 85, 86, 90, 129, 173, 174, 175, 176, 177, 178, 193, 194, 199, 214, 215, 531
White v. Mellin [1895] AC 154 ... 1029
White v. Metropolitan Police Commissioner *The Times* 24 Apr. 1982 ... 66
White v. St Albans City and District Council *The Times* 12 Mar. 1990 ... 366
Whitehouse v. Jordan [1981] 1 WLR 246 ... 57, 226, 233
Whiteley v. Adams (1863) 15 CB (NS) 392; 143 ER 838 ... 800
Whitfield v. H. & R. Johnson (Tiles) Ltd. [1990] 3 All ER 426 ... 390
WHPT Housing Association Ltd. v. Secretary of State for Social Services [1981] ICR 737 ... 670
Wickens v. Champion Employment Agency [1984] ICR 365 ... 671, 672, 676
Wicks v. Fentham (1791) 4 TR 247; 100 ER 1000 ... 477
Wieland v. Cyril Lord Carpets [1969] 3 All ER 1006 ... 268
Wiffen v. Bailey [1915] 1 KB 600 ... 475
Wilchick v. Marks and Silverstone [1934] 2 KB 56 ... 538
Wilkes v. Wood (1763) Lofft. 1; 98 ER 489 ... 945
Wilkinson v. Downton [1897] 2 QB 57 ... 93, 451, 455, 471, 472, 473, 855
William Coulson & Sons v. James Coulson and Co. [1887] 3 TLR 846 ... 830, 831
Williams v. A. & W. Hemphill Ltd., 1966 SLT 259 ... 682
Williams v. BOC Gases [2000] PIQR Q253 ... 961
Williams v. Mersey Docks [1905] 1 KB 804 ... 1009

Williams v. Natural Life Ltd. [1998] 1 WLR 830 ... 167
Williams v. Reason [1988] 1 WLR 96 ... 784
Williams v. Trimm Rock Quarries (1965) 109 SJ 454 ... 1036
Williamson v. Thornycroft [1940] 2 KB 658 ... 1016
Willson v. Ministry of Defence [1991] 1 All ER 638, 641 ... 969, 970
Wilsher v. Essex Area Health Authority [1987] QB 730; [1988] AC 1074 ... 82, 120, 231, 247, 248, 250, 254, 256, 257
Wilson v. Donaldson [2004] EWCA Civ 972, (2004) 148 SJLB 879 ... 633, 636
Wilson v. Lombank Ltd. [1963] 1 WLR 1294 ... 484
Wilson v. Pringle [1987] QB 237 ... 451, 452, 454
Wilson v. Tyneside Window Cleaning Co. [1958] 2 QB 110 ... 660
Wilsons & Clyde Coal Co. Ltd. v. English [1938] AC 57 ... 612, 653, 697, 700, 907
Winkfield, The [1902] P 42 ... 485, 486
Winkworth v. Hubbard [1960] 1 Lloyd's Rep. 150 ... 979, 980
Winnik v. Dick (1984) SLR 185 ... 910
Winter Garden Theatre (London) Ltd. v. Millenium Productions Ltd. [1948] AC 173 ... 504
Winterbottom v. Wright (1842) 10 M & W 109 ... 114, 704
Wise v. Kaye [1962] 1 QB 638 ... 1001, 1002
With v. O'Flanagan [1936] Ch. 75 ... 165
Withers v. Henley (1614) Cro. Jac. 379; 79 ER 324 ... 470
Withers v. Perry Chain Co. Ltd. [1961] 1 WLR 1314 ... 658
Wong v. Parkside Health NHS Trust [2001] EWCA Civ 1721 ... 474
Wood v. Bentall Simplex Ltd. [1992] PIQR P332 ... 1019
Wood v. Manley (1839) 11 A & E 34; 113 ER 325 ... 504
Woodar Investment Development Ltd. v. Wimpey Construction (UK) Ltd. [1980] 1 WLR 227 ... 194, 724
Woodhouse AC Israel Cocoa Ltd. v. Nigerian Produce Marketing Co. Ltd. [1972] AC 741 ... 565
Woodley v. Metropolitan District Railway Co. (1887) 2 Ex. D 384 ... 908
Woodrup v. Nicol [1993] PIQR Q 104 ... 980, 992, 993
Woods v. Durable Suites Ltd. [1953] 1 WLR 857 ... 662
Woods v. Winskill [1913] 2 Ch. 303 ... 381
Woodward v. Hutchins [1977] 1 WLR 760 ... 846
Woodward v. Mayor of Hastings [1945] KB 174 ... 361
Wooldridge v. Sumner [1963] 2 QB 43 ... 224, 228, 906, 912
Woollerton & Wilson Ltd. v. Richard Costain Ltd. [1970] 1 WLR 411 ... 496, 545, 1030
Woolwich Building Society v. Inland Revenue Commissioners [1993] AC 70 ... 80, 108, 433
World Beauty, The [1969] P 12 ... 1023
Wormald v. Cole [1954] 1 QB 614 ... 636
Worsley v. Tambrands Ltd. [2000] PIQR P95 ... 737
Wright v. British Railways Board [1983] 2 AC 773 ... 978
Wringe v. Cohen [1940] 1 KB 229 ... 555, 556
Wroth v. Tyler [1974] Ch. 30 ... 279
Wrotham Park Estates Co. Ltd. v. Parkside Homes Ltd. [1974] 1 WLR 798 ... 1033
Wyatt v. Hillingdon LBC (1978) 76 LGR 727 ... 388
Wyngrove v. Scottish Omnibuses 1966 SC 47 (HL) ... 240

X (A woman formerly known as Mary Bell) v. SO [2003] EWHC 1101; [2003] EMLR 37 ... 840
X Health Authority v. Y [1988] RPC 379 ... 839, 844
X (Minors) v. Bedfordshire County Council [1995] 2 AC 633 ... 133, 136, 154, 201, 203, 210, 211, 388, 398, 399, 401, 410, 411, 412, 414, 415, 418, 419, 420, 421, 422, 425, 433, 444, 445, 700, 701
X, Re [1984] 1 WLR 1422 ... 827
X v. Y [2001] QB 967 ... 843

Y (Mental Incapacity: Bone Marrow Transplant), Re [1996] 2 FLR 787 ... 459
Yewens v. Noakes (1880) 6 QBD 530 ... 668
Yianni v. Edwin Evans & Sons [1982] QB 438 ... 168
Yorkshire Dale SS Co. v. Minister ofWar Transport [1942] AC 691 ... 893
Youell v. Bland Welch & Co. Ltd. (No. 2) [1990] 2 Lloyd's Rep. 431 ... 28
Young & Marten Ltd. v. McManus Childs Ltd. [1969] 1 AC 454 ... 730
Young and Woods v. West [1980] IRLR 201 ... 674
Youssoupoff v. Metro-Goldwyn-Mayer Pictures Ltd. (1934) 50 TLR 581 ... 754, 757

Yuen Kun Yeu v. Attorney-General of Hong Kong [1988] AC 175 . . . 123, 128, 129, 203, 211, 398, 401, 404

Zalwalla & Co. v. Waila [2002] IRLR 697 . . . 942

Ziemniak v. ETPM Deep Sea Ltd. [2003] EWCA Civ 636 . . . 386

Zoernsch v. Waldock [1964] 1 WLR 675 . . . 33

TABLE OF CASES FROM OTHER JURISDICTIONS

AUSTRALIA

Agar v. Hyde [2000] HCA 41 ... 420
Allen v. Roughley (1955) 94 CLR 98 ... 501
Australian Broadcasting Corporation v. Lenah Game Meats [2001] 208 CLR 199; HCA 63 ... 843

Beaudesert Shire Council v. Smith (1966) 120 CLR 145 ... 393, 394, 592, 593s
Benning v. Wong (1969) 122 CLR 249 ... 627
Bondarenko v. Summers (1969) 69 SR (NSW) 269 ... 924
Brodie v. Singleton Shire Council (2001) 206 CLR 512 ... 415
Bryan v. Maloney (1995) 128 ALR 163 ... 128
Bunyan v. Jordan (1937) 57 CLR 1 ... 472
Burnie Port Authority v. General Jones Pty. (1994) 68 ALJR 331 ... 627

Caltex Oil (Aust.) Pty. Ltd. v. The Dredge Willemstad (1976) 136 CLR 529 ... 47, 159, 188
Cattanach v. Melchior [2003] HCA 38 ... 130
Chapman v. Hearse [1961] SASR 51; 106 CLR 112 ... 219
Chappel v. Hart (1998) 195 CLR 232 ... 456
Cook v. Cook (1986) 68 ALR 353 ... 230, 231
Crimmins v. Stevedoring Industry Financing Committee (1999) 167 ALR 1 ... 420

D'Agruima v. Seymour (1951) 69 WN (NSW) 15 ... 635
Deaton's Property Ltd. v. Flew (1949) 79 CLR 370 ... 681
Dow Jones v. Gutnick [2002] HCA 56 ... 777

Graham v. Baker (1961) 106 CLR 340 ... 958

Hahn v. Conley [1972] ALR 247 ... 204
Hawkins v. Clayton (1988) 164 CLR 539 ... 935
Hollis v. Vabu Pty. Ltd. (2001) 207 CLR 21 ... 667

Insurance Commissioner v. Joyce (1948) 77 CLR 39 ... 910

Jackson v. Harrison (1978) 138 CLR 438 ... 923, 924
Jaensch v. Coffey (1984) 155 CLR 549 ... 141, 145, 146

Kenny & Good Pty. Ltd. v. MGICA (1992) Ltd. (1999) 163 ALR 611 (HC of Australia) ... 278
Kitano v. Commonwealth of Australia (1974) 129 CLR 151 ... 593
Kondis v. State Transport Authority (1984) 55 ALR 225; (1984) 154 CLR 672 ... 661, 696, 698

McHale v. Watson (1966) 115 CLR 199 ... 229
Malec v. J. C. Hutton Pty. Ltd. (1990) 64 ALJR 316 ... 260, 261, 263
March v. E. & M. H. Stamare Pty. Ltd. (1991) 171 CLR 506 ... 245

National Insurance Co. of New Zealand v. Espagne (1961) 106 CLR 569 ... 958
Northern Territory v. Mengel (1995) 185 CLR 307 ... 592

Perre v. Apand Pty. Ltd. (1999) 198 CLR 180 ... 128, 186
Pyrenees Shire Council v. Day (1998) 192 CLR 330 ... 209, 415, 417

Rogenkamp v. Bennett (1950) 80 CLR 292 ... 910

Seale v. Perry [1982] VR 193 ... 174
Shaddock and Associates Pty. Ltd. v. Paramatta City Council (No. 1) (1981) 150 CLR 225 ... 427
Shell Co. of Australia Ltd. v. Federal Commissioner of Taxation [1931] AC 275 ... 792
Skusa v. Commonwealth of Australia (1985) 62 ALR 108 ... 352
Smith v. Jenkins (1970) 44 ALJR 78 ... 924
Smith v. Leurs (1945) 70 CLR 256 ... 205
Smiths Newspapers v. Becker (1932) 47 CLR 279 ... 787
Stevens v. Brodribb Sawmilling Co. Pty. Ltd. (1986) 160 CLR 16 ... 698

Sullivan v. Moody (2000) 75 ALJR 1570; [2001] HCA 59 … 128, 417
Sutherland Shire Council v. Heyman (1985) 60 ALR 1; (1985) 157 CLR 424 … 128, 181, 413, 416, 934

Trident Insurance Co. Ltd. v. MacNiece Bros. Pty. Ltd. (1988) 165 CLR 107 (HC of Australia) … 194

Watt v. Rama [1972] VR 353 … 117, 217

CANADA

Aldridge v. Van Patter [1952] 4 DLR 93 … 621

Bank of Nova Scotia v. Hellenic Mutual War Risks Association (Bermuda) Ltd. [1990] 1 QB 818 … 28
Barrette v. Franki Compressed Pile Co. of Canada Ltd. (1955) 2 DLR 665 … 609
Bazley v. Curry (1999) 174 DLR (4th) 45 … 665, 691, 699, 700
Bielitski v. Obadiak (1922) 65 DLR 627 … 472
Burgess v. Woodstock [1955] 4 DLR 615 … 530

Canadian National Railway Co. v. Norsk Pacific Steamship Co., 11 CCLT (2d) 1 (1992); (1992) 91 DLR (4th) 289 (Supreme Ct of Canada) … 124, 158, 159, 160, 186, 188, 189, 192, 197, 282, 295, 417
Canadian Pacific Hotels Ltd. v. Bank of Montreal (1988) 40 DLR (4th) 385 … 28
Casey v. Automobiles Renault of Canada (1965) 54 DLR (2d) 600 … 477
Central Trust Co. v. Rafuse (1986) 31 DLR (4th) 481 … 192
Children's Foundation v. Bazley (1999) 174 DLR (4th) 45 … 679
City of Kamloops v. Nielsen [1984] 2 SCR 2 … 416
Committee for the Commonwealth of Canada v. Canada (1991) 77 DLR (4th) 385 … 498
Cook v. Lewis [1951] SCR 830 … 252
Cooper v. Hobart [2000] SCC 79 … 128, 417

Devon Lumber Co. Ltd. v. MacNeill (1988) 45 DLR (4th) 300 … 531, 534
Duval v. Séguin (1973) 40 DLR (3d) 666 … 117

Gershman v. Manitoba Vegetable Producers' Marketing Board (1976) 69 DLR (3d) 114 … 430

Hart v. Dominion Stores (1968) 67 DLR (2d) 675 … 730

Jacobi v. Boys' and Girls' Club of Vernon (1999) 174 DLR (4th) 71 … 679, 691

Kamloops v. City of Nielsen [1984] 2 SCR 2 … 935
Kaplan v. Canada Safeway (1968) 68 DLR (2d) 627 … 342
Kroeker v. Jansen (1995) 123 DLR (4th) 652 … 981

McKinnon Industries Ltd. v. Walker [1951] 3 DLR 577 … 525
McLean v. Brett (1919) 49 DLR 162 … 636
Mann v. Saulnier (1959) 19 DLR (2d) 130 … 495, 556
Montreal Tramways v. Leveille [1933] 4 DLR 337 … 217
Motherwell v. Motherwell (1976) 73 DLR (3rd) 1427 … 531

Nancy B v. Hôtel-Dieu de Québec (1992) 86 DLR (4th) 385 … 456
Nor-Video Services Ltd. v. Ontario Hydro (1978) 84 DLR (3rd) 221 … 521, 1020
Norsk Pacific Steamship Co. Ltd. v. Canadian National Railway Co. (1992) 91 DLR (4th) 289 (Supreme Court of Canada) … 13, 33, 45, 46, 47, 48, 49, 108, 226, 626

Ogopogo, The [1970] 1 Lloyd's Rep. 257; [1971] 2 Lloyd's Rep. 410 … 202, 203, 220, 227

R in the Right of Canada v. Saskatchewan Wheat Pool (1983) 143 DLR (3d) 9 … 383
Rivtow Marine Ltd. v. Washington Iron Works [1974] SCR 1189 … 180, 185, 737
Roncarelli v. Duplessis [1959] SCR 121 … 430

Snell v. Farrell (1990) 72 DLR (4th) 289 … 251, 252

Triangle Steel & Supply Co. v. Korean United Lines Ltd. (1986) 63 BCLR 66 (Sup.C. of BC) … 186

Urbanski v. Patel, (1978) 84 DLR (3d) 650 … 220, 998

Vaughan v. Halifax Dartmouth Bridge Commission (1961) 29 DLR (2d) 523 … 530

Winnipeg Condominium Corp. No. 36 v. Bird Construction Co. Ltd. (1995) 121 DLR (4th) 193 ... 128

EUROPEAN COURT OF HUMAN RIGHTS

A v. United Kingdom (1998) 27 EHRR 611 ... 856

Bromiley v. United Kingdom, Application No. 33747/96, Judgment of 23 Nov. 1999 ... 134

Clunis v. United Kingdom, Application No. 45049/98, Judgment of 11 Sept. 2001 ... 134, 924, 925

Commission v. United Kingdom, Case C–300/95; [1997] ECR I-2649; [1997] All ER (EC) 391 ... 715, 719, 739, 748

E v. United Kingdom (2002) 36 EHRR 519 ... 422

Friedl v. Austria (1995) 21 EHRR 83 ... 847

H v. United Kingdom (1987) 10 EHRR 95; (1988) 13 EHRR 449 ... 106

Handyside v. United Kingdom (1976) 1 EHRR 737 ... 853

Hatton v. United Kingdom (2002) 34 EHRR 1 ... 542

HL v. United Kingdom, Application No. 45508/99; (2005) 40 EHRR 32 ... 464, 468, 469

Ivison v. United Kingdom, Application No. 39030/97, Judgment of 16 Apr. 2002 ... 134

Keegan v. United Kingdom [2006] ECtHR 764; Application No. 28867/03, Judgment of 18 July 2006 ... 104, 105, 106, 107, 136, 444, 445, 479

Khatun & 180 Others v. United Kingdom (unreported, 1 July 1998) ... 533

K.M. v. UK, Application No. 28945/95 ... 103, 107

Laskey, Jaggard and Brown v. United Kingdom (1997) 24 EHRR 39 ... 462

Lopez Ostra v. Spain (1994) 20 EHRR 277 ... 532

L.T.P. v. UK, Application No. 28945/95 ... 107

Malone v. United Kingdom (1984) 7 EHRR 14 ... 825

Niemietz v. Germany (1992) 16 EHRR 97 ... 823

Osman v. United Kingdom (1998) 29 EHRR 245 ... 34, 103, 104, 118, 129, 133, 134, 135, 136, 212, 399, 412, 421, 443

P, C and S v. United Kingdom (2002) 35 EHRR 1075 ... 422

Peck v. UK (2003) EHRR 287 ... 846, 847, 848

PG and JH v. UK, ECtHR 25 Sept. 2001 ... 848

Pretty v. United Kingdom [2002] 2 FLR 45 ... 461

Roche v. United Kingdom (2006) 42 EHRR 30 ... 421, 444

Thoma v. Luxembourg (ECtHR, 29 Mar. 2001 (Application no. 00038432/97), unreported) ... 784

Tolstoy Miloslavsky v. UK (1995) 20 EHRR 442 ... 808

Venema v. The Netherlands [2003] 1 FLR 552 ... 422

Von Hannover v. Germany (2005) 40 EHRR 1 ... 848, 849, 852, 853, 854

Z v. United Kingdom [2001] 2 FLR 612; (2002) 34 EHRR 3; Application No 29392/95 ... 35, 103, 118, 129, 133, 134, 135, 136, 212, 399, 411, 412, 421, 444

EUROPEAN COURT OF JUSTICE

Angonese v. Cassa di Risparmio di Bolzano SpA [2000] ECR I-4139, Case C–281/98 ... 437

Banks v. British Coal Corporation [1994] ECR I-1209 ... 437

Brasserie du Pêcheur v. Federal Republic of Germany, Case C–46/93 ... 405, 435, 437

Courage plc v. Crehan [2001] ECR I-6297, Case C–453/99 ... 437

Criminal Proceedings against Luciano Arcaro [1996] ECR I-4705, Case C–168/95 ... 395

Dillenkofer v. Federal Republic of Germany [1996], Cases C–178/94, C–179/94, C–188/94, C–189/94 and C–190/94; ECR I-4845; [1996] All ER (EC) 917 ... 435

Francovich and Bonifaci v. Italian Republic [1991] ECR I-6911, Joined Cases C–6/90 and C–9/90, ECR I-5357 . . . 405, 435, 436, 437

Haim v. Kassenzahnärztliche Vereinigung Nordrhein ('Haim (No. 2)') [2000], Case C–424/97; ECR I-5123 . . . 436

Hoechst AG v. Commission of the European Communities [1989] ECR 2859 . . . 823

ICI v. Colmer [1998] ECR I-4695, Case C–264/96 . . . 395

Manfredi v. Lloyd Adriatico Assicurazioni SpA, Joined Cases C–295 to 298/04, (not yet reported, judgment of 13 July 2006) . . . 437

Marshall (No. 2), Case C-271/91; [1993] ECR I-4367 . . . 438

Marshall v. Southampton and SW Hants AHA (No. 1), Case 152/84; [1986] ECR 723 . . . 438

O'Byrne v. Sanofi Pasteur MSD Ltd. Case C172/04, [2006] ECR I-1313; [2006] 1 WLR 1606 . . . 746

Pfeiffer v. Deutsches Rotes Kreuz Kreisverband Waldshut eV [2004] ECR I-3325, Joined Cases C–397 to 403/01 . . . 395

R v. Secretary of State for Trade and Industry *ex parte* Factortame Ltd. (No. 3), Case C–48/93; [1996] ECR I-1029 . . . 405, 435

Skov AEG v. Billa Lavprisvarehus, Case C–402/03 [2006] ECR I-199 . . . 715, 717

EUROPEAN COMMISSION ON HUMAN RIGHTS

S v. France (1990) 65 DR 250 (ECommHR) . . . 518

GERMANY

Caroline cases . . . 854

Lebach case . . . 826

HONG KONG

Cheng v. Tse Wai Chun [2000] 3 HKLRD 418 . . . 790, 805

IRELAND

Bell v. Great Northern Railway Co. of Ireland (1890) 26 LR Ir. 428 . . . 141

Brian Morgan v. Park Developments Ltd. [1983] ILRM 156 . . . 935

NETHERLANDS

B v. Bayer Nederland BV, 9 Oct. 1992 NJ 1994, 535 . . . 253

NEW ZEALAND

A v. Bottrill [2003] 1 AC 449 (PC) . . . 948

Autex v. Auckland City Council [2000] NZAR 324 . . . 615

Awa v. Independent News Auckland [1995] 3 NZLR 701 . . . 756

Bell-Booth Group Ltd. v. AG [1989] 3 NZLR 148 . . . 783

Bowen v. Mount Paramount Builders (Hamilton) Ltd. [1977] 1 NZLR 394 . . . 935

Christian v. Johannesson [1956] NZLR 664 . . . 350

Everitt v. Martin [1953] NZLR 298 . . . 484

Hamilton v. Papakura District Council [2000] 1 NZLR 265; [2002] UKPC 9; [2002] 3 NZLR 308 . . . 528

Invercargill City Council v. Hamlin [1996] AC 624 (PC) . . . 180, 416, 934

Invercargill v. Hamlin [1994] 3 NZLR 513 (NZCA) . . . 128

Lange v. Atkinson [2000] 3 NZLR 385 . . . 800, 816

Mount Albert BC v. Johnson [1979] 2 NZLR 234 . . . 935

Nobilo v. Waitemata County [1961] NZLR 1064 . . . 512

Petterson v. Royal Oak Hotel Ltd. [1948] NZLR 136 . . . 681

UNITED STATES OF AMERICA

Aafco Heating & Air Conditioning Co. v. Northwest Publications, Inc., 321 NE 2d 580 (1974) (Indiana App.), cert. denied 424 US 913, 96 SCt. 1112 (1976) ... 876

Aas v. Superior Court, 24 Cal. 4th 627, 12 P 3d 1125 (2000) ... 299

A.C. Excavating v. Yacht Club Homeowners Ass'n 114 P 3d 862 (Col. 2005) ... 299

Adams v. Bullock, 81 125 NE 93 (1919) ... 238

Adams v. State, 357 So. 2d 1239 (La. App. 1978) ... 306

Ammerman v. Hubbard Broadcasting Co., 91 NM 250, 572 P2d 1258 (1977) (New Mexico App.), cert. denied 436 US 906, 98 SCt. 2237 (1978) ... 871

Amphitheaters v. Portland Meadows (1948) 198 P 2d 847 ... 524

Anderson v. Fisher Broadcasting Co. Inc., 300 Or. 452, 712 P 2d 803 (1986) ... 888

Anderson v. Minneapolis, St. Paul & St. Ste. Marie Railway, 146 Minn. 430, 179 NW 45 (1920) ... 324

Appley Brothers v. United States, 164 F 3d 1164, 1175 (8th Cir. 1999) (ND law) ... 320

Armstrong v. Paoli Memorial Hospital, 430 Pa. Super. 36, 633 A 2d 605 (1993) ... 307

Bachchan v. India Abroad Publications, 154 Misc. 2d 228, 585 NYS 2d 661 (1992) (NYS) ... 882

Ballard Shipping Co. v. Beach Shellfish, 32 F 3d 623 (1st Cir. 1994) ... 296

Banks v. Hyatt Corporation, 722 F 2d 214, 220 (5th Cir. 1984) ... 323

Barker v. Lull Engineering Co. 573 P 2d 443 (1978) ... 719, 733

Bartnicki v. Vopper, 532 US 514, 121 SCt. 753 (2001) ... 887

Basko v. Sterling Drug Inc., 416 F 2d 417 (2d Cir. 1969) ... 324

Bass v. Nooney Co., 646 SW 2d 765 (No. 1983) ... 302, 304

Basso v. Miller, 386 NYS 2d 564, 352 NE 2d 868 (1976) ... 341, 363

Baxter v. Ford Motor Co., 12 P 2d 409 (1932) ... 710, 712, 726

Baylor University v. Bradshaw, 52 SW 2d 1094 (Tex. App. 1932) ... 329

Beauharnais v. Illinois, 343 US 250, 266, 72 SCt. 725, 735 (1952) ... 869

Becken v. Manpower Inc., 532 F 2d 56 (7th Cir. 1976) (Ill. law) ... 314

Biakanja v. Irving, 49 Cal. 2d 647, 320 P 2d 16 (1958) ... 298

Biddle v. Warren, 86 Ohio St. 3d 395, 715 NE 2d 518 (1999) ... 336

Bily v. Arthur Young and Co., 834 P 2d 745 (1992) ... 167

Bloxom v. Bloxom, 512 So. 2d 839, 950–51 (La. 1987) ... 323

Blumenthal v. Drudge, 992 F Supp. 44 (DCDC) (1998) ... 868

Boehner v. McDermott, 441 F 3d 1010 (DC Cir. 2006) ... 887

Bonome v. Kaysen, 17 Mass, 695, 32 Media L Rep. 1520 (Mass. Super. Ct. Mar. 3 2004) ... 883

Bonsignore v. City of New York, 683 F 2d 635 (2nd Cir. 1982) (NY law) ... 314

Boomer v. Atlantic Cement Co., 257 NE 2d 870 (1970) ... 547

Bosley v. Andrews, 393 Pa. 161, 142 A 2d 263 (1958) ... 302, 303

B.P. Chemicals Ltd. v. Jiangsu Sopo Corp.,.285 F 3d 677, 685 (8th Cir. 2002) ... 334

Bradley Center v. Wessner, 250 Ga. 199, 296 SE 2d 693 (1982) ... 318

Brady v. Hopper, 751 F 2d 329 (10th Cir.1984) (Col. law) ... 321

Braun v. Chronicle Pub. Co., 5 Cal.App. 4th 1036 (1997) ... 880

Breunig v. American Family Insurance Co., 173 NW 2d 619 (1970) ... 231

Brown v. Tesack, 556 So. 2d 84 (La. App. 1989) ... 319

Browning-Ferris Industries of Vermont Inc. v. Kelco Disposal Inc., 492 US 257 (1989) ... 721

Bryant v. Beary, 766 So. 2d 1157, 1160 (Fla. App. 2000) ... 310

Butts v. Curtis Pub. Co.; Walker v. Associated Press, 388 US 130, 87 SCt. 1975 (1967) ... 872

Camacho v. Honda Motor Co., 741 P 2d 1240 (1987) ... 720

Campbell v. Animal Quarantine Station, 632 P 2d 1066 (Haw. 1981) ... 306

Cantrell v. Forest City Publishing Co., 419 US 245, 95 SCt. 465 (1974) ... 886

Carlisle v. Fawcett Publications Inc., 201 Cal.App. 2d 733, 20 Cal. Rptr. 405 (1962) ... 885

Carson v. Allied News Co., 529 F 2d 206 (7th Cir. 1976) ... 872

Carson v. Here's Johnny Portable Toilets Inc., 698 F 2d 831 (6th Cir. 1983) ... 887

Central Hudson Gas & Elec. Corp. v. Public Serv. Comm'n, 447 US 557, 100 SCt. 2343 (1980) ... 876

Chair King Inc. v. GTE Mobilnet Inc., 135 SW 2d 365 (2004) ... 484

Chapadeau v. Utica Observer-Dispatch Inc., 38 NY 2d 196, 379 NYS 2d 61, 341 NE 2d 569 (1975) ... 876

Chaplinsky v. New Hampshire, 315 US 568, 62 SCt. 766 (1942) ... 869

Child Protection Group v. Cline, 350 SE 2d 541 (1986) ... 884

Christensen v. Superior Court, 54 Cal. 3d 868, 820 P 2d 181 (1991) ... 153, 293, 297, 298, 306

City of Pinellas Park v. Brown, 604 So. 2d 1222, (Fla. 1992) ... 310, 312

Clawson v. Longview Pub. Co. 589 P 2d 1223 (1979) (Washington) ... 871

Clinton v. Commonwealth Edison Co., 36 Ill. App. 3d 1064, 344 NE 2d 509 ... 287

Coca-Cola Bottling Works v. Lyons (1927) 111 So. 305 ... 709

Cohen v. Cabrini Medical Center, 94 NY 2d 639, 730 NE 2d 949 (2000) ... 307

Cole v. D.J. Quirk Inc., 2001 Mass. App. Div. 139, 2001 WestLaw 705730 ... 304

Collins v. Eli Lilly Co., 116 Wis. 2d 166, 342 NW 2d 37 (1984) ... 325

Conley v. Boyle Drug Co., 570 So. 2d 275 (Fla. 1990) ... 325

Consolidated Rail Corp. v. Gottshall, 512 US 532, 114 SCt. 2396 (1994) ... 302

Conway v. O'Brien, 111 F 2d 611 (1940), 612 ... 224

Council of Co-Owners v. Whiting-Turner Contracting Co., 308 Md. 18, 517 A 2d 336 (1986) ... 299

Cox Broadcasting Corp. v. Cohn, 420 US 469, 95 SCt. 1029 (1975) ... 885

Craig v. Driscoll, 64 Conn. App. 699, 781 A 2d 440 (2001) ... 316

Curtis Pub. Co. v. Butts, 388 US 130, 87 SCt. 1975 (1967) ... 876

Dalehite v. US, 346 US 15 (1953) ... 408

Dart v. Wiebe Manufacturing Inc., 709 P 2d 876 (1985) ... 720

Davis v. Monsanto Co., 627 F Supp. 418 (1990) ... 884

Dempsey v. National Enquirer, 702 F Supp. 934 (1989) ... 885

DePass v. United States, 721 F 2d 203 (7th Cir. 1983) ... 288, 290

Dewey v. R. J. Reynolds Tobacco Co., 577 A 2d 1239 (1990) ... 736

Dias v. Oakland Tribune Inc., 139 Cal. App. 3d 118, 188 Cal. Rptr. 762 (1983) ... 884

Dietemann v. Time Inc., 449 F 2d 245 (9th Cir. 1971) ... 886

Dillon v. Legg, 68 Cal. 2d 728, 441 P 2d 912 (1968) ... 305

Dillon v. Twin State Gas & Electric Co., 85 NH 449, 163 A 111 (1932) ... 260, 332

Dilworth v. Dudley, 75 F 3d 307 (7th Cir. 1996) ... 879

Doe v. America Online Inc., 783 So. 2d 1010 (2001) (Florida) ... 868

Dolcefino v. Randolph, 19 SW 3d 906 (Tex. App. 2000) ... 868

Dudas v. Glenwood Golf Club, 261 Va. 133, 135 SE 2d 129 (2001) ... 311

Dun & Bradstreet, Inc., v. Greenmoss Builders, Inc., 472 US 749, 105 SCt. 2939 (1985) ... 875

East River Bocre Leasing Corp. v. General Motors Corp., 645 NE 2d 1195 (NY 1995) ... 284

East River Steamship Corp. v. Transamerica Delaval Inc., 476 US 858, 106 SCt. 2295 (1986) ... 180, 283, 284, 293, 299, 300, 706

Edson v. Walker, 573 So. 2d 545 (La. App. 1991) ... 316

Edwards v. Honeywell Inc., 50 F 3d 484, (7th Cir. 1995) (Ind. law) ... 292

Edwards v. Lee's Administrator, 96 SW (2d) 1025 (1936) ... 53

E.I. du Pont de Nemours & Co. Inc. v. Rolfe & Christopher 431 F. 2d 1012 (Fifth Cir. 1970), cert. denied 400 US 1024 (1971) ... 839

El Chico Corp. v. Poole, 732 SW 2d 306 (Tex. 1987) ... 315

Ellenwood v. Exxon Shipping Co., 795 F Supp. 31, 34 (D Me. 1992) ... 305

Elmore v. American Motors Corp. (1969) 451 P 2d 84 ... 713

Escola v. Coca-Cola Bottling Co. of Fresno (1944) 150 P 2d 436 ... 707, 711

Estate of Amos v. Vanderbilt University, 62 SW 3d 133 (Tenn. 2001) ... 305

Estate of Heck v. Stoffer, 752 NE 2d 192 (Ind. App. 2001) ... 314

Estates of Morgan v. Fairfield Family Counseling Ctr., 77 Ohio St. 3d 284, 673 NE 2d 1311 (1997) ... 321

Evangelical United Brethren Church of Adna v. State ofWashington, 407 P 2d 440 (1965) ... 408

Exxon Co. v. Sofec Inc., 517 US 830, 116 SCt. 1813 (1996) ... 288

Factors Etc. Inc. v. Pro Arts Inc., 579 F 2d 215 (2nd Cir. 1978), cert. denied 440 US 908, 99 SCt. 1215 (1979) ... 888

Fanelle v. LoJack, Corp., 2000 WL 1801270 (ED Pa. 7 Dec. 2000) ... 877

Farwell v. Boston and Worcester Railroad Corp., 4 (Met) 49 (1842) ... 56, 652, 907

Farwell v. Keeton, 396 Mich. 281, 240 NW 2d 217 (1976) ... 320, 322

Feldman v. Lederle Laboratories, 479 A 2d 374 (1984) ... 720, 739

Fellows v. National Enquirer Inc., 42 Cal. 3d 234, 721 P 2d 97, 228 Cal. Rptr. 215 (1986) ... 886

Feng v. Metropolitan Transp. Auth., 285 A 2d 447, 727 NYS, 2d 470 (2001) ... 288

F.F.P. Operating Partners v. Duenez, 69 SW 3d 800, 804 (Tex. App. 2002) ... 308, 313

Fifield Manor v. Finston, 54 Cal. 2d 354, 632P 2d 1073 (1960) ... 296

Fithian v. Reed, 204 F 3d 306 (1st Cir. 2000) ... 287

Florida Star, The v. BJF, 491 US 524, 109 SCt. 2603 (1993) ... 883, 885

Follett v. Jones, 252 Ark. 950, 481 SW 2d 713 (1972) ... 328

Ford Motor Co. v. Lonon, 398 SW 2d 240 (1966) ... 726

Funchess v. Cecil Newman Corp., 632 NW 2d 666 (Minn. 2001) ... 320

Gaines-Tabb v. ICI Explosives, 160 F 3d 613 (10th Cir. 1998) (Okla. law) ... 307

Galella v. Onassis, 487 F 2d 986 (2nd Cir. 1973) ... 886

Gammon v. Osteopathic Hospital of Maine Inc., 534 A 2d 1282 (Me. 1987) ... 306

Gertz v. Robert Welch Inc., 418 US 323, 94 SCt. 2997 (1974) ... 865, 872, 874, 875, 876, 877

Ghassemieh v. Schafer, 52 Md.App. 31, 447 A 2d 84 (1982) ... 334

Gilbert v. Medical Economics Co., 665 F 2d 305 (1981) (10th Cir.) ... 885

Gill v. Hearst Publishing Co., 253 P. 2d 441 (1953) ... 845

Global Green v. CBS, Inc., 286 F 3d 281 (5th Cir. 2002) ... 868

Global Relief Foundation Inc. v. New York Times Co., 390 F 3d 973 (2d Cir. 2004) ... 868

Grant v. American National Red Cross, 745 A 2d 316, 321 n. 5 (2000) (DC) ... 326

Green v. America Online, Inc., 318 F 3d 465 (3d Cir. 2003) ... 868

Green v. State, 91 So. 2d 153 (La. App. 1956) ... 318

Greenbelt Cooperative Publishing Ass'n. v. Bressler, 398 US 6, 90 SCt. 1537 (1970) ... 879

Greenberg v. Barbour, 322 F Supp. 745 (ED Pa. 1971) ... 321

Greenman v. Yuba Power Products Inc. 377 P 2d 897 (1963) ... 711, 722

Grimes v. Kennedy Krieger Institute, 366 Md. 29, 782 A 2d 807 (2001) ... 337

Grimshaw v. Ford Motor Co. 119 Cal. App. 3d 757 (1981) ... 720

Griswold v. Connecticut, 381 US 479, 85 SCt. 1678 (1965) ... 883

Grotts v. Zahner, 115 Nev. 339, 989 P 2d 415 (1999) ... 305

Grover v. Stechel, 45 P 3d 80 (NM App. 2002) ... 321

Guth v. Freeland, 28 P 3d 982 (Haw. 2001) ... 306

Hamil v. Bashline, 481 Pa. 256, 392 A 2d 1280 (1978) ... 325

Hamilton v. Beretta USA Corp., 96 NY 2d 222, 750 NE 2d 1055 (2001) ... 308, 325

Hardy v. Brooks, 103 Ga. App. 124, 118 SE 2d 492 (1961) ... 317

Hardy v. Southwestern Bell Telephone Co., 910 P 2d 1024 (Ok. 1996) ... 327

Harris v. Pizza Hut, 455 So. 2d 1364 (La. 1984) ... 320

Haught v. Maceluch, 681 F 2d 291 (5th Cir. 1982) (Tex. law) ... 305

Heath v. Playboy Enterprises Inc., 732 F Supp. 1145 (1990) ... 884

Hembree v. State, 2001 WestLaw 575561 (Tenn. App.) ... 318

Henningsen v. Bloomfield Motors Inc.161 A 2d 69 (1960) ... 710, 722

Henry v. Collins, 380 US 356, 85 SCt. 992 (1965) ... 871

Hercules Carriers Inc., In Re, 720 F 2d 1201 (11th Cir. 1983) ... 294

Herskovitz v. Group Health Co-Operative of Puget Sound, 664 P 2d 474 (1983) ... 264, 326

Hicks v. US, 368 F 2d 626 (1966) (4th Circuit Court of Appeals) ... 264

Hirsch v. S. C. Johnson & Son Inc., 90 Wis. 2d 379, 280 NW 2d 129 (1979) ... 887

Hockensmith v. Brown, 929 SW 2d 840 (Mo. App. 1996) ... 334

Hoffman v. Red Owl Stores Inc., 133 NW 2d 267(1965) ... 164

Holt v. Rowell, 798 So. 2d 767 (Fla. App. 2001) ... 302

Holton v. Mem'l Hosp., 679 NE 2d 1202 (Ill. 1997) ... 326

Holtz v. Holder, 101 Ariz. 247, 418 P 2d 584 (1966) … 330, 331
Howard v. Des Moines Register Co., 283 NW 2d 289 (1979) (Iowa), cert. denied 445 US 904, 100 SCt. 1081 (1980) … 884
Hubert v. Harte-Hanks Texas Newspapers Inc., 652 SW 2d 546 (1983) … 885
Hustler Magazine, Inc. v. Falwell, 485 US 46, 108 SCt. 876 (1988) … 878
Hutchinson v. Proxmire, 443 US 111, 99 SCt. 2675 (1979) … 873
Hymnowitz v. Eli Lilly and Co., 73 NY 2d 487, 539 NE 2d 1069 (1989) … 325

Immuno AG v. Moor-Jankowski, 77 NY 2d 235, 567 NE 2d 1270 (1991), 566 NYS 2d 906 (1991), cert. denied 500 US 954, 111 SCt. 2261 (1991) … 879
Indian Towing Co. v. US, 350 US 61 (1955) … 408
Irvine v. Akron Beacon Journal, 30 Media L. Rep. 2008 (Ohio Ct. App. 2002) … 885

Jacob E. Decker & Sons v. Capps, 164 SW 2d 828 … 711, 712
Jacobsen v. Oliver, 201 F Supp. 2d 93 (DDC 2002) … 292
Jacron Sales, Inc. v. Sindorf, 276 Md. 580, 350 A 2d 688 (1976) … 876
J'Aire Corp. v. Gregory, 598 P 2d 60 (1979) (Sup. C. Cal.) … 173, 297, 298
Janklow v. Newsweek, Inc., 788 F 2d 1300 (1986) (9th Cir.) … 879
Jaubert v. Crowley Post-Signal Inc., 375 So. 2d 1386 (1979) … 845
Johnson v. State of California, 447 P 2d 352 (1968) … 408
Johnson v. State of New York, 37 NY 2d 378, 334 NE 2d 590 (1975) … 306
Jorgenson v. Vener, 616 NW 2d 366 (2000) … 326
Joseph v. State, 26 P 3d 459 (Alas. 2001) … 313, 322

Kapellas v. Kofman, 1 Cal. 3d 20, 81 Cal. Rptr. 360, 459 P 2d 912 (1969) … 885
Kelly v. Gwinell, 96 NJ 538, 476 A 2d 1219 (1984) … 207, 315
Kentucky Fried Chicken v. Superior Court, 14 Cal. 4th 814, 927 P 2d 1260 (1997) … 293
Kermarec v. Compagnie Générale Transatlantique, 358 US 625, 79 SCt. 406, 3 L Ed. 2d 550 (1959) … 283, 364
Kitchen v. K-Mart Corp., 697 So. 2d 1200 (Fla. 1997) … 308
Knievel v. ESPN, 393 F 3d 1068 (9th Cir. 2005) … 867
Kotlikoff v. Community News, 89 NJ 62, 444 A 2d 1086 (1982) … 879
Kramer v. Lewisville Mem'l Hosp., 858 SW 2d 397 (1993) (Tex.) … 326
KTRK Television v. Felder, 950 SW 2d 100 (Tex. App. 1997) … 868
Kurczi v. Eli Lilly & Co., 113 F 3d 1426 (6th Cir.1997) (Ohio law) … 324

Lamoureaux v. Totem Ocean Trailer Express Inc., 632 P 2d 539 (1981) (Alas.) … 332
Landers v. East Texas Salt Water Disposal Co., 151 Tex. 251, 248 SW 2d 731 (1952) … 330
Lawlor v. Orlando, 795 So. 2d 147 (Fla. App. 2001) … 287
Lee v. GNLV Corp., 22 P 3d 209 (Nev. 2001) … 287
Lee v. State Farm Mut. Ins. Co., 272 Ga. 583, 533 SE 2d 82 (2000) … 305
Leppke v. Segura, 632 P 2d 1057 (Col. App. 1981) … 316
Lewis v. Time Inc., 710 F 2d 549 (9th Cir. 1983) … 879
Lloyd's Leasing Ltd. v. Conoco, 868 F 2d 1447 (5th Cir. 1989) … 301
Lohrenz v. Donnelly, 350 F 3d 1272, 1274 (DC Cir. 2003) … 873
Lord v. Lovett, 146 NH 232, 770 A 2d 1103 (2001) … 326
Louisiana ex rel. Guste v. M/V Testbank, 752 F 2d 1019 (5th Cir. 1985) … 295, 296, 300, 301
Louisville & NR Co. v. M/V Bayou Lacombe, 597 F 2d 469 (5th Cir. 1979) … 296
Lovgren v. Citizens First National Bank, 126 Ill. 2d 411, 534 NE 2d 987 (1989) … 886
Lugtu v. California Highway Patrol, 26 Cal. 4th 703, 28 P 3d 249 (2001) … 314
Lunney v. Prodigy Services Company, A 2d 230 (1998) … 778

McBride v. General Motors Co., 737 F Supp. 1563 (1990) … 721
McCarthy v. Olin Corporation, 119 F 3d 148 (2d Cir. 1997) (NY law) … 292, 310
MacPherson v. Buick Motor Co., 217 NY 382, 111 NE 1050 … 705, 706
Maddux v. Donaldson, 362 Mich. 108, 425 NW 2d 33 (1961) … 252, 330, 331

Martin Luther King Jnr., Centre for Social Change Inc. v. American Heritage Products Inc., 250 Ga. 135, 296 SE 2d 697 (1982) ... 888

Martin v. Abbott Laboratories, 102 Wash. 2d 581, 689 P 2d 368 (1984) ... 325

Masson v. New Yorker Magazine Inc., 501 US 496, 111 SCt. 2419 (1991) ... 871, 878

Mattingly v. Sheldon Jackson College, 743 P 2d 356 (Alas. 1987) ... 297

Maule v. NYM Corp., 54 NY 2d 880 (1981) (sports writer) ... 872

Medico v. Time Inc., 643 F 2d 134 (3d Cir. 1981) ... 868

Meetze v. Associated Press, 230 SC 330, 95 SE 2d 606 (1956) ... 884

Mellon Mortgage Co. v. Holder, 5 SW 3d 654 (Tex. 1999) ... 311

Melvin v. Reid, 112 Cal. App. 285, 297 P 91 (1931) ... 826, 884

Metro-North Commuter R Co. v. Buckley, 521 US 424, 117 SCt. 2113 (1997) ... 304

Meyering v. General Motors Corp., 275 Cal. Rptr. 346 (Cal. App. 1990) ... 290, 309

Miami Herald v. Ane, 458 So. 2d 239 (1984) (Florida) ... 876

Michaels v. Internet Entertainment Group Inc., 1998 US Dist. LEXIS 20786 (CD Cal. 1998) ... 885

Midler v. Ford Motor Co., 849 F 2d 460 (9th Cir). 1988, cert. denied 503 US 951, 112 SCt. 1513 (1997) ... 887

Milkovich v. Lorain Journal, 497 US 1, 110 SCt. 2695 (1990) ... 878

Miller v. Transamerican Press Inc., 621 F 2d 721 (5th Cir. 1980), cert. denied 450 US 1041, 101 SCt. 1759 (1981) ... 880

Miskovsky v. Oklahoma Pub. Co., 654 P 2d 587 (1982) (Oklahoma) cert. denied 459 US 923, 103 SCt. 235 ... 879

Mokry v. University of Texas Health Science Center, 529 SW 2d 802 (Tex. App. 1975) ... 306

Moldea v. New York Times Co., 22 F 3d 310 (2d) Cir. (1994) cert. denied 513 US 875, 115 SCt. 202 ... 879

Molien v. Kaiser Foundation Hospitals, 27 Cal. 3d 916, 616 P 2d 813 (1980) ... 305

Monitor Patriot Co. v. Roy, 401 US 263, 91 SCt. 602 (1961) ... 871

Moore v. Shah, 458 NYS 33 (1982) ... 220

Morris v. Maryland Cas. Co., 657 So. 2d 198 (La. App. 1995) ... 304

Motschenbacher v. R. J. Reynolds Tobacco Co., 498 F 2d 821 (9th Cir. 1974) ... 887

Muchow v. Lindblad, 435 NW 2d 918 (ND 1989) ... 305

Murrey v. United States, 73 F 3d 1448, 1454 (7th Cir. 1996) ... 327

Namath v. Sports Illustrated., 80 Misc. 2d 531, 363 NYS 2d 279 (1975) (SCt.), aff'd. 48 A 2d 487, 371 NYS 2d 10, 352 NE 2d 584 (1976) ... 888

Nash v. Keene Pub. Corp., 214 NH 127, 498 A 2d 348 (1985) ... 875

Nelson v. Metro-North Commuter RR, 235 F 3d 101 (2d Cir. 2000) ... 289

New York Times Co. v. Sullivan, 376 US 254, 84 SCt. 710 (1964) ... 865, 869, 870, 871, 872, 873, 874, 875, 876, 877

Newman v. Sathyavaglswaran, 287 F 3d 786 (9th Cir.) ... 336

Niederman v. Brodsky, 436 Pa. 401, 261 A 2d 84 (1970) ... 304

Nixon v. Mr. Property Management Co., 690 SW 2d 546 (Tex. 1985) ... 313, 319

Norfolk & Western Ry. Co. v. Ayers, 538 US 135, 123 SCt. 1210 (2003) ... 303

Novak Heating & Air Conditioning v. Carrier Corp., 622 NW 2d 495 (Iowa 2001) ... 324

Novak v. Rathnam, 153 Ill.App. 3d 408, 505 NE 2d 773 (1987) ... 288, 311

O'Brien v. Muskin Corp., 463 A 2d 298 (1982) ... 720

O'Connor Agency Inc. v. Brodkin, 99 Cal. App. 4th 588, 120 Cal. Rptr. 2d 336 (2002) ... 292

Oliver v. Miles, 144 Miss. 852, 110 So. 666 (1927) ... 324

Ollman v. Evans, 750 F 2d 970 (1984) (DC Cir.) (en banc), cert. denied 471 US 1127, 105 SCt. 2662 (1985) ... 879

Onassis v. Christian Dior-New York Inc., 122 Misc. 2d 603, 472 NYS 2d 254 (1984), aff'd., 110 A 2d 1095, 488 NYS 2d 943 (1985) ... 887

Ornelas v. Fry, 727 P 2d 918 (1986) ... 220

Osterlind v. Hill, 160 NE 301 (1928) ... 201

Otis Engineering Corp. v. Clark, 668 SW 2d 307, 318 (Tex. 1983) ... 311, 316

Pacific Mutual Life Insurance Co. v. Haslip, 111 SCt. 1032 (1991) ... 721

Palko v. Connecticut, 302 US 319, 327 (1937) ... 824

Palsgraf v. Long Island Railroad Co., 248 NY 339, 162 NE 99 (1928) ... 275, 288

Panagakos v. Walsh, 434 Mass. 353, 749 NE 2d 670 (2001) ... 316, 317
Panama R. Co. v. Johnson, 264 US 375, 44 SCt. 391 (1924) ... 283
Pang v. Ming, 53 Ohio St. 3d 186, 559 NE 2d 1313 (1990) ... 330, 331
Parsons v. Crown Disposal Co., 15 Cal. 4th 456, 936 P 2d 70 (1997) ... 293
Patrick v. Employers Mut. Cas. Co., 745 So. 2d 641 (La. App. 1999) ... 320
Pavesich v. New England Life Insurance Co., 122 Ga. 190, 50 SE 68 (1905) ... 887
Peavy v. WFAA-TV Inc., 221 F 3d 158 (5th Cir. 2000) ... 887
Peck v. Tribune, 214 US 185 (1909) ... 754
Pence v. Ketchum, 326 So. 2d 831 (La. 1976) ... 316
Pennfield Corp. v. Meadow Valley Electric Inc., 413 Pa. Super. 187, 604 A 2d 1082 (1992) ... 324
People Express Airlines v. Consolidated Rail Corporation, 100 NJ 246, 495 A 2d 107 (1985) ... 295, 296, 297
Perez v. Lopez, 74 SW 3d 60, 69 (Tex. App. 2002) ... 312
Perry-Rogers v. Obasaju, 282 A 2d 231, 723 NYS 2d 28 (2001) ... 306
Philadelphia Newspapers, Inc. v. Hepps 475 US 767, 106 SCt. 1558 (1986) ... 877, 878, 880
Philips v. Kimwood Machine Co., 525 P 2d 1033 ... 711
Phillips ex rel. Phillips v. Roy, 431 So. 2d 849 (La. App. 1983) ... 315
Pierce v. So. Pacific Transp. Co., 823 F 2d 1366 (9th Cir. 1987) ... 302
Piercefield v. Remington Arms Co., 133 NW 2d 129 (1965) ... 712
Piner v. Superior Court, 192 Ariz. 182, 962 P 2d 909 (1998) ... 329, 330, 331
Piscitelli v. Friedenberg, 87 Cal. App. 4th 953, 105 Cal. Rptr. 2d 88 (2001) ... 287, 292
Ponticas v. K.M.S. Investments, 331 NW 2d 907 (Minn. 1983) ... 314
Potere v. City of Philadelphia, 380 Pa. 581, 112 A 2d 100 (1955) ... 303
Potts v. Little, 171 Ariz. 98, 828 P 2d 1239 (1991) ... 331
PPG Industries Inc. v. Bean Dredging, 447 So. 2d 1058 (La. 1984) ... 296
Procanik v. Cillo, 97 NJ 339; 478 A 2d 755 (1984) (NJ Sup. Ct) ... 7, 83
Procter & Gamble Co. v. Amway Inc., 242 F 3d 539 (5th Cir. 2001) ... 876
Project Creation Inc. v. Neal, 2001 Tenn. App. Lexis 624 (21 Aug. 2001) ... 881
Public Citizen Health Research Group v. Young, 909 F 2d 546 (DC Cir. 1990) ... 323

Quackenbush v. Ford Motor Co., 153 NYS 131 (NY App. 1915) ... 284

Rabideau v. City of Racine, 243 Wis. 2d 486, 627 NW 2d 795, 807 (2001) ... 307
Ramirez v. Plough Inc., 6 Cal. 4th 539, 863 P 2d 167 (1993) ... 293
Randy Knitwear Inc. v. American Cyanamid Co., 181 NE 2d 399 (1962) ... 726
Renwick v. The News and Observer Pub. Co., 312 SE 2d 405 (1984), cert. denied 469 US 858, 105 SCt. 187 (1984) ... 886
Robbins v. Kaas, 163 Ill. App. 3d 927, 516 NE 2d 1023 (1987) ... 304
Robblee v. Budd Services Inc., 136 NC App. 793, 525 SE 2d 847 (2000) ... 306, 320
Robins Dry Dock & Repair Co. v. Flint, 275 US 303, 48 SCt. 134 (1927) ... 185, 294, 296, 300
Rodrigues v. State, 472 P 2d 509 (Haw. 1970) ... 303, 306
Roe v. Wade, 410 US 113, 93 SCt. 705 (1973) ... 7, 883
Rosen v. State Farm Gen. Ins. Co., 70 P 3d 351 (Cal. 2003) ... 299
Rosenblatt v. Baer, 383 US 75, 86 SCt. 669 (1966) ... 871
Rosenbloom v. Metromedia, Inc. 403 US 29, 91 SCt. 1811 (1971) ... 874
Rowland v. Christian, 443 P 2d 561 (1968) ... 341, 363, 364
Ruiz-Troche v. Pepsi Cola of Puerto Rico, 161 F 3d 77 (1st Cir. 1998) ... 87, 288

Saelzer v. Advanced Group 400, 25 Cal. 4th 763, 23 P 3d 1143 (2001) ... 311
St Amant v. Thompson, 390 US 727, 88 SCt. 1323 (1968) ... 870
St Hill v. Tabor, 542 So. 2d 499 (La. 1989) ... 316
Sanders v. Acclaim Entertainment Inc., 188 F Supp. 2d 1264 (D.Col. 2002) ... 307
Saratoga Fishing Co. v. J. M. Martinac & Co., 520 US 875, 117 SCt. 1783 (1997) ... 299
Saunders Sys. Birmingham Co. v. Adams, 217 Ala. 621, 117 So. 72 (1928) ... 327
Schoneweis v. Dando, 231 Neb. 180, 435 NW 2d 666 (1989) ... 884
Schultz v. Barberton Glass Co., 4 Ohio St. 3d 131, 447 NE 2d 109 (1983) ... 304

Seely v. White Motor Co., 403 P 2d 145 (1965) . . . 706
Shihab v. Express-News Corp., 604 SW 2d 204 (1980) (Texas App.) . . . 868
Shulman v. Group W Productions, 18 Cal. 4th 200, 74 Cal. Rptr. 843, 955 P 2d 469 (1998) . . . 883, 886
Sidis v. F. R. Publishing Corp., 113 F 2d 806 (2nd Cir. 1940). cert. denied 311 US 711, 61 SCt. 393 (1940) . . . 884
Simonsen v. Thorin, 120 Neb. 684, 234 NW 628 (1931) . . . 317
Sindell v. Abbott Laboratories, 26 Cal. 3d 588, 607 P 2d 924 (1980) (Supreme Ct of California) . . . 253, 254, 325, 741
Sipple v. Chronicle Publishing Co., 154 Cal. App. 3d 1040, 201 Cal. Rptr. 665 (1984) . . . 884
Smith v. Cutter Biological Inc., 823 P 2d 717 (Haw. 1991) . . . 325
Smith v. English, 586 So. 2d 583 (La. App. 1991) . . . 312
Smith v. Lockheed Propulsion Co., 247 CA 2d 774, 56 Cal. Rptr. 128 (1967) . . . 624
Smith v. State Dept. of Health, 676 So. 2d 543 (La. 1996) . . . 326
Socony-Vacuum Oil. Co. v. Marshall, 222 F 2d 604 (1st Cir. 1955) . . . 287
Soileau v. State, 724 So. 2d 834 (La. App. 1998) . . . 288
Sprecher v. Adamson Companies, 30 Cal. 3d 358, 636 P 2d 1121 (1981) . . . 314
Stagl v. Delta Airlines, 52 F 3d 463 (2d Cir. 1995) . . . 290, 291
State v. Perry, 610 So. 2d 746 (La. 1992) . . . 284
State of Louisiana ex rel Guste v. M/V Testbank, 752 F 2d 1019 (5th Cir.) (1985) . . . 12, 226
Stephenson v. Universal Metrics Inc., 251 Wis. 2d 171, 641 NW 2d 158 (2002) . . . 315, 319
Stevenson v. East Ohio Gas Co., 73 NE 2d 200 (Ohio App. 1946) . . . 160, 296
Stoddard v. Davidson, 355 Pa. Super. 262, 513 A 2d 419 (1986) . . . 304
Stone v. Essex County Newspapers, 367 Mass. 849, 330 NE 2d 161 (1975) . . . 876
Strait v. Hale Constr.Co., 26 Cal. Ap. 3d 941, 103 Cal. Rptr. 487 (1972) . . . 676
Stratton Oakmont Inc. v. Prodigy Services Co., 1995 WL 323710 (NY Supp., 24 May 1995) . . . 867
Sullivan v. Durham, 161 NY 290, 55 NE 923 (1900) . . . 624
Summers v. Tice, 33 Cal. 2d 80, 199 P 2d 1 (1948) . . . 252, 253, 259, 324
Sutowski v. Eli Lilly & Co., 82 Ohio St. 3d 347, 696 NE 2d 187 (1998) . . . 325
Sweeney v. Patterson, 76 US App D C 23, 24 (1942) . . . 865

T. J. Hooper, The, 60 F 2d 737, 739 (2d Cir. 1932) . . . 328
Taco Bell v. Lannon, 744 P 2d 43 (Col. 1987) . . . 308
Taira Lynn Marine Ltd., In Re, 444 F 3d 371 (5th Cir. 2006) . . . 301
Tarasoff v. University of California, 17 Cal. (3d) 425 (1976) . . . 203, 204
Technical Chemical Company v. Jacobs, 480 SW 2d 602 (Tex. 1972) . . . 323
Telnikoff v. Matusevitch, 347 Md. 561, 702 A 2d 230 (1997) . . . 882
Terre Haute First National Bank v. Stewart, 455 NE 2d 262 (1984) . . . 230
Terrell v. Wallace, 747 So. 2d 748 (La. App. 1999) . . . 311
Texas Industries Inc. v. Radcliff Materials Inc., 451 US 630, 101 SCt. 2061 (1981) . . . 284
Thing v. LaChusa, 48 Cal. 3d 644, 771 P 2d 814 (1989) . . . 305
Thomas v. Winchester, 6 NY 397 (1852) . . . 705
Thompson v. County of Alameda, 614 P 2d 728 (1980) . . . 204
Thompson v. Skate America Inc., 261 Va. 121, 540 SE 2d 123 (2001) . . . 311
Thrasher v. Leggett, 373 So. 2d 494 (La. 1979) . . . 316
Time Inc. v. Firestone, 424 US 448, 96 SCt. 958 (1976) . . . 873
Time Inc. v. McLaney, 406 F 2d 565 (5th Cir 1969.), cert. denied 395 US 922, 89 SCt. 1769 (1969) . . . 873
Torrack v. Corpamerica Inc., 51 Del. 254, 144 A 2d 703 (1958) . . . 319
Town of Alma v. Azco Construction Inc., 10 P 3d 1256 (Col. 2000) . . . 299
Tucker v. American States Insurance, 747 So. 2d 620 (La. App. 1999) . . . 287
Tuttle v. Buck 119 NW 946 (1909) . . . 573

Ultramares Corp. v. Touche, Niven and Co., 255 NY 170, 174, NE 441, 444 (1931) . . . 161
Union Oil Co. v. Oppen, 501 F 2d 558 (9th Cir. 1974) . . . 295
United States v. Carroll Towing Co., 159 F 2d 169, 173 (1947) . . . 224, 720
United States of America v. Silk, 331 US 704 (1946) . . . 672

Vallere v. Louisiana Health Systems, 722 So. 2d 418 (La.App. 1998) ... 304
Virgil v. Sports Illustrated, 424 F Supp. 1286 (SD. Cal. 1976) ... 884
Virgil v. Time Inc., 527 F 2d 1122 (9th Cir. 1975), cert. denied 425 US 998 (1976) ... 884
Vitale v. National Lampoon, 449 F Supp. 442 (1978) ... 873

Wagner v. International Railway Co., 232 NY 176 (1921) ... 219, 220
Wakley v. Cooke and Healey [1849] 4 Exch. 511, 517; 154 ER 1316, 1318 ... 868
Wakulich v. Mraz, 203 Ill. 2d 223, 785 NE 2d 843 (2003) ... 335
Waldbaum v. Fairchild Publications, Inc., 627 F 2d 1287 (2d Cir. 1980), cert. denied 449 US 898, 101 SCt. 266 (1980) ... 875
Wassell v. Adams, 865 F 2d 849 (7th Cir. 1989) (Ill. law) ... 323
Weitz v. Lovelace Health System Inc., 214 F 3d 1175 (10th Cir. 2000) ... 321
Werwinski v. Ford Motor Co., 286 F 3d 661 (3d Cir. 2002) (Pa. law) ... 294, 298
Wheeler v. Green, 286 Or. 99, 593 P 2d 777 (1979) ... 876
Wickens v. Oakwood Healthcare System, 465 Mich. 53, 631 NW 2d 686 (2001) ... 326
Williams v. Pasma, 656 P 2d 212 (1982) (Montana), cert. denied 461 US 945, 103 SCt. 2122 (1983) ... 873
Wilson v. Department of Public Safety, 576 So. 2d 490 (La. 1991) ... 318
Wolf v. Regardie, 553 A 2d 1213 (1989) (DC App.) ... 884
Wynn v. Smith, 16 P 3d 424 (2001) (Nevada) ... 870

Yania v. Bigan, 397 Pa. 316, 155 A 2d 343 (1959) ... 334, 335
Young v. Players Lake Charles, L.L.C., 47 F Supp. 2d 832 (SD Tex. 1999) ... 315
Young v. Telegraph Co., 107 N.C. 370, 11 SE 1044 (1890) ... 306

Zeran v. America Online Inc., 129 F 3d 327 (4th Cir.) (1997), cert. denied 118 SCt. 2341 (1998) ... 867

TABLE OF UNITED KINGDOM LEGISLATION

Page references in bold indicate that the section is reproduced in full.

Administration of Justice Act 1969 ... 977

Administration of Justice Act 1982 ... 95, 143, 1004, 1009, 1011, 1013, 1018
- s.1(a)–(b) ... 1004
- s.3 ... 143, 1004, 1012, 1013
- s.3(2) ... 1010
- s.4 ... 999
- s.4(1) ... 1007
- s.5 ... 993, 997
- s.6 ... 968, 969
- s.8 ... 995
- s.10 ... 959
- s.15 ... 977
- Sch.1 ... 977

Administration of Justice Act 1985, s.57 ... 928

Agriculture Act 1967 ... 586

Alkali Act 1863 ... 559

Animals Act 1971 ... 95, 631, 632, 633, 634, 637, 639, 640, 642, 646
- s.2 ... 638, 644, 645, 903
- s.2(1) ... 637, 638
- s.2(2) ... 638, 639, 640, 641, 642, 643, 644, 645
- s.2(2)(a) ... 631, 638, 639, 640, 641
- s.2(2)(b) ... 631, 638, 639, 640, 641, 642, 643
- s.2(2)(c) ... 642, 643
- s.3 ... 646, 647, 903
- s.4 ... 634, 635, 903
- s.4(1) ... 634, 636
- s.4(1)(a) ... 636
- s.5 ... 636, 643
- s.5(1) ... 636, 644, 645
- s.5(2) ... 644, 645, 913
- s.5(3) ... 644, 645
- s.5(4) ... 647
- s.5(5) ... 635
- s.5(6) ... 634, 636
- s.6(1) ... 637
- s.6(2) ... 638
- s.6(3) ... 637, 643
- s.6(4) ... 643
- s.7 ... 503, 635
- s.7(1) ... 503
- s.8(1) ... 633, 635
- s.8(2) ... 633
- s.9 ... 647
- s.10 ... 636
- s.10(1) ... 903
- s.11 ... 634, 636, 637

Banking Act 1979, s.47 ... 490

Banking Act 1987, s.1(4) ... 398, 402

Betting and Lotteries Act 1934, s.11(2) ... 379

Bill of Rights 1688, art.9 ... 791, 792

Bills of Exchange Act 1882, s.64(1) ... 491

Bills of Lading Act 1855, s.1 ... 24

Broadcasting Act 1996
- s.110 ... 822
- s.111 ... 822
- s.111(1)–(2) ... 822

Building Act 1984, s.38 ... 344, 353, 373

Building Societies Act 1986, s.13 ... 168

Cable and Broadcasting Act 1984, s.28 ... 757

Carriage of Goods by Sea Act 1992 ... 24

Chancery Amendment Act 1858 ... 394, 541, 546
- s.2 ... 1032

Children Act 1975, Sch.1, para.3(1) ... 1011

Civil Aviation Act 1982 ... 496
- s.76(1)–(2) ... 496

Civil Evidence Act 1968
- s.11 ... 241
- s.13(2A) ... 785

Civil Jurisdiction and Judgments Act 1982 ... 746

Civil Liability (Contribution) Act 1978 ... 1035, 1036, 1037, 1040
- s.1(1) ... 693, 1035
- s.1(2) ... 1035
- s.1(3) ... 1035, 1036
- s.1(4) ... 1035
- s.1(5) ... 1036
- s.1(6) ... 1035, 1036
- s.2(1)–(2) ... 1036
- s.2(3) ... 1037
- s.3 ... 1033
- s.4 ... 1034
- s.6(1) ... 1035

Civil Partnership Act 2004 ... 1012

Civil Procedure Act 1997, s.7(1) ... 834

Clean Air Act 1956, s.16 ... 563

Coal Industry Act 1994, s.7 ... 497

Coal Industry (Nationalisation) Act 1946 ... 497

Companies Act 1985
- s.236 ... 166
- s.395 ... 486

Companies Acts ... 166, 413
Compensation Act 2006 ... 6, 95
s.1 ... 120, 225, 240, 241
s.3 ... 256, 1039
Competition Act 1998 ... 574, 603
Compulsory Purchase Act 1965, s.10 ... 541
Congenital Disabilities (Civil Liabilities) Act 1976 ... 95, 117, 217, 218, 744, 901
s.1(3) ... 217
s.1(4) ... 218
s.1(7) ... 901
s.1A ... 218
s.2 ... 217, 218
Conspiracy and Protection of Property Act 1875 ... 598, 599
Consumer Credit Act 1974 ... 1023
Consumer Protection Act 1987 ... 93, 243, 434, 657, 659, 703, 704, 708, 714, 719, 720, 727, 728, 729, 731, 732, 733, 734, 735, 737, 741, 742, 743, 745, 746, 747, 927, 928, 932, 937, 946, 964
Part I ... 718, 745
Part II ... 718, 738
s.1(2) ... 728, 730
s.1(3) ... 729
s.2(1) ... 727, 741
s.2(2) ... 727, 728
s.2(2)(b) ... 728
s.2(2)(c) ... 729
s.2(3) ... 729
s.2(4) ... 728
s.3 ... 732
s.3(1) ... 733, 747
s.3(2) ... 734, 737
s.3(2)(b) ... 745
s.4 ... 732, 747
s.4(1)(a)–(b) ... 738
s.4(1)(c) ... 729
s.4(1)(d) ... 738
s.4(1)(e) ... 718, 719, 738, 739, 740, 742
s.4(1)(f) ... 738
s.4(1)(f)(i) ... 729
s.5 ... 727
s.5(1) ... 727, 742
s.5(2) ... 743
s.5(3) ... 742, 743
s.5(3)(a)–(b) ... 728
s.5(4) ... 742
s.6(1)(a) ... 744
s.6(2)–(3) ... 744
s.6(4) ... 741
s.6(7) ... 746
s.7 ... 745, 915
s.9(2) ... 434
s.11A ... 928
s.13(1) ... 738
s.41(1)(e) ... 719
s.45 ... 727, 730
s.46(4) ... 731
Consumer Safety Act 1978 ... 718
s.6 ... 718
Consumer Safety (Amendment) Act 1986 ... 718
Contagious Diseases (Animals) Act 1869 ... 392
Contempt of Court Act 1981, s.10 ... 800
Contracts (Applicable Law) Act 1990 ... 746
Contracts of Employment and Redundancy Payments Act (Northern Ireland) 1965, s.4(1)(d) ... 380
Contracts (Rights of Third Parties) Act 1999 ... 25, 26, 94, 173, 174, 194, 199, 355, 357, 358, 922, 993
s.1(1)(a) ... 25
s.1(1)(b) ... 25, 26
s.1(2) ... 25, 922
s.1(3) ... 922
s.1(6) ... 356, 922
s.6(5) ... 922
Control of Pollution Act 1974 ... 563
Copyright, Designs and Patents Act 1988
s.8 ... 838
s.97(2) ... 948
s.180 ... 387, 395
s.194 ... 395
Countryside and Rights of Way Act 2000 ... 347, 365
s.1 ... 365
s.2 ... 365, 499
s.13 ... 347
s.13(2)–(3) ... 365
Sch.2 ... 499
Courts Act 2003 ... 967, 974
ss.100–101 ... 973
Courts and Legal Services Act 1990 ... 765
s.8 ... 814
s.8(2) ... 765, 808, 881
s.69(2) ... 792
Criminal Evidence Act 1898, s.1(f)(ii) ... 755
Criminal Injuries Compensation Act 1995 ... 62, 64
Criminal Justice Act 1972, s.1 ... 66
Criminal Justice Act 1982, s.67 ... 66, 67, 68
Criminal Justice Act 1987 ... 827
Criminal Justice Act 1988 ... 63
s.104(2) ... 66
ss.108–117 ... 63
Criminal Justice and Public Order Act 1994 ... 495
s.68 ... 495
ss.70–71 ... 495
Criminal Law Act 1967, s.3 ... 462, 505

Criminal Law Act 1977 ... 495, 503
s.12(3) ... 503
Crown Immunity Act 1947, s.10 ... 217
Crown Proceedings Act 1947 ... 33, 95, 118, 208, 398, 434, 435
s.2(1) ... 398, 434
s.2(2) ... 434
s.2(5) ... 435, 471
s.4 ... 434
s.10 ... 134
Crown Proceedings (Armed Forces) Act 1987 ... 217, 435

Damages Act 1996 ... 95, 967, 969, 971, 973
s.2 ... 965, 971, 973
s.3 ... 969
s.4 ... 971, 974
s.6 ... 974
Dangerous Wild Animals Act 1976 ... 631
Sch ... 637
Data Protection Act 1984 ... 825
Data Protection Act 1998 ... 93, 825
s.13 ... 845
Defamation Act 1952 ... 95, 796
s.4 ... 780, 781
s.4(3) ... 811
s.7 ... 783, 792, 795
s.9(1) ... 795
s.16(1) ... 757
Sch. ... 795
Part II ... 783
para.9 ... 792
Defamation Act 1996 ... 95, 756, 781, 791, 796
s.1 ... 757, 778, 779
s.2 ... 759, 780
s.2(4) ... **780**, 881
s.2(5) ... 781
s.3 ... 780
s.3(5) ... 782
s.4 ... 756, 780, 781, 970
s.4(3)–(5) ... 781
s.5 ... 756, **784**, 785
s.6 ... 756, 788
s.8 ... 756, 810, 814
s.8(2)–(3) ... 810
ss.9–10 ... 756, 810
s.12 ... **810**
s.12(1) ... 785
s.13(1) ... 791, 792
s.13(4) ... 791
s.14 ... 796
s.14(3) ... 792
Sch.1 ... 796
Defective Premises Act 1972 ... 94, 131, 197, 198, 345, 370, 373, 374, 434, 731, 935
s.1 ... 374
s.1(1) ... 370, 373, 374
s.1(2) ... 373, 374
s.2 ... 373
s.2(5) ... 197
s.3 ... 369, 370, 373
s.3(c)(iii) ... 731
s.3(1) ... **369**, 370
s.3(2) ... 369
s.4 ... **370**, 371
s.4(1) ... 370, 538
s.4(3)–(5) ... 371
s.5 ... 434
s.6(3) ... 370
Disability Discrimination Act 1995 ... 1007
Dramatic and Musical Performers' Protection Act 1958 ... 387, 394

Education Act 1944, s.10 ... 344
Education Act 1968, s.3(3) ... 344
Education Acts ... 586
Education (Miscellaneous Provisions) Act 1948, s.7 ... 344
Employers' Liability Act 1880 ... 908, 909
Employers' Liability (Compulsory Insurance) Act 1969 ... 69, 70, 651
Employers' Liability (Defective Equipment) Act 1969 ... 657, 659, 660
s.1 ... 659
s.1(1) ... 657, 696
s.1(1)(a) ... 657
s.1(3) ... 657, 660
Employment Act 1980, s.17 ... 584
Employment Act 1982 ... 600
Employment Protection (Consolidation) Act 1978
s.1 ... 380
s.58 ... 667
Employment Rights Act 1996 ... 239
s.1 ... 380
s.86 ... 579
Environmental Protection Act 1990 ... 563
s.79 ... 563

Factories Act 1937
s.14(1) ... 662
s.61 ... 391
Factories Act 1961 ... 384, 389, 662
s.14 ... 378, 390, 392
s.14(1) ... 389
s.28 ... 389
s.28(1) ... 662
s.29 ... 389
s.72 ... 390
Factory Acts ... 434

Factory and Workshop Act 1878 ... 382, 383, 386
Factory and Workshop Acts ... 386, 387
Fair Trading Act 1973 ... 421
Family Law Act 1996 ... 531
Family Law Reform Act 1969, s.8 ... 457
Fatal Accidents Act ... 931, 964, 998, 999
Fatal Accidents Act 1846 ... 909, 1004, 1007, 1008, 1009, 1015
s.2 ... 1009
s.5 ... 1009, 1010
Fatal Accidents Act 1959 ... 1018
Fatal Accidents Act 1976 ... 1008, 1009, 1010, 1012, 1018, 1019
s.1 ... 744
s.1(1) ... 1009
s.1(2)–(3) ... 1011
s.1(4) ... 1012
s.1A ... 143, 744, 1004
s.2 ... 1011
s.2(3) ... 1011
s.3(1)–(1A) ... 1013
s.3(2) ... 1011, 1013
s.3(3)–(3A) ... 1016
s.3(4) ... 1013
s.4 ... 1018, 1019
s.5 ... 901, 1009, **1010**
Finance Act 1995, s.142 ... 971
Finance Act 1996 ... 971
Financial Services and Markets Act 2000 ... 566
s.19(1) ... 398
Sch.1 ... 398
Fire and Rescue Service Act 2004, s.44(2) ... 348
Fox's Libel Act 1792 ... 764, 766

Government of Wales Act 1998, s.77 ... 791
Guard Dogs Act 1975 ... 645
s.1 ... 645
s.5(2) ... 383

Health and Safety at Work Act 1974 ... 383, 662
s.2 ... 662
s.2(1) ... 384
s.47(1)(a) ... 383, 384
s.71 ... 353
Highways Act 1959 ... 391
s.41 ... 391
s.154 ... 390
Highways Act 1980 ... 365, 554, 555
s.41(1)–(1A) ... 554
s.58 ... 554
s.58(1)–(2) ... 554
s.137(1) ... 497
Highways (Miscellaneous Provisions) Act 1961 ... 365, 554
s.1(1) ... 391
Housing (Homeless Persons) Act 1977 ... 388, 426, 432
Human Rights Act 1998 ... 34, 100, 101, 102, 103, 212, 217, 405, 412, 428, 435, 438, 439, 440, 441, 442, 443, 446, 461, 464, 498, 517, 518, 519, 532, 535, 536, 542, 548, 623, 629, 815, 824, 827, 835, 842, 845, 846, 848, 851, 853, 855, 856, 857, 858, 859, 883
s.1 ... 439
s.3 ... 101, 439, 542
s.6 ... 101, 421, 422, 439, 518, 533, 542, 855
s.6(1) ... 438, 532, 856
s.6(2) ... 439
s.6(3) ... 101, 856
s.6(3)(a) ... 439, 532, 857
s.7 ... 438, 442, 855
s.8 ... 101, 137, 212, 438, 442, 855
s.8(1) ... 440, 855
s.8(3) ... 440, 441
s.9 ... 107
s.12 ... 855, 1032
s.12(3) ... 1032
s.12(4) ... 845, 850, 851, 857, 1032
s.12(4)(a)(ii) ... 850

Inheritance (Provision for Family and Dependants) Act 1975 ... 1012
Interception of Communications Act 1985 ... 825

Land Compensation Act 1973, s.1 ... 541
Landlord and Tenant Act 1985
s.11 ... 371
s.12 ... 371
Landlord and Tenant Act 1988, s.1(3) ... 946
Latent Damage Act 1986 ... 198, 374, 434, 927, 930, 932, 933, 935
s.1 ... 928
s.3 ... 928, 932
s.3(7) ... 434
s.4 ... 928, 932
s.5 ... 928
Law Reform (Contributory Negligence) Act 1945 ... 89, 95, 248, 266, 268, 269, 270, 271, 392, 636, 891, 892, 894, 896, 899, 900, 901, 902, 903, 904, 905, 922, 1036, 1037
s.1 ... 895, 897, 900, 901, 902, 1037
s.1(1) ... 270, 271, **893**, 1010
s.1(2) ... 269
s.4 ... 897, 899, 900, 901, 903, 904, 905
s.14(5) ... 540
Law Reform (Husband and Wife) Act 1962 ... 678

Law Reform (Limitation of Actions etc.) Act 1954 ... 398
Law Reform (Married Women and Joint Tortfeasors) Act 1935 ... 693, 1033
Law Reform (Miscellaneous Provisions) Act 1934 ... 999, 1007, 1009
s.1(1)–(1A) ... 1007
s.1(2)(c) ... 1008
s.1(4) ... 1007
s.1(5) ... 1008
Law Reform (Miscellaneous Provisions) Act 1971 ... 1010, 1016
Law Reform (Personal Injuries) Act 1948 ... 398, 891, 963, 964
s.1 ... 382, 652, 907
s.1(1)–(2) ... 909
s.2(1) ... 962
s.2(4) ... 980, 993
Legal Aid Act 1971
s.7 ... 881
Sch.1, Part II(1) ... 881
Libel Act 1843
s.1 ... 811
s.2 ... 811
Libel Act 1845 ... 811
Libel Act 1879 ... 811
Limitation Act 1623, s.5 ... 504
Limitation Act 1939 ... 928
s.26 ... 928, 929
Limitation Act 1963 ... 930
Limitation Act 1975, s.2B(3) ... 1011
Limitation Act 1980 ... 122, 436, 927, 931, 935, 936
s.2 ... 928
s.3 ... 937, 1036
s.10 ... 1036
s.11 ... 928, 929
s.11(1)–(2) ... 931
s.11(4)–(6) ... 931
s.11A ... 745, 932
s.11A(3) ... 937
ss.12–13 ... 929, 931
s.14 ... 928, 929
s.14(1)–(3) ... 931
s.14A ... 928, 930, 932, 933, 935
s.14A(4)(a)–(b) ... 932
s.14B ... 928, 930, 932, 935
ss.28–28A ... 936
s.33 ... 928, 936
s.33(1) ... 932
s.38(3) ... 936
Limitation Acts ... 927, 935
Local Authorities Social Services Act 1970, s.7 ... 418
Local Government Act 1972
s.222 ... 560
s.235 ... 562
Local Government Act 1988
s.17 ... 384
s.19(7) ... 384
Lord Cairns' Act *see* Chancery Amendment Act 1858
Lord Campbell's Act *see* Libel Act 1843
Lord Tenterden's Act *see* Statute of Frauds (Amendment) Act

Magistrates' Courts Act 1980, s.40 ... 66
Marine Insurance Act 1906 ... 567
Maritime Conventions Act 1911, s.1 ... 896
Matrimonial Homes Act 1967 ... 531
Matrimonial Homes Act 1983 ... 531
Mental Health Act 1983 ... 463
Part IV ... 458
Mines and Quarries Act 1954 ... 662
s.157 ... 389, 662
Misrepresentation Act 1967 ... 94
s.2 ... 709
s.2(1) ... 164, 280, 568, 725, 731, 905
s.2(2) ... 731

National Assistance Act 1948, s.26 ... 961
National Health Service Act 1946 ... 993
National Insurance Act 1946 ... 671
National Insurance Act 1965 ... 671, 672
s.1(2)(b) ... 670
National Parks and Access to the Countryside Act 1949, s.60 ... 363
Noise Abatement Act 1960, s.1 ... 563
Northern Ireland Act 1998, s.50 ... 791
Northern Ireland (Emergency Provisions) Act 1978, s.14 ... 465
Nuclear Installations Act 1965 ... 383, 618
s.12(1)(b) ... 383
Nuisance Removal Act 1846 ... 559

Occupiers' Liability Act 1957 ... 95, 98, 341, 343, 344, 345, 346, 347, 350, 357, 358, 359, 363, 365, 368, 398, 434
s.1(1) ... 343
s.1(1)(c) ... 359
s.1(2) ... 343, 346
s.1(3) ... 358
s.1(3)(a) ... 341, 343, 346
s.1(3)(b) ... 346
s.2 ... 352, 357, 358
s.2(1) ... 351, 356, 359, 915
s.2(2) ... 343, 351

s.2(3) ... 352, 355
s.2(3)(b) ... 354, 355
s.2(4) ... 347, 360
s.2(4)(a) ... 355, 359
s.2(4)(b) ... 360, 361, 362, 696
s.2(5) ... 355, 912
s.2(6) ... 347, 357
s.3(1) ... 357
s.5 ... 347
s.5(1) ... 347
s.6 ... 434
s.11(3) ... 358

Occupiers' Liability Act 1984 ... 95, 98, 341, 343, 344, 345, 347, 358, 359, 363, 365, 367, 368, 371, 398, 434
s.1 ... 367
s.1(1) ... 366, 367
s.1(3) ... 366
s.1(3)(a)–(b) ... 366
s.1(4) ... 366
s.1(6) ... 367
s.1(8) ... 367
s.1A ... 365
s.3 ... 434

Offices, Shops and Railway Premises Act 1963 ... 384, 662

Parliamentary Papers Act 1840
s.1 ... 792
s.2 ... 792
s.3 ... 795

Partnership Act 1890, s.10 ... 689

Petroleum (Production) Act 1934 ... 497

Police Act 1964, s.49 ... 774

Police and Criminal Evidence Act 1984 ... 459, 467, 927
Part IX ... 774
s.1 ... 834
s.8 ... 485, 834
ss.9–16 ... 485
s.17 ... 348, 485
s.18 ... 485
s.19 ... 485, 834
ss.20–22 ... 485
s.28 ... 467

Post Office Act 1710 ... 825

Post Office Act 1969, s.14 ... 825

Powers of Criminal Courts Act 2000
s.35 ... 66, 67
ss.130–134 ... 66

Prison Act 1952 ... 470
s.12(1) ... 469

Private Security Industry Act 2001, s.3(2)(j) ... 504

Proceedings Against Estates Act 1970
s.1 ... 1008
s.1(2)(a) ... 1008
s.1(2)(c) ... 1008

Proceeds of Crime Act 2002 ... 487
s.329 ... 487

Protection from Harassment Act 1997 ... 473, 534, 535, 654, 692, 693, 827, 835
s.1(1)–(2) ... 473
s.1(3)(c) ... 473
s.3(2)–(9) ... 473
s.5 ... 473
s.7 ... 473

Public Authorities Protection Act 1893 ... 398, 403

Public Health Act 1875 ... 387, 559

Public Health Act 1936 ... 409, 562, 563
s.31 ... 618
s.92(1) ... 562
s.107(1) ... 562
s.343(1) ... 563

Public Health Acts ... 378

Public Order Act 1986 ... 498
s.14A ... 497

Race Relations Act 1976 ... 679, 681, 1007
s.32(1) ... 679
ss.53–55 ... 383
ss.56–57 ... 383, 943

Railways and Transport Safety Act 2003, s.111 ... 554

Rehabilitation of Offenders Act 1974 ... 785, 826
s.8(3) ... 785

Reservoirs Act 1975
s.28 ... 618
Sch.2 ... 618

Riding Establishments Act 1964 ... 631

Riding Establishments Act 1970 ... 631

Rivers Pollution Act 1876 ... 559

Road Traffic Act 1930 ... 70, 386, 387
s.35 ... 381

Road Traffic Act 1972 ... 70
s.143 ... 70
s.148(3) ... 356
s.148(4) ... 70
s.149 ... 71

Road Traffic Act 1974, s.20 ... 68

Road Traffic Act 1988 ... 898, 911
s.15 ... 897
s.16(2) ... 898
s.143 ... 386
s.149 ... 911
s.149(3) ... 911
s.157 ... 980

Road Traffic Acts ... 229

Road Traffic (NHS Charges) Act 1999 . . . 993, 994

Safety of Sports Grounds Act 1975, s.13 . . . 383
Sale of Goods Act 1893
s.12 . . . 708
s.14 . . . 708
sale of Goods Act 1979 . . . 730, 742
s.2(5) . . . 730
s.12 . . . 18, 708
s.13 . . . 18, 745
s.14 . . . 18, 708, 723, 730, 745
s.14(3) . . . 703
s.15 . . . 18, 745
s.22 . . . 489
s.24 . . . 489
s.53 . . . 731
s.55 . . . 18
s.61(1) . . . 730
Sch.2 . . . 745
Scotland Act 1998, s.41 . . . 791
Sex Discrimination Act 1975 . . . 383, 1007
s.41 . . . 679
ss.62–66 . . . 383
ss.65–66 . . . 943
Sexual Offences Act 1967, s.1 . . . 755
Sexual Offences (Amendment) Act 1976
s.4 . . . 826
s.7(2) . . . 826
Sexual Offences (Amendment) Act 1991 . . . 827
Slander of Women Act 1891 . . . 759
s.1 . . . 759
Social Security Act 1975 . . . 670
Social Security Act 1989 . . . 962, 964
Social Security Acts . . . 414
Social Security Administration Act 1992 . . . 650, 717, 964
Social Security (Contributions and Benefits) Act 1992 . . . 650
Social Security (Recovery of Benefits) Act 1997 . . . 955, 956, 962, 963, 964, 968, 1018
s.1(1)(a) . . . 963
s.1(4)(b) . . . 963
s.3 . . . 964
s.29 . . . 963
Sch.1
Part I . . . 963
Part 2 . . . 964
Sch.2 . . . 963
Solicitors' Act 1974, s.37 . . . 70
Southern Rhodesian Act 1965 . . . 385
Statute of Frauds (Amendment) Act 1828 . . . 567
s.6 . . . 567
Suicide Act 1961 . . . 461
s.2(1) . . . 456, 461
Supply of Goods (Implied Terms) Act 1973
s.8 . . . 18
ss.9–11 . . . 18, 745
supreme Court Act 1981
s.32A . . . 969
s.50 . . . 541, 1032
s.51 . . . 942
s.69(1) . . . 814, 947, 977
s.69(3) . . . 814, 977

Theatres Act 1968, s.4(1) . . . 757
Theft Act 1968, s.9(1)(b) . . . 350
Theft Act 1978, s.3(4) . . . 467
Third Parties Against Insurers Act 1930, s.1 . . . 69
Torts (Interference with Goods) Act 1977 . . . 483, 485, 490, 491, 492
s.1 . . . 483
s.1(a) . . . 492
s.2 . . . 488
s.2(1) . . . 483
s.3(2)–(3) . . . 491
s.4 . . . 491, 492
ss.5–6 . . . 491
s.7 . . . 491, 1030
s.7(2) . . . 485
s.8 . . . 485, 490, 491, 1030
s.10 . . . 490
s.11(1) . . . 485, 490, 903
s.11(3) . . . 488
Trade Descriptions Act 1968 . . . 67
Trade Disputes Act 1906 . . . 574, 598, 599
s.3 . . . 596, 597, 598
ss.4–5 . . . 598
Trade Union Act 1871 . . . 598
Trade Union and Labour Relations Act 1974 . . . 595, 599
s.13(1) . . . 583
s.13(2) . . . 596, 600
Trade Union and Labour Relations (Consolidation) Act 1992 . . . 599
Part V . . . 574
s.145 . . . 384
s.152 . . . 667
s.219 . . . 586, 600
s.219(1) . . . 583, 600
s.219(2) . . . 600
s.220 . . . 499, 601
s.221 . . . 601, 1031
s.221(2) . . . 601
ss.222–234 . . . 601
s.244(1) . . . 600
Trade Union Reform and Employment Rights Act 1993 . . . 599, 600
Tramways Act 1870 . . . 555
Transport Act 1962, s.43(7) . . . 357

Unfair Contract Terms Act 1977 ... 95, 169, 170, 190, 192, 197, 356, 357, 358, 359, 370, 674, 744, 745, 891, 906, 915, 916, 917, 918, 920, 1037, 9906
s.1 ... 358
s.1(3) ... 170, 359, 915
s.2 ... 359, 675, 745, 917, 918, 920
s.2(1) ... 915, 920
s.2(2) ... 163, 169, 170, 357, 359, 675, 915, 917, 920
s.2(3) ... 915
s.3 ... 745, 918
ss.5–7 ... 915, 918
s.8 ... 918
s.12 ... 745
s.13 ... 675
s.13(1) ... 917, 918
s.20 ... 18
Sch.1, para.4 ... 920
Unsolicited Goods and Services Act 1971 ... 488

Water Industry Act 1991 ... 618
s.18 ... 519
s.22 ... 519
s.94(1) ... 519
Waterworks Clauses Act 1847 ... 387
s.35 ... 387
s.47 ... 387
Workmens' Compensation Act 1897 ... 650

SECONDARY LEGISLATION

Abrasive Wheels Regulations 1970 (SI 1970/535), reg.3 ... 389

Bereavement (Variation of Sum) (England and Wales) Order 2002 (SI 2002/644) ... 1004, 1013

Building Regulations 1976 (SI 1976/1676) ... 353
Building Regulations 2000 (SI 2000/2531) ... 353

Civil Procedure Rules 1998 (SI 1998/3132) ... 434, 765, 766
Part 1 ... 434
Part 6, r.6.20(5)–(8) ... 21
Part 24 ... 434
r.24.2 ... 765
Part 41, rr.41.4–41.10 ... 973
Part 54 ... 403, 404, 432, 433
r.54.4 ... 404, 434
r.54.20 ... 404, 434

Damages (Personal Injury) Order 2001 (SI 2001/2301) ... 988
Damages (Variation of Periodical Payments) Order 2006 ... 973

Electronic Commerce (EC Directive) Regulations 2002 (SI 2002/2013) ... 778
reg.17 ... 778
regs.18–19 ... 779

Legal Services (England and Wales) Conditional Fee Agreements Regulations 2000 (SI 2000/692) ... 881

National Health Service (General Medical Services) Regulations (SI 1992/635), Sch.3, para.4(h) ... 201

Prison Rules 1964 ... 386, 428, 469, 470
Provision and Use of Work Equipment Regulations 1998 ... 395, 396

Rules of the Supreme Court (SI 1978/579)
Ord.15
r.1 ... 502
r.10A ... 485
Ord.22, r.1 ... 881
Ord.29
Part II ... 968
r.11 ... 968
Ord.33, r.3 ... 760, 764
Ord.37, rr.7–12 ... 969
Ord.53 ... 403, 432, 433, 434
Ord.62 ... 942
SI 1982/1201, reg.5 ... 898
SI 1982/1202 ... 897
SI 1982/1342 ... 897
SI 1989/1219 ... 897
SI 1992/1336 ... 827
SI 1997/200, reg.2(2)(a) ... 964
SI 1997/2205 ... 963
reg.2(2)(a) ... 1018
regs.3–6 ... 964
sI 2001/1118, reg.2 ... 963

Town and Country (Use Classes) Order 1987 (SI 1987/764) ... 562

Workplace (Health, Safety and Welfare) Regulations 1992 (SI 1992/3004) ... 662

TABLE OF LEGISLATION FROM OTHER JURISDICTIONS

SOUTH AFRICA

Bill of Rights, s.8 ... 855

CANADA

Constitution, s.52 ... 855

FRANCE

Civil Code
  Art.9 ... 846
  Art.1382 ... 30

Napoleonic Code 1804, Art.1384 1 CC ... 92

GERMANY

Civil Code
  para.823 ... 651
  para.831 ... 652

Strict Liability Act 1978 ... 628

UNITED STATES OF AMERICA

Alien Act ... 870

Black Lung Act 30 U.S.C., s.901 ... 336

Cal.Code Civ.Proc., para.425.16 ... 880
Californian Civil Code, s.1708.8 ... 887
Clean Water Act 33 U.S.C., s.1251 ... 295
Comprehensive Environmental Response, Compensation, and Liability Act, 42 USC 9601 *et seq* ... 296
Constitution ... 336, 883
  First Amendment ... 779, 824, 845, 869, 878, 882, 884, 886, 887
  Fourth Amendment ... 721

Dramshop Act, 235 ILCS 5/6–21 (Ill.) 315 ... 335

Federal Employers' Liability Act (FELA) 45 U.S.C., paras.51–60 ... 283
Federal Tort Claims Act 1946 ... 408

Jones Act 46 U.S.C., para.688 ... 283

National Childhood Vaccine Injury Act 42 U.S.C., s.300aa ... 336

Oil Pollution Act, 33 U.S.C.2701 ... 295

Privacy Act 1974, 5 USC, s.552(a) (1992) ... 883

Restatement (Second) of Contracts, Art.90 ... 164
Restatement (Second) of Torts ... 287, 312, 314, 628, 713
  § 37–44 ... 314
  § 282 ... 334
  § 314 ... 313, 314
  § 314A ... 314
  § 314B ... 314
  § 315–319 ... 314
  § 321–324 ... 314
  § 324A ... 314
  § 344 ... 323
  § 402A ... 712, 713, 716, 736, 747
  § 402A(1) ... 712
  § 402A(2) ... 713
  § 519 ... **626**
  §§ 552A–552B ... 294
  § 652D 1977 ... 884
  § 766C ... 298
  § 822 ... 521
  § 833(c) ... 557
Restatement (Third) of Torts ... 286, 287, 292, 293, 310, 312, 314, **316**, 317, 714, 729, 730, 732
  § 1 ... 714
  § 1(b) ... 336
  § 2(a)–(c) ... 714
  § 6 ... 305
  § 18 ... 455
  § 19 ... 308, 316
  § 19(a) ... 730
  § 28 ... 325

§ 29 ... 308
§ 34 ... 308
§ 39 ... **317**
§ 40 ... 322
§ 41 ... 308, **320**, 321
§ 42 ... **320**
Rhode Island Environmental Injury Compensation Act ... 296
Rivers and Harbours Appropriation Act 33 U.S.C., s.401 ... 296

Sedition Act ... 870

Tex.Alco.Bev. Code Ann.
para.2.02 ... 315, 316
para.2.03 ... 315

Uniform Commercial Code, s.2–318 ... 709, 712

Wis. Stat., para.125.035(2) ... 315

TABLE OF INTERNATIONAL INSTRUMENTS

Brussels Convention on Jurisdiction and the Enforcement of Judgments in Civil and Commercial Matters 1968 ... 717, 746

EC Directive 73/239/EEC (Insurance) ... 438

EC Directive 77/780/EEC (First Banking Co-ordination) ... 437, 438

EC Directive 80/778/EEC ... 561

EC Directive 85/337/EEC (Environmental Impact Assessment) ... 629

EC Directive 85/374/EEC (Product Liability) ... 93, 657, 703, 704, 714, 715, 717, 718, 719, 730, 735, 737, 747, 723, 727, 728
- Preamble ... 715, 717
- Art.1 ... 715
- Art.2 ... 715, 728
- Art.3 ... 715, 737
- Art.3(2) ... 715, 738
- Arts.4–5 ... 715
- Art.6 ... 734
- Art.6(1) ... 715
- Art.7(e) ... 718, 719, 739
- Art.7(1)(a)–(d) ... 716
- Art.7(1)(e) ... 715, 717
- Art.8(1) ... 717
- Art.9 ... 716
- Art.12 ... 716
- Art.13 ... 717
- Art.15(1)(a) ... 716
- Art.15(1)(b) ... 717, 738
- Art.15(2) ... 717

EC Directive 89/391/EC (Framework, Health and Safety) ... 396, 662

EC Directive 89/655/EC (Work Equipment) ... 396

EC Directive 95/46/EC (Data Protection) ... 93, 825
- Recital 10 ... 825

EC Directive 97/11/EC ... 629

EC Directive 2000/31/EC (E-Commerce) ... 778
- Art.12 ... 778
- Art.13 ... 779
- Art.22(1) ... 778

EC Directive 2004/35/EC (Environmental Liability) ... 563, 629
- Recital 11 ... 563, 629
- Art.1 ... 563
- Art.2(1) ... 563
- Art.3(3) ... 563, 629

EC Directive (Product Safety) ... 738

EC Treaty ... 395, 405, 438
- Art.28 ... 430, 435
- Art.42 ... 943
- Art.43 ... 436
- Art.81 ... 395, 574, 603
- Art.82 ... 574, 603

European Convention for the Protection of Human Rights ... 101, 102, 103, 104, 129, 136, 137, 212, 422, 438, 439, 440, 441, 442, 444, 446, 464, 469, 479, 498, 520, 542, 629, 756, 839, 851, 853, 856, 857, 858, 859, 885, 1032
- Art.2 ... 136, 405, 439, 444, 461, 840
- Art.3 ... 136, 137, 405, 412, 422, 439, 444, 445, 461
- Art.4 ... 405, 439
- Art.5 ... 101, 405, 439, 443, 463, 464, 468
- Art.5(1)(b) ... 468
- Art.5(1)(c) ... 443
- Art.5(1)(e) ... 464, 468
- Art.5(3) ... 443
- Art.5(5) ... 443
- Art.6 ... 105, 133, 134, 135, 136, 399, 405, 412, 421, 435, 439, 443, 444, 445, 925, 929
- Art.6(1) ... 34, 103, 421, 435, 444
- Art.7 ... 405, 439
- Art.8 ... 101, 103, 104, 105, 136, 137, 405, 422, 439, 441, 442, 444, 445, 461, 479, 517, 519, 532, 533, 535, 536, 542, 548, 623, 629, 820, 823, 825, 836, 843, 847, 848, 851, 852, 856, 858, 1006
- Art.8(1) ... 532
- Art.8(2) ... 461
- Art.9 ... 405, 439
- Art.10 ... 405, 439, 498, 551, 768, 771, 784, 800, 815, 851, 856, 858
- Art.10(1) ... 851
- Art.10(2) ... 808, 851
- Art.11 ... 101, 405, 439, 498, 551
- Art.12 ... 405, 439
- Art.13 ... 104, 848
- Art.14 ... 439
- Art.66 ... 212, 213
- Protocol 1
  - Art.1 ... 101, 439, 441, 517, 519, 533, 836

Art.2 ... 101, 103, 439
Art.3 ... 439
Protocol 6, Arts.1–2 ... 439

Rome Convention on the Law Applicable to Contractual Obligations ... 746

Universal Declaration of Human Rights 1948, Art.12 ... 820

Vienna Convention on Diplomatic Relations ... 794

PART I

SETTING THE SCENE

1 Introduction
2 Some General Warnings for the Novice Tort Lawyer

1

INTRODUCTION

1. TORT AT THE CROSSROADS

Today the law of tort is mainly, though by no means exclusively, concerned with 'accidents' arising in countless ways. Most, however, happen at the workplace or on the roads. In 2003 for instance 3,200 deaths in Britain were linked to car accidents—a high number, but much lower than in the past. The total number of deaths caused by accidents was 11,300. By comparison, during the same year, work accidents caused 230 deaths. The number of work-related injuries however, was substantially higher. Thus, in 2004, 151,000 accidents were *recorded* as having taken place at work. In the same year, the number of *recorded* injured in traffic accidents totalled about 278,000. These figures refer to 'recorded' accidents; if one includes tort claims arising from unrecorded and unreported accidents, the total then increases by about 70 per cent. There is uncertainty as to the exact figure of purely property damage caused by traffic accidents but the figure could be as high as six times as much as that given above for personal injuries.

The trend in tort claims has gone up since Pearson reported in 1978 an estimated figure of approximately 250,000 claims per annum (and of these 213,000 received some of their compensation through tort law). By 1988, the Civil Justice Review estimated that the figure had risen to close to 340,000 claimants. Among these, car-related claims had gone up, but figures for work-related accidents had dropped, partly because of improvements in workplace safety but largely because of the decline of high-risk manufacturing industry. Medical negligence claims, which attracted next to no attention thirty or forty years ago, now often make the headlines, but this may be partly because they have tended to involve serious incidents and partly because the medical profession (and their insurers) have proved adept in publicising this trend, even though medical negligence injury claims still represent only 1 per cent of all tort claims.

Statistics can be very misleading, partly because one may not be comparing 'apples with oranges', partly because one is not adjusting figures for inflation, and partly because what is counted and the way 'things' are counted may differ. Details are not for this book, though one matter must be clarified at the outset. When comparing figures we must distinguish between claims raised (first step if the claimant is informed that he can try to make another person liable for his hurt and takes the chance of doing so), writs issued (the next stage when the claimant ups the stakes), settlements reached without concluding the judicial process (third stage) and final verdicts (last step). How much the actual figures change as the potential claimant moves from stage one to stage four can be seen at the figures given by Pearson in 1978. It was thus said there that 86 per cent of claims are disposed of without legal proceedings being commenced. Of the remaining 14 per cent, a further 11 per cent will be settled before a date for trial has been fixed. The remaining (approximately) 3 per cent *may* proceed to full trial—the 'may' suggests that depending on the nature of the dispute the figure may be as low as 1 per cent—though how many of these claims will then end in a verdict for the plaintiff or the defendant is yet another matter. So, the curve from complaint, threat of action, writ, trial and victory slopes downward and does so very steeply! Winning through litigation is thus a very 'chancy' business!

Notwithstanding the above caveats the tort-related claim numbers are high; and the incidents to which they relate cause much pain and cost much money to individuals and society as a whole. However one reads them, they can thus cause concern—personal and institutional. But as Professor Cane has rightly observed, they must also be put in perspective. He thus noted that

In 2002, the male death rate from cancer in England was 275.3 per 100,000, and from circulatory disease 385.2 per 100,000; while the male death rate from 'all accidents and adverse events' was only 23.1 per 100,000 and from road accidents, 9.2 per 100,000.[1]

The overall conclusion is thus not in doubt. Out of the total number of persons who die or are injured every year only a small percentage of them will get compensated and only a fraction of them will receive their compensation through the law of torts. As already indicated the Pearson Committee reported that the number of people who obtained compensation through this source was just over 213,000 a year.[2] This represents a small fraction—6.66 per cent to be precise—of the total number of injuries, estimated, at that time, to be in the region of 3 million. Yet, this 6.66 per cent of the total number of annual victims of accidents, ended up by obtaining through the tort system about 25 per cent of the total amount of compensation paid to accident victims from *all* sources of compensation.[3] Thus, for the years 1971–6 the total tort compensation was £202 million per annum. Of this amount, £69 million was paid to victims of work-related injuries and £118 million to road accident victims. The true measure of this figure becomes obvious when one realises that this £202 million is almost half the total value of moneys distributed through the social security system to approximately 1.5 million recipients in this period.[4]

The above represent the so-called 'private costs', i.e. the sums *transferred* from the defendant (or his insurer) to the claimant to 'compensate' the latter for his injuries. In addition, however, one must bear in mind that there are additional 'social costs'. These

[1] *Atiyah's Accidents, Compensation and the Law* (7th edn., 2006), 18, 20 ff.

[2] Cmnd. 7054-I, table 4.

[3] No study as thorough as that conducted by the Pearson Committee has taken place since the publication of that Report. But such, mainly circumstantial, evidence that is available suggests that the general trends remain unchanged and, hence, the Pearson Committee figures retain considerable interest.

[4] For diverse reasons, the remaining 1.3 million injured persons received no compensation for their injuries. The reasons for this include ignorance, no one to blame, lack of initiative to pursue matters further, impecuniosity, etc.

include the administrative costs needed to make the transfer payments. The amounts of these administrative costs are high and, indeed, in the cases considered above amounted to nearly double the sums actually paid over to the victims. Thus, 'the administrative costs of making the annual payments of £202 million averaged some £175 million during the same period'.[5]

Though the tort system has been accused, probably fairly, as being slow, cumbersome and capricious in its outcome it is, above all, expensive. This is because it entails the above-mentioned serious transaction or social costs (such as fees from lawyers, actuaries, expert witnesses, investigations, court-related expenses and the like[6]) all of which help increase the total bill for redressing the results of the accident. Seen from a different optic, however, the study of the subject also presents both intellectual and practical significance, especially when an attempt is made to relate it properly to the other systems of compensation.[7] This means that these, in turn, must be compared with the tort system and evaluated not only in terms of costs but also in terms of how politically realistic it is to envisage them taking over the function of tort law. Ideologically inclined academics invariably underplay this point.

As an intellectual subject tort law may be said to be both demanding and exciting. Indeed, it is more than just 'exciting'; it can also become fascinating as its study increasingly demands wider reading, made necessary by the subject's growing cohabitation with (English) administrative law and European law (in the sense of law coming from the two European courts of Luxembourg and Strasbourg).[8]

The continuing importance of the law of tort is due not only to the increase in the number of accidents nor, even, to its growing complexity caused by its interaction with other branches of the law. To these legal and comparative dimensions, one must add what, for lack of a better term, one might be called the sociological dimension. This is associated with the very contemporary trend of citizens feeling 'entitled' to protection against any of the vicissitudes of modern life. Here, we thus move beyond the usual realm of personal injury and enter the modern and complex topics of discrimination—sex, race, age and so on—which modern societies attempt to stamp out. The result is a society more willing than ever to look sympathetically at a wider spectrum of complaints, many of which would have been unimaginable, say, fifty years ago. This, however, also comes at a high cost; and here we are not envisaging financial costs but the cost of restricting freedom of expression in the pursuit of the reduction—eradication is the utopians' dream—of all the unacceptable forms of discrimination. A second and parasitic consequence of this modern legislation is the increase in the regulatory regime that controls how business, government agencies of all kinds and, indeed, universities work.

5 Cane, *Atiyah's Accidents, Compensation and the Law* (Select Bibliography), 396.

6 It has been estimated that it takes the tort system 85p to deliver £1 of compensation compared to between 8 and 12p to deliver £1 of benefit via the social security system. For more details on this see Cane (Select Bibliography), 466.

7 More about this in Section 7.

8 These observations will be fully justified when we turn to chs. 7, 8, 20, 21 and 22. This does not mean that other areas of tort law have remained immune to these influences. In ch. 2 we explain why these points must be brought out more clearly in university classes.

These are, as yet, largely unquantifiable costs, but perhaps more serious than most have yet to accept.

A so-called 'compensation culture' appears to be growing in Europe (including the UK[9]) but seems particularly pronounced in the United States, where one knowledgeable observer once remarked that: '[f]ew Americans, it seems, can tolerate more than five minutes of frustration without submitting to the temptation to sue'.[10] Though the picture seems to have changed in the 1990s, and the pro-plaintiff verdicts apparently decreased significantly both in numbers and in the size of their awards, tort reform is still a lively issue in the United States and very often this is really needed. The recent shift alluded to above has not yet been adequately noticed in our country.

Combined, all of the above factors invite speculation on tort law and tort reform and much ink has flown to this end. The product of such speculation has varied from the idealistic, the utopian, the opportunistic, and the patchy; rarely, however, does it nowadays embody really new thinking. Arguably, the most novel way of approaching tort reform has been via the little studied subject of civil procedure. Reorganising the jurisdiction of the civil courts—in England this has largely meant pushing more cases into the Crown Courts and out of the High Court—toying with varying forms of contingent fee systems, removing legal aid from personal injury cases, have all provided new yet indirect ways to address problematic areas of tort law. Yet this move, as well, has its price and that is the need to widen one's knowledge to include civil procedure before one can begin understanding modern tort law in action.

Yet, at the end of the day, it is the politicisation of the subject that has managed to preserve its wide interest at a time when new subjects are beginning to dominate as never before the law curriculum. This underlying political agenda of tort law, along with the personalities of those who pursue it—be they judges or academics—contributes immensely to the stimulation (as well as the annoyance) that the subject can generate in the reader's mind. Somehow, this combination can be found in some branches of the law—constitutional law in its widest sense is the obvious example—but seems to be less pronounced in others such as property law, which arguably induce a calmer frame of mind.

The best, short account that a student can find about the successive but, at best, only partially successful ideas to reform tort law can be found in chapter 18 of Professor Cane's aforementioned seventh edition of the Atiyah monograph. His summary is learned, admirably impartial and cerebral in tone. If it suffers from a 'defect'—and most traditional scholars would not see it in that way at all—it is that it has stripped the debate of the underlying political and academic passions alluded to above, making the subject and its exposition appear to be somewhat dry. This book will try to make its readers more alive to these political or para-legal aspects of the subject since they so often provide the real arguments which propel these debates. The attentive student

[9] For evidence of a compensation culture, or at least of the perception of it by politicians, see the Parliamentary debates surrounding the passage of the Compensation Act 2006.

[10] Quoted by J. Fleming, *The American Tort Process* (Select Bibliography), 2.

should thus keep his highlighter handy when reading common-law judgments. For unlike his civilian colleagues, he will be privileged to find many of these clues in the judgments themselves.

The United States offers, in its judgments and in its academic literature, excellent illustrations for many of the observations made above; and this is why we have devoted in this book two long specialised chapters in order to bring out the differences as well as its similarities that this related system presents with our own. For every time some attempt is made to reorganise tort law in the United States—in practice this takes the form of either capping damages for non-pecuniary losses or moving more cases out of the jurisdiction of State courts and into Federal courts (the latter being staffed by appointed and not elected judges, reputedly less sympathetic to claimants)—the whole country is convulsed. Democrats tend to see in such moves an attempt to stifle the rights of the poor and a step towards affording greater protection to large and rich corporations, Republicans making the exact opposite claims, invoking the danger of making large corporations less competitive in a globalised economy which includes countries (such as China and India) who operate with minimal labour costs.

The politicisation of law in the United States is, in fact, even more deep in areas such as family law, homosexual marriage or partnerships, abortion and the death sentence, where the views of the population on such matters can often take precedence over the state of the economy or the (chaotic) state of American foreign policy and thus even decide the outcome of general elections. But it would be a mistake to see these as topics unrelated to tort law proper, for the law these days is a seamless web and strict compartmentalisation does not work (if, indeed, it ever did). Thus, substantial areas of tort law, e.g. the relatively new causes of action for wrongful life and wrongful birth are all by-products of the liberalisation of the law of abortion which took place in 1973;[11] and the debates about punitive damages or workers' compensation schemes are also inextricably linked to various constitutional provisions. This list could be made much longer.

This cohabitation of law and politics is thus not only a widespread phenomenon, it also gives American law a very special flavour. On the positive side, it promotes (more than it does in this country) the examination of law in an interdisciplinary manner. Arguably, however, it also presents some drawbacks, notably that it also contributes to the legal discourse losing much of the doctrinal rigour one finds in other systems, ours for instance and even more so the German, as the emphasis sometimes can shift too much in the opposite direction.

In Britain the position is different; but not *so* different and, arguably, still in a state of evolution. For here, as well, we find professionals of all kinds and even highly placed judges expressing worries about the size and cost of tort litigation. But if the problem is detected, the diagnosis of its causes and, even more so, the proposed remedies, are not shared by everyone. Yet the national temperament and judicial caution in England are different from those in the United States and are thus likely to ensure that we never

[11] *Roe* v. *Wade*, 410 US 113, 98 SCt. 705. The important decision of the Supreme Court of New Jersey in *Procanik* v. *Cillo*, 478 A 2d 755 (1984) acknowledged this link openly.

quite emulate the more extreme elements of the American system. Besides, the American system possesses some special features (such as the use of juries in civil trials and the almost total absence of a welfare-state safety net) that are absent from our system and may thus ensure a more balanced approach towards the problem of accident compensation. Finally, the reduced willingness of the English system to award punitive damages (at all, to say nothing of at American levels) is yet a third reason why we should not be too concerned about American storms reaching our shores with any great destructive force.

Yet having said this, one cannot deny the existence of conscious or subconscious tendencies. And it is a fact of contemporary life that whereas in days gone by ideas travelled 'with the sun' from east to west, nowadays they are increasingly born in America, one might even suggest in the Pacific rim, and then, with a jet lag of a few years, reach us in Europe. This is true of fast food, clothing, music, general tastes and, arguably, law as well. Thus, the politicisation of tort law is thus becoming obvious in our system as well as the patchy nature of our reforms clearly reflect either the impact that pressure groups have on the generation of 'partial' legislation or even the introduction of legislation which openly admits as its first objective the desire to save the NHS money (even if the long term effects of this reform remain openly uncertain).[12] The desire to protect public funds being dissipated by pro-claimant awards is another interesting development, not uninfluenced by underlying beliefs about the proper role of judges (which not everyone will find congenial). Thus, many would argue—indeed have argued in many systems not so different from ours—that it is not for judges to take decisions which have as their prime aim to protect public finances, this being a matter more suitably left to the legislator.

Notwithstanding such 'restrictive tendencies' one can find in our kaleidoscopic society quite a few tort lawyers speaking openly and with horror of what they describe as the emergence of a 'compensation culture'. The author of one the most idiosyncratic but also influential and thought-provoking case books—Tony Weir—is among the scholars who have persistently attacked this trend. Such consistency in views always attracts admiration and complements his vivacious style. But whereas the works of Mr Weir forty years ago[13] would use his most elegant written style to spark off new ideas, more recent works exude much pessimism, repeatedly attacking his *bêtes noires*. These seem to be increasing in number and now include payments made by the welfare system, the rapacity of insurance companies, and human-rights lawyers as a group, all of the above being accompanied by a good dose of euroscepticism. This, for instance, is how this learned author put these ideas himself in his address at the David Hume Institute in Scotland in 2003:

> The best ways to get money *to which you are not entitled* just by asking for it are (a) to get social security payments or relief, (b) to claim on an insurance policy, and (c) to bring a tort suit.[14]

[12] These points will be elaborated further when we look at the gradual expansion of the Criminal Injuries Compensation Scheme or the reforms authorising periodical payment of damages.

[13] For instance in P. Catala and J. A. Weir, 'Delict and Tort: A Study in Parallel' (1963) 37 *Tul. LR* 573 and (1964) 38 *Tul. LR* 663 and 702.

[14] See http://www.davidhumeinstitute.com/ (emphasis added).

If one reads on it becomes moderately clear that what this author is *really* castigating is the abuse of these systems through fraudulent behaviour. But if fraud exists—and it always has and always will continue to do so in the future—you battle it as best you can but do not blame the aims which the system tries to achieve through welfare payments, insurance and tort litigation. Yet that is what the quoted sentence does. Confusing the underlying idea, and the mechanisms devised to implement it, with the way it can be abused—and even Mr Weir admits that the figures that support his accusations are 'soft'—thus only muddies the debate. A differently phrased sentence could have avoided this impression. But a more complete account might have destroyed the effect of an attention-catching phrase. Writing for effect and writing to impart knowledge may not always go together.

So, if in a lecture entitled 'The Compensation Culture' you wish, for instance, to cite examples, as Mr Weir does, of cases such as *Revill* v. *Newbury* [15] in order to suggest that tort law has gone crazy by punishing the householder who shot the burglars who tried to burgle him, you might also have regard to the proper context of the case. One should thus also emphasise (a) that these cases such as that one represent numerically a tiny minority of cases and thus do not add to the tort crisis, and (b) one should also say that drawing the lines of permissible self-defence is neither easy nor yet achieved definitively by any legal system. The conclusion thus would seem to be that if one case draws the line 'wrongly', it does not mean that the underlying idea of asking the court to decide what constitutes reasonable self-defence is wrong. The result may thus be that decisions such as this may not appeal to the general public; but this is neither the first nor the last tort decision that will have this effect; nor is it sufficient to support the thesis of a compensation culture or a tort law in crisis. But Mr Weir's critical presentation does not stop there.

For the critic of such decisions should, at the same time as mentioning his worries about them, also be pointing out that there is a host of other cases which, under the influence of individual judges—and this, too, has to be stressed—have established vast areas of immunity for a variety of defendants such as local authorities, statutory bodies, the police, the fire brigade and so on. Likewise, using statistics to suggest the rising cost of tort litigation, for instance in medical malpractice cases, must be accompanied by the necessary clarification that the cost of medical care is growing much faster than inflation, and the cost of treatment under the NHS is not only rising but often—very often—is unavailable, or being cut back severely. Likewise, mistakes—often not only gross but also repetitive—made by various social welfare services are the reasons for these claims being brought even though they are almost invariably unsuccessful.[16]

Claims for compensation through damages may also be due in part to the cutting back on the resources of the central and local public services. If the state does this for reasons of economy, political dogma, or both—and it's worth pondering over the

[15] [1996] 1 All ER 291.

[16] For a case involving not just an isolated error but a cascade of negligent acts see *Lawrence* v. *Pembrokeshire CC* [2006] EWHC 1029 (QB), [2007] PIQR P1.

influence that a handful of thinkers (Hayek, Friedman) or politicians (Reagan or Thatcher) have had on this topic—should it then also be allowed to use the resulting shortfall in personnel to 'excuse' its errors and avoid liability? Strangely enough, those who mistrust the American tort scene should learn in this context a lesson or two from it. For the main lesson is, in our view, the fact that in the USA the lack, almost total, of any efficient system of social security has not only totally deprived 50 million of its citizens of all medical coverage, it has also forced tort law to step in the gap in an attempt to fashion an acceptable solution. For it is no longer politically acceptable to leave a victim of negligently caused harm uncared for if he is not rich enough to carry personally (or through insurance) the inevitable costs of our industrial society. So if society does not care, the tort system will—indeed must—move in and fill the gap.

One should not be surprised that the discussion of these issues has now become part of the tort scene. When our tort law was formed, it was shaped to meet the needs of a primitive society. A primitive legal system, because of its lack of techniques and inclination, concerns itself mainly with the murderer, the footpad and those who disturb the 'King's peace'. By the same token, in the Middle Ages civil liability for nervous shock received no attention in a world accustomed to unbelievable physical suffering. Liability for intentional false statements was unthought-of until much later; and liability for careless false statements was not generally accepted until 1963 (and we are still struggling to keep it within reasonable bounds). Likewise, liability for injury on the highway was limited to falling into potholes, easily repayable by the local community, by taking care of the surface of the highway. The notion that the source of danger may lie underneath the surface of a modern concreted road was, quite simply, unthinkable when the early law placed on the shoulders of the local community the task of maintaining the highway. The legal system was, correspondingly, untuned to deal with such problems. The recovery of damages for disappointment over a ruined holiday[17] today represents a very advanced stage of development, which not everyone would regard as 'progress'. Generally speaking, the law reflects its society; and clinging to past rules when society has been transformed radically, especially during the last one hundred years, is a recipe for legal disaster. Readers of this book, especially law students, should constantly test the relevance of the rules they are taught against the need of their environment. As a result, the law has changed to meet these needs and it would be wrong to condemn this shift as being part of a compensation culture. We see it as an organic growth of the law.

There are many reasons for this trend to seek to be compensated when injured through the fault of others and they have little to do with the situation in the United States or the changes, technological and economic, of our society. This time we are thinking of changes linked to deeper psychological factors, namely the change of mentality among our citizens. Here, the change may be less welcome, though it would be wrong, again, to equate it with a growth of the 'compensation culture'. For now we are talking of a wider phenomenon: one that could be described as the emergence of the

[17] *Ichard* v. *Frangoulis* [1977] 1 WLR 556; *Jackson* v. *Horizon Holidays Ltd.* [1975] 1 WLR 1468 (a contract action).

'rights and entitlements' culture. This has been a slowly growing phenomenon which has taken place since the end of World War II and has been encouraged by a long period of relative peace coupled with a period of unprecedented prosperity in the richer countries of the world. In the 1990s, the 'mood change' received a boost from an unexpected quarter with the publication (by Conservative governments) of the various so-called 'Citizen's Charters'. A few years later it was transformed (by the Labour governments) into legislation of the most varied kind. Thus, even though all political parties have assisted this development, nowadays it is mainly those of conservative inclination who deplore the results. It is too late to do anything about it.

For even if the 'rich', the 'stiff upper lip', the 'pull-yourself-together', the 'neo-conservative' type of characters may condemn this new reality—and, indeed, there may be much to condemn in this 'softening' up of characters and the decline of the kind of self-sufficiency of bygone days—it is here to stay. Moreover, the loss of those virtues that are now missed must be weighed against the fact that our society has acquired a social conscience of sorts. In France they call it 'socialisation of risks'; and the legal consequences of this view is that society, as a whole, has obligations towards its more vulnerable members, which is reflected in many rules of tort and administrative law. One may thus like or dislike this social trend; think that it has gone too far or not far enough. But the tort legislator, the judge or the practitioner should not think that through his actions alone—judging, writing and teaching—he can single-handedly reverse this trend in a significant way for the foreseeable future. What we must learn to do, therefore, is not rail against this new world but try to tame it as much as possible or shape it in a way that achieves a balanced attribution of risks and costs.

Understanding how all these changes came about may be the beginning of inventing effective strategies to deal with some of the less desirable side effects. Thus, the weakening of family, religious and neighbourhood bonds may be making people less able to cope with the ordinary vicissitudes of life. Tort law (along with criminal and social law) should learn to handle the consequences of these phenomena not only by reacting to deviance but also by trying to avoid it. This includes not only punishing or ordering the payment of damages for the usual kind of physical injury—on the road, near the pub, in badly policed neighbourhoods—it may require the law to take an attitude towards the more modern and potentially more catastrophic activities of our times. These may emanate from corporations; and regulating their activities—physical as well as financial to minimise abuse stemming from greed—must not be ruled out a priori because powerful financial interests may demand this. In short, dealing with accidents may require a judicious mix of prevention as well as cure; and tort books traditionally only addressed the latter. It may also mean that the problems of tort are not so much caused by trying to help the affected 'little guy' but by being less protective of the large corporation. But this does not mean that the reaction should not be a balanced one.

Take, for instance, toxic torts and widespread pollution. The traditional attempt to deal with this problem though the tort of nuisance is, clearly, inadequate. Zoning laws, planning permission and other preventive regulatory regimes must be combined with traditional criminal or tort sanctions. The academic must strive to find the right balance, unaffected by personal ideologies and pressure from vested economic interests.

Digging in a populous area with a mechanical excavator where cables and pipelines lie beneath the surface of a road is also likely to cause more damage to others than the old-fashioned digging with a pickaxe did one hundred years ago. Likewise, avoiding imposing liability on a local authority for bad 'maintenance' of a highway must proceed on the basis that contemporary roads are sophisticated structures, concealing below their surface, cables, pipes, ducts and other man-made structures, and if a local authority has not maintained all of these properly in a way that causes damage to others, liability should be a possibility. Excluding it on the grounds that the statutes which have imposed liability on local authorities are 'consolidating' statutes, i.e. statutes consolidating existing practice and not envisaging new liabilities, is simply a fig leaf that hides judicial reluctance to expand tort liability. The idea that this liability need be extensive is wrong and it is wrongly invoked as an excuse against the imposition of liability. The experience of other systems, socio-economically similar to ours, shows clearly that the recognition of liability in principle does not mean that it will always be found or that it will be economically crushing.[18] One must, in short, expose the cluster of arguments invoked to avoid liability, all of which have one common and essentially political basis: that regulation harms the working of the market. This is true if it is excessive; but it is also true to attest that the market harms the market when it is left unbridled in its pursuit not of profit but greed.

Another reason for avoiding liability even in principle is the danger that it will open the floodgates of litigation. One of the greatest tort lawyers of the common law—the late Professor Fleming—called this the flagship of the timorous. But it still weighs heavily on judges; and does so in many areas of the law of torts. Thus, not that long ago the Court of Appeal of the Fifth Circuit in the United States was called upon to decide a case of a spillage of a toxic chemical which led to the 'closing' by the authorities of a vast area of the Mississippi estuary. The closure had disastrous effects on the business interests of such local concerns as restaurants, commercial fishermen, cargo-terminal operators and bait and tackle shops.[19] In the event only forty-one suits were brought against the polluter. Presumably, they were 'test' actions; and thousands more might have followed had the original claimants been successful; but one cannot be sure. This was portrayed as a typical example of a 'floodgates' dispute.

Yet once again some of these damage-producing events can be minimised through preventive activity, regulatory control, especially in the financial sector, licensing laws and other such mechanisms. They can also be handled *ex post* through mutually set up funds by operators of modern bulk carriers that will provide out of these funds automatic compensation for harm to people and the environment caused by this massive transportation of goods. This is not going to be cheap; but the profits made by

[18] B. Markesinis and J. Fedtke, 'Authority or Reason? The Economic Consequences of Liability for Breach of Statutory Duty in a Comparative Perspective' [2007] *Eur. Bus. LR* 5.

[19] *State of Louisiana* v. *M/V Testbank*, 752 F 2d 1019 (1985) discussed by Atiyah in (1985) 3 *OJLS* 485.

the industry, the oil industry in particular, are phenomenally large and can carry the consequences of its activities.

At the other end of the spectrum, many of the victims of such mass disasters can more easily and more cheaply carry first party insurance against the feared event occurring than placing the liability on the shoulders of the tortfeasor and thus forcing him to obtain liability insurance which is likely to be more expensive. Householders, for instance, often carry at very low extra cost insurance coverage for power cuts which might affect the contents of their freezers. On the right occasion, the law can, does and should send out clear signals that this should happen more widely.

We shall examine another such case later in this introduction, this time from Canada,[20] and suggest that even if its approach does not commend itself to everyone, it provides a superb teaching tool which can make students think about these problems in different ways. But our system and the prevailing method of legal instruction in most law schools has made such lateral thinking impossible as students are forced to treat the legal concepts they are taught in their classrooms as ways of surmounting a number of legal hurdles. Glance at the editions of the major English tort books twenty or thirty years ago, and you will find none of this new reasoning.

Incidentally, though many of these claims alluded to above involved pure financial loss—a type of harm which, we shall see, causes much concern to common lawyers—this opening of the 'floodgates of litigation' can also occur where personal injury has occurred. Thus, the American manufacturers of the intra-uterine contraceptive device the Dalcon Shield were sued by over 200,000 women—including 4,000 in Britain. They complained of suffering serious pelvic infection, sterility or ectopic pregnancies as a result of a defect in the product (there were also a few instances of death). The product was withdrawn from sale in 1974; by 1985 the manufacturers had been forced into bankruptcy; and by the end of that decade an offer for £1.3 billion had been made to the victims as part of a financial reorganisation plan for the manufacturers.

Similar claims for physical injuries, suffered as a result of, say, defective heart valves, have also been the subject of vast, worldwide settlements. And even more recently, hundreds of thousands of women who had silicone prostheses implanted in their bodies to improve their physical appearance ended up suing Dow Corning for a variety of complaints, some real, others exaggerated. In these cases, no one ever raised the floodgates argument, which makes one wonder whether there is some other reason which makes the 'economic loss' claims so controversial. The increase in tort claims is not only due to our greater ability to cause more and greater harm and our reduced willingness to put up with the normal vicissitudes of life.

Other factors are also at play. Competition among multinational pharmaceuticals leads to the temptation to get a product on the market before it has been thoroughly tested. Gaining such an edge over competition may mean millions if not billions of dollars in gains. Sometimes, however, it also leads to extensive harm, huge compensation claims, many frustrated victims and a few well-paid lawyers. The market brings the best

20 *Norsk Pacific Steamship Co. Ltd.* v. *Canadian National Railway Co.* (1992) 91 DLR (4th) 289.

as well as the worst out of human beings; but finding the right balance seems to have eluded us all up to now.

The greater likelihood and potential magnitude of such losses have also encouraged people to seek to spread them as widely as possible, especially since modern insurance makes it easier to do this.[21] Modern insurance, developed mainly in order to protect defendants, has ended up also assisting and encouraging claimants. Insurance has thus made the imposition of liability more frequent in certain areas of the law—especially traffic accidents and products liability—and has induced some strange twists in traditional concepts as a consequence. As we shall point out below, some authors[22] have criticised this trend and have argued that, in any event, the courts are ill-equipped to undertake such very specialised exercises. Yet, overall, there is no denying the fact that, as a result of modern insurance practices, the notions of 'duty' (and causation) are at times used to conceal insurance dictates and the term 'negligence' is employed in contexts where the defendant could not humanly have avoided the accident in question. Thus, in Section 4 below (and in other parts of this book), we shall be arguing that, despite the difficulties inherent in such exercises, our courts would be well advised (and our students well served) to consider these insurance arguments more openly. For not only has this approach gained acceptance in modern life, whether we like it or not, it also provides a useful tool (along with others) in solving the problems posed by modern tort cases.

Despite these changes in people's expectations—and Mr Weir is right in saying that it is only *reasonable* expectations that should be satisfied—our law is currently in a conservative mode. It seems to be striking at the 'little guy', not the rich corporation. Even more, many would like to see this tort law retrenched even further. However, it would not be at all surprising if this trend were reversed by the time of a new edition of this book. For no tort lawyer can deny the fact that tort law is cyclical, vacillating between adopting the claimant's view and that of the defendant. It always was like that and it will remain so.

The law of tort also faces another crisis. The French refer to this branch as the law of *individual responsibility*; but how much of this area can truly be described as an *individual* responsibility? As a result of insurance and the extension of vicarious liability, a large number of actual wrongdoers, especially drivers and employees, are rarely called upon to meet the consequences of their conduct since these are shouldered by some insurance company or by the employers, usually companies. Today the law of torts is thus largely concerned with the liability of 'innocent absentees'. To some extent this development is inevitable, and even desirable. But it also represents a change of emphasis and direction for the law of torts from a branch of the law conceived to deal with human beings to a complex set of rules regulating impersonal legal entities or the possible

[21] Though in the so-called 'cable cases' (below, Section 3) it is not clear who that person should be, whether the contractor/defendant or the property-owner/plaintiff.

[22] Most recently, J. Stapleton, 'Tort, Insurance and Ideology' (1995) 58 *MLR* 820. Cf. B. Hepple, 'Negligence: The Search for Coherence' (1997) 50 *CLP* 69, esp. at 81 ff.

liability of innocent absentees. As we shall see in Section 5, developments such as these have thrown into doubt the fault basis of tortious liability, though one still finds tort lawyers who are willing to justify most tort rules by reference to rules of morality.[23] To be more precise, while it is right that fault should lead to liability, the converse, that there should be no liability in the absence of fault, is today in doubt. This shift from individual to corporate litigants has also played havoc with our law of defamation. We can summarise this section by saying that tort law is nowadays at a crossroads. In the words of a leading comparative lawyer:

> In some respects people are more responsible than ever. Their capacity to cause damage, as indeed their capacity to come to the aid of their neighbour, has been greatly increased as a result of scientific and technological progress. On the other hand, given the increased importance of social security and insurance, their (individual) responsibility is in decline.[24]

Two more preliminary points need to be made to put what will be found in the following chapters in perspective. The first is general and related to law reform; the second is purely didactic.

Tort law is becoming by the day a more complex set of rules than it ever was, where national law mixes with legal ideas which emanate from foreign jurisdictions. Tort law rules are also becoming intermingled with those from other branches of English law. Equity, criminal law and administrative law are the prime contributors of such rules. Finally, its interrelationship with the complex rules of social security rules is such that only a few tort experts can pronounce on this with any sense of authority. The time when one person could master this entire area of the law once known as tort law has gone and gone forever.

Yet all this pales into insignificance when one starts enquiring about the funding of the system. In one sentence, this, too, is getting out of control. Is this to be solved by limiting the scope or ambit of tort law? Or is it by controlling somehow the level of awardable damage? Or should we place rather more emphasis on procedural rules aiming to devise a simpler, cheaper, quicker way of trying the more routine kind of cases? We know of little contemporary work that has explored empirically the feasibility of the second option; though the Woolf Reforms[25] took some bold and welcome steps in the context of the last of the above-mentioned points. But we do note that over 80 per cent of all claims over, approximately, £250,000 refer to future economic losses. Second, we also know that during the same period (early 2002) only 1 per cent of cases ended with payments in excess of £100,000, yet these resulted in 32 per cent of the total compensation received by claimants.[26] Third, we know that a substantial proportion of the general damages awarded to the claimant are damages for future medical expenses and these tend to increase more rapidly than the inflation rate. Finally, liability insurers

[23] For instance Peter Cane in *The Anatomy of Tort Law* (1997).

[24] Tunc (Select Bibliography), 7.

[25] As a result of *Access to Justice, Final Report* (HMSO 1996).

[26] R. Lewis, 'The Politics and Economics of Tort Law: Judicially Imposed Periodical Payments of Damages' (2006) 69 *MLR* 418, 422.

remain the predominant payers for all awards in excess of £100,000. 'For claims of this size in that year [2001–2] liability insurers paid out more than over £2.26 billion, almost six times as much as the NHS's £0.4 billion.'[27] These are figures that cannot/will not be addressed by the kinds of reforms lawyers, especially academic lawyers, usually talk about. These are figures that one day will call for a new and fundamental review of the future funding of the tort system. Could that be the time we should be preparing for? And should we then be prepared to think seriously of moving out of the tort system and, indeed, the court system the vast majority of accidents which involve minor, self-healing injuries and which, in practice, attract modest awards? It is impossible to predict without empirical studies what this could save in terms of money; but it cannot be in doubt that it could seriously reduce transaction costs, delays in settlements and, just as importantly, time wasted by the courts on matters that do not need a high level of intellectual effort. Though we cannot assess the wisdom of the idea we raise it in the hope that others might decide to explore the issue further.

Second, a supplementary conclusion for the novice reader might be worth voicing. Quite simply it is this: we are in this book dealing with a subject which is so fluid that one could find support, both judicial and academic, for almost any proposition one might wish to put forward. That is why some have accused tort law of being a subject void for uncertainty. We shall be arguing in this book that this uncertainty accounts for the subject's special intellectual fascination. For the litigant, however, it is a cause of great and legitimate concern.

SELECT BIBLIOGRAPHY

ATIYAH, P. S., *The Damages Lottery* (1997).

CANE, P., *Atiyah's Accidents, Compensation and the Law* (7th edn., 2006).

FLEMING, J. G., *An Introduction to the Law of Torts* (2nd edn., 1985), ch. 1.

—*The American Tort Process* (1988), chs. 1, 2 and 4.

HARLOW, C., *Understanding Tort Law* (2nd edn., 1995), chs. 1 and 2.

HEPPLE, B., 'Negligence: The Search for Coherence' (1997) 50 *CLP* 69.

LEWIS, R., 'The Politics and Economics of Tort Law: Judicially Imposed Periodical Payments of Damages' (2006) 69 *MLR* 418.

RABIN, R. L., *Perspectives on Tort Law* (1976).

ROYAL COMMISSION, *On Civil Liability and Compensation for Personal Injury* (The Pearson Committee Report) (Cmnd. 7054–I, 1978), chs. 3 and 4.

TUNC, A., *Int. Enc. Comp. L.* xi, ch. 1, Introduction (updated in French under the title *La Responsabilité civile* (1981)).

WILLIAMS, G. L., and HEPPLE, B. A., *Foundations of the Law of Tort* (2nd edn., 1984).

27 R. Lewis, 'The Politics and Economics of Tort Law: Judicially Imposed Periodical Payments of Damages' (2006) 69 *MLR* 418, 441.

2. TORT AND CONTRACT

It is customary to compare and contrast the notion of tort with those of contract, crime and trust,[28] but little of practical value is gained by the kind of abstract and cursory comparisons often attempted in introductory chapters. To say, for example, that crime and tort share a common past but are now subject to different rules and pursue different aims adds little to knowledge. In any case, compensation and punishment surface when we talk about the purposes of the law of torts and again when we consider penal damages. Given the limitations of space, such discussions can be avoided without much loss and the reader is referred to some of the older editions of tort textbooks for further details. However, the relationship between tort and contract is conceptually more difficult to define and can have important practical implications; it may also help to explain and, perhaps, reinstate some of the tort rules that were formulated mainly in the late 1970s and are currently under attack. For clarity's sake, the material in this section can be divided into three parts: (1) the theoretical division between contract and tort; (2) the escape 'into' tort prompted by a rather rigidly conceived law of contract and the recent resurgence of contract; and (3) the attempt to escape 'out' of contract into the domain of tort.

(A) THE DIVISION BETWEEN CONTRACT AND TORT

In his oft-quoted definition of tortious liability, Winfield laid stress upon the fact that liability in tort arises from the breach of an obligation primarily fixed by law, whereas in contract it is fixed by the parties themselves.[29] This distinction may have been acceptable when contract liability was regarded as stemming from an exchange of promises only and not, as may be the case today, from the mere fact that the claimant has conferred a benefit on the defendant, or has incurred loss by relying upon the latter's behaviour. But basing contractual obligations exclusively on the prior promises of the parties is questioned by some influential modern contract lawyers; and to the extent that this new approach is correct, it makes the division between voluntarily assumed and legally imposed obligations[30] an 'oversimplification' of the issue.

It is not only contract lawyers who doubt this conceptual division. Tort lawyers, too, have experienced difficulties in dealing with certain cases of liability that are regarded as tortious, but in which the duties imposed upon the defendant flow from the fact that he and the claimant have entered into a particular relationship. For example, the

[28] One might also add unjust(ified) enrichment, since its relationship with tort can give rise to interesting areas of overlap. But, as Birks observed: '[t]he bulk of [that] law . . . is not concerned with the menu of remedies available for wrongs but with the causes of action which, not being wrongs, nevertheless entitle a plaintiff to restitution of enrichment received by the defendant at his expense': see his *Civil Wrongs: A New World*, Butterworth Lectures 1990–1 (1992), 109 and, generally, his *Unjust Enrichment* (2nd edn., 2005). An excellent illustration can be found in the case of payment made by mistake. Unjust enrichment gives the claimant the right to recover, but this right is not based on a wrong committed by the defendant. More is said about the relationship with restitutionary remedies in Section 5, below.

[29] *The Province of the Law of Tort* (1931), 32.

[30] Atiyah (Select Bibliography), *passim*.

relationship between an occupier of land and his lawful visitors gives rise to a duty in the former to take care. In the absence of consideration (e.g. payment of a fee), the relationship cannot be regarded as contractual. However, there is an agreement or understanding between the parties in so far as the entrant is permitted to be there, so it is impossible to say that the will of the parties is totally irrelevant to the existence of the obligation to take care. Similarly, the maker of a gratuitous but careless false statement may be liable, partly because he voluntarily undertook to offer advice and partly because the claimant, to his knowledge, relied upon it.[31] The reliance element here plays a crucial role, but since it can be found increasingly both in contract and tort situations it makes the dividing line between these two concepts very vague.[32]

Another reason for scepticism about the decisive role of consent in contract and its absence in tort is that contracts are concluded or avoided on the strength of objective criteria and impersonal considerations. Moreover, even the presumed intention of the parties is losing ground in areas such as frustration where, for a long time, it had exercised considerable influence.[33] Conversely, consent may play an important role in tort, even where there is no overlap with contract. For example, a hurt sustained in the course of sport and in accordance with the rules of the game will not always be actionable. Whether consent can remove tortious liability in all cases of grievous bodily harm is doubtful and one can envisage a number of borderline areas (e.g. emergency surgical operations) that would call for a more cautious answer.[34] Still, consent may in this type of case prevent liability arising in tort.

A subtler approach to this distinction is to say that it is not the *existence* of the duty, but its *content*, that is determined by the law in tort and by the parties in contract. There is a great deal of truth in this, since in a contract for the sale of goods, for example, the quantity, price and other terms will be determined in accordance with the declared or presumed intention of the parties, whereas the duties in tort are fixed by law. Even this variation, however, is not wholly convincing. This is because the content of tort duties can be avoided or varied by means of consent, warnings, etc. (i.e. by some manifestation of the will of the parties). Additionally, an increasing number of statutes require that certain obligations be implied by law in certain contracts, for example sale of goods or hire purchase.[35] In fairness to Winfield, however, it should be pointed out that he said

[31] *Hedley Byrne & Co. Ltd.* v. *Heller and Partners Ltd.* [1964] AC 465. The way we now understand the notions of 'assumption of responsibility' by the defendant and 'reliance' by the plaintiff may have taken this process further, notably by extending liability towards certain third parties. See the discussion of *Henderson* v. *Merrett Syndicates Ltd.* [1995] 2 AC 145 and *White* v. *Jones* [1995] 2 AC 207 in ch. 3, below.

[32] Another area where tort and contract come close to a complete overlap is that of defective products, as is seen most clearly in American and French law. See, generally, J. Stapleton, *Product Liability* (1994) and S. Whittaker, *Liability for Products: English Law, French Law, and European Harmonization* (2005).

[33] Again, similar points about presumed intentions and implied contracts could be made with regard to the history of unjust enrichment and restitutionary remedies in English law: see, generally, P. B. H. Birks's books *An Introduction to the Law of Restitution* (1985, repr. with additions, 1989) and *Unjust Enrichment* (2nd edn., 2005).

[34] P. D. G. Skegg, 'Consent to Medical Proceedings on Minors' (1973) 36 *MLR* 370; *idem.*, 'A Justification for Medical Procedures Performed without Consent' (1974) 90 *LQR* 512.

[35] E.g. Sale of Goods Act 1979, ss. 12–15, 55; Supply of Goods (Implied Terms) Act 1973, ss. 8–11; Unfair Contract Terms Act 1977, s. 20.

only that tortious liability arises out of the breach of a duty *primarily* fixed by law. Hence, even in his day a distinction between tort and contract along the lines we have been discussing was only an approximate one.

Winfield's second distinction, that tort duties are owed to the world at large (duties *in rem*) whereas in contract they are owed to a specific person (*in personam*), also needs careful examination. For although at the primary level, that is to say before a tort has been committed, this distinction is certainly valid, it is of rather academic importance. For a tort comes into existence only where there has been a breach of primary duty, which then brings into play the duty to pay damages, and this is as much *in personam*, i.e. owed to a specific person (the victim), as any contractual duty.

To establish a distinction between the two concepts on the basis of the differences in their avowed aims is perhaps more promising. For this may help to explain, though not necessarily to justify, the reluctance of the common law of tort (a) to impose liability for omissions and (b) to provide compensation for pure economic loss. Thus, tort law primarily aims at protecting life and property, whereas the law of contract is, in a sense, there to promote the further development of a person's interests. As Weir[36] has expressed this idea: '[c]ontract is productive, tort law protective. In other words, tort-feasors are typically liable for making things worse, contractors for not making them better.' If this statement is taken to be descriptive of a certain attitude of the English common law, it is accurate. However, that author's frequently expressed opposition to the use of tort law as a way of compensating negligently inflicted economic loss lends credence to the interpretation that he would also like his readers to take it prescriptively: this is what has been happening *and is how things should remain*. We have here, therefore, a theoretical reason why we should leave the compensation of pure economic loss to contracts, which supports some of the more pragmatic objections (e.g. the 'floodgates' argument) against the compensability through tort of pure financial harm.

One wonders, however, whether economic loss can be really placed so firmly on the one side of this apparently rigid divide. Weir was conscious of the difficulties of his proposed division, so he cautiously added the word 'typically' in his statement. In fact he went further by admitting that 'a man who makes a thing worse is also not making it better'. This, however, does not go far enough since it fails to address another question, namely: 'is a man who is not making a thing better making it in any sense worse?' The reader need not spend much time on these tongue-twisters but should merely reflect on some of the cases that we will encounter later on. In the legal malpractice situation, has the intended beneficiary who has through the lawyer's negligence lost the benefit of the will made by the testator been made poorer or not made richer? Similarly in the construction type of contract, which was at the basis of the *Junior Books* v. *Veitchi Co. Ltd.*[37] litigation, has the negligence of the subcontractor that has affected the employer made the latter poorer or has it merely failed to make him richer? The same doubts can be raised in the context of shipping cases such as *The Aliakmon*[38]—discussed in Chapter 3—and thus make one wonder about the universal validity of the proposed basis for distinction.

[36] Weir (Select Bibliography), 5. [37] [1983] 1 AC 520. [38] [1986] AC 785.

Still, it is reasoning such as the above (and historical reasons coupled with nineteenth-century ideological beliefs) that also accounts for another important tort rule, namely that, statute apart, contract alone can create affirmative duties of action.[39] For contract's avowed aim to promote the claimant's desire to increase his wealth can explain why a defendant who has promised to do something in this respect will be made to pay damages if he fails to keep his promise. A glance at contract textbooks, however, will show that contract law protects not only expectations, but also reliance interests; and, as stated, Weir's formulation refers to tortfeasors being *typically* liable for making things worse and contractors *typically* liable for not making things better. We are, in other words, again talking of the traditional paradigm contract[40]—the executory sale—where failure by the seller to deliver the goods will deprive the buyer of a gain. This approach, however, fails to pay adequate heed to the case which is both breach of contract and a tort, for example, a dentist who has extracted the wrong tooth or a carrier who has damaged the goods being transported. Where contractual liability is imposed because of detrimental reliance by the claimant, the latter is likely to complain that he is left worse off rather than not being made richer. Can it really be said that where there is such overlap between tort and contract the solution should in all instances be governed by formal categories shaped by tradition and that the claimant's rights should depend upon whether his action was framed in the one branch or the other? An affirmative answer does not commend itself; and it becomes ludicrous when one remembers that until recently the choice between the contractual or tortious set of rules was determined in a manner which, though historically explicable,[41] was little short of being capricious. The recent tendency to allow claimants a choice between the contractual or tortious remedies[42] must be seen as a move towards attenuating the difference between contract and tort. The even more recent attempt to assimilate the rules on remoteness of damage in certain cases[43] could also be seen in the same light. Yet, as we shall see, the judicial pronouncements do not all point in one direction and there undoubtedly exist different tendencies among different judges.

Why then, in view of these doubts, are contract and tort still kept so rigidly apart? A number of explanations could be offered. The first is that traditional thinking takes time to wear out.[44] Moreover, extensive government intervention in the economy is a comparatively modern phenomenon.[45] The inevitable time lag between political and

39 The historical reasons behind this distinction are examined by S. F. C. Milsom, 'Not Doing Is No Trespass' [1954] *CLJ* 105.

40 Not now accepted by everyone: see Atiyah (Select Bibliography).

41 See Poulton (Select Bibliography).

42 *Esso Petroleum Co. Ltd.* v. *Mardon* [1976] QB 801, 819; *Batty* v. *Metropolitan Property Realizations Ltd.* [1978] QB 554, 566; *Midland Bank Trust Co. Ltd.* v. *Hett, Stubbs & Kemp* [1979] Ch. 384; *Henderson* v. *Merrett Syndicates Ltd.* [1995] 2 AC 145.

43 *Parsons (Livestock) Ltd.* v. *Uttley Ingham & Co. Ltd.* [1978] QB 791.

44 This is a theme of a series of essays by A. Watson, *Society and Legal Change* (1977). A. W. B. Simpson, in his most readable *Invitation to Law* (1988), 85, states most appositely: '[w]ays in which the law was classified in the past tend to persist, even though they may not be ideal for the conditions of today. . . . For everything in the law, like everything in literature, is affected by the past.'

45 Weir (Select Bibliography), 4.

social change, on the one hand, and consequential change in the law, on the other, may partly explain the slowness of the reaction against the traditional schematisation. A second and more technical reason is that, despite the modern tendency to accept that at the *primary* level the frontier between the two notions is no longer that clear, at the *secondary* level (i.e. that of consequences) the law still contains a number of different rules for contract and tort. Two can be mentioned here briefly, though others do exist.[46]

The first is that the period of time after which a cause of action is barred starts to run in contract from the moment of the conduct constituting breach, whereas in tort it starts to run from the, often much later, moment when the claimant sustains his damage. The second rule relates to the service of writs outside the jurisdiction.[47] Such service depends upon permission being granted by the High Court and the Rules of the Supreme Court generally make it easier to obtain leave to serve a writ outside the jurisdiction if an action is framed in contract rather than in tort.

Another reason advanced in favour of keeping separate the treatment of contract and tort has that the fusion of the two notions would create an 'unmanageably large' course and, by implication, an unmanageably large book. This is true. But quite apart from the fact that a pedagogic reason of this kind should not impede the development of the law, the fact remains that the value of such 'pragmatic' objections can also be exaggerated. For, first, one is not necessarily talking of a complete overlap of the two breaches of the law of obligations. Thus, some sections of contract, for example, offer and acceptance, need have no place in such a course. Second, a book need not be exhaustive. This is self-evident, though it must, at least, lay down the right signposts warning its readers of the uncertain boundaries of its subject. Thus, we shall note further down that this is not the only frontier area of tort law that is vague. The old jurisdictional battles between common law and equity have also left outside the area of tort many 'wrongs' that have for traditional reasons been handled by the law of trusts—typically the area of constructive trusts, although in the privacy sphere it is clear that the vehicle of choice for developing protection in recent years has been the equitable doctrine of breach of confidence. But let us return to the relation between contract and tort that is the main focus of this discussion.

It is arguable that a more unified approach in one book (and one course) would be of benefit to the student (and, even, practitioner)—even at the price of losing some detail. For example, let us not forget the difficulties that have resulted from the fact that both courts and the legislature have shared this traditional division of the law of obligations. One has only to see the changes in the law concerning negligent statements to see how these two agents of law reform approached the problem independently and with little effort to co-ordinate the new sets of rules. It is submitted, therefore, that a rigid distinction between

[46] For instance, the range of remedies is greater for breach of contract than for the commission of a tort; the measure of damages is different for these two notions; the liability of the Crown is wider in contract than it is in tort; conversely, in the case of minors public authorities' tortious liability can be more extensive than their liability in contract. But in practice it is the two procedural issues discussed in the text above which have tested most the attempt to bring the two notions closer to one another.

[47] Civil Procedure Rules, r. 6.20(5)–(7) (contract) and (8) (tort).

contract and tort, and their separate exposition in separate courses, is becoming unfashionable and inadvisable. As stated, however, this applies only to those aspects where there is overlap. Where none exists, contract and tort must continue to be treated separately. In the remaining part of this section we shall thus focus on two particular ways in which the interaction between contract and tort has taken place. When many of these cases come up for reconsideration in Part II (on negligence) the reader would be well advised to bear these preliminary points in mind.

In the first group of cases, the courts are discovering tort duties where they could be promoting contractual solutions. Here the flight 'into tort' is taking place simply because the tort rules provide the least resistance to the creation of a remedy which the court's 'sense of justice' requires. It could be strongly argued that in most of these cases the less 'open-ended' contract law would have provided the better peg on which to hang the legal solution demanded by justice and proposed by our courts. However, the rigidity of the doctrine of consideration made this impossible. So tort has been 'stretched' to make up for the rigidity of contract. But this subterfuge should not surprise us. For our tort law is accustomed to performing this residual, gap-filling role, as Lord Devlin himself acknowledged in precisely this context in his classic judgment in *Hedley Byrne & Co.* v. *Heller & Partners*.[48]

In the second group of cases we see the reverse. There is an attempt by the claimant to 'escape' into tort as a way of going 'beyond' what has been agreed in the contract. This is a far more problematic area of the law; and the dangers of abusing the advantages of a flexible approach towards the problem of demarcation are considerable. To make matters worse, the proposed division between these two types of cases is not waterproof. It is also fair to admit to the reader the fact that the multiple *dicta* on the subject are irreconcilable. While this will not come as a surprise to seasoned tort lawyers, students may find it disconcerting to be warned of such uncertainty in such a crucial area of the law of negligence. Yet false certainty is bad certainty. For, as Birks remarked, '[w]hen people follow a course, their vision is forever affected by what they are told at the start'.[49] The decisions typically advocated by textbooks have not so much formed the legal mind over decades as sometimes deceived it into underdevelopment.

(B) THE ESCAPE 'INTO' TORT PROMPTED BY A RIGIDLY CONCEIVED LAW OF CONTRACT

Traditionally, in common law systems a person cannot enforce a promise that is not under seal unless he can show that he (the promisee) has suffered some detriment or, conversely, that he has conferred some benefit on the promisor. For this purpose, mutual promises of future performance are deemed to be sufficient. This is the

48 [1964] AC 465, though from time to time academic lawyers forget this and suggest that other parts of the law (e.g. the law of succession) might serve as a better vehicle for law reform. Thus, see J. A. Weir, 'The *Damnosa Hereditas*' (1995) 111 *LQR* 357, and for criticism of this see S. M. Cretney, 'Negligent Solicitors and Wills: A Footnote' (1996) 112 *LQR* 54.

49 *Civil Wrongs: A New World*, Butterworth Lectures 1990–1 (1992), 110.

requirement of *consideration* that evinces the presence of a bargain, which according to traditional thinking at least, justifies the enforcement of promises. One important side effect of this is that a person who is not a 'party' to the bargain, in the sense of having personally given consideration, cannot enforce it. Strict adherence to this notion by the English (but not American) common law thus meant that contracts in favour of third parties were not valid in the sense that they gave no rights to the third party to demand that the promisor carried out his promise. This rather rigid structuring of the English law of contract, explicable though it is in historical terms, contrasted sharply with other (e.g. modern European and Commonwealth) systems. More importantly, it accounts for some interesting fluctuations in the boundaries between contract and tort—hence the inclusion of this topic in the present discussion.

Generally speaking, one could say that in earlier times contract used to expand to make up for the fact that tort law was still in a state of (relative) infancy. In *De La Bere* v. *Pearson Ltd.*,[50] for example, the defendants advertised in their newspaper that their finance editor was willing to answer relevant inquiries by the readers. The plaintiff asked for the name of a stockbroker and was inadvertently given that of an undischarged bankrupt who misappropriated the plaintiff's money. A contractual action against the defendants succeeded even though it is by no means obvious that the doctrine of consideration was satisfied. In reality the presence of a contract was assumed, for without it the plaintiff would have been without a remedy. On other occasions contracts were discovered during the pre-contractual phase when, by definition, there should not be one. So in *Dick Bentley Productions Ltd.* v. *Harold Smith (Motors) Ltd.*[51] the plaintiffs told the defendants that they were looking for a 'well-vetted' car. The defendants showed them a Bentley with an (apparently) low mileage (20,000 miles) which the plaintiffs bought. The statement as to the mileage turned out to be false, the car was unsatisfactory, so the plaintiffs claimed and were awarded damages for breach of contract. The difficulty about this case was that the statement on which the claim was based was made prior to the conclusion of the contract; and it was by no means clear that it had been turned into a contractual term. Salmon LJ overcame the difficulty by arguing that:

> In effect [the defendant had] said: 'If you enter into a contract to buy this motor car from me . . . I undertake that you will be getting a motor car which has done no more than twenty thousand miles since it was fitted with a new engine and new gearbox.' This device is known as a 'collateral contract'.[52]

Contract theory was here advancing into the pre-contractual phase achieving results almost identical to those of a negligence action.[53] In yet other instances, contracts have been invented in order to extend to third parties the operation of contractual exemption clauses;[54] or in order to correct the defect of specific legislative provisions such as

50 [1908] 1 KB 280.
51 [1965] 1 WLR 623.
52 *Ibid.*, 629.
53 See *Esso Petroleum* v. *Mardon* [1976] QB 801.
54 *New Zealand Shipping Co. Ltd.* v. *A. M. Satterthwaite and Co. Ltd. (The Eurymedon)* [1975] AC 154.

section 1 of the Bills of Lading Act 1855.[55] Finally, contractual reasoning was employed in what, in today's terms, would be described as a product liability case to make the manufacturer of a product which did not possess the advertised qualities liable to its ultimate purchaser.[56] Other cases—typically of more recent vintage—have revealed the opposite trend: a preference for hanging the solution on the peg(s) of the law of torts which, as we shall note in the next chapter, has witnessed in the post-war years an unprecedented growth. *De la Bere*'s case, for example, would nowadays almost certainly be handled as a tort case falling under the rule in *Hedley Byrne & Co. Ltd.* v. *Heller & Partners Ltd.*[57] Other examples where the plaintiff succeeded in tort include *Ross* v. *Caunters*[58] and *Junior Books Ltd.* v. *Veitchi Co. Ltd.*[59] and, of course, the offshoots of *Donoghue* v. *Stevenson*,[60] which switched the entire law of product liability from contract to tort.[61] *Leigh and Sillivan Ltd.* v. *The Aliakmon Shipping Co. Ltd.* (*The Aliakmon*),[62] on the other hand, offers an intriguing but unsuccessful attempt by the plaintiff to base his action in tort. The non-availability of a contractual answer in this case led to the kind of vacuum which legal systems dislike and, in the event, a statutorily-based solution.[63] All of these cases will be discussed in greater detail in Chapter 3, below, as they form part of the complicated fabric of the law of negligence in the 1980s. Here we shall limit our observations to a few comments relevant to the topic under discussion, namely the relationship between contract and tort. Student readers, however, may be well advised to reconsider these comments after they have read the text of Chapter 3.

Ross v. *Caunters* [64] offers a good illustration.[65] In that case a solicitor was hired by a testator to prepare his will. He did so and sent it to him for execution, failing to warn him that the will would be invalid if witnessed by the spouse of one of the beneficiaries. This is precisely what occurred and, when the plaintiff was deprived of the benefits under the will, he sued the solicitor for his admitted negligence. Sir Robert Megarry V-C gave judgment for the plaintiff, relying upon the wider *dicta* of *Donoghue* v. *Stevenson* [66] rather than the narrower rule in *Hedley Byrne & Co. Ltd.* v. *Heller & Partners Ltd.*[67] The differences between the two will be explained in Chapter 3. Here suffice it to say that the successful course of action was framed in tort. The same result (but through different reasoning) was more recently reached by the House of Lords in *White* v. *Jones*.[68] A contractual approach would have avoided the open-endedness of the notion of duty of care. It would also have ensured that any exemption clauses available to

[55] *Brandt* v. *Liverpool Brazil and River Plate Steam Navigation Co.* [1924] 1 KB 575.

[56] *Carlill* v. *Carbolic Smoke Ball Co.* [1892] 2 QB 484; [1893] 1 QB 256.

[57] [1964] AC 465. [58] [1980] Ch. 297.

[59] [1983] 1 AC 520. [60] [1932] AC 562.

[61] That the law of product liability could have gone down the contractual (instead of tort) path can be seen from most of the early decisions on the subject both in the USA (which started from the common-law position) and French law (which was unencumbered by consideration) and chose to base its early product liability law on an expanded notion of the contract of sale. [62] [1986] AC 785.

[63] Carriage of Goods by Sea Act 1992. See, also, the discussion in B. S. Markesinis and H. Unberath, *The German Law of Torts: A Comparative Treatise* (4th edn., 2002), 303.

[64] [1980] Ch. 297. [65] As does the much maligned decision in *Junior Books* v. *Veitchi* [1983] 1 AC 520.

[66] [1932] AC 562. [67] [1964] AC 465. [68] [1995] 2 AC 207.

protect the negligent attorney/promisor in a (possible) action by his client (promisee) would have also protected him in an action by the plaintiff (third-party beneficiary).[69] Finally, it would have avoided the criticisms levelled against the majority judgment for using the (vague) notion of 'assumption of responsibility'. But for practical reasons the case was not pleaded in contract; and it was, clearly, decided in tort. For present purposes, however, these cases are particularly illuminating examples of the thesis advanced in this section: if considerations of justice require that a remedy be found, and one cannot be based on contract because of the rigidity engendered by the doctrine of consideration, then our courts will be tempted to resort to tort in order to fill the vacuum.[70] Academic purists are then left to vent their disagreement in learned journals in the hope that next time around they might bring greater doctrinal clarity to a subject that remains so endearingly casuistic.

Of course, this thesis is subject to modification as and when the rules of contract law are relaxed, either by judicial interpretation or legislative intervention. Recent years have, indeed, seen examples in both of these categories which will bring some reduction in the frequency of 'escapes' into tort with regard to claims for economic loss in the tort of negligence.

The first important development to consider is legislative: the enactment of the Contracts (Rights of Third Parties) Act 1999 has allowed the third party to bring a direct action in contract against the promisor.[71] This amounts to the introduction of a further exception to the doctrine of privity of contract and operates most clearly where the parties to the contract expressly confer a benefit on the third party (s. 1(1)(a)).

[69] In one sense, the crux of these decisions is not so much whether the defendant (solicitor, subcontractor in the *Junior Books* case) should be liable towards the claimant (third-party beneficiary or site-owner), but whether he should be made to pay more to him than he would have had to pay had he been successfully sued by his co-contractor (testator, main contractor). This point was clearly identified by Goff LJ (as he then was) in his judgment in *The Aliakmon* in the Court of Appeal. A contractual explanation (some kind of contract in favour of third parties) solves this problem instantly. For in such contracts the promisor (attorney, subcontractor) can rely against the third party (beneficiary, site-owner) upon all the exemptions and defences that he has against the promisee (testator, contractor). The contractual explanation also helps to ensure that the nature of the relationship between claimant and defendant (in our examples owner/subcontractor, beneficiary/lawyer) is the same (contractual rather than tortious) as that of the defendant and his co-contractor (in our examples subcontractor/contractor, lawyer/testator). For if the two sets of relationships were different then they might be subject to different rules concerning such matters as jurisdiction, damages, limitation period, liability for omissions, and many others. These points have yet to receive proper consideration by our highest court.

[70] Some authors have argued that the solution to the problem of the disappointed, intended legatee should be found in the law of succession. Thus, J. A. Weir, 'A *Damnosa Hereditas*' (1995) 111 *LQR* 357. There may be something in this idea *de lege ferenda*; but *de lege lata* it does not seem to be supportable. See the remarks in S. M. Cretney, 'Negligent Solicitors and Wills: A Footnote' (1996) 112 *LQR* 54–5. Thus, not for the first time, our law of torts has been called upon to rectify the deficiencies—real or perceived—in different parts of our private law.

[71] A full discussion of this Act is not appropriate here. The reader is referred, *inter alia*, to the following sources for further discussion: A.S. Burrows, 'The Contracts (Rights of Third Parties) Act 1999 and the Implications for Commercial Contracts' [2000] *LMCLQ* 540; M. Dean, 'Removing a Blot on the Landscape: The Reform of the Doctrine of Privity' [2000] *JBL* 143; and T. Roe, 'Contractual Intention under Section 1(1)(b) and 1(2) of the Contracts (Rights of Third Parties) Act 1999' (2000) 63 *MLR* 887. For comparative consideration, see B.S. Markesinis, H. Unberath and A. Johnston, *The German Law of Contract: A Comparative Treatise* (2006), 181–6 and, generally, ch. 4.

Section 1(1)(b), however, would seem to be of much wider application: under it, a third party can enforce the contract where the relevant contractual term 'purports to confer a benefit on him'. Without more, this could conceivably cover a very wide range of situations in which a third party might be said to be benefited by such a contract, in the sense that the defective performance of the contract might *affect* the third party (such as in the *White* v. *Jones* scenario).[72] However, the 1999 Act goes on to clarify that section 1(1)(b) 'does not apply if on a proper construction of the contract it appears that the parties did not intend the term to be enforceable by the third party': this reflects the evident intention of the Law Commission to exclude situations where the contract is merely 'incidentally of benefit' to the third party.[73] It thus seems that this will exclude most of the tort cases on negligent misstatements from the ambit of the 1999 Act so that, while the impact of the Act will be significant, it will not allow an action in contract to all third parties whose interests are affected by the defective performance of a contract. As a result, tort cases such as *White* v. *Jones* and *Henderson* v. *Merrett Syndicates*[74] will remain crucial in the establishment of any such liability towards many third parties. Nevertheless, it is clear that this expansion of contract law may render the escape into tort less attractive and, indeed, less frequently necessary.

The second major development in the contract sphere concerns the availability of a remedy for a promisee in respect of a loss which has actually been suffered by a third party. The case law is discussed in more detail in Chapter 3,[75] but is clearly key to any assessment of the evolving relationship between contract and tort, especially since the developments have taken place in the field of the construction industry and are (at least to some extent) a direct result of the retreat from negligence in *Murphy* v. *Brentwood District Council*.[76] This is because, prior to that case, third parties to a building contract (for instance third party purchasers) could often avail themselves of the *Anns* type of remedy and recover pure economic loss in tort. One way around the *Murphy* decision was, where possible, to get a 'duty of care deed' signed by all the parties, including the third party who would not otherwise have been a party to the original contract. This granted a direct action for the third party against the builder for defects in the building, and thus could avoid difficult questions of privity or the extension of the tort of negligence. These more recent cases,[77] however, have allowed a contractual claim to lie against the builder of the building at the suit of a promisee claimant who did not own the development site at the time at which the breach of the building contract occurred (such as subsequent purchasers or tenants). However, in *Panatown* the majority in the House of Lords then went on to deny recovery to that promisee under the original contract where the third party would have been able to maintain an action in its own

[72] [1995] 2 AC 207.

[73] See Law Commission, *Privity of Contract: Contracts for the Benefit of Third Parties*, No. 242 (Cm. 3329, 1996), paras. 7.17–7.52, esp. para. 7.25, n. 22.

[74] [1995] 2 AC 145.

[75] See below, ch. 3, Section 3(c).

[76] [1991] 1 AC 398.

[77] *St Martins Property Construction* v. *Sir Robert McAlpine Ltd.* [1994] 1 AC 85 (HL) (*St Martins*), *Darlington BC* v. *Wiltshier Northern Ltd.* [1995] 1 WLR (CA) and *Alfred McAlpine Construction Ltd.* v. *Panatown Ltd.* [2001] 1 AC 518 (HL) (*Panatown*).

right under the duty of care deed. The loss which is being compensated in these cases could be characterised as that of the third party (in that it is that party which will have to pay the cost of curing any defects in the building) or that of the promisee claimant (in that he did not get what he bargained for under the contract—a building according to the contractual specifications—and thus did suffer damage in his own right).[78] If the latter interpretation is the correct one then it is somewhat difficult to see why the existence of the duty of care deed in favour of the third party should affect the promisee's right to sue the builder under the original contract.

Thus, post-*Murphy*, English law appears to be undergoing something of a renaissance in the utility of contractual principles to deal with difficult three-party situations. However, it is as well to note that the interrelationship between tort and contract principles has by no means run all one way in the past twenty years. Some areas that were traditionally covered by contract were never relinquished to tort: carriage of goods remained resolutely contractual in flavour, despite the attempts of Robert Goff LJ (as he then was) in *The Aliakmon*—this position was underlined by the statutory developments in that area in 1992. Furthermore, these new developments in contract law, while adding welcome flexibility and responsiveness to the law's armoury, would not seem to apply to some of the most awkward three-party situations which have, until now, been treated under tort law: i.e. negligent misstatements. In Chapter 3, the complex case law on *Hedley Byrne* and its progeny is discussed in depth: these recent contractual developments, it is submitted, have not diminished the importance of the tort case law in this area, although the increased willingness to find flexible solutions may yet presage a further realignment in the contract–tort relationship in the future. There remains room for significant development and for learning from the experience of other jurisdictions in dealing with similar problems—and our highest courts have shown themselves increasingly open to hearing and using such material.[79]

(C) THE ESCAPE 'OUT' OF CONTRACT AND INTO THE DOMAIN OF TORT

It is here that the contract–tort overlap has proved even more complicated; and wide *dicta* from some judges have not, it is submitted, helped to clarify matters. For example, in *Tai Hing Cotton Mill Ltd.* v. *Liu Chong Hing Bank Ltd.*[80] Lord Scarman maintained that:

> Their Lordships [did] not believe that there [was] anything to the advantage of the law's development in searching for a liability in tort where the parties are in a contractual relationship.

[78] For the latter view, see Lord Griffiths in *St Martins* [1994] 1 AC 85 and Lord Goff in *Panatown* [2001] 1 AC 518.

[79] For further discussion of the *Panatown* case, see B. Coote, 'The Performance Interest, *Panatown* and the Problem of Loss' (2001) 117 *LQR* 81, G. H. Treitel, 'Damages in Respect of a Third Party's Loss' (1998) 114 *LQR* 527, I. N. D. Wallace, 'Third Party Damage: No Legal Black Hole?' (1999) 115 *LQR* 394 and H. Unberath, 'Third Party Losses and Black Holes: Another View' (1999) 115 *LQR* 535. For further and comparative discussion, see B. S. Markesinis and H. Unberath, *The German Law of Torts: A Comparative Treatise* (4th edn., 2002), esp. 59–67, 300–6 and 330–9.

[80] [1986] AC 80, 107.

This was a bank–customer dispute, and his Lordship was eager to stress that his above-quoted comment was 'particularly' apt to commercial relationships. But unfortunately, it is submitted, later judgments seemed to have paid less attention to this proviso. So, in *Johnstone* v. *Bloomsbury Health Authority*[81] Sir Nicolas Browne-Wilkinson (as he then was) felt that the *Tai Hing* case showed that where there is a contractual relationship between the parties their respective rights and duties *have to be* analysed wholly in contractual terms and not as a mixture of duties in tort and contract.[82] Below, when we discuss the case in the context of the employer's liability towards his employees,[83] we shall argue that this approach, *in the context of that type of relationship*, may be particularly dangerous. For, if accepted and taken to its logical extremes, it could completely displace the law of employers' liabilities and put their employees at a disadvantage that may not be acceptable to modern society. In other words, the principle that in *commercial* transactions the contractual allocation of risks should not be disturbed by a subsequent escape 'out of contract' and 'into tort' (as has happened in many instances and with unfortunate consequences in the United States[84]) may be fully acceptable.[85] The same is true where the claimant is attempting to expand the defendant's duties beyond what is envisaged both by the express and implied terms of the contract *and* the accepted boundaries of the law of torts. So, in *Reid* v. *Rush & Tompkins Group plc*[86] an attempt to saddle employers with tortious liability for failing to provide their employee (who was working overseas) with personal accident insurance[87] was not successful, since no such duty arose from contract nor could it be based on any existing tort rule. But the escape out of the contract regime into tort may be justifiable in other contexts where what one could call 'public policy' arguments would not favour the exclusion by the law of contract of rules deriving from the existing general law.[88] Another area where Lord Scarman's pronouncement may also carry less weight (and, thus, recourse to the potentially more generous tort rules may be allowed) is that of concurrent contractual and tortious liability. This could be especially significant in the context of relationships between professionals and clients, for example, solicitors,[89] doctors,[90] insurance brokers[91] and the like; and this position does not seem to have been undermined by wider *dicta* in such important House of Lords' decisions as *Pirelli*[92] and

[81] [1992] 1 QB 333. [82] *Ibid.*, 350 (emphasis added). [83] See ch. 18, below.

[84] For a brief discussion see J. G. Fleming, *The American Tort Process* (1988), *passim*.

[85] E.g. *National Bank of Greece SA* v. *Pinios Shipping Co. (No. 1)* [1989] 3 WLR 185 (reversed on grounds not affecting this point: [1990] 1 AC 627), *Bank of Nova Scotia* v. *Hellenic Mutual War Risks Association (Bermuda) Ltd.* [1990] 1 QB 818; cf. *Canadian Pacific Hotels Ltd.* v. *Bank of Montreal* (1988) 40 DLR (4th) 385.

[86] [1989] 3 All ER 228.

[87] Or, alternatively, to advise him to obtain such insurance himself.

[88] The aforementioned *Johnstone* case offers an example. The same justification can be found in cases dealing with the liability of professionals (discussed in the next para. in the text) for, as was correctly observed in *Clerk and Lindsell on Torts* (18th edn., 2000): '[i]t is highly unlikely that most plaintiffs in any sense voluntarily agree to forfeit such a benefit [i.e. deriving from the tort rules] when they enter into the relevant contract'.

[89] *Midland Bank Trust Co. Ltd.* v. *Hett, Stubbs & Kemp* [1979] Ch. 384.

[90] *Thake* v. *Maurice* [1986] QB 644.

[91] *Youell* v. *Bland Welch & Co. Ltd. (No. 2)* [1990] 2 Lloyd's Rep. 431, 459.

[92] *Pirelli General Cable Works Ltd.* v. *Oscar Faber and Partners* [1983] 2 AC 1.

Murphy.[93] On the contrary, the concurrence rule was reaffirmed by the House of Lords in the important decision of *Henderson* v. *Merrett Syndicates Ltd.*[94] where Lord Goff said that:

> . . . in the present context, the common law is not antipathetic to concurrent liability and . . . there is no sound basis for a rule which automatically restricts the claimant to either a tortious or a contractual remedy. The result may be untidy; but given that the tortious duty is imposed by the general law, and the contractual duty is attributable to the will of the parties, I do not find it objectionable that the claimant may be entitled to take advantage of the remedy which is most advantageous to him, subject only to ascertaining whether the tortious duty is so inconsistent with the applicable contract that, in accordance with ordinary principle, the parties must be taken to have agreed that the tortious remedy is to be limited or excluded.[95]

SELECT BIBLIOGRAPHY

Atiyah, P. S., 'Contracts, Promises and the Law of Obligations' (1978) 94 *LQR* 93.

Bartlett, A. V. B., 'Concurrent Liability after *Murphy*' (1991) 7 *PN* 20.

Burrows, A., 'Solving the Problem of Concurrent Liability' [1995] *CLP* 103 ff.

Fridman, G. H. L., 'The Interaction of Tort and Contract' (1977) 93 *LQR* 422.

Guest, A. G., 'Tort or Contract?' (1961) 3 *Malaya LR* 191.

Hadden, T., 'Contract, Tort and Crime: The Forms of Legal Thought' (1971) 87 *LQR* 40.

Holyoak, J., 'Tort and Contract after *Junior Books*' (1983) 99 *LQR* 591.

—'Concurrent Liability in Tort and Contract' (1990) 6 *PN* 113.

Markesinis, B. S., 'An Expanding Tort Law: The Price of a Rigid Contract Law' (1987) 103 *LQR* 354.

—'Doctrinal Clarity in Tort Litigation' (1992) 25(1) *The International Lawyer* 953–66.

Poulton, W. D. C., 'Tort or Contract' (1966) 82 *LQR* 346.

Reynolds, F., 'Tort Actions in Contractual Situations' (1985) II *NZULR* 215.

Weir, J. A., 'Complex Liabilities' in Zweigert, K. and Droknig, U. (eds.), *International. Encyclopedia of Comparative Law* (1976), xi, ch. 12.

Winfield, P. H., *The Province of the Law of Tort* (1931).

—'The Foundation of Liability in Tort' (1927) 27 *Col. LR* 1 (repr. in *Select Legal Essays*, 3 (1952)).

93 *Murphy* v. *Brentwood District Council* [1992] 1 AC 378.

94 [1995] 2 AC 145 at 93–4. The reasoning of Oliver J (as he then was) in *Midland Bank Trust Co.* v. *Hett, Stubbs & Kemp* [1979] Ch. 384 was reaffirmed and the ambit of the Scarman *dicta* from *Tai Hing* further circumscribed.

95 *Concurrent* thus does not imply that the two sets of duties (arising from contract and tort) will also be *co-extensive*; and it is precisely because the tort duty may be wider than the contract duty that the claimant may wish to rely upon it in preference to the contractual duty. This will be allowed provided there is nothing in the contract excluding such a tortious duty. See *Holt* v. *Payne Skillington (a firm)*, *The Times*, 22 Dec. 1995.

3. ELEMENTS OF WRONGDOING AND THE ROLE OF POLICY

The phrase 'law of contract' refers to the characteristics shared by every contract and not to the details of different types of contract. It is not possible to speak of a 'law of torts' in a similar sense. Though every tort is the breach of some legal duty, this gives little indication of the requirements of any particular tort. 'Duty' means a prohibition of a certain form of behaviour in a given kind of situation (e.g. you ought not to injure a person by a careless act, which means that the law recognises that there *could* be liability in a given kind of situation). 'Breach of duty' is constituted by the defendant's conduct violating this prohibition, which generally (but not always) has to be blameworthy in some way.

In view of these vagaries, therefore, it might be thought appropriate to speak of a 'law of torts' rather than a 'law of tort', for there is no common set of characteristics which every tort has to possess. A few torts are complete without damage, for example, trespass and libel. These are said to be actionable *per se* and the absence of damage is not relevant to liability since, in these instances, the prime function of tort law is to vindicate private rights and not necessarily to compensate the victim. (Of course, if the victim has suffered actual damage he will also be awarded damages.) Other torts are complete without fault (blameworthiness) although, as we shall see, liability without fault remains the exception rather than the rule.

The majority of torts are complete and compensation must be made when there is conduct, causation, fault and damage—an equation enshrined in a programmatic way in the famous Article 1382 of the French Civil Code. What each of these elements means will be discussed as we proceed in appropriate sections of this book: it will suffice here to make two general points with regard to conduct.

The first is that 'conduct' covers acts and omissions. An act in law is a bodily movement controllable by will, sometimes described as 'voluntary', as opposed to an unwilled movement that is involuntary. 'Voluntary' does not connote willingness, but only controllability. It is a basic element of liability that an act should be voluntary in this sense. Thus, in one case a man who was carried onto the plaintiff's land did not act and so was not liable in trespass; whereas a man who was induced by threats to do so was liable because, although he acted under threat, his mind still controlled his movement.[96] The second point is that the common law, unlike the modern civil-law systems, has, up to now, evinced a marked reluctance to assimilate liability for omissions into liability for wrongful acts. The matter will be discussed more fully in Chapter 3, where it presents its greater interest, though it is also of importance to the law of nuisance.

With regard to fault—which, incidentally, is not a term of art in English law—one should note that it assumes three forms: malice, intention (including recklessness) and

[96] Compare *Smith* v. *Stone* (1647) Style 65; 82 ER 533 (not liable) and *Gilbert* v. *Stone* (1647) Style 72; 82 ER 539 (liable).

negligence. The first, the most reprehensible state of mind, has assumed different meanings in different contexts, but it could broadly be equated to spite. Only a few torts make malice an ingredient of liability, though proof of it in others can increase the claimant's compensation, while in some torts, for example defamation, it can negate one of the accepted defences. Intention signifies the state of mind of a person who foresees and desires a particular result (or is deemed to have foreseen and desired an inevitable result). It is often bracketed with recklessness where the actor foresees, but does not desire, a particular result that is not regarded as inevitable.

Negligence, discussed in Chapter 3, in one sense refers to the state of mind of a person who fails to advert to the foreseeable consequences of his conduct, as a reasonable man would have done. In another sense it refers to careless behaviour, which is the failure to act as a reasonable man who, having foreseen the consequences, would have acted. Yet a third use of 'negligence' denotes a separate tort of that name (and, in this book, whenever confusion might arise over the use of the term in this sense, we have capitalised the word). It is with the last two meanings that the law of tort is mainly concerned. These terms are not always used in the same way or with precision by writers or by courts and the student should learn to understand the meaning of each term in its context.

English law, unlike other systems, does not recognise gross (or very bad) negligence; and equating this with recklessness is, for the reasons already given, not conceptually possible. Yet there are times when the defendant's conduct is not just bad but repeatedly bad. When he is not guilty of the kind of lapse of attention which afflicts us all, but keeps doing the wrong thing over and over again. Should not the law treat such persons differently? Some systems do, for instance, the French using the term *faute lourde.* Though it might be breaking with tradition, there might be something to be said in favour of making some use of a notion shaped along these lines; indeed Lord Bingham has come close to hinting that he would favour something along these lines in order to express the law's disapproval for repeated bad behaviour. The advantage of this idea, especially useful in the context of liability for breaches of statutory duties, is that it offers a compromise between those who resolutely refuse to make statutory bodies libel for the negligence of the servants and those who, in appropriate circumstances, would like to see the possibility being at least considered. The case of *Lawrence* v. *Pembrokeshire County Council*[97] which we shall encounter with others like it in Chapters 7 and 8, is an example in point and suggests to all but the most closed minded that there can be instances where statutory bodies can be visited with liability without this result bankrupting them financially.

The pattern of liability resulting from the complex interplay of the above requirements is difficult to grasp. It may therefore be helpful in conveying at least a general idea to present it in diagrammatic form (see Fig. 1.1).

[97] [2006] EWHC 1029 (QB), [2007] PIQR P1.

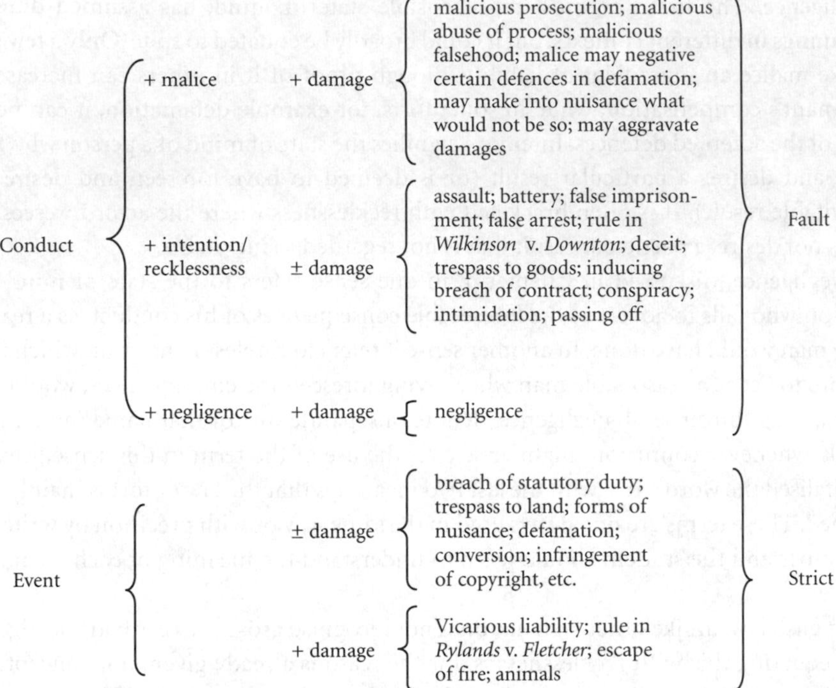

Fig. 1.1 Patterns of Liability

The important feature of the common law of tort is that even if the requirements of conduct, fault, causation and damage are present, it still does not follow that there will be liability.[98] For instance, the kind of harm suffered by the claimant may not be recognised as attracting liability. Thus, mental suffering (in the form of mere pain or grief), as distinguished from nervous shock, has, traditionally, not been recognised and hence it has not been compensated; and even shock was recognised by the courts only step by step. Yet, on the other hand, our law, with its unique ability to raise inconsistency to a supreme virtue, is able to conceive mental distress more broadly when it is dealing with its compensation within the context of the Criminal Injuries Compensation Scheme.

Generally speaking, the same has been true of pure economic loss, though, as we shall see in Chapter 3, courts have vacillated on this matter and have now moved towards a mixed regime, abandoning the 'all or nothing' approach some would have liked to adopt. Alternatively, one or other of the parties to the action may not be recognised by the law. For policy reasons the 'Queen's enemies' are not recognised as capable of suing

[98] This point was the subject of a debate between Salmond, who talked of a law of torts, and Winfield, who believed in a law of tort. The history of the dispute, along with a suggested compromise, can be found in G. Williams, 'The Foundation of Tortious Liability' [1939] *CLJ* 111.

in respect of injuries inflicted on them. More significantly, as we shall see in Part III, no one can sue in respect of a breach of statutory duty unless it can be shown that the statute in question recognises the category of persons to which that person belongs. For historical reasons, until the enactment of the Crown Proceedings Act 1947, the Crown could not be liable in tort. Trade unions used to enjoy extensive immunity from tortious liability when acting in contemplation or furtherance of trade disputes, but this was considerably reduced by several Acts of Parliament in the 1980s.[99] Barristers, too, enjoy immunity in respect of work done in court, though this immunity may be on its way out, especially in view of the fact that liability insurance is now obligatory. If diplomats commit torts they cannot be sued, but their insurance companies can be made liable.[100] International comity demands that diplomats shall remain immune from suit;[101] justice demands that victims shall receive compensation; and insurance makes it possible to give effect to both considerations via the legal device of the 'unenforceable duty'—a striking example of the manipulation of concepts to give effect to policy decisions.

It will be noted that in all these cases the courts were not concerned with individual claimants or defendants, but were expressing a dictate of general policy that there is to be no *prima facie* liability. The device used by the common law to embody policy decisions as to whether liability should even be countenanced in the kind of situation in question is that of 'duty' or 'duty-situation'. In Professor Fleming's words:

> Though fashions have shifted . . . the prevailing pattern is to express in terms of 'duty' judicial policies of a more or less generalised nature . . . leaving to 'remoteness of damage' the evaluation of more contingent and random features of each particular case.[102]

The student can find many examples where liability was not imposed because, as the courts put it, there was no legal 'duty'. The notion of 'duty' has thus played a cardinal role in the common law of torts, but since it is talked about most frequently in relation to the law of negligence, namely, as a 'duty to take care', its detailed consideration will be deferred until Chapter 3. Yet, as will become clearer in Chapters 3 and 4, duty, carelessness and remoteness are nothing more than verbal devices that help courts in formulating decisions, but do not really explain them. What is important is that the student should realise that all these concepts are tools to be used as necessary; they are means towards an end, not the end itself. Attachment to concepts as such, to the exclusion of the socio-economic pressures that guide the way in which they are used, can distract lawyers from the real policy issues that lie behind them. The brief discussion we have included in Section 4 on the important Canadian decision of *Norsk Pacific Steamship Co. Ltd.* v. *Canadian National Railway Co.* will make these points more obvious and facilitate the treatment of this subject in Chapter 3 (on negligence).

[99] See ch. 15.

[100] *Dickinson* v. *Del Solar* [1930] 1 KB 376, *Zoernsch* v. *Waldock* [1964] 1 WLR 675.

[101] A diplomat is under a legal duty to pay, which is unenforceable against him, but such a duty is a sufficient basis on which to ground the liability of the insurance company.

[102] *The Law of Torts* (8th edn., 1992), 136.

In accordance with what has just been said, we shall point out in Chapter 3 that which concept is chosen to justify a particular result will often (though not always) be a matter of personal choice by the judge. In some cases, however, a particular aim may dictate the adoption of one concept instead of another. *Rondel* v. *Worsley*[103] shows that an important reason (allegedly) in favour of a barrister's immunity from liability for his conduct of a case is the danger that action against him might be an indirect retrial of the previous case, which has exhausted the possibility of appeal. This aim could only be achieved through the terminology of 'no duty-situation'. If the 'lack of care' approach had been adopted instead of 'duty', as the plaintiff had urged upon the court, the result in that particular case might still have been the same (since it was by no means clear that the defendant barrister had been careless). However, the overall policy aim of not clogging up the courts with claims from disgruntled clients would not have been achieved. For it would have left open the possibility that some other frustrated litigant might sue his legal adviser and concentrate on the latter's lack of care, thereby bringing in the rights and wrongs of the earlier decision.

Another case of importance is *Smith* v. *Littlewoods Corp.*,[104] which will be discussed later in the chapters on negligence and nuisance. Here suffice it to say that Lord Mackay LC decided the case on what, in textbook terms, could be described as the element of carelessness, whereas Lord Goff relied upon the notion of duty of care. The practical difference between these two judgments is that the first does not exclude in categorical terms the possibility of recovery in the case of omissions (in general), whereas the second one, which has prevailed in practice, does.

Nowadays writers and (common law) judges are increasingly prepared to bring policy issues into the open. For example, the so-called 'floodgates' argument used to play a dominant role in denying liability for nervous shock[105] and economic loss.[106] One can understand the fear that if such losses were to become automatically compensatable, the courts might be inundated with claims. This kind of argument, however, is questionable when it leads to a *blanket*[107] denial of justice. Also, it can be accorded more significance than it deserves, since experience has shown that even where liability has

103 [1969] 1 AC 191.

104 [1987] AC 241 Discussed by B. S. Markesinis in 'Negligence, Nuisance and Affirmative Duties of Action' (1989) 105 *LQR* 104.

105 See now *McLoughlin* v. *O'Brian* [1983] 1 AC 410.

106 E.g. *Spartan Steel & Alloys Ltd.* v. *Martin & Co. (Contractors) Ltd.* [1973] QB 27, 38–9, per Lord Denning MR.

107 As will be noted in ch. 3, below, English law has a tendency to create 'blanket' immunities and then to justify them by reference to various policy factors. This is, nowadays, happening with increasing frequency in the case of various public authorities such as the social security services, local authorities, the police, the Crown Prosecution Service, etc. It remains to be seen, however, whether they will survive a challenge—inevitable we believe—under Strasbourg law or the Human Rights Act 1998. The first pronouncement of the Strasbourg Court on this matter came in *Osman* v. *United Kingdom* (2000) 29 EHRR 245, and was related to the (apparently) blanket immunity given to the police under the House of Lords' ruling in *Hill* v. *Chief Constable of West Yorkshire Police* [1989] AC 53. This suggested that such immunities might be seen as a 'disproportionate restriction on [a litigant's] right of access to a court, in breach of Article 6(1) of the European Convention on Human Rights'.

been recognised (thus creating new duty-situations) the corresponding increase in litigation has not, on the whole, been as great as had been feared. For the courts do possess other means of keeping liability under control. We shall see, for example, that allowing trespassers an action in negligence against occupiers of land does not deprive the courts of their ability to refuse claims by non-meritorious entrants.[108] But it has enabled them to do justice in other instances where in the past this was not possible because trespassers used not to be recognised as capable of suing in negligence at all. Some decisions of the House of Lords in the early 1980s on nervous shock and economic loss suggest that this 'floodgates' argument was losing favour with the courts,[109] though more recent decisions show that the fears associated with it have not yet been eradicated. The so-called 'cable cases' offer a good illustration of how policy arguments can help determine the outcome of litigation. The 'floodgates' argument has been successfully invoked in these cases.

Another policy factor at work has been the role of insurance practice. Again the *Norsk* case contains one of the best discussions currently available on this subject; and it is to be regretted that we have no equivalent decision from a British court to hold out to our students as a model of a stimulating analysis of the law. Generally speaking, however, it would appear highly advisable that before extensions (or limitations) of liability are considered one should study their economic and insurance implications and weigh these against the advantage of making the negligent person liable.

All such matters, however, cannot be evaluated properly as long as we do not look beyond the formal conceptualism of the law—something that British judges and academics seem averse to doing. Overwork may be a reason; but not an entirely convincing one—at any rate as far as our highest court is concerned (and, certainly, not convincing as far as academics are concerned). Having said that, however, we should at the same time never lose sight of the fact that all extra-legal dimensions only become meaningful in the light of the law itself. While a study of the law alone will yield but an incomplete picture of the problem with which it has to deal, to wander into the economic and social surroundings without a clear grasp of the rules and limits of the law will fail even to reveal what those problems are. So nothing we have said thus far should be understood to diminish the prime need to know the law and to acquire a sufficient mastery of its techniques. The purpose of this Introduction is to give some idea of the wider context, an appreciation of which, we contend, is essential for the full understanding and further sensible development of the law.

However, subsequent case law (especially *Z* v. *UK* [2001] 2 FLR 621) has suggested the need for greater care, both at home and in Strasbourg, in the use of this argument. We shall return to this topic in chs. 3 and 8, but here we draw the reader's attention to the growing 'Europeanisation' of our tort law.

[108] Ch. 3, below.

[109] *McLoughlin* v. *O'Brian* [1983] 1 AC 410; *Junior Books Ltd.* v. *Veitchi Co. Ltd.* [1983] AC 520. The fear, however, has resurfaced in more recent cases.

SELECT BIBLIOGRAPHY

EHRENZWEIG, A. A., 'Assurance Oblige: A Comparative Study' (1950) 15 *Law and CP* 445.

—and THORNTON, J.K., 'The Impact of Insurance on the Law of Torts' (1950) 15 *Law and CP* 431.

FLEMING, J. G., 'Remoteness and Duty: The Control Devices in Liability for Negligence' (1953) 1 *Can. BR* 471.

GREEN, L., 'Tort Law Public Law in Disguise' (1959) 38 *Texas LR* 257.

JAMES, F., 'Accident Liability Reconsidered: The Impact of Liability Insurance' (1948) 57 *Yale LJ* 549.

MARKESINIS, B. S., 'Policy Factors and the Law of Torts', *The Cambridge Lectures* (1981) 99.

SYMMONS, C. R., 'The Duty of Care in Negligence: Recently Expressed Policy Elements' (1971) 34 *MLR* 394, 528.

4. ECONOMIC ANALYSIS OF TORT LAW

(A) SOME GENERAL REMARKS

In the last few years, common-law courts, particularly in the United States, have made increasing use of techniques of economic analysis in decision-making.[110] These techniques derive from welfare economics, which see the legal system as a potential means of enhancing the efficient allocation of society's resources. From this point of view, the law is 'a giant pricing machine' in which 'laws act as prices or taxes which provide incentives',[111] thereby complementing the allocative mechanisms of the market. The law of tort, and specifically the torts of nuisance and negligence, was the focus for many of the early breakthroughs in the economic theory of law[112] and it has continued to provide fertile ground for scholarship and debate throughout the common-law world. However, little of this academic effort has filtered through to the English courts, although this might (just conceivably) begin to change. Certainly, the judgment of Lord Hoffmann in *Stovin* v. *Wise*,[113] which used economic reasoning to help explain the limited extent of duties of affirmative action in the tort of negligence, could serve as a model for further imitation.

[110] For a prediction of the growing influence of economic analysis in legal doctrine, see B. Ackerman, *Reconstructing American Law* (1984).

[111] C. G. Veljanovski, *The Economics of Law: An Introductory Text*, Institute of Economic Affairs, Hobart Paper 114 (1990).

[112] See, in particular, G. Calabresi, 'Some Thoughts on Risk Distribution and the Law of Torts' (1961) 70 *Yale LJ* 400, and *The Cost of Accidents: A Legal and Economic Analysis* (Select Bibliography); and R. Posner, 'A Theory of Negligence' (Select Bibliography). Ronald Coase used examples from nuisance law in his seminal article 'The Problem of Social Cost' (Select Bibliography).

[113] [1996] 1 AC 923, 944.

There may be good reasons for this limited judicial reception of economic ideas. A great deal of economic writing in this area is difficult for non-specialists to penetrate. Having said that, there are now several texts and articles that are clearly written and reasonably accessible to the non-specialist.[114] A more serious objection is that the line taken in particular by the Chicago School and its followers has proved controversial in the wider legal profession, among practitioners and academics alike. The 'law and economics movement' has been variously criticised for applying economic principles in an inconsistent and deficient way.[115] It has also been accused of failing to recognise the value judgements that are inherent in economic analysis;[116] and for seeking to advance a right-wing political agenda at the expense of other points of view.[117] Whatever the rights and wrongs of these claims, under these circumstances it is far from clear that the economic approach to law could be adopted by the bench, which in this respect is no better qualified than academics are to choose between the competing claims of the protagonists.

To take this view would, however, make the mistake of identifying just one school of thought—the Chicago School—as encompassing the whole field of law and economics. In reality this field is extremely diverse and the pioneering work of writers such as the Nobel Laureate Ronald Coase has been applied in a wide range of contexts.[118] At the same time, most analysts share enough common ground to make the application of economic techniques a realistic possibility in certain parts of the law. It is not necessary to share Judge Richard Posner's view (expressed in his academic capacity) that economic analysis can be a universal solvent for legal and ethical problems,[119] to see that for some issues at least economic techniques can provide a useful, additional tool to courts. One of Judge Posner's more forceful critics has written that 'economic analysis by itself, unencumbered by value choices, can be an effective aid in analysing the issues presented in legal disputes, clarifying when a value choice must be made, and identifying what choices are available'.[120]

114 In particular, in this field, see W. M. Landes and R. A. Posner, *The Economic Structure of Tort Law* (Select Bibliography).

115 G. Cohen, 'Posnerian Jurisprudence and the Economic Analysis of Law: The View from the Bench' (Select Bibliography).

116 This is a point frequently made by the critical legal studies school. See e.g. M. Kelman, 'Consumption Theory, Production Theory, and Ideology in the Coase Theorem' (Select Bibliography).

117 L. Caplan, 'Does Good Economics Make Good Law?', *California Lawyer* (May 1985), 28, cited in B. White, 'Coase and the Courts: Economics for the Common Man' (Select Bibliography) 577, 579.

118 For discussion of Coase's work and its relationship to the Chicago School see R. Ellickson, 'The Case for Coase and against "Coaseanism"' (1989) 99 *Yale LJ* 611, discussing J. J. Donahue III, 'Diverting the Coasean River: Incentive Schemes to Reduce Unemployment Spells' (1989) 99 *Yale LJ* 549. See also G. Calabresi, 'The Pointlessness of Pareto: Carrying Coase Further' (1991) 100 *Yale LJ* 1211, for discussion of the tensions between regulatory and libertarian aspects of Coase's work.

119 See in particular *The Economics of Justice* (1981) for an attempt to make a wide ethical justification for the use of economic analysis in law.

120 White (Select Bibliography), 579.

(B) THE 'COASE THEOREM' AND THE CONCEPT OF TRANSACTION COSTS

The starting-point for economic analysis of law is the proposition known as the 'Coase Theorem', which can be stated as follows: the assignment of legal rights and liabilities has no implications for economic efficiency as long as the parties involved in a particular dispute can bargain costlessly, that is to say, with *zero transaction costs*, to resolve that dispute. This surprising result—surprising, at least, to lawyers—is explained by Coase by the example of a rancher whose cattle trespass on to the adjoining land of a farmer, damaging his crops. If the right to graze cattle is worth more to the rancher than the farmer's right to keep his crops free from interference is worth to him, it is irrelevant that a court might give the farmer the legal right to enjoin the cattle trespass. In a world without transaction costs the party valuing the right the most highly will buy it from the other. Such an exchange will lead to a welfare gain since, by definition, it will make both parties better off than they were before the exchange. The court's assignment of legal liability has *distributional* implications and so will affect the relative *private* wealth of the two parties, but it does not, under these assumptions, affect the net *social cost* of the activity one way or the other.[121]

To appreciate this point it is necessary to bear in mind that economic analysis of the law focuses on the net cost to society *both* of certain harmful activities *and* of the legal intervention designed to offset them. Free exchange, based on contract, is seen as the normal means of enhancing the value of economic resources. This, of course, is on the (important) assumption that both parties to the exchange are acting rationally to pursue their own self-interest, and that their contract is not vitiated by force or fraud. Then, the exchange will necessarily make them both better off than they were before. Tort law, by contrast, sets up a series of income transfers from one party to another through liability rules requiring the payment of compensation. An income transfer, dictated by a court, cannot be assumed to create economic surplus value in the same way that a contract would. Indeed, because of the administrative costs of income-transfer systems such as tort law or social security, it is possible that it will impose a net cost on society. Tort is therefore supplementary to contract in ensuring an efficient allocation of economic resources; but the primacy of contract does not necessarily hold in a situation where market-based exchange is inhibited by high transaction costs.

The Coase Theorem, then, reminds lawyers that decisions on legal liability are only the starting-point of a process of resource allocation, which is continued via the

[121] See Coase (Select Bibliography), 104: 'It is necessary to know whether the damaging business is liable or not for damage caused, since without the establishment of this initial delimitation of rights there can be no market transactions to transfer and recombine them. But the ultimate result (which maximizes the value of production) is independent of the legal position if the pricing system is assumed to work without cost.' If the assumption of zero transaction costs is maintained, any *wealth effect* which results from the transfer of legal liability to one side as opposed to another will, in the end, be unable to counter the movement of resources to their most efficient use: see G. Calabresi, 'Transaction Costs, Resource Allocation and Liability Rule: A Comment' (1968) 11 *J Law & Econ.* 67; and R. Coase, 'Notes on the Problem of Social Cost', ch. 6 in his *The Firm, the Market and the Law* (1988), at 170–4.

market. As a proposition, the theorem is essentially tautologous, in that it follows from the way in which Coase appears to define 'transaction costs' very widely to include all barriers to private exchange. However, it is clear that Coase did not set out just to restate the basic axioms of welfare economics. His point in using the model of costless exchange was to illustrate the economic functions of legal rules in the real-life situations where transaction costs are high:

If market transactions were costless, all that matters (questions of equity apart) is that the rights of the various parties should be well defined and the results of legal actions easy to forecast. But as we have seen, the situation is quite different when market transactions are so costly as to make it difficult to change the arrangement of rights established by the law. In such cases the courts directly influence economic activity. It would therefore seem desirable that the courts should understand the economic consequence of their decisions and should, in so far as this is possible without creating too much uncertainty about the legal position itself, take these consequences into account when making their decisions.[122]

Thus the concept of transaction costs is central to Coasean analysis. In terms of contracting *process*, transaction costs may usefully be described as the costs of arriving at an agreement, monitoring it during performance, and enforcing it through legal or other sanctions.[123] More fundamentally, though, transaction costs include anything that prevents a competitive market equilibrium being arrived at through exchange: they include externalities, information costs, strategic behaviour, monopoly, 'small numbers bargaining', adverse selection, and all the other causes of incomplete or failed exchange identified by economic theory.[124] The Coase Theorem may look like a tautology, but this is irrelevant since the purpose of the concept of transaction costs is not, in the end, to examine the state of competitive equilibrium. Its purpose is, instead, to direct attention to the institutional arrangements that arise by virtue of the failure of the free market to arrive at this state unaided.

Coase's 1960 paper 'The Problem of Social Cost' laid out a basic framework for analysing the way in which different types of legal intervention interact with economic activity. This was later extended and developed by Guido Calabresi and Douglas Melamed in a paper entitled 'Property Rules, Liability Rules and Inalienability: One View of the Cathedral'.[125] At one level, the state can facilitate private exchange simply by instituting a system of *property rights*, which then form the subject-matter of private agreements.[126] If an 'entitlement' is protected by a 'property rule' in the form of an injunction or criminal sanction against interference, the effect is that it may be appropriated from its owner only through exchange. This is the least intrusive level of state intervention since it remains up to the parties to set the value of the entitlement. By

122 Coase (Select Bibliography), 119.

123 C. J. Dahlman, 'The Problem of Externality' (1979) 22 *J Law & Econ.* 148, approved by Coase, *The Firm, the Market and the Law* (1988), 6.

124 H. Hovenkamp, 'Marginal Utility and the Coase Theorem' (1990) 75 *Cornell LR* 783, 787.

125 (1972) 85 *Harv. LR* 1089.

126 This is the theme of Coase's 1959 paper, 'The Federal Communications Commission' (1959) 2 *J Law & Econ.* 1.

contrast, in the case of a 'liability rule' the asset may be taken in return for the payment of damages representing what a court considers to be its value. In the case of an 'inalienable' entitlement, the law prevents its sale even between willing buyers and sellers; thus rules such as the ban on personal servitude simultaneously 'protect' the entitlement while limiting its grant. Transaction-cost analysis can help to indicate why certain entitlements receive these particular forms of legal protection. Accident law protects the right to life and limb through liability rules, on the whole, because of the prohibitive costs of pre-accident bargaining between, for example, all road users and pedestrians. High transaction costs may mean that an accurate market evaluation cannot be made—the market assessment 'is either unavailable or too expensive compared to a collective valuation'[127]—and that bargaining over the entitlement is impossible, so that 'an initial entitlement, though incorrect in terms of economic efficiency, will not be altered in the marketplace'.[128] In these cases a liability rule is preferable to a property rule which could cement in place an inefficient allocation. This model has been used for the analysis of nuisance and other areas of tort and property law.

Legal intervention, then, can enhance efficiency in situations where private bargaining will not lead to an optimal outcome. Coase is vague as to how the courts should achieve this goal and proceeds by way of examples drawn from nuisance law, rather than through the formulation of a single, general principle. However, in his discussion of the cases, it is possible to discern the rule later formulated more precisely by Judge Posner, namely that in circumstances of high transaction costs the court should allocate a legal right to *the party who values it the most highly*. In this way the court reproduces the outcome which the market would have arrived at under circumstances of pure competition (and which will therefore be welfare-maximising).[129] Finally, Coase considers the possibility that the state will act through regulation or criminal legislation, restricting the scope of private activity. The point is not that regulation is necessarily illegitimate, but rather that it must be shown to be superior to the use of other methods in achieving the intended goal:

> From these considerations it follows that direct governmental regulations will not necessarily give better results than leaving the problem to be solved by the market or the firm. But equally, there is no reason why, on occasion, such governmental administrative action should not lead to an improvement in economic efficiency. This would seem particularly likely when, as is normally the case with the smoke nuisance, a large number of people is involved and when therefore the costs of handling the problem through the market or the firm may be high.[130]

[127] G. Calabresi and A. D. Melamed, 'Property Rules, Liability Rules, and Inalienability: One View of the Cathedral' (1972) 85 *Harv. LR* 1089, 1110.

[128] *Ibid.*, 1089, 1119.

[129] See Coase, 'Notes on The Problem of Social Cost', ch. 6 in his *The Firm, the Market and the Law* (1988), 119–33; Posner, *Economic Analysis of Law* (1972), 13–14, 45; and see the critique of White (Select Bibliography).

[130] Coase (Select Bibliography), 118.

(C) ACCIDENT COMPENSATION AND INTERNALISATION

Legal intervention may affect economic behaviour by, amongst other things, 'internalising' the social costs of dangerous and harmful activities to those responsible for them:

> Externalities are situations where the costs influencing individual behaviour diverge significantly from the costs to society. As a result the actions of rational individuals lead to inefficient outcomes—those activities which impose (uncompensated) external costs are over-expanded and those which supply uncompensated external benefits are underexpanded. The law, by shifting these costs and by creating incentives, can cause individuals to consider these external effects ('internalise' them). In the case of external harms the efficiency goal of the law is to impose third-party losses on those who could bear them most cheaply.[131]

The result is a price structure which more accurately reflects the net costs of various kinds of economic activity. In this regard, Calabresi's book *The Costs of Accidents* illustrates the variety of goals that may be imputed to the law of negligence. Instead of viewing tort law in the conventional way as a means of satisfying the claims of individual accident victims to compensation for their injuries, Calabresi insists that 'apart from the requirements of justice [it is] axiomatic that the principal function of accident law is to reduce the sum of the costs of accidents and the costs of avoiding accidents'.[132] The costs of avoidance and the costs of administering compensation systems must be taken into account, just as much as the injuries and economic losses sustained by victims. The goal of overall cost-reduction can be achieved through a variety of means—spreading the risk of loss as widely as possible, imposing liability on defendants with 'deep pockets', or seeking to deter careless behaviour through market incentives ('general deterrence')—and through a variety of systems of compensation: fault-based liability with private insurance, social insurance, enterprise liability or regulation. For Calabresi, the purpose of economic analysis is not to dictate any particular system of compensation, but to 'indicate the questions we must ask in deciding whether one system is preferable to another'.[133]

One way in which tort law may promote allocative efficiency is by identifying the 'least cost avoider' as the appropriate party to be assigned liability. This frequently means assigning liability to the 'deep pocket' defendant or 'best briber', since he or she will have the resources to initiate further exchanges in the market if the court cannot make a definitive allocation based on efficiency. Given the limited information that the court has available, this is more likely than not to be the case. For example, where an enterprise causes pollution damage to residents of a district, it may be more feasible to envisage the enterprise buying out the residents rather than vice versa. If the right to enjoin the pollution is accorded to the residents, the enterprise will buy them out if it values the right to pollute more highly than they do. But if the court grants the

[131] D. Harris and C. G. Veljanovski, 'Liability for Economic Loss in Tort', in M. Furmston (ed.), *The Law of Tort: Policies and Trends in Liability for Damage to Property and Economic Loss* (1986), 48.

[132] Calabresi (Select Bibliography), 26.

[133] *Ibid.*, 312–13.

enterprise the right to carry on polluting, it is unlikely that the residents, given their lack of resources and access to contracting expertise, will bargain to buy the right from the enterprise even if they do value it more highly.

Calabresi does not insist on giving primacy to market solutions. Distributional questions are seen as important, not just because the law may have goals other than allocative efficiency, but because an unequal distribution of resources places constraints upon the effectiveness of any market-based approach. He thus maintains that 'unless the distribution of income—and therefore of goods and services—is satisfactory, it may be foolish to say that society is better off if all consumers can choose what they want for themselves after seeing what the true costs of their possible choices are'.[134] *The Costs of Accidents* concludes with a substantial indictment of the fault system, which is found to be defective both as a loss spreader and as a system of primary cost control.

(D) THE THEORY OF THE INHERENT EFFICIENCY OF THE COMMON LAW

The work of Judge Richard Posner demonstrates how price-theoretic economic techniques can be applied to non-market situations, such as family relations, crime and punishment, and the administration of the legal system. It is this wide-ranging and novel application of economic analysis, beyond the traditional areas of anti-trust and market regulation, which is said to account for the distinctive character of the 'new law and economics'.[135] Posner's second distinctive claim is to have revealed the implicit 'economic structure' or logic of the common law. In contrast to Calabresi's open discussion of policy-making, Posner aims to provide a 'positive' economic theory of the law. Central to this is his argument that the common-law courts tend to pursue the goal of welfare efficiency, even if they do not necessarily do so explicitly. One illustration is the fault principle in negligence, the 'dominant function' of which, Posner suggests, 'is to generate rules of liability that if followed will bring about, at least approximately, the efficient—the cost-justified—level of accidents'.[136] More precisely, the so-called 'Hand formula'[137] provides a mechanism for setting standards of care, which serves to minimise the total costs to society of any accident. The principles of causation and contributory negligence, and the calculation of damages, can also be seen as maximising the relevant incentives on parties to take the appropriate level of care, although here Posner criticises twentieth-century statutory developments reducing the importance of

[134] Calabresi (Select Bibliography), 78; see also G. Calabresi and P. Bobbit, *Tragic Choices* (1976), 32.

[135] C. G. Veljanovski, *The Economics of Law* (1990), 14–15.

[136] 'A Theory of Negligence' (Select Bibliography), 33. This thesis is developed more systematically with William S. Landes in R. A. Posner and W. S. Landes, *The Economic Structure of Tort Law* (1987). An early analysis which contradicts the focus of Landes and Posner on the fault principle is J. P. Brown, 'Toward an Economic Theory of Liability' (1973) 2 *Jo. LS* 323; and see also S. Shavell, *Economic Analysis of Accident Law* (1987); I. Ayres, 'A Theoretical Fox Meets Empirical Hedgehogs: Competing Approaches to Accident Economics' (1988) 82 *NWUL Rev.* 387.

[137] Which measures breach of a duty of care by comparing the cost of precautions with the magnitude of the harm and likelihood of its occurring.

contributory negligence and altering the basis for calculating damages for wrongful death.[138] The answer to the question why the common law should produce positive outcomes for efficiency when legislation, by and large, does not, lies in the nature of legal process, which can itself be analysed in an economic way. The case-law system in effect creates a 'market' for legal ideas in which concepts and rules are thrown into competition with each other (precedents are a 'capital stock'). The possibility of litigation means that parties themselves will seek to have inefficient rules overturned. Courts do not have the power to issue general rules of redistribution and litigation generally takes the form of the assertion of individual rights, not general group interests. By contrast, Posner uses the arguments of the 'public choice' school to argue that the legislative process encourages collective action by pressure groups to bring about redistributive measures at the expense of the general good.[139]

Posner uses criteria of efficiency borrowed from welfare economics. According to the criterion of 'Pareto efficiency', a reallocation of resources will be welfare enhancing if it makes at least one person better off without making anyone else worse off. By definition, this will normally be achieved through exchange. An allocation is 'Pareto optimal' when no further change is possible without making somebody worse off, a kind of 'unanimity principle'. For most of his analyses Posner utilises a variation of the Pareto principle known as 'Kaldor–Hicks efficiency'. According to this principle, an allocation is efficient if it leads to a net welfare gain out of which winners could compensate the losers if they chose to (hence the use of the expression 'potential Pareto efficiency' to describe Kaldor–Hicks).[140] The use of Kaldor–Hicks is justified by the restrictiveness of the Pareto 'unanimity' principle. However, its use takes Posner a long way from libertarian positions on the value of freedom of contract; if the courts are applying some version of the Kaldor–Hicks principle, then 'the efficient solution is coercively imposed after some third party determination of costs and benefits'.[141] Following the direction hinted at by Coase, Posner argues that welfare will be maximised in a situation of high transaction costs by a court transferring the right in question to the party who values it most highly. For this purpose value is defined by willingness to pay, so that in effect the right is allocated to the party who can make the highest bid for it. In this way the court 'mimics' the outcome of the market. The result may well be (in most cases, must be) to redistribute income from poor to rich. This analysis has been criticised as tending to define away questions of distribution and inequality. The result is that: 'the transfers that come about against a background of wealth inequality are fine; any that come about against a background of inequality in strength, or the power to organise and apply strength, are unjustifiable. Some

[138] Posner, 'A Theory of Negligence' (Select Bibliography); and *Economic Analysis of Law*, ch. 6.

[139] *Economic Analysis of Law*, chs. 19–20. For criticism, see A. I. Ogus, 'Legislation, the Courts and the Demand for Compensation' in R. C. O. Matthews (ed.), *Economy and Democracy* (1986), ch. 6.

[140] *Economic Analysis of Law*, 12–15.

[141] C. G. Veljanovski, 'The New Law and Economics: A Research Review', Oxford Centre for Socio-Legal Studies (1982), repr. in A. I. Ogus and C. G. Veljanovski (eds.), *Readings in the Economics of Law and Regulation* (1984), 21.

inequalities are apparently more equal than others—and all without reference to any apparent normative criterion at all.'[142] Posner's work remains the most comprehensive and thought-provoking, but also the most controversial application of economic techniques to the analysis of law.

(E) EMPIRICAL STUDIES OF THE EFFECTS OF TORT LAW

The pioneering studies of the economics of tort law were largely conceptual and theoretical. Increasingly, though, the emphasis within tort law scholarship has turned towards empirical studies. Some of these are referred to in later chapters of this book. In 1996 a major study by lawyers and economists from the University of Toronto was published which draws together the diverse evidence on the economic effects of tort, making it possible for the first time to assess the overall impact of economic research in this field.[143] The authors conclude that, taken as whole, tort law does not perform well when evaluated against the three normative criteria of deterrence, compensation and corrective justice. Where tort performs a deterrent function, it tends to do so in conjunction with certain aspects of the insurance system (such as the varying of insurance premiums according to the risk of damage occurring).[144] Similarly, tort, on its own, fails to ensure effective compensation, particularly for the consequences of product-related accidents and medical injuries. But, as the authors accept, 'tort cannot be meaningfully valuated except by reference to its alternatives'[145] and it is not always clear that no-fault compensation schemes or social insurance, taken in the round, can be said to perform better. Although they argue that tort law systems of the kind which prevail in most common-law jurisdictions should shrink, to be replaced by no-fault insurance schemes and wider dependence on universal health service provision, changes of this kind require legislative intervention which, in most systems, does not seem imminent. Moreover, legislative interventions may lead to problems of their own, including high administrative costs and the blunting of deterrence effects. Concerns such as these led to retrenchment, in the early 1990s, of the New Zealand scheme, which in the 1970s had replaced tort law with a form of state-backed social insurance as the principal source of compensation for accidents.

142 A. A. Leff, 'Economic Analysis of Law: Some Realism about Nominalism' (1974) 60 *Virginia LR* 451, at 481 and 459 respectively.

143 Dewees, Duff and Trebilcock, *Exploring the Domain of Accident Law* (Select Bibliography).

144 For scepticism concerning the possibility that tort law has a deterrent effect on behaviour, see H. Luntz, (2001) 9 *Tort Law Journal* 311, 315, reviewing the work of two of the present authors and their colleagues (B. Markesinis, J.-P. Auby, D. Coester-Waltjen and S. Deakin, *Tortious Liability of Statutory Bodies: A Comparative and Economic Analysis of Five English Cases* (1999)). In our view, the body of empirical evidence in favour of tort law having some behavioural effect is now sufficiently extensive to withstand such scepticism, although we agree with Luntz that the question must be, in the final analysis, resolved by empirical evidence, and that not all studies point in the same direction. For an argument that tort law studies should be sensitive both to economic analysis and to empirical work, see S. Deakin, 'The Evolution of Tort' (1999) 19 *OJLS* 537.

145 Dewees, Duff and Trebilcock (Select Bibliography), 12.

(F) ECONOMIC ANALYSIS IN THE CONTEXT OF ONE TORT CASE: THE *NORSK* DECISION[146]

(i) The Facts of *Norsk*

The New Westminster Railways Bridge, which spans the Fraser River near Vancouver and carries a single railway track, is owned by the Department of Public Works of Canada (PWC). A barge, towed by a tug owned by the defendants (Norsk), and negligently navigated by its captain, damaged the bridge, necessitating its closure for several weeks. As a result, the Canadian National Railway (CNR), which was the plaintiff in this action, had to reroute traffic over another bridge, incurring considerable additional expense. CNR, which accounted for 86 per cent of the use of the bridge, had a licence contract with PWC which, *inter alia*, obliged them to provide PWC with inspection, consulting, maintenance and repair services of the bridge as and when requested by PWC and at PWC's expense. Since the marine traffic using the Fraser River was, at the site of the bridge, heavy and had, in the past, occasioned structural damage to the bridge leading to its closure, the licence agreement between CNR and PWC provided that the former could not claim damages from the latter in the event of closure of the bridge in an emergency. CNR owned the land (and tracks) on either side of the bridge (but not the bridge itself or the rails on it). Because they did not own the bridge itself, the loss they suffered was entirely 'economic' or financial. The question, therefore, arose whether they were owed a duty of care in tort in respect of these losses. CNR's tort action for its economic losses was accepted at first instance, by the Court of Appeal, and by four judges out of seven in the Supreme Court of Canada.

(ii) The Majority and Concurring Opinions

The majority (McLachlin, Stevenson, L'Heureux-Dubé and Corry JJ) and minority (LaForest, Sopinka and Iacobucci JJ) were in agreement on several points. Thus, first, *both* agreed that the 'more flexible approach' to economic loss set out by the House of Lords in *Anns* v. *Merton London Borough Council* was preferable to the reasoning in *Murphy* v. *Brentwood District Council*, in which the approach of *Anns* had been repudiated. *Murphy* was expressly stated as not representing the law in Canada.[147] LaForest J, who delivered the minority judgment, said: 'I fully support this court's rejection of the broad bar on recovery of pure economic loss . . . .'[148] The dispute thus centred around what was termed 'relational economic loss', that is to say economic loss suffered by the plaintiff (CNR) as a result of property damage caused to a third party (here, PWC). Second, all the judges agreed that 'the law of tort does not permit recovery for *all* economic loss'.[149] Third, there was full agreement that cases like *Norsk* required

[146] *Norsk Pacific Steamship Co. Ltd.* v. *Canadian National Railway Co.* (1992) 91 DLR (4th) 289 (Supreme Court of Canada).

[147] *Ibid.*, 303 (LaForest J), 367 (McLachlin J), 380 (Stevenson J). The decisions in *Anns* ([1978] 1 AC 728) and *Murphy* ([1991] 1 AC 398) are discussed in ch. 3, below.

[148] *Ibid.*, 303.

[149] *Ibid.*, 377 (McLachlin J).

a discussion of the underlying economic and wider policy considerations.[150] Fourth, all three judgments implicitly accepted Stevenson J's view that 'the case at bar is a good example of how useful comparative law can be'.[151]

For the majority, McLachlin J essentially adopted the two-pronged test which Lord Wilberforce enunciated in *Anns*.[152] If there were negligence, foreseeable loss, and sufficient proximity between negligent act and the loss, liability should follow *unless* 'pragmatic' considerations dictated the opposite result. 'Proximity may consist of various forms of closeness—physical, circumstantial, causal or assumed—which serve to identify the categories of cases in which liability lies.'[153] Further down she added that:

> The meaning of proximity is to be found . . . in viewing the circumstances in which it has been found to exist and determining whether the case at issue is similar enough to justify a similar finding.

The learned judge had no illusions that if this approach is followed 'new categories of case will from time to time arise', and that for a time: 'It will not be certain whether economic loss can be recovered in these categories until the courts have pronounced on them.' But she then continued:

> During this period, the law in a small area of negligence may be uncertain. Such uncertainty, however, is inherent in the common law generally. It is the price the common law pays for flexibility.[154]

Moreover, the feared open-endedness of the law, which might result if one were to abandon the rigid exclusionary rule (favoured by the House of Lords in cases such as *Murphy*), had not materialised either in Canada, where the courts had since the mid-1970s moved towards a more liberal rule. (Nor has this occurred in those civil-law systems which have always opted for a liberal approach to the problem of economic loss.) What then of McLachlin J's pragmatic considerations, notable among which were the insurance and loss-spreading arguments? Did they militate in favour of the non-liability rule?

First, consider the insurance argument that the plaintiff was in a better position to obtain cheaper insurance cover for his loss. McLachlin J thought this was based on 'questionable assumptions'.[155] Quoting Bishop,[156] the learned judge took the view that such an approach reduced the tortfeasor's incentive to take care and thus, in the long run, would result in more accidents and, thereby, eventually increase insurance costs.

[150] The way the Canadian judges considered insurance arguments must be contrasted with the reference made to this factor by both majority and minority in *Marc Rich & Co. AG* v. *Bishop Rock Marine Co. Ltd.* [1996] AC 211. Such a comparison suggests that, at the very least, English students if not English litigants, will emerge better informed about the underlying issues if they study carefully the Canadian opinions. This, however, should not be taken as saying that an economic analysis of a case can solve all difficulties; all it is meant to imply is that it can provide yet another tool of analysis and exegesis.

[151] (1992) 91 DLR (4th) 289, 384.

[152] [1978] AC 728, 751–2.

[153] *Norsk* (1992) 91 DLR (4th) 289, 369.

[154] *Ibid.*, 386.

[155] *Ibid.*, 372.

[156] 'Economic Loss in Tort' (1982) 2 *OJLS* 1.

The reaction to the 'loss-spreading argument' was just as hostile. For, first: '[w]here losses are spread by relieving the tortfeasor of liability we can expect more accidents, and so more losses. Second, some of the victims must sustain large losses not small ones . . . '. Finally, 'the loss-spreading rationale cannot justify the numerous cases where *there is only one victim*'.

There was a third, pragmatic, argument against the imposition of liability in this case: the law of negligence has no role to play in cases such as the present one where the parties could have made provision in their contract allocating such losses. McLachlin J found this argument, too, unconvincing for three reasons. First, it assumes that all persons organise their affairs in accordance with the laws of economic efficiency. Second, it presupposes that the parties to the transaction share an equality of bargaining power which will result in the effective allocation of the risk (but was there not such a balance here?). Finally, it overlooks the significance that personal fault plays in our tort systems and its role in limiting harm to innocent parties.

Stevenson J's concurring judgment is, with respect, the least effective of the three, even though it was the 'swing' judgment that won the case for the plaintiff. There are two reasons for this harsh characterisation. The first lies at the core of his decision which is, essentially, a variation of the views of Gibbs and Mason JJ of the High Court of Australia in *Caltex Oil (Aust.) Pty. Ltd.* v. *The Dredge Willemstad*.[157] The effect of them was that the plaintiff could recover because the defendant knew or ought to have known that 'a specific individual . . . as opposed to a general or un-ascertained class of the public' was likely in this instance to suffer the foreseeable kind of loss.[158]

The *Caltex* origins of the approach should, it is submitted, have alerted the learned judge to the major weakness of the Australian case that stems from the fact that its judges did not speak with one voice. Stevenson J's proposed solution also suffers from the fact that it 'places [an unwarranted] premium on notoriety'.[159]

But Stevenson J not only advanced a view that has failed to command wider support; he also weakened the overall result of the case by expressly disapproving of McLachlin J's proximity test.[160] The most disturbing aspect of this case as a whole is thus that it has not left us with a clear *ratio decidendi*. For the proximity test advocated by the majority is espoused only by three justices out of seven. And if one looks at the case purely from the common-law point of view, and removes from the majority camp the vote of the Quebec judge (L'Heureux-Dubé J), one is left with only two justices out of six advocating proximity as the appropriate controlling device.

(iii) The Minority

LaForest J's judgment is a veritable *tour de force* which students should read carefully after they have studied the discussion of negligence in Chapter 3. Four areas of his judgment should be singled out for consideration, though, for obvious reasons, the last one will not be reviewed in this book. First, his doubts about the suitability of

157 (1976) 136 CLR 529.

158 *Norsk* (1992) 91 DLR (4th) 289, 387.

159 *Ibid.*, 377; and for more criticism see 339–43.

160 *Ibid.*, 387.

the proximity test; second, his reply to McLachlin J's treatment of the economic considerations; third, his emphasis on the contractual relationship between CNR and PWC; and finally his use of comparative law.

LaForest J doubted McLachlin J's view that deciding cases solely on the basis of proximity would lead to the gradual formation of categories of recovery that made sense in policy terms. It is almost impossible to assert which of the two justices is right on this point. But doctrinally LaForest J is on firmer ground when, quoting Feldthusen's work, he insists: 'that different types of factual situations may invite different approaches to economic loss and it seems to . . . be at best unwise to lump them all together for purposes of analysis'.[161] Precedents from the public authorities cases, negligent misstatements, defective rather than dangerous products, and relational economic-loss cases should thus not be used (as they have been by the House of Lords) interchangeably, since they raise different policy issues. The section of the judgment entitled 'The Need to Re-Centre the Analysis on Contractual Relational Economic Loss'[162] thus deserves careful study and may hold the key to the emerging compromise between the 'all' or 'nothing' schools of thought.

LaForest J also countered McLachlin J's economic analysis. The latter's view, that a non-liability rule would encourage risk-takers, cause more accidents, and ultimately raise insurance costs, was countered by the argument that risk-takers would be deterred by the fact that their liability would still be engaged *vis-à-vis* the owners of the damaged property (here the owners of the bridge). This response was also used to counter McLachlin J's rejection of the loss-spreading argument, though no specific reply was given for those accidents that involved only one victim. McLachlin's concern, that plaintiffs in such cases may be unable to obtain insurance, was also doubted. This was largely on the ground that their losses in these instances were more akin to loss of *business* rather than to loss of *profits* (for which business-interruption insurance was widely available and cheaper than liability insurance). One must admit that, in *this type of case*, LaForest J's views seem appealing. However, one must also agree with him when he urges lawyers to 'inform themselves about fundamental matters of insurability'.[163] Yet there are at least two problems with this approach. First, there is inadequate empirical interdisciplinary work to aid judges in this difficult task. Second, in England at any rate, there seems to be little inclination on the part of our judges to address these points or to address them openly so that the legal community can engage in a more meaningful discussion of the real issues.

A third and critical difference between majority and minority was the significance the latter attributed to the contractual bond between CNR and PWC. First of all, one should note CNR's 'overwhelming superior risk capacity' since they could protect themselves through contracts both with the property owner (PWC) and their own clients, suppliers, etc., and thus 'combine to minimise the impact of losses once they occur'.[164] Moreover, for reasons which are more fully explained in the judgment, LaForest J argued that if the

161 *Norsk* (1992) 91 DLR (4th) 289, 299.
162 *Ibid.*, 299–301.
163 *Ibid.*, 350.
164 *Ibid.*, 352.

majority's view prevails, '*both* parties [i.e. CNR and PWC] [will have to] insure at considerable additional social cost. The only gain will be a slight reduction in the plaintiff's first party insurance costs to take into account the possibility that the insurance company will recover from a tortfeasor under the new doctrine.'[165]

SELECT BIBLIOGRAPHY

CALABRESI, G., *The Costs of Accidents: A Legal and Economic Analysis* (1970).

—and HIRSCHOFF, J. T., 'Toward a Test for Strict Liability in Torts' (1972) 81 *Yale LJ* 1055.

COASE, R., 'The Problem of Social Cost' (1960) 3 *J Law & Econ.* 1.

COHEN, G. M., 'Posnerian Jurisprudence and the Economic Analysis of Law: The View from the Bench' (1985) 133 *U Pa. LR* 1117.

DEAKIN, S., 'Law and Economics' in Thomas, P. A. (ed.), *Legal Frontiers* (1996), ch. 3.

DEWEES, D., DUFF, D. and TREBILCOCK, M., *Exploring the Domain of Accident Law: Taking the Facts Seriously* (1996).

LANDES, W. M., and POSNER, R. A., *The Economic Structure of Tort Law* (1987).

MARKESINIS, B. S., AUBY, J.-P., COESTER-WALTJEN, D., and DEAKIN, S., *Tortious Liability of Statutory Bodies: A Comparative and Economic Analysis of Five English Cases* (1999).

OGUS, A. I., 'Economics and Law Reform: Thirty Years of Law Commission Endeavour' (1995) 111 *LQR* 407.

—*Costs and Cautionary Tales: Economic Insights for the Law* (2006).

POSNER, R. A., *Law and Economics* (4th edn., 1993).

—'A Theory of Negligence' (1972) 1 *Jo. LS* 29.

WHITE, B., 'Coase and the Courts: Economics for the Common Man' (1987) 72 *Iowa LR* 577.

5. FUNCTIONS OF TORT

The aims of the law of tort have changed throughout its history: appeasement, justice, punishment, deterrence, compensation and loss-spreading can be counted amongst them. None of them has offered a complete justification for the law. Indeed, due to the traditional dualism between law and equity, the 'restitutionary' functions that are (and have for a long time now been) performed by the law of torts have often been seriously underplayed by academics and confusingly handled by the courts. Overall, however, it can be said with some measure of confidence that at different stages of development of tort law one of its functions may have been more prominent than the rest. Moreover, each in its historical setting reveals something about the socio-economic and philosophical trends of the day.

165 *Norsk* (1992) 91 DLR (4th), 352.

Appeasement, for example, aims at buying off the victim's vengeance. To the extent that it gives effect to feelings for revenge it now tends to take a back seat, though one still finds some lawyers (e.g. Ehrenzweig) who believe that the 'pay' can be a significant rationale of tort liability; and in so far as appeasement evinces the policy of preventing the prosecution of private feuds its role is in part satisfied by the aim of deterrence discussed below. The idea that 'justice' also requires the tortfeasor to 'pay' has its problems, too. For, to the extent that justice or moral condemnation embodies the idea of 'ethical retribution', it also seems to have small appeal these days. If, on the other hand, justice means 'ethical compensation', that is to say the moral need to compensate the victim, then this task seems to be performed by the 'compensation' aim without entering into *moral* arguments, which play little or no role whenever liability is not based on moral guilt (i.e. when it tends to be strict, and even in many cases of negligence). Punishment is also, arguably, an aim which is best left to another branch of the law (criminal law). In Chapter 25, however, we shall note that the English common law has accepted a *limited* number of instances in which punitive damages may be awarded to the aggrieved party. In these cases it is thus permissible to look not only at the claimant's loss, but also at the defendant's reprehensible behaviour, and increase the damages accordingly. But the 'punitive' element in tort litigation remains minimal in English law (and non-existent in most civil-law systems). This is partly because modern dogma believes in a (fairly) rigid distinction between crime and tort, but also because it fears that the presence of punitive elements in a civil action, unaccompanied by the evidential and other procedural safeguards of the criminal trial, can be excessively dangerous to any defendant.[166]

Deterrence is another function attributed to tort law. As traditionally understood, it plays an interesting but subsidiary part in modern tort law. This is because the deterrent or admonitory effect of money compensation is generally less than that of the corporal punishment of criminal law (e.g. imprisonment). The lighter consequence of a successful tort action, therefore, blunts its deterrent value. (This is certainly true whenever the defendant is insured; and as we shall note in Chapter 25, courts seem willing to allow, under certain circumstances, even insurance for punitive awards.) Further, as already indicated, tort damages do not, in principle, correspond exactly to the gravity of conduct (as they tend to do in criminal law). The amount of damages is *generally* speaking the same whether the tort was committed negligently or intentionally (though some rules, e.g. those concerning 'remoteness of damage', are different); and the triviality of the fault bears little relation to the possible enormity of its financial consequences.[167]

166 This objection, however, can be seriously overstated, as Professor Birks, 'Civil Wrongs: A New World' (Select Bibliography), 80, among others, pointed out. For it ignores the fact that many civil (uninsured or inadequately insured) defendants can be financially ruined by a huge award made against them, given that in tort (unlike crime) the 'punishment' is not always proportionate to the tortfeasor's bad state of mind. This result is, in fact, so unacceptable to some authors that they have tried to explain the non-liability rule in cases of pure economic loss by invoking the injustice of huge liability flowing from a minor inattention (for example, severing an electrical cable while drilling in a street).

167 That is why it is unconvincing to attribute the non-liability rule in the 'cable cases' to tort law's dislike of disproportionate consequences.

Similarly, deterrence in the form of monetary payment is hardly effective if the tortfeasor is too poor to pay, or is not insured.

The greatest objection to the deterrence theory, however, is that it is inapplicable in those numerous cases where the claimant's injury is the result of error rather than blameworthiness. This is particularly true of traffic accidents, the vast majority of which result from regrettable, but statistically inevitable, lapses of attention. Traffic accidents, of course, are only one way of causing personal injury and property damage so it might be dangerous to erect a theory on one form of tortuous activity. Yet we noted in Section 1 of this chapter how statistically important traffic-related accidents are to the law of torts, so it is important to look at this example with care.

It is thus interesting to note in this respect the empirical studies carried out by the US Department of Transportation in the early 1970s. These suggested that in Washington the average good driver (defined as one who had not been involved in any traffic accident during the preceding four years) commits approximately nine driving errors of four different kinds during every five minutes of driving![168] In such cases, how can it be said that the threat of a tort action will deter a potential tortfeasor when it appears humanly unavoidable to continue making such errors, and when it is clear that even consideration for the tortfeasor's own safety and the threat of criminal proceedings against him cannot prevent the harmful results? That such errors are actionable as 'negligence' is not because this will deter others from committing them, but most likely because, as a result of compulsory insurance, it is the easiest, if not the only, way of affording the innocent victim compensation without ruining the defendant or unduly burdening the state with the financial consequences of an accident.

Yet having made the above point we must also remind the reader that the deterrent element may be important in some torts, such as defamation, deceit or, even, negligent statements. Indeed, even in the area of 'accidents', the law can have a deterrent function, for example, where the tortfeasor is truly negligent or is prone to commit an unusually large number of errors. For an unusually high incidence of errors points towards an unusually careless person whose conduct needs to be controlled. This could, for example, happen by increasing his insurance premiums or even refusing to insure him altogether and thereby, in exceptional cases, even denying him the right to exercise a particular trade or profession. The admonitory factor may also be significant in those cases (e.g. medical malpractice) where an adverse judgment can be seen as a negative statement about the tortfeasor's professional competence or integrity; but this kind of malpractice situation is statistically rare.

Yet, however, 'fair-minded' one may strive to be, giving the reader all the 'pros and cons' of deterrence theory the fact is that the doubts about deterrence persist. One further reason for this is that it is not regarded as being very effective to tell people what not to do, or simply to tell them that they must behave carefully. One must also give them clear guidance as to the kinds of precautions and measures potential tortfeasors

168 *Driver Behaviour and Accident Involvement Implications for Tort Liability* (1970), 177–8.

should take to avoid the accident; and this, on the whole, the law of torts does not do. In many instances criminal sanctions, government regulation, and economic incentives can promote accident prevention more efficiently than tort law itself. So, again, deterrence takes second place.

Deterrence could, however, be approached in a different way. This is what the modern economists/tort lawyers have done; and their views as well as their significance for modern tort law were summarised in the previous section.

So we come to compensation, which many would regard as a prime function of modern tort law, even though the term, itself, may need clarification.[169]

The need to compensate victims of modern accidents is obvious; and throughout this book we shall see how many of the detailed tort rules have been shaped by this compensatory principle. Yet this approach must not be overstressed, for two reasons. First, as we shall see in Section 7 of this chapter, the compensation of accidents is by no means left only to the law of torts. On the contrary, as we noted in Section 1 of this chapter, the bulk of the compensation money comes from other sources, not tort law. Other systems of compensation have developed over the years and, in fact, overall play a more significant role in catering for the needs of accident victims than does the law of tort. Second, and from a theoretical point of view just as important, is the fact that the emphasis on compensation has led many lawyers (academics and judges) to underplay the importance of 'restitutionary damages' in the law of torts. Thus, it is submitted, one commentator was right in criticising a leading treatise on tort for its 'continuing failure . . . to subject restitutionary damages to coherent and systematic analysis'.[170] If the only consequence of this were doctrinal opaqueness, not all (English) lawyers would complain. But as the same commentator has maintained,[171] and Birks demonstrated,[172] this (old-fashioned) 'analysis enables courts . . . to conclude (wrongly) that there is something "anomalous" or "exceptional" about restitutionary damages', and even to refuse to grant them on the grounds that they are unknown to tort law.[173] So how important are restitutionary damages to the law of tort?

A number of cases show that such restitutionary damages are, indeed, awarded by our courts. In *Reading* v. *Attorney-General*,[174] for example, Sergeant Reading often travelled in lorries involved in smuggling illicit goods. In all these instances he wore his army uniform, which helped the lorries go through army checkpoints unchecked. When he was eventually arrested and tried, the court held that the proceeds of his wrongdoing should go to the state. The aim of the award in this case was not compensation, since the state had suffered no loss, but recoupment of the unjust enrichment made by the defendant, and this was quantified by reference to the gain made by the defendant.

[169] On which see Peter Cane, *Atiyah's Accidents, Compensation and the Law* (Select Bibliography), 411 ff.

[170] E. McKendrick, 'Review of *Clerk and Lindsell on Tort* (16th edn., 1989)' in (1991) 54 *MLR* 162.

[171] *Ibid.*, 163.

[172] 'Civil Wrongs: A New World' (Select Bibliography).

[173] E.g. *Stoke-on-Trent CC* v. *W. & J. Wass Ltd.* [1988] 1 WLR 1406, 1415 (per Nourse LJ).

[174] [1951] AC 507.

Other instances can be given. For example, the question of restitutionary damages for trespass to land has caused much discussion in this country,[175] but the colourful American case of *Edwards* v. *Lee's Administrator*[176] shows how just it is to allow an action in equity for an account of profits from trespass to land. In that case, Edwards discovered on his land an entrance to a marvellous underground cave of onyx formations. He built a hotel on his land and turned the cave into a flourishing tourist business. The problem was that the most attractive part of the cave lay under his neighbour's land and, eventually, Lee brought an action claiming a share of these profits, which he obtained from the court.

In his Butterworth Lecture, Peter Birks gave many examples of such actions that are not technically torts but are hidden in the interstices of the law of trusts. In his view:

> The dominant position of compensation for loss is protected [indeed, preserved in tort books] by banishing the account of profits from the books on damages, by marginalizing the wrongs for which an account is most commonly sought, and by the persistence of the old notion of waiver[177] with its implication that the common law gives restitution for a wrong only when the wrong has been transmogrified into something else.[178]

The result, as the author explained in detail, is an unsatisfactory dichotomy of treatment of the subject of civil wrongs (under at least two courses: tort and equity). If that were all, it would not really matter. But there are more drawbacks. Thus, first, there is uncertainty about the existence and ambit of new torts (e.g. is breach of confidence a tort?[179] Is 'knowing assistance' in a fraudulent misapplication of funds[180] a tort?). Second, we have been landed with a theoretically underdeveloped law dealing with the civil liability of accessories. Finally, we are, on occasion, faced with the rejection of the claimant's (just) claim because of the difficulties which our courts are faced with when asked to come to terms with a gain-based rather than loss-based action for damages. The case of *Stoke-on-Trent City Council* v. *W. & J. Wass Ltd.*[181] illustrates this last point perfectly.

In *Wass* the eponymous defendants ran an open market without permission, thus infringing the appropriate planning law. Their activity was also a nuisance to the markets held by the plaintiff city which was, by law, entitled to have its monopoly protected within a radius of six and three-quarters miles from each of its own markets. The defendants' technique was to run their markets without permission and, when they had exhausted every avenue of appeal against refusal of their application, they would close their 'unlicensed' market and then reopen it nearby and the process would start anew.

[175] See e.g. *Phillips* v. *Homfray* (1883) 24 Ch. D 439, and W. M. C. Gummow, 'Unjust Enrichment, Restitution and Proprietary Remedies', in P. Finn (ed.), *Essays on Restitution* (1990), 60–7.

[176] 96 SW 2d 1025 (1936).

[177] 'When the common law itself allows the victim of a tort to claim the tortfeasor's gain, it traditionally does so by saying that the victim waives the tort. The message is plain. The tort being waived, the restitutionary remedy is given for something that is not a tort at all': Birks (Select Bibliography), 68.

[178] *Ibid.*, 74.

[179] *Ibid.*, 101. Yet note how it was underused in the *Gorden Kaye* case [1992] FSR 62, discussed in ch. 22, below.

[180] Cf. *Agip (Africa) Ltd.* v. *Jackson & Co.* [1990] Ch. 265.

[181] [1988] 1 WLR 1406.

In Birks's words they were thus 'not so much [set] to defy the law [but] to derive the maximum advantage from its delays'.[182] The city's application for an injunction and the sum it would have charged for a licence succeeded at first instance. But in the Court of Appeal the money claimed was reduced to a nominal sum since no actual loss could be shown. Nourse LJ's concluding words deserve to be quoted in full:

> I rest my decision in this case on the simple ground that where no loss has been suffered no substantial damages of any kind can be recovered . . . It is possible that the English law of tort, more especially the so-called 'proprietary torts', will in due course make a more deliberate move towards recovery based not on loss suffered by the plaintiff but on the unjust enrichment of the defendant . . . But I do not think that the process can begin in this case and I doubt whether it can begin at all at this level of decision.[183]

This statement is indicative of the point made above, namely that the effective concealment of restitutionary damages behind a variety of stratagems or historical accidents can mislead judges and adversely affect deserving claimants, not to mention the danger of hampering the efficient and clear development of its law. As one commentator has observed: 'Can we continue to allow the historical division between equity and law to play tricks on us to the extent that it has fooled us into locating equitable wrongs in a course which has nothing to do with wrongs but with the institution of a trust?'[184]

Rhetorical though the question is, it must be emphatically answered in the negative. Tort textbooks must openly admit that compensation has an important role to play in the law of torts. But it is not a monopolistic one. Restitutionary damages are available for many wrongs which can (or should) also be considered as torts. And that their further integration into the subject under review must continue apace, even if considerations of space may mean that (for a time at least) they will not receive in *tort* textbooks the attention that is customarily accorded to some torts, e.g. negligence. In the years to come students should thus expect more developments along these lines.

SELECT BIBLIOGRAPHY

ATIYAH, P. S., *The Damages Lottery* (1997).

BIRKS, P. B. H., 'Civil Wrongs: A New World', *Butterworth Lectures 1990–1* (1992), 55–112.

CANE, P., *Atiyah's Accidents, Compensation and the Law* (7th edn., 2006), ch. 17.

—*Tort Law and Economic Interests* (2nd edn., 1996).

—*The Anatomy of Tort Law* (1997).

EHRENZWEIG, A. A., 'Negligence without Fault' (1966) 54 *Cal. LR* 1422.

ENGLARD, I., 'The System Builders: A Critical Appraisal of Modern American Tort Theory' (1980) 9 *Jo. LS* 27.

EPSTEIN, R. A., 'A Theory of Strict Liability' (1973) 2 *Jo. LS* 151.

182 Birks (Select Bibliography), 58.
183 [1988] 1 WLR 1406, 1415.
184 E. McKendrick, *Tort Textbook* (5th edn., 1991), 3.

FLEMING, J. G., 'More Thoughts on Loss Distribution' (1966) 4 *Osgoode Hall LJ* 161.

—'Is There a Future for Tort?' (1984) 58 *Aust. LJ* 131.

—*An Introduction to the Law of Torts* (2nd edn., 1985), 1.

FLETCHER, G. P., 'Fairness and Utility in Tort Theory' (1972) 85 *Harv. LR* 537.

MCGREGOR, H., 'Compensation versus Punishment in Damages Awards' (1965) 28 *MLR* 629.

WILLIAMS, G. L., 'The Aims of the Law of Tort' [1951] 4 *CLP* 137.

6. FAULT AS THE BASIS OF TORTIOUS LIABILITY

The importance attached to fault largely depends upon the functions that a legal system is prepared to assign to its tort law. Since, as we have noted, these have changed over the years, the role of fault as the basis of liability has in turn been ignored, glorified, and questioned. We need not involve ourselves in the problems of whether liability was historically based on fault or simply on damage and causation.[185] The fact remains that by the middle of the nineteenth century it became increasingly accepted that 'sound policy lets losses lie where they fall, except where a special reason can be shown for interference'.[186] Apart from a few exceptional situations such special reason was the tortfeasor's fault in one or other of the meanings explained earlier. A person at fault was guilty not only of a legal wrong but also of an ethical wrong.[187] As Professor Fleming has put it: 'the triumph of fault liability was well-nigh complete and marked a singular judicial triumph in remoulding ancient precedents in the image of a radically different era'. [188]

The moral, social and economic reasons behind this approach blended so well at that particular historical period that the result appeared attractive. To nineteenth-century moralists the idea that bad people should pay and that very bad people should pay more had obvious appeal. It was thus reflected in a number of rules—intended consequences are never too remote, malice defeats certain defences, a plaintiff was deprived of compensation if he had contributed to his own hurt, etc. Tort law, however, had a deterrent and not only an admonitory function to perform. At a time of a weak or non-existent insurance market the compensation of the victim came out of the tortfeasor's pocket. To quote again from Professor Fleming: 'Personal fortune was regarded as the primary source of compensation, so that the deterrent lash would be at once real and ineluctable.'[189]

[185] For different views see J. B. Ames, 'Law and Morals' (1908) 22 *Harv. LR* 97; C. H. Fifoot, *History and Sources of the Common Law* (1949), ch. 9; O. W. Holmes, *The Common Law* (1923), ch. 1; J. H. Wigmore, 'Responsibility for Tortious Acts: Its History' (1894) 7 *Harv. LR* 315.

[186] Holmes, n. 185, 50 and, in greater detail, 94 ff.

[187] Tunc (Select Bibliography), 75.

[188] *Introduction to the Law of Torts* (2nd edn., 1985), 6.

[189] *Ibid.*

Yet there was more in this moralistic movement than one might surmise at first sight. For in logic and law the reverse of a proposition usually commands the same respect as the proposition itself. This meant that persons not at fault could not be liable for the damage they caused. It is here that economic expediency blended in with current morality and created the nineteenth-century legacy of fault,[190] which subsequent generations have found difficult to shake off. For insistence upon fault, and (just as importantly) the need for a plaintiff to prove it, meant that during the period of industrial expansion and increased industrial accidents, an enterprise could be shielded against the costs of accidents. In human terms the result was appalling for the injured workers, who were indirectly called upon to subsidise production at the expense of life and limb. In economic terms any other solution could have ruined enterprises in their infancy. One can find more evidence of this type of economic reasoning in nineteenth-century American cases[191] than in their English counterparts, but it represents part, at least, of the truth for English law as well. Finally, fault had educational and social value in so far as it helped to balance one's freedom of action against the duties and responsibilities arising from such action. People should be allowed some freedom of action and should not be made to pay for the damage they cause if they have not fallen below a certain minimum standard of proper behaviour; nor should they recover if their fault in any way contributed to their own hurt.

Continuing growth of industry, the emergence of modern insurance and the social effects of two world wars soon encouraged increasing opposition to these arguments. Even moralists were quick to stress that no human being can really sit in moral judgement on the acts of another human being; which, in any event, was not the function of a court of law. As votes started to matter as the electorate became politically organised, the social consciousness of the state became increasingly apparent. Indifference to the weak and the needy was something that few politicians could afford to display. Besides, insurance was making the absorption of losses easier than in the past, and the need to protect nascent industrialisation was no longer there. Economic analyses of the law of tort also started to reveal how costly a system based on fault could be, and, above all, the role of fault in imposing liability became increasingly attenuated.

First of all one should note the large number of 'overlooked faults', such as those which are undiscovered or not pursued through lapse of time or expense, as well as social faults, such as pollution, or exploitation through tobacco, alcohol or pornography.[192] In the light of so long a list one is justified in asking what is left of the principle that requires a person to answer for damage caused by his fault.

There is also another reason behind this attenuation of the fault principle, which is simply that a very large number of the people who are actually at fault are never called

190 See C. Woodard, 'Reality and Social Reform: The Transition from Laissez-Faire to Welfare State' (1962) 72 *Yale LJ* 286.

191 E.g. *Farwell* v. *Boston and Worcester Railroad Corp.* 45 Mass. 4 (Met) 49 (1842).

192 Tunc (Select Bibliography), 66.

upon to meet the economic consequences of their wrongdoing. As Professor James has pointed out,[193] those who have to pay are 'innocent absentees', namely, employers and insurance companies; and the ultimate burden of insurance is borne in the end indiscriminately by the just and the unjust.[194]

This allusion to insurance reveals yet another weakness of a fault-based theory of liability. As Professor Tunc has said:

> Liability insurance, apart from automobile insurance and professional insurances, is very cheap . . . If liability for fault is the foundation of society and morality, one must admit that this foundation is strangely cheap.[195]

The last, but by no means least significant, sign of abandonment of the fault principle that followed the change of emphasis of tort law from loss-shifting to loss-spreading is the transformation of the notion of negligence from a concept with strong moral overtones into a legal notion in which wider policy considerations determine the existence of a duty to take care, its breach, and even the extent of the consequences. The extension of 'negligence' to include cases of unavoidable error has caused a certain amount of conceptual confusion, but it has been prompted by sympathy for the victim and has been facilitated by the availability of insurance. Nevertheless, not all cases lend themselves to this kind of analysis.

In the medical malpractice case of *Whitehouse* v. *Jordan*,[196] an attempt was made to hold an obstetrician liable for allegedly misusing the forceps during delivery and thereby injuring the infant plaintiff. Had the court treated the unfortunate error of the doctor as 'negligence' it would have compensated the plaintiff by holding the doctor liable, and so imposed an additional burden on some hospital authority. On the other hand, the actual decision that the doctor had not been negligent avoided such an outcome, but left the innocent victim without redress. These doubts about fault, however, should not lead us to the opposite extreme of advocating the complete abandonment of fault as a criterion of liability. For truly blameworthy conduct liability should, in principle, be imposed. In these instances fault can be useful. Where, however, one is talking of accidents resulting from statistically inevitable errors, fault is an unsatisfactory criterion of compensation.[197] Fault-orientated liability should here yield to loss-spreading techniques, some of which we have looked at briefly. Only in cases of faults in a narrow sense should civil liability be reintroduced.

193 'Tort Law in Midstream' (Select Bibliography), 331.

194 'An Evaluation of the Fault Concept' (Select Bibliography), 398.

195 Tunc (Select Bibliography), 67.

196 [1981] 1 WLR 246.

197 The diverging cases of *Roberts* v. *Ramsbottom* [1980] 1 WLR 823 and *Mansfield* v. *Weetabix Ltd.* [1998] 1 WLR 1263 offer a good illustration of the point made in the text. Unfortunately, both made little use of insurance arguments and, instead, chose to focus (mainly) on the relevance of some criminal law cases to tort law.

SELECT BIBLIOGRAPHY

CANE, P., *The Anatomy of Tort Law* (1997).

FLEMING, J. G., 'The Role of Negligence in Modern Tort Law' (1967) 53 *Virginia LR* 815.

FLETCHER, G. P., 'Fairness and Utility in Tort Theory' (1972) 85 *Harv. LR* 537.

ISON, T. G., *The Forensic Lottery* (1967).

JAMES, F., 'Tort Law in Midstream: Its Challenge to the Judicial Process' (1959) 8 *Buffalo LR* 315.

—'An Evaluation of the Fault Concept' (1965) 32 *Tenn. LR* 394.

—'The Future of Negligence in Accident Law' (1967) 53 *Virginia LR* 911.

MALONE, W. S., 'Ruminations on the Role of Fault in the History of the Common Law of Torts' (1970) 31 *Louis. LR* 1.

STOLJAR, S., 'Accidents, Costs and Legal Responsibility' (1973) 36 *MLR* 233.

TUNC, A. (ed.), *International Encyclopedia of Comparative Law*, xi: *Torts* (1972), ch. 1, 63–86.

7. ALTERNATIVE SYSTEMS OF COMPENSATION

So far we have talked only incidentally about other methods of compensation, such as social security and private insurance. That the well-established tort books should place emphasis on compensation at law is understandable and in keeping with tradition. On the other hand, an entirely legalistic approach, despite some merits, also has its drawbacks, for it tends to present only one part of the whole picture of the system of compensation for harm and injury. Thus, no lawyer, practising or academic, must be allowed to forget that, in the words of the Pearson Committee Report, tort law has been reduced to the role of 'junior partner' in the whole compensation system.

Second, the attempt to compensate victims through tort, without taking into account other available sources of compensation, may encourage lawyers into making artificial distinctions. For instance, in *Jobling* v. *Associated Dairies Ltd.*,[198] the court had to decide whether damage sustained as a result of a *tort* should be assessed without regard to a subsequent *non-tortious event*, which supervened and obliterated its effects. In the earlier case of *Baker* v. *Willoughby*,[199] where the *subsequent* event was an independent tort, the House of Lords, applying *causal* language, compensated the victim in respect of the first injury to the full extent as if the subsequent injury had never taken place. In *Jobling*, on the other hand, where the subsequent event was not tortious (supervening illness), the defendant's responsibility for the first injury was limited to the consequences of his prior tort until the moment when the subsequent illness obliterated its effect. This difference

[198] [1982] AC 794 (mainly a causation case, and this aspect will be discussed in ch. 4).
[199] [1970] AC 467.

between the two cases could explain the different outcome, though it might be possible to sustain a counter-argument. Yet, just as noteworthy is the House of Lords' desire to underplay the role of causation and emphasise the role played by the Criminal Injuries Compensation Board, when fixing the compensation payable in tort. The relevant passage from Lord Wilberforce's judgment deserves to be quoted in full.

> The fact, however, is that to attempt a solution of these and similar problems, where there are successive causes of incapacity in some degree, upon classical lines ('the object of damages for tort is to place the plaintiff in as good a position as if the tort had not taken place,' '... the defendant must compensate for the loss caused by his wrongful act—no more,' 'the defendant must take the plaintiff as he finds him', etc.) is, in many cases, no longer possible. We live in a mixed world where a man is protected against injury and misfortune by a whole web of rules and dispositions, with a number of timid legislative interventions. To attempt to compensate him upon the basis of selected rules without regard to the whole must lead either to logical inconsistencies, or to over- or under-compensation. As my noble and learned friend, Lord Edmund-Davies, has pointed out, no account was taken in *Baker* v. *Willoughby* of the very real possibility that the plaintiff might obtain compensation from the Criminal Injuries Compensation Board. If he did in fact obtain this compensation he would, on the ultimate decision, be over-compensated.[200]

In *Hill* v. *Chief Constable of West Yorkshire* [201] we can find an example where the possibility of compensation under the Criminal Injuries Compensation scheme influenced not the element of causation but that of duty of care. *Hill* is one of those cases that was decided during the mid-1980s when legal thinking was increasingly affected by the hostility towards the Wilberforce formula concerning the existence of a duty of care enunciated in *Anns* v. *Merton London Borough Council*.[202] This debate will be discussed more fully in Chapter 3. Here suffice it to say that the argument centred on the stage of the inquiry at which policy considerations would be introduced in order to determine whether there was a duty of care. Thus, should policy be used to negative a *prima facie* duty arising whenever there is 'sufficient relationship of proximity or neighbourhood' between the tortfeasor and the victim 'such that, in the reasonable contemplation of the former, carelessness on his part may be likely to cause damage to the latter' (*Anns*)? Or should policy factors be used at the first stage in order to determine whether it was 'just and reasonable' (*Peabody*)[203] to impose such a duty?[204] In *Hill*'s case, Fox LJ opted for the second approach, and denied that the police were under a duty towards potential victims of a dangerous criminal to apprehend him before he committed a crime. As the learned

200 [1982] AC 794, 803–4.

201 [1988] QB 60 (CA); approved by the House of Lords in [1989] AC 53.

202 [1978] AC 728.

203 *Governors of the Peabody Donation Fund* v. *Sir Lindsay Parkinson* [1985] AC 210, 240.

204 In the subsequent case of *Stovin* v. *Wise* [1996] AC 923, 949, Lord Hoffmann suggested that 'provided ... the considerations of policy etc. are properly analysed, it should not matter whether one starts from one or the other'. A few lines further down, however, the learned judge made clear his own preference for non-liability rules. Though not without much merit, such a starting-point—the Law Lord, using computer language, calls it the 'default position'—is not without its difficulties. These are alluded to later on in this chapter but discussed in greater detail in the next.

judge put it: 'If the state [had] made no provision at all for criminal injuries [through the Criminal Injuries Compensation Board], that might be a reason for imposing a legal duty of care upon the police in the conduct of their investigations . . . .'[205]

Cases such as the above can be taken to suggest that the courts, when interpreting concepts with a strong normative content,[206] are likely to take into account the availability of, *inter alia*, alternative sources of compensation before deciding whether to impose (or discover) a duty of care. Such an approach is, it is submitted, both illuminating and acceptable *provided* the alternative remedies envisaged by the judges are *genuinely available and effective*. In the *Hill* case, the options available to the plaintiff under the Criminal Injuries Compensation Scheme were, if not ideal, good enough. In subsequent cases, however, where much use was made of *Hill*, our courts seemed to have lost sight of the significance of the italicised words and thus, effectively, left very deserving victims uncompensated.[207]

A third and major objection to the complete separation of various available systems of compensation is that this encourages their independent and uncoordinated development. The Pearson Committee recognised this when it said that:

> . . . the two systems have for too long been permitted to develop in isolation from each other, with regard to the fact that, between them, they meet many needs twice over and others not at all.[208]

However, its suggestions to overcome this isolationist approach were modest; and even these now look unlikely ever to be implemented.[209] A similar objection could be made to the traditional unwillingness to consider openly and in detail the impact of insurance on the law of torts. We shall return to this point briefly in the next chapter, though we also referred to what has already been said about the different ways different types of insurance can operate (and the different types of messages they can send out to the market) in the law of tort.

In recent times, however, there have been (mainly academic) stirrings against an over-legalistic approach to the law of tort. They owe much to the economic analysis of law which started in the United States and which we described briefly earlier in this chapter. This awareness of the need for a new direction in the teaching of tort law is already reflected in introductory works.[210] And Professor Atiyah's pioneering book on *Accidents, Compensation and the Law* for over thirty years now has been both an impetus in this direction and a veritable mine of ideas. In this Introduction we shall touch on

205 [1988] QB 60, 73.

206 Such as legal cause and, even more, duty of care.

207 Thus in *Elguzouli-Daf and Another* v. *Commissioner of Police of the Metropolis* [1995] QB 355, the plaintiffs were kept in custody for 25 and 85 days respectively and then the Crown Prosecution Service discontinued proceedings against them. The claims for tort damages for malicious prosecution and false imprisonment failed, the Court of Appeal setting great store by the *Hill* judgment. In these cases, however, the remedies left to the plaintiffs, though available on paper, were hardly effective in practice as Steyn LJ appeared to admit in his judgment.

208 Cmnd. 7054-I (1978), para. 271.

209 For further details, see ch. 25, below.

210 Williams and Hepple (Select Bibliography); Harlow (Select Bibliography).

only some of these wider issues and return to some of them in greater detail in later parts of this work as and when the need arises. This will be especially necessary when discussing compensation in Chapter 25.

It will be remembered that earlier, in Section 3, we spoke of 'loss distribution' and 'loss allocation' as aims for modern tort law. They are indeed often thought of in such terms. Equally, however, it is obvious that which method of distributing losses or allocating risks is chosen will very largely depend upon the kind of political choices one is prepared to make. Broadly speaking, there is a choice between two approaches (which can be ingeniously combined in certain cases).

The first is the free-market system, which tends to make people who cause damage pay for it. The other is a more collectivist approach, which lays greater emphasis on equality of treatment and places a greater burden on the state itself. If economic efficiency is something one should aim at, the tort system is expensive, for its administration costs (investigating claims, costs of litigation, etc.—economists usually call them 'transfer payments') represent a very large percentage of the total amounts available for compensation. Thus, the Pearson Committee estimated that it cost 85p to deliver £1 in net benefits to the victim; and, in Professor Fleming's words: 'Studies in the United States raise operating costs to $1.07 for automobile and $1.25 for product liability. In the protracted asbestos litigation it has cost $1.59 in combined litigation expenses to deliver $1 to the average plaintiff.'[211] In that sense tort law could be described as wasteful.

On the other hand, the social security system tends to have lower administrative costs, though the wider cost of the state and local-authority bureaucracy has not yet been accurately worked out. Though the social security system in many respects is just as complicated as the tort system, it does make its awards reach victims more quickly and often without the uncertainty that accompanies litigation. On the other hand, although social security compensation may be speedier, it also tends to be lower than the amount of a victim's actual loss and less likely to be tailored to his particular injury and needs—especially in the case of serious injuries.[212]

Apart from purely economic criteria, ideological and political decisions are also involved in deciding which of these systems should be adopted and to what extent, if any, the one should displace the others. Ours, being a mixed economy, strives for a balance, which of course leaves many unsatisfied. The structure that has resulted from this compromise may be divided into three levels. (In this chapter we shall merely describe the general outline; but we shall return to the question of compensation in Chapter 25, Section 2.)

At the first level the state assumes directly a primary, if not sole, responsibility to provide compensation. At the second level the state role is additional to that played by tort law and/or insurance. Finally, at the third and last level the compensation system—state or private—is at its weakest, leaving potential claimants with few, if any, rights. We can use this division for the brief remarks that conclude this section.

211 J. Fleming, *The American Tort Process* (1988), 19; Pearson Report, i, para. 261.

212 See ch. 25, Section 4.

(A) FIRST LEVEL

As stated, at the first level the role of the state is most developed.[213] It provides sickness and unemployment benefits and other compensation for accidents at work, based upon the principle of social insurance that entitlement rests on each individual's contributions while in employment. All these benefits can be accompanied by income support for those in further need. In many cases of personal injury, the state is the only provider of relief. In other cases, however, the state system of benefits may coexist alongside the tort rules. What form this coexistence takes will be discussed in Chapter 25. Here suffice it to say that whereas in the past these awards could (in part or in whole) be cumulated with the tort awards, the current trend is to restrict this right almost to a vanishing point. Though the principle pursued by these (new) rules—the avoidance of double compensation of the claimant—is a laudable one, the way it has been implemented in practice has been neither flawless nor notable for its clarity.[214]

(B) SECOND LEVEL

At the second level of the compensation system come those injuries for which the victim must seek satisfaction by prosecuting a tort claim. The money here will come in most cases from insurance of some kind, or from the defendant who, in the case of a corporation, may then pass on the costs of its general overheads. The state's role here is limited to providing *additional* compensation (through what one can broadly describe as the welfare system) as well as the coercive system (courts, policemen, bailiffs, etc., all of which cost money) that helps the victim to obtain his compensation. Additionally, it supplies the kind of regulatory background to ensure that certain potential defendants conduct their business properly, carry insurance, offer financial services properly, and so on. But in recent times, the state has also come up with some additional or supplementary schemes that can be of crucial importance to potential claimants. These include Criminal Injuries Compensation schemes and the Compensation Orders that can be made by criminal courts. Finally, they include a number of *ex gratia* payment schemes. We shall discuss them in turn.

(i) Criminal Injuries Compensation Schemes[215]

The state's role here can be crucial since it provides direct and, *in practice* invariably exclusive, assistance to victims of crimes of violence through the Criminal Injuries Compensation Board or, after the Criminal Injuries Compensation Act 1995 came into force,[216] by the Criminal Injuries Compensation Authority. Before describing this

213 The classic account of the gradual growth of the role of the state in providing for injury and disease is found in W. R. Cornish and G de N. Clark, *Law and Society in England* 1750–1950 (1989).

214 For further details, see ch. 25, below.

215 For more details see P. Rock, *Helping Victims of Crime* (1990) and D. Miers, *State Compensation for Criminal Injuries* (1997).

216 This deals with all complaints received after 1 Apr. 1996.

regime a few preliminary words are necessary about the vagaries of politics and how they have affected this scheme. If one word were to be used, it would be 'badly'; if a phrase is allowed: 'unprincipled inconsistency'.

The scheme was originally set up as a result of ideas canvassed in the late 1950s and early 1960s. But the theoretical foundations of the scheme have always been in doubt and never really sorted out. *Justice*, in a report published in 1962, probably provided the widest range of possible justifications. They varied from an attempt to argue that victims of violence are in a position that is analogous to victims of war, to the view that the state has a moral duty towards towards its citizens when it has failed to protect them.[217] Then there was the idea of 'balance': if criminals deserved a more caring treatment by the state, their victims should receive compensation that went further than the inadequate limits of assistance received from the social security system. None of these reasons ever explained adequately why a new scheme was needed rather than, say, enhancing the existing levels of state support if this was, indeed, inadequate. Nor has there ever been an explanation for carving out another category of victims for preferential treatment. Professor Cane has explored[218] in detail these inconsistencies so we need not cover the same ground. Suffice thus to say that the scheme was, in the end, essentially based on vague but widespread notions of sympathy and compassion.[219]

In 1964 the (Labour) government of the day accepted that public sympathy required that such victims should be helped by the state, but (attempted) to disguise the lack of a well-thought-out justification for the scheme by ordaining that the payments made under it would be *ex gratia*. By the 1980s the prevailing opinion in both political parties had moved towards the position that such payments should be placed on a statutory basis; and sections 108–17 of the Criminal Justice Act 1988 embodied this new conception of the state's own duties towards victims of crime. But almost immediately fears began to be expressed about the Board being inundated by claims and by huge delays becoming inevitable in the processing of these claims. The operation of the new scheme was thus suspended and an interim (and revised) administrative scheme was brought into application to deal with all claims made after 1 February 1990. This was nowhere near as thorough and well thought out as the 1988 Act,[220] as the absence of a definition of what amounted to a 'crime of violence' (which triggered off the application of the scheme), about which more in the next paragraph.

By the early 1990s, however, new concerns began to emerge about the cost of the scheme, especially its tendency to calculate the amount of damages awarded by following the usual tort rules. The then Home Secretary Michael Howard (subsequently, a short-lived leader of

217 Can any state ever really effectively, protect its citizens? Such an amorphously phrased sentence invites a negative reply. But the reality is even harsher. For our courts have held that the police are not liable even when they know of a specific threat to commit a crime imminently. This was the essence of *Osman* v. *Ferguson* [1993] 4 All ER 344; and this result was used by exploiting the device of 'duty of care', backed by economic thinking that argued that the police should be spared the expense of being held liable, even when their behaviour was blatantly faulty.

218 In *Atiyah's Accidents, Compensation and the Law* (7th edn., 2006), ch. 12, with rich further references.

219 P. Duff, 'Criminal Injuries Compensation: the Symbolic Dimension' [1955] *Juridical Review*, 102.

220 The provisions of which were described in the previous edition of the book.

the Conservative Party) thus opted for a tariff scheme based on a list of injuries. The new scheme was challenged in the courts and was held by the House of Lords to be illegal.[221] This, eventually, led to an enhanced tariff scheme which was embodied in the latest of the Acts, the Criminal Injuries Compensation Act 1995 which in due course, also gave way to yet another version in 2001. In keeping with the patchy way of dealing with this issue, the new version of the statute demonstrated even greater generosity both in the direction of sums paid in the case of multiple injuries but also in allowing these awards to be claimed, in the event of fatal accidents, by the surviving same-sex partners of the victim of violence. Home Office legislation, it would seem, whether on technical matters such as the above, or on wider issues of law and order, can never get matters right in their first attempt.

As already noted, the scheme is based on the idea of compensation being paid for injuries suffered by 'crimes of violence' as a result of intentional or reckless activities.[222] One does not always expect statutes to provide definitions; but one does hope for a modicum of consistency and rationality. Not so in this case. The Act thus includes in its purview arson, fire-raising and poisoning but not injuries caused by breach of health and safety legislation. Perhaps, the omission can be justified on a variety of grounds, one of which would be that these injuries are rarely the result of intentional (or reckless) activities. But what about a depressed person who throws himself on the path of an oncoming train, thereby causing the driver of the train severe anxiety and trauma? In 1987 the Court of Appeal held[223] that this was not a crime of violence; but the government, acting under pressure from the train-drivers' union, extended the scheme to cover this event. Drivers of motor cars on the other hand do not have unions to argue their case so, presumably, a similarly placed driver of a vehicle would have no claim under this scheme.

There are other cases of injuries attributable to an 'offence'[224] which, however, may not be able to generate compensation under this scheme. Imagine another depressed person— twentieth-century society has been quite efficient in increasing the numbers of citizens who feel depressed and dejected—deciding to commit suicide by cutting off the gas pipes in a house. A passing policeman, literally, smells something suspicious, enters the premises to investigate, and in the course of his search is injured or killed by a gas explosion. The Divisional court, which dealt with such a case, held—by majority—that there was no liability under the scheme; but the wording of the decision suggests that a change of facts might justify a different result.[225]

221 *R* v. *Secretary of State for the Home Department, ex parte Fire Brigades' Union* [1995] AC 513.

222 Despite the emphasis on intention or recklessness, compensation under the Scheme can also be obtained in the case of accidentally caused injuries. This is typically the case where law enforcement activities are taking place. For more details see: K. Williams, 'Compensation for Accidental Shooting by Police' [1991] *NLJ* 231.

223 *R.* v. *Criminal Injuries Compensation Board ex parte Webb* [1987] QB 74.

224 But what if the person causing the injury is excused from criminal responsibility because, for instance, he or she is under the age of 10, or is insane, or enjoys diplomatic immunity? The Scheme provides for compensation to be paid. For further details on all these points see the more specialised works referred in the Select Bibliography at the end of this section.

225 *R.* v. *Criminal Injuries Compensation Board ex parte Clowes* [1977] 1 WLR 1353.

Excluded from the interim scheme were such matters as acts of domestic violence, mainly to avoid collusion between members of the same family, injuries arising from the use of motor cars which would be covered by the Motor Insurers' Bureau (discussed below) or minor injuries, where compensation would be below a certain level—these days the amount being £1,000. The Authority in charge of the administration of the Scheme is also given wide powers to weigh carefully (and if necessary reduce) the amount of the award in order to take into account the conduct of the claimant. The idea behind these discretionary powers is similar to that found in the institution of contributory negligence though, in practice, it is innovatively wider in so far as it allows the Authority to take into account not only the conduct of the claimant but also his general character.

A number of supplementary observations about the new scheme may also be in order. Thus, first, the Scheme does not apply to rescuers claiming for psychiatric injuries nor to members of the emergency services for accidental injuries suffered in the course of their work. Second, claims by persons entitled to use the new scheme must be made within two years (instead of the previous three) from the date of the injury. Third, in fatal accident cases, compensation may include (in addition to lost dependency) funeral expenses and a bereavement sum of £10,000 (which must be shared by all dependants). Finally, compensation under the scheme can include damages for 'mental injury'. But whereas in the normal tort cases mental distress means psychiatric injury (as defined and delimited by the courts[226]) in the case of the Scheme it is defined more widely to include 'temporary medical anxiety, medically verified, or a disabling mental illness confirmed by psychiatric diagnosis'.[227]

The possibility of an award being made under this heading is also wider under the Scheme than it is under the common law of tort in so far as it also *seems*[228] to allow for mental injury suffered as a result of being told of the harm-inflicting event provided always the claimant's harm is 'directly attributable to a crime of violence'. This divergence between the rules of the common law of tort and the rules established by the Scheme is intriguing and not entirely easy to explain for it shows those who set up the scheme to be entirely unaware or unconcerned by the common-law rules which restrict so emphatically the possibility of recovery. Whether this is due to the fact that, as has happened in other cases of tort law, the legislator and the courts have not shown an excessive degree of co-ordination or whether it is made possible by the low and, on the whole, controlled levels of award made by the scheme is a matter which can be left to speculation. But if the second reason has something to do with this divergence of philosophies it may contain ideas worth imitating in the main part of tort law. To put it

226 For which see our discussion in ch. 3, below.

227 Para. 9 of the 2001 Scheme.

228 We have italicised this word for in one case where parents were told of their child being indecently assaulted and suffering as a result, an acute form of depression, the claim failed. The judge, however, also suggested that if the description of the assault had been graphic and occurred soon after it took place a claim might be allowed on the grounds that it would be 'directly attributable to the crime'. Thus, see, *R.* v. *Criminal Injuries Compensation Board ex parte Kent and Milne* [1998] PIQR Q98.

differently—and consistently with a theme that runs throughout this book—the level of possible awards may be one reason which leads our courts to avoid confronting this issue by shutting the possibility out completely through the (over)use of the notion of duty of care.

One final point remains to be made and it concerns the effect which these developments have had on the law of torts. Since most cases of intentional physical harm result from perpetrators who cannot be tracked down or, more likely, are financially not worth suing, the effect of the schemes has been to reduce significantly the number of cases dealing with trespass to the person which used to figure in tort books. But that should not be taken to mean that the Criminal Injuries Compensation Schemes have abolished tort law; rather, they have tried to supplement it for the benefit of the victim. Thus, claimants under the schemes may be penalised if, in appropriate cases, they fail to take advantage of the tort rules; and if they receive any tort award this will be deducted in full from any money paid under the scheme. Last, but by no means least, there are still cases where the use of the action of trespass, for instance against the police for assault or false imprisonment, can yield punitive awards[229] which, as stated, cannot be made under the schemes.

(ii) Compensation Orders[230]

One of the most interesting and relatively recent ways devised by the state to assist victims of crimes is the power granted to criminal courts to make *compensation* orders for damage resulting from the commission of an offence. This innovation, first introduced by section 1 of the Criminal Justice Act 1972,[231] can now be found in sections 130–4 of the Powers of Criminal Courts Act 2000. This gives the courts—typically magistrates and Crown Court judges—the power to order *convicted*[232] offenders to pay compensation to their victims. Sadly, however, the criminal courts do not have the power to issue compensation orders against defendants convicted of road traffic offences. The only (minimal) deviation from this rule can be found in section 104(2) of the Criminal Justice Act 1988. This allows a compensation order to be made in the case of an injury resulting from a road traffic offence whenever the offender is uninsured and the Motor Insurance Bureau will not pay.

Such awards can, according to the better view, be combined with custodial orders and/or an order to pay a fine but in practice they rarely are. This may be partly due to the fact that such a combination may be considered as unnecessarily severe but also, perhaps, because the enforcement of such orders might, in such circumstances be more

[229] For instance *White* v. *Metropolitan Police Commissioner, The Times*, 24 Apr. 1982; *Taylor* v. *Metropolitan Police Commissioner, The Times*, 6 Dec. 1989.

[230] For a discussion of the notions of 'reparation' and 'punishment' and the relationship of these two notions see Lucia Zedner, 'Reparation and Retribution: Are they Reconcilable?' (1994) 57 *MLR* 228.

[231] Which was re-enacted as s. 35 of the Powers of Criminal Courts Act 1973 and amended by s. 40 of the Magistrates' Court Act 1980 and s. 67 of the Criminal Justice Act 1982.

[232] A difference here with the Criminal Injuries Compensation schemes which never required a criminal conviction before payments could be made under those schemes.

difficult.[233] The idea that compensation (which is typically the remedy of a civil wrong) should not be treated in these cases as merely an appendage of the criminal sanction is reinforced by section 67 of the Criminal Justice Act 1982. This makes it clear that if the offender is incapable of paying both the fine and the compensation, priority should be given to the latter. The compensation order is in respect of 'any personal injury, loss or damage, resulting from [an] *offence*' and in no way depends upon the existence of any civil liability (arising from breach of contract or the commission of any tort which is also a criminal offence). The amount to be paid is left to the court's discretion having regard to all the evidence submitted to the court. In theory the Crown Court can, subject to what will be said below, award unlimited compensation. Magistrates' courts on the other hand have, since 1984, been subject to an upper limit of £2,000.[234] In practice, however, the awards seem to be very low. In 1983, for example, 'nearly half of the 122,000 awards in magistrates' courts were for £25 or less; only 18 exceeded £1,000. The pattern was comparable in 1984';[235] and by the end of the 1980s the *average* amount of such orders had gone up only slightly to £134 for magistrates' courts and £901 for the Crown Court.

In numerical terms most compensation orders are made in cases of theft and handling stolen goods; but the chances of obtaining such an order seem to be at their highest in cases of criminal damage. Section 35 orders, it seems, have not been used adequately in favour of consumers in the context of violations of the Trade Descriptions Act 1968. Indeed, the number of orders made under this heading seems to be falling. And the average amount awarded in 1981 was £308—a poor record which prompted Sir Gordon (now Lord) Borrie, the Director-General of the Office of Fair Trading at the time, to remark that 'surely it is timely for a little more boldness to be encouraged'.[236]

Michael Ogden QC, the former chairman of the Criminal Injuries Compensation Board, also expressed the hope that section 67 of the Criminal Justice Act 1982 would prompt the courts to make greater use of this power.[237] The possibility of making such orders, as a convenient and rapid means of avoiding the expense of resort to civil litigation is, in fact, well known and well developed in other systems. This is typically true wherever the device of class actions (enabling one person to bring an action on behalf of a group of injured consumers, each of whom has suffered a relatively small loss that discourages him personally from hazarding litigation) is unknown, or where resort to the usual contractual or tortious remedies is likely to be time-consuming and costly, and thus dissuade victims from asserting their rights. In this country, however, the innovation has had only a modest success, with the magistrates' courts making the fuller use of these powers (113,000 compensation orders made, compared to just under 7,000 ordered by the Crown Court).

[233] On this see M. Ogden, 'Compensation Orders in Cases of Violence' [1985] *Crim. LR* 500; Home Office Consultation Paper, *Compensation and Support for Victims of Crime* (2004), 11 and 12.

[234] Criminal Penalties (Increase) Order (SI No. 1984/447).

[235] S. Weatherill, 'The Powers of Criminal Courts to Make Compensation Orders' (1986) 136 *NLJ* 459, 464.

[236] G. Borrie, *The Development of Consumer Law and Policy: Bold Spirits and Timorous Souls*, The Hamlyn Lectures (1984), 69.

[237] 'Compensation Orders in Cases of Violence' [1985] *Crim. LR* 500.

The relative novelty of the innovation can provide only a partial answer, even allowing for the fact that sentencing habits may take time to change. But with the passage of time and the decline in the number of orders issued, it cannot be considered as a serious explanation. Another reason may be the fact that whereas (rightly) the initiative is left to the prosecution, the rights of the injured person to intervene in the proceedings and quantify his loss seem to be too uncertain. The impecuniosity of most convicted may be a more substantive reason for the lack of use of this remedy. Last and by no means least is the effect of *dicta* in a pre-1982 court decision that courts should refrain from making such orders where there is substantial uncertainty as to the extent of the loss. Decisions of the Court of Appeal in the 1970s also suggested that judges—in practice, as we have seen with magistrates—should be slow in involving themselves in cases where the causation issue was too complicated. The wording of section 67 of the Criminal Justice Act 1982 provides some hope to those who would like to see courts making a more liberal use of their powers; but legal conservatism may also make courts hesitant to intervene, especially where there is substantial uncertainty over issues of causation and remoteness.

The above reasons, individually and cumulatively, may explain the steady decline of compensation orders. Thus, limiting our observations to compensation orders issued by magistrates' courts, we note that in 1990 such orders were made in 29 per cent of cases. This figure declined to 19 per cent in 1996 and 15 per cent by 2003.

(iii) The Motor Insurers' Bureau

Victims of car accidents where the driver is either uninsured or unknown have, since 1946 and 1968 respectively, been given a new form of protection. Such claims can now be met, subject to certain technical conditions, by the Motor Insurers' Bureau, which was set up just after World War II by an agreement between the government and insurance companies.

The Motor Insurers' Bureau is a company limited by guarantee and financed by a levy on member companies in proportion to their motor premium incomes. Under the agreement, the Bureau will meet judgments against uninsured motorists. Its obligations are contractual towards the government and not statutory and, in theory, they could deny payment made for claims submitted by third parties. In practice, of course, this never occurs. Usually, a settlement is negotiated but if none is reached, the Bureau will then defend the case on behalf of the uninsured defendant. What is covered are claims for death, injury or property damage.

With regard to the untraced, hit-and-run motorists, the Bureau has, since 1968, agreed to give sympathetic consideration to making *ex gratia* payment to victims suffering personal injury if it is satisfied that the motorist concerned would have been held liable had he been traced and sued. The scheme was revised in 1972 and now all authorised motor insurers are required to be members of the Bureau.[238] In 2003 the

[238] Road Traffic Act 1974, s. 20. For further details see D. B. Williams, *The Motor Insurance Bureau* (2nd edn., 1972).

coverage has been extended to cover property damage if the offending vehicle has been identified (even if its driver cannot be traced). In all these cases, compensation is assessed in accordance with the normal tort principles.

The overall protection thus given to traffic-accident victims is considerable. Certainly, it is greater than that given to employees suing their employers under the 1969 Act, since in this latter case there is no statutory right to claim the amount of an unsatisfied judgment directly from the insurer. Such a right of direct access is provided by section 1 of the Third Parties Against Insurers Act 1930 only in the event of a tortfeasor being insolvent. Where that works, it offers the victim the advantage of receiving the whole of the insurance money directly and does not force him to compete with the other creditors of a *bankrupt* tortfeasor for a share of his estate.

The regime just described is, obviously, of great importance to many victims who would otherwise be left uncompensated. The reader, however, must note once again its anomalous features—e.g. its contractual rather than statutory nature—as well the preferential treatment it gives to a particular (albeit very significant) group of claimants.

(iv) Special *Ex Gratia* Payment Schemes

These schemes rarely fall to be discussed in tort classes, even less examined. They do, however, from part of the growing and complex system of compensation for accident or misfortune and, for the sake of relative completeness, a few words must be said about them. The main schemes we have in mind are: (i) the vaccine damage scheme; (ii) the HIV scheme; (iii) the hepatitis scheme; and (iv) the variant-CJD scheme.

Broadly speaking, all of the above have some common features. Thus, first, they all involve payments made by trust set up by the government to make *ex gratia* payments for certain types of harm. Second, their theoretical basis is, as with the schemes discussed above, debatable and, probably, they should be seen as gestures of sympathy and support manifested after public pressure was applied on the government of the day. In that sense they represent yet another example of what organised pressure, invariably accomplished with the aid of the media, can force governments to do. Third, all these schemes involve making payments without the need to establish fault on the part of anyone. In this sense, they thus all represent a departure from the fault system which has traditionally supplied the best reason for shifting the loss from the shoulders of the person who suffered it on to the shoulders of the person whose fault caused it in the first place. Fourth, all these schemes provide more or less predetermined sums which, moreover, are modest by comparison to sums that could have been obtained through a tort action (assuming the problems of fault and causation could be overcome). Finally, the amounts awarded by most of these schemes have been repeatedly adjusted upwards, providing yet another sign of the effectiveness of public pressure being brought to bear on governments and the civil service. Most of these points touch upon the interrelationship of tort law and real-world politics which, as we say repeatedly in this book, is inadequately explored by those who prefer looking at our subject in a black letter law kind of way. But the interested tutor and reader should seize on these hints and explore them further himself with a view to discovering how 'living' law is shaped.

(C) THIRD LEVEL

Finally, at the third level of the compensation system one finds those interferences that the system cannot afford to compensate. Compensation for them through the courts will be denied because in a world of limited resources they come too low in any scale of allocation of resources. Nervous shock cases, for example, have until recently received little attention at law for this reason, as well as for their assumed propensity to lead to increased litigation. Put differently (and more bluntly), there is not enough money to go around for every injury, so 'marginal' cases have to be left out. In these the victim is left to bear the loss himself or through his own first-party insurance coverage. As already stated, social security payments and their relationship to tort awards will be considered in Chapter 25. The last part of this section will, thus, briefly touch on the remaining possible source of compensation: insurance.

Insurance presents a number of advantages for all parties concerned. For the victim it represents a considerable guarantee that funds will be available to compensate him if he succeeds in his action. For the party inflicting the injury it means that if his conduct is held to be an actionable wrong, this will not spell economic ruin for him. For the insurers themselves, there is, of course, the possibility of profitable business—one rarely hears of poor insurers—by means of insurance premiums. Moreover, there is something that appears, at first sight at least, to be very unfair. That is the insurer's right, after he has paid the victim, to take over his rights by way of subrogation. This gives insurers the right to have their cake and eat it (except where it can be shown convincingly that sums recouped through subrogation are used to keep premiums low). The social interest, too, is served by insurance that enables members of society to obtain compensation through law without thereby ruining others. Further, in certain types of harm the insurance system makes a positive contribution towards accident prevention by inhibiting shortcomings through higher premiums, loss of no-claims bonuses or, even, by refusing to insure altogether unless certain standards of safety are scrupulously maintained. Indeed, so successful has insurance been that during this century it has been made compulsory in certain areas. Since 1976, for example, any solicitor practising in England or Wales is obliged to take out insurance under a special scheme organised by the Law Society.[239] (Recently the Bar has approved a scheme for compulsory mutual insurance.) Seven years before that the Employers' Liability (Compulsory Insurance) Act 1969 made it obligatory for employers to take out insurance coverage for liability for bodily injury, including death and disease. However, by far the most important instance of compulsory insurance is the earliest of them all, dealing with liability for death or injury arising from the use of a vehicle on a road (introduced in 1930 and now regulated by the Road Traffic Act 1972).[240] This is no place to discuss the technical rules on this matter though one should state that, despite the doctrine of privity of contract, any person who is covered by the insurance policy may enforce it against the insurer even though he has supplied no consideration for the coverage.[241] Equally,

[239] Solicitors Act 1974, s. 37. [240] Road Traffic Act 1972, ss. 143 ff. [241] *Ibid.*, s. 148(4).

the victim may, subject to certain formalities, claim from the insurer the amount plus interest and costs for which a court has condemned the tortfeasor.[242]

Non-compulsory insurance can be divided into two broad categories. First-party insurance is taken out by victims to cover themselves against the chance of harm being inflicted on them. Third-party liability insurance, on the other hand, protects tortfeasors against the harm they inflict on others. This latter type can take a number of forms, each with special rules: for example, employers' liability insurance, products liability insurance, motor insurance (additional to what is compulsory), libel insurance, etc. First-party insurance involves two parties, the insurer and the insured, whereas third-party liability insurance involves three: the insurer, the insured and the victim. This difference may have important consequences. For example, in first-party insurance the insured victim will obtain his insurance money once the insured risk materialises without the uncertainty of litigation (subject, of course, to the insurance policy being valid). On the other hand, in third-party liability insurance the insurer will pay the victim only if the insured has been found guilty of a tort. Indeed, insurance companies tend to take over such actions and by utilising their superior financial resources and expertise they can often drag out, or even frustrate, the compensation process. Another consequence is that, in first-party insurance, premiums are easier to quote, hence lower in some cases. In the 'cable cases', for example, a factory owner who is trying to obtain insurance coverage for the loss that might flow from a power failure should be able to inform the insurer of the precise amount of cover he wishes to purchase. He should also be in a position to tell him what means, if any, he has at his disposal to minimise the effect of a power failure (e.g. an additional electrical generator). A contractor, on the other hand, may find it difficult to name a sum for which he wishes to be covered should he be held liable to the factory owner, especially if he cannot obtain accurate plans of the area in which he is working. Additionally, third-party insurance invariably involves higher transaction costs; for it will be remembered that the insurer in this kind of insurance will not pay unless and until his client (the insured) is found 'guilty' of the tort he is accused of having committed. On the other hand it could be argued that in some cases an extension of liability might help to make such activities safer since insurance companies, which will inevitably be drawn into the picture, are virtually certain to insist on stringent precautions being taken before they extend insurance coverage.[243] This illustration, incidentally, shows not only how insurance actually operates, but also how it could be used[244] to determine the most reasonable and efficient allocation of resources.

242 *Ibid.*, s. 149.

243 This point is made by H. Kötz, in K. Zweigert and H. Kötz, *An Introduction to Comparative Law* (trans. J. A. Weir, 1977), ii, 273. Given that the position in German law presents considerable similarity with ours, the view deserves careful consideration.

244 Contrast J. Stapleton, 'Tort Insurance and Ideology' (1995) 55 *MLR* 820, where she doubts whether (a) insurance *is* taken into account by the courts and (b) whether it *should* be taken into account at all. Growing evidence seems to suggest that the learned author is unconvincing on (a) but may find some support for (b) among those who still believe that tort law performs an important role in corrective justice.

SELECT BIBLIOGRAPHY

ALLEN, D. K., BOURN, C. J. and HOLYOAK, J. H. (eds.), *Accident Compensation after Pearson* (1979).

ATIYAH, P. S., *The Damages Lottery* (1997).

BURN, S., 'Injury Tariff ' (1996) 93(12) *LSG* 22.

CANE, P., *Atiyah's Accidents, Compensation and the Law* (7th edn., 2006), chs. 1, 11–18.

DAVIES, M., 'The End of the Affair: Duty of Care and Liability Insurance' (1989) 9 *Leg. Stud.* 67.

FRANKLIN, M. A., 'Replacing the Negligence Lottery: Compensation and Selective Reimbursement' (1967) 53 *Virginia LR* 724.

GREER, D., *Criminal Injuries Compensation* (1991).

HARLOW, C., *Understanding Tort Law* (1987).

HOWARTH, D., 'Three Forms of Responsibility: On the Relationship between Tort Law and the Welfare State' [2001] *CLJ* 553.

MIERS, D., *State Compensation for Criminal Injuries* (1997).

PEARSON COMMITTEE, *Report of the Royal Commission on Civil Liability and Compensation for Personal Injury*, Cmnd. 7054–I (1978), chs. 4–7.

STAPLETON, J., 'Tort, Insurance and Ideology' (1995) 58 *MLR* 820.

WIKELEY, N., OGUS, A. I., and BARENDT, E. M., *The Law of Social Security* (6th edn., 2002).

WILLIAMS, D. B., *Criminal Injuries Compensation* (2nd edn., 1986).

WILLIAMS, G. L., and HEPPLE, B. A., *Foundations of the Law of Tort* (2nd edn., 1984), chs. 5 and 6.

2

SOME GENERAL WARNINGS FOR THE NOVICE TORT LAWYER

1. GENERAL COMMENTS

It is unusual, indeed we believe it is unique, to find a section such as this in any tort textbook. That is one reason why the authors of this book originally agonised over whether to include it or not. The majority of thoughtful (and anonymous) 'feedback' reviews, sent to the publishers before the preparation of the last and the present edition from colleagues using this book, strongly backed the aims and contents of that sub-section, so it appears once again and, what is more, in a reinvigorated form in a chapter of its own. But why do we feel the need to make these observations? The starting-point is the realisation that this is a students' textbook and is thus concerned not only with imparting knowledge but also suggesting a methodology for understanding tort law. Nowadays, this may involve going beyond describing and analysing legal concepts and precedents.

Academic instruction, during the teaching life of the present authors, has striven for a readable, systematic and analytical presentation of the material. Though the trend is slowly evincing a shift of emphasis, for a long time the material included in tort textbooks was almost all exclusively legal. Legal and, at its best, admirably analytical was the way tort was taught. But it was not only that: it could also be dry, separated as it was from life, real suffering and its protagonists' outlook and beliefs. Thus, for years Professor Atiyah's *Accidents and Compensation and the Law* formed the solitary exception to such method of instruction in trying to discuss torts with the aid of statistics, looking at law in action, and by paying due attention to such underlying formative factors as insurance. As Professor Twining, the editor of the series in which Atiyah's book first appeared, said at the time: the book 'won almost instant recognition as a brilliantly designed and executed departure from tradition'. Now, thirty-seven years later and in its seventh edition, meticulously updated by Professor Peter Cane, the book still provides an invaluable reference aid. But it may not appeal to all students; nor has it supplanted the traditional textbook and casebook, both of which have, indeed, even multiplied in numbers. To be too much ahead of one's time is as bad as failing to catch up with it.

This book has tried to learn from the strengths and the weaknesses of the Atiyah experiment. From the outset it tried to innovate and, in terms of coverage, to go for a midway house between what one could call—in substance as well as written style—the traditional and the modern. This has meant a number of things such as: (a) slowly decreasing the attention paid to certain topics which, in practical terms, are of little importance; (b) openly warning students that the idea that through analytical ingenuity they can reconcile *all* the cases is an unrealistic dream as well as an exercise which is simply not useful; and (c) gradually enhancing the extra-legal material which forms part of the presentation of the subject-matter by enlarging the range of topics which caught Atiyah's attention but which we feel are still important to understanding how tort law is 'formed'. So, the evolution that has affected tort law involves and conceals many other factors; and it is for us to begin preparing newcomers to learn how to detect them and to learn how to handle them for themselves. We would not be surprised if it takes a decade or more before this way of looking at torts percolates through to decisions and academic writings.

These background factors range from the overtly political—note, for instance, the reform introduced to save the public purse of much needed cash by authorising periodical payments[1]—to the highly technical and multidisciplinary, such as the role and capabilities of the insurance industry to meet claims. They extend from the international dimension (and thus often neglected in an introspective country such as ours), for instance the growing importance of the impact of the judgments of European Community and European Court of Human Rights law upon our domestic law, to, finally, the role that can be played by the 'psychobiography' of judges who decide the cases we have to discuss. All of these sub-topics are increasingly studied in other countries, especially the United States which remains the main source of ideas—good and bad—but are overdue in ours.

We think that the time has come to usher in gently more changes in what we teach and how to teach it. For although some may think that the average (and higher) student may no longer possess the broad culture one would wish him to have, he or she is certainly more sophisticated than most of his or her predecessors. It is our opinion that today's students are thus more willing to seek out the real causes of a decision while being less willing to accept 'authority' as the only 'reason' that makes it acceptable. The world, in short, including the academic world we live in, has changed dramatically during the twenty years this book has been in the bookshops and the book must therefore reflect these changes—to be sure in a measured and controlled way—but reflect them nonetheless it must. We think we are innovating by attempting to do just that in the entire book; and also explaining our themes and reasons in these introductory chapters.

At this early stage of their study we thus believe there is a need to warn students off some misapprehensions that are common to beginners. For students tend to assume that tort law in practice is that which they find in the books: neat, systematic, doctrinal

[1] Discussed in ch. 25, below.

and legalistic. They also assume that our judges are gifted in argument and analysis—which, undoubtedly, they are—and doctrinally widely read—which, surprisingly, not all of them are. The following propositions may thus be borne in mind as the reader goes through the pages that follow and encounters criticism of individual rules, decisions and academic opinions. We have certainly tried to pick these themes up consistently and repeatedly as the narrative progressed so here we merely highlight them and explain why we think they are important.

2. JUDICIAL MENTALITY AND OUTLOOK, AND HOW IT AFFECTS DECISION-MAKING

Every true professional practises his art according to its rules, stricter or more elastic as the case may be, and with absolute honesty and integrity. But no one has ever doubted that the way these professionals work, as well as the final product they produce, reflects in different ways and to varying degrees their mentality, outlook, training, idiosyncrasies, environment and other beliefs. The freedom each has to draw on these often hidden and certainly less widely studied factors may, of course, vary from profession to profession; but to pretend that this is not the case in law, and with judges in particular, is something that would not appear to be convincing. Indeed, it would be not just unreasonable to assume the contrary but also incompatible with human nature to suggest that our judges would not take advantage of the vagueness of the key concepts they themselves have fashioned to develop the law of torts—notably the amorphous formula of 'fair, just and reasonable'[2]—in order to introduce in the deciding process some of these personal characteristics which we are here trying to single out for discussion.

If what we suggest is novel to our legal landscape, it most assuredly is not novel elsewhere. Certainly, the volume of material attempting such complex studies in growing by the day. Judge Posner, for instance, is among the many (and respected) jurists who, writing most recently in the *Harvard Law Review* observed that:

> It is no longer open to debate that ideology (which I see as intermediary between a host of personal factors, such as upbringing, temperament, experience, and emotion—even including petty resentments toward one's colleagues—and the casting of a vote in a legally indeterminate case, the ideology being the product of the personal factors) plays a significant role in the decisions even of lower court judges when the law is uncertain and emotions aroused. It must play an even larger role in the Supreme Court, where the issues are more uncertain and more emotional and the judging less constrained.[3]

Yet statements such as these are not only found in the United States, a jurisdiction which we never tire of describing as being close to ours (even though often it is not).

[2] Only very recently, as we shall observe in ch. 3, have our judges tried to demystify somewhat the importance of this formula; but there is still much to be done. Thus, see, *H.M.'s Commissioners of Customs and Excise* v. *Barclays Bank plc* [2006] UKHL 28, [2006] 3 WLR 1.

[3] 'The Supreme Court 2004 Term Foreword: A Political Court', (2005) 119 *Harv. LR* 32, at 48–9 and notes.

They are appearing even in 'different' systems where judges, in their judgments, have traditionally eschewed open discussion of policy and have, on the contrary, idolised the power of abstract concepts and notions, giving the (erroneous) impression that judges there mechanically apply their deductive reasoning to reach their conclusions. So there, too, we see a growing admission of this phenomenon—the admission that the judge's personal outlook and mentality play a part in the final judgment—and there, too, we see academics being urged to study these influences and try to understand better how they affect the decision process. Thus, the recently retired President of the German Constitutional Court, Professor Jutta Limbach, had this to say on the subject in a lecture given at the Humboldt University of Berlin in 1996:

> (I)f formally approached, it is of course the duty of the *Bundesverfassungsgericht* [the Constitutional court] to answer authoritatively the question whether a certain provision is constitutional. The Court must, however, be aware of the fact that the answer to this question is the result of highly complex considerations involving a balancing of interests and values. There is no absolutely correct decision; at least such a decision cannot be achieved by us on this earth. The dissenting opinions of judges are, in many cases, proof of this fact. Conflicting views between judges do not materialise from thin air. In addition to different historical and cultural perspectives which play a role, judges also have diverging opinions concerning social values. We know that individuals have an a priori understanding of certain issues which more or less affects the legal solutions they opt for. *This has nothing to do with prejudice or bias. We are all determined by certain basic views which are independent of the process of applying the law and which are formed by intuition rather than by rational analysis. This is a mixture of moral, legal, philosophical, and political convictions, and it includes an individual's understanding of the world that we live in.*[4]

Whichever the system under examination, the conclusion thus seems to be the same. One cannot expect a judge to shake off completely his training, academic specialisation, ethnic and religious background and general political (if not necessarily party political) outlook, when deciding borderline cases. What is difficult is not making this assertion but proving beyond doubt its veracity.

Happily, we live in an era which has seen our contemporary common law judges falling over themselves to accept to give public lectures, publish collections of their essays, or even take part in a prestigious named lecture series (such as the Hamlyn Lectures) which expect from their speakers not just 'description' but 'creativity and originality'. Thus, the more thoughtful these lectures are, the more clues they give us about the judge/speaker's general philosophy about life and the law. This is so, notwithstanding the great effort which judges often make to avoid, in their extra-judicial musing, language which might impede their future judicial work. These extra-judicial writings thus provide us with information that can also be found in their judicial opinions, previous or subsequent to the date of the delivery of the said lecture, suggesting an interesting interrelationship.

But this is outlook and mentality influencing their judgment. It is not bias. The importance of the Limbach quotation, italicised above, lies precisely in the fact that it

[4] *Das Bundesverfassungsgericht als politischer Machtfaktor* (1996). The emphasis is ours.

shows that this phenomenon is also found in Germany *and* that it should *not* be seen as evidence of bias. Certainly the Germans (and the Americans), who have been conscious of this for some time now, see it simply as an interesting and understandable by-product of the judge's life, education, mentality, professional environment and general outlook and, as such, must be taken into account. If that is, indeed, the case, it merits careful study for the valuable clues it can give us in understanding the decision-making process; in telling us a little bit more than he has as to why he decided a particular case they way he did; perhaps, even, in supplying us with a strong predictive element about future judicial behaviour. In our view we ignore such studies at our peril.

So, is the background, training, general outlook and life philosophy of our judges reflected in their judgments and, more crucially, does it help shape them? The first is becoming easier to prove; the latter must remain a matter of conjecture. This is no place to elaborate the thesis in detail[5] though the danger that the 'theorist' (such as us) may be seeing more things than are actually there is real. A small number of illustrations connected with tort law can, however, be given, if only to get the debate started among students and their teachers. The latter can then encourage their students to find other illustrations of this kind or, conversely, if more conventionally minded, guide them away from such heresies.

Thus can, for instance, a judge as learned as Lord Rodger of Earlsferry ever conceal his lifelong devotion to Roman law, in his case evidenced by the fact that he is a second-generation Roman lawyer, and the resulting support he has given to the subject extra-judicially in order to keep it alive in the university curriculum? It would be unreasonable to expect otherwise.[6] More importantly, however, his feelings (and our view of what we believe them to be) seem to receive some support from his judgment in the *Fairchild*[7] case where he was the only judge to refer at Roman law before switching to a more detailed consideration of contemporary German law.[8] If, as the learned judge admitted, the latter is much more detailed than the former (and chronologically closer to us, thus avoiding the risks which arise from missing or corrupt texts), why use space and time talking about Roman law? Moreover, in that case his Lordship had the good fortune to have before him Sir Sydney Kentridge QC who, as a jurist experienced in the law of South Africa, cleverly introduced the points that suited his client's case, including Roman law texts which he must have known were likely to appeal to Lord Rodger's

[5] For more details and, above all references to literature, see B.S. Markesinis, 'Judicial Mentality: Mental Disposition or Outlook as a Factor Impeding Recourse to Foreign Law' (2006) 86 *Tul. LR*. 1325.

[6] Though one might regret his own admission in his Kelly Lecture—'Savigny in the Strand' (1995) 28–30 *Ir. Jur.*, 1, 18—that he feels a 'certain personal ambivalence towards comparative law because of its tendency in the past to attract away scholars from the field of Roman law'.

[7] [2006] 1 AC 32, at paras. 119 ff.

[8] Which Lord Rodger himself described (at para. 167) as 'being even more instructive'. This is entirely understandable given the discussion these topics have received in German law. And since these are more detailed and, chronologically closer to us, why include references to Roman law? The argument that it shows that the problem before their Lordships has occupied jurists for generations strikes one as too weak to justify an excursus into a dead system whose language few can nowadays master. It is, in other words, likelier that it is an indication of the point made in the text, above.

interest in that field. But this may well be a near-unique coincidence; for how many members of the present Bar, let alone their successors in years to come, will have the expertise or predilection to delve into the mysteries of classical Roman law?

Let us move to the troubling issue of pure economic loss and whether it should, as a rule, be recoverable in an action based on the tort of negligence. Teachers, if not (yet) students, will know that some academics hold very strong negative views on this topic while others (including ourselves) believe that a nuanced view must be—indeed is—taken by the courts. Do we really believe that a judge, especially a learned and strong-minded judge, can, on his appointment to the Bench, divest himself from a life's habits and beliefs, on whichever side of this intellectual divide they may fall? Felix Frankfurter, an immensely gifted (and opinionated) Justice of the United States Supreme Courts in the 1940s and 1950s once wrote that when a man (and now a woman) is admitted to the Supreme Court he

> . . . brings his whole experience, his training, his outlook, his social, intellectual, and moral environment with him when he takes a seat on the supreme bench.[9]

Is this not clearly reflected in Lord Hoffmann's judgments on the subject of economic loss? Is this not also obvious in his many decisions on liability of local authorities for breach of statutory duties and whether these can give rise to a civil action?[10] It is, we feel, permissible to see these judgments as a superb illustration of *advocacy* as much as judgment; advocacy of his views attested by constant cross-referencing to his own earlier views, refined but essentially restated over the years, but always emanating from a three-line statement in his majority opinion in *Stovin* v. *Wise*.[11] For it was there that he first boldly stated that

> The trend of authorities has been to discourage the assumptions that anyone who suffers loss is prima facie entitled to compensation from the person . . . whose act or omission can be said to have caused it. The default position is that he is not.

'The trend' . . . but what trend? The late 1960s and 1970s, under the leadership of Lord Denning and Lord Reid, saw an 'opening' of our law—both the law of torts and administrative law—towards a regime that was not opposed to liability, including state liability. In the late 1970s Lord Wilberforce—another great judge—was not following the trend identified by Lord Hoffmann in *Stovin* v. *Wise* but, arguably, was trying to move negligence in the opposite direction. Lord Roskill tried to do the same in the early 1980s. The trend to which Lord Hoffmann is alluding, though not without its supporters during the preceding years of tort expansion (notably, Lord Brandon) really took off in the mid-1990s when his own presence began to become felt on the scene. So it would be more accurate to talk not—impersonally—of a trend but of Lord Hoffmann's 'own philosophical view of the law of torts' which, one is tempted to suggest, he is trying

[9] P. Elman (ed.), *Felix Frankfurter: Of Law and Men—Papers and Addresses of Felix Frankfurter* (1956), 38.

[10] For a fuller discussion of the Hoffmann factor in these cases see B. Markesinis and J. Fedtke, 'Authority or Reason? The Economic Consequences of Liability for Breach of Statutory Duty in a Comparative Perspective' (2007) *Eur. Bus. LR* 5.

[11] [1996] 3 WLR 388, 411.

to entrench for future generations as his own retirement is fast approaching. This, then, could be seen as nothing less than a battle of ideas, even if the official language used by the battling judges would underplay any personalisation of the disagreements.

Lord Hoffmann's quotation, moreover, is not an ordinary *obiter dictum* but in its amplitude and boldness a summary of his basic belief about the role of tort law in the twenty-first century. This, again, is one of his many talents. For in a media-dominated era, he knows how to shape an attention-catching phrase, whether he does it in a case dealing with wrongful incarceration of terrorists, libel and media freedom or ordinary lacklustre tort law. And, again, this is not our interpretation of a series of tort judgments, bolstering through repetition the force of declaration of principle, but one that is borne out by Lord Hoffmann's subsequent judicial history which shows how committed he has remained to this basic proposition.[12] After all it encapsulates a—his?—wider philosophical belief which many people—lawyers and non-lawyers—share: namely, that tort law must be 'reined in'.

But if seen in this way, it is no longer a sentence in a judgment which, in theory, is considered from judgment to judgment, inductively leading to the concluding climax, but a wider, overriding, boldly expressed stance which *must* lead him to shape the facts of each subsequent case in a way that is compatible with this honestly held, deep and quite legitimate conviction. When we examine his judgments in the area of tortious liability for breach of statutes we shall say more about this phenomenon. The issue here is whether it is academically proper to raise this issue and invite its further examination.

Certainly, this would be a plausible and proper analysis to adopt if we were looking at the writings of an academic. Why *must* it be essentially different in the case of a strong-minded judge? If a student is made to believe that the judicial oath can somehow separate the judge from his life's honest beliefs, temperamental outlook, cultural and religious ideas, *in an absolute and permanent manner*, we submit such a student should, at the very least, be encouraged to consider the alternative. Indeed, we simply do not believe (on the basis of discussions with judges and not just hunches) that a creative judge cannot, in most instances, mould his material in the direction he wishes his case to go.

Our judges, of course will never admit openly to such 'weaknesses'[13]—if, indeed, that is what they are—even less do they like to admit that they are wrong. So when they are ignored, overruled and more rarely openly told that they were wrong, they will again, over a period of time, change or qualify the original view in the hope that the 'shift' is as little noticed as possible. Again, we will see examples of this in some of Lord Hoffmann's judgments—for instance in *Stovin* [14] and *Gorringe* [15] dealing with statutory duties, or in privacy versus speech cases—for instance in *R v. Central Independent Television plc* [16]

[12] His judgment in *Gorringe* v. *Calderdale MBC* [2004] 1 WLR 1057 offers a good illustration.

[13] Though in his extra-judicial writings Lord Mustill, with his usual candour and stylistic elegance, comes close to adopting such a position. More on this point in the next sub-section.

[14] *Stovin* v. *Wise* [1996] AC 923.

[15] See *Gorringe v. Calderdale MBC* [2004] 1 WLR 1057, at para. 26.

[16] [1994] Fam. 192, 203. Subsequently, however, the learned judge had to 'explain away' extra-judicially (in his 1996 Goodman Lecture) the exact meaning of part of this part of his judgment.

and the *Campbell* [17] cases—where the shifts can easily be missed amidst the torrent of words found in multi-opinion decisions. But however smooth, low-key and imperceptible they may be to the untrained eye, such shifts are there, and young lawyers must be prepared to expect them and trained to detect them.

For changes of emphasis and hue are not only (welcome) signs that judges are as human as the rest of us; they also provide the material on which future changes of the law will be based. Indeed, the smoother the transition, the better, on the whole, it is for the entire legal order, which abhors sudden or violent shifts. We shall thus see in our discussion of privacy (in Chapter 22) how substantial changes in this part of the law have been wrought under the pressure of new circumstances (which include the growing importance of the European Court of Human Rights in Strasbourg). Law, in other words is anything than static and understanding its dynamics also involves understanding the personalities of those who interpret it and make it.

Our judges may hide their own shifts; politeness (among other things) also leads them to differ from their American counterparts and often try to convince the reading public that their internal differences are minimal. This certainly makes for a more civilised, indeed attractive, discourse. But it can also lull the student—perhaps even the time-pressured practitioner—to fail to pick up major differences in the intellectual foundations of a multi-opinion decision. We shall note, for instance in the privacy chapter how true this is in the *Campbell* judgment of the House of Lords. Baroness Hale, for instance, argued that there was substantial agreement over the 'horizontal effect issue' between herself and the opinions of the other judges.[18] How misleading this particular emphasis on 'unanimity' is—on this crucial underlying issue of this case—is explained at great length by the authors of an excellent new media law textbook[19] to which the reader is referred for further details. What thus remains to be done here is for some practitioner to pick this divergence up and use it in some future case to his advantage. If and when this is done, the semblance of unity will have been shattered.

Common-law judges thus love to conceal more than to reveal. In a sense this is a paradox, since one finds in their judgments more references to policy arguments propelling them towards answer A or B than in any decision of the courts of all major civil-law systems. Yet the judges not only conceal—cover up might be another word—the evolution of their own thought, they also cover up the academic sources of their inspiration. In *White* v. *Jones*,[20] for instance, Lord Mustill delivered a judgment which is not only brilliant, it is also profoundly influenced by foreign ideas about the borderline of contract and tort. But there is no reference to this except a general and anonymous expression of gratitude for the help thus received. In what is probably the leading restitution case of the last twenty years—*Woolwich*[21]—the contrast is even more striking when one compares the judgments of Lord Keith (total absence of reference to academic

17 [2004] 2 WLR 1232. 18 *Ibid.*, para. 126.

19 H. Fenwick and G. Phillipson, *Media Freedom under the Human Rights Act* (2006), esp. 132–40.

20 [1995] 2 AC 207.

21 *Woolwich Building Society* v. *Inland Revenue Commissioners* [1993] AC 70.

opinion) and Lord Goff (open acknowledgment of the fact that the change was propelled by the pioneering work of Professors Birks and Cornish). There is a long tradition behind such attitudes. *Taylor* v. *Caldwell*,[22] a major decision by a great judge—Blackburn J—gave its author the chance to use his foreign law (and Roman law learning) without any open attribution to the works that contained the basic idea.[23] But times have changed. What happened in Blackburn's time is no longer acceptable now. And Blackburn had a further excuse: he was simply failing to cite himself writing extra-judicially; to fail to cite others is not the same.

There is, finally, one more type of concealment that common-law judges like to attempt. It is prompted by 'political' and pragmatic considerations which a modern civil-law judge might find difficult to understand. But the reason, to English eyes, is as obvious as it is interesting: conceal the innovation and no one will be disturbed, worried, puzzled, start thinking, and so on. Lord Blackburn's classic decision in *Rylands* v. *Fletcher*[24] offers one example. For there he took great pains to make his innovation look as if it represented an application—at worst a simple analogical extension—of existing law. Another and, until recently less widely known, was Lord Atkin's use of Scottish ideas in his famous opinion in *Donoghue* v. *Stevenson*[25] (though their origin was, in the final version of his judgment suppressed): this was fairly recently revealed fully and discussed convincingly by a Scottish academic.[26] But the help apparently given by Professor Percy Winfield to Lord Atkin in the same case has never, to our knowledge, been fully documented.

Once again, the picture is no different in the United States which is why we described this taste for concealment as being commonly found in the common law world. This can only help to strengthen the force of the point made in the text. Thus, the late Professor Grant Gilmore, one of the greatest private lawyers of the United States once said the same thing about Cardozo, probably the greatest stylist of American law. Gilmore thus wrote that

> (T)he more innovative the decision to which he had persuaded his brethren on the court, the more the opinion strained to prove that no novelty—not the slightest departure from prior law—was involved.[27]

What American's call 'judicial psychobiography' has helped bring all of these features into the open. This does not mean that the growing volume of books and articles is all of high quality. Some would argue that quality is the exception not the rule. But the poor quality of some (many?) of these works does not mean that this little-known genre of legal scholarship is without its merits. For, if properly pursued, it can teach the student much about the decision-making process, the importance of the personality of

22 (1863) 32 LJQB 164.

23 To his own *Treatise on the Effect of the Contract of Sale on the Legal Rights of property and possession of Goods, Wares and Merchandises* (1845) which the late C. H. S. Fifoot described as 'an early essay in comparative law'. See *Judge and Jurist in the Reign of Queen Victoria* (1959) at 16.

24 (1866) LR 1 Ex. 265 at 279–80.

25 [1932] AC 562.

26 R. Evans-Jones, 'Roman Law in Scotland and England and the Development of One Law for Britain', (1999) 115 *LQR* 605.

27 *The Ages of American Law* (1977), 75.

the participating judge and the need to avoid placing too much faith in the concepts that he or she is taught at law schools. These are words that help to formulate judgments, but not the reasons that dictate them. And for the practitioner, absorbing the significance of these ideas might also give him some useful clues as to how to handle his case when he is standing before the court. Every little bit that can assist him in presenting his case better can help; and it is not a convincing reason to shut such ideas of studying law out of one's mind in an a priori manner simply because they have never up to now been tested in our country.

3. ACADEMIC INTERESTS AND PRACTITIONERS' CONCERNS: CLOSE OR FAR APART?

Many examples to support the implied message of this heading can be given; suffice it to mention but a few.

Causation could be the first example. The Germans and Americans have produced a considerable literature on this subject. Indeed, a well-known French legal writer, paraphrasing Voltaire, once remarked that if the subject did not exist it would have to be invented so as to give the Germans a topic on which to exercise their legal minds. This observation is not meant to belittle the subject. Hart and Honoré's monograph on causation[28] is an example of erudition and style combined in discussing a difficult subject; the wealth of citations that this book receives attest to its continued value. Decisions such as those delivered in the cases of *Hotson*,[29] *Wilsher*[30] and, most recently, *Fairchild*[31] (discussed below in Chapters 3 and 4) show how complicated this topic can be. Yet it is also worth reminding the reader of what three leading American tort lawyers had to say at the end of the 100 pages that they devoted to this subject in their best-selling casebook:

> The problem [of legal cause] is a difficult one, but the length of the treatment in this casebook and the time allotted it in most courses may perhaps give an exaggerated impression of its importance. In the great majority of negligence cases, the problem does not arise at all . . . [32]

So, by all means let us study causation cases (and other topics of particular theoretical import) since they can help sharpen the mind; but let us also remember to keep the problem in perspective; and let us warn our students about this.

The same point can be made about many medical malpractice cases. They, too, make our point in so far as they raise points that interest philosophers but are also numerous in practice. The point is that the issues that concern mostly the philosophers may not be the ones that occupy the practitioners involved in medical malpractice litigation.

[28] *Causation in the Law* (2nd edn., 1985).

[29] *Hotson* v. *East Berkshire AHA* [1987] AC 750.

[30] *Wilsher* v. *Essex AHA* [1988] AC 1074.

[31] *Fairchild* v. *Glenhaven Funeral Services Ltd.* [2003] AC 32.

[32] W. L. Prosser, J. W. Wade and V. E. Schwartz, *Torts: Cases and Materials* (7th edn., 1982), 364.

This is not to deny these are enriching in the sense that the former are of little use to lawyers. In educational terms they can encourage students—especially those who receive nowadays more of a black-letter law training than, perhaps, ever before—to look at law, as an eminent American jurist once put it, 'from without' as well as 'from within'.[33] Nevertheless, a note of warning is needed. For when judicial statements in this part of the law are couched in philosophical or even metaphysical terms, a strong case could be made for the argument that the court is unsure what the answer should be and is thus seeking refuge behind jurisprudential or philosophical shibboleths in order to avoid giving a clear or bold solution. We shall, for example, see in the so-called 'wrongful life' cases that many of the judges have stated that impaired life is preferable to no life at all.[34] The chances are that statements such as the above will be returned to the domain of philosophers when (rather than if) the courts come to recognise that a claim for damages in such cases is not as inconceivable as they currently seem to think, for it really involves finding a way to help a family hit by misfortune to handle, at least, its financial aspects and does not mean saying that we—as a society living according to the law—value impaired life differently. Until such shifts occur, the courts will remain undecided on the matter, as the philosophers have always been.[35]

Let us turn now to a third illustration, linked to the example already alluded to in the previous sub-section—pure economic loss.

The question whether negligently inflicted pure economic loss should be compensated through tort law has literally captivated academic writers in England, America and Germany but has left totally unmoved lawyers from many other major legal systems such as the French, Spanish or Italian. This is understandable, since the theoretical importance of the subject is enhanced by the fact that it is in the borderline zone of contract and tort and thus invites, as it were, the applicability of different rules.[36] In addition, it has given so many jurists the chance to explain the (prevalent) non-liability rule by having recourse to insurance practices and economic analysis. Yet the pages devoted to this subject in the various textbooks, monographs and articles are in no way an accurate reflection of the number of times these points come before the higher courts. Of course, some supporters of the present non-liability rule might be

33 R. Pound, *The Spirit of the Common Law* (1921), 212.

34 'Man, who knows nothing of death or nothingness cannot possibly know whether that is so,' per Stephenson LJ in *McKay* v. *Essex AHA and Another* [1982] QB 1166. A much more meaningful discussion of the real issues behind these cases can be found in the decision of the Sup. Ct. of New Jersey in *Procanik* v. *Cillo*, 97 NJ 339, 478 A 2d 755 (1984)—a decision which, incidentally, also reveals how the wider legal background can affect the outcome of the litigation.

35 Strange as it may seem the question whether non-existence is preferable to life (with or without impairments) received much attention by some of the greatest Greek philosophers and tragedy writers and, on the whole, preference was shown for the former. Though the debate has not died, and has puzzled authors as varied as Shakespeare, Nietzsche and Jean-Paul Sartre, modern times, largely perhaps as a result of Nazi atrocities, have become loath to pronounce on this issue and, especially, to suggest that life with impairments is worse than non-life.

36 See B. S. Markesinis, 'An Expanding Tort Law: the Price of a Rigid Contract Law' (1987) 103 *LQR* 354. One of the most thoughtful discussions on this topic can be found in Lord Mustill's article cited in the Select Bibliography.

tempted to attribute such a (relative) dearth of case law to the strictness of the non-liability rule. But this hardly is convincing given that the systems where liability is acknowledged have an equally slender body of case law when one would expect the opposite. Extensive comparative reading has never produced, for us at least, a satisfactory explanation so, at the end of the day, the differences may be due to lawyers in general and judges in particular being conservative by nature.[37] This could mean that they prefer the devil they know (injustice and artificiality in some cases)[38] to the devil they do not know but are invited to let in their courtrooms (uncertainty) if they were ever to relax the existing rules. This issue will occupy us in the next chapter; but its practical frequency when compared, for instance, with accidents at work or traffic accidents, is minimal.

This gap between academic tort law and judges' tort law is also made obvious by the absence of any real dialogue—at any rate until recently—between the Bench and universities of the kind which, for historical reasons, we find in other countries.[39] This lack of effective communication is aggravated by three factors.

First, academics in this country, unlike in the United States, are too quick to accept without questioning judicial utterances on a particular subject.[40] One writer of a learned monograph on the workings of the House of Lords observed that the fact that academic opinion fails to impress judges is in part because of their 'own reticence at expressing [their] criticism in a forceful manner lest it be perceived as disrespectful'.[41] To this, as the same author remarked, the 'editors of the prestigious journals'—themselves academics—have also contributed greatly for they have been known to exercise serious censorship on texts that they perceive as being disrespectful rather than simply critical. Finally, the academic environment is also not without its share of blame, young lecturers often instilling in their students an unwarranted degree of deference to judges. All of the above, if not wrong, is, at the very least, not in tune with the spirit of our times (as well as wise past sayings) which (rightly) have always encouraged thinking people 'to probe everything and keep the best'.[42]

Second, academic criticism is rarely read unless it is published in the literally one or two journals that most judges read (or glance at?). Otherwise, such writings are unlikely to come to the attention of most judges, unless counsel put these works before them in court. Remedying this shortcoming is not easy, even though in the last twenty or thirty years we have seen a growing number of judges interested in academic law and, indeed,

37 For an interesting comparative examination of this subject see M. Bussani and V. V. Palmer, *Pure Economic Loss in Europe* (2003).

38 See e.g. Edmund-Davies LJ's dissenting judgment in *Spartan Steel & Alloys* v. *Martin & Co.* [1973] QB 27, and Lord Devlin's views about economic loss in *Hedley Byrne & Co. Ltd.* v. *Heller and Partners Ltd.* [1964] AC 465. Cf. Lord Hoffmann's observations in *White* v. *Chief Constable of South Yorkshire Police* [1999] 2 AC 455, [1998] 3 WLR 1510.

39 The best account in English of this fascinating subject can be found in J. P. Dawson's *The Oracles of the Law* (1967).

40 The point is forcefully made by, among others, P. S. Atiyah and R. S. Summers, *Form and Substance in Anglo-American Law* (1987), ch. 14.

41 Alan Paterson, *The Law Lords: How Britain's Top Judges See their Role* (1982), 19.

42 St. Paul, II Epistle to the Thessalonians.

themselves contributing to it. The main difficulty here is probably time, or more accurately the lack thereof. For the bulk of litigation, especially at first instance, is conducted under such pressurised conditions that in practice the only chance to introduce new ideas and invite the judge to reflect on an issue is at the level of the House of Lords. At that stage, however, one may come across the other difficulty already described, namely that the senior judge has formed a view about a wider issue and, just as importantly, an opinion about the salience of his own views on that subject. Neither attribute is conducive to honest dialogue.

There is more to this paradox than meets the eye. For no one can explain—to us at least—why in some cases our highest judges may have shown an interest in academic views, including views on foreign law, whereas in others they have ignored them completely. An example of the first is the *Fairchild* case; and illustration of the second can be found in the *East Berkshire* case. We shall encounter this last case in the chapter which deals with liability of statutory and governmental bodies[43] though, for the time being, it is a matter of some puzzlement why our courts are not willing even to consider foreign empirical evidence on this subject, especially in the light of the fact that little or no indigenous information is available about the effect which the level of damages may have on preserving the non-liability rule.[44]

Finally, the insights that judges and academics have into the law are very different. Thus, Lord Goff—one of the small number of judges who, through his own work judicially and extra-judicially, has tried hard to bridge this gap—had this to say of this phenomenon:

> The judge's vision of the law tends to be fragmented; so far as it extends, his vision is intense; and it is likely to be strongly influenced by the facts of the particular case . . . jurists on the other hand, do not share the fragmented approach of the judges. They adopt a much broader approach, concerned not so much with the decision of a particular case, but rather with the place of each decision in the law as a whole. They do not share our intense view of the particular; they have rather a diffused view of the general. This is both their weakness and their strength.[45]

One could interpret this as a plea for greater co-operation; but, as far as the practising Bar is concerned it is, on the whole, still falling on deaf ears. Not so, however, with some of our current judges. This, for example, is what Steyn LJ had to say on the subject when, as a Court of Appeal judge, he had to hear *White* v. *Jones*:

> The question decided in *Ross* v. *Caunters* [and which had to be reconsidered in the instant case] was a difficult one. It lies at the interface of what has traditionally been regarded as the separate domains of contract and tort. It is therefore not altogether surprising that the appeal in the present case lasted three days, and that *we were referred to about forty decisions of English and foreign courts*. Pages and pages were read from some of the judgments. But we were not referred to a single piece of academic writing . . . . Traditionally counsel make very little use of

[43] See ch. 8, below.

[44] For a detailed analysis (with figures) see B. Markesinis and J. Fedtke, 'Authority or Reason? The Economic Consequences of Liability for Breach of Statutory Duty in a Comparative Perspective' (2007) *Eur. Bus. LR* 5.

[45] In his Maccabean Lecture to the British Academy (Select Bibliography), 183–4.

academic materials . . . . In a difficult case it is helpful to consider academic comment on the point. Often such writings examine the history of the problem, the framework into which a decision must fit, and countervailing policy considerations in greater depth than is usually possible in judgments prepared by judges who are faced with a remorseless treadmill of cases that cannot wait. And it is arguments that influence decisions rather than the reading of pages upon pages from judgments . . .[46]

Yet, the combination of the textbook and the learned article should progressively become an instrument that attempts to combine the vision of the particular and of the general. Lord Goff, again in the Childs Lecture at Oxford University, proclaimed that 'we now live in the age of the legal textbook'.[47] This sounds more like a hope or a prophecy than a statement of fact; but, given the form of contemporary legal education, this looks like a prophecy that might, one day, be fulfilled. And if textbooks are to succeed in this mission, they must start by admitting that both in content and style they must be adapted to appeal to a new and different generation of lawyers.

Yet this plea for greater co-operation between the academic and practising sides of the profession cannot be left without an important postscript; and the contents of this postscript are simple. Though, surprisingly, not all academics have been quick to embrace this crusade[48] for a stronger influence on the final direction of a judgment, judges, themselves, are slowly moving in this direction. Thus, one needs no footnotes to show that references to academic literature have increased dramatically during the last ten years or so, even though it still does not reflect properly or adequately the extent of judicial debt to academic writings.

This is not all that has come out of our judges' recent involvement in academic writing. Some of the most thoughtful are now telling us what we have been suspecting for some time, namely that:

One cannot always be sure, as regards an individual judge, that the reasons published in a judgment are in fact his reasons for the decision.[49]

The statement comes from Lord Mustill, a judge with unusual and multiple talents. He thus continued:

They [the reasons] may have been constructed after the event to reconcile the decision with legal materials which appeared to stand in its way, and which played no part in his formation of the conclusion, or to call up support from favourable materials for a decision arrived at without recourse to them (for example a decision made intuitively, or on grounds of policy).

Further down, the learned judge concluded:

Many judges would, I believe, if pressed acknowledge that the outcome of a difficult case may be evolved by an unperceived background working of mechanisms quite different from those employed when he sits down with the rule-book and seeks to apply it to a simple situation.[50]

46 [1995] 2 AC 207, 235 (where the judgments of the Court of Appeal are reproduced before the opinions of the Law Lords) (our emphasis).

47 'Judge, Jurist and Legislature' (Select Bibliography), 92.

48 See, for instance, the cautious note of P. Cane ('What a Nuisance!') in (1997) 113 *LQR* 515, esp. 518–19.

49 Lord Mustill, 'What Do Judges Do?', (1995–6) 3 *Särtryck ur Juridisk Tidskrift* 611 at 620.

50 *Ibid.*, 623.

The final example of diverging interests between academics and practitioners comes from the law of damages. Again, one is forced to note not only the divergence but also the lack of effort to try and develop an interest in each other's concerns. An academic with an unusually deep knowledge of the law of damages was thus right to complain recently that

> Tort scholarship is very partial. It is extraordinary how much attention is focused upon issues of liability as opposed to the quantum of damages. Practitioners are bemused by the preoccupation of academics with the rules of fault: they are aware that liability is infrequently challenged by insurers—being raised as a preliminary issue in only about 20 per cent of their cases—whereas the amount of compensation is almost always open to some negotiation.[51]

We again feel forced to remind our readers of such paradoxes and invite their teachers to discuss them with them and, even, ask then to try to explain them. But one possible explanation is the great—one might even call it lamentable—lack of co-operation that exists between judges, practitioners and academics. It would be wrong to blame one of these groups more than another; but one is tempted to fly an academic kite and suggest that as the old, monastic centres of learning discover the need to rely more and more upon the funds of the private sector, including law firms, they may be forced to accept the need to work with industry and the law firms more than they did before. Indeed, this is one of the many, background factors which have affected university life enormously during the last twenty years or so; and the contact with the real world may already be reflected in the appearance of new courses and posts which simply were unheard of in the not too distant past.

4. IVORY TOWER NEATNESS V. THE UNTIDINESS OF THE REAL WORLD

This is another facet of the troubled relationship between cloister and court mentality discussed above. But the fact that academics are listened to by contemporary judges to a greater extent than they were in the past does not mean that the natural predilection of the former for neatness and consistency has been adopted by the real world. Indeed, where there is excessive theorising, neatness and structure found in their work, it may have the opposite effect on judges. The point is made here since, as stated at the very beginning of this section, many an unfortunate student will be pushed in his or her studies to fit the decisional law within the particular theory or framework that appeals to their teacher. Such exercises are not devoid of academic merit to the extent that they stretch the student's mind and also try to make him see how the various parts of the law come together. But the student should be warned that, in some cases, such effort and its result will bear little resemblance to what happens in the real world. Many academic

51 R. Lewis, 'The Politics and Economics of Tort Law: Judicially Imposed Periodical Payments of Damages' (2006) 69 *MLR* 418.

attempts[52] to bring order to the untidy tort of negligence could be cited to support our provocative statement but, because of lack of space, two will suffice.

The first comes from the late Peter Birks, one of Oxford University's most productive and learned jurists. Birks's great appeal owed much not only to his learning but also to the passion with which he pursued his theories (and engaged with those who doubted them). He held the Chair which was once meant to give pride of place to 'civil'—in the sense of non canon—law, though his main claim to fame was through his work on restitution. But Roman law left its mark on him and he, in turn, tried to structure modern law around Roman ideas of classification. Birks's passion led him to advocate his views on structure and education in many pieces; and one of these pieces appeared in a collection of essays edited by one of the present authors.[53] In that piece, his desire for structure led him to produce a diagram which he called 'the institutional map' which proceeded to divide and categorise law and its various branches in a way inspired by Roman law—law, for instance is, in his view 'either public or private', a proposition tracing back its origins to Roman and medieval law but ignoring the modern constitutionalisation of private law. In this structured world, reminiscent in its rigidity and preoccupation with logical order of the nineteenth-century German Pandectist School, Birks also deals with the case of *Spring* v. *Guardian Assurance*.[54] This is a difficult case, which touches both on the law of negligence and the law of defamation; and we shall deal with it under the former heading (i.e. in Chapter 3) for the ruling of the House of Lords has now firmly placed it there. But Birks, focusing on classification, was deeply troubled by and also critical of the decision; and his views, naturally, deserve attention. Yet in reaching a final view on them, the critical teacher and student should also factor in two other considerations before finally reaching a conclusion about the proper placing of the case and the attractiveness of Birks's views.

The first factor is derived from the American practice (slowly gaining acceptance in European academic centres of learning) of looking at the effect that such writings have on others in the field. This tends to be measured by counting (nowadays easily done with the aid of computers) the number of citations received by a particular piece. This kind of work, known at times under the inelegant name of 'reputology', does not attempt to measure 'scholarship' but the effect of scholarship on others. By that measure, Birks's piece has, literally, had no effect whatsoever. The pursuit of theory and structure not only left the courts unmoved; it also found few takers in the academic world.[55] Everyone is free to write what they wish; readers, however, must also learn to recognise what kind of writing has an impact.

52 And the eldest of the authors of this book has, himself, committed this sin in his younger days.

53 'The Heap of Good Learning: The Jurist in the Common Law Tradition' in B.S. Markesinis (ed.), *Law Making, Law Finding and Law Shaping: The Diverse Influences, the Clifford Chance Lectures* (1997) II, 112 ff.

54 [1995] 2 AC 296.

55 Thus on a manual search of six leading English law journals during the years 1980–2000 Birks received 143 citations for the totality of his work but the said piece only one. Between 2000 and 2004, the total number of citations went up to 163 but, again, this piece only received one note reference. A computer search of nearly one thousand American law journals for the years 2001–2005 revealed a total of 352 citations but only two to this essay. By the way, the vast number of citations is devoted to Birks's work as a restitution lawyer and not as

The second point the careful teacher and student should consider is not just to reflect upon the taxonomy advocated by Birks but on the kind of modern, policy-oriented arguments invoked in favour of the decision by Lord Cooke of Thorndon (often referred to with admiration as the 'antipodean Denning' since he was Chief Justice in New Zealand before he was invited to sit in the House of Lords) in a learned article published in a collection of Essays in honour of the late John Fleming.[56] Such a comparison is not meant to suggest that one view is 'right' and the other is 'wrong', for in our subject rarely are these characterisations really meaningful. But what it does suggest is how much more contemporary and, we submit, relevant, is the optic adopted by the practitioner. Those who live in cloisters sometimes—not always—miss this dimension; students should not be allowed to do so.

Professor Stapleton's work also seems to fall into the category of deep (perhaps too deep?) theorising, even though her work has found favour with judges who share her 'conservative' views about the proper ambit and scope of tort law: minimal! For instance, some years ago in her feisty 'In Restraint of Tort', she rightly criticised the current trend of our courts to decide cases by first slipping them into a 'relevant pocket of liability'. She then continued:

> Yet for this to produce stability and coherent outcomes two fairly obvious conditions must be satisfied. First, it must be clear what it is about the new case which characterises it and which indicates the relevant earlier case law 'pocket' within which it needs to be judged... [and second] the boundaries of existing pockets must make sense.[57]

The criticism becomes that much more obvious and convincing when, for instance, she forces her readers to ask themselves:

> why is it that what is important about the facts of *Smith* v. *Bush* is the form of the defendant's carelessness (negligent professional advice) so that it can be associated with earlier case law allowing a duty of care (*Hedley Byrne*)? Why was not the relevant fact that the plaintiff suffered the economic loss through the acquisition of defective property so that the case would be placed in the *D & F Estates/Murphy* 'pocket' of case law with the result that a duty of care would be denied?[58]

At this stage the scholarly ability to criticise gives way to the teacher's predilection to become a system builder. Thus Professor Stapleton succumbs to the temptation to erect her own edifice where liability will be imposed if certain positive factors are found to exist and other negative factors are not present. Her 'agenda of countervailing concerns', which militate against the imposition of liability, thus includes assurances on the following points: that the imposition of liability does not produce a 'specific unattractive

a Roman law lawyer. For fuller details see: Sir Basil Markesinis, 'Understanding American Law by Looking at It through Foreign Eyes: Towards a Wider Theory for the Study and Use of Foreign Law' (2006) 81 *Tul. LR* 123 ff.

[56] 'The Right of *Spring*', in P. Cane and J. Stapleton (eds.), *The Law of Obligations: Essays in Celebration of John Fleming* (1998).

[57] Stapleton (Select Bibliography), 85–6.

[58] *Ibid.*, 85; references omitted. The complete beginner may wish to return to these comments after he or she has read about these cases in ch. 3, below.

socio-economic impact'; that the claimant has adequate and appropriate alternative means of protection; that the claimant is not seeking to use tort to evade an understanding of where risks should fall; that assisting the claimant would not bring the law into disrepute.

In purely doctrinal terms, the proposed criteria do not seem to be able to produce the desired results. For instance, Professor Stapleton has not concealed her unhappiness with the decision or the reasoning of the majority in *White* v. *Jones*. Yet would observance of her 'countervailing concerns' lead to a different result? By giving a remedy to the disappointed beneficiary, did *White* v. *Jones* bring the law into disrepute? Or was there an alternative way—*de lege lata*—for the plaintiff to protect himself? Or can one really argue that potential beneficiaries are best placed to take out insurance instead of placing this obligation (as so many systems do) on the lawyers who carry out these transactions (and make much money out of them)? One need not labour the point further. Any attempt to apply these elaborate criteria to different factual situations shows that sometimes they work and in others they simply make no sense at all.[59]

Yet even if this critique is unduly harsh, one still has to ask oneself whether such a highly structured approach will prove more popular to our courts than their existing (and not always satisfactory) techniques? Time alone will answer this question. But the history of the tort of negligence thus far suggests that our courts are likely to continue shifting from one *mutually inconsistent doctrine* to another as they grapple with the immensely complex problems that confront them under the heading of the tort of negligence. The italicised words are, in fact, not ours but Lord Mustill's who, after noting that the House of Lords has, in the last sixty years, 'embraced six mutually inconsistent doctrines on a field of great theoretical and practical importance', concluded with the statement:

> it involves no disloyalty on my part to the legal system in which I have spent my working life, or to past, present and future colleagues to say that the picture thus painted is not one of unqualified success . . . . *The root of the problem is I believe a reluctance on the part of the judges to accept inwardly, and afterwards to acknowledge outwardly, that decisions in this field are essentially concerned with social engineering.*[60]

Expecting structure, order or theoretical consistency from our courts or any underlying theory for tort recovery is perhaps asking for too much from them. Courts do not see themselves as being expected to provide this or even being equipped to perform such a task. Pragmatism and incrementalism are the words that matter and the maintenance of a tolerable level of consistency through the system of precedent in order to

[59] This is particularly obvious from Professor Stapleton's article entitled 'Duty of Care Factors: a Selection from the Judicial Menus', in P. Cane and J. Stapleton (eds.), *The Law of Obligations: Essays in Celebration of John Fleming* (1998), 59 ff. For here we find a revamped list of factors which the learned author feels ought to determine the discovery (or not) of a duty of care. Yet she, herself, admits (at 87) that these factors may not be applicable to new factual configurations and, more devastatingly for her theory, may be differently evaluated by different judges. Such exercises, therefore, though highly stimulating for legal theorists, are not likely to have much effect in the bulk of tort litigation.

[60] Mustill (Select Bibliography), 23, 24 (emphasis added).

secure stability and predictability in legal transactions. An academic may be doing a useful service to his students, at least in their starting years, by giving them a starting-point to tackle the vast mass of material that they will gradually have to master. But if he thinks that this work will have a constant or enduring impact on our courts or on law in action, he is likely to be disappointed. Structure, consistency and order are virtues that have traditionally been more valued by civilian systems; and any one even remotely familiar with their updating processes will have already become aware that there, too, the complexity of modern law, emanating from national as well as supra-national sources, has led to a degree of flux, uncertainty and untidiness that once was mostly associated with the common law. The way in which our own law has developed a limited and *sui generis* law of liability for omissions in the context of neighbouring properties but not in the context of saving lives or preventing personal injury is one still living example of the irrationality of the contemporary common law. The rationally minded judge, academic or student will try to invent an explanation; occasionally he may even convince himself that he has squared the circle. In the common-law universe, rarely will he be right for long.

Tort lawyers, especially beginners, should thus revert to these points and reconsider them in the light of the suggested further reading. Above all, however, they should bear all these points in mind when absorbing the more technical arguments which are advanced in the chapters that follow, especially Chapters 3 and 4 which deal with that most amorphous and most important of torts—Negligence—to which most of the issues discussed above belong.

5. TORT'S STRUGGLE TO SOLVE MODERN PROBLEMS WITH OLD TOOLS

This is another truth that has not quite sunk into the consciousness of lawyers, academic and practitioners, who cling to rules and notions that once made sense but are struggling to provide answers to a world that is very different from that in which they were born. The longevity of some tort rules and concepts is, indeed, as admirable as it is remarkable. Thus, in this country, in many legal cases much of what we do and how we think today can be traced back to the Middle Ages. Even the way the text in our books is divided into chapters can, in some instances, be attributed to the forms of action which, as Maitland put it, we have buried but which still rule us from their graves. The same is true of what is included in a tort book and what is often left outside because it once formed part of the work of the Courts of Equity.

In the continent of Europe one can go back even further to the law of ancient Rome—parts of the modern French or German law being shaped on the basis of often erroneous beliefs of what Roman law used to be. To a large extent this survival is due to the flexible, if not amorphous, content of some of these concepts as they came to be formulated by the School of Natural Law.

This adaptability cannot conceal the fact that many of these rules—both in the common and civil law—were devised for human beings (the plaintiffs and defendants of the past) rather than corporations or legal entities (the typical claimants and defendants of today). They were also developed at a time when risk-spreading techniques (like insurance) were weak or unknown; and had as their prime aim the shifting of losses at a time when a weak social conscience attributed no role to the state in the context of accidents at work and disease. One must also remember that they were built on, or at least flourished around, the idea of fault; and made a crucial distinction (not necessarily supportable in our times) between harm resulting from accident and from disease[61] (e.g. cerebral haemorrhage resulting from cranial injuries or high blood pressure). It is, as stated, a tribute to these concepts' adaptability that they have survived for so long. Indeed, it is almost amazing that the tort of negligence can be used to tackle the careless manufacturer who allows a snail to slip into a ginger-beer bottle; an obstetrician who makes an error in the process of a complicated delivery of a child by forceps; and the driver who causes multiple injuries as a result of an unexpected brain haemorrhage which causes him to lose control of his faculties. The same could be said of the medieval tort of nuisance and more recent attempts to use it for zoning functions or to combat environmental pollution—a problem certainly not new, but new in its dimensions.

The problem of adapting tort law of the past to a new world has not been unique to this system. A great French jurist—Jean Carbonnier—referring to the ingenious efforts to use an amorphous provision of the Napoleonic Code of 1804 (Article 1384 1 CC) to cope with car accidents, has described them as an immense waste of time and intelligence. For nearly twenty years now the French have had a statute which, essentially, made much of their traffic-accident law independent of fault. It certainly has not solved all the problems; but it did represent a fresh attempt to solve a problem that had hitherto been tackled by provisions devised in the era of horse-and-buggy and no insurance; and did show that the French codal system could prove, at the end of the day, more flexible and more adaptable than our case-law system. The reader of tort textbooks should thus not content himself or herself with the criticism of individual decisions but should question constantly the suitability of tort as a means of compensating injuries and other harms.

This inadequacy—especially the centrality of the notion of fault—is obvious in the case of medical accidents from which both doctors and patients come out as losers. The ability to shake off a fault-based system of compensation is as strange here as it is in another great generator of tort litigation: traffic accidents. In such cases, building a compensation system around the notion of fault can only increase blame attribution (which, in turn leads to defensive action instead of an attempt to solve the case), costs and uncertainty and, what is more, does all this in the context of the vast majority of injuries which are minor, transient, self-healing and not really costly.

[61] The subject of Jane Stapleton's interesting and important work, *Disease and the Compensation Debate* (1986).

Using old torts to deal with modern and complex cases of personal injury is not the only area where antiquarianism is rife. The medieval tort of nuisance has often been pressed into action to perform zooming functions or to help defeat environmental pollution. The (ultimately unsuccessful) invocation of a very rarely used rule—the rule in *Wilkinson* v. *Downton* [62]—in order to find a solution to a horrific example of disregard for human dignity[63]—is another instance of legal disingenuousness to which counsel, less than a few years ago, had to resort in order to combat the slow recognition that we need a more modern way to protect human dignity and privacy. All of these problems have yet to be solved definitively. This leads us to the next point: reform. Where does it come from: the legislature? The courts? Transnational sources? Or all three (with possible issues of incomparability)? This is another source of difficulty which makes reliance on past experience often seem far less relevant.

6. TORT LAW NEEDS TO BE REFORMED BUT SYSTEMATIC REFORM REMAINS UNLIKELY

The mid-1970s were dominated by the Pearson Committee and its Report. It worked hard and in 1978 produced three interesting volumes. The Report contained empirical data and interesting ideas. It was also the first and last major attempt to look at the entire field of tort and consider whether it was working as well as it should or could. Its fate has been what most sanguine observers at the time it was appointed had always expected. For a variety of reasons nothing could come out if it. Its volumes have thus been gathering dust ever since on some official shelf, confirming A. P. Herbert's cynical remark that Royal Commissions are sometimes set up as lightning conductors to allay the well-founded suspicion that nothing is actually going to be done about the matter in question.[64] Reform of this type of law is rarely by the requisite political will to push it through, so the creation of such reports might be viewed (with hindsight) as a waste of public funds.

If systematic reform is lacking, piecemeal change has been the rule. Sometimes the push to change came from Parliament, though this tended to be on rather narrow topics, usually highlighted following public outcry or concern. The Vaccine Damages Scheme falls in this category. On other occasions, it was prompted by the EC, which speaks from the clouds of Brussels and then expects its pronouncements to be painlessly incorporated into the corpus of national law—not always an easy task (although one that might be eased were our respective national governments to take the negotiation and drafting process of such legislation at the EC level rather more seriously and carefully). Our Consumer Protection Act 1987 is the local outgrowth of the Directive[65]

[62] [1897] 2 QB 57. [63] *Wainwright* v. *Home Office* [2004] 2 AC 406; see ch. 9, below.

[64] *Anything but Action*, Hobart Paper No. 5 (1960).

[65] Students of drafting techniques should compare the text of the 1987 Act with the EEC Directive 85/374/EEC [1985] *OJ* L210/29 that it is meant to implement. Another example is the Data Protection Act 1998 the genesis of which must be sought in Directive 95/46/EC [1995] *OJ* L281/31.

which, when being enacted, gave rise to much anxiety but has given rise to little case law since. Yet in other cases, the statutory reform mainly referred to another (neighbouring) branch of the law but, indirectly, also affected tort law. The long overdue Contracts (Rights of Third Parties) Act 1999 is an example which challenged the doctrine of privity of contract. For by relaxing our traditional rules it removed some of the pressure built up (especially in the 1980s and early 1990s) to expand the law of tort at the expense of the law of contract.

The patterns of legislative reform are almost infinite but they are at their most confusing when Parliament's willingness to intervene is combined with the courts' urge to reform, each carrying out their task in splendid isolation from the other. We shall encounter such examples when we discuss the Misrepresentation Act 1967 and *Hedley Byrne* v. *Heller*[66]—another area where contract and tort come close together—as well as when we look at a more 'pure' tort problem and see how it was dealt with by the Defective Premises Act 1972 and *Dutton* v. *Bognor Regis*[67] and its progenies.

The complexities of legislative reform do not stop there. There are times when the legislator cannot stop tinkering with a subject. For instance, at the time of writing a government which has been in office for just under ten years has passed nearly forty 'law and order bills' and still cannot seem to get it right. The (then) Prime Minister thus recently told the Press that

> The criminal justice system is *the* [sic] public service *most distant* [sic] from what most reasonable people want.[68]

This is hardly a statement that inspires confidence in the machinery of justice and, indeed, the self-confidence of the nation.

In the area closer to home—tort law—the legislature keeps fine-tuning its solutions on the coexistence of tort law and social security.[69] The changes wrought to the law of damages, in 1996 and again in 2003, have affected the form in which they should be paid and form the latest (and possibly most important) reform in this part of the law: it will be discussed in Chapter 25. The problem with this particular part of the law is not just that it is complex; it is the source of the complexity that is particularly troublesome. For the compensation derives from different sources—basically the state and the private sector—and each of these systems is imbued with a different philosophy. Making sense of the how the two work together is the privilege of the few with the result that they often get short shrift in tort courses.

The kind of changes alluded to above were not unimportant. Indeed, they often demanded from both the teacher and the student a change of frame of mind. But the way of dealing with these topics also encouraged confusion. They thus provide another example, if one were needed, of our earlier thesis: namely, that real life does not reflect the order and system that academics expect of it. This, incidentally, raises another and

66 [1964] AC 465. 67 [1972] 1 QB 373.

68 *The Times*, 16 May 2006, p. 6.

69 See, for instance, our discussion in ch. 25 about the deductibility of social security benefits from tort awards.

wider issue. Since most of these tort problems do not involve headline-catching issues nor bring in votes for politicians, the chances that Parliament will decide to intervene to rectify anomalies tend to be slim.

Significant tort reform is likely to remain statutory in form for the foreseeable future. Unlike in the United States, the modernisation of the law of torts has, in our country, been achieved by the legislator and not the courts. Thus, from World War II onwards we find—and will examine in the chapters that follows—such important enactments as the Contributory Negligence Act 1945, the Crown Proceedings Act 1947, the Defamation Acts of 1952 and 1996, the Occupiers Liability Acts 1957 and 1984, the Animals Act 1971, the Congenital Disabilities (Civil Liability) Act 1976, the Unfair Contract Terms Acts 1977, the Administration of Justice Act 1982, the Damages Act 1996 and the Compensation Act 2006. Each of these statutes has greatly changed the law, making Britain the country in Europe that has the largest number of tort statutes which are also the lengthiest in size!

If that is the case, what role has been preserved by our courts? In an era when so much of the common law is found in statutes one must ask to what extent our courts remain a major source of new law. More specifically, to what extent should they strive to retain a creative function? While studying his tort cases, the critically minded student should constantly ask himself if legislation is the only or best way to achieve reform. To quote Lord Goff again:

For all practical purposes, textbooks are as informative as any code could be, indeed more so; and they lack all the defects of codes, since they can be changed without difficulty—as the law develops, and they encourage, rather than inhibit, the gradual development of the law. To put it shortly; propositions of law in a textbook need not aspire to completeness; they may be changed without legislation; and judges are at liberty to depart from them, if persuaded that it is right to do so.[70]

Once again, therefore, the plea can be made for the exposition and development of tort law through a partnership between case law and academic writing rather than the fossilising and distorting effect that piecemeal legislation can have on the development of the law.[71] So, does court-induced reform, with or without academic assistance in the background, have a future in our country?

In a system essentially created by court decisions this should be the first item that should have been examined under this heading of tort reform. This is a difficult question to answer without flying an academic kite and suggesting—very tentatively—a distinction between liberalising and restraining innovation.

For in the first group our judges seem to have lost their appetite to give the lead to law reform. Thus, a student reading *Launchbury* v. *Morgans*[72] (discussed in Chapter 19) must ask himself whether the House of Lords was right to castigate Lord Denning's attempt in the Court of Appeal[73] to introduce the doctrine of the family car. Or was the

70 'Judge, Jurist and Legislature' (Select Bibliography), 92. 71 *Ibid.*, 89.
72 [1973] AC 127. 73 [1971] 2 QB 245.

House of Lords right in *Pirelli* [74] (discussed in Chapter 24) right to apply a rule which their Lordships believed to be patently unjust? In this case the legislature conveniently obliged,[75] but what happened to the Practice Direction of 1966 in which their Lordships gave themselves the right to deviate from some of their earlier opinions? And what about the rule of privity of contract, which Lord Reid held back in 1967 from reforming because legislation was imminent?[76] (In fact it only came thirty-two years later.) The delay of *legislative action* could be taken to suggest that either our system is atherosclerotic or, if you are conservatively minded, to claim that our system had, in multiple, complex and oblique ways, already found a solution around the biggest problems of privity of contract. The era of *Rylands* v. *Fletcher*,[77] *Donoghue* v. *Stevenson*,[78] *Hedley Byrne* v. *Heller*,[79] *Home Office* v. *Dorset Yacht* ,[80] *McLoughlin v. O' Brian*[81] and *Anns* v. *Merton Borough Council*[82] seems to have gone. And what calibre of judges made this law!

The days of confidence have thus given way to retrenchment. This fits in with our times of doubt, widespread attack on all our public institutions, and a form of collective uncertainty as we decide whether we belong to Europe, we should serve America or, somehow, float in the Atlantic on our own. Retrenchment is dominated by fears that liability will make our civil servants afraid to act and nightmares of massive local authority bankruptcies for being made to pay not for slight errors but repeated and grossly negligent behaviour.[83] These fears would merit most serious consideration if there were supported by figures, empirical evidence and decisional law coming from sister jurisdictions. But the judges who raise such fears with great perspicacity have failed to answer them with data, preferring hunches instead. Today, many of our judges are thus putting to use their formidable talents in the service of particular ideals: to carve out immunities for all sorts of statutory bodies, to reduce the rights of minority shareholders, to slow down (if they cannot stop) the development of a law of privacy. These aims they have pursued relentlessly since about the mid-1990s and, arguably, have done all this in the belief that a liberalisation of the rules of liability would carry unbearable economic consequences. This is not an insignificant belief. It is shared by many and has much to be said for it. But it may be doubted whether it contains the answer needed by our times. And one thing must surely be beyond dispute: it is a move driven by a political philosophy and not pure legal reasoning.

The retrenchment has also come with an enhanced zeal for casuistry at the expense of the search for any underlying principles. The progressive, unprincipled, piecemeal expansion of the law of breach of confidence in order to achieve in all but name something approaching a law of privacy is one illustration of this.[84] It is difficult to believe

[74] *Pirelli General Cable Works Ltd.* v. *Faber (Oscar) and Partners* [1983] 2 AC 1.

[75] By passing the Latent Damage Act 1984. [76] [1968] AC, 58, 72.

[77] (1865) 3 H & C 774; 159 ER 737 (Court of Exchequer); LR 1 Ex. 263 (Court of Exchequer Chamber).

[78] [1932] AC 562. [79] [1964] AC 465.

[80] [1970] AC 1004. [81] [1983] 1 AC 419.

[82] [1978] AC 728.

[83] See for instance the facts of *Lawrence* v. *Pembrokeshire CC* [2006] EWHC 1029 (QB), [2007] PIQR P1 and *AD and OH (a child: by AD his litigation friend)* v. *Bury MBC* [2006] EWCA Civ. 1, [2006] 1 WLR 917.

[84] Discussed in ch. 22, below.

that all the judicial contortions found there were due to principle or caused by respect for tradition—both would have been acceptable, if perhaps unconvincing, reasons. One is, however, seriously tempted to suggest that even our judiciary—well paid, widely respected and protected by tenure—may be more concerned at the reaction of some sections of the Press than their high standing and dignity warrant. Their prevarications may owe something to this extra-legal factor; and if this is plausible, why not make the student conscious that 'deciding' is not something that is done in a legal vacuum?

The final verdict on this transformation of judicial law has yet to be pronounced. In the meantime, however, one can lament the decline in the creative function of our courts, a decline taking place at a time when other courts, in Israel, in Germany, in South Africa, in Canada, in Australia, are producing creative innovations over a wide area of private as well as public law. Those who like us believe that law moves in a cyclical way, await with impatience the new cycle and remain bemused at the way learned colleagues seize upon aberrant decisions here and there to complain that tort law is getting out of control. It is doing nothing of the kind, but is instead grappling with the problem that it has had to face from its earliest years: how to reconcile in a meaningful manner the competing interests of claimants and defendants.

7. ARE LIABILITY RULES RESTRICTED BECAUSE THE DAMAGES RULES HAVE BEEN LEFT UNREFORMED OR BECAUSE THE RELATIONSHIP BETWEEN LIABILITY AND DAMAGES HAS BEEN NEGLECTED?

Tort law in general and its most important heading of liability—negligence—are always split up into component parts and also tend to be examined in a particular sequence. In the tort of negligence, for instance, we ask first whether there is a duty of care and, if the answer is affirmative, we proceed to examine whether this was carelessly breached and whether this carelessness was the cause of the claimant's damage. If it is, we finally reach the crucial question of calculating the reparation needed to make him, again, whole. The rules appropriate to this phase of this inquiry are examined in Chapter 25; and their complexity is greatly enhanced by the fact that they have to be combined with the rules appropriate to other sources of compensation which may be available to the injured party.

The problem with this approach is that it tends to conceal the fact that what happens in the last phase of our inquiry may, on occasion, have an open or (which is likelier), a concealed effect on what we do in the first. There is little doubt, for instance, that in the United States, where damages are in the exclusive domain of juries, judges (and some academics) place considerable, often exaggerated, emphasis on the notion of duty of care (which is within judicial control). This enables them to control litigation and keep many frivolous (and, one should add, some meritorious) claims from being considered by the jury and ending up with substantial awards.

In our system, though juries are no longer used, one often is left with the impression that the duty question is also influenced by the assumption that if the claimant wins on this point (and satisfies all other requirements) his damages *must, of necessity*, be very high. The consequences may be unpredictable and even catastrophic for the defendant. We have already stated our belief that this is the prime reason behind the extensive immunities currently accorded by our courts to defendants who are in breach of statutory obligations. This is a vital and highly complex area of our law and we devote to it one whole chapter below[85] so little more need be said at this stage.

Let us also suggest that the same fear may lie behind our excessively restrictive rules that govern our law of psychiatric injuries. Conservative academics may invoke high-sounding expressions—such as the dignity of the law being endangered if such claims were to be met. We remain unconvinced. The ability to separate the fictitious from the real claim has greatly improved with the progress of medical science. The cost of litigation is a sufficient disincentive to chance litigation with a real complaint. The absence of juries means that we do not run the risks which, on this topic, have made American law even more cautious than ours. In short, it is shocking to see our law in the entangled mess it is in; and painful to read when a senior judge tells us that it has by now become so complex that only the legislator can untangle the mess.

Taken individually, the above arguments seem to us to be quite compelling. But, taken cumulatively, they become even more persuasive to those at least who do not share the apocalyptic view that the discovery of a duty of care in such cases will ruin many local authorities. This overall assessment is supported by the evidence that exists—admittedly not complete or detailed enough to warrant total confidence but, nonetheless, of considerable interest.

8. TORT LAW IS, IN PRACTICE, OFTEN INACCESSIBLE TO THE ORDINARY VICTIM

The multitude of cases that a student will encounter in tort textbooks may lead him to believe that victims of accidents have easy and frequent recourse to this branch of the law. In reality, nothing could be further from the truth; and this misapprehension is encouraged further by the fact that the operation of tort law in practice tends to be ignored by traditional books and cases. The reality is that most victims of accidents do not even go as far as consulting a lawyer about what their rights are, let alone pursue them to a successful conclusion. Accidents at home[86] offer an example where legal action is rarely pursued because, quite simply, there is no legal action to pursue (e.g. slipping in the bathtub or scalding in the kitchen). On other occasions, however, no action is sought (though one, for example, might be possible under the Occupiers' Liability Acts) because the victims are unaware of their possible rights or, ignorant of

[85] See ch. 8.

[86] On which see Hazel Genn's *Meeting Legal Needs?* (Select Bibliography).

the possible role of insurance, would consider it unsociable to sue the owner/host of the premises.

But even where there are no such inhibiting factors, many victims are left without a remedy, either because they never bothered to ascertain their rights or because they were discouraged from doing so by the fear of becoming entangled in a lengthy and costly legal process. The figures are, in fact, quite worrying. The Oxford Socio-Legal Studies Group, in its *Compensation and Support for Illness and Injury*, has claimed that out of the representative sample of 1,711 victims questioned by them, 444 (26 per cent) considered claiming damages, 392 (23 per cent) thought a claim was possible, 247 (14 per cent) actually consulted a lawyer, and 198 (12 per cent) actually obtained damages.[87] These figures suggest that most potential claims are defeated at the outset: the accident victim does not realise that a legal remedy might be available or, even if he does, other constraining factors prevent him from consulting a solicitor about bringing a claim.[88] Among these constraining factors, costs are the most pervasive fear, with the Legal Aid scheme being unavailable to all but the poorest and in some cases, such as defamation, not being available at all.

The unavailability of the class-action mechanism or the (limited possibility of) undertaking litigation on a contingency fee system (both possible in the United States) thus enables culpable defendants not only to discourage litigation but also, if one starts, to drag it out so as to force weaker claimants into disadvantageous settlements. Both these weaknesses of the English system are periodically reviewed, but it is difficult to predict when and what type of relief will come to address this grave problem. Victims are also discouraged from having recourse to tort law because costs are not only great but also unpredictable (unlike many European systems where, for example, they are fixed in various ways in advance and can be estimated by the prospective litigant). The unpredictability is, of course, also an element of the litigation process that is increased by some of the legal rules that we shall discuss in this book. Prominent among them is the defence of contributory negligence that may lead to the victim's damages being reduced in an often totally unpredictable way. The retention of this defence may appear to be morally sound for, according to this view, why should a victim who has been at fault be in a position to increase through his own fault the extent of the tortfeasor's liability? Yet in reality this argument is considerably weakened where—as in the cases of road-traffic accidents—an insurance company is the ultimate payer and, in many cases, the victim's fault in substance consists of some minor inattention, inevitable in some kinds of claimants, like young children or old people. To this objection the defenders of the *status quo* would counter that the abolition of the defence of contributory negligence would oblige insurers to pay out larger amounts and thus force them to put up the premiums. Even this fear, however, has not been substantiated after the relatively recent reform of the traffic-accident law in France that effectively reduced, and in many

[87] D. Harris *et al.* (eds.), *Compensation and Support for Illness and Injury* (Select Bibliography), 46.
[88] *Ibid.*, 47.

cases totally eliminated, this defence. The French innovations are thus worth a closer look, although this is not the right place to discuss them.

The outcome of litigation is further complicated and made uncertain by the necessity for the claimant to prove the tortfeasor's fault and/or to establish the causal link between the fault or harmful conduct and the damaging result. The system only partially helps the victim through such devices as *res ipsa loquitur*; in many areas, however, the claimant's position is unenviable. Actions against the pharmaceutical industry offer a good example. In this country there has not been a single successful action against a drug manufacturer. This bizarre result must surely be as undesirable as the opposite extreme, found in the United States, where many manufacturers—especially of contraceptive devices—have been forced either into bankruptcy or out of the development or distribution of such products.[89]

The overall picture provided by the modern sociological surveys of the operation of the tort system in practice is a grim one. The Oxford Socio-Legal Studies Group likened the position of victims of accident to participants in:

> a compulsory, long-distance obstacle race. The victims, without their consent, are placed at the starting line, and told that if they complete the whole course, the umpire at the finishing line will compel the race promoters to give them a prize; the amount of the prize, however, must remain uncertain until the last moment because the umpire has discretion to fix it individually for each finisher. None of the runners is told the distance he must cover to complete the course, nor the time it is likely to take. Some of the obstacles in the race are fixed hurdles (rules of law), while others can, without warning, be thrown into the path of the runner by the race promoters, who obviously have every incentive to restrict the number of runners who can complete the course. As the runners' physical fitness, and their psychological preparedness for the race, varies greatly the relative difficulty of the obstacles also varies from runner to runner. In view of all the uncertainties . . . many runners drop out; others press on. . . . . After waiting to see how many runners drop out at the early obstacles without any inducement, the promoters begin to tempt the remaining runners with offers of money to retire . . . most runners accept. . . . . The few hardy ones who actually finish may still be disappointed with the prize money.[90]

9. HUMAN RIGHTS LAW IS SET TO INFLUENCE TORT LAW, BUT THIS INFLUENCE IS LIKELY TO BE GRADUAL AND INDIRECT

The passage of the Human Rights Act 1998 was a momentous event for the UK constitution. At the same time it is bound to have far-reaching implications for the evolution of private law, including the law of tort.[91]

[89] Fleming (Select Bibliography), 15.

[90] Harris *et al.* (Select Bibliography), 132–3.

[91] See generally J. Wright, *Tort Law and Human Rights* (2001).

A number of Convention rights appear to have immediate implications for tort law: these include the right to life in Article 2, the right to liberty and security in Article 5, the right to access to the court in Article 6, the right to respect for private and family life in Article 8, the right to freedom of expression in Article 10, the right to freedom of assembly and association in Article 11, the right to protection of property in Article 1 of the First Protocol to the Convention and the right to education in Article 2 of the First Protocol to the Convention. However, for various reasons we were originally told that we should not expect to see tort law transformed overnight. Was this a prediction, an expectation or, merely, a set of comforting words for those fearing the worst from this overdue innovation? On the whole, we take the view that the progress made has been more substantial than many of us had hoped for and this is thanks to a number of judges espousing the new regime with an open mind. It was thus left to sections of the political world and the Press to do their respective best (worst, perhaps one should say) to distort the Act's beneficial effects and to exaggerate unpopular decisions, many unrelated to the Act itself.[92]

As is well known, the Act did not incorporate the European Convention on Human Rights *directly* into domestic UK law. Rather, under section 3 of the Act, the courts must interpret legislation 'so far as it is possible to do so' in such a way as to render it compatible with Convention rights. Under section 8, damages may be awarded against public authorities which act in contravention of a Convention right. Finally, and most importantly for our purposes, section 6 of the Act provides that it shall be unlawful for public authorities, *including courts*, to act in ways that are incompatible with Convention rights.

This is all good and true; but is it not also true to say that the main focus of human-rights jurisprudence is on relations between private citizens and the state? This is commonly known as the 'vertical' application of Convention (or constitutional) rights; and that is how things were when the human-rights culture originally became part of the world of litigation. However, starting in Germany[93] in the early to middle 1950s the argument was articulated that (weak) individuals could be exploited not only by the all-powerful state but also by modern and powerful entities such as trade unions, multinational companies and, of course, the Press. A number of jurisdictions thus began to recognise the possibility that human rights may also have a 'horizontal' effect, in the sense of giving rise to legal rights and obligations in relations between private persons or entities. Section 6(3) of the Human Rights Act, by characterising a court as a public authority, creates the possibility that in UK law, too, it may be possible to apply human-rights considerations to disputes arising between private individuals. The key issue here is how the courts will come to interpret section 6. From a comparative constitutional perspective, 'horizontality' might be defined in a number of different

92 For instance, decisions dealing with early releases from prison which, if wrong or leading to fateful events, could only be blamed on how the Parole Boards applied the relevant rules and were nothing to do with the Human Rights Act itself.

93 See B. S. Markesinis, 'Privacy, Freedom of Expression and the Horizontal Effect of the Human Rights Bill: Lessons from Germany' (1999) 115 *LQR* 47.

ways.[94] At one end of the spectrum are those who argue for 'full horizontality', that would imply an obligation on the courts to develop the common law in a way that is consonant with Convention rights.[95] At the other extreme are those who insist that the purpose of the Act is to control the power of the state over the individual. Proponents of this view, therefore, anticipate that the influence of Convention rights over private law will be at most 'tangential'.[96]

The structure and wording of the Act, together with the record of the Parliamentary debates, suggest that it is not open to the courts to adopt 'full horizontality', that is, the view that Convention rights should be given effect in all private law litigation. But it would be surprising if the courts came down in favour of a restrictive reading of the Act which confined its force to regulating relations between citizens and the state. One reason for this is that certain 'private' persons, such as large corporations and economic associations, are just as capable in practice of the abusive exercise of power as state organs. The UK courts had, in any event, begun to consider the contents of the Convention when developing common law torts in such contexts as freedom of expression[97] and freedom of association. So it now seems more than likely that the passage of the Act will reinforce this process: certainly the evidence to date is very largely in support of such an interpretation. This indeed has happened to some extent in the area of privacy; and it is in the chapter on privacy that we shall examine in greater detail the effect of the *Campbell* v. *MGN Ltd.*[98] judgment which contains one of the most interesting (though inconclusive) discussions of this issue.

There are other areas in which Convention rights which are likely to have a growing, indirect influence on the common law though more time is needed before we can assess the full effect.

The first relates to the general area of tortious interference with the person. The torts of battery, assault and false imprisonment already define a set of rights to personal autonomy.[99] A rights-based conception of these torts would require a strict reading of those defences that can be invoked to justify interference. There are indeed signs that the courts, without invoking the Act directly, are taking a restrictive view of the justification defence in the context, for example, of false imprisonment.[100]

The second main area where we may expect to see tort law shifting under the influence of human rights law relates to the tort of negligence. Traditionally, the tort of

[94] See R. Clayton and H. Tomlinson, *The Law of Human Rights* (2000), ch. 5, at paras. 5.74–5.99 and M. Hunt, 'The Effect on the Law of Obligations' in B. S. Markesinis (ed.), *The Impact of the Human Rights Bill on English Law* (1998), ch. 12.

[95] See H. W. R. Wade, 'Horizons of Horizontality' (2000) 116 *LQR* 217, supported by J. Morgan, 'Questioning the "True Effect" of the Human Rights Act' (2002) 22 *Leg. Stud.* 259.

[96] Sir Richard Buxton, 'The Human Rights Act and Private Law' (2000) 116 *LQR* 48, perhaps exemplified by his views in *Wainwright* v. *Home Office* [2004] 2 AC 406 (see ch. 22 below).

[97] See, e.g., *Derbyshire CC* v. *Times Newspapers* [1993] AC 534.

[98] [2004] 2 AC 457.

[99] See ch. 9, below.

[100] See *R* v. *Governor of Brockhill Prison, ex parte Evans (No. 2)* [2000] 4 All ER 15, discussed in ch. 9, below; T. Hickman, 'Tort Law, Public Authorities and the Human Rights Act 1998', in D. Fairgrieve, M. Andenas and J. Bell (eds.), *Tort Liability of Public Bodies in Comparative Perspective* (2002).

negligence has recognised and defended a discrete set of interests: in historical terms, property rights were the first focus of protection, followed by rights to physical integrity and, more recently, purely economic or financial interests. The Convention rights point the way to new categories of claims in negligence, based for example on access to educational provision (as referred to in Article 2 of the Protocol) or to respect for family life (under Article 8). As we shall see in our discussion of the tort of negligence, the law is still a long way from recognising such claims fully or even adequately.[101] If the 1998 Act is to have an effect in this area, it is most likely to be felt gradually and indirectly, as the courts develop existing lines of argument within the common law in ways which are broadly in line with human-rights jurisprudence. In practical terms, this tendency is likely to be particularly relevant in relation to the tortious liability of public bodies.[102]

The question of liability in negligence and/or for breach of statute is one of the most fashionable pet-hates of the common law. Another is its dislike of awarding damages for what was once called nervous shock and is nowadays described as psychiatric injury. As we shall note in the next paragraphs, the two may come closer together as a result of human rights law.

Strasbourg has already flexed its muscle in this area of negligence in *Osman* v. *UK*.[103] There, it expressed its disapproval of the use of the notion of duty of care in order to create extended areas of immunity for certain types of defendants (e.g. the police). This decision, which appeared just before the fourth edition of this book saw the light of day, caused shock waves in our country not only because it was seen as a European intervention in our law but also because it showed how this European Court, comprising—some noted with dismay—in many cases not 'proper judges' but retired politicians, had misunderstood our love affair with the notion of duty of care.[104] In the rush to condemn the decision, little notice was paid to the fact that the English judge on that Court had concurred with the result. More importantly, little was said of the fact that during the preceding years, under the tutelage of, literally, a handful of judges in the Court of Appeal and the House of Lords, the extensive use of the notion of duty of care had led to the creation of extensive areas of immunities covering the police, the public prosecution service, social services in local authorities departments, the fire brigade, the lifeboat service and so on. The Strasbourg Court took the view that preventing the case being heard at such an early stage of the proceedings was incompatible with Article 6(1) of the Convention.

A most 'skilful campaign' was then mounted by the British legal establishment to 'persuade' Strasbourg to backtrack. Strasbourg did just that in *Z* v. *UK* and *T.P. and K.M.* v. *UK*,[105] and those English judges and academics who were (are) consumed by the fear of an explosion in litigation could, once again, breathe freely. But is this issue dead? With the threat from Strasbourg removed, English courts seem to have returned to their

[101] See ch. 3, below. [102] See ch. 8, below.

[103] *Osman* v. *United Kingdom* (1998) 29 EHRR 245.

[104] An essential ingredient of the tort of negligence, discussed in ch. 3, below.

[105] Application Nos. 29392/95 and 28945/95.

old (bad?) ways. Thus in *D* v. *East Berkshire Community Health NHS Trust and others*; *MAK and another* v. *Dewsbury Healthcare NHS Trust and another*; *RK and another* v. *Oldham NHS Trust and another*[106] a majority of the House of Lords was, again, emphatic in rejecting the possible liability of a local authority.

But is the *Osman* kind of idea completely dead or could we be faced one day with an *Osman* Mark II?

This is too big an issue to be discussed in the first chapter of this book so it will receive a fuller treatment in Chapter 8, below. Yet we cannot but note the astuteness of Lord Bingham in alluding to this background factor in his dissenting judgment in *D* v. *East Berkshire Community Health NHS Trust*. More importantly, he predicted that if the common law refused to evolve, Strasbourg might strike again. He thus said that

> the question does arise whether the law of tort should evolve, analogically and incrementally, so as to fashion appropriate remedies to contemporary problems or whether it should remain essentially static, making only such changes as are forced upon it, leaving difficult and, in human terms, very important problems to be swept up by the Convention. I prefer evolution.[107]

Less than a year after this statement was made, Strasbourg in fact returned to the fray in the case of *Keegan* v. *United Kingdom*.[108] The Fourth Section of the Court held that an action should be possible under Article 13 of the Convention if local law denied it. The dispute arose as a result of a botched investigation by the Liverpool police, whose officers early one morning broke into the claimant's home, believing it to be the home of a known and dangerous criminal. Strasbourg took the view that the facts of the case amounted to a violation of Article 8 of the Convention. They also took the view that Article 13 of the Convention required that a remedy be given in domestic law if the grievance in question could be regarded as 'arguable' in terms of the Convention. Naturally, the Court admitted that this did not amount to a guarantee that a remedy would be given, since under the Contracting State's laws an effective remedy should be provided in principle. English law, however, did not allow such a remedy to be considered unless the police had acted with malice, which they had not. The absence of a remedy for negligence, however, denied the courts the chance to examine the proportionality and reasonableness of the police activity: the national law setting in such cases had set the balance in favour of protecting the police. Damages were thus accorded to the claimants, the amount being fixed at levels higher than those that the defendants thought justifiable.

The facts of the case make it clear that it is not—yet—as threatening as *Osman*. But, in our view, it has the potential of growing further and justifying, if a case with appropriate facts came before the Court, Strasbourg questioning the continued reluctance to hold the police and other statutory bodies liable for their negligently caused harm. This time round, the English citadel may fall more easily since very senior judges—such as Lords

[106] [2005] 2 AC 373.

[107] *D.* v. *East Berkshire Community Health NHS Trust and* others; *MAK and another* v. *Dewsbury Healthcare NHS Trust and another*; *RK and another* v. *Oldham NHS Trust and another* [2005] 2 AC 373, at para 50.

[108] Application No. 28867/03.

Bingham and Nicholls—have now joined those who have always argued that the notion of duty of care is a blunderbuss weapon.[109] More importantly, however, *Keegan* illustrates the importance of this new tort/human-rights linkage which will, sooner or later, be resolved from abroad if the local courts persist in their refusal to adapt English law to the demands of its present-day environment. So the question which must be asked is whether our courts can persist for much longer in denying the European[110] realities? If, some might even say when, they succumb, the change of heart will represent one of the biggest influences of human-rights law upon internal tort rules.

Though our courts are currently sending out clear negative signals to claimants, litigation is not halting. The most recent batch of decisions,[111] dealing with the recurring problem of *alleged* child abuse leading to the separation from their parents, seem to be trapped by the *East Berkshire*[112] ruling. What is striking about these two decisions is not the unnecessarily long regurgitation of the *dicta* from the majority in *East Berkshire* but the minimal lack of attention to two elements of these cases: first, the fact that the local authorities and their officials were guilty of *repeated and gross violations* of their duties. These could/should have prompted the lower judges to consider, or at least to reflect on, Lord Bingham's safety-valve device of contemplating the imposition of liability only in cases of serious fault along the lines of the French notion of *faute lourde*. This did not happen because of *dicta* in the Lords in *East Berkshire* which assumed that the interests of the child and the interests of the parents were in conflict, which made the task of social workers making these delicate assessments unenviable if not impossible.

Yet should our judges be allowed to disguise their deep-rooted suspicion of tort liability by pretending that the interests of the child meant that they should 'single-mindedly'[113] ignore the interests of the parents? For even if this were convincing in all cases (which we submit it is not), surely we must accept that the interests of the child are not simple and easily defined interests, but are rather interests endowed with multiple facets, at least one of which is coterminous with that of its parents, namely the interest in keeping the family unit together?

This is nothing more nor less than the interest envisaged in Article 8 of the Convention; and its unjustifiable violation should lead to the award of damages especially if, as in

109 Thus in *Phelps* v. *Hillingdon CC* [2001] 2 AC 619, 667: Lord Nicholls of Birkenhead, referring to the way the notion of duty of care works, poignantly remarked that ' "Never" is an unattractive absolute in this context.' This is precisely what the judges in Strasbourg could not understand and did not like.

110 Law emanating from the European Court of Justice in Luxembourg is, of course, now part of own legal system, so its existence cannot be denied nor its influence on our law (and, just as importantly, on the way our judges interpret law) belittled. But Strasbourg law, it is often argued, is less binding in its detail since the Convention, to which we signed up almost half a century ago, only sets out our 'minimal' obligations and allows much room for variation in detail. Yet how realistic such an analysis is, given the existence of a central court charged with the creation of a uniform interpretation of the articles of the Convention, and given also this Court's widening jurisdiction, is open to much debate.

111 *Lawrence* v. *Pembrokeshire CC* [2006] EWHC 1029 (QB), [2007] PIQR P1 and *AD and OH (a child: by AD his litigation friend)* v. *Bury MBC* [2006] EWCA Civ. 1, [2006] 1 WLR 917.

112 *D.* v. *East Berkshire Community Health NHS Trust and Others*; *MAK and Another* v. *Dewsbury Healthcare NHS Trust and Another*; *RK and Another* v. *Oldham NHS Trust and Another* [2005] 2 AC 373.

113 This pair of words appears repeatedly in Field J's judgment in *Lawrence*. For the reasons we give in the text, we find them unfortunate.

this instance, the errors that led to the splitting up of the family kept happening with hair-raising regularity.[114] Surely, in such cases the public interest is not solely and always on the side of shielding local authorities from the economic consequences of their shoddy behaviour; it also encompasses the need to send out a signal to them that mistakes are one thing, while repeated negligence is quite another, and intolerable, form of behaviour. But such subtlety of evaluation is eliminated if one chooses to work with a notion—duty of care—that operates on the basis of 'all or nothing'. That is why Lord Nicholls was so right in calling this an 'unacceptable alternative'.

Second, let us retain this optic of looking at what happened in this case and not let us fall into the trap of describing the parental claim as one arising out of emotional or psychiatric distress. For such an analysis would not only be wrong; it would also lead the conservative judges back into our law and encourage them to invoke the messy state of the law of nervous shock in order to come back to what is frequently their default starting-point: immunity!

So, instead, let us recognise that here we are here dealing with a new situation of human-rights torts where the monetary compensation awarded is a sign that society values a certain state of affairs—here family life, including family union—and expresses its disapproval when it has been disturbed—especially, one might add, if it has been disturbed by its own agents and officials. After all, English tort law is not a stranger to moving into action even in the absence of any quantifiable damage, if what it is really doing is helping to vindicate a right—like, for instance, the human freedom of locomotion in the case of false imprisonment or reputation in the case of libel—from being violated in an unwarranted manner. Again, the most recent Strasbourg case law would favour, we think, such an approach; and it is, itself,[115] suggesting the award of damages that we would find both reasonable and by no means excessive nor would consider as ruinous; and if it ever were to become part of the legal orthodoxy in this country, it would then be another illustration of human-rights law (emanating from abroad) shaping our national tort law rules.

Strasbourg is already thinking along these lines. As long ago as the 1980s a mother was separated from her child, which child was made a ward of court in order to protect it against the alleged violence of the mother's partner. When the mother's conditions improved she applied to re-establish access to the child which, in the meantime, had been put up for adoption by the council. The local council's delay in producing the relevant documentation that would determine the mother's right of access to her child was described as 'deplorable' by the English judge hearing the case; but the child ended up being adopted and the mother being denied access to it. Since, in effect, there was no other real remedy left to the mother, she began proceedings in Strasbourg complaining that the delay in determining her right of access to her child amounted to a violation of Articles 6 and 8 of the Convention. She won on both grounds.[116]

The case presented many novel points, and they are still with us today.

[114] See [1]–[17] of Field J's judgment in *Lawrence*.

[115] As the *Keegan* case suggests.

[116] *H* v. *United Kingdom* (1987) 10 EHRR 95; (1988) 13 EHRR 449.

First, awards against delays in court proceedings cannot be made according to section 9 of the Human Rights Act 1998. But the delays of a local authority can result in it having to face monetary consequences.

Second, since that case was decided the Strasbourg Court has sent out signals that it is not likely to succumb to the tempting siren voices which convinced it to backtrack from *Osman* and set the level of damages at demeaningly low levels.[117] On the contrary, Strasbourg seems determined to send just about the right signal to local authorities and its agents that sloppy behaviour simply will not be tolerated. The *Keegan* case shows that they are sticking to their guns or, rather, their own figures—not too high, but neither too low to be meaningless.

Third, it is clear that whatever the nature of this remedy, it resembles more what Lester and Pannick have described as a 'new public law tort of acting in breach of the victim's rights'[118] and this, as already stated in the previous paragraph, can only mean that the foundations are being laid for evading other restrictive rules of English tort law such as the rules on nervous shock.

The human rights dimension of these cases is thus crucial, indeed innovative, for all sorts of reasons. For, first, not only does it suggest that the system of remedies developing under our recent human rights legislation is different and not easily reconcilable with those found in domestic law; it also shows that judges in Strasbourg are likely to continue their own development of the law, and in doing this they may not be able to provide English law with the more finely tuned approach that our courts could develop were they freed from the conservative tendencies of the House of Lords.

This brief discussion will, perhaps, make more sense to the novice tort lawyer after he or she has read the accounts in Chapters 3 and 8 and then returns to ponder these wider reflections. So here suffice it to say or, simply, repeat that intelligent lawyers will get much mileage out of looking at tort cases from the new perspective of human rights. Tort law is thus, once again, changing; and the stimulus is coming from the contact with foreign—or should we say better 'transnational' sources. For those who believe that a dialogue between 'relevant' legal cultures is enriching, this must be an exciting moment.

10. MISCELLANEOUS MATTERS

Some of the points we make here are certainly not limited to tort law; though in the course of writing a long, detailed book on this subject we thought they were particularly pronounced in its sphere. Another point that troubled us was: why raise these points here? We came to the conclusion that we should, in the belief that, despite limitations in

117 Thus in *Z.* v. *UK* and *T.P. and K.M.* v. *UK*, Application Nos. 29392/95 and 28945/95 (2002) 34 EHRR 3, see Arden LJ's concurring opinion suggesting an award in line with those recommended by the guidelines of the Judicial Studies Board.

118 A. Lester and D. Pannick, 'The Impact of the Human Rights Act on Private Law: The Knight's Move' (2000) 116 *LQR* 380, at 382.

time and space, the student should not be presented with the rudiments of a particular branch of the law in a compartmentalised way but, every now and then, should be asked to consider the 'details' against the broader fabric of English justice. In one sense this might lead to a more jurisprudential approach to tort law; but then what is wrong with that?

All except those following one-year law courses must surely favour a more broadly based instruction in the law, even allowing for the fact that most students who are likely to use this book will be in their first or second year of study. So here are some general observations to be tested against the more detailed study of the material provided in this book.

(i) Our law of torts is increasingly dominated by statute. An (admittedly) quick study of the laws of Western Europe suggests that we have more and longer statutes on torts than any other system in Western Europe. In itself this may not be a defect; but it becomes a problem given (1) the long-winded nature of English legislative drafting; (2) the lack of proper training in statutory construction; and (3) the lack of co-ordination between the courts and the legislature when dealing with law reform.

(ii) Our case law—especially on tort—is the second headache. On the whole, judgments have been getting longer, to some extent inevitably, given the growing complexity of the law. But the length of our judgments compared with the length of judgments from other Commonwealth jurisdictions, arguably, reveals an excessive use of citation in lieu of substantive reasoning. To give one example: anyone who reads *Murphy* and *Norsk*, two more-or-less contemporaneous decisions of the House of Lords and the Supreme Court of Canada on the question of economic loss, will immediately notice a difference in styles, sources of inspiration and techniques. For the student at least, *Norsk* provides an excellent functional analysis of an as-yet unresolved problem, whereas *Murphy* seems bogged down in a dry and often not fully thought-out consideration of precedents. Anathema though it may seem to some, it is equally true to say that today most of the exciting ideas in tort law are coming from the Supreme Court of Canada and the High Court of Australia and not from the House of Lords.[119]

[119] In this we agree with Ewan McKendrick, 'Restitution of Unlawfully Demanded Tax' (1992) *LMCLQ* 88, 92: '[t]he last decade in the House of Lords has generally been witnessed by great conservatism and undue deference to Parliament. It is now rather difficult to maintain that the House of Lords is the most influential court in the common law world.' McKendrick, in his discussion of the House of Lords' decision in *Woolwich Building Society* v. *IRC* [1993] AC 70, expressed the hope that in that case and others, 'there are now some signs that the House of Lords may rediscover its role'. We leave it to the reader to decide, in the light of our discussion above, whether in the decade and a half since these remarks were written, whether there has indeed been a resurgence in English appellate jurisprudence.

SELECT BIBLIOGRAPHY

BURMAN S., and GENN, H. (eds.), *Accidents in the Home* (1977).

CANE, P., *Atiyah's Accidents, Compensation and the Law* (7th edn., 2006), chs. 3–11.

CLAYTON, R., and TOMLINSON, H., *The Law of Human Rights* (2000).

CONAGHAN, J., and MANSELL, W., *The Wrongs of Tort* (1994).

FLEMING, J. G., *The American Tort Process* (1988).

FRIEDMANN, D., and BARACK-EREZ, D. (eds.), *Human Rights in Private Law* (2001), esp. chs. 7, 14, 15 and 16.

GENN, H., *Meeting Legal Needs? An Evaluation of a Scheme for Personal Injury Victims* (1982).

—*Hard Bargaining: Out of Court Settlement in Personal Injury Actions* (1987).

GOFF OF CHIEVELEY, LORD, 'The Search for Principle', Maccabean Lecture in Jurisprudence (1983) 69 *Proceedings of the British Academy* 169.

— 'Judge, Jurist and Legislation' (1987) 2 *Denning LJ* 79.

HARLOW, C., *Understanding Tort Law* (1987), ch. 3.

HARRIS, D. *et al.* (eds.), *Compensation and Support for Illness and Injury* (1984).

HICKMAN, T., 'Tort Law, Public Authorities and the Human Rights Act 1998' in Fairgrieve, D., Andenas, M., and Bell, J. (eds.), *Tort Liability of Public Bodies in Comparative Perspective* (2002).

MARKESINIS, B. S., 'Privacy, Freedom of Expression and the Horizontal Effect of the Human Rights Bill: Lessons from Germany' (1999) 115 *LQR* 47.

MUSTILL, LORD, 'Negligence in the World of Finance' (1992) 5 *The Supreme Court* [Malaysia] *Journal* 1.

STAPLETON, J., 'In Restraint of Tort' in Birks, P. B. H. (ed.), *The Frontiers of Liability* (1994), ii, 83 ff.

WRIGHT, J., *Tort Law and Human Rights* (2001).

PART II

THE TORT OF NEGLIGENCE

3 Establishing Liability in Principle
4 Other Elements of Liability
5 An American Perspective on Negligence Law

3

ESTABLISHING LIABILITY IN PRINCIPLE

1. THE DUTY CONCEPT AND THE ELEMENTS OF THE TORT OF NEGLIGENCE

(A) THE CONCEPTUAL STRUCTURE OF NEGLIGENCE

The tort of negligence forms one of the most dynamic and rapidly changing areas of liability in the modern common law. Its expansion, in particular in the course of the twentieth century, reflects the pressures that the rise of an industrial and urban society have brought to bear upon the traditional categories of legal redress for interference with protected interests.[1] The growth and increasing sophistication of insurance have also contributed to this expansion.[2] A doctrinal examination of negligence must not lose sight of this wider social and economic context within which the tort has developed, which is reflected in fluidity of the central legal concepts and the courts' ever-increasing recourse to 'policy' as an explanation for their decisions.

The conceptual structure of negligence is highly flexible and capable of general application. These features have allowed the courts to utilise the tort in the context of novel claims for compensation. The evolution of the tort, however, has not always favoured the expansion of liability, and in recent years courts in most common law systems have placed restrictions on its scope. It would be wrong to see the tort of negligence as set upon some predetermined path of enlargement, as some authors have suggested.[3] The experience of the last twenty years or so if anything suggests a dialectical process of evolution with many, often inexplicable, tergiversations.

Duty, breach, causation and damage are the elements which together make up any successful negligence claim.[4] Their requirements may be rephrased as a series of

[1] See J. G. Fleming, 'Remoteness and Duty: the Control Devices in Liability for Negligence' (Select Bibliography), 471–2.

[2] See M. Davies, 'The End of the Affair: Duty of Care and Liability Insurance' (1989) 9 *Leg. Stud.* 967; although a more sceptical view on the role of insurance in the development of the tort is expressed by J. Stapleton, 'Tort, Insurance and Ideology' (Select Bibliography).

[3] T. Weir, 'The Staggering March of Negligence' (Select Bibliography).

[4] See *Lochgelly Iron and Coal Co.* v. *McMullan* [1934] AC 1, 25; the tort of negligence 'properly connotes the complex of duty, breach and damage thereby suffered by the person to whom the duty was owing' (per Lord Wright).

questions, each of which must be answered affirmatively if the claimant is to win: does the law recognise liability in this type of situation (duty)? Was the defendant careless in the sense of failing to conform to the standard of care set by law (breach)? Has the claimant suffered harm (damage) for which the law regards the defendant as responsible either in whole or in part (causation)? This chapter, together with Chapter 4, will address each of these questions in turn. The question of how the court puts a monetary value on the damage suffered by the claimant for the purpose of awarding compensation or *damages* is a separate issue which is considered in Chapter 25.

The British courts did not recognise the existence of a general duty in tort imposing liability for careless behaviour across a range of situations and relationships until the 1930s. The turning point was the decision of the House of Lords in *Donoghue* v. *Stevenson*.[5] Prior to this decision, legal liability for carelessness was clearly established only in a number of separate, specified situations, which lacked a unifying principle. A duty to take care was attached by law to certain traditional categories of status, as in the case of the duty owed to a customer by an innkeeper or common carrier, or the duty of an artisan to use the customary degree of skill and care in his work. Other situations that gave rise to a duty of care without the need for a specific promise or undertaking included the holding of certain public offices and the bailment of goods.[6] Road and rail accidents and maritime collisions caused by carelessness could also lead to liability in tort, although in many such cases legal responsibility was limited by the operation of the defences of contributory negligence and consent. In the nineteenth century the courts added the category of liability for 'things dangerous in themselves', such as a loaded firearm.[7] In such cases the law recognised 'a peculiar duty to take precaution imposed upon those who send forth or install such articles when it is necessarily the case that other parties will come within their proximity'.[8]

Beyond this the courts declined to go. This was partly on the ground that duties of care, which originated in *contract*, were confined in their effect to the parties to a particular agreement. To use tort to extend the liability of a landlord, builder or manufacturer to remote third parties would undermine the strict common-law principle of 'privity of contract'.[9] For example, a landlord who contracted to repair the floor of a house and then failed to do so owed no duty of care to the tenant's wife injured when the floor gave way beneath her, since 'there was but one contract, and that was made with the husband. The wife cannot sue upon it.'[10]

This emphasis on privity of contract amounted to a view that in the area of negligence, tort was subordinate to contract as a source of civil liability. However, as we have seen, some exceptions to privity of contract had long been recognised. The restriction of tort claims came to be seen as outmoded because the courts could no longer find a coherent

[5] [1932] AC 562. [6] See P. Winfield, 'Duty in Tortious Negligence' (1934) 34 *Col. LR* 41, 45.

[7] *Langridge* v. *Levy* (1837) 2 M & W 519; (1838) 4 M & W 337.

[8] *Dominion Natural Gas Co. Ltd.* v. *Collins* [1909] AC 640, 646 (Lord Dunedin).

[9] *Winterbottom* v. *Wright* (1842) 10 M & W 109 is generally taken to be the origin of this strict insistence on privity of contract.

[10] *Cavalier* v. *Pope* [1906] AC 424, 430 (Lord James).

explanation for the admission of some exceptions and the denial of others. The treatment of claims for compensation was perceived as having become arbitrary and unjust.[11]

These doubts set the scene for the decision in *Donoghue* v. *Stevenson*,[12] which finally established the duty of a manufacturer to an ultimate consumer to ensure that goods put into circulation were free from defects that he should have foreseen might cause physical injury or damage to property. In that case the appellant alleged that she had been poisoned by drinking the contents of a bottle of ginger beer manufactured by the respondent and purchased for her by a friend from a retailer. The opaque surface of the bottle concealed, it was alleged, the remains of a decomposed snail, which the appellant discovered only after she had consumed most of the bottle's contents. She claimed as a result to have contracted gastroenteritis. On a preliminary matter of law (and with the allegations never proved) the House of Lords held, by a bare majority, that the manufacturer owed a duty of care to the ultimate consumer, thus overturning the old cases which had limited the scope of duty in the ways described above.

In his judgment, Lord Atkin addressed the question of how to formulate a 'general conception of relations giving rise to a duty of care, of which the particular cases found in the books are but instances', in the following terms:

> The rule that you are to love your neighbour becomes in law: You must not injure your neighbour and the lawyer's question: Who is my neighbour? receives a restricted reply. You must take reasonable care to avoid acts or omissions which you can reasonably foresee would be likely to injure your neighbour. Who then in law is my neighbour? The answer seems to be persons who are so closely and directly affected by my act that I ought reasonably to have them in contemplation as being so affected when I am directing my mind to the acts or omissions which are called into question.[13]

This statement of the 'neighbour principle' remains controversial, not least because Lord Atkin made no reference to the distinction between physical harm—personal injury or property damage—and pure economic or financial loss, which has since become an important marker of the limits of tort liability. Its status is at best that of a guideline of general principle; in no sense is it a formula that can be mechanically applied to determine the incidence of liability. Nevertheless, in its decisive rejection of the traditional, narrow formulation of duty situations it marks the starting-point for analysis of the modern tort.

According to Lord Atkin, the decision in *Donoghue* v. *Stevenson* supplied a legal remedy to meet an obvious 'social wrong', thereby giving legal expression 'to a general public sentiment of moral wrongdoing'.[14] Fault, in this sense, is at the basis of negligence liability; the claimant has to show that the defendant's behaviour was

[11] See, in particular, the doubts expressed by Scrutton LJ in *Hodge* v. *Anglo-American Oil Co.* (1922) 12 Ll. L Rep. 183, 186, and by Greer LJ in *Bottomley* v. *Bannister* [1932] 1 KB 458, 478–9. On the other hand, the early attempt of Brett LJ to formulate a general principle of liability in *Heaven* v. *Pender* (1883) 11 QBD 503, 509, did not meet with general favour: see Cotton and Bowen LJJ in the same case at 516–17; Brett MR himself, Bowen and A. L. Smith LJJ in *Le Lievre* v. *Gould* [1893] 1 QB 491, 497, 502, 504; and Greer and MacKinnon LJJ in *Barnes* v. *Irwell Valley Water Board* [1939] 1 KB 21, 33, 46.

[12] [1932] AC 562.

[13] *Ibid.*, 580.

[14] [1932] AC 562, 538, 580, respectively.

careless. Damage is also an essential requirement. Unlike, for example, in the torts of libel, trespass and false imprisonment, which are said to be actionable *per se*,[15] in negligence the claimant must prove that he sustained a loss or injury as a result of the defendant's negligence. Fault, causation and damage are necessary but not sufficient conditions of liability, however, as they appear to be in other legal systems (e.g. the French). In the old Roman-law terminology *damnum sine iniuria* is not enough to justify the imposition of liability. Since the modern expansion of negligence began, the very generality of the notion of liability for fault has made it necessary for the courts to have resort to 'control devices' whose purpose is to confine what would otherwise be an overextensive legal liability.[16] While to some extent the courts have achieved this by references to causation, including the concept of 'remoteness' or 'legal cause', it is above all the concept of *duty of care* which they have used to shape the tort of negligence.

(B) THE DUTY CONCEPT

The notion of duty of care has been called 'superfluous', the result of an 'historical accident',[17] and the 'fifth wheel on the coach'.[18] In other systems, particularly the civil-law systems of the European mainland, the concept has no precise equivalent, causation or other notions being used to perform the functions duty accomplishes in our law. Thus, though roughly the same process of classifying legal claims as admissible or not inevitably takes place, it is achieved through other means such as delimiting in advance the list of protected interests or using the notions of 'fault' (as a legal term of art), causation and damage (both of the latter being understood in a normative sense).[19] If the concept of duty in the common law serves a useful purpose, this must be found in its capacity to synthesise the numerous different criteria used by the courts to determine the boundaries of negligence liability. Additionally, it also presents a distinct advantage over causative notions in so far as it makes those who are deciding issues of liability fully conscious of the fact that policy determines the final outcome.

The issue of *duty* is thus essentially concerned with whether the law recognises in principle the possibility of liability in a given type of situation. To put it differently, it helps demarcate the range of people, relationships and interests that receive the

[15] See chs. 23 and 9, respectively.

[16] See Fleming, 'Remoteness and Duty' (Select Bibliography). How arbitrary the 'controlling devices' can be may be seen from the latest decision of the House of Lords in the matter of psychiatric injury. Thus, see *White* v. *Chief Constable of South Yorkshire Police* [1999] 2 AC 455, especially Lord Hoffmann's opinion.

[17] P. Winfield, 'Duty in Tortious Negligence' (1932) *Col. LR* 41, 66.

[18] W. W. Buckland, 'The Duty to Take Care' (1935) 51 *LQR* 637. On the historical circumstances that gave rise to the separation of 'duty' from the other elements of the tort of negligence, see D. J. Ibbetson, *An Historical Introduction to the Law of Obligations* (1999), ch. 9. For a claim that the concept of duty of care fulfils a 'moral' purpose in today's tort law, see N. McBride, 'Duties of Care: Do They Really Exist?' (2004) 24 *OJLS* 417, and the reply by D. Howarth, 'Many Duties of Care: Or a Duty of Care? Notes from the Underground' (2006) 26 *OJLS* 449–72.

[19] See generally F. H. Lawson, 'Duty of Care: A Comparative Study' (1947) 22 *Tul. LR* 111; B. S. Markesinis and H. Unberath, *The German Law of Torts: A Comparative Treatise* (4th edn., 2002). Professor Hepple, 'Negligence: The Search for Coherence' (Select Bibliography) is the latest writer to express doubts about the continuing need for the notion of duty of care. His proposed solution would bring English law much closer to the French model.

protection of the law from the effects of negligently inflicted harm. Thus, even where the defendant's carelessness can be shown to have caused damage to the claimant, the law may nevertheless not acknowledge the existence of a 'duty situation', thereby refusing to impose liability.

This may happen for a number of reasons, the most important being that the law does not grant equal protection to different *kinds of damage*. Thus, whereas physical injury and damage to tangible property interests are normally within the scope of the duty of care, financial or 'pure economic' losses, which are not directly connected to physical damage, may not be. The precise extent to which the law recognises liability for economic loss has been one of the most difficult questions to face the courts in the past few years. In its decision in *Murphy* v. *Brentwood District Council* [20] the House of Lords formulated a narrow rule limiting the scope for recovery in this area, but economic loss remains recoverable in a number of other situations. Another kind of damage which the tort of negligence only partially encompasses is 'nervous shock'—nowadays usually referred to as 'psychiatric injury' or 'mental distress'.[21] One commonly occurring example of this is the medical condition known as post-traumatic stress disorder which may arise in reaction to the death or injury of a close relative or friend, especially if this occurred in gruesome circumstances. The courts have only slowly, and because of progress in medical science, come to accept that 'nervous shock' constitutes a physical condition for which compensation may be appropriate. Even then, as the House of Lords' decision in *Alcock* v. *Chief Constable of South Yorkshire* [22] indicates, liability will tend to be limited to a small class consisting for the most part of immediate relatives of the victim present at the scene of a particular accident or its immediate aftermath.

The concept of duty is also used to categorise claims for compensation by reference to *classes of claimants and defendants*. For example, the common law at one stage failed to recognise the unborn child or embryo in the womb as a potential claimant for these purposes,[23] and statutory intervention was required for this rule to be reversed.[24] The courts have since changed their minds on the question of the availability of an action by a child born alive for injuries sustained in the womb,[25] but for most purposes the (English) common law has now been ousted by the Congenital Disabilities (Civil Liability) Act 1976. Conversely, certain categories of defendants—in particular those involved in the administration of justice[26] and in the public service

[20] [1992] 1 AC 398.

[21] For an overview see P. Gilliker, 'A "New" Head of Damages: Damages for Mental Distress in the English Law of Torts' (2000) 20 *Leg. Stud.* 19.

[22] [1992] 1 AC 310. The current trend is, if anything, becoming more restrictive. See *White* v. *Chief Constable of South Yorkshire Police* [1999] 2 AC 455 and the more detailed discussion in this chapter, below.

[23] *Walker* v. *Great Northern Railway* (1891) 28 LR Ir. 69.

[24] In the form of the Congenital Disabilities (Civil Liability) Act 1976. Courts in other common-law jurisdictions took a different view: see in particular the decisions of the Supreme Court of Victoria in *Watt* v. *Rama* [1972] VR 353 and of the Ontario Court of Appeal in *Duval* v. *Séguin* (1973) 40 DLR (3d) 666.

[25] *Burton* v. *Islington HA* [1993] 2 QB 204.

[26] The scope of barristers' immunity from civil action has been greatly reduced by *Arthur J. S. Hall & Co.* v. *Simons* [2002] 1 AC 615, not following the earlier HL judgment of *Rondel* v. *Worsley* [1969] 1 AC 191; on the liability of judicial officers, see *Sirros* v. *Moore* [1975] QB 118.

generally[27]—have what amounts to a qualified protection from being subjected to negligence actions.

Finally, the concept of duty is concerned with the important distinction between *acts* and *omissions*.[28] Liability for positive acts of carelessness is well recognised, but liability for failure to act is treated differently, with 'duties of affirmative action' being imposed only in exceptional circumstances. Of these, two of the most important are the duties owed by occupiers of premises to lawful visitors and by employers to their employees. For what are mainly historical reasons these areas of law, which have been heavily influenced by statutory intervention, have developed separately from the mainstream of negligence liability, and for this reason they are the subject of special treatment in Chapters 6 and 18 respectively. These chapters must thus be read in conjunction with the present one.

It is sometimes said that where the law does not acknowledge a duty situation the defendant, effectively, has *immunity* from liability for damage caused by his negligence.[29] This was also the view taken by the European Court of Human Rights in *Osman* v. *United Kingdom*,[30] a ruling which opened up the possibility that many of the 'blanket immunities' which derive from the duty concept could be challenged on human rights grounds, in particular for infringing an aggrieved person's access to a judicial procedure for resolving their complaint. In a later decision, *Z* v. *United Kingdom*,[31] the Court took a much more cautious view of this issue, as part of which it accepted that the absence of a duty of care in English law does not normally provide a defendant with immunity from a claim which would otherwise exist; rather, it means that the claim is not made out in the first place. As we shall see below,[32] following *Z*, the scope for mounting a human-rights challenge to a finding of 'no duty' on the grounds that it amounts to an unjustifiable 'immunity' is now very limited, but it has not completely disappeared. It would thus not be unwise to predict that this is one of those cyclical problems that will reappear, especially given the ongoing renewal of the membership of the House of Lords and the signs of unease, especially among some judges of the Court of Appeal, with the current tendency to use the 'no duty' approach to create large areas of 'no-go' for the law of tort.

(C) DUTY, FORESEEABILITY AND FAULT

The notion of duty is sometimes used in a separate and more specific sense, namely that for there to be a duty of care in a particular case the harm in question must have been foreseeable to the *individual* claimant.[33] In *Bourhill* v. *Young* Lord Wright explained that

[27] The immunity of the Crown is now limited by the Crown Proceedings Act 1947. Local government authorities and similar bodies benefit from a certain degree of immunity in the exercise of their discretionary powers. See ch. 8, Section 5, below.

[28] Lord Goff extensively discusses this in his judgment in *Smith* v. *Littlewoods Organisation Ltd.* [1987] AC 241.

[29] See D. Howarth, 'Negligence after *Murphy*: Time to Rethink' (Select Bibliography).

[30] (1998) 29 EHRR 245. [31] [2001] 2 FLR 621.

[32] See Section 5(a)(i), below.

[33] See R. W. M. Dias, 'The Breach Problem and the Duty of Care' (Select Bibliography), 376, 380 ff.

foreseeability 'is always relative to the individual affected. This raises a serious additional difficulty in the cases where it has to be determined not merely whether the act itself is negligent against someone but whether it is negligent *vis-à-vis* the plaintiff.'[34] In this case the House of Lords held that a motorist who was killed in a collision brought about by his own carelessness owed no duty of care to a pedestrian in the vicinity of the accident who suffered nervous shock and a terminated pregnancy as a result of hearing the sound of the crash and witnessing its aftermath. Rather than say that the particular plaintiff was an 'unforeseeable claimant' to whom, as an individual, no duty was owed, this case may now be more accurately explained by saying that she was not within the general class of claimants who were able to recover for damage of this kind, namely nervous shock. In order to keep conceptual confusion to a minimum, it is normally better to regard duty as giving rise to a *general* or '*notional*' question of this kind, and to leave the issue of whether a *particular* claimant can recover against a particular defendant to the question of causation or remoteness of damage. This is the approach which will be taken in this book.

This does not mean that the individual relationship between claimant and defendant does not matter when it comes to ascertaining whether a duty of care arose between them. In some circumstances the nature of their *pre-tort relationship*—that is to say, the nature of undertakings or assumptions of responsibility made by one party to the other before the damage occurred of which the claimant is complaining—may be essential. This is frequently the case, for example, with regard to recovery for financial losses and with regard to liability for pure omissions—two areas in which a duty of care rarely arises between strangers in the same way that it does, for example, in respect of physical damage inflicted by one user of the highway on another.

However, it is important to stress that even where the particular individual circumstances of claimant and defendant are significant for establishing the existence and scope of a duty of care, the test is hardly ever concerned with foreseeability as such. Foreseeability alone is, in fact, entirely inadequate as a test for establishing a duty of care. As Lord Goff recently pointed out: '[i]t is very tempting to try to solve all problems of negligence by reference to an all-embracing criterion of foreseeability, thereby effectively reducing all decisions in this field to questions of fact. But this comfortable option is, alas, not open to us.'[35]

Although Lord Atkin's 'neighbour principle' stresses foreseeability or 'reasonable contemplation' of harm as a preliminary test of duty, the use of this criterion fails to explain why many kinds of non-physical damage[36] which are entirely foreseeable nevertheless lie outside the scope of negligence liability. It may be just as foreseeable, for example, that careless driving on a busy road may result in physical injury and in damage to the property of other road users—both these kinds of damage are in principle recoverable in negligence—as that it will result in financial losses to road users who are

[34] [1943] AC 92, 108. See also *Alcock* v. *Chief Constable of South Yorkshire* [1992] 1 AC 310, 319.

[35] *Smith* v. *Littlewoods Organisation Ltd.* [1987] AC 241, 280.

[36] And, as we shall see below, even some cases of physical injury or property damage.

merely delayed following the accident and who, without suffering any injury or damage to property, may as a result forfeit wages or a valuable business opportunity. These financial losses, however, will not normally be recoverable through a negligence action,[37] thanks to the rule limiting liability for what is termed 'pure economic loss'.[38]

Again, foreseeability is only one part of the concept of *breach* of duty. A breach of duty arises where the conduct of the defendant is 'unreasonable' in the sense of failing to reach the appropriate standard of care. This will be the standard of normally careful behaviour in the profession, occupation or activity in question. In applying this standard in what is sometimes a rough-and-ready way, the courts frequently balance the degree of foreseeability or *risk* of harm against the *costs* to the defendant of avoiding the harm and the wider *benefits* foregone if a certain activity cannot be carried on.[39] The level at which the standard is set is an evaluative question which the courts have acknowledged involves, once again, issues of policy and judgement, and not a question that can be addressed solely by asking whether the particular harm was foreseeable in the circumstances. Thus, is a cricket club at fault if a batsman hits a six and the ball lands on and injures a passer-by? The answer may depend on the likelihood of such an injury occurring and the extent of the precautions—which might range from building a higher fence to stopping cricket being played altogether on that site—that could have prevented it.[40]

It can be seen from this discussion that an important distinction exists between *negligence as a state of mind* and the *tort of negligence*. Negligence as a state of mind, distinct from both intention and recklessness, denotes the failure to foresee the consequences of one's actions in terms of the risk of harm they create to others. While negligence in this sense is a necessary condition of liability in tort, it is very far from being sufficient, even assuming the existence of a causal link between the defendant's lack of care and the resulting damage. To assess whether the negligence is *tortious* in character one has to know not only whether the damage in question is of a type which the courts recognise as recoverable in principle (duty), but also whether the defendant could have avoided the harm by taking precautions which the law regards, in the circumstances, as an acceptable burden (breach).

(D) CAUSATION AND DAMAGE

Questions of *causation* also require the courts to make value judgements about the ascription of legal responsibility for damage. Where damage results from multiple causes the courts often resort to the test of 'but-for cause'—would the loss have been incurred but for the defendant's negligence?[41] This notion is based on the view that a defendant should be liable only to the extent that it can be shown that his conduct was

37 Though they might be recoverable under public nuisance—a result explicable if one bears in mind the effects of history on modern law.

38 J. Stapleton, 'Duty of Care and Economic Loss: A Wider Agenda' (1991) 107 *LQR* 249, 254.

39 *Latimer* v. *AEC Ltd.* [1953] AC 643, an approach to some extent also reflected in s. 1 of the Compensation Act 2006, discussed below in ch. 4, Section 1(c)(ii).

40 See *Bolton* v. *Stone* [1951] AC 850.

41 *Wilsher* v. *Essex AHA* [1988] AC 1074.

a condition of the claimant's hurt. Thus, if a hospital negligently fails to diagnose and treat a patient's condition, following which he dies, the hospital will escape liability if it can show that the patient's condition was untreatable and that he would have died from it no matter how much care had been taken.[42] An employer whose negligence causes an employee to suffer a career-limiting injury will incur only limited liability if he can show that the employee would have retired early anyway, thanks to a quite separate and independent illness which develops after the injury but before the employee's case comes to trial. According to the House of Lords, the employer will be liable only for the *additional* consequences, in terms of premature loss of wages and career, which can be attributed to the injury suffered at work.[43] On the other hand there are cases in which the 'but-for' test tends to break down, in particular where the courts have difficulty distinguishing the causal responsibility of multiple tortfeasors. The test cannot be mechanically applied, as a matter of logic, to every instance, and policy considerations may, once again, openly be factored into the equation.[44]

Another area in which evaluative judgements of this sort are made concerns the question of remoteness: should a defendant be liable for a greater extent of damage than he could reasonably have foreseen would occur as a result of his negligence? The courts have held that the *extent of damage* need not have been foreseeable as long as there was foreseeability of the *kind of damage* sustained by the claimant. An illustration is the so-called 'eggshell skull' principle, which grants recovery in full to a claimant who is unusually vulnerable or susceptible to the consequences of a particular kind of injury. An employee who sustains a life-threatening disease when an accident at work triggers a condition that would otherwise have lain dormant will recover damages in full for the consequences of the illness, even though the accident itself was comparatively minor and its consequences could not have been predicted.[45] This outcome can be seen as striking a compromise between the idea that the extent of the defendant's legal liability should be strictly limited to his degree of personal responsibility and the idea that he should be made fully liable for the consequences, in terms of the increased risk of harm to others, of his behaviour. It is significant that the courts yet again treat this issue of remoteness differently according to whether injury to the person or interference with economic interests is at stake, with the latter being accorded less extensive protection.[46]

Of the conceptual elements of the tort of negligence the fourth, *damage*, is by far the least developed—perhaps because until recently the use of juries meant that all aspects pertaining to this notion were left for them to determine. Questions of the definition and categorisation of damage, which in other legal systems (because of the absence of the notion of duty of care) are essential determinants of negligence liability, tend to be

42 *Barnett* v. *Chelsea and Kensington Hospital* [1969] QB 428.

43 *Jobling* v. *Associated Dairies Ltd.* [1982] AC 794.

44 See in particular the complex and controversial judgments of the House of Lords in *Fairchild* v. *Glenhaven Funeral Services Ltd.* [2003] 1 AC 32 and *Barker* v. *Corus UK Ltd.* [2006] 2 WLR 1027, discussed in ch. 4, Section 2, below.

45 *Smith* v. *Leech, Brain & Co. Ltd.* [1962] 2 QB 405.

46 See below, ch. 4, Section 3(e)–(f).

dealt with in English law under different headings. As we have just seen, the distinction between physical and economic loss is addressed under the headings of duty of care and (to a lesser extent) remoteness of damage. The subsuming of damage questions into other conceptual categories does not end there. As Jane Stapleton has pointed out:

> A fundamental question ... in determining the outer limit of the scope of the tort of negligence is that of what damage is or could be recognised as constituting the minimum for an actionable claim. Is it necessary, for example, to show that palpable and deleterious physical changes have occurred to the person or property of the claimant because of the defendant's fault, or is it enough to show the certainty, probability or possibility that such changes will occur in the future? ... Another major question is this: on the basis of a requirement of actionable damage, how do and how should courts deal with a fact situation where the essence of the claimant's complaint (such as defective house foundations) could be formulated in terms either of physical damage or of economic loss? A third important question is this: what is the relationship between the court's formulation of the damage which can form the gist of an action and the level of proof required of the claimant in establishing a causal connection between that damage and the defendant's fault? Clearly these sorts of issues are crucial to an understanding of the limits of negligence, yet the courts rarely address them.[47]

To some extent it will not matter under which particular heading the courts address questions of this kind. The point, however, is that a certain lack of conceptual clarity may adversely affect the way in which these questions are formulated and dealt with. The question, for example, whether a claimant should be able to recover for the loss of a chance of avoiding physical injury arose in a case where carelessness by employees of a hospital materially increased the risk that a patient would fail to make a full recovery from a prior accident (which was not itself the responsibility of the hospital). The plaintiff's condition worsened, but it could not be shown that his initial injuries would not have led to the same result in any case. By approaching the issue exclusively in terms of whether, on the balance of probabilities, the defendants' carelessness caused the plaintiff's final condition, the House of Lords appeared to sideline the question whether 'loss of a chance' fell within the definition of compensatable damage.[48]

Another area where conceptual difficulty has arisen concerns the identification, for the purposes of the limitation of actions, of the precise time at which actionable damage occurs. Statutes limit the bringing of actions to a period of a few years after the damage arises,[49] but the period of limitation may start to run before the claimant is aware that the loss has been incurred. Suppose, for example, that the claimant buys a house which, unknown to him or to the seller, is constructed on defective foundations as a result of the combined negligence of the builder and the local authority inspector whose job it was to inspect the foundations during construction. At what point does the claimant suffer loss?[50] Is it when he pays more for the house than it is truly worth?

47 J. Stapleton, 'The Gist of Negligence' (Select Bibliography), 213.

48 *Hotson* v. *Berkshire AHA* [1987] AC 750.

49 See generally the Limitation Act 1980.

50 See *Anns* v. *Merton LBC* [1978] AC 728; *Pirelli General Cable Works Ltd.* v. *Oscar Faber & Partners* [1983] 2 AC 1; *Murphy* v. *Brentwood DC* [1991] 1 AC 398; E. McKendrick, '*Pirelli* Re-Examined' (1991) 11 *Leg. Stud.* 326; ch. 24, Section 9 below.

Or when the foundations begin to cause cracks in the structure of the house? Is it, alternatively, when he has the house valued by a surveyor, perhaps many years later when he wishes to sell it, only to find that it is worth a fraction of what he assumed? These questions, which are of the utmost importance to all the parties concerned and their insurers, continue to receive an uncertain answer from the courts. In part this is because of the lack of a clear conception of what constitutes 'damage' in this instance and where the boundaries lie between 'physical' losses, which are normally recoverable in the tort of negligence, and those which are 'purely economic', and which are much less likely to be recoverable.

(E) THE UTILITY OF EXISTING CONCEPTS

The fluidity and equivocation of the basic concepts of negligence make it important to avoid too rigid an insistence on finding the 'correct' technical form in which to phrase an issue. Some questions may equally well be put in terms of either duty or causation (and, in particular, remoteness of damage). In the United States, where most negligence actions are tried with a jury, the labelling of an issue in terms of either duty or remoteness plays an important role in determining the extent of the judge's powers. For, whereas the question of duty is one for him alone to determine, the question of remoteness must, at least in part, go to the jury.[51] This point does not arise in England, where the jury no longer plays a significant part in negligence litigation and both duty and remoteness are questions for the judge. In this regard, Lord Denning once remarked:

> The more I think about these cases, the more difficult I find it to put each into its proper pigeonhole. Sometimes I say: 'There was no duty.' In others I say: 'The damage was too remote.' So much so that I think the time has come to discard these tests which proved so elusive. It seems to me better to consider the particular relationship in hand, and see whether or not, as a matter of policy, economic loss should be recoverable, or not.[52]

Few judges would take *quite* so iconoclastic a view. In recent decisions of the appellate courts there has, if anything, been a reassertion of the need for conceptual precision and an attempt to avoid direct appeals to 'policy'.[53] Unfortunately, this renewed emphasis upon technical rigour has not led to greater clarity in the use of concepts. This is partly because some of the concepts now in fashion (such as 'proximity' or the even vaguer

[51] See Professor Robertson's 'American Perspective', ch. 5, below. Even in that system, however, leading academics (and some judges) have acknowledged how interchangeable are the basic notions of the tort of negligence. Thus, see Prosser on *Torts* (4th edn., 1971), 244.

[52] *Spartan Steel and Alloys Ltd.* v. *Martin & Co. (Contractors) Ltd.* [1973] 1 QB 27, 37. To similar effect, in the context of duty of care, is Lord Steyn in *Rees* v. *Darlington Memorial NHS Hospital Trust* [2004] 1 AC 309, 323.

[53] See, in particular, the decisions of the House of Lords which led to the gradual abandonment and final abrogation of the doctrine enunciated in *Anns* v. *Merton LBC* [1978] AC 782, especially *The Mineral Transporter* [1986] AC 1; *The Aliakmon* [1986] AC 785; *Yuen Kun Yeu* v. *A-G of Hong Kong* [1988] AC 175; *Caparo Industries plc* v. *Dickman* [1990] 2 AC 605; and *Murphy* v. *Brentwood DC* [1991] 1 AC 398, discussed by B. S. Markesinis and S. Deakin, 'The Random Element of their Lordships' Infallible Judgment' (Select Bibliography); and see now the more recent, and highly significant, judgment of the House of Lords in *Customs and Excise Commissioners* v. *Barclays Bank plc* [2006] 3 WLR 1, discussed later in this chapter.

'fair, just and reasonable') are, on closer examination, just as elusive as the ones they are meant to replace (e.g. 'foreseeability'). Moreover, some were invented in the area of economic loss where there has been wider unease at the prospect of compensation but, subsequently, extended to instances of physical harm without this (policy-dictated) expansion ever being fully or adequately explained. Lack of clarity may also be the result of a continued attempt by our courts to conflate the phrase 'duty of care' with 'breach of duty', in the sense that the absence of carelessness is sometimes taken to indicate the absence of a duty.[54] The fact that one conceptual basis for a ruling (no duty) can often be exchanged for another (remoteness of damage) without making any difference to the outcome inevitably leads one to question whether the existing conceptual structure of the tort of negligence is serving a useful purpose. Faced with such uncertainties one must ask whether the present preoccupation with formal subdivisions of the duty concept is not obscuring the real issues. Thus, some have argued for the replacement of the duty concept by concepts based on causation, such as the notion of remoteness of damage, as a means of determining the boundaries of liability.[55] Yet these views as well are open to the objection that the causation concepts are not sufficiently clear or robust to subsume all such questions. Causative devices also suffer from the fact that, while pretending to make results appear to flow almost effortlessly from the application of rules of natural science they, too, conceal policy-based value judgements. The courts will thus continue using the duty concept to filter out certain claims before issues of fault, causation and damage are considered.[56]

While the achievement of conceptual clarity must be acknowledged as a goal in its own right, it is also necessary for the purpose of enabling policy issues to be properly identified and addressed by the courts. What is needed is a frank acknowledgement that policy choices are being made all the time in difficult cases which lie at the boundaries of negligence liability, and that in this area the outcome of decisions cannot be predicted in advance by the mechanical application of verbal formulae. As stated in Chapter 2, Lord Mustill is one of a very small number of judges who have boldly stated extra-judicially that judging involves a considerable degree of 'social engineering' and that judges first decide a case and then find the verbal formulae that express their conclusions on paper. There are signs, however, that other judges are becoming more inclined to admit to exercising such powers,[57] and that the members of our highest appellate court are becoming dissatisfied with the verbal formulae developed in the 1990s around the duty concept.[58]

54 There are many recent examples of this, discussed by D. Howarth, 'Negligence after *Murphy*' (Select Bibliography); and for similar examples in the law of the USA, see ch. 5, below.

55 See W. Tetley, 'Damages and Economic Loss in Marine Collision: Controlling the Floodgates' (1991) 13 *J Maritime Law & Com.* 539; B.A. Hepple, 'Negligence: The Search for Coherence' [1999] *CLP* 69.

56 *Canada National Railway* v. *Norsk Pacific Steamship Co.* (1992) 91 DLR (4th) 289, 320 (LaForest J).

57 Thus see Lord Mustill, 'Negligence in the World of Finance' (1992) 5 *The Supreme Court Journal* 1, at 24, and also his remarks in 'What Do Judges Do?', 3 (1995–6) *Särtryck ur Juridisk Tidskrift*, 611 at 620 and the discussion in ch. 2, above. See, however, Lord Browne-Wilkinson's comments in 'The Impact on Judicial Reasoning' in B. S. Markesinis (ed.), *The Impact of the Human Rights Bill on English Law* (1998), 21 ff.: '[t]he judge looks for what are called "the merits" and having found them seeks to reach a result, consistent with legal reasoning, whereby the deserving win and the undeserving lose'.

58 See *Customs and Excise Commissioners* v. *Barclays Bank plc* [2006] 3 WLR 1.

2. FORMULATING THE DUTY OF CARE

(A) BEFORE AND AFTER *ANNS*

The question whether a duty of care exists in a given situation is a question of law upon which the appellate courts are the final arbiters. In *Donoghue* v. *Stevenson* Lord Macmillan asserted that 'the categories of negligence are never closed',[59] in the sense that the courts possess the power to create new duty situations expanding the area of liability. In that case Lord Atkin's formulation of the 'neighbour principle' was not qualified by reference to particular kinds of loss nor to the distinction between acts and omissions. Subsequent courts, however, interpreting the *Donoghue* opinions, soon came to the conclusion that their scope was limited to personal injury and damage to property. The broad 'neighbour principle' was treated as an *obiter dictum*, with the *ratio* limited to the particular case of the duty owed by a manufacturer to an ultimate consumer.[60]

The dialectic evolution of English law—two steps forwards, one step backwards—thus manifested itself almost immediately after its leading case was decided and has continued ever since. How important it is for the reader to absorb this deeply (and draw the appropriate conclusions from this inbuilt doctrinal inconsistency of our highest court) can be seen from the following extra-judicial statement made by one of its most academically learned members—Lord Mustill. Thus, referring to these doctrinal tergiversations of the law lords during the sixty years following the publication of *Donoghue* v. *Stevenson*, tergiversations be it noted which have spread from the issue of pure economic loss to other areas of the negligence liability, he wrote:

> We can thus see that in the space of sixty years the courts have successively embraced six mutually inconsistent doctrines in a field of great theoretical and practical importance... it involves no disloyalty on my part to the legal system in which I have spent my working life, or to past, present and future colleague, to say that the picture thus painted is not one of unqualified success.[61]

But to return to the evolution of *Donoghue* v. *Stevenson*,[62] in *Hedley Byrne & Co. Ltd.* v. *Heller and Partners Ltd.*, decided in 1963,[63] the House of Lords recognised for the first time the possibility of an action in the tort of negligence for financial loss suffered through reliance on a misstatement. However, this case was not regarded as giving rise to a general duty of care in relation to pecuniary losses. The misstatement cases were seen as a category on their own, separate from the broad terms of the 'neighbour principle'.[64]

59 [1932] AC 562, 619.

60 See *Farr* v. *Butters Bros. & Co.* [1932] 2 KB 606, 613–14 (Scrutton LJ); *Haynes* v. *Harwood* [1935] 1 KB 146, 167–8 (Roche LJ); *Old Gates Estate Ltd.* v. *Toplis & Harding & Russell* [1939] 3 All ER 209, 217 (Greer LJ); *Barnett* v. *Packer* [1940] 3 All ER 575, 577 (Singleton J); *Deyong* v. *Shenburn* [1946] KB 227, 233 (Du Parcq LJ); *Howard* v. *Walker* [1947] KB 680, 683 (Lord Goddard); and see the view of Lord Atkin himself in *East Suffolk Rivers Catchment Board* v. *Kent* [1941] AC 74, 89.

61 'Negligence in the World of Finance' (1992) 5 *The Supreme Court Journal* 1, 23.

62 [1932] AC 352. 63 [1964] AC 465.

64 *Home Office* v. *Dorset Yacht Co.* [1970] AC 1004, 1061 (Lord Diplock).

Two further judgments of the House of Lords then set the law, for a while, on a more expansive path. In *Dorset Yacht Co.* v. *Home Office* (not an economic-loss case) Lord Reid commented of the neighbour principle, 'the time has come when we can and should say that it ought to apply unless there is some justification or valid explanation for its exclusion'.[65] This approach effectively appeared to be shifting onto defendants the onus of justifying the restriction of liability for economic loss and for omissions. It was confirmed by the House of Lords in *Anns* v. *Merton London Borough Council* where Lord Wilberforce said:

The position has now been reached that in order to establish that a duty of care arises in a particular situation, it is not necessary to bring the facts of that situation within those of previous situations in which a duty of care has been held to exist. Rather the question has to be approached in two stages. First one has to ask whether, as between the alleged wrongdoer and the person who has suffered damage there is a sufficient relationship of proximity or neighbourhood such that, in the reasonable contemplation of the former, carelessness on his part may be likely to cause damage to the latter, in which case a *prima facie* duty of care arises. Secondly, if the first question is answered affirmatively, it is necessary to consider whether there are any considerations which ought to negative, or to reduce or limit the scope of the duty or the class of person to whom it is owed or the damages to which a breach of it may give rise.[66]

Dorset Yacht was concerned with liability for omissions and with responsibility for the acts of third parties, *Anns* with omissions and with the boundary between property damage and pure economic loss. *Anns* established, for a while, that a local authority could be liable in tort for the negligence of its inspectors in failing to exercise with due care the statutory power to check the foundations of houses in the course of construction. The House of Lords held that the duty was owed to occupiers of houses which, as a consequence of such defective construction, had become uninhabitable. The nature of the loss suffered here was ambiguous: the courts classified it as physical, material damage to the house. As Lord Denning, who had begun the whole process in his judgment in *Dutton*, later admitted when writing extra-judicially, that this was incorrect; the loss suffered should properly have been seen as pecuniary or pure economic loss.[67] Because the house is *built* defectively, the occupier does not suffer property damage as a result of the council's negligence. He takes an interest in property which is *already damaged* and therefore suffers a loss which is purely financial, in the form either of a reduced value of the property compared to what he paid for it, or the expenditure required to put it right. Property damage, in other words, is making something worse than it was, and not making it bad to begin with. This truth and the underlying legal analysis, correctly carried out by the German Supreme Court as early as 1963,[68] was not to become part of the English orthodoxy until the mid to late 1980s.

It is possible that the loss was categorised as property damage in order to make the extension of liability in *Anns* (and in the earlier decision of the Court of Appeal, *Dutton* v.

65 [1970] AC 1004, 1027. 66 [1978] AC 728, 751–2.

67 *The Discipline of Law* (1979), 255–61.

68 B. S. Markesinis and H. Unberath, *The German Law of Torts: A Comparative Treatise* (4th edn., 2002), 615 ff.

Bognor Regis Urban District Council)[69] seem less revolutionary. After all, it must be in the interest of a judge who is conscious of the extent of his innovations to try to disguise them as far as possible in order to ensure their longevity. But in *Junior Books Co. Ltd.* v. *Veitchi Co.*,[70] the House of Lords went one step too far, this time by explicitly allowing in wide *dicta* a claim in negligence for financial expenditure. In that case, negligence by a building subcontractor led to the installation of a defective floor in a factory. The floor had to be repaired, at substantial cost to the owner of the factory. For a variety of reasons (not all of which are entirely clear), the owner chose not to sue the main contractor in contract as he might have been expected to do, but instead to pursue the subcontractor in tort. The House of Lords allowed an action in terms that gave substantial encouragement to claims for financial loss. Perhaps because of the explicit nature of the expansion of duty in *Junior Books*, a reaction against it set in almost immediately (though, given the facts of the case, the actual result may not be unjust). Two principal objections to a wide rule of recovery presented themselves. First was the fear of indeterminate liability, or the prospect of releasing a large number of unmeritorious and potentially oppressive claims for compensation. Second, there was concern that the traditional relationship between tort and contract was being disrupted, with adverse consequences for legal and commercial certainty. Criticism of *Junior Books*—which peaked when, only a few years after it was decided, it led a Court of Appeal judge to doubt whether it was worth even citing as authority beyond its own facts[71]—thus began to affect *Anns* itself. The turning point came with *Murphy* v. *Brentwood District Council* where a seven-judge House of Lords formally overruled *Anns*, invoking the 1966 Practice Statement in order to do so. According to Lord Keith of Kinkel, *Anns* 'did not proceed on any basis of established principle'.[72]

(B) THE THREE-STAGE TEST

What is left of economic-loss recovery and recovery for omissions after *Murphy* is considered later in our analysis. At this point it is necessary to examine how *Murphy* affects the general formulation of the test of duty of care. At the basis of the overruling of *Anns* is a rejection of Lord Wilberforce's so-called 'two-stage' test of liability. It is no longer sufficient, if it ever was, to establish a *prima facie* duty of care by reference simply to foreseeability of harm. Nor is it enough to prove, as Lord Wilberforce once put it, 'a sufficient relationship of proximity or neighbourhood', leaving it only to considerations of policy to narrow down the *prima facie* duty defined in such general terms. This

69 [1972] 1 QB 373. 70 [1983] AC 520.

71 *Simaan General Contracting Co.* v. *Pilkington Glass Ltd. (No. 2)* [1988] QB 758.

72 [1991] 1 AC 398, 471. One must not, however, forget that in the *Junior Books* case Lord Keith, unlike Lord Brandon, came very close to the overall position of the majority judgment, which relied heavily on *Anns*. Cf. Lord Hoffmann's opinion in *White* v. *Chief Constable of South Yorkshire Police* [1999] 2 AC 455, especially at 511, where the learned Law Lord seems less concerned with principle and more concerned 'to preserve the general perception of the law as [a] system of rules which is fair between one citizen and another'. Astute students and ingenious practitioners could make much of these real or apparent contradictions in stated philosophy; but a textbook can do no more than note them.

is partly because the courts no longer consider that the reference to 'policy' in Lord Wilberforce's formulation is sufficiently precise; an Australian judge has called the considerations that would have to come into play here 'indefinable'.[73] Instead, the House of Lords, adopting language used in the High Court of Australia, stated that in 'novel' cases courts should not make a general assumption of *prima facie* duty but should, instead, seek to develop the law 'incrementally and by analogy with established categories' of already decided cases. The courts thus turned their back on the broad formulations adopted in *Anns* and *Dorset Yacht* and confined *Donoghue* v. *Stevenson* to cases of physical damage. Incrementalism, however, has come to acquire a much more rigid and narrow form in the English common law than it has in other parts of the Commonwealth where it is seen as a means of preserving flexibility and not as a limiting tool.[74]

In place of the two-stage test, we now have a three-stage test through which claims for the extension of duty of care must proceed. In addition to foreseeability, it is necessary to show that claimant and defendant were in a relationship of 'proximity' *and* that it would be 'fair, just and reasonable' to impose a duty on one party for the benefit of the other.[75] A separate and additional requirement of 'policy' is mentioned in some cases,[76] but in most situations it is difficult to distinguish this heading from the requirement that imposition of a duty should be 'fair, just and reasonable'.

The concept of proximity is not new to the law of negligence. The term is mentioned both in late-nineteenth-century attempts to formulate the test of duty of care[77] and by Lord Atkin in *Donoghue* v. *Stevenson*[78] and by Lord Wilberforce in *Anns* v. *Merton LBC*[79] in their respective formulations of the test. What is new, after the line of cases culminating in *Murphy*, is the emphasis placed on proximity as a central control device within the definition of duty of care. In so far as this rather ambiguous term can be given a general meaning, it normally signifies the presence of a pre-tort relationship of some kind between claimant and defendant arising *prior to* the infliction of damage.

[73] Brennan J in *Sutherland Shire Council* v. *Heyman* (1985) 157 CLR 424, 480: 'it is preferable, in my view, that the law should develop categories of negligence incrementally and by analogy with established categories, rather than by a massive extension of a *prima facie* duty of care restrained only by indefinable "considerations which ought to negative, or to reduce or limit the scope of the duty or the class of person to whom it is owed"'.

[74] For more flexible approaches, see *Bryan* v. *Maloney* (1995) 128 ALR 163 (Australia); *Winnipeg Condominium Corp. No. 36* v. *Bird Construction Co. Ltd.* (1995) 121 DLR (4th) 193 (Canada); *Invercargill* v. *Hamlin* [1994] 3 NZLR 513 (New Zealand). Recent Commonwealth decisions are also notable for a more explicit and detailed consideration of competing policy factors than is normal in the appellate courts of the UK, and a rejection of the terminology of the three-stage test. See in particular *Perre* v. *Apand Pty. Ltd.* (1999) 198 CLR 180 and *Sullivan* v. *Moody* (2000) 75 ALJR 1570 (High Court of Australia, discussing economic loss and the liability of public authorities respectively) and *Cooper* v. *Hobart* [2000] SCC 79 (Supreme Court of Canada, reaffirming that *Anns* still applies in Canada while aligning the test more closely to the 'incremental' approach: see J. Neyers, 'Distilling Duty: The Supreme Court of Canada Amends *Anns*' (2002) 118 *LQR* 221; P. Gilliker, 'Revisiting Pure Economic Loss: Lessons to be Learnt from the Supreme Court of Canada' (2005) 25 *Leg. Stud.* 49).

[75] See, in particular, *Governors of the Peabody Donation Fund* v. *Sir Lindsay Parkinson & Co.* [1985] AC 210, 240–1 and *Yuen Kun Yeu* v. *A-G of Hong Kong* [1988] AC 175, 183 (Lord Keith of Kinkel); *Davies* v. *Radcliffe* [1990] 1 WLR 821, 826 (Lord Goff); *Caparo Industries plc* v. *Dickman* [1990] 2 AC 605, 617–18 (Lord Bridge).

[76] See, in particular, *Hill* v. *Chief Constable of West Yorkshire* [1988] QB 60; [1989] AC 53.

[77] See *Le Lievre* v. *Gould* [1893] 1 QB 491, 497 (Lord Esher MR), 504 (A. L. Smith LJ).

[78] [1932] AC 562, 580–1.

[79] [1978] AC 728, 751.

It is far from clear, however, that either proximity or the 'fair, just and reasonable' head is a requirement of the duty of care in cases of physical damage involving positive acts. The better view is that 'a defendant who, by his own positive act, has carelessly caused physical damage to the claimant or his property is *always* held to owe a duty of care to the victim'.[80] This is why, where physical damage is concerned, liability can arise between strangers, as it does between users of the highway. It is principally in cases of economic loss and liability for negligent misstatements, by contrast, that the courts have said that it is necessary to show either that the claimant and defendant were personally known to each other prior to the commission of the tort or that the claimant formed part of a small class of people, which should have been within the contemplation of the defendant.[81] Similar considerations apply in relation to liability for omissions. Here, even liability for physical damage is not, in principle, available unless the parties were in a pre-tort relationship, giving rise to a duty to act, such as that of parent and child.[82] This is also true of certain situations in which the identity of the parties is relevant to the definition of duty of care; hence the notion of whether liability would be fair, just and reasonable is invoked to explain why the police, for example, are protected against liability for negligence arising in the course of the operational performance of their statutory responsibilities.[83] The scope of that protection has come into question in the past decade as a result of a series of decisions of the European Court of Human Rights which, applying various articles of the European Convention, have called into question the limits of the duty concept. It nevertheless remains the case that the issue of liability for omissions in general, and that of public and statutory defendants in particular, raises distinct questions in the context of the concept of duty of care.[84]

Considerations of policy, sometimes coming under the heading of the 'fair, just and reasonable' criterion, limit the duty of care in exceptional circumstances where the criterion of proximity is satisfied, but where there is, nevertheless, an overriding public or general interest in denying a particular type of claim. The leading example of this effect is *MacFarlane* v. *Tayside Health Board*,[85] in which the House of Lords denied a

[80] J. Stapleton, 'Duty of Care Factors' (Select Bibliography), 72. In *Marc Rich & Co. AG* v. *Bishop Rock Marine Co. Ltd., The Nicholas H* [1996] AC 211, 235, Lord Steyn said that 'the elements of foreseeability and proximity as well as considerations of fairness, justice and reasonableness are relevant to all cases whatever the nature of the harm sustained by the plaintiff'. Not only was there no clear authority for this statement; it contradicts *Donoghue* v. *Stevenson*, as Lord Lloyd pointed out in his dissent in that case. Lord Steyn's *dictum* can be regarded as relevant only to the special circumstances of *The Nicholas H*, which involved a defendant in a quasi-public or regulatory position: see our discussion below, Section 5(a)(iv). See also the discussion of this point by Hobhouse LJ in *Perrett* v. *Collins* [1998] 2 Lloyd's Rep. 255 and of Ian Kennedy J and the Court of Appeal in *Watson* v. *British Boxing Board of Control* [2001] QB 1134; see also C. Witting, 'Physical Damage in Negligence' (Select Bibliography).

[81] On economic loss, contrast *White* v. *Jones* [1995] 2 AC 207 with *Yuen Kun Yeu* v. *A-G of Hong Kong* [1988] AC 175, and on misstatements (in a case involving physical harm), *Sutradhar* v. *NERC* [2006] UKHL 33.

[82] *Smith* v. *Littlewoods Organisation Ltd.* [1978] AC 241 (Lord Goff); *Hill* v. *Chief Constable of West Yorkshire* [1989] AC 53.

[83] See *Hill* v. *Chief Constable of West Yorkshire* [1989] AC 53.

[84] Beginning with *Osman* v. *United Kingdom* (1998) 29 EHRR 455 and continuing with *Z* v. *United Kingdom* [2001] 2 FLR 621. The significance of these and other cases are considered further below; see Section 5(a)(i), and in ch. 8.

[85] [2000] AC 59.

claim brought by parents for the costs of bringing up a healthy child born as a result of the failure of a vasectomy operation which the defendants had negligently carried out on the father. Although, for reasons we shall explore in more detail below,[86] the case was categorised (by the majority) as one of pure economic loss, and therefore one in which a duty of care might not necessarily arise in any event, there was a high degree of proximity between the parties, in the sense that they were in a pre-tort relationship involving elements of reliance and an assumption of responsibility on the part of the defendants. The parents were, after all, relying on the surgeon's skill in carrying out the operation successfully. On this basis, the case was analytically indistinguishable from *Hedley Byrne* v. *Heller*.[87] However, a duty of care was denied on the 'fair, just and reasonable' or 'policy' ground, with Lord Steyn taking the lead in suggesting that considerations of 'distributive justice', or 'the just distribution of losses and benefits among the members of a society', should prevail; more bluntly, 'the law of tort has no business to provide legal remedies consequent upon the birth of a healthy child, which all of us would regard as a valuable and good thing'.[88] In *Rees* v. *Darlington Memorial Hospital NHS Trust*[89] the House of Lords, by bare majority in a seven-member court, applied *MacFarlane* to rule that a disabled mother, who gave birth to a healthy child despite having had a sterilisation operation designed to make conception impossible, had no claim for the extra costs of raising the child that were specific to her disability; however, she was allowed to recover £15,000 as a 'conventional' award recognising that because of the defendants' negligence, she had been denied the opportunity to plan her life as she had wished. This was a doubly controversial decision: Lord Steyn, this time in the minority, argued that the considerations of policy which ruled out recovery in *MacFarlane* had no application in a case where either the mother or the child was disabled, while the conventional award granted by the majority was both 'contrary to principle' and 'a backdoor evasion of the principle enunciated in *MacFarlane*'.[90]

MacFarlane and *Rees* show how difficult it can be to predict the outcome of applying the three-stage test. Many critics have pointed to the conceptual uncertainty which surrounds it. In the earlier case of *Stovin* v. *Wise*, Lord Nicholls in particular had this to say about the notion of proximity:

> Proximity is a slippery word. Proximity is not legal shorthand for a concept with its own, objectively identifiable characteristics. Proximity is convenient shorthand for a relationship between two parties, which makes it fair, and reasonable one should owe the other a duty of care. This is only another way of saying that when assessing the requirements of fairness and reasonableness regard must be had to the relationship of the parties.[91]

Although the test was recently reaffirmed by the House of Lords in *Customs & Excise Commissioners* v. *Barclays Bank plc*,[92] Lord Bingham noted that the test 'provides no

[86] In our discussion of pure economic loss, see Section 3(c), below.
[87] [1964] AC 465. [88] [2000] AC 59, 82.
[89] [2004] 1 AC 309. The High Court of Australia reached a different conclusion, allowing a mother's claim on similar facts to Macfarlane, in *Cattanach* v. *Melchior* [2003] HCA 38.
[90] [2004] 1 AC 309, 328. [91] [1996] AC 923, 932.
[92] [2006] 3 WLR 1.

straightforward answer to the vexed question whether or not, in a novel situation, a party owes a duty of care',[93] while Lord Hoffmann considered that the phrases used in the test 'are often illuminating but discrimination is needed to identify the factual situations in which they provide useful guidance'.[94] According to Lord Walker of Gestingthorpe, there was an 'increasingly clear recognition that the threefold test... does not provide an easy answer to all our problems, but only a set of fairly blunt tools'.[95] The best that can be said for the test is, perhaps, that it marks the start of analysis, not the end of it. Alternatively, and in accordance with the views, cited above, of Lord Mustill, it could be seen as yet another phase in the unending process to provide workable underpinnings to the evolving law of negligence. Other critics, however, have gone even further in expressing their doubts about the utility of this mechanism. Thus, according to Nicholas Mullany, the three-stage test is analytically obscure: 'the supposedly separately identifiable second and third limbs of the "new" post-*Anns* duty test are, in truth, one chameleon-like criterion... a facet sufficiently malleable to accommodate any desired result'. Proximity thus becomes yet another entry point for policy considerations, but 'is too impoverished a concept adequately to subsume' the policy issues involved.[96]

But the picture changes if we look at what the courts do and not just at what they say. For then it becomes clear that the *approach* to the formulation of the duty of care has changed considerably as a result of the demise of *Anns*. Thus, first, more attention is now paid to the likely impact of any potential extension of the duty concept on other areas of law, such as public law, statutory duties, contract law and the law of property.[97] Second, attempts to formulate a general test for establishing duty of care are now discouraged, in favour of a much closer consideration of what Lord Bridge called 'the more traditional categorisation of distinct and recognisable situations as guides to the existence' of a duty.[98] This means that the duty concept will only be applied, or 'extended', to novel or previously unconsidered situations if this can be done by analogy with the existing categories of potential liability. In his judgment in *Stovin* v. *Wise*,[99] Lord Hoffmann expressed the contrast between the approaches of the courts pre- and post-*Anns* as follows:

Lord Wilberforce, who gave the leading speech [in *Anns*], first stated the well-known two-stage test for the existence of a duty of care. This involves starting with a *prima facie*

[93] *Ibid.*, 7. [94] *Ibid.*, 14.

[95] *Ibid.*, 25.

[96] N. J. Mullany, 'Proximity, Policy and Procrastination' (Select Bibliography), 80, 82.

[97] The existence of possible alternative remedies in the form of statutory actions against the builder under the Defective Premises Act 1972 was a factor in the decision to reject negligence liability in *Murphy* v. *Brentwood DC* [1991] 1 AC 398. So was the concern to avoid a situation in which public authorities could be made liable for the negligent but good faith exercise of their public-law powers. The debate on recovery of economic loss (discussed below) illustrates the general concern that tortious liability might be undermining principles of contract law (*Banque Financière de la Cité SA* v. *Westgate Insurance Co.* [1991] 2 AC 249) and property law (see *Downsview Nomines Ltd.* v. *First City Corp.* [1993] 3 All ER 937). See T. Weir, 'The Staggering March of Negligence' (Select Bibliography).

[98] *Caparo Industries plc* v. *Dickman* [1990] 2 AC 605, 618. [99] [1996] AC 923, 949.

assumption that a duty of care exists if it is reasonably foreseeable that carelessness may cause damage and then asking whether there are any considerations which ought to 'negative, or to reduce or limit the scope of the duty or the class of person to whom it is owed or the damages to which a breach of it may arise'. Subsequent decisions in this House and the Privy Council have preferred to approach the question the other way round, starting with situations in which a duty has been held to exist and then asking whether there are considerations of analogy, policy, fairness and justice for extending it to cover a new situation.... The trend of authorities has been to discourage the assumption that anyone who suffers loss is *prima facie* entitled to compensation from a person (preferably insured or a public authority) whose act or omission can be said to have caused it. The default position is that he is not.

In practice, this means that, as Lord Oliver has explained, the discussion of duty of care should be located by reference to those specific areas—such as negligent misstatements, the distinction between acts and omissions, liability for the acts of third parties and the exercise of statutory duties and powers—that represent the outermost boundaries of liability.[100] The problem with this approach is that it assumes that a new case can be easily slotted into an existing pocket of liability. This is not always so in practice. For, as Professor Stapleton has observed:

the fundamental flaw in the pre-judged pockets approach, which makes it so unsatisfactory, is that any case may have more than one factor, which is juridically significant. The case may involve a local authority defendant, a problematic kind of loss, conduct consisting of an omission... and so on. By focusing without explanation on only of them—so that, for example, the case is designed at the outset as one 'about negligent misstatement'—courts de-emphasise and run the risk of ignoring other factors to which in other contexts they do give considerable attention. Analytical method needs to be richer than this.[101]

This is a grave objection, but for the time being at least, the courts continue to approach the application of the law relating to duty of care by breaking it down into a series of categories, which give rise to distinct issues. Our analysis will follow this general approach by focusing, in turn, on the kind of damage that is suffered; the manner of infliction of harm; and the position of certain special claimants and defendants. Before we look at these categories in detail, however, we need to consider the implications of human rights law for the conceptual structure of the duty of care in negligence.

(C) THE IMPACT OF HUMAN RIGHTS LAW ON THE DUTY CONCEPT

We have already seen that one of the principal purposes of the duty concept is to restrict certain claims where there are good grounds for believing that tort-based litigation

100 *Caparo Industries plc* v. *Dickman* [1990] 2 AC 605, 618, 635.

101 'In Restraint of Tort' in P. B. H. Birks (ed.), *The Frontiers of Liability* (1994), 83 ff. To illustrate her case she refers to *Smith* v. *Bush* which if treated as a negligent misstatement case is grouped under *Hedley Byrne* and leads to liability, but if treated as a case of economic loss resulting from defective property must then be slotted into the *Murphy* pocket and result in no liability.

would not be in the public interest. This is particularly the case with public authorities, whose operational autonomy has been preserved by the courts through restrictions on the scope of duty of care. In *Osman* v. *United Kingdom*[102] this line of thinking was called into question by a startling judgment of the European Court of Human Rights. The Court held that a breach of Article 6 of the European Convention on Human Rights had occurred as a result of the failure of English law to recognise the possibility of a cause of action in the following situation: the police, having been warned of the relevant danger, had failed to take steps to protect the plaintiff and his family from threats of violence from a third party, who went on to injure the plaintiff and kill his father. On these facts, the First Instance Court and Court of Appeal had held that the police owed no duty of care to the plaintiff and his father,[103] applying the principle laid down in *Hill* v. *Chief Constable of West Yorkshire*.[104] The main basis of *Hill* is the recognition that the potential imposition of negligence liability for failure to prevent a particular crime could lead to a misallocation of the necessarily limited resources which the police have at their disposal.[105] In its ruling in *Osman*, however, the European Court of Human Rights treated the outcome of the litigation as tantamount to granting the police a blanket immunity from civil liability for operational errors, in contravention of Article 6's guarantee of access to the courts for the determination of civil rights and obligations.

The *Osman* ruling had the potential to open up to human rights scrutiny many apparently similar 'exemptions' from liability accorded to professional groups and public authorities by the operation of the duty concept.[106] However, this prospect receded as a result of the European Court of Human Rights' later ruling in *Z* v. *United Kingdom*.[107] Here, a number of children (and in some cases their parents) made claims for psychiatric harm arising from alleged negligence committed by local authorities in the exercise of their powers of child protection. In most of the cases, it was argued for the children that the authorities had negligently failed to take steps to protect them from parents who were causing them physical and mental harm, thereby causing the children long-term psychiatric illness; in others, it was claimed that the authorities had acted negligently in exercising the power to remove children from their parents, causing psychiatric harm to the children and parents alike. The House of Lords, in *X (Minors)* v. *Bedfordshire County Council*,[108] had rejected these claims on the ground that in exercising the powers in question, the local authorities did not owe a duty of care with regard to the relevant interests of the claimants. As in *Hill*, the essence of the argument here was the need to protect the operational autonomy of public bodies acting with limited resources. Backtracking from *Osman*, the European Court of Human Rights in *Z* ruled that the judgment of the House of Lords in *X (Minors)* could not be regarded as imposing

102 (1998) 29 EHRR 245.
103 *Osman* v. *Ferguson* [1993] 4 All ER 344.
104 [1989] AC 53, reaffirmed by the HL in *Brookes* v. *Commissioner of Police of the Metropolis* [2005] 1 WLR 1495.
105 See below, Section 5(a)(i).
106 See T. Weir, 'Down Hill-All the Way?' [1999] *CLJ* 4; C. Gearty, 'Unravelling *Osman*' (2001) 64 *MLR* 159.
107 [2001] 2 FLR 621, (2002) 34 EHRR 3. See also *T.P. and K.M.* v. *United Kingdom* [2001] 2 FLR 246.
108 [1995] 2 AC 633.

an immunity or 'exclusionary rule': 'the inability of the applicants to sue the local authority flowed not from an immunity but from the applicable principles governing the substantive right of action in domestic law'. This was in part because, as the Court recognised, the English law of negligence 'includes the fair, just and reasonable criterion as an intrinsic element of the duty of care'.[109] It could be argued with some measure of plausibility that *Osman* was overruled by Strasbourg, itself, as a result of a concerted pressure exerted on it by various sections of the English legal establishment.

The upshot of *Z* is that Article 6 is of only very limited use in attacking the restrictions placed on the liability in tort of public and similar bodies by the duty of care concept. In *Z*, the Court made it clear that Article 6 is not concerned with the definition of rights and obligations under substantive law; it operates only on procedural bars against the enforcement of rights which are acknowledged to exist. Hence where claims are rejected on substantive grounds—for example, because the proximity necessary for a duty of care is lacking,[110] or on the basis of the defence of illegality[111]—there is no infringement of Article 6. The Court did not overrule *Osman*, however, and so the issue arises of precisely how far Article 6 constrains the exclusionary use of the duty concept.

Two stages of inquiry are relevant here. First, the court must determine whether the exclusionary rule in question is an 'immunity' in the sense required by the Article. It is possible that certain very sweeping or 'blanket' protections for defendants could come under this heading. An example of this could be the immunities conferred on certain persons involved in the administration of justice, in particular judges and witnesses. In *Arthur J. S. Hall* v. *Simons*[112] Lords Hope, Hutton and Millett thought that Article 6 was relevant in this context; Lord Hoffmann thought that it was not; and the other three judges offered no view on the matter. The exemption of the Crown from certain civil liabilities arising out of the operation of the armed forces, as provided for by section 10 of the Crown Proceedings Act 1947, looks at first sight as if it must fall under the ambit of Article 6, but this was recently held not to be the case in *Matthews* v. *Ministry of Defence*:[113] section 10 imposes a substantive rather than a procedural bar on an action for negligence. If *Matthews* is any guide, Article 6 is unlikely to provide much help to litigants frustrated by the restrictive ambit of the duty concept in English law.

Notwithstanding the above comments, which we hope convey accurately the law as it now stands, it is difficult to deny that, whatever the terminology, the adoption of the duty concept to resolve legal disputes at an early stage and without a full trial does not amount to the conferment of wide-ranging immunities on certain types of defendants. Consider, for instance, Lord Nicholls's view when confronted in *Phelps* v. *Hillingdon London Borough Council*[114] with the argument that if a duty of care were found in that case, other councils would, likewise, be subjected to such claims. The implication was

109 (2001) 34 EHRR 2, at para. 100.

110 See *Bromiley* v. *United Kingdom*, Application No. 33747/96, Judgment of 23 Nov. 1999 and *Ivison* v. *United Kingdom*, Application No. 39030/97, Judgment of 16 Apr. 2002.

111 *Clunis* v. *United Kingdom*, Application No. 45049/98, Judgment of 11 Sept. 2001.

112 [2002] 1 AC 615; see below, Section 5(a)(ii).

113 [2002] 1 WLR 2621 (CA), affirmed [2003] 1 AC 1163 (HL).

114 [2001] AC 619.

clearly that the only way to avert this 'evil' was to cut off this avenue by using the notion of duty of care. To this he replied:

I am not persuaded by these fears. I do not think they provide sufficient reason for treating work in the classroom *as territory which the courts must never enter. 'Never' is an unattractive absolute in this context. This would bar a claim, however obvious it was that something had gone badly wrong, and however serious the consequences for the particular child.* If a teacher carelessly teaches the wrong syllabus for an external examination, and provable financial loss follows, why should there be no liability? *Denial of the existence of a cause of action is seldom, if ever, the appropriate response to fear of its abuse.* Rather, the courts, with their enhanced powers of case-management, must seek to evolve means of weeding out obviously hopeless claims as expeditiously as is consistent with the court having a sufficiently full factual picture of all the circumstances of the case.

We have italicised some words and sentences in the above quotation in order to stress our conviction that the use of the duty, despite terminological niceties, does indeed lead to widespread immunities; and this is not altered by the fact that those who opt for this method of controlling litigation do so with the best of motives. Equally, and in support of our earlier statement, we cite the words of Lord Nicholls, for they received most recently the strong approval of Lord Bingham, the Senior Law Lord, in the *East Berkshire* case.[115] It would be inappropriate to pursue this argument further at this point. But we feel it is, once again, essential to make the reader—especially the beginner—fully conscious of the fact that there is no judicial unanimity on this matter, just as an ever-changing set of judicial coalitions continue to pursue the common aim of all judges: namely, the erection of a system of justice which satisfies both the requirements of fairness and predictability.

But we must return to the post-*Osman* situation in our country. If a court finds that it is faced with an 'immunity' in the true, 'procedural' sense, it moves to the second stage of inquiry, which requires it to apply a proportionality test as allowed by the 'margin of appreciation' stated in the wording of Article 6 itself. The court must see if 'the limitation imposed impaired the essence of the right and in particular whether it pursued a legitimate aim and there was a reasonable relationship of proportionality between the means employed and the aim sought to be achieved'.[116] Under this heading, the European Court of Human Rights has held that statutory limitation periods, orders for security for costs and the exclusion of claims on the grounds of lack of civil capacity may be acceptable.[117] Thus even if the possibility remains that Article 6 can be invoked in a duty case, it is open to a court to hold that the exclusion of liability passes the proportionality test.[118]

115 *D* v. *East Berkshire Community NHS Trust* [2005] 2 AC 373, discussed further, below.

116 See *Z* v. *United Kingdom* [2001] 2 FLR 612, (2002) 34 EHRR 3, at para. 93.

117 *Ibid.*

118 See also the judgment of Lord Hutton in *Arthur J.S. Hall* v. *Simons* [2002] 1 AC 615, arguing that the granting of immunities to defence counsel in criminal proceedings would fall under the margin of appreciation in Art. 6. As it was, the majority of the House of Lords held that the immunity of counsel in criminal proceedings should in any event be ended, reversing *Rondel* v. *Worsley* [1969] 1 AC 191; Lord Hutton's reasoning is however of relevance for the question of whether remaining immunities, such as those enjoyed by judges and witnesses, are compatible with Art. 6.

But while this part of *Osman* may have 'unravelled',[119] the impact of human-rights law on the duty concept, far from having ended, is only just beginning. Other provisions of the Convention, such as Article 2 concerning protection of the right to life,[120] Article 3 concerning subjection to degrading treatment[121] and Article 8 concerning the protection of private life,[122] may be relevant in defining the range of interests which are safeguarded by the tort of negligence.

At present, the duty concept recognises three main 'interests' which are protected from unreasonable harm: the physical integrity of the person; interests in tangible property; and purely economic or financial interests. The notion of what constitutes a recognised 'type of harm' in this sense is increasingly coming under challenge from novel claims. One possibility is that the courts could recognise a wider notion of psychiatric or mental well-being than is currently the case. As we shall see below,[123] this category of harm is not currently regarded as synonymous with physical harm to the person, and can give rise to a duty of care only under restricted circumstances. This could prove crucial in those cases where a parent claims damages for his or her 'suffering' as a result of being forcefully separated from his or her child as a result of a local authority negligently reaching the conclusion that the child was being abused by its parents. To phrase this claim as one of mental distress or psychiatric injury would lead to failure under English law. But if it comes to be seen as a harm resulting from the breach of a human right, for instance, based on Article 8 of the Convention which safeguards family life, then the outcome could be different.[124]

In the *X (Minors)*[125] litigation, the courts focused on whether the special position of the public authorities gave them protection against liability which other defendants did not have. However, a further, challenging aspect of the case was the nature of the damage which formed the basis of the claim. In his leading speech, Lord Browne-Wilkinson held that professional employees, such as teachers and psychologists, owed a duty of care to children in their care not just with regard to their physical safety and health and psychiatric well-being, both of which are heads of loss recognised as coming within the concept of duty of care, but also with regard to their educational needs, which the common law has not traditionally recognised as covered by the duty concept.[126]

[119] See C. Gearty, '*Osman* Unravels' (2002) 67 *MLR* 87; M. Lunney, 'Never Say Never Again' [2001] *KCLJ* 244; T. Hickman, 'Negligence and Article 6: The Great Escape' [2002] *CLJ* 13.

[120] For a recent case in which Art. 2 was applied, see *Van Colle* v. *Chief Constable of Hertfordshire* [2006] EWHC 360, discussed further in Section 5(a), below.

[121] As in *Z* v. *United Kingdom* [2001] 2 FLR 621 itself, in which the European Court of Human Rights ordered damages to be paid to the claimants on this ground.

[122] On which, see the judgment of the European Court of Human Rights in *Keegan* v. *United Kingdom* [2006] ECHR 764, suggesting that where Convention rights under Art. 8 were at stake in a case of alleged wrongful procurement of a search warrant, the claimants should not be required to prove malice (as required by the tort of misfeasance in a public office and the absence of a duty of care in negligence).

[123] See Section 3(b), below.

[124] On this, see the judgment of the Court of Appeal in the *East Berkshire* case ([2004] QB 558), discussing the implications of human rights law for an action brought by the child as opposed to the parent in that case; on whether the human-rights claim could be extended to the parent in future, see our discussion of the *East Berkshire* case later in this chapter and in ch. 8, below.

[125] [1995] 2 AC 633.

[126] [1995] 2 AC 633, 766.

In *Phelps* v. *Hillingdon London Borough Council*[127] the House of Lords affirmed this principle and refused to strike out a claim based on the direct responsibility of a local authority for a child's educational needs (as opposed to its vicarious liability for negligence committed by one or more of its employees). As a result, the principle of a school's responsibility for the general well-being of a child which it accepts, including the educational development of that child, is in the course of becoming well established.[128]

It is not completely clear where this type of harm fits into the existing categories of damage under the duty of concept. It has been suggested that a child's educational needs, rather than being a separate head of harm in this sense, should be placed under the heading of pure economic loss.[129] Whether this categorisation is watertight remains to be seen. It perhaps reflects a desire on the part of the courts to expand existing categories of harm, rather than creating wholly new ones; but the alternative approach would have the merit of spelling out more explicitly that society places a particular value on the interests embodied in Convention rights and seeks to prevent them from being disturbed.[130]

There are a number of approaches which the courts can take on this question, ranging from developing the common law in the light of Convention rights, to maintaining the law of negligence in its pre-existing state and allowing claims for breach of the Convention to proceed under the Human Rights Act.[131] In his judgment in *D* v. *East Berkshire NHS Community Health Trust*,[132] Lord Bingham posed the question of 'whether the law of should evolve, analogically and incrementally, so as to fashion appropriate remedies to contemporary problems or whether it should remain essentially static, making only such changes as are forced upon it, leaving difficult and, in human terms, very important problems to be swept up by the Convention'; adding, 'I prefer evolution'. Lord Bingham was in a minority of one in this instance, with the result that the law of tort currently refuses to recognise a duty of care owed by social workers to the parents of children wrongly accused of abusing them. Whether that rule is compatible with Articles 3 and 8 of the Convention remains to be seen. Notwithstanding the outcome in *D*, it seems unlikely that the interests protected by the tort of negligence can be sealed off from the growing body of human rights jurisprudence.[133] With this caveat in mind, we now turn to a closer examination of the kinds of damage recognised by the existing law.

127 [2001] 2 AC 619.

128 See *Gower* v. *London Borough of Bromley* [1999] ELR 356, 359; *Bradford-Smart* v. *West Sussex CC* [2002] EWCA Civ. 7, [2002] 1 FCR 425 (CA); *Carty* v. *Croydon LBC* [2005] 1 WLR 2312; *Marr* v. *London Borough of Lambeth* [2006] EWHC 1175; D. Fairgrieve, 'Pushing Back the Boundaries of Public Authority Liability: Tort Law Enters the Classroom' [2000] *PL* 288.

129 *Bradford-Smart* v. *West Sussex CC*, EWCA Civ. 7, at para. 31 (Judge LJ).

130 See B. S. Markesinis and J. Fedtke, 'Authority or Reason? The Economic Consequences of Liability for Breach of Statutory Duty in Comparative Perspective' [2007] *EBLR* 5, at 36, arguing that claims by parents for psychiatric harm following mistakes made by public authorities in child care cases could better be framed as claims under Art. 8 of the European Convention (protection of family life).

131 Section 8 of that the Human Rights Act allows, among other things, a claim for damages against a public authority for breach of Convention rights. See our discussion, below, ch. 8, Section 8.

132 [2005] 2 AC 373, 400.

133 On this see further T. Hickman, 'Tort Law, Public Authorities and the Human Rights Act 1998', in D. Fairgrieve, M. Andenas and J. Bell (eds.), *Tort Liability of Public Authorities in Comparative Perspective* (2002).

3. KINDS OF DAMAGE

(A) PHYSICAL (BODILY) HARM AND DAMAGE TO PROPERTY

After *Donoghue* v. *Stevenson* the law recognised a general duty of care protecting the personal safety and health and tangible property interests of the claimant. The general duty in relation to physical and property harm has not been affected by the overruling of *Anns*. Liability for physical harm caused by negligent misstatements or the negligent performance of a service is well established as part of the *Donoghue* duty.[134] Recovery for physical harm may, however, be qualified in relation to certain types of claimants, such as trespassers, or may conversely be specially extended to cover deserving claims such as those of rescuers; these issues are considered below and in later chapters. Certain defendants, such as public authorities and others serving the collective interest, may benefit from a qualified protection from liability in respect of physical harm.[135] The limited nature of liability for omissions also affects the protection accorded to physical interests. Finally, it must be remembered that, despite the existence of a general duty of care, claims for compensation for physical loss may be limited by other considerations such as remoteness and causation, as well as by the manner in which damages for loss are calculated in different cases.

More difficulty is encountered when the limits of what is meant by 'physical harm' are considered. In *MacFarlane* v. *Tayside Health Board*,[136] the majority of the House of Lords held that a woman who became pregnant unexpectedly following the failure of a vasectomy operation carried out on her husband should succeed in a claim for pain and suffering arising from the birth (while rejecting her claim for economic losses flowing the costs of raising her child). The focus of discussion was on whether the claim for pain and suffering should be ruled out, as the minority thought, on policy grounds, using the 'fair, just and reasonable' head. However, an important dimension of the decision was the implicit finding that the claimant had suffered physical damage. While it is undeniably the case that she endured physical inconvenience and pain during the pregnancy and birth, and that her physical autonomy could be said to have been compromised by the unwanted pregnancy which it was the purpose of her husband's vasectomy to prevent, it is not so clear that the pregnancy and birth could be described as 'damage' in the normal sense of injury to the person. This is not to say that the decision was wrong. As Christian Witting argues, *MacFarlane* is one of a number of cases in which the courts have 'shifted attention away from the examination of actual changes in physical

[134] See *Sharp* v. *Avery and Kerwood* [1938] 4 All ER 85; *Dutton* v. *Bognor Regis UDC* [1972] 1 QB 373, 410.

[135] We suggest that a principle of this kind offers the best explanation for the otherwise puzzling decision of the House of Lords in the property-damage case of *Marc Rich & Co. AG* v. *Bishop Rock Marine Co. Ltd.* [1996] 1 AC 211, discussed below, Section 5(a)(iv).

[136] [2000] 2 AC 59; see also *Greenfield* v. *Irwin* [2001] 1 WLR 1279. This aspect of *MacFarlane*, along with others, was affirmed in the later House of Lords decision of *Rees* v. *Darlington Memorial Hospital NHS Trust* [2004] 1 AC 309.

structures or states of persons and property and towards a more context-specific inquiry into social perceptions of damage'.[137] The notion of 'physical harm', in other words, is approached from the point of view of prevailing notions of what constitutes the autonomy and integrity of the person (and, it may be added, of tangible property).

(B) PSYCHIATRIC INJURY AND ILLNESS

As we have seen, the duty concept draws a distinction between physical harm to the person, on the one hand, and psychiatric harm, on the other: the latter is recoverable only under exceptional circumstances. However, the validity of this approach has given rise to considerable debate. Advances in scientific understanding and shifts in the social perception of damage make the divide between physical and psychiatric harm increasingly difficult to draw with conviction.

The courts were slow to accept that psychiatric injury or 'nervous shock' could constitute a head of damage for which the tort of negligence provided compensation, in particular where it was caused by harm or the threat of harm to a person other than the claimant. It is now generally understood, in the words of Lord Bridge in *McLoughlin* v. *O'Brian*,[138] 'that an acute emotional trauma, like a physical trauma, can well cause a psychiatric illness in a wide range of circumstances and in a wide range of individuals whom it would be wrong to regard as having any abnormal psychological make-up'. But despite the progress which the courts have gradually made over the course of more than a century of litigation towards the recognition of this head of damage, there remain severe restrictions on the scope of recovery. Psychiatric illness is therefore not yet placed on a par with bodily injury or the loss of a limb.

(i) Defining Psychiatric Harm

The starting-point is to specify what is meant by psychiatric harm. Damages cannot be recovered for mere grief or emotional distress caused by the injury or death of another, even of a loved one: 'in English law no damages are awarded for grief or sorrow caused by a person's death,'[139] except for a limited, conventional amount known as a claim for bereavement which we shall discuss in Chapter 25 when describe the law of damages.

Closer to the point examined here, we note that there is, in principle, a distinction between mere grief and a more serious, prolonged psychiatric or psychological condition which may be identified with the help of expert medical testimony. Medical science now recognises a condition known as 'post-traumatic stress disorder', which may occur as a result of witnessing or being involved in a catastrophic event or in reaction to the violent or unexpected death of a close relative or friend.[140] In *Alcock* v. *Chief Constable of South Yorkshire*, relatives and friends of spectators who were crushed to death inside

[137] 'Physical Damage in Negligence' (Select Bibliography).

[138] [1983] 1 AC 410, 433.

[139] *Hinz* v. *Berry* [1970] 2 QB 40, 42 (Lord Denning MR).

[140] Older terms for similar conditions include neurasthenia, shell shock and nastalgia: see [1990] 1 AC 310, 317.

a football stadium as a result of police negligence brought actions for damages based on psychiatric illness suffered in reaction to the event. Some had witnessed the scene at the ground. Others had seen it transmitted live on national television. Yet others had not seen the event but had suffered reactions from, amongst other things: fear that a close friend or relative had been killed or injured; being told that such a person had indeed been killed; and identifying the body at the temporary mortuary set up near the ground. The nature of the condition from which the plaintiffs were suffering was described in court as follows:

> It is classified as an anxiety disorder. It follows on a painful event, which is outside the normal human experience, the disorder involves preoccupation with the event—that is intrusive memories—with avoidance of reminders of the experience. At the same time there are persistent symptoms of increased arousal—these symptoms may be experienced in the form of sleep difficulty, irritability or outbursts of anger, problems with memory or concentration, startled responses, hyper-vigilance and over-reaction to any reminder of the event.... Many [of the plaintiffs] described an inability or difficulty in carrying out normal life activities such as work, family responsibilities or any activity normally engaged in before the disaster.... All those in whom post-traumatic stress disorder was identified appear to have undergone a personality change, the significant features of which [included] being moody, irritable, forgetful and withdrawn within themselves, [and] frequent unprovoked outbursts of anger and quarrelsome behaviour were reported.[141]

All of the plaintiffs were suffering from more than one specific and identifiable psychiatric illness, including depression. The nature of this condition is such that the need to identify an illness of a serious kind would probably, in itself, solve many of the problems associated with the floodgates argument. In *Hevican* v. *Ruane*[142] it was described as 'no more than the most remote of possibilities'; and in *Ravenscroft* v. *Rederiaktiebolaget Transatlantic*,[143] in a judgment for the plaintiff which was later overruled as incompatible with *Alcock*,[144] the judge referred to a 'small but significant range of the population' being liable to a reaction of this kind. For the purposes of determining whether a significant psychiatric injury has been suffered, the Court of Appeal in *Vernon* v. *Boseley (No. 1)*[145] ruled that there was no significant distinction between post-traumatic stress disorder, as just defined, and 'pathological grief disorder' which the court understood to mean an abnormal degree of grief giving rise to a psychological condition. Damages were recoverable for the latter as long as it could be shown that the other conditions for recovery were met.

(ii) Primary Victims

The next step in the analysis involves a fundamental distinction within the law between 'primary' and 'secondary' victims of psychiatric harm. A 'primary victim' may be defined as one who suffers psychiatric injury after being directly involved in an accident

141 [1992] 1 AC 310, 317.
142 [1991] 3 All ER 65, 72.
143 [1991] 3 All ER 73, 79.
144 [1992] 2 All ER 470.
145 [1997] 1 All ER 577.

and is *either* himself physically injured *or* put in fear of injury. A 'secondary victim', by contrast, suffers psychiatric injury as a consequence of witnessing or being informed about an accident, which involves another. As far as primary victims are concerned, it is well established that an accident victim who is physically injured through the negligence of another may, in principle, recover damages for the psychiatric as well as the physical consequences of the accident, subject to the normal rules of causation and remoteness of damage.[146] Equally, if the claimant's person is negligently endangered and he is placed in fear of an injury which does not actually occur, the early cases[147] clearly indicate that there will be liability.

These decisions were reaffirmed by the House of Lords in *Page* v. *Smith*.[148] The defendant, driving carelessly, caused a collision between his car and that being driven by the plaintiff. The latter, although receiving no physical injury at the time or later, subsequently suffered a reaction which led to the revival of the condition ME (myalgic encephalomyelitis) which left him chronically ill and unable to work. In his leading judgment, Lord Lloyd said that in the case of a primary victim such as the plaintiff—that is to say, one directly involved in an accident—it was not necessary to consider whether psychiatric injury had been foreseeable. It was enough that injury of some kind—either physical or psychiatric—was foreseeable.

Although *Page* v. *Smith* has been the subject of some well-aimed criticism,[149] it remains good law until such time as the House of Lords chooses to reconsider it. Its main effect is to limit the category of primary victims to those who, in addition to suffering psychological harm, also suffer physical harm as a result of an injury-threatening event caused by the defendant's negligence, or fall within the 'zone of danger' of such an event. Because primary victims, unlike secondary ones, are not subject to the wide range of 'control devices' put in place by the courts to limit liability for psychiatric harm,[150] efforts are constantly being made to stretch the category of 'primary victim' so that it can embrace additional types of claim. In *White* v. *Chief Constable of South Yorkshire*[151] the category was held to include rescuers who feared for their own safety while at the scene of the event, and in *Salter* v. *UB Frozen and Chilled Foods Ltd.*[152] it was held to cover the case of a fellow employee who regarded himself as the involuntary cause of the victim's death. In *W* v. *Essex County Council*[153] Lord Slynn refused to rule out the possibility that parents who felt guilt at having (through no fault of their own)

[146] In the unusual case of *Meah* v. *McCreamer (No. 1)* [1985] 1 All ER 367, the plaintiff recovered damages for the consequences of a car crash which included a personality change and his subsequent imprisonment following conviction of offences of rape and assault. See also the Australian case of *Jaensch* v. *Coffey* (1984) 155 CLR 549, discussed by F. A. Trindade, 'The Principles Governing the Recovery of Damages for Negligently Caused Nervous Shock' [1986] *CLJ* 476, 477.

[147] *Bell* v. *Great Northern Railway Co. of Ireland* (1890) 26 LR Ir. 428, not following *Victorian Railway Commissioners* v. *Coultas* (1888) 13 App. Cas. 222; *Dulieu* v. *White* [1901] 2 KB 669.

[148] [1996] 1 AC 155. For an application of *Page* see *Nobles* v. *Schofield*, CA Judgment of 14 May 1998, discussed by N. J. Mullany, 'English Psychiatric Injury Law: Chronically Depressing' (1999) 115 *LQR* 30.

[149] See the judgment of Lord Goff of Chieveley in *White* v. *Chief Constable of South Yorkshire* [1999] 2 AC 455.

[150] See our analysis in the next sub-section, 'Secondary Victims'.

[151] [1999] 2 AC 455. [152] 2003 SLT 1011. [153] [2001] 2 AC 592.

exposed their children to the risk of sexual assault by a foster child whom they had taken into their care and who then physically abused their natural children, were primary victims for the purposes of a psychiatric injury claim. This decision is perhaps at the outer limits of the concept of primary victim. The 'zone of danger' proviso in *Page* has, by contrast, been narrowly interpreted. In *Rothwell* v. *Chemical & Insulating Co. Ltd.*[154] the Court of Appeal held that it did not assist an employee who, having been exposed to asbestos dust through the negligence of his employer, suffered depression as a result of his fear of contracting asbestosis or an asbestos-related disease, without in fact having done so. It is surprising that the claimant's depression was not regarded as closely analogous to the development of the plaintiff's ME in *Page*.

(iii) Secondary Victims

Even greater difficulties begin when the claimant himself was neither physically injured nor threatened with injury. Such claimants were termed 'secondary victims' by Lord Lloyd in *Page* v. *Smith*.[155] The victim may have suffered a psychological reaction after witnessing the scene of an accident where another is killed or injured, or through fear of injury to another, which does not then materialise. Witnessing a scene may take the form of being present at the event itself, seeing it relayed through television or hearing about it on the radio, or coming on the scene in its immediate aftermath. Alternatively, the reaction may have been brought about by being informed of another's death or injury in particular circumstances. Psychiatric injury could occur without a 'shock' of any kind being sustained, for example through the burden of caring for an injured relative. The nature of the relationship between the claimant and the person suffering the injury in question could range from that of a close family tie to the relations of friendship or employment; the claimant could be a rescuer or a mere bystander. At a further extreme, damage to property, such as a house, or to a much-loved pet, could induce a reaction of this kind. In each of these cases the psychological reaction suffered by the claimant may be entirely foreseeable. However, for secondary victims, foreseeability of psychiatric damage being inflicted on the claimant is a necessary but not sufficient condition of establishing a duty of care.[156] If, for these purposes, the law regarded psychiatric harm as equivalent to physical harm, there would be no difficulty about a duty of care arising and liability would then depend on questions of fault, causation and remoteness. Many cases might fail at these later stages, particularly on questions of causation. But the common law does not currently take this view.

The prevailing view instead is that the extent of the duty of care is limited by a number of essentially arbitrary factors. In particular, the claimant will have to show, in

154 [2006] EWCA Civ. 27. 155 [1996] 1 AC 155.

156 In some early decisions the courts denied recovery to what would now be classified as 'secondary victims' who were not in the likely area of *physical* impact: see *Behrens* v. *Bertram Mills Circus Ltd.* [1957] 2 QB 1 and *King* v. *Phillips* [1953] 1 QB 429, where the judges were divided on the reason for denying recovery. In *Bourhill* v. *Young* [1943] AC 92, Lords Wright and Porter argued for the test of foreseeability of shock or psychiatric damage, and this was accepted by the Privy Council in *The Wagon Mound (No. 1)* [1961] AC 388. These *dicta* should not now be read as referring to primary victims following the judgment of Lord Lloyd in *Page* v. *Smith* [1996] AC 155 (see in particular at 189).

general, that his illness or condition was caused by a 'shock' of some kind; that he either witnessed the event directly or came upon its immediate aftermath; and that his relationship with the accident victim was sufficiently 'proximate' in the sense defined by the judges. These requirements were reasserted in *Alcock* v. *Chief Constable of South Yorkshire*,[157] where Lord Oliver argued that the policy of the common law was, on the whole, to confine any action in negligence to the 'primary' accident victim. The (inevitable) consequence of this is that any claim for loss by 'secondary' victims is, by its nature, exceptional. He thus maintained that:

The infliction of an injury on an individual, whether through carelessness or deliberation, necessarily produces consequences beyond those to the immediate victim. Inevitably the impact of the event and its aftermath, whether immediate or prolonged, is going to be felt in greater or lesser degree by those with whom the victim is connected whether by ties of affection, of blood relationship, of duty or simply of business. In many cases those persons may suffer not only injured feelings or inconvenience but adverse financial consequences as, for instance, by the need to care for the victim or the interruption or non-performance of his contractual obligations to third parties. Nevertheless, except in those cases which were based upon some ancient and now outmoded concepts of the quasi-proprietorial rights of husbands over their wives, parents over their children or employers over their menial servants, the common law has, in general, declined to entertain claims for such consequential injuries from third parties . . .[158]

Thus statute has abolished the right of a husband to sue for loss of consortium upon the death of his wife or the right of a parent to sue for loss of services of a child.[159] In their stead, a more modern but limited right has emerged; and it is given to a former spouse or a child under the age of majority to sue for bereavement damages.[160] Other examples of the rights of secondary victims to sue, such as the right of dependants of the deceased to sue for financial compensation for the loss of their breadwinner, are supplied by statute[161] and not by the common law. Once this point of view is taken, what is unusual is not that there are arbitrary limits on the right of a victim of psychiatric injury to receive compensation, but that the law permits him an action at all. As Lord Oliver put it:

What is more difficult to account for is why, when the law in general declines to extend the area of compensation to those whose injury arises only from the circumstances of their relationship to the primary victim, an exception has arisen in those cases in which the event of injury to the primary victim has been actually witnessed by the plaintiff and the injury claimed is as stemming from that fact.[162]

An alternative view would be to acknowledge that psychiatric harm is a form of injury in its own right, and to cease viewing the sufferer as a 'secondary victim'. In such

157 [1992] 1 AC 310. 158 *Ibid.*, 408–9.

159 Administration of Justice Act 1982; see also *Best* v. *Samuel Fox & Co. Ltd.* [1952] AC 716.

160 Section 1A of the Fatal Accidents Act 1976, inserted by the Administration of Justice Act 1982, s. 3.

161 See generally the Fatal Accidents Act 1976.

162 *Alcock* v. *Chief Constable of South Yorkshire* [1992] 1 AC 310, 410.

cases one would then use as limiting devices (*a*) the requirement that there should be evidence of the seriousness of the psychiatric injury in question and (*b*) the need for a clear causal connection to be established.[163] Additionally, it would be reasonable to assume that the cost of modern litigation would also act as a *de facto* barrier against the bringing of entirely frivolous claims. The medical understanding of psychiatric illness has arguably reached the stage at which this approach is feasible and therefore preferable to the admittedly arbitrary and illogical distinctions[164] currently operating in this area.

In *White* v. *Chief Constable of South Yorkshire*[165] the House of Lords rejected arguments of the kind just made. The leading judgments were delivered by Lord Hoffmann and Lord Steyn. Lord Steyn offered four reasons for treating psychiatric harm as a special area of liability. First, the task of identifying those categories of psychiatric harm that are recognised by law is a highly complex one which involves both sides calling expert medical advice. Second, there is the risk that, as his Lordship put it, 'litigation is sometimes an unconscious disincentive to rehabilitation'—in other words, the prospect of recovering damages prevents the claimant's condition from improving. We may note before moving on that these factors could also be present in many cases involving purely physical injury, where no question of denying a duty of care arises. Lord Steyn's third reason was the traditional 'floodgates' argument, namely that 'a relaxation of the special rules governing the recoverability of damages for psychiatric harm would greatly increase the class of persons who can recover damages in tort'. His final reason was that potential defendants would be exposed to a risk of liability, which would be 'disproportionate to tortious conduct involving perhaps momentary lapses of concentration, e.g. in a motor car accident'.[166] Again, it could be argued that this is not a factor which is unique to cases involving psychiatric harm.

Moreover, one could produce widely accepted counter-arguments against each of Lord Steyn's four propositions. For instance, it could be said that the proportionality of the consequences of the tort and the gravity of the tortfeasor's fault are linked in criminal law but not in the law of torts. The floodgates argument is also, in practice, often based on judicial hunches; and these hunches have tended to underestimate the disincentive that high litigation costs and the unavailability of legal aid have on commencing litigation even where there is a real need for it, let alone when it is known to be baseless. 'Accident neurosis' is a well-known and recognised state of affairs, but medical and other evidence suggests that it is a rare phenomenon; and the idea of depriving deserving victims of compensation because the chance of compensating them might have an adverse effect on a few of them seems a very weak argument. Lord Steyn's first

[163] See generally H. Teff, 'Liability for Psychiatric Illness after Hillsborough' (Select Bibliography); N.J. Mullany and P. Handford, *Tort Liability for Psychiatric Damage* (Select Bibliography). For the position in American jurisdictions, see ch. 5 below. Various options for reform of English law are laid out in Law Commission Consultation Paper No. 137, *Liability for Psychiatric Illness* (1995) and in the final report stemming from the same inquiry, Law Commission, *Liability for Psychiatric Illness* (Law Com. No. 249, 1998). For a proposal to abolish entirely tortious liability for nervous shock, see J. Stapleton, 'In Restraint of Tort', in P. B. H. Birks (ed.), *The Frontiers of Liability* (1994).

[164] On the lack of logic in these distinctions, see Lord Oliver in *Alcock* [1992] 1 AC 310, 410.

[165] [1999] 2 AC 455.

[166] [1992] 1 AC 310, 494.

argument is, finally, also becoming less convincing as medical science progresses and defines both the symptoms of these illnesses and the ways to ascertain their onset. The truth of the matter is thus that the present harsh law will remain in force for as long as past ideas about nervous shock still hold sway over the minds of conservative judges. Yet predicting a day when all these arguments will collapse may be neither foolhardy nor undesirable. For the answer to this problem (as well as so many others of the law of negligence which proceed on the basis of no duty and hence non-liability) may lie in a combination of a skilful use of medical evidence and a restrained approach on the question of quantum of damages.

Having made these points, one must, however, admit that whatever the merits or demerits of this approach, the effect of *White* v. *Chief Constable of South Yorkshire* is that the House of Lords has set its face against the assimilation of psychiatric harm to other kinds of injury, at least for the time being and as far as secondary victims are concerned. It is therefore necessary to consider the special requirements for recovery for this kind of harm.

(a) The Claimant Must Not Have Been Abnormally Susceptible to Psychiatric Illness. In order to recover, a secondary victim must show that he was *not* unusually susceptible to psychiatric harm of the kind in question.[167] The nature of the claimant's particular relationship with the accident victim will be taken into account: in one case a test of a 'reasonably strong-willed mother' was adopted.[168] Thus an unduly hypersensitive person will not recover damages unless a person of normal fortitude would have suffered shock under the same circumstances which means that, once again, the innate conservatism of the law has suspended in this area the application of the well-known principle of the 'eggshell skull' rule. But once that requirement is met, the rule that the defendant 'takes the claimant as he finds him' applies and the unusually sensitive claimant can recover in full.[169]

(b) The Psychiatric Harm Must Have Occurred Through 'Shock'. Notwithstanding advances in medical understanding, the courts continue to maintain that for recovery under this head to be achieved, the claimant must in the first place have suffered a 'shock' of some kind. The shock does not have to be induced by a single, catastrophic event: in *North Glamorgan NHS Trust* v. *Walters*[170] damages were awarded in the case of a pathological grief reaction brought about by a series of misdiagnoses and medical errors over a period of thirty-six hours, which together resulted in the death of the claimant's son. More controversially, liability has been imposed under this heading in cases of medical negligence leading to unnecessary medical treatment, which then caused psychiatric harm to the relatives of the immediate victim. In *Froggatt* v. *Chesterfield and North Derbyshire Royal Hospital NHS Trust*[171] damages were awarded to the husband and son of a woman who was misdiagnosed as suffering from breast cancer, and who had a

167 Lord Wright in *Bourhill* v. *Young* [1943] AC 92, 110.

168 *Kralj* v. *McGrath* [1986] 1 All ER 54.

169 *Jaensch* v. *Coffey* (1984) 54 ALR 417; *Page* v. *Smith* [1996] AC 155.

170 [2002] EWCA Civ. 1792.

171 High Court, QBD, 13 Dec. 2002.

mastectomy as a result. The husband suffered what the court referred to as 'sudden trauma' when seeing his wife immediately after the operation. The son, likewise, suffered post-traumatic stress disorder on being told by his mother of the (false) diagnosis. In the light of this decision, it is all the more strange that 'psychiatric illnesses caused in other ways, such as by the experience of having to cope with the deprivation consequent upon the death of a loved one, attract no damages'.[172] It seems, for example, that one who suffers psychiatric damage from the cumulative stress of caring for a loved one who is seriously injured or mentally impaired by an accident will have no claim against the person whose negligence caused the initial injury.[173] But why this should be so is far from clear. The question could well be regarded as more suitable for analysis through causation rather than duty. Why should a family member who undertakes to care for the accident victim be unable to recover for an illness triggered by the stress of such a task, in a case where the circumstances were particularly distressing? The range of claimants likely to be able to sue in this kind of action is unlikely to be very extensive.

(c) The Claimant Must Have Been in Physical Proximity to the Accident or its Aftermath. This requirement is related to the one that we have just considered, and means that the claimant must either have been present at the scene itself or have arrived in the aftermath of the death or injury occurring. In *McLoughlin* v. *O'Brian*[174] one of the plaintiff's children was killed in a car crash in which two of her other children and her husband were injured. The plaintiff was at home at the time and learned of the crash about an hour after it had happened from a friend who had witnessed it, and who then drove her to a nearby hospital where she saw the surviving members of her family. The scenes at the hospital 'were distressing in the extreme and were capable of producing an effect going well beyond that of grief and sorrow'.[175] The House of Lords held that the plaintiff had a claim for nervous shock. Although it is normally necessary to have been within sight or earshot of the event giving rise to the injury, exceptions do exist. Thus, according to Lord Wilberforce 'an exception from, or I would prefer to call it an extension of, the latter case has been made where the plaintiff does not see or hear the incident but comes on its immediate aftermath'; *McLoughlin*'s case was 'on the margin' of recovery. To similar effect is the decision of the High Court of Australia in *Jaensch* v. *Coffee*,[176] another case in which the plaintiff suffered shock after a visit to the hospital where, in this case, her husband had been taken after being involved in an accident.

The law draws a clear dividing line between witnessing an accident and simply being told about it. According to the Court of Appeal in *Hambrook* v. *Stokes Bros.*[177] and to Lord Wilberforce in *McLoughlin*, there can be no recovery in a case where a third party brought about the shock through communication. By contrast, in *Hevicane* v. *Ruane*[178]

172 *Alcock* v. *Chief Constable of South Yorkshire* [1992] 1 AC 310, 403 (Lord Ackner).

173 See *Jaensch* v. *Coffey* (1984) 155 CLR 549, 569 (Brennan J), cited with approval by Lord Ackner [1992] 1 AC 310, 403. See also *Pratt and Goldsmith* v. *Pratt* [1975] VR 378, discussed by Trindade, 'The Principles Governing the Recovery of Damages for Negligently Caused Nervous Shock' [1986] *CLJ* 476, 479.

174 [1983] 2 AC 410.

175 Lord Wilberforce [1983] AC 410, 417.

176 (1984) 155 CLR 549.

177 [1925] 1 KB 141.

178 [1991] 3 All ER 65.

liability was established in a case where the father of a boy killed in a car accident was told of his death at a police station and then identified the body at a mortuary. In *Ravenscroft* v. *Rederiaktiebolaget Transatlantic*[179] the plaintiff, who suffered a depressive reaction following the death of her son in an industrial accident and who did not actually see the body, was allowed to recover at first instance. The Court of Appeal, however, reversed this judgment on the grounds that this ruling was incompatible with the House of Lords' ruling in *Alcock*. It seems unlikely that the ruling in *Hevicane*'s case would have gone the same way if it had come after *Alcock*.

In *Alcock*[180] a variety of cases were brought to test the limits of the law. Some plaintiffs witnessed the scene of the disaster from other stands inside the stadium. One of the plaintiffs, sitting in a coach outside the ground, saw the events unfolding on a television in the coach. He then went to find his son, who turned out to have died in the stadium. Yet other plaintiffs, who were at home on the day, heard of the events on the radio or saw television pictures, which were being transmitted live. The television pictures did not pick out individuals; this would have been excluded by broadcasting conventions which, said Lord Keith of Kinkel, would have been known to the defendant, although the relevance of this point is somewhat obscure.[181] The judge excluded claims by those who heard the news on radio but allowed claims by those relatives who had suffered shock after seeing the television reports and later receiving news of the deaths, but on this last point he was reversed by the higher courts. According to Lord Keith:

> The viewing of these scenes cannot be equiparated with the viewer being within 'sight or hearing of the event in question' to use the words of Lord Wilberforce [in *McLoughlin* v. *O'Brian*], nor can the scenes reasonably be regarded as giving rise to shock, in the sense of a sudden assault on the nervous system. They were capable of giving rise to anxiety for the safety of relatives known or believed to be present in the area affected by the crush, and undoubtedly did so, but that is very different from seeing the fate of the relative or his condition shortly after the event.[182]

This view is related, then, to the idea that liability arises only where the illness is induced by shock, in the sense of what Lord Ackner called 'the sudden appreciation by sight or sound of a horrifying event, which violently agitates the mind'.[183] But there seems no reason, in principle, why an 'agitation of the mind' cannot come about through witnessing scenes on television or even through a combination of communications, such as the hypothetical case given by Lord Bridge in *McLoughlin* v. *O'Brian*[184] of a mother who knows that her husband and children are staying in a hotel which, she learns, has burned down. Newspapers show pictures of the victims shouting for help, and she then finds out that all her family died in the fire. She then suffers psychiatric injury as a result of the 'imagination of the agonies of mind and body in which her family died'. As Harvey Teff points out, the most important element triggering a psychiatric illness in such a case is not the 'direct perception' of the event but the close relationship between

179 [1991] 3 All ER 73, overruled [1992] 2 All ER 470. See also *Hunter* v. *British Coal Corporation* [1999] QB 140.

180 [1992] 1 AC 310.

181 *Ibid.*, 398.

182 [1992] 1 AC 310, 398.

183 *Ibid.*, 401.

184 [1983] 1 QB 410, 442.

the plaintiff and the accident victim; the precise manner in which the horror of the event is conveyed may be irrelevant.[185] In *Alcock* the House of Lords was persuaded to maintain this restriction by fear of the floodgates opening, but this objection could have been dealt with more effectively by insisting on evidence of a serious medical condition. Another way of looking at the means of communication is to regard the intervention of the broadcast media as a *novus actus interveniens*, or the act of a third party, which breaks the chain of causation. Alternatively,[186] one can treat the damage as being too remote,[187] or treat the television medium as removing the claimant from the category of 'proximate' persons:

> I do not consider that a claimant who watches a normal television programme which displays events as they happen satisfies the test of proximity. In the first place a defendant could normally anticipate that in accordance with current television broadcasting guidelines shocking pictures of persons suffering and dying would not be transmitted. In the second place, a television programme such as that transmitted from Hillsborough involves cameras at different viewpoints showing scenes all of which no one individual would see, edited pictures and a commentary superimposed.[188]

The notion of the defendant being aware that the television authorities would not show pictures of individuals is, in itself, a somewhat peripheral consideration in the circumstances. It seems more relevant to point out that the defendant would have been aware of the near certainty that some television pictures showing unspecified dead and dying spectators would be transmitted, and that relatives of those present at the ground would immediately be concerned. Many of the *Alcock* plaintiffs suffered a reaction from a series of events, of which the television pictures formed only part. It is entirely foreseeable that the accumulation of hearing news of the disaster, wondering whether a close relative was involved, and then, in some cases, being required to identify the body of the deceased in the temporary mortuary after nearly an entire day spent searching for him, should have triggered a psychological reaction. Yet the insistence that there should be 'direct, immediate perception' of the event ruled out these claims.[189]

A difficult question concerns the availability of an action against a defendant whose own negligence is the cause of his injury. In *Bourhill* v. *Young*[190] the plaintiff sued the estate of a motorcyclist who had been killed in an accident. She claimed to have heard the crash and seen blood on the road; she subsequently had a miscarriage. The claim failed, as it clearly should have done, since the plaintiff had no relationship of any kind with the dead man and had not even witnessed the accident. A clearer case is the one discussed in *Bourhill*:[191] what would happen if a pregnant woman witnessed a window-cleaner falling to his death on spiked railings, suffered shock, and then miscarried? In *Alcock*, Lord Ackner thought that 'there must be a limit at some reasonable point to the extent of the duty of care owed to third parties which rests upon everyone in his

185 'Liability for Psychiatric Illness after Hillsborough' (Select Bibliography).

186 [1992] 1 AC 310, 362 (Parker LJ).

187 *Ibid.*, 387 (Nolan LJ).

188 *Ibid.*, 423 (Lord Jauncey of Tullichettle).

189 *Ibid.*, 387 (Nolan LJ).

190 [1943] AC 92.

191 In the Court of Session: 1941 SC 395, 399.

actions'.[192] Other uncertainties arise from the continuing tendency of the courts to view the claimant as a 'secondary victim' of the accident. In particular, will the defendant escape on the grounds that the initial victim has been contributorily negligent?

The fault of the initial victim cannot be imputed to the claimant, and the duty of care is owed to the claimant in respect of his 'shock' independently of any duty owed to the initial victim. But the causation aspect of contributory negligence must be considered as well. Normally contributory negligence is not regarded as completely breaking the chain of causation;[193] but it could be open to a court to find that the initial victim's error rendered the loss suffered by the claimant too remote.[194]

Greatorex v. *Greatorex*[195] is a recent judgment of the High Court which has provided some answers to these questions. The facts of the case were relatively simple. For in that case a young man, whom we shall henceforth call D2, was injured in an accident caused by his own grossly negligent driving.[196] P, his father, a professional fire officer stationed nearby, suffered serious post-traumatic stress disorder as a result of attending his unconscious son at the scene of the accident. The question was whether the father could claim damages for his own harm from the driver/injured son (D2) or, since he was uninsured, from the Motor Insurance Bureau, which stepped into the gap and became the second defendant in the action (D3)?

Since all negligence reasoning starts with a discussion of the notion of duty of care, *Greatorex* naturally had to grapple with the question whether a victim of self-inflicted injuries owes a duty of care to a third party not to cause him psychiatric injury. Cazalet J acknowledged that there was no binding authority on the question of duty. For guidance he was thus directed to German law, among other systems, and his conclusion was, undoubtedly, influenced by a decision of the German Federal Supreme Court (BGH) of 11 May 1971, cited to him by counsel for the Motor Insurance Bureau. To that question the BGH had given a negative reply. In the opinion of the Federal Court the imposition of such a duty would unduly restrict the person's (D2's) right to self-determination. Cazalet J expressly followed the reasoning of the BGH and regarded the argument

192 [1992] 1 AC 310, 403.

193 See below, ch. 4, Section 3(b) and ch. 24, Section 2.

194 By extension of *McKew* v. *Holland & Hannen & Cubitts (Scotland) Ltd.* [1969] 3 All ER 1621, discussed below, ch. 4, Section 3(b).

195 [2000] 1 WLR 1976.

196 We call in this case the primary victim D2 in order to stress that in many instances there may also be a D1—another tortfeasor—who contributes to causing D's injuries. In a car accident case such as *Greatorex* D2 would, typically, be another driver whose fault, along with that of D1, contributed to D1's injuries. Where such a D1 exists, he may well be the first to be sued by P, typically because he may (unlike D2 in *Greatorex*) be a stranger to P. The problem then arises whether, if D1 is sued by P, he will be liable to him for the whole of his damage or only for his—D1's—share? If D1 and D2 are joint tortfeasors *vis-à-vis* P, the answer should be that each of them pays the full amount and then has a right to seek a contribution or an indemnity from the other. But what if D2 enjoys, as result of the law or a contract, an immunity towards P; can D1 also take advantage of this and pay only his share of the harm to P? Or will he, alternatively, have to shoulder all the loss even though he caused only part of it, perhaps a very small part? *Greatorex*, because of its facts, did not discuss these points, but there is much American (and German) material on this point which, if the point ever arises, counsel may wish to explore before an English court. For further details see: B. S. Markesinis, 'Foreign Law Inspiring National Law: Lessons from *Greatorex* v. *Greatorex*' [2000] *CLJ* 386.

derived from the right to self-determination as enunciated in the German case as 'powerful'. Matters would be different where, by harming himself, D2 causes damage other than nervous shock to another person. It thus seems that in German and possibly English law, the ethical duty not to harm oneself becomes a legal duty as soon as the self-harming activity also causes *physical* harm to another person. From this perspective D2's immunity from liability for nervous shock (suffered by others) constitutes an exception. In other words, D2's right to self-determination prevails only if we regard this injury as special. Cazalet J's constant reference to 'policy' lends credence to this view and illustrates, once again, our legal system's difficulty in coping with the ramifications of nervous shock and emotional injuries.

(d) The Claimant Must Have Had a Close Personal or Familial Relationship with the Accident Victim. Among 'secondary victims', the class of potential claimants is limited, by and large, to those in a close relationship to the accident victim. These will normally be family relatives. Traditionally the category of close relatives clearly included spouses and parents of the accident victim, but excluded those in other relationships such as brothers and sisters. In *McLoughlin* v. *O'Brian* Lord Wilberforce said:

> As regards the class of persons, the possible range is between the closest of family ties—of parent and child, or husband and wife—and the ordinary bystander. Existing law recognises the claims of the first; it denies that of the second, either on the basis that such persons must be assumed to be possessed of fortitude sufficient to enable them to endure the calamities of modern life, or that defendants cannot be expected to compensate the world at large . . . other cases involving less close relationships must be very carefully scrutinised. I cannot say that they should never be admitted. The closer the tie (not merely in relationship, but in care) the greater the claim for consideration. The claim, in any case, has to be judged in the light of the other factors, such as proximity to the scene in time and place, and the nature of the accident.[197]

This suggests that if the event is particularly traumatic, there will be a wider range of potential claimants. In *Alcock* v. *Chief Constable of South Yorkshire*[198] the House of Lords rejected claims brought by brothers, brothers-in-law, uncles, grandparents and friends of the deceased. However, Lord Keith considered that 'reasonable foreseeability should be the guide' to the class of potential claimants. 'The kinds of relationship which may involve close ties of love and affection are numerous, and it is the existence of such ties which leads to mental disturbance when the loved one suffers a catastrophe.'[199] The degree of closeness can therefore be presumed in some cases (the relationship between parent and child and that between fiancés were given by Lord Keith as examples). In others, it is open to being established by the claimant through appropriate evidence; while it might also be possible, conversely, to rebut the presumption of proximity between, for example, husband and wife who had been separated for many years. It is doubtful whether this approach opens up the danger of indeterminate liability, since in a peripheral case the burden of proof will be on the claimant, and this burden may be

[197] [1983] 1 AC 410, 422. [198] [1992] 1 AC 310. [199] [1992] 1 AC 310, 397.

considerable. The cases of husband and wife and the parents of children remain the 'core' examples of the nature of relationship required, by reference to which other claims will be judged. There seems no reason why the boyfriend or girlfriend of the deceased, or a fiancé, could not recover. One of the *Alcock* plaintiffs, a fiancée of a young man who died in the disaster, almost certainly would have recovered had she been present at the scene; as it was she failed because she had been elsewhere when the disaster took place. Whether a claim by a mistress or paramour of a married victim could be barred by public policy, on the other hand, remains to be seen.

It follows from what has just been said that mere bystanders, who have no ties of love or affection to the main accident victim, will almost certainly have no claim in nervous shock caused by witnessing the event in question. Lord Keith in *Alcock* thought that liability could not be 'entirely excluded' if 'the circumstances of a catastrophe occurring very close to him were particularly horrific',[200] but since this exception was not invoked in the circumstances of the *Alcock* litigation it is plainly very narrow in scope. The position of rescuers who suffer nervous shock is more problematic. At one time there seemed to be a judicial policy of accommodating their claims, on the ground that nothing should be done to discourage rescuers from acting in an emergency. In *Chadwick* v. *British Railways Board*[201] the plaintiff suffered a long-term psychiatric illness after helping out in the aftermath of the 1957 Lewisham railway disaster, which occurred a short distance from where he lived. He was allowed to recover damages for his loss. However, in *White* v. *Chief Constable of South Yorkshire*[202] the House of Lords took a much more restrictive line. In this case, the plaintiffs were police officers who had been closely involved in the events surrounding the Hillsborough stadium disaster. Some of them had been present at the ground and had taken part in attempts to rescue the accident victims; others had witnessed highly distressing scenes in the aftermath of the disaster. The plaintiffs suffered psychiatric harm and brought actions for damages against the Chief Constable (their own employer) on the grounds of his vicarious liability for the conduct of their own fellow officers, whose negligence had caused the deaths and injuries of the spectators concerned.

The House of Lords, by a majority, ruled against the plaintiffs on the grounds of the absence of a duty of care. The majority judges were plainly influenced by the injustice of allowing claims by police officers to succeed after many of those brought by relatives of those who died had been rejected in *Alcock*. However, in their concern to avert this injustice, their Lordships introduced a number of new conceptual problems into the law. We consider in Chapter 18 below the problems raised by the fact that the plaintiffs in *White* were suing their own employer. Considered as *secondary* victims, the ruling of the House of Lords was that the plaintiffs were in no better position than bystanders. Plainly they had no close personal or familial ties to the main accident victims; the key to this part of the judgment was the finding that they had no special status as rescuers. According to the judges in the majority, *Chadwick* was a case of a 'primary' victim—the plaintiff had himself been in physical danger when administering help to those injured

200 *Ibid.*, 397. 201 [1967] 1 WLR 912. 202 [1999] 2 AC 455.

in the train crash. This was not so in *White*. On this interpretation of *Chadwick*, then, a rescuer can only recover if, as a result of his physical proximity to the scene of the accident, he had been in fear of physical injury. However, the reclassification of *Chadwick* as a case of a primary victim makes little sense. The harm he suffered was a result of the distressing scenes he witnessed, not of any fear he might have had for his own safety. The majority ruling in *White* also leads to peculiar results, as Lord Goff pointed out in his dissent in that case. The majority might have distinguished *Chadwick* on a different ground, namely that the rescuers in *White* were professionals who were trained to carry out the tasks in question rather than concerned members of the public (such as Mr Chadwick). But this route is not without its difficulties either. To reject claims by professional rescuers *simply* because of their status as fire or police officers—the so-called 'fireman's rule' which is observed in some US jurisdictions—would arguably be too inflexible, as Lord Hoffmann's judgment in *White* recognised. Nor does it follow, once the possibility of liability is admitted, that a claim by professional rescuers must fail on the basis that the training they receive makes it unlikely that they will suffer a psychiatric injury; in a particularly horrific situation, such an injury is foreseeable.

Drawing the line between professionals and volunteers, then, probably leads to more problems than it solves. But the effect of *White* is effectively to end the special protection which rescuers as a class had previously enjoyed in this area of the law; in future, even a volunteer will have to show that he was a 'primary' victim of the accident.

(iv) A 'Relational' Duty of Care with Regard to Psychiatric Well-Being

So far we have been considering the cases of 'primary victims' who are either injured as a result of a catastrophic event or find themselves within the 'zone of danger' surrounding it, and 'secondary victims' who witness such an event or its aftermath. In neither set of cases is it relevant that the claimants are not known to or identifiable by the defendant prior to the event. Different considerations arise, however, in cases where the claimant and defendant are in a pre-tort relationship or are otherwise known to each other in advance, and, in particular, where the defendant can be regarded as having assumed a responsibility to the claimant to take care not to expose him to the risk of psychiatric harm. These cases are sometimes referred to as involving 'primary victims', but it seems to us that the confusing terminology of primary and secondary victims is best avoided altogether in this situation, so that the focus can shift to the issue of whether the elements of a 'relational' duty of care are present: 'what has to be determined is the nature and potential scope of the duty of care in the light of the relationship between the claimant and defendant'.[203]

The presence of a pre-tort relationship is, we suggest, the best explanation for cases which appear to allow recovery for shock induced by damage to the property of the claimant which, when considered alongside *Alcock* and other decisions disallowing the claims of relatives of the victims of accidents, are otherwise difficult to explain. For example, in *Attia* v. *British Gas*[204] the plaintiff's house was burned down as a result of

203 *Butchart* v. *Home Office* [2006] EWCA Civ. 239, at [20] (Latham LJ).
204 [1988] QB 304.

negligence by the defendant's workmen who were carrying out a job in the house; the defendant sought to have the claim struck out, but it was allowed to stand. In this case there was a high level of proximity between the parties as a result of their already being in a commercial relationship prior to the tort being committed. The possibility of recovery for distress at the death of a favourite pet cat or dog was considered in *Owens* v. *Liverpool Corporation*.[205] This case, in which a tramcar hit a hearse with the result that the coffin it was carrying was overturned, causing distress to the mourners, can be regarded as confined to the particular circumstances of distress arising from injury to a corpse, for which there are also precedents in other common law systems.[206] However, a better view would be that the very thing the undertakers were employed to do was to avoid causing anxiety and upset of this kind to those who attended the funeral. The case is analogous to those decisions in the area of recovery for pure economic loss, which enable third parties, external to a contract, to claim compensation for losses which it was the intention of the contract to avoid.[207]

The same idea seems to be behind a *dictum* of Nolan LJ in *Alcock* to the effect that 'if a publicity seeking organisation made arrangements for a party of children to go up in a balloon, and for the event to be televised so that their parents could watch, it would be hard to deny that the organisers were under a duty to avoid mental injury to the parents as well as physical injury to the children'.[208] A similar case, from this point of view, is *Al-Kandari* v. *Brown*,[209] in which a solicitor acting for the plaintiff's husband in matrimonial proceedings was held responsible for setting in course a chain of events which culminated in the husband arranging the kidnapping and assault of the plaintiff and the abduction of their children. The plaintiff was awarded damages against the solicitor both for her physical injuries and for her psychiatric reaction to these events. In this case there was physical harm, but the psychiatric illness was brought about as much by the abduction of her children as by her own treatment. Had the facts been slightly different and no physical harm had befallen the plaintiff, her claim could have been denied on the authority of *Alcock*, but this result seems entirely artificial.

The potential confusion which is created by the distinction between 'primary' and 'secondary' victims of psychiatric harm is illustrated by *W* v. *Essex County Council*.[210] The council, in breach of a specific undertaking, sent a known sexual abuser to live with the plaintiffs as a foster child; he then abused the plaintiffs' children. The Court of Appeal allowed an action by the children but ruled out liability to the parents on the ground that they were 'secondary victims' who did not witness the events that gave rise to the 'primary' harm. It is arguable, however, that the council assumed a specific responsibility to the parents to avoid the harm which might be expected to befall them—which would inevitably take the form of psychiatric injury—if their own children were abused. When the case reached the House of Lords, an appeal was allowed which in this context meant that the defendant's claim that the facts disclosed no cause

205 [1939] 1 KB 394.

206 Cf. *Alcock* [1992] 1 AC 310, 347 (Hidden J); *Christensen* v. *Superior Court* (1991) 820 P 2d 181.

207 See below, Section 3(c).

208 [1992] 1 AC 310, 386–7.

209 [1980] QB 665.

210 [1999] Fam. 90; [2001] 2 AC 592.

of action was rejected. This is not the same thing as saying that a cause of action was made out. Moreover, Lord Slynn did not base his ruling on the argument that an assumption of responsibility had been made to the parents. Rather, he seems to have thought that the parents could be regarded either as 'primary victims' or as 'secondary victims' who had been sufficiently close in time and space to the physical harms inflicted on their (natural) children to come under the *McLoughlin* principle.[211]

The confusion over primary and secondary victims is fortunately absent in one area where liability for psychiatric harm has been more clearly recognised, namely the responsibility owed by schools and educational authorities to children in their care or under their control. This principle of the responsibility of the individual teacher to his students was accepted by the House of Lords in *X (Minors)* v. *Bedfordshire County Council* [212] and in *Phelps* v. *Hillingdon London Borough Council* the House of Lords refused to strike out an action based on the direct duty owed by a public authority with responsibility for educational services.[213] The potential for the application of this principle is apparent from a decision of the Court of Appeal, *Bradford-Smart* v. *West Sussex County Council*,[214] in which an action was brought against the defendant for not taking steps to prevent the bullying of the claimant by some of her schoolmates. The bullying took place out of school, but it was argued that the defendant should have taken steps to discipline the perpetrators. It was found, on the facts, that the school had not acted negligently, but the existence of a duty of care was recognised by the court.

The principle of assumption of responsibility may be taken further to cover cases involving doctor–patient relationships. The case of *In Re Organ Retention Group Litigation* [215] concerned claims for psychiatric harm brought by parents of deceased children whose organs had been removed, retained and disposed of in the course of post-mortem examination, without the parents' knowledge or consent (although consent to the post mortems themselves had been granted). Gage J held that clinicians who had sought the parents' consent to the post mortems had been under a duty of care to inform them of the possibility of organ retention and to seek their consent to it; the parties were in a medical relationship with was akin to a contractual one. The presence of a medical relationship can also have the effect of imposing upon the defendant can a duty of care to transmit distressing information to the plaintiff in a sensitive way. In *AB* v. *Tameside and Glossop Health Authority*[216] the defendant sent out letters warning former patients that a health worker from whom they had previously received obstetric treatment had been tested positive for HIV, leading to the risk that they would contract the disease. The letters were sent by standard post and no arrangements were made for

[211] To similar effect is *Froggatt* v. *Chesterfield and North Derbyshire Royal Hospital NHS Trust*, QBD, 13 Dec. 2002, discussed above.

[212] [1995] 2 AC 633, 766 (Lord Browne-Wilkinson).

[213] [2001] 2 AC 619.

[214] [2002] EWCA Civ. 7; [2002] 1 FCR 425 (CA); see also *Gower* v. *Bromley LBC* [1999] ELR 356; P. Giliker, 'A "New" Head of Damages: Damages for Mental Distress in the English Law of Torts' (2000) 20 *Leg. Stud.* 272.

[215] [2004] EWHC 644; see also *Stevens* v. *Yorkhill NHS Trust* 2006 SLT 889.

[216] [1997] 8 Med. LR 91.

counselling (although these were later put in place). Claims in respect of psychiatric injury caused by the way in which the news of the possible risk to health was transmitted were rejected by the Court of Appeal, but only after counsel for the defendants had conceded the existence of a duty of care. As Mullany has argued, this concession seems justified: there was a pre-existing relationship and psychiatric harm was foreseeable.[217] The existence of a duty of care need not depend upon the information being false. Nevertheless, it should be borne in mind that even if a duty is established, there may be problems of causation: the claimant will have to show that the shock would not have been suffered anyway.

What if *false* information is negligently conveyed to a potential victim of psychiatric harm? The possibility of liability here is indicated by cases in Australia, New Zealand and the United States concerning false death notices in newspapers.[218] Thus an incorrect report to the effect that persons at the scene of a disaster have been killed or injured could give rise to liability. In *Allin* v. *City and Hackney Health Authority*[219] the defendants were found liable for negligently telling a patient who had just given birth that her baby had died. In this case, the closeness of the pre-tort relationship between the parties was a factor weighing heavily in favour of liability. The responsibility of the broadcast media to remote third parties is much less clear. One possibility is that the visual media could negligently induce shock in viewers, perhaps by focusing on the fate of particular individuals in breach of broadcasting guidelines. Such cases aside, can an organisation be deemed negligent to near relatives of the deceased for showing distressing scenes of a disaster? To hold it liable would raise problems of an infringement of free speech and the need to take into account the countervailing interest of the public at large in receiving the information in question. These issues have yet to come before the English courts.

(v) Employees

The courts have had considerable difficulty in classifying the claims of employees who witness traumatic deaths or injuries of colleagues. In *Dooley* v. *Cammell Laird & Co. Ltd.*,[220] an employee was allowed to recover for the fear that his workmates might have been injured when the crane he was operating, through no fault of his own, dropped a load into the hold of a ship. In *Alcock*[221] Hidden J considered that it was the nature of the activity or the task undertaken by the employee, and not the relationship he might have with the accident victim, that determined liability. This seems to be the best approach: the liability of the employer in most cases should depend on the duty of care

217 N. J. Mullany, 'Liability for Careless Communication of Traumatic Information' (1998) 114 *LQR* 380. Mullany also suggests that even if there is no pre-existing relationship, a duty of care can arise from the assumption of responsibility which is inherent in the transmission of bad news (see at 383). This would go further than the proposition outlined in the text. See also *Andrews* v. *Secretary of State for Health* (2000) 54 BMLR 111, discussed by N. J. Mullany, 'English Psychiatric Injury Law: Chronically Depressing' (1999) 115 *LQR* 30, 36.

218 See Fleming, *Torts* (7th edn., 1987), at 147, and see also ch. 5, below.

219 [1996] 7 Med. LR 167; N. J. Mullany, 'Liability for Careless Communication of Traumatic Information' (1998) 114 *LQR* 380.

220 [1951] 1 Lloyd's Rep. 271. See also *Galt* v. *British Railways Board* (1983) 133 NLJ 870.

221 [1992] 1 AC 310, 346–7.

which he owes to employees not to expose them to undue risk of harm, either physical or psychiatric. An employee will be able to claim as a *secondary* victim only if he comes within one of the categories of protected close friends or relatives outlined in *Alcock*.[222] In the *White* litigation, no clear distinction appears to have been drawn between the two different types of claim which were open to the plaintiffs, namely their claims as secondary victims and their claims as employees. The claim of an employee arises from the pre-tort relationship which he has with his employer, and is shaped by the nature of that relationship, which, in this case, is one of mutual trust and confidence.[223] This claim is not, therefore, parasitic on witnessing a particular event, which causes harm to another. Indeed, for the purposes of this claim (in contrast to an employee's claim as a secondary victim) it is neither necessary nor sufficient that the employer's negligence (or that of an employee of the employer) should have led to the event in question. It is not necessary, for the reason that case law suggests that the employer has a duty to avoid causing psychiatric harm to his employee in a number of situations, many of which do not involve catastrophic injuries. But nor is it sufficient, since an employer may expect employees to withstand a certain level of exposure to stress. In particular, an employer is arguably entitled to expect that employees who are trained in rescue services will be able to withstand a greater degree of exposure to shock than ordinary members of the public. Thus, in such situations, police and fire officers may expect to have greater difficulty in showing that their employer has been *in breach* of the personal duty of care, which he owes them.

This last point is highly relevant to the facts of *White* v. *Chief Constable of South Yorkshire*.[224] From the point of view of employer's liability, it cannot be argued that the Chief Constable was in breach of that duty *simply* for exposing his officers to the harrowing scenes that they witnessed. If the disaster had occurred through the fault of a third party, it seems inconceivable that a reasonable police authority would, in the circumstances, have withdrawn its officers from the scene. Does it make any difference that the employer, in *White*, was responsible for the accident occurring in the first place? At this point, difficult issues of causation arise. It is possible to argue that the plaintiffs in *White* suffered *additional* distress and abuse from the crowd and from relatives during and after the events in the stadium because of the role of their fellow officers in causing the deaths of the victims. More generally, the accumulation of circumstances—the employer's initial responsibility for the disaster together with the highly stressful situation in which the plaintiffs were then placed—could be seen as placing the employer in breach of his duty to have regard to both their physical and their psychiatric health and safety, as Lord Goff argued in his dissent.

Unfortunately, the approach taken by the majority in *White* was to question whether the employer owed his employees a duty of care at all in the situation which arose in that

222 See *Macfarlane* v. *EE Caledonia Ltd.* [1994] 2 All ER 1; *Robertson and Rough* v. *Forth Bridge Joint Board* [1995] IRLR 251; *Keen* v. *Tayside Contracts Ltd.* 2003 SLT 500.

223 See below, ch. 18.

224 [1999] 2 AC 455.

case. According to Lord Steyn, the liability of the employer to his employees depended on general principles of tort law, which limited the degree to which psychiatric damage was compensable; there was nothing to be gained, then, from formulating the claim as one of employer's liability. If this approach is taken, then a major restriction has been placed on the extent of the employer's personal liability. Lord Hoffmann, on the other hand, seemed to accept that earlier cases,[225] which had held that an employer could be liable for causing certain types of psychiatric harm to an employee, had been correctly decided. However, his Lordship seems to have considered that this line of authority was of no relevance in a case where the psychiatric harm in question was sustained through witnessing the death or injury of another,[226] although why this exception should be carved out of the general law of employer's liability is not clear. Later decisions have confirmed that *White* does not upset the earlier line of cases, and that the relationship of employment is one of those which can give rise to a duty of care to have regard for psychological well-being.[227] We will consider these decisions in more detail in the chapter on employers' liability.[228]

(C) 'PURE' ECONOMIC LOSS

Personal injury and property damage may both have economic consequences. A person who sustains an injury may lose not simply the use of a limb but also the earning capacity which goes with it. In such a case, he will receive compensation for loss of future earnings as well as for loss of the limb and facility in question. As far as property damage is concerned, the courts will have primary regard to the market value of the property in question when assessing compensation for its loss. In these cases the law of tort provides compensation for economic losses *arising directly* out of physical loss; this is not controversial.[229] What is disputed and will be discussed in this section is the possible use of tort law to provide compensation for losses that are merely financial or pecuniary in nature. These, then, are losses that have no connection to personal or physical harm suffered by the claimant and are sometimes termed 'pure' economic losses. Such losses

225 In particular *Walker* v. *Northumberland CC* [1995] 1 All ER 737.

226 To similar effect is the judgment of Lady Paton in *Keen* v. *Tayside Contracts* 2003 SLT 500; however, a similar claim was not struck out in *Harrhy* v. *Thames Trains Ltd.* [2003] EWHC 2120.

227 In particular, *Hatton* v. *Sutherland* [2002] EWCA Civ. 76 and *Barber* v. *Somerset CC* [2004] 1 WLR 1089, applied in *Hartman* v. *South Essex Mental Health and Community Care Trust* [2005] EWCA Civ. 6, a decision which casts doubt on the denial of a duty of care in *French* v. *Sussex CC* [2004] EWHC 3217. See further our analysis in ch. 18, below.

228 See below, ch. 18.

229 The need to establish a direct causal relationship does not normally give rise to much difficulty in a case where the plaintiff has suffered physical harm—at any rate when the harm has resulted from an act rather than an omission—and the extent of compensation will be determined by reference to the principles of computation of damages. An instance of the link being insufficiently direct is *Pritchard* v. *Cobden* [1988] Fam. 22, where an accident victim failed to recover damages for the financial consequences of his divorce which, the court held, was a foreseeable consequence of his injuries. The division of assets between the plaintiff and his wife was too remote from the initial injury to be the subject of compensation. See also *Meah* v. *McCreamer (No. 2)* [1986] 1 All ER 943.

might include financial loss or expenditure incurred as a result of the defendant's negligence, interruption to an expected stream of income such as wages or rents, or failure to make a gain as expected from a valuable contract or from an expected legacy under a will. For the most part an 'exclusionary rule' bars recovery in these cases; liability being the exception. The logic of this position may not be immediately obvious; nor, indeed, is it shared by many other legal systems.[230] Why should recovery for economic loss be made to depend upon the fortuitous event that it is sustained through the medium of physical or property damage? It is not plausible to say that pure economic losses are, for this purpose, less easily quantified than those flowing from physical damage. The courts compute as a matter of course the future lost earnings of claimants in personal injury cases. These losses are often no easier to estimate accurately than those claimed in cases of pure economic loss, and in some cases they may be more difficult to establish.[231]

On the other hand, few would argue with the proposition that the law should provide greater protection to personal safety and health than to purely economic interests. A general duty of care to avoid causing foreseeable physical injury or disease seems widely accepted. But this does not explain why, *nowadays*, interests in tangible property should be so much better protected than mere financial interests.[232] Historically, the protection of property rights was one of tort law's principal functions, at least as much as the protection of life and limb.[233] But this historical feature of the law cannot, on its own, any longer provide a satisfactory explanation for the current sharp distinction between physical and economic losses, especially as societies and their hierarchy of values change subtly over the passage of time. Another reason why such a sharp differentiation in favour of tactile forms of wealth is no longer supportable is due to the fact that nowadays the wealth of many (if not most) people takes the form of bank accounts, equities

230 E.g. France, Italy, the Netherlands.

231 See generally ch. 25 below, and in particular the discussion of how to assess the claimant's claim for lost future wages, taking into account the impact of taxation and of collateral benefits such as pensions and insurance.

232 See *Canadian National Railway* v. *Norsk Pacific Steamship Co.* (1992) 91 DLR (4th) 289, 383 (Stevenson J): 'Some argue that there is a fundamental distinction between physical damage (personal and property damage) and pure economic loss and that the latter is less worthy of protection . . . but I am left unconvinced. Although I am prepared to recognise that a human being is more important than property and lost expectations of profit, I fail to see how property and economic losses can be distinguished.' The same kind of dated 'hierarchy of values' has also been advanced in the related topic of compensation for psychiatric injury where some have argued against it on the grounds that '[i]t is widely felt that trauma to the mind is less [serious] than lesion to the body' (T. Weir, *A Casebook on Tort* (7th edn., 1992), 88). Such views are not only debatable; they also show how lawyers and the law fail to adapt to changing social conditions and, in this last example, take note of great progress in medical science which seriously undermines such scientific basis as there ever was in favour of these dated misconceptions.

233 It may plausibly be argued that the nineteenth-century common law conferred greater protection upon property (both real and personal) than upon the person. Aside from the well-established liability for trespass, liability for non-trespassory interferences with land was, in many cases, strict, both in nuisance and under the principle of *Rylands* v. *Fletcher* (see below, chs. 12, 13 and 16), while even negligent harm to the person would quite frequently not give rise to liability as a result both of the limited scope of the duty of care pre-*Donoghue* v. *Stevenson* [1932] AC 562 and of the operation of the defences of contributory negligence, assumption of risk (consent) and common employment (see below, ch. 24).

and 'entitlements' (such as pension or alimony rights, social payments and the like), the latter sometime being known under the term 'new forms of property'. So, the justification for the law's disadvantageous protection afforded to pure economic interests must be sought elsewhere.

In this context, a factor frequently mentioned by the courts is the fear that without the exclusionary rule the 'floodgates' of liability would open, exposing defendants to an endless series of actions. Though widely invoked, this is an argument which has yet to be explored (or exploded) completely. Thus, to begin one should note that if this argument has any force it is one of 'administrative convenience' and, in essence, unrelated to the idea of justice, which is what the courts should be dispensing. To be sure, the rather modest in size English judiciary (compared to its European counterparts) may—understandably—make our judges wary of making access to the courts so easy as to harm their efficacy. But this fear, one feels, underestimates the cost and uncertainty of litigation; and assumes all too quickly that English litigants would be as quick as their American counterparts in commencing litigation the moment an untoward event occurred. Thus, for instance, we know from sociological studies that a fair number of medical malpractice suits start because claimants are really seeking an explanation for what went wrong rather than out of a desire to seek vengeance or make money out of their hurt.

Second, the 'floodgates' argument, if valid, is invoked in a selective manner. For extensive liability does, nowadays, result from defective products (the Dalcon Shield inter-uterine device, the Dow Corning silicone breast prostheses, the Shelley-Borg defective heart valves), asbestos-related injuries, toxic torts and the like, involving hundred of thousands of victims and yet no one has ever raised this argument in this context. Conversely, we find cases involving pure economic loss suffered—to the knowledge of all concerned—by one person only,[234] and yet even in such cases, where clearly there is no danger of opening the floodgates of litigation, the claims are treated with suspicion if not hostility.

A (slightly) better argument is that an open-ended duty of care in relation to economic losses creates the danger of indeterminate (not simply extensive) liability, that is to say, liability the extent of which would be unpredictable in terms of both the size of claims and the number of potential claimants and thus difficult to insure.[235] This element of uncertainty would, so the argument runs, have a deterrent effect in relation to activities that are socially necessary or beneficial, which might not be carried on in the light of the risk of 'crushing liability' for economic damage. An example frequently given concerns liability for the consequences of a road accident. If a careless driver were potentially liable not simply to those immediately involved in a collision but to all persons whose businesses or earnings were affected by, for example, a traffic jam resulting from the crash, the costs of motoring (and in particular the cost of liability insurance)

[234] For instance in *Caltex Oil (Australia) Pty. Ltd.* v. *Dredge Willemstad* (1976) 136 CLR 529.

[235] On the important distinction between liability which is indeterminate and therefore unpredictable, on the one hand, and indefinite (large-scale) liability, see *Canadian National Railway* v. *Norsk Pacific Steamship Co.* (1992) 91 DLR (4th) 289, 338 (LaForest J).

would become prohibitive for all road-users.[236] Since liability has to stop somewhere, a rule excluding recovery for pure economic loss has the pragmatic benefit of promoting a degree of legal and commercial certainty. 'The solution to cases of this type is necessarily pragmatic and involves drawing a line that will exclude at least some people who have been undeniably injured owing to the [defendant's] admitted failure to meet the requisite standard of care.'[237]

The exclusionary rule has also been based on a preference for contract, rather than tort, as a means of protecting financial interests. Claimants, it is said, should seek to cover economic losses by contracting directly with potential tortfeasors or, if this is not possible, by taking out first-party insurance. Parties may allocate the risk of economic loss between themselves in a number of ways, most importantly by establishing particular standards of contractual performance and by excluding or limiting liability in damages. Where the parties have agreed contractual terms of this kind, there may be little or no justification for the law imposing different standards of performance and liability rules through a general tort duty. Where they have not so contracted, it is said that the law should be prepared to let the loss lie where it falls.[238] These are plausible arguments for restricting liability at least where business entities are concerned although, as we shall note further below, they do not provide satisfactory explanations of all aspects of the case law.

We thus feel that the system should be seeking—indeed we believe it has found—a *via media*. The all or nothing approach seems to hold few attractions. Instead, as Professor Feldthusen[239] has argued convincingly, we should avoid discussing all cases of pure economic loss under one heading. We should, instead, be trying to distinguish between a number of separate areas—we could call them different factual configurations—'the differences among [which] . . . are every bit as significant as the initial distinction from physical damage'. Feldthusen thus identified the following specific areas: liability of public authorities; responsibility for negligent misstatements; negligence in the performance of a service; recovery of economic loss caused by defective products and buildings; 'relational' economic losses arising from damage to the property of a third party; and negligence in the performance of a service. The question of the overlap between tort and contract as sources of obligation also deserves special treatment. The liability of public bodies is considered in more detail in Chapter 8 below. The remaining categories are analysed in what follows.

(i) Liability for Negligent Misstatements

Notwithstanding *Murphy* v. *Brentwood DC*, it remains possible to recover financial losses in respect of negligent misstatements, under the principle enunciated by the

236 J. Stapleton, 'Duty of Care and Economic Loss: A Wider Agenda' (1991) 107 *LQR* 249, 254; *Stevenson* v. *East Ohio Gas Co.* (1946) 73 NE 2d 400.

237 *Canadian National Railway* v. *Norsk Pacific Steamship Co.* (1992) 91 DLR (4th) 289, 302 (LaForest J).

238 This view is expounded by LaForest J in his dissenting judgment in the *Norsk* case, *ibid.* See also Markesinis and Deakin (Select Bibliography).

239 'Economic Loss in the Supreme Court of Canada' (Select Bibliography). Professor Feldthusen's classification was adopted by LaForest J in his dissenting judgment in the *Norsk* case (1991) 91 DLR (4th) 289.

House of Lords in the earlier case of *Hedley Byrne & Co.* v. *Heller & Partners*.[240] In that case, the plaintiffs were considering supplying advertising services to a potential client, Easipower, and through their bank sought from Easipower's bankers, the defendants, a credit reference for Easipower. The defendants replied 'without responsibility' to the effect that Easipower was financially sound. In fact, shortly afterwards, Easipower went into liquidation and the plaintiffs, who had relied on the reference, lost a large amount of money. The House of Lords held that the defendants would have owed a duty of care to the plaintiffs and would have been liable but for the disclaimer that their remarks were made without responsibility.

Once it is accepted that tort law recognises liability for careless words as well as careless behaviour, there is a clear need for a control device to deal with the threat of *indeterminate*[241] liability. Whereas 'it is at least unusual casually to put into circulation negligently made articles which are dangerous... words can be broadcast with or without the consent or the foresight of the speaker or writer'.[242] From time to time, a number of potential tests have been put forward as the basis of negligence liability in this area of the law. Thus, in some cases, the judges speak of the need for a 'voluntary assumption of responsibility' by the person making the statement. In *Hedley Byrne* itself, the defendants avoided liability precisely because they told the plaintiffs that their statement was made 'without responsibility'. In other decisions, the 'reasonable reliance' of the claimant on the other's advice appears to be of central importance. It has been said that 'these two concepts are, in fact, closely related'[243]—a view supported by a *dictum* of Lord Morris in *Hedley Byrne* to the effect that a duty of care will arise where 'a person takes it upon himself to give information or advice to, or allows his information or advice to be passed on to, another person who, as he knows or should know, will place reliance on it'.[244]

There are, nevertheless, some serious problems in defining the scope of *Hedley Byrne* liability by reference to the twin concepts of assumption of responsibility and reasonable reliance. A person will rarely be placed under a duty of care for simply 'taking it upon himself 'to offer advice (as Lord Morris put it); nor will it necessarily be accurate to term the relevant assumption a 'voluntary' one. The advice may be given voluntarily, in the sense that the *claimant* will not normally have contracted to receive the information in question.[245] But the defendant will, in many cases of *Hedley Byrne* liability, have a contractual obligation with a *third party* that may require him to take care in divulging the advice or information to the claimant. Alternatively, he will have some kind of professional obligation, which similarly places him under a duty to take care. In

[240] [1964] AC 465.

[241] We stress 'indeterminate', as Cardozo CJ did in his famous judgment in *Ultramares Corp.* v. *Touche, Niven and Co.*, 255 NY 170, 174, NE 441, 444 (1931), for the danger in these cases arises not so much from the possibility of an extended liability but from its indeterminate nature. For insurance companies can cope—at the right premium—with extended liability; but it is much more difficult to fix a premium with open-ended liability.

[242] Lord Reid in *Hedley Byrne* [1964] AC 465, 483.

[243] E. McKendrick, *Tort Textbook* (5th edn., 1991), 52.

[244] [1964] AC 465, 503.

[245] Although it may be the case that there are concurrent duties in contract and tort in a particular situation: see *Pirelli General Cable Works Ltd.* v. *Oscar Faber & Partners* [1983] 2 AC 1.

these circumstances it is entirely unhelpful to refer to there having been a voluntary assumption of responsibility. As Lord Oliver said in *Caparo Industries plc* v. *Dickman*, this phrase 'was not intended to be a test for the existence of the duty for, on analysis, it means no more than that the act of the defendant in making the statement or tendering the advice was voluntary and that the law attributes to it an assumption of responsibility... [but] it tells us nothing about the circumstances from which such attribution arises'.[246]

What matters, instead, is that the information or advice in question has been issued in a specific commercial or professional context, and it is this context which often provides the vital clue to the extent of the defendant's liability in tort. This idea is often summed up by saying that the central requirement for a duty of care is the existence of a 'special relationship' between the parties. Prior to *Hedley Byrne* it was understood that, apart from instances of fiduciary duty, such as that owed by a solicitor to a client, liability for misstatements could arise only for fraud or for breach of a contractual undertaking. The Court of Appeal had thus in the 1950s ruled against a duty of care arising in negligence.[247] However, considering the earlier judgments, Lord Devlin argued that:

> there is ample authority to justify your Lordships in saying now that the categories of special relationships, which may give rise to a duty to take care in word as well as deed, are not limited to contractual relationships or to relationships of fiduciary duty, but include also relationships which... are 'equivalent to contract', that is, where there is an assumption of responsibility in circumstances in which, but for the absence of consideration, there would be a contract.[248]

The duty in this case arose from the purpose for which the information had been supplied. Although the information was given gratuitously, in the sense that the claimants did not pay to receive it, the bank was, nevertheless, acting in a commercial context and knew that the information would be passed on to the claimants by their bank and relied upon for their business. The defendants would certainly have been expected, as a matter of business practice, to give references of this kind, since without them their own clients might be unable to get business. As Lord Devlin observed, 'it would discourage the customers of the bank if their deals fell through because the bank had refused to testify to their credit when it was good'.[249] On the other hand, the defendants were entitled, in the absence of a contract, to the protection of the disclaimer:

[246] [1990] 2 AC 605, 607. In *Customs & Excise Commissioners* v. *Barclays Bank plc* [2006] 3 WLR 1(HL) the presence of a voluntary assumption of responsibility was described as a 'sufficient but not necessary condition of liability' by Lord Bingham (at 6) but as 'critical' by Lord Hoffmann (at 14); Lord Rodger considered that 'although it may be decisive in many situations, the presence or absence of a voluntary assumption of responsibility does not necessarily provide the answer in all cases' (at 20); while Lord Mance said that '[a]ssumption of responsibility is on any view a core area of liability for economic loss' (at 28). Notwithstanding these differences of emphasis, the absence of an assumption of responsibility in this particular case (which concerned the liability of a bank for failing to stop payments out of two accounts which had been frozen by order of the Customs and Excise) was clearly an important aspect of the outcome, which went in the defendant's favour.

[247] Most notably in *Candler* v. *Crane, Christmas & Co.* [1951] 2 KB 164, in which the majority overrode a vigorous dissent from Denning LJ. On fiduciary duty, see *Nocton* v. *Lord Ashburton* [1914] AC 932; on fraud, *Derry* v. *Peek* (1889) 14 App. Cas. 337.

[248] [1964] AC 465, 528–9. [249] *Ibid.*, 529.

'If the inquirers chose to receive and act upon the reply they cannot disregard the definite terms upon which it was given.'[250] Such a disclaimer would, nowadays, have to pass a 'reasonableness' test under section 2(2) of the Unfair Contract Terms Act 1977.[251]

Where the context in which advice is given is, by contrast, a casual or social occasion, a duty will not normally arise. *Chaudhry* v. *Prabhakar*,[252] which may have been wrongly decided, provides an exception. For there, the Court of Appeal held that advice seriously given between friends might give rise to liability. In that case, the defendant took it upon himself to advise the plaintiff in her purchase of a second-hand motor car. He failed to notice that the car he recommended had previously been involved in an accident. A few months after the plaintiff bought the car it was declared unroadworthy and she sued him successfully for the loss of value. It is unlikely that this decision will be extended to produce a general liability for gratuitous advice, though. The existence of a duty was conceded by counsel at first instance and was not the subject of a full argument in the Court of Appeal.

In *Mutual Life & Assurance Co.* v. *Evatt* [253] the Privy Council laid down a further restriction on liability, namely that the duty of a professional adviser was limited to information or advice which he held himself out as qualified to give or which he was in the business of giving. In this case, an assurance company was held not liable for a reply it gave to the plaintiff, a policyholder, concerning the financial soundness of an associated company in which the plaintiff then decided to invest. This decision has not, on the whole, been followed by the English courts. In the recent case of *Lennon* v. *Commissioner of Police of the Metropolis*[254] the Court of Appeal held that it was sufficient for there to be an assumption of responsibility by the defendant, coupled with reliance by the claimant on the exercise by the defendant of due care and skill. Here, a police officer was able to recover compensation for negligent advice from his employer, concerning the impact on his terms and conditions of employment of his transfer from one police force to another. The Court of Appeal had earlier declined to follow *Evatt* in *Esso Petroleum Co.* v. *Mardon*,[255] where it had held that Esso owed a pre-contractual duty of care to a potential tenant of a petrol station to prepare accurate estimates of the likely business which the station would generate. This decision is perhaps explicable by reference to the difficulty that Mr Mardon would have had in finding out the necessary information from any other source. Normally there will be no duty of care under *Hedley Byrne* between business parties negotiating at arm's length; each side will have to rely on its own judgement or obtain the opinion of a third party. Thus, with reason, the courts take the view that parties to precontractual

[250] *Ibid.*, 504 (Lord Morris of Borth-y-Gest).

[251] See below, ch. 24, and see *Smith* v. *Eric S. Bush* [1990] 1 AC 829, discussed below.

[252] [1989] 1 WLR 29. [253] [1971] AC 793.

[254] [2004] 1 WLR 2594.

[255] [1976] QB 801. In *Howard Marine & Dredging Co.* v. *A. Ogden & Sons (Excavations) Ltd.* [1978] QB 574 a majority of the Court of Appeal (Lord Denning and Shaw LJ) rejected the majority judgment of the Privy Council in *Lovatt.*

negotiations will primarily look to their own interests and not to those of each other. As Glidewell LJ has put it:

> liability in tort for economic loss by reliance on a statement which in the event is shown to be wrong arises only within the confines of the *Hedley Byrne* principle. It does not apply in the common situation . . . as between parties negotiating for a prospective contract. They cannot have a right of action in tort if during the course of those negotiations something is said on which they rely and in the event a contract does not result. If, as often happens, one party to negotiations is concerned to protect his or its position but, should the contract in the end not be achieved and, if the passage of time is likely to give rise to damage, then that party must seek to protect its position by obtaining a promise from the other, a promise upon which either a right of action in contract for breach of the promise may be brought or, at the very least, it can be suggested that an estoppel can arise.[256]

In cases where a contract does result from negotiations it will not, normally, be necessary to use *Hedley Byrne* to determine liability for pre-contractual misstatements. Under section 2(1) of the Misrepresentation Act 1967 the victim of a misrepresentation which leads to contractual relations between him and the person making the statement may sue the other party for damages representing his loss, unless the other can show that he took all reasonable care up to the time of contracting to ensure that the information was true. This is, then, a form of statutory tort, which is dependent for its operation on the misstatement inducing a contract. When this condition has been satisfied, section 2(1) provides a superior basis for compensation than *Hedley Byrne* since it does not require the existence of a special relationship and it effectively reverses the burden of proving negligence.[257] Damages under section 2(1) will also be more extensive, being calculated on the basis of the tort of deceit where the rules of remoteness of damage are less restrictive than those which operate in negligence.[258]

Even if advice is given in a professional or commercial context, the mere knowledge that it will be passed on to or used by third parties does not suffice to establish a duty of care under *Hedley Byrne*, in the absence of an assumption of responsibility. This is clear from the recent House of Lords decision in *Sutradhar* v. *National Environmental Research Council*,[259] a decision which, moreover, concerned liability for physical harm

256 *Glen-Mor Fashions Ltd.* v. *Jaeger Company Shops Ltd.* (unreported, transcript on LEXIS), Court of Appeal, 20 Nov. 1991. There are alternatives to *Hedley Byrne* for framing liability for disappointed pre-contractual expectations, but these are rarely, if ever, available in English law. As far as estoppel is concerned, there is no equivalent to the wide-ranging Art. 90 of the American Restatement (2d) of Contracts which has been used as a basis for imposing liability for reliance losses: see *Hoffman* v. *Red Owl Stores Inc.*, 133 NW 2d 267 (1965); cf. *Combe* v. *Combe* [1951] 2 KB 215. The only protection offered by English law is therefore the device of a collateral contract. This will, by its nature, be rare, but see *Blackpool and Fylde Aero Club* v. *Blackpool BC* [1990] 1 WLR 1195; and on 'lock out' agreements, *Walford* v. *Miles* [1992] AC 128.

257 See e.g. *Howard Marine & Dredging Co.* v. *Ogden* [1978] QB 574.

258 *Royscott Trust Co.* v. *Rogerson* [1991] 3 All ER 294; but cf. the criticism of this decision by R. Hooley, 'Damages and the Misrepresentation Act 1967' (1991) 107 *LQR* 547.

259 [2006] UKHL 33. A similar decision, stressing the need for proximity, in the context of economic loss, is *West Bromwich Albion FC* v. *El Safty* [2005] EWHC 2866, in which a surgeon treating a football player owed no duty of care to his club.

and not simply pure economic loss. The claim was based on the alleged failure of the defendant, an agency of the UK government, to take due care in preparing a research report which stated that water in certain areas of Bangladesh was drinkable. The report was made available to the government of Bangladesh but otherwise had limited circulation. The claimant allegedly suffered arsenical poisoning after drinking water from wells which the defendant had reported were safe. The claim was struck out on the grounds that the element of proximity, required for a duty of care, was lacking; the defendant was in the same position as the author of a newspaper article or textbook, who makes no assumption of responsibility to the hundreds or thousands who might read his work.[260]

Hedley Byrne does not necessarily apply to a failure to speak, at least in cases where a potential tort duty of this kind would overlap with the rules of contract law, which limit liability for non-disclosure. This is the effect of *Banque Financière de la Cité SA* v. *Westgate Insurance Co.*,[261] a case that arose out of a complex insurance fraud. The plaintiff banks were fraudulently misled by the defendant's manager into believing that they were fully covered by an insurance policy negotiated with the defendant. The plaintiffs attempted to make the defendant liable in negligence for the failure of one of the manager's colleagues, who knew about the fraud, to notify them of it. The House of Lords held that, under these circumstances, there was no liability in tort for a mere failure to speak out as opposed to an active misstatement. During pre-contractual negotiations, the law of contract imposes a duty of disclosure only under exceptional circumstances; and even then it does not grant an action for damages but simply a right to rescind the contract. In the *Banque Financière* case the House of Lords took the view that the rules of contract law should not be circumvented by the use of a negligence action. This places a substantial restriction on the potential development of *Hedley Byrne* to cover omissions. But care must be taken to define what is here meant by an omission: there could well be liability in tort, as there is in contract, for a failure to correct a misleading impression created by an ambiguous statement[262] or one which becomes false at a later point in time.[263]

The *Hedley Byrne* principle was re-examined by the House of Lords in *Caparo Industries plc* v. *Dickman*.[264] Caparo made a takeover bid for a company, Fidelity, in which it already had a sizeable shareholding. When the takeover was completed it emerged that Fidelity was effectively worthless and that a false impression of its business value had been created. Caparo brought an action against Touche Ross, Fidelity's auditors, claiming that the takeover had been launched in reliance on the accounts prepared by the auditors, which had shown Fidelity making a large profit in the preceding tax year when in fact it had made a loss. The House of Lords held that no duty of care

260 [2006] UKHL 33, at [36] (Lord Hoffmann).

261 [1991] 2 AC 249.

262 This is well established in contract cases on misrepresentation: see e.g. *Notts, Patent Brick and Tile Co.* v. *Butler* (1886) 16 QBD 778.

263 *With* v. *O'Flanagan* [1936] Ch. 75.

264 [1990] 2 AC 605.

was established on these facts. Lord Bridge held that the central distinction was that between cases in which 'the defendant giving advice or information was fully aware of the nature of the transaction which the plaintiff had in contemplation' and those in which 'a statement is put into more or less general circulation and may foreseeably be relied on by strangers to the maker of the statement for any one of a variety of different purposes which the maker of the statement has no specific reason to contemplate'.[265] Even though a takeover bid was known to be highly probable, to hold the auditors liable for the consequences of an investment decision, which went wrong, would open up the prospect of an open-ended liability. According to Lord Oliver, no logical distinction could be made between existing shareholders such as Caparo, who extended their shareholding in reliance on the report, and members of the public who could have read the report and bought shares or lent to the company after having read it.[266]

At the basis of *Caparo* is the House of Lords' view of the purpose of the annual audit of accounts of a publicly listed company. Under the Companies Acts, the auditor, once appointed by the company in general meeting, is required to examine the company accounts to see if they give a 'true and fair view' of the company's finances.[267] The auditor's report must be sent to each one of the shareholders. According to Lord Bridge, the purpose of this is not to protect individual shareholders in their investment decisions, but rather to safeguard the collective interest of the shareholders in ensuring that the company is effectively managed. In the event of a breach of duty by the auditor, any losses would, said Lord Bridge, be recouped by an action brought by the company, thereby making an action in tort by individual shareholders unnecessary and inappropriate.

This last point is open to the objection that it is most unlikely that the company will have an action for contract damages in circumstances such as those in *Caparo*, for the reason that it suffers no loss. The overvaluation in this case harmed only the takeover bidder, who paid too much, and not the company itself, or indeed the other shareholders, who were bought out at a premium. Indeed, once their action in the tort of negligence failed, the new owners of Fidelity started an action in the company's name for breach of contract against the auditors; but this action did not make any progress.[268]

Caparo does not mean that auditors and accountants can never incur liability in tort to those who rely on their statements. In the pre-*Hedley Byrne* decision of *Candler* v. *Crane, Christmas*,[269] a statement of accounts was prepared for the specific purpose of enabling an investor to decide whether or not to put money into the company. The relationship between the parties here was much closer, and the purpose of the advice much more specifically related to a particular transaction, than it was in *Caparo*, and it seems

265 [1990] 2 AC 605, 620–1.

266 *Ibid.*, 650–2.

267 Companies Act 1985, ss. 235 ff. See now Companies Act 2006, Part 16, Ch. 1. See also A. McGee, 'The "True and Fair View" Debate: A Study in the Legal Regulation of Accounting' (1991) 54 *MLR* 874.

268 See M. Percival, 'After *Caparo*: Liability in Business Transactions Revisited' (1991) 54 *MLR* 739, 743. For a suggestion that the ruling in *Caparo* may not survive changes in the liability of auditors under European Community law, see P. Burbidge, 'Liability of Statutory Auditors to Third Parties: Is the European Writing on the Wall for *Caparo* v. *Dickman*?' (2002) 18 *PN* 40.

269 [1951] 2 KB 164.

likely that a duty would now arise if similar facts occurred today. Thus, in *Morgan Crucible Co. plc* v. *Hill Samuel & Co. Ltd.*,[270] decided after *Caparo*, the Court of Appeal refused to strike out a claim brought by a successful takeover bidder against directors and auditors of the target company which, when he took it over, turned out to be less valuable than he had been led to believe. Here, statements had been made with the avowed purpose of influencing the conduct of an *identified* bidder: the director and auditors could accordingly have owed him a duty of care. At present, however, this appears to be as far as the law will go. If the statement is made to a large class of recipients, or for a number of purposes only one of which is related to the transaction which subsequently goes wrong, a tort claim will not be likely and the claimant will be limited to whatever contractual rights he may have.[271]

The House of Lords' view of the limited purpose of the annual audit has been called 'an artificial interpretation, which takes no account of commercial reality'.[272] The annual audit is one of the few reliable means shareholders have of obtaining information concerning the internal operation of a company. The fear of the floodgates also appears to have been misplaced in that instance. If a company's shares are boosted by false information in advance of a takeover bid, any loss will tend to be concentrated on the successful takeover bidder who ends up with the overvalued shares. Even then, the claimant will have to prove that the report was a material factor in his decision to launch the bid. He may be required to show that he would not have bought the shares but for the report, which may be difficult to do in practice. The auditor may also be able to refute allegations of a lack of care in preparing the account. These are illustrations of the point that the imposition of a duty of care does not, by itself, lead inevitably to liability; indeed, Bingham LJ, in the Court of Appeal, thought that the plaintiffs might well fail at the full trial of the action on one of these grounds.[273] In relation to policy, the prospects of 'defensive accounting', excessive liability insurance premiums, and accountancy firms going out of business if a duty of care were imposed were all raised in argument in *Caparo*. But the experience of other legal systems—such as Germany,[274]

270 [1991] Ch. 295; *Galoo Ltd. (in liquidation)* v. *Bright Grahame Murray* [1994] 1 WLR 1360; cf. *James McNaughton Paper Group Ltd.* v. *Hicks Anderson & Co.* [1991] 2 QB 113, where a similar kind of claim failed on the facts.

271 See in particular the judgment of Neill LJ in *James McNaughton Paper Group Ltd.* v. *Hicks Anderson & Co.* [1991] 2 QB 113; and see Percival, 'After *Caparo*' (1991) 54 *MLR* 739. It also follows that the director of a company cannot be liable under *Hedley Byrne* for a negligent misstatement made by that company, unless he has assumed a personal responsibility to the recipient of the information in such circumstances as to give rise to a duty of care: *Williams* v. *Natural Life Ltd.* [1998] 1 WLR 830. The law in the USA, allowing for the divergences among state jurisdictions, seems to be the same. See *Bily* v. *Arthur Young and Co.*, 834 P 2d 745 (1992)—a case that also raises a point not yet made in England. This is the idea of 'informational asymmetry' between accountant and audited company, which, ultimately, has more information about its affairs than the auditing accountant. There is no reason, however, why in such cases accountants should not state precisely the information given to them by their clients and limit their liability to their interpretation of it.

272 Percival, 'After *Caparo*' (1991) 54 *MLR* 739 at 742.

273 [1989] QB 653, 690.

274 German law, in particular, may contain a borrowable idea for at least certain types of audit (the so-called compulsory audits such as the formation audit, the annual audit, etc.) where the accountant's liability is capped to the tune of $4 million (approximately) per audit in cases of publicly listed companies. Though the figure

the Netherlands and a few states of the USA—which have flirted with the imposition of a more extensive liability, suggests that these fears may have been greatly exaggerated. A knowledgeable American judge has thus observed that: 'The sky has not fallen on the accounting profession'[275] as a result of making auditors potentially liable for their faults. Here, however, as in so many other instances of tort (negligence) liability,[276] we are faced with statements, which are rarely supported by solid empirical evidence available to us all.

This tendency of English judges to express views on the economic aspects of the cases they are hearing based on hunches rather than empirical or other scientifically assembled evidence is, arguably, unfortunate and one might even suggest that it should be discouraged. If an example is needed to make the point, it can be found in Lord Hoffmann's judgment in *Stovin* v. *Wise*.[277] There he thus said:

> It would not be surprising if one of the consequences of the *Anns* case . . . was that local council inspectors tended to insist upon *stronger* [our italics] foundations than were necessary.

There are at least two difficulties with such statements. First, if they are based on hearsay evidence or a hunch they may start one thinking along new and original lines; but hunches cannot, by themselves, justify a switch in justifications or legal results. Second, why should the potential risk of legal liability lead to excessively strong instead of 'appropriate' foundations being laid? One could thus counter Lord Hoffmann's point by suggesting that while the post-*Anns* regime led to unnecessarily strong and expensive foundations, the post-*Murphy* situation may have encouraged the sloppy verification of building calculations. What the law must, surely, be encouraging is neither excessive caution not unnecessary sloppiness; and the latter may well follow a signal from the courts that they favour a non-liability rule just as the former may flow from a rule which seems to invite litigation. Such a battle of 'hunches' and 'intuitive guesses' may be useful in the classroom but, it is submitted, forms a very suspicious basis for a court judgment.

In contrast to *Caparo* is another decision of the House of Lords in two cases heard together, *Smith* v. *Eric S. Bush* and *Harris* v. *Wyre Forest DC*.[278] These concerned the common situation in which a surveyor prepares a valuation report for a building society (or a local authority) which is considering advancing a loan to a prospective purchaser on the security of the property. Building societies are required by legislation to obtain a valuation report before they make such loans.[279] The report is intended only

could, of course, be varied, the idea that many of the problems of the modern law of torts may be linked more to the growing quantum of damages rather than to the expansion of the liability rules. We have touched on this in ch. 1; and we come back to it briefly at the end of this chapter as well as in ch. 25.

[275] Judge Richard Posner, writing extra-judicially in *Cardozo: A Study in Reputation* (1990), 112.

[276] Our judges' rejection of a doctrine of 'informed consent' in medical cases is also based on (empirically) unsubstantiated fears about what might follow if patients were given more information than the paternalistic English legal system is at present prepared to grant them. In this area, however, there has been some movement in favour of claimants and a corresponding abandonment of medical paternalism.

[277] *Stovin* v. *Wise* [1996] AC 923.

[278] [1990] 1 AC 831. See also *Yianni* v. *Edwin Evans & Sons* [1982] QB 438.

[279] Building Societies Act 1986, s. 13.

to establish the value of the house as security; it is not a full structural survey. However, the prospective purchaser effectively pays for the report, by advancing a fee to the building society, which then engages the surveyor, and he normally receives a copy of the report. In *Smith*'s case both the mortgage-application form signed by the plaintiff and the report itself carried a disclaimer of liability by the surveyor, which amongst other things stated that the report 'is not, and should not be taken as, a structural survey'. A similar disclaimer was issued in the *Harris* case; and the report was not even passed on. In both cases the plaintiffs relied on favourable valuations to go ahead with their purchases, only to find that the properties contained defects which required considerable expenditure to put right. In *Smith*'s case the surveyor's report should have identified a structural weakness in the chimney flue; the chimney subsequently collapsed, causing widespread damage to the rest of the house. In *Harris*'s case the report failed to warn of the possibility of settlement of the house. When this was discovered after an interval of a few years, the house was saleable for only a fraction of the price the plaintiffs had paid for it.

Two questions arose: whether, in these circumstances, there was a duty to the purchaser to take care in the preparation of the report; and whether the disclaimer was invalidated by the Unfair Contract Terms Act 1977, which regulates exclusion clauses of this kind.[280] The House of Lords unanimously held that a duty of care did arise: the surveyor should have known that a purchaser in this position was unlikely to take out an additional survey, and would instead rely on the valuation report as evidence of the property's structural soundness. Evidence was led to the effect that fewer than 10 per cent of homeowners took out their own surveys prior to the purchase of their property. Like *Hedley Byrne*, this case was close to contract; Lord Templeman thought that 'the relationship between the valuer and the purchaser is "akin to contract". The valuer knows that the consideration he receives derives from the purchaser and is passed on by the mortgagee, and the valuer also knows that the valuation will determine whether or not the purchaser buys the house.'[281] The duty arises, according to Lord Griffiths, notwithstanding the explicit denial of responsibility by the surveyor: his Lordship rejected the use of the phrase 'voluntary assumption of responsibility' as a general test of liability.[282] The fact that the plaintiff was, in effect, paying at least in part for the advice he received makes *Smith* v. *Bush*, if anything, an even stronger case than *Hedley Byrne* itself.[283]

280 Unfair Contract Terms Act 1977, s. 2(2); see below, ch. 24.

281 [1990] 1 AC 831, 846.

282 *Ibid.*, 864.

283 The problem with this approach, however, is, why is *Smith* v. *Bush* a *Hedley Byrne* type of case and not a *D. & F. Estates/Murphy* case, leading to non-liability? As Professor Stapleton has put it convincingly, if 'the boundaries of existing pockets [of liability are to be used, then] they must make sense'. In practice, however, the pockets overlap as *Smith* v. *Bush* clearly shows. For, if one focuses on the negligent professional advice, one then slots the case into the *Hedley Byrne* pocket and liability flows almost automatically. If, however, one looks at the nature of the plaintiff's loss (economic loss resulting from the acquisition of defective property), then one is pushed into the *Murphy* non-liability rule. On all this see J. Stapleton, 'In Restraint of Tort' in P.B.H. Birks (ed.), *The Frontiers of Liability* (1994), 85–6.

The second question, concerning the scope of the Unfair Contract Terms Act was also answered in favour of the claimants. The defence of exclusion is considered in more detail in Chapter 24; it is sufficient at this stage to note the potential impact of the Act in misstatement cases. Under section 2(2) of the Act, an exclusion of liability for negligence in relation to property damage or economic loss must be 'reasonable'. This provision applies to all cases of 'business liability', that is to say liability arising out of the course of a business or from the occupation of business premises.[284] Section 2(2) is therefore applicable to the normal range of *Hedley Byrne* cases, arising as they do out of the performance of professional duties. However, the decision on 'reasonableness' in *Smith* v. *Bush* is not necessarily applicable to all disclaimers under *Hedley Byrne*. *Smith* v. *Bush* involved a business-consumer relationship in which the consumer had little or no scope to renegotiate the terms: in Lord Griffiths's words, 'the disclaimer is imposed on the purchaser who has no effective power to object'. The House of Lords also took judicial notice of the fact that the surveyor was likely to be insured against liability. They also noted that the liability in question was unlikely to be extensive, as the duty was limited to those buying 'modest houses' such as 'young first time buyers [who] are likely to be under considerable financial pressure'. Claimants with the capacity for renegotiation or for contracting for the desired service elsewhere are unlikely to benefit from this approach to disclaimers.

Leaving the question of exclusion to one side and focusing simply on duty of care, it is not easy to reconcile *Smith* v. *Bush* with the restrictive approach taken by the House of Lords in the *Caparo* and *Murphy* cases. The most convincing attempt to do so has been that of Hoffmann J in his judgment in *Morgan Crucible* v. *Hill Samuel*. According to his Lordship,[285] the different outcomes in *Caparo* and *Smith* 'consist in the different economic relationships between the parties and the nature of the markets in which they were operating'. In *Smith* the mortgagor 'is a person of modest means and making the most expensive investment of his or her life', whereas the takeover bidder in *Caparo* 'is an entrepreneur taking high risks for high rewards'. The prospective homeowner is far more vulnerable to economic risk and more likely, as a result, to act in reliance upon the information he receives, rather than relying upon his own judgement.[286] This explanation is, of course, one based on policy rather than on conceptual grounds; and many commentators remain highly critical of the distinction drawn by the courts in these cases. Thus, not unnaturally, it has left some academic commentators unhappy.

So far we have been considering cases in which the claimant incurred economic loss as a result of his own reliance on the defendant's misstatement. There exists a related category of cases in which the courts have imposed liability where the claimant's loss

284 Unfair Contract Terms Act, s. 1(3).

285 [1991] Ch. 295, 302.

286 Even then there are doubts that the judgments in *Caparo* paid adequate attention to the 'asymmetry of information' between the company and the shareholders: see Markesinis and Deakin (Select Bibliography), 628–9. The basic idea was used by the Court of Appeal in *Merrett* v. *Babb* [2001] 3 WLR 1 in a factual context that produced a harsh result since the liability fell on the surveyor personally, since his employing company had gone bankrupt and its insurance had been discontinued.

has been caused by the reliance of a third party. In *Ministry of Housing and Local Government* v. *Sharp*,[287] a clerk in a local authority registry carelessly stated that certain land was free of charges when answering a request from solicitors acting for a prospective purchaser. In fact a charge had been registered by the Ministry, giving it the right to demand a sum from the owner of the land in return for the granting of planning permission. The land was sold under the assumption that no charge existed; the legal effect of this was to deprive the Ministry of the right to the sum in question. The Court of Appeal held that it was entitled to recover this sum from the local authority. This cannot be regarded as a *Hedley Byrne* case because the statement was not directed to the claimant; as such it falls outside the area of misstatement liability and must be judged under the general principles limiting recovery for pure economic loss after *Murphy*. It is possible that the same result would be reached today, given that the plaintiff was foreseeable as an individual and that there is no danger of indeterminate liability arising.

In *Spring* v. *Guardian Assurance Ltd.*[288] the House of Lords held that when writing a reference for an existing or former employee, an employer owes a duty to avoid careless misstatements which might result in him being unable to find subsequent employment. This is not an easy case to resolve. For, first, one is faced with pure economic loss in which the role of reliance is at best indirect. Second, to impose a duty in these circumstances could be seen as undermining the well-established rule of the law of defamation. According to this, an employer writing a reference letter is protected by a defence of qualified privilege and thus should not be liable for untrue statements as long as he acted in good faith (without malice). These grounds led the Court of Appeal to deny liability. As Glidewell LJ put it, in relation to defamation and malicious falsehood 'a substantial section of the law regarding these two associated torts would be emasculated'[289] if a duty of care in negligence were imposed. For similar reasons the court rejected the implication of a term into the employee's contract of employment which would have placed the employer under a similar duty to take care. However, in the House of Lords, Lord Goff took the view that

> it must often be very difficult for an employee to obtain fresh employment without the benefit of a reference from his present or a previous employer . . . it is plain that the employee relies on him to exercise due skill and care in the preparation of the reference before making it available to the third party.[290]

In other words, it is relevant that the employee has no alternative but to rely on the employer in this situation. The fact that employer and employee are in a pre-tort relationship with implied obligations of mutual trust and confidence is also crucial to the outcome in *Spring*.[291]

287 [1970] 2 QB 223.
288 [1995] 2 AC 296.
289 [1993] 2 All ER 273, 294.
290 [1995] 2 AC 296, 319.
291 *Spring* therefore complements developments in employment law which have seen the expansion of the employer's obligation to act in good faith towards the employee: see Lord Cooke of Thorndon, 'The Right of *Spring*', in P. Cane and J. Stapleton (eds.), *The Law of Obligations: Essays in Celebration of John Fleming* (1998), and our discussion of *Spring* in the context of employers' liability, ch. 18, below.

Between them, these control factors suggest that the principle in *Spring* can be adequately confined. It certainly does not follow from *Spring* that any inaccurate statement affecting the reputation of an individual or product will give rise to liability if it leads to foreseeable economic loss. In the absence of a close pre-tort relationship between the parties, it is highly unlikely that a duty of care in negligence will arise. Fears that *Spring* will fatally undermine the defence of qualified privilege in defamation are also questionable. That defence is as broad as it is partly because defamation is a tort to which strict liability applies; it is not necessary to prove fault. Following *Spring*, the defence of qualified privilege will continue to protect employers who do not act carelessly. Where an action is brought in negligence, proof of carelessness, and the establishment of a causal link between fault and damage, will often be problematic. Where, conversely, fault and causation are established, the case for remedying a clear injustice to the claimant will be particularly strong. Thus it is strongly arguable that in *Spring* the right balance was struck between protecting the interests of the employee in maintaining his reputation and preserving a cost-effective system of employment-based references.

(ii) Negligence in the Performance of a Service

In *Henderson* v. *Merrett Syndicates Ltd.*[292] the House of Lords held that the *Hedley Byrne* principle extended beyond liability for financial harm caused by misstatements to cover a wider set of cases of economic loss brought about by negligence in the performance of a service. According to Lord Goff, this wider principle 'rests upon a relationship between the parties, which may be general or specific to the particular transaction, and which may or may not be contractual in nature'.[293] If the services were performed in a commercial context,

> the concept provides its own explanation why there is no problem in cases of this kind about liability for pure economic loss; for if a person assumes responsibility to another in respect of certain services, there is no reason why he should not be liable in damages for that other in respect of economic loss which flows from the negligent performance of those services.[294]

For this reason, his Lordship considered that once the necessary 'special relationship' was established, it was not open to the defendant to resist the imposition of a duty of care on the 'fair, just and reasonable' ground. As with *Hedley Byrne* itself, however, the outcome might be different if services were performed outside a commercial setting or there was a disclaimer. In the context of the *Henderson* litigation, Lord Goff's ruling meant that Lloyd's Names (in effect, investors in the Lloyd's insurance market) were able to establish that a duty of care was owed to them by the managing agents who had held themselves out 'as possessing a special expertise to advise the Names on the suitability of risks to be underwritten'.[295]

[292] [1995] 2 AC 145. [293] *Ibid.*, 180. [294] *Ibid.*, 181.

[295] *Ibid.*, 182. For subsequent litigation arising out of the losses of Lloyd's Names, see *Brown* v. *KMR Services Ltd.* [1995] 4 All ER 598; *Aiken* v. *Stewart Wrightson Members Agency Ltd.* [1995] 1 WLR 1281; *Jaffay and Others* v. *Society of Lloyds* [2002] EWCA Civ. 1101; (2002) 146 SJLB 214 (CA).

This wider principle of liability was also used in *White* v. *Jones*.[296] In that case a majority of the House of Lords held that a solicitor could be liable in negligence for failing to prepare timeously a new will, thereby depriving the claimants/intended beneficiaries of the benefits intended by the testator. Lord Goff, giving again the leading judgment, held that:

> the assumption of responsibility by the solicitor towards his client should be held in law to extend to the intended beneficiary who (as the solicitor can reasonably foresee) may, as a result of the solicitor's negligence, be deprived of his intended legacy in circumstances in which neither the testator nor his estate will have a remedy against the solicitor.[297]

The House of Lords thereby approved the result in the earlier case of *Ross* v. *Caunters*[298] but rejected the reasoning of Sir Robert Megarry V-C who had based his ruling on the wider neighbour principle of *Donoghue* v. *Stevenson*.[299] *White* v. *Jones* is, thus, conceptually akin (but not identical) to the notion of a contract in favour of third parties, used in some United States jurisdictions (and Germany) to solve this kind of problem. For in this type of situation, conferring a benefit on the third party is, in Cardozo J's words, the 'end and aim' of the entire transaction.[300]

Tort law in this case meets an important need. If the solicitor negligently breaches his contract with the testator, the estate of the deceased, which inherits the latter's contractual rights, will have no effective action in contract for anything more than nominal damages. This is because the solicitor's negligence has caused nothing other than nominal damage to the estate. (In practice this should be equal to the solicitor's 'wasted' fee.) This, it is submitted, is an unfair result; and it is due to the rigid privity-of-contract rule, the basis of which is that a party (in this case, the beneficiary) which has not provided consideration (value) for a promise (by the solicitor) cannot sue for its breach.[301] But in the absence of any tort action, the privity rule would in the instant situation have the effect that no person could demand legal sanctions from the negligent solicitor—an outcome that is neither just nor economically efficient.[302] Like *Hedley Byrne*,[303] this is properly understood not as an invitation to the opening of the floodgates, but as a solution to a dilemma. For, if no remedy is granted in this case, the person who has the

296 [1995] 2 AC 207. For a full discussion of the case, including its intricate background, see B. S. Markesinis, 'Five Days in the House of Lords: Some Comparative Reflections on *White* v. *Jones*' (1995) 3 *Torts LJ* 169.

297 [1995] 2 AC 207, 268.

298 [1980] Ch. 297; and see the roughly analogous case of *J'Aire Corp.* v. *Gregory*, 598 P 2d 60 (1979) (Sup. C. Cal.).

299 [1932] AC 562.

300 This and the other reasons given in the text above explain why the plaintiff's attempt to rely on *White* v. *Jones* in the subsequent case of *Goodwill* v. *British Pregnancy Advisory Service* [1996] 1 WLR 1397 was legally unconvincing. See, on the other hand, *Carr-Glynn* v. *Frearsons (a firm)* [1998] 4 All ER 225, and Chadwick LJ's ingenious expansion (at 231–2) of *White* v. *Jones* to cover the facts of that case.

301 *Tweddle* v. *Atkinson* (1861) 1 B & S 393; *Dunlop Pneumatic Tyre Co. Ltd.* v. *Selfridge & Co. Ltd.* [1915] AC 847; *Scruttons Ltd.* v. *Midland Silicones Ltd.* [1962] AC 446. Though the old 'privity rule' has now been modified by the Contracts (Rights to Third Parties) Act 1999, the *White* v. *Jones* situation was expressly left outside the purview of the new Act: Law Com. No. 242, *Contracts for the Benefit of Third Parties* (Cm. 3329, 1996) 214, n. 22.

302 In principle it is inefficient because the party undertaking the obligation is under-deterred from breaching the contract. See Markesinis and Deakin (Select Bibliography) for general discussion.

303 [1964] AC 465, above.

right to demand a remedy (the testator) has suffered no loss and the person who has suffered the loss (the beneficiary) has no right. Moreover, as Lord Goff was eager to stress, the extent of the *tort*[304] duty is shaped by the underlying contract (here between the testator and the defendant). Finally, in this particular factual configuration, there is no risk of placing the solicitor in a position of conflict since the interests of his client and of the intended beneficiary overlap completely.[305]

However, it seems that, in part because of these considerations, *White* v. *Jones* will apply only in a narrow range of situations. This is illustrated by decisions in which the intention of the contractor (promisee) to benefit the third party as an individual was less obvious and recovery in tort was denied. In the earlier case of *Clark* v. *Bruce, Lance*,[306] the Court of Appeal concluded that the interests of the client who had contracted for the services potentially conflicted with those of the claimant who claimed to have been the intended beneficiary of the contractual performance. This case concerned the granting by a lessor to a lessee of an option to purchase the freehold upon the death of the lessor or of his wife, whichever was later. The terms of the option were not particularly favourable to the lessee, and he claimed that the lessor's solicitor had been negligent in not pointing this out to his client. The court, distinguishing *Ross* v. *Caunters*, held that the solicitor's principal responsibility lay to his client, and that to impose upon him the suggested duty of care in tort with regard to the claimant was not compatible with this responsibility.

Another restriction on *White* v. *Jones* is that it may have no application in a situation where the estate does suffer a loss as a consequence of the solicitor's negligence. In *Carr-Glynn* v. *Frearsons*[307] it was said at first instance that to allow an action under such circumstances would be to expose the solicitor to an unacceptable risk of separate and cumulative claims being brought (one by the personal representatives of the deceased, the other by the frustrated beneficiary) in respect of the same wrong. However, an appeal was allowed on the grounds that the solicitor's duty to the plaintiff was complementary to his duty to the testator.

Nor does *White* v. *Jones* imply that a solicitor will, in general, be liable to third parties for a failure to provide an effective service to his own client. One very obviously different kind of case is that in which a solicitor is sued by his client's opponent in litigation: here, there is normally no duty of care even for situations of loss which is not purely economic.[308] Slightly different is the situation in which the negligence of a solicitor

[304] *White* v. *Jones* excluded, in *obiter dicta*, the possibility of an action based upon a contract in favour of third parties (or some other contractual variant). But as we shall explain below when discussing the *Panatown* case, the shift is now back to contract with the (ultimate) result that the pressures to expand tort to meet the rigidity of old (i.e. pre-1999 Act) contract law may now ease off.

[305] Cf. the denial of recovery in the Australian case of *Seale* v. *Perry* [1982] VR 193 on the ground that the interest of the frustrated beneficiary was not substantial enough to merit protection, and the dissent of Lord Mustill in *White* v. *Jones* [1995] 2 AC 207, in particular at 289–91.

[306] [1988] 1 WLR 881.

[307] [1997] 2 All ER 614; [1998] 4 All ER 225; see also *Chappell* v. *Somers & Blake* [2004] Ch. 19, in which it was held that an executor was not liable to the sole beneficiary of an estate for failure to proceed promptly to probate, partly on the grounds that the executor had a cause of action on these facts.

[308] See *Al-Kandari* v. *J. R. Brown & Co.* [1988] QB 665.

acting for a seller of land causes economic loss to the buyer. In *Gran Gelato Ltd.* v. *Richcliff (Group) Ltd.*,[309] an error by the solicitor led to his own client making an innocent misrepresentation which caused substantial loss to the plaintiff once the transaction was completed. The Vice-Chancellor rejected the plaintiff's claim on the ground that, in this case, the solicitor's duties were owed only to his own client. The result seems contrary to principle, since there is no danger of indeterminate liability here and a tort claim would avoid the multiplicity of actions. As Professor Andrew Tettenborn has explained, the ruling in *Gran Gelato*:

> necessitates two actions where one ought to do: Purchaser v. Vendor (for damages) and Vendor v. Solicitor (for an indemnity…). Since (i) the vendor is normally not at fault at all, and (ii) everyone accepts that the loss ought ultimately to be borne by the solicitor who is, there seems little point in not allowing this whole long-winded process to be short-circuited by a direct action against the solicitor, saving time and money all round.[310]

Since *White* v. *Jones*[311] was decided there has been a further twist to the question what happens if one contracting party violates his contractual obligations but it is a third party (and not his co-contractor) who suffers the loss. The case in point here is *Alfred McAlpine Construction Ltd.* v. *Panatown Ltd.*[312] The decision marks a shift from tort to contract reasoning; and its origins go back seven years to the decision of *St Martins Property Corporation Ltd.* v. *Sir Robert McAlpine Ltd.*[313] The story is a long and complicated one, so here suffice it to mention some of its salient points.[314]

In *St Martins Property Corporation Ltd.* v. *Sir Robert McAlpine Ltd.* the principle in *The Albazero* was transferred to construction law. The essence of this development was an increasingly liberal attitude towards contractual claims by which a promisee is not suing for loss sustained by himself but is seeking to recover damages on behalf of a third party. The key decisions for this development were first *St Martins*, *Darlington BC* v. *Wiltshier Northern Ltd.*,[315] and, most recently, *Alfred McAlpine Construction Ltd.* v. *Panatown Ltd.* In these cases contractual remedies were extended to cover situations where a building employer is not the owner of the development site at the time of the breach of the building contract and, as a result (arguably), suffers no financial loss. Indeed, the builder/defendant in these cases based his defence on the 'no loss argument'. However, the courts allowed recovery of substantial damages in contract in respect of the site owner's loss. To hold otherwise, they stressed, would mean allowing a meritorious claim to disappear into a 'legal black hole'. The need for a contractual solution, or, more crucially, the very danger of the 'black hole', can be traced to the change of heart by the House of Lords in *Murphy* towards the builder's liability in tort. For, prior to that case, third parties to a building contract (for instance third-party purchasers) could often avail themselves of the *Anns* type of remedy and recover pure economic loss in tort.

309 [1992] Ch. 560.
310 'Enquiries before Contract: The Wrong Answer?' [1992] *CLJ* 415, 417.
311 [1993] 2 AC 207. 312 [2001] 1 AC 518.
313 [1994] 1 AC 85.
314 For a full and critical account see H. Unberath, *Transferred Loss* (2003), 56, 205.
315 [1995] 1 WLR 68.

In the seminal case of *Panatown* this reorientation towards and rediscovery of contract principles reached a new peak. For not only was the contract route to recovery reinforced; but by a majority their Lordships laid the foundation for an even more flexible approach to contractual actions where the performance of a service benefits as a matter of fact a third party. This new approach lays emphasis on the fact that a building employer is entitled to substantial damages because he does not get what he bargained for, whether or not he suffered a financial loss as a result of the breach.[316] In the present context it is, of course, impossible to appreciate fully the impact of this remarkable decision.[317] A few remarks, however, may help bring out more clearly some basic points and speculate on future developments.

There is little doubt that the *Panatown* line of cases reopens contractual avenues in the area of construction law and in this sense puts an end to the attempts made by our courts, in cases such as *Junior Books* v. *Veitchi*,[318] to expand tort law given the rigidity of contract law. For the line of cases enabled promisees to recover substantial damages even though they were not the owners of the development site at any material time and, arguably, did not suffer a financial loss as a result of the breach. Whether this remedy is more satisfactorily analysed as a remedy whereby one recovers a third party's loss (or his own) cannot be decided here. For this depends on a series of intricate points such as the promisee's accountability to the third party, the relevance of direct third-party rights, and so forth. Suffice it to say, however, that a majority in *Panatown* denied recovery of damages on both grounds where the third party could sue himself, regardless of the theoretical basis of the promisee's remedy. In the present instance, the building owner could have sued on the basis of a so-called duty-of-care deed. This result seems somewhat harsh. For that limited, direct right of action was merely meant to fill the gap left by *Murphy* and provide protection to subsequent purchasers or tenants,[319] but arguably not to substitute liability under the building contract itself.[320] *St Martins* also presents an ironical twist. For Lord Clyde saw it as an example of Lord Goff 's theory of 'transferred loss'.[321] The latter, though the inventor of the theory (in *The Aliakmon*), and user of it in *White* v. *Jones*, abandoned it in *Panatown* in the belief that he had not used the term with 'any great accuracy'.[322] One wonders, however, whether the principle of transferred loss should be discarded without more, since it performs a useful function.[323]

[316] See Lord Griffiths' speech in *St Martins*, H. Beale, 'Privity of Contract: Judicial and Legislative Reforms' (1995) 9 *J Contract L* 103 and B. Coote, 'Contract Damages, *Ruxley* and the Performance Interest' [1997] *CLJ* 537.

[317] For further details of this development see J. Cartwright, 'Damages, Third Parties and Common Sense' (1996) 10 *J Contract L* 244, B. Coote, 'The Performance Interest, *Panatown* and the Problem of Loss' (2001) 117 *LQR* 81, G. H. Treitel, 'Damages in Respect of a Third Party's Loss' (1998) 114 *LQR* 527 and I. N. D. Wallace, 'Third Party Damage: No Legal Black Hole?' (1999) 115 *LQR* 394.

[318] [1983] 1 AC 520.

[319] Cf. D. Lewis, 'Investigating the JCT Standard Forms of Agreement for Collateral Warranty' (1997) 13 *Constr LJ* 305.

[320] Cf. the dissents of Lords Millett and Goff in the *Panatown* case [2001] 1 AC 518.

[321] *Ibid.*, at 529.

[322] See [2001] 1 AC 518, 557.

[323] See H. Unberath, 'Third Party Losses and Black Holes: Another View' (1999) 115 *LQR* 535.

Lord Goff's hesitation to base his decision on a concept that allowed recovery of third-party loss must, however, be understood in the light of his overall strategy in the latter case. For he preferred to explain the promisee's remedy as being founded on loss suffered by the promisee himself rather than by the building owner. The employer did not get what he bargained for: a building according to the specifications of the contract. It would be 'absurd' if he could not recover substantial damages (measured by the cost of cure) as a result. Thus Lord Goff followed the direction indicated by Lord Griffiths in *St Martins*; and, seen in this light, his reluctance to adhere to a principle 'invented' by him in *The Aliakmon* for taking care of third-party losses was understandable.[324]

Finally, it is important to stress that Lord Clyde, as well, drew comparisons with German law (as did Lord Goff both in the instant case and in his earlier judgment in *White* v. *Jones*). Lord Clyde referred to German law in order to underline that the concept of a contract for the benefit of a third party may provide a satisfactory solution in certain so-called 'homely' examples, for instance in the notorious *Jackson* v. *Horizon Holidays Ltd.*[325] situation.[326] Lord Clyde's comments must be welcomed. For English law, after its overdue abolition of the traditional doctrine of privity, can benefit from the experience that German law has gained by working on this concept over many decades.

A more specific difficulty in applying the principle in *White* v. *Jones* lies in cases of wrongful conception which, while capable of being categorised as instances of the negligent performance of professional service, give rise special considerations of their own. In *Goodwill* v. *British Pregnancy Advisory Service*[327] the plaintiff sued the defendants in negligence for advising her partner that his vasectomy operation had been successful when this was not the case. In reliance on her partner's assertion that they could not have children, she gave up her own contraception arrangements. She subsequently became pregnant and gave birth to a child. Her claim, which was brought in respect of the costs of raising the child, justifiably failed, largely because her relationship with her partner began some time after the operation had been carried out. Under these circumstances, the Court of Appeal held that the defendant owed her no duty of care. According to Thorpe LJ,

> the plaintiff is no nearer the doctor adviser than one who some three and half years after the operation commenced a sexual relationship with his patient... the class to which the plaintiff belongs is in my judgment potentially excessive in size and uncertain in character.[328]

Gibson LJ, on the other hand, thought that it would not be 'fair, just and reasonable' to impose a duty of care and bring this case under the *White* v. *Jones* heading.[329]

As already stated, this is a commendable result. Juridically, however, this result could have been achieved in a more convincing manner if the vague concepts—proximity, and

324 B. S. Markesinis and H. Unberath, *The German Law of Torts: A Comparative Treatise* (4th edn., 2002), 304.

325 [1975] 1 WLR 1468.

326 Cf. Law Com. No. 242, *Contracts for the Benefit of Third Parties* (Cm. 3329, 1996) para. 7.40.

327 [1996] 1 WLR 1397.

328 [1996] 1 WLR 1397, 1406.

329 *Ibid.*, 1403.

the 'fair, just and reasonable' head—used by the learned judges had been avoided. This could have happened if the learned judges had distinguished *Goodwill* from *White* v. *Jones* by stating that in the former the claimant's interests were emphatically not the 'end and aim' of the transaction (the vasectomy operation).[330] To put it differently, if contractual concepts had been available to English law, one would have described the plaintiff in *Goodwill* as an 'incidental' but not the 'intended' beneficiary of the contract and thus easily defeated her claim.

This argument cannot, however, explain the outcome in *MacFarlane* v. *Tayside Health Board*,[331] another case of a failed vasectomy operation which gave rise to an unwanted pregnancy. Here, the claimants were husband and wife; in addition to a claim for pain and suffering endured by the wife during the pregnancy and birth, they brought a claim for the expenses of raising the healthy child to which the wife gave birth. The House of Lords rejected this second claim on policy grounds. According to Lord Steyn, 'the traveller on the Underground would consider that the law of tort has no business to provide legal remedies consequent upon the birth of a healthy child, which all of us regard as a valuable and good thing'.[332] On this basis, he rejected the claim on the 'fair, just and reasonable' ground, as did Lords Slynn and Hope. Other possible arguments against liability—offsetting the emotional and psychological benefits of parenthood against the financial costs of raising the child, or regarding the conception or the subsequent omission to abort the child as an intervening cause—were rejected in favour of this sweeping policy ground. Lords Clyde and Millett would have gone further, also ruling out aspects of the mother's claim for damages for physical harm leading to pain and suffering on grounds related to policy.

The reasoning and outcome in *MacFarlane* were not without difficulty, as subsequent cases showed. In *Parkinson* v. *St James and Seacroft University Hospital NHS Trust*[333] the Court of Appeal upheld a claim for economic loss in a case where the child was born disabled; the parents, it was held, were entitled to recover the additional costs that arose from the child's disability. In the view of the Court of Appeal, the 'fair, just and reasonable' ground did not rule out a duty of care in this case. Then, in *Rees* v. *Darlington Memorial Hospital NHS Trust*,[334] a majority of the Court of Appeal (Waller LJ dissenting) held that a disabled mother could recover for the extra costs she incurred, as a result of her disability, in raising the child. However, this ruling was reversed by a seven-member House of Lords.[335] The majority judges regarded themselves as bound by the policy argument relied on in *MacFarlane*: as Lord Millett put it, the essence of that decision was that 'the House considered it to be morally repugnant to award

330 Cf. *Carr-Glynn* v. *Frearsons (a firm)* [1998] 4 All ER 225.

331 [2000] 2 AC 59; to similar effect is *Greenfield* v. *Irwin* [2001] 1 WLR 1279. On these cases see T. Weir, 'The Unwanted Child' [2000] *CLJ* 238; M. Jones, 'Bringing Up Baby' (2001) 9 *Tort LR* 14; O. Radley-Gardner, 'Wrongful Birth Revisited' (2002) 118 *LQR* 11.

332 [2000] 2 AC 59, 82.

333 [2002] QB 266; see also the earlier Court of Appeal decision in *Emeh* v. *Kensington and Chelsea and Westminster AHA* [1985] QB 1012.

334 [2002] 2 WLR 1483.

335 [2004] 1 AC 309.

damages for the birth of a healthy child'.[336] Lord Bingham, more prosaically, suggested that had the House of Lords decided *MacFarlane* differently, 'it is . . . hard to think that . . . its decision would have long survived the first award to well-to-do parents of the estimated cost of providing private education, presents, clothing and foreign holidays (even if at no more expensive a level than the parents had provided for earlier, wanted children) against a National Health Service found to be responsible, by its negligence for the birth of the child'.[337] To allow an exception to *MacFarlane* in a case where the mother was disabled would open up 'anomalies' of the kind pointed out by Waller LJ in his dissent in the Court of Appeal:[338] according to Lord Millett, 'ordinary people would feel uncomfortable that a disabled person should recover the costs of looking after a healthy child when a person not suffering from a disability who through no fault of her own was no better able to look after such a child could not'.[339] The majority nevertheless went on to hold that it was appropriate to award the claimant a 'conventional sum' of £15,000, to represent the denial of the mother's right 'to live her life in the way that she wished and planned'.[340]

The basis for making this award was that the defendant, while not liable for the costs of raising the child, remained liable, on normal tort law grounds, for the pain and suffering attendant on the pregnancy and birth as well as for associated expenses and financial losses. In other words the 'conventional sum' awarded in *Rees* is simply an aspect of the claim for damages for the consequences of the physical harm suffered by the mother. As Lord Bingham put it, the conventional award in such a case 'would not be, and would not be intended to be, compensatory . . . But it would not be a nominal, let alone, a derisory award. It would afford some measure of recognition of the wrong done.'[341]

The minority judges in Rees argued that policy reasons pointed to the need to qualify *MacFarlane* in a case where the mother was disabled: '[b]y allowing the seriously disabled parent to recover the extra costs of child-rearing which are due to her disability the law will be doing its best to enable her to perform this task on equal terms with those who are not affected by the impairment'.[342] They also argued that the conventional award proposed by the majority was contrary to authority and went beyond 'limits to permissible creativity for judges'.[343] Following the judgments in *Rees*, the status of *Parkinson* (the case of the child born disabled) is unclear: each of the minority judges supported the outcome in that case, while Lord Millett, in the majority, expressly left the point open; the other three majority judges expressed doubt about the *Parkinson* result.

MacFarlane and *Rees* are arguably no different from other cases involving the negligent performance of a service: the claim arose from the very category of loss which it was the purpose of the service in question (the vasectomy operation or sterilisation) to prevent. Reflection may suggest that it is difficult to find a principled legal basis for

336 *Ibid.*, 345.
337 *Ibid.*, 316.
338 [2003] QB 20, 34–5
339 [2004] 1 AC 309, 349.
340 *Ibid.*, 317 (Lord Bingham).
341 *Ibid.*, 317.
342 *Ibid.*, 332 (Lord Hope).
343 *Ibid.*, 328 (Lord Steyn).

the outcome in these cases, which perhaps is why the courts have had to fall back on open-ended policy justifications of the kind (dubiously) associated with the notion of 'distributive justice'. Many other European systems have acknowledged the possibility of liability in this kind of situation, particularly where the child is born disabled.[344] After decisions such as *Fairchild* v. *Glenhaven Funeral Services Ltd.*[345] it is no longer fanciful to suggest that our supreme court may well be interested in the views taken on such 'world issues' by other, major legal systems. But it is also likely that the philosophical predisposition of individual judges will, in the end, win the day, even if it is thinly disguised by reference to Aristotle or the 'person in the Underground'. This is an aspect of tort law which, it is submitted, neither students nor practitioners have adequately studied; but this is not the place to try to address it in any detail.

(iii) Pure Economic Loss Arising from Defects in Buildings and Products

As we have seen, potential liability for articles which actually cause personal injury or damage to property is not in doubt following *Donoghue* v. *Stevenson*.[346] There is, on the other hand, no liability in tort for producing an article which is found to be merely defective, and therefore worth less than the claimant paid for it; the claimant will have to depend on contract for compensation in such cases. After a period of some uncertainty, this rule was clearly reasserted in *Murphy* v. *Brentwood District Council*.[347]

An intermediate category arises where an article is both defective and *dangerous*. Can the owner of the article recover from the producer the costs of alleviating the risk of danger or, alternatively, the loss in value as a result of ceasing to use the article? Following *Murphy* the answer is almost certainly not: these losses are characterised as pure economic loss and therefore as outside the range of recovery, just as much as those which arise where an article is merely defective.[348]

English law has reached this position as a result of *Murphy* overruling the potentially wide-ranging (and somewhat ambiguous) decision of the House of Lords in *Anns* v. *Merton London Borough Council*.[349] A principal difficulty facing the courts after *Anns* was the correct characterisation of the damage in that case. The action was brought against the council by the occupiers of the properties in question who had bought houses on long leases in ignorance of the defective foundations. Lord Wilberforce

[344] For a full comparative discussion see B. S. Markesinis and H. Unberath, *The German Law of Torts: A Comparative Treatise* (4th edn., 2002), especially 178–91 and 194–8.

[345] [2003] 1 AC 32.

[346] [1932] AC 562.

[347] [1991] 1 AC 398. See also *Invercargill CC* v. *Hamlin* [1996] AC 624, in which the Privy Council took a somewhat different approach to the issue of relational economic loss in the context of an appeal from New Zealand.

[348] In *East River Steamship Corp.* v. *Transamerica Deleval Inc.*, 476 US 858 (1986), the US Supreme Court rejected a claim for pure economic loss arising from a defective product, but this was not viewed as a case of a *dangerously defective* product and may be of doubtful relevance in *Murphy*, despite being cited by Lord Keith as authority for the general exclusionary rule. On the *East River* case generally see the discussion in ch. 5, below. See also the decision of the Supreme Court of Canada in *Rivtow Marine Ltd.* v. *Washington Iron Works* [1974] SCR 1189, discussed below.

[349] [1978] AC 728.

referred to their loss as 'material, physical damage'.[350] For reasons that are now generally accepted, however, it cannot be said that they suffered property damage, since at the time they entered into their leases the damage to the structure of the houses had already occurred. As Deane J of the High Court of Australia explained in *Sutherland Shire Council* v. *Heyman*:

the only property, which could be said to have been damaged in such a case, is the building, itself. The building itself could not be said to have been subjected to 'material, physical damage' by reason merely of the inadequacy of its foundations since the building never existed otherwise than with its foundations in that state. Moreover, even if the inadequacy of its foundations could be seen as physical, material damage to the building, it would be damage to property in which a future purchaser or tenant had no interest at all at the time when it occurred.[351]

Lord Keith adopted this passage in *Murphy*.[352] In that case a house was built with a defective concrete raft foundation which began to crack, fracturing a gas pipe and causing other structural faults to occur. The plaintiff, who had bought the house new from the original builders, was unable to carry out the necessary repairs and sold the house for £35,000 less than its market value without the defects. His cause of action, according to the members of the House of Lords, originated in this economic loss, and not in the defects in either the raft or the pipes. If it could not be accurately characterised as property damage, the loss in *Anns* might nevertheless be described as economic loss consequential upon the threat to health and safety posed by the defective foundations. In *Anns* Lord Wilberforce said,

what is recoverable is the amount of expenditure necessary to restore the dwelling to a condition in which it is no longer a danger to the health or safety of persons occupying and possibly (depending on the circumstances) expenses arising from the necessary displacement.[353]

Likewise, in *Peabody Donation Fund* v. *Sir Lindsay Parkinson & Co.*, Lord Keith spoke of damages 'as representing expenditure necessary to avert injury to safety and health'.[354]

This notion of damages as 'preventive' compensation has not, however, survived *Murphy*, and it is arguable, in retrospect, that it did not add much to the clarification of the issues at stake. It allowed a link with physical harm to be maintained without there being a clear acceptance that mitigation or prevention of this kind did not affect the nature of the loss but simply made the recovery of the expenditure more justifiable in policy terms. In *Murphy* the correct identification of the loss as 'purely economic', was, for Lord Keith, of itself enough to cast fatal doubt on *Anns*. According to his Lordship:

It is difficult to draw a distinction in principle between an article which is useless or valueless and one which suffers from a defect which would render it dangerous in use but which is discovered by the purchaser in time to avert any possibility of injury. The purchaser may incur expense in putting right the defect, or, more probably, discard the article. In either case the loss is purely economic.[355]

350 *Ibid.*, 759.
351 (1985) 60 ALR 1, 60–1.
352 [1991] 1 AC 398, 468.
353 [1978] AC 728, 759.
354 [1985] AC 210, 242.
355 [1991] 1 AC 398, 470.

If an action for 'preventive' economic loss was allowed, there was, according to Lord Keith, nothing to stop courts extending liability to cover merely defective products, and 'that would open on an exceedingly wide range of claims'.[356] In similar vein Lord Oliver described the suggested distinction as 'fallacious'.[357] Although there are strong arguments on the other side,[358] *Murphy* has settled the question, at least for the time being.

While the rulings in *Anns* and *Murphy* were immediately concerned with the question of the liability of local authorities for the consequences of failure to inspect building foundations, they also extended to the liability of builders for defective premises and to that of manufacturers for defective products. *Murphy* was applied to deny a claim in tort for pure economic loss by a commercial owner against the original builder in *Department of the Environment* v. *Thomas Bates & Sons*;[359] and it implicitly confirmed two earlier decisions on manufacturers' liability. Thus, in *Muirhead* v. *Industrial Tank Specialities Ltd.*[360] a manufacturer of an electrical pump was liable for property damage incurred by the ultimate user when the pump, which was used to aerate his lobster tanks, failed to work as intended. But the manufacturer was held not liable for loss of profits for the period when the tanks were out of action. In *Simaan General Contracting* v. *Pilkington Glass (No. 2)*[361] the plaintiff had no action for economic losses arising from a defect of quality caused by a subcontractor; he was limited to his rights against the main contractor. To similar effect is the Scottish case of *Scott Lithgow Ltd.* v. *GEC Electrical Projects Ltd.*[362]

The House of Lords in *Murphy* also cast doubt on the 'complex structure theory', which had been canvassed in the earlier case of *D. & F. Estates* v. *Church Commissioners of England* [363] as a way out of the difficulties created by *Anns*. In *D. & F. Estates* Lord Bridge maintained that: 'it may well be arguable that in the case of complex structures . . . one element of the structure should be regarded . . . as distinct from another element so that damage to one part of the structure caused by a hidden defect in another may qualify to be treated as damage to "other property"'.[364] If this argument had been accepted, it could have been applied both to chattels (e.g. a car with defective brakes, the failure of which causes the vehicle to crash) and to buildings (e.g. defective foundations, which cause cracks to appear in the roof and walls of the house). In *Murphy*, however, both Lord Bridge and Lord Oliver rejected this theory as 'artificial'.[365]

356 [1991] 1 AC 398, 469.

357 *Ibid.*, 488.

358 See Sir Robin Cooke, 'An Impossible Distinction?' (1991) 107 *LQR* 46, and R. O'Dair, 'A House Built on Firm Foundations?' (1991) 54 *MLR* 561, both discussing American law and its use in *Murphy*.

359 [1991] 1 AC 499; to similar effect are a number of more recent cases including *Samuel Payne* v. *John Setchell Ltd.* [2002] BLR 489; *Mirant-Asia Pacific* v. *OAPIL* [2004] EWHC 1750; *Horbury Building Systems Ltd.* v. *Hampden Insurance NV* [2004] EWCA Civ. 418; and *Holding and Management (Solitaire) Ltd.* v. *Ideal Homes North West Ltd.* [2004] EWHC 2408.

360 [1986] QB 507.

361 [1988] QB 758.

362 1992 SLT 244.

363 [1989] 1 AC 177.

364 *Ibid.*, 207.

365 [1991] 1 AC 398, 470 (Lord Keith), 476–9 (Lord Bridge).

The matter does not quite end there, as the judgments in *Murphy* contain a number of references to 'exceptional' instances of liability which bear a certain resemblance to the complex-structure idea. Lord Bridge gave the examples of subcontractors fitting a boiler which subsequently catches fire and burns the building in which it is installed, and of electrical wiring which is defectively installed with the same result. Lords Keith and Jauncey gave similar examples. Lord Oliver, on the other hand, expressed some scepticism about the idea.[366] In the examples given by Lords Keith, Bridge and Jauncey, the existence of an action appears to depend upon the factor that responsibility for the separate parts of the building rests with different persons. It is not clear whether it is also necessary to have regard to the degree of integration of the subcontractor's work into the whole, or the feasibility of physically separating the different components.[367] The incoherence of these apparent exceptions makes it unlikely that much can be made of them in future. Thus in *Bellefield Computer Services Ltd.* v. *E. Turner & Sons Ltd.*[368] the Court of Appeal took the view that it was bound by *Murphy* to reject the complex-structure theory, and to disallow a claim for damage to a building caused by a fire which, thanks to the negligent failure of the defendant builder to construct an effective firebreak, was much worse than it would have otherwise been. It was with some embarrassment that, at the same time as rejecting the claim for damage to the structure, the court allowed a claim for plant and equipment which was damaged in the same fire; Schiemann LJ wondered 'whether if, for instance, the present case had preceded *Murphy*, the principled parts of the speeches would have been expressed differently'.[369]

But the greatest problem to arise from the rejection of liability in *Murphy* is the question where this leaves the principle enunciated in *Hedley Byrne*. As already noted, not only is *Hedley Byrne* still good law; its *ratio* is also apparently capable of being extended to cover cases which, on first sight, seem to have little connection with negligent misstatements. One such case is (the earlier case of) *Pirelli General Cable Works Ltd.* v. *Oscar Faber & Partners*,[370] in which the owners of a factory site sued consulting engineers who were responsible for the defective design and construction of a chimney on the site. The chimney had to be partially demolished and replaced when the material chosen by the defendants for its inner lining proved to be inappropriate, causing cracks in the chimney's structure. The judges who decided *Pirelli* clearly regarded the damage in question as physical damage to the structure of the chimney; however, according to Lord Keith in *Murphy*, the loss should properly be regarded as economic. Since the defendants had been employed to advise on the choice of the material and design structure of the chimney, *Pirelli* should be seen as coming within the scope of *Hedley Byrne*. Lord Keith also suggested that *Junior Books* v. *Veitchi Co.*[371] could be seen as a

366 *Ibid.*, 470 (Lord Keith), 478 (Lord Bridge), 497 (Lord Jauncey), 489 (Lord Oliver).

367 For discussion, see I. N. Duncan Wallace, '*Anns* beyond Repair' (1991) 107 *LQR* 228, 235.

368 [2000] BLR 97; I. N. Duncan Wallace, '*Donoghue* v. *Stevenson* and "Complex Structure": *Anns* Revisited?' (2000) 116 *LQR* 530.

369 [2000] BLR 97, 104. See also the discussion of the *Bellefield* case in *Offer-Hoare* v. *Larkstore Ltd.* [2005] EWCA 2742, at paras. 87–8.

370 [1983] 2 AC 1.

371 [1983] AC 520; see above, Section 2.

Hedley Byrne case.[372] All of which brings us back to Professor Stapleton's point, namely that all these major cases have complex juridical elements which can easily place them in one category instead of another and thus alter the ultimate result. How does the judge decide which pigeonhole is appropriate? And are we back again to Lord Mustill's view (discussed in Chapter 2) that, consciously or unconsciously, the judge decides first and then searches for the most suitable justification?

The effect of all this is that while under *Murphy*[373] the careless builder is free of liability for economic loss in tort, consulting engineers, architects or surveyors who carelessly give poor advice to site-owners or purchasers of property may face liability under *Hedley Byrne*. This is an odd result for a number of reasons. First, the elements of reliance and proximity are just as likely to be present in the one case as in the other. Second, there seems to be no good reason from the point of view of policy for imposing a more extensive duty of care for negligent speech than for negligent conduct or, if there is, this reason has not been stated. Third, the distinction between careless words and careless acts is difficult to draw in practice, as *Pirelli* illustrates. Was that case really about negligent advice, or was it simply an illustration of a service that was negligently performed? Lord Keith's explanation of *Pirelli* as an instance of negligent misstatement seems to be a rather opportunistic, *ex post* rationalisation of the earlier decision. His placing of *Junior Books* in the same category also contradicts his own earlier judgment in *Junior Books* where he had said that *Hedley Byrne* was not in point.[374]

It is doubtful whether the notion of reliance, as developed in the *Hedley Byrne* line of cases, can adequately account for these distinctions. Reliance 'is an extremely slippery concept [which] is unlikely to provide a secure foundation for a coherent development of the law'.[375] These difficulties are clearly illustrated by *Nitrigin Eireann Teoranta* v. *Inco Alloys Ltd*.[376] In that case the defendants manufactured and supplied to the plaintiffs some alloy steel tubing which turned out to be defective. The plaintiffs discovered cracking in the structure of which the tubing formed part, but could not identify the cause. The tubing then ruptured, causing an explosion and resulting in damage to the plaintiffs' chemical works. The judge held that this was not a case of liability under *Hedley Byrne*: the cause of action in tort (as opposed to contract) accrued only when the explosion took place and caused physical damage to the plant. This was because the manufacture and supply of the component did not bring the parties into a special pre-tort relationship of the kind required for *Hedley Byrne* liability. Although the defendants were specialist manufacturers who could be taken to have known of the plaintiffs' particular requirements, 'that is neither a professional relationship in the sense in which the law treats professional negligence nor a *Hedley Byrne* relationship'.[377]

372 [1991] 1 AC 398, 466. See generally E. McKendrick, '*Pirelli* Re-Examined' (1991) 11 *Leg. Stud.* 326.

373 And the earlier House of Lords decision of *D. & F. Estates* v. *Church Commissioners for England* [1989] 1 AC 177.

374 [1980] 1 AC 520, 535. See N. J. Mullany, 'Limitation of Actions: Where Are We Now?' [1993] *LMCLQ* 34, 36.

375 McKendrick, '*Pirelli* Re-Examined' (1991) 11 *Leg. Stud.* at 332.

376 [1992] 1 All ER 854.

377 *Ibid.*, 860.

While this must be correct, it seems to follow that, in the absence of liability for pure economic loss caused by dangerously defective products, had the plaintiffs discovered the cause of the cracking before the explosion took place and had then taken steps to remove the danger, they could not have recovered for this expenditure. In this way *Murphy* creates a powerful disincentive to take the necessary precautions to avoid both property damage and potential danger to life and limb. This result may appear to some as 'logical', once the nature of the damage is correctly identified; but it can be reconciled only with difficulty with the important aim of minimising the net costs of accidents and of accident prevention.[378]

It seems unlikely that the House of Lords could reconsider in the near future the sweeping nature of the *Murphy* ruling, and insert into it the important distinction between merely defective products and those which are dangerous. At best it is possible that the apparent exceptions to the rule against recovery mentioned in the judgments of Lords Keith, Bridge and Jauncey could be developed in favour of a claimant who takes steps to mitigate likely future damage. From a doctrinal point of view, however, this would be less than completely satisfactory. In *Rivtow Marine Ltd.* v. *Washington Iron Works*[379] the Supreme Court of Canada, over a strong dissent by Laskin J who would have granted recovery, rejected a claim for expenditure to remedy a dangerous defect in a crane. But it did allow the plaintiff's claim on the more limited ground that the defendants had breached an implied duty to warn the plaintiff of the defect in question. This precise point did not arise in *Murphy* or in *Inco Alloys*, but, given some of the broad *dicta* (examined above) against economic-loss recovery in non-*Hedley Byrne* situations, it has long seemed unlikely that even the majority judgment in *Rivtow* would not be followed in England, and this has now been confirmed by the Court of Appeal in *The Rebecca Elaine*.[380]

(iv) Relational Economic Loss Arising from Damage to the Property of a Third Party

This category of cases concerns the situation in which the claimant suffers economic loss by virtue of damage caused by the defendant to the property of a third party with whom the claimant is in some kind of relationship, contractual or otherwise. The normal rule is that relational losses of this kind are not recoverable: the claimant must show damage to *his* property before he can recover anything. As recently restated by Lord Brandon in *The Aliakmon*,[381] there is a long line of authority for a principle of law that, in order to enable a person to claim in negligence for loss caused to him by reason of loss of or damage to property, he must have had either the legal ownership or

[378] See generally A. Grubb and A. Mullis, 'An Unfair Law for Dangerous Products: The Fall of *Anns*' [1991] *Conv.* 225.

[379] [1974] SCR 1189.

[380] *Hamble Fisheries Ltd.* v. *L. Gardner & Sons Ltd., The Rebecca Elaine* [1999] 2 Lloyd's Rep. 1; to similar effect is *Amiri Flight Authority* v. *BAE Systems plc* [2003] EWCA Civ. 1447.

[381] [1986] AC 785, 809, recently reaffirmed and applied by the HL in *Owners of Cargo Lately Laden on Board the Ship or Vessel 'Starsin'* v. *Owners and/or Demise Charterers of the Ship or Vessel 'Starsin'* [2003] UKHL 12. On the relevant US law, see *Robins Dry Dock & Repair Co.* v. *Flint*, 275 US 303 (1927), discussed in ch. 5 below.

a possessory title to the property concerned at the time when the loss or damage occurred, and it is not enough to have had only contractual rights in relation to such property which have been adversely affected by the loss of or damage to it.

This is the prime example of a 'bright line rule' which aims to place a clear limit on tort recovery in the interests of certainty. As LaForest J of the Supreme Court of Canada put it, 'since most claims of this nature occur in the commercial area, the requisite certainty should exist before the accidents occur'.[382] The rule is also justified by the argument that those with merely relational interests of this kind should be encouraged to protect themselves by a contract with the property owner (with whom they may be in a pre-existing relationship). They should thus be discouraged from relying on a tort claim, on the basis that allocation of liability and adjustments of risk may most easily take place between parties who are already in a proximate economic relationship.

An example of rights over property falling short of rights of ownership or possession was provided in *The Mineral Transporter*.[383] Time charterers of a ship who suffered economic loss when it was out of action following a collision were unable to recover in tort for their loss, since at the time of the collision they had no possessory right in the ship, having merely a right to its use under the terms of the sub-charter. Similarly, in *The Aliakmon* goods being shipped by sea were damaged by the carelessness of the carrier, with the result that the buyer suffered a financial loss equivalent to the difference between the contract price and the value of the goods when he took possession of them. At the time the damage occurred the goods were still owned by the seller but they were at the risk of the buyer—that is to say, he was required by the contract of sale to take the goods and to pay the full price for them regardless of damage. The buyer sued the carrier in tort for the resulting loss but the action failed precisely because he had no possessory right in relation to the goods when the damage occurred.

The facts of *The Aliakmon* were rather unusual: the initial cost-and-freight contract[384] for the sale of the goods had been varied to give the buyer more time to pay, with the seller retaining ownership of the goods until he did. The buyer would normally have sued the carrier in contract by virtue of holding the shipping documents, but he had pledged these back to the seller as security for the price. Under these circumstances

382 LaForest J, in *Canadian National Railway* v. *Norsk Pacific Steamship Co.* (1992) 91 DLR (4th) 289, 337. For further support for the rule against recovery in relational cases, see B. Feldthusen, 'Pure Economic Loss in the High Court of Australia: Reinventing the Square Wheel?' (Select Bibliography), criticising the decision of the High Court in *Perre* v. *Apand Pty. Ltd.* (1999) 198 CLR 180 for failing to pay sufficient attention to the different categories of economic loss claim.

383 [1986] AC 1.

384 A cost-and-freight contract and (slightly different) a cost-insurance-freight contract are specialised types of contract for the international sale of goods, under which the seller undertakes to transfer certain shipping documents to the buyer while the goods are in transit. Normally the risk passes to the buyer on shipment, but the transfer of documents gives him rights of action against the carrier for any negligence and also the benefit of the insurance policy covering the goods. This correspondence of risk and rights of action broke down in *The Aliakmon* for the reasons explained in the text. On international sales contracts generally see R. Goode, *Commercial Law* (3rd edn., 2004), chs. 32–6. *The Aliakmon* overruled *The Irene's Success* [1982] QB 481, but cf. *Triangle Steel & Supply Co.* v. *Korean United Lines Ltd.* (1986) 63 BCLR 66 (Sup. C. of BC declining to follow *The Aliakmon*).

Lord Brandon considered that the normal exclusionary rule had to apply: the buyer should have protected himself by contracting for the seller to assign to him any rights of action he might have against the carrier for negligence. However, the seller would have had no significant contract action to assign: since he was entitled to full payment of the price from the buyer, he would not have suffered any loss and would therefore have been unable to sue the carrier for contract damages. Lord Brandon's decision effectively means that the carrier was liable to neither the seller nor the buyer for the consequences of his negligence.[385] On this particular point of maritime law the effect of the House of Lords' decision has now been reversed by statute,[386] but the decision remains of importance for the wider issue of tort law that it decided.

The exclusionary rule has been applied in a number of other contexts. Claimants failing to recover have thus included a contractor unable to complete a building job when the defendant flooded the land he was working on,[387] a tug owner who lost a valuable towage contract when the defendant damaged and sank the ship he was towing,[388] and insurers who were required to pay out when the defendant sank and damaged a ship they had insured.[389] These decisions were reaffirmed in *Spartan Steel & Alloys Ltd.* v. *Martin & Co. (Contractors) Ltd.*,[390] where the defendant contractors carelessly cut through a cable supplying electricity to an industrial estate, with the result that the plaintiff steelmakers had to shut down production for a period. The plaintiffs were able to recover for damage actually inflicted to their property, namely to the materials that were being mixed in the furnace at the time of the power cut and which had to be removed at a loss before the melt could be completed. However, they were unable to recover the net profits from the four further melts that they would have normally carried out during the period when the electricity was cut off; these losses were purely economic in nature.

A recognised exception to this rule of non-recovery in tort arises out of the maritime-law principle of 'general average contribution'. This is a device for pooling risk, under which owners of goods in a ship's hold undertake in advance to pay a proportion of the costs of any damage caused to the cargo during the voyage, regardless of whether their own share of the cargo is damaged. In *The Greystoke Castle*,[391] the House of Lords held that cargo-owners in this position were engaged in a 'joint venture' which made it appropriate for those whose property was undamaged, and whose loss was therefore merely economic, to recover this amount from the defendant responsible for the

385 See B. S. Markesinis, 'An Expanding Tort Law: The Price of a Rigid Contract Law' (1987) 103 *LQR* 359, for extensive discussion.

386 Carriage of Goods by Sea Act 1992. The main impetus, however, to change the law and pass the Act was not the decision in *The Aliakmon* but difficulties arising from modern forms of carriage, in particular the carriage of goods in bulk. On this see F. M. B. Reynolds, 'The Significance of Tort in Claims in Respect of Carriage by Sea' [1986] *LMCLQ* 97.

387 *Cattle* v. *Stockton Waterworks* (1875) LR 10 QB 453.

388 *SA de Rémorquage à Hélice* v. *Bennetts* [1911] 1 KB 243.

389 *Simpson & Co.* v. *Thomson* (1887) 3 App. Cas. 279.

390 [1973] 1 QB 27.

391 [1947] AC 265.

collision. However, the notion of a joint venture between the property owner and those with a relational interest in the property has not been extended beyond this specific case.

Although the English courts have consistently rejected attempts to circumvent the exclusionary rule in cases of this kind, a more flexible approach has been adopted elsewhere in the Commonwealth. In *Caltex Oil (Australia) Pty. Ltd.* v. *Dredge Willemstad*,[392] the defendants negligently damaged an oil pipeline belonging to a third party. The plaintiffs, who made use of the pipeline, incurred losses by virtue of the need to make alternative arrangements for transporting their oil. The High Court of Australia allowed an action for damages. A number of potential bases for the decision were advanced in the judgments of the High Court. One of the most important was the 'known plaintiff' principle, to the effect that recovery is permissible where the claimant is foreseeable as an *identifiable individual* who would be likely to suffer the loss in question. This deals with the problem of indeterminate liability, and could have led to a different result in *Spartan Steel*[393] if the plaintiff had been the only user affected by the rupture of the cable. In general, though, the 'known plaintiff ' exception creates the paradox that the more extensive the harm caused by the defendant, the less likely he is to be liable, and for this reason it has not been generally accepted as sufficient basis for determining the existence of a duty of care.

The relevant policy and doctrinal arguments were fully analysed in the decision of the Canadian Supreme Court in *Canadian National Railway* v. *Norsk Pacific Steamship Co.*[394] The Supreme Court allowed, by the barest of majorities,[395] an action where the defendant's steamship negligently collided with a railway bridge spanning the River Fraser in British Columbia, causing the plaintiff, the main user of the bridge, expenditure for rerouting its trains while the bridge was being repaired. The bridge was owned by a public-works commission, which entered into contracts for its use with several companies of which the plaintiff was the predominant one, accounting for over 80 per cent of the use of the bridge. The majority judgment of McLachlin J emphasised the strong element of proximity in this situation and the absence of dangers associated with the 'floodgates' argument: the plaintiff's 'position for practical purposes, *vis-à-vis* the tortfeasor, is indistinguishable from that of the owner of the damaged property'.[396]

The difficulty with this approach lies in the use made of the concept of proximity, which, according to LaForest J's dissenting opinion in *Norsk*, is too vague to support a departure from the normal rule of non-liability.[397] Nor is it clear why liability should rest upon whether the plaintiff is individually ascertainable or one of a very small class, or in some kind of physical propinquity to the defendant. While these may be relevant factors in rebutting the 'floodgates' argument, they do not provide in themselves an

392 [1976] 136 CLR 529.

393 [1973] 1 QB 27.

394 (1991) 91 DLR (4th) 289.

395 Stevenson J issued an opinion concurring in the result but offering different reasons from those of McLachlin, L'Heureux-Dubé and Cory JJ. LaForest, Sopinka and Iacobucci JJ dissented.

396 (1992) 91 DLR (4th) 289, 376.

397 See the discussion above, Section 2(b).

independent justification for allowing recovery; something more is needed. On the other hand, if it can be shown that the plaintiff rather than the defendant was in the best position to minimise or avert the loss,[398] policy factors could justify rejecting the plaintiff's claim if the case is otherwise evenly balanced. In *Norsk* the plaintiff could have sought better protection against the risk of damage to the bridge in its contract with the owner. As it was, this contract specifically provided that the railway company was to have no right of indemnity from the public-works commission for the costs of diverting traffic in the event that the bridge was closed for repairs. There is a strong argument for saying that, in these circumstances, the court should have let the loss lie where it fell, and that a tort action would upset the allocation of risk which the exemption clauses in the contract between the railway and the public-works commission embodied. As LaForest J put it: 'In contracts between sophisticated parties such as those in [*Norsk*], who are well advised by counsel, such exclusions of liability often result from determinations regarding who is in the best position to insure the risk at the lowest cost.'[399]

(v) Overlapping and Concurrent Duties in Contract and Tort

A theme which runs throughout the cases examined so far concerns the difficulties which arise when a given duty situation could be governed by obligations in either contract or tort. The degree to which tort duties should be shaped or perhaps negated altogether by contract is one with which the courts have had to grapple from the time *Donoghue* v. *Stevenson* began the modern expansion of the tort of negligence. As far as physical injury and damage to property are concerned, the position is now fairly clear: the law imposes a general duty of care in tort based not upon the breach of an undertaking or promise but upon failure to comply with an objective standard of care. In *Donoghue* v. *Stevenson* Lord Macmillan explained this principle in the following important passage:

> Where, as in cases like the present, so much depends upon the avenue of approach to the question, it is very easy to take the wrong turning. If you begin with the sale by the manufacturer to the retail dealer, then the consumer who purchases from the retailer is at once seen to be a stranger to the contract between the retailer and manufacturer and so disentitled to sue upon it. There is no contractual relation between the manufacturer and the consumer, and thus the plaintiff if he is to succeed is driven to try to bring himself within one or other of the exceptional cases.... If, on the other hand, you disregard the fact that the circumstances of the case at one stage include the existence of a contract of sale between the manufacturer and the retailer and approach the question by asking whether there is evidence of carelessness on the part of the manufacturer and whether he owed a duty to be careful in a question with the party who has been injured in consequence of his want of care, the circumstance that the injured party was not a party to the incidental contract of sale becomes irrelevant and his title to sue the manufacturer is unaffected by this circumstance.[400]

[398] Either by making alternative arrangements in advance or by taking out loss insurance.

[399] LaForest J at (1992) 91 DLR (4th) 289, 302.

[400] [1932] AC 562, 611. The passage is discussed by Lord Mustill writing extra-judicially, in 'Negligence in the World of Finance' (1992) 5 *The Supreme Court Journal* 1.

This was Lord Macmillan's answer to the dissenting judges, who argued that as the appellant was a stranger to the contracts for the manufacture and sale of the article, she could have no cause of action. If the manufacturer undertook any duties in respect of his products, these were confined to the contracts he had with his distributors. Thus to grant recovery to the ultimate consumer, with whom he had no contractual link, was in Lord Buckmaster's words 'simply to misapply to tort doctrines applicable to sale and purchase'.[401] In rejecting this point the majority effectively reversed the priority of contract over tort: at least where physical loss is concerned, the presence alongside a duty of care of a contract setting a narrower obligation becomes, in Lord Macmillan's word, 'irrelevant' to the tort action. Subsequent cases decided that the defendant can in certain circumstances protect himself against liability in tort by expressly contracting with the plaintiff for the benefit of an exclusion or limitation clause, or, in the case of occupiers' liability, by bringing such a restriction of liability to the claimant's notice.[402] Yet even this possibility is now subject to regulation by the Unfair Contract Terms Act 1977.

With pure economic or financial loss it is a different matter; for reasons analysed above it is not possible to place it on a par with physical damage, and there may be good arguments for allowing the rules of contract to prevail over tort in allocating legal responsibility. The first situation to consider here is that in which the parties were brought into a pre-tort relationship of proximity as a result of entering into a contract with each other. If tort is allowed to dictate the outcome of a claim for damages after the event, the parties' capacity to make their own allocation of risk in advance, and set the price accordingly, may be seriously undermined. The contract may indeed have set a different standard of care from that of liability for negligence, or have specified more or less precise obligations than those which tort law would impose upon the parties. Contract damages are calculated on different principles from those applicable to tort, and the limitation periods for bringing an action also differ. The price paid for the service or performance in question is likely to have reflected these factors. Particularly in commercial transactions between business entities, then, the courts should respect the parties' own choice of contractual form. This appears to be what Lord Scarman had in mind in *Tai Hing Cotton Mill Ltd.* v. *Liu Chong Hing Bank Ltd.*[403] In that case, speaking on behalf of the Privy Council, he said that in a case concerning the relationship between banker and customer:

> their Lordships believe it to be correct to adhere to the contractual analysis: on principle because it is a relationship in which the parties have, subject to a few exceptions, the right to determine their obligations to each other, and for the avoidance of confusion because different consequences do follow according to whether liability arises from contract or tort...

For these reasons the failure of the parties to agree upon a particular contract term may constitute good grounds for the court to refuse to impose a duty of care where that would have an equivalent effect to the missing term. This would be giving the claimant

[401] [1932] AC 562, 577 (Lord Buckmaster).
[402] *Ashdown* v. *Samuel Williams* [1957] 1 QB 504.
[403] [1986] AC 80, 107.

the benefit of a term which he had been unable to insert into the contract through negotiation. In *Greater Nottingham Co-operative Society* v. *Cementation Piling and Foundation Ltd.*[404] the owner of a site sued a subcontractor for negligence in the course of construction. Although the action was brought in tort, the parties had already agreed a contract for the work in question, which contained undertakings by the subcontractor as to the quality of the basic design and the materials to be used. But no warranty as to the standard of the actual building work had been given. The court refused to imply a duty of care to meet the absence of a contractual remedy.

This principle has also been applied in cases concerning the employment relationship and the relationship between a school and one of its pupils. In *Reid* v. *Rush and Tompkins Ltd.*[405] an employee sued his employer for failing to advise him to take out insurance cover for a period of work overseas. The employee had been injured in a car accident in Ethiopia while in the course of his employment. His claim was not for the injuries he suffered but for his economic loss. This resulted from the fact that while overseas he was not covered by the employer's insurance and, in the absence of any scheme of residual liability insurance such as that provided for the United Kingdom by the Motor Insurers' Bureau, was left to bear the financial costs of his injury. Nor was he able to bring an action against the driver whose carelessness was responsible for his injuries. His claim against his employer failed because, according to Ralph Gibson LJ, it was not open to the court to impose a duty of care which was not 'contained in any express or implied term of the contract'. Similarly, in *Scally* v. *Southern Health and Social Services Board*[406] the House of Lords held that an employer's duty to inform his employees about their rights to certain financial benefits under the complex provisions of a pension scheme arose, if at all, in contract. But there was no duty of care in tort. *Van Oppen* v. *Trustees of Bedford School*[407] was another case concerning a failure to extend insurance cover, in this case arising out of a rugby accident which left a school student disabled. It was held that in the absence of any express undertaking the school owed no duty in tort to extend its insurance to cover students in this way.

These last three decisions are open to the criticism that it may be unrealistic to expect employees, on the one hand, or the parents of school students, on the other, to enter into contractual bargaining on this kind of matter. These are contracts in which the employer or the school frequently imposes the terms but no individual bargaining takes place. The presumption of a rough equilibrium of bargaining power, which the courts are prepared to make in cases involving business entities such as *Tai Hing*, simply does not hold here. The view that contractual allocations of risk will necessarily be efficient has been said by McLachlin J of the Supreme Court of Canada to rest on a series of 'questionable assumptions', including the assumption that all parties to a transaction share an equality of bargaining power, which will result in the effective allocation of risk. It is not considered that certain parties who control the situation (e.g. the owners of an indispensable bridge) may refuse to indemnify against the negligence of those over whom they have no

404 [1989] QB 71.
405 [1990] 1 WLR 212.
406 [1991] ICR 771.
407 [1990] 1 WLR 235.

control, or may demand such an exorbitant premium for this indemnification that it would be more cost effective for the innocent victim to insure itself.[408]

Arguably, similar considerations are relevant in a situation where the claimant is relying on the defendant for advice, or is relying on his professional expertise in the performance of a service. In these circumstance, the decision of the House of Lords in *Henderson* v. *Merrett Syndicates Ltd.*[409] shows that a duty of care in respect of pure economic loss can coexist with a complex matrix of contractual obligations. In that case, relationships between the Lloyd's Names and the managing agents were mediated in some cases by a direct contractual relationship, while in other cases there were a series of intermediary contracts between the Names and the managing agents upon whose advice they relied. Lord Goff adopted the reasoning of Oliver J in the earlier case of *Midland Bank Trust Co.* v. *Hett, Stubbs and Kemp*.[410] He thus held that the extended *Hedley Byrne* form of liability for negligence in the performance of a service 'may arise not only in cases where the relevant services are rendered gratuitously, but also where they are rendered under a contract'.[411] At the same time, it was accepted that, in the words of Lord Browne-Wilkinson, 'the agreement of the parties evidenced by the contract can modify and shape the tortious duties which, in the absence of contract, would be applicable'.[412] In particular, the tort duty will not extend to permitting 'the plaintiff to circumvent or escape a contractual exclusion or limitation of liability for the act or omission that would constitute the tort'.[413] A clear exclusion of this kind could only be defeated by the application of the Unfair Contract Terms Act 1977.

The second case to consider is one in which the parties to a tort claim were not in a contractual relationship with each other when the tort took place. Here, the argument made above applies again: if the parties have failed to contract at all, the claimant will be getting something for nothing if the court now allows him a negligence claim in essentially the same terms as a contract would have provided for. This is the essential basis of the rule of privity of contract, that only one who is a party to a contract may maintain an action for its breach. In the pre-*Murphy* building case of *Portsea Island Mutual Co-operative Society Ltd.* v. *Michael Brashier Associates Ltd.*, a claim for economic loss caused by negligent design by a firm of architects failed on the grounds that 'Portsea was in effect seeking to recover in negligence sums which they might well have been entitled to claim under a collateral agreement. Portsea could have invited Brashiers to enter into a collateral warranty in respect of the superstore when, for suitable Consideration, they might have agreed to do so.'[414]

408 McLachlin J in *Canadian National Railway* v. *Norsk Pacific Steamship Co.* (1992) 91 DLR (4th) 289, 374.

409 [1995] 2 AC 145.

410 [1979] Ch. 384.

411 [1995] 2 AC 145, 193.

412 *Ibid.*, 206.

413 This was the formulation of Le Dain J in the Supreme Court of Canada case of *Central Trust Co.* v. *Rafuse* (1986) 31 DLR (4th) 481, 522, which was adopted by Lord Goff in *Henderson* v. *Merrett Syndicates Ltd.* [1995] 2 AC 145, 191.

414 (1990) 6 *Const. LJ* 63, 70.

However, the simple absence of a contract between the parties cannot be the decisive reason for a court denying the existence of a duty of care; otherwise the tort of negligence would have no role at all in the compensation of financial loss. As we have seen, one way of explaining cases such as *Hedley Byrne* [415] and *White* v. *Jones* [416] is to view them as legitimate but limited exceptions to the privity rule in contract law. The source of the duty to take care lies in a contract to which the claimant is not a party, but of which he is effectively the intended beneficiary. In *Hedley Byrne* the contract between the bank and its customer would probably have contained an implied term to the effect that the bank would avoid carelessly releasing false information about its client. In *Ross* the contract for services between the solicitor and the testator would contain an undertaking by the latter to perform with reasonable care and skill. In the event of breach, however, no contractual action will lie, since the defendant's co-contractor is unlikely to have suffered any loss. Thus in *White* v. *Jones* the loss is suffered not by the estate but by the disappointed beneficiary. In *Caparo Industries* v. *Dickman* [417] the result of the auditor's negligence is not to harm the company, which contracts for their services, but the shareholders who rely on the information contained in the audited accounts. And in *The Aliakmon* [418] breach of contract by the carrier will not harm the seller, who expects to receive payment in full from the buyer in any event, but rather the buyer who takes the goods in a damaged condition. If all other things were equal there would seem to be good reasons for allowing a tort action in this type of case: otherwise the performing party is relieved from the normal legal incentives for the performance of his undertaking.[419]

The Aliakmon illustrates one reason why all other things may not be equal: under the contract the performing party may have been given the benefit of exclusion or limitation clauses which would restrict his liability in the event of his being sued by the defendant. If he cannot take advantage of these clauses in any tort action brought against him by the claimant, he may face a much greater liability than he could possibly have contemplated when he entered into the contract. The tort action, then, risks upsetting the allocation of risk between the parties, which would normally have been reflected in the price the defendant charged for his services.[420]

This problem is difficult to deal with if the claimant's action is seen as tortious rather than contractual in nature. There are few signs that the English courts are prepared to allow even a narrow departure, here, from the privity rule. In *The Aliakmon* Lord

415 [1964] AC 465.
416 [1995] 2 AC 207.
417 [1990] 2 AC 605.
418 [1986] AC 785.
419 One means by which the parties themselves can attempt to ensure that the benefit of any contract claim is passed on from one party to another is through the assignment of the benefit of contract terms. This is plausible in certain situations of building contracts, but it is an extremely complex and even precarious means of achieving the desired result. See J. Cartwright, 'The Assignment of Collateral Warranties' (1990) 6 *Const. LJ* 14; I. N. Duncan Wallace, 'Assignment of Rights to Sue for Breach of Construction Contracts' (1993) 109 *LQR* 82.
420 It may be noted that this is a completely different situation from that which occurred in the case of *The Nicholas H* [1996] AC 211. In that case, the plaintiff entered into a contract with a third party, the shipowners, which contained a limitation clause, but this clause did not purport to protect the defendant classification society. See Lord Lloyd's dissent, [1996] AC 211, 223.

Brandon rejected an argument to the effect that the plaintiff's claim could be viewed as contractual on the basis of the doctrine of 'transferred loss'—a proposal put by Robert Goff LJ in the Court of Appeal.[421] In other cases, however, courts have found ways of effectively extending the benefit of exclusion and limitation clauses to cover actions for negligence brought in tort by third parties. In these cases the presence of exclusion clauses in the underlying contract have been used to deny the existence of a duty of care in tort to the third party.[422] This was done in *Norwich City Council* v. *Harvey*,[423] even though the loss in question was damage to property, and therefore within the scope of the normal duty of care. More generally, the complete denial of a duty of care does not provide an answer to the situation (as in *The Aliakmon*) in which a duty is *partially* modified, or a liability *partially* excluded, by the terms of the underlying contract. As the law presently stands the outcome is either all or nothing.

In *White* v. *Jones* the Court of Appeal, in particular, was explicit about the shortcomings of the privity-of-contract rule and of the methods used to limit its effects. Sir Donald Nicholls V-C considered 'whether a remedy for breach of contract could be shaped whereby, the client having lost the opportunity to make a gift to the intended beneficiary, (1) his estate should be regarded as having lost a sum equal to the amount of the intended gift, and (2) the executors should hold that sum, when recovered from the solicitor, upon trust for the intended beneficiary'.[424] In the event he concluded that a solution in tort, which could avoid these complexities, was preferable. Steyn LJ considered the argument that the scope of the duty of care should, in such a case, be largely determined by the nature of the obligations in the underlying contract, including any exclusion and limitation clauses. He concluded that where such clauses were present, 'it seems to me unavoidable that the duty will have to be limited in the way suggested by Robert Goff LJ' in *The Aliakmon*.[425] In the House of Lords in *White* v. *Jones*, Lord Goff considered *obiter* that a contractual solution, however desirable, was impossible to achieve short of parliamentary intervention.[426] But he admitted that the tort action, which he was prepared to fashion in order to avoid injustice, would be shaped by the underlying contractual relationship between testator and solicitor. In its result,

[421] [1986] AC 785, 819–20, rejecting the approach outlined at [1985] 1 QB 350, 397.

[422] *Southern Water Board* v. *Carey* [1985] 2 All ER 1077; *Norwich City Council* v. *Harvey* [1988] 1 WLR 828; *Pacific Associates Inc.* v. *Baxter* [1990] QB 993; cf. *Precis (521) plc* v. *William M. Mercer Ltd.* [2004] EWCA Civ. 414 (stressing the need for knowledge of the exclusion clause on the part of the defendants). See generally, B. S. Markesinis, 'Doctrinal Clarity in Tort Litigation: A Comparative Lawyer's Viewpoint' (1991) 25 *The International Lawyer* 953.

[423] [1989] 1 WLR 828.

[424] [1995] 2 AC 207, 224. One solution to the privity problem is the remedy of a trust of the promise, but this has not been widely used in English law since the judgment of Lord Wright in *Vandepitte* v. *Preferred Accident Insurance Co. of New York* [1933] AC 70, while the possibility of the promisee suing for substantial damages on behalf of the third party was limited by *Woodar Investment Development Ltd.* v. *Wimpey Construction (UK) Ltd.* [1980] 1 WLR 227. For a radically different approach (or series of approaches) to the question from that adopted by the House of Lords, see *Trident Insurance Co. Ltd.* v. *MacNiece Bros. Pty. Ltd.* (1988) 165 CLR 107 (HC of Australia). The reform of the privity doctrine raises wider questions going beyond those with which the law of negligence is concerned. See Law Commission Consultation Paper No. 121, *Privity of Contract: Contracts for the Benefit of Third Parties* (1991), and the Contracts (Rights of Third Parties) Act 1999.

[425] [1995] 2 AC 207, 239.

[426] *Ibid.*, 266.

therefore, the legal remedy now available to such claimants comes very close to the contractual model discussed above.

(vi) Insurance Considerations and Related Aspects of Policy

Closely allied with the view that contract, rather than tort, should provide the basis for recovery in cases of economic loss is the argument that the court should let the loss lie where it falls in a situation where the claimant has taken out first-party or loss insurance or, alternatively, where he could have done so relatively cheaply. If the court imposes a duty of care in these circumstances it will be effectively forcing the defendant to carry liability insurance, which will increase his costs and perhaps require him to raise his prices. The result will be a potentially wasteful, double insurance. Alternatively, if liability insurance is not available, the defendant may decide to give up the activity in question. Under the law of subrogation the insurance company which has extended loss insurance to the claimant is entitled to bring an action in his name to recover the damages in tort from the defendant. The consequence of this is that the resulting action may not benefit the claimant as an individual one way or the other. In the past the English courts regarded the availability of insurance as more or less irrelevant to the question whether a duty of care arises on a given set of facts.[427] In *Murphy* v. *Brentwood District Council*, however, Lord Keith of Kinkel clearly thought it relevant that the plaintiff's loss had been met by his insurance company and that the company was now seeking to recoup this payment by way of the tort action. It is certainly not self-evident why the insurance company, which has been paid to take the risk of the loss occurring, should have a right of action against the council, who will have to bear the loss in some form by passing it on in the form of higher local taxes or a reduction in public services.[428]

Similar considerations influenced the majority of the House of Lords in *Marc Rich & Co. AG* v. *Bishops Rock Marine Co. Ltd., The Nicholas H.*[429] The plaintiff was the owner of cargo, which was lost following the sinking of a ship which the employee of the defendant, a shipping classification society, had negligently passed fit to sail. Although, in this case, the damage was physical harm (damage to property), it was held that the classification society owed no duty of care to the cargo owners. One ground relied on by the majority was the need to avoid upsetting the complex system of loss insurance and liability insurance which operated under arrangements made by cargo owners and ship owners. As Lord Steyn explained:

> Cargo owners take out direct insurance in respect of the cargo. Ship owners take out liability risks insurance in respect of breaches of their duties of care in respect of the cargo. The insurance system is structured on the basis that the potential liability of ship owners to cargo

[427] See e.g. *Lamb* v. *Camden LBC* [1981] QB 625.

[428] See Lord Keith [1991] 1 AC 358, 458–9, 472; T. Weir, 'Governmental Liability' [1989] *PL* 40. The subrogation rule which, in practice, often allows insurance companies to have their cake and eat it, may well be one of the reasons that judges are reluctant in many of these cases to allow a cause of action. Thus, see, Lord Hoffmann's views in *Stovin* v. *Wise* [1996] AC 923, 955.

[429] [1996] AC 211. This decision may be contrasted with *Watson* v. *British Boxing Board of Control* [2001] QB 1134, in which a regulatory body was held liable in negligence notwithstanding its lack of insurance to cover the loss in question; see further our discussion in Section 5(a)(iv), below.

owners is limited under Hague Rules and by virtue of tonnage limitation provisions. And insurance premiums payable by owners obviously reflect such limitations on the ship owners' exposure... The result of a recognition of a duty of care in this case will be to enable cargo owners, or rather their insurers, to disturb the balance created by the Hague Rules and Hague–Visby Rules as well as by tonnage limitation provisions, by enabling cargo owners to recover in tort against a peripheral party to the prejudice of ship owners under the existing system.[430]

This case illustrates, like so many other recent ones,[431] that insurance factors weigh heavily in the minds of some judges. The case, however, also illustrates the dangers in the courts seeking to make judgements about the insurance implications of their rulings on the basis of limited evidence. As Lord Lloyd pointed out in his powerful dissent, there was no evidence to suggest that classification societies did not already carry liability insurance. Moreover, the imposition of liability might have the effect of raising standards in an area of legitimate concern to the 'shipping community at large'.[432] Such a clash of views does not, it is submitted, reduce either the reality or the utility of insurance reasoning; but it does make one ask for a more substantial discussion of these issues.

Similarly, the cost of liability insurance for professionals and the difficulty of obtaining full cover have been raised in cases concerning accountants and architects. But in *Caparo Industries* v. *Dickman*, Bingham LJ considered, with commendable frankness, that it was impossible to draw any conclusions from such arguments on the ground that the court did not have before it the relevant information on the state of insurance markets.[433] In practice, courts may well find it difficult to make a definitive judgement on the question of which of the two parties is best placed to take out insurance. At the same time, there is (mainly anecdotal) evidence to suggest that recent large-scale claims arising out of product liability and natural disasters have depleted the spare capacity of insurance markets. An awareness of this growing problem may thus help explain (even when it does not always justify) the increasingly cautious approach of the courts to the development of new duty situations.[434] The plea for increased empirical and interdisciplinary study of these problems thus remains valid.

On the other hand, the arguments against letting the loss lie where it falls are not all one way. First, there is the possibility that denying a duty of care simply on the ground that the claimant is protected by insurance will remove the normal legal incentives on the defendant to avoid causing the loss or damage in question.[435] Second, the insurer's rights of subrogation *may* reduce the premiums he charges to potential claimants. Furthermore, insurance may not cover all losses suffered by a claimant. Under these

430 [1996] AC 211, 239, 240.

431 For instance, Lord Griffiths in *Smith* v. *Bush* [1990] 1 AC 831, 858–9; Hoffmann J in *Morgan Crucible Co.* v. *Hill Samuel* [1991] Ch. 295, 302–3; Lord Hoffmann in *Stovin* v. *Wise* [1996] AC 923, 958; and Lord Mance in *Customs & Excise Commissioners* v. *Barclays Bank plc* [2006] 3 WLR 1, 34–36. Many of Lord Denning's judgments also contain illuminating references to insurance considerations.

432 [1996] AC 211, 228–9.

433 [1989] QB 653, 688. See also Lord Hoffmann's judgment in *White* v. *Chief Constable of South Yorkshire Police* [1999] 2 AC 455.

434 M. Davies, 'The End of the Affair: Duty of Care and Liability Insurance' (1989) 9 *Leg. Stud.* 967.

435 W. Bishop, 'Economic Loss in Tort' (1982) 2 *OJLS* 1.

circumstances subrogation enables him to share the risk and expense of litigation with the insurance company, which will normally bear the greater part of the costs.[436] This is a relevant factor in cases involving consumers, such as Messrs Anns and Murphy. If both claimant and defendant are business entities, the court would seem to be justified in posing the question whether the most efficient outcome, in terms of the net costs of the accident, would have been for the claimant to have protected himself through either contract or insurance. The importance of this point was stressed by LaForest J in his dissenting judgment in the *Norsk* case. Referring to the need 'to bring insurance considerations into the open', LaForest J argued that of the three parties involved in the accident, the plaintiff was better placed than both the defendant and the owner of the bridge to protect itself against the consequences of an accident. It would have known the value to its own operations of the bridge being open and the likely costs of closure. The defendant would have had no means of assessing these costs. More generally, the plaintiff was in a good position to use its expertise, resources and bargaining power to find a contractual or insurance-based solution; in this regard: 'It is hard to imagine a more sophisticated group of plaintiffs than the users of railway bridges. These parties have access to the full range of protective options: first party commercial insurance or self-insurance, contracts with both the bridge owner and with the railway's customers.'[437]

The situation may well be different where consumer liability is concerned. Here, a realistic approach on the court's part would be to recognise that individual consumers of goods and services are most unlikely to have access to either the resources or the contracting expertise needed effectively to protect themselves against a risk of large-scale loss. This is arguably one of the most serious weaknesses of the House of Lords' decision in *Murphy*: for the purposes of denying a duty of care, the position of home-owners and residents was equated with that of sizeable construction companies and property developers. A different approach is evident in *Smith* v. *Bush*,[438] where the House of Lords, in formulating the duty of care, appears to have been influenced by the aims of consumer protection contained in the Unfair Contract Terms Act 1977. Had the plaintiff been acting in a business capacity (as in *Hedley Byrne*) it is most unlikely that a duty of care could have arisen in circumstances where a clear disclaimer of liability was brought to his notice. In such a case, the court would have been justified in asking why he had not sought to contract for the information in question.

(vii) The Respective Roles of Parliament and the Courts

In *Murphy* one reason given for denying a duty of care in tort was the availability of a statutory framework for consumer protection under the Defective Premises Act 1972.[439] This remedy is, however, less than fully effective, thanks to the short limitation period laid down for actions under the Act.[440] At the same time the members of the

436 R. O'Dair, '*Murphy* v. *Brentwood DC*: A House Built on Firm Foundations?' (1991) 54 *MLR* 561.

437 (1992) 91 DLR (4th) 289, 349.

438 [1990] 1 AC 831.

439 See [1991] 1 AC 398, 472 (Lord Keith), 480 (Lord Bridge) and 491 (Lord Oliver).

440 The limitation period begins to run from the date on which the building is completed or the time at which the relevant work is completed: s. 2(5). The benefits of the extended period allowed for by the Latent

House of Lords also appear to have been unaware of important changes to the National House Building Council insurance scheme, which have greatly expanded the availability of actions under the Defective Premises Act which were previously barred.[441] If in future the courts are to deny the existence of a duty situation solely on the ground that Parliament has legislated in the area concerned, the scope of the tort of negligence would be considerably reduced. In the context of claims for negligent construction, the presence of the Defective Premises Act as an alternative to the common law is offset by the Latent Damage Act 1986, the terms of which appear to assume that *Anns* was correctly decided.[442] Indeed, *Murphy* seems to remove much of the rationale for this Act.[443]

A more specific argument expressed in recent decisions is that the courts should defer to Parliament in areas where the social and economic effects of a decision extending liability are difficult to assess, or where opposing policy arguments are finely balanced. It is thus true to assert that the courts are immediately concerned with the resolution of the particular dispute before them and with the enunciation of rules which allow as far as possible for doctrinal clarity and ease of application. Parliament, on the other hand, is better equipped to collect evidence on the wider consequences of liability rules and to confront questions of policy head-on. A recent example is *Islington London Borough Council* v. *University College London Hospital NHS Trust*,[444] in which the Court of Appeal rejected an attempt by a local authority to recover costs of residential care in respect of a victim of medical negligence on the part of the defendants: it was 'quite impossible for a court to know, within the confines of a particular case and with the benefit only of a sparse amount of evidence and its own commonsense, what are the wider implications of the move that it is being asked to make'.[445]

Whatever the merits of this point of view in the *Islington* case, at various times the judges have taken a more robust view on the basis that the common law should not be unduly constrained. There are enough previous examples of judicial innovation in areas raising complex questions of policy to suggest that deference to Parliament can easily be overcome in cases seen by the judges as appropriate for this purpose. Moreover, this may also be a desirable course to take if, as has often happened in practice, one is faced with a situation where Parliament is either unable or unwilling to intervene.

(viii) Economic Loss: A Summary and Conclusion

It may be useful to summarise and review this examination of the case law on economic loss. As the law now stands, the situations in which the law recognises a duty of care in relation to 'pure' economic loss are tightly circumscribed. The one area where liability

Damage Act 1986 do not appear to apply to claims under the Defective Premises Act 1972: see *Warner* v. *Basildon DC* (1991) 7 *Const. LJ* 146, and on limitation generally see ch. 24, Section 9, below.

[441] On this, see I. N. Duncan Wallace, '*Anns* beyond Repair' (1991) 107 *LQR* 228, 243; and see ch. 6, Section 2(g)(ii).

[442] See below, ch. 24, Section 9.

[443] See J. Stapleton, 'Duty of Care and Economic Loss' (1991) 107 *LQR* 249.

[444] [2005] EWCA Civ. 596.

[445] [2005] EWCA Civ. 596, at para. 37 (Buxton LJ).

is clearly established concerns negligent misstatements and negligence in the performance of a service, where *Hedley Byrne & Co. Ltd.* v. *Heller & Partners Ltd.* [446] continues to be good law. Indeed, as already stated, it has been extended by the decisions of the House of Lords in *Henderson* v. *Merrett Syndicates Ltd.* [447] and *White* v. *Jones*.[448] Between them these cases represent important inroads into the non-liability rule; and these may well be extended further as contract law moves into the field, either as a result of the Contracts (Rights of Third Parties) Act 1999 or the *Panatown* decision, whose full import has not yet been fully gauged. As far as the other categories of economic loss are concerned, only in the most exceptional cases will 'relational' loss arising from damage to another's property be compensated, even with the assistance of the proximity test. Economic loss arising from defects in products and buildings is also outside the scope of the tort of negligence. *Murphy* v. *Brentwood District Council* [449] has been described as giving rise to a 'negative orthodoxy'.[450] This amounts to denying the existence of a duty of care going beyond the 'traditional categorisations', but offers no set of principles or clear statement to guide the courts in their treatment of situations lying on the boundary of liability. There also remains the difficulty of reconciling *Murphy* with the continuing authority of *Hedley Byrne*, and, within the misstatement cases, of explaining how the restrictive judgment in *Caparo Industries* v. *Dickman* [451] fits together with decisions such as *Smith* v. *Bush*.[452]

From this rather unpromising situation there are two possible developments, the beginnings of which may already be discerned. The first is that the courts will begin to distinguish more closely between the types of claimants and defendants involved in economic-loss claims. In particular this could mean acknowledging the different positions of business entities on the one hand, and private consumers of goods and services on the other, when it comes to the capacity to control the risk of economic loss without resort to tort law. The second is that the courts will pay greater regard to the role of contractual standards in this area of the law in shaping the scope and level of tort obligations. Beyond that, it is difficult to predict the future and the topic is likely to remain a fertile ground for dispute and controversy.

4. THE MANNER OF INFLICTION

(A) ACTS AND OMISSIONS

According to Lord Goff in *Smith* v. *Littlewoods Organisation Ltd.*, 'the common law does not impose liability for what are called pure omissions'.[453] This means that there is no

446 [1964] AC 465.
447 [1995] 2 AC 145.
448 [1995] 2 AC 207.
449 [1991] 1 AC 398.
450 Howarth (Select Bibliography).
451 [1990] 2 AC 605.
452 [1990] 1 AC 831.
453 [1987] 2 AC 241, 271; see also the judgment of Lord Hoffmann in *Stovin* v. *Wise* [1996] AC 923, 943–4.

general duty of care in tort to prevent harm occurring to another. The normal mechanism for creating such 'affirmative duties of action' is contract (or statute). The hostility of the common law to the concept of affirmative duties in tort is longstanding, the product, it has been said, of 'values of an era in which private selfishness was elevated to the rank of a public virtue'.[454] Though the socio-economic environment is changing, there are few signs that the courts are currently prepared to abandon their unwillingness to treat omissions like acts.

Although the distinction between acting and failing to act—between *misfeasance* and *non-feasance*—is said to be fundamental to this area of the law, in practice it may be difficult to discern. As two academic lawyers have observed, 'there are many situations in which it is impossible to draw any clear line'.[455] Thus, in *Donoghue* v. *Stevenson*,[456] was it the manufacturer's act of putting a dangerous product into circulation or his failure to check the contents of the bottle which caused the plaintiff's illness? In situations like this the courts normally have little difficulty in establishing a causal link between the positive act of the defendant giving rise to a risk of harm and the damage which subsequently ensued. Potentially much more difficult are situations in which the damage is brought about through the actions either of a third party or of the plaintiff himself. If the defendant could have acted to avert the harm but failed to do so, it is then that the question of legal responsibility for omissions arises in an acute form.

In his speech in *Smith* v. *Littlewoods Organisation Ltd.*,[457] Lord Goff was careful to stress the absence of a *general* duty of affirmative action in tort. For the law does recognise certain *specific* situations in which affirmative duties in tort may arise. Two of the most important concern the duties of occupiers to ensure that their property is safe for lawful visitors and the duties of employers in relation to the health and safety of their employees while at work. These are considered separately in Chapters 6 and 18 of this book. The point about these specific instances is that the duty to act arises from the existence of a pre-tort relationship (and very possibly a contract) between the parties. Other relationships with the potential to give rise to affirmative duties are those between parents and their children;[458] between a school and the children in its care;[459] between a host and his guests;[460] and between prison authorities and similar institutions and those in their charge.[461] In each case the scope of the potential duty imposed on the responsible person is twofold: on the one hand, to see to the safety of the other person in the relationship and, on the other, to see that the other does not cause harm to third parties. These various instances may, no doubt, be drawn together under

[454] B. S. Markesinis, 'Negligence, Nuisance and Affirmative Duties of Action' (Select Bibliography), 112.

[455] P. Cane, *Atiyah's Accidents, Compensation and the Law* (7th edn., 2006), 72–3.

[456] [1932] AC 562.

[457] [1987] AC 241.

[458] This also includes a foster-parent looking after the child: see *Surtees* v. *Kingston-upon-Thames BC* [1992] 2 FLR 559.

[459] *Barnes* v. *Hampshire CC* [1969] 1 WLR 1563. This duty now extends to the psychological and educational well-being of the child: see *Bradford-Smart* v. *West Sussex CC* [2002] FSR 425.

[460] *The Ogopogo* [1971] 2 Lloyd's Rep. 410.

[461] *Ellis* v. *Home Office* [1953] 2 QB 135.

the general umbrella of 'proximity'. The use of 'proximity' is only the beginning of the analysis, however, since the precise scope and extent of the duty will differ from one situation to another; but without some pre-tort relationship of this kind, it is unlikely that an affirmative duty of any degree can be imposed.

(i) A Duty to Rescue?

This is the main reason for the absence of any general duty to come to the rescue of another who is in a situation of danger. A parent who sees his child drowning is under an obligation to come to his aid,[462] but no such duty arises between strangers. An illustration of this is the US case of *Osterlind* v. *Hill*,[463] in which the defendant, a strong swimmer who had rented out a canoe to the deceased, sat on the shore and watched him drown when the canoe overturned. He was held to have owed no duty of care. The fact that the deceased rented the canoe from the defendant could be viewed as creating a relationship between them of the kind which would give rise to a duty of affirmative action;[464] but the matter is unclear and it is entirely possible that an English court would follow *Osterlind* v. *Hill* today. In *Barrett* v. *Ministry of Defence*,[465] for example, the Court of Appeal held that there was no duty to rescue in a case where the deceased, a naval airman serving on a remote Norwegian base, drank himself to death. The military authorities were under no duty to ensure that the deceased did not put his own life in danger in this way, even though they were aware that he had a drink problem.

There are suggestions in *Barnett* v. *Chelsea and Kensington Hospital*[466] that a National Health Service casualty department is under a duty to take in a patient who presents himself in an emergency, and NHS general practitioners are placed under a separate statutory duty to provide certain services to local patients.[467] But English law does not in general require specialists such as doctors or ambulancemen and women to come to the aid of stricken accident victims they happen to encounter, unless there is some prior assumption of responsibility. This position has been implicitly confirmed by the recent House of Lords' decisions in *X (Minors)* v. *Bedfordshire County Council*[468] and *Stovin* v. *Wise*.[469] In the latter case, Lord Hoffmann argued that the failure of a public authority to act under its statutory powers for the benefit of the plaintiff could not give rise to liability unless the statute clearly indicates 'a policy which confers a right to financial compensation if the power has not been exercised'.[470] This approach has been applied to hold that rescue services such as the coastguard[471] and the fire brigade[472] (and, by extension, the providers of health and medical services) are under no duty at common

[462] *Carmarthenshire CC* v. *Lewis* [1955] AC 549. [463] 160 NE 301 (1928).

[464] By analogy with *The Ogopogo* [1970] 1 Lloyd's Rep. 257; [1971] 2 Lloyd's Rep. 410. *Osterlind* v. *Hill* would not now be followed in the majority of US jurisdictions: see ch. 5, Section 6 below.

[465] [1995] 3 All ER 87. [466] [1969] 1 QB 428.

[467] National Health Service (General Medical Services) Regulations (SI No. 1992/635), Sch. 3 para. 4(h).

[468] [1995] 2 AC 633. [469] [1996] AC 923.

[470] *Ibid*., 955. [471] *OLL* v. *Secretary of State for Transport* [1997] 3 All ER 897.

[472] *Capital and Counties plc* v. *Hampshire CC* [1997] QB 1004; for an empirical study of the effects of this decision, J. Hartsthorne, N. Smith and R. Everton, '"*Caparo* Under Fire": A Study into the Effects upon the Fire Service of Liability in Negligence' (2000) 63 *MLR* 502.

law to come to the rescue of a member of the public. Indeed, if they do so, they can only be liable for making matters worse than they would otherwise have been, or for undertaking an assumption of responsibility to act.[473] In adopting this rather extreme position, the law apparently takes no account either of the magnitude of the danger to be averted or of the potential cost to the rescuer, even though the former may be considerable and the latter relatively insignificant. This is the effect of denying the existence of any duty of care, as opposed to admitting the existence of a duty and then seeking to establish whether in all the circumstances the failure of the defendant to act was reasonable. The latter may well be the case if, for example, he could only have acted at the risk of endangering his own safety or that of a third party. Just as with economic loss, to admit a duty of care merely widens the scope of the court's inquiry to cover questions of fault and causation; it does not, in itself, lead to a finding of liability.

In *Smith* v. *Littlewoods Organisation Ltd.*,[474] the principal speeches, by Lords Goff and Mackay, approached the question of affirmative duties from different angles. The case arose from Littlewoods' failure to protect their property, a large derelict cinema awaiting redevelopment, from the entry of vandals, who caused a fire which spread to the adjoining properties of the plaintiffs. Lord Goff, as we have seen, formulated his judgment for the defendants in terms of the absence of duty. Lord Mackay, on the other hand, avoided relying on the act-omission dichotomy and argued instead that the defendants had not in the circumstances acted unreasonably, a position which assumes the prior existence of a duty of care. The other members of the House of Lords appear to have taken the same approach as Lord Mackay, although the judgments are not altogether clear on this point. Littlewoods had insufficient knowledge of the presence of trespassers on their property and the threat of a fire was small when set against the enormous cost of averting the danger, which in this case would have required a twenty-four-hour watch on the premises. However, it is clear from Lord Mackay's speech that liability might have been imposed had the risk of fire been clearer in advance. His Lordship's judgment may therefore be read as leaving open the possibility that affirmative duties of action may arise in an appropriate case.

A relationship such as that between a host and his guests may give rise to a duty to rescue, as in the Canadian case of *The Ogopogo*.[475] In the course of a boat party one of the guests fell overboard. The host attempted to reverse the boat back to the spot in question but failed to place the boat in the right position, with the result that a second guest dived in to rescue the first. Both were drowned. The Canadian Supreme Court held that the defendant owed a duty of care as host to do what he could to rescue his guests, but that in the circumstances he had not behaved negligently. In this case there was an additional source of duty in respect of the second guest, namely the failure to achieve an effective rescue of the first: this created the situation of additional danger in

473 *Kent* v. *Griffiths* [2000] 2 WLR 1158; T. Hickman, '"And That's Magic!" Making Public Bodies Liable for Failing to Confer Benefits' [2000] *CLJ* 432; R. Bagshaw, 'The Duties of Care of Emergency Service Providers' [1999] *LMCLQ* 71; K. Williams, 'Medical Samaritans: Is There a Duty to Treat?' (2001) 21 *OJLS* 393.

474 [1987] AC 241.

475 [1970] 1 Lloyd's Rep. 257; [1971] 2 Lloyd's Rep. 410.

which the second guest put his own life at risk. *The Ogopogo* illustrates the effect of a court taking a wide view of duty: the focus of attention shifts to the question of fault, that is, to whether the defendant acted reasonably, taking into account the resources at his disposal, and the danger to himself and to the other guests. Taking these factors into account, rescuers will not normally be held to a high *standard* of care. But in a case of an egregious failure to act, the prior existence of a duty leaves open the possibility of a liability.

The Ogopogo raises a further point, namely that a rescuer who is under no duty to begin with may assume a duty of care by starting to come to the victim's aid, and in particular may be under a duty not to make things worse. In *East Suffolk Rivers Catchments Board* v. *Kent*[476] the House of Lords implicitly accepted the principle that a defendant exercising his powers in aid of the plaintiff could be made liable for making his predicament worse. As we have just seen, this principle has survived the retrenchment of *Anns* which follows from the more recent decisions of the House of Lords in the *X (Minors)* and *Stovin* cases. In this case the defendants avoided liability as they were able to show that their failure to repair the plaintiff's floodwall had left him as badly off as he was before. In *Barrett* v. *Ministry of Defence*[477] the Court of Appeal held that the military authorities were under no initial duty to protect the plaintiff's husband against the consequences of excessive drinking. However, once they began to care for him (after he had collapsed through drunkenness) they were under a duty to exercise due care in doing so. On this basis, damages were awarded to the plaintiff (although reduced for the contributory negligence of the deceased). However, *The Ogopogo* is a signal that rescuers are likely to escape liability on the ground that only the most serious errors will be deemed to constitute a breach of duty.

(ii) Failure to Warn

A failure to warn another of an impending danger is treated in the same way as a failure to come to his rescue. In certain exceptional circumstances a duty to warn may be implied; such a duty normally arises, for example, in the context of statutory products liability, between a manufacturer and ultimate consumers, as far as physical harm and damage to consumer property is concerned.[478] Otherwise, a close relationship between the parties of the kind already mentioned will be necessary. It is not enough that harm to the defendant is foreseeable; there is no liability in negligence, according to Lord Keith of Kinkel, 'on the part of one who sees another about to walk over a cliff with his head in the air, and forebears to shout a warning'.[479]

A close relationship between the parties is not at first sight so obvious in the American case of *Tarasoff* v. *University of California*,[480] in which a psychiatric patient spoke of his intention to kill his former girlfriend during conversations with his

476 [1941] AC 74.

477 [1995] 3 All ER 87.

478 See below, ch. 20, Section 3(c)(ii).

479 *Yuen Kun Yeu* v. *Attorney-General of Hong Kong* [1988] AC 175, 192.

480 17 Cal. (3d) 425 (1976).

psychiatrist. The psychiatrist failed to pass on any warning, and the patient later murdered the girlfriend. The court found the psychiatrist liable in an action brought by the victim's parents. An English court would have to go well beyond existing authority in order to follow *Tarasoff*. The decision seems supportable when one compares the scale of the threat and the fact that it was taken seriously with the relative ease with which the girlfriend could have been informed. But it also raises difficult problems of confidentiality between doctor and patient and has not been widely followed in the United States, having subsequently been interpreted as a case in which there *was* a close relationship between the psychiatrist and the girlfriend, whose precise identity was known to him.[481]

(iii) Failure to Take Adequate Precautions

Persons with responsibility for looking after those in their care may be liable in tort for their failure to do so. In *Kirkham* v. *Chief Constable of Manchester*[482] the police were held responsible for a failure to pass on information to the prison authorities concerning the suicidal tendencies of a prisoner on remand, who subsequently killed himself. An infants' school which let young children out to go home several minutes before the normal time incurred liability to a child who was injured crossing a busy road, on the ground that her mother would have met her in time had she been released as normal.[483] The same principles appear to apply to parents and their own children. Public policy does not prevent a child suing its own parent in tort, and if the parent is insured there may be a good reason to do so. However, the duty of care does not arise if the parent does not in practice control the child and bear responsibility for its safety and welfare on a day-to-day basis. Nor is the duty one to maintain the 'duties of conscientious parenthood' in terms of general upbringing, but simply to 'protect the child against foreseeable danger' to life and limb.[484]

A duty to safeguard another's property can arise on the basis of an *ad hoc* relationship, as in *Stansbie* v. *Tromans*,[485] in which a decorator failed to safeguard the house he was painting from entry by thieves. The householder with whom he had contracted succeeded in an action against him for the value of the stolen property. Aside from these instances of pre-existing relationships, a duty to act has also been imposed upon defendants who have created a situation of public danger. Such a case was *Haynes* v. *Harwood*,[486] where this took the form of failing to control a horse in a street where children were playing; the plaintiff, a policeman, was injured trying to control the horse.

481 *Thompson* v. *County of Alameda* 614 P 2d 728 (1980). See ch. 5, Section 5, below.

482 [1990] 2 QB 283; *Reeves* v. *Commissioner of Police of the Metropolis* [2000] 1 AC 360; but cf. *Orange* v. *Chief Constable of South Yorkshire* [2002] QB 347 (no duty owed where suicide was not foreseeable; but this case may be better explained as one in which the defendant was not in breach of duty).

483 *Barnes* v. *Hampshire CC* [1969] 1 WLR 1563.

484 *Hahn* v. *Conley* [1972] ALR 247, 251 (Barwick CJ).

485 [1948] 2 KB 48.

486 [1935] 1 KB 146.

(B) LIABILITY FOR THE ACTS OF THIRD PARTIES

(i) Parents and Children

The intervention of a third party in the chain of events raises particular difficulties in ascribing legal responsibility for damage. The courts could have dealt with these questions through concepts of causation alone; instead, they have consistently applied the concept of duty to exclude liability at the outset.[487] The law was summarised by Dixon J in the Australian case of *Smith* v. *Leurs*:

> It is... exceptional to find in the law a duty to control another's actions to prevent harm to strangers. The general rule is that one man is under no duty of controlling another to prevent his doing damage to a third. There are, however, special relations, which are the source of a duty of this nature. It appears now to be recognised that it is incumbent upon a parent who maintains control over a young child to take reasonable care so to exercise that control as to avoid conduct on his part exposing the person or property of others to unreasonable danger. Parental control, where it exists, must be exercised with due care to prevent the child inflicting intentional damage on others or causing damage by conduct involving unreasonable risk of injury to others.[488]

The responsibility of parents and teachers for the behaviour of children was confirmed by the House of Lords in *Carmarthenshire County Council* v. *Lewis*.[489] A child of four years old was allowed to wander out of a nursery school on to a busy road. The plaintiff's husband, who happened to be driving by at the time, swerved to miss the child and crashed into a lamp-post. He was killed in the collision. The defendant authority was found to be at fault for having failed to install a more effective gate to keep the children inside during school hours. The scope of this duty will clearly vary according to the age of the children in question and to the particular risk which they are likely to pose.

(ii) Custodial Authorities

Prison authorities owe a duty of care to safeguard inmates against the foreseeable risk of injury from fellow prisoners. In *Ellis* v. *Home Office*[490] negligence by warders was established, but the standard of care imposed will clearly be limited by the extent to which there was knowledge of the risk of injury and the nature of the precautions taken to avoid it. In addition, prison authorities may owe a duty of care to an inmate to avoid placing him in circumstances where he is exposed to an undue risk of psychiatric illness, as occurred in a case where a remand prisoner, who was known to be in a depressed and suicidal condition, was placed in a cell with another prisoner who was making threats of suicide, which he subsequently carried out, thereby exacerbating the claimant's depression.[491]

487 See *Topp* v. *London Country Bus (South West) Ltd.* [1993] 1 WLR 976.
488 (1945) 70 CLR 256, 261–2.
489 [1956] AC 549.
490 [1953] 2 QB 135.
491 *Butchart* v. *Home Office* [2006] EWCA Civ. 239.

Custodial authorities may also be liable to third parties for damage caused by escapes. In *Dorset Yacht* v. *Home Office*[492] a number of borstal boys escaped from custody while working on Brownsea Island off the coast of Poole and attempted to make their escape by boarding a yacht for the mainland. They collided with and then boarded the plaintiff's yacht, which was damaged as a consequence. The borstal officers were held to have been in breach of a duty of care in permitting the boys to escape—'the borstal boys were under the control of the Home Office's officers, and control imports responsibility'.[493] The damage suffered by the plaintiff was also held to be within the scope of this duty since it was foreseeable that the boys would seek to escape from the island and that they would attempt to use the yacht to do so.

(iii) Landowners

The principles of the tort of nuisance recognise the possibility of liability for omissions in relations between adjoining landowners. In *Sedleigh-Denfield* v. *O'Callaghan*[494] a trespasser laid a pipe in a ditch belonging to the defendants in such a way as to block the drainage of water off the defendants' land. In a subsequent rainstorm the plaintiff's land was flooded. The defendants were liable for their failure to act, since they were aware of the danger of flooding from their own land on to the plaintiff's but did nothing about it. Landowners have also been held liable in nuisance for permitting a fire to catch hold and spread,[495] and for failing to prevent a landslip on to neighbouring land.[496] In these cases the risk of damage to property arose from a combination of natural events, the defendant's failure to act, and, in *Sedleigh-Denfield*, a third party's intervention. In *Smith* v. *Littlewoods Organisation Ltd.*,[497] on the other hand, no natural event was involved, and the courts treated the issue as whether the defendants could be liable in negligence for the consequences of the fires started by the trespassing vandals. Lord Mackay formulated the relevant test in the following terms: '[w]hat the reasonable man is bound to foresee in a case involving injury or damage by independent human agency, just as in cases where such agency plays no part, is the probable consequences of his own act or omission, but . . . in such a case, a clear basis will be required on which to assert that the injury or damage is more than a mere possibility'.[498] As we have seen, Lord Mackay's speech assumes the possibility of a duty of care in this case by focusing on the separate and logically dependent question of breach of duty. In the circumstances, Littlewoods had no knowledge of the acts of the trespassers concerned and the risk of fire was slight when set against the considerable cost of mounting a twenty-four-hour security guard. Lord Goff rejected outright the existence of a duty of care. Although he was in a minority of one in this regard, it is not clear from the other judgments quite what is the extent of landowners' affirmative duties to avoid damage to adjoining land. *Smith* confirms a series of authorities in the lower courts suggesting that

[492] [1970] AC 1004.
[493] Lord Pearson, *ibid.*, 1055.
[494] [1940] AC 80.
[495] *Goldman* v. *Hargrave* [1967] 1 AC 645.
[496] *Leakey* v. *National Trust* [1980] QB 485.
[497] [1987] AC 241.
[498] [1987] AC 241, 261.

householders would only in the most extreme circumstances face liability to their neighbours for the acts of third parties, such as thieves and vandals, on their property. Lord Goff justified the outcome in the following terms: '[t]he practical effect is that it is the owner of the damaged premises (or, in the vast majority of cases, his insurers) who is left with a worthless claim against the vandal, rather than the occupier of the property which the vandal entered (or his insurers), a conclusion which I find less objectionable than one which may throw an unreasonable burden on ordinary households'.[499] The victims of theft and vandalism had not, on the whole, succeeded in obtaining damages from adjoining landowners through whose unoccupied property the thieves gained access to that of the plaintiffs.[500] One factor behind these decisions was the feeling that, since the plaintiff householders were likely to be insured, their loss would be met in full, while to extend liability further would force all householders to carry a new and expensive form of liability insurance. More generally, on the evidence of several recent cases,[501] it seems unlikely that the House of Lords as currently constituted will countenance extensions of the duty concept into novel areas of liability. But the tort of negligence is known for its volatility and this is an issue to which the appellate courts are sure to return.

(iv) A Wider Principle?

A form of liability which has arisen in several American state jurisdictions is that of the host who serves alcohol to customers or to guests who then drive home drunk. The host owes a duty to road-users injured by the drunk drivers. At first the imposition of a duty of care was limited to the owners of bars and restaurants, 'commercial hosts', but in the New Jersey case of *Kelly* v. *Gwinnell*[502] it was recently extended to cover the 'social host' who plies his party guests with alcohol. Aside from the difficulties of setting the appropriate standard of care for a host who may not know when his guests are over the limit, this form of liability carries the practical difficulty that the host is most unlikely to be insured against the loss in question. This has the unfortunate effect of enabling the insurance companies of both the driver and the victim to shift some of the loss, which they were paid to bear, on to a party whose responsibility for the accident was at best indirect. It is most unlikely that either commercial or social hosts will be made liable in this way in the English courts. This is because of the clear rejection of foreseeability of harm as the principal criterion of duty coupled with the use by the courts of policy arguments, and in particular arguments concerning insurance, to narrow the scope of duty.[503]

499 *Ibid.*, 279.

500 *Lamb* v. *Camden LBC* [1981] 1 QB 625; *Perl* v. *Camden LBC* [1984] 1 QB 342; *King* v. *Liverpool CC* [1986] 1 WLR 890.

501 In particular *Murphy* v. *Brentwood DC* [1991] 1 AC 398; *Alcock* v. *Chief Constable of South Yorkshire* [1992] 1 AC 310.

502 476 A 2d 1219 (1984).

503 J. Horder, 'Tort and the Road to Temperance: A Different Kind of Offensive against the Drinking Driver' (1988) 51 *MLR* 735. On the insurance point raised in the text, see further ch. 5, below.

5. PARTIES

In addition to considering the kind of damage and the manner in which it was inflicted, we now examine the way in which the notion of duty confines liability by reference to the nature of the parties involved. In some cases there exist classes of protected defendants, parties who by virtue of their identity may qualify for a certain degree of immunity from a negligence action: public bodies, certain persons involved in the administration of justice, and certain professional groups fall into this category. Conversely, in other cases the duty concept has been extended by either legislative or judicial action to include certain groups of plaintiffs within the scope of protection; two such groups requiring particular mention are the children born disabled as the result of prenatal injuries, and rescuers.

(A) PROTECTED DEFENDANTS

(i) Public Bodies

The Crown used to enjoy a general immunity from tort action, but this is now subject to the Crown Proceedings Act 1947, under which the Crown can, for the most part, be sued in tort for the actions of its servants and agents.[504] Outside the Act the Crown continues to be immune and the Monarch retains her personal immunity from suit.

Local government authorities and health authorities and certain other bodies with public responsibilities do not enjoy a general immunity from tort action, but as a matter of policy they are treated differently from private citizens and corporations for the purposes of the duty of care in negligence. The reasons for this, and the scope of the resulting protection enjoyed by public authorities, are examined in more detail later in this book.[505] Here we will provide a brief overview of the factors which make public bodies a special case for the purposes of duty of care.

A first point, which is perhaps obvious but also important, is that (certain specific statutory immunities aside) there is nothing to prevent a public or statutory body being liable just like any other person for foreseeable physical injury or similar harm brought about by a positive act. The contentious cases nearly all relate to situations in which the damage in question either does not involve physical harm to the person (psychiatric harm, property damage or pure economic loss), or arises from an omission or failure to act.

Second, bodies whose powers derive from statute, which is the case with public-sector organisations, are for this reason in a special position. Out of respect for the intentions of Parliament, the courts have held that statutory bodies will not incur liability in tort merely for failing to perform a *duty* imposed upon them by legislation,

[504] See *Pearce* v. *Secretary of State for Defence* [1988] AC 755.
[505] See ch. 8, below.

still less for failing to exercise a statutory *power*. Either the statute in question must be read as giving rise to a private action for breach of statutory duty (the tests for which are difficult to meet) or the existence of a common law duty of care must be independently established. Cases of breach of statutory duty aside, where a public body does not come under a common law duty of care, it cannot be held liable in negligence for failing to exercise statutory powers in such a way as confer a benefit upon the claimant; however, it can be liable, on general tort law grounds, for making matters worse by virtue of its intervention. In *Gorringe* v. *Calderdale MBC*[506] Lord Hoffmann encapsulated this rule when he said, 'I find it difficult to imagine a case in which a common law duty can be founded simply upon the failure (however irrational) to provide some benefit which a public authority has power (or a public law duty) to provide.' The idea that statutory bodies can only be liable for making matters worse goes back to the pre-*Anns* decision of *East Suffolk River Catchment Board* v. *Kent*.[507] It has become linked to the principle that hospitals, the fire brigade and other emergency services cannot be liable for failing to act in response to a request for help; their liability is confined to situations where they choose to respond and thereby make an assumption of responsibility.[508] Where they intervene, they can be held liable only for the additional damage which they cause. Other jurisdictions pay some regard to the idea that where there is general reliance by members of the public upon a particular service, it should be possible for an aggrieved individual to bring an action against a public body for failing to provide it.[509] This principle has not been accepted by the British courts.

It follows from what has just been said that a critical issue is when, precisely, a common law duty of care can arise in circumstances involving the provision of services by public bodies. In cases involving liability of public authorities for the repair and maintenance of the highway, the courts have repeatedly held that no affirmative duty of action arises at common law, referring to an apparently long-standing line of authority.[510] When coupled with the finding that relevant statutory powers cannot be interpreted in such a way as to give rise to a private action for breach of statutory duty, the inevitable conclusion has been to deny claims brought by motorists injured as a result, it is claimed, of the dangerous state the highway. By contrast, in cases involving liability to children taken into care or provided with certain educational services, the courts have accepted that a common law duty of care can arise, because the elements needed to establish a pre-tort relationship between the parties, including assumption of responsibility

[506] [2004] 1 WLR 1057, 1067. See also his judgment in *Stovin* v. *Wise* [1996] AC 923, 949.

[507] [1941] AC 74.

[508] See our discussion above, at Section 4(a)(i).

[509] See S. Todd, 'Liability in Tort of Public Bodies', in N. J. Mullany and A. Linden (eds.), *Torts Tomorrow: A Tribute to John Fleming* (1999), discussing *Pyrenees Shire Council* v. *Day* (1988) 102 CLR 330, where the idea was accepted by a minority of the High Court of Australia, the majority reaching the same result on different grounds. The idea was discussed but rejected by the Court of Appeal in *Capital & Counties plc* v. *Hampshire CC* [1997] QB 1004.

[510] The most important recent decisions are *Goodes* v. *East Susssex CC* [2000] 1 WLR 1356; *Stovin* v. *Wise* [1996] AC 923; *Gorringe* v. *Calderdale MBC* [2004] 1 WLR 1057; *Sandhar* v. *Secretary of State for Transport, Environment and the Regions* [2005] 1 WLR 1632.

and reasonable reliance, are present.[511] On this view, these two sets of cases—the highway cases and the children's cases—do not contradict each other.[512]

Third, even in situations where a common law duty of care does arise independently of the statutory origin of the power or duty in respect of which the public body is acting, the statute may frame the scope of that common law duty, and in particular may narrow it down. For example, the purpose for which the particular statutory duty or power was granted may restrict the potential class of plaintiffs. In the pre-*Murphy* case of *Peabody Donation Fund* v. *Sir Lindsay Parkinson & Co.*,[513] the House of Lords held that any duty owed by a local authority under *Anns* to take care in the inspection of foundations of new dwellings was restricted to loss suffered by private individuals and householders. This was because the latter constituted the class for whose protection the Public Health Acts, which were the source of the councils' powers in this instance, had been passed. No action was available, by contrast, in the case of loss suffered by a property speculator or construction company.

More generally, where a statutory duty gives rise to a discretion as to how and when it should be performed, the defendant will not *normally* be liable for decisions taken within the range of that discretion. However, it remains open to a claimant to argue that the defendant's decision was wholly unreasonable in the circumstances, and therefore outside the scope of the discretion provided by statute,[514] while there are also suggestions that the notion of a statutory discretion will not necessarily protect the defendant.[515]

Fourth, allowing again for the possibility of a common law duty of care on grounds not related to the statutory origin of the powers or duties of the public body in question, the courts will not hold public bodies liable in tort if to do so involves entering into areas of policy which are not properly *justiciable*. Thus the courts will not expand the duty concept in a way which will interfere with certain quasi-judicial or regulatory functions of statutory bodies, such as the health and safety inspectorate.[516] A separate but related idea is that the courts will not interfere with decisions involving *policy* as opposed to the *operation* of services and activities.

The notion of justiciability was discussed at length by Lord Browne-Wilkinson in *X (Minors)* v. *Bedfordshire County Council*[517] as a ground for concluding that a local

[511] *X (Minors)* v. *Bedfordshire CC* [1995] 2 AC 633; *Barrett* v. *Enfield LBC* [2001] 2 AC 550; *Phelps* v. *Hillingdon LBC* [2001] 2 AC 619.

[512] See *Gorringe* v. *Calderdale LBC* [2004] 1 WLR 1057, 1068–9 (Lord Hoffmann), 1078–9 (Lord Scott of Foscote), 1082–3 (Lord Rodger of Earlsferry), 1086 (Lord Brown of Eaton-under-Heywood). This aspect of *Gorringe* was applied in *Carty* v. *Croydon LBC* [2005] 1 WLR 2312 to find that a local authority education officer could owe a common law duty of care in respect of the provision of special educational needs to the claimant, which operated alongside a statutory duty which was not in itself actionable; however, the court found that no breach had occurred.

[513] [1985] AC 210.

[514] *X (Minors)* v. *Bedfordshire CC* [1995] 2 AC 633, 732–3 (Lord Browne-Wilkinson); see also P. P. Craig and D. Fairgrieve, '*Barrett*, Negligence and Statutory Powers' [2000] *PL* 626.

[515] *Barrett* v. *Enfield LBC* [2001] 2 AC 550, 586 (Lord Hutton); *Phelps* v. *Hillingdon LBC* [2001] 2 AC 619, 652–3 (Lord Slynn); *Gorringe* v. *Calderdale LBC* [2004] 1 WLR 1060–1 (Lord Steyn).

[516] *Harris* v. *Evans* [1998] 1 WLR 1285.

[517] [1995] 2 AC 633; see also the judgment of Hale LJ in *A* v. *Essex CC* [2004] 1 WLR 1881 (in which it was held that while an adoption agency was not under a general duty of to provide information to prospective foster

authority owed no duty for failing properly to exercise its power to take a child who was the victim of abuse into its care. Relevant factors here included the need to avoid imposing a common law duty which would cut across a complex statutory scheme for such decisions, the risk of 'defensive' practice on the part of the authorities concerned, and the danger of interfering with the difficult exercise of judgement by the professional employees concerned. By contrast, in *Barrett* v. *Enfield London Borough Council*,[518] the House of Lords declined to strike out a set of claims relating to alleged negligence by local authorities with regard to the treatment of children who had already been taken into care. Lord Slynn's judgment indicates a preference for treating many of the factors raised by Lord Browne-Wilkinson as issues of breach and causation, rather than duty of care. Then in *Phelps* v. *Hillingdon London Borough Council*[519] the House of Lords held that a local authority could under certain circumstances owe a duty of care in respect of the provision of educational services to children in its schools, further confirming the movement back towards an expansive view of liability. However, in the most recent decision of the House of Lords in this series, *D* v. *East Berkshire Community NHS Trust*,[520] it was held that doctors and social workers owed no duty of care to parents wrongly suspected of child abuse, on the grounds that such a duty would interfere with the principal responsibility of medical and social work professionals to have regard to the interests of the child in a case where abuse was suspected.

Like the notion of justiciability, the policy-operation distinction is intended to protect the policy autonomy of public bodies charged with the responsibility for allocating scarce resources between competing needs. The basic idea is that a decision to allocate resources to one activity or service as opposed to another will not normally be a matter about which a particular individual or group should be able to complain. By contrast, negligence in the performance of a service or activity which the authority has decided to supply may give rise to liability. The idea of a policy–operation distinction has never, it seems, enjoyed the unequivocal support of the courts, and it has often been suggested that it does not provide a clear-cut basis for deciding whether a duty of care should exist, particularly at the striking-out stage when the court has to proceed on the basis of assumed facts.[521] However, the aim of the distinction remains a legitimate one, namely to limit private actions by individuals against bodies with responsibility for looking after the interests of the public as a whole, or of a wide class of persons. It is thought that large-scale liabilities in tort, if widely imposed on local authorities for example, will enable a small group of favoured plaintiffs to benefit at the expense of the community as a whole.[522]

parents concerning children being considered for adoption, when it undertook to provide such information, it was under a duty to take care in doing so).

518 [2001] 2 AC 550. 519 [2001] 2 AC 619.

520 [2005] 2 AC 373.

521 See, in particular, the judgments of the House of Lords in *Barrett* v. *Enfield LBC* [2001] 2 AC 550 and *Phelps* v. *Hillingdon LBC* [2001] 2 AC 619.

522 See, in particular, *Yuen Kun Yeu* v. *A-G of Hong Kong* [1988] AC 175, *X (Minors)* v. *Bedfordshire CC* [1995] 2 AC 633 and *Stovin* v. *Wise* [1996] AC 923.

Finally, there are certain areas of public-sector activity which appear to have attracted protection on specific grounds of policy; the most important of these is the rule that the police will not be liable for negligence in the course of investigation and preventing crime. In *Hill* v. *Chief Constable of West Yorkshire* an action was brought against the police in the name of the last victim of a serial killer for their failure to make an earlier arrest. The claim was struck out on policy grounds, including those elaborated in the following way by Glidewell LJ in the Court of Appeal:

> Investigative police work is a matter of judgement, often no doubt dictated by experience or instinct. The threat that a decision, which in the end proved to be wrong, might result in action for damages would be likely to have an inhibiting effect on the exercise of that judgement.... While no doubt many such actions would fail, preparing for and taking part in the trial of such an action would inevitably involve considerable work and time for a police force, and thus either reduce the manpower available to detect crime or increase expenditure on police services.[523]

This does not mean that the police or prison officers may not be liable in a case in which there was a close pre-tort relationship with the claimant or some form of undertaking of responsibility. The *Dorset Yacht* case is just about at the limit of this version of 'proximity'. A clearer case is *Kirkham* v. *Chief Constable of Manchester*,[524] in which the police failed to pass on to prison authorities information concerning the suicidal tendencies of a remand prisoner who subsequently hanged himself while in custody. Similarly, the police have been held to owe a duty to informers not to release their identity in a way which would expose them to threats of violence,[525] and to have a duty to protect complainants and prosecution witnesses from threats of physical violence arising in connection with a criminal investigation.[526] On the other hand, the effect of *Hill* is that the police owe no duty of care to a suspect of a crime to avoid negligence in the course of their investigation, since this would 'prejudice the fearless and efficient discharge of [this] vitally important public duty',[527] even where the victim is known to the police and the circumstances disclose what might, in other contexts such as those involving the emergency services, be regarded as an assumption of responsibility.[528]

523 [1988] QB 60, 75–6; the decision of the Court of Appeal was confirmed by the House of Lords [1989] AC 53. *Hill* has been applied in a number of cases to deny claims brought in negligence against the police: see in particular *Alexandrou* v. *Oxford* [1993] 4 All ER 328; *Ancell* v. *McDermott* [1993] 4 All ER 355.

524 [1990] 2 QB 283; see also *Reeves* v. *Commissioner of Police of the Metropolis* [2001] 1 AC 360 (duty owed to person held overnight in police custody); cf. *Orange* v. *Chief Constable of West Yorkshire* [2002] QB 347.

525 *Swinney* v. *Chief Constable of Northumbria* [1997] QB 464.

526 *Van Colle* v. *Chief Constable of Hertfordshire* [2006] EWHC 360, a case decided under the Human Rights Act 1998 (using the power in s. 8 to award damages for breach of a Convention right), but which the judge said could have been decided the same way at common law.

527 *Calveley* v. *Chief Constable of Merseyside Police* [1989] 1 All ER 1025, 1030 (Lord Bridge).

528 See, in particular, *Osman* v. *Ferguson* [1993] 4 All ER 344. Although, in *Osman* v. *United Kingdom* (1998) 25 EHRR 245, the European Court of Human Rights held that the outcome in *Osman* v. *Ferguson* placed the UK in breach of Art. 6 of the ECHR, the Court's later decision in *Z* v. *United Kingdom* (2002) 34 EHRR 3, severely limits the scope for arguing that *Hill* and the case law to which it has given rise involve a breach of Art. 6 of the Convention; see our discussion below, ch. 8, Section 8, and P. Giliker, '*Osman* and Police Immunity in English Law of Torts' (2000) 20 *Leg. Stud.* 372.

Hill has been applied in numerous cases.[529] It was recently reaffirmed, although with apparent hesitation, in *Brooks* v. *Commissioner of Police of the Metropolis*.[530] Here the House of Lords held that when investigating a crime, the police did not owe a duty of care to have regard to the psychological well-being of witnesses or potential victims of the crime, where that might be affected by the way in which the investigation was conducted. According to Lord Steyn,

> A retreat from the principle in Hill's case would have detrimental effects for law enforcement. Whilst focusing on investigating crime, and the arrest of suspects, police officers would in practice be required to ensure that in every contact with a potential witness or a potential victim time and resources were deployed to avoid the risk of causing harm or offence. Such legal duties would tend to inhibit a robust approach in assessing a person as a possible suspect, witness or victim. By placing general duties of care on the police to victims and witnesses the police's ability to perform their public functions in the interests of the community, fearlessly and with despatch, would be impeded. It would, as was recognised in Hill's case, be bound to lead to an unduly defensive approach in combating crime.[531]

Although it was said in the Court of Appeal in *Brookes* that it would be inappropriate 'to describe the police as having in every case an "immunity from suit" in respect of allegations of negligent investigation of crime',[532] the pattern of the decided cases suggests that of all the decisions in the area of duty of care, *Hill* comes closest to providing a 'safe haven' for public bodies in the exercise of certain functions. Following the *Phelps* and *Barrett* decisions, and even in the light of the more recent denial of a duty to have regard to the interests of parents in child-care cases in *D* v. *East Berkshire NHS Trust*,[533] no such safe haven can be said to operate for local authorities and other public bodies in respect of the exercise of their child-care and educational responsibilities; the factors determining whether a duty of care arises are of such subtlety and complexity that it is not possible to insulate defendants from an entire class of claims as *Hill* appears to do. *Hill* therefore appears as something of an anomaly, and it may be asked how much longer it will enjoy this unusual status.

(ii) Persons Involved in the Administration of Justice

Judges and arbitrators may not be sued in tort for negligence committed in the course of their judicial duties.[534] Nor, until recently, could a client sue his barrister or solicitor for negligence in respect of court work and preparatory work closely connected

529 See ch. 8, below, for a review of this case law.

530 [2005] 1 WLR 1495. Lord Bingham (at 1497) said that he would be 'reluctant to endorse the full breadth of what *Hill* ... has been thought to lay down' and Lord Nicholls (at 1498) said that he 'was not to be taken as endorsing the full width of all the observations in *Hill*', but neither judge thought that *Hill* had been wrongly decided.

531 [2005] 1 WLR 1495, 1509–10.

532 *Brooks* v. *Commissioner of Police for the Metropolis* [2002] EWCA Civ. 407, at para. 73 (Kennedy LJ). Such an immunity would, in a formal sense, be difficult to reconcile with Art. 6 of the European Convention on Human Rights, for the reasons we have just noted.

533 [2005] 2 AC 373.

534 *Sirros* v. *Moore* [1975] AC 118; nor may arbitrators, when acting in their arbitral capacity: *Arenson* v. *Arenson* [1977] AC 405.

with the court appearance.[535] However, this last immunity was abolished by a seven-member House of Lords in *Arthur J. S. Hall* v. *Simons*,[536] invoking the 1966 Practice Statement in order to do so. Three main reasons had been given for the existence of this immunity: the 'cab-rank' principle, whereby the barrister cannot choose his client; the overriding duty which the barrister owes as an officer of the court, and the possibility of conflict between this and the fear of litigation from clients; and the fear that actions against barristers will result in the costly relitigation of disputes.[537] In *Arthur Hall*, there was general agreement that as far as the cab-rank principle was concerned, legal advocates were in the same position as many other professionals who cannot easily refuse clients, but who do not enjoy immunity from litigation. Nor was it likely, in the view of the court, that an advocate's duty to the court could excuse incompetence. The danger of costly relitigation and related disruption to the administration of justice caused the greatest difficulty and led a minority of judges to argue that the immunity should be retained for criminal cases. One answer to this concern is that appropriate control devices are available at the stage of determining issues of breach and causation.

As we have seen, as a consequence of decisions including *White* v. *Jones*,[538] solicitors may under certain circumstances be liable to their own clients in both contract and tort and to third parties in tort. However they have an immunity from suit where the litigation against them amounts to an abuse of the process of the court, in the sense of being an attempt to relitigate or attack the previous decision of a court on a matter of criminal responsibility.[539] Very occasionally a duty may extend to the adversary of the client, as in *Al-Kandari* v. *J. R. Brown*.[540] This case, however, was unusual in that the solicitor had undertaken a responsibility to his client's opponent—his wife, with whom his client was engaged in matrimonial proceedings—to look after the client's passport. The passport, however, was used by the client to flee the country taking with him the (common) children.[541] Normally, however, there will be no duty towards an adversary to take care in the conduct of litigation, for example by making sure that a winding-up order is sent to the right address.[542]

The potential liability in negligence of the Crown Prosecution Service appears to be heavily qualified both by its involvement in the administration of justice and by its status as a publicly funded body. This, at least, is the impression given by the decision of the Court of Appeal in *Elguzouli-Daf* v. *Commissioner of Police of the Metropolis*.[543] There, two plaintiffs alleged negligence in the processing of their cases by the CPS, which resulted in their imprisonment on remand being needlessly prolonged. (In one

535 *Rondel* v. *Worsley* [1969] 1 AC 191; *Saif Ali* v. *Sydney Mitchell & Co.* [1980] AC 198.

536 [2000] 3 WLR 543; see M. Seneviratne, 'The Rise and Fall of Advocates' Liability' (2001) 21 *Leg. Stud.* 644.

537 See *Rondel* v. *Worsley* [1969] 1 AC 191.

538 [1995] 2 AC 207.

539 *Smith* v. *Linskills* [1995] 3 All ER 326.

540 [1987] QB 514.

541 After arranging for his wife to be kidnapped!

542 *Business Computers International Ltd.* v. *Registrar of Companies* [1987] 3 All ER 465.

543 [1995] QB 335; cf. *Welsh* v. *Chief Constable of the Merseyside Police* [1993] 1 All ER 692.

case the incarceration lasted for eighty-five days.) Assuming the allegations to be true for the purposes of a striking-out action, the Court of Appeal held that the CPS owed them no duty of care. According to Steyn LJ, in such a case 'there are compelling considerations, rooted in the welfare of the whole community, which outweigh the dictates of individualised justice'. The considerations to which he referred included the danger of prosecutors taking a defensive approach to the performance of their duties. Also relevant was the time and energy which would have to be devoted to guarding against the risks of lawsuits. Finally there was the danger of the CPS being enmeshed in continuous litigation—'a spectre that would bode ill for the efficiency of the CPS and the quality of our criminal justice system'.[544] As against these factors, however, one must also mention the fact that this case, unlike *Hill*, was a case of misfeasance not non-feasance. More importantly, the plaintiff's interest that was at stake was his personal freedom—an interest which, in these days of more pronounced human rights awareness, should be handled with greater sensitivity. It is submitted, therefore, that in such circumstances one should be slow in sacrificing such interests to the altar of administrative convenience and that cases such as *Elguzouli* should be reconsidered at the earliest possible opportunity in the light of the new climate created by cases such as *Barrett* and *Phelps*.

(iii) Other Professionals

The decisions in *Hedley Byrne* v. *Heller*, *Henderson* v. *Merrett Syndicates Ltd.* and *White* v. *Jones* opened up the possibility of extensive professional liability for accountants, surveyors and solicitors. Other groups, including stockbrokers and architects,[545] also once enjoyed immunity in tort, but this cannot survive the expansion of liability for negligence in the performance of a service.

(iv) Regulatory Bodies

Similar considerations apply to regulatory bodies as to other organisations performing public duties; the courts aim to limit the range of matters over which negligence suits may be brought in order not to divert such bodies from the efficient performance of their allotted tasks. This means in practice that regulatory bodies are unlikely to incur liability for omissions and, moreover, that they may escape liability even where they would otherwise be vicariously liable for misstatements made by employees. Thus in *Harris* v. *Evans*[546] the Court of Appeal held that a health and safety inspector owed no duty of care to the plaintiff, the owner of a bungee-jumping business, when he told a local authority that the crane used by the plaintiff was not safe. However, it reached a different conclusion in *Perrett* v. *Collins*[547] in imposing liability upon a private association responsible for checking the construction of a light aircraft which subsequently crashed, injuring the plaintiff. Likewise, in *Watson* v. *British Boxing Board of*

[544] [1995] QB 335, 349.

[545] *Jarvis* v. *Moy Davies & Co.* [1936] 1 KB 399.

[546] [1998] 1 WLR 1285; although cf. *Welton* v. *North Cornwall DC* [1997] 1 WLR 570.

[547] [1998] 2 Lloyd's Rep. 255.

Control[548] it imposed liability upon the defendant regulatory body for failing to ensure that adequate medical care was made available to a boxer following the end of the fight. What appears to distinguish these two cases from *Harris* is that they both involved physical harm to the person.

The leading House of Lords authority in this area is *Marc Rich & Co. AG* v. *Bishop's Rock Marine Co. Ltd., The Nicholas H.*[549] Here a shipping classification society was held to have no liability for the decision of one of its surveyors to pass as seaworthy a vessel which was not in a fit condition to sail, with the result that the vessel later sank with the loss of the plaintiff's cargo. Of the various grounds given for this decision, the most convincing (we would suggest) is the suggestion that the defendant was performing a public function which was analogous to that of a public regulatory body: the classification societies, according to Lord Steyn:

> act in the public interest... [the defendant] is an independent and non-profit-making entity, created and operating for the sole purpose of promoting the collective welfare, namely the safety of lives and ships at sea. In common with other classification societies, [the defendant] fulfils a role which in its absence would have to be fulfilled by states.[550]

The same principle has been applied to hold that a government department with responsibility for certifying shipping vessels could not be held liable to the owners of a vessel which was negligently classified as meeting minimum safety requirements, with the result that the plaintiffs invested in it as a business asset, only for the vessel later to be reclassified as unfit for use, the plaintiffs then losing their investment.[551]

Yet even this type of argument has its flaws. And the *Marc Rich* result underscores these dangers once one recalls that this was a case where policy arguments—important but not, necessarily, overpowering—were used to trump a claim for damage to property and not merely pure economic loss. In the light of the above, it is submitted that the danger that these cases present is not simply that an inappropriate result may be reached in a given factual situation. By far the greatest danger lies, in our view, in the indiscriminate subsequent use of wider *dicta* and policy arguments which may be compelling for one kind of dispute but considerably weaker for another.

(v) The Armed Forces

The military authorities cannot be made vicariously liable for the harm caused by the negligence of a member of the armed forces under battle conditions. This was the finding of the Court of Appeal in *Mulcahy* v. *Ministry of Defence*.[552] The basis for the court's approach was public policy and, specifically, the perception that 'it would be highly detrimental to the conduct of military operations if each soldier had to be

548 [2001] QB 1134; J. George, '*Watson* v. *British Boxing Board of Control*: Negligent Rule-Making in the Court of Appeal' (2002) 65 *MLR* 106.

549 [1996] AC 211.

550 [1996] AC 211, 241.

551 *Reeman* v. *Department of Transport* [1997] 2 Lloyd's Rep. 648.

552 [1996] QB 732.

conscious that, even in the heat of battle, he owed such a duty to his comrade'.[553] Under such conditions, no duty is owed either to civilians or to their property, or to fellow soldiers. However, this does not rule out the possibility of liability under less abnormal circumstances; the armed forces do not enjoy a complete immunity from suit.[554]

(B) PROTECTED CLAIMANTS

We have already encountered a number of situations in which a duty of care is limited by law to a particular class of claimants. Normally only the owner of property has an action in negligence for its damage; only the near relatives of those involved in an accident who are also eyewitnesses of the events surrounding it can sue for psychiatric injury. In this part we are concerned with two further cases in which the status of protected claimants has been clarified.

(i) Injuries Sustained by the Embryo in the Womb

An embryo in the womb or 'unborn child' *en ventre sa mère* may sustain injury as the result of an accident affecting the mother or through other means, such as the negligent prescription of a course of drugs or a blood transfusion. One objection to any claim brought on the embryo's behalf for compensation is that it was not at the time the injury was sustained a legal person, capable of being owed a duty of care. This was answered in *Burton* v. *Islington Health Authority* by the argument that the duty of care, which is merely 'contingent' or potential at the time of the injury, then 'crystallises' upon the birth of the child.[555] In respect of births taking place after 22 July 1976 the matter is now governed by the Congenital Disabilities (Civil Liability) Act 1976. For the child to have an action at all it must be born alive. The Act then provides a 'derivative' action, to the effect that the child has an action against a defendant who owed a duty of care in tort to either one of the parents and would have been liable to them in tort had they suffered actionable injury or damage.[556] If one of the parents was contributorily negligent, this will go to reducing the child's damages.[557] In the case of events which preceded conception (an example might be exposure of one of the parents to a

[553] [1996] QB 732, 750 (Sir Ian Glidewell).

[554] Under the Crown Proceedings Act 1947, s. 10, the armed forces had a blanket immunity in precisely the circumstances which arose in *Mulcahy*'s case, namely negligence occurring under battle conditions. The Crown Proceedings (Armed Forces) Act 1987 removed this immunity from most situations while giving the Secretary of State the power to reinstate it by order for particular purposes. The immunity was not restored for the purposes of the Gulf War, which makes it surprising that the court in *Mulcahy* should have interpreted the common law the way it did, even though such a route was clearly open to it. For an unsuccessful attempt to challenge the remaining immunity under the Human Rights Act 1998, see *Matthews* v. *Ministry of Defence* [2003] 1 AC 1163.

[555] [1993] QB 204, following the Australian decision in *Watt* v. *Rama* [1972] VR 353 and the Canadian decision in *Montreal Tramways* v. *Leveille* [1933] 4 DLR 337. In *Re S* (*Adult: Refusal of Medical Treatment*) [1992] 3 WLR 806, the president of the Family Division held that a doctor had lawful authority to carry out a caesarean section operation on a patient who had refused her consent where this was thought to be the only way to save the unborn child; see P. R. Glazebrook, 'What Care Must Be Taken of an Unborn Baby?' [1993] *CLJ* 20.

[556] Congenital Disabilities (Civil Liability) Act, s. 1(3).

[557] *Ibid.*, s. 2.

substance which affected their reproductive capacity), the defendant has a defence if either or both of the parents knew at the time of conception that there was a risk of any child they had being born disabled, unless the defendant is the father and he alone knew of the risk.[558]

In the light of the *Islington Health Authority* case[559] and Commonwealth authorities which established the embryo's right of action without recourse to statute, the main effect of the Act is to provide an extensive immunity to the mother of the child. She owes no duty except in the one case of her driving a motor vehicle when she either knew or should reasonably have known that she was pregnant.[560] If she commits a breach of duty by driving carelessly, which results in injury to the embryo, she may then be the subject of an action. This exception indicates the impact of insurance considerations on the extent of negligence liability, since when the mother is driving (as opposed to simply riding in the car as a passenger) she will normally have the benefit of liability insurance.

In a 'wrongful life' action the child sues for the pain and suffering caused by being born disabled as a consequence, for example, of a doctor's failure to diagnose or to treat a disease or illness of the mother during pregnancy. In *McKay* v. *Essex Health Authority*[561] the Court of Appeal rejected the possibility of this action by the child on the grounds of public policy, both under the common law and (by way of *obiter dicta*) under the 1976 Act. The gist of a 'wrongful birth'[562] action, by contrast, is that had a correct diagnosis of the child's condition been carried out the mother would have aborted it, thereby avoiding pain and suffering during birth and the subsequent costs of raising a disabled child. In *Rance* v. *Mid-Downs Health Authority*[563] this type of claim was rejected, the judge holding that there was no duty on policy grounds. Finally there are the 'wrongful conception cases', the most important of which is the House of Lords' decision in *MacFarlane* v. *Tayside Health Board.*[564] The upshot of *MacFarlane* is that in the case of an unwanted pregnancy brought about by failure of contraception or sterilisation treatment, the mother is able to bring a claim based on physical harm (pain and suffering during the pregnancy and birth), but that neither she nor the father can sue for the cost of rearing a healthy child, this head of loss being ruled out on policy grounds. If, however, the child is born disabled,[565] the court can award damages for the

558 Congenital Disabilities (Civil Liability) Act, s. 1(4). Note also s. 1A of the Act, under which a child may have an action against a doctor who caused it to be born disabled through negligent selection of sperm or gametes used to bring about the creation of the embryo.

559 To which the Act was inapplicable because the plaintiff was born before it came into force.

560 Congenital Disabilities (Civil Liability) Act, s. 2.

561 [1982] QB 1166.

562 *Rance* v. *Mid-Downs HA* [1991] 1 All ER 801.

563 *Ibid.*

564 [2000] 2 AC 59, applied in *Greenfield* v. *Irwin* [2001] 1 WLR 1279. See also the earlier cases of *Udale* v. *Bloomsbury AHA* [1983] 1 WLR 1098, *Emeh* v. *Kensington and Chelsea and Westminster AHA* [1985] 1 QB 1012, *Thake* v. *Maurice* [1986] QB 644, *Gold* v. *Haringey HA* [1988] QB 481, *Allan* v. *Bloomsbury HA* [1993] 1 All ER 651, *Walkin* v. *South Manchester HA* [1995] 1 WLR 1543, *Goodwill* v. *British Pregnancy Advisory Service* [1996] 1 WLR 1397 and *Allan* v. *Greater Glasgow Health Board* 1998 SLR 580.

565 *Parkinson* v. *St James and Seacroft University Hospital NHS Trust* [2002] 2 QB 26.

extra cossts of raising the child although no claims arises if the mother herself is disabled and thereby incurs extra costs; instead she may be awarded a sum representing her loss of opportunity to plan her life as she had wished.[566]

(ii) Rescuers

The courts have long ago set aside decisions treating rescuers as a class of parties beyond the contemplation of defendants and have also rejected the application of the defence of *volenti non fit injuria* to defeat their claims. Nor will the rescuer's intervention normally be treated as breaking the chain of causation. The duty is owed to the rescuer as such and is not dependent on the defendant having owed some prior duty of care to the victim. 'Professional rescuers', such as doctors, policemen and firemen, may fall within the scope of the duty of care just as much as individuals acting out of altruism, and the subject of the rescue can be property as well as people. Thus in *Ogwo* v. *Taylor* [567] the defendant, whose negligence started a blaze on his premises, was liable to a fireman who was injured in the course of attempting to control the fire.

Cardozo CJ's argument in the New York case of *Wagner* v. *International Railway Co.*[568] to the effect that 'danger invites rescue.... The wrong that imperils life is a wrong to the imperilled victim; it is also a wrong to his rescuer', was followed by the English Court of Appeal in *Baker* v. *T. E. Hopkins.*[569] According to Wilmer LJ, 'assuming the rescuer not to have acted unreasonably... it seems to me that he must normally belong to the class of persons who ought to be within the contemplation of the wrongdoer as closely and directly affected by the latter's act'. The duty arises in relation to the rescuer even though the defendant owed no duty of care in relation to the primary accident victim, for example, because the latter was a trespasser. It is unnecessary, moreover, for the precise form of physical harm to the rescuer to be foreseen. On the other hand, it could be that the rescuer suffers an injury entirely through his own fault or otherwise in a way that could not have been foreseen. In *Crossley* v. *Rawlinson*[570] the plaintiff, running with a fire extinguisher to put out a blaze in a lorry, tripped up and fell. The judge held that the manner of his injury was unforeseeable. The case raises a difficult issue of causation; but surely it is entirely foreseeable that, in the heat of the moment, a rescuer who puts himself at risk will suffer an injury which he might otherwise have avoided. For similar reasons, it is unlikely that a defence of contributory negligence will defeat a rescuer. Or, if the defence does apply, the reduction in his damages is likely to be small. Finally, there is no reason in principle to deny a duty of care as between the victim of a self-inflicted accident or injury and one who comes to his rescue.[571]

An interesting development in a number of Canadian, American and German cases concerns the potential liability of a doctor who, through his negligence, endangers a patient, with the result that a close relative then agrees to 'donate' an organ, such as a

566 *Rees* v. *Darlington Memorial Hospital NHS Trust* [2004] 1 AC 309.

567 [1988] AC 431.

568 232 NY 176, 180 (1921).

569 [1959] 1 WLR 966.

570 [1982] 1 WLR 369.

571 *Harrison* v. *BRB* [1981] 3 All ER 650, *Chapman* v. *Hearse* [1961] SASR 51; 106 CLR 112 although, in the context of psychiatric harm, see *Greatorex* v. *Greatorex* [2001] 1 WLR 1976, discussed above, Section 3(b)(iii).

kidney, in a life-saving operation. Can the relative sue the doctor on the basis that he is a rescuer who has himself been endangered by the initial act of negligence? An action was allowed in the Canadian case of *Urbanski* v. *Patel*.[572] The requirement of foreseeability is satisfied, given that this is a common type of operation, and an argument from the floodgates seems implausible here as one is not talking about an indeterminate group of potential plaintiffs. In some American cases[573] liability has been denied on the ground, for example, that the plaintiff has time to reflect on his intervention. But it is arguable that this is a too-literal reading of Cardozo CJ's reference, in *Wagner* v. *International Railway Co.*,[574] to there being no liability where the act of rescue is 'wanton'. Nor should the defence of consent be available here, any more than it is generally as far as rescuers are concerned.[575]

SELECT BIBLIOGRAPHY

AMES, J. B., 'Law and Morals' (1908) 22 *Harv. LR* 97.

CANE, P., 'Taking Disagreement Seriously: Courts, Legislatures and the Reform of Tort Law' (2005) 25 *OJLS* 393.

COOKE, SIR ROBIN, 'An Impossible Distinction?' (1991) 107 *LQR* 46.

DIAS, R. W. M., 'The Duty Problem in Negligence' [1953] *CLJ* 198.

—'The Breach Problem and the Duty of Care' (1956) 30 *Tul. LR* 376.

FELDTHUSEN, B., 'Economic Loss in the Supreme Court of Canada: Yesterday and Tomorrow' (1991) 17 *Can. Bus. LJ* 356.

—'Pure Economic Loss in the High Court of Australia: Reinventing the Square Wheel?' (2000) 8 *Tort LR* 33.

FLEMING, J. G., 'Remoteness and Duty: The Control Devices in Liability for Negligence' (1953) 31 *Can. BR* 471.

—'Requiem for *Anns*' (1990) 106 *LQR* 525.

—'Economic Loss in Canada' (1993) 1 *Tort LR* 68.

HEPPLE, B., 'Negligence: The Search for Coherence' [1997] *CLP* 69 ff.

HOWARTH, D., 'Negligence after *Murphy*: Time to Rethink' [1991] *CLJ* 58.

LAWSON, F. H., 'Duty of Care: A Comparative Study' (1947) 22 *Tul. LR* 111.

MARKESINIS, B. S., 'An Expanding Tort Law: The Price of a Rigid Contract Law' (1987) 103 *LQR* 354.

—'Negligence, Nuisance and Affirmative Duties of Action' (1989) 105 *LQR* 104.

—and DEAKIN, S., 'The Random Element of Their Lordships' Infallible Judgment: An Economic and Comparative Analysis of the Tort of Negligence from *Anns* to *Murphy*' (1992) 55 *MLR* 619.

MULLANY, N. J., 'Proximity, Policy and Procrastination' (1992) 9 *Aust. Bus. LJ* 80.

—and HANDFORD, P., *Tort Liability for Psychiatric Damage* (1993).

572 (1978) 84 DLR (3d) 650.

573 See *Moore* v. *Shah*, 458 NYS 33 (1982); *Ornelas* v. *Fry*, 727 P 2d 918 (1986).

574 232 NY 176 180, (1921).

575 See generally B. S. Markesinis, *The German Law of Torts* (2nd edn., 1990), 486–8.

Rodger, A., 'Lord Macmillan's Speech in *Donoghue* v. *Stevenson*' (1992) 108 *LQR* 236.

Stapleton, J., 'The Gist of Negligence' (1988) 104 *LQR* 213, 389.

—'Tort, Insurance and Ideology' (1995) 58 *MLR* 820.

—'Duty of Care: Peripheral Parties and Alternative Opportunities for Deterrence' (1995) 111 *LQR* 301.

—'Duty of Care Factors: A Selection from the Judicial Menus' in Cane, P., and Stapleton, J. (eds.), *The Law of Obligations: Essays in Honour of John Fleming* (1998), ch. 4.

Teff, H., 'Liability for Psychiatric Illness after Hillsborough' (1992) 12 *OJLS* 440.

Weir, T., 'Abstraction in the Law of Torts: Economic Loss' (Oct. 1974) *City of London LR* 15.

—'Tort: Liability for Defective Foundations' [1991] *CLJ* 24.

—'The Staggering March of Negligence' in Cane, P., and Stapleton, J. (eds.), *The Law of Obligations: Essays in Honour of John Fleming* (1998), ch. 6.

Witting, C., 'Physical Damage in Negligence' [2000] *CLJ* 189.

—'Duty of Care: An Analytical Approach' (2005) 25 *OJLS* 33.

4

OTHER ELEMENTS OF LIABILITY

1. BREACH OF DUTY: NEGLIGENCE AS FAULT

In this chapter we are concerned with the two principal elements of the cause of action in negligence apart from duty of care—which was discussed in the previous chapter—that is to say, *breach of duty* and *causation of damage*.[1] The issue of breach of duty is concerned with whether the defendant was careless, in the sense of failing to conform to the standard of care applicable to him. The level at which the standard is set is a question of law, but this question is posed in the most general terms. In *Hazell* v. *British Transport Commission* [2] Pearson J said that:

> the basic rule is that negligence consists in doing something which a reasonable man would not have done in that situation or omitting to do something which a reasonable man would have done in that situation, and I approach with scepticism any suggestion that there is any other rule of law, properly so called, in any of these cases.

The standard of the 'reasonable person'—the man (or, nowadays) the man and woman 'on the Clapham omnibus'[3]—is that of the ordinary citizen. In practice, this is little more than the anthropomorphic conception of justice as perceived by judges or juries. The law thus expects the defendant to act upon 'those considerations which ordinarily regulate the conduct of human affairs'.[4] Secondly, the test is objective and, with one or two exceptions such as infants, is said to treat all defendants equally, with

[1] It is a matter of some dispute where one should commence one's inquiry: with duty or damage. In practical terms, the latter makes much sense; for without harm in this case there is no tort of negligence. On the other hand, the purpose of the previous chapter was to show that not every harm that is carelessly caused leads to an obligation to compensate. Seen in this way, the question of duty, i.e. the notion which determines the range of relationships and interests which are protected by the law, is logically anterior to that of harm. The dilemma is more theoretical than real; and, as we shall note, policy intrudes in the elements discussed in this chapter and often determines how they will be decided. The duplication of effort that this leads to is both unfortunate but, it seems also, inevitable.

[2] [1958] 1 WLR 169, 171.

[3] See *Hall* v. *Brooklands Racing Club* [1933] 1 KB 205, 224. In his judgments (such as in *MacFarlane*) Lord Steyn seems to have moved the reasonable man into the Underground. But the less attractive environment does not seem to have altered the fact that he remains in Lord Radcliffe's beautiful imagery, the 'anthropomorphic conception of justice': *Davis Contractors Ltd.* v. *Fareham UDC* [1956] AC 686, 728.

[4] *Blyth* v. *Birmingham Waterworks Co.* (1856) 11 Ex. 781, 784 (Alderson B).

the effect that an inexperienced defendant will normally be held to the level of skill of one with the normal level of experience for the job in question.[5] Thirdly, as far as specialist defendants—such as doctors or accountants—are concerned, the standard is that of the reasonably competent person in the profession in question or the particular branch of it. In practice this means that the courts defer very substantially (although not quite completely) to the standards set by and widely observed in the profession itself at any particular time.[6] Fourthly, the standard of care may be varied to meet special circumstances such as situations of rescue or sport.[7]

References to 'justice', in an abstract or even concretised form, are attractive but not always focused enough to be helpful. A more far-reaching effort to inject some substance into the basic negligence standard was thus made by Learned Hand J in a series of American cases. According to the 'Hand formula', the standard of care may be expressed in terms of three variables: the probability that harm will result to the claimant from the defendant's act or omission (P); the gravity of the loss or harm (L); and the cost or burden of preventing it (B). A breach occurs where the cost to the defendant of taking the necessary precautions is outweighed by the magnitude of the risk and the gravity of the possible harm to the claimant: or where 'B is less than L multiplied by P: i.e., $B < PL$'.[8] In *Conway* v. *O'Brien* Learned Hand J described his approach in these terms:

> The degree of care demanded of a person by an occasion is the resultant of three factors: the likelihood that his conduct will injure others, taken with the seriousness of the injury if it happens, and balanced against the interest which he must sacrifice to avoid the risk. All these are practically not susceptible of any quantitative estimate, and the second two are generally not so, even theoretically. For this reason a solution always involves some preference, or choice between incommensurables, and it is thought most likely to accord with commonly accepted standards, real or fancied.[9]

Advocates of the economic analysis of law see the 'Hand formula' as an economically efficient rule, which sets the optimum standard of care for the avoidance of accidents. It suggests that society will tolerate a certain level of accidents, where the costs of avoidance would outweigh the gains in terms of reduced risk. It is also suggested that 'Hand was purporting only to make explicit what had long been the implicit meaning of negligence'.[10] The nature of the risk is certainly a factor taken into account by English and Scottish courts. So, in *Glasgow Corporation* v. *Muir* Lord Macmillan said: 'There is no absolute standard, but it may be said that the degree of care required varies directly with the risk involved.'[11]

[5] *Nettleship* v. *Weston* [1971] 2 QB 691.

[6] *Bolam* v. *Friern Hospital Management Committee* [1958] 1 WLR 582.

[7] *Wooldridge* v. *Sumner* [1963] 2 QB 43.

[8] *US* v. *Carroll Towing Co.*, 159 F 2d 169 (1947). [9] 111 F 2d 611, 612 (1940).

[10] W. M. Landes and R. A. Posner, *The Economic Structure of Tort Law* (1987) (Select Bibliography) 85.

[11] [1943] AC 448, 456. See also the Scottish case of *Mackintosh* v. *Mackintosh*, 2 M 1357, 1362–3: 'in all cases the amount of care which a prudent man will take must vary infinitely according to circumstances. No prudent man in carrying a lighted candle through a powder magazine would fail to take more care than if he was going through a damp cellar. The amount of care will be proportionate to the degree of risk run and to the magnitude of the mischief that may be occasioned'; Landes and Posner (Select Bibliography), 87.

In *Paris* v. *Stepney Borough Council* [12] an employer was found to be negligent in failing to supply a workman, who was sighted in only one eye, with goggles to protect his remaining eye. As the plaintiff was already partially sighted the consequences of any injury to his remaining eye were sufficiently great to require the employer to take special steps for his protection. The House of Lords, reversing the Court of Appeal on this point, held that both the scale of the potential harm and the magnitude of the risk had to be taken into account. Lord Simonds said: 'I see no valid reason for excluding as irrelevant the gravity of the damage which the employee will suffer if an accident occurs, and . . . I cannot accept the view, neatly summarised by Asquith LJ [in the Court of Appeal], that the greater risk of injury is, but the risk of greater injury is not, a relevant circumstance.'[13]

It is less clear whether the English courts always have regard to the other aspect of the 'Hand formula', namely the cost of prevention. In *Bolton* v. *Stone*[14] a cricket ball hit for six struck the plaintiff on a street outside the ground. The House of Lords regarded the central question as whether the risk of this happening was sufficiently substantial, and was not so concerned with the costs of prevention. In other decisions, however, the costs of prevention have been more explicitly considered.[15] In the recent case of *Shine* v. *Tower Hamlets London Borough Council*,[16] *Bolton* v. *Stone* itself was interpreted as authority for the proposition that there has to be 'a balance between the likely severity of the accident and the cost of putting it right'. It is fair to say that the 'Hand formula', loosely conceived, has long been an approach followed by the English courts in appropriate cases.[17]

In determining for this purpose which issues raise questions of law and which raise questions of fact, the *setting* of the standard needs to be distinguished from its *application* in a particular case. These are logically separate processes although they are sometimes confused in judgments. As we have seen, the law determines the level at which the standard is set—the standard, in most cases, of the reasonably careful person in the situation or occupation in question—but its application in a particular case will be a question of 'fact and degree'.[18] For instance, the question whether a given form of medical treatment constitutes a lack of due care for the patient is to be judged by reference to the 'standard of the ordinary skilled man exercising and professing to have that special skill'. In applying this standard to a particular defendant the issue may become 'whether he is, in following that practice, doing something which no competent medical practitioner using due care would do, or whether, on the other hand, he is acting in accordance with a perfectly well-recognised school of thought'.[19] Questions of

12 [1951] AC 367.

13 *Ibid.*, 375.

14 [1951] AC 850.

15 In particular, *Latimer* v. *AEC Ltd.* [1953] AC 643, *Smith* v. *Littlewoods Ltd.* [1987] AC 241 and *Shine* v. *Tower Hamlets LBC* [2006] EWCA Civ. 852.

16 [2006] EWCA Civ. 852 at [25] (Buxton LJ).

17 On the relevance in this context of s. 1 Compensation Act 2006, see this chapter, below, section 1(c)(ii).

18 *Qualcast (Wolverhampton) Ltd.* v. *Haynes* [1959] AC 743.

19 *Bolam* v. *Friern Hospital Management Committee* [1957] 1 WLR 582, 585, 592 (McNair J).

this last kind were traditionally put to the jury. Now that jury trials no longer take place in England and Wales for personal injury and other negligence claims, it is a matter for the trial judge. Decisions on the application of the reasonableness standard do not normally give rise to legal precedents binding courts for the future. However, the appellate courts have the power to overturn the judge on the inferences to be drawn from the facts and to make their own assessment of the various factors to be weighed in the balance. In this context, one should note that decisions that do not create strictly binding precedents may nevertheless indicate in broad terms the kind of approach which courts are likely to take in future.

The complexity of this balancing process makes the notion of fault underlying negligence liability a highly relative one. If the carelessness of defendants' behaviour is to be judged, at least in part, by undertaking a calculus of the wider social costs and benefits of imposing liability, the result is to dilute the idea of fault based on individual responsibility. In *Nettleship* v. *Weston* Megaw LJ remarked that 'tortious liability has in many cases ceased to be based on moral blameworthiness'.[20] In this case a learner driver was held liable for the consequences of a lack of care in driving which was, in the circumstances, probably all that could have been expected of her; the court was influenced, however, by the fact that she was covered by third-party insurance.[21] A finding of negligence allowed the plaintiff to be compensated and the loss to be spread through the means of insurance. *Nettleship* illustrates the tendency for negligence to verge towards strict liability in areas such as road traffic and employers' liability where the courts see defendants (or their insurers) as better equipped than claimants to absorb or shift the losses in question.

To the extent that this can be shown to be widely the case, it amounts to an important departure from traditional principle, *viz.*, that the incidents of insurance are not meant to affect the imposition of liability. Though this principle still has its adherents, especially those who do not believe that the judges are equipped to weigh correctly the consequences of insurance practice,[22] the fact is that it is obviously taking place; and examples of such an open allusion to insurance practice can be found in leading decisions of many courts around the world.[23] Where, however, this is deemed not to be the case, the attitude of the courts to liability can be considerably more restrictive, the courts invoking (indirectly or directly) insurance arguments in order *not* to impose liability. The best example of this cautious attitude can be found in cases examining whether medical professionals have been negligent.[24] These points were also considered in Chapter 1 so we shall not return to them again here.

[20] [1971] 2 QB 691, 709–10.

[21] *Ibid.*, 699 (Lord Denning).

[22] J. Stapleton, 'Tort Insurance and Ideology' (1995) *MLR* 820.

[23] *Norsk Pacific Steamship Co. Ltd.* v. *Canadian National Railways Co.* (1992) 91 DLR (4th) 289 (Supreme Court of Canada) and *State of Louisiana* v. *M/V Testbank*, 752 F 2d 1019 (1985), being two of the most interesting illustrations of this 'new' trend.

[24] *Bolam* v. *Friern Hospital* [1957] 1 WLR 582, *Whitehouse* v. *Jordan* [1981] 1 WLR 246, *Sidaway* v. *Bethlem Royal Hospital* [1985] AC 871; see this chapter, below, section 1(b).

(A) THE OBJECTIVE STANDARD

(i) The Standard of the Reasonable Person

The standard is that of the 'ordinary citizen' and not that of the defendant himself; an especially careful defendant will not be deemed negligent for merely contravening his own, higher standards. Conversely, one whose personal conception of what is reasonable fails to match up to that of the court will have no defence based on his subjective belief that he acted carefully. As Professor Landes and Judge Posner put it, 'the information cost of determining each injurer's intelligence and ability to make judgments of this sort would be too great to justify departing from the reasonable-man standard'.[25]

The 'ordinary citizen' is not normally required to display the skill or expertise of a professional person in a given area. If he holds himself out to others as possessing a particular skill he would be held to that higher standard, but this does not mean that in every case it is necessary to reach the levels of competence achieved by professionals. In *Wells* v. *Cooper*[26] the plaintiff was injured when a door handle, which had been fitted by the defendant occupier himself, came away from the door. According to Jenkins LJ, 'the degree and skill required of him must be measured not by reference to the degree of competence in such matters which he personally happened to possess, but by reference to the degree of care and skill which a reasonably competent carpenter might be expected to apply to the work in question'.[27] The notion of a 'reasonably competent carpenter' appears to refer not to the standard set by a professional artisan but to that of a reasonably competent do-it-yourself enthusiast; the court held that the defendant had displayed the necessary skill and the plaintiff's action failed.

(ii) Negligence Distinguished from 'Mere Errors'

The standard of the reasonable person is not one of extraordinary care or vigilance. Since most people are susceptible to the occasional error of judgement, mere errors will not necessarily signify negligence, although this will depend on the context. Errors of judgement committed in an emergency will not normally be classified as negligence. Thus in *The Ogopogo*[28] the defendant's decision to reverse the boat back to the point at which the first guest had fallen overboard was a mistake; the court decided that it would have been more effective to have manoeuvred the boat back round in an arc. However, the Supreme Court of Canada also held that in the circumstances of a rescue this was not an error of a sufficiently serious kind to amount to negligence. The courts' attitude to rescuers seems to be to avoid, as far as possible, imposing upon them potential liabilities that will deter assistance or make it more expensive. It seems unlikely, therefore, that a volunteer or non-specialist will be held to a high standard of care. In the case of a qualified rescuer, such as a fireman or police officer, it is more likely that the courts

[25] See *The Economic Structure of Tort Law*, n. 10 (see also Select Bibliography), 127.
[26] [1958] 2 QB 265. [27] *Ibid.*, 271.
[28] [1971] Lloyd's Rep. 410.

would apply the standard of care of the professional group in question. One who is trained to deal with emergency situations may reasonably be expected to meet a higher standard of care.[29]

Even then, there are cases, not involving rescue as such, in which the courts have judged the actions of the police leniently on the ground that they cannot be expected, in the heat of the moment, to act with the normal regard for the safety of others. Chasing a suspected criminal may count as an emergency for this purpose. In *Marshall* v. *Osmond*,[30] a suspect was struck by a police car as he got out of his own vehicle to make his escape. The police officer driving the car was held to have committed an error of judgement, but the court refused to say that he had been negligent. The extent to which an emergency justifies taking risks will be one of degree. In *Rigby* v. *Chief Constable of Northamptonshire*[31] the police were held to have acted negligently by firing a CS canister into a shop belonging to the plaintiff, with the aim of flushing out a dangerous psychopath. The police had no fire-fighting equipment at their disposal, and in the resulting fire the plaintiff's shop and stock were damaged.

For the same reasons a misjudgement committed in the course of sporting activity is unlikely to amount to carelessness. In *Wooldridge* v. *Sumner*[32] the plaintiff, who was taking photographs at a horse show, was seriously injured when one of the horses got out of its rider's control and collided with him. The plaintiff alleged that the rider had been negligent in rounding a corner too quickly and in attempting to get back on to the track when he knew spectators were in his path. According to Diplock LJ:

> It cannot be suggested that the participant, at any rate if he has some modicum of skill is, by the mere act of participating, in breach of his duty of care to a spectator who is present for the very purpose of watching him do so. If, therefore, in the course of the game or competition, at a moment when he really has no time to think, a participant by mistake takes a wrong measure, he is not, in my view, to be held guilty of any negligence.[33]

The defendant was not liable. In establishing the standard in this case, Diplock LJ considered that the reasonable spectator would expect the sportsman to 'concentrate his attention on winning'. The reasonable expectations of the *victim* of injury were a relevant factor in determining the standard of care to be imposed upon the defendant.

What is reasonable behaviour between sporting participants will depend in part upon how far the sport has a common understanding of the limits to physical commitment and competition. In *Condon* v. *Basi*[34] an amateur footballer was held liable for breaking an opponent's leg in a tackle which was expressly held not to be malicious, although it was dangerous. This case is perhaps explicable by the fact that the participants

29 See *Cattley* v. *St John Ambulance Brigade* (1990, unreported); T. Weir, *A Casebook on Tort* (7th edn., 1992), 158.

30 [1983] QB 1034.

31 [1985] 1 WLR 1242.

32 [1963] 2 QB 43.

33 [1963] 2 QB 43, 68. But the result may be different if the harm is inflicted as a result of a clear contravention of the rules of the game. See further our discussion in the text, below.

34 [1985] 1 WLR 866; see also *Blake* v. *Galloway* [2004] 1 WLR 2844 and *Sharp* v. *Highland and Islands Fire Board* 2005 SLT 855.

were playing in a local league where injuries of this kind are quite rare. In professional soccer and rugby such injuries are common and it is difficult to see how a court could hold a defendant liable for negligence except in extreme circumstances: those who play the sport at this level know that there is a high possibility of serious injury to a limb. The issue cannot turn solely or even principally on whether there was a breach of the game's own rules. A breach of the rules may be minor (a technical foul) or incidental to the injury in question (soccer and rugby players have been known to suffer broken legs in lawful tackles). It is a different matter if the defendant *intended* to injure the plaintiff; except in a sport such as boxing, an action for battery will lie, and consent will not be a defence.[35]

Errors of judgement are routinely classified as negligence in road-traffic accidents. The courts have had regard to the imposition, under successive Road Traffic Acts, of compulsory third-party insurance covering owners and drivers of vehicles against liability for both personal injury and, now, property damage. The intention of this is to ensure that all victims of accidents are, as far as possible, in a position to receive full compensation; in a case where no defendant can be found, compensation is normally available through the Motor Insurers' Bureau. This system of loss-shifting would not work if the courts were not prepared to make findings of liability in the vast majority of cases.

(iii) General or Variable?

It is said that the objective standard applies regardless of the individual abilities or disabilities of defendants. One clear exception to this arises in the case of children. In the Australian case of *McHale* v. *Watson* the principles were stated as follows:

> The standard of care being objective, it is no answer for [a child], any more than it is for an adult, to say that the harm he caused was due to his being abnormally slow-witted, quick-tempered, absent minded or inexperienced. But it does not follow that he cannot rely in his defence upon a limitation upon the capacity for foresight or prudence, not as being personal to himself, but as being characteristic of humanity at his stage of development and in that sense normal.[36]

In this case a twelve-year-old boy accidentally injured a nine-year-old girl. What happened was that a sharpened steel rod thrown by the boy ricocheted off a post and hit the girl in the eye. The court held that the defendant should be held to the standard of an ordinary boy of twelve, and not to the higher 'degree of sense and circumspection which nature ordinarily withholds till life has become less rosy'. Recovery was denied. The relevant standard here is that of a child of roughly the same age and maturity as the defendant; this last point takes into account the fact that children of the same age are frequently at different stages of development. American decisions also indicate that where children are involved in activities normally undertaken only by adults—such as

[35] On the defence of *volenti* in relation to the torts of intentional interference, see ch. 24, Section 3, below.

[36] (1966) 115 CLR 199.

driving—they will then be held to the normal adult standard of care.[37] English courts have followed the same approach. In *Mullin* v. *Richards*[38] the plaintiff, a fifteen-year-old schoolgirl, was injured by a schoolfriend in a mock fight with plastic rulers. It was held that, by the standard of the ordinarily prudent fifteen-year-old schoolgirl, she had not acted carelessly.

Conversely, the vulnerability of children means that those responsible for their care will be held to a higher standard than would otherwise be the case: '[a] measure of care, appropriate to the inability or disability of those who are immature or feeble in mind or body is due from others, who know of or ought to anticipate the presence of such persons within the scope of hazard of others'.[39] An ice-cream-van driver has to take special care of the possible danger to children on the road, although he need not necessarily take extreme precautions, such as driving along at a virtual snail's pace.[40] Parents are responsible for ensuring their children's safety in the home by, for example, keeping dangerous household items such as electrical goods out of their reach or, at an appropriate age, instructing them in their use.[41] In *Surtees* v. *Kingston upon Thames BC* the plaintiff sued her foster-parents for injuries she sustained when, at the age of two years, she scalded her foot in hot water. The action failed for lack of proof of negligence. Sir Nicolas Browne-Wilkinson VC considered that 'we should be slow to characterise as negligent the care which ordinary loving and careful mothers are able to give to individual children, given the rough-and-tumble of home life'.[42]

The case of infants aside, the English courts have rejected arguments to the effect that inexperienced defendants should be held to a lower standard of care. In *Nettleship* v. *Weston* the Court of Appeal held a learner driver to the same standard of care as an experienced road-user. In the view of Megaw LJ:

> if this doctrine of varying standards were to be accepted as part of the law on these facts, it could not logically be confined to the duty of care owed by learner drivers. . . . The disadvantages of the resulting unpredictability, uncertainty and, indeed, impossibility of arriving at fair and consistent decisions outweigh the advantages. The certainty of a general standard is preferable to the vagaries of a fluctuating standard.[43]

The opposing view was adopted by the High Court of Australia in *Cook* v. *Cook*.[44] As in *Nettleship*, an amateur driving instructor brought the action against the learner driver. The High Court of Australia explained why the standard expected of the defendant would differ as between the plaintiff, who knew of her inexperience, and third parties, who would not:

> it is the very absence of skill, which lies at the heart of the special relationship between the driving instructor and his pupil. In such a case, the standard of care, which arises from the relationship of pupil and instructor, is that which is reasonably to be expected of an unqualified

[37] See *Terre Haute First National Bank* v. *Stewart*, 455 NE 2d 262 (1984); Landes and Posner, n. 10 (see also Select Bibliography), 128–9.

[38] [1998] 1 WLR 1304.

[39] *Latham* v. *R. Johnson* [1913] 1 KB 398, 416.

[40] *Kite* v. *Nolan* [1982] RTR 253.

[41] *Jauffer* v. *Abkar*, *The Times*, 10 Feb. 1984.

[42] [1992] 2 FLR 559, 584.

[43] *Ibid.*

[44] (1986) 68 ALR 353.

and inexperienced driver in the circumstances in which the pupil is placed. The standard of care remains an objective one. It is, however, adjusted to the special relationship under which it arises.[45]

The defendant is not necessarily held to the *same* standard in regard to particular plaintiffs: the normal standard of care may be adjusted where the parties were in a pre-tort relationship within which their particular characteristics were known to each other. This issue is separate from the question whether defences such as *volenti* or contributory negligence should be available. The outcome in *Nettleship* v. *Weston*[46] is still explicable using this approach: the instructor in that case specifically checked in advance to see whether the defendant was covered by liability insurance, and presumably would have refused to go out with her if she had not been. In *Wilsher* v. *Essex Area Health Authority*[47] a trainee hospital doctor was held to the same standard in relation to a patient's care as the court would have applied to an experienced doctor. In relation to his colleagues or his supervisors, who would have been more aware of the consequences of his lack of experience, a different standard could plausibly have applied. Similarly, if in *Marshall* v. *Osmond*[48] the police had injured a third party rather than the suspect whom they were chasing, the decision could well have been different. There is no reason why the police should be held to the same standard of care in the case of bystanders as in the case of the suspect. But there is no clear English authority for this approach.

We have already noted the stringent view taken in relation to negligence on the highway. The apparent policy aim of ensuring the maximum coverage of liability seems to explain decisions such as *Roberts* v. *Ramsbottom*[49] and *Broome* v. *Perkins*,[50] in which the drivers concerned could not plausibly be said to have driven carelessly, having suffered respectively a heart attack and a diabetic attack while at the wheel. A different rule is adopted in several American states, which holds the defendant to the standard of a normal person suffering the condition in question.

In *Breunig* v. *American Family Insurance Co.*[51] the defendant had a sudden mental blackout and drove her car into the back of another vehicle. She was held to have been careless only because she had received prior warning of the likely effects of her mental illness; her negligence lay in the act of driving itself. Had she not received these warnings, the court would not have made a finding of negligence. Without adopting this rule as such, the Court of Appeal in *Mansfield* v. *Weetabix Ltd.*[52] reiterated that liability in negligence is based on fault, even in road-traffic cases. It thus held that a lorry driver who crashed his lorry after losing consciousness at the wheel as a result of a condition (hypoglycaemia) which he was unaware he had and had no reason to believe he suffered from, was not liable for the damage caused. The relevant standard to apply, in the view of the court, was that of the reasonably careful driver who was unaware that he was suffering from a condition that impaired his ability to drive safely.

45 *Ibid.*, 358 (Mason, Wilson, Deane and Dawson JJ).
46 [1971] 2 QB 691.
47 [1987] QB 730.
48 [1983] QB 1034.
49 [1980] 1 WLR 823.
50 [1987] RTR 321.
51 173 NW 2d 619 (1970).
52 [1998] 1 WLR 1263.

(B) PROFESSIONAL STANDARDS

Professional men and women are governed by the standard of care of a normal person of their occupation or specialism: 'the test is the standard of the ordinary skilled man exercising and professing to have that special skill'.[53] An extension of this is the so-called *Bolam* test, by virtue of which a professional person is exonerated if he can show that his practice accorded with a substantial and respectable body of opinion in his field. Thus, 'he is not guilty of negligence if he has acted in accordance with a practice accepted as proper by a responsible body of medical men skilled in that particular art'. Conversely, 'putting it the other way round, a man is not negligent, if he is acting in accordance with such a practice, merely because there is a body of opinion who would take a contrary view'.[54] The facts of *Bolam* illustrate this: medical opinion at the time was divided on the practice of administering electroconvulsive therapy without physically restraining the patient, and evidence suggested that there were risks either way. After hearing McNair J's direction, the jury found for the defendant.

An important aspect of the *Bolam* test is that the court will not expect the defendant to have anticipated future developments in knowledge or practice: he will be judged by the state of knowledge of the normal professional at the time of the alleged tort. This was illustrated in *Roe* v. *Ministry of Health*.[55] Each of the plaintiffs was paralysed when a contaminated anaesthetic was administered to them in the course of an operation. Tiny and undiscoverable cracks in the ampoules in which the liquid anaesthetic was kept were the cause of the contamination. In the view of Lord Denning, the anaesthetist 'did not know that there could be undetectable cracks, but it was not negligent for him not to know it at that time. We must not look at the 1947 accident with 1954 spectacles.'[56] The court dismissed the plaintiffs' appeals.

Where professional opinion is divided, it is not surprising that judges (who have now taken over the jury's function of applying the reasonableness test to the facts) normally consider themselves in no better position than the professionals to resolve the matter. If one body of opinion is against a technique but another, which is also sizeable and respectable, is for it, the normal finding is one of no negligence. It is more straightforward when the defendant departed from general practice. Liability was admitted, for example, in *Kralj* v. *McGrath*[57] when a 'horrific' technique was employed to deliver a twin baby.

Other factors have led the courts to take a broadly pro-defendant line in medical malpractice cases (though there are areas—such as those involving the vexed question of 'informed consent' where the courts have, in recent times, moved more towards the position of claimants, perhaps influenced by the 'rights' culture that has accompanied the growth of the human rights law). Thus, one argument frequently invoked is that the

[53] *Bolam* v. *Friern Hospital* [1957] 1 WLR 582, 586. The particular specialism or skill which the defendant holds himself out as having is relevant here: *Shakoor* v. *Situ* [2001] 1 WLR 410.

[54] [1957] 1 WLR 582, 587.

[55] [1954] 2 QB 66.

[56] *Ibid.*

[57] [1986] 1 All ER 54.

profession itself can bring sanctions to bear against inefficient doctors, and through its own internal procedures can maintain high standards more effectively than the courts can. A second is the fear of 'defensive medicine' and the frequent complaints of medical professionals themselves that the threat of legal liability and the cost of insurance coverage are inhibiting the development of new surgical techniques. The courts have accordingly said that, in the context of medical negligence, a 'mere' error of judgement is unlikely to amount to carelessness, despite the potentially grave consequences of such an error.[58] How much empirical evidence supports the validity of these arguments (which militate against liability) is, however, a highly debatable point, not least because of the fact that many of the (empirical) surveys carried out on these points may have been 'sponsored' or otherwise 'encouraged' by interested parties.

The *Bolam* test was considered and broadly confirmed by the House of Lords in *Sidaway* v. *Bethlem Royal Hospital*.[59] This concerned the question of 'informed consent' and the extent of the doctor's obligation to inform the patient of significant risks attached to a particular course of treatment. In this case the defendant's surgeon omitted to tell the plaintiff of a small risk, put by the trial judge at 1–2 per cent, that a back operation could lead to damage to the spinal cord and hence to a degree of paralysis. The operation was performed with full care and skill, but as a result of interference with the spinal cord the plaintiff was paralysed. The plaintiff's complaint was that the surgeon had been negligent in not warning her of the risk, and that had she known of it she would not have consented to the operation. In the view of Lord Bridge (with whom Lord Keith of Kinkel agreed), 'the appellant's expert witnesses' agreement that the non-disclosure complained of accorded with a practice accepted as proper by a responsible body of neurosurgical opinion afforded the respondents with a complete defence to the appellant's claim'. However, Lord Bridge did not accept that the *Bolam* test would apply in every instance:

> even in a case where, as here, no expert witness in the relevant medical field condemns the non-disclosure as being in conflict with accepted and responsible medical practice, I am of opinion that the judge might in certain circumstances come to the conclusion that disclosure of a particular risk was so obviously necessary to an informed choice on the part of the patient that no reasonably prudent medical man would fail to make it.[60]

Such a case might be one in which there was 'an operation involving a substantial risk of grave adverse consequences'; the degree of persistence of the patient in seeking information also had to be taken into account. The implication is that in *Sidaway* itself the risk of injury, estimated at around one chance in 100, was not great enough. Lord Diplock, likewise, thought that *Bolam* would normally apply, except in a case where the court was clear that the particular practice was not 'responsible'.

[58] *Whitehouse* v. *Jordan* [1981] 1 WLR 246.

[59] [1985] AC 871. See also the discussion of *Sidaway* in *Chester* v. *Ashfar* [2005] 1 AC 134, 150–4 (Lord Hope of Craighead).

[60] [1985] AC 871.

In subsequent cases *Sidaway* has been interpreted as providing general support for the *Bolam* test. However, if this is correct, the degree to which the courts review professional standards objectively is extremely limited; those standards are simply rubber-stamped for the purposes of defining carelessness. Alone of the judges in *Sidaway*, Lord Scarman thought it relevant to ask what the reasonable *patient* would have expected to receive by way of information. As we have seen, there is authority for the view that the plaintiff's reasonable expectations are relevant in setting the standard of care where (as here) the parties in a duty relationship are not strangers, but were in a close pre-tort relationship akin to contract.[61] In the case of many hospital treatments the patient may not know the right question to ask, or may expect to be informed without asking about specific risks. According to Lord Scarman, there might be cases in which fears for the patient's health could justify the doctor's silence, for example, where information concerning a risk of failure could increase stress on the patient. This would be a matter for the court to judge, however, and not solely a question of medical opinion.[62] This approach would no doubt be opposed by those who consider that the courts should not put themselves in such a position, but it does at least have the merit of avoiding the appearance of simply rubber-stamping professional practice. If a doctor is expressly asked about the risks of a particular treatment and still declines to inform the patient, it is more likely that a finding of negligence would be made, although even here some consider that the *Bolam* test alone should apply.

In *Bolitho* v. *City and Hackney Health Authority*[63] the House of Lords confirmed the general position that while the *Bolam* test was still good law, there remained some scope for the judges to depart from the standard set by general professional practice when setting the relevant legal standard. According to Lord Browne-Wilkinson:

> the court is not bound to hold that a defendant doctor escapes liability for negligent treatment or diagnosis just because he leads evidence from a number of medical experts who are genuinely of opinion that the defendant's treatment or diagnosis accorded with sound medical practice... the court has to be satisfied that the exponents of the body of opinion relied upon can demonstrate that such opinion has a logical basis. In particular in cases involving, as they so often do, the weighing of risks against benefits, the judge before accepting a body of opinion as being responsible, reasonable or respectable, will need to be satisfied that, in forming their views, the experts have directed their minds to the question of comparative risks and benefits and have reached a defensible conclusion on the matter.[64]

This may not advance the law much, however, since his Lordship also remarked that 'it will very seldom be right for a judge to reach the conclusion that views genuinely held by a competent medical expert are unreasonable'.[65] On the other hand, we return to the

[61] There is normally no contract between the patient and either the hospital or the doctor treating him in the case of NHS treatment, but a contract will normally arise between patient and doctor in private practice.

[62] [1985] AC 871, 889.

[63] [1998] AC 232. The House of Lords has also reasserted the importance of the *Bolam* test as a control device in the context of decisions expanding the duty of care of professional workers in the public sector (in particular, *Barrett* v. *Enfield LBC* [2001] 2 AC 550 and *Phelps* v. *Hillingdon LBC* [2001] 2 AC 619), and this approach was recently applied by the Court of Appeal in *Carty* v. *Croydon LBC* [2005] 1 WLR 2312.

[64] [1998] AC 232, 241–2. [65] *Ibid.*, 243.

point made earlier on namely, that the fact that we live in a society increasingly affected by a rights and entitlements culture may well continue to propel the law in the direction of claimants, something which might even gain further momentum by the declining efficiency of the national health-care system in this country.

It is important to note that, outside the medical area, the courts have often declined to allow common practice to be a defence. This has happened in cases of employers' liability, although here it is also possible that negligence may consist in failing to take preventive action only once the scale of the threat to occupational health is known and protective equipment has become available, as in *Thompson* v. *Smiths Ship Repairers (North Shields) Ltd.*[66] In *Lloyds Bank* v. *Savory*[67] it was not a defence to show that the defendants had followed general banking practice in their procedures for handling cheques. Nor can the common-practice defence be invoked in a case where the exercise of professional skill or judgement was not in issue, and the court feels able to determine whether there has been a lack of competence without referring to a body of professional opinion.[68] On the other hand, the courts have shown that in emerging areas of negligence law, such as the liability of local government officials for negligence in respect of the provision of special educational needs, they will not easily infer breach of duty if generally observed practices and procedures have been followed.[69] This last example comes from an area which has become so controversial, as well as being affected by other areas of the law—administrative law, EC law, the law of the ECHR—that it is the subject of a special chapter in this book.[70]

(C) WEIGHING THE RISK AND GRAVITY OF HARM AGAINST THE COST OF PREVENTION

As we have seen, the essence of the 'Hand formula' is weighing the magnitude and scale of the risk of harm against the cost of prevention. The approach has been criticised on the ground that it is both invidious and impractical to compare, for example, the consequences to the plaintiff in terms of the loss of a limb or pain and suffering against what may only be a financial cost to the defendant. Personal injury can never be 'fully compensated' despite the efforts of the tort system to do so, and placing an economic value on the risk of such injury is a process fraught with difficulty. The same objection does not arise with regard to property damage, and here the use of cost–benefit analyses is less contentious.[71] One argument for the use of cost–benefit comparisons even for personal injury is that many socially desirable or necessary activities cannot be carried on without some risk of causing personal injury. Transport is one obvious example.

66 [1984] QB 145.

67 [1933] AC 201. See also *Edward Wong Finance Co. Ltd.* v. *Johnson Stokes & Master* [1984] AC 296.

68 See *J. D. Williams & Co. Ltd.* v. *Michael Hyde & Associates Ltd.* [2001] BLR 99, [2000] Lloyd's Rep. PN 823; cf. *Adams* v. *Rhymney Valley DC* [2001] PNLR 68.

69 *Carty* v. *Croydon LBC* [2005] 1 WLR 2312.

70 Ch. 8, below.

71 For discussion of these and related issues, see R. Abel, 'Should Tort Law Protect Property against Accidental Loss?' in M. Furmston (ed.), *The Law of Tort: Policies and Trends in Liability for Damage to Property and Economic Loss* (1985), ch. 8, in particular at n. 182.

The level of care required in relation to a given activity may be a highly contentious question of policy, and one in which Parliament has stepped in to set standards through statutory regulation for areas such as employers' liability. There will, however, inevitably be cases (including many in the field of employment) to which no statutory standard is relevant, and here the courts cannot avoid the task of weighing the different interests involved.

Assessing the risk of harm has, as we have seen, two related aspects: the court must consider both the *degree of probability* of the risk being realised and the *gravity* of the potential injury itself. If serious injury is a possibility, even a comparatively small risk may weigh heavily in the balance. On the other side, in examining the cost of prevention the court has to consider not simply the potential *expenditure* to the defendant of taking additional steps to prevent the harm. It must also bear in mind the *benefit foregone* if, as may be possible, the activity in question has to be abandoned, as will be the case if the cost to the defendant of carrying on outweighs the gains. Nor is it simply the cost to the defendant that the court has to consider. It may be that the claimant is in the best position to take the necessary steps to avert the danger in question. If, in economic terminology, the claimant were the 'least cost avoider', social cost as a whole would be minimised by a no-liability rule, which would leave it up to the claimant to act. An essential qualification to the test adopted by Learned Hand J is made by Landes and Posner. According to these authors, what matters in the comparison is not the total or average values but the *marginal* costs and benefits of eliminating a particular risk: 'the court asks, "What additional care inputs should the defendant have used to avoid this accident, given his existing level of care?"'[72] If an incremental gain in safety can only be made at enormous expense, failure to take this precaution is unlikely to amount to negligence in the sense applied by the courts.

These considerations are not always spelled out in the judgments of the English courts. However, they often seem to underlie the judges' apparently intuitive notions of what is reasonable in a particular case, and there are some signs that their use is becoming more explicit.

(i) Risk and Foreseeability of Damage

The relationship between the risk of injury and the degree of foreseeability was considered by the House of Lords in *Bolton* v. *Stone*,[73] the facts of which were described above. The chances of a passer-by being struck by a cricket ball hit out of the ground were found to be very small. Balls had been hit out of the ground only six times in the preceding thirty years, and the street (in which the plaintiff was a resident) was fairly quiet and unfrequented. The House of Lords allowed an appeal by the owners of the ground from findings of liability in the lower courts. Lord Reid approached the case by asking whether the risk was sufficiently substantial and rejected a test based on foreseeability alone: 'on the theory that it is foreseeability alone that matters it would be irrelevant to consider how often a ball might be expected to land in the road and it

[72] Note 10 (see also Select Bibliography), 87. [73] [1951] AC 850, 518; *Ibid.*, 866–7.

would not matter whether the road was the busiest street or the quietest country lane. The only difference between these cases is in the degree of risk.' The correct test was: 'what a man must not do, and what I think a careful man tries not to do, is create a risk which is substantial'. In this case the risk was 'extremely small'.[74]

The question in each case, then, is not whether a particular injury was foreseeable, but whether, in the first place, the risk was *sufficiently* substantial, and this is a matter of degree. This is only the first step in the argument, though; the only way to assess whether a risk is sufficiently substantial is to measure it against both the gravity of the resulting injury and the cost of prevention to the defendant. In this regard, Lord Reid said: 'In considering that matter I think that it would be right to take into account, not only how remote is the chance that a person might be struck, but also how serious the consequences are likely to be if a person is struck, but I do not think that it would be right to take into account the difficulty of remedial measures.'[75] This is, in effect, to consider only one half of the equation. In the same case, Lord Radcliffe appeared to take a different view. He thus said: 'It seems to me that a reasonable man, taking account of the chances against an accident happening, would not have felt himself called on either to abandon the use of the ground for cricket or to increase the height of his surrounding fences.'[76] A seven-foot-high fence surrounded the ground, which was itself ten feet below the level of the street outside. One way of explaining the outcome, then, is to say that the costs to the defendants of taking *extra* precautions—of building a higher fence, for example—were considerable in relation to the *extra* degree of safety which would thereby have been achieved. The only way of really being sure that no one could have been hit by a cricket ball would have been to stop playing cricket on the site altogether. This considerable cost to the defendants would have far outweighed the removal of the comparatively small risk of passers-by being struck by a flying cricket ball.

It is not clear, however, that this was the basis for the decision in *Bolton* v. *Stone*. For only Lord Radcliffe's judgment referred, obliquely, to the factor of the cost of prevention, and, as we have just seen, Lord Reid expressly ruled it out as a factor to be taken into account. In *The Wagon Mound (No. 2)*[77] he explained *Bolton* v. *Stone* as a case in which 'the risk was so small that in the circumstances a reasonable man would have been justified in disregarding it and taking no steps to eliminate it'.

On the other hand, Lord Reid's judgment in *The Wagon Mound (No. 2)* explicitly considered the cost of prevention. In this case oil discharged into Sydney harbour from the defendant's vessel was ignited, most probably by a piece of hot metal which fell into the water from welding work going on in one of the wharfs. In the resulting fire the plaintiffs' vessels were damaged. The likelihood of the oil catching fire was very low—oil of the kind in question, on the surface of water, is 'extremely difficult to ignite in the open'—but there was a risk, however small. The gravity of any damage that would then occur was enormous, but also relevant was the lack of justification for the initial

[74] *Ibid.*, 866–7.
[75] *Ibid.*, 867.
[76] *Ibid.*, 869.
[77] [1967] 1 AC 617, 642.

spillage: to have avoided the risk would have 'presented no difficulty, involved no disadvantage and required no expense'.[78]

The limited relevance of foreseeability of harm as a test is illustrated by the case of *Paris* v. *Stepney Borough Council*, which was analysed above.[79] We also see this in *Haley* v. *London Electricity Board*,[80] where workmen employed by the defendant excavated a hole in a London street and, by way of warning to pedestrians, simply placed a shovel across it. This would have been sufficient, it was said, for sighted pedestrians, but the defendant, who was blind and who frequently walked down that street on his way to a bus stop, missed the shovel with his white stick and fell into the hole. He was seriously injured and lost his hearing. The Electricity Board defended itself on the ground that this course of events was not reasonably foreseeable; but this was answered by evidence of the large number of blind people who lived in London and who would be used to walking unaccompanied.

Perhaps more to the point in this case was the low cost to the defendants of minimising the risk to the plaintiff: a light fence around the hole could easily have been provided. The defendants possessed such fences and would have used one in this case but for a delay in it being made available. By contrast the cost to the plaintiff would have been considerable: he had taken the normal precaution for a blind person of carrying his stick with him, and could have protected himself further only by walking accompanied or by staying at home.

(ii) Assessing the Costs of Prevention

A case cited to illustrate the importance of the cost of prevention is the American decision of *Adams* v. *Bullock*.[81] The defendant company ran trolley-buses under wires which were not insulated. Unlike electric wires, the trolley wires could not be protected by insulation. The plaintiff, a young boy, was injured when he dangled a wire on to one of the trolley-bus wires from a bridge several feet above it. According to the court, the only way this injury could have been avoided was to have run the wires underground. The remote possibility of injury occurring in this way did not justify such an expense. Landes and Posner have explained the outcome in this way:

> This is a clear statement of the proposition that the optimal level of care is a function of its cost, other things being equal. On the one hand, even if the probability of harm is slight, if the cost of avoiding the harm is also slight the failure to avoid may be negligence. On the other hand, even if the probability and magnitude of harm are the same for trolley and electric wires, electric companies may be liable in negligence and trolley companies not, simply because the cost of care is lower for electric companies.[82]

Two decisions in which the House of Lords has had express regard to the costs of prevention are *Latimer* v. *AEC Ltd.*[83] and *Smith* v. *Littlewoods Ltd.*[84] In the *Latimer* case the

78 [1967] 1 AC 617, 643–4.
79 See above.
80 [1965] AC 778.
81 125 NE 93 (1919).
82 n.10 (see also Select Bibliography), 87–8.
83 [1953] AC 634.
84 [1987] AC 241.

defendant's factory was flooded by heavy rain. Sawdust was placed on the worst-affected areas. However, many areas of the floor remained damp and the plaintiff slipped on one of them, breaking his ankle. The judge found that the employers had done everything necessary short of shutting down the factory for the duration of the shift in question; the House of Lords held that a reasonably prudent employer would not have shut down the works completely in these circumstances. The cost, both to the employer and to the workmen who would have forfeited their wages, outweighed the potential risk: the plaintiff was the only worker to have 'experienced any difficulty'.[85]

The decision seems questionable when it is borne in mind that both tort (through the employer's personal duty of care to his employees[86]) and contract (through the express and implied terms of the contract of employment) place on the employer the principal onus of ensuring that the factory is a safe place in which to work.[87] It is far from clear as a matter of contract law that the employer would not have had to compensate the employees for any closure of the factory, and such an obligation could now arise under statute.[88] *Latimer* illustrates the extent to which these decisions raise difficult questions of degree, in which openly evaluative judgements may have to be made. *Smith* v. *Littlewoods*[89] concerned the liability of the owners of a large derelict cinema for the acts of vandals who entered the premises and set fire to them, causing damage to adjoining properties. Only property damage was in issue here, then. The gravity of the potential harm was substantial in financial terms. Unlike in *Latimer*, however, the loss was property damage and not personal injury, and the likelihood of such an event occurring was found to be low: the defendants were not aware of the presence of vandals on the site and had no reason to assume that they constituted a significant threat. Nor, it seemed, were the adjoining owners particularly concerned, since none of them complained to Littlewoods prior to the fire of the potential danger to their own property. Finally, the defendants had taken certain precautions against illicit entry. Short of posting a continuous guard over the property they would not have been in a position to prevent the vandals getting in. Since the plaintiffs were either covered by loss insurance or could easily have been so, they may be regarded as best placed to bear the loss and to shift it.

What is reasonable may depend upon the resources of the defendant. Although, as we have seen, the courts are said to apply a general standard which takes little or no regard of individual disabilities, there may be cases in which it would be pointless to impose too onerous a burden on the defendant. This is particularly so where affirmative duties of action are concerned. In *Goldman* v. *Hargrave*[90] Lord Wilberforce argued that:

> the standard ought to be to require of the occupier what it is reasonable to expect of him in his individual circumstances. Thus, less must be expected of the infirm than of the able-bodied: the owner of a small property where a hazard arises which threatens a neighbour with

[85] [1953] AC 643, 659.

[86] See ch. 18, below.

[87] *Johnstone* v. *Bloomsbury HA* [1992] 1 QB 333. In practice this, of course, means the management of the enterprise.

[88] Under the 'guarantee pay' provisions of the Employment Rights Act 1996.

[89] [1987] AC 241.

[90] [1967] 1 AC 645, 663.

substantial interests should not have to do as much as one with larger interests of his own at stake and greater resources to protect them . . .

This argument may have less force, though, outside the specific context in which Lord Wilberforce was addressing it. Normally the burden of care will not be displaced from one party to the other *simply* because of a disparity of income and resources between them; the relevant question is which of them can act at the least cost. Duties of affirmative action, however, may become unenforceable if the mere ownership of land is taken to carry with it extensive duties to act for the protection of near neighbours.

Another area in which the balancing of costs and benefits gives rise to difficult issues is that of 'negligence in design'. The costs to a company or utility of altering an existing design in order to achieve incremental protection to consumers or users of the service in question may be enormous. In *Wyngrove* v. *Scottish Omnibuses*[91] the complaint concerned the defendants' failure to fit a vertical pillar on the rear platform of their buses. The absence of the pillar allegedly caused the plaintiff to fall out of the bus when attempting to exit from it, as a result of which he sustained serious injuries. Various other handholds had been provided. In the view of Lord Reid, the fact that thousands of journeys had been safely made without a similar accident occurring entitled the bus company to conclude that their system was adequate: the chance of injury occurring in the way alleged was 'very remote'.

Watt v. *Hertfordshire County Council*[92] illustrates the importance of weighing the risk against the benefit that would be forgone by excessive preventive measures. A fireman sued his employers for negligence when he was injured by heavy lifting gear in the course of a journey by lorry to rescue a woman trapped under a vehicle. The court held that the unusual risk being run by not waiting for a more suitable vehicle in which to carry the lifting gear was justified by the exceptional end in view, namely that of saving the life of the woman; and the plaintiff's action failed.

Given the substantial body of case law in which the courts had explicitly taken into account the costs of precautions, broadly defined, in determining whether there was a breach of duty, it is far from clear why Parliament felt it necessary to enact section 1 of the Compensation Act 2006. This provides that:

A court considering a claim in negligence or breach of statutory duty may, in determining whether the defendant should have taken particular steps to meet a standard of care (whether by taking precautions against a risk or otherwise), have regard to whether a requirement to take those steps might—

(a) prevent a desirable activity from being undertaken at all, to a particular extent or in a particular way, or

(b) discourage persons from undertaking functions in connection with a desirable activity.

The justification given for this measure was a government report in 2004[93] which suggested that there was 'a common misperception' of the strictness of the 'breach' test,

91 1966 SC 47 (HL).

92 [1954] 1 WLR 835; see also *Daborn* v. *Bath Tramways Motor Co.* [1946] 2 All ER 333.

93 Better Regulation Taskforce, *Better Routes to Redress* (May 2004).

which was leading to 'a disproportionate fear of litigation and consequent risk-averse behaviour'.[94] Section 1 'is intended to contribute to improving awareness of this aspect of the law; providing reassurance to the people and organisations who are concerned about possible litigation; and to ensuring that normal activities are not prevented because of the fear of litigation and excessively risk-averse behaviour'.[95] Whether it will make any difference to the way in which the courts approach their task remains to be seen, but this may be doubted, for two reasons: the provision is permissive, not mandatory (the court 'may' have regard to the considerations set out in limbs (a) and (b)), and, as we have seen, it adds nothing to the common law, which certainly permits and arguably requires the court to consider the costs of prevention.

Can a defendant be made liable for failing to take into account the possibility that another will fail to take due care for his own safety in the sense of being contributorily negligent? The courts have said that this can amount to negligence by the defendant,[96] even though it might seem that the law is thereby requiring the defendant to undertake a degree of prevention which is socially wasteful in the sense that the claimant was the 'least cost avoider'. One difficulty in practice, however, is that the court may have insufficient information to make such a categorical judgment about relative fault. Moreover, as far as employer's liability is concerned, the employer's superior resources, his power to direct the pace and form of the work, and his greater loss-shifting capacity, may all point in the direction of imposing on him the responsibility of ensuring that employees are, as far as possible, safeguarded against the consequences of a lack of attention or misjudgment, even if the latter could amount to contributory negligence.

(D) PROOF OF CARELESSNESS

In a civil action the plaintiff is required to prove his case on a balance of probabilities; in so far as proof of carelessness is concerned this means adducing facts from which the courts may make the necessary inference of a lack of care. If the defendant has been convicted of a criminal offence, that may be admitted in evidence in the civil action by virtue of the Civil Evidence Act 1968.[97] This is especially useful in road-traffic cases. Once evidence is admitted of a conviction which could only have been secured where the defendant was negligent, the normal burden of proof is reversed and the defendant has to displace the presumption against him.

More generally the claimant may be able to invoke the doctrine known as *res ipsa loquitur* or 'the event speaks for itself'. This means that under certain circumstances the claimant may raise a presumption of negligence simply by detailing the manner in which the accident or the loss in question occurred. Negligence will be presumed where the means by which the damage was inflicted were under the defendant's sole control or

94 Explanatory Note to the Compensation Act 2006, para. 7.

95 *Ibid*., para. 10.

96 *Grant* v. *Sun Shipping Co. Ltd.* [1948] AC 549, 567; *London Passenger Transport Board* v. *Upson* [1949] AC 155, 173.

97 Section 11.

where, on first sight, no explanation other than carelessness by the defendant is possible. The practical effect is that the claimant does not need to 'prove precisely what was the relevant act of omission which set in train the events leading to the accident'.[98]

According to Lord Griffiths, speaking for the Privy Council in *Ng Chun Pui* v. *Lee Chuen Tat*,[99] this does not mean that the burden of proof is formally reversed. The claimant has the burden throughout of establishing his case on the balance of probabilities, and the judge must make an assessment of whether there has been a lack of due care on all the evidence presented to him. Another way of putting this is to say that the defendant does not formally have the burden of *disproving* lack of care on the balance of probabilities simply because *res ipsa loquitur* has been successfully raised against him. All *res ipsa loquitur* does is to assist the claimant in establishing his case[100] and to raise a *prima facie* finding of lack of care against the defendant. But in practice the application of *res ipsa loquitur* may effectively settle a case where neither side can offer a convincing explanation of the event in question. Here, although the burden of proof is not reversed *as such*, the effect is not dissimilar.[101]

The classic statement of principle is that of Erle CJ in *Scott* v. *London and St Katherine Docks Co.*:[102]

> There must be reasonable evidence of negligence. But where the thing is shown to be under the management of the defendant or his servants, and the accident is such as in the ordinary course of things does not happen if those who have the management use proper care, it affords reasonable evidence, in the absence of explanation by the defendants, that the accident arose from want of care.

What amounts to sole control is a question of fact in each case, but some examples may serve to illustrate the scope of the idea. Control of a motor vehicle on the part of the owner or driver is frequently inferred. If a lorry's brakes fail without warning, the owner (but not the driver) has to show that the cause was a hidden defect or some external cause.[103] Thus in *Henderson* v. *Henry E. Jenkins*[104] the defendants failed to show that the cause of the brakes corroding was not their own use of the lorry, and so they were held liable. In *Bennet* v. *Chemical Construction (GB) Ltd.*[105] the doctrine did apply when two panels being worked on by the defendant's employees fell on top of a fellow-worker. They must have fallen as a result of the carelessness of those handling them. On the other hand, in *Easson* v. *London & North Eastern Railway Co.*[106] it was decided that *res ipsa loquitur* did not apply in a case where a child fell out of the offside door of an express train. The door could have flown off, but it was equally possible that a passenger could have interfered with or opened it. In *Ng Chun Pui* v. *Lee Chuen Tat*[107] the

98 *Lloyde* v. *West Midlands Gas Board* [1971] 1 WLR 749, 755 (Megaw LJ).

99 [1988] RTR 298.

100 D. R. Howarth and J. A. O'Sullivan, *Hepple, Howarth and Matthews' Tort Cases and Materials* (5th edn., 2000), at 295, helpfully refer to *res ipsa loquitur* as a potential aid to the claimant in discharging the burden of proof.

101 A good example of this is *Ward* v. *Tesco Stores Ltd.* [1976] 1 WLR 810.

102 (1865) 3 H & C 596, 601.

103 [1970] AC 282.

104 *Ibid.*

105 [1971] 1 WLR 1571.

106 [1944] KB 421.

107 [1988] RTR 298.

defendant's coach swerved across the central reservation of a highway and collided with a bus coming in the opposite direction. The defendant escaped liability by showing that an unidentified car had cut across in front of him, causing him to brake and skid. His reaction of braking was not negligent but an understandable response in an emergency.

In *Ward* v. *Tesco Stores Ltd.*[108] a shopper slipped on a pool of liquid yoghurt lying on the floor of the defendant's store. The judges of the Court of Appeal disagreed on whether the yoghurt could have got there only as a result of the store's negligence. The only evidence of carelessness led by the plaintiff was to the effect that on another occasion a pool of orange juice had been allowed to stand on the floor for a period of a quarter of an hour. The issue was how long the yoghurt might have been there before the plaintiff slipped on it. Ormrod LJ thought it possible that 'had some customer knocked it off the shelf a few moments before, then no reasonable system which the defendants could be expected to operate would have prevented this accident'.[109] Lawton LJ, with whom Megaw LJ agreed, thought that as the floor was under the defendant's control an explanation of how the yoghurt got there was required; and none had been forthcoming.

The defendant may rebut the *prima facie* finding of fault by showing that he was not in sole control of the means of the accident. In *The Kite*[110] the plaintiff's goods were on a barge being towed by the defendants' tug. The defendants were able to show that those in charge of the barge were also responsible for its steering. Alternatively, the defendant may produce a different explanation for the events, which in no way involves their own carelessness. It is no answer that an explosion in an oxygen pipe could have been caused by the entry of particles into the pipe, if they could have got in there by virtue of the negligence of the defendant's employees.[111]

The effect of *res ipsa loquitur* is to shift the standard of care towards a form of stricter liability, and it is therefore appropriate that its main application lies in areas such as road traffic and employers' liability where a high standard of care has in any case been imposed.[112] In principle, though, it is concerned with inferences from the facts and not with the legal imposition of a stricter standard. In the area of common-law liability for defective products which cause injury or other loss to ultimate consumers, courts from *Donoghue* v. *Stevenson*[113] onwards have rejected the application of *res ipsa loquitur* and required proof of fault by the manufacturer to be established.[114] Statute, in the form of the Consumer Protection Act 1987, has now imposed a form of stricter liability for certain kinds of damage caused by defective products which in many respects is akin to a legal reversal of the burden of proof.[115]

108 [1976] 1 WLR 810.

109 *Ibid.*

110 [1933] P 154.

111 *Colvilles Ltd.* v. *Devine* [1969] 1 WLR 475.

112 Its application to cases of pure economic loss is likely to be highly restricted: see *Stafford* v. *Conti Commodity Services Ltd.* [1981] 1 All ER 691; Hepple, Howarth and Matthews, n. 100, 288.

113 [1932] AC 562, 622–3 (Lord Macmillan).

114 Although *Grant* v. *Australian Knitting Mills Ltd.* [1936] AC 85 shows that the courts may be prepared to make certain inferences in the plaintiff's favour, in other cases the need to show fault has led to the rejection of the plaintiff's claim in negligence. See our analysis in ch. 20 below.

115 See ch. 20, below.

SELECT BIBLIOGRAPHY

Ehrenzweig, A. A., 'Negligence without Fault' (1966) 54 *Cal. LR* 1422.

James, F., 'Accident Liability Reconsidered: The Impact of Liability Insurance' (1948) 57 *Yale LJ* 549.

Landes, W. M. and Posner, R. A., *The Economic Structure of Tort Law* (1987), chs. 3, 4 and 5.

Posner, R. A., 'A Theory of Negligence' (1972) 1 *Jo. LS* 29.

Tunc, A., 'Tort Law and the Moral Law' [1972] *CLJ* 247.

2. CAUSATION OF DAMAGE

(A) THE NATURE OF THE CAUSAL INQUIRY

The defendant's carelessness must be shown to have caused the loss or damage in question. The finding of a sufficient causal link is an essential ingredient in all forms of tort liability (with the exception of torts actionable without proof of damage).[116] Most of the case law, however, has arisen in connection with the tort of negligence and it is convenient to deal with the issue generally at this point.

It has become customary in the English law of torts to analyse the question of causation in two stages.[117] The first, which is sometimes referred to as 'factual causation', 'cause in fact' or 'but-for cause', is essentially concerned with whether the defendant's fault was a necessary condition of the loss occurring. This 'but-for' test consists of posing the question: would the loss have been sustained but for the relevant act or omission[118] of the defendant? If it would, the defendant is normally (but not always) absolved at this point. If, alternatively, the claimant is able to show on the balance of probabilities that he would not have suffered the harm in question, the defendant may still succeed by establishing the absence of what is called a 'legal cause'. At this second stage the courts make an assessment of whether the link between the conduct and the ensuing loss was sufficiently close. To put it differently, judges decide which of the conditions of the claimant's harm should also be regarded in a legal sense to be its causes. Judges ask whether a particular event 'broke the chain of causation', and use terms such as 'direct', 'proximate', 'foreseeable', or (alternatively) 'remote' to describe the relation

[116] Even here, causation will have to be established if the claimant is seeking to show that they have suffered special damage.

[117] See A. Honoré, 'Causation and Remoteness of Damage', ch. 7 in A. Tunc (ed.), *Int. Encl. Comp. L.* (1983), xi, 67 (Select Bibliography), referring to the similar 'bifurcation' of analysis in the American common law and in German law.

[118] Proving that an omission was the cause of the claimant's loss can, however, be particularly problematic; see our discussion, below.

between an act or omission and its consequences. A but-for cause which does not pass one of these tests of (legally relevant) causal proximity may be termed a 'mere condition'. It is, in other words, a factor 'without which' the loss would not have been incurred, but it is a factor to which, for one reason or another, the law attaches no causal responsibility in terms of liability in damages.

The separation of these two stages of inquiry and the use of the terms 'factual' and 'legal' cause to describe them is by no means free of controversy. One may question, for example whether the issues, which come under the rubric of 'legal cause' really have very much to do with causation in the sense of describing the relations between particular events in time and space.[119] The courts appear to be using (or possibly misusing[120]) the language of cause to decide (yet again) questions of policy, such as which of the parties is best placed to shift the loss in question or which outcome will best promote loss prevention in that context in the future. The issue of insurability is never far away,[121] and conceptual divisions which are familiar from other areas of the law of tort, such as the division between economic loss and other categories of damage, come into play here too.[122] Conversely, it would be wrong to assume that the issues discussed under the first phase of the causation inquiry—the so called cause in fact—are purely factual issues, totally disassociated from policy considerations. We shall return to this point very soon.

Certainly the terms used, such as 'direct' or 'proximate', have no precise scientific or logical meaning. As Professor Honoré has said, they 'are not taken literally. They do not refer to what is far or near in space or time. They are simply a shorthand use to denote all those considerations, causal or other, which may make the connection between the tortfeasor and the damage legally sufficient.'[123] But this does not necessarily mean that the question of causation could or should be restricted to a basic application of the but-for test, with the rest dismissed as camouflage for policy. Professor Honoré significantly refers to considerations 'causal or other'. In their monograph *Causation and the Law*,[124] Professors Hart and Honoré argued that, in addition to policy, important notions of personal responsibility for the consequences of one's conduct play a role in this area, and that these are to be found underlying many of the judgments of the courts. These 'common sense' notions of causation, which are revealed both in everyday and in legal usages of language, are to be found embedded in the law, together with more openly policy-based perspectives. What is not acceptable, according to Hart and Honoré, is either the confusing intermingling of the one with the other, or the adoption

[119] See the dissenting judgment of McHugh J of the High Court of Australia in *March* v. *E. & M. H. Stamare Pty. Ltd.* (1991) 171 CLR 506, discussed by N. J. Mullany, 'Common Sense Causation: An Australian View' (1992) 12 *OJLS* 431 (Select Bibliography). See also Lord Denning MR in *Lamb* v. *Camden LBC* [1981] QB 625.

[120] On this see the pertinent remarks of Professor David Robertson in his account of American law given in ch. 5, below.

[121] See *ibid.*

[122] See our discussion of *The Liesbosch* [1933] AC 449 and *Lagden* v. *O'Connor* [2004] 1 AC 1067 in this chapter, below, Section 3(e)–(f).

[123] 'Causation and Remoteness of Damage', n. 117 (see also Select Bibliography), 4.

[124] 1st edn., 1957; 2nd edn., 1985 (Select Bibliography).

of one of a number of 'reductionist' positions that see the ordinary usages of causation concepts, and the notions of responsibility that they reflect, as largely irrelevant to the question of legal cause. Their own position has itself been criticised as underplaying the importance of policy considerations in this area;[125] but there is no doubt that their work, in addition to sparking off an unending debate among academic writers,[126] has influenced both directly and indirectly trends in judicial thinking in this area.

One unfortunate consequence of the customary division between 'factual' and 'legal' cause is, as already suggested, the misleading impression that the first stage of inquiry is, by and large, a simply technical or evidentiary one, from which policy factors are absent, in contrast to an apparently more evaluative and normative second stage when policy comes to the fore.[127] That this is not the case is amply demonstrated by the numerous significant instances in which the apparent absence of 'factual cause' does not, as predicted, end up absolving the defendant. It may seem obvious that the claimant's action must be at least a *conditio sine qua non* of the loss, that is to say an event 'without which' the harm would not have happened. However, there are instances, most notably involving multiple tortfeasors, in which the but-for test breaks down as a guide to liability. If two defendants out hunting, acting negligently, both fire shots which strike the claimant in the leg, is he to be denied damages from either defendant on the ground that his injury would have been sustained in any event by virtue of the negligence of the other? Understandably, perhaps, most courts posed a question of this kind to allow the claimant to recover against one or, in an appropriate case, both defendants.[128]

Cases raising similar issues have arisen in English law. In *Baker* v. *Willoughby*,[129] a literal application of the but-for test would have left the plaintiff recovering only part of his loss in respect of two independently tortious injuries. The House of Lords carved out an exception to the test to allow the claimant more complete recovery of damages. In *Fairchild* v. *Glenhaven Funeral Services Ltd.*[130] the House of Lords again qualified the but-for test to allow recovery in a case where it was impossible on the state of scientific evidence to determine which one or more of several employers, all admittedly in breach

[125] For a review of the second edition of *Causation and the Law* which also examines the large critical literature which followed the publication of the first edition, see D. Howarth (1987) 96 *Yale LJ* 1389.

[126] As a famous French author once remarked, 'if the topic of causation did not exist it would have to be invented so that lawyers would have something on which to exercise their legal minds'. However, the volume of academic writing on the subject should not allow us to forget what the authors of a major American tort case book had to say about this subject: 'The problem [of causation] is a difficult one, but the length of the treatment in this casebook and the amount of time allocated it in most courses may perhaps give an exaggerated impression of its importance. In the great majority of negligence cases, the problem does not arise at all; it comes up only in the fraction of negligence actions that involve unusual fact situations' (Prosser, Wade and Schwartz, 11th edn., by V. Schwartz, K. Kelly and D. Partlett (2005), 355). This, then, is another example of a point made in ch. 2 above, namely that what fascinates academics (and some judges) is not always what concerns the practice of the law.

[127] For refinement of this division see W. S. Malone, 'Ruminations on Cause-in-Fact' (1956) 9 *Stan. LR* 60; and see generally R. W. Wright, 'Causation in Tort Law' (1985) 73 *Cal. LR* 1735.

[128] We discuss this hypothetical case in our discussion of 'indeterminate' cause, below.

[129] [1970] AC 467; discussed below in our analysis of 'supervening' causes.

[130] [2003] 1 AC 32.

of duty, had caused the claimant to suffer a fatal illness. In doing this, the House drew on comparative evidence, including German law, to show policy factors dictated a departure from the normal rule.[131] These cases suggest that although the but-for test is based on notions of the limits of individual responsibility, and in particular on the precept that the defendant should not be liable for a loss which he personally did not cause, such a principle may come into conflict with the aim of ensuring that the victim of tortious conduct is fully compensated for losses caused by fault. As Lord Nicholls of Birkenhead recently said:

> Even the sophisticated versions of the 'but-for' test cannot be expected to set out a formula whose mechanical application will provide infallible threshold guidance on causal connection for every tort in every circumstance. In particular, the 'but-for' test can be over-exclusionary.[132]

The courts have also had to deal with the question of the burden of proof and with whether the defendant may be liable, in the absence of conclusive proof under the but-for test, for increasing the risk of particular damage occurring. This possibility has been raised in order to reduce the considerable odds against certain claimants establishing the necessary causal link in industrial-injury and medical-malpractice cases. However, in *Wilsher* v. *Essex Area Health Authority* [133] the House of Lords reaffirmed the centrality of the but-for test to issues of causation in negligence,[134] while in *Hotson* v. *East Berkshire Health Authority*[135] and *Gregg* v. *Scott*[136] it declined to develop the law in favour of the idea that the claimant can recover for the diminished prospect or 'loss of a chance' of avoiding harm. Courts in other parts of the common law world have taken a more flexible view of these questions, albeit with controversial results.[137] Although these decisions make it clear that difficult policy questions are involved in the but-for test, the formal division between 'factual' and 'legal' cause is too well established (and perhaps too convenient from a doctrinal point of view) to be abandoned. However, some confusion might be avoided if the phrase 'but-for cause' were used in preference to 'factual cause' or 'cause in fact', and that will be the approach taken in this book.

Turning now to the most vexed aspect of causation, that of legal cause, we find that in *The Wagon Mound (No. 1)*[138] the Privy Council stressed the importance of reasonable foreseeability as opposed to 'directness' as a basis for determining 'remoteness' of damage. This test of legal cause is applicable both to the 'threshold' situation in which the court is trying to establish whether the defendant is liable at all, and in the situation in which it is concerned with establishing the *extent* of liability of one who has caused tortious damage.

131 See the judgments of Lord Bingham [2003] 1 AC 32, 58–66, and Lord Rodger [2003] 1 AC 32, 113–18.

132 *Kuwait Airways Corp.* v. *Iraqi Airways Co. (Nos. 4 and 5)* [2002] 2 AC 883, 1092.

133 [1988] AC 1074, discussed below.

134 The qualification subsequently made to the but-for test in *Fairchild* v. *Glenhaven Funeral Services Ltd.* [2003] 1 AC 32 was limited, in its turn, by a further HL decision, *Barker* v. *Corus UK Ltd.* [2006] 2 AC 572. See our discussion in Section 2(b)(iii) of this chapter, below.

135 [1989] AC 750, discussed below

136 [2005] 2 AC 176.

137 These are discussed by Professor J. G. Fleming in his 'Probabilistic Causation in Tort Law' (1989) 68 *Can. BR* 661 (Select Bibliography).

138 [1961] AC 388.

The test of reasonable foreseeability, like that of the but-for cause, is plainly based on the courts' perception that an individual should not be made liable in tort for damage beyond the scope of his personal responsibility. Thus, if damage ensues in an unexpected or unusual way, it may be that the 'chain of causation' has been broken, absolving the defendant from liability for damage occurring after that point.

Since the judgment in *The Wagon Mound (No. 1)*, it has become increasingly clear that the test of foreseeability of damage is no more *conclusive* in regard to causation than it is as a test for duty and breach, and that numerous other considerations will come into play, in particular where physical damage, as opposed to economic loss, is the basis of the claim.[139] As far as extent is concerned, *The Wagon Mound (No. 1)* itself established that once the *kind* of damage in question can be seen to have been reasonably foreseeable, its *extent* is then irrelevant: the defendant is liable even though all the consequences could not have been predicted. In this way English law, in common with other systems, favours the claimant as against a defendant who is responsible for causing tortious damage of some kind. Once the initial threshold of liability is passed, unless the ensuing damage is of a different 'kind', the risk of greater than expected damage occurring, or of damage occurring in an unexpected way, lies on the defendant.[140] In English law there has been an active debate over what precisely is meant by 'kind of damage' in the context of the rule in *The Wagon Mound (No. 1)*. This has largely been resolved in favour of a liberal interpretation, which favours claimants in cases of physical injury or disease, and a more restrictive test for property damage and economic loss.

Notwithstanding the importance of notions of personal responsibility, it is impossible to give an account of this area without returning over and over again to certain central issues of policy which are to be found throughout the tort of negligence and which affect other torts involving damage. These include the search for an economically efficient framework of liability and, in conjunction or sometimes in competition with this, for a system of loss shifting and loss spreading which reflects social values and concerns about the allocation of risks and responsibilities. In a doctrinal sense, it is impossible to write about causation without acknowledging that inherent in the law's account of causation is also a view of what constitutes *fault*.[141] This is clearly so, for example, when the court is considering making an apportionment of legal responsibility between claimant and defendant, as in the case of contributory negligence under the Law Reform (Contributory Negligence) Act 1945.

More controversially, the same is true of 'loss of a chance' cases such as *Hotson* v. *East Berkshire Area Health Authority*[142] and *Gregg* v. *Scott*[143] and of cases of probabilistic cause such as *Wilsher* v. *Essex Area Health Authority*[144] and *Fairchild* v. *Glenhaven Funeral Services Ltd.*[145] Similarly, in deciding, as in *Smith* v. *Leech, Brain & Co. Ltd.*,[146]

[139] See the judgment of Watkins LJ in *Lamb* v. *Camden LBC* [1982] QB 625, discussed below.

[140] See, in particular, *Hughes* v. *Lord Advocate* [1963] AC 837 and *Smith* v. *Leech, Brain & Co. Ltd.* [1962] 2 QB 405, discussed below.

[141] The converse is true, as Howarth has pointed out: n. 125, 1419–20.

[142] [1987] AC 750.

[143] [2005] 2 AC 176.

[144] [1988] AC 1074.

[145] [2003] 1 AC 32; [2002] 3 WLR 89.

[146] [1962] 2 QB 405, discussed below, Section 4(c).

that an employer who has negligently put his employees' safety at risk should be liable for the unforeseeable consequence in terms of a life-threatening disease which results in the case of one particular employee whose vulnerability is greater than that of his fellow-workers, the court is evidently making a policy judgement based on the importance of the claimant's interest and upon the employer's superior capacity to control and minimise the risk in question.

(B) BUT-FOR CAUSATION

Under the but-for test the claimant must prove the existence of a causal link on the balance of probabilities, which is taken to mean a likelihood of more than 50 per cent. If the court finds that it was as likely as not that the injury would have occurred without the defendant's negligence, the action will fail even if there is an admission of carelessness. An illustration of this is *Barnett* v. *Chelsea and Kensington Hospital*.[147] The action was brought by the estate of the plaintiff, who died after doctors at the hospital negligently failed to diagnose that he was suffering from arsenic poisoning. The court held that even with a correct diagnosis the plaintiff's condition was too far advanced for the hospital to have saved him.

A gloss on the 'but-for' test was made in *Bolitho* v. *City and Hackney Health Authority*,[148] namely that '[a] defendant cannot escape liability by saying that the damage would have occurred in any event because he would have committed some other breach of duty thereafter'.[149] This is perhaps best regarded as simply saying that the court will seek to establish, as best it can, what would have happened but for negligence *both actual and hypothetical* of the defendant.

(i) 'Probabilistic Cause': Questions of Risk and Proof

Difficulties arise where there are several alternative explanations of the events leading up to the damage, some innocent and some traceable to the defendant's fault. In *McGhee* v. *National Coal Board*[150] the plaintiff contracted dermatitis after working in a kiln. The immediate cause of the dermatitis was brick dust with which he came into contact while at work. The defendants were not at fault through exposing him to the dust; this was an inevitable feature of the work he was employed to do. However, they were in breach of their common law duty of care in failing to provide washing facilities at the place of work. The question facing the court was whether the plaintiff had shown that his condition was caused by the absence of washing facilities. Medical evidence could not clearly establish that he would not have contracted it anyway, as a result of the exposure to the dust during working hours. The House of Lords nevertheless allowed his appeal from decisions of the lower courts in favour of the defendant. The judgment

147 [1969] 1 QB 428; see also *McWilliams* v. *Sir William Arroll & Co. Ltd.* [1962] 1 WLR 295.

148 [1998] AC 232.

149 *Ibid.*, 240 (Lord Browne-Wilkinson).

150 [1973] 1 WLR 1; E. Weinrib, 'A Step Forward in Factual Causation' (1975) 38 *MLR* 518 (Select Bibliography).

of Lord Wilberforce appears to accept the possibility that in the absence of conclusive proof of a link between fault and damage, liability may be imposed upon a defendant whose negligence increases the risk of a particular loss occurring, if that risk is subsequently realised. 'It is a sound principle', he said, 'that where a person has, by breach of duty of care, created a risk, and injury occurs within the area of that risk, the loss should be borne by him unless he shows that it had some other cause.'[151]

In effect this shifts the burden of proof on to the defendant. The basis for doing so is the inherent difficulty facing the plaintiff in a case where medical opinion cannot establish definitively that the damage is attributable to one potential cause of harm rather than another. In these circumstances 'if one asks which of the parties, the workman or the employers, should suffer from this inherent evidential difficulty, the answer as a matter of policy or justice should be that it is the creator of the risk who, *ex hypothesi*, must be taken to have foreseen the possibility of damage, who should bear its consequences'.[152] The superior resources of the defendant in this case and the high standard of care imposed on employers in relation to their employees may help to explain why liability might be shifted in this way. Another, more general rationale for reversing the burden of proof in cases such as this has been suggested by Professor J. G. Fleming on the basis of a comparative review of the relevant case law: this is that the defendant's admitted fault may be the very reason the claimant cannot prove his case on the balance of probabilities.[153]

Nevertheless, in either case, the defendant is being made liable for damage which *on the normal application of the but-for test* it cannot be proved he personally caused.[154] The mere fact that he was at fault in the sense of breaching a duty of care is, we would suggest, not a good reason for imposing liability. To do so may be to impose a powerful incentive for careful behaviour on the part of defendants. But this runs up against the objection that it is not the role of the tort of negligence to penalise careless behaviour *as such*. If this is seen as desirable, there may be an argument for leaving it to Parliament to achieve through statutory regulation of the kind which is widespread in relation to employer's liability.[155]

In *Wilsher* v. *Essex Area Health Authority*[156] the House of Lords was highly critical of the approach set out by Lord Wilberforce, while leaving intact the authority of *McGhee* and explaining it as a case in which there was sufficient evidence to make the necessary inference of a causal link between fault and damage. In *Wilsher* the plaintiff, who was born three months prematurely, suffered blindness in one eye and near-blindness in the

151 [1973] 1 WLR 1, 6.

152 *Ibid.* In *McGhee* Lord Wilberforce relied on the earlier House of Lords' judgment in *Bonnington Castings Ltd.* v. *Wardlaw* [1956] AC 613, but there are difficulties with this since *Wardlaw*'s case was one of possible cumulative causes, one tortious and one not, whereas the two possible causative factors in *McGhee* were apparently alternative: see J. Stapleton, 'The Gist of Negligence. Part II' (1988) 104 *LQR* 389, 402.

153 See J. Fleming, 'Probabilistic Causation in Tort Law', n. 137 (see also Select Bibliography), 668, 671, discussing, in particular, the use of this idea in German law.

154 See J. Stapleton, 'The Gist of Negligence: Part II' (1988) 104 *LQR* 389, 404 (Select Bibliography).

155 See generally ch. 18, below.

156 [1988] AC 1074.

other as a result of a condition known as retrolental fibroplasia. He claimed that this was caused by the carelessness of a hospital doctor who failed to notice that a device for measuring the dosage of oxygen to the blood had been wrongly attached to a vein and not, as it should have been, to an artery. As a result the plaintiff had received an excessive dose. Medical evidence established no fewer than six separate potential causes of the plaintiff's blindness, all of which, with the exception of the excessive dose of oxygen, were inherent in his condition as a premature birth. The House of Lords, reversing the Court of Appeal, held that causation had not been adequately established: 'a failure to take preventive measures against one out of five possible causes is not evidence as to which of those five caused the injury'.[157]

In the Court of Appeal in *Wilsher*[158] Mustill LJ had taken the following view of *McGhee*:

> If it is an established fact that conduct of a particular kind creates a risk that injury will ensue; and if two parties stand in such a relationship that the one party owes a duty not to conduct himself in that way; and if the first party does conduct himself in that way; and if the other party does suffer injury of the kind to which the risk related; then the first party is taken to have caused the injury by his breach of duty, even though the existence and extent of the contribution made by the breach cannot be ascertained.

According to Lord Bridge, however, this was a misreading of *McGhee*:[159]

> The conclusion I draw is that *McGhee* laid down no new principle of law whatever. On the contrary, it affirmed the principle that the onus of proving causation lies on the pursuer or plaintiff. Adopting a robust and pragmatic approach to undisputed primary facts of the case, the majority concluded that it was a legitimate inference of fact that the defender's negligence had materially contributed to the pursuer's injury. The decision, in my opinion, is of no greater significance than that, and to attempt to draw from it some esoteric principle which in some way modifies, as a matter of law, the nature of the burden of proof of causation, which a plaintiff or pursuer must discharge once he has established a relevant breach of duty is a fruitless one.

Similarly, in *Snell* v. *Farrell*[160] the Supreme Court of Canada, while accepting that 'the legal or ultimate burden remains with the plaintiff', suggested that 'in the absence of evidence to the contrary adduced by the defendant, an inference of causation may be drawn, although positive or scientific evidence of causation has not been adduced'.[161] In this case the plaintiff was blinded in one eye during the course of an operation which was carried out negligently by the defendant. There was a chance that blindness could have resulted however much care was taken. As in *McGhee* the medical evidence was equivocal rather than, as in *Wilsher*, sharply divided, and the Supreme Court decided that there was sufficient evidence to find for the plaintiff. *Snell* v. *Farrell* indicates that

157 [1987] QB 739, 779 (Sir Nicolas Browne-Wilkinson V-C, approved by Lord Bridge at [1988] AC 1074, 1091).
158 [1987] QB 730, 771–2.
159 [1988] AC 1074, 1090.
160 (1990) 72 DLR (4th) 289.
161 *Ibid.*, 301.

the question of causation is ultimately one for the court to determine on its own assessment of the medical evidence, intuitive as this may be. In practice much will depend on how the medical evidence is presented to the court and to the weight it feels able to give to differing accounts.

The difficulty with Lord Bridge's formulation of the but-for test is its excessive rigidity. *Snell* and *McGhee* were cases in which courts felt compelled to take flexible approaches to the issues of causation by virtue of the limited nature of the scientific evidence available to them. Other situations, such as those involving multiple defendants each of which commits a potentially tortious act, pose even sharper problems for the but-for test.

(ii) 'Indeterminate Cause': Cases involving Multiple Defendants

So far we have been considering situations in which the defendant's fault competes with one or more 'innocent' explanations of the claimant's injury. More problematic are cases in which there is no 'innocent' explanation for the injury; the claimant's injury could only have occurred through the fault of one or more of a number of defendants. In these cases, the strict application of the but-for test has been modified to avoid a result which under-compensates the claimant.

The principal situation to consider is that in which the claimant's injury could only have been caused by the fault of one out of several careless defendants, in circumstances where the individual in question cannot be identified: this may be called the case of 'indeterminate cause'. The best illustration is provided by two similar cases decided in the United States and Canada respectively, *Summers* v. *Tice*[162] and *Cook* v. *Lewis*.[163] In each case the plaintiff was shot by one bullet which was fired by one of two defendants out hunting, each of whom had been careless in aiming his gun in the plaintiff's direction. There was no means of telling from whose gun the shot was fired. The courts adopted the solution of reversing the burden of proof, so that each defendant had to show that he did not cause the injury. In the absence of such proof, both defendants were held liable.

A variant of this situation arises where the claimant is struck by two bullets, fired by each of the two defendants. If his injuries would have resulted from one bullet only, each defendant is entitled to say that 'but for' his own personal carelessness, the claimant would still have sustained his loss. This result would leave the claimant 'falling between two stools', and it is therefore likely that were this case to come before an English court it would find the defendants jointly liable, perhaps varying the damages payable by each according to their degree of responsibility. This is analogous to what happened in *Fitzgerald* v. *Lane*.[164] The plaintiff walked onto a pelican crossing without looking and was struck by a car driven by the first defendant, thrown into the air, and

162 119 P 2d 1 (1948).

163 [1951] SCR 830.

164 [1987] QB 781; affirmed on different grounds [1989] AC 328. See the similar US case of *Maddux* v. *Donaldson*, 108 NW 2d 33 (1961), discussed in ch. 5, below.

struck again by a car being driven in the opposite direction by the second defendant. Each of the two drivers was driving too quickly and was held to have been in breach of the duty of care they owed to the plaintiff. The plaintiff sustained tetraplegia as a result of the accident, but it could not be established that the second collision contributed to his injury. The second defendant claimed that the first impact alone would have been sufficient, on the balance of probabilities. The Court of Appeal held both of them liable and made an award of damages based on an assessment that they were equally to blame with the plaintiff for the accident. The basis for finding them both liable was the principle enunciated by Lord Wilberforce in *McGhee* v. *National Coal Board*,[165] namely that each one had materially increased the risk of such injury by his negligence and should, as a consequence, have the burden of disproving a causal link.

Joint tortfeasors are held liable *in solidum*, that is to say each one is potentially responsible for the full amount of the loss. A defendant held liable to the full extent might then seek contribution from the other; but that is a separate matter. The result seems just, since it enables the claimant to receive full compensation and shifts his loss to the two defendants jointly, but it cannot be reconciled with a strict application of the balance-of-probabilities test.

In *Sindell* v. *Abbott Laboratories* the Supreme Court of California adopted a more radical departure from the traditional analysis.[166] The case concerned the liability of manufacturers of a defective pregnancy drug, which induced a cancerous condition in the female children of the mothers taking it. This condition did not appear until the children reached puberty, and it was impossible to show which of several hundred manufacturers had produced the particular drug which had been taken by the plaintiffs' mothers. It was known, however, that the defect was inherent in the design of the drug, so that any one of the manufacturers could have been responsible in each case. The court rejected the solution of imposing joint and several liability as in *Summers* v. *Tice*,[167] partly because only a few of the potential defendants were before the court and it was considered unfair to make those who were present responsible to the full extent. Instead, the court held each defendant liable according to the degree of its share of the market for the drug at the relevant time, on the basis that this was the best approximation the court could make of their likely responsibility. Of the many objections to *Sindell*, Professor Fleming suggests, 'by far the most formidable is that it departs from the prior art not merely by lacking all precedent but by being incompatible with the traditional notion of tort as a system of individual responsibility. This was not corrective but distributive justice.'[168] Nor can the economic argument for imposing such liability, on the ground that it increases incentives to take care, be easily justified here. Such a goal is most likely better achieved through general regulation, and only the absence of

[165] [1973] 1 WLR 1.

[166] 607 P 2d 924 (1980). See also the decision of the Dutch Hoge Raad, *B* v. *Bayer Nederland BV*, 9 Oct. 1992, NJ 1994, 535, discussed by Lord Bingham of Cornhill in *Fairchild* v. *Glenhaven Funeral Services Ltd.* [2003] 1 AC 32, 62–3.

[167] 119 P 2d 924 (1948).

[168] 'Probabilistic Causation in Tort law', n. 137 (see also Select Bibliography), 668.

effective regulation could justify a common-law court engaging in such a far-reaching form of loss shifting.

(iii) Exposure to Risk as a Basis for Establishing a Causal Link

English law has seen no precise equivalent to the *Sindell* case, but a decision which has proved equally controversial for the way in which it appears to depart from general principles of causation is *Fairchild* v. *Glenhaven Funeral Services Ltd.*[169] Here, a number of claims were brought by victims of mesothelioma, a fatal disease which is contracted by inhaling asbestos dust. It was accepted in each case that the claimant had been negligently exposed to asbestos dust by several successive employers.[170] However, it was not possible to show which employer had caused the exposure which led to the claimant's illness. Nor was it possible to show whether the illness had been caused by a single exposure or by the cumulative effect of exposure over more than one employment. Thus the court could not even be sure whether it was dealing with a case of a single material cause (*Sindell*) or multiple causes (*Fitzgerald*).[171]

As in *Fitzgerald*, the *Fairchild* litigation was resolved in favour of the claimants, but only on appeal to the House of Lords, the Court of Appeal having rejected the possibility of liability on the authority of *Wilsher*, and in particular Lord Bridge's discussion of *McGhee.* In the House of Lords, *Wilsher* was shown to be distinguishable, on the ground that in that case there were several potentially innocent explanations of the plaintiff's injury. In *Fairchild*, on the other hand, as in *Fitzgerald*, the courts took the view that the damage could only have occurred through the fault of one or more of the defendants. It was therefore felt necessary to adapt the but-for test in order to avoid a plainly unjust result, using Lord Wilberforce's judgment in *McGhee* (now fully rehabilitated) for this purpose. Lord Bingham of Cornhill said:

> it seems to me just and in accordance with common sense to treat the conduct of A and B in exposing C to a risk to which he should not have been exposed as making a material contribution to the contracting by C of a condition against which it was the duty of A and B to protect him.[172]

Lord Nicholls also acknowledged that the 'court is applying a different and less stringent test' from the normal but-for threshold.[173] According to Lord Hoffmann, in

169 [2003] 1 AC 32.

170 As Professor Jane Stapleton has pointed out, this conclusion is strange in that it is at odds with what is known about asbestos exposure, namely that the general population is exposed to asbestos dust, to a degree which may (we cannot be sure in the present state of knowledge) give rise to the disease of mesothelioma. See her article 'Lords A'Leaping Evidentiary Gaps' (2003) 10 *Tort LR* 276 (Select Bibliography).

171 For a slightly different reading of *Fairchild*, suggesting that it was (or perhaps should have been) regarded as a case of a single material cause, on the basis that exposure to a single particle of asbestos dust may, under certain circumstances, lead to the contraction of mesothelioma, see T. Weir, 'Making It More Likely versus Making It Happen' [2002] *CLJ* 519 (Select Bibliography). For a critique of this view, see B. S. Markesinis and J. Fedtke, 'Authority or Reason? The Economic Consequences of Liability for Breach of Statutory Duty in a Comparative Perspective' [2007] *EBLR* 5.

172 [2003] 1 AC 32, 68, at para. 34.

173 *Ibid.*, at para. 45.

the circumstances of the case, 'a rule requiring proof of a link between the defendant's asbestos and the claimant's disease would, with the arbitrary exception of single employer cases, empty the [employer's] duty of content'; on this basis, it was open to the court 'to formulate a different causal requirement in this class of case'.[174] Lord Rodger of Earlsferry thought that 'the decision in *McGhee* undoubtedly involved a development of the law relating to causation', the important point in both cases being that 'the state of scientific knowledge makes it impossible for the victim to prove on the balance of probabilities that his injury was caused by the defenders' or defendants' wrongdoing'.[175]

The standing of *Fairchild* was, however, very soon called into question in another House of Lords case, *Barker* v. *Corus UK Ltd.*[176] The main issue here was whether, in a case where the principle in *Fairchild* (the '*Fairchild* exception') was applied, the defendants should be held jointly liable, in which case each one would be liable for the whole of the claimant's loss if the others were insolvent or could not be traced; or whether, because of the exceptional nature of liability under *Fairchild*, justice and fairness demanded that each defendant should only be held liable in proportion to their degree of fault, as measured by the duration and intensity of the exposure for which they were responsible. The House of Lords, by a majority (Lord Rodger dissenting), held in favour of proportionate liability, and in so doing offered a novel interpretation of what *Fairchild* had decided. This was that the damage suffered by the claimant under *Fairchild* was not the disease itself, but the increased risk of contracting it. As Lord Hoffmann put it, *Fairchild* did not proceed on the basis of 'the fiction that a defendant who had created a material risk of mesothelioma was deemed to have caused or materially contributed to the contraction of the disease'.[177] Instead, 'the *Fairchild* exception treats the risk of contracting mesothelioma as the damage'.[178]

There are numerous problems with this view. One, as Lord Rodger explained in his judgment, is that it involves 'not so much reinterpreting as rewriting the key decisions in *McGhee* and *Fairchild*'.[179] Nor does the new solution have the advantage of clarifying the law: instead, 'it will tend to maximize the inconsistencies in the law by turning the *Fairchild* exception into an enclave where a number of rules apply which have been rejected for use elsewhere in the law of personal injuries'.[180] These rules are of a fundamental kind: they include the rule that the claimant in personal injury case must have suffered physical injury or disease in order to have a cause of action in negligence, and the principle of *in solidum* liability itself. Lord Rodger would have applied the principle

174 *Ibid.*, at 74.

175 *Ibid.*, 111–12. Of the five members of the House of Lords in *Fairchild*, only Lord Hutton thought that *McGhee* did not lay down an exception to the regular but-for test: *ibid.*, 91–2.

176 [2006] 2 AC 572.

177 *Ibid.*, 579.

178 *Ibid.*, 593. See, to similar effect, Lord Scott of Foscote, at 598, and Lord Walker of Gestingthorpe, at 613.

179 [2006] 2 AC 572, 601. Baroness Hale of Richmond agreed with Lord Rodger's interpretation of *Fairchild* but sided with the other majority judges on the question of whether the liability of the defendants should be proportionate to the period of exposure for which they were responsible.

180 [2006] 2 AC 572, 606.

of *in solidum* liability in *Barker* on fairness grounds. We will return to the question of the implications of *Barker* for the law of joint liability in a later chapter;[181] here it is sufficient to note that the outcome in *Barker*, in so far as it related to the apportionment of liability between joint tortfeasors, was almost immediately reversed by legislation, in the form of section 3 of the Compensation Act 2006, which restored the principle of *in solidum* liability in mesothelioma cases. The question for us to consider at this point is the impact of *Barker* on general principles of causation in the tort of negligence.

According to *Barker*'s reinterpretation of *Fairchild*, the critical concept is the nature of the risk to which the claimant is exposed. As Lord Hoffmann put it in *Barker*, 'the purpose of the *Fairchild* exception is to provide a cause of action against a defendant who has materially increased the risk that the claimant will suffer damage and may have caused that damage, but cannot be proved to have done so because it is impossible to show, on a balance of probability, that *some other exposure to the same risk* may not have caused it instead' (emphasis added).[182] Later in his judgment he said, 'it is an essential condition for the operation of the exception that the impossibility of proving that the defendant caused the damage arises out of the existence of another potential causative agent which operated in the same way'. Thus the exception would not apply, for example, 'when the claimant suffers lung cancer which may have been caused by exposure to asbestos or some other carcinogenic matter but may also have been caused by smoking and it cannot be proved which is more likely to have been the causative agent'.[183] On this basis, *McGhee* is explicable on the grounds that both the initial exposure to brick dust and the subsequent failure to provide washing facilities were 'causative agents' which 'operated in the same way' to expose the plaintiff to the 'same risk', namely the risk of dermatitis. *Wilsher*, by contrast, was a case in which 'a number of very different causative agents were in play'.[184]

This is an acknowledgement that the ground given, in *Fairchild*, for distinguishing *Wilsher*—namely, that in *Wilsher* some of the potential causes were innocent whereas, in *Fairchild*, all were tortious—was not convincing. *McGhee*, after all, was a case in which the loss could have been caused by either a 'tortious' or an 'innocent' factor. In line with this approach, Lord Hoffmann went on to hold that the claim in *Barker* was not ruled out on the grounds that not all the potential causative agents could be ascribed to the negligence of the defendants. In this case, the claimant's own carelessness or lack of self-care, in respect of one particular period of employment, was a possible cause of his exposure; but as Lord Hoffmann put it, in applying the *Fairchild* exception 'it should be irrelevant whether the other exposure was tortious or non-tortious, by natural causes or human agency or by the claimant himself'.[185]

[181] See ch. 26, below.

[182] [2006] 2 AC 572, 585.

[183] *Ibid.*, 587; see also, on this point, the judgment of Lord Rodger in *Fairchild*, [2003] 1 AC 32, 118–19. In *McTear* v. *Imperial Tobacco Ltd.* 2005 2 SC 1, a decision preceding *Barker*, the Outer House of the Court of Session declined to apply *McGhee* or *Fairchild* to assist the claimant in a case of the kind described by Lord Hoffmann.

[184] [2006] 2 AC 572, 587 (Lord Hoffmann).

[185] *Ibid.*, 585.

However, the doctrinal solution arrived at in *Barker* was unnecessary to achieve this end,[186] and in general it has little to commend it. It remains to be seen whether it will stand the test of time. Lord Hoffmann's suggestion that the *Fairchild* principle should apply where the exposure to risk is caused by different causative agents which 'operate in the same way' is unlikely to contribute to legal clarity.[187] The House of Lords might have taken a different path, viewing *Fairchild* and *McGhee* as illustrations of a principle which courts in numerous other jurisdictions have adopted, to the effect that the 'but-for' test should be applied flexibly in cases where it is precisely the defendant's own fault which prevents the claimant from establishing his case on the normal balance-of-probabilities test. Where this is the case and all the other elements of liability are present—duty of care, breach and damage of the kind which the imposition of the duty of care was aimed at preventing—the burden of proof can shift, in an appropriate situation, from claimant to defendant.[188] In this context, talk of 'fictions' to describe exceptions to the but-for test is, we would suggest, inappropriate. The but-for test is simply one of a number of conceptual devices that the courts use to establish what Professor Honoré has called, as we have seen, a 'sufficient legal connection' between victim and tortfeasor.[189] There is no reason, in principle, why the test should not yield, under certain circumstances, to wider considerations of what constitutes an adequate causal link. Policy factors play a role here; thus it is perhaps no accident that both *McGhee* and *Fairchild* were cases of employer's liability, a context in which the law has long acknowledged that policy places a strong emphasis on the maintenance by the employer of workplace health and safety,[190] whereas *Wilsher* was a case of medical negligence, an area where the courts have, on the whole, sought to avoid doctrinal innovations which might, as they see it, lead to excessive liabilities.[191]

(iv) Supervening or Overtaking Causes

Into this category fall cases in which the causal effect of the defendant's fault is nullified by a later event or by the subsequent emergence of a latent condition. In each case the overtaking cause is unrelated to the initial tort. In *Baker* v. *Willoughby*[192] the plaintiff's leg, which was injured in a car accident caused by the negligence of the defendant, was

186 As we have pointed out, *McGhee* was a case in which there were both 'innocent' and 'tortious' causes, and there is no good reason why either that case or *Fairchild* should be read as suggesting that the exception made to the but-for test can only work in a context where all potential causes are tortious. As it is, the formulation of liability on the basis of exposure to risk has the odd result, according to Lord Hoffmann, that the claimant's lack of self-care does not constitute contributory negligence, since 'a defendant is liable for the risk of disease which he himself has created and not for the risks created by others, whether they are defendants, persons not before the court or the claimant himself' (at para. 593); see also the discussion of this point by Lord Walker of Gestingthorpe, at 614–15, and our analysis of contributory negligence in ch. 24, Section 2, below.

187 J. Scherpe, 'A New Gist?' [2006] *CLJ* 487.

188 See Fleming, 'Probabilistic Causation in Tort Law', n. 137 (see also Select Bibliography).

189 'Causation and Remoteness of Damage', n. 117 (see also Select Bibliography), at 4, discussed above.

190 See ch. 18, below.

191 Hence the rejection of the 'loss of a chance' theory in *Hotson* v. *East Berkshire AHA* [1987] AC 750 and *Gregg* v. *Scott* [2005] 2 AC 176.

192 [1970] AC 467.

later amputated after a separate and unrelated incident in which he was shot by robbers at the scrap-metal merchants where he worked. The House of Lords held that the defendant was liable for the full consequences of the injury *he* caused regardless of the second incident; he therefore had to pay damages based on the plaintiff's losses *beyond* the point at which the leg was amputated. The causal effect of the accident therefore continued notwithstanding the fact that the use of the leg would have been lost anyway as a result of the amputation. In *Jobling* v. *Associated Dairies*,[193] by contrast, the House of Lords reached what appears at first sight to be a contradictory result. Here, the plaintiff's back was injured as a result of his employer's negligence, but before the trial of the action it became clear that the plaintiff was suffering, quite independently, from a back complaint which would have curtailed his working life in any event. The defendant was held liable for pain and suffering and loss of earnings only up to the time at which the effects of the second cause, the disease, would effectively have overtaken those of the first, the injury.

Baker v. *Willoughby*[194] has to be seen as an exception to the normal application of the 'but-for' rule, justified by the principle of fully compensating the plaintiff for damage tortiously inflicted. Had the two events—the car accident and the shooting—been related, as they might have been, for example, if the plaintiff's initial incapacity had prevented him from getting away from the robbers, the first defendant (as he may be called for convenience) could have been held responsible for the cumulative consequences of both injuries. As it was, the second injury arose from a wholly unrelated sequence of events. Under these circumstances, it was open to the first defendant to argue that his liability should be confined to the plaintiff's losses up to the point at which the leg was shot. If the court, when applying the but-for test, is required to take into account the possibility that the plaintiff's loss would have occurred regardless of the defendant's fault, then it must also be required to take into account events which have actually taken place before the trial of the action. As Lord Pearson put it, 'the present state of disablement, with the stump and the artificial leg on the left side, was caused wholly by the supervening event and not at all by the original accident. Thus the consequences of the original accident have been submerged and obliterated by the greater consequences of the supervening event.'[195]

This solution would, however, have left the plaintiff significantly under-compensated. If a claim had been made against the robbers as second defendants it would have covered only the *additional* damage they caused, that is to say, the extra loss of facility and the additional lost earnings over and above those caused by the first defendant. The same would have been true of any claim made by the plaintiff before the Criminal Injuries Compensation Board.[196] This point is illustrated by *Performance Cars Ltd.* v. *Abraham*.[197] If a car, which has already been involved in a collision with one defendant and requires a repaint, is involved in a further collision with a second defendant, the

193 [1982] AC 794.
194 [1970] AC 467, 495.
195 *Ibid.*
196 See, E. McKendrick, *Tort Textbook* (5th edn., 1991), 94.
197 [1961] 1 QB 33; *Performance Cars* was recently reaffirmed by the Court of Appeal in *Halsey* v. *Milton Keynes General NHS Trust* [2004] EWCA Civ. 576.

second defendant can be held liable only for any additional damage which he has caused. He has damaged a car which is already damaged. The same principle applies to personal injuries: the defendant takes the plaintiff as he finds him, and cannot be liable for greater losses than he has inflicted. If, then, the liability of the first defendant, in *Baker* v. *Willoughby*,[198] had been limited to the period prior to the shooting, a part of the plaintiff's loss—the continuing effect of the initial incapacity—would have remained uncompensated. He would have 'fallen between two defendants'. Because of this 'manifest injustice', there can be no room for the application of the but-for rule in this case. But this is no more than saying that where the initial and supervening causes are both tortious, the but-for test is inapplicable, for the same reasons as it breaks down in *Summers* v. *Tice*,[199] *Fitzgerald* v. *Lane*[200] and *Fairchild* v. *Glenview Funeral Services Ltd.*,[201] where multiple tortfeasors are involved.

Lord Reid offered two different explanations. The first was that the second injury did not diminish any of the consequences, in terms of the loss of facility, of the first one: 'so why should it be regarded as having obliterated or superseded them?' Lord Reid's second argument explained the plaintiff's disability 'as having two causes'.[202] These arguments, however, fail to do justice to the basic point of the but-for test, namely that since the plaintiff lost his leg anyway through an event unconnected with the first accident, the first defendant cannot be held responsible for what happened after that point in time. Nor were the two events concurrent causes of the plaintiff's total disability: the first tort had nothing to do with the complete loss of the leg. In *Jobling* v. *Associated Dairies*[203] Lord Wilberforce suggested that Lord Reid's reasoning was unsustainable, and that Lord Pearson's explanation of the outcome was to be preferred. *Jobling*'s case was decided on a strict application of the but-for test. Since the plaintiff would have lost the use of his back regardless of the defendant's fault, the latter could only be held responsible for the consequences up to the point when the underlying condition would have made itself felt independently of that fault. Again, it would have been different if the employer's lack of care had triggered or accelerated the underlying back complaint; but this was not the case. In the words of Lord Bridge:

> When the supervening illness or injury, which is the independent cause of the loss of earning capacity, has manifested itself before trial, the event has demonstrated that, even if the plaintiff had never sustained the tortious injury, his earnings would now be reduced or extinguished. To hold the tortfeasor, in this situation, liable to pay damages for a notional continuing loss of earnings attributable to the tortious injury is to put the plaintiff in a better position than he would be in if he had never suffered the tortious injury.[204]

It is also important to distinguish *Jobling* from *Performance Cars* v. *Abraham*[205] (or, more precisely, from its equivalent in terms of personal injury). *Jobling* was not a case in which the plaintiff was suffering from a *pre-existing* condition or disease; the condition

198 [1970] AC at 467.
199 119 P 2d 1 (1948).
200 [1987] QB 781.
201 [2003] 1 AC 32.
202 [1970] AC 467, 492.
203 [1982] AC 794.
204 *Ibid.*, 820.
205 [1962] 1 QB 33.

from which the disease sprang was dormant at the time of the injury and the disease did not begin to take effect until after the injury took place. Had the plaintiff's disease already begun to take effect when the injury took place, *Jobling* would not have given rise to the arguments which it in fact presented. As Lord Wilberforce put it, it was found that 'the myelopathy was not a condition existing, but dormant, at the date of the original injury; it was a disease supervening after that event. If it has been dormant but existing it is not disputed that it would have had to be taken into account in the actual condition found to exist at the trial. But the appellant submits that a different result follows if the origination of the disease takes place after the accident....'[206]

Jobling may usefully be compared, in this context, with the American decision of *Dillon* v. *Twin State Gas and Electric Co.*[207] In this case the deceased, a young boy, fell from a bridge and was electrocuted by wires left negligently positioned by the defendant when he was only seconds from hitting the ground. Damages were based on the deceased's limited life expectancy of no more than a few seconds. Here, the threat to the boy was sufficiently serious at the time of the accident for the court to treat it as analogous to a pre-existing medical condition, which was going to lead to loss of life in any event. Similarly, in *Cutler* v. *Vauxhall Motors Ltd.*[208] the plaintiff, who had varicose veins, won damages when he suffered a graze as a result of the defendant's negligence and had to undergo an operation to treat the veins, as a result of which he suffered further complications. But the court reduced his award on the basis that he would have had to undergo this operation in any event at some point in the future. In *Jobling*, the condition was not pre-existing as such, but there was compelling reason to treat it as if it were. The outcome, however, might seem unfair to the claimant when his position is compared to that of a similar victim of an occupational disease, whose underlying condition does not manifest itself until after the trial. His damages cannot be reduced in the light of later events, although in assessing them in the first place the court will have taken into account the need to make a discount for future contingencies. The answer to this is that the court has to take into account what it knows at the date of the trial, and that as far as the plaintiff whose condition emerges later is concerned, it would be costly and inconvenient to have a rule which permitted the court to re-open damages awards. As Lord Keith of Kinkel put it, 'the court will not speculate when it knows, so that when an event within its scope has actually happened prior to the trial date, that event will fall to be taken into account in the assessment of damages'.[209]

In *Jobling* the court was satisfied that the defendant's act and the onset of the plaintiff's condition were wholly unrelated, and that the plaintiff would certainly have suffered the loss in question whether or not the defendant had been negligent: after the relevant date, therefore, his damage was not compensatable. In a case like this the but-for test is applied on the balance of probabilities. A different approach was followed in a decision of the High Court of Australia, *Malec* v. *J. C. Hutton Pty. Ltd.*[210] The High

206 [1982] AC 794, 802.

207 163 A 2d 111 (1932); R. Peaslee, 'Multiple Causation and Damage' (1934) 47 *Harv. LR* 1127.

208 [1971] 1 QB 418.

209 [1982] AC 794, 813. See, for further discussion, ch. 25, below.

210 (1990) 64 ALJR 316.

Court essentially took the view that when attempting, under the but-for test, to assess the likelihood that a particular course of events would have ensued in the absence of fault by the defendant, the normal test of the balance of probabilities should be modified. In respect of actual past events, the balance-of-probabilities test would be applied, and an event to which the court allotted a probability of 50 per cent or more would be treated as having occurred. But in the case of an event which it is alleged would or would not have occurred, or might or might not yet occur, the approach of the court is different:

> The future may be predicted and the hypothetical may be conjectured. But questions as to the future or hypothetical effect of physical injury or degeneration are not commonly susceptible of scientific demonstration or proof. If the law is to take account of future hypothetical events in assessing damages, it can only do so in terms of the degree of probability of the events occurring.... Where proof is necessarily unattainable, it would be unfair to treat as certain a prediction which has a 51 per cent probability of occurring, but to ignore altogether a prediction which has a 49 per cent chance of occurring. Thus the court assesses the degree of probability that an event would have occurred, or might occur, and adjusts its award of damages to reflect the degree of probability.[211]

The plaintiff, as in *Jobling*, was the victim of an occupational disease for which his employer was responsible but, it was held, was more likely than not to have contracted his depressive condition in any case. Rather than awarding him nothing beyond a certain date, however, the High Court awarded him damages in full for the effects of the disease, subject only to a reduction for the chance (which was less than 100 per cent) that he would have contracted it anyway. This approach opens up the wider issue of recovery for loss of a chance which, as we shall now see, has given rise to a considerable body of discussion in the English case law.

(v) Loss of a Chance

The approach in *McGhee* v. *National Coal Board*[212] risks imposing liability for the full extent of the loss on a defendant who cannot be shown to have been personally responsible for the damage under normal principles of causation. An alternative is to hold the defendant liable only for a portion of the loss, based upon the extent of his responsibility for it. The issue arises above all in medical malpractice cases where the defendant fails, through negligence, to improve a pre-existing condition of the plaintiff. If losing a less than 50 per cent chance of recovery is recognised as a form of legal damage in its own right, the plaintiff can recover compensation for this 'loss of a chance'. Causation is established on the balance of probabilities for the loss of the chance even if not for the injury which the plaintiff actually sustained. The result is similar to the *McGhee* principle in enabling a plaintiff to overcome the formidable difficulties of proof in medical-malpractice and industrial-injury cases, but it differs in offering an alternative to the 'all-or-nothing' solution of holding the defendant liable either in full or not at all.

[211] *Ibid.*, 318. [212] [1973] 1 WLR 1.

The issue came before the English courts in *Hotson* v. *East Berkshire AHA*.[213] The plaintiff, a boy of 13, was injured when he fell out of a tree. He was taken to the defendant's hospital, where medical staff failed to make a correct diagnosis of his condition. He was sent home and returned only five days later, in some considerable pain, when a correct diagnosis was made and an operation carried out. The plaintiff was left with necrosis of the hip joint. Medical evidence established that even if the hospital had correctly diagnosed his condition on the first occasion and treated it promptly, there was still a 75 per cent likelihood that the plaintiff would have gone on to develop the necrosis. Another way of putting this is to say that for every 100 patients admitted in this condition, twenty-five could be expected to make a full recovery. The plaintiff's claim was that he might have been one of these twenty-five, but that the opportunity of recovery was denied him by the defendant's carelessness.

The House of Lords decided for the defendant on the apparently straightforward ground that causation had not been established on the balance of probabilities. Lord Ackner stressed that this 'was a relatively simple case concerned with the proof of causation, on which the plaintiff failed, because he was unable to prove, on the balance of probabilities, that his deformed hip was caused by the authority's breach of duty in delaying over a period of five days a proper diagnosis and treatment'.[214] In the view of Lord Bridge: '[u]nless the plaintiff proved on a balance of probabilities that the delayed treatment was at least a material contributory cause of the avascular necrosis he failed on the issue of causation and no question of quantification could arise'.[215] In taking this line the House of Lords more or less ducked the question whether the loss of a chance is an appropriate subject-matter for recovery in its own right.[216] Only Lord Mackay gave the question prolonged consideration, and he declined to 'lay it down as a rule that a plaintiff could never succeed by proving loss of a chance in a negligence action'.[217] The tenor of his judgment was, however, against allowing this type of recovery as a matter of course. Lords Bridge and Ackner, by denying that any issue other than causation was involved, would effectively deny any role to loss of a chance of recovery in this context.[218]

The trial judge in *Hotson* argued that in awarding a sum based upon the extent of the injury discounted by the chance that it would have occurred anyway, he was merely following established practice in the quantification of damages. In particular, when the court awards damages for personal injury it reduces the sum representing future loss of earnings by a figure meant to represent the chance or contingency that the claimant's working life might have been foreshortened by some other event, for which the defendant cannot be held responsible. There is thus a standard reduction for 'normal vicissitudes' of

[213] [1987] AC 750.

[214] *Ibid.*, 793.

[215] *Ibid.*, 782.

[216] See Stapleton, 'The Gist of Negligence: Part II', n. 154 (see also Select Bibliography).

[217] *Hotson* v. *East Berkshire AHA* [1987] AC 750, 786.

[218] The other two Law Lords agreed with all three judgments.

life and a greater reduction will be made if there is a higher-than-normal chance that the plaintiff would not have carried on working until the standard retirement age.[219] Thus:

in the end the problem comes down to one of classification. Is this on true analysis a case where a claimant is concerned to establish causative negligence or is it rather a case where the real question is the proper quantum of damage? Clearly the case hovers near the border. Its proper solution in my judgment depends on categorising it correctly between the two. If the issue is one of causation then the health authority succeeds since the claimant will have failed to prove his claim on the balance of probabilities. He will be lacking an essential ingredient of his cause of action. If however, the issue is one of quantification, then the claimant succeeds because it is trite law that the quantum of a recognised head of damage must be evaluated according to the chances of the loss occurring.[220]

This argument from quantification can be dealt with, however, by pointing out that when calculating the quantum of damages, the court has already established causation on the balance of probabilities, and is now making the best assessment it can of the present value of the claimant's future losses flowing from his injury. It has to make a guess as to what might have happened in the absence of injury, since there is no alternative way of proceeding. But how the court approaches the issue of quantification of damages for the loss of a limb, for example, has no necessary bearing upon the separate question of whether the claimant can recover at all for the loss of a chance of keeping that limb. This was the essence of Lord Bridge's judgment in *Hotson*.[221]

A more radical argument, however, is that the strict balance-of-probabilities test is itself inappropriate in a case where the court has to make an estimate of the effect of alternative hypothetical causes. The court has to make a guess, which may be more or less accurate. Under these circumstances the difference between 51 per cent and 49 per cent will be somewhat arbitrary, and the consequences of treating a 51 per cent likelihood as a certainty will be more arbitrary still. This appealed to the High Court of Australia in *Malec* v. *J. C. Hutton Pty. Ltd.*,[222] but was effectively brushed aside by the House of Lords in *Hotson*. Another argument is that the courts have in some instances awarded compensation for lost expectations of financial gain, even though the claimant could only show that he had a chance of making such a gain. In *Kitchen* v. *Royal Air Force Association*,[223] for example, damages were awarded against a solicitor based on the lost chance of bringing a civil action for damages. Again, in *Allied Maples Group Ltd.* v. *Simmons & Simmons*[224] the plaintiffs won damages against their solicitors for the loss of an opportunity to bargain over the allocation of rights and liabilities under a lease. These and similar cases do not establish that loss of a chance of *physical recovery* is a form of compensatable damage in its own right; but they do indicate that the courts are capable of providing compensation for a variety of different forms of loss.

219 See below, ch. 25.
220 Per Simon Brown J [1985] 1 WLR 1036, 1044.
221 [1989] AC 750.
222 (1990) 64 ALJR 316, discussed above.
223 [1958] 2 All ER 241; *Chaplin* v. *Hicks* [1911] 2 KB 786.
224 [1995] 1 WLR 1602.

The principal argument for loss-of-chance recovery is that the claimant has been deprived of something tangible. Prior to the defendant's breach of duty, the claimant had a real, if indeterminate, *prospect* of recovery. Professor Joseph King has argued that, 'but for the defendant's tortious conduct, it would not have been necessary to grapple with the imponderables of chance. Fate would have run its course.'[225] Another way of putting it is to say that 'when a defendant's negligent action or inaction has effectively terminated a person's chance of survival, it does not lie in the defendant's mouth to raise conjectures as to the measure of the chances that he has put beyond the possibility of realisation. If there was any substantial possibility of survival and the defendant has destroyed it, he is answerable.'[226] This view, expressed in an *obiter dictum* by the US 4th Circuit Court of Appeals, has been followed in a line of cases allowing lost-chance recovery. However, such recovery has been rejected in a majority of American jurisdictions.[227] The issue has given rise to a lively debate, with opponents arguing that departures from the traditional causation rule 'adversely impact the cost and quality of health care and exacerbate the problems of defensive medicine and cost containment'.[228] A more specific concern is that lost-chance recovery will lead to a multiplicity of new claims, giving rise to fresh evidential difficulties and complicating the relationship between different heads of damage. This version of the familiar 'floodgates' argument appears to have influenced Lord Mackay in *Hotson*.[229]

The House of Lords revisited the same issues more recently in *Gregg* v. *Scott*,[230] but arrived at essentially the same conclusion as in *Hotson*. In *Gregg*, a negligent diagnosis led to a delay in treatment for cancer. On the basis of statistical evidence presented to him, the judge found that the delay had reduced the claimant's chances of making a full recovery from around 40 per cent to 25 per cent. Because the claimant had not had a better-than-even chance of surviving the illness in the first place, his claim for reduced life expectancy had to fail. According to Lord Nicholls of Birkenhead, 'a patient should have an appropriate remedy when he loses the very thing it was the doctor's duty to protect', that is to say, a correct diagnosis. The law should therefore 'recognise the existence and loss of poor and indifferent prospects as well as those more favourable', a result that would be impossible if the all-or-nothing approach of the balance of probabilities were applied.[231] However, Lord Nicholls was in a minority of one in clearly arguing for loss

225 'Causation, Valuation, and Chance in Personal Injury Torts Involving Pre-existing Conditions and Future Consequences' (1981) 90 *Yale LJ* 1353, 1378 (Select Bibliography).

226 *Hicks* v. *US*, 368 F 2d 626, 632 (1966) (4th Circuit Court of Appeals).

227 For a comprehensive review, see L. Perrochet, S. Smith and U. Colella, 'Lost Chance Recovery and the Folly of Expanding Medical Malpractice Liability' (1992) 27 *Tort and Insurance LJ* 615.

228 *Ibid.*, 628.

229 [1987] AC 750, citing doubts expressed in the Supreme Court of Washington in *Herskovitz* v. *Group Health Co-operative of Puget Sound*, 664 P 2d 474 (1983) (Brachtenbach J, dissenting).

230 [2005] 2 AC 176.

231 [2005] 2 AC 176, 189.

of a chance recovery,[232] and the majority judgments in *Gregg* express the normal kinds of judicial scepticism with regard to claims of this kind, namely that the introduction of loss of a chance recovery would disturb the conceptual structure of tort law, introduce uncertainty into the application of the law, and impose an excessive burden of liability on medical professionals and health care providers.

In *Chester* v. *Ashfar*,[233] decided the year before *Gregg*, the House of Lords took a much more flexible approach to application of the but-for test. The defendant negligently failed to warn the claimant that there was a very small risk, 1–2 per cent, of her suffering a serious disability as a result of an operation designed to cure her of back pain. The operation was performed with due care and attention, but the disabling condition nevertheless occurred. The claimant was unable to show that she would not have chosen to have the operation if she had been informed of the risk, but it was accepted that, had she been warned of the risks of the procedure as she should have been, she would have taken further advice and, at the very least, delayed having the operation. On this basis, the House of Lords, by a majority of three to two, held that she should recover for the effects of the disability. The majority regarded this as a case in which the but-for test had to be modified on the grounds of policy, in order to reflect 'the fundamental importance of a surgeon's duty to warn a patient in general terms of significant risks';[234] the case can be seen as one in which the claimant was wrongfully denied a chance to avoid serious harm. The decision is a problematic one, however, not just because of the rather sweeping way in which the normal rules of causation were evaded, but also because, as Professor Jane Stapleton has convincingly argued,[235] it is far from clear that the but-for test was correctly applied here: because the chances of the operation going wrong were so slight, the claimant had a good argument to the effect that, if she had taken advice and postponed the procedure to a later date, it was more likely than not that she would not then have suffered the disability for which she was claiming. The case should therefore have been decided on the grounds of remoteness, rather than a lack of 'factual' causation. If that route had been followed, the outcome would arguably have been the same, because of the flexible way in which the remoteness rules are applied in physical injury cases;[236] from the point of view of the doctrinal coherence of the law, this alternative route would have been preferable.

[232] Lord Hope of Craighead also dissented in *Gregg*, but offered a slightly different basis for his judgment, suggesting that the claimant was entitled to recover on the alternative grounds of a loss of a chance and the physical harm he suffered, in the form of the spread of the disease, as a result of the false diagnosis (see his judgment at [2005] 2 AC 176, 208–9). Baroness Hale of Richmond, in her judgment, also pointed out that 'on conventional principles' the claimant could have recovered for 'any extra pain, suffering, loss of amenity, financial loss and loss of expectation of life which may have resulted from the delay' ([2005] 2 AC 176, 230), but that this possibility had not been examined at the trial stage and so was not before the House in *Gregg*.

[233] [2005] 1 AC 134. [234] [2005] 1 AC 134, 146 (Lord Steyn).

[235] J. Stapleton, 'Occam's Razor Reveals an Orthodox Basis for *Chester* v. *Ashfar*' (2006) 122 *LQR* 427 (Select Bibliography).

[236] See our discussion in this chapter, below, section 3(c).

3. REMOTENESS OF DAMAGE

(A) INTERVENING ACTS OF THIRD PARTIES

The question of intervening acts generally arises at the so-called second stage of the causal inquiry, once a but-for relationship has already been established between the claimant's loss and the defendant's conduct. Courts speak of the 'chain of causation' between fault and damage being broken by some external event or by the act of a third party, or of a *novus actus interveniens*. Alternatively, an act of the claimant himself may suffice; this could either break the chain of causation completely or be regarded instead as contributory negligence in circumstances where the court will then make an apportionment of responsibility under the Law Reform (Contributory Negligence) Act 1945, reducing the claimant's damages accordingly.

An act of nature, such as a storm, could also be seen as breaking the chain of causation in an appropriate case, as in *Carslogie Steamship Co.* v. *Royal Norwegian Government.*[237] The degree to which the intervening act is foreseeable is a relevant but not decisive test. In *Dorset Yacht Co.* v. *Home Office*[238] Lord Reid said that an act of a third party 'must have been something very likely to happen if it is not to be regarded as *novus actus interveniens* breaking the chain of causation. I do not think that a mere foreseeable possibility is or should be sufficient.' In this case it was to be expected that the borstal boys would seek to escape from the island and would use a yacht to do so, since there were few other means available; it was the 'very kind of thing' likely to happen. In *Lamb* v. *Camden London Borough Council* Lord Denning criticised both this test and the test of reasonable foreseeability as too wide and liable to 'extend the range of compensation far too widely'. He gave the following example, based on *Dorset Yacht* and the analysis by the Law Lords in that case, to illustrate his point:[239]

> Suppose that, by some negligence of the staff, a Borstal boy—or an adult prisoner—escapes over the wall or from a working party. It is not only foreseeable—it is, as we all know, very likely—that he will steal a car in the immediate vicinity. He will then drive many miles, abandon the car, break into a house and steal clothes, get a lift in a lorry, and continue his depredations. On Lord Diplock's test [confining duty to persons in the immediate vicinity of the escape]—and it may be of Lord Morris of Borth-y-Gest and Lord Pearson also—the Home Office would owe a duty to the owner of the stolen car but to none of the others who suffered damage. So the owner of the car could sue but the others could not. But on Lord Reid's test of 'very likely' to happen, the Home Office would be liable not only to the owner of the stolen car, but also to all the others who suffered damage: because it was very likely to happen.

In *Lamb*, contractors working for the defendant council caused the plaintiff's house to be flooded, with the result that her tenant had to move out. The plaintiff, who was

[237] [1952] AC 292.
[238] [1970] AC 1004, 1030.
[239] [1985] QB, 625, 635.

living abroad at the time, moved her furniture out of the house and squatters subsequently moved in, causing extensive damage. The plaintiff failed to show that the council was responsible for the damage inflicted by the squatters. According to Lord Denning, this was because the principal responsibility for keeping them out lay with the plaintiff and she had to bear the loss. But this outcome could not be explained by a test of foreseeability, no matter that it might be qualified by requiring a high degree of foreseeability. Policy, and in particular the availability of insurance to the plaintiff, was decisive.[240]

Oliver LJ, on the other hand, thought the test was 'not what is foreseeable as a possibility but what would the reasonable man actually foresee if he thought about it', and that in the case of a third-party intervention a 'stringent' test of likelihood would be applied.[241] Watkins LJ regarded evidence of reasonable foreseeability as the minimum the plaintiff had to show, and that the court would take into account a range of features including 'the nature of the event or act, the time it occurred, the place where it occurred, the identity of the perpetrator and his intentions, and responsibility, if any, for taking measures to avoid the occurrence and matters of public policy'. In this case it would be wrong to make the defendants pay for the 'antisocial and criminal' behaviour of the squatters.[242]

These two cases indicate that the relationship between the defendant and the third party may be as important as the nature of the intervening act. In *Dorset Yacht* the borstal boys were in the care of the officers, but there was no such relationship in *Lamb*, no matter how foreseeable it was that squatters might enter an empty house and cause damage to it.[243] Nor was there any such relationship in *Topp* v. *London Country Bus (South West) Ltd.*[244] when, again, it was highly foreseeable that the defendant's bus might be stolen when it was left unattended with the keys in the ignition. The Court of Appeal held that the defendant owed no duty to a remote claimant who was killed by the careless driving of the third party who stole the bus. Equally, the nature of the relationship between the claimant and defendant will be important. The defendant may be held to have undertaken a duty of care specifically to the claimant as in *Stansbie* v. *Troman*,[245] in which a decorator was liable for allowing thieves into the plaintiff's house which he was painting at the time after he had been warned of this very danger. The

240 Policy also seems to be the best explanation of *Meah* v. *McCreamer (No. 2)* [1986] 1 All ER 943. The plaintiff, who had been injured in a road accident by the defendant's negligence, recovered damages for a personality disorder brought on by the effects of the accident and which led to him committing a number of vicious criminal assaults, for which he was imprisoned. He was then sued by the victims of his assaults, and brought a further action to recover this sum from the original defendant. Woolf J rejected his claim on the ground of 'remoteness'.

241 [1981] QB 625, 642.

242 *Ibid.* See also *Perl (Exporters) Ltd.* v. *Camden LBC* [1984] QB 342, *Ward* v. *Cannock Chase DC* [1985] 3 All ER 537.

243 For this reason the question may be better treated as raising a question at the stage of formulating the duty of care, rather than as an aspect of remoteness of damage. See our discussion of *Smith* v. *Littlewoods Organisation Ltd.* [1987] AC 241 in ch. 3, Section 4(a), above.

244 [1993] 1 WLR 976.

245 [1948] 2 KB 48.

intervention of a rescuer will hardly ever be taken to have broken the chain of causation, although if he acts particularly foolishly he could be held to have been contributorily negligent, which will go to reduce his damages.[246]

In cases of rescue and emergency the foreseeability test may be entirely irrelevant. In *The Oropesa*[247] the defendant's ship of that name collided with the *Manchester Regiment*, causing it serious damage. The captain of the *Manchester Regiment* set out in a lifeboat to consult the captain of *The Oropesa* on the means of saving his crew; the lifeboat capsized and many lives were lost. Although this sequence of events was not easily foreseeable, the action of the captain was reasonable in the circumstances and did not break the chain of causation. A contrasting case is *Knightley* v. *Johns*,[248] in which the defendant negligently overturned his car in a tunnel. In dealing with the situation thus created, a police officer ordered a police motorcyclist to close the tunnel and the latter drove against the traffic in order to do so. The police motorcyclist was involved in a collision with another motorist. The defendant was not held liable for this second incident, as the behaviour of both of the police officers was, in the circumstances, entirely unreasonable.

Where the defendant has, through his fault, created an unjustifiable and unusual risk of danger, the fact that the precise chain of events by which that danger is realised is unpredictable may not absolve him of legal responsibility. This may explain *Philco Radio and Television Corp.* v. *Spurling*,[249] in which the defendant mistakenly delivered some highly inflammable film material to the plaintiff's premises, where it was left lying around. It was then ignited by one of the plaintiff's employees 'as a lark'. The defendants were held liable for the damage to the plaintiff's premises in the ensuing explosion and fire.

(B) ACT OF THE CLAIMANT

An act of the claimant may be classified as a *novus actus* without necessarily amounting to contributory negligence, which implies a failure to take due care for one's own safety. Paradoxically, while contributory negligence is only a partial defence under the Law Reform (Contributory Negligence) Act 1945, a complete defence will be made out if the claimant's own act is shown to have broken the chain of causation. In *McKew* v. *Holland and Hannen and Cubitts (Scotland) Ltd.*[250] the plaintiff, who had temporarily lost the full use of his leg following an injury caused by the negligence of the defendants, sustained further injury when his leg gave way on a steep flight of stairs which had no handrail. He was held to have been the sole cause of this additional injury, by placing himself in a position where he might be in danger. The similar case of *Wieland* v. *Cyril Lord Carpets*[251] was decided the other way, on the ground that the plaintiff in that case had taken sufficient regard for her own safety.

246 *Harrison* v. *British Railways Board* [1981] 3 All ER 639.

247 [1943] P 32.

248 [1982] 1 WLR 349.

249 [1949] 2 All ER 882.

250 [1969] 3 All ER 1621. In occupier's liability cases involving injury to children, it is far less likely that the defence of *novus actus* will succeed: see e.g. *Jolley* v. *Sutton LBC* [2000] 1 WLR 1082.

251 [1969] 3 All ER 1006.

In other cases positive acts of the plaintiff have been held not to break the chain of causation; in *Pigney* v. *Pointer's Services*[252] an accident left the plaintiff suffering from a form of neurosis, as a result of which he took his own life. The defendants were held liable for his death. Similarly, in *Reeves* v. *Commissioner of Police for the Metropolis*,[253] the Police Commissioner was held liable for the suicide of a prisoner in custody under circumstances where inadequate steps had been taken to deal with this risk. In this case, it was inappropriate to view the chain of causation as broken by the deceased's voluntary act, since the police were under a duty of care to avoid the very harm which occurred. This case is a reminder that the scope of the underlying duty will play a major role in determining whether a particular event is regarded as an intervening cause.[254]

In *Emeh* v. *Kensington, Chelsea and Fulham Area Health Authority*[255] the plaintiff underwent a sterilisation operation which, thanks to the negligence of the surgeon who carried it out, reversed itself with the result that she became pregnant again. In an action to recover damages for the pain and suffering of the birth and for the costs of raising the child, the defendant argued that the plaintiff could have avoided these costs by having the child aborted. The court held that in this case, where there was no medical reason for the pregnancy to be terminated, the plaintiff's decision not to have an abortion could not be regarded as a *novus actus*. Similar decisions have been reached in other 'wrongful conception' cases.[256]

The defence of contributory negligence, which is considered in greater detail in Chapter 24 below,[257] depends to a certain extent on the specialised application of the principles of causation, although it was clear before the Law Reform (Contributory Negligence) Act 1945 that contributory negligence was a defence in its own right. Since the Act transformed the defence from a total bar into a partial defence only, going to the reduction of damages, the approach to cause has been closely bound up with the court's task of adjusting the loss between the parties according to their relative fault. Contributory negligence operates to reduce the claimant's damages in a case where his lack of care for his own safety contributed to his loss. The claimant is held to the standard of a reasonably careful person in his position, but he does not have to owe a duty of care to the defendant; the duty issue is irrelevant since the defendant is not claiming that he has suffered loss, but rather that the claimant is the victim of his own carelessness. A causal link between the claimant's lack of self-care and the damage he suffers is therefore required. Prior to the Act of 1945 a complex case law developed on the precise circumstances under which the claimant's own fault was deemed to be a relevant causal factor. Now, under the Contributory Negligence Act, the claimant's claim is not to be defeated only 'by reason of the fault of the person suffering the

252 [1957] 1 WLR 1121.

253 [2000] 1 AC 360.

254 See in particular Lord Hoffmann's judgment in *Reeves* and also in the *SAAMCO* case on remoteness of damage in negligent misrepresentation, *South Australia Asset Management Co.* v. *York Montague Ltd.* [1997] AC 191.

255 [1985] QB 1012.

256 See, in particular, *MacFarlane* v. *Tayside Health Board* [2000] 2 AC 59.

257 See Section.

damage, but the damages recoverable in respect thereof shall be reduced to such extent as the court thinks just and equitable having regard to the defendant's share in the responsibility for the damage'.[258] The courts have interpreted this as meaning not simply that they may now adjust the claimant's damages award to take into account the degree to which he was at fault, where before it was all or nothing, but that much of the old case law on the particular meaning given to contributory negligence as cause is no longer applicable. In particular, the old doctrine of 'last opportunity', under which the party who had the last chance to avoid the accident was deemed to be entirely responsible for it, has apparently disappeared from the law.[259]

Thus, while it remains possible for a court to hold that a claimant's lack of care for himself was the sole cause of his loss, or, on the other hand, that it was causally insignificant, the tendency now is to use the Act to apportion responsibility between the parties according to their degree of fault. In the words of Lord Porter in *Stapley* v. *Gypsum Mines Ltd.*,[260] the Act 'enables the court . . . to seek less strenuously to find some ground for holding the plaintiff free from blame or for reaching the conclusion that his negligence played no part in the ensuing accident in as much as owing to the change in the law the blame can now be apportioned equitably between the two parties'. Causation is still a requirement of the defence's application, as the wording of section 1(1) indicates.

This means, in the first place, that the claimant's act must be shown to have been one of the operative causes of the damage in the sense of being a but-for cause, and, secondly, that it must also be a 'proximate' or legal cause. In *Jones* v. *Livox Quarries Ltd.*[261] the plaintiff, a worker on a construction site, rode on the back of a vehicle contrary to instructions and was injured when it was involved in a collision. He was held to have been contributorily negligent and a reduction of one-fifth was made to his damages award. According to Lord Denning:

> if the plaintiff while he was riding on the tow bar, had been hit in the eye by a shot from a negligent sportsman, I should have thought that the plaintiff's negligence would in no way be a cause of his injury. It would only be a circumstance in which the cause operated. It would only be a part of the history. But I cannot say that in the present case. The man's negligence here was so much mixed up with the injury that it cannot be dismissed as mere history. His dangerous position on the vehicle was one of the causes of his damage.[262]

As in the case of intervening acts of third parties, in determining what is an 'operative cause' of damage a number of policy factors may come into play. In the context of contributory negligence the court's power to apportion blame has clearly influenced its approach to the issue of weighing causal responsibility. Prior to the Act, in Lord Denning's view, the negligence of the driver in *Jones* would have been regarded as the 'predominant cause' and the plaintiff would have recovered in full, but now 'we have regard to all the causes, and one of them undoubtedly was the plaintiff's negligence in riding on the tow bar'.[263]

[258] Section 1(1).
[259] See e.g. *Cakebread* v. *Hopping Brothers (Whetstone) Ltd.* [1947] KB 641.
[260] [1953] AC 663, 677.
[261] [1952] 2 QB 608.
[262] *Ibid.*
[263] *Ibid.*

The power to make an apportionment between claimant and defendant could not, it seems, have been derived from the common law with its all-or-nothing approach, but had to be provided by statute. Once the Act was passed the courts were quick to give it a wide interpretation which provided them with a broad discretion to adjust damages awards to take into account the relative fault of the parties. When they do this, the courts perform the same kind of balancing act with which the debate over 'loss of a chance' and probabilistic cause are concerned. As we have seen, in these two areas the English courts have retained the all-or-nothing approach, in part out of fear of introducing uncertainties into the law and its application. Yet a similar modification of the common law in the area of contributory negligence has become a fully accepted part of the judicial function. In this respect, the decision in *McKew*—where the Contributory Negligence Act was ignored and the claim rejected completely on the grounds of causation—seems contrary not simply to recent practice but also, on one interpretation, to the Act itself, which in section 1(1) appears to bar the total exclusion of damages and to insist upon apportionment in circumstances where the damage caused is partly the result of the fault of the claimant and partly of the defendant.[264] On the other hand, there is the view of Watkins LJ in *Lamb* v. *Camden London Borough Council*:[265]

I prefer to regard *McKew* as a good example of a determination to bring realistic consideration to bear upon the question of fresh damage arising from an event or act occurring subsequently to the initial negligent act in the context of remoteness of damage. The plaintiff McKew had caused fresh damage to himself as a result of taking an unreasonable risk. That he would be likely or quite likely to do this was said to have been reasonably foreseeable. Yet because he had behaved unreasonably in the doing of it, his act was found to be a *novus actus interveniens* which freed the defendants from all liability for it.

(C) FORESEEABILITY OF THE EXTENT OF DAMAGE

We now turn to the question of the extent of legal liability of a defendant who has caused tortious damage to the claimant. A major limitation on recovery following the decision of the Privy Council in *The Wagon Mound (No. 1)*[266] is the principle that the defendant will not be liable for a *kind of damage* which he could not reasonably have foreseen. However, once foreseeability of the kind of damage is established, the *extent* of loss is irrelevant and the defendant will be liable in full. Where this is the case, it is said that the defendant 'must take the claimant as he finds him', with all his particular susceptibilities. The difficulty here lies in knowing what is meant by the 'kind of damage' which the defendant should have foreseen.

In *The Wagon Mound (No. 1)*[267] an engineer on the defendant's ship negligently discharged a quantity of furnace oil into Sydney harbour, fouling the wharf owned by the plaintiffs and halting repair work on two other ships, the *Corrimal* and the *Aubrey D.*

264 See *Pitts* v. *Hunt* [1991] QB 24 for this view of s. 1(1) of the Act.
265 [1981] QB 625, 646.
266 [1961] AC 388.
267 *Ibid.*

After they were advised that the oil could not be ignited, the plaintiffs resumed welding work, but the oil was ignited by a piece of molten metal and the wharf and the two ships were consumed in the resulting fire. The plaintiff's action for the damage to the wharf failed on the ground that while damage by pollution was reasonably foreseeable, damage by fire was not. The Privy Council rejected the test apparently laid down by the Court of Appeal in the earlier case of *Re Polemis* under which the defendant was liable if there was a direct link between his carelessness and the resulting damage. Viscount Simonds said:

> It does not seem consonant with current ideas of justice or morality that, for an act of negligence, however slight or venial, which results in some trivial foreseeable damage, the actor should be liable for all consequences, however unforeseeable and however grave, so long as they can be said to be 'direct'. It is a principle of civil liability, subject only to qualifications which have no present relevance, that a man must be considered to be responsible for the probable consequences of his act. To demand more of him is too harsh a rule, to demand less is to ignore that civilised order requires the observance of a minimum standard of behaviour.[268]

As this *dictum* indicates, the decision in *The Wagon Mound* was based on a strong assertion that the extent of the defendant's liability should be proportionate to his fault. In elevating foreseeability to be a main test of remoteness, Viscount Simonds was influenced by *Donoghue* v. *Stevenson* and in particular by Lord Atkin's expressed view that liability should be modelled upon a 'general public sentiment of moral wrongdoing for which the offender must pay'.[269] Yet this is only one of a number of possible ways of looking at negligence liability; it takes a wholly exaggerated view of the degree to which the legal concept of carelessness is based on moral fault and pays no regard at all to the aims of loss shifting and accident prevention. These considerations, almost completely absent from Viscount Simonds's judgment, have nevertheless influenced other courts in their treatment of *The Wagon Mound (No. 1)*, and account to a large degree for a steady decline in its influence over the past forty years.

In *Re Polemis and Furness, Withy & Co.*,[270] a stevedore employed by the defendant charterers carelessly dropped a plank into the hold of the plaintiff's ship while it was being unloaded. The hold contained petrol vapour, which was ignited by a spark struck by the falling plank; in the ensuing fire the ship was completely destroyed. The arbitrators found that 'the causing of the spark could not have been anticipated from the falling of the board, though some damage to the ship might reasonably have been anticipated'. The defendants were held liable for the full loss, the Court of Appeal rejecting an argument that they should not have to pay for damage of a kind they could not have foreseen: if the act would or might probably cause damage, the fact that the damage it in fact causes is not the exact kind of damage one would expect is immaterial, so long as the damage is in fact caused sufficiently directly by the negligent act and not by the operation of independent causes having no connection with the negligent act, except

268 [1961] AC 388, 422–3.
269 [1932] AC 562, 580.
270 [1921] 3 KB 560.

that they could not avoid its results. Once the act is negligent, the fact that its operation was not foreseen is immaterial.[271]

These wide *dicta* of Scrutton LJ were rejected in *The Wagon Mound (No. 1)* in favour of the test of foreseeability of the kind of damage. The difference between the cases is based, then, upon their respective approaches to the definition of 'kind of damage'. In *The Wagon Mound* damage by pollution was deemed to be a different 'kind' of damage from damage by fire. On this basis the outcome in *Re Polemis* would presumably now be reversed. *Polemis* could be reconciled with *The Wagon Mound* only if 'kind of damage' were construed sufficiently widely to cover any form of property damage.

This is broadly what has happened to *The Wagon Mound (No. 1)* as far as *physical injury* to the person is concerned: the courts have reached a position where, as long as some kind of injury or harm to the person was foreseeable, its extent does not matter. Nor is any distinction drawn for this purpose between physical injury and psychiatric harm; these are not separate 'kinds of damage'.[272] Possibly this approach does less than full justice to the *Wagon Mound* principle, but it conforms to long-standing precedents and also has the advantage of respecting the principle of fully compensating the victim of tortious damage. In *Smith* v. *Leech Brain & Co. Ltd.*[273] the plaintiff was burned on the lip by hot molten metal. The burn induced a cancer from which he died. The defendants, who were in breach of duty by not providing him with a protective shield, were held liable for his death. This case exemplifies the 'eggshell skull' principle, which is to the effect that the defendant takes the victim as he finds him. The defendant cannot deny liability for the full extent of the plaintiff's loss on the ground that he was unusually vulnerable to a particular disease or condition.

Smith v. *Leech Brain & Co. Ltd.*[274] has since been followed in other cases of physical injury, both in England and in other Commonwealth jurisdictions. A rare exception is the first-instance decision in *Tremain* v. *Pike.*[275] A farm-worker contracted a rare disease, Weil's disease, after coming into contact with rats on his employer's farm. The defendant was held to be in breach of the employer's duty to provide his employee with safe working conditions, but the extent of his liability was limited on the ground that injury through rat-bites was foreseeable, but contracting Weil's disease was not. The decision seems anomalous and unsatisfactory given the high *standard* of care, verging on strict liability, to which employers are held. The Court of Appeal implicitly rejected *Tremain* v. *Pike* in *Parsons* v. *Uttley Ingham*,[276] in which the plaintiff recovered for the consequences of an unusual illness contracted by his pigs after they were fed mouldy nuts from a hopper installed by the defendant. As this decision concerned damage to property (the pigs) there would be a compelling case for it to be followed where personal safety and health were the interests affected, since by general consent the protection of life and limb ranks above that of tangible and intangible property.

[271] *Ibid.* [272] *Page* v. *Smith* [1996] 1 AC 955.

[273] [1962] QB 405.

[274] See in particular *Bradford* v. *Robinson Rentals* [1967] 1 WLR 337, *Robinson* v. *Post Office* [1974] 1 WLR 1176.

[275] [1969] 3 WLR 1556. [276] [1978] QB 791.

In the case of property damage generally the trend is less clear, but there are signs that the courts will take a flexible view of what is meant by 'kind of damage'. In *The Wagon Mound (No. 2)*[277] the owners of the two ships damaged in the fire sued the owners of the *Wagon Mound*. This time the judge found as a fact that there was a small but significant risk of damage by fire, and the Privy Council held that this was sufficient for the jury to hold the defendants liable for the full amount of the loss. It might appear that the second *Wagon Mound* case reversed the first.[278] Yet the decisions are probably compatible, since in *The Wagon Mound (No. 1)* it was found that damage by fire was not foreseeable; in each case the premise was that a *specific* kind of property damage had to be foreseeable, and not just property damage of *any* kind.[279] In *Vacwell Engineering Co.* v. *BDH Chemicals Ltd.*[280] the defendants supplied a chemical to the plaintiffs without warning that it was liable to explode in water. An employee of the plaintiffs placed a consignment of the chemical in a sink; this set off a chemical reaction, which caused a huge explosion. The judge held that the magnitude and extent of the explosion were irrelevant, as long as the explosion itself and the type of damage to property which it could cause were foreseeable. There is no clear authority indicating that for the purpose of *The Wagon Mound (No. 1)* test, all kinds of property damage are deemed to be as good as each other. On the contrary, it appears that the test of remoteness for property damage (and, by extension, for pure economic loss) is stricter than for interferences with physical safety and health. The precise limits to recovery can probably only be established on a case-by-case basis. But in general, the restrictive approach to property and economic loss may be justified both by the higher priority accorded to protecting bodily integrity and by the widespread availability of loss insurance for property damage.

(D) FORESEEABILITY OF THE CAUSAL SEQUENCE

A further qualification to the test in *The Wagon Mound (No. 1)* is that if the type of damage suffered was foreseeable, the precise sequence of events by which the injury was brought about need not have been. In *Hughes* v. *Lord Advocate*[281] the defendants left a manhole uncovered and protected only by a tent and paraffin lamp. A child climbed down into the hole and, as he was re-ascending, kicked over one of the lamps, which fell into the hole, causing an explosion in which he was burned. The Court of Session denied liability on the ground that although injury by burning was foreseeable as the boy might have come into contact with one of the lamps, burning by means of this sequence of events was not. The House of Lords reversed on the ground that the precise chain of events was immaterial. In contrast is the decision of the Court of Appeal in *Doughty* v. *Turner Manufacturing Co. Ltd.*[282] Here the court drew a distinction between burning caused by a splash of hot liquid, which was deemed to be foreseeable, and burning caused by an explosion, which was not. An employee of the defendants

277 [1967] 1 AC 617.

278 See generally the important discussion of R. W. M. Dias, 'Trouble on Oiled Waters: Problems of the *Wagon Mound (No. 2)*' [1967] *CLJ* 62 (Select Bibliography).

279 E. McKendrick, *Tort Textbook* (5th edn., 1991), 101.

280 [1971] 1 QB 88.

281 [1963] AC 837.

282 [1964] 1 QB 518.

carelessly tipped the asbestos cover of a molten metal container into the metal, setting off a chain reaction which caused an explosion in which the plaintiff, who was standing nearby, was injured, suffering bad burns. The court held that the manner and extent of his injuries were not foreseeable. The case is hard to reconcile with *Hughes*.[283]

The celebrated American case of *Palsgraf* v. *Long Island Railroad Co.*,[284] which is frequently (but mistakenly) thought to turn on the absence of any duty of care to an unforeseeable plaintiff, is better regarded as raising an issue which an English court would today treat as one of remoteness. Nor is it obvious that Cardozo J's judgment would be followed, bearing in mind the decision of the House of Lords in *Hughes* v. *Lord Advocate*.[285] In *Palsgraf* the plaintiff was standing on the defendant's railway platform, waiting for a train, when another train stopped to collect passengers. As it was about to pull out again a passenger tried to climb on board; he was assisted by two guards who dislodged a package he was carrying. Unknown to them it contained fireworks, which ignited on contact with the tracks, setting off an explosion which tipped over a set of scales on to the plaintiff. Her action for damages failed on appeal in the New York Court of Appeals.

A first point to note is that whatever was intended by Cardozo J and other judges of the majority, the case does not turn on the absence of a duty of care as that term is now understood.[286] The plaintiff was within the class of persons to whom the railway owed a general duty of care to avoid exposure to physical harm. Moreover, the standard of care imposed was a high one since the plaintiff was not a stranger but a passenger who had purchased a railway ticket. The case is properly classified as turning on causation rather than the anterior question of duty, and the relevant question is whether injury of the kind in question was too remote. Since it was conceivably foreseeable that the scales might cause physical injury if they fell over, the issue resolves itself into the foreseeability of the precise sequence of events through which this took place. Following *Hughes*, the unforeseeability of this precise sequence would not matter and the defendants would be held liable.

The same analysis offers the best explanation for the outcome in *Jolley* v. *Sutton London Borough Council*.[287] The defendant council was held to be in breach of its duty as an occupier by virtue of having left a derelict boat on council land for over two years. Two boys took it upon themselves to repair the boat; while they were carrying out work on it, the structure collapsed, trapping one of them and causing him severe injuries. In the Court of Appeal it was held that 'it was not reasonably foreseeable that an accident could occur as a result of the boys deciding to work under a propped boat',[288] but the House of Lords restored the judge's finding of liability, on the basis that some risk of harm to the children from the presence of the structure was foreseeable. The result is

283 E. McKendrick, *Tort Textbook* (5th edn., 1991), argues that the remarks of the Court of Appeal concerning remoteness were *obiter*, since it was not in fact foreseeable that any injury could have occurred from the employee's initial act.

284 162 NE 99 (1928).

285 [1963] AC 837.

286 W. Prosser, '*Palsgraf* Revisited' (1953) 52 *Mich. LR* 1 (Select Bibliography).

287 [2000] 1 WLR 1082.

288 [1998] 1 WLR 1546.

within the limits of recognised principle, in that it takes a broad view of 'kind of damage' in physical injury cases for the purposes of the remoteness stage of inquiry, and *Jolley* could also be read as a *Hughes*-like case in which nothing was allowed to turn on the argument that the precise causal sequence was not foreseeable, although a close reading of the House of Lords' judgments might indicate that sufficient foreseeability had been established on the facts.[289]

(E) REMOTENESS AND DAMAGE TO PROPERTY

An exception to the 'eggshell skull' rule may apparently operate in relation to certain economic losses. In *The Liesbosch*[290] the plaintiffs' dredger was sunk outside Patras harbour by the defendants' ship. All the plaintiffs' capital was tied up in the contract it had to dredge the harbour, and in order to complete this work it had to hire another dredger. This turned out to be more expensive than buying a substitute. The House of Lords denied a claim for this additional expense on the ground (as expressed by Lord Wright) that 'the appellants' actual loss in so far as it was due to their impecuniosity arose from that impecuniosity as a separate and concurrent cause, extraneous to and distinct in character from the tort'.[291]

It is not clear why this form of economic vulnerability—in the sense that impecuniosity here is the equivalent of the 'eggshell skull' principle—should be analysed differently from physical vulnerability. The only plausible explanation is the argument of policy to the effect that the law places a higher value on physical interests, and in particular on personal health and safety.

But if this is so, the result in *The Liesbosch* is still hard to understand since that case did not concern pure economic loss, but economic loss flowing from property damage. For most purposes of the tort of negligence (and in particular the categorisation of kinds of damage for the purposes of determining the duty of care) physical damage to the person and damage to tangible property are on the same footing. Lord Wright's reference to causation as the explanation for *The Liesbosch* is unconvincing since it does not explain the different outcome in a case of physical injury such as *Smith* v. *Leech Brain & Co. Ltd.*[292] It would be open to the courts to take a different approach in property-damage cases on policy grounds. However, the policy argument does not explain everything. If the plaintiff's economic losses in the sense of lost earning capacity are unusually extensive—if, for example, he is a particularly highly paid earner—the defendant will, nevertheless, be required to meet his loss in full. Why then must a tortfeasor 'take his victim as he finds him in terms of exceptionally high or low profit earning capacity, but not in terms of pecuniosity or impecuniosity which may be their manifestations'?[293] Doubts such as these have confined *The Liesbosch* to cases where the

[289] See R. Williams, 'Remoteness: Some Unexpected Mischief' (2001) 117 *LQR* 30.

[290] *Liesbosch Dredger* v. *SS Edison* [1933] AC 449.

[291] *Ibid.*, 460.

[292] [1962] 2 QB 405.

[293] *Dodd Properties (Kent) Ltd.* v. *Canterbury CC* [1980] 1 All ER 928, 940 (Donaldson LJ).

plaintiff failed to mitigate his losses when it would have been reasonable to do so, as opposed to cases where he could have done so but chose, for good reasons, not to.[294]

In *Alcoa Minerals of Jamaica Inc.* v. *Broderick*[295] the Privy Council declined to apply *The Liesbosch* in a case of property damage caused by pollution. The plaintiff's damages had been augmented because he had been unable to pay for repairs at a critical time. The Privy Council held that there was no absolute rule barring consideration of the plaintiff's impecuniosity, and that in this case it was foreseeable, given the scale of the pollution, that a householder in the plaintiff's position might not be able to take immediate steps to repair the damage.

The authority of *The Liesbosch* was further diminished—indeed, restricted almost to vanishing point—by the judgment of the House of Lords in *Lagden* v. *O'Connor*.[296] The claimant's car was damaged by the negligent driving of the defendant, and had to be repaired. The claimant could not afford to pay for the hire of a replacement car because he was unemployed; he therefore entered into an arrangement with a credit hire company, under which they provided him with a credit facility under which he had the use of a car free of charge for twenty-six weeks, in return for enabling the credit hire company to recover their costs from the defendant's insurers, together with an insurance policy which would meet those costs if the action against the defendant failed. The overall result, while more flexible for the claimant, was also more expensive than the simple hire of a car would have been. The House of Lords held that, notwithstanding *The Liesbosch*, the impecuniosity of the claimant was a factor that it could take into account where, as here, he had acted reasonably in mitigating his loss, and where his impecuniosity was foreseeable; it was foreseeable that some road users might, by virtue of their lack of resources, have to have resort to a credit hire arrangement.

(F) REMOTENESS AND PURE ECONOMIC LOSS

The issue of how to treat consequential economic losses arising from a breach of the duty of care which arises under *Hedley Byrne* v. *Heller*[297] and *Henderson* v. *Merrett Syndicates*[298] was one of the issues which arose for decision in the House of Lords in *South Australia Asset Management Corp.* v. *York Montague Ltd.* (generally known as the *SAAMCO* case).[299] The claimants advanced a loan to a third party in return for taking security over property which the defendants had negligently over-valued. The plaintiffs would not have made the loan in the first place had a correct valuation been made. After the transaction was made, there was a fall in the market, leaving the claimants with an even greater loss than before. The point to be decided was whether the additional loss caused by the fall in the market could be recovered from the defendants. The House of Lords held that it could not. Lord Hoffmann went on to specify that the claimant's loss

294 See, in particular, *ibid.*; *The Savand* [1998] 2 Lloyd's Rep. 97.
295 [2002] 1 AC 371.
296 [2004] 1 AC 1067.
297 [1964] AC 465.
298 [1995] 2 AC 145.
299 [1997] AC 191.

was confined to the 'loss of coverage', that is, the difference between the actual value (as it later appeared) of the property at the time the loan was made and the value which the defendant had incorrectly placed on it.[300]

While this result may well be correct from the point of view of both policy and principle, confusion arose from the way in which the case was argued. At first instance and in the Court of Appeal it was described as a 'measure of damages' case, while Lord Hoffmann's leading judgment in the House of Lords describes it as turning on the 'scope of duty'. According to Lord Hoffmann, '[i]n the present case, there is no dispute that [a] duty was owed to the lenders. The real question in this case is the kind of loss in respect of which the duty was owed'.[301] In this context, '[a] correct description of the loss for which the valuer is liable must precede any consideration of the measure of damages'.[302] In a case involving a misstatement or negligent performance of a service, where the defendant's liability necessarily arises from an assumption of responsibility or undertaking which is then relied upon by the claimant, the nature of the initial assumption or undertaking is an important factor limiting the defendant's legal duty, just as it would be in the parallel case of a contractual undertaking. Thus in *SAAMCO* it was essential to bear in mind that the defendant undertook to provide information about the property in question, not to advise the claimant on whether or not to enter into the transaction.

However, this point does not completely resolve the issue in *SAAMCO* since we are still left with the problem of how to apply rules on foreseeability and remoteness in the context of consequential loss, which is normally described as an issue of causation and not as one relating to duty of care. According to Lord Hoffmann, '[r]ules which make the wrongdoer liable for all the consequences of his wrongful conduct are exceptional and need to be justified by some special policy'. In so far as this statement can be read as referring to principles of remoteness, it must be placed in context. It should not be read as applying to cases of physical injury where, as we have seen, a line of cases beginning with *Hughes* v. *Lord Advocate*[303] has tempered the approach laid down in *The Wagon Mound (No. 1)*[304] by imposing liability in cases where harm of a foreseeable kind occurred to an extent or in a manner that was not itself foreseeable. Nor does it seem to apply to property damage, in particular now that *The Liesbosch*[305] has been, to put it at its lowest, severely qualified by *Lagden* v. *O'Connor*.[306] In the context of pure economic loss, however, there are good reasons for taking a stricter approach, not least because it

300 This part of the *SAAMCO* ruling has given rise to considerable discussion and difficulty in later cases. See *Kenny & Good Pty. Ltd.* v. *MGICA (1992) Ltd.* (1999) 163 ALR 611 (HC of Australia), discussed by D. McLaughlan and C. Rickett, '*SAAMCO* in the High Court of Australia' (2000) 116 *LQR* 1; *Platform Home Loans Ltd.* v. *Oyston Shipways Ltd.* [2000] 2 AC 190, discussed by J. Stapleton, 'Risk-Taking by Commercial Lenders' (1999) 115 *LQR* 527 and D. Howarth, 'Complexity Strikes Back: Valuation in the House of Lords' (2000) 8 *Tort LR* 85, and in ch. 24, Section 2, below, in our examination of contributory negligence.

301 [1997] AC 191, 212. 302 *Ibid.*, 211.

303 [1963] AC 837; see also *Jolley* v. *Sutton LBC* [2000] 1 WLR 1082; M. Staunch, 'Risk and Remoteness of Damage in Negligence' (2001) 64 *MLR* 191.

304 [1961] AC 388. 305 [1033] AC 449.

306 [2004] 1 AC 1067.

is only in exceptional circumstances that a duty of care in respect of this kind of damage can arise. The outcome in *SAAMCO* is perhaps best understood in this light.

(G) REMOTENESS OF DAMAGE IN CONTRACT AND TORT

In principle the rules of remoteness are more generous in the tort of negligence than they are in contract. The tort test, even after *The Wagon Mound (No. 1)*,[307] holds that if the kind of damage suffered was foreseeable, the extent need not be. In contract those losses arising 'naturally . . . according to the usual course of things' are recoverable, subject to a more extensive liability arising if the claimant made the defendant aware of special circumstances before entering into the agreement.[308] According to Lord Reid in *The Heron II*,[309] a higher degree of foreseeability is required for recovery of consequential damage flowing from breach of contract than is the case in tort; moreover, the relevant point at which foreseeability is judged is the time at which the contract was made and not the point at which, as in tort, the relevant duty is breached. The basis for this more restrictive rule may be that in contract the parties are brought together by their own agreement, and should be able to rely upon their own allocation of risk or that which would implicitly attach to a contract of that kind. However, in *H. Parsons (Livestock) Ltd.* v. *Uttley, Ingham & Co. Ltd.*[310] Lord Denning suggested that, regardless of the origin of a particular obligation in contract or tort, the tort rule should apply in cases of physical injury or property damage. This would leave the contract rule to apply only in cases of pure economic loss. There is much to be said for this, at least as far as injury to the person is concerned. In relation to the contract of employment, for example, it would be unusual if the employer's general duty of care in tort to his employees could be implicitly cut down by the existence of a contract term setting a lower standard of care and, according to one reading of the broad *dicta* of *The Heron II*, a more restrictive conception of remoteness of damage.[311] In relation to property damage, Lord Denning's *dicta* in *Parsons* were rejected by the majority of the Court of Appeal, although they reached the same result in that case, holding the defendant liable for the full extent of the harm caused to the pigs.

As far as pure economic loss is concerned, the *Hadley* v. *Baxendale* rule in contract clearly places limits on recoverability which would involve the drawing of distinctions within the general category of 'economic loss' as a kind of damage. In *Wroth* v. *Tyler*[312] an unexpectedly large loss suffered following the collapse of a house sale was recovered on the ground that the *type* of loss had been foreseeable; this seems hard to reconcile with the normal contract rule, and may also have been a misapplication of the normal tort rule. As we have just seen, the *SAAMCO* case is authority for the proposition that, when it comes to determining remoteness of damage, all types of pure economic loss should not be treated in the same way. Because the duty of care in tort to avoid causing

307 [1961] AC 388.

308 *Hadley* v. *Baxendale* (1854) 9 Exch. 341.

309 [1969] 1 AC 350, 385.

310 [1978] QB 791.

311 See the discussion of this point in the context of *Johnstone* v. *Bloomsbury HA* [1992] QB 333; see ch. 18, below.

312 [1974] Ch. 30.

pure economic loss is derived from an undertaking or assumption of responsibility of some kind (which is not the case for physical injury or damage to tangible property), it seems correct that the scope of the duty undertaken should play a part in determining the extent of the defendant's liability, just as it does in contract.

One area where the different contract and tort rules on remoteness may make a substantial impact concerns liability for misrepresentation. The *Wagon Mound (No. 1)* principle of foreseeability applies to liability in negligence under *Hedley Byrne & Co. Ltd.* v. *Heller*.[313] But in the tort of deceit the 'directness' test of *Re Polemis*[314] applies, on the ground of the greater fault of the defendant. This more extensive basis for recovery also applies to claims brought under section 2(1) of the Misrepresentation Act 1967,[315] thanks to the reading of section 2(1) adopted by the Court of Appeal in *Royscott Trust Co.* v *Rogerson*.[316]

SELECT BIBLIOGRAPHY

DIAS, R. M. W., 'Trouble on Oiled Waters: Problems of the *Wagon Mound (No. 2)*' [1967] *CLJ* 62.

EPSTEIN, R. A., 'A Theory of Strict Liability' (1973) 2 *Jo. LS* 151.

FLEMING, J. G., 'Probabilistic Causation in Tort Law' (1989) 68 *Can. BR* 661.

—'Probabilistic Causation in Tort Law: A Postscript' (1991) 70 *Can. BR* 137.

FRASER, J., and HOWARTH, D., 'More Concern for Cause' (1984) 4 *Leg. Stud.* 131.

HART, H. L. A., and HONORÉ, A. M., *Causation and the Law* (2nd edn., 1985).

HONORÉ, A. M., 'Causation and Remoteness of Damage', in Tunc, A. (ed.), *Int. Encl. Comp. L* (1983), xi, ch. 7.

KING, J., 'Causation, Valuation, and Chance in Personal Injury Torts Involving Pre-existing Conditions and Future Consequences' (1981) 90 *Yale LJ* 1358.

MULLANY, N. J., 'Common Sense Causation—An Australian View' (1992) 12 *OJLS* 431.

PROSSER, W., '*Palsgraf* Revisited' (1953) 52 *Mich. LR* 1.

STAPLETON, J., 'Law, Causation and Common Sense' (1988) 8 *OJLS* 111.

—'The Gist of Negligence: Part II' (1988) 104 *LQR* 389.

—'Lords A'Leaping Evidentiary Gaps' (2003) 10 *Tort LR* 276.

—'Occam's Razor Reveals an Orthodox Basis for *Chester* v. *Ashfar*' (2006) 122 *LQR* 426.

WEINRIB, E., 'A Step Forward in Factual Causation' (1975) 38 *MLR* 518.

WEIR, T. 'Making It Happen versus Making It More Likely' [2003] *CLJ* 219.

313 [1964] AC 465. 314 [1921] 3 KB 560.

315 *Doyle* v. *Olby Ironmongers* [1969] 2 QB 158; *East* v. *Maurer* [1990] 2 All ER 737.

316 [1991] 3 All ER 294; R. Hooley, 'Damages and the Misrepresentation Act 1967' (1991) 107 *LQR* 547.

4. THE TORT OF NEGLIGENCE: A SUMMARY AND CONCLUSION

As we have seen in our review of the tort of negligence in the past two chapters, the evolution of this tort since it was synthesised in *Donoghue* v. *Stevenson* has consisted of a search for 'control devices' and mechanisms which could set limits to the scope of the tort and prevent it encroaching on other areas of civil obligation.[317] At various times, both duty and causation have served this need,[318] with the former gradually becoming the focus of attention and, it must be admitted, controversy. Within the case law on duty there has been a gradual move away from general conceptual formulae, and the adoption instead of more specific criteria, many of them explicitly policy-orientated, to guide the courts. Thus, as we have seen, the courts have come to make increasing reference to arguments based on insurability, the deterrent effects of liability, the possibilities of loss shifting, and the dangers of unwelcome or 'defensive' reactions to extensions of the duty concept. Notions of fault have also been affected by the concern to ensure that the perceived goals of tort law, in particular ensuring effective compensation, have been met.

The overall result is a mixed one, with tort law in general and negligence in particular brimming with antithetic decisions reflecting different philosophies. For the litigant this is unsatisfactory, for the judge it must often be baffling, for the practitioner, no doubt, a boon. Such a state of affairs cannot be a source of pride but a sense of puzzlement and dissatisfaction. This is reflected in frequent judicial confessions that the case law has become so complex that only legislative intervention can save it from its internal contradictions and conflicts.

That this should be so is, in one sense, inevitable. The growth of sloppy, if not downright negligent, behaviour understandably leads to demands for proper redress. At the same time, a widening of liability, especially if coupled with unwarranted and uncontrollable awards, also justifies calls for control and restraint. One way out of this mess might well be in relooking at the law of damages rather than the rules of liability. Better still might be radical intervention that removed from the scope of tort litigation such costly areas of tort law as medical liability and even accidents at work. The truth of the matter, however, is that at present even making such suggestions is tantamount to disturbing a hornet's nest. But the hornets need not worry; for we do not live in times when there is the political will to attempt proper reform. And yet the present state of affairs cannot go on for ever.

On a conceptual level, it is clear that the issues involved in setting the boundaries to liability are too complex to be adequately captured by such open-ended terms as 'proximity', 'foreseeability', and, worst of all, the 'fair, just and reasonable' test. At the same

[317] Whether they have been successful is open to debate. See T. Weir, 'The Staggering March of Negligence', ch. 5 in P. Cane and J. Stapleton (eds.), *The Law of Obligations: Essays in Honour of John Fleming* (1998).

[318] See D. Howarth, *Textbook on Tort* (1995), 114–18.

time, there is legitimate concern that negligence lacks an adequate conceptual structure, a framework of principle within which the complex balancing of different factors can be placed. Unadorned references to 'policy' are unappealing; so is the judicial tendency to make assumptions concerning the possible consequences of decisions which are based on judicial hunches rather than empirical evidence. A degree of conceptual fluidity, and perhaps some confusion, thus seems unavoidable; and may well be preferable to the solution of freezing the law in its present state, leaving the existing categories of recovery as they are and refusing to add to them when justice so demands. In that sense we may leave the last word to McLachlin J, speaking on behalf of the majority of the Canadian Supreme Court in the *Norsk* case, in terms which describe a particular attitude both to the specific question of economic loss but also to the tort of negligence as a whole:

> The fact is that situations arise, other than those falling within the old exclusionary rule, where it is manifestly fair and just that recovery of economic loss be permitted. Faced with these situations, courts will strain to allow recovery, provided they are satisfied that the case will not open the door to a plethora of undeserving claims. They will refuse to accept injustice merely for the sake of the doctrinal tidiness, which is the motivating spirit of *Murphy*. This is in the best tradition of the law of negligence, the history of which exhibits a sturdy refusal to be confined by arbitrary forms and rules where justice indicates otherwise.[319]

[319] (1991) 91 DLR (4th) 289, 365.

5

AN AMERICAN PERSPECTIVE ON NEGLIGENCE LAW[1]

by D. W. Robertson[*]

1. FUNDAMENTAL DIFFERENCES IN LEGAL CULTURE

English readers of decisions by courts in the United States need to consider three major differences between the legal cultures of the two countries before drawing any firm conclusions about the American picture. These differences combine to make it greatly more important in the United States than in England that the basic law of negligence—its conceptual apparatus and essential vocabulary—be as firm, clear, and simple as possible.[2]

First, the United States has no unified law of negligence, but rather at least fifty-three discrete systems.[3] Each of the fifty states has its own tort law. The legislature and highest court in each state constitute the supreme authority as to that state's private law. The federal maritime law is a distinct fifty-first system, and the Federal Employers' Liability Act[4] a fifty-second; here the Congress and the United States Supreme Court share the supreme authority.[5] The fifty-third system is a federal common law of torts that

[*] W. Page Keeton Chair in Tort Law, University Distinguished Teaching Professor, University of Texas.

[1] The topics treated in this chapter are a sampling from a large field. For broader studies of negligence law in the United States, see D. B. Dobbs, *The Law of Torts* (2000); *Restatement (Third) of Torts: Products Liability* (1998); *Restatement (Third) of Torts: Apportionment of Liability* (2000); *Restatement (Third) of Torts: Liability for Physical Harm* (forthcoming) (Proposed Final Draft No. 1, 6 Apr. 2005). See also *Restatement (Second) of Torts* (1965). The three new *Restatements (Third)* replace some but not all of the *Restatement (Second)*.

[2] See generally D. W. Robertson, 'The Vocabulary of Negligence Law' (1997) 58 *La. LR* 1; D. W. Robertson, 'Allocating Authority among Institutional Decision Makers' (1997) 57 *La. LR* 1079.

[3] Probably there are others. Professor Shapo characterises 'a conglomerate of statutory and common law dealing with the tort liability of the federal government' as a discrete system: M. S. Shapo, *Towards a Jurisprudence of Injury* (1984), 2–21. And the District of Columbia has its own local tort jurisprudence.

[4] This Act, 45 USC §§51–60, deals with interstate railroads' tort duties to their employees. It is a bare-bones statute, leaving a multitude of tort-law details to the United States Supreme Court and the lower federal courts.

[5] See, e.g., the Jones Act, 46 USC app. §688(a); *Panama R. Co.* v. *Johnson*, 264 US 375, 44 SCt. 391, 393 (1924); *Kermarec* v. *Compagnie Générale Transatlantique*, 358 US 625, 79 SCt. 406 (1959); *East River S.S. Corp.* v. *Transamerica Delaval, Inc.*, 476 US 858, 106 SCt. 2295 (1986).

supplements national legislation on matters such as antitrust.[6] Each of these systems is operated and proclaimed by judges, many of whom exercise the authority to issue published opinions that are then studied by those who must discern what the controlling law is on a particular point in a particular jurisdiction. (In the United States at present there are at least eighteen hundred judges with the authority to issue published decisions.) And each of these systems is continually subject to the possibility of legislative change, which sometimes seems to come virtually at whim. If one is looking for uniformity, clarity, and predictability, the tort law of the United States is not a pretty picture.

One point calls for some emphasis: The decisions of the federal courts, including the United States Supreme Court, are not authoritative on issues of private state law, but merely persuasive.[7] This means that a decision of the United States Supreme Court on a point of federal maritime law is no more (and no less) representative of the American law of negligence than a decision on a similar point of New York law by that state's highest court. It is thus a technical mistake to say that a United States Supreme Court maritime decision has "destroy[ed] the authority" of an earlier New York state-law decision on a similar point.[8] New York's law remains that reflected in the decisions of its own courts unless and until those courts are persuaded by the United States Supreme Court's reasoning—or by the reasoning in some persuasive decision from the House of Lords or a court in another of the United States—to change it.[9]

The fifty-plus American negligence systems are in the foregoing senses independent of one another. Moreover, they are operated by many thousands of judges and lawyers whose educational backgrounds, even within a single jurisdiction, are often significantly divergent from one another's in coverage and quality. At the same time, these disparate negligence systems share common policy goals and generally strive for common outcomes. Thus, authorities from one system are routinely cited as persuasive in another. If a court in Florida is to understand and evaluate the decision and reasoning of a court in Montana, the conceptual structure of negligence law needs to be as uniform as we can make it. From this point of view the American law of negligence is intra-national comparative law, and the conceptual apparatus of negligence law is its essential vocabulary. In the United States we accept, however regretfully, that we will never achieve a uniform national law of torts; indeed, some analysts have perceived a "growing divergence" among the American states' tort laws.[10] This is all the more reason to try especially hard to speak a uniform national language of torts.

6 See, e.g., *Texas Industries, Inc.* v. *Radcliff Materials, Inc.*, 451 US 630, 101 SCt. 2061 (1981).

7 See, e.g., *State* v. *Perry*, 610 So. 2d 746, 751 (La. 1992) (stating that the Supreme Court of Louisiana 'is the final arbiter of the meaning of the state constitution and laws').

8 *Murphy* v. *Brentwood DC* [1991] AC 398, 469 (Lord Keith of Kinkel), 494 (Lord Jauncey of Tullichettle).

9 This in fact happened in New York. For many years *Quackenbush* v. *Ford Motor Co.*, 153 NYS 131 (NY App. 1915), stood for the proposition that the purchaser of a product that is defective in such a way as to damage itself has a cause of action in tort against the manufacturer. In *East River S.S. Corp.* v. *Transamerica Delaval, Inc.*, 476 US 858, 106 SCt. 2295 (1986), the United States Supreme Court (without paying any particular attention to New York law) held that there is no such cause of action under federal maritime law. Subsequently the highest court in New York found the reasoning of *East River* to be 'persuasive' and changed New York law to conform to the resolution in *East River*. *Bocre Leasing Corp. v. General Motors Corp.*, 645 NE 2d 1195 (NY 1995).

10 T. W. Reavley and J. W. Wesevich, 'An Old Rule for New Reasons' (1992) 71 *Tex. LR* 1, 3 n. 4.

The second fundamental difference between England's and America's legal cultures is America's pervasive use of juries in negligence cases. In a bench-trial system like England's—where experienced judges who have been selected for office on merits-based criteria determine issues of fact as well as issues of law—the law of negligence can perhaps be fairly subtle and fairly flexible and still serve its functions of forecasting outcomes and guiding the judges and lawyers in their handling of disputed cases. In jury-trial systems like forty-nine[11] of the American states the situation is far different. The American trial judge's major tasks are determining which issues are for the jury and how to instruct the jury on those issues. If there is to be any consistency and predictability in the way these tasks are performed by the huge number of trial judges who perform them on a daily basis throughout the United States, the governing negligence law needs to be as firm, clear, and simple as can be achieved. An approach to a particular legal problem that an English jurist might properly decry as conceptualism might be regarded in the United States as necessary and welcome guidance for the often bewildered participants in a litigation system that is to some extent inevitably kaleidoscopic.

The third important difference of legal culture stems from the American system of compensating plaintiffs' lawyers. Normally the American tort plaintiff pays his lawyer nothing out of pocket. Instead the client and lawyer agree that the lawyer will take a percentage of whatever can be recovered by judgment or settlement from the defendant. Such a contingency fee agreement would be illegal in England and most other countries. It is legal and proper throughout the United States.[12] The chief virtue of the contingency fee system is enabling the downtrodden to approach the halls of justice. This is a considerable virtue. But it may be outweighed by the flood of silly, vindictive, or purely mercenary litigation that could ensue if plaintiffs' lawyers do not exercise rigorous discipline as to the kinds of cases they will accept. There are many thousands of plaintiffs' lawyers in the United States, and not all of them have as much work as they would like. In such a country a major goal of the law of negligence must be furnishing clear guidance to lawyers as to which cases are *not worth pursuing*. This goal is achievable only by rules of tort law that are broad, clear, and definite enough to instruct trial judges to dismiss some types of actions virtually as soon as they are brought to court. This is because any case that can survive this initial procedural stage—even though it may be fairly clear that the case can never lead to a judgment in the plaintiff's favour—has some settlement value and will therefore be pursued if the plaintiff is persistent enough in searching for a lawyer to take it. Again this difference argues for a firmer, clearer, and simpler doctrinal apparatus than may be necessary or appropriate in England.

[11] Louisiana is the exception. Litigants in that state have a right to jury trial, but a jury's findings of fact—including even its assessment of damages—are exposed to fairly sweeping appellate review. Thus, many litigants determine that there is no advantage in jury trial and elect to try their cases to the bench.

[12] For informative and entertaining reflections on this difference, see R. L. Abel, 'An American Hamburger Stand in St Paul's Cathedral' (2001) 51 *DePaul LR* 253.

2. THE QUEST FOR CONCEPTUAL CLARITY: THE TRADITIONAL MODEL

On the conceptual outlines of the cause of action in negligence there has been broad general agreement: the plaintiff in a negligence action cannot succeed without satisfying the five elements of duty, breach of duty, factual causation, legal causation, and damages.[13]

The *duty* inquiry is a matter for the judge's determination. It asks whether there is a rule of law or a discernible principle or policy that should shield the defendant from liability even when it is apparent that unacceptable conduct on the part of the defendant has been a factual and a legal cause of cognisable harm.[14]

The other four elements present jury questions—matters for the jury's determination under limiting instructions given by the judge—unless reasonable minds could not differ. The *breach* issue addresses whether the defendant's conduct was unacceptable, *viz.*, unreasonable under the circumstances. Other names for the breach issue are the substandard conduct issue and the negligence issue.[15] The *factual causation* issue inquires whether the harmful event of which the plaintiff complains would probably have been avoided if the defendant's conduct had been reasonable under the circumstances. If the harmful event would probably have occurred regardless of the defendant's wrongful conduct, then such conduct was not a cause-in-fact of the injuries of which the plaintiff complains. The *legal causation* inquiry (which is also variously called the scope

[13] See D. B. Dobbs, *The Law of Torts* (2000), 269; D. W. Robertson *et al.*, *Cases and Materials on Torts* (3rd edn., 2004), 76; W. P. Keeton, *et al.*, *Prosser and Keeton On Torts* (5th edn., 1984), 164–5. The legal causation issue is often termed the 'proximate cause' issue. Because the latter term carries a great deal of confusing historical baggage, legal causation is the preferable term.

[14] The American Law Institute is in the final process of formulating the *Restatement (Third) of Torts: Liability for Physical Harm*. Proposed Final Draft No. 1 (6 Apr. 2005) states in §7:

> (a) An actor ordinarily has a duty to exercise reasonable care when the actor's conduct creates a risk of physical harm.
> (b) In exceptional cases, when an articulated countervailing principle or policy warrants denying or limiting liability in a particular class of cases, a court may decide that the defendant has no duty or that the ordinary duty of reasonable care requires modification.

This formulation reflects the traditional thinking emanating from *Heaven* v. *Pender* (1883) 11 QBD 503, 509:

> [W]henever one person is by circumstances placed in such a position with regard to another that every one of ordinary sense who did think would at once recognise that if he did not use ordinary care and skill in his own conduct with regard to those circumstances he would cause danger of injury to the person or property of the other, a duty arises to use ordinary care and skill to avoid such danger.

The *Restatement (Third's)* articulation of the duty element reinforces the *Heaven* v. *Pender* principle by requiring judges who would depart from it to confine the departure to 'particular class[es] of cases' and to justify the departure on 'articulated [grounds of] principle or policy'. The *Restatement (Third)* formulation disapproves of *ad hoc* (i.e., one-case-at-a-time) declarations of no duty. See D. W. Robertson *et al.*, *Cases and Materials on Torts* (3rd edn., 2004), 216–8, 295–7. For examples of cases that declare new no-duty rules in ways that seem acceptable under the *Restatement (Third)* criteria, see *ibid.*, 296.

[15] It would be conducive to better understanding of the terminology if the word 'negligence' took a capital 'N' when referring to the law of negligence or to the cause of action in negligence and a lower-case 'n' when referring to the substandard conduct element of such a cause of action.

of liability issue or the proximate cause issue)[16] addresses whether the injury the plaintiff suffered was so remote or attenuated a consequence of the defendant's wrongful conduct that imposing liability seems unfair or otherwise inappropriate. In general the legal causation requirement seeks "to confine the liability of a negligent actor to those harmful consequences which result from the operation of the risk, or of a risk, the foreseeability of which rendered the defendant's conduct negligent".[17] The *damages* issue addresses whether the particular consequences for which the plaintiff seeks compensation are attributable to the harmful event for which the defendant is responsible. It also seeks to set an appropriate monetary equivalent for such injurious consequences.

The broad agreement on the conceptual model entails recognition that the five elements must be defined with care and kept separate. But in practice several varieties of confusion or conceptual mistakes have sometimes occurred.[18] *First*, judges and lawyers often say "no duty" when a more careful articulation would be "no breach".[19] This confusion is sometimes harmless, but it can have the unintended or unjustified effect of awarding the trial judge additional power over an issue that is normally assigned to the jury.[20] *Second*, the vocabulary of duty is sometimes used to address the

[16] The *Restatement (Third) of Torts* is departing from the *Restatement (Second)* by dropping the legal cause label. The *Restatement (Third)* treats this issue in Ch. 6, titled 'Scope of Liability (Proximate Cause)'. The heart of Ch. 6 is §29, which is captioned 'Limitations on Liability for Tortious Conduct' and states: 'An actor's liability is limited to those physical harms that result from the risks that made the actor's conduct tortious.'

[17] *Socony-Vacuum Oil. Co.* v. *Marshall*, 222 F 2d 604, 610 (1st Cir. 1955).

[18] The remainder of this section deals with seemingly random conceptual mistakes. The immediately following section addresses an apparently purposive pattern whereby some judges have set out to alter the traditional model.

[19] See e.g. *Clinton* v. *Commonwealth Edison Co.*, 36 Ill.App. 3d 1064, 344 NE 2d 509, 514–15 (1976) (upholding a trial judge's decision that the defendant power company 'had no duty' to insulate a high-voltage transmission line near the plaintiff's house). The no-duty phrasing is potentially misleading because no one doubted that the power company owed a general duty of care under the broad principle of *Heaven* v. *Pender* ((1883) 11 QBD 503). A more careful phrasing of the Illinois court's thought (no duty to insulate) would have been that under the particular circumstances it was clear that the power company's duty of reasonable care was not breached by the failure to insulate. For a judicial recognition (and rejection) of the mistake of phrasing no-breach arguments in no-duty language, see *Piscitelli* v. *Friedenberg*, 87 Cal.App. 4th 953, 105 Cal. Rptr. 2d 88, 109 (2001). For an example of exactly that mistake, see *Lawlor* v. *Orlando*, 795 So. 2d 147, hn. 5 (Fla.App. 2001) (upholding a grant of summary judgment for the defendant on the ground that 'psychotherapist did not owe duty to outpatient who committed suicide, where patient showed no sign of suicidal tendencies, there was no evidence of prior suicide attempts or threats, and suicide screening a few months before patient's suicide showed no risk of suicide'). For further examples, see D. W. Robertson *et al.*, *Cases and Materials on Torts* (3rd edn., 2004), 296.

[20] Because the negligence (breach) issue is assigned to the jury, it is '[o]nly in that small percentage of cases where reasonable minds could not differ on the outcome of balancing all of the factors [that] summary judgment [on the breach issue is] appropriate': *Tucker* v. *American States Insurance*, 747 So. 2d 620, 628 (La.App. 1999). But judges should not let their concern for control over the jury tempt them into mislabelling no-breach determinations as no-duty determinations. A judge can enter a no-breach determination at the summary judgment stage whenever she can persuasively demonstrate that 'the facts lead ineluctably to [but one] outcome': *Fithian* v. *Reed*, 204 F 3d 306, 309 (1st Cir. 2000) (Mass. law) (upholding summary judgment that a homeowner was not negligent in failing to guard against the risk that discharge from his neighbour's snow-blower would break the homeowner's window and injure a child); see also *Lee* v. *GNLV Corp.*, 22 P 3d 209 (Nev. 2001) (upholding summary judgment that a restaurateur was not negligent in failing to administer the Heimlich manoeuvre to a choking customer).

problem of legal causation.[21] Again the effect is an artificial accretion of power to the judge and a corresponding inroad into the normal province of the jury.[22] *Third*, courts often conflate the issues of factual causation and legal causation.[23] This third type of confusion always entails muddled analysis and the use of inappropriate precedents. Also, it usually suppresses any discussion of the policy considerations that actually influence judges' answers to difficult legal causation questions. *Fourth*, courts sometimes transfer the issue of the victim's fault from the realm of affirmative defences (where it belongs) into the legal cause issue, for example stating that the plaintiff's "extraordinary negligence was the superseding and sole proximate [legal] cause" of the injuries in suit.[24] It is sometimes convenient to call this mistake the *sole proximate cause fallacy*. *Fifth*, certain problems that are normally treated under the issue of damages are sometimes mistakenly lumped into the factual causation inquiry. The effect of this last type of confusion is to hold the plaintiff to a much higher standard of proof than is normally thought to be appropriate.[25]

The antidote to the first two types of confusion (using "no duty" to mean "no breach" or "no legal causation") is confining the vocabulary of duty to its proper place. The traditional hallmarks of a true issue of duty involve *categories* of defendants (e.g., land occupier), of plaintiffs (e.g., trespasser), of conduct (e.g., nonfeasance), or of types of harm (e.g., pure economic damage or purely psychic harm). If the asserted impediment

[21] See, e.g., *Palsgraf* v. *Long Island R. Co.*, 248 NY 339, 162 NE 99, 100 (1928) (concluding that a railroad had 'no duty' to use reasonable care to prevent its employees' dangerous activities at one end of the station platform from causing unforeseeable injury to a passenger at the other end). According to one analyst, here the no-duty articulation was not just potentially misleading but 'unnerving and potentially quite deceiving': S. D. Sugarman, 'Assumption of Risk' (1997) 31 *Val. U LR* 833, 842. This criticism reflects the view that a railroad clearly owes an intending passenger a duty of reasonable care—indeed, arguably a duty of highest care under the traditional treatment of innkeepers and common carriers. What the *Palsgraf* court meant was that under the particular circumstances, the duty's scope of protection did not extend to the plaintiff's situation. Nowadays it is widely recognised that the scope-of-protection inquiry is merely an alternative way of phrasing the legal causation inquiry. See, e.g., D. B. Dobbs, *The Law of Torts* (2000), 273.

[22] See D. W. Robertson *et al.*, *Cases and Materials on Torts* (3rd edn., 2004), 214–15.

[23] See e.g. *Novak* v. *Rathman*, 153 Ill.App. 3d 408, 505 NE 2d 773, 776 (1987) (finding 'no causal connection' between the defendant's conduct in releasing a dangerous psychotic from incarceration and a murder later committed by the psychotic). The court's 'no causal connection' finding is facially implausible because plainly the psychotic could not have committed the murder if he had been kept locked up.

[24] *Exxon Co.* v. *Sofec, Inc.*, 517 US 830, 116 SCt. 1813, 1817 (1996) (federal maritime law). In this case the victim's fault was seen as so egregious that the court approved a trial in which only that issue was presented; the plaintiff was not even permitted to put on evidence of the defendant's fault. See also *Feng* v. *Metropolitan Transp. Auth.*, 285 AD 2d 447, 727 NYS, 2d 470, 471 (2001) (holding that conduct of a man who was struck by a train was so egregiously negligent as to be deemed 'a superseding cause necessarily relieving the [railroad] of liability'); *Soileau* v. *State*, 724 So. 2d 834, 839 (La.App. 1998) (holding that the duty to maintain highways in reasonably safe condition 'does not extend to protect motorists against harm which would not have occurred but for their grossly negligent operation of a motor vehicle'); cf. *Ruiz-Troche* v. *Pepsi Cola of Puerto Rico*, 161 F 3d 77, 87 (1st Cir. 1998) (discussing a so-called 'absorption theory' of Puerto Rico law whereby 'if one tortfeasor is only slightly responsible, the overwhelming negligence of the other tortfeasor "absorbs" the minimal negligence of the former and the latter bears all liability').

[25] See *DePass* v. *United States*, 721 F 2d 203, 208–9 (7th Cir. 1983) (Posner J, dissenting, taking his colleagues to task for forgetting the factual causation/damages distinction and for holding the plaintiff to an inappropriately heavy burden of proof as to the extent of his injuries).

to the plaintiff's recovery—the particular defensive argument under consideration—is not a categorical claim but instead depends upon factual details or nuances, the problem should not be regarded as one of duty but rather as one of breach of duty or of legal causation.[26]

The antidote to the third type of confusion (the conflation of the factual causation and legal causation elements) is careful delimitation of the factual causation inquiry.[27] The plaintiff satisfies the law's factual causation requirement by producing evidence from which a reasonable person could conclude that the harmful event forming the basis for the lawsuit probably would not have happened in the absence of the defendant's wrongful conduct. On the basis of such evidence the jury is free to determine that the defendant's wrongful conduct was a factual cause of the harm. Obviously other forces, often including the negligent conduct of tortfeasors other than the defendant, will also compete for attention as putative causes of the harm. The existence of such other forces may present difficulties to be dealt with under the duty, breach, or legal causation inquiries, but these difficulties form no proper part of the factual causation issue. Put in the simplest possible terms, the key idea is this: the plaintiff's factual causation burden is satisfied by showing that the defendant's wrongful conduct was probably *a* cause of the harmful event; requiring proof that it was *the* cause would burden the plaintiff's case far too greatly.

The antidote to the fourth type of confusion (the sole proximate cause fallacy) is the realisation that in a system that has made the general determination to use the fault of the victim to reduce rather than to bar recovery—*viz.*, a "comparative fault" or "comparative responsibility" system—it will always be inappropriate to conclude in a particular case that the victim's negligent conduct is so egregious that it prevents the defendant's negligent conduct from being a legal cause of the harm. If the defendant was guilty of negligent conduct that was a factual cause of the harm and that (putting the victim's fault to one side) would be regarded as a legal cause of the harm, then the defendant should pay something, no matter how negligent the victim may have been.[28]

26 Whether the alleged impediment goes to breach of duty or to legal causation does not matter as much, since both are classified as jury issues unless reasonable minds could not differ. Generally speaking, if at its core the defensive argument asserts that the defendant's behaviour was acceptable under the circumstances, it is a breach argument. If it implicitly concedes unacceptable behaviour but insists that the injury was too remote a consequence thereof, it is a legal causation argument. A more precise way to look at the difference is to note that the legal cause inquiry is focused on the foreseeability of the particular event that harmed the plaintiff, whereas the breach inquiry asks whether the defendant's conduct was substandard in light of the full array of foreseeable risks that the evidence shows were created or exacerbated by his conduct. See *Nelson* v. *Metro-North Commuter RR*, 235 F 3d 101, 106 (2d Cir. 2000) (Calabresi J, noting that 'the proposed *Restatement (Third) of Torts* takes the (generally accepted) position that the harm whose severity should be considered [as part of the breach inquiry] is not [just] the particular harm incurred by the plaintiff, but whatever harms are rendered more likely by the actor's conduct') (citation and internal quotation marks omitted).

27 See generally D. W. Robertson, 'The Common Sense of Cause in Fact' (1997) 75 *Tex. LR* 1765.

28 A legal system wishing to bar egregiously negligent victims from all recovery can do so straightforwardly, by adopting a 'modified' comparative fault system in which a plaintiff whose degree of fault exceeds a specified level (usually 50 or 51 per cent) is barred by the affirmative defence of contributory negligence: D. W. Robertson *et al.*, *Cases and Materials on Torts* (3rd edn., 2004), 381–2. Well over half of the American states have done this. See D. B. Dobbs, *The Law of Torts* (2000), 505.

Dealing with the fifth type of confusion (the intermingling of factual causation and damages considerations) once again entails careful delimitation of the factual causation inquiry. As was observed above, the factual causation issue asks whether the defendant's wrongful conduct was among the causes of the harmful event on which the lawsuit is based. Once that element is satisfied, whether particular injurious consequences are attributable to that event is properly approached under the damages inquiry, where the plaintiff's burden of proof has traditionally been less demanding than at the factual causation stage. In traditional judicial thinking we must guard against holding a defendant responsible when he has caused no harm; this is the appropriate province of the factual causation issue. But once we know that the defendant has caused some legally cognisable harm, we need not worry as much about perhaps making him pay a bit too much. "[T]he extent of [the plaintiff's] injury [is] an issue on which courts traditionally do not impose a heavy burden of proof on plaintiffs .... Doubts are resolved against the tortfeasor."[29]

Once the five elements of the negligence cause of action are properly delimited and the recurrent confusions sorted out and put to one side, the resultant model—the traditional model—works fairly well to direct the trial judge's attention to the right questions and to provide a workable indication of which issues should be decided by the judge and which, if any, left to the jury. And it must never be thought that the model is dispensable in bench-trial systems. There, too, it is the fundamental grammar of negligence law, necessary for focusing the attention of an appellate court on the asserted or actual flaws in a lower court's determination of the case, and for effective communication among judges, lawyers, scholars, and others charged with the tasks of rationalising, explaining, and trying to improve a system's negligence jurisprudence.

In the next section we will look at recent (and to this author regrettable) efforts by some courts to revise the traditional model. In those that follow we will use the traditional model to analyse American decisions in several areas of negligence law that are innately troublesome or challenging.

3. RECENT EFFORTS TO REVISE THE TRADITIONAL MODEL[30]

Guido Calabresi J, who was a stellar torts teacher and scholar before he ascended to the federal bench, has provided us with a powerful demonstration of the traditional model's intended function in delimiting the roles of trial judge and jury. In *Stagl* v.

[29] *DePass* v. *United States*, 721 F 2d 203, 208–9 (7th Cir. 1983) (Posner J, dissenting).

[30] At one level the judicial disagreements revealed in this section are political. For the most part the defenders of the traditional model want to resist erosion of plaintiffs' rights, while the revisers want to cut back on tort law's coverage. At times the debate becomes overtly political and heated. Often each side accuses the other of judicial legislation. See, e.g., *Meyering* v. *General Motors Corp.*, 275 Cal. Rptr. 346 (Cal. App. 1990) (holding, over a bitter dissent, that an automobile maker's obligation to use reasonable care in designing and manufacturing sunroofs is not obviated by hooligans' dropping a chunk of concrete from a highway overpass onto the car).

Delta Airlines,[31] the plaintiff was a 77-year-old woman who was injured while trying to reclaim her luggage after a commercial airline journey from Florida to New York. The flight was late in arriving, and the passengers were consequently hurried and impatient. At the luggage-retrieval area provided by the airline company (Delta) at LaGuardia Airport, the plaintiff suffered a broken hip when an unidentified man knocked suitcases from the baggage carousel onto her. She sued Delta for negligence in failing to take any crowd-control measures or to provide a safer way for elderly and disabled people to retrieve their luggage. The district (i.e. trial) judge granted Delta's motion for summary judgment, holding that Delta had 'no duty' to control the crowd at the luggage-retrieval area or to designate a separate area for elderly passengers.

Reversing and remanding the case for trial, Calabresi J's opinion for the United States Court of Appeals for the Second Circuit explained that the trial judge had made a negligence-law mistake by transmogrifying a breach issue into a duty issue:

There is no question that Delta, as an owner or occupier of the premises, owed a duty to take reasonable steps in maintaining the safety of its baggage retrieval area.... [Yet the district judge] refused to impose an obligation upon Delta to safeguard passengers against the foreseeable risks caused by its concentration of allegedly unruly travelers around a congested baggage carousel. In the district [judge's] opinion, such a duty would "offer little if any real public benefit, and yet would impose upon the airline burdensome and costly obligations". Although we appreciate that...the existence and scope of an alleged tortfeasor's duty is usually a policy-laden declaration reserved for judges..., we also note that...*courts do not exercise this authority on an ad hoc basis.*

To the contrary, the judicial power to modify the general rule that "whenever one person is by circumstances placed in such a position with regard to another that every one of ordinary sense who did think would at once recognise that if he did not use ordinary care and skill in his own conduct with regard to the circumstances he would cause danger of injury to the person or property of the other, a duty arises to use ordinary care and skill to avoid such danger" is reserved for very limited situations.... [It is true that courts have occasionally] conducted *fact-specific duty analyses.* But where, as here, the applicable duty relationship [the premises owner–invitee relationship] is well established, we do not...condone[]...the limitation of a familiar liability rule simply to avoid placing a disproportionate burden on a defendant in a particular case. The law deals with that problem *not by redefining the defendant's duties in each case, but by asking whether—considering all the circumstances of the particular case—the defendant breached its duty of care.*[32]

Calabresi J's warnings against "fact-specific" or "*ad hoc*" duty analyses reflects the traditional view that "an actor ordinarily has a duty to exercise reasonable care when the actor's conduct creates a risk of physical harm", and that judges should depart

[31] 52 F 3d 463 (2d Cir. 1995) (NY law).

[32] *Ibid.*, 467–9 (citations omitted; emphasis supplied). The internal quotation in the first paragraph is from the trial judge's decision in *Stagl*. The internal quotation in the second paragraph is of course from *Heaven* v. *Pender* (1833) 11 QBD 503.

from that norm only "when an articulated countervailing principle or policy warrants [such a departure for] a particular class of cases".[33]

But despite the eloquence (and authority) of Calabresi J's warnings, some courts seem to be increasingly tempted to *ad hoc* limitations on defendants' duties. For example, in *McCarthy* v. *Olin Corporation* Calabresi J's own court upheld the dismissal of a complaint against the manufacturer of "Black Talon" bullets—bullets that are "designed to bend upon impact into six ninety-degree angle razor-sharp petals or 'talons' that increase the wounding power of the bullet by stretching, cutting and tearing tissue and bone as it travels through the victim"—that were used by a deranged person to commit a massacre.[34] The complaint alleged that the manufacturer was negligent in advertising the bullets so as to make them attractive to dangerous persons and in failing to restrict the marketing of the bullets to law-enforcement agencies. The trial judge dismissed the complaint on "no duty" grounds. Affirming over Calabresi J's dissent, the appellate court stated:

> To impose a duty on ammunition manufacturers to protect against criminal misuse of its product would likely force ammunition products—which legislatures have not proscribed, and which concededly are not defectively designed or manufactured and have some socially valuable uses—off the market due to the threat of limitless liability. Because Olin did not owe a legal duty to plaintiffs to protect against Colin Ferguson's horrible action, appellants' complaint does not state a cause of action for negligence and the claim was properly dismissed.[35]

Richard Posner J—who, like Calabresi J had a brilliant academic career before becoming a federal appellate judge—has cogently explained that *ad hoc* or fact-specific duty doctrines (like those rejected in *Stagl* and accepted in *McCarthy*) are attractive to judges who want "to rein in juries".[36] But the price is high. The jury's traditional role is being usurped on a selective basis and without principled explanation. And the law of negligence is in danger of becoming rigidified in the areas in which courts have uttered their authoritative "no duty" declarations. For example, recent decisions of the California Supreme Court have held that the manufacturer of an over-the-counter

[33] As we saw above in n. 14, this is the way the *Restatement (Third) of Torts: Liability for Physical Harm* is phrasing the tradition stemming from *Heaven* v. *Pender* (1883) 11 QBD 503. For examples of courts declaring a new no-duty rule respecting a discrete class of cases on policy grounds, see D. W. Robertson *et al.*, *Cases and Materials on Torts* (3rd edn., 2004), 296. See also *Piscitelli* v. *Friedenberg*, 87 Cal.App. 4th 953, 105 Cal. Rptr. 2d 88, 108–9 (2001) (articulating a public policy argument for holding that a plaintiff in a legal malpractice action cannot recover the punitive damages that he would have recovered if the attorney had not botched the underlying lawsuit). (The *Piscitelli* court couched its ruling in no-legal-causation terms, but its categorical holding precluding legal causation as a matter of law was functionally a no-duty ruling.) For disagreement with *Piscitelli* as having overstepped judicial boundaries in the direction of 'judicial legislation', see *O'Connor Agency, Inc.* v. *Brodkin*, 99 Cal.App. 4th 588, 120 Cal. Rptr. 2d 336, 339 (2002). For disagreement with the content of the *Piscitelli* court's particular no-duty rule, see *Jacobsen* v. *Oliver*, 201 F Supp. 2d 93 (DDC 2002) (holding that the punitive damages that would have been recovered if the attorney had not botched the underlying lawsuit are part of the compensatory damages that must be awarded in the legal malpractice action if the plaintiff is to be made whole).

[34] 119 F 3d 148, 152 (2d Cir. 1997) (NY law).

[35] *Ibid.*, 157.

[36] *Edwards* v. *Honeywell, Inc.*, 50 F 3d 484, 488 (7th Cir. 1995) (Ind. law).

medication marketed for children had no duty to label the product with Spanish-language warnings of serious risks;[37] that a rubbish-disposal operator had no duty to design or operate its machine so as to minimise noises calculated to frighten horses on nearby bridle paths;[38] and that the operator of a business had no duty to open the cash register to an armed robber who was threatening to shoot a customer unless the robber's demands were complied with.[39] As a dissenting California justice has noted, no matter how desirable may be the public policy effectuated by these judicial determinations, they are subject to criticism on two fundamental fronts:

By framing [these issues] as [questions] of duty, the majority usurps the jury's historic function in a negligence case to determine the reasonableness of defendant's conduct under the surrounding circumstances.[40]

* * *

It is always possible to recast any question of whether the standard of care has been breached as a question of "duty".... If a court does so, however, it abandons the flexibility inherent in the application of the reasonable person standard and instead dictates a rigid, inflexible rule of conduct that applies not only to the defendant in the case before it but also to all defendants in future cases who are confronted by a risk of the same type of harm to another, regardless of differences in the surrounding circumstances.[41]

4. PURE ECONOMIC DAMAGE[42]

All legal systems impose "limits on tort actions for intangible injuries".[43] One recurrent type of intangible injury is "pure economic loss", defined as financial loss that is not accompanied by a physical injury to the plaintiff's person or property. Courts in the United States approach the issue of negligence liability for such intangible economic losses under the influence of two broad policy concerns: proper maintenance of the tort/contract boundary and avoiding the floodgates problem.

Courts feel that the tort/contract boundary should be policed because tort law's central concern is human safety, whereas contract law is often better designed to control the shifting of financial losses. They worry that permitting negligence actions for economic losses may cause "contract law [to] drown in a sea of tort".[44]

37 *Ramirez* v. *Plough, Inc.*, 6 Cal. 4th 539, 863 P 2d 167 (1993) .

38 *Parsons* v. *Crown Disposal Co.*, 15 Cal. 4th 456, 936 P 2d 70 (1997).

39 *Kentucky Fried Chicken* v. *Superior Court*, 14 Cal. 4th 814, 927 P 2d 1260 (1997).

40 *Ibid.*, 1272 (Kennard J, dissenting).

41 *Ibid.*, 1276 (Kennard J, dissenting).

42 As its title signals, the new *Restatement (Third) of Torts: Liability for Physical Harm* does not treat the problem of pure economic loss. A separate *Restatement (Third)* directed at that problem alone is in the early stages of preparation.

43 *Christensen* v. *Superior Court*, 54 Cal. 3d 868, 820 P 2d 181, 206 (1991) (Kennard J, concurring and dissenting).

44 *East River S.S. Corp.* v. *Transamerica Delaval, Inc.*, 476 US 858, 106 SCt. 2295, 2300 (1986).

One cogent evocation of the particular floodgates concerns that arises in economic-loss cases runs as follows:

In cases of physical injury to persons or property, the task of defining liability limits is eased, but not eliminated, by the operation of the laws of physics. Friction and gravity dictate that physical objects eventually come to rest. The amount of physical damage that can be inflicted by a speeding automobile or a thrown fist has a self-defining limit. Even in chain reaction cases, intervening forces generally are necessary to restore the velocity of the harm-creating object. These intervening forces offer a natural limit to liability. The laws of physics do not provide the same restraint for economic loss. Economic relationships are intertwined so intimately that disruption of one may have far-reaching consequences. Furthermore, the chain reaction of economic harm flows from one person to another without the intervention of other forces. Courts facing a case of pure economic loss thus confront the potential for liability of enormous scope, with no easily marked intermediate points and no ready recourse to traditional liability-limiting devices such as intervening cause.[45]

The tort/contract problem and the floodgates problem combine to instil great caution in the American courts' approach to economic-loss cases. Indeed, a leading treatise propounds it as a general rule that "[w]hen commercial or economic harm stands alone, divorced from injury to person or property, courts have not imposed a general duty of reasonable care".[46] But not all courts agree, and even those that do generally agree nevertheless may perceive many exceptions to the generalisation. Perhaps the most widely recognised exception is liability for negligent misstatements by those whose regular commercial or professional activities or particular transactions put them in the information-supplying business.[47] (This area of the law is often called "negligent misrepresentation", and the bulk of it traces its lineage to the writ of deceit.[48])

In cases in which the plaintiff's pure economic loss arose from some form of conduct other than an information-supplying transaction, there is much current ferment in the United States. We cannot even agree on an organisational framework within which to classify these cases.[49] The subsections below ((b)–(e)) reflect one of many possible organisational schemes. Here we are subdividing the large conglomeration of cases in which a defendant's negligent conduct has brought about financial harm to the plaintiff into four subcategories: cases in which the economic loss was caused by (i) harm to a public resource, (ii) harm to the person or property of another, (iii) lapses in the defendant's performance of a service, and (iv) defects in buildings and products.

45 H. S. Perlman, 'Interference with Contract and Other Economic Expectancies' (1982) 49 *U Chi. LR* 61, 71–2.

46 D. B. Dobbs, *The Law of Torts* (2000), 1282.

47 See *Restatement (Second) of Torts* (1977), §§552, 552A, 552B.

48 Those who understand the significance of this history may find discussions of whether there is an 'intentional fraud exception' to 'the economic loss doctrine' to be hopelessly muddled: *Werwinski* v. *Ford Motor Co.*, 286 F 3d 661, 674 (3d Cir. 2002) (Pa. law).

49 The selection of an organising scheme can be a bit of subtle (or sometimes not so subtle) advocacy for a particular position on the appropriate size and shape of the prohibition against economic loss recovery. See, e.g., *In re Hercules Carriers, Inc.*, 720 F 2d 1201, 1203–4 (11th Cir. 1983) (Clark J, concurring specially and arguing for a two-part organisational system that would place cases like Justice Holmes's decision in *Robins Dry Dock* (see n. 62 below) in a category of negligent interference with contractual relations and all cases that lack contractual

(A) THE PURE ECONOMIC LOSS PROBLEM VIEWED GENERALLY[50]

Courts sometimes approach the problem of economic loss in a global fashion and try to devise principles that can be applied without particular reference to whether the loss arose from harm to a public resource, from harm negligently inflicted on the person or property of someone other than the plaintiff, from negligence in the defendant's performance of a service, or from a defect in a building or product. The two leading cases of this type are probably the decision of the United States Court of Appeals for the Fifth Circuit in the maritime case of *Louisiana ex rel. Guste* v. *M/V Testbank* [51] and the New Jersey Supreme Court's decision in *People Express Airlines* v. *Consolidated Rail Corporation.*[52]

These two elaborately reasoned decisions point in opposite directions. In the *Testbank* decision ten members of the fifteen-judge court held that a vessel whose negligent navigation led to a collision with another vessel and the spilling of a chemical into the lower Mississippi River, causing great disruption to shipping, fishing, and other activities in a huge surrounding area, had no duty to anyone (other than commercial fishermen[53]) whose losses were not accompanied by physical damage to tangible property. The key to the majority's reasoning was the view that a "bright-line rule"[54] denying all liability for economic loss not accompanying physical harm to the plaintiff's person or tangible property best serves the law's administrative and economic concerns. The five dissenters urged that in the *Testbank* context (economic loss caused by negligent harm to a public resource) such a bright-line rule of no duty was too clumsy, too arbitrary, and most of all too unfair. The dissenters would have sorted among the interests damaged by the defendant's negligence by using familiar principles of legal causation with the modification that losses must be foreseeable in a "particular" sense in order to be recoverable.[55]

In *People Express* the unanimous New Jersey Supreme Court took an approach virtually identical to the *Testbank* dissenters' in upholding a negligence cause of action

entanglements in the other category). The four-part organisation used in this chapter is not inspired by advocacy; we are simply looking for a way to sort the large number of cases into piles of manageable size.

50 Whether the area can usefully be viewed generally is subject to vigorous debate. See *Canadian National Railway Co.* v. *Norsk Pacific Steamship Co.*, 11 CCLT (2d) 1, 58 (1992) (LaForest J, dissenting): 'To phrase the key issue in this case as a simple one of "is pure economic loss recoverable in tort" is misleading. I do not doubt that pure economic loss is recoverable in some cases. It does not follow, however, that all economic loss cases are susceptible to the same analysis, or that cases of one type are necessarily relevant to cases of another .... The fact is that different types of factual situations may invite different approaches to economic loss, and it seems to me at best unwise to lump them all together for purposes of analysis.'

51 752 F 2d 1019 (5th Cir. 1985) (en banc) (federal maritime law).

52 100 NJ 246, 495 A 2d 107 (1985).

53 Many courts (including the trial court in *Testbank*) have held on historical and policy grounds that commercial fishermen are not subject to the 'pure economic loss' prohibition. See, e.g., *Union Oil Co.* v. *Oppen*, 501 F 2d 558 (9th Cir. 1974) (federal maritime law). No claims by commercial fishermen were before the Fifth Circuit in *Testbank*; the portion of the trial court's decision applying the fishermen's rule was not appealed.

54 752 F 2d at 1029.

55 *Ibid.*, 1049.

on behalf of an airline forced to suspend operations at its passenger terminal because of the threat of an explosion at the defendant's nearby rail yard. The *People Express* court was sharply critical of the physical injury requirement, stating that it "capriciously showers compensation along the path of physical destruction, regardless of the status or circumstances of the individual claimants".[56] A better limiting principle, the court said, would allow recovery to "[a]n identifiable class of plaintiffs [that is] particularly foreseeable in terms of the types of persons or entities comprising the class, the certainty or predictability of their presence, the approximate numbers of those in the class, as well as the type of economic expectations disrupted".[57]

(B) ECONOMIC LOSS CAUSED BY NEGLIGENT HARM TO A PUBLIC RESOURCE

The *Testbank* and *People Express* decisions can be placed in a large subcategory of economic loss cases in which the plaintiffs' losses stemmed from damage to the air, to the public's drinking water, or to a public highway, bridge, waterway, or other public resource. In these cases the law of negligence is criss-crossed by the law of public nuisance[58] and by numerous statutes.[59] Prohibiting recovery of pure economic loss is especially controversial in these cases, because it leaves innocent victims without recourse and often lets seriously culpable polluters and the like go scot free. The commercial fishermen's exception[60] is explained in part by these concerns, as are some of the statutory responses.[61]

(C) ECONOMIC LOSS CAUSED BY NEGLIGENT INJURY TO THE PERSON OR PROPERTY OF ANOTHER

Under the influence of a maritime decision authored by Oliver Wendell Holmes J,[62] most courts in the United States have denied recovery for economic loss flowing from negligent injury to the person or property of someone other than the plaintiff.[63] Probably this is the area within the economic loss field where the American courts have

[56] 495 A 2d at 111.

[57] *Ibid.*, 116.

[58] See generally D. B. Dobbs, *The Law of Torts* (2000), 1334–8.

[59] See, e.g., the Rivers and Harbors Appropriations Act, 33 USC §§401 ff.; the Clean Water Act, 33 USC §§1251 ff.; the Oil Pollution Act, 33 USC §§2701 ff.; the Comprehensive Environmental Response, Compensation, and Liability Act, 42 USC §§9601 ff.

[60] See n. 53 above.

[61] See, e.g., *Ballard Shipping Co.* v. *Beach Shellfish*, 32 F 3d 623 (1st Cir. 1994) (treating the federal Oil Pollution Act and the Rhode Island Environmental Injury Compensation Act).

[62] See *Robins Dry Dock & Repair Co.* v. *Flint*, 275 US 303, 48 SCt. 134 (1927) (holding that under federal maritime law a vessel's time charterer (a type of lessee) could not recover from the dry dock whose negligence damaged the vessel and caused the charterer to lose the use of it).

[63] See e.g. *Louisville & NR Co.* v. *M/V Bayou Lacombe*, 597 F 2d 469 (5th Cir. 1979) (federal maritime law); *PPG Industries, Inc.* v. *Bean Dredging*, 447 So. 2d 1058 (La. 1984); *Fifield Manor* v. *Finston*, 54 Cal. 2d 632, 354 P 2d 1073 (1960); *Stevenson* v. *East Ohio Gas Co.*, 73 NE 2d 200 (Ohio App. 1946).

been the most conservative.[64] An interesting deviation was *Mattingly* v. *Sheldon Jackson College*,[65] in which the court recognised a cause of action on behalf of an employer who suffered "losses of business income and profit and increases in expenses" as a result of the defendant's negligent injury to three of the plaintiff's employees (one of whom was the plaintiff's son).[66] (In this portion of the opinion the *Mattingly* court relied extensively on the reasoning in *People Express*.) Then in a separate section of the opinion the *Mattingly* court stated: "We now adopt the modern rule that employers may not recover simply for the loss of their employees' services or for loss of profits arising from the negligent injury of their employees by a third person."[67] The court did not explain the inconsistency between its two announced holdings. *Mattingly* thus stands as a kind of monument to the general confusion that seems to pervade the economic loss field.[68]

(D) ECONOMIC LOSS CAUSED BY NEGLIGENCE IN THE PERFORMANCE OF A SERVICE

The three leading American treatises describe a broad consensus that recovery in tort should ordinarily be denied for economic losses caused by the defendant's negligence in the performance of a service or undertaking.[69] This viewpoint is offset to a considerable degree by the fact that American contract law often allows the loss-suffering party to bring a successful action either as a party to the contract whereby the defendant agreed to perform the service or as a third-party beneficiary of that contract.[70] Furthermore,

64 See *Christensen* v. *Superior Court*, 54 Cal. 3d 868, 820 P 2d 181, 189 (1991) (listing as two factors explaining the conservatism (*a*) the fact that in these cases "the plaintiff had no preexisting relationship" with the defendant and (*b*) "the defendant had not previously assumed a duty of care beyond that owed to the public in general"); *J'Aire Corp.* v. *Gregory*, 24 Cal. 3d 799, 598 P 2d 60, 65 (1979) (allowing recovery for economic loss caused by the negligent performance of a service and distinguishing the cases involving negligent harms to the person or property of others); D. W. Robertson, "Recovery in Louisiana Tort Law for Intangible Economic Loss" (1986) 46 *La. LR* 737, 753 (stating that courts are "more reluctant to award recovery" in cases involving harms to the person or property of others than in other types of economic loss cases).

65 743 P 2d 356 (Alas. 1987).

66 *Ibid.*, 359–61.

67 *Ibid.*, 363.

68 One writer has suggested that *People Express* and *Mattingly* belong to an exceptional category of cases in which recovery for pure economic loss is justified because "the defendant [was] engaging in some unusually dangerous activity". Note, "Limited Recovery Rule as a Dam" (1989) 31 *Ariz. LR* 959, 971. (Recall that the activity of the *People Express* defendant threatened a massive explosion. That of the *Mattingly* defendant caused a ditch to cave in and bury the workers.) While the factual characterisation of the cases is perhaps plausible enough, an "unusually dangerous activity" exception to the general no-duty rule in this area of the law would probably not be manageable. Viewed in hindsight after the injury-producing event, whatever conduct has led to it is likely to strike many observers as having been unusually dangerous. Thus the exception would continually strain toward swallowing the rule.

69 See D. B. Dobbs, *The Law of Torts* (2000), §452; W. P. Keeton *et al.*, *Prosser and Keeton on Torts* (5th edn., 1984), §129; *Restatement (Second) of Torts* (1977), §766C.

70 See W. P. Keeton *et al.*, *Prosser and Keeton on Torts* (5th edn., 1984), 1000. See also *Hale* v. *Groce*, 304 Or. 281, 744 P 2d 1289 (1987) (holding that an intended beneficiary of a will whose expectancy was thwarted by the negligence of an attorney in preparing the will had a cause of action against the attorney as a third-party beneficiary of the contract between the testator and the attorney as well as a negligence cause of action against the attorney).

there is a significant number of decisions allowing recovery for negligently inflicted economic loss without regard to the requirements of contract law when "a benefit to the plaintiff was the purpose of the contract [whereby defendant undertook to perform the service] and the damage was foreseeable."[71]

Some authorities suggest that the conceptual thread uniting these successful negligence claims is that the defendant "renders a service or has some other contractual relationship in which he owes a duty to use reasonable care to avoid a risk of pecuniary loss to the person with whom he is directly dealing, and that same duty is held to extend to another person whom he knows to be pecuniarily affected by the service rendered."[72] Others believe that the only unifying principle is a much more general "limitation to specifically foreseeable plaintiffs."[73] In truth the decisional law is uncertain to a highly unsatisfactory degree. When the defendant's negligent performance consists of a misstatement of commercial or professional information, liability may be reasonably likely.[74] When it consists in some other kind of conduct, the recognition of a duty of care will turn on "various factors, among which are the extent to which the transaction was intended to affect the plaintiff, the foreseeability of harm to him, the degree of certainty that the plaintiff suffered injury, the closeness of the connection between the defendant's conduct and the injury suffered, the moral blame attached to the defendant's conduct, and the policy of preventing future harm."[75] Factors of such generality and elasticity do not have much predictive, resolving, or explanatory power. The factors overlap one another considerably, and there is no way to tell whether it takes just one, some, or all of them to do the trick. Perhaps tort law would do better to leave this area to the law of contract.

(E) ECONOMIC LOSS CAUSED BY DEFECTS IN BUILDINGS AND PRODUCTS

When a negligently made building, structure, or product manifests its defectiveness through physical symptoms—when it collapses, breaks, catches fire, explodes, etc.—the disappointed owner can plausibly characterise the situation as a physical damage case. But that characterisation will not be accepted in jurisdictions that embrace the

[71] *Christensen* v. *Superior Court*, 54 Cal. 3d 868, 820 P 2d 181, 194 (1991). The leading case for this 'exception' has been *J'Aire Corp.* v. *Gregory*, 24 Cal. 3d 799, 598 P 2d 60, 65 (1979) (allowing the lessee of a restaurant whose commercial expectations were disappointed because of the defendant's delay in performing a repair contract with the owner of the building to recover under negligence law on the seemingly fairly lenient grounds that (*a*) there was 'a special relationship' between the repair contractor and the lessee, (*b*) 'the risk of harm [was] foreseeable and [was] closely connected with the defendant's conduct', (*c*) the 'damages [were] not wholly speculative', and (*d*) 'the injury [was] not part of the plaintiff's ordinary business risk').

[72] *Restatement (Second) of Torts*, §766C, *cmt.* e.

[73] W. P. Keeton *et al.*, *Prosser and Keeton on Torts* (5th edn., 1984), 1001.

[74] See *Restatement (Second) of Torts*, §766C *cmt.* e. See also text and nn. 47–8 above. But see *Werwinski* v. *Ford Motor Co.*, 286 F 3d 661, 674–81 (3d Cir. 2002) (Pa. law) (suggesting that the law of negligent misrepresentation may be eroding).

[75] *Biakanja* v. *Irving*, 49 Cal. 2d 647, 320 P 2d 16, 19 (1958).

economic loss rule. In these jurisdictions, there will generally be no cause of action in tort unless the defective thing, in the process of damaging itself, also causes physical harm to other property or to a person.

In this regard, courts generally make no distinction between defective buildings and structures and defective products.[76] But some courts do take dwellings as a special case. In some states that embrace the economic loss rule, homeowners can sue negligent builders for losses connected with physical defects in the home.[77] (Clear doctrinal or policy explanations for this homeowners' exception are hard to find in the case law, but on the political level the explanation seems apparent.) Other states take the opposite view and deny a negligence remedy to disappointed home buyers who have not sustained personal injury or physical damage to property other than the defective structure.[78] A third group of states has found a middle ground that allows recovery against a negligent builder for the costs of remedying building defects that threaten personal injury.[79] Other permutations and compromise positions can also be found in the jurisprudence and literature.

The most influential American decision on the problem of economic loss caused by defects in products has been that of the United States Supreme Court in the maritime case of *East River S.S. Corp.* v. *Transamerica Delaval Inc.*,[80] in which the charterers (lessees) of ships whose engines failed were denied recovery against the manufacturer of the defective engines for the monetary losses caused by the ships' unfitness for service. The decision's holding is that "a manufacturer in a commercial relationship has no duty under either a negligence or strict products-liability theory to prevent a product from injuring itself."[81] The Supreme Court noted a wide divergence among the American courts that had considered the point and justified its resolution by invoking the two broad policies discussed at the beginning of this section.[82]

Turning first to the tort/contract boundary-maintenance issue, the court noted that the paramount concern of the law of negligence is human safety, a concern that is not centrally implicated when a product injures only itself:

> The tort concern with safety is reduced when an injury is only to the product itself. When a person is injured, the cost of an injury and the loss of time or health may be an overwhelming misfortune, and one the person is not prepared to meet. In contrast, when a product injures itself, the commercial user stands to lose the value of the product, risks the displeasure of its

76 See, e.g., *Town of Alma* v. *Azco Construction, Inc.*, 10 P 3d 1256 (Col. 2000) (economic loss rule barred recovery of costs of replacing leaky water lines).

77 See, e.g., *A.C. Excavating* v. *Yacht Club Homeowners Ass'n*, 114 P 3d 862 (Col. 2005).

78 See, e.g., *Aas* v. *Superior Court*, 24 Cal. 4th 627, 12 P 3d 1125 (2000). Subsequently the California legislature partially overruled *Aas* by enacting 'legislation establishing a limited new cause of action for certain specified housing defects'. *Rosen v. State Farm Gen. Ins. Co.*, 70 P 3d 351, 356 (Cal. 2003).

79 See e.g. *Council of Co-Owners* v. *Whiting-Turner Contracting Co.*, 308 Md. 18, 517 A 2d 336, 344–5 (1986).

80 476 US 858, 106 SCt. 2295 (1986).

81 106 SCt. at 2302. The *East River* rule contemplates tort recovery when the defective product injures other property but not when the damage is confined to the 'product itself'. Distinguishing between 'the product itself 'and 'other property' can be tricky. See, e.g., *Saratoga Fishing Co.* v. *J. M. Martinac & Co.*, 520 US 875, 117 SCt. 1783 (1997) (federal maritime law).

82 See the text above at nn. 42–5.

customers who find that the product does not meet their needs, or, as in this case, experiences increased costs in performing a service. Losses like these can be insured. Society need not presume that a customer needs special protection. The increased cost to the public that would result from holding a manufacturer liable in tort for injury to the product itself is not justified.[83]

Moreover, if tort liability were extended too far, "contract law would drown in a sea of tort,"[84] which would be unfortunate because:

Contract law, and the law of warranty in particular, is well suited to commercial controversies of the sort involved in this case because the parties may set the terms of their own agreements. The manufacturer can restrict its liability, within limits, by disclaiming warranties or limiting remedies. In exchange, the purchaser pays less for the product. Since a commercial situation generally does not involve large disparities in bargaining power, we see no reason to intrude into the parties' allocation of the risk.[85]

The *East River* court then turned to a discussion of the floodgates problem, stating:

In products-liability law, where there is a duty to the public generally, foreseeability is an inadequate brake. Permitting recovery for all foreseeable claims for purely economic loss could make a manufacturer liable for vast sums. It would be difficult for a manufacturer to take into account the expectations of persons downstream who may encounter its product. In this case, for example, if the charterers—already one step removed from the transaction—were permitted to recover their economic losses, then the companies that sub-chartered the ships might claim their economic losses from the delays, and the charterers' customers also might claim their economic losses, and so on. "The law does not spread its protection so far."[86]

(F) POSTSCRIPT: BRIGHT-LINE RULES SELDOM STAY BRIGHT FOR LONG

The Fifth Circuit's opinion in *Testbank*[87] claimed clarity and predictability as the chief virtues of the prohibitory rule it was announcing, stating: "The bright line rule of damage to a proprietary interest ... has the virtue of predictability."[88] But what, exactly, is the bright-line rule? The *Testbank* opinion is not entirely clear whether the rule limits economic-loss recovery to damages *caused by* physical harm to a proprietary interest of the plaintiff (such a rule would indeed have fairly bright edges) or whether it is enough that the economic loss is sustained in an accident that involved physical harm to a proprietary interest of the plaintiff.[89] Subsequent decisions by the Fifth Circuit indicate

83 106 SCt. at 2302 (citations and internal quotation marks omitted).

84 *Ibid.*, 2300.

85 *Ibid.*, 2303 (citations omitted).

86 *Ibid.*, 2303–4 (citations omitted). The concluding internal quotation is from Justice Holmes's opinion in *Robins Dry Dock* (n. 62 above), 275 US at 309.

87 See n. 51 above.

88 752 F 2d at 1029. The 'bright line' characterisation runs throughout the majority's opinion; see *ibid.*, 1023, 1026.

89 Most of the *Testbank* court's language suggests the latter, more lenient answer. See, e.g., *ibid.*, 1020 ('physical damage to a proprietary interest [is] a prerequisite to recovery for economic loss'); *ibid.*, 1021 ('claims for economic loss unaccompanied by physical damage to a proprietary interest [are] not recoverable in maritime tort'). But other language in the opinion at least hints that the rule requires a causal link between the physical

that the latter, more lenient, characterisation is the correct reading of *Testbank*.[90] The result is some demonstrable fading of the proclaimed bright lines, some conspicuous fuzziness.

For example, in *Lloyd's Leasing Ltd. v. Conoco*,[91] a three-judge panel of the Fifth Circuit had to decide whether hotels in Galveston, Texas could recover for business losses brought about when oil negligently spilled by the defendant into the Gulf of Mexico washed up on Galveston's beaches and chased tourists away. The *Testbank* rule afforded no clear answer because the hotels claimed physical damage—oil tracked onto carpets by the few tourists who stayed around—stemming from the same accident. Two members of the panel made the case simple for themselves by emphasising that the oil was spilled 70 miles from Galveston and announcing that it was wholly unforeseeable that it would spread so far. On this view, none of the plaintiffs' damages were recoverable.

The third member of the panel in *Lloyd's Leasing* was Judge Patrick Higginbotham, who four years earlier had been the author of *Testbank*. Judge Higginbotham could not accept the panel majority's unforeseeability proclamation,[92] which led him to the conclusion that the hotels should recover for the physical harm to their carpets. But he agreed with the panel majority that there should be no recovery for the hotels' loss of tourist trade, explaining:

> Our insistence [in *Testbank*] upon physical injury to a proprietary interest was a forthright pragmatic limit on the doctrine of foreseeability. Undoubtedly many persons suffered some foreseeable physical loss [from the accident in *Testbank*] and yet were not allowed to recover general economic losses. These physical losses were not a direct consequence of the collision and spill but were the secondary consequences of shipping delays.
>
> *Testbank* limits which parties can recover for foreseeable injuries. In this appeal, the [hotels'] only physical injury is two parties removed from the most immediate *Testbank* plaintiff, the [state of Texas as] owner of the affected shore property. The spillage came to rest upon the property of one party, and was then removed by a second party—the sticky-footed interlopers—onto the property of still a third party, the plaintiffs in this case. Arguably such injury is a foreseeable consequence of the spill, but its nexus with the spill is a step removed, as so the plaintiffs are beyond the ambit of permissible claimants under *Testbank*.
>
> I would hold that these [hotels] cannot recover general economic losses attributed to the general loss of custom attending the spill because they have no physical injury within the meaning of *Testbank*.[93]

In the jurisprudential system here envisaged by *Testbank*'s author, we see the *Testbank* rule entailing two different "foreseeability" inquiries in the cases it affects: The rug

harm and the economic damages being sought. See *ibid.*, 1022 ('[a] prevailing rule denie[s] a plaintiff recovery for economic loss if that loss resulted from physical damage to property in which he had no proprietary interest').

[90] See , e.g., *In re Taira Lynn Marine Ltd.*, 444 F 3d 371, 377 (5th Cir. 2006) ('the law of this circuit does not allow recovery of purely economic claims absent physical injury to a proprietary interest'). See also *Lloyd's Leasing*, discussed in the text just below.

[91] 868 F 2d 1447 (5th Cir. 1989).

[92] See *ibid.*, 1450 ('I am persuaded that spilling millions of gallons of crude oil into the sea eleven miles off the gulf coast created a direct and foreseeable risk of tainting the coastline. It is no answer that the precise coastal point to be hit was not foreseeable; it is enough that the risk realized be within the set of foreseeable risks.')

[93] 868 F 2d at 1451.

damage was foreseeable enough to be recovered for but not foreseeable enough to count as a physical-harm ticket to pursue general economic losses. This is an intelligible, coherent, and perhaps even a wise formulation. But it is hardly a "bright-line" rule.

5. PSYCHIATRIC INJURY (NERVOUS SHOCK)

In the United States psychiatric injury (the earlier English decisions called this "nervous shock") is more often called mental or emotional distress. One leading treatise announces that "[n]o general agreement has yet been reached on many of the issues involving liability for negligence resulting in fright, shock, or other mental or emotional harm, and any resulting physical consequences".[94] Such statements should not lead the reader to conclude that chaos wholly reigns. The area is complex, and there are thousands of reported cases, so that inevitably confusion will be found in the language and reasoning of some of the opinions. Still, when one considers the actual results of the reported cases there seems to be broad agreement among the American states on the general outlines of this body of law.[95]

In virtually all of the states, the law (as represented by the results of the cases, not necessarily their language) reflects the view that the policies of the law of negligence would be ill-served by allowing recovery for all emotional harms that foreseeably result from negligent conduct. This conservatism is deplored by some analysts, who "contend that courts . . . have not only perpetuated an outmoded [physical/emotional] dualism[96] but have devalued the importance of emotional life by their caution in granting recovery".[97] Despite such views, it seems to be fairly common ground that the floodgates problem, the problem of easily fabricated and easily exaggerated injuries, and the need to avoid

[94] W. P. Keeton *et al.*, *Prosser and Keeton on Torts* (5th edn., 1984), 359–60.

[95] See generally *Consolidated Rail Corp.* v. *Gottshall*, 512 US 532, 114 SCt. 2396 (1994); D. B. Dobbs, *The Law of Torts* (2000), 821–4, 835–52; D. W. Robertson *et al.*, *Cases and Materials on Torts* (3rd edn., 2004), 235–53.

[96] Not many of us who generally support the courts' present approach think that physical and emotional injuries constitute a duality. But neither do we think that recognition of practical differences between the two is outmoded. See generally D. W. Robertson, 'Liability in Negligence for Nervous Shock' (1994) 57 *MLR* 649. However, it must be acknowledged that the cases reflect considerable difficulty in drawing the distinction between non-problematic physical injury cases and cases in which the law presumes against recovery because the plaintiff's physical problem stems from a traumatic event perceived as having initially attacked the emotions. Compare *Bosley* v. *Andrews*, 393 Pa. 161, 142 A 2d 263 (1958) (denying recovery for a heart attack that resulted from shock and fright when the plaintiff was chased by the defendant's Hereford bull) with *Pierce* v. *So. Pacific Transp. Co.*, 823 F 2d 1366 (9th Cir. 1987) (characterising a heart attack caused by workplace stresses as a physical injury). Also compare *Holt* v. *Rowell*, 798 So. 2d 767 (Fla.App. 2001), *rev'd on other grounds*, 850 So.2d 474 (Fla. 2003) (denying recovery to a man whose lawyer's negligence caused him to be wrongly jailed for ten days on the theory that being imprisoned is not itself a physical injury) with *Bass* v. *Nooney Co.*, 646 SW 2d 765 (Mo. 1983) (allowing recovery for the emotional injuries flowing from being trapped in a malfunctioning elevator for about thirty minutes).

[97] D. B. Dobbs, *The Law of Torts* (2000), 822 (reporting the views of L. Bender, 'Feminist (Re)torts' (1990) 39 *Duke LJ* 848, and N. Levit, 'Ethereal Torts' (1992) 61 *Geo. Wash. LR* 136).

encouraging or validating undue sensitivity[98] all point in the direction of retaining some special duty limitations on recovery for emotional harm. In a legal system depending upon vigilant screening by trial judges so that dubious cases do not reach juries (see Section 1 above), such limitations seem especially important tools.

All of the states have long allowed recovery for negligently inflicted emotional harm when it is "parasitic to" (caused by) a compensable physical injury.[99] For example, a negligent injury to the hand of an amateur violinist will lead to liability for the emotional harm stemming from the plaintiff 's inability to pursue his avocation. When one moves away from this classic case of "parasitic" emotional harm, the courts' reasoning and rhetoric begin to develop divergent tendencies. However, common policies and themes are visible.

On two fundamental matters there seems to be complete agreement. All courts try to restrict recovery to serious emotional distress; pursuit of claims for transient or slight distress is actively discouraged.[100] (There is not much agreement on the criteria for seriousness. Some jurists believe that seriousness in this context requires a showing of physical or medically recognisable psychological consequences. Others would treat such a showing as centrally relevant but not always essential.) Courts also agree that the precipitating event must have been one that would produce serious emotional distress in what Lord Ackner has called "a reasonably strong-nerved person".[101] In sum: "[T]he plaintiff can recover only if a normally constituted person would suffer, and the plaintiff in fact suffered, severe distress."[102]

With those two fundamental background requirements in mind, we can see that most of the reported cases in which plaintiffs have been successful in recovering for negligently inflicted emotional distress that is not parasitic to a physical injury fall into the following four categories (the first three of which are set out in roughly the chronological order of their acceptance).

First (under what is usually called *the impact rule*), most of the states have long allowed recovery for emotional injury incurred in an accident in which the plaintiff sustained compensable physical harm[103] or suffered an impact upon his

98 See *Bosley* v. *Andrews*, 393 Pa. 161, 142 A 2d 263, 266–7 (1958) (stating that many 'every-day events can cause or aggravate . . . nervous shock' and that awarding compensation in such cases 'may cause normal people, as well as nervous persons and persons who are mentally disturbed or mentally ill, to honestly believe that the sudden and unexpected event caused them fright or nervous shock or nervous tension with subsequent emotional distress or suffering or pain or miscarriage or heart attack, or some kind of disease'). See also D. B. Dobbs, *The Law of Torts* (2000), 823 (suggesting that the law needs to avoid encouraging 'maladaptive attitudes about distress').

99 In a narrowly divided (5–4) decision, the US Supreme Court has recently held that railway workers who contract the occupational disease asbestosis can seek damages (from their employers under the Federal Employers' Liability Act, n. 4 above) for fear of future cancer on the view that the cancer-fear damages are parasitic to the disease. *Norfolk & Western Ry. Co.* v. *Ayers*, 538 US 135, 123 SCt. 1210 (2003).

100 See e.g. *Rodrigues* v. *State*, 472 P 2d 509, 520 (Haw. 1970): 'It is universally agreed that there are compelling reasons for limiting the recovery of the plaintiff to claims of *serious* mental distress.' Emphasis in original.

101 *Alcock* v. *Chief Constable of South Yorkshire* [1991] 3 WLR 1057, 1106.

102 D. B. Dobbs, *The Law of Torts* (2000), 836.

103 See e.g. *Potere* v. *City of Philadelphia*, 380 Pa. 581, 112 A 2d 100 (1955), in which a lorry fell into a 19-foot-deep hole in the street, causing the driver to sustain minor physical injuries as well as an 'anxiety neurosis'. The anxiety neurosis was not a 'parasitic' emotional harm, because it was caused by the frightening fall and not by the minor physical injuries. Nevertheless, recovery for the anxiety neurosis was allowed.

person.[104] For example, when the defendant allowed a large sheet of glass to fall off its lorry and smash into the windscreen of a following car, the following driver, though physically unhurt, was allowed to recover for the emotional distress that he suffered as a result of having his windscreen shattered and being showered with glass fragments.[105]

Second (under what is usually called the *zone-of-danger rule)*, many states also allow recovery for emotional trauma produced by the plaintiff's fear for his or her own physical safety, provided the plaintiff suffered such fright while in a zone of physical danger created by the defendant's negligent conduct.[106]

Along with the requirements that the emotional harm must flow from the plaintiff's fear for her own physical safety and be incurred in the zone of danger created by the defendant's negligent conduct, many of the states require in addition that the emotional harm for which recovery is sought has manifested itself in physical symptoms or illness.[107] In states where this "physical manifestation" requirement applies and is treated with respect, the requirement is seen as a useful guarantee that the emotional distress was genuine and serious. For example, in one recent case the physical manifestation requirement precluded recovery on behalf of an otherwise deserving victim whose allegations of physical symptoms were "[frequent] crying, sleeplessness, [and] increased migraine headaches".[108] In other states little more than lip service is paid to the physical manifestation requirement; in these jurisdictions allegations of sleeplessness and migraine headaches would suffice to meet the requirement. In recognition

[104] There is wide divergence as to how significant the impact must be. The spectrum includes both *Metro-North Commuter R Co.* v. *Buckley*, 521 US 424, 117 SCt. 2113, 2117 (1997) (holding that 'simple physical contact with a substance [asbestos] that might cause a disease at a substantially later time' was not an impact in the relevant sense) and *Stoddard* v. *Davidson*, 355 Pa.Super. 262, 513 A 2d 419 (1986) (holding that the jostling of occupants of a vehicle as it ran over a corpse in the roadway sufficed for impact).

However it is construed, the impact rule can often be perceived as under-inclusive. See e.g. *Niederman* v. *Brodsky*, 436 Pa. 401, 261 A 2d 84, 85 (1970) (where the court seems to congratulate itself on 'remov[ing] this ancient roadblock' from the state's law). On the other hand, the impact rule can sometimes seem over-inclusive. See e.g. *Morris* v. *Maryland Cas. Co.*, 657 So. 2d 198, 200 (La.App. 1995) (holding that a locomotive engineer had a cause of action for emotional distress against the estate of a motorist who was struck and killed by the train because the engineer 'was a participant in the accident'). The court did not analyse its concept of participancy, but probably it is best seen as a generous version of the impact rule.

The perception that the impact rule can be over-inclusive may help to explain cases that seem to treat actions for negligently induced fear of AIDS as a discrete category of emotional harm cases with its own special set of rules. See e.g. *Cole* v. *D.J. Quirk, Inc.*, 2001 Mass.App.Div. 139, 2001 WestLaw 705730, in which the court declined to allow a recovery for fear of AIDS brought about when the plaintiff was cut by negligently discarded and potentially contaminated surgical tweezers. The court stated that the fear-of-AIDS cases fall into two groups—those in which courts insist on a showing of 'actual exposure' to the disease and those in which the courts apply a 'reasonable fear' criterion—and opted to join the former group. For a contrasting case, see *Vallere* v. *Louisiana Health Systems*, 722 So. 2d 418 (La.App. 1998) (allowing an action for fear of AIDS and hepatitis stemming from exposure to inadequately disinfected surgical instruments).

[105] *Schultz* v. *Barberton Glass Co.*, 4 Ohio St. 3d 131, 447 NE 2d 109 (1983).

[106] See e.g. *Niederman* v. *Brodsky*, treated in n. 104 above.

[107] For discussion of the 'requirement that the emotional distress result in (although it need not be caused by) physical injury' see *Bass* v. *Nooney Co.*, 646 SW 2d 765, 771 (Mo. 1983).

[108] *Robbins* v. *Kaas*, 163 Ill.App. 3d 927, 516 NE 2d 1023, 1027 (1987).

that the physical manifestation requirement has a tendency to become trivialised under the pressure of plaintiffs' counsel's ingenuity, a number of states have jettisoned it altogether.[109] In some jurisdictions it has been replaced by a "special proof" rule requiring the presentation of "expert medical or scientific proof" of the existence and severity of the emotional distress.[110]

Third (under the *uninjured-bystander rule*), many states have fairly recently come to allow recovery for emotional injury produced by the plaintiff's having witnessed injury or death to a loved one,[111] provided the plaintiff can satisfy three criteria of having been at or near the scene, sustaining the emotional distress through direct and contemporaneous perception of the harm to the loved one, and having a close relationship with the loved one. (Here, too, as in the zone-of-danger cases, many states add a physical manifestation requirement.) For a time after the landmark California decision[112] allowing emotional suffering recovery in this situation, some courts treated the three criteria as mere guidelines to be used in deciding whether the emotional distress was a foreseeable enough consequence of the defendant's negligent conduct for recovery to be appropriate.[113] But recently the three criteria are coming to be regarded as doctrinal requirements[114]—part of the duty rule whose ingredients the plaintiff must satisfy—such that failing to satisfy any one of them is fatal to recovery.[115]

Fourth, two long-standing exceptions to the normal rule denying recovery for negligently inflicted emotional distress have allowed such recovery to persons aggrieved by

109 See e.g. *Molien* v. *Kaiser Foundation Hospitals*, 27 Cal. 3d 916, 616 P 2d 813, 819–21 (1980). According to Comment, 'Is the Injury Requirement Obsolete in a Claim for Fear of Future Consequences?' (1994) 41 *UCLA LR* 1337, 1355, at least fifteen states have jettisoned the physical manifestation requirement. But the court in *Muchow* v. *Lindblad*, 435 NW 2d 918, 923 (ND 1989) emphasises that this is still 'the minority view', and the court in *Ellenwood* v. *Exxon Shipping Co.*, 795 F Supp. 31, 34 (D Me. 1992) states that '[t]he nationwide movement toward a standard allowing recovery for wholly emotional injury without some physical manifestation has been halting'.

110 *Estate of Amos* v. *Vanderbilt University*, 62 SW 3d 133, 134, 136 (Tenn. 2001).

111 What we are calling *uninjured bystander* cases are stand-alone claims for emotional injuries, to be distinguished from the functionally similar claims that are traditionally embedded in actions for wrongful death and for loss of consortium (see n. 126 below). One similarity is that all of these claims are 'derivative' in the sense that they depend upon harm to another. In actions asserting wrongful death and loss of consortium claims, it is well settled that the primary victim's negligence is attributable to the plaintiff for purposes of diminishing or perhaps barring recovery. See *Restatement (Third) of Torts: Apportionment of Liability* §6 (2000). Some analysts would treat uninjured bystander plaintiffs the same way. See *ibid.*, *cmt.* b. On this point there are very few cases, and they are divided. See *ibid.*, Reporters' Note.

112 *Dillon* v. *Legg*, 68 Cal. 2d 728, 441 P 2d 912 (1968).

113 See e.g. *Haught* v. *Maceluch*, 681 F 2d 291 (5th Cir. 1982) (Tex. law).

114 See e.g. *Grotts* v. *Zahner*, 115 Nev. 339, 989 P 2d 415, 416 (1999) (overruling an earlier decision and denying recovery to a woman who witnessed her fiancé's fatal injury because 'any non-family "relationship" fails, as a matter of law, to qualify for NIED standing'); *Thing* v. *LaChusa*, 48 Cal. 3d 644, 771 P 2d 814 (1989) (turning all three *Dillon* criteria from 'foreseeability factors' into firm doctrinal requirements).

115 For the most part, courts have dealt with the growing perception that a general foreseeability approach that is merely 'informed' by use of the three *Dillon* criteria is too flexible and open-ended by making those criteria into rules of law, as was done in the cases treated in n. 114 above. For another approach, see *Lee* v. *State Farm Mut. Ins. Co.*, 272 Ga. 583, 533 SE 2d 82 (2000) (insisting that Georgia law has not moved beyond the impact rule while at the same time managing to interpret that rule so as to allow a mother to recover for witnessing her child's death).

negligence in the transmission of a telegram or similar message regarding a serious illness or death in the family[116] or by being a witness to or otherwise directly affected by the defendant's negligent handling of the corpse of a loved one.[117] (Not many courts require physical manifestation of these types of emotional distress.[118]) The principle that accounts for the courts' leniency in this small sub-area is elusive, but "[i]n both kinds of case, the contractual relationship and its implicit undertakings undoubtedly play a large part in liability."[119]

In cases falling outside the foregoing four categories, most of the states deny recovery for negligently inflicted emotional suffering except when it is parasitic to a compensable physical injury. Looked at in the large, the *results* (not the language) of the reported cases seem relatively harmonious. But there is an important qualification, necessitated by the fact that in scattered decisions throughout the country courts seem from time to time simply to forget entirely the normal rules regulating recovery for emotional harm.[120] For example, decisions can be found allowing recovery for emotional suffering incident to negligence in the disposal of body parts,[121] in the treatment and handling of pets,[122] and in the destruction or damage of property.[123]

Moreover, the rapid expansion of the capabilities of medical science is creating new situations where the courts sometimes seem to feel that the rules just do not fit. One recent New York decision upheld the pursuit of recovery by a couple whose embryo was mistakenly implanted in another woman's uterus for their "emotional distress over the possibility that the child that they wanted so desperately, as evidenced by their undertaking the rigors of in vitro fertilisation, might be born to someone else and that they might never know his or her fate".[124] Another recent New York decision denied recovery

[116] See e.g. *Johnson* v. *State of New York*, 37 NY 2d 378, 334 NE 2d 590 (1975); *Young* v. *Telegraph Co.*, 107 N.C. 370, 11 SE 1044 (1890).

[117] See e.g. *Christensen* v. *Superior Court*, 54 Cal. 3d 868, 820 P 2d 181 (1991); *Gammon* v. *Osteopathic Hospital of Maine, Inc.*, 534 A 2d 1282 (Me. 1987).

[118] See W. P. Keeton *et al.*, *Prosser and Keeton on Torts* (5th edn., 1984), 361–2; *Guth* v. *Freeland*, 28 P 3d 982, 983 (Haw. 2001) (holding that a deceased's children who complained of negligent corpse desecration stated a cause of action although they made no 'claim that they suffered physical injury as a result of the incident or that their emotional distress was manifested in a physical injury or illness').

[119] D. B. Dobbs, *The Law of Torts* (2000), 837.

[120] The usual result of this kind of 'forgetfulness' is the allowance of recovery when the rules seem to forbid it. But for the other side of the coin, see *Robblee* v. *Budd Services, Inc.*, 136 NC App. 793, 525 SE 2d 847 (2000) (upholding a summary judgment dismissing the action of a woman who was badly frightened when she narrowly escaped being shot by a deranged man on premises where the defendant was responsible for security services). The court's only explanation for summarily rejecting the woman's claim was the puzzling statement that the woman did not have a sufficiently foreseeable emotional injury. Perhaps attention to the zone of danger/fear for self criterion would have produced a different judicial attitude. (But see Section 6 below.)

[121] See *Mokry* v. *University of Texas Health Science Center*, 529 SW 2d 802 (Tex.App. 1975) (defendant negligently lost a human eyeball that had been sent to it for testing).

[122] See *Campbell* v. *Animal Quarantine Station*, 632 P 2d 1066 (Haw. 1981) (dog).

[123] See *Adams* v. *State*, 357 So. 2d 1239 (La.App. 1978) (pecan tree); *Rodrigues* v. *State*, 472 P 2d 509 (Haw. 1970) (flooded home). The Hawai'ian legislature responded to the holding in *Rodrigues* by enacting a statute precluding recovery for emotional distress caused by property damage unless 'serious emotional distress or disturbance results in physical injury . . . or mental illness'. See HRS §663–8.9(b) as quoted in *Guth* v. *Freeland*, 28 P 3d 982, 985 (Haw. 2001).

[124] *Perry-Rogers* v. *Obasaju*, 282 AD 2d 231, 723 NYS 2d 28, 29 (2001).

to a woman whose emotional life was badly damaged when a negligent medical procedure virtually destroyed her husband's fertility.[125] Neither court offered much of an explanation for its conclusion. Arguably the divergence between the two results could have been explained by stating that the first couple had a decent argument under the uninjured-bystander rule on the analogy that their situation was much like that of a parent who witnesses a child being kidnapped. No such analogy was apparent in the second case.[126]

In summary: even though there may be persuasive policy arguments in favour of more generous treatment of emotional injuries,[127] the simple truth is that no jurisdiction could afford to treat emotional injuries on the same basis as physical injuries. In reality there are bound to be duty limits, and the courts are not doing their job if they do not articulate those limits in a clear enough fashion to inform counsel for potential plaintiffs that only limited types of emotional claims can be allowed.[128] In this area many analysts feel that firmer rules would be welcome. For example, "no pets".[129]

6. LIABILITY FOR THE CRIMES AND INTENTIONAL HARMS OF THIRD PARTIES[130]

Criminals and intentional tortfeasors are very often uninsured and impecunious and thus not worth suing in tort. Crime and intentional tort victims will therefore frequently try to impose responsibility on some other person or entity whose negligence arguably set the stage for the injuries or in some other fashion contributed to them.[131]

125 *Cohen* v. *Cabrini Medical Center*, 94 NY 2d 639, 730 NE 2d 949 (2000).

126 Note also that the wife in *Cohen* had a claim for loss of consortium—i.e., a traditionally well-recognised claim for the impairment to her husband's usefulness as such—which the court left undisturbed. See 730 NE 2d at 951. For discussion of the cause of action for loss of consortium and of its relationship with and differences from actions for negligently inflicted emotional distress, see D. B. Dobbs, *The Law of Torts* (2000), 839–41.

127 For an array of such arguments, see N. J. Mullany and P. R Handford, *Tort Liability for Psychiatric Damage* (1993); see also text at nn. 96–7 above. For an assessment of their persuasiveness, see D. W. Robertson, 'Liability in Negligence for Nervous Shock' (1994) 57 *MLR* 649.

128 For a particularly vivid example of an emotional-injury plaintiff whose life was adversely affected by her lawyer's overly optimistic view of the controlling law, see *Armstrong* v. *Paoli Memorial Hospital*, 430 Pa.Super. 36, 633 A 2d 605 (1993).

129 See *Rabideau* v. *City of Racine*, 243 Wis. 2d 486, 627 NW 2d 795, 807 (2001) (Abrahamson CJ, concurring and stating: 'For purpose of recovery for negligent infliction of emotional distress, this court treats the death of a dog the same as it treats injury to or death of a best friend, a roommate, or a nonmarital partner: It allows no recovery.')

130 See generally D. B. Dobbs, *The Law of Torts* (2000), 874–903; D. W. Robertson, 'Negligence Liability for Crimes and Intentional Torts Committed by Others' (1992) 67 *Tul. LR* 135.

131 Dramatic examples include *Gaines-Tabb* v. *ICI Explosives*, 160 F 3d 613 (10th Cir. 1998) (Okla. law) (exonerating the manufacturer of the explosive that was used to blow up the government office building in Oklahoma City on the view that the terrorists' actions constituted the sole proximate cause of the tragedy); *Sanders* v. *Acclaim Entertainment, Inc.*, 188 F Supp. 2d 1264 (D.Col. 2002) (exonerating the purveyors of violence-glorifying movies and video games that may have inspired the students who massacred their fellow students at Columbine High School in Colorado on a mélange of grounds including no-duty, no-breach,

It will facilitate discussion if we think of these as cases in which the plaintiff seeks to hold the defendant liable for the defendant's own negligent conduct that permitted or facilitated the commission of a crime or intentional tort by *X*, using *X* to signify the immediate perpetrator. It will sometimes be convenient to use the tag *X-crimes litigation* to refer to this group of cases.[132] Please note that we are not here concerned with vicarious liability.[133] In the cases under consideration here, the immediate perpetrator of the injury *(X)* is not in such a relationship with the defendant that defendant can be made vicariously liable for *X*'s conduct.

All *X*-crimes cases—in which defendants are being sued for their negligence respecting harms immediately perpetrated by someone else—present defendants with obvious legal causation arguments. In addition, many (though by no means all) of them implicate the settled common-law reluctance to "impose liability for what are called pure omissions"[134] or "nonfeasance".[135] Because of the way in which legal causation arguments and arguments over the nonfeasance (no-duty-to-act) issue tend to become intertwined and to dominate discussion in *X*-crimes cases, *X*-crimes cases constitute a discrete area within the law of negligence.[136]

The *X*-crimes cases are a discrete area for another reason as well: Here legal doctrine often seems markedly at odds with deeply held sentiments of large numbers of citizens and jurists. The "enabling" or "facilitative" contribution of the defendant's arguably negligent conduct will often strike the observer's emotions as pale and remote when

no-cause-in-fact, and sole proximate cause); *Hamilton* v. *Beretta USA Corp.*, 96 NY 2d 222, 750 NE 2d 1055 (2001) (holding that the manufacturers of cheap pistols have no duty to keep them from falling into irresponsible hands); *Kitchen* v. *K-Mart Corp.*, 697 So. 2d 1200 (Fla. 1997) (holding that a department store could be liable for selling a rifle to a drunken man who then used the weapon intentionally to shoot the plaintiff); *Taco Bell* v. *Lannon*, 744 P 2d 43 (Col. 1987) (upholding recovery against a restaurant by a customer who was shot by a gunman during the course of an armed robbery).

132 As the title to this section suggests, the class of cases with which we are concerned are sometimes called 'third-party claim[s]': *F.F.P. Operating Partners* v. *Duenez*, 69 SW 3d 800, 804 (Tex.App. 2002). The term 'third party' has many other applications, so one must be very careful with it.

133 'Vicarious liability is liability for the tort of another person': D. B. Dobbs, *The Law of Torts* (2000), 905. 'When *A* is held *vicariously* liable for damages done by *B*, the liability is not based on any view that *A* has been at fault; it is imposed solely on the basis that *B* was at fault and that the relationship between *A* and *B* justifies holding *A* responsible. The most important instance of vicarious liability... is the liability of an employer ("master") for the tort of an employee ("servant") who was acting in the scope of the employment': D. W. Robertson *et al.*, *Cases and Materials on Torts* (3rd edn., 2004), 314 (emphasis in original). In this section, we are not talking about vicarious liability but about cases in which the defendant's own fault is the focus. Occasional statements to the effect that a liquor seller, for example, can sometimes be held 'vicariously liable for the damages caused by an intoxicated person' are misuses of the terminology of vicarious liability. See, e.g., *F.F.P. Operating Partners* v. *Duenez*, 69 SW 3d 800, 805 (Tex.App. 2002).

134 *Smith* v. *Littlewoods Organisation Ltd.* [1987] AC 241, 271 (Lord Goff).

135 W. P. Keeton *et al.*, *Prosser and Keeton on Torts* (5th edn., 1984), 373. See D. B. Dobbs, *The Law of Torts* (2000), 854 (stating that the nonfeasance rule is 'embedded in the question whether the defendant owes a duty to protect the plaintiff from harms inflicted by others').

136 The *Restatement (Third of Torts): Liability for Physical Harm* (Proposed Final Draft No. 1, 6 Apr. 2005) does not treat these cases as a discrete area. Instead it focuses on the *X*-crimes problem periodically as it moves through the elements of negligence liability. See §19, *cmts.* c through h; §29, *cmt.* d, *illus.* 8; §34, *cmt.* d, *illus.* 1, *cmt.* e, *illus.* 3, 4, *cmt.* g, *illus.* 6, 7, 9; §41.

contrasted with the immediate, direct, and typically egregious blameworthiness of the actual perpetrator (*X*); there will often be emotional resonance to the defendant's figurative plea, "never mind me, it's all *his* fault."

A particular vivid demonstration of this sentiment in operation is provided by *Meyering* v. *General Motors Corp.*,[137] in which a motorist was injured when a chunk of concrete thrown by two juvenile hooligans from a highway overpass penetrated the sunroof of the motorist's car. The injured motorist sued the car's manufacturer (GM), alleging that the plexiglass sunroof was negligently thin and weak. The trial court dismissed the motorist's complaint on the ground that "the criminal conduct of the two juveniles constituted an unforeseeable intervening act which the manufacturer and seller of the vehicle had no duty to guard against".[138] The court of appeal reversed and remanded the case for trial on the merits, explaining that "well-established precedent"[139] provided as follows:

> [M]anufacturers must design their products to perform in a reasonably safe manner. This obligation includes taking into account the possibility that foreseeable negligence or misconduct of the user or third persons may contribute to causing the injury.[140]
>
> * * *
>
> [I]t is not necessary that GM anticipate that someone might throw a rock off a freeway overpass. Rather, in designing the Corvette's sunroof, it is only necessary that GM foresee the possibility that objects could fall from above a car and thus pose a danger to its occupants. [In one reported case, an auto manufacturer was held liable when a horse fell on the top of the car, collapsing the roof.] [O]bjects can fall from trucks onto cars below; roadside signs frequently warn of the danger of falling rocks; indeed, the rock in question here could have been accidentally or negligently kicked off the overpass and onto a passing car. In addition, it may well be that the sunroof in question would provide inadequate protection to the car's occupants during rollover accidents. It is certainly a question of fact [for trial on the merits] as to the extent of the risk posed by the sunroof's design and whether GM was negligent in failing to use stronger materials.[141]

A dissenting judge in *Meyering* violently disagreed with the majority's analysis. This judge accused the majority of "elect[ing] to expand the scope of tort liability in California".[142] He went on to make an overtly political argument:

> The majority's decision expands the current limits of liability. It is clearly a policy decision favoring recovery by plaintiffs from remote actors, increasing the potential scope of liability for manufacturers, and fostering claims and litigation. Is this the direction in which we are presently headed in the California judiciary? I think not.... We are in a trend of restriction, not expansion, of litigation rights. This, I suggest, is in harmony with enlightened legal thought.[143]

Perhaps because of the unusual heat of the dissenting opinion, the California Supreme Court subsequently designated the *Meyering* decision as unsuitable for publication.[144]

137 275 Cal. Rptr. 346 (Cal.App. 1990).
138 *Ibid.*, 347.
139 *Ibid.*, 351, n. 4.
140 *Ibid.*, 349.
141 *Ibid.*, 348.
142 *Ibid.*, 352.
143 *Ibid.*, 356–7.
144 See 819 P 2d 842.

(A) A TAXONOMIC CHOICE

The frequency of *X*-crimes litigation does not seem to be diminishing, yet the results of the reported cases in the aggregate leave the impression that plaintiffs fail far more often than they succeed. These phenomena have led the author of an excellent treatise to posit the existence of a general no-duty rule—"the defendant has no duty to control others"—that "is subject to significant exceptions".[145] But such a broadly phrased no-duty rule[146] would be a huge subtraction from the traditional principle of *Heaven* v. *Pender* (which is being strongly reaffirmed in the forthcoming *Restatement (Third) of Torts*).[147] Therefore, the organisation of the *X*-crimes area in this chapter will maintain the traditional view that *Heaven* v. *Pender* is still good law: one who engages in affirmative conduct that creates or exacerbates risks of physical harm to others generally owes a duty of reasonable care to mitigate such risks. Under this approach the only legitimate no-duty issue in *X*-crimes cases is the applicability of the general no-duty-to-act rule. (We will call this the *nonfeasance* rule.) In cases that fall outside the nonfeasance rule, discussions of a no-duty-to-control-others rule are seen to be either mechanisms for reaching *ad hoc* no-duty determinations[148] or awkward ways of talking about breach or

145 D. B. Dobbs, *The Law of Torts* (2000), 875. By setting up his organisation of the *X*-crimes area in that way, Professor Dobbs signals his belief that the gist of this legal area is most accurately conveyed by positing a no-duty rule in the foreground and 'significant exceptions' in the background. In contrast, this chapter reflects the belief that the more informative approach is to posit *Heaven* v. *Pender* ((1883) 11 QBD 503) as the foreground with a very significant miscellany of inroads in the background. This is a familiar kind of dispute among legal analysts: '[S]ome of the more interesting and intractable problems in legal theory inhere in the difficulty of distinguishing foreground from background': S. L. Winter, 'An Upside-Down View of the Countermajoritian Difficulty' (1991) 69 *Tex. LR* 1881, 1881.

146 From one point of view, a statement that one generally has no duty to control the behaviour of others is a trivial truism. But in the Dobbsian sense the formulation subtracts from *Heaven* v. *Pender* (see nn. 14 and 145 above) by implying that the involvement of another's active wrongdoing in bringing about the injury furnishes the more passively involved defendant with something like a presumption against responsibility.

Professor Dobbs's formulation is questionable for another reason as well: in the *X*-crimes cases the defendant is only occasionally being sued for failing to control *X*, and never for merely that. The core allegations of any even remotely plausible *X*-crimes case will be that the defendant had enough pre-tort involvement in the dangerous situation to be required to use reasonable care in respect to it. No competently-represented *X*-crimes plaintiff will assert that the defendant had a free-standing duty to control others' behaviour.

147 See n. 14 above.

148 Courts that purport to base their exoneration of particular *X*-crimes defendants on a rule of no-duty-to-control-others are frequently seen to be engaged in the creation of *ad hoc* no-duty rules. See, e.g., the discussion of *McCarthy* v. *Olin Corp.*, above at nn. 34–5. See also *Bryant* v. *Beary*, 766 So. 2d 1157, 1160 (Fla.App. 2000) (summarily exonerating a policeman whose high-speed pursuit of a 16-year-old traffic violator caused the boy to wreck his car and kill himself with the statement that '[c]ommon sense and all rational notions of public policy dictate that a violator fleeing law enforcement who injures himself as a result of his own criminal misconduct should not be able to bring an action for negligence against the law enforcement officer trying to detain him'). This no-duty declaration is baldly political and definitely would not meet the 'principle or policy' criterion for duty denials imposed by the forthcoming *Restatement (Third)*. See n. 14 above. That the court in *Bryant* (an intermediate appellate court in Florida) was simply arrogating to itself the authority to make up new rules is made all the more clear when one considers the earlier Florida Supreme Court decision in *City of Pinellas Park* v. *Brown*, 604 So. 2d 1222, 1225 (Fla. 1992), in which the court held policemen liable for a high-speed chase that killed an innocent motorist and reaffirmed the principle of *Heaven* v. *Pender* in the strongest of terms.

causation issues.[149] At the same time, it must be kept centrally in mind that the courts display a genuine reluctance to allow recovery in *X*-crimes cases, and that they emphasise their reluctance by continually talking about a no-duty-to-control-others rule as well as by such techniques as setting an impossibly high cause-in-fact barrier,[150] or affirming summary dismissal of claims on the basis of no-breach reasoning couched in no-duty terms,[151] or engaging in questionable legal causation reasoning.

(B) THE LEGAL CAUSATION ISSUE

Legal (proximate) causation arguments leap to the forefront in *X*-crimes decisions because it is so obvious that the most immediate and direct cause of the harm was the bad conduct of *X* rather than the (by comparison) more "background" or "remote" contribution of the defendant. Sometimes the drama of this contrast is so great that it leads courts to manipulate the cause-in-fact burden in the defendant's favour[152] or even into outright mistakes about factual causation. For example, one court found "no causal connection" between an Illinois mental institution's negligent release of a dangerous schizophrenic from custody and a murder committed by the schizophrenic in Florida fourteen months later.[153] But obviously there *was* a causal connection; if the schizophrenic had remained locked up in Illinois he would not have been able to get to Florida to commit the murder. The court's choice of a cause-in-fact articulation completely obscured the actual basis for its decision to exonerate the institution, whatever that might have been.

Similarly obscurant is a shibboleth that the provider of liquor is not liable for harms caused by an intoxicated consumer "because the law deem[s] the consumption rather than the serving of liquor as the proximate cause of an accident".[154] This liquor-provider causation shibboleth is a no-duty rule disguised in the raiment of legal

[149] That no-duty language in these cases frequently means no breach may be illustrated by two decisions handed down by the Virginia Supreme Court on the same day. In *Dudas* v. *Glenwood Golf Club*, 261 Va. 133, 540 SE 2d 129 (2001), the court held that an operator of a golf course had no duty to protect a golfer from an armed robbery. In *Thompson* v. *Skate America, Inc.*, 261 Va. 121, 540 SE 2d 123 (2001), it held that the operator of a skating rink did have a duty of reasonable care to protect a skater from a criminal assault. These were both principled decisions; factual differences between the two cases readily account for the divergent results. But these factual differences addressed whether the requirements of reasonable care had been *satisfied*, not whether a duty to behave reasonably *existed*.

[150] See, e.g., *Saelzer* v. *Advanced Group 400*, 25 Cal. 4th 763, 781, 23 P 3d 1143, 1155 (2001) (a 4–3 decision upholding a summary judgment that an apartment complex's lax security could not be said to have been a cause-in-fact of an attack on a delivery person. Kennard J's dissent noted that the holding 'places a virtually insurmountable burden in the path of any plaintiff seeking to recover damages for injuries allegedly suffered as a result of a property owner's unreasonable failure to provide security to protect against foreseeable third party criminal acts').

[151] See, e.g., *Mellon Mortgage Co.* v. *Holder*, 5 SW 3d 654 (Tex. 1999); *Terrell* v. *Wallace*, 747 So. 2d 748 (La.App. 1999); see also the cases treated above in n. 149.

[152] See n. 150 above.

[153] *Novak* v. *Rathnam*, 153 Ill.App. 3d 408, 505 NE 2d 773, 776 (1987).

[154] *Otis Engineering Corp.* v. *Clark*, 668 SW 2d 307, 318 n. 3 (Tex. 1983) (McGee J, dissenting). See also La. RS 9:2800.1(A) (quoted in pertinent part in n. 177 below).

causation. If the disguise were removed the rule could not so easily be set forth as somehow self-justifying. As the *Restatement (Third)* reminds us,[155] such situation-specific no-duty rules traditionally have called for policy justifications.

The *Restatement (Third) of Torts* makes no attempt to provide a general rule or principle of legal causation for *X*-crimes cases.[156] The *Restatement (Second)* did so, but it handled the matter in a schizophrenic fashion by setting forth a general rule against recovery virtually in the same breath as a potentially huge exception:

> The act of a third person in committing an intentional tort or crime is a superseding cause of harm to another resulting therefrom, although the actor's negligent conduct created a situation which afforded an opportunity to the third person to commit such a tort or crime, *unless* the actor at the time of his negligent conduct realized or should have realized the likelihood that such a situation might be created, and that a third person might avail himself of the opportunity to commit such a tort or crime.[157]

If the *Restatement (Second)*'s "unless" clause is not to swallow entirely the clause that precedes it, the inquiry must boil down to whether the risk that *X* would harm the plaintiff in some fashion broadly similar to that which occurred was a foreseeable enough risk of the defendant's conduct to call for reasonable precautions on the defendant's part. This is obviously a highly flexible inquiry to which judicial responses will differ depending on factual nuances. Predicting courts' responses in particular cases is assisted to only a modest degree by realising that "legal causation tends to become more inclusive as the degree of defendant's fault increases. Legal causation also tends to be more inclusive in cases of physical harm to human beings than in cases involving other types of damage."[158]

Almost always there will be a large overlap between the legal causation and negligence (breach-of-duty) issues in these cases, and sometimes the two issues will virtually coalesce.[159] Suppose a citizen who sees that his automobile is being driven away by a thief commandeers another vehicle to engage in high-speed pursuit through a densely populated area. During the chase the thief, determined to escape, drives recklessly and at high speed and runs down a pedestrian. Should the citizen be liable to the pedestrian?[160] The duty and cause-in-fact issues are not problematic in this case: obviously the citizen owes a duty to use reasonable care in all respects in operating a vehicle on a public roadway, and equally obviously the pedestrian would not have been injured if the citizen had not instituted the chase. The pivotal issue in this case is the

155 See n. 14 above. 156 See n. 136 above.

157 *Restatement (Second) of Torts* §448 (emphasis supplied).

158 D. W. Robertson, 'Negligence Liability for Crimes and Intentional Torts Committed by Others' (1992) 67 *Tul. LR* 135, 139.

159 See, e.g., *Perez* v. *Lopez*, 74 SW 3d 60, 69 (Tex.App. 2002) (couching the conclusion that the defendants had no reason to anticipate that a juvenile would use a rifle to kill himself in no-legal-cause terms when the true meaning was probably that the defendants were guilty of no substandard conduct). In a case like *Perez*, the parties may care deeply whether the court is holding the defendant blameless (not negligent) as opposed to exonerating the defendant on some other basis such as legal cause or victim fault. So courts are always to be faulted for not clarifying their decisional grounds, regardless of whether in a particular instance legal analysts will much care. See D. W. Robertson *et al., Cases and Materials on Torts* (3rd edn., 2004), 207.

160 See *City of Pinellas Park*, n. 148 above (imposing liability on police pursuers of traffic violator); *Smith* v. *English*, 586 So. 2d 583 (La.App. 1991) (imposing liability on civilian pursuers of car thief).

breach-of-duty issue. Was it unreasonable for the citizen to chase the thief? Given the obvious risks that high-speed pursuits present to other roadway users, would a reasonable person have sought police assistance, thereby taking the substantial risk that he would never see his car again, in lieu of high-speed pursuit through crowds of his neighbours? Rationally answering this question turns almost entirely on the degree of foreseeability that the chase would lead to a traffic accident. Once this risk is determined to be high enough to lead to the conclusion that the citizen was guilty of negligence, there is little remaining work to be done on the issue of legal cause.[161]

Similarly, suppose that an abandoned urban building—one that presents no appreciable risk of fire or tumbling-down damage to persons in the vicinity—is used by a sociopath as a hiding place for molesting children. Whether the building owner is negligent for failing to lock up or otherwise secure the building against intruders depends in major part on the degree of foreseeable risk that the building will be used for such purposes.[162] If the owner is found guilty of negligence, there is really nothing further to be said about legal causation.

It follows from the foregoing discussion that legal causation is seldom a truly dispositive issue in the present context. In most of these cases "tortious or criminal action by a third party is . . . the 'very kind of thing' "[163] that made it arguably negligent for the defendant to act or fail to act as it did. Legal causation defences are routinely invoked in these cases, but they usually turn out to be a contrived or confused way of saying something about duty or breach of duty. If the risk that *X* will commit a crime or intentional tort is one of the reasons the defendant's conduct appears negligent, then *X*'s fault cannot sensibly be regarded as an intervening or superseding cause that insulates the defendant from liability.[164] If the defendant is to be absolved in this situation, some other reason must be found.

(C) THE NONFEASANCE ISSUE

The common-law precept, sometimes known as the no-duty-to-act rule, that excludes liability for what is variously called "nonfeasance" or "pure omissions"[165] is firm but

161 Note that, while the negligence and legal cause issues largely overlap in the case posed, they do not completely coalesce, because the foreseeable risks that may lead to the conclusion that the citizen's conduct was negligent included not only the risk that the thief would run down someone but also the risk that the citizen himself would. See n. 26 above.

162 Cf. *Nixon* v. *Mr. Property Management Co.*, 690 SW 2d 546 (Tex. 1985) (basing liability on the building owner's violation of a city ordinance).

163 *Dorset Yacht Co. Ltd.* v. *Home Office* [1970] AC 1004, 1030 (Lord Reid).

164 See e.g. *Joseph* v. *State*, 26 P 3d 459, 465–6, 471 (Alas. 2001) (exposing the mutual inconsistency of jury instructions (*a*) that a jailer had a duty of reasonable care to protect an intoxicated prisoner against intentionally self-inflicted injury but (*b*) that the prisoner's intentional suicide would be a superseding cause of his death); *F.F.P. Operating Partners*, n. 133 above, 69 SW 3d at 809 (rejecting an argument that a negligent liquor-provider should be exonerated because the drunken driver's conduct was the 'sole proximate cause' of the plaintiff's injuries).

165 See nn. 134–5 above. See also *Restatement (Second) of Torts* §314: 'The fact that the actor realizes or should realize that action on his part is necessary for another's aid or protection does not of itself impose upon him a duty to take such action.'

narrow. How narrow depends in the first place on what is regarded as a pure omission[166] and in the second place on the exceptions that courts are willing to devise to the basic nonfeasance rule. Judicial views have changed on these matters over the years. "Merely" owning real estate was at one time regarded as bearing such a close resemblance to doing nothing whatever that the landowner could rarely be held liable for injuries caused by conditions on the land. From this point of view the modern law of landowners' and land occupiers' liability began with the law's willingness to recognise something that laymen had perhaps suspected all along, *viz.*, that owning land is itself an activity that has societal implications.[167]

Analysis of the *X*-crimes cases is facilitated by first separating out the ones that do not involve any significant nonfeasance issue (subsection (i) below) and then by grouping those that do involve nonfeasance issues (subsections (ii) through (v) below) into the categories of the recognised exceptions to the nonfeasance rule.[168]

(i) Liability Based on Affirmative Negligent Conduct ('Misfeasance')

When the defendant contributes to the injuries caused by *X* in some active way, such as chasing a fleeing automobile thief under circumstances likely to cause the thief to injure others, liability for negligence may readily be imposed.[169] Such cases present no nonfeasance problem; liability flows from "misfeasance",[170] defined as affirmative negligent conduct that is a cause-in-fact and a legal cause of the plaintiff's injuries. The same can be said of cases in which an employer negligently hires or retains an unsuitable person for a job presenting unusual opportunities or temptations to commit crimes. Here again the basis of liability is affirmative negligent conduct, *viz.*, putting the unsuitable person into contact with the foreseeable victim.[171]

166 For a good discussion of the difference between nonfeasance (pure omission) and misfeasance (doing something wrong), see *Lugtu* v. *California Highway Patrol*, 26 Cal. 4th 703, 28 P 3d 249, 256–7 (2001) (rejecting the defendant's 'nonfeasance' characterisation of a motorcycle patrolman's conduct in directing a speeding motorist to stop his car on the central reservation of the multilane highway rather than on the shoulder and then being unable to prevent another speeding vehicle from striking the first speeder's car). For a decision that tends to obscure the distinction, see *Estate of Heck* v. *Stoffer*, 752 NE 2d 192 (Ind.App. 2001) (treating defendants' keeping a pistol in the house as nonfeasance), *rev'd*, 786 NE 2d 265 (Ind. 2003).

167 See the discussion in *Sprecher* v. *Adamson Companies*, 30 Cal. 3d 358, 636 P 2d 1121, 1125–8 (1981).

168 The treatment of the nonfeasance rule and its exceptions in the *Restatement (Second) of Torts* was repetitious and not well organised. The basic nonfeasance rule was treated in §314, the prior conduct exception in §§321 and 322, the volunteer exception in §§323, 324, and 324A, the relationship-with-the-perpetrator exception in §§315–19, and the relationship-with-the-victim exception in §§314A and 314B. The *Restatement (Third) of Torts: Liability for Physical Harm* (Proposed Final Draft No. 1, 6 Apr. 2005) has a more orderly and efficient presentation at §§37 through 44.

169 See n. 160 above.

170 W. P. Keeton *et al.*, *Prosser and Keeton on Torts* (5th edn., 1984), 373.

171 See e.g. *Bonsignore* v. *City of New York*, 683 F 2d 635 (2nd Cir. 1982) (NY law) (holding a police department liable to the victim of a shooting by a disturbed policeman who should not have been assigned to street duty); *Becken* v. *Manpower, Inc.*, 532 F 2d 56 (7th Cir. 1976) (Ill. law) (holding a furniture-moving company liable for thefts from customers by temporary employees who should not have been hired because they had arrest records for theft); *Ponticas* v. *K.M.S. Investments*, 331 NW 2d 907 (Minn. 1983) (holding an apartment complex liable for the rape of a tenant by the apartment manager).

One large group of misfeasance cases involves what is sometimes called "negligent entrustment".[172] When the defendant entrusts *X* with a dangerous instrumentality such as a pistol[173] or a bottle of whisky[174] under circumstances in which a reasonable person would have refrained from doing so, the defendant can be liable for the injuries *X* causes by reason of having been provided with the dangerous instrument or substance.

Liquor-provider or "dram shop" liability raises special problems, but not because there is any conceptual difficulty in classifying the defendant's conduct as misfeasance and not because of any legitimate legal causation difficulties. Liquor-provider liability is a special problem because of societal factors. Injuries caused by intoxicated persons are prevalent. Many of the intoxicated persons who cause these injuries turn out to be impecunious and uninsured. Taverns, other sellers, and social hosts of all kinds often dispense alcoholic beverages under circumstances that a moment's reflection would reveal as endangering highway users and others. Yet numbers of people evidently do not regard such conduct as wrongful, at least not unless the circumstances are egregious. Furthermore, liquor, beer, and wine are major industries with considerable financial and political power; it is not disrespectful to note that courts and legislatures are not blind to such factors.

As a result of this complex of factors, all of the United States are struggling with the liquor-provider problem. Apparently a dwindling few recognise a common-law duty of reasonable care that can hold both liquor sellers and social providers of alcohol liable for alcohol-induced injuries.[175] Others have "dram shop" statutes that impose liability on liquor sellers under certain (generally fairly limited) circumstances.[176] Quite a few states have gone even further and enacted statutes designed to preclude liquor-provider liability altogether[177] or setting low ceilings on the damages that can be owed by negligent liquor providers.[178]

Various middle grounds may be seen. In many states one can be liable for injuries that result from providing liquor to a minor, because doing so is a misdemeanour and

172 W. P. Keeton *et al.*, *Prosser and Keeton on Torts* (5th edn., 1984), 197.

173 See e.g. *Phillips ex rel. Phillips* v. *Roy*, 431 So. 2d 849 (La.App. 1983) (liability for selling pistol to deranged man).

174 See e.g. *El Chico Corp.* v. *Poole*, 732 SW 2d 306 (Tex. 1987) (liquor-seller liability for traffic accident).

175 See e.g. *Kelly* v. *Gwinell*, 96 NJ 538, 476 A 2d 1219 (1984) (a recognition of social-liquor-purveyor liability that was subsequently superseded by NJSA 2A:15–5.7, immunising social hosts from responsibility for providing adults with liquor).

176 See e.g. Tex.Alco.Bev. Code Ann. §§2.02, 2.03.

177 One outspoken jurist has decried such statutes as 'appalling... special interest' legislation: *Young* v. *Players Lake Charles, L.L.C.*, 47 F Supp. 2d 832, 834, 837 (SD Tex. 1999). See, e.g., La. RS 9:2800.1(A) (providing that 'the consumption of intoxicating beverages, rather than the sale or serving or furnishing of such beverages, is the proximate cause of any injury, including death and property damage, inflicted by an intoxicated person upon himself or upon another person'); *Stephenson* v. *Universal Metrics, Inc.*, 251 Wis. 2d 171, 641 NW 2d 158, 165–6 (2002) (holding that the provisions of Wis. Stat. §125.035(2) that '[a] person is immune from civil liability arising out of the act of procuring alcohol beverages for or selling, dispensing or giving away alcohol beverages to another person' conferred immunity on a bar-room customer who 'procured' liquor for his drunken friend by falsely promising the bartender he would drive the friend home).

178 See, e.g., 235 ILCS 5/6–21 (Ill.).

is in any event generally regarded as wrongful.[179] As to liability for injuries resulting from providing liquor to adults, there is considerable variety. In some states liquor-provider liability is limited to grossly negligent[180] or reckless[181] conduct on the part of the provider. Other states might impose liability for the consequences of providing liquor "to any intoxicated person, or to any habitual drunkard".[182] Some states have developed a rule that, while one cannot be liable for providing the liquor, there remains the possibility of liability for affirmative acts over and above providing the liquor, such as ejecting a helplessly intoxicated customer from a tavern near a busy highway[183] or "jump-starting" the automobile of an obviously liquor-impaired man to enable him to try to drive home from the tavern.[184]

One frequent line of argument against liquor-provider liability should be identified so as to explore and question its premises. This is the view that holding the liquor provider liable will somehow "erode... the concept that an individual is responsible for his or her own actions"[185] by shifting responsibility away from the drunken immediate perpetrator of the harm onto the more indirectly responsible liquor provider. The *Restatement (Third)* offers a rebuttal to that viewpoint:

> It is sometimes suggested that imposing liability on the [liquor-providing or other similarly situated] defendant for failure to adopt precautions against [*X*'s] misconduct unduly diminishes the basic responsibility of [*X*]. This argument is largely unpersuasive. Insofar as [*X*'s] misconduct is criminal, [*X*] remains fully subject to whatever criminal punishments the law imposes. If that misconduct is tortious, recognizing the liability of the... defendant does not significantly diminish the potential tort liability of [*X*]. So long as [*X*] is solvent, the plaintiff will generally much prefer to bring a tort claim against [*X*] directly, since the tortious quality of [*X*'s] conduct is typically much easier to recognize and prove than the negligence of the [defendant]. Moreover, even if the plaintiff both sues and recovers from the... defendant, [the] defendant has an appropriate claim for contribution or indemnification against [*X*].... It is only when [*X*] is insolvent that the plaintiff will prefer the claim against the... defendant, and [the] defendant will be unable to collect reimbursement from [*X*]. While [*X*'s] insolvency is of course not uncommon, in such situations [*X*] as a practical matter escapes tort liability regardless of whether the law recognizes the liability of the... defendant.[186]

[179] See, e.g., *St. Hill* v. *Tabor*, 542 So. 2d 499 (La. 1989) (social host who provided liquor to minors held liable without reference to misdemeanour statute); *Edson* v. *Walker*, 573 So. 2d 545 (La.App. 1991) (liability imposed on violator of statute prohibiting sale of alcohol to minors). Some courts have trouble deciding how to treat harms caused by so-called 'adult but underage' drinkers (i.e., persons between 18 and 21). See *Panagakos* v. *Walsh*, 434 Mass. 353, 749 NE 2d 670, 672 (2001).

[180] See, e.g., Tex.Alco.Bev. Code Ann. §2.02 (liquor seller liable only if 'it was *apparent* [that the customer] was *obviously* intoxicated to the extent that he presented a *clear* danger to himself and others') (emphasis added).

[181] See *Craig* v. *Driscoll*, 64 Conn.App. 699, 716, 781 A 2d 440 (2001) (noting that Michigan recognises 'a cause of action for the sale of liquor to an intoxicated alcoholic sounding in intentional or reckless misconduct').

[182] See *ibid.* (quoting a Connecticut statute criminalising sales to habitual drunkards and indicating that the statute could be used as a basis for 'an action sounding in negligence per se').

[183] See *Pence* v. *Ketchum*, 326 So. 2d 831 (La. 1976), overruled in part by *Thrasher* v. *Leggett*, 373 So. 2d 494 (La. 1979).

[184] See *Leppke* v. *Segura*, 632 P 2d 1057 (Col.App. 1981).

[185] *Otis Engineering Corp.* v. *Clark*, 668 SW 2d 307, 319 (Tex. 1983) (McGee J, dissenting).

[186] *Restatement (Third) of Torts: Liability for Physical Harm*, §19, *cmt.* d (Proposed Final Draft No. 1, 6 Apr. 2005).

It might be added that, in the recurrent situation in which *X* (the drunk driver) is impecunious and has little or no liability insurance, the real choice is between saddling the injured person with the loss or placing it on the liquor provider. In the usual case, the injured person is a stranger to the drunk driver and had no way of diminishing the risk of another motorist's inebriation. The liquor provider, by hypothesis negligent in entrusting the drunk driver with the liquor, could have avoided it by meeting the law's requirement of exercising reasonable care. If the liquor provider has to insure against such liability, the cost of liquor will go up. Perhaps fewer people will buy and use it. And in any event, the price of liquor will more accurately reflect its costs.

(ii) Liability Based on the Defendant's Failure to Take Reasonable Steps to Alleviate Dangers Created by the Defendant's Prior Conduct

The immediately preceding subsection discusses cases that base liability on affirmative negligent conduct and thus fall outside the nonfeasance (no-duty-to-act) rule. We now turn to the first of the recognised exceptions to that rule. In a leading decision from the state of Nebraska, the court refused to find an automobile driver negligent when his vehicle struck a trolley pole and knocked it across the roadway, but held him liable for thereafter failing to take steps to warn or otherwise protect other motorists against hitting the downed pole.[187] A very similar decision from Georgia held that a motorist who was "innocent"' in striking a cow in the roadway nevertheless could be held liable for failing to use reasonable care to warn other motorists of the danger created by the cow's carcass.[188] The principle of these decisions has come to be fairly generally recognised. Section 39 of the *Restatement (Third) of Torts* offers the following summary:

> When an actor's prior conduct, even though not tortious, creates a continuing risk of physical harm of a type characteristic of the conduct, the actor has a duty to exercise reasonable care to prevent or minimize the harm.[189]

The principle is often called the "prior conduct"' or "prior innocent conduct" exception to the nonfeasance rule. (The latter term is useful as a reminder that the prior conduct need not be negligent or otherwise tortious, but because the principle covers both innocent and negligent prior conduct,[190] we will use the broader *prior conduct* tag.) The prior-conduct principle is simple and easy to accept: certainly if the defendant's previous activities, albeit without fault, have contributed to the dangerous situation in which the plaintiff is found, the defendant should have a duty of reasonable care to alleviate the danger.[191]

[187] *Simonsen v. Thorin*, 120 Neb. 684, 234 NW 628 (1931).

[188] *Hardy v. Brooks*, 103 Ga.App. 124, 118 SE 2d 492 (1961).

[189] *Restatement (Third) of Torts: Liability for Physical Harm*, §39 (Proposed Final Draft No. 1, 6 Apr. 2005).

[190] Those who work in this area of the law must be alert to the distinction between using 'prior conduct' as a basis for misfeasance liability and using it as the predicate of the 'prior conduct' exception to the nonfeasance rule. Prior conduct might be negligent and still not present a suitable basis for misfeasance liability because of legal causation problems or immunity doctrines. See D. W. Robertson *et al., Cases and Materials on Torts* (3rd edn., 2004), 232–3.

[191] But see *Panagakos* (n. 179 above), in which the prior-conduct principle did not prove robust enough to overcome the judicial tendency to immunise liquor-procurer liability.

Many of the situations in which defendants have been held liable for failing to guard against the risk that *X* will commit an intentional tort or a crime potentially fall into the prior-conduct category. The House of Lords decision in *Dorset Yacht* v. *Home Office*[192] is a good example. In this case seven borstal boys escaped from custody while working on Brownsea Island off the coast of Poole and tried to get away by boarding a yacht for the mainland. They collided with and then boarded the plaintiff's yacht, causing damage. The prior-conduct rule readily explains the decision holding the borstal officers liable. These boys might or might not have presented dangers to society while they were at large before being incarcerated. However that may be, when the defendants incarcerated the boys and put them to work off the coast of Poole, they created a new danger by putting the boys together in a kind of critical mass and in the plaintiff's vicinity under circumstances in which an escape attempt was a distinct possibility. When the boys escaped and damaged the boat, the defendants were liable for having failed to take reasonable steps to guard against dangers that the defendants' own prior conduct had created. On the other hand, if the plaintiff's boat had been stolen or damaged by bad boys who needed to be but never had been locked up, no basis for the defendants' liability would have been found.[193]

The American cases involving harms done by escaped prisoners reflect the same analysis.[194] The courts' opinions often indicate that liability turns on whether the injury occurred "during, or as an integral part of, the process of escaping".[195] The quoted phrase is a cryptic way of saying that in order to fall within the scope of the prior-conduct exception to the nonfeasance rule, the harm must have been among the risks created by the incarceration situation, as opposed to the general risks that result from the existence of criminally inclined persons in society.

The prior-conduct principle provides a useful perspective for examining the different approaches taken in the judgments of Lord Mackay and Lord Goff in *Smith* v. *Littlewoods Ltd.*,[196] in which the defendants were charged with failing to take reasonable steps to guard against the risk that vandals would start a fire in the defendants' abandoned cinema and thereby damage neighbouring property. The House of Lords concluded that the defendants should not be held liable. Lord Mackay's judgment seemed to recognise that the defendants owed a duty of reasonable care, but concluded

[192] [1970] AC 1004.

[193] See *Green* v. *State*, 91 So. 2d 153, 155 (La.App. 1956): 'An institution's duty to restrain a convicted criminal is not based upon the purpose of protecting the general public from all harms that the prisoner might inflict if he were allowed to escape. A convicted person may be as dangerous on the day of his legal release as he was on the first day that he was confined.... There is no more reason for the State to be civilly responsible for the convict's general misconduct during the period of his escape than for the same misconduct after a legal release, unless there is some further causal relationship than the release or escape to the injuries received.'

[194] For the most part, escaped-prisoner cases are treated as nonfeasance cases in which the plaintiff cannot succeed without making out an exception to the nonfeasance rule. But in cases in which the defendant is alleged to have been negligent in deliberately releasing a dangerous person from custody, the courts often proceed as though the nonfeasance rule is not in play because misfeasance has been alleged. See e.g. *Bradley Center* v. *Wessner*, 250 Ga. 199, 296 SE 2d 693 (1982); *Hembree* v. *State*, 2001 WestLaw 575561 (Tenn.App.).

[195] *Wilson* v. *Department of Public Safety*, 576 So. 2d 490, 493 (La. 1991).

[196] [1987] AC 241 (HL).

that under the circumstances the duty had not been breached. Lord Goff, on the other hand, appeared to conclude that no duty of care was owed. The divergence between the two approaches can usefully be viewed as stemming from differences over the scope of the prior-conduct exception to the nonfeasance rule. When *Smith* v. *Littlewoods* is viewed in that light it will be seen that Lord Mackay was willing to recognise the ownership or occupancy "of property, particularly property of the tenement type"[197] as itself sufficient prior conduct to give rise to a duty of care to guard against foreseeable risks that vandals would use the property to harm others. Lord Goff, on the other hand, viewed the case as one in which the plaintiffs were seeking to "impose liability for pure omissions".[198] For Lord Goff, the ownership of "property of the tenement type" did not constitute prior conduct that was itself sufficient to generate a duty of reasonable care. In his view only when the owner of such property "has knowledge or means of knowledge that a third party has created or is creating a risk of fire, or indeed has started a fire, on his premises"[199] would a duty of reasonable care to alleviate such risks arise.[200]

The American decisions that are analogous to *Smith* v. *Littlewoods* are divided in their results. Far too frequently the courts discuss the issue of liability *vel non* under the rubric of legal causation, using formulas that obscure the true policy grounds of the decision.[201] Breach and duty considerations also tend to become commingled in ways that obfuscate. But one thing at least emerges with reasonable clarity: in the modern American cases the ownership of real estate counts as an activity[202] that can itself be sufficient under the prior-conduct rule to give rise to a duty of care under appropriate circumstances to alleviate dangers created by vandals and similar trespassers on the premises.[203]

(iii) Liability Based on the Defendant's Failure to Carry Through after Volunteering Assistance

The second recognised exception to the nonfeasance rule holds one who undertakes or volunteers to provide safety precautions or assistance to persons in peril to a duty of reasonable care in carrying out the undertaking.[204] This principle is fairly broad in its application to landlords and similar businesses who may have no initial duty to guard against the risks of crime associated with their operations but who can become liable

[197] *Ibid.*, 262 (Lord Mackay of Clashfern, quoting with approval the judgment of Lord Wylie in *Evans* v. *Glasgow District Council*, 1978 SLT 17, 19).

[198] *Ibid.*, 271. [199] *Ibid.*, 274.

[200] For further discussion of the possible reasons for Lord Goff 's refusal to recognise the ownership of real property as itself sufficient to amount to 'prior innocent conduct', see the text surrounding n. 218 below.

[201] See e.g. *Brown* v. *Tesack*, 556 So. 2d 84, 87 (La.App. 1989), *rev'd* 566 So. 2d 955 (La. 1990).

[202] See text at nn. 166–7 above.

[203] See e.g. *Nixon* v. *Mr. Property Management Co.*, 690 SW 2d 546 (Tex. 1985) (abandoned apartment used as refuge by rapist); *Torrack* v. *Corpamerica, Inc.*, 51 Del. 254, 144 A 2d 703 (1958) (arsonist set fire to abandoned building).

[204] See D. B. Dobbs, *The Law of Torts* (2000), 860–73; *Stephenson* v. *Universal Metrics, Inc.*, 251 Wis. 2d 171, 641 NW 2d 158 (2002) (holding that a bar-room customer who falsely promised the bartender he would drive a drunken friend home, thereby persuading the bartender to serve more liquor to the friend, would have been liable under the volunteer principle to the friend's drunk-driving victims but for an 'immunity' conferred by the liquor-provider statute treated above in n. 177).

for holding out an assurance of security measures that are then not properly carried out. For example, a restaurant that had an armed security guard on the premises was held liable for a criminal's acts in shooting patrons during a robbery on the basis that "[a] duty of protection which has been voluntarily assumed must be performed with due care".[205] But not everyone agrees. The Minnesota Supreme Court recently noted a division of authority "on whether a landlord's provision of security measures can give rise to liability for harms to tenants that results from a failure to maintain those measures" and stated that it was "not inclined to establish a rule that would discourage landlords from [providing or] improving security".[206]

Many of the cases that base liability upon the volunteer principle state that the defendant's duty is limited to using reasonable care not to worsen the situation.[207] Other cases ignore that limitation entirely.[208] In any event it is a limitation that usually seems fairly easy to meet.[209] If the other requisites for liability are in place, usually the court will be persuaded by an argument that the victim could have made other provisions for avoiding or alleviating the danger, such as by looking to others for help, had the defendant not purported to provide it.[210]

(iv) Liability Based on a Pre-Existing Special Relationship between the Defendant and *X*[211]

Section 41 of the *Restatement (Third) of Torts* spells out an exception to the nonfeasance rule based on the defendant's pre-tort special relationship with *X*, the immediate perpetrator of the harm:

> (a) An actor in a special relationship with another owes a duty of reasonable care to third persons with regard to risks posed by the other that arise within the scope of the relationship.
> (b) Special relationships giving rise to the duty provided in Subsection (a) include:
> (1) a parent with dependent children,
> (2) a custodian with those in its custody,

[205] *Harris* v. *Pizza Hut*, 455 So. 2d 1364, 1369 (La. 1984); see also *Patrick* v. *Employers Mut. Cas. Co.*, 745 So. 2d 641 (La.App. 1999) (holding a shopping centre with a security service responsible for a crime in its parking lot). But see *Robblee*, n. 120 above.

[206] *Funchess* v. *Cecil Newman Corp.*, 632 NW 2d 666, 674–5 (Minn. 2001).

[207] See e.g. *Farwell* v. *Keeton*, 396 Mich. 281, 240 NW 2d 217, 220 (1976): 'Without regard to whether there is a general duty to aid a person in distress, there is a clearly recognized legal duty of every person to avoid any affirmative acts which may make a situation worse.' See also *Restatement (Third) of Torts: Liability for Physical Harm* §42 (Proposed Final Draft No. 1, 6 Apr. 2005): 'An actor who undertakes to render services to another that the actor knows or should know reduce the risk of physical harm to the other has a duty of reasonable care to the other in conducting the undertaking if: (a) the failure to exercise such care increases the risk of harm beyond that which existed without the undertaking, or (b) the person to whom the services are rendered or another relies on the actor's exercising reasonable care in the undertaking.'

[208] See W. P. Keeton *et al.*, *Prosser and Keeton on Torts* (5th edn., 1984), 381–2.

[209] The decisions often skate over the 'worsening' issue with an indication that the plaintiff 'reasonably relied' on the defendant's assistance: *Appley Brothers* v. *United States*, 164 F 3d 1164, 1175 (8th Cir. 1999) (ND law). And 'courts are willing to accept very sparse evidence of reliance': D. B. Dobbs, *The Law of Torts* (2000), 860.

[210] See D. W. Robertson *et al.*, *Cases and Materials on Torts* (3rd edn., 2004), 223–5.

[211] It will be remembered that we are ruling out of the discussion relationships between the defendant and *X* that would suffice to make the defendant vicariously liable for *X*'s torts. See text and n. 133 above.

(3) an employer with employees when the employment facilitates the employee's causing harm to third parties, and
(4) a mental-health professional with patients.[212]

The Reporters' Note accompanying this section presents a number of cases in support of the described "relationship-with-perpetrator" exception.[213] But there are many cases in which courts have looked with disfavour on any such exception to the nonfeasance rule.[214] The *Restatement* acknowledges that the existence of this "relationship-with-perpetrator" exception is far from assured, stating in *Comment b* to §41 that "court[s] may decide, based on special problems of principle or policy" to refuse to apply it.[215] The *Restatement* also acknowledges that the group of relationships it lists as covered by the exception has no strong natural coherence or obvious boundary, stating in *Comment i* that "the list of special relationships provided in [§41] is not exclusive. Courts may decide that additional relationships [between the defendant and the perpetrator] justify exceptions to the [nonfeasance rule]."[216]

Many of the cases that can be cited in support of the "relationship with perpetrator" exception are susceptible of explanation on other grounds.[217] Asking about the relationship between the defendant and *X* can sometimes be a useful way of asking whether the defendant has engaged in affirmative negligent conduct that was a legal cause of the harm and, if not, whether the defendant has engaged in prior conduct contributing to the situation in a way that obligates the defendant to take reasonable steps to alleviate the danger. If neither question can be answered affirmatively, the existence of some kind of previous relationship between the defendant and *X* may or may not persuade the court that the defendant should be responsible for taking steps to guard against *X*'s torts.

In truth there is a large element of arbitrariness to any particular method of organising the decisions in which a defendant is sought to be held liable for the results of a crime or intentional tort committed by *X*. The misfeasance/nonfeasance line itself is far from bright, and the lines between the various exceptions to the nonfeasance rule are frequently blurred. For example, *Dorset Yacht* could with approximately equal facility be explained (as suggested above) as resting liability on the defendants' failure to take reasonable steps to guard against dangers created by their prior conduct, or as resting

212 *Restatement (Third) of Torts: Liability for Physical Harm*, §41 (Proposed Final Draft No. 1, 6 Apr. 2005).

213 See also *Greenberg* v. *Barbour*, 322 F Supp. 745 (ED Pa. 1971), where, without even acknowledging the nonfeasance (no-duty-to-act) issue, the court imposed a duty on a hospital staff doctor whose failure to admit a mental patient into the hospital for treatment resulted in the patient's attacking the plaintiff.

214 See, e.g., *Grover* v. *Stechel*, 45 P 3d 80 (NM App. 2002) (holding that a mother did not have a special relationship with her drug-addicted and violent adult son, and that her contributing to his financial support was not to be regarded as prior conduct that had contributed to the danger that he would stab someone); *Weitz* v. *Lovelace Health System, Inc.*, 214 F 3d 1175 (10th Cir. 2000) (NM law) (holding that a psychiatric service had no duty to guard against murders committed by a dangerous outpatient); *Brady v. Hopper*, 751 F 2d 329 (10th Cir. 1984) (Col. law) (holding that the psychiatrist of the man who wounded the plaintiffs during an attempt to assassinate President Reagan had no duty to the plaintiffs).

215 *Restatement (Third) of Torts: Liability for Physical Harm*, §41, *cmt.* b (Proposed Final Draft No. 1, 6 Apr. 2005).

216 *Ibid.*, *cmt.* i.

217 See, e.g., *Estates of Morgan* v. *Fairfield Family Counseling Ctr.*, 77 Ohio St. 3d 284, 673 NE 2d 1311 (1997) (defendant psychiatric institution had a close relationship with both the patient who murdered his parents and the parents themselves). See also n. 214 above.

liability on a special relationship between the defendants and *X*, the borstal boys. In *Smith* v. *Littlewoods* Lord Goff took the latter view.[218] This led him to reject the persuasiveness of *Dorset Yacht* in the *Smith* v. *Littlewoods* situation, because the *Smith* defendants had no relationship at all with the vandals who started the fire in the abandoned cinema. Had Lord Goff viewed *Dorset* as falling under the prior-conduct exception as opposed to the "relationship-with-perpetrator" exception, he might then have been led to examine his unstated premise that owning property is not itself an activity.

The "relationship with perpetrator" explanation of cases like *Dorset Yacht* seems inferior to the prior-conduct explanation in two senses. In the sense just indicated, the "relationship with perpetrator" explanation is too narrow; it directs one's attention away from a useful comparison of the amount of actual involvement of the defendant in the circumstances leading up to the harm. In another sense it is too broad; it fails to provide a basis for explaining why the *Dorset Yacht* defendants should not be liable for all of the crimes and torts done by the boys after their escape, even when they have left the immediate area of the prison and been absorbed back into society. Yet we all know intuitively and without a moment's hesitation that the *Dorset Yacht* defendants would not have been found liable had the boys made good their escape, gone home, and then set forth a month later to steal or vandalise a boat. The "relationship with perpetrator" concept does not afford a felicitous explanation for this intuition, but the prior-conduct concept does. As indicated above, the prior-conduct principle carries with it the explanation that liability is limited to the risks that were created by the defendant's having incarcerated the boys.

(v) Liability Based on a Pre-Existing Relationship between the Defendant and the Victim

In all of the American states certain pre-tort relationships between the victim and the eventual defendant are viewed as sufficient to give rise to a general duty of protection that is broad enough to include protection against foreseeable risks of injury through the crimes and intentional torts of others. This may be the most frequently invoked of the exceptions to the nonfeasance rule. A mother must take reasonable care to protect her children; a school, its pupils; a jail, its prisoners;[219] a hospital, its patients; an employer, its employees; a common carrier, its passengers; and an innkeeper, his guests.[220] This listing is by no means exhaustive; the details of the putative pre-existing relationship will always be important. Thus, while most states would probably hold as a general matter that the relationship between a host and a social guest does not itself suffice to call upon the host to take affirmative steps to protect his guest, one of the leading cases held that two friends out for an evening of carousing owed each other a duty of reasonable care to guard against foreseeable risks of injury from others' intentional torts.[221]

[218] [1987] AC at 272: '[A] duty may arise from a special relationship between the defender and the third party, by virtue of which the defender is responsible for controlling the third party: see, for example, *Dorset Yacht*...'.

[219] See e.g. *Joseph* v. *State*, 26 P 3d 459 (Alas. 2001).

[220] See generally *Restatement (Third) of Torts: Liability for Physical Harm* §40 (Proposed Final Draft No. 1, 6 Apr. 2005).

[221] *Farwell* v. *Keeton*, 396 Mich. 281, 240 NW 2d 217 (1976).

There is a split of authority on the extent of the duty that an ordinary business owes to protect its customers against the risks of crimes and intentional torts. Some states recognise a full-blown duty of reasonable care that is sufficient to require the business to provide security precautions against generally foreseeable risks of crimes.[222] Others limit the duty to situations in which "the business has actual or imputed knowledge of an *impending* assault and the opportunity to prevent it".[223] In the latter group of states, hotels are treated differently than other businesses. A hotel in a high-crime area would owe a duty to protect its guests against the risks of injury from generally foreseeable crimes and intentional torts,[224] but an ordinary business in the same area would have no responsibility to a customer until seeing a specific criminal threat in the process of developing. "The distinction [between hotels and ordinary businesses] is no doubt rooted in the belief that business patrons of innkeepers, like those of common carriers and unlike those of other businesses, have entrusted their personal security to the innkeeper."[225]

7. RECURRENT PROBLEMS OF FACTUAL CAUSATION AND DAMAGES[226]

(A) FACTUAL CAUSATION IN GENERAL

In all torts cases (including not only negligence cases but also those based on intentional tort or strict liability) the plaintiff must normally prove by a preponderance of the evidence that identified substandard conduct on the defendant's part was *a* factual cause of the harm or result complained of. It is important to emphasise that the plaintiff is not required to prove that defendant's conduct was *the* cause of the harm. This would be an impossible burden, because "[e]ver since the first cause brought the world into being, no event has had a single cause".[227] The cause-in-fact burden is satisfied if the plaintiff shows that it was more likely than not that the defendant's substandard conduct was one of the causes of the accident or other result that the plaintiff complains of.

Usually the factual causation issue is solved by application of the but-for test, under which the defendant is not responsible for an injury that would have occurred regardless of whether the defendant had engaged in the wrongful conduct with which he is charged. For example, in a lawsuit claiming that the plaintiff's injuries resulted from an inadequate warning in an automobile operator's manual, the plaintiff's admission that he had never read any part of the manual was fatal to his case.[228]

222 See *Restatement (Second) of Torts* (1965), §344.

223 *Banks* v. *Hyatt Corporation*, 722 F 2d 214, 220 (5th Cir. 1984) (discussing Fla. and La. law) (emphasis added).

224 See, e.g., *Wassell* v. *Adams*, 865 F 2d 849 (7th Cir. 1989) (Ill. law).

225 *Ibid.*, 221.

226 See generally D. W. Robertson, 'The Common Sense of Cause in Fact' (1997) 75 *Tex. LR* 1765.

227 *Public Citizen Health Research Group* v. *Young*, 909 F 2d 546, 550 (DC Cir. 1990).

228 *Bloxom* v. *Bloxom*, 512 So. 2d 839, 950–51 (La. 1987). See also *Technical Chemical Company* v. *Jacobs*, 480 SW 2d 602 (Tex. 1972).

When *Baker* v. *Willoughby* came before the House of Lords, Lord Pearson responded to a defensive argument based on the but-for test by stating: "[I]t is formidable. But it must not be allowed to succeed, because it produces manifest injustice."[229] Lord Pearson was reminding us that occasionally the courts perceive that they must relax the but-for test in the plaintiffs' favour. This happens when that test would exonerate a defendant as to whom our sense of justice cries out that his causal contribution was sufficient to impose responsibility. In these situations the courts have at their disposal a number of familiar techniques for relaxing the but-for test. The relaxation may take the form of shifting to a "substantial factor" test.[230] It may take the form of shifting the burden of proof on the issue of factual causation to the defendant.[231] Or it may take the form of "unitising" two or more tortfeasors by treating each as vicariously responsible—for cause-in-fact purposes only—for the other's contribution to the injury as well as directly responsible for his own.[232] Each of these techniques for relaxing the but-for test is well settled in the decisional law. But each is narrowly limited to a specific range of situations. In almost all cases, the normal operation of the but-for test—which in its standard operation requires the plaintiff to prove by a preponderance of the evidence that, more likely than not, proper conduct on the defendant's part would have avoided the injury in suit—is deemed perfectly satisfactory, and whatever answer it yields is controlling on the issue of factual causation.[233]

(B) THE MARKET SHARE THEORY

Occasionally the but-for test will produce a strong sense of "manifest injustice" by exonerating a defendant under circumstances where none of the familiar relaxation techniques seems to work. American judicial responses to such situations have varied. Often the sense of "manifest injustice" will be suppressed and the defendant exonerated.[234] But

[229] [1970] AC 467, 495 (HL).

[230] See D. W. Robertson *et al.*, *Cases and Materials on Torts* (3rd edn., 2004), 126–30; *Basko* v. *Sterling Drug, Inc.*, 416 F 2d 417 (2d Cir. 1969); *Anderson* v. *Minneapolis, St. Paul & St. Ste. Marie Railway*, 146 Minn. 430, 179 NW 45 (1920); R. Peaslee, 'Multiple Causation and Damage' (1934) 47 *Harv. LR* 1127.

[231] See D. W. Robertson *et al.*, *Cases and Materials on Torts* (3rd edn., 2004), 130–5; *Pennfield Corp.* v. *Meadow Valley Electric, Inc.*, 413 Pa.Super. 187, 604 A 2d 1082 (1992); *Summers* v. *Tice*, 33 Cal. 2d 80, 199 P 2d 1 (1948).

[232] See D. W. Robertson *et al.*, *Cases and Materials on Torts* (3rd edn., 2004), 135–42; *Oliver* v. *Miles*, 144 Miss. 852, 110 So. 666 (1927).

[233] See, e.g., *Novak Heating & Air Conditioning* v. *Carrier Corp.*, 622 NW 2d 495 (Iowa 2001) (exonerating both the seller of an air-conditioning unit and the independent trucker who delivered the unit to the plaintiff in a damaged condition because, while the damage must have been caused by one or the other, the plaintiff could not show by a preponderance of the evidence that either defendant was more likely than not to have done it). Probably some courts would have solved this case differently by relaxing the 'exclusive control' requirement of the *res ipsa loquitur* doctrine. See D. W. Robertson, 'The Common Sense of Cause in Fact' (1997) 75 *Tex. LR* 1765, 1783–4. Doing so would have permitted the trier of fact to infer that each defendant was guilty of negligent conduct. The cause-in-fact issue could then have been addressed by the burden-shifting technique associated with *Summers* v. *Tice*, n. 231 above.

[234] See, e.g, *Kurczi* v. *Eli Lilly & Co.*, 113 F 3d 1426 (6th Cir. 1997) (Ohio law) (rejecting the 'market share' causation theory); *Novak*, n. 233 above.

some courts have been attracted to creative new approaches to the factual causation issue.

For example, a recurrent problem in the product liability context has involved the plaintiff who can show that she was injured by using a particular drug or other product; that the product was unreasonably dangerous and caused injuries to hundreds or thousands of consumers; and that the product was manufactured and distributed by a number of different companies whose identities are known. But the plaintiff has no way of showing which of these companies actually supplied the particular product that caused her individual injuries. In this situation an application of the but-for test in the normal way would exonerate any of the companies the plaintiff chooses to sue. To meet this "manifest injustice", several states adopted a "market share" causation theory, whereby a manufacturer can be held liable based on its proportional share of the overall distribution of the product.[235] The theory is controversial,[236] and some recent signals suggest that it may prove short-lived.[237]

(c) 'Probabilistic causation' and 'lost opportunity' theories

Another situation in which some courts perceive "manifest injustice" in the normal operation of the but-for test involves victims of medical malpractice who are unable to produce expert testimony that the wrongful conduct of the defendant probably caused the patient's death or other injury in question. Often the medical experts whose opinion testimony is necessary to establish causation in malpractice and similar cases will insist on expressing their opinion in the form of percentages. For example, rather than saying that the malpractice probably caused the patient's death, the expert may prefer to state that the malpractice deprived the patient of a 75 per cent chance of surviving.[238] When the medical opinion testimony is to the effect that the malpractice deprived the patient of a chance of surviving (or of avoiding whatever other undesirable consequences form the basis of the lawsuit) that was greater than 50 per cent, most courts are willing to "translate" this into an opinion that the malpractice probably caused the death (or other undesirable consequence).[239]

[235] See *Smith* v. *Cutter Biological, Inc.*, 823 P 2d 717 (Haw. 1991); *Conley* v. *Boyle Drug Co.*, 570 So. 2d 275 (Fla. 1990); *Hymnowitz* v. *Eli Lilly and Co.*, 73 NY 2d 487, 539 NE 2d 1069 (1989); *Martin* v. *Abbott Laboratories*, 102 Wash. 2d 581, 689 P 2d 368 (1984); *Collins* v. *Eli Lilly Co.*, 116 Wis. 2d 166, 342 NW 2d 37 (1984); *Sindell* v. *Abbott Laboratories*, 26 Cal. 3d 588, 607 P 2d 924 (1980).

[236] See generally D. B. Dobbs, *The Law of Torts* (2000), 430–2.

[237] See *Hamilton* v. *Beretta US Corp.*, 96 NY 2d 222, 750 NE 2d 1055, 1066–8 (2001) (significantly narrowing the New York version of the theory); *Sutowski* v. *Eli Lilly & Co.*, 82 Ohio St. 3d 347, 696 NE 2d 187, 187 (1998) (holding that '[i]n Ohio, market-share liability is not an available theory of recovery'); cf. *Restatement (Third) of Torts: Liability for Physical Harm* §28, *cmt.* o (Proposed Final Draft No. 1, 6 Apr. 2005) (discussing the virtues and drawbacks of the market-share theory and taking no position on its future).

[238] See *Hamil* v. *Bashline*, 481 Pa. 256, 392 A 2d 1280 (1978).

[239] See D. W. Robertson *et al.*, *Cases and Materials on Torts* (3rd edn., 2004), 146–7.

The real difficulty arises when the most the expert will say is that the medical malpractice made a less than 50 per cent chance still lower. Many courts will conclude against causation in such cases, on the view that the expert's statement amounts to an opinion that the malpractice probably did not cause the injury. But many other judges and commentators have perceived "manifest injustice" in this situation. Two techniques have been proposed for dealing with it. The first, called "probabilistic causation", is radical; it would hold the defendant whose wrongful conduct is shown to have cost the victim an appreciable but lower than 50 per cent chance of avoiding the injury in question liable for full damages.[240] Only a small minority of analysts think this approach has much promise.

The second approach is called the "lost chance" or "lost opportunity" theory.[241] It would allow partial recovery against a medical defendant who probably did not cause a physical injury but whose wrongful conduct can be shown to have damaged the patient's chances of avoiding the injury by treating the "opportunity" as itself a valuable interest, so that injuring *it* is redressable under the law of negligence.[242] The point bears emphasis: the theory classifies the loss of opportunity—i.e., the "reduction in likelihood of a more favourable outcome"[243]—as itself the injury for which recovery can be had.[244] The question of any recovery for the patient's and the patient's family's emotional suffering from learning of the squandered opportunity is an entirely separate matter.[245]

Courts in the United States are divided as to the validity of the "lost opportunity" theory.[246] The arguments over its desirability are coherent and respectable on both sides. Many observers believe that fairness and corrective justice arguments weighs rather heavily in favour of accepting the theory.[247] There is also a strong economic argument in the theory's favour:

A loss is a loss even if it is only probable, as are most things in life. No doubt Murrey [the deceased hospital patient in the case under discussion] would have paid a lot (if he had a lot

[240] In *Herskovits* v. *Group Health Co-Op.*, 99 Wash. 2d 609, 664 P 2d 474 (1983), the experts agreed that the malpractice reduced the victim's chances of survival from 39 per cent to 25 per cent. Two of the justices would have allowed full wrongful death damages in this situation. According to Professor Dobbs, there is a 'group of courts' that do this. D. B. Dobbs, *The Law of Torts* (2000), 435.

[241] See generally D. W. Robertson *et al., Cases and Materials on Torts* (3rd edn., 2004), 143–9.

[242] Four members of the *Herskovits* court (see n. 240 above) adopted this theory, whereby the defendant's liability would be calculated at 14 per cent of wrongful death damages.

[243] D. B. Dobbs, *The Law of Torts* (2000), 435.

[244] See n. 252 below for further elaboration of this point.

[245] See *Wickens* v. *Oakwood Healthcare System*, 465 Mich. 53, 631 NW 2d 686, 691 (2001) (Cavanaugh J, agreeing with the majority's refusal to allow a patient to recover for medical malpractice that reduced her chances of surviving cancer from 55 per cent to 15 per cent, but insisting that the patient should be allowed to recover for 'injuries suffered as a result of learning of her reduced life expectancy').

[246] See *Smith* v. *State Dept. of Health*, 676 So. 2d 543, 547 (La. 1996) (stating that the lost-opportunity theory 'has been recognised by a majority of the states'); *Grant* v. *American National Red Cross*, 745 A 2d 316, 321 n. 5 (2000) (DC) (stating that '[t]he majority of jurisdictions . . . have refused to recognize 'loss of chance' as a doctrine lessening required proof of causation'); *Kramer* v. *Lewisville Mem'l Hosp.*, 858 SW 2d 397, 400 (1993) (Tex.) (stating that seventeen states had accepted the lost-opportunity theory while eight had rejected it).

[247] For recent adoptions of the theory, see *Lord* v. *Lovett*, 146 NH 232, 770 A 2d 1103 (2001); *Jorgenson* v. *Vener*, 2000 SD 87, 616 NW 2d 366 (2000); *Holton* v. *Mem'l Hosp.*, 679 NE 2d 1202 (Ill. 1997) (Ill.).

to pay) for a 5 per cent chance of survival if the alternative was a certainty of immediate death. This shows that he lost something by being deprived of that chance. If 200 people were in Murrey's situation and received improper care, we would expect 10 to have survived if all 200 had received proper care, so that if none of the 200 was entitled to any damages the hospital would have escaped liability for malpractice that had caused a number of deaths in a realistic sense of "cause." Damages for loss of a chance are necessary to prevent the underdeterrence of medical negligence.[248]

On the other side of the debate are legitimate political and administrative concerns. In the United States medical malpractice liability is widely viewed as having helped to drive up health-care costs to an unacceptable level; presumably widespread adoption of the "lost-opportunity" theory would add to this burden. And the "lost opportunity" theory is potentially very complex. Its effect is to translate doubts about factual causation into a damages-reduction technique. Once this begins to be done, the courts may find it very hard to find a stopping place.[249]

(D) MULTIPLE TORTFEASORS GENERALLY

The presence of multiple tortfeasors often makes it easier for courts to solve problems of "manifest injustice" that are perceived to follow from the normal operation of the but-for test. For example, the technique of treating each tortfeasor as vicariously responsible (for causation purposes) for the other's wrongful conduct[250] is obviously confined to multiple tortfeasor situations.

For another example, consider a hypothetical case that is famous in academic circles. *A* negligently failed to repair the brakes on a car it had leased to *B*; *B* then failed to apply the brake pedal and ran down the plaintiff.[251] If the two cases are viewed entirely separately, the but-for test will exonerate each tortfeasor: But for *A*'s wrongful failure to repair the brakes, the plaintiff would still have been run down, because *B* did not try to use the brakes. But for *B*'s wrongful conduct in not using the brakes, the plaintiff would still have been run down, because the brakes would not have worked even if *B* had tried to use them. The solution to this situation is the insight that each tortfeasor's wrongful conduct has deprived the plaintiff of a viable cause of action against the other. If *A* had properly repaired the brakes, *B*'s failure to apply the brake pedal would then have been a clear factual cause of the injuries. Similarly, if *B* had applied the brake pedal, *A*'s failure to repair the brakes would then have been a clear factual cause of the injuries. Each tortfeasor's wrongful conduct has therefore damaged or defeated the plaintiff's cause of action against the other tortfeasor; each should therefore be liable for the plaintiff's

248 *Murrey* v. *United States*, 73 F 3d 1448, 1454 (7th Cir. 1996) (Posner J).

249 See e.g. *Hardy* v. *Southwestern Bell Telephone Co.*, 910 P 2d 1024 (Ok. 1996) (holding that the lost opportunity theory can apply only in medical malpractice actions).

250 See text and n. 232 above.

251 The hypothetical is based on *Saunders Sys. Birmingham Co.* v. *Adams*, 217 Ala. 621, 117 So. 72 (1928) (reversing a judgment against the rental company; the driver was not sued). See D. W. Robertson, 'The Common Sense of Cause in Fact' (1997) 75 *Tex. LR* 1765, 1787 and n. 97.

loss.[252] An alternative expression of this theory asserts that a tortfeasor whose wrongful conduct has created a serious or fatal defect in the plaintiff's potential case against another tortfeasor should be estopped from asserting the same defect in the case against himself.

The technique just described helps to explain the House of Lords' decision in *Baker* v. *Willoughby*.[253] First the defendant, a motorist, hurt Mr Baker's leg through negligent driving. Later a robber shot that same leg, necessitating its amputation. Visualise each of Mr Baker's potential lawsuits separately. Had Mr Baker sued the robber who shot his leg, the robber would have defended by saying that the leg was already damaged and virtually useless when he shot it. When Mr Baker sued the motorist who initially hurt his leg, the motorist responded by saying that we now know that the leg was soon to be lost in any event. Each of these defensive arguments, taken by itself, is valid.[254] But when they are viewed together, each of the two tortfeasors is seen to have greatly damaged Mr Baker's potential cause of action against the other; each should therefore be liable for the full value of the leg.[255]

The situation of the plaintiff in *Jobling* v. *Associated Dairies Ltd.*[256] was very similar to Mr Baker's, *except* that the second injury in *Jobling* did not emanate from a second tortfeasor but from implacable nature. This difference was crucial. The *Jobling* defendant negligently hurt the plaintiff in 1973. The injury disabled the plaintiff from working. Then in 1976 the plaintiff was overwhelmed by a new illness, unrelated to the injury caused by the defendant, that prevented him working and would have done so regardless of the defendant's injury. The trial occurred in 1979. In the House of Lords no respectable technique for avoiding the normal operation of the but-for test could be found. Inasmuch as it was known at the trial that the plaintiff would have been disabled

[252] The above-sketched approach has sometimes been called a 'deprivation-of-cause-of-action' approach. D. W. Robertson, 'The Common Sense of Cause in Fact' (1997) 75 *Tex. LR* 1765, 1787–9. Another name for it is the 'remedy-impairment' theory. D. W. Robertson *et al., Cases and Materials on Torts* (3rd edn., 2004), 134. Some commentators see the approach as too contrived or clever to be useful. See, e.g., R. Wright, 'Causation in Tort Law' (1985) 73 *Cal. LR* 1735, 1787, 1801. But the approach is familiar thinking in many analogous areas. See generally R. Peaslee, 'Multiple Causation and Damage' (1934) 47 *Harv. LR* 1127; see also *The T. J. Hooper*, 60 F 2d 737, 739 (2d Cir. 1932) (Learned Hand J, sketching the remedy-impairment approach). Moreover, it has a modern analogy in the 'lost opportunity' cases treated above in Section 7(c). Both the remedy-impairment technique and the lost-opportunity technique enable plaintiffs to bypass insurmountable difficulties in proving factual causation of a physical harm by recharacterising the injury in suit as harm to an expectation. (The analogy reveals an unexplored difficulty, though: perhaps both theories are incompatible with the rules (treated above in Section 4) that generally prohibit recovery in negligence for pure economic loss.)

[253] [1970] AC 467.

[254] The robber's is a standard 'preexisting condition' argument of the sort that is typically accepted. See, e.g., *Follett* v. *Jones*, 252 Ark. 950, 481 SW 2d 713 (1972) (holding that the wrongful death damages awardable against a road-traffic tortfeasor who negligently struck a man with terminal cancer must be limited to the extent, if any, by which the traffic accident further shortened the victim's already much-shortened life expectancy). The motorist's is the 'looming threat' variation of that argument. See D. W. Robertson *et al., Cases and Materials on Torts* (3rd edn., 2004), 162–3; J. King, 'Causation, Valuation, and Chance in Personal Injury Torts involving Preexisting Conditions and Future Consequences' (1981) 90 *Yale LJ* 1353. For further discussion of the relationship between these two types of defensive arguments see Section 7(f) below.

[255] For a similar explanation of *Baker*, see Lord Keith's speech in *Jobling* v. *Associated Dairies Ltd.* [1982] AC 794, 815.

[256] [1982] AC 794.

from working regardless of the injury inflicted by the defendant, the defendant could not be said to be a factual cause of the lost earnings except for the interval between the 1973 injury and the manifestation of the 1976 illness. Had the 1976 illness resulted from the negligence of a second tortfeasor, the *Baker* technique would have been available as a way of awarding full compensation.

(E) JOINT AND SEVERAL LIABILITY

Another approach to the factual causation issue that is confined to multiple tortfeasor situations is provided by a doctrine of "joint and several liability". In its standard operation this doctrine does not address the issue of factual causation. This subsection looks at cases where it does.

(i) The Standard Operation of the Doctrine of Joint and Several Liability

The standard operation of the joint and several liability doctrine is illustrated by a case in which a passenger on a coach is hurt in a collision between the coach and a railway train.[257] Neither the coach operator nor the locomotive engineer is keeping a proper lookout. Both are liable to the plaintiff, because each is guilty of negligent conduct that was a but-for cause of the plaintiff's harm, *viz.*, each could have avoided the collision by using reasonable care. There is no need for resort to any causation test other than the but-for test in standard form. Once factual causation (and the other four elements of negligence liability) are seen to be established against each of the defendants, only then does the joint and several liability doctrine come into play. Its role is to provide that, while the plaintiff is entitled to receive no more than his total assessed damages, each of the defendants is responsible for that total. This means that the plaintiff can collect the total from either of them or from the two of them in any combination. (They may then be able to adjust the loss as between themselves through actions for contribution.)

The coach passenger case is the easy, standard case for joint and several liability. In that standard operation, the joint and several liability doctrine is not affecting the cause-in-fact issue. It is simply providing that the risk of insolvency of one of the judgment debtors rests on the other judgment debtor and not on the plaintiff. In recent times many states have altered the law of joint and several liability by using comparative fault principles in various ways to limit the ultimate exposure of each tortfeasor.[258] These changes do not affect the analysis of factual causation in multiple tortfeasor cases[259] and are not of immediate relevance to the present discussion.

(ii) Using a 'Joint and Several Liability' Approach to Solve Cause-in-Fact Problems

As we saw just above, the standard operation of the joint and several liability doctrine has nothing to do with the plaintiff's burden of establishing cause in fact. Nevertheless

257 See *Baylor University* v. *Bradshaw*, 52 SW 2d 1094 (Tex.App. 1932).

258 See D. W. Robertson *et al.*, *Cases and Materials on Torts* (3rd edn., 2004), 438–48.

259 See *ibid.*, 150–7; *Piner* v. *Superior Court*, 192 Ariz. 182, 962 P 2d 909 (1998).

the doctrine—or perhaps it would be more precise to say a very similar doctrine with the same name—has sometimes been put to the task of helping the plaintiff with the issue of factual causation. In the coach passenger case, the plaintiff sustained a single indivisible injury. But cases often arise in which the conduct of several tortfeasors has combined to cause injuries that are divisible in nature. When the facts provide a basis whereby the injuries can be segregated and causally apportioned among the defendants, this must and will be done. But when the injuries are theoretically apportionable among the defendants but not so as a practical matter—i.e. when the facts provide no basis whereby causal apportionment can occur—application of the joint and several liability doctrine provides a way whereby the plaintiff can meet an otherwise insuperable factual causation burden. For example, when pollution from two independent negligent sources drained into the plaintiff's lake, rendering it useless for watering cattle and killing the fish,[260] it seemed clear that each tortfeasor was a but-for cause of part but not all of the damage. Requiring the plaintiff to prove how much of the damage was caused by each tortfeasor would have resulted in exonerating the defendants, because as a practical matter the evidence necessary to apportion was simply not available. In such cases most American courts will agree that while the trier of fact should try very hard to apportion the separate damages between or among the tortfeasors whenever that is feasible, when apportionment is simply not possible the tortfeasors should be held jointly and severally liable for the entire damage.[261]

Note that the effect of using the joint and several liability doctrine against the tortfeasors in the polluted lake case is to hold each of them liable for some damages that we know the tortfeasor did not cause. If we were talking about tortfeasors who had somehow acted in concert in causing the pollution, the factual causation problem would be readily solvable by "unitising" them, i.e. by holding each tortfeasor liable for his own pollution and at the same time vicariously responsible (for cause-in-fact purposes) for the other's pollution.[262] But in the cases under discussion the tortfeasors are strangers to one another, and there is no honest way to construct a concert-of-action or other vicarious-responsibility treatment of them. Nevertheless, by treating the cluster of theoretically apportionable injuries that cannot as a practical matter be apportioned as though they constituted a single indivisible injury, the application of joint and several liability means that each tortfeasor can be made to pay for more harm than he actually caused.

A leading American case showing the reach of the joint and several liability doctrine to impose liability upon a tortfeasor for such a cluster of injuries is *Maddux* v. *Donaldson*.[263] Mrs Maddux suffered multiple injuries when her automobile was struck by Donaldson's vehicle and knocked into the path of Bryie's vehicle; the impact with Bryie's vehicle occurred about 30 seconds after the original collision. Mrs Maddux sued both Donaldson

[260] *Landers* v. *East Texas Salt Water Disposal Co.*, 151 Tex. 251, 248 SW 2d 731 (1952).

[261] See *Piner* v. *Superior Court*, 192 Ariz. 182, 962 P 2d 909 (1998); *Pang* v. *Ming*, 53 Ohio St. 3d 186, 559 NE 2d 1313 (1990); *Holtz* v. *Holder*, 101 Ariz. 247, 418 P 2d 584 (1966); *Maddux* v. *Donaldson*, 362 Mich. 425, 108 NW 2d 33 (1961).

[262] See text and n. 260 above.

[263] 362 Mich. 425, 108 NW 2d 33 (1961).

and Bryie but then discontinued the suit against Donaldson. The trial court dismissed the suit against Bryie because of the lack of evidence showing which of Mrs Maddux's multiple injuries were caused by the impact for which Bryie was responsible.[264] Reversing, the Michigan Supreme Court held that joint and several liability should be imposed, stating:

> [I]f there is competent testimony, adduced either by plaintiff or defendant, that the injuries are factually and medically separable, and that the liability for all such injuries and damages, or parts thereof, may be allocated with reasonable certainty to the impacts in turn, the jury will be instructed accordingly and mere difficulty in doing so will not relieve the triers of the facts of this responsibility [of apportionment]. But if, on the other hand, the triers of the facts conclude that they cannot reasonably make the division of liability between the tortfeasors,... we have, by their own finding, nothing more than an indivisible injury [for which the tortfeasors are jointly and severally liable].[265]

In other words, if it is impossible as a practical matter to apportion the various parts of a cluster of theoretically separable injuries, the cluster will be treated as though it were a single indivisible injury.[266]

Viewed through American eyes, *Fitzgerald* v. *Lane*[267] appears to be functionally indistinguishable from *Maddux*. The House of Lords' determination to hold each of two motorists liable for Mr Fitzgerald's full damages (less a reduction to reflect his own contributory fault) would not strike most American judges or commentators as in any way problematic. The law of negligence strives with some diligence to avoid extracting damages from a tortfeasor whose conduct has probably caused *no* harm, no matter how faulty the conduct. But a defendant whose tortious conduct is known to have caused some significant harm to the plaintiff can sometimes be held liable for additional harm without unduly offending judicial sensibilities.[268]

(F) PRE-EXISTING CONDITIONS AND LOOMING THREATS

"Every victim of tortious conduct inevitably brings to the transaction a tangle of preexisting conditions."[269] It is common ground in England and the United States that the tortfeasor should not be held liable for the effects of the pre-existing conditions.

264 In a suit against Donaldson this problem would not have arisen. Donaldson's negligent conduct was a but-for cause of both the original impact with his vehicle and of the subsequent impact with the Bryie vehicle. Bryie, of course, made no causal contribution to the original impact.

265 108 NW 2d at 36–8.

266 In the multiple-car-wreck context a recurrent question will be how close in time the impacts or accidents must be to legitimate the use of the joint-and-several-liability technique to cure the plaintiff's factual causation problem. As noted above, the two impacts in *Maddux* were about thirty seconds apart. The court in *Holtz* v. *Holder*, 101 Ariz. 247, 418 P 2d 584 (1966), used the technique when the two collisions were five to ten minutes apart. In *Piner* v. *Superior Court*, 192 Ariz. 182, 962 P 2d 909 (1998), the technique was used when plaintiff's tangle of injuries stemmed from two rear-ending incidents separated by four or five hours. In *Potts* v. *Little*, 171 Ariz. 98, 828 P 2d 1239 (1991), the court thought thirteen days was too much separation. But the court in *Pang* v. *Ming*, 53 Ohio St. 3d 186, 559 NE 2d 1313 (1990), applied the technique against traffic tortfeasors responsible for three separate wrecks spread over a five-month period.

267 [1989] AC 328 (HL).

268 See text and n. 29 above.

269 J. King, 'Causation, Valuation, and Chance in Personal Injury Torts involving Preexisting Conditions and Future Consequences' (1981) 90 *Yale LJ* 1352, 1354.

Thus in a typical case in which a roadway accident injured the shoulder of a man who already had shoulder problems, the court stressed that the damages assessed against the defendant should not include the original condition but only the new effects of the accident for which the defendant was responsible, stating that "courts recognize that a defendant whose acts aggravate a plaintiff's preexisting condition is liable only for the amount of harm actually caused by the negligence."[270] Thus also, in *Jobling* v. *Associated Dairies*[271] Lord Wilberforce began his analysis of the issue presented in that case by stating that if the 1976 illness had been the result of a dormant condition that pre-existed the injury brought about by the defendant in 1973, "it is not disputed that it would have had to be taken into account."[272]

The complication in *Jobling* was that the 1976 illness was *not* the result of a condition that pre-existed the original injury "but a [new] disease supervening after that event."[273] In other words, at the point in time at which the defendant's negligent conduct hurt the plaintiff, the 1976 illness was not a pre-existing condition but merely a future contingency or threat. In both England and the United States the judicial treatment of such contingencies or threats has been somewhat less clear than the firm rule that holds that the defendant should not be made to pay for the effects of actual conditions that pre-existed the tort. But the following discussion will show that the two problems raise identical policy issues and should take the same treatment.

If an innocent pedestrian is killed by a negligent motorist as the pedestrian is walking to board an aeroplane that later takes off on time and crashes, killing all aboard, traditional judicial attitudes will be quite impatient with the negligent motorist's argument that the life he took was essentially worthless because his victim was only a short aeroplane ride away from dying in any event. On the other hand, if a skydiver whose parachute has failed to open should happen to be shot by a negligent sportsman just a second before hitting the ground, the sportsman will probably end up owing no tort damages.[274] The difference between the two situations is easy to grasp intuitively;[275] some threats are far enough advanced at the time the defendant's wrongful conduct harms the plaintiff to demand to be taken into account, and others are not. "The operative line—roughly speaking, the line between future contingencies [that can be ignored] and imminent threats [that have to be factored in]—cannot be described with precision, but the rule is roughly this: We will take into account only those threats that

270 *Lamoureaux* v. *Totem Ocean Trailer Express, Inc.*, 632 P 2d 539, 544 (1981) (Alas.). See also n. 254 above.

271 See n. 256 above.

272 [1982] AC at 802.

273 *Ibid.*

274 The leading case in the United States is *Dillon* v. *Twin State Gas & Electric Co.*, 85 NH 449, 163 A 111 (1932), in which (on one view of the facts) the defendant's negligent conduct electrocuted a boy after he was already in the process of falling to his certain death from a high bridge. The court reasoned that on that factual scenario the defendant's conduct had not deprived the boy of anything of value. A member of the court that decided *Dillon* later wrote a celebrated law review article based on the case. See R. Peaslee, 'Multiple Causation and Damage' (1934) 47 *Harv. LR* 1127.

275 See W. P. Keeton *et al.*, *Prosser and Keeton on Torts* (5th edn., 1984), 353: 'There is a clear distinction between a person who is standing in the path of an avalanche when the defendant shoots to kill, and one who is about to embark on a steamship doomed later to strike an iceberg and sink. The life of the latter has value at the time, as any insurance company would agree, but that of the former has none.'

are so far advanced and so nearly certain at the time of the accident that any attempt to ignore their functional identity with preexisting conditions would seem dishonest."[276] With relief, we ignore other contingencies. "The retrospective conjuring up of events contingent at the time of injury would open the door to absurd results. Allowing such contingencies to affect valuation would create a rule that could not be administered."[277]

In 1973, when the defendant's negligent conduct injured the victim in *Jobling* v. *Associated Dairies*, the 1976 illness was far in the unknowable future and hence wholly contingent. Had the trial occurred in 1975, no court would have regarded the possibility that some illness other than the one the defendant caused might soon disable the plaintiff as calling for any significant limitation of the plaintiff 's damages. But at the time of trial in 1979, the 1976 illness could no longer be regarded as a contingency because "a court must not speculate when it knows the facts, and must therefore have regard to relevant events, which have occurred before trial."[278] That principle was also recognised in *Baker* v. *Willoughby*: "There is no doubt that it is proper to lead evidence at the trial as to any events or developments between the date of the accident and the date of the trial which are relevant for the proper assessment of damages."[279]

The *Jobling* victim's later illness and the *Baker* victim's later shooting injuries, each highly contingent at the time of the injury, were both fully certain by the time of the trial. This certainty meant that the effects of the later event were indistinguishable in principle from the effects of a medical condition that pre-existed the events in which the defendant injured the victim. The now-known-to-be-certain future events had to be taken into account, just as pre-existing conditions (and imminent threats) have to be taken into account, in order to avoid offending the principle that a tortfeasor should not be made to pay for something that we know he had nothing to do with. It was only because the future event in *Baker* emanated from a potential tortfeasor that the court was able to find a way (and perceive it as fair) to make the defendant pay for the effects of that event.

8. THREE POSTSCRIPTS

(A) THE RELATIONSHIP BETWEEN INTENTIONAL TORTS AND NEGLIGENCE

The traditional model (see Section 2 above) defines negligent conduct as any conduct that is unreasonable under the circumstances. This definition includes no requirement of inadvertence or accident. Thus, no conceptual or definitional barrier prevents the

276 D. Robertson, 'The Common Sense of Cause in Fact' (1997) 75 *Tex. LR* 1765, 1798.

277 J. King, 'Causation, Valuation, and Chance in Personal Injury Torts involving Preexisting Conditions and Future Consequences' (1981) 90 *Yale LJ* 1353, 1358.

278 [1982] AC at 807 (Lord Edmund-Davies). See also *ibid.*, 813: '[T]he court will not speculate when it knows, so that when an event within its scope has actually happened prior to the trial date, that event will fall to be taken into account in the assessment of damages' (Lord Keith of Kinkel).

279 [1970] AC at 490 (Lord Reid).

victim of a deliberate punch in the nose (a classic case of the intentional tort of battery) from calling the assailant's conduct negligence if he so chooses. As Professor Dobbs has recently emphasised, "the plaintiff can assert that *any* conduct counts as negligence."[280] This does not mean that by doing so the plaintiff can defeat an insurance-policy exclusion of coverage for assault and battery,[281] or a shorter statute of limitations for battery than for negligence,[282] or a statute immunising the defendant from liability for claims arising out of assault and battery.[283] But there is no need to characterise such limitations as emanating from a different realm of governance than the law of negligence. On the contrary, they merely carve part of the realm of negligence (that part that is overlapped by the realm of intentional torts) away for special treatment in limited respects. One frequently encounters the view that "[t]he theories of negligence and intentional tort are contradictory and mutually exclusive."[284] The view is easy to sympathise with because of the vernacular meaning of the word negligence. But it introduces a conceptual difficulty that can induce confusion[285] and serves no useful purpose.

(B) IN THE LIFE OF THE LAW THERE IS SOMETIMES PROGRESS

In 1959 the Supreme Court of Pennsylvania handed down its decision in *Yania* v. *Bigan*,[286] an infamous case for its exoneration of "morally reprehensible conduct"[287] and for being perhaps the "wors[t]" of the nonfeasance (no-duty-to-act) cases.[288] The parties to this case were both engaged in strip-mining operations for coal. These operations created deep water-filled pits that required periodic pumping out. After Yania had finished helping Bigan repair Bigan's water-removal pump, Bigan through "urging, enticing, taunting and inveigling" caused Yania to jump into the pit.[289] Bigan then stood by and watched as Yania struggled and drowned. Upholding the trial court's dismissal of Yania's widow's and children's wrongful death action, the court exonerated Bigan from responsibility for negligence in taunting and enticing Yania into the water by stating without explanation that "such conduct directed to an adult in full possession of all his mental faculties [simply cannot] constitute . . . actionable negligence."[290] (Presumably this was the court's version of the sole proximate cause fallacy treated above in Section 2.) The court then exonerated Bigan from responsibility for failing to help Yania once it

280 D. B. Dobbs, *The Law of Torts* (2000), 258 (emphasis in original).

281 See generally E. S. Pryor, 'The Stories We Tell: Intentional Harm and the Question for Insurance Funding' (1997) 75 *Tex. LR* 1721.

282 See e.g. *Ghassemieh* v. *Schafer*, 52 Md.App. 31, 447 A 2d 84 (1982).

283 See e.g. 28 USC §2680(h).

284 *B.P. Chemicals Ltd.* v. *Jiangsu Sopo Corp.*, 285 F 3d 677, 685 (8th Cir. 2002) (quoting *Hockensmith* v. *Brown*, 929 SW 2d 840, 845 (Mo.App. 1996), and citing *Restatement (Second) of Torts* (1965), §282, *cmt.* d).

285 See, e.g., *Ghassemieh* v. *Schafer*, 52 Md.App. 31, 447 A 2d 84 (1982).

286 397 Pa. 316, 155 A 2d 343 (1959).

287 W. P. Keeton *et al.*, *Prosser and Keeton on Torts* (5th edn., 1984), 535.

288 *Ibid.*, 375 n. 22.

289 397 Pa. at 319 (quoting the plaintiffs' complaint).

290 *Ibid.*, 320. Incidentally, the court's statement, while bizarre in its specific content, does help to corroborate that negligence is routinely conceived as potentially embracing deliberate conduct. See Section 8(a) above.

became evident that he was drowning by stating that "[t]he mere fact that Bigan saw Yania in a position of peril in the water imposed upon him no legal, although a moral, obligation or duty to go to his rescue."[291] (This shows that the prior-conduct principle—treated above in Section 6(c)(ii)—was not yet recognised in Pennsylvania.)

In 2003 the Supreme Court of Illinois court produced a decision on facts that were remarkably evocative of *Yania*'s. A 16-year-old girl named Elizabeth Wakulich went to visit two men friends (aged 18 and 21), who "by offering monies, by goading, and by applying great social pressure" induced Elizabeth to drink an entire quart of liquor.[292] The men then did virtually nothing for Elizabeth as she lapsed into unconsciousness, vomited copiously, and died. The court exonerated the men from responsibility for causing Elizabeth to drink the liquor on concluding that "[t]hrough its passage and continual amendment of the Dramshop Act, the [Illinois legislature] has preempted the entire field of alcohol-related liability."[293] (The Illinois Dramshop Act includes a provision that "[n]othing in this Act shall be construed to confer a cause of action for injuries to the person or property of the intoxicated person."[294] Here we are perhaps reminded of the human and social impact of what some jurists have decried as "appalling special interest legislation."[295]) The court then turned to Elizabeth's mother's alternative theory of liability: that the defendants' failure to help Elizabeth after she became ill and lost consciousness was actionable under the volunteer exception to the nonfeasance rule (see Section 6(c)(iii) above).[296] The court upheld the viability of this cause of action, indicating that if the facts alleged in the plaintiffs' complaint were true, the defendants had voluntarily undertaken to care for Elizabeth after she became unconscious and then failed to exercise due care in the performance of that "undertaking." The court handled the volunteer exception's "worsening" requirement as follows:

> Here, plaintiff has alleged that defendants failed to summon aid by contacting Elizabeth's parents, failed to otherwise obtain medical assistance that evening or the following morning when she was still unconscious, and prevented other persons from obtaining aid, proximately causing her death. These allegations, liberally construed, sufficiently allege that defendants' conduct "increased the risk of harm" to Elizabeth.[297]

(C) THE SOCIO-POLITICAL ROLE OF NEGLIGENCE LAW

It is widely recognised that in the United States court-administered tort law is used to address a broad range of social and political problems that other societies remit to different mechanisms. The present reality in this respect is complex. While many

[291] *Ibid.*, 321–2.
[292] *Wakulich* v. *Mraz*, 203 Ill. 2d 223, 785 NE 2d 843, 846 (2003).
[293] 751 NE 2d at 848.
[294] 235 ILCS 5/6–21(a).
[295] See n. 177 above.
[296] The prior-conduct exception (see Section 6(c)(ii) above) would seemingly have been a stronger theory, but it was evidently not urged and was not considered by the court.
[297] 785 NE 2d at 856.

"important socio-political issues [that] have come to the fore in the second half of the twentieth century [would seem to be] grist for the tort law mill, . . . often tort law has been [replaced] as the central mechanism by which [American] society deals with the problem."[298] Some of the replacement mechanisms are extra-legal, perhaps reflecting an emerging awareness that "[l]aw cannot effectively solve all problems. Even issues capable of legal resolution are sometimes resolved outside the law by community standards and practices that do not depend heavily upon formal tort law."[299]

Moreover, other forms of legal regulation have been devised for some problems that might have been left to the law of negligence.[300] An evocative example of an alternative legal mechanism may be seen in the recent decision of the United States Court of Appeals for the Ninth Circuit in *Newman* v. *Sathyavaglswaran*,[301] in which parents complained that the Los Angeles County Coroner's office had harvested their dead children's corneas without permission. Viewed most straightforwardly, this was a case of negligent (or perhaps intentional[302]) infliction of emotional distress. But the plaintiffs instead successfully characterised the wrong to them as an unconstitutional taking of their property without due process of law.[303]

Another example is *Biddle* v. *Warren*,[304] in which a hospital shared the confidential medical records of thousands of its patients with an avaricious lawyer who wanted to file claims in the patients' names for government-funded medical payments. The court said this breach of confidentiality was a "palpable wrong" but that efforts to make it fit within "traditional or accepted legal theories", such as negligence, were like "trying to fit a round peg into a square hole."[305] The court's solution was to create what it viewed as a brand-new tort, stating: "We hold that in Ohio, an independent tort exists for the unauthorized, unprivileged disclosure to a third party of nonpublic medical information that a physician or hospital has learned within a physician–patient relationship."[306]

298 S. D. Sugarman, 'A Century of Change in Personal Injury Law' (2000) 88 *Cal. LR* 2403, 2416.

299 D. B. Dobbs, *The Law of Torts* (2000), 257. While in some respects the realisation that law cannot solve all problems may fairly be characterised as emergent, it is also true (and always has been) that the majority of Americans have never seen the inside of a lawyer's office and wisely shudder at the prospect.

300 Professor Dobbs sketches a wide range of these (*ibid.*, 1097–113), including workers' compensation, social security disability benefits, and specialised statutes such as the Black Lung Act, 30 USC §901 ff. and the National Childhood Vaccine Injury Act, 42 USC §300aa–1 ff.

301 287 F 3d 786 (9th Cir.), *cert. denied*, 537 US 1029 (2002).

302 The requirement of *intent* is satisfied for most intentional torts by showing that the defendant must have known that his conduct would cause the harmful or forbidden consequence. See *Restatement (Third) of Torts: Liability for Physical Harm* §1(b) (Proposed Final Draft No. 1, 6 Apr. 2005).

303 42 USC §1983 provides in pertinent part that '[e]very person who, under color of any statute, ordinance, regulation, custom, or usage, of any State . . . , subjects . . . any citizen of the United States . . . to the deprivation of any rights, privileges, or immunities secured by the Constitution and laws, shall be liable to the party injured in an action at law'. The potential advantages this theory offered to the *Newman* plaintiffs included side-stepping tort law's restrictions on recovery for nervous shock (see Section 5 above), defeating any immunity from tort liability the Coroner may have enjoyed as an agent of government under state law, and providing a basis for invoking the jurisdiction of a federal rather than a state court.

304 86 Ohio St. 3d 395, 715 NE 2d 518 (1999). 305 715 NE 2d at 522.

306 *Ibid.*, 523. The court's only explanation for not placing this 'new' tort within the realm of negligence law was the observation that 'negligence [is] designed to protect . . . interests that only coincidentally overlap with

The existence and evolution of a variety of legal and extra-legal mechanisms that may be viewed as supplementing[307] or even as displacing[308] the law of negligence is an extremely important point, but we should conclude with a reminder that because of its inherent flexibility and capacity for growth and adaptation, "[t]he concept of negligence and the set of rules that go with that concept dominate the law of torts."[309] *Grimes* v. *Kennedy Krieger Institute*[310] is dramatically illustrative. This started out as two separate cases in which the parents of children who had been harmfully exposed to the dangers of lead paint in low-income housing sued a research institute connected with the Johns Hopkins University for failing to warn them of dangers well known to the researchers, who were studying various lead-paint abatement methodologies, looking for the most cost-effective. The facts were complicated, but the gist of the lawsuits was that the researchers had stood by and watched as some of the children suffered levels of exposure that the parents could have avoided had they been told. Both trial judges viewed the matter as a nonfeasance case (see Section 6(c) above) in which the researchers had no duty to the children.

The two cases were appealed by the plaintiffs and consolidated for argument and decision in the Maryland Supreme Court. In an emphatic reversal of the trial courts' no-duty holdings, the Maryland high court said the researchers had used the children like "the canaries in the [coal] mines."[311] The court held that the relationship between "a research entity conducting an ongoing nontherapeutic scientific study [and] minor volunteer participant[s]" in the study is a "special relationship" giving rise to affirmative duties of reasonable care, which could well include the responsibility for giving an appropriate warning of known or reasonably anticipatable dangers.[312] Taking some pains to make sure that its broad message was heard and understood, the court emphasised:

> We . . . hold . . . that the very nature of nontherapeutic scientific research on human subjects can, and normally will, create special relationships out of which duties arise. Since World War II the specialness or nature of such relationships has been frequently of concern in and outside of the research community.[313]

that of protecting patient confidentiality': *ibid.*, 522. One might translate this as saying that the patients' injury was outside the normal boundaries of negligence law because it was neither a personal injury (they did not claim emotional suffering, just a right to confidentiality) nor an injury to tangible property.

307 See D. B. Dobbs, *The Law of Torts* (2000), 1096 (stating that the alternatives 'do not displace the tort system over a wide spectrum' but instead 'supplement it').

308 See S. D. Sugarman, 'A Century of Change in Personal Injury Law' (2000) 88 *Cal. LR* 2403, 2416: (stating that 'often tort law has been eclipsed as the central mechanism . . . ').

309 D. B. Dobbs, *The Law of Torts* (2000), 257.

310 366 Md. 29, 782 A 2d 807 (2001).

311 782 A 2d at 813. Raker J, concurring in the result only, thought the majority's criticisms of the researchers too extreme. See also L. F. Ross, 'In Defense of the Hopkins Lead Abatement Studies' (2002) 30 *Journal of Law, Medicine and Ethics* 50.

312 782 A 2d at 818–19.

313 *Ibid.*, 834–5.

PART III

SPECIAL FORMS OF NEGLIGENCE

6 Liability for Occupiers and Builders
7 Breach of Statutory Duty
8 Liability of Public and Statutory Bodies

6

LIABILITY FOR OCCUPIERS AND BUILDERS

1. INTRODUCTORY REMARKS

Until fairly recently the liability of occupiers towards persons injured whilst on premises was subject to a special regime. Its independence (as a topic and as a chapter in tort books) was largely due to the fact that its original rules evolved before *Donoghue* v. *Stevenson*[1] set the tort of negligence on its modern, expansive, mode and reflected a judicial desire to control legislation that fell under this heading. Today, occupier's liability is, essentially, part of the law of negligence in *statutory form*[2] which has materialised in the shape of successive legislative accretions. This means that prime importance must be attached to the wording of the statutes, assisted wherever necessary by reference to the preparatory publications of the Law Commission. In some respects the interrelationship of these statutory rules with those emanating from other areas of the common law, contract or negligence, must also be considered.[3] In practice, however, our topic, though largely in statutory form, has effectively been absorbed by the general principles of negligence[4] and the separate treatment accorded to it in this chapter largely reflects custom and convenience.

The law discussed in this subsection regulates the liability of an occupier of *premises*[5] towards persons *on* the premises and not to those outside them. Liability to the latter is often based on the common law rules of negligence, but may also overlap with nuisance (private or public), which will be dealt with in Chapter 13.

The Occupiers' Liability Acts of 1957 and 1984 are at present the governing statutes though, as will be seen, the protection they afford is by no means identical. The philosophy

[1] [1932] AC 562.

[2] Something which did not occur in the USA where, first in California—*Rowland* v. *Christian* 443 P 2d 561 (1968)—and then in New York—*Basso* v. *Miller* 352 NE 2d 868 (1976), moved the subject in the direction of the English reforming statutes but by assimilating the subject to the general law of negligence.

[3] See, for instance, *Maguire* v. *Seton MBC and Another* [2006] 1 WLR 250.

[4] And, indeed, the common law may still be relevant for liability under certain fact situations: see *Fairchild* v. *Glenhaven Funeral Services Ltd.* [2002] 1 WLR 1052 (CA).

[5] The word is given a very special and broad meaning by s. 1(3)(a) of the Occupiers' Liability Act 1957 so that it applies also to ladders, electricity pylons, grandstands, or diving boards, lifts, aeroplanes, and so on. See *Monarch Airlines Ltd.* v. *London Luton Airport Ltd.* [1998] 1 Lloyd's Rep. 403: it seems that 'premises' may include an airport runway.

of the common law, before it was reformed and (largely) rendered in statutory form, was the preservation of the freest use and enjoyment of land by the occupier—a cherished idea to the landowning class in England during the period when these ideas were being developed.[6] This led to a gradation of standards of care varying with the status of a person coming on to the land (which depended upon the purpose of the visit) rather than with the nature of the land, the risks encountered on it or the occupier's ability to obviate them.

Thus, the occupier's standard of care was at its highest towards *contractors*, that is, those who entered under a contract. Liability was based on an implied warranty that the premises were fit for the purpose contemplated by the contract. The standard was less onerous towards *invitees*, that is, those who shared with the occupier a mutual interest of a business or material nature, for example, customers in a shop. Towards them an occupier had to 'use reasonable care to prevent damage from unusual danger, which he knew *or ought to have known*'.[7] Towards *licensees*—a misleading term since a friend *invited* to a meal is not an invitee but a licensee—the standard was lower still. These were persons with permission to enter premises for some purpose of their own, as distinct from a mutual interest, or, where there was a mutual interest, one which was not of a business or material nature. The occupier was obliged only to warn them of any *concealed danger* or trap of which he *actually* knew. Obviously the dividing line between liability to invitees and licensees was far from easy to draw. For the twin requirements of mutuality of interest and its business or material nature created permutations which tended to be ignored, while the distinction between 'unusual dangers' and 'traps' defied elucidation. Also, 'actual knowledge' of traps was often stretched to mean 'ought to have known', thus blurring still further the distinction between invitees and licensees.[8]

Towards 'uninvited' persons (not covered by these three categories) the occupier used to owe no duty in negligence. The 'hostility' towards these persons, prompted by the nineteenth-century attachment to land and the belief to bolster its unfettered use and enjoyment, is clearly illustrated by the use of the biblical term 'trespassers' even though with the passage of time it became increasingly obvious that most of these unfortunate entrants were unattended children, anything but morally blameworthy or 'bad'. Later developments in the common law,[9] especially the passing of the Occupiers'

[6] See F. Bohlen, *Studies in the Law of Torts* (1926), 46.

[7] Per Willes J in *Indermaur* v. *Dames* (1866) LR 1 CP 274, 288. This increased protection is really the result of the mid-nineteenth-century idea that only 'bargains' could give rise to duties of affirmative action. But Willes J made it clear that the 'protection does not depend upon the fact of a contract being entered into . . .' (*ibid.*, at 287–8); and Canadian cases have extended this higher protection to a young child accompanying its mother on a shopping expedition: *Kaplan* v. *Canada Safeway* (1968) 68 DLR (2d) 627.

[8] See e.g. Asquith LJ's interpretation of 'actual knowledge' in *Pearson* v. *Lambeth BC* [1950] 2 KB 353, 364. *Stowell* v. *The Railway Executive* [1949] 2 KB 519 shows how licensees were sometimes turned into invitees, while *Fairman* v. *Perpetual Investment Building Society* [1923] AC 74 illustrates the strange results that were created by these distinctions.

[9] *British Railways Board* v. *Herrington* [1972] AC 877. In the past uninvited entrants were frequently and indiscriminately referred to as trespassers, but the implication that they were 'wrongdoers', undeserving of legal protection, was frequently not justified by the facts.

Liability Act 1984, considerably improved the position of such 'uninvited' entrants without opening the floodgates of recovery for unworthy claimants.

The above-mentioned capricious distinctions produced, not, reduced unnecessary litigation. They also became increasingly untenable as the socio-economic environment changed. With the passage of time they became virtually meaningless as a result of fictions invented by the courts in order to bypass them. So, in 1957 the legislature stepped in and removed many of the peculiarities of the old law. The 1984 Act has nearly completed this process. As stated, however, the changes have come in the form of successive waves and this accounts for a degree of complexity in the law which is unknown to systems that are outside the sphere of the common law and, doctrinally at least, have adopted a less rigid application of the liability rules dependant on the status of the entrant.

2. THE OCCUPIERS' LIABILITY ACTS 1957 AND 1984

(A) THE SCOPE OF THE ACTS

The drawback of the common law was that it fixed different standards of care *vis-à-vis* different types of visitors. With the passage of time and in order to avoid some of the unfairness thus created, judges began to distinguish between 'occupancy duties' and 'activity duties'. The former, which concerned the state of the premises, were indeed graded in the way described above; but the latter were concerned with what an occupier did on his premises rather than their state or condition and here the ordinary rules of negligence applied uniformly to entrants regardless of categories.[10] This distinction did not go far enough, so the first Occupiers' Liability Act 1957 (which according to s. 1(3)(a) applies to premises and movable structures) rolled contractors, invitees and licensees into a single category of 'lawful visitors' to whom an occupier now owes 'the common duty of care'.[11] Subsequently the 1984 Act provided further protection to entrants other than those covered by the 1957 Act.

[10] *Dunster* v. *Abbott* [1954] 1 WLR 58. See also *Riden* v. *A. C. Billings & Son Ltd.* [1957] 1 QB 46; affirmed [1958] AC 240. As some distinguished American tort lawyers have observed: '[t]hroughout the judicial consideration of these duties to trespassers, licensees, and invitees, the distinction between misfeasance and nonfeasance is recurrently drawn, and a duty of care is more readily found where defendant's conduct is viewed as involving dangerous activity than where it is looked on as a mere failure to take affirmative steps for plaintiff' protection': F. Harper, F. James and O. Gray, *The Law of Torts* (2nd edn., 1986), ii, 131.

[11] There has been some doubt whether this common duty of care replaced only the 'occupancy duty', or the 'activity duty' as well. The wording of s. 1(1) of the Act suggests the latter, whereas s. 1(2) suggests the former. The interpretation based on s. 1(2) (i.e. abolition of 'occupancy duty') should be preferred, for the Act was clearly meant to remove the subtle distinctions of the common law and it is clear that it deals with liability for dangers arising from the state of the premises, i.e. the occupancy duty. Activities remain unaffected, since in this instance there was no need for statutory intervention as the gradation between contractors, invitees and licensees was never relevant. *Dicta* by Brown LJ in *Ogwo* v. *Taylor* [1988] 1 AC 431, 438, support this interpretation. So does the judgment of Lord Goff in *Ferguson* v. *Welsh* [1987] 1 WLR 1553, 1563 (though he reached this conclusion by interpreting the wording of s. 2(2) of the 1957 Act). In the same case, however, Lord Keith, relying on the same section, took the view that: 'The safety referred to [in this section] is safety not only from dangers

One final point is that, in the words of Lord Gardiner LC in *Commissioner for Railways* v. *McDermott*,[12] 'occupation of premises is a ground of liability and is not a ground of exemption from liability'. This implies that there may be situations in which a claimant, suffering injury through the defective condition of premises controlled by the defendant, might recover for breach of a duty imposed on him *in some capacity other than that of occupier*.[13] Conversely put this means that the words 'state of the premises' limits the application of the Act[s] to breach of the occupancy duties. So a claimant, like the one in *Tomlinson* v. *Congleton Borough Council and another*[14]—injured because of his own misjudgement in attempting to dive in shallow water in an artificial lake on the occupier's premises despite the presence of prohibitive notices warning of the dangers—will not be able to complain that the injury was due to the 'state of the premises' and recover by relying on the Act[s].[15] He should find another ground for complaint which, in this case, he could not and thus failed.

(B) OCCUPIER

There is no definition in either Act of who is an 'occupier' so the common-law rules still apply. As one learned judge put it, the word 'occupier' is only a convenient label for the kind of relationship that gives rise to a duty of care.[16] Like all labels, however, it must be treated with caution. For example, a person may not be in 'occupation' as the word is understood in the law of property or landlord or tenant, but he may nonetheless be an 'occupier' for the purposes of one of the Acts. Nor is the owner of premises necessarily its 'occupier' under the Act.

What is decisive is *control*, which can exist with or without complete physical possession of the premises. Equally, merely irregular maintenance activities[17] or control over

due to the state of the premises but also known dangers due to things *done or omitted to be done* on them' (*ibid.*, 1559, italics supplied). Despite this divergence of opinion, the difference between the two views may, in practice, not be so important since the standard of care at common law and under the Act is the same. The view propounded in the text was recently reaffirmed by Neill LJ in *Revill* v. *Newberry* [1996] 1 All ER 291, at 297–8 (though the pronouncements of the learned judge are in the context of the 1984 Act, discussed below) and *Fowles* v. *Bedfordshire CC* [1995] PIQR P380.

12 [1967] 1 AC 169, 186.

13 E.g. occupiers carrying out structural alterations to buildings may be additionally liable for failure to comply with s. 38 of the Building Act 1984 (not yet in force). Sometimes these statutory duties may be strict duties. See e.g. the Education Act 1944, s. 10 (as amended by Education (Miscellaneous Provisions) Act 1948, s. 7 and Education Act 1968, s. 3(3) imposing on those in charge of schools a duty to keep them in good repair. *Reffell* v. *Surrey CC* [1964] 1 WLR 358 held this to be an 'absolute' duty).

14 [2004] 1 AC 46, [2003] 3 WLR 705, [26], [27].

15 In *Tomlinson*, after some discussion, especially in the Court of Appeal—[2003] 2 WLR 1120, 1137—it was decided in that case that the claimant was a trespasser on the defendant's land. This means that the observations in that case are, technically speaking, relevant only to the 1984 Act. The overall reasoning of Lord Hoffmann in the House of Lords in particular, however, suggests that the same ideas apply to the 1957 Act.

16 *Wheat* v. *Lacon & Co. Ltd.* [1966] 1 QB 335, 366, per Diplock LJ (affirmed [1966] AC 552). The existing case law understandably refers to the 1957 Act. In this context, however, there is no difference between the 1957 and 1984 Acts.

17 Such as cutting the grass outside a set of properties: *Prentice* v. *Hereward Housing Association* (unreported, 28 Apr. 1999; overturned by the Court of Appeal on other grounds: [2001] 2 All ER (Comm.) 900).

the main means of access to premises belonging to another[18] will not suffice as sufficient control to make out occupier status. The absence of sufficient 'control' thus explains why a landlord is not liable under the Occupiers' Liability Act (though he may, as we shall note further down, be liable under the Defective Premises Act 1972). The same is true of a time charterer[19] and, apparently, the chairman and secretary of a club.[20] There are, however, recent cases where the courts have allowed a claim to be brought against individual members of clubs as 'representative' of the club membership as a whole.[21]

A detailed discussion of who is an occupier in this branch of the law can be found in *Wheat* v. *Lacon & Co. Ltd.*[22] The defendants, who owned a public house, entrusted it to a manager under a service agreement that required him, *inter alia*, to sell their drinks on the ground floor. The manager was granted a licence to live on the first floor and to take in paying guests. There was no direct access between the ground floor and the accommodation on the first floor and there were separate entrances to the two parts of the building. A paying guest of the manager was fatally injured while descending an unlit and defective staircase on the first floor. His widow sued and the main issue was who was in occupation of that part of the premises.

On the construction of the agreement, the House of Lords held that there was nothing to prevent two or more persons from being occupiers of the same premises if they shared control. In such a case, each would come under the duty to lawful visitors depending on his degree of control.[23] In *Ferguson* v. *Welsh*[24] Lord Goff further suggested that if land is in the occupation of two (or more) persons, then an entrant can, in appropriate circumstances, be regarded as a lawful visitor *vis-à-vis* one occupier but not with regard to the other.

The possibility of joint occupation is well illustrated in *AMF International* v. *Magnet Bowling Ltd. and Another*.[25] Magnet Bowling, the first defendants, decided to build a number of bowling alleys. This was an expensive operation and it was agreed, *inter alia*, that AMF would retain property in all equipment and raw materials brought into any of these centres until the installation was completed. Magnet Bowling also instructed a firm of architects, the second defendants, to erect the buildings and agreed to send for AMF to build the alleys 'when the centre shall be ready to accept delivery of the said goods'. Following such notice AMF moved in, but its equipment was damaged by rainwater which entered the building through an imperfectly completed doorway.

[18] Access to a roof above a supermarket, through the defendant's window: *Bailey* v. *Armes* [1999] ECGS 21 (CA).

[19] *Ellis* v. *Scruttons Maltby Ltd. and Cunard Steamship Co.* [1975] 1 Lloyd's Rep. 564.

[20] *Robertson* v. *Ridley* [1989] 2 All ER 474. This case, however, poses a question that does not arise in the preceding two illustrations, namely, if the 'officers' of a club are not 'in control' of its premises, who is?

[21] *Murray* v. *Hibernian Dance Club* [1997] PIQR P46 (CA) and *Grice* v. *Stourport Tennis Club* [1997] CLY 3859 (CA).

[22] [1966] AC 552, especially in Lord Denning's speech.

[23] *Fisher* v. *CHT Ltd. (No. 2)* [1966] 2 QB 475 is a good illustration, as is *Andrews* v. *Initial Cleaning Services Ltd.* [2000] ICR 166 (CA).

[24] [1987] 1 WLR 1553, 1562–3.

[25] [1968] 1 WLR 1028.

Claims were made in contract (which is not relevant here) and in tort. One issue was who should be treated as occupier of the premises. The court took the view that both defendants were occupiers, and that the standard of care owed by each depended on their respective degrees of control. The point that there can be more than one occupier of premises is well settled, as is the rule that the degree of control will determine the level of care that will have to be attained by each occupier before the duty is deemed to have been discharged.[26]

Absentee ownership may not deprive the owner of 'control'. In *Harris* v. *Birkenhead Corporation* [27] the first defendant was a local authority carrying out a slum-clearance programme. Its practice was to brick up the ground-floor openings in all the houses it acquired so as to prevent vandals from entering and damaging the property. The house in question had been owned by the second defendant, managed for her by a reputable firm of estate agents, and occupied by a tenant, who kept it in a first-class condition. In July 1967 the local authority served on the second defendant a notice to treat and a notice of entry, but agreed to allow the tenant to remain until 23 December. The tenant left on the agreed date and within a few days the house became a prey to vandals. Before the local authority's employees entered the property the infant plaintiff entered through a smashed door, went to the top floor and fell out of a broken window, sustaining brain injuries. The court distinguished *Wheat* v. *Lacon* [28] on the ground that in the present case no one was in physical occupation of the premises after the tenant's departure and refused to hold the first and second defendants liable as joint occupiers. Since the immediate supervision and control and the power to permit or prohibit entry had passed to the local authority, it alone was deemed to be the occupier even though it had not actually or symbolically taken possession of the house.[29]

One may summarise the law by saying that the decision in each case, therefore, as to who is an occupier depends on the particular facts, the nature and extent of the occupation and the control exercised by the defendants over the premises in question.[30] Actual physical possession of the premises, however, may not always be necessary even though its presence tends to reinforce the existence of control.

(C) LAWFUL VISITOR UNDER THE 1957 ACT

According to section 1(2) of the Act the common duty of care is owed to 'lawful visitors' and also in respect of lawful visitors' property (s. 1(3)(b)). This section merely defines the *extent* of the occupier's duty, so one has to see whether a particular entrant exercising

[26] For a more recent confirmation of the rule, see *Collier* v. *Anglian Water Authority, The Times*, 26 Mar. 1983. But a self-employed painter who, while employed by a contractor, fell off the roof of the building he was meant to paint could not sue the contractor *inter alia* under the 1957 Act, since the latter did not 'occupy' the roof: *Page* v. *Read* (1984) 134 New LJ 723.

[27] [1975] 1 WLR 379. See also *Hawkins* v. *Coulsdon and Purley UDC* [1954] 1 QB 319 (requisitioning authority).

[28] [1966] AC 552.

[29] For another example see *Clare* v. *L. Whittaker & Son (London) Ltd.* [1976] ICR 1.

[30] See also *Bunker* v. *Charles Brand & Sons Ltd.* [1969] 2 QB 480. This case, involving a tunnel-boring machine, illustrates the wide definition of 'premises' given by s. 1(3)(a) of the 1957 Act.

a right would have been a 'contractor', invitee or licensee at common law and hence a lawful visitor.

A visitor entering premises pursuant to a contract is entitled to claim any higher protection that the contract may confer upon him. It is submitted, however, that the occupier's duty is, essentially, a tort duty and, therefore, the occupier should be allowed the defence of contributory negligence. [31]

A case that recently raised in an interesting manner the question of the possibility of a high contractual standard taking over from the lower, negligence-based 'common duty of care' is *Maguire* v. *Stefan Metropolitan Council and another*.[32] In that case, a local council (the first defendant) operated a leisure centre which included some exercise machines. Before entering a service contract with the manufacturers' local agents (second defendants), the council invited one of the latter's employees to inspect the machines which were found to be in good order with the result that a service contract was concluded between first and second defendants. Subsequently, a visitor at the centre was injured when one of the machines malfunctioned and he brought an action against both defendants. The action against the second defendant succeeded in negligence and no appeal was taken against this judgment. But the council was also found to be liable to the claimant on the basis of a warranty that the machine would be safe for the use it was designed. An appeal against this part of the decision of first instance was successful on the grounds that the judge had erred in implying a term into the contract between the claimant and the council which differed—was, in effect, stricter—than the terms of the common duty of care implied by section 5 of the 1957 Act. Citing *Sole* v. *W. J. Hallt Ltd.*[33] Rix LJ observed in *Maguire*:

> As I understand the purpose of this section [[34]], it is designed to *reduce* what was at common law the higher duty of an occupier to such persons entering by right of contract and equate them in this respect with other visitors.[35]

Persons entering *as of right* are also lawful visitors even though the occupier may object to their presence (s. 2(6)).[36]

[31] A visitor entering premises pursuant to a contract is entitled to claim any higher protection that the contract may confer upon him. It is submitted, however, that the occupier's duty is, essentially, a tort duty and, therefore, the occupier should be allowed the defence of contributory negligence. This is certainly the case where the claimant pleads his case in tort: *Sole* v. *Hallt* [1973] QB 574; and, arguably, should be so irrespective of how the action is pleaded: *Sayers* v. *Harlow UDC* [1958] 1 WLR 623 and *Forsikringsaktieselskapet Vesta* v. *Butcher* [1989] AC 852 (affirmed by the House of Lords, *ibid.*, 890 ff.).

[32] [2006] 1 WLR 2550.

[33] [1973] QB 574, 578.

[34] Section 5(1) states: 'Where persons enter or use, or bring or send goods to, any premises in exercise of a right conferred by contract with a person occupying or having control of the premises, the duty he owes them in respect of dangers due to the state of the premises or to things done or omitted to be done on them, in so far as they duty depends on a term to be implied in the contract by reasons of its conferring that right, shall be the common duty of care.' The first defendant in *Maguire* had not breached this 'common duty of care' having asked a reputable—indeed the most appropriate person—to inspect the machinery.

[35] [2006], 1 WLR 2550 [19]. Emphasis added.

[36] N.B. those entering in exercise of 'rights to roam' under the Countryside and Rights of Way Act 2000 (as and when it enters into force) are not owed a duty under the 1957 Act but fall instead under a modified version of the regime of the 1984 Act: see s. 13 of the 2000 Act, which amends the current s. 2(4) of the 1957 Act.

Examples include policemen entering premises in execution of a search warrant (or in pursuit of fugitive offenders),[37] firemen attending a fire,[38] employees of public utilities (gas and electricity board employees entering to read meters), etc., properly pursuing their lawful duties. Where entry is the result of an invitation or express provision, the question concerning the entrant's status is simple and the main problem is usually whether the requisite standard of care has been satisfied. However, an entrant may be a lawful visitor even if he has entered the premises on an implied permission, and this can present considerable difficulties. The implied licence test is not easy to apply in practice. In *Lowery* v. *Walker*[39] the defendant owned a plot of unfenced land, which members of the public, including the plaintiff, used as a short cut. Although the defendant had often protested, he had never taken any serious action because most of the people involved were customers for his milk. The plaintiff was attacked by a wild horse which had been let loose in the field without notice. It was held that he was a licensee, not a trespasser, by virtue of implied permission to be there and so entitled to recover.

On the other hand, in *Great Central Railway Co.* v. *Bates* [40] a policeman on duty saw the door of X's warehouse open and a bicycle inside the premises. He went in with a view to removing the bicycle to safer quarters and fell into an uncovered hold. The court refused to entertain the idea of implied permission on the facts and hence he was not entitled to recover. The harshness of the decision can be explained, if at all, only by reference to the importance that the law attaches to the privacy of one's premises and the wish to discourage entries without properly executed warrants. Only in exceptional circumstances, for example a crime actually taking place, is even a policeman allowed to enter the premises. Atkin LJ's judgment[41] implies that the result *might* have been different had this been the case.

The willingness of courts, as in *Lowery* v. *Walker*,[42] to imply permission was often due to the severity of the common law towards trespassers prior to *Herrington* v. *British Railways Board*.[43] Along with the tendency to ascribe liability to an 'activity' of the occupier rather than to the 'state' of his premises, which made the status of an entrant irrelevant, they created a fictitious permission so that they could treat an entrant as a licensee rather than as a trespasser.[44] Now that trespassers, too, can recover in negligence, it may well be that implied permission will no longer be inferred so readily. However, even before the position of trespassers was improved, judges had begun to voice anxiety against undue eagerness to infer permission. In *Edwards* v. *Railway Executive*,[45] for example, Lord Goddard stressed that 'repeated trespass itself confers no licence' and a few years later Devlin J repeated the idea in *Phipps* v. *Rochester Corporation*.[46] 'Knowledge', he said, 'is not of itself enough to constitute a licence; there is a distinction between toleration and permission.'

37 Police and Criminal Evidence Act 1984, s. 17.
38 For instance Fire and Rescue Services Act 2004, s. 44 (2).
39 [1911] AC 10.
40 [1921] 3 KB 578.
41 *Ibid.*, at 581–2.
42 [1911] AC 10.
43 [1972] AC 877.
44 *Pannett* v. *P. McGuiness & Co. Ltd.* [1972] 2 QB 599, 605–6.
45 [1952] AC 737.
46 [1955] 1 QB 450, 455.

Difficulties arise when the claimant enters with the permission not of the occupier but of one of his employees. What kind of protection will the entrant receive if the employee acted contrary to instructions in giving permission? Suppose, for example, that an au pair girl, contrary to her employer's instructions, lets her boyfriend into the house one night. While going upstairs, he is injured through a defective tread. His rights might be affected by his status as a lawful visitor or as a trespasser, which will turn on the employer's 'right' to invite him to enter the premises. Thus in the analogous context of *Stone* v. *Taffe*[47] the entrant was treated as a lawful visitor and allowed to recover from the occupier. The Court of Appeal took the view that in such circumstances, provided the entrant was *bona fide*, he should be treated as a visitor rather than a trespasser, since the employee, though breaking his employer's instructions, was 'still in the course of his employment' according to the rules of vicarious liability. So long as the claimant *bona fide* believes that he is entitled to be on the premises, it might be more appropriate to use the terminology found in the law of agency. It might thus be more appropriate to say that he relied on the employee's *apparent authority* to invite him on the premises, rather than to put the emphasis on 'course of employment', which can be a vaguer concept. This, in fact, was the approach taken by the House of Lords in *Ferguson* v. *Welsh*. In that case an occupier A contracted with B to demolish property and to allow subcontractors on to the land *only* with A's consent. Acting *without* A's consent, B employed a subcontractor whose employee (the plaintiff) was injured while on the site. It was held that A had clothed B with ostensible authority to 'invite' the plaintiff. As a result, the plaintiff was the lawful visitor of A.[48] But if the plaintiff was aware, or ought to have been aware, of a prohibition and entered or remained on the premises despite this, he would become a trespasser.

Related to this problem is that of permissions limited by (a) space (or area), (b) time or (c) purpose of entry.

A person who has permission only to enter a certain part of premises has no permission to go to another part. In Scrutton LJ's words: '[w]hen you invite a person into your house to use the stairs, you do not invite him to slide down the banisters'.[49] The question, as always, must be approached with common sense. For example, a customer of a public house may use its lavatory and remains a lawful visitor while making a reasonable search for it.[50] Perhaps more controversially, a visitor who swam in a pond near a stately home on a National Trust estate seems to have been treated as a lawful visitor, due to the fact that his original entry on to the property was allowed and that the only notice declaring that bathing was not allowed was in the car park and was not prominently displayed.[51]

[47] [1974] 1 WLR 1575.

[48] [1987] 1 WLR 1553. In the event, however, the plaintiff's claim failed since the court took the view that the common duty of care had not been breached.

[49] *The Carlgarth* [1927] P 83, 110.

[50] *Gould* v. *McAuliffe* [1941] 2 All ER 527.

[51] *Darby* v. *National Trust* [2001] PIQR P27 (CA), although liability was rejected eventually because the risks of swimming there were so obvious that there had been no duty to warn about them.

Common sense should also be shown with regard to limitations in time. Thus, a customer who stays in a pub beyond closing hours and without the permission of the publican becomes a trespasser.[52] Occupiers of dwellings, for example, are usually taken to give implied licence to members of the public pursuing their lawful business to walk up the drive, for example, to sell goods.[53] If a licence is revoked the entrant must be given reasonable time to leave;[54] and, in any event, the revocation of the licence must be clear and unambiguous. Thus, in *Snook* v. *Mannion*[55] a policeman followed a motorist up the driveway of his house and asked to breathalyse him. The occupier turned and said 'Fuck off'. The Divisional Court took the view that the words that were uttered—which must be taken to have referred to the policeman's presence on the motorist's premises rather than merely to the attempt to breathalyse him—were *not* sufficiently clear to amount to a revocation of the licence usually implied allowing members of the public (including the police) to proceed from the (outer) gate to the door of a house on legitimate business. The existence of such a licence, however, may be in doubt if entry is expressly forbidden; notices like 'Private' or 'Keep out' may not be sufficient.[56]

Finally, an example of a limitation on the purpose of entry is *R* v. *Jones and Smith*,[57] where a son entered his father's premises and stole some goods. He was charged with burglary and the question concerned the application of section 9(1)(b) of the Theft Act 1968, which states that 'a person is guilty of burglary if having entered any building as a trespasser he steals or attempts to steal anything in it'. Given that the son had a general permission to enter his father's home, the question was whether he was a trespasser for the purposes of section 9(1)(b). The court held that he was, since he entered the premises knowing or being reckless as to whether his entry was in excess of any permission given to him.

A more recent example can be found in the aforementioned case of *Tomlinson* v. *Congleton Borough Council*.[58] There the claimant was injured while taking a plunge in an ornamental lake which was not meant to be used for swimming—and notices brought this to the attention of potential swimmers—though it could be used for the purposes of canoeing, kayaking and the like. The claimant who chose to dive thus became a trespasser. This can still leave unanswered the question 'at which point in time did the claimant become a trespasser?' When he started to paddle, decided to swim (if this was, indeed, possible) or took the plunge? If there is a duty (which can be discharged meaningfully) to stop the entrant from doing the prohibited act (which results in his injury), it could be argued that the injured entrant was, up until that moment a lawful visitor and may have be owed (the higher?) duty owed under the 1957 Act. Yet Lord Hoffmann was right to avoid this conundrum by arguing

> that the incidence and content of the duty should not depend on the precise moment at which [the claimant] crossed the line between the status of lawful visitor and that of trespasser. But there is no dispute that the act in respect of which [the claimant] says that he was owed a duty,

[52] *Stone* v. *Taffe* [1974] 1 WLR 1575.
[53] *Dunster* v. *Abbot* [1954] 1 WLR 58.
[54] *Robson* v. *Hallett* [1967] 2 QB 939.
[55] [1982] Crim. LR 601.
[56] *Christian* v. *Johannesson* [1956] NZLR 664, 666. Cf. *Snook* v. *Mannion* [1982] Crim. LR 601.
[57] [1976] 1 WLR 672.
[58] [2003] 3 WLR 705.

namely, diving into the water, was to his knowledge prohibited by the terms upon which he had been admitted to the park.[59]

The status of children gives rise to special difficulties. Infancy raises two problems: first, when does it convert a child into a licensee where an adult would be a trespasser? Second, assuming that the child is a lawful visitor, does infancy affect the standard of duty owed to him? The latter point is more appropriately discussed under the next heading, so here we shall discuss only the former.

In *Glasgow Corporation* v. *Taylor*[60] Lord Sumner said that 'infancy as such is no more a status conferring rights, or a root of title imposing obligations on others to respect it, than infirmity or imbecility'. The mere fact that the occupier has on his premises a dangerous object attractive to children does not make him liable to a trespassing child who meddles with it and gets injured. Yet the presence of such an object in a place accessible to children may aid the inference of an implied licence.[61] Prior to *British Railways Board* v. *Herrington*,[62] which recognised that trespassers, too, were entitled to some protection by the law of negligence, the courts often relied on this 'allurement doctrine' in order to imply licences. This enabled them to circumvent the old rule refusing a remedy to trespassers, and enabled them to compensate injured children. However, now that trespassers can recover in negligence, the 'allurement' doctrine is likely to be absorbed into the general consideration of what is reasonable in the circumstances (which will include the foreseeability of children) in the light of any attraction presented to them.[63]

(D) COMMON DUTY OF CARE

Section 2 of the Occupiers' Liability Act provides:[64]

> (1) An occupier of premises owes the same duty, the 'common duty of care', to all his *visitors*, except in so far as he is free to and does extend, restrict, modify, or exclude his duty to any *visitor* or *visitors* by agreement or otherwise.
>
> (2) The common duty of care is a duty to take such care as in all the circumstances of the case is reasonable to see that the visitor *will be reasonably safe* in using the premises for the purposes for which he is invited or permitted by the occupier to be there.

The duty imposed by subsection (2) was described by Lord Denning in *Wheat* v. *Lacon*[65] as 'simply a particular instance of the general duty of care which each man owes to his "neighbour"'.

59 *Ibid.*, [13]–[15]. 60 [1922] 1 AC 44, 67.

61 See Law Reform Committee Third Report, *Occupiers' Liability to Invitees, Licensees and Trespassers*, Cmnd. 9305 (1953). 62 [1972] AC 877.

63 This is not to say that the 'allurement' doctrine is now completely irrelevant. For a recent application of the doctrine, see *Jolley* v. *Sutton LBC* [1998] 1 Lloyd's Rep. 433 (upheld by the House of Lords on ground that the damage suffered was of a reasonably foreseeable type: [2000] 1 WLR 1082; [2000] 2 Lloyd's Rep. 65. N.B. that the Court of Appeal had expressly approved the reasoning of the judge at first instance on the allurement issue: [1998] 1 WLR 1546; [1998] 2 Lloyd's Rep. 240).

64 The italicised words make it clear that it is the visitor (not the premises) that must be reasonably safe.

65 [1966] AC 552, 578. For litigated illustrations see *Clerk and Lindsell on Torts* (18th edn., 2000) ss. 10–26 to 10–28; see, most recently, *Laverton* v. *Kiapasha (t/a Takeaway Supreme)* [2002] EWCA Civ. 1656; (2002) 146

Whether the duty, which—and this must be stressed given the general reluctance in Negligence to impose liability for omissions—covers acts *and* omissions, has been fulfilled is a matter of fact to be decided according to the circumstances. What was said about this in Chapter 3 applies here too. The magnitude of the risk, the likelihood of injury, the cost of avoiding it, the existence of warnings, the state of lighting or fencing, etc. will be taken into account.[66] But however widely defined, the duty cannot be expected to cover all possible 'defects' in the premises.[67] Moreover, two general observations must be made—and stressed.

First, no occupier owes a duty to protect entrants against risks that are patently obvious to any reasonable visitor.[68] Second (and conversely) there is, equally, no duty to protect visitors against of ordinary risks resulting from activities which they choose to engage in while on someone else's land. To do so, would be an unacceptable form of paternalism over an individuals freedom to engage in risky pastimes or activities.[69]

In *appropriate* circumstances an occupier may also be liable to one of his visitors for harm caused to him by another visitor. This is particularly likely to happen where the conduct of the wrongdoing visitor can be seen as a foreseeable consequence[70] of a breach of duty by the occupier himself. So, for example, in *Cunningham* v. *Reading Football Club Ltd.*[71] the defendants were held liable to police officers injured by hooligans who broke off loose pieces of concrete from the football ground and (as had happened in the past) hurled them at the police.

Section 2(3) specifically mentions two special factors: (*a*) an occupier must be prepared for children to be less careful than adults; and (*b*) an occupier is entitled to

SJLB 266; [2002] NPC 145 (CA) for a majority decision on the appropriate standard of care to require of a take-away shop owner in keeping his floor clear of excess water during a busy night's trading.

66 For a recent illustration, see *Murphy* v. *Bradford MBC*, *The Times*, 11 Feb. 1991. Whether lighting has been adequate gives rise to certain problems. The cases do not support a general rule putting an occupier of land under a duty to provide lighting at all times of darkness. The answer depends on the circumstances and, in particular, upon whether the visitor was invited to use the premises in the dark or not. So, a hotel visitor who was injured while searching in the dark for the lavatory was held entitled to recover: *Cabell* v. *Shelborne Hotel* [1939] 2 KB 534. But the claimant may have his damages reduced if wandering in the dark amounts to contributory negligence: see *Ghannan* v. *Glasgow Corporation*, 1950 SLT 2.

67 *Berryman* v. *Hounslow LBC* [1997] PIQR P83 (CA): broken lift in premises forced resident to walk up stairs carrying his shopping and thereby injure his back. Held: absence of a working lift was not a breach of s. 2 of the 1957 Act.

68 E.g. *Staples* v. *West Dorset District Council* [1995] PIQR P439.

69 A point stressed by Lord Hoffmann in *Tomlinson* v. *Congleton BC* [2004] 1 AC 46, [2003] 3 WLR 705, [46] where, in his own inimitable style, he also expressed forcefully his disagreement with the philosophically different stance adopted by Sedley LJ in his judgment in the same case in the Court of Appeal: [2003] 2 WLR 1120, 1135 at [45] where he said that it is 'only where the risk is so obvious that the occupier can safely assume that nobody will take it that there will be no liability'. The judgments of these two judges, which most commentators would agree are equally learned but philosophically positioned on the different sides of the conservative/liberal divide, offer interesting material for evaluating the linkage between political philosophy and opinion writing. Traditionally minded judges would play this link down if not deny out outright. We believe the matter deserves closer scrutiny.

70 This is why the court in *Skusa* v. *Commonwealth of Australia* (1985) 62 ALR 108 was right in refusing to hold the defendants liable as occupiers of a courtroom when a disgruntled litigant decided to shoot one of the lawyers in that case.

71 [1992] PIQR P141.

expect that a person exercising his calling will appreciate and guard against special risks 'ordinarily incident to it'.

With regard to (*a*), if a child is a lawful visitor he is owed the common duty of care, but reasonable care requires the occupier to take the characteristics of children into account. In the words of Hamilton LJ in *Latham* v. *R. Johnson & Nephew Ltd.*,[72] he should appreciate 'that in the case of an infant, there are moral as well as physical traps. There may accordingly be a duty towards infants not merely not to dig pitfalls for them, but not to lead them into temptation.'

In *Glasgow Corporation* v. *Taylor*[73] a seven-year-old boy died as a result of eating poisonous berries off a shrub in a public park. It was alleged that the local authority knew that the berries were poisonous and presented a temptation to young children. The corporation was held liable. As one would expect, every case turns on its own facts.[74] What is not a danger to an adult may well be one to a child. In *McGinlay or Titchener* v. *BR Board*[75] Lord Fraser said that 'the duty will tend to be higher in a question with a very young or very old person than in the question with a normally active and intelligent adult or adolescent'. For example, in *Moloney* v. *Lambeth London Borough Council*[76] an occupier was held liable to a four-year-old boy who fell through the bars of a balustrade. Since a person of the plaintiff's size was liable to go through the gaps, the staircase was held not to comply with the occupier's duty of care to a child of that age.

In the case of children another relevant circumstance is the degree of care which the occupier may assume will be exercised by parents.[77] In *Phipps* v. *Rochester Corporation*[78] the plaintiff, aged five, was walking across a piece of land which was being developed by the defendants. He fell into a trench which was obvious enough to an adult. Evidence was adduced to the effect that children frequently played there and that the defendants had done nothing to prevent it. Devlin J held that the plaintiff was a licensee, but refused to hold the defendants liable since he took the view that in measuring the care taken by the occupiers the habits of prudent parents should also be taken into account[79] along with all other relevant circumstances. The *Phipps* reasoning was applied more recently in *Simkiss* v. *Rhondda Borough Council*,[80] a case that shows that claimants may sometimes find themselves in a no-win situation. The action in *Simkiss* was brought by a seven-year-old girl who fell off a steep slope of land that lay opposite the block of flats where she lived with her family. In fact her father had left her there to picnic with a

[72] [1913] 1 KB 398, 415. [73] [1922] 1 AC 44.

[74] For illustration, see *Clerk and Lindsell on Torts* (19th edn., 2006), 12, ss. 12–34.

[75] [1983] 1 WLR 1427, 1432–3.

[76] [1966] 198 EG 895. Cf. the Building Regulations 1976 (SI No. 1976/1676), which imposed strict liability under s. 71 of the Health and Safety at Work Act 1974 (an enactment which imposes stringent requirements in this respect) (now to be found in s. 38 of the Building Act 1984, which has yet to be brought into force). See now the new regulations (SI No. 2000/2531) for further details.

[77] See, in similar vein, *B* v. *McDonald's Restaurants Ltd.* [2002] EWHC 490, where the court found that the vast majority of purchasers of hot tea and coffee would be of at least teenage years and thus well aware of the dangers of such hot drinks and their possible spillage, so that there was no duty to warn of such dangers, even where the injury was actually sustained by a child (paras. 63–9). [78] [1955] 1 QB 450.

[79] *Ibid.*, at 472. [80] (1983) 81 LGR 461.

friend since, according to his evidence, he had described the slope as not dangerous, adding that many children used to picnic on the spot. The plaintiff and her friend sat on a blanket they had with them and, apparently, were trying to slide down the slope when the accident occurred. The action against the local authority (occupiers of the land) for alleged negligence in failing to fence the area and to warn off the plaintiff was dismissed. The Court of Appeal took the view that this was not a concealed trap. If the plaintiff's father did not consider the area dangerous, the defendants could not be asked to achieve a higher standard of care. As stated, the claimant's position under the *Phipps* test is that he should carry the prime responsibility for leaving his child there without warning and adequate protection. On the other hand, if he states that the area is safe, then the implication is that in failing to take precautions to avoid the accident he cannot complain that the occupier was negligent.

This unfortunate predicament can and should be avoided if we accept that the father's assessment of the possible dangers is one but not the only crucial factor. The fact that the father may be unduly casual in assessing the degree of danger should not be sufficient to absolve the occupier. The dangerous state of his premises and the degree of care required to make them safe must be assessed objectively. But if the father's carelessness or indifference was a factor in the realisation of the child's harm, then the occupier's liability should be reduced rather than completely avoided, so as to avoid leaving the hapless child without any compensation whatsoever. When one considers how generous courts are these days towards *trespassing* children, the *Simkiss* judgment stands out as a rather harsh decision.

Section 2(3)(b) mentions the second consideration which is relevant when determining the occupier's standard of care: the occupier is entitled to assume that persons exercising a particular calling, trade or profession will guard against risks ordinarily incidental to it. For example, in *General Cleaning Contractors Ltd.* v. *Christmas*,[81] the plaintiff, a window-cleaner, was employed to clean windows. While he was standing on the outside of the wall and holding on to one sash of a window for support, the other sash came down on his fingers, causing him to let go and fall to the ground. He failed in his action against the occupiers. The decision might have been different had he been injured through some defect of the staircase when going upstairs in the ordinary way to reach the upper windows, for this would not be regarded as a risk ordinarily incidental to his job. Similarly, in *Roles* v. *Nathan*[82] two chimney-sweeps were killed by carbon monoxide fumes while sealing up a sweep-hole in a vertical shaft on the defendant's premises. Lord Denning said that:

> The occupier here was under no duty of care to these sweeps, at any rate in regard to the dangers that caused their deaths. If it had been a different danger, as for instance if the stairs

[81] [1953] AC 180. Note the words 'ordinarily incidental'. Thus, in *Bird* v. *King Line* [1970] 2 Lloyd's Rep. 349, a foreman scaler who tripped over empty bottles on the deck of a ship was allowed to recover for his injuries since the risk that had caused his injuries could not be described as ordinarily incidental to his job.

[82] [1963] 1 WLR 1117. See also *Phillips* v. *Perry & Dalgety Agriculture Ltd.* (unreported, CA), 6 Mar. 1997 and *Hannington* v. *Mitie Cleaning (South East) Ltd.* [2002] EWCA Civ. 1847, 26 Nov. 2002 (CA).

leading to the cellar gave way, the occupier might no doubt be responsible, but not for these dangers which were special risks ordinarily incidental to their calling.[83]

Special skills possessed by the entrant will not, however, automatically absolve the occupier of all liability. Indeed, a number of recent decisions dealing with injured firemen could be taken to suggest a certain judicial reluctance to utilise section 2(3)(b) and absolve too quickly, as some American courts do, the negligent occupier of all liability towards, for example, the injured fireman.

Thus, in *Salmon* v. *Seafarer Restaurants Ltd.*[84] a fireman entered a fish-and-chip shop to extinguish a fire. He was injured as a result of an explosion caused by leaking gas which, in turn, was the result of the heat generated by the fire melting seals on gas meters, leading to an escape of gas. The defendant/occupier attempted to argue that towards an entering fireman his duty was to protect him against some 'special, exceptional or additional risk' and not the ordinary risks that are a necessary part of his job. The court refused to accept this argument. Instead, it took the view that, though the fireman's special skills and training were relevant in determining liability, where it was foreseeable that (though exercising these skills) he would be injured through the negligence of the occupier, the latter was in breach of his duty of care. In such cases, the occupier should thus be liable to the claimant.

Among the various defences open to an occupier, section 2(5) of the Act expressly preserves consent (*volenti non fit injuria*)[85] and section 2(3) implies the defence of contributory negligence. Since both these are generally available in other torts, they will not be discussed here. But mention must be made of two defences peculiar to this branch of the law, namely warning and exclusion of liability.

Due warning may in appropriate circumstances discharge the occupier's duty of care; in others it may raise the defence of *volenti* or contributory negligence.[86] In all instances it must be adequate in order to have the desired effect and this is obviously a matter of fact. In *London Graving Dock Co.* v. *Horton*[87] the House of Lords had given the impression that if a visitor recognised the significance of a warning, the occupier would be absolved altogether. Section 2(4)(a) of the Act, however, negatives so wide a proposition by providing that regard must be had to all the circumstances in each case and a warning should not be treated as automatically absolving the occupier from liability.[88]

[83] [1963] 1 WLR 1117, at 1123–4.

[84] [1983] 1 WLR 1264 applied in *Ogwo* v. *Taylor* [1988] 1 AC 431 and approved by the House of Lords [1988] 1 AC 443 (another fireman's case), although distinguished in *Simpson* v. *A.I. Dairies Farms Ltd.* [2001] NPC 14 (rationalised by *Clerk and Lindsell on Torts* (18th edn., 2nd supp., 2002), para. 10–32 because the risk in question was not obviously something to do with the trade or calling concerned). In the joinery context, see a similar approach in *Eden* v. *West & Co.* [2002] EWCA Civ. 991; [2003] PIQR Q2 (CA).

[85] Invoked against a fifteen-year-old boy in *McGinlay* v. *British Railways Board* [1983] 1 WLR 1427. Compare *Simms* v. *Leigh Rugby Football Club* [1969] 2 All ER 923 and *Slack* v. *Glenie* (unreported, CA, 19 Apr. 2000) concerning how far a visitor can be taken willingly to accept the risks inherent in certain sporting or leisure activities.

[86] *Slater* v. *Clay Cross Co. Ltd.* [1956] 2 QB 264, 271 (per Denning LJ).

[87] [1951] AC 737.

[88] For illustration see *Stone* v. *Taffe* [1974] 1 WLR 1575. In *Bunker* v. *Brand (Charles) & Sons Ltd.* [1969] 2 QB 480, the plaintiff's damages were reduced by one half and in *Bird* v. *King Line Ltd.* [1970] 2 Lloyd's Rep. 349, by two-thirds.

The presence of an adequate warning is thus one of many circumstances in determining whether the occupier has discharged his duty of care. Therefore a warning in an unusual language,[89] or in an unsuitable place[90] or one not given in a serious manner[91] will not suffice. Likewise, in circumstances of excessive danger the presence of a warning—however appropriately phrased—may not be sufficient, the occupier being expected to take additional precautions to avoid injury to the claimant.[92] Equally, the absence of a warning about one kind of danger will not assist the claimant if he suffers injury due to another type of danger.[93] At the other end of the spectrum we find cases where the risk is obvious to the visitor. In such cases, the need of a warning may be dispensed with altogether. Thus, in *Staples* v. *West Dorset District Council*[94] the court took the view that the defendants, who were occupiers of a famous sea wall in Lyme Regis known as 'the Cobb', which was covered in algae and seaweed and obviously very slippery, were under no duty to warn users of its inherent dangers.[95]

What about a notice which is appropriate to an ordinary adult but unintelligible to the particular claimant because he is, for example, a very young child? Older cases seemed to take the view that in these instances permission to be on the premises depended on the plaintiff being accompanied by a competent guardian. This notion of conditional licence was rejected as unduly complicated by Devlin J in *Phipps* v. *Rochester Corporation*,[96] and perhaps the answer here, too, is that one has to consider all relevant factors (including parental responsibilities towards children) before deciding whether or not the warning was adequate. However, in view of the generous attitude towards child trespassers the importance of the problem can be exaggerated.

The second defence, found in section 2(1), concerns the possibility of excluding liability and this remains open to some extent even after the Unfair Contract Terms Act 1977. After the Contracts (Rights of Third Parties) Act 1999, it is also possible to exclude by contract the liability of someone who is not a party to that contract.[97] Exclusion can apply to liability arising from the occupation of premises that are *not* used as business premises and thus fall outside the 1977 Act. But the same can be true of business premises, provided the exclusion term satisfies the requirement of the reasonableness laid down in

[89] *Geier* v. *Kujawa, Weston and Warne Bros., Transport* [1970] 1 Lloyd's Rep. 364 suggests that a notice to be valid may have to be translated to a party who is known not to comprehend the language in which it is expressed. Probably, the same is true of a notice erected in a public place—e.g. a beach—known to be frequented by foreigners (e.g. tourists). On the other hand, the notice in *Geier*'s case would, nowadays, be invalidated by s. 148(3) of the Road Traffic Act 1972.

[90] *Coupland* v. *Eagle Bros. Ltd.* [1969] 210 EG 581.

[91] *Bishop* v. *J. A. Starnes & Sons Ltd.* [1971] 1 Lloyd's Rep. 162. Cf. *White* v. *Blackmore* [1972] 2 QB 651, where the warning was held to be adequate.

[92] *Rae* v. *Mars (UK) Ltd.* [1990] 3 EG 80 at 84.

[93] *Darby* v. *National Trust* [2001] PIQR P27 (CA): failure to warn of the risks of catching Weil's disease through swimming in the defendant's pond did not lead to liability for death by drowning in that pond.

[94] (1995) 93 LGR 536. See also *Cotton* v. *Derbyshire Dales DC, The Times*, 20 June 1994 (danger of walking at the edge of a steep cliff).

[95] See also *Darby* v. *National Trust* [2001] PIQR P27 (CA).

[96] [1955] 1 QB 450.

[97] Section 1(6) of the 1999 Act.

section 2(2) of the 1977 Act and the action does not relate to personal injury or death. For simplicity's sake we can describe the occupier who is subject to the 1957 Act as the *private* occupier and use the words *business occupiers* for those subject to the 1977 Act.

In *Ashdown* v. *Samuel Williams and Sons, Ltd.*[98] the second defendants occupied industrial premises surrounded by land owned by the first defendants. Access to the second defendants' land was by two roads, one of which was safe while the other, a short cut, could be used at the user's risk. There were notices to that effect, which an employee of the second defendants saw when using the short cut. She was injured by railway trucks being negligently shunted along the line and claimed damages. It was held that the second defendants were not liable, since they had provided the plaintiff with a reasonably safe way of reaching her work in so far as it was necessary for her to traverse the premises of the first defendants. It was held further that the first defendants were not liable, since they could exclude their liability by a properly phrased notice.

Now, there is nothing illogical in saying that if I can exclude you from my property altogether, I can permit you to enter upon my terms.[99] This proposition, though logical, was seriously curtailed by the Unfair Contract Terms Act 1977, which refers to 'business occupiers' and which will be considered presently. Further, it is clear from *Ashdown* and *White* v. *Blackmore* [100] that what matters is not whether the entrant knew of the risk, but whether the occupier had made all reasonable effort to inform him of it.[101] Following *Ashdown*[102] and section 2 of the Occupiers' Liability Act, the occupier's liability can still be excluded by contract, by an adequate notice, or 'otherwise'. This refers, for example, to rules and regulations made and published under bye-laws or other statutory authority, which are binding whether they are 'agreed to' by the visitor or not. An example could be found in a condition limiting the liability of the British Railways Board towards holders of railway platform tickets set out in section 43(7) of the Transport Act 1962.

Finally, an occupier's duty may be limited, excluded, etc., 'in so far as he is free' to do so. Until recently the only limitation on his power to restrict or exclude his duty altogether was in section 3(1) of the Occupiers' Liability Act. This states that an occupier cannot by contract with one person (*X*) *reduce* the common duty of care he owes to third parties (e.g. *X*'s employees), though he may *extend* it for their benefit. This includes situations where the occupier is bound to let third parties enter his premises. Since he cannot prevent them from entering in the first place, it would be inconsistent if he were able to restrict his duty towards them. The precise impact of the Contracts (Rights of Third Parties) Act 1999 upon section 3(1) remains to be seen: on the one hand, it seems to be broader than the 1957 Act because it applies to *any* third party, not just one whom the occupier is bound by contract to admit to his premises.[103] On the

[98] [1957] 1 QB 409.

[99] It would follow that if the occupier cannot exclude entry—e.g. to visitors covered by s. 2(6) of the 1957 Act—he should not be able to exclude his liability either.

[100] [1972] 2 QB 651.

[101] *Ibid.*, 674. This may cause undue hardship, however, to infants, blind persons and illiterate persons.

[102] [1957] 1 QB 409.

[103] *Clerk and Lindsell on Torts* (19th edn., 2006), para. 10–55, which describes s. 3(1) of the 1957 Act as 'now largely redundant'.

other hand, to take advantage of the 1999 Act, the third party will need to show that the term in question purported to confer a benefit upon him.[104]

Such is the regime that governs the position of private occupiers subject to the Occupiers' Liability Act 1957. Today, however, most important cases are likely to be concerned with *business occupiers* and thus affected by the Unfair Contract Terms Act 1977 which, in one deep scoop, undermined the *laissez-faire* thinking which had dominated the law until its coming into force. If the old law attached undue importance and protection to landownership, the new law may have gone too far the other way.

The relevant provisions of this Act, which in some respects appear to be inadequately thought out and ill drafted, apply only to cases of 'business liability'. According to section 1(3) this means liability for breach of obligations or duties arising *either* from things done by a person 'in the course of business' *or* 'from the occupation of premises used for business purposes of the occupier'. This last part is crucial but vague and a number of questions are likely to arise. Should the Act apply only to premises which are 'mainly used' for business purposes by their occupier, or only 'exclusively' used for such purposes? Where the use of premises for business is only minor or incidental the application of the Act should, arguably, be excluded. What if a doctor uses his sitting room as an overflow waiting room? And what if the entire premises are used for private purposes except for one hour every morning? Would the Act apply for that hour and for the rest of the day would we revert to the old law? Other problems will no doubt arise. While the *Ashdown* situation would now call for a different solution, what answer should be given if the facts were similar to those in *White* v. *Blackmore*,[105] where a fee was charged for entrance on land, the proceeds going to a charitable purpose? What if a student or employee of a college (which is a charity) is injured on its premises? (Section 2 of the Occupiers' Liability Act 1984, amending s. 1 of the 1977 Act, may provide an answer to this last hypothetical case.) If the scope of the 1977 Act turns out to be too wide, it would not be surprising to see courts placing a narrow interpretation on this section.

Once it has been decided that the premises are business premises, attention focuses on section 2, which states unequivocally that in cases of personal injury or death it is not possible to exclude liability resulting from the negligence of the occupier (s. 2(1)). The important point to note is that for this purpose negligence is defined in section 1(1)(c) as including, *inter alia*, the breach of the common duty of care imposed by the Occupiers' Liability Act 1957 (s. 1(1)(c)). As for other kinds of loss, for example, damage to property, exclusion is possible only if it is reasonable in view of all the circumstances obtaining when the liability arose (s. 11(3)).

The effect of all this is that liability for breach of the common duty of care under the Occupiers' Liability Act 1957 can no longer be excluded, *vis-à-vis* lawful visitors at any rate. What about trespassers? Liability to them does not arise under this Act, but initially

104 W. V. H. Rogers (ed.), *Winfield and Jolowicz on Tort* (17th edn., 2006), para. 9–23, which states that 'in practice the 1957 Act may continue to be relied upon . . .'.

105 [1972] 2 QB 651.

arose at common law (and subsequently under the Occupiers' Liability Act 1984) when there has been a breach of the 'duty of common humanity'. As we shall see, the difference between these two notions—common duty of care, duty of common humanity—is not one of law but one of fact, depending on the factual situation of each case. Yet differences may remain in practice. For example, it seems that due to defective drafting of the 1984 Occupiers' Liability Act the occupier can exclude his liability towards persons covered by that Act, whereas the 1977 Unfair Contract Terms Act makes such an exclusion impossible towards the type of lawful entrants covered by the 1957 Occupiers' Liability Act. One hopes, however, that such a solution would not prevail and the courts, if the opportunity arose, would hold that the duty owed under the 1984 Act is non-excludable. Two arguments might support such a construction. The 1984 Act, unlike the 1957 Act, makes no provision for 'contracting out'; and the omission must have been intentional since it was provided for in the Law Commission's Draft Bill on which the 1984 Act was based. Second, duties owed to trespassers are really minimal duties and, therefore, as a matter of public policy they should not be excludable. An interesting point arises out of the definition of 'negligence' in section 1(1)(c) as including the breach of common duty of care imposed by the 1957 Act. Once this has been breached, liability for it cannot be excluded according to the Unfair Contract Terms Act. If, of course, the duty has been fulfilled and has not been breached, there is no liability to be excluded. Now, we have seen that according to the Occupiers' Liability Act warning notices may, in certain circumstances, prevent the duty from arising altogether (s. 2(1)), or discharge the occupier's duty towards his visitor (s. 2(4)(a)). For a time, one could have argued that such notices do not offend against the Unfair Contract Terms Act 1977, since section 2 of this Act refers to notices excluding or limiting *liability for breach*, as distinct from notices which show that there has been no breach in the first place. If this way of looking at section 2 of the 1977 Act had prevailed,[106] it would have limited the application of the Act considerably, and in that sense it could be seen as being contrary to the intentions of the legislator.

However, in the light of the recent decision of the House of Lords in *Smith* v. *Bush*,[107] this view no longer seems tenable. This means that a disclaimer of liability would be ineffective under section 2(2) of the 1977 Act unless it satisfied the requirement of reasonableness provided by section 1(3) of the same statute.

(E) LIABILITY FOR INDEPENDENT CONTRACTORS

An occupier will, of course, be vicariously liable for torts committed by his servants in the course of their employment, whatever it may be. What if work were to be performed by an independent contractor? On principle the employer of an independent contractor is not vicariously liable so that an occupier would not be answerable for his

[106] As suggested by *Harris* v. *Wyre Forest DC* [1988] QB 835 (reversed by HL in *Smith* v. *Bush* [1990] 1 AC 831).

[107] [1990] 1 AC 831, especially at 848 (per Lord Templeman), 857 (per Lord Griffiths). The factual context of *Smith* v. *Bush* is different from that discussed in the text above, but, it is submitted, the reasoning of the House of Lords is applicable to both situations. For further discussion of this case, see below, ch. 24, Section 4.

independent contractor. Yet in *Thomson* v. *Cremin*[108] the House of Lords appeared to say that the occupier owed his invitees a personal, non-delegable duty to see that care was taken, which he could not avoid by entrusting its performance to an independent contractor. His liability was not vicarious, but personal. This has now been altered by section 2(4)(b) of the Occupiers' Liability Act, which states that:

> Where damage is caused to a visitor by a danger due to the faulty execution of any work of construction, maintenance or repair by an independent contractor employed by the occupier, the occupier is not to be treated without more as answerable for the danger if in all the circumstances he had acted reasonably in entrusting the work to an independent contractor and had taken such steps (if any) as he reasonably ought in order to satisfy himself that the contractor was competent and that the work had been properly done.

Three points should be noted about this section: first, it is a particular application of the general rule set out in section 2(4) according to which the standard of care owed by an occupier towards lawful visitors is determined after all surrounding circumstances are taken into account.

It follows, second, that in the case of work done by an independent contractor the questions to be answered before an occupier is deemed to have attained the requisite standard include, in appropriate circumstances, the following: (*a*) did the occupier act reasonably in entrusting the work to an independent contractor? (*b*) did he select him with reasonable care? (*c*) circumstances permitting, did he supervise him properly while the work was being done? and (*d*) did he check its completion? In this last context, the words of Mocatta J in *AMF International* v. *Magnet Bowling*[109] are important:

> In the case of the *construction of a substantial building* or of a ship . . . the building owner, if he is to escape subsequent tortious liability for faulty construction, should not only take care to contract with a competent contractor or shipbuilder, but also to cause that work to be supervised by a properly qualified professional man such as an architect surveyor, or a naval architect or Lloyd's surveyor. Such cases are different in fact and in everyday practice from having a flat rewired.[110]

It is submitted that the italicised words must be read with caution and that everything must in the end depend on the nature and complexity of the work that is undertaken and the other surrounding circumstances. Thus in *Ferguson* v. *Welsh*, Lord Keith observed:

> It would not ordinarily be reasonable to expect an occupier of premises having engaged a contractor, to supervise the contractor's activities in order to ensure that he was discharging his duty to his employees to observe a safe system of work. In special circumstances, on the other hand, when the occupier knows or has reason to suspect that the contractor is using an unsafe system of work, it might well be reasonable for the occupier to take steps to see that the system was made safe.[111]

Given the facts of that case, Lord Keith here was, of course, speaking of injury to the contractor's employees; naturally, however, the same principle applies towards all third parties.

[108] [1956] 1 WLR 103.
[109] [1968] 1 WLR 1028.
[110] *Ibid.*, at 1044.
[111] [1987] 1 WLR 1553 (another construction/demolition case), at 1560.

The concluding words from the *AMF* citation distinguish cases such as *Green* v. *Fibreglass Ltd.*,[112] where an occupier, who employed an independent contractor to rewire his office, was held not liable to a charwoman who received severe electrical burns as a result of faulty rewiring. In *Woodward* v. *Mayor of Hastings*,[113] on the other hand, a pupil at a school injured himself on an icy step left in a dangerous condition by a negligent cleaner. Even on the assumption that the cleaner was an independent contractor of the corporation, the latter was liable as its officers could have inspected the way she had done the job. 'The craft of the charwoman may have its mysteries', said du Parcq LJ,[114] 'but there is no esoteric quality in the nature of the work which the cleaning of a snow-covered step demands.' The occupier in this case was therefore under a duty to select a competent person and to inspect the work. On the other hand, in *Haseldine* v. *Daw*[115] the plaintiff was injured when the lift that he was wiring collapsed to the bottom of its shaft as a result of negligent repairs by a firm of independent contractors. The occupier was not liable, for 'to hold him responsible for the misdeeds of his independent contractor would be to make him insure the safety of his lift. That duty can only arise out of contract...'.

This reference to insurance leads us to an important issue which has only just arisen in the case law. Is it a part of the occupier's duty under section 2(4)(b) to check that an independent contractor is adequately insured to cover any risks that might eventuate while the contractor is operating on the occupier's premises? Although the Court of Appeal in *Gwilliam* v. *North Hertfordshire Hospital NHS Trust*[116] ultimately found that the occupier hospital was not liable for injuries sustained by a visitor using a game provided by an independent contractor during a fund-raising event, the majority seemed to take the view that there *was* a duty upon the occupier to inquire into whether or not the contractor had adequate insurance.[117] On the facts, the majority were satisfied that a simple inquiry coupled with an assurance from the contractor would be sufficient to discharge this duty.

Sedley LJ dissented strongly on the reasoning applied by the majority to reach the result. He would have found there to be no such duty, viewing the imposition of such an obligation upon occupiers as a duty entirely separate from any general duty arising by analogy with section 2(4)(b) and arguably of equal application in situations beyond the facts of the case (such as private occupiers who allow the public on to their land or even occupiers whose contractors' activities harm their neighbours, rather than the public).[118]

112 [1958] 2 QB 245.
113 [1945] KB 174.
114 *Ibid.*, at 183.
115 [1941] 2 KB 343.
116 [2002] 3 WLR 1425.
117 *Ibid.*, paras. 15 and 16 (Lord Woolf CJ) and para. 40 (Waller LJ). Both judges in the majority seemed to view the checking up on insurance as essential to determining the competence and standing of the contractor, so that it was relevant to the reasonableness of the occupier's behaviour in selecting and supervising the contractor. The factual point in the case was, of course, that such insurance cover had expired before the relevant accident occurred.
118 *Ibid.*, paras. 55 and 57. As *Clerk and Lindsell on Torts* (19th edn., 2006), 12–58, puts it: 'The common duty of care is to see that visitors will be reasonably safe, words that do not readily translate into an additional obligation to safeguard the visitor's right to compensation.'

Furthermore, the learned judge took the view that even if there had been such a duty, he would then have found it to have been breached on the facts of the case.[119]

This result has now been achieved thanks to the decision of the Court of Appeal in *Naylor* v. *Paling*.[120] So a night-club owner was relieved of all liability for having failed to check whether the independent doorman carried insurance for the injury he caused to one of the club's patrons though the overzealous performance of his assigned duties. The result is to be welcomed for the reasons already given but one should nonetheless use it with caution. For lack of insurance could be an indication of uninsurability of the independent contractor, presumably because of his bad record; and in such cases the possibility of the occupier being held liable for breach of his own personal duty would then have to be considered again.

Finally, one should draw attention to the vagueness of section 2(4)(b). Is work not involving 'work of construction, maintenance or repair' excluded from it? What comes under these words? In *AMF International* v. *Magnet Bowling Ltd*.[121] it was held that a builder's failure to take adequate precautions against flooding should come under this section even though it was strenuously argued that at most he was guilty of nonfeasance rather than misfeasance. Mocatta J said:

> It seems to be that if a builder in the course of constructing a building fails to take adequate precautions against flooding and that causes damage to the property of a visitor, it would be altogether too technical to hold this not within the true construction of the words 'a danger due to the faulty execution of any work of construction, maintenance or repair'.[122]

Lord Woolf CJ has held, in *Gwilliam* (discussed above), that section 2(4)(b) is to be treated as one example of how an occupier can discharge his duty under the 1957 Act, so that (where no issue of 'construction, maintenance or repair' arose) section 2(4)(b) could at best be applied by analogy.[123] However, the majority in *Gwilliam* did go on to use the essence of section 2(4)(b) in its discussion of the duty owed. Thus, it seems that the courts may be willing to extend the ideas behind section 2(4)(b) to situations which fall beyond its strict wording.

119 Because it would have been straightforward to require a simple copy of the insurance certificate to have been faxed or sent to the hospital to check on the adequacy of the insurance policy: [2002] 3 WLR 1425, [48].

120 [2004] PIQR P615.

121 [1968] 1 WLR 1028.

122 *Ibid*., at 1043. In *Ferguson* v. *Welsh* [1987] 1 WLR 1553, 1560, Lord Keith thought that s. 2(4)(b) required 'a broad and purposive interpretation' which led him to the conclusion that the word 'construction' embraces also the word 'demolition'. With the greatest respect this seems a strained interpretation, at any rate in cases when pure demolition work is involved. By contrast, a stronger case can be made for applying s. 2(4)(b) in those instances where demolition has to precede construction.

123 [2002] 3 WLR 1425, [10] and [11]. See also Waller LJ, [39] and [40] (agreeing with Lord Woolf CJ in the result, but preferring to reach that result via the common law, asking whether the imposition of such a duty was fair, just and reasonable).

(F) PROTECTED ENTRANTS UNDER THE 1984 ACT

(i) The Development of the Common Law

The common law and the 1957 Act had little time for persons who were not included in any of the three types of entrants which together made up the category of 'lawful visitor', namely, contractors, invitees and licensees. If they were injured while on other persons' premises due to the defective state of these premises they had only themselves to blame. This group of persons, who were beyond the pale of the law of negligence, came under four subcategories. First were persons exercising *private* rights of way. Then we had entrants under section 60 of the National Parks and Access to the Countryside Act 1949—sometimes referred to as 'authorised ramblers'. A third category included persons exercising *public* rights of way. Finally we had trespassers. It was, in fact, this last category that attracted the full wrath of the traditional common law and led to most of the litigation.

A trespasser is a person who has no permission, express or implied, to be where he is. The common law's traditional severity towards trespassers was exemplified by *Robert Addie & Sons (Collieries)* v. *Dumbreck*.[124] In that case it was held that an occupier was not liable for injury to trespassers unless he had acted intentionally[125] or recklessly. As late as 1964 the Privy Council found occasion to reaffirm this rule in *Commissioner for Railways* v. *F. J. Quinlan*.[126]

The policy reasons behind such a harsh rule may have been a desire to leave owners of land free to use it as they wished, especially at a time when freedom of property was as sacrosanct as freedom of the person. American authors and courts have, on the whole, been more forthright than their English counterparts in acknowledging the importance attached traditionally to land, the dominance of landowners and the heritage of feudalism.[127] Such considerations progressively lost their appeal. The Supreme Court of California was thus surely right to argue that the classifications into trespassers, licensees and invitees bore no relation 'to the factors which ought to determine the liability of an occupier. These should include the connection between the injury and the occupier's conduct, his moral blameworthiness, the need to prevent future harm and the prevalence and availability of insurance.'[128]

124 [1929] AC 358.

125 In *Revill* v. *Newberry* [1996] 2 WLR 239—a case much discussed in the popular press of the time—the defendant was thus held liable to the plaintiff/burglar whom he shot while he was trespassing on his grounds. The latter's damages were, however, reduced by two-thirds to account for his own crime.

126 [1964] AC 1054. The *Quinlan* case even rejected an attempt made a year earlier in *Videan* v. *British Transport Commission* [1963] 2 QB 650 to limit the *Addie* ruling to breaches of the 'occupancy duties'.

127 *Rowland* v. *Christian*, 443 P 2d 561, 564–5 (1968) decided by the Sup. Ct. of California. The conclusion was that an occupier owed the common duty of care towards all persons—including trespassers—who came on to his land. One of the latest converts to this rule is New York: see *Basso* v. *Miller*, 386 NYS 2d 564, 352 NE 2d 868 (1976); and some authors have already argued that occupiers of business premises should be under strict liability towards those on their premises. Thus, see E. Ursin, 'Strict Liability for Defective Business Premises: One Step beyond *Rowland* and *Greenman*' (1975) 22 *UCLALR* 820.

128 *Rowland* v. *Christian*, 443 P 2d 561, at 567.

Another argument in favour of the old harsher treatment of trespassers derived from the nineteenth-century moral judgement that a trespasser was a wrongdoer deserving of his plight. This argument, however, is no more convincing than the previous one, as Lord Dunedin himself admitted in the *Addie* case:

The term trespasser... is a comprehensive one; it covers the wicked and the innocent; the burglar, the arrogant invader of another's land, the walker blithely unaware that he is stepping where he has no right to walk, or the wandering child—all may be dubbed as trespasser.[129]

In this country, however, the injustice of the Victorian attitudes was only gradually appreciated. Thus, in the beginning only indirect attempts were made to avoid the harshness of the old rule, for example, by resorting to the implied permission and the allurement doctrines.[130] Powerful doubts about the correctness of the law were, however, voiced by the Court of Appeal in *British Railways Board* v. *Herrington* and on appeal the House of Lords[131] heeded them by making it possible for occupiers to be liable in negligence to trespassers. It said that the *Addie* case would be decided differently today and that it was no longer an exclusive statement of the law. The facts in that case were that the plaintiff, aged six, was electrocuted by the defendant's railway line after crossing a gap in the fence bordering it. The fencing had been in a dilapidated condition for some time. The local stationmaster was aware of this and of the fact that children were in the habit of passing through, but he took no steps. The House of Lords held that, although the plaintiff was a trespasser, he could recover in negligence.

Lord Pearson drew attention to the changes that have taken place in the socio-economic conditions and said that the time had come to abandon the old rule and to mitigate the plight of trespassers.[132] Accordingly, by applying the 'neighbour' principle, a new duty situation was created with regard to them. However, although they deserved more compassionate treatment than hitherto, the House of Lords was unable to extend its compassion as far as to abandon the interests of occupiers. Concern for the former is essential; but it was felt that this should not result in an unbearable burden being placed on the latter. A fair balance was sought by saying that the new duty—dubbed the duty 'of common humanity'—was less onerous than the common duty of care in (possibly) two respects: first, that the presence of a trespasser in most cases will not be reasonably foreseeable;[133] second, the standard of care required of the occupier would, in such cases, be less exacting than that towards a lawful visitor.[134]

Herrington was a turning-point in the law; but the way the humanitarian duty was described gave rise to considerable discussions in the 1970s about how this differed

129 [1929] AC 358, 371.

130 Similar methods were adopted in the USA. See *Kermarec* v. *Compagnie Générale Transatlantique*, 358 US 625, 630–1, 79 SCt. 406, 3 L Ed. 2d 550 (1959) (refusing to accept the common-law rules for the law of admiralty); *Rowland* v. *Christian*, 443 P 2d 561, 565–7 (1968). The Victorian attitudes towards trespassers, however, still retained some support: see, for instance, J. A. Weir, *Casebook on Tort* (2nd edn., 1970), 68–99.

131 [1971] 2 QB 107; [1972] AC 877.

132 *Ibid.*, at 929.

133 *Ibid.*, at 941 (per Lord Diplock).

134 *Ibid.*, at 898–9 (per Lord Reid).

from the common duty of care. But while the battle of semantics raged, the courts in England and in other common law jurisdictions made it increasingly clear that at least child trespassers were not to be left without protection.[135] Only in exceptional situations, where the cost of keeping the young trespasser out of the potentially dangerous premises was exorbitant, would the courts deny liability.[136] As for the totally unmeritorious trespasser—e.g. the thief—the courts felt confident that an impressive array of concepts and maxims—foreseeability, *volenti*, *ex turpi causa non oritur actio*—still enabled them to exclude recovery where justice so demanded.

(ii) The Intervention of the Legislator: The 1984 Act[137]

The 1984 Act, though mainly concerned with ameliorating the protection afforded to trespassers has, in fact, achieved the same result for two of the three other categories of entrants who were not lawful visitors under the 1957 Act. These are the persons exercising private rights of way[138] and the 'authorised ramblers'. It should be noted that, on its entry into force, the Countryside and Rights of Way Act 2000 created a general right of access to 'access land' for 'open-air recreational purposes' (ss. 1 and 2). Such ramblers are to be treated as falling within the protection of the Occupiers' Liability Act 1984, albeit that any duty owed to them is excluded in respect of

'(a) a risk resulting from the existence of any natural feature of the landscape, or any river, stream, ditch or pond whether or not a natural feature, or (b) a risk of [the rambler] suffering injury when passing over, under or through any wall, fence or gate, except by proper use of the gate or of a stile'.[139]

On the other hand, those using public rights of way have not been included in the Act and do not enjoy the rights given by it.[140] Their exclusion was prompted by the fear that any contrary decision would have resulted in large expenditure being incurred by the owners of the servient land. Users of those public highways *adopted* by local authorities do, however, enjoy the protection afforded to them by the Highways (Miscellaneous Provisions) Act 1961 (now the Highways Act 1980).[141]

135 Thus, see *Pannett* v. *McGuiness* [1972] 2 QB 599, *South Portland Cement* v. *Cooper* [1974] AC 623.

136 *Penny* v. *Northampton BC* (1974) 72 LGR 733.

137 For a discussion of the Act, see R. A. Buckley, 'The Occupiers' Liability Act 1984: Has *Herrington* Survived?' [1984] *Conv.* 413.

138 See *Vodden* v. *Gayton* [2001] PIQR P4 for a recent example.

139 Section 1(6A) of the 1984 Act, as inserted by s. 13(2) of the 2000 Act. In fixing any duty owed to such ramblers, the 2000 Act requires regard to be had to '(a) the fact that the existence of that right ought not to place an undue burden (whether financial or otherwise) on the occupier, (b) the importance of maintaining the character of the countryside, including features of historic, traditional or archaeological interest, and (c) any relevant guidance given under' any code of conduct issued by the Countryside Agency (s. 1A of the 1984 Act, as inserted by s. 13(3) of the 2000 Act). See the website of the Department for the Environment, Food and Rural Affairs (DEFRA) for further details on the Act and its entry into force; see also P. H. Kenny 'Is New Right to Roam Final Straw?' [2001] *Conv.* 296.

140 Nor are they regarded as 'visitors' of the owner of the subsoil: *McGeown* v. *N.I. Housing Executive* [1995] 1 AC 233; *Campbell* v. *N.I. Housing Executive* [1996] 1 BNIL 99. But other avenues of redress may be open to them. Thus, see *Thomas* v. *British Rail Board* [1976] QB 912.

141 For discussion, see chs. 7 and 8, below.

The existence of a duty under the Act is covered by section 1(3) and, unlike the 1957 Act, is only meant to provide protection against the infliction of personal injury.[142] According to this section a duty will arise if three requirements are satisfied. First, the defendant must be '*aware* of the danger' or 'have reasonable grounds to believe that it exists' (s. 1(3)(a)). Second, he must '*know*' or have 'reasonable grounds to believe that the entrant is in the vicinity of the danger . . . or that he may come into the vicinity of the danger' (s. 1(3)(b)). Finally, 'the risk is one against which, in all the circumstances of the case, he may reasonably be expected to offer the other some protection'.

The criteria mentioned by the Act are ambiguous, in that whereas the last of the three is, clearly, objective, the first two (contained in s. 1(3)(a) and (b)) could be seen as being subjective (note the italicised words) *or* objective (reasonable awareness, etc.). This lack of clarity, particularly annoying given the difficulties experienced by the courts (and scholars) during the post-*Herrington* years, is unfortunate; and it has hardly been rectified by *White* v. *St Albans City and District Council*.[143] In that case the Court of Appeal held that an occupier who had taken measures to keep the public off his dangerous premises should not, by that reason alone, be deemed to have reason to believe that persons were likely to be in the vicinity of the danger for the purposes of section 1(3)(b). Rather, the answer should be made to depend on all the facts of the case, including the state of the land. This suggests that knowledge that the entrant is in the vicinity of the danger will be more readily imputed where the fencing around the occupier's land was defective and evidence could be adduced to show that persons used the land, for example, as a short cut to their work. If, on the other hand, the occupier's land was properly fenced, it would be wrong to impute to the occupier any knowledge that the plaintiff may have entered the danger zone. This 'objective' formulation—liability depends on constructive knowledge—seems to have been replaced by a more 'subjective' test. Thus, according to the decision of the Court of Appeal in *Swain* v. *Buri*,[144] the words 'has reasonable grounds to believe', found in section 1(3)(b) of the 1984 Act, must be taken to refer to 'actual knowledge of the facts that would lead a reasonable man to expect the presence of a trespasser; mere culpable ignorance, or constructive knowledge, [will] not do'.[145] In that case an owner of an empty warehouse abutting on a council estate was thus absolved from all liability towards an agile but mischievous small boy who climbed on the roof and then fell through a skylight.

When one turns to the *contents* of the duty (discovered only once the preceding requirements have been satisfied), matters seem more straightforward. Thus, section 1(4) of the 1984 Act, adopting the familiar negligence standard, expects the occupier 'to take such care as is reasonable in all the circumstances'. Would this exclude a consideration of

142 Section 1(1) alluding to persons 'suffering injury'. Property damage may also be protected through the (unintended) survival of the duty of common humanity imposed by the *Herrington* judgment of the House of Lords: [1972] AC 877. There is a hint of this possibility in *Tutton* v. *A. D. Walter* [1986] QB 61 but we are unaware of a judgment on the point.

143 *The Times*, 12 Mar. 1990.

144 [1996] PIQR P442.

145 *Clerk and Lindsell on Torts* (17th edn., 2nd supp., 1995), para. 10–74.

the resources of the occupier? The Law Commission certainly wanted to prevent recourse to this,[146] thus removing doubts sown in *Herrington* about the relevance of such resources,[147] but the Court of Appeal in *Ratcliff* v. *McConnell* seems to suggest that resources may still be relevant.[148] Section 1(6), essentially, requires the courts to consider the defence of *volenti non fit injuria* at the same time as they consider whether a duty arises under the 1984 Act. For, if the trespasser willingly accepted the risk, no duty of care will arise. Thus, as a result of such reasoning, the Court of Appeal recently held[149] that the occupiers of a college open-air swimming pool owed no duty of care under section 1 to a student trespasser who was seriously injured after climbing over a locked gate one night and then diving head first into the school pool knowing that it was closed for the winter and its water levels kept low. The decision, though unfortunate for the plaintiff, shows that the fears expressed in the 1960s and 1970s that the recognition of a duty of care towards trespassers would bring indeterminate liability have proved unfounded. More generally, one might thus argue that this case law provides an illustration of the ability of the courts to keep liability within reasonable bounds and avoid the apocalyptic consequences that conservative lawyers fear every time liberalisation of our tort rules is mentioned through the abandonment of the device of duty of care. That said, the recent comments (*obiter*) of Simon Brown LJ in *Scott* v. *Associated British Ports* [150] and the result in *Tomlinson* v. *Congleton Borough Council*[151] suggested that, in fact situations where clear knowledge on the part of the occupier can be shown concerning the use made of their premises by others which 'imperils' such trespassers, such knowledge may lead to the imposition of liability. This is provided that fairly straightforward remedial measures could, to the occupier's knowledge, have been taken to prevent the problem and seems to be in spite of the fact that warning notices may have been used and that the danger may have been an obvious one (as in *Tomlinson*). Finally, to return to the 1984 Act, section 1(8) limits the duty of the occupier to personal injury suffered by the entrant. Property damage is thus excluded *under the 1984 Act*. But the wording of section 1(1) and 1(8) of the Act *may* not have excluded any residual liability the occupier may have towards a trespasser's property under the rule in *Herrington*'s case.[152]

Reasonable knowledge that the trespasser may be in the vicinity must not be understood in too precise a manner. It is enough that the occupier has reasonable grounds of believing that the trespasser will be on his land at some *times* not others so that, for

[146] Law Commission, *Report on Liability for Damage or Injury to Trespassers and Related Questions of Occupiers' Liability* (Select Bibliography).

[147] *British Railways Board* v. *Herrington* [1972] AC 877, 941 (per Lord Diplock), *viz.*, the court should consider 'the expense involved in giving effective warning of it to the kind of trespasser likely to be injured, in relation to the occupier's resources in money or in labour'.

[148] *Ratcliff* v. *McConnell* [1999] 1 WLR 670, 680. [149] *Ibid.*

[150] Unreported, 22 Nov. 2000 (CA), para. 20.

[151] [2003] 2 WLR 1120. However, see now *Donoghue* v. *Folkestone Properties Ltd.* [2003] 2 WLR 1138 (CA).

[152] See the quaint case of *Tutton* v. *A. D. Walter* [1986] QB 61. On the other hand, E. McKendrick, *Tort Textbook* (5th edn., 1991), 150, argues that the *Herrington* test was designed to deal with personal injuries and not property damage.

instance, if the injury occurs during a midnight swim in an area known to be frequented by trespassers in the daytime, no liability will ensure.[153] The same immunity may result where the injury occurred in a part of the property not known to be frequented by trespasser.[154]

To sum up, a trickle of cases during the last four or five years has established three main guidelines as to how the courts are likely to decide such cases. The first is among the surrounding circumstances likely to be carefully scrutinised by the courts is the seriousness of the likely injury to the trespasser. Second, youthful trespassers are likely, once again, to be treated more leniently though, having said this, one notes a number of recent cases where trespassing youths, seriously injured while on unauthorised land (or making unauthorised use of it), have failed to succeed in their actions.[155] The third point, largely but not always necessarily related to this result, is the fact that our courts refuse to impose liability on the occupiers for obviously dangerous activities freely undertaken by the injured trespassers. The liberalisation of the law in favour of trespassers has thus not, apparently, led to an unlimited right to win compensation, a result which must not only be welcomed in principle but also praised for having being achieved in a suitably legal and flexible manner.

(G) LIABILITY OF NON-OCCUPIERS: VENDORS, LANDLORDS, BUILDERS, LOCAL AUTHORITIES

Any of the above *may* be occupiers in the sense described in the previous paragraphs, in which case their liability could be engaged under the Occupiers' Liability Act(s). Where, however, this is not the case, their liability may arise under statute, the evolving common law, or both. We shall discuss the liability of each of these potential defendants in turn.

(i) Vendors and Landlords

Purchasers or lessees of premises might first consider suing vendors or landlords in contract. However, the rule of *caveat emptor* ('buyer beware', arguably eroded in recent times)[156] makes it unlikely that such actions will succeed. In the case of land, therefore, implied obligations about the quality of the premises are considerably narrower than those found in the case of sale of chattels.[157]

153 *Donoghue* v. *Folkstone Properties Ltd* [2003] 2 WLR 1138. Time here means not only time of the day but also time of the year. Thus, as the *Donoghue* case shows that an occupier of a harbour may owe a duty of care towards trespassers whom he knew swam in it in the summer did not mean that such a duty was also owed towards the odd swimmer who swam in the harbour waters in the winter. In that case the claimant, a professional driver, was injured when he dived from one of the slipways in the winter and around midnight, striking his head on a grid pile under the water. The decision at first instance in favour of the claimant was reversed by a strong Court of Appeal.

154 *Higgs* v. *Foster (t/a Avaion Coaches)* [2004] EWCA Civ. 843.

155 Thus, see: *Swain* v. *Pearl* [1996] PIQR P442; *Price* v. *City of Nottingham*, unreported, 1 July 1998 (CA); *Ratcliff* v. *McConnell* [1999] 1 WLR 670; *Tomlinson* v. *Congleton BC* [2004] 1 AC 46, [2003] 3 WLR 705.

156 See L. Gleeson and E. McKendrick, 'The Rotting Away of *Caveat Emptor*?' [1987] *Conv.* 121.

157 Nevertheless, in the context of commercial property and thanks to recent decisions at the highest judicial levels, the law of contract may still have a significant role to play, especially where claims are made by subsequent

At common law, tort rules were equally unfavourable to plaintiffs. *Cavalier* v. *Pope* [158] established precisely such an immunity for landlords as far back as 1906; and less than thirty years later, the same immunity was conclusively given to vendors.[159] In the years that followed, various attempts were made to restrict these immunities but, subject to what will be said in the next paragraphs, their success was only marginal.[160]

The immunity of landlords and vendors for acts or omissions before letting or selling the premises thus persisted until the 1970s when it was frontally assaulted by *Dutton* v. *Bognor Regis UDC*.[161] The best interpretation of this decision is that it abolished the immunity of landlords and vendors for dangers *positively*[162] created *before* the sale or demise of the premises, thus extending the ruling in *Billings* but not totally avoiding (as it could not) the effect of *Cavalier* v. *Pope*.[163] As noted in Chapter 3, *Dutton* was subsequently approved (in most respects) by *Anns* v. *Merton London Borough Council*.[164] The case law of the House of Lords subsequent to *Anns* has, however, cast so much uncertainty on the *Dutton* type of reasoning that it is doubtful whether this line of attack will offer great chances to future claimants. Happily for them, legislative intervention in the form of section 3 of the Defective Premises Act 1972 has reached results very similar (though not identical[165]) to those foreshadowed by *Dutton*, so the old-fashioned immunities of landlords and vendors have, for most intents and purposes, been interred by statute.

Section 3(1) provides that

> where work of construction, repair, maintenance or demolition or any other work is done on or in relation to premises, any duty of care owed, because of the doing of the work, to persons who might reasonably be expected to be affected by defects in the state of the premises created by the doing of the work shall not be abated by the subsequent disposal of the premises by the person who owed the duty.[166]

The main effect of the section is to abolish the common law immunity of a vendor or lessor in negligence in respect of damage caused by the dangerous state of the premises

transferees of the property concerning such defects. See the discussion of *Alfred McAlpine Construction Ltd.* v. *Panatown Ltd.* [2001] 1 AC 518 and associated cases in ch. 3, above.

158 [1906] AC 428.

159 *Bottomley* v. *Bannister* [1932] 1 KB 458.

160 Thus, in *A. C. Billings & Son* v. *Riden* [1958] AC 240 the House of Lords abolished the landlord's immunity for dangers positively created after the demise of the premises; and in *Rimmer* v. *Liverpool City Council* [1985] QB 1 it was held that a landlord, who designed or built premises, owed a duty of care to persons who might reasonably be expected to be affected by the condition of the premises.

161 [1972] 1 QB 373.

162 Liability for non-feasance was not, however, possible. See, for instance, *Boldack* v. *East Lindsey DC* (1999) 31 HLR 41.

163 The continued vitality of *Cavalier* v. *Pope* was illustrated by *Boldack* v. *East Lindsey DC* (1999) 31 HLR 41 (CA), which was a case where the 1972 Act was held not to apply and so the common law rules precluded recovery.

164 [1978] AC 728.

165 For further details on the changes brought about by case law and statute, see J. Spencer, 'The Defective Premises Act 1972' (Select Bibliography).

166 Section 3(2) goes on to specify the situations when the section does *not* apply.

sold or let by him. The way this section was designed to operate was explained by the Law Commission:

> Any person who does work on land is under a duty of care at the time when he does the work, but if he subsequently sells or lets the premises on which he did the work, his potential liability for breach of that duty comes to an end. The transaction of sales or letting alone confers this immunity. It is only, therefore, necessary to provide that a sale or letting shall have no effect upon a pre-existing duty arising from the doing of the work and the general principles of negligence will apply.[167]

The Act achieves this result in a cumbersome and ambiguous way; and it also raises two further points.

First, unlike *Dutton*, section 3(1) does not impose liability for misfeasance generally, but only for misfeasance by 'work of construction, repair, maintenance or demolition or *any other work*' (emphasis added). The italicised words may provide a way to widen the application of the Act if they are not construed as being limited to works of construction, repair, and maintenance; and in the context of occupiers' liability Mocatta J attempted a broad definition of similar terms.[168] Even a wide interpretation might still leave outside the scope of the section some activities, such as spraying a field with poisonous fertiliser. If this were to be so, then a vendor or lessor who did the spraying would not be liable to the purchaser. Second, the section appears to restrict the landlord's immunity to damage created 'on or in relation to premises', which could limit its applicability to buildings unless the term 'premises' is understood in a broad sense.

It will be clear from what has been said so far that neither *Dutton* nor section 3 renders a landlord liable for careless omissions, in particular an omission to carry out necessary repairs.[169] This has been achieved (at any rate as far as omitted repairs are concerned, for there is still no liability for failing to warn of existing dangers not created by himself) by section 4, which states:

> Where premises are let under a tenancy which puts on the landlord an obligation to the tenant for the maintenance or repair of the premises, the landlord owes to all persons who might reasonably be expected to be affected by defects in the state of the premises a duty to take such care as is reasonable in all the circumstances to see that they are reasonably safe from personal injury or from damage to their property caused by a relevant defect.

First, the landlord's duty is additional to any other duty imposed on him by contract or statute, and it cannot be excluded or restricted in any way.[170] Second, the duty is owed to all those 'who might reasonably be expected to be affected'[171] by the defects in the

[167] Law Commission, *Civil Liability of Vendors and Lessors for Defective Premises*, No. 40 (HC 184, 1970) s. 46.

[168] *AMF International Ltd.* v. *Magnet Bowling Ltd.* [1968] 1 WLR 1028. In *Andrews* v. *Schooling* [1991] 1 WLR 783 the Court of Appeal held that the words 'taking on work' of s. 1(1) of the Act (which deals with the liability of builders discussed later) also extends to non-feasance.

[169] See the *Boldack* decision ((1999) HLR 41) though compare the Irish case of *Ward* v. *McMaster* [1985] IR 29 denying *Cavalier* v. *Pope* [1906] AC 428 of all validity.

[170] Section 6(3) of the 1972 Act. This must now be read in conjunction with the Unfair Contract Terms Act 1977.

[171] Section 4(1).

premises and they include not only tenants[172] and 'visitors' but also neighbours, users of the highway and even trespassers. Nowadays this protection must be analogous to that offered by the *Herrington* rule and the Occupiers' Liability Act 1984. Third, liability is imposed only for damage due to 'a relevant defect', which section 4(3) defines as:

> a defect in the state of the premises existing at or after the material time and arising from, or continuing because of, an act or omission by the landlord which constitutes or would, if he had had notice of the defect, have constituted a failure by him to carry out his obligation to the tenant for the maintenance or repair of the premises...

It has been clarified by the *Sykes* v. *Harry* case[173] that it is not vital in a claim under section 4 to prove that the landlord had notice, actual or constructive, of the actual defect which gave rise to the injury. It would be sufficient to show that he had failed to take such care as was reasonable in all the circumstances to see that the claimant was reasonably safe from personal injury caused by a relevant defect of which he ought in all the circumstances to have known. It will be noticed that a 'relevant defect' exists only if the landlord is in breach of his express or implied obligation to repair: express if it derives from an express undertaking to repair, implied if it derives, for example, from statute.[174] As to the latter, sections 11 and 12 of the Landlord and Tenant Act 1985 provide for implied covenants by a lessor to *repair* the structure and exterior of dwelling-houses (and certain installations in them) where the lease is for less than seven years.[175] Further, section 4(4) of the 1972 Act in effect provides that, save in one exceptional circumstance, whenever a landlord has a right to 'enter the premises to carry out any description of maintenance or repair', that is, has a power to repair, he will be deemed to be under an obligation to do so. This last sentence of section 4(4) makes clear that for the purposes of section 4 the landlord's power to effect repairs is transformed into a *sui generis obligation* to repair. We say *sui generis* for a tenant cannot force a landlord to exercise this power, but he can sue him for damage resulting from the failure to exercise it. This represents a potential widening of a landlord's obligations, especially since the Court of Appeal decided in *Mint* v. *Good*[176] that such an implied power exists in any situation in which a landlord may reasonably be expected to enter and carry out repair. This is now the rule as far as weekly tenancies are concerned.

(ii) Builders

At common law, builders who built on *other* peoples' land would be held liable in negligence. However, if they built on their *own* land they were treated as vendors and

172 *Sykes* v. *Harry* [2001] QB 1014 (CA), at 1025, in spite of the fact that the landlord already had a contractual obligation toward the tenant.

173 [2001] QB 1014 (CA).

174 Section 4(5).

175 But this duty does not require the landlord to correct defects that existed from the time the building was put up, let alone to make the house fit for human habitation: *Quick* v. *Taff Ely BC* [1986] QB 809. It was s. 11 of the 1985 Act that had created the confusion in *Sykes* v. *Harry* [2001] QB 1014, given the limitation of the landlord's obligation to repair only defects of which he has actual or constructive notice.

176 [1951] 1 KB 517.

thus enjoyed the immunity of the latter.[177] This immunity was undermined[178] by *Dutton* (where two members of the Court of Appeal proceeded to hold a *local authority* liable for negligent inspection of the foundations of a house), and it was definitely withdrawn by subsequent cases.[179] But an unfortunate 'coupling' of the two liabilities (i.e. that of builders and local authorities) had been made;[180] and when, in more recent times, the House of Lords overruled *Anns* in a case involving a local authority,[181] the liability of builders was further redefined in a restrictive way following the trend set by the slightly earlier decision in *D. & F. Estates* v. *Church Commissioners for England*.[182] The end result thus seems to be that a builder may be liable to a third party (be he the owner, occupier, visitor or passer-by) on the principle of *Donoghue* v. *Stevenson* but only if (*i*) a *latent* defect causes the claimant to suffer (*ii*) *physical* injury.[183] To put it differently, the builder will not be liable if: (*a*) the harm suffered by the claimant is purely economic loss (e.g. expenditure to prevent a collapse of the roof) or (*b*) if the occupier becomes aware of the defect before further damage occurs, for at that stage it ceases to be latent and, according to Lord Keith again, it is 'the latency of the defect which constitutes the mischief'.[184] On this kind of reasoning, therefore, it is the occupier of the premises who must be sued.

Taking conclusions to their logical extremes may not, however, always make practical sense. Thus in *Targett* v. *Torfaen BC*[185] Sir Donald Nicholls V-C (as he then was) rightly pointed out that:

> ... knowledge of the existence of a danger does not always enable a person to avoid the danger. In simple cases it does. In other cases, especially where buildings are concerned, it would be absolutely unrealistic to suggest that a person can always take steps to avoid a danger once he knows of its existence, and that if he does not do so he is the author of his own misfortune.

The *Targett* judgment thus proposes an attenuation of the *Murphy* ruling as far as personal injury or damage to other property is concerned. It thus seems sensible to suggest that the builder remains liable for the harm (as defined above) suffered by the claimant (be he the occupier or visitor of the premises) when it would be unreasonable

[177] *Bottomley* v. *Bannister* [1932] 1 KB 458, *Otto* v. *Bolton & Norris* [1936] 2 KB 46.

[178] *Dutton* v. *Bognor Regis DC* [1972] 1 QB 373. It was subsequently argued that since the builder was not a party to the action, the removal of his immunity was only contained in *dicta*. The acceptance of *Dutton* by later cases such as *Anns* and *Batty* made this debate an academic one. See next note for references.

[179] *Anns* v. *Merton LBC* [1978] AC 728, *Batty* v. *Metropolitan Properties Ltd.* [1978] QB 554.

[180] P. Cane, *Tort Law and Economic Interests* (1991), 513, also doubted the wisdom of making the liabilities of builders and local authorities 'co-extensive'. Contrast Lord Oliver's views in *Murphy* [1991] 1 AC 398, 483.

[181] *Murphy* v. *Brentwood DC* [1991] 1 AC 398. See ch. 3, above, for extensive discussion.

[182] [1989] AC 177.

[183] See e.g. the observations in *Murphy* of Lord Keith at [1991] 1 AC 398, 462, and Lord Bridge at 475. Thus, if damage to *other property* is caused by a negligently built building then liability will attach to the negligent defendant: see *Bellefield Computer Services* v. *E. Turner & Sons* [2000] BLR 97 (CA) and *Baxall Securities Ltd.* v. *Sheard Walshaw Partnership* [2001] BLR 36 (QBD). (The *Baxall* decision was overturned on causation grounds, while acknowledging the design error made by the architect: [2002] BLR 100 (CA).)

[184] [1991] 1 AC 398, 464.

[185] [1992] 3 All ER 27 at 37.

to expect the occupier to remove the patently obvious defect but not unreasonable for the claimant to run the risk of harm through that danger.[186]

A second way one might attempt to make a builder liable would be to argue that the builder was in breach of one of the many statutory duties contained, for example, in section 38 of the Building Act 1984. This could open new vistas to disappointed claimants. However, at the time of writing this section has not yet been brought into force and there is, therefore, no case law to enable one to predict how such actions might fare in practice.

The third and final way for rendering builders liable to third parties may be found in the Defective Premises Act 1972. Section 3 of that statute has already been discussed when the liability of builders/vendors was being considered, so little need be added here. However, section 1 of the same enactment has recently acquired enhanced significance and, despite its limitations, may yet offer the best chance of making builders liable to persons affected by their negligent work. Section 1(1) of the 1972 Act provides that:

> A person taking on work or in connection with the provision of a dwelling... owes a duty: (*a*) if the dwelling is provided to the order of any person, to that person; and (*b*) without prejudice to paragraph (*a*) above, to every person who acquires an interest (whether legal or equitable) in the dwelling, to see that the work which he takes on is done in a workmanlike or, as the case may be, professional manner, with proper materials and so that as regards that work the dwelling will be fit for habitation when completed.

A number of points should be made about this section (in conjunction with s. 1(2) and s. 2 of the same Act).

First, by a person 'taking on work...' one understands—and, in the absence of case law on the Act, this and the points that follow can only represent academic speculation—builders, architects, engineers, surveyors and all kinds of subcontractors. Local authorities and their subcontractors and surveyors are, most likely, excluded from this section (see subsection (iii), below).

Second, the duty is owed to those commissioning the work and anyone who subsequently acquires a legal or equitable interest in the land.

Third, the duty is higher than the ordinary duty in negligence; one knowledgeable commentator has thus described it as 'a wide-ranging "due care" tortious warranty of suitability in favour of purchasers and their successors'.[187]

Fourth, the duty applies only to dwellings and, debatably, excludes other types of buildings such as factories, shops, etc. Further, it covers misfeasance as well as nonfeasance;[188] and, arguably, allows compensation for pure economic loss,[189] which is, however, excluded by the common law.

[186] In *Targett* the plaintiff, a tenant of a council house, successfully sued the designer/builder of the premises when he fell down some external steps which were unlit and had no handrail to make them safe. A 25 per cent reduction in the amount of damages was, however, made on the grounds of contributory negligence.

[187] I. N. Duncan Wallace, '*Anns* beyond Repair' (Select Bibliography), 242.

[188] *Andrews* v. *Schooling* [1991] 1 WLR 783. In *Jacobs* v. *Morton* (1994) 72 BLR 92 at 105, the court took the view that this statutory duty did not apply to the rectification of an existing building.

[189] *Andrews* v. *Schooling* [1991] 1 WLR 783. Contrast *Murphy* v. *Brentwood DC* [1991] 1 AC 398. It is submitted that if the text, above, is correct, it leads to diverging results depending upon whether a cause of action can be framed under the Act or the common law which may not be very logical.

Fifth, the person who takes on work in accordance with section 1(1) may enjoy the defence given him in section 1(2) of the Act. In effect this excuses him from liability if he agreed to do the work in accordance with instructions given by the other party (for whom he is doing the work). The defence does not apply if he owes a duty to warn the other party of any defects in the instructions.

Sixth, actions under the Act are subject to an arguably very brief limitation period of six years. Moreover, this limitation period in effect runs from the date of completion of the work. Surprisingly, the alternative discoverability periods provided by the Latent Damage Act 1986 do not seem to apply.[190]

Finally, and most importantly, in the early years of the Act, dwellings covered by an 'approved scheme'—typically by the National House Builders Protection Scheme—were excluded from the purview of section 1. Surprisingly, at some unspecified date prior to 1988 an agreement was reached between the government and the NHBC that made it possible to utilise the section 1 remedy against builders. This agreement, however, was never publicised; and apparently both our courts and the practitioners in the field remained unaware of it, at least until late in 1990.[191] Two points would follow from this. First, this ignorance did not really matter to plaintiffs while their *Anns* rights remained alive; but, now that the *Anns* rights have been taken away by *Murphy*, the 1972 Act acquires much greater significance. Second, if the courts (including the House of Lords) were indeed unaware of the 1988 change of practice (which made it possible to use section 1 of the 1972 Act against builders), how could they have been reassuring litigants (and themselves) that the 'abolition' of the common-law remedies did not really matter given the existence of the statutory remedies? In this context, therefore, the most that one can say of *Murphy* is that it is consistent with the current mode of their Lordships to leave 'consumer protection' to statute law and not undertake this task themselves. This attitude may satisfy those who believe in the separation of powers; but, in practice, it allows powerful pressure groups to intervene in the legislative process and dilute consumers' rights.

(iii) Local Authorities

The liability of local authorities is discussed in more detail in Chapter 8, below. Here, suffice it to say that after *Murphy* they are not liable for any economic harm (e.g. repair costs) suffered by owners of premises. Surprisingly, their Lordships were also eager to stress that they were also leaving open the question of liability for physical injury to persons (or damage to other property) under the usual *Donoghue* v. *Stevenson* principle. As for damage to other property, the High Court[192] has refused to hold a local

[190] *Warner* v. *Basildon DC* (1991) 7 Const. LJ 146, 154; and see the discussion of the Latent Damage Act 1986 in ch. 8, below.

[191] Thus in *Warner* v. *Basildon DC* (1991) 7 *Const. LJ* 146 at 154, Gibson LJ believed that 97 per cent of houses built in any year were covered by the NHBC scheme 'and, in consequence, the section 1 remedy [of the 1972 Act] is excluded'. There is little concrete evidence that in *Murphy* their Lordships were better informed.

[192] In *Tesco Stores Ltd.* v. *Wards Construction (Investment) Ltd.* (1995) 76 BLR 94.

authority liable for damages caused by its failure to detect a defect in the property which was the result of the builder's failure to comply with building regulations. The result was largely achieved by invoking the elusive device of 'fair, just and reasonable'; and it may even be regarded as dubious in so far as it introduces a distinction—unknown to the common law—between personal injuries and physical damage to property. As stated, the recoverability of the former has yet to be determined whenever compensation for the latter seems to have been excluded.

SELECT BIBLIOGRAPHY

DUNCAN-WALLACE, I. N., '*Anns* Beyond Repair' (1991) 107 *LQR* 228.

GRAVELLS, N.P., 'Defective Premises: Negligence Liability of Builders' (1979) 43 *Conv.* (NS) 97.

JAMES, F., 'Tort Liability of Occupiers of Land: Duties Owed to Licensees and Invitees' (1954) 63 *Yale LJ* 605.

LAW COMMISSION, *Liability for Damage or Injury to Trespassers and Related Questions of Occupier's Liability*, No. 75, Cmnd. 6428 (1976).

LAW REFORM COMMITTEE, Third Report, *Occupier's Liability to Invitees, Licensees and Trespassers*, Cmnd. 9306 (1954).

MCMAHON, B. M. E., 'Conclusions on Judicial Behaviour from a Comparative Study of Occupiers' Liability' (1975) 38 *MLR* 39.

MESHER, J., 'Occupiers, Trespassers and the Unfair Contract Terms Act 1977' (1979) 43 *Conv.* (NS) 58.

NEWARK, F. H., 'The Occupiers' Liability Act (Northern Ireland) 1957' (1958) 12 *NILQ* 203.

NORTH, P. M., *Occupiers' Liability* (1971).

PEARSON COMMITTEE, *Royal Commission on Civil Liability and Compensation for Personal Injury*, Cmnd. 7054–1 (1978), ch. 28.

ROGERS, W. V. H., and CLARKE, M. G., *The Unfair Contract Terms Act 1977* (1978).

SPENCE, J., 'The Defective Premises Act 1972: Defective Law and Defective Law Reform' [1974] *CLJ* 307; [1975] *CLJ* 48.

7

BREACH OF STATUTORY DUTY

1. THE NATURE OF THE ACTION

The action for breach of statutory duty enables the claimant to recover compensation for losses brought about by the defendant's failure to comply with a statutory obligation. Increasing areas of commercial and business activity are regulated by legislation designed to protect the health and safety of employees, consumers, and road-users; regulation may also have the aim of protecting certain property and financial interests. It is unusual for a regulatory statute explicitly to create a private, civil right of action; more frequently, they simply create criminal offences that are sanctioned by fine or imprisonment. It is also possible for a statute to be entirely silent on the question of remedies, making no reference to either civil or criminal sanctions. Unless the statute is explicit on the presence or absence of a private action, it is the task of the court to determine whether, on its proper construction, a civil action arises by implication.[1] A common instance of such an action is the claim of an employee who has been injured at work as a result of the employer's failure to comply with the provisions of health and safety legislation, such as that which requires machinery to be securely fenced. However, a private action for damages will not be inferred automatically. On the contrary, the rules of construction are strict and normally require the claimant to show that he belongs to a class of persons whom the statute was passed to protect. Together with other presumptions of statutory interpretation, this has the effect of substantially restricting the availability of the action for breach of statute.

The action for breach of statutory duty is conceptually separate from the general tort of negligence. The modern view was expressed by Lord Wright in *London Passenger Transport Board* v. *Upson*,[2] where he said that the action for breach of statute was

> a special common law right which is not to be confused in essence with a claim for negligence. The statutory right has its origin in the statute, but the particular remedy of an action for damages is given by the common law in order to make effective for the benefit of the injured

[1] *Cutler* v. *Wandsworth Stadium Ltd.* [1949] AC 398.

[2] [1949] AC 155, 168; *Caswell* v. *Powell Duffryn Associated Collieries Ltd.* [1940] AC 152, 177–8.

party his right to the performance by the defendant of the defendant's statutory duty. It is not a claim in negligence in the strict or ordinary sense.

It follows that the availability and scope of the private action for breach of statute are, in each case, a matter for the construction of the relevant legislation.

It is vital, as a consequence, to distinguish between the action for breach of statute and the action sometimes known as negligence in the exercise of a statutory power.[3] The latter is an instance of negligence at common law, and while the statutory origin of the power in question may help to shape the common law duty, the statute is not, in principle, the *origin* of the action. Thus the celebrated case of *Anns* v. *Merton London Borough Council*[4] was not an action for breach of statutory duty even though the Public Health Acts were used in that case to set the limits to the duty owed by the council; it was an action at common law. Although *Anns* has now been overruled on the precise point of negligence law which it decided,[5] the principle that statutory bodies may be liable for the negligent exercise of their powers remains good law and will be considered in a subsequent chapter.[6]

Although the view expressed by Lord Wright represents the modern consensus, there is some authority for a contrary position according to which the true basis for the action is the idea of 'statutory negligence'. According to this view, the action for statutory breach retains the essential features of the general negligence action. There is, however, one exception. The *standard* of care is no longer set by the common law through the notion of the 'reasonable man' but by the particular statute which 'concretises', or makes more specific, the standard of behaviour required.[7] For example, while an employer is under a general duty of care at common law to have regard to the health and safety of his employees, a provision such as section 14 of the Factories Act 1961 would specify more precisely the content of this obligation by requiring him to fence dangerous machinery.

The question is of more than just theoretical interest. Under the statutory negligence approach, the court is relieved of the need to look for what is almost certainly a fictitious parliamentary intent to grant a private cause of action. There is also a clear acknowledgement that the general law on the scope of the duty of care is relevant to the existence of a statutory claim. The general law on causation and defences (such as consent and contributory negligence) also comes into play. Finally the question of fault is affected and it might become possible, under certain circumstances, for a defendant to avoid liability if he can show that his breach of the statute was not due to fault (either intention or carelessness) on his part.[8]

[3] See P. P. Craig, 'Negligence in the Exercise of a Statutory Power' (1978) 94 *LQR* 240; S. Arrowsmith, *Civil Liability and Public Authorities* (1992), ch. 6.

[4] [1978] AC 728.

[5] *Murphy* v. *Brentwood DC* [1991] 1 AC 398.

[6] Ch. 8, below.

[7] G. L. Williams, 'The Effect of Penal Legislation in the Law of Tort' (Select Bibliography).

[8] German law adopts an essentially similar position under Art. 823 II BGB: if liability under the statute could arise without fault, civil liability will nonetheless be imposed only if the defendant was at fault. See B. S. Markesinis and H. Unberath, *The German Law of Torts* (4th edn., 2002), at 885–8; B. S. Markesinis and J. Fedtke, 'Authority or Reason? The Economic Consequences of Liability for Breach of Statutory Duty in Comparative Perspective' [2007] *Eur. Bus. LR* 6, at 38–43.

The incorporation of breach of statutory duty actions into the general law of negligence is accepted in numerous jurisdictions in the United States, where two theories have developed. Thus, one argues that a breach of statute is *evidence* of negligence on the part of the defendant, whereas the other suggests that such a breach is negligence *per se*. In each case the scope of the private action is limited to a situation where the common law already recognises a duty of care between the parties. This would, for example, happen in a case of physical injury sustained by an employee as a result of his employer's negligence but would not, necessarily, be the case if the damage fell into the category of pure economic loss. In his seminal article on the subject, Thayer suggested that breach of the statute might be negligence *per se* for the reason that no reasonable person commits a crime.[9] This could, on the other hand, lead to a situation in which a minor breach of a criminal regulation, punishable perhaps by a small fine, gives rise to a much more extensive liability to pay tort compensation, which could ruin the defendant financially. The extent of liability might be out of all proportion to the degree of fault involved, in particular if the claimant would not otherwise have incurred a duty of care towards the defendant.[10] The view that the statute provides evidence of negligence in a situation where a general duty of care is already imposed by virtue of the common law received the support of Professor Glanville Williams. This great scholar argued persuasively for the adoption of the statutory negligence theory in English law, finding support for this position in a number of nineteenth century cases.[11]

As the law currently stands, the action for breach of statutory duty is closer to strict liability than to liability for negligence. In particular, in the context of accidents at work the employer's fault is normally irrelevant if there has been a breach of a statutory health and safety regulation for which he is responsible. This approach could be justified by the policy of providing employers with strong incentives to perform these particular duties. In other cases, as we shall see, the courts have given statutes a reading that implies the need to show fault. Though it has been suggested that 'the language used in legislation seems to be largely haphazard . . . it is upon the accident of language that the issue is made to turn'.[12]

Numerous decisions ostensibly applying the test of 'legislative intention' for deciding the presence of an action could be just as well and perhaps better explained using the statutory negligence approach. In the leading case of *Cutler* v. *Wandsworth Stadium*[13] the plaintiff, a bookmaker, sued the occupier of the stadium for breach of section 11(2) of the Betting and Lotteries Act 1934. This made it an offence for the occupier of a licensed dog-racing track to exclude any bookmaker if a lawful totalisator was being operated on the track. The House of Lords held that the purpose of the statute was to

[9] 'Public Wrong and Private Action' (Select Bibliography).

[10] See C. Morris, 'The Role of Criminal Statutes in Negligence Actions' (Select Bibliography); G. Fricke, 'The Juridical Nature of the Action on the Statute' (Select Bibliography).

[11] Williams (Select Bibliography); see *Blamires* v. *Lancashire & Yorkshire Railway* (1873) LR 8 Ex. 283, *Cayzer, Irvine & Co.* v. *Carran Co.* (1884) LR 9 App. Cas. 873.

[12] Williams (Select Bibliography), 243.

[13] [1949] AC 398.

protect the public by preventing the tote having a monopoly, and not to protect the livelihood of the bookmakers. Another way of looking at the case would be to point out that the plaintiff's claim was for financial or pure economic loss, and as a result outside the normal scope of the duty of care in negligence. A similar case is the recent decision of the House of Lords in *Scally* v. *Southern Health and Social Services Board.*[14] Here, several junior doctors sued for financial losses suffered as a result of their employers' failure to notify them of options available under the complex terms of an occupational pension scheme. By the time the doctors found out about these rights, their opportunity to exercise them had expired. This was a breach by the employer of the obligation under employment protection legislation to provide full information concerning terms and conditions of employment.[15] In rejecting a claim for damages in tort for breach of statutory duty the courts pointed to the existence of an alternative remedy under the Act itself, namely an application to an Industrial (now Employment) Tribunal for rectification of the written statement of contract terms.[16] Yet this judgment also reflects the current preference of the courts for a contractual rather than a tort-based remedy for pure economic losses.[17]

To similar effect is *Pickering* v. *Liverpool Daily Post*,[18] which concerned an action for damages brought by a mental patient for the release, contrary to regulations, of information concerning his application for discharge before a mental health tribunal. This was, in essence, a claim for damages for a breach of privacy, and as such outside the normal range of interests protected by tort law. The Court of Appeal allowed the claim for damages on the ground that the regulations were designed to protect applicants from unwelcome publicity, but the House of Lords reversed their decision on the basis that there is

> no authority where a statute has been held... to give a cause of action for breach of statutory duty when the nature of the statutory obligation or prohibition was not such that a breach of it would be likely to cause to a member of the class for whose benefit or protection it was imposed either personal injury, injury to property or economic loss. But publication of unauthorised information about proceedings on a patient's application for discharge to a mental health review tribunal, though it may in one sense be adverse to the patient's interest, is incapable of causing him loss or injury of a kind for which the law awards damages.[19]

The view that the law of tort is inherently incapable of providing damages for breach of privacy is questionable.[20] But the *Pickering* decision nevertheless illustrates an increasing tendency for the courts to deny actions for statutory breach if the effect

14 [1991] 4 All ER 563, noted by M. R. Freedland, 'Individual Contracts of Employment and the Common Law Courts' (1992) 21 *ILJ* 135.

15 See Employment Protection (Consolidation) Act 1978, s. 1 ff. (now contained in the Employment Rights Act 1996, s. 1 ff.), and the equivalent provision for Northern Ireland which was considered in *Scally*, Contracts of Employment and Redundancy Payments Act (Northern Ireland) 1965, s. 4(1)(d).

16 See the judgment of Kelly LJ in the Northern Ireland Court of Appeal [1991] 4 All ER 563.

17 Freedland, 'Individual Contracts' (1992) 21 *ILJ* 135.

18 [1991] 4 All ER 622.

19 *Ibid.*, at 632.

20 See ch. 22 below.

would be to recognise new types of claim. A more recent decision of the House of Lords, *Cullen* v. *Chief Constable of the Royal Ulster Constabulary*,[21] is to similar effect. The plaintiff, who had been arrested under statutory powers derived from prevention of terrorism legislation, was denied immediate access to a solicitor in accordance with those powers; however, in contravention of the relevant statute, he was not given the reasons for the deferral of access. The House of Lords held by a majority that he had no claim for breach of statutory duty. According to Lord Hutton, 'damages are awarded for a breach of statutory duty in order to compensate a person for loss or damage suffered by him by reason of the breach of duty'. Here, 'not only did the plaintiff suffer no personal injury, injury to property or economic loss, but there was no evidence of any harm sustained by him'.[22] Lords Bingham and Steyn argued in a dissenting judgment that the statute 'was apt to create private law rights'[23] which, because of their constitutional nature, should be regarded as actionable *per se*, that is, without the need to show damage. The failure of this argument in *Cullen* is an indication of how restrictive the courts' approach to the tort of breach of statutory duty has become.

The courts were not always so reluctant to develop the tort. Appeals to precedent aside, a strong argument against the 'statutory negligence' theory is that confining liability to cases where the common law has already recognised the existence of a duty situation, and where the defendant can be shown to have been at fault, would unduly restrict the development of the law of tort. The courts, it is said, should be able to grant a private action for damages going beyond the existing common law in areas where Parliament has recognised the importance of the interests at stake.[24] Recovery for financial loss developed in this way, through actions for breach of statutory duty, before the decision in *Hedley Byrne & Co. Ltd.* v. *Heller & Partners Ltd.*[25] which established a non-contractual duty of care at common law in respect of economic loss caused by financial misstatements. The most striking decision is *Monk* v. *Warbey*,[26] in which the Court of Appeal allowed the victim of a road accident an action for damages against the owner of the car who had permitted another to drive it uninsured, contrary to section 35 of the Road Traffic Act 1930. This was a claim for financial losses flowing from the inability of the plaintiff to claim on the defendant's insurance; it was not a claim to the effect that the plaintiff had caused the physical injuries himself.

In reality, the growth of a nominate tort separate from the general tort of negligence can only be accounted for by an historical rather than a conceptual perspective. The action for breach of statutory duty developed as it did in the final quarter of the nineteenth century precisely in order to avoid the restrictiveness of the then common law in the area of employers' liability. As we shall note in Chapter 18, for most of the nineteenth century it had been possible to defeat common law claims for personal injury through one or more of the three defences of consent, contributory negligence,

21 [2003] 1 WLR 1763. 22 *Ibid.*, at 1779.

23 *Ibid.*, at 1770.

24 R. A. Buckley, 'Liability in Tort for Breach of Statutory Duty' (Select Bibliography), 208.

25 [1964] AC 465; see *Woods* v. *Winskill* [1913] 2 Ch. 303.

26 [1935] 1 KB 75.

and common employment.[27] The action for breach of statutory duty was a means of overcoming these defences. In *Groves* v. *Lord Wimborne*[28] the Court of Appeal held that common employment was no defence to a claim based on the employer's failure to fence dangerous machinery under the Factory and Workshop Act 1878. It was later held that consent could be no defence to a claim based on statute either.[29] The rationale for this was that no one could effectively grant his consent to the breach of an obligation imposed by Parliament. But the defences could not have been sidestepped in this way had the courts perceived the action as originating in the common law. But for *Groves* v. *Wimborne*,[30] the action for breach of the statute would most likely have been consigned to a 'history of total obscurity' and 'haphazard applications'.[31]

The scope of these defences is, today, substantially reduced (common employment was abolished altogether in 1948[32]), largely removing the rationale for treating the action for breach of statutory duty any differently from common law negligence. It should be stressed, at the same time, that the action for breach of statute, if not part of the tort of negligence, is nevertheless 'tortious in character'.[33] Principles of causation apply in the normal way[34] and there is modern authority to suggest that consent and contributory negligence may be partially applicable as well.[35] But if the separation of the statutory action from general principles of negligence is, more than anything else, an historical accident, a strong case for its reintegration exists in terms of doctrinal clarity and predictability of application. Nor has its separation from the tort of negligence allowed the action for breach of statute to develop into new areas of liability. On the contrary, the action for breach of statute has declined to the point where the courts scarcely recognise the possibility of an Act or regulation creating a new private action unless it does so explicitly. This is partly because, when the courts are seeking the necessary parliamentary intention, they are 'looking for what is not there'.[36] The fiction of legislative intention, which formerly made the law of statutory breach unpredictable, now simply tends to make it restrictive, as the decisions in *Scally* v. *Southern Health and Social Service Board*[37] and *Pickering* v. *Liverpool Daily Post*[38] only too clearly illustrate. As a consequence the modern action for statutory breach is really of much significance only in the areas of industrial health and safety and accidents on the highway, where the courts have freely inferred its existence in a range of situations. Outside this area the instances of civil liability for statutory breach are few and far between.

[27] Which barred any action against the employer where the plaintiff was injured through the negligence of a fellow worker.

[28] [1898] 2 QB 402.

[29] *Wheeler* v. *New Merton Board Mills Ltd.* [1933] 2 KB 669.

[30] [1898] 2 QB 402.

[31] K. M. Stanton, *Breach of Statutory Duty in Tort* (Select Bibliography), 3.

[32] Law Reform (Personal Injuries) Act 1948, s. 1.

[33] *American Express Co.* v. *British Airways Board* [1983] 1 WLR 701, 709 (Lloyd J).

[34] See e.g. *McWilliams* v. *Sir William Arrol* [1962] 1 WLR 295; below, Section 2(c).

[35] See respectively, *Imperial Chemical Industries* v. *Shatwell* [1965] AC 656 and *Caswell* v. *Powell Duffryn Associated Collieries Ltd.* [1940] AC 152.

[36] Williams (Select Bibliography), 244.

[37] [1991] 4 All ER 563, above.

[38] [1991] 4 All ER 622.

When the Canadian Supreme Court had the chance to reconsider the nature of breach of statutory duty in *R in the Right of Canada* v. *Saskatchewan Wheat Pool*[39] it decisively rejected the current position of English law. Reviewing the authorities, Dixon J contrasted American developments assimilating the tort of statutory breach into general negligence with the 'painful emergence' in England of the separate nominate tort. He also rejected Thayer's view that breach of statutory duty should amount to negligence *per se* in favour of the more flexible view that it was only evidence of negligence, at least in cases not involving industrial health and safety. In this case, the breach by the defendants of a regulation prohibiting the discharge of infected grain from an elevator did not, in the absence of proof of a lack of care, give the plaintiff authority for an action for damages for the costs of fumigating the two ships which had been loaded with the grain.

2. THE COMPONENTS OF LIABILITY

It is necessary, in the first place, to determine whether a private action arises under a particular statute, and then second to see whether the claim falls under the scope of the action in question.

(A) THE AVAILABILITY OF A CIVIL REMEDY

In some cases a statute will state explicitly whether or not a private action lies for its breach. Private actions of any kind may be completely excluded.[40] Alternatively, as in the Nuclear Installations Act 1965, the scheme of compensation provided by the Act may be stated to be exhaustive. Section 12(1)(b) states that compensation for breach of the Act's provisions is payable only in accordance with the terms of the Act itself, and that 'no other liability shall be incurred by any person in respect of that injury or damage'. The Sex Discrimination Act 1975 sets up a scheme of remedies, including damages, administered by Employment Tribunals. The regular courts are excluded by a provision to the effect that 'no proceedings, whether civil or criminal, shall lie against any person in respect of an act by reason that the act is unlawful by virtue of a provision of this Act'.[41]

A third possibility is to provide for enforcement through a specially created action for breach of statutory duty. The Health and Safety at Work Act 1974 provides that 'breach of a duty imposed by health and safety regulations . . . shall, so far as it causes damage, be actionable except in so far as the regulations provide otherwise'.[42] Regulations made under the Act are gradually modernising and in some cases replacing

[39] (1983) 143 DLR (3d) 9.

[40] See e.g. Safety of Sports Grounds Act 1975, s. 13; Guard Dogs Act 1975, s. 5(2).

[41] Section 62; on remedies more generally see ss. 63–6. Parallel provisions operate in the context of other prohibited grounds of discrimination (see e.g. Race Relations Act 1976, ss. 53–7).

[42] Section 47(1)(a).

regulations under the Factories Act 1961 and Offices, Shops and Railway Premises Act 1963, although many of the latter remain in force. However, it should be noted that the *general* duty of an employer 'to ensure, so far as is reasonably practicable, the health, safety and welfare of his employees' under section 2(1) of the Health and Safety at Work Act does not give rise to a private action for damages.[43] Had it done so it could have rendered obsolete most of the employer's general duty of care at common law and pushed employers' civil responsibility farther in the direction of stricter liability.[44]

A variety of statutory formulae may be used explicitly to create a private action. For example, section 145 of the Trade Union and Labour Relations (Consolidation) Act 1992, which prohibits a refusal to deal with a prospective supplier of goods and services on the grounds related to his employment of trade unionists, is enforced as follows:

> The obligation to comply with this section is a duty owed to the person with whom there is a refusal to deal and to any other person who may be adversely affected by its contravention; and a breach of the duty is actionable accordingly (subject to the defences and other incidents applying to actions for breach of statutory duty).

Yet another model is provided by the Local Government Act 1988, section 17 of which governs the terms of commercial contracts agreed by local authorities with commercial suppliers. Failure to comply with section 17 is stated not to be a criminal offence, but it is 'actionable by any person who, in consequence, suffers loss or damage'.[45]

The difficulties begin when the statute is silent on the question of civil liability. The Law Commission has proposed the enactment of a general presumption to the effect that in these circumstances a breach of statutory duty will be actionable in damages,[46] but this has not been taken up. In the absence of such a measure, the courts' approach is that expressed by Viscount Simonds in *Cutler* v. *Wandsworth Stadium Ltd*. There, the learned judge stated that 'the only rule, which in all the circumstances is valid, is that the answer must depend on a consideration of the whole Act and the circumstances, including the preexisting law, in which it was enacted'.[47]

In *Cutler*'s case the House of Lords rejected the notion of a general presumption of civil liability for statutory breach which was raised by Greer LJ in *Monk* v. *Warbey*.[48] In *Monk* Greer LJ had said that:

> *prima facie* a person who has been injured by breach of a statute has a right to recover damages from the person committing it, unless it can be established by considering the whole of the Act that no such right was intended to be given.

Although there are nineteenth-century precedents for the view that the common law provides 'an action on the case for special damage sustained by the breach of a public

43 Health and Safety at Work Act 1974, s. 47(1)(a).

44 On employer's liability in general, see ch. 18, below.

45 Section 19(7).

46 Law Commission, *The Interpretation of Statutes: Report by the Two Commissions* (Select Bibliography).

47 [1949] AC 398, 407.

48 [1935] 1 KB 75, 81.

duty',[49] this approach is not generally followed today. The law was restated by Lord Diplock in *Lonrho Ltd.* v. *Shell Petroleum Co. Ltd. (No. 2)*. The normal rule, according to his Lordship, was to the effect that a civil action was excluded in any case where the statute provided for a criminal sanction as the means of enforcing the relevant duty. To this there were two exceptions:

> the first is where on the true construction of the Act it is apparent that the obligation or prohibition was imposed for the benefit or protection of a particular class of individuals.... The second exception is where the statute creates a public right (i.e. a right to be enjoyed by all those of Her Majesty's subjects who wish to avail themselves of it) and a particular member of the public suffers what Brett J in *Benjamin* v. *Storr*[50] described as 'particular, direct and substantial' damage 'other and different from that which was common to all the rest of the public'.[51]

If anything, Lord Diplock's second exception states the law rather broadly; there are very few examples of such a wide principle being invoked to grant a civil action for breach of statutory duty other than in the context of public nuisance.[52] In this case, Lonrho complained that the defendants' alleged supply of oil and gas in breach of sanctions orders made under the Southern Rhodesia Act 1965 had caused it a loss of business. For it had maintained the illegal Rhodesian regime in power and postponed the resumption of normal oil supplies through the plaintiff's pipeline. The action was misconceived, said Lord Diplock, because the orders neither were passed for the protection of a group of which the plaintiffs formed part nor had they conferred a benefit on the public generally: they simply imposed a prohibition on activity which had previously been lawful. The implication is that a measure passed for the protection of the public as a whole may give rise to a private action for damages by a person who suffers special damage. This second category is wider, however, than any envisaged by the House of Lords in *Cutler* v. *Wandsworth Stadium Ltd.*,[53] and it is difficult to reconcile with the approach taken in other leading authorities.[54] It also rests on the difficult distinction between an Act that is read as conferring a public benefit, on the one hand, and one that is read as simply prohibiting an activity, on the other.

It must normally be shown, then, that the statutory duty was imposed for the benefit of a particular class of persons separate from the public at large. In *Cutler* v. *Wandsworth*

[49] *Couch* v. *Steel* (1854) 3 El & Bl. 402, 415 (Lord Campbell CJ), in which a merchant seaman who fell ill at sea successfully sued his employer for damages arising from breach of legislation requiring ships to carry medicines on board. This case would now quite easily be interpreted as a case of a statute designed for the protection of a particular group.

[50] (1874) LR 9 CP 400, 407.

[51] [1982] AC 173, 182.

[52] As Lord Diplock put it ([1982] AC 173, 182), 'most of the authorities about this second exception deal not with public rights created by statute but with public rights existing at common law, particularly in respect of use of highways': *Boyce* v. *Paddington BC* [1903] 1 Ch. 109 is 'one of the comparatively few cases about a right conferred on the general public by statute' (*ibid.*).

[53] [1949] AC 398.

[54] *Atkinson* v. *Newcastle Waterworks Co.* (1877) 2 Ex. D 441; *Phillips* v. *Britannia Hygienic Laundry Co.* [1923] 2 KB 832.

Stadium Ltd.[55] the House of Lords, as we have seen, decided that regulations providing for bookmakers' access to licensed racing tracks were imposed in the interests of ensuring choice for the public and not to protect the bookmakers' economic interests. More recently, in *R* v. *Deputy Governor of Parkhurst Prison, ex parte Hague*[56] the House of Lords held that the Prison Rules 1964 were essentially regulatory in character. Thus, they did not give rise to a private right of action on the part of a prisoner who was confined in breach of the Rules. Conversely, the initial expansion of employers' civil liability for statutory breach took place because the courts saw the Factory and Workshop Acts as clearly passed for the benefit of the industrial workforce. In *Groves* v. *Lord Wimborne*[57] A. L. Smith LJ had this to say of the Factory and Workshop Act 1878:

The Act... is not in the nature of a private legislative bargain between employers and workmen as the learned judge seemed to think, but is a public Act passed in favour of the workers in factories and workshops to compel their employers to do certain things for their protection and benefit.

As a guide to construction, however, the 'recognisable class of claimants' test has not always proved easy to apply consistently. In *Phillips* v. *Britannia Hygienic Laundry Co.*[58] the Court of Appeal held that no right of action arose out of breach of a vehicle use and construction order which produced a defective condition in the defendant's van. The defect led to an accident in which the plaintiff's van was damaged. According to Bankes LJ, 'the public using the highway is not a class; it is the public itself and not a class of the public'.[59] The decision cannot be reconciled with *Monk* v. *Warbey*,[60] in which breach of a vehicle owner's obligation to take out appropriate liability insurance under the Road Traffic Act 1930 was held to create a right of private action on the part of an accident victim. Of the two decisions *Monk* v. *Warbey* now seems anomalous, given the restrictive modern approach to allowing statutory actions. The courts' protective attitude towards victims of industrial accidents is at odds, however, with the approach taken with regard to those injured on the highway. Another restrictive decision is *McCall* v. *Abelesz*,[61] in which the Court of Appeal denied a private action to residential tenants in a case where the breach of statutory duty amounted to the crime of harassment. It is not clear why this group could not have constituted a relevant class for whose protection the regulations were passed. More recently the courts have had to consider claims for damages for breach of legislation prohibiting the unauthorised recording and distribution of musical performances by 'bootleggers'. After some debate, it was held that actions for damages could be brought by the performers and musicians affected but not by their record companies. Yet the latter would undoubtedly suffer loss, as contracts

55 [1949] AC 498.

56 [1992] 1 AC 58, 159–61 (Lord Bridge of Harwich), 178–9 (Lord Jauncey of Tullichettle). See also *Calveley* v. *Chief Constable of Merseyside* [1989] AC 1228, 1237 (Lord Bridge of Harwich).

57 [1898] 2 QB 402, 406. For discussion of *Groves* and its continuing relevance on this point, see *Ziemniak* v. *ETPM Deep Sea Ltd.* [2003] EWCA Civ. 636.

58 [1923] 2 KB 832, 840. 59 *Ibid.*

60 [1935] 1 KB 75; the relevant provision is now contained in the Road Traffic Act 1988, ss. 143 ff.

61 [1976] QB 585.

with the artists for their exclusive recording rights would be made less valuable as a result of the illegitimate competition of the bootleggers.[62]

The provision by the Act of a criminal penalty or other remedy for its breach has been seen in numerous cases as having some bearing on the availability of the civil remedy, but it is difficult to draw any clear conclusion either way as to the effect it might have. The presence of criminal penalties under the nineteenth-century Factory and Workshop Acts did not stop the courts from developing employers' liability for statutory breach. Divergent conclusions, however, have been reached in cases concerning utilities and public authorities. *Atkinson* v. *Newcastle and Gateshead Waterworks Co.*[63] was an early decision restricting liability. In that case a waterworks company had failed to maintain the necessary water pressure, in contravention of legislation,[64] with the result that firemen were unable to put out a fire which then damaged the plaintiff's house. The court held that the £10 fine prescribed by the Act was meant to be an exclusive remedy. In *Dawson & Co.* v. *Bingley Urban District Council*,[65] on the other hand, the defendant council was held liable in a civil action for the consequences of placing an inaccurate direction to a fire plug in breach of the Public Health Act 1875. For, as a result of this misdirection, the fire brigade had been delayed in putting out a fire on the plaintiff's premises. *Atkinson* was distinguished on the unconvincing grounds that the Act of 1875 provided for no separate penalty, and that the defendant in *Atkinson* was a private company. The decision in *Atkinson* is more easily explicable as a justified attempt to avoid the imposition of 'floodgates' liability on utilities, and to shift the burden of fire insurance on to householders.[66] Legislation regulating the privatised utilities now provides for them to compensate consumers affected by the interruption to supplies of gas, water and electricity.[67]

Atkinson was, again, distinguished in *Read* v. *Croydon Corporation*,[68] a case involving the same Act, the Waterworks Clauses Act 1847, but a different section which placed the defendants under a duty to supply clean water.[69] As a result of their breach, the plaintiff's infant daughter contracted typhoid. The case was not, as it might appear, one of damages for injury and disease. The action was, instead, brought by the father in his capacity as a ratepayer and therefore a member of a protected class, and compensation was awarded for pure economic loss, namely his expenses incurred as a result of the child's illness.

62 *RCA Corporation* v. *Pollard* [1983] Ch. 135; *Rickless* v. *United Artists Corporation* [1988] QB 40; see also *Ex parte Island Records* [1978] Ch. 122 and *Lonrho Ltd.* v. *Shell Petroleum Co. Ltd.* [1982] AC 175, discussed further below. The relevant legislation, the Dramatic and Musical Performers' Protection Act 1958, has now been replaced by the Copyright, Designs and Patents Act 1988, ss. 180 ff., which provides protection for both performers and those with exclusive recording rights.

63 (1877) LR 2 Exch. D 441.

64 The Waterworks Clauses Act 1847, s. 47.

65 [1911] 2 KB 149.

66 Buckley (Select Bibliography); see also *Clegg, Parkinson & Co.* v. *Earby Gas Co.* [1896] 1 QB 592.

67 Both the utility itself and third persons who induce a breach of its statutory duty may be liable in tort. See generally the discussion in G. S. Morris, 'Industrial Action in Essential Services: The New Law' (1991) 20 *ILJ* 89.

68 [1938] 4 All ER 631.

69 Section 35.

A potentially significant extension of the liability of local authorities for statutory breaches was made in *Thornton* v. *Kirklees Metropolitan Borough Council*,[70] in which the Court of Appeal held that a person wrongfully denied relief under the Housing (Homeless Persons) Act 1977 could sue the authority in damages. The court was influenced by the absence of any specified penalty for breach of the Act. Where, by contrast, the statute provides for a distinct adjudicative procedure for determining eligibility for a public benefit, as it does for social security payments, a separate civil action for damages will normally be excluded.[71] *Thornton* was criticised as 'quite out of line with other cases regarding civil liability for breach of statutory duty'[72] and as a 'puzzling' decision which 'may have to be reconsidered at some future date'.[73] Decisions since *Thornton* suggest that even in a case where there is a recognisable class of claimants, the courts will lean against finding a private cause of action where the statutory provisions in question confer broad discretionary powers on public bodies. In *X (Minors)* v. *Bedfordshire Country Council*[74] the House of Lords ruled out claims for breach of statutory duty brought by victims of child abuse against local authorities who, it was alleged, had failed to take adequate steps to protect them. In particular, it was argued that the defendants had failed to act in accordance with their statutory duties to initiate proceedings to take them into care. Lord Browne-Wilkinson concluded, on the basis of a close reading of the relevant legislation, that:

> the section itself points out the basic tension which lies at the root of so much child protection work: the decision whether to split the family in order to protect the child. I find it impossible to construe such a statutory provision as demonstrating an intention that even where there is no carelessness by the authority it should be liable in damages if a court subsequently decided with hindsight that the removal, or failure to remove, the child from the family either was or was not 'consistent with' the duty to safeguard the child.[75]

This approach was applied in *O'Rourke* v. *Camden London Borough Council*,[76] in which *Thornton* was finally overruled. According to Lord Hoffmann, it was inappropriate to infer the existence of a private cause of action given the wide discretion which the Act conferred upon the council when making decisions on the allocation of resources to deal with homelessness.[77]

[70] [1979] 1 WLR 637. See also *West Wiltshire DC* v. *Garland* [1995] Ch. 297, in which the same factor led the Court of Appeal to hold that a local council had a cause of action against district auditors for their failure to fulfil their statutory obligation to audit the council's accounts.

[71] See *Jones* v. *Department of Employment* [1989] QB 1.

[72] J. A. Weir, 'Governmental Liability' [1988] *PL* 40, 52. Cf. *Wyatt* v. *Hillingdon LBC* (1978) 76 LGR 727, 723: 'a statute . . . which is dealing with the distribution of benefits . . . does not in its very nature give rise to an action by the disappointed . . . person' (Geoffrey Lane LJ).

[73] *X (Minors)* v. *Bedfordshire CC* [1995] 2 AC 633, 748 (Lord Browne-Wilkinson).

[74] [1995] 2 AC 633; see also *Clunis* v. *Camden and Islington HA* [1998] QB 978.

[75] [1995] 2 AC 633, 747–8.

[76] [1998] AC 189.

[77] See the argument against this line of reasoning in R. Carnwath, 'The *Thornton* Heresy Exposed' (Select Bibliography).

(B) THE SCOPE OF THE CIVIL REMEDY

Once the existence of the action is established, it remains to see whether the claimant's claim falls within its scope. Here, three issues are relevant: whether the defendant's conduct infringed the standard set by the Act; whether the claimant was a member of the class protected by the Act; and whether the damage occurred in the manner against which the Act was meant to guard. These requirements are strictly enforced and frequently result in the failure of actions for breach of statutory duty.

It is axiomatic, first of all, that the terms of the relevant provision must have been broken. Criminal statutes are strictly construed. In *Chipchase* v. *British Titan Products Co. Ltd.*[78] a regulation required a platform more than six feet six inches from the ground to be at least thirty-four inches wide if there was a danger of a workman falling from it. The plaintiff fell from a platform that was nine inches wide but only six feet above the ground. On this basis no claim could arise under the statute, although a claim in general negligence could be argued.

In conformity with the view that the right to bring the action derives from the particular statute which creates the obligation and not from the general law of negligence, the appropriate standard for judging the defendant's behaviour can only be arrived at by a process of statutory construction. Certain provisions have been interpreted as giving rise to strict liability, such as the requirement in section 14(1) of the Factories Act 1961 that 'every dangerous part of any machinery... shall be securely fenced'. Thus, in *John Summers & Sons Ltd.* v. *Frost*[79] this provision was used to impose liability for an injury caused by the unfenced part of a grinding-wheel, even though the machine could not have been used at all if completely fenced in. In effect, it was impossible to comply with the statute except by removing the machine from service, which was unlikely to have been the aim of the Act. The effect of the decision had to be reversed by statutory order.[80]

In other cases the otherwise unconditional words of the statute are qualified by the use of a phrase requiring the employer to maintain a safe workplace 'as far as reasonably practicable', a standard which comes close to that of negligence liability.[81] In *Nimmo* v. *Alexander Cowan & Sons*[82] a bare majority of the House of Lords held that the use of this phrase in section 29 of the Factories Act 1961 placed the onus on the employer of showing that he had taken all reasonable precautions. Sometimes the word 'practicable' appears on its own, which may be taken as indicating a standard midway between negligence and strict liability; thus section 157 of the Mines and Quarries Act 1957 enables the employer to avoid liability where 'it was impracticable to avoid or prevent the contravention'. There is little consistency in the way provisions such as these are drafted,

[78] [1956] 1 QB 545.

[79] [1955] AC 740. See also the imposition of strict liability for breach of regulations relating to the use of asbestos in *Cherry Tree Machine Co. Ltd. and Shell Tankers (UK) Ltd.* v. *Dawson* [2001] PIQR P19.

[80] Abrasive Wheels Regulations 1970 (SI No. 1970/535), reg. 3.

[81] See e.g. ss. 28 and 29 of the Factories Act 1961 (obligation to keep floors, etc. and means of access free of obstruction).

[82] [1968] AC 107.

and 'often it is difficult to find any reason' for one formulation being preferred over another.[83]

The approach taken to interpreting section 14 of the Factories Act is something of an exception, explicable perhaps by the historical importance of that section in the development of the statutory action and its practical importance for workplace safety. In interpreting other provisions the courts normally manage to avoid finding an employer or occupier strictly liable if he has been wholly blameless. In *Scott* v. *Green & Sons*[84] the plaintiff, who was injured when a cellar flap on the pavement gave way beneath him, failed in an action against the owner for breach of section 154 of the Highways Act 1959. The flap had been damaged shortly before when an unidentified lorry driver had driven his vehicle on to it; the defendants had not had time to become aware of the damage, let alone to have done anything about it. To similar effect is *Whitfield* v. *H. & R. Johnson* (*Tiles*) *Ltd.*[85] There, the plaintiff sued her employer for breach of section 72 of the Factories Act 1961, which provides that 'a person shall not be employed to lift, carry or move any load so heavy as to be likely to cause injury to him'. Unknown to either party the plaintiff was suffering from a latent back condition which was triggered when she lifted a load that would normally have given her no difficulty. In rejecting the claim, the Court of Appeal held that section 72 did not require the employer to take the plaintiff as he found her. The section, according to the court, was 'intended to make sure that the weight of the load was appropriate to the sex, build and physique, or other obvious characteristic, of the employee in question'.[86] The employer was protected against liability for a concealed risk of injury without the court finding, as such, that the standard was less than strict. But the decision can be questioned since had it been a negligence action the 'eggshell skull' principle—that the defendant takes the plaintiff as he finds her—would most likely have resulted in a finding for the plaintiff in this case.

The second issue to consider is whether the claimant falls into the class of persons protected by the Act. In *Knapp* v. *Railway Executive*[87] an accident occurred when a level-crossing gate that had been insecurely locked swung back across the railway line when a train was approaching, as a result of which its driver was injured. This was a breach of a regulation requiring gates to be kept closed to the road when a train was approaching and closed to the railway at all other times. The driver's claim for damages for breach of statutory duty failed. The Court of Appeal found that the purpose of the regulation was the protection of the road-using public and not the employees of the railway. 'The conflict of interest,' said the court, 'with which the legislature is here dealing is clearly a conflict between the road-using public . . . and the railway company . . . and the whole purport of the section is to protect the road-using public against the railway company, it being assumed that the railway company, having got its power of running over the railway, will so manage its affairs that its traffic can proceed in safety.'[88]

If the principle is clear, however, its application here is open to question. There is no reason why the regulation should not have sought to protect the safety of those on the

[83] [1968] AC 107 (Lord Reid). [84] [1969] 1 WLR 301. [85] [1990] 3 All ER 426.
[86] *Ibid.*, 434–5 (Beldam LJ). [87] [1949] 2 All ER 508. [88] *Ibid.*, 515 (Jenkins LJ).

train, both employees and passengers, as well as those using the highway. Also open to question is *Hartley* v. *Mayoh & Co.*[89] A fireman was electrocuted in the course of fighting a blaze at the defendant's factory. His injury was brought about by a breach of electricity regulations passed for the protection of 'persons employed' in factories and workshops. It was held that a fireman was not a person employed in a factory, and so an action for damages for statutory breach failed. The result is the consequence of seeing the statutory breach in isolation from any wider tort duty. It also stems directly from the 'statutory interpretation' approach, which as explained above, ascribes the existence of the damages claim to a fictitious Parliamentary intention as opposed to a pre-existing duty of care at common law.

A narrow approach to statutory interpretation is also evident in cases involving the duty of local authorities to maintain the highway in a state of repair. This duty is of pre-modern origin, but a private action for its breach only became available in 1961, thanks to a provision which has now become under section 41 of the Highways Act 1980.[90] This refers to a duty to 'maintain the highway'. In *Goodes* v. *East Sussex County Council*[91] the House of Lords held that this did not extend to a duty to remove ice and snow from the road, a decision subsequently reversed by Parliament. In *Gorringe* v. *Calderdale Metropolitan Borough Council*[92] the House of Lords maintained its restrictive view of section 41, holding that it did not impose a duty to provide adequate warning signs. By contrast, in *Department for Transport, Environment and the Regions* v. *Mott, MacDonald Ltd.*,[93] where the problem emanated under the surface of the road, the Court of Appeal held that there was a violation of the duty under the Highways Act.

(C) CAUSATION, REMOTENESS AND DEFENCES

'But-for' or 'factual' causation must be established in the normal way. Thus in *McWilliams* v. *Sir William Arrol & Co. Ltd.*[94] the employer successfully defended a claim for damages brought by the widow of the deceased employee, who had fallen from a platform 70 feet above ground while not wearing a safety harness as required by legislation.[95] The defendant's defence succeeded because he was able to show that the employee would not have worn a harness even if one had been provided. The claimant's claim will thus fail if the only reason for the employer's breach of the statutory duty was the claimant's own act of carelessness. To put it differently: the victim can have no claim if he was the sole cause of

89 [1954] 1 QB 383.

90 It was originally contained in the Highways (Miscellaneous Provisions) Act 1961, s. 1(1).

91 [2000] 1 WLR 1356.

92 [2004] 1 WLR 1057. For discussion, see Markesinis and Fedtke, 'Authority or Reason?' [2007] *Eur. Bus. LR* 6, at 16.

93 [2006] EWCA Civ. 1089, [2006] 1 WLR 3356. Carnwath LJ's speech is an interesting example of the Court of Appeal limiting the application of what it clearly considers an unreasonable House of Lords authority where the latter is problematic in the way it deals with case law authority and with statutory interpretation.

94 [1962] 1 WLR 295.

95 Factories Act 1937, s. 61: 'Where any person is to work at a place from which he is liable to fall a distance more than ten feet, then . . . means shall be provided, so far as is reasonably practicable, by fencing or otherwise for ensuring his safety.'

his own loss.[96] For the same reason, contributory negligence used to be a total defence before the law was modified by the Law Reform (Contributory Negligence) Act 1945. The position was summarised by Lord Atkin in *Caswell* v. *Powell Duffryn Associated Collieries*:

> The person who is injured, as in all cases where the damage is the gist of the action, must show not only a breach of duty but that his hurt was due to the breach. If his damage is due entirely to his own wilful act no cause of action arises as, for instance, if out of bravado he puts his hand into moving machinery or attempts to leap over an unguarded cavity. The injury has not been caused by the defendants' omission but by the plaintiff's own act.[97]

Lord Atkin went on to say that where the employers' breach and the plaintiff's lack of care for himself combine to cause the injury, the defence of contributory negligence would apply to defeat the plaintiff's claim. This, however, must now be read subject to the 1945 Act and the interpretation subsequently placed upon it, namely that in such a case of concurrent causes the court will apportion the responsibility of the two parties and award the claimant a reduced measure of damages.[98] For the employee's own breach of statutory duty constitutes 'fault' for the purposes of the Act of 1945.[99]

The most severe limitation of the action for statutory breach is the principle, laid down in *Gorris* v. *Scott*,[100] that the loss or damage must have been of the kind which the statute was passed to prevent and must have occurred in the manner the statute contemplated. An order made under the Contagious Diseases (Animals) Act 1869 required cattle to be placed in separate pens of a certain size when being transported by ship. The plaintiff's cattle were carried on board a ship without pens of any kind, as a result of which they were washed overboard in heavy seas. An action on the statute failed as the court found that its purpose was to control the spread of disease and not to prevent the cattle from being washed away. While breach and damage were undoubtedly linked in the sense of *but-for cause*, the damage here could not be said to be within the scope of the risk envisaged by the statute. Hence, to use the language of negligence liability, it was *too remote* as far as the statutory action was concerned.

The application of *Gorris* v. *Scott* to industrial injury cases has been controversial. In particular, the courts have interpreted the duty to fence machinery in section 14 of the Factories Act 1961 and its predecessors as intended to cover a situation in which an employee puts his hand into a moving machine, and not one in which an employee is injured by a part of an unfenced machine flying out and hitting him.[101] It is not obvious that this interpretation of section 14 is the correct one.[102] But assuming that it is correct, the strictness with which the 'risk principle' is applied in statutory cases of personal injury contrasts with the much looser approach we find in the general law of

[96] *Ginty* v. *Belmont Building Supplies Ltd.* [1959] 1 All ER 414, *Boyle* v. *Kodak Ltd.* [1969] 1 WLR 661.
[97] [1940] AC 152, 164.
[98] *Jones* v. *Livox Quarries Ltd.* [1952] 2 QB 608.
[99] See the judgment of Lord Diplock in *Boyle* v. *Kodak Ltd.* [1969] 1 WLR 661.
[100] (1874) LR 9 Exch. 125.
[101] See in particular, the decision of the House of Lords in *Close* v. *Steel Company of Wales Ltd.* [1962] AC 367, and the authorities cited there.
[102] See the vigorous dissent of Lord Denning, *ibid.*

negligence. For in the latter case, it is not open to a defendant to claim that injury of a foreseeable kind occurred in a *manner* which was not foreseeable.[103] If *Gorris* v. *Scott* is essentially the application of remoteness rules in the context of statutory actions, there is much to be said for adopting the approach of the common law and drawing a distinction between property damage, where liability is narrowly confined to the envisaged risk, and personal injury cases, where a far more flexible approach is taken.

Many statutes that have given rise to the possibility of a private action expressly prevent the application of exclusion and limitation clauses.[104] Rather more uncertainty surrounds the defence of consent. It was suggested earlier that this defence should apply to a statutory claim as to any other claim in tort. But since the action for breach of statutory duty was separated from the common law of negligence in large part because of the need to limit the scope of the defence of consent,[105] its application remains in some doubt.[106] As the defence has been narrowed considerably since the 1890s there is probably now no good reason to exclude it. Nevertheless, the House of Lords was appropriately cautious in allowing a partial application of the defence in *ICI Ltd.* v. *Shatwell.*[107] Lords Reid and Pearce both suggested that the defence would be inapplicable if the employer either in person or, if a corporation, through its managerial or supervisory employees, were directly implicated in the breach of statutory duty. However, the defence of *volenti* could apply where the employer was liable for breach of statutory duty solely by virtue of his vicarious liability for a breach committed by the claimant. This was the case in *Shatwell*, where the plaintiff clearly consented to running the risk of the danger in question. According to Lord Pearce:

> the defence should be available where the employer was not himself in breach of statutory duty and was not vicariously in breach of any statutory duty through the neglect of some person who was of superior rank and whose commands the plaintiff was bound to obey (or who had some different and special duty of care...).[108]

This creates an area of difficulty since it may be far from clear what, in any given case, the phrase 'employee of superior rank' really means.

(D) A WIDER PRINCIPLE OF CIVIL LIABILITY?

The feeling has persisted that in *Cutler* v. *Wandsworth Stadium Ltd.*[109] the House of Lords clarified the law of liability for statutory breach in an unduly restrictive way. Nonetheless, no clear agreement has emerged on the possibility of a wider principle of liability. In *Lonrho Ltd.* v. *Shell Petroleum Co. (No. 2)* [110] the House of Lords rejected the so-called *Beaudesert* principle announced by the High Court of Australia, to the effect that 'a person who suffers harm or loss as the inevitable consequence of the unlawful,

103 *Hughes* v. *Lord Advocate* [1963] AC 837. 104 See Stanton (Select Bibliography), 123–4.
105 *Baddeley* v. *Earl Granville* (1887) 19 QBD 423.
106 *Wheeler* v. *New Merton Board Mills Ltd.* [1933] 2 KB 669.
107 [1965] AC 656. 108 *Ibid.*, 687.
109 [1949] AC 398, discussed above. 110 [1982] AC 173, 188 (Lord Diplock).

intentional and positive act of another is entitled to recover damages from that other'.[111] This goes too far in two ways. First, as we have seen, it is not the case that every breach of a statute must give rise to civil liability. Second, liability for the economic tort of causing loss by unlawful means normally requires the defendant's illegal act to have been directed at the claimant.[112]

A likelier candidate is the equitable principle that an injunction (and possibly damages) will be available in respect of a breach of a penal statute that infringes a substantial economic or 'property' interest of the plaintiff. The leading modern case is *Ex parte Island Records*,[113] in which performers and recording companies won injunctions to restrain the sale and distribution by 'bootleggers' of unauthorised concert recordings, made contrary to the Dramatic and Musical Performers' Protection Act 1958. Lord Denning rejected the normal analysis in terms of the action for breach of statutory duty—'the dividing line between the pro-cases and contra-cases is so blurred and so ill-defined that you might as well toss a coin to decide it'. Instead, equity would intervene 'to protect a private individual in his rights of property, and in aid of this would grant an injunction to restrain a defendant from committing an unlawful act, even though it was a crime punishable by the criminal courts, and would supplement its jurisdiction in this regard by its power under Lord Cairns' Act to award damages in lieu of or in addition to an injunction'.[114] The basis of the action was interference with a private right, over and above injury to the public as a whole.[115] Waller LJ agreed with grant of an injunction but did not support Lord Denning's view on the availability of damages; Shaw LJ dissented on the grounds that the statute provided no private cause of action.[116]

In *Lonrho Ltd.* v. *Shell Petroleum Co. Ltd. (No. 2)*[117] Lord Diplock rejected any 'wider general rule, which does not depend on the scope and language of the statute by which a criminal offence is committed'. This amounts to a reassertion of what many now regard as the fiction of parliamentary intent as the crucial test. The difficulty with Lord Diplock's approach is that it fails to deal with some far from insignificant nineteenth-century authorities in which the availability of equitable relief to restrain breaches of the criminal law threatening property and commercial interests was clearly recognised.[118] At the same time, it would be anomalous if breach of a criminal statute could be restrained by way of injunction as to the future, while no action for damages for past

[111] *Beaudesert Shire Council* v. *Smith* (1966) 120 CLR 145, 160.

[112] P. Elias and A. Tettenborn, 'Crime, Tort and Compensation in Private and Public Law' [1981] *CLJ* 230.

[113] [1978] Ch. 122.

[114] *Ibid.*, 135.

[115] Where the applicant for an injunction does not suffer special damage, the action may only be brought with the consent of the Attorney-General through his relator action: *Gouriet* v. *Union of Post Office Workers* [1978] AC 435.

[116] In the later case of *Rickless* v. *United Artists Corporation* [1988] QB 40, a different Court of Appeal held that the statute did confer an action for breach of statutory duty on the performers, although not on the record companies (see above).

[117] [1982] AC 173, 188.

[118] See in particular, *Springhead Spinning* v. *Riley* (1868) LR 6 Eq. 551; Lord Wedderburn, 'Rocking the Torts' (1983) 46 *MLR* 224.

losses could be brought in respect of the same legal wrong. In the different context of civil liability for breach of European Community law Lord Diplock himself has said that if an injunction lies in equity to restrain an unlawful act threatening economic loss to the plaintiff, a damages action must follow in respect of the same breach 'at any rate since 1875 when the jurisdiction conferred upon the Court of Chancery . . . passed to the High Court'.[119] Statute has now intervened to deal with the specific situation of 'bootlegging' by granting an action for statutory damages both to performers and those to whom they grant exclusive recording rights.[120] But until the House of Lords has a further opportunity to reconsider it, the general status of the *Island Records* principle is likely to remain somewhat confused.

(E) LIABILITY FOR BREACH OF OBLIGATIONS ARISING UNDER EUROPEAN COMMUNITY LAW

Developments in European Community law over the past decade have made it increasingly possible for private actions for damages to be brought against defendants, particularly public authorities, which act in breach of obligations arising under Treaties, directives, and other sources of EC law. There is some authority[121] to suggest that this form of liability is best described as a form of the tort of breach of statutory duty. We consider the scope of this tort, and its nature, in relation to the liability of public bodies, in Chapter 8. Only a few areas in which private-sector defendants may be liable in tort for breaches of EC law have so far been recognised, but one such case is that of breach of the competition law provisions of the EC Treaty.[122]

It is also possible[123] for EC law to used as an aid to interpretation of domestic statutes whose scope, in the context of a breach of statutory duty case, is unclear. In *Robb* v. *Salamis (M & I) Ltd.*[124] the House of Lords had to consider whether there had been a breach of the Provision and Use of Work Equipment Regulations 1998 in circumstances where the pursuer, a scaffolder working on an oil and gas production platform, suffered

[119] *Garden Cottage Foods Ltd.* v. *Milk Marketing Board* [1984] AC 130, 144.

[120] Copyright, Designs and Patents Act 1988, ss. 180 ff.; s. 194 creates a private right of action for breach of this Part of the Act.

[121] *R* v. *Secretary of State for Transport, ex parte Factortame (No. 7)* [2001] 1 WLR 942.

[122] See, e.g., the recent ruling of the House of Lords, in *Crehan* v. *Inntrepreneur Pub Co. (CPC)* [2007] ICR 1344, on the meaning and application of Art. 81 of the EC Treaty in the context of tort-like claims for the effects of anti-competitive agreements and practices.

[123] And, indeed, necessary, if the result would otherwise lead to a breach of a provision of the EC Treaty: see Case C-264/96 *ICI* v. *Colmer* [1998] ECR I-4695. However, with regard to interpretation consistently with Directives, this interpretive obligation may not impose an obligation upon a private party if the only source of that obligation were the directive (i.e. where national law was not capable of interpretation in that manner). This is because this would amount to achieving horizontal direct effect of directives, which the ECJ has consistently rejected. See Case C-168/95 *Criminal Proceedings against Luciano Arcaro* [1996] ECR I-4705 (esp. para. 45) and Joined Cases C-397 to 403/01 *Pfeiffer* v. *Deutsches Rotes Kreuz Kreisverband Waldshut eV* [2004] ECR I-3325. This point was correctly perceived by the House of Lords as long ago as 1988 (*Duke* v. *GEC Reliance Systems Ltd.* [1988] AC 618) despite some more recent wobbles (*Webb* v. *EMO Air Cargo Ltd (No. 2)* [1995] 1 WLR 1454).

[124] 2007 SLT 158, 181.

injury when the ladder he was using to descend from a bunk bed gave way. The question was whether the ladder was 'suitable'. In deciding that it was not, Lord Hope relied upon the Directives which the 1998 Regulations were adopted to implement.[125]

SELECT BIBLIOGRAPHY

BUCKLEY, R. A., 'Liability in Tort for Breach of Statutory Duty' (1984) 100 *LQR* 204.

CARNWATH, R., 'The *Thornton* Heresy Exposed: Financial Remedies of Breach of Public Duties' [1998] *PL* 407.

FRICKE, G. L., 'The Juridical Nature of the Action upon the Statute' (1960) 76 *LQR* 240.

LAW COMMISSION, *The Interpretation of Statutes*: *Report by the Two Commissions*, Scot. Law Com. No. 11 (HC 256) (1969).

MORRIS, C., 'The Role of Criminal Statutes in Negligence Actions' (1949) 49 *Col. LR* 21.

STANTON, K., *Breach of Statutory Duty in Tort*, Modern Legal Studies Series (1986).

THAYER, E. R., 'Public Wrong and Private Action' (1914) 27 *Harv. LR* 317.

WILLIAMS, G. L., 'The Effect of Penal Legislation in the Law of Tort' (1960) 23 *MLR* 233.

125 Namely, the Framework Health and Safety Directive (89/391/EEC, [1989] *OJ* L183/1) and the Work Equipment Directive (89/655/EEC, [1989] *OJ* L393/13). For discussion of the 'interpretive obligation' (also known as the principle of 'indirect effect'), see (e.g.) A. M. Arnull *et al.*, *Wyatt & Dashwood's European Union Law* (5th edn., 2006), paras. 5–015, 5–029 and 5–030.

8

LIABILITY OF PUBLIC AND STATUTORY BODIES

1. THE DISTINCTIVE NATURE OF THE LIABILITY OF THE GOVERNMENT, PUBLIC AUTHORITIES AND STATUTORY BODIES

(A) HISTORICAL DEVELOPMENT

In principle, liability in tort may attach to the acts or omissions of a statutory utility, local authority or government department in just the same way as it would to those of a private person. Public authorities, their agents and employees enjoy no general immunity from civil liability. Dicey noted that 'the Reports abound with cases in which officials have been brought before the courts, and made, in their personal capacity, liable to punishment, or to the payment of damages, for acts done in their official character but in excess of their lawful authority'.[1] He regarded this general application of the 'ordinary' principles of civil liability as a fundamental aspect of the rule of law. Many of the important cases in the torts of trespass to the person, false imprisonment and trespass to property, which are considered in later chapters,[2] have been actions brought to attack the abuse of governmental authority. In the field of negligence, the liability of public bodies was clearly established in the middle of the nineteenth century,[3] and then consolidated in a series of actions brought against utilities and other statutory undertakings for negligent interference with property.[4] These cases are normally considered under the rubric of 'negligence in the exercise of a statutory power'. In relation to liability for personal injury, it has long been clearly established that both the general duty of care arising under *Donoghue* v. *Stevenson*[5] and the more specific duties imposed, for example, on occupiers and employers, apply without distinction to public authorities.

In certain other respects, however, this picture of the general application of the principles of tortious liability has to be qualified. For immunities for both central and local government have operated at various times. Historically the Crown was immune

[1] *An Introduction to the Study of the Law of the Constitution* (1885), 1979 reprint, 193.

[2] See below, ch. 9. [3] *Mersey Docks & Harbour Board* v. *Gibbs* (1866) LR 1 HL 93.

[4] Most notably, *Geddis* v. *Proprietors of the Bann Reservoir* (1878) 3 App. Cas. 430.

[5] [1932] AC 562.

from both civil and criminal liability, with the effect (amongst others) that central government bodies could not be sued directly in tort. A way round this was found in the form of actions brought against state officials, but the government departments and offices of state for which they worked were not, strictly speaking, vicariously liable for the torts committed by their servants and agents. It was normal, however, for any damages awarded by a court against such officials to be paid by the Crown and for cases to be settled when it was thought that a private employer would have been vicariously liable. But these practices did not rest upon any legal principle and some considered them to be illegal.[6] The Crown Proceedings Act 1947 formally removed this immunity and made the Crown liable for the torts of its servants and agents as 'if it were a person of full age and capacity'.[7] Since then it has also become common practice for legislation extending or clarifying tort duties (such as the Occupiers' Liability Acts of 1957 and 1984), or altering the scope of defences (such as the Law Reform (Personal Injuries) Act 1948), to contain express provisions binding the Crown formally. Nowadays, there are thus few if any areas in which a significant Crown immunity remains.[8]

The liability of local authorities was, likewise, limited for a time by statute, in the form of the Public Authorities Protection Act 1893. This imposed time limits of six months or, in some cases, a year, on any actions against public bodies acting by way of the exercise of statutory duties or powers. The origins of this Act are obscure and it was repealed, without great objection, in 1954.[9] More recently, the decision of the House of Lords in *Anns* v. *Merton London Borough Council*[10] appeared to herald a significant expansion of governmental liability, justified, it seemed, by the 'deep pockets' theory of public defendants. *Anns* implied that local authorities could be liable for, amongst other things, negligent failure to ensure compliance with bye-laws, thereby causing pure economic loss to remote parties.[11] Though the House of Lords attempted to preserve an area of immunity in relation to decisions of 'policy' involving the balancing of competing interests, it abolished immunity for any 'operational' negligence occurring in the course of day-to-day administration. This distinction, however, was criticised as unclear and difficult to apply in practice. The formal demise of *Anns* came with *Murphy* v. *Brentwood District Council*[12] after a series of earlier decisions had substantially restricted its application to statutory bodies.[13] Following *Murphy*, the liability of public bodies was further restricted in *X (Minors)* v. *Bedfordshire County Council*,[14] in which

[6] See C. Harlow, *Compensation and Government Torts* (Select Bibliography), ch. 2.

[7] Section 2(1).

[8] The Crown Proceedings Act 1947 preserves the immunity in a small number of areas, discussed later in this chapter. A new immunity was introduced for the Bank of England as a banking supervisor in the Banking Act 1987, s. 1(4), and this has been extended to different financial market regulators, the major provision is today in Sch. 1, s. 19(1) of the Financial Services and Markets Act 2000, see M. Andenas and D. Fairgrieve, 'Misfeasance in Public Office, Governmental Liability and European Influences' (Select Bibliography), 760.

[9] The Law Reform (Limitation of Actions etc.) Act 1954. See T. Weir, 'Governmental Liability' (Select Bibliography), 48.

[10] [1978] AC 728.

[11] In this case, homeowners who bought properties which had been constructed on defective foundations after the council had failed to carry out an adequate inspection of them.

[12] [1991] 1 AC 398.

[13] See in particular, the judgments of Lord Keith in *Peabody Donation Fund* v. *Sir Lindsay Parkinson & Co.* [1985] AC 210, *Yuen Kun Yeu* v. *Attorney-General of Hong Kong* [1988] AC 175 and *Rowling* v. *Takaro Properties* [1988] AC 473, discussed below.

[14] [1995] 2 AC 633.

their Lordships struck out as disclosing no cause of action a number of claims brought against local authorities in respect of alleged failures to perform statutory duties relating to the care, protection, and education of children. The trend to restrict liability was continued in *Stovin* v. *Wise (Norfolk County Council, third party)*,[15] where the House ruled (by a bare majority) that a highway authority did not owe a duty of care to a road-user to exercise its statutory powers in such a way as to maintain the highway in a safe condition. Since then, the pendulum has swung back and forth. A turning-point was the judgment of the European Court of Human Rights in *Osman* v. *United Kingdom*,[16] which ruled that a no-duty rule for public bodies was contrary to the right to a fair hearing under Article 6 of the European Convention. Although the Court drew back from the full implications of this ruling in its later decision in *Z* v. *United Kingdom*[17] (a case arising from the *X (Minors)* litigation), *Osman* impelled the House of Lords to look again at the duty issue, and its decisions in *Barrett* v. *Enfield London Borough Council*[18] and *Phelps* v. *Hillingdon London Borough Council*[19] widened again the scope of the duty of care in relation to the negligent performance of public services. However, in *D* v. *East Berkshire Community NHS Trust*[20] the House of Lords rejected a claim brought by the parents of children who were wrongly taken into care, but there was no challenge to the finding of the Court of Appeal in the *D* case[21] to the effect that a duty was owed to the child; on this point, in particular because of the impact of the judgments of the European Court of Human Rights, *X (Minors)* could not stand. Whether the distinction drawn in this case between the parents' claim and that of the child can be maintained in the future is an issue to which we return below.

(B) REASONS FOR THE DISTINCTIVE NATURE OF GOVERNMENTAL LIABILITY

Several reasons have been advanced for treating governmental liability as a special case within negligence.[22] If *substantial*[23] claims for economic compensation are made by a

15 [1996] AC 923; to similar effect is the later decision of the House of Lords in *Gorringe* v. *Calderdale MBC* [2004] 1 WLR 1057.

16 (1998) 29 EHRR 245.

17 [2001] 2 FLR 612.

18 [2001] 2 AC 550.

19 [2001] 2 AC 619.

20 [2005] 2 AC 373.

21 [2004] QB 558.

22 See generally the discussion in B. S. Markesinis, J.-P. Auby, D. Coester-Waltjen and S. Deakin, *Tortious Liability of Statutory Bodies: A Comparative and Economic Analysis of Five English Cases* (Select Bibliography), and Law Commission, *Remedies against Public Bodies: A Scoping Report* (2007), at paras. 3.18–3.21; cf. S. Bailey and S. Bowman, 'Public Authority Negligence Revisited' (Select Bibliography), who, following a comprehensive review of the case law to that point, suggest that 'public authorities should not per se be different from other kinds of defendant' (at 131). See also their earlier analyses, 'Negligence in the Realms of Public Law: A Positive Obligation to Rescue' [1984] *PL* 277, and 'The Policy/Operational Dichotomy: A Cuckoo in the Nest' [1986] *CLJ* 430. On the theoretical foundation for judicial restraint and the erection and dismantling of different 'public law hurdles', see M. Andenas and D. Fairgrieve 'Sufficiently Serious? Judicial Restraint in Tortious Liability for Public Authorities and the European Influence' (Select Bibliography), at 286–313.

23 We stress *substantial* for, in keeping with the views expressed in earlier chapters, we feel that inadequate attention has thus far been paid to a desirable distinction between liability grounds and quantification of damages. Thus, in the Court of Appeal phase of the *Phelps* litigation Otton LJ suggested a number of reasons why these claims, even if successful, should not lead to huge awards: the cost of providing (privately if necessary)

particular group of claimants, the cost has to be met either by a diversion of resources away from general expenditure or by an increase in taxation. It is not obvious that the loss is better borne by the local authority (or by the taxpayers or community at large) than by the plaintiffs. Indeed, the latter may (in some but not all cases) be in a better position to cover the risk in question through additional precautions or through insurance. This seems to have been the case in *Anns* [24] and *Murphy*,[25] where actions nominally brought in the names of the occupiers and owners of the properties were, in essence, actions brought by their insurers by virtue of the doctrine of subrogation. This enables the liability insurer, after having indemnified his insured, to step into his shoes and sue the tortfeasor for the initial loss caused to the plaintiff. Tony Weir has summed up the relevant issues in the following way:

> Now it hardly needs saying (any more) that a local authority does not normally have to pay companies which suffer merely pecuniary loss as a result of their carelessness, as the Norwich Union did in this case, and it is hard to imagine anybody less deserving of a dip in the public trough than the insurer who profits from taking the risk that houses may collapse.... But our absurd law on subrogation to tort claims means that the public must bail out private insurers.[26]

Similarly, in *Stovin* v. *Wise* [27] Lord Hoffmann noted that: 'denial of liability [in that case] does not leave the road user unprotected' since not only do drivers of vehicles owe each other a duty of care, but 'if, as in the case of [the defendant], they do not, there is compulsory insurance to provide compensation to victims'. There is however, still the question of whether displacing costs, through insurance premiums, on to road users in this way, provides the right incentives on the highway authority to maintain the road in a safe condition.

A second reason for granting some kind of immunity is the wish to avoid the situation in which public authorities become inundated with frivolous and unmeritorious claims. This is a real possibility because, unlike commercial entities or individual defendants, local authorities cannot (normally) become insolvent or bankrupt. An important practical bar to speculative litigation therefore does not apply. *Anns*[28] illustrates the danger (subject to evaluating the cost risks attendant to unsuccessful litigation) of making local authorities 'defendants of last resort': the most obvious action, by the householder against the builder whose negligence the local authority failed to correct, is frequently

alternative training to the 'impaired' child, plus a modest amount for pain and suffering resulting from its diminished self-esteem, might well be appropriate in such a case. See *Phelps* v. *Hillingdon LBC* [1999] 1 WLR 500.

24 [1978] AC 728.

25 [1991] 1 AC 398.

26 Weir (Select Bibliography), 43. The obvious flaw in this argument is that Weir's focus is on the individual case and not on the rule. Eventually, the cost of this rule is borne by the insured, through higher premiums. The liability rules will either place the cost on the local authority or on the owners of the property. Another way of approaching the policy question is to ask if the local authority is better placed to enforce the compliance with the technical standards, and if liability would provide proportionate incentives for effective enforcement. Most would say that what Weir calls 'our absurd law on subrogation' is based on sound legal and economic principles, and it is not only 'our law' but that of most other countries.

27 [1996] AC 923, 958.

28 [1978] AC 728.

ruled out by insolvency of the firm in question. Under *Anns* the local authority and the builder were joint tortfeasors, with the builder being assessed for the predominant part of liability; but the difficulty, in practice, of getting the builder to pay anything would normally lead to the local authority paying everything. In this context the argument that, given the difficulties of proving carelessness, few claims will actually succeed in practice may be of debatable force. For, as Lord Browne-Wilkinson noted in *X(Minors)* v. *Bedfordshire County Council*,[29] if a common-law duty of care is held to exist, there is a very real risk that many hopeless (and possibly vexatious) cases will be brought. This would expose authorities to great expenditure of time and money in their defence.

A third factor is the fear of courts unduly restricting the policy-making functions of the body in question and interfering with decisions that are not susceptible to judicial control. As Lord Keith of Kinkel recognised in his judgment in *Yuen Kun Yeu* v. *Attorney-General of Hong Kong*,[30] many decisions taken by regulatory bodies may end up favouring one group against another or elevating the public interest above that of a particular interest group. If that group is able to demand automatic compensation for its losses, the regulatory body may be unable to act in the general interest. Nor will the court have the expertise or the information to judge whether one group should be favoured over another. For instance, if a regulatory authority shuts down a bank that has been involved in fraud it thereby protects future, would-be investors at the possible expense of those who have already made deposits. This latter group, who may well lose all or most of their savings, may feel particularly aggrieved since they can claim that the reason they kept their money in the bank was the reassurance they felt they had from the regulatory authority that all was well with the bank.[31] One approach would be to argue that since, in these circumstances, the court is said to lack the criteria by which to assess negligence, it should deny a duty of care altogether. The opposite approach is that the regulatory body must subject the question to particularly careful scrutiny, as the complexity of the issues involved and the range of interests at stake alike require that a high level of care be taken. The mere fact that *competing* interests at stake cannot be decisive; the law often deals with conflicting duties of care, and it cannot limit public authority liability for that reason alone.[32]

A fourth consideration is the fear that the threat of legal liability will give rise to 'defensive' or wasteful practices by potential defendants. This has to be weighed against any 'deterrent' effect or raising of standards of performance which judicial intervention may bring in its wake. In *Stovin* v. *Wise*,[33] Lord Hoffmann said that 'it was important to consider, before extending the duty of care owed by public authorities, the cost to the

29 [1995] 2 AC 633, 762.

30 [1988] AC 175.

31 This was one of the issues to arise out of the Bank of England's closure of the London arm of the Bank of Commerce and Credit International in 1990. In litigation arising from the collapse of BCCI, the House of Lords declined to strike out a claim against the Bank in respect of the tort of misfeasance in a public office: *Three Rivers DC* v. *Bank of England (No. 3)* [2003] 2 AC 1, discussed below, Section 4(b).

32 See the cases discussed in Section 2(b) below, *Barrett* v. *Enfield LBC* [2001] 2 AC 550, *Phelps* v. *Hillingdon LBC* [2001] 2 AC 619 and *D* v. *East Berkshire Community NHS Trust* [2005] 2 AC 373.

33 [1996] AC 923, 958. See also *X (Minors)* v. *Bedfordshire CC* [1995] 2 AC 633, 748 (Lord Browne-Wilkinson).

community of the defensive measures which they are likely to take in order to avoid liability'. The existence of a duty of care would, he thought, distort the priorities of local authorities, which would be bound to play safe by increasing their spending on road improvements rather than risk enormous liabilities for personal injury accidents. As a result they would spend less on education or social services. This consideration can be used against any form of governmental liability or enforcement of the legal obligations of public authorities. The alternative way of putting this is to ask if the benefits to the community of this pressure on public authorities to comply with their duties and not behaving negligently outweigh the costs.

In addition to these considerations of policy, there are specific legal reasons for recognising the distinctive nature of governmental liability. The analysis of the common law duty of care is complicated by the presence of statutory powers and duties. With the exception of the Crown, which possesses various inherent prerogative powers,[34] most of the activities of public bodies are underpinned by statute in this way. The presence of statute means, in the first place, that an alternative ground of liability may arise, namely a liability for breach of statutory duty. As we have seen,[35] the action for breach of statutory duty is conceptually separate from negligence liability. But it is also normally harder to establish, in the sense that the plaintiff must show that the statute was meant to create a private cause of action for a particular group, of which he is part. The relationship between the action for breach of statutory duty and the separate, common law liability for negligence in the exercise of a statutory power is far from clear. In particular, it is uncertain how far the absence of any private action for statutory breach should prevent the court imposing a parallel duty of care at common law. Some decisions suggest that the fit between these two separate areas of liability may be very close.[36]

In the second place, it is possible for a statute to create a specific immunity from common law liability in tort. This may be the case where liability in nuisance or under the tort of *Rylands* v. *Fletcher*[37] is concerned. The principles governing statutory immunity for these torts of interference with property are considered separately in a later chapter.[38] It is rare, however, if not completely unknown, for a statute to grant immunity for *negligence*;[39] and there is a presumption that liability for negligence will arise if an authorised activity is carried on in a negligent manner.[40]

In addition it is necessary to consider the overlap between the liability of public bodies to pay damages for tortious injury and the separate question of the validity of

[34] See H. W. R. Wade and C. F. Forsyth, *Administrative Law* (Select Bibliography), 44 ff. and 215–21.

[35] Ch. 7, above.

[36] Above all, the highway cases of *Stovin* v. *Wise* [1996] AC 923 and *Gorringe* v. *Calderdale MBC* [2004] 1 WLR 1057.

[37] (1866) LR 1 Ex. 265 (1868) LR 3 HL 330.

[38] See Ch. 13, below.

[39] New immunities were introduced for banks and financial market regulators under the Banking Act 1987, s. 1(4). See Andenas and Fairgrieve, 'Misfeasance in Public Office' (Select Bibliography), 760.

[40] *Geddis* v. *Proprietors of the Bann Reservoir* (1878) 3 App. Cas. 430.

their acts under administrative law.[41] Thus, a person affected by an administrative decision can challenge it on the ground that it was taken in excess of the relevant statutory powers, that is to say, was *ultra vires*.[42] The decision can be quashed (or nullified) by a quashing order. Alternatively, an action may lie to compel a public body to perform a statutory duty (a mandatory order) or to prevent it from acting in breach of such a duty (a prohibiting order). These remedies, called the prerogative orders, must now be sought under a specially designated procedure known as the application for judicial review, under the Civil Procedure Rules (CPR), Part 54. It is vital to stress, however, that no action for damages lies either in tort law or in administrative law on the ground simply that a statutory authority has acted *ultra vires*.[43] The relevant principles of administrative law are concerned solely with the question of the validity of the act in question, and not with liability to pay damages to one who is affected by it. Conversely, however, it may be that an authority cannot be liable in the tort of negligence unless the act or omission in question was *ultra vires*.[44]

In this sense, the scope of the *vires* principle in administrative law is potentially important for the scope of common law liability in negligence. In addition, there is a significant procedural point concerning the form of damages actions brought against public bodies. As a result of the House of Lords' decision in *O'Reilly* v. *Mackman*,[45] actions of a 'public law' nature may only be brought by way of the application for judicial review. To proceed by way of a writ in the High Court is an abuse of process. This means that where an action for damages is bound up with a challenge to the validity of an administrative act, it may have to be brought as a public law action under CPR Part 54 (which has replaced RSC Order 53).[46] While CPR Part 54 permits damages claims to be combined with a claim for one or more of the prerogative orders, the limitation period is extremely short (three months). Additionally, it could be argued that the procedure is not entirely suitable for the argument of a claim for compensation as opposed to a challenge to validity. For this reason, the procedural separation of public-law and private-law issues may have resulted in the grant to statutory bodies of a kind of limited immunity, similar to that of the old Public Authorities Protection Act 1893, from certain kinds of claims for damages. However, the extent of any such immunity has been considerably narrowed as a result of the more recent decisions of the House of Lords in *Roy* v. *Kensington and Chelsea and Westminster Family Practitioner Committee*[47] and Court of Appeal in *Clark* v. *University of Lincolnshire and Humberside*.[48] In addition,

[41] It is important to note, at the same time, that administrative law is undergoing rapid expansion. The reach and intensity of judicial review of administrative action is developing all the time. Today there is practically no area that is not subject to some level of review, and the review of administrative discretion is becoming much more intrusive, considerably strengthening the protection of the rights of private parties against public administration.

[42] For an introduction to the *ultra vires* principle see Wade and Forsyth (Select Bibliography), 35–42.

[43] *Gorringe* v. *Calderdale MBC* [2004] 1 WLR 1057, 1067.

[44] See in particular, Lord Diplock's judgment in *Dorset Yacht Co.* v. *Home Office* [1970] AC 1004, 1068.

[45] [1983] 2 AC 237.

[46] *Cocks* v. *Thanet DC* [1984] 2 AC 286.

[47] [1992] 1 AC 625.

[48] [2000] 1 WLR 1998; T. Hickman, '*Clark:* The Demise of *O'Reilly* Completed?' [2000] *JR* 178.

the practical significance of *O'Reilly* has been much reduced by the inclusion in CPR Part 54 of a two-way power to transfer cases between the public-law and private-law procedures.[49]

Another motivation for limiting liability is that where negligence, in the sense of maladministration by central government departments or local government, is concerned there is an alternative remedy to civil litigation. This can take the form of intervention by the Parliamentary Commissioner for Administration or 'Parliamentary Ombudsman'.[50] The Ombudsman can sometimes make a substantial impact on the availability of compensation in circumstances where a negligence claim, although possible, would face considerable difficulties in terms both of establishing a duty of care and proving causation. A good illustration of this can be found in the Ombudsman's report on the Barlow Clowes affair. In that case a large number of investors lost their savings following the collapse of a fraudulent investment company which had been licensed to trade by the Department of Trade and Industry. The report led to the government paying out to the investors around £16 million in *ex gratia* sums.[51] In this case, a claim in negligence would have been both difficult to mount and time-consuming to pursue, not least in the light of the ruling of the Privy Council in *Yuen Kun Yeu* v. *Attorney-General of Hong Kong*.[52]

But the government does not always pay out sums in compensation following a ruling of the Ombudsman. In 2006 it refused to meet claims made by members of occupational pension schemes whose retirement benefits had been lost when their schemes were wound up by their employers. The Ombudsman found that government departments had issued misleading advice in the 1990s on the security of occupational schemes. The government responded by arguing that the sheer size of the claims made it impossible to meet them; it would be tantamount to underwriting all occupational pension schemes for the period in question. This led to litigation in which the claimants sought to establish that the decision not to pay compensation was irrational and hence *ultra vires*.[53] The claimants were successful at first instance but, at the time of writing (the spring of 2007), the government has indicated that it will appeal from this finding.

So far we have been considering factors, in some cases policy-related and in others juridical in nature, which argue for restricting the liability of governmental and statutory bodies. However, the past few years have seen the emergence of a new rationale for *extending* governmental liability, according to which compensation should be paid for

[49] CPR Pts. 54.4, 54.20.

[50] The powers of the Parliamentary Ombudsman derive from the Parliamentary Commissioner Act 1967. It is not possible to make a direct complaint to the Parliamentary Ombudsman but this is possible in the case of the Local Government Ombudsman who has jurisdiction over a wide range of governmental and statutory bodies. Several ombudsman schemes also operate in the private sector, some of them with statutory backing. See generally P. Cane, *Tort Law and Economic Interests* (2nd edn., 1996), at 366 ff.

[51] *Ibid.*, 389.

[52] [1988] AC 475. It is unclear how far this area of law is in need of some reassessment, particularly in the light of the case law decided since the *Yuen Kun Yeu* case, discussed in Section 2(b) of this chapter, below.

[53] *Secretary of State for Work and Pensions* v. *Parliamentary Commissioner for Administration* [2007] EWHC 242 (Admin), *The Times*, 27 Feb. 2007.

the effects of action by governmental or statutory bodies which interferes with certain fundamental rights of individuals. Thus thanks to a series of decisions of the European Court of Justice and the House of Lords, it is now accepted that an action in damages may lie against a public authority for the effects of a breach of European Community law. This will be so if the provision in question was intended to confer rights on individuals, if the breach was sufficiently serious, and if there is a direct causal link between the breach and the damage sustained by the claimants.[54] This principle has been used to explore the contours of government liability for interference with a range of social and economic rights guaranteed by Treaty provisions and directives. In addition, public authorities now face the possibility of liability in damages under the Human Rights Act 1998 for interference with Convention rights, that is, the rights contained in Articles 2–12 of the European Convention on Human Rights and certain of its Protocols as defined by the 1998 Act. It is not yet completely clear how these novel forms of state liability should be aligned with existing causes of action dealing with the abuse of governmental power, in particular the torts of breach of statutory duty and misfeasance in a public office. What is clear is that the area of governmental liability in tort could well be reshaped yet again as a result of these developments.

To explore these issues, we now turn to a more detailed consideration of governmental liability in negligence and other torts. We shall examine in turn the extent of common law liability in negligence; liability for breach of statutory duty; public law as a source of liability and, alternatively, of immunity; and Crown proceedings. We will then conclude by examining the possible impact on this area of law of the principle of state liability under European Community law, and the obligation upon public authorities to observe the provisions of the European Convention on Human Rights and of a number of its Protocols, under the Human Rights Act 1998.

2. THE LIABILITY OF STATUTORY BODIES IN NEGLIGENCE

(A) THE RECOGNITION OF A COMMON LAW ACTION

Two decisions in the middle of the nineteenth century clearly established that public bodies could be liable in tort for negligence occurring in the performance of activities authorised by statute. In *Mersey Docks and Harbour Board Trustees* v. *Gibbs*[55] the dock trustees were held liable for their failure to maintain a clear passage into a harbour, with the result that the ship carrying the plaintiff's cargo ran aground. The House of Lords,

[54] See Joined Cases C-60/90 and C-9/90, *Francovich and Bonifaci* v. *Italian Republic* [1991] ECR I-6911; Case C-46/93, *Brasserie du Pêcheur* v. *Federal Republic of Germany* and Case C-48/93, *R* v. *Secretary of State for Trade and Industry, ex parte Factortame Ltd. (No. 3)* [1996] ECR I-1029; *R* v. *Secretary of State for Transport, ex parte Factortame Ltd. (No. 5)* [2000] 1 AC 524.

[55] (1866) LR 1 HL 93.

adopting an opinion of Blackburn J, rejected an argument to the effect that the trustees were covered by Crown immunity. Such bodies, which performed commercial and related activities for profit, should be subject to a liability 'co-extensive with that imposed by the general law on the owners of similar works'.[56] In *Geddis* v. *Proprietors of the Bann Reservoir*[57] Lord Blackburn confirmed this result. He said:

> It is now thoroughly well established that no action will lie for doing that which the legislature has authorised, if it be done without negligence, although it does occasion damage to anyone; but an action does lie for doing that which the legislature has authorised, if it be done negligently.

In this case the defendants, who had statutory authority to undertake public works for the supply of water, in diverting various rivers failed to clear one of them of obstructions, with the result that it overflowed and flooded the plaintiff's land. His action for damages was successful. Lord Blackburn's approach was thus to treat statutory bodies like any others for the purposes of negligence. Only if the statute clearly specified a defence would a negligence action be defeated. Similarly, the fact that the negligence was that of a statutory body was not, in itself, an additional ground of liability. The action originated at common law, and was governed by the rules normally applicable to a negligence claim; it was not a special form of liability in the same sense as the (entirely separate) action for breach of statutory duty.

The prospect of a limited immunity for statutory bodies was raised again, however, by the later judgment of the House of Lords in *East Suffolk Rivers Catchment Board* v. *Kent*.[58] In that case the plaintiff's land was flooded following a high tide and a breach in a floodwall. The defendants, acting under statutory powers, attempted to mend the breach in the wall but negligently failed to do so, with the result that the plaintiff's land remained flooded far longer than it would otherwise have done. Viscount Simon LC, noting that the defendants were under no statutory duty to act, held that they could not be liable for merely failing to improve the situation. He thus adopted the view of du Parcq LJ in the Court of Appeal that the Rivers Catchment Board could not be held liable for damage suffered through failure to exercise its powers adequately, or at all, even though the damage might have been averted or lessened by the exercise of reasonable care and skill.[59] Similarly Lord Romer held that:

> Where a statutory authority is entrusted with a mere power, it cannot be made liable for any damage sustained by a member of the public by reason of a failure to exercise that power. If, in the exercise of their discretion, they embark upon an execution of that power, the only duty they owe to any member of the public is not thereby to add to the damage which he would have suffered had they done nothing.[60]

56 (1866) LR 1 HL 93, at 107 (Blackburn J). See Harlow (Select Bibliography), 23–4.

57 (1878) 3 App. Cas. 430, 455–6.

58 [1941] AC 74. See also the earlier case of *Sheppard* v. *Glossop Corp.* [1921] 3 KB 132, discussed by P. Craig, 'Negligence in the Exercise of a Statutory Power' (Select Bibliography), 431–2.

59 [1940] 1 KB 319, 337.

60 [1941] AC 74, 102. Lords Porter and Thankerton also held in favour of the Rivers Catchment Board.

Since some of the judges in the majority appeared to decide the case on the grounds of causation as much as on the nature of the duty of care, the *ratio* of *East Suffolk* has not been entirely clear. But Lord Romer's formulation enjoyed general support at least until the decision of the House of Lords in *Anns* v. *Merton London Borough Council* [61] was handed down.

In the *East Suffolk* case Lord Atkin gave one of the two[62] major dissenting judgments of his career.[63] As always, Lord Atkin started by stating the issues clearly or, in this case, complaining that:

> I cannot help thinking that the argument did not sufficiently distinguish between two kinds of duties: (1) A statutory duty to do or abstain from doing something.[64] (2) A common law duty to conduct yourself with reasonable care so as not to injure persons liable to be affected by your conduct.

For present purposes, therefore, the central question was not whether the board was under a pre-existing statutory duty to act, but whether the relationship between the two parties was sufficiently close to give rise to a duty of care at common law. In his view, once the board had gone on to the plaintiff's land and undertaken the responsibility of closing the breach in the floodwall, they came under a duty to take care in the way the work was executed. This was an application of the general principle laid down in *Donoghue* v. *Stevenson*[65] in the formulation of which he had, nine years earlier, played such a vital part.

(B) A QUALIFIED PROTECTION FROM LIABILITY?

The apparent *ratio* of the *East Suffolk* case has been criticised as resting on a *non sequitur*. It does not necessarily follow from the fact that a public body has been granted a statutory discretion (as opposed to a duty) to act that it may not be liable for common law negligence if it decides to do so and then goes on to execute its powers carelessly. The correct distinction, from this point of view, is between, on the one hand, negligence in the formulation of general policy or planning[66] and, on the other, negligence in the operation or implementation of the policy decision.[67] As Professor Paul Craig has explained:

> The . . . dichotomy between planning and operation can be applied to the *East Suffolk* case. On the facts it appeared that the catchment board could not afford the most sophisticated machinery (or the most skilled labourers) but that the greater part of the damage resulted from using the wrong technique to repair the wall. The best approach to the case would, it is

61 [1978] AC 728.

62 The other was, of course, in *Liversidge* v. *Anderson* [1942] AC 206.

63 [1941] AC 74, 88–94.

64 A duty primarily owed to the state and not necessarily to an individual.

65 [1932] AC 562.

66 When the body is called upon to make decisions concerning the distribution of resources which the court is ill-equipped to second-guess.

67 When adequate criteria for judging negligence are much more likely to exist.

submitted, have been to ask: 'given the limited resources possessed by the board (the planning decision) did the workmen use reasonable dispatch?' The answer would appear to be that on the facts they did not. Even taking account of the limited resources, the work took far too long due to administrative inefficiency and use of the wrong technique.[68]

The distinction between 'policy' and 'operational' decisions originates in the federal law of the United States, where legislation of 1946 abolishing sovereign immunity substituted a more limited immunity for negligence committed by agencies or officials in the exercise of a discretionary function.[69] One example of a policy decision includes the decision of the federal government to export a highly dangerous fertiliser, which exploded when it was being shipped.[70] Another can be found in the maintenance by a state government of 'open house' in a reform school for young offenders, from which an inmate escaped to burn down the plaintiff's property.[71] By contrast, where the federal government allocated resources to provide a lighthouse and a lifeguard service it was liable to the owners of a vessel which sank as a result of the failure of the lifeguards to ensure that the lighthouse was working properly.[72] And in another case, a state that placed a youth with foster parents was liable for failing to warn them of his violent tendencies with the result that he assaulted the mother.[73]

In *Anns* v. *Merton London Borough Council*[74] the policy–operation distinction won the approval of Lord Wilberforce, with whose judgment three of the other Law Lords agreed. The apparent *ratio* of the *East Suffolk* case, to the effect that a statutory body may only be liable for additional damage caused by its negligence as opposed to a failure to prevent harm, was rejected. Lord Wilberforce recognised that the liability of public bodies had to be formulated with regard both to the statutory origin of their powers and to the discretion with regard to policy that these powers conferred. The court could not neglect the 'essential factor' that

> the local authority is a public body, discharging functions under statute; its powers and duties are definable in terms of public not private law. The problem which this type of action creates, is to define the circumstances in which the law should impose over and above, or perhaps alongside, these public-law powers and duties, a duty in private law towards individuals so that they may sue for damages in a civil court.[75]

Lord Wilberforce's judgment in effect fused the argument from policy (to the effect that the courts should not interfere with planning decisions) with the more conceptual

68 Craig (Select Bibliography), 434–5.

69 The Federal Tort Claims Act 1946. See Craig (Select Bibliography), 442 ff. Subsequently the distinction found its way into the laws of several states, which either adopted this provision in legislation or had it read in by decision of courts.

70 *Dalehite* v. *US*, 346 US 15 (1953).

71 *Evangelical United Brethren Church of Adna* v. *State of Washington*, 407 P 2d 440 (1965).

72 *Indian Towing Co.* v. *US*, 350 US 61 (1955).

73 *Johnson* v. *State of California*, 447 P 2d 352 (1968).

74 [1978] AC 728.

75 *Ibid.*, 754.

point concerning the statutory origins of the council's powers and the need to ensure that private and public law remedies should not come into conflict. He thus said:

Most, probably all, statutes relating to public authorities or public bodies, contain in them a large area of policy. The courts call this 'discretion', meaning that the decision is one for the authority or body to make, and not for the courts. Many statutes, also, prescribe or at least presuppose the practical execution of policy decisions: a convenient description of this is to say that in addition to the area of policy or discretion, there is an operational area. Although this distinction between the policy area and the operational area is convenient, and illuminating, it is probably a distinction of degree; many 'operational' powers or duties have in them some element of 'discretion'. It can safely be said that the more 'operational' a power or duty may be, the easier it is to superimpose on it a common law duty of care.[76]

The House of Lords' earlier decision in *Home Office* v. *Dorset Yacht Co.*[77] had already recognised this distinction implicitly. Lord Reid had argued that the prison officers had not been granted any discretion in relation to the borstal boys who were under their care; they had simply failed to carry out their instructions, with the consequence that the boys escaped. There was no question, on the other hand, of making the Home Office liable for the consequences of adopting a policy of allowing borstal boys to be given work experience outside the detention centre, or for setting up an 'open borstal'.[78] In *Anns* Lord Wilberforce paid considerable attention to the form and aims of the particular statute under which the council's powers arose. The Public Health Act 1936 was intended 'to provide for the health and safety of owners and occupiers of buildings, including dwelling-houses, by, *inter alia*, setting standards to be complied with in construction, and by enabling local authorities, through building bye-laws, to supervise and control the operations of builders'.[79] The Act consisted mainly of powers and imposed few statutory duties on authorities; the manner in which they carried out building inspections, the number of inspectors employed, and the manner in which tests were to be carried out were matters for the councils themselves to decide. However, the mere fact that the Act created a power to inspect, rather than a duty to do so, was not, according to Lord Wilberforce, relevant because 'they were under a duty to give proper consideration to the question whether they should or not'.[80] As far as the actual inspection was concerned, this was 'heavily operational' and the inspector, once appointed, was under a duty to take care to ensure that the bye-laws were complied with. Even this, however, being a duty originating under statute, carried with it a small element of discretion, and a corresponding area of immunity for the purposes of any private law action for negligence.

The notion of the council's 'duty to give consideration' was arguably unnecessary here. Even in the absence of such a duty, it could be said that once the decisions to make

[76] *Ibid.* [77] [1970] AC 1004.

[78] *Ibid.*, 1031, discussing *Greenwell* v. *Prison Commissioners* (1951) 101 LJ 486; see also Lord Diplock at [1970] AC 1004, 1069.

[79] [1978] AC 728, 753. [80] *Ibid.*, 755.

bye-laws and to enforce them through the appointment of inspectors had been taken it was irrelevant that there was no pre-existing statutory duty requiring the council to do so. A common law duty could arise from the expectation of potential occupiers that the foundations of the houses they bought had been checked by the inspectors at an early stage of construction. The only relevant question then would be whether the negligence of the inspectors was 'operational' in the sense described above. If the action is clearly seen as arising at common law, subject only to a limited immunity for policy decisions, there is no need to search for a pre-existing statutory duty as opposed to a power. Lord Wilberforce seemed to recognise this when he said, in relation to the *East Suffolk* case, that:

quite apart from such consequences as may flow from an examination of the duties laid down by the particular statute, there may be room, once one is outside the area of legitimate discretion or policy, for a duty of care at common law. It is irrelevant to the existence of this duty of care whether what is created by the statute is a duty or a power: the duty of care may exist in either case.[81]

This also follows from Lord Wilberforce's explanation of *East Suffolk*,[82] namely that the judges in that case, with the exception of Lord Atkin, had not fully recognised the potential scope of the 'neighbour principle' as an independent basis for common law liability across a range of situations.

The effect of *Anns* may therefore be summarised as follows: the issue of whether the defendant was acting under a statutory duty or by way of a mere power is irrelevant to liability, once a common law duty of care has been established on the basis of general principles. However, the common law recognises a limited protection from liability for public bodies based on the distinction between decisions of policy, which are non-justiciable, and operational negligence; and in determining the scope of the immunity for policy, the aims and form of the relevant statute are factors to be taken into account.

One of the effects of the House of Lords' decision in *Murphy* v. *Brentwood District Council*,[83] overruling *Anns*, was to restrict the class of situations in which a general common law duty of care will arise. In particular, the House of Lords held that *Anns* had gone too far in recognising a potentially open-ended liability for pure economic loss and for omissions. Following *Murphy* these categories of liability are much more tightly drawn up, and will certainly not extend to the case of a council compensating occupiers for pure economic loss caused by its failure to inspect building foundations.[84]

The later decisions of the House of Lords in the *X(Minors)* and *Stovin* cases went further still in casting doubt on the principles enunciated in *Anns* for determining the liability of public bodies. In *Stovin* [85] Lord Hoffmann said that 'the distinction between policy and operations is an inadequate tool with which to discover whether it is inappropriate to impose a duty of care or not'. This was because, in practice, the distinction is 'often elusive'. Lord Hoffmann, however, went further. He suggested that even in a case where the distinction could be clearly applied, the mere fact that the performance of the

[81] [1978] AC 728, 758. [82] [1941] AC 74.
[83] [1991] 1 AC 398. [84] See above, ch. 3. [85] [1996] AC 923, 951.

duty or, as the case might be, the exercise of the power in question fell under the category of 'operations' did not suffice to establish liability (all other things being equal). In the same vein, Lord Browne-Wilkinson in *X(Minors)*[86] held that, separately from the policy–operation dichotomy, it was not permissible for a court to impose a common law duty of care where its observance 'would be inconsistent with, or have a tendency to discourage, the due performance by the local authority of its statutory duties'.

However, the wide protection granted to public authorities in *X (Minors)* proved to be vulnerable to further litigation.[87] In *Barrett* v. *Enfield London Borough Council*[88] the House of Lords marked the first retreat. For in that case it accepted that local authorities could be held liable in tort for failure to discharge their responsibility towards children in their care (as opposed to those who might be taken into care, which was the equivalent issue in *X (Minors)*). At first blush, the decision could be seen to mark a small step forward, its slightly different set of facts justifying a different appreciation of the policy factors invoked by Lord Browne-Wilkinson to justify his decision in *X (Minors)*. But it is also possible to discern the indirect influence of the European Court of Human Rights in Strasbourg, which set the new thinking in motion through its *Osman* decision (see below) (which it subsequently saw fit to overrule in its essential part[89]). This new thinking was boldly manifested in *Phelps* v. *Hillingdon London Borough Council*,[90] especially in the judgments of Lords Nicholls and Clyde. This decision made it clear that a duty of care could arise in relation to the delivery of a range of educational services by public authorities. It is thus now clear that *X (Minors)* was the high-water mark of judicial restriction of the duty of care in this area. With the dawn of the new century, the attempt (if such it was) to provide public authorities with a 'safe haven' from such claims had failed.

The one exception to this recent loosening of the approach to duty of care is the decision of the House of Lords in *D* v. *East Berkshire Community NHS Trust*,[91] rejecting the possibility of a claim by parents who were wrongly accused of physically abusing their children. In the light of the decision of the Court of Appeal in this case to the effect that a duty of care *was* owed to the *child*, declining to follow *X (Minors)*, the House's decision in *D* is arguably unsustainable. This anomalous exception aside, the effect of *Phelps* and *Barrett* is that cases have to be examined in detail to see whether, in the circumstances of the case, a duty of care has been assumed. The opening of the floodgates that some feared would result[92] has not materialised.

86 [1995] 2 AC 633, 739.

87 See the discussion of the 'public law hurdles' in *X (Minors)* and the earlier case law in Andenas and Fairgrieve 'Sufficiently Serious?' (Select Bibliography), at 286–313, and also the extensive analysis in C. Booth and D. Squires, *The Negligence Liability of Public Authorities* (Select Bibliography).

88 [2001] 2 AC 550; P. Craig and D. Fairgrieve, '*Barrett*, Negligence and Discretionary Powers' (Select Bibliography).

89 In *Z* v. *United Kingdom* [2001] 2 FLR 612, discussed in ch. 3, Section 2(c), above.

90 [2001] 2 AC 619.

91 [2005] 2 AC 373.

92 See e.g. 'Schools face explosion of litigation', *The Times*, 14 May 2002.

The reassessment of *X (Minors)* was triggered by the much-debated ruling of the European Court of Human Rights in *Osman* v. *United Kingdom*.[93] This appeared to suggest that a broad immunity-like treatment of public bodies in the tort of negligence was contrary to the right of access to the Court contained in Article 6 of the European Convention on Human Rights. Following the later decision of the European Court of Human Rights in *Z* v. *United Kingdom*,[94] however, it is now unlikely that Article 6 will prove to be a significant constraint on the restriction by the courts of the notion of duty of care, for reasons we have already explored.[95] However, with all its weaknesses *Osman* had proved the growing influence which outside forces—in this case Strasbourg—can have (and will increasingly have) on the development of our domestic law. Following *Barrett* and *Phelps*, the law is proceeding down a new path. Only the police still enjoy this kind of wide-ranging protection, as a result of the doctrine developed in *Hill* v. *Chief Constable of West Yorkshire*,[96] which had at one time seemed likely to cover the whole public sector; and even here, the possibility that a duty of care to the victims of crime will arise in particular cases has been recognised in a claim brought under the Human Rights Act.[97]

Extracting relevant principles from these various decisions is far from straightforward. With the aim of imposing some kind of order, we may suggest that two broad sets of issues arise. The first set of issues is concerned with the significance, for the common law negligence claim, of the *statutory origins* of the legal duties and powers which are exercised by the class of public or governmental defendants. The second set of issues is concerned with whether the distinctive *functions* of this class of defendants justify restricting their duty of care: in the language of duty of care, these concerns go under the headings of *policy* and *justiciability*.

(i) The Statutory Context

The courts have long recognised the relevance in this context of the statutory origins of the duties and powers exercised by public bodies. However, there are a number of different views of the precise significance of the statutory context.

(a) Statute as the Source of the Private-Law Action. At one extreme are *dicta* suggesting that unless the legislation in question can be construed as giving rise to a cause of action for breach of statutory duty at the suit of the injured party, no common law action for damages for breach of the obligation in question can lie. This was the view of Brennan

93 (1998) 29 EHRR 245; see above, ch. 3, Section 2(c).

94 [2001] 2 FLR 612.

95 See ch. 3, Section 2(c) above. The European Court of Human Rights has since held the UK liable for breach of the *substantive* human rights (including Art. 3) involved instead of basing the outcome on the procedural rights (access to court) in Art. 6. Article 6 still bars immunities, and the UK argument has been that there was no immunity in the cases before the Court.

96 [1989] AC 53; although see also the comment of the Court of Appeal in *Brooks* v. *Commissioner of Police for the Metropolis*: 'we do not think that it is appropriate to describe the police as having in every case an "immunity from suit" in respect of allegations of negligent investigation of crime' ([2002] EWCA Civ. 407, at para. 73).

97 *Van Colle* v. *Chief Constable of Hertfordshire Police* [2006] EWHC 360.

and Deane JJ in the Australian case of *Sutherland Shire Council* v. *Heyman*.[98] The plaintiffs, as in *Anns*, bought property containing a hidden defect that the council had failed to discover through inspection when the house was being constructed. However, the plaintiffs failed to make inquiries of the council or seek from it a compliance order giving details of the property and of its inspection, as they could have done. The minority (Gibbs CJ and Wilson J) held that the council owed a duty of care but that there was no evidence of negligence in its exercise of the discretionary power to inspect. The majority denied the existence of a duty of care, but gave different reasons for that conclusion. Mason J held that the plaintiffs could not show that they had relied on the council's power to inspect, and on this basis he concluded that the council owed no duty of care to the plaintiffs. In Brennan J's view, by contrast, it was not open to a court to impose a common law duty of care in relation to the exercise of a statutory power, in a case where the statute in question could not be read as impliedly imposing a duty which sounded in private damages by an injured party. He said:

> Before the repository of a statutory power can be liable in negligence for a failure to exercise it, the statute, must (either expressly or by implication) impose a duty to exercise the power and confer a private right of action in damages for a breach of the duty so imposed. The question whether Parliament has conferred a private right of action depends upon the interpretation of the statute.[99]

Having decided that the relevant legislation was not intended to create a private cause of action for breach of statutory duty, Brennan J went on to say that:

> If the court ascertains from the Act and Ordinance that Parliament did not intend to impose on the council any other duty to future purchasers of property, it is not open to the court to remedy a supposed deficiency by superimposing a general common law duty on the council to prevent any damage that future purchasers of property might suffer in the event of a non-exercise or a careless exercise of their statutory powers. To superimpose such a general common law duty on a statutory power would be to 'conjure up' the duty in order to give effect to judicial ideas of policy. The common law does not superimpose such a duty on a mere statutory power.[100]

Similarly, Deane J argued against liability on the grounds that:

> protection of the owner of land from the mere economic loss which might be sustained by reason of a defect in a building erected upon his or her land is not part of the purpose for which the relevant legislative powers and functions were conferred upon the Council.[101]

The English case law contains similar views on the inadmissibility of a common law duty of care in cases where the statute does not disclose an intention to provide private parties with a civil action for its breach. The observations of O'Connor LJ and Lord Oliver in *Caparo Industries plc* v. *Dickman* concerning the relationship between the auditor's statutory duty under the Companies Acts and the plaintiff's common law

98 (1985) 157 CLR 424.
99 *Ibid.*, 482.
100 *Ibid.*
101 *Ibid.*, 511.

claim for negligent misstatement provide one example of this,[102] as do the majority judgments in *Stovin* v. *Wise*.[103]

However, the difficulty with this approach is that the tests for determining the circumstances under which an action for breach of statutory duty arise are extremely strict.[104] If the courts took the view that a common law negligence action could not be countenanced in a situation where the tests for an action based on the implied intention of the statute were not satisfied, very few actions of this kind would succeed. This is not to deny that there are certain circumstances under which a statute can be read as excluding a common law claim. A statute will, for example, normally be read as impliedly excluding a private law action in tort if it makes separate provision for the adjudication or resolution of disputes arising out of administrative action. Thus claimants for social security benefits have to pursue appeals through the adjudicative procedure laid down by the Social Security Acts, and will not have a separate common law claim for compensation for negligence.[105] However, these are, in the present context, somewhat exceptional cases; in most of the instances we are considering here, the statute is silent on the question of remedies and procedures.

(b) Aligning Public-Law and Private-Law Tests for Determining the Legitimate Exercise of Statutory Powers. A second possibility is that the scope of any common law duty of care is limited by principles of public law which determine the limits of the decision-making powers of statutory bodies. Thus according to Lord Browne-Wilkinson in *X (Minors)* v. *Bedfordshire County Council*, the statutory context is important because '[w]here Parliament has conferred a statutory discretion on a public authority, it is for that authority, not for the courts, to exercise the discretion: nothing which the authority does within the ambit of the discretion can be actionable at common law'.[106] In a similar vein, in *Stovin* v. *Wise* Lord Hoffmann expressed the view that in order for a common law duty to exist, there has to be a 'public law duty to act' in the sense that the failure to do so would amount to irrationality, for example on the grounds that it was '*Wednesbury* unreasonable'.[107] On this basis, although it would not be necessary in all cases to find that the statutory provision in question conferred a duty as opposed to a power, it would nevertheless be necessary to show, in the case of a mere power, that the actions (or omissions) of the authority constituted an abuse of that power from

[102] [1989] QB 653, 714 and [1990] 2 AC 605, 653–4, respectively. The majority judgments in this case had limited support in authority for the restriction of liability, and they fit into a pattern of activist judgments limiting liability. They are at least as clear examples of 'judicial activism' as any of judgments we have discussed that expands liability. See also C. Harlow, *Understanding Tort Law* (1988), 132: 'today the cases of statutory power and statutory duty are as far as possible being aligned'; for criticism of this trend, see S. Todd, 'The Negligence Liability of Public Authorities: Divergence in the Common Law' (1986) 102 *LQR* 370, 396–7.

[103] [1996] AC 923.

[104] See ch. 7, above.

[105] *Jones* v. *Department of Employment* [1989] QB 1; see also the use of a separate right of appeal to defeat a negligence claim in *Mills* v. *Winchester Diocesan Board of Finance* [1989] Ch. 428.

[106] [1995] 2 AC 633, 738.

[107] *Stovin* v. *Wise* [1996] AC 923, 953. A decision is '*Wednesbury* unreasonable' if it is so unreasonable that no reasonable authority could have taken it.

a public law point of view, in order for a duty of care to arise.[108] This argument has particular force in cases, such as *Stovin* and (arguably) *X (Minors)*, which arise from an omission or failure to act. To hold a statutory body liable for failure to do a certain act when that act was not compelled by public law—or in other words, fell within the discretionary powers of the statutory body concerned—could be seen as upsetting the scheme of powers and duties established by the relevant statute and undermining the accepted principles of judicial review of administrative action.[109]

But this argument also has its difficulties. The claim that public law should *necessarily* confine the scope of the private-law negligence claim has not won the general approval of the courts. In the Australian case of *Pyrenees Shire Council* v. *Day*,[110] the High Court of Australia allowed an action for negligence to proceed against the council for its failure to warn occupiers of a fire risk in property which it had inspected under statutory powers. Kirby J discussed the test laid down by Lord Hoffmann in *Stovin* in the following terms:

> Although such a test might have the attraction of reconciling principles of the law of negligence and administrative law, it would impose on a claimant a burden more onerous than the law of negligence typically does. It may be 'fair, just and reasonable' to impose on a public authority a duty of care to exercise relevant statutory powers in given circumstances although a refusal to do so would not have attracted the epithet 'irrational'. This would be especially so where the beneficiaries of the power 'could not guard themselves' or where the defects said to call forth the exercise of the power are dangerous and even life-threatening.[111]

Similarly, in *Barrett* v. *Enfield London Borough Council* [112] Lord Slynn considered that a common-law negligence action should not necessarily be ruled out merely because 'an act [is] being done subject to the exercise of [an] overriding statutory power'.

(c) Statute as Framing the Common-Law Duty of Care. A third possible approach is to argue that a common law action can arise from the exercise of a statutory duty or power as long as the general conditions for a duty of care are present, but that the aims and contents of the statute frame the scope of that duty. This was the line taken by the

108 This is not quite the same as saying that an *ultra vires* act is either a necessary (or sufficient) condition for the existence of a common law duty; it is enough that the public body has failed properly to exercise its discretion. See Lord Browne-Wilkinson in *X (Minors)* v. *Bedfordshire CC* [1995] 2 AC 633, 736, and see also the judgment of Hale LJ in *A* v. *Essex CC* [2004] 1 WLR 1881, 1893, suggesting that 'the exercise of statutory discretion only gives rise to liability in tort if it is so unreasonable that it falls outside the ambit of the discretion'.

109 The review of administrative discretion is rapidly developing, considerably strengthening the protection of the rights of private parties against public administration. While *Wednesbury* unreasonableness (in the strict sense) as traditionally understood and applied did not entail a great intensity of review, the potentially stricter head of proportionality review is replacing *Wednesbury* in wide areas of administrative law. These include, in particular where a human right under the ECHR is in issue (by virtue of the Human Rights Act 1998) and where EC law is relevant; whether it is spreading further is a matter for ongoing conjecture. The reader is referred to books on administrative law for consideration of such matters: see, e.g., P. P. Craig, *Administrative Law* (5th edn., 2003) and Wade and Forsyth (Select Bibliography).

110 (1998) 192 CLR 330.

111 *Ibid.*, 426. See also the judgment of Hayne J in *Brodie* v. *Singleton Shire Council* (2001) 206 CLR 512, 628–9.

112 [2001] 2 AC 550, 571. See also the speech of Lord Hutton [2001] 2 AC 550, 577–87, and the speech of Lord Slynn in *Phelps* v. *Hillingdon LBC* [2001] 2 AC 619.

majority of courts in the line of decisions which followed *Anns* in exploring the liability of local authorities for negligent building inspection. In an early post-*Anns* decision, *Governors of the Peabody Donation Fund* v. *Sir Lindsay Parkinson & Co.*[113] a local council failed to exercise a statutory power to halt work for the installation of an unauthorised drainage system on land that the plaintiff/company was developing. Two years later the plaintiff had to reconstruct the system at a considerable financial loss. It brought an *Anns*-style action against the council. But it failed in the House of Lords on the ground that the statutory power in question had been conferred for the purposes of protecting the health and safety of future occupiers and their families, and not the financial interests of companies involved in the construction work.[114] In *Murphy* itself, a duty was denied even in a case where the claimants were occupiers who had incurred an economic loss in moving out of property which had apparently become dangerous to live in once the hidden defect was revealed. According to Lord Oliver:

> there is nothing in the terms or purpose of the statutory provisions which support the creation of a private law right of action for breach of statutory duty. There is equally nothing in the statutory provisions, which even suggests that the purpose of the statute was to protect owners of buildings from economic loss. Nor is there any easily discernible reason why the existence of the statutory duties, in contradistinction to those existing in the case of other regulatory agencies, should be held in the case of a local authority to create a special relationship imposing a private law duty to members of the public....[115]

In contrast to the decisions in *Sutherland* and *Murphy*, the Canadian Supreme Court decided, in *City of Kamloops* v. *Nielsen*,[116] to allow an *Anns*-style action for negligence against a local authority. By a bare majority, it rejected an argument to the effect that the relevant legislation must be found to impose a private-law duty on the defendant. However, Wilson J suggested that the private-law remedy must be 'impliedly sanctioned' by the legislature:

> In order to obtain recovery for economic loss the statute has to create a private law duty to the plaintiff alongside the public law duty. The plaintiff has to belong to the limited class of owners or occupiers of the property at the time the damage manifests itself.... Finally, and perhaps this merits some emphasis, economic loss will only be recoverable if as a matter of statutory interpretation it is a type of loss the statute intended to guard against.[117]

More recently the *Kamloops* decision has been described by the Canadian Supreme Court as based on the principle that 'the statute has to create a private law duty to the plaintiff alongside the public law duty.... Economic loss will only be recoverable if *as*

113 [1985] AC 210. See also *Curran* v. *Northern Ireland Co-Ownership Housing Association Ltd.* [1987] AC 718.

114 See also the discussion of the Court of Appeal in *Investors in Industry Commercial Properties Ltd.* v. *South Bedfordshire DC* [1986] QB 1034, another case restricting *Anns* which was later overtaken by *Murphy*.

115 [1991] 1 AC 318.

116 [1984] 2 SCR 2. See also the decision of the Privy Council in the New Zealand appeal of *Invercargill CC* v. *Hamlin* [1996] AC 624, in which, perhaps surprisingly, their Lordships declined to follow *Murphy* on the ground that different policy considerations were relevant to the determination of the duty of care in the context of a claim from New Zealand.

117 [1984] 2 SCR 35.

a matter of statutory interpretation it is a type of loss the statute was intended to guard against.'[118]

Courts following this approach have been particularly sceptical of the claim that a duty of care can be established on the basis of 'general reliance' or 'a general expectation on the part of the community' that a statutory power will be exercised in a certain way. Although the notion of 'general reliance' was mentioned by Lord Hoffmann in his judgment in *Stovin* v. *Wise*,[119] later English case law has been sceptical of the idea.[120] In *Pyrenees Shire Council* v. *Day* the majority of the High Court of Australia rejected 'general reliance' in favour of an approach which was more sensitive to the framing role of the statute. In the words of Brennan CJ:

> If community expectation that a statutory power will be exercised were to be adopted as a criterion of a duty to exercise the power, it would displace the criterion of legislative intention. In my respectful opinion, if the public law duty of a public authority to exercise a power is relevant to its liability in damages for a failure to exercise that power, the appropriate criterion is legislative intention.[121]

Thus recent decisions in a number of Commonwealth jurisdictions point to the importance of a 'statutory framing' analysis. However, the statutory context will not always point away from liability. In *Phelps* v. *Hillingdon London Borough Council*[122] the issue was whether the defendant council owed a common law duty of care with regard to the educational development of children in its schools. Lord Clyde noted that 'the present claims all arise in the public sector where there is a very obvious statutory context', deriving from provisions of various Education Acts which aimed to ensure the provision of educational services to children with special needs. In His Lordship's view, 'the existence of a statutory background against which the professionals are exercising their particular skills should not inhibit the existence of a common law duty of care'.[123] On the other hand, sensitivity to the statutory framework of child protection led the High Court of Australia in *Sullivan* v. *Moody*[124] to deny a claim for negligence brought by parents who alleged they had been wrongly accused of abuse towards their children: since this legislation 'required the respondents to treat the interests of the children as paramount' it would be 'inconsistent with the proper and effective discharge of those responsibilities that they should be subjected to a legal duty, breach of which would sound in damages, to take care to protect persons who were suspected of being the sources of that harm'.[125] This approach was followed by the House of Lords in *D.* v. *East Berkshire Community NHS Trust*, with the same result: it would be inconsistent with the

[118] *Canadian National Railway* v. *Norsk Pacific Steamship Co.* (1992) 91 DLR (4th) 289, 314 (LaForest J). See also the Supreme Court of Canada's discussion of issues relating to the liability of regulatory bodies in *Cooper* v. *Hobart* [2001] SCC 79.

[119] [1996] AC 923, 953–5.

[120] See in particular *Capital and Counties plc* v. *Hampshire CC* [1997] QB 1004; *OLL Ltd.* v. *Secretary of State for Transport* [1997] 3 All ER 897.

[121] (1998) 192 CLR 330, 344.

[122] [2001] 2 AC 619.

[123] *Ibid.*, 673.

[124] [2001] HCA 59.

[125] *Ibid.*, at para. 62 (Gleeson CJ, Gaudron, McHugh, Hayne and Callinan JJ).

'proper and effective discharge' of the 'professional and statutory responsibilities of doctors and other health professionals' to impose a duty of care to the parents of a child alleged to have suffered physical abuse at their hands.[126] A relevant factor here, which was much relied on by the majority judgments in *East Berkshire*, was the ministerial guidance *Working Together* issued under section 7 of the Local Authority Social Services Act 1970; however, Lord Bingham showed in his dissenting judgment that this guidance could be interpreted as assisting the parents' claim. Although it stated that in the event of conflict the interests of the child should prevail, it also stressed, among other things, 'involving the parents', 'partnership with the parents' and 'the need for a high degree of cooperation with parents'.[127] Thus it is arguable that the statutory context in *East Berkshire* was by no means as clear cut as the majority assumed.

(ii) Justiciability and Public Policy

(a) Weighing Justiciability and Policy: General Considerations The question of justiciability goes to the inability of the courts to assess complex policy issues of the kind which public bodies are required to make. This idea overlaps to a certain extent with the 'policy' element of the policy–operation dichotomy, and with the concept of 'policy' as one of the factors to be weighed in the balance in determining the existence of a duty of care.[128] According to Lord Browne-Wilkinson:

> Since what are under consideration are discretionary powers conferred on public bodies for public purposes the relevant factors will often include policy matters, for example social policy, the allocation of finite financial resources between the different calls made upon them or (as in *Dorset Yacht*) the balance between pursuing desirable social aims as against the risk to the public inherent in so doing. It is established that the courts cannot enter upon the assessment of such 'policy' matters.[129]

However, the application of the 'policy' test has gone far beyond what was said in *Anns*, as justiciability has become entwined with a separate line of authority associated with the decision of the House of Lords in *Hill* v. *Chief Constable of West Yorkshire*.[130] These cases suggest that certain categories of *operational* negligence cannot be the subject of common law claims for damages, where the effect would be to distort decisions on the distribution of resources by public bodies. In *Hill* the estate of the last victim of a serial killer brought an action against the police for negligence in failing to identify and apprehend the murderer at an earlier date. The action was struck out. According to Lord Keith:

> The manner of conduct of such an investigation must necessarily involve a variety of decisions to be made on matters of policy and discretion, for example as to which particular line of inquiry is most advantageously to be pursued and what is the most advantageous way to deploy the available resources. Many such decisions would not be regarded as appropriate by the court to be called into question.[131]

126 [2005] 2 AC 373, 407 (Lord Nicholls of Birkenhead).
127 *Ibid.*, 395. 128 See ch. 3, above.
129 *X (Minors)* v. *Bedfordshire CC* [1995] 2 AC 633, 737.
130 [1989] AC 53. 131 *Ibid.*, 63.

Similarly, in the case of *X (Minors)* v. *Bedfordshire County Council*[132] Lord Browne-Wilkinson regarded the complexity of decisions relating to child protection orders as one reason for denying the existence of a duty of care. He cited similar factors in ruling that local authorities could not be sued for alleged breaches of duty under legislation governing the provision of services for children with special educational needs.

The notion of justiciability has been invoked to enable public bodies exercising regulatory and prosecutorial functions also to escape liability. Thus, in *Elguzouli-Daf* v. *Commissioner of Police of the Metropolis and Another*[133] the plaintiffs sued the Crown Prosecution Service for negligently processing their prosecutions, with the result that they were detained in custody (on remand) for lengthy periods. The actions were struck out, on the ground that 'there are compelling considerations, rooted in the welfare of the whole community, which outweigh the dictates of individualised justice'. These included the risk of 'defensive' action by CPS prosecutors and the diversion of resources away from their principal functions. In this context, according to Steyn LJ, the application of the policy–operation distinction would be 'impractical, unworkable and not capable of avoiding... adverse consequences for the CPS'.[134] In *Harris* v. *Evans*[135] the plaintiff's business was temporarily shut down when a Health and Safety inspector decided (allegedly on the basis of a mistaken understanding of HSE policy) that the mobile crane which he used to provide bungee jumping was unsafe. His action for damages for lost profits was struck out. Said the Vice Chancellor:

> it would be seriously detrimental to the proper discharge by enforcing authorities of their responsibilities in respect of public health and safety if they were to be exposed to potential liability in negligence at the suit of the owners of the businesses adversely affected by their decisions.[136]

In related contexts, *Hill* has been cited in a string of cases to deny liability on the part of the police to the victims of crimes and accidents. Hence the owner of a shop could not sue the police for losses allegedly caused by their negligent failure to catch a burglar.[137] The estate of a victim of a road-traffic accident had no cause of action against the police for failing to alert road-users to the presence of slippery diesel oil left on the highway by a third party,[138] nor was there a cause of action where a government department allegedly failed to take the necessary steps to deport a non-UK citizen with a violent criminal record, following which he went on to commit further crimes.[139]

132 [1995] 2 AC 633.

133 [1995] QB 335. Cf. *Welsh* v. *Chief Constable of the Merseyside Police* [1993] 1 All ER 692.

134 [1995] QB 335, 349–50.

135 [1998] 1 WLR 1285. Cf. *Welton* v. *North Cornwall DC* [1997] 1 WLR 570.

136 [1998] 1 WLR 1285, 1301 (Sir Richard Scott VC).

137 *Alexandrou* v. *Oxford* [1993] 4 All ER 328.

138 *Ancell* v. *McDermott* [1993] 4 All ER 355. Nor did the police owe a duty of care to avoid causing psychological harm to a potential murder witness who was wrongly suspected of the crime: *Brooks* v. *Commissioner of Police of the Metropolis* [2005] 1 WLR 1495.

139 *K* v. *Secretary of State for the Home Department* [2002] EWCA Civ. 983; see also *Palmer* v. *Tees AHA* (2000) 2 LGLR 69; [2000] PIQR P1.

A similarly wide protection has been applied to public rescue services, such as the fire service and the coastal rescue. Thus, such bodies are under no private-law duty to respond to emergency calls, and cannot be liable for an omission to act when carrying out a rescue.[140]

These decisions hark back to the majority judgments in *East Suffolk*.[141] Indeed, in cases concerning alleged failures of the emergency services, recent decisions have rehabilitated the idea that a public authority can only be liable for *making things worse*. Thus, in *Capital and Counties plc* v. *Hampshire County Council*,[142] the defendant fire authority was held to be liable for the carelessness of fire officers in switching off the automatic sprinkler system in the plaintiff's factory as part of a failed attempt to keep it from going up in flames. The intervention of the fire service, in this instance, had actively exacerbated the situation.

Difficult issues arise where there is evidence of an assumption of responsibility by the defendant authority to a particular person or group of persons. In some cases, this has been enough to tip the balance in favour of a finding of a duty of care. Thus it seems to be generally agreed that the police owe a duty of care to take steps to ensure the safety of arrested persons who are known to be at risk of committing suicide.[143] Similarly, the police may owe a duty of care to conceal the identity of their informants and to protect the confidentiality of the information that they provide, so as to minimise the risk of retaliation against them.[144] Likewise, an ambulance service was held liable for failing to come to the aid of the claimant's husband after initially accepting responsibility for responding to an emergency call.[145] An adoption agency does not owe a general duty of care in relation to the information that it chooses to disclose to prospective adopters, but once it decides to provide certain information, it may come under a duty of care to ensure that it is given and received.[146] A regulatory authority, which would not otherwise be liable for failing to have regard to the economic interests or more general welfare of the claimant, may incur liability for negligent misstatements. This would be the case if the existence of a pre-tort relationship, based on reliance by or an assumption of responsibility to a particular individual, can be established.[147]

[140] *Capital and Counties plc* v. *Hampshire CC* [1997] QB 1004; *OLL Ltd.* v. *Secretary of State for Transport* [1997] 3 All ER 897.

[141] [1941] AC 74.

[142] [1997] QB 1004.

[143] *Reeves* v. *Commissioner of Police of the Metropolis* [1998] 2 WLR 401.

[144] *Swinney* v. *Chief Constable of Northumbria Police Force* [1997] QB 464; see also *L* v. *Reading BC* [2001] 1 WLR 1575 in which the Court of Appeal refused to strike out a claim in a case where a police officer judged (wrongly) that the claimant had sexually abused his daughter, on the basis that a legal assumption of responsibility could have arisen on the facts.

[145] *Kent* v. *Griffiths* [2000] 2 WLR 1158; T. Hickman, '"And That's Magic!" Making Public Bodies Liable for Failing to Confer Benefits' [2000] *CLJ* 432.

[146] *A* v. *Essex CC* [2004] 1 WLR 1881.

[147] *T* v. *Surrey CC* [1994] 4 All ER 577, *Welton* v. *North Cornwall DC* [1997] 1 WLR 570, *X (Minors)* v. *Bedfordshire CC* [1995] 2 AC 633, 763–4. See also three cases in which regulatory bodies were held to have incurred a duty of care to take steps to avoid physical harm to the claimant, in circumstances where an assumption of liability could be inferred: *Perrett* v. *Collins* [1998] 2 Lloyd's Rep. 255, *Watson* v. *British Boxing Board of Control* [2001] QB 1134, and, in the HC of Australia, *Crimmins* v. *Stevedoring Industry Financing Committee* (1999) 167 ALR 1; although cf. *Marc Rich & Co. AG* v. *Bishop Rock Marine, The Nicholas H* [1996] 2 AC 211; *Agar* v. *Hyde* [2000] HCA 41.

But even here, it is possible that the plaintiff's claim will be defeated by policy considerations. In *Osman* v. *Ferguson*[148] the relationship between the police and the family of the murder victim was, prior to the killing, sufficiently close for the Court of Appeal to consider that there might have been a special pre-tort relationship sufficient to give rise to a duty of care. However, the court decided that *even if this had been the case*, it would be against public policy for a duty of care to be imposed on the police with regard to the safety of a particular individual or group of individuals.[149]

In contrast stand a number of decisions in which the courts rejected arguments based on non-justiciability. In *Lonrho plc* v. *Tebbit*[150] Sir Nicolas Browne-Wilkinson V-C declined to strike out an action for damages brought by Lonrho in respect of alleged negligence by the Secretary of State for Trade and Industry in the exercise of powers under the Fair Trading Act 1973 governing takeovers and mergers. The alleged negligence lay in failing to release Lonrho from an undertaking not to mount a takeover bid for the House of Fraser until after the point at which another bid had been made, successfully, by the Fayed brothers. According to Lonrho, there was no reason to delay the release of the undertaking once the Monopolies and Mergers Commission had reported that a takeover by Lonrho would not be contrary to the public interest. Sir Nicolas held that no issue of policy arose, since 'the timing of the release did not involve the allocation of resources or the distribution of risks'; nor were there any other obvious public policy considerations. Accordingly the matter was justiciable.[151] This decision points to the need to keep the justiciability exception within tightly defined bounds.

Moreover, the post-*X (Minors)* case law emphasises that there are limits to the use of the justiciability exception in the context of statutory claims in respect of the psychological and educational treatment of children. In *Barrett* v. *Enfield London Borough Council*,[152] *X (Minors)* was distinguished on the ground that the courts were better placed to judge the conduct of local authorities with regard to children already in their care than they were with regard to the decision to take them into care in the first place; according to Lord Slynn, the factors that swayed Lord Browne-Wilkinson in *X (Minors)* did not 'have the same force individually or cumulatively in the present case' where '[t]he decision to remove the child from care is already taken and the authority has

[148] [1993] 4 All ER 344.

[149] It was this finding which later persuaded the ECtHR to hold that in the *Osman* litigation there had been a denial of the claimant's right of access to the court under Art. 6 ECHR (*Osman* v. *United Kingdom* (1998) 29 EHRR 455). After the Court's later decision in *Z* v. *United Kingdom* [2001] 2 FLR 612, the scope for invoking Art. 6 in such a case is much reduced, but in *Van Colle* v. *Chief Constable of Hertfordshire* [2006] EWHC 360 Art. 2 was applied to ground a finding of liability under the Human Rights Act 1998, s. 6, in a case where the police failed to take adequate steps to protect a prosecution witness. See our discussion in ch. 3, above, and in Section 8 of this chapter, below. See also *Roche* v. *United Kingdom* (2006) 42 EHRR 30, where the European Court of Human Rights held by the barest majority, nine votes to eight, that there had been no violation of Art. 6(1) of the Convention. This case indicates that there remains a fundamental disagreement on the applicability of Art. 6 on immunities and duties of care in English law.

[150] [1991] 4 All ER 973; [1992] 4 All ER 280.

[151] [1991] 4 All ER 973, 980. The Vice-Chancellor's judgment was upheld in the Court of Appeal: [1992] 4 All ER 280.

[152] [2001] 2 AC 550.

statutory powers in relation to the child which do not necessarily involve the exercise of the kind of discretion involved in taking a child from its family into care'.[153]

In *D* v. *East Berkshire Community NHS Trust*[154] the Court of Appeal declined to follow *X (Minors)*, and held that a duty of care was owed to children in respect of a decision to take them into care following allegations of abuse by their parents. The Court concluded that in the light of the case law of the European Court of Human Rights after *X (Minors)* had been decided,[155] a claim of this kind, when brought by a child under Article 3 or Article 8 of the European Convention (concerning the right not to be subjected to degrading and inhumane treatment and the right to the protection of family life respectively), necessarily gave rise to factual questions of various kinds which made a no-duty rule inappropriate. A claim under Article 3 would require the court to consider whether the local authority in question knew, or should have known, that its intervention was called for, and a claim under Article 8 would give rise to the issue of whether, in the light of the conduct of parties involved in a case of suspected child abuse, action was 'necessary in a democratic society'. Claims could be brought against the relevant public authorities under section 6 of the Human Rights Act and substantial damages were, in principle, awardable if professional misconduct or maladministration could be shown. Under these circumstances, the no-duty rule could not stand: in a striking example of the impact that human-rights law can now have on the development of the common law, the Court ruled that 'given the obligation of the local authority to respect a child's Convention rights, the recognition of a duty of care to the child on the part of those involved should not have a significantly adverse effect on the way in which they perform their duties'.[156]

(b) *Recent Approaches to Justiciability and Policy: Comparing Phelps and East Berkshire*

The *Phelps* litigation concerned a school's failure to diagnose dyslexia in one of its children, thereby leaving the child without appropriate educational training. Dyslexia is a medically recognised disorder manifested by difficulty in learning to read despite conventional instruction.[157] It is dependent upon fundamental cognitive disabilities, which are frequently of constitutional origin. Until comparatively recently, the disorder was not medically recognised and the courts, here as in cases of psychiatric injury, took a sceptical attitude towards this disability, often associating its deleterious effects to environmental factors connected with the child/claimant's life or to lack of intelligence.[158] The difficulties of diagnosis also delayed its admission into the law as a plausible form of tortious harm. It is thus not entirely surprising that the Court of

153 [2001] 2 AC 550, 568.

154 [2004] QB 558. See also *S* v. *Gloucestershire CC* [2001] Fam. 313.

155 The relevant cases include *E* v. *United Kingdom* (2002) 36 EHRR 519, an Art. 3 case, and two Art. 8 cases, *P, C and S* v. *United Kingdom* (2002) 35 EHRR 1075 and *Venema* v. *The Netherlands* [2003] 1 FLR 552.

156 [2004] QB 558, 590 (Lord Phillips of Worth Matravers MR).

157 See *Diagnostic and Statistical Manual of Mental Disorders* (4th edn., 1995), 46–53.

158 This then is not the first time that medical uncertainties have encouraged judicial timidity. This is partly because these harms appear as unreal, easily faked, and, generally, not deserving the protection of the law. The medical view on the matters has changed; but the law is still lagging behind.

Appeal in *Phelps* was inclined to take a hostile view to these claims by invoking a barrage of arguments in order to stop the case going to trial.[159] These arguments varied from the opinion that the claimant had suffered no recoverable loss to the view that the educational psychologist, who had failed to discover the child's disability, had assumed no responsibility towards the child itself, but only towards her employers. The Court of Appeal went so far as to deny vicarious liability on the ground that it would introduce liability through the 'back door'. In reversing the Court of Appeal on these various points, the House of Lords confirmed the direction taken in *Barrett*, at the heart of which was a more nuanced approach to issues of policy and justiciability. Thus Lord Clyde was 'not persuaded that the recognition of a liability upon employees of the education authority for damages for negligence in education would lead to a flood of claims, or even vexatious claims, which would overwhelm the school authorities, nor that it would add burdens and distractions to the already intensive life of teachers'. Nor, in his view, would it 'inspire some peculiarly defensive attitude in the performance of their professional responsibilities. On the contrary, it may have the healthy effect of securing that high standards are sought and secured.' Lord Clyde was also sceptical of arguments based on the feasibility of alternative remedies, noting that 'even if there are alternative procedures by which some form of redress might be obtained, such as resort to judicial review or to an ombudsman or the adoption of such statutory procedures as are open to parents, which might achieve some correction of the situation for the future, it may only be through a claim for damages at common law that compensation for the damage done to the child may be secured for the past as well as the future'.[160]

Lord Nicholls's speech is particularly notable for its explicit consideration of the possible implications of litigation relating to educational malpractice. In an attempt to dispel the fears that a pro-claimant judgment would open the floodgates of litigation he made the following observations:

> Let me consider three instances. Take a case where an educational psychologist is employed by an education authority... When carrying out the assessment and advising the education authority, [does] he owe a duty of care to the child?... I confess I entertain no doubt on how that question should be answered.... This seems to me to be, on its face, an example par excellence of a situation where the law will regard the professional as owing a duty of care to a third party as well as his own employer... My second illustration concerns a teacher. Does a teacher owe a common law duty of care to a pupil who is obviously having difficulty and not making the progress he should?... A teacher must exercise due skill and care to respond appropriately to the manifest problems of such a child... [and] if he does not do so, he will be in breach of the duty he owes the child... My third illustration raises a particularly controversial issue. It cannot be that a teacher owes a duty of care only to children with special educational needs. The law would be in an extraordinary state if, in carrying out their teaching responsibilities, teachers owed duties to some for their pupils but not to others. So the question which arises, and cannot be shirked, is whether teachers owe duties of care to all their pupils in respect of the way they discharge their teaching responsibilities... I can see no escape from the conclusion that teachers do, indeed owe such duties....[161]

[159] [1999] 1 WLR 500. [160] [2001] 2 AC 619, 672. [161] [2001] 2 AC 619, 665–7.

But does this open the door to claims based on poor quality of teaching? While it is one thing to award damages in cases of manifest incompetence or negligence comprising specific, identifiable mistakes, it is arguably quite another to countenance claims of a more general nature, to the effect that the child did not receive an adequate education. Lord Nicholls was conscious of the need to stress this difference so he said:

> ... proof of under performance by a child is not by itself evidence of negligent teaching. There are many, many reasons for under performance... suffice it to say, the existence of a duty of care owed by teachers to their pupils should not be regarded as furnishing a basis on which generalised 'educational malpractice' claims can be mounted.[162]

Phelps therefore shifted the emphasis away from duty of care as a control factor. As Lord Nicholls put it, fears of a defensive reaction to the possibility of litigation do not

> provide sufficient reason for treating work in the classroom as territory, which the courts must never enter. 'Never' is an unattractive absolute in this context. This would bar a claim, however obvious it was that something had gone badly wrong.... Denial of the existence of a cause of action is seldom, if ever, the appropriate response to fear of its abuse.[163]

The logic of this approach is that the courts will scrutinise carefully claims that substandard performance led to actionable damage.[164] *Phelps* thereby marks a significant move away from the sweeping protection aimed at by *Hill*, in particular by making it near impossible to regard the justiciability and policy exceptions as offering a form of safe haven to public defendants; instead, cases will have to be taken on a one-by-one basis and closely examined to see if a striking-out order is justified.

How far do the judgments in *East Berkshire* mark a move back to a more restrictive approach? As we have seen, the issue before the House of Lords was whether medical professionals owed a duty of care to the parents of children who were alleged to have suffered physical abuse. The parents claimed that, because of negligent diagnoses, they had been wrongly accused of child abuse, and that they had suffered psychiatric loss as a consequence of the false accusations and of the taking of their children into care which resulted from them. The Court of Appeal had already held that a duty of care was owed to the children, and no appeal was made against this finding. For the majority in the House of Lords, the presence of a duty of care with regard to the children was a critical factor in rejecting the parents' claims. Lord Nicholls, while accepting that the principle of the protection of family life was a factor which placed a parent in a stronger position, for these purposes, than a non-family member facing accusations of child abuse, nevertheless concluded that it would be wrong to allow the parents' claim given

162 *Ibid.*, 668; Lord Jauncey, at 665, agreed.

163 *Ibid.*, 667. Lord Slynn of Hadley agreed: *ibid.*, 654–5.

164 For a case applying *Phelps* which suggests this approach, see *Bradford-Smart* v. *West Sussex CC* [2002] 2 FCR 425, and see D. Fairgrieve, 'Pushing Back the Boundaries of Public Authority Liability: Tort Law Enters the Classroom' (Select Bibliography).

'the seriousness of child abuse as a social problem [which] demands that health professionals, acting in good faith in what they believe are the best interests of the child, should not be subject to potentially conflicting duties when deciding when a child may have been abused'.[165] According to Lord Brown of Eaton-under-Heywood, a no-duty rule was preferable, in this context, to a shift in focus to the question of breach:

> There is always a temptation to say in all these cases that no one, whether a doctor concerned with possible child abuse, a witness or a prosecutor will ever in fact be held liable unless he has conducted himself manifestly unreasonably; it is unnecessary, therefore, to deny a duty of care, better to focus on the appropriate standard by which to judge whether it is breached. That, however, is to overlook two fundamental considerations: first, the insidious effect that his awareness of the proposed duty would have upon the mind and conduct of the doctor (subtly tending to the suppression of doubts and instincts which in the child's interests ought rather to be encouraged), and second, a consideration inevitably bound up with the first, the need to protect him against the risk of costly and vexatious litigation, by no means invariably soundly based.[166]

However, a powerful counter-argument was mounted by Lord Bingham in his dissenting judgment. After reviewing the statutory context of the UK law on child protection and the relevant case law of the European Court of Human Rights, he argued that 'far from presuming a conflict between the interests of the child and parent the law generally presumes that they are consonant with each other, or at any rate, if not consonant, not so dissonant that healthcare professionals should proceed without fully informing and consulting the parents'.[167] He also suggested, in the light of evidence that the law in other European jurisdictions would not rule out the parents' claim without a consideration of the facts of the case, that a shift from duty to breach as a control factor would be appropriate: 'the concept of duty has proved itself a somewhat blunt instrument for dividing claims which ought reasonably to lead to recovery from claims which should not'.[168] In the light of these considerations and of the growing influence of European human rights law, we venture to suggest that the no-duty ruling in *East Berkshire* will prove to be no more durable than that in *X (Minors)* turned out to be. It has already been challenged in litigation which suggests that, regardless of the common law position, it will be difficult to insulate public authorities from claims by both the parent and the child under the Human Rights Act.[169] If that proves to be the case, the common-law rule will start to look highly anomalous.

165 [2005] 2 AC 373, 407.

166 [2005] 2 AC 373, 422.

167 *Ibid.*, 396.

168 *Ibid.*, 400. On the position in certain other European jurisdictions, see B.S. Markesinis and J. Fedtke, 'Authority or Reason? The Economic Consequences of Liability for Breach of Statutory Duty in a Comparative Perspective' (Select Bibliography), 38–49 (Germany); Andenas and Fairgrieve, 'Misfeasance in Public Office' (Select Bibliography) and D. Fairgrieve, *State Liability in Tort* (Select Bibliography), ch. 4 (France).

169 *L* v. *Pembrokeshire CC* [2006] EWHC 1029, [2007] PIQR P1; see also *Fairlie* v. *Perth and Kinross Healthcare NHS Trust* [2004] SLT 400.

3. LIABILITY FOR BREACH OF STATUTORY DUTY

The general principles concerning the action for breach of statutory duty have already been considered.[170] Conceptually, the action is seen as arising under the statute by virtue of an implied legislative intent. It is, therefore, distinct from the common law action for negligence in the exercise of a statutory power, even if the tendency of the courts in cases such as *Peabody*[171] and, in particular, *Stovin* v. *Wise*[172] has been, as Professor Carol Harlow puts it, to 'align' the two.[173]

The tests for identifying the necessary statutory intent are restrictive. It will normally be necessary for the plaintiff to show that he fell within a particular class of persons whom the statute was passed to protect, tests that are difficult to surmount.[174] The effect of the decision in *Atkinson* v. *Newcastle Waterworks*[175] was felt for a long time to restrict the potential liability of utilities and statutory bodies under this head of liability. To some extent this assumption was challenged by the much-criticised[176] decision in *Thornton* v. *Kirklees Metropolitan Borough Council*,[177] in which the Court of Appeal accepted the possibility of statutory action for damages arising under the Housing (Homeless Persons) Act 1977. However, the *Thornton* case did not give rise to a spate of statutory actions against public bodies, in part because of the procedural changes introduced into public law which limited the availability of private law actions for administrative negligence and it was formally overturned in 1998.[178]

The principal significance of the statutory action in the present law seems to be to restrict the potential scope of negligence liability. As we have just seen, the House of Lords, especially in the 1990s, took the view that no common law duty may be imposed in a case where it is not possible to imply an intention to create a statutory action. As the statutory action is only rarely available, this could be said to have created a certain presumption against liability, although in *Phelps* v. *Hillingdon London Borough Council*[179] the House of Lords accepted the possibility of common law duties of care while ruling out an action for breach of statutory duty.

4. PUBLIC LAW AS A SOURCE OF LIABILITY

(A) DAMAGES FOR *ULTRA VIRES* ACTS?

Judicial review may be available to challenge an administrative act that is *ultra vires*. This could be on the grounds that the authority in question failed to take into account relevant considerations, failed to direct itself correctly on the law, or did not observe the

170 In ch. 7, above. 171 [1985] AC 210. 172 [1996] AC 923.
173 C. Harlow, *Understanding Tort Law* (1988), 132.
174 For a recent example, see *Goodes* v. *East Sussex CC* [2000] 1 WLR 1365.
175 (1877) LR 2 Ex. D 441. 176 See in particular, Weir (Select Bibliography), 52.
177 [1979] 1 WLR 637. 178 *O'Rourke* v. *Camden LBC* [1998] AC 189. 179 [2001] 2 AC 619.

requirements of natural justice (or 'due process'). As we have already noted, however, a finding of *ultra vires* does not necessarily entail liability for damages in negligence.[180] It is one thing to have an act declared invalid, thereby restoring the *status quo*, but quite another for the authority to find itself indemnifying a potentially wide range of people for various losses. In the former case the plaintiff or applicant is required to show only that he has a sufficient interest to challenge an excess of authority by the relevant body; in the latter, he must show that that a private-law right of his had been infringed.[181]

The relationship between *vires* and claims for damages was considered by Lord Keith of Kinkel in *Rowling* v. *Takaro Properties Ltd.*[182] A minister exercised powers under statute to prevent the issue of shares in Takaro to a foreign company, with the result that a rescue plan for Takaro failed. The minister's action was later held to be *ultra vires* and an action was brought against him for compensation for the economic losses arising from the failure of the share deal. The Privy Council, overruling the New Zealand courts, found for the minister. Lord Keith noted that the normal consequence of an *ultra vires* act will simply be delay, as the act or decision can be nullified by proceedings for judicial review or its equivalent. In itself this is not much of an argument against granting damages for *ultra vires* acts, since in commercial matters even a short delay may cause considerable loss; and this was precisely the case in *Takaro*. Lord Keith went on, however, to argue that 'in the nature of things, it is likely to be very rare indeed that an error of law of this kind by a minister or other public authority can properly be categorised as negligent'.[183] A misinterpretation of powers, on its own, is unlikely to be actionable in damages; there must be something more, such as the elements of knowledge or malice required for the tort of misfeasance in a public office,[184] or an assumption of responsibility in the context of the kind of pre-tort special relationship which can give rise to a duty of care in negligence under *Hedley Byrne & Co. Ltd.* v. *Heller & Partners Ltd.*[185]

(B) THE TORT OF MISFEASANCE IN A PUBLIC OFFICE

Damages may nonetheless be available for an *ultra vires* act if an official *knowingly* acts in excess of his powers or acts with *malice* towards the plaintiff. This is the tort of

180 The improper exercise of statutory powers does not, by itself, give rise to any civil liability in English law: *Lonrho plc* v. *Tebbit* [1991] 4 All ER 973, 978 (Sir Nicolas Browne-Wilkinson VC). See also *Bourgoin SA* v. *Ministry of Agriculture* [1986] 1 QB 785, per Parker LJ. For further discussion of damages for invalid acts, see P. Craig, 'Compensation and Public Law' (Select Bibliography), 435–43; Law Commission, *Remedies against Public Bodies: A Scoping Report* (2006), paras. 3.57–3.68.

181 See J. Beatson, '"Public" and "Private" in English Administrative Law' (1987) 103 *LQR* 34. Beatson J (as he now is) was referring here to a 'Hohfeldian' right, meaning one which is the corollary of an obligation owed in private law by the authority to the claimant or applicant individually.

182 [1988] AC 473. 183 [1988] AC 473, 502.

184 Section 4(b), see below.

185 [1965] AC 465. See also *Shaddock and Associates Pty. Ltd.* v. *Paramatta City Council (No. 1)* (1981) 150 CLR 225, *Davy* v. *Spelthorne BC* [1984] AC 262, *Ministry of Housing and Local Government* v. *Sharp* [1970] QB 223. See the discussion of this case by Lord Oliver of Aylmerton in *Murphy* v. *Brentwood DC* [1991] 1 AC 398. See also *Lonrho plc* v. *Tebbit* [1991] 4 All ER 975; [1992] 4 All ER 280 (courts refusing to strike out action for

misfeasance in a public office. Lord Diplock described the tort as 'well established',[186] and it has been frequently and recently applied in England and other Commonwealth jurisdictions. The essence of liability is the abuse of public office, leading to damage to the claimant. The need for the claimant to show special damage, over and above the consequences of the breach of duty for the public as a whole, was confirmed in *Watkins* v. *Secretary of State for the Home Department*.[187] The claimant, a convicted prisoner, alleged that correspondence with his legal advisers had been interfered with by prison officers acting in bad faith and in breach of the (statutory) Prison Rules. The House of Lords rejected his claim on the grounds that he had not suffered any actionable damage in the form of physical or property damage or economic loss, reversing the Court of Appeal, which had held that the tort was made out in a case where 'constitutional rights', such as the right at issue in this case, were interfered with. The facts of the case occurred before the Human Rights Act 1998 came into force and it is possible that a successful claim for breach of a Convention right would now be available under the Act.[188] Given the possibility of a human-rights-based claim, it is surprising that the House of Lords did not consider *Walker* an appropriate case in which to extend the common law along the lines suggested in the Court of Appeal, particularly since *Ashby* v. *White*[189] had decided as long ago as 1703 that the tort was committed in a case involving knowing interference with the right to vote. According to Lord Bingham, *Ashby* v. *White* was a 'highly politicized decision' which it would be anachronistic to treat as having decided that the character of the right invaded [was] determinative, in the present context, of whether material damage need be proved'.[190] The outcome in *Walker* may be contrasted with *Karagozlou* v. *Commissioner of Police for the Metropolis*,[191] where the damage suffered by the claimant, who was also a convicted prisoner, was his reassignment from a category D open prison to a more restrictive category prison. The Court of Appeal held that he had suffered actionable damage—loss of residual liberty—within the meaning of *Walker*.

Although damage is an essential part of the tort, it is not necessary for the claimant to show that he was a member of a class which the public duty or power in question was aimed at protecting, or that he was identifiable as an individual who was likely to be harmed by the defendant's conduct. In *Akenzua* v. *Secretary of State for Home Department*[192] a claim was brought in respect of the decision by officers acting for the

compensation for pure economic loss arising out of a minister's exercise of powers in respect of mergers and takeovers).

186 *Dunlop* v. *Woollahra Municipal Council* [1982] AC 158, 172; see Craig, 'Compensation and Public Law' (Select Bibliography), 426–8; See also *Cullen* v. *Morris* (1819) 2 Stark. 577, *Tozer* v. *Child* (1857) 7 El. & Bl. 377, *Farrington* v. *Thomson and Bridgland* [1959] VR 286, *David* v. *Abdul Cader* [1963] 1 WLR 834, 839–40 (Viscount Radcliffe); and, generally, the review of the history of the tort in the judgments of Lord Bingham of Cornhill, Lord Rodger of Earlsferry, Lord Walker of Gestingthorpe and Lord Carswell in *Watkins* v. *Secretary of State for the Home Department* [2006] 2 WLR 807.

187 [2006] 2 WLR 807.

188 See the judgment of Lord Bingham, at [26]. A claim of this sort failed on its facts in *Francis* v. *Home Office* [2006] EWHC 3021.

189 (1703) 1 Smith's LC 253.

190 [2006] 2 WLR 807, at para. 25.

191 [2006] EWCA Civ. 1691.

192 [2003] 1 WLR 741.

defendant to release a dangerous criminal from detention in order to enable him to act as a police informer. He subsequently carried out a murder which was unrelated to his activities as an informer. The claim brought by the estate of the murdered woman was rejected at first instance on the grounds that she had not been an identifiable in advance as a potential victim, but the Court of Appeal reversed on the grounds that this was not a material ingredient of the tort. The case serves as a reminder that control devices, such as the requirement of a pre-tort relationship or an assumption of responsibility, which apply in the context of the tort of negligence, have no relevance here, since 'a claim in misfeasance postulates that the claimant can prove altogether more blame-worthy conduct than in a negligence action; it is unsurprising that the law should decline to impose a further limiting requirement'.[193]

It has been said that the power alleged to have been abused must have a statutory or public origin,[194] but this requirement is loosely interpreted. A public body exercising a private-law power will not escape the application of the tort. In *Jones* v. *Swansea City Council*[195] the plaintiff alleged that a council resolution turning down her application to amend the terms of a lease between herself and the council was actuated by malice. The ruling party on the council appeared to be opposed to the change of user because the plaintiff's husband had previously been a councillor for an opposing party. The council attempted to argue that the power in question arose under private law as part of the council's general contractual capacity. This was rejected on the ground that a power exercised by a public officer or by a statutory body collectively should only be exercised for the public good: 'it is not the juridical nature of the relevant power but the nature of the council's office which is the important consideration'.[196]

It is now clearly established that either knowledge that the relevant act was taken in excess of powers or malice towards the plaintiff will suffice to establish the necessary mental element. The authorities were recently reviewed in *Three Rivers District Council* v. *Bank of England (No. 3)*,[197] a case arising out of the BCCI affair in which depositors who had lost out as a result of BCCI's collapse sued the Bank of England, as the principal regulator concerned, for failing to take steps to close the bank down sooner.[198] According to Lord Steyn:

> The case law reveals two different forms of liability for misfeasance in public office. First there is the case of targeted malice by a public officer, i.e. conduct specifically intended to injure a person or persons. This type of case involves bad faith in the sense of the exercise of public power for an improper or ulterior motive. The second form is where a public officer acts knowing that he has no power to do the act complained of and that the act will probably injure the plaintiff. It involves bad faith inasmuch as the public officer does not have an honest belief that his act is lawful.[199]

193 *Ibid.*, 751 (Simon Brown LJ).

194 *Jones* v. *Swansea City Council* [1990] 1 WLR 54, 71 (Slade LJ).

195 [1990] 1 WLR 54, 1453.

196 *Ibid.*, 71 (Slade LJ).

197 [2003] 2 AC 1.

198 For a full discussion and analysis of this case, see Andenas and Fairgrieve, 'Misfeasance in Public Office' (Select Bibliography).

199 [2003] 2 AC 1, 191.

This formulation of the second form of liability indicates that while foreseeability is not sufficient, subjective recklessness in the sense of turning a blind eye to the consequences of the act is enough to establish the requisite mental element of the tort; an omission may also suffice. On this basis, the House of Lords, by a majority, refused to strike out the depositors' claims as disclosing no cause of action: the claimants would succeed if they could show, on the facts, that the Bank had failed to take the necessary remedial action to close down BCCI after the point when the fraud was known to it and the consequences to depositors of failing to act must have been clear.

The outcome of the *Three Rivers* case suggests that the tort of misfeasance may have a more important role to play in controlling abuse of discretion than has been the case until now. Few earlier decisions have resulted in success for the plaintiff. In *Bourgoin SA* v. *Ministry of Agriculture*[200] the action concerned the decision by the minister to ban the import of French turkeys into the United Kingdom, contrary to Article 28 (ex 30) EC which prohibits such restrictions on free trade within the European Community. It was alleged that the minister's motive was to protect British turkey farmers from competition. The plaintiff, whose business was affected by the ban, brought an action for damages. His claim for breach of statutory duty failed, but both Mann J and the Court of Appeal held that an action for misfeasance would lie if it could be shown that the minister had knowingly acted in excess of his powers. According to the judge:

> There is no sensible distinction between the case where an officer performs an act which he has no power to perform with the object of injuring A . . . and the case where an officer performs an act which he knows he has no power to perform with the object of conferring a benefit on B but which has the foreseeable and actual consequence of injury to A.[201]

The Ministry settled the case and so it is not known if the tort could actually have been established.

In practice, plaintiffs are likely to face considerable difficulties of proof. The action succeeded before the Supreme Court of Canada in *Roncarelli* v. *Duplessis*,[202] in which the Prime Minister of Quebec had ordered a liquor licence to be withdrawn from a restaurant apparently as punishment for its owner's support for the Jehovah's Witnesses. This clear case may be contrasted with *Jones* v. *Swansea City Council*,[203] in which the plaintiff failed to show that a vote of councillors on a planning matter had been actuated by malice. The Court of Appeal and the House of Lords agreed that an action would lie if it could be shown that a majority of councillors, voting at a particular meeting, did so when motivated by malice. The Court of Appeal ordered a retrial of the action but the House of Lords overturned this decision.

200 [1986] 1 QB 716.

201 *Ibid.*, 740.

202 [1959] SCR 121; see also *Gershman* v. *Manitoba Vegetable Producers' Marketing Board* (1976) 69 DLR (3d) 114.

203 [1990] 1 WLR 54 (CA) and 1453 (HL).

5. PUBLIC LAW AS A SOURCE OF IMMUNITY

(A) VALIDITY OF ADMINISTRATIVE ACTION AS A PRIVATE-LAW DEFENCE

The classic position of English law is that the invalidity of an administrative act does not establish fault for the purposes of tortious liability, and that a valid act does not exclude it. In *Dorset Yacht Co.* v. *Home Office* [204] Lord Diplock argued for it being a defence to a claim in negligence that the act or omission giving rise to liability was taken within the relevant statutory powers. The *ultra vires* principle was one means by which the courts were kept out of areas which were non-justiciable in the sense of providing 'no criterion by which a court can assess where the balance lies between the weight to be given to one interest and that to be given to another'. To cross the boundary of *ultra vires* and allow a negligence action for acts within the authority's statutory discretion would undermine its policy-making function:

It is, I apprehend, for practical reasons of this kind that over the past century the public law concept of *ultra vires* has replaced the civil law concept of negligence as the test of the legality, and consequently of the actionability, of acts or omissions of government departments or public authorities done in the exercise of a discretion conferred upon them by Parliament. According to this concept Parliament has entrusted to the department or authority charged with the administration of the statute the exclusive right to determine the particular means within the limits laid down by the statute by which its purpose can best be fulfilled. It is not the function of the court, for which it would be ill-suited, to substitute its own view of the appropriate means for that of the department or authority by granting a remedy by way of a civil action at law to a private citizen adversely affected by the way in which the discretion has been exercised. Its function is confined in the first instance to deciding whether the act or omission complained of fell within the statutory limits imposed upon the department's or authority's decision. Only if it did not would the court have jurisdiction to determine whether or not the act or omission, not being justified by the statute, constituted an actionable infringement of the plaintiff's rights in civil law.[205]

To a large extent this immunity for *intra vires* acts has now been subsumed into the policy–operation dichotomy and into the courts' reluctance to adjudicate on 'non-justiciable' matters of discretionary judgment. Where a policy decision is taken *ultra vires*, it is still up to the claimant to establish a breach of a duty of care: as we just saw, damages are not automatically available for an *ultra vires* act. Even if both fault and invalidity are established it is highly likely that the courts will still decline to intervene in the policy-making area.[206] Where, on the other hand, negligence is operational in

204 [1970] AC 1004, 1068.

205 *Ibid.* See also to the same effect, *Fellowes* v. *Rother DC* [1983] 1 All ER 513 (Robert Goff J); *Lonrho plc* v. *Tebbit* [1991] 4 All ER 973, 980 (Sir Nicolas Browne-Wilkinson VC).

206 Craig, 'Negligence in the Exercise of a Statutory Power' (Select Bibliography) considers various circumstances in which a finding of *ultra vires* might be of assistance in overcoming the policy–operation dichotomy: see 447–52.

character—such as a failure to carry out an inspection with due care—the carelessness of the employee concerned will almost certainly amount to an *ultra vires* act. As far as validity is concerned, most statutory powers must be exercised with due care: where a body exercises powers negligently it will almost certainly have exceeded its powers.[207]

(B) PROCEDURAL IMMUNITY UNDER CPR PART 54

Where a claim for damages in tort (either in negligence or for breach of statutory duty) directly raises the question of the validity of an act or omission in administrative law under the *ultra vires* rule, it may be necessary for the damages claim to be brought by way of proceedings for judicial review under Part 54 of the Civil Procedure Rules (formerly Rules of the Supreme Court, Order 53) rather than through the normal method of a writ issued in the High Court. This has a number of important procedural consequences, not least that the action must be begun within a short limitation of three months, in contrast to the normal six-year limitation period for civil claims in tort.[208] It is also necessary to seek the permission of the court to proceed with an application for judicial review. The application is likely to be decided on the basis of affidavit evidence with limited opportunity for cross-examination. These restrictions, designed to protect public bodies from harassment, make sense when the *validity* of an act is under challenge and there is a need for a speedy decision which avoids delay and the consequent harmful effects on public administration. What is less obvious is whether they serve any purpose when a claim for damages is being brought after the event, unless it is the aim, which has some support,[209] of returning to the days of the Public Authorities Protection Acts when local authorities enjoyed a similar kind of procedural immunity from suit.

The rule that questions of public law should be raised exclusively by means of an application for judicial review originated in the judgment of the House of Lords in *O'Reilly* v. *Mackman*.[210] It was held that if a 'public law' action was begun by writ, it would be struck out as an abuse of process. The implication for tort claims was made clear at once in the twin decision of *Cocks* v. *Thanet District Council*.[211] The plaintiff sued in the county court for a mandatory injunction requiring the council to grant him permanent accommodation under the Housing (Homeless Persons) Act 1977, and coupled this with a claim for damages for breach of statutory duty under *Thornton* v. *Kirklees Metropolitan Borough Council*.[212] The action was struck out on the ground that an essential step or 'necessary condition precedent' in establishing the private-law claim for damages was a public law finding that the council had acted in excess of its powers under the Act.[213] It was therefore appropriate for the council to invoke the procedural

207 *Ibid.*, 453.
208 On limitation generally, see ch. 24, Section 9, below.
209 See generally Weir (Select Bibliography).
210 [1983] 2 AC 237.
211 [1983] 2 AC 286.
212 [1979] QB 626, now overruled by the House of Lords in *O'Rourke* v. *Camden LBC* [1998] AC 189.
213 [1983] 2 AC 286, 294 (Lord Bridge).

protections of Order 53 and to require the plaintiff to bring his claim as an application for judicial review.

Later decisions have, however, substantially qualified the potential scope of this ruling, and changes to the Civil Procedure Rules Part 54 (the successor of Rules of the Supreme Court Order 53) have removed much of its practical significance. *Roy* v. *Kensington and Chelsea and Westminster Family Practitioner Committee*[214] was concerned with a claim by a general practitioner in the National Health Service that the Committee (a statutory body with responsibilities in relation to local health-care services) had wrongfully withheld part of his salary. He began an action by writ for payment of the sum in question, only to be met by a defence that he should first have to bring proceedings for judicial review to establish the impropriety of the Committee's decision. Rejecting the defence, Lord Lowry described the plaintiff as having 'a bundle of rights, which should be regarded as his individual private law rights against the committee, arising from the statute and regulations and including the very important private law right to be paid for the work which he has done'.[215] Lord Lowry distinguished *Cocks* v. *Thanet District Council*[216] on the ground that 'Mr. Cocks was simply a homeless member of the public . . . whereas Dr. Roy had already an established relationship with the committee' when the dispute arose. This is unconvincing: Mr Cocks was seeking to establish a private-law right to damages which would have been just as much a 'right' as that asserted by Dr Roy. Nevertheless, the impression was given that *Cocks* would not be followed in decisions which did not relate to claims of the kind that arose in that case.

In *Roy*[217] Lord Lowry distinguished between two possible approaches to the relationship between private rights and the principle laid down by the House of Lords in *O'Reilly* v. *Mackman*.[218] First, a broad approach, according to which *O'Reilly* 'did not apply generally against bringing actions to vindicate private rights in all circumstances in which those actions involved a challenge to a public law act or decision, but . . . merely required the aggrieved person to proceed by judicial review only when private law rights were not at stake'. Second, a narrow approach which 'assumed that the rule applied generally to *all* proceedings in which public law acts or decisions were challenged, subject to some exceptions when private law rights were involved'. His Lordship expressed a preference for the broad view as being consonant with principle and having the 'practical merit of getting rid of a procedural minefield', but did not feel compelled formally to adopt it as the basis for the rejection of the Committee's defence. Nevertheless, a clear enough signal had been given for future courts in this area.[219] In *X (Minors)*[220] Lord Browne-Wilkinson confirmed the trend of the case law by commenting that a

214 [1992] 1 AC 625. 215 *Ibid.*, 647–8.

216 [1983] 2 AC 286.

217 [1992] 1 AC 625.

218 *Ibid.*, 651.

219 *Roy* has been followed in a number of cases involving claims in tort, contract, and restitution. See *Woolwich Equitable Building Society* v. *IRC* [1993] AC 70, *Mercury Communications Ltd.* v. *Director-General of Telecommunications* [1996] 1 WLR 48, *British Steel plc* v. *Customs and Excise Commissioners* [1997] 2 All ER 366, *Trustees of the Dennis Rye Pension Fund* v. *Sheffield CC* [1997] 4 All ER 747, and *Andreou* v. *Institute of Chartered Accountants of England and Wales* [1998] 1 All ER 14.

220 [1995] 2 AC 633, 736.

private-law action for negligence would not normally have to be brought under Order 53 (as it then was). The decreasing significance of *O'Reilly* v. *Mackman* has been further reinforced by changes to the Civil Procedure Rules which allow protection for public bodies against abuse of process in actions begun by writ[221] and also facilitate the transfer of cases from the procedures for an ordinary action to those for judicial review and vice versa.[222] Thus, '[e]xclusivity, as defined in *O'Reilly* v. *Mackman*, now seems abandoned',[223] leaving only a few exceptional situations in which claims begun by ordinary action may be halted on the grounds of abuse of process.[224]

6. CROWN PROCEEDINGS IN TORT

Central government departments and certain other bodies exercising state functions, such as the armed forces, are viewed for the purposes of liability in contract and tort as exercising the powers of the Crown. Until the Crown Proceedings Act 1947 this meant that they could take advantage of the Crown's general immunity from suit. In practice, actions in tort would be brought against an individual civil servant. While the Crown was, in theory, not responsible for the torts committed by its agents and employees, it was the practice for it to pay any damages awarded against those acting on its behalf. The anomaly of immunity in tort was formally removed by section 2(1) of the 1947 Act. This provides that the Crown shall be subject to the normal liability in tort in three cases: first, where torts are committed by its servants or agents;[225] second, in respect of a breach of the employer's personal common law duty of care to his employees; finally, in respect of a breach of common-law duties attaching to the ownership, occupation, possession or control of property. Section 2(2) provides that the Crown shall be liable for breach of statutory duty in a case where the duty in question does not bind the Crown alone. This means that the Crown is caught by the most common kind of statutory action, namely for breach of employers' duties under the Factory Acts.[226] In addition, a number of specific statutes providing for particular duty situations and particular defences have specifically included the Crown in their scope. These include the Occupiers' Liability Acts 1957[227] and 1984,[228] the Defective Premises Act 1972,[229] the Latent Damage Act 1986[230] and the Consumer Protection Act 1987.[231] The 1947 Act makes provision for statutory provisions concerning contributory negligence, joint liability, and contribution and indemnity to apply to the Crown.[232] Immunities

[221] See CPR Pt. 1 and Pt. 24; *Clark* v. *University of Lincolnshire and Humberside* [2000] 1 WLR 1998.

[222] CPR Pt. 54.4, 54.20.

[223] T. Hickman, '*Clark*: The Demise of *O'Reilly* Completed?' [2000] *JR* 178, 182.

[224] *Ibid.*, 182–3.

[225] On the relevant definition of a Crown servant, see s. 2(6).

[226] See *Nicholls* v. *Austin (Leyton) Ltd.* [1946] AC 493; *Sparrow* v. *Fairey Aviation Co. Ltd.* [1964] AC 1019. See also the discussion of s. 2(2) of the 1947 Act in the context of liability for breach of European Community law in Oliver LJ's dissenting judgment in *Bourgoin SA* v. *Ministry of Agriculture, Fisheries and Food* [1986] 1 QB 716.

[227] Section 6.

[228] Section 3.

[229] Section 5.

[230] Section 3(7).

[231] Section 9(2).

[232] Section 4.

retained by the 1947 Act in respect of activities of the armed forces were repealed in 1987, subject to a power on the part of the Secretary of State to revive them in the event of war or national emergency.[233] The Crown retains immunity in respect of the discharge of judicial responsibilities.[234]

7. LIABILITY FOR BREACHES OF EUROPEAN COMMUNITY LAW

As we have seen,[235] one of the few areas of growth for the action for breach of statutory duty in recent years concerns liability in damages for breach of a provision of European Community law. Here, too, there are policy arguments for restricting the potential liability of governmental bodies. As Nourse LJ put it in *Bourgoin SA* v. *Ministry of Agriculture, Fisheries and Food*:

> In this country the law never allowed that a private individual should recover damages against the Crown for an injury caused him by an *ultra vires* order made in good faith. Nowadays this rule is grounded not in procedural theory but on the sound acknowledgement that a minister of the Crown should be able to discharge the duties of his office expeditiously and fearlessly, a state of affairs which could hardly be achieved if acts done in good faith, but beyond his powers, were to be actionable in damages.[236]

Nourse and Parker LJJ held that Community law did not require the fashioning of a new remedy which would effectively extend potential liability for breach of statutory duty to the point where an *ultra vires* act of an official or statutory body would automatically give rise to a damages claim. By contrast, Oliver LJ argued that a remedy of this kind was necessary to protect the plaintiff's European Community law rights under Article 30 (now Article 28) of the EC Treaty, and that there was no basis consonant with European law for protecting the Minister's discretion as a matter of domestic public policy.

However, in a series of judgments beginning with *Francovich and Bonifaci* v. *Italy*,[237] the European Court of Justice has fashioned a principle according to which the government

[233] Crown Proceedings (Armed Forces) Act 1987. In *Matthews* v. *Ministry of Defence* [2003] 1 AC 1163 the House of Lords rejected an argument under the Human Rights Act 1998 to the effect that the remaining immunity under this Act was contrary to the Convention right contained in Art. 6 ECHR, ruling that the protection provided was a 'substantive' and not a 'procedural' immunity; see also the decision of the European Court of Human Rights in *Roche* v. *United Kingdom* (2006) 42 EHRR 30, where the European Court of Human Rights held by the barest majority, nine votes to eight, that there had been no violation of Art. 6 (1) of the Convention.

[234] Crown Proceedings Act 1947, s. 2(5). For further detail on Crown proceedings see Wade and Forsyth (Select Bibliography), ch. 21.

[235] See Section 4 above.

[236] [1986] 1 QB 716, 790.

[237] Cases C-6/90 and C-9/90, *Francovich and Bonifaci* v. *Italian Republic* [1991] ECR I-5357; Case C-46/93, *Brasserie du Pêcheur* v. *Federal Republic of Germany* and Case C-48/93, *R* v. *Secretary of State for Trade and Industry, ex parte Factortame Ltd. (No. 3)* [1996] ECR I-1029; Cases C-178/94, C-179/94, C-188/94, C-189/94 and C-190/94, *Dillenkofer* v. *Federal Republic of Germany* [1996] ECR I-4845, [1996] All ER (EC) 917. Lord Goff has suggested that *Francovich* may have effectively reversed *Bourgoin*: see *Kirklees MBC* v. *Wickes* [1992] 3 WLR

of a Member State could be held liable in damages to one of its citizens for loss caused by the Member State's breach of Community law. For this to happen, three conditions must be satisfied. First, the provision in question must be designed to confer individual rights. Second, the breach in question must be sufficiently serious in the sense of amounting to a manifest and grave disregard by the authority concerned of the limits on its discretion. Finally, there must be a sufficient causal link between the breach of Community law and the loss suffered by the individual.[238]

The *Francovich* judgment itself concerned the failure to implement a Directive. Its applicability in the sphere of domestic English law was recognised in *R*v. *Secretary of State for Transport, ex parte Factortame (No. 5)*,[239] in which the House of Lords held that an action for damages lay against the UK government in respect of the passage of legislation affecting the trade and livelihood of the claimants, when it was known that there was a substantial risk that the legislation in question was contrary to what is now Article 43 of the European Community Treaty on freedom of establishment. But the terms in which the judgment was delivered, together with subsequent decisions of the European Court of Justice, indicate that the principle is not confined to acts of a legislature, but can also extend to breaches of Community law committed by public authorities.[240] It is true that many directly effective EC law provisions will already grant rights exercisable by private parties directly against such public authorities, for which national law must provide remedies in a manner no less favourable than to comparable breaches of national law and to ensure that the exercise of the relevant EC law right is not rendered practically impossible. However, where there are limitations upon enforcement of such rights by private parties (either where national law is not open to interpretation consistently with the EC law rule, or because the provision is not directly effective (as in *Francovich* itself) or because the limitations upon national remedies are acceptable under EC law) then such private claimants may also wish to rely upon a *Francovich*-style claim against a public authority. Of course, to succeed in those circumstances the claimant must clear the extra hurdle of showing that the failure to secure its EC law rights amounted to a sufficiently serious breach, in the sense described above.[241] It is

170, 188; and see generally R. Caranta, 'Governmental Liability after *Francovich*' [1993] *CLJ* 272; S. Arrowsmith, *Civil Liability and Public Authorities* (1992), 254–7.

238 For discussion of the scope of this liabiltiy, see P. P. Craig, 'The Domestic Liability of Public Authorities in Damages: Lessons from the European Community?'; M. Hoskins, 'Rebirth of the Innominate Tort'; and J. Allison, 'Transplantation and Cross-Fertilisation', all in J. Beatson and T. Tridimas (eds.), *New Directions in European Public Law* (1998); C. Lewis, 'The Right to an Effective Remedy', in M. Andenas (ed.), *English Public Law and the Common Law of Europe* (1999).

239 [2000] 1 AC 524; see however *R* v. *Secretary of State for Transport, ex parte Factortame (No. 7)* [2001] 1 WLR 942, ruling that as these were claims in tort (specifically, the tort of breach of statutory duty), they were time-barred under the Limitation Act 1980.

240 See W. van Gerven, 'Bridging the Unbridgeable: Community and National Tort Laws after *Francovich* and *Brasserie*' (1996) 45 *ICLQ* 507. See, further, Case C-424/97 *Haim* v. *Kassenzahnärztliche Vereinigung Nordrhein ('Haim (No. 2)')* [2000] ECR I-5123 (discussed by G. Anagnostaras, 'The Allocation of Responsibility in State Liability Actions for Breach of Community Law: a Modern Gordian Knot?' (2001) 26 *ELR* 139).

241 This is clearly not the place to provide a detailed discussion of the intricacies of EC law on this topic: for details, the reader should refer to A. M. Arnull *et al.*, *Wyatt & Dashwood's European Union Law* (5th edn., 2006) and P. P. Craig and G. de Búrca, *EU Law: Text, Cases, and Materials* (3rd edn., 2004).

also possible that Community law rights can give rise to liabilities on the part of individuals and entities in the private sector, where those provisions are capable of creating 'horizontal direct effect' between private parties;[242] thus far, however, the areas where such a remedy can clearly be said to be a requirement of the substantive EC law rule (rather than the application of national remedies to the breach of an EC law right) are by no means clearly demarcated.[243]

The basis of the *Francovich* line of cases is the principle that effective judicial remedies should be made available within national legal systems for the protection of rights established by Community law, and this may have the result that liability can be imposed in a wider range of situations than those so far recognised by the English courts. For example, the restrictions placed on liability for the tort of breach of statutory duty by *Bourgoin* may no longer hold, in particular the distinction drawn by the English case law between measures passed in the interests of a particular group[244] and those passed in the interests of the public.[245] This could cease to be tenable with respect to liability for breach of a Community law obligation. The European case law also has the potential to undercut the limitations placed upon liability for the tort of misfeasance in a public office by the decision of the House of Lords in *Three Rivers District Council* v. *Bank of England*.[246] In particular, it is not clear whether the criterion of a 'sufficiently serious breach' requires evidence of knowledge of a lack of statutory authority on the part of the relevant body as the House of Lords insisted, or whether a looser test of foreseeability, or even, in some circumstances, strict liability might suffice.[247] In *Three Rivers District Council* the courts considered whether an action lay against the Bank for failure to follow the terms of the First Banking Co-Ordination Directive;[248]

242 See W. van Gerven, 'Bridging the Unbridgeable: Community and National Tort Laws after *Francovich* and *Brasserie*' (1996) 45 *ICLQ* 507, 530 ff., discussing Case C-128/92, *Banks* v. *British Coal Corporation* [1994] ECR I-1209.

243 Two possible contenders are the rules on the free movement of workers (see Case C-281/98 *Angonese* v. *Cassa di Risparmio di Bolzano SpA* [2000] ECR I-4139, where the horizontal direct effect of Article 39 EC seems to have been acknowledged by the Court of Justice) and the EC competition rules (see Case C-453/99 *Courage plc* v. *Crehan* [2001] ECR I-6297 and Joined Cases C-295 to 298/04 *Manfredi* v. *Lloyd Adriatico Assicurazioni SpA* (not yet reported, judgment of 13 July 2006) (and see A.G. Geelhoed's Opinion, paras. 52 to 58)). The competition law issue has been the subject of intense debate as to whether the damages remedy, overcoming the 'illegality bar' in English law, amounted to a remedy *mandated by EC law* in a way similar to that in *Francovich* (for discussion, see G. Cumming, '*Courage* v. *Crehan*' [2002] *ECLR* 199 and J. Edelman and O. Odudu, 'Compensatory Damages for Breach of Article 81' (2002) 27 *EL Rev* 327). While the issue has yet satisfactorily to be resolved, there is at least one clear difference from the *Francovich* and *Brasserie du Pêcheur* case law: there is no criterion that any such breach of the competition rules by the party in the stronger bargaining position must have been 'sufficiently serious' in the same way (which is only logical, given that that formulation is specifically designed to deal with Member States' actions in the EC law field, rather than those of private parties).

244 Which may give rise to a private tort action.

245 Which may not give rise to such an action.

246 [2003] 2 AC 1.

247 There may be strict liability where the validity of an administrative act or decision, rather than a legislative measure, is in question, and where the right infringed is particularly clear and important (such as the right to free movement of goods): see Case C-5/94, *R* v. *Ministry of Agriculture, Fisheries and Food, ex parte Hedley Lomas* [1996] 3 WLR 787.

248 Directive 77/780/EEC [1977] *OJ* L322/30.

however, it was ruled in the House of Lords that, under the terms of the Directive, no rights of the kind suggested were conferred on individual depositors, so that this claim failed under the first of the three criteria laid down by the European Court of Justice.[249]

Development of this new head of liability may well have important implications for those substantive areas where rights are well established under EC law. These include not just competition law and the law of the single market, but also, for example, employment and discrimination law, health and safety law and areas of environmental law. Within these areas, national courts could be seen as coming under a duty to develop existing causes of action so as to ensure the effectiveness of Community law. This could imply changes to, for example, the components of the tort of breach of statutory duty or, as the case may be, the tort of misfeasance in a public office. Further, certain procedural and/or remedial limitations that currently apply under English law could be held to be insufficiently effective in securing the enforcement of EC law rights.[250] It could also be argued that if extensions to these torts take place within the context of Community law, it would be anomalous (and unjust) not to make parallel extensions in areas of common law liability not touched on by Community law.

Finally, one should bear in mind one further point. Given the principle of the supremacy of Community law over domestic law, the scope of the changes needed to bring the common law into line with the EC Treaty would be an issue that would, ultimately, have to be decided by the European Court of Justice and not the domestic courts alone.[251]

8. LIABILITIES ARISING UNDER THE HUMAN RIGHTS ACT 1998

As we have seen,[252] under the Human Rights Act 1998 it is 'unlawful for a public authority to act in a way which is incompatible with a Convention right'.[253] Under section 7 of the Act, victims of the breach of a Convention right by a public authority may bring proceedings against that authority under the 1998 Act. In the event of breach, section 8

[249] To similar effect is *Poole* v. *HM Treasury* [2006] EWHC 2731, a decision on the Insurance Directive (73/239/EEC [1973] *OJ* L228/3).

[250] Such judgments have already been delivered in some fields: for a well-known example, see the saga of Mrs Marshall: Case 152/84 *Marshall v. Southampton and SW Hants AHA (No. 1)* [1986] ECR 723 and Case C-271/91 *Marshall (No. 2)* [1993] ECR I-4367, where the latter case saw the ECJ hold that the principle of an effective remedy precluded the statutory limit upon the amount of compensation that Mrs Marshall could receive for her dismissal from her employment on grounds that amounted to sex discrimination (discriminatory retirement ages, which had themselves been enshrined in statute and had been held unlawful in *Marshall (No. 1)*). For a wide range of illustrations and discussion, see M. Dougan, *National Remedies before the Court of Justice* (2004).

[251] See generally the full discussions of van Gerven, 'Bridging the Unbridgeable' (1996) 45 *ICLQ* 507, and Dougan, *National Remedies before the Court of Justice* (2004).

[252] See above, ch. 2, Section 9.

[253] Human Rights Act 1998, s. 6(1).

empowers the court to grant such relief or remedy, including damages, as it sees fit. 'Convention rights' are the specified rights identified by the 1998 Act from among those which are contained in the European Convention on Human Rights and various of its Protocols.[254] These consist of Articles 2–12 and 14 of the Convention, which concern the right to life, the prohibition of torture, the prohibition of slavery and forced labour, the right to liberty and security, the right to a fair trial, no punishment without law, the right to respect for private and family life, freedom of thought, religion and conscience, freedom of expression, freedom of assembly and association, the right to marry, and the prohibition of discrimination. Also included are Articles 1–3 of the First Protocol (the right to protection of property, the right to education and the right to free elections) and Articles 1–2 of the Sixth Protocol (these concern the death penalty). In most cases these rights are qualified by a 'margin of appreciation' which invites courts to engage in a proportionality test in order to determine whether, in a particular case, there has been a breach of the provision. Because courts and tribunals are themselves public bodies for this purpose,[255] they are required to interpret and give effect to both primary and subordinate legislation, as far as possible, in such a way as to avoid acting incompatibly with Convention rights. This provision, however, does not affect the validity or effect of any primary legislation that is incompatible with Convention rights.[256] A public authority is relieved of the obligation to act in accordance with the Convention rights if, as a result of primary legislation, it could not have acted differently. The same result applies if a public authority was acting in order to give effect to primary legislation which cannot be read or given effect to in such a way as to be compatible with Convention rights.[257]

Thus the Human Rights Act seems likely to have a particular impact in the field of governmental liability. In the first place this is because it is public authorities, in the first instance, which are required to respect Convention rights. In principle, these rights only have 'vertical effect'—in other words, they do not give rise to obligations that are binding on private individuals or entities. By imposing specific obligations on public authorities and creating the possibility of damages awards and other remedies being applied against them, the Act has special significance for public authorities. In addition, the influence of the Convention and, now, the Act on the general law of tort is already obvious in certain areas, such as privacy[258] and freedom of expression.[259] Thus public authorities and private entities alike will be affected in so far as the evolution of the general law of tort is influenced by the passage of the 1998 Act.

A first issue to consider is the definition of 'public authority' under the Act. The definition adopted here differs from the notion of an organ of the state which has been adopted in EC law for the purposes of determining the extent of state liability. Under section 6 of the Act, a public authority includes 'any person certain of whose functions

254 *Ibid.*, s. 1. 255 *Ibid.*, s. 6(3)(a).
256 *Ibid.*, s. 3. 257 *Ibid.*, s. 6(2).
258 See below, ch. 22, Section 3.
259 See *Middlebrook Mushrooms Ltd.* v. *Transport and General Workers Union* [1993] IRLR 232.

are functions of a public nature'. This definition may not include, for example, privatised corporations in the regulated utilities that tend to fall within the public sector for the purposes of determining the vertical direct effect of European Community Directives.[260] Moreover, the Act states that 'in relation to a particular act, a person is not a public authority . . . if the nature of the act is private'. A public body, such as a local authority, could therefore have mixed public and private functions; the precise boundary between them is not clear. While there is still, at the time of writing, little case law addressing these problems,[261] the potential for the Act to reshape aspects of governmental liability in tort is also apparent.

The second issue to consider is the scope of remedial intervention under the 1998 Act for breach of Convention rights by public authorities. As we have just seen, there is a discretionary element in the award of damages, since the court is empowered by section 8(1) to award such remedy 'as it sees fit'. Under section 8(3) of the Act, the court can only award damages if it 'is satisfied that the award is necessary to afford just satisfaction to the person in whose favour it is made'. It must take account of the existence of 'any other relief or remedy granted, or order made, in relation to the act in question' and 'the consequences of any decision (of that or any other court) in respect of that act'. Thus while the right to award damages has been described by the Law Commission as a new type of action for breach of statutory duty,[262] and by learned commentators as a new tort of acting in breach of Convention rights,[263] it may be more correct to describe it as a new statutory power to award damages under the 1998 Act, since '[i]t is difficult to describe this new action as a public law tort if there is no right to monetary compensation'.[264] As the case law currently stands, the contours of the new action are not clear, but it is possible to argue that it should develop by analogy with the action for breach of a European Community obligation. If this is so, the focus of attention will be on the meaning in this context of a 'grave and manifest' breach by the defendant of the victim's Convention rights.[265]

The potential reach of the new action was demonstrated in the early case of *Marcic* v. *Thames Water Utilities*.[266] The claimant's property was regularly flooded as a result of the failure of the defendant to carry out drainage works which would have prevented this. At first instance, the court found that the defendant was liable to pay damages under the Human Rights Act for breach of the claimant's Convention rights in respect

260 See *Griffin* v. *South West Water Services Ltd.* [1995] IRLR 15; *Cameron* v. *Network Rail Infrastructure Ltd.* [2007] 1 WLR 163.

261 The leading case so far is *R (On the application of Heather)* v. *Leonard Cheshire Foundation* [2002] HRLR 30, holding that a private-sector provider of long-term residential care was not a public authority under s. 6(3) of the Act.

262 Law Commission, *Damages Under the Human Rights Act 1998*, No. 266 (Scot. Law Com. No. 180) (Cm. 4853, 2000).

263 A. Lester and D. Pannick, 'The Impact of the Human Rights Act on Private Law: the Knight's Move' (2000) 116 *LQR* 380, 382.

264 See Fairgrieve, 'The Human Rights Act 1998 (Select Bibliography), 704.

265 See generally, *ibid.*, also M. Amos, 'Damages for Breach of the Human Rights Act 1998' [1999] *EHRLR* 178, and 'Extending the Liability of the State in Damages' (2001) 21 *Leg. Stud.* 1.

266 [2001] 3 All ER 698; [2002] QB 929; J. Morgan, 'Nuisance, Property and Human Rights' (2002) 118 *LQR* 27.

of the protection of private and family life (Article 8) and peaceful enjoyment of possessions (Article 1 of the First Protocol). The judge, applying a proportionality test, ruled that the defendant had failed to show that its decision to deploy resources elsewhere was fair in the circumstances. The decision illustrates dramatically the potential for the Human Rights Act to open up areas of public decision-making to judicial scrutiny: there was no liability at common law, and separate legislation had also attempted to rule out a private cause of action. However, when the case was appealed, the Court of Appeal ruled that there had after all been a common nuisance, and that while the claimants' Convention rights had been infringed, common law damages were a sufficient remedy. This basic approach to such questions was confirmed by the House of Lords, but on the facts their Lordships held that the relevant statutory regime covered the field and provided a remedial avenue for the claimant which was sufficient to secure his Convention rights.[267] The fact that the claimant had not chosen to use that statutory regime was not sufficient to allow him to avoid its procedures by bringing a claim in nuisance.[268]

The *Marcic* litigation, together with other recent decisions including the judgment of the Court of Appeal in the *East Berkshire* case,[269] confirms the suggestion that the *indirect* influence of the Human Rights Act on the common law is likely to be considerable.[270] To the extent that this is so, there may be less need for the courts to rely directly upon the remedies provided by the Act itself for interference with Convention rights. But where no common law tort remedy is possible, the Act will begin to come into its own. Thus in *R (On the application of Bernard)* v. *Enfield London Borough Council*[271] substantial damages were awarded under section 8(3) of the Act for psychiatric harm arising from a breach of the claimant's rights to the protection of family and private life under Article 8 of the Convention, in a case where the defendant council had acted unlawfully in failing to provide the claimant, who was disabled, with adequate accommodation for her needs. In *Anufrijeva* v. *Southwark London Borough Council*,[272] a claim based on alleged maladministration in the context of the provision of housing to the families of asylum-seekers, the Court of Appeal ruled that Article 8 of the Convention was capable of imposing upon public authorities a positive duty to take steps to ensure respect of family life. In his judgment, Lord Woolf CJ suggested that 'the discretionary exercise of deciding whether to award compensation under the [Human Rights Act] is not to be compared to the approach adopted where damages are claimed for breach of an obligation under the civil law', but that the level of damages awarded in respect of a tort claim, together with the level of awards made by the Criminal Injuries Compensation Board and the Parliamentary and Local Government Ombudsmen, 'may all provide some rough guidance where the consequences of the infringement of

[267] [2004] 2 AC 42.
[268] The judgments in the House of Lords and their ramifications are discussed more fully in ch. 13, below.
[269] [2004] QB 558. See our discussion in this chapter, Section 2, above.
[270] Hickman, 'Tort Law, Public Authorities and the Human Rights Act 1998' (Select Bibliography).
[271] [2003] HRLR 4.
[272] [2004] QB 1124.

human rights are similar to that being considered' in the case before the court.[273] In *Anufrijeva* there was no closely analogous claim in tort, and the Court suggested that damages in a case of a breach of the positive obligation under Article 8 should be 'modest' since 'resources are limited and payments of substantial damages will deplete the resources available for other needs of the public',[274] an argument of the kind frequently deployed, as we have seen in this chapter, to narrow down the tortious liability of statutory and public bodies.

The third issue to consider concerns the possible impact of the Human Rights Act on the general law of tort and in particular, for present purposes, on the principles governing the liability of public authorities. As we have seen in this chapter, there has been intense judicial discussion since the late 1970s of the position of public bodies in relation to the tort of negligence. The focus of the current law on the issue of the defendant's conduct, and specifically with the linked issues of duty, fault and causation, has made it possible for the courts to weigh up a range of competing legal and policy factors. The Human Rights Act marks a shift in the conceptual orientation of the law: within human rights jurisprudence, the focus is on the claimant's rights, and the language of reasonableness is replaced by a test of proportionality which arguably imposes stricter limits on the degree to which open-ended policy considerations can be brought into play in the defendant's favour.[275]

The advent of the Human Rights Act does not, however, imply that the human rights approach will necessarily prevail over that followed until now by the tort of negligence. A court, as a public authority, must not act incompatibly with a Convention right, but this does not mean that a court is *compelled* in all instances to develop the common law in such a way as to provide a remedy to those whose Convention rights have been infringed.[276] In the present context, the existence of a separate and distinct cause of action for breach by public authorities of Convention rights under sections 7 and 8 of the 1998 Act might lead the courts to conclude that the common law of negligence should continue its evolution as before. At the other extreme, it is possible that the courts will, over time, seek to align the negligence action with human rights jurisprudence. In between these two alternatives is a further possibility, namely that the courts will 'maintain a clear separation between the negligence enquiry and any enquiry into whether a Convention right had actually been violated. These enquiries may well reach different conclusions, but the presence of the [Human Rights Act] would permeate the underlying policy considerations intrinsic to the negligence determination.'[277] By these means, rights that are currently applied only in a 'vertical' sense may come increasingly to influence the content of tort law.

The possibility of a horizontal application of Convention rights has, thus far, divided commentators on the 1998 Act.[278] But, it is submitted, our courts are already moving in

273 [2004] QB 1124, at 1160. 274 *Ibid.*

275 See generally, Hickman (Select Bibliography).

276 See generally our discussion of the relationship between tort law and the Human Rights Act 1998 in ch. 1, above. 277 Hickman (Select Bibliography), 49.

278 From the growing literature one thus notes that Sir William Wade ('Horizons of Horizontality' (2000) 116 *LQR*, 217 ff. with references to his earlier works on the subject) and Murray Hunt ('The Horizontal Effect

that direction. And once it is fully appreciated that the need to afford protection to individuals extends not only against an all-powerful state but also against potential intrusive and oppressive entities (such as the press, trade unions, or powerful multinationals), the ambiguous wording of the 1998 Act will be made to yield the result herein predicted.

Until now, the case law on governmental liability has made very little mention of rights-based considerations. Thus, in *Elguzouli-Daf* v. *Commissioner of Police of the Metropolis*,[279] no account appears to have been taken of the extended and, in the event, unnecessary infringement of the personal liberty of the plaintiffs. Article 5 of the European Convention, which must now be observed by a prosecuting authority, states that 'no-one shall be deprived of his liberty' save in a number of specified cases, one of which is 'the lawful arrest or detention of a person effected for the purpose of bringing him before the competent legal authority on reasonable suspicion of having committed an offence . . . '.[280] But in relation to such arrest or detention, the person arrested 'shall be brought promptly before a judge or other officer authorised by law to exercise judicial power and shall be entitled to trial within a reasonable time or to release pending trial'.[281] Persons who are detained in contravention of this provision 'shall have an enforceable right to compensation'.[282]

It is possible, but not inevitable, that *Elgozouli-Daf* would not now be decided the same way. In that case, the effect of the Court of Appeal's decision was that the substance of the plaintiffs' claims could not even be addressed. To rule out a duty of care was to prevent the plaintiffs from making their respective cases on the merits, and to deny them compensation even on the assumption that their allegations of negligence were true. This seems incompatible with the requirements of Article 5 of the Convention. However, for the reasons we have just discussed, the passage of the Human Rights Act does not *automatically* translate into a requirement for the courts to adjust the common law.

The most direct impact to date of human rights jurisprudence on the tort of negligence arose from the decision of the European Court of Human Rights in *Osman* v. *United Kingdom*.[283] The Court ruled that as a consequence of the Court of Appeal's ruling in *Osman* v. *Ferguson*,[284] there had been a breach of Article 6 of the European

of the Human Rights Act' [1998] *PL* 423) favour (some form) of the German doctrine being adopted by our law while Buxton LJ ('The Human Rights Act and Private Law' (2000) 116 *LQR* 48) seems to regard it with suspicion, given that human rights (originally at any rate) were meant to be protected against encroachments by the superior power of the state. An account (in English) of the German doctrine of *Drittwirkung* can be found in B. S. Markesinis, 'Privacy, Freedom of Expression and the Horizontal Effect of the Human Rights Bill: Lessons from Germany', The Wilberforce Lecture (1999) 115 *LQR*, 47–88. The Wade/Buxton controversy can, by the way, also be found in Israel where Barak CJ, following the German cases, has introduced the *Drittwirkung* doctrine into Israeli contract law. On this, see Professor Shalev's comments in 'Constitutionalisation of Contract Law' in A. Gambaro and A. M. Rabello (eds.), *Towards a New European* Ius Commune (1999), 205 ff. We mention this information briefly and in passing, for we very much doubt that English law will be able to avoid this important and wide-ranging issue for long.

279 [1995] QB 335.
280 ECHR, Art. 5(1)(c).
281 *Ibid.*, Art. 5(3).
282 *Ibid.*, Art. 5(5).
283 (1998) 29 EHRR 455.
284 [1993] 4 All ER 344.

Convention on Human Rights, which guarantees a person's right to have a claim relating to his civil rights and obligations brought before a court or tribunal. The Court ruled that although the principle of protecting the police from litigation which would encourage defensive and wasteful practices was a potentially legitimate one under the Convention, the Court of Appeal's ruling resulted in a 'blanket immunity' which could not be regarded as proportionate to this objective. In the Court's view, it should have been open to a court to weigh other public-interest considerations in the balance, and to have taken account of the proximity of the parties and of the seriousness of the harm which occurred in that case. Yet in the later case of *Z* v. *United Kingdom*,[285] the Court ruled that there had been no breach of Article 6 arising from the House of Lords' judgment in *X (Minors)* v. *Bedfordshire County Council*:[286] the denial of a duty of care on the ground that it was not 'fair, just and reasonable' to impose such a duty could not be equated with an 'immunity' against litigation. As we saw in Chapter 3, the effect of *Z* is to reinstate a strict test for what constitutes an immunity under Article 6: it must be shown that the rule in question operates as a procedural bar against the action in question, rather than a substantive denial that a particular right or claim exists. As a result, it is not clear that the wide protection outlined in *Hill* v. *Chief Constable of West Yorkshire*[287] and applied in *Osman* v. *Ferguson*[288] is contrary to Article 6, whereas it could be contrary to the substantive rights of the Convention, including Articles 2 and 3.[289]

The wider potential of human rights jurisprudence to outflank *Hill* has been illustrated in two recent cases. In *Van Colle* v. *Chief Constable of Hertfordshire*,[290] a claim against the police for failure to take steps to protect a prosecution witness succeeded under the Human Rights Act, by reference to the right to life under Article 2 of the Convention. *Keegan* v. *United Kingdom*[291] is a potentially highly significant judgment of the European Court of Human Rights. Here the police used force to enter the claimant's home having obtained a search warrant to look for stolen property in the premises in question. Had the police made proper inquiries, they would have discovered that the person they suspected had no connection with the property. The claimant was unable to bring a claim for negligence thanks to the *Hill* and *Osman* line of cases, so he sought damages instead for the tort of malicious procurement of a search warrant,[292] a tort analogous to that of malicious prosecution which we consider in Chapter 10. His claim failed before the English courts on the grounds that malice had not been made out.[293] The European Court of Human Rights, however, held in his favour, on the grounds that it should not be necessary to show malice in a case where there was a clear case of interference with family life under Article 8. Substantial damages were awarded. The

285 [2001] 2 FLR 612.

286 [1995] 2 AC 633.

287 [1989] AC 53.

288 [1993] 4 All ER 344.

289 There remains a fundamental disagreement on the applicability of Art. 6 on immunities and duties of care in English law, see *Roche* v. *United Kingdom* (2006) 42 EHRR 30, where the European Court of Human Rights held by the barest majority, nine votes to eight, that there had been no violation of Art. 6(1) of the Convention.

290 [2006] EWHC 360.

291 [2006] ECtHR 764.

292 *Gibbs* v. *Rea* [1998] AC 786.

293 *Keegan* v. *Chief Constable of Merseyside Police* [2003] 1 WLR 2187.

ruling can be seen as a further qualification of *Hill*, since it was the absence of a remedy for negligence which denied the national courts the possibility of examining the proportionality and reasonableness of the conduct of the police.[294]

As we have seen in this chapter, the Court of Human Right's ruling in *Osman* had a considerable indirect impact on the evolution of the law of negligence as applied to statutory bodies. However, the use of Article 6 in this instance was both controversial and also unexpected. In future, the key issue is likely to relate to the effects of certain substantive Convention rights, such as those relating to freedom of expression and protection of private and family life, on the common law of tort. While it is too early to be confident of the outcome, it will probably not be long before influence of human rights jurisprudence is brought to bear on the common law of tort. Thus we have already seen that the case law of the European Court of Human Rights under Article 3 (the right not to be subjected to inhuman or degrading treatment) and Article 8 (the right to the protection of private and family life) has had a substantial impact on the tort of negligence, leading to the rejection of the *X (Minors)* approach in the decision of the Court of Appeal in the *East Berkshire* case.[295] By no means all areas of the law of tort are moving in this direction; the decision of the House of Lords in *Watkins* v. *Secretary of State for the Home Department*[296] not to extend the tort of misfeasance in a public office to cover cases of interference with 'constitutional rights' where no special damage, in the sense of economic loss, property damage or physical injury, could be shown, is a clear indication of that. By contrast, the recent decision of the European Court of Human Rights in *Keegan*,[297] to the effect that it should not be necessary to show malice in an action against the police for violent conduct amounting to interference with the right to family life, highlights just how far removed the law of torts currently is from providing effective protection for certain fundamental rights. Over time it seems inevitable that the law governing the liability of statutory governmental bodies will be increasingly influenced by developments such as this within human rights jurisprudence.

9. TOWARDS A SYNTHESIS OF THE LAW RELATING TO GOVERNMENTAL LIABILITY?

The law relating to governmental liability has, in recent years, been subject to conflicting pressures. In this it has not been any different from the mainstream tort of negligence, although in our presentation of the case law we have suggested that certain special factors apply in relation to the liability of the government, local authorities and public officials in general. Thus, on the one hand, we have seen attempts by the courts to contain the consequences of *Anns* by providing a qualified protection for public

[294] Markesinis and Fedtke (Select Bibliography), at p. 34.
[295] [2004] QB 558.
[296] [2006] 2 WLR 807.
[297] [2006] ECtHR 764.

bodies from liability for omissions. On the other, we are beginning to see the effects of developments in European Community law and in human rights law. Though these do not always move in tandem, they have this in common: a tendency to open up new areas of liability in line with the prevailing culture of rights and entitlements (which is also affecting medical liability law) and current calls for greater accountability and transparency in the administration of public affairs.

Under these circumstances it would be premature to speak of an emerging synthesis of the principles of liability let alone of a clear map for the future. However, we can identify the questions around which the legal debates seem likely to coalesce.

First, what precisely is the rationale for treating public authorities as a special case? The courts have identified several factors in the course of the long retreat from *Anns*, most notably the danger of opportunistic litigation against defendants of last resort and the diversion of resources into wasteful 'defensive' practices aimed at warding off litigation. Whether these factors, and their tendency to produce blanket exclusions of liability, will withstand the onslaught of the human rights legislation is another matter. We may also legitimately ask whether these are factors that are unique to the public sector and, indeed, whether it makes any sense for this purpose to classify all public bodies (police, rescue services, regulators, local councils, government departments) in the same way.

Another factor that has weighed heavily in the minds of some judges is that the intrusion of tort law into this area challenges democratic accountability. Yet it is interesting to note that in other countries—such as France, Germany, Italy and the Netherlands—the very opposite conception prevails. And this sees in the judge the right organ to control the errant behaviour of public officials. This school of thought likewise does not consider it right for judges to act as protectors of public finances. One may not come to share these views; but one should at the very least be made aware of the fact that there exists a respectable body of opinion in countries that share our basic values that does not coincide with what some judges would wish us to think is the only and obvious answer to these problems.

Second, if, despite the above, there is a case for treating public bodies in a distinct way, where is the boundary to be drawn between the public and the private? This is a particular problem given the current lack of a legal common definition of the public sector across the different areas of tort law, European Community law and human rights law. The possibility of, eventually, giving increased horizontal effect to the new human rights legislation must also not be excluded; and if or when this occurs, and we submit it has already started to happen, it could affect large areas of the law of obligations.

Third, how are the courts to resolve clashes between the instrumental or efficiency-based considerations that have dominated recent decisions limiting the scope of the duty of care, and the jurisprudence of human rights which derives from the European Convention on Human Rights and the Human Rights Act 1998? The cross-fertilisation of tort law with emerging concepts of citizenship may yet prove to be one of the most productive areas for doctrinal development in the years to come. In all this, we may well see more and interesting examples of a phenomenon of recent vintage: the constitutionalisation of private law. But this is not the place, and certainly not the time, to go into this fascinating subject in any further detail.

Fourth and finally, few can argue that over the last few decades the ways of making the state liable for various forms of mishap and disaster have grown immensely.[298] This growth may not all, of course, be in the form of pro-claimant decisions in actions for damages. But things cannot be looked at in such an isolated manner. For, in addition to a certain expansion of the liability rules, we have seen a proliferation of other statutory compensation schemes, not all of which may require litigation. Finding a common thread that links them all may not be something common lawyers may relish, wedded as they apparently are to *ad hoc* ways of solving problems and a suspicion of general principle. Yet this growth of 'compensation schemes' cannot continue in an unchecked and uncoordinated manner for too long before it leads to problems of its own. Drawing a parallel with the development of the law of restitution, one could argue that the same thing happened in the 1960s until the arrival of the leading cases of the 1980s and 1990s which finally found in the idea of unjustified enrichment an underlying principle. Could it not be said that the same thing might happen in this area where public law and private law coalesce? And could it not be that this idea is what the mainland Europeans sometimes refer to as the socialisation of risks? To put it differently, when some harm befalls a citizen through no fault of his own, could it not be said that *within measure* his loss should be carried by the community? If this sounds like politics and not law, it should not be seen as a sign of weak legal analysis. For the student as much as the advocate must never forget how close the two disciplines are in the area covered by this book.

SELECT BIBLIOGRAPHY

ANDENAS, M., and FAIRGRIEVE, D., 'Misfeasance in Public Office, Governmental Liability and European Influences' (2002) 51 *ICLQ* 757.

—'Sufficiently Serious? Judicial Restraint in Tortious Liability for Public Authorities and the European Influence' in Andenas, M. (ed.), *English Public Law and the Common Law of Europe* (1998) 285.

BAILEY, S., and BOWMAN, S., 'Public Authority Negligence Revisited' [2000] *CLJ* 85.

BEATSON, J., and TRIDIMAS, T. (eds.), *New Directions in European Public Law* (1998).

BOOTH, C., and SQUIRES, D., *The Negligence Liability of Public Authorities* (2006).

CRAIG, P., 'Negligence in the Exercise of a Statutory Power' (1978) 94 *LQR* 428.

—'Compensation and Public Law' (1980) 96 *LQR* 413.

—and FAIRGRIEVE, D., '*Barrett*, Negligence and Discretionary Powers' [1999] *PL* 626.

298 The growth of liability runs in parallel with the expansion of judicial review in administrative law and the public law remedies. A clearer principle of legality has been developed and administrative discretion is more intensively reviewed, in favour of the private party. There is practically no form of administrative action that is not subject to some form of judicial review.

Fairgrieve, D., 'The Human Rights Act 1998, Damages and Tort Law' [2001] *PL* 695.

—'Pushing Back the Boundaries of Public Authority Liability: Tort Law Enters the Classroom' [2002] *PL* 288.

—*State Liability in Tort* (2004)

Harlow, C., *Compensation and Government Torts* (1982).

—*State Liability: Tort Law and Beyond* (2004)

Hickman, T., 'Tort Law, Public Authorities and the Human Rights Act 1998', in Fairgrieve, D., Andenas, M., and Bell, J. (eds.), *Tort Liability of Public Authorities in Comparative Perspective* (2002), ch. 2.

Markesinis, Sir Basil, and Fedtke, J., 'Authority or Reason? The Economic Consequences of Liability for Breach of Statutory Duty in a Comparative Perspective' [2007] *Eur. Bus. LR* 5.

Markesinis, B.S., Auby, J.-P., Coester-Waltjen, D., and Deakin, S., *Tortious Liability of Statutory Bodies: A Comparative and Economic Analysis of Five English Cases* (1999).

Wade, H.W.R., and Forsyth, C.F., *Administrative Law* (9th edn., 2004), chs. 20, 21.

Weir, J.A., 'Governmental Liability' [1989] *PL* 40.

PART IV

INTERFERENCE WITH THE PERSON

9 Intentional Interference
10 Malicious Prosecution

9

INTENTIONAL INTERFERENCE

1. INTRODUCTION: THE MEANING OF INTENTIONAL INTERFERENCE

English law does not acknowledge a single tort of 'intention' in the same sense that it acknowledges the existence of the tort of negligence. One reason for this is historical. Until the middle of the nineteenth century and before the forms of action were abolished, wrongdoing was remedied by variants of trespass or case. Liability for intentional conduct was distributed among these two, and over the years some forms of liability for intention acquired particular names, such as assault, battery, and so on. This did not happen with careless conduct, which fell under trespass or case depending on whether the resulting harm was direct or consequential. After the forms of action disappeared it became possible gradually to collate the nameless instances of liability for carelessness under the rubric 'negligence'. In this way the new tort of negligence made its appearance. This was not possible with intention, however, since liability for intentional harm had already crystallised into the specific nominate torts which still exist today.

Intentional physical interference with the person may occur by way of an act that threatens violence (assault), amounts to unlawful contact (battery), or constitutes the deprivation of liberty (false imprisonment). There is, in addition, a residuary and uncertain form of liability for the intentional infliction of physical harm, known as the rule in *Wilkinson* v. *Downton*.[1] These torts are normally actionable without proof of damage and they also involve a sharp distinction being drawn between an act and an omission: the latter will not normally suffice to ground liability. Malice is not a necessary ingredient of liability, but the defendant must have had the relevant intention. Although there are some equivocal *dicta*,[2] modern case law takes the view on the whole

1 [1897] 2 QB 57.

2 E.g. *Wilson* v. *Pringle* [1987] QB 237, 249: 'it is the act and not the injury that must be intentional. An intention to injure is not essential to an action for trespass to the person. It is the mere trespass itself which is the offence' (Croom-Johnson LJ). This statement is ambiguous in that it refers to 'injury' rather than 'interference'. It is clear that intention to injure is not necessary since injury itself is not necessary, trespass being actionable *per se*. 'Interference' in the sense of unlawful contact is the gist of the tort of battery, with or without damage, and it seems in the light of other authorities (cited in the text) that the defendant must have intended the interference, in this sense.

that the defendant must not simply intend to commit the act in question; he must also intend the consequence, that is to say, the interference in question. This represents a change from the traditional point of view which effectively imposed *strict* liability once it had been shown that the interference derived directly from a positive act of the defendant, leaving the defendant to show that his case fell under one of a number of defences.[3] The need to show fault was first clearly articulated in nineteenth-century decisions concerning accidents on the highway, and it has since been normal to analyse collision cases in terms of negligence and not in terms of trespass.[4] Since then the extension of negligence liability following *Donoghue* v. *Stevenson* [5] has reinforced this tendency. In *Fowler* v. *Lanning*[6] the plaintiff simply alleged that the defendant had shot him, without alleging either intention or negligence. Diplock J held that this did not constitute a cause of action, on the basis that 'trespass to the person does not lie if the injury to the plaintiff, although the direct consequence of the act of the defendant, was caused unintentionally and without negligence on the defendant's part'. Diplock J would have preserved a category of negligent trespass to the person; Lord Denning MR went one step further in *Letang* v. *Cooper*[7] by suggesting that: 'when the injury is not inflicted intentionally, but negligently, I would say that the only cause of action is negligence and not trespass. If it were trespass, it would be actionable without proof of damage; and that is not the law today.' Certain questions of limitation of actions aside,[8] the practical consequences of *Fowler* v. *Lanning* and *Letang* v. *Cooper* may not be so very great, since few actions are started where no damage has been sustained. However, these two decisions significantly narrow the scope of the 'interference' torts in comparison to negligence. The preponderance of the tort of negligence in the modern law of torts is a reflection of the tendency to focus on loss-spreading and to use the 'fault principle' as a basis for judging activity that causes damage. It should be stressed, however, that the function of the interference torts is not to engage in loss-spreading as such but to affirm the fundamental importance of certain interests, such as personal bodily integrity and freedom of movement, *in their own right*. In this sense the torts of trespass to the person are similar in nature to the torts of interference with land and with chattels, which still bear clear signs of their origins as torts of strict liability.[9]

[3] See P. H. Winfield, 'The Myth of Absolute Liability' (1926) 42 *LQR* 37; A. L. Goodhart and P. H. Winfield, 'Trespass and Negligence' (1933) 49 *LQR* 37; H. J. Prichard, 'The Rule in *Williams* v. *Holland*' [1964] *CLJ* 234, 237.

[4] See *Fletcher* v. *Rylands* (1866) LR 1 Ex. 1 265, 268 (Blackburn J), *River Wear Commissioners* v. *Adamson* (1977) 2 App. Cas. 743 (Lord Blackburn), *Holmes* v. *Mather* (1875) LR 10 Ex. 261 (Bramwell LJ); see generally J. G. Fleming, *Torts* (7th edn., 1992), 18 ff.

[5] [1932] AC 562.

[6] [1959] 1 QB 426, following *Stanley* v. *Powell* [1891] 1 QB 86.

[7] [1965] 1 QB 232, 240, applied by the Court of Appeal in *Wilson* v. *Pringle* [1987] QB 237.

[8] *Letang* v. *Cooper* was argued in the tort of battery in order to take advantage of the longer limitation period of six years, as opposed to three years for negligence, in force at that time. On the present law of limitation, see ch. 24, Section 9 below.

[9] See P. Cane, *The Anatomy of Tort Law* (1997), in particular chs. 2 and 3. See also U. Burnham, 'Negligent False Imprisonment: Scope for Re-emergence' (1998) 61 *MLR* 573.

2. ASSAULT

The conduct forbidden by this tort is an intentional act that threatens violence, or in other words one that produces in the claimant a reasonable expectation of immediate, unlawful force.[10] The tort is actionable *per se*. Assault is both a tort and a crime; the relevant principles of law apply to both. The actual application of force is known as the tort of 'battery', and the term 'assault' is used in both ordinary and (sometimes) in legal speech to refer to both the threat and the application. The two torts are distinct, however, in that there may be an assault without an actual blow[11] and a battery without an assault where, for example, a sleeping person is hit or there is a blow from behind.

The threat must relate to *immediate* force; a threat of more remote future force is not enough.[12] The reaction induced in the claimant need not be fright as such, merely the apprehension of force.[13] As long as the claimant reasonably expects immediate force, the defendant's ability actually to apply it is not essential. It follows that the necessary intention is the intention to produce an expectation that force is about to be used, or recklessness as to this consequence.[14] Pointing an unloaded gun at the claimant is common-law assault if he does not know it is unloaded;[15] and it is still assault even though the claimant manages to escape in time,[16] or if the defendant is restrained before actually hitting him.[17] Words by themselves do not constitute an assault.[18] They could be used, however, to invest an otherwise innocuous act with menace, as when a person strolls up to another uttering threats; conversely words may negative the threat which would otherwise have arisen. In *Tuberville* v. *Savage*[19] the defendant laid his hand on his sword, saying as he did so: 'if it were not assize time, I would not take such language from you'. Since the words made it clear that the threat would not be carried out, this was held not to be an assault. On the other hand, words that do not negative a threat as such but which make it conditional in some way will not prevent there being an assault. In *Read* v. *Coker*[20] the menacing gesture was accompanied by a threat to break the plaintiff's neck unless he 'got out', and the defendant was held liable for assault. The need for a threat of force means that mere passive obstruction is not assault, as when a person simply stands in front of another in order to obstruct him, but without touching or threatening him.[21]

10 *R* v. *Beasley* (1981) 73 Cr. App. R 44.
11 *Jones* v. *Sherwood* [1942] 1 KB 127.
12 *Mbasogo* v. *Logo Ltd. (No. 1)* [2005] EWHC 2034.
13 *R* v. *Norden* (1755) Fost. 129.
14 See *R* v. *Venna* [1976] QB 421.
15 *R* v. *St George* (1840) 9 C & P 483, 493.
16 *Mortin* v. *Shoppee* (1828) 3 C & P 373.
17 *Stephens* v. *Myers* (1830) 4 C & P 349.
18 *Mead's* v. *Belt's Case* (1823) 1 Lew. CC 184; 168 ER 1006.
19 [1669] 1 Mod. Rep. 3; 86 ER 684.
20 (1853) 13 CB 850.
21 *Innes* v. *Wylie* [1844] 1 C & K 257.

3. BATTERY

(A) CONTACT

The tort of battery consists of a direct act of the defendant resulting in an undesired contact with the person of the claimant. The contact must be intentional. At the same time, though, it need only be nominal: 'the least touching of another in anger is a battery'.[22] For example, in *Ashton* v. *Jennings*[23] an act of placing a hand on another to assert social precedence was held to be a battery.

In *Wilson* v. *Pringle*[24] the Court of Appeal held that the touching has to be 'hostile', but this seems contrary to authority and is probably incorrect. The need to find some element of hostility was thought to arise in order to avoid the conclusion that incidental contact on the street or in a crowd can constitute battery. However, in *Re F*[25] Lord Goff, invoking an earlier judgment of his own in *Collins* v. *Wilcock*,[26] argued that an

> exception has been created to allow for the exigencies of everyday life: jostling in a street or some other crowded place, social contact at parties and such like. This exception has been said to be founded on implied consent, since those who go about in public places, or go to parties, may be taken to have impliedly consented to bodily contact of this kind. Today this rationalization can be regarded as artificial: and, in particular, it is difficult to impute consent to those who, by reason of their youth or mental disorder, are unable to give their consent. For this reason I consider it more appropriate to regard such cases as falling within a general exception embracing all physical contact which is generally acceptable in the ordinary conduct of everyday life.

The requirement that a touching be 'hostile' was incompatible, according to Lord Goff, with the basic principle that 'any touching of another's body is, in the absence of lawful excuse, capable of amounting to a battery and a trespass'. Other authorities suggest that what Holt CJ called 'anger' should not be taken literally. Stealing a kiss is a battery even though the intention may be far from 'hostile'.[27] Lord Goff's test of what is acceptable in everyday life would exclude from liability the case of a person touching another in the course of conversation or slapping a person on the back by way of congratulation. In *Wainwright* v. *Home Office*[28] Lord Hoffmann confirmed Lord Goff's approach, defining a battery as 'a touching of the person with what is sometimes called hostile intent but which [Lord Goff] redefined as meaning any intentional physical contact which was not "generally acceptable in the ordinary conduct of human life"'.

[22] *Cole* v. *Turner* (1704) 6 Mod. Rep. 149; 87 ER 907.

[23] [1674] 2 Lev. 133; 83 ER 485.

[24] [1987] QB 237.

[25] [1990] 2 AC 1.

[26] [1984] 1 WLR 1172, 1177.

[27] *R* v. *Chief Constable of Devon and Cornwall, ex parte Central Electricity Generating Board* [1982] QB 458, 471 (Lord Denning MR, citing R. F. V. Henston and R. A. Buckley, *Salmond and Henston's Law of Torts* (19th edn., 1987), 133); *KD* v. *Chief Constable of Hampshire* [2005] EWHC 2550 (unwelcome cuddling).

[28] [2004] 2 AC 406, 417.

The contact must be direct. In *Dodwell* v. *Burford*[29] the defendant struck the horse on which the plaintiff was riding and he was thrown off; the court held that there had been a battery. It is arguable, however, that the plaintiff's fall was consequential, for which the appropriate action at that time would have been in case and not in trespass. With the abolition of the forms of action it no longer matters whether the claim is framed as case or trespass, but some difficulty remains over the precise scope of the modern tort of battery. It seems that there could be liability where the interference is brought about intentionally but indirectly, as, for example, by daubing the inside of the claimant's hat with filth as a joke so that he dirties his hair. Winfield referred to this category as 'intentional physical harm other than trespasses to the person', but the American *Restatement of Torts*[30] includes it within the scope of battery; this would extend the tort to cover wilful acts of the kind which may lie within the rule in *Wilkinson* v. *Downton*.

The need for the contact to be intentional has already been noted. It has been held that the intention need not be present at the commencement of the relevant act, provided it is formed while the act is still continuing. In *Fagan* v. *Metropolitan Police Commissioner*[31] the defendant unintentionally stopped his car on a policeman's foot. When told to get off he deliberately delayed doing so. He was held guilty of criminal assault because his later intention to inflict an unlawful contact was directed to a continuing act.

Since assault and battery are crimes as well as torts, statute has made provision for avoiding unnecessary double process. Criminal proceedings will be a bar to further civil proceedings where the hearing was a summary one and ended, after a hearing on the merits, either with a certificate of dismissal or with the accused being convicted and either being imprisoned or paying the fine levied on him.[32] However, these provisions do not prevent civil actions being brought in respect of more serious crimes tried on indictment; nor do they prevent action being brought against those who, for one reason or another, are not prosecuted.[33]

(B) DEFENCES

Consent operates as a defence to the tort of battery, within certain limits. This issue is particularly important in cases of medical treatment. As Lord Browne-Wilkinson put it in *Airedale NHS Trust* v. *Bland*,[34] in general 'any treatment given by a doctor to a patient which is invasive (i.e. involves any interference with the physical integrity of the patient) is unlawful unless done with the consent of the patient: it constitutes the crime of battery and the tort of trespass to the person'. However, this statement is simply the beginning of the analysis. It is necessary, first, to consider what amounts to consent, and

29 (1670) 1 Mod. Rep. 24; 86 ER 703.

30 Section 18.

31 [1969] 1 QB 439; see also *R* v. *Miller* [1983] 2 AC 161.

32 See Offences Against the Person Act 1861, ss. 42–5; *Ellis* v. *Burton* [1975] 1 WLR 386.

33 As in *Halford* v. *Brookes* [1991] 1 WLR 428.

34 [1993] 1 All ER 821, 881.

whether apparent agreement can be vitiated. Consent must be 'real' in the sense of not being induced by fraud or misrepresentation. This does not mean that a doctor who fails to give a patient full information prior to an operation will necessarily be liable in trespass. His liability in negligence will depend on the so-called *Bolam* [35] test, which asks whether his practice conformed with that of a respectable body of opinion within the relevant part of the medical profession, with the rider, added by the House of Lords in *Sidaway* v. *Bethlem Royal Hospital*,[36] that there might be circumstances in which the nature of the risks in question would dictate disclosure regardless of the normal practice. However, the question whether the defendant conformed to the necessary standard of care in advising the patient is separate from the question whether the patient has given his consent to surgery: 'justice requires that in order to vitiate the reality of consent there must be a greater failure of communication between doctor and patient than that involved in a breach of duty' in negligence.[37] In *Chatterton* v. *Gerson* Bristow J thought that 'once the patient is informed in broad terms of the nature of the procedure which is intended, and gives her consent, that consent is real, and the cause of action on which to base a claim for failure to go into the risks and implications is negligence, not trespass'.[38] It might be different, perhaps, if a surgeon, through error, carried out a circumcision on a patient when he was meant to undertake a tonsillectomy.[39] The point is that the patient's consent to being operated on is broadly effective to protect the surgeon in respect of that type of operation. If the surgeon makes an error leading to the failure of the operation, the claimant's complaint is not that he was operated on against his will but that the outcome of the operation was detrimental to him.[40] Additional protection for the surgeon derives from the ruling in *Freeman* v. *Home Office (No. 2)*[41] to the effect that the burden of proving that consent to treatment was not given lies on the patient.

Subject to the need to show proof of consent, then, an adult of sound mind is entitled to refuse to agree to medical treatment. A doctor who respects this wish does not commit the crime of aiding and abetting a suicide if the patient dies as a result;[42] indeed, he would normally be liable in trespass if he continued the treatment against the patient's wishes. This means, for example, that a patient on a life-support system can, if in full possession of his faculties and if properly informed, insist that the life-support system be switched off.[43] It is also possible that a patient might indicate his wishes in

[35] *Bolam* v. *Friern Hospital* [1957] 1 WLR 582; ch. 3 above.

[36] [1985] AC 871.

[37] *Chatterton* v. *Gerson* [1981] QB 432 (Bristow J).

[38] [1981] QB 432, 443. [39] *Ibid.*

[40] See *Hills* v. *Potter* [1984] 1 WLR 641, *Sidaway* v. *Bethlem Royal Hospital* [1985] AC 871, *Freeman* v. *Home Office (No. 2)* [1984] QB 524, *F* v. *R* (1984) 33 SASR 189, *Chappel* v. *Hart* (1998) 195 CLR 232, *Chester* v. *Ashfar* [2003] QB 356.

[41] [1984] 1 QB 524, 537–9 (McCowan J), 557 (Sir John Donaldson MR).

[42] For this crime, see Suicide Act 1961, s. 2(1); *Pretty* v. *DPP* [2002] 1 AC 800.

[43] *Airedale NHS Trust* v. *Bland* [1993] AC 789, 866 (Lord Goff of Chieveley), approving the Canadian decision in *Nancy B* v. *Hôtel-Dieu de Québec* (1992) 86 DLR (4th) 385, *Re AK (Medical Treatment: Consent)* [2001] FLR 129, *Re B (Adult: Refusal of Medical Treatment)* [2002] 2 All ER 449.

advance of falling unconscious or being unable to express his will clearly, although the court would have to be sure that the conditions for the removal of medical treatment had been met and that the prior expression of will remained fully effective.[44]

As far as medical treatment of children is concerned, much depends on whether the child is old enough to appreciate the significance of what is being proposed, but this is subject to the court's inherent power to make a child a ward of court and to take decisions on his or her behalf in what are deemed the child's best interests. The starting-point is section 8 of the Family Law Reform Act 1969 which provides that a child over the age of 16 may consent to medical treatment without seeking the consent of his parent or guardian. In *Gillick* v. *West Norfolk Area Health Authority*[45] the House of Lords held that a child under the age of sixteen who possessed 'sufficient understanding and intelligence' could consent to the receipt of contraceptive advice and treatment without the consent of her parents. For young children the consent of the parents is usually necessary and sufficient. Where there is doubt or the views of the parents are in conflict, the child can be made a ward of court and the doctor can then seek the court's permission to carry out the operation. In *Re P (A Minor)*[46] a child's father objected to the termination of her pregnancy. Her local authority made her a ward of court and the court's consent to the operation was granted. In *Re B (A Minor)*[47] a child of seventeen with a mental age of five or six was made a ward of court, following which the court gave leave for her to be sterilised with the agreement of her mother and of the local authority. In some cases, however, the courts have gone further and used their inherent jurisdiction to consent to medical treatment on a child's behalf, even though the child was of an age where she was competent to refuse consent.[48] Once the child is a ward of court, the court will, in effect, decide what is in 'his best interests', having regard to appropriate medical opinion and the views of parents even though they may be in conflict with those of the child.[49]

In *Re A (Children) (Conjoined Twins: Surgical Separation)*[50] the court was called on to exercise its wardship jurisdiction in deciding whether to authorise an operation to separate conjoined twins. If the operation was carried out, one of the twins (Jodie) stood a good chance of surviving, but the other (Mary) was certain to die within minutes. If the operation was not carried out, the life expectancy of both of the twins was limited to a few months at most. The parents refused to give their approval to the operation; thus, without the court's intervention, the operation to separate them would have amounted to a battery. Both at first instance and in the Court of Appeal, it was held

44 As in the case of a Jehovah's Witness: *Re T (Adult: Refusal of Medical Treatment)* [1992] Fam. 95.

45 [1986] AC 112.

46 (1981) 80 LGR 301.

47 [1988] AC 199.

48 *Re W (A Minor) (Wardship: Medical Treatment)* [1991] 4 All ER 177, *Re W (A Minor) (Wardship, Medical Treatment)* [1991] 4 All ER 627.

49 See *Re B (A Minor) (Wardship; Sterilisation)* [1988] AC 199, *Re C (A Minor) (Wardship, Medical Treatment)* [1990] Fam. 26, *Re J (A Minor) (Wardship, Medical Treatment)* [1991] Fam. 33, *Airedale NHS Trust* v. *Bland* [1993] AC 789, 808–9 (Sir Thomas Bingham MR).

50 [2001] Fam. 147.

that the balance of interests of the twins lay in favour of granting permission to carry out the operation. The court also considered whether there would be a breach of the criminal law if the operation went ahead. Ward LJ considered that, by intervening, the surgeons would be coming to Jodie's defence; the same argument would presumably have been available to defeat any civil-law claim of trespass to the person. Brooke LJ, again considering this issue in the context of the criminal law, held that the defence of necessity was made out on the facts. While the case has limited significance for tort law by comparison to its momentous importance for medical and criminal law, it indicates the growing importance attached to the defence of necessity in cases of medical treatment.[51]

Thus the defence of necessity is increasingly to the fore in cases involving medical treatment administered to adults without their consent, where the wardship jurisdiction is irrelevant.[52] It is well established that necessity may be a defence in the context of an emergency that compels a rescuer to act. In *Re F* Lord Goff said: 'to fall within the principle, not only (1) must there be a necessity to act when it is not practicable to communicate with the assisted person, but also (2) the action taken must be such as a reasonable person would in all the circumstances take, citing in the best interests of the assisted person'. 'Officious' intervention would not therefore be protected, but action taken by rescuers or carers in an emergency would be. Where, following a railway accident, passengers are trapped in the wreckage, 'it is this principle which may render lawful the actions of other citizens, railway staff, passengers or outsiders, who rush to give aid and comfort to the victims: the surgeon who amputates the limb of an unconscious passenger to free him from the wreckage; the ambulance man who conveys him to hospital; the doctors and nurses who treat him and care for him while he is unconscious'.[53] Similarly, 'it very commonly occurs that a person, due to accident or some other cause, becomes unconscious and is thus not able to give or withhold consent to medical treatment. In that situation it is lawful, under the principle of necessity, for medical men to apply such treatment as in their informed opinion is in the best interests of the unconscious patient.'[54]

Legislation[55] governs the circumstances under which treatment can be administered to mental patients in respect of their mental health, but the legality of other forms of treatment falls to be determined by the common law. In *Re F* the House of Lords invoked the principle of necessity to authorise a sterilisation operation to be carried out on a woman of 36 whose mental age was such that she could not give her consent to the operation. According to Lord Brandon, 'a doctor can lawfully operate on, or give other

[51] On this see also the judgment of Lord Goff of Chieveley in *R* v. *Bournewood Community and Mental Health NHS Trust, ex parte L* [1999] AC 458.

[52] The *parens patriae* jurisdiction formerly exercised by the courts in the case of adults, such as mental patients, unable effectively to express their will or consent to medical treatment, has been repealed by statute: see *Re F* [1990] 2 AC 1, *Airedale NHS Trust* v. *Bland* [1993] AC 789, 857 (Lord Keith of Kinkel).

[53] [1990] 2 AC 1, 76.

[54] *Airedale NHS Trust* v. *Bland* [1993] AC 789, 857 (Lord Keith of Kinkel).

[55] Principally in the form of the Mental Health Act 1983, Pt. IV.

treatment to, adult patients who are incapable, for one reason or another, of consenting to his doing so, provided that the operation or other treatment concerned is in the best interests of such patients',[56] the notion of 'best interests' being decided according to the *Bolam* test of respectable medical practice.[57] In *Re Y (Mental Incapacity: Bone Marrow Transplant)*[58] this principle was extended to a case in which permission was sought to carry out a bone marrow transplant on the defendant, who was mentally incapacitated, for the benefit of her sister. The court granted permission on the basis that the defendant's own interests, in the context of a very tight-knit family, would be served by her sister's survival.

But the idea that necessity can overcome the absence of consent does not, it seems, cover cases in which an adult patient of sound mind consciously refuses medical treatment. In *St George's Healthcare NHS Trust* v. *S*[59] the defendant, who was pregnant, was diagnosed with a condition which was life-threatening both to herself and to her unborn child. She was advised to agree to delivery of the child by caesarean section but she declined. The plaintiff NHS Trust obtained a court order authorising it to carry out the operation against the defendant's wishes, which it then proceeded to do, successfully. On appeal from the initial ruling, the Court of Appeal ruled that the judge had been wrong to grant the hospital's application, since even consideration of the right to life of the unborn child did not justify, in this case, interference with the mother's right to self-determination and physical autonomy. In general, necessity is much less likely to apply as a defence to the torts of trespass to the person than it is to the torts of trespass to property. Although 'the necessity for saving life has at all times been considered a proper grounds for inflicting such damage as may be necessary upon another's property',[60] it does not follow that interference with physical integrity can so easily be justified. In *Leigh* v. *Gladstone*[61] force-feeding a prisoner, in this case a suffragette, was held to be lawful; but since that time (1909) the practice has not been carried on by the prison authorities and this first instance judgment almost certainly does not now represent the law.[62] It is also doubtful whether lawful authority will amount to a defence in cases of physical interference beyond the clear cases in which specific statutory authority is provided, for example, for the exercise of police powers.[63]

In *Airedale NHS Trust* v. *Bland*[64] the courts were faced not with the question whether treatment could be administered to a patient without his consent, but whether it could

56 [1990] 2 AC 1, 55.

57 See *Simms* v. *Simms* [2002] EWHC 2734 (Fam) (in which the court authorised the treatment of patients suffering from vCJD using new, untested drugs).

58 [1996] 2 FLR 787.

59 [1998] 3 All ER 673.

60 *Southport Corp.* v. *Esso Petroleum Co.* [1954] 2 QB 182 (Devlin J).

61 (1909) 26 TLR 169.

62 See *Secretary of State for the Home Department* v. *Robb* [1995] Fam. 127.

63 The question of police powers under the Police and Criminal Evidence Act 1984 and related legislation lies outside the scope of this book.

64 [1993] AC 789. There have since been many applications of this ruling. The authorities were recently reviewed by the Court of Appeal in *Portsmouth NHS Trust* v. *Wyatt* [2005] EWCA Civ. 1181.

be withheld under circumstances where it was impossible to ascertain what the patient's wishes were. The patient sustained injuries that caused him to suffer brain damage, as a result of which he was unable to respond to any external stimuli. He had to be fed by a tube inserted into his nose and stomach, and medical staff were required to take steps to ensure that he remained free of infections which would otherwise have been fatal to him. In the words of the President of the Family Division,[65] 'there is simply no possibility whatsoever that he has any appreciation of anything that takes place around him'. Doctors treating him, who were unanimously of the opinion that he had no prospect of recovery, made an application for a declaration that medical treatment could lawfully be withdrawn notwithstanding the patient's inability to give his consent; the application was supported by the patient's parents.

There was no question in this case of applying the wardship jurisdiction; the patient, who was 17 when he sustained his injuries, was aged 21 at the time the case was brought to court. Lord Goff, giving the leading judgment in the House of Lords,[66] said that there was no absolute rule that a patient's life had to be prolonged by treatment or care regardless of all the circumstances; the patient's right of self-determination, which meant that he could withhold consent for medical treatment, qualified the principle of the 'sanctity of life'. It was, moreover, inconsistent with the principle of self-determination that the law should provide no means of enabling treatment to be lawfully withheld in a case where the patient was in no condition to indicate whether or not he consented to treatment being continued. The difficulty was whether the doctor could be held civilly or criminally liable for his failure to treat the patient. In this regard, Lord Goff considered that there was a fundamental difference between a case in which a doctor sought to bring life to an end by a positive act of commission—by, for example, administering a fatal overdose—and one in which he discontinued life-saving treatment. The latter could be accurately characterised as an omission, and could give rise to liability only in circumstances where the doctor was under an affirmative duty of action. The central question, then, concerned the precise extent and scope of the doctor's duty to his patient in these circumstances. This was to act according to the 'patient's best interests' in accordance with the *Bolam* test, subject to the need to seek the court's opinion by obtaining a declaration on an originating summons, the procedure laid down for such cases in *Re F*.

The House of Lords unanimously agreed that the declarations sought should be granted on the basis that it was in the patient's best interests that the treatment should be discontinued. There was no support for the approach taken in certain American cases, namely to seek a 'substituted view' of the patient's wishes based on evidence either of his own personal attitude, in the past, to the question of termination of life in the event of incurable illness, or on a number of different factors such as his former character and feelings. As Lord Mustill said, such an approach to fictive consent 'is surely meaningless'.[67]

65 [1993] AC 789, 825 (Sir Stephen Brown P).

66 Lords Keith and Lowry expressed their broad concurrence with the reasoning adopted by Lord Goff.

67 [1993] 1 All ER 821, 892.

On the other hand, the view that it was in the patient's best interests for the treatment to be terminated was based on the problematic distinction, in this context, between acts and omissions, which seems less than convincing as a basis for granting the declarations requested. Lord Mustill also cast doubt on the appropriateness of using the *Bolam* test of medical practice in this context: 'I accept without difficulty that this principle applies to the ascertainment of the medical raw material such as diagnosis, prognosis and appraisal of the patient's cognitive functions. Beyond this point, however, it may be said that the decision is ethical, not medical, and that there is no reason in logic why on such a decision the opinions of doctors should be decisive.'[68]

In *NHS Trust A* v. *M*[69] the *Bland* decision was challenged on grounds deriving from the Human Rights Act 1998. Specifically, it was argued that the withdrawal of treatment from patients in a permanent vegetative state contravened the right to life in Article 2 of the European Convention, and that a breach of Article 3, concerning the prohibition on inhuman and degrading treatment, would also occur during the interval between the ending of treatment and the death of the patient. However, the President of the Family Division, Dame Elizabeth Butler-Sloss, ruled that a responsible decision by a medical team to withhold treatment which passed the *Bolam* test would not amount to the intentional deprivation of life as required by Article 2. Nor would there be a breach of Article 3 if the decision was shown to be in the best interests of the patient.

But the *Bolam* test does not apply in a case where a terminally ill patient wishes to end his own life with the assistance of another. Here, the patient's consent is deemed irrelevant on public-policy grounds; the issue of what amounts to generally acceptable medical practice does not arise; and the person who helps the patient to die will be subject to both civil and (more relevant in practice) criminal sanctions. Assisting suicide is a crime under the Suicide Act 1961. In *Pretty* v. *DPP*[70] the House of Lords ruled that this statutory prohibition was not contrary to the Human Rights Act 1998. The plaintiff, Diane Pretty, suffered from a fatal degenerative condition, motor-neurone disease, and wished to end her life, but was not in a position to do so simply by refusing to receive medical treatment. She sought a declaration that her husband would not face prosecution under section 2(1) of the Suicide Act 1961 if he helped her to commit suicide. Her application was denied. The House of Lords rejected her argument that under Article 2 of the Convention the right of self-determination implied a right to assistance in ending her life; it also ruled out her claim that the prohibition on assisted suicide infringed her right to dignity and the protection of private life under Article 8. The European Court of Human Rights subsequently reached a similar conclusion: although Article 8 was applicable in this case, it was permissible under Article 8(2) to qualify the protection of private life by reference to a countervailing interest, here the need to safeguard the terminally ill against pressure to consent to an assisted death.[71]

Consent and necessity may arise as defences to trespass to the person in other contexts. Consent may be a defence to a criminal conviction for assault, but again this

[68] *Ibid.*, 895. [69] [2001] 2 FLR 367.
[70] [2002] 1 AC 800. [71] *Pretty* v. *United Kingdom* [2002] 2 FLR 45.

is subject to the possibility that consent will be negatived by public policy. In *Re F* Lord Griffiths said that 'although the general rule is that the individual is the master of his own fate the judges through the common law have, in the public interest, imposed certain constraints on the harm that people may consent to being inflicted on their bodies'. Examples include participation in a prize-fight, fighting in circumstances likely to give rise to actual bodily harm, and serious bodily injury inflicted as part of sexual practices.[72] In *Bland* Lord Mustill referred to consent being a defence both to criminal assault and to a claim in tort 'at the bottom end of the scale'. He then suggested that 'whatever the scope of the civil defence of *volenti non fit injuria* there is a point higher up the scale than common assault at which consent in general ceases to form a defence to a criminal charge.... If one person cuts off the hand of another it is no answer to say that the amputee consented to what was done.'[73]

The defendant may also invoke self-defence in an appropriate case. The force used by the defendant to defend himself must not be out of proportion to the force exerted against him, as it was in *Lane* v. *Holloway* where a provocative blow by the plaintiff did not excuse a savage retaliation;[74] nor will the defence avail one who, in seeking to defend himself, strikes an innocent bystander.[75] In this regard it is relevant to note section 3 of the Criminal Law Act 1967, which provides that a person has the right to use 'such force as is reasonable in the prevention of crime'.

The relevance of contributory negligence in this context is not completely clear. It had no application in *Lane* v. *Holloway*,[76] but in *Murphy* v. *Culhane*[77] it was suggested that the defence would have applied in circumstances where the plaintiff initiated a criminal affray in the course of which he was killed, had not total defences been available in the form of consent and illegality. But there is authority pointing to a very restricted application of contributory negligence in the context of the intentional torts,[78] and on principle it would seem to have little role to play, since the process of shifting loss through apportionment does not have the relevance here that it does in relation to the tort of negligence.

4. FALSE IMPRISONMENT

The tort of false imprisonment consists of the complete restriction of the claimant's freedom of movement without lawful excuse or justification. The tort is actionable *per se*, that is, without proof of damage.

72 [1990] 2 AC 1, 70, citing, respectively, *R* v. *Coney* (1882) 8 QBD 534, *Attorney-General's Reference (No. 6 of 1980)* [1981] QB 715, and *R* v. *Donovan* [1934] 2 KB 498; and see also *R* v. *Brown* [1994] 1 AC 212, *Laskey, Jaggard and Brown* v. *United Kingdom* (1997) 24 EHRR 39.

73 [1993] 1 All ER 821, 889. See also the judgment of Lord Hobhouse in *Pretty* v. *DPP* [2002] 1 AC 800.

74 [1968] 1 QB 379.

75 *The Case of Thorns* (1466) YB 6 Ed. fo. 7 pl. 18, *Lambert* v. *Bessey* (1681) T. Ray 421.

76 [1968] 1 QB 379.

77 [1977] QB 94.

78 See the judgments of Lord Hoffmann and Lord Rodger in *Standard Chartered Bank* v. *Pakistan National Shipping Corp.* [2002] 3 WLR 1547, a case concerning liability in the tort of deceit.

(A) CONFINEMENT

The restriction of the claimant need not take the form of confinement in a room or prison cell: according to the *Termes de la Ley*, 'imprisonment is the restraint of a man's liberty, whether it be in the open field, or in the stocks, or in the cage in the streets or in a man's own house, as well as in the common gaole'.[79] Moreover, imprisonment does not have to involve seizure of the claimant; touching and informing him that he is under arrest are sufficient.[80]

However, the restraint must be complete; that is to say, the claimant's freedom of movement has to be impeded in every direction. There is a distinction to be drawn here between *confinement* and *obstruction*. It is not sufficient to prevent a person from going forward if he is free to go back, or vice versa. In *Bird* v. *Jones*[81] a section of Hammersmith Bridge was temporarily fenced off. The plaintiff, who insisted on climbing over the fence to go forward, was prevented from doing so, but was told he could go back instead. The court held that he had not been falsely imprisoned and held that his attempt to go forward was a breach of the peace, for which he had been lawfully arrested. By contrast, in *Austin* v. *Metropolitan Police Commissioner*, there was a clear case of containment where the police, fearing a breach of the peace, confined several hundred people for several hours in a 'closed cordon' around Oxford Circus in central London, an area of only fifty metres in diameter.[82]

In *Bird* v. *Jones*, an avenue of escape was available. To avoid a finding of imprisonment on these grounds, the escape route in question must be reasonably accessible and safe. Thus it would not normally be false imprisonment to turn the key on a person in a room on the ground floor from which he could easily escape by stepping out of a window, but it would be a different matter if the room were several storeys up in a block of flats.

In *R*v. *Bournewood Community and Mental Health NHS Trust, ex parte L*[83] the House of Lords held by a bare majority that there was no false imprisonment in a case where an 'informal' mental patient was kept on an unlocked ward in a mental hospital under circumstances where he showed no desire to leave. His consultant would have applied for an order for his detention under the Mental Health Act 1983 had he tried to leave the hospital. The majority held that he was not being detained against his will. On this point, the decision seemed highly dubious; as Lords Nolan and Steyn pointed out in their dissents, the patient was kept under sedation and would have been physically restrained from leaving had he attempted to.

Perhaps not surprisingly, the *Bournewood* case was the subject of a subsequent claim for a breach of Article 5 of the European Convention on Human Rights. This Article provides that 'Everyone has the right to liberty and security of the person' and stipulates that 'No one shall be deprived of his liberty' save in one of a number of specified cases

79 Section v 'Imprisonment'.

80 *Hart* v. *Chief Constable of Kent* [1983] RTR 484.

81 (1845) 7 QB 742.

82 [2005] EWHC 480.

83 [1999] AC 458.

and according to a procedure prescribed by law. These include, under Article 5(1)(e), 'the lawful detention of... persons of unsound mind'. In *HL* v. *United Kingdom*[84] the European Court of Human Rights held that the applicant had been detained contrary to Article 5. The Court decisively rejected, as inappropriate in respect of the Convention, the narrow reading of the concept of containment which had prevailed in the House of Lords:

Considerable emphasis was placed by the domestic courts, and by the [UK] Government, on the fact that the applicant was compliant and never attempted, or expressed the wish, to leave. The majority of the House of Lords specifically distinguished actual restraint of a person (which would amount to false imprisonment) and restraint which was conditional upon his seeking to leave (which would not constitute false imprisonment). The Court does not consider such a distinction to be of central importance under the Convention. Nor, for the same reason, can the Court accept as determinative the fact relied on the by the Government that the regime applied to the applicant (as a compliant incapacitated patient) did not materially differ from that applied to a person who had the capacity to consent to hospital treatment, neither objecting to their admission to hospital. The Court reiterates that the right to liberty is too important in a democratic society for a person to lose the benefit of Convention protection for the single reason that he may have given himself up to be taken into detention... especially when it is not disputed that that person is legally incapable of consenting to, or disagreeing with, the proposed action.

The Court went on to find that the UK government had failed to make out a defence under Article 5(1)(e), on the grounds that there were insufficient procedural safeguards to protect against an arbitrary deprivation of liberty (a point we return to below).

The House of Lords' judgment is highly significant for opening up an apparent gap between the common law tort of false imprisonment and the right not to be deprived of liberty and security of the person under Article 5. In particular, the common law concept of confinement is, on the face of it, significantly narrower than that of deprivation of liberty. In contrast to the common law's insistence on the need for complete restraint of movement, the starting-point under Article 5 'must be the concrete situation of the individual concerned and account must be taken of a whole range of factors arising in a particular case such as the type, duration, effects and manner of implementation of the measure in question'; thus, 'the distinction between a deprivation of, and a restriction of, liberty is merely one of degree of intensity and not one of nature or substance'.[85] It follows that in cases involving public defendants such as the police or mental health authorities, claims under the Human Rights Act 1998 are in the process of superseding the common law tort of false imprisonment; since it is also possible that in certain circumstances, tortious liability may be more extensive than that under the Convention, the two types of claim may have to argued in tandem.[86]

84 Application No. 45508/99, Judgment of 5 October 2004, at p. 30; also reported at (2005) 40 EHRR 32.

85 *HL* v. *United Kingdom*, Judgment of 5 October 2004, at p. 29.

86 See, e.g. *Austin* v. *Commissioner of Police of the Metropolis* [2005] HRLR 20; *Connor* v. *Chief Constable of Merseyside Police* [2006] EWCA Civ. 1549.

As far as the tort is concerned, it is not necessary that the claimant should have been aware of his imprisonment at the time of confinement. This point has given rise to some difficulty in the case law. In *Herring* v. *Boyle*[87] a mother went to fetch her son from a private school, but was not allowed to remove him until she had paid the bill. The court held that the boy had not been falsely imprisoned because there was nothing to show that 'the plaintiff was at all cognisant of any restraint'. What is not clear from the report, however, is whether the boy was imprisoned at all, quite apart from the question of his knowledge. In *Meering* v. *Graham-White Aviation Co. Ltd.*[88] the Court of Appeal held that knowledge of confinement was not necessary, but the authority is impaired by the failure of the court to cite *Herring* v. *Boyle*. *Meering* is preferable on the ground of policy, however: not only is there a general interest in upholding individual liberty which goes above and beyond individual circumstances, but the individual concerned may feel equally aggrieved to find out after the event that he was the subject of an unjustified confinement. This view was endorsed by the House of Lords in *Murray* v. *Ministry of Defence*.[89] The plaintiff was detained in her house for half an hour by soldiers, who were searching for terrorist suspects, without being told that she was under arrest, following which she was further detained at a screening centre. She failed in her action for false imprisonment because the defendants had lawful authority to act as they did under section 14 of the Northern Ireland (Emergency Provisions) Act 1978. On the point of knowledge, Lord Griffiths stated *obiter* that: 'if a person is unaware that he has been falsely imprisoned and has suffered no harm, he can normally expect to recover no more than nominal damages... [but] the law attaches supreme importance to the liberty of the individual and if he suffers a wrongful interference with that liberty it should remain actionable even without proof of special damage'.

A person may be restrained by the defendant either acting personally or through someone else, usually an official. In the latter case a distinction was drawn in a number of nineteenth-century cases between a 'ministerial' act and a 'judicial' act.[90] A 'ministerial' act, in this sense, consists of an act of the official where he is merely the instrument or agent of the defendant, so that it is the latter who will be liable for the imprisonment.[91] A 'judicial' act is one where the official exercises his own judgement:[92] in this case the person who initiated the process is not normally liable for false imprisonment although he may be liable for malicious prosecution or for malicious abuse of process.[93]

The basic distinction between these categories of cases was reaffirmed by the Court of Appeal in *Davidson* v. *Chief Constable of North Wales and Another*.[94] The second defendant, a store detective, gave information to the police that led to the arrest of the plaintiff

87 (1834) 1 CM & R 377; 149 ER 1126.

88 (1919) 122 LT 44.

89 [1988] 1 WLR 692.

90 See *Austin* v. *Dowling* (1870) LR 5 CP 543, 540.

91 *Hopkins* v. *Crowe* (1836) 4 A & E 774; 111 ER 974.

92 *Brown* v. *Chapman* (1848) 6 CB 365; 136 ER 1292.

93 See below, ch. 10; *Lock* v. *Ashton* (1842) 12 QB 871; 116 ER 1097, *Lea* v. *Carrington* (1889) 23 QBD 45.

94 [1994] 2 All ER 597.

on suspicion of shoplifting. She and a friend were detained by the police for two hours until they were released when it became clear that the store detective's suspicions had been unfounded. The plaintiff's claim against the store detective for false imprisonment was struck out as disclosing no cause of action, a ruling that was upheld on appeal: according to Sir Thomas Bingham MR, 'what distinguishes the case in which a defendant is liable from a case in which he is not is whether he has merely given information to a properly constituted authority on which that authority may act or not as it decides or whether he has himself been the instigator, promoter and active inciter of the action that follows'.[95]

It is not altogether clear whether 'intention' in the tort of false imprisonment refers to an intention to confine the plaintiff or an intention to perform the act that results in imprisonment. If the defendant commits an act resulting in imprisonment without realising what he is doing, but in circumstances where he could be described as negligent, is he liable for the tort of false imprisonment which, in contrast to negligence, is actionable *per se*? Although the point remains open, there is a case for saying that the need to uphold personal liberty requires the broadest possible interpretation to be given to false imprisonment. On the other hand, modern decisions on the mental element in the tort of battery, while not strictly in point, suggest that there is no tort in a case where the defendant neither intended the consequences of his act nor was reckless or negligent with regard to them.[96]

Some guidance on this point may be inferred from *R* v. *Governor of Brockhill Prison, ex parte Evans (No. 2)*.[97] The claimant was sentenced to several concurrent terms of imprisonment, the longest of which was a sentence of two years for burglary. In calculating the length of her imprisonment, the prison governor took into account the time she had spent in custody on remand in relation to that sentence alone. In proceedings for judicial review, it was established that this was an error; the correct approach was to aggregate the periods spent on remand in relation to all the relevant offences, and deduct that from the period of imprisonment. On this basis, the applicant had been detained in excess of just over two months, in respect of which she brought an action of false imprisonment. The House of Lords upheld her claim: although the prison governor had acted in good faith on the basis of earlier case law, he had, objectively speaking, confined the applicant without lawful justification. Several judgments refer to false imprisonment as a tort of strict liability. This suggests that once the objective conditions of confinement are met, it is no defence for the defendant to argue that he did not intend the outcome.

(B) DEFENCES

(i) Consent

Consent is a defence to false imprisonment, but the problem lies in determining when the claimant's consent may be inferred. *Sunbolf* v. *Alford*[98] held that there can be no

[95] *Ibid.*, 602.
[96] *Fowler* v. *Lanning* [1959] 1 QB 426, *Letang* v. *Cooper* [1965] 1 QB 232; see our discussion, above.
[97] [2001] 2 AC 19.
[98] (1838) 3 M & W 248; 150 ER 1135.

private power of arrest for debt or breach of contract, but later cases have appeared to erode the effects of this rule. One such case is *Robinson* v. *Balmain New Ferry Co. Ltd.*,[99] in which the plaintiff paid one penny to enter a wharf in order to board a ferry. He then decided not to wait for the ferry and sought to go back through the turnstile. Above the turnstile on both sides of the barrier was a notice requiring payment of a penny by any person entering or leaving the wharf. The plaintiff refused to pay and was prevented from leaving. The Privy Council held that he had no claim in false imprisonment. Lord Loreburn argued that the plaintiff had contracted to leave the wharf via the ferry and that the defendants were under no obligation to let him leave by any other way. In effect, this was imprisonment for breach of contract; *Sunbolf* v. *Alford* was not cited. A better explanation for the outcome may be that Robinson could have escaped his confinement by taking the ferry: assuming that this means of exit was a reasonable one, he was not subject to the requisite degree of confinement.

A second difficult case is *Herd* v. *Weardale Steel, Coal and Coke Co. Ltd.*[100] The plaintiff, a miner, descended a mine at the usual time but when he got to the pit bottom he declined to carry on working and asked to be returned to the surface in the cage. The defendants refused to let him take an empty cage that was available and he had to wait a further twenty minutes until the end of the shift before he was allowed to return. The House of Lords held that the employer had the defence of consent, but this is extremely dubious as not only was there no express agreement to this effect but the judgment again goes against *Sunbolf* v. *Alford*. However, the outcome may be explained by the distinction between acts and omissions: it could be argued that the defendants had simply failed to take steps to release the plaintiff in a situation where there was no affirmative duty upon them to do so.

(ii) Justification and Necessity

Imprisonment is authorised by statute in circumstances of lawful arrest and the confinement of persons remanded in custody pending the hearing of a criminal charge and of those convicted and sentenced to a term of imprisonment. The issue of the extent of the statutory powers of arrest of the police and of private citizens is outside the scope of this book.[101] However, a development which is of considerable importance for the law of tort is the growing use of the common law defence of necessity to buttress these statutory powers. In *Thames Valley Police* v. *Hepburn*, decided as recently as 2002, Sedley LJ said:

> It is a bedrock of our civil liberties that a citizen's freedom of person and movement is inviolable except where the law unequivocally gives the state power to restrict it. If a person obstructs

[99] [1910] AC 295. [100] [1915] AC 67.

[101] The reader is referred to specialist texts on constitutional law and the law of civil liberties. The principal legislation in this area is the Police and Criminal Evidence Act 1984; other legislation, such as the Theft Act 1978, s. 3(4), is also relevant, as is the common-law power to arrest for a breach of the peace. On the information which must be given to a person upon his arrest or as soon as practicable thereafter, see *Christie* v. *Leachinsky* [1947] AC 573, *John Lewis & Co.* v. *Tims* [1952] AC 676, and the Police and Criminal Evidence Act 1984, s. 28. The fact that an arrested person later pleads guilty to a charge is not conclusive evidence that his initial

a police officer in the execution of his or her duty an offence is committed and a power of arrest arises. That, and not an implied power to detain or manhandle people who are doing nothing wrong, is how the law protects officers executing a search warrant from interference.[102]

However, later cases have cast doubt on this proposition, both with regard to the specific case of police searches, and in the wider context of the intentional torts including false imprisonment. In *Connor* v. *Chief Constable of Merseyside Police*[103] the police, in the course of executing a search warrant, carried out a raid on the claimants' property, having had grounds to believe that they would find illegal firearms there; they failed to find any. In order to carry out the search they removed the occupants of the house and placed them in police cars for periods of up to an hour. The judge found rejected claims of trespass to the person, false imprisonment and infringement of human rights on various grounds including the availability of a necessity defence. The Court of Appeal upheld this ruling, on the grounds that the police, genuinely believing that firearms were present and that shots might be fired, were entitled to remove the occupants from the house and to detain them while the search continued. Although 'the burden on the police justifying an interference with civil liberties of the kind we have here is a heavy one',[104] it had been discharged in this case. The Court also found that the police had a defence to the human-rights claim under the provisions of Article 5(1)(b) of the Convention, which applies where a person is arrested or detained 'in order to secure the fulfillment of any obligation prescribed by law'.

The defence of necessity was also invoked in *Austin* v. *Commissioner of Police of the Metropolis*.[105] Here, the police, in dealing with an unauthorised political demonstration involving several thousand people in central London, had cordoned off an area around Oxford Circus and detained several hundred people for a period of hours in a confined space, fifty metres in diameter. Conditions were physically uncomfortable. The judge found that the police had acted 'to prevent serious injury, and possible death, to persons for whom they were responsible, including police officers, members of the crowd and third parties, as well as to protect property'. Under such circumstances, 'the police can take measures for the protection of everyone, and a likely measure, involving minimum use of force, is to detain the crowd until dispersal can be arranged safely'.[106] A claim under Article 5 failed on the same grounds.

Notwithstanding these decisions, there are grounds for thinking that the defence of necessity should be construed strictly in relation to Article 5 claims. In *HL* v. *United Kingdom* the issue, as we have seen, was whether the confinement of the applicant in a mental hospital could be justified under paragraph 1(e) of Article 5. The European Court of Human Rights held that the defence was not made out. After considering the

confinement by the police was lawful, according to the Court of Appeal in *Hill* v. *Chief Constable of South Yorkshire* [1990] 1 All ER 1046.

[102] [2002] EWCA Civ. 1841.
[103] [2006] EWCA Civ. 1549.
[104] *Ibid.*, at [65] (Waller LJ).
[105] [2005] EWHC 480.
[106] *Ibid.*, at [577] (Tugendhat J).

scope of the common law defence of necessity, it stated that 'the relevant national law must meet the standard of "lawfulness" set by the Convention which requires that the law be sufficiently precise to allow the citizen—if need be with appropriate advice—to foresee, to a degree that is reasonable in the circumstances, the consequences which a given action might entail'.[107] Although the defence of necessity provided a basis for determining when detention might occur on the grounds of protecting persons of unsound mind from harming themselves and others, there was an absence, in this case, of the procedural safeguards which would have been needed to protect against 'arbitrary deprivations of liberty'.[108] It remains to be seen what impact this strict test will have on the development of the common law defence, but it may well be the case here, as in other contexts, that there is an alignment over time of the common law approach with that prevailing under the Convention.

Statutory authorisation for the imprisonment of persons convicted of offences is found in section 12(1) of the Prison Act 1952;[109] the Prison Rules, which are made pursuant to statutory powers, lay down in greater detail the manner in which the prison regime is to be arranged. The tort of false imprisonment would seem to have little role to play in this area following the decision of the House of Lords in two joined cases, *R* v. *Deputy Governor of Parkhurst Prison, ex parte Hague* and *Weldon* v. *Home Office*.[110] In each case prisoners who had been lawfully detained following conviction complained of mistreatment alleged to be contrary to the Prison Rules; in the *Hague* case this consisted of segregation, in *Weldon*, of confinement in a 'strip cell'. In *Weldon* in the Court of Appeal Ralph Gibson LJ accepted that 'there is no reason... why the nature of the tort, evolved by the common law for the protection of personal liberty, should be held to be such as to deny its availability to a convicted prisoner, whose residual liberty should, in my judgment, be protected so far as the law can properly achieve unless statute requires otherwise'.[111] However, the notion that a convicted prisoner has a 'residual liberty' in this sense was rejected by the House of Lords.[112] In the view of Lord Bridge:

> the concept of the prisoner's 'residual liberty' as a species of freedom of movement within the prison enjoyed as a legal right which the prison authorities cannot lawfully restrain seems to me quite illusory. The prisoner is at all times lawfully restrained within closely defined bounds and if he is kept in a segregated cell, at a time when, if the rules had not been misapplied, he would be in the company of other prisoners in the workshop, at the dinner table or elsewhere, this is not the deprivation of his liberty of movement, which is the essence of the tort of false imprisonment, it is the substitution of one form of restraint for another.[113]

[107] Application No. 45508/99, Judgment of 5 October 2004, at [114].

[108] *HL*, Judgment of 5 October 2004, at [124].

[109] 'A prisoner, whether sentenced to imprisonment or committed to prison on remand or pending trial or otherwise, may be lawfully confined in any prison.'

[110] [1992] 1 AC 58. [111] [1992] 1 AC 58, 139.

[112] The House of Lords thereby repudiated *dicta* to the contrary of Ackner LJ in *Middleweek* v. *Chief Constable of Merseyside* (1985) [1992] 1 AC 179, 186 (Note).

[113] [1992] 1 AC 58, 163.

According to Lord Jauncey, the prisoner

> is lawfully committed to a prison and while there is subject to the Prison Act 1952 and the Prison Rules 1964. His whole life is regulated by the regime. He has no freedom to do what he wants, when he wants. His liberty to do anything is governed by the prison regime. Placing Weldon in a strip cell and segregating Hague altered the conditions under which they were detained but did not deprive them of any liberty that they had not already lost when initially confined.[114]

Any action for mistreatment has to be brought instead in negligence (which requires proof of fault) or via a public law remedy; alternatively, the House of Lords accepted that a personal action for false imprisonment would lie against a prison officer who acted in abuse of his powers or against a fellow prisoner. However, Lord Bridge thought that the prison authorities would not be vicariously liable for any such abuse of power by an officer.[115]

There are several difficult aspects to this decision. The notion that the prisoner has no 'residual liberty' within the terms set down by the Prison Rules is disturbing enough, according as it does a narrow and formal meaning to the concept of imprisonment and unduly widening the scope of the lawful-authority defence, which effectively now applies even when the Prison Rules have been breached. It is also the case that few of the arguments put forward for restricting the tort in this context are particularly compelling. It cannot be the case, for example, that the tort of false imprisonment should be narrowed down on the ground, suggested by Lords Bridge and Jauncey, that a contravention of the Prison Rules cannot be construed as giving rise to a private action for breach of the statutory duty. The question of the availability of a private action for breach of the statute is a logically separate matter with no bearing on the scope of the false imprisonment tort. The suggestion that the prison authorities would not be liable for an officer acting in abuse of his powers is a contentious reading of the difficult concept of an employer's vicarious liability for torts committed by an employer in the 'course of his employment'.[116] Nor is it the case that a prisoner able to show that his confinement had passed the bounds of legality would be able, in the event of there being false imprisonment, to walk out of the prison, as Lord Bridge suggested; it would simply be the case that the additional and unlawful confinement to which he had been subjected would have to be discontinued.

In contrast to the approach taken in *Hague* and *Weldon*, long-standing authorities on the tort of false imprisonment which suggest that the wrongful continuation of an originally lawful imprisonment is actionable,[117] more recent case law also establishes that a prison governor may be liable for false imprisonment in a case where the prisoner is

[114] [1992] 1 AC 58, 176.

[115] *Ibid.*, 164.

[116] See our discussion in ch. 19, below. Since *Hague* and *Weldon* were decided, the scope of the employer's liability for intentional torts has been considerably clarified by the decisions in *Lister* v. *Hesley Hall Ltd.* [2001] 2 AC 215 and *Majrowski* v. *Guy's and St. Thomas's NHS Trust* [2006] 3 WLR 125.

[117] *Withers* v. *Henley* (1614) Cro. Jac. 379; 79 ER 324, *Mee* v. *Cruikshank* (1902) 86 LT 708, although cf. *Olutu* v. *Home Office* [1997] 1 All ER 385, 391–2.

detained beyond the correct time for her release. Thus, as we have seen, in *R* v. *Governor of Brockhill Prison, ex parte Evans (No. 2)*[118] the House of Lords held that, in such circumstances, it was irrelevant that the governor was acting in good faith on a widely held understanding of the law which was later judged by a court to be incorrect. No defence of justification was available under such circumstances. The *Brockhill* case was however given a very narrow reading in *Quinland* v. *Governor of Swaleside Prison*,[119] where the mistake in calculating the sentence was made by the judge at the original trial, not by the governors of the prison. The governors escaped liability on the grounds that they were executing a prison warrant that was valid on its face, and the judge was found to have immunity under section 2(5) of the Crown Proceedings Act 1947.

5. RESIDUARY TRESPASS AND HARASSMENT: THE TORT IN *WILKINSON* V. *DOWNTON* AND THE PROTECTION FROM HARASSMENT ACT 1997

The boundaries of liability under the tort in *Wilkinson* v. *Downton*[120] are notoriously clear. Broadly speaking, this cause of action can be said to cover the intentional and indirect infliction of physical injury or psychiatric harm upon another. In the case itself a practical joker falsely told the plaintiff that her husband had broken both his legs in an accident. She suffered nervous shock and fell ill. The court allowed her claim for damages. She could not sue in trespass because the damage to her was inflicted indirectly through words, and at that time the courts were not prepared to award damages for nervous shock as such. Wright J nevertheless held the defendant liable on the basis that he had 'wilfully done an act calculated to cause physical harm to the plaintiff—that is to say, to infringe her legal right to personal safety, and has in fact thereby caused physical harm to her. That proposition without more appears to me to state a good cause of action, there being no justification alleged for the act.'[121]

Wilkinson v. *Downton* has only been followed twice in England. In *Janvier* v. *Sweeney*[122] the defendants, private detectives, were held liable to the plaintiff for threatening, without any justification, to denounce her fiancé, a German internee, to the authorities as a spy, causing her to fall ill. The defendants had clearly acted without justification, in the sense of threatening her in order to obtain private letters belonging to her mistress. This decision suggests that the tort is not confined to situations in which false or misleading statements are made.

In the second English authority, *Khorasandjian* v. *Bush*,[123] the defendant repeatedly made unwanted and harassing telephone calls to the plaintiff, placing her under

[118] [2001] 2 AC 19. [119] [2003] QB 306. [120] [1897] 2 QB 57.
[121] [1897] 2 QB 57. [122] [1919] 2 KB 316.
[123] [1993] QB 727. It should also be noted that an *employer* will owe a personal duty of care to his employees to avoid circumstances under which they are exposed to sexual, racial or other forms of harassment in the

considerable stress, but not inflicting any physical injury as such. The Court of Appeal, upholding the judgment of Judge Stockdale QC, decided that it was appropriate to grant an injunction against the defendant under the rule in *Wilkinson* v. *Downton*.[124] According to Dillon LJ, although there was no evidence of the plaintiff having suffered any physical or psychiatric condition, 'there is... an obvious risk that the cumulative effect of continued and unrestrained further harassment such as she has undergone would cause such an illness';[125] on this basis, a *quia timet* injunction could be issued. It is important that the defendant was taken to have intended the plaintiff to have suffered the harm in question; had he merely been negligent, he presumably could not have been held liable under *Wilkinson* v. *Downton*. The question of his possible liability in the tort of negligence was not considered by the court.[126]

Wilkinson v. *Downton* was approved in Australia in *Bunyan* v. *Jordan*,[127] although it was distinguished on the facts, since the words in question were not uttered in the defendant's presence. According to Latham CJ, 'none of the cases has gone so far as to suggest that a man owes a duty to a person who merely happens to overhear statements that are not addressed to them'. Where the defendant knows, however, that it is almost certain that the plaintiff will overhear a statement addressed to a third party, and intends her to be harmed as a consequence of doing so, there would seem to be no reason why he should not be held liable.[128]

The widest rule that can be gleaned from *Wilkinson* v. *Downton* is that of a general principle of residuary liability outside the nominate torts of intentional interference. It is unlikely that it could be used as a basis for creating a generalised tort of intentional interference of a physical or economic kind. Despite some wide *dicta* in *Rookes* v. *Barnard*,[129] the courts have preserved the separate heads of liability in this area.[130] In *Wainwright* v. *Home Office*[131] the House of Lords distinguished *Wilkinson* v. *Downton* almost to vanishing point. The claimants in *Wainwright*, a mother and son, were subjected to a strip search when they visited a relative in prison, on the grounds that they might be bringing drugs into the prison. The search, as such, was authorised by the Prison Rules, but the prison officers deviated from the established procedure in a number of ways, not least by subjecting the son to a battery. That part of his claim

workplace or in work-related environments, as well as, under certain circumstances, being vicariously liable for torts of harassment committed by employees against their fellow employees: see *Waters* v. *Metropolitan Police Commissioner* [2000] 1 WLR 1607; J. Conaghan, 'Law, Harm and Redress: A Feminist Perspective' (2002) 22 *Leg. Stud.* 319.

124 The Court of Appeal also held that an injunction could lie on the basis of a cause of action in private nuisance, but this is no longer good law following the decision of the House of Lords in *Hunter* v. *Canary Wharf* [1997] AC 655.

125 [1993] QB 727, 736.

126 On liability in negligence for physical harm resulting from statements (both true and false), see ch. 3, above.

127 (1937) 57 CLR 1.

128 As in the Canadian case of *Bielitski* v. *Obadiak* (1922) 65 DLR 627.

129 [1964] AC 1129.

130 *Lonrho* v. *Shell Petroleum Co. Ltd.* [1982] AC 173.

131 [2004] 2 AC 406, noted by A. Johnston, 'Putting the Cart Before the Horse? Privacy and the Wainwrights' [2004] *CLJ* 15.

succeeded. In addition, both claimants argued that they had a cause of action for trespass to the person for the distressing and humiliating manner in which the search had been carried out. This claim failed. According to Lord Hoffmann, the tort in *Wilkinson* v. *Downton* 'has nothing to do with trespass to the person',[132] and as such required actual damage in the form of physical harm or recognised psychiatric illness. Moreover, an intention to harm the claimant had to be shown. For this purpose, an imputed intention was insufficient: 'the defendant must actually have acted in a way which he knew to be unjustifiable and either intended to cause harm or at least acted without caring whether he caused harm or not'.[133] Since the prison officers had neither intended to cause distress 'or realized that they were acting without justification in asking the Wainwrights to strip'[134] they could not be liable. Even if an intention had been established, Lord Hoffmann doubted that a cause of action lay for intentionally causing distress as opposed to a recognised psychiatric illness.

However, the law in relation to vexations and disturbing behaviour has been strengthened by the Protection from Harassment Act 1997. This Act makes it a tort (as well as a crime) for a person to pursue a course of conduct amounting to harassment of another, and which he knows or ought to know amounts to harassment of another.[135] For this purpose, 'the person whose course of conduct is in question ought to know that it amounts to harassment of another if a reasonable person in possession of the same information would think the course of conduct amounted to harassment of another'.[136] It is a defence, among other things, for the defendant to show that 'in the particular circumstances the pursuit of the course of action was reasonable'.[137] A 'course of conduct' involves 'conduct on at least two occasions' and 'conduct' includes 'speech'.[138] The victim has the right to seek damages for '(among other things) any anxiety caused by the harassment and any financial loss resulting from the harassment'.[139] In addition, in the case of either an actual or an apprehended breach of this part of the Act, a court can grant an injunction to restrain the defendant from harassing the claimant.[140] If the terms of the injunction are broken, the claimant may seek a warrant for the arrest of the defendant.[141] If the defendant has committed a crime under either section 2 (harassment) or section 4 (the separate offence of 'putting people in fear of violence'), it can issue a restraining order prohibiting the defendant from 'doing anything described in the order'.[142]

The critical difference made by the Act is that a claim can be made for 'anxiety' falling short of a recognised category of psychiatric harm such as post-traumatic stress

132 [2004] 2 AC 406, 426.
133 *Ibid.* 134 *Ibid.*
135 Protection from Harassment Act 1997, s. 1(1), (2).
136 *Ibid.*, s. 1(2).
137 *Ibid.*, s. 1(3)(c).
138 *Ibid.*, s. 7.
139 *Ibid.*, s. 3(2).
140 *Ibid.*, s. 3(3).
141 *Ibid.*, s. 3(4)–(5). Breach of the injunction is also an offence: s. 3(6)–(9).
142 *Ibid.*, s. 5.

disorder. However, the claim will only lie if there is a course of conduct amounting to harassment. As Lord Hoffmann put it in *Wainwright*, 'the requirement of a course of conduct shows that Parliament was conscious that it might not be in the public interest to allow the law to be set in motion for one boorish incident'; he went on, 'it may be that the development of the common law should show similar caution'.[143] The practical effect of the judicial self-restraint shown in *Wainwright* is to increase the importance of the Act as a source of protection. Successful claims have been brought in relation to, among other things, a campaign of harassment waged by animal-rights activists against employees of a company carrying out medical research (although the company itself had no cause of action),[144] and intrusive police questioning, over a period of months, of the mother of a child who had allegedly been assaulted by the claimant's partner.[145] The practical value of the tort has also been enhanced by the ruling of the House of Lords in *Majrowski* v. *Guy's and St. Thomas's NHS Trust*,[146] to the effect that an employer may be vicariously liable for a breach of the Act committed by an employee in the course of their employment.

SELECT BIBLIOGRAPHY

Cane, P., '*Mens Rea* in Tort Law' [2000] *OJLS* 533.

Handford, P. R., 'Tort Liability for Threatening or Insulting Words' (1976) 54 *Can. BR* 563.

Kodilinye, G., 'False Imprisonment through Ministerial Officers: The Commonwealth Experience' (1979) 28 *ICLQ* 766.

North, P. M., 'Civil and Criminal Proceedings for Assault' (1966) 29 *MLR* 16.

Prosser, W. L., 'False Imprisonment: Consciousness of Confinement' (1955) 55 *Col. LR* 847.

Trindade, F. A., 'Some Curiosities of Negligent Trespass to the Person: A Comparative Study' (1971) 20 *ICLQ* 706.

—'Intentional Torts: Some Thoughts on Assault and Battery' (1982) 2 *OJLS* 211.

Turner, J. W. C., 'Assault at Common Law', in Radzinowicz, L., and Turner, J. W. C. (eds.), *The Modern Approach to Criminal Law* (1945), ch. 18.

Williams, G. L., 'Two Cases on False Imprisonment', in Holland, R. H. C., and Schwarzenberger, G. (eds.), *Law, Justice and Equity: Essays in Tribute to G. W. Keeton* (1967), ch. 5.

143 [2004] 2 AC 406, 426. See also the judgment of Hale LJ in *Wong* v. *Parkside Health NHS Trust* [2001] EWCA Civ. 1721.

144 *Daiichi* v. *Stop Huntingdon Animal Cruelty* [2004] 1 WLR 1503.

145 *KD* v. *Chief Constable of Hampshire* [2005] EWHC 2550.

146 [2006] 3 WLR 125; see further ch. 19, below.

10

MALICIOUS PROSECUTION

To succeed in an action for malicious prosecution the claimant must show: (1) that the defendant prosecuted him; (2) that the prosecution ended in the defendant's favour; (3) that there was no reasonable and probable cause for the prosecution; and (4) that the defendant was actuated by 'malice'. Damage is also a necessary ingredient. The interests protected by the tort were described by Holt CJ in *Savill* v. *Roberts*:[1] 'there are three sorts of damages, any one of which is sufficient to support this action. First, damage to [the claimant's] fame, if the matter whereof he be accused be scandalous. Second, to his person, whereby he is imprisoned. Third, to his property, whereby he is put to charges and expenses.' A further possibility is damage sustained through the seizure of the claimant's property. Damage to 'fame' appears to mean the harm done to reputation by charging a person with a crime of a dishonourable nature.[2] Damage to the person has been held to include the threat of imprisonment and not just actual imprisonment.[3] In *Gregory* v. *Portsmouth City Council* Lord Steyn commented that the tort is 'narrowly defined', for the following reasons:

> The fear is that a widely-drawn tort will discourage law enforcement: it may discourage not only malicious persons but honest citizens who would otherwise carry out their civic duties of reporting crime. In the result malevolent individuals must receive protection so that responsible citizens may have it in respect of the hazards of litigation. The tort of malicious prosecution is also defined against the backcloth that there are criminal sanctions, such as perjury, making false statements to the police, and wasting police time, which discourage the mischief under consideration. Moreover, the tort must be seen in the context of overlapping torts, such as defamation and malicious falsehood, which serve to protect interests of personality.[4]

We will now consider the ingredients of the tort.

[1] (1698) 12 Mod. 208; 88 ER 1267; see *Berry* v. *BTC* [1962] 1 QB 306.
[2] *Rayson* v. *South London Tramways Co.* [1893] 2 QB 324, *Wiffen* v. *Bailey* [1915] 1 KB 600.
[3] *Ibid.*
[4] [2000] 1 AC 419, 426.

1. THE DEFENDANT INITIATED A PROSECUTION

In false imprisonment the defendant acts directly to restrain the plaintiff; in malicious prosecution he does this indirectly by setting the official process in motion. Therefore the distinction between ministerial and judicial acts of officials which is relevant to false imprisonment is also relevant here.[5] That apart, the wrongful continuation of a prosecution after the defendant comes to know that it is baseless is sufficient, unless he informs the court of the facts which have come to his attention.[6]

For the purposes of this tort a criminal charge includes 'all indictments involving either scandal to reputation or the possible loss of liberty to the person'.[7] The tort may also extend to certain forms of abuse of civil process.[8] These include the malicious presentation of a winding-up order or petition in bankruptcy;[9] malicious execution against property;[10] malicious arrest, based on evidence in other proceedings;[11] and malicious procurement of a search warrant.[12] In *Gregory* v. *Portsmouth City Council*,[13] the House of Lords ruled that the tort did not apply where the plaintiff, a local councillor, was removed from membership of certain council committees after an inquiry found him guilty of the misuse of confidential information. Not only did the tort not extent to internal disciplinary proceedings of this kind; in Lord Steyn's view it should not be widened to cover types of civil claim in addition to those already well established, since 'any manifest injustices arising from groundless and damaging civil proceedings are either already adequately protected under other torts or are capable of being addressed by any necessary or desirable extensions of other torts'.[14] In particular, the torts of malicious falsehood and defamation were, he felt, more appropriate for protecting individuals against the negative consequences in terms of harm to the claimant's reputation.

Preferring a complaint is not sufficient by itself: the test is whether proceedings have reached a stage at which they damage the plaintiff.[15] Signing a charge sheet is not necessarily the start of a prosecution;[16] but in *Malz* v. *Rosen*[17] signing the charge sheet and

[5] See ch. 9, Section 4.

[6] *Tims* v. *John Lewis & Co. Ltd.* [1951] 2 KB 459, 472 (reversed on other grounds [1952] AC 676).

[7] *Quartz Hill Consolidated Gold Mining Co.* v. *Eyre* (1883) 11 QBD 674, 691 (Bowen LJ).

[8] According to Lord Steyn, giving the leading judgment of the House of Lords in *Gregory* v. *Portsmouth City Council* [2000] 1 AC 419, 427, there is no *separate* tort of malicious abuse of process, since, quoting J. G. Fleming, *The Law of Torts* (9th edn., 1998), cases involving civil process 'resemble the parent action too much to warrant special treatment'.

[9] *Chapman* v. *Pickersgill* (1762) 2 Wils. KB 145; 95 ER 734, *Johnson* v. *Emerson & Sparrow* (1872) LR 6 Ex. Ch. 329, *Quartz Hill Consolidated Gold Mining Co.* v. *Eyre* (1883) 11 QBD 674.

[10] *Clissold* v. *Cratchley* [1910] 2 KB 244.

[11] *Roy* v. *Prior* [1971] AC 470.

[12] *Elsee* v. *Smith* (1822) 1 D & R 97, *Everett* v. *Ribbands* [1952] 2 QB 191, 205, *Reynolds* v. *Commissioner of Police of the Metropolis* [1985] QB 881, 885, *Gibbs* v. *Rea* [1998] AC 786.

[13] [2000] 1 AC 419.

[14] *Ibid.*, 432.

[15] *Mohammed Amin* v. *Bannerjee* [1947] AC 322.

[16] *Austin* v. *Dowling* (1870) LR 5 CP 534.

[17] [1966] 1 WLR 1008, 1012–13.

being prepared to give evidence were held to be sufficient. The fact that the defendant was bound over to attend does not of itself indicate that he was the prosecutor.[18] Similarly, the preparation of a medical report at the behest of the police has been held not to amount to setting the legal process in motion.[19]

Normally, merely providing information to the prosecuting authorities would not be enough to give rise to liability. However, in circumstances where the facts in question could be known only to the defendant, and raise a matter of such seriousness that the prosecutor has no effective discretion, it is possible for the tort to be committed if the information was provided falsely and maliciously. This was the case in *Martin* v. *Watson*,[20] where the defendant maliciously made a groundless accusation of indecent exposure against the plaintiff who was subsequently prosecuted. Lord Keith of Kinkel, delivering the single judgment of the House of Lords, ruled that:

> Where an individual falsely and maliciously gives a police officer information indicating that some person is guilty of a criminal offence and states that he is willing to give evidence in court of the matters in question, it is properly to be inferred that he desires and intends that the person he names should be prosecuted. Where the circumstances are such that the facts relating to the alleged offence can be within the knowledge only of the complainant, as was the position here, then it becomes virtually impossible for the police officer to exercise any independent discretion or judgment, and if a prosecution is instituted by the police officer the proper view of the matter is that the prosecution has been procured by the complainant.[21]

It should also be noted that notwithstanding the introduction in 1985 of the Crown Prosecution Service[22] it is still possible for the police to be the prosecutors for the purposes of this tort, since they continue to have a role in determining the stage at which the proceedings may be said to cause damage to the plaintiff.

2. THE PROSECUTION FAILED

The prosecution must end in the claimant succeeding. This is a fundamental rule that is designed to avoid the retrial, by civil means, of the criminal action.[23] It does not matter how the proceedings ended in the claimant's favour. The magistrate's refusal to commit for trial will suffice, even if a new charge may then be brought.[24] Nor does it matter what the ground of acquittal was: it could be a 'technicality' not related to innocence or guilt on the merits[25] or it could be the discontinuance of the prosecution[26]

[18] *Brown* v. *Stradling* (1836) LJPC 295; cf. *Fitzjohn* v. *Mackinder* (1861) 9 CB (NS) 505; 142 ER 99.

[19] *Evans* v. *London Hospital Medical College* [1981] 1 WLR 184.

[20] [1996] 1 AC 74.

[21] *Ibid.*, 86–7.

[22] By virtue of the Prosecution of Offences Act 1985.

[23] *Gilding* v. *Eyre* (1861) 10 CB (NS) 592.

[24] *Delegal* v. *Highley* (1861) 3 Bing. NC 950; 132 ER 677.

[25] *Wicks* v. *Fentham* (1791) 4 TR 247, 248; 100 ER 1000.

[26] See the Canadian case of *Casey* v. *Automobiles Renault of Canada* (1965) 54 DLR (2d) 600.

or the quashing of the conviction on appeal. On the other hand, once there is no further appeal the fact of conviction will defeat the claimant, even if it is clear that the conviction was obtained by fraud.[27]

3. ABSENCE OF REASONABLE AND PROBABLE CAUSE

This is a formidable obstacle for the claimant to surmount; in effect he has to prove a negative. The following definition of reasonable and probable cause, given by Hawkins J in *Hicks* v. *Faulkner*,[28] was quoted with approval by Lord Atkin in *Herniman* v. *Smith*:[29] 'an honest belief in the guilt of the accused based upon a full conviction, founded upon reasonable grounds, of the existence of a state of circumstances, which, assuming them to be true, would reasonably lead any ordinarily prudent and cautious man, placed in the position of the accuser, to the conclusion that the person charged was probably guilty of the crime imputed'. In other words, there must be both an honest belief and objective facts on which to base it. As far as the defendant's belief is concerned, the question is 'did he honestly believe in the plaintiff's guilt?', not 'did he honestly believe that there was reasonable and probable cause?'[30] The defendant's knowledge of facts negating the plaintiff's guilt is relevant to the honesty of his belief,[31] as is taking legal advice, which may be evidence of an honest belief if all the relevant facts are made known to the legal adviser.[32] The same applies if the true facts were stated to the police, who then advised that an offence had been committed.[33] On the other hand, the mere fact that a prosecution has been initiated by the Director of Public Prosecutions does not of itself preclude an action for malicious prosecution: 'there may be cases where there has been, even by a responsible authority, the suppression of evidence which has led to a false view being taken by those who carried on a prosecution and by those who ultimately convicted'.[34] Nor is the conviction of the claimant at first instance—then quashed on appeal—necessarily evidence of reasonable and probable cause, since it could, for example, have been procured by perjured evidence which comes to light later.[35]

[27] *Basébé* v. *Matthews* (1867) LR 2 CP 684.

[28] (1878) 8 QBD 167, 171.

[29] [1938] AC 305, 316.

[30] *Tempest* v. *Snowdon* [1952] 1 KB 130, 137. The question whether reasonable and probable cause is shown is, in the end, a question of law for the judge: see *Herniman* v. *Smith* [1938] AC 305, 315 (Lord Atkin), *Glinski* v. *McIver* [1962] AC 726.

[31] *James* v. *Phelps* (1840) 11 A & E 483; 113 ER 499.

[32] *Hewlett* v. *Crutchley* (1813) 5 Taunt. 277; 128 ER 696.

[33] *Malz* v. *Rosen* [1966] 1 WLR 1008.

[34] *Riches* v. *Director of Public Prosecutions* [1973] 1 WLR 1019, 1026 (Stephenson LJ).

[35] *Herniman* v. *Smith* [1938] AC 305 has impliedly overruled the old case of *Reynolds* v. *Kennedy* (1784) 1 Wils. KB 232; 95 ER 591, on this point.

4. MALICE

Malice here refers to the defendant's motive, and includes any motive other than the desire to secure the ends of justice. The requirement is separate from the requirement of reasonable and probable cause; even though lack of a reasonable cause may be *evidence* of malice it is not conclusive.[36] The onus of proof of malice is on the claimant and it is a matter for the jury,[37] although if there is no evidence of a motive that is potentially malicious the judge will not permit the matter to go to the jury.[38]

In *Gibbs* v. *Rea*,[39] a case of maliciously procuring a search warrant, a majority of the Privy Council felt able to infer malice in a case where there was no evidence that the police officer in question had reasonable grounds for suspecting the plaintiff of any crime. If the defendant had persuaded a judge to issue a warrant by suggesting that there were grounds for suspicion when he knew there were none, 'to procure the warrants in that state of mind was to employ the court process for an improper purpose (such as simply a fishing expedition)'.[40] On that basis, the lower court (the Court of Appeal of the Cayman Islands) had been entitled to make a finding of malice. As the dissenting judgment of Lord Goff and Lord Hope makes clear, this comes close to equating malice with the separate requirement of an absence of reasonable cause for the procurement of the warrant. In two other recent cases where police searches have failed to find evidence to incriminate suspected criminals, *Keegan* v. *Chief Constable of Merseyside Police*[41] and *Connor* v. *Chief Constable of Merseyside Police*,[42] the courts have been reluctant to infer malice. *Keegan* was subsequently the subject of a claim for breach of Article 8 of the European Convention on Human Rights; the Strasbourg Court upheld the claim, ruling that it should be sufficient, in such a case, to show that the search warrant had been obtained in the absence of reasonable grounds.[43] This decision has highly significant implications for the scope of the liability of public authorities in the tort of negligence, suggesting, as it does, that the wide *de facto* immunity enjoyed by the police in respect of claims arising from the negligent exercise of their powers is not compatible with the Convention;[44] to that extent it may reduce the need for claimants to make out a case based on malice.

36 See *Wershof* v. *Metropolitan Police Commissioner* [1978] 3 All ER 540.

37 *Mitchell* v. *Jenkins* (1835) 5 B & Ad. 588, 595; 110 ER 908.

38 *Brown* v. *Hawkes* [1891] 2 QB 718.

39 [1998] AC 786.

40 [1998] AC 786, 800.

41 [2003] 1 WLR 936.

42 [2006] EWCA Civ. 1549.

43 *Keegan* v. *United Kingdom*, Application No. 28867/03, Judgment of 18 July 2006.

44 See our discussion in ch. 8, above.

SELECT BIBLIOGRAPHY

Harper, F. W., 'Malicious Prosecution, False Imprisonment and Defamation' (1937) 15 *Tex. LR* 157.

Shelbourn, C., 'Compensation for Detention' [1978] *Crim. LR* 22.

Winfield, P. H., *The History of Conspiracy and Abuse of Legal Procedure* (1921).

—*The Present Law of Abuse of Legal Procedure* (1921).

PART V

LAND, CHATTELS AND INTENTIONAL INTERFERENCE WITH ECONOMIC INTERESTS

11 Interference with Chattels
12 Land
13 Lesser Interferences with Land: Nuisance
14 Deceit
15 The Economic Torts

11

INTERFERENCE WITH CHATTELS

1. INTRODUCTION

The present law of trespass to chattels is governed by the Torts (Interference with Goods) Act 1977, which introduces a collective term 'wrongful interference with goods' to cover trespass, conversion, negligence and any other tort resulting in damage to goods or to an interest in goods.[1] The Act abolishes the tort of detinue,[2] but otherwise has little or no impact on the principles of liability developed by the common law: thus, the nomenclature and substantive scope of the common law claims remain significant to this day in understanding the legal rules in this area and their use should not be dismissed as 'old-fashioned' or obsolete.[3]

2. TRESPASS TO GOODS

Any direct interference with possession of goods amounts to a trespass. It appears that liability is strict, but there is some uncertainty over this. In the case of collisions on the highway the rule has long since evolved that even if the claimant sues in trespass, he has to prove negligence.[4] The same is true of trespass to the person, where it has even been suggested that the trespass will not lie for a non-intentional interference, with the result that the claimant must bring the action in negligence and prove both fault and damage.[5] In cases not involving collisions there is authority to suggest that as long as there is voluntary conduct directed at the thing in question, that is to say an intention in relation to the goods, the defendant is liable even though he thought the thing was his

1 Section 1.

2 Section 2(1). Except for one case, the scope of detinue had already been taken over by conversion, and that one case has now been made into a case of conversion: see below, Section 3.

3 W. V. H. Rogers, *Winfield & Jolowicz on Tort* (17th edn., 2006), para. 17–2, n. 16; cf. Longmore LJ in *HSBC Rail (UK) Ltd. v. Network Rail Infrastructure Ltd.* [2006] 1 WLR 643, at [1].

4 *Holmes v. Mather* (1875) 133 LT 361.

5 *Letang v. Cooper* [1965] 1 QB 232; see above, ch. 9, Section 1.

or did not realise that he was committing a trespass.[6] To this extent, liability is strict in the sense that absence of fault is no defence. Where, on the other hand, the defendant interferes unintentionally with the claimant's thing without being aware of its presence, he may escape liability altogether if he has not been negligent. In *National Coal Board* v. *J. E. Evans & Co. (Cardiff) Ltd.*[7] the defendants, without negligence on their part, damaged a cable belonging to the plaintiff which ran beneath land owned by a local authority. The presence of the cable was unknowable since the plaintiff's predecessors had laid it without notifying the landowner. The defendants consciously performed the act of digging a trench, but the court found in their favour on the basis of their lack of knowledge of the cable. This case appears to decide that liability is strict when the defendant knows of the presence of the thing, but based on fault if he neither knows nor could be expected to know.

It is not altogether clear whether liability is based on damage or whether the tort is actionable *per se*.[8] It may be possible to distinguish between deliberate touchings, which are actionable *per se*,[9] and unintended or careless acts of touching, which require damage.[10] If no damage is suffered damages will only be nominal,[11] unless the interference is carried out by agents of government in which case there is constitutional justification for awarding aggravated damages.[12] The recent *Transco* case[13] has further assumed that pure economic loss is recoverable under a claim for trespass to goods (albeit alongside a parallel claim in negligence).

The interference must be direct. Looking at a letter or listening in to a private conversation does not amount to a trespass.[14] On the other hand, it is not necessary to show that the thing was physically moved or transported; deliberate damage, if inflicted directly, will be a trespass.[15]

Since trespass is an invasion of possession, the possessor of the goods at the time is the person who has the right to sue. It is not easy to generalise from the numerous particular instances of possession. A bailee always has possession. When the bailment is terminable at will the bailor who can terminate the bailment at any time has an immediate right to possession; this right to immediate possession is treated as being

[6] *Wilson* v. *Lombank Ltd.* [1963] 1 WLR 1294.

[7] [1951] 2 KB 861. See also *Transco Plc* v. *United Utilities Water Plc* [2005] EWHC 2784 (QBD), where both negligence and trespass to goods were pleaded and found to be made out.

[8] In the recent *Transco* case (*ibid.*), the employee of a water company turned off the claimant's gas tap while conducting under street repairs. Damage was found (at [22]) by virtue of the loss suffered by preventing gas from flowing along that pipe: the claimant had expended large sums tracking down the problem and in compensating its customers for interrupted supply.

[9] *Leitch & Co.* v. *Leydon* [1931] AC 90, 106.

[10] *Everitt* v. *Martin* [1953] NZLR 298 and *Vine* v. *Waltham Forest LBC* [2000] 1 WLR 2383 (CA).

[11] *Kirk* v. *Gregory* (1876) 1 Ex. D 55 (one shilling).

[12] *Entick* v. *Carrington* (1765) 19 St. Tr. 1030; 95 ER 807.

[13] *Transco Plc* v. *United Utilities Water Plc* [2005] EWHC 2784 (QBD), at [18], [19] and [23].

[14] See *Malone* v. *Metropolitan Police Commissioner* [1979] Ch. 344, 374–6. Compare the Texan case of *Chair King Inc.* v. *GTE Mobilnet Inc.* 135 SW 2d 365 (2004), in which the court thought that sending junk faxes might constitute the tort of trespass.

[15] *Fouldes* v. *Willoughby* (1841) 8 M & W 540.

the same thing as possession itself.[16] In this situation the bailee at will can also sue.[17] If the bailee sues for the whole loss, the bailor is precluded from bringing an action.[18] Where, on the other hand, the bailment is for a period of time, the bailor has no immediate right of possession and only the bailee has the right to sue for trespass to the goods.[19] The right to possess is also treated as possession in the case of trustees, executors, and administrators and owners of franchises. As far as the employment relationship is concerned, the employee is normally said only to have 'custody' of the thing so that the employer retains possession, but there is some authority to suggest that the employee may also have the right to sue in trespass in certain instances.[20] Things attached to or beneath land are possessed by the landowner,[21] but things left lying loose on land fall into the possession of the person who picks them up.[22] Things lost continue for this purpose to be possessed by the loser.[23]

Interference with possession being the gist of trespass, a defence of *jus tertii*—to the effect that a third party has a better right than the claimant (except in a case where the defendant acts on behalf of, or with the authority of, that party)—was not available. The 1977 Act, section 8, now provides that in any action for wrongful interference with goods a defendant may show, in accordance with rules of court, that a named third party has a better right than the claimant. This is designed to prevent a defendant being doubly liable.[24] Rules of Court made under the Act[25] generally oblige a claimant to furnish particulars of his title and to identify any other person who, to his knowledge, has or claims an interest in the thing. The defendant may apply for directions on whether the third party so named should be joined to the action. The Act states that contributory negligence is no defence to proceedings based on *intentional* trespass to goods,[26] leaving open the possibility of the defence applying in cases of negligent interference.

Sections 8–22 of the Police and Criminal Evidence Act 1984 govern the powers of the police to search for and seize property.[27] A consideration of these provisions, however, lies outside the scope of this book.

[16] See *United States of America and Republic of France* v. *Dolfus Mieg et Cie SA and Bank of England* [1952] AC 582, 605 (Viscount Jowitt), *Towers & Co. Ltd.* v. *Gray* [1961] 2 QB 351, 361 (Lord Parker CJ).

[17] *Burton* v. *Hughes* (1824) 2 Bing. 173, 175; 130 ER 272.

[18] *The Winkfield* [1902] P 42, as modified by the 1977 Act, s. 8.

[19] *HSBC Rail (UK) Ltd.* v. *Network Rail Infrastucture Ltd.* [2006] 1 All ER 343 (CA), because the bailor's right in such circumstances was a bare proprietary right carrying with it no right to possession: the bailor may only claim where he can prove permanent injury to his reversionary proprietary interest, which was not established by the claimant in this case.

[20] See generally *Meux* v. *Great Eastern Railway Co.* [1895] 2 QB 387.

[21] *Elwes* v. *Brigg Gas Co.* (1886) 33 Ch. D 562, *South Staffordshire Water Co.* v. *Sharman* [1896] 2 QB 44, *City of London Corp.* v. *Appleyard* [1963] 1 WLR 982.

[22] *Bridges* v. *Harkesworth* (1851) 15 Jur. 1079, *Parker* v. *British Railways Board* [1982] QB 1004; cf. the different approach of criminal law: *R* v. *Foley* (1889) 17 Cox 142 (Ir.); 93 ER 379.

[23] *R* v. *Thurborn* (1849) 1 Den. 387; 169 ER 293.

[24] Section 7(2). It will also normally restrict the damages payable to claimants with a limited interest in the goods to the value of that interest.

[25] RSC Ord. 15, r. 10A (SI No. 1978/579).

[26] Section 11(1).

[27] For a recent discussion of these provisions see *R* v. *Chesterfield Justices, ex parte Bramley* [2000] QB 576; [2000] 1 All ER 411 (esp. at 587–8 on the use of an action for trespass to goods to allow a judge to determine whether or not legal professional privilege had validly been claimed in relation to certain seized documents).

3. CONVERSION

The gist of conversion (known originally as trover) is any dealing with another's property in a way which amounts to a denial of his right over it, or an assertion of a right inconsistent with his right, by wrongfully taking, detaining or disposing of it. The defendant does not have to assert ownership as such or intend to acquire the thing for himself: the point is that the defendant's conduct must amount to 'so extensive an encroachment on the rights of the owner as to exclude him from use and possession of the goods'.[28] For example, in *Tear* v. *Freebody*[29] the defendant took certain goods of the plaintiff with the intention of taking a lien over them; this was held to be conversion. On the other hand, a case where there was trespass but no conversion was *Fouldes* v. *Willoughby*:[30] the defendant wrongfully refused to carry two horses of the plaintiff after the defendant had boarded his ferry and proceeded to take the horses ashore when the plaintiff refused to do so. This amounted to an unjustified interference with the plaintiff's property but not a denial of his right of ownership.

In order to be able to sue, the claimant must have the right to any one of ownership,[31] possession, or the immediate right to possess,[32] or a lien or equitable title;[33] however, a mere contractual right will not suffice.[34] A reversionary interest may become a right to immediate possession if the act of conversion by the possessor is inconsistent with the terms on which he holds the possession.[35] The finder of a chattel gets possession of it by taking it and retaining it; the question is whether he has a better right than anyone else. A person with a prior right to possession will defeat one whose right is acquired later in time. The finder therefore has a better right than total strangers and those whose rights are derived from him. In *Armory* v. *Delamirie*[36] a chimney-sweep's boy who found

28 *Kuwait Airways Corp.* v. *Iraqi Airways Co. (Nos. 4 and 5)* [2002] 2 AC 883 (HL) at [39] (per Lord Nicholls).

29 (1858) 4 CB (NS) 228.

30 (1841) 8 M & W 540.

31 *A* v. *Leeds Teaching Hospital NHS Trust (Re Organ Retention Group Litigation)* [2005] QB 506: no such right of ownership or right to possession existed with regard to the organs of the children who had died once the post-mortem had been completed.

32 *The Winkfield* [1902] AC 42. See *Smith (Administrator of Cosslett (Contractors) Ltd.)* v. *Bridgend CC* [2001] 3 WLR 1347, which emphasises that this right to immediate possession must exist at the time of the conversion. Thus, although no such right was held by the insolvent contractor when it attempted to enter the defendant's land to retrieve machinery, there *was* such a right at the time when that machinery was disposed of (due to the intervention of the administrator and the impact of s. 395 of the Companies Act 1985) and so a claim in conversion was made out.

33 *International Factors Ltd.* v. *Rodriguez* [1979] QB 35, although note the application of the *dicta* in that case—concerning an equitable right to property which was *not* in possession—have since been rejected in *MCC Proceeds Ltd.* v. *Lehman Brothers* [1998] 4 All ER 675 and subsequent cases have followed *MCC* (see, e.g., *Hounslow LBC* v. *Jenkins* [2004] EWHC 217 (Ch), which emphasised that a common law possessory title was required to sustain an action in conversion (at [12] and [15]).

34 *Rogers* v. *Kennay* (1846) 9 QB 592 and *OBG Ltd.* v. *Allan* [2005] QB 762. The recent case of *On Demand Information plc (In Administrative Receivership)* v. *Michael Gerson (Finance) plc* [2001] 1 WLR 155 (CA) (reversed on other grounds [2002] 2 WLR 919 (HL)) illustrates that a careful examination of the precise consequences of a contract is required, before such rights are dismissed as 'merely' contractual.

35 *Union Transport Finance Ltd.* v. *British Car Auctions Ltd.* [1978] 2 All ER 385, 389.

36 (1721) 1 Stra. 505; 93 ER 664.

a jewel (possibly in a chimney) succeeded in an action for conversion against a jeweller to whom he had handed the jewel for valuation and who refused to return it to him. The owner could not be found.[37] This reasoning has been held to apply even to a stolen car, which had been in the claimant's possession when taken by police in the course of investigations: *Costello* v. *Chief Constable of Derbyshire*.[38] It was acknowledged by the claimant that the car was stolen (although the claimant himself had not stolen it), but it could not be shown who was the true owner and the claimant did not have to rely upon any specific illegal transaction to establish his prior possession of the car. Thus, the refusal of the police to return the car amounted to conversion. Whether or not this conclusion can survive after the entry into force of the Proceeds of Crime Act 2002 (and in particular its s. 329, which establishes it as a criminal offence for a person to be in possession of property that amounts to a benefit derived from his criminal conduct) remains to be seen, and will depend upon the use by the Assets Recovery Agency of its extensive powers to take civil proceedings to recover such property.[39]

Liability in conversion is strict, in the sense that all that is needed is an intention to do the act in question and not an intention to bring about the consequences, namely the interference with the claimant's title. Ignorance or mistake is no defence, as the numerous cases involving sales by rogues and others who have obtained the goods by deception indicate: the original owner can always sue the third party in conversion as long as title has not passed to the rogue.[40] Similarly, an auctioneer who sells and delivers an article on behalf of a client who has no title will be liable to the owner.[41]

There must be an act of some kind; an omission will not suffice. The act need not be a sale as such. In *Ashby* v. *Tolhurst*[42] the attendant at a car park allowed a stranger to take away the plaintiff's car. His employers were held not liable for conversion, for although the attendant had been negligent, he had not done any act.[43] Similarly, a mere contract of sale of a third person's property, without delivery having taken place, does not

37 The position of a finder against the owner or occupier of land will depend on the latter's implied or express intention to retain a better right than those who come on to his land: see *Bridges* v. *Hawkesworth* (1851) 15 Jur. 1079, *Parker* v. *British Airways Board* [1982] QB 1004.

38 [2001] 1 WLR 1437 (CA), relying upon *Webb* v. *Chief Constable of Merseyside* [2000] QB 427 (CA) (noted by D. Fox, 'Enforcing Possessory Title to a Stolen Car' [2002] *CLJ* 27 and G. Battersby, 'Acquiring Title by Theft' (2002) 65 *MLR* 603). *Costello* has been followed by subsequent judgments in *Gough* v. *Chief Constable of the West Midlands* [2004] EWCA Civ. 206 and *Settelen* v. *Metropolitan Police Commissioner* [2004] EWHC 217.

39 For details on this legislation and its application, see E. Rees QC and R. Fisher, *Blackstone's Guide to the Proceeds of Crime Act 2002* (2nd edn., 2005).

40 E.g. *Hollins* v. *Fowler* (1875) LR 7 HL 757. The doctrine of fundamental mistake in contract law may frequently operate to prevent the rogue taking good title: *Cundy* v. *Lindsay* (1878) 3 App. Cas. 459; cf. *Lewis* v. *Averay* [1982] 1 QB 198.

41 *Consolidated Co.* v. *Curtis* [1892] 1 QB 495. And it is for the auctioneer to prove that he has acted in good faith and without notice of the fact that the person who had put the goods up for auction was not the true owner: *Marcq* v. *Christie Manson & Woods Ltd. (t/a Christie's)* [2002] 4 All ER 1005 (QBD), upheld on appeal: [2004] QB 286 (CA). Naturally, if the true owner had claimed the painting from the auctioneers earlier, then the auctioneers would have been on notice, and a decision nevertheless to return to the painting to the person who had put it up for auction *would* have amounted to conversion.

42 [1937] 2 KB 242.

43 There might, instead, have been liability for breach of contract or breach of occupier's duty.

constitute conversion either by the buyer or by the seller:[44] section 11(3) of the Act now declares that 'denial of title is not of itself conversion'. An exception to the requirement for an act as well as a denial of title is in the case of a bailee who, in breach of his duty to the bailor, allows the thing to be lost or destroyed. This used to give rise to liability in detinue as opposed to conversion, but section 2 of the Act abolishes detinue and subsumes this case into conversion. It now seems to be the case that if there is neither loss nor destruction of a thing but merely detention, there is no liability as there was previously in detinue. But this would be so only where possession was obtained without some wrong being committed and would not apply in the case of a bailee who does not have a right to possess as against the bailor once the latter demands the return of the goods.[45]

Acts denying title may assume many forms, the most obvious being a taking of the thing. Although taking possession is not essential, should this occur then conversion could overlap with trespass: 'the distinction between the actions of trespass and trover [or conversion] is well settled: the former is founded on possession; the latter on property'.[46] Thus a mere taking, which does not amount to a denial of the claimant's title, is a trespass, not conversion; so is mere possession. This may matter, as the means of computing damages will differ according to which tort is committed. Despite the abolition of detinue, however, detention could amount to conversion if it is adverse to the claimant. In *Howard E. Perry & Co. Ltd.* v. *British Railways Board*[47] the defendant carrier held the plaintiffs' steel in depots. During a strike by steelworkers the defendants, fearing sympathy-strike action by their own employees if the plaintiffs were allowed to remove the steel, refused to let them do so. This was held to be conversion: once a bailee refuses to restore goods on the bailor's demand he commits conversion,[48] even though without such a demand he would only be liable for breach of the contract of bailment.

Mere receipt of the thing may amount to conversion. With regard to pledge, section 11(2) states that 'receipt of goods by way of pledge is conversion if the delivery of the goods is conversion'. Apart from pledge, the case of the 'involuntary bailee' deserves attention. No person can be regarded as a bailee, involuntary or otherwise, if he is unaware that he has the thing.[49] An involuntary bailee is not liable for the loss of the thing through mere negligence, nor for making a reasonable attempt to return it to its owner.[50] He is only liable if he intentionally damages or destroys it, although even here he will not be liable for disposing of perishable goods.[51]

44 *Douglas Valley Finance Co. Ltd.* v. *S. Hughes (Hirers) Ltd.* [1969] 1 QB 738.

45 See below.

46 *Ward* v. *Macauley* (1791) 4 Term Rep. 489, 490; 100 ER 1135 (Lord Kenyon CJ).

47 [1980] 1 WLR 1375.

48 *Clayton* v. *Le Roy* [1911] 2 KB 1031.

49 *Lethbridge* v. *Phillips* (1819) 2 Stark. 544; 171 ER 731.

50 *Elvin and Powell Ltd.* v. *Pummer Roddis Ltd.* (1933) 50 TLR 158.

51 Under the Unsolicited Goods and Services Act 1971 the recipient may, in certain circumstances, treat unsolicited goods as unconditional gifts after six months or thirty days from notice to the sender, so long as the sender does not take possession in the meantime and the recipient does not unreasonably refuse him permission to do so.

Conversion can also consist of wrongful delivery of possession of a thing to a third party. In *Hollins* v. *Fowler*[52] a broker who had received goods obtained fraudulently without notice of the fraud was liable in conversion to the owner even though he acted in good faith. *A fortiori* a person is liable if he confers a good title on the third party, for example by a sale in market overt or by sale or delivery by a seller in possession.[53] However, a distinction has to be drawn between these cases and those in which the defendant acts purely in an instrumental capacity, innocently and without notice of the claimant's right. For example, an innocent depositee of the claimant's article will not be liable simply because he restores it to the depositor.[54] Nor in all probability will an innocent holder of a thing be liable for delivering the thing to a third party at the order of the person from whom he received it, provided he is unaware that such delivery is in pursuance of a transaction that could affect title and he acts purely in an instrumental capacity. As Blackburn J said in *Hollins* v. *Fowler*:

> On principle, one who deals with goods at the request of the person who has actual custody of them in the bona fide belief that the custodian is the true owner, or has the authority of the true owner, should be excused for what he does if the act is of such nature as would be excused if done by the authority of the person in possession, if he was the finder of the goods or entrusted with their custody.[55]

Apart from taking or delivering possession unlawfully, the abuse of possession could also be conversion. For this reason a carrier (bailee) who goes against instructions (for example, by delivering to the consignee after notice of stoppage *in transitu*) commits conversion.[56] In *Moorgate Mercantile Co. Ltd.* v. *Finch and Read* [57] F hired a car under a hire-purchase agreement and lent it to R, who transported goods in it which had not cleared customs. The customs authorities forfeited and sold the car. F having disappeared, the hire-purchase company recovered damages for conversion from R, who was deemed to have realised that forfeiture was likely to result from his conduct. If a thing is destroyed, that could amount to conversion, but if it is simply damaged it is possible that the action must lie in trespass. Changing a thing's character, for example, making wine out of grapes (as in the Roman *specificatio*) would amount to conversion.[58]

[52] (1875) LR 7 HL 757. See the recent example of *Motis Exports Ltd.* v. *Dampskibsselskabet AF 1912, Aktieselskab* [1999] 1 Lloyd's Rep. 837, where delivery by a bailee to a person who presented a forged bill of lading was held *prima facie* to amount to conversion even where the shipowner had acted innocently and without any negligence.

[53] Sale of Goods Act 1979, ss. 22, 24.

[54] *Hollins* v. *Fowler* (1875) LR 7 HL 757, 767 (Blackburn J).

[55] (1875) LR 7 HL 757, 766. See also 18th Report of the Law Reform Committee, *Conversion and Detinue* (Cmnd. 4774, 1971), paras. 46–50.

[56] *The Tigress* (1863) 32 LJ Adm. 97, *Booth Steamship Co. Ltd.* v. *Cargo Fleet Iron Co. Ltd.* [1916] 2 KB 570.

[57] [1961] 1 QB 701.

[58] But it may also entitle the original owner to claim that he owns the resulting product. See, most recently, the judgment of Moore-Bick J in *Glencore International AG* v. *Metro Trading International Inc.* [2001] 1 Lloyd's Rep. 284 (QBD), at 328: 'the owner of goods which are wrongfully taken and used to make a new commodity can recover them from the wrongdoer, even in their altered form, if he can identify them in that new commodity and show that it is wholly or substantially composed of them'. See the case note by J. Ulph, 'Retaining Proprietary Rights at Common Law through Mixtures and Changes' [2001] *LMCLQ* 449.

As between co-owners, each owns the whole so that one co-owner is guilty of conversion if he destroys the goods or disposes of them in a way that gives good title to the entire property, or destroys the other's interest.[59] This includes anything that is equivalent to destruction, including forceful exclusion of the other from the enjoyment of possession or of the fruits of the property.

Defences include the exercise of a right of distress, which is discussed below,[60] and *jus tertii* under section 8 of the Act. A bailee is estopped from denying his bailor's lack of title on the grounds that he either never had it or has lost it.[61] But under section 8 the bailee may seek to join to the action a third party who he believes has better title than the bailor, in order that the third party may assert this superior right. Consent is a defence but contributory negligence is not, by virtue of section 11(1) of the Act. Prior to the 1977 Act, the House of Lords appeared to suggest in *Moorgate Mercantile Co. Ltd.* v. *Twitchings*[62] that there could be, in principle, a duty of care on the part of the claimant owner to the defendant third party to register the hire-purchase agreement, and he would be estopped from asserting his title if he negligently failed to do so. It is unclear whether the possibility of estoppel survives as a means of outflanking section 11(1). The possibility of contributory negligence is retained in the specific case of actions against banks.[63]

The traditional remedy for conversion is an action for damages in which the claimant recovers the market value of the thing and any special loss that has resulted.[64] As one would expect, there is also a duty on the claimant to mitigate his loss.[65] It had recently been held that the test for remoteness of damage in conversion is one of reasonable foreseeability;[66] thus, a possible claim to recover damages for the claimant's inability to deliver the converted goods under a contract of sale already concluded with a third party would only succeed if the defendant were aware of the existence of that contract.[67] However, in *Kuwait Airways* v. *Iraqi Airways (Nos. 4 and 5)*,[68] the majority of the House of Lords followed Lord Nicholls in distinguishing between claims for consequential loss

59 Section 10 of the 1977 Act. 60 See below, ch. 12.

61 See *Biddle* v. *Bond* (1865) 6 B & S 225; 122 ER 1179, *Rogers, Sons & Co.* v. *Lambert & Co.* [1891] 1 QB 318.

62 [1977] AC 890. 63 By virtue of the Banking Act 1979, s. 47.

64 *BBMB Finance (Hong Kong) Ltd.* v. *Eda Holdings Ltd.* [1991] 2 All ER 129; see also *IBL Ltd.* v. *Coussens* [1991] 2 All ER 133. The recent House of Lords judgment in *Kuwait Airways Corp.* v. *Iraqi Airways Co. (Nos. 4 and 5)* [2002] 2 AC 883 (HL) provides detailed discussion of the application of the 'but-for' test as a threshold causation issue: 'was the wrongful conduct a necessary condition of the occurrence of the harm or loss[?]' (para. 73, per Lord Nicholls). In the context of conversion, this test 'calls for consideration of whether the plaintiff would have suffered the loss in question had he retained his goods and not been unlawfully deprived of them by the defendant. The test calls for a comparison between the owner's position had he retained his goods and his position having been deprived of his goods by the defendant. Loss which the owner would have suffered even if he had retained the goods is not loss "caused" by the conversion. The defendant is not liable for such loss' (at [83], per Lord Nicholls). See P. Cane, 'Causing Conversion' (2002) 118 *LQR* 544.

65 See, e.g., *Greer* v. *Alstons Engineering Sales and Services Ltd.* [2003] UKPC 46.

66 *Saleslease Ltd.* v. *Davis* [1999] 1 WLR 1644 (CA), *Kuwait Airways Corp.* v. *Iraqi Airways Co. (Nos. 4 and 5)* [2001] 3 WLR 1117 (CA) and *Sandeman Coprimar SA* v. *Transportes Integrales SL* [2003] QB 1270 (CA).

67 *Saleslease Ltd.* v. *Davis* [1999] 1 WLR 1644 (Schiemann LJ dissenting on the application of this test to the facts). Of course, such a claim would be attractive only if the pre-existing contract were concluded at a price above what the available market rate would be at the time of the conversion.

68 [2002] 2 AC 883 (HL) (noted by P. Cane, 'Causing Conversion' (2002) 118 *LQR* 544).

where the defendant has acted dishonestly and those where he has not. Where dishonesty could be shown, their Lordships required the application of the test used in deceit: the defendant would be held liable for all of the consequences which directly and naturally flowed from the wrongful conduct.[69] There is a special rule that where a document such as a cheque or other negotiable instrument represents a sum of money, the measure of damages will be that sum and not the value of the piece of paper.[70] Where damages paid represent the whole of the claimant's interest, or such sum as has been agreed in settlement, payment extinguishes his title which then vests in the defendant.[71] Because of the open-ended nature of the conversion and the multiple interests that may operate in respect of a particular article, the statute seeks to protect a defendant against double liability by requiring the claimant to identify any other person who, to his knowledge, has an interest in the goods.[72] The Act also apportions damages between the different claimants, with provision for restitution to the defendant in the event of unjust enrichment,[73] and also requires the claimant to make an allowance to an innocent improver or to a subsequent transferee from such a person.[74] Finally, it has recently been held[75] that exemplary damages may also be available in appropriate circumstances,[76] where: 'the tortious conduct persisted in with complete indifference to the harm it was causing and in defiance of repeated interventions by the law [and] was calculated (in the sense . . . of likely) to make a profit beyond what would probably be recovered in cash or in kind by legal process'. In such circumstances, deterrence of the criminal conduct was justified by awarding exemplary damages beyond the loss incurred by the claimant to recover the profit made by the thief.

Self-help is permissible as long as it is peaceful and involves no more force than is reasonable in the event of opposition, although given the great sensitivity of such a reasonableness test to the relevant context, certainty as to exactly how far someone can go in exercising this right is notoriously difficult to establish.[77] The common law did not possess a real action for the recovery of chattels to correspond to the Roman law *vindicatio*, but specific restitution could be provided for in equity. Section 3(2) and (3) now provide for the court to grant specific delivery and damages at its discretion, with the possibility also of an interlocutory order for delivery pending the full trial.[78] If the

[69] In order to place the *Kuwait Airways* case in the wider context of causation in tort law, see our discussion of it in ch. 4, Section 2, above.

[70] See *Lloyds Bank Ltd.* v. *The Chartered Bank of India, Australia and China* [1929] 1 KB 40, 55–6 (Scrutton LJ). However, this will only apply where the negotiable instrument remains a valid security at the time of conversion: *Smith* v. *Lloyds TSB Bank plc* [2001] QB 541 (CA) (noted by C. Hare, 'Loss Allocation for Materially Altered Cheques' [2001] *CLJ* 35). Thus, if a cheque has undergone unauthorised alterations then it will be null and void under s. 64(1) of the Bills of Exchange Act 1882 and no cause of action in conversion will lie for the sum represented.

[71] Section 5.

[72] Section 8.

[73] Section 7.

[74] Section 6.

[75] *Borders (UK) Ltd.* v. *Commissioner of Police of the Metropolis* [2005] EWCA Civ. 197.

[76] See, generally, our discussion in ch. 25, Section 2(d), below.

[77] Most modern English cases relate to attempts to free cars from wheel-clamps, causing damage to said clamp. Facing a prosecution for criminal damage, defendants have relied upon recaption of their car as a lawful excuse. Usually, the car has in fact not been lawfully parked in any case, thus disentitling any defence of lawful excuse: see, e.g., *R* v. *Mitchell* [2003] EWCA Crim. 2188, [2004] RTR 14.

[78] Section 4.

court does not order this, the claimant can choose whether to claim damages only (including consequential damages) or to ask for specific delivery, in which case the defendant has the alternative of paying the value of the goods and any consequential damages.

The common law had a remedy known as *replevin* in a case where an article was taken out of another's possession by a trespassory act for the purpose of distraining it for rent, rates, damage feasant or some other similar reason. *Replevin* allowed the latter to regain provisional possession pending a decision on title. Section 4 of the Act, by providing for interim possession pending a decision as to title, appears to have left little scope for the common-law *replevin* action whose scope is, as a result, unclear.

4. NEGLIGENCE

Wrongful interference overlaps with the tort of negligence. Section 1(a) of the Act extends its scope to 'negligence in so far as that results in damage to goods or to an interest in goods'. This implies that the procedural and remedial provisions of the Act could apply in cases of carelessly inflicted damage. In practice there is unlikely to be much overlap, as the court is unlikely to exercise its discretion in favour of an order for specific delivery in a case of mere negligence.

SELECT BIBLIOGRAPHY

BURNETT, H. W., 'Conversion by an Involuntary Bailee' (1960) 76 *LQR* 364.

DERHAM, D. P., 'Conversion by Wrongful Disposal as Between Co-Owners' (1952) 68 *LQR* 507.

ELLIOTT, J. H. S., 'Damages in Detinue and Conversion' (1951) 9 *NILQ* 157.

FLEMING, J. G., 'Tort Liability for Damage to Hire Purchase Goods' (1958) 32 *Aust. LJ* 267.

GOLDRING, J., 'The Negligence of the Plaintiff in Conversion' (1977) 11 *MULR* 91.

GOODHART, A. L., 'Three Cases on Possession', in Goodhart, A. L., *Essays in Jurisprudence and the Common Law* (1937), ch. 4.

GORDON, D. M., 'Anomalies in the Law of Conversion' (1955) 71 *LQR* 346.

GUEST, A. G., 'Accession and Confusion in the Law of Hire-Purchase' (1964) 27 *MLR* 505.

LAW REFORM COMMITTEE, *Conversion and Detinue*, 18th Report (Cmnd. 4774, 1971).

MARSHALL, O. R., 'The Problem of Finding' (1949) 2 *CLP* 68.

MILSOM, S. F. C., 'Not Doing is No Trespass' [1954] *CLJ* 105.

PALMER, N. E., 'The Application of the Torts (Interference with Goods) Act 1977 to Actions in Bailment' (1978) 41 *MLR* 629.

—'The Abolition of Detinue' [1981] *Conv. (NS)* 62.

PATON, G. W., *Bailment in the Common Law* (1952).

PEDEN, J. R., 'Measure of Damages in Conversion and Detinue' (1970) 44 *Aust. LJ* 65.

PROSSER, W. L., 'The Nature of Conversion' (1957) 42 *Cornell LR* 168.

SIMPSON, A. W. B., 'The Introduction of the Action on the Case for Conversion' (1959) 74 *LQR* 364.

SLATER, R. B., '*Accessio*, *Specificatio* and *Confusio*: Three Skeletons in the Closet' (1959) 37 *Can. BR* 597.

TAY, A. E. S., 'Possession and the Modern Law of Finding' (1964) 4 *Syd. LR* 383.

TETTENBORN, A. M., 'Damages in Conversion: The Exception or the Anomaly?' [1993] *CLJ* 128.

THORNLEY, J. W. A., 'Transfer of Title to Chattels by Non-Owners' [1966] *CLJ* 186.

—'New Torts for Old or Old Torts Refurbished?' [1977] *CLJ* 248.

WARREN, E. H., 'Qualifying as a Plaintiff in an Action for Conversion' (1936) 49 *Harv. LR* 1084.

12

LAND*

1. TRESPASS TO LAND *QUAERE CLAUSUM FREGIT*

Any direct interference with land in the possession of another is trespass and is actionable *per se*.[1] It is not a crime except where statute has made it so.[2] 'Interference' may take the form of entering land or part of it, or of remaining there after the withdrawal of permission, or of dispossessing the occupant. It also implies that the defendant acted without the permission of the occupier; permission is therefore a defence and is considered below.

The distinction between direct and indirect or consequential interference is a legacy of the old distinction between trespass and case: direct intrusion constituted trespass, consequential interference with the occupier's use and enjoyment amounted at best to nuisance. In a Canadian case, *Mann* v. *Saulnier*,[3] a fence properly constructed by the defendant, and which when constructed did not intrude into the plaintiff's land, began to lean over it after a while. This was held to be a nuisance, not trespass, since it was the consequence of erecting the fence. What is 'direct' and 'consequential' is no more clear-cut here than it is with trespass to the person, however. In *Gregory* v. *Piper*[4] a quantity of rubbish was dumped near the plaintiff's wall without touching it. When it dried out, some of it rolled up against the wall and this was held to be trespass. In contrast to this is *Southport Corporation* v. *Esso Petroleum Co. Ltd.*[5] The master of an oil tanker, which had been stranded in an estuary, jettisoned a quantity of oil to lighten the vessel. This drifted ashore and polluted the foreshore of the plaintiff. Denning LJ in the Court of Appeal and Lords Radcliffe and Tucker in the House of Lords treated the damage as consequential;[6] Morris LJ in the Court of Appeal treated it as direct.[7]

* This chapter draws on parts of the text prepared by R. W. M. Dias for the 2nd edn. of this book.

1 *Entick* v. *Carrington* (1765) 19 St. Tr. 1029, 1066; 95 ER 807. However, recent cases show that, in the absence of any actual damage suffered by the claimant, damages for such a trespass that causes no actual damage to the claimant's land are likely to be nominal only: see *Nelson* v. *Nicholson, The Independent*, 22 Jan. 2001 and *BRB (Residuary) Ltd.* v. *Cully* (QBD (T & CC), unreported, 1 Aug. 2001).

2 See the Criminal Law Act 1977, as modified by the Criminal Justice and Public Order Act 1994 (esp. s. 68, which introduces an offence of 'aggravated trespass', and ss. 70 and 71, which created the concept of 'trespassory assemblies'; see the discussion of *DPP* v. *Jones* [1999] 2 AC 240 below on trespassory assemblies on the highway).

3 (1959) 19 DLR (2d) 130.

4 (1829) 9 B & C 591.

5 [1954] 2 QB 182; [1956] AC 218.

6 [1954] 2 QB 182, 196; [1956] AC 218, 242, 244.

7 [1954] 2 QB 182, 204.

Trespass can be committed in various ways. Entry on to land is simply the most obvious example; placing things on land or inducing animals[8] to enter are also potentially trespassory. As was stated in *Gregory* v. *Piper*,[9] 'if a single stone had been put against the wall it would have been sufficient'. Interference with possession in other ways may also amount to trespass: a recent example is the discharge of water into the flowing watercourse of another.[10] With regard to entry into the airspace, a distinction has to be drawn between entry within the area of ordinary user and outside it. An illustration of the former is *Kelsen* v. *Imperial Tobacco Co. (of Great Britain and Ireland) Ltd.*,[11] in which an advertisement sign projected into the airspace above the plaintiff's shop; this was held to be a trespass. Likewise, in *Laiqat* v. *Majid* the installation on the defendants' property of an extractor fan which protruded 75 centimetres into the claimants' garden at a height of 4.5 metres was held, on appeal, to amount to a trespass.[12] A trespass is also committed when the jib of a crane swings over the claimant's airspace, even though it causes no damage of either a physical or economic kind. An injunction will normally be available to protect the claimant's rights in his property.[13] By contrast, in *Bernstein of Leigh* v. *Skyviews & General Ltd.*[14] the defendant's activity took place above the area of ordinary user and was held not to be a trespass. Here, an aircraft flew hundreds of feet above the plaintiff's property in order to take photographs of it. In connection with aircraft, the provisions of the Civil Aviation Act 1982 should be noted. Section 76(1) states that it is not a trespass for aircraft to fly at a reasonable height having regard to wind, weather and all the circumstances prevailing at the time. Section 76(2) states that loss or damage caused by civil (not military) aircraft, or by a person or article carried on one, while in flight or landing or taking-off, is to be compensatable without proof of fault. In the litigation stemming from the December 1999 crash of a Korean Airlines flight shortly after take-off from Stansted Airport, coming down in Hatfield Forest near Great Hallingbury in Hertfordshire, it was clarified[15] that this loss or damage included psychiatric harm (albeit subject to the application of ordinary common law rules regarding foreseeability and remoteness of damage as they apply to such injuries).[16]

Continuing trespass, usually by things placed on land, is actionable from day to day;[17] and this is so even if the original claimant transfers the land to a third party, who is then entitled to sue for the continuation.[18] If a thing is lawfully on land to begin with,

8 But not bees, according to *Tutton* v. *A. D. Walter Ltd.* [1986] QB 61.

9 (1829) 9 B & C 591, 594; 109 ER 220; see also *Westripp* v. *Baldock* [1939] 1 All ER 279.

10 *British Waterways Board* v. *Severn Trent Water* [2002] Ch. 25 (CA), at [38]. Thus, on the expiry of a previous licence and in the absence of any statutory authority for the defendant's act, the discharge of water from its sewerage operations into the claimant's canals amounted to a trespass.

11 [1957] 2 QB 334.

12 [2005] EWHC 1305, [2005] 26 EGCS 130.

13 *Woollerton & Wilson Ltd.* v. *Richard Costain Ltd.* [1970] 1 WLR 411, *Anchor Brewhouse Developments Ltd.* v. *Berkly House (Docklands Developments) Ltd.* [1987] 2 EGLR 187; P. Cane, *Tort Law and Economic Interests* (2nd edn., 1996), 52–4.

14 [1978] QB 479.

15 *Glen* v. *Korean Airlines Co. Ltd.* [2003] QB 1386, at [14], [18] and [33].

16 *Ibid.*, at [35]–[39]; see our discussion of the common-law requirements in ch. 3, Section 3(b), above.

17 *Holmes* v. *Wilson* (1839) 10 A & E 503; 113 ER 190.

18 *Hudson* v. *Nicholson* (1839) 5 M & W 437; 151 ER 185.

but then the permission to keep it there has been withdrawn, continuation of its presence thereafter is a trespass.[19] The position is the same if a person's permission to be on land is withdrawn, and if he fails to leave within a reasonable time he then becomes a trespasser. Trespass can be committed to the subsoil. Normally, possession of the surface carries with it the subsoil and the things embedded in it.[20] It is possible, however, for one person to possess the surface and another to possess the minerals beneath, so that there could be trespass to both or to the owner of the minerals alone.[21]

With regard to the highway, it is not trespass against the owner of the subsoil for persons to pass along the highway in the course of ordinary passage and take part in activities incidental to that, but it is trespass if that purpose is exceeded. In *Hickman* v. *Maisey*[22] the defendant committed trespass by using the highway for the purpose of spying on the performance of racehorses on the plaintiff's land. The extent of the lawful use of the highway was considered by the House of Lords in the case of *Director of Public Prosecutions* v. *Jones*.[23] Under section 14A of the Public Order Act 1986,[24] an order was in force banning all trespassory assemblies around Stonehenge, with the intention of protecting the ancient monument from possible damage due to various groups which gathered there for the summer solstice. The assembly which led to the prosecution was held on the grass verge of the highway beside Stonehenge and was in protest against the ban itself. The Director of Public Prosecutions argued that such a march was caught by the ban under section 14A. Thus, the case turned on whether or not the defendants' assembly on the highway amounted to a 'trespassory' one within section 14A and so, to determine this, the common law of trespass had to be examined. The House of Lords was divided on the matter, concluding by a narrow majority that such use did not amount to trespass. Lord Irvine LC considered that the public's right to use the highway is not simply restricted to a right of passing and re-passing and ancillary activities. Rather, it is a right to use the highway for such reasonable and usual

19 *Lonskier* v. *B. Goodman Ltd.* [1928] 1 KB 421.

20 *Elwes* v. *Brigg Gas Co.* (1886) 33 Ch. D 562.

21 See *Cox* v. *Glue* (1848) 5 CB 533; 136 ER 987. Petroleum is vested in the Crown by virtue of the Petroleum (Production) Act 1934 and coal was vested in the British Coal Corporation by virtue of the Coal Industry (Nationalisation) Act 1946 (although see now the Coal Industry Act 1994, s. 7). The Crown also has prerogative rights in gold and silver.

22 [1900] 1 QB 752.

23 [1999] 2 AC 240.

24 It should be noted that it is an offence to commit any act that *wilfully obstructs* the free passage along a highway, 'without lawful authority or excuse' (s. 137(1) of the Highways Act 1980). In *Hirst and Agu* v. *Chief Constable of West Yorkshire Police* (1987) 85 Cr. App. R 143, the Divisional Court held that 'lawful... excuse' could cover a use of the highway that was reasonable in all the circumstances (see Glidewell LJ, at 150–1 and Otton J at 151: the latter explicitly referred to the need to strike a balance between the right to free speech and to demonstrate on the one hand and the need for peace and good order on the other). In *DPP* v. *Jones* itself, Lord Irvine LC and Lord Hutton explicitly welcomed that the result of the majority's interpretation of the common law of trespass accorded with this case law on the 1980 Act, while the dissenting minority (Lords Slynn and Hope) specifically excluded the 1980 Act and its case law from their analysis of the issue. It is submitted that the majority's view is preferable on this point (see esp. Lord Hutton at 291); otherwise, a defence of lawful excuse would be available in cases of actual physical obstruction of the highway and yet not in cases of assembly where no obstruction was caused.

activities as are consistent with and do not obstruct the general public's 'primary' right of passage along the highway. Such reasonable and usual uses could include peaceful assemblies such as the one in issue in the case. Lord Hutton and Lord Clyde adopted a similar conclusion, although they were careful to emphasise that this did not amount to a ruling that *all* peaceful, non-obstructive assemblies would be justifiable in this way: the assessment would depend strongly upon the facts of the case and seems to preserve the idea in *Hickman* v. *Maisey* that a purpose which was neither reasonable nor usual would still amount to a trespass.

One of the most interesting aspects of the case was the different weight accorded to human rights considerations by their Lordships.[25] Lord Irvine LC, while basing himself largely on a reading of certain passages in the earlier authorities,[26] did refer to a fear that the common law of trespass on the highway might not satisfy the ECHR if it remained as narrowly confined as the minority had argued.[27] Lords Slynn and Hope, however, refused to take the ECHR into account, since they felt that there was neither statutory ambiguity in the 1986 Act nor any vagueness in the common law rules which was in need of clarification.[28] The clearest discussion of these issues is to be found in the judgment of Lord Hutton,[29] who emphasised that the common law right to assembly would be unduly restricted unless it could in some circumstances be exercised on the public highway. Indeed, this right to assemble and protest about important public issues is intimately connected to having a public space in which to do so and Lord Hutton was keen to make this connection between freedom of expression and the common-law right of assembly. Now that the Human Rights Act 1998 has come into force, one would expect similar reasoning to infuse other areas of the common law;[30] nevertheless, it is interesting that the *Director of Public Prosecutions* v. *Jones* case showed a willingness among some of the senior judiciary to face these issues under the more traditional common-law reasoning process.

Although there is a right to navigate in tidal waters and anchor temporarily, there is no right to establish permanent moorings if the soil is privately owned.[31] Picketing may

25 Of particular relevance here are Arts. 10 and 11 ECHR, which deal with freedom of expression and freedom of assembly respectively.

26 [1999] 2 AC 240, 253–8 (see also Lord Hutton, *ibid.*, 291–4).

27 *Ibid.*, 259. See the discussion of the area, including the impact of the recent Strasbourg court judgment in *Appleby* v. *UK* (2003) 37 EHRR 38, by J. H. Rowbottom, 'Property and Participation: A Right of Access for Expressive Activities' [2005] *EHRLR* 186. *Appleby* concerned a group of people who sought to collect signatures and distribute leaflets in a privately owned shopping mall to oppose local authority plans to build on a local park and the ECtHR held that neither Article 10 nor Article 11 ECHR required that the UK ensure that such access be provided.

28 [1999] 2 AC 240, 265 and 277–8 respectively.

29 *Ibid.*, 287–8, citing in particular the (on this point dissenting) judgment of Lord Denning MR in *Hubbard* v. *Pitt* [1976] QB 142, esp. 178–9, and Lamer CJ in *Committee for the Commonwealth of Canada* v. *Canada* (1991) 77 DLR (4th) 385, 394.

30 See our discussion of various issues of defamation and privacy in chs. 21 and 22 respectively, as well as recent developments in title to sue in nuisance (later in this chapter) and under the rule in *Rylands* v. *Fletcher* (in ch. 16).

31 *Fowley Marine (Emsworth) Ltd.* v. *Gafford* [1967] 2 QB 808, 823.

amount to trespass of the highway subsoil if it falls outside the right to take part in peaceful picketing at one's own place of work under section 220 of the Trade Union and Labour Relations (Consolidation) Act 1992.

Finally, there is trespass *ab initio*. Where a person enters land under the authority of law and abuses that authority by a positive act of misfeasance, he is deemed to become a trespasser *ab initio*, that is, from the moment of his original, authorised entry. This doctrine is thus likely to be of particular relevance to particular statutory authorisations of entry, such as those contained in section 2 and Schedule 2 of the Countryside and Rights of Way Act 2000. In *The Six Carpenters' Case* the defendants entered a tavern and, having consumed food and drink, refused to pay. Mere failure to pay being an omission as opposed to an act, they were held not liable for trespass *ab initio*. If the abuse is independent of the authority under which a person enters, it does not constitute trespass *ab initio*.[32] This antiquated doctrine has been criticised by Lord Denning amongst others,[33] but he made use of it in *Cinnamond* v. *British Airways Authority*[34] to hold that minicab drivers unlawfully touting for business had abused the authority given them by law and were therefore trespassers *ab initio*.

Trespass requires voluntary conduct. The necessary intention is the intention to perform the act that amounts to interference, and it is immaterial that the defendant was unaware that he was trespassing or that he was genuinely mistaken. In *Smith* v. *Stone*[35] the defendant, who had been deposited on the plaintiff's land by a gang of men, was held not liable in trespass since he had committed no voluntary act. In *Gilbert* v. *Stone*,[36] on the other hand, where the defendant had been forced by threats to enter the plaintiff's land, he was held liable since his presence there was the result of his conscious act. This indicates that once an act of this kind can be identified, liability in trespass to land is strict in the sense that it does not depend upon intention or negligence as to the consequences of the act. Whether the complete absence of fault could be a defence, as it appears to be in the case of interference with chattels,[37] is unclear.

As with trespass to goods, it is the possessor who is entitled to sue. This includes a person with the immediate right to possess. Just as possession is *prima facie* evidence of ownership, it appears that the converse is true.[38] Acts of enjoyment of land, for example, the cultivation of crops or building on the land, constitute evidence of possession.[39] Occupation of buildings is also evidence and simply having means of access, such as a key, may also be sufficient.[40] However, licence rights for access to land only will not be

32 *Ellis* v. *Pasmore* [1934] 2 KB 164.

33 See his judgment in *Chic Fashions (West Wales) Ltd.* v. *Jones* [1967] 2 QB 299, 313, 317, 320.

34 [1980] 1 WLR 582, 588.

35 (1647) Style 65; 82 ER 533.

36 (1647) Style 72; 82 ER 539.

37 As in *National Coal Board* v. *J. E. Evans & Co. (Cardiff) Ltd.* [1951] 2 KB 861, discussed above, ch. 11, Section 1.

38 *Hebbert* v. *Thomas* (1835) 1 Cr. M & R 861, 864 (Parke B).

39 *Jones* v. *Williams* (1837) 2 M & W 326; 150 ER 781. And this is also true of the situation where the claimant has been granted the right to grow crops on another's land: *Monsanto plc* v. *Tilly* [2000] Env. LR 313 (CA).

40 *Jewish Maternity Home Trustees* v. *Garfinkle* (1926) 95 LJKB 766.

sufficient evidence of possession or occupation to give standing to sue in trespass against protestors occupying that land.[41] By virtue of the doctrine of 'trespass by relation', when a person with a right to possess enters the land his possession is 'related back' to the time when his right accrued so that he can sue for trespass between such accrual and his entry. A trespasser has no right to possess and cannot acquire one simply by entry; at best he can do so only after acquiescence by the owner,[42] for example, by delay. A tenant or subtenant, as distinct from a lodger or licensee,[43] does have possession. A reversioner can sue in respect of permanent damage to the reversion. As between co-owners, each possesses the whole,[44] so it is only in a case of total exclusion of one by the other that the former can sue. A party in possession can sue in trespass for damages and *jus tertii* in a third person is no defence.[45] The claimant's possession will only yield to ownership in the defendant himself or if the latter acted on the authority of the owner.[46]

On the other hand, an owner who has been dispossessed has to recover his land by an action for recovery. This used to be known as the action for ejectment. It finds a place in a work on torts by virtue of the fact that this proprietary action evolved out of the law of trespass with the aid of one of the most famous fictions of English law. Questions of title used to be decided by ancient real actions beside which the action by way of trespass was speedy. To enable these questions to be decided under the guise of trespass a fictitious ploy was used. This involved the pretence, which a defendant was not allowed to challenge, that the plaintiff had demised or leased the land to an imaginary character, John Doe, who had been ejected by another imaginary character, Richard Roe. The plaintiff brought his action with John Doe as nominal plaintiff against Richard Roe, who disclaimed any interest in the land and advised the real defendant to defend it himself. The action took the name of *Doe d. A* v. *B*. The principle on which the issue was decided has remained more or less the same. This is that a claimant out of possession has to establish a better right to possess than the defendant and he has to win by the strength of his own title and not by the weakness of that of the defendant.[47] It is here that the vexed question arises whether, in an action for recovery of land, a defendant can set up the defence of *jus tertii*, even though he is unable to do so in the ordinary case of trespass to land. It would seem that if a claimant has to win by virtue of the strength of his own title, then evidence that someone else has a better title should

[41] *Manchester Airport plc* v. *Dutton* [2000] QB 133 (CA), applied in *Countryside Residential (North Thames) Ltd.* v. *T (A Child)*, *The Times*, 4 Apr. 2000, [2000] 2 EGLR 59: to eject such protestors, a licensee would require occupation rights. See E. Paton and G. Seabourne, 'Unchained Remedy: Recovery of and by Licensees' [1999] *Conv.* 535.

[42] By analogy from standing to sue in nuisance, see *Pemberton* v. *Southwark LBC* [2000] 1 WLR 1672 (CA).

[43] *Hill* v. *Tapper* (1863) 2 H & C 121. Although cf. *Mehta* v. *Royal Bank of Scotland* [1999] 3 EGLR 153, where occupancy of a hotel room for a very extended period seems to have made out sufficient possession for a claim to be brought.

[44] *Murray, Ash and Kennedy* v. *Hall* (1849) 7 CB 441; 137 ER 175.

[45] *Nicholls* v. *Ely Beet Sugar Factory Ltd.* [1931] 2 Ch. 84.

[46] *Delaney* v. *T. P. Smith Ltd.* [1946] KB 393, 397.

[47] *Martin d. Tregonwell* v. *Strachan* (1744) 5 Term Rep. 107 n; 101 ER 61.

prevail, so that the defence of *jus tertii* would indeed be available. This was the view of the court in *Doe d. Carter* v. *Barnard*,[48] but there are strong authorities the other way.[49] Even so, if the defendant acquired possession from a person with defective title he cannot seek to establish a better title in someone else as against the person from whom he acquired or his successors.[50] Nor may he do so if his acquisition of possession was wrongful as against the claimant.[51]

In addition to the action for recovery of land, a claimant also has an action for mesne profits in respect of the loss he has suffered through being kept out of possession.[52] Mesne profits include not just rents and gains from possession and exploitation of the land but also damage caused by deterioration of the land and the costs of regaining possession. The basis for calculating damages is known as the 'user principle'. In *Inverugie Investments Ltd.* v. *Hackett*[53] Lord Lloyd stated this as follows:

> The plaintiff may not have suffered any *actual* loss by being deprived of his use of the property. But under the user principle he is entitled to recover a reasonable rent for the wrongful use of his property by the trespasser. Similarly, the trespasser may not have derived any *actual* benefit from the use of the property. But under the user principle he is obliged to pay a reasonable rent for the use that he has enjoyed. The principle need not be characterised as exclusively compensatory, or exclusively restitutionary; it combines elements of both.[54]

In this case, the defendants, who held the freehold of a hotel complex, had unlawfully ejected the plaintiff, the tenant, and run the hotel for a period of years at an average occupancy rate of between 35 and 40 per cent. The House of Lords held that for the period in question, the plaintiff was entitled to compensation based on a reasonable rent[55] for the continuous use of all the apartments in the complex and not just for those apartments actually used by the defendant, nor even for those which the plaintiff was likely to have been able to fill. By comparison, in the case of *Amec Developments Ltd.* v. *Jury's Hotel Management (UK) Ltd.*,[56] the court assessed damages on the basis that, had the parties negotiated for the defendant to make use of the claimant's land to build its

[48] (1849) 13 QB 945.

[49] *Asher* v. *Whitlock* (1865) LR 1 QB 1, 6, *Perry* v. *Clissold* [1907] AC 73, 79–80, *Allen* v. *Roughley* (1955) 94 CLR 98. See S.A. Wiren, 'The Plea of *Jus Tertii* in Ejectment', A.D. Hargreaves, 'Terminology and Title in Ejectment', and W.S. Holdsworth, 'Terminology and Title in Ejectment: A Reply' (Select Bibliography).

[50] *Doe d. Johnson* v. *Baytup* (1835) 3 A & E 188; 111 ER 384.

[51] *Davison* v. *Gent* (1857) 1 H & N 744; 156 ER 1400.

[52] On the availability of injunctions, see ch. 26, Section 1, below. In *Horsford* v. *Bird* [2006] UKPC 3, the Privy Council upheld an award of damages in lieu of an injunction where one landowner had fenced off land and thereby annexed 455 square feet of the claimant's property. Damages were assessed so as to include the standard valuation of such undeveloped land, plus an uplift for the increased amenity value that the annexation had brought to the defendant's property (at [12] and [13]).

[53] [1995] 1 WLR 713.

[54] *Ibid.*, 718.

[55] This was treated as the starting-point by the court in *Davies* v. *Ilieff* (Ch. D, unreported, 21 Dec. 2000), although the judge went on to distinguish the *Inverugie* case due to its status as commercial premises. In *Davies* v. *Ilieff*, the property in question had been the claimant's home, so the court awarded 'general damages in addition, to reflect the insult of the trespass', to the value of an extra £1,500.

[56] [2001] 1 EGLR 81 (Ch. D).

hotel, the claimant would have been a willing seller. This illustrates that a careful consideration of the surrounding circumstances will be necessary in any assessment of an appropriate monetary award in these cases.[57] In the recent Privy Council judgment in *Horsford* v. *Bird*,[58] yet another approach was taken: their Lordships held that the 'quantum of the claim [for mesne profits] should... be assessed on a yearly basis as a percentage of the capital value of the piece of land in question', at an annual rate of return of 7.5 per cent. This again reflected the context of the case, in that the defendant had fenced off land that included 455 square feet of the claimant's property and had had use of it for eight years and three months before the lower court's judgment had awarded damages in lieu of an injunction.

It used to be the case that, before he could bring an action for mesne profits, the plaintiff first had to regain possession and then use the doctrine of trespass by relation to backdate his possession to cover the period during which he was excluded. This is now largely unnecessary, after an amendment to the Rules of the Supreme Court that allows the claimant to join his claim for mesne profits to the action for recovery.[59] If the claimant's interest in the land has come to an end, he can still sue for mesne profits.[60]

Self-help may be used in certain circumstances, but the law does not encourage resort to self-help and so these are hedged about with restrictions. A party actually in possession may use reasonable force to resist wrongful entry, or attempted entry, by a trespasser. His possession must be legal. In *Holmes* v. *Bagge*[61] it was held that cricketers were not in possession of the playing area and were thus not entitled to eject the plaintiff, a substitute player, who had refused to leave when ordered to do so by the captain. Second, the force used must be reasonable. In *Collins* v. *Renison*[62] the defendant found a trespasser up a ladder placed on his land and, according to his plea, 'gently shook the ladder, which was a low ladder, and gently overturned it and gently threw the plaintiff from it upon the ground'. The force used was held to be unreasonable. If trespass is peaceful, the trespasser must be asked to leave before force is used, unless he turns violent. Third, a person ousted by a trespasser may regain possession by using reasonable force.[63] Subject to this requirement, an owner can expel squatters or demonstrators taking part in a 'sit-in'. If he re-enters peacefully, he should first request the trespasser to

[57] The result of this case might be thought to be inconsistent with Lord Lloyd's reasoning in *Inverugie*, given that a wrongful use also occurred in *Amec* and yet the court there seemed to be willing to allow Amec's apparent willingness to negotiate for a price for such use to be held against it in the assessment of a 'reasonable rent' for the use enjoyed. Alternatively, it might be argued that Lord Lloyd's own application of the idea of a 'reasonable rent' in *Inverugie* was somewhat harsh and that the *Amec* approach represents a finer balance. That said, the parties in *Amec* had agreed that the assessment of damages should be based upon the price which Amec could reasonably have demanded from Jury during the negotiations.

[58] [2006] UKPC 3. Their Lordships also acknowledged that aggravated damages were in principle available in such claims too, but held that no case had been made out for their award on the facts (at [14]).

[59] RSC Ord. 15, r. 1.

[60] *Mount Carmel Investments Ltd.* v. *Peter Thurlow Ltd.* [1988] 1 WLR 1978; see also *Southport Tramways Co.* v. *Ganey* [1897] 2 QB 66.

[61] (1853) 1 E & B 782; 118 ER 629, *Dean* v. *Hogg* (1834) 10 Bing. 345; 131 ER 937.

[62] (1754) 1 Sayer 138; 96 ER 830.

[63] *McPhail* v. *Persons, Names Unknown* [1973] Ch. 447, 465–7 (Lord Denning MR).

leave, and on refusal use reasonable force.[64] However, against one who has possession, an owner out of possession commits a criminal offence if he uses force to re-enter. The old Statutes of Forcible Entry and Detainer have been replaced by the Criminal Law Act 1977, which makes it a criminal offence to resort to force, however reasonable, except in the case of a 'displaced residential occupier' or 'protected intending occupier'.[65] The criminal law goes further than the civil law, since an owner who uses reasonable force to re-enter will not commit a tort and yet might be liable to conviction under legislation.[66] Entry on to the land of another may be lawful for other purposes: a person may enter the land of a neighbour to abate a nuisance[67] or, in some cases, to retake a chattel, at least where it was wrongfully taken by the landowner.[68]

Another form of self-help is distress damage feasant. If a chattel is unlawfully on land and is doing damage, the landowner may impound it until the owner pays, or offers to pay, compensation for the damage done. At common law this power applied to trespassing things and to animals. Distrained animals had to be fed and watered and cows milked; the distrainor was liable for any damage resulting from his failure to do this. Section 7 of the Animals Act 1971 abolishes the common law power in relation to 'livestock' in favour of a more or less equivalent statutory power that includes a power of sale. The Act may have inadvertently abolished the common law power of distraint in respect of 'any animal' unless this phrase in section 7(1) can be read as confined to livestock. A modern application of the law relating to distress damage feasant occurred in *Arthur* v. *Anker*.[69] The lessees of a private car park employed the defendants to clamp the wheels of vehicles that were parked there without permission. The defendants refused to release vehicles except on payment of a fee. Notices on the land indicated that unauthorised vehicles would be clamped and that a specified release fee would be charged. The Court of Appeal, Hirst LJ dissenting, held that in a case such as this a landowner could only invoke distress damage feasant to clamp unauthorised vehicles if they were causing damage. According to Sir Thomas Bingham MR:

> It is plain that physical damage to the land or anything on it is not necessary to found a claim to distress damage feasant. But I do not think a mere technical trespass, mere unlawful presence on the land, is enough. Actual damage would be shown if the party entitled to the use of the land were denied, or obstructed in, the use of it . . . Thus if any of the leaseholders, or any of the leaseholders' licensees (including suppliers seeking to make deliveries), were unable to use the car park, or prevented from unloading, by a trespassing car, that would amount to actual damage. But there is no evidence and no finding of any such evidence in the present case.[70]

His Lordship rejected the proposition that the cost of towing away the car could, in itself, constitute 'damage' for this purpose. He also cast doubt on the use of flat-rate fines for the release of vehicles. Even if damage is suffered—and the landowner thereupon

[64] *Green* v. *Goddard* (1704) 2 Salk. 641; 91 ER 540. [65] Section 12(3).

[66] See *Hemmings* v. *Stoke Poges Golf Club* [1920] 1 KB 720.

[67] See below, ch. 13, Section 6(b).

[68] See *Anthony* v. *Haney and Harding* (1832) 8 Bing. 186, and the 18th Report of the Law Reform Committee, *Conversion and Detinue* (Cmnd. 4774), paras. 116–26.

[69] [1996] 2 WLR 602. [70] *Ibid.*, 610.

becomes entitled to retain the chattel as security for a claim for compensation—the flat-rate charge levied by the wheel-clamper is paid to augment the latter's profits and not to compensate the landowner. Neill LJ gave a concurring judgment; Hirst LJ, however, dissented on the basis that since the tort of trespass itself is actionable *per se*, damage should be presumed for the purposes of the remedy. While there is much to be said for this view, the policy factors referred to by Neill LJ in his judgment should also be borne in mind. As he stated, the remedy of distress damage feasant 'had its origins in medieval times and provided a convenient form of self-help in agricultural communities', but in the context of motor vehicles:

the courts should do nothing to encourage the use of clamping without notice. One can anticipate that many disputes would be likely to arise if clamps were applied to motor vehicles without any prior warning. . . . Pending some control by Parliament it seems to me that the matter can be satisfactorily dealt with by means of clearly worded notices and by the application of the doctrine of *volenti*.[71]

The *volenti* defence was, then, the route adopted by the majority to finding in the defendants' favour: the plaintiffs were taken to have consented to the clamping of their vehicles and to the payment of a fee in return for their release.

In general, a trespasser's liability is clear; as far as licensees are concerned, a bare licensee comes under a duty to leave as soon as his licence is revoked and if he refuses or fails to leave within a reasonable time he becomes a trespasser.[72] Depending upon the terms of the contract, a contractual licence may be revocable, in which case the licensee becomes a trespasser even if the revocation is actionable as a breach of contract.[73] This is subject, however, to an exception where a contract is specifically enforceable and the licensee has conducted himself properly.[74] Nor can a licence be revoked if it is coupled with an interest, whether in land or in chattels.[75]

2. DEFENCES

The Limitation Act 1623, section 5, which is the oldest surviving tort law statute, provides that if the defendant pleads disclaimer of title to the land and if 'the trespass was by negligence or involuntary' and he makes a tender of sufficient amends, action

[71] *Ibid.*, 615. N.B. section 3(2)(j) of the Private Security Industry Act 2001, which makes it an offence to attach wheel clamps to cars without holding the necessary licence (this provision entered into force on 28 February 2005 for England and Wales, and 6 July 2006 for Scotland).

[72] But note that a failure to follow certain procedures in a public law context may invalidate a revocation of a licence. Thus, the failure to offer a parent the chance to make representations before excluding her from school grounds amounted to a procedural error which vitiated the revocation of her licence to remain and which could be relied upon as a defence to a claim in trespass: *Wandsworth LBC* v. *A* [2000] 1 WLR 1246 (CA).

[73] *Kerrison* v. *Smith* [1897] 2 QB 445.

[74] *Hurst* v. *Picture Theatres Corp.* [1915] 1 KB 1, *Winter Garden Theatre (London) Ltd.* v. *Millenium Productions Ltd.* [1948] AC 173, 189 (Viscount Simon); cf. *Thompson* v. *Park* [1944] KB 408.

[75] *Wood* v. *Manley* (1839) 11 A & E 34; 113 ER 325.

against him shall be barred. 'Involuntary' here should be taken to mean 'unintentional', since if there is no act the tort of trespass is not made out in any event; however, the effect of the statute was nullified by interpreting it narrowly to mean 'no act' in *Basley* v. *Clarkson* in 1681.[76] The defence of *jus tertii* has already been touched upon, as has that of mistake and the defence of one's own property.

The claimant's consent is always a defence in the sense that it constitutes 'leave and licence'.[77] It is, however, a trespass to exceed the terms of a licence: 'where you invite a person into your house to use the stairs you do not invite him in to slide down the bannisters'.[78] Certain licences, such as the licence of traders and canvassers to walk up a garden path to call on the occupier, may be implied subject to the landowner's power to exclude them by advance notice, while others are regulated by law such as the powers of entry of the police. Rights of entry are also affected by rights of way, easements and immemorial customary rights, as well as by numerous statutes. These matters are outside the scope of this book and the reader is referred to texts on civil liberties and on land law for the details.

The defence of necessity may also be available under certain limited circumstances. In *Re F*[79] Lord Goff identified three situations in which the defence might apply. First, there are cases of public necessity such as the destruction of property to prevent the spread of fire, as in the Great Fire of London of 1666 or the case of *Dewey* v. *White*,[80] in which firemen threw down a chimney stack which was threatening to fall damaging the plaintiff's house; second, cases of private necessity, as in *Cope* v. *Sharpe (No. 2)*[81] where the defendant went on to the plaintiff's land to prevent a fire spreading to neighbouring land over which his employer had shooting rights; and, third, a category of cases in which action is taken as a matter of necessity to come to the aid of another whose person or property is in imminent danger. In this last category, 'to fall within the principle not only (1) must there be a necessity to act when it is not practicable to communicate with the assisted person, but also (2) the action taken must be such as a reasonable person would in all the circumstances take, acting in the best interests of the assisted person'.[82] If anything the modern tendency is to restrict the scope of this defence. In *Southwark London Borough Council* v. *Williams*,[83] a case in which squatters attempted to argue that their unlawful occupation of an empty house was justified by their need to find shelter for homeless families, Lord Denning MR had this to say about the matter. 'Necessity would open a door which no man could shut.... The plea would

[76] 3 Lev. 37.

[77] *Thomas* v. *Sorrell* (1674) Vaughan 330; 124 ER 1098. For a possible defence of acquiescence (and an emphasis that mere delay in bringing an action does not, without more, amount to acquiescence) see *Jones* v. *Stones* [1999] 1 WLR 1739 (CA).

[78] *The Carlgarth* [1927] P 93, 110.

[79] [1990] 2 AC 1, 74.

[80] (1827) M & M 56; 173 ER 1079.

[81] [1912] 1 KB 496.

[82] *Re F* [1990] 2 AC 1, 75 (Lord Goff). See also the Criminal Law Act 1967, s. 3, which enables a member of the public to use 'such force as is reasonable in the prevention of crime', a provision which draws no distinction between defence of oneself or of another.

[83] [1971] 1 Ch. 734, 744.

be an excuse for all sorts of wrongdoing. So the courts must, for the sake of law and order, take a firm stand. They must refuse to admit the plea of necessity to the hungry and the homeless; and trust that their distress will be relieved by the charitable and the good.' Meanwhile, in *Monsanto plc* v. *Tilly*,[84] the issue of trespassory protests against genetically modified crops was raised. The Court of Appeal emphasised that the danger claimed to be faced by others must be so immediate as to amount to an emergency. Further, even in such emergency situations such trespass could not be justified where a public body already existed to protect those very public interests. Finally, the court gave significant weight to the motives of the protesters in their attempt to change government policy by drawing publicity to the issue of genetically modified crops: such changes to policy must be sought through lawful means in a democratic society,[85] so that any violations of private rights which are committed in an attempt to gain publicity for a particular cause could not escape censure.

Where necessity is a defence to trespass there may remain the possibility that it will not cover liability in another tort, such as negligence. In *Rigby* v. *Chief Constable of Northamptonshire*[86] the police fired a CS-gas canister into the plaintiff's shop in order to flush out a dangerous psychopath who had taken refuge in the shop. The shop was burned out. The court held that necessity was a good defence to the plaintiff's claim of trespass, but that the police were nonetheless liable in negligence for firing the canister into the shop without arranging for any fire-fighting equipment to be present.

A final possibility open to the defendant is to plead 'inevitable accident'. This is tantamount to a denial of fault and its scope is limited given that the tort of trespass to land is essentially based on strict liability.[87]

[84] [2000] Env. LR 313 (CA)—an application by Monsanto for summary judgment and a permanent injunction against the protestors to prevent further trespass to land and goods.

[85] Indeed, their Lordships were concerned that the issues raised (upon which the pleading of the defence of necessity would require them to rule) were of an inherently non-justiciable nature under public law (per Stuart-Smith LJ, at 330). The Court of Appeal was, in any case, unhappy about offering any view on these matters in an entirely private law (and summary) action, without the presence of any of the relevant public authorities (such as the licensor for Monsanto's activities, the Department of the Environment, Transport and the Regions) to make the case in favour of such crop trials (per Mummery LJ, at 340). Indeed, their Lordships were concerned that the issues raised (upon which the pleading of the defence of necessity would require them to rule) were of an inherently non-justiciable nature under public law (per Stuart-Smith LJ, at 330). The Court of Appeal was, in any case, unhappy about offering any view on these matters in an entirely private law (and summary) action, without the presence of any of the relevant public authorities (such as the licensor for Monsanto's activities, the Department of the Environment, Transport and the Regions) to make the case in favour of such crop trials (per Mummery LJ, at 340).

[86] [1985] 1 WLR 1242.

[87] See *Southport Corp.* v. *Esso Petroleum Co. Ltd.* [1953] 2 All ER 1204, 1212 (Devlin J).

SELECT BIBLIOGRAPHY

DENNING, A. T., 'Re-Entry for Forfeiture: The Case of *Elliott* v. *Boynton*' (1927) 43 *LQR* 53.

HARGREAVES, A. D., 'Terminology and Title in Ejectment' (1940) 56 *LQR* 376.

HOLDSWORTH, W. S., 'Terminology and Title in Ejectment: A Reply' (1940) 56 *LQR* 479.

MITCHELL, J. D. B., 'Learner's Licence' (1954) 17 *MLR* 211.

RICHARDSON, J. E., 'Private Property Rights in the Air Space at Common Law' (1953) 31 *Can. BR* 116.

SHAWCROSS, C. N., and BEAUMONT, K. M., *Air Law* (3rd edn., 1966), ch. 25.

SMITH, J., 'Liability for Substantial Physical Damage to Land by Blasting: The Rule of the Future' (1920) 33 *Harv. LR* 542, 667.

WADE, H. W. R., 'What Is a Licence?' (1948) 64 *LQR* 57.

WILLIAMS, G. L., 'A Strange Offspring of Trespass *Ab Initio*' (1936) 52 *LQR* 106.

WIREN, S. A., 'The Plea of *Jus Tertii* in Ejectment' (1925) 41 *LQR* 139.

SELECT BIBLIOGRAPHY

13

LESSER INTERFERENCE WITH LAND: NUISANCE

1. DEFINITION

'There is perhaps no more impenetrable jungle in the entire law', wrote Dean Prosser, 'than that which surrounds the word nuisance.'[1] Nuisances may be private or public. Because of the vagaries of history[2] and the connection between the two forms, private nuisance has come to cover different types of conduct on the part of defendants.[3] Indeed, beyond saying that all these instances are actionable because they are intolerable inconveniences, the only other common element is that they affect the claimants' use or enjoyment of their land. Private nuisance is therefore commonly defined as any substantial and unreasonable interference with the claimant's land or any right over or in connection with its enjoyment.

2. BASIS OF LIABILITY

The gist of liability is unreasonable interference with the claimant's interest. This is sometimes referred to as the 'principle of reasonable user' which is (rightly) seen as the main controlling mechanism of this tort. But the words 'reasonable' and 'reasonableness' must be used with some caution in order to avoid confusion with the tort of negligence where they can also be found. Thus, in nuisance the law does not concentrate so much on the quality of the 'doing' (unreasonableness of the defendant's conduct) as on the quality of the 'deed' (unreasonableness of the result to the claimant). The two considerations are by no means mutually exclusive (for the unreasonableness of the

[1] W. L. Prosser and W. P. Keeton on *Torts* (5th edn., 1984), 616.

[2] The early history of the tort is traced by P. H. Winfield, 'Nuisance as a Tort' (Select Bibliography) and F. H. Newark, 'The Boundaries of Nuisance' (Select Bibliography) and W. A. McRae Jr., 'Development of Nuisance in the Early Common Law' (1948) 1 *U Fla. LR* 27. For the nineteenth-century developments see J. F. Brenner, 'Nuisance Law and the Industrial Revolution' (1974) 3 *Jo. LS* 403 and, more recently, John McLaren's excellent article on nuisance law, 'Nuisance Law and the Industrial Revolution' (Select Bibliography).

[3] *Goldman* v. *Hargrave* [1967] 1 AC 645, 657, per Lord Wilberforce.

defendant's conduct is often a factor which makes the resulting interference unreasonable);[4] but the different optics adopted in the two torts can produce different results.

The defendant may interfere with the claimant's interests by: (*a*) affecting materially his land (encroaching on to, or causing physical damage to, it); or (*b*) affecting his use or enjoyment of it: or (*c*) interfering with servitudes and similar rights over the land. The second type of interference can pose interesting problems of delimitation, while the last is more the concern of books on property than on tort,[5] so it will be omitted from this account.

The distinction between material interference with property and interference with use or enjoyment was sanctioned by the House of Lords in *St Helens Smelting Co.* v. *Tipping*[6] in 1865. The plaintiff bought an estate near a smelting factory and later complained that noxious fumes from it were damaging his trees and crops. The defendants contended that the whole neighbourhood was devoted to similar manufacturing purposes and that, therefore, the smelting operations should be allowed to continue with impunity. Dismissing this argument, the Lord Chancellor, Lord Westbury, pointed out that when interference with a plaintiff's enjoyment is alleged, the surrounding circumstances are relevant, but that different considerations apply when the alleged interference concerns material injury to property.

In descending order of significance, three reasons could be advanced for this distinction (which appears to be restricted to the common law systems). The first is that property and, in particular, tangible, material interference with it, generally receives greater protection than the enjoyment derived from it.[7] This argument would certainly have commended itself to earlier generations. Nowadays, however, it may appear less attractive, especially since a clear-cut distinction between property damage and mere interference with enjoyment is not always easy to make.

Second, it might be said that property damage is more easily assessable and quantifiable than mere interference with enjoyment.[8] The answer to this is that difficulty in quantifying damages has not prevented courts from awarding them in personal injury

[4] We shall return to this point below, Section 3(b)(iv).

[5] *Gale on Easements* (17th edn., 2002); P. Jackson, *Law of Easements and Profits* (1978), C. Harpum, S. Bridge and M. Grant (eds.), *Megarry and Wade: The Law of Real Property* (6th edn., 1999). Some of these nuisances are actionable *per se*. See *Nicholls* v. *Ely Beet Sugar Factory Ltd.* [1936] Ch 343. The deviation from the rule (which requires damage as an element of nuisance) may be due to the close analogy with trespass and the fact that both actions are, in such circumstances, aimed at vindicating rights and not necessarily compensating the claimant. Thus, R. A. Buckley, *The Law of Nuisance* (Select Bibliography), 105.

[6] (1865) 11 HLC 642, 650; 11 ER 1483, 1486, per Lord Westbury LC.

[7] On this idea of hierarchy of values in the law of torts, see B. S. Markesinis, 'Policy Factors and the Law of Torts', *The Cambridge Lectures* (1981) 199, 204 ff. For an economic explanation and criticism (with further references), see A. I. Ogus and G. M. Richardson, 'Economics and the Environment' (Select Bibliography), 299 ff.

[8] An illustration of this can be found in *Bone* v. *Seale* [1975] 1 WLR 797, where, in a nuisance action provoked by smells emanating from a nearby pig farm, the court held that the damages should be fixed by analogy with damages for loss of amenity in personal injury actions. This approach was convincingly criticised by Lord Hoffmann in his opinion in *Hunter* v. *Canary Wharf Ltd.* [1997] 2 WLR 684 at 708, where he argued that the damages in such cases should be calculated either by reference to the diminished capital value of the land

cases, so there is no reason why it should justify a rigid distinction here between two types of interference.

Third, the distinction may represent an attempt by the House of Lords to reconcile two conflicting earlier decisions. In *Hole* v. *Barlow*[9] the Court of Common Pleas had held that a defendant would not be liable if he carried on his activity in a 'convenient and proper' location. In *Bamford* v. *Turnley*[10] the Court of Exchequer Chamber disapproved of this decision on the ground that it was too favourable to defendants. The suggested reconciliation is that the relevance of locality should be confined to cases of discomfort (*Hole*) as distinct from property damage (*Bamford*).[11]

All three arguments may partially explain the distinction between the two kinds of interferences, though it would be a mistake to accept Lord Westbury's opinion as creating a *sharp* legal dichotomy between them. Indeed, in the case of *Hunter* v. *Canary Wharf*,[12] the House of Lords and, especially, Lord Hoffmann, were keen to dispel the impression that Lord Westbury's distinction created two separate torts.[13] Three reasons could be given why Lord Westbury's dichotomy should not be overstressed.

The first has already been mentioned: the distinction between material damage and discomfort is not always easy to draw. Thus, noise and smells may (*a*) inconvenience the claimant, (*b*) affect his business and (*c*) even reduce the value of his property. While (*a*) would not qualify as material damage to property, (*b*) and (*c*) pose greater difficulty. It is by no means clear that (*c*), for example, could be included in Lord Westbury's definition and the absence of conclusive authority leaves the point open to argument.[14]

The second reason was forcefully advanced by Lord Hoffmann in his penetrating opinion in the *Hunter* case.[15] In his view, Lord Westbury's dichotomy resulted in a tendency to regard cases falling in the second category as being 'actions in respect of the discomfort or even personal injury which the plaintiff has suffered . . .'. This was an unintended and unacceptable side effect of the dichotomy. For even in cases '"productive of sensible personal discomfort" the action is not for causing discomfort to the person but, as in the case of the first category, for causing injury to the land. True it is that the land has not suffered "sensible" injury, but its utility has been diminished by the existence of the nuisance.'

A correct appreciation of this fact thus has important consequences for two further issues: (*a*) the rule that claimants in nuisance must have an interest in the land in

(which could not be proved in the *Bone* case) or by calculating the 'diminution in the amenity value of the property during the period for which the nuisance persisted'. That this (second) instance involved 'placing a value on intangibles' did not worry his Lordship, especially in the light of what was said in *Ruxley Electronics and Construction Ltd.* v. *Forsyth* [1996] AC 344.

[9] (1858) 4 CB (NS) 334; 140 ER 1113.

[10] (1860) 3 B & S 62; 122 ER 25.

[11] For the suggestion of a *via media*, see Buckley (Select Bibliography), 7–8.

[12] *Hunter* v. *Canary Wharf Ltd.* [1997] 2 WLR 684.

[13] *Ibid.*, 709.

[14] For the difficulties generally, see Ogus and Richardson (Select Bibliography), 229; J.P.S McLaren, 'The Common Law Nuisance Actions' (Select Bibliography), 534.

[15] [1997] 2 WLR 684, 708.

question and (*b*) the way that damages should be calculated in nuisances of this second kind. We will discuss both of these matters further below.

The final reason that a rigid distinction should be avoided is that it could convey the belief that it would suffice to prove any material injury to property in order to establish an actionable nuisance, which would be wrong. For not every 'fleeting or evanescent'[16] interference will be an actionable nuisance, but only one that is substantial and unreasonable. Thus, when water flowed over the plaintiff's land but caused only 'trivial injury', the claim in nuisance was rejected.[17] The same conclusion was reached when the defendant's land was subject to minor subsidence causing the plaintiff no 'appreciable harm'.[18]

There is also some authority to suggest that the pervading notion of 'reasonableness' is not restricted to nuisances resulting from discomfort, but is also relevant in cases of material damage to the claimant's property. So, in *Watt* v. *Jamieson*,[19] where the defendant's vent-pipe discharged vapour on the plaintiff's land and thereby caused, *inter alia*, dry rot (material damage to property), Lord President Cooper took the view that 'the critical question is whether what he [the plaintiff] was exposed to was *plus quam tolerabile* when due weight has been given to *all the surrounding* circumstances of the offensive conduct and its effects'. The plaintiff's action was dismissed. Similarly, in *Stearn* v. *Prentice Brothers*[20] the defendants collected manure on their land, thereby attracting rats which attacked the plaintiff's crops. The plaintiff's action was again dismissed since it was held that what the defendants had done was, in the circumstances of that case, neither excessive nor unusual.

Despite these arguments the distinction between property damage and interference with enjoyment or use cannot be totally ignored. For the requirement of substantial and unreasonable interference is more easily satisfied in cases of material interference with property and, as one leading tort lawyer put it, 'English courts remain chary of protecting trifling personal discomforts falling short of physical injury.'[21] Further, the nature of the locality is a factor seriously taken into account when nuisance takes the form of interference with enjoyment of the land, but it is ignored when the nuisance materially affects the claimant's land. Finally, the availability of injunctive relief and the rules for calculating damages may not be the same in both instances. So, despite the fact that no clear-cut distinction between the two types of interference is possible, the distinction between material damage to property and interference with use and enjoyment is still of some importance in English law.

16 *Benjamin* v. *Storr* (1874) LR 9 CP 400, 407, per Brett J.

17 *Nobilo* v. *Waitemata County* [1961] NZLR 1064, 1067.

18 *Mitchell* v. *Darley Main Colliery Co.* (1884) 14 QBD 125, 137; affd. (1886) 11 App. Cas. 127.

19 1954 SC 56.

20 [1919] 1 KB 394.

21 J. Murphy, *Street on Torts* (12th edn., 2007), 434.

3. UNREASONABLE INTERFERENCE

(A) MATERIAL DAMAGE TO PROPERTY

In addition to what has been said so far it should be noted that even material interference can take different forms: for example, a lightning strike not properly dealt with by the defendant,[22] flooding,[23] encroachment by roots,[24] contamination by sewage,[25] and so on. What is interesting about all these are the reasons which have led to the gradual imposition of affirmative duties of action on the landowners from whose land danger emanates and the devices adopted by courts towards this end. Four cases call for particular comment: *Sedleigh-Denfield* v. *O'Callaghan*,[26] *Goldman* v. *Hargrave*,[27] *Leakey* v. *National Trust*[28] and *Holbeck Hall Hotel* v. *Scarborough Borough Council*.[29]

In the first, the plaintiff's land was flooded because the drainage system in the defendant's land became blocked through the act of a trespasser; the defendants were held liable because they were aware of the cause of the flooding, but had failed to take reasonable steps to abate it.

In the second case a tree on the defendant's land was struck by lightning. Though the defendant felled it, he did not extinguish the fire after doing so in the belief that the fire would eventually burn itself out. It kept smouldering, however, and, fanned by a sudden gust of wind, spread to the plaintiff's land. The Privy Council held that the rule in *Sedleigh-Denfield* v. *O'Callaghan* applied to cases such as this where the danger arose not from the act of a trespasser, but from an operation of nature on something on the defendant's land.

In the third case the defendant, the National Trust, owned and occupied land on which there was a large mound known as 'Burrow Mump'. Because of its geological structure, known by the defendant, this was prone to subsidence. After an unusually dry summer followed by a very wet autumn, the mound developed cracks, which eventually caused a substantial earth-slip on to the plaintiff's adjoining property. The defendant, though warned by the plaintiff of the possibility of an impending collapse, refused to do anything about it and merely gave the plaintiff permission to abate the cause of the nuisance at his own expense. Nor was it willing to remove the fallen debris after the subsidence or to compensate the plaintiff, arguing that there was no liability in law for an occurrence of this sort. O'Connor J at first instance and a unanimous Court of Appeal

22 *Goldman* v. *Hargrave* [1967] 1 AC 645.

23 *Fletcher* v. *Smith* (1877) 2 App. Cas. 781. But not if the flooding occurs because water is diverted before it reaches the defendant's land: *Home Brewery plc* v. *William Davis & Co. (Loughborough) Ltd.* [1987] 1 All ER 637.

24 *Davey* v. *Harrow Corp.* [1958] 1 QB 60, *Masters* v. *Brent LBC* [1978] QB 841, *Solloway* v. *Hampshire CC* (1981) 79 LGR 449, *Delaware Mansions* v. *Westminster City Council* [2002] 1 AC 321 (HL).

25 *Humphries* v. *Cousins* (1877) 2 CPD 239, *Marcic* v. *Thames Water Utilities Ltd.* [2002] QB 929 (CA).

26 [1940] AC 880.

27 [1967] 1 AC 645.

28 [1980] QB 485.

29 [2000] QB 836 (CA).

held otherwise. In the light of *Sedleigh-Denfield* v. *O'Callaghan* and *Goldman* v. *Hargrave*, the extension in *Leakey* was as inevitable as it was just. *Sedleigh-Denfield* had held a landowner liable, in certain circumstances, for the act of a trespasser. *Goldman* v. *Hargrave* extended that rule to dangers arising by operations of nature affecting something on the land. Finally, *Leakey* completed the process by including dangers arising out of operations of nature on the land itself. Ingenious distinctions, which in the past had stood in the way of enlarging the duty of occupiers of land, had been criticised by judges and writers for something like fifty years before being abandoned.[30] But such criticisms used to be brushed aside as being only *obiter dicta* or the product of academic thinking. *Leakey* put an end to all this and in so doing cast upon occupiers of land a general, though measured, duty to take care in relation to hazards on their land, whether natural or artificial.[31] The technique of imposing liability in *Leakey* is also known. In substance this was a case of non-feasance, so a duty to act had to be 'discovered' by the court. Subsuming omissions under the bad performance of activities and thereby imposing liability where previously there would be none, is not new.[32] Such duties to take positive action, though on the increase, have not developed into a general duty to act in favour of another. Yet in this limited area of the law we do appear to be moving towards such a general duty.

More noteworthy than the reasoning techniques is the reason behind the extension of liability. *Leakey* reveals in part the policy factors that determine the final result but which are often concealed behind the legal jargon. For in this, as in so many other cases, the court was faced with a clash of interests. For, on the one hand, we have the interest of the occupier to protect himself against liability resulting from the natural use of his land. On the other hand, however, there is also the neighbour to be protected against potential dangers arising from the land of the other occupier. For a long time the law was satisfied with the conception of separate and autonomous proprietors, each of whom was entitled to exploit his territory in a natural manner and none of whom was obliged to restrain or direct the operations of nature in the interest of avoiding harm to his neighbour. In that era, which elevated the pursuit of private interest to the level of a public virtue, the emphasis was on the landowner's right to use or not use his land as he chose and to avoid making him liable if at all possible.

Today, however, the emphasis is more on accident prevention and loss distribution and both of these policy arguments may be seen in play here. For accident prevention suggests that the owner of land on which a cause of interference arises will usually be in a better position to prevent or control it.

In *Leakey*'s case this may not have been entirely true, since the National Trust was prepared to allow the plaintiff to enter on its land and abate the danger, so it was not the

[30] E.g. Wright J in *Noble* v. *Harrison* [1926] 2 KB 332; Lord Wright in *Sedleigh-Denfield* [1940] AC 880 at 910; A. L. Goodhart, 'Liability for Things Naturally on Land' (Select Bibliography).

[31] On this point, see *Green* v. *Lord Somerleyton* [2003] EWCA Civ. 198, [2004] 1 P & CR 33, where Jonathan Parker LJ concluded that the *Leakey* duty also applied to naturally flowing water, pointing out (at [81]) that 'in the context of the English landscape a distinction between "natural" and "artificial" features is an inherently uncertain foundation on which to rest a decision as to the existence of liability in nuisance'.

[32] See ch. 3, Section 4(a) above.

only entity that could have prevented the harm. Arguably, however, it was best placed to bear the cost of such preventive action. This leads to the second policy argument that focuses on a benefit–burden analysis.

The occupier of land on which the nuisance arises no doubt derives benefit from its use and, so runs the argument, he should also shoulder the corresponding burden, especially if this is likely to be modest. This is particularly true in this type of situation since what we are ultimately talking about is the (modest) cost of insurance against such risks, as against the cost of cure of the resulting harm, which may run into thousands of pounds. The extension of the duty of positive action is, however, accompanied by the rider that the standard of care to be shown by a landowner is not the objective standard of the 'reasonable man', but a more subjective one.[33] For the standard is tailored to the abilities and resources of the particular defendant who has a hazard thrust upon him through no seeking or fault of his own. This probably is right (though if the policy reasons given in the previous paragraph are convincing, then they could be taken to justify the imposition of the usual, objectively determined, duty of care). Interestingly, however, in *Leakey* the defendants attempted to exploit quite subtly this requirement that the standard of care should take into account the financial position of the defendant (and, perhaps, by implication of the plaintiff as well). For they argued that in this case it should determine not merely the standard of duty, but also its very existence. They argued, in other words, that this kind of balancing operation was almost bound to lead to such delays and complexities that it would be better if the court refused to discover a duty altogether. The Court of Appeal, however, remained unimpressed. A lighter, subjective standard of care did not appear to create problems when it was applied to liability towards trespassers in the post-*British Railways Board* v. *Herrington* era.[34] And it had caused no difficulties after *Goldman* v. *Hargrave*; so there was little reason to suppose that it might do so if adopted in this instance. Policy thus favoured the imposition of liability; and there was no contrary reason why this should not be so.

These principles were recently revisited[35] in the case of *Holbeck Hall Hotel Ltd.* v. *Scarborough Borough Council*,[36] where the erosion of a cliff had caused part of the plaintiff's hotel atop it to collapse—the rest of the hotel was then unsafe and had to be

33 Although it seems that in cases of public nuisance arising due to forces of nature, the standard remains an objective one: see *Wandsworth LBC* v. *Railtrack plc* [2002] QB 756 (CA), concerning the disturbance to passers-by caused by a large number of pigeons roosting under a bridge owned by the defendant. The claimant had been given permission to pigeon-proof the bridge itself, but succeeded in arguing that the defendant was liable to abate the nuisance.

34 [1972] AC 877: see ch. 6 for discussion, above.

35 See also *Bybrook Barn Garden Centre* v. *Kent CC* [2001] Env. LR 30, where the Court of Appeal applied *Leakey* to hold the defendant council liable in nuisance for its failure, as highway authority, to enlarge a drainage culvert to ensure that it could carry the extra water from a local steam. When it flooded and damaged the claimant's premises, and since the defendant had known of the inadequacy of the culvert, the court held the defendant liable. While remedying the defect would have been at some cost, it would have been easy to achieve and there was even an argument that the defendant, as the highway authority, would have been under a statutory duty so to act, had an appropriate notice been served on it. On the facts, therefore, *Bybrook* was a case where the application of the measured duty of care was a good deal more straightforward than in the *Holbeck Hall Hotel* case ([2000] QB 836 (CA), discussed in the text which follows).

36 [2000] QB 836 (CA).

demolished. The defendant local authority owned the base of the cliff and the plaintiff claimed damages in nuisance for the defendant's failure to take remedial action to prevent the landslip. The Court of Appeal agreed that the *Leakey* principle also applied to a danger caused due to a lack of support by the defendant's land of the plaintiff's property, but went on to analyse the scope of the 'measured duty' owed by the defendant in the light of whether or not such extensive damage had been reasonably foreseeable to the defendant, given their knowledge of the cliff and expert reports on its state. Stuart-Smith LJ held that:

> I do not think it is just and reasonable in a case like the present to impose liability for damage which is greater in extent than anything that was foreseen or foreseeable (without further geological investigation), especially where the defect and danger existed as much on the plaintiffs' land as Scarborough's.[37]

Many other important considerations which might have provided future guidance on how to assess the operation of the measured duty of care were, thus, not given authoritative consideration in the case. So, how should the parties be required to apportion expenditure if the defendant is not to be responsible for all costs of abatement?

The judge at first instance had suggested that a deduction should be made for what the plaintiff would have agreed to contribute towards such works, had agreement been reached between the parties. Alternatively, if it could be shown that the defect in the soil which led to the landslip was present in the properties of *both* parties, then should expenses be split in the ratio of how much of the defect is on each one's side of the boundary? Stuart-Smith LJ did provide some guidance on one matter: he considered (*obiter*) that the defendant's duty in this case might not even have extended to having to carry out expensive remedial works to prevent damage to the plaintiff's property which *had been* foreseeable: depending upon all the circumstances, the defendant may have been bound to do no more than 'to warn . . . neighbours of such risk as they were aware of or ought to have foreseen and shar[e] . . . such information as they had acquired relating to it'.[38] This illustrates just how flexibly the courts may be willing to interpret the measured duty of care in more extreme fact situations, in an attempt to 'do justice' as between the parties to the case. In such difficult cases, on the basis of the policy discussion developed above, one might argue that in *Holbeck Hall Hotel* the arguments concerning who was best placed to remedy the problem and/or bear the cost thereof were much more finely balanced than had been the case in the earlier cases discussed above, which led the court to take very great care in framing the appropriate scope of the duty.

[37] [2006] QB 836 (CA), para. 51, explicitly using principles derived from negligence cases such as *Marc Rich & Co. v. Bishop Rock Marine Co. Ltd.* [1996] AC 211, to determine the scope of this measured duty of care and thus departing from the standard rule that foreseeability of the relevant *type* of damage attracts liability to pay damages for the full *extent* of damage of that type which actually occurs.

[38] *Ibid.*, para. 54. Likewise, in *Green v. Lord Somerleyton* [2003] EWCA Civ. 198, [2004] 1 P & CR 33, Jonathan Parker LJ held (in finding no breach of the *Leakey* duty by the defendant) that it was significant that at no stage did the claimant make clear to the defendant what the latter was to do to address the flooding problem, nor did the claimant initiate any possible joint action to address it (at [106]–[109]).

Though the court in *Leakey* held that it mattered not whether the case was pleaded in negligence or nuisance, we see here a certain similarity to the method of approach advocated by the leading negligence cases in the 1970s (though under attack since the mid-1980s). For, if harm is foreseeable, there will be liability so long as there is no special policy reason why there should be none. The cases discussed in the previous paragraphs could have further and, it is submitted, unexplored implications for the law of negligence. For, as we have noted already, in nuisance the courts have shown a greater willingness to impose liability for omissions than they have done in the law of negligence.

This becomes particularly obvious if one compares the nuisance cases just discussed with another set of cases, this time pleaded in negligence: *Lamb* v. *Camden London Borough Council*,[39] *P. Perl (Exporters) Ltd.* v. *Camden London Borough Council*[40] and *Smith* v. *Littlewoods Organisation Ltd.*[41] For in these negligence cases the defendants, occupiers of empty premises, were held *not* liable to their neighbours (the plaintiffs) for harm caused by third parties/strangers who entered the plaintiffs' premises after having obtained easy access into the defendants' (occupiers') premises. Originally the justification given for this result was that A could not be made liable to C for the acts of B who was neither A's servant, child, nor other person for whom A had to answer. Eventually, however, it became clear that the real reason was the reluctance of our law to impose liability for pure omissions in the context of the tort of negligence. Yet such a liability could be imposed if the action could be brought under the heading of *Sedleigh-Denfield* v. *O'Callaghan*—something that in the *Smith* case was considered theoretically possible by both Lords Mackay and Goff.[42] This could be taken to suggest that the newly found liability for non-feasance in pure nuisance situations could, with a minimum of ingenuity, spread to nuisance–negligence cases once the courts have worked out the necessary safeguards for such an extension of the law.[43] But our courts have not, thus far, taken this step; and until that happens, nuisance may offer claimants opportunities for compensation that negligence still does not. These opportunities may even be enhanced by the advent of the Human Rights Act 1998 and the requirement that the courts and other public bodies take Article 8 ECHR and Article 1 of the First Protocol to the ECHR into account.[44]

The recent case of *Marcic* v. *Thames Water Utilities Ltd.*[45] proceeded on the basis of the *Leakey* principle: the Court of Appeal held the defendant liable for damage caused by repeated flooding from its drainage system, which had become inadequate in the face of the increasing demands on the system. This involved ruling that the older cases, which had denied the liability of sewerage operators which inherited systems, on the

[39] [1981] QB 625. [40] [1984] QB 342.

[41] [1987] 2 WLR 480. [42] [1987] 2 WLR 480, 497. See also Lord Goff's speech at 510.

[43] On this see B. S. Markesinis, 'Negligence, Nuisance and Affirmative Duties of Action' (1989) 105 *LQR* 104.

[44] Article 1 of the First Protocol to the ECHR relates to the protection of property: thus, at first instance, the judge discussed whether the result of the flooding amounted to a partial deprivation of the plaintiff's property, assessing whether or not a (substantial) reduction in the value of the property counted as partial deprivation under Art. 1 of the First Protocol (*Marcic*, [56] and [93] (at 953 and 962 respectively) (QBD)).

[45] [2002] QB 929 (CA).

basis that liability would only arise for cases of misfeasance and not non-feasance had not survived *Goldman* v. *Hargrave* and *Leakey*.[46] The defendant also failed to convince the Court of Appeal that it had acted reasonably in its failure to abate the floods.[47] At first instance, however, the judge made an extensive examination of the alternative claim against the defendant for a breach of the claimant's human rights.[48] The Court of Appeal dealt with the matter more briefly, but emphasised that the human rights dimension of a case might have consequences for the assessment of the measured duty of care. Thus, even if substantial expenditure to abate a nuisance could not be justified (e.g. if only one house were at risk of flooding every five years), this did not necessarily mean that:

> it is just that the householder should receive no compensation for the damage done. The flooding is a consequence of the benefit that is provided to those making use of the system. It seems to us at least arguable that to strike a fair balance between the individual and the general community, those who pay to make use of a sewerage system should be charged sufficient to cover the cost of paying compensation to the minority who suffer damage as a consequence of the operation of the system.[49]

On Thames Water's appeal to the House of Lords, however, a radically different analysis was adopted. First, it was acknowledged that, in the time between the Court of Appeal's judgment and that of their Lordships, Thames Water had completed work upgrading the sewerage system in the area of the claimant's house, which had served to remove the sewage flooding problems that Mr Marcic had been experiencing. The costs of this work (along with other work to address sewer flooding in other areas under Thames Water's authority) were then taken into account by the regulator when fixing sewerage charges for the subsequent reference period (2005–2010).[50] Thus, the only

46 [2002] QB 929, [100]. The older cases included *Glossop* v. *Heston and Isleworth Local Board* (1879) 12 Ch. D 102 (CA).

47 It had argued that its system of prioritising work was a reasonable way to cope with many such problems, given its limited resources. However, the court took the view that the reasonableness of the defendant's conduct had to be assessed in the light of all of the possible courses of action open to it, including its statutory powers-the *Leakey* duty could even extend to requiring the defendant to exercise its statutory powers of compulsory purchase. Given the defendant's considerable resources and its failure to take *any* action to prevent the flooding, the court refused to accept that its system of work met the reasonableness standard required ([2002] QB 929, [87] and [96]).

48 Since the defendant was a statutory sewage undertaker and a public authority for the purposes of s. 6 of the Human Rights Act 1998, it was possible for Mr Marcic to bring a direct claim against Thames Water for violation of his Convention rights.

49 [2002] QB 929, [113] (CA). On this point, the Court of Appeal expressly disagreed with the judge at first instance, who had held that the defendant's priorities system might be 'entirely fair', even if it resulted in no work ever being done to remedy the flooding to the plaintiff's land One suggestion of the court on how to achieve this compliance with the ECHR was to extend *Rylands* v. *Fletcher* to cover such escapes of sewage, requiring a modification of the current position that this is 'such a use as is proper for the general benefit of the community' and is on that ground exempt from the rule in *Rylands* v. *Fletcher* (see, further, the discussion in ch. 16, below, in particular concerning the case of *Transco plc* v. *Stockport MBC* [2004] 2 AC 1). That such a modification might be required by the ECHR was suggested to be due to the decision in *S* v. *France* (1990) 65 DR 250 (ECommHR): '[w]hen a state is authorised to restrict rights or freedoms guaranteed by the Convention, the proportionality rule may well require it to ensure that these restrictions do not oblige the person concerned to bear an unreasonable burden' (at 263).

50 [2003] UKHL 66, [2004] 2 AC 42, [27]–[28] (per Lord Nicholls).

question that remained was whether Mr Marcic was also entitled to damages. This was the second key facet of their Lordships' judgments. Far greater emphasis was placed upon the existence of a detailed statutory scheme for securing the enforcement of Thames Water's duties with regard to the provision of appropriate sewers under section 94(1) of the Water Industry Act 1991. This was because those duties were only enforceable by the Director General of Water Services ('the Director') under section 18 of the 1991 Act, by means of enforcement orders. Had such an order been made against Thames Water, and the company had failed to comply, then it is clear that Mr Marcic would have been able to rely upon that order to bring proceedings for compensation for loss or damage as a result of a breach of any such order.[51] Since, however, no complaint had been made by Mr Marcic to the Director, nor had any enforcement order been issued, he had to rely upon the application of either the common law of nuisance or the Human Rights Act 1998 to allow him to 'sidestep the statutory enforcement code'.[52] Their Lordships were not willing to allow him to succeed in this endeavour.

Lord Nicholls[53] was at pains to reject the approach of the Court of Appeal to the impact of *Leakey* and *Goldman* v. *Hargrave*, pointing out that Thames Water was no ordinary occupier of land, but a sewage undertaker appointed by statute. It was thus impossible to understand Thames Water's obligations with regard to those sewers without careful appreciation of that statutory regime, and he held that the attempt to impose obligations upon Thames Water under the common law of nuisance would be inconsistent with the statutory scheme. Mr Marcic's claim was basically that Thames Water should build more sewers, yet the statutory scheme was specifically designed to prevent the possibility of an individual householder bringing proceedings against a sewage undertaker for failure to provide efficient sewers. The addition of a common law claim 'would set at nought the statutory scheme. It would effectively supplant the regulatory role the Director was intended to discharge when questions of sewer flooding arise.'[54] Lord Hoffmann took a similar approach, emphasizing strongly the difficulty of requiring a court to rule upon the difficult questions of prioritisation of such works, especially in the light of the wide range of broader public interest questions that had to be addressed by the Director in fulfilling his regulatory functions. 'These,' he said, 'are decisions which courts are not equipped to make in ordinary litigation. It is therefore not surprising that for more than a century the question of whether more or better sewers should be constructed has been entrusted by Parliament to administrators rather than judges.'[55]

This approach meant that the focus upon Human Rights considerations was relocated to the question of whether Mr Marcic's rights under Article 8 and Article 1 of the First Protocol to the ECHR could found a direct cause of action against Thames Water.

[51] Because s. 22 of the Water Industry Act 1991 specifically provides for this possibility, since the company's duty under an enforcement order is 'a duty owed to any person who may be affected by a contravention of the order'.

[52] [2003] UKHL 66, [2004] 2 AC 42, [22] (per Lord Nicholls).

[53] *Ibid.*, [29]–[36], with whose judgment Lords Scott, Hope and Steyn concurred.

[54] *Ibid.*, at [35]. [55] *Ibid.*, at [64].

Here, too, Mr Marcic was unsuccessful, which should not be surprising in the light of their Lordships' emphasis upon the significance and force of the statutory regulation and enforcement scheme. First, the direct claim against Thames Water was rejected for being similarly inconsistent with the statutory regime.[56] This then raised the issue whether or not the statutory scheme for regulation and enforcement was itself compatible with Mr Marcic's rights under the Convention: again, their Lordships were unanimous in holding that no breach[57] of his Convention rights had been established. The existence of the mechanism for making a complaint to the Director, with the possibility of enforcement orders and judicial review of the Director's decision on such a complaint, provided adequate protection for such rights. Here, again, the complex range of public interest issues at stake and the need to balance individual rights with the broader needs of the community were stressed in the judgments of their Lordships: there was no evidence that Parliament had adopted a balance that was inappropriate in the circumstances.[58] Thus, overall, the outcome of the *Marcic* litigation shows that great case must be taken in expanding arguments based on the measured duty of care into areas where statutory regulation and enforcement regimes play the major role. In such circumstances, potential claimants are well advised to make use of all possible statutory complaints procedures in good time and providing as much detailed evidence to the regulator as possible about such nuisances.

(B) INTERFERENCE WITH USE OR ENJOYMENT OF LAND

The claimant's enjoyment of land may be affected in various ways. Most typically this happens as a result of noise, smells or interference with his rights to light, air and uninterrupted view. However, while 'English law had long recognized the duty of occupiers of land not to offend their neighbour's sense of smell or hearing, it has left them lamentably free to offend their neighbour's sense of sight'.[59] To the extent that this statement refers to a right of uninterrupted view, it is correct, since no such right has ever been recognised. But a claimant's right to the free passage of light (for purposes of illumination and heating)[60] can be protected according to the usual rules of nuisance[61] so long as it exists as an easement. The right to the free access of air will be protected in an even more limited way, the main requirement being that it is flowing from defined or limited openings.[62] The same (non-liability) rule was recently held to apply to interferences with television reception caused by the defendant erecting on his land a huge tower block. As Lord Hoffmann put it: 'The general principle is that at common law

[56] *Ibid.*, [38]–[39] (per Lord Nicholls), [71] (per Lord Hoffmann) and [87] (per Lord Hope).

[57] Although see *ibid.*, [44] (per Lord Nicholls), where a note of concern is sounded with regard to the consistent availability under the statutory regime of compensation for external flooding.

[58] See, e.g., *ibid.* at [42] (per Lord Nicholls).

[59] *McVittie* v. *Bolton Corp.* [1945] KB 281, 283, per Scott LJ.

[60] *Allen* v. *Greenwood* [1980] Ch. 119.

[61] *Colls* v. *Home and Colonial Stores Ltd.* [1904] AC 179 (the deprivation of light must not be trivial).

[62] *Bass* v. *Gregory* (1890) 25 QBD 481.

anyone may build whatever he likes upon his land. If the effect is to interfere with the light, air or view of his neighbour, that is his misfortune. The owner's right to build can be restrained only by covenant or the acquisition (by grant or prescription) of an easement of light or air . . . for the benefit of windows or apertures on adjoining land.'[63] The claimant's main protection thus lies in the observance of the planning system.[64] Any detailed discussion of interference with light and air would require an extended excursion into the law of servitudes and this lies outside the scope of this book.

Not every interference with enjoyment of property will be actionable.[65] The following statement from the Vice-Chancellor's judgment in *Walter* v. *Selfe*[66] conveys in substance (if not in modern language) the kind of standard courts are likely to apply. The inconvenience must thus be

> considered in fact as more than fanciful, more than one of mere delicacy or fastidiousness, as an inconvenience materially interfering with the ordinary comfort . . . of human existence, not merely according to elegant or dainty modes and habits of living, but according to plain and sober and simple notions among the English people.

In order to determine this in practice, the courts often find themselves weighing more openly a variety of factors in the process of determining the 'unreasonableness' of the situation. As always, the basic requirement is that the interference must be objectively unreasonable and, if it is not, the claimant's claim will fail, however opprobrious the defendant's conduct may be. As Knight-Bruce V-C's statement implies, people must learn to put up with the 'give and take' which is part of social co-existence, and only to this extent will the law protect interferences. Protection ceases when this limit is exceeded and interferences beyond it become actionable as nuisances.[67] So judges have here to strike a balance, so far as possible, between the conflicting interests of the occupier of land and his neighbour.[68]

Paradoxically, it seems that the more 'advanced' a society becomes the likelier it is that a growing number of interfering activities may be regarded as reasonable. So, what is reasonable depends upon the facts of each case, and the tests that have been periodically suggested are, inevitably, flexible. As Lord Wright put it in *Sedleigh-Denfield* v. *O'Callaghan*, echoing in less flowery language the above-quoted statement of Knight-Bruce V-C:

> A balance has to be maintained between the right of the occupier to do what he likes with his own, and the right of his neighbour not to be interfered with. It is impossible to give any

63 *Hunter* v. *Canary Wharf Ltd.* [1997] 2 WLR 684, 711.

64 Which in this case, however, was for business and economic reasons seriously truncated—an element which exacerbates the, arguably, unfair result. Contrast *Nor-Video Services Ltd.* v. *Ontario Hydro* (1978) 84 DLR (3rd) 221.

65 Indeed, the courts can refuse to characterise a particular situation as relating to the enjoyment of the land at all: see *Anglian Water Services Ltd.* v. *Crawshaw Robbins Ltd.* [2001] BLR 173, where Stanley Burton J doubted whether the loss of gas supply due to flooding amounted to anything more than an interference with the use of the appliances, rather than the land itself (see esp. paras. 124 and 142).

66 (1851) 4 De G & Sm. 315; 64 ER 849, per Knight-Bruce V-C.

67 Succinctly explained in the American *Restatement (Second) Tort* (1979), para. 822, note *g*.

68 Expressed e.g. by Veale J in *Halsey* v. *Esso Petroleum Co. Ltd.* [1961] 1 WLR 683, 698, echoing Knight-Bruce V-C in *Walter* v. *Selfe* (1851), 4 De G & Sm. 315, 322; 64 ER 849, 852.

precise or universal formula. Broadly speaking it may be said that a useful test is perhaps what is reasonable according to the ordinary usages of mankind living in society, or, more correctly, in a particular society.[69]

'Reasonableness', therefore, has come to depend upon a variety of factors of which the most important are the duration of the interference, the sensitivity of the plaintiff, the character of the neighbourhood and the fault of the defendant.

(i) Duration of Interference

The general rule is that for an interference to be thought unreasonable it has to be of appreciable duration. As Talbot J put it in *Cunard* v. *Antifyre Ltd.*:[70] 'Private nuisances, at least in the vast majority of cases, are interferences for a substantial length of time by owners or occupiers of property with the use or enjoyment of neighbouring property.' What amounts to 'substantial length' is a matter of fact, though in *Crown River Cruises Ltd.* v. *Kimbolton Fireworks Ltd.*[71] a firework display on a moored vessel which lasted for about a quarter of an hour and caused a fire to another vessel moored nearby was deemed capable of giving rise to liability in nuisance.

Harrison v. *Southwark and Vauxhall Water Co.*[72] shows that an activity which could otherwise be characterised as a nuisance may be excused because of its temporary and useful nature.[73] The defendants, in the exercise of their statutory powers, sank a shaft in land adjoining the plaintiff's house. The operation entailed a certain amount of noise and vibration in respect of which the plaintiff brought an action in nuisance. It was held that, as the disturbance was only temporary and for a lawful object, it was not a nuisance. These *dicta*, however, seem more relevant to nuisance involving interference with the use and enjoyment of land rather than with occurrences leading to physical injury where isolated events have resulted in liability. A long line of cases involving personal injury caused by falling masonry or other projections supports this view. And the same scepticism about 'continuity' or 'recurrence' as an essential element of nuisance liability is also appropriate in cases involving property damage. In delivering the judgment of the court in *Clift* v. *Welsh Office*,[74] Sir Christopher Slade held that

> when one is dealing with temporary and normal operations, such as demolition and building, there are good reasons why, as a matter of policy, the law should expect neighbours to put up with a certain amount of discomfort and inconvenience; provided that precautions are taken to see that the nuisance is reduced to a minimum. However, we see no sufficient reason why as a matter of policy the law should expect the neighbour, however patient, to put up with actual

[69] [1940] AC 880, 903.

[70] [1933] 1 KB 551, 557. See also *AG* v. *PYA Quarries Ltd.* [1957] 2 QB 169, 192, per Denning LJ.

[71] [1996] 2 Lloyd's Rep. 533.

[72] [1891] 2 Ch. 409, esp. 413–14. See also *Andreae* v. *Selfridge & Company Ltd.* [1938] Ch. 1 (CA), which was discussed and distinguished in relation to cases concerning property damage in *Clift* v. *Welsh Office* [1999] 1 WLR 796 (CA).

[73] But not if the nuisance is ongoing and the interference is significant: see *Dennis* v. *Ministry of Defence* [2003] EWHC 793 (QB), [2003] Env LR 34.

[74] *Clift* v. *Welsh Office* [1999] 1 WLR 796 (CA). Presumably, in such a case, one would have to argue that reasonable user of the defendant's land only extends to non-material interferences with the land of the claimant.

physical damage to his property in such circumstances. Where there is physical damage, the loss should in our judgment fall on the doer of the works rather than his unfortunate neighbour.

Many of the cases focus upon the fact that there exists a dangerous state of affairs which leads to the damage. This is well illustrated by *Midwood & Co. Ltd.* v. *Manchester Corporation*[75] where the electric mains installed by the defendants fused. For three hours inflammable gas had accumulated and an explosion occurred, setting fire to the plaintiff's adjoining premises. The defendants were held liable on account of the dangerous state of affairs. The event itself was serious and the fact that it was isolated did not matter. The need for a potentially dangerous state of affairs was also stressed in *Spicer* v. *Smee*,[76] where, on facts similar to those in the *Midwood* case, the court held that it was the defective wiring rather than the resulting fire that rendered the defendant liable. By contrast, in *Bolton* v. *Stone*[77] both the trial court and the Court of Appeal held that the isolated escape of a ball from a cricket field was not a nuisance because the evidence showed that there was no dangerous state of affairs. As Jenkins LJ said: 'The gist of such a nuisance . . . is the causing or permitting of a state of affairs from which damage is likely to result.'[78]

Perhaps, therefore, the position is that an isolated interference, unlikely to be repeated in the future, will not amount to a nuisance.[79] For if there were no physical interference there would be no question of damages under *St Helens Smelting Co.* v. *Tipping*[80] and there would also be no point in seeking an injunction.[81] But if there is a state of affairs suggesting that the interference may not remain an isolated event, then an action in nuisance (and probably in negligence) may lie. Indeed, in the *Bolton* v. *Stone* situation the fact that the cricket balls had reached the public road only very exceptionally in the past indicated that there was no dangerous state of affairs to justify an action in nuisance.[82]

75 [1905] 2 KB 597. See also Lawton J in *British Celanese* v. *A. J. Hunt Ltd.* [1969] 1 WLR 959, 969. According to Professor Fleming, *The Law of Torts* (8th edn., 1992), 420, n. 93: 'The origin of the idea that nuisance must be continuous or recurring apparently lay in the assize of nuisance, the object of which was abatement. This led the courts to regard nuisance as a condition capable of abatement after it was known to be injurious, but the modern trend is away from this requirement.'

76 [1946] 1 All ER 489.

77 [1951] AC 850.

78 [1950] 1 KB 201, 208. The House of Lords eventually decided the case on negligence, nuisance having been dropped by the plaintiff.

79 But it may give rise to liability in negligence or under the rule of *Rylands* v. *Fletcher*. Although cf. the discussion of the cases in *Anglian Water Services Ltd.* v. *Crawshaw Robbins Ltd.* [2001] BLR 173, paras. 128–44, in which Stanley Burnton J decided that the interruption of gas supplies would not qualify as an actionable nuisance because it 'did not involve an invasion of any substance or form of energy on to the claimant's land. It is not one of the exceptional cases of liability in nuisance without such an invasion. A homeowner or tenant does not have a property right in the supply of gas. His or her protection lies in his or her rights against the gas supplier' (para. 143).

80 (1865) 11 HLC 642; 11 ER 1483.

81 And if one is sought the court will be slow in granting it. *Swaine* v. *Great Northern Ry. Co.* (1846) 4 De GJ & S 211; 46 ER 899.

82 Contrast this case with the later and, in this respect, different cricket case of *Miller* v. *Jackson* [1977] QB 966, where the balls landed regularly like 'thunderbolts from the heavens' (per Cumming-Bruce LJ at 988).

(ii) Sensitivity

In determining whether an interference is reasonable or not the courts will refuse to take account of any abnormal sensitivity of the claimant himself or his property which renders an otherwise innocuous activity of the defendant harmful to him. As Lord Robertson said in *Eastern and South African Telegraph Co. Ltd.* v. *Cape Town Cos. Ltd.*:[83] 'A man cannot increase the liabilities of his neighbour by applying his own property to special uses, whether for business or pleasure'.

In *Robinson* v. *Kilvert*[84] the landlord of certain premises let a floor to the plaintiff to be used as a paper warehouse, but retained the cellar immediately below. He himself manufactured products in the cellar that required the air to be hot and dry, and this was achieved by means of special apparatus. The plaintiff sought an injunction to restrain the landlord from producing these conditions on the ground that the heat damaged his own paper. At the time of the contract the landlord did not know that the plaintiff intended to store a very sensitive kind of paper. The injunction was refused; and the result would, probably, accord with common sense, given the facts of the case. In other instances, however, the balancing of competing interests may make it difficult to decide how to evaluate the claimant's particular sensitivity. Thus, in the American case of *Amphitheaters* v. *Portland Meadows*[85] the court refused to grant an injunction to the owners of an open-air cinema affected by the floodlights of their neighbours who operated a racetrack. Though the case cannot be taken as stating categorically that shedding light on the claimant's land can never be a nuisance, it does suggest that in that instance the court felt that the exceptionally sensitive use to which the claimant had put his land did not entitle him to protection against his neighbour putting his land to an equally legitimate use.

In the recent English case of *Network Rail* v. *Morris*,[86] the claimant Morris ran a recording studio located some 80 metres from mainline railway tracks operated by the defendant. After the defendant had replaced track circuits on the line near the studio, the claimant complained of noise interference with the amplifiers in his recording studio and claimed he had lost £60,000 of business as a result. Despite efforts by the defendant to address the problem, no solution was found and a claim was brought in nuisance by Morris. The Court of Appeal declined to hold that this use of Morris's property fell within the category of such abnormal sensitivity as to exclude it from the protection of the law of nuisance.[87] However, Buxton LJ specifically doubted whether there remained 'any further life in some particular rules of the law of nuisance, such as for instance the concept of "abnormal sensitiveness" drawn from *Robinson* v. *Kilvert*... That rule was developed at a time when liability in nuisance, for damaging a neighbour by use of one's own land, was thought to be strict.'[88] Things were now different because

[83] [1902] AC 381, 393. See also *Heath* v. *Brighton Corporation* (1908) 98 LT 718, 721.

[84] (1889) 41 Ch. D 88, esp. at 97, per Lopes LJ.

[85] (1948) 198 P 2d 847.

[86] [2004] EWCA Civ. 172; [2004] Env LR 41.

[87] *Ibid.*, [19] (per Lord Phillips MR) and [36] (per Buxton LJ).

[88] *Ibid.*, [35].

both he and the Master of the Rolls preferred to treat the case wholly on the basis of whether or not it was foreseeable that the type of damage involved here would be suffered by this claimant, in the light of the approach taken by Lord Goff in *Cambridge Water*.[89] On the facts, the damage involved was held not to have been foreseeable and so no claim in nuisance could be made out. This case is a further illustration of growing reliance upon the notion of foreseeability to cover all of the balancing elements under discussion here, and also of a judicial tendency to associate the 'modern' law of nuisance more explicitly with the law of negligence. This is a theme to which we will return later in this chapter.[90]

Assuming that it still survives, the sensitivity rule in these cases must not be misinterpreted so as to extend to the remoteness-of-damage phase of the inquiry. If a claimant succeeds, on grounds other than special sensitivity, in establishing an actionable nuisance he will then be compensated even for damage that was the result of the particular sensitivity of his property. Thus, in *McKinnon Industries Ltd.* v. *Walker*[91] sulphur dioxide emitted from the defendant's factory damaged the plaintiff's commercially grown orchids. His claim for his damage was successful even though the defendants argued that the growing of these plants was a particularly sensitive horticultural activity.

(iii) Character of the Neighbourhood

In *St Helens Smelting Co*[92] it was held that the character of the neighbourhood was not to be taken into account in cases of physical damage to property, but might be a relevant factor in cases of interference with enjoyment or use. In *Sturges* v. *Bridgman*[93] Thesiger LJ said:

> Whether anything is a nuisance or not is a question to be determined, not merely by an abstract consideration of the thing itself, but in reference to its circumstances; what would be a nuisance in *Belgrave Square* would not necessarily be so in *Bermondsey*; and where a locality is devoted to a particular trade or manufacture carried on by the traders and manufacturers in a particular established manner not constituting a public nuisance, Judges and juries would be justified in finding, and may be trusted to find, that the trade or manufacture so carried on in that locality is not a private or actionable wrong.

This 'locality' principle, however, should not be taken to mean that courts would automatically sanction an interference merely because it is typical in a particular area.[94] *Rushmer* v. *Polsue & Alfieri Ltd.*[95] in fact shows that the locality principle will rarely be applied against a meritorious claimant. For in that case both the Court of Appeal and

89 *Ibid.*, [24]–[28] (per Lord Phillips MR) and [35]–[38] (per Buxton LJ).

90 See Section 8, below.

91 [1951] 3 DLR 577. The case is pre-*Wagon Mound*, but it is unlikely that a different result would be reached today.

92 (1865) 11 HLC 642; 11 ER 1483.

93 (1879) 11 Ch. D 852, 865.

94 For a discussion of the difficult issue of the impact of a grant of planning permission on the nature of the locality, see Section 5 of this chapter, below.

95 [1906] 1 Ch. 234, esp. Cozens-Hardy LJ at 250–7; affd. [1907] AC 121. The decision is criticised by Ogus and Richardson (Select Bibliography), 298, as economically inefficient: see Section 9(a), below.

the House of Lords accepted the plaintiff's claim for an injunction to restrain the use of the defendant's printing presses at night, even though the premises were in the printing area of London.

(iv) Fault

Is a defendant liable only if he knew or ought to have known of the cause of a nuisance; or could he be liable irrespective of the fault? This may well be the most vexed question in the tort of nuisance. Unfortunately, even though it appears to have attracted much academic attention it still appears to be an unresolved question, largely because one can cite judicial *dicta* which support both strict and fault liability. Thus, in *Goldman* v. *Hargrave* Lord Wilberforce said that 'the tort of nuisance, uncertain in its boundary, may comprise a wide variety of situations, in some of which negligence plays no part, in others of which it is decisive.'[96] The *dictum* appears to confirm the view that some forms of nuisance are strict[97] while others are fault-based; but it does not clarify the *standard* of duty that is appropriate to the different kinds of situations.[98]

To decide this important issue the traditional view favoured a distinction between the creator of a nuisance and one who continued or adopted an existing nuisance. In the first case the liability was said to be strict, while in the second it depended upon whether the defendant knew or ought to have known of the nuisance in the first place.

The idea that the liability of the creator of a nuisance was strict was encouraged by older *dicta* to the effect that carelessness was not necessary for liability. Many of these cases, however, were decided before the modern development of liability for negligence, and should therefore be treated with caution.[99] Other *dicta* come from cases primarily concerned with the availability of an injunction where considerations of the nature of the defendant's duty were irrelevant. For example, in *Rapier* v. *London Tramways Co.*[100] Lindley LJ said: 'If I am sued for nuisance and nuisance is proved it is no defence to say and to prove that I have taken all reasonable care to prevent it.' The action was for an injunction for excessive noise and smell coming from the defendant's large and overcrowded stables. This *dictum* should be understood in context as suggesting that evidence that the defendant had done all he could was no reason for denying the

96 *Goldman* v. *Hargrave* [1967] 1 AC 645, 657.

97 See the differing views of the Court of Appeal and House of Lords on this point in *Cambridge Water Co.* v. *Eastern Counties Leather plc* [1994] 2 WLR 53. See J. A. Weir, 'The Polluter Must Pay—Regardless' [1993] *CLJ* 17.

98 Indeed the case adds, as already noted, a further dimension of uncertainty. For where the nuisance is the result of an act of nature (or, possibly, of a third party) the defendant's standard of care will be fixed by reference to his particular circumstances, i.e. it will be 'subjective'. On the other hand, where the nuisance develops out of a *prima facie* lawful activity by the defendant, then he will be liable only if he failed to foresee what the reasonable man would have foreseen in his position. Here, in other words, we are back to the 'objective' standard which normally prevails in negligence.

99 J. M. Eekelaar, 'Nuisance and Strict Liability' (Select Bibliography) regards *Humphries* v. *Cousins* (1877) 2 CPD 239 as a good example of this group of cases. *Clerk and Lindsell on Torts* (18th edn., 2000), para. 19.29 thus warn that: 'It [is] important . . . to be guided by the more recent cases and to treat with caution statements concerning the standard of duty to be found in the older cases.'

100 [1893] 2 Ch. 588, 600. Similar *dicta* can be found in *Midwood* v. *Manchester Corporation* [1905] 2 KB 597, *Charing Cross Electricity Supply Co.* v. *Hydraulic Power Co.* [1914] 3 KB 772.

plaintiff his injunction for an activity which did amount to a nuisance. But depriving the defendant of this defence does not imply that he was not aware of the likely consequences of the state of affairs existing on his land. As one writer has put it, '[i]t is quite consistent to deny a defendant the defence that he has taken every precaution against an invasion yet insist that his liability depends on actual or presumed knowledge of its likelihood and indeed to hold him liable if he has such knowledge. Prevention must not be confused with detection.'[101] A defendant who has to have actual or presumed knowledge of the likely consequences of his activity can hardly be said to be liable strictly. The important point is that it is unsafe to make the 'fault/strict liability' question depend on the 'creating/continuing a nuisance' dichotomy. For, as we said, it is *implicit* in most cases where the creator of the nuisance was held liable that he knew of the invasion. Only where it cannot be assumed that the creator of nuisance was aware of the consequences of his activity will the state of his knowledge be relevant. But this is equally true for him who creates the nuisance as it is for him who continues it.

The above position was recently reaffirmed by Lord Goff in the *Cambridge Water*[102] case. He there said:

> ...that in this field we must be on our guard, when considering liability for damages in nuisance, not to draw inappropriate conclusions from cases concerned only with a claim for an injunction. This is because, where an injunction is claimed, its purpose is to restrain further action by the defendant which may interfere with the claimant's enjoyment of his land, and *ex hypothesi* the defendant must be aware, if and when the injunction is granted, that such interference may be caused by the act which he is restrained from continuing. It follows that these cases provide no guidance on the question whether foreseeability of harm of the relevant type is a prerequisite of the recovery of damages for causing such harm to the plaintiff.

In attempting to resolve the role that fault (and, more precisely, foreseeability) plays in the tort of nuisance we must, nowadays, look at the wider picture of modern tort law. Thus, in our analysis we must include not only the tendency of the tort of negligence to encroach upon the domain of other torts, but also the possibility of intermediate positions between the possible 'extremes' of strict and negligence liability. The current judicial tendency to treat the principle of 'reasonable user' as the main controlling mechanism for the tort of nuisance must also be borne in mind. The combination of these considerations thus leads us easily into Lord Goff's most recent pronouncement on the subject that can be found in the *Cambridge Water* case. There he said:

> ... it is still the law that the fact that the defendant has taken all reasonable care will not of itself exonerate him from liability, the relevant control mechanism being found within the principle of reasonable user. But it by no means follows that the defendant should be held liable for damage of a type which he could not reasonably foresee. The development of the law of negligence in the past 60 years points strongly towards a requirement that such foreseeability should be a prerequisite of liability in damages for nuisance, as it is of liability in negligence.[103]

101 Eekelaar (Select Bibliography), 197.

102 *Cambridge Water Co. v. Eastern Leather plc* [1994] 2 WLR 53, 75.

103 *Ibid.*, at 75.

Lord Goff was speaking here of cases where the nuisance was created by the defendant himself or by a person for whose actions he is responsible.[104] When the nuisance is caused by natural causes or by the act of persons for whom the defendant is *not* responsible, the liability of the latter will be determined by cases such as *Sedleigh Denfield* v. *O'Callaghan* and *Goldman* v. *Hargrave*. The forward march of the tort of negligence (and its individual criteria) is thus discernable, making it increasingly difficult to deny that strict liability is, in this area of the law as well, in retreat. Nevertheless, care must be taken in the approach to such cases, as it seems that matters relating to the burden of proof upon each of the parties may be the key issue in nuisance claims. If, as Lord Goff suggests, the control mechanism for liability is 'reasonable user', then if such user is shown to be unreasonable it will be incumbent upon the defendant to show that reasonable steps were taken to prevent the nuisance.[105] The New Zealand Court of Appeal in *Hamilton* v. *Papakura District Council*[106] preferred to treat this task for the defendant as the raising of a defence, while the Court of Appeal in *Marcic* v. *Thames Water Utilities Ltd.* was willing to apply the maxim *res ipsa loquitur* to furnish sufficient proof that the defendant had not taken sufficient steps to prevent the nuisance shown.[107] Thus, strict liability in the absolute sense is undoubtedly in retreat in this area and the available defences do make use of concepts which are strongly influenced by the law of negligence, but the total assimilation of nuisance into negligence has yet to occur in this field.

(v) Malice

Another form of fault is malicious behaviour and here the question is whether a lawful act becomes unlawful if done maliciously. In *Bradford Corporation* v. *Pickles*[108] the defendant, annoyed by the plaintiff's refusal to buy his land at the inflated price he demanded, maliciously prevented water percolating in unknown and undefined channels under his land from reaching the plaintiff's adjoining land. The abstraction of water as such was lawful and the House of Lords refused to hold that the defendant's act became unlawful because of his bad motive. This case has traditionally[109] been taken to

[104] And his view was applied robustly by the Court of Appeal in *Savage* v. *Fairclough* [2000] Env. LR 183, denying recovery for contamination of the plaintiff's drinking water by the defendant's activities on his neighbouring pig farm, because the 'hypothetical good farmer' in those circumstances would not have foreseen the type of damage suffered (at 190–2). Meanwhile, in *Jan de Nul (UK)* v. *NV Royale Belge* [2000] 2 Lloyd's Rep. 700, Moore-Bick J held that liability could apply to the foreseeable siltation of the properties adjoining the estuary, in spite of the fact that those responsible 'had taken all reasonable precautions to avoid such damage' (at 713 (para. 36)).

[105] See *Anthony* v. *The Coal Authority* [2005] EWHC 1654 (QB), [133]–[135] and [161] and cf. *Arscott* v. *The Coal Authority* [2004] EWCA Civ. 892, [2005] Env LR 6.

[106] [2000] 1 NZLR 265, para. 74 (a point not addressed by the Privy Council on appeal: [2002] UKPC 9, [2002] 3 NZLR 308).

[107] [2002] QB 929. Contrast *Green* v. *Lord Somerleyton* [2003] EWCA Civ. 198, [2004] 1 P & CR 33, where the Court of Appeal refused to adopt a similar approach to the assessment of a possible breach of the *Leakey* measured duty of case when floodwater flowed on to neighbouring Norfolk marshland (at [105]), since those marshes were the 'natural receptor' for such water flows.

[108] [1895] AC 587.

[109] But see Buckley (Select Bibliography), 16. It must be remembered, of course, that the defendant in that case was not motivated by any spite against the people of Bradford, but was merely trying to obtain the highest possible price for his land. See also G. H. L. Fridman 'Motive in the English Law of Nuisance' (Select Bibliography).

give a negative answer to the question 'does a lawful act become unlawful because it is done with malice?' For, although it concerns water rights with regard to which special rules apply, it contains *dicta* of wider import that, with other subsequent and equally wide pronouncements, influenced the development of English law on this subject. On the other hand, it could be argued that the water which Pickles abstracted was only a *prospective* amenity as far as the plaintiffs were concerned, from which it might follow that a malicious interference with a *present* amenity could be actionable. Two cases lend some support to this contention.

In *Christie* v. *Davey*[110] the plaintiff, a music teacher, lived in a semi-detached house next to the defendant. The latter, annoyed by the plaintiff's piano lessons, started to produce loud noises designed to make life intolerable for the plaintiff. An injunction was granted. *Christie* v. *Davey* was followed in *Hollywood Silver Fox Farm Ltd.* v. *Emmett*,[111] where the defendant, whose premises adjoined the plaintiff's silver fox farm, maliciously procured his son to discharge guns on his own land as near as possible to the breeding pens so as to prevent the silver foxes from breeding and thus cause damage to the plaintiffs. He, too, was held liable.[112] This shows how the defendant's malice may characterise the interference with the plaintiff as unreasonable. For in the absence of malice this could well have been treated as a case of undue sensitivity.

These cases, however, do not establish any broad proposition that a claimant is entitled to success whenever a defendant maliciously interferes with an existing amenity of his.[113] For, as far as water rights are concerned at any rate, there is authority[114] to the effect that abstraction of water, even in the claimant's land (a present amenity), is still not actionable (though the particular case does not deal specifically with malicious abstraction). These unsatisfactory distinctions are the result of the piecemeal approach of the common law as well as the absence of a general and coherent theory of abuse of rights.

110 [1893] 1 Ch. 316, esp. at 326–7, per North J.

111 [1936] 2 KB 468, noted in 52 *LQR* 461, and 53 *LQR* 1–3. Another possible way of reconciling the *Pickles* case with *Christie* v. *Davey* and *Hollywood Silver Fox Farm* is to say that in the latter two cases the interference was capable of being regarded as a nuisance (even absent of malice) but that this was not so in *Pickles*. A slightly different explanation is offered by *Salmond and Heuston on the Law of Torts* (20th edn., 1992), 66.

112 In *Hunter* v. *Canary Wharf Ltd.* [1997] 2 WLR 684 at 722, Lord Cooke said (*obiter*) that he did 'not think... that the view that malice is irrelevant would have wide acceptance today'.

113 Lord Denning is one of the few judges who has consistently tried to build a more generalised theory of abuse of rights. For example, in *Secretary of State for Employment* v. *ASLEF (No. 2)* [1972] 2 All ER 949, 967, he said: '[t]here are many branches of our law when an act which would otherwise be lawful is rendered unlawful by the motive or object with which it is done'. This bold approach goes back to his dissenting judgment in *Chapman* v. *Honig* [1963] 2 QB 502, 510. Malice, of course, plays an important part in the law of defamation in the sense that, when proved, it can destroy certain defences (see ch. 21, below).

114 *Popplewell* v. *Hodkinson* (1869) LR 4 Exch. 248. For a discussion of the 'water cases' see J. G. Fleming, *The Law of Torts* (7th edn., 1987), 400–1. See also *Stephens* v. *Anglian Water Authority* [1987] 3 All ER 379 (no action in negligence either).

4. WHO CAN SUE AND WHO CAN BE SUED?

(A) WHO CAN SUE

The traditional position of English law has been that only those who have a legal interest in the land affected can sue in private nuisance.[115] An alternative way to put this is to say that only those with an exclusive possession of the land can bring an action in nuisance. In practice this means freehold owners,[116] but it also includes tenants in occupation,[117] licensees with exclusive possession,[118] reversioners if they can prove permanent injury to their interests[119] and even a person who has no title to the land but has exclusive possession of it.[120] This last category has been held by the Court of Appeal in *Pemberton* v. *Southwark London Borough Council*[121] to include 'tolerated trespassers',[122] because such occupants did have exclusive possession right up until the moment that they were evicted.[123] Intriguingly, reference was also made to the importance of Article 8 ECHR in determining this issue: Clarke LJ specifically stated that 'I regard [Article 8 ECHR] as a relevant factor in determining whether a tolerated trespasser has a sufficient right to sue the council in trespass or nuisance.' We will return to this point below.

Mere visitors, on the other hand, cannot bring an action. At common law the same was true of the tenant's wife. So, when in *Malone* v. *Laskey*[124] vibrations on the defendant's premises caused the collapse of a cistern and consequent injury to the wife of the occupier of the adjoining premises, she was denied an action in nuisance because she had no proprietary or possessory interest in the land.[125] This rule has, nowadays, been

115 *Malone* v. *Laskey* [1907] 2 KB 141 is the decision most influential for this point of view; and it has been followed by *Nunn* v. *Parkes & Co.* (1924) 59 LJ 806, *Cunard* v. *Antifyre* [1933] 1 KB 551 (esp. at 557 per Talbot J), *Metropolitan Properties Ltd.* v. *Jones* [1939] 2 All ER 202 (esp. 205 per Goddard LJ).

116 Co-owners can sue each other: *Hooper* v. *Rogers* [1975] Ch. 43, 51.

117 *Jones* v. *Chappell* (1875) LR 20 Eq. 539 (weekly tenant), *Burgess* v. *Woodstock* [1955] 4 DLR 615, at 619 (tenant at will). The same applies to tenants wishing to sue their landlord: *Vaughan* v. *Halifax Dartmouth Bridge Commission* (1961) 29 DLR (2d) 523.

118 *Newcastle-under-Lyme Corp.* v. *Wolstanton Ltd.* [1947] Ch. 92, at 106–8. But not those without such possession: see *Jan de Nul (UK)* v. *NV Royale Belge* [2000] 2 Lloyd's Rep. 700, 719, where contracts which granted only the right to put down a mooring on the land of another (and which could be cancelled by the landowner at any time) did not provide such exclusive possession. However, as discussed below (Section 7), these parties in *Jan de Nul* had the fallback position of a claim in public nuisance.

119 *Colwell* v. *St Pancras BC* [1904] 1 Ch. 707, 713, per Joyce J. What if the nuisance merely interferes with use or enjoyment but does not affect the property? Older cases, e.g. *Simpson* v. *Savage* (1856) 1 CB (NS) 347; 140 ER 143, seemed to deny the reversioner any right of action, but the judge in *Hampstead & Suburban Properties Ltd.* v. *Diomedous* [1969] 1 Ch. 248 seemed to find this distinction unattractive.

120 *Foster* v. *Warblington UDC* [1906] 1 KB 648.

121 [2000] 1 WLR 1672 (CA).

122 Who have breached the terms of a possession order (e.g. by failing to continue rent instalment payments, which have been agreed to pay off a previous debt owing to the landlord) and are liable to be evicted at any time that the local authority obtains a warrant for possession.

123 In so holding, the court rejected the argument that possession had to be of the character that would found a claim for adverse possession against the owner of the property.

124 [1907] 2 KB 141 (not overruled on this point by *Billings AC & Sons* v. *Riden* [1958] AC 240, 254, 264).

125 Her action in negligence also failed though, nowadays, it would succeed.

modified by the Matrimonial Homes Act 1967 (consolidated by amendments in the Matrimonial Homes Act 1983) and the Family Law Act 1996, which give *spouses* a statutory right of occupation which, if properly registered, is enforceable against all the world.[126] But cohabiting partners, children, other relatives and guests cannot, in English law, bring an action for nuisance in the absence of exclusive possession as defined above.[127]

By re-confirming the validity of the above restrictive interpretation of the list of possible claimants, the majority decision of the House of Lords in *Hunter* v. *Canary Wharf Ltd.*[128] has gone against a number of Commonwealth judgments[129] as well as a bold attempt by a majority of our own Court of Appeal[130] to liberate our law from its past. Nonetheless, the majority decisions embody a rigorous analysis of the existing case law (as well as the history of the tort) and in this sense provide interesting insights into how differing judicial philosophies and techniques can affect the outcome of a dispute.

The examination—necessarily brief—of this aspect of this case must start by quoting an interesting observation by Lord Cooke. The learned Lord thus stressed, it is submitted correctly, that:

> . . . in logic more than one answer can be given [to this problem]. Logically it is possible to say that the right to sue for interference with the amenities of a home should be confined to those with proprietary interests. . . . No less logically the right can be accorded to all who live in the home. *Which test should be adopted . . . is a question of the policy of the law. It is a question not capable of being answered by analysis alone. All that analysis can do is to explore the alternatives. . . .* The reasons why I prefer the alternative [to the position adopted by the majority] . . . is that it gives better effect to widespread conceptions concerning the house and family.[131]

Lord Cooke would thus have been willing to respond to the appeal of textbook writers[132] to attempt 'a degree of modernisation' in the law 'while freeing it from undue reliance upon the technicalities of land law'. One suspects that such an approach to case-law development would have appealed to judges such as Lord Denning or pioneering jurists such as Professor John Fleming of the Berkeley Law School. But it was doomed to failure in the current climate that prevails in our highest court where, for instance, Lord Hoffmann boldly stated that 'the development of the common law should be rational and coherent. It should not distort its principles and create anomalies merely as an expedient to fill a gap.'[133] Once this is accepted as the cornerstone of

126 For fuller details, Kodilinye, 'Standing to Sue in Private Nuisance' (Select Bibliography). See, also, *Hunter* v. *Canary Wharf Ltd.* [1997] 2 WLR 684 at 696 (per Lord Goff) and 710 (per Lord Hoffmann).

127 As a matter of common law, this is now beyond dispute as a result of the *Hunter* decision; however, see the discussion of the *McKenna* v. *British Aluminium* case in the subsequent text.

128 [1997] 2 WLR 684.

129 E.g. *Motherwell* v. *Motherwell* (1976) 73 DLR (3rd) 62, *Devon Lumber Co. Ltd.* v. *MacNeil* (1987) 45 DLR (4th) 300.

130 In *Khorasandjian* v. *Bush* [1993] QB 727.

131 *Ibid.*, 719, emphasis added.

132 Led by *Clerk and Lindsell on Torts* (17th edn., 1995), paras. 910 and 911.

133 [1933] QB 709. Echoes, here, of Lord Mustill's dissent in *White* v. *Jones* [1995] 2 AC 207.

the philosophy of the majority, the resolution of the dispute acquires a certain legalistic tone. Thus, the question (implicitly) becomes what technical arguments can be found in favour of the *status quo*. Between them, the majority had little difficulty in finding three; and one cannot deny their force (once one accepts the basic premise that one is not free to break free from the existing technicalities of land law). Thus, Lord Goff argued that the current state of the law could claim 'certainty' and 'efficiency' on its side.[134] To these two points one must add Lord Hoffmann's analysis of Lord Westbury's views discussed above. For once one accepts the view that in his *St Helens* judgment Lord Westbury did not intend to create two separate torts (one dealing with material interference and one with interference with enjoyment), it follows logically and inexorably that only those with an interest in land can sue. The decision in *Hunter* thus does more than tackle, for the time being at least, a particular problem area of the law in nuisance: it gives us some revealing insights into the views our judges have about the interplay of interpretation and development of the law.

However, it is possible that there is an alternative means by which to break these shackles: Article 8 ECHR and the Human Rights Act 1998. As discussed above, the Court of Appeal in *Pemberton* was willing to refer to considerations of a right to a private and family life to bolster its conclusion that a tolerated trespasser did have standing to sue in nuisance. Furthermore, Lord Cooke's dissenting opinion in *Hunter* relied explicitly on the European Convention on Human Rights, as well as on the United Nations Convention on the Rights of the Child, in reaching the conclusion that we should be 'treating residence as an acceptable basis of standing at common law in the present class of case'.[135] The recent case of *McKenna* v. *British Aluminium*[136] suggests that, in the light of the duty of the courts (as a public authority under s. 6(1)(3)(a) of the Human Rights Act 1998) 'not to act in a way which is incompatible with a Convention right', Article 8 ECHR may have the potential to liberalise the rules on who can sue in nuisance. The case concerned claims by permanent residents against a neighbouring factory for the infliction of mental distress and physical harm over a period of time, which was still continuing. On a motion to strike out the claims of those who were children and thus permanent residents but lacking any proprietary interest in the land, Neuberger J refused to dismiss the possibility that an extension to the standing rule might be needed in the light of Article 8 ECHR. While acknowledging that it might be thought inappropriate to extend a 'property-based claim' such as nuisance (or *Rylands* v. *Fletcher*) to cover this fact situation, he held that:

> There is obviously a powerful case for saying that effect has not been properly given to Article 8.1 [ECHR] if a person with no interest in the home, but who has lived in the home for some time and had his enjoyment of the home interfered with, is at the mercy of the person who owns the home, as the only person who can bring proceedings.

[134] *Ibid.*, 696.

[135] [1997] AC 655, 713–15, citing in particular the important case of *Lopez Ostra* v. *Spain* (1994) 20 EHRR 277, which found that fumes and smells from a waste treatment plant could amount to a breach of Art. 8 ECHR.

[136] [2002] Env. LR 30.

This argument may be bolstered by the fact that, in the follow-up to *Hunter* under the ECHR, the European Commission of Human Rights considered the position of all of the *Hunter* applicants to be protected by Article 8 ECHR, not just those with proprietary rights in the land in question.[137] While *McKenna* was only a case heard on a motion to strike out, the parties provided very full argument on these difficult issues and it may be that Neuberger J's careful judgment will reopen this debate in the years ahead. Of course, where the defendant is a public authority (under section 6 of the Human Rights Act 1998) then a direct action against that defendant will lie at the suit of anyone who holds Article 8 and/or Article 1 of the First Protocol rights under the Convention, whether or not they satisfy the proprietary interest criterion laid down in *Hunter.*[138]

What is the legal position if the damage occurred before the claimant acquired an interest in the property? *Prima facie*, the answer should be that the claimant would have no remedy unless he proved that the damage resulted from a continuing nuisance; in which case he could recover whether the loss began before or after his acquisition of the premises. This proposition is supported and illustrated by *Masters* v. *Brent London Borough Council*,[139] where the plaintiff's father was the leasehold owner of premises which developed cracks because of the encroaching roots of a line of trees planted by the defendant local council in the vicinity of his house. Unable to meet the cost of repairs, the plaintiff's father sold the premises to him in order to enable him to raise a mortgage and, *inter alia*, meet the repair costs with the mortgage money. This, the plaintiff did and then sued the local authority, which unsuccessfully argued that since the damage had occurred before the plaintiff had acquired an interest in the premises, he should not be compensated.

This result was endorsed by the House of Lords in *Delaware Mansions Ltd.* v. *Westminster City Council*,[140] where the plaintiffs had acquired the property and had had to have remedial work done to prevent further damage to the property due to encroaching tree roots.[141] An engineer's report had been secured and passed to the defendant,

137 *Khatun & 180 Others* v. *United Kingdom* (unreported, 1 July 1998) However, it should be noted that the Commission went on to find that the development in Canary Wharf was necessary in response to the pressing social need for development and regeneration of the area and the impact which it had upon television reception was proportionate to achieving that goal and thus the interference with the right was justified under Art. 8(2) ECHR.

138 *Dennis* v. *Ministry of Defence* [2003] EWHC 793 (QB), [2003] Env LR 34, where Buckley J recognised that an interference with the claimants' rights under both Art. 8 ECHR and Art. 1 of the First Protocol to the ECHR had occurred ([55] ff.) and that the claimant's wife would have had a separate claim under that heading ([91]). However, since he had included loss of amenity to the whole family within the damages awarded for nuisance, he would have deducted any separate award to Mrs Dennis from the overall total for nuisance in any case (at [91]). See also *Andrews* v. *Reading Borough Council* [2005] EWHC 256, [2006] RVR 56.

139 [1978] QB 841. The case, however, has atypical facts in so far as it involved a sale by one member of a family to another, which may have been accompanied by a discount in the purchase price. For without such a discount the hazards of litigation would make such a transaction dubious, to say the least.

140 [2002] 1 AC 321.

141 Recent tree-root cases have tended to turn on difficult evidentiary questions of causation and foreseeability where multiple possible causes for the damage are involved. In such circumstances, the factor relevant to the defendant's duty in nuisance must be the 'effective' cause or have 'materially contributed' to the damage:

which carried out some pruning of the tree roots but had declined to remove the tree. In a claim for the cost of the remedial work, Lord Cooke of Thorndon held that, so long as double recovery was not an issue, 'where there is a continuing nuisance of which the defendant knew or ought to have known, reasonable remedial expenditure may be recovered by the owner who has had to incur it'.[142] The subsequent case (on a motion to strike out) of *Kirk* v. *Brent London Borough Council*[143] has made clear that there is no pre-condition to a claim for damages that notice must be given to the local authority before carrying out such remedial works. However, the absence of such notice may have an impact upon the assessment of the extent of any damage that may be recovered at trial.

As stated, nuisance liability primarily protects interests in land, though damages in respect of chattels on the land can also be recovered.[144] Until not long ago it would have also been possible to argue that personal injury, incidentally suffered by the occupier, might also be compensatable. There was no English case that had allowed recovery of damages for personal injuries in an action of *private* nuisance, though the court in the Canadian case of *Devon Lumber Co. Ltd.* v. *MacNeill*[145] did do so. The recovery of pure economic loss by means of an action in *private* nuisance also seems uncertain, especially in these days when this kind of loss receives short shrift in the context of the tort of negligence. Yet there was some (slender) authority to support recovery.[146]

But the current trend of House of Lords decisions suggest that such claims should be entertained under our 'fully developed law of negligence'[147] and are thus unlikely to fare well if pleaded in nuisance. Disturbance of health, comfort and enjoyment might, likewise, be actionable in those nuisances that come under the heading of 'interferences with enjoyment and use'. As Professor Fleming[148] remarked, 'certain sophisticated interests of personality which, standing alone, receive only limited protection by our law, are most amply vindicated if asserted in the title of the free use and enjoyment of land, where such factors as personal taste and sensibilities are accorded fuller protection'. Yet, once again, one must remind the reader of the current hostile climate towards such expanding views. This may explain the disapproval shown in *Hunter* towards the majority view in *Khorasandjian* v. *Bush*,[149] which had enabled a plaintiff to rely upon the tort of nuisance in order to obtain redress for persistent telephone harassment by the defendant.[150] However, more recently Neuberger J in *McKenna* v. *British Aluminium*

Loftus-Brigham v. *Ealing London Borough Council* [2003] EWCA Civ. 1490 (noted by S. Brown and S. Lindsay, 'Seeing the Wood for the Trees: *Loftus-Brigham* and the apportionment of damage' (2005) 21 *Const. LJ* 431), applied in *Eiles* v. *Southwark London Borough Council* [2006] EWHC 1411 (T & CC).

142 *Ibid.*, para. 38. Lord Cooke also pointed out that, '[a]lthough counsel evidently preferred a more insular approach, it can be useful to remember that there is a common law world elsewhere which may provide some help, particularly on issues where English law is not yet settled', before going on to consider certain American and Australasian authorities which supported a similar conclusion.

143 [2005] EWCA Civ. 1701.

144 *Halsey* v. *Esso Petroleum Co. Ltd.* [1961] 1 WLR 683.

145 (1988) 45 DLR (4th) 300.

146 See *British Celanese Ltd.* v. *A. H. Hunt Ltd.* [1969] 1 WLR 959, *Ryeford Homes Ltd.* v. *Sevenoaks District Council* (1989) 16 *Const. LR* 75.

147 *Hunter* v. *Canary Wharf Ltd.* [1997] 2 WLR 684, 695.

148 *Torts* (8th edn., 1992), 417.

149 [1993] QB 727.

150 That defect in our law has now been cured by the enactment of the Protection from Harassment Act 1997 (see ch. 9, Section 5, above). The potential of the *Khorasandjian* judgment goes beyond what is now covered by the

was not prepared to rule out that a claim for physical injury and mental distress might be brought in nuisance (or *Rylands* v. *Fletcher*): again, one might argue that a reading of Article 8 ECHR would require a more flexible application of the common law rules in this area on what is recoverable in such claims.[151] Whether the case law will develop further in this direction depends upon the courts' interpretation of their duties under the Human Rights Act 1998 *vis-à-vis* the common law.

The case of *Dennis* v. *Ministry of Defence* provides clear evidence of the potential of such arguments under the 1998 Act, but also creates difficulties.[152] Buckley J awarded damages for loss of amenity, including a sum to cover the enjoyment of the property by the whole family, not just the property owner.[153] While the reasoning behind the inclusion of the whole family in assessing the award is not clear, it could certainly be argued that this approach only makes sense if it is considered as the infusion of the common law of nuisance with principles derived from the rights to be protected under the Convention, thus permitting departure from the strictures of the approach in *Hunter*.[154]

(B) WHO CAN BE SUED

In most private nuisances the activity complained of will emanate from the defendant's land and the person who will be sued is its owner or occupier. We have seen that in rare cases the cause of the interference may be a floating barge,[155] could occur on the public highway[156] or could emanate from the sea,[157] neither of the last two being in private ownership. That an action will lie in such cases is not in dispute; but whether it is to be dubbed private or public nuisance seems to be less settled.[158] One commentator has argued that it would be 'unduly restrictive and illogical to limit the scope of private

1997 Act, but its continued vitality must be in doubt even though in *Hunter* Lord Hoffmann was careful not to say that the case was 'wrongly decided' ([1997] 2 WLR 684 at 709); and Lord Cooke was not against it at all: *ibid.*, at 719.

151 [2002] Env. LR 30 (paras. 49–53). See, further, *Ribee* v. *Norrie* [2001] PIQR P8 (CA), a case concerning an occupier's liability for the escape of fire which caused property damage and physical injury to his neighbour. While the case turned on the question of the occupier's responsibility for a fire that was probably started by one of his tenants, the action seems to have proceeded on the basis that damages for personal injury were recoverable under the common law cases concerning the escape of fire.

152 [2003] EWHC 793 (QB), [2003] Env. LR 34 (noted by J. Elvin, 'The Law of Nuisance and the Human Rights Act' [2003] *CLJ* 546, 548).

153 [2003] EWHC 793 (QB), [2003] Env. LR 34, at [91]. Contrast the view taken by W. V. H. Rogers, *Winfield and Jolowicz on Tort* (17th edn., 2006), para. 14–15 (although *Dennis* is not there cited on this point).

154 Buckley J recorded some concern that his conclusion on the existence of nuisance might not directly be covered by authority, and that 'save where it may be considered more appropriate to leave the matter to legislation, the common law should develop in line with European decisions on human rights' ([2003] EWHC 793 (QB), [2003] Env. LR 34, at [49]), but did not return to this point when dealing with the assessment of damages at common law.

155 *Crown River Cruises Ltd.* v. *Kimbolton Fireworks Ltd.* [1996] 2 Lloyd's Rep. 533.

156 E.g. *Midwood & Co. Ltd.* v. *Manchester Corporation* [1905] 2 KB 597. For Canadian authorities, see McLaren, 'The Common Law Nuisance Actions' (Select Bibliography), 505, 519, n. 64.

157 *Southport Corp.* v. *Esso Petroleum Co. Ltd.* [1953] 3 WLR 773 (affd. in the House of Lords [1956] AC 218).

158 Compare Devlin J's views in the *Southport* case [1953] 3 WLR 773, 776, with those of Denning LJ in the Court of Appeal [1954] 2 QB 182, 196–7. See also *Hubbard* v. *Pitt* [1976] QB 142.

nuisance to disputes between neighbouring landowners'.[159] In such cases, however, the person sued is clearly the *creator* of the nuisance and that had long seemed sufficient to establish his liability subject, of course, to the other requirements of liability being satisfied. However, the recent decision of the Court of Appeal in *Hussain* v. *Lancaster City Council*[160] has cast doubt upon this apparently straightforward proposition. The plaintiffs owned a shop and lived on a council housing estate and had been subjected to a severe and prolonged campaign of harassment (often racially motivated) by (*inter alia*) other tenants on the council estate which was owned by the defendants. They claimed damages and an injunction requiring the council to act to curb these activities of its tenants. The Court of Appeal ruled that their claim had rightly been struck out, holding that there was no nuisance because, although 'the acts complained of unquestionably interfered persistently and intolerably with the plaintiffs' enjoyment of the plaintiffs' land, . . . they did not involve the tenants' use of the tenants' land'.[161] This extra restriction would have the undesirable consequence of protecting an independent contractor from liability where, for example, he creates a nuisance on the land of one party while working on the land of another, where he does not have possession of that other party's land.[162] Furthermore, it is difficult to reconcile with certain earlier cases, including some House of Lords authority which assumed that this was not an issue.[163] A preferable way of dealing with the facts of the *Hussain* case was, it is submitted, given by the Court of Appeal in *Lippiatt* v. *South Gloucestershire County Council*:[164]

> The disturbance complained of in *Hussain*'s case was a public nuisance for which the individual perpetrators could be held liable, and they were identified as individuals who lived in council property; but their conduct was not in any sense linked to, nor did it emanate from, the homes where they lived.[165]

Where the occupier of the land is held liable for his own conduct, the situation is straightforward. But liability may also attach to the occupier for his failure to rectify the unreasonable conduct or state of affairs created by his predecessor, or even a trespasser, provided that he knew or ought to have known of it; provided, in other words, he knowingly or negligently *continued* the nuisance.

In *Sedleigh-Denfield* v. *O'Callaghan*,[166] for example, the plaintiff's field was flooded as a result of the blockage of the drainage system in the defendant's land by a trespasser.

159 Buckley (Select Bibliography), 5. 160 [2000] QB 1.

161 *Ibid.*, 23 (per Hirst LJ).

162 W. V. H. Rogers, *Winfield and Jolowicz on Tort* (17th edn., 2006), para. 14–17.

163 E.g. *Southport Corp.* v. *Esso Petroleum Co. Ltd.* [1953] 3 WLR 773 (affd. in the House of Lords [1956] AC 218-see esp. 224–5 (per Lord Devlin)). See, further, M. Davey, 'Neighbours in Law' [2001] *Conv.* 31.

164 [2000] QB 51, 61 (per Evans LJ).

165 It should also be noted that Art. 8 ECHR may have an impact upon even this rationalisation (even though the Court of Appeal in *Mowan* v. *Wandsworth London Borough Council* [2001] 3 EGCS 133 rejected any such challenge on facts prior to the entry into force of the Human Rights Act 1998): public authorities are under a positive duty to act to protect citizens' human rights under the Convention and it is possible that local authority landlords in such situations will be forced at the very least to establish procedures to assess whether or not any action should be taken against such tenants and, if so, how much: see D. Rook, 'Property Law and the Human Rights Act 1998: A Review of the First Year' [2002] *Conv.* 316. 166 [1940] AC 880.

The defendants were liable, for they were aware, or ought to have become aware through one of their servants, of the possibility of flooding and had done nothing to prevent it. Similarly, with regard to nuisance created by third parties after the defendant's occupation has begun, he will be liable if he knew or ought to have known of it[167] or if he adopted it, for example, by making use of it.[168] Generally speaking, however, failure to remedy an inherited state of affairs tends to be judged more leniently and the occupier's circumstances and resources may be taken into account. As Lord Wilberforce said in *Goldman* v. *Hargrave*:[169]

> the law must take account of the fact that the occupier on whom the duty is cast has, ex hypothesi, had this hazard thrust upon him through no seeking or fault of his own. His interest and his resources, whether physical or material, may be of very modest character either in relation to the magnitude of the hazard, or as compared with those of his threatened neighbour. A rule that required of him in such unsought circumstances in his neighbour's interest a physical effort of which he is not capable, or an excessive expenditure of money, would be unenforceable or unjust.

An occupier is, of course, liable for nuisance caused by his servants committed in the course of their employment; but his possible liability for independent contractors requires separate consideration. The general rule is that in the absence of carelessness in choosing a competent independent contractor, the employer is not liable for a contractor. Yet in nuisance there seem to be a number of exceptions,[170] which is not surprising, since occupiers may be liable even for the acts of strangers. The precise extent of this wider liability is not clear. In *Bower* v. *Peate*[171] Cockburn LJ proclaimed that anyone who orders work to be done, the natural consequences of which are likely to be injurious, cannot escape liability by relying on someone else to do what is necessary to avoid harm. *Bower* v. *Peate* was a case of withdrawal of support from the plaintiff's adjoining premises. It could thus be argued[172] that Cockburn LJ's *dictum* is too wide and should be restricted to withdrawal of support or, at least, to nuisance which produces dangers to property rather than occasional discomfort and annoyance to the plaintiff. Withdrawal of support cases, however, are not the only instances of the liability of occupier for the torts of independent contractors.

Moreover, any restriction of this wider liability to nuisances affecting materially the claimant's property would be incompatible with *Matania* v. *National Provincial Bank Ltd.*,[173] where the defendants were held liable for the discomfort and annoyance caused to the plaintiff as a result of dust and noise being produced by independent contractors

[167] And this holds true even where trespassers based on the occupier's land commit acts amounting to a nuisance on the neighbouring claimant's land: *Lippiatt* v. *South Gloucestershire CC* [2000] QB 51.

[168] For a recent example, see *Marcic* v. *Thames Water Utilities Ltd.* [2002] QB 929 (CA), para. 83.

[169] [1967] 1 AC 645, 663.

[170] *Spicer* v. *Smee* [1946] 1 All ER 489, 495, per Atkinson LJ.

[171] (1876) 1 QBD 321, 326.

[172] See e.g. *Hughes* v. *Percival* (1883) 8 App. Cas. 443, 447, per Lord Blackburn.

[173] [1936] 2 All ER 633. For the most recent discussion, see *Johnson (Trading as Johnson Butchers)* v. *B. J. W. Property Developments Ltd.* [2002] 3 All ER 574 (QBD (T & CC)), [52] ff. (a case concerning an occupier's vicarious liability for a contractor's negligence in fitting a fireplace in a fire breast built into the party wall).

working in the defendants' flat. The better view may be that an occupier of land is under a so-called 'non-delegable duty', which perhaps also gives the clue to the possible escape from liability. For a non-delegable duty does not impose strict liability, but merely a duty to ensure that care is taken.[174] So, if the occupier can show that neither he nor his independent contractor was at fault, he is not liable. There is also Scottish authority[175] to support the view that an occupier may avoid liability if he can show that his independent contractor had exclusive control of the premises at the time of the occurrence of the nuisance.

Finally, the liability in nuisance of landlords and tenants towards (*a*) neighbours and (*b*) passers-by creates difficulties. Generally it is the occupier (invariably the tenant[176]) who is liable in nuisance—in public nuisance, if injury or damage is sustained by a passer-by on the street (discussed in Section 7); and in private nuisance, if injury is sustained by a neighbouring occupier.[177] But to this rule there are exceptions that render the landlord liable, even though he is not the occupier. This happens if: (*a*) he had authorised the nuisance;[178] (*b*) he had let the premises knowing of the nuisance;[179] (*c*) he ought to have known of the nuisance before he let the premises;[180] (*d*) he is under a duty to repair;[181] (*e*) though not bound to repair, he has expressly reserved the right to enter and inspect the premises;[182] and (*f*) he has an implied right to enter and inspect.[183]

It should be noted, however, that before the enactment of section 4(1) of the Defective Premises Act 1972 the landlord's liability in nuisance extended only to occupiers of adjoining premises and not to members of their families and/or their lawful visitors.[184] These persons, however, now receive the same protection as the occupier and, indeed, any other reasonably foreseeable claimant.

[174] See *The Pass of Ballater* [1942] P 112, 117, per Langton J; *Morris* v. *C. W. Martin & Sons Ltd.* [1966] 1 QB 716, 725, per Lord Denning MR.

[175] *Gourock Ropework Co.* v. *Greenock Corp.*, 1966 SLT 125, where it is said that there was no difference in this respect from English law.

[176] Lack of effective control is, invariably, the reason why landlords are not held liable. Thus, in *Habinteg Housing Association* v. *James* (1995) 27 HLR 299, the landlord—a housing association—was not held liable to one of its tenants for a cockroach infestation which may have started in another part of the estate owned by the association.

[177] And, of course, if the actions of the tenant do not amount to an actionable nuisance, then no such nuisance is created merely by proceeding against the landlord instead: *Southwark London Borough Council* v. *Mills* [2001] 1 AC 1 (HL), where the ordinary use of adjoining flats in a building with poor sound-proofing did not amount to a nuisance.

[178] *Harris* v. *James* (1876) 45 LJQB 545, *Sampson* v. *Hodson-Pressinger* [1981] 3 All ER 710, noted by M. Owen, 'Authorised Nuisances' [1982] *CLJ* 38.

[179] *Roswell* v. *Prior* (1701) 12 Mod. Rep. 635; 88 ER 1570. This includes where it is the *ordinary and necessary consequence* of the permitted act or perhaps even where the nuisance is the foreseeable consequence: *Tetley* v. *Chitty* [1986] 1 All ER 663 (noise from go-karting track leased by local authority) for this purpose.

[180] *Brew Bros. Ltd.* v. *Snax (Ross) Ltd.* [1970] 1 QB 612, 636, per Sachs LJ, 644, per Phillimore LJ.

[181] *Payne* v. *Rogers* (1749) 2 HBL 350; 126 ER 590.

[182] *Wilchick* v. *Marks and Silverstone* [1934] 2 KB 56.

[183] *Mint* v. *Good* [1951] 1 KB 517.

[184] E.g. *Malone* v. *Laskey* [1907] 2 KB 141.

5. DEFENCES

The following are good defences:

(i) Inevitable accident is a defence in cases where negligence is essential to liability. Where negligence is not essential, only act of God or secret operations of nature will suffice. The practical significance of this defence is minimal.[185]

(ii) Act of trespasser will not, as already stated, be a defence. The occupier will only be liable if he knowingly or negligently continued the nuisance.[186]

(iii) Ignorance of the state of affairs will be a defence unless it is due to a failure to use reasonable diligence to know of it. In *Ilford Urban District Council* v. *Beal*[187] the defendant built a wall on her land eight or nine feet above a sewer belonging to the plaintiff, which cracked as a result. She was held not liable in negligence or even in nuisance, because she was unaware of the existence of the sewer and could not reasonably have been expected to know of it.

(iv) Prescription applies to (private) nuisances which, if legalised, could be the subject of servitudes. Time starts to run not when the defendant begins his activity, but when it begins to interfere with the claimant. This follows from the fact that the gist of nuisance is the result to the claimant not the activity of the defendant. Thus, in *Sturges* v. *Bridgman*[188] the defendant's premises adjoined those of the plaintiff, a medical practitioner. For over twenty years the defendant had been using noisy machinery, which had not interfered with the plaintiff's use of his land until the latter built a consulting room at the bottom of his garden near the defendant's machinery and then complained of the noise. Prescription was pleaded as a defence but failed, since the nuisance commenced only when the new building was erected, since before then there was no right of action. This defence rarely succeeds in practice.[189]

(v) Contributory negligence could be a defence except, possibly, when the consequence was intended by the defendant. *Dicta* in *Trevett* v. *Lee*[190] (a case of

[185] In *Lord Chesham* v. *Chesham UDC* (1935) 79 *SJ* 453, the defence was pleaded but rejected. Where the activity is actionable both as a nuisance and under *Rylands* v. *Fletcher* the defence may succeed, e.g. *Nichols* v. *Marsland* (1876) 2 Ex. D 1.

[186] *Sedleigh-Denfield* v. *O'Callaghan* [1940] AC 880, 897, *Page Motors Ltd.* v. *Epsom and Ewell Borough Council* (1982) 80 LGR 337.

[187] [1925] 1 KB 671. Cf. *Humphries* v. *Cousins* (1877) 2 CPD 239, *National Coal Board* v. *Evans (J. E.) & Co. (Cardiff) Ltd.* [1951] 2 KB 861.

[188] (1879) 11 Ch. D 852. Cf. *Harvey* v. *Walters* (1873) LR 8 CP 162 (right to discharge water from eaves on adjoining land), *Hulley* v. *Silversprings Bleaching Co.* [1922] 2 Ch. 268 (acquired right to pollute watercourse), *Jones* v. *Pritchard* [1908] 1 Ch. 630 (emission of smoke). Prescriptive rights cannot, apparently, be acquired for the creation of noise, smell, or for the encroachment of branches and roots: *Lemmon* v. *Webb* [1894] 3 Ch. 1; [1895] AC 1.

[189] For a recent illustration of the difficulties, see *Dennis* v. *Ministry of Defence* [2003] EWHC 793 (QB), [2003] Env LR 34, [50]–[54].

[190] [1955] 1 WLR 113. See also *Caswell* v. *Powell Duffryn Associated Collieries Ltd.* [1940] AC 152, 165 (per Lord Atkin).

public nuisance) appear to support this. However, authority is scant, which seems to suggest that the practical significance of this defence is minimal,[191] even though section 14(5) of the Contributory Negligence Act 1945 seems to be clear about the availability of the defence.

(vi) Statutory authority.[192] The general principles of this defence will be discussed later. For the present, suffice it to say that in an action for nuisance statutory authorisation will be a defence only if it can be shown that the interference with the claimant's rights was permitted by express wording in the statute or by necessary implication. It was held in *Metropolitan Asylum District Managers* v. *Hill*[193] that authority to purchase land and erect buildings for the poor and sick could not be regarded as authorisation to site a smallpox hospital in an area so as to interfere with adjoining landowners. The argument that, because there was authority to erect a smallpox hospital, it could be erected anywhere was tantamount to saying that the statute gave a licence to commit any nuisance by means of the hospital, which was clearly unacceptable.

The whole question of statutory authorisation as a defence to nuisance was considered by the House of Lords in *Allen* v. *Gulf Oil Refining Ltd.*,[194] the facts of which were as follows. In 1965 Gulf Oil secured a private Act of Parliament, which stated in its preamble that 'because of increasing public demand for the company's products in the UK... it was essential that further facilities for the importation of crude oil and petroleum products and for their refinement should be made available'. Strangely, though the Act contained specific provisions relating to the acquisition of the necessary land by Gulf Oil and the construction of a refinery and certain subsidiary works, it contained no express authority for the use and operation of the refinery once it had been built. Their Lordships unanimously took the view that the essential problem was one of statutory construction. They also agreed with Lord Dunedin in *Corporation of Manchester* v. *Farnworth*,[195] where he said: 'When Parliament has authorised a certain thing to be made or done in a certain place, there can be no action for nuisance caused by the making or doing of that thing if the nuisance is the inevitable result of the making or doing so authorised. The onus of proving that the result is inevitable is on those who wish to escape liability for nuisance...'.

Agreement, however, ended here. Lord Keith was inclined to construe the Act in accordance with the *contra proferentem* rule, i.e. against the party offering a document

[191] Winfield (Select Bibliography), 200, maintained that the defence is never available in nuisance; G. Williams, *Joint Torts* (1951), 203–5, believed the opposite; R. F. V. Heuston and R. A. Buckley, *Salmond and Heuston on the Law of Torts* (20th edn., 1992), 75, state that it would be unlikely for the defence to succeed while J. G. Fleming, *The Law of Torts* (9th edn., 1998), 491–2, adopts a subtler approach.

[192] A. M. Linden, 'Strict Liability, Nuisance and Legislative Authorization' (1966) 4 *Osgoode Hall LJ* 196. See, generally, ch. 8, Section 5 above.

[193] (1881) 6 App. Cas. 193.

[194] [1981] AC 1001. But if a nuisance is created through the exercise of statutory powers the creator will be liable if he exercised the powers in a negligent manner: see *Tate and Lyle* v. *Greater London Council* [1983] 2 AC 509. Useful guidelines can be found in *Fellowes* v. *Rother District Council* [1983] 1 All ER 513. These points are also discussed below in ch. 24.

[195] [1930] AC 171, 183.

in support of his case,[196] and took the view that the purpose of the Act was merely to confer powers of compulsory purchase of land and not to authorise the operation of a refinery. The rest thought otherwise. True, the Act touched but lightly on the matter of operation and use of the refinery; but they felt that it was unlikely that Parliament merely intended to authorise the acquisition of land and the construction of certain works and not their operation as well. As Lord Diplock put it: 'Parliament can hardly be supposed to have intended the refinery to be nothing more than a visual adornment to the landscape in an area of natural beauty. Clearly the intention of Parliament was that the refinery was to be operated as such . . .'.[197] Lord Wilberforce took a similar view. If the plaintiff were to be granted an injunction, he reasoned, this would mean that the refinery could not be operated, thereby leaving Gulf Oil as owners of land that they had compulsorily acquired but could not use.[198]

Such a result seemed so absurd that the majority felt they had to accept (*a*) that the Act, by necessary implication, not only authorised the building of the refinery, but also its operation and use and (*b*) that it thereby bestowed immunity on Gulf Oil from any 'non-negligent' interferences. Point (*a*) is an understandable and desirable reading of the wording of the enabling Act, but (*b*) is more open to doubt, especially if it leads to a large number of innocent and detrimentally affected citizens being left without legal redress. The difficulty which prevented the majority from separating (*a*) and (*b*) was the belief that if liability for a 'non-negligent' interference were accepted, a claimant would then be more or less 'entitled' to an injunction. This would lead to the closure of the refinery—a result that their Lordships considered to be undesirable. The reasons for this reluctance of the courts to rely on the power given by Lord Cairns's Act (now s. 50 of the Senior Courts Act 1981) and to 'downgrade the plaintiff's remedy from an injunction to mere damages'[199] will be discussed presently. Here suffice it to stress the fear of English courts that such a solution might amount to buying a licence to continue with an interfering activity. Quite apart from the fact that 'interference' in the context of nuisance is a relative concept, the point is whether English law should be more willing, in appropriate circumstances, to award compensation for damage caused even by a lawful activity. As things stand at the moment this can, apparently, only be done by express statutory authority. The Land Compensation Act 1973, section 1, offers an apt example. It provides *inter alia* for compensation to be paid for the depreciation in the value of land by physical factors caused by 'public works'.[200] Gulf Oil's works could not be described as 'public works', though they indirectly benefited the public. Would it not be possible, therefore, to use such enactments by way of analogy so as to provide

[196] [1981] AC 1001, 1020.

[197] *Ibid.*, at 1014.

[198] *Ibid.*, at 1013.

[199] J. A. Jolowicz, 'Should Courts Answer Questions? Does Statutory Authority to Build Confer Immunity from Liability for Use?' [1981] *CLJ* 226, 228–9.

[200] On this, and related matters, see P. Craig, 'Compensation in Public Law' (1980) 96 *LQR* 413. See also s. 10 of the Compulsory Purchase Act 1965, which provided the background to the claim in *Clift* v. *Welsh Office* [1999] 1 WLR 796 (CA).

compensation for deserving claimants without jeopardising the useful activities of certain defendants? If English law wishes to remain committed to the principle that, in the absence of express authorisation, compensation for damage caused through lawful conduct cannot be paid, then it should be prepared to find some way in which to widen the ambit of existing enactments to cover cases such as this. In this vein, such statutes will now have to be interpreted in the light of the Human Rights Act 1998: section 3 provides that '[s]o far as it is possible to do so, primary legislation and subordinate legislation must be read and given effect in a way which is compatible with the Convention rights' and, where this is not possible, the courts must (under section 4) declare the legislation incompatible with the Convention. Thus, it is possible to argue that any future construction of a statute such as the one at issue in *Allen* v. *Gulf Oil* will need to pay much closer attention to the justifiability of any restriction upon the right to a private and family life under Article 8 ECHR. The same balance will still have to be made between the general economic welfare of the country and the individual interest(s) of those affected by such projects, but the onus of proving the justifiability of any intrusion upon those individual interests will fall upon the party seeking so to intrude.[201] Finally, insofar as the defendant accused of an interference with Article 8 ECHR rights is a public authority under section 6 of the Human Rights Act 1998, claimants may proceed with a claim for damages based directly upon Article 8 ECHR. These considerations may have a significant impact upon the interpretation of the defence of statutory authorisation of a nuisance.

The following are ineffectual as defences:

(i) It is no defence that the claimant came to the nuisance.[202] This was confirmed by a majority of the Court of Appeal in *Miller* v. *Jackson*,[203] when Geoffrey Lane LJ stated: 'It is no answer to a claim in nuisance for the defendant to show that the plaintiff brought the trouble on his own head by building or coming to live in a house so close to the defendant's premises that he would inevitably be affected by the defendant's activities where no one had been affected previously.' Lord Denning MR, however, remained unimpressed. The Millers, he felt, came to the nuisance with their eyes open, they had bought a house with a pleasant view of a green and the accompanying disadvantage of being hit occasionally by a cricket ball. There are echoes here of the defence of *volenti* (consent), which the

201 See the recent ruling of the ECtHR in *Hatton* v. *United Kingdom* (2002) 34 EHRR 1, which emphasised the failure of the UK government to provide a procedural regime which allowed interested parties to object to increased levels of (night) flights at busy airports such as Heathrow. However, in the Grand Chamber judgment in *Hatton* v. *United Kingdom* (2003) 37 EHRR 28 the earlier ruling on the facts was overturned and the Court stressed that the UK's actions had not exceeded its margin of appreciation under the ECHR: 'in matters of general policy, on which opinions within a democratic society may reasonably differ widely, the role of the domestic policy maker should be given special weight' (at [97]). Of course, there is nothing to prevent the UK courts from adopting a stricter standard of scrutiny *within* that margin when applying the ECHR rules at national level: see, e.g., H. Fenwick, *Civil Liberties and Human Rights* (3rd edn., 2003), at (e.g.) 184–5.

202 *Bliss* v. *Hall* (1838) 4 Bing. NC 183; 132 ER 758, *Sturges* v. *Bridgman* (1879) 11 Ch. D 852.

203 [1977] QB 966, 987.

courts have recently resurrected from the quiescence into which the defence of contributory negligence had reduced it.[204] However, this kind of reasoning runs counter to the decision in *Sturges* v. *Bridgman*, which Lord Denning regarded as no longer binding. But authority cannot just be ignored and some explanation of why it is not binding should be forthcoming. So the position is that *Sturges* v. *Bridgman* is by no means dead and Lord Denning's view must remain, at the very least, debatable.

(ii) It is also no defence that the defendant's activity is a useful one. In *Adams* v. *Ursell*[205] the defendant was prevented from maintaining a fried-fish shop in a fashionable neighbourhood, even though it was argued on his behalf that to prevent him from doing so would cause hardship both to him and to the poorer inhabitants. Likewise, in *Dennis* v. *Ministry of Defence* the court did not accept that the need to train pilots so as to maintain a functioning national air force for defence reasons could amount to a defence to a claim in nuisance.[206]

(iii) It is not a valid defence to allege and prove that the nuisance resulted from the *combined acts* of different people and that the act of the defendant alone was not a nuisance.[207]

(iv) Planning permission. Unlike statutory authorisation, the granting of planning permission does not provide a defence to committing a nuisance—hence the inclusion of this topic in this section. But in *Gillingham Borough Council* v. *Medway (Chatham) Dock Company Ltd.* a local authority was denied an injunction that it sought against an operator of a large port to which it had previously granted planning permission. In that case, Buckley J stated that 'where planning consent is given for a development or change of use, the question of nuisance will thereafter fall to be decided by reference to a neighbourhood with that development or use *and not as it was previously*'.[208] The italicised words give the impression that the implementation of planning permission could affect the standard of what would be a nuisance by changing the nature of the locality. In the subsequent case of *Wheeler* v. *J. J. Saunders*[209] the court reaffirmed the general view that planning permission did *not* amount to a defence in nuisance. But the court also doubted whether the *Gillingham* view (about the effect that the granting of consent could have on the neighbourhood) could apply to planning permissions that, as in the instant case, merely involved an intensification of an existing use.[210] This (real or apparent) back-pedalling from the *Gillingham*

[204] E.g. *Cummings* v. *Granger* [1977] QB 397, *Murphy* v. *Culbane* [1977] QB 94.

[205] [1913] 1 Ch. 269. [206] [2003] EWHC 793 (QBD), [2034] Env. LR 34.

[207] *Thorpe* v. *Brumfit* (1873) LR 8 Ch. 650, 656 (per James LJ), *Blair and Sumner* v. *Deakin* (1887) 57 LT 522.

[208] [1993] QB 343 at 361, emphasis added.

[209] [1995] 2 All ER 697; see also *Hunter* v. *Canary Wharf Ltd.* [1997] AC 655 (CA), per Pill LJ at 669 (reversed on other grounds (HL), but see at 710 (Lord Hoffmann) and 712–22 (Lord Cooke of Thorndon) for support for the critique of the *Gillingham* position).

[210] In *Wheeler* the planning permission had enabled the defendant to increase the number of pigs that he held on his farm.

position has had the unfortunate effect of establishing two types of planning permission—those which can affect the locality and those which cannot—without providing clear criteria for distinguishing the one type from the other. The confusing case law can be explained (if not justified) by discovering the policy concerns that lie behind these decisions. Thus, as a leading environmental practitioner has observed, there is an unexpressed public policy behind these disputes: '[i]f we have a complete system of planning law, under which decisions are taken to allow or promote developments which will have an important regenerative effect, ought a limited number of affected people be able to stop them by claiming injunctions for nuisance?'[211] If our courts had a more flexible approach towards nuisance, and were more readily willing to grant damages in lieu of injunctions in cases of proven nuisances, these dilemmas might be reduced if not totally avoided. But, as will be stated in the next section, our courts have not yet taken this bull by the horns.

6. REMEDIES

A claimant in a nuisance action has a choice between three remedies: damages, injunction and a limited form of self-help known as 'abatement'. Damages are discussed in Chapter 25. The general requirements for an injunction will also be discussed below (in Chapter 26), but it is necessary to make a few remarks here concerning injunctions in the context of nuisance.

(A) INJUNCTION[212]

More often than not a claimant will be anxious to stop a defendant from continuing his activity. This interest of the claimant will generally be matched by a corresponding willingness on the part of the defendant to pay damages (if found guilty of nuisance) rather than give up his activity. Injunctions, being discretionary remedies, are well suited to balancing these conflicting interests. This balancing operation, however, gives rise in practice to considerable difficulties and uncertainties. The availability of an injunction in the case of an established nuisance was discussed in *Miller* v. *Jackson*[213] and *Kennaway* v. *Thompson*,[214] to which we now turn.

Assuming that the majority in *Miller* v. *Jackson* was right on the issue of liability, the question that then had to be determined was whether the plaintiff should be granted an

[211] S. Tromans, 'Nuisance and Planning Control' [1995] *CLJ* 494, at 496.

[212] For further details see Buckley (Select Bibliography), 118 ff.; J. A. Jolowicz, 'Damages in Equity: A Study of Lord Cairns' Act' [1975] *CLJ* 224; B. S. Markesinis and A. M. Tettenborn, 'Cricket, Power Boat Racing and Nuisance' (Select Bibliography) and S. Tromans, 'Nuisance: Prevention or Payment' (Select Bibliography).

[213] [1977] QB 966.

[214] [1981] 1 QB 88.

injunction. For an affirmative answer to the issue of liability does not automatically decide the question whether or not to grant an injunction. Leaving aside Geoffrey Lane LJ's judgment as being in this respect a dissenting judgment, Cumming-Bruce LJ thought an injunction should be refused despite the defendant's liability and Lord Denning MR would have thought likewise had he held the defendants liable, which he did not. Two factors influenced them: first, the defendants' actions were reasonable and even beneficial; and second, the plaintiff had bought her house with her eyes open and had 'come to' the nuisance. Though Cumming-Bruce LJ was not prepared to go along with Lord Denning in saying that this negated liability altogether, he was nevertheless prepared to let it militate against the grant of an injunction.[215]

In *Kennaway* v. *Thompson*[216] the plaintiff, who did not come to the nuisance, was disturbed in her lakeside home by powerboat racing organised by the defendants. The defendants rightly admitted liability in nuisance, but contested the plaintiff's claim to an injunction, saying that the activities were just as beneficial as in *Miller* v. *Jackson* and therefore ought not to be restrained. This time Lawton LJ for the Court of Appeal discounted the idea of allowing the merits, social or otherwise, of the defendants' conduct to stand in the way of the plaintiff's right to an injunction. Even meritorious defendants, he argued, could be restrained from carrying on activities that substantially invaded other people's right to peace and quiet.

Three points arise out of these two cases. First, the plaintiff's case in *Kennaway* was, it could be argued, weaker than in *Miller* because she had suffered no 'sensible material injury' to her property; there had only been interference with her enjoyment of it. That the plaintiff succeeded in *Kennaway* but not in *Miller* is thus all the more remarkable.

Second, Lawton LJ in *Kennaway* did not actually say that the court in *Miller* had been wrong to refuse the plaintiff his injunction. Yet his decision is not easily reconcilable with the first ground in *Miller* v. *Jackson* that the playing of cricket is a good thing and ought not to be stopped. Does this mean that the other ground, namely that claimants who come to nuisances should be refused injunctions at the court's discretion, is sound and justifies that decision on its facts?[217] It is submitted that, although *Sturges* v. *Bridgman*[218] may be hard to justify today, courts should not mitigate, or even subvert entirely, the effects of established cases which they dislike by way of equitable discretion: yet this result was indeed the effect of *Miller* v. *Jackson*. If such cases are no longer to be followed, their rejection should be effected by forthright judicial reversal or by legislation.[219]

Third, a more serious point about *Kennaway* is that behind the statement that the grant of an injunction is at the discretion of the court there lurk some fairly rigid rules

215 Another possibility considered was granting an injunction but postponing its operation for a year to give the defendants time to rectify the situation.

216 [1981] QB 88.

217 In granting an injunction in *Tetley* v. *Chitty* [1986] 1 All ER 663, 675, McNeill J took account of the fact that the plaintiff had lived there for some time before the nuisance began.

218 (1879) 11 Ch. D 852.

219 Stamp J expressed doubts on just this use of equitable discretion: see his comments in *Woollerton & Wilson Ltd.* v. *Costain Ltd.* [1970] 1 WLR 411, 413, and see the views of Russell LJ in *Charrington* v. *Simons & Co. Ltd.* [1971] 1 WLR 598, 602.

governing even the exercise of discretion. Thus, in *Shelfer* v. *City of London Electric Lighting Co.*[220] A. L. Smith LJ, at the instance of a publican, restrained the defendant company from causing excessive vibration, even though the result was to deprive many Londoners of a desirable service, namely the provision of electricity. To a claim by the defendant that the plaintiff should be limited to damages in lieu of an injunction under Lord Cairns's Act, his Lordship stated that only in exceptional circumstances should a plaintiff who proved a tangible invasion of his rights be deprived of an injunction to protect them. However beneficial a defendant's activity, if it were a nuisance, courts would not let him 'buy the right to commit it'. Later decisions confirmed this attitude. In *Cowper* v. *Laidler*,[221] for instance, a plaintiff who bought property with its appurtenant right to light as a pure speculation in order to extract as much money as possible from the defendant for the release of his rights when the latter wanted to redevelop his own neighbouring land, was held entitled to an injunction to prevent the redevelopment. Similarly, the plaintiff in *Marriott* v. *East Grinstead Gas and Water Co.*[222] was able to restrain the defendants from passing their pipes under his land, even though the general gain from doing so was considerable and the plaintiff's resulting prejudice nil. The principle was further emphasised by the Court of Appeal in *Pride of Derby and Derbyshire Angling Association Ltd.* v. *British Celanese Ltd.*,[223] where the court granted an injunction that interfered drastically with the defendant's disposal of municipal sewage by preventing its discharge directly into the River Derwent.

On the other hand, the courts have at times departed from this attitude, especially where adherence to it would benefit unreasonable and unmeritorious claimants. Thus, in *Llandudno Urban District Council* v. *Woods*[224] a local authority failed to restrain an undoubted, though technical, trespass on its land; and in a similar case, *Behrens* v. *Richards*,[225] the owner of a Cornwall cliff-top was denied an injunction to prevent its longstanding use by walkers. Admittedly, when confronted with *Shelfer*'s case, a court can generally find special circumstances to justify departing from it;[226] as, indeed, Cumming-Bruce LJ did in *Miller* v. *Jackson*. But it could be argued that that kind of development is undesirable. The point about *Shelfer* is that a court's discretion to refuse an injunction is highly circumscribed, and is not to be exercised merely because of the (perceived) merits of a case: this point was strongly reiterated by Mummery LJ in the recent case of *Regan* v. *Paul Properties*.[227] The importance of both *Kennaway* and *Regan* is that they reiterated the *Shelfer* principle in the face of recent tendencies to undermine it in favour of greater discretion. In *Regan*, indeed, Mummery LJ specifically

220 [1895] 1 Ch. 287. 221 [1903] 2 Ch. 337.

222 [1909] 1 Ch. 70. 223 [1953] Ch. 149.

224 [1899] 2 Ch. 705. 225 [1905] 2 Ch. 614.

226 See *Jaggard* v. *Sawyer* [1995] 1 WLR 269, per Millett LJ; and see *Marcic* v. *Thames Water Utilties Ltd. (No. 2)* [2002] QB 1003, para. 10, where the judge emphasised that in this case the claimant wanted damages while the defendant was arguing for an injunction—in such circumstances, no guidance could be provided by the *Shelfer* criteria. (N.B. the damages in lieu of the injunction related specifically to the claim for a breach of Mr Marcic's human rights, although there seems to be no reason why similar considerations would not apply to a claim in nuisance on those facts.)

227 *Regan* v. *Paul Properties DPF No. 1 Ltd.* [2006] 3 WLR 1131 (CA), [35]–[36] and subsequent discussion.

rejected the approach of the judge at first instance, who had required the claimant to discharge the onus of showing why he should not be left to a remedy in damages.[228]

Of course, there are cases where the effects of granting an injunction would be so extreme or catastrophic that no one would advocate it: for instance, closing a major industry. So far such situations have been relatively few and courts have developed various means to avoid such results. Thus, the operation of the injunction may be suspended for a period of time (and even extended further) in order to give the defendant the chance of avoiding or minimising the effects of the nuisance.[229] Another way is to qualify the injunction: for example, by limiting its operation to a certain time.[230] Such solutions may not go far enough; but arguably they do make the present law less unacceptable than some critics try to make out.

It could be said, therefore, that English courts more or less take the view that in the case of a proven nuisance an injunction should issue as a matter of course, though not as of right, but that the desirability of such an approach is increasingly in doubt. The point is that in determining the availability of injunctive relief one should not balance the claimant's interest only against that of the defendant, but also weigh his interest in obtaining an injunction against the wider implications of such a course of action (e.g. closure of a major industry).[231] The law of nuisance, in other words, could be used as a kind of compulsory purchase of private enterprise, by awarding damages generously but injunctions sparingly where the activity sought to be restrained has some wider social value. The net result, so it could be argued, would be to allow a valuable enterprise to flourish while making sure that it pays the costs in terms of loss of amenity.[232] In the light of contemporary social and economic conditions this view may gain wider acceptance, but so far it does not represent the prevailing English practice[233] and, indeed, may present certain problems of its own.

[228] *Ibid.*, at [57]–[60].

[229] E.g. *Pennington* v. *Brinsop Hall Coal Co.* (1877) 5 Ch. D 769, *Shoreham UDC* v. *Dolphin Canadian Proteins Ltd.* (1972) 71 LGR 261.

[230] E.g. *Kennaway* v. *Thompson* [1981] QB 88. Contrast *Tetley* v. *Chitty* [1986] 1 All ER 663 (a blanket ban on go-karting).

[231] For a recent *public interest* example, see *Dennis* v. *Ministry of Defence* [2003] EWHC 793 (QB), [2003] Env. LR 34, where Buckley J held that 'a nuisance is established but that the public interest clearly demands that RAF Wittering should continue to train pilots' (at [48], and see [44]–[47]) and thus proceeded to assess damages rather than grant any injunction or declaration ([64] ff.).

[232] See J. G. Fleming, *Introduction to the Law of Torts* (2nd edn., 1985), 188–9. This view, which is gaining ground in the USA, is epitomised by *Boomer* v. *Atlantic Cement Co.*, 257 NE 2d 870 (1970). On these environmental aspects of the problems in nuisance, see the articles by McLaren, Ogus and Richardson, and Tromans (Select Bibliography).

[233] Thus, in *Shelfer* v. *City of London Electric Lighting Co.* [1895] 1 Ch. 287, 316, Lindley LJ said: 'Neither has the circumstance that the wrongdoer is in some sense a public benefactor (e.g. a gas or water company or a sewer authority) ever been considered a sufficient reason for refusing to protect by injunction an individual whose rights are being persistently infringed. Expropriation, even for a money consideration, is only justifiable when Parliament has sanctioned it. Courts of Justice are not like Parliament, which considers whether proposed works will be so beneficial to the public as to justify exceptional legislation, and the deprivation of people of their rights with or without compensation'. This approach has, apparently, been accepted by Canadian judges; McLaren, 'The Common law Nuisance Actions' (Select Bibliography), 552 ff.

In the first place, control of development in this way through private law (as is often the case in the United States) appears to be needed less urgently in this country. For we are more accustomed to a system of development control which takes place in advance through the use of administrative procedures than to a system of *ex post facto* control by a judiciary which, one would have thought, is not the best body to resolve zoning issues.

Second, even apart from this, there is still something to be said for a social philosophy that allows (in some instances at least) the interests of even an eccentric or over-sensitive individual to prevail over public interest, which is often rather nebulous. In some ways this is a mark of a liberal society and the law of nuisance in particular exists, *inter alia*, in the interest of minorities.[234] Nor is this entirely an individualistic view. For not only are the 'social costs' of pollution or other interferences with amenity notoriously difficult to compute (thus making an analysis of economic efficiency rather impracticable), but also any price put on the deprivation of amenity is bound to be artificial. Many people would not agree to be deprived of the peace and quiet of their home at any price; hence a person whose house is rendered uninhabitable by the act of another may have a justifiable complaint, whatever compensation he is offered. Further, despite the theory that everything has its value, a house subject to some serious disadvantage may turn out to be unsaleable in fact; so an award of damages reflecting the supposed reduction in the value of a house due to a nuisance may prove to be inadequate in practice.

Third, *Kennaway* v. *Thompson* shows that certainty may well be no less desirable even in the context of 'discretionary' remedies than elsewhere in the law. There is no reason why such relief should be regarded as less important in this respect than an award of damages and hence to be granted or refused according to a court's perception of the merits of the individual case. Indeed, in a tort like nuisance, whose effectiveness depends largely upon the availability of injunctive relief, some certainty in the principles on which injunctions are granted is more important than elsewhere.[235]

(B) ABATEMENT

Abating a nuisance is a form of self-help and as such not favoured as a remedy.[236] This attitude underlies three rules. The first is that while abatement may take the form of

[234] See R. A. Buckley, 'Cricket and the Law of Nuisance' (1978) 41 *MLR* 334, 337.

[235] And one possible future avenue of argument is that the exercise of the court's discretion to award damages in lieu of an injunction may yet have to be scrutinised under the Human Rights Act 1998 to ensure that it gives sufficient respect to a claimant's rights under Art. 8 ECHR to a private and family life and a home. This could provide greater certainty by forcing a clarification of the conditions upon which injunctions will be available, but it could also create a situation of even greater flexibility in the use of such remedies, if such a balancing exercise forces the courts into an increasingly *ad hoc* approach. Such developments are to be awaited with interest and no little trepidation.

[236] *Lagan Navigation Co.* v. *Lambeg Bleaching, Dyeing and Finishing Co. Ltd.* [1927] AC 226, 242, per Lord Atkinson. For the abator, however, it may present three distinct advantages: first, it may offer a cheap way of eliminating a cause of interference without going to court; second, in cases of emergency it may be the most efficient remedy; and third, it may be available in cases where no actionable nuisance exists. Thus, encroaching roots and branches which cause no damage are not actionable, but may nevertheless be severed by the abator: *Lemmon* v. *Webb* [1894] 3 Ch. 1; [1895] AC 1. See *Clerk and Lindsell on Torts* (15th edn., 1988), 304–7.

removing an obstruction or other nuisance emanating from the neighbour's land (e.g. cutting off intruding roots, etc.), it cannot normally take the form of other positive acts, such as erecting structures on the latter's land. This, at any rate, appears to be established in public nuisance affecting, for example, the right of access to the highway. In *Campbell Davys* v. *Lloyd*[237] there was a public right of way over the plaintiff's land and a decrepit bridge, which spanned a nearby river. While rebuilding the bridge, the defendant was forced to place piles on the plaintiff's land and, when sued in trespass, replied that he was abating a nuisance (interference with the right of way as a result of the state of the bridge). The defence was rejected, *inter alia*, for the reason stated. However, this reluctance to sanction positive acts of repair and maintenance does not apply quite so clearly in private nuisance. For example, the owner of a dominant tenement has the right to maintain and improve the surface of a road on which he has a private right of way; and the same is true if he is seeking to preserve an easement of support.[238] The precise ambit of these rights, however, is uncertain and it is unlikely that it extends to major works on servient property.

The second limitation can be seen in the exhortation of Eyre CJ in *Kirby* v. *Sadgrove*,[239] where he said: '[a]batement ought only to be allowed in clear cases of nuisance where the injury is apparent at the first view of the matter, the abator makes himself his own judge and proceeds at his own hazard to destroy the thing which he considers as an infringement of his right'. In other words, where the existence of a nuisance rests on a delicate balance between competing interests, this type of self-help is inappropriate. Finally, if abatement requires, as may often be the case, the abator to enter another person's land, he must generally give notice to that person.[240] However, precisely *when* notice has to be given is not clear. In *Jones* v. *Williams*[241] Parke B suggested that notice to the plaintiff is necessary if the nuisance was caused by his predecessor in title and he only continued it. In that case, the abator's claim that he had lawfully entered the plaintiff's land in order to remove a heap of manure, which constituted a nuisance by smell, was rejected because he did not state that notice was given, nor that the plaintiff was himself the wrongdoer. Notice is also unnecessary in cases of 'emergency',[242] but when this exists has not been clearly defined.

Whether notice is necessary or not, the abator must in all cases ensure that his action does not affect the property of the other in excess of what is absolutely necessary in the circumstances.[243] So, if branches from a tree on A's land overlap B's land, B may be

237 [1901] 2 Ch. 518, 523.

238 *Newcomen* v. *Coulson* (1877) 5 Ch. D 133, *Jones* v. *Pritchard* [1908] 1 Ch. 630, 638 (per Parker J). For further details, see P. Jackson, *The Law of Easements and Profits* (1978).

239 (1797) 3 Anst. 892, 896; 145 ER 1073, 1074.

240 No notice is required for a man to cut off branches overhanging his own land: *Lemmon* v. *Webb* [1895] AC 1, 5, per Lord Herschell. The abator, however, cannot retain the branches for that would be to convert them: *Mills* v. *Brooker* [1919] 1 KB 555.

241 (1843) 11 M & W 176, 181–2; 152 ER 764, 766–7.

242 *Earl of Lonsdale* v. *Nelson* (1823) 2 B & C 302, 311–12; 107 ER 396, 400, per Best J. Immediate danger to life or health is an emergency: *Lemmon* v. *Webb* [1895] AC 1.

243 *Roberts* v. *Rose* (1865) LR 1 Ex. 82.

allowed to enter A's land and cut them back to the point of encroachment. B will not be allowed to keep the severed branches nor to break down A's fence, for example, in order to get on his land and cut the branches; nor will he be permitted to cut down the whole tree.

7. PUBLIC NUISANCE

So far we have spoken of private nuisance. But there is the other type of nuisance, known as public nuisance, which is an amorphous and unsatisfactory area of the law covering an ill-assorted collection of wrongs, some of which have little or no association with tort and only appear to fill a gap in the criminal law. The definition of public nuisance given by the classic book *Archbold's Criminal Pleading and Practice* confirms this. This runs as follows:[244] 'A person is guilty of a public nuisance . . . who *(a)* does an act *not warranted by law*, or *(b) omits to discharge a legal duty*, if the effect of the act or omission is to endanger life, health, property, morals, or comfort of the public, or to obstruct the public in the exercise or employment of rights common to all Her Majesty's subjects.' As one commentator put it: '[w]ith such a broad concept in existence, backed with such broad remedies, what need have we of any other criminal offence?—or torts?—or remedies in administrative law?'[245] The mess that public nuisance is in is partly due to the haphazard and piecemeal growth of a legal system developed solely by practitioners without the kind of doctrinal backing that universities provided to the law of the Continent of Europe.

Unfortunately, the result is not just an intellectual mess; it also offends all contemporary notions of certainty and precedent in criminal law and must thus be regarded as dangerous.[246] In this subsection we shall focus on one particular category of public nuisance cases which we could generically describe as 'abuses of the highway'.

Public nuisance in this sense refers to interference with members of the public in the exercise of their common rights on the highway. For example, in *Hubbard* v. *Pitt*[247] the defendants were picketing on the road outside the plaintiffs' offices. An interlocutory injunction was granted to the plaintiffs on the ground that picketing on the highway, other than in pursuance of a trade dispute, was unlawful and a public nuisance. In the Court of Appeal the plaintiffs laid more emphasis upon their allegation that the defendants' conduct constituted a private nuisance and there was some doubt whether the

244 (2007), para. 31–40 (emphases added). See also *R* v. *Soul* (1980) 70 Cr. App. R 295, *R* v. *Madden* [1975] 1 WLR 1379.

245 J. Spencer, 'Public Nuisance' (Select Bibliography).

246 And, one might have thought, vulnerable to challenge as an offence not sufficiently 'prescribed by law' to satisfy the requirements of the European Convention on Human Rights: but this allegation, and one that the crime so defined also offended against common law principles, was unanimously rejected by the House of Lords in *R* v. *Rimmington and Goldstein* [2006] 1 AC 459.

247 [1976] QB 142.

facts supported the existence of either a private or a public nuisance.[248] But the Court of Appeal, by a majority, felt that they should apply the test laid down by the House of Lords in the *American Cyanamid* case[249] and decided on a balance of convenience. In the majority's view this required that the injunction be maintained.[250] In another case, *Attorney-General* v. *Gastonia Coaches Ltd.*,[251] coach operators parked sixteen coaches outside their offices and these inevitably interfered with the passage of traffic. Gastonia were found guilty of public nuisance and were restrained from parking their coaches on the highway. They were also made to pay damages to private litigants who had suffered particular harm from the emission of exhaust gases.

Public and private nuisance, apart from the name, do not have much else in common. Public nuisance is a crime triable summarily or on indictment, which can also give rise to civil liability towards anyone suffering special damage. Private nuisance, on the other hand, is only a tort. Public nuisance affords protection to persons other than those with an interest in land. Private nuisance is concerned with interferences with the use and enjoyment of land. In public nuisance, damages for personal injury[252] and even economic loss can be recovered, while in private nuisance it is primarily damage to land which is compensated and, perhaps, damage to goods. Finally, prescription is a defence to an action in *private nuisance* but it is not in the case of public nuisance.[253]

As stated, the same activity may constitute both forms of nuisance and, despite the differences, their overlap and the terminological similarity have led many to discuss these two types of liability together, with resulting confusion to both.[254] The connection with negligence might also be mentioned at this stage. Public nuisance differs from negligence in two respects. First, though the point is not free of doubt, the better view seems to be that fault is an ingredient in actions of public nuisance, but, even so, its presence is presumed and it is for the defendant to excuse himself. In negligence, on the other hand, the burden of proof lies squarely on the claimant's shoulders.[255] Second, the tort of negligence remedies primarily physical damage, but public nuisance, which includes dangers on the highway, also extends to mere obstruction.

Public nuisance is first and foremost a crime because, as Denning LJ put it:[256] 'a public nuisance is a nuisance which is so widespread in its range or so indiscriminate in

[248] There is no reason in principle why it cannot be both: *Halsey* v. *Esso Petroleum Co. Ltd.* [1961] 1 WLR 683 at 699 ff.

[249] *American Cyanamid Co.* v. *Ethicon Ltd.* [1975] AC 396.

[250] Given the connection with the defendants' rights to free expression and freedom to assemble under Arts. 10 and 11 ECHR respectively, allied with the impact of s. 12 of the Human Rights Act 1998, it seems strongly arguable that at least the reasoning process, and quite possibly also the result, in *Hubbard* v. *Pitt* would be different if decided today. See, also, *DPP* v. *Jones* [1999] 2 AC 240, discussed in ch. 12, above.

[251] [1977] RTR 219.

[252] Although note the doubts expressed by Lord Goff on this point in *Hunter* v. *Canary Wharf* [1997] AC 655, 692, citing Newark (Select Bibliography) and suggesting that such cases are better dealt with in negligence.

[253] The reason is that 'it cannot have a lawful beginning by licence or otherwise, being an offence against the common law': *Dewell* v. *Sanders* (1618) Cro. Jac. 490; 79 ER 419, *R* v. *Cross* (1812) 3 Camp. 224; 170 ER 1362.

[254] *Hubbard* v. *Pitt* [1976] QB 142.

[255] This solution is appropriate if the claimant is seeking damages for personal injury. Where an injunction is sought, the position is likely to be analogous to that of private nuisance where a fault-based approach seems to be irrelevant.

[256] *A-G* v. *PYA Quarries* [1957] 2 QB 169, 191.

its effect that it would not be reasonable to expect one person to take proceedings on his own responsibility to put a stop to it, but that it should be taken on the responsibility of the community at large'. The prosecution must prove that the acts complained of affected a considerable number of persons or a section of the public. So a person who makes a bogus telephone call falsely giving information as to the presence of explosives may have committed this offence. This requires that 'the public, which means a considerable number of persons or a section of the public, was affected, as distinct from individual persons'. In *R* v. *Madden*[257] the appellant's conviction for committing public nuisance in the above manner was quashed, *inter alia*, on the ground that his hoax message had reached only the telephonist who received it and eight policemen who were involved in searching for the bomb. By contrast, in *Jan de Nul* v. *NV Royale Belge*[258] the court emphasised that 'where there is physical interference with a right of [navigation over the whole of an estuary] the fact that it is actually exercised by very few members of the public does not prevent the obstruction from constituting a public nuisance'. Thus, the siltation caused in the estuary by Jan de Nul's dredging operations, which had affected some of the berths of yacht clubs and wharves, was held to have had a sufficiently significant effect on access to parts of the estuary to amount to a public nuisance.

Further, the act must have caused that considerable number of people making up the 'public' to have suffered a 'common injury'. This requirement was emphasised strongly in the recent case of *R* v. *Rimmington and Goldstein*,[259] where Lord Bingham stated that

> central to the content of the crime was the suffering of common injury by members of the public by interference with rights enjoyed by them as such ... To permit a conviction of causing public nuisance to rest on an injury caused to separate individuals rather than on an injury suffered by the community or a significant section of it as a whole was to contradict the rationale of the offence and pervert its nature, in Convention terms to change the essential constituent elements of the offence to the detriment of the accused.[260]

This clarification has brought a welcome limit to the use of public nuisance in the criminal field to impose greater penalties than those available under explicit statutory provisions or to criminalise conduct where the prosecutor could not think of anything else with which to charge the defendant.[261] It will, likewise, have a concomitant impact upon the range of cases where public nuisance may give rise to claims in tort. As Lord

[257] [1975] 1 WLR 1379. In *A-G* v. *PYA Quarries* [1957] 2 QB 169 the Court of Appeal refused to state how many people were needed to constitute a 'class of Her Majesty's subjects'. The question was one of fact, with the result that the Court of Appeal would rarely interfere with the findings of the trial judge.

[258] [2000] 2 Lloyd's Rep. 700, 713 (QBD). This finding was not challenged on appeal: *Jan de Nul (UK)* v. *AXA Royale Belge SA (formerly NV Royale Belge)* [2002] 1 Lloyd's Rep. 583 (CA).

[259] [2006] 1 AC 459 (noted by A. Ashworth, 'Public Nuisance: Elements of Offence—Requirement of Common Injury' [2006] *Crim. LR* 153).

[260] *Ibid.*, [6] and [37]. As a result, their Lordships agreed that certain earlier cases (on which see [23]–[28]), such as *R* v. *Norbury* [1978] *Crim. LR* 435 (where the defendant had made 605 obscene telephone calls to 494 different women over a period of some four years) and *R* v. *Johnson* [1997] 1 WLR 367 (hundreds of obscene calls to thirteeen different women over a number of years) had been wrongly decided.

[261] Spencer (Select Bibliography), at 77 and *R* v. *Rimmington and Goldstein* [2006] 1 AC 459, [37] (per Lord Bingham).

Bingham stated, 'the circumstances in which, in future, there can properly be resort to the common law crime of public nuisance will be relatively rare'.[262]

Even with the welcome retrenchment effected by *R* v. *Rimmington and Goldstein*, however, it would be unreasonable if in such circumstances, and without more ado, the law allowed every person who was inconvenienced by such a public nuisance to bring an action in tort. But, as already indicated, the crime may become a tort as well if the complainant can prove special loss over and above the inconvenience suffered by the public in general. So, in order to sue in tort the claimant has to prove special (or, perhaps more accurately, particular) damage which is 'particular, direct and substantial' to himself.[263] What this means exactly remains obscure.[264] One line of thought insists that the claimant must prove damage that is not merely different in degree from that suffered by the general public, but also different in kind. On the facts in the *Jan de Nul* case,[265] both of these elements could be said to have been present, since 'the injury suffered by the public at large is limited to the interference with the freedom of navigation in the estuary generally. In those circumstances any significant interference with an individual's commercial operations or the enjoyment of private rights resulting from the obstruction to navigation would ... represent damage over and above that suffered by the public at large and would be sufficient to support an action.'[266] It was not just general navigation along the estuary which was obstructed for the particular claimants, but also use of berths, wharves and jetties with which they made a living.

A different and more liberal approach, which probably prevails nowadays, is to allow the action whenever the claimant can show that the right he shares with others has been appreciably more affected by the defendant's behaviour.[267] So a barge-owner, navigating a creek obstructed by the defendant's barges, could successfully claim from the latter his extra costs for unloading his cargo off his barges and transporting them by land to the place of ultimate destination, for in Lord Ellenborough's view he had suffered greater damage than other members of the public who might have been contemplating using the creek.[268]

The most obscure point, however, is the requirement that special damage has to be 'direct'. Apparently, the test of this is narrower than that for damage elsewhere. Thus,

262 [2006] 1 AC 459, [31].

263 'The requirement of particular damage was strictly insisted on in the mid-nineteenth century, lest the construction of railways, which was necessarily disruptive, became too expensive' (*Ricket* v. *Metropolitan Ry. Co.* (1867) LR 2 HL 175; J. A. Weir, *A Casebook on Tort* (10th edn., 2004), 206).

264 This issue is examined by G. H. L. Fridman, 'The Definition of Particular Damage in Nuisance' (1953) 2 *UWALR* 490–503 and G. Kodilinye, 'Public Nuisance and Particular Damage in the Modern Law' (1986) 6 *Leg. Stud.* 182.

265 [2000] 2 Lloyd's Rep. 700.

266 *Ibid.*, per Moore-Bick J at 715.

267 Which might be an equally plausible interpretation of the position of those businesses in *Jan de Nul* which, while using the same rights of navigation as any other member of the public, were commercially reliant upon being able to do so without hindrance.

268 *Rose* v. *Miles* (1815) 4 M & S 101, 103; 105 ER 773. The decision which, it will be noticed, allows recovery for pure economic loss has impeccable origins that can be traced back to *Iveson* v. *Moore* (1699) 1 Ld. Raym. 486; 91 ER 1224 (another case allowing recovery for pure economic loss resulting from highway obstructions).

Lord Reid said that in public nuisance the question is 'whether the damage caused to the plaintiff by the nuisance was other and different from the damage caused by the nuisance to the rest of the public. When the word "direct" is used in determining that question, its meaning or connotation appears to be narrower than when it is used in determining whether damage is too remote.'[269] In what sense it is 'narrower' or 'different' is left unexplained, and the matter must be left open. Indeed, in the recent *Jan de Nul* case,[270] Moore-Bick J seems not to have applied the criterion of 'directness' separately at all.

In *Jacobs* v. *London County Council*[271] Lord Simonds accepted the definition of nuisance on the highway 'as any wrongful act or omission upon or near a highway, whereby the public are prevented from freely, safely, and conveniently passing along the highway'. Generally speaking, nuisance on the highway can be produced either by the condition of the highway itself or by obstructions thereon.[272] As to the first, at common law highway authorities were not liable for non-feasance—failure to keep the highway in repair—though they could be liable for misfeasance—damage caused by some wrongful action. The Highways Act 1980 (re-enacting the provisions of the Highways (Miscellaneous Provisions) Act 1961) abolishes this distinction and makes highway authorities liable (under s. 41(1)) for damage resulting from failure to maintain (adopted) highways. This duty had been interpreted to apply only to the physical or structural condition of the highway and not to keeping it clear of ice and snow,[273] which led to the result that any liability would thus be denied *even if* the authority could reasonably have prevented the formation of such ice or could reasonably have removed the ice or snow. This position seems to have been reversed by the insertion of section 41(1A) into the 1980 Act.[274] Nor does the section 41(1) duty extend to the authority's failure to improve the highway (e.g. by adding warning signs, etc.).

However, section 58(1) of the 1980 Act gives them a defence if they prove that they have taken such care as is reasonable in the circumstances. In order to assist the courts, section 58(2) of the 1980 Act has specified a number of factors to be taken into account in deciding the issue. 'The character of the highway', 'the standard of maintenance appropriate for a highway of that character', 'the state of repair in which a reasonable person would have expected to find that highway' and the highway authority's

[269] *Wagon Mound (No. 2)* [1967] 1 AC 617, 636.

[270] *Jan de Nul (UK)* v. *NV Royale Belge* [2000] 2 Lloyd's Rep. 700, 715 (QBD).

[271] [1950] AC 361, 375, quoting J. T. Pratt and W. W. Mackenzie, *Law of Highways* (18th edn., 1967), 107.

[272] Although see *Wandsworth LBC* v. *Railtrack plc* [2002] QB 756 (CA), concerning the disturbance to passers-by caused by a large number of pigeons roosting under a bridge owned by the defendant.

[273] *Goodes* v. *East Sussex CC* [2000] PIQR P148 (HL). *Gorringe* v. *Calderdale MBC* [2004] UKHL 15, [2004] 1 WLR 1057 (noted by J. Morgan, 'Slowing the Expansion of Public Authorities' Liability' (2005) 121 *LQR* 43 and E. J. Russell, 'Effect of Statutory Duties and Powers on Common Law Liability' [2005] *SLT* 27). *Sandhar* v. *Department of Transport, Environment and the Regions* [2004] EWCA Civ. 1440, [2005] 1 WLR 1632 confirmed that no such duty existed at common law, despite attempts to rely upon an 'assumption of responsibility' by the relevant authority to ensure that all trunk roads would be salted in freezing conditions. (On the notion of 'assumption of responsibility' generally, see the discussion in ch. 3, Section 3(c), above.)

[274] By s. 111 of the Railways and Transport Safety Act 2003, although the operation of this new duty in conjunction with the s. 58 defence (discussed in the subsequent text) is by no means clear as yet.

knowledge (actual or presumed) will be among the circumstances which will be weighed by the courts in deciding whether the authority is in breach of its duty. Parenthetically, it might be noted that the Act provides an example of statutory liability for the acts of independent contractors.[275]

With regard to obstruction on the highway, not every obstacle will be a nuisance and the all-important test of reasonableness has to be applied. Obviously, whether an obstruction is unreasonable will be a matter of opinion based on fact.[276] Obstruction or injury caused by *projections* into the highway form a particularly unsatisfactory and unsettled part of the law. A distinction between *natural* and *artificial* projections is invariably adopted, the latter being more severely treated than the former. The distinction is not easy to explain or justify. One commentator has asked: 'what are the grounds for distinction between a tree and a bit of a house? Is it that a house is used and a tree is not? Is it because a house is always built and a tree is not always planted? . . . Is it because people are supposed to know about houses and not about trees, trees being subject, as houses are usually not, to *secret unobservable processes of nature*?'[277] Whatever the reason for the distinction, the fact is that it is made. With regard to *natural* projections, the rule is that damage caused by the collapse of branches protruding from land adjacent to the highway will be actionable only if the occupier was negligent, that is, if he knew or should have known of the defect that caused the collapse. In *Noble* v. *Harrison*[278] a branch of a tree growing on the defendant's land and overhanging a highway suddenly broke and damaged the plaintiff's vehicle. It was found that the fracture occurred owing to a latent defect not discoverable by a reasonable and careful inspection. It was held that the mere fact that the branch overhung the highway did not make it a nuisance since it did not obstruct free passage along the highway. Although, in the event, the branch proved to be a danger, the defendant was not liable since he had not created the danger and had no knowledge, actual or implied, of its presence.

With regard to *artificial* projections, for example a protruding lamp-bracket, the authorities are in confusion. According to one view, liability is based on negligence, as with natural projections. A contrary view imposes on the defendant a stricter form of liability, except where the collapse occurred through the act of a trespasser or by a secret and unobservable operation of nature, such as a subsidence under or near the foundations of the premises. In *Wringe* v. *Cohen*[279] a part of the defendant's premises collapsed because of want of repair. The plaintiff was held entitled to damages. Atkinson J formulated the rule in the terms stated above. It should be noted that the exceptions formulated by the Court of Appeal deprive the rule of much of its significance. For, to

275 Further, as illustrated by *Roe* v. *Sheffield City Council and Others* [2003] EWCA Civ. 1, [2004] QB 653, such claims against the highway authority may also involve concurrent claims against other defendants (here, a claim for breach of a statutory duty owed by the tram company under the Tramways Act 1870).

276 Thus, see *Trevett* v. *Lee* [1955] 1 WLR 113.

277 J. A. Weir, *A Casebook on Tort* (10th edn., 2004), 208 (italics in the original).

278 [1926] 2 KB 332. On similar facts the House of Lords reached the same conclusion in *Caminer* v. *Northern and London Investment Trust Ltd.* [1951] AC 88.

279 [1940] 1 KB 229, 233.

quote Friedman, 'it can hardly be imagined that any damage caused neither by the act of a third person nor by a latent defect could be due to anything but knowledge or negligence of the occupier'.[280]

Though the effect of the exceptions is probably that the rule in *Wringe* v. *Cohen* has been substantially assimilated to ordinary fault liability, it remains true to say that the onus of proof has been reversed. Once the claimant proves that the defendant was in control of the premises and that he suffered injury because of their dangerous condition, it will be for the defendant to prove, for example, that this resulted from a secret and unobservable operation of nature.

As already stated, a public nuisance becomes actionable as a tort if the claimant proves special damage to himself. In cases like those discussed above this poses few difficulties. Problems do, however, arise in cases where custom is lost as a result of an unlawful obstruction of the highway, for example, by theatre queues preventing access to nearby shops. In *Lyons, Sons & Co.* v. *Gulliver*[281] the plaintiff's shop was obstructed by crowds, at times five deep, queuing daily from 2.30 p.m. to 6.20 p.m. to enter the defendant's variety theatre. It was held that the obstruction amounted to an actionable public nuisance and an injunction was granted.

8. NUISANCE AND OTHER FORMS OF LIABILITY

Nuisance liability overlaps with trespass, negligence and the rule in *Rylands* v. *Fletcher*.[282] It may be helpful to consider its relationship to trespass and negligence, leaving discussion of *Rylands* v. *Fletcher* until Chapter 16, below.

The main difference from trespass is the historical distinction between actions in trespass and in case.[283] As indicated in the previous chapter, trespass lay where the invasion was a *direct* interference, an action on the case lay where the interference was *consequential*. So, in *Mann* v. *Saulnier*[284] a fence, which had been properly constructed by the defendant, began to lean over towards the plaintiff's land after a period of time. This was treated as a nuisance, since the leaning was only a consequence of the act of erecting the fence. However elusive and unattractive to the modern mind this distinction may be, it 'is still attended with practical significance. For the one [trespass] there is liability without actual harm, for the other [nuisance] damage is essential; [moreover] every trespassory intrusion is tortious unless privileged, while a nuisance is never actionable unless it is unreasonable.'[285]

[280] (1940) 3 *MLR* 305. [281] [1914] 1 Ch. 631.

[282] (1866) LR 1 Ex. 265; (1868) LR 3 HL 330, on which see ch. 16, below.

[283] Another difference is that trespass applies to 'things'; nuisance also covers intangible interferences, e.g. fumes, vibrations, noise, etc. See further P. Keeton, 'Trespass, Nuisance and Strict Liability' (Select Bibliography) and Winfield (Select Bibliography).

[284] (1959) 19 DLR (2d) 130.

[285] J. G. Fleming, *The Law of Torts* (9th edn., 1998), 465. Proof of damage in nuisance is *generally* essential, since without it there is only a potential nuisance. However, whenever damage is inevitable the courts will

By far the most significant and obscure relationship, however, is that between negligence and nuisance. The issue is not thereby clearly formulated for, as indicated previously, the term negligence refers either to the defendant's careless conduct or to the independent tort of negligence in which carelessness is but one element of liability. The role played in nuisance by carelessness, which is an aspect of fault, has already been dealt with,[286] but something has still to be said of the overlap with the tort of negligence. If, as discussed earlier on, nuisance is not, or at least not always, a form of strict liability, then there is a tendency to assimilate those nuisances that are not intentional with the tort of negligence. This view has, indeed, been advanced on the ground that in both cases 'reasonableness' is the standard by which the defendant's behaviour is tested and it deserves careful consideration, not least because of the reputation of its advocates.[287]

Yet at present it is difficult to identify the two torts for the following reasons. *First*, as regards reasonableness, it must be stressed that the gist of nuisance is the 'deed' not the 'doing', i.e. it is primarily the result suffered by the claimant rather than the defendant's activity that is scrutinised by the courts.[288] This result is the unreasonable interference with the claimant's land or his use and enjoyment of it, and the defendant's wrongdoing may be one factor along with others which, in certain circumstances, can make an interference unreasonable.

By contrast, the gist of negligence lies in the unreasonableness of the defendant's conduct, i.e. his wrongdoing. Unreasonableness, therefore, is viewed differently in these two torts. In negligence, the issue whether the defendant's conduct is unreasonable will be judged by its foreseeable consequences; in nuisance it is primarily the unreasonableness of what has happened to the claimant which is in issue. In these cases 'a negligent interference with the use and enjoyment of land is private nuisance in respect to the *interest invaded*, and negligence in respect to the type of *conduct* that causes the invasion'.[289]

There is never any talk of intentional interferences falling under a form of liability called 'intention'; instead, with reference to the interest invaded they are often called private nuisances. The same goes for those instances of nuisance, if any, where liability may be truly strict. Thus Prosser has argued that 'nuisance is not a separate tort... subject to rules of its own. Nuisances are types of damage—the invasion of two quite

presume it: *Fay* v. *Prentice* (1845) 1 CB 828; 135 ER 769 (rainwater dripping over the plaintiff's garden from a projecting cornice). In cases of discomfort, the inconvenience *is* the damage and there must be evidence of this.

286 Above, Sections 3(a) (on the 'measured duty of care') and 3(b)(iv) (on 'fault').

287 Thus G. Williams and B. A. Hepple, *Foundations of the Law of Torts* (2nd edn., 1984), 127 state: 'Whether the tort is called nuisance or negligence, the question is whether the defendant has acted "reasonably"'. See also Lord Denning MR in *Miller* v. *Jackson* [1977] QB 966, 980.

288 This test was adopted by Geoffrey Lane LJ in *Miller* v. *Jackson* [1977] QB 966, 985, where he asked: 'Was there here a use by the defendants of their land involving an unreasonable interference with the plaintiffs' enjoyment of *their* land?' Academic writers have taken a similar view.

289 *Restatement (Second) Torts*, para. 833(*c*) (italics supplied). Lord Denning in *Miller* v. *Jackson* [1977] QB 966, 980, said: 'It is the very essence of a private nuisance that it is the unreasonable use *by a man of his land* [italics supplied] to the detriment of his neighbour.' To place emphasis on the 'doing' rather than on the 'deed' is, at the very least, unorthodox. Cf. Geoffrey Lane LJ, *dictum* at 985, quoted in preceding note.

unrelated kinds of interests, by conduct that is tortious because it falls into the usual categories of tort liability.'[290] This is why he describes nuisance as 'a field of tortious liability rather than *a type* of tortious conduct'. It may be that much of our own confusion on the subject has been generated by our failure to appreciate this fact and to look upon nuisance as a type of liability independent of other torts.

A *second* reason nuisance cannot be assimilated to the tort of negligence is that the two torts afford protection to different interests. The difference is due to history since they represent different stages in the development of the law of civil responsibility. Nuisance, the earlier of the two, protected interests in land and only a person with an interest in the affected land[291] could succeed in this tort. Negligence, on the other hand, is the more modern and, in some respects, the wider of the two torts.

Third, in cases involving neighbouring landowners English law has shown greater willingness to impose liability in negligence for omissions than it has in other areas of the tort of negligence.[292] Cases like *Goldman* v. *Hargrave*[293] and *Leakey* v. *National Trust*[294] show that for a variety of reasons courts are willing to acknowledge the special relationship between neighbouring landowners and to impose a general, though measured, duty of care in order to ensure that landowners are protected by the law of negligence from dangers emanating from their neighbour's land. *Smith* v. *Littlewoods Organisation Ltd.*[295] has blurred further the borderline between nuisance and negligence; and the Lord Chancellor's judgment certainly does not appear to be rigidly opposed to liability for omissions.[296]

Even if the above arguments are unconvincing, it still remains to be shown what advantage, conceptual or otherwise, would be gained by treating those nuisances in which fault is relevant as a sub-category of the tort of negligence. As Shaw LJ said in *Leakey* v. *National Trust*: 'I do not for myself... see how the difficulty [of resolving nuisance cases] is disposed of by transmuting a liability in nuisance (however occasioned) into a duty to do what can reasonably be done in the circumstances of a particular case to prevent or to diminish the consequence of a nuisance. This formulation may, so it seems to me, create fresh problems and the derivative problems may defy resolution.'[297]

At present, therefore, the identification of the torts of nuisance and negligence thus seems wrong, or at least premature, for, of course, one should never forget the tendency of the tort of negligence to absorb older torts. *Smith* v. *Littlewoods Organisation Ltd.* suggests that this may well come about; but this has not yet occurred.

290 *Torts* (4th edn., 1971), 577. Prosser talks of 'two unrelated interests', referring thereby to the interests protected by public and private nuisance. This point is made clear in his *Selected Topics on the Law of Torts* (1953), 164.

291 Although see the discussion above (Section 4(a)) concerning 'who can sue' in the light of the reasoning in *McKenna* v. *British Alumnium* [2002] Env. LR 30.

292 On this see B. S. Markesinis, '*Leakey* v. *National Trust*' [1980] *CLJ* 259 ff.

293 [1967] 1 AC 645.

294 [1980] QB 485. See also *Holbeck Hall Hotel* v. *Scarborough BC* [2000] QB 836 (CA), discussed in the text above (Section 3(a)) for a particularly sensitive example.

295 [1987] AC 241.

296 [1987] AC 241 discussed by B. S. Markesinis, 'Negligence, Nuisance and Affirmative Duties of Action' (1989) 105 *LQR* 104. See, further, the recent case of *Johnson (Trading as Johnson Butchers)* v. *B. J. W. Property Developments Ltd.* [2002] 3 All ER 574 (QBD (T & CC)), in which HH Judge Thornton QC explicitly dealt with liability for escapes as a situation where negligence and nuisance had been assimilated (para. 47 ff.).

297 [1980] QB 485, 529. In a similar vein, see Geoffrey Lane LJ in *Miller* v. *Jackson* [1977] QB 966, 985.

9. NUISANCE AND PROTECTION OF THE ENVIRONMENT

Nuisance is an old tort; environmental pollution, though an old concern,[298] has only recently been appreciated as a real problem. As reliance upon fuels like oil and coal is threatened or diminishes, new sources of energy are brought into use, carrying with them hitherto unthought-of hazards. But this is not the only risk to the environment. Massive and often ill-planned industrialisation and new methods of bulk transportation of goods like crude oil have meant that land, air and sea can be seriously affected, often through the activity of one polluter only.[299] Concern about destruction of the environment is a product of the material rise in standards of living. Clearly, such problems can be resolved by concerted action by politicians, lawyers, economists and other experts.

Unfortunately, such co-operation is not always forthcoming. For a solution commending itself to an expert may be unattractive to vote-seeking politicians and solutions offered by lawyers have often failed to take account of the ideas of economists. These dimensions are not within the purview of this book, but the student should at least be made aware of their connection with the tort of nuisance. We shall, therefore, discuss briefly two related problems: the economic efficiency of the action in nuisance in achieving pollution control and measures taken by the state to combat this problem.

(A) EFFICIENCY OF THE ACTION IN NUISANCE

Protection of the environment suggests that our first reaction should be to consider the possibility of public rather than private nuisance. This, however, is rather limited for a number of reasons. The first is the requirement of special damage which, as we have seen, has to be proved before an individual can sue in respect of public nuisance. Absence of 'special damage', however, is not fatal to proceedings, since a private citizen could always try a 'relator action', that is, obtain the permission of the Attorney-General to lend his name to the suit. This is straightforward from a purely legal point of view and many of these cases, especially the older ones, were cases where the Attorney-General appears as the nominal plaintiff.[300] Though this procedure overcomes the requirement of 'special damage', it presents another drawback: would a private citizen, who has not suffered 'special damage', hazard the risk and cost of modern litigation for

[298] It seems that the first Act on this matter was passed in the reign of Edward I, banning, in certain circumstances, the use of coal as being detrimental to health matters. Not until Victorian times did systematic legislation start to appear, e.g. Nuisance Removal Act 1846, Alkali Act 1863, Public Health Act 1875 and Rivers Pollution Act 1876. For a review of these developments, see J. F. Brenner, 'Nuisance Law and the Industrial Revolution' (1974) 3 *Jo. LS* 403.

[299] E.g. the extensive destruction caused by the grounding of one oil-tanker, *Amoco Cadiz*, near the north coast of France.

[300] See, e.g., *A-G* v. *PYA Quarries Ltd.* [1957] 2 QB 169.

the benefit of the general public? A private person is unlikely to take that risk, though some pressure group (e.g. for preserving the environment) might well be willing to do so. Here again there are doubts and difficulties: doubts, because some statutory nuisances (discussed below) offer a speedier method of solving these problems; difficulties, because many modern activities which are great polluters (building refineries, factory zones, railway depots, etc.) are increasingly sanctioned by private Acts of Parliament which, as in the *Gulf Oil* case, tend to be construed so as to confer immunity for non-negligent interferences. For these reasons, the action for public nuisance has not played a dominant role in the battle against environmental pollution.[301]

What of private nuisance? It would certainly be intriguing if a tort which evolved out of the problems of neighbourhood in the later Middle Ages could be assigned such a modern function, but then tort concepts are remarkably pliable and have adapted to changes in the socio-economic environment. There are indeed lawyers[302] who argue that private nuisance has considerable potential in this respect,[303] because, first, 'the conceptual framework of nuisance is sufficiently malleable to allow the injection of the environmental perspective' and, second, 'judges who have been faced with private nuisance litigation which involved pollution problems have been prepared to recognize that fact'.

Third, and related to the above, in their selection of remedies courts have often shown willingness to 'use the law of nuisance to make polluters change their ways'.[304] Though there is force in, and some support for, these arguments, it is undeniable that the English law of nuisance has not played a primary role in pollution control. Indeed, it has been seriously doubted whether the tort of nuisance is economically the most efficient way to achieve this goal. For Ogus and Richardson, who have done the most detailed study of this type in this country, the reasons for these doubts are three:

The first is the principle of justice which postulates that existing property rights must be protected even where the result will impose greater costs on society at large. The second is the private law's limited ability to deal with generally inferior environmental conditions, both because it can intervene only where there has been a perceptible change (damage) and because the system of control presupposes an interest in neighbouring land. Finally, enforcement of standards created by private law is only to be selective.[305]

301 N.B., however, the powers of local authorities to bring proceedings for an injunction under s. 222 of the Local Government Act 1972, where they 'consider it expedient for the promotion or protection of the interests of the inhabitants of their area'. The possible utility of this power in the environmental field (for a recent example in a related area, see *Wandsworth LBC* v. *Railtrack plc* [2002] QB 756 (CA)) does not seem to have been much tested and will depend upon whether or not the local authority itself supports the activity of which the local citizenry complains.

302 McLaren, 'The Common Law Nuisance Actions' (Select Bibliography); M. Katz, 'The Function of Tort Liability in Technology Development' (1969) 38 *U Cinn. LR* 587.

303 McLaren, 'The Common Law Nuisance Actions' (Select Bibliography), 560.

304 See e.g. Denning LJ in *Pride of Derby and Derbyshire Angling Association Ltd.* v. *British Celanese Ltd.* [1953] Ch. 149, 192: '[t]he power of the courts to issue an injunction for nuisance has proved itself to be the best method so far devised of securing the cleanliness of our rivers'.

305 Ogus and Richardson (Select Bibliography), 324.

This statement and the account preceding it suggest that the requirements and characteristics of private nuisance make it a clumsy device for controlling pollution. For example, the requirement that claimants must have an interest in land is difficult to rationalise in terms of efficiency. Thus *Malone* v. *Laskey*,[306] which denied the tenant's wife a right of action, left the loss on the person who was clearly less able to bear it and totally incapable of preventing it. The distinctions between interferences with property and amenity, which were criticised earlier, are also dubious, if not indefensible, on any economic ground.[307]

The use of the locality principle in *Rushmer* v. *Polsue and Alfieri*[308] can also be doubted on economic grounds. Commenting on the decision in this case to order the printers to cease their night operations for the sake of the *only* resident in that part of Fleet Street, Ogus and Richardson suggest that 'the decision may accord with the justice notion that the plaintiff should be protected against adverse changes in the environment but on pure efficiency criteria it probably resulted in the printer subsidising the milkman's [plaintiff's] use of his land'.[309]

The *Cambridge Water*[310] case also illustrates the severe limitations on the use of nuisance actions to secure an efficient level of environmental protection. The defendants ran a tanning business that involved the use of certain chemicals. These chemicals entered the water supply and contaminated a borehole that was purchased by the plaintiff, a statutory water company, in 1976. The contamination was not thought to be serious in nature and the plaintiff was satisfied, before it bought the borehole that the water was 'wholesome', in the sense of conforming to the legislative standards which applied at that time.

However, in 1980 an EC Directive (80/778) laid down a higher standard, with the result that the plaintiff could no longer use the borehole to supply water for human consumption. It thus had to shut down is operations and purchase another well, at a cost of around £1 million which it then claimed from the defendants. The judge rejected its claim on two grounds. First, liability under *Rylands* v. *Fletcher* was excluded, since the defendants' use had been natural (the location, Sawston, having been an 'industrial village' since at least the nineteenth century). Second, there could be no liability in nuisance or negligence since the defendants had not been in any way at fault. The loss suffered by the plaintiff was not foreseeable at the time the spillages occurred. Indeed, the defendants had taken steps to reduce the spillages in the 1970s and had even been praised for achieving a good environmental record. All of this was of no avail in the Court of Appeal, which allowed an appeal on the basis that liability in nuisance was strict in the case of interference with a 'natural' incident of ownership, such as the right of a landowner to

306 [1907] 2 KB 141.

307 Ogus and Richardson (Select Bibliography), 299.

308 [1906] 1 Ch. 234; affd. [1907] AC 121.

309 Ogus and Richardson (Select Bibliography), 298.

310 *Cambridge Water Co.* v. *Eastern Counties Leather plc* [1994] 2 WLR 53; J.A. Weir, 'The Polluter Must Pay—Regardless' [1993] *CLJ* 17. See also the report of the judgment of Ian Kennedy J in (1992) 4 *J Env. Law* 81 and the note by N. Atkinson.

naturally occurring water which comes underneath his land through underground channels. The decision is both unjust and inefficient, since it imposes upon potential defendants a degree of responsibility that is out of all proportion to the level of care that they could reasonably be expected to take with regard to the environment. In this case, not only was liability strict, but it extended many years beyond the initial spillage. This type of potential liability cannot be insured against effectively; and the consequences for the defendants in *Cambridge Water* were that they were in danger of being put out of business until the Court of Appeal's ruling was reversed by the House of Lords.

Finally, the *dicta* of Lindley LJ in the *Shelfer*[311] case, which has so influenced the English law on injunctions in this context, may accord with the prevailing philosophy of the time, and even of today, that in such matters the courts should not usurp the role of the legislature. But this attitude also shows how the choice of remedy is determined by preferring individual rights to general social welfare.

All this suggests that nuisance has been either too capricious in its application, or too insensitive towards wider economic considerations, to serve as the main weapon in protecting the environment and achieving the economically optimum result for society in general.

However, though these considerations cast doubts on the usefulness of nuisance in protecting the environment, they do not impair its value in other respects. For, not only in some cases may it provide the only method of compensation for pollution victims, but it may also afford those individuals an opportunity to air legitimate grievances and even succeed in condemning wrongful activities which affect others as well.[312]

(B) STATUTORY NUISANCES

Where the common law proved to be ineffective or slow, the legislator has intervened in two ways: either by controlling the activity in advance or by providing expeditious methods of dealing with some of their obnoxious side effects.

The first method is to require certain trades (referred to as 'offensive trades' and described in Acts of Parliament or local bye-laws[313]) to be licensed in advance by the local authority. These requirements will often be related to planning regulations now to be found in the Town and Country (Use Classes) Order 1987[314] and, alone or together with other rules, they may go a long way towards preventive control. The second method is to describe certain unacceptable states of affairs as statutory nuisances and to provide summary remedies for them. For instance, section 92(1) of the Public Health Act 1936 described certain matters as 'statutory nuisances' if they were nuisances at

311 [1895] 1 Ch. 287, 317.

312 The importance of not underestimating this consideration was stressed by J. L. Sax, *Defending the Environment: A Strategy for Citizen Action* (1970), 112.

313 Section 107(1) of the Public Health Act 1936 provides a list of such trades (e.g. fat-extractor, fat- or glue-maker, soap- or tallow- or tripe-boiler), all of which are likely to cause obnoxious fumes or smells, while other provisions of the Act (as well as the Local Government Act 1972, s. 235) enable local authorities to extend the scope of the legislation to other trades or business, subject to confirmation by the Secretary of State.

314 SI 1987/764.

common law, *or* were 'prejudicial to health' (described by s. 343(1) as 'injurious or likely to cause injury to health'). Run-down or defective premises, whether an actionable nuisance or not, may come under statutory nuisance prejudicial to health; and the same qualification may apply to the keeping of animals and to accumulations or deposits, such as manure or refuse. The Clean Air Act of 1956, section 16, also provided that the emission of smoke might, in certain circumstances, be treated as a statutory nuisance for the purposes of the Public Health Act 1936. The Control of Pollution Act 1974, in effect incorporating section 1 of the older Noise Abatement Act of 1960, also provided for summary proceedings in addition to any common law remedy for noises amounting to a nuisance. Incidentally, turning certain 'noisome trades' into statutory nuisances may mean removing them from the cumbersome area of public nuisance to which they traditionally belonged. The Environmental Protection Act 1990 was passed to consolidate much of this material and the current matters which amount to a statutory nuisance are to be found in its section 79.

Where a statutory nuisance has been committed, it will be usual for the local authority to serve an abatement notice which, if not complied with, will result in proceedings before magistrates. If nuisance is proved, they will make such order as they think fit, and failure to comply with it will be an offence. In other circumstances, however, for example in noise nuisance, the procedure may be even simpler, in that failure to comply with the original abatement notice may itself be an offence without the need for a nuisance order. These nuisance orders or notices will be directed to the person whose act or default causes the nuisance, although in certain circumstances the local authority will itself be empowered to abate the nuisance. It will be clear, however, that all such technical matters are matters of administrative law and this is no place to enter into their detail.[315] Nevertheless, it should be stressed that a large proportion of the legal activity relating to questions of nuisance (and social and environmental issues in particular) takes place under statutory provisions rather than the common law. This is an important aspect in considering the common law rules on nuisance discussed in this chapter. Indeed, as and when the EC Directive on Environmental Liability[316] is implemented in the United Kingdom, it may be that this trend will only increase.

[315] A brief account can be found in Buckley (Select Bibliography), 151–72. See, for fuller treatment, R. Malcolm and J. Pointing, *Statutory Nuisance: Law and Practice* (2002).

[316] Directive 2004/35/EC [2004] *OJ* L143/56, requiring Member States to establish a regime on environmental liability with regard to the prevention and remedying of 'environmental damage' (as defined in Art. 2(1), including 'any damage that significantly adversely affects the ecological, chemical and/or quantitative status and/or ecological potential . . . of the waters concerned' and 'any land contamination that creates a significant risk of human health being adversely affected as a result of the direct or indirect introduction, in, on or under land, of substances, preparations, organisms or micro-organisms'). This regime requires the establishment of competent national authorities to recover such environmental damage from the relevant operators, and thus relies upon state enforcement to secure respect for the principle that 'the polluter pays' (Art. 1). While those EC rules expressly do not confer any right upon private individuals to sue for compensation for environmental damage covered by the Directive (Art. 3(3)), the Directive also expressly applies without prejudice to 'relevant national legislation' (Art. 3(3)) or to civil liability regimes for 'traditional damage' under any international agreement (rec. 11). At the time of writing, the UK is conducting a consultation (separately in Scotland and England & Wales) on the implementation of the Directive.

SELECT BIBLIOGRAPHY

BUCKLEY, R. A., *The Law of Nuisance* (1981).

BURROWS, P., 'Nuisance, Legal Rules and Decentralised Decisions: A Different View of the Cathedral Crypt', in Burrows, P., and Velijanovski, C. G. (eds.), *Economic Approach to Law* (1981).

BUXTON, R. J., 'Nuisance and Negligence Again' (1966) 29 *MLR* 676.

—'The Negligent Nuisance' (1966) 8 *Malaya LR* 1.

CALABRESI, G., and MELAMED, A. D., 'Property Rules, Liability Rules and Inalienability: One View of the Cathedral' (1972) 85 *Harv. LR* 1089.

CAMPBELL, D., 'Of Coase and Corn: a (Sort of) Defence of Private Nuisance' (2000) 63 *MLR* 197.

CANE, P., 'Justice and Justification for Tort Liability' (1982) 2 *OJLS* 30, 51–61.

DAVEY, M., 'Neighbours in Law' [2002] *Conv.* 31.

DIAS, R. W. M., 'Trouble on Oiled Waters. Problems of the *Wagon Mound (No. 2)*' [1967] *CLJ* 62.

EEKELAAR, J. M., 'Nuisance and Strict Liability' (1973) 8 *Ir. Jur.* 191.

FRIDMAN, G. H. L., 'Motive in the English Law of Nuisance' (1954) 40 *Virginia LR* 583.

GEARTY, C., 'The Place of Private Nuisance in a Modern Law of Torts' [1989] *CLJ* 214.

GOODHART, A. L., 'Liability for Things Naturally on the Land' [1930–2] 4 *CLJ* 13.

KEETON, P., 'Trespass, Nuisance and Strict Liability' (1959) 59 *Col. LR* 457.

KIDNER, R., 'Television Reception and the Tort of Nuisance' [1989] *Conv.* 279.

—'Nuisance and Rights of Property' [1998] *Conv.* 267.

KODILINYE, G., 'Public Nuisance and Particular Damage in Modern Law' (1986) 6 *Leg. Stud.* 182.

—'Standing to Sue in Private Nuisance' (1989) 9 *Leg. Stud.* 284.

LEE, M., 'What is Private Nuisance?' (2003) 119 *LQR* 298.

MARKESINIS, B. S., and TETTENBORN, A. M., 'Cricket, Power Boat Racing and Nuisance' (1981) 131 *NLJ* 108.

MCLAREN, J. P. S., 'The Common Law Nuisance Actions and the Environmental Battle: Well-Tempered Swords or Broken Reeds?' (1972) 10 *Osgoode Hall LJ* 505.

—'Nuisance Law and the Industrial Revolution: Some Lessons from Social History' (1983) 3 *OJLS* 155.

NEWARK, F. H., 'The Boundaries of Nuisance' (1949) 65 *LQR* 480.

OGUS, A. I., and RICHARDSON, G. M., 'Economics and the Environment: A Study of Private Nuisance' [1977] *CLJ* 284.

SPENCER, J., 'Public Nuisance: A Critical Examination' [1989] *CLJ* 55.

STEELE, J., 'Private Law and the Environment: Nuisance in Context' (1995) 15 *Leg. Stud.* 236.

TROMANS, S., 'Nuisance: Prevention or Payment' [1982] *CLJ* 87.

WINFIELD, P. H., 'Nuisance as a Tort' [1930–2] *CLJ* 189.

14

DECEIT*

The common-law rules concerning liability for dishonesty were synthesised to create the tort of deceit at the end of the eighteenth century in *Pasley* v. *Freeman*,[1] and the tort takes its modern form from the decision of the House of Lords in *Derry* v. *Peek*[2] in 1889. Most of the cases concern non-physical damage, that is to say, financial or pure economic loss, although the tort can also extend to cover personal injuries[3] and damage to property. The requirements of liability are as follows: the defendant must make (1) a false statement (2) of existing fact (3) with knowledge of its falsity and with the intention that the claimant should act on it, with the result (4) that the claimant acts on it to his detriment.[4]

1. A FALSE STATEMENT

A false statement may be made orally or in writing or by conduct. In *R* v. *Barnard*[5] the accused entered a shop in Oxford wearing academic dress to which he was not entitled, thereby representing himself as a member of the university. He was held to be guilty of obtaining goods by false pretences. If a statement is ambiguous the claimant has to show that the false sense was the one which the defendant wished him to understand.[6] Silence can render a person liable only if he was under a duty to speak or to correct a misleading impression.[7] Sometimes the defendant may be held liable for stating a half-truth: if what was left unsaid would have negated what was said, there may be liability.[8] In some cases statute has created a special duty of disclosure, as in the provisions of

* This chapter draws on parts of the text prepared by R. W. M. Dias for the 2nd edn of this book.

[1] (1789) 3 Term Rep. 51; 100 ER 450.

[2] 14 App. Cas. 337.

[3] See *Langridge* v. *Levy* (1837) 2 M & W 519; 150 ER 863.

[4] For a judicial summary of these requirements see *Bradford Third Equitable Benefit Building Society* v. *Borders* [1941] 2 All ER 205, 211.

[5] (1837) 7 C & P 784; 173 ER 342.

[6] *Gross* v. *Lewis Hillman Ltd.* [1970] Ch. 445; see also *Smith* v. *Chadwick* (1884) 9 App. Cas. 187, *Woodhouse AC Israel Cocoa Ltd.* v. *Nigerian Produce Marketing Co. Ltd.* [1972] AC 741.

[7] *Schneider* v. *Heath* (1813) 3 Camp. 506; 170 ER 1462; *Arkwright* v. *Newbold* (1881) 17 Ch. D 301, 318.

[8] *Peek* v. *Gurney* (1873) LR 6 HL 377.

financial services legislation which place companies under certain duties of disclosure in respect of company prospectuses.[9] The statement must normally be made by the defendant himself, but there is some authority for the suggestion that one who uses a false impression created in the claimant's mind by a third party in order to profit by it can then be made liable.[10]

A statement of fact that was true when made but which becomes untrue later will ground liability provided the defendant learned of the falsity and then chose not to warn the claimant.[11] Equally, if the statement was false when made but the defendant believed it to be true at the time and later discovered that it was false, it seems that he would be liable in deceit if he failed to notify the claimant.[12] What happens if a false statement was made fraudulently but, before the claimant can act upon it, it becomes true? Here there is no liability.[13] On the other hand, if the statement becomes true only after the claimant has acted on it—by, for example, entering into a contract in reliance on the statement—there will be liability since the statement was still false when the cause of action accrued.

2. A STATEMENT OF EXISTING FACT

The statement has to be of existing fact. Promises and declarations of future purpose are not, generally speaking, actionable unless they are contained in a contract supported by consideration. Sometimes it is difficult, however, to distinguish between a statement of fact and a promise. A declaration of future intention may be treated as a representation of a present state of mind. In *Edgington* v. *Fitzmaurice*[14] a misstatement concerning the objects for which debentures were issued was held sufficient to give rise to liability; Bowen LJ said that 'the state of man's mind is as much a fact as the state of his digestion'.[15] Thus a false opinion made deliberately will be actionable since it is a misrepresentation of the mind of the person giving it.[16] By contrast, in *Wales* v. *Wadham*[17] a wife's statement that she intended not to remarry following the divorce was held to be an opinion as to the future and not a representation of fact. Statements of law may be statements either of opinion or of fact. A statement of what a legal rule might be, based on ambiguous words in a statute or on a difficult matter of

[9] The relevant legislation is now contained in the Financial Services and Markets Act 2000. These provisions, and their predecessors, effectively reverse the House of Lords' judgment in *Derry* v. *Peek* (1889) 14 App. Cas. 337 on the narrow point of company law with which it was concerned.

[10] *Bradford Building Society* v. *Borders* [1941] 2 All ER 205, 208.

[11] *Incledon* v. *Watson* (1862) 2 F & F 841; 175 ER 1312.

[12] This seems to follow from *Briess* v. *Woolley* [1954] AC 333.

[13] *Ship* v. *Croskill* (1870) LR 10 Eq. 73.

[14] (1885) 29 Ch. D 459.

[15] *Ibid.*, 483.

[16] *Anderson* v. *Pacific Insurance Co.* (1872) LR 7 CP 65, 69, *Bissett* v. *Wilkinson* [1927] AC 177, 182.

[17] [1977] 1 WLR 199.

interpretation, will be a statement of opinion, but a deliberate misstatement of a statutory provision's meaning will be treated as a statement of fact. In *West London Commercial Bank Ltd.* v. *Kitson*[18] a false statement to the effect that the defendants had power to accept bills of exchange was held to give rise to liability.

There is a special rule concerning representations about the creditworthiness of third parties. Section 6 of the Statute of Frauds (Amendment) Act 1828 (Lord Tenterden's Act) provides that a fraudulent misrepresentation as to 'the character, conduct, credit, ability, trade or dealings of any other persons, to the intent or purpose that such other person may obtain credit, money, or goods upon' has to be made in writing and signed by the defendant for any action to lie. A company can make a written representation through a duly authorised agent acting within the scope of his authority or through an employee acting in the course of his duties.[19] The Statute applies only to actions in deceit and not to negligence;[20] this creates the odd situation, following the expansion of negligence liability,[21] that in the absence of writing there might be liability in negligence even though there would be none if the misstatement had been made intentionally.[22] Another difficulty is that the Act affects only actionability and not liability. This has repercussions for the principle of the employer's vicarious liability for the torts of his employee: the employee might, in a case of an unwritten misstatement, invoke the Act to avoid being sued, but since he is still *liable* an action could conceivably lie against his employer.[23]

3. THE DEFENDANT'S STATE OF MIND

The relevant mental state is that the defendant must either have known that the statement was false or must have been reckless as to its truth or falsity. Recklessness here includes indifference as to whether a statement is true or false, in the sense of a defendant not caring if it is true or having no belief in its truth.[24] This could cover a situation in which the defendant has a sense of unease about the truth of a statement, and deliberately refrains from inquiring whether it is true or not.[25] If the defendant acts dishonestly in this sense, lack of a fraudulent motive is not a defence, nor is any justification

[18] (1884) 13 QBD 360, 363 (Bowen LJ).

[19] *UBAF Ltd.* v. *European American Banking Corp.* [1984] QB 713.

[20] *Banbury* v. *Bank of Montreal* [1918] AC 626.

[21] In *Hedley Byrne & Co. Ltd.* v. *Heller & Partners Ltd.* [1964] AC 465.

[22] See *W. B. Anderson & Sons Ltd.* v. *Rhodes (Liverpool) Ltd.* [1967] 2 All ER 850, *Diamond* v. *Bank of London and Montreal Ltd.* [1979] QB 333.

[23] See *Brown* v. *Morgan* [1953] 1 QB 397.

[24] *GE Commercial Finance Ltd.* v. *Gee* [2005] EWHC 2056, at [104] (Tugendhat J).

[25] *Ibid.*, at para. 107 (Tugendhat J), referring to the judgment of Lord Scott of Foscote in *Manifest Shipping Co. Ltd.* v. *Uni-Polaris Shipping Co. Ltd.* [2003] 1 AC 469, a case not on the tort of deceit but on liability under the Marine Insurance Act 1906 to which similar principles apply.

defence available.[26] On the other hand, if the defendant *carelessly but honestly* makes a false statement, he will not be liable for deceit.

In the leading case of *Derry* v. *Peek*[27] an Act of Parliament incorporating a tramway company provided that it could operate steam-driven carriages with the consent of the Board of Trade. The directors issued a prospectus declaring that they had the right to use steam, on the faith of which the plaintiff bought shares in the company. The Board of Trade subsequently refused the necessary permission. The House of Lords held that there was no action in deceit since the defendants had honestly believed that permission was a formality; they had merely been careless. This principle still holds. In *Thomas Witter Ltd.* v. *TBP Properties Ltd.*[28] the vendor of a business was alleged to have failed to check whether a profit forecast was accurately based. Jacob J held that in the absence of evidence of dishonesty, the defendant could not be liable in deceit.

Derry v. *Peek* established that carelessness was not sufficient for the action of deceit; later, in *Hedley Byrne & Co. Ltd.* v. *Heller & Partners Ltd.*,[29] the House of Lords held that carelessness might, in certain circumstances, give rise to liability for breach of a duty of care in negligence. Section 2(1) of the Misrepresentation Act 1967 also provides for damages for the victim of reliance on a misstatement that induces a contract with the representor. The representor has the duty of, in effect, disproving negligence. Much of the significance of the distinction between liability for deceit and the near-strict liability provided for by section 2(1) has been effaced by the decision of the Court of Appeal in *Royscott Trust Ltd.* v. *Rogerson*[30] to the effect that the measure of damages under section 2(1) is the same as it is for deceit.[31]

The defendant must intend the claimant to act on the statement. In *Peek* v. *Gurney*[32] the plaintiff, who bought shares in the open market in reliance on fraudulent misstatements in a company prospectus, was held to have no action since the intention behind the prospectus was to induce persons to apply for shares, not to buy them in the market. As long as the defendant intends the claimant to act on his statement, it does not matter that it is made to a third party. In *Langridge* v. *Levy*[33] the defendant sold a gun to a father for use by him and his son, having knowingly made a false statement about its manufacture. When the son used the gun, it burst and injured him. He was able to maintain an action against the defendant for fraud.

4. CAUSATION

The claimant must act on the statement in the sense of being induced by it to enter into a particular transaction. Clearly, if no causal link is established—if, for example, the claimant disregarded the advice or information given by the defendant—there can be

[26] *Standard Chartered Bank* v. *Pakistan National Shipping Corp.* [2000] 1 Lloyd's Rep. 218; *GE Commercial Finance Ltd.* v. *Gee* [2005] EWHC 2056.

[27] (1889) 14 App. Cas. 337.

[28] [1996] 2 All ER 573.

[29] [1964] AC 465.

[30] [1991] 3 All ER 294.

[31] See generally the discussion in ch. 3, above.

[32] (1873) LR 6 HL 377.

[33] (1837) 2 M & W 519.

no question of liability.[34] But recent cases have shown that the test of reliance or inducement is more liberal here than it is in the context of liability in negligence. In particular, in cases of deceit the claimant is not required to show that he would not have entered into the transaction if the statement had either not been made or had not been made fraudulently. It is enough if the defendant's conduct was one of the factors which induced the claimant to act as he did; if he was, in addition, influenced by other considerations including independent advice, this is not necessarily fatal to his claim.[35] The justification for this approach lies in the policy of the law in discouraging fraud.

5. DAMAGE, DAMAGES AND DEFENCES

Loss is an essential element of the tort. In principle the claimant is entitled to be placed in the position he would have been in had the fraudulent misrepresentation not been made. Damages for lost expectation, or lost bargain, are not normally available, since this would involve placing the claimant in the position he would have been in if the statement had attained the status of a contractual warranty. However, if the claimant can show that, in the absence of the fraud, he would have entered into a transaction with the defendant or another which would have generated a particular income stream, a legitimate claim for lost profits may be made out.[36]

In relation to remoteness, damages are calculated not on the basis of foreseeability and the *Wagon Mound (No. 1)*[37] test in negligence but, instead, on the basis of a test of directness. The defendant will thus be liable for all damage directly flowing from the misstatement, even if certain losses and certain kinds of damage were not foreseeable.[38] One consequence is that the defendant takes the risk of the claimant's loss being augmented by events occurring after the fraud took place that were outside the control of either party, such as a fall in the market which further devalues the property which was the subject of the transaction between them. The basis for taking this approach to intentional wrongdoing is, as Lord Steyn has explained, twofold:

First it serves a deterrent purpose in discouraging fraud... in the battle against fraud civil remedies can play a useful and beneficial role. Second, as between fraudster and the innocent

34 *Central Railway of Venezuela* v. *Kisch* (1867) LR 2 HL 99.

35 See *Downs* v. *Chappell* [1997] 1 WLR 426 (Hobhouse LJ), *Smith New Court Securities Ltd.* v. *Scrimgeour Vickers (Asset Management) Ltd.* [1997] AC 254 (Lord Steyn), *Hagen* v. *ICI Chemicals and Polymers Ltd.* [2002] IRLR 31 (Elias J, noting the difference between deceit and negligence); see also long-standing authority for this approach in *Edgington* v. *Fitzmaurice* (1885) 29 Ch. D 459, 483 (Bowen LJ), itself a case of fraudulent misrepresentation.

36 *East* v. *Maurer* [1991] 1 WLR 461, *Downs* v. *Chappell* [1997] 1 WLR 426, *Smith New Court Securities Ltd.* v. *Scrimgeour Vickers (Asset Management) Ltd.* [1997] AC 254, *Clef Aquitaine SARL* v. *Laporte Materials (Barrow) Ltd.* [2001] QB 488.

37 [1961] AC 388.

38 *Doyle* v. *Olby (Ironmongers) Ltd.* [1969] 2 QB 158, *Downs* v. *Chappell* [1996] 3 All ER 344, *Smith New Court Securities Ltd.* v. *Scrimgeour Vickers (Asset Management) Ltd.* [1997] AC 254.

party, moral considerations militate in favour of requiring the fraudster to bear the risk of misfortunes directly caused by his fraud.[39]

The same policy underlies the House of Lords' ruling in *Standard Chartered Bank* v. *Pakistan National Shipping Corporation*[40] to the effect that contributory negligence is not a defence to this tort, and the principle that any attempt to exclude or limit liability for deceit will be strictly construed.[41]

SELECT BIBLIOGRAPHY

Fullagar, W. K., 'Liability for Representations at Common Law' (1951) 25 *Aust. LJ* 278.

Keeton, R. E., 'Fraud: Misrepresentations of Law' (1937) 15 *Tex. LR* 409.

[39] *Ibid.*, 279–80. The result in *Smith New Court* may be contrasted with the decision of the House of Lords in the *Banques Bruxelles Lambert* case (*sub nom. South Australia Asset Management Corp.* v. *York Montague Ltd.* [1997] AC 191) which concerned *negligent* misrepresentation.

[40] [2002] 3 WLR 1547.

[41] *HIH Casualty and General Insurance Ltd.* v. *Chase Manhattan Bank Ltd.* [2001] 2 Lloyd's Rep. 483.

15

THE ECONOMIC TORTS

1. THE FRAMEWORK OF THE ECONOMIC TORTS

The purpose of the economic torts is to protect a person in relation to his trade, business or livelihood. However, he will only be protected from certain kinds of interference, principally those inflicted intentionally or deliberately. Nor will an intention to harm suffice, on its own, to ground liability. For the interference to be actionable some additional element of unlawfulness must normally be present. Most of the cases fall into one of two categories: those involving wrongful interference with a *pre-existing legal right* of the claimant, and those involving the use of *independently unlawful means*. The only exception to the principle just stated arises in the tort of conspiracy to injure, where the act of combination or association between the defendants, when coupled with an intention to harm the claimant, is sufficient for liability even though lawful means are used.

The fact that the economic torts are restricted in this way illustrates the lower priority which the law of tort accords to the protection of 'pure economic' or financial interests, as opposed to the protection of physical integrity and of property rights.[1] The torts of trespass to the person and trespass to goods and to land are actionable *per se*, that is to say without proof of damage, upon evidence of an intentional act of interference. With the economic torts, by contrast, not only is damage or the threat of damage a necessary ingredient of liability, but the mere intention to harm another's economic interests cannot give rise to liability if the losses were inflicted through lawful means. Conversely, the defendant will not be liable for foreseeably but unintentionally causing economic loss, even where unlawful means are used.[2]

These basic principles were laid down in a series of decisions dating from the turn of the last century, in which the English courts rejected the notion of a *prima facie* liability in tort for the infliction of economic losses through 'unfair competition'. In *Mogul Steamship Co. Ltd.* v. *McGregor, Gow & Co.*[3] the plaintiffs complained that they had been driven out of the market for the shipping of tea from the Chinese ports by the concerted acts of the defendants acting as a 'shipping conference'. The defendants had sought to monopolise the trade by, amongst other things, offering uneconomic rates to the local

[1] See J.A. Weir, *Economic Torts* (Select Bibliography), 8–13, for a restatement of this distinction.

[2] *Ibid.*, 14–20.

[3] (1889) LR 23 QBD 598; [1892] AC 25.

shippers and giving local agents special rebates in return for an agreement to deal exclusively with the defendants. The plaintiffs' claim failed on the grounds that no unlawful act had been committed and that the defendants had simply been acting in pursuit of their own economic self-interest through collective action. The distinction between means and ends emerged clearly in the speech of Bowen LJ in the Court of Appeal:

[A trader's] right to trade freely is a right that the law recognises and encourages but it is one which places him at no special advantage as compared with others. No man, whether trader or not, can, however, justify damaging another in his commercial business by fraud or misrepresentation. Intimidation, obstruction and molestation are forbidden; so is the intentional procurement or violation of individual rights, contractual or other, assuming always that there is no just cause for it... [but] the defendants have been guilty of none of these acts. They have done nothing more against the plaintiffs than pursue to the bitter end a war of competition waged in the interest of their own trade.[4]

The same principle was applied to labour disputes in the great case of *Allen* v. *Flood*.[5] Boilermakers employed at a shipbuilding yard discovered that the plaintiffs, who were working in the yard as shipwrights, had previously worked as boilermakers at another yard without being members of the boilermakers' trade union. An official of the union, Allen, indicated to the employers that the boilermakers would go on strike in protest at the employment of the plaintiffs unless they were dismissed, and they were duly dismissed later the same day. The House of Lords allowed Allen's appeal from the findings of liability of the lower courts. The case turned on the absence of any unlawful means. The contracts of employment of the men working at the yard were effectively 'contracts at will', that is to say, they could be terminated on notice of an hour or so. This meant that Allen's threat of a strike did not amount to a threat to induce a breach of the men's contracts with their employer; had the strike gone ahead, they would have given lawful notice to walk off the job. Equally, Flood's dismissal was not a breach of contract: the employers were not required to give him any more notice than he in fact received. Although Allen intended to inflict economic harm on Flood, he did so without upsetting any pre-existing right of Flood to continuing employment and without threatening independently unlawful means. The House of Lords held this distinction between lawful and unlawful means to be vital. Lord Davey said:

The right which a man has to pursue his trade or calling is qualified by an equal right of others to do the same and compete with him, though to his damage. And it is obvious that a general abstract right of this character stands on a different footing from such a private particular right as the right to performance of a contract into which one has entered. A man has no right to be employed by any particular employer, and no right to any particular employment if it depends on the will of the employer.[6]

Lord Shand saw the case as 'one of competition in labour, which... is in all essentials analogous to competition in trade, and to which the same principles apply'.[7]

[4] (1889) LR 23 QBD 598, 614. [5] [1898] AC 1.
[6] *Ibid.*, 173. [7] *Ibid.*, 164.

The majority therefore rejected the view that 'malice' against the plaintiff was a sufficient basis for liability. They did so largely through concern that the notion of 'malice' was too vague to be applied consistently by courts, and in particular (at that time) by juries. The meaning of malice in the law of torts is not always clear. It denotes something more than an intention to hurt the claimant, but it is not necessarily synonymous with an illegitimate motive. The absence of any factor justifying the defendant's behaviour, when coupled with the intention to harm the claimant, comes close to capturing the essence of the concept.

Professor Richard Epstein has suggested the following definition in the context of the economic torts: 'Malice in its pure form means more than an intention to inflict some injury. All competition, and most economic activity, will do that. Instead, it refers to actions done out of spite or ill will, whereby someone is prepared to impose costs upon himself solely to make someone else worse off.'[8] An example of this concept of malice is the American case of *Tuttle* v. *Buck*,[9] in which liability was imposed upon the defendant, a wealthy industrialist, who drove the plaintiff out of business by setting up a rival barber to him in his home town, for reasons related entirely to a personal grudge. This case would not be followed in England because the means used were lawful and the defendant acted alone. In some American jurisdictions the requirement that the defendant should disprove an implication of malice by showing that he acted out of economic self-interest has given rise to the notion of a '*prima facie* tort liability'. English law recognises a form of this only in the isolated case of conspiracy to injure. In *Quinn* v. *Leathem*,[10] decided three years after *Allen* v. *Flood*, the House of Lords held that acts carried out by a combination of workers with the aim of driving out of business an employer who took on non-union labour could be tortious, if the actions were motivated by ill will against the plaintiff personally, as opposed to the economic self-protection of the defendants. For some time it was not clear whether this decision had implicitly qualified *Allen* v. *Flood*, but in due course it was decided that the principle of *Quinn* v. *Leathem* was confined to cases of combination and, moreover, that the defence of justification would normally be available to trade unionists acting, for example, to defend their trade against non-union competition.[11]

Conspiracy aside, then, the English common law has adopted a *formal* criterion—the presence of an element of unlawfulness, in the sense of a crime or a civil wrong such as a breach of contract or possibly breach of a statutory obligation—as opposed to *substantive* criteria for identifying illegitimate or unfair competition. Writing extra-judicially,[12] Lord Devlin complained that *Allen* v. *Flood* had thereby dammed up a stream of liability which could have developed within the common law, although he warned that 'only a tenuous barrier' held it back. As it is, *Allen* v. *Flood* remains (just)

[8] R. A. Epstein, 'A Common Law for Labour Relations: A Critique of the New Deal Legislation' (1983) 92 *Yale LJ* 1357, 1368.

[9] 119 NW 946 (1909).

[10] [1901] AC 495.

[11] See *Sorrell* v. *Smith* [1925] AC 700, *Crofter Hand Woven Harris Tweed Co.* v. *Veitch* [1942] AC 435, *Lonrho Ltd.* v. *Shell Petroleum Co. Ltd.* [1982] AC 173.

[12] *Samples of Lawmaking* (1962).

good law, and with the common law abandoning the task of working out the limits of legitimate competition the responsibility has gradually been assumed by Parliament. In the commercial sphere, matters such as predatory pricing, retail-price maintenance, and exclusive dealing are dealt with by legislation that includes the Competition Act 1998. This legislation has largely displaced the common law of tort in favour of a number of administrative and judicial procedures for regulating anti-competitive arrangements; it is underwritten, in its turn, by European Community legislation deriving from Articles 81 and 82 of the EC Treaty. A consideration of this body of law lies outside the scope of this book.[13] The common law of tort retains its importance in employment cases, however, where it operates in conjunction with legislation concerning the scope of lawful trade disputes now to be found in Part V of the Trade Union and Labour Relations (Consolidation) Act 1992, and as a residual form of redress in cases of competition between businesses.[14]

The absence of any unifying principle drawing together the different heads of economic tort liability has often been remarked upon. There is no equivalent in this area of law to the role played by *Donoghue* v. *Stevenson* in the tort of negligence.[15] Attempts to provide a general theory have tended to break down against the reluctance of the courts to engage in the kind of synthesis needed.[16] It is probably futile to expect such a synthesis to emerge in the near future. This is because of the context in which most of the modern case law arises, that is to say, industrial disputes involving trade unions and employers. Since the Trade Disputes Act 1906 Parliament has conferred extensive immunities on trade unions, their members and others involved in the organisation of strike action which would otherwise be tortious. This immunity was felt to be necessary if the purposes of trade unionism were to be rendered lawful and an equilibrium established in industrial relations.[17] However, following the decision of the House of Lords in *Rookes* v. *Barnard* in 1964[18] the courts embarked on an expansion of

[13] See R. Whish, *Competition Law* (4th edn., 2003) and P. J. Slot and A. Johnston, *An Introduction to Competition Law* (2006) for a systematic treatment of the principles of both UK and EC competition law.

[14] Important non-labour cases of the past few years include *CBS Songs Ltd.* v. *Amstrad Consumer Electronics plc* [1988] AC 1013; *Lonrho plc* v. *Fayed* [1992] 1 AC 448; *Stocznia Gdanska SA* v. *Latvian Shipping Co.* [2002] 2 Lloyd's Rep. 436; and the trilogy of cases decided by the House of Lords in 2007, *OBG Ltd.* v. *Allan*, *Douglas* v. *Hello! Ltd (No. 3)* and *Mainstream Properties Ltd.* v. *Young* [2007] UKHL 21.

[15] See Lord Wedderburn, 'Rocking the Torts' (1983) 46 *MLR* 223, 229.

[16] An important article which provides perhaps the best attempt at a general explanation is Weir, 'Chaos or Cosmos? *Rookes*, *Stratford* and the Economic Torts' [1964] *CLJ* 225. See also P. Elias and K. Ewing, 'Economic Torts and Labour Law: Old Principles and New Liabilities' [1982] *CLJ* 321; and H. Carty, 'Intentional Violation of Economic Interests: The Limits of Common Law Liability' (1988) 104 *LQR* 250. P. J. Sales, 'The Tort of Conspiracy and Civil Secondary Liability' [1990] *CLJ* 491 offers an altogether different perspective, suggesting that many of the cases are best explained in terms of a principle of secondary liability for aiding or assisting a civil law wrong; but cf. the judgment of Lord Slynn in *Crédit Lyonnais Bank Nederland NV* v. *Export Credits Guarantee Department* [2000] 1 AC 486.

[17] Numerous labour law texts provide an account of the background to the enactment of the immunities and their relationship to the industrial relations system. See, in particular, O. Kahn-Freund, *Labour and the Law* (3rd edn., by P. Davies and M. Freedland, 1983), ch. 1, and Lord Wedderburn, *The Worker and the Law* (3rd edn., 1986), ch. 1.

[18] [1964] AC 1129.

economic tort liability which had the effect of 'outflanking' the immunities provided by statute through the creation of new, nominate torts. In particular, this period saw: the development of the general tort of interference with trade by unlawful means; the extension of the tort of inducing breach of contract to cover a wider category of acts of interference with contractual performance; the acceptance of the tort of inducing breach of statutory duty as a new head of liability; and the evolution of economic duress as a ground for recovery of money and, in the view of some, as a tort in its own right. At times it has seemed that the courts (and the Bar) were engaged in a battle of wits with the parliamentary draftsman, to see which side could develop the optimal formula for widening or for narrowing liability respectively. To some extent this tension (or the potential for it) still exists, despite a change in labour law policy since 1979 which has seen Parliament, rather than the courts, take the lead in the narrowing down of the immunities.[19] From an historical perspective, the dynamic quality of the economic torts, which makes them so resistant to synthesis, was undoubtedly a reaction to Parliament's attempts since 1906 to neutralise this area of common law liability. There are signs, in recent non-labour cases,[20] that the courts are rowing back from some of the expansionary decisions of earlier decades, but how far this signifies a broader retrenchment of the economic torts remains to be seen.

Notwithstanding the complexity of this area of the law, some degree of classification is nevertheless possible. There are three broad sub-categories of liability: those torts based on the defendant's wrongful interference with the claimant's pre-existing legal rights (inducing breach of contract and inducing breach of statutory duty, in particular); the tort of interference with trade or business by unlawful means; and the tort of conspiracy. These will now be considered in turn, to be followed by an outline of the statutory immunities in relation to trade disputes.

2. WRONGFUL INTERFERENCE WITH THE CLAIMANT'S PRE-EXISTING RIGHT

Where the defendant intentionally and knowingly interferes with a pre-existing right of the claimant to receive income, goods or services, with the result that the claimant suffers economic damage, liability in tort may arise. The right in question may exist under a contract or by virtue of a fiduciary relationship, or it may, more exceptionally, arise under a statutory obligation. The classic instance is the tort of inducing breach of contract; since that tort was given its modern form in the nineteenth century, various additions have been made by the courts.

[19] See generally S. Deakin and G. Morris, *Labour Law* (4th edn., 2005), ch. 11.

[20] Above all, in the recent decision of the House of Lords in *OBG Ltd.* v. *Allan/Douglas* v. *Hello! Ltd. (No. 3)/Mainstream Properties Ltd.* v. *Young* [2007] UKHL 21.

(A) INDUCING BREACH OF CONTRACT

It is a tort for the defendant (A) intentionally knowingly to persuade a third party (B) to break his contract with the claimant (C), to the damage of C. This tort was established in *Lumley* v. *Gye*[21] and confirmed by the House of Lords in *Allen* v. *Flood*[22] and, more recently, in *OBG Ltd.* v. *Allan*.[23] In *Lumley* v. *Gye* the plaintiff had a contract for the exclusive services of the opera singer Johanna Wagner, who was then lured away by the defendant to sing at his theatre for a higher fee. The defendant was aware of the terms of the contract between Lumley and Wagner. The plaintiff sued for damages and the Court of Queen's Bench decided by a majority that he had a good cause of action.[24] It was irrelevant, according to Erle J, that the plaintiff could also sue Miss Wagner for damages for breach of contract (in fact this action was brought separately).[25] The remedy on the contract might be inadequate, in the sense that damages might be restricted by the duty to mitigate or by the rule of remoteness in contract law. Under these circumstances, 'he who procures the damage maliciously might justly be made responsible beyond the liability of the contractor'. The essence of the tort, then, lies in what Erle J called malice but which is now thought of, more precisely, as the knowing or deliberate procurement of the breach. The status of the tort was unclear for a long period until *Allen* v. *Flood* was decided. It was made clear in that case that there could be no liability for persuading someone not to enter into a contract.[26] The crucial dividing line was between the case in which the plaintiff had a legal right to performance, protected by contract, and the case in which he merely had a moral or commercial expectation of some kind which was not embodied in contractual form.

Lumley v. *Gye* concerned an employment contract, and the authorities relied on by the majority as precedents were mainly cases arising out of actions by masters for the enticement away of their servants, an area heavily regulated at that time by statute. However, the modern tort has been extended beyond employment contracts, and the original statutory context in which the action for enticement arose has also been forgotten. The tort has been applied to contracts for the commercial supply of goods,[27] contracts of hire[28] and exclusive dealing contracts.[29] The contract in question must be a valid one: it must not be illegal or in restraint of trade,[30] nor, it seems, capable of being rescinded.[31] Damage is necessary, but business losses of some kind flowing from a breach of contract are frequently assumed.[32]

21 (1853) 2 E & B 216. 22 [1898] AC 1.

23 [2007] UKHL 21.

24 The judgment of the dissenting judge, Coleridge J, is perhaps the most convincing of the four.

25 *Lumley* v. *Wagner* (1852) 1 De GM & G 604; 42 ER 687.

26 [1898] AC 1, 121 (Lord Herschell).

27 *Temperton* v. *Russell* [1893] 1 QB 715.

28 *J. T. Stratford & Son Ltd.* v. *Lindley* [1965] AC 269.

29 *Jasperson* v. *Dominion Tobacco Co.* [1923] AC 709.

30 *Joe Lee Ltd.* v. *Damleny* [1927] 1 Ch. 300, *De Francesco* v. *Burnum* (1890) 43 Ch. D 165, *Greig* v. *Insole* [1978] 1 WLR 302.

31 *Ibid.*, 341.

32 See *Exchange Telegraph Co.* v. *Gregory & Co.* [1896] 1 QB 147, *Goldsoll* v. *Goldman* [1914] 2 Ch. 603.

The relevant mental state is that of intention: the defendant must intend to interfere with the claimant's contractual rights, in the sense of doing so knowingly. Malice, in the separate sense of a personal animus against the defendant or an illegitimate motive, is not part of the modern tort;[33] on the other hand, mere carelessness is evidently not sufficient.[34] The defendant must either know of the contract[35] in question, or turn a blind eye to its existence. It will, however, suffice if he is reckless as to the consequences of his actions, in the sense of knowingly creating a risk of breach and being indifferent whether or not it happens.[36]

However, it seems that it is not necessary that the defendant should have been aiming to hurt the claimant *as such*. This is a requirement of the separate tort of interference with trade or business by unlawful means; but here what matters is the intention to interfere with the claimant's contractual right and not the desire to cause him loss.[37] The normal form of the tort involves direct persuasion being brought to bear on the contract breaker. According to some authorities, it is possible to commit it where A and B enter into a contract which, to A's knowledge, is incompatible with B's contract with C.[38] The passing-on of information, for example to the effect that a given company is being boycotted by the union, may also be sufficient.[39]

It may also be possible to induce breach by 'direct prevention' of performance, as in *GWK Ltd.* v. *Dunlop Rubber Co. Ltd.*,[40] where A clandestinely arranged for tyres manufactured by C to be removed from B's vehicles, leaving B in breach of his contract with C. In the same way, it was suggested in *D.C. Thomson Ltd.* v. *Deakin* that hiding an employee's tools might be inducing breach of his contract with his employer.[41] At the same time, many commentators insist that a firm line should, in principle, be drawn between cases in which the defendant intends to interfere with the contractual rights of the claimant and those situations in which he merely prevents the performance of the contract in question.[42] According to this point of view, *merely* assisting in or facilitating a breach of contract should not, in itself, give rise to tortious liability. However, in *Millar* v. *Bassey*[43] the Court of Appeal came close to holding otherwise. The singer Shirley Bassey was sued by the plaintiffs on the grounds that by deliberately refusing to perform a contract which she had made with a record production company, Dreampeace, she

[33] *Quinn* v. *Leathem* [1901] AC 495, 510 (Lord Macnaghten).

[34] E.g. *Cattle* v. *Stockton Waterworks Co.* (1875) LR 10 QB 453.

[35] As in *Stratford* v. *Lindley* [1965] AC 269.

[36] *Torquay Hotel Co. Ltd.* v. *Cousins* [1969] 2 Ch. 106, 138 (Lord Denning), *Emerald Construction Co. Ltd.* v. *Lowthian* [1966] 1 WLR 691.

[37] See *Smithies* v. *NATSOPA* [1909] 1 KB 310, 316, *D. C. Thomson Ltd.* v. *Deakin* [1952] Ch. 646, 696–7 (Jenkins LJ), 702 (Morris LJ), *Edwin Hill & Partners* v. *First National Finance Corp.* [1989] 1 WLR 225, 234 (Stuart-Smith LJ).

[38] *British Motor Trade Association* v. *Salvadori* [1949] Ch. 556.

[39] As in *Stratford* v. *Lindley* [1965] AC 269, *Torquay Hotel* v. *Cousins* [1969] 2 Ch. 106; but cf. *Thomson* v. *Deakin* [1952] Ch. 646.

[40] (1926) 42 TLR 376.

[41] *Thomson* v. *Deakin* [1952] Ch. 646, 686 (Evershed MR).

[42] See D. R. Howarth, *Textbook on Tort* (1995), 479–84; Weir, *Economic Torts* (Select Bibliography), 35–42.

[43] [1994] EMLR 44.

made it impossible for Dreampeace to perform the contracts which it had made with the plaintiffs, who were session musicians hired to work on that recording. It was alleged that Ms Bassey knew about the contracts made with the plaintiffs and was aware that they would be broken by Dreampeace as a consequence of her own breach. At first instance the claim was struck out as disclosing no cause of action, but the Court of Appeal, Peter Gibson LJ dissenting, reversed this decision and allowed the claim to proceed. The judgment which most clearly supports the view that the law should be clarified in favour of liability in such a case was that of Beldam LJ, who said:

> If it is actionable to cause loss to the plaintiff by enticing or persuading another to break his contract with the plaintiff, can it be said to be unarguable that it is actionable to cause such loss by voluntarily and deliberately refusing to perform a contract knowing that such refusal will make it impossible for the other party to fulfil his obligations to the plaintiff? I do not think so.[44]

Peter Gibson LJ, by contrast, maintained that it was a requirement of the tort that the defendant should have intended to interfere with the contract in question. Ralph Gibson LJ agreed and said that '[i]n a case where the defendant has done nothing more than refuse to perform her positive obligations under the contract with the co-defendant, the requirement as to intention may indeed be more than mere knowledge that her refusal will render her co-defendant incapable of performing its contract with the plaintiffs'.[45] Nevertheless, his Lordship went on to hold that the case should proceed to trial so that the principle of law involved could be properly tested. Thus only one judge, Beldam LJ, clearly decided in favour of the extension of liability argued for by the plaintiffs; however, the failure of the Court of Appeal to uphold the judgment of first instance left the scope of the tort decidedly unclear.

This line of decisions has now been cast in doubt by the decision of the House of Lords in *OBG Ltd.* v. *Allan*.[46] Lord Hoffmann, giving the leading judgment, held that

> to be liable for inducing breach of contract, you must know that you are inducing a breach of contract. It is not enough to know that you are procuring an act which, as a matter of law or construction of the contract, is a breach. You must actually realize that it will have this effect. Nor does it matter that you ought reasonably to have done so.[47]

On this basis, his Lordship took the view that *Millar* v. *Bassey* had been wrongly decided, and that the true basis for the *GWK* case was not inducing breach of contract, but the separate tort of causing loss by unlawful means. The critical issue, following Lord Hoffmann's judgment, is the precise nature of the knowledge required for the tort to be committed. His Lordship confirmed the view, set out in earlier decisions, that turning a blind eye to the possibility of breach or acting recklessly in the sense of not caring whether there was a breach or not would be sufficient. In this regard, 'if someone knowingly causes a breach of contract, it does not normally matter that it is the means by which he intends to achieve some further end or even that he would rather been able

[44] [1994] EMLR 44, 55. [45] *Ibid.*, 72.
[46] [2007] UKHL 21. [47] [2007] UKHL 21, at [39].

to achieve that end without causing a breach'.[48] But there was vital distinction between that situation and one in which 'the breach of contract is neither an end in itself nor a means to an end, but merely a foreseeable consequence' of the defendant's conduct.[49]

In one of the cases decided by the House of Lords in the *OBG* trilogy, *Mainstream Properties* v. *Young*[50] the claimant company brought an action for inducing breach of contract against a third party who had provided finance for two of its directors to exploit a commercial opportunity which properly belonged to the claimant. The defendant argued that he had believed that the opportunity had been waived by the claimant, and that the two directors were therefore free to act as they did, without acting in breach of their contracts of employment. In fact, the defendant had been given false information on this point by the two directors, information which he had not checked with the claimant company. The judge dismissed the claim for inducing breach of contract and the Court of Appeal upheld his ruling on the basis that the necessary degree of subjective knowledge had not been made out. Perhaps somewhat surprisingly, given that an interference of recklessness was by no means implausible on the facts of the case and would not have been out of line with previous authorities,[51] the House of Lords confirmed this result.

The recent cases narrowing the *Lumley* v. *Gye* tort all involve commercial disputes. In so far as they indicate a more restrictive approach to the definition of ingredients of the tort, they may not necessarily have much impact in the context of industrial action. There, the union official who organises strike action will almost certainly commit the tort of inducing breach of the employment contracts of his members (and will therefore have to show that he has the protection of the trade-dispute immunity, considered below). In part this is because, contrary to what happened in *Allen* v. *Flood*,[52] contracts of employment now normally require notice of several weeks to be given for the contract to be terminated lawfully,[53] and knowledge of this fact on the part of the strike organiser is unlikely to be difficult to establish. Even if the union gives the employer extensive strike notice (and in practice this is unusual), this is most unlikely to amount to notice on behalf of the members to lawfully terminate their contracts. The union is not normally authorised to act as agent of the members for this purpose.[54] It is theoretically possible that the members could give the union the necessary authority, but the practical difficulties of proceeding in this way are probably too great to make it worthwhile. Another point to bear in mind is that employees who go on strike rarely intend to put an end to the employment relationship: almost invariably, they intend to return to work once the dispute is settled. This makes it unrealistic to regard strike notice as evidence of an intention to terminate the employment relationship as opposed to suspending it. However, the common law does not recognise the possibility that the

48 [2007] UKHL 21, at [42].
49 *Ibid.*, at [43].
50 [2005] EWCA Civ. 861; [2007] UKHL 21.
51 In particular, *Greig* v. *Insole* [1978] 1 WLR 302.
52 [1898] AC 1.
53 See, in this regard, Employment Rights Act 1996, s. 86 ff.
54 See *Boxfoldia Ltd.* v. *NGA* [1988] IRLR 383.

contract of employment could be lawfully suspended for the duration of the dispute: going on strike will almost certainly amount to a repudiatory breach of the contract of employment by the striker.[55]

The common law does recognise a limited justification defence to this tort, but its scope is so limited as to be practically meaningless, at least in cases of labour disputes. In *South Wales Miners' Federation* v. *Glamorgan Coal Co. Ltd.*[56] the House of Lords rejected an argument to the effect that a union could be justified in organising strike action where it was in the economic interests of its members, although a similar defence was later to prove acceptable in the context of conspiracy to injure. The difference lies, perhaps, in that conspiracy to injure does not involve the use of unlawful means. Something exceptional is required to invoke the defence, such as the argument, accepted by the court in *Brimelow* v. *Casson*,[57] that industrial action taken to raise the wages of chorus girls was the only means available to save them from resort to prostitution. It may be easier to establish justification in non-labour cases. In *Edwin Hill & Partners* v. *First National Finance Corp.*[58] the Court of Appeal accepted that justification would be made out in a case where the defendant had an equal or superior right to that of the plaintiff. In this case the defendant had rights as a secured creditor over certain land, having lent money to the developer. The plaintiffs, a firm of architects, had a contract with the developer. The defendant could have called in its loan, with the result that the plaintiff would immediately have lost any right it had to insist on its contract with the developer. Instead, the defendant arranged a re-financing deal as part of which the developer had to agree to appoint new architects and dismiss the plaintiffs. The Court of Appeal held that the defendant had been acting in pursuance of its own rights over the property and therefore had a defence to an action of inducing breach of the plaintiff's contract.

(B) OTHER FORMS OF INTERFERENCE WITH CONTRACT

In the classic form of the tort exemplified by *Lumley* v. *Gye*, it was essential that the inducement be *direct* and that it should lead to a *breach* of the relevant contractual obligation. These requirements were watered down in the middle decades of the last century in a number of controversial decisions, before being reconsidered by the House of Lords in *OBG Ltd.* v. *Allan*,[59] which has restored some orthodoxy to this part of the law.

55 *Simmons* v. *Hoover Ltd.* [1977] QB 284; the attempt of Lord Denning to argue the contrary in *Morgan* v. *Fry* [1968] QB 710 has not found favour.

56 [1905] AC 239. See also *Smithies* v. *NATSOPA* [1909] 1 KB 310, *Pratt* v. *British Medical Association* [1919] 1 KB 244, *De Jetley Marks* v. *Lord Greenwood* [1936] 1 All ER 863, *Camden Nominees* v. *Forcey* [1940] Ch. 352.

57 [1924] 1 Ch. 302.

58 [1989] 1 WLR 225. See also *SOS Kinderdorf International* v. *Bittaye* [1996] 1 WLR 987, 993–4: 'circumstances such as to justify an employer in dismissing an employee cannot, except perhaps in exceptional circumstances, constitute justification for a third party interfering with the contract' (Lord Keith of Kinkel).

59 [2007] UKHL 21.

(i) 'Indirect' Interference with Contract

Indirect interference occurs when, in the course of a strike, the organisers of the strike put the employer in a position where he cannot perform commercial contracts with third parties. No direct inducement to the breach of these contracts has taken place; breach comes about indirectly, because the employer's workforce is temporarily unavailable to him. Although it is not possible to talk about direct inducement, the courts have held that the third-party employer may complain about indirect inducement to breach of the commercial contract in question. This tort first made its appearance in *D. C. Thomson & Co. Ltd.* v. *Deakin*.[60] The union NATSOPA was conducting a boycott of Thomsons, which did not permit union members to be among its workforce. In sympathy with NATSOPA, members of the Transport and General Workers' Union (TGWU) who were employees of Bowaters, a firm which supplied printing material under contract to Thomsons, told their employer that they would not be willing to supply material to Thomsons in pursuance of this contract. Subsequently Bowaters failed to supply the material and Thomsons sued officials of the TGWU for an injunction. The Court of Appeal held that liability in tort could arise where the interference, although indirect, came about through unlawful means. The requirements, according to Jenkins LJ, were as follows. The defendant must have known of the existence of the commercial contract and must have intended to procure its breach; he must have induced breach of the employment contracts of the relevant workforce; and there must have been, as a necessary consequence of this, a breach of the commercial contract. Jenkins LJ thought that the withdrawal of labour had to be 'comparable, for practical purposes, to a direct invasion of the contractual rights' of the plaintiff. On the facts found by the court, Thomsons' action failed because Bowaters' employees did not break their contracts of employment: Bowaters did not actually require its employees to undertake the necessary deliveries. This was a rather exceptional case. By contrast, in *J. T. Stratford & Son Ltd.* v. *Lindley*[61] the union action in question was unlawful, in the sense that an instruction issued by the union amounted to inducing breach of the employment contracts of its members. This was enough to establish the tort of indirect interference.

The tort of 'indirect interference' is, in truth, a hybrid of the tort of inducing breach of contract and the tort of interference with business by unlawful means (considered below). Because the interference is not direct, it cannot be regarded as a straightforward application of *Lumley* v. *Gye* and so it is necessary to find some other element of unlawful means: 'indirect interference is only unlawful if unlawful means are used'.[62] However, the tort also differs from the normal situation of interference by unlawful means. It is an element of that tort that the defendant should have been 'aiming at' the claimant, in the sense of intending to cause him economic damage;[63] but this does not appear to be an element of the tort of 'indirect interference'. With indirect interference, it is sufficient that the defendant should have intended to procure the relevant breach of

60 [1952] Ch. 646. 61 [1965] AC 269.

62 *Torquay Hotel* v. *Cousins* [1969] 2 Ch. 106, 138 (Lord Denning MR); see also *Stocznia Gdanska SA* v. *Latvian Shipping Co.* [2002] 2 Lloyd's Rep. 436, 460 (Rix LJ).

63 *Hadmor Productions Ltd.* v. *Hamilton* [1983] 1 AC 191.

contract; the claimant can sue if he is denied performance even if he is not the person against whom the defendant was aiming. In addition to being unsatisfactory from a doctrinal point of view, this is a potentially considerable extension of liability since it opens a wider range of potential claimants who may well be the incidental and unintended victims of industrial action.

It also has implications for commercial cases. In *Stocznia Gdanska SA* v. *Latvian Shipping Co.*[64] the principle was invoked in a case where the defendants, by withdrawing funds in breach of contract from one of their subsidiary companies, made it impossible for the company to perform its contract with the claimant. It was held that since this did not amount to direct inducement, the *Lumley* v. *Gye* tort was not made out. However, the defendants were held to have committed the 'indirect' version of the tort. The difficulty with this ruling is that the defendant was liable even though it could not be shown that it was 'aiming at' the claimant.

The problems inherent in extending tortious liability in this way were also evident in *Middlebrook Mushrooms Ltd.* v. *Transport and General Workers' Union.*[65] Members of the trade union distributed leaflets outside supermarkets with the aim of persuading members of the public not to buy mushrooms produced by the plaintiff (which was in dispute with a number of its employees who were members of the union). The Court of Appeal lifted an injunction that had been granted at first instance on the ground, among others, that there was no clear intention to induce breach of the contracts that the supermarkets might have had with the plaintiffs. Although such a breach *might* have been a consequence of the defendant's conduct, this was not a case of direct inducement, since at no stage did the defendant approach the supermarket managers with the aim of persuading them to break an existing contract. Nor, in the context of indirect interference, were unlawful means used in seeking to convince members of the public not to buy the plaintiff's products. However, the issues at stake were sufficiently unclear for the judge hearing the case to have granted an injunction that severely disrupted the defendant's efforts to organise industrial action in defence of its members' interests.

In *OBG Ltd.* v. *Allan*[66] Lord Hoffmann, giving the leading judgment of the House, reconsidered these cases and came to the conclusion that 'the distinction between direct and indirect interference is unsatisfactory', the result of an 'unnatural union' between the tort of inducing breach of contract and the tort of causing loss by unlawful means. In the light of this clear guidance, it seems unlikely that the indirect interference tort will be regarded, in future, as an aspect of *Lumley* v. *Gye* liability; instead, it will be subsumed under the tort of causing loss by unlawful means, for the purposes of which the claimant must show that the defendant intended to cause him damage.

(ii) 'Bare' Interference with Contractual Performance

At one time it appeared to be the case that the claimant did not have to show that the contractual obligation in question was actually broken. It was enough to show that there was an interference with performance, falling short of breach but causing loss to

[64] [2002] 2 Lloyd's Rep. 436. [65] [1993] IRLR 232. [66] [2007] UKHL 21, at [38].

either party (B or C) to the contract in question. This notion of liability for 'bare' interference falling short of inducing breach started life in *Torquay Hotel Co. Ltd.* v. *Cousins*.[67] The defendants succeeded in interrupting supplies of fuel to the hotel, with which their members were in dispute. The contract for the supply of the fuel contained a *force majeure* clause, according to which neither side was to be liable if performance was prevented by factors outside their control, such as industrial action. The owners of the hotel nevertheless succeeded in getting an injunction on the basis that their right to receive contractual performance had been interfered with, even though they could not themselves have brought an action against the supplier for damages for breach of contract. Lord Denning said: 'There must be *interference* in the execution of a contract. The interference is not confined to the procurement of a *breach* of contract. It extends to a case where a third person *prevents* or *hinders* one party from performing his contract, even though it be not a breach.'[68]

This decision has been criticised as going against *Allen* v. *Flood*, since that case decided that some element of independent unlawfulness is a precondition of economic tort liability (conspiracy aside).[69] *Torquay Hotel* was nevertheless confirmed by the House of Lords in *Merkur Island Shipping Corp.* v. *Laughton*,[70] in which the relevant commercial contract contained a similar *force majeure* clause. Lord Diplock cited the judgment of Jenkins LJ in *Thomson* v. *Deakin* (discussed above), but omitted to say that Jenkins LJ spoke at each relevant point about the inducement of a *breach* of contract and not of mere interference with contract *falling short of breach*. Lord Diplock also said that since Parliament, in the relevant legislation at that time,[71] had granted immunity in certain circumstances (of which this was not one) from liability for the tort of interference with contract, this was some evidence that the tort did indeed exist at common law. Since it is clear that the drafter included this provision just in case the tort invented by Lord Denning in *Torquay Hotel* might, in the future, be seen as legitimate, in order that it should then be immunised, Lord Diplock's interpretation can only be regarded as perverse. His approach could conceivably be justified on the basis that the exclusion clause does not prevent there being a breach of the *primary* contractual obligation to perform; its effect is confined to excluding the *secondary* liability to pay damages arising out of breach. This distinction is developed in Lord Diplock's own judgment in *Photo Production Ltd.* v. *Securicor Transport Ltd.*[72]

The House of Lords relied on the tort of interference in slightly different circumstances in *Dimbleby & Sons Ltd.* v. *National Union of Journalists*.[73] The union was conducting a boycott of a third-party company, TBF Ltd., in pursuance of a trade dispute. Dimbleby had a contract for some printing to be carried out by another company in the TBF group. The union called on its members employed at Dimbleby to 'black' the TBF contract. It was held that the union had thereby committed the tort of interfering with

[67] [1969] 2 Ch. 106. [68] *Ibid.*, 138.

[69] See in particular Weir, *Economic Torts* (Select Bibliography), 36–8. [70] [1983] 2 AC 570.

[71] Trade Union and Labour Relations Act 1974, s. 13(1); now Trade Union and Labour Relations (Consolidation) Act 1992, s. 219(1).

[72] [1980] AC 827. [73] [1984] 1 WLR 427.

the commercial contract between Dimbleby and the TBF company, and Dimbleby was granted an injunction.[74] This is not as straightforward as it might seem, since Dimbleby was the party whose performance was being interfered with (B), not the party to whom performance was owed (C). Moreover, Dimbleby did actually perform its contract, but at greater expense to itself. It seems that once the tort is extended from inducement of breach to interference with contractual performance, either party to the contract can sue without necessarily being the person against whom the defendant was 'aiming'. The potential range of the tort was thrown into sharp relief by the county court decision of *Falconer* v. *Aslef.*[75] Because of a rail strike called by the defendant unions in pursuance of a trade dispute, the plaintiff was unable to make a return journey from London to the North of England as he had planned and had to stay in a hotel in London for a further two days. He successfully sued the unions for damages representing his expenses. His return ticket incorporated an exclusion clause exempting British Rail from liability, but this did not prevent him from suing for interference. The case was also distinctive in that the plaintiff was not being 'aimed at' by the defendant: his loss was foreseeable but he was not the intended victim of pressure.

The entire line of authority which began with *Torquay Hotel* now seems destined for oblivion as a result of the decision of the House of Lords in *OBG Ltd.* v. *Allan.*[76] According to Lord Hoffmann, 'one cannot be liable for inducing a breach unless there has been a breach'. Thus the *Merkur Island* and *Dimbleby* cases should have been decided on the basis of the tort of causing loss by unlawful means. This conclusion is entirely correct in principle, but it is nevertheless rather remarkable that two quite recent decisions of the House of Lords should have sidestepped in this way. For reasons that have nothing to do with tort law but which turn on the relationship between the economic torts and the statutory immunities for those organising trade disputes, the *Merkur Island* and *Dimbleby* cases would not have been decided as they were, in favour of the plaintiffs, had they had to rely on the tort of causing loss by unlawful means.[77]

Be that as it may, it would seem that the concept of liability for bare interference cannot stand after the decision of the House of Lords in the *OBG* case. The principal claimant was an engineering company which had been the subject of an invalid receivership. The receivers, acting under the belief that their appointment was valid, had terminated commercial contracts between the claimant and various third parties, and had settled a number of outstanding claims at what was found by the trial judge to

[74] There was no immunity on account of the secondary action provisions of s. 17 of the 1980 Employment Act: see B. Simpson, 'The Employment Act 1990 in Context' (1991) 54 *MLR* 418.

[75] [1986] IRLR 331. *OBG Ltd.* v. *Allan* [2005] EWCA Civ. 106, discussed above, was another case in which liability, at first instance, was established on the basis of a 'bare' interference with contract; the decision was reversed on appeal. See also *SOS Kinderdorf International* v. *Bittaye* [1996] 1 WLR 987 in which the Privy Council, on appeal from the Court of Appeal of The Gambia, held, rather surprisingly, that the first defendant's act of cutting off the power to the plaintiff's residence and depriving him of the use of his car amounted to the tort of interference with his contract of employment with the second defendant. Somewhat unsatisfactorily, the interference point received only the briefest of consideration by Lord Keith ([1996] 1 WLR 987, 993).

[76] [2007] UKHL 21.

[77] On the reasons for this, see S. Deakin, 'The Uneasy Case for Synthesis in the Economic Torts', Blundell Property Law Lecture delivered in London on 16 June 2006.

have been an undervalue. The claimant had then gone into liquidation. One of the bases on which its case was argued was that the receivers, as well as the creditor by whom they had been (purportedly) appointed had committed the tort of wrongful interference with contractual relations. The judge held in favour of the claimant but the Court of Appeal, by a majority, reversed, on the grounds that the defendants had not intentionally and knowingly interfered with the contracts in question. The House of Lords rejected an appeal on the grounds, as Lord Hoffmann put it, that 'there was no breach or non-performance of any contract'; nor was this a case in which unlawful means had been employed or in which there had been an intention to cause loss.[78]

(iii) Making a Contract Less Valuable

This is *not* a tort, nor does it constitute unlawful means, in the absence of interference with a contractual obligation. The point was discussed in *RCA Corp.* v. *Pollard*,[79] one of the 'bootlegger' cases concerning claims brought by performers and record companies against distributors of recordings of concert performances made illegally. The illegal activities of the bootleggers undoubtedly diminished the value to the record companies of their exclusive recording contracts with the performers, but this was held to be insufficient on its own to form the basis for a cause of action: a person cannot be held liable in tort for knowingly making certain contractual rights less valuable, without actually bringing about a breach of the contractual obligations in question.

(C) INDUCING BREACH OF FIDUCIARY DUTY

In principle, contractual rights are not the only rights which may be protected from interference by an action in tort. Inducing breach of a fiduciary duty was found to be tortious in *Prudential Assurance Co.* v. *Lorenz*,[80] a case of a strike of insurance agents. However, there may be a limit to how far tortious liability may be incurred through inducing or assisting in a breach of an equitable obligation, not least because the intervention of tort could upset rules of equity in this area. For this reason the Court of Appeal in *Metall und Rohstoff AG* v. *Donaldson, Lufkin Jenrette Inc.*[81] held that assisting in the breach of a constructive trust did not give rise to liability in tort (although it may be noted that the *Prudential Assurance* case was not cited to the court). As a result of these contradictory decisions, the precise scope of tortious liability for interference with equitable obligations is unclear.[82]

(D) INDUCING BREACH OF STATUTORY DUTY

In *Meade* v. *Haringey London Borough Council*[83] the Court of Appeal held that, in principle, a person affected by the failure of an employer to maintain a service which he

[78] [2007] UKHL 21, at para. [86]. [79] [1983] 1 Ch. 135.

[80] (1971) 1 KIR 78. In this case, the tort was committed when a strike of insurance agents was called.

[81] [1990] 1 QB 391. See also *Law Debenture Trust Ltd.* v. *Ural Caspian Oil Corp.* [1995] 1 All ER 157, 167 (no liability in tort for interference with a contingent equitable right to the return of property), discussed by Weir, *Economic Torts* (Select Bibliography), 30.

[82] For discussion, see *ibid.*, 31–2, in particular n. 29. [83] [1979] ICR 494.

was required to maintain by virtue of a statutory obligation could bring an action against the employer for breach of statutory duty and also against the union which had *induced* the breach of statute. In this case a trade union had called a strike of caretakers and others employed in the council's schools. The council ordered the schools to close on the day of the strike. Lord Denning suggested that the council was in breach of its statutory duty to parents under the Education Acts and that the union could have been liable for inducing this breach. In the event no injunction was issued, since the strike had come to an end by the time the case reached the Court of Appeal. However, the principle established in *Meade* has since gained more general acceptance.[84] This is particularly significant for labour dispute cases, since unlike the torts of interference with contract there is no statutory immunity for this particular tort.[85]

The development of the principle of liability for a breach of an obligation imposed by European Community law[86] has also increased the scope of liability. In *Barretts & Baird (Wholesale) Ltd.* v. *Institution of Professional Civil Servants*[87] there was a strike by civil servants employed by the Meat and Livestock Commission, a body with a statutory duty to operate a guaranteed price system both under the Agriculture Act 1967 and under European Community law. The judge found that on the facts the employer had not been placed in breach of the relevant obligation, but had it been he was prepared to grant an injunction to meat producers who would have been affected by the strike.

The idea that 'bare interference' with a statutory duty will suffice to establish liability, by analogy with the *Torquay Hotel* principle,[88] will presumably not survive the rejection of *Torquay Hotel* by the House of Lords in *OBG Ltd.* v. *Allan.*[89] Likewise, authorities suggesting that the statutory duty in question has to be independently actionable at the suit of the claimant, in the sense of satisfying the test laid down in *Cutler* v. *Wandsworth Stadium Ltd.*,[90] would appear to be vindicated by *OBG*.

3. INTERFERENCE WITH THE CLAIMANT'S TRADE OR BUSINESS BY UNLAWFUL MEANS

(A) INTENTION TO HARM THE CLAIMANT

In the tort of causing loss by unlawful means it is necessary to show that the defendant had an 'intent to injure' the claimant, or that he was 'aiming at him' as the object of the

[84] In particular in *Associated British Ports* v. *TGWU* [1989] IRLR 305 (CA), discussed below.

[85] Cf. Trade Union and Labour Relations (Consolidation) Act 1992, s. 219.

[86] *Garden Cottage Foods Ltd.* v. *Milk Marketing Board* [1984] AC 130.

[87] [1987] IRLR 3; noted by B.W. Napier, 'Breach of Statutory Duty and Unlawful Means in Strike Law' [1987] *CLJ* 222.

[88] See *Associated British Ports* v. *TGWU* [1989] IRLR 305 (CA).

[89] [2007] UKHL 21.

[90] [1949] AC 398. See above, ch.7. The view that the economic tort of inducing breach of statutory duty would be limited in this way is based on *Lonrho Ltd.* v. *Shell Petroleum Co. Ltd.* [1983] AC 173 and *Barretts &*

economic pressure he was seeking to exert or the damage he was seeking to inflict. By contrast, in the *Lumley* v. *Gye* tort, the claimant has to show that the defendant knew of the existence of the relevant contract and intended to induce its breach (or was reckless with regard to the possibility of breach). It therefore has to be borne in mind *both* that the economic torts are torts of intention, *and* that the focus of intention differs from one tort to another. With inducing breach of contract and related torts, the claimant must intend to bringing about a break of the obligation in question; with causing loss by unlawful means, he must intend to inflict economic damage on the claimant as such.

The issue of intention in the context of this tort was the focus of the recent judgments of the Court of Appeal and House of Lords in *Douglas* v. *Hello! Ltd (No.3)*.[91] This claim arose from the various actions brought against Hello! magazine by Michael Douglas and Catherine Zeta-Jones for the wrongful publication of photographs covertly taken at their wedding reception, and by *OK!* magazine, with whom they had an exclusive deal for the publication of photographs which they had approved. The Douglases had entered into a contract for the exclusive publication of these photographs by *OK!*; and *OK!* was a direct rival of *Hello!* The owners of *OK!* sued *Hello!* for (among other things) the tort of intentional interference with business by unlawful means, on the basis that *Hello!*'s wrongful acts had deprived them of the opportunity of exploiting to the full their agreement with the Douglases. In the Court of Appeal this claim failed on the grounds that *Hello!* had not intended to cause economic harm to *OK!* Nor had the *Lumley* v. *Gye* tort been committed here, since the Douglases had taken all the precautions they could to keep *OK!*'s exclusive deal secure.

In the House of Lords, the importance of intention in the tort of causing loss by unlawful means was reiterated in each of the judgments (including those of Lord Nicholls of Birkenhead and Lord Walker of Gestingthorpe, who were in the minority on the outcome of *Douglas* v. *Hello! Ltd.(No.3)*). However, their Lordships took a different view of the meaning of 'intention' in this context to that of the Court of Appeal. Lord Hoffmann, with whom Baroness Hale of Richmond and Lord Brown of Eaton-under-Heywood agreed, held that *OK!*'s action should succeed on the grounds that the photographs published by *Hello!* had been obtained in breach of confidence. He did not decide the case on the grounds of liability in the economic torts, since, in his view, the necessary ingredient of unlawful means was not present in this case.[92] However, Lord Hoffmann made it clear that on this point he held otherwise on the unlawful means point, he would have found that in favour of the claimant had: the element of intention was present since 'the injury to OK! was the

Baird v. *IPCS* [1987] IRLR 3. See also *Wilson* v. *Housing Corp.* [1998] ICR 151, in which Dyson J held that there was no cause of action for inducing another to commit an unfair dismissal of an employee. See also *Michaels* v. *Taylor Woodrow Developments Ltd.* [2001] Ch. 493, 515 (Laddie J).

91 [2005] EWCA Civ. 595; [2007] UKHL 21.

92 See our discussion of this point in the text, Section 3(b) ('Unlawful Means') below.

means of attaining [*Hello!*'s] desired end and not merely a foreseeable consequence'.[93] In his judgment, Lord Nicholls put the matter as follows:

Intentional harm inflicted against a claimant... satisfies the mental ingredient of this tort. This is so even if the defendant does not wish to harm the claimant, in the sense that he would prefer that the claimant were not standing in his way... Take a case where a defendant seeks to advance his own business by pursuing a course of conduct which he knows will, in the very nature of things, be injurious to the claimant. In other words, a case where loss to the claimant is the obverse side of the coin from gain to the defendant. The defendant's gain and the claimant's loss are, to the defendant's knowledge, inseparably linked. The defendant cannot obtain the one without bringing about the other. If the defendant goes ahead in such a case in order to obtain the gain he needs, his state of mind will satisfy the mental ingredient of the unlawful interference tort.[94]

In the light of the outcome in *Douglas* v. *Hello! Ltd.(No.3)*, the views of Lord Hoffmann and Lord Nicholls on this point may, strictly speaking, be regarded as *obiter*, but they will surely be regarded as highly persuasive, expressing as they do the considered and unanimous opinion (on this point) of the House of Lords.

(B) UNLAWFUL MEANS

The tort of causing loss by unlawful means expanded considerably following the decision of the House of Lords in *Rookes* v. *Barnard*.[95] The categories of unlawful means became, for a while at least, very wide. An influential view, associated in particular with Lord Denning, was that the term 'unlawful means' signified *acts which the defendant was not at liberty to commit* or, by virtue of the tort sometimes called 'intimidation', *threats* to commit such acts. The notion of 'not being at liberty'[96] to commit a given act covered restraints imposed by the law of tort (including fraud and misrepresentation) and by contract; more uncertainly, it appeared, at least according to some authorities, to extend to obligations derived from the criminal law and from statutory duties.[97] The wrong in question did not need to be independently actionable. In this sense, the tort of causing loss by unlawful means had a much broader scope than torts based on interference with the claimant's pre-existing rights.

All that now has to be reconsidered in the light of the decision of the House of Lords in the *OBG* trilogy of cases. In his leading judgment, Lord Hoffmann said this:

In my opinion, and subject to one qualification, acts against a third party count as unlawful means only if they are actionable by that third party. The qualification is that they will also be unlawful means if the only reason why they are not actionable is because the third party has

[93] [2007]1 UKHL 21, at [134].

[94] [2007] UKHL 21, at [165], [167].

[95] [1964] AC 1129.

[96] This is the phrase used by Lord Denning in numerous cases: e.g. *Torquay Hotel Co.* v. *Cousins* [1969] 2 Ch. 106, 139. See also the judgment of Lord Reid in *Rookes* v. *Barnard* [1964] AC 1129, 1168–9, discussed by Lord Nicholls of Birkenhead in *OBG Ltd.* v. *Allan* [2007] UKHL 21, at [150].

[97] See generally Carty, 'Intentional Violation of Economic Interests' (Select Bibliography), 265 ff., for a discussion of the concept of unlawful means and of possible alternatives to the test of the defendant 'not being at liberty' to commit a particular act. The argument that only breaches of the civil law should constitute unlawful

suffered no loss. In the case of intimidation, for example, the threat will usually give rise to no cause of action by the third party because he will have suffered no loss. If he submits to the threat, then, as the defendant intended, the claimant will have suffered loss instead. But the threat must be to do something which would have been actionable if the third party had suffered loss.[98]

Later in his judgment Lord Hoffmann offered this formulation:

Unlawful means consists . . . of acts intended to cause loss to the claimant by interfering with the freedom of a third party in a way which is unlawful as against that third party and which is intended to cause loss to the claimant. It does not in my opinion include acts which may be unlawful against a third party but which do not affect his freedom to deal with the claimant.[99]

This represents a considerable narrowing of the tort. Lord Hoffmann's view was supported by Baroness Hale and Lord Brown; Lords Nicholls and Walker dissented on this point, Lord Nicholls suggesting that the majority view represented a 'radical departure from the purpose for which this tort has been developed' which would result in 'an unjustified and unfortunate curtailment of the scope of this tort'.[100] It is not completely clear what the majority judgment implies for each of the potential categories of unlawful means, as we shall now see.

(i) Physical Threats

The application of physical force or violence, or the threat of such violence, is the classic case of unlawful means.[101] A threat of violence made by a striker to a worker crossing a picket line would suffice for the tort of intimidation, for example.[102] This basic principle should still stand after *OBG Ltd.* v. *Allan*: such a threat would amount to an unlawful interference with the freedom of a third party to deal with the claimant.

(ii) Fraud and Misrepresentation

The use of fraud or misrepresentation will also constitute unlawful means. The tort was used to enforce a price maintenance agreement in *National Phonograph Co. Ltd.* v. *Edison Bell Co. Ltd.*[103] The defendants had been placed by the plaintiff on the 'suspended list' for failure to sell at the set price of the plaintiff's products, with the result that they could not buy from the plaintiff or its agents. The defendants nonetheless obtained the plaintiff's products by deception, by having their employees act as independent dealers. This placed the plaintiff's dealers, unknowingly, in breach of their contracts with the plaintiff. The plaintiff succeeded in its action against the

means is related to the idea that many (although not all) of the economic torts cases can be explained in terms of a more general theory of secondary civil liability: P. Sales, 'The Tort of Conspiracy and Civil Secondary Liability' [1990] *CLJ* 491.

98 *OBG Ltd.* v. *Allan* [2007] UKHL 21, at [49].

99 [2007] UKHL 21, at [51].

100 [2007] UKHL 21, at [155].

101 As in the old case of *Tarleton* v. *McGawley* (1793) Peake NP 270; 170 ER 153.

102 See *Messenger Group Newspapers* v. *NGA* [1984] ICR 397.

103 [1908] 1 Ch. 335.

defendants on the grounds that the latter had used unlawful means, namely a fraudulent misrepresentation, to impose a loss on them. The facts of this case clearly satisfy Lord Hoffmann's test.[104]

The point also arose in *Lonrho plc* v. *Fayed*.[105] Lonrho argued that it had incurred damage as a result of an alleged fraud perpetrated on the Secretary of State for Industry by Fayed, which led to the Secretary of State permitting Fayed to make a bid for the department store Harrods when Lonrho had previously been prevented from doing so. Lonrho's claim under the tort of interference with trade was struck out as disclosing no cause of action, but the Court of Appeal, affirmed by the House of Lords on this point, reinstated the claim. The Court of Appeal accepted that 'the unlawful act was in some sense directed against the plaintiff or intended to harm the plaintiff', but rejected a proposition that it was necessary, in addition, to show that the 'predominant purpose' of the defendant was to injure the plaintiff. They also rejected an argument that the unlawful means—here, the alleged fraud—had to be independently actionable. This point would now be subject to the new test. However, in Lord Hoffmann's view the outcome would be the same since the allegations concerned fraudulent misrepresentations made to third parties who would have had a civil claim if they had suffered loss.[106]

(iii) Breach of Contract and Inducing Breach of Contract

The central issue decided by *Rookes* v. *Barnard* was that a threat of breach of contract or of inducement to breach of contract could constitute unlawful means and, therefore, that the scope of unlawful means was not confined to physical threats and fraud. Prior to *Rookes* there was clear authority only for the proposition that certain criminal or tortious acts and threats of physical violence or coercion could constitute unlawful means,[107] although the notion that a threatened breach of contract would suffice is implicit in several of the judgments in *Allen* v. *Flood*.[108]

In *Rookes* the plaintiff, a draughtsman employed by BOAC, left the draughtsmen's union after a dispute. His colleagues threatened to strike unless he was dismissed, and the employer duly suspended and then dismissed him by giving him the necessary notice under his contract of employment. Because he received notice of his dismissal, he could not take advantage of the tort of inducing breach of contract: BOAC had not committed a breach. However, the threat made by his colleagues had been unlawful, in the sense that a strike would have involved them in a breach of their contracts of employment. This was the crucial difference between *Rookes* and *Allen* v. *Flood*. In *Allen*, the threat to strike had been lawful: the notice required to quit was so short that no breach of contract would have been involved. In *Rookes*, by contrast, not only was the notice required to be given to terminate the contracts of employment much longer (several weeks) but, on one reading of the case, the contracts had incorporated a 'no-strike'

104 See the judgment of Lord Hoffmann in *OBG Ltd.* v. *Allan* [2007] UKHL 21, at [49].

105 [1990] 2 QB 479 (CA); [1992] 1 AC 448 (HL).

106 *OBG Ltd.* v. *Allan* [2007] UKHL 21, at [50].

107 Hence the judgment of the Court of Appeal which found for the defendants: [1963] 1 QB 623.

108 [1898] AC 1.

clause which bound the individual employees. It was the case, of course, that Rookes himself could not have sued BOAC for breach of contract; but this was not fatal to his claim. Because BOAC had responded immediately to pressure of an unlawful kind from the defendants, and because the defendants were intending to injure Rookes in the sense of aiming their pressure at him as a non-union member, the tort of intimidation was established. What Rookes was suing for was, as Lord Reid put it, 'loss caused to him by the use of an unlawful weapon against him—intimidation of another person by unlawful means'. In this respect, a breach of contract was as much unlawful means as a threat of physical harm. Lord Reid said:

I agree with Lord Herschell [in *Allen* v. *Flood*] that there is a chasm between doing what you have a legal right to do and doing what you have no legal right to do, and there seems to me to be the same chasm between threatening to do what you have a legal right to do and threatening to do what you have no legal right to do. It must follow from *Allen* v. *Flood* that to intimidate by threatening to do what you have a legal right to do is to intimidate by lawful means. But I see no good reason for extending that doctrine. Threatening a breach of contract may be a much more coercive weapon than threatening a tort, particularly when the threat is directed against a company or corporation, and, if there is no technical reason requiring a distinction between different kinds of threats, I can see no other ground for making such a distinction.[109]

The House of Lords went on to confirm the nature of this tort. In *Stratford* v. *Lindley*[110] the defendants committed the tort of interference with business by the unlawful means of inducing breach of the employment contracts of their members, thereby placing the plaintiff in breach of numerous commercial contracts and causing him loss. In *Hadmor Productions Ltd.* v. *Hamilton*[111] action taken to boycott the plaintiff's business by inducing the union's members not to deal with it, in breach of their contracts of employment, amounted to interference by unlawful means. The test set out by Lord Hoffmann in *OBG Ltd.* v. *Allan*[112] would clearly have been satisfied in these two cases.

There are, nevertheless, some unexpected consequences of treating a breach of contract or, above all, a *threatened* breach of contract as unlawful means. This is the case in so-called two-party intimidation where the claimant and defendant are parties to the same contract. If one threatens the other with breach of contract, it might seem odd to allow the victim to sue in tort rather than in contract, thereby permitting him to avoid rules of contract law (such as the mitigation and remoteness rules) which limit the extent of contract damages in comparison with tort. For this reason it has been suggested that breach of contract should only be treated as unlawful means for the purposes of three-party intimidation, that is to say the position in *Rookes* v. *Barnard* and in most labour dispute cases, and that for two-party intimidation the claimant should have to show a physical threat of some kind.[113]

109 [1964] AC 1129, 1168–9.
110 [1965] AC 269.
111 [1983] 1 AC 191. See also, in the context of a commercial dispute, *Stocznia Gdanska SA* v. *Latvian Shipping Co.* [2002] 2 Lloyd's Rep. 436.
112 [2007] UKHL 21.
113 See Carty, 'Intentional Violation of Economic Interests' (Select Bibliography), 260–2. In *OBG Ltd.* v. *Allan* [2007] UKHL 21 Lord Hoffmann reserved his position on whether there should be liability in situations of two-party intimidation (at [61]).

(iv) Crime

The extent to which non-violent activity that involves a breach of a regulatory statute providing for criminal sanctions constitutes unlawful means is not altogether clear. Even if it does, for the claimant to have an action in tort he must show not simply that the activity in question has caused him harm; he must also show that he was the intended as opposed to the incidental victim. In *Lonrho Ltd.* v. *Shell Petroleum Co. Ltd.*[114] Lonrho sued the oil companies Shell and BP for losses it had occurred as a consequence of alleged sanctions-busting by the defendants, consisting of the supply of oil to the illegal Rhodesian regime contrary to orders made under legislation. Sanctions-busting was said to have maintained the illegal regime in power, thereby preventing Lonrho making profits from its own legitimate activities in that part of Africa. The action was struck out on the basis that even if the allegation were true, no cause of action arose, since it had not been shown that Shell and BP had any intention to injure Lonrho. Had Lonrho been able to show that the statute in question created an implied action for breach of statutory duty on its part, it could have brought an action under this head of liability. However, the House of Lords found that, under the established tests, no implied action for breach of statute arose in this case. Lonrho also argued that the principle enunciated in *Gouriet* v. *Union of Post Office Workers* [115] could form the basis of a claim in damages. In this case the plaintiff sued for an injunction to prevent the union carrying out a boycott of post destined for South Africa, which would have been in breach of various criminal statutes. The House of Lords held that a statutory obligation which confers an interest on the public as a whole (as opposed to one conferring protection upon a particular group, in the sense used in *Cutler* v. *Wandsworth Stadium Ltd.*[116]) could be enforced by a plaintiff who by virtue of the breach had suffered special damage over and above that of the general public. In *Gouriet* itself the plaintiff failed since he had not attempted to post a letter to South Africa; he was simply a concerned member of the public.[117] However, the principle laid down in *Gouriet* was then taken up by Lord Denning in *Ex parte Island Records Ltd.*,[118] in which the Court of Appeal granted an injunction to performers and record companies for the enforcement of legislation prohibiting the unauthorised recording of dramatic performances by 'bootleggers'. However, in *Lonrho* v. *Shell* Lord Diplock cast doubt on the existence of any such principle, at least in so far as it could be said to extend to granting a plaintiff a right to damages as opposed to an injunction. He also formally rejected the proposition advanced by the High Court of Australia in *Beaudesert Shire Council* v. *Smith*[119] that an action for damages may be brought by one who suffers damage 'as the inevitable consequence of the unlawful, intentional and positive act of another'. This proposition, it is true, has no authority of any substance in its favour and

[114] [1982] AC 173. [115] [1978] AC 435.

[116] [1949] AC 398. [117] He was a member of a group known as the National Association for Freedom.

[118] [1978] Ch. 122.

[119] (1966) 120 CLR 145. On the status of *Beaudesert* in Australian law, see *Northern Territory* v. *Mengel* (1995) 185 CLR 307; N. Mullany, '*Beaudesert* Buried' (1995) 111 *LQR* 583; Weir, *Economic Torts* (Select Bibliography), 13.

has not been followed.[120] In particular, it is deficient in failing to consider whether the statute in question was meant to confer a civil action on the claimant or whether the claimant was the intended victim of the defendant's acts. However, Lord Diplock's broad *dicta* go much further than a rejection of *Beaudesert*. If *Gouriet* is correct (and there is no reason to assume it is not) the odd situation arises of an injunction being made available to an individual damaged by unlawful action, but damages nevertheless being unavailable in respect of the same wrong.[121]

In *RCA Corporation* v. *Pollard*[122] the Court of Appeal found a solution in the context of the 'bootlegging' statutes by reinterpreting the relevant legislation to give performers (but not their record companies) an action for breach of statutory duty under the principles in *Cutler* v. *Wandsworth Stadium*. But *Cutler* remains authority, in general, for the courts taking a restrictive approach to the discovery of the implied action for breach of statute.[123]

The narrow definition of unlawful means set out by the majority of the House of Lords in *OBG Ltd.* v. *Allan*[124] would seem to exclude the possibility of liability in tort in a case where the defendant, without more, commits a crime in the course of taking business away from the claimant. Their Lordships discussed with counsel a hypothetical case in which a courier service gained a competitive edge over its rivals by ordering its motorcyclists to exceed speed limits and ignore traffic lights; as Lord Nicholls put it, this would not be a tort since 'the couriers' criminal conduct is not an offence committed against the rival company in any realistic sense of that expression'.[125] However, his Lordship was also 'far from satisfied that, in a two-party situation, the courts would decline to give relief to a claimant whose economic interests had been deliberately injured by a crime committed against him by the defendant'.[126] On Lord Hoffmann's narrower test, which had the support of the majority, such conduct would seem to be insufficient to give rise to liability, unless the crime was independently actionable as a civil wrong (or would have been had the claimant suffered loss).

(v) Interference with Statutory Obligations

A related question is how far interference with the performance of an obligation imposed by statute, which might have nothing to do with any criminal offence, can constitute unlawful means. We have already seen that inducing breach of a statutory duty owed to a third party is almost certainly a tort in its own right; by analogy with breach of contract, is there any reason why a breach of statute or threatened breach of statute should not also be unlawful means? In numerous cases it has been suggested that for the purposes of the tort of causing loss by unlawful means, it does not matter whether the breach of statute is independently actionable as a tort.

120 See *Kitano* v. *Commonwealth of Australia* (1974) 129 CLR 151, *Dunlop* v. *Woollahra MC* [1982] AC 158.

121 There is important nineteenth-century authority supporting the principle invoked in *Gouriet:* see *Springhead Spinning Co.* v. *Riley* (1868) LR 6 Eq. 551. See also *Department of Transport* v. *Williams* [1993] TLR 367, discussed by Weir, *Economic Torts* (Select Bibliography), 19.

122 [1983] Ch. 135.

123 See above, ch. 3, Section 4(a).

124 [2007] UKHL 21.

125 *Ibid.*, at [160].

126 *Ibid.*, at [161].

Rookes v. *Barnard*[127] can be invoked as authority for this proposition. The unlawful means in that case (the threatened breach of contract by Rookes's colleagues) was not actionable by Rookes since it was only a threatened breach. Lord Reid's notion of unlawful means as an act that the defendant was 'not at liberty to commit' could certainly cover a breach of statute *as such*, whether or not a third party could bring an action in respect of the loss. This reasoning persuaded the Court of Appeal to grant an injunction in *Associated British Ports* v. *Transport and General Workers' Union*,[128] a case in which a threatened strike would have involved the workers concerned acting in breach of an obligation to work normally which was contained in regulations incorporating the National Dock Labour Scheme. The House of Lords overturned the grant of the injunction on the narrow ground that the regulations in question did no more than repeat the *contractual* duty of the workers under their contracts of employment; since the unlawful means of inducing breach of the contract of employment was covered by the relevant statutory immunity, the injunction was lifted.[129]

Whether the decision of the Court of Appeal in the *Associated British Ports* case would be followed today raises a critical issue concerning the scope and rationale of the House of Lords' ruling in *OBG Ltd.* v. *Allan*. If Lord Hoffmann's test of what constitutes unlawful means is applied by analogy, the breach of statute in question would have to be independently actionable at the suit of the claimant, or be such as to give rise to liability if he had suffered damage. It is arguable that Lord Hoffmann's test is not compatible with what Lord Reid said in *Rookes* v. *Barnard*, but the point is unclear at best. As Lord Nicholls noted in his dissenting judgment in *OBG*, complications arise in cases 'where the civil rights of a third party infringed by the defendant are statute-based', whichever interpretation is adopted.[130] In view of the outcome in *OBG* and the reasoning adopted by the majority in that case, there must be doubt over the correctness of the Court of Appeal's analysis in *Associated British Ports*.

(vi) Other Categories

Other categories of unlawful means have been invoked from time to time. One possibility is contempt of court, although the authorities here are equivocal.[131] In *Associated Newspaper Group* v. *Wade*[132] Lord Denning thought that 'interference with the freedom of the press' might qualify, but this is thought to be incorrect: the defendant's freedom of action must be restrained by a specific legal obligation. It appears to follow from *Mogul Steamship* v. *McGregor, Gow*[133] that restraint of trade is not unlawful means for

127 [1964] AC 1129.

128 [1989] IRLR 305. For a discussion of this issue which leans in favour of a requirement of actionability, see the judgment of Laddie J in *Michaels* v. *Taylor Woodrow Developments Ltd.* [2001] Ch. 493.

129 [1989] IRLR 399.

130 [2007] UKHL 21, at [156].

131 In *Acrow (Automation) Ltd.* v. *Rex Chainbelt Inc.* [1971] 3 All ER 1175 Lord Denning MR thought that it could be unlawful means on the ground that contempt of court involved acts which the defendant was not at liberty to commit, but cf. *Chapman* v. *Honig* [1963] 2 QB 502 (in which Lord Denning MR dissented).

132 [1979] ICR 664.

133 [1892] AC 25.

this purpose. All such miscellaneous categories must now be read in the light of Lord Hoffmann's judgment in *OBG Ltd.* v. *Allan.*[134]

(C) ECONOMIC DURESS

Economic duress is another area in which the boundaries of liability are being tested. In *The Universe Sentinel*[135] the House of Lords allowed the plaintiff to recover money which it had paid over to the union under duress, in order to free its ship from blacking. To establish economic duress, it must be shown first that the defendant brought pressure to bear on the plaintiff in such a way as to vitiate his will or consent, and secondly that the pressure was of a kind 'which the law does not regard as legitimate'.[136] It is not necessary to find independently unlawful means. In commercial cases, even where duress involves a threat to break a pre-existing contractual obligation, the courts have sometimes been reluctant to apply the doctrine if that would mean invalidating arm's-length commercial transactions.[137] In cases of labour disputes, the House of Lords held in *The Universe Sentinel* that what counts as 'legitimate' is to be decided by reference to the statutory trade-dispute immunities, a rare and controversial example of the common law borrowing from legislation. 'This was judicial legislation, for there was no immunity in [the Trade Union and Labour Relations Act 1974] for economic duress (for the good reason that Parliament in 1974 had no idea that any such liability could possibly arise in trade disputes).'[138] In general, economic duress acts as a basis for a restitutionary action for the return of money or for rescission of a contract at the option of the victim of the pressure. In *The Universe Sentinel*, however, Lord Scarman expressed the view that it could be 'actionable as a tort'.[139] If this view is more widely adopted, *Allen* v. *Flood* will be substantially undermined.

(D) DEFENCES

In *Rookes* v. *Barnard*[140] the House of Lords rejected any possibility of a justification defence. This follows from the use of unlawful means: pressure intentionally exercised through unlawfulness is not capable of being justified by any superior motive of the defendant. However, it may be that there is a limited justification defence by way of analogy with the defence which is available in cases of inducing breach of contract, namely that the defendant was asserting a pre-existing legal right which was at least the equal of the right he was interfering with.[141]

134 [2007] UKHL 21.

135 *Universe Tankships Inc. of Monrovia* v. *International Transport Workers' Federation* [1983] 1 AC 366; see also *Dimskal Shipping Co.* v. *International Transport Workers' Federation, The Evia Luck* [1991] 4 All ER 871.

136 *The Universe Sentinel* [1983] 1 AC 366, 384 (Lord Diplock).

137 See *Pao On* v. *Lau Yiu Long* [1980] AC 614 (PC), *The Atlantic Baron* [1979] QB 705.

138 Lord Wedderburn, *The Worker and the Law* (3rd edn., 1986) 653.

139 [1983] 1 AC 366, 400.

140 [1964] AC 1129.

141 See *Ibid.*, 1206, 1209 (Lord Devlin).

4. CONSPIRACY

It is necessary to distinguish two senses of the tort of conspiracy: conspiracy to injure, which does not require an element of independent unlawfulness, and conspiracy to use unlawful means.

(A) CONSPIRACY TO INJURE

This tort is based on an agreement amongst several persons to combine together with the aim of injuring the plaintiff, with resulting damage. No unlawful means are required, but there is a wide justification defence: the defendants will avoid liability if they can show that their purpose in combining together was legitimately to advance their own self-interests. In *Quinn* v. *Leathem*[142] the jury found that the motive of the defendants in boycotting the plaintiff's business was 'to injure the plaintiff in his trade as distinguished from the intention of legitimately advancing their own interests'. On its facts the decision to award the plaintiff damages was problematical, since it could have been argued that the defendants, by placing pressure on the business of a non-union employer, were seeking to advance their own economic self-interest at the expense of non-union competitors. Parliament was sufficiently concerned to enact the wide-ranging 'second limb' of section 3 of the Trade Disputes Act 1906, according to which, within the scope of the trade-dispute formula, a simple act of interference with the trade or business of another was not to be actionable in tort. This turned out to be unnecessary when the House of Lords confined *Quinn* v. *Leathem* to a case in which the defendants had exhibited malice towards the plaintiff, that is to say, their interest in doing him down outweighed their own interest in preserving their share of the trade.[143]

The tort of conspiracy to injure received a further narrowing in *Crofter Hand Woven Harris Tweed Co.* v. *Veitch*.[144] This concerned an agreement between officials of a trade union and a group of employers, with whom it operated a closed shop, to boycott the supplies of the plaintiff and other employers on the island of Harris who were outside the closed-shop agreement. The union in question (the Transport and General Workers' Union) had members both in the mills and in the docks at Stornoway, the island's main port. The plaintiff's claim in conspiracy was rejected on the ground that the predominant purpose of the defendants was to protect their own economic interests. Lord Wright said: 'The true contrast is between the case where the object is the legitimate benefit of the combiners and the case where the object is deliberate damage without any such just cause. The courts have repudiated the idea that it is for them to determine whether the object of the combiners is reasonably calculated to achieve that

142 [1901] AC 495.

143 *Sorrell* v. *Smith* [1925] AC 700. The successor provision to the 'second limb', s. 13(2) of the Trade Union and Labour Relations Act 1974, was repealed in 1982, but the best view is that this makes no difference in practice to the scope of the immunities.

144 [1942] AC 435.

benefit.'[145] *Crofter*, decided in 1942, represents the high-water mark of judicial abstention in industrial disputes and of the courts' acceptance of the essential legitimacy of trade-union organisation. The test of whether the action is intended to further the defendants' self-interest is a *subjective* one: the court does not make its own assessment of whether the action was, from an *objective* point of view, proportional to the end in question. It is also necessary for the aim in question to be an economic one. Malice of a personal kind will give rise to liability;[146] but the notion of an economic motive is sufficiently broad to include action against a discriminatory 'colour bar' operated by certain employers, which harmed the members of the union who were thereby excluded from employment.[147]

In *Lonrho Ltd.* v. *Shell Petroleum Co.*[148] and again in *Lonrho plc* v. *Fayed*[149] the House of Lords has confirmed the existence of the tort, but on each occasion doubts were expressed as to its rationale. Why should two persons be made liable for doing together what each one would have had a lawful right to do if he had done it separately? The answer to this undoubtedly is that the act of combination with the purpose of inflicting unjustified harm on a third party amounts to an abuse of the right in question.[150] The extensive scope of the justification defence will tend to limit the practical significance of this tort.

(B) CONSPIRACY USING UNLAWFUL MEANS

Where the combiners intend to use unlawful means as the mechanism for inflicting harm, there can be no defence of justification. It is therefore unnecessary to show that the combiners had the 'predominant purpose' of harming the claimant as opposed to benefiting themselves. It is enough that they intended to hurt the claimant in the sense generally used in the tort of causing loss by unlawful means, that it to say of directing or aiming their pressure at him.[151] The existence of the tort of conspiracy using unlawful means may, in a given case, provide a basis for significantly widening the category of defendants. In *Rookes* v. *Barnard*[152] a trade union official (Silverthorne) who participated in the threat of the strike was not employed by BOAC and could not therefore have threatened to break his contract of employment; he was nevertheless held liable in conspiracy.[153]

Given the widening effect of the tort of unlawful means conspiracy, it is vital to establish whether the unlawful means used have to be independently actionable. As we have seen in the context of our discussion of *Rookes* v. *Barnard*,[154] that case can be read

[145] *Ibid.*, 469. [146] *Huntley* v. *Thornton* [1957] 1 WLR 321.

[147] *Scala Ballroom (Wolverhampton) Ltd.* v. *Ratcliffe* [1958] 1 WLR 1057.

[148] [1982] AC 173. [149] [1992] 1 AC 448.

[150] T. Weir, *A Casebook on Tort* (7th edn., 1992), 601; see now the 10th edn. (2004) at 622.

[151] *Lonrho plc* v. *Fayed* [1992] 1 AC 448, overruling on this point *Metall und Rohstoff AG* v. *Donaldson Lufkin and Jenrette Inc.* [1990] 1 QB 391. See generally P. J. Sales, 'The Tort of Conspiracy and Civil Secondary Liability' [1990] *CLJ* 491. [152] [1964] AC 1129.

[153] He could of course have been held liable for the tort of inducing breach of the employment contracts of others, but this possibility was removed by s. 3 of the Trade Disputes Act 1906.

[154] [1964] AC 1169.

as establishing that the category of unlawful means includes any act which the defendant was 'not at liberty to do' rather than one which was actionable as an independent civil wrong. There is merit in the proposition that, for the sake of consistency, this approach should be adopted as well in the context of unlawful means conspiracy. Nevertheless, there are *dicta* to suggest that in this context, the unlawful means used must have been independently actionable against at least one of the conspirators.[155] It is difficult to square this with *Rookes* v. *Barnard*, where the unlawful means relied on were threats to break contracts of employment—not actual breaches of contract, nor the tort of inducing breach of contract. However, it would be compatible with the more narrow definition of unlawful means adopted more recently by the House of Lords in *OBG Ltd.* v. *Allan*.[156]

5. THE TRADE DISPUTE IMMUNITY

A full account of the law relating to the trade-dispute immunity must be left to texts on labour law.[157] Here the main outlines of the immunity will be noted. The organisation of strike action will almost certainly involve the commission of one or more of the economic torts. Parliament's response to this has been to enact a statutory *immunity* from liability in tort for industrial action which falls within the *trade-dispute formula*. The precise terms of this formula and its scope have varied considerably since it was first introduced, in the context of criminal conspiracy, in the Conspiracy and Protection of Property Act 1875. The rapid expansion of economic-tort liability in the last quarter of the nineteenth century, coupled with the decision of the House of Lords in *Taff Vale Railway Co.* v. *Amalgamated Society of Railway Servants*[158] which allowed an action in damages to be brought against the trade union in its registered name,[159] led to the passage of the Trade Disputes Act 1906. This gave trade unions a *complete* immunity from liability in tort (s. 4) and gave individual organisers of strikes a more limited immunity in respect of the tort of inducing breach of the contract of employment where the act was done 'in contemplation or furtherance of a trade-dispute' (s. 3). Section 5 defined a trade dispute as 'any dispute between employers and workmen, or

155 See *Crédit Lyonnais Bank Nederland NV* v. *Export Credit Guarantee Department* [1998] 1 Lloyd's Rep. 19, 32 (Stuart Smith LJ), *The Rialto* [1998] 1 Lloyd's Rep. 322, 334 (Toulson J, going even further to suggest that the wrong has to be independently actionable at the suit of the claimant, which seems incorrect in the light of *Rookes* v. *Barnard*) and *Michaels* v. *Taylor Woodrow Developments Ltd.* [2001] Ch. 493 (Laddie J); the opposing view was expressed by Waller LJ in *Surzur Overseas Ltd.* v. *Koros* [1999] 2 Lloyd's Rep. 611, 617.

156 [2007] UKHL 21. The conspiracy torts were not, however, discussed by the House of Lords in the *OBG* trilogy of decisions.

157 See S. Deakin and G. Morris, *Labour Law* (4th edn., 2005).

158 [1901] AC 426.

159 That is to say, the name under which the union was registered under the Trade Union Act 1871. Strictly speaking the trade union did not acquire legal personality by virtue of such registration. See generally Lord Wedderburn, *The Worker and the Law* (1986), 526 ff.

between workmen and workmen, which is connected with the employment or non-employment, or the terms of the employment, or with the conditions of labour, of any person', while 'workmen' meant 'all persons employed in trade or industry, whether or not in the employment of the employer with whom a trade-dispute arises'. Section 2 enacted a right to take part in peaceful picketing 'merely for the purpose of peacefully persuading or communicating information, or of peacefully persuading any person to work or abstain from working'. Finally the protection contained in the Conspiracy and Protection of Property Act was extended to cover both criminal and tortious conspiracy.

These immunities were meant to establish an equilibrium in labour relations by allowing trade unions to organise and to mobilise their members in support of collective bargaining over pay and conditions without the constant threat of illegality.[160] In the *Crofter* case the House of Lords essentially accepted the legitimacy of this aim—the right to strike, said Lord Wright, was 'an essential element in the principle of collective bargaining'[161]—and were undoubtedly influenced by it in placing a narrow interpretation on the tort of conspiracy to injure. However, for most of its history the trade-dispute immunity has been regarded with hostility by the courts, according to a principle that legislation affecting to oust the common law should be construed strictly.[162] In *Rookes* v. *Barnard*[163] judicial acquiescence in the application of the trade-dispute formula effectively came to an end. That decision turned not so much on the extension of economic-tort liability as on an exceptionally narrow reading of the immunity contained in the 1906 Act, which admittedly extended to a case of inducing breach of contract but which the House of Lords held did not cover a *threatened breach of contract*. After *Rookes* the second great expansion of economic-tort liability, comparable to that of the 1890s and 1900s, got under way. In the Trade Union and Labour Relations Act 1974[164] Parliament, under a Labour government, re-enacted the immunities in what was meant to be a stronger and clearer form. However, there followed several years of uncertainty until the House of Lords clarified their meaning in *Duport Steels Ltd.* v. *Sirs* in 1980.[165] By this stage a Conservative government had taken office, and Parliament began a gradual process of rolling back the extensive immunities granted in 1906 and reaffirmed in 1974. The major landmarks in this process were the abolition of the 'blanket' immunity of the trade union (1982) and the placing of restrictions on the remaining trade-dispute immunity, including bans on 'secondary' or solidarity strikes (1980, 1982 and 1990), the restriction of issues coming within the definition of a trade dispute (1982), the outlawing of strike action in support of the closed shop (1988), and the introduction of trade union ballots and majority support for strike action as preconditions of obtaining immunity (1984, 1988, 1990 and 1993).

The relevant statutory provisions are now contained in the Trade Union and Labour Relations (Consolidation) Act 1992 (as amended by the Trade Union Reform and

160 See generally O. Kahn-Freund, *Labour and the Law* (3rd edn., 1983) and in particular ch. 1.

161 [1942] AC 435.

162 *Valentine* v. *Hyde* [1919] 2 Ch. 129, 153 (Astbury J).

163 [1964] AC 1129.

164 As amended in the Trade Union and Labour Relations (Amendment) Act 1976.

165 [1980] 1 WLR 142.

Employment Rights Act 1993). Section 219 re-enacts the trade-dispute formula protecting action in contemplation or furtherance of a trade dispute; however, the only torts covered by this are conspiracy,[166] inducing breach of contract and interference with contract (as well as threats of inducement or interference).[167] The tort of interference with business by unlawful means is not mentioned as such; however, it is almost certainly the case that any tortious act that is immunised by section 219(1)–(2) cannot be unlawful means for the purpose of that tort.[168] The most important omission concerns breach of statutory duty. The failure of Parliament to extend the scope of the provisions now consolidated in section 219 after the courts began to develop this novel head of tort liability means that once this tort is established (whether independently or as part of the tort of interference with business by unlawful means) the immunity is inevitably lost. Nor is there any mention of economic duress in section 219. The requirement of 'contemplation or furtherance' essentially means that the dispute, if not actually going on, must be reasonably imminent and not far off in the future.[169] The concept of trade dispute is contained in section 244(1) of the Act. A dispute must be between workers and *their own employer*[170] and must be related *wholly or mainly* to one of the following:

(a) terms and conditions of employment, or the physical conditions in which any workers are required to work;

(b) engagement or non-engagement, or termination or suspension of employment or the duties of employment, of one or more workers;

(c) allocation of work or the duties of employment between workers or groups of workers;

(d) matters of discipline;

(e) a worker's membership or non-membership of a trade union;

(f) facilities for officials of trade unions; and (g) machinery for negotiation or consultation, and other procedures, relating to any of the above matters, including the recognition by employer or employers' associations of the right of a trade union to represent workers in such negotiation or consultation or in the carrying out of such procedures.

It can be seen from this that strikes of a purely political nature are not (and never have been) protected. Where there is a great deal of uncertainty, on the other hand, is in the application of the 'wholly or mainly' test to a case where there are mixed motives. In

166 Section 219(2). 167 Section 219(1).

168 This was the view of Lord Diplock in *Hadmor Productions Ltd.* v. *Hamilton* [1982] IRLR 102; hence it is probably irrelevant that Parliament has repealed (in the Employment Act 1982) s. 13(2) of the Trade Union and Labour Relations Act 1974, which sought to make a declaration to this effect 'for the avoidance of doubt'. It was also specified that breach of contract could not be unlawful means either. On the effects of this repeal see *Barretts & Baird (Wholesale) Ltd.* v. *IPCS* [1987] IRLR 3.

169 *Bent's Brewery Co. Ltd.* v. *Hogan* [1945] 2 All ER 570.

170 This is a change from the 1906 formula which means that workers cannot lawfully be in dispute with *another* employer over the terms and conditions of *his* workers (as they might well be if he is a non-union employer).

Mercury Communications Ltd. v. *Scott-Garner*[171] the Court of Appeal held that a dispute in which British Telecom workers sought to boycott British Telecom's non-unionised competitor, Mercury, was a politically motivated dispute concerning the union's campaign of privatisation and not, as the union suggested, a dispute over possible future redundancies. On the other hand, the 1989 docks strike was found to be based on a dispute over the form of collective bargaining following the abolition of the statutory National Dock Labour Scheme, and not a political strike aimed at halting the Scheme's demise.[172]

The great General Strike of 1926 was almost certainly based on a trade dispute, since it involved workers striking in sympathy with the mineworkers who were then in dispute with their employers over pay.[173] This type of 'secondary' action has now been made unlawful by the withdrawal of immunity. Secondary action means action taken which involves an interference with the contracts of employment of workers who are not employed by the employer in the trade dispute.[174] Other cases of exceptions to the trade dispute immunity include action taken to enforce trade union membership;[175] action taken because of the dismissal of a worker following his participation in unofficial industrial action;[176] and pressure to impose union recognition.[177] The effect of a failure of the union to ballot its members in accordance with the requirements of the Act[178] will also be to remove the statutory immunity. The right to picket has also been confined by recent legislation. Section 220 of the Act now limits protection to peaceful picketing at the worker's own place of work, thereby opening up the likelihood of liability for 'secondary picketing'.[179]

An employer or worker who suffers damage as a result of tortious industrial action may bring an action for an injunction or for damages against the individual or union concerned. The circumstances under which the union will be liable for the acts of officials and members are laid down in the Act, as are upper limits to the damages which may be awarded against a trade union in tort in respect of each claimant's claim.[180] The principles governing the grant of an injunction are laid down in section 221: amongst other things, the court is required, in exercising its discretion,[181] to take into account the likelihood of a trade dispute defence succeeding at a full trial of the action.[182]

171 [1974] ICR 74.

172 *Associated British Ports* v. *Transport and General Workers Union* [1989] IRLR 291.

173 See A. L. Goodhart, 'The Legality of the General Strike in England' (1926) 36 *Yale LJ* 464; cf. the view of Astbury J in *National Sailors' and Firemen's Union of Great Britain and Ireland* v. *Reed* [1926] Ch. 536, 539–40.

174 Trade Union and Labour Relations (Consolidation) Act 1992, s. 224.

175 *Ibid.*, s. 222.

176 *Ibid.*, s. 223.

177 *Ibid.*, s. 225.

178 *Ibid.*, ss. 226–34.

179 On picketing generally see *Thomas* v. *NUM (South Wales Area)* [1985] IRLR 136, *News Group Newspapers Ltd.* v. *Sogat (82)* [1986] IRLR 336, *Rayware Ltd.* v. *TGWU* [1989] IRLR 134, *Union Traffic Ltd.* v. *TGWU* [1989] IRLR 127.

180 Trade Union and Labour Relations (Consolidation) Act 1992, ss. 20–3.

181 Under *American Cyanamid Co.* v. *Ethicon Ltd.* [1975] AC 396; see below, ch. 26, Section 1.

182 Trade Union and Labour Relations (Consolidation) Act 1992, s. 221(2); *NWL* v. *Woods* [1979] ICR 867, *Associated British Ports* v. *TGWU* [1989] IRLR 291, 305, 399.

6. THE FUTURE OF THE ECONOMIC TORTS

The removal of large parts of the statutory immunity for industrial action in the 1980s and 1990s has given new life to the common law heads of liability. A greater role has been accorded to the courts in protecting the interests of employers, consumers, and workers affected by trade disputes. They have responded by introducing the notion of liability for economic duress and by expanding the tort of interference with business by unlawful means, in particular in cases involving interference with statutory obligations. Partly as a consequence of these trends, the treatment of the economic torts in labour or industrial cases is diverging from their treatment in commercial cases. In industrial cases it seems that the courts are far more willing to protect 'bare' expectations and intangible economic interests. In commercial cases, on the other hand, they have insisted on the traditional need to show independently unlawful means, refusing to supply a remedy for bare interference with contractual expectations[183] and restricting the application of economic duress.[184]

The narrowing of the immunities in the 1980s and 1990s might have led the courts to take a more limited view of the scope for expansion of the economic torts, on the ground that innovation in the common law is no longer needed to outflank the much broader parliamentary immunity of the 1970s. There is little evidence, as yet, that they see it this way.[185] Nor have they come close to evolving a synthesis of the different heads of economic-tort liability. The preservation of separate heads of nominate torts and separate categories of unlawful means is likely for the immediate future. From time to time proposals are put forward for the replacement of the system of common law liabilities and statutory immunities by a framework of 'positive' rights to engage in industrial action.[186] Such a framework would no doubt have to specify in some detail the circumstances in which these rights could be exercised, and the limitations upon them. This would mean moving closer towards the type of labour law regulation found in some mainland European systems, in which the correlative rights and obligations of employers and trade unions have been systematically developed over time by courts and by legislatures. Whether assimilation of this kind will gradually take place, perhaps as part of the United Kingdom's membership of the European Union, remains to be seen.

183 As in *Lonrho Ltd.* v. *Shell Petroleum Co.* [1982] AC 173 , *RCA Corp.* v. *Pollard* [1983] Ch. 135 and the recent *OBG* trilogy of cases [2007] UKHL 21.

184 *Pao On* v. *Lau Yiu Long* [1980] AC 614.

185 Although see the decision of the House of Lords in *Associated British Ports* v. *TGWU* [1989] IRLR 399. Even then, the union won on the interpretation of the relevant statutory obligation without being able to get the House of Lords to consider the wider *dicta* laid down in the Court of Appeal on the scope of the tort of interference with business by unlawful means, with the result that these *dicta* still stand; however, they may well prove to be incompatible with the approach taken by the House of Lords in *OBG Ltd.* v. *Allan* [2007] UKHL 21, for the reasons discussed earlier in this chapter.

186 See generally K. D. Ewing, *The Right to Strike* (1990).

The role of the economic torts in regulating competition in commercial relations seems likely to remain a marginal one.[187] With the passage of the Competition Act 1998, the United Kingdom has the makings of a systematic and integrated approach to competition law. The 1998 Act, rather than taking its inspiration from the common law, effectively extends into domestic law the principles laid down in Articles 81 and 82 of the EC Treaty. These principles recognise substantive grounds for legal intervention going far beyond those acknowledged by the law of tort. The impact of this legislation on the law of tort itself, however, is unlikely to be at all substantial, because of the insulation of the common law from statutory influences which has been a feature of the approach of the courts in this area.[188]

SELECT BIBLIOGRAPHY

ARDEN, Dame M., 'Economic Torts in the Twenty-First Century' (2006) 41 *The Law Teacher* 1.

CARTY, H., 'Intentional Violation of Economic Interests: The Limits of Common Law Liability' (1988) 104 *LQR* 250.

—*An Analysis of the Economic Torts* (2001).

CLERK, J. F., and LINDSELL, W. H. B., *On Torts* (17th edn., 1996), ch. 17.

ELIAS, P., and EWING, K., 'Economic Torts and Labour Law: Old Principles and New Liabilities' [1982] *CLJ* 321.

HEYDON, J. D., *Economic Torts* (2nd edn., 1978).

HOWARTH, D., 'Against *Lumley* v. *Gye*' (2005) 68 *MLR* 195.

STILITZ, D., and SALES, P., 'Intentional Infliction of Harm by Unlawful Means' (1999) 115 *LQR* 411.

WEDDERBURN, K. W., 'The Right to Threaten Strikes' (1961) 24 *MLR* 572.

—*The Worker and the Law* (3rd edn., 1986), chs. 7 and 8.

WEIR, J. A., 'Chaos or Cosmos: *Rookes*, *Stratford* and the Economic Torts' [1964] *CLJ* 225.

—*Economic Torts* (1997).

[187] This is even more clearly the case now that the House of Lords has upheld the restrictive approach taken in the *OBG* trilogy of cases discussed above (*OBG Ltd.* v. *Allan/Douglas* v. *Hello! Ltd.(No.3)/Mainstream Properties Ltd.* v. *Young* [2007] UKHL 21).

[188] See Weir, *Economic Torts* (Select Bibliography), 27 (esp. 19).

PART IV

STRICTER FORMS OF LIABILITY

16 The Rule in *Rylands* v. *Fletcher*
17 Liability for Animals
18 Employer's Liability
19 Vicarious Liability
20 Product Liability

16

THE RULE IN *RYLANDS* V. *FLETCHER*

1. GENERAL OBSERVATIONS

Anyone who in the course of 'non-natural' use of his land 'accumulates' thereon for his own purposes anything likely to do mischief if it escapes is answerable for all direct damage thereby caused. This is the rule in *Rylands* v. *Fletcher*,[1] the facts of which were as follows. The defendants employed independent contractors to construct a reservoir on their land, which was separated from the plaintiff's colliery by intervening land. Unknown to them, beneath the site of the reservoir there were some disused shafts connecting their land with the plaintiff's mine. The independent contractors were negligent in failing to discover this. Water from the reservoir burst through the shafts and flooded the plaintiff's mine. The defendants were held personally liable, despite the absence of blame in themselves.

This liability could not have been based on any of the then-existing torts. Since the flooding was not direct and immediate, trespass could not lie,[2] and since the activity was not continuous or recurring[3] it could not have been, as the law then stood,[4] an actionable nuisance. Nor at that time was any liability for the negligence of an independent contractor accepted.[5] The existing law was extended to cover the situation by means of analogies. Blackburn J in the Court of Exchequer Chamber said:

We think that the true rule of law is, that the person who for his own purposes brings on his lands and collects and keeps there anything likely to do mischief if it escapes, must keep it in at his peril, and, if he does not do so, is *prima facie* answerable for all the damage which is the

[1] (1865) 3 H & C 774; 159 ER 737 (Court of Exchequer); (1866) LR 1 Ex. 265 (Court of Exchequer Chamber); (1868) LR 3 HL 330 (House of Lords).

[2] See Martin B in *Fletcher* v. *Rylands* (1865) 3 H & C 774, 796; 159 ER 737, 746.

[3] Which was then regarded as essential to a nuisance action. For another reason why it could not be treated as a nuisance, see Martin B, *ibid.* Cf., however, the more recent case of *British Celanese* v. *A. H. Hunt* [1969] 1 WLR 959 where the judge, following *Midwood & Co. Ltd.* v. *Manchester Corp.* [1905] 2 KB 597, said, probably *obiter*, that 'an isolated happening by itself can create an actionable nuisance' (*ibid.*, 969).

[4] It is implicit in Professor Newark's thesis (Select Bibliography) that one of the reasons behind the *Rylands* rule was the need to deal with isolated escapes, a view endorsed most recently by Lord Goff in *Cambridge Water Co.* v. *Eastern Leather plc* [1994] 2 AC 264, 299 and 304, [1994] 2 WLR 53, 74 and 80.

[5] *Bower* v. *Peate* (1876) 1 QBD 321, was the first inroad into this principle.

natural consequence of its escape.... The general rule, as above stated, seems on principle just. The person whose grass or corn is eaten down by the escaping cattle of his neighbour, or whose mine is flooded by the water from his neighbour's reservoir, or whose cellar is invaded by the filth of his neighbour's privy, or whose habitation is made unhealthy by the fumes and noisome vapours of his neighbour's alkali works, is damnified without any fault of his own; and it seems but reasonable and just that the neighbour, who has brought something on his own property which was not naturally there, harmless to others so long as it is confined to his own property, but which he knows to be mischievous if it gets on his neighbour's, should be obliged to make good the damage which ensues if he does not succeed in confining it to his own property.[6]

The judgment is noteworthy, because it is an outstanding example of a creative generalisation.[7] As Wigmore wrote, this epoch-making judgment owes much of its success to 'the broad scope of the principle announced, the strength of conviction of its expounder, and the clearness of his exposition'.[8]

The simplicity and lucidity of Blackburn J's statement is the second noteworthy feature of this judgment, for not only is it virtually impossible to improve on its careful phraseology, but it also conceals the fact that the foundations of new law were being created behind a screen of not-always-convincing analogies.[9] In any event, *Rylands* v. *Fletcher* undoubtedly opened a new chapter in the law of torts and one which could have evolved into a comprehensive theory of strict liability for escaping things and also for independent contractors. That this did not happen is largely due to the fact that there was, almost from the outset, and certainly at the turn of the nineteenth century and the first half of the twentieth century, a concomitant desire to restrict, for ideological reasons,[10] the ambit of the rule. So it was that, on appeal to the House of Lords, Lord

[6] (1866) LR 1 Ex. 265, 279–80.

[7] Such generalisations, however, are rare. Another famous example is Lord Atkin's speech in *Donoghue* v. *Stevenson* [1932] AC 562. A 'negative' generalisation occurs in *Bradford Corp.* v. *Pickles* [1895] AC 587, 594, 598–9, per Lords Halsbury, Watson and Ashbourne. The style of the Blackburn judgments, short and uncluttered by citations, should be compared with contemporary judgments in the House of Lords; and more advanced students should ask themselves why a long string of citations is used to replace cogent legal reasoning. For further thoughts on this topic (in the context of negligence litigation) see B. S. Markesinis and S. F. Deakin, 'The Random Element of their Lordships' Infallible Judgement: an Economic and Comparative Analysis of the Tort of Negligence from *Anns* to *Murphy*' (1992) 55 *MLR* 619, 642.

[8] J. H. Wigmore, *Selected Essays in the Law of Torts* (Select Bibliography), 78.

[9] Some contemporary authors have argued that Blackburn was not 'aware ... that he was extending the law in any significant way' (E. McKendrick, *Tort Textbook* (5th edn., 1991)) thus, essentially, repeating Professor Newark's view (Select Bibliography) and, indeed, Blackburn himself in *Ross* v. *Fedden* (1872) 26 LT 966, 968. Yet, as Professor Simpson has remarked (*Leading Cases in the Common Law* (Select Bibliography), at 199) '[this explanation] signally fails to make sense of the case's status as a leading case'. This, in turn, raises a wider (and fascinating) point namely, what matters most: the judge's original understanding or the way his judgment has been interpreted by subsequent generations of judges, including himself? We shall return to this point briefly in the last part of this chapter. A further point which students may wish to ponder is this: does a judge who makes new law admit this openly? Or has he, effectively, made new law and then tried to cover up the tracks?

[10] This may explain, in part at least, the fact that such fervent supporters of the fault principle as F. Pollock (*The Law of Torts* (1887), 398) and O. W. Holmes (*The Common Law* (1881), lectures 3 and 4) experienced such difficulty with this decision. See, also, P. J. Ames, 'Law and Morals' (1908) 22 *Harv. LR* 97.

Cairns adopted Blackburn J's formulation but with a limitation thereof to 'non-natural users' of land, a point which will be considered later.

Third, Blackburn's judgment conceals whatever policy reasons may lie behind it. Indeed, Prosser has suggested that it is futile to search for them.[11] There is certainly nothing in the judgments to suggest any specific policy aims; and a consideration of the background of the judges[12] makes it unlikely that they were favouring, as some have suggested, the dominant landed gentry at the expense of the middle-class-based developing industry.[13] On the other hand, there is little doubt that the case is best understood if seen in its proper historical and socio-economic context and this, perhaps, explains why there have been so many theories attempting to explain the case and to promote (or prevent) its subsequent adoption in various parts of the United States. Thus, Roscoe Pound's explanation of the case, that it was an attempt to subject 'the landowner to a liability at his peril, in the interest of the general security',[14] shows greater concern for public welfare than might have existed in the mid-nineteenth century. Leon Green's view[15] that, in deciding that the surface industrialist should be saddled with the loss since he, rather than the subterranean land owner, was better able to prevent the risk, could also be accused of ascribing to the nineteenth century an accident-prevention approach more typical of our times. Whether any theory represents the truth, or even part of it, must remain unsolved. Their study, however, certainly adds perspective to the decision and may possibly explain its subsequent fate. It also raises the possibility that some (leading) Victorian judges (and, besides Blackburn J, himself, one counts among them Willes J) were coming to view that strict liability was the rule rather than the exception.[16] This last point may be a crucial one. For, if correct, it undermines the most recent attempts of the House of Lords to buttress their preference for fault (and the tort of Negligence) with arguments which ascribe to Blackburn himself such a predilection. More about this point, however, at the end of this chapter.

The rule in *Rylands* v. *Fletcher* has been interpreted to cover a variety of things 'likely to do mischief' on escape irrespective of whether they are dangerous *per se*. These include, *inter alia*, water,[17] electricity,[18] explosions,[19] oil,[20] vibrations[21] and at one time

[11] W.L. Prosser, 'The Principle of *Rylands* v. *Fletcher*'. (Select Bibliography), 139.

[12] Thus R. T. Molloy, '*Rylands* v. *Fletcher*: A Re-Examination of Juristic Origins' (Select Bibliography) and R. Pound, 'The Economic Interpretation and the Law of Torts' (Select Bibliography).

[13] So F.H. Bohlen, whose interpretation ('The Rule in *Rylands* v. *Fletcher*') (Select Bibliography) is accepted by F. P. Harper and F. James, *The Law of Torts* (2nd edn., 1986), ii, 793.

[14] *Interpretations of Legal History* (1923), 109.

[15] 'Tort Law: Public Law in Disguise' (Select Bibliography), 5. Green also argues that any contrary decision would have hurt the mining industry which at that time was more important to the English economy than the surface-based milling industry which required the storage of extra quantities of water. In support of this he recites the hostile reception of *Rylands* v. *Fletcher* in the US eastern seaboard, where the milling industry was clearly more important than mining. This last point, however, has been doubted by others, e.g. Pound and Prosser (both: Select Bibliography).

[16] See Simpson (Select Bibliography), 198.

[17] *Rylands* v. *Fletcher* (1868) LR 3 HL 330.

[18] *National Telephone Co.* v. *Baker* [1893] 2 Ch. 186.

[19] *Rainbam Chemical Works* v. *Belvedere Fish Guano Co.* [1921] 2 AC 465.

[20] *Mulholland & Tedd Ltd.* v. *Baker* [1939] 3 All ER 253.

[21] *Hoare & Co.* v. *McAlpine* [1923] 1 Ch. 167; but cf. *Barrette* v. *Franki Compressed Pile Co. of Canada Ltd.* (1955) 2 DLR 665.

even gypsies.[22] Stallybrass reviewed the older cases and suggested that the common thread running through them is the question:

Was the risk one which the defendant was entitled to take only on condition of paying compensation to those injured thereby irrespective of negligence on his part? And the answer to that question will not depend upon whether the thing in question was dangerous *per se*, but upon whether it was dangerous in the circumstances of the particular case.[23]

However, we must note at this stage that the recent judgments of the House of Lords in the case of *Transco plc* v. *Stockport Metropolitan Borough Council*,[24] while acknowledging the continued existence of this area of strict liability, have circumscribed its potential scope of application. The basic facts of the case were as follows. The defendant council used a three-inch water pipe to supply water to a block of flats which it owned, and large quantities of water leaked from that pipe, flowed on to another part of the defendant's land and caused subsidence and a landslip at the base of a former railway embankment on that land. This had the effect of washing away the support for a 27-metre section of the claimant's gas main, which had been constructed within the embankment, and meant that the claimants had to expend £93,681 to restore the support and cover the pipe so as to avoid a gas leak. The claimants sought to recover this sum from the defendant council under the rule in *Rylands* v. *Fletcher*.

Even Lord Bingham's general formulation of the rule in his judgment shows a tendency to restrict its ambit:

An occupier of land who can show that another occupier of land has brought or kept on his land an exceptionally dangerous or mischievous thing in extraordinary or unusual circumstances is in my opinion entitled to recover compensation from that occupier for any damage caused to his property interest by the escape of that thing, subject to defences of act of God or of a stranger, without the need to prove negligence.[25]

In the light of this, Lord Bingham subsequently suggested that the notion of what counts as a sufficiently 'dangerous thing' should 'not . . . be at all easily satisfied':

It must be shown that the defendant has done something which he recognised, or judged by the standards appropriate at the relevant place and time, he ought reasonably to have recognised, as giving rise to an exceptionally high risk of danger or mischief if there should be an escape, however unlikely an escape may have been thought to be.[26]

In what follows, account must be taken of the impact of this most recent ruling of the House of Lords on the scope and operation of the rule in *Rylands* v. *Fletcher*. We will return to the more general implications of *Transco* for the future in the concluding section of this chapter.

22 *A-G* v. *Corke* [1933] Ch. 89; but cf. *Smith* v. *Scott* [1973] Ch. 314. The last two categories in the list (vibrations and gypsies) are questionable: the recent case of *Lippiatt* v. *South Gloucestershire Council* [2000] QB 51 suggests that liability for the acts of people on the land may, nowadays, be more properly founded in nuisance, since a landlord in possession of the property could be said to be responsible for the acts of his licensees.

23 'Dangerous Things' (Select Bibliography), at 387.

24 [2004] 2 AC 1 ('the *Transco* case' or '*Transco*'), noted by K. Amirthalingam, '*Rylands* Lives' [2004] *CLJ* 273 and R. Bagshaw, '*Rylands* Confined' (2004) 120 *LQR* 388.

25 [2004] 2 AC 1, at [11].

26 *Ibid*., at [10].

2. THE REQUIREMENTS OF LIABILITY

(A) THE THING MUST BE BROUGHT ON TO THE DEFENDANT'S LAND (I.E. 'ACCUMULATED')

Such accumulation must be voluntary, so that an occupier will not be liable for things naturally on his land[27]—such as spontaneous accumulations, for example, rainwater flowing by gravity on to the plaintiff's land.[28] Nor will he be liable for the side effects of normal operations on his land. In *Smith* v. *Kenrick*,[29] rainwater accumulated naturally in a subterranean lake surrounded by a bar of coal. It was obvious that if the coal were mined the water would be released and would flow into the plaintiff's mine; which indeed occurred. Cresswell J, delivering the judgment of the court, refused to hold the defendant liable, on the ground that: 'It would seem to be the natural right of each of the owners of two adjoining mines . . . to work his own in the manner most convenient and beneficial to himself, although the natural consequence may be, that some prejudice will accrue to the owner of the adjoining mine . . . .'

But what if something naturally on the defendant's land is deliberately released by him on the claimant's land? If the release is deliberately aimed at the claimant, the best cause of action may well be trespass;[30] but the *Rylands* rule may be relevant where the release is intentional though not deliberately aimed at the claimant.[31]

(B) ESCAPE

There is a distinction between an escape of a thing already *on* the land and the diversion of a thing or substance *away from* the land. There is no liability for the latter, even though this inflicts damage on a neighbour. In *Gerrard* v. *Crowe*,[32] in order to prevent water from a boundary river from flooding his land, the defendant erected a wall on his own land, thereby diverting the water and increasing the flow over the plaintiff's land. The House of Lords held that no action lay. In *Read* v. *J. Lyons & Co. Ltd.*[33] Viscount

27 Such as self-sown weeds on the defendant's land blowing on to the plaintiff's land: *Giles* v. *Walker* (1890) 24 QBD 656. *Goldman* v. *Hargrave* [1967] 1 AC 645 and *Leakey* v. *National Trust* [1980] QB 485 may now suggest that an occupier of land may be under a measured duty of care to protect his neighbours from harm arising naturally from his own land. In such cases, however, liability would not be based on the *Rylands* rule: see our discussion of the 'measured duty of care' in ch. 13, section 3(a), above.

28 *Pontardawe RDC* v. *Moore-Guyn* [1929] 1 Ch. 656, *Neath RDC* v. *Williams* [1951] 1 KB 115; cf. A. L. Goodhart, 'Liability for Things Naturally on the Land' [1930–2] *CLJ* 27–8.

29 (1849) 7 CB 515; 137 ER 205. The case was extensively considered in *Rylands* v. *Fletcher* where it was obvious that the plaintiff could only succeed by distinguishing *Smith* v. *Kenrick*, hence his insistence on artificial accumulation. In all of these cases, however, liability may be arguable on some other ground, e.g. negligence or nuisance. See *Leakey* v. *National Trust* [1980] QB 485.

30 *Rigby* v. *Chief Constable of Northamptonshire* [1985] 1 WLR 1242.

31 *Crown River Cruises* v. *Kimbolton Fireworks Ltd.* [1996] 2 Lloyd's Rep. 533 (*obiter*, Potter J).

32 [1921] 1 AC 395. For a recent discussion of similar issues in the context of a claim for an easement, see *Palmer* v. *Bowman* [2000] 1 All ER 22.

33 [1947] AC 156, 168. Lord Macmillan defined it in even narrower terms: 'there must be the escape of something from one man's close to another man's close' (at 181). The escape will usually be unintentional and

Simon said that: '"Escape"... means escape from a place where the defendant has occupation of or control over land to a place which is outside his occupation or control.' In that case while an employee of the Ministry of Supply was performing her duties in a munitions factory managed by the defendants on behalf of the Ministry, a shell exploded and injured her. The House of Lords refused to hold the defendants liable since she was inside the premises at the time, which meant that her injury had not resulted from any 'escape' therefrom. As to this, it should be noticed, *first*, that though there are in this decision *dicta* on many aspects of the rule in *Rylands* v. *Fletcher* (liability for personal injuries, non-natural user, etc.), the main issue was that of escape. *Second*, the House of Lords had no doubt that there is no special rule about 'dangerous' things and the only thing that can be said these days about this is that the more dangerous a substance or thing is the likelier it is to help to characterise the use of the land as 'non-natural'. *Third*, counsel's argument that 'escape' could also mean escape from control and not only escape 'out' of the defendant's land was rejected, thus preventing any further extension of the rule to other cases.[34] *Fourth*, the case was argued exclusively on *Rylands* v. *Fletcher*, i.e. strict liability. Nowadays a negligence argument might, in some circumstances, succeed, aided by the doctrine of *res ipsa loquitur*. But in *Read* negligence was not argued. The reason this tort was not argued might be related to the fact that the injurious event was caused by the fault of a fellow worker and this, according to the then-prevailing doctrine of common employment, would have prevented the employer being vicariously liable to one employee for the fault of another employee.[35]

In most cases, the thing which by escaping causes harm is situated on land which belongs to the defendant. There do exist, however, some rather isolated exceptions to this statement. Thus, cases like *Midwood* v. *Manchester Corporation*[36] suggest that where a dangerous thing is brought on the highway, or interferes with any dangerous thing already there, and causes damage to adjoining property (but not to other users of the

involuntary. Arguably, *Rylands* v. *Fletcher* cannot apply to a deliberate and voluntary escape: *Rigby* v. *Chief Constable of Northamptonshire* [1985] 2 All ER 983, 996, per Taylor J (but cf. *Crown River Cruises* v. *Kimbolton Fireworks Ltd.* [1996] 2 Lloyd's Rep. 533).

34 Yet see Lord Hoffmann's formulation in the *Transco* case ([2004] 2 AC 1, at [34]), which would include 'escape from the defendant's land *or* control' (emphasis added) as a key element.

35 If this interpretation of *Read* is correct, it is not entirely clear why the employer's non-delegable duty to provide a safe place of work, which had earlier circumvented the inconvenience of common employment, was not invoked. However, it must be remembered that this duty was not expressly mentioned in Lord Wright's speech in *Wilson*'s case [1938] AC 57, and it took the courts some time to give it more precise content. See below, ch. 18. Moreover, it should be borne in mind that the plaintiff in *Read* was, on one view, not directly employed by the defendant in such a way as to bring her under the scope of the duty of care. The question of her employment status is highly complex: the defendant employer was deemed to be the 'agent' of the Ministry for the purposes of carrying out munitions work, while the claimant was directed to work as an inspector by a labour exchange under wartime national service legislation. Whatever the reason, the way that the issue was framed in *Read* proved to be of historic significance for the tort in *Rylands* v. *Fletcher*.

36 [1905] 2 KB 597. See also *Powell* v. *Fall* (1880) 5 QBD 597. In *Rigby* v. *Chief Constable of Northamptonshire* [1985] 2 All ER 983, 995–6, Taylor J expressed the view (*obiter*) that *Rylands* v. *Fletcher* could apply to unintentional escapes from the highway as well as from private land. On this see the cases discussed by J. Spencer, 'Motor-cars and the Rule in *Rylands* v. *Fletcher*: A Chapter of Accidents in the History of Law and Motoring' [1983] *CLJ* 65.

highway), he who introduced it there will be liable without proof of negligence, unless he can prove that the accident was due to the act of a stranger or to the act of God. In that case the defendants had laid a defective electrical cable, which fused and caused inflammable gas to escape from the highway into the plaintiff's house, resulting in an explosion and fire. For this they were held liable in damages. Nearly ten years later the Court of Appeal extended this in *Charing Cross Electricity Supply Co.* v. *Hydraulic Power Co.*[37] by holding that *Rylands* v. *Fletcher* applied as between two companies using the same highway. The defendant water company was held liable for damage to the electrical cables of the plaintiff company caused by water escaping from broken mains.

In *Transco*, however, there was an absence of agreement among their Lordships as to whether or not a qualifying 'escape' had taken place to fall within the scope of the rule in *Rylands* v. *Fletcher*. Since the water escaped from a pipe on one part of the defendant's land and flowed across it, eventually causing a landslip on another part of that land, Lord Scott took the firm view[38] that no escape from the defendant's land had taken place at all. Both he and Lord Hobhouse doubted whether the fact that the claimant had an easement over that part of the land (for the purpose of maintaining the gas main) made any difference to this conclusion, while Lord Hoffmann was 'willing to assume'[39] that that easement provided a sufficient proprietary basis for the claim advance by Transco. Lord Bingham did not advert to this point specifically, although it is submitted that, had he done so, its seems that he would have been likely to agree with the position of Lords Scott and Hobhouse, given Lord Bingham's express approval of the approach of the House of Lords in *Read* v. *Lyons* on this point.[40] Lord Walker, meanwhile, does not seem to have considered the point specifically at all.

3. CONTROLLING MECHANISMS

Providing workable limits to tort liability has been a concern of tort law from Roman times to this day. The reason for this is obvious: the spectrum of open-ended and uncontrolled liability is not one that any society can tolerate. This policy attitude is reflected in every tort where we find appropriately crafted concepts and mechanisms that perform such limiting functions. Since their common aim is to control liability, we call them here 'controlling mechanisms'. In the tort of Negligence, for instance, the concept of duty of care performs this task, though the bounds of liability are also kept in check through the notions of causation, remoteness and, of course, through a fluctuating standard of care that defendants are expected to display in their daily lives. In the tort of nuisance the controlling function is, primarily, performed through the notion of 'reasonableness' (which, as we have noted in Chapter 13, is understood differently in nuisance from in the tort of Negligence); and in *Rylands* v. *Fletcher* we find

[37] [1914] 3 KB 772. [38] [2004] 2 AC 1, at [77]–[79].
[39] *Ibid.*, at [47]. [40] *Ibid.*, at [9].

three controlling mechanisms: 'non-natural user', foreseeability (as has now been interpreted by the House of Lords in the *Cambridge Water* case) and a special list of defences. Each of these three mechanisms must now be examined in turn.

(A) 'NON-NATURAL USE' OF LAND

This is the most flexible and elusive[41] of the ingredients of liability. Blackburn J most probably understood 'natural' to refer to things 'naturally on the land and not artificially created'.[42] In the House of Lords, however, uncertainty crept in for the first time as a result of Lord Cairns's paraphrase of Blackburn J's formulation. It is, again, a matter of some dispute whether he intentionally or inadvertently introduced the additional requirement of 'non-natural user'. Indeed, Professor Newark believed that Lord Cairns did not introduce any additional requirement at all since, according to him, 'Lord Cairns' non-natural user is . . . merely an expression of the fact that the defendant has artificially introduced on to the land a new and dangerous agent.'[43]

Through a series of subsequent historical accidents, the courts took a different view and have come to look upon 'natural' as signifying something that is ordinary and usual even though it may be artificial, instead of non-artificial. Thus, what to Blackburn would have been non-natural simply because it was artificial would now be regarded as non-natural if it were abnormal, excessive or inappropriate to its location. As Lord Moulton put it in *Rickards* v. *Lothian*:[44] 'It is not every use to which land is put that brings into play that principle [i.e. of *Rylands* v. *Fletcher*]. It must be *some special use bringing with it increased danger to others*, and must not merely be the ordinary use of land or such a use as is proper for the general benefit of the community.' The italicised words may amount to an 'alternative criterion' for deciding what is non-natural. Thus, something that benefits the community might not easily be regarded as non-natural.[45] Indeed, in the *Cambridge Water* case the judge at first instance took the view that the activity in question could not be characterised as non-natural. In the House of Lords, however, Lord Goff was, it is submitted correctly, hesitant about the value of the criterion. But neither was he willing to accept the argument that 'the creation of employment as such . . . is sufficient of itself to establish a particular use as constituting a natural and ordinary use of land'.[46]

41 In the *Cambridge Water* case Lord Goff thought the expression to be 'lacking in precision' but did not feel that the facts of the case before him called for 'any redefinition': [1994] 2 AC 264, 309, [1994] 2 WLR 53, 82–3. In the *Transco* case ([2004] 2 AC 1), this was the element that received most attention, in terms of analysis, from each of their Lordships in their respective judgments.

42 According to Newark (Select Bibliography), 560, he was contrasting 'the immunity from liability in the case of natural accumulations, such as a water pond, with the *Rylands* v. *Fletcher* liability in the case of artificial accumulations, such as constructed reservoirs'. In the judgment itself, as Newark points out, the words 'natural' and 'naturally' are not used consistently.

43 *Ibid.*, 561. 44 [1913] AC 263, 280.

45 For a good recent example, see the judgment of the Court of Appeal in *British Gas* v. *Stockport Metropolitan Borough Council* [2001] Env. LR 44, where the use of a mains water pipe to provide water to a block of flats was held not to fall within the category of 'non-natural user' of the land.

46 [1994] 2 AC 264, 309 [1994] 2 WLR 53, 83.

What is 'natural' is thus viewed differently in different cases. In the words of Lord Porter, whether use is 'natural' or 'non-natural' is

> a question of fact subject to a ruling of the judge as to whether the particular object can be dangerous or the particular use can be non-natural, and in deciding this question I think that all the circumstances of the time and place and practice of mankind must be taken into consideration so that what might be regarded as dangerous or non-natural may vary according to those circumstances.[47]

The latter part of his *dictum* indicates that there is no objective test for determining what is 'non-natural'. This varies from place to place and time to time, which may explain why an explosives factory was considered to be a non-natural use of land in 1921, but natural in 1946.[48] On this point, we can compare *British Gas* v. *Stockport Metropolitan Borough Council*[49] with the earlier case of *Collingwood* v. *Home & Colonial Stores Ltd.*[50] In *Collingwood*, a distinction had been drawn between 'ordinary' pipes and 'mains' pipes, the latter being a means of carriage in bulk for the purposes of the party carrying the water and thus a non-natural user of the land. In *British Gas*, Schiemann LJ[51] made explicit reference to the status of such pipes in 'current conditions' and went on to emphasise that the mains pipe was nothing out of the ordinary—it was 'of a type of which there must be hundreds if not thousands of examples round the country'.[52]

On appeal to the House of Lords, the *British Gas* case became *Transco* and their Lordships upheld the conclusion of the Court of Appeal that such use made of the land by the defendant's pipe did not satisfy this requirement of the rule in *Rylands* v. *Fletcher*. Regrettably, however, their Lordships' judgments were not at all consistent *inter se* on the precise test to be applied under this heading. Criticism was made by some of the notion of 'non-natural user'[53] and of 'ordinary use',[54] yet Lord Scott consistently combined notions of 'ordinary' and 'natural' use throughout his judgment.[55] Lord Bingham, meanwhile, would have asked whether the use of the land was 'extraordinary or unusual'[56] and although Lord Walker stated his agreement with this approach, he himself also referred to asking whether there had been a 'special' use of the land[57] to satisfy this criterion.

Beyond these differences in terminology, their Lordships in *Transco* also suggested further relevant criteria which should be considered under this heading. First, Lords

47 *Read* v. *J. Lyons & Co. Ltd.* [1947] AC 156, 176.

48 Compare *Rainbam Chemical Works* with *Read* v. *Lyons*.

49 [2001] Env. LR 44.

50 [1936] 3 All ER 200.

51 [2001] Env. LR 44, at [35].

52 On this point, compare *British Gas* with the (minority) judgment of Keith and Blanchard JJ in *Autex* v. *Auckland City Council* [2000] NZAR 324—one could view the cost of damages incurred by victims of water escaping from the public supply system as simply another cost of the provision of such a system. This point may have more force in the context of privatised utilities.

53 [2004] 2 AC 1, at [11] (per Lord Bingham) and [63] (per Lord Hobhouse).

54 *Ibid.*, at [37] (per Lord Hoffmann, with which Lord Walker concurred) and [62] (per Lord Hobhouse).

55 *Ibid.*, at [84], [85], [88] and [90].

56 *Ibid.*, at [11].

57 *Ibid.*, at [103], [106] and [108].

Walker and Hoffmann held the exceptional nature of the risk of danger of mischief to be relevant to determining the nature of the use to which the land was put;[58] by contrast, for Lord Bingham this requirement seemed to operate separately as part of the examination of the nature of the thing accumulated on the defendant's land and its propensity to cause mischief were it to escape. The distinction is important: as Bagshaw has pointed out,[59] it could lead to different results where an escape occurred in a locality where otherwise dangerous activities were commonplace, such as an industrial area containing a number of neighbouring chemical plants.

Second, Lord Hoffmann suggested that a key question to ask when determining whether or not the user was 'non-natural' was whether or not 'the damage which eventuated was something against which the occupier [that is, the claimant] could reasonably be expected to have insured himself'.[60] Thus, the fact that the relevant risk here was not thought to be greater than that ordinarily arising from such pipes was, for Lord Hoffmann, buttressed by the fact that this risk of damage was one against which people can and commonly do insure themselves, and this was particularly true of a party like Transco.[61] Lord Hobhouse, however, expressly dissociated himself from this suggestion, in a paragraph which is worthy of fuller quotation:

> The existence of an insurance market does not mean that such insurance is available free of charge: premiums have to be paid. Some risks may only be insurable at prohibitive rates or at rates which for the proposer are not commercially viable and so make the risk, for him, commercially uninsurable. (Indeed, in recent times it has been the experience that some insurers will not cover certain risks at all, *e.g.* loss or damage caused by flooding.) The rationale, he who creates the risk must bear the risk, is not altered at all by the existence of an insurance market. It is an application of the same concept, an acknowledgement of risk. The economic burden of insuring against the risk must be borne by he who creates it and has the control of it. Further, the magnitude of the burden will depend upon who ultimately has to bear the loss: the rule [in *Rylands* v. *Fletcher*] provides the answer to this. The argument that insurance makes the rule unnecessary is no more valid than saying that, because some people can afford to and sensibly do take out comprehensive car insurance, no driver should be civilly liable for his negligent driving. It is unprincipled to abrogate for all citizens a legal rule merely because it may be unnecessary as between major corporations.[62]

One thing, however, upon which a majority of their Lordships did seem to agree was that the suggestion of Lord Moulton in *Rickards* v. *Lothian* that 'such a use as is proper

[58] [2004] 2 AC 1, at [46] (per Lord Hoffmann) and [103] (per Lord Walker). It seems that Lord Hobhouse ultimately adopted a similar approach in dismissing the appeal—see [67]—although arguably his approach could also be aligned with that of Lord Bingham as relating to the dangerous nature of the thing accumulated.

[59] '*Rylands* Confined' (2004) 120 *LQR* 388, 390.

[60] [2004] 2 AC 1, at [46].

[61] *Ibid.*, at [49].

[62] *Ibid.*, at [60]. In the subsequent case of *LMS International Ltd.* v. *Styrene Packaging & Insulation Ltd.* [2005] EWHC 2065 (TCC), [2006] BLR 50, Judge Peter Coulson QC opined (at [228]): 'given that this was a matter on which Lord Hoffmann and Lord Hobhouse expressly disagreed, it would, I think, be a mistake for me to attach any real significance to the point at all', before recording ('with great diffidence') that he favoured Lord Hobhouse's position on the question.

for the general benefit of the community'[63] did not provide an adequate guide[64] and risked involving the court in ultimately fruitless attempts to identify the overall social welfare created or harmed by the relevant use of the land by the defendant. Instead, it was important to adhere to the circumstances prevailing in modern society when addressing this question.

All this would still seem to mean that the requirement of non-natural use embodies an evaluation of risk along lines similar to those in negligence where, *inter alia*, the gravity of the harm threatened is weighed against the utility of the defendant's conduct, etc.[65] This merger of notions has, indeed, been advocated by some lawyers; and first-instance judgments such as that of Mackenna J in *Mason* v. *Levy Auto Parts of England Ltd.*[66] can, arguably, be seen in this light, since the kinds of factors that led the judge to find that there had been a non-natural use of the land (and thus impose liability under the *Rylands* rule) were precisely the kind of factors that would also have to be considered to find negligence liability. Yet not all judgments support such an approach;[67] and it is thus best to regard the requirement that the land is not put to a non-natural use as one of the controlling mechanisms of this 'strict' liability tort. Having said this, however, one must also note that, now that the House of Lords has accepted that foreseeability of harm of the relevant type is a prerequisite of liability in damages under the *Rylands* v. *Fletcher* rule, our courts may be less tempted to extend the use of the concept of (non-)natural user in order to avoid imposing liability. Thus, in the *Cambridge Water* case the defendants' storage of substantial quantities of chemicals for their business was characterised as 'almost a classical case of non-natural use'.[68] Nevertheless, because the plaintiff's harm was unforeseeable no liability was imposed.

(B) FORESEEABILITY

We know, both from *Rylands* v. *Fletcher* itself and the *Cambridge Water* decision, that liability in this tort is strict in the sense that, where the requirements of the tort are satisfied (accumulation, escape, etc.), the defendant will be liable even if he exercised all reasonable care to prevent the escape from taking place.[69] To put it differently, the strictness here is complete if we look at it from the point of view of the level of care required. But if we look at things from the angle of extent of damage, the strictness may depend upon the exact meaning we attribute to the notion of foreseeability.[70] The question which thus arises at this stage is the following: should we say that the defendant is liable only for foreseeable damage *provided the escape itself was also foreseeable by the reasonable*

63 [1913] AC 263, 280.

64 [2004] 2 AC 1, at [11] (per Lord Bingham), [37] (per Lord Hoffmann), [105]–[106] (per Lord Walker).

65 Prosser (Select Bibliography), 179, 185; and see above, ch. 4.

66 [1967] 2 QB 530.

67 See e.g. *British Celanese* v. *A. H. Hunt* [1969] 1 WLR 959.

68 [1994] 2 AC 264, 309 [1994] 2 WLR 53, 83, per Lord Goff.

69 *Ibid.*

70 On which see D. Wilkinson, '*Cambridge Water Company* v. *Eastern Counties plc*: Diluting Liability for Continuing Escapes' (1994) 57 *MLR* 799, 803 ff.

person? Or is it better to say that the escape, itself, is taken for granted (i.e. we do not inquire whether it was foreseeable) and limit our inquiry to the question whether the damage in suit was foreseeable? In *Cambridge Water*, Lord Goff seemed to place considerable emphasis on the fact that the seepage that occurred in that case was not foreseeable;[71] and that could suggest that he was opting for the first of the two possibilities given above—namely, that there could be no liability if the escape was not also foreseeable. This approach, however, does not square easily with either the *dicta* of Blackburn J in *Rylands* v. *Fletcher* or the result itself, since it will be remembered that in that leading case liability was imposed even though the escape was not foreseeable.[72] Not surprisingly, therefore, the preponderance of academic opinion has come down in favour of the view that what needs to be foreseen is the harm in suit but not the escape itself.[73] This, too, seems to have been the view of Lord Bingham in the *Transco* case, where although he emphasised that an 'exceptionally high risk of danger or mischief' was required, he also explicitly qualified this with the phrase 'however unlikely an escape may have been thought to be'.[74]

(C) DEFENCES

Whenever liability can be easily incurred, its *extent* tends to be limited in various ways. One way of achieving this is by increasing the number of exceptions and defences applicable to the rule. To put that proposition in a slightly different form, we may say that where there are few restrictions at the point of 'duty', there tend to be many more at the point of 'causation'.[75] Thus it is a matter of no surprise, though arguably one of regret, to see that a number of defences have sapped the rule of *Rylands* v. *Fletcher* of much of its vitality. We shall here briefly describe five.

(i) Statutory Authority

Statute may exclude liability that would otherwise arise.[76] In *Smeaton* v. *Ilford Corporation*,[77] the court interpreted section 31 of the Public Health Act 1936 as affording the defendants

[71] [1994] 2 AC 264, 294, 305–6 and 307 [1994] 2 WLR 53, 67, 69 and 81.

[72] As Professor Fleming was quick to point out in his note on the *Cambridge Water* case in (1995) 3 *Tort LR* 56.

[73] Thus, for instance, *Salmond and Heuston on The Law of Torts* (21st edn., by R. A. Buckley, 1996), 314; *Winfield and Jolowicz on Torts* (17th edn. by W. V. H. Rogers, 2006), para. 15–6 (albeit seeing some connection between contemplation of escape and the consequences of that escape, on the one hand, and the harm involved, on the other).

[74] [2004] 2 AC 1, at [10]; see, also, Lord Hoffmann's endorsement of this approach at [33].

[75] This can be seen most clearly in other legal systems (e.g. the French) where one finds more instances of strict liability than one does in the English common law.

[76] E.g. Nuclear Installations Act 1965. Statutes may also restrict the extent of the defence. See, for instance, the Reservoirs Act 1975, s. 28 and Sch. 2.

[77] [1954] Ch. 450. The position *vis-à-vis* local authorities, however, has not been clarified. Compare Lord Evershed MR's views with those of Denning LJ in *Pride of Derby etc.* v. *British Celanese Ltd.* [1953] Ch. 149, 172–7, 189–90. The recent judgment of the House of Lords in *Marcic* v. *Thames Water Utilities Ltd.* [2004] AC 42 has upheld the general approach of the earlier sewerage cases to the relevance of the (now more complex) statutory scheme (under the Water Industry Act 1991): this led to their Lordships' unanimous denial that

a complete defence to liability under *Rylands* v. *Fletcher* for the escape of sewage which they had accumulated under the Act.

As one might expect, the question whether the rule in *Rylands* v. *Fletcher* has been excluded is largely one of construction of the statute in question.[78] In *Green* v. *The Chelsea Waterworks Co.*,[79] for example, Parliament authorised the defendants to lay a water pipe which burst without the defendant's negligence and flooded the plaintiff's premises. Since the defendants were under a statutory duty to maintain a continuous supply of water through the pipes, it was held that by necessary implication they were exempt from all liability where the damage was not due to their negligence. But in *Charing Cross Electricity Co.* v. *Hydraulic Co.*,[80] where the facts were similar, the plaintiff succeeded in his claim. The difference can be explained on the ground that in the second case the defendant had only the *power* to supply water and keep pumping it through the mains, but no duty to do so.

The rules that apply to Nuisance with regard to statutory authority are also relevant here.

(ii) Consent of the Claimant[81]

This is a specific application of the defence of *volenti non fit injuria* and need not be discussed in detail. In practice, it has been often invoked when water from the top floor of a building affects the occupants of lower floors (e.g. overflowing cisterns, bathtubs, etc.). In many cases, however, it may not really be necessary to fall back on this defence, for the defendant can always argue that the existence of normal amounts of water is not a 'non-natural use'. An extension of the idea of consent is that it is a defence that the cause of danger is maintained for the common benefit of both defendant and claimant. In *Carstairs* v. *Taylor*,[82] for example, the plaintiff occupied the ground floor of a building, the top floor of which was occupied by the defendant. Rainwater from the roof was collected in a specially constructed box from which it was discharged into the drains. A rat gnawed a hole in the box and water drained into the plaintiff's premises and damaged his goods. The defendant, not being negligent in any way, was held not liable.[83]

(iii) Act of Third Party

In *Rickards* v. *Lothian* [84] property on the second floor of a building was damaged by an overflow of water from a basin on the top floor because the tap had been turned on and

Mr Marcic had any claim in (there) nuisance without making proper use of the various statutory complaints procedures. This case is discussed further in ch. 13, above.

[78] On this point see now *Allen* v. *Gulf Oil Refining Ltd.* [1981] AC 1001 (a nuisance action); above, ch. 13, Section 5.

[79] (1894) 70 LT 547, *Geddis* v. *Proprietors of Bann Reservoir* (1878) 3 App. Cas. 430.

[80] [1914] 3 KB 772.

[81] *A-G* v. *Cory Brothers & Co. Ltd.* [1921] 1 AC 521, 539.

[82] (1871) LR 6 Ex. 217.

[83] See also *Anderson* v. *Oppenheimer* (1880) 5 QBD 602. The collection of water in a cistern has been considered as a natural use of land: *Rickards* v. *Lothian* [1913] AC 263. *Contra* industrial water under pressure: *Charing Cross Electricity Supply Co.* v. *Hydraulic Power Co.* [1914] 3 KB 772.

[84] [1913] AC 263.

the waste pipe plugged by some third person. It was held that, by having on his premises a reasonable supply of water, the defendant was only making an ordinary and proper use of his house, and that he was not responsible for the wrongful act of a third party.

It has been suggested[85] that the defence should be limited to the 'mischievous, deliberate and conscious act of a stranger', as in *Rickards* v. *Lothian*. Such a restrictive view has little to commend it, for, as Jenkins LJ pointed out in *Perry* v. *Kendricks*,[86] the basis of the defence is the absence of any control by the defendant over the acts of a stranger on his land and therefore the nature of the stranger's conduct is irrelevant. It is for the defendant to satisfy the court that on a balance of probabilities the escape was caused by the *unforeseeable*[87] act of a stranger.

Who counts as a 'stranger' in this context is not always easy to determine. A trespasser clearly is. A servant acting in the course of his employment will, however, render his master liable and cannot be treated as a stranger. But *Stevens* v. *Woodward*[88] shows that a servant, when acting outside the course of his employment, may be a stranger. Likewise, the occupier will be liable for the negligence of his independent contractors and perhaps of lawful visitors, provided he has some control over their acts. Finally, no uniform answer is possible as far as members of the defendant's family are concerned. The degree of control over such persons may hold the key to discovering the right answer.

(iv) Act of God

This ill-defined defence is, probably, available whenever an escape is caused by the operation of natural forces beyond human anticipation or avoidance. Despite its name, it is a defence destitute of any theological connotation and the term *vis major* is preferable. An illustration is *Nichols* v. *Marsland*,[89] where the defendant created some artificial ornamental lakes by damming up a natural stream. He was held not liable when rainfall 'greater and more violent than any within the memory of witnesses' caused the embankments to collapse and the escaping water destroyed four nearby bridges. Nowadays, however, there is a tendency to restrict the ambit of this defence, not least because of the increased ability to predict such occurrences.[90] The enhanced degree of foreseeability may have also contributed to the decline of this defence.

[85] Per Singleton LJ in *Perry* v. *Kendricks* [1956] 1 WLR 85, 87.

[86] *Ibid.*, 90.

[87] If the act of the third party is foreseeable then the defendant will, probably, be liable in negligence. Contrast *Greenock Corporation* v. *Caledonian Railways Co.* [1917] AC 556.

[88] (1881) 6 QBD 318: a servant used a private lavatory against instructions and did not turn off the tap; it was held that the master was not liable for the flooding.

[89] (1876) 2 Ex. D 1. Cf. *Greenock Corp.* v. *Caledonia Railways Co.* [1917] AC 556.

[90] See the criticism *ibid.*, where it was held that the 'criterion is no longer whether the event can reasonably be anticipated, but whether or not human foresight and prudence can reasonably recognise the possibility of such an event'.

(v) Default of the Claimant

This defence, recognised by Blackburn J himself in his judgment in *Rylands* v. *Fletcher*, is applicable if the damage to the claimant is due entirely to his act or default.[91] Where this amounts to his own contributory negligence, then his damages will be reduced in accordance with general principles.[92]

4. WHO IS PROTECTED AND FOR WHAT?

What interests does the rule protect? Can a claimant whose interests in land have been violated recover in respect of consequential damage to chattels or to his person? In 1868 Blackburn J allowed a claim for damage to chattels[93] and subsequent judges have followed his example. With regard to personal injury, the position used to be less clear. In *Read* v. *J. Lyons*[94] Lord Macmillan denied liability *obiter*; but he failed to refer to the earlier decision in *Hale* v. *Jennings Bros.*,[95] where an *occupier* of land was awarded damages for personal injuries under this rule. So Lord Macmillan may only have been condemning an extension of *Rylands* v. *Fletcher* to injury suffered by *non-occupiers*. *Shiffman* v. *Order of St John*[96] was such a case. The plaintiff there was awarded damages for an injury inflicted by a falling flagpole in Hyde Park. This liability followed a finding of negligence, but the court stated *obiter* that the defendants would have been liable under *Rylands* v. *Fletcher* even if negligence had not been proved. Arguably, it was this extension of the rule that was being attacked by Lord Macmillan and not the application of the rule to cases of personal injury suffered by occupiers of land. Until recently, therefore, one could plausibly argue that Lord Macmillan's view was an isolated one, having found favour neither with his fellow Law Lords in *Read* v. *Lyons*[97] nor with the subsequent decision of the Court of Appeal in *Perry* v. *Kendricks Transport Ltd.*[98] In English law, even more doubtful was (and is) the position of a non-occupier and this despite favourable *dicta* in some English cases[99] and even more encouraging authority from Canada.[100]

[91] *Dunn* v. *Birmingham Land Co.* (1872) LR 7 QB 244, 246. If the plaintiff's conduct merely contributed to his harm then this damage may be reduced accordingly under s. 1 of the Law Reform (Contributory Negligence) Act 1945.

[92] But contrast *Martins* v. *Hotel Mayfair* [1976] 2 NSWLR 15, 67.

[93] *Jones* v. *The Festiniog Ry. Co.* (1868) LR 3 QB 733; see now *Halsey* v. *Esso Petroleum Co. Ltd.* [1961] 1 WLR 683; but a non-occupier cannot: *Cattle* v. *Stockton Waterworks Co.* (1875) LR 10 QB 453.

[94] [1947] AC 156, 170–1.

[95] [1938] 1 All ER 579. Likewise in *Miles* v. *Forest Rock Granite Co.* (1918) 34 TLR 500.

[96] [1936] 1 All ER 557.

[97] [1947] AC 156.

[98] [1956] 1 WLR 85.

[99] *Miles* v. *Forest Rock Granite Co. (Leicestershire) Ltd.* (1918) 34 TLR 500 and *Perry* v. *Kendricks Transport Ltd.* [1956] 1 WLR 85.

[100] *Aldridge* v. *Van Patter* (1952) 4 DLR 93.

These expansive interpretations, using *Rylands* v. *Fletcher* as a possible cause of action for personal injuries (suffered by an occupier or non-occupier of land) must now be reconsidered and regarded as being less persuasive in the light of the recent decisions of the House of Lords in the *Cambridge Water* case,[101] in *Hunter* v. *Canary Wharf*[102] and in *Transco*.[103] For all three decisions, adopting a distinctly historical approach, see a closer relationship between the two torts of nuisance and the rule in *Rylands* v. *Fletcher*, and place them unequivocally within the context of measures which are meant to vindicate violations of interests in land.[104] This optic, coupled with the equally undoubted contemporary tendency to restrict the field of application of *Rylands* v. *Fletcher*, must make reliance on the above-mentioned case law of doubtful wisdom.[105] The fact that the wisdom of the identical *dicta* mentioned above has rarely[106] been expressly challenged[107] allows little room for optimism for any practitioner who would wish to go against this modern trend (as exemplified by *Transco*, *Hunter* and *Cambridge Water*). The other aspect of the reasoning of their Lordships in both *Cambridge Water* and *Transco* that was used to buttress this conclusion was explicit reference to the existence of a number of statutory schemes for the imposition of strict liability. For Lord Goff in *Cambridge Water*, the statutory route was the preferred method for any expansion in the scope, or expansive application, of strict liability: this would allow the precise identification of the nature of the activity and the criteria for any such liability.[108] *Transco* took this one stage further: their Lordships cited the range of specific statutory schemes which now exists to show that this was an area where Parliament was willing to act to deal with particular risks.[109] Yet these statutes clearly cover personal injury as well as property damage: Parliament, apparently, does not view only proprietary interests as worthy of such protection. Indeed, as Nolan has recently reminded us,[110] the result of the restrictive approach of their Lordships in *Cambridge Water*, *Hunter* and *Transco* would seem to be to afford 'greater protection... to proprietary interests than to personal interests, and... this would appear to be

[101] [1994] 2 AC 264: a *Rylands* v. *Fletcher* case.

[102] [1997] AC 655: a private nuisance case.

[103] [2004] 2 AC 1.

[104] See, most recently, *ibid.*, at [11] (per Lord Bingham), [39] and [46] (per Lord Hoffmann), [54] and [60] (per Lord Hobhouse), [78]–[80] (per Lord Scott); Lord Walker recorded (at [116]) his concurrence with the Opinions of Lords Bingham and Hoffmann.

[105] See, e.g., the judgment of Ward LJ in *Ribee* v. *Norrie* [2001] PIQR P8, at [30], where he strongly doubted whether a claim for personal injury under the rule in *Rylands* v. *Fletcher* could survive the reasoning of Lord Goff in *Cambridge Water*. This point seems only to have been strengthened after *Transco*.

[106] Judge Anthony Thornton QC has recently doubted both the assimilation of *Rylands* into a sub-species of nuisance (*Johnson* v *B. J. W. Property Developments Ltd* [2002] EWHC 1131 (TCC); [2002] 3 All ER 574, at [17]) and the requirement of an interest in land to be able to sue under the rule (*Re-Source American International Ltd* v *Platt Service Ltd* [2003] EWHC 1142 (TCC) at [171]).

[107] In spite of the valid point that 'no member of the House of Lords in *Transco* sought to explain why it might be sensible to compel those who undertake hazardous activities to internalise only real property damage costs' (R. Bagshaw, '*Rylands* Confined' (2004) 120 *LQR* 388, 389).

[108] [1994] 2 AC 264, 305.

[109] See, e.g., [2004] 2 AC 1, at [6] (per Lord Bingham) and [42] and [45] (per Lord Hoffmann).

[110] D. Nolan, 'The Distinctiveness of *Rylands* v. *Fletcher*' (Select Bibliography), 440.

indefensible. Indeed, it has been said that for the law to privilege real property interests in this way is suggestive of an "alarming retrogressive tendency,"[111] a throwback to a more primitive stage of the law's development.'

However, the recent case of *McKenna* v. *British Aluminium*[112] raises the possibility of an alternative challenge to the more restrictive approach of *Cambridge Water*, *Hunter* v. *Canary Wharf* and *Transco*, in the form of Article 8 ECHR and the Human Rights Act 1998. In so far as this requirement of an interest in land fails to respect a right to a private and family life, it may yet be that the courts will have to revisit the question of who can sue (both in nuisance and under *Rylands* v. *Fletcher*)—Neuberger J in *McKenna* was certainly not prepared to hold that any such reasoning was unarguable.[113] It is certainly possible that an appropriate protection of such interests under Article 8 ECHR may require not only a more relaxed approach to the question of standing to sue under the rule in *Rylands* v. *Fletcher* (and, indeed, the tort of nuisance), but also that heads of damage must be available that secure an adequate protection of the proper scope of such Article 8 interests.

Academics, furthermore, are entitled to doubt the wisdom of this high-level judicial retreat from strict liability evinced in *Cambridge Water*, *Hunter* v. *Canary Wharf* and now *Transco*—hence the concluding section of this chapter. Before we come to this, however, a few words must be said about the relationship of the *Rylands* rule to the tort of nuisance.

5. *RYLANDS* V. *FLETCHER* AND NUISANCE[114]

The distinction between the two torts is not easy to draw and in practice it is not uncommon for the two torts to be pleaded together.[115] Furthermore, recent authority in the House of Lords has persisted in viewing the rule in *Rylands* v. *Fletcher* as a

111 Quoting FV. Harper and F. James, *Law of Torts* (1956), at 806.

112 [2002] Env. LR 30 (cited to their Lordships in the *Transco* case, but not referred to in any of their opinions). The concerned claims by permanent residents against a neighbouring factory for the infliction of mental distress and physical harm over a period of time which was still continuing. On a motion to strike out the claims of those who were children and thus permanent residents but lacking any proprietary interest in the land, Neuberger J held that the *Cambridge Water* case meant that an interest in land was now a necessary condition for the bringing of a claim under *Rylands* v. *Fletcher* (at [21]). But see the point on the Human Rights Act 1998 and Art. 8 ECHR in the subsequent text.

113 *Ibid.*, [39] ff., which meant that he refused to strike out their claims. Interestingly, in the light of the discussion in the text above concerning personal injury claims under *Rylands* v. *Fletcher*, one of the arguments advanced against the use of Art. 8 ECHR by counsel in *McKenna* was that it would be inappropriate to extend nuisance or *Rylands* v. *Fletcher* to cover personal injury claims when they are essentially property torts: see [46] ff. (and esp. [49]).

114 For recent discussion highlighting the distinctions that do exist between the two torts, see Nolan (Select Bibliography).

115 See Newark (Select Bibliography) and also W. A. West, 'Nuisance or *Rylands* v. *Fletcher*' (1966) 30 *Conv. (NS)* 95. In *McKenna* v. *British Aluminium Ltd* [2002] Env. LR 30, Neuberger J inclined to the view that, after *Cambridge Water* and *Hunter* v. *Canary Wharf*, 'when considering a claim in *Rylands* v. *Fletcher* one should treat

'sub-species' (or similar) of nuisance, with consequences for the way in which the tort has (been) developed. Yet differences do exist, at least at the conceptual level. Thus, first, *Rylands* v. *Fletcher* is a tort of strict liability (in the sense described in the previous paragraphs) whereas the meaning of 'strictness' in nuisance is, as we have seen, far less clear. Second, in *Rylands* v. *Fletcher* liability depends upon 'non-natural use' of land by the defendant; in nuisance even 'natural use' may give rise to liability. Third, nuisance, unlike *Rylands* v. *Fletcher*, does not require 'accumulation' and 'escape'. Fourth, some nuisances, for example obstruction of light or noise, are not covered by *Rylands* v. *Fletcher*. Fifth, prescription may legalise certain types of *private* nuisance. Finally, in *Rylands* v. *Fletcher* the defendant is strictly liable for his independent contractors; in nuisance the position is not clear.[116]

6. *RYLANDS V. FLETCHER* AND THE FUTURE OF STRICT LIABILITY IN GENERAL

Rylands v. *Fletcher* gave the common law one of its most widely discussed and, arguably, most influential generalisations. Not for the first time, an English seed was borrowed by America, combined with indigenous elements and brought to full bloom under the doctrine of liability for extra-hazardous activities.[117] On the other hand, in its country of origin the idea had a mixed reception almost from the very beginning. Originally, it looked as if it had the kind of future ahead of it which was, subsequently, destined for another bold judicial generalisation: that found in Lord Atkin's opinion in *Donoghue* v. *Stevenson*. Yet after a moderately welcoming start, given to it by some Victorian judges, the rule was progressively emasculated of all its potential as it struck at the heart of another Victorian favourite: fault. For the Victorian era became (progressively) moralistic and thus any legal rule that encouraged tort to depart from this favoured shibboleth was suspicious, to say the least. In fact it was both suspicious and dangerous in so far as it also challenged the hypocrisy of the age. This is because the fault rule—as it came to be applied by the end of the nineteenth century—served this hypocrisy as well, since it protected nascent industries at a time of weak, if not non-existent, insurance practices. For by this time the fault rule had acquired a double aspect: not only did it mean that if you are at fault you must pay; it was also (less convincingly) understood to require

it effectively as an extension or branch of the law of nuisance. Not in the sense that it is an extension in a number of possible directions, including an extension to the identity and nature of persons who can sue, but an extension in the sense that an isolated incident, which might not have been regarded in the nineteenth century (and might not even be regarded in the twentieth or twenty-first century) as being a nuisance, can, if it involves an escape of the relevant nature, give rise to a claim in what amounts to nuisance' at [22].

116 For a recent discussion of this issue in the context of liability for fire, see the judgment of Judge Thornton QC in *Johnson (Trading as Johnson Butchers)* v. *B. J. W. Property Developments Ltd.* [2002] 3 All ER 574, at [52] ff.

117 See, e.g., *Sullivan* v. *Durham* 161 NY 290, 55 NE 923 (1900) and *Smith* v. *Lockheed Propulsion Co.*, 247 CA 2d 774, 56 Cal. Rptr. 128 (1967).

that if you are not at fault, you need not pay.[118] This clash of philosophies, evident in a number of traffic-accident cases decided during the first twenty-odd years of the twentieth century,[119] came to a head with the decision of *Read* v. *Lyons & Co. Ltd.*[120] where the adherents of the fault principle won their most decisive battle. In the words of Professor John Fleming: '[t]he most damaging effect of [that] decision [was] that it prematurely stunted the development of a general theory of strict liability . . . .'[121]

The focus on the fault principle is, however, alive and well in the most recent ruling of the House of Lords: *Transco*. While their Lordships rejected a direct invitation from counsel for the defendants to abrogate the independent existence of the *Rylands* rule and assimilate it to the tort of negligence, Lord Hoffmann did expressly remark that:

> the cases in which there is an escape which is not attributable to an unusual natural event or the act of a third party will, by the same token, usually give rise to an inference of negligence. . . . It is perhaps not surprising that counsel could not find a reported case since the Second World War in which anyone had succeeded in a claim under the rule.[122]

It should be noted, as did the judge in the recent case of *LMS International Ltd.* v. *Styrene Packaging & Insulation Ltd.*,[123] that Lord Hoffmann's comment concerning the lack of successful claims was not strictly accurate, as it had not taken into account the cases on the escape of fire where liability had been established[124]—since *Transco* related to the escape of water, those cases had not been cited to their Lordships by counsel in argument. Equally, it should be noted that in most of these cases the court found the requirements of both negligence and the *Rylands* rule to be satisfied on the facts, as indeed did the judge in *LMS International* itself (as well as the claim in nuisance).

Yet the retreat back into fault has had more casualties than the lost opportunity for our law to formulate a generalised principle of strict liability. Most notable among them was our law of traffic accidents, in which the fault requirement became firmly embedded, and thus missed the opportunity of being based on some strict or no-fault liability scheme (as so many other European systems are) and thereby sparing our courts a large chunk of their daily (and unnecessary) workload.[125] But it also led our judges to attempt a bold reinterpretation of the notion of fault in a way which has not only stripped it of most, if not all, of its moral content but has also led it to be understood (as noted in Chapter 1, above) in different ways in different factual situations.

[118] In practice this, of course, also included cases where the plaintiff could not prove the defendant's fault, something which happened frequently as growing industrialisation increased the number of what the French at the time aptly called 'anonymous accidents'—often exploding boilers in various industrial settings.

[119] And beautifully described by Professor John Spencer in 'Motor Cars and the Rule in *Rylands* v. *Fletcher*: A Chapter of Accidents in the History of Law and Motoring' [1983] *CLJ* 65.

[120] [1947] AC 156.

[121] *The Law of Torts* (9th edn., 1998), 383.

[122] [2004] 2 AC 1, 19.

[123] [2005] EWHC 2065 (TCC), [2006] BLR 50 (Judge Peter Coulson QC).

[124] Such as *Mason* v. *Levy Auto Parts Ltd.* [1967] 2 QB 530, *Balfour* v. *Barty-King* [1957] 1 All ER 156 and *E. Hobbs (Farms) Ltd.* v. *The Baxenden Chemical Co. Ltd.* [1992] 1 Ll. L Rep. 54.

[125] This is ironic, of course, since those who opposed the *Rylands* rule believed that its adoption would increase the volume of litigation. See ch. 3 of the 4th edn of this work for more details on the law on traffic accidents.

So how have our courts (and our legal system as a whole) achieved the demolition of the *Rylands* rule, given that they are loath to give us openly their policy and philosophical objections? Three avenues of thought were followed.

First, the Pearson Committee, objecting to the American developments, argued that general pronouncements (of the kind found in para. 519 of the American *Restatement (Second) on Torts*)[126] entail 'important change[s] in the substance of liability [by means of] . . . a long drawn-out process of judicial legislation'.[127]

At least three possible objections could be advanced against this argument. First, is not the common law accustomed and well attuned to growth through well-understood judicial incrementalism that is, inevitably, the result of disputes being litigated before some tribunal?[128] Second, has our tendency to push cases (which could be handled more easily through strict liability regimes) into the tort of Negligence avoided the feared increase in litigation?[129] And, third (and in a related way), does not a properly conceived regime of strict liability (unencumbered by multiple layers of defences and exceptions) lead to speedy compensation and avoid excessive recourse to our courts?

The second line of reasoning pursued by our courts (in refusing to develop a generalised rule of strict liability) stresses the argument that for a decision to go down that route would entail unfathomed economic consequences for our society. More precisely, it would mean that 'the cost of damage resulting from such operations would have to be absorbed as part of the overheads of the relevant business rather than be borne (where there is no negligence) by the injured person or his insurance, or even by the community at large'.[130] The fact that attempts such as the one favoured by the authors of this book have, in fact, taken place in other countries (the United States and the Commonwealth), and have also been advocated by experienced tort experts such as Professor Fleming, has not carried much weight in our country since our judges are, undeniably, uncomfortable when asked to employ economic reasoning to tort disputes.[131] Thus, from a practitioner's point of view an economic/insurance approach seems to hold out little promise of appeal. In the classroom, however, such an analysis of the underlying problems holds out rich rewards as well as the opportunity to

[126] This reads as follows: '(1) One who carries on an abnormally dangerous activity is subject to liability for harm to the person, land or chattels of another resulting from the activity, although he has exercised the utmost care to prevent the harm. (2) This strict liability is limited to the kind of harm, the possibility of which makes the activity abnormally dangerous.' This principle is severely qualified by the numerous exceptions found in §§520–4A.

[127] Cmnd. 7054–I (1978), §647. It is submitted that the use of the word 'legislation', instead of (the more obvious) 'decision', itself betrays the hostility towards the idea of allowing the rule to develop through case law.

[128] McLachlin J's observations in *Norsk Pacific Steamship* v. *Canadian National Railway Co.* (1992) 91 DLR (4th) 289, make the same point in the context of the tort of Negligence.

[129] Given the point made previously—that the fault notion has been applied in different ways in different factual situations so as to accommodate its application—it is perhaps unsurprising that such litigation has continued to be frequent, as each claimant tries to establish that a more favourable approach should apply to *his* particular situation.

[130] Per Lord Goff in the *Cambridge Water* case: [1994] 2 AC 264, 304.

[131] This is well illustrated by the disagreement between Lords Hoffmann and Hobhouse in *Transco* as to the relevance of the availability of insurance to the assessment of the nature of the use of the land: see the text at nn. 61 and 62, above for details.

experience the refreshing effect of other common-law judgments which have shown less attachment to our more legalistic and avowedly historical judicial reasoning.[132]

Indeed, this avowedly historical approach of the recent decisions of the House of Lords is the third and last feature of this current trend to merge the *Rylands* rule with the tort of nuisance (and, perhaps, also negligence).[133] In two recent decisions of the House of Lords[134] we thus saw Lord Goff relying heavily upon an article which, though obviously learned, was written sixty years ago and was based on (mainly) nineteenth- and early twentieth-century cases, in order to forestall attempts to make old torts serve modern environmental concerns. In the most recent instalment (*Transco*) of the contributions of the House of Lords to the judicial development of the rule in *Rylands* v. *Fletcher*, all of their Lordships endorsed the position taken by Lord Goff in *Cambridge Water* and *Hunter* v. *Canary Wharf* with regard to the question of foreseeability, and strove further to restrict the scope of application of the *Rylands* rule (as discussed above).

In this struggle to minimise the effect of the *Rylands* rule, courts and academics that oppose its survival have not hesitated even to imply that its creator, one of the common law's greatest judges, was 'unconscious' of its import. Indeed, they have shrewdly used (misused?) his own subsequent *dicta* to suggest that he had never intended to bring about any legal revolution. The fact that he may have deliberately attempted to minimise the full effect of his innovation, precisely in order to give it a good start in life, has thus not even been considered by academic or practising lawyers, even though nowadays we have increasing evidence that 'creative' judges are not averse to such techniques.[135] Nor has it been widely noticed that in *Rylands* v. *Fletcher* Willes J—the outstanding common lawyer of his time—(as well as Keating and Montague Smith JJ) came round to Blackburn's view of strict liability even though they had, three months earlier, taken a leading hand in deciding in *Indermauer* v. *Dames*[136] that the negligence principle should apply to an accident which occurred on private premises.[137] Nor, finally, have any of the modern commentators paid sufficient attention to another reality—namely, that whatever Blackburn's real views about strict liability, subsequent judges (and legal historians) in this country and abroad saw his judgment as one that contained a great potential for growth. The demolition of the strict liability rule may

132 Thus in *Benning* v. *Wong* (1969) 122 CLR 249, Windeyer J said: 'to regard negligence as the normal requirement of responsibility in tort, and to look upon strict liability as anomalous and unjust, seems to me to mistake present values as well as past history. In an age when insurance against all forms of liability is commonplace, it is surely not surprising or unjust if the law makes persons who carry on some kind of hazardous undertaking liable for the harm they do, unless they can excuse or justify it on some recognised grounds.'

133 Something which the High Court of Australia had the courage to do more openly than our House of Lords: see *Burnie Port Authority* v. *General Jones Pty* (1994) 68 ALJR 331.

134 The *Cambridge Water* case [1994] 2 AC 264 and the *Hunter* v. *Canary Wharf* case [1997] AC 655.

135 Cf. Lord Denning MR's judgment in *Dutton* v. *Bognor Regis Urban District Council* [1972] 1 QB 373 at 396, with the views he subsequently expressed in one of his books—*The Discipline of the Law* (1979) at 264—about the nature of the harm suffered by Mrs Dutton. See, also, Lord Mustill's observations on this point in his recent lecture 'What Do Judges Do?' (1995) 96(3) *Särtryck ur Juridisk Tidskrift*, 611.

136 (1866) LR 1 CP 274; affirmed (1867) LR 2 CP 311.

137 A point stressed by Professor Simpson (Select Bibliography).

thus be neither as (historically) obvious nor as desirable as the House of Lords has recently made it out to be. About this, history as much as modern realities allows plenty of room for doubt.

Yet notwithstanding the intellectual appeal which the historical analysis holds out to anyone who uses it, it is unlikely to be able to displace the modern courtroom trend to subsume *Rylands* under the tort of negligence and/or nuisance.[138] So, if the history of *Rylands* v. *Fletcher* holds any lessons for us today they must be different ones. In our view it must surely be that we cannot go on using torts devised hundreds of years ago to meet the more complex problems which confront our modern society. To be able to tackle these problems we need new approaches, new ideas and new techniques. Thus, it may well be that in these days of 'common law fatigue' the initiative must pass on to the legislator. Indeed, this is Lord Goff's final conclusion in the *Cambridge Water* case, though unfortunately it, too, is not without serious problems. Here are two.

First, at what level of generality should such legislation be pitched? The Pearson proposal[139] was, probably, narrower than that found in the American *Restatement*; yet it, too, was subject to the same objections that were levelled against the American document. Moreover, many academics argued at the time that the Commission's proposals would, in practice, lead to many irrational distinctions being drawn. This would be even likelier to happen if we were to opt for the kind of approach that one finds in Germany and which, in Lord Goff's words, enables each, specific statute to 'lay down precise criteria and the incidence and scope of such liability'.[140] All these points are, of course, worthy of further discussion but this book is not the place to attempt it.

Second, even if specific statutory intervention holds the answers for the future, the question is: will it come about and when? To this question the answer must be pessimistic in tone since, invariably, tort reform holds out no prospect of votes for busy politicians; and, if it does—as problems with environmental connotations do—it is likely to run into considerable difficulties with vested interests and the currently prevailing philosophy which is ideologically opposed to government regulation and intervention. Such intervention as we may get is thus likely to be sporadic and limited to high-visibility cases; and its patchy nature will, inevitably, also reveal unprincipled differences and verbal ambiguities that run the risk of creating more litigation. Sooner

138 Acknowledging a similar trend with regard to the influence of negligence upon the tort of nuisance: discussed in ch. 13, above.

139 Its main thrust was for a statutory scheme which would impose strict liability on the 'controllers of things or operations . . . which by their unusually hazardous nature require close, careful and skilled supervision', or on controllers of things or operations 'which, although normally by their nature perfectly safe, are likely, if they go wrong, to cause serious and extensive casualties': Cmnd. 7054–I (1978), §1643.

140 *Cambridge Water* [1994] 2 AC 264, 305, [1994] 2 WLR 53, 80. For materials on the German Strict Liability Act 1978 (the '*Haftpflichtgesetz*'), see B. S. Markesinis & H. Unberath, *The German Law of Torts: A Comparative Treatise* (4th edn., 2002), 853–6 (for the text of the Act) and 859–61 (for discussion and references).

or later, our law is also likely to come into conflict with international treaties that are increasingly regulating matters that affect the environment and consumer expectations. One might expect some pressure from the European Convention for the Protection of Human Rights and Fundamental Freedoms, particularly since the entry into force of the Human Rights Act 1998: certainly, although nascent, the potential impact of Article 8 ECHR has begun to be raised regularly in cases in this area, as evinced by the comments of Neuberger J in the *McKenna* case.[141] In the more specific field of environmental protection and liability, the European Community has been particularly active over the years in establishing procedural protection on matters such as environmental impact assessment,[142] and EC legislation is now in place requiring Member States to establish a regime on environmental liability with regard to the prevention and remedying of 'environmental damage'.[143] This regime requires the establishment of competent national authorities to recover such environmental damage from the relevant operators, and thus relies upon state enforcement to secure respect for the principle that 'the polluter pays'. While those EC rules expressly do not confer any right upon private individuals to sue for compensation for environmental damage covered by the Directive,[144] the Directive also expressly applies without prejudice to 'relevant national legislation'[145] or to civil liability regimes for 'traditional damage' under any international agreement.[146] Once again, we may thus be faced with the task of importing 'foreign' regimes instead of being able to show that our indigenous ones are just as good as or better than the foreign models. For modern claimants, the recent decisions of the House of Lords thus hold out little hope. It thus seems likely that it will be from the European scene that the next boost to their rights will have to come; and faint traces of this prospect can even be found in the *Cambridge Water* case itself. That said, the recent explosion at the Buncefield Oil depot in Hertfordshire[147] may yet lead to litigation in the English courts in which the rule in *Rylands* v. *Fletcher* will once again be placed under the microscope. We have yet to hear the last word on the subject of this much-debated tort.

141 [2002] Env. LR 30, [39] and [46] ff.

142 Directive 85/337/EEC [1985] *OJ* L175/40, as amended by Directive 97/11/EC [1997] *OJ* L73/5.

143 Directive 2004/35/EC [2004] *OJ* L143/56, which is required to have been implemented by Member States by 30 April 2007.

144 *Ibid*., Art. 3(3).

145 *Ibid*., which (in spite of the unfortunate phrasing) presumably would also cover pre-existing common-law rights such as those under *Rylands* v. *Fletcher*.

146 Directive 2004/35/EC [2004] *OJ* L143/56, rec. 11.

147 Which occurred early in the morning of Sunday 11 December 2005, causing 40 injuries and a huge fire which burned for a number of days (see, e.g., the various reports from 12 December 2005 in *The Times* and the *Guardian* (for the latter's ongoing coverage of the damage, investigation, environmental aspects, etc, see: http://www.guardian.co.uk/buncefield)). The Health and Safety Commission has set up an independent investigation into the incident: see http://www.buncefieldinvestigation.gov.uk/index.htm for details.

SELECT BIBLIOGRAPHY

BOHLEN, F. H., 'The Rule in *Rylands* v. *Fletcher*' (1911) 59 *U Pa. LR* 423 (repr. in *Studies in the Law of Torts* (1926), ch. 7).

FRIDMAN, G. H. L., 'The Rise and Fall of *Rylands* v. *Fletcher*' (1956) 34 *Can. BR* 810.

GREEN, L., 'Tort Law: Public Law in Disguise' (1959) 38 *Tex. LR* 257.

HEUSTON, R. F. V., 'Judges and Judgments' (1986) 20 *UBCLR* 33.

LAW COMMISSION, *Civil Liability for Dangerous Things and Activities*, Report No. 32 (1970).

LINDEN, A. M., 'Whatever Happened to *Rylands* v. *Fletcher*', in Klaz, L. (ed.), *Studies in Canadian Tort Law* (1977), 325 ff.

MOLLOY, R. T., '*Rylands* v. *Fletcher*: A Re-Examination of Juristic Origins' (1942) 9 *U Chi. LR* 266.

MORRIS, C., 'Hazardous Enterprises and Risk Bearing Capacity' (1952) 61 *Yale LJ* 1172.

MURPHY, J., 'The Merits of *Rylands* v *Fletcher*' (2004) 24 *OJLS* 643.

NEWARK, F. H., 'Non-Natural User and *Rylands* v. *Fletcher*' (1961) 24 *MLR* 557.

NOLAN, D., 'The Distinctiveness of *Rylands* v. *Fletcher*' (2005) 121 *LQR* 421.

POUND, R., 'The Economic Interpretation and the Law of Torts' (1940) 53 *Harv. LR* 365.

PROSSER, W. L., 'The Principle of *Rylands* v. *Fletcher*', in Prosser, W. L., *Selected Topics on the Law of Torts* (1953), ch. 3.

SIMPSON, A. W. B., 'Legal Liability for Bursting Reservoirs: The Historical Context of *Rylands* v. *Fletcher*' (1984) 13 *Jo. LS* 209, reprinted (in a slightly different form) in Simpson, A. W. B., *Leading Cases in the Common Law* (1995), ch. 8.

STALLYBRASS, W. T. S., 'Dangerous Things and the Non-Natural User of Land' [1929] *CLJ* 376.

WIGMORE, J. H., *Selected Essays in the Law of Torts* (1924), 78 ff.

WILLIAMS, D. W., 'Non-Natural Use of Land' [1973] *CLJ* 310.

17

LIABILITY FOR ANIMALS

1. APPLICATION OF THE GENERAL LAW

Damage by animals is a familiar mischief in agricultural communities and, not surprisingly, it attracted the attention of the law from very early times. Even today a large number of injuries (in the late 1970s the Pearson Committee Report estimated 50,000 a year), together with a very small number of deaths, are attributable to animals, mainly dogs or horses.[1] These figures, however, paint a somewhat distorted picture of the importance of this part of law. Since the 1971 Animals Act, the wording of which has been judicially described as 'cumbersome', 'inept' and 'difficult to construe',[2] a relatively small number of cases[3] has been decided under it, a fact which seems to indicate that in the numerically frequent, but relatively trivial, cases no litigation follows, while the more serious injuries tend to be litigated, if at all, under the rules of negligence.[4]

Although the subject has reduced significance today, at any rate when compared with the tort of negligence, this was not always the case. The richness of the common law,[5] which is still sometimes relevant for the understanding of the modern law, testifies to the venerable ancestry of the subject. For characteristic of primitive systems is the tendency to identify the owner with his animals, and even inanimate property,[6] and to hold him liable irrespective of fault. This has now changed, but it explains why strict liability has remained acceptable in this field of law. One could argue, of course, that with the growth of the law of negligence since the middle of last century, the old rules of strict liability could have been abandoned. However, this did not happen since

[1] In the late 1970s, there were about six million dogs and half-a-million horses in the UK: Cmnd. 7054–1 (1978), para. 1597. Very few injuries appear to be caused by wild animals.

[2] Sections 2(2)(a) and (b) have given rise to particular problems. Thus, see: *Smith* v. *Ainger*, *The Times*, 5 June 1990, *Curtis* v. *Betts* [1990] 1 All ER 769, *Jaundrill* v. *Gillett*, *The Times*, 30 Jan. 1996.

[3] Of which the most important are probably *Cummings* v. *Granger* [1977] QB 397 and *Mirvahedy* v. *Henley* [2003] 2 AC 491, [2003] 2 WLR 882; although it should be noted that the frequency of reliance upon the Act in cases that are actually litigated to judgment seems to be on the increase in recent years.

[4] In some cases (e.g. Dangerous Wild Animals Act 1976, Riding Establishments Acts 1964 and 1970) there are provisions for compulsory insurance against liability for damage caused, and here the compensation of victims tends to come through insurance companies, not the courts. There has been some doubt whether these Acts are meant to provide unlimited insurance cover: see Cmnd. 7054–1 (1978), paras. 1627, 1628.

[5] On which see the magisterial and still highly instructive volume, *Liability for Animals* by G.L. Williams (Select Bibliography).

[6] See *R* v. *The Eastern Counties Ry. Co.* (1842) 10 M & W 58; 152 ER 380.

modern views of policy came to their aid. For, notwithstanding the usefulness of animals, their ability for independent locomotion, coupled with their propensity for causing harm, justifies the imposition upon the owner of a duty to protect the public, at least against the typical risks involved in keeping animals for his own benefit. Cattle trespass and liability for dangerous animals is thus but an instance, indeed historically the earliest, of wider principles of strict liability.

Though every legal system has developed special rules of liability for animals, this has nowhere resulted in the exclusion of the ordinary law. A host of ordinary torts, therefore, can be committed through animals. If I choose to teach my parrot to utter defamatory words and it does so in the presence of a third person, I shall be responsible for the defamation as if I had spoken it myself. More realistically, if I drive livestock on the highway and cause an obstruction, I am liable in public nuisance.[7] In *Pitcher* v. *Martin*[8] the defendant, who was walking with a dog on a long lead, carelessly let it escape from control. The lead became entangled with the plaintiff's legs and tripped her up. It was held that a dog with a long lead loose upon the road was a nuisance, and the plaintiff also succeeded in negligence. Again, anyone who incites an animal to attack will be liable in assault and battery as if he himself had assaulted the claimant. And in *League against Cruel Sports* v. *Scott*[9] the court took the view that a master of hounds would be held liable in trespass if he knew that there was a real danger of his hounds entering prohibited land, provided he intended this to happen or negligently failed to prevent it. In the instant case, such an intention could be inferred from the fact that in the circumstances it was effectively impossible to prevent entry by the hounds. Thus, in all these cases the ordinary tort rules may apply concurrently with the provisions of the 1971 Act.

With regard to liability in negligence, the special rules concerning liability for animals in no way affect the ordinary duty to take care,[10] not only when doing something with an animal, but also by allowing it to be in such a place as to give rise to a foreseeable risk. Thus, in *Draper* v. *Hodder*[11] the infant plaintiff was savaged by a pack of Jack Russell terrier puppies that suddenly dashed from the defendant's premises next door. The dogs had not previously misbehaved apart from frequently raiding the adjoining premises in scavenging expeditions. It was impossible to prove knowledge of a dangerous propensity in any of the animals, not only because none of them had done such a thing before, but also because it was impossible to show which dog or dogs actually took part in the attack. The strict liability claim for damage inflicted by dangerous animals, which will be dealt with shortly, was therefore rejected. However, the owner was held responsible in negligence for allowing the dogs to escape. As an

[7] *Cunningham* v. *Whelan* (1917) 521 LT 67. In *Leeman* v. *Montagu* [1936] 2 All ER 1677, the noise made by cockerels from about two o'clock every morning was held to be a private nuisance.

[8] [1937] 3 All ER 918.

[9] [1985] 2 All ER 489.

[10] *Fardon* v. *Harcourt-Rivington* (1932) 146 LTR 391, 392, per Lord Atkin. In *Smith* v. *Prendergast, The Times*, 18 Oct. 1984, the Court of Appeal held the defendant liable for negligently failing to discover the vicious propensities of an Alsatian which he had decided to keep as a guard dog when it strayed on to his land a mere three weeks before it attacked the plaintiff.

[11] [1972] 2 QB 556.

experienced dog-breeder, he should have known the propensity of Jack Russells, when in a pack, to attack moving persons or objects; and though aware of their habit to dash next door, he had neither kept them in a compound nor maintained a fence. Once some kind of damage was foreseeable, then according to the ordinary rules of negligence neither its extent nor precise method of infliction needed to be foreseeable.[12] In the present case it was enough that some kind of injury to the toddler next door was foreseeable, for example, by being bowled over and scratched rather than being bitten all over his body.

There was, however, one example of a common law refusal to extend to animals the principles of negligence: an owner or occupier used to owe no duty to users of the highway to prevent livestock from straying from his land *on to* the highway and causing damage to its users. This rule, which originated before the great enclosure movement of two centuries ago and before the advent of fast-moving vehicles, may have been reasonable in those times, because in view of the prevailing traffic conditions it was deemed not to be unreasonable to let livestock stray upon the road. However, this gradually hardened into an arbitrary rule and was reaffirmed in 1946 by the House of Lords in *Searle* v. *Wallbank*.[13] This decision meant that, irrespective of the type of road and the volume of traffic on it, adjoining landowners could not be liable to injured users of the highway; it amounted to a kind of subsidy to farmers at the expense of road-users.

This immunity has now happily been abolished by section 8(1) of the Animals Act 1971 (the only section of the Act which, according to Lord Hailsham, was really worth enacting).[14] So now, when damage is caused by animals straying on the highway, liability will be decided in accordance with the ordinary rules of negligence.[15] Section 8(2), however, goes on to provide that:

> where damage is caused by animals straying from unfenced land to a highway a person who placed them on the land shall not be regarded as having committed a breach of the duty to take care by reason only of placing them there if: *(a)* the land is common land, or is land situated in an area where fencing is not customary, or is a town or a village green; and *(b)* he had a right to place the animals on that land.

The Act thus does not require landowners to fence in against the highway. In *Davies* v. *Davies*[16] it was held that the defendant, who had a licence to graze sheep on a certain piece of land, could avail himself of this defence and thus avoid liability to the owner of a car who collided with some of his animals on the highway. However, in the recent case of *Wilson* v. *Donaldson*,[17] the Court of Appeal upheld the trial judge's conclusion that

[12] Above, ch. 4.

[13] [1947] AC 341.

[14] HL Debs, vol. 312, cols. 887–8 (12 Nov. 1970).

[15] If the defendant's negligence enabled third parties to release horses from his field on to the highway and while there cause danger on the highway, the defendant may be liable to the injured user of the highway. See: *Jaundrick* v. *Gillett*, *The Times*, 30 Jan. 1996.

[16] [1975] QB 172; but cf. *Rees* v. *Morgan* [1976] CL para. 245: cow straying on the highway.

[17] [2004] EWCA Civ. 972, (2004) 148 SJLB 879. See also *Hole* v. *Ross-Skinner* [2003] EWCA Civ. 774, in which the Court of Appeal overturned the trial judge's findings on both breach of duty and causation to hold the defendant not liable where the escape of horses from the defendant's stud farm was due to the actions of unknown trespassers who had cut the fence and left the gate open.

negligence had been shown where cows had strayed on to the road by walking from the defendant's field, across an intervening field owned by another farm and along an unfenced track on to the road. It was critical in this case that the defendant farmer was well aware that a heavily used public footpath used the gate between his land and that of the neighbouring farm, and knew that the neighbouring farm was dilapidated and unoccupied, with no fencing to prevent access to the road. The judge found, and the Court of Appeal agreed, that there was a foreseeable risk that a careless walker might leave open the defendant's gate, thus allowing the cattle to reach the road, and the defendant's failure to take greater precautions to prevent this eventuality (in spite of the evidence that there had been no instance of livestock straying on to the road in the thirty-six years that the defendant had been farming there) led to his liability in negligence.

We move next to the special rules of strict liability under the Act which we shall examine under three headings: liability for straying livestock, liability for 'dangerous animals', and liability for dogs.

2. LIABILITY FOR STRAYING LIVESTOCK

This is one of the oldest forms of strict liability and the most important progenitor of the *Rylands* v. *Fletcher*[18] rule. It is now regulated by section 4 of the 1971 Act. 'Livestock' is defined in section 11 to include cattle, horses, asses, mules, hinnies, sheep, pigs, goats and poultry, as well as deer not in a wild state. Dogs and cats, however, were never included under this heading and remain excluded from this part of the Act, probably on the ground that it is impossible to control them to the same degree as one can control cattle, but also because their propensity for causing damage during transient intrusions is negligible.

According to section 4(1), the livestock must 'stray' (a word that still awaits authoritative definition) 'on to land' in the ownership or occupation of another and, under the common law, which still remains valid, this includes even the 'slightest degree of entry', such as reaching over a fence or putting a hoof through a hedge.[19] The fact that entry could have been prevented if the claimant had fenced his own land and so stopped animals from straying in will not be a defence, for in general there is no duty to fence out. But if a duty to fence out livestock is indeed imposed upon the claimant occupier,[20] by way of contract or easement or ancient custom,[21] but is ignored and, as a result, animals stray on to his land, he will not be allowed to complain (s. 5(6) of the 1971 Act). As already noted, this strict rule of liability cannot be invoked by travellers on the

[18] (1868) LR 3 HL 330, on which see ch. 16, above.

[19] *Ellis* v. *The Loftus Iron Co.* (1874) LR 10 CP 10.

[20] But the duty need not be owed to the defendant whose livestock strays on to the claimant occupier's land; it may, for instance, be owed by the claimant occupier to his landlord (e.g. a duty to maintain the fences of the leased land). At common law, the defendant could not take advantage of such breach, since no duty to fence was owed to him. The wording of the 1971 Act now suggests a different solution, with the result that the defendant may be absolved. On this see P. M. North, *The Modern Law of Animals* (Select Bibliography), 136 ff.

[21] As was the case in *Egerton* v. *Harding* [1975] QB 62.

highway who are injured by livestock straying *from adjoining land* on to the highway; liability here is based in negligence.

It is still not entirely clear whether the liability is strict or is based on negligence when livestock escapes from land on to the highway and thence on to adjacent property. An Australian court has favoured strict liability,[22] whereas our Court of Appeal touched upon (but, it is submitted, did not entirely solve) this problem not that long ago in its decision in *Matthews* v. *Wicks*.[23] In that case the plaintiff's sheep, while lawfully grazing on common land, strayed on to the highway where they were left to wander freely before moving on to the defendant's land, causing damage to his plants. The defendant, relying on section 7 of the 1971 Act, retained the sheep until proper compensation was paid to him.[24] The plaintiff, regarding the defendant's request for monetary compensation as exorbitant, began proceedings for the return of the sheep. The defendant counter-claimed damages, relying on section 4 of the 1971 Act. To this point the plaintiff's answer was section 5(5) of the 1971 Act, which excludes liability under section 4 whenever the livestock strays from a highway 'and its presence there was a lawful use of the highway'. In the opinion of the Court of Appeal the presence of the sheep on the highway was not, in those circumstances, lawful so the defence of section 5(5) was not available to the plaintiff's case.

It *appears* that English law has, in effect, now opted for the view taken by the Australian court. For, since the defendant has based his counter-claim on section 4 and the plaintiff had lost his argument on section 5(5), it could be said that an action under section 4 can be maintained in cases where animals stray from land on to the highway and from there on to someone else's land. But the only published report of this case does not suggest that the court was asked to decide this wider question, but only to consider the availability in such circumstances of the defence of section 5(5). If that is so, then the main point remains undecided; and one hopes that if the point ever arises again, strict liability under section 4 will not be available for this type of cattle trespass. For if it is, it will result in 'the anomaly that the travelling public must accept the risk of such strays[25] while abutting landowners need not; and that an owner of stock trespassing from the highway is liable only for negligence if he put them on the road, yet strictly liable if they strayed thither to start with. None of this makes a great deal of sense.'[26]

The defence of section 5(5), mentioned in the preceding paragraphs, is justified by the belief that the escapes it refers to (i.e. of animals lawfully on the highway) should be treated as normal hazards incident to the use of the highway and should be repressible only on proof of negligence. It thus only codifies the common law rule exemplified by

22 *D'Agruima* v. *Seymour* (1951) 69 WN (NSW) 15.

23 *The Times*, 25 May 1987.

24 The old remedy, known as distress damage feasant, is now limited to cases where the detention of the trespassing chattel is needed to secure compensation for damage actually caused. Thus, according to the majority of the Court of Appeal in *Arthur* v. *Anker* [1996] 2 WLR 602, wheel-clamping of cars unlawfully parked on private property cannot normally be justified by recourse to this defence. The restriction of the ambit of the medieval remedy seems in keeping with the tendency of modern courts to look with disfavour upon most forms of self-redress.

25 For in such cases it is for the injured claimant to prove negligence under s. 8(1) of the Act.

26 J. G. Fleming, *The Law of Torts* (9th edn., 1998), 397.

Tillet v. *Ward*,[27] which defeated the claim of an ironmonger into whose shop an ox strayed from the highway, causing a fair amount of damage before getting out again.

Originally, cattle trespass supported only claims for damage to the surface of the land and depasturing of crops. The range of protection gradually widened to include injury to the plaintiff's livestock through the spread of disease carried by strays[28] and misbreeding resulting from a trespassing 'scrub' bull serving a thoroughbred heifer.[29] Even bodily injury was included at common law.[30] Section 4(1)(a) abolishes this last extension (i.e. bodily injury), so the kind of damage recoverable under the section is limited to damage to land or property on it. This restriction is welcome, since it is consonant with the nature of the action to confine redress to those consequences which are typical of the tasks involved in trespass, rather than to extend its range to situations which are adequately covered by the rules of negligence or liability for dangerous animals.[31]

The defences available to a defendant are the following:

(i) under section 5(1) he will not be liable if the damage is due wholly to the fault of the person suffering it; lack of adequate fencing, however, may be evidence of fault in the claimant but will not, in the absence of a duty to fence, amount to fault in itself (s. 5(6));

(ii) contributory negligence (s. 10, applying the Law Reform (Contributory Negligence) Act 1945);

(iii) under section 5(5) there will be no liability for livestock straying from a highway so long as its presence on the highway was lawful—a point already noted when *Matthews* v. *Wicks*[32] was discussed above;

(iv) finally, on the analogy of *Rylands* v. *Fletcher*, it could be argued that the defendant is not responsible for the act of a stranger (e.g. leaving a gate open).[33] But the authority, such as it is, is not convincing; given the wording of sections 4(1) (liability arises 'except as otherwise provided by *this Act*') and 5 of the Act, the better view would be not to recognise this defence.

3. LIABILITY FOR 'DANGEROUS ANIMALS'

The common law distinguished between animals *ferae naturae* (wild by nature) and animals *mansuetae naturae* (tame animals), but the distinction is more appropriate to describe who owns the animal than who should be made liable for the damage it causes,

[27] (1882) 10 QBD 17. A person who has animals on the highway will be liable in negligence if they stray off it due to his carelessness: *Gaylor* v. *Davies* [1924] 2 KB 75.

[28] *Theyer* v. *Purnell* [1918] 2 KB 333. [29] *McLean* v. *Brett* (1919) 49 DLR 162.

[30] *Wormald* v. *Cole* [1954] 1 QB 614.

[31] The wider definition of damage contained in s. 11 should, for present purposes, thus be ignored.

[32] *The Times*, 25 May 1987.

[33] *M'Gibbon* v. *M'Curry* (1909) 43 ILT 132. Compare the position reached by the Court of Appeal in the general law of negligence in the two recent cases of *Wilson* v. *Donaldson* [2004] EWCA Civ. 972 and *Hole* v. *Ross-Skinner* [2003] EWCA Civ. 774, discussed in Section 1 of this chapter, above.

so it might be preferable to distinguish between 'dangerous' and 'harmless' animals. Rabbits and pigeons, for example, are classed as 'wild', but they are not dangerous. Though the Act adopts the latter distinction, it does not introduce in practice any *significant* deviation from the old common law. The older cases are thus still relevant, though in the last resort it is the wording of the Act that must prevail.[34]

Liability for dangerous species is governed by section 2(1) of the Act, is imposed upon the 'keeper' of the animal[35] and is strict. According to section 6(1), a dangerous species is a species which is *(a)* not commonly domesticated in the British Isles *and* *(b)* whose fully grown animals normally have such characteristics that they are likely, unless restrained, to cause damage, or that any damage they may cause is likely to be severe.

The use of the words 'not commonly domesticated' in Britain makes it clear that dangerous species include not only animals such as bears, tigers and lions, which are not indigenous, but also animals such as foxes, which can be found in the British Isles but not in captivity and mostly in a wild state. The definition of dangerous animals, it will be noted, can be wider than the old common law definition of animals *ferae naturae*. For camels, though clearly not *ferae naturae*,[36] will be regarded as dangerous and the fact that they are domesticated elsewhere in the world (e.g. in Arabia) will not affect the question in English law.[37] Second, according to section 11, no distinction is made between sub-species or individual animals within a species. In *Behrens* v. *Bertram Mills Circus Ltd.* [38] it was held that since an Indian elephant belongs to a species which is *ferae naturae* (dangerous), it was of no avail to the defendant to show that the particular elephant was docile. Finally, it should be noted that whether or not an animal is dangerous is a matter of law. In most cases the common law characterisation will be followed. In some instances there is now also statutory guidance: for example, animals included in the Schedule to the Dangerous Wild Animals Act 1976[39] will almost certainly be regarded as dangerous for the purposes of the 1971 Act.[40] Omission from the Schedule to the 1976 Act, however, is not conclusive.

It is not enough that an animal is not domesticated in this country; there must *also* be a likelihood of severe injury or damage, either because of the mischievous or dangerous nature of the particular species or because any injury or damage which this species is likely to cause will be severe. In other words, the characterisation of 'dangerous' turns either on the 'great risk of harm' or 'the risk of great harm'. An elephant, for

[34] Though the Act defines 'dangerous' and 'non-dangerous' animals, nowhere does it define 'animals'. The term should undoubtedly be taken to include birds and reptiles. Insects should also be included, but not, it is submitted, bacteria. See North (Select Bibliography), 22.

[35] Section 6(3) Animals Act 1971: this includes ownership or possession of the animal, or being the head of a household in which a person under 16 years of age holds such ownership or possession of the animal.

[36] *McQuaker* v. *Goddard* [1940] 1 KB 697.

[37] *Tutin* v. *Mary Chipperfield Promotions Ltd.* (1980) 130 *NLJ* 807.

[38] [1957] 2 QB 1.

[39] An interesting feature of this enactment is that it lays down the rule that a licence to possess an animal to which that Act applies will be granted only on condition that the licensee is insured against liability for any damage caused by the animal in question. The quantum of the available insurance, however, has not been defined.

[40] *Quaere* whether 'vipers and adders' listed in the Schedule are 'not commonly domesticated'? (See HL Debs., vol. 305, col. 1433 (27 Nov. 1969), Lord Wilberforce.)

example, is not particularly likely to cause harm, but if it does, the harm is likely to be great. In the main, the test appears to require special danger to mankind to be shown. But the wording of section 6(2) is neutral and, therefore, despite the customary emphasis upon the risk of personal injury, there is no reason to believe that liability under section 2 would not extend to property damage.

4. LIABILITY FOR NON-DANGEROUS ANIMALS

Liability for non-dangerous animals is regulated by section 2(2). It provides that liability will be incurred provided that the claimant can show that *each* of these three requirements is satisfied in turn:

1. the damage is of a kind which either
   (*a*) 'the [particular] animal, unless restrained, was *likely*[41] to cause'; *or*
   (*b*) 'if caused by [that] animal, was likely to be severe';[42] *and*
2. the likelihood[43] of the damage or its severity was because the particular animal had characteristics which are either
   (*a*) not normally found in members of its species;[44] *or*
   (*b*) not normally so found except at particular times, or in particular circumstances (for example, the vicious disposition of cats which have just given birth);[45] *and*
3. these characteristics were known to the 'keeper', *or*
   (*a*) to a person under 16, who has the animal and is a member of the keeper's household; *or*
   (*b*) to anyone employed by the keeper who is in charge of the animal.

[41] In *Smith* v. *Ainger*, *The Times*, 5 June 1990, the Court of Appeal suggested that this word should not, necessarily, be taken to refer to 'high probability' of the harmful event happening; it was sufficient that 'there [was] a material risk that it [would] happen'.

[42] Notice that the likelihood of damage being caused or of its being severe refers to the tendency of this particular animal in s. 2(2) and not 'fully grown' examples of the species generally, as in s. 2(1).

[43] Which seems to cover events 'reasonably to be expected' and not to require as much as that they be 'more likely than not' to occur: per Lord Scott in *Mirvahedy* v. *Henley* [2003] 2 AC 491, at [95].

[44] E.g. a dog which attacks people carrying handbags: *Kite* v. *Napp*, *The Times*, 1 June 1982. The recent case of *Gloster* v. *Chief Constable of Greater Manchester Police* [2000] PIQR P114 raised the issue of whether a dog which has been *trained* to bite in 'limited and defined circumstances' falls under the heading of having characteristics not normally found in members of its species. Pill LJ took the view that it was a German shepherd dog's ability to respond to training which was the relevant characteristic, rather than the propensity to bite—he thus found the case to fall outside s. 2(2)(b). It seems that Hale LJ would have held this dog to be included within s. 2(2)(b), since its training was what did make it act differently from other dogs, including German shepherd dogs which had not been trained; however, she decided the case on the basis that (on the facts) the dog in question was not likely to have caused that damage if unrestrained, so that the case did not meet the requirements of s. 2(2)(a).

[45] See the examples given by the Court of Appeal in *Cummings* v. *Grainger* [1977] QB 397, per Ormrod LJ: it was held that an Alsatian dog which barked and ran around guarding its territory and then bit the plaintiff was exhibiting characteristics not normally found except in particular circumstances such as this, and was therefore within s. 2(2). See, also, *Jaundrill* v. *Gillett*, *The Times*, 30 Jan. 1996: horses released from the defendant's land through the intervention of third parties and bolting towards the plaintiff's oncoming car in the dark could not be brought under s. 2(2)(b). Additionally, the harm in that case was held to have been caused by the release of the horses on to the highway and not their alleged abnormal characteristics.

From reading this section, one thing seems reasonably clear: in cases of a non-dangerous animal, the keeper will not be held strictly liable unless he was actually aware of its dangerous characteristics.[46] Beyond that, much uncertainty exists and several judges have condemned the phrasing of the Act as either 'cumbrously worded'[47] or 'inept'.[48] Most recently, Lord Nicholls has described 'the language of section 2(2) [as] . . . opaque. In this instance the parliamentary draftsman's zeal for brevity has led to obscurity.'[49]

The difficulties caused by the wording of this section became obvious in *Curtis* v. *Betts*[50] when a bull mastiff (usually lazy and docile) attacked the young plaintiff (who had been friendly with him all his life) while the latter went up to talk to the dog as it was being loaded into the rear of a Land Rover in order to be taken for a walk. The Court of Appeal took the view that section 2(2)(a) was satisfied since the harm caused by the mastiff was 'likely to be severe'. The court further held that the opening words of section 2(2)(b) ('the likelihood of the damage or of its being severe') were awkward and, probably, included by mistake. In the view of the court the words 'the damage' should replace the existing, inept phrase and, if this were done, it would be clear that this subsection merely required that a causal link be established between the characteristic of the animal and the damage.[51] In the instant case the crucial characteristic was the animal's known tendency to act in a menacing and aggressive manner when protecting its territory (which, here, included the rear of the Land Rover). The keepers of the dog were thus held liable.

However, this conclusion raises a point of common difficulty with section 2(2)(b): in deciding in this way in *Curtis* v. *Betts*, the Court of Appeal effectively ruled that there could be liability for a characteristic of an animal which was *normal in the circumstances in question* (even if not in the usual course of events). Pill LJ took the view in the *Gloster* case[52] that 'the section is not concerned with animals behaving in a perfectly normal way for animals of the species or subspecies'. In that same case, however, Hale LJ did not agree and, in the more recent case of *Mirvahedy* v. *Henley*, after an analysis of the parliamentary debates, she ruled that such behaviour *was* specifically intended to be covered by the 1971 Act.[53] The House of Lords rejected the appeal from the judgment

46 *Wallace* v. *Newton* [1982] 1 WLR 375 at 381. Park J held that s. 2(2)(b) of the 1971 Act did not require the plaintiff to prove that the animal was vicious. The words were to be given their ordinary natural meaning so that the animal had particular characteristics not normally found in animals of the same species. Park J held that a horse called 'Lord Justice', which was unpredictable and unreliable in its behaviour, fell within s. 2(2) when it injured the plaintiff's arm when being loaded into a horsebox.

47 *Cummings* v. *Granger* [1977] QB 397, 404, per Lord Denning MR.

48 *Curtis* v. *Betts* [1990] 1 WLR 459, 468, per Nourse LJ.

49 *Mirvahedy* v. *Henley* [2003] 2 AC 491, [2003] 2 WLR 882, at [9]; although note that Lord Hobhouse was far less critical of the drafting of the wording in section 2(2)(b): at [65] and [69].

50 [1990] 1 All ER 769.

51 In *Gloster* v. *Chief Constable of Greater Manchester Police* [2000] PIQR P114, Hale LJ clearly took the view (at P121) that these comments in *Curtis* v. *Betts* were *obiter* and did not seem convinced of the validity of this approach, although no decision on the point was necessary to dispose of the *Gloster* case.

52 *Gloster* v. *Chief Constable of Greater Manchester Police* [2000] PIQR P114, P117–118, relying upon the judgment of Lloyd LJ in the Court of Appeal in the unreported case of *Breeden* v. *Lampard* (21 Mar. 1985).

53 [2002] QB 769, at [22] ff. This view of s. 2(2)(b) was also supported by North (Select Bibliography), 51: it seems that the intention was to include such situations in a change from the pre-existing position at common law.

of the Court of Appeal,[54] albeit only after a total addition of 163 further judicial paragraphs to the debate on the appropriate interpretation of section 2(2) of the Act, and only by a 3:2 majority.

A number of points of interest and importance arise from the judgments of their Lordships in *Mirvahedy*. The case involved a claim for damages for injuries suffered by the claimant in a collision on the dual carriageway stretch of a road (the A380 in Devon) between the claimant's car and a horse owned by the defendants. The horse was one of three of the defendants' horses that had taken fright on the night in question and had stampeded out of their field, pushing over an electric fence and the surrounding wooden fence, and forcing their way through tall bracken and other vegetation before fleeing along a track and then approximately a mile on to the A380, where the collision took place. The first point of note is that it was conceded that section 2(2)(a) was satisfied on the facts: the damage was of a kind that escaping horses were likely to cause or it was likely to be severe. Yet Lord Scott raised understandable doubts about this concession: he suggested that 'a horse loose on the highway does not usually result in damage to third parties, that if damage to third parties does result the damage is not usually severe, no more, perhaps, than a dent to a car, and that the cases in which serious injury or damage results are fortunately few and far between'.[55] Indeed, paying more careful attention to the operation of section 2(2)(a) on the facts of any given case could remove some of the pressure from the controversial question of the proper ambit of section 2(2)(b).[56]

Second, the case provided a forum at the highest judicial level for the expression of the conflicting possible approaches to the vexed question of the meaning of section 2(2)(b) and their respective merits and shortcomings. Lord Nicholls acknowledged that he had found it difficult to decide between the two approaches discussed above, but ultimately came down in favour of the approach in *Cummings* v. *Granger* and *Curtis* v. *Betts*:[57] first, this accorded better with the language of section 2(2)(b) itself; second, adopting the approach that had commended itself in *Breeden* v. *Lampard* and to Pill LJ in the *Gloster* case would amount to a radical departure from the scheme originally proposed by the Law Commission and his Lordship was not convinced that this had been Parliament's intention in the minor changes that had been made to that proposal by the wording of the 1971 Act; third, the *Cummings* v. *Granger* approach did not empty section 2(2)(b) of all content, as:

Some forms of accidental damage are instances where this requirement could operate. Take a large and heavy domestic animal such as a mature cow. There is a real risk that if a cow

[54] [2003] 2 AC 491, [2003] 2 WLR 882. See C. F. Sharp, 'Normal Abnormality? Liability for Straying Horses under the Animals Act 1971: *Mirvahedy* v. *Henley* [2003] UKHL 16' [2003] *JPIL* 172: Mr Sharp QC appeared for the claimant in the case.

[55] [2003] 2 AC 491 at [98] (and see generally his discussion at [95]–[101].

[56] See, e.g., *E (A Child)* v. *Townfoot Stables* [2004] CLY 169 (a child of eight being thrown from a pony while attending a riding school did not suffer damage of a kind which a pony was likely to cause or, if caused, was likely to be severe).

[57] *Ibid.*, [44]–[47].

happens to stumble and fall onto someone, any damage suffered will be severe. This would satisfy [section 2(2)(a)]. But a cow's dangerousness in this regard may not fall within [section 2(2)(b)]. This dangerousness is due to a characteristic normally found in all cows at all times. The dangerousness results from their very size and weight. It is not due to a characteristic not normally found in cows 'except at particular times or in particular circumstances'.[58]

In *Mirvahedy* itself, however, the relevant characteristic had been that the horses had been terrified (rather than that they were large and heavy animals) and it had been this that caused the collision on the road. The subsequent judgment of the Court of Appeal in *Clark* v. *Bowlt*[59] has made clear that the relevant characteristic under consideration under section 2(2)(a) (in relation to the kind of damage caused) must then be the basis for consideration under section 2(2)(b). Thus, the fact that the weight of the horse in question meant that if it were to move into the path of a car it would be likely to cause severe damage did satisfy section 2(2)(a), but failed to meet the requirements of section 2(2)(b), because this weight was a normal characteristic of the species in question.[60] Meanwhile, the (different) characteristic that the judge had taken into account for the purposes of section 2(2)(b)—the propensity of a horse to assert an inclination to move otherwise than directed by its rider—did not satisfy the test of section 2(2)(a) because the damage caused was not of a type likely to be occasioned unless the horse had been restrained.[61]

Lord Hobhouse and Lord Walker delivered judgments that concurred with that of Lord Nicholls and based upon essentially the same reasons: as Lord Hobhouse pointed out, '[I]t is true that there is an implicit assumption of fact in s. 2(2) that domesticated animals are not normally dangerous. But the purpose of paragraph (b) is to make provision for those that are.'[62]

However, it is the practical operation of this argument that forms the crux of the dissents of Lord Scott and Lord Slynn: they were both convinced by the force of the argument that

To impose strict liability on the keeper of an ordinary domesticated animal, or of a non-dangerous wild animal held in captivity, for damage done by the animal when responding normally, as any member of its species would respond, to some external stimulus seems...

58 *Ibid.*, [46].

59 [2006] EWCA Civ. 978, (2006) 150 SJLB 886, at [11]–[13] (per Lord Phillips CJ).

60 Although, as D. Howarth has noted, arguably even this point relates only to 'particular times or... circumstances', since the extent of the weight of the animal 'usually appertain[s] only to fully-grown animals' 'The House of Lords and the Animals Act: Closing the Stable Door' [2003] *CLJ* 548, at 550.

61 (2006) 150 SJLB 886, at [14]–[17]. Lord Phillips CJ recorded (at [11]) that 'I am afraid that in this rather difficult area of the law the judge has got into a muddle': one can, it is respectfully submitted, only sympathise with the judge.

62 *Ibid.*, [71]. This ground has been described by Howarth as a 'rather more convincing... reason' for adopting the view taken by the majority, focusing upon the cases where the assumption is false that domestication of an animal means that it is not dangerous. However, as he also pointed out, the requisite knowledge under s. 2(2)(c) relates only to the animal's characteristics, rather than the relevant 'particular times or... circumstances'—this undermines the force of this ground somewhat, and is a further proof of the unfortunate drafting of section 2(2) of the 1971 Act (D. Howarth, 'The House of Lords and the Animals Act: Closing the Stable Door' [2003] *CLJ* 548).

inconsistent with the apparent intention of the Act to draw a distinction between dangerous and non-dangerous animals and inconsistent, in particular, with the apparent purpose of paragraph (b) to limit strict liability for non-dangerous animals to damage attributable to abnormal characteristics.[63]

This is based upon the understanding that Parliament's intention was to leave a general negligence liability regime in place with regard to the keepers of 'non-dangerous' animals, while extending a strict liability regime to 'dangerous' ones.

Finally, it is noteworthy that their Lordships were directed to a number of extracts from Hansard during the passage of the Bill that led to the 1971 Act,[64] and counsel also made extensive reference to the Law Commission's views in its report and draft bill that presaged the Bill that eventually went before Parliament. However, a number of their Lordships explicitly found them not to have been helpful in divining the proper approach to section 2(2),[65] either due to their lack of clarity, to changes wrought to the Law Commission's proposals or due to apparent misunderstandings in some of the statements made by Ministers to Parliament during the passage of the Bill.

The result of the *Mirvahedy* case is to require great care to be taken in the definition of what amounts to 'particular times or . . . circumstances' within section 2(2)(b): if this category were to be construed too broadly then the statutory scheme would absorb many situations where liability might be thought to arise only on the negligence of the keeper. It seems unlikely that this outcome would be one which Parliament had intended when it passed the 1971 Act. Indeed, the absence of any duty under section 2(2)(b) clearly does not preclude the possibility of a duty under the general law of negligence, as discussed above.[66]

The requisite knowledge[67] that the keeper of the animal must have (under section 2(2)(c)) must relate to the particular propensity that caused the damage.[68] Thus, it was held in *Glanville* v. *Sutton*,[69] where a horse bit a man, that it was not sufficient to prove that it was known to have bitten other horses. But it is not necessary to prove that the animal has actually done the particular kind of harm on a previous occasion; it is sufficient if, to the defendant's knowledge, it has manifested a tendency to do that kind of harm.[70] A mere propensity to cause mischief through playfulness or the display of some other non-aggressive characteristic shared by the rest of its species will not be sufficient,

[63] [2003] 2 AC 491, [2003] 2 WLR 882, at [118] (per Lord Scott).

[64] In reliance upon *Pepper* v. *Hart* [1993] AC 593.

[65] See, e.g., [2003] 2 AC 491, [2003] 2 WLR 882, per Lord Slynn at [60], Lord Hobhouse at [65], Lord Scott at [102] and Lord Walker at [158]–[160].

[66] In *Mirvahedy* itself, this argument was also made before the county court judge, but it was not found to be made out and no appeal was pursued against that finding before the appellate courts: see *ibid.*, at [4].

[67] And what is required is 'actual' (rather than constructive) knowledge: see *Chauhan* v. *Paul* [1998] CLY 3990 (CA).

[68] And in the case of characteristics which are only exhibited at particular times or in particular circumstances, the knowledge required of the owner is only that of the characteristic and *not* of the accompanying circumstances (Hale LJ in *Mirvahedy* v. *Henley* [2002] QB 769, at [31]).

[69] [1928] 1 KB 571.

[70] Thus, see *Kite* v. *Napp*, *The Times*, 1 June 1982 (the owner of a dog which had a known propensity to bite people carrying bags was held liable to plaintiff who was carrying a bag when attacked by the dog).

though it may attract a duty to take care in negligence.[71] *Hunt* v. *Wallis* [72] made it clear that, when deciding whether the dog had characteristics not normally found in animals of the same species, comparisons should be made with the same breed and not with dogs in general.

In *Mirvahedy*, Lord Scott's dissenting judgment pointed out certain difficulties with the view of the majority when read in conjunction with the requirements of section 2(2)(c): the danger is that 'a professional keeper of animals will have a more extensive strict liability than an ignorant amateur. . . . I find it quite impossible to understand what legislative policy could be served by allowing a keeper's ignorance of the normal characteristics of the animal in his charge to permit him to escape the strict liability imposed on a responsible keeper who had made himself aware of those characteristics.'[73] This, for him, was a further reason why a more restrictive construction of the strict liability imposed under section 2(2)(b) would have been desirable.

Liability under the Act attaches to the '*keeper*' of the animal, who is defined in section 6(3) as the person who owns the animal, or has it in his or her possession, or who is the head of a household of which a member under the age of 16 owns the animal or has it in his possession. In *Flack* v. *Hudson*[74] a keeper of a horse was thrown from it after the horse had been frightened by farm machinery—the keeper died in the accident. The owner was aware that the horse did have a propensity to take fright in this way, but the keeper was not. Her widower sued the owner of the horse, arguing that the owner was subject to strict liability as owner and keeper of the horse. The Court of Appeal held that there was no restriction on those who could bring an action against the keeper of an animal, so that another keeper could validly do so. As Keene LJ pointed out, 'The owner has his protection in the requirement that knowledge on his part of the dangerous characteristic of the animal must be proved if he is to be liable under section 2(2) and he also has the potential protection in appropriate cases of the section 5 defences.' A person remains the keeper, even if he has lost control over it, until another person becomes its keeper in accordance with the rules given above. But section 6(4) provides that where the animal is taken into and kept in possession for the purpose of preventing it from causing damage or of restoring it to its owner, a person is not a keeper by virtue only of that possession.

Ultimately, in any assessment of the operation of these provisions, one may be forced to agree with the observations of Lord Walker in *Mirvahedy* that the very general terms in which section 2(2) of the 1971 Act is expressed means that it must cover an enormous amount of ground concerning 'the whole range of incidents involving animals of species classified as non-dangerous'.

That range includes (i) physical injury to humans by biting (especially by dogs) or kicking or knocking down (especially by horses); (ii) injuries caused to livestock (such as a dog worrying

[71] *Draper* v. *Hodder* [1972] 2 QB 556.
[72] *The Times*, 10 May 1991, [1994] PIQR P128.
[73] [2003] 2 AC 491, [2003] 2 WLR 882, [119]–[120] (per Lord Scott).
[74] [2001] QB 698.

a neighbour's sheep, or a cat killing a neighbour's chickens); (iii) road traffic accidents, especially those caused by animals straying on the highway; (iv) damage caused by livestock getting out onto neighbouring land and destroying crops or gardens; and (v) injury or damage caused by the spread of animal infection or by the smell or noise of animals (a class which shades off into cases normally classified as nuisance). So section 2(2) has a lot of work to do. It is expressed in general, abstract terms and it has to be applied to a wide range of disparate incidents.[75]

This vast range suggests that any interpretation of section 2(2) is liable to cause difficulties when applied to the great variety of factual situations that may come before any legal adviser or judge. A more nuanced examination of these various circumstances might lead to calls for a more carefully focused design for the scope of strict liability for incidents relating to animals, divided according to the risks attaching to particular animals and/or particular circumstances or locations.[76] Alternatively, a simpler overarching strict liability regime could be established by statutory reform, focusing upon the potential harmful consequences of animals' behaviour, rather than on artificial distinctions relating to (innate) dangerousness.[77] Either way, a more careful focus upon the competing policy arguments at stake will be required in any future reform process.

5. DEFENCES

The defences under section 5(1) and (2), which have been mentioned in connection with straying livestock, apply here too. Thus, assumption of risk is a defence and so is proof that the damage suffered by the claimant was wholly due to his own fault: in a case involving a suspect being chased and sought by the police, it was held that 'a suspect who ignores clear warnings to come out or a dog will be sent to find him has only himself to blame if he suffers injury as a result'.[78] Contributory negligence is also a defence in the sense that it will reduce the claimant's damages.

The defence under section 5(3), however, needs closer attention. This reads:

> A person is not liable under section 2 of this Act for any damage caused by an animal kept on any premises or structure to a person trespassing there, if it is proved either:
> (*a*) that the animal was not kept there for the protection of persons or property; or
> (*b*) (if the animal was kept there for the protection of persons or property) that keeping it there for that purpose was not unreasonable.

75 [2003] 2 AC 491, [2003] 2 WLR 882, at [135].

76 E.g. some form of economic analysis: see, e.g., the brief suggestions of D. Howarth [2003] *CLJ* 548 at 549.

77 E.g., C. Sharp, 'Normal Abnormality? Liability for Straying Horses under the Animals Act 1971: *Miruahedy* v. *Henley* [2003] UKHL 16' [2003] *JPIL* 172, 181, and K. Amirthalingam, 'Animal Liability: Equine, Canine and Asinine' (2003) 119 *LQR* 563, 567.

78 *Dhesi* v. *Chief Constable of the West Midlands Police*, *The Times*, 9 May 2000 (CA), per Stuart-Smith LJ.

Keeping a lion for the purpose of protection would thus certainly be characterised as 'unreasonable', whereas keeping a dog, even a fierce one, may be considered reasonable in the circumstances. Moreover, though section 5(3) may provide a defence to an action under section 2 in strict liability, it does not affect any liability that may be imposed upon the defendant as *occupier* of the premises in accordance with the ordinary rules of negligence.

In *Cummings* v. *Granger*[79] the defendant was the occupier of a breaker's yard, which was locked at night, and his untrained Alsatian dog was turned loose inside it to deter intruders. One night an associate of the defendant, who had the key, unlocked a side gate and entered the gate accompanied by his girlfriend. The dog attacked her and caused serious injuries. In her action under section 2 the main issue was whether the defendant could rely on any of the defences in section 5. The court of first instance and the Court of Appeal thought that the case came under section 2(2), since *(a)* the damage likely to be caused was severe; *(b)* the dog would run around and bark guarding its territory, and this was not characteristic of Alsatians except in circumstances where they are used as guard dogs, which constituted 'particular circumstances' within the meaning of the subsection; and *(c)* these characteristics were known to the defendant. As for possible defences, the Court of Appeal took a different view from that of the High Court. Section 5(1) was inapplicable since the attack was not wholly, but only partly, due to the plaintiff 's fault. Section 5(2), however, could apply, for the plaintiff knew of the risk and had decided to take it.[80]

The Court of Appeal also felt that even the defence under section 5(3) could apply, since keeping a dog as a means of protecting the premises was, in the circumstances, a reasonable way of preserving one's property. In this context mention must now be made of section 1 of the Guard Dogs Act 1975, which provides that a guard dog cannot be allowed to roam about in premises unless it is under the control of its handler.[81] In *Cummings* v. *Granger* the Guard Dogs Act did not apply, since the incident had occurred before this Act came into force. Contravention of the Guard Dogs Act only entails criminal liability to a fine up to £400, but the Act does not confer a right of civil action. It could, however, indirectly affect the civil action because such contravention may show that this was an unreasonable method of protecting persons or property.[82] If this were so, the defence of section 5(3) would disappear in the case of guard dogs, though in the present case the defendant would still have escaped liability under section 5(2) by virtue of the plaintiff 's voluntary acceptance of the risk.

79 [1977] QB 397.

80 On which see *Ilott* v. *Wilkes* (1820) 3 B & Ald. 304, 313; 106 ER 674, 678, per Bayley J.

81 If not it must be chained up: see *Hobson* v. *Gledhill* [1978] 1 All ER 945. The court held that it would depend upon all the circumstances (including the purpose of having a guard dog) whether a twelve-foot chain prevented a dog being at liberty so as to 'go freely about the premises' which the Act prohibits.

82 *Quaere* where the dog is both a pet and a guard dog: e.g. an Alsatian kept by an old lady.

6. REMOTENESS OF DAMAGE AND STRICT LIABILITY

There is nothing in the Act concerning remoteness and the position at common law is not clear. Both the *scienter* as well as the cattle-trespass rule have a strong affinity with *Rylands* v. *Fletcher*,[83] which was expressly excluded from the foreseeability test in *The Wagon Mound (No. 1)*.[84] One might infer, therefore, that directness, not foreseeability, is the test in such cases. Assuming that this is so, does it mean that the keeper's liability extends to all injury resulting from the animal's vicious propensity? We have already noted *Granville* v. *Sutton*[85] and the rule that in the case of non-dangerous animals the keeper will only be liable if an animal causes harm of the kind that is expected from its known vicious characteristics. The owner of a biting dog will not, therefore, be liable for every harm it causes, although he will be liable for such damage that flows from the expected harm. Is the rule the same in the case of dangerous animals and is recovery limited to typical injury? American courts have, on the whole, taken the view that here, too, responsibility should be confined to such consequences as lie within the special risk warranting strict liability. English courts, on the other hand, appear to have adopted the more stringent position that liability is not limited to savage acts but applies equally to all acts. Thus liability was imposed when a scared elephant ran after a barking dog;[86] and according to Devlin J (as he then was) the same would apply where a person suffered a heart attack on seeing an escaped tiger, however amiable, sitting on his bed. *Brook* v. *Cook* [87] offers a contrary example. The plaintiff, aged 61, saw her neighbour's pet monkey, twelve inches high, suddenly jump on to the wall dividing their gardens. She took fright and while rushing indoors slipped and broke her wrist. She claimed that the monkey was an animal *ferae naturae* and that its owner was therefore under a strict duty for any damage suffered through its activity. After deciding that it was an animal *ferae naturae*, Lord Evershed MR held that there was no liability because this was not a case of an injury resulting from an attack of any sort of animal. Unfortunately, the judgment is not fully reported so the wider rule of remoteness probably prevails.[88]

7. LIABILITY FOR DOGS

Section 3 of the Act states that 'where a dog causes damage by killing or injuring livestock,[89] any person who is a keeper of the dog is liable for the damage, except as otherwise provided by this Act'. The defences are assumption of risk, fault of the claimant

[83] (1868) LR 3 HL 330. [84] [1961] AC 388, 426–7.

[85] [1928] 1 KB 571. Except if one takes the view that foreseeability is not necessary for the imposition of liability, but is still the test of remoteness once liability has attached.

[86] *Behrens* v. *Bertram Mills Circus Ltd.* [1957] 2 QB 1. [87] (1961) 105 SJ 684.

[88] There is little convincing authority. In *Eustace* v. *Eyre* [1947] LJNCCR 106, a county court held the owner of a cow which strayed into the plaintiff's field liable for injury to the latter's bull, which broke its leg trying to mate with her.

[89] Which here, by contrast with s. 4, includes pheasants, partridges and grouse, while in captivity.

and contributory negligence; the latter, of course, only reduces the amount of the damages awarded to the claimant. Section 5(4) provides an additional defence, namely that 'a person is not liable under section 3 of this Act if the livestock was killed or injured on land on to which it had strayed and either the dog belonged to the occupier or its presence on the land was authorised by the occupier'.

There is also the provision of section 9 of the Act, which entitles a person to kill a dog if this is necessary to protect his livestock or crops.[90] The defence is available if:

(*a*) . . . the defendant acted for the protection of any livestock and was a person entitled to act for the protection of that livestock; and

(*b*) . . . within forty-eight hours of killing or injury notice thereof was given by the defendant to the officer in charge of a police station.

A person is entitled to act for the protection of livestock if either the livestock, or the land on which it is, belongs to him or to any person under whose express or implied authority he is acting and it is not a case covered by section 5(4) of the 1971 Act. Such authority is deemed to exist whenever the defendant believes or has reasonable ground to believe that the dog is worrying or is about to worry the livestock and there are no other reasonable means of ending or preventing the worrying; or when the dog has been worrying livestock, has not left the vicinity, and is not under the control of any person and there are no means of ascertaining to whom it belongs.

SELECT BIBLIOGRAPHY

North, P. M., *The Modern Law of Animals* (1972).

Williams, G. L., *Liability for Animals* (1939).

90 The common-law rule is crystallised in *Creswell* v. *Sirl* [1948] 1 KB 241.

18

EMPLOYERS' LIABILITY

1. INTRODUCTION

The term 'employment' is ambiguous; a person can be said to be 'employed' either as an employee or as an independent contractor, and the law is very different in the two cases. For a long time it has been customary to use the term 'servant' rather than 'employee', and some judges continue to do so to this day. This use, however, has become incorrect and anachronistic. The term 'servant' denoted, in the nineteenth century, a particular status for workers which was derived from certain statutes, the last of which was repealed in 1875. Then the practice changed and, for a time, statutes used the term 'workman'. The modern expression is 'employee'; and this term will be used here since it signifies that the employment relationship originates in contract and is no longer based principally on forms of status derived from statute.[1]

The liability of an employer to an employee has two aspects. There is his liability to employees for harm *suffered by them*, and his liability for harm *caused by them* in the course of their employment (vicarious liability). Both represent forms of stricter liability. This is true of the first aspect, where an employer owes a 'non-delegable' duty to his employees; and is certainly true of most statutory duties imposed in the interests of safety of employees. It is also true of the second aspect (vicarious liability) in that an innocent employer can in certain instances be made to pay for the torts of his employees.[2] Yet in all these instances (save perhaps in the case of statutory duties which can be truly strict) the term *stricter* (rather than strict) form of liability has been chosen because negligence is not altogether irrelevant. Thus, as previously explained, a non-delegable duty is not strict or absolute, but is a duty to see that care is taken, so that if there is no want of care by anyone the employer is not liable. In the case of vicarious liability one must never forget that a tort of the employee (be it negligence or any other) is the basis of action, so that if the employee is not liable, neither is the employer; and if the employee has a good defence the employer will enjoy the vicarious benefit of it.[3]

[1] See generally S. Deakin, 'The Contract of Employment: A Study in Legal Evolution' (2002) 11 *Historical Studies in Industrial Relations* 1.

[2] We consider vicarious liability in ch. 19, below.

[3] *ICI Ltd.* v. *Shatwell* [1965] AC 656.

2. THE EMPLOYER'S LIABILITY TO HIS EMPLOYEES

According to the Pearson Committee Report in the late 1960s,[4] in the United Kingdom every year some 1,300 people were killed and over 700,000 were injured at work. Since that time, the number of deaths caused by workplace accidents has declined considerably, but injuries are still running at a high level, and the impact of occupational diseases is considerable. Health and Safety Commission figures for 2005–6 indicate that 212 people were killed at work in the United Kingdom, and that there were 328,000 reportable workplace injuries. In the same period, 1,629 people died of mesothelioma, and several thousand more from other occupational cancers and lung diseases.[5]

The practical significance of this subject is therefore considerable. Since it tends to be dealt with by specialised works, here we shall deal with it only in outline. Before we do so, however, we should stress the complexity of the subject. This is largely (but not exclusively) due to the fact that the injured employee's rights to compensation may derive from many sources that are not mutually exclusive. Diagrammatically this can be depicted as in Figure 18.1.

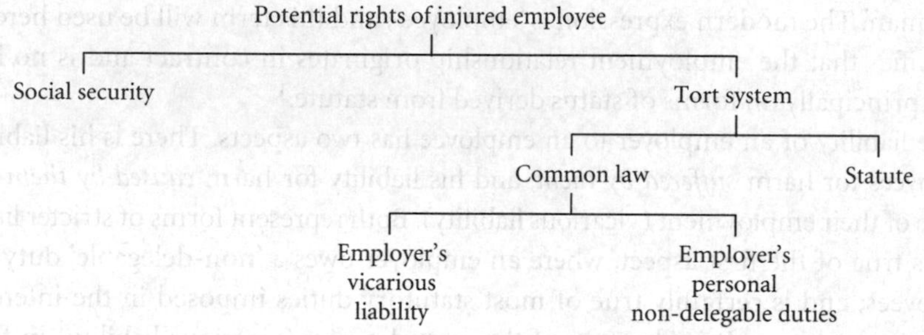

Fig. 18.1 Employee's rights to compensation

(A) SOCIAL SECURITY

Injured workmen have enjoyed limited no-fault benefits since the first Workmen's Compensation Act of 1897. Most of these rights can now be found integrated and, at times, enlarged in the Social Security Contributions and Benefits Act 1992 and the Social Security Administration Act of the same year. These enactments have created a national insurance system that provides benefits for injuries arising out of and in the

[4] Vol. i, para. 958; for further details, see ii, paras. 154 ff.

[5] Health and Safety Commission, *Health and Safety Statistics 2005–6*. The precise number of deaths from all occupational cancers and lung diseases is not known; it is thought to be in a range from 3,000 to 12,000 per year (*ibid.*, at p. 8).

course of insurable employment. Both employers and employees contribute to a common fund and claims are made against the state, not the employer. Since entitlement to payment in no way depends upon proof of fault or breach of duty by the employer, the system substantially favours the victim for obvious reasons. Though persons injured at work fare, on the whole, better than other accident victims (with the possible exception of victims of traffic accidents in those cases in which they succeed), their damages in most cases do not amount to full compensation.[6] As a result, the Pearson Commission estimated that approximately 12 per cent of those injured at work turn to the law of tort for additional compensation despite the risks, costs and delays that accompany tort litigation. This resort to tort law was particularly strengthened by the (gradual) weakening of the so-called 'unholy Trinity', namely, (*a*) the doctrine of common employment, (*b*) the abandonment of the rule that contributory negligence is a *complete defence*, and (*c*) the weakening of the defence of *volenti non fit injuria*. The trend towards tort litigation was also strengthened by the Employers' Liability (Compulsory Insurance) Act 1969, which made liability insurance compulsory for all employers[7] (except for nationalised industries, local authorities and the police). This system of automatic compensation, combined with the possibility of extra tort damages (which, incidentally, is unknown on the whole in most civil law systems), caused some concern in this country in the 1970s, and its abolition was considered by the Pearson Committee.[8] In the end, however, this step was rejected, since the no-fault scheme and its proposed improvements were not thought to provide an adequate alternative that would justify the abandonment of the tort remedy. Thus, considerable sums are paid annually and will continue to be paid through the tort system to the most seriously injured employees.

(B) TORT LAW SYSTEMS

The tortious liability of an employer for his employee's hurt can be based either on common-law rules or on the breach of specific statutory provisions. Liability at common law can, as already stated, be subdivided into vicarious liability for the tort of one

[6] Yet, as the Pearson Committee noted (i, para. 182), one should not underestimate the possible value of social security benefits which, in the case of severe disablement of a young worker, could produce inflation-proofed payment exceeding the damages in a suit against his employer.

[7] Failure to insure is a criminal offence. But in *Richardson* v. *Pitt-Stanley* [1995] ICR 303 the Court of Appeal (by majority) refused to entertain a *civil* action by the plaintiff (an injured employee) who sued the directors and secretary of the company for their failure to take out insurance, thus frustrating his efforts to claim damages from the uninsured company which, because of its subsequent liquidation, had no assets to satisfy the judgment which he had obtained against it. The diverging judgments are interesting as much for their rigour as for revealing the haphazard nature of trying to discover the legislator's intent concerning the availability of a civil remedy in addition to the expressly provided criminal sanction. The provision of the German Civil Code—§823 II BGB—that a culpable violation of a criminal statute also provides a civil remedy for those whom it intended to protect against the damage in suit, thus seems to avoid both the unnecessary complexity and unfairness of the English decision. See also *Naylor* v. *Paylings* [2004] EWCA Civ. 560, in which the Court of Appeal held that an employer was not in breach of its duty of care for failing to ensure that its subcontractors had liability insurance (in a case of personal injury caused to a customer).

[8] Vol. i, ch. 17.

employee committed against a fellow worker,[9] and primary liability of the employer himself under a non-delegable duty. Various explanations have been put forward for their distinction. Professor Atiyah, for example, believes that the distinction between primary and vicarious liability may have something to do with the much older distinction between misfeasance and non-feasance (traditionally 'condemned' less frequently by the law of torts).[10] Others[11] feel that the distinction may be linked to some failure of the managerial system on the one hand (for which primary liability is appropriate) and casual acts of negligence on the other (where vicarious liability is applicable). A third explanation (which, incidentally, also finds some support from the study of other legal systems) may be historical: primary liability rules may have been multiplied where vicarious liability proper was either non-existent (see, for example, §831 of the German Civil Code) or seriously affected by doctrines (such as that of 'common employment') developed to shield modern industry (at its formative stage) from excessive claims. At the end of the day, however, the search for a theoretical explanation may be unnecessary and all that a contemporary lawyer should remember is that different rules apply to cases of primary and vicarious liability.

Since the doctrine of 'common employment' is still (occasionally) mentioned in decisions and the literature, the student should be told briefly of the reasons which led to its rise and fall. Thus in the mid-nineteenth century, for reasons connected with the need to protect nascent industries (at a time of weak or non-existent insurance markets) the rule developed that masters would not be vicariously liable for the harm caused by one of their servants to another.[12] As stated, this doctrine was abolished by section 1 of the Law Reform (Personal Injuries) Act 1948 and an employer's liability for the tort of one employee against another of his employees is now part of the ordinary law of vicarious liability, discussed in sub-section (iii) below. The belated abolition of the doctrine is largely due to the fact that the courts in England (and in the United States) had already found ways of circumventing its application once industry was firmly on its feet and modern insurance had enabled such losses to be absorbed by liability insurance. The chief way[13] for avoiding the harshness of the doctrine of 'common

[9] Such actions were made possible by the abolition of the doctrine of common employment (referred to above) by s. 1 of the Law Reform (Personal Injuries) Act 1948. But there may still be instances where an injured employee cannot succeed, e.g. where the tortfeasor was not acting within the course of his employment. In such cases, the employer's personal, 'non-delegable duty' (discussed below) may provide a remedy to the injured co-employee.

[10] *Vicarious Liability in the Law of Torts* (1967), 217.

[11] M. A. Jones, *Textbook on Torts* (5th edn., 1996), 218.

[12] The socio-economic conditions are discussed by Friedman and Ladinsky (Select Bibliography). *Priestley* v. *Fowler* (1837) 3 M & W 1; 150 ER 1030, is the *fons et origo* of the doctrine in England. Its American counterpart, more explicit in its invocation of policy, is *Fazwell* v. *Boston and Worcester Ry. Corp.*, 45 Mass. (4 Met.) 49 (1842). See the discussion in ch. 24, below.

[13] But not the only one. A second inroad was made fairly early in the day by excluding the application of the doctrine of common employment in cases of breach of statutory duties: *Groves* v. *Lord Wimborne* [1898] 2 QB 402. Just as important was the insistence of the House of Lords that the doctrine of *volenti non fit injuria* would only be considered where the employee had truly consented to running the risk (that injured him) and was not merely aware of it: *Smith* v. *C. Baker & Sons* [1891] AC 325; see ch. 24, Section 3.

employment' was by developing the notion of non-delegable duty so that an employer could delegate the performance of his own duty to another, but he could not rid himself of the answerability for its bad performance. The responsibility is personal to him, that is to say non-delegable.

The classic exposition of the non-delegable duty principle is in *Wilsons and Clyde Coal Ltd.* v. *English*,[14] where the estate of a miner sued his employers, the question being whether they were liable for his death since they had entrusted to a competent servant the task of providing a reasonably safe system of working in the mine, which he had failed to do. The House of Lords held them liable, not vicariously, but for breach of their non-delegable duty, the exposition of which is to be found in the speech of Lord Wright.[15] This duty, he said, is threefold: to see that reasonable care is taken to provide competent staff, adequate material and a proper system, including effective supervision. To these a fourth should be added: a safe place of work. Convenient as these categories are, they are only aspects of the broad duty to see that reasonable care is taken. Moreover, as in all cases where the imposition of a duty is being considered by a court, wider policy considerations may militate against such a result. Thus, in *Mulcahy* v. *Ministry of Defence*[16] the Court of Appeal held that it would not be 'fair, just and reasonable' to impose a duty of care 'on one soldier in his conduct towards another when engaging the enemy during hostilities'. Nor were the defendants under any duty in such circumstances to maintain a 'safe system of work'. Their liability on vicarious primary liability grounds was denied.

Traditionally, the employer's duty was one to protect, so far as it is reasonable in the circumstances, the employee's *physical* safety. Recent decisions have however recognised the employer's responsibility to safeguard the employee against certain kinds of psychiatric harm as part of a growing recognition that the employment relationship is one of mutual trust and confidence between the parties.[17] In *Walker* v. *Northumberland County Council*[18] it was held that the defendant employer could be liable for exposing the plaintiff, who had been the manager of a social-work department, to a nervous breakdown caused by overwork. It was relevant here that the plaintiff had, to the employer's knowledge, suffered a previous breakdown because of overwork; hence the risk of him suffering significant work-related stress a second time was a foreseeable one. In stress cases of this kind, the employer will not be liable where the employee's adverse reaction was not foreseeable;[19] in the case of a managerial or professional employee, in particular, the employer may be able to argue that it was entitled to expect the employee to be able to withstand a certain level of occupational pressure. The defence of *volenti non fit injuria* may also be available to the employer if, for example, the employee agrees to undertake a job that requires long hours and/or heavy responsibilities,[20] although the

[14] [1938] AC 57. [15] *Ibid.*, 78; see too Lord Maugham at 86.

[16] [1996] 2 All ER 758.

[17] See L. Dolding and R. Mullender, 'Law, Labour and Mental Health' (1996) 59 *MLR* 296.

[18] [1995] 1 All ER 737.

[19] *Petch* v. *Customs and Excise Commissioners* [1993] ICR 789.

[20] See *Johnstone* v. *Bloomsbury Area Health Authority* [1991] 1 WLR 1314; [1992] 1 QB 333.

precise scope of the defence in this context is unclear.[21]The principle of liability for psychiatric harm may also arise in other contexts. Thus in *Waters* v. *Commissioner of Police for the Metropolis*,[22] damages were awarded for psychiatric harm caused to the plaintiff by her employer's failure properly to investigate her claim that she had been sexually assaulted, outside working hours, by a fellow police officer, and by its failure subsequently to protect her from victimisation and harassment.

The question whether the employer has a duty to protect its employees against psychiatric harm has also arisen in the context of claims brought by employees suffering from post-traumatic stress disorder after having witnessed or participated in traumatic or catastrophic events. If the principle in *Walker* v. *Northumberland County Council* accurately states the law, an action may lie *whether or not the employer was responsible for the accident* if the employee can show that the employer unreasonably exposed him to the risk of post-traumatic stress disorder. Unfortunately, the decided cases have tended to confuse these two bases of liability, which conceptually are quite separate, with the result that the law in this area lacks clarity. In *Macfarlane* v. *E. E. Caledonia*[23] the plaintiff, who witnessed at close hand the aftermath of the explosion on the oil rig Piper Alpha, which led to very heavy loss of life, failed in a claim for negligence against his employer, in part because he was off duty at the time the explosion occurred; he was in no better position than a bystander who happened to be on the scene at the time. By contrast, in *Frost* v. *Chief Constable of South Yorkshire* the Court of Appeal allowed a number of claims by policemen and women who had been present during and immediately after the Hillsborough stadium disaster, when, as a result of negligence on the part of senior police officers who were responsible for crowd control, ninety-six football spectators were crushed to death. According to Rose LJ:

> Once it is accepted that there is no justification for regarding physical and psychiatric injuries as different kinds of injury, when an employer negligently causes physical injury to one employee, it seems to me to be impossible to contend that he is not equally *liable* to a fellow employee of normal fortitude working on the same task who sustains psychiatric injury, whether through fear for himself or through witnessing what happens to his fellow workmen... whereas in cases outwith the master and servant relationship [sic] the courts have found it necessary, in identifying those to whom a duty of care is owed, to draw a distinction between primary and secondary victims and to impose limiting criteria to determine those within the second category who can recover, in the master and servant context a duty of care exists by reason of that relationship.[24]

[21] See our discussion of the *volenti* defence below, ch. 24, Section 3.

[22] [2000] IRLR 70; B. Barrett, 'Harassment at Work: A Matter of Health and Safety' [2000] *JBL* 343. In *Waters*, the liability of the employer was personal. By contrast, in *Green* v. *DB Group Services Ltd.* [2006] IRLR 764 the employer was found to be *vicariously* liable for an employee's conduct in negligently causing psychiatric illness to a fellow employee, through harassment. On vicarious liability generally, see ch. 19, below. The problem here is that it is not clear that there is authority for the proposition that one employee owes another a duty of care in negligence to avoid causing psychiatric harm to another, separately from the possibility of liability under the Protection from Harassment Act 1997, although a case can be made for this (see D. Brodie, 'Deterring Harassment at Common Law' (2007) 36 *ILJ* 213).

[23] [1994] 2 All ER 1. See also *Robertson and Rough* v. *Forth Bridge Joint Board* [1995] IRLR 251.

[24] [1997] IRLR 171, 177.

However, when the case reached the House of Lords under the name *White* v. *Chief Constable of South Yorkshire*,[25] the Court of Appeal's ruling was overturned and liability to the plaintiffs denied. The essence of the House of Lords' decision was that employees were owed no special duties as secondary victims of accidents, even if they were acting as rescuers. Unfortunately, the leading judgments of Lords Steyn and Hoffmann did not deal fully with the point that the cause of action for breach of the employer's personal duty of care is conceptually distinct from any claim which the employee might have as a secondary victim. Lord Steyn appears to have thought that the same principles which limit recovery for nervous shock in cases involving secondary victims should also limit the scope of the employer's personal duty of care. If this is so, it seems doubtful that *Walker* v. *Northumberland County Council* can remain good law. More cautiously, Lord Hoffmann thought that *Walker* had no application in a case where the employee's psychiatric harm was caused by witnessing physical harm to another. The reason for this was the need to avoid causing an anomaly in the treatment of employees and relatives in nervous shock cases. However, the result could have been a highly anomalous exception to the scope of the employer's personal duty to have regard to the health and safety of his employees.

That outcome appears to have been avoided by the more recent affirmation by the House of Lords of the correctness of the approach followed in *Walker* v. *Northumberland County Council*. In *Barber* v. *Somerset County Council*[26] the House held that an employer did owe a duty of care with regard to the psychiatric, and not simply the physical, well being of its employees, and that the relevant test of breach was whether the employer had acted in a reasonable and prudent way, taking positive steps to have regard for the safety and well being of its workers in the light of what it either knew or should have known. This is basically the same test that has long been applied in physical injury cases.[27] In *Hartman* v. *South Essex and Mental and Community Care NHS Trust*[28] the Court of Appeal, while broadly following the approach as in *Barber*, took the opportunity to stress the importance of finding that the psychiatric harm in question was foreseeable; it was not enough to show that the employer had been in breach of its general duty to have regard to the safety and well being of the employee and that psychiatric illness had then ensued.

One of the six cases decided in *Hartman*, *Melville* v. *Home Office*, concerned a claim by a prison health-care officer, one of whose tasks included recovering the bodies of prisoners who had committed suicide. In the course of his career, he had to deal with several such incidents. On the final occasion, he had to perform this task in a case where he had cut down the body, removed a ligature, and unsuccessfully attempted to revive the prisoner. He subsequently suffered nightmares and flashbacks and took early retirement on the grounds of ill health. He sued his employer for negligence on the grounds that a procedure which had been put in place, under which a prison care team was meant to contact members of staff who had to deal with suicides in order to offer them

[25] [1992] 2 AC 455. [26] [2004] IRLR 475.

[27] *Stokes* v. *Guest, Keen and Nettlefield (Bolts and Nuts) Ltd.* [1968] 1776; see also *Petch* v. *Customs and Excise Commissioners* [1993] ICR 789.

[28] [2005] IRLR 293.

support and counselling, had not been operated in his case. The judge found in his favour and this ruing was upheld on appeal. This case suggests that employees who are exposed, as part of their work, to a high risk of psychiatric disease may have a claim if the employer, having accepted the need for a counselling procedure to protect them against the risk of such harm, does not then implement it. *Melville* does not establish under what circumstances the employer may be liable for failing to provide such support (in the form of training or counselling) in the first place. However, it is a welcome indication that the courts are prepared to distinguish between claims arising from the relationship of employment itself, and claims, of the type rejected in *White* v. *Chief Constable of South Yorkshire*, which depend upon an employee being classed as a 'secondary victim'.

The scope of the employer's duty with regard to pure economic loss has also been expanded by recent decisions. In *Reid* v. *Rush & Tompkins Group plc*[29] the Court of Appeal refused to hold that an employer was under a duty to warn an employee posted overseas to take out personal accident insurance. In the event, the employee was involved in a hit-and-run traffic accident while working for his employer in Ethiopia and was left uncompensated, since that country has nothing equivalent to the UK Motor Insurers' Bureau. This decision must now be seen in the light of two House of Lords' decisions, *Spring* v. *Guardian Assurance Ltd.*[30] and *Scally* v. *Southern Health and Social Services Board.*[31] In *Spring* it was held that an employer could be liable to an employee (or ex-employee) in respect of economic losses caused by a negligently prepared reference, while in *Scally* the employer was held liable for loss caused by its failure to provide employees with information concerning valuable occupational pension rights. It is not clear how far these cases can be used as the basis for a widening of the employer's personal duty of care to its employees. *Spring* can be seen as an extension of the principle of *Hedley Byrne* v. *Heller*,[32] since it involves the voluntary assumption by the employer of a particular responsibility to the employee; but it is not a conventional *Hedley Byrne* case, since it was not the employee but rather the third-party employer who relied on the false information provided by the defendant. *Scally* was argued on the basis of an implied term in contract rather than the employer's duty of care in tort; however, in this context there may be little merit in distinguishing between obligations taking the form of implied terms in the contract of employment and those deriving from the employer's tortious duty. According to Lord Woolf in *Spring*,'[33] just as in the earlier authorities the courts were prepared to imply by necessary implication a term imposing a duty on an employer to exercise due care for the physical well-being of his employees, so in the appropriate circumstances would the court imply a like duty as to his economic well being'.

[29] *Reid* v. *Rush & Tompkins Group plc* [1990] 1 WLR 212. It might be different if it could be shown that the employer voluntarily assumed responsibility (in the sense of *Hedley Byrne*) for the employee's economic welfare.

[30] [1994] 3 All ER 129.

[31] [1992] 1 AC 294.

[32] [1964] AC 465; see above, ch. 2.

[33] [1994] 3 All ER 129, 178.

Some further features of the employer's duty should be noted. First, it only applies when the relationship of employer and employee exists. An independent contractor employed to do a piece of work cannot rely on such a duty and sue his employer. Second, the responsibility, as already noted, is personal to the employer in the sense that he is not relieved of it even though he delegates performance to a third party, however competent, including an independent contractor. What is personal, therefore, is not performance of the obligation, but responsibility for *bad* performance, so that the employer remains liable for the breach of the obligation. Thus, it is not enough to show that the employer has personally taken care, for example, by engaging a competent third party; he has to ensure that care is taken by that party.[34] All the same, though, this duty requires more than simply taking reasonable care oneself, it is not strict.[35] For in most cases it is a defence to show that proper care has been taken by everyone, the employer and the person engaged by him.

Apart from the provision of adequate materials, an employer is only liable for the defaults of persons actually engaged by him. With regard to defective materials, however, the Employers' Liability (Defective Equipment) Act 1969 makes him answerable for the default of anyone (that is, a manufacturer, supplier, and so on), whether engaged by him or not, which renders equipment defective. *Davie* v. *New Merton Board Mills Ltd.*[36] had held that an employer who bought a badly manufactured tool in open market was not liable to his employee because neither the manufacturer nor the seller had been 'engaged' by him to make or supply the tool. This case was overruled by the Act of 1969 so that, with regard to equipment, liability became (in theory) wider than it used to be, in that an employer became answerable even for the default of persons not engaged by him. On the other hand the Act preserves the employer's right to recover a more-or-less complete indemnity from the party actually to blame. Despite fears expressed at the time of the passing of the Act that it would cast a great burden on employers, this has not in fact occurred. Indeed, the rather limited case law, most of it, interestingly enough, unreported,[37] revealed the two main weaknesses of the Act:[38] (*a*) the difficulties encountered by employees to prove that the third party had been at *fault*, and (*b*) the difficulty of proving that the accident was *caused* by the third party's fault. As a result of the Consumer Protection Act 1987, giving effect to the European Community's Directive on Products Liability,[39] the claimant's first burden may have now been considerably eased. But the second hurdle (connected with causation) remains and will continue to prejudice injured workers until such time as the courts reverse the onus of

34 Cf. Langton J in *The Pass of Ballater* [1942] P 112, 117: 'The point may perhaps be crystallized by saying that he has not merely a duty to take care but a duty to provide that care is taken.'

35 Note, however, Viscount Simond's opinion in *Davie* v. *New Merton Board Mills Ltd.* [1959] AC 604, 620, that at times 'the subject-matter may be such that the taking of reasonable care may fall little short of absolute obligation'.

36 [1959] AC 604.

37 Which is discussed and criticised by Lang (Select Bibliography).

38 Other weaknesses are: (*a*) that it does not apply to borrowed employees (s. 1(1)(a) combined with s. 1(3)); (*b*) that the word 'defect' used in s. 1(1) probably does not include design faults.

39 Discussed below, ch. 20.

proof and oblige the employer to show, on the balance of probabilities, that the defective equipment was *not* the cause of the injury. This result appears particularly sensible in this situation, since it would facilitate the compensation of the injured employee without placing the financial burden on his employer, who would be insured and who, in any event, would be able in most cases to reclaim his costs from the guilty third party.

The employer's non-delegable duty is owed to each employee individually and, therefore, each employee's particular circumstances, which are known or ought to be known to the employer, will determine the degree of precaution required. Thus, in *Paris* v. *Stepney Borough Council*[40] an employer was held liable to his employee for not having provided him with goggles when he knew that that employee had only one eye and was running a risk of greater injury in consequence. But although the employer is required to show a high standard of care, there are limits. As *Withers* v. *Perry Chain Co. Ltd.*[41] shows, the law does not require an employer to dismiss the employee even if this might be the only way of avoiding the risk of harm.

Finally, it is not entirely clear to what extent these common-law duties may be modified (in favour of the employer) through the *express* terms of the contract of employment. In *Johnstone* v. *Bloomsbury Health Authority*[42] the plaintiff, a junior doctor, was employed by the defendants and undertook to work forty hours a week in addition to making himself available for a further forty-eight hours on average a week over a specified period. For this he now sued the defendants, in essence claiming that this express duty under the contract violated the employer's common-law duty to take care for his safety and well-being. In the light of the facts of that particular case the plaintiff, by a majority, succeeded in his action. However, on the important *legal* issue involved, the Court of Appeal was divided in a different way. For the dissenting judge (Leggatt LJ) and one of the majority judges (Sir Nicolas Browne-Wilkinson V-C) thought that the common-law duty to take care of the employee would have to cede precedence to a clearly defined express term that gave the employer a right (and not just a discretion) to call upon the plaintiff (employee) to provide up to an additional forty-eight hours per week. To the other (majority) justice (Stuart Smith LJ), however, the answer depended on the interaction of the two sets of rules (the tort rules and the terms of the contract), and this meant that the defendant could only exercise his discretion to ask the plaintiff to do the additional hours if this could be done without breaching the common-law duty to take care of the employee's health. This last view seems preferable, for otherwise the entire law of negligence, dealing with the employer's liability to his employees, could be swallowed up (and thus avoided) by carefully drafted contracts of employment which would be seriously disadvantageous to employees.

40 [1951] AC 367, followed in Scotland in *Porteous* v. *NCB*, 1967 SLT 117 (SC).

41 [1961] 1 WLR 1314, 1320.

42 [1992] QB 333. The court felt that it was not necessary to decide whether the duty to take care of the employee's health derived from tort or arose by implication of law into the contract of employment. See also our discussion of this case in ch. 24, below.

As already stated, the employer's duty to see that reasonable care is taken falls into four categories.

(i) Competent Staff

In *Hudson* v. *Ridge Manufacturing Co. Ltd.*[43] an employee was injured as a result of a foolish prank practised upon him by a fellow employee, whose propensity for mischief had been known to the employers for a long time. The latter were held liable for a breach of their *personal* duty[44] to see that safe fellow employees were provided. Streatfield J said:

> Here is a case where there existed, as it were in the system of work a source of danger, through the conduct of one of the defendants' employees, of which they knew, repeated conduct which went on over a long period of time, and which they did nothing whatever to remove, except to reprimand and go on reprimanding to no effect. In my judgment, therefore, the injury was sustained as a result of the defendants' failure to take proper steps to put an end to that conduct.[45]

(ii) Adequate Materials

The Employers' Liability (Defective Equipment) Act 1969 puts this aspect of the duty into statutory form. Section 1 says that if the employee suffers personal injury in the course of his employment as a result of a defect in equipment provided by his employer for the purposes of the latter's business, and he, the employee, can prove that it is attributable wholly or partly to the fault of a third party, then the employee's injury will also be attributable to the negligence of the employer without prejudice to the latter's right to contribution or a complete indemnity from the party at fault. But the employer's obligation is not absolute. Reasonable care is taken if the appliances are of the type usual for the work in question,[46] but this does not imply that the employer must always adopt the latest improvements available in the market. Nor will he be liable if the employee fails to make proper use of the equipment. In *Parkinson* v. *Lyle Shipping Co. Ltd.*[47] the plaintiff was injured while attempting to relight a boiler. His action in negligence failed because the court took the view that the injury was not the result of defective equipment, but of the manner in which the plaintiff used it. The weaknesses of this enactment have already been mentioned; so has the possible relief that may come in the guise of the Consumer Protection Act 1987.[48]

43 [1957] 2 QB 348. Cf. *Smith* v. *Crossley Bros. Ltd.* (1971) 95 SJ 655; and see also next footnote.

44 The importance of stressing the employer's personal liability is that a practical joke by one employee against another is rarely considered to fall within the course of the former's employment so as to render the employer vicariously liable. See *O'Reilly* v. *National Rail and Tramway Appliances Ltd.* [1966] 1 All ER 499, *Coddington* v. *International Harvester Co. of Great Britain* (1969) 6 KIR 146. *Chapman* v. *Oakleigh Animal Products* (1970) 8 KIR 1063 appeared an exception to this tendency. *Harrison* v. *Michelin Tyre Co. Ltd.* [1985] 1 All ER 918 may be read as signalling a willingness to render employers vicariously liable for the horseplay of their employees where the incident is 'part and parcel of the employment'. The test for determining that question was said to be 'a reasonable approach' (*ibid.*, at 920) which is sufficiently amorphous to enable future judges to extend vicarious liability for practical jokes in their (presumed) desire to aid victims.

45 [1957] 2 QB 348 at 351.

46 *Roberts* v. *Alfred Holt & Co.* (1945) 61 TLR 289.

47 [1964] 2 Lloyd's Rep. 79.

48 Discussed below, ch. 20.

From the above, it will have been noticed that the Act obliges the employer to supply his employees with safe 'equipment'. Somewhat surprisingly, section 1(3) of the Act defines equipment to include 'any plant and machinery, vehicle, aircraft and clothing'. The extent of this wide definition was, however, tested in the case of *Coltman* v. *Bibby Tankers Ltd.*[49] when the Court of Appeal had to decide whether a ship could be included in the above definition of equipment. The House of Lords, giving the lie to the widely held view that English courts invariably give effect to the clear wording of statutes, adopted a purposive interpretation of the Act and, contrary to the view of the Court of Appeal, held that there was no reason to exclude vessels from the ambit of the 1969 statute.

(iii) Safe Place of Work

Whether the place of work is safe or not depends on the circumstances and the nature of the place. The requisite standard is that of the reasonably prudent employer. A place originally safe may subsequently become unsafe because of some new factor. It was held in *Latimer* v. *AEC Ltd.*[50] that the defendants' liability depended on whether they had taken the appropriate steps which a reasonably prudent employer would have taken. In the circumstances they had done so, and the fact that the floor of the factory had become slippery did not warrant the closure of the factory. Not only must the premises where the work takes place be safe but also the access to them.[51] Moreover, the duty is not discharged by the mere issuing of warnings to the employees. Finally, one cannot generalise on the effect, if any, that the plaintiff/employee's knowledge of the danger will have on his claims. The answer must, overall, depend on all the circumstances of each case, though the protective philosophy that the courts have adopted towards employees may well work in his favour.[52]

The duty with regard to a safe place of work applies even when the employee is not working on his employer's premises, although, as a matter of common sense, the requisite standard may vary and the discharge of the duty may be easier. In *Wilson* v. *Tyneside Window Cleaning Co.*[53] the defendants sent their employee to clean windows of a client. Owing to their dangerous condition he fell and injured himself. It was alleged on his behalf that the defendants had failed to take reasonable care not to expose him to unnecessary risk. It was held that though an employer owes his employees a duty even in respect of work done outside his premises, in the present case it had been fulfilled. If, however, the risk that exists at the place where the work has to be done has been encountered on previous occasions, then the employer may be under a duty to devise a safe system of work and may be liable if he does not.[54] Although an employer is, in most cases, under no duty to inspect the premises where his employee will have to work, he is

49 [1988] AC 276. The same broad approach to the Act was adopted by the Court of Appeal in *Knowles* v. *Liverpool City Council*, *The Times*, 2 July 1992, when it held that equipment included a flagstone on which the employee was working.

50 [1953] AC 634.

51 *Ashdown* v. *Samuel Williams & Sons Ltd.* [1957] 1 QB 409.

52 *McCafferty* v. *Metropolitan Police District Receiver* [1977] 1 WLR 1073.

53 [1958] 2 QB 110. For variations in the standard of care, see the *dictum* by Pearce LJ at 121–2. See also *Smith* v. *Austin Lifts Ltd.* [1959] 1 WLR 100.

54 Cf. *General Cleaning Contractors* v. *Christmas* [1953] AC 180.

still under a duty to provide proper instructions and the necessary implements;[55] nor will he be necessarily absolved of liability if he proves that the employee was aware of the danger and had not objected to it.[56]

(iv) Proper System

This is probably the most important, but ill-defined, aspect of the employer's duty. It includes special instructions and reasonably effective supervision to ensure that the system and instructions are adhered to. In the words of Lord Reid:

> It is the duty of the employer to consider the situation, to devise a suitable system, to instruct his men what they must do and supply any implements that may be required... No doubt he cannot be certain that his men will do as they are told when they are working alone. But if he does all that is reasonable to ensure that his safety system is operated he will have done what he is bound to do.[57]

This, too, was a case where a window-cleaner sued his employers in respect of injuries sustained while cleaning a window. The House of Lords held them liable because they had failed to devise a safe system of work providing for an obvious danger. In leaving it to the initiative of individual workmen to take appropriate precautions, the defendants had failed in their duty. But:

> where there is a recognised and general practice which has been followed for a substantial period in similar circumstances without mishap [the employer] is entitled to follow it, unless in the light of common sense or newer knowledge, it is clearly bad: but, where there is developing knowledge, he must keep reasonably abreast of it and not be too slow to apply it; and where he has in fact greater than average knowledge of the risks, he may be thereby obliged to take more than the average or standard precautions.[58]

It is a question of fact whether: (*a*) a system should be devised (a recurring danger will, for instance, be a strong reason for devising a system to deal with it) and (*b*) whether the one devised is effective. An employer will not necessarily be relieved of liability merely by issuing orders not to do certain things;[59] indeed, in cases of extreme risk he will be expected to issue absolute and explicit instructions against doing a particular job in a certain manner and will be saddled with part (at least) of the consequences if he does not.[60] Finally, although the discharge of the duty may involve a measure of supervision, this does not imply that 'an employer is bound, through his foreman, to

55 *Ibid.*

56 *McCafferty* v. *Metropolitan Police District Receiver* [1977] 1 WLR 1073. See also, *McDermid* v. *Nash Dredging and Reclamation Co. Ltd.* [1987] AC 906. Lord Brandon (esp. at 919) held the defendants liable for the negligence of the tug skipper in operating the system for casting off. He required no more than this for the defendants to be in breach of their non-delegable duty. Is this consistent with a notion that an employer's duty is to take reasonable care that care is taken? If not, then the employer's liability seems strict. See the explanation of Mason J in the Australian High Court case of *Kondis* v. *State Transport Authority* (1984) 55 ALR 225.

57 *General Cleaning Contractors Ltd.* v. *Christmas* [1953] AC 180, 194.

58 *Stokes* v. *GKN* [1968] 1 WLR 1776, 1783 (per Swanwick J) followed by Mustill J in *Thompson* v. *Smiths Ship Repairers (North Shields) Ltd.* [1984] QB 405; 1 All ER 881, 889.

59 E.g. *Baker* v. *T. E. Hopkins & Son Ltd.* [1959] 1 WLR 966.

60 *King* v. *Smith* [1995] ICR 339.

stand over workmen of age and experience every moment they are working and every time that they cease work, in order to see that they do what they are supposed to do'.[61]

(C) STATUTORY DUTIES

The various statutory duties of an employer towards his employees need only be discussed in the form of a few general points. The first is that in theory the common-law duty of the employer, emanating as it does from the employment relationship, is of a general nature, whereas statutory duties depend on the specific statute creating them.[62] In practice employers are subjected to an ever-growing number of duties designed to improve the health and safety at work.

Second, liability in these instances is often absolute and, therefore, a statutory duty facilitates the employee's task of establishing his employer's liability. So, for example, in *John Summers and Sons Ltd.* v. *Frost*[63] the House of Lords interpreted section 14(1) of the Factories Act 1937 (providing for the fencing of every dangerous part of machinery) as giving rise to an absolute liability even where it could be shown that fencing would render the machine inoperable. Even when phrases such as 'so far as reasonably practicable' appeared in a statute (for example section 28(1) of the Factories Act 1961), the courts held that it was for the employer[64] to prove that it was not reasonably practicable to avoid the results.[65]

Third, the various enactments tend, as a rule, to amplify and give effect to one or other aspect of the *Wilsons* case, namely, safe equipment, safe place of work, or safe system. The Factories Act 1961, the Mines and Quarries Act 1954, the Offices, Shops and Railway Premises Act 1963 and the Health and Safety at Work Act 1974 are examples of statutory intervention in this area. The Acts of 1954, 1961 and 1963 have over the past few years gradually been replaced by regulations which, among other things, implement the EC Framework Directive on Health and Safety[66] and various 'daughter directives'.[67] The reader is referred to specialist works on health and safety for a more detailed treatment of this legislation.

[61] *Woods* v. *Durable Suites Ltd.* [1953] 1 WLR 857, 862, per Singleton LJ.

[62] Section 2 of the Health and Safety at Work Act 1974, however, casts upon employers a general duty to ensure, as far as possible, the health, safety, and welfare at work of all their employees. Breach of this duty entails only penal, not civil, sanctions.

[63] [1955] AC 740.

[64] *Nimmo* v. *Alexander Cowan and Sons Ltd.* [1968] AC 107.

[65] It is not clear whether 'reasonably practicable' introduces the test of 'reasonable care' of negligence. In yet other instances the term 'practicable' (rather than 'reasonably practicable') has been used; see s. 157 of the Mines and Quarries Act 1954. Since everything ultimately depends on the construction of the wording of the relevant statute it is to be regretted that the relevant language appears often to have been chosen haphazardly.

[66] Directive 89/391 [1989] *OJ* L183/1.

[67] Thus the Workplace (Health, Safety and Welfare) Regulations (SI No. 1992/3004) replaced many of the provisions of the Factories Act 1961 and the Office, Shops and Railway Premises Act 1963 relating to the provision of a safe workplace and system of work. See generally A. Redgrave, J. Hendy and M. Ford, *Health and Safety* (3rd edn., 1998).

SELECT BIBLIOGRAPHY

FLEMING, J. G., 'Tort Liability for Work Injury', in *Int. Encl. Comp. L* xv (1975), ch. 9.

FRIEDMAN, L. M., and Ladinsky, J., 'Social Change and the Law of Industrial Accidents' (1967) 67 *Col. LR* 50.

LANG, B., 'The Employer's Liability (Defective Equipment) Act: Lion or Mouse?' (1984) 47 *MLR* 48.

MCKENDRICK, E., 'Vicarious Liability and Independent Contractors: A Re-Examination' (1990) 53 *MLR* 770

NEWARK, F. H., 'Bad Law' (1966) 17 *NILQ* 469.

WILLIAMS, G., 'The Effects of Penal Legislation in the Law of Tort' (1960) 23 *MLR* 233.

19

VICARIOUS LIABILITY

Vicarious liability is liability imposed on an employer to a third party for the tort of his employee committed in the course of employment. This means that a relationship of employer and employee, as distinct from employer and independent contractor, has to exist. A few apparent exceptions to this rule are not really such. First, however, it needs to be pointed out that vicarious liability is another instance of stricter liability in the sense that the employer who is not at fault is made responsible for the employee's default. It thereby gives the injured party compensation from the person who is better able to pay and spread the cost of the injury, namely the employer. Some justification for this departure from the fault principle was needed and many reasons have in fact been offered. Some have an air of fiction about them, such as the 'control' test, which attributes to the employer the ability to control the behaviour and precise manner of working of his employee. Others base liability on an analogy with causation in that the employer set the whole thing in motion[1] and that, therefore, he should bear the consequences if a third party suffers through the employee's wrongful conduct. The 'deeper pocket' justification has economic overtones: the employer is richer so he should pay; which also suits the victim since the employer is invariably in a better position to pay than his employee.[2] Economic and moral considerations also seem to be satisfied by those who advocate that the person who derives a benefit from the activity of another should also bear the risk of damage inflicted by those acts.[3] Yet another economic variant is that the employer is in a better position to spread the loss through insurance or the price of his products. Though the theoretical justifications of vicarious liability vary, this is not a problem that has often worried the English courts. Lord Pearce's remark that the doctrine of vicarious liability has not grown from any clear logical or legal principle but from social convenience and rough justice[4] is typical of their

[1] *Hutchinson* v. *The York, Newcastle and Berwick Rly. Co.* (1850) 5 Exch. 343, 350; 155 ER 150, 153, per Alderson B.

[2] Inference from Alderson B, *ibid.*, at 350 (Exch.), 153 (ER).

[3] Would this not be a good reason for making parents liable vicariously for the torts of their minor children as in French law?

[4] *ICI Ltd.* v. *Shatwell* [1965] AC 656, 685. See also *Duncan* v. *Findlater* (1839) 6 Cl. & F 894, 910; 7 ER 934, 940, per Lord Brougham, *Longdon-Griffiths* v. *Smith* [1950] 2 All ER 662, 667, per Slade J, *Broom* v. *Morgan* [1953] 1 QB 597, 608, per Denning LJ, and *Lister* v. *Hesley Hall Ltd.* [2001] 2 AC 215, 242, per Lord Hobhouse; cf. the explicit discussion of policy considerations in the leading Canadian Supreme Court case *Bazley* v. *Curry* (1999) 174 DLR (4th) 45, and the discussion by P. Cane, 'Vicarious Liability for Sexual Abuse' (Select Bibliography).

pragmatic approach to the question. Perhaps it should also be taken to suggest that, although no single theory can explain the rule, its basis cannot be dismissed entirely. As Professor Glanville Williams wrote:

> Vicarious liability is the creation of many judges who have had different ideas of its justification or social policy, or no idea at all. Some judges may have extended the rule more widely or confined it more narrowly than its true rationale would allow; yet the rationale, if we can discover it, will remain valid so far as it extends.[5]

Anyone who wishes to hold an employer vicariously liable must prove: (*a*) that the offender was his employee; (*b*) that he committed a tort; and (*c*) that he committed it in the course of his employment.

1. IDENTIFYING THE 'EMPLOYEE' AND HIS 'EMPLOYER'

The determination of the nature of the work relationship (employee/independent contractor) is normally said to be a question of mixed fact and law, although where the discovery of the correct status depends on the construction of written documents it may be a pure question of law.[6] It has been said that 'the . . . evaluation of the factual circumstances in which the work is performed . . . is a question of fact to be determined by the trial court'.[7] The construction of the relevant document must thus be undertaken 'in its contractual matrix',[8] something which gives the trial court considerable power in weighing the plethora of (usually) conflicting elements but also gives the process a certain impressionistic character.[9] But let us now move to specifics. It is sometimes said that where there is a contract of service or of employment, there is necessarily an employer–employee relationship and the employer will be liable for the employee's tort; where the contract is for services, this is an employer–independent contractor relationship and the employer is not vicariously liable for the torts of the other. This criterion, however, like so many others, only restates the problem rather than solves it. What one has to do is to marshal various tests, which cumulatively point either towards an

[5] 'Vicarious Liability and the Master's Indemnity' (Select Bibliography), 231. See also W. A. Seavey, 'Speculations as to "Respondeat Superior"' (Select Bibliography) and Fleming James, 'Vicarious Liability' (Select Bibliography).

[6] *Davies* v. *Presbyterian Church of Wales* [1986] 1 WLR 323.

[7] *Lee Tin Sang* v. *Chung Chi-Keung* [1990] 2 AC 374, 414, per Lord Griffiths.

[8] *McMeechan* v. *Secretary of State for Employment* [1995] IRLR 461, 463. See also the judgment of the Court of Appeal in this case at [1997] IRLR 353.

[9] These factors are sometimes so evenly divided between them that the trial court's power to assess them *qualitatively* may, in the end, be influenced by the wider policy desire to afford greater protection to the victim. This can be achieved by granting the claimant the status of employee and thus according him the benefits invariably reserved by special statutes to employees but not independent contractors. See, for instance, *Lane* v. *Shire Roofing Company (Oxford) Ltd.* [1995] IRLR 493.

employer–employee relationship, or away from one. Before discussing the various criteria used by the courts to decide whether there is an employer–employee relationship a note of warning about the rich case law may not be out of place. It will be noticed that the cases that follow do not always deal with the existence of an employer–employee relationship, in the context of the *potential liability* of the employer for his employees' torts. Many of them, on the contrary, are concerned to discover the true nature of the relationship for the purposes of tax obligations and duties and, as already alluded to, the applicability of employment-protection laws. An employee, for example, enjoys greater employment security than an independent contractor. Are the courts likely to draw the distinction between employees and independent contractors in the same way, irrespective of the wider context of the dispute? Some commentators think so,[10] whereas others[11] warn against a mechanical use of decisions rendered in one context (i.e. employment-protection laws) in the very different situation where the liability of the employer might be at issue.

The case of *O'Kelly* v. *Trusthouse Forte plc*[12] offers a good illustration of the attractiveness of the second view. In that case the defendants, owners of the Grosvenor House Hotel, operated a hotel and restaurant business for which they employed permanent staff. Additionally, they also hired out rooms for private functions for which they provided catering facilities. This part of the business was in need of casual staff some of whom were known as 'regulars' and who were rostered in preference to other casual staff (though they were free to refuse these more frequently offered jobs). When the plaintiff (and two other regulars) were 'dismissed', allegedly for belonging to a trade union, they brought an action for unfair dismissal under section 58 of the Employment Protection Consolidation Act 1978 (now section 152 of the Trade Union and Labour Relations (Consolidation) Act 1992). The court held that they were not employees for the purposes of the employment-protection legislation, because the necessary element of mutuality of obligation was absent from their relationship with the employer.[13] As Professor Ewan McKendrick points out, however,[14] the result would surely have been different if one of them had spilt wine over a hotel customer and the employer–employee relationship was being investigated for the purposes of rendering the hotel (employers) liable to the customers.[15]

[10] *Winfield and Jolowicz on Tort* (15th edn., 1998), 696.

[11] E. McKendrick, *Tort Textbook* (5th edn., 1991), 18.

[12] [1984] QB 90.

[13] On the mutuality test, which has been significant mainly in the context of employment protection legislation and which has given rise to an extensive case law, see S. Deakin and G. Morris, *Labour Law* (4th edn., 2005), at paras. 3.46–3.52, and our further discussion below.

[14] 'Vicarious Liability and Independent Contractors: A Re-Examination' (Select Bibliography).

[15] See also *Hollis* v. *Vabu Pty. Ltd.* (2001) 207 CLR 21, in which the High Court of Australia, in a case similar to the one discussed by McKendrick (here, a courier whose contract appeared to indicate that he was self-employed knocked down a pedestrian), held that the employer was vicariously liable; however, the court reached this conclusion by ruling that the correct analysis of the employment relationship in this case pointed towards employee status for all purposes and not solely for third party claims in tort. See A. Stewart, 'Redefining Employment? Meeting the Challenge of Contract and Agency Labour' (2002) 15 *Australian Journal of Labour Law* 235.

The traditional criterion for distinguishing employees from independent contractors is the degree and right of control.[16] Bramwell LJ regarded a servant as anyone who was subject to the command of the employer as to the manner in which he was to do his work.[17] On the other hand, if the employer only determined 'what' was to be done rather than 'how' it was to be done, then the person working for him would be an independent contractor. In *Honeywill and Stein Ltd.* v. *Larkin Brothers Ltd.*[18] Slesser LJ expressed this idea as follows:

The determination whether the actual wrongdoer is a servant or agent on the one hand or an independent contractor on the other depends on whether or not the employer not only determines what is to be done, but retains the control of the actual performance, in which case the doer is a servant or agent; but if the employer while prescribing the work to be done, leaves the manner of doing it to the control of the doer, the latter is an independent contractor.

In *Performing Rights Society Ltd.* v. *Mitchell and Booker (Palais de Danse) Ltd.*[19] the defendants engaged a band for their dance hall. The agreement stipulated that the musicians should not infringe the plaintiff's copyright, which they did. The liability of the defendants depended on whether the musicians were their servants and it was held that they were.

The control test was more appropriate to the social conditions of an earlier age. For, as Professor Kahn-Freund put it, the distinction between servant and independent contractor on the basis of the control test 'reflects a state of society in which the ownership of the means of production coincided with the possession of technical knowledge and skill and in which that knowledge and skill was largely acquired by being handed down from one generation to the next by oral tradition and not by being systematically imparted in institutions of learning'.[20] As specialist skills of employees increased, the unskilled employer was less and less able to control their work. While it might be thought that the control test might be preserved by saying that the employer would have the right to control their work if he possessed the necessary skill. This, however, begs the question, since saying that the defendant has the right to control work results from the decision *already* made that he is an employer. Moreover, the term 'servant', as it was used in the nineteenth-century cases, does not necessarily correspond to the modern term 'employee'. The term 'servant' denoted, on the whole, manual workers as opposed to clerical and professional employees. This distinction is of practically no relevance in the modern law.[21] The increasing subtlety of the employment relationship makes the control test, however modified, inadequate. As Lord Parker CJ put it:

Superintendence and control cannot be the decisive test when one is dealing with a professional man, or a man of some particular skill and experience. Instances of that have been given

[16] For an oft-quoted statement, see *Short* v. *J. & W. Henderson Ltd.* (1946) 62 TLR 427, 429, per Lord Thankerton. For an elaborate examination of the tests for identifying the employment relationship, see Atiyah, *Vicarious Liability in the Law of Torts* (Select Bibliography), 31 ff.

[17] *Yewens* v. *Noakes* (1880) 6 QBD 530, 532–3.

[18] [1934] 1 KB 191, 196. [19] [1924] 1 KB 762.

[20] 'Servants and Independent Contractors' (Select Bibliography), 505.

[21] See A. Merritt, 'Control v. Economic Reality: Defining the Contract of Employment' [1982] *Aust. Bus. LR* 105.

in the form of the master of a ship, an engine driver, or a professional architect . . . In such cases, there can be no question of the employer telling him how to do work, therefore the absence of control and direction in that sense can be of little, if any, use as a test.[22]

To this list one should add doctors. Indeed, it was in this context that the courts experienced their earliest difficulties with the control test. This implied that hospitals could not be liable for the torts of medical experts, who could hardly be dictated to by hospital authorities as to how they should exercise their calling.[23] A change in attitude appeared in the early 1940s. In *Gold* v. *Essex County Council*[24] the Court of Appeal held that a radiographer was a servant of the hospital that employed him and thus rendered it vicariously liable for his negligence in the course of his duty, even though the hospital authorities were not competent to dictate to him how he should exercise his skill. In *Cassidy* v. *Ministry of Health*[25] a hospital's liability for the professional negligence of its permanent medical staff was unequivocally established. In that case it was unclear whether the negligence that resulted in the plaintiff's injury was that of the whole-time assistant medical officer, the house surgeon, or one of the nurses. The Court of Appeal was not deterred by this in holding the hospital liable to the plaintiff. All three judges felt that it was unnecessary to pinpoint whose negligence had caused the harm; the hospital was vicariously liable for the professional negligence of its staff.

In addition to the shortcomings of the control test, another factor behind the change that came about was the change in the social and economic environment. In the past, when hospitals were supported by voluntary contributions, it was essential to preserve their valuable services as much as possible by avoiding liability so as to safeguard their slender resources from being depleted by payment of heavy damages. Accordingly, courts distinguished between torts committed by doctors and nurses in the course of routine and administrative functions, for which hospitals were vicariously liable, and in the course of exercising professional skill, for which they were not liable. However, once hospitals came to rest on a more secure financial basis, especially after the introduction of the National Health Service, courts became more willing to hold them liable. So today a hospital authority would be liable except in cases where a surgeon or consultant treats a patient under private contract.

The emphasis placed on control has thus been reduced, but not abandoned. It has become a kind of residuary test in the sense that it can be outweighed by other considerations; but, these being equal or inconclusive, the control test will decide the issue. *Argent* v. *Minister of Social Security and Another*[26] offers a good example. In that case the applicant worked as a part-time teacher in a drama school but he combined this with

[22] *Morren* v. *Swinton and Pendlebury BC* [1965] 1 WLR 576, 582.

[23] *Hilyer* v. *St Bartholomew's Hospital* [1909] 2 KB 820.

[24] [1942] 2 KB 293. The judgments also indicate reliance on a breach of the hospital's 'non-delegable' duty to ensure that care is taken of the patient.

[25] [1951] 2 KB 343. *Roe* v. *Minister of Health* [1954] 2 QB 66 has probably added staff anaesthetists. See further C. J. Hamson, 'Liability of Hospitals for Negligence' (Select Bibliography).

[26] [1968] 1 WLR 1749, 1758–9. To similar effect see McCardie J in *Performing Rights Society* v. *Mitchell and Booker (Palais de Danse) Ltd.* [1924] 1 KB 762, 767.

work as a full-time actor with various theatre companies. The school did not prescribe a syllabus and in no way interfered with his teaching. On being classified as a self-employed person within section 1(2)(b) of the National Insurance Act 1965, he appealed, alleging that he was a servant, not an independent contractor, and that consequently he should be regarded as an employed person. His contention was rejected. Roskill J said:

> If one studies the cases... a number of tests have been propounded over the years for resolving the problem that I have to solve. For example, in the earlier cases it seems to have been suggested that the most important test, if not the all-important test, was the extent of the control exercised by the employer over the servant.... But it is also clear that as one watches the development of the law in the first 60 years of this century and particularly the development of the law in the last 15 or 20 years in this field, the emphasis has shifted and no longer rests so strongly upon the question of control. Control is obviously an important factor. In some cases it may still be the decisive factor, but it is wrong to say that in every case it is the decisive factor. It is now, as I venture to think, no more than a factor, albeit a very important one.

More recent decisions continue to show the secondary role attached by some judges to the control test. In *WHPT Housing Association Ltd.* v. *Secretary of State for Social Services*[27] an architect worked on a freelance basis for the plaintiff's association and eventually sought to be included as a member of its permanent staff for the purposes of the Social Security Act 1975. Despite a considerable degree of integration in the business and the fact that his work was subject to fairly close and regular control by the association's chief architect, he was found to be self-employed because he had retained control over the issue of how many hours of service he would offer his employer. Nourse J put it in this way: '[i]n a contract of service... the principal obligation undertaken by the employee is *to provide himself to serve*: whereas in a contract for services the principal obligation is not to provide himself to serve the employer *but his services for the use of the employer*.'[28]

The difficulties that accompany the control test have led other judges to propose alternative approaches. One is the integration test proposed by Denning LJ in *Stevenson Jordon and Harrison Ltd.* v. *MacDonald and Evans*,[29] where he said that 'under a contract of service, a man is employed as part of the business, and his work is done as an integral part of the business; whereas, under a contract for services, his work, although done for the business, is not integrated into it but is only accessory to it'.

The idea of looking to the underlying economic nature of the relationship between the parties was extended in *Market Investigations Ltd.* v. *Minister of Social Security*,[30] where an appellant company was engaged in market research employing a few full-time workers and many part-time interviewers selected from a panel of nearly 500 people. In 1966 the company asked the minister to decide whether a part-time interviewer was

[27] [1981] ICR 737.

[28] *Ibid.*, 748.

[29] [1952] 1 TLR 101, 111. Also see Denning LJ in *Bank voor Handel en Scheepvaart NV* v. *Slatford* [1953] 1 QB 248, 295: 'whether the person is part and parcel of the organization'.

[30] [1969] 2 QB 173, esp. at 184.

employed for the purposes of the National Insurance Acts 1946 and 1965. The minister's conclusion was that the particular interviewer worked under a contract of service (or contract of employment) and not, as the company contended, a contract for services; and his decision was upheld on appeal. In the opinion of Cooke J, control, though relevant, was not decisive. What mattered more was whether the interviewer could be said to be in business on her own account, or as an employee working for an agreed wage whose employer took the risk of loss and the chance of profit. The relevance of this 'economic reality' test has since been accepted by the Privy Council.[31]

A further approach is to examine closely the nature of the 'contractual matrix' affecting worker and employer, in order to establish whether there exists the 'mutuality of obligation' which is needed to identify a contract of employment.[32] If the existence of mutual obligations to provide work (in the case of the employer) and to accept any work which is offered (in the case of the worker) is in doubt, the relationship may be classified as one of self-employment, or otherwise outside the scope of the 'employee' concept. This means that home-workers,[33] agency workers,[34] 'zero-hours' contract workers,[35] and workers in casualised trades or occupations[36] may not qualify for social or employment protection. In principle, it should follow that their employer is also exempt from vicarious liability from any torts which such workers may commit in the course of their employment. However, as we have seen in the context of our earlier discussion of *O'Kelly* v. *Trusthouse Forte plc*,[37] there is a strong argument here to the effect that victims of torts, as strangers to the contract of employment, should not be adversely affected by contract terms which have the effect of denying employee status to the worker. So far this argument has not been tested in the English courts.[38] If it were accepted, it would mean that a worker could be regarded as an employee for one purpose (vicarious liability) while remaining self-employed for others (social security and employment law). While legislation can (and does) bring about this result, it is not clear that the common law would accept the idea of 'divisible' status.

It seems that none of these tests, on its own, is conclusive. The courts, indeed, have from time to time explicitly espoused an impressionistic, multi-factor approach to the

[31] *Lee Ting Sang* v. *Chung Chi-Keung* [1990] 2 AC 374.

[32] For particularly strong assertions of the importance of the contractual matrix, see *Hewlett Packard Ltd.* v. *Murphy* [2002] IRLR 4, *Stevedoring & Haulage Services Ltd.* v. *Fuller* [2001] IRLR 627.

[33] *Airfix Footwear Ltd.* v. *Cope* [1978] ICR 1210, *Nethermere (St Neots) Ltd.* v. *Taverna and Gardiner* [1984] IRLR 240.

[34] *Wickens* v. *Champion Employment Agency* [1984] ICR 365; *Ironmonger* v. *Movefield Ltd.* [1988] IRLR 461 (both cases involving the relationship between the worker and the agency; on the possibility that the user may be liable for torts committed by the employee, see below).

[35] *Clark* v. *Oxfordshire Health Authority* [1998] IRLR 125.

[36] *O'Kelly* v. *Trusthouse Forte plc* [1983] IRLR 369, *Carmichael* v. *National Power plc* [1998] IRLR 301.

[37] [1983] IRLR 369; see above, and McKendrick, 'Vicarious Liability and Independent Contractors' (Select Bibliography).

[38] Although it has been suggested that victims of unlawful discrimination and, by extension, tort victims should not be affected by a claim that the contract between the worker and the employer was tainted by illegality, see *Hall* v. *Woolston Hall Leisure Ltd.* [2000] IRLR 578. On the relevant Australian case law, see A. Stewart, 'Redefining Employment? Meeting the Challenge of Contract and Agency Labour' (2002) 15 *Australian Journal of Labour Law* 235.

question of identifying the employment relationship. A full discussion of this topic can be found in *Ready Mixed Concrete (South East) Ltd.* v. *Minister of Pensions and National Insurance*,[39] where a concrete-manufacturing company agreed with the owner of a lorry to pay him a fixed mileage rate for transporting concrete. The contract described him as an independent contractor, and he was obliged to maintain his vehicle in good order and at his own expense. He was also free to employ a competent driver whenever necessary. He, on the other hand, undertook to make his lorry available whenever the company wanted it, to have it painted in the company's colours, and to wear the company's uniform. The company also prescribed a special way in which he should present the accounts. The question whether he was an employed person within the National Insurance Act 1965 turned on whether or not he was under a contract of service. MacKenna J, after a lengthy review of the authorities, decided that he was an independent contractor. He laid down the conditions of a contract of service as follows:

(i) the servant agrees that, in consideration of a wage or other remuneration, he will provide his own work and skill in the performance of some service for his master;
(ii) he agrees, expressly or impliedly, that in the performance of that service he will be subject to the other's control in a sufficient degree to make that other master; and
(iii) the other provisions of the contract are consistent with its being a contract of service.

In this case, the driver owned the lorry and bore the financial risk, and 'he who owns the assets and bears the risk is unlikely to be acting as an agent or servant. If the man performing the service must provide the means of performance at his own expense and accept payment by results, he will own the assets, bear the risk, and be to that extent unlike a servant.'[40] The lorry owner's contract was thus one of services, not of service.

MacKenna J's conditions must not be applied rigidly—successive judges have warned against the risks of doing so. In *Market Investigations Ltd.* v. *Minister of Social Security* Cooke J said: 'No exhaustive list has been compiled and perhaps no exhaustive list can be compiled of the considerations which are relevant in determining that question, nor can strict rules be laid down as to the relative weight which the various considerations should carry in particular cases.'[41] What emerges from all this is that courts will take into account a variety of tests to determine the nature of the relationship between the tortfeasor and his employer. How much weight will attach to each test depends on each case; and, as already stated, the determination may vary depending upon whether the court is ultimately deciding the issue in a, say, tax or liability situation.[42] If on balance the multiple factors point towards one type of relationship, then the courts will

[39] [1968] 2 QB 497, 515, 525.

[40] In the United States this is sometimes referred to as the 'economic reality' argument. See *United States of America* v. *Silk*, 331 US 704 (1946), referred to by our Court of Appeal in *Lane* v. *Shire Roofing* [1995] IRLR 493.

[41] [1969] 2 QB 173, 184–5; approved by McNeill J in *Warner Holidays Ltd.* v. *Secretary of State for Social Services* [1983] ICR 440, 453–4 and by Nolan J in *Wickens* v. *Champion Employment* [1984] ICR 365, 369.

[42] Describing the 'worker' as an independent contractor may confer upon him tax benefits; but it may also decrease his protection if his claim for compensation for personal injury is at stake. See, for instance, *Lane* v. *Shire Roofing* [1995] IRLR 493 (CA). But, it seems, the courts will rarely admit this openly.

accept it even if the parties themselves have given a different label to their relationship. So, in *Ferguson* v. *John Dawson & Partners (Contractors) Ltd.*[43] the plaintiff worked on the defendant's building site and was described as a subcontractor working as part of the 'lump' labour force.[44] He was injured, and argued that he was an employee for the purposes of statutory safety duties owed by employers to their employees. The defendant's contention, that the parties had characterised their relationship as that of employer-independent contractor and that the statutory duties were thus not owed to the plaintiff, was rejected, since in the court's view all the other circumstances pointed towards a relationship of employer and employee. Where, however, the surrounding circumstances point towards a relation of either employer–employee or employer–independent contractor and there is no underlying illegality, there is no reason why the courts should not strive to give effect to the label that the parties have attached to their relationship.[45]

The preceding paragraph may be an over—simplification of the law in so far as it implied that in the absence of any illegality the will of the parties-as manifested in the negotiated terms—may be paramount. In reality, however, it appears that the courts go beyond the declared will of the parties and take into account wider societal interests whenever they conclude that the label chosen by the parties, however honestly chosen, must give way to the true realities of each situation.[46] So, in *Warner Holidays Ltd.* v. *Secretary of State for Social Services* [47] McNeil J said:

> When the community has an interest . . . in the collection of contributions for social security purposes, while the intention of the parties as to the nature of the contract they intend is itself important, it is not necessarily conclusive. The parties to a contract of employment cannot, by private arrangement, exclude from the arrangement public and community obligations.

43 [1976] 1 WLR 1213. To similar effect, see the recent decision of the Privy Council in *Lee Ting Sang* v. *Chung Chi-Keung* [1990] 2 AC 374.

44 Such characterisation can bring legal and illegal advantages to both contracting parties. In the case of a self-employed person, for example, the employer is spared the trouble of making deductions in respect of income tax and paying National Health Insurance contributions. It can also mean that in a case like *Ferguson* v. *Dawson* the employer will not be liable for breach of certain statutory duties, which are meant to ensure the safety of employees. For a worker, his description as a self-employed person may enable him to deduct certain expenses from his pay-packet and generally place him in a better tax position, and it may also give him the opportunity illegally to evade tax obligations, since as a self-employed person he is responsible for his own tax declarations.

45 *Massey* v. *Crown Life Insurance Co.* [1978] 1 WLR 676. It will be noted that in this case there was no suspicion of tax impropriety. For a more recent decision suggesting that the courts will regard illegality arguments with scepticism in the context of tort claims and certain statutory claims, see *Hall* v. *Woolston Hall Leisure Ltd.* [2000] IRLR 578. The status of home-workers and part-time workers can also have important consequences as far as payment of social-security contributions, withholding of taxes, and the law of unfair dismissal is concerned. The case law gives no unequivocal guidance on this. There is a very large case law, discussed by S. Deakin and G. Morris, *Labour Law* (5th edn., 2005), paras. 3.29–3.32.

46 'The question [whether the plaintiff is an employee or an independent contractor] is not determined by the label which the parties themselves put on the relationship': per Mummery J in *McMeechan* v. *Secretary of State for Employment* [1995] IRLR 461, 463.

47 [1983] ICR 440, 454; although cf. *Calder* v. *H. Kitson Vickers (& Sons) Engineers Ltd.* [1988] ICR 232, 250 (Ralph Gibson LJ).

It may be reasonable, therefore, to assume that in that case the state's interest in collecting national insurance contributions from the employer may have influenced the court's decision to hold that the contractual terms of entertainers engaged at a holiday camp for a summer season should be interpreted as making the entertainers 'employed earners'. In other instances, however, the courts may have been influenced in their characterisation of the relationship by other factors such as the desire to protect employees from contracting out of the advantages given to them by employment legislation. So, in *Young and Woods* v. *West*[48] a skilled metal-worker who had clearly opted in favour of being described as 'self employed' (since this gave him a legitimate tax advantage) was, nevertheless, held to be an employee when he was dismissed and then (successfully) blew 'hot and cold' and invoked statutory employment rights. Thus the dividing line between all these cases is often a fine one; and the partial concealment by the courts of the true reasons that motivate their decisions make it difficult to state the law with any greater degree of authority.

Before leaving this topic some mention should be made of 'borrowed' employees, which is best illustrated by *Mersey Docks and Harbour Board* v. *Coggins and Griffith (Liverpool) Ltd.*[49] A harbour authority hired out to X, a firm of stevedores, a mobile crane with its operator. The contract expressly provided that the operator was to work for the time being as the employee of X, although the harbour authority retained the power of dismissal. The question was whether it or X was vicariously liable to the plaintiff, who was injured by the negligence of the operator. It was held that the harbour authority was liable as it still controlled the manner in which the crane was worked. This case is one of a number dealing with the same problem, but it probably contains the clearest enunciation of the applicable principles. Though obviously a number of factors have to be considered in deciding which of the two masters will be liable, the courts still attach significance to the control test as an ultimate resort. Other factors include the type of machinery that has been loaned (the more complicated it is, the more likely the permanent employer will remain liable), the duration of the service under the temporary employer, and such general matters as who pays, who pays his national insurance contributions, who retains the power of dismissal, and whether the two employers themselves have attempted to regulate this matter.

The general employer's ability to shift liability on to the shoulders of the temporary employer may, however, be seriously restricted by the Unfair Contract Terms Act 1977 (UCTA) as two interesting and, apparently, contradictory cases suggest: *Phillips Products* v. *Hyland*[50] and *Thompson* v. *T. Lohan (Plant Hire) Ltd.*[51] *Phillips* and *Thompson* had, for all intents and purposes, similar facts. They both involved owners hiring out JCBs along with their operators. Both contracts of hire made, according to their clauses 8, the hirers

48 [1980] IRLR 201.

49 [1947] AC 1, 61. It was further said, at 13–14, that the question which of the two employers would be liable for the tort of the borrowed servant was not determined by any agreement between them.

50 [1987] 1 WLR 659. Despite the year of publication this decision was, in fact, decided two and a half years earlier than *Thompson*.

51 [1987] 1 WLR 649.

(temporary employers) and not the owners of the machinery (permanent employers) liable for the negligent conduct of the machine operators. In both cases the operators' negligence caused harm—in *Phillips* it damaged the hirer's property; in *Thompson*'s case it killed the plaintiff's husband who was also employed by the owner of the machinery. In *Phillips* the plaintiffs (hirers) sued the owners of the machinery for the damage to their property. The owners relied on clause 8 of the contract (with the hirers) and attempted to deny liability for the operator's negligence. The Court of Appeal took the view that clause 8 was caught by section 2(2) of UCTA and would protect the owners if the clause satisfied the requirement of reasonableness as set out in section 13 of UCTA. In the court's view it did not, and hence the clause transferring liability to the hirers (and, in effect, exonerating the owners) was held to be void.

In *Thompson*, by contrast, the plaintiff's widow sued the owner of the machinery (permanent employer of the negligent operator) and recovered damages. In third-party proceedings the owner then tried to shift the loss on to the hirer (temporary employer of the negligent operator). Not unnaturally the defendants (hirers) tried to invoke UCTA in order to avoid the application of clause 8 which, if valid, would transfer liability to them. This move, though—as we have seen, successful in *Phillips*—failed in *Thompson*.

The different treatment of clause 8 by the two courts raises a number of questions. Arguably, however, the different treatment of the same clause can be explained by the fact that if it had been validated in *Phillips* it would, in effect, have denied a remedy to the victims of the negligent act, whereas in *Thompson* the validation of clause 8 did not deny the victim (Mrs Thompson) any remedy but merely stopped the owner of the machinery (first defendant) from shifting the loss to the hirer (second defendant). Such an interpretation (and reconciliation of the two cases)[52] thus makes the validity of such indemnity clauses depend on how they affect the primary victim. 'If the victim's claim is prejudiced by an indemnity clause, then section 2 [of the UCTA] applies (as in *Phillips*) [and makes the transfer of liability to the temporary employer void]; if the victim's claim is not prejudiced, then section 2 [of the UCTA] does not apply [and the clause is valid, transferring ultimate liability on to the shoulders of the temporary employer].'[53]

In view of the above it is, therefore, safe to assert that, overall, the courts place a heavy burden of proof on the permanent employer before they will allow him to shift responsibility on to the shoulders of the temporary employer.[54] There may, however, be much to be said for the view taken by some American courts which allows the plaintiff to sue *both* employers and have them subsequently sort out among themselves which of them

[52] This is the explanation offered by J. N. Adams and R. Brownsword, 'Double Indemnity–Contractual Indemnity, Clauses Revisited' (Select Bibliography), and it seems convincing, not least since it derives some support from Fox LJ's judgment in *Thompson* v. *T. Lohan (Plant Hire) Ltd.* [1987] 1 WLR 649, 657.

[53] Adams and Brownsword (Select Bibliography), 149.

[54] This is certainly true where skilled workers are left with complicated machinery. In theory, however, it should be different where unskilled labour is hired out. See *Bhoomidas* v. *Port of Singapore Authority* [1978] 1 All ER 956, 960.

should bear the cost.[55] This approach was recently been adopted by the Court of Appeal in *Viasystems (Tyneside) Ltd.* v. *Thermal Transfer Northern Ltd.*[56] According to Rix LJ,

what one is looking for is a situation where the employee in question, at any rate for relevant purposes, is so much a part of the work, business or organisation of both employers that it is just to make both employers answer for his negligence. What has to be recalled is that the vicarious liability in question is one which involves no fault on the part of the employer. It is a doctrine designed for the sake of the claimant imposing a liability incurred without fault because the employer is treated by the law as picking up the burden of an organisational or business relationship which he has undertaken for his own benefit.[57]

The basis for his Lordship's approach was an openly functional one:

The concept of vicarious liability does not depend on the employer's fault but on his role. Liability is imposed by a policy of the law upon an employer, even though he is not personally at fault, on the basis, generally speaking, that those who set in motion and profit from the activities of their employees should compensate those who are injured by such activities even when performed negligently. Liability is extended to the employer on the practical assumption that, inter alia because he can spread the risk through pricing and insurance, he is better organised and able to bear that risk than the employee, even if the latter himself of course remains responsible; and at the same time the employer is encouraged to control that risk.[58]

So-called 'triangular' employment relationships in which a worker is hired out by an employment agency to work for a 'user' employer for a period of time, are a major source of difficulty in this area of law. *Viasystems* offers one solution—imposing dual vicarious liability. But there are other issues. It may not be clear that the worker has a regular employment relationship with either employer. Normally the worker will have a contract with the agency, which may not necessarily be a contract of employment; if work is only provided on an intermittent basis, it may only be a contract for services,[59] in which case the agency may not be vicariously liable for any torts committed by the worker. Nor will the user employer be liable if, as will often be the case, it can show that there was no contractual nexus of any kind between him and the worker. Recent case law suggests that such a contract may be implied in an appropriate case, but that it is not permissible to do so unless such an implication is necessary in order to give legal effect to the intentions of the parties, and that the mere presence of control by the user employer is not enough.[60]

55 *Strait* v. *Hale Constr. Co.*, 26 Cal. Ap. 3d 941, 103 Cal. Rptr. 487 (1972) and for further references to US views, see J. A. Henderson and R. N. Pearson, *The Torts Process* (1981), 177–9; and for an analysis of the parallel problem in UK labour law, see S. Deakin, 'The Changing Concept of the "Employer" in Labour Law' (2001) 30 *ILJ* 72.

56 [2005] EWCA Civ. 1151; see also *Horley* v. *Luminar Leisure Ltd.* [2006] IRLR 817. Prior to *Viasystems*, the general view of the English courts had been that dual vicarious liability was impossible on the grounds that 'a servant cannot have two masters' (see the judgment of Littledale J in *Lather* v. *Pointer* (1826) 5 B & C 547).

57 *Viasystems (Tyneside) Ltd.* v. *Thermal Transfer (Northern) Ltd.* [2005] EWCA Civ. 1151, para 79 (Rix LJ).

58 *Ibid.*, para 55 (Rix LJ).

59 See e.g. *Wickens* v. *Champion Employment Agency* [1984] ICR 365; *Ironmonger* v. *Movefield Ltd.* [1988] IRLR 461, noted above in our discussion of mutuality of obligation.

60 See *Dacas* v. *Brook Street Bureau (UK) Ltd.* [2004] IRLR 368; *Cable and Wireless plc* v. *Muscat* [2006] IRLR 354; *Cairns* v. *Visteon Ltd.*, EAT, Appeal No. UKEAT/0494/06/JOJ, 29 November 2006 (discussing the

Another special case of vicarious liability is 'casual delegation', where, for example, one person drives another's car with his permission and, partly at least, in his interest. In these cases there is no employment relationship and the courts use the terms 'principal' and 'agent' rather loosely. Whatever the terminology, the fact is that the courts are prepared to hold the owner of a vehicle liable for the negligence of its driver when the latter is driving with the owner's permission and, partly at least, in the latter's interests. In *Ormrod* v. *Crosville Motor Services Ltd.*,[61] A asked B to drive his (A's) car from England to the South of France where eventually they were to have a joint holiday. While still in England B negligently caused an accident for which A was held vicariously liable, even though B was not A's employee, because B was pursuing not only his own interests but A's as well. Subsequently, the Court of Appeal in *Morgans* v. *Launchbury*[62] attempted, largely out of insurance considerations, to widen this type of vicarious liability by applying it to the authorised use of cars even where the owner had no interest or concern in the use; but the House of Lords[63] reversed the decision and reinstated the traditional rule. In that case the defendant wife owned a car, which was treated as a 'family' car. Her husband promised her that he would get a friend to drive should he ever have too much to drink. One day the husband got drunk and asked C, a friend, to drive him and the plaintiffs back home. Owing to C's negligence a collision occurred in which the husband was killed and the plaintiffs were injured. The Court of Appeal by a majority held that the defendant should be vicariously liable since she had allowed the use of her car. The House of Lords unanimously reversed the decision on the ground that mere permission to drive without the owner having some concern or interest in the use of the car was insufficient to render her vicariously liable. But the defendant/owner of the loaned car (or other chattel) must have a specific and identifiable interest in the use of the car.[64]

2. THE EMPLOYEE MUST COMMIT A TORT

This requirement seems obvious since vicarious liability is, by definition, liability imposed on one person for the wrongdoing of another. It has been challenged by the so-called 'employer's tort' theory, according to which an employer is liable because the employee's wrongdoing is the employer's own tort, i.e. liability is primary, not vicarious.[65] Whatever its merits, this theory was repudiated by the House of Lords in *Staveley Iron and Chemical Co. Ltd.* v. *Jones*,[66] which restored the traditional view, namely that vicarious

relevance of *Viasystems* in this context); *James* v. *Greenwich LBC*, EAT, Appeal No. UKEAT/0006/06/ZT 21 December 2006.

[61] [1953] 1 WLR 1120. Cf. *Hewitt* v. *Bonvin* [1940] 1 KB 188, where the defendant, who lent his car to his son entirely for the latter's use, was not held responsible for damage negligently caused by him.

[62] [1971] 2 QB 245. [63] [1973] AC 127. [64] *Norwood* v. *Navan* [1981] RTR 457.

[65] G. L. Williams, 'Vicarious Liability: Tort of the Master or of the Servant?' (Select Bibliography); cf. the language of Denning LJ in e.g. *Cassidy* v. *Ministry of Health* [1951] 2 KB 343, 361.

[66] [1956] AC 627.

liability is indeed vicarious and an employer can only be liable provided his employee commits a tort. A mere procedural bar, however, preventing action against the employee does not relieve the employer, because the employee remains guilty of a tort, albeit one for which *he* cannot be sued. So, in *Broom* v. *Morgan*[67] the plaintiff and her husband were employed by the defendant. The plaintiff was injured through her husband's negligence and she sued the defendant who disputed vicarious liability, contending that, as the law then stood, husbands and wives could not sue each other in tort, and that if the husband was not liable to his wife, he could not be liable either.[68] The Court of Appeal, however, held him liable, since the husband's immunity was only from suit, not from responsibility for a tort. This was also the *ratio* of *Smith* v. *Moss*,[69] where the plaintiff recovered damages from her mother-in-law, who was held vicariously liable for the negligent driving of her son, the husband of the plaintiff, since on the facts he was acting as her agent *ad hoc*.

The traditional theory received further support in *Imperial Chemical Industries Ltd.* v. *Shatwell*.[70] Two brothers, George and James, were employed as shot-firers. Safety regulations, imposed on them personally, required that tests of electrical circuits for shot-firing should only be conducted from behind cover, but rather than inconvenience themselves by having to comply with regulations, they agreed to test a circuit in the open. An explosion followed, injuring both of them. George sued the company, alleging that it was vicariously liable for the negligence and breach of regulations by his brother James. The House of Lords held the company not liable on the ground of consent. Since James himself would not have been liable to George for this reason, the employers were entitled to the vicarious benefit of that defence just as they would have had to carry the vicarious liability in its absence. Lord Pearce put the point succinctly: '[u]nless the servant is liable the master is not liable for his acts; subject only to this, that the master cannot take advantage of an immunity from suit conferred on the servant.'[71]

3. COURSE OF EMPLOYMENT[72]

The most vexed requirement is that an employee has to commit his tort 'in the course of his employment'. The problem is to devise suitable criteria for determining this, and to apply these to particular situations. Unfortunately, the plethora of often irreconcilable authorities does not make the task of exposition easy. As Comyn J said: 'the large body of case law... is notable for one thing, its inconsistency very often with an immediately preceding case'.[73] However, without detracting from the wisdom of that warning, one is

67 [1953] 1 QB 597.

68 The husband-and-wife rule has since been abolished by the Law Reform (Husband and Wife) Act 1962.

69 [1940] 1 KB 424.

70 [1965] AC 656. The regulations have since been altered so as to impose the obligation on the master.

71 *Ibid.*, at 686.

72 For a thorough discussion, see Atiyah (Select Bibliography), 171–285. See also James (Select Bibliography), 173 ff.

73 *Harrison* v. *Michelin Tyre Co. Ltd.* [1985] 1 All ER 918, 920.

tempted to suggest that the courts tend to expand the notion of 'course of employment' if by doing so they are serving better an 'important purpose'.

(A) POLICY FACTORS

One such important purpose, for which admittedly there seems to be little express textual support, can be found in the courts' desire to secure a source of compensation for the victim of the tort.[74] A wider understanding of the notion of course of employment has this effect since it provides the victim of the tort with a solvent and creditworthy person (the employer) to sue. Equally, the courts are increasingly aware of the importance of economic factors in this context. Thus one justification for widening the scope of vicarious liability is the employer's superior capacity to spread certain risks through insurance. Conversely, vicarious liability may be seen as providing employers with incentives to control and limit such risks in the face of potential legal liability. These ideas are at the core of the 'enterprise risk' theory of vicarious liability which has been influential in a number of recent British and Commonwealth decisions. As Lord Nicholls put it in *Dubai Aluminium Co. Ltd.* v. *Salaam*:[75]

> The underlying legal policy is based on the recognition that carrying on a business enterprise necessarily involves risk to others. It involves the risk that other will be harmed by wrongful acts committed by the agents through whom the business is carried on. When those risks ripen into loss, it is just that the business should be responsible for compensating the person who has been wronged.

Another important purpose of vicarious liability which is reflected in the 'course of employment concept' is related to the protection of human rights, such as the right not to be discriminated against on the grounds of race, sex or disability. Thus, in *Jones* v. *Tower Boot Co. Ltd.*[76] the Court of Appeal, after stating that the meaning of 'course of employment' should be given a wider meaning whenever the Race Relations Act 1976 was involved, proceeded to hold an employer liable for the actions of his employees which violated section 32(1) of the 1976 Act.[77]

74 One could further refine this *speculation* by saying that the courts will enlarge the course of employment if they are anxious to secure compensation for physical injuries suffered by the victim, but they will be less likely to do the same thing if he has suffered only pure economic loss. Cf., for instance, two decisions: *Vasey* v. *Surrey Free Inns* (1995) 10 CL 641 (employer liable for assault committed by his employee) and *Generale Bank Nederland NV* v. *Export Credit Guarantee Department* [1998] 1 Lloyd's Rep. 19 (employer not liable for employee's fraudulent acts which were not within his ostensible authority).

75 [2002] 3 WLR 1913 at [21]. The enterprise risk theory prominently featured in the two landmark decisions of the Supreme Court of Canada in *Children's Foundation* v. *Bazley* (1999) 174 DLR (4th) 45 and *Jacobi* v. *Boys' and Girls' Club of Vernon* (1999) 174 DLR (4th) 71. By contrast, the decision of the House of Lords in *Lister* v. *Hesley Hall Ltd.* [2001] 2 AC 215, while arriving at the same outcome as *Bazley*, made less use of this notion. See our discussion of *Lister* below, Section (e).

76 [1997] ICR 254.

77 One is inclined to think that the same would apply to the corresponding s. 41 of the Sex Discrimination Act 1975. However, for a sceptical view of the claim that cases such as *Jones* v. *Tower Boot* should influence the common law of tort, see Lord Clyde in *Lister* v. *Hesley Hall Ltd.* [2001] 2 AC 215, 234.

(B) TESTS BASED ON IMPLIED AUTHORITY

Let us return to the main point discussed in this subsection. That an employer is liable for acts that he expressly authorises is obvious; but this is primary, not vicarious, liability. Clearly, it is impractical to require that an employer should specifically authorise each and every action of his employee. So from early times it was sought to justify the employer's vicarious liability on the hypothesis of implied authority. The difficulty was to fix the limits of this, and the solution was to say that authority is deemed to extend only so far as the scope of the employment. Was implied authority, then, the test of the scope of employment, or vice versa? It was neither; and it only helped to confuse matters, for in reality it was little more than a justification for the decision to make employers liable for the torts of employees. Nonetheless, the language of implied authority as the test of scope of employment has been used.

In *Poland* v. *Parr & Sons*[78] the employee of a company reasonably believed that some children were stealing a company's property and he struck one of them, who was seriously injured. It was held that although his act was unreasonable it was still within the course of his employment, because, in the words of Bankes LJ: 'As a general rule a servant has an implied authority upon an emergency to endeavour to protect his master's property if he sees it in danger or has reasonable ground for thinking that he sees it in danger.' The case involved assault and battery by the servant, and the difficulty of holding such acts as being in the course of his employment is obvious. The notion of implied authority was here clearly of some use, for if the act complained of could be regarded as one which the employee has discretion to do, then the employer can be held liable even for the wrongful exercise of that discretion. In *Poland* v. *Parr* such discretion to protect the employer's property was readily applied, but Atkin LJ was also eager to state its limits:

> where the servant does more than the emergency requires, the excess may be so great as to take the act out of the class. For example, if Hall [the employee] had fired a shot at the boy, the act might have been in the interest of his employers, but that is not the test.[79]

Thus an employee who wrongly arrests someone after a supposed attempt at theft has ceased is not regarded as acting within the limits of implied authority because his motive is no longer protection of property but vindication of justice.[80]

In another case[81] the employer of a garage attendant who out of personal vengeance attacked one of the customers was not liable. Similarly, a bus passenger who complained of a bus conductor's language and found himself assaulted by the conductor as a result cannot render the latter's employer liable.[82] However, the employer of a person put in

[78] [1927] 1 KB 236, 240.

[79] *Ibid.*, at 245. Does an employee have a discretion to protect the property of a third party entrusted to the care of his master? Liability for an employee's assault is discussed by F. D. Rose in 'Liability for an Employee's Assaults' (Select Bibliography).

[80] *Hanson* v. *Waller* [1901] 1 QB 390.

[81] *Warren* v. *Henlys Ltd.* [1948] 2 All ER 935.

[82] *Keppel Bus Co. Ltd.* v. *Sa'ad bin Ahmad* [1974] 1 WLR 1082. In an earlier case, however, a tram company was held liable when one of the conductors pushed a passenger off the tram: *Smith* v. *North Metropolitan*

charge of premises (e.g. a public house) or of a vehicle (or vessel) will be liable for the reasonable force used by such a person to maintain order on the premises, car or vessel, and may even be liable (though, it is submitted less justifiably so) where the wrongful act was primarily motivated by malice or spite.[83] Such extensions of liability, however, though explicable, perhaps, by reference to 'deep pocket' theories, must not be undertaken lightly if the doctrine of vicarious liability is not to be totally distorted. On the whole, therefore, in such cases it is better to try to base liability on the employer's own fault in selecting an aggressive or irresponsible employee or some other grounds of liability.

Several cases establish that it is not enough that the employment merely gave the employee the opportunity to commit the wrong. That is why a firm of cleaners will not be liable if one of its employees uses the plaintiff's telephone while cleaning the latter's premises and runs up high bills as a result of making unauthorised calls.[84] In *General Engineering Services Ltd.* v. *Kingston and Saint Andrew Corp.*[85] the plaintiff's house was burnt down because the local firemen had an industrial dispute with their employers (defendants) and operated a 'go slow' policy as a result of which it took them seventeen minutes (instead of three) to cover the distance from the fire brigade's offices to the plaintiff's home. The Privy Council refused to hold the employers vicariously liable. It is unclear whether this ruling would also cover the situation in which the employees were involved in an all-out strike rather than performing their work badly in pursuance of an industrial dispute.

It is significant, in this context, that tests of the employer's vicarious liability under statutes such as the Race Relations Act 1976, which are meant to have an educative or exemplary effect upon employers, are beginning to diverge from the common-law test. In *Irving* v. *The Post Office*[86] the Court of Appeal held that the Post Office was not vicariously liable under the Race Relations Act for racially abusive words written on an envelope by one of their employees who bore a grudge against the plaintiffs (who were his neighbours) who were of Jamaican origin. However, in the later case of *Jones* v. *Tower Boot Co. Ltd.*,[87] the Court of Appeal, as we have seen, took a broader view of the 1976 Act. Here, an employer took no action to prevent racial taunts and assaults that were directed by his employees against one of their fellow workers. The Employment Appeal Tribunal held that the employer was not vicariously liable under the Act for the

Tramways Co. (1891) 55 JP 630. For a more recent decision (imposing liability) see *Vasey* v. *Surrey Free Inns* [1995] 10 CL 641.

83 *Petterson* v. *Royal Oak Hotel Ltd.* [1948] NZLR 136. This and other related cases are discussed by Rose (Select Bibliography).

84 *Heasmans* v. *Clarity Cleaning Co. Ltd.* [1987] ICR 949.

85 [1989] 1 WLR 69.

86 [1987] IRLR 289. See also *Deaton's Property Ltd.* v. *Flew* (1949) 79 CLR 370: the employers of a barmaid were not held responsible when she threw a glass of beer at a customer.

87 [1997] IRLR 168. See also the Race Relations Act case of *Burton* v. *De Vere Hotels Ltd.* [1996] IRLR 596, dealing with the statutory equivalent to the employer's personal duty of care, and taking a broad view of liability which was, however, doubted in the subsequent House of Lords decisions in *MacDonald* v *Advocate General for Scotland*, *Pearce* v. *Governors of Mayfield Secondary School* [2003] IRLR 512.

actions of his employees, but the Court of Appeal reversed on the ground that this would produce the perverse result that 'the more heinous the act of discrimination, the less likely it will be that the employer would be liable'.[88] In this case, the court took the view that the statutory background in this case justified it taking a view of the employer's vicarious liability that went beyond the common-law approach. However, it is not inconceivable that innovations in statutory interpretation, such as this, can also have an influence on the development of the common law, just as the common law plainly influences to some degree the interpretation of the statute.[89]

At common law it nevertheless remains the case that the definition of 'scope of employment' is crucial though, unfortunately, numerous decided cases show it cannot be reduced to a concise and workable formula. As Finnemore J remarked: 'I think the answer to much of the argument on both sides is that there is no one test which is exhaustive by which this particular problem can be solved.'[90] Notwithstanding the above statement, courts often appear to find less difficulty with this issue than writers who keep striving to reconcile the irreconcilable. There seems to be only one simple rule: if an employee committed his tort within the scope of his employment, the employer is liable; if he acted outside it, the employer is not liable. The question whether an act was within or outside the scope of employment is one of fact. As the Lord President put it in the leading Scottish case of *Kirby* v. *National Coal Board*: [91] 'It is probably not possible, and it is certainly inadvisable, to endeavour to lay down an exhaustive definition of what falls within the scope of the employment. Each case must depend to a considerable extent on its particular facts.'

(C) DISTINGUISHING BETWEEN 'AUTHORISED ACTS' AND 'UNAUTHORISED MODES'

So how do the courts approach this task? It appears that the position is analogous to that in negligence where likewise there is a simple rule; if a person has behaved carelessly, he is liable (subject to certain other conditions being fulfilled); if he was not careless, he is not liable. The question whether his behaviour was careless or not is one of fact. Just as there are guidelines (not rules) to help in determining carelessness, so too there are only guidelines that help in determining scope of employment. The decision is ultimately impressionistic. Leaving aside the 'implied authority' fiction, the test is simply: was this what the employee was employed to do? was it a bad way of doing it? The courts have in fact frequently used Salmond's formulation[92] as a starting-point,

88 [1997] IRLR 168, 172.

89 See S. Deakin, 'Private Law, Economic Rationality and the Regulatory State' in P. B. H. Birks (ed.), *The Classification of Obligations* (1997).

90 *Staton* v. *NCB* [1957] 1 WLR 893, 895.

91 1958 SC 514, 532 quoted with approval by the House of Lords in *Williams* v. *A. & W. Hemphill Ltd.*, 1966 SLT 259, 260 (another deviation case containing interesting *dicta*).

92 R. F. V. Heuston and R. A. Buckley, *Salmond and Heuston on Torts* (19th edn., 1987), 521. In *Harrison* v. *Michelin Tyre Co. Ltd.* [1985] 1 All ER 918, 920, Comyn J suggested a paraphrase which, in some cases, might prove more helpful: 'was the incident [complained of] part and parcel of the employment in the sense of being

according to which a wrongful act is deemed to be in the course of employment 'if it is either (1) a wrongful act authorised by the master, or (2) a wrongful and unauthorised mode of doing some act authorised by the master'. From there on, the process is one of applying these guidelines to the facts in a way that conforms to the judge's overall appreciation of the merits of the case and without attaching too much importance to available precedents.

Under this approach, an employer may sometimes be liable even for an act which he has forbidden. An obvious reason for this harsh possibility is that if the law were otherwise, an employer need only issue appropriate instructions to evade liability. There are, however, different kinds of prohibitions. One kind may delimit the scope of employment so that if the employee disobeys he acts outside it. Another kind may only limit the manner in which a job is to be done without limiting the job itself. The distinction is easier to grasp than apply. A general statement of it was made by Lord Dunedin in *Plumb* v. *Cobden Flour Mills Co. Ltd.*:[93]

> There are prohibitions which limit the sphere of employment, and prohibitions which only deal with conduct within the sphere of employment. A transgression of a prohibition of the latter class leaves the sphere of employment where it was, and consequently will not prevent recovery of compensation. A transgression of the former class carries with it the result that the man has gone outside the sphere.

An early case applying this test was *Bayley* v. *The Manchester, Sheffield and Lincolnshire Railway Co.*[94] A porter in the company's service forcibly removed the plaintiff from the train, erroneously believing that he was in the wrong carriage. It was the duty of porters to ensure that passengers were in their right carriages. The company was held liable. The porter's tort was held to have been committed within the scope of his employment, since he was doing clumsily what he was employed to do, namely to see that passengers were in the right carriages. Kelly CB said: 'It is obviously very likely that the servant may, while acting in the performance of the general duty cast upon him, neglect any particular direction as to the mode of doing it. But it appears to me that he will be none the less acting within the scope of his employment.'

One cannot, therefore, generalise, nor should one dissect the employee's task into its component activities. In Diplock LJ's words, 'the matter must be looked at broadly'[95] and all the surrounding circumstances carefully taken into account. The various ways in which an employee can be said to perform his duty wrongfully, and so make his employer liable, are truly infinite. For instance, in *Century Insurance Co. Ltd.* v. *Northern Ireland Road Transport Board*,[96] the driver of a petrol lorry negligently threw down

incidental to it although and albeit unauthorized or prohibited? . . . or was it so divergent from the employment as to be plainly alien to and wholly distinguishable from the employment? A "reasonable approach" must be adopted in answering these questions.'

93 [1914] AC 62, 67.

94 (1873) LR 8 CP 148, esp. at 153, per Kelly CB. Blackburn J seemed to hint that the company was liable for its own negligence in failing to select a good servant.

95 *Ilkiw* v. *Samuels* [1963] 1 WLR 991, 1004. See also *Duffy* v. *Thanet District Council* (1984) 134 *NLJ* 680, *Harrison* v. *Michelin Tyre Co. Ltd.* [1985] 1 All ER 918.

96 [1942] AC 509.

a lighted match while petrol was being transferred from the lorry to a tank. An explosion and fire ensued. Viscount Simon had no doubt that his act was in the course of employment; and the way he stated it was that 'negligence in starting smoking and throwing away a lighted match in that moment is plainly negligence in the discharge of the duties upon which he was employed'.[97]

Two cases illustrate the point. In *Limpus* v. *London General Omnibus Co.*[98] the defendants forbade drivers of buses to race on the road. One driver disobeyed instructions and caused a collision. The defendants were held liable as the driver was still acting within the scope of his employment. On the other hand, in *Conway* v. *George Wimpey & Co. Ltd.*[99] the defendants provided transport for their workmen to distant parts of a construction site. As other firms were also working there, the defendants gave specific directions to the drivers of their lorries not to transport any workmen employed by other firms. One driver gave a lift to the plaintiff, who was employed by another firm, but the driver was not aware of this. The plaintiff was injured by the driver's negligence, but the Court of Appeal held the defendants not liable, one reason being that the driver was acting outside the scope of his employment. The distinction between these two is that in *Limpus* the driver was doing the job he was employed to do, namely to drive a bus for public transport; disobeying the instructions not to race only made it a bad way of doing that job. In *Conway*, on the other hand, the driver was employed to transport only the defendants' workmen; when he gave a lift to a workman employed by another firm, he was not doing that job. But Asquith LJ did not even attempt to distinguish; he simply brushed *Limpus* aside with the remark: 'I am not unaware that a prohibition has been held in some cases not to curtail the scope of employment, as in *Limpus* v. *London General Omnibus Co.*, but I think it does so in this case.'[100]

The statement is revealing in that it shows that judges appear to treat this matter as a question of fact and are not disposed to worry over much about nice distinctions. But though judges treat these matters as ultimately questions of fact, they have on several occasions tried to formulate general guidelines and have warned against the risk of applying too narrow a test in deciding whether the act complained of is a different act or a bad way of performing an authorised act. Thus in *Ilkiw* v. *Samuels*[101] Diplock LJ argued that:

> where there is an express prohibition, the decision into which of these two classes the prohibition falls seems to me to involve first determining what would have been the sphere, scope, course... of the servant's employment if the prohibition had not been imposed. As each of these nouns implies, the matter must be looked at broadly, not dissecting the servant's

[97] *Ibid.*, at 514.

[98] (1862) 1 H & C 526; 158 ER 993.

[99] [1951] 2 KB 266.

[100] [1951] 2 KB at 276. See also *Ricketts* v. *Thomas Tilling Ltd.* [1915] 1 KB 644, where a retrial was ordered as there was evidence that the bus-driver was negligent in letting the conductor turn it round—i.e. that it was a bad way of doing his job of driving a bus. Cf. *Beard* v. *London General Omnibus Co.* [1900] 2 QB 530, where a conductor who decided to drive the bus himself was acting outside the course of his employment. This was not his job.

[101] [1963] 1 WLR 991, 1004.

task into its component activities... by asking, what was the job on which he was engaged for his employer? and answering that question as a jury would.

In *Rose* v. *Plenty*[102] a milkman, contrary to an express prohibition, took a young boy with him on his milk round. Partly owing to the boy's own carelessness, but mainly owing to the milkman's negligent driving, the boy was injured. Despite the express prohibition, the majority of the Court of Appeal had no doubt about holding the employer vicariously liable; the employee was still performing the duty he had been employed to perform, even though he was carrying it out in a bad way. The decision is in tune with the prevailing tendency to give a generous interpretation to course of employment; but, despite Scarman LJ's efforts, it is not easily reconcilable with earlier cases. In both *Twine* v. *Bean's Express Ltd.*[103] and *Conway* v. *Wimpey*[104] the employers were held not liable when their employees, through their negligent driving, injured passengers whom they should not have allowed into the vehicles. Perhaps, in view of what we have said, such a reconciliation is neither always possible nor even desirable, since decisions in this area of the law should not be used like tintacks with which to nail down particular solutions, but simply as starting-points in a process of reasoning by analogy, by the use of contrasting examples, guided by common sense. Nevertheless, one possible reconciliation can be found in Lord Denning MR's judgment, which stressed that in *Rose* v. *Plenty*, by contrast with *Twine* and *Conway*, the unauthorised passenger was furthering the purposes of the employer (i.e. by helping to distribute the milk).[105]

(D) ROAD-TRAFFIC CASES: DETOUR, DEVIATION AND TRAVEL TO AND FROM WORK

Considerable difficulty has also arisen in cases where drivers of vehicles depart from the authorised routes. The question whether they are still within the scope of employment while on detour is again not easily answered. The classical formulation is that of Parke B in *Joel* v. *Morrison*:[106] '[i]f he [the driver] was going out of his way, against his master's implied commands, when driving on his master's business, he will make his master liable; but if he was going on a frolic of his own, without being at all on his master's business, the master will not be liable.' This test is devoid of guidance since it begs the question. To call an action a 'frolic' is not to give a reason why it is outside the course of employment; it only expresses a decision already made that it is outside. The real question is, why is it a 'frolic'? The answer is purely a matter of impression, and much

102 [1976] 1 WLR 141.

103 (1946) 62 TLR 458, an ambiguously phrased judgment, especially at first instance, scrutinised by F. H. Newark, '*Twine* v. *Bean's Express Ltd.*' (Select Bibliography).

104 [1951] 2 KB 266.

105 A presumed benefit which the employer obviously did not desire if it were accompanied by corresponding liability.

106 (1834) 6 C & P 501, 503; 172 ER 1338, 1339. '[A] memorable phrase [that] has been the subject matter of innumerable questions in Law examinations for the last 150 years': per Comyn J in *Harrison* v. *Michelin Tyre Co. Ltd.* [1985] 1 All ER 918, 919.

depends on the way in which the factual statement is phrased. Often a decision turns on which of two alternative ways of stating the same activity is more plausible, one form of words making it fall within the course of employment, the other making it fall outside. For instance, in *Storey* v. *Ashton*[107] Cockburn CJ said:

> I am very far from saying, if a servant when going on his master's business took a somewhat longer road, that owing to this deviation he would cease to be in the employment of the master, so as to divest the latter of all liability; in such cases, it is a question of degree as to how far the deviation could be considered a separate journey. Such a consideration is applicable to the present case, because here the cabman started on an entirely new and independent journey which has nothing at all to do with his employment.

The reasoning in the concluding sentence again begs the question. Similarly, in *Hilton* v. *Thomas Burton (Rhodes) Ltd.*[108] the plaintiff's husband was killed while being driven in the defendant's car by a fellow employee. They were returning after having refreshment in a coffee shop. Diplock J held that although the driver was using the car with the defendant's permission, he was doing something he was not employed to do and, therefore, the defendants were not vicariously liable. This is simply an opinion on those facts.

Detour cases are inconclusive; so are cases involving travel by car to and from work. In this last context, however, the case of *Smith* v. *Stages*[109] contains a number of guidelines. According to Lord Lowry:

> The paramount rule is that an employee travelling on the highway will be acting in the course of his employment if, and only if, he is at the material time going about his employer's business. One must not confuse the duty to turn up for one's work with the concept of already being 'on duty' while travelling to it.[110]

His Lordship proceeded to illustrate the application of this test through a series of further propositions:

> 1. An employee travelling from his ordinary residence to his regular place of work, whatever the means of transport and even if it is provided by the employer, is not on duty and is not acting in the course of his employment, but, if he is obliged by his contract of service to use the employer's transport, he will normally, in the absence of an express condition to the contrary, be regarded as acting in the course of his employment while doing so.
>
> 2. Travelling in the employer's time between workplaces (one of which may be the regular workplace) or in the course of a peripatetic occupation, whether accompanied by goods or tools or simply in order to reach a succession of workplaces (as an inspector of gas meters might do), will be in the course of the employment.
>
> 3. Receipt of wages (though not receipt of a travelling allowance) will indicate that the employee is travelling in the employer's time and for his benefit and is acting in the course of his employment, and in such a case the fact that the employee may have discretion as to the mode and time of travelling will not take the journey out of the course of his employment.

[107] (1869) LR 4 QB 476, 479–80. [108] [1961] 1 WLR 705.

[109] [1989] AC 928. The Court of Appeal's decision, especially Glidewell LJ's judgment, printed in [1988] ICR 201, also deserves careful reading. [110] [1989] AC 928, 955–6.

4. An employee travelling *in the employer's time* from his ordinary residence to a workplace other than his regular workplace or in the course of a peripatetic occupation or to the scene of an emergency (such as a fire, an accident or a mechanical breakdown of plant) will be acting in the course of his employment.
5. A deviation from or interruption of a journey undertaken in the course of employment (unless the deviation or interruption is merely incidental to the journey) will for the time being (which may include an overnight interruption) take the employee out of the course of his employment.
6. Return journeys are to be treated on the same footing as outward journeys.

All the foregoing propositions are subject to any express arrangements between the employer and the employee or those representing his interests. They are not, I would add, intended to define the position of salaried employees, with regard to whom the touchstone of payment made in the employer's time is not generally significant.

The emphasis here, then, is on the notion of what counts as the employer's time, and on the use of the employment contract (and in particular the methods of calculating wages) for determining this.

(E) INTENTIONAL TORTS AND THE TEST OF 'SUFFICIENT CONNECTION'

This category of cases has given rise to more difficulty than any other. Theft and fraud by employees raise particular problems, for it might be thought that, cases of dishonest employers aside, no employee is employed to be dishonest.[111] Earlier cases in fact took this view, but the modern approach is much more *nuancé*. Cases involving sexual assault have seen a similar evolution towards a greater acceptance of the possibility of vicarious liability. It is in these contexts that the courts have moved beyond the traditional distinction between 'authorised acts' and 'unauthorised modes' and have applied a test of 'sufficient connection' between the wrong committed and the scope of the employee's employment.

(i) Theft

In *Morris* v. *C. W. Martin & Sons Ltd.*[112] the plaintiff took her fur coat to a furrier to be cleaned. The furrier did not undertake this type of work, so with the plaintiff's consent, but without acting as her agent, he subcontracted the work to a firm of cleaners, who handed it to one of their employees to clean. The employee stole it and the firm was held liable to the plaintiff. The firm's liability was not for any carelessness in the choice of employee, for there was no reason to suspect his honesty. Instead, its liability was based on the breach of its non-delegable duty as bailee for reward. This duty, as we have said, is not strict or absolute; it is simply a duty to see that care is taken. Lord Denning pointed out[113]

111 *Cheshire* v. *Bailey* [1905] 1 KB 237.

112 [1966] 1 QB 716, approved in *Port Swettenham Authority* v. *T. W. Wu & Co.* [1979] AC 580.

113 [1966] 1 QB 716, at 726.

that if the firm could show that it had taken care and that its employees had also exercised due diligence and, despite this, the coat had been stolen, it would have been absolved from liability. In the event, however, the firm could not establish the second part of the proposition, so it was held liable for breach of its own duty and not vicariously. The same, *primary*, liability would, probably, arise if it could be shown that the employer had negligently employed the employee who stole the plaintiff's property.

In *Nahhas* v. *Pier House (Cheyne Walk) Management Ltd.*[114] the defendant negligently hired an ex-'professional thief' to work as a porter in a block of flats. The porter, using the key entrusted to him by one of the tenants, entered the latter's flat and stole some jewellery. The employer was held primarily liable for the theft. The same would probably be true if, for instance, a security company employed an ex-thief to patrol and guard premises and the guard used his position to commit a new theft. But it would be extending liability too far if such a rule were applied indiscriminately whenever an ex-criminal was hired by an employer to do some work, for the adoption of such a wide rule of (potential) liability would defeat the general and, it is submitted, justifiable interest that society has to assist the rehabilitation of offenders.

If we return to *Morris*, however, we notice that the same result could have been achieved equally well through the doctrine of vicarious liability. For in that case the employee who stole the coat was in fact the employee who had been asked to look after it, so he could be said to have done badly what he had been asked to do properly, thereby acting in the course of his employment and rendering his employer vicariously liable.[115] On the other hand, if the coat had been stolen by another employee (for example, the night porter or a guardsman) who had not been entrusted with its care, then the employer's vicarious liability would probably have been excluded, though his primary liability under the non-delegable duty would still have been possible.

(ii) Deceit

There used to be a similar judicial reluctance to make employers liable for the fraud of their employees. It was not until the middle of the nineteenth century[116] that the possibility vicarious liability was accepted here too, though for many years it seemed that this would only have been where the employer and not just the employee benefited from the fraud. This qualification was laid to rest by the House of Lords in *Lloyd* v. *Grace, Smith & Co.*,[117] where a solicitor was held liable for the fraud of his managing clerk who, having fraudulently persuaded a client to hand over some title deeds, disposed of the property for his own benefit. The decision is important not only for its ruling, but also for its terminology. Fraud in cases such as this involves a deception of the victim by the employee, and it is impossible to say whether this deception was in the employee's course of employment before one determines the extent of his authority, whether actual or apparent, to do such acts. In *Lloyd* v. *Grace, Smith & Co.* there was such

114 [1984] 270 EG 328.

115 See also the view of Lord Steyn in *Lister* v. *Hesley Hall Ltd.* [2002] 1 AC 215, 228, that *Morris* v. *Martin* cannot be dismissed as simply a bailment case.

116 *Barwick* v. *English Joint Stock Bank* (1867) LR 2 Ex. 259.

117 [1912] AC 716.

apparent authority, for the solicitor, who took little interest in his firm's affairs, had allowed the clerk to deal with such matters and thereby represented that he had authority to do what he actually did. The conclusion, therefore, seems to be that in some cases at least—notably fraud—the employer will be vicariously liable for the employee's fraud only when the latter has acted within his ostensible authority.

For, in reality, in such cases a decision whether the employee committed a fraud 'in the course of his employment' can be made only after it has been ascertained with what authority, actual or apparent, the employee is clothed. But in torts which involve no *reliance* by the claimant upon representation by the employee, but involve other wrongs (e.g. intentional or negligent physical acts by the employee), the ostensible authority of the employee does not provide the criterion for his employer's possible vicarious liability.[118] It follows from the above that in cases where the claimant was deceived by the employee, the claimant must prove that he relied on the employee's ostensible authority and, therefore, his action will fail if, for example, he was aware that the fraudulent employee did not work for the defendants.[119]

However, there may be situations in which the employer will be vicariously liable for the employee's fraud even in the absence of actual or apparent authority. In *Dubai Aluminium Co. Ltd.* v. *Salaam*[120] the issue was whether a firm of solicitors was vicariously liable for the conduct of its senior partner who, without the knowledge of his partners, drafted a series of documents which enabled clients of the firm to defraud the claimant. The action came before the courts on the issue of contribution between the firm of the solicitors, which had settled the action brought by the claimants, and the fraudsters, and proceeded on the assumption (which was never in fact tested) that the senior partner had committed the equitable wrong of dishonestly assisting a breach of fiduciary duty.[121] The House of Lords had to decide whether the senior partner had acted 'in the course of the ordinary business of the firm' so as to make the firm vicariously liable for his wrong under section 10 of the Partnership Act 1890. Lord Nicholls, giving the leading judgment, held that this was not a case of reliance upon actual or ostensible authority, since at no point had the firm made any representation to the claimants. Nor could the conduct of the senior partner, since it was fraudulent, be said to have been authorised by his partners. However, Lord Nicholls considered that vicarious liability could be established in a case where 'the wrongful conduct [was] so closely

118 *Armagas Ltd.* v. *Mundagas SA, The Ocean Frost* [1985] 3 WLR 640 (with a most illuminating judgment by Goff LJ). For a more recent illustration see *Generale Bank Nederland NV* v. *Export Credit Guarantee Department* [1998] 1 Lloyd's Rep. 19.

119 *Kooragang Investments Property Ltd.* v. *Richardson and Wrench Ltd.* [1982] AC 462; see *Dubai Aluminium Co. Ltd.* v. *Salaam* [2002] UKHL 48, [2003] 2 AC 366, at [28]: '[t]he critical feature in this type of case is that the wronged person acted in reliance on the ostensible authority of the employee' (Lord Nicholls). Apparent authority can result only from a representation made by the principal and not the agent. For details see B. S. Markesinis and R. J.C. Munday, *An Outline of the Law of Agency* (3rd edn., 1994).

120 [2002] UKHL 48, [2003] 2 AC 366.

121 Strictly speaking, then, this was not a tort case. However, the judgments of the House of Lords proceeded on the assumption that, for this purpose, the law relating to the vicarious liability of a partnership for an equitable wrong committed by one of its partners was the same as that which would apply to the vicarious liability of an employer for a tort committed by one of its employees.

connected with acts the partner or employee was authorised to do that, for the purposes of the liability of the firm or the employer to third parties, the wrongful conduct may *fairly and properly be regarded* as done by the partner while acting in the ordinary course of the firm's business or the employee's employment'. On this basis, since the senior partner was authorised to draft documents of the type which formed the basis of the wrong in this case, the firm was vicariously liable for his wrongs.

(iii) Sexual and Other Assaults

The test of 'sufficient connection' was also used by the House of Lords in the leading case on the liability of an employer for torts involving sexual assault by an employee, *Lister* v. *Hesley Hall Ltd.*[122] Here, the warden of a children's home committed a number of sexual assaults on children who were in his care. His employer was unaware of the assaults at the time they were committed; the victims made the relevant complaints, leading to the warden's conviction and imprisonment, after an interval of several years. Prior to the case reaching the House of Lords, it was held that the employer was not vicariously liable for the assaults,[123] on the ground that the warden's acts of sexual abuse could not be regarded as an unauthorised mode of carrying out his authorised duties. The House of Lords reversed the lower courts on this point and overturned an earlier authority to the same effect by the Court of Appeal.[124] According to Lord Steyn (with whom Lord Hutton concurred), the correct approach 'is to concentrate on the relative closeness of the connection between the nature of the employment and the particular tort'.[125] Since, in this case, 'the sexual abuse was inextricably interwoven with the carrying out by the warden of his duties', it was fair and just to hold the employers vicariously liable.[126] Lord Millett would, similarly, have imposed vicarious liability 'where the unauthorized acts of the employee are so connected with acts which the employer has authorized that they may properly be regarded as falling within the scope of his employment'. The advantage of this test, in his Lordship's view, was that of 'dispensing with the awkward references to "improper modes" of carrying out the employee's duties; and by focusing attention on the connection between the employee's duties and his wrongdoing it would accord with the underlying rationale of the doctrine and be applicable without straining the language to accommodate cases of intentional wrongdoing'.[127]

In his judgment, Lord Clyde suggested that in applying the test of sufficient connection the following three factors should be considered.[128] First, a broad approach should be taken to construing the employee's duties, so that 'it becomes inappropriate to concentrate too closely on the particular act complained of.' Thus an intentional wrong can be seen as one aspect of a larger pattern of conduct which falls within the employee's

122 [2002] 1 AC 215.

123 At first instance, the judge held the employer liable for the warden's failure to report to the employer his intention to commit wrongful acts and the harmful consequences of those acts for the victims. This extremely artificial ground of liability was rejected by the Court of Appeal.

124 *Trotman* v. *North Yorkshire CC* [1999] LGR 584.

125 [2002] 1 AC 215, 229.

126 *Ibid.*, 230.

127 *Ibid.*, 245.

128 *Ibid.*, 235–6.

scope of employment. Second, the time and place at which a particular wrong is committed are relevant but not conclusive. Thus there might be circumstances under which an employer could be vicariously liable for an act committed outside working hours and away from the place of employment while, conversely, 'the fact that the act in question occurred during the time of employment and in the place of employment is not enough in itself'. Third, it is not enough that the employment merely provided the employee with the opportunity to commit the wrong: for example, 'there must be some greater connection between the tortious act of the employee and the circumstances of his employment than the mere opportunity to commit the act which has been provided by access to the premises which the employment has afforded'.

In making a finding of vicarious liability on the facts of *Lister* v. *Hesley Hall* the House of Lords was following the lead three years earlier of the Supreme Court of Canada in the very similar case of *Bazley* v. *Curry*.[129] However, the rationale for the decision in *Bazley* was much more clearly based on an explicit consideration of the policy factors underlying vicarious liability. According to MacLachlin J, giving the judgment of the court, '[t]he question in each case is whether there is a connection or nexus between the employment enterprise and that wrong that justifies imposition of vicarious liability on the employer for the wrong, in terms of fair allocation the consequences of the risk and/or deterrence'.[130] This formulation makes use of the notion of a 'sufficient' or (in some versions) 'strong' connection,[131] then, but is subtly different from that put forward by the House of Lords. In *Lister*, the relevant connection is between the employee's wrong and the duties which he was expressly or impliedly required, under the terms of his contract of employment, to undertake. In *Bazley*, on the other hand, the connection is between the wrong and the risks which are inherent in the enterprise undertaken by the employer. As a result, 'the test for vicarious liability for an employee's sexual abuse of a client should focus on whether the employer's enterprise and empowerment of the employee materially increased the risk of sexual assault and hence the harm'.[132]

In their application, the two tests are by no means poles apart, since, under *Bazley*, the court must pay regard to the nature of the employee's responsibilities, under his employment, towards the victim, while factors of time and space may also be relevant. Nor will the *Bazley* test necessarily result in liability in a wider range of cases. Both *Lister* and *Bazley* were cases in which sexual abuse was committed against children in a residential setting. In the companion case to *Bazley*, *Jacobi* v. *Boys' and Girls' Club of Vernon*, the Supreme Court of Canada denied liability in a case where sexual assaults were committed in the course of outings from a non-residential club and in the employee's home outside working hours.

Nevertheless, the 'enterprise risk' approach of the Supreme Court has the advantage over *Lister*'s more formalistic analysis of encouraging an open discussion of the

129 (1999) 174 DLR (4th) 45.

130 *Ibid.*, 62.

131 The *strong* connection test was emphasised by the court when applying *Bazley* in *Jacobi* v. *Boys' and Girls' Club of Vernon* (1999) 174 DLR (4th) 71.

132 *Bazley* (1999) 174 DLR (4th) 45, 63.

economic and social effects of a finding of vicarious liability. *Lister* simply replaces one verbal formula (the distinction between 'authorised acts' and 'unauthorised modes') with another ('sufficient connection') which in the long run may prove no more adequate to the task in hand.

Lister has since been applied in a series of cases involving assaults by police officers. These decisions illustrate the limit of the Lister test. In *Attorney-General of Virgin Islands* v. *Hartwell*[133] a police officer who was off duty at the time and acting out of a personal vendetta fired his police revolver into a crowded bar, injuring the plaintiff, a tourist. The Privy Council held that there was an insufficiently close connection between the tort and police officer's regular duties. By contrast, vicarious liability was established in *Bernard* v. *Attorney-General of Jamaica*,[134] when a police officer, announcing his status, demanded that the plaintiff give him a public telephone which he was using at the time. When the plaintiff refused, the police officer shot him, using his service revolver, rendering him unconscious, and proceeded to arrest him. An important factor here was that the defendant was holding himself out as acting with the authority of a police officer at the point when the tort was committed. On the other hand, vicarious liability was denied in *N.* v. *Chief Constable of Merseyside Police*,[135] a case in which the claimant was drugged and raped by an off-duty police officer. Although he had given the claimant the impression that he was on duty at the time he had offered her assistance, and was wearing his police uniform, the court held that this was a 'mere opportunity' case.

(iv) Harassment

The question of whether an employer can be vicariously liable for torts committed by an employee under the terms of the Protection from Harassment Act 1997 was given an affirmative answer by the House of Lords in *Majrowski* v. *Guy's and St. Thomas's NHS Trust*.[136] The issue was not clear-cut, since the torts of harassment created by the Act have no common-law equivalent, and the Act is silent on the issue of the employer's liability. Lord Nicholls considered the policy justifications for the doctrine of vicarious liability, referring to its compensatory, deterrent and risk-shifting functions, and suggested that 'with these policy considerations in mind, it is difficult to see a coherent basis for confining the common law principle of vicarious liability to common law wrongs'.[137] The same considerations justified the view, according to his Lordship, that the correct approach to take in this case was not to ask whether the Act could be read as creating a cause of action based on vicarious liability, but whether there were grounds to believe that, expressly or impliedly, it had excluded it, a difficult hurdle for the defendant to overcome. He went on to argue that the policy and context of the 1997 Act justified a finding in the claimant's favour:

> Vicarious liability for an employee's harassment of another person, whether a fellow employee or not, will to some extent increase employers' burdens. That is clear. But, here again, this does

133 [2004] 1 WLR 1273.
134 [2005] IRLR 398. See also *Brown* v. *Robinson* [2004] UKPC 56.
135 [2006] EWHC 3041.
136 [2006] ICR 1129.
137 [2006] ICR 1129, 1202.

not suffice to show Parliament intended to exclude the ordinary common law principle of vicarious liability. Parliament added harassment to the list of civil wrongs. Parliament did so because it considered the existing law provided insufficient protection for victims of harassment. The inevitable consequence of Parliament creating this new wrong of universal application is that at times an employee will commit this wrong in the course of his employment. This prompts the question: why should an employer have a special dispensation in respect of the newly-created wrong and not be liable if an employee commits this wrong in the course of his employment? The contemporary rationale of employers' vicarious liability is as applicable to this new wrong as it is to common law torts.[138]

Lord Hope of Craighead reached the same conclusion on the rather different ground that the structure and wording of the Act, and in particular the provisions which were specific to Scottish law, indicated that the legislator had intended to allow a claim based on vicarious liability. Baroness Hale of Richmond agreed with this approach and gave a judgment which was sceptical of the policy arguments advanced in favour of liability; Lord Carswell and Lord Brown of Eaton-under-Heywood expressed similar doubts. Thus the decision in *Majrowski* can be understood as turning on a narrow point of statutory interpretation, and might easily have gone the other way. Nevertheless, the case of the 1997 Act aside, *Majrowski* helpfully establishes that 'the principle of vicarious liability is applicable where an employee commits a breach of a statutory obligation sounding in damages while acting in the course of his employment unless the statute expressly or impliedly indicates otherwise'.[139]

4. CONTRIBUTION BETWEEN EMPLOYER AND EMPLOYEE

There has been little doubt that where an employee commits a tort for which his employer is vicariously liable, the two of them are to be treated as joint tortfeasors. It follows from this that if the employer were held liable for the tort of his employee in the course of employment, he would have a right to recover a complete indemnity.[140] The proposition was, indeed, asserted on a number of occasions, yet never actually tested until the Law Reform (Married Women and Tortfeasors) Act 1935 created a new statutory right.[141] This right is now to be found in section 1(1) of the Civil Liability (Contribution) Act 1978, which allows any person who is liable for damages suffered by

138 [2006] ICR 1129, 1206.

139 [2006] ICR 1129, 1220 (Lord Brown of Eaton-under-Heywood). It is also possible for an employer to be held vicariously liable for the negligent infliction of psychiatric harm on one employee by another (although *quaere* whether a duty of care can truly be said to exist between employees): *Green* v. *DG Group Services Ltd.* [2006] IRLR 764; D. Brodie, 'Deterring Harassment at Common Law' (2007) 36 *ILJ* 213.

140 The common law rule of *Merryweather* v. *Nixon* (1799) 8 TR 186; 101 ER 1337, prohibiting contribution or indemnity between joint tortfeasors, did not apply to cases where one of them was completely innocent.

141 See Denning LJ's remarks in *Jones* v. *Manchester Corp.* [1952] 2 QB 852, 870.

another to recover a contribution from any other person liable in respect of the same damage (the contribution between the joint tortfeasors being determined by the court, taking into account both the relative blameworthiness of the parties and the causative potency of their respective conducts in producing the harm in suit). In the typical vicarious liability case this would mean the employer (in effect, his insurers) claiming a complete indemnity from the culpable employee.[142]

Apart from this statutory right, however, the House of Lords held in *Lister* v. *Romford Ice and Cold Storage Co.*[143] that an employer was entitled to an indemnity from his wrongdoing employee on the ground that the latter impliedly undertook in his contract of employment to perform his contractual duties with due care. This common-law (as distinct from the statutory) right to an indemnity is lost (*a*) where the employee, though acting in the course of his employment, was actually carrying out a task other than the specific task for which he was employed,[144] or (*b*) where the employer was personally liable, or liable through other employees.[145]

The right to an indemnity, whether statutory or common law, has had supporters, especially in the past, on the basis that 'the person who caused the damage is the person who must in law be called on to pay damages arising therefrom'.[146] Retribution apart, the rule also seemed to be supported by policy considerations. It was argued, for example, that any contrary ruling would involve the creation of a special class of person to whom the ordinary rules of liability for negligence do not apply;[147] and perhaps, even make employees more slap-happy in the execution of their work. Yet this rule, which is not shared by most civil-law systems, may have more disadvantages than advantages, at least in cases involving torts based on negligence. On moral grounds the prevailing view is unacceptable when severe consequences flow from minor lapses;[148] different considerations may apply where an intentional tort is committed.[149] On economic grounds (cases of intentional torts aside) it makes little sense to shift the loss from the person who can best bear it and place it on the person who cannot bear it and is, in practice, unlikely to be insured. On pragmatic grounds the existing rule can only contribute to bad industrial relations.[150] Finally, on theoretical grounds the right of subrogation or indemnity should not be a concern of the law of torts, which exhausts its function once

[142] See, e.g., *KD* v. *Chief Constable of Hampshire* [2005] EWHC 2550. Where, on the other hand, the employee is a joint tortfeasor along with one or more other defendants, the employer who is vicariously liable for the employee's tort cannot claim to be completely innocent for the purposes of apportioning liability between himself and those other defendants. For this purpose, the employer steps into the employee's shoes and so the extent of the employee's responsibility, for apportionment purposes, is therefore attributed to him. See *Dubai Aluminium Co. Ltd.* v. *Salaam* [2002] UKHL 48, [2003] 2 AC 366.

[143] [1957] AC 555.

[144] *Harvey* v. *O'Dell Ltd.* [1958] 2 QB 78.

[145] *Jones* v. *Manchester Corp.* [1952] 2 QB 852.

[146] *Semtex Ltd.* v. *Gladstone* [1954] 1 WLR 945, 953, per Finnemore J; similarly J. A. Jolowicz, 'Right to Indemnity between Master and Servant' (Select Bibliography) ('reason and justice alike seem to call for the liability').

[147] *Ibid.*, 107.

[148] Which, of course, is a general criticism of the fault system.

[149] See *KD* v. *Chief Constable of Hampshire* [2005] EWHC 2550.

[150] See Lord Denning MR's remarks in *Morris* v. *Ford Motor Co. Ltd.* [1973] QB 792, 801.

the victim has been compensated.[151] That these objections do have force is evident from the aftermath of *Lister* v. *Romford Ice*.[152] For it became clear that in practice a person suing for the indemnity was not really the employer but his insurance company; and if it is wrong for the reasons suggested to allow an employer to sue his employees, it must be more objectionable to allow his insurers to take over his rights. Insurance companies are paid to cover risks, and if they were allowed to claim damages through subrogation when those risks materialised, they would, in effect, be having their cake and eating it.[153]

The upshot of this storm was a 'gentlemen's agreement' by which liability insurers agreed not to exercise their subrogation rights in such circumstances unless there was evidence of collusion or wilful misconduct. The 'gentlemen's agreement', however, does not cover all eventualities, and the ruling in *Lister* is still, technically, the law. This means that, on occasion, it has to be evaded by means that add little to the clarity and simplicity of the legal system.[154] Since legislative intervention appears unlikely in the foreseeable future, one must hope that the House of Lords will, on the first available opportunity, remedy this defect. *De lege ferenda*, therefore, it would be best to limit such a right to an indemnity to cases where the employee intentionally inflicted the loss on the victim.

5. LIABILITY FOR THE TORTS OF INDEPENDENT CONTRACTORS

We have noted that an employer is not vicariously liable for the torts of his independent contractors. He may, however, be primarily liable if he is in breach of his own duty, and this may happen in one of two ways:

(i) He may authorise the commission of a tort, in which case he is liable as a joint tortfeasor along with the independent contractor. This is not vicarious liability. The main problem in such cases lies in deciding what constitutes authorisation.

(ii) He will be liable for a breach of his own non-delegable duty, which requires him to see that care is taken. This, as already indicated, goes further than personally taking care, for however carefully he may have selected and instructed the contractor, he will remain answerable for the latter's default.

[151] J. A. Weir, 'Subrogation and Indemnity: A Note on *Morris* v. *Ford Motor Co. Ltd.* [1973] QB 792' (a privately published case note).

[152] [1957] AC 555.

[153] Insurance companies might counter this by saying that by exercising such subrogation rights they can keep premiums at affordable levels. There seems to be no published empirical evidence to support this; and the premiums do not appear to have gone up as a result of giving up the right to exercise the subrogation claims following the 'gentlemen's agreement'.

[154] See the tortuous ways employed by the majority in *Morris* v. *Ford Motor Co. Ltd.* [1973] QB 792, to deny the plaintiffs, who were not insurers, their right of subrogation.

Unfortunately, it is not at all clear when and why[155] the law determines that such non-delegable duties will arise. Very often non-delegable duties are created by statutes and whether this is so will depend on the construction of the statute in question. For example, section 1(1) of the Employers' Liability (Defective Equipment) Act 1969 renders an innocent employer liable for injury suffered by his employee as a result of supplying him with equipment in a defective state 'attributable wholly or partly to the fault of a third person'.[156] Section 2(4)(b) of the Occupiers' Liability Act 1957 also shows that in certain circumstances an occupier may be liable for dangers due to the faulty execution of any work of construction, maintenance or repair, even when this has been done by an independent contractor. Little difficulty also arises in cases of strict, or near strict, liability where non-delegable duties are generally discovered without much difficulty. It has been noted, for example, that possibly in all cases of nuisance the duty is non-delegable;[157] and in *Rylands* v. *Fletcher*,[158] where liability is truly strict, the defendant did not escape liability for the negligence of his independent contractors. But these are not the only instances where the common law has imposed non-delegable duties. *Bower* v. *Peate*[159] suggests that such a duty arises in cases of withdrawal of support from neighbouring land. Other cases are operations involving extra-hazardous acts,[160] and the liability of bailees for reward.[161] It should, however, be stressed that even in non-delegable duty situations the employer's liability does not extend to the independent contractor's 'collateral negligence'. This is negligence unconnected with the job that the independent contractor was engaged to perform; but its application is not easier than the application of 'course of employment'.[162]

155 J. A. Jolowicz, 'Liability for Independent Contractors in English Law: A Suggestion' (Select Bibliography), has suggested that the value of the interest protected and the 'character of the risk' created may be significant factors. He thus concludes that, whereas the considerations which led the courts to introduce vicarious liability 'are founded upon the assured social desirability of giving an injured plaintiff a defendant worth powder and shot and do not depend in any way upon the degree of protection ordinarily afforded by the law to the particular interest affected, or upon the magnitude of the risk involved, the considerations leading to the imposition of liability for independent contractors are essentially legalistic. They are founded not upon any assumed social policy, but upon the preconceived ideas of value to which familiarity with the law gives rise'. See also the discussion of the situation when such duties arise by Mason J in *Kondis* v. *State Transport Authority* (1984) 154 CLR 672 (employer/employee; adjoining landowners; hospital/patient; school authority/pupil; occupier of land/visitor). Mason J thought a common thread was the undertaking of responsibility by one party over the person or property of another. Why should this give rise to a duty not only to take care but also to ensure that care is taken? Is this really no more than an attempted *ex post facto* rationalisation of a random group of cases?

156 What if the defect is attributable wholly to ordinary wear and tear (i.e. no one's fault), but the third party's fault lies in failing to put it right? The answer requires a creative interpretation of the words of the Act for it to apply.

157 Certainly public nuisance on or adjoining the highway (e.g. *Tarry* v. *Ashston* (1876) 1 QBD 314 but not work *near* the highway: *Salsbury* v. *Woodland* [1970] 1 QB 324). *Matania* v. *National Provincial Bank Ltd.* [1936] 2 All ER 633 suggests that the same rule may apply to private nuisance as well.

158 (1866) LR 1 Exch. 265: (1868) LR 3 HL 330.

159 (1876) 1 QBD 321, 326. The *dicta* are of wider import than withdrawal of support and are generally held to be too wide: *Hughes* v. *Percival* (1883) 8 App. Cas. 443, 447.

160 *Honeywill & Stein Ltd.* v. *Larkin Bros. Ltd.* [1934] 1 KB 191, *Balfour* v. *Barty-King* [1957] 1 QB 496.

161 *Morris* v. *C. W. Martin & Sons Ltd.* [1966] 1 QB 716. *British Road Services Ltd.* v. *Arthur Crutchley & Co. Ltd.* [1968] 1 All ER 811, suggests that a bailee for reward will even be liable for the torts of the servants of his independent contractor. Similarly *Riverstone Meat Co. Ltd.* v. *Lancashire Shipping Co. Ltd.* [1961] AC 807.

162 *Padbury* v. *Holliday & Greenwood Ltd.* (1912) 28 TLR 494.

6. THE CHANGING CONTOURS OF EMPLOYERS' LIABILITY: AN EPILOGUE

We have noted that the two doctrines of the employer's personal and non-delegable duty of care to its employees and its vicarious liability for the torts of its employees are intertwined, only partially capable of being subject to a coherent justification, and constantly witnessing an expansion of the scope of their application. This latter characteristic is in tune with the current trend, prevalent in modern tort law, liberally to compensate physical injuries at the same time as widening the category of risks for which defendants with 'deep pockets' can be deemed responsible. The law relating to employers' liabilities is also subject to shifting notions of the boundaries of the enterprise. These various tendencies are reflected in the following tensions in the sphere of legal doctrine.

(A) THE GRADUAL AND UNSYSTEMATIC EXPANSION OF THE NON-DELEGABLE DUTIES

It is becoming increasingly common for organisations to hive off their 'non-core' activities to subcontractors or third parties, thereby testing the legal notion of the unitary enterprise on which the idea of employer's liability ultimately rests. One response has been for the courts to expand the categories of the employer's non-delegable duties. In *McDermid* v. *Nash Dredging and Reclamation Co. Ltd.*[163] the plaintiff was an inexperienced deck hand employed by the company of the defendants. While working on a tug (owned by the parent company of the defendants) he was injured as a result of the negligence of the master of the tug. Since the master of the tug was not an employee of the defendants, the latter could not (according to traditional doctrine) be held liable vicariously for his wrongs. They were, however, held liable on non-delegable grounds. The House of Lords (unlike the Court of Appeal) appeared to think that the ruling involved no real extension of the law. Yet, in reality, the effect of the case is that the employer's duties to *provide* competent staff, a safe place of work, safe equipment and a safe system of work (discussed earlier on) were extended to include a non-delegable duty to ensure the proper *operation* of the devised system of work.[164] It is easy to treat this as yet another common law extension of the list of non-delegable duties. Yet this new non—delegable duty—unlike the traditional four that have followed *Wilsons and Clyde Coal Ltd.* v. *English*[165]—was hardly within the defendant's (employer's) control, so 'the effect was as if vicarious liability had been imposed for the tort of an independent contractor',[166] even though the language used by the House of Lords was that of non-delegable duties.

[163] [1987] AC 906.
[164] In this case the courts felt that the system of work devised was safe but its operation had not been adequate.
[165] [1938] AC 906.
[166] McKendrick, 'Vicarious Liability And Independent Contractors' (Select Bibliography), at 773–4, where one can find an excellent discussion of this emerging topic.

Notwithstanding this point, however, the ruling marks an extension of the protection afforded to the injured party even though subsequent case law has limited the applicability of the *McDermid* rule to cases where the victim/claimant is an employee of the defendants.[167]

(B) EXTENDING THE NOTION OF EMPLOYEE STATUS

A further response to the same phenomenon is to impose vicarious liability upon the employer for the wrongs of individuals who would not, for other legal purposes, be regarded as his employees. We have already noted that, in principle, there is nothing illogical in saying that a person might be treated as an employee of another person for one purpose (for example, civil liability) but not for another (for example, employment protection or tax and social security). If this view were to gain wider acceptance than it currently enjoys, it could well be used to justify the liability of the 'employer' of the 'flexible' workforce of casual and temporary workers. This view would, *de lege lata*, find some support in the judgment of Staughton J in his *McDermid*[168] decision and, as stated, in the result (but *not* the judgments) of the House of Lords in the same case. The point, however, is not yet finally resolved; and, as stated, the legitimate wish to compensate the victims should not hurry lawyers into imposing unlimited liability on employers who should not always be assumed to have deeper pockets or, necessarily, be in a better position to obtain effective insurance cover.

(C) IMPOSING ADDITIONAL AFFIRMATIVE DUTIES ON EMPLOYERS

This can be seen happening in some foreign systems;[169] and there may even be some scattered *dicta* in our case law supporting, in some instances, primary duties of supervision,[170] co-ordination[171] and even control of the activities of third parties.[172] There are also hints of the existence of a more general doctrine of assumption of responsibility to third parties. Though this principle cannot yet be claimed to be part of English law it has found a clear exposition in the Australian case of *Kondis* v. *State Transport Authority*[173] where Mason J said:

> It appears that there is some element in the relationship between the parties that makes it appropriate to impose on the defendant a duty to ensure that reasonable care and skill is taken for the safety of the persons to whom the duty is owed... [I]n these situations the special duty arises because the person on whom it is imposed has undertaken the case, supervision or

[167] Thus, see *Watts* v. *Lowcur Ltd.*, quoted and discussed by McKendrick, *ibid.*

[168] *McDermid* v. *Nash Dredging & Reclamation Co. Ltd.*, *The Times*, 31 July 1984, noted by J. Murdoch in (1985) 1 *Professional Negligence* 119.

[169] E.g. the German, the reason being that in that system the rules of vicarious liability are weak.

[170] See e.g. Lord Bridge in *D. & F. Estates Ltd.* v. *Church Commissioners for England* [1989] AC 177, 209.

[171] See *Stevens* v. *Brodribb Sawmilling Co. Pty. Ltd.* (1986) 160 CLR 16 (but not yet accepted by English law).

[172] *Smith* v. *Littlewoods Organisation Ltd.* [1987] AC 241 provides the best starting-point but, it must be admitted, this development is still in an embryonic stage.

[173] (1984) 154 CLR 672, 687.

control of the person or property of another or is so placed in relation to that person or his property as to assume a particular responsibility for his or its safety, in circumstances where the person affected might reasonably expect that due care will be exercised.

(D) PURPOSIVE EXTENSION OF THE VICARIOUS LIABILITY RULES

It is in the area of the employer's vicarious liability for intentional torts that the limits of legal principle have been most severely tested in recent years. In the sexual abuse cases, *Lister* v. *Hesley Hall Ltd.*[174] and *Bazley* v. *Curry*,[175] the courts were aware of the argument that the vicarious liability doctrine had been developed 'to provide a just and pragmatic remedy to people who suffer as a consequence of wrongs perpetrated by an employee'. This had to be balanced by due regard for the need to avoid relegating the employer 'to the status of an involuntary insurer'. The solution developed by the Supreme Court of Canada was the 'enterprise risk' test, which was also invoked by the House of Lords in the post-*Lister* decision of *Dubai Aluminium Co.* v. *Salaam*.[176] In her far-sighted judgment in *Bazley* v. *Curry*, McLachlin J argued that 'enterprise risk' was the common factor capable of explaining the otherwise inchoate case law on the liability of employers for unauthorised acts of employees: '[t]he common theme resides in the idea that where the employee's conduct is closely tied to a risk that the employer's enterprise has placed in the community, the employer may justly be held vicariously liable for the employee's wrong'. This led her to engage in an exercise of balancing pro-liability factors, such as the deterrence and risk-shifting effects of liability, against factors adverse to liability including the danger of claims chilling socially useful activities. In strong contrast is the judgment of Lord Hobhouse in *Lister* v. *Hesley Hall Ltd.*: while *Bazley* v. *Curry* contained 'a useful and impressive discussion of the social and economic reasons for having vicarious liability as a part of the law of tort which extends to embrace acts of child abuse', his Lordship insisted that '[l]egal rules have to have a greater degree of clarity and definition than is provided by simply explaining the reasons for the existence of the rule and the social need for it'.[177] In line with this attitude, the judgments in *Lister* eschewed an explicit policy analysis. Whether, at the end of the day, the result is greater clarity in the formulation and application of the law may be open to question. In the words of McLachlin J in *Bazley* v. *Curry*:

> A focus on policy is not to diminish the importance of legal principle. It is vital that the courts attempt to articulate general legal principles to lend certainty to the law and guide future applications. However, in areas of jurisprudence where changes have been occurring in response to policy considerations, the best route to enduring principle may lie through policy. The law of vicarious liability is just such a domain.[178]

174 [2001] 2 AC 215.
175 (1999) 174 DLR (4th) 45.
176 [2003] 2 AC 366, at [23] (Lord Nicholls).
177 [2001] 2 AC 215, 242.
178 (1999) 174 DLR (4th) 45, 58.

(E) SYNTHESIS OF THE EMPLOYER'S VICARIOUS AND PERSONAL DUTIES?

As the law is tested by novel forms of claim, we may be seeing the integration of the employer's personal and vicarious liabilities. Vicarious liability has never been an entirely satisfactory solution to the need to fashion a set of principles for determining the liability of the enterprise for the risks it creates. Treating the employer as liable for another's tort rather than as personally responsible for the risk inherent in the enterprise produces the problem of joint liability which *Lister* v. *Romford Ice and Cold Storage Co. Ltd.*[179] so signally failed to solve. The doctrine of the employer's personal liability to his employees developed in the *Wilsons*[180] case as a way round the inadequacies of vicarious liability, and above all the restrictive and doctrinally dubious defence of common employment. The co-existence of the two forms of liability continues to cause confusion. Thus, as we have seen, in *McDermid* v. *Nash Dredging & Reclamation Co.*,[181] the extension of the employers' non-delegable duty was hard to distinguish, in terms of its effects, from a holding that the employer was vicariously liable for the tort of an independent contractor.

In *Lister* v. *Hesley Hall Ltd.*,[182] Lord Hobhouse's judgment also came close to eliding the two ideas. According to his Lordship, the employer's *vicarious* liability in that case 'derives from [his] voluntary assumption of the relationship towards the plaintiff and the duties that arise from that relationship and their choosing to entrust the performance of those duties to their servant'. In such a situation, 'the motive of the employee and the fact that he is doing something expressly forbidden and is serving only his own ends does not negative the vicarious liability for breach of the "delegated" duty'. This formulation of the test for vicarious liability, in referring to an assumption of responsibility to the claimant by the *employer* rather than by the employee, is certainly unorthodox, and cannot be said to form part of the *ratio* of *Lister* v. *Hesley Hall Ltd.* However, there is much to be said for an analysis here which focuses on the defendant's overall responsibility for the care of the claimant. If the facts had been altered slightly and the claimant had been an employee, it is not hard to see that the defendant could have been held *personally* liable by analogy to decisions such as *Waters* v. *Commissioner of Police of the Metropolis.*[183] In view of such decisions, it is striking that the personal liability of the defendant, for example for failing to ensure safe and competent staff, did not feature more prominently in the discussions in *Bazley* and *Lister*.

The very same policy factors, involving an assessment of the deterrent effects of liability, risk-shifting through insurance, and the danger of adverse 'defensive' practices, apply in both sets of cases. When the House of Lords invoked such factors to limit the personal duty of care of defendants in cases involving child care and educational provision, as it did in *X (Minors)* v. *Bedfordshire County Council*,[184] it then faced near-insurmountable difficulties in explaining why this denial of duty could not be circumvented by a claim based on the defendant's vicarious liability for the alleged

179 [1957] AC 555.
180 *Wilsons and Clyde Coal Co. Ltd.* v. *English* [1938] AC 57.
181 [1987] AC 906.
182 [2001] 2 AC 215.
183 [2000] IRLR 70.
184 [1995] 2 AC 663.

negligence of its employees. One reason for the retreat from *X (Minors)* in the later *Barrett*[185] and *Phelps*[186] cases was indeed the perception that there was no clear reason for denying that the individual teachers and medical professionals in those cases had been acting in the course of their employment when the alleged wrongs were committed. What these cases demonstrate is the need for consistency in the courts' approach to cases of vicarious liability, on the one hand, and the scope of the personal duty of care of organisational defendants on the other. Thus we suggest that, regardless of whether the trend in future is to extend or diminish the scope of these duties of care, there is likely to be increasing pressure to align the principles of vicarious and personal liability, most likely along the lines of the 'enterprise risk' approach of the Supreme Court of Canada.

SELECT BIBLIOGRAPHY

Adams, J. N., and Brownsword, R., 'Double Indemnity–Contractual Indemnity Clauses Revisited' [1988] *JBL* 146.

Atiyah, P. S., *Vicarious Liability in the Law of Torts* (1967).

Barak, A., 'Mixed and Vicarious Liability: A Suggested Distinction' (1966) 29 *MLR* 60.

Brill, R. L., 'The Liability of an Employer for the Wilful Torts of his Servants' (1968) 45 *Chicago-Kent LR* 1.

Cane, P., 'Vicarious Liability for Sexual Abuse' (2000) 116 *LQR* 21.

Hamson, C. J., 'Liability of Hospitals for Negligence', in Hamson, C. J., *The Law in Action* (1954), 19.

—'Master and Servant–Duty of Master-Defective Tool' [1959] *CLJ* 157.

James, F., Jr., 'Vicarious Liability' (1954) 28 *Tul. LR* 161.

Jolowicz, J. A., 'The Right to Indemnity between Master and Servant' [1956] *CLJ* 101.

—'Liability for Independent Contractors in the English Common Law: A Suggestion' (1957) 9 *Stan. LR* 690.

Kahn-Freund, O., 'Servants and Independent Contractors' (1951) 14 *MLR* 504.

McKendrick, E., 'Vicarious Liability and Industrial Action' (1989) 18 *ILJ* 161.

—'Vicarious Liability and Independent Contractors: A Re-Examination' (1990) 53 *MLR* 770.

Morris, C. R., Jr., 'Enterprise Liability and the Actuarial Process: The Insignificance of Foresight' (1961) 70 *Yale LJ* 554.

Newark, F. H., '*Twine* v. *Bean's Express Ltd.*' (1954) 17 *MLR* 102.

Rose, F. D., 'Liability for an Employee's Assault' (1977) 40 *MLR* 420.

Seavey, W. A., 'Speculations as to "*Respondeat Superior*"', in Pound, R. (ed.), *Harvard Legal Essays* (1934), 433.

Stevens, R., 'A Servant of Two Masters' (2006) 122 *LQR* 201.

Williams, G. L., 'Vicarious Liability: Tort of the Master or of the Servant?' (1956) 72 *LQR* 522.

—'Vicarious Liability and the Master's Indemnity' (1957) 20 *MLR* 220.

[185] *Barrett* v. *Enfield LBC* [2001] 2 AC 550.

[186] *Phelps* v. *Hillingdon LBC* [2001] 2 AC 619.

20

PRODUCT LIABILITY

1. INTRODUCTION

The emergence in England of a body of 'product liability law' is comparatively recent. Its development can be traced to EC Directive 85/374 and to the Consumer Protection Act 1987 that aimed to implement the principles contained in the Directive. Before this it was not possible to speak of 'product liability law' as such, but only of various laws relating to liability for defective products.[1] A consumer who was injured or whose property was damaged by a product that he had bought could bring an action against the retailer for damages for breach of contract. The standard here was and is strict: where goods are sold in the course of a business the Sale of Goods Act implies into the contract of sale a term (amongst others) to the effect that the goods will be fit for the purpose intended.[2] The doctrine of privity of contract, however, prevents an action for contract damages being brought by a third party even though it might be entirely foreseeable that a defective product would cause harm, for example, to a member of the purchaser's family or to an employee. Nor can the person who has bought the goods sue for the losses sustained by that other person unless they in turn cause loss to him.[3] Contract actions are also limited in the sense that they normally lie only against the retailer who sold the product and not against the manufacturer whose default was most likely responsible for its defective state. In *Donoghue* v. *Stevenson*[4] the House of Lords cut through these limitations by acknowledging the possibility of an action in negligence by the ultimate consumer against the manufacturer. There remained the difficulty, however, of proving negligence. The EC Directive and Consumer Protection Act 1987 address this by imposing a form of strict liability not just upon manufacturers but upon all those, including distributors and retailers, in the supply chain. In doing so they have incorporated into English law a model of extended liability borrowed largely from the law of the United States.

A number of justifications have been offered for the imposition of strict liability on manufacturers and other producers. One is that producers are best able to *spread* the risk of damage through the adoption of insurance or through pricing of products;

[1] Lord Griffiths *et al.*, 'Developments in English Product Liability Law' (Select Bibliography), 355.

[2] Sale of Goods Act 1979, s. 14(3).

[3] *Priest* v. *Last* [1903] 2 KB 148.

[4] [1932] AC 562.

another is that producers are in the best position to *minimise* the risks of damage by taking precautions at the design and manufacturing stages of production. These efficiency-based considerations rest upon insights of economic analysis which have themselves been challenged by critics of the strict liability principle, who argue that it loads excessive costs of precaution upon manufacturers, stifles innovation, and threatens to lead to an 'insurance crisis'. An alternative, non-consequentialist rationale for strict liability has been proposed by Professor Jane Stapleton, namely 'a moral argument that if, in seeking to secure financial profit, an enterprise causes certain types of loss, it should be legally obliged to pay compensation to the victim';[5] this idea, she suggests, links together most of the areas of strict liability in tort (such as the employer's vicarious liability for the torts of employees) although she also accepts that it does not explain all aspects of modern product liability law.[6]

In this area, then, the principles of the common law tort of negligence overlap with stricter forms of liability derived from contract law and from legislation. These different sources of civil liability have not as yet been synthesised into a single, coherent body of doctrine. They provide alternative and possibly cumulative bases for a cause of action in damages. The Consumer Protection Act 1987 has provided rights to consumers over and above those provided by the common law of tort and contract, without in any way removing the protection which the common law already conferred. Because of the limited scope of the Act, however, the claimant may, in certain circumstances, have to frame the cause of action in negligence or breach of contract. To gain a full view of this field, therefore, it will be necessary to examine and compare the separate bases for civil liability and to see how they differ in regard to such questions as: who are the potential plaintiffs and defendants to the action? What degree of fault is required for liability? What kinds of loss can be compensated? Which defences are available? And how are damages to be computed? A detailed examination of these questions will be preceded by an overview of the law's historical development in England and America. The American law is important to an understanding of the strict liability principle that underlies the 1985 Directive and the Consumer Protection Act.

2. THE EVOLUTION OF PRODUCT LIABILITY LAW IN ENGLAND AND AMERICA

(A) THE REJECTION OF THE 'PRIVITY OF CONTRACT FALLACY'

As an earlier chapter has already explained,[7] the scope of liability for negligence was limited in the nineteenth century by the idea that obligations that originated in contract could not be extended beyond the scope of a particular agreement. The attitude of the courts was epitomised by *Winterbottom* v. *Wright* in which Lord Abinger complained

[5] *Product Liability* (Select Bibliography), 186. [6] *Ibid.*, 204. [7] See above, ch. 3.

that any other rule would produce 'the most absurd and outrageous consequences, to which I can see no limit'.[8] The plaintiff was the driver of a horse-drawn coach who was injured in an accident brought about, it was alleged, by the failure of the defendant to maintain the coach in a good state of repair as required by a contract with the coach's owner. The case was not much of an authority in itself, being an instance of an omission to take due care rather than one of active misfeasance;[9] nonetheless it was widely relied on as a basis of a rule of non-liability for manufacturers. Two exceptions were however recognised in the case of 'things inherently dangerous', such as a bottle of poison[10] or an explosive device, and fraudulent misrepresentation made directly to the plaintiff. *Langridge* v. *Levy*,[11] in which a gun which was falsely represented to be safe went off in the plaintiff's hand and injured him, illustrates both lines of authority. The wider privity rule was first abandoned in the United States where the overwhelming majority of state jurisdictions adopted the rule formulated by Cardozo J for the New York Court of Appeals in *MacPherson* v. *Buick Motor Co.* in 1916.[12] In this case the plaintiff was injured when a wheel on the car he was driving, and which he had bought from a retailer, fell to pieces, causing the car to crash. He brought an action for negligence against the manufacturer. The court upheld the plaintiff's claim on the ground that liability 'is not limited to poisons, explosives, and things of like nature, to things which in their normal operation are implements of destruction. If the nature of a thing is such that it is reasonably certain to place life and limb in peril when negligently made, it is then a thing of danger. Its nature gives warning of the consequences to be expected.'[13] The court found 'nothing anomalous in a rule which imposes upon A, who has contracted with B, a duty to C and D and others according as he knows or does not know that the subject-matter of the contract is intended for their use'.

The equivalent decision for English and Scots law was that of the House of Lords in *Donoghue* v. *Stevenson*[14] where the plaintiff was poisoned by the contents of a ginger beer bottle bought for her by a friend. By a bare majority the House of Lords allowed an action in negligence direct against the manufacturer. Lord Buckmaster's vigorous dissent would have confined any liability to the immediate contracting parties. Lord Atkin, by contrast, focused on the manufacturers' knowledge and intention that the goods would eventually reach consumers beyond the end of the contract chain: 'I confine myself to articles of common household use, where everyone, including the manufacturer, knows that the articles will be used by persons other than the actual ultimate purchaser—namely, by members of his family and his servants, and, in some cases, his guests.'[15] Lord Macmillan asserted the priority of negligence over the privity rule and expressed the manufacturer's duty in similar terms:

a person who for gain engages in the business of manufacturing articles of food and drink intended for consumption by members of the public in the form in which he issues them is

[8] (1842) 10 M & W 109, 114.

[9] See F. H. Bohlen, *Studies in the Law of Torts* (1926), 236–7.

[10] *Thomas* v. *Winchester*, 6 NY 397 (1852).

[11] (1837) 2 M & W 519.

[12] 217 NY 382, 111 NE 1050.

[13] *Ibid.*, at 389 (NY), 1053 (NE).

[14] [1932] AC 562; see above, ch. 3.

[15] [1932] AC 562, at 583.

under a duty to take care in the manufacture of those articles. That duty, in my opinion, he owes to those whom he intends to consume his products. He manufactures his commodities for human consumption; he intends and contemplates that they shall be consumed. By reason of that very fact he places himself in a relationship with all the potential customers of his commodities, and that relationship, which he assumes and desires for his own ends, imposes upon him a duty to take care to avoid injuring them. He owes them a duty not to convert by his own carelessness an article which he issues to them as wholesome and innocent into an article which is dangerous to life and health.[16]

In the United States the *MacPherson* judgment became the basis for 'a general rule imposing negligence liability upon any supplier, for remuneration, of any chattel'.[17] English law has broadly followed the same route. Liability has been extended to products and articles of all kinds, ranging from tombstones[18] to defective hair dyes[19] and contaminated underwear.[20] The scope of the duty has been extended beyond manufacturers *qua* producers to embrace all those who handle the goods in a business capacity along the chain of supply; those potentially liable include makers of component parts, assemblers, distributors and retail sellers, as well as those doing installation work, repairs and contract work of various kinds.[21] Potential claimants include all those coming into contact with the goods either as ultimate consumers or users; employees of the purchaser, members of his family, subsequent purchasers and even 'bystanders' exposed to danger may sue.[22] The one general restriction on the scope of liability is that it remains confined to physical injury or property damage caused by contact with the goods; 'pure economic' loss is not normally recoverable either in England or in most US jurisdictions.[23]

The most serious restriction on the use of the tort of negligence for consumer protection, however, is the need to show fault. This could be overcome, in an appropriate case, by an inference of negligence in the claimant's favour. In *Grant* v. *Australian Knitting Mills Ltd*[24] the plaintiff caught dermatitis from a suit of underwear manufactured by the defendants. The underwear had been infected with an 'irritant chemical' at some stage in the manufacturing process. The Privy Council, allowing an appeal, held the manufacturers liable in negligence:

According to the evidence, the method of manufacture was correct; the danger of excess sulphites being left was recognised and was guarded against; the process was intended to be foolproof. If excess sulphites were left in the garment, that could only be because someone was

16 [1932] AC 562, at 620.

17 W. Prosser, 'The Assault upon the Citadel (Strict Liability to the Consumer)' (Select Bibliography), 1102.

18 *Brown* v. *Cotterill* (1934) 51 TLR 21.

19 *Parker* v. *Oloxo Ltd.* [1937] 3 All ER 524.

20 *Grant* v. *Australian Knitting Mills Ltd.* [1936] AC 85.

21 See the cases cited below, Section 2(a).

22 See below, *ibid.*

23 *Murphy* v. *Brentwood District Council* [1991] 1 AC 398, *East River Steamship Corp.* v. *Transamerica Delaval Inc.*, 476 US 858 (1986). It should be noted, however, that some American jurisdictions do allow limited recovery for pure economic loss caused by defective chattels, on a theory of liability for breach of warranty: see *Seely* v. *White Motor Co.*, 403 P 2d 145 (1965); J. Phillips, 'Misrepresentation and Products Liability' (1991) 20 *Anglo-Am. LR* 327; see also the discussion in the text, below.

24 [1936] AC 85.

at fault. The appellant is not required to lay his finger on the exact person in all the chain who was responsible or to specify what he did wrong. Negligence is found as a matter of inference from the existence of the defects taken in connection with all the known circumstances; even if the manufacturers could by apt evidence have rebutted that inference they have not done so.[25]

In numerous American decisions, courts have taken the view that product liability is an appropriate area for the application of the doctrine of *res ipsa loquitur*, effectively reversing the burden of proof. *Res ipsa loquitur* applies where it can be shown that the defendant had exclusive control of the thing which caused the accident and where no explanation other than the defendant's negligence is forthcoming.[26] While 'control' is normally taken in English law to refer to control at the time the accident occurred, American courts have been prepared to extend the relevant time back to the process of manufacture itself. In *Escola* v. *Coca-Cola Bottling Co. of Fresno*[27] the defendants were held liable on the assumption that for a cola bottle to explode in the hands of a waitress, it must have been defectively manufactured and inadequately inspected. The defendants were in control of the manufacturing and inspection of the bottles and there was no evidence that the bottle had been interfered with or mishandled after leaving the factory. Although *res ipsa* can be answered by a defendant showing that the defect could not have been avoided by reasonable care, the leading commentator on the American case law wrote in 1960 that 'such cases are so extremely rare as to be almost negligible'.[28]

The English courts have not allowed the formal use of *res ipsa loquitur* in claims for product liability based on negligence, instead insisting upon the claimant's obligation to prove fault.[29] In practice they have achieved much the same result by making an 'inference of negligence' of the kind used by Lord Wright to decide *Grant* v. *Australian Knitting Mills Ltd.*[30] However, this is not an automatic aid to the claimant, and courts have from time to time declined to make the inference in his favour. In *Evans* v. *Triplex Safety Glass Co. Ltd.*[31] a manufacturer of 'toughened safety glass' fitted into the windscreen of a car avoided liability for injuries suffered by the drivers and passengers when the glass shattered without warning. The court held that the fault might have occurred when the glass was fitted, and that suppliers had had sufficient time to check the glass. The possibility of intermediate examination and the length of time between the manufacturing process and the accident prevented an inference of negligence being drawn. The English courts have also taken conflicting views on the question whether a manufacturer can escape liability by showing that he had a rigorous manufacturing and inspection process.[32]

Even in the United States, where as we have seen *res ipsa* was flexibly applied to assist the plaintiff, dissatisfaction with the negligence remedy led courts to develop forms of

25 *Ibid.*, 101 (Lord Wright). 26 See above, ch. 4.
27 (1944) 150 P 2d 436. 28 Prosser, 'The Assault upon the Citadel' (Select Bibliography), 1115.
29 Finnemore J, *Mason* v. *Williams and Williams Ltd.* [1955] 1 All ER 808, relying on *Donoghue* v. *Stevenson* [1932] AC 562. 30 [1936] AC 85.
31 [1938] 1 All ER 283.
32 Cf. *Daniels and Daniels* v. *R. White & Sons* [1938] 4 All ER 258, *Hill* v. *James Crowe (Cases) Ltd.* [1978] ICR 298; see below, Section 2(c).

strict liability. The central point was that only strict liability would allow the plaintiff to sue all those who had handled the goods down the length of the supply chain. As Dean Prosser explained:

It is here that negligence liability breaks down. The wholesaler, the jobber and the retailer are simply not negligent. They are under no duty to test or inspect the chattel, and they do not do so; and when, as is usually the case today, it comes to them in a sealed container, examination becomes impossible without destroying marketability. No inference of negligence can arise against these sellers, and res ipsa loquitur is of no use at all.[33]

As a result there began a movement towards strict liability along two routes: initially through the concept of a transmissible warranty or representation that the goods were free of any hidden defects, and then increasingly through the imposition of a strict tort duty. In England, by contrast, the courts rejected such far-reaching conceptual solutions within the common law, leaving it to statute to introduce a measure of stricter liability in the form of the 1987 Act.

(B) FROM NEGLIGENCE TO STRICT LIABILITY

(i) Liability for Breach of Warranty

After the destruction of the 'privity of contract fallacy', broadly two types of action were available to the consumer: an action in negligence against the manufacturer and an action for breach of contract against the retailer. Sales law implied into contracts for the sale of goods terms or warranties to the effect that the goods complied with the contract description, were fit for the purpose intended and were of merchantable quality.[34] If a defective product injured a consumer, the seller would be held liable for breach of one of these contract terms. Moreover, the courts awarded the injured consumer damages according to the foreseeable extent of his injuries; he was not limited to claiming the difference between the contract price of the goods and their real value.[35] These actions for breach of warranty have been described by Professor Waddams as essentially tortious in nature. Certainly, in the nineteenth century it was not obvious that liability depended on breach of promise or that the warranty in question had to be contained in a contract between the manufacturer and the consumer.[36] It was only in the course of the nineteenth century that the action for warranty came to be regarded as exclusively contractual in nature, with the result that (in the absence of fraud) representations made outside a contract would not give rise to an action for damages.[37]

Whereas the English courts stuck rigidly to the idea that representations and warranties could give rise to liability only where the parties were in privity of

[33] Prosser, 'The Assault upon the Citadel' (Select Bibliography), 1117.

[34] In England, ss. 12 and 14 of the Sale of Goods Act 1893, which codified the common law (now ss. 12 and 14 of the Sale of Goods Act 1979).

[35] *Brown* v. *Edgington* (1841) 2 Man. & G 279; 133 ER 751.

[36] S. J. Waddams, 'The Strict Liability of Suppliers of Goods' (Select Bibliography), 155–7.

[37] *Heilbut, Symons* v. *Buckleton* [1913] AC 30.

contract,[38] in the United States courts began to impose strict liability upon manufacturers according to various notions of extended liability for breach of warranty. The imposition of strict liability began with cases of contaminated food and drink, and developed from there to include products of all kinds.[39] One idea was that the manufacturer's warranty to the initial purchaser ran with the goods in a manner similar to restrictive covenants over land.[40] In other cases the courts brought the manufacturer and the consumer into privity by (somewhat fictitiously) regarding the retailer as the agent of one or the other. Alternatively, as in the famous English contract case of *Carlill* v. *Carbolic Smoke Ball Co.*,[41] they deemed the manufacturer to have made an implied unilateral offer to the consumer that the latter accepted by purchasing the goods from the retailer.[42]

In due course the notion of an extended liability for breach of warranty came to be embodied in section 2–318 of the Uniform Commercial Code, which was adopted by all the state jurisdictions with the exception of Louisiana. This provides that: 'A seller's warranty whether express or implied extends to any natural person who is in the family or household of the buyer or who is a guest in his home if it is reasonable to expect that such person may use, consume or be affected by the goods and who is injured in person by breach of the warranty. A seller may not exclude or limit the operation of this section.' A comment to the section provided that 'the section is neutral and not intended to enlarge or restrict the developing case law on whether the seller's warranties, given to his buyer who resells, extend to other persons in the distributive chain'. This limitation on the potential doctrinal significance of the section, and the apparently illogical restriction of the right of action to members of the purchaser's household,[43] operated as substantial constraint on the scope of the provision. There were, however, other difficulties with using warranty as the basis of liability. Thus contract damages might be more limited than those available in tort, in particular in a case of wrongful death. Warranty law also required the consumer to show that he had relied on the representation, which might be problematic in a case where the goods were purchased by someone else and the ultimate consumer was ignorant of or indifferent to their precise origin.[44] Then, the warranties in question might be excluded or limited by a clause in one or more of the contracts in the supply chain. Finally, at least in cases where the warranty was regarded as running with the goods, one who did not

[38] English law currently takes a broader view of potential liability for negligent misrepresentation, under the principle enunciated in *Hedley Byrne & Co. Ltd.* v. *Heller & Partners Ltd.* [1964] AC 465, while as between contracting parties there are increased opportunities to sue for damages for a non-contractual representation under the Misrepresentation Act 1967, s. 2: see below, Section 2(c).

[39] Prosser, 'The Assault upon the Citadel' (Select Bibliography), 1103 ff.

[40] *Coca-Cola Bottling Works* v. *Lyons* (1927) 111 So. 305.

[41] [1893] 1 QB 256.

[42] See generally C. W. Gillam, 'Products Liability in a Nutshell' (1957) 37 *Oregon LR* 119.

[43] Waddams (Select Bibliography), 159.

[44] Prosser gave the following example: 'The husband or guest who eats a plate of beans seldom asks the housewife whose product they are, and still less often at what store she bought them': 'The Assault upon the Citadel' (Select Bibliography), 1128.

actually gain title to them at any point, such as an employee or guest of the purchaser, could not recover. Some of these difficulties could be avoided in a case where a manufacturer's promotional literature or advertising could be construed as a set of representations made direct to the final consumer. If a product advertised as safe turned out to be dangerously defective an action either for deceit or for negligent misrepresentation might lie, as in a case where glass fitted into a car windscreen was described by the manufacturer as 'shatterproof'.[45] Unless deceit was proved or assumed, however, this action was subject to some of the difficulties already mentioned. As Prosser noted at the time, 'what all this adds up to is that "warranty" as a device for the justification of strict liability to the consumer, carries far too much luggage in the way of undesirable complications, and is leading us down a very thorny path'.[46]

(ii) Strict Liability in Tort

The restrictions on the warranty action were confronted in a series of judgments in America in the early 1960s, from which there emerged the principle of strict liability in tort for harm caused by a defective product. In *Henningsen* v. *Bloomfield Motors Inc.*[47] the Supreme Court of New Jersey enlarged the scope of the transmissible warranty of quality by reference to general considerations of public policy. The action, against both the manufacturer and the retailer, was initiated by the wife of the purchaser of a Chrysler Plymouth car who was injured while driving it. There was no evidence of any negligence. The court offered the following justification for the imposition of strict liability without regard to privity:

> where the commodities sold are such that if defectively manufactured they will be dangerous to life and limb, then society's interests can only be protected by eliminating the requirement of privity between the maker and his dealers and the reasonably expected ultimate consumer. In that way the burden of losses consequent upon use of defective articles is borne by those who are in a position to either control the danger or make an equitable distribution of the losses when they do occur . . . Accordingly, we hold that under modern marketing conditions, when a manufacturer puts a new automobile in the stream of trade and promotes its purchase by the public, an implied warranty that it is reasonably suitable for use as such accompanies it into the hands of the ultimate purchaser. Absence of agency between the manufacturer and the dealer who makes the ultimate sale is immaterial.[48]

The scope of this principle, the setting-aside of the technical limitations of sales law, and the court's insistence that exclusion or limitation of liability by contract would not be permitted had important consequences. Notably, it led to the belief that the basis of liability should lie not in contract, as the *Henningsen* court had suggested, but in terms of strict liability in tort. This view was, indeed, subsequently articulated by the Supreme

[45] *Baxter* v. *Ford Motor Co.*, 12 P 2d 409 (1932); cf. the similar English law case of *Evans* v. *Triplex Safety Glass Co. Ltd.* [1938] 4 All ER 283, in which the action was brought in negligence under *Donoghue* v. *Stevenson* [1932] AC 562 and the action failed for lack of proof of fault in the process of manufacture.

[46] Prosser, 'The Assault upon the Citadel' (Select Bibliography), 1133.

[47] 161 A 2d 69 (1960).

[48] *Ibid.*, 81, 84.

Court of California in *Greenman* v. *Yuba Power Products Inc.*[49] In that case the defendant raised a defence available under sales law, namely that the plaintiff had failed to give prompt notice of the breach of warranty and therefore forfeited any contract action. The court excluded the defence of lack of notice as far as the warranty action was concerned and then went on to impose a more general strict liability upon the manufacturer in tort:

A manufacturer is strictly liable in tort when an article he places on the market, knowing that it is to be used without inspection for defects, proves to have a defect that causes injury to a human being. Recognised first in the case of unwholesome food products, such liability has now been extended to a variety of other products that create as great or greater hazards if defective. Although in these cases strict liability has usually been based on the theory of an express or implied warranty running from the manufacturer to the plaintiff, the abandonment of the requirement of a contract between them, the recognition that the liability is not assumed by agreement but imposed by law, and the refusal to permit the manufacturer to define the scope of its own responsibility for defective products make clear that the liability is not one governed by the law of contract warranties but by the law of strict liability in tort. Accordingly, rules defining and governing warranties that were developed to meet the needs of commercial transactions cannot be invoked to govern the manufacturer's liability to those injured by their defective products unless those rules also serve the purposes for which such liability is imposed.[50]

At this time the courts put forward a number of justifications for moving towards strict liability in tort. One, emphasised by Traynor J in *Yuba*[51] and in his earlier concurring opinion in *Escola* v. *Coca-Cola Bottling Co. of Fresno*,[52] was the manufacturer's superior capacity to absorb the risks of injury and to spread the costs either through insurance or through adjusting the prices of his products. 'The cost of an injury and the loss of time or health may be an overwhelming misfortune to the person injured, and a needless one, for the risk of injury can be insured by the manufacturer and distributed among the public as a cost of doing business.'[53] A second argument was based on the notion of the manufacturer's ability to control risk of defects arising, and the likelihood that strict liability would lead it to take additional precautions at the various stages of the production process.[54] In addition to these utilitarian or efficiency-based justifications, the courts rationalised strict liability in terms of general appeals to public protection. The ultimate consumer was normally unable to analyse or scrutinise the product for safety, and implicitly took it on trust that it would not be dangerous to life and limb.[55] Doctrinally this led to a new suggestion. The manufacturer could be seen

49 377 P 2d 897 (1963). 50 *Ibid.*, 901 (Traynor J).
51 *Ibid.* 52 150 P 2d 436 (1944). 53 *Ibid.*, 440.
54 *Philips* v. *Kimwood Machine Co.*, 525 P 2d 1033, 1041–2 (1974). This development was linked to the economic analysis of Guido Calabresi, and in particular the idea that the manufacturer's strict liability was based upon it being the 'least cost avoider': see G. Calabresi and J. Hirschoff, 'Towards a Test for Strict Liability in Torts' (Select Bibliography).
55 *Jacob E. Decker & Sons* v. *Capps*, 164 SW 2d 828, 829 (1942). The same point can be put in economic terms: if the consumer is systematically unable to assess the degree of risk involved in the use of products, a strict

as representing the safety of the product in question, not only because of the kind of promotional activities which had given rise to liability in *Baxter* v. *Ford Motor Co.*[56] but also by virtue of the fact that he was putting the product on the market.[57]

There were also thought to be significant reasons relating to litigation and process costs for imposing strict liability. An action in tort making all those in the supply chain strictly liable could be seen as a means of 'short-circuiting' the successive actions for breach of contract of consumer against retailer, retailer against distributor, and so on, stretching back to the manufacturer. This process was not simply wasteful of resources; it was capable of being disrupted if at any point in the supply chain one of the parties was insolvent, out of the jurisdiction or protected by an exclusion or limitation clause.[58] Second, tort liability extended the scope of potential plaintiffs in such a way as to remove some of the anomalies that had attached to liability for warranty. It was no longer necessary for the victim to have acquired title to the goods or to show reliance on the defendants' warranty of safety, and the artificial restraints of UCC section 2–318 were no longer applicable. This meant that not simply employees of the purchaser but also bystanders who were injured simply by virtue of being in the vicinity of the defective product could recover.[59] This was the consequence of the important change of emphasis brought about by framing the cause of action in tort:

> If the philosophy of the strict liability is that all injured plaintiffs are to be compensated by holding the suppliers of products to strict liability for all the harm they do in the world, and in expecting them to insure against the liability and pass the cost on to society by adding it to the price, then there is no reason whatever to distinguish the pedestrian hit by an automobile with bad brakes from the injured driver of the car. If the supplier is to be held liable because of his representation of safety in marketing the goods, then the pedestrian stands on quite a different footing. He is not the man the supplier has sought to reach, and no implied representation has been made to him that the product is safe for use; nor has he relied on any assurance of safety whatever.[60]

Most American jurisdictions subsequently moved to adopt the version of strict tort liability contained in section 402A of the Restatement (Second) of Torts which was drawn up by the American Law Institute in 1965:

Special Liability of Seller of Product for Physical Harm to User or Consumer

(1) One who sells any product in a defective condition unreasonably dangerous to the user or consumer or to his property is subject to liability for physical harm thereby caused to the ultimate user or consumer, or to his property, if (a) the seller is engaged in the business of selling such a product, and (b) it is expected to and does reach the user or consumer without substantial change in the condition in which it is sold.

liability regime which places the responsibility for risk assessment clearly on the producer is appropriate. See D. Dewees, D. Duff and M. Trebilcock, *Exploring the Domain of Accident Law* (1996), at 204.

56 12 P 2d 409 (1932), discussed above.

57 *Jacob E. Decker & Sons* v. *Capps*, 164 SW 2d 828, 832–3 (1942); Prosser, 'The Assault on the Citadel' (Select Bibliography), 1123.

58 *Ibid.*, 1124.

59 *Piercefield* v. *Remington Arms Co.*, 133 NW 2d 129 (1965).

60 W. Prosser, 'The Fall of the Citadel (Strict Liability to the Consumer)' (Select Bibliography).

(2) The rule stated in Subsection (1) applies although (a) the seller has exercised all possible care in the preparation and sale of his product, and (b) the user or consumer has not bought the product from or entered into any contractual relation with the seller.

The definition of 'seller' here therefore applied to all those engaged in handling the goods in a business capacity along the length of the supply chain; it therefore includes manufacturers, distributors, wholesalers and retailers. As far as the range of plaintiffs was concerned, in imposing liability to the user or consumer, section 402A apparently excluded an action brought by a mere bystander; however, this further extension was later accepted by the courts of several state jurisdictions, including California. In *Elmore* v. *American Motors Corp.*[61] the Supreme Court of California suggested that, 'if anything, bystanders should be entitled to greater protection than the consumer or user where injury to bystanders from the defect is reasonably foreseeable'. The reason was that bystanders have no opportunity of any kind to inspect for defects or to limit their purchases to those of reputable manufacturers.

The imposition of strict liability relieved the plaintiff of the burden of proving fault. However, it did *not* entail the manufacturer (or subsequent handler in the supply chain) becoming an automatic insurer for any damage caused by the product. Attention was shifted away from the quality of the defendant's conduct and from the scope of his duty of care towards the nature of the 'defect' and to the availability of defences. The central concept in section 402A was that of a product which reached the consumer 'in a defective condition unreasonably dangerous'. This formulation was not equivalent to reading a requirement of negligence back into the section, since the test was whether the product was unreasonably dangerous from the point of view of the consumer, not whether the manufacturer was at fault in the process of producing it. Comment (*i*) to section 402A stated that 'the article sold must be dangerous to an extent beyond that which would be contemplated by the ordinary consumer who purchases it, with the ordinary knowledge common to the community as to its characteristics'.

This was the basis for the 'consumer expectation test' which courts in a number of American jurisdictions went on to apply. But at the same time the formulation used was designed to avoid a situation in which *absolute* liability, without the possibility of any defences, was imposed on the manufacturer. In particular, this led some courts to develop a separate 'risk–utility defence' which sought to measure the costs and benefits of product innovation, with particular reference to product design, in a way potentially more favourable to manufacturers.[62] It should be noted that despite its emphasis on no-fault liability, section 402A also made extensive provision for defences: in particular, the defendant would not be liable if the product left his hands in a safe condition and was subsequently mishandled by another.[63] Nor did section 402A make any reference to liability for pecuniary or 'pure economic' loss.

[61] (1969) 451 P 2d 84, 89.

[62] S. Birnbaum, 'Unmasking the Test for Design Defect: From Negligence [to Warranty] to Strict Liability to Negligence' (1980) 33 *Vand. LR* 593, 600.

[63] Restatement (Second) of Torts, s. 402A, comment (g).

The law moved on again with the adoption of the Restatement (Third) of Torts: Product Liability in 1998, when section 402A was replaced by a new definition of liability which distinguishes between manufacturing defects, design defects, and failures to warn. Section 1 of the Third Restatement now states that '[o]ne who is engaged in the business of selling or otherwise distributing products who sells or distributes a defective product is subject to liability for harm to persons or property caused by the defect'. Under section 2(a), a product is 'defective' when 'at the time of sale or distribution, it contains a manufacturing defect, is defective in design, or is defective because of inadequate instructions or warnings'. A manufacturing defect occurs under section 2(b) 'when the product departs from its intended design even though all possible care was exercised in the preparation and marketing of the product'. A design defect occurs 'when the foreseeable risks of harm posed by the product could have been reduced or avoided by the adoption of a reasonable alternative design by the seller or other distributor, or a predecessor in the commercial chain of distribution, and the omission of the alternative design renders the product not reasonably safe'. Finally, under section 2(c) a product may be defective 'because of inadequate instructions or warnings when the foreseeable risks of harm posed by the product could have been reduced or avoided by the provision of reasonable instructions or warnings by the seller or other distributor, or a predecessor in the commercial chain of distribution, and the omission of the instructions or warnings renders the product not reasonably safe'.

According to the comment to section 1 of the Third Restatement, sections 2(b) and 2(c) recognise that the strict liability principle established for manufacturing defects is inappropriate for defects of design and failures to warn, and, as a result, return the law 'to a reasonableness test traditionally used in determining whether an actor has been negligent'. This reflects the courts' earlier development of the risk–utility defence for these types of design defect. Nevertheless, the comment goes on to state 'that many courts insist on speaking of the liability based on the standards described in sections 2(b) and 2(c) as being strict', since for some purposes the focus of analysis is on the product rather than the manufacturer. Moreover, non-manufacturer sellers in the chain of supply are still held to a strict standard. Nevertheless, the Third Restatement represents a certain move back towards principles of negligence away from those of strict liability. As the comment notes, ' "strict products liability" is a term of art that reflects the judgment that products liability is a discrete area of tort law which borrows from both negligence and warranty', that is, from contract law. In the sense in which we have used the phrase in this chapter, products liability involves *stricter* forms of negligence liability.

(iii) Directive 85/374/EEC and the Consumer Protection Act 1987

Proposals for a European Community Directive on Products Liability were first considered in the 1970s and, after slow progress, finally led to the adoption by the Member States of the present Directive in 1985. Independently of the Community the Council of Europe adopted a Convention on Product Liability in January 1977; this has remained unratified with the later development of the Community's proposal, but it provided a useful model for a harmonising measure. The Council of Europe Convention is stronger, in that it does not contain any version of the 'state of the art' or 'development risks' defence that the Directive allows to Community Member States.[64] However, states such as Sweden and Finland, while still outside the EC, chose to use the Directive rather than the Convention as the basis for recent products-liability legislation.[65]

The Directive was the first significant attempt to achieve the harmonisation of an area of private law at Community level. The preamble seeks to justify the approximation of laws by arguing that divergences between the laws of different Member States 'may distort competition and affect the movement of goods within the common market and entail a differing degree of protection of the consumer'. In other words, different liability regimes may distort the market by subsidising producers in some states and penalising others.[66] An argument directed more clearly to the kind of social-policy factors that influenced the American debate in the 1950s and 1960s is the assertion in the following paragraph of the preamble. According to this, 'liability without fault on the part of the producer is the sole means of adequately solving the problem, peculiar to our age of increasing technicality, of a fair apportionment of the risks inherent in modern technological production'.[67]

The Directive accordingly provides in its first Article that 'the producer shall be liable for damage caused by a defect in his product'. The category of producer effectively includes all those in the supply chain from the manufacturer down (including the manufacturer of a component part). Also included is any person who 'presents himself as a producer' by putting his name, trademark or other distinguishing feature on the product, as are other suppliers unless they can notify the consumer of the identity of the producer.[68] Those made responsible in this way are jointly and severally liable for damage caused.[69] In addition, the person responsible for importing the product into the European Community (although not into the particular Member State, unless otherwise liable) will be deemed to be a producer for this purpose.[70] 'Products' include all movables except primary agricultural produce and game; electricity is also specifically included in the Directive.[71]

The claimant is required to prove defect and damage and the causal link between them.[72] The definition of defect is contained in Article 6(1):

A product is defective when it does not provide the safety which a person is entitled to expect, taking all circumstances into account, including:

(*a*) the presentation of the product;
(*b*) the use to which it could reasonably be expected that the product would be put;
(*c*) the time when the product was put into circulation.

64 Art. 7(1)(e); see below.

65 See D. G. Smith, 'The European Community Directive on Product Liability' (Select Bibliography), 103.

66 It was on this basis that the ECJ decided, in Case C-402/03 *Skov AEG* v. *Billa Lavprisvarehus* [2006] ECR I-199, that Danish law was not compatible with Directive 85/374 insofar as it imposed a greater liability upon suppliers than provided for by the directive.

67 See also the judgment of Tesauro AG in Case C-300/95 *Commission* v. *United Kingdom* [1997] ECR I-2649; [1997] All ER (EC) 391, in particular at [16]–[17].

68 Art. 3.

69 Art. 5.

70 Art. 3(2).

71 Art. 2.

72 Art. 4.

This reflects to some degree the 'consumer expectation' test initially developed for manufacturing defects under section 402A of the American Restatement (Second) of Torts. However, the reference to the reasonable expectation of the use to which the product would be put and to the time it was put into circulation also brings in elements associated with the 'risk–utility' test. Moreover, the Directive refers to the safety which 'a person', not necessarily the ultimate consumer, is 'entitled to expect'. This can be read as incorporating the risk–utility test for cases of defective design as opposed to defective manufacture (a product failing to match up to the intended specification).[73] Nonetheless, the Directive is probably more favourable to the consumer than section 402A was because it does not require him to prove that the product is both defective and 'unreasonably dangerous'.[74]

'Damage' under the Directive is defined as personal injury and death, on the one hand, and damage to property used for private use or consumption, on the other; 'pure economic loss' and business losses are thereby excluded. Damage to the product itself is also excluded and there is a 500 Euro minimum threshold for property-damage claims, which is designed to prevent a flood of minor claims.[75] Contracting-out through exclusion or limitation clauses is prohibited.[76] A number of defences are spelled out: amongst others, these arise where the producer can prove that he did not put the product into circulation; that the defect did not exist when he put it into circulation; and that the defect arose out of his compliance with public regulations.[77] The Directive also contains a general exemption for non-business producers.[78]

The validity of the 'economic argument' for harmonising product liability law through a directive has been called into question. Prior to the Directive, all the Member States had laws concerning product liability.[79] It is far from clear what the effects upon producer prices would be of moving to a general strict liability regime; it is possible that the difference would be barely discernible.[80] Even on the assumption that a common strict liability standard might have a significant impact on prices, the Directive as drafted is most unlikely to achieve the levelling-out of the conditions of competition. One reason for this is that it does not seek to harmonise the remedies available to the consumer in the various Member States. The level at which damages are payable, in particular, is left up to Member States by virtue of a provision making it possible, but not obligatory, for national legal systems to impose a maximum limit on damages awards of 70 million Euros. Second, the Directive allows Member States two further derogations by providing that they may extend the scope of protection beyond industrial products to include agricultural products and game.[81] Member States may also

[73] C. Newdick, 'The Future of Negligence in Product Liability' (Select Bibliography), 300.

[74] G. M. Whitehead and G. Scott, 'A Comparison of Product Liability Law in the United States and the European Community' (Select Bibliography), 172.

[75] Art. 9.

[76] Art. 12.

[77] Art. 7(1)(a), (b) and (d) respectively.

[78] Art. 7(1)(c).

[79] For a review, see F. Albanese and L. F. del Duca, 'Developments in European Product Liability' (Select Bibliography).

[80] S. Whittaker, 'The EEC Directive on Product Liability' (Select Bibliography), 235.

[81] Art. 15(1)(a).

make their own legislative provisions for a 'state of the art' defence.[82] According to this defence, a producer is exempted if he can show that the defect could not have been discovered given the state of scientific and technical knowledge at the time the product was put into circulation. Third, the Directive does not seek to iron out significant potential differences between the laws of different Member States. It preserves existing principles of contractual or non-contractual liability already in force in Member States,[83] and permits, but does not require, the use of contributory negligence as a defence.[84] It explicitly preserves the existing national laws on contribution by joint tortfeasors.[85] Nor does the Directive address the matter of the different approaches taken by the Member States to the question whether state social insurance institutions are subrogated to the claims of accident victims, differences which can substantially affect the level of damages payable by the defendant.[86] These divergencies raise the possibility of 'forum-shopping' by plaintiffs seeking out the most advantageous jurisdiction in which to bring their action.[87]

Certain of these derogations were apparently included in the Directive as the price of gaining unanimous agreement for its adoption.[88] With regard to the derogations, the Directive provides for a review procedure under which the Commission is required to submit a report to the Council of Ministers on the operation of the derogation provisions ten years after the adoption of the Directive.[89] The Directive itself acknowledges that the harmonisation it achieves 'cannot be total at the present stage, but opens the way towards greater harmonisation'.[90] This could have been read as suggesting that the rationale for the Directive was not to ensure uniformity of laws throughout the Community, but to entrench a certain *minimum* level of social protection for consumers, below which no Member State would be permitted to fall. Yet this goal may potentially come into conflict with the economic argument for ensuring parity of producers' costs across the single market. With this economic goal in mind, the Directive could instead be interpreted as laying down *maximum* standards of protection; with all its limitations, it could paradoxically come to have a restrictive effect on the development of consumer-protection law in the Member States.[91] That this interpretation of the Directive is the correct one has now been confirmed by the judgment of the ECJ in *Skov AEG* v. *Billa Lavprisvarehus*,[92] in which Danish legislation imposing strict liability upon

82 Art. 7(1)(e) and Art. 15(1)(b). 83 Art. 13.
84 Art. 8(1). 85 *Ibid.*
86 T. Weir, 'Governmental Liability' [1988] *PL* 40, 42; although under the scheme of recoupment contained in the Social Security Administration Act 1992, the position in English law is now closer to the position in systems which subrogate the state to the victim's claim. See below, ch. 8.
87 Forum shopping is regulated by the rules of private international law and, within the European Community, by the Brussels Convention on Jurisdiction and Enforcement of Judgments in Civil and Commercial Matters of 1968. See R. Atree, 'Jurisdiction, Enforcement of Judgment and Conflicts of Laws' in P. Kelly and R. Atree (eds.), *European Product Liability Law* (Select Bibliography), ch. 17.
88 See Smith (Select Bibliography), 106–7. 89 Art. 15(2).
90 Preamble, final para.
91 See J. Stapleton, 'Three Problems with the New Product Liability' (Select Bibliography) and for further discussion see her *Product Liability* (Select Bibliography), 60–5.
92 Case C-402/03, [2006] ECR I-199.

suppliers under circumstances which went beyond those set out for supplier liability in the Directive, was for that reason ruled to be incompatible with the Directive.

The Directive was incorporated into English law by virtue of Part I of the Consumer Protection Act 1987. Earlier calls for the imposition of strict liability, for defective products had been made in the aftermath of the thalidomide affair, in which children were born with congenital disabilities after their mothers had taken the thalidomide drug during pregnancy. The difficulties of proving negligence on the part of the company that had manufactured the drug gave rise to a wide public debate on the question of product liability. Both the English and Scottish Law Commissions made proposals for the introduction of strict liability and these were later echoed by the Pearson Commission in the late 1970s.[93] Some limited progress was made by the Consumer Safety Act 1978 which now, as amended,[94] forms Part II of the Consumer Protection Act 1987. This imposed certain regulatory requirements upon manufacturers in the area, in particular, of information and warnings relating to dangerous products put into circulation, and in addition to criminal sanctions provided for persons affected by a breach of the Act to bring a private action for breach of statutory duty.[95] However, this legislation fell a long way short of imposing a general private-law liability upon producers for dangerously defective products. It took the adoption of the Directive for the UK Parliament to introduce general liability of this kind, in the form of Part I of the Consumer Protection Act 1987.

The details of the Act are considered below; at this point certain features of its relationship with the Directive may be noted. The language used by the Act departs from that contained in the Directive in a number of respects. One justification for this could be the abstract and general quality of the language used in the Directive. However, there was an argument for leaving it up to the English courts (with appropriate guidance, where necessary, from the European Court of Justice) to resolve any ambiguities of drafting.[96] As it is, not only does the Act make provision for the optional 'state of the art' or 'development risks' defence in Article 7(e) of the Directive, but it could be read as significantly expanding its scope. Article 7(e) allows a defence where the producer shows that: 'the state of scientific and technical knowledge at the time when he put the product into circulation was not such as to enable the existence of the defect to be discovered'. Section 4(1)(e) of the Act, by contrast, provides for a defence where: 'the state of scientific and technical knowledge at the relevant time was not such that a producer of products of the same description as the product in question might be expected to

[93] Law Commission, *Liability for Defective Products*, No. 82 (Scots Law Com. No. 45) (Cmnd. 6831, 1977); Pearson Commission, *Report of the Royal Commission on Civil Liability and Compensation for Personal Injury* (Cmnd. 7054–1, 1978), ch. 22.

[94] By the Consumer Safety (Amendment) Act 1986.

[95] Consumer Safety Act 1978, s. 6; see now, Consumer Protection Act 1987, s. 41(1); on breach of statutory duty generally, see ch. 7, above. The theoretical availability of this private action has had little impact on the development of consumer protection law. See the account of the law in A. Bell, 'Product Liability Damages in England and Wales' (1991) 20 *Anglo-Am. LR* 371.

[96] C. Newdick, 'Risk, Uncertainty and "Knowledge" in the Development Risk Defence' (1991) 20 *Anglo-Am. LR* 309, 326.

have discovered the defect it if had existed in his products while they were under his control'. By apparently making the relevant standard that of the producer in the field and not the expectation of the consumer of the product, the Act arguably tilted the relevant test even further away from the consumer-expectation model towards the American risk–utility test, with its emphasis on adjusting the costs and benefits of innovation. The test is similar to that of negligence, except that the burden of proof is reversed.[97]

In the early 1990s the European Commission started infringement proceedings against the United Kingdom in respect of section 4(1)(e) of the 1987 Act,[98] but in 1997 the ECJ rejected the Commission's argument. The Court held that:

in order to have a defence under Art. 7(e) of the Directive, the producer of a defective product must prove that the objective state of scientific and technical knowledge, including the most advanced state of such knowledge, at the time when the product in question was put into circulation was not such as to enable the existence of the defect to be discovered. Further, in order for the relevant scientific and technical knowledge to be successfully pleaded against the producer, that knowledge must have been accessible at the time when the product was put into circulation.[99]

The Court went on to hold that section 4(1)(e) placed the burden of proof on the producer, as required by the Directive, and did not impose a limit on the state and degree of scientific knowledge to be taken into account. Nor did it make the defence dependent upon the subjective knowledge of the producer. Finally, the Court considered that any ambiguities in section 4(1)(e) could be resolved by national courts interpreting the Act in line with the wording and purpose of the Directive, as required by EC law.

(iv) Return to Negligence?

As we have seen, the European Community Directive closely resembles the form of strict liability that has evolved in the United States. Somewhat ironically, the Directive's adoption and implementation have coincided with signs of a change of mood towards the strict liability principle in the United States. This is evident first of all in the growing use of the risk–utility test in preference to the test of consumer expectation. Thus, in *Barker* v. *Lull Engineering Co.*[100] the Supreme Court of California adopted a 'two-pronged' test under which the plaintiff, if she could not win on the basis of consumer expectations, could then try to establish that the manufacturer failed to pass the risk–utility test. In other words she was asked 'to prove, in light of the relevant factors, that on balance the benefits of the challenged design outweigh the risk of danger inherent in such design'.[101] The court denied that the risk–utility test was one which 'rings of

97 *Ibid.*, 310.

98 G. G. Howells, 'Europe's Solution to the Product Liability Phenomenon' (1991) 20 *Anglo-Am. LR* 205, 218.

99 Case C-300/95, *Commission* v. *United Kingdom* [1997] ECR I-2649; [1997] All ER (EC) 391. For comment, see C. Hodges, 'Development Risks: Unanswered Questions' (1998) 61 *MLR* 560; M. Mildred and G. Howells, 'Comment on "Development Risks, Unanswered Questions"' (1998) 61 *MLR* 570.

100 573 P 2d 443 (1978).

101 *Ibid.*, 452.

negligence' in the sense of inviting the court to balance the cost of prevention against the magnitude of the harm and the risk of its occurring, as in the 'Hand test' for determining breach of duty.[102] It differed from negligence in that it 'explicitly focuses the trier of fact's attention on the adequacy of the product itself, rather than on the manufacturer's conduct, and places the burden on the manufacturer, rather than the plaintiff, to establish that because of the complexity of, and trade-offs implicit in, the design process, an injury-producing product should nevertheless not be found defective'.[103]

Nonetheless, courts have been at pains to point out that this test does not convert the manufacturer into an automatic insurer for consumer injury or damage, and in practice it may not be too difficult for a manufacturer to present enough evidence to meet the presumption against him. Moreover, courts in several jurisdictions started in the early 1980s to use the risk–utility test not as an alternative to consumer expectation, but as the principal determinant of liability in cases of defective design where, it was said, 'the consumer simply does not have adequate information to know what to expect'.[104] A review of the American case law around this time suggested that in most jurisdictions consumer expectation was retained only for cases of manufacturing defect (meaning products that are badly manufactured according to their specification, such as a car with faulty brakes). In some states the plaintiff had a choice of pursuing one route or the other. Some jurisdictions had also diluted the strict-liability element in the tests for applying the 'state of the art' defence, allowing manufacturers' compliance with the general practice of a particular industry to be advanced as a defence.[105]

A second area of contention in contemporary US law concerns awards of punitive damages against manufacturers, which may dwarf the compensatory award paid to the consumer in respect of the costs of personal injury or property damage. Under English law the grounds for the award of punitive or exemplary damages are highly restricted,[106] and one of the first decisions under the Consumer Protection Act confirmed this approach for cases of statutory product liability. The most significant category for present purposes concerns cases in which the defendant calculated that the gains he would make from committing a tort would outweigh compensatory damages he might have to pay to the plaintiff. By contrast, US jurisdictions recognised the possibility of punitive damages for a variety of purposes including the case of the 'calculating' defendant but also embracing the reckless or intentional commission of a wrong or malice against the plaintiff.[107] In the celebrated case of *Grimshaw* v. *Ford Motor Co.*[108] the defendants were

[102] Above, ch. 4, Section 1; *United States* v. *Carroll Towing Co.*, 159 F 2d 169, 173 (1947).

[103] 573 P 2d 443, 456 (1978).

[104] *O'Brien* v. *Muskin Corp.*, 463 A 2d 298, 308 (1982); see also discussion of the consumer-expectation test in *Dart* v. *Wiebe Manufacturing Inc.*, 709 P 2d 876 (1985) and *Camacho* v. *Honda Motor Co.*, 741 P 2d 1240 (1987); and see generally, Birnbaum, 'Unmasking the Test for Design Defect' (1980) 33 *Vand. LR* 593; Newdick, 'The Future of Negligence in Product Liability' (Select Bibliography); N. P. Terry, 'State of the Art Evidence: From Logical Construct to Judicial Retrenchment' (1991) 20 *Anglo-Am. LR* 285.

[105] See Terry, *ibid.; Feldman* v. *Lederle Laboratories*, 479 A 2d 374 (1984).

[106] See the judgment of Lord Devlin in *Rookes* v. *Barnard* [1964] AC 1129, discussed in ch. 25, below.

[107] G. C. Christie, 'Current Trends in the American Law of Punitive Damages' (1991) 20 *Anglo-Am. LR* 349.

[108] 119 Cal. App. 3d 757 (1981).

aware of a design defect in one of their car models which rendered the vehicle liable to burst into flames when hit in the rear. Nevertheless, they declined to fix it because the costs of doing so were thought to outweigh the risk of litigation. They were held liable in a wrongful death action for punitive damages of $125 million (reduced on appeal to $3.5 million) as against compensation of nearly $3 million. There are numerous other cases in which punitive damages have far outstripped compensatory awards. In America the measure of damages is a jury matter, and appellate courts are reluctant, on the whole, to interfere with the jury's decision. In some states, legislatures have responded by passing Acts to limit both the availability of punitive damages and the scale on which they may be awarded. Defendants have also challenged high punitive awards on a variety of constitutional grounds, so far with little success.[109] Statutes limiting the operation of punitive awards have themselves been challenged on grounds of alleged unconstitutionality. Again the courts are generally reluctant to interfere, although there is a developing trend towards declaring such measures unconstitutional on the ground of their potentially arbitrary effects in differentiating between the claims of different plaintiffs.[110]

Empirical research suggests that the courts are moving away from high damages claims of their own accord, and are at the same time taking a more restrictive view of the scope of manufacturers' liability. A study of judgments of appellate courts in product-liability cases carried out by Professors Henderson and Eisenberg found that the success rate for plaintiffs began to fall in the early 1980s. This was largely because courts were setting an increasingly pro-defendant standard of responsibility and dismissing a larger number of claims at pre-trial hearings on questions of law, pre-empting the role of the jury which tends to be more strongly pro-plaintiff.[111] These findings cast doubt on the idea of a 'product liability crisis' in America, or at least indicate that the American courts are moving gradually towards their own solution to the initial mushrooming of liability following the strict-liability principle.

There are a number of justifications for moving away from the strict-liability test back towards some kind of negligence standard. In the first place there is an economic argument about which party, plaintiff or defendant, is best equipped to bear the damage or injury or the risk of it. Economic analysis suggests that the risk of loss should be imposed on the 'least cost avoider', that is to say, the person who can most effectively take steps either to avoid the risk of damage or to minimise its effects. The explicit

109 The US Supreme Court has rejected such challenges under the excessive-fines clause of the US Constitution (*Browning-Ferris Industries of Vermont Inc.* v. *Kelco Disposal Inc.*, 492 US 257 (1989)) and under the due-process clause of the Fourteenth Amendment to the Constitution (*Pacific Mutual Life Insurance Co.* v. *Haslip*, 111 SCt. 1032 (1991)).

110 E.g. by allowing punitive damages to be awarded only once, in effect favouring the first plaintiff to get judgment. The first plaintiff may be one of many if the defect caused a large-scale disaster or a string of accidents. See *McBride* v. *General Motors Co.*, 737 F Supp. 1563 (1990), discussed by Christie, 'Current Trends' (1991) 20 *Anglo-Am. LR* 349.

111 'The Quiet Revolution in Products Liability' (1991) 20 *Anglo-Am. LR* 188. See also the longer account, 'The Quiet Revolution in Products Liability: An Empirical Study of Legal Change' (1990) 36 *UCLA LR* 479, and for general discussion of American trends in this and related areas J. G. Fleming, *The American Tort Process* (1988).

assumption of the judges in such cases as *Henningsen* v. *Bloomfield Motors*[112] and *Greenman* v. *Yuba Products*[113] was that the manufacturer could most effectively avoid the defect through taking greater care in the process of production, and that businesses throughout the length of the supply chain were better placed than the ultimate consumer to spread the costs of prevention either through insurance or through increased prices. This view has been challenged by arguments to the effect that manufacturers may, in certain circumstances, be no more able than consumers to assess the nature of certain risks.[114] Some risks are unavoidable, in particular in relation to hidden design defects. A strict liability regime which holds the manufacturer automatically liable for the resulting harm may lead to manufacturers taking *excessive* amounts of care, pushing prices up beyond a level which reflects the potential costs to society of product defects, driving producers out of the market, or inhibiting innovation. It has also been suggested that product innovation may be stymied by the threat of high damages awards based on strict liability.[115]

Nor is it clear that the manufacturer is always best placed to take out the relevant insurance. Certainly as far as physical damage to property is concerned, the consumer, who has more information about the value of the property in question and the uses to which it is put, is in a better position to take out insurance covering the potential loss. Since household property is by and large covered by first-party or loss insurance, strict liability, by imposing upon the manufacturer what is in essence a requirement to carry third-party or liability insurance, may be creating the circumstances for a wasteful double-insurance of the loss in question. There are also signs that high damages awards have made it increasingly difficult for American producers to obtain the necessary liability insurance.[116]

These arguments do not seem so convincing in the case of personal injury, where the preventive or deterrent aim of strict liability may seem more clearly justified. However, if it is accepted that a certain level of risk is unavoidable as the price of product innovation, the interests of victims of injury are arguably better served by a system of collective health-care provision, buttressed by social-security benefits in relation to sickness and invalidity, than by a system which loads costs almost exclusively on to producers. In contrast to the United States, most European Community countries have some degree of collective health-care and social-insurance provision of this kind. It has thus been argued that for these countries strict product liability of the American kind, where compensation is assured through the costly court system, is both unnecessary and, in so far as it diverts economic resources from more worthwhile ends, undesirable.[117]

Whether these arguments will over time come to influence European courts and the European Community itself to weaken the strict liability principle contained in

[112] 161 A 2d 69 (1960). [113] 377 P 2d 897(1963).

[114] For a discussion and critique of the different economic theories, see Stapleton, *Product Liability* (Select Bibliography), ch. 5. [115] See C. Hodges, 'Development Risks: Unanswered Questions' (1998) 61 *MLR* 560.

[116] See the discussion of Howells, 'Europe's Solution to the Product Liability Phenomenon' (1991) 20 *Anglo-Am. LR* 204; Stapleton, *Product Liability* (Select Bibliography), in particular ch. 6.

[117] A. Bernstein, 'A Duty to Warn: One American View of the EC Products Liability Directive' (1991) 20 *Anglo-Am. LR* 224.

the Products Liability Directive remains to be seen. The less desirable features of the American system may well be the result not of strict liability as such, but rather of the prominent role of the jury, the possibility of stratospherically high damages awards, and the incentive to litigation provided by the contingency fee system.[118] In these respects, none of the product liability regimes of the EC Member States is truly comparable to the American system. However, it may well be that the Product Liability Directive itself, through the test of defect that it provides and through its acknowledgment of a development risks defence, comes closer to setting a modified negligence standard, or 'stricter' form of negligence liability, than would appear at first sight.

3. THE CAUSES OF ACTION AND COMPONENTS OF LIABILITY

We now turn to a more detailed analysis of the components of liability under the different potential causes of action in contract, tort and statute respectively. We will examine in turn the parties to the various actions; the types of products covered; the standard of care and of responsibility imposed upon the defendant and the availability of particular defences; the relevant principles of causation and remoteness; the concept of damage and the measurement of damages; and exclusion and limitation of liability.

(A) THE PARTIES TO THE ACTION

Here the fundamental point, referred to above, is the limited nature of the contract action for breach of warranty. Only a buyer who is in a direct contractual relation with a seller can sue for breach of an express or implied warranty of fitness. It is useful to distinguish here between 'vertical' contracts between businesses in the supply chain and 'horizontal' links involving consumers at the end of the chain (see Fig. 20.1).[119] Goods will normally pass through the hands of several commercial entities—the manufacturer, distributor(s) and retailer—before they reach the consumer. Each commercial supplier could have an action against the person or entity from which it bought the goods if it suffers loss as a result of a defect in the product. The last 'horizontal' contract between the retailer and the consumer will also contain, in addition to any express terms, the obligations of merchantable quality and fitness for the purpose intended which are implied by the Sale of Goods Act in any case of a sale made in the course of a business (although not to private sales).[120] Liability for breach of these obligations is strict, so the retailer will have no defence by claiming that the original defect was the responsibility of the manufacturer.

[118] See Fleming, *The American Tort Process* (1988).
[119] See R. M. Goode, *Commercial Law* (2nd edn., 1995).
[120] Section 14.

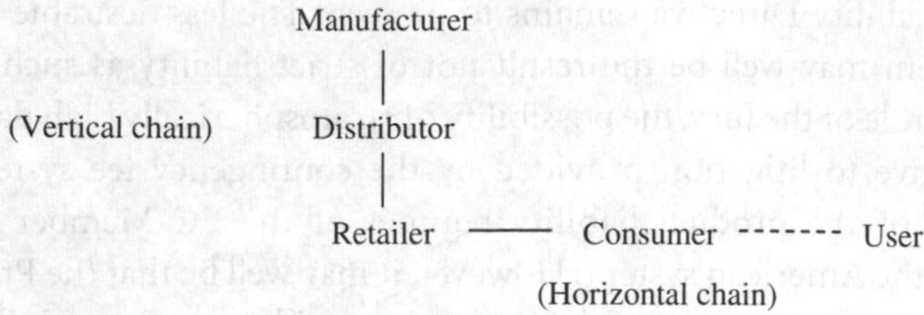

Fig. 20.1 Vertical and horizontal chains of supply

However, no contract action will arise if the person who purchased the product hands it on to a friend as a gift—as in *Donoghue* v. *Stevenson*[121]—or if the product injures another member of his household, as in *Priest* v. *Last*,[122] where a husband bought a hot-water bottle which burst and scalded his wife. In that case he recovered damages only because he had met the expenses arising from her injuries. Still less will any contract claim arise if the injury or other loss is sustained by a bystander who has no relation of any kind with the person who bought the goods. Although a breach of contract has taken place, in that defective goods have been supplied, the person suffering the loss is not the contracting party. The privity rule prevents the third party who has suffered the loss from bringing the action, on the ground that he has not supplied the consideration for the contract in question.[123] Nor can the person who made the contract bring an action for the third party's loss, unless that loss in some way caused additional actionable damage to him.[124]

It might nevertheless be possible in some situations for liability for the original defect to be transmitted back up the length of the supply chain. This could happen where a consumer (who is also the final purchaser) brings an action in contract against the retailer from whom he bought the product, and that retailer then sues the distributor for breach of contract, and so on back to the manufacturer. This, however, is an inefficient solution to the problem. For not only does it involve a multiplicity of parties and actions; more importantly it will not work if one of the parties in the chain is uninsured, insolvent, out of the jurisdiction, or protected by an exclusion clause. In that event, the liability will thus not get passed back up the chain.

Nor will it necessarily be possible for the retailer to leapfrog over an insolvent or unreachable supplier to one further up the supply chain, or back to the manufacturer itself, by bringing an action in tort. Even if negligence can be established, the retailer's claim is classified as 'pure economic loss' because he has not suffered physical harm of any sort. The physical harm has been suffered by the consumer and the retailer's only

[121] [1932] AC 562. [122] [1903] 2 KB 148.

[123] *Dunlop Pneumatic Tyre Co.* v. *Selfridge & Co. Ltd.* [1915] AC 847.

[124] *Woodar Investment Development Ltd.* v. *Wimpey Construction UK Ltd.* [1980] 1 WLR 277. See the discussion of the Law Commission, *Liability for Defective Products*, No. 82 (Scots Law Com. No. 45) (Cmnd. 6831, 1977), on the question of privity and liability for defective products.

damage is the pecuniary loss suffered by virtue of his liability in contract to the consumer. In *Lambert* v. *Lewis*[125] the Court of Appeal rejected such an action by a retailer against the manufacturer, on the ground that under *Spartan Steel and Alloys Ltd.* v. *Martin & Co. (Contractors) Ltd.*[126] it was necessary to show that the economic loss arose directly out of physical damage to the plaintiff, that is to say, injury to the plaintiff or damage to goods in which he had a proprietary or possessory interest when they were damaged. The House of Lords rejected an appeal on different grounds, and in doing so stated that it was *not* deciding that economic loss could not be recovered in these circumstances. Since then, the decisions of the House of Lords in *The Aliakmon*[127] and *Murphy* v. *Brentwood District Council*[128] have further emphasised the exceptional nature of recovery in negligence for pure economic loss. There is a case for saying that where physical damage occurs at *some point* in the supply chain, it is artificial to regard the resulting economic losses of contractors higher up the chain as a case of 'pure economic loss'.[129]

But when a similar point was made in *The Aliakmon* the House of Lords responded unsympathetically to that suggestion.[130] The manufacturer and consumer may be directly linked through contract if the retailer acts as the manufacturer's agent for the purposes of the sale to the consumer or, alternatively, as the agent of the consumer. Perfectly conceivable in principle, an agency relationship is unlikely in practice and will not be inferred by a court unless there is the clearest evidence of an intention to create it.[131] Alternatively, the manufacturer may make a representation direct to the consumer that gives rise to liability in contract. In *Carlill* v. *Carbolic Smoke Ball Co.*[132] the manufacturer's representation,[133] made through advertising, was taken to be a promise constituting an offer for a unilateral contract. The consumer accepted by taking the tablets for the period prescribed. This case, too, must be regarded as somewhat exceptional. It was not an action brought for misrepresenting the nature of the product as such, but a 'reward case' brought for the enforcement of the promise to pay the sum of money in the event that the tablets did not work.

Advertising statements will not normally give rise to legal liability for misrepresentation, on the grounds that they are just 'puffing up' the product.[134] Moreover, even when liability in damages for a misrepresentation can be established, for example, under section 2(1) of the Misrepresentation Act 1967, an action for damages will lie only if the statement in question induced a contract between the two parties. While an action for misrepresentation against the retailer is therefore entirely plausible,[135] it is unlikely to

[125] [1982] AC 225. [126] [1973] 1 QB 27.

[127] [1986] AC 785. [128] [1991] 1 AC 398.

[129] *The Kapetan Georgis* [1988] 1 Lloyd's Rep. 352, 356 (Hirst J).

[130] See the discussion of this point in ch. 3, Section 3(c)(iv) above.

[131] On the circumstances in which an agency relationship will be implied from commercial dealings, see *New Zealand Shipping Co. Ltd.* v. *A. M. Satterthwaite & Co. Ltd., The Eurymedon* [1975] AC 154 (PC).

[132] [1893] 1 QB 256.

[133] That he would pay a sum of money to anyone who was not protected against influenza after taking its tablets for the duration of the prescribed course.

[134] *Dimmock* v. *Hallett* (1866) LR 2 Ch. App. 21. [135] E.g. *Andrews* v. *Hopkinson* [1957] 1 QB 229.

arise between the manufacturer and ultimate consumer. It is possible that a collateral contract might arise in an appropriate case, as in *Shanklin Pier Ltd.* v. *Detel Products Ltd.*[136] where the plaintiff bought the paint manufactured by the defendant following a visit from one of its representatives who made various statements about its qualities. The paint was bought from a retailer, and the act of entering into this separate contract of sale was seen as the consideration for a collateral contract containing the defendant's warranties as to the quality of the paint. However, this is a somewhat artificial solution about which the courts have traditionally been sceptical. And it will only be used where there is clear evidence of contractual intent on the part of the manufacturer,[137] which will normally be lacking when the statements are made through general advertising as opposed in a face-to-face meeting. In so limiting liability for misrepresentations English law is far more rigid than its American counterpart, which admits the possibility of liability for public misrepresentations, including advertisements, in the absence of privity.[138]

It may, however, be possible to establish a separate duty of care in tort to avoid making careless statements that could endanger the consumer or otherwise cause his loss. Where the statement could cause the consumer physical harm, a duty of care is clearly established. Thus, liability has been imposed on the supplier of a volatile chemical in flasks whose labels carelessly failed to give an adequate warning of its properties;[139] on the distributor of a hair dye who gave a false assurance of its safety to a hairdresser, one of whose customers contracted dermatitis when it was applied;[140] and on a retailer who sold a cleaning fluid without testing to see whether it was correctly labelled.[141] Where economic loss is concerned, the claimant has the more difficult task of framing an action within the principles laid down by the House of Lords in *Hedley Byrne & Co. Ltd.* v. *Heller & Partners*,[142] with its limiting requirement of a pre-tort 'special relationship' between the parties.

Economic loss aside, the negligence action which the House of Lords recognised in *Donoghue* v. *Stevenson*[143] cut through the difficulties imposed by the privity rule by imposing a duty of care directly upon the manufacturer to the ultimate consumer, whether or not that person had any contractual rights against a retailer. Any person suffering physical injury or property damage can sue, including 'bystanders' and others not in a relation of any kind with the final purchaser, as long as the normal tests of causation and remoteness are satisfied. Nor are manufacturers the only potential defendants. Those who are responsible for assembling the different parts of a product[144]

[136] [1951] 2 KB 584; see also *Wells (Merstham) Ltd.* v. *Buckland Sand & Silica Co. Ltd.* [1965] 2 QB 170.

[137] *Heilbut Symons & Co.* v. *Buckleton* [1913] AC 30.

[138] *Baxter* v. *Ford Motor Co.*, 12 P 2d 409 (1932), *Randy Knitwear Inc.* v. *American Cyanamid Co.*, 181 NE 2d 399 (1962), *Ford Motor Co.* v. *Lonon*, 398 SW 2d 240 (1966).

[139] *Vacwell Engineering Co. Ltd.* v. *BDH Chemicals Ltd.* [1971] 1 QB 88.

[140] *Watson* v. *Buckley, Osborne, Garret & Co.* [1940] 1 All ER 174; although cf. *Holmes* v. *Ashford* [1950] 2 All ER 76, where manufacturers were held to have given an adequate warning: see R. Bradgate, 'Misrepresentation and Product Liability in English Law' (1991) 20 *Anglo-Am. LR* 334, 341.

[141] *Fisher* v. *Harrods Ltd.* [1966] 1 Lloyd's Rep. 500.

[142] [1964] AC 465. [143] [1932] AC 562.

[144] *Malfroot* v. *Noxal Ltd.* (1935) 51 TLR 551.

or who supply a defective component part are included.[145] Repair work[146] and installation work[147] may similarly give rise to liability, and it is also possible that a distributor[148] or a seller on hire purchase[149] may come under a duty of care in negligence to the consumer.

As we have seen, the principal difficulty in the negligence action concerns the need to show fault. This is difficult enough in an action against the original manufacturer, although the plaintiff is normally given the benefit of certain inferences in his favour.[150] For others in the supply chain, such as distributors and retailers, it may be impossible to prove negligence as they are not responsible for the production process itself, although it might be possible to hold them liable for failing to inspect the goods for obvious signs of defects. Strict liability independently of contract is needed if the consumer is to have the possibility of an action against all the business parties in the supply chain. Under the Consumer Protection Act 1987, section 2(1), 'where any damage is caused wholly or partly by a defect in a product, every person to whom subsection (2) below applies shall be liable for the damage'. The Act does not spell out who may sue except in so far as this is implicit in the definition of 'damage' in section 5. 'Damage' means death, personal injury or damage to property (but not business property), including land and excluding damage to the product itself.[151] Those suffering physical harm are, therefore, included, although it is possible that as with the tort of negligence and even in the case of American jurisdictions recognising strict liability, those who suffer injury as 'mere' bystanders will only recover if their presence was foreseeable. Users and consumers will come under the category of 'foreseeable claimants' without much difficulty, but it is not clear how a court would deal with the problem of remoteness which arises where physical harm occurs in a *manner* which could not have been contemplated.[152] It is unclear whether the Act extends to 'nervous shock' recovery: section 45 of the Act provides that personal injury includes 'any disease and any other impairment of a person's physical or mental condition'. Although pure economic loss appears to be excluded this is not so obvious as it might be. These questions are discussed further below, in the analysis of 'damage'.

There is also difficulty over the definition of property damage. In the first place the aim of the Act (and of the Directive) is to prevent claims for damage to commercial property being brought under the strict liability principle. This accords with the general orientation of products liability towards the protection of consumer interests as opposed to business interests. For property damage to be actionable, therefore, the property must first of all have been of a type ordinarily intended for private use and consumption. Second, it must actually have been intended by the person suffering the

145 *Barnes* v. *Irwell Valley Water Board* [1939] 1 KB 21.

146 *Stennett* v. *Hancock and Peters* [1939] 2 All ER 578.

147 *Hartley* v. *Mayoh & Co.* [1952] 2 All ER 525 (affirmed on a different point [1954] 1 QB 383).

148 *Watson* v. *Buckley, Osborne, Garrett & Co. Ltd.* [1940] 1 All ER 174.

149 *Andrews* v. *Hopkinson* [1957] 1 QB 229, 236 (McNair J).

150 *Grant* v. *Australian Knitting Mills Ltd.* [1936] AC 85.

151 Section 5(1).

152 As in *Hughes* v. *Lord Advocate* [1963] AC 837. For discussion, see Whittaker, 'The EEC Directive on Product Liability' (Select Bibliography), 264–5.

loss or damage to be used 'mainly for his own private use, occupation or consumption'.[153] The overall result of this is to exclude actions by business entities in respect of business losses. Consumers can sue, but only in respect of damage to property intended for 'private' use; 'private' use appears to mean 'non-business' use. Where someone buys, for example, a car or a word processor for a mixture of personal and business uses, the court will have the task of identifying whether the product was intended 'mainly' for personal use. If not, the claimant will have to rely on common law negligence to recover any property damage caused by the defective product.

The Act, following the Directive, provides for an extensive list of potential defendants.[154] First of all there is the category of *producers*:

'producer', in relation to a product, means—

(*a*) the person who manufactured it;
(*b*) in the case of a substance which has not been manufactured but has been won or abstracted, the person who won or abstracted it;
(*c*) in the case of a product which has not been manufactured, won or abstracted but essential characteristics of which are attributable to an industrial or other process having been carried out (in relation to agricultural produce), the person who carried out that process...[155]

A product is defined as 'any goods or electricity' and includes a product, whether a raw product or a manufactured component, which is included in another product. The crucial point here is the extent to which the definition extends beyond the obvious categories of industrial manufacturers. Products 'won or abstracted' under paragraph (*b*) could include, for example, minerals (such as coal, gas and oil) and water, so that mining and oil companies and water companies are included under the Act. Farmers, however, are not included since under section 2(4) there is an exemption for those who supply agricultural produce ('any produce of the soil, of stock-farming or of fisheries')[156] before it undergoes industrial processing. The concept of an 'industrial or other process' under paragraph (*c*) is also important. The Directive refers by contrast to 'products which have undergone initial processing'.[157] If paragraph (*c*) receives a purposive interpretation[158] to give effect to the clear intention of the Directive to maximise the number of potential defendants, it would seem that any person who processes primary agricultural produce by, for example, cleaning or packaging it with a view to consumption will be caught by the Act. The only clear exemption that the Act and the Directive provide is for the farmer or other 'primary producer' who does not himself process the produce in this way.

The second group includes those who put their brand or trade mark on the goods: 'any person who, by putting his name on the product or using a trade mark or other distinguishing mark in relation to the product, has held himself out to be the producer of the product'.[159] The purpose of extending liability in this way is to catch those who

153 Section 5(3)(a)–(b).
154 Section 2(2).
155 Section 1(2).
156 *Ibid.*
157 Art. 2.
158 This is necessary under the doctrine of the 'indirect effect' of Directives: *Litster* v. *Forth Dry Dock & Engineering Co. Ltd.* [1990] 1 AC 456.
159 Section 2(2)(b).

represent the goods as their own, on the basis that by doing so they should assume the same responsibility to the class of consumers as those who manufacture the goods.

The third group consists of those responsible for importing the goods into a Member State of the Community, in the course of a business.[160] In so far as this provision is designed to deal with the problem that the manufacturer and even the 'brand-name' dealer may both be outside the jurisdiction of the consumer, it does not do so very effectively. For the consumer may well have come into contact with the product in a Community Member State other than the one into which the product was initially imported. It would have been more effective had the Directive and the Act imposed liability on the person responsible for importing the product into the Member State where the loss occurred or where the consumer was domiciled.

Suppliers along the length of the vertical chain who do not fall into one of these three categories will also be liable to the consumer unless they can identify to the consumer the person who supplied the goods to them. The consumer must make the request within a reasonable time of the damage occurring and at a time when it is not reasonably practicable for him to make the necessary identification.[161] For the supplier to escape liability, it is not necessary that the person he identifies be solvent or insured. This provision is therefore narrower than its equivalent in American law; the Restatement imposes liability on suppliers without the possibility of this defence of 'identification' of the producer. Nor does the Act clearly cover repairers, installers and others who work on a product. It seems that actions against this group will have to be brought in contract or negligence as before.

As far as suppliers of components or of raw materials that go to form part of a defective product are concerned, the Act provides that they are not for this reason alone to be treated as supplying the product in question.[162] They also have a defence if they can show that the defect was not attributable to them but was wholly attributable to the producer of the subsequent product.[163] However, there is no defence where a component itself is defective and is then incorporated in a larger product. A supplier of faulty brakes that are incorporated into a car will be potentially liable along with the manufacturer of the car itself.

In common with the contractual and tortious forms of liability at common law, the Act confines its liability to business producers and suppliers. This is the effect of section 4(1)(c) which provides a defence to suppliers who can show that the supply took place otherwise than in the course of their business. The same is true of producers, brand-namers and importers who can show that the production or other such activity was 'done otherwise than with a view to profit'. This excludes the case of the producer of home-made cakes who gives them to her friends. The position of charities, however, is not so clear. If cakes are produced for and sold from a charity stall, are they supplied in the course of a business and produced with a view to profit? Where a producer distributes free samples to help generate trade, that is clearly within the Act.

160 Section 2(2)(c).
161 Section 2(3).
162 Section 1(3).
163 Section 4(1)(f)(i).

Governmental bodies are included within the Act by virtue of section 45, which defines business as including the activities of 'a local authority or other public authority', and the provisions of the Act concerning product liability bind the Crown.[164]

It may be noted, finally, that where more than one of these potential defendants is found liable, liability is joint.[165]

(B) THE 'PRODUCTS' COVERED

The Sale of Goods Act 1979 defines goods as 'personal chattels other than things in action and money', including growing crops but excluding real property (land).[166] The terms implied into a sale of goods contract by section 14 of the Act may equally well arise by implication in a contract to supply combined goods and services, as in the case of a building contract.[167] The categories of articles and substances to which a tort action in negligence has been applied are equally broad, if not broader. These include a tombstone,[168] underwear,[169] hair dyes,[170] motor vehicles,[171] lifts,[172] bottles[173] and chemicals.[174]

Under the Consumer Protection Act, as we have seen, a product includes 'any goods or electricity and... includes a product which is comprised in another product, whether by virtue of being a component part or raw material or otherwise'.[175] Under section 45, goods include 'substances, growing crops and things comprised in land by virtue of being attached to it and any ship, aircraft or vehicle'. Manufactured drugs and other pharmaceutical products are therefore within the Act.

In *A* v. *National Blood Authority*[176] counsel for the defendants conceded that processed blood, used in transfusions, was a product under the Act; although prior to this point the issue was unclear (and had been debated in academic writings), this concession seems correct, particularly in the light of parallel US case law on the meaning of 'product'. Under the Restatement (Third), there is a specific exclusion for blood; otherwise, '[h]uman blood and human tissue both satisfy the formal requisites of section 19(a) [of the Restatement]'. The reason for the exclusion is that 'legislatures and courts alike have concluded that public policy concerns behind the availability of both human blood and human tissue outweigh the risks inherent in their supply'. However, there is no such exclusion under Directive 85/374 (nor, by extension, under the Consumer Protection Act 1987).

[164] Section 9. Thus NHS Trusts responsible for the administration of blood infected with hepatitis C to patients in their care were held liable under the Act in *A* v. *National Blood Authority* [2001] 3 All ER 289.

[165] Section 2(5). [166] Section 61(1).

[167] See *Young & Marten Ltd.* v. *McManus Childs Ltd.* [1969] 1 AC 454.

[168] *Brown* v. *Cotterill* (1934) 51 TLR 21.

[169] *Grant* v. *Australian Knitting Mills Ltd.* [1936] AC 86.

[170] *Parker* v. *Oloxo Ltd.* [1937] 3 All ER 524.

[171] *Herschtal* v. *Stewart and Arden Ltd.* [1940] 1 KB 155.

[172] *Haseldine* v. *C. A. Daw Ltd.* [1941] 2 KB 343.

[173] *Hart* v. *Dominion Stores* (1968) 67 DLR (2d) 675.

[174] *Vacwell Engineering Co. Ltd.* v. *BDH Chemicals Ltd.* [1971] 1 QB 88.

[175] Section 1(2). [176] [2001] 3 All ER 289.

The exemption for primary agricultural produce has already been noted. Land itself is not included in the definition of 'product'. Although the Act could be clearer on this point, it seems likely that claimants suffering loss through defects in buildings will have to bring an action against the builder either under the Defective Premises Act 1972 or under common law negligence.[177] The building itself, being an immovable, is part of the 'land' and not something simply attached to it. Where, however, the claimant is injured by a defective product which is incorporated into a house—such as bricks or roof tiles—he will have an action against the manufacturer of that product and others in the supply chain who fall within the definition of 'producer'. He will only rarely have an action against the builder. Although a builder will frequently contract to give title both to the land and to the materials which make up the building, section 46(4) of the Consumer Protection Act provides that where the supply of the materials takes the form of the disposal or creation of an interest in land, the supplier has a defence to any action under the Act. The builder will only be liable under the Act, therefore, in the event of supplying materials without also conferring title to the property.

(C) THE SCOPE AND STANDARD OF RESPONSIBILITY

Liability for breach of the implied terms in a contract for sale of goods is strict, enabling the buyer, under certain circumstances, to terminate the contract for breach of condition and return the goods, or alternatively to sue for damages.[178] Liability for misrepresentation is strict where the warranty in question is incorporated into the contract as a term, or forms a collateral contract; the buyer will have the normal range of contractual remedies. Where the misrepresentation is not incorporated into a contract in this way, damages are not available for a purely innocent misrepresentation (that is to say, one which is neither fraudulent nor negligent).[179] However, if the misrepresentor cannot show that he had reasonable grounds for making the statement he will be liable for damages under section 2(1) of the Misrepresentation Act 1967. These will be calculated according to the measure for the tort of deceit.[180]

Liability in negligence rests, as we have seen, on proof of fault, normally without the benefit of *res ipsa loquitur*. Notwithstanding Lord Wright's willingness in *Grant* v. *Australian Knitting Mills*[181] to make an inference of negligence from the mere existence of contamination in the product, in other decisions the English courts have refused to find negligence simply from the fact that a product failed to conform to an expected standard of safety, or to the one advertised. This can be seen in the case of a lemonade bottle which fractured when the plaintiff picked it up,[182] or the case of the car

[177] On liability for defective buildings, see ch. 3, Section 3(c)(iii) above.

[178] Sale of Goods Act, s. 53.

[179] The buyer will, however, be able to rescind the contract and claim restitution and indemnity (or he may, alternatively, be awarded damages in lieu of rescission under s. 2(2) of the Misrepresentation Act 1967), but the right to rescind may be lost by, e.g., lapse of time (*Leaf* v. *International Galleries* [1950] 2 KB 86) or affirmation (*Long* v. *Lloyd* [1958] 1 WLR 753), or by resale of the goods to a third party.

[180] *Royscot Trust Co.* v. *Rogerson* [1991] 3 All ER 294.

[181] [1936] AC 85.

[182] *Daniels* v. *R. White & Sons Ltd.* [1938] 4 All ER 258.

windscreen made of 'toughened safety glass' which shattered without warning.[183] Lord Atkin's original formulation in *Donoghue* v. *Stevenson* also emphasised the role of fault, in that he would have imposed liability on a manufacturer who sold products 'in such a form as to show that he intends them to reach the ultimate consumer in the form in which they left him with no possibility of intermediate examination'.[184] In *Donoghue*'s case there was no possibility of intermediate examination as the bottle was opaque and concealed its contents. The courts soon tightened this aspect of the test, substituting 'probability' for 'possibility' of intermediate examination.[185] The failure of an intermediary to make an effective examination will not exempt the manufacturer if no such examination was anticipated.[186]

In *Donoghue* v. *Stevenson*,[187] however, clear limits were set to the manufacturer's responsibility, in the sense that once he ceased to have 'control' of the item, he would cease to be liable for the consequences of its use. In *Evans* v. *Triplex Safety Glass*[188] the court was persuaded by an argument that the fault in the windscreen might have occurred when it was fitted, by a third party, and not during the process of manufacture. Where the product is mishandled by the consumer himself this does not, in itself, absolve the manufacturer, but it may provide a basis for a defence of contributory negligence.[189]

Under the Consumer Protection Act, liability is strict but, as under American law, this does not mean absolute or automatic liability. The boundaries to the producer's liability are set, above all, by the concept of 'defect' contained in section 3 of the Act, by the duties which are implicit in this definition, and by the defences which feature in section 4.

(i) The Concept of Defect

As we have seen, American law recognises three kinds of possible defect, and these can also be found in the extensive English case law. First are those that occur at the design stage, as in the production of a drug with unanticipated side effects or a model of a motor vehicle with a tendency to swerve unexpectedly. Then we encounter those occurring in the process of manufacture itself which prevent the product complying with its specification, such as the snail in the bottle in *Donoghue* v. *Stevenson*.[190] Finally, we have those deriving from a failure to give adequate warnings or instructions about the product, as in *Vacwell Engineering* v. *BDH Chemicals*.[191] Under US law (as summarised and codified in the Third Restatement), the consumer-expectation test applies to manufacturing defects, and the risk–utility test to the other two.

A strict test based on the consumer-expectation model makes most sense when the defect takes the form of a defect in the manufacturing process. No reasonable or

183 *Evans* v. *Triplex Safety Glass Co. Ltd.* [1938] 1 All ER 283.
184 [1932] AC 562, 599.
185 *Paine* v. *Colne Valley Electricity Supply Co. Ltd.* [1938] 4 All ER 803, 808–9 (Goddard LJ).
186 See *Clay* v. *A. J. Crump & Sons Ltd.* [1964] 1 QB 533, *Herschtal* v. *Stewart and Ardern Ltd.* [1940] 1 KB 155.
187 [1932] AC 562; see in particular the judgment of Lord Macmillan.
188 [1938] 1 All ER 283.
189 *Farr* v. *Butters Brothers & Co.* [1932] 2 QB 606.
190 [1932] AC 562.
191 [1971] 1 QB 88.

'ordinary' consumer expects to find a snail in a bottle of ginger beer. Beyond such cases, the statutory test poses difficulties in terms of the different expectations which particular groups of consumers might have. How far should a manufacturer or distributor have to take into account the possibility of the product being used by a child or by a consumer who might suffer an allergic reaction? While it is generally expected that coffee on sale in a restaurant will be served hot, so that the restaurant owner is not, without more, liable under the Act for injury caused by a spillage, should this apply if the injury is sustained by a young child who may not have been aware of the danger? In *B* v. *McDonald's Restaurants Ltd.*[192] it was held that, since most users of the restaurant were either teenagers or adults, the product was not defective in the sense of being contrary to the expectations of safety of 'persons generally'. In *Tesco Stores Ltd.* v. *Pollard*[193] the Court of Appeal held that the test to apply to a 'child-proof' bottle of dishwasher powder was whether 'the bottle would more difficult to open than it had an ordinary screwtop',[194] which the Court found it was. The Court rejected an argument to the effect that relevant test was whether the bottle complied with the relevant British Standard certificate for the product (on the facts as found, it did not) on the grounds that the Act should not be read as imposing a warranty on every producer to the effect that 'the product fulfills its design standards'.[195]

The sharpest criticism of the consumer-expectation test has come in the area of design defects. The test is said to be incoherent, since 'in many situations... the consumer would not know what to expect, because he would have no idea how safe the product could be made'.[196] The risk–utility test, by contrast, enables the court to engage in a balancing act, weighing the social utility of the product against the risk and seriousness of any injury that might occur from its use. More specifically, the test may be centred on the notion of the 'reasonably prudent manufacturer', enabling the court to take into account the manufacturer's capacity to eliminate the defect and his capacity to spread the risk through insurance or through price variations. Alternatively, it might take into account the role of the consumer by considering whether an alternative product was available, how far the consumer was aware of the danger in question, and how far he could have avoided it.[197] There is no uniform approach, as courts in different jurisdictions place different emphases on the various aspects of the test.

By contrast to this differentiated approach, the 1987 Act does not formally distinguish between the three types of defect. Nor does the Directive, and now the Act, unequivocally adopt one test or the other. Instead, the Act simply states in section 3(1) that 'there is a defect in a product for the purposes of this Part if the safety of the product is not such as persons generally are entitled to expect; and for those purposes "safety", in relation to a product, shall include safety in relation to products comprised in that product and safety

192 [2002] EWHC 490. 193 [2006] EWCA Civ. 393.

194 *Ibid.*, at para. 18. 195 *Ibid.*, at para 17.

196 J. W. Wade, 'On the Nature of Strict Tort Liability for Products' (1973) 44 *Miss. LJ* 825, cited by the Sup. Ct. of California in *Barker* v. *Lull Engineering Co.*, 573 P 2d 443, 454 (1978).

197 See S. Birnbaum, 'Unmasking the Test for Design Defect' (1980) 33 *Vand. LR* 593; Whitehead and Scott (Select Bibliography).

in the context of risks of damage to property, as well as in the context of risks of death or personal injury'. A crucial notion here is the standard of 'what persons generally are entitled to expect'. Section 3(2) broadly follows Article 6 of the Directive, but uses different language, by specifying that this standard shall be determined by reference to 'all the circumstances . . . including' the following three factors:

(*a*) the manner in which, and purposes for which, the product has been marketed, its get-up, the use of any mark in relation to the product and any instructions for, or warnings with respect to, doing, or refraining from doing, anything with or in relation to the product;
(*b*) what might reasonably be expected to be done with or in relation to the product; and
(*c*) the time when the product was supplied by its producer to another.

Section 3(2) also provides that a defect shall not be inferred from the mere fact that a safer product is put into circulation at a later date.

The Act refers to the expectations which 'persons generally', not just consumers, are 'entitled' to have, not just those which they might happen to have. To that extent, then, it could be read as departing from the consumer-expectation approach. On the other hand, the manufacturer's expectations are clearly not conclusive, even if reasonable: the standard is therefore stricter than that implied by the foreseeability test used in the tort of negligence. This emerges from one of the very few cases so far decided under the Act, *Iman Abouzaid* v. *Mothercare (UK) Ltd.*[198] Here the Court of Appeal upheld a finding of liability for injury caused to the plaintiff when an elasticated strap on a fleece-lined sleeping bag, intended to be attached to a pushchair, recoiled while he was fitting it, and struck him in the eye. According to Chadwick LJ, under the Directive and the Act 'the product is to be judged by the standard persons generally are entitled to expect in all the circumstances'. Thus the relevant test was not whether the product was fit for use but whether it reached the level 'of safety which the public at large are entitled to expect'.[199] The decision is particularly significant since the Court of Appeal held that there was no claim for common law negligence: the nature of the injury had been unforeseeable.

This aspect of the meaning of 'defect' was also the subject of extensive analysis by Burton J in *A* v. *National Blood Authority*.[200] The claimants had received blood transfusions while undergoing surgery. In each case the blood in question had been received from donors who were infected with hepatitis C, a virus which causes inflammation of the liver; this virus was then transmitted to the claimants. At the relevant time, although it was known in the medical profession that a form of hepatitis could be transmitted through blood transfusions, the hepatitis C virus had not been identified as the relevant agent. The discovery of the hepatitis C virus was made in May 1988. During 1989 a screening test was made commercially available; this was adopted in the UK National

198 *The Times*, 20 Feb. 2001.

199 *Ibid.*, para. 22.

200 [2001] 3 All ER 289. There is a fascinating account of the background to the litigation in this case, which refers to the use of comparative legal materials in the preparation of the arguments and to the judge's response to academic discussion of his approach, in M. Brooke QC and I. Forrester QC, 'The Use of Comparative Law in *A and Others* v. *National Blood Authority*'; N. Underhill QC, 'Postscript' and Mr Justice Burton, 'Afterword', in G. Canivet, M. Andenas and D. Fairgrieve (eds.), *Comparative Law before the Courts* (Select Bibliography), 57 ff.

Health Service during 1991. The claims at issue related to infections which occurred after the coming into force of the Consumer Protection Act 1987 (on 1 March 1988) and the introduction of screening (liability was accepted in the case of those who were infected after 1 April 1991). The defendants included the suppliers of blood and the NHS Trusts which had performed the relevant medical operations.

Burton J held that the relevant expectation was that of 'the public at large'; however, what was relevant here was not what the public 'actually expected' but, rather, 'what is legitimately to be expected, arrived at objectively',[201] and this was for the court to decide. The defendants argued that the court should have regard to the question whether the risk, in this case, was avoidable. Since, in this case, avoiding the risk of harm completely was not possible, the public was not entitled to expect that blood would be completely free of contamination: '[t]he most that they could legitimately expect was that all legitimately expectable (reasonably available) precautions—or in this case tests—had been carried out'. By contrast, the claimants argued that consideration of the conduct of the producer was irrelevant. Holding in favour of the claimants, Burton J ruled that the avoidability or otherwise of the risk was not, in this case, a relevant circumstance, and that the 'public at large' had a legitimate expectation that the blood would be 100 per cent safe. A relevant factor, in his view, was that the risk of infection, while known to medical professionals, was barely known at all among the public at large. According to Burton J, it 'is as inappropriate to propose that the public should not "expect the unattainable"—in the sense of tests or precautions which are impossible—at least until it is informed as to what is unattainable or impossible, as it is to reformulate the expectation as one that the producer will not have been negligent or will have taken all reasonable steps'.[202]

This case therefore comes down squarely on the side of the consumer-expectation test. In the words of Burton J, 'the Directive was intended to eliminate proof of fault or negligence' and 'to make it easier for claimants to prove their case'. Since neither the Directive nor the Act draws a clear distinction between cases of manufacturing defects and other cases, this decision could be interpreted as rejecting the risk–utility test for those cases. However, while rejecting as irrelevant in this context the US distinction between manufacturing and design defects, Burton J did accept that the contaminated blood was a 'non-standard product', that is, one 'different from the norm which the producer intended for use by the public'.[203] In that context, he suggested that '[w]here, as here, there is harmful characteristic in a non-standard product, a decision that it is defective is likely to be straightforward'.[204]

It would be premature to infer from the silence of the Directive on this point that the English courts will not take something from the American practice of setting a

201 [2001] 3 All ER 289, [31]. 202 *Ibid.*, [56].

203 *Ibid.*, [65].

204 *Ibid.*, [66]. Although this was not the view of Ian Kennedy J in *Richardson* v. *LRC Products Ltd.* [2000] PIQR P164: the fact that a condom burst during sexual intercourse did not, he ruled, in itself give rise to an actionable 'defect'. It is not clear what test of 'defect' the court was applying in this case and as a result it is difficult to assign it much weight as an authority.

consumer-expectation standard for manufacturing defects and a broader risk–utility calculus for design defects and failures to warn. In a case of defective design, would the court take no account of the utility of, for example, a prescription drug capable of alleviating or eliminating an otherwise intractable disease, by comparison to one whose effects were purely cosmetic? This would not be reintroducing negligence by the back door.[205] Significantly, the Act directs attention to the packaging of a product and to the way it is presented and marketed. Expectations engendered by a product's promotion (for example, concerning the safety aspects of a vehicle design or of a new drug) could influence the standard to which the manufacturer is required to conform.[206]

A question which has been much addressed in the American courts is whether producers should bear liability for products which are inherently dangerous, for example, through over-consumption, but in respect of which full and adequate warnings have been given and no alternative is feasible. The Restatement (Second) of Torts took the view that 'many products cannot be made entirely safe for all consumption, and any food or drug necessarily involves some risk or harm, if only through over-consumption', but that 'good tobacco is not unreasonably dangerous merely because the effects of smoking may be harmful'.[207] This view has been challenged in litigation against cigarette companies by smokers who, while aware of the risks of smoking, nevertheless contracted diseases through long-term consumption of tobacco products; the matter has still to be clearly resolved.[208]

(ii) Special Duties: Duty to Warn and Post-Sale Duties

A duty to warn may arise as part of negligence. This may be limited by the circumstances of the original sale. This is the implication, at least, of *Hurley* v. *Dyke*[209] in which a car, sold at auction in a dangerously defective condition, was involved in an accident in which a third-party passenger was injured. Because the car was sold 'as seen and with all its faults' the House of Lords held that the seller was not liable. The decision seems surprising in view of the possible danger to one who did not know the circumstances in which the car was sold. On the other hand, a manufacturer may come under a continuing duty to warn once the goods leave his hands, in particular if brand-naming or advertising concerning the product creates a misleading impression. This was the case

205 Thus in *A* v. *National Blood Authority* [2001] 3 All ER 289, Burton J went on to consider whether the claimants should succeed on the facts, in the event that the relevant test of defect was that claimed by the defendants, namely that the avoidability of the risk should be taken into account. On the basis of twenty days of medical evidence, he concluded that the defendants had still failed to show that they had taken the minimum necessary steps to avoid the harm. This was because of the failure to put in place 'surrogate tests' which had been in use in some other countries prior to the discovery of the hepatitis C virus (these worked by screening out those thought most at risk of passing on infected blood, such as drug addicts), and the delay in implementing the test for identifying hepatitis C once it became available.

206 In this context it is perhaps relevant that *Iman Abouzaid* v. *Mothercare (UK) Ltd.*, *The Times*, 20 Feb. 2001, in which the Court of Appeal imposed liability under the Act, was a case of negligent design.

207 Section 402A, comment (i).

208 For a critical view of the Restatement position in this context, see *Dewey* v. *R. J. Reynolds Tobacco Co.*, 577 A 2d 1239 (1990).

209 [1979] RTR 265. See also *Kubach* v. *Hollands* [1937] 3 All ER 907.

in *E. Hobbs Farms Ltd.* v. *Baxenden Chemical Co. Ltd.*, where a manufacturer failed to correct a statement to the effect that insulation foam was 'self-extinguishing' after it became clear that this might not be the case. The customer succeeded in an action for negligent misrepresentation when the foam caught fire, causing extensive damage. According to Deputy Judge Ogden QC, 'a manufacturer who realises that omitting to warn past customers about something which might result in injury to them must take reasonable steps to attempt to warn them, however lacking in negligence he may have been when the goods were sold'.[210] It should be borne in mind that the parties in this case had been in direct contractual privity, though.

The Consumer Protection Act's reference in section 3(2) to the promotion and packaging of the product impliedly creates a duty to warn consumers generally of possible dangers. A duty to warn is also implicit in the test of 'such safety as persons are entitled to expect'. This would certainly include a duty to warn about dangers that were either known to the manufacturer or reasonably foreseeable when the product was marketed; it could also include a duty to warn against foreseeable but unintended uses and misuses.[211] It is not clear, though, how far, if at all, this marks an improvement on the position in negligence. Thus *Worsley* v. *Tambrands Ltd.*,[212] the manufacturer of a tampon avoided liability for the extremely serious physical effects of 'toxic shock syndrome' on the ground that the box in which the tampon was contained had given a clear and adequate warning of this danger. In line with US jurisprudence in duty-to-warn cases, Ebsworth J expressly applied the risk–utility test to support her ruling.[213]

Neither the Act nor the Directive spells out in any detail a post-sale duty to keep consumers informed about newly discovered defects in a product. It is possible that such an obligation could arise as part of the duty of care in negligence.[214] Section 3(2) of the Act requires the court to take into account the time when the product left the manufacturer's hands, that is to say, when he supplied it to another producer, not when it was supplied to the consumer. This is apparently designed to safeguard the manufacturer against liability brought about through wear and tear to the product. It could also be read as limiting the extent of any post-sale duty to warn where, for example, information concerning a defect comes to the manufacturer's attention some time after the product left the factory gate. Under these circumstances it is arguable that the manufacturer *should be* under a duty to issue a public warning about the product and, possibly, to pay the costs of withdrawing the product from the market and replacing those items sold to consumers. This is a developing area of liability in the United States.[215] It has only an implicit presence, at best, within Article 3 of the Products Liability Directive.

210 [1992] 1 Lloyd's Rep. 55, 65.

211 Whitehead and Scott (Select Bibliography), 173.

212 [2000] PIQR P95.

213 *Ibid.*, P102.

214 See *Rivtow Marine Ltd.* v. *Washington Iron Works* [1974] SCR 1189, where the Sup. Ct. of Canada discussed the liability of a crane manufacturer to inform the user of a possible danger arising after the sale. Such liability was rejected by the Court of Appeal in the context of a pure economic loss claim in *The Rebecca Elaine* [1999] 2 Lloyd's Rep. 1.

215 Discussed by Whitehead and Scott (Select Bibliography).

The more recent Product Safety Directive is more specific on this matter.[216] And Part II of the Consumer Protection Act 1987 is also important since it enables the Secretary of State to issue a duty to warn, requiring a manufacturer to issue a notice to warn consumers of a possible danger.[217] The Product Safety Directive will require the provisions of Part II of the 1987 Act to be extended, giving rise to the possibility of actions for breach of statutory duty being brought by consumers suffering loss or injury as a result of failure to comply with these provisions.

(iii) The Producer's Defences

Some of these are uncontroversial and closely follow the Directive. Thus, the producer will have a defence if he can show that the defect was attributable to compliance with a legal requirement;[218] that he did not at any point supply the product to another, as, for example, in a situation where it was put into circulation after being stolen from him;[219] that the defect did not exist when he parted with it;[220] and, in the case of a component supplier, that the defect was contained not in his component but in the final product, and that it was the result either of the design of the final product or of compliance with instructions from the manufacturer of that product.[221]

Much more controversial is the so-called 'state of the art' or development-risks defence in section 4(1)(e). Inclusion of this was optional under the Directive.[222] Not only does the Act make provision for this defence, but it apparently widens its scope by providing that the producer will be exempted if he can show that 'the state of scientific and technical knowledge at the relevant time was not such that a producer of products of the same description as the product in question might be expected to have discovered the defect if it had existed in his products while they were under his control'. By contrast, the Directive provides a defence where 'the state of scientific and technical knowledge at the time when he put the product into circulation was not such as to enable the existence of the defect to be discovered'. The central difference is that the Act appears to set up as the relevant standard that of producers within the industry in question, whereas the Directive appears to envisage an external standard which could be set higher than that prevailing as a matter of practice within the industry at any given time.

The Act can be read as injecting an element of subjectivity into the otherwise objective test laid down by the Directive. This may be defensible on the ground that the court otherwise has no clear standard against which to judge the producer's liability.[223] The UK government took the view, during the passage of the Act, that the form of section 4(1)(e) was justified by the need to avoid restricting innovation in design. It could, however, be argued that where innovation has been chilled in America this is the result of high punitive damages awards and not strict liability as such. The German experience may well support this thesis.

[216] Art. 3(2).
[217] Section 13(1).
[218] Section 4(1)(a).
[219] Section 4(1)(b).
[220] Section 4(1)(d).
[221] Section 4(1)(f).
[222] Art. 15(1)(b).
[223] Newdick (Select Bibliography), 310.

In *Commission* v. *United Kingdom*,[224] the ECJ upheld section 4(1)(e) against a challenge mounted by the European Commission, and at the same time cast some light on the scope of the defence contained in Article 7(e) of the Directive. The Court took the view that section 4(1)(e) could not be read as establishing, as the relevant test, the subjective knowledge of the producer at the time the product was circulated. It was also confident that the UK courts would interpret section 4(1)(e) purposively, in line with both the wording and intent of the Directive. With regard to Article 7(e), the Court, following Advocate General Tesauro, held that the producer must be aware of the *most advanced* state of *accessible* scientific and technical knowledge in the relevant field at the point when the product was circulated. In many respects this is a stringent test. According to the Advocate General:

since [Article 7(e)] refers solely to the 'scientific and technical knowledge' at the time when the product was marketed, it is not concerned with the practices and safety standards in use in the industrial sector in which the producer is operating. In other words, it has no bearing on the exclusion of the manufacturer from liability that no one in that particular class of manufacturer takes the measures necessary to eliminate the defect or prevent it from arising if such measures are capable of being adopted on the basis of the available knowledge.[225]

The relevant knowledge is that of 'an expert in the sector', that is, the industry in question, but for this purpose knowledge may include even 'isolated opinions to the effect that [the product] is defective [even if] most academics do not take that view'. The justification for this extensive definition of scientific knowledge is that once the opinion has been put into circulation, even though it may not yet represent a scientific consensus, the risk of damage or injury is no longer unforeseeable.[226] The relevant knowledge must, on the other hand, be available in a language that is reasonably accessible and in a form that is subject to a reasonably high degree of circulation.[227]

The inclusion of a broad 'state of the art' defence aligns the apparently strict standard of the Act more closely to that of negligence, albeit with the burden of proof reversed: the producer has the burden of showing that the defence is made out. An essential aspect of the strict-liability standard in the United States is that it judges the product and not the producer. If this principle is observed, it is arguably irrelevant to liability that the producer could not have known about the defect at the time the product was put into circulation. Moreover, industry *practice* is less relevant than industry *capability*, or the potential for greater safety, in judging whether a 'state of the art' defence is made out.[228]

224 Case C-300/95, [1997] ECR I-2649; [1997] All ER (EC) 391.

225 Advocate General's Opinion, at para. 20.

226 *Ibid.*, para. 22. For discussion, see C. Hodges, 'Development Risks: Unanswered Questions' (1998) 61 *MLR* 560, and the reply by M. Mildred and C. Howells, 'Comment on "Development Risks: Unanswered Questions"' (1998) 61 *MLR* 570.

227 Advocate General's Opinion, at para. 23.

228 See the discussion of N. P. Terry, 'State of the Art Evidence' (1991) 20 *Anglo-Am. LR* 285. Some recent US case law marks a retreat from the strict liability standard in favour of a more explicit 'reasonably prudent manufacturer' test in the context of litigation over exposure to asbestos: *Feldman* v. *Lederle Laboratories*, 479 A 2d 534 (1984).

Section 4(1)(e) puts this in doubt for English law. At the same time, it should be borne in mind that the test of design defect in the tort of negligence might itself set a stringent standard for producers, requiring them to carry out research into the possible implications of design innovations. In *IBA* v. *EMI Electronics Ltd.*[229] the designer of a radio mast that collapsed in conditions of high winds and ice was found liable for failing to investigate fully the possible effects of such conditions on the structure.

Section 4(1)(e) is not, in so many words, confined to cases of defects in design. However, its application to manufacturing defects is likely to be limited by the terms in which it is phrased and by the ruling of the ECJ in the infringement proceedings brought against the United Kingdom. Moreover, it should clearly have no application in a case where the defendant knew of the defect in question; as Burton J ruled in *A* v. *National Blood Authority*,[230] the producer, in such a case, supplies at his own risk.

(D) CAUSATION AND REMOTENESS

The rules of causation and remoteness which apply in the tort of negligence may pose a significant barrier in practice to product liability claims brought under the common law. This is illustrated by the Scottish case of *McTear* v. *Imperial Tobacco Ltd.*,[231] the only British claim so far to reach a full hearing on the potential liability of cigarette manufacturers for causing lung cancer in smokers. The case was argued in negligence before the Outer House of the Court of Session. Lord Nimmo Smith rejected counsel's submission that, given the widespread scientific consensus that smoking is a cause of cancer, this was a 'relatively straightforward' product liability claim. He held, after a review of the relevant scientific evidence that takes up several hundred pages of his judgment, that the pursuer had failed to establish, as a matter of general causation, that there was a causal link. The scientific evidence consisted of inferences drawn from epidemiological studies which, in the judge's view did not permit a finding of causation, as opposed to statistical correlation. The judge then went on to find that individual causation, in the sense of a link between cigarette smoking and the pursuer's cancer, had not been made out either, given the possibility that he could have contracted lung cancer from one of a number of different sources. It could not be shown, on the balance of probabilities, that the pursuer would not have contracted lung cancer had he not been exposed to tobacco smoke from the defender's cigarettes.

In striking contrast to *McTear*, Stanley Burnton J had very little difficulty in finding a causal link between smoking and cancer in the context of a *defence* of contributory negligence in *Badger* v. *Ministry of Defence.*[232] Medical witnesses for both sides were agreed that 'Mr. Badger's smoking was a substantial cause of his death',[233] in addition to the exposure to asbestos which was found to be the fault of his employer. The judge was also able to establish, on the basis of an Appendix to his judgment consisting of just

229 (1981) 14 BLR 1.
230 [2001] 3 All ER 289.
231 2005 2 SC 1.
232 [2005] EWHC 2941.
233 *Ibid.*, at [17].

a few pages, that 'by 1971, when the first health warnings were put on cigarette packets, it was reasonably foreseeable by a reasonably prudent man that if he smoked he risked damaging his health'.[234]

The Consumer Protection Act 1987 does not deal explicitly with the questions of causation and remoteness of damage, and so it is likely that the courts have had to apply the tests of but-for cause and 'legal cause' derived from general principles.[235] However, principles that operate mainly in the context of negligence liability should, arguably, be adapted in a strict liability tort. Section 2(1) states that a causal link between defect and damage must be established, impliedly putting the onus on the claimant. Given the policy of the Directive and of the Act there may be an argument for the use of principles of 'probabilistic cause', involving a partial reversal of the burden of proof,[236] if not necessarily the revolutionary 'market share' approach to apportioning liability.[237] In *Sindell* all those manufacturers who could have been responsible for producing a defective drug were held liable in proportion to their share of the relevant market at the time it was marketed. As far as remoteness is concerned, there is an argument for limiting the principle enunciated in *The Wagon Mound (No. 1)*,[238] namely that the defendant will not be liable if the damage was of a type of harm that was not reasonably foreseeable, to cases of negligence, since the idea that foreseeability should play a role in limiting the extent of the defendant's liability is out of place in a strict liability action. Alternatively, if the foreseeability test is to be applied there is a good case for ensuring that the relevant notion of 'type of damage' is broadly defined at least for cases of personal injury.[239]

In *Tesco Stores Ltd.* v. *Pollard*[240] the claimant, a child of thirteen months at the relevant time, suffered personal injury when he removed the top from a bottle containing dishwasher powder and began to ingest the contents. The Court of Appeal ruled out a negligence claim on the grounds that it had been unforeseeable that the claimant could have removed the top, which was in principle 'childproof' and was in any event much more difficult to remove than a normal bottle top, as he was assumed to have done. For the purposes of the common-law claim the defendant was also entitled to assume that the child's mother would have taken steps to prevent him having access to the bottle, which she had failed to do (although a claim by the child against his mother for negligence also failed on the facts). The statutory claim failed on the grounds that the product was not defective, and so the issue of causation under the Act did not arise.

Where damage is caused partly by a defective product and partly by the claimant's own fault the defence of contributory negligence will be available, by virtue of section 6(4) of the Act. Again, applying the defence of contributory negligence in a situation

234 *Ibid.*, at para. 44.

235 See above, ch. 4.

236 J. G. Fleming, 'Probabilistic Causation in Tort Law' (1989) 68 *Can. BR* 661; *Fairchild* v. *Glenhaven Funeral Services Ltd.* [2003] 1 AC 32; see above, ch. 4.

237 Adopted in the California products-liability case of *Sindell* v. *Abbots Laboratories*, 607 P 2d 924 (1980).

238 [1961] AC 388.

239 Whittaker, 'The EEC Directive on Product Liability' (Select Bibliography), 254.

240 [2006] EWCA Civ. 393.

where the defendant may be liable without fault could be seen as contradictory.[241] As it is, where the defence applies the court will be able to make an apportionment of liability based not on relative blame but on the relative causal responsibility for the damage in question of claimant and defendant. The Act's failure to clarify the way in which causation and contributory negligence will operate could pose a far more significant restriction, in practice, upon successful claims for compensation than even the inclusion of the 'state of the art' defence in section 4(1)(e).

(E) THE CATEGORIES OF RECOVERABLE 'DAMAGE'

Injury to the person and damage to the property of the consumer are recoverable both for breach of warranty under the Sale of Goods Act and under the common law of negligence. An example of a case in which the two actions were combined was *Grant* v. *Australian Knitting Mills*.[242] There, the plaintiff, who contracted dermatitis from a suit of underwear that had been contaminated in the process of manufacture, successfully sued both the manufacturer in the tort of negligence and the retailer for breach of contract.

The Consumer Protection Act defines damage in section 5(1) as 'death or personal injury or any loss of or damage to any property (including land)'. On normal principles, liability for personal injury includes liability for direct economic consequences, including loss of earnings. The Act limits the relevant scope of property damage to non-business property, that is to say property both ordinarily intended for private use, occupation or consumption and actually used for these ends by the person suffering the loss or damage.[243] The effect is to allow recovery of the financial cost of replacing damaged property but to rule out claims for consequential losses such as lost profits. Small property claims are also excluded by section 5(4), which requires the plaintiff to have suffered property damage (excluding interest) amounting to more than £275.

The greatest uncertainty concerns recovery for 'pure' economic loss, that is to say economic losses that do not flow directly out of either personal injury to the consumer or damage to his property. For breach of warranty it is axiomatic that consequential economic losses of this kind *are* recoverable, subject to the normal rules of remoteness of damage in contract.[244] In negligence the scope for recovery of pure economic loss has been greatly reduced by the decision of the House of Lords in *Murphy* v. *Brentwood District Council*.[245] Although this case concerned defective property, the broad principles laid down by the House of Lords are entirely applicable to the question of defective products. The distinction drawn by the House of Lords between property which is in a dangerous state and that which is merely defective has been criticised as 'impossible', in particular in cases where the economic loss consists of steps taken to avoid a potential danger to life and limb.[246] The reader is referred to Chapter 3 above for a more detailed account of the issues arising out of *Murphy*.

241 Whittaker, 'The EEC Directive on Product Liability' (Select Bibliography), 251–3.

242 [1936] AC 86.

243 Section 5(3).

244 *Hadley* v. *Baxendale* (1854) 9 Exch. 341: see G. H. Treitel, *Law of Contract* (11th edn., 2003), 965 ff.

245 [1991] 1 AC 398.

246 Sir Robin Cooke, 'An Impossible Distinction?' (1991) 107 *LQR* 46.

The only area in which pure economic loss is now clearly recoverable in negligence concerns liability for negligent misstatement under *Hedley Byrne & Co. Ltd.* v. *Heller & Partners*.[247] This could well be relevant in cases of product liability, where loss may be incurred as a result of misleading labels on articles or, more speculatively, through misleading advertising and promotion. The difficulty will lie in establishing the necessary proximity between the parties for a 'special relationship' to be established. Recent decisions are not encouraging in this regard.[248]

The Consumer Protection Act provides that damage to the 'product itself' as a result of the defect is not property damage within the meaning of the Act, so ruling out a claim in pure economic loss for a merely defective product.[249] The meaning of the 'product itself' here may give rise to the kind of difficulties encountered over the meaning of 'complex structure' prior to *Murphy* v. *Brentwood District Council*, when the House of Lords did its utmost to restrict the use of the idea in that context.[250] The Act refers to there being no liability for 'the loss of or any damage to the product itself or for the loss of or any damage to the whole or any part of any product which has been supplied with the product in question comprised in it'. Is a car tyre, manufactured by a component supplier, 'comprised in' a motor vehicle so that if it bursts, causing the car to crash, the only damage is to the 'product itself'? If the car is not the 'product itself' but 'other property', recovery would seem possible. Are a defectively manufactured cork, supplied by a third party, and the wine in the bottle which is damaged by the cork's defectiveness part of the same property?[251] Given the House of Lords' scepticism about the value of drawing fine distinctions between different components of a complex structure, it seems highly likely that the different parts will be seen as the same whole for this purpose, denying the consumer recovery for damage to the product as a whole.

Section 5(3) of the Consumer Protection Act requires there to be damage to property that the person suffering the loss intends for his own private use. It does not expressly require the person suffering the loss to have a proprietary or possessory right over the property at the moment it is damaged as the common law of negligence does. The categories of recoverable economic loss may therefore be broader under the Act than in cases arising under the common law such as *The Aliakmon*,[252] where the property was damaged before the plaintiff acquired (or resumed) ownership of the goods. In practice, however, the most significant limitation on the recoverability of pure economic losses is the exclusion of business property from the scope of the Act. While some economic loss cases involve consumer interests, with *Murphy*[253] and its predecessors being the most obvious examples, the greater number tend to arise out of business losses of various kinds.

[247] [1964] AC 465.
[248] In particular *Caparo Industries plc* v. *Dickman* [1990] 2 AC 605.
[249] Section 5(2).
[250] See above, ch. 3.
[251] See *M/S Aswan Engineering Establishment Co. Ltd.* v. *Lupdine Ltd.* [1987] 1 WLR 1, 23 (Lloyd LJ).
[252] [1986] AC 785.
[253] [1991] 1 AC 398.

Damages for distress or unhappiness are rarely available for breach of warranty in the context of a sale-of-goods contract as opposed to a contract the purpose of which is to avoid distress or to provide some form of contentment.[254] In negligence the grounds of recovery for 'nervous shock' are limited in comparison with the general admission of recovery for physical harm.[255] Nervous shock is not mentioned as such in the Act, but the definition of personal injury in section 45 extends to 'any disease and any other impairment of a person's physical or mental condition'. The latter part of the definition appears to correspond to nervous shock as it is currently defined by the courts for the purposes of negligence, in the sense of a particular psychological condition.[256]

Where the consumer suffers shock of this kind as a consequence of his own injury or as a result of damage to his property[257] then, by analogy with negligence, there should be recovery. Where a third party suffers shock as a consequence of witnessing an injury to another caused by a defective product, the matter is more difficult. In negligence the circumstances under which the third party can recover are strictly limited; there must normally be a close family or personal tie between the plaintiff and the injury victim, and the plaintiff must witness the accident or come on the scene shortly afterwards.[258] The Act makes no mention of these restrictions and it is entirely plausible to read it as imposing a general responsibility for psychological harm to a third party, as long as a causal link between such harm and the defect is established.[259]

Where a defective product causes death, the dependants of the deceased may bring an action for damages based on their economic dependency by virtue of section 6(1)(a) of the 1987 Act. This deems the death to have been caused by a 'wrongful act, neglect or default' for the purposes of section 1 of the Fatal Accidents Act 1976.[260] By extension it also becomes possible for an action of bereavement to be brought under section 1A of the 1976 Act. Again, a plaintiff born after receiving injuries while in the womb as a consequence of a defective product may bring an action under the Congenital Disabilities (Civil Liability) Act 1976, by virtue of section 6(3) of the 1987 Act.

(F) EXCLUSION AND LIMITATION OF LIABILITY

The availability of an exclusion clause in actions based on contract and tort is limited by the Unfair Contract Terms Act 1977, which is considered in more detail in Chapter 24 below. A contract term excluding business liability for death or personal injury caused by negligence is void; a term covering property damage or economic loss must be

254 See e.g. *Hayes* v. *Dodd* [1990] 2 All ER 815 for the general approach in contract.

255 See above, ch. 3.

256 See *McLoughlin* v. *O'Brian* [1983] AC 410.

257 *Attia* v. *British Gas Corp.* [1988] QB 304.

258 *Alcock* v. *Chief Constable of South Yorkshire* [1993] 1 AC 310; see above, ch. 3.

259 See the discussion of Whittaker, 'The EEC Directive on Product Liability' (Select Bibliography), 273–4, suggesting that a requirement of proximity analogous to that prevailing under the common law of negligence should be adopted in the Act, a suggestion which was not taken up.

260 See also Consumer Protection Act, s. 6(2), dealing with the supplier's liability in the event of death.

'reasonable'.[261] The Act is particularly protective of consumers in circumstances where they contract with business entities. A 'consumer' under the Act is one who does not contract in a business capacity or who does not hold himself out as doing so, where the other party is one who does contract in a course of a business.[262] Under section 3 exclusion and limitation clauses in business–consumer contracts must pass a test of reasonableness; this also applies between business entities where the contract is on written standard terms of the person protected by the clause. With specific regard to product liability, section 6 of the Act prevents a business entity excluding or limiting its liability to a consumer in regard to the implied terms of compliance with contract description, fitness for intended purpose, and merchantability under sections 13–15 of the Sale of Goods Act 1979 and to the corresponding terms implied into a hire-purchase contract.[263] Where two businesses contract with each other, any exclusion or limitation of these terms is subjected to a test of 'reasonableness'.[264]

The Consumer Protection Act, which as we have seen is concerned only with the liability of business entities to consumers, contains a clear policy of prohibiting exclusions or limitations: liability under the Act cannot be excluded or limited by any contract term, notice, or any other provision.[265] The defence of *volenti non fit injuria*, or the claimant's voluntary assumption of risk, is only rarely available in claims based on the tort of negligence. This is because it is necessary to show not simply that the claimant was aware of a particular danger but that he consented to the defendant being careless in the sense of acting in breach of a duty of care.[266] The modern tendency has been for the courts to use contributory negligence to apportion responsibility between the parties rather than invoke the defence of *volenti*, which excludes the claim completely. It is likely that a similar approach would be taken under Part I of the Consumer Protection Act. It should be noted, however, that the claimant's conduct might be taken into account at the earlier stage of analysis when assessing whether the product is defective. For under section 3(2)(b), the court must consider 'what might reasonably be expected to be done with or in relation to the product'. If, therefore, the consumer uses a product that he knows to be dangerous, perhaps having received a warning to that effect from the producer, the product might no longer be regarded as defective for the purposes of the Act.[267]

(G) LIMITATION OF ACTIONS

The general principles of limitation of actions apply,[268] with two exceptions as far as the Consumer Protection Act is concerned.[269] In the first place, the limitation period for

[261] Section 2. [262] Section 12.

[263] By ss. 9, 10 and 11 of the Supply of Goods (Implied Terms) Act 1973.

[264] For this purpose 'reasonableness' has the special meaning ascribed to it by Sch. 2 to the Act.

[265] Section 7. [266] *Dann* v. *Hamilton* [1939] 1 KB 509.

[267] See, in the context of a discussion of Directive 85/374, Whittaker, 'The ECC Directive on Product Liability' (Select Bibliography), 261.

[268] See ch. 24 below, Section 9.

[269] See Limitation Act 1980, s. 11A, inserted by the Consumer Protection Act 1987.

claims of damage to property under the Act is three years (the same as for personal injury), as opposed to the normal six-year period. Second, actions under the Act are subject to a special 'long-stop' of ten years (as opposed to the normal fifteen) from the time the producer in question supplies the product to another. This long-stop is an absolute bar to liability. In *O'Byrne* v. *Sanofi Pasteur MSD Ltd.*[270] the ECJ held that the equivalent provision in the Directive, which refers to the point at which the producer puts the product into circulation, should be interpreted as referring to the point at which the product 'leaves the production process operated by the producer and enters a marketing process in the form in which it is offered to the public in order to be used or consumed'. This was a case in which the claimant was severely injured after being given a vaccine manufactured by the defendant. The defendant argued that the product had been put into circulation when it had been transferred by it to one of its subsidiary companies prior to its distribution. The claimant, on the other hand, argued that the product had not been put into circulation until the subsidiary supplied it to the hospital nominated to receive it by the Department of Health. The ECJ's ruling was broadly favourable to the position of the claimant, but it was left up to the national court to decide how precisely to apply it to the facts of the case.

(H) CHOICE OF LAW

The complex rules concerning the applicable law for a particular tort or contract action are likely to be of great importance in practice. Actions under the Consumer Protection Act are classified as tort actions for this purpose.[271] The search by claimants for the most advantageous jurisdiction is regulated within the European Community by the 1968 Brussels Convention on Jurisdiction and the Enforcement of Judgments, which was incorporated into English law by the Civil Jurisdiction and Judgments Act 1982 with effect from 1987.[272] An account of the effect of these Conventions, and of choice of law rules within the Member States of the European Community, lies outside the scope of this book.[273]

4. CONCLUSION

It may be useful to summarise the main points of this presentation of product liability law. We have seen how liability evolved from an initial position in which the law of negligence played a minor role in compensating victims of dangerously defective products,

[270] Case C-172/04, [2006] ECR I-1313, [2006] 1 WLR 1606. [271] Section 6(7).

[272] And, to a lesser degree as far as products liability is concerned, by the Rome Convention on the Law Applicable to Contractual Obligations, which takes effect in English law by virtue of the Contracts (Applicable Law) Act 1990.

[273] For an account of this area see R. Atree, 'Jurisdiction, Enforcement of Judgments and Conflicts of Laws', ch. 17 in Kelly and Atree (Select Bibliography).

thanks largely to the 'privity of contract fallacy'. *Donoghue* v. *Stevenson*[274] put an end to this and ushered in the modern, all-embracing duty of care as far as physical injury and property damage are concerned. The major weakness of *Donoghue* v. *Stevenson* was that, far from doing away with the need to show fault on the part of the producer, the judgments of the majority in that case (most notably Lord Macmillan) confirmed it by excluding the use of *res ipsa loquitur* to assist the plaintiff. While American courts developed a number of dynamic solutions to deal with this problem,[275] the English common law continued to be shaped by the traditional conceptual categories of civil liability, and in particular by a rigid demarcation between tort and contract.

With the adoption of Directive 85/374/EEC and its subsequent implementation in the form of the Consumer Protection Act 1987, a form of strict or 'stricter' liability based on the American model was incorporated into English law. The standard laid down by the Consumer Protection Act is, however, close to fault-based liability. The notion of 'defect' in section 3(1) and the wide defences made available to producers in section 4 make it clear that the producer is very far from being made an automatic insurer for losses caused by products put into circulation. Other restrictions on liability, such as the short limitation period and the confinement of recoverable damage to physical injury and non-business property losses, mean that the common law of contract and tort will continue to play a distinct and important role in this area.

Wider questions concerning the value and efficacy of product liability law are currently being posed. In the United States a reaction has set in against the expansion of civil liability which began in the late 1950s and continued for the next twenty-five years or so. Many of the features of American law which have given cause for concern, such as stratospheric levels of punitive damages awarded against producers, would not apply to the forms of strict liability now found in the United Kingdom and other European countries. However, more general doubts about strict liability have led many American courts to curtail the use of the consumer expectation test in favour of the more open-ended risk–utility approach, in particular with regard to cases of defects in design, in what may be seen as at least a partial 'return to negligence'. The factors that have prompted this move include the concern that manufacturers are finding it increasingly difficult to obtain adequate third-party insurance cover and the fear that excessive liability is inhibiting innovation. Nor is it clear that the move to strict liability has led to any increase in the safety of products.[276] There is a perception that the best interests of both producers and consumers may not be served by a system which is so heavily reliant on civil litigation, and that it is necessary to find a more appropriate balance between civil liability and regulatory controls.

Yet despite the doubts expressed by commentators, the first few cases to be decided under the Directive and the Act suggest that this new cause of action will prove to be

274 [1932] AC 562.

275 Ranging from the use of misrepresentation law and the notion of a transmissible warranty to the solution of strict liability in tort (adopted by s. 402A of the Second Restatement of Torts).

276 See Dewees, Duff and Trebilcock, *Exploring the Domain of Accident Law* (1996), ch. 4, for a review of the empirical evidence relating to the impact of product liability law.

distinguishable from negligence. The no-fault basis of liability was strongly emphasised by the ECJ in its ruling in *Commission* v. *United Kingdom*,[277] and, following this lead, the English courts have imposed liability in circumstances where there would have been no possibility of a common law claim in negligence.[278] In the landmark case of *A* v. *National Blood Authority*,[279] the consequences were far-reaching: to hold, as the judge did, that it was irrelevant to consider how far the risk of harm was avoidable, is questionable when set against the overwhelming public benefit which is derived from maintaining a regular supply of donated blood. The decision is all the more striking when it is borne in mind that many US states have passed legislation exempting suppliers of human blood and tissue from this form of liability. Since this is not an option available under the terms of the Directive, the responsibility for ensuring that a workable rule emerges in the UK context rests with the courts (both at UK and EC level) alone.

SELECT BIBLIOGRAPHY

Symposium on Product Liability Law (1991) 20(2) *Anglo-Am. LR*.

ALBANESE, F., and DEL DUCA, L., 'Developments in European Product Liability' (1987) 5 *Dickinson J Int. Law* 193.

BORRIE, G., 'Product Liability in the EEC' (1987) 9 *Dublin University* LJ 82.

BROOKE QC, M., and FORRESTER QC, I. 'The Use of Comparative Law in *A and Others* v. *National Blood Authority*'; UNDERHILL QC, H., 'Postscript'; and MR JUSTICE BURTON, 'Afterword', in Canivet, G., Andenas, M., and Fairgrieve, D. (eds.), *Comparative Law before the Courts* (2004).

CALABRESI, G., and HIRSCHOFF, J., 'Towards a Test for Strict Liability in Torts' (1972) *Yale LJ* 1054.

GRIFFITHS, LORD, DE VAL, P., and DORMER, R. J., 'Developments in English Product Liability Law: A Comparison with the American System' (1988) 62 *Tul. LR* 353.

HOWELLS, G., *Comparative Product Liability* (1993).

HUBER, P., *Liability: the Legal Revolution and its Consequences* (1988).

KELLY, P., and ATREE, R. (eds.), *European Product Liability Law* (1992).

NEWDICK, C., 'The Future of Negligence in Product Liability' (1987) 103 *LQR* 288.

PRIEST, G., 'The Invention of Enterprise Liability: A Critical History of the Intellectual Foundations of Modern Tort Law' (1985) 143 *Jo. LS* 461.

PROSSER, W., 'The Assault upon the Citadel (Strict Liability to the Consumer)' (1960) 69 *Yale LJ* 1099.

—'The Fall of the Citadel (Strict Liability to the Consumer)' (1966) 50 *Minn. LR* 791.

SMITH, D., 'The European Community Directive on Product Liability: A Comparative Study of its Implementation

[277] Case C-300/95, [1997] ECR I-2649; [1997] All ER (EC) 391.

[278] *Iman Abouzaid* v. *Mothercare (UK) Ltd., The Times*, 20 Feb. 2001; *A* v. *National Blood Authority* [2001] 3 All ER 289.

[279] *Ibid.*

in the UK, France and West Germany' [1992] *LIEI* 101.

STAPLETON, J., 'Products Liability Reform: Real or Illusory?' (1986) 6 *OJLS* 392.

—'Three Problems with the New Product Liability', in Cane, P. and Stapleton, J. (eds.), *Essays for Patrick Atiyah* (1991).

—*Product Liability* (1994).

WADDAMS, S. J., 'The Strict Liability of Suppliers of Goods' (1974) 37 *MLR* 154.

WHITEHEAD, G., and SCOTT, G., 'A Comparison of Product Liability Law in the United States and the European Community' (1991) 2 *Eur. Bus. LR* 171.

WHITTAKER, S., 'The EEC Directive on Product Liability' (1985) 5 *YEL* 233.

—*Liability for Products: English Law, French Law, and European Harmonization* (2005).

PART VII

PROTECTION OF HUMAN DIGNITY (IN PRIVATE LAW)

21 Defamation and Injurious Falsehood

22 The Protection of Human Privacy

23 Defamation and Privacy: An American Perspective

21

DEFAMATION AND INJURIOUS FALSEHOOD

1. DEFAMATION: INTRODUCTION

(A) THE MEANING OF 'DEFAMATORY'

No exhaustive definition of 'defamatory' emerges from the cases. This should come as no surprise for, as Lord Reid once said, it is not for the judges to 'frame definitions or to lay down hard and fast rules. It is their function to enunciate principles and much that they say is intended to be illustrative or explanatory and not to be definitive.'[1] One can nevertheless achieve a working description by combining two statements, namely: a defamatory statement is one which injures the reputation of another by exposing him to hatred, contempt or ridicule, or which tends to lower him in the esteem of *right-thinking* members of society.[2]

In defamation the defendant need not have ascertained beforehand the likely effect of his words as long as his speech or writing was voluntary. What is relevant is that the words were understood by others in a defamatory sense. As Russell LJ put it: '[l]iability for libel does not depend on the intention of the defamer; but on the fact of defamation'.[3] Courts treat the meaning of the words as a matter of construction rather than evidence, to be interpreted objectively in their context, with reference to the opinion of right-thinking members of society. Such a test is vague and unsatisfactory. In *Rubber Improvements Ltd.* v. *Daily Telegraph Ltd.*,[4] Lord Devlin said that the test was the effect on the 'ordinary' and not the 'logical' man.[5] It has been decided, for instance, that

[1] *Cassell & Co. Ltd.* v. *Broome* [1972] AC 1027, 1085. The Faulks Committee recommended the following definition: 'Defamation shall consist of the publication to a third party of matter which in all circumstances would be likely to affect a person adversely in the estimation of reasonable people generally.' This may well avoid some difficulties, but might give rise to others, so on balance it may be better to avoid any statutory definition.

[2] *Parmiter* v. *Coupland and Another* (1840) 6 M & W 105, 108; 151 ER 340, 342 (per Parke B), and *Sim* v. *Stretch* [1936] 2 All ER 1237, 1240 (per Lord Atkin). Italics supplied.

[3] *Cassidy* v. *Daily Mirror Newspapers Ltd.* [1929] 2 KB 331, 354.

[4] [1964] AC 234, 285 (henceforth referred to as *Lewis* v. *Daily Telegraph*).

[5] In *Hartt* v. *Newspaper Publishing plc, The Independent*, 27 Oct. 1989; CLY 1989, 2246, the court took the view that the yardstick should be the 'hypothetical reader who is not unduly suspicious, but who can read between the lines. He might think loosely, but is not avid for scandal, and will not select one bad meaning where other non-defamatory meanings are available.' See, also, *Skuse* v. *Granada Television* [1996] EMLR 278.

a person alleged to be insane,[6] or a woman alleged to have been raped,[7] has been defamed, probably because such accusations lead them to being 'shunned and avoided'. This sounds more like the reaction of a (very) 'ordinary' and not 'logical' person. But if 'ordinary' persons still think in this way, can they be described as 'right-thinking' members of society?

Various attempts have been made to explain what this last term means. Professor Street equated this with a 'substantial and respectable proportion of society'.[8] From a moral point of view the test is neither flawless nor convincing; but at least it is pragmatic, for the law largely depends on what the majority of people actually think, rather than on what they should think. In an increasingly pluralistic society, however, the designation of one or more sections as 'right-thinking' results in difficulties. For example, I call a workman a 'blackleg', a statement which would lower him in the eyes of his striking colleagues, but might raise him in the esteem of other members of the public who are inconvenienced by the strike. Is the test of defamation what right-thinking persons belonging to the class to which the statement is published think? Or right-thinking persons *generally*? The view, which has prevailed for some time now, is the latter one;[9] and two older cases bring out this point clearly.

In *Byrne* v. *Deane*,[10] automatic gambling machines, unlawfully kept by the defendants on their club premises, were removed by the police after someone informed them of their illegal presence. The following day someone put on the notice-boards of the club a typewritten paper containing a verse which ended with the lines: 'But he who gave the game away may he burn in hell and rue the day'—burn being originally spelt 'byrnn'. The issue was whether the plaintiff (named Byrne) was correct in alleging that the verse was defamatory of him in so far as it implied that he had been disloyal to the club. The Court of Appeal decided that 'to allege of a man...that he has reported certain acts, wrongful in law, to the police, cannot possibly be said to be "defamatory", because a "good and worthy subject of the King" would not regard such an allegation to be defamatory'.

In *R* v. *Bishop*[11] the appellant appealed against a criminal conviction for burglary on the ground that the jury were wrongly allowed to hear evidence in cross-examination of his previous convictions. Charged with burglary by stealing from X, the appellant sought to explain the presence of his fingerprints in X's premises by saying that he had entered on X's invitation for homosexual purposes. The prosecution applied for leave to ask the appellant questions relating to his previous convictions, relying on proviso

[6] *Morgan* v. *Lingen* (1863) 8 LT 800.

[7] *Youssoupoff* v. *Metro-Goldwyn-Mayer Pictures Ltd.* (1934) 50 TLR 581.

[8] *On Torts* 10th edn., by Margaret Brazier and John Murphy (1999), 440. Cf. the views of Holmes J in the American case of *Peck* v. *Tribune*, 214 US 185 (1909), where reference was made to the reactions of 'a *considerable* and *respectable* class in [the plaintiff's] community' to test whether the plaintiff had been defamed. Interestingly enough, though the italicised words used by Holmes can be subjected to the same criticisms of Street's choice of words, they were inserted by the great American judge as a means of ensuring the opposite result namely, that 'liability [was not treated as] a question of majority vote'.

[9] Thus, see, *Tolley* v. *Fry* [1930] 1 KB 467 at 479 (per Greer LJ) and, more recently, *Gillick* v. *BBC* [1996] EMLR 267.

[10] [1937] 1 KB 818, esp. Slesser LJ at 833. [11] [1975] QB 274.

(f)(ii) to section 1 of the Criminal Evidence Act 1898, which states: 'A person charged or called as a witness ... shall not be asked ... any question tending to show that he had committed or been convicted of ... any offence other than wherewith he is then charged ... unless ... (ii) ... the nature of conduct of the defence is such as to involve imputations on the character of the prosecutor or the witnesses for the prosecution.' The request was granted and the appellant's previous convictions were revealed in cross-examination. On appeal, it was argued on his behalf that the jury was wrongly allowed to hear this evidence. For, after the enactment of section 1 of the Sexual Offences Act 1967, it is no longer an offence to commit a homosexual act in private with another consenting man over 21. In the light of this, it was not an imputation on X's character to say that he was homosexual. Stephenson LJ, disagreeing with this argument, said that an allegation of conduct which is not illegal may still be an allegation of immorality:

If Mr Price were to sue the appellant in respect of his allegation if repeated outside a court of law, we venture to think that a submission that the words were incapable of a defamatory meaning would be bound to fail and a jury would generally be likely to find them defamatory. We believe that we are not behind the times in considering that Mr Price's character was clearly impugned by the allegation of homosexual conduct made against him by the defendant in the particular circumstances of that case. It is also however submitted that a substantial proportion, and perhaps a majority, of the population would probably still consider an allegation of homosexuality as being defamatory. However, it is also clear that an (arguably) growing minority of citizens might not share such a view, which may at some point in the near future become the majority opinion. Who in such a case are the 'right-thinking' members of society? If the view of the current minority opinion is preferred, is there not a concern here that it might be high-handed to disregard the majority perspective, even if it may appear to be increasingly problematic? Certainly in cases like *Byrne*, where *illegal* acts are involved, the attitudes of the average, law-abiding citizen should provide the proper yardstick for comparison. But in the second type of situation where religious or moral issues are touched upon, the answer may be less clear.[12]

In a more recent decision[13] the case seems to have proceeded on the basis that the relevant 'community' was the 'hypothetical ordinary reasonable reader of the newspaper' in question. Since this was published in Arabic, reference was made in the judgment to how the Muslim society takes a particularly dim view of allegations of a sexual nature, especially when made against women. This flexibility seems sensible, in the circumstances; and the Court of Appeal did not question this approach. Yet it is not without its own difficulties, since this could lead to the same statement having certain consequences for one section of the population of one state but not for other citizens of the very same state.

Affecting the sensibilities of one racial or religious section of society is one thing, but would the average, reasonable person treat a statement that he was 'hideously ugly' as

[12] *Ibid.*, at 281.

[13] *Al-Fagih* v. *H. H. Saudi Research & Marketing (UK)* (QBD, 28 July 2000, unreported) (overturned on other grounds [2002] EMLR 13).

defamatory? The actor and director Stephen Berkoff did; and was (unusually, one is tempted to suggest) willing to chance litigation. A majority of the Court of Appeal was of the view that the words were capable of being defamatory and thought the matter should be left for a jury to decide.[14] Such a deferential attitude to the rights of juries seems unconvincing (though, as we shall note below, a number of important recent dicta still recognise the importance of the jury role *in determining whether the statement is defamatory*). We take this view partly because courts have, on other occasions involving more serious statements, taken a different view of their rights[15] but, mainly, because the judgment seems to place excessive limitations upon the desired ability to describe people or even to poke fun at them in everyday life. It is submitted, therefore, that decisions such as *Berkoff* must be treated with suspicion. This is because of (*a*) the current and understandable wish (manifested *mainly in the area of damage awards*) to diminish the role of juries[16] and (*b*) the tendency of our courts to ascribe, especially under the growing influence of the European Convention on Human Rights, greater importance to free speech. In the instant case, therefore, one must welcome the later decision of the Court of Appeal in *Norman* v. *Future Publishing*,[17] where *Berkoff* was distinguished by differentiating between mere insults (on the one hand) and words used with the deliberate intention of holding the claimant up to mockery and ridicule (on the other), with the consequence that the matter was not left to the jury.

(B) LIBEL AND SLANDER

Defamation consists of libel and slander. The first is usually written, the second is oral. The distinction, unknown to Roman law, Scots law and the modern civilian systems, has an historical origin. Libel evolved out of statements considered in Tudor times to be prejudicial to the state. For this reason, they were criminally punished by the Court of Star Chamber. This, being a prerogative court, gave preference to the interests of the state. Governmental suspicion of the press required that injurious publications should be suppressed at all costs.[18] On the other hand, the remedy for spoken words had been evolving in the common law courts from an earlier time and represented a development from the older ecclesiastical jurisdiction. Indeed, the main peculiarity of slander—that it is actionable only upon proof of special damage (pecuniary loss)—provided the temporal justification for the common law courts in taking over from the ecclesiastical courts. After the abolition of Star Chamber, libel was handed over to the common law courts.

[14] *Berkoff* v. *Burchill* [1996] 4 All ER 1008 (with a lengthy consideration of the various meanings of defamatory by Neill LJ at 1011–17).

[15] Cf. *Shanson* v. *Howard* [1997] 4 CL 237, *Awa* v. *Independent News Auckland* [1995] 3 NZLR 701.

[16] Jury involvement in defamation cases is also likely to decrease as a result of the new 'offer of amends' defence (ss. 4–6) and (possibly) the new summary procedure (ss. 8–10) introduced by the Defamation Act 1996. On the other hand, the new Act refused to adopt a frontal attack on the jury system that is still seen in this country (and the United States) as an important constitutional guarantee. Thus, see *Hansard*, HL Debs., vol. 570, cols. 592–5, 597–8 (8 Mar. 1996). See, also, *Kirby-Harris* v. *Baxter* [1995] EMLR 516.

[17] [1999] EMLR 325.

[18] Suspicion is still reflected in criminal prosecutions for libel where truth is no defence.

The distinction between these two forms of defamatory statements remained too deeply ingrained to be discarded easily[19] and, irrational though it is, we must begin by explaining them.

The main distinction is that libel consists of a defamatory statement or representation in 'permanent form', which, according to Professor Street,[20] must also be visible. Anything temporary and audible only is slander. Statements in books, articles, newspapers, letters are libels; and in *Monson* v. *Tussauds Ltd.*[21] the making and placing of a waxwork of the plaintiff (a person prosecuted but not convicted for a criminal offence) near the 'Chamber of Horrors' was held to be a libel. Spoken words by themselves constitute slander. What if they are taped or included in a film reel? In *Youssoupoff* v. *Metro-Goldwyn-Mayer Pictures Ltd.*[22] a Russian princess sued a film company, alleging that a film about Rasputin published pictures and words suggesting that he had seduced her. The company was held liable. However, it is doubtful whether the case conclusively decided whether permanence is the sole test of libel or whether the defamatory matter must be visible as well. Slesser J suggested that both elements should be applied:

> There can be no doubt that, so far as the photographic part of an exhibition is concerned, that is a permanent matter to be seen by the eye, and is the proper subject of an action for libel, if defamatory. I regard the speech which is synchronised with the photographic reproduction and forms part of one complex, common exhibition as an ancillary circumstance, part of the surroundings explaining that which is to be seen.[23]

If this is so, then a defamatory anecdote in a film, heard but not accompanied by visible presentation, would be slander and not libel, although it is in permanent form; and the same would apply to a gramophone record.

Written and spoken words are clear illustrations of the distinction between libel and slander, but there are other examples. Broadcasting, radio, television and theatrical performances used to pose nice problems, but they are now statutorily treated as publication in permanent form by section 1 of the Defamation Act 1952. Section 16(1) goes on to provide that 'words shall be construed as including a reference to pictures, visual images, gestures and other methods of signifying meaning'. Section 28 of the Cable and Broadcasting Act 1984 extends the same rule to cable programme services. Finally, in like vein, section 4(1) of the Theatres Act 1968 states that 'the publication of words in the course of a performance of a play shall . . . be treated as publication in permanent form'.

What of 'skywriting' by an aeroplane, or dictating a telegram over the telephone? Perhaps the dictation is slander, while the reproduction in telegram form is libel for which the person dictating would be liable as he authorises its publication. The Faulks Committee suggested that skywriting would be libel because the vapour takes some time to disperse.[24] Another possible argument in favour of this view might be the fact

[19] The Faulks Committee, unlike its predecessor (the Porter Committee), recommended the abolition of the distinction in civil proceedings: Cmnd. 5909 (1975), para. 91.

[20] *On Torts* 10th edn, by Margaret Brazier and John Murphy (1999), 451.

[21] (1934) 50 TLR 581.

[22] *Ibid.*

[23] *Ibid.*, at 587.

[24] *Gulf Oil (GB) Ltd.* v. *Page* [1987] Ch. 327 came close to the imaginary example since it involved an aerial display of a sign defamatory of the plaintiffs. The libel/slander dichotomy was not considered as the legal dispute focused on the ability to obtain an interim injunction where there was a strong *prima facie* case that the display

that skywriting, in common with theatre or radio performances, can reach a very wide public. If this were to be considered as a decisive criterion then a plausible case could be made that this is a case of libel. Similar uncertainty apparently also surrounds records and taped recordings. The fact that their contents are in 'permanent' form suggests that they should be treated (if defamatory) as libels, even though they are not 'communicated' until they are played. On the whole, however, such distinctions do little credit to the law and civilian systems are no worse off for ignoring them.

Other differences between libel and slander are:

(i) Libel is both a tort and a crime; the older limitation that it was criminal only where there was a danger of a breach of the peace appears to have been abandoned since the 1930s.[25] Slander is only a tort, though spoken words may, of course, constitute other crimes, for example sedition, blasphemy, criminal conspiracy.

(ii) Libel is actionable *per se*. This means that once publication of a libel referring to the plaintiff has been proven damages will be presumed. As Goddard LJ thus put it:

> A plaintiff can, if he likes, by way of aggravating damages, show that he has suffered actual damage, which he can prove, but in every case he is perfectly entitled to say 'Here is a serious libel on me. The law assumes I must have suffered damage and I am perfectly entitled to substantial damages'.[26]

Slander, on the other hand, requires proof of special damage. Special damage here means material loss capable of estimation in money. Loss of marriage prospect, however,[27] and of consortium[28] have been held to be 'special' damage. In four exceptional cases, which can again be explained by reference to history, slander is actionable *per se*. This is because they are 'either so obviously damaging to the financial position of the victim that pecuniary loss is almost certain; or so intrinsically outrageous that they ought to be actionable even if no pecuniary loss results'.[29]

The four cases are:

(i) Imputation of a criminal offence punishable with imprisonment in the first instance—the true basis of action being that allegations of such types of misconduct are likely to cause the person defamed to be shunned and excluded from society.[30]

(ii) Imputation of un-chastity or adultery to a woman or girl. This was not actionable *per se* at common law, since immoral conduct used to come under the spiritual

of the material was part of a conspiracy to injure the plaintiff without just cause. The Court of Appeal granted an injunction, contrary, it seems, to the longstanding practice not to grant interim injunctions in defamation cases.

[25] *R* v. *Wicks* [1936] 1 All ER 384, followed by *Goldsmith* v. *Pressdram Ltd.* [1977] QB 83. On this and related matters see J. R. Spencer, in 'Criminal Libel in Action: the Snuffing of Mr. Wicks' [1979] *CLJ* 60, 67 ff., and in P. R. Glazebrook (ed.), *Reshaping the Criminal Law: Essays in Honour of G. L. Williams* (1978), 266 ff.

[26] *English and Scottish Co-operative Properties Mortgage and Investment Society Ltd.* v. *Odhams Press Ltd.* [1940] 1 All ER 1, at 12–13.

[27] *Speight* v. *Gosnay* (1891) 60 LJQB 231.

[28] *Lynch* v. *Knight* (1861) 9 HLC 577; 11 ER 854.

[29] Per Asquith LJ in *Kerr* v. *Kennedy* [1942] 1 KB 409, 411.

[30] *Gray* v. *Jones* [1939] 1 All ER 798: 'You are a convicted person. I will not have you here. You have a conviction.'

courts and the common law courts insisted on proof of 'temporal loss'. Section 1 of the Slander of Women Act 1891, however, dispensed with this need for special damage. The Act does not go all the way, since imputation of immorality, provided that it falls short of the carnal knowledge, is without a remedy.[31]

(iii) Imputation of certain diseases, which are exceedingly ill-defined. (Venereal diseases and leprosy are included, but not smallpox. There is no clear authority on what the position is concerning 'new' diseases such as AIDS, even though such allegations may have drastic consequences in, for example, the area of employment law. This heading of slander is so antiquated that it is better to avoid extending it. If, on the other hand, new forms of diseases such as AIDS do lead the average person to shun and avoid sufferers, then a case could be made for extending this heading to include them and thus 'deter' those persons who make such allegations.)

(iv) Imputation 'calculated to disparage the plaintiff in any office, profession, calling, trade or business', so long as the calling or profession is lawful, no matter how humble. In *Foulger* v. *Newcomb*[32] it was held that a gamekeeper whose job it was to preserve foxes in a certain area could succeed against the defendant, who accused him of poisoning foxes. A qualification at common law was that it was not sufficient to show that the statement was likely to harm the plaintiff in his occupation; it had to be directed against him 'in the way of his calling'. Thus, an accusation that a schoolmaster had committed adultery on the school premises was held not to be actionable *per se*,[33] though an imputation of impropriety with a pupil might be.[34] After section 2 of the Defamation Act it now suffices that the words are likely to injure the plaintiff in his calling.

2. DEFAMATION: ELEMENTS OF LIABILITY

(A) THE ALLEGATION MUST BE DEFAMATORY

Something has already been said about the meaning of 'defamatory'.[35] It should now be added that spoken words which are merely abusive, understood as vituperation or uttered in a fit of temper, are not defamatory.[36] The reason is that abuse is only meant to give vent to one's own feelings rather than to injure the claimant. Also, abuse may damage the claimant's self-esteem. This is not the concern of defamation, which protects the esteem in which *others* hold him. The manner in which the words are spoken

[31] The main difficulty is defining 'un-chastity'. *Kerr* v. *Kennedy* [1942] 1 KB 409, 412, said that it includes lesbianism.

[32] (1867) LR 2 Ex. 327.

[33] *Jones* v. *Jones* [1916] 2 AC 481.

[34] *Thompson* v. *Bridges*, 273 SW 529 (1925), cf. *Hopwood* v. *Muirson* [1945] KB 313.

[35] Above, Section 1(a).

[36] *Fields* v. *Davis* [1955] CLY 1543 (defendant calling the plaintiff, a married woman, a 'tramp').

and the surrounding circumstances are crucial and a speaker takes the risk that his audience may construe his words as defamatory. On the other hand, it is doubtful whether written words can ever be dismissed as mere abuse.

In most cases it is easy to decide whether words are defamatory. A straightforward allegation of dishonesty or immorality or other dishonourable behaviour raises few problems. But other allegations might also affect the claimant's reputation in a prejudicial manner. As Lord Pearson put it,

> words may be defamatory of a trader or businessman or professional man, though they do not impute any moral fault or defect of personal character. They can be defamatory of him if they impute lack of qualification, knowledge, skill, capacity, judgment or efficiency in the conduct of his trade or business or professional activity.[37]

It is thus defamatory to refer to someone as a crook, coward, liar, hypocrite, a fanatic, a habitual drunkard, a drug addict or drug dealer, dishonest, a cheat.

Often the words used by the defendants may be innocuous in themselves but the general picture they paint of the claimant may damage his reputation. In *Liberace* v. *Daily Mirror Newspapers*[38] a journalist described Liberace, a well-known entertainer, as: 'the summit of sex—the pinnacle of masculine, feminine, and neuter. Everything that he, she or it can ever want to be . . . a deadly, winking, sniggering, snuggling, chromium-plated, scent impregnated, luminous, quivering, giggling, fruit flavoured, ice-covered heap of motherly love.' The judge held that these words, taken together, were capable, in their ordinary and natural sense, of meaning that Liberace was a homosexual and the jury agreed that they were defamatory.

The search is therefore for the meaning that words would convey to the ordinary man. This, as already stated, is a matter of construction, not evidence, but of construction in a non-technical sense. For the ordinary man does not live in an ivory tower and he is not inhibited by the knowledge of the rules of construction. So, though he is essentially a fair and reasonable person, he can and does read between the lines in the light of his general knowledge and experience of worldly affairs and is even allowed a certain amount of loose thinking.[39] In the ultimate analysis, therefore, the test of the 'ordinary man' is what the jurors think about the words published about the claimant.

The reverse situation may also occur; namely, the claimant may be tempted to select libellous statements, which are taken from a text which, however, as a whole, proves that there is no defamation. Thus, in *Charleston* v. *News Group Newspapers Ltd.*[40] the two plaintiffs, who played a 'respectable' married couple in a well-known Australian soap opera, sued the *News of the World* for a photomontage which consisted of their

[37] *Drummond-Jackson* v. *British Medical Association* [1970] 1 WLR 688, 698–9.

[38] *The Times*, 17 and 18 June 1959. According to RSC Ord. 33, r. 3 there is jurisdiction to try as a preliminary issue the question whether words complained of in an action for defamation are capable of having a particular meaning. This should be availed of where it is obvious that it would save costs without occasioning delay: *Keays* v. *Murdoch Magazines (UK) Ltd. and Another* [1991] 1 WLR 1184.

[39] *Lewis* v. *Daily Telegraph* [1964] AC 234, 258, per Lord Reid. For a more recent confirmation of this approach see: *Skuse* v. *Granada Television* [1996] EMLR 278. See, also, Lord Reid's views in *Morgan* v. *Odhams Press Ltd.* [1971] 1 WLR 1239 at 1245.

[40] [1995] 2 All ER 313.

faces superimposed on naked bodies performing sex. Though the photograph was accompanied by an eye-catching title, the supporting text made it clear that the pictures had been reproduced from a computer game in which the image of the plaintiffs had been used without their knowledge and consent. The plaintiffs complained that the picture and headline title were defamatory in so far that they implied that they had posed for the pictures. The action failed on the ground that the title and picture could not be seen in isolation and that the final decision whether the tort of defamation had been committed depended on the words being seen in the total context. Though this result is in tune with the prevailing tendency not to inhibit free expression, the actual outcome comes very close to giving tabloids a licence to hurt people through sensational reporting which is 'neutralised' or 'corrected' by an accompanying text, invariably in smaller print. Lord Nicholls was the only judge to draw attention to such practice;[41] but it remains to be seen whether his cautionary warning to news editors to avoid going down such a road will have any effect.

Matters become more complicated when the claimant argues that the words bear an inner meaning which renders them defamatory; he says, in other words, that even if they are not defamatory on the surface, they are so because of an innuendo. This depends on factors known to the recipient of the statement at the time of publication and is something which the claimant must plead and prove (if he does not do so, his pleadings will be struck out). Even if he fails to prove such facts to support an innuendo, he may still revert to the natural meaning of the words. It should be made clear, however, that when a defamatory meaning is derived from the words themselves, this is not an innuendo.[42]

Innuendoes form an important part of defamation. Thus, in *Tolley* v. *J. S. Fry & Sons Ltd.*,[43] the plaintiff, an amateur golfer, was pictured on a poster with a slab of the defendants' chocolate protruding from his pocket. The accompanying caddy in doggerel verse compared the excellence of the chocolate with the excellence of the plaintiff's stroke. The plaintiff alleged an innuendo by the defendants that he had agreed to the advertisement for gain and had thus prostituted his reputation as an *amateur* (i.e. not as a professional playing for money) golfer. It was held that this was defamatory and that the plaintiff could recover.

It is immaterial whether or not the defendant knows of the external facts that transform an innocent statement into a defamatory one. We shall say more about unintentional defamation later, but for present purposes *Cassidy* v. *Daily Mirror Newspapers Ltd.*[44] can be given as an illustration. The defendants published a photograph of Mr Cassidy with Miss X and announced their engagement. In fact Mr Cassidy was already married, though he lived apart from his wife. The information on which the defendants based their statement came from Mr Cassidy himself, though they made no further attempt to ascertain its accuracy. Mrs Cassidy then brought an action alleging an innuendo that, since the paper had published the statement that Cassidy was unmarried, she must be regarded as his mistress. The court upheld her contention and awarded her £500.

41 *Ibid.*, at 320.
42 *Lewis* v. *Daily Telegraph* [1964] AC 234.
43 [1931] AC 333.
44 [1929] 2 KB 331.

It will be clear from the little that has already been said that the line between an ordinary meaning and an innuendo might not always be easy to draw. A derogatory implication may be so near the surface that it is hardly hidden at all, or it may be more difficult to detect. If it is said of a man that he is a fornicator, the statement cannot be enlarged by innuendo. If it is said of him that he was seen going into a brothel, the same meaning would probably be conveyed to nine men out of ten. But the lawyer might say that in the latter case a derogatory meaning was not a necessary one, because a man might go to a brothel for an innocent purpose. An innuendo pleading that the words were understood to mean that he went there for an immoral purpose would not, therefore, be ridiculous.[45]

This last type of innuendo is the so-called 'false innuendo' and, as Lord Hodson put it in *Lewis* v. *Daily Telegraph*, 'it is no more than an elaboration or embroidering of the words used without proof of extraneous facts'. But then one could say that one saw X entering a named house, which could have a derogatory implication for anyone who knew that house was a brothel, but not for anyone who did not. This type of innuendo, known as a 'true' or 'legal' innuendo, is derived not from an elaboration of the words, but from extrinsic evidence associated with the statement. In the last example, therefore, the claimant has to prove that the person to whom the statement was made knew that the particular house was a brothel and understood the claimant was entering it for an immoral purpose. The distinction between these types of innuendo was once important for pleading purposes, but since 1972[46] it has ceased to be significant because a claimant now should give particulars of all such meanings.

Lewis v. *Daily Telegraph*[47] illustrates these points. The *Daily Telegraph* reported that the Scotland Yard Fraud Squad was inquiring into the affairs of the Rubber Improvement Co. Ltd. and its Chairman, Mr Lewis. They sued in defamation, claiming (*a*) that the words were defamatory in their ordinary and natural meaning and (*b*) that the words meant or could be understood to mean that the plaintiffs were guilty of fraud and dishonesty. The defendants did not deny that the words in their ordinary meaning were defamatory, but pleaded justification. As to (*b*), they denied that the words meant or were capable of meaning that the plaintiffs were guilty of or suspected of fraud. The crux of the matter, therefore, was whether the words could be understood by an 'ordinary reasonable man' to bear the meaning alleged by the plaintiffs; or whether such defamatory meaning would be apparent only to readers who possessed special and additional knowledge of the question. The judge at first instance decided in favour of the first view and left the issue to the jury, which found for the company and awarded it £100,000. The Court of Appeal and the House of Lords by a majority favoured the second view, namely that being investigated for fraud was not the same thing as being guilty of fraud, the latter requiring additional facts.[48] A new trial was thus ordered.

45 *Lewis* v. *Daily Telegraph* [1964] AC 234, 278, per Lord Devlin.
46 *Allsop* v. *Church of England Newspaper Ltd.* [1972] 2 QB 161.
47 [1964] AC 234.
48 See, also, *Mapp* v. *News Group* [1998] 2 WLR 260.

In his judgment Lord Reid considered how the judge should approach this task of deciding between a range of possible meanings:

Ordinary men and women have different temperaments and outlooks. Some are unusually suspicious and some are unusually naive. One must try to envisage people between these two extremes and see what is the most damaging meaning they would put on the words in question . . . What the ordinary man, not avid for scandal, would read into the words complained of must be a matter of impression. I can only say that I do not think that he would infer guilt of fraud merely because an inquiry is on foot. And, if that is so, then it is the duty of the trial judge to direct the jury that it is for them to determine the meaning of the paragraph but that they must not hold it to impute guilt of fraud because as a matter of law the paragraph is not capable of having that meaning.[49]

In the event, since the words used in the article could not be given a defamatory meaning otherwise than by 'some strained or forced or utterly unreasonable interpretation',[50] they could become defamatory *only* by pleading additional, extraneous facts known to the recipient of the statement[51] and showing that they were in fact understood in the sense claimed by the plaintiff. No such (true) innuendo was pleaded and no evidence adduced to this effect, so the judge was wrong in not telling the jury that, whatever the words meant, as a matter of law they did not mean that the plaintiffs were fraudulent. This part of the case reveals that an innuendo constitutes a separate cause of action, which in the present context means that had it been pleaded and proved the plaintiffs would have succeeded in their action, even though the defendant had a defence on the first cause of action. Second, it follows that separate verdicts should be returned and separate damages should be assessed in respect of innuendoes.[52]

In *Lewis* the position with regard to false innuendoes was left open. In *Allsop* v. *Church of England Newspaper Ltd.*,[53] however, it was made clear that the same rules should apply to both. Thus, where the words complained of have various meanings or overtones outside the dictionary definitions, it is desirable and necessary that the claimant should give particulars of all such meanings. Lord Denning MR offered two reasons for this: 'in the first place, so that the defendant should know the case which he has to meet and to decide whether to plead justification or fair comment, or apologise: and, in the second place, so that the trial can be properly conducted'.[54]

Pleading an innuendo is not only important for the defendant, it may also be important to the claimant. For when the claimant does not plead an innuendo limiting the scope of possible defamatory meanings of the words complained of, the scope of the defence of justification is correspondingly widened. In *London Computer Operators Training Ltd.* v. *BBC*[55] the BBC was sued by the plaintiffs, who alleged that an entire

[49] [1964] AC 234, at 259–60.

[50] *Jones* v. *Skelton* [1963] 1 WLR 1362, 1370, per Lord Morris.

[51] At the time of publication for facts discovered after publication cannot support an innuendo: *Grappelli* v. *Derek Block (Holdings) Ltd.* [1981] 2 All ER 272.

[52] [1964] AC 234, 273, per Lord Hodson.

[53] [1972] 2 QB 161.

[54] *Ibid.*, 167. See also *Fullam* v. *Newcastle Chronicle and Journal Ltd.* [1977] 1 WLR 651.

[55] [1973] 1 WLR 424.

broadcast concerning their operations at a computer operators' school had defamed them. The original defence was justification and fair comment, and the particulars pleaded were that students who had paid high fees had never been able to get a job, etc. At a subsequent date the BBC applied for leave to amend their defence by adding to the particulars of justification a certificate of the criminal record of the founder of the plaintiff company, which contained particulars of previous convictions for theft, larceny and obtaining by false pretences. The Master granted leave, but the Judge in Chambers allowed only the part of the record that was relevant to the defence of justification. On further appeal the Court of Appeal restored the Master's decision. Since no innuendo had been pleaded, the court was entitled to examine the full width of the meanings that the jury might reasonably put upon the words. The greater the conceivable width, the greater the scope of the particulars of justification.[56]

Who decides whether a statement is defamatory or not—the judge or the jury? (Defamation actions can still be tried before a jury at the option of either party.) Since the passing of Fox's Libel Act in 1792 (which was meant to apply to criminal trials, but has also been followed in civil trials) the task of deciding whether words are defamatory is left to the jury, the judge merely directing or advising the jury. Indeed, the rationale of jury trial (such as it is) would disappear if the jurors were to cease being the final arbiters of meaning. In practice, however, the role is shared with the judge. For, whether the words in question are defamatory or not is for the jury to decide; but whether they are even 'capable' of bearing a defamatory meaning is for the judge to decide and in this way he can exercise some control over the matter.[57] So (*a*) a judge may decide to leave the matter to the jury, in which case he must explain to them what defamation means in law; (*b*) if the words are obviously defamatory, he may indicate to them that the evidence submitted to the court can only be interpreted in one way. If, despite this, the jury finds for the defendant, a new trial may be ordered on appeal, though such a course will appear to be an interference with the functions of the jury and in practice has very rarely been taken; (*c*) if he believes that no reasonable man would consider the words to be defamatory, he must withdraw the case from the jury, but, once again, such a course will be taken only in very clear cases.

In *The Capital and Counties Bank Ltd.* v. *G. Henty & Sons*[58] the defendants quarrelled with the manager of a branch of the plaintiff bank. They circularised some of their customers, who knew nothing of the dispute and who in turn showed the circular to

[56] [1973] 1 WLR 424, at 428, per Cairns LJ. See also *S. & K. Holdings Ltd.* v. *Throgmorton Publications Ltd.* [1972] 1 WLR 1036.

[57] *Morgan* v. *Odhams Press Ltd.* [1971] 1 WLR 1239, 1251, per Lord Morris. In its recent Report (Select Bibliography), 28, the Supreme Court Procedure Committee saw 'no reason . . . why all necessary rulings on whether the words are 'capable' of any given meaning should not be dispensed of as early as possible, [for] in practice this would lead to earlier and cheaper settlements . . .'. Apparently, such a procedure already exists in Scots law. It is too early to predict what effect cases like *Keays* v. *Murdoch Magazines (UK) Ltd. and Another* [1991] 1 WLR 1184 will have on a future practice. In that case the Court of Appeal held that there was jurisdiction under RSC Ord. 33, r. 3 to try as a preliminary issue the question whether the words complained of were capable of bearing a particular meaning. This should be exercised where it was apparent that it would save costs without occasioning delay. See, now, *Mapp* v. *News Group Newspapers Ltd.* [1998] 2 WLR 260, esp. 265.

[58] (1882) 7 App. Cas. 741.

others, informing them that the defendants would not receive in payment cheques drawn at any of the branches of the plaintiff. The latter claimed damages on the ground that the circular imputed insolvency. The House of Lords, after enunciating the principle just stated, proceeded to hold by majority that the words in question were not defamatory in their natural meaning and that the suggested innuendo was not one that any reasonable man would draw. Thus, despite the fact that the defendants' statement did cause a run on the plaintiff's bank, our highest court was of the view that the words that had caused such havoc did not warrant a referral to the jury. The defendants were thus entitled to judgment.[59]

How slow one should be in quashing a jury verdict for perversity is demonstrated by the *Grobbelaar* litigation. In that case the well-known goalkeeper of the English team was accused by the *Sun* newspaper for being bribed to 'fix' games on the basis of intrusive and unsavoury techniques used to obtain evidence of the footballer's guilt. Leaving aside other issues that arose in that case (such as the availability of the defence of qualified privilege to which we shall return later) we note here that the jury found for the claimant and awarded him damages of £85,000 damages. The Court of Appeal set this verdict aside on the grounds that it was perverse, only to see its own decision quashed by the House of Lords, Lord Bingham (restating) the orthodox position, namely:

> the task of an appellate court, whether the Court of Appeal or the House, is to seek to interpret the jury's decision and not, because of justifiable dissatisfaction at the outcome, to take upon itself the determination of factual issues which lay within the exclusive province of the jury.[60]

Two further cases, decided in 2001, also considered the circumstances under which the judge could withdraw the case from the jury. In the first—*Safeway Stores* v. *Tate*[61]—due to an administrative slip no jury was empanelled for the day of the hearing and the claimant then applied for a summary dismissal of the case under Civil Procedure Rules 24.2, claiming that the defendant had no real defence. The old CPR rules on the matter expressly excluded libel actions from the court's jurisdiction to grant summary judgments but the (new) ones which had to be applied in this instance, were silent leaving it to the judge's discretion whether the defendant had any real prospect of defending the actions. Exercising this discretion, the trial judge reached the conclusion that the words complained of could not really be held to be defamatory and, accordingly, granted the claimant's request for summary dismissal. The decision was quashed by Otton LJ speaking for the Court of Appeal, when he stated that

> it is beyond the power of the Civil Procedure Rule Committee to limit the right to trial by jury or the right to have the question 'libel or no libel' determined by the jury, by its general powers to reform the rules of practice and procedure of the courts.

[59] An analogous and more recent case—*Aspro Travel Ltd.* v. *Owners Abroad Group plc* [1996] 1 WLR 132—applied the same principle but on this point reached, it is submitted, the right result.

[60] *Grobbelaar* v. *News Group Newspapers Ltd* [2002] 1 WLR 3024, at 3037, [26]. The claimant's award was, however, reduced to £1. By so doing, the House of Lords also, incidentally, resolved the uncertainty that had hitherto existed as to whether it was entitled, under s. 8(2) of the Courts and Legal Services Act 1990, to exercise the power given by that Act to the Court of Appeal and substitute its own sum for that awarded by the jury.

[61] [2001] QB 1120.

The underlying reason is clear and, it is submitted convincing. Trial by jury has, as the learned Justice observed, been sanctioned since Fox's Libel Act and could only be removed by statute and not by delegated delegation (such as the CPR rules). But if this meant that the judge could not decide questions of fact, nor remove them from the jury on the grounds that he felt that they *might* decide them perversely,[62] it did not mean that he could not decide whether the words were capable of defamatory meaning.

These fine (but important) distinctions are confirmed by the subsequent case of *Alexander* v. *Arts Council of Wales*[63] where the claimant, complained that he was libelled by the Arts Council of Wales (a non-governmental body distributing lottery money) and its chief executive. The defendants invoked, *inter alia*, qualified privilege and the claimant riposted with the allegation that the chief executive (and thus the Arts Council of Wales) was activated by malice (and thus, as we shall note below, lost his defence). The judge ruled that no jury, if properly directed, could find malice and thus withdrew the issue from the jury and gave judgment for the defendants. Their appeal, on the grounds that the finding of malice depended on findings of fact which the judge should have left to the jury, was dismissed. The decision thus appears to be irreconcilable with the *Safeway* case. In reality, however, the two decisions can be reconciled on the grounds that in the *Alexander* case the judge had reached the conclusion that there was no evidentiary basis to support the claimant's case for malice and that thus this defence was *bound* to fail. As May LJ said:

> *Safeway Stores plc* v. *Tate* is thus a decision binding on this court to the effect that, if there is a material issue of fact in a libel case, section 69 of the Supreme Court Act 1981 entitles a party to have the issue decided by the jury. It is, however, for the judge to decide whether there really is such an issue.[64]

As the judge further added:,

> The critical question for the judge was whether there was any evidence, taken at is highest, on which a jury properly directed could properly infer that the second defendant subjectively did not honestly believe that what she intended to say... was true...[65]

His decision was that there was not; and in reaching it he was perfectly within his rights, even though it was prudent to be restated that such action should be taken only in the clearest of cases in order to avoid the likely risk that costly appeals will follow.

(B) THE DEFAMATORY STATEMENT MUST REFER TO THE CLAIMANT

The words have to be defamatory of the claimant and not of some other person, real or imaginary. However, if a statement does not refer to the claimant but a subsequent one sheds light on the first (thus making the identification clearer), then it may be taken

[62] [2001] QB 1120, at 1128 H. Emphasis added to bring out the difference with the point made in the *Alexander* case discussed immediately below.
[63] [2001] 1 WLR 1840.
[64] *Ibid.*, at 1853A.
[65] *Ibid.*, at p. 1854, [42].

into account.[66] The identification of the claimant depends upon whether reasonable people would believe that the words complained of referred to him.[67] The reasonable man, here as elsewhere in defamation, tends to be renamed the 'ordinary' man in order to take into account a 'certain amount of loose thinking'[68] and the inevitable tendency, especially when reading newspaper reports, to skim through the accounts without concentrated attention or second reading.

In *Morgan* v. *Odhams Press*,[69] G, a journalist, while investigating a dog-doping conspiracy, came across Miss M, who was a kennel-maid at a greyhound track and was involved in the doping of the dogs. She confessed in the presence of the police and she was likely to be a key witness in any proceedings that might ensue. In the light of this, it was agreed that she would remain in the care of G. Later, while in G's company, she met the plaintiff and spent some time with him before being persuaded to return to G. Subsequently the *People* published the story, which included a photograph of Miss M. One day later, the *Sun*, which, like the *People*, was owned by the defendant company, produced a follow-up article stating that the 'dog-doping girl was kidnapped last week by members of the gang and kept in a house in Finchley'. Miss M, while staying with the plaintiff, had on several occasions been seen in his company and his house was on the border of Finchley. He sued, alleging that his friends, on reading the second article, had understood him to be one of Miss M's kidnappers. The key issue was whether the reasonable reader would understand the article as referring to the plaintiff. The Court of Appeal took the view that the case should not have been allowed to go to the jury. Two reasons were given for this. First, because the ordinary man must be envisaged as reading the article carefully, so that the discrepancies contained therein would prevent him from reading it as referring to the plaintiff; and second, because the article itself *must* contain some pointer indicating that it referred to the plaintiff. In the opinion of the court the article in question failed to satisfy both requirements. The House of Lords by a majority overruled the Court of Appeal and held that in determining the impression on the mind of the reader, regard should be had to the character of the article and the class of reader likely to read it. Lord Donovan once said that the ordinary sensible man reading an article in a popular newspaper is not expected to analyse it like a Fellow of All Souls.[70] The relevant impression to be taken into consideration was that which would be conveyed to an ordinary sensible man, having knowledge of the circumstances, reading the article casually and not expecting a high degree of accuracy. Such a man could well reach the conclusion that the article referred to the plaintiff and hence the judge was right to leave the matter to the determination of the jury. Nor did their

66 *Bruce* v. *Odhams Press Ltd.* [1936] 1 KB 697, 705, per Greer LJ. In the case of two publications, where words used in the first are defamatory of the claimant and were understood to be aimed at him (even though they did not expressly identify him), the jury are allowed to look at the second publication to see to whom the first publication referred: *Hayward* v. *Thompson* [1982] QB 47.

67 *Hayward* v. *Thompson* [1982] QB 47.

68 Per Lord Reid in *Morgan* v. *Odhams Press Ltd.* [1971] 1 WLR 1239, 1245. See also Lord Pearson at 1269–70. See, also, *Skuse* v. *Granada Television* [1996] EMLR 278.

69 [1971] 1 WLR 1239.

70 *Ibid.*, 1264.

Lordships feel that it was necessary to discover a pointer referring to the plaintiff, though in this case it was felt that there was one.

The emphasis on how the ordinary man would interpret the defendant's statement means that at common law—now subject to what will be said below about 'unintentional defamation'—the latter's own knowledge of or intention to refer to the claimant is irrelevant.[71] In *Newstead* v. *London Express Newspaper Ltd.*[72] the defendants' newspaper stated that 'Harold Newstead, a thirty-year-old Camberwell man' had been convicted of bigamy. This was true of a Camberwell barman of that name, but not of the plaintiff, a barber, who was also aged about thirty and lived in Camberwell. The plaintiff's contention that the words were capable in law of being understood to refer to him was upheld, while the defendant's contention, that if words were true of one person they could not in law be defamatory of another, was rejected. In *E. Hulton & Co.* v. *Jones*[73] the defendants published a story of the discreditable doings in Dieppe of a fictitious character called Artemus Jones, who was said to be a churchwarden in Peckham. The plaintiff, who had been baptised Thomas Jones but called himself Thomas Artemus Jones (abbreviated to Artemus Jones), was a barrister not a churchwarden; he did not live in Peckham, nor had he visited Dieppe. He had, however, contributed articles to the very newspaper that published the fictitious story. He sued its proprietors for libel, was awarded £1,750 and the House of Lords upheld the decision.

Different problems arise when the defendant's statement refers to a class of people to which the claimant belongs. The question whether the words can be said to refer to him splits into two parts: one of law—are the words capable of referring to the claimant; one of fact—did reasonable people, who knew the claimant, believe the words to refer to him? It is generally accepted that the test for identification here is the same as for defamatory meanings: would a sensible ordinary reader identify the claimant as the person defamed?

In the leading case of *Knupffer* v. *London Express Newspaper Ltd.*,[74] the defendants published an article about a Young Russian political party, which had a British branch consisting of twenty-four members led by the plaintiff. The party was an international one with several thousand members and the article referred mainly to its activities in America and France. The plaintiff alleged that it was particularly applicable to Britain and, since the libel concerned the person responsible for the politics of the party, that it

[71] Although cf. *O'Shea* v. *Mirror Group Newspapers* [2001] EMLR 40, concerning the use of a photograph of a woman to advertise pornographic internet services. The claimant alleged that the woman in the photograph was the 'spit and image' of her and that this amounted to defamation, since it implied that she was associated with the promotion of the service in question. Morland J agreed that this would have made out liability at common law for 'unintentional defamation', but went on to hold that this conclusion could not stand in the face of Art. 10 ECHR. He held that it 'would impose an impossible burden on a publisher if he were required to check if the true picture resembled someone else who because of the content of the picture was defamed' (para. 43 of the judgment). For commentary, see J. Coad, 'Pressing Social Need and Strict Liability in Libel' [2001] 12 *Ent. LR* 1999 and P. Milmo *et al.* (eds.), *Gatley on Libel and Slander* (10th edn., 2005), para. 7.5.

[72] [1940] 1 KB 377.

[73] [1910] AC 20. The rigour of the common law, as exemplified by these two cases, is now modified by ss. 4–6 of the Defamation Act 1996.

[74] [1944] AC 116.

personally affected him. Rejecting this contention, the House of Lords laid down the general rule that where a class of persons is defamed, no one person can succeed unless he proves that the defamatory statement (*a*) was capable of referring to him and (*b*) was in fact understood to refer to him. In the present case the plaintiff failed on (*a*). 'In deciding this question', said Lord Porter, 'the size of the class,[75] the generality of the charge and the extravagance of the accusation may well all be elements to be taken into consideration, but none of them is conclusive. Each case must be considered according to its own circumstances.'[76] The actual decision of the House of Lords in that case thus suggests an inclination to construe narrowly the first of these requirements. *Le Fanu* v. *Malcolmson*,[77] however, shows that a general statement or reference to a class may be actionable by a particular claimant if the words in the surrounding circumstances can be taken to refer to him. A local newspaper published a letter denouncing the alleged cruelty with which factory operatives were treated. The House of Lords upheld the verdict of the jury awarding damages to the owners of the factory, since there were special circumstances which enabled the jurors to identify the plaintiff's factory. To decide otherwise, it was said, 'would be opening a very wide door to defamation'.

Are the rules any different if the claimant is a legal (i.e. artificial) rather than a human entity? Since Lord Esher MR boldly asserted in *South Hetton Coal Co. Ltd.* v. *North-Eastern News Association Ltd.*[78] that 'the law of libel is one and the same as to *all* plaintiffs', the answer has, in general terms,[79] been negative. Whether this is correct is arguable.[80] For, authority apart,[81] it is by no means obvious that the quite exceptional rules of defamation should be applicable to non-human entities. Defamation protects reputation and good name in order to uphold an individual's dignity and social esteem: this is the basis of the developing law and accounts for the rule that an individual's reputation is protected without him having to prove the falsity of the accusation or incurring any loss. (As we shall note further below, the defendant can avoid liability if he can prove the accuracy of his statement.)

[75] *Aspro Travel Ltd.* v. *Owners Abroad Group plc* [1996] 1 WLR 132 provides an illustration of this: allegations that a 'family' company was about to go bust were defamatory of its directors on the ground that they were allowing it to trade though (apparently) insolvent. *Quaere* whether the statement referred to the directors of a large, public company.

[76] Per Lord Porter at 124. For a more recent illustration see *Schloimovitz* v. *Clarendon Press, The Times*, 6 July 1973. But what if the defamatory statement refers to either one of two persons in the alternative? There seems to be no recent English authority on this point but, perhaps, the better solution is to say that both may sue.

[77] (1848) 1 HLC 637, 9 ER 910; *Orme* v. *Associated Newspapers Ltd., The Times*, 4 Feb. 1981. (A critical article referring to the activities of the Unification Church (the Moonies) held by the judge to be capable of referring to their leader. After a six-month trial the jury agreed, but also found that it was true.)

[78] [1894] 1 QB 133, 138 (italics supplied).

[79] For more details, see C. Duncan and B. Neill, *Defamation* (Select Bibliography), ch. 9.

[80] For trenchant criticism, see J. A. Weir, 'Local Authority v. Critical Ratepayer: A Suit in Defamation' [1972] *CLJ* 238 ff., whose views are here partly adopted.

[81] This comes in two forms. First, the unambiguous *South Hetton* ruling which has been followed many times since—e.g. *Shevill* v. *Presse Alliance SA* [1996] AC 959; *Steel* v. *McDonald's Corp* [1999] All ER 384 D—and was recently reconfirmed by a majority of the House of Lords in the *Jameel* case (see discussion in the text, below). Second but indirectly, the fact that Parliament refused to enact the full changes recommended by the Faulks Committee on Defamation (in § 336 of its Report of March 1975 (Cmnd 5909)) was influenced by Lord Reid's words in *Lewis* v. *Daily Telegraph* [1964] AC 234, 262 as well as Mr Weir's case note.

It is thus arguable that when the rules are extended to legal entities,[82] they lose this justification. For example, to award (as the jury did) £100,000 to the Rubber Improvement Company is absurd, for it had no feelings to be injured nor any social relations that might have been impaired by the publication of the statement that its affairs were being investigated by the Fraud Squad. The *only* harm that it could have suffered, and which would have deserved compensation if it actually had been incurred, was, *arguably*, harm to its commercial relations. 'Harm of that sort however, had it occurred, could be proved and therefore should be proved';[83] but it was not. All of which goes to show that what is here challenged is not an institution's right to compensation for loss resulting from a false statement made by the defendant and actionable under some such tort as injurious falsehood, but its right to take advantage of rules designed to protect *human* reputation and esteem.

This objection is not without serious merit. Like most arguments, however, it is subject to counter-arguments. Most recently, Lord Bingham expressed them forcefully in his *Jameel* decision when he said:

Should the corporation be entitled to sue in its own right only if it can prove financial loss? I do not think so, for two main reasons. First, the good name of a company, as that of an individual, is a thing of value. A damaging libel may lower its standing in the eyes of the public and even its own staff, make people less ready to deal with it, less willing or less proud to work for it. If this were not so, corporations would not go to the lengths they do to protect and burnish their corporate images. I find nothing repugnant in the notion that this is a value which the law should protect. Nor do I think it an adequate answer that the corporation can itself seek to answer the defamatory statement by press release or public statement, since protestations of innocence by the impugned party necessarily carry less weight with the public than the prompt issue of proceedings which culminate in a favourable verdict by judge or jury. Secondly, I do not accept that a publication, if truly damaging to a corporation's commercial reputation, will result in provable financial loss, since the more prompt and public a company's issue of proceedings, and the more diligent its pursuit of a claim, the less the chance that financial loss will actually accrue.[84]

In *Jameel* v. *Wall Street Journal Europe*[85] the rule that that defamed legal entities can claim damages without having to prove that they suffered any provable harm was extended to foreign corporations, as well, even though they did not trade in England but had a trading reputation in this country. The case was most recently decided by the House of Lords which, reversing the decisions of Eady J in the High Court as well as the Court of Appeal, gave judgment for the defendant newspaper following a detailed (but

[82] Though, as we shall note below, a distinction has emerged between legal entities which exist for profit and legal entities through which the central and local government perform their essentially political functions.

[83] Weir, 'Local Authority v. Critical Ratepayer' [1972] *CLJ* 238, at 240. Cf. Lord Reid in *Lewis* v. *Daily Telegraph* [1964] AC 234, 262: 'A company cannot be injured in its feelings, it can only be injured in its pocket. Its reputation can be injured by a libel but that injury must sound in money. The injury need not necessarily be confined to loss of income. Its goodwill may be injured.'

[84] *Jameel (Mohamed) and Another* v. *Wall Street Journal Europe Sprl* [2006] 3 WLR 642, [25] and [26].

[85] [2004] 2 All ER 92 at [26].

not entirely unanimous) re-examination of the *Reynolds* defence of 'responsible journalism'.[86] But the question whether a trading corporation could invoke the rule of 'presumed damages' reared its face again and split their Lordships three to two. The dissentients on this point—Lord Hoffmann and Baroness Hale—invoked arguments very similar to those mentioned in our text above. Indeed, Baroness Hale thought that the time was ripe for the House of Lords to take their *Derbyshire*[87] ruling (which, on free speech grounds, prohibited central and local government from suing in defamation) one step further and include, in the absence of special damage, trading companies, thus preventing them from profiting from the special rules of the law of defamation. Yet the majority of the lords—*viz.* Lords Bingham, Hope and Scott—thought otherwise; and in §§11–27 of Lord Bingham's opinion one will find the most sustained argument thus far available in favour of the *status quo.*[88]

There is thus, at present, little doubt that the rule in *South Hetton Coal Co. Ltd.* v. *North-Eastern News Association Ltd*[89] still stands with the result that a trading corporation and company can sue for defamation affecting its business or trading reputation. This statement, however, must be understood to be subject to two caveats. First, it, gives the corporation no right to sue for defamatory statements, which reflect solely upon individual officers or members. And, second, one could argue that their Lordships opinions in *Jameel* suggest that they favour the retention of this rule so long as the damages awarded are 'modest' and not excessive or punitive, probably because if they were that might trigger the successful application of Article 10 of the European Convention.

So far we have been talking of trading corporation but what about non-trading legal entities? The same rule about presumed damages was, in the 1970s, extended to entities, such as local authorities.[90] However, this extension of the *South Hetton* rule to cover local councils (and, presumably, other government departments with corporate status such as the Secretaries of State for defence, education and science, energy, environment and social services) rightly came to be seen as illogical and untenable. For this is not a simple extension of the rule from trading to non-trading corporations, but an unhappy assimilation of the notions of trading companies and government. For a local council is more than just a non-profit-making corporation; it is a kind of government department performing public functions and a citizen's right to criticise its functioning should not

86 Which will be considered in greater detail below. In this part of the chapter, we will only deal with the question of damages.

87 [1993] AC 534.

88 Any summary of the learned Law Lord's arguments would require painting in excessively broad brushstrokes, so it suffices here to draw the readers' attention to the fact that (a) he did not find the Weir objections convincing; (b) explained why he did not feel Art. 10 of the European Convention made such a change necessary and (c) gave powerful reasons why, despite the current trend towards an enhanced protection of freedom of expression, retention of the current rule was advisable.

89 [1894] 1 QB 133.

90 *Bognor Regis UDC* v. *Campion* [1972] 2 QB 169, 175, per Browne J. In *Electrical, Electronic, Telecommunication and Plumbing Union* v. *Times Newspapers Ltd.* [1980] QB 585, O'Connor J held that a trade union could not sue for defamation. The earlier and opposite case of *National Union of General and Municipal Workers* v. *Gillian* [1946] KB 81, however, was not followed because of a technical point. In the opinion of the judge, the Trade Union and Labour Relations Act 1974 removed from unions the status of a separate legal personality.

be stifled by the technical rules of defamation which, in this case, impermissibly stifle political speech. Thus in *Derbyshire County Council* v. *Times Newspapers*,[91] the House of Lords overruled this line of reasoning. Lord Keith, speaking for all their Lordships, followed the decision in *Attorney-General* v. *Guardian Newspapers Ltd. (No. 2)*[92] (a case not of defamation but concerning confidentiality), and held that:

> there are rights available to private citizens which institutions of central government are not in a position to exercise unless they can show that it is in the public interest to do so. The same applies . . . to local authorities. In both cases I regard it as right for this House to lay down that not only is there no public interest favouring the right of organs of government, whether central or local, to sue for libel, but that it is contrary to the public interest that they should have it. It is contrary to the public interest because to admit such actions would place an undesirable fetter on freedom of speech.[93]

This extract[94] suggests that in *Derbyshire* the House of Lords stopped short of according a similar immunity to statements criticising elected politicians[95] and other, unelected, officials who, presumably, can still sue their political tormentors (provided they can satisfy the usual elements of the tort). The rationale of *Derbyshire*, however, suggests that this could be the next step to be taken by our courts.[96] However, if our courts were minded to move in that direction, it might be preferable if they were to accord greater immunity to the *nature and content* of the speech (e.g. political speech v. titillating gossip) rather than make immunity hang on whether the person criticised was a politician or public (rather than a private) figure. For this would avoid the definitional difficulties which US law has encountered as a result of adopting the second approach while also achieving the laudable aim of protecting political speech. The case of *Reynolds* v. *Times Newspapers*[97] goes some way towards achieving this development by means of an extension of the defence of qualified privilege and we shall be looking at it in greater detail in the defences section.

(C) PUBLICATION

In *Pullman* v. *W. Hill & Co. Ltd.*[98] Lord Esher MR described publication as: 'The making known of the defamatory matter after it has been written to some person *other* than the person of whom it is written.'

91 [1993] AC 534. 92 [1990] 1 AC 109.

93 *Ibid.*, at 458. Unlike the Court of Appeal [1992] 3 WLR 28, which reached the same result by boldly relying on the ECHR, their Lordships chose to place more faith on American materials as well as Lord Goff's judgment in *Attorney-General* v. *Guardian Newspapers Ltd. (No. 2)* [1990] 1 AC 109, 283–4, where the view was expressed that in the field of freedom of speech there was no difference in principle between English law on the subject and Art. 10 of the Convention. 94 And, indeed, the wording of Lord Keith's judgment.

95 But the *Derbyshire* reasoning applies to political parties and justifies withholding from them the right to sue: *Goldsmith* v. *Bhoyrul* [1998] 2 WLR 435, 438.

96 In accord Sir Brian Neill, 'The Media and the Law' (Select Bibliography), 14–15. See also Lord Lester, 'Defaming Politicians and Public Officials' [1995] *PL* 1 ff.

97 [2001] 2 AC 127; see the text under Section 3(e)(ii), below, for detailed discussion.

98 [1891] 1 QB 524, 527.

If a statement is sent to the person of whom it is written, there is no publication of it, for one cannot publish a libel of a man to himself. Lord Esher's statement is equally true of spoken words. Communication to the claimant alone is thus insufficient to ground liability, because the law is concerned with the esteem that *third* parties have of the claimant. In criminal libel, on the other hand, publication to the prosecutor alone will suffice.

Communication of the defamatory statement to one person (other than the defamed) will suffice. Typically, this takes place as a result of a positive act (writing or telling something to B about C) but, exceptionally, one may also be liable for not taking positive steps to prevent the publication by someone else. This, it will be remembered, was the case of the managers of the club in *Byrne* v. *Dean* who were held liable for not having removed the defamatory poem from the club's notice-boards. (One might be tempted to draw an analogy between this rule and liability for 'adopting' a nuisance.)

A special rule is that a communication between spouses about a third party is not publication. This used to be explained by reference to the fiction of unity between husband and wife. It would, however, be better to accept that there is either an arbitrary rule that there can be no publication between spouses, or that there is a publication but that such communications are protected by absolute privilege. However, a communication by a third party to one spouse about the other is publication.[99] Another special rule is that by dictating a defamatory letter to his secretary an employer commits slander, though, as we shall see, he will probably be covered by the defence of qualified privilege. If she reads it back to him or hands it back typed, she is not making a fresh publication.[100] A statement not heard by the recipient because, for example, he is deaf, or is not understood because it is written in a language he does not know or because it is not obviously referable to the claimant[101] is not treated as having been published. Nor is a person liable if a third party on his own initiative hears or sees the defamation. However, he will be liable for statements which he intended a third party to know or should have foreseen might come to his attention. So, in *Huth* v. *Huth*[102] the opening of a letter by a butler, acting out of curiosity and in breach of his duties, was held not to amount to publication by the defendant. But a defendant should anticipate that a husband might, at least in some circumstances, open his wife's letters.[103] Equally, a letter addressed to a businessman is likely to be opened by a secretary and, therefore, the correspondent will be liable for the resulting publication to the secretary unless the letter was clearly marked 'personal' or 'private'.[104] A guiding test given by Harman LJ in *Theaker* v. *Richardson*[105] was the following: 'The question of publication of a libel

[99] *Theaker* v. *Richardson* [1962] 1 WLR 151.

[100] See *Osborn* v. *Boulter* [1930] 2 KB 226, 231, *Eglantine Inn Ltd.* v. *Smith* [1948] NI 29, 33.

[101] *Sadgrove* v. *Hole* [1901] 2 KB 1.

[102] [1915] 3 KB 32.

[103] Though in *Theaker* v. *Richardson* [1962] 1 WLR 151, 157, the court said that it would not treat this as normal practice and take judicial notice of it.

[104] *Pullman* v. *W. Hill & Co. Ltd.* [1891] 1 QB 524.

[105] [1962] 1 WLR 151, 157–8.

contained in a letter will depend on the state of the defendant's knowledge, either proved or inferred, of the conditions likely to prevail in the place to which the libel is destined.'

The burden of proving publication rests on the claimant, but in many instances it is considerably eased by certain rebuttable presumptions of fact. An open postcard or 'telemessage', for example, is deemed to have been published to those who would normally see it in the course of transmission; spoken words are deemed to have been published to persons within earshot. Equally, if it can be shown that a letter has been properly addressed, the publication to the addressee is presumed. In the case of defamatory innuendoes the claimant must prove that the words complained of were published to a specific person or persons possessed of the special facts which enabled them to understand the innuendo.

Interdepartmental 'memos' raise interesting questions with regard to publication. In *Riddick* v. *Thames Board Mills Ltd.*,[106] the plaintiff was dismissed for incompetence with two months' salary. Then, as if he had been guilty of some misconduct, he was escorted to a waiting car by the two company officials who dismissed him, made to sit between them, and driven away. He brought an action for false imprisonment that was settled for £251. In the course of that action an interdepartmental memorandum of the *defendants* was disclosed. The document was the result of an inquiry made by R, the chief personnel manager, to his assistant, F, and composed by F on the basis of information derived from the two people who had dismissed and escorted the plaintiff. F dictated his report to his secretary and sent it to R who, having read it, filed it away. As a result of this disclosure the plaintiff brought a second action for defamation based on this report. The jury found that the two people who had dismissed the plaintiff in the first place and escorted him to the car had acted maliciously and had given a wrong account. They also found that the words in the memos, based on their account, were defamatory and awarded damages to the plaintiff. On appeal the decision was reversed. One ground on which the judges agreed was that a party (the company) disclosing a document on discovery should be entitled to the protection of the court against any use of it otherwise than in the action in which it was disclosed. However, the judges held different views on whether a report by one employee to another amounted to publication for the purposes of making the employer liable for defamation. Lord Denning MR argued that there was no publication, for the act of the employee making the report would be the act of the employer; and the act of the other employee in receiving it would also be the act of the employer. This would be, in effect, the employer making a publication to himself. Stephenson and Waller LJJ, on other hand, disagreed and held that communications between employees, usually involving communications with secretaries, had for a long time been treated as publications. However, Stephenson and Waller LJJ disagreed

[106] [1977] QB 881. A written complaint made against a police officer under s. 49 of the Police Act 1964 (now Part IX of the Police and Criminal Evidence Act 1984) could be used by a police officer to found an action in defamation against the complainant: *Conerney* v. *Jacklin* [1985] *Crim. LR* 234. But statements made in the course of the investigation of the complaint would be protected from discovery: *Hehir* v. *Commissioner of Police for the Metropolis* [1982] 1 WLR 715.

between themselves on another point: Waller LJ felt that though there was publication the company was protected by qualified privilege, while Stephenson LJ felt that the defence did not apply. The only clear *ratio* of this unsatisfactory case is that relating to the disclosure of documents.

Difficult questions can arise with regard to repetition and republication by a third party. One thing seems reasonably clear: 'It is no justification to a person, in giving currency to that which is injurious to the character of another, for him to say that he heard the statement made by another person.'[107] More difficult is the question: how far is the original publisher liable for subsequent repetitions or republications of the defamatory statement?

The starting-point must be clear: the original publisher is not liable for damage ensuing from republication of his statement if this is the voluntary act of a third party over which he has no control.[108] Where, however, he authorised the republication there is no doubt that he is liable for both the original publication and the republication;[109] and there is little doubt that the same would be true if the original publisher intended republication.[110] Even an unauthorised repetition may make the original publisher liable. This would be whenever publication was made to a person who, to the knowledge of the original publisher, was under a legal or moral duty to repeat the words to a third person;[111] and, arguably, if repetition is the natural and probable consequence of the original publication.[112] It may be otherwise, however, where there is voluntary republication by a third party. The law on this has undergone some subtle changes.

Originally, such republications were treated as being causally unconnected with the original statements. In principle, there is nothing to prevent a modern court from adopting a similar line if the facts of the particular case justify this. In general, however, it is unlikely that the original publisher will be absolved, at any rate for utterances whose repetition he had reason to anticipate. The decision of the Court of Appeal in *Slipper* v. *British Broadcasting Corporation*[113] could be taken to support this view. In that case the defendants made a film which dealt with the plaintiff's effort to get one of the great train robbers extradited from Brazil where he had sought refuge after he had escaped from an English jail. The plaintiff alleged that the film contained defamatory material about him and sued the BBC for damages that, he claimed, should take into account the fact that the reviews of the film in the national press essentially reproduced the sting of the libel. The defendants failed in their attempt to strike out the paragraph in the

107 *Watkin* v. *Hall* (1868) LR 3 QB 396, at 403, per Lush J. Cf., however, *dicta* in *Aspro Travel* v. *Owners Abroad plc* [1996] 1 WLR 132 (and the discussion below of the defence of 'truth', Section 3(c)).

108 A long line of cases starting with *Ward* v. *Weeks* (1830) 7 Bing. 211, at 215.

109 *Speight* v. *Gosnay* (1819) 60 LJQB 231 at 232 (per Lopes LJ). There may thus be two causes of action. However, the claimant may recover for both publications, even if he only sues for the first. See *Cutler* v. *McPhail* [1962] 2 QB 292, 299, per Salmond J.

110 For a beautiful illustration taken from Sheridan's *School for Scandal*, Act 1, Sc. 1, see A. M. Dugdale (ed.), *Clerk and Lindsell on Torts* (18th edn., 2000) para. 22–200, n. 46.

111 *Derry* v. *Handley* (1867) 16 LT 263, *Kendillon* v. *Maltby* (1842) Car. & M 402 at 408; 174 ER 342 per Lord Denman CJ.

112 *Speight* v. *Gosnay* (1891) 60 LJQB 231, *Ward* v. *Lewis* [1955] 1 WLR 9 (*dicta*).

113 [1991] 1 QB 283.

plaintiff's statement of claim that complained of the republication of the libel by the press. In Bingham LJ's words:

Defamatory statements are objectionable not least because of their propensity to percolate through underground channels and contaminate hidden springs. Usually, in fairness to a defendant, such effects must be discounted or ignored for lack of proof. But here, where the further publications (although not republication) are provable and are said to have been foreseeable, natural, provable and perhaps even intentional results of the publication sued upon, I see no reason in logic or policy why those effects need be ignored if the factual premises are established. Nor do I see any threat whatever to freedom of expression, which (I accept) the courts must be vigilant to protect.[114]

This analysis was taken further in *McManus* v *Beckham*.[115] In that case, while in the plaintiff's shop (where autographed memorabilia by well-known people were sold), the wife of the well-known footballer made statements to various customers about the authenticity of some of her husband's signed pictures, advising them not to buy them. The plaintiffs complained that the slanders caused damage to his business as a result of the negative press coverage that this incident received in the national press and that Mrs Beckham, known to court publicity in professional and private life must have known or foreseen that her comments would be widely reported. Mrs Beckham's attempt to strike out the plaintiff's particulars that she should have foreseen the publicity and resulting harm succeeded at first instance but was rejected by the Court of Appeal. In turning down the idea of an absolute rule that the unauthorised repetition of a defamatory statement could never be seen as the natural and probably consequence of the defendant's conduct, the learned justices argued that the question was, essentially, one of reasonable foreseeability. However, the justices were also conscious of the vagueness of this term so, instead, they strove to advocate a balance between the view that that the defendant should be liable for all the consequences set in train by his conduct and the opposing need to limit his liability to his own actions. Waller LJ formulated the test as follows:

What the law is striving to achieve in this area is a just and reasonable result by reference to the position of a reasonable person in the position of the defendant. If a defendant is actually aware (i) that what she says or does is likely to be reported, and (ii) that if she slanders someone that slander is likely to be repeated in whole or in part, there is no injustice in her being held responsible for the damage that the slander causes via that publication. I would suggest further that if a jury were to conclude that a reasonable person in the position of the defendant should have appreciated that there was a significant risk that what she said would be repeated in whole or in part in the press and that would increase the damage caused by the slander, it is not unjust that the defendant should be liable for it. Thus I would suggest a discretion along the above lines rather than by reference to 'foreseeability'.[116]

Another point is that every repetition is a fresh publication that gives rise to a fresh cause of action against each successive publisher.[117] This also holds for publication on

114 [1991] 1 QB 283, at 300.
115 [2002] 1 WLR 2982.
116 *Ibid.* at [34].
117 '*Truth*' *(NZ) Ltd.* v. *P. N. Holloway* [1960] 1 WLR 997, 1002–3.

the internet, despite counsel's forceful arguments in favour of the 'single publication' rule adopted in the United States[118] for Internet publications.[119] Thus, not only the author of an article, but the editor, printer and publisher are also liable. Moreover, even mechanical distributors, such as bookstalls, could be liable. To avoid excessive harshness, however, the law distinguishes between republication and mere dissemination. Thus, in *Vizetelly* v. *Mudie's Select Library Ltd.*,[120] the owners of a circulating library were liable for allowing people to use books which the publishers had asked them to return as they might contain libellous material. Romer LJ laid down the rule that distributors would not be liable if they proved the following points: first, that they were innocent of any knowledge of the libel contained in the work in question: second, that there was no reason for them to be aware that the work contained libellous material; third, that they were not negligent in failing to know that the work was libellous. Scrutton LJ subsequently abridged the test when he restated by asking the question: 'Ought the defendant to have known the matter was defamatory?'[121] In *Goldsmith* v. *Sperrings Ltd.*,[122] Lord Denning MR, relying on his own research, doubted the validity of the above. The fact that both parties had conducted the case on the assumption that secondary distributors can be sued (subject to the defence of innocent dissemination)

118 The main reason for the adoption of this rule in the United States appears to have been to prevent the possibility of multiple actions in different US states arising out of the same, single publication of a defamatory statement on the internet. For commentary on these aspects, see W. L. Prosser, 'Interstate Publication' (1953) 51 *Mich LR* 959; L. A. Wood, 'Cyber-Defamation and the Single Publication Rule' (2001) 81 *Boston ULR* 895; and N. Shanmuganathan, 'Liability of Online Publishers following *Gutnick*' (2002) 152 *NLJ* 1040. In Australia, see the extensive recent discussion of some of the legal and policy issues behind this debate in *Dow Jones* v. *Gutnick* [2002] HCA 56, in which the High Court declined to adopt a single publication rule. On this case see N. Shanmuganathan and L. Caddy (2003) 153 *NLJ* 383–4 and 386, and the brief discussion in ch. 23 below.

119 See *Loutchansky* v. *Times Newspapers (Nos 2, 3, 4 and 5)* [2002] EMLR 14, where the Court of Appeal upheld Gray J's adherence to the traditional rule in the context of limitation periods, seeing no reason to depart from the Court of Appeal decision in *Berezovsky* v. *Forbes (No. 1)* [1999] EMLR 278.

120 [1900] 2 QB 170.

121 *Sun Life Assurance Co. of Canada* v. *W. H. Smith & Sons Ltd.* (1934) 150 LT 211.

122 [1977] 1 WLR 478, 487. The facts were as follows. Sir James Goldsmith sued *Private Eye* and 37 of its distributors for a series of defamatory articles. Actions against some of the distributors were settled on the understanding that they would no longer sell *Private Eye*. Negotiations with the others, including the publishers and editors, continued, and the plaintiff agreed to discontinue all actions and not to impede the sales of the magazine once his terms had been accepted. The compromise negotiation failed and action against the remaining distributors continued. The question was whether this should be allowed, or whether the proceedings represented an abuse of the judicial process. For Lord Denning MR the latter was the correct view. This is partly because the learned judge refused to accept that an action lay against secondary distributors, but also because the plaintiff's predominant purpose in suing all the distributors was to shut off the channels of distribution, and this would seriously affect the notion of freedom of the press. Nor would the plaintiff derive any special benefit from such process except that it would be oppressive for the distributors. However, the majority of the Court of Appeal felt otherwise, taking the view that in an action for libel the plaintiff has a course of action against any distributor of the alleged libel. It would be a denial of justice to stay such an action at an interlocutory stage, unless there was strong evidence to show that the plaintiff's purpose in bringing these actions was not to protect and vindicate his reputation but to destroy the paper. The evidence, particularly that relating to the terms on which the plaintiff had offered to settle his dispute, made it clear that his purpose was to vindicate his reputation and prevent further anticipated attacks upon it. If in doing these things a danger resulted for the freedom of the press, then it was not the plaintiff's fault, but the result of a defect in the law which only Parliament could rectify.

was, in Lord Denning's view, irrelevant and the court should remedy the error. Scarman and Bridge LJJ, however, refused to accept this view. It was wrong for a judge to conduct his own researches, especially in interlocutory proceedings. More important, before such a view could be accepted it needed to be argued by counsel for both sides. Counsel for the defence had not been heard on this point and to decide it against him would violate the rule that both sides must be heard.

The harshness of the old rule (concerning distributors, sellers, broadcasters of live programmes and Internet operators), criticised by Lord Denning in the above case, has now been mitigated[123] by section 1 of the Defamation Act 1996.

This gives the above 'type'[124] of (possible) defendants a statutory defence if they can show that they took all reasonable care in relation to the publication of the statement complained of and did not know (nor could have known) that what they did caused or contributed to the publication of a defamatory statement.

Publication through radio or television can give rise to nice problems, as can the Internet. It is clear from the case of *Godfrey* v. *Demon Internet*[125] that Internet Service Providers (ISPs) can be held liable for the 'publication' of defamatory material, if they store that material on their servers where it is accessible to its customers. ISPs were not simply the owners of an electronic device through which information was transmitted; in so holding, Morland J preferred the analogy with cases such as *Vizetelly*, rather than with the position of a telephone company as a mere conduit for the transmission of such information.[126] The defence of section 1 of the 1996 Act was not available to Demon Internet, since the relevant libel had been drawn to their attention and yet they had not removed the message from the newsgroup until two weeks after they had learnt of the libel. It is important to note that the implementation of the EC E-Commerce Directive[127] in the United Kingdom has required certain changes to the current state of the law with regard to 'mere conduits' for the transmission of information,[128] 'caches'

[123] But see P. Milmo, 'The Defamation Bill' (1995) 145 *NLJ* 1340 and 'Fast Track or Gridlock?' (1996) 146 *NLJ* 222, arguing that in one sense at least the position of potential defendants may have become worse.

[124] The full list is provided by the statute. But 'authors', 'editors' and 'publishers' are excluded from the purview of this defence and are thus subject to the normal common law rules.

[125] [1999] 4 All ER 342.

[126] See the recent decision by the New York Court of Appeals in *Lunney* v. *Prodigy Services Company*, AD 2d 230 (1998), upheld by the Supreme Court in its decision of 1 May 2000 (see R. Chandrani, 'USA: Defamation—First Major Ruling on Defamation in Cyberspace' [2000] 11 *Ent. LR* N104). Two points should be noted: first, the New York Court of Appeals did acknowledge that ISPs who monitored their notice-boards and exercised some form of editorial control might not avail themselves of this 'conduit' argument so easily and, second, the means used to achieve this result (of no liability for the ISP) was the granting of the protection of qualified privilege to ISPs, as is also made available to telephone companies in the United States. See, further, N. Cannon, 'Internet Libel: Who is Responsible?' (2000) 150 *NLJ* 90.

[127] Directive 2000/31/EC [2000] *OJ* L178/1, which should have been implemented in the Member States by 17 Jan. 2002 (see Art. 22(1) of the Directive). Implementation in the UK was made by the Electronic Commerce (EC Directive) Regulations 2002 (SI No. 2013): see www.legislation.hmso.gov.uk/si/si2002/20022013.htm for the text.

[128] Art. 12 of Directive 2000/31/EC, which requires Member States to exempt the ISP from liability provided that the ISP does not initiate the transmission, select the recipient of the transmission, and does not select or modify the information contained in the transmission—see r. 17 of the UK Regulations.

which store information[129] and ISPs which act as 'hosts' for third parties' websites.[130] A detailed discussion of all of these instances (e-mail, bulletin boards, web pages and blogs, etc.), possible conditions (actual knowledge, negligence in failing to monitor web pages, caches, etc.) and their interrelationship with the defence in section 1 of the Defamation Act 1996 is beyond the scope of this book,[131] although it should be noted that these provisions are not limited to liability for defamation but extend to liability under rules relating to pornographic content or where others' activity using Internet intermediaries amounts to a breach of a claimant's intellectual property rights.

The tort is committed wherever the statement is heard or the programme received. The same, of course, is true of publications through newspapers, journals and the Internet. This may give the claimant a chance to choose the most convenient forum to litigate. Factors that will influence this decision will include legal costs (contingency fee system, availability of legal aid), likely measure of damages (as a general rule much higher in common-law than in civil-law jurisdictions) and the impact that the constitutional background may have on the likely success of the defamation action.[132] But simultaneous litigation in different countries is rightly discouraged; and damages awarded by the courts of one country should, it is submitted, be taken into account whenever the same statement is the subject of litigation in more than one system.

3. DEFENCES

Only the defences peculiar to defamation are discussed here; general defences which apply elsewhere as well are not included, though a brief reference will be made to 'consent'.

(A) UNINTENTIONAL DEFAMATION

It will be evident from the foregoing that at common law the fact that the maker of a statement was unaware of the circumstances making it defamatory does not absolve him from liability. Thus, in *Hulton* v. *Jones*[133] the defendants were liable for a statement

[129] Art. 13 of the Directive, which requires Member States to exempt ISPs from liability where the sole purpose of the storage of the information is to ease its efficient onward transmission. This is provided that, in particular, the ISP does not modify the information and that it acts expeditiously to remove or disable access to the stored information if it becomes aware that the source of the information has been removed from the network or that a court has ordered such removal—see r. 18 of the UK Regulations.

[130] Art. 14 of the Directive, which requires the ISP's exemption from liability for the information stored, provided that the ISP lacks actual knowledge of illegal activity or information (or facts from which this is apparent) and acts expeditiously to remove the information when such knowledge is acquired—see r. 19 of the UK Regulations.

[131] For helpful discussion in context, see M. Collins, *The Law of Defamation and the Internet* (2nd edn., 2005).

[132] E.g. in the United States the First Amendment provides preferential treatment to free speech at the expense of reputation.

[133] [1910] AC 20, especially Lord Loreburn LC at 23. Cf. the vigorous and attractive dissenting views of Fletcher-Moulton LJ in the Court of Appeal.

which they believed was about a fictitious person. In *Newstead* v. *London Express Newspapers Ltd.*[134] the rule was extended to make a defendant liable for a libel which was true of one person and honestly aimed at and intended for him, but which could reasonably be attributed to the plaintiff. Indeed one may go further and argue that if one combines these cases with *dicta* in *Morgans* v. *Odhams Press* we may have authority for the proposition that 'a person may be sued for making a true statement about X which anyone can, despite its terms, suppose to be a false statement about Y'.[135]

Cases like these added 'terror to authorship' and led to growing pressures for reform. This was attempted by section 4 of the Defamation Act 1952, which enabled a defendant to make an 'offer of amends' for an innocent defamation which, if accepted, would be the end of the dispute and, if not accepted, would provide a defence in any subsequent litigation. But the way the offer had to be made was hedged by so many qualifications[136] and technical requirements that the defence failed to assist many defendants; indeed, it appears that only one case of significance was ever decided under this section.[137] While not entirely abandoning the mould of the earlier statute, sections 2–4 of the Defamation Act 1996[138] contain many novel features which are designed to breathe new life into the defence and remove some of the harshness of the common law.

An offer of amends must be in writing, expressed to be an offer under section 2 of the 1996 Act and state whether it is qualified or not.[139] According to section 2(4):

An offer to make amends under this section is an offer—

(a) to make a suitable correction of the statement complained of and a sufficient apology to the aggrieved party,
(b) to publish the correction and apology in a manner that is reasonable and practicable in the circumstances, and
(c) to pay to the aggrieved party such compensation (if any), and such costs, as may be agreed or determined to be payable.

Two important differences from the old section 4 must be noted thus far.

First, unlike the old law, the new Act requires that the offer be accompanied by an offer of monetary compensation. This follows the views of the Neill Committee, which had rightly pointed out that it would be:

unsatisfactory that defendants should have a defence available, based on their reasonable behaviour after publication, which would leave the plaintiff with no compensation at all, in respect to hurt feelings or injury to reputation, to take account of what was ex hypothesi a defamation. Indeed, it could well be a serious defamation, and we see no overriding public interest in depriving plaintiffs of all compensation merely because the defendants have seen the error of their ways.[140]

134 [1940] 1 KB 377.

135 J. A. Weir, *A Casebook on Tort* (5th edn., 1983), 446.

136 Described in the fourth edition of this book.

137 *Ross* v. *Hopkinson, The Times*, 17 Oct. 1956.

138 These sections came into force on 28 Feb. 2000.

139 The offer may either be general (i.e. refer to the statement generally) or qualified to a specific defamatory meaning of the statement which the defendant accepts that it conveys.

140 §VII, 17.

Second, no time limit is any longer set on the making of the offer of amends. The old requirement that the offer be made promptly was thus discarded, since it was seen as imposing on potential defendants an undesirable choice of either moving too quickly, even before a proper investigation of the matter, or losing the right to invoke the defence (and thus avoiding litigation). The offer may thus be made at any time until the defendant has served a defence: section 2(5). The idea that once a defence has been served, the offer of amends procedure has, essentially, lost its *raison d'être*, can also be seen in section 4(4). This states that 'the person who made the offer need not rely on it [in the event that it is not accepted] by way of defence,[141] but if he does he may not rely on any other defence'. As a result of this arrangement, defendants may have to take some strategic decisions and decide whether to plead a defence (e.g. truth) which *if* it succeeds[142] will absolve them of all liability or go for the offer of amends which, though it may involve losing face, provides the comfort of limiting the financial consequences of their statement.

A further innovation of the new section 4 can also be seen in the consequences of the offer of amends being accepted or not. If it is, then, as with the old section 4, that will be the end of the matter and litigation will have been avoided or be brought to an end.[143] But if the offer *is not accepted*,[144] then the offer of amends will provide a defence to defamation proceedings subject to section 4(3) of the Act. But the new section 4(3) represents an improvement in the position of the defendant for, unlike the old regime, *he* is no longer obliged to prove that his words were published 'innocently', the burden now falling on the claimant to show that the person who made the offer (i.e. the defendant)

> *knew or had reason to believe* that the statement complained of—
>
> (a) referred to the aggrieved party or was likely to be understood as referring to him, and
> (b) was both false and defamatory of that party; but it shall be presumed until the contrary is shown that he did not know and had no reason to believe that was the case.

Indeed, the defendant's position might be further improved depending upon how the italicised words of section 4(3) are interpreted. For, if the words are understood to be equated with recklessness, the defence will have a greater chance of surviving than if it is enough for the claimant to prove that the defendant failed to take reasonable care. The determination of this fell to be decided by the case of *Milne* v. *Express Newspapers*[145] which produced interesting judgments at first instance by Eady J (who had been a member of the Neill Committee which paved the way for the enactment of the 1966

141 But even if he does not rely on it as a defence he may use it in mitigation of damages: s. 4(5).

142 And if it fails, land them with substantial costs.

143 As against the person who made the offer. Thus, if the defamatory statement is contained in a book, an offer of amends made by the printer and accepted by the claimant will prevent him from proceeding against the printer but not against the author.

144 The words are italicised in order to stress the fact that the requirements set out in s. 4(3) are only taken into account in cases where the offer is refused. It is irrelevant that the offeror does not satisfy these requirements if his offer is accepted.

145 [2003] 1 WLR 927.

Act) and the Court of Appeal. At first instance, Eady J concluded that mere proof that the defendant had been negligent would not deprive him of the defence. He thus noted:

> The main purpose of the statutory regime [of 1996] is to provide an exit route for journalists who have made a mistake and are willing to put their hands up and make amends. In the absence of agreement, the offer of amends also signifies a willingness to place oneself *in the hands of the court for assessing the appropriate steps to be taken by way of vindication and compensation*. It would thus make no sense at all to interpret the wording to mean that journalists would be deprived of the defence if they had been negligent....[146]

The italicised words lead us naturally to the last issue to be discussed under this heading: the assessment of damages after the acceptance of the offer. For the making of the offer is not the end of the story as far as the claimant is concerned. The judgment that went a long way towards clarifying these issues was, again, delivered by Eady J this time in the case of *Abu* v. *MGN Ltd.*[147] The governing provision is, in this respect, section 3(5) of the 1996 Act which begins by stating that 'if the parties do not agree on the amount to be paid by way of compensation, it shall be determined by the court on the same principles as damages in defamation proceedings.' As Eady J observed in the *Abu* v. *MGN Ltd* litigation:

> The principles to be applied, whether in the course of libel proceedings or without action having been brought, must be taken as intended to be precisely the same as on any assessment of damages in such proceedings. Those principles take account of such issues as mitigation, aggravation and causation of loss.[148]

Defendants will thus be free in raising an allegation of general bad reputation, to offer evidence that some element of damage has been caused by factors other than the libel complained of and, to the extent that the damages are 'at large' invite the court to take the broad circumstances into account. Reading the full judgment thus makes it clear that there it would be wrong to assume that damages awarded under this procedure cannot be significant or that going doing the 'offer of amends' path will, in all cases, lead to a cheap or speedy resolution of the dispute.

(B) CONSENT

Consent is a general defence, in no way peculiar to the tort of defamation, and little need be said about it. Perhaps one example will suffice. In *Chapman* v. *Lord Ellesmere*[149] a horse-trainer was allowed by the stewards of the Jockey Club to train horses and his licence was subject to a number of conditions. One of these was that his licence might be withdrawn by the stewards—acting at their absolute discretion—and such withdrawal (or suspension) might be published in the *Racing Calendar*, the recognised

[146] [2003] 1 WLR 927, at para. 41, approved by the Court of Appeal in [2005] 1 WLR 772.
[147] [2003] 1 WLR 2201.
[148] *Ibid*. at [13].
[149] [1932] 2 KB 431, *Tadd* v. *Eastwood* [1985] ICR 132.

organ of the Jockey Club, for any reason which might seem proper to them. At a subsequent race, a horse was found doped and was thus disqualified. This decision, as well as 'a warning' to its trainer, was published in the *Racing Calendar* and by *The Times*. The statement was held to involve a defamatory innuendo about the trainer, but its publication in the *Racing Calendar* was not actionable because the plaintiff had consented to publication of the steward's decision in *that* journal. The fact that it was published in such a way as to carry a defamatory innuendo was a risk which the trainer, by consenting to a report of the decision being published, had elected to run. However, publication in *The Times* was without his consent and, as the law then stood,[150] was not covered by privilege; so it was actionable.

(C) JUSTIFICATION OR TRUTH

A peculiarity of the English (but not American) common law, which favours the claimant,[151] is that *he* does not have to prove that the statement complained of was false. If he proves that the allegations against him are defamatory then they will be *presumed* to be untrue. The burden is thus on the defendant to prove that the allegations are true. On the strength of Commonwealth authority,[152] there is no duty in negligence[153] to take care *not* to publish injurious statements which are *true*.

One ludicrous side effect of this rule is that a claimant may leave court with substantial compensation, but with his name not necessarily cleared. For this award does not necessarily imply that what the defendant said of him was false, but only that he (the defendant) failed to prove that it was true. A second and more general drawback is that it may inhibit free speech. For, as Lord Keith (among others) has observed: '[q]uite often the facts which would justify a defamatory publication are known to be true, but admissible evidence capable of proving those facts is not available'.[154]

Truth is a defence because 'the law will not permit a man to recover damages in respect of an injury to a character which he either does not, or ought not to possess'.[155] The defendant must establish the truth of the precise charge that has been made, which is ultimately a matter of interpretation of the facts. Repeating a rumour will not amount to justification, even if it is honestly believed. 'If you repeat a rumour you cannot say it is true by proving that the rumour in fact existed; you have to prove that the subject matter of the rumour is true.'[156]

150 The publication might now be covered by s. 7 and Part II of the Sch. to the Defamation Act 1952.

151 Less so now than in the past. See the concluding comments to the defamation section of this chapter.

152 *Bell-Booth Group Ltd.* v. *AG* [1989] 3 NZLR 148.

153 Though the tort of Negligence has penetrated the tort of defamation where *untrue* statements are concerned, made in the context of a negligently prepared reference: see *Spring* v. *Guardian Assurance plc* [1994] 3 All ER 129. See also the comments below concerning *Reynolds* v. *Times Newspapers* [2001] 2 AC 127 and qualified privilege relating to false statements.

154 *Derbyshire County Council* v. *Times Newspapers Ltd.* [1993] 1 All ER 1011, 1018.

155 *McPherson* v. *Daniels* (1829) 10 B & C 263, 272; 109 ER 448, 451 per Littledale J.

156 *Cookson* v. *Harewood* [1932] 2 KB 478 at 485, per Greer LJ, approved by Lord Devlin in *Lewis* v. *Daily Telegraph* [1964] AC 234 at 283–4. See *Stern* v. *Piper* [1996] 3 WLR 715 (containing an exhaustive discussion of

In *Wakley* v. *Cooke and Healey*[157] the defendants called the plaintiff a 'libellous journalist' and proved that he had once been convicted of such a charge. The court took the view that these words did not mean 'that the plaintiff has been guilty, upon one occasion only, of having published a libel, but that he had been guilty of gross misconduct as a journalist, by the habit of libelling others'. The defence of truth accordingly failed. The Court of Appeal has also held[158] that the defendant may plead justification to any meaning of the published statement which a jury, properly directed, might reasonably find to be the real meaning of the words complained of and thus is not restricted to justifying the meaning pleaded by the plaintiff. The defendant must, however, plead his justification with sufficient particularity to enable the claimant to know precisely what case he has to meet.[159]

At common law, where a statement contained more than one charge and only part of the libel was justified, the defendant had to pay damages in respect of the part not justified.[160] That rule of partial justification has now been extended by section 5 of the Defamation Act, which provides that:

> In an action for libel or slander in respect of words containing two or more distinct charges against the plaintiff, a defence of justification shall not fail by reason only that the truth of every charge is not proved if the words not proved to be true do not materially injure the plaintiff's reputation having regard to the truth of the remaining charges.

Where the words complained of are not severable, or contain only one charge, the position is more complicated. Suppose, for example, that the defendant accuses the claimant of rape, whereas in fact he had been convicted only of indecent assault.

the so-called 'repetition rule') and, for the latest restatement and application of this rule, see *Shah* v. *Standard Chartered Bank* [1998] 3 WLR 592, esp. at 610. It was thought possible that *Thoma* v. *Luxembourg* (ECtHR, 29 Mar. 2001 (Application no. 00038432/97), unreported) would require a reassessment of the repetition rule (see the doubts of Eady J in *Lukowiak* v. *Unidad Editorial* [2001] EMLR 1043, [58]), but the UK courts have rejected the argument that there is any inconsistency between the rule and the Convention: see, most recently, *Mark* v. *Associated Newspapers (No. 1)* [2002] EMLR 38, [33]–[35] (per Simon Brown LJ). The Court of Appeal in *Mark* distinguished between the repetition rule (and its concern for establishing the *meaning* of the words in question) and the application of qualified privilege (where the precise terms and circumstances of the repetition come into play), holding that *Thoma* and Art. 10 ECHR are relevant to the question of privilege only, not to the meaning of the words used. This interpretation tends to lend support to the view (adopted below in Section 3(e)(ii)) that the courts will seek to use *Reynolds* privilege increasingly widely in the coming years, as a response to claims that *prima facie* liability in defamation restricts freedom of expression disproportionately, by stressing the availability of defences such as qualified privilege.

157 (1849) 4 Exch. 511, 517; 154 ER 1316, 1318.

158 *Prager* v. *Times Newspapers Ltd.* [1988] 1 WLR 77. If the words complained of are capable of a wider meaning than that pleaded by the claimant, the defendant is allowed to attempt to justify the words in that wider meaning. (The judgments of Purchas and Nicholl LJJ contain interesting pronouncements on justification.) See *Williams* v. *Reason* [1988] 1 WLR 96. (Evidence that the plaintiff, an amateur rugby player, had received 'boot money' (from Adidas, the manufacturers of sports equipment) was relevant to justifying the wider charge of 'amateurism'.)

159 *Lucas-Box* v. *News Group Newspapers Ltd.* [1986] 1 WLR 147, *Prager* v. *Times Newspapers Ltd.* [1988] 1 WLR 77. The claimant, too, is under a similar obligation to be specific in his pleadings when the meaning of the words complained of is not clear.

160 *Clarke* v. *Taylor* (1836) 2 Bing. NC 654, 665; 132 ER 252, 256, per Tindall CJ.

Section 5 of the Defamation Act would clearly not avail the defendant. It would, however, be unfair to allow the claimant to recover damages as if he had not been convicted of any offence involving indecency at all. [161]

It is for the defendant who wishes to rely on this statutory defence to raise it and the judge is under no obligation, when dealing with a defence of justification, to draw the jury's attention to section 5.[162]

If a statement carries a defamatory innuendo the defendant must prove the truth of this in order to escape liability.[163] Statements to the effect that the claimant had committed a criminal offence used to create a difficulty because a conviction in the criminal trial was not *prima facie* evidence for the purposes of the civil action so that guilt had to be proved over again. Section 13(2)(A)[164] of the Civil Evidence Act 1968 has now altered the position so that, in an action in which it is necessary to establish whether the *claimant* did or did not commit a criminal offence, proof of a previous conviction is conclusive evidence that he did commit the crime in question.

One difference between justification and the two defences that follow used to be that even malice on a defendant's part did not deprive him of the defence of truth. This is no longer wholly true. For a modification has been introduced by the Rehabilitation of Offenders Act 1974, which provides that after certain periods of time, depending on the length of sentences imposed on offenders, their convictions are to be treated as 'spent' and, therefore, as if they had not occurred. Section 8(3), however, adds that in actions for defamation based on imputations of such offences, justification shall continue to be a defence by proof of the convictions except where 'the publication is proved to have been made with malice'. However, whether this rebuttal of the defence requires proof of spite or includes other improper motives has not been decided.

(D) FAIR COMMENT

This defence stems from the belief that honest and fair criticism is indispensable in every freedom-loving society. The law weighs the interest of the claimant against freedom of speech and, on the whole, comes down in favour of the latter. It is for the judge to rule whether the matter is one of public interest[165] and for the jury (ultimately) to

[161] Another difficulty arises whenever there are several defamatory allegations but all contain a 'common sting'. In such cases it will be enough to justify the sting: *Khashoggi* v. *IPC Magazines Ltd.* [1986] 1 WLR 1412, *Polly Peck* v. *Trelford* [1986] QB 1000.

[162] *Moore* v. *News of the World Ltd.* [1972] 1 QB 441.

[163] For a recent review of the vital link between the precise meaning of the words of which the claimant complains and the operation of defences such as justification and fair comment, see the Court of Appeal's decision in *Cruise* v. *Express Newspapers* [1999] QB 931.

[164] Inserted by s. 12(1) of the 1996 Defamation Act.

[165] *Telnikoff* v. *Matusevitch* [1990] 3 WLR 725, 730; [1992] 2 AC 343, 354–7, 363. Likewise, in the context of the defence of qualified privilege it is the judge who decides whether the occasion is privileged.

decide whether the statement is one of fact or is an opinion and, if the latter, whether it is honest and fair. The requirements of this frequently invoked defence are as follows:

(i) Public Interest

The comment must refer to matters of public interest. In *London Artists Ltd.* v. *Littler*[166] Lord Denning MR said: 'Whenever a matter is such as to affect people at large, so that they may be legitimately interested in, or concerned at, what is going on; or what may happen to them or to others; then it is a matter of public interest on which everyone is entitled to make fair comment.' The reference to 'people at large' should not be taken to suggest that if the statement complained of refers to one person or a few persons only it can never be of public interest. Thus, in *South Hetton Coal Co.* v. *North-Eastern News Association Ltd.*,[167] a colliery company owned most of the cottages in a certain village. The defendant published a long article describing some of the cottages owned by the plaintiff company as being, for the most part, unfit for habitation owing to a complete lack of decent sanitation, inadequate accommodation and want of sufficient water supply. It was held that the condition of these cottages was a matter of public interest, which would have given the defendants a defence, but that they had gone beyond the limits of fair and *bona fide* comment. Here the public was legitimately *concerned*.

In *London Artists* v. *Littler* the public was legitimately *interested*.[168] The defendant, an impresario, wrote and published at a press conference a letter suggesting that the plaintiff organisers in the entertainment business had taken part in what appeared to be a plot to force the end of a successful play, which the defendant was producing, by arranging for four leading players to give identical notices to leave. This was likely to stop the play. The defendant's letter was written after he had received the players' notices simultaneously as well as a notice from the theatre-owners that they were planning to transfer another play to the theatre that he himself had rented from them. In the ensuing action for libel the defendant pleaded, *inter alia*, fair comment, but the trial judge held that the plea failed as the matter was not one of public interest. The defendant's appeal was dismissed, but on a different ground. His comments were, undoubtedly, on a matter of public *interest*, but 'fair comment', as we shall see, presupposes correct basic facts on which the comments and inferences are based.[169] In the present case one of the basic facts which the defendant had failed to prove was the existence of a plot between the plaintiffs to put an end to his play.

Matters of government, national or local, management of public and religious institutions, the conduct of foreign policy, etc. can obviously be brought under the heading of 'public interest'. Even the private behaviour of, for example, the Prime Minister or other ministers may fairly be commented on if this sheds light on matters of honesty and integrity, which are qualities of holders of public office. On the other hand, it has been held that the management by a parish clergyman of a charitable society is not

166 [1969] 2 QB 375, 391.
167 [1894] 1 QB 133.
168 [1969] 2 QB 375.
169 On which see Lord Denning, *ibid.*, 391.

necessarily the subject of public comment, so as to excuse the publication of injurious matter regarding the clergyman in relation to the charity.[170]

(ii) True Facts

The comment must be an opinion on true facts. There is, however, one instance where facts, though untrue, can be the subject of opinion and protected as fair comment. This is whenever the facts themselves, though untrue, are protected by privilege. Thus: 'If a statement made by a witness is fairly and accurately reported, and attributed to the witness who made it, then, no doubt, although the evidence given by the witness is afterwards shown to be false, the statement reported can be made the subject of fair comment.'[171]

The importance of ensuring that the facts are true can be seen from *London Artists Ltd.* v. *Littler*,[172] where, although the comment was in the public interest, the defence failed because the defendant could not prove the correctness of the underlying facts. These were that the theatre-owners (plaintiffs) wanted to get the defendant's play out of their theatre, that all the leading stars gave notice simultaneously and that there was a plot between the owners and the actors to end the play. The first and second were proved, but not the last. There was some argument whether the allegation of a plot was a fact or a comment and the court took the view that, on balance, it was a fact. Even if this allegation were treated as comment, it would arguably not have helped the defendant since there were not enough facts to lead an honest man to have made such a comment.[173] Obviously the distinction is not clear-cut, as the next case demonstrates.

In *Dakhyl* v. *Labouchere*,[174] the plaintiff described himself as a 'specialist for the treatment of deafness, ear, nose and throat diseases' and the defendant described him as 'a quack of the rankest species'. Was this a comment (as the court was inclined to believe) or a statement of fact? Further, to say that A failed his examinations is an allegation of fact; to say that he is a fool because he failed is a comment on the fact. And what of a statement that the claimant is a 'sinner' or an 'immoral' person? There is no obvious answer to such questions; and in all cases it must depend on the facts which may, in appropriate circumstances, be gleaned from all the surrounding circumstances and not just discovered in the document complained of.[175]

Two qualifications should be added to what has been said. First, it is not always essential that:

the facts upon which the comment is based should themselves be stated in the alleged libel. The question is whether there is a sufficient substratum of facts stated or indicated in the

170 *Gathercole* v. *Miall* (1846) 15 M & W 319; 153 ER 872.

171 *Grech* v. *Odhams Press Ltd.* [1958] 2 QB 275, 287, per Jenkins LJ. See also *Mangena* v. *Wright* [1909] 2 KB 958, 977, per Phillimore J. It is for the defendant to prove that the statement was made on a privileged occasion and that his report of it was fair and accurate: *Brent Walker Group plc* v. *Time Out Ltd.* [1991] 2 QB 772.

172 [1969] 2 QB 375.

173 On which see Lord Denning MR's observations *ibid.* at 392–3.

174 [1908] 2 KB 325; cf. *Smiths Newspapers* v. *Becker* (1932) 47 CLR 279.

175 In *Telnikoff* v. *Matusevitch* [1990] 3 WLR 725, 731, the Court of Appeal had, it is submitted more convincingly, taken the view that the facts should be gleaned from all the relevant surrounding circumstances. But

words which are the subject matter of the action and whether the facts or subject matter on which comment is made, are indicated with sufficient clarity to justify comment being made. The substratum of fact, facts, or subject matter may be indicated impliedly in the circumstances of the publication.[176]

In *Kemsley* v. *Foot*,[177] for example, the defendant published an article referring to one of the Beaverbrook newspapers and described it as 'lower than Kemsley' (Lord Kemsley being the owner of another group of papers). Was this an allegation of fact (in which case justification would be the right defence) or an expression of opinion? If the defendant states what some public man has done and then says that it is disgraceful, this is an expression of an opinion. But if he asserts that the claimant has been guilty of disgraceful conduct, and does not state what the conduct was, this is an allegation of fact. The same is true if he states an inference without the facts on which it is based, unless, as in this case, the basic facts are indicated in the words complained of. The House of Lords took the view that the defence of fair comment was available, given that the conduct of the Kemsley Press was the fact on which the comment was made.[178]

Second, according to section 6 of the Defamation Act: 'In an action for libel or slander in respect of words consisting partly of allegations of fact and partly of expression of opinion, a defence of fair comment shall not fail by reason only that the truth of every allegation of fact is not proved if the expression of opinion is fair comment having regard to such facts alleged or referred to in the words complained of as are proved.'

From the above it will be clear that 'fair comment' differs from 'justification' in that it is directed to expressions of opinion, whereas justification applies to fact. In fair comment, the defendant must prove that the opinion was honestly held, whereas in justification honest belief is irrelevant. The two defences are, therefore, different and should be pleaded in the alternative.

(iii) Fairness

The comment must be fair: it is crucial that a jury could hold that it is one that an honest-minded person could make on the facts. However, it is not for the jury to substitute its own judgement as to what is fair. 'The question which the jury must consider', said Lord Esher in *Merivale* v. *Carson*,[179] 'is this—would any *fair man*, however prejudiced

this part of its judgment was reversed by the House of Lords: [1992] 2 AC 343 (Lord Ackner dissenting). The result in that case was that the decision whether the defendant's reply to a previously published article by the plaintiff in the same newspaper was fact or comment should be decided by looking at his letter alone and ignoring the earlier article. The final decision unduly restricts the defence of fair comment. It also produces the strange result that if the defendant pleads (as he had) fair comment as a defence, his reply will be read in isolation. But if he also pleads justification, his reply will be looked at in conjunction with the earlier piece that prompted his letter. This hair-splitting does not, it is submitted, inspire much confidence in the law! The decision is criticised by A. Mullis, 'Tort' [1991] *All ER Rev.* 390–1.

176 W. V. H. Rogers (ed.), *Winfield and Jolowicz on Tort* (12th edn., 1984), 326. See now the 17th edn. (2006), 555 (para. 12–32).

177 [1952] AC 345.

178 Provided, of course, that the jury felt that this was the type of comment an honest man might make.

179 (1888) 20 QBD 275, 281 (italics supplied): the test is objective—how the words would be understood, not how they were intended. Applied in *Cornwell* v. *Myskow* [1987] 1 WLR 630. The same case held that if

he may be, however exaggerated or obstinate his views, have said that which this criticism has said?'[180] Lord Denning MR appeared to put it more subjectively. For he said: '[n]o matter that it was badly expressed so that other people read all sorts of innuendoes into it; nevertheless, he has a good defence of fair comment. His honesty is the cardinal test.'[181] The ambiguity seemed to have been settled by the Court of Appeal in *Telnikoff* v. *Matusevitch*.[182] For the court took the view (and, in this context was approved by the House of Lords) that fairness is to be judged objectively (as defined in section (*c*), above), so that once the defendant has demonstrated this, then his comment will be presumed to be honest unless and until the *claimant* can then prove that it was motivated by malice.[183] However, the comments of Lord Nicholls in *Reynolds* v. *Times Newspapers*[184] seem to have reopened the matter:

> the time has come to recognise that in this context the epithet 'fair' is now meaningless and misleading. Comment must be relevant to the facts to which it is addressed. It cannot be used as a cloak for mere invective. But... [t]he true test is whether the opinion, however exaggerated, obstinate or prejudiced, was honestly held by the person expressing it....

As Eady J noted in *Branson* v. *Bower (No. 2)*,[185] if fair comment is indeed a defence which promotes freedom of expression, and if such freedom is necessary even for the protection of unreasonable opinions, then it seems inappropriate to use phrases such as 'reasonable' and 'fair' to test the comment's suitability for protection.

The position may be different if the defendant attributes bad motives to the claimant rather than merely criticising his work. *Campbell* v. *Spottiswoode*[186] held that it was actionable to suggest, however honestly, that Dr Campbell, the editor of a religious magazine, in advocating a scheme for missions to the heathen was an impostor and that his alleged aim of propagating the gospel was 'a mere pretext for puffing his obscure magazine'.

This approach, which is not without support from earlier authority,[187] implies that imputations of base or dishonourable motives can *never* be protected by fair comment. Other cases, however, can suggest that in these cases the test of fair comment is

justification is not pleaded by the defendant, evidence of the plaintiff's actual reputation at the date of the trial is irrelevant and should not be considered by the jury.

180 The italicised words can cause some difficulties. For can a 'fair' man be obstinate and prejudiced? Many have thus argued that the defence should simply be called 'comment', the word 'fair', being dropped from the heading.

181 *Slim* v. *Daily Telegraph Ltd.* [1968] 2 QB 157, 170.

182 [1990] 3 WLR 725, 741.

183 As pointed out in P. Milmo *et al.* (eds.), *Gatley on Libel and Slander* (10th edn., 2005), para. 12.22, the result of this analysis seems to be 'asking the jury, "(1) Has the defendant satisfied you that an honest person could have made this statement? (2) If yes, has the claimant satisfied you that the defendant was dishonest (*i.e.* not expressing his real opinion)?" which might be thought likely to confuse'.

184 [2001] 2 AC 127, 193, citing Diplock J's judgment in *Silkin* v. *Beaverbrook Newspapers* [1958] 1 WLR 743, 747. It should be noted, however, that Lord Nicholls made no reference (in his *dicta* on the issue of fair comment) to the *Telnikoff* cases, so, at present, there is some uncertainty about the precise position as a matter of precedent.

185 [2002] 2 WLR 452 ([17]–[20] of the judgment).

186 (1863) 3 B & S 769, esp. at 776–7: 122 ER 288, 290–1, per Cockburn CJ: 'A man has no right to impute to another, whose conduct may be fairly open to ridicule or disapprobation, base, sordid and wicked motives, unless there is so much ground for the imputation that a jury shall find, not only that he had an honest belief in the truth of his statements, but that his belief was not without foundation.'

187 E.g. *Hunt* v. *The Star Newspaper Co. Ltd.* [1908] 2 KB 309, 320, per Fletcher-Moulton LJ.

available, but applied more strictly, in that the writer's opinion must not only be honestly held, but must also be a reasonable inference from the facts.[188] It is doubtful, however, whether this 'reasonableness' test is workable in practice and is compatible with the general purpose of fair comment. Nowadays, therefore, it may be true to say that even imputations concerning motives are governed by the ordinary test and constitute fair comment when put forward as the expression of opinion. There is some authority for this,[189] especially if the test is the 'objective' one propounded by Lord Esher MR in *Merivale* v. *Carson*.[190]

(iv) Absence of Malice

The defence will be defeated by the claimant proving that the statement was made with malice which, in this instance, was always equated with evil motive or spite. In *Thomas* v. *Bradbury, Agnew & Co. Ltd.*[191] the Court of Appeal held that a book reviewer[192] for *Punch* was hostilely motivated against the plaintiff's books, which was evident not only by the review he wrote but also by his behaviour in the witness box. His malice negated a plea of fairness. However, the recent ruling in *Branson* v. *Bower (No. 2)*[193] suggests that, to defeat the defence of fair comment, the claimant must show that 'the defendant did not genuinely believe the opinion he expressed'.[194] This is a more restricted test for malice than that applied in qualified privilege cases, effectively removing the 'improper motive' limb from consideration in fair comment cases. The justification for this shift has been explained in terms of freedom of expression: 'Commentators, of all shades of opinion are entitled to 'have their own agenda... The defence of fair comment envisages that everyone is at liberty to conduct social and political campaigns by expressing his own views, subject always... to the objective safeguards which mark the limits of the defence.'[195] In the light of these recent developments concerning the 'fairness' of the comment and the requirements for showing malice, it has been suggested that this defence is now better regarded as one of 'honest comment on a matter of public interest'.[196]

(E) PRIVILEGE

There are two kinds of privilege: *absolute*, which is limited in scope but affords complete protection; and *qualified*, which is wider in its ambit but can be defeated by malice. The first category represents the triumph of speech rights over reputation.

[188] Buckley LJ in *Peter Walker & Sons Ltd.* v. *Hodgson* [1909] 1 KB 239, 253.

[189] *Broadway Approvals Ltd.* v. *Odhams Press Ltd. (No. 2)* [1965] 1 WLR 805. See, most recently, Eady J's acceptance in *Branson* v. *Bower (No. 2)* [2002] 2 WLR 452 (at [22]) that there is no special rule for these cases.

[190] (1888) 20 QBD 275, 281. [191] [1906] 2 KB 627.

[192] The writer's malice may not, however, infect the publisher who, in such cases, will be allowed to plead the defence: *Lyon* v. *Daily Telegraph* [1943] KB 746.

[193] [2002] 2 WLR 452 (esp. [7] and [23]–[28]), applying the principles laid down by Lord Nicholls sitting in the Hong Kong Court of Final Appeal in *Cheng* v. *Tse Wai Chun* [2000] 3 HKLRD 418.

[194] *Cheng* v. *Tse Wai Chun* [2000] 3 HKLRD 418, 438, per Lord Nicholls. [195] *Ibid.*, 430.

[196] See D. R. Howarth and J. A. O'Sullivan, *Hepple, Howarth, Matthews' Tort: Cases and Materials* (5th edn., 2000), 964.

(i) Absolute Privilege

Freedom of speech is so important on certain *occasions* that complete immunity is accorded to the maker of a statement, even if it is untrue and he was motivated by malice. Every communication on such occasions is protected. The occasions may be divided into three broad categories: parliamentary, judicial and executive.

(a) Parliamentary Privilege (1) Statements made in Parliament. Article 9 of the Bill of Rights 1688 states that

> the freedom of speech and debates or proceedings in Parliament ought not to be impeached or questioned in any court or place out of Parliament.[197]

For centuries Parliament was, of course, taken to refer to the national parliament housed at the Palace of Westminster. The devolution of powers however, that took place in the late 1990s in the United Kingdom, created legislatures in Scotland, Wales and Northern Ireland, each with a slightly different range of powers to act. Provision thus had to be made for similar privilege for the Scottish Parliament and the Welsh and Northern Irish Assemblies.[198] One limiting factor is that such privilege for these legislatures has only been granted 'for the purposes of the law of defamation', raising questions about liability for malicious falsehood after statements made in the regional assemblies

In *Church of Scientology of California* v. *Johnson-Smith*[199] it was held that a plaintiff cannot even use statements in Parliament to show malice so as to defeat fair comment on statements made outside Parliament. Similar privilege extends to petitions to Parliament[200] and letters written *by* MPs to the Speaker[201] but not, it seems, letters written *to* MPs.[202]

Until recently, the effect of Article 9 of the Bill of Rights was that an MP's right to sue could be affected as much as the right to be sued for something he had said in Parliament. This problem came to a head when an MP brought a defamation against the *Guardian*.[203] The action was stayed by the court because the newspaper's wish to plead justification by reference to things said by the MP in the course of Parliamentary proceedings was prohibited by Article 9 of the Bill of Rights. The considerable debate that surrounded this issue[204] centred mainly on the idea that the purpose of the Bill of Rights was to prevent MPs being sued for opinions expressed during Parliamentary proceedings, not from vindicating their own rights as claimants. So, in the end, the Defamation Act 1996,[205] while reaffirming the traditional immunity (s. 13(4)), in

[197] On this see P. Milmo *et al.* (eds.), *Gatley on Libel and Slander* (10th edn., 2005), para. 13.28.

[198] See s. 41 of the Scotland Act 1998, s. 77 of the Government of Wales Act 1998 and s. 50 of the Northern Ireland Act 1998 for details.

[199] [1972] 1 QB 522.

[200] *Lake* v. *King* (1668) 1 Wms. Saund. 120; 85 ER 128.

[201] *Rost* v. *Edwards* [1990] 2 QB 460.

[202] *Rivlin* v. *Bilainkin* [1953] 1 QB 485.

[203] *Hamilton* v. *Guardian, The Times*, 22 July 1995. See, also, *Allason* v. *Haines* [1995] EMLR 143.

[204] See, for instance, HL Debs., vol. 572, cols. 24–52 (7 May 1996). An account of this incident, from the newspaper's angle (with some interesting insights as to how s. 13(1) of the Defamation Act 1996 came about), can be found in D. Leigh and E. Vulliamy, *Sleaze: The Corruption of Parliament* (1997).

[205] An excellent illustration of the well-known principle that in English law a 'constitutional enactment' can be amended by ordinary legislation.

section 13(1), also gives MPs the right to waive Article 9 so that proceedings in Parliament can be used in evidence in court. Ironically, after the law was changed in the way described in the text the two MPs withdrew their libel actions!

(2) Reports, papers, proceedings, etc. ordered to be published by Parliament.[206]

(b) Judicial Privileges (1) Statements by a judge, jury, advocates or witnesses in any judicial or quasi-judicial proceedings.[207] As Fry LJ explained: 'It is not a desire to prevent actions from being brought in cases where they ought to be maintained that has led to the adoption of the present rule of law; but it is the fear that if the rule were otherwise, numerous actions would be brought against persons who were merely discharging their duty.'[208] Judicial proceedings means proceedings before any superior or inferior court, including county court, bankruptcy registrar, magistrate, professional disciplinary committees[209] or tribunals exercising functions equivalent to those of an established court of justice,[210] so long as certain criteria are satisfied.[211]

(2) Communications between solicitor and client relating to judicial proceedings. The privilege is far-reaching and can even cover communications between (opposing) solicitors (when one makes a defamatory statement about the other's client) provided they have an 'immediate link' with possible legal or quasi-legal proceedings.[212] Communications that are not related to judicial proceedings are also privileged, though it is uncertain whether this is of the absolute or qualified variety.[213]

(3) Fair and accurate newspaper reports of judicial proceedings publicly heard before any court specified by section 14(3) of the Defamation Act 1996,[214] provided they are published *contemporaneously* with such proceedings. This privilege is now unequivocally treated as absolute, though qualified privilege would have served just as well.[215]

(4) Fair and accurate reports of proceedings at a public meeting under section 7 of and paragraph 9 of the Schedule of the Defamation Act 1952. This is another of those

[206] Parliamentary Papers Act 1840, ss. 1 and 2.

[207] *Royal Aquarium and Summer and Winter Garden Society Ltd.* v. *Parkinson* [1892] 1 QB 431, 451, per Lopes LJ.

[208] *Munster* v. *Lamb* (1883) 11 QBD 588, 607. Cf. *Rondel* v. *Worsley* [1969] 1 AC 191, 269, per Lord Pearce.

[209] E.g. *Addis* v. *Crocker* [1961] 1 QB 11.

[210] *O'Connor* v. *Waldron* [1935] AC 76, 81, per Lord Atkin. Evidence given at official conciliation proceedings does not attract absolute privilege: *Tadd* v. *Eastwood* [1985] ICR 132 (CA).

[211] What these criteria are is not entirely clear, and there is ample authority on what has to be considered under this heading. See *Shell Co. of Australia Ltd.* v. *Federal Commissioner of Taxation* [1931] AC 275, *Lincoln* v. *Daniels* [1962] 1 QB 237. Communications with the European Commission may attract absolute privilege: *Hasselblad (GB) Ltd.* v. *Orbinson* [1985] 2 WLR 1 and this even though the procedure adopted by the Commission to investigate complaints is more administrative than judicial in nature. Licensing justices, however, have not been included. See *Attwood* v. *Chapman* [1914] 3 KB 275.

[212] Which the Court of Appeal thought did *not* exist in *Waple* v. *Surrey* [1998] 1 WLR 860. The court there stressed that one 'should be slow to extend the scope of this privilege'. See at 864–5 (per Brooke LJ).

[213] *More* v. *Weaver* [1928] 2 KB 520 (absolute); cf. *Minter* v. *Priest* [1930] AC 558 (which left the matter open). The communication must be fairly referable to the relationship of solicitor and client.

[214] They include any court in the UK, the European Court of Justice (or any court attached to that Court), the European Court of Human Rights and any international criminal tribunal established by the UN Security Council or by an international agreement to which the UK is a party. See, also, Courts and Legal Services Act 1990, s. 69(2).

[215] Indeed, qualified privilege may still apply if the statutory requirements have not been fulfilled.

variations on the theme of public hearings—earlier for instance we referred to court proceedings—where a person's conduct is somehow mischaracterised or criticised. Any newspaper report of these would, at common law, amount to an actionable republication. The provision in question makes sure that such publications, if carried out in a 'fair and accurate manner' are not actionable. The question here is what does 'public meetings' mean? In *McCartan Turkington Breen (A Firm)* v. *Times Newspapers Ltd*[216] the House of Lords had the occasion to make some useful clarifications.

In that case the plaintiffs were a Northern Irish firm of solicitors who had represented an English serviceman who had been convicted of serious criminal offences allegedly committed while he was serving in Northern Ireland. An informal committee was formed to secure the release of the convicted serviceman and, to this end, the held a press conference at the home of one of the committee members. Invitations were sent out to the Press to attend and, indeed, others were present (though not by invitation). Attendance was in no way restricted not any attempt was made to check the identity or the credentials of those attending. The defendants published a story about the meeting along with parts of a press release making critical references of the plaintiff's. In an action for defamation they invoked the qualified privilege defence of section 7 and the prime question to be decided was the meeting one that could properly be described as a 'public meeting'. The High Court and the Court of Appeal thought that it was not. In the subsequent successful appeal to the House of Lords, Lord Bingham gave a number of reasons why he disagreed with this result, key among which is the following sentences:

> The object [of the meeting] was to stimulate public pressure to rectify what the committee as promoters of the conference saw as a grave miscarriage of justice, and publicity was the essence of the exercise. A general invitation to attend was issued to the press. While the attendance of other members of the public was not solicited, not was admission denied to anyone . . . Both journalists and other members of the public in fact attended in significant numbers.[217]

In the instant case, therefore, the press was not probing but reporting an event: 'in a very literal sense, [it was acting] as a medium of communication'. The meeting was public because those who organised it had manifested their desire that the proceedings of their meeting be communicated to the wider public. The defence invoked under the statute was thus valid.

The significance of the decision lies not so much in its definition of what amounts to a 'public meeting' but in that it shows that the statutory defence of privilege can be wider than that of the common law defence of qualified privilege (which we shall consider below). For the latter will succeed only if the defendant can demonstrate that he took all reasonable steps to verify his story whereas in the case of the statutorily based defence all that has to be shown was that that the report of what occurred was 'fair and accurate'.

216 [2001] 2 AC 277. 217 *Ibid.*, at [5].

(c) Executive Privileges. The key issue concerns statements made by one officer of the state to another in the course of duty.[218] In *M. Isaacs & Sons Ltd. v. Cook,*[219] it was made clear that it does not make any difference if the report in question is related to commercial matters. There is some doubt, however, about the scope of this privilege; in particular, how high-ranking the official has to be in order to claim immunity.[220]

(ii) Qualified Privilege

Qualified privilege becomes a live issue only where a statement is found to defamatory and untrue. This defence, known in US law as 'conditional privilege', resembles fair comment, in that it, as well, can be defeated by malice. However, it differs from *absolute* privilege in that here it is the communication that contains the statement complained of that is privileged, not the entire occasion on which the statement was made. In cases of absolute (unlike qualified) privilege no investigation is allowed into the communicator's conduct or attitude. Instances of this privilege, which may be very widely invoked, may be grouped under four traditional headings ((a) to (d), below) which will be examined seriatim. To these four heading, one must now add a new one, created by the important decision of the House of Lords in *Reynolds* v. *Times Newspapers* [221] and which concerns publications in the mass media. Though it helps present the rich material in this 'structured' manner, it must be made clear that these subdivisions do not represent watertight compartments. However, they do share one characteristic—that is, they exist for 'the common convenience and welfare of society',[222] or as another judge put it:

> It was in the public interest that the rules of our law relating to . . . privilege communications were introduced because it is in the public interest that persons should be allowed to speak freely on occasions when it is their duty to speak, and to tell all they know or believe, or on occasions when it is necessary to speak in the protection of some (self or) common interest.[223]

The four (traditional) headings have one thing in common. For the defence of privilege to succeed there had to be a legal, moral or social duty to make the statement *and* an interest in receiving it. 'This reciprocity is essential.'[224] The defendant has to

[218] *Chatterton* v. *Secretary of State for India* [1895] 2 QB 189. A different kind of privilege is the privilege against production of a document. In this case the claimant is not claiming protection against a possible defamation action but is attempting to prevent the publication of a confidential (usually official) document on which an action of defamation might be based. The matter is best discussed in books on evidence, though one may remind the reader that since *Conway* v. *Rimmer* [1968] AC 910 the courts have clearly asserted their right to override ministerial objections and ask to inspect the relevant documents. This right, however, is sparingly exercised. See *Air Canada* v. *Secretary of State for Trade* [1983] 2 AC 394.

[219] [1925] 2 KB 391.

[220] Compare *Merricks* v. *Nott-Bower* [1965] 1 QB 57, and *Richards* v. *Naum* [1967] 1 QB 620. In *Fayed* v. *Al-Tajir* [1988] QB 712 internal documents of a foreign embassy were treated as attracting absolute privilege. The Vienna Convention on Diplomatic Relations may have played an important part in the outcome of this case.

[221] [1999] 4 All ER 609; [2001] 2 AC 127.

[222] *Toogood* v. *Spyring* [1834] 1 CM & R 181, 193; 149 ER 1044, 1049–50 per Parke B. It is for the judge to decide whether the occasion is privileged and the communication was made with reference to that occasion.

[223] *Gerhold* v. *Baker* [1918] WN 368 at 369, per Bankes LJ. For a similar approach see *Henwood* v. *Harrison* (1872) LR 7 CP 606 at 622, per Willes J.

[224] *Adam* v. *Ward* [1917] AC 309 at 334, per Lord Atkinson.

establish the facts necessary to create the privilege; but whether the situation is one that attracts qualified privilege is for the judge to determine. As stated, this privilege will be lost if the claimant shows that the defendant was motivated by malice; and this will be the final sub-heading of this section as it applies to all types of qualified privilege. Finally, the jury will have the last word on whether the defendant acted in good faith. In short, all of the defamation protagonists (claimant, defendant, judge and jury) may have a role to play in this defence.

The following five sub-headings deal with more specific situations in which qualified privilege has been found to exist.

(a) Matters of Public Interest. These included fair and accurate reports of Parliamentary proceedings. At common law this was finally settled in 1868 in *Wason* v. *Walter* [225] and is justified by the idea that the advantages of such publicity outweigh the possible injury to the claimant's reputation. However, as Lord Denning said in *Associated Newspaper Ltd.* v. *Dingle*,[226] if the newspaper 'adds its own spice and prints a story to the same effect as the parliamentary paper, and garnishes and embellishes it with circumstantial detail, it goes beyond the privilege and becomes subject to the general law'. Privilege will also be granted to a sketch of parliamentary proceedings 'if it is made fairly and honestly with the intention of giving an impression of the impact made on the hearer'.[227]

The Parliamentary Papers Act 1840, section 3, as extended by section 9(1) of the Defamation Act 1952, confers a similar privilege on *extracts* or *abstracts* of reports or proceedings, etc., published by order of either House of Parliament.

Qualified privilege is also enjoyed by 'fair and accurate'[228] reports of judicial proceedings that the public may attend. Though this includes the proceedings of *any* court, the proceeding must be in public. No privilege extends to publication of obscene or prohibited matter. As regards proceedings in foreign courts, these, under the current regime, are privileged only so far as their matter is of legitimate interest to the public in *this* country.[229] Qualified privilege may also protect people making statements to the proper authorities in order to procure the redress of public grievances. Finally, section 7 of the Defamation Act 1952 affords qualified privilege to numerous kinds of reports in newspapers and broadcasts of public meetings provided they were not made with malice. This section and the Schedule to the Act distinguish between statements privileged without any explanation or contradiction and statements privileged subject to explanation or contradiction. In the latter group the defence will be lost if it is shown that the defendant failed to publish in an appropriate manner any letter or statement offered by the claimant by way of explanation or contradiction of the remarks made by the defendant.

225 (1868) LR 4 QB 73.

226 [1964] AC 371, 411.

227 *Cook* v. *Alexander* [1974] QB 279, 288, per Lord Denning MR.

228 The fairness and accuracy of the report are matters to be decided by the jury; the judge should decide this issue only in the most obvious of cases: *Kingshott* v. *Associated Kent Newspapers Ltd.* [1991] 1 QB 88.

229 *Webb* v. *Times Publishing Co. Ltd.* [1960] 2 QB 535.

The above (mixed, i.e. common law and statutory) regime, though not explicitly abrogated, has in practice been overtaken by the regime in the Defamation Act 1996 (especially Sch. 1). A detailed consideration (and comparison) of the wording of the lengthy (1952 and 1996) Schedules would not be appropriate to this book.[230] Still, one must note that the new regime, though it builds on the old scheme of things, also represents a rationalisation of it. Thus, first, section 14 of the 1996 Act, as we have seen, accords *absolute* privilege to fair and accurate reports before a court to which this section applies (i.e. mainly the UK courts and the two European Courts in Luxembourg and Strasbourg), if published contemporaneously with the proceedings. Second, qualified privilege is granted by Schedule 1 to the 1996 Act to fair and accurate reports of proceedings in public of a legislature or court *anywhere in the world.* Thus, these reports need not be contemporaneous with the proceedings, nor are they limited to legislatures or courts 'in one of Her Majesty's dominions outside Great Britain' (as was the case with the 1952 Act). Nor, finally, is the statutory privilege under the 1996 Act limited (as it was under the old regime) to publications in newspapers and broadcasts. But, as is the case with the regime which the 1996 Act replaces,[231] the reports must be fair and accurate (though this does not mean that they must be verbatim); and the protection of the Schedule does not cover the publication of material prohibited by law.

(b) Matters of Interest to the Publisher. In *Turner* v. *Metro-Goldwyn-Mayer Pictures Ltd.* [232] Lord Oaksey said:

> There is ... an analogy between the criminal law of self-defence and a man's right to defend himself against written or verbal attacks. In both cases he is entitled, if he can, to defend himself effectively, and he only loses the protection of the law if he goes beyond defence and proceeds to offence. That is to say, the circumstances in which he defends himself, either by acts or by words, negative the malice, which the law draws from violent acts or defamatory words.

Thus, brewers who answered a complaint by a publican of poor-quality beer supplied to him by voicing a suspicion that he had watered it were covered by privilege.[233] In such cases not only is the business communication itself treated as being privileged, but also the incidents of the transmission and treatment of that communication, which are in accordance with the reasonable and usual course of business. This includes dictation to a secretary or typist.[234]

(c) Matters of Interest to Others. Common examples of the privilege under this heading are found in character references given by former employees to prospective employers.[235] This heading is not free of difficulties. For example, though it will be easy for a judge to

230 For details, see P. Milmo *et al.* (eds.), *Gatley on Libel and Slander* (10th edn., 2005), chs. 14 and 15.

231 It should be noted that the new Act does not expressly abrogate any existing privileges (see s. 15(4)(b)) but simply makes most of them redundant in practice.

232 [1950] 1 All ER 449, 470–1.

233 *Osborn* v. *Boulter* [1930] 2 KB 226.

234 See *ibid.* and *Bryanston Finance* v. *de Vries* [1975] QB 703, below.

235 The rich casuistry is considered in P. Milmo *et al.* (eds.), *Gatley on Libel and Slander* (10th edn., 2005), ch. 14.

decide when there is a *legal* duty to communicate the defamatory matter, it may be less easy to decide if or when the defendant has a *moral* or *social* duty. Lindley LJ thought that 'the question of moral or social duty' is for 'each judge to decide as best he can for himself'.[236] But Scrutton LJ wondered whether in so doing a judge should merely 'give his own view of moral and social duty', or should 'endeavour to ascertain what view 'the great mass of right minded men' would take'.[237] Perhaps a compromise between these two would be the right answer.

The limitation on this category of qualified privilege is illustrated by *Watt* v. *Longsdon*.[238] A director of a company informed the chairman of his suspicion that the plaintiff, an employee, was misbehaving with women; and he also informed the plaintiff's wife. It was held that communication to the chairman was privileged, but not to the wife, for although she had an interest in hearing about the allegation, he had no moral or social duty to inform her.

This part of the law of defamation, though still valid, must be constantly scrutinised against the expansion of the tort of negligence following the decision in *Spring* v. *Guardian Assurance plc*.[239] For though their Lordships were anxious to emphasise that the two torts occupy different ground and cater for different interests, the new possibility of suing the referee in negligence may well overtake current practice.

(d) Common Interest. Qualified privilege also applies in cases where two parties have an interest in a statement about the claimant other than those falling under any of the above categories. Thus, it has been held that an employer and his employees have a common interest in the reason for the dismissal of an employee.[240] So, too, in *Watt* v. *Longsdon* the communication to the chairman of the company was privileged because both publisher and receiver had a common interest in the matter.

Is the dictation of a letter to a secretary covered by original privilege arising out of the dictation of the business letter? Or is it an ancillary privilege dependent upon whether privilege covers communication to the intended recipient? Lord Denning MR in *Bryanston Finance Ltd.* v. *de Vries*[241] thought that it is an original privilege because of the common interest in getting the letter written. This means that communications to secretaries do not depend upon whether or not the publication to the ultimate recipient of the letter would have been privileged. The converse is true if one accepts Lawton LJ's view[242] that the privilege is ancillary and depends upon whether the communication to the recipient was privileged or not. This second view does not exclude instances of common interest between employer and secretary so as to render such dictation privileged *per se*. Nowadays a great number of matters connected with the survival and

236 *Stuart* v. *Bell* [1891] 2 QB 341.

237 *Watt* v. *Longsdon* [1930] 1 KB 130, 144. But in the case of newspaper publications 'public interest and public benefit are necessary . . . but not enough without more. There must be a duty to publish to the public at large and an interest in the public at large to receive the publication': per Stephenson LJ in *Blackshaw* v. *Lord* [1983] 3 WLR 283, 301.

238 [1930] 1 KB 130.

239 [1995] 2 AC 296.

240 *Hunt* v. *Great Northern Railway Co.* [1891] 2 QB 189.

241 [1975] QB 703, 719.

242 *Ibid.*, 736–8.

prosperity of the business will be a matter for mutual concern for both employer and employee and in such cases all relevant communications will be privileged.

This, in fact, was a major issue in *Bryanston Finance* v. *de Vries*. The defendant and a colleague, who were involved in litigation over financial matters with a loan bank and its chairman, prepared a circular and letters accusing the chairman of the plaintiff company of various improprieties. They also threatened to send these documents to: (*a*) the shareholders of the plaintiff; (*b*) the Department of Trade and Industry; (*c*) the Stock Exchange; and (*d*) various other organisations, including the national press, unless they reached a favourable settlement. Upon receipt of the letter and documents the chairman obtained an injunction to restrain their publication to the above-mentioned bodies and then sued for libel. So far there had been publication only to the secretary, which the defendant claimed was privileged. The issue was whether it was original privilege or depended upon communication to the recipients being privileged. If the second view is taken to be the common denominator of all three judgments, one would say that communication to the shareholders, the Department of Trade and the Stock Exchange would be privileged because of common interest, but communication to the press would not be so.

Watts v. *Times Newspapers*[243] recently highlighted a different difficulty. If a person makes a defamatory statement about X he may, as we saw, be led to publish an apology. This, indeed, was the situation in *Watts*, where the defendant newspaper published two pieces concerning plagiarism by X, but to the second piece attached a photograph of Y (who had the same name as X). The paper agreed to publish a (neutral) apology. Unfortunately, it ended by publishing an apology which was largely drafted by Y's solicitor and which again made reference to the plagiarism by X. X then sued the newspaper for the contents of the apology and the paper, in its turn, added Y's solicitor (the draftsman of the text) as a third party. Y's position (and that of his solicitor) was deemed to be covered by privilege since he was, essentially, responding to an attack made on him. But the paper itself did not share in the privilege. This was because it was the paper that had defamed Y and could thus not be seen to be taking advantage of his self-defence. But the court also held that the paper could not plead privilege (for the communication prepared by Y) since a simple, unembellished apology (without the references to X) would have been perfectly sufficient. The case thus suggests that though in some cases the defence of privilege may be available where an apology to A actually refers to B this will not always be so.[244]

(*e*) *Journalistic Privilege: The* Reynolds *Breakthrough*.[245] The defence of qualified privilege, as described above, was in practice of little use to the mass media for in most cases that concerned them the publication was made not to a particular person but to the

243 [1996] 2 WLR 427.

244 This problem does not arise when the apology is made in open court, for then it is covered by absolute privilege.

245 Sometimes referred to as 'responsible journalism privilege'.

world at large.[246] The media were thus 'agitating' for a generic type of privilege that would discard the 'reciprocal duty/interest' test. The publication by the *Sunday Times* in the mid-1990s of a shortened version of a story concerning the Irish Prime Minister Mr Albert Reynolds, who had recently resigned from his office, was destined to bring this issue to the fore.

The story concerned allegations that Mr Reynolds had misled the Irish Parliament on a particular issue. The version of the story published in Ireland had included an account of Mr Reynolds's version of events, while the UK version had omitted his explanation. Mr Reynolds sued in defamation and one of the defences pleaded was qualified privilege. Thus, the question facing the courts was whether publication to the world at large satisfied the 'duty/interest' test and could thus attract qualified privilege. It would, if it was in the public interest that the matter should be made public.[247] In the Court of Appeal[248] it was held that:

> the common convenience and welfare of society in a modern, British democracy, required the ample dissemination to the public of information concerning, and vigorous discussion of matters relating to the public life of the community and to those who participated in it.[249]

This suggested a clearer commitment to the value of free expression, especially in relation to 'public life'. However, whether this is, indeed, the end result of the case depends upon a more detailed analysis of the judgments. The quick answer is a 'qualified yes'.

In order to move in this direction, so close one is tempted to say to the learned justice's overall philosophy (as evidenced by his judgments in this area of the law), Lord Bingham developed a third limb to the restricting reciprocal 'interest/duty' test discussed above. He called it the 'circumstantial test'. According to this test, the court must also ask itself the following question. Were the nature, *status* and source of the material, and the circumstances of the publication, such that the publication should in the public interest be protected in the absence of proof of express malice?

'Status' in this respect denoted 'the degree to which information on a matter of public concern may (because of its character and known provenance) command respect.' He continued:

> The higher the status of a report, the more likely it is to meet the circumstantial test. Conversely, unverified information from unidentified and unofficial sources may have little or no status. So, where defamatory statements of fact are to be published to the widest audience on the strength of such sources, the publisher undertakes a heavy burden in showing that the publication is 'fairly' warranted by any reasonable occasion or exigency.

246 The decision of the Court of Appeal in *Blackshaw* v. *Lord* [1984] QB 1, as discussed by Brooke LJ in *Loutchansky* v. *Times Newspapers Ltd*. [2001] 3 WLR 404, showed how 'discouraging' it was to newspapers contemplating the possibility of relying upon it.

247 While earlier cases had recognised this possibility of publication to the world at large attracting qualified privilege, it should be noted that its scope had been strictly confined. See Stephenson LJ in *Blackshaw* v. *Lord* [1984] QB 1, at 27: '[t]here may be extreme cases where the urgency of communicating a warning is so great, or the source of the information so reliable, that publication of suspicion or speculation is justified; for example, where there is danger to the public from a suspected terrorist or the distribution of contaminated food or drugs . . .'.

248 [2001] 2 AC 127, esp. 167 ff. 249 *Ibid*., 176.

It was for this reason that the defendant newspaper's plea of qualified privilege failed on this occasion. Privilege should be accorded to such communications because: 'It is in the general interest of society that correct information should be obtained as to the character of persons in whom others have a legitimate interest.'[250] It follows that an inquiry about a person out of curiosity will not clothe the answer with privilege.[251] Communications made to the inquirer subsequent to the first reply—perhaps correcting or amplifying the contents of the latter in the light of new information available to the maker of the statement—will also be covered by the privilege.[252] This reasoning has attracted some criticism.[253]

Some thus suggest that the focus on status and source of the material to be published carries the danger of skewing the qualified privilege defence in favour of protecting certain types of information and of deserting others. For, if the source were neither identified[254] nor official then it would be unlikely to be held to be sufficiently authoritative to attract qualified privilege. Thus, the New Zealand Court of Appeal has stated that 'in the marketplace of ideas it seems... invidious and dangerous to make judgments that free speech is not served except by those with special knowledge'.[255]

It might also be argued that the reference to obtaining 'correct' information is too restrictive. It is clear that there already exists a defence of fair comment on public-interest matters, so long as such comment is based on facts which are true. Surely, the key area in the balance between freedom of expression and the protection of reputation in these circumstances concerns 'false defamatory statements of fact, and comment thereon, on matters of public interest'.[256] The Court of Appeal's test in *Reynolds* might thus seem inclined to protect such false statements only where their source is authoritative.[257]

Whatever the imperfections of the ruling in the Court of Appeal, the fact is that the 'ball was set rolling'. It is thus not surprising that when the case moved to the House of Lords the starting-point was, again, the importance of freedom of expression, both 'to disseminate and to receive information on political matters'. Lord Steyn could not have been more emphatic:

The starting point is now freedom of expression, a right based on a constitutional or higher legal foundation. Exceptions to freedom of expression must be justified as being necessary.

250 *Whiteley* v. *Adams* (1863) 15 CB (NS) 392; 143 ER 838 (per Erle CJ).

251 See, for instance, Hamilton LJ's *dicta* in *Greenlands* v. *Wilmshurst* [1913] 3 KB 507 at 541.

252 *Gardner* v. *Slade* (1849) 18 LJQB 334 at 336, per Lord Denman CJ and per Coleridge J.

253 See, e.g., I. Loveland, *Political Libels: A Comparative Study* (Select Bibliography), 165–9.

254 Itself raising questions often dealt with under s. 10 of the Contempt of Court Act 1981 concerning a journalist's right not to reveal his sources, except in 'exceptional circumstances', such as 'in the interests of justice': see, most recently, *Ashworth Hospital Authority* v. *MGN* [2001] 1 WLR 515 (CA) and [2002] 1 WLR 2033 (HL), dealing with issues under Art. 10 ECHR.

255 *Lange* v. *Atkinson* [1998] 3 NZLR 424, at 434.

256 J. G. Fleming, *The Law of Torts* (9th edn., 1998), 629–30.

257 In dismissing the arguments of the *Sunday Times*, one of the important planks of Lord Bingham's reasoning was that the source of the information was a relatively junior aide of Mr Spring (Reynolds' coalition partner in the government at the time): 'a member of the staff of one of Mr. Reynolds's leading political opponents could scarcely be judged an authoritative source for so serious a factual allegation' ([2001] 2 AC 127, at 179). It should, however, be pointed out that this was only one of the considerations upon which his

In other words, freedom of expression is the rule and regulation of speech the exception requiring justification.[258]

In a *tour de force* opinion Lord Nicholls took the same position when he argued that:

the court should [above all] have particular regard to the importance of freedom of expression.... The court should be slow to conclude that a publication was not in the public interest and, therefore, the public had no right to know, especially when the information is in the field of political discussion. Any lingering doubts should be resolved in favour of publication....[259]

On the other hand, care was taken to stress that '[r]eputation is an integral and important part of the dignity of the individual... Protection of reputation is conducive to the public good.'[260] Lord Nicholls, with whose speech Lord Cooke and Lord Hobhouse expressed their 'full agreement', rejected the Court of Appeal's development of a separate, 'circumstantial test'. Instead, in his view, 'these factors are to be taken into account in determining whether the duty–interest test is satisfied'.[261] The learned Law Lord then provided the following *non-exhaustive* list of relevant circumstances:

1. the seriousness of the allegation. The more serious the charge, the more the public is misinformed and the individual harmed if the allegation is not true; 2. the nature of the information, and the extent to which the subject matter is a matter of public concern; 3. the source of the information. Some informants have no direct knowledge of the events. Some have their own axes to grind, or are being paid for their stories (presumably if sources are being paid this will increase the risk that the information is not accurate—although this point was not elaborated); 4. the steps taken to verify the information; 5. the status of the information. The allegation may already have been the subject of an investigation which commands respect; 6. the urgency of the matter. News is often a perishable commodity; 7. whether comment was sought from the defendant. He may have information others did not possess or have not disclosed. An approach to the defendant will not always be necessary. The requirement that a comment is sought was not however to be elevated into a rigid rule of law to be followed in every case; 8. whether the article contained the gist of the claimant's side of the story; 9. the tone of the article (a newspaper can raise queries or call for an investigation. It need not adopt allegations as statements of fact); 10. the circumstances of publication, including the timing.[262]

The determination of whether a particular statement attracts qualified privilege is thus conducted on a case-by-case basis by the judge, taking these factors into account. *Reynolds* may not have marked out a category of 'political information' which will always attract qualified privilege. Nor was the view adopted that freedom of expression should, in all cases, unhesitatingly prevail. Some commentators may have been disappointed with the result.[263] Yet striving to balance the two competing rights namely, that of the press to publish the statement and that of politicians to safeguard their reputation, is consistent with the values always adopted in this country and, indeed, those legal

judgment was based: others included the paper's failure to record Reynolds' version of events and to contact Reynolds for observations on the highly damaging statements made in the article (*ibid.*).

258 *Ibid.*, at p. 208A.

259 *Ibid.*, at 205.

260 *Ibid.*, at 201, per Lord Nicholls.

261 *Ibid.*, at 195.

262 *Ibid.*, at 205.

263 Loveland, *Political Libels* (Select Bibliography), 173.

systems which have not gone down the American path of protecting one human value at the expense of all others. The Nicholls 'balancing' approach thus represents a broader application of qualified privilege to claims to publish matters in the public interest to the world at large;[264] and it looked as if it would be easier to establish when it concerned statements regarding the political arena. If the privilege is held to exist, the jury must then determine whether or not the defendant acted in good faith. The result, as Lord Phillips subsequently said,[265] was the development of a new '*sui generis*' defence, albeit built on 'an orthodox foundation.'

In making this balance, a key question (which was not given a completely clear answer by the *Reynolds* decision) was the *standard* of conduct which the publisher would have to satisfy to be able to claim a defence of qualified privilege. This fell—to some extent—to be decided by the next decision namely, *Loutchansky* v. *Times Newspapers (Nos. 2, 3, 4 and 5).*[266]

In that prolonged dispute the essence of a number of consolidated claims was that the defendants had libelled the plaintiff by accusing him of money-laundering. The former never even invoked the defence of truth but, instead, squarely based their case on qualified privilege: the matters concerned, they argued, were of great importance so they had a duty to publish them while the general public had an interest to know. Though the judge at first instance held that the defence of qualified privilege did not succeed he, nonetheless, gave leave to appeal on the grounds that the case raised the important issue 'namely what standards the courts should apply when deciding whether there was a duty to publish defamatory words to the world at large'.

Drawing largely on a dictum of Lord Nicholls in *Reynolds*,[267] the Court of Appeal held that the standard is that of the 'responsible journalist'. This standard should be set neither too low (for fear of encouraging 'too great a readiness to publish defamatory matter') nor too high (as this 'would deter newspapers from discharging their proper function of keeping the public informed'). There is a clear recognition in the *Loutchansky (Nos. 2, 3, 4 and 5)* judgment that (some) factual inaccuracy of such statements may be tolerated, particularly due to the likely deterrent effect that a harsher line might have on future publications of truthful information.

A further difficulty may be that the line has been blurred between finding the existence of the privilege and deciding whether the defendant was actuated by malice. This was the basis of Lord Hope's dissent in *Reynolds* itself and is underlined by the judgment of the Court of Appeal in *Loutchansky* v. *Times Newspapers (Nos. 2, 3, 4 and 5)*, since the publisher's conduct is clearly relevant to establishing the existence of the privilege. Once that has been assessed and found not to exclude the privilege,

> [i]t is a little difficult to see how the same enquiries which objectively sustained the occasion as privileged would be capable of contributing to a conclusion that subjectively she was recklessly indifferent to the truth or falsity of her publication.[268]

[264] See Lord Phillips MR in *Loutchanksy* v. *Times Newspapers (Nos. 2, 3, 4 and 5)* [2002] 2 WLR 640, [31] and [32].

[265] *Ibid.*, at para. 32.

[266] *Ibid.*, [35]–[41].

[267] *Reynolds* v. *Times Newspapers* [2001] 2 AC 127, at 202.

[268] *GKR Karate (UK) Ltd.* v. *Yorkshire Post Ltd.* [2001] 1 WLR 2571, at 2580. See further *Loutchansky* v. *Times Newspapers (Nos 2, 3, 4 and 5)* [2002] EMLR 14, [33] and [34].

This has at least two interesting consequences.

First, it will be for the defendant to show that its conduct has satisfied the standard of 'responsible journalism' so as to rely upon the privilege (whereas it is the claimant who must prove malice). Second, it will be for the judge to weigh these competing factors in deciding upon the existence of the privilege (whereas it is for the jury to decide, as a matter of fact, whether or not malice is present). Again, depending upon one's wider ideological views, this could be criticised for placing excessive hurdles in the way of free expression and making the availability of the qualified privilege defence unpredictable, with all of the 'chilling effect' upon free expression that this could entail. Alternatively, it might be argued that these burdens upon the press to satisfy a reasonable standard avoid encouraging irresponsible journalism and ensure that the quality of the information which is put into circulation is of a high standard.

The post-*Reynolds* cases show, in our view, that, in theory, our courts were conscious of the need to liberalise the defence of privilege without encouraging irresponsible journalism. This last point is evident in the decision in the prolonged *Grobbelaar*[269] litigation.

It will be recalled that the *Grobbelaar* case arose after the Sun accused in an unrestrained manner the well-known footballer for 'fixing' games. The trial of the case held after the publication of the Court of Appeal decision in *Reynolds* (but before the House of Lords judgment was handed down) refused to accept the newspaper's plea of qualified privilege. The paper's appeal was dismissed, in no small measure because the publication campaign against the claimant was 'massive and relentless' and the 'language used... in the highest degree emotive'.[270]

The *Grobbelaar* case illustrates many things: first, how 'the absurd reversal of the normal burden of proof encourages claimants to sue even when they know that what the defendant said was perfectly correct'.[271] Second, how unwise it is to try to set aside a jury verdict. Third, how the Nicholls test in *Reynolds* might begin to work in practice. Finally, how judges can do justice by reducing unmerited awards to nothing.

Whatever the intentions of the inventor of the *Reynolds* test, the extent of innovation and liberalisation that it contained made it likely to receive an uneven start. The *Grobbelaar* case may show an understandable dislike for irresponsible journalism; but there was also the danger that first instance judges might see Lord Nicholls's tests not as 'pointers which might be more or less indicative... [but] as a series of hurdles to be negotiated by a publisher before he could successfully rely on qualified privilege'.[272] This case law was thus in need for an early corrective and it came in the form of the *Jameel* case, to which we must now turn our attention.

269 *Grobbelaar* v. *News Group Newspaper Ltd.* [2002] 1 WLR 3024.

270 [2001] 2 All ER 437, [34]–[37] (per Simon Brown LJ). Interestingly enough, however, there was no disapproval of unsavoury techniques used to obtain the evidence against Mr Grobbelaar. Surprisingly, however, the Court of Appeal quashed the jury verdict in favour of the plaintiff only to see its own decision quashed. But the plaintiff's success was Pyrrhic for his damages were reduced to £1 on the grounds that 'his reputation as a sportsman ha[d] been destroyed by his corrupt dealing. To award him anything more would be an affront to sport, public justice and public policy' [2002] 1 WLR 3024, at [36] (per Lord Steyn).

271 J. A. Weir, *Tort Law* (2002), at p. 168.

272 *Jameel (Mohamed) and another* v. *Wall Street Journal Europe Sprl* [2006] 3 WLR 642 (henceforth referred to as *Jameel*), [33]; noted by J. H. Rowbottom, 'Libel and the Public Interest' [2007] *CLJ* 8.

Jameel involved a publication in the reputable *Wall Street Journal*—the European sister of the New York-based paper—a few months after the attack on the Twin Towers of New York on September 11th, 2001. The horrific event, the realisation that a majority of the suicide bombers were of Saudi Arabian origin, the public outcry in reaction against this new, indiscriminate, and devastating form of terrorism were such that the USA Regulatory Authorities resolved to survey international financial transactions which might involve the transfer of large amounts of money to sources sympathetic to world terrorism. Such activities were clearly covert; and they also attracted much interest and support world-wide. The public at large was certainly (legitimately) interested to know which of the Arab countries supported these measures.

The litigation in the instant case arose as a result of a story carried on the front page of the said newspaper written by a responsible journalist specialising in these issues and reporting that the accounts of the claimant and one of the companies of which he was president and general manager was thus being secretly monitored. The extent to which the journalist who wrote the story verified his story (before publishing it) proved less extensive than he had originally claimed. Likewise, an attempt made by him to seek the reactions of Mr Jameel prior to publication of the story also appeared to be ineffective, if not left for the last minute. On the other hand their Lordships were also eager to point out that, given the nature of this surveillance (if, indeed, it existed) Mr Jameel would not have been aware of it nor could he have reacted meaningfully to the news contained in the imminent publication.[273] The jury at first instance found the story to be defamatory, the trial judge (Eady J) refused to apply the *Reynolds* test, largely on the grounds that the publishers had failed to delay the publication of their story long enough for the respondents to reply, and the Court of Appeal rejected (albeit on narrow grounds) the appeal against Eady J's judgment. The House of Lords reversed the Court of Appeal, revisited their *Reynolds* test, castigated (in varying degrees) the practice followed by the courts of first instance up that point, and arguably differed as to the full consequences of their decision in *Jameel*. For all these reasons this is a seminal judgment for this part of the law. Here we shall limit our observations to three points.

First, all of the judges in the *Jameel* case were eager to stress that the Nicholls tests (given above) were not tests, certainly not hurdles, that should all be surmounted one by one but simply a list 'of ten non-exhaustive matters which should in suitable cases be taken into account'.[274] Treating them as hurdles, as Eady J had done,[275] gave the impression that *Reynolds* had changed nothing and this was patently wrong.

Second, the view of the trial judge that the failure to give the claimant an adequate chance to rebut the points made against him—assuming, which in this case was

[273] This is true for if Mr Jameel did not know that he was under surveillance he could not have reacted meaningfully to the (prime) allegation that his accounts were being monitored. On the other hand, he could have reacted to the underlying allegation that he was involved in financing terrorism; and, in that sense, it may have been somewhat facile on the part of their lordships to dismiss the paper's failure to contact him on the ground that there was nothing meaningful he could have said. This is a fine but not insignificant point that was missed, presumably in the 'excitement' to establish the journalistic freedom to investigate and publish.

[274] *Jameel* [2006] 3 WLR 642, per Lord Hoffmann at [56].

[275] The trial judge came in for some very severe criticism from Lord Hoffmann. Thus, see *ibid.* his [55] and [56].

impossible, that he could meaningfully do this—was not fatal in this case.[276] The assessment whether the story was in the public interest should be made by the judge looking at it as a whole. It would in principle be left to editorial judgement to decide whether a defamatory statement was allowed to enter the story though, again in principle, 'the more serious the allegation, the more important it is that it should make a real contribution to the public interest element of the article'.[277] In Lord Bingham's words, it was 'a very narrow ground on which to deny the [*Reynolds*] privilege'. Lord Hoffmann put it in even stronger terms when he said:

In the present case, the inclusion of the names of large and respectable Saudi businesses was an important part of the story. It showed that co-operation with the United States Treasury's requests was not confined to a few companies on the fringe of Saudi society but extended to companies which were by any test within the heartland of the Saudi business world. To convey this message, inclusion of the names was necessary. Generalisations such as 'prominent Saudi companies', which can mean anything or nothing, would not have served the same purpose.[278]

Finally, there was some disagreement (though its extent is not obvious, because the participating judges chose to remain cryptically silent whenever they disagreed with the brother judges) which concerns the full consequences of this judgment for the future (given that as far as the facts of this case in particular all judges felt that the *Reynolds* privilege justified the quashing of the judgment of the Court of Appeal). To some extent this may be linked to whether one sees *Jameel* (reading *Reynolds*) as a 'development of qualified privilege based on the requirement of a reciprocal duty and interest between the publisher and the recipient of the statement in question'[279] or seeing it, as Lord Hoffmann did, as 'a different jurisprudential creature from the traditional form of privilege from which it sprang'.[280] For him this meant that not only one should recognise this by giving the defence a new name—he opted for 'the *Reynolds* public interest defence'; but also accepting that in future one would not have to enquire whether there was a duty to communicate information and an interest to receive it but merely to begin by satisfying itself that the disputed material presented a public interest. If that were satisfied then the inquiry would shift 'to whether the steps taken to gather and publish the information were responsible and fair'.[281]

It might be unwise to hazard a guess whether this turns out to be a battle over semantics or not. But one can see the greater potential that Lord Hoffmann is giving to his reading of the *Reynolds* case, in particular if one rereads the *Reynolds* judgements where the participating Law Lords do not appear to have rejected the duty/interest approach.[282]

(f) Qualified Privilege Is Defeated by Malice. Malice, a term which can be misleading, should not be taken to mean only spite or wish to inflict harm for its own sake.[283] Lack

[276] *Ibid.*, per Lord Bingham at [35]. [277] *Ibid.*, per Lord Hoffmann at [51]. [278] *Ibid.*, at [52].

[279] *Ibid.*, per Lord Bingham at [29]–[30]. [280] *Ibid.*, at [46].

[281] *Ibid.*, at [53]. On this inquiry, see most recently *Roberts* v. *Gable* [2007] EWCA Civ 721, which develops the application of the *Reynolds* approach to Cases of 'reportage', in the context of political infighting and allegations within the British National Party in London.

[282] [2001] 2 AC 127. Thus, see Lord Nicholls, at 194–5, 197, 204; Lord Steyn, at 213; Lord Cooke of Thorndon, at 217, 224, 227; Lord Hope of Craighead, at 229, 235; Lord Hobhouse of Woodborough, at 237, 239.

[283] The discussion above concerning malice in the defence of fair comment, clarifying that proving malice in fair comment relates only to honesty of belief, not to motivations: as Lord Nicholls explained in *Cheng* v. *Tse*

of honest belief in his statement will deprive a defamer of his defence, provided, of course, that he acted intentionally or recklessly when publishing the defamatory matter. As Lord Diplock said in *Horrocks* v. *Lowe*,[284] despite the imperfection of the mental process by which the belief is arrived at (such as carelessness, impulsiveness, irrationality, prejudice, reliance on intuition), it may still be 'honest', that is, a positive belief that the conclusions one has reached are true. The law demands no more.[285]

The privilege may also be lost if there is 'excessive' communication, for instance where a privileged occasion is misused for a purpose other than that given by the law (e.g. giving the statement wider publication than was necessary). At the risk of some repetition we should remind the reader that in the *Reynolds* type of privilege, the issue of malice is wrapped up with the finding of public interest and proper journalistic behaviour. As Lord Phillips MR thus put it in the *Loutchansky* case:

> once *Reynolds* privilege attaches, little scope remains for any subsequent finding of malice. Actual malice in this context has traditionally been recongised to consist of either recklessness, i.e. not believing the statement to be true or being indifferent as to its truth, or of making it with the dominant motive of injuring the claimant. But the publisher's conduct in both regards must inevitably be explored when considering Lord Nicholls's ten factors, i.e., in deciding whether the publication is covered by qualified privilege in the first place.[286]

4. DEFAMATION: DAMAGES

Subject to what will be said at the end of this section, damages are awarded by juries. Moreover, until recently, most lawyers (and, certainly, judges) would have agreed with Lord Hailsham who, in *Cassell & Co. Ltd.* v. *Broome*,[287] warned that the judiciary should avoid at any level substituting itself for a jury, unless the award is manifestly too large or too small. This reluctance to interfere with the role of juries has already been noted in

Wai Chun [2000] 3 HKLRD 418, the reason for this difference is that the qualified privilege defence is predicated on the idea that the defendant fulfils a duty or protects an interest by his publication of the statement. Thus, 'if... a person's dominant motive is not to perform this duty or protect this interest, he is outside the ambit of this defence' (at 433). Using the occasion 'for a purpose other than that for which the occasion was privileged' will defeat the defence of qualified privilege (at 438).

284 [1975] AC 135, 150. On this see Duncan and Neill (Select Bibliography), ch. 18.

285 However, it should be noted that this reasoning cannot apply to the *Reynolds* privilege discussed above. As the Court of Appeal made clear in *Loutchansky* v. *Times Newspapers (Nos. 2, 3, 4 and 5)* ([2002] 2 WLR 640, [37] and [38]), such a finding of 'carelessness' (etc.) would be fatal to a newspaper's claim under several of the *Reynolds* factors. Indeed, as noted in the text above, there seems to be little room for a finding of malice under *Reynolds* privilege, given the assessment of the defendant's conduct which is essential to the finding of the privilege in the first place. Furthermore, their Lordships in *Reynolds* did little to clarify the meaning of malice for the purposes of the qualified privilege or fair comment defences: see D. R. Howarth and J. A. O'Sullivan, *Hepple, Howarth and Matthews' Tort: Cases and Materials* (5th edn., 2000), 988–9.

286 *Loutchansky* v. *Times Newspapers (Nos. 2, 3, 4 and 5)* [2002] 2 WLR 640, [30].

287 [1972] AC 1027, 1065. See also *Blackshaw* v. *Lord* [1983] 3 WLR 283, 302 ff. *Cassell* is the leading case concerning punitive damages; and further guidance on their award in the context of defamation cases was given by the Court of Appeal in *Riches* v. *News Group Newspapers* [1986] QB 256.

the first part of this chapter where we discussed the judicial reluctance to substitute its verdict for that of the jury. Here we see the same problem but not in the context of 'libel or no libel' but that of the appropriate measure of damages. This 'reluctance' to intervene and adjust has, in the course of the past twenty-five years, been questioned. Many reasons have provoked these doubts.

The first and most troublesome was the fact that many juries have made some very substantial awards which, coupled with high costs,[288] have led many (and, of course, not least the newspaper industry) to complain about the state of the law. The reasons why such high awards were made are not entirely clear. In part this may be because juries were not given any real guidance as to what they should award. The size of the awards may also have reflected a dislike of the tabloid press, totally unrestrained in our country by a patchy law of privacy (on which see below, Chapter 22). Discontent reached a peak in *Sutcliffe* v. *Pressdram Ltd.*,[289] when a jury awarded £600,000 to Sonia Sutcliffe, the wife of the 'Yorkshire Ripper', for a libel published by *Private Eye*.

A second reason was the growing concern felt by many that defamation awards were seriously overtaking awards for serious cases of physical injury. This, some thought, might be closely liked with the fact that juries were not really given any guidance as to the amount of money they could award. The judgments in the Court of Appeal the *Sutcliffe* case offered interesting guidelines that could be used to direct juries in awarding *reasonable* amounts. Juries were thus asked to consider the weekly or monthly sum that a huge capital award would yield. Equally a large award would tempt defendants to appeal and thus cause claimants delays, expenses and anxiety. This is certainly true in many American cases where awards are often reduced as a result of remittiturs, appeals or other post-trial settlements. But juries should not be given information about awards in other libel actions (since this might result in unseemly 'over'- or 'under'-bidding). The proposals seemed to have had little impact in practice; and they certainly did not address the concern here mentioned (i.e. their superiority over personal-injury awards) since comparisons with the latter were deemed to be 'inappropriate'.

As the law moved into the 1990s and the pressure to enact the European Convention of Human Rights into internal law grew, a third concern was voiced: excessive damages infringed the right of freedom of speech. In *Rantzen* v. *Mirror Group Newspapers (1986) Ltd.*,[290] the Court of Appeal was strongly influenced by Article 10 ECHR. It felt that 'the common law . . . requires the courts to subject large awards of damages to a more searching scrutiny than has been customary in the past'.[291] The reduction of the

[288] E.g. in 1987 the *Daily Star* had to pay Jeffrey Archer £500,000 after he won a libel action that cost an estimated £300,000. In the same year, Lieut. Cdr. Packard was awarded £450,000 in an action against a newspaper (which had sold a mere 40 copies in this country). In 1988 Koo Stark was awarded £300,000 in an action that cost an estimated £100,000, and in 1989 Count Tolstoy was ordered to pay Lord Aldington £1.5 million after prolonged hearings that were said to have cost close to £1 million. These figures are small in comparison with those found in successful American libel actions, but they are huge in comparison with European standards; and until the (slow) introduction of structured settlements, they meant that libel actions could often produce higher awards than many cases of serious physical injury. These huge awards, however, by no means constitute the norm, as a helpful appendix in P. Carter-Ruck, *Libel and Slander* (5th edn., 1997) depicting all awards made between 1951 and 1997, shows.

[289] [1991] 1 QB 153.

[290] [1993] 2 WLR 953.

[291] *Ibid.*, 972.

plaintiff's damages in that case from £250,000 to £110,000 was an obvious sign of the newly found confidence to intervene and reduce jury awards. But the situation was still not satisfactory, in that it meant that additional time and expenditure had to be used in order to achieve a fairer result.

By the 1990s, the patchy and slow pace of case law reform was moving the law in the right direction (at any rate for those who believed that speech needed greater protection); but, as stated, it was still not enough. So Parliament was forced to intervene. As a result, section 8(2) of the Courts and Legal Services Act 1990 states that 'rules of court may provide for the Court of Appeal, in such class of case as may be specified in the rules, to have power, in place of ordering a new trial, to substitute for the sum awarded by the jury such sum as appears to the court to be proper'. It was thought that the combination of guidelines and a statutory right to reduce the amount would provide, on paper, an effective doubled-pronged attack to the perceived abuses of the older law. But juries were still awarding high damages; and concern was voiced from outside as well as inside the UK. Thus, in *Tolstoy Miloslavsky* v. *UK*[292] the European Court of Human Rights held that while the use of juries to award damages was 'prescribed by law' as required under Article 10(2) ECHR, the size of the award (there, £1.5 million), combined with the absence of any provision allowing the Court of Appeal to review awards which were arguably disproportionate in size, amounted to a breach of Article 10. Matters, it was thought, could be improved if the trial judge had the power—which superior courts had hitherto denied him—to give guidance to juries on the right level of awards. This might include drawing their attention to levels of compensation found in personal injury (but not other defamation) cases. This last step was, indeed, taken by the Court of Appeal in *John* v. *Mirror Group Newspapers Ltd.*[293] and reduced the damages awarded to the singer Elton John for an allegation that he had been bulimic from £350,000 to £50,000.[294]

Cases such as *Kiam* v. *MGN Ltd.*[295] illustrate that the ideal balance has not yet been achieved; that our courts are, for historical reasons, reluctant to interfere with jury awards unless they are manifestly 'excessive'; and powerful dissents can still be found demanding that a measure of comparability be found between libel and personal injury awards. With the newspaper industry having a big stake in this matter, one cannot exclude another attempt to legislate when the political climate becomes more propitious.

The damages awarded in defamation cases are also said to be 'at large'. Lord Hailsham explained this in the following way:

> Quite obviously, the award must include factors for injury to the feelings, the anxiety and uncertainty undergone in the litigation, the absence of apology, or the reaffirmation of the truth of the matters complained of, or the malice of the defendant. The bad conduct

[292] (1995) 20 EHRR 442 [293] [1997] QB 586.

[294] In the Law Commission's Final Report on *Damages for Personal Injury: Non-Pecuniary Loss*, No. 257 (1999), the suggestion of a statutory cap on damages for non-pecuniary loss in defamation was considered and rejected: see paras. 4.24–4.30, which list some of the practical problems, such as the danger of making particularly egregious libels more likely, since such a cap would effectively set the cost beforehand.

[295] [2003] QB 281.

of the plaintiff himself may also enter into the matter, where he had provoked the libel, or where perhaps he has libelled the defendant in reply. What is awarded is thus a figure which cannot be arrived at by any purely objective computation.... In other words the whole process of assessing damages where they are 'at large' is essentially a matter of impression and not addition.[296]

It follows that invariably, if not inevitably, such 'damages are in their nature punitive or exemplary in the loose sense' of the words. Since *Rookes* v. *Barnard*,[297] there is in this country, as there has always been in America, a clear distinction between compensatory damages, which can include an enlarged award (aggravated damages) in cases of outrage, and punitive or exemplary damages, which go beyond compensation and attempt to 'punish the defendant'. One such case is where the defendant decides to publish a libel, calculating that possible damages will be outweighed by the profit accruing[298] from the sale of, for example, the book and the publicity. This was the case in *Cassell* v. *Broome*, which was deemed to be a proper case for punitive damages in order to teach the defendant that tort does not pay. In such cases it is felt that over and above the figure awarded for loss of reputation an additional sum is needed to vindicate the strength of the law and act as a supplement to its strictly penal provisions.

The desirability of punitive elements in civil cases is a hotly disputed issue and is discussed more fully in Chapter 25, Section 2(d), below. In the context of defamation, however, this presents a further problem. This stems from the fact that they are often pleaded *in terrorem* in circumstances that do not really fit the strict criteria set out in the House of Lords cases of *Rookes* and *Cassell*. In such cases, however, it is not easy to persuade the court *in advance of the trial* that the case is so unarguable as to deserve striking out. As a result, a claimant may gain a considerable tactical advantage by 'threatening' criminal sanctions on a defendant without any of the safeguards that usually accompany criminal proceedings. No doubt some would find this a just counterpart, especially for media defendants who tend to be in a financially stronger position when compared to legally unaided claimants. But if the scales of justice are unevenly tipped in defamation cases (first in favour of defendants and then, if claimants turn out to be sufficiently resilient, in their favour), the balance should arguably be restored by means other than resorting to the rather anomalous device of punitive awards.[299]

A further important point that must be made in this context is the following. Many, if not most, defamatory statements are published by one or more defendants in one or

296 *Broome* v. *Cassell & Co. Ltd.* [1972] AC 1027, at 1071.

297 [1964] AC 1129.

298 Which raises the often vexed question of the availability of restitutionary damages, measured by reference to the gain made by the defendant by having committed the wrong. See, further, the Law Commission's Final Report on *Aggravated, Exemplary and Resitutionary Damages*, No. 247 (1997), esp paras. 3.48 ff. concerning the relationship between restitutionary and exemplary damages, particularly in situations where the defendant's conduct showed a 'deliberate and outrageous disregard of the plaintiff's rights'.

299 Of the £350,000 originally awarded to Mr (now Sir) Elton John, £275,000 consisted of exemplary damages—a proportion which may both show how unguided the jury was and be taken as a sign of the average juror's dislike of the behaviour of the tabloid press. This part of the award was reduced by the Court of Appeal to £5,000.

more newspapers, etc. Clearly, the claimant cannot be allowed to recover damages several times over. Section 12 of the Defamation Act provides: 'In any action for libel or slander the defendant may give evidence in mitigation of damages that the plaintiff has recovered damages, or had brought action for damages, for libel or slander in respect of the publication of words to the same effect as the words on which the action is founded, or has received or agreed to receive compensation in respect of any such publication.' Referring to the facts of *Lewis* v. *Daily Telegraph*,[300] where similar libels were published in two additional newspapers on the same day, each being dealt with by a different jury, Lord Reid said:

> I do not think it is sufficient merely to tell each jury to make such allowances as they may think fit. They ought, in my view, to be directed that in considering the evidence submitted to them, they should consider how far the damage suffered by the plaintiffs can reasonably be attributed solely to the libel with which they are concerned and how far it ought to be regarded as the joint result of the two libels. If they think that some part of the damage is the joint result of the two libels they should bear in mind that the plaintiffs ought not to be compensated twice for the same loss. They can only deal with this matter on very broad lines and they must take it that the other jury will be given a similar direction.

The above comments about the jury's role in assessing defamation awards will have to be read in conjunction with the new procedure for the summary disposal of defamation claims laid down by sections 8, 9 and 10 of the Defamation Act 1996.[301] This innovative procedure, the brainchild of Lord Hoffmann, will be available to the court and allow it to 'dispose summarily' of the claimant's claim when it appears to have 'no realistic prospect of success'.[302] This could be either because there is no real likelihood that the cause of action will be established or because of the apparent strength of the merits of the defence. Equally, section 8(3) of the 1996 Act also gives the court the power to give judgment for the claimant and grant him summary relief. This, according to section 9, can include damages of up to £10,000—if, in the court's view, 'there is no defence to the claim which has a realistic prospect of success and . . . there is no other reason why the claim should be tried'. This power to exclude juries from the award of damages, coupled with the aforementioned power to intervene to alter the level of their awards, thus represents a further inroad to trial by jury[303] and one which it is hoped will help streamline and expedite defamation trials in this country.[304]

300 [1964] AC 234, 261.

301 These sections came into force on 28 Feb. 2000.

302 Section 8(2) of the Defamation Act 1996.

303 In the Law Commission's Final Report on *Damages for Personal Injury: Non-Pecuniary Loss*, No. 257 (HC 344, 1999), it was accepted that a split of function between judge and jury (the former deciding quantum and the latter deciding liability) would be workable (para. 4.20). However, the Report declined to recommend such a change, suggesting that defamation law needed time to settle after many recent changes and that any such reorganisation needed to be viewed in the wider context of how defamation actions as a whole should be tried.

304 To date, there are few examples of the use of the new summary disposal procedure: see *Milne* v. *Telegraph Group* [2001] EMLR 30, where the defendant requested the use of the procedure, waiving a defence of qualified privilege and being held liable to the tune of £5,000 for reporting in a newspaper article a statement (made by a third party) which alleged the plaintiff was a compulsive liar. See the brief comments reported in Law

5. DEFAMATION: MITIGATION OF DAMAGE

(A) APOLOGY

The making, or offer, of an apology is not a defence to liability, but goes towards mitigating damages. Section 1 of the Libel Act 1843 (Lord Campbell's Act) enables a defendant in any action for defamation to give evidence that he has made, or offered, an apology either before, or as soon as possible after, the commencement of proceedings. But he must notify the claimant in writing of his intention to lead such evidence. In the case of publications in newspapers and periodicals, section 2 of the Act (as amended by the Libel Acts of 1845 and 1879) enables a defendant to plead that the libel was published without malice or gross negligence and that a full apology has been published. Such a plea must be accompanied by a payment into court by way of amends.

Apology is also relevant in making an 'offer of amends' for unintentional defamation under section 4(3) of the Defamation Act 1952 or, once it comes into force, the new defence of unintentional defamation. These were discussed earlier so we do not need to return to them again.

(B) CLAIMANT'S REPUTATION

In mitigation of damages the defendant is entitled to adduce evidence of the claimant's *general* bad reputation prior to the publication of the libel. This is a controversial plea. In a leading modern case, *Plato Films* v. *Speidel*,[305] Viscount Simonds questioned why, if none of the other numerous and adequate defences is available, any further indulgence should be shown to a defendant; and the other judges were prepared to give this a measure of support. Despite their Lordships' reservations, the law was settled in 1882 in *Scott* v. *Sampson*[306] and none of them was prepared to disturb the long-standing rule. In that case Cave J said *obiter* that *general* evidence of bad reputation is in principle admissible, as immediately and necessarily connected with the question of damages. A plaintiff complains of loss of reputation[307] and that he has been deprived of his character by the defendant. Why should not the defendant then be permitted to show that the plaintiff's character was previously tainted or that he had little character or reputation to lose? He then quoted Starkie on *Slander and Libel*:

To deny this would be to decide that a man of the worst character is entitled to the same measure of damages with one of unsullied and unblemished reputation. A reputed thief

Commission, *Aspects of Defamation Procedure: A Scoping Study* (May 2002), para. 13(2) (available on the Internet at www.lawcom.gov.uk/library/lcspecial-1/defamation.pdf).

305 [1961] AC 1090. 306 (1881) 8 QBD 491, 503.

307 In *Singh* v. *Gillard* (1988) 138 *NLJ* 144, 145, Lord Donaldson MR stated that the defendant 'can prove that the plaintiff is of bad character and so has little or no reputation to be damaged. But the rules as to what evidence can be called in support of such a plea are highly restrictive' (relying on Neill LJ in *Pamplin* v. *Express Newspapers (No. 2)* [1988] 1 All ER 282, 286: 'an admitted master of the law and practice relating to claims for defamation'. Despite the date of the report, *Pamplin* was decided in Feb. 1985).

> would be placed on the same footing with the most honourable merchant, a virtuous woman with the most abandoned prostitute. To enable the jury to estimate the probable quantum of injury sustained a knowledge of the party's previous character is not only material but seems to be absolutely essential. [308]

Only evidence showing the claimant's actual reputation prior to or at the time of publication of the libel can be submitted. Specific evidence revealing his character and disposition (i.e. of the reputation he ought to have) is not admissible. To put it differently: the defendant can lead evidence about the claimant's publicly known behaviour in order to show that the claimant did not have much reputation to lose. But he cannot lead evidence in order to remake the claimant's reputation. For, it is said, it would be intolerable if a jury, learning long after of this or that discreditable episode in a person's life, could diminish his current public esteem. Other reasons have been given against the admission of evidence of *specific* instances of misconduct. If such allegations were allowed in evidence it would open the door to collateral issues, which have only an indirect bearing on the main question in the case. This would, inevitably, prolong the trial and tend to confuse the jury by distracting their attention from the main issue. The result might be that a trial in which the truth and falsity of one allegation was being investigated might degenerate into trials of the truth or falsity of other allegations not strictly relevant to the subject-matter of the trial, introduced by the defendants simply to mitigate damages. It would also place an undue burden on the plaintiff, who would have to support with evidence his entire conduct through life rather than prove his general reputation. All these arguments against admitting evidence of particular facts concerning the claimant's life drew a great deal of support from the facts of *Plato* v. *Speidel*, though the case also brought out the deficiencies of the present law and the need for its reform.

In that case General Speidel claimed damages from the distributors of a film which depicted him as a party to the murder of King Alexander of Yugoslavia. The defendants pleaded justification and, alternatively, in mitigation of damages, allegations demonstrating that the general had been guilty of war crimes, persecuting the Jews, espionage while attached to the German Embassy in Paris in 1934, and so forth. The Court of Appeal struck out the plea and rephrased it as follows: 'Alternatively in mitigation of damages the defendants will at the trial of the action give evidence in chief that the plaintiff had a bad reputation as a man who was a party to and/or responsible for acts which were crimes against humanity and/or atrocities.' The defendants appealed, but the House of Lords, on the grounds already mentioned, upheld the Court of Appeal's refusal to allow evidence of specific facts concerning the general's past. What the defendants thus had to prove was that the plaintiff had a '*general* bad reputation', rather than that he committed acts A, B and C, and the jury would be left to decide what reputation he deserved. In practice, this is notoriously difficult to achieve and that is why defendants can rarely use this weapon and, instead, choose to invoke one of the substantive defences including wide-ranging pleas of justification, sometimes based upon attaching imaginative or even ingenious meanings to the words complained of.

[308] From the 2nd edn. of that work (1830), ii, at 88 (cited at [1961] QC 1090, 1137).

The position of the present law is thus unequivocal: it does not wish to hinder the claimant's attempt to vindicate himself by the fact that he has committed other misdemeanours or indiscretions not directly associated with the acts or omissions attributed to him in the words complained of. However, in the view of the Supreme Court Procedure Committee: 'It is... not necessary for the purpose of effective vindication, nor consonant with justice, that a plaintiff who *has* misconducted himself in the same sector of his life as that to which the libel relates should recover damages on exactly the same generous basis as one who truly has an unblemished record in the relevant area of activity.'[309] The Committee thus concluded[310] that it 'would be a significant improvement upon the present position if it were possible for defendants to rely upon specific instances of misconduct on the plaintiff's part, for the purpose of mitigating damages rather than by way of defence, provided that the allegations related to the same sector of the plaintiff's life (e.g. business probity, conduct towards his family, etc.) and provided proper and specific notice was given in the defence'.[311] The Committee's proposals were noted in the 1996 Defamation Bill but the relevant clause, which would have changed the law, was lost at the Committee stage of the House of Commons.

6. DEFAMATION: EPILOGUE

Defamation: what a tort! One specialist has called this body of law 'absurd, complex and unfair'.[312] Writing earlier, a distinguished judge thought its rules had 'passed beyond redemption'.[313] Just over twenty years later, another learned judge thought that 'the practice and procedure attendant upon the administration of justice in the context of claims for defamation is the last refuge of complexity and technicality in the law'.[314] The national press (more in the right in the case of this tort than in the case of privacy cases) has groaned repeatedly under its repressive rules, while undeserving (and, invariably, wealthy) plaintiffs have been happy to exploit them.[315] It is a tort that bears the scars of history; and in the survival of the distinction between libel and slander shows, we find another argument for those who see in the past not only a source of pride but also an encumbrance. Eccentricity comes with uniqueness. Sometimes this is justified, as with the rule that provides that the cause of action is extinguished with the death of either party and with the rule that the action must be brought within one year (instead

309 *Report on Practice and Procedure in Defamation* (Select Bibliography), 34.

310 *Ibid.*, 35.

311 The committee acknowledged that, if accepted, its proposal would (as indicated in the text, above) lead to 'a widening of issues and... increase the length and cost of the inquiry'. However it regarded this as 'a legitimate price to pay for the avoidance of unduly high awards and, more importantly, for the avoidance of the court being allowed to assess the plaintiff's career and reputation on a false or misleadingly incomplete footing': *ibid.*, 37.

312 T. Weir, *Casebook on Tort* (10th edn., 2004), at 522.

313 Lord Diplock's judgment in *Slim* v. *Daily Telegraph Ltd.* [1968] 2 QB 157, 179.

314 *Singh* v. *Gillard* [1988] 138 *NLJ* 144, Lord Donaldson MR.

315 The late Robert Maxwell is one of many inhabiting this pantheon.

of the usual three). On other occasions—think of the rule that forces the defendant to prove that what he said was true rather than the claimant to prove that it was said of him was false—encourages undeserving plaintiffs to chance litigation. The absence of legal aid makes this a rich man's tort; and the unrestricted—until recently—jury awards allowed popular attachment to a potentially flawed method of trial[316] to produce some vary dubious awards. Many of these peculiarities have been whipped out by other systems which owe their law to ours (e.g. American) while others, as old as ours, were wise enough never to adopt them. To this list of accusations comes the last and, arguably, the most serious one: excessive technicality. For this is a branch of the law which is so complex, so fine in its minutiae, at times so unclear, that it helps fortify the popular mistrust towards law and those who serve it. Can, therefore, anything good be said of this tort and this branch of the law? In fact we think two points can be singled out for attention, if not commendation, allowing us to end this chapter on a note of optimism which was absent from earlier editions of this book.

The first admirable feature of this branch of tort law is that it brings into relief a theme that runs throughout this subject and thus this book. Law is about competing values, drawing lines, striking a balance between competing interests—that of the plaintiff who complains that he has been wronged and that of the defendant who feels that he, too, has rights and should thus not be made to sacrifice them completely or without proper balancing. In negligence we see this happening in every page of the book; but it can be concealed by the vague, often protean concepts that our judges use and which we the teachers burn on to the minds of impressionable youth concealing the real struggle that lies hidden by them. In defamation (and privacy, which we discuss below[317]) that is rarely possible since the clash between free speech and reputation is rarely out of sight and out of the arguments of counsel and judges. Indeed, what is involved here is more than a clash but a true confrontation of equally important titanic values. For we must never allow ourselves to forget that human dignity, of which reputation, honour and privacy are but obvious manifestations, is every bit as important to any democratic order as is free expression. If this real confrontation leads teacher and student alike to condemn the rules they have to learn and use, it should also gives them occasion to remember that they must never opt for one at the expense of the other but try to reconcile them striking the balance on a fact sensitive basis and not in an a priori manner. This leads to the second point that is good about this part of the law.

For, by hook or by crook, case law or statutory reform, the personal influence of great defamation lawyers who once sat on the bench or chaired reform committees, our law is changing and changing for the better. This does not mean forgetting the list of

316 *Beta Construction v. Channel Four Television Co. Ltd.* [1990] 1 WLR 1042 contains some useful guidelines on which cases are suitable to be tried by judge alone under s. 69(1) and (3) of the Supreme Court Act 1981. Jury trial should thus be avoided if (*a*) their involvement would entail a 'substantial' prolongation of the trial, or (*b*) 'significantly' increase costs or (*c*) involve the jury in the examination of complicated or extensive documents (such as corporate accounts). Section 8 of the Courts and Legal Services Act 1990 may well, in due course, assist those who would like to see a reduction of jury involvement in defamation trials. So will s. 8 of the 1996 Act.

317 See ch. 22.

grievances summarised above; but neither does it call for the concealment of the fact that progress has been made. For this, our old, venerable and introverted culture has a surprising source to thank: foreign influences. Thus, the internationalisation of our legal culture has much to claim to its credit, though traditionalists have pretended (and no doubt will continue to argue in writings as well as in judgments) that our law of human rights has always been as good and as efficient as that of other lands. We think that it has not and, more importantly, neither does the Senior Law Lord. Thus, writing extra-judicially, he had this to say about the relevant part of the *Spycatcher* case:

An additional argument sometimes heard is that incorporation is unnecessary since the Convention rights are already protected by the common law. The House of Lords recently held in the field of freedom of speech there is no difference in principle between English law and Article 10 of the Convention. Lord Goff of Chieveley said the same thing in the *Spycatcher* judgment. But the House of Lords' earlier *Spycatcher* decision has itself been held to have violated the Convention, as of course have other of their Lordships' decisions. If in truth the common law as it stands were giving the rights of United Kingdom citizens the same protection as the Convention—across the board, not only in relation to Article 10—one might wonder why the United Kingdom's record as a Strasbourg litigant was not more favourable.[318]

The reference to the American experience and its hallowed preference for free expression is discussed in the next chapter and need not detain us at this stage. Though it has its adherents in this country as well, we note that the solutions of that legal culture are not all of unmitigated success, as our American colleague is at pains to show in his learned contribution in Chapter 23 of this book. More importantly, the United States is no longer seen, in this country as, indeed, elsewhere, as the only source of new legal ideas. Since this book first saw the light of day just over twenty years ago the significance of the European Convention on Human Rights has become of paramount importance. It is one which will continue to grow now that its rules and ideas have been 'repatriated' home by the Human Rights Act 1999.

In a textbook one can only quote extracts from judgments and, alas, even less of the arguments of counsel before a court. Yet it would not take much for the attentive reader to notice not only the impact that this case law is having on our legal rules but also to appreciate the hugely important shift in legal borrowings. For inspiration is no longer sought from (other) common law courts but also from those which are geographically closer to us. Europe, as a whole, is a repository of fascinating ideas and solutions; and, one day, we may also not just discover but also admit that 'Europe' is found not just in the decisions of the Courts of Luxembourg and Strasbourg but also in the decisions of the courts of France, Germany, the Netherlands or Italy which have influenced so much the emergence of the new European jurisprudence. In the meantime, however, we can reflect on the accuracy of these concluding observations by collating the numerous dicta from such landmark decisions as *Reynolds* or *Loutchansky* or *Grobbelaar* and

318 Lord Bingham, 'The European Convention on Human Rights: Time to Incorporate' in R. Gordon and R. Wilmot-Smith (eds.), *Human Rights in the United Kingdom* (1996) ch. 1, 1, 9 (references omitted).

noting the progress that we have made in the direction of free speech. By reflecting on Commonwealth decisions which, for instance, have refused to follow the *Reynolds* ruling on the grounds that it had an impact on the role of juries,[319] we may take our thoughts even further. For nowadays are we not branching out in new directions rather than insisting on the 'uniformity' of the common law? And as the *Derbyshire* litigation shows (especially at the Court of Appeal level where the human-rights breakthrough came about[320]), are not these new directions *truly* new in that the authors of professional books on defamation[321] had *not* even envisaged them when they were speculating in very legalistic ways whether cases like *Bognor Regis District Council* v. *Campion*[322] were going to prevail? Defamation (and privacy as we shall see) is thus offering lawyers of all kinds—students, academics, practitioners and judges—the chance to innovate and improve; it is up to them to seize it.

7. INJURIOUS FALSEHOODS AND PASSING OFF

The distinction between defamation and injurious falsehoods (a term coined by Salmond) is that in the former the defendant's allegation is against the claimant, whereas in the latter it is against his goods. Lord Esher MR said:[323] '[i]n such a case a jury would have to say which sense the libel really bore; if they thought it related to the goods only, they ought to find that it was not a libel; but if they thought it related to a man's conduct of business, they ought to find it was a libel.' This statement shows that often it will be advisable for a claimant to sue on both grounds.[324] Indeed, the case of *Joyce* v. *Sengupta*[325] shows that if the facts will support an action under this heading the court will consider it even if the claimant's real aim in proceeding under this tort was to obtain legal aid which, as we saw, is not available if the action is phrased in defamation. This is clearly an advantage as far as the claimant is concerned; but it may also deprive him of advantages that would be available to him if he were proceeding under defamation. Thus, in malicious falsehood, the claimant will have to prove the falsity of the words rather than enjoy the benefit (given to defamation claimants) of placing on the defendant the onus of proving the truth of the statement. Moreover, in cases of malicious falsehood it is for the claimant to prove the defendant's malice (which, probably, means dishonest or improper motive)[326] and also show that he has suffered actual

319 *Lange* v. *Atkinson* [2000] 3 NZLR 385.

320 [1992] QB 770, CA.

321 P. Carter Ruck, *Libel and Slander* (4th edn., 1992), 73. R.W.M. Dias (ed.), *Clerk and Lindsell on Torts* (16th edn., 1989), paras. 2–43, 21–18, 21–25, was, if anything, more anodyne, offering no ideas for the future. Likewise P. Lewis (ed.), *Gatley on Libel and Slander* (8th edn., 1981), paras. 958, 959.

322 [1972] 2 QB 169.

323 *South Hetton Coal Co. Ltd.* v. *North-Eastern News Association Ltd.* [1894] 1 QB 133, 139.

324 E.g. *Griffiths* v. *Benn* (1911) 27 TLR 346, 350.

325 [1993] 1 WLR 337.

326 *Serville* v. *Constance* [1954] 1 WLR 487, 490. In *Joyce* v. *Motor Surveys* [1948] Ch. 252, the view seemed to be that an intention to injure without just cause or excuse would suffice.

loss.[327] Loss here means pecuniary damage; though injury to feelings may also be compensated as aggravated damages if this is linked to the injury caused to the claimant's financial interests.[328] If, however, the claimant succeeds[329] on all of the above three points, an action will lie against the defendant or his estate (unlike defamation, where the cause of action is extinguished by death of either party).[330]

Passing off constitutes another form of unfair competition taking the form of a misrepresentation of the claimant's business. The following felicitous statement by Professor Fleming captures the essential difference from the tort described in the previous paragraph: '[w]hile it is injurious falsehood for a defendant to claim that your goods are his, it is passing off for him to claim that his goods are yours.'[331] Many of the peculiarities of this tort must be sought in the common law; but its potential for growth, especially as it expands to encompass 'unfair trading' in general, suggests that it has as much of a future as it has a past.[332] It is not, however, discussed in traditional tort courses, so its further consideration must be left to more specialised works.[333]

SELECT BIBLIOGRAPHY

BARENDT, E., 'Libel and Freedom of Speech in English Law' [1993] *PL* 449.

CARTER-RUCK, P., and STARTE, H.N.A., *On Libel and Slander* (5th edn., 1997).

DUNCAN, C., and NEILL, B., *Defamation* (2nd edn., 1983).

FLEMING, J.G., 'Retraction and Reply: Alternative Remedies for Defamation' (1978) 12 *UBCLR* 15.

HOLDSWORTH, SIR WILLIAM, 'Defamation in the 16th and 17th Centuries' (1925) 41 *LQR* 13.

JOHNSTON, I.D., 'Uncertainties in the Defence of Fair Comment' (1978) 8 *NZULR* 359.

KAYE, J.M., 'Libel and Slander: Two Torts or One?' (1975) 91 *LQR* 524.

KENNEDY, T.P., and REED, A., 'The Europeanisation of Defamation' (1996) 5 *JEL* 201.

LLOYD, LORD, 'Law and the Press' (1966) 19 *CLP* 43.

—'Reform of the Law of Defamation' (1976) 29 *CLP* 183.

327 *Royal Baking Powder Co.* v. *Wright Crossley & Co.* (1901) 18 RPC 95, 99. The loss must also be monetary in nature; injured feelings will not be compensated through this tort: *Fielding* v. *Variety Incorporated* [1967] 2 QB 841. On the other hand, proof of a general loss of custom, rather than loss of identifiable customers, may be enough: *Ratcliffe* v. *Evans* [1892] 2 QB 524. The plaintiff's failure to prove pecuniary loss was the reason why in *Allason* v. *Campbell, The Times*, 8 May 1996, the claim in malicious falsehood failed.

328 *Khodaparast* v. *Shad* [2000] 1 All ER 545.

329 E.g. it is likely that all privileges that are recognised in the law of defamation are also relevant to this tort. Equally, liability may be avoided if the statements made are *bona fide* or are made pursuant to a duty imposed on their maker.

330 The same difference exists with 'active transmissibility', that is, that in malicious falsehood the cause of action is inherited by the claimant's estate, whereas in the case of defamation his right is extinguished by death.

331 *The Law of Torts* (8th edn., 1992), 714.

332 Note, e.g., *Warnink* v. *Townend* [1979] AC 731.

333 See, e.g., C. Wadlow, *The Law of Passing-Off: Unfair Competition by Misrepresentation* (3rd edn., 2004).

LOVELAND, I., 'Defamation of Government: Taking Lessons from America' (1994) *Leg. Stud.* 206.

—*Political Libels: A Comparative Study* (2000).

NEILL, SIR BRIAN, 'The Media and the Law' [1993] *Yearbook of Media and Entertainment Law* 1.

ROGERS, W. V. H. and MILMO, P. (eds.), *Gatley on Libel and Slander* (9th edn., 1998, and First Supplement to the 9th edn., 2002).

RUBENSTEIN, M. (ed.), *Wicked, Wicked Libels* (1972).

SHARLAND, A. and LOVELAND, I., 'The Defamation Act 1966 and Political Speech' [1997] *PL* 113.

SUPREME COURT PROCEDURE COMMITTEE, *Report on Practice and Procedure in Defamation* (1991).

SYMMONS, C. R., 'The Problem of Hidden Reference in Defamation' (1974) 3 *Anglo-Am. LR* 98.

WATKINS, A., *A Slight Case of Libel* (1990).

WILLIAMS, K., '"Only Flattery is Safe"; Political Speech and the Defamation Act 1996' (1997) 60 *MLR* 388.

22
THE PROTECTION OF HUMAN PRIVACY

Besmirching the claimant's honour and reputation, discussed in the previous chapter, is not the only way in which one may interfere with his personality. Other invasions are possible, but they are less effectively prohibited by our legal order. And the gaps in our system, which are once again largely the result of the piecemeal and gradual development of our law, as well as the product of multiple and by no means identical judicial *dicta* which often emerge from a single case, are beginning to reveal our system as one which is not only patchy and unprincipled but also dangerously complex.

This subject has always been sensitive to the competing forces of openness and freedom of expression on the one hand and, on the other hand, the legitimate desire to keep away from public gaze certain aspects of one's private life.[1] It would be foolish to deny how vitally important both of these interests are. It is this competition which gives the subject and the chapter its intellectual edge; it also gives these rules of law their growing practical significance. But there is more to this area of law than this.

There is an underlying concern about the erosion of certain expectations of privacy that have hitherto been taken for granted, which flows from our growing ability to collect, collate and disseminate information about individuals. This has been enhanced as a result of technological advances which make such information-gathering potentially far-reaching and intrusive. And as if all this were not enough, nowadays one must also cope with another challenge—a challenge that is felt across our law and not just the law of privacy. This is linked to the fact that British lawyers—and this includes students—can no longer advise on these matters by relying solely on national law, values and ideas. Foreign law is seeping into our system on a regular basis; and Europe (in the form mainly of the case law of the Strasbourg court) has been becoming the 'brooding omnipresence in the sky'. We may resent it, we may dislike it; but notwithstanding some loose bravura talk on behalf of some politicians, it is probably here to stay, so we should better learn how to master it.

The sketch that follows in this chapter deals almost exclusively with violations of human privacy by private individuals and organisations. It does not deal with violations

[1] For the question to what extent these formulations include the private affairs of incorporated bodies, see the discussion below.

by the state, which may be challenged under human rights law. Nor does it go into a detailed analysis of various statutory regimes such as the data protection legislation, important though they can be to a potential claimant. A textbook on a common law subject must take space into account when allocating the treatment it gives to its topics; and it is with the common law that it must mainly deal with, even though the legislator—national and European—and the Strasbourg court have amply demonstrated their intention to retain their role as key sources of the law. With the above in mind, the material has thus been divided into five subheadings: (1) the difficulties of defining privacy; (2) the casuistic protection afforded by English law; (3) the protection afforded in the most important types of cases; (4) the growth of breach of confidence after the entry into force of the Human Rights Act; (5) Europe and beyond.

1. DEFINITIONAL DIFFICULTIES AND OTHER OBJECTIONS TO RECOGNISING A WIDER PROTECTION OF PRIVACY

The abundance of definitions that exist of the concept of privacy could be taken to suggest that none of them is entirely satisfactory. Winfield, for example, who was one of the first academics in this country to urge the courts to make a tort of all offensive invasions of personal privacy, defined 'infringement of privacy' as an 'unauthorised interference with a person's seclusion of himself or of his property from the public'.[2] Earlier, a well-known American academic and subsequently judge—Thomas Cooley—coined the oft-quoted phrase 'the right to be let alone'.[3] Westin's definition is wider, in so far as it includes legal entities. 'Privacy', he has thus argued, 'is the claim of individuals, *groups, or institutions* to determine for themselves when, how, and to what extent information about them is communicated to others.'[4] On the international level the Universal Declaration of Human Rights of 1948 provides in its Article 12 that 'no one shall be subjected to arbitrary interference with his privacy, family, home or correspondence ...'.[5] No definition of privacy is given; but the interests protected are clearly envisaged in wide terms. Other definitions, containing subtly different verbal variations, can be found.[6] On the whole it is perhaps accurate to say that those who favour a *general* right of privacy have tried to supply a definition and are in a slight numerical majority over those who have opposed it. On the other hand, we also note that in general terms those

[2] See Winfield, (Select Bibliography), 24.

[3] *Law of Torts* (2nd edn., 1888), 29.

[4] See Westin, *Privacy and Freedom* (Select Bibliography), 7 (italics supplied).

[5] The emphasis on 'home' and 'private and family life' also appears in Art. 8 ECHR. As Hale LJ observed in *R* v. *Broadcasting Standards Commission, ex parte British Broadcasting Corporation* [2001] QB, 885, at para. 42, '[w]hile "private life" life may bring with it certain nuances it is not obvious that "privacy" should always do so'.

[6] See the literature in the Select Bibliography.

who have opposed a general right of privacy have had rather more success in showing that a workable definition may be difficult to frame than they have had in stopping the *gradual* expansion of the protected areas of human personality.

The above comments are not meant to deny that legitimate concerns do not exist against an enlarged protection of privacy, especially if it is brought about through the creation of a new, general rule. Marshall, for example, referring to Cooley J's definition, has asked what the 'right to be let alone' means. Does it give a claimant to privacy the right 'to go on battering the baby, or cheating the Inland Revenue, or poisoning the customers?'[7] Marshall's rhetorical question does more than challenge a well-known definition. Through his examples the author reveals vividly that the right of one person to stop revelations about his affairs may conflict with the right of another person to his freedom of expression and, even more importantly, the right of the general public to be informed about a particular state of affairs. Here, as in the law of defamation, this clash of values is the crux of the matter.

Yet the difficulty lies not so much in the kind of examples that Marshall has adduced in order to make his point against over-generalised definitions; none of the instances which he gives deserve to be protected against the glare of publicity. The value of Marshall's point lies rather in the fact that it makes us aware of the undoubted difficulty of devising a test that defines what information must remain private. For, clearly, not everything that interests the public should be published in the public interest. But the difficulty in drawing lines in some marginal cases is not a reason for not trying to draw them at all, as the press seems to suggest, no doubt because many in the press would prefer the freedom to draw those lines for themselves, as and when they see fit. Yet the press is on no firmer ground when it asserts that it alone should be left with the task of regulating its conduct (in the sense of deciding what should be published and what the consequences of wrongful publication should be). For the argument that no one else (e.g. the legislator, or the courts) can do the job better than the press can do it by itself is hardly convincing, quite apart from the fact that the remedies for violation of 'codes of conduct' provided to 'aggrieved parties' under the existing self-regulatory regime neither 'satisfy' them nor 'deter' the habitual offenders! Self-regulation has, thus far, prevailed not because it has proved to be successful but because our press has, especially by exploiting the 'sleaze culture' of recent times, gained such an unhealthy stranglehold over our politicians. The problem may thus lie, in part at least, in the effort to devise a definition that will cover all circumstances, rather than allow circumstances to help to delimit on an *ad hoc* basis what deserves protection and what calls for exposure. The British press has exploited this difficulty and has managed to remain largely judge and jury of its own misbehaviour, a state of affairs which is rarely considered to be commendable.

One aspect of this definitional difficulty concerning privacy was recently addressed by our Court of Appeal in *R* v. *Broadcasting Standards Commission, ex parte British Broadcasting Corporation*;[8] and it was approached in a manner which turned more on

[7] See Marshall, 'The Right to Privacy' (Select Bibliography), 243.

[8] [2001] QB 885 ('the *Dixons* case').

the wording of the applicable statute and less on whether it was desirable to find a solution of principle. Nonetheless, the three brief but interesting judgments in that case illustrate that the difficulties posed by the main issue which confronted the Court of Appeal in that case and which is best treated as remaining unresolved. This was whether privacy, as a concept, is wide enough to cover similar or analogous rights of incorporated bodies.

In *R* v. *Broadcasting Standards Commission, ex parte British Broadcasting Corporation*, a move towards a wider interpretation of the notion of privacy to cover the rights of both types of 'persons'—human and incorporated—was made. The claimant's (Dixons Ltd.) contention that its rights of privacy (as an incorporated body) had been infringed by the BBC's investigative journalism[9] were infringed was contested by the latter, *inter alia*, on the grounds that as an incorporated body Dixons did not enjoy any privacy rights, a notion more appropriate to human rather than legal persons. In the Court of Appeal, and overruling the judge at first instance, this argument was rejected, largely on the basis of the wording of the applicable statute.[10] Lord Woolf MR in fact went further when he held that he was prepared to allow a corporation to sue under that Act because he was, in principle, unwilling to accept that European Convention rights, arguably limited to humans, could be used to 'cut down' the avowedly wider protection afforded in this case by the English statute.[11] Presumably, this kind of reasoning suggests that the same result would be reached if a few courts had to construe a similarly (unambiguously) phrased statute, thus turning the whole issue into a simple one of statutory construction. Such an approach would entail the courts never even considering the appropriateness of a distinction being made between the two types of 'person'.

Such an interpretation seems to emerge only from Lord Woolf's judgment. How far this ruling goes towards recognising privacy rights to incorporated bodies may be less clear. The three judgments in the case contain interesting *dicta*, which make it strongly arguable that the final answer must still be in doubt. Thus, though Hale LJ (as she then was), who gave the second (and shorter) judgment in that case, *appeared* to favour a more general application of this wider meaning of privacy,[12] at the end of this very same paragraph she also stated that:

> [t]here may well be contexts in which the concept should be limited to human beings, whose very humanity is defined by their own particular consciousness of identity and individuality, their own wishes and their own feelings. But that debate is for another day.

[9] Filming—as part of a consumer-affairs programme—surreptitiously in its stores with a view to showing that the firm was selling old products as new.

[10] Sections 110 and 111 of the Broadcasting Act 1996. Section 111(1) in particular provides that '[a] fairness complaint may be made [to the Broadcasting Standards Commission = BSC] by an individual or a body or persons, whether incorporated or not, but, subject to subsection (2), shall not be entertained by the BSC unless made by the persons affected or by a person authorized by him to make the complaint for him'. Interpreting this wording, Mr Pannick (who appeared for the BBC) suggested that 'if the complaint had been made by Dixons on behalf of their staff, the BSC would have had jurisdiction to adjudicate the dispute. But if the complaint had been made by Dixons itself, it should fail since a company has no privacy to protect.' This interpretation of the statutory wording was rejected by Lord Woolf as a 'very restricted interpretation of section 111(1)' (*ibid.*, at [31]).

[11] See *ibid.*, [17].

[12] See *ibid.*, [44].

This part of her argument would thus seem to incline in favour of the view that in many cases privacy should be treated as a notion more appropriate to human rather than legal persons and that therefore, legislation (and case law) should reflect this more clearly. We read these words to suggest that, perhaps, a future answer may thus depend more upon the context than upon the wording of whatever statute had to be considered.

It was, however, left to Lord Mustill, sitting as the third judge, to articulate most thoughtfully the idea that the concept of privacy cannot easily apply to impersonal corporate bodies. Thus, though European guidance on this matter is scanty or, rather, contradictory,[13] the following extract from Lord Mustill's judgment should receive careful consideration in the future and avoid, as has happened without much intellectual dispute in the law of defamation, the equation of legal and physical persons. He thus said:

I do, however, wish to emphasise the degree to which this conclusion is dependent on the language and purpose of this particular statute, for in general I find the concept of a company's privacy hard to grasp. To my mind the privacy of a human being denotes at the same time the personal "space" in which the individual is free to be itself, and also the carapace, or shell, or umbrella, or whatever other metaphor is preferred, which protects that space from intrusion. An infringement of privacy is an affront to the personality, which is damaged both by the violation and by the demonstration that the personal space is not inviolate. The concept is hard indeed to define, but if this gives something of its flavour I do not see how it can apply to an impersonal corporate body, which has no sensitivities to wound, and no selfhood to protect.

There will, it is true, be many occasions where grounds for complaint maintainable by a company will be of the same kind as those which could be presented by an individual as a breach of privacy. For example the clandestine copying of business documents would be actionable by a company and an individual alike as civil wrongs, amounting to a breach of confidentiality, copyright and the like. But privacy and confidentiality are not the same. For example, the reading and copying of personal diaries, letters to relatives or lovers, poems and so on could ground not only an allegation of tortious conduct but also an additional complaint that the privacy of the writer and perhaps also of the recipient have been intruded upon. Such conduct is specially objectionable, not because legal rights have been infringed but because of the insult done to the person as a person. No such complaint would, I believe, be feasible when made by a company, not for the obvious reason that a corporation does not create documents of this kind, but because an intrusion into such matters has an extra dimension, in the shape of the damage done to the sensibilities of a human being by exposing to strangers the workings of his or her inward feelings, emotions, fears and beliefs—a damage which an artificial "person", having no sensibilities, cannot be made to suffer. A company can have secrets, can

[13] Whether Art. 8 of the ECHR includes under the term privacy the rights of legal entities (as well as human beings) is undecided: *Niemietz* v. *Germany* (1992) 16 EHRR 97 contains *dicta* which *could* be seen as being the first steps in that direction, given that it held that Art. 8 of the ECHR applied to business premises as well as homes. *Contra*, on this narrower point, the Court of Justice of the European Communities in its earlier decision in Joined Cases 46/87 and 227/88, *Hoechst AG* v. *Commission of the European Communities* [1989] ECR 2859, 2893. But that is not the same point as the one which confronted the Court of Appeal in the *Dixons* case.

have things which should be kept confidential, but I see this as different from the essentially human and personal concept of privacy.[14]

Returning to privacy in general, we note that other objections, besides definitional difficulties, have been voiced against the recognition of a new general right. The fear that the recognition of a general right would trigger endless litigation is one such argument put forward by opponents of privacy. Empirical evidence, however, from countries (such as Germany) which recognise a general right of privacy does not support this assertion.[15] Why would the English public, which is (in)famous for its dislike of 'making a fuss', change its natural character? Indeed, why would it go a step further and resort to litigation, especially since this is not an area where legal aid applies and the costs of going to court can be notoriously high? To put it differently, if the volume of litigation in Germany is low, even though access to the courts is cheap (by English standards), why would it be high in our country where costs are prohibitively high?

That the aforementioned objection, too, is not well founded can be seen by the fact that it is usually coupled with another one: the recognition of wider privacy rights would have a chilling effect on the press.[16] This is an objection that deserves to be taken seriously for, in the words of Cardozo J, 'freedom of expression is the matrix, the indispensable condition of nearly every other form of freedom'.[17] However, foreign empirical evidence—and not just hearsay propaganda used by opponents of a privacy right in England—once again proves how unsubstantiated this fear has proved to be in practice, at any rate in countries such as ours. Germany, to use the illustration again since it comes from a country with a highly developed law of privacy, nowadays protects speech rights in a manner that is entirely comparable to that found in the United States and certainly more effectively than we do through our law of defamation.[18] That, surely, proves that a balance between the competing interests can be found by, for instance, giving preference to political speech but preferring privacy over salacious and titillating revelations or intrusions which mainly serve the financial interests of the publisher.

So the picture that emerges from this sketch is far less clear-cut and convincing than opponents of privacy would like us to believe. The debate on the need for a general right of privacy is thus likely to continue, especially now that the Human Rights Act 1998 has entered into force. But while the 1998 Act has already given our courts the occasion to

[14] [2001] QB 885, [48] and [49].

[15] For some statistical information see B. S. Markesinis and H. Unberath, *The German Law of Torts: A Comparative Treatise* (4th edn., 2002), 476–88. Nor is it convincing to say that privacy actions, though controllable in the Federal Republic of Germany, have got out of hand in the United States. Although it is true that in the American system there is a large corpus of case law under this heading, many of the cases could have been litigated under some other tort heading. And many other instances have, in fact, received even less protection than they do in Britain because of the preponderance given in American law to First Amendment rights (free expression).

[16] See, for instance, Lord Wakeham, HL Debs., vol. 583, col. 772 (24 Nov. 1997). That this has not happened in Germany is shown in Markesinis and Unberath, n. 15 above, 472–8.

[17] *Palko* v. *Connecticut*, 302 US 319, 327 (1937).

[18] See B. S. Markesinis, 'Privacy, Freedom of Expression, and the Horizontal Effect of the Human Rights Bill: Lessons from Germany' (1999) 115 *LQR* 47. American comparatists agree.

reconsider the actual law, the exact extent of its impact is still unclear. For present purposes one must thus admit that a final resolution to the position of principle awaits a definitive pronouncement from the House of Lords, even though the last few years have seen our law make a significant progress towards protecting human privacy.

2. THE PROTECTION AFFORDED BY ENGLISH LAW: CASUISTRY VERSUS PRINCIPLE

Human privacy is not left unprotected by English law. Indeed, there is a rich variety of available remedies reflecting a willingness to enlist tort, contract, crime and equity to achieve the end result. And the remedies are not only found in the common law but also secreted in a growing number of statutes which deal with a growing number of activities which affect aspects of human privacy and which are now proscribed or regulated.

Concern for privacy can thus also explain a series of statutory enactments such as the Post Office Act 1710,[19] which imposed criminal penalties for the unauthorised opening of letters. Analogous enactments have imposed confidentiality requirements in the context of handling of telegraphic messages.[20] Although as late as 1979, Megarry V-C rejected[21] the existence of a common-law remedy for interception of telephonic conversations, the legislature intervened again (prompted as so often is the case by the fact that the *Malone* judgment was successfully challenged before the European Court of Human Rights).[22] The Interception of Communications Act 1985 thus created certain criminal offences in an attempt to remedy this gaping hole in the fabric of the protection of privacy.

More or less at the same time, the European Community was also showing concerns about the effects that databanks could have by storing private information which could then affect adversely our public lives. The Data Protection Act 1998, which replaced an indigenous product with the same name and of earlier vintage (1984), was born out of the need to implement a European Directive[23] which was self-avowedly concerned with the protection of human privacy.[24]

19 Currently s. 14 of the Post Office Act 1969.

20 For fuller references see Seipp (Select Bibliography), 338 ff.

21 In *Malone* v. *Metropolitan Police Commissioner* [1979] Ch. 344.

22 *Malone* v. *United Kingdom* (1984) 7 EHRR 14 (one should note that the position taken by Megarry V-C in *Malone* [1979] Ch. 344 has long been questioned by constitutional lawyers as inconsistent with cases such as *Entick* v. *Carrington* (1765) 2 Wils. KB 275; 19 Howell's St Tr 1029; 95 ER 807). If the interception is carried out by an unofficial person for unofficial purposes an action may lie for breach of confidence: *Francome* v. *Mirror Group Newspapers Ltd.* [1984] 1 WLR 892.

23 Directive 95/46/EC of the European Parliament and of the Council of 24 Oct. 1995 on the protection of individuals with regard to the processing of personal data and on the free movement of such [1995] *OJ* L281/31.

24 See, in particular, the tenth Recital to Directive 95/46/EC, *viz.*: 'the object of the national laws on the processing of personal data is to protect fundamental rights and freedoms, notably the right to privacy, which is recognised both in Article 8 of the European Convention for the Protection of Human Rights and Fundamental

The anonymity of persons who attracted publicity much against their will has also raised issues of privacy. More precisely, should the identities of such persons be made public freely? Two categories of persons fell into this group, the first apparently less deserving than the second. But, notwithstanding this first reaction, they both raised delicate issues.

First, then, there were criminals who had served their time and had repaid their debt to society: should they be allow to melt into the background and have, as the Gospel so emphatically urges us to do, their sins forgiven and forgotten? The Rehabilitation of Offenders Act 1976 was passed to deal with this issue; but, drafted as it is in a very technical way, it also has its limitations. Not all offences are erased; their seriousness will determine which can and which cannot be protected. Nor does this happen immediately, the passage of time again being an important element in calculating when privacy protection will accrue. The nuanced approach is perfectly understandable, even if one could argue that, at times, the wider societal interest in the reintegration of people who have offended society's rules is also a value worth bearing in mind and, with measure, promoting. Comparison with the California case of *Melvin* v. *Reid*[25] shows English law in a bad light. For some ex-criminals, their past is never forgiven and forgotten. A day's sensational journalism may thus destroy a rehabilitation that would have taken years to accomplish.

It is not only United States law that differs from English law in this respect. The West German Constitutional Court handed down a classic judgment in the *Lebach* case,[26] stating that it is the function of the courts to weigh the value of free speech on the one hand against privacy on the other. That court then went on to lay down criteria that the lower courts should apply in making that assessment: e.g. the purpose of publication (educational, prevention of crime, sensationalism); how long after the event does the disclosure take place; the need to help to reintegrate offenders into society; the extent of publication, etc. Only the traditional insularity of common-law practitioners can explain why the experience of foreign systems, often as casuistic in their approach as that of the common law, has failed to have been noticed by our courts.

The identification of victims of sexual offences was another area where human anonymity was granted by the legislator rather than by the courts. The development of the law in this area is typical of the incremental growth of the law in common-law systems such as ours.

At first, no anonymity whatsoever was granted to these unfortunate victims. Then section 4 of the Sexual Offences (Amendment) Act 1976 granted anonymity to victims of rape offences (as defined narrowly by s. 7(2) of the Act). Victims of 'lesser' sexual

Freedoms and in the general principles of Community law; . . . for that reason, the approximation of those laws must not result in any lessening of the protection they afford but must, on the contrary, seek to ensure a high level of protection in the Community'.

25 297 P 91 (1931).

26 Reproduced in translation in B. S. Markesinis and H. Unberath, *The German Law of Torts: A Comparative Treatise* (4th edn., 2001), 423–9. See also B. S. Markesinis, 'Conceptualism, Pragmatism and Courage: A Common Lawyer Looks at Some Judgments of the Federal Supreme Court' (1986) 34 *Am. J Comp. L* 349.

offences (such as unlawful sexual intercourse, incest or buggery), anxious to be left alone to forget their traumatic experiences, were, in fact, left unprotected as far as their privacy was concerned. The Criminal Justice Act 1987 extended anonymity to cases involving conspiracy to rape and burglary with intent to rape; but in the House of Lords, the minister from the Home Office thought that any further extension of the anonymity laws would be 'the thin end of the wedge'. The Calcutt Report disagreed, but the Home Office was, mysteriously it seems, adamant. And then, quite unexpectedly and with very little publicity, the official attitude changed. The Sexual Offences (Amendment) Act 1991 made it possible to extend by statutory instrument anonymity to all cases of sexual offences; and Statutory Instrument No. 1992/1336 brought this protection into existence in October 1992. In this branch of the law, the incremental growth of English law has, surely, not been one of its strengths; and the adverse consequences that both the media and anonymous government circles feared would follow any extension of the anonymity laws have failed to materialise.

The Harassment Act 1997 followed;[27] and, a year later, came the most important of statutes, the Human Rights Act 1998, which laid the foundations for a seismic change in this part of the law. There are complex reasons, to be alluded to later on, which explain why this did not quite happen in the form that some had hoped.

Moving now from the statutory fabric to where the common law has been pressed into service, we note, again, a huge variety of circumstances in which some limited form of relief against intrusions into personal privacy is provided.

Defamation is one; and we shall look at it again below when we discuss *Tolley* v. *Fry*,[28] and examine the particular wrong which American law books describe as 'appropriation of likeness'.

Trespass and nuisance can also help. Again, we shall look at this briefly below when discussing the *Bernstein* case, which will reveal the limitations of these torts in this area. It should be also be noted that the attempt of a majority of the Court of Appeal in *Khorasandjian* v. *Bush*[29] to 'twist' the tort of nuisance to offer greater protection against intrusions upon personal privacy was rejected by the House of Lords in *Hunter* v. *Canary Wharf Ltd*.[30]

Re X,[31] a wardship case, shows once again not only the inventiveness of British lawyers but also—again—the limited utility of using tools devised to perform different functions in an attempt to protect privacy interests in a circuitous manner. In this decision, anonymity was given to an ex-murderess in order to protect the anonymity of

27 Discussed in ch. 9, above.

28 [1931] AC 333. The limitations of this decision were revealed in *Gorden Kaye* v. *Andrew Robertson and Sport Newspapers* [1991] FSR 62, also reprinted in App. I to the Calcutt Report. The facts of the case are given below.

29 [1993] QB 727.

30 [1997] 2 WLR 684. Whether the result produced by *Hunter* is a fair one is another matter (which is discussed more broadly in the general context of the law of nuisance in ch. 13, above). Doctrinally the *Khorasandjian* (majority) judgment is suspect, as the dissenting judge (Sir Peter Gibson as he then was) was quick to point out. Yet in practice, the decision represents a laudable attempt to protect privacy—something which now may be (partly) achieved by the Protection from Harassment Act 1997 (on which see above, ch. 4).

31 [1984] 1 WLR 1422.

her newly born child. But it must not be forgotten that this way of protecting the mother's anonymity is only incidental. It is also limited in time; for when the wardship ends—through the death of the child or when it reaches the age of majority—the protection will disappear. Moreover, now that the recent media furore over this case has shown that the child, for whom the anonymity was primarily granted, has become aware of its mother's past, the case of their privacy continuing to receive protection has become more dubious; had it been protected by a law of privacy, the chances are that it would not have been lifted.

Nowhere, however, do we find more clearly the limitations of the casuistic approach than in the case of *Gorden Kaye (by Peter Froggatt his next friend)* v. *Andrew Robertson and Sport Newspapers Ltd.*,[32] a case which had a great impact upon the contents of the Calcutt Report.

Mr Kaye played the lead in the well-known and popular television sit-com, *'Allo 'Allo*. His sufferings started with the 1989 winter storms. He was then severely injured by a detached piece from an advertisement hoarding. For three days after this incident he was on a life-support machine; another seven days followed in intensive care. His condition remained critical throughout this period. Visits were severely restricted, not least in order to limit the risk of infection. As is usual, complete calm and peace were ordered to facilitate recovery; and so as to ensure that those medical decisions were observed, a special notice was pinned on the door of his hospital room to this effect.

The two defendants were the editor and owning company of the *Sunday Sport*—a weekly publication which the judge at first instance described as having 'a lurid and sensational style'. The photo of Mr Kaye lying asleep (or, probably, unconscious) in bed was printed on the same page as a photo of a scantily clad woman; but that only added to the bad taste of the contents of the front page. Disregarding the notice on the door, the defendants' agents entered Mr Kaye's hospital room where they photographed him with a flashlight and took an interview of sorts. At the trial the editor admitted—proudly one suspects—that his staff had achieved 'a great old-fashioned scoop'. He also accepted that other publications might well be willing to 'pay large sums of money for the privilege' of talking to and photographing Mr Kaye. Though the defendants claimed Mr Kaye had consented to all this, the available medical evidence suggested that he was, at best, only in very limited control of his faculties. Indeed, a quarter of an hour after the alleged 'voluntary' interview had taken place, Mr Kaye had no recollection of the event. Though in the subsequent publication the defendants claimed to have been motivated by a desire to inform Mr Kaye's fans of the state of his health, the facts described above (and given more fully in the judgment) point in another direction. For the average reader, this lurid and sensational journalism may well have had much baser motives.

Porter J issued a series of orders, in effect banning the publication of the story (in its original form). The defendants appealed and Glidewell, Bingham and Legatt LJJ

[32] [1991] FSR 62. In the light of the most recent developments sketched out above some judges are now saying that the case would be decided differently. Thus see *Naomi Campbell* v. *Mirror Group Newspapers* [2002] EWHC 499; [2002] EMLR 30 (QBD), [167].

essentially upheld the plaintiff's claim but, as a result of their careful review of our patchy law, had to issue a more restricted order. Basically, this allowed the defendants to publish some photos and their story, provided they made it clear that neither had been obtained with Mr Kaye's consent. The reasoning of their Lordships, as well as the reduced level of protection (to their obvious regret) which they were able to give to Mr Kaye, clearly reveals two points. First, it shows the legal contortions which have to be made in order to protect deserving victims and, second, it illustrates the need to establish some wider principle of privacy that will enable us to close unacceptable gaps in our law. Indirectly, the case and judgments also show how inadequate are the press's current attempts to demonstrate that they can police themselves on this matter.

The leading judgment was delivered by Glidewell LJ; but the other two Lords Justice delivered concurring opinions of particular interest, not least because of their comparative content. In these judgments, four causes of action were considered. In inverse order of likely success they were: passing off, trespass to the person, libel and malicious falsehood.

Passing off was dealt with briefly. It was rejected since the case was not considered to be covered by the House of Lords' decision in *Warnink* v. *Townend and Sons.*[33] The plaintiff's claim seemed to have foundered mainly on the ground that he was 'not in the position of a *trader* [italics supplied] in relation to his interest in his story about his accident'. True—but an extension of the tort could have been made, indeed, it was almost made in the case of *Sim* v. *Heinz.*[34] This case, which was not, apparently, cited to or by the court in either *Warnink* or *Kaye*, shows that an extension of this very 'commercial' tort could be attempted in order to avoid the 'grave defect in the law [of allowing one] party, for the purpose of commercial gain, to make use of the voice of another party without his consent'.[35] And if that could be done for the voice of an actor, why not for his image, especially when the appropriation of his likeness is used to enrich another person?

The attempt to use trespass to the person[36] to protect Mr Kaye did not fare much better. Two reasons were given, the first more convincing than the second. The first was that no case could be found to support the view that the taking of the flashlight photograph amounted to battery. The second was that there was no causal evidence to show that, as a result of their act, Mr Kaye had suffered distress and a setback in his recovery. In Glidewell LJ's words there was 'no evidence that the taking of the photographs did in fact cause him [Mr Kaye] any damage'. The second point is, it is submitted, not very telling since battery is a tort actionable *per se* and will succeed without proof of any damage. But the first point presented a greater obstacle given that, apparently, 'there can

33 [1979] AC 731. 34 [1959] 1 WLR 313.

35 *Sim* v. *Heinz* [1959] 1 WLR 313, 317.

36 The tort of trespass to land was not considered. According to P. Prescott, '*Kaye* v. *Robertson*: A Reply' (Select Bibliography), it could have been used if the hospital had been willing to lend its name to the action. Damages would have been very difficult to estimate, but an injunction to prevent publication of the so-called interview might have been granted. The new criminal offences recommended by the Calcutt Report (ch. 6) would, if implemented, make such activities actionable.

be no battery unless there is *contact* with the plaintiff'.[37] Flashlight contact might be treated as sufficiently close to physical contact to justify, as Glidewell LJ was willing to entertain, an extension of the tort of battery. It must be noted, however, that in novel situations the current tendency is to resort to the tort of negligence rather than expand the older tort of battery and even to bypass the latter tort by having resort to criminal law. Why not then try negligence? This ever-growing tort, unlike battery, requires proof of the existence of a duty of care—something which would have caused no problem in the instant case; but it also requires proof of damage which, as stated, was not forthcoming. It may thus be that the two elements of the two torts were inadvertently telescoped into one. Clearly, the learned judge regarded this part of his judgment as secondary to the main thrust of his arguments that came in his discussion of the remaining two causes of action: libel and malicious falsehood.

Libel was, according to Glidewell and Bingham LJJ, strongly arguable. *Tolley* v. *J. S. Fry and Sons Ltd.*[38] was the authority that persuaded the judge who heard the application at first instance; and it also appealed to the judges in the Court of Appeal. If it was not used in the end, it was because of the rule in *William Coulson & Sons* v. *James Coulson and Co.*[39] which held that interim injunctions are to be used sparingly in libel actions—a rule confirmed in *Herbage* v. *Times Newspapers Ltd. and Others* (unreported), despite the decision of the House of Lords in *American Cynamid* v. *Ethicon*.[40] So, though the judges felt that the publication was libellous, they also felt that a jury might well not take the same view and, in the circumstances, a general injunction should not be, and was not, granted.

But was the publication libellous on the authority of *Tolley* v. *Fry*? *Tolley* succeeded because an innuendo was discovered. It was, in 1931—but would it still be now?—defamatory for an amateur golfer to give the impression that he had 'prostituted his amateur status for gain'. But, as stated, the *ratio* of the case would not have covered a professional golfer even though he, too, needs (perhaps even more strongly than the amateur) to prevent the unauthorised use of his image. So where is the innuendo here? Given the nature of the publication in question, one could argue that any respectable member of society who appears to be associated with the *Sunday Sport* is, automatically, defamed. But the learned judge, hinting, perhaps, at this suggestion, was right in taking the view that such 'a conclusion is [not] inevitable'. And if a jury were to decide that there was no defamation, which would be the end of Mr Kaye's interest to be left in peace in his hospital bed. Yet, as Bingham LJ said: '[i]f ever a person has a right to be let alone by strangers with no public interest to pursue, it must surely be when he lies in hospital recovering from brain surgery and in no more than partial command of his faculties'. And yet this right, *de lege lata*, depends upon the quaint facts of *Tolley* v. *Fry*; and the result, judging from the Court of Appeal judgment in *Tolley*,[41] was not so obvious even in those halcyon days of the 1930s when sportsmen played for their sport and not for money.

[37] *Street on Torts* (10th edn., 1999), 33.
[38] [1931] AC 333.
[39] [1887] 3 TLR 846.
[40] [1975] AC 395.
[41] [1930] 1 KB 467.

In the end Mr Kaye succeeded by the skin of his teeth but then, again, only in a very limited way, because the judges were able to rely upon the tort of malicious falsehood. This is not an easy tort, as any reading of a textbook will reveal; nor is it frequently used. But at least it avoided the injunction problems of *Coulson* v. *Coulson*. For in malicious falsehood, the test of that case[42] applies only to the requirement that the claimant must show that the words are false; and the (original) statement by the *Sunday Sport* that the photos and interview were taken with Mr Kaye's consent was, clearly, false.

The casuistry of English law has not come to an end. Currently, the most widely used way to protect privacy is through the ever-expanding equitable action to restrain breaches of confidence. This has become so important in modern practice that it will be the subject of its own subsection below. But what we said thus far (and what will be added later) can already support an unfavourable conclusion: English law is excessively patchy, messy and unprincipled. It is the methodology that is really wanting.

If all of the above shows clearly that many aspects of human privacy are adequately protected, it does not mean that this laudable aim is achieved is in the best way. We say this because the protection is neither complete nor principled. More importantly, it has become chaotically complex: this is partly because of the common law way of updating the law—slowly, patchily, and via contradictory *dicta*, successive accretions of decisions, dithering judgments—but also and above all because of a good dose of Strasbourg law which seems to be galloping ahead without mature reflection or planning. This book, which in its first edition twenty years ago was the first among the larger textbooks to devote specific space to the tort of privacy, now finds itself admitting that because of all these factors the law has now become too complex to be compatible with the idea of justice. Are matters as bad or as complex elsewhere? France may have gone overboard in protecting human privacy even in cases that seem to cry out for a different solution; but Germany reveals a state of affairs which is not only balanced but also achieved not though their Code but through court activity, and which is thus usable by us as well, if only to signal what could be achieved by judicial development of the law in this area.

The picture in countries such as Germany shows that (whatever may be the starting-point of the inquiry) protection there is also dependent upon the facts of each case: in that sense the protection of privacy in Germany can also be seen as patchy. The damnation of our law thus comes more from the persistent attempts of English judges to afford such protection as they see fit by means of expanding medieval torts by putting them on a procrustean bed and stretching them in a way that satisfies neither modern logic nor contemporary feelings of justice. What makes the German practice so different is the fact that their judges have tried to develop logical criteria that will help them determine on which side of the line new cases will fall. Thus, in Germany in cases where speech clashes with privacy, we find German courts weighing such factors as: (*a*) the motives of the publisher which, in the context of privacy protection, has been taken to mean that if the invasion was motivated by a wish to make money at the expense of the claimant, damages should be assessed in a way that would deprive the tortfeasor of his

42 [1887] 3 TLR 46. For an outline of the law in this area, see ch. 21, Section 7, above.

ill-gotten gains; (*b*) the importance of the speech (e.g. does it advance knowledge and public debate or merely benefit the speaker financially?); (*c*) the way in which the information about the claimant was obtained: e.g. where illegal means or a telephoto lens are used (indicating to the 'intruder' that the claimant wished to be left alone); (*d*) the extent of the dissemination of the information; (*e*) the accuracy of the statement or whether it was fabricated by a news medium; (*f*) the breadth of the restriction which the claimant wishes to place upon the defendant's speech rights; (*g*) other, wider societal objectives which may be involved in the dispute; and so on. The courts also take the view that a severe attack may justify an otherwise excessive counter-attack. This 'balanced' approach is not just to our liking. Here is what one of our greatest judges[43] had to say on this very topic:

> The German approach shows us the way, avoiding the brutal simplicity of the [US] First Amendment, to work out a balance between the right of free speech and the right of privacy—it being noted . . . that German courts have, in some contexts, affirmed the primacy of speech as strongly as it has been done in the USA.

Those of our learned judges who thus see serious 'conceptual problems' with the development of a 'blockbuster' tort of privacy[44] might thus offer us a fuller version of their concerns so that we can address them individually. Most importantly, however, they might wish to take note that what some of us are calling for is not the creation of a 'blockbuster' tort but the evolution of rational criteria to decide the expansion of the afforded legal protection which everyone sees coming. Judging from the most recent cases such as *A* v. *B plc and another*, the series of *Douglas* v. *Hello!* and *Campbell* decisions, etc., we may, indeed, be seeing such a reorientation of our legal thinking, namely, from the barren attempt to stretch medieval torts to perform modern functions (as described above) to the gradual development of rational criteria which are 'thrown into the melting pot' where the balancing of the competing values takes place. Thus, in all of the above cases, one notes statements which stress the need to afford some residual rights of privacy even to public figures, observations that the surreptitious taking of photographs, e.g. through telephoto lenses, is an indication which must be weighed in the balancing process and may even be a strong pointer that there is an actionable invasion,[45] repeated statements that some distinction has to be made between permanent and transient sexual relationships (the latter receiving lesser protection), and many other statements of this type. These criteria have nothing in common with earlier attempts to expand trespass, nuisance or passing off, but bear greater resemblance to the reasoning processes of continental European courts. If our judges—or some of them at least—do not wish to 'learn' from systems such as the above,[46] which have been

[43] Lord Wilberforce in his Foreword to B. S. Markesinis, *Always on the Same Path: Essays in Foreign Law and Comparative Methodology* (2001), ii, p. xiii.

[44] For instance Mummery LJ in *Wainwright* v. *Home Office* [2002] 3 WLR 405, 419.

[45] For instance, *R* v. *Broadcasting Standards Commission, ex parte British Broadcasting Corporation* [2001] QB ('the *Dixons* case'), [37], per Lord Woolf MR.

[46] Or at least acknowledge in their judgments when and how foreign law has guided them to their conclusions. In the *Dixons* case, discussed above, Lord Woolf MR accepted (at [17]) unequivocally that it is 'perfectly

operating under the kind of wider statutory-style regime which we, too, must now observe, that is their choice. But such a preference for reinventing the wheel cannot conceal the fact that important changes are taking place in this area of the law which are bringing our law closer to that of our geographical neighbours.

3. THE PROTECTION AFFORDED BY ENGLISH LAW IN THE MOST IMPORTANT TYPES OF CASES

The absence of a tort of privacy in English law does not mean that privacy interests are left totally unprotected. In fact, a combination of statutes and the common law have in their own pragmatic way gone a long way—especially in recent times—to close many of the most worrisome gaps. For didactic purposes the cases can be grouped under three broad headings: (*a*) privacy interests violated by intrusions into one's private sphere; (*b*) appropriation of personality and likeness; and (*c*) public disclosures of true private facts, nowadays protected mainly through remedies available under the equitable doctrine of breach of confidence.

(A) INTRUSIONS

The starting-point here is the idea that property carries for the owner the right to exclude others and, hence, from early times the torts of trespass and nuisance have proved sufficient to cope with most intrusions, however motivated. Indeed, such is the extent of protection afforded to the owner (but probably not to a licensee)[47] that the law, in the case of trespass, allows the claimant to succeed without proof of any damage[48] and, in appropriate cases, has even granted aggravated damages.[49] The narrow construction of

appropriate to have regard to the jurisprudence of the European Court of Human Rights, the European Court of Justice *and of other countries*' (emphasis added).

47 The law on this may not be entirely clear. Is a guest in the home of his host entitled to rely on trespass to protect his privacy while in his room? Does a female employee of the master of the house have such rights? (Arguably yes, according to Lord Denman in *Lewis* v. *Ponsford* (1838) 8 Car. & P 687; 173 ER 674.) And what of an occupier of a hotel room or a hospital bed in circumstances such as those litigated in *Gorden Kaye* v. *Andrew Robertson and Sport Newspapers Ltd.* (reproduced in App. I to the Calcutt Report)? The last two examples have not been tested in this country though, according to Prescott (Select Bibliography), an action by the hospital authority in the *Kaye* case would have succeeded. Clearly, in such instances we are not talking of an action for damages (since the hospital has suffered none) but an action for an injunction restraining the publication of any photos or interviews. Not surprisingly, then, a number of recent *dicta* have suggested that the *Kaye* case would nowadays be decided differently. See, for instance, Morland J in *Naomi Cambell* v. *Mirror Group Newspapers* [2002] EWHC 499; [2002] EMLR 30 (QB), [67].

48 *Entick* v. *Carrington* (1765) 2 Wils. KB 275; 95 ER 807, 817, per Lord Camden CJ.

49 *Merest* v. *Harvey* (1814) 5 Taunt. 442; 128 ER 761. There is, however, little modern authority on this point. Calculating damages in trespass actions would also present difficulties so, in many cases, the remedy might be an injunction restraining the publication of any photograph taken or recording made during the 'intrusion'. The Calcutt proposals, discussed below, seem to offer a much clearer starting-point, unconnected with the

police powers to enter and search premises has also been explained by Lord Denning in *Ghani* v. *Jones*[50] as depending upon the individual's right that his 'privacy and his possessions... [be not] invaded except for the most compelling reasons'. The same privacy interests have been invoked by the courts as justification for a narrow construction of various statutes to prevent official searches of premises unless explicitly authorised.[51] But developments under the so-called 'Anton Piller' order,[52] giving the police under certain circumstances considerable powers of search and seizure in civil suits, represent, from a privacy point of view, an unfortunate retreat.[53]

Nuisance is another tort that could help a claimant whose privacy was interfered with by activities taking place outside his land. In *Walker* v. *Brewster*,[54] for example, the plaintiff sought to enjoin his neighbours from holding large fêtes on their grounds which adjoined his own. These fêtes attracted large crowds and destroyed his privacy. *Constant* aerial surveillance has also been described as a 'monstrous invasion of privacy' and might thus, in appropriate circumstances, amount to an actionable nuisance.

Bernstein v. *Skyviews*[55] involved another attempt to use nuisance to protect privacy interests. There, the owner of land photographed from the air involved a miscellany of torts such as nuisance and trespass to make the photographer liable. But an action for trespass failed because the owner of the land has no unlimited rights over the airspace above his property (and, anyway, the picture was shown to have been taken from an angle so that there had been no 'invasion' of the airspace above his land). Nuisance likewise fails if, as here, there is no dangerous or continuing state of affairs, which clearly there is not in the case of an isolated flight near the claimant's land.[56] But nuisance would also fail if the claimant had no interest in the land in question, e.g. if he happened to be a lodger or a guest photographed by the flying plane while sunbathing unaware in the nude. Such an interference with this hypothetical claimant's self-image should not be left 'unpunished'; but nuisance would certainly fail to provide a remedy since he would have no interest in the land. This particular 'defect' of the old tort of nuisance—inevitable since nuisance was invented hundreds of years ago to deal with pig farms and brick-builders causing their distinct kind of pollution to medieval Englishmen—was not really designed to deal with the modern plague of the paparazzi. The attempt of

technical rules of the ancient tort of trespass. For discussion of the law of tort relating to trespass to land, see ch. 12, above.

50 [1970] 1 QB 693, 708.

51 See *Inland Revenue Commissioners* v. *Rossminster Ltd.* [1980] AC 952, *Morris* v. *Beardmore* [1981] AC 446.

52 *Anton Piller KG* v. *Manufacturing Processes Ltd.* [1976] Ch. 55; now known as 'search orders' and with a statutory footing: see s. 7(1) Civil Procedure Act 1997.

53 See also the powers of search and seizure granted the police by the Police and Criminal Evidence Act 1984, ss. 1, 8 and 19.

54 (1876) LR 5 Eq. 25, 26.

55 *Bernstein* v. *Skyviews & General Ltd.* [1978] QB 479

56 It might be otherwise if there were constant air surveillance or observance of what was happening on the claimant's land through the erection of mirrors on the observer's land. For discussion of the tort of nuisance, see ch. 13 above.

a majority of the Court of Appeal in *Khorasandjian* v. *Bush*[57] to 'twist' the tort of nuisance was thus rejected by the House of Lords in *Hunter* v. *Canary Wharf Ltd.*[58]

(B) APPROPRIATION OF PERSONALITY

This may take such forms as an unauthorised use of another person's name, voice or image, the last type of violation being the most common and, historically (in both the United States and the Federal Republic of Germany), one of the earliest types of privacy litigation to arise.

The appropriation of one's likeness typically occurs by the use of a picture without permission and is the commonest form of this type of privacy invasion. It involves no free-speech implications for the defendant and it should not be condoned by society, especially where the claimant's image is used to the commercial advantage of the defendant. In *Tolley* v. *Fry*[59] and in a number of other unreported cases in the 1930s,[60] the English courts were able to make an ingenious use of the tort of defamation to combat the commercial appropriation of personality. Thus, as already noted, the plaintiff was able to succeed in his claim for damages because the court fastened on his 'amateur' status in order to assert that this was prejudiced by the innuendo that he had allowed his picture to be used 'for financial gain'. However, as we shall see, the overall protection afforded to victims of such violations is not sufficient and the claim for protection in such cases is strong. Many legal writers have supported this point of view[61] and judicial systems such as those of the United States and Germany that have taken steps (by means of statutes, judicial decisions or both) to deal with the problem and to provide a remedy in such cases do not appear to have suffered in any way.

Sim v. *H. J. Heinz Co. Ltd.*[62] offers another example of legal ingenuity. In this case the claimant complained about the unauthorised impersonation (by another well-known actor) of his characteristic voice in a television advertisement promoting the defendants' products. The plaintiff argued, *inter alia*, that his voice as an actor was part of his stock-in-trade and, therefore, was something which he was entitled to protect as part of his goods. This was, in effect, an invitation to the court to extend analogically the remedy available for the tort of passing off. In the Court of Appeal Hodson LJ said that

57 [1993] QB 727.

58 [1997] 2 WLR 684. As discussed previously, it can be questioned whether the result produced by *Hunter* is a fair one, given that *Khorasandjian* was a laudable attempt to protect privacy, that now is achieved (partly) by the Protection from Harassment Act 1997 (on which see above, ch. 9). On nuisance generally, see ch. 13 above.

59 [1931] AC 333.

60 Quoted by J. G. Fleming, *The Law of Torts* (8th edn., 1992), 605, n. 44.

61 E.g. T. Frazer, 'Appropriation of Personality: A New Tort?' (1983) 99 *LQR* 281; Prescott (Select Bibliography), at 456. The latter author, however, seems to limit the protection to cases where the likeness is used for 'promoting a commercial product or service'. This would mean that the use of one's image to promote a political party or other, non-contentious, cause might not be actionable and such a result would appear of dubious merit. Furthermore, the protection offered by passing off claims such as *Irvine* v. *Talksport Ltd.* [2002] 2 All ER 414 is dependent upon the existence of goodwill in the claimant's image, which may tend to limit this more to the commercial sphere as well (unless an argument can be made (with or without the Human Rights Act 1998) that such 'goodwill' needs protection even in non-commercial endorsement cases).

62 [1959] 1 WLR 313.

this was 'an arguable case'. But passing off has its own limitations, since the remedy has typically been available only to persons engaged in some common field of activity. In the event, the plaintiff's request for an injunction was turned down.

However, the recent *Irvine* v. *Talksport Ltd.*[63] decision suggests that this 'common field of activity' limitation will no longer prevent celebrities, with significant goodwill or reputation in their image, from using passing off to enjoin apparent endorsements by them of products or services. Nevertheless, as far as English law is concerned, these cases are really little more than further examples of the ingenuity that legal advisers have to resort to in order to overcome the absence of well-accepted action in such cases.[64]

(C) PUBLIC DISCLOSURE OF TRUE PRIVATE FACTS[65]

(i) The Growth of the Action for Breach of Confidence

This is by far the most difficult, though the most common, category of invasion of privacy and the one that brings out most clearly the clash between one person's right to be left alone and another person's right to speak and to be informed. It must be remembered, of course, that we are here envisaging cases involving the disclosure of private (not public) facts. This division is not, however, as easy as it appears to be at first sight. For instance, something that happens at a party or in a restaurant may be witnessed by many people: is this public? Would the characterisation differ if the scene witnessed were in a part of the restaurant reserved for 'private' dining? Can the taking of a picture of an intimate moment in a public place be, of itself, an indication of a private intrusion if it were taken with a telephoto lens[66] Finally, this subject is further complicated by our

[63] [2002] 1 WLR 2355, [2002] 2 All ER 414. It should be noted, however, that Mr Irvine was awarded only £2,000 in damages (see [2003] EMLR 6) and, since this was a lower figure than Talksport's original offer of £5,000, also had to pay Talksport's costs (totalling approximately £30,000—something of a Pyrrhic victory). However, the Court of Appeal ruled ([2003] EWCA Civ. 423, [2003] 2 All ER 881, [2003] EMLR 26) that the basis of assessment of damages should have been what Talksport would have had to pay lawfully to secure Mr Irvine's endorsement (rather than what Talksport would have been willing to pay). This upped the award to £25,000, which shifted the burden of paying the costs back to Talksport. Further, the ruling as it stands seems not to apply to character-merchandising cases where a claimant's likeness is used: Laddie J ruled that such merchandising does not necessarily entail the public thinking that the celebrity whose image is used actually endorses the product. Yet this may also be characterised as an appropriation of personality: see K. Sloper and B. Cordery, 'Personality Endorsement: New Brands Hatch?' [2002] 13 *Ent. LR* 106, 108–9.

[64] One interesting point which was argued but not reported in the *Irvine* case ([2002] 2 All ER 414) is the possible human-rights dimension to such cases, especially concerning Art. 8 (on the right to a private and family life) and Art. 1 of the First Protocol (on the protection of property): as Laddie J stated '[h]ad I come to the conclusion that passing off had not developed sufficiently to cover false endorsements it would have been necessary to go on to consider whether this new strand of law was effective, to use the words of Sedley LJ in *Douglas* v. *Hello! Ltd* [2001] FSR 732, to "give the final impetus" to reach that result' (para. 77). Whether this may presage a more generalised approach in future cases remains to be seen.

[65] The fullest discussion can be found in F. Gurry, *Breach of Confidence* (1985).

[66] Many systems (e.g. the German and French) have held that the fact that a number of people have witnessed an event does not, by itself, mean that it can be recorded and repeated with impunity to the world at large. Certainly the use of a telephoto lens may now lead to trouble, as even the Press Council's own guidelines recognise. See also the early recognition of this issue by Laws J in *Hellewell* v. *Chief Constable of Derbyshire* [1995] 1 WLR 804.

system's apparent inability to distinguish in legal terms between those who seek publicity (politicians, actors) and those who have had publicity unwillingly thrust upon them. Though putting up with intrusive observance is, generally speaking, likelier to be expected from members of the first group rather than the second, we have now, finally, reached the stage in this country where we accept than even public figures are entitled to some degree of privacy. A different but not unrelated issue is the extent to which a public figure can control the degree of observation and exposure which he actually gets.

The case law, a trickle for the better part of the twentieth century, burgeoned substantially as the new century dawned and has become a veritable torrent in recent years. This decisional explosion was, no doubt, prompted by the ability of the tabloid press to feed the appetite of its readers for scurrilous gossip. *Beckham* v. *MGN* [67] involved an injunction to stop the publication of photographs taken at the home of that most high profile of celebrity couples; *Blair* v. *Associated Newspapers Ltd.* [68] sought an injunction against various parties to stop the publication of the domestic arrangements made by the Prime Minister's wife. *Holden* v. *Express Newspapers Ltd.*[69] concerned the banning of photos of the actress and her husband relaxing at their home swimming pool. Angus Deayton likewise sought an injunction against the publication of intimate details.[70] Sara Cox obtained substantial damages as settlement from the *Sunday People* for being photographed in the nude with her husband while on their honeymoon. The court's judgment in *Archer* v. *Williams*[71] granted the wife of the (in)famously disgraced politician an injunction against her former employee who had revealed many stories about her, including the fact that she had had a facelift. In *Jagger* v. *News of the World*, Jade Jagger sought and gained an injunction to prevent pictures of her embracing someone in front of a West End nightclub. *Douglas and Zeta Jones* and *OK!* v. *Hello!* has already (at the time of writing) generated a number of major decisions because the couple sold the pictures of their wedding to one magazine but another rival managed to publish first its own surreptitiously taken pictures.[72] The list seems endless; the dignity of the law was, it could be argued, never more seriously challenged than by having to deal with such antics; the lawyers, as always, were the biggest winners.[73] This list also

[67] 28 June 2001, Eady J. (unreported).

[68] Case no. HQ0001236 (2001) (unreported, transcript available on Westlaw).

[69] 7 June 2001, referred to in M. Tugendhat and I. Christie, *The Law of Privacy and the Media* (Select Bibliography), 218.

[70] *The Guardian*, 10 June 2002.

[71] [2003] EMLR 38. Note that in this case a contractual basis (the employment relationship) was used found the claim to protect such private information.

[72] *Douglas* v *Hello! Ltd.*: *(No. 1)* [2001] QB 967; *(No. 2)* [2003] EWCA Civ. 139, [2003] EMLR 28; *(No. 3)* [2006] QB 125, to name but a few (a Westlaw search showed ten separate cases relating to the matter): the ruling of the House of Lords on appeal from the last of these was handed down on 2 May 2007 (see [2007] UKHL 21).

[73] The costs incurred in some of these cases have been substantial, while the damages awarded have typically been rather minimal, and very minimal by comparison with the costs expended: see, e.g., the award in *Douglas* v. *Hello! (No. 3)* [2006] of £14,500 to Michael Douglas and Catherine Zeta-Jones (and nothing at all to *OK!* Magazine)—costs are already well into seven figures and no doubt continue to rise. However, on appeal the House of Lords (by a 3:2 majority) restored the order of Lindsay J at first instance, which awarded £1,033,156 to *OK!*. Even this award, however, is substantially below the level of costs expended by the claimants in this litigation to date.

shows that, in the absence of legal aid, it is those who thrive on publicity—celebrities—who complain whenever the information published about them has not been suitably airbrushed and/or sanitised by their staff. But enough of the unacceptable face of the law; let us now return to the legal reasons given to justify these decisions.

In order to prevent the disclosure of private information such as the above the courts have, once again, been shown not to be short of ingenuity. This time, however, it was not the law of torts that was mined for useful nuggets but equity. The old equitable remedy of breach of confidence proved malleable enough to fill this growing need.

An early start had been made during the nineteenth century in *Prince Albert* v. *Strange*.[74] It involved the publication of some drawings made by the royal couple, which was enjoined on the grounds that the sanction was necessary to protect property rights in literary and artistic creations. However, it is clear that the judge did not base his reasoning solely upon this ground: 'breach of trust, confidence or contract' was also invoked and, indeed, presumed by the judge in the absence of contrary evidence from the defendant. This line of reasoning seemed moderately promising, so invoking the notion of breach of an implied contract, as in the case where a photographer was stopped from using photographs taken of a customer without the latter's consent, was tried in a different case.[75] Later still, the device of breach of an implied obligation of confidence was tried in *Argyll* v. *Argyll*,[76] where a man was not allowed to disclose information given to him by his ex-wife during their marriage and concerning her private affairs.

But the equitable remedies available for breach of confidence had their own limitations. In particular three requirements had to be satisfied[77] before a remedy might become available (and then it could be defeated if the public interest required that the information be published).[78] Thus, *first*, the information 'betrayed' must have had 'the necessary quality of confidence about it'; *second*, it 'must have been imparted in circumstances importing an obligation' of confidence; and *third*, it 'must have been used in an unauthorised way to the detriment of the [confider]'.[79]

[74] (1848) 2 De G & Sm. 652; 64 ER 293. The point with regard to breach of confidence was made more explicitly in *Morison v. Moat* (1851) 8 Hare 241, 68 ER 482, affd. (1852) 21 LJ Ch. (NS) 248.

[75] *Pollard* v. *Photographic Co.* (1888) 40 Ch. D 345. Much the same result is reached under modern copyright law, which grants the person who commissioned the photograph 'for private and domestic purposes' the right to prevent it being shown to the public (s. 85 of the Copyright, Designs and Patents Act 1988).

[76] [1967] Ch. 302. The parties involved were the Duke and Duchess of Argyll.

[77] Conveniently summarised in *Coco* v. *A. N. Clark (Engineers) Ltd.* [1969] RPC 41, 47. See, also, *A-G* v. *Guardian Newspapers* (No. 2) [1990] 1 AC 109.

[78] To date, this defence has typically related to relatively straightforward cases, such as preventing future crimes (*Weld-Blundell* v. *Stephens* [1920] AC 956), breaches of statute (*Initial Services* v. *Putterill* [1968] 1 QB 396—breach of competition laws), or matters detrimental to the public interest (*Lion Laboratories* v. *Evans* [1984] 2 All ER 417). Equally, the courts have been keen to stress that just because the public may be interested in knowing about something, that will not necessarily make it 'in the public interest' that it should be disclosed, warning the Press that it is 'peculiarly susceptible to the error of confusing the public interest with their own interest' (per Sir John Donaldson MR in *Francome* v. *Mirror Group Newspapers* [1984] 2 All ER 408).

[79] *Malone* v. *Commissioner of Police of the Metropolis (No. 2)* [1979] Ch. 344 at 375, per Megarry V-C. See, also, *Saltman Engineering Co. Ltd.* v. *Campbell Engineering Co. Ltd.* (1948) 65 RPC 203, *Coco* v. *A. N. Clark (Engineers) Ltd.* [1969] RPC 41, 47, per Megarry J. It is worth noting, however, that in recent years the courts have been increasingly willing to dispense with the requirement of showing detriment (see, e.g. the Court of

In the nearly 40 years that have elapsed since these conditions were specified, our judges have proceeded to reshape these requirements, especially the second one, or water them down in response to the unremitting pressures to do something about privacy[80] without going to the (as they saw it) extreme option of accepting the need to create a tort of privacy. The result was to call meat 'fish' and thus make it edible on a Friday with one's conscience kept at bay. The evolution of our law had to happen spontaneously, using local ingredients and ideas, and without having recourse to foreign wisdom. There is long tradition behind this kind of intellectual chauvinism[81] and, unconvincing though it is, it is only to be expected in a major legal system.

So let us start with the second of the *Coco* requirements, in practice the most crucial of the three.[82] When did the circumstances impose an obligation of confidence? In the beginning the answer was obvious: if there was a pre-existing identifiable, intimate relationship between confider and confidant that made such confidence essential. Where more obviously to find this than in a relationship involving trust[83] or marriage?[84] Founding liability on such grounds would—clearly—not work where 'the wrong complained of was deliberate and even surreptitious taking [of information] with a view to publication';[85] and such were the bulk of cases we mentioned earlier on. But in *Stephens* v. *Avery*[86] the mould began to crack. Sir Nicolas Browne-Wilkinson V-C (as he then was) thus held that while there must exist a relationship between the confider and the confidant, it need not amount to a pre-existing legal relationship. So, where information relating to sexual conduct had been communicated to another person expressly in

Appeal's judgment in *Federal Bank of the Middle East* v. *Hadkinson* [2000] 2 All ER 395, 413–14). Alternatively, the courts have been prepared to find detriment very readily: see, e.g., Rose J's decision in *X Health Authority* v. *Y* [1988] RPC 379, 391–2.

80 Although it must be acknowledged that some similar pressures were also felt in a more commercial context: e.g. where information arrived in the hands of third parties who were not somehow privy to the original relationship of confidence (e.g. *Millar* v. *Taylor* (1769) 4 Burr 2303; and the position of the newspapers in the *Spycatcher* saga—see *A-G* v. *Guardian Newspapers Ltd.* [1988] 3 WLR 776, 805 (per Lord Goff)) or where some form of 'commercial espionage' led to confidential information being taken surreptitiously (e.g. *E.I. du Pont de Nemours & Co. Inc.* v. *Rolfe & Christopher* 431 F 2d 1012 (Fifth Cir., 1970), cert. denied 400 US 1024 (1971); *Franklin* v. *Giddens* [1978] Qd R. 72 and *Francome* v. *Mirror Group Newspapers Ltd.* [1984] 2 All ER 408). See, generally, J. Stuckey, 'The Liability of Innocent Third Parties Implicated in Another's Breach of Confidence' (1981) 4 *UNSWLJ* 73 and G. Wei, 'Surreptitious Takings of Confidential Information' (1992) 12 *Leg. Stud.* 302.

81 Lord Goff, for instance, argued along such lines in the context of free speech but Lord Bingham, writing extra-judicially, was, we think more candid when he asked how could this stand up to the fact that the UK had repeatedly been held to have violated the European Convention.

82 We shall discuss the erosion of the other two requirements in the following sub-section.

83 *W* v. *Edgell* [1990] Ch. 59 (doctor/patient) or *A-G* v. *Guardian Newspapers Ltd.* [1987] 1 WLR 1248 (employer/employee).

84 *Duchess of Argyll* v. *Duke of Argyll* [1967] Ch. 302.

85 M. Richardson, 'The Private Life after *Douglas* v. *Hello*' [2003] *Singapore Journal of Legal Studies*, 311, 326.

86 *Stephens* v. *Avery and Others* [1988] Ch. 449. The later case of *WB* v. *H. Bauer Publishing* [2002] EMLR 8 (another 'motion to strike out' case) was even more open when it admitted that '[o]ne of the inhibiting factors about this aspect of the law, hitherto, has been that it was traditionally necessary to establish a duty of confidence—most frequently associated with a prior relationship of some kind. It is becoming easier now, however, to establish that an obligation of confidence can arise (in equity) without the parties having been in any such prior relationship; the obligation may be more readily inferred from the circumstances in which the information came to the defendant's attention' (per Eady J, para. 30).

confidence and that other person expressly disclosed that information to another, the court would intervene and enjoin such publication. The proposition that, in the absence of a legally enforceable contract or a pre-existing relationship (such as employer–employee or doctor–patient), it was not possible to enforce a legal duty of confidence had become 'plainly wrong' even though everyone until then had regarded it as obviously right. Though this was a judgment delivered on a striking-out motion, and the Vice-Chancellor refused to be drawn into the question of where and how the borderlines should be drawn, it is clearly a decision that some judges at least were begin to show sensitivity to the need to set limits to aggressive intrusions by the press into private lives of individuals.

Another way of creating an obligation of confidence was to say that it arose out of an agreement of confidentiality, either expressly or mutually implicitly assumed by the parties. But this, too, showed that breach of confidence, though a useful substitute for privacy could not cover the archetypal case of violation of human privacy which arises when one person surreptitiously obtains pictures or recording of another without the latter's permission. Yet this requirement that an agreement existed was watered down as well in the 1990s, as the case of *Shelley Films Ltd.* v. *Rex Features Ltd.*[87] shows. For the agreement of confidentiality found its way into the dealing of the parties, not because of an implied agreement being reached between them to that effect, but because 'a reasonable person in the position of the defendant would have assumed such an obligation'. After all, in the *Shelley* case one would have assumed as much given the plethora of notices on the set prohibiting photography. So something 'extra' still had to exist, beyond the quality of the information itself, to put on notice the potential violator of the confidence that he was assuming an obligation of confidence. Protection under this heading would still not work in many cases of violation of privacy. The true turning point came in *Venables* v. *News Group Newspapers*,[88] where the President of the Family Division, Dame Elizabeth Butler Sloss, delivered one of her characteristically bold (and controversial) judgments when she issued injunctions *contra mundum* preventing the publication of material which might reveal the identity of the killers of the young Jamie Bulger. The judgment finally sat the *Coco* requirement on its head. For here there was no information imparted in circumstances of confidence. The confidentiality was imposed regardless of how it was obtained. It was there because of the notoriety of the killer and the danger—obvious and real—to his life; information which, if made public would endanger the child's life which deserved protection under Article 2 ECHR. The Court of Appeal in the *Douglas* v. *Hello! (No. 3)* case could not have put it more clearly when it said:

> A remarkable feature of the *Venables* case was that the nature of the information alone gave rise to the duty of confidence regardless of the circumstance in which the information might come to the knowledge of a person who might wish to publish it.[89]

[87] [1994] EMLR 134. (Publication of pictures taken surreptitiously on film set was prohibited by court order.)

[88] [2001] 1 All ER 908. This was soon followed by a similar order to protect Mary Bell and the by now adult child (once protected by the wardship order we encountered earlier on in our treatment (see n. 31 and the associated text, above): see *X (A woman formerly known as Mary Bell))* v. *SO* [2003] EWHC 1101, [2003] EMLR 37.

[89] *Douglas* v. *Hello!* [2006] QB 125, at [69].

The crucial requirement of the action of breach of confidence had finally watered down to nothing. Perhaps, that is the wrong way of putting the monumental shift. A far better way and relevant to this chapter is the one adopted by Helen Fenwick and Gavin Phillipson in their excellent treatise[90] where they have written:

Venables thus specifically affirms that a court may grant an injunction against a publication of information, regardless of the circumstances in which it is obtained, based solely upon the damage that disclosure of the information in question may do to the Convention rights of the person to whom the information relates.

This liberating process for the action for breach of confidence was encapsulated in an important (*obiter*) *dictum* in the case of *A* v. *B plc*[91] where it was said that

A duty of confidence will arise whenever the party subject to the duty is in a situation where he either knows or ought to know that the other person can reasonably expect his privacy protected.

The case which came as close as any court has in recognising a tort of privacy—always under the name of breach of confidence—was *Campbell* v. *MGN Ltd.*[92] It involved the surreptitious taking of photographs of the model Naomi Campbell in the street outside the premises of Narcotics Anonymous where she was undergoing counselling. The need to secure the tempestuous model some free space to cure herself of her harmful habit was, of course, downplayed by the paper reproducing the pictures, the excuse, as always, being its wish to inform the public who had a 'right to know'. The Court of Appeal judgment had already espoused this new line by accepting that the confidentiality arose not because one person had confided to another but because it related 'to an aspect of an individual's private life which he does not choose to make public'. Lord Phillips MR, with his typical intellectual honesty, added that '[w]e consider that the unjustifiable publication of such information would better be described as breach of privacy rather than breach of confidence'.[93] What remained to be done was for the House of Lords to put the coping stone to this long process, delayed for so long by the greedy parts of our press industry finding willing assistants in timorous judges. But the House of Lords in fact went even further than any other case before it, since on the facts of *Campbell*, unlike those of *Shelley* or *Douglas*, there were no obvious indications that the photographed scene was not to be photographed. As Fenwick and Phillipson have thus correctly observed:

This was . . . the first time that an English appellate court had imposed liability for use of personal information in the absence of any circumstances imposing the obligation save for the nature of the information itself. That is the value underlying this cause of action.[94]

90 *Media Freedom under the Human Rights Act* (Select Bibliography), 732.

91 [2002] 2 All ER 545, at 551B.

92 [2004] 2 AC 457.

93 Fenwick and Phillipson (Select Bibliography), 663.

94 *Ibid.*, 739. See, also, their review of the aspects of the case which dealing with horizontality at p. 134 ff. where Lord Hoffman's confused and confusing judgment comes in for some very trenchant criticism.

In *Campbell* their Lordships skirted around the terminological issue but, it might be argued, only to save face by not admitting that what they had denied for decades now existed. 'This tort', declared Lord Nicholls who, along with Lord Hoffmann, was in the dissent, 'however labelled, affords respect for one aspect of an individual's privacy. That is the value underlying this cause of action.'[95] Despite his foot-dragging, Lord-Hoffmann also had to attribute the protection afforded not to breach of confidence or good faith (which, for years, was seen as the foundation of the confidence action) but to the need to protect the human dignity and personality. He thus said:

> the new approach takes a different view of the underlying value which the law protects. Instead of the cause of action being based upon the duty of good faith applicable to confidential personal information and trade secrets alike, it focuses upon the protection of human autonomy and dignity....

For those who have an interest in encouraging a debate between comparable legal cultures, this is a remarkable statement. What is remarkable is not so much that we now have in all but name a tort of privacy, but that some of our judges cannot say so openly and boldly lest they be asked 'why then have they been opposed to it for so long?' Is it because their opposition to ideas or reform is often based on 'instinct' or 'hunches' rather than empirical evidence? Or is it, at any rate in the case of Lord Hoffmann (who, extra-judicially, also happens to be the President of the Anglo-German Lawyers Association) that they would find it difficult to admit that what they have now discovered to lie at the basis of the action is something which German lawyers declared in their Constitution (and their subsequent case law) over fifty years ago? This is no matter of idle academic speculation but one related to Lord Hoffmann's attitude towards to case law of Strasbourg which he seems to view as based on different 'values'. His quotation above would suggest that the values are quite similar, which is as one would expect from two Western European countries of similar socio-economic development and cultures of comparable richness and antiquity.

(ii) What Is Protected? Continuing the Move away from Confidence and towards Privacy

The association of the new right to the old equitable remedy carried for a time another unwelcome consequence. For the earlier cases dealt mainly with the confidentiality of *commercial* information and the question was how and to what extent the old ambit of the remedy could/would expand to encompass *personal* information. Not surprisingly it did; and just before the Human Rights Act came into force and, of course, after it, an extended range of information of a personal nature came to be covered by the new rules. This sub-section this deals with the erosion of the first of the *Coco* requirements: what information enjoys the required degree of confidence?

A long line of decisions has expanded the list and the courts have thus held that facts concerning sexual relations, even extra-marital ones,[96] were protected as was

[95] [2004] 2 AC 457, at [15]. [96] *A* v. *B plc* [2003] QB 195.

photographs of the interior of a person's home,[97] his address,[98] whether he/she had had a facelift,[99] receiving advice in order to shake off drug a habit,[100] or even a child's face used by a local authority on a brochure warning of the dangers of AIDS without the permission of the child's parents.[101] Data found in medical records has, of course, enjoyed protection from an even earlier time.[102] But it is the *way* that the courts have come to look at the use of photos which, in a sense, moves the new approach *in name based on confidentiality* away from that equitable remedy and *closer to the notion of privacy*. For, at around this time, our courts, after some hesitation, also took two other important decisions.

First, in *Campbell* v. *MGN Ltd.*[103] the House of Lords refused to follow the important case of *Australian Broadcasting Corporation* v. *Lenah Game Meats*,[104] which had laid down the rule that the first thing that a court would have to do would be to investigate whether the disclosure of such information would be 'highly offensive', the term being understood in an objective sense.[105]

The majority of their Lordships refused to give the offensiveness test the prime importance which the Australian Chief Justice and the Court of Appeal in *Campbell* had given to it. In Lord Hope's words:

> If the information is obviously private, the situation will be one where the person to whom it realities can reasonably expect his privacy to be respected, So there is *normally* no need to go on and ask whether it would be highly offensive for it to be published.[106]

We have italicised the word 'normally' for it suggests that though the offensiveness test cedes primacy to Article 8 ECHR and, moreover, it is to be understood in a 'subjective as well as objective sense', it may be thrown into the balance in dubious or marginal cases. Lord Hope's powerfully expressed view also received support in this context from the (dissenting) opinion of Lord Nicholls, who remarked on this point that:

> [The Gleeson] formulation should be used with care, for two reasons. First, the 'highly offensive' phrase is suggestive of a stricter test of private information than a reasonable expectation of privacy. Second, the 'highly offensive' formulation can all too easily bring into account, when deciding whether the disclosed information was private, considerations which go more properly to issues of proportionality; for instance, the degree of intrusion into private life, and the extent to which publication was a matter of proper public concern. This could be a recipe for confusion.[107]

[97] *Beckham* v. *MGN Ltd.* 28 June 2001 (unreported).

[98] *Mills* v. *News Group Newspapers Ltd.* [2001] EMLR 41.

[99] *Archer* v. *Williams* [2003] EMLR 38.

[100] *Campbell* v. *MGN Ltd.* [2004] 2 AC 457.

[101] *A (A Child)* v. *Newham LBC* (2001) WL 1612596 (unreported, transcript available on Westlaw).

[102] See, for instance, *R v. Department of Health ex parte Source Informatics* [2001] QB 424 and *X* v. *Y* [2001] QB 967.

[103] [2004] 2 WLR 1232.

[104] [2001] 208 CLR 199, HCA 63, see, especially, [54].

[105] On this basis, however, the Court of Appeal in *Campbell* v. *MGN Ltd.* [2003] 2 WLR 80, esp. [63] ff., treated the publication of the photos of Miss Campbell as being of 'peripheral' importance, failing to balance this notion against the importance of Art. 8 of the ECHR.

[106] *Campbell* v. *MGN Ltd.* [2004] 2 WLR 1233, [96].

[107] *Ibid.*, [22].

The frequent appearance of the word privacy in these judgments—which in theory are dealing with breach of confidence—is, we think, indicative of what is going on in the minds of the judges. Indeed, Lady Hale who arguably gave the most closely reasoned opinion of all five Law Lords involved in that case was both blunt and clear when, on this point she, she wrote:

An objective reasonable expectation [of privacy] test is much simpler and clearer than the test sometimes quoted from the judgments of Gleeson CJ. [108]

Second, it is important to see how our courts have come to appreciate the significance of photographs (such as those taken of Miss Campbell as she was coming out of the clinic where she was receiving treatment for her addiction). For it is clear that they are not trying to discover the nature of the information revealed by the photos—whether, for instance, it went further than the story told by the accompanying words—but are instead examining the effect they had or could have upon the claimant. This is not just a difference in semantics but one which suggests that, whereas the purpose of the enquiry in the first case is to determine the degree of confidential information contained in the pictures, in the second it was a privacy-oriented approach focusing on the double and appropriate notions of intrusion and harm. Again, one could prolong the size of this chapter unnecessarily by including a substantial sample of citations illuminating this difference, but two will suffice. The first comes from the (dissenting) opinion of Lord Nicholls and reveals the confidence-oriented approach (even though elsewhere he, too, used privacy language); the second comes from Baroness Hale's opinion which, as stated, seems to have maintained over this broad range of issues examined in this chapter the greater degree of scholarly consistency. Lord Nicholls remarked that: 'the fact that the photographs were taken surreptitiously adds nothing to the only complaint made.'[109]

Baroness Hale, however, observed that the publication of the photographs:

[a]dded to the potential harm, by making Campbell think that she was being followed or betrayed, and deterring her from going back to the same place again.[110]

(iii) Weakening the Last of the *Coco* Requirements (Detriment)

The third and final of the *Coco* ingredients had no better fate than the other two and was watered down with the passage of time. We see this in the courts' increasing willingness either to dispense altogether with the requirement that 'detriment' be shown in order to make out a claim for breach of confidence or, at the very least, to find detriment very readily.[111] This is closely connected to the recent recognition that damages for injury to

[108] *Campbell* v. *MGN Ltd.* [2004] 2 WLR 1233, [135].

[109] *Ibid.*, [155].

[110] *Ibid.*, [30].

[111] *Federal Bank of the Middle East* v. *Hadkinson* [2000] 2 All ER 395, 413–14; *X Health Authority* v. *Y* [1988] RPC 379, 391–2. It is interesting to note that this move away from a requirement of detriment is not confined to classic 'privacy' cases, but has also occurred in the more traditional, commercial sphere of breach of confidence.

feelings may be recovered in a breach of confidence claim,[112] a recognition which accords, in principle, with the idea of using confidence to protect privacy interests.[113]

(iv) Information in the Public Domain

In this sub-heading we deal with two interrelated problems. The first is whether information available to 'some' people can deny it its 'confidential' label, leading it to being branded as being already in the public domain and thus not deserving of the protection of the law. This is a point which has particular bearing on requests for injunctions, always treated warily by the courts out of fear that they might have—or be seen to have—an inhibiting effect upon freedom of speech.[114] Thus, section 12(4) of the Human Rights Act 1998 instructs the court to:

> have particular regard to the importance of... freedom of expression and, where the proceedings relate to material which the respondent claims, or which appears to the court, to be journalistic, literary or artistic material..., to
> (a) the extent to which—
> (i) the material has, or is about to, become available to the public...

The second problem is, in one sense, a variant of the first: can information obtained in a public location or from a public incident ever be treated as 'confidential' and thus, once again, be denied legal protection? It is in this last type of cases that we see most clearly how even the modern notion of confidence, even when distorted beyond recognition from its ancestor, does not overlap entirely with the notion of privacy.

To our first question, different legal systems have given different answers. American cases[115] and academic writers[116] heavily incline to the view that what is already known or takes place in public location cannot be protected as being private and confidential. This solution, largely influenced by the underlying American reverence for free expression as protected by the famous First Amendment to their Constitution, also has in its favour the virtues of simplicity and certainty. Yet it also lacks the nuance and flexibility of approach that life in its infinite complexity seems to require. No wonder, then, that

[112] *Cornelius* v. *De Taranto* [2000] EMLR 12 (Morland J). Although this was admittedly a claim for breach of a contractual confidence, there seems little reason why the same principles should not apply across the board for breach of confidence: indeed, Morland J went on in *Campbell* v. *Mirror Group Newspapers* [2002] EMLR 30 to award damages for distress and injured feelings under both breach of confidence and breach of s. 13 of the Data Protection Act 1998. He also implied that, in appropriate circumstances, even aggravated damages might be awarded. Though much of Morland J's ruling was overturned by the Court of Appeal [2003] WLR 80, and his conclusion that liability could sound under the 1998 Act was rejected, the Court of Appeal did acknowledge that, on the facts, Morland J's conclusion about aggravated damages would have stood had liability been shown.

[113] See W. R. Cornish, *Intellectual Property: Patents, Copyright, Trademarks and Allied Rights* (4th edn., 1999), para. 8.48, quoted with apparent approval by Morland J in *Cornelius* v. *De Taranto* [2000] EMLR 12; see also *Campbell* v. *Frisbee* [2003] EMLR 76. (For the same point in the current edition, see W. R. Cornish and D. Llewellyn, *Intellectual Property: Patents, Copyright, Trademarks and Allied Rights* (5th edn., 2003), para. 8–49.)

[114] For brief discussion of these issues, see ch. 26, Section 1(d) below.

[115] *Jaubert* v. *Crowley Post-Signal Inc.*, 375 So. 2d 1386 (1979); *Gill* v. *Hearst Publishing Co.*, 253 P 2d 441 (1953).

[116] W. L. Prosser, 'Privacy' (1960) 48 *Cal. LR* 383, 394–5.

other major legal systems—for instance the Canadian,[117] the German[118] and the French[119]—have taken the opposite position. This is the position which, in recent times, English law also seems to have adopted. As far back as *Attorney-General* v. *Guardian Newspapers (No. 2)*[120] it was said that

It may be more difficult to establish that confidentiality has gone for all purposes, in the context of personal information, by virtue of its having come to the attention of certain categories of readers.

In *A* v. *B plc*[121] an attempt by the defendant to argue that the amorous antics of a footballer published by the former should not be considered as confidential and thus deserving of protection was rejected by the court partly because these antics were conducted in public (a point to which we return in the next sub-section) but also because they were already known to a limited number of people. The same fate was also reserved for a similar claim by the defendants in the *Campbell* case. For there, too, her predicament and the treatment she was receiving for it was known to a number of people, including of course other addicts who received the same counselling as the model herself. It is interesting, however, to note that by the time that the *Campbell* litigation reached the House of Lords, the point discussed here had become so well established[122] that it was not even addressed by any of the judgments of their Lordships.

The question, however, remains: how many people have to be aware of this information before a court takes the view that this has deprived the information of its 'confidential' or 'private' nature?[123] The flexibility of the approach inherent in the English approach can encourage litigation though, having voiced this concern, one must also note that the test seems to be applied very loosely. Thus, in the *Cherie Blair* case[124] the details of her domestic arrangements had already appeared in one print run of the *Mail on Sunday* so, presumably, the offending article had already been read by thousands of readers. Yet further publication was banned on the grounds that the information retained its confidential character.

The decision of the European Court of Human Rights in *Peck* v. *UK*[125] has reconfirmed this approach in a judgment with facts which may generate more litigation in

117 *Les Editions Nice Versa Inc.* v. *Aubry* [1999] 5 BHRC 437.

118 BGH 19 Dec. 1995, BGHZ 131, 322 (and many others since).

119 Because the right under Art. 9 of the *Code Civil* is explicitly one to privacy and the protection of one's private life: see, e.g., CA Paris 15 May 1970, *Ferrat*, D. 1970, jur, 466 (and many others). See, for helpful comparative discussion, H. Beverley-Smith, A. Ohly and A. Lucas-Schloetter, *Privacy, Property and Personality: Civil Law Perspectives on Commercial Appropriation* (2005), ch. 5 and generally.

120 [1990] 1 AC 190.

121 [2002] EWCA 337, [2002] 3 WLR 542.

122 An aberrant decision seems to be *Theakston* v. *MGN* [2002] EWHC 137, [2002] EMLR 22—the story of the exploits of a television presenter in a brothel written by the prostitute with whom he had an affair; publication was allowed on the grounds that the information was already in the public domain—must, after the decision in *Peck* v. *UK* , Case No. 44647/98 (2003), now be regarded as 'suspect'.

123 The issue is by no means novel to the post-Human Rights Act 1998 era: see, e.g., *Woodward* v. *Hutchins* [1977] 1 WLR 760, at 764 per Lord Denning MR: 'in this case the incident on this Jumbo Jet was in the public domain. It was known to all the passengers on the flight.'

124 Case No. HQ0001236 (2001) (unreported, transcript available on Westlaw).

125 (2003) EHRR 287 (App. No. 00044647/98).

the future as public surveillance through CCTV cameras, in times of increased criminality and terrorism, is practised in literally tens of thousands of public places up and down the country.

In *Peck* the applicant to the Strasbourg court was captured by CCTV cameras wandering carrying a knife soon after he had tried to commit suicide. The pictures were, in due course but without any malice or bad faith, passed by the *local authority*[126] to various local newspapers which published recognisable still photographs of Mr Peck. A TV programme known as *Crime Beat* also showed extracts of the CCTV footage. A failed attempt to have this decision judicially reviewed led Mr. Peck to take the case to Strasbourg, complaining of violations of his Article 8 ECHR rights. One of the defences put forward by the UK government was, predictably, that the information was already in the public domain. The key sentence in the judgment of the Strasbourg court was that:

> As a result [of showing the footage], the relevant moment was viewed to an extent which far exceeded any exposure to a passer-by or to security observation . . . and to a degree surpassing that which the applicant could possibly have foreseen when he walked in Brentwood on 20 August 1995.[127]

The decision of the Strasbourg court in *Peck* thus recognised that there is:

> a zone of interaction of a person with others, even in a public context, which may fall within the scope of 'private life'.[128]

Important though the judgment is, it does not mean that the Strasbourg court was willing to allow the extension of the law to run riot. Thus in *Peck* it was prepared to draw a distinction for the purposes of privacy between different sets of factual circumstances where the events in question occur in a public place: the public nature of the place and activity in question was balanced against the subsequent disclosure of the intrusive CCTV footage without any attempt to conceal Mr Peck's identity. The judgment also suggests that foreseeability on the part of the subject as to whether the privacy of their actions in a public place would be respected will be an important consideration. A participant in a public demonstration caught by the police cameras would thus not be allowed to complain of an Article 8 violation, the older case of *Friedl* v. *Austria* [129] retaining all its force. In this context the court thus stated:

> The present applicant was in a public street but he was not there for the purposes of participating in any public event and he was not a public figure. It was late at night, he was deeply perturbed and in a state of some distress . . . the footage was disclosed to the media for further broadcast and publication purposes . . . The applicant's identity was not adequately, or in some cases not at all, masked in the photographs and footage so published and broadcast. He was recognised by certain members of his family and by his friends, neighbours and colleagues . . .

[126] It is thus important to note that this was a straightforward application of the Convention regulating the relations between state and individuals. It is, however, believed that the same result would be reached if the cameras belonged to a private company or the television transmission had taken place by a private and not public company.

[127] (2003) 36 EHRR 41, [53].

[128] *Ibid.*, [57].

[129] (1995) 21 EHRR 83.

This aspect of the decision appears to shift considerably the boundaries of what is regarded as private life under Article 8, and to recognise that intrusion into personal privacy cannot be justified simply by virtue of that intrusion occurring while the person concerned was present in a public place.[130] The importance of this statement and, indeed, the judgment as a whole, cannot thus be underestimated, though, consistently with his judicial and general legal ideology, in *Wainwright* Lord Hoffmann did try to limit the decision to its facts.[131] But quite apart from the fact that the result of the *Wainwright* decision was, itself, most recently held by the Strasbourg to be a violation of the Convention,[132] the judgments of the majority of their Lordships in *Campbell* seem to suggest that the *Peck* ruling remains intact. Thus Lord Hope was among those who regarded the taking of the photographs in a street as normally leading to no legal action if they simply happen to capture an individual in the process. But if the picture is, as was the case here, so taken as to obscure others but emphasise the claimant,[133] and did so in a way that was surreptitious and particularly hurtful to her, legal consequences would follow.

This would thus leave us with the following conclusion. Though mere covert photography is not (yet?) actionable in itself, if what is being photographed is private and, particularly if it is done surreptitiously, it will be actionable.[134] The fact that all of this happened in a public place will then not be enough to prevent that interest from being protected by the law. This seems entirely in keeping with the common denominator of all three of the majority judgments to shift the court's scrutiny away from 'locational' factors to the nature and effect of the publicised acts. But does this go far enough to satisfy the even newer pronouncement on the subject by Strasbourg in the *von Hannover* case?[135] We shall consider this in Section 4 below but for the time being are content to say that this is by no means clear.

[130] See also *PG and JH* v. *UK*, ECtHR 25 Sept. 2001 and *R* v. *Loveridge* [2001] EWCA Crim. 973.

[131] *Wainwright* v. *Home Office* [2003] UKHL 53, [2004] 2 AC 406, at [33], arguing that the Strasbourg court was only concerned with the need to regulate the CCTV regime. This is not just a piece of brilliant but, it is submitted, unconvincing advocacy on the part of a judge who at times appears to be inimical to the Strasbourg jurisprudence; it also one which disregards the crucial role of the Strasbourg jurisprudence in establishing norms and requirements as to what interests a national legal system should protect. It also attempts to ignore the reality that, in identifying the absence of adequate legal protection for Mr Peck, the Strasbourg court has identified a systemic failure to address privacy issues of which the *Peck* decision is merely one instance.

[132] *Wainwright* v. *The United Kingdom* (Application No. 12350.04), Strasbourg 26 Sept. 2006, *The Times* 3 Oct. 2006, (2006) 156 *NLJ* 1524, holding the UK in violation of Arts. 8 and 13 of the Convention. It should be noted that, on the facts of *Wainwright*, the claimant would now be able to proceed directly against the relevant public body by virtue of the Human Rights Act 1998.

[133] *Campbell* v. *MGN Ltd.* [2004] 2 AC 457, [122]–[123].

[134] This position is confirmed by the recent majority judgment of the House of Lords in *Douglas* v. *Hello!* [2007] UKHL 21, [122] (per Lord Hoffmann) and [329] (per Lord Brown). It should be noted, however, that the minority placed great emphasis upon the issue of whether the information embodied in the photographs had sufficiently entered the public domain in reaching their conclusion that the appeal should be dismissed (see [255]–[259] (per Lord Nicholls) and [292]–[299] (per Lord Walker)).

[135] *Von Hannover* v. *Germany* (2005) 40 EHRR 1.

(v) Public Figures, Public Officials, Public Functions

There is little doubt that law should, and in recent times has come to, distinguish between public figures and private individuals who are, often by accident, caught up in a publicity-generating event and find themselves in the headlines. Few would also dissent from the general proposition that those who seek publicity should receive less protection (if the media whose attention they court exceeds the permissible limits of observance or intrusion) than those who have chosen not to live in the limelight. The difficulty, however, has been to decide how much privacy (if any) such public figures should be granted. Further, what we have thus far described generically as 'public figures' could be subdivided into three categories: *(a)* public figures in general; *(b)* public officials, which is a narrower category than the first insofar as it would not, for instance, include an actor or famous sportsman; and *(c)* public figures (or officials) performing official functions, who, so the argument then goes, should be spared the glare of publicity when not on official duty. Those obsessed with categorisations could proceed to make further subdivisions.[136] For instance, we could have permanent public figures—e.g. the Beckhams or the McCartneys—who figure in the media on a daily basis, and those who attain public notoriety only as a result of an isolated event—e.g. a robbery or murder or great invention—and then, eventually, return to 'normality'. For present purposes, however, we shall simplify our account by limiting our observations to the privacy rights of public figures (whether officials or not) and also consider the even more protective device produced by the Strasbourg court in *von Hannover*:[137] namely, removing the protection of anonymity only when the actor is actually performing his or her official duties.

Acceptance that public figures also deserved protection came late in English law. One of the fullest discussions, even if not without flaws, can be found in the decision of the Court of Appeal in *A* v. *B plc*, the so-called *Flitcroft* decision.[138]

In the *Flitcroft* case, the Court of Appeal developed an approach to the position of 'public figures' and their privacy. The court held that the position of public figures should lead them to realise that their conduct will be subject to greater media scrutiny and that even trivial facts relating to a public figure can be of great interest to readers and other observers of the media. Conduct which, in the case of a private individual, would not be the appropriate subject of comment can be the proper subject of comment in the case of a public figure. The public figure may hold a position where higher standards of conduct can rightly be expected by the public. The public figure may be a role model whose conduct could well be emulated by others. He may set the fashion. The higher the profile of the individual concerned, the likelier that this will be the position. Whether you have courted publicity or not you may be a legitimate subject of

[136] See, e.g., the approach in Germany, as helpfully explained in H. Beverley-Smith, A. Ohly and A. Lucas-Schloetter, *Privacy, Property and Personality: Civil Law Perspectives on Commercial Appropriation* (2005), ch. 4. For the American approach, see the contribution by Professor David Anderson in ch. 23 of this book, below.

[137] *Von Hannover* v. *Germany* (2005) 40 EHRR 1.

[138] *A* v. *B plc and Another* [2002] 2 All ER 545.

public attention. If you have courted public attention then you have less ground upon which to object to the intrusion which follows. Tellingly, Lord Woolf CJ held that:

In many of these situations it would be overstating the position to say that there is a public interest in the information being published. It would be more accurate to say that the public have an understandable and so a legitimate interest in being told the information. If this is the situation then it can be appropriately taken into account by a court when deciding on which side of the line a case falls. The courts must not ignore the fact that if newspapers do not publish information which the public are interested in, there will be fewer newspapers published, which will not be in the public interest. The same is true in relation to other parts of the media.[139]

When this paragraph is put into the context of the breach of confidence action, it reads as a significant relaxation of the public interest defence: in the *Flitcroft* case, the 'public's interest' in the information was deemed to be sufficient justification for refusing to prevent its publication, bolstered by the consideration that the press is an important conduit through which the important freedom of expression is exercised. This is in spite of the courts' warnings of the tendency of the press to confuse the public interest with its own.[140] Apparently, the broader, systemic public interest in the continued publication of newspapers is sufficiently important to run the many risks inherent in this approach, although it will be possible to argue against this presumption on the facts of each individual case.[141]

After the judgment in the *Flitcroft* case was handed down, it appeared at first difficult to decide to what extent the courts were slowly moving towards recognising an extended right of confidence but were coupling it with a tacit or indirect hint that speech should be given preference whenever it clashed with what one might call—though the courts did not then use this term—privacy rights. If the *Flitcroft* decision suggested a strong *leaning* towards freedom of expression in cases involving public figures, this could, arguably, be ascribed to the very liberal philosophy of the Lord Chief Justice (who delivered the judgment of the Court of Appeal). It was also in tune with the views of another judge—Lord Hoffmann—who had famously declared some eight years earlier[142] that 'freedom of speech is a trump card which always wins'.

139 *A* v. *B plc and Another* [2002] 2 All ER 545, [11], point (xii).

140 Per Sir John Donaldson MR in *Francome* v. *Mirror Group Newspapers* [1984] 2 All ER 408; it is also in spite of the wording of s. 12(4)(a)(ii) of the Human Rights Act 1998: see para. 11(v) of the judgment in *A* v. *B plc and Another* [2002] 2 All ER 545, where Lord Woolf CJ took the view that s. 12(4) 'does not mean that the court is justified in interfering with the freedom of the press where there is no identifiable special public interest in any particular material being published. Such an approach would turn section 12(4) upside down. Regardless of the quality of the material which it is intended to publish *prima facie* the court should not interfere with its publication. Any interference with publication must be justified.'

141 E.g., per Lord Woolf CJ, where 'unlawful means' are used to obtain the information (such as by bugging or phone tapping (para. 11(x) of the *A* v. *B plc and Another* [2002] 2 All ER 545)).

142 *R* v. *Central Independent Television plc* [1994] Fam. 192, 203. Subsequently, however, the learned judge had to 'explain away' extra-judicially (in his 1996 Goodman Lecture) the exact meaning of his sentence, something which he has been forced to do on at least one further occasion namely in *Gorringe* v. *Calderdale Metropolitan Borough Council* [2004] 1 WLR 1057 para. 26, where he, again, had to explain away his earlier *dicta* in *Stovin* v. *Wise* [1996] AC 923.

But the momentum was slowly building up in the opposite direction, as evinced by Sedley LJ's pioneering judgment in *Douglas* v. *Hello!*,[143] where he had said that:

the qualifications set out in Article 10(2) [ECHR] are as relevant as the right set out in Article 10(1). This means that, for example, the reputations and rights of others—not only but not least their Convention rights—are as material as the defendant's right of free expression.[144]

Sedley LJ's weighing in favour of a balancing of the Convention Rights—Articles 8 and 10 in particular—was one of the most significant turning points of the post-Human Rights Act law on this subject. For not only did it counter the attempt (implicitly) made by section 12 (4) of the Human Rights Act presumptively to focus attention on the importance of Article 10 of the Convention (speech rights) at the expense of Article 8 (privacy); but, it also and on the contrary managed to reintroduce Article 8 into the equation, thus laying down, as it were, the foundations of what has now become the accepted orthodoxy: namely, a proper balancing of the competing values.[145] In this, it is believed, it echoed better the emerging trend among British legal opinion, which, unlike the American, seems always to have preferred a balancing process to a single-minded preference for one value over another. But whether because of the judgment of Sedley LJ or because of what we call the British preference for balancing values, the fact is that less than a year after the *Flitcroft* judgment was handed down, a differently constituted Court of Appeal, sitting in the case of *Campbell* v. *MGN Ltd.*,[146] was at pains to point out that

[w]hen Lord Woolf spoke of the public having 'an understandable and so a legitimate interest in being told' information, even including trivial facts, about a public figure, he was not speaking of private facts which a fair-minded person would consider it offensive to disclose. That is clear from his subsequent commendation of the guidance we would observe that the fact that an individual has achieved prominence on the public stage does not mean that his private life can be laid bare by the media. We do not see why it should necessarily be in the public interest that an individual, who has been adopted as a role model, without seeking this distinction, should be demonstrated to have feet of clay.

What followed in the *Campbell* decision at the House of Lords level has now put this issue beyond all dispute and, incidentally, placed English law firmly in the European (and not American) camp so far as concerns the refusal to give precedence to speech over other competing rights such as privacy. Significantly, this positioning is found not only in the opinions of the members of the majority—such as Lord Hope[147] and

143 [2001] 2 WLR 992, 1020 ff.

144 One interesting consequence of the Act's reference to 'any relevant privacy code' was highlighted by Brooke LJ in *Douglas* v. *Hello!*, where he suggested that any newspaper which flouts the Code of Practice (ratified by the Press Complaints Commission) would be 'likely in those circumstances to have its claim to an entitlement to freedom of expression trumped by Article 10(2) considerations of privacy'.

145 Which might, perhaps, have been taken too literally by the Court of Appeal in *McKennitt* v. *Ash* [2006] EWCA Civ. 1714, [2007] EMLR 4, at [11], *viz.*: Arts. 8 and 10 ECHR 'are now not merely of persuasive or parallel effect but . . . are the very content of the domestic tort that the English court has to enforce' (per Buxton LJ).

146 [2003] 2 WLR 80; [2003] 1 All ER 224 (CA), [40]–[41].

147 *Campbell* v. *MGN Ltd.* [2003] 2 WLR 80, at [113].

Baroness Hale[148]—but also of those who dissented, namely Lord Nicholls[149] and Lord Hoffmann,[150]—the latter being the author of the 'trump card' formulation who in this case was willing to state that:

There is... no question of automatic priority. Nor is there a presumption in favour of one rather than the other.

The last word on the subject is, at the time of writing, to be found in Lord Steyn's judgment in *Re S* where, delivering the judgment of the entire House, he explained the process to be followed when he said:

First, neither article has such precedence over the other. Secondly, where the values under the two articles are in conflict, an intense focus on the comparative importance of the specific rights being claimed in the individual case is necessary. Thirdly, the justifications for interfering with or restricting each right must be taken into account. Finally, the proportionality test must be applied to each.[151]

4. EUROPE: THE BROODING OMINPRESENCE IN THE SKY

This position reached at a national level on the significance of the photographed or recorded events taking place in a public area has not, as we noted, been without its 'internal' critics; but it also sits uncomfortably with the *von Hannover* decision[152] of the Strasbourg court which seems to afford even greater protection than either English or, indeed, German law do for such interests. For in that decision, the Strasbourg court held that Germany, despite its most sophisticated law on privacy, was in violation of Article 8 of the Convention in the context of a long line of cases which dealt with Princess Caroline of Monaco and her long-standing crusade against the world, and mainly the German Press, not to photograph her and her family on every conceivable occasion. To understand the long judgment, one must examine the rich casuistry of incidents which the court had to consider. These photographs involved her sometimes lunching in a private section of a public restaurant with her (former) lover, sometimes showed her with her young children in a public areas, and sometimes depicted her

148 *Campbell* v. *MGN Ltd.* [2003] 2 WLR 80, at [138]. 149 *Ibid.*, at [12]. 150 *Ibid.*, at [55].

151 *Re S* [2005] 1 AC 593, at [17]. For those hoping that the House of Lords would bring greater clarity to this area in its judgment on the *Douglas* v. *Hello!* appeal ([2007] UKHL 21), the opinions of the majority of their Lordships in upholding *OK* !'s appeal add but little to this debate. The majority explicitly denied the relevance of privacy and Art. 8 ECHR to what they considered to be a case which concerned purely a 'commercial confidence' since it concerned *OK!*'s attempt 'to protect commercially confidential information and nothing more' (at [118] (per Lord Hoffmann)). The minority took a similar view, also accepting that the claim did not concern 'privacy' but only confidentiality (see, e.g., [255] (per Lord Nicholls)).

152 *Von Hannover* v. *Germany* (2005) 40 EHRR 1.

doing her shopping or performing the kind of humdrum chores that ordinary human beings carry out on a daily basis. Yet, among the many novel and controversial aspects of this very broad—in our view too broad—opinion, one notes the emphasis placed by the court upon the fact that, when photographed in most of these instances, the Princess was not performing any official functions. It would seem this was the prime reason why the court took the view that she should not have to put up with the incessant surveillance by the Press.

If one were to analyse the case in the way a common lawyer would, one might be tempted not to read too much into this linking of anonymity with the question whether the observed person was performing official functions or not. One could, in other words, argue that this point arose only because the court was dealing with the facts before it and what all had in common was that they did not involve her acting in any way as a Princess of the Principality of Monaco. So any statements that went beyond these facts could and would be dismissed as *obiter*.

But European decisions do not recognise the distinction between *ratio decidendi* and *obiter dicta*; and the wording of the judgment clearly gives the impression that its kernel is to be found not in the distinction between public versus private figures but in this idea of whether the persons 'observed' were performing their official functions (which could be observed, described and criticised) or simply leading their normal lives. If that, indeed, were to prevail it would, it is submitted, be too narrow a distinction from which to allow a new outgrowth of the law of privacy. For information, even private, insignificant or indirect, about a human being's life, lifestyle, manner, behaviour and outlook, can be not just newsworthy but also important, especially if the person observed, photographed (etc.) is a public figure. For behaviour 'off guard', as it were, could give real clues about the public figure's true beliefs and attitudes. So how should a future English court react to the suggestion that *von Hannover* afforded significantly more extensive protection to privacy than, say, *Campbell*?

One's starting-point must, of course, be that the Strasbourg decisional law is not, unlike the judgments on EC law handed down by the Court of Justice of the European Communities, *directly* binding upon English courts as a matter of national constitutional law. This is due to the drafting of the Human Rights Act 1998 and the duties which it imposes upon national courts. The Strasbourg court, too, has acknowledged some scope for divergent national commensurations of the competing interests that must often be balanced under ECHR analysis, under the heading of the 'margin of appreciation' afforded to each state under the Convention. This is because the Strasbourg court has acknowledged that the national level is better placed to judge the balance of individual rights with competing societal interests, especially given that the Convention is said to perform a subsidiary role to that of the national legal system when it comes to the protection of human rights.[153] Indeed, it has (and it is submitted highly persuasively) been argued that the kind of value judgement involved in the *von Hannover*

[153] See, e.g., *Handyside* v. *United Kingdom* (1976) 1 EHRR 737, [48]. On the margin of appreciation generally, see (e.g.) H. Fenwick, *Civil Liberties and Human Rights* (3rd edn., 2002), 34–7.

case—with regard to the appropriate level of privacy protection to be afforded to such public figures—is *precisely* the kind of issue which would normally have fallen within that very margin of appreciation.[154] After *Campbell* it is also difficult to deny that English law has made important strides forward, so long as the majority judgments are not surreptitiously eroded by those traditionally hostile to the reasoning that they contain. A second arguably saving point would be to stress another feature of the *von Hannover* case (to which we have thus far alluded only indirectly). This is its emphasis upon the persistent harassment of Princess Caroline by the press. An English court could thus plausibly make the case that, in the absence of such persistent harassment of the claimant, the extraordinary additional protection enunciated by Strasbourg was as unnecessary as was its decision making the protection dependent upon the performance of special duties. Shifting the debate back to the public/private figures basis could thus not only be welcome, but also be argued to be compatible with the practice of most legal systems.[155]

To conclude, the problem with the *von Hannover* judgment is that the protection afforded to privacy may have now swung in the opposite direction and may have become excessive. This is so for two reasons.

First, if the person photographed or otherwise depicted by the defendant is not performing public functions, then the result of *von Hannover* seems to be that photographing him (etc.) may be prohibited irrespective of whether he or she is a public official or celebrity of any kind.

Second, such photography (etc.) may end up being prohibited even if the content of what is captured on the lens or the activity depicted is entirely innocuous and part of everyday life. This protection will, as stated, go beyond the German *Caroline* cases of the 1990s, since in those judgments protection in a public space was extended only under fairly carefully defined criteria which seem to have disappeared in the Strasbourg court's judgment in the *von Hannover* case.[156]

No doubt practising lawyers will invent ways to bypass such results; but for those who seek to set up Strasbourg as a useful centre for inspiration, this decision may represent a step too far. The law—ours as well as the European—thus awaits the desired synthesis.

[154] See H. Beverley-Smith, A. Ohly and A. Lucas-Schloetter, *Privacy, Property and Personality: Civil Law Perspectives on Commercial Appropriation* (2005), 220–2. Note, however, that it has also been argued that just because the state is given such a margin by the Strasbourg court by no means *requires* the national courts to use all of that margin to deny protection to Convention rights if those national courts, being closer to the issues raised, take the view that more protection is indeed warranted. See, e.g., frequent references to this argument throughout H. Fenwick, *Civil Liberties and Human Rights* (3rd edn., 2002) on the application of various Convention rights in the national courts.

[155] *Von Hannover* still being relatively 'hot off the presses', it has not received the in-depth analysis that it deserves, at any rate in this country. But see Fenwick and Phillipson (Select Bibliography), at 677 ff. which, once again, provides the best descriptive and analytical account of the subject.

[156] For the view that a 'coherent framework for the protection of privacy in public places' is beginning to emerge in English law, see N. A. Moreham, 'Privacy in Public Places' [2006] *CLJ* 606.

5. THE REACH OF THE HUMAN RIGHTS ACT 1998

In the summer of 1998 the Labour Party's electoral promise to 'repatriate human rights'—a soundbite slogan meant to stress the fact that Britain's failure to incorporate the European Convention which it had helped draft forty years earlier was, finally, to be rectified—became a reality. Section 6 of the new Act makes it illegal for any public authority to act in a way which is incompatible with the Convention while, in the event of such a violation, sections 7 and 8 give the courts the right to make any order they think fit to put right the breach in question.[157]

Our courts were never considered likely to create a new *general* cause of action; and thus far they have not done this (even though they have, as we have seen, given the old equitable remedy a similar kind of amplitude). The Act did not authorise the creation of a new tort; nor would this have been compatible with the way our judges see their role as interpreters of the law.[158] But this does not mean that the new Act has not had a profound effect upon our law of privacy,[159] for it provided the stimulus to expand the remedy for breach of confidence and, in the process, change or re-define so many of its old requirements which had kept it for most of its life restrained and minimally effective. But for all this to happen, our courts had to determine whether the Act applied only 'vertically' (i.e. regulating the relations of state and citizen) or also had a 'horizontal' role to play (i.e. regulating the activities of private bodies such as the Press, trade unions, multinational corporations, all of whom had, in the contemporary world, just as much the opportunity to oppress private individuals as the state did). For political reasons, the government failed to define this itself, departing in this respect from the constitutional practice of other systems.[160] Yet in this context it did ensure that two things occurred. First and most significantly, it defeated an amendment introduced in the House of Lords by Lord Wakeham (in his capacity as Chairman of the Press Complaints Commission) explicitly ruling out horizontal effect.[161] Second, it offered a 'sweetener' to the Press by adding section 12 to the Human Rights Act, which was intended to

[157] Section 8(1). This could include damages and accounts of profits—important remedies for the subject under consideration. Injunctive relief will also be available, although our courts will have to take note of the Strasbourg jurisprudence that has adopted a sceptical stance towards any form of 'prior restraint'.

[158] See, for instance, the views of the judges in the Court of Appeal judgment in *Wainwright* v. *Home Office* [2001] EWCA Civ. 2081; [2002] 3 WLR 405, a decision which, incidentally, spent much effort in contemplating the expansion of a curious tort rule contained in the old case of *Wilkinson* v. *Downton* [1897] 2 QB 57 and finally reached a result which all three judges seemed to regret. In *Wainwright*, as in the *Kaye* and the *Douglas* cases, one sees how a wider tort of privacy could have helped. One also sees in *Wainwright*—as indeed in the *Douglas* case—how breach of confidence (as traditionally understood) cannot always provide the desired remedy. Yet how wedded some of our judges are to the practices they know best can be seen from the opening statements of Mummery LJ (at 419 in *Wainwright*). The judgment of the House of Lords in *Wainwright* [2004] 2 AC 406 (on which see A. Johnston, 'Putting the Cart Before the Horse? Privacy and the Wainwrights' [2004] *CLJ* 15) sidestepped these difficulties and confirmed a restrictive approach to such questions, although the subsequent, post-HRA case law has shown a somewhat bolder attitude, as discussed above.

[159] See, for instance, the Lord Chancellor's remarks in HL Debs., vol. 583, cols. 784–7 (3 Nov. 1997).

[160] For instance, s. 52 of the Canadian Constitution or s. 8 of the South African Bill of Rights.

[161] HL Debs., vol. 583, col. 771, 24 Nov. 1997.

ensure that the courts when deciding such cases had 'particular regard' to the importance attached by the Convention to freedom of information. As already mentioned however, thanks to Sedley LJ's masterly sleight of hand in the *Douglas* case, the competing Article 8 of the Convention re-entered into the picture. For, as his Lordship observed,

> You cannot have particular regard to Article 10 without having equally particular regard at the very least to Article 8.[162]

The issue of horizontality is one of those which raises important theoretical issues as well as practical problems. Ultimately it is about the reach of public law in the realm of private law, and asks the questions whether some such reach is needed and whether that public law reach poses dangers for private law. Unsurprisingly, it has received most attention in Germany where under the name of *Drittwirkung der Grundrechte*—literally third-party effect of basic rights—it has produced some fascinating writings, but also decisions which have been almost verbatim transplanted into the legal systems of countries as far away and as diverse as Brazil, Israel and South Africa, to mention but a few. In England, even the term was widely unknown until the mid-1990s; and although the Human Rights Act gave birth to a fairly substantial literature it was, as most such discussions tend to be in this country, centred on the wording of the statute and the debates that had preceded it in the two Houses of Parliament. Sadder still is the fact that the interaction of the judges with the academic literature was occasional if not even superficial; and a reading of the judgments in the House of Lords in *Campbell* shows this.[163] We can thus limit the consideration of this literature to the minimum that is needed in order to understand the revolutionary work that our judges have carried out during the early years of the Human Rights Act ('HRA').

The issue is whether the HRA allows the court to proceed to a horizontal application of human rights provisions found in the Convention. Logically prior is, of course, the question whether the Strasbourg court has, itself, given such a horizontal effect to provisions of the Convention. If one limits oneself only to the first of the issues mentioned above—permissibility by the HRA[164]—one can, conveniently, attempt to bypass the work already done by the Strasbourg court and this has accepted the horizontality idea.[165] So, does the HRA allow/permit/require our courts to give a horizontal effect to Convention rights?

The late Professor Wade claimed that it did;[166] indeed, he argued in favour of a duty imposed on our courts to do so *directly*. The fact that the HRA in its section 6(1) and (3) clearly talked of public authorities (including the courts) not acting incompatibly with

162 [2001] 2 WLR 992, para. 135.

163 The discussion in Fenwick and Phillipson (Select Bibliography), esp. 123 ff., shows this amply, so the interested reader is referred to this work for further material on the matter.

164 As Lord Hoffmann seemingly did in his *Campbell* judgment: [2004] 2 AC 457, [49].

165 For an important decision affecting the UK, see *A* v. *United Kingdom* (1998) 27 EHRR 611.

166 H.R. Wade, 'The United Kingdom's Bill of Rights' in J. Beatson, C.F. Forsyth and I. Hare (eds.), *Constitutional Reform in the United Kingdom: Practice and Principles* (1998), 62–4. See, also, his 'Horizons and Horizontality' (2000) 116 *LQR* 224 and, in the same vein, J. Morgan, 'Questioning the True Effect of the HRA' (2002) 22 *Leg. Stud.* 259.

Convention rights was, to the learned Professor, of no real significance since the courts were obliged to give effect to Convention rights. The problem with this reading was that it flatly ignored the wording of the HRA and what the Lord Chancellor had said in the debates in the House of Lords when talking about the aims of the Act.[167] The exact opposite view was taken by Buxton LJ (writing extra-judicially),[168] a position which seemed to be in direct conflict with Parliament's resounding rejection of the Wakeham Amendment which had attempted to ensure precisely this result—i.e. exclude horizontality—as well as with section 12(4) of the HRA.

Neither of these theories has gained court support.[169] As often happens, the theory which has attracted most support—certainly in academic circles but, arguably also, among judges—has come from a practitioner with impeccable academic credentials; and it avoids the extreme formulations of both of the above-mentioned theories.

This *via media* came in an important article by Mr Murray Hunt,[170] who argued—it should be noted incidentally, along lines not that much removed from the currently prevailing German practice[171]—that the Act, following section 6(3)(a), had an *indirect* effect obliging judges to interpret law in a way that was compatible with Convention rights. Indeed, according to Mr Hunt, our courts were 'under an absolute duty' to do so—hence his theory of indirect application has been described as the 'strong indirect horizontality'—whereas other authors[172] argued merely for an 'obligation to take into account' the Convention principles ('weak indirect horizontality'). Our courts have ignored the two extreme theories of Wade and Buxton and have opted for the indirect horizontality theory in one or the other of its forms, their (perhaps?) understandable dislike for theorising having prevented them from being too specific as to which form precisely—the strong or the weak—they have adopted.

Thus in *Douglas* v. *Hello! Ltd.*[173] we find Brooke LJ informing us that the courts must 'take into account'[174] Strasbourg law, and Keene LJ arguing that the courts must be 'informed'[175] by the jurisprudence of the Convention—language suggesting an adherence to a weak indirect horizontality. Yet in the same case we see, not surprisingly perhaps, Sedley LJ telling us that the courts '*must* themselves act compatibly . . . with the Convention'[176]—words suggesting a preference for strong indirect application. In the

[167] 'The Convention has its origins in a desire to protect people from the misuse of power by the state, rather than from the actions of private individuals', HL Debs., vol. 582, col. 1232, 3 Nov. 1997.

[168] 'The Human Rights Act and Private Law' (2000) 116 *LQR* 48.

[169] The most clearly phrased renunciation of the Wade theory can be found in the judgment of Lord Phillips CJ in *Douglas* v. *Hello! Ltd. (No. 3)* [2006] QB 125, [50]. The Buxton thesis was roundly rejected in *Venables and Another* v. *News Group Newspapers* [2001] 1 All ER 908, 916.

[170] 'The Horizontal Effect of the Human Rights Act' (1998) *PL* 423.

[171] The leading judgment remains that of the Constitutional Court in *Lüth* of 1957, BVerfGE 7, 198, reproduced in translated form by B. S. Markesinis and H. Unberath, *The German Law of Torts: A Comparative Treatise* (4th edn., 2002), 392 ff.

[172] G. Phillipson, 'The Human Rights Act, "Horizontal Effect" and the Common Law: a Bang or a Whimper?' (1999) 62 *MLR* 824.

[173] [2001] 2 WLR 992, the first of the *Douglas* cases.

[174] *Ibid.*, at [91].

[175] *Ibid.*, at [166].

[176] *Ibid.*, at [128] (emphasis added).

Court of Appeal's decision in *Campbell*, Lord Phillips MR also used language compatible with the notion of weak indirect application, talking of the courts 'having regard' to Articles 8 and 10 of the Convention.[177] In the same case, but at the House of Lords level, we find what in common language could only be described as 'pretty slight' analysis. Baroness Hale is the only one who, perhaps because of her academic background, took a fully considered and consistent position on this point and came down in favour of a strong indirect view when she said:

> The 1998 Act does not create any new cause of action between private persons. But if there is a relevant cause of action applicable, the court as a public authority must act compatibly with both parties' Convention right.[178]

Lord Hope's detailed consideration of the Strasbourg case law likewise suggests that he is, in effect, siding with Baroness Hale's view that the English courts are bound to take into consideration how the Convention rights have been shaped in practice by the Strasbourg court. Both of these judges thus seem to be disagreeing with Lord Hoffmann who, it would appear, is in the minority on this point as well. Indeed, arguably, his position is a cause of some confusion since in one passage he seems to be against the any idea of horizontality whereas in another he seems to suggest the opposite. Thus, in para. 49 of his opinion he informs us that:

> Although the Convention, as an international instrument, may impose upon the United Kingdom an obligation to take some steps (whether by statute or otherwise) to protect rights of privacy against invasion by private individuals, it does not follow that such an obligation would have any counterpart in domestic law.

It would appear that Lord Hoffmann is here making the distinction to which we alluded earlier, between the Strasbourg court giving Convention rights a horizontal effect and the national court, interpreting the HRA, and being free to do the opposite. This last stance would be perfectly compatible with what we called the Buxton approach, which excludes horizontality under the HRA. The problem with such a stance, however, is not only that the Buxton approach has found no favour in academic and, more importantly court circles; the real problem comes in the next paragraph of Lord Hoffmann's judgment where he tells us:

> What human rights law has done is to identify private information as something worth protecting as an aspect of human autonomy and dignity. And this recognition has raised inescapably the question of why it should be worth protecting against the state but not against a private person. I can see no logical ground for saying that a person should have less protection against a private individual than he would have against the state for the publication of personal information for which there no justification.

It is, at the very least, difficult to understand how these two statements come together and, maybe, Lord Hoffman will himself one day tell us how, or will otherwise explain

177 *Campbell* v. *MGN Ltd.* [2003] 2 WLR 80, at [42].

178 *Campbell* v. *MGN Ltd.* [2004] 2 WLR 1232, at [132] (emphasis added).

the ambiguity of how they do not contradict each other. In the first statement, he seems to tell us that the national statute may deviate from the Strasbourg law, yet then in the second he tells us why, in this case at least, he sees no reason why this should be so. The latter statement seems to accept horizontality even though this seems not to be linked either to the ECHR or the HRA.

It is not the role of a textbook to labour too closely points that depend so much upon the use of words or concepts. It may be wrong to argue that, under the pressures of modern judging, it would be misleading to attribute too much emphasis to words such as 'take into account', 'be informed', 'must apply' and so on, or seek to impose too much consistency among the judgments of five, learned and strong-minded judges of our highest court. It might thus be best simply to alert the reader to what are, arguably, divergences and inconsistencies and let him—if he be a student, with the help of his teacher—try to resolve them. For present purposes, it will thus suffice to say once again that progress has been made in this area as well, even if this may frustrate those members of the Press who find it advantageous to expose true private facts concerning other persons for no legitimate rhyme or reason. But then, this is as much a personal view as is the opposite, and in the end we rely upon our courts to strike the right balance between privacy and speech.

6. THE DEVELOPMENT OF ENGLISH LAW: LESSONS THAT WILL NOT BE LEARNT

If there is one lesson that emerges from this (very) summary account, it is that English law has reached the position of recognising a tort of privacy in all but name. Some judges had advocated this open approach. Laws LJ was, chronologically speaking, among the first to call a spade a spade,[179] though even earlier Lords Denning[180] and Scarman[181] had described human privacy as a 'fundamental right'. Lord Keith added his weight to this call for intellectual honesty when, in *Attorney-General* v. *Guardian Newspapers*,[182] he said that in that case 'breach of confidence involve[d] no more than an invasion of privacy'. Even more recently, Lord Nicholls, in his judgment in *R* v. *Khan*,[183] asked himself the question 'whether the present, piecemeal protection of privacy has now developed to the extent that a more comprehensive principle can be seen to exist'. Yet though our judges have stripped the equitable doctrine of breach of confidence of many of its original (and limiting) requirements and, not infrequently in their judgments, used terminology that is compatible only with the notion of privacy, no English judge has yet shown the willingness to give the (new) cause of action the

179 See *Hellewell* v. *Chief Constable of Derbyshire* [1995] 1 WLR 804,7.

180 *What Next in the Law* (1982), Part six—Privacy and confidence.

181 In his judgment in *Morris* v. *Beardmore* [1980] 2 All ER 753, at 763.

182 [1990] 1 AC 109, 205.

183 [1997] AC 558, 583.

name that most fits its aim and scope—privacy—choosing, instead, to hide behind antiquated notions and concepts. Why?

One reason is that habits stemming from education and one's professional environment help to shape a judge's outlook, mentality and terminology, and these die hard.[184] Mummery LJ's declared preference in *Wainwright* for going on using old torts,[185] which were devised to perform different functions in a now forgotten era, is an example of this attitude. One can understand it; but one finds it difficult to accept. We may, in other words, be faced here with a generational difference which a new group of judges will find less difficult to stomach. We can only wait and see.

Another objection to adopting and developing a tort openly called 'privacy' may be linked to the idea that it would bring a flood of claims in its wake. Large parts of our law of torts are based on such judicial hunches, even though they remain uncorroborated by empirical evidence and even though most judges, talented legal technicians though they are, would find it very difficult to deal with material and evidence coming from other social sciences. Yet evidence there exists; and it comes from Germany where figures are available (if only the judges were willing to consider them) and which show that that system, unlike the French, has successfully avoided a flood of claims and has not devalued speech. This conclusion was, instinctively, shared by the Lord Chancellor's Department in its 1993 paper;[186] and since it reached the same end point without having relied upon figures from other systems, it can only help to support the view that this fear of opening the floodgates is unwarranted. Indeed, why should it happen in our system where going to court is so expensive and where there is no legal aid available for these types of cases when it has not happened elsewhere where recourse to courts is both easy and cheap?

So one comes to a third possibility: the judges' fear of taking on the Press openly on an issue it seems to care deeply about. It would be unacceptable as well as deeply worrying if this were, indeed, the case. But we do not think it needs to be seen to be so, for when one is talking about the Press one should recognise that much of the serious Press seems to have few or no real concerns about this issue of privacy, being more preoccupied—and justly so—with some of the antique features of our law of defamation. So that leaves us with the Murdoch press, and tabloids such as the *Sun* or the *News of the World*; and it is no coincidence that this same newspaper group is also the one which is most opposed (though on different grounds) to Europe and European integration. A law textbook cannot begin to solve legal issues once they 'degenerate' so openly into political disputes over power and money. But it can, at the very least, alert its readers to the underlying issues.

Be that as it may, have we reached a happy end? 'Yes and no' is the only correct answer. On the plus side, although those of us who started this campaign over twenty years ago

184 On which see B. S. Markesinis, 'Judicial Mentality: Mental Disposition or Outlook as a Factor Impeding Recourse to Foreign Law' (2006) 80 *Tul. LR.* 1325.

185 See n. 155, above.

186 Lord Chancellor's Department and Scottish Office: Joint Consultation Paper, *Infringement of Privacy*, HC 291-1 (1993).

seemed—initially—to be unable to make any headway whatsoever, the Younger Report being waved at us like a cross barring the road to an advancing vampire, the position for victims of shameful intrusions into their private lives is better now than it ever was in the past. Yet why, instead of celebrating this improvement, do we also express concern about the current state of affairs in this area of the law? The reasons are two.

First, the shaping of the law of privacy is not yet complete. We are not here referring to the nomenclature to be used to represent the result that we wished to achieve but which has (nearly) come about, notwithstanding the attachment to an antiquated term. What remains to be done is to convince our judges to develop rational criteria for determining the extent of possible protection given by the law and to abandon the old-fashioned, and essentially unhelpful, manner of fixing the limits of liability and protection through antiquated conceptualism and terminology.

Second, the development of rules of compensation which will achieve a reasonable level or recompense and avoid gold-digging actions still remains to completed. For while we do wish to see Naomi Campbell or Catherine Zeta-Jones protected from a rapacious Press, at the same time neither do we wish to encourage rapacity in these celebrities. All this could, in theory, be achieved through legislation (an idea which we find unattractive since it invites horse-trading rather than rational compromises between competing lobbies), self-regulation (which has been conclusively proved to be a toothless and inadequate way of reining in the worse elements of the Press) or, finally, court-induced reform. We prefer the latter approach and sincerely hope that it will continue.

The other main complaint that has sometimes been made is the price that we have paid for this progress.

The tort of privacy, which hardly figured in tort textbooks when ours first appeared on the national scene, has now become so extended, so complex and so confusing that one full chapter (the size of two law review articles) can do nothing more than whet the students' appetites. Is this because we made the mistake of recognising a tort of privacy or widened the notion of breach of confidence? 'No' is the emphatic answer. For change has come despite the repeated attempts of many judges to block change and reform. So it is not because the path of change was opened up that this complexity we are complaining about has crept into our law (and our account of it), but because endless judges and practitioners, using their formidable skills and ingenuity, helped bring it about through their inability or unwillingness to co-ordinate their efforts. For, by trying to be faithful to their incremental, hesitant, cautious way of developing the law through multi-opinion judgments, there has been a refusal to cut the Gordian knot by acknowledging the existence of a general principle and then leaving it to the courts to shape its contours on a case-by-case basis on the basis of rational criteria, instead of applying the outmoded conceptual framework of the old-fashioned torts.

To this, it will be objected that the beauty (and strength) of the common law lies in its many-faceted judgments, in the talent and ability to extract working rules through the careful analysis of the cases that call for resolution and, very rarely, synthesise its casuistic law. In any event, its dislike of principle and its attachment to casuistry and pragmatism are unchangeable features and only academics or foreigners or both would dare question the utility of these basic features of the common-law system.

Maybe these are, indeed, all attributes that have contributed to the glory of the common law. Undoubtedly, they are ingredients that have added to its intellectual appeal and to the refining of thousands of legal minds throughout the centuries. But they have come at a price: a highly convoluted law; endless misery for victims of press prying; and much wealth to rapacious newspaper moguls who make money at the expense of others. And the end result is a position reached which is very similar to that adopted by other major systems which could have, through intellectual dialogue were we open to it, have influenced us and saved us much time and effort. But we ignored this route and now foreign institutions—such as the courts in Luxembourg and (particularly in this field) Strasbourg—are in many ways influencing, and sometimes even dictating, the shape and pace of change of our law. Whether politicians are more to blame than lawyers for this sorry state of affairs cannot be answered here. But today's students are mature enough to realise the irresistible force of globalisation and the attraction, intellectual as well as professional, of working together with other cultures and learning from each other.

SELECT BIBLIOGRAPHY

BINGHAM OF CORNHILL, LORD, 'Should There Be a Law to Protect Rights of Personal Privacy?' [1996] *EHRLR* 450.

CALCUTT, SIR D., *Review of Press Self-Regulation*, Cmnd. 1102 (1990).

—*Review of Press Self-Regulation*, Cmnd. 2135 (1993).

EADY, B., 'Opinion: A Statutory Right to Privacy' [1996] *EHRLR* 243.

FELDMAN, D., 'The Developing Scope of Article 8 of the European Convention on Human Rights' [1997] *EHRLR* 266.

—'Secrecy, Dignity or Autonomy? Views of Privacy as a Civil Liberty', 47 (2) CLR 42.

FENWICK, H., and PHILLIPSON, G., *Media Freedom under the Human Rights Act* (2006).

HUNT, M., 'The 'Horizontal Effect' of the Human Rights Act' [1998] *PL* 423.

LESTER OF HERNE HILL, LORD, and PANNICK D., *Human Rights Law and Practice* (2nd edn., 2004).

LORD CHANCELLOR'S DEPARTMENT AND THE SCOTTISH OFFICE, *Infringement of Privacy: A Consultation Paper* (1993).

MACCORMICK, N., 'A Note upon Privacy' (1973) 89 *LQR* 23.

MARKESINIS, B. S., 'The Right to Be Let Alone versus Freedom of Speech' [1986] *PL* 67.

—(ed.), *Protecting Privacy* (1999).

—'O'CINNEIDE, C., FEDTKE, J., and HUNTER HENIN, M., 'Concerns and Idea about the Developing English Law of Privacy (and How Knowledge of Foreign Law Might Be of Help)' (2004) 52 *Am. J Comp. L* 133.

MARSHALL, G., 'The Right to Privacy: A Sceptical View' (1975) 21 *McGill LJ* 242.

MATRIX MEDIA AND INFORMATION GROUP, *Privacy and the Media: The Developing Law* (2002).

NAISMITH, S. H., 'Photographs, Privacy and Freedom of Expression' [1996] *EHRLR* 150.

PERRI 6, *The Future of Privacy*, 2 vols. (1998).

PHILLIPSON, G., and FENWICK, H., 'Breach of Confidence as a Privacy Remedy in the Human Rights Act Era' (2000) 63 *MLR* 660.

PRESCOTT, P., '*Kaye* v *Robertson*: A Reply' (1991) 54 *MLR* 451.

ROSEBERG, J., *Privacy and the Press* (2004).

SANDERSON, M. A., 'Is *von Hannover* a Step Backward?' [2004] 6 *EHRLR* 631.

SEIPP, D.J., 'English Judicial Recognition of a Right to Privacy', (1983) 3 *OJLS* 325.

TUGENDHAT, M., and CHRISTIE, I., *The Law of Privacy and the Media* (2002).

WACKS, R., *Privacy and the Law* (1993), ii.

WESTIN, A., *Privacy and Freedom* (1967).

WINFIELD, P., 'Privacy' (1931) 47 *LQR* 23.

YOUNGER, K., *Report of the Committee on Privacy*, Cmnd. 5012 (1972).

23

DEFAMATION AND PRIVACY: AN AMERICAN PERSPECTIVE

Professor David A. Anderson[*]

1. ENGLISH AND AMERICAN DEFAMATION LAW COMPARED

Chapter 21 eloquently embraces the central conviction of the English law of defamation: that reputation and freedom of expression are equally important values. Unspoken, but no less central, is the belief that the two can be successfully balanced so that neither need be subordinated to the other. For better or worse, the American law of defamation sees the matter differently. It views protection of reputation and freedom of expression as conflicting values that often cannot both be honoured. The American assumption is that 'Whatever is added to the field of libel is taken from the field of free debate.'[1] When one value has to be chosen over the other, the American law usually chooses to protect speech. The Supreme Court recognises that this 'exacts a correspondingly high price from the victims of defamatory falsehood',[2] but considers it necessary because of

> a profound national commitment to the principle that debate on public issues should be uninhibited, robust, and wide-open . . .[3]

The American 'hallowed preference for free expression', as it is called in Chapter 21, has reduced defamation litigation in the United States to practical insignificance when compared with the frequency and importance of libel litigation in England. In the past quarter-century, on average fewer than twenty libel cases against *media* have gone to trial per year in the entire United States.[4] The law of defamation simply is no longer

* Fred and Emily Marshall Wulff Centennial Chair in Law, The University of Texas at Austin.

1 *New York Times Co.* v. *Sullivan*, 376 US 254, 272 (1064) (quoting *Sweeney* v. *Patterson*, 76 US App D C 23, 24 (1942)).

2 *Gertz* v. *Robert Welch, Inc.*, 418 US 323, 342 (1974).

3 *New York Times Co.* v. *Sullivan*, 376 US 254, 270 (1964).

4 *See* Press Release, Media Law Res. Ctr., MLRC Annual Study of Media Trials: 14 Trials in 2005: 7 Wins, 7 Losses, Relatively Modest Damage Awards, http://www.medialaw.org/Content/NavigationMenu/About_

a major threat to the press in America.[5] It retains somewhat more vitality in cases against non-media defendants, such as employers who defame employees in the course of firing them, but in these cases the defamation claim is often secondary to another tort claim, such as wrongful discharge, and thus even in these cases the law of defamation does not play as central a role in protecting reputation as it does in England. To the American observer, it seems remarkable that although successful libel suits are more frequent in England, they do not seem to produce the level of self-censorship that American courts have assumed the common law of defamation would generate.[6] Possibly the litigation difficulties that defamation victims face in England give the press some of the protection that doctrine denies them in that country.

Although the American law of defamation has descended from that of England, it has diverged so greatly that nowadays the resemblance is largely superficial. In practice the law works quite differently because of differences in the way defamation litigation is financed and conducted and because of the impact in America of constitutional free-speech principles. Doctrinally, the American law is far more protective of speech than the English law. It offers virtually all of England's common-law protections, plus a succession of constitutional restrictions designed to thwart suits that could survive the common law barriers.

The common-law rules are similar. American law observes the English law's distinction between libel and slander and the related rules regarding slander *per se* and presumed harm. As in England, the essence of the tort is harm to reputation; insults and affronts to honour, actionable in some continental legal systems, generally do not suffice in the United States. The same elaborate structure of absolute and conditional privileges protects many kinds of defamatory but socially useful communications. There are many minor differences, however, a few of which are significant enough to warrant mention here.

Thus, the liberal pleading rules of American courts generally do not require plaintiffs to identify specifically the words of which they complain or the precise defamatory meaning they claim the words convey. Typically, the plaintiff merely alleges that he or she is defamed by the defendant's published article or broadcast. The defendant is then forced either to defend against all possible defamatory meanings that might be found in the material or engage in wasteful preliminary skirmishes attempting to pin down the plaintiff. The English rules requiring claimants to plead innuendo go a long way toward eliminating such unnecessary confusion, and ought to be emulated in the United States.

American courts vigorously protect satire and other varieties of humour by refusing to find defamatory meaning in statements that sometimes seem more defamatory than funny. An example is a case in which the television network ESPN posted on its web site a photo of the retired motorcycle daredevil Evil Knievel taken at an 'extreme sports' banquet hosted by ESPN. The photo showed Knievel with one arm around his wife and

MLRC/News/2006_Bulletin_No_1.htm (March 2, 2006) (noting that the were an average of 27 trials per year in the 1980s, 18.8 trials per year in the 1990s, and 13.8 trials per year thus far this decade).

[5] From 1980 to 1998 the total of all final judgments against media in the United States was $21 million, or 0.01% of media revenues for *one year*. See D. A. Anderson, 'Freedom of the Press' (2002) 80 *Tex. LR* 429, 484 n. 298.

[6] E. Barendt *et al.*, *Libel and the Media: The Chilling Effect* (1997).

his other arm around a young woman. The caption said 'Evil Knievel proves you're never too old to be a pimp.' A US Court of Appeals held that the caption was not actionable because the general content on the web site would alert readers that the word 'pimp' was a sophomoric attempt at humour rather than a reference to the usual meaning of the word. A dissenting judge argued that a jury should have been allowed to determine how the average person in the community would have interpreted the photo and caption.[7]

A major new issue for every country is the scope of liability for Internet defamation. Internet defamation challenges some of the fundamental notions of defamation law. For example, the Internet makes it possible to forward defamatory messages with unprecedented ease. How many of those involved in such transmissions should be treated as having 'published' the defamation? American common law employs the same republication rules as the English common law.[8] Under these rules, a company that provides computer bulletin-boards on which a subscriber posts a defamatory message accessible to all other subscribers would be liable as a republisher, at least if the company were aware of the defamation. So would a reader who forwarded the message to someone else, and possibly the service provider that facilitated the transmissions. After a decision indicating that the conventional concept of publication would apply to all of these,[9] the Internet industry persuaded Congress to pass a statute that has been construed to grant complete immunity to all except the originator of the message. The stated purpose of the statute was to encourage Internet service providers (ISPs) to screen material transmitted on their systems to keep out obscenity. The companies had argued that such screening of content would subject them to liability as publishers.

The statute states that 'No provider or user of an interactive computer service shall be treated as the publisher or speaker of any information provided by another information content provider.'[10] Although the statute was presented to Congress as a solution to the specific problem that arose from treating an ISP as a publisher for purposes of defamation law, the courts have viewed it as creating an absolute immunity for ISPs. Under English law, and in the United States until passage of this statute, an ISP that merely transmitted someone else's defamation would be treated as a distributor, and thus not liable unless it knew or should have known of the defamation,[11] but once it was notified of the defamatory material, if it failed to remove the material it would be treated as a publisher.

The statute obliterates the distinction between publication and distribution, so far as the Internet is concerned. The statute protects a provider even if it is notified of a posting, knows that it is false and defamatory, and agrees that it should have been removed.[12] The statute may even protect a provider who induces a contributor to post

7 *Knievel* v. *ESPN*, 393 F 3d 1068 (9th Cir. 2005).

8 See above, ch. 21, Section 2(c).

9 *Stratton Oakmont, Inc.* v. *Prodigy Services Co.*, 1995 WL 323710 (NY Supp., 24 May 1995).

10 47 USCs. 230 (1996).

11 See above, ch. 21, Section 2(c).

12 *Zeran* v. *America Online, Inc.*, 129 F 3d 327 (4th Cir.) (1997), *cert. denied* 118 SCt. 2341 (1998).

defamatory matter.[13] It protects a service provider from negligence claims that do not sound in defamation.[14] Despite the statute's stated anti-obscenity purpose, one decision interpreted the language so as to protect a service provider from civil liability arising from obscenity.[15] Each of these decisions is authoritative only in the jurisdiction of the court that rendered it, and it is possible that eventually the Supreme Court may construe the statute in a manner more consistent with the limited purpose for which it was enacted. But another possibility is that other republishers, such as newspapers that run letters-to-the-editor or radio stations that broadcast call-in shows, may persuade courts or legislatures that they should have the same immunity that ISPs have been given. As matters stand, the statute greatly restricts the influence of the law on what may be the most important source of defamation for the future. Such a sweeping immunity is not a solution that England or any other legal system should emulate unadvisedly.

While the English courts require defendants to establish the precise truth of the defamatory accusation, the American courts usually accept a rough approximation. For example, evidence showing that the plaintiff, a journalist, had fabricated one story was held sufficient to preclude liability for a statement that the journalist had been fired for repeatedly fabricating stories.[16] This result is quite at odds with the very similar English case described above.[17]

The common law privileges in the United States are generally similar to those in England, but the privilege to report public proceedings appears to be broader. It applies not only to legislative and judicial proceedings and public meetings, but also has been applied to written reports, public officials' statements to the press, and even to material leaked from official files.[18] A few courts have expanded this to a general privilege to repeat defamatory allegations, even by private persons, provided the allegations are accurately reported.[19] This expansion may be the result of misunderstanding of the common law,[20] but it is indicative of the tendency to protect accurate repetition.

[13] See *Blumenthal* v. *Drudge*, 992 F Supp. 44 (DCDC) (1998) (holding a service provider immune even though the originator of the defamation was paid by the provider). This is a trial court decision that need not be followed by other courts.

[14] See *Green* v. *America Online, Inc.*, 318 F 3d 465 (3d Cir. 2003)(holding that statute provided immunity against claims of negligent failure to police content of material transmitted on ISP's network).

[15] *Doe* v. *America Online, Inc.*, 783 So. 2d 1010 (2001) (Florida).

[16] *Shihab* v. *Express-News Corp.*, 604 SW 2d 204 (1980) (Texas App.).

[17] See *Wakley* v. *Cooke and Healey* [1849] 4 Exch. 511, 517; 154 ER 1316, 1318. The case is described at ch. 21, Section (3)(c) above.

[18] See, e.g., *Medico* v. *Time, Inc.*, 643 F 2d 134 (3d Cir. 1981).

[19] See *Global Green* v.*CBS, Inc.*, 286 F 3d 281 (5th Cir. 2002) (extending the privilege to a private attorney's allegations in a television broadcast that plaintiff had fabricated accusations against her husband to get his lottery winnings).

[20] The court in *Green* relied on two Texas decisions holding that media defendants can establish substantial truth by showing that the allegations they are reporting were in fact made. See *Dolcefino* v. *Randolph*, 19 SW 3d 906 (Tex. App. 2000); *KTRK Television* v. *Felder*, 950 SW 2d 100 (Tex. App. 1997). But of course the most that accurate reporting can establish is privilege; to establish substantial truth the defendant must show that the underlying charge is true, not merely that the charge was made. The conflating of privilege with substantial truth is not merely a local phenomenon, however. In *Global Relief Foundation Inc.* v. *New York Times Co.*, 390 F 3d 973 (2d Cir. 2004), the court held that a newspaper report that an Islamic charity was being investigated by

These differences are minor, however, when compared with the differences introduced by American constitutional law. The American courts have concluded that the shared common-law principles do not give speech—or at least speech about matters of public concern—the degree of protection required under the free-speech-and-press clauses of the First Amendment to the US Constitution. They have created a body of federal constitutional defamation law that supplements, and in some instances supplants, the common law rules. The effects are pervasive, introducing new rules with respect to fault, damages, burdens of proof, and appellate review.

2. PUBLIC OFFICIALS

All of this constitutional development has taken place since 1964. Until then, the US Supreme Court adhered to the position that defamatory falsehoods 'are no essential part of any exposition of ideas'[21] and thus are 'not . . . within the area of constitutionally protected speech.'[22]

The court abandoned that notion in *New York Times Co.* v. *Sullivan*,[23] one of the most dramatic and far-reaching decisions in American constitutional law. The effect of the common law on speech could not be ignored, even though truth was a complete defence, because

> would-be critics of official conduct may be deterred from voicing their criticism, even though it is believed to be true and even though it is in fact true, because of doubt whether it can be proved in court or fear of the expense of having to do so.[24]

These worries were likely to induce self-censorship. The court quoted James Madison, the primary draftsman of the First Amendment:

> Some degree of abuse is inseparable from the proper use of every thing; and in no instance is this more true than in that of the press.[25]

Although the rationale of *New York Times* v. *Sullivan* seemed to apply generally to libels occurring in discussions of public issues, the case did not require the court to go so far. Rather, the court fashioned a cluster of new constitutional defamation rules dealing only with libels against public officials. Sullivan was the elected official in charge of police in Birmingham, an Alabama city beset with racial violence. The *New York Times* published an advertisement by a group seeking to raise funds for civil-rights demonstrators in the South. The advertisement accused the Birmingham police of brutal and

the government for funding terrorism was substantially true without regard to whether there was any basis for the government's suspicions.

21 *Chaplinsky* v. *New Hampshire*, 315 US 568, 572, 62 SCt. 766, 769 (1942).

22 *Beauharnais* v. *Illinois*, 343 US 250, 266, 72 SCt. 725, 735 (1952).

23 376 US 254, 84 SCt. 710 (1964).

24 *Ibid.*, 279.

25 *Ibid.*, 271, quoting *Elliot's Debates on the Federal Constitution* (1876), iv, 571.

unlawful treatment of Dr Martin Luther King, Jr. and other civil-rights activists. It did not name Sullivan, but he claimed he was necessarily implicated because only he had power to authorise the police actions alleged. The Alabama courts, applying common-law principles similar to those of England and most of the other American states, awarded Sullivan $500,000 in damages against the *New York Times* and four black Alabama clergymen who had signed the advertisement. The defendants urged the Supreme Court to hold that liability could never be imposed for criticism of the official conduct of a public official. Such liability, they argued, would be a species of seditious libel, which had been universally condemned in the United States since the notorious Alien and Sedition Acts expired in 1801. But the majority of the justices were unwilling to go that far. Instead, they adopted a

> federal rule that prohibits a public official from recovering damages for a defamatory falsehood unless he proves that the statement was made with 'actual malice'—that is, with knowledge that it was false or with reckless disregard of whether it was false or not.[26]

The court analogised this to a state law rule, recognised only in a minority of the states, which expanded the common law privilege of fair comment to cover false statements of fact about the conduct of public officials. It soon became apparent, however, that the *New York Times* rule went beyond anything known to the common law anywhere. The 'actual malice' needed to satisfy the *New York Times* rule can be shown only by proving that the defendant published despite

> a high degree of awareness of probable falsity. . . . There must be sufficient evidence to permit the conclusion that the defendant in fact entertained serious doubts as to the truth of his publication.[27]

This requirement is administered with such rigour that omitting the word 'serious' from the jury instruction on this issue may require a new trial.[28]

Had the court stopped with the announcement of the 'actual malice' rule, the case would have gone back to Alabama for retrial. For all its stringency, the test would only have raised a jury issue, and had a new jury found that the *New York Times* published with the requisite subjective awareness of falsity Sullivan might yet have won. To prevent this, the court promulgated several rules ancillary to the 'actual malice' requirement.

First, the court announced that 'actual malice' must be established with 'convincing clarity', rather than the preponderance of evidence usual in civil cases.

Second, the court asserted that since the factual issue of 'actual malice' was one upon which constitutional rights depended, the jury's fact finding would be scrutinised more closely than usual. The court would '"make an independent examination of the whole record," so as to assure ourselves that the judgment does not constitute a forbidden intrusion on the field of free expression'.[29] Engaging in such a review of the Alabama

[26] 376 US 254, 84 SCt. 710 (1964), at 279–80.

[27] *St Amant* v. *Thompson*, 390 US 727, 731, 88 SCt. 1323, 1325 (1968).

[28] See *Wynn* v. *Smith*, 16 P 3d 424 (2001) (Nevada).

[29] 376 US at 285, 84 SCt. at 729 (1964) (citation omitted).

trial record, the court concluded that a jury could not properly find that the *New York Times* published with knowing or reckless falsity, even though there was evidence that its secretary suspected that one of the allegations was false, and even though material in the *New York Times*'s own files would have shown several of the statements to be false.

We think the evidence against the *Times* supports at most a finding of negligence in failing to discover the misstatements, and is constitutionally insufficient to show the recklessness that is required for a finding of actual malice.[30]

This language made clear that it would be futile to retry the case under the new 'actual malice' standard; the Supreme Court would ultimately hold the evidence insufficient.

Finally, the court drove a stake through the heart of Sullivan's lawsuit by holding unconstitutional his theory that criticism of his police officers defamed him. This theory smacked of seditious libel,

transmuting criticism of government, however impersonal it may seem on its face, into personal criticism, and hence potential libel, of the officials of whom the government is composed.[31]

Thus, although the 'actual malice' rule is usually thought of as the key holding in *New York Times* v. *Sullivan*, in fact the rule is the least of its products. Had the decision merely announced the 'actual malice' rule, the American courts probably would have continued to apply something very similar to the English law of defamation, with an additional jury issue in public-official cases. What assured a decisive break with the English tradition was the court's demonstrated willingness to supervise the administration of state libel law, to make sure that the preference for 'wide open, robust debate' was observed in practice as well as in theory.

The decision in the *New York Times* case was not the only example of that commitment: in the next ten years, eleven libel cases were decided by the Supreme Court and in only one of those was a judgment for the plaintiff able to surmount the substantive and procedural barriers erected by the court. Even with the more conservative bent of the court in recent years, it has adhered steadfastly to the basic principles of the *New York Times* case.[32] The 'public official' category, of course, includes elected officials (local, state and national) like Sullivan. But it also encompasses candidates for public office,[33] appointed officials[34] and 'those among the hierarchy of government employees who have, or appear to the public to have, substantial responsibility for or control over the conduct of government affairs'.[35] Officers as lowly as the superintendent of the county motor pool[36] and a deputy sheriff[37] have been subjected to the *New York Times* rules.

[30] *Ibid.*, 288.

[31] *Ibid.*, 292.

[32] See e.g. *Masson* v. *New Yorker Magazine, Inc.*, 501 US 496, 111 SCt. 2419 (1991).

[33] *Monitor Patriot Co.* v. *Roy*, 401 US 263, 91 SCt. 602 (1961).

[34] *Henry* v. *Collins*, 380 US 356, 85 SCt. 992 (1965).

[35] *Rosenblatt* v. *Baer*, 383 US 75, 86 SCt. 669 (1966).

[36] *Clawson* v. *Longview Pub. Co.*, 589 P 2d 1223 (1979) (Washington).

[37] *Ammerman* v. *Hubbard Broadcasting Co.*, 91 NM 250, 572 P 2d 1258 (1977) (New Mexico App.), *cert. denied* 436 US 906, 98 SCt. 2237 (1978).

3. PUBLIC FIGURES

The primary rationale of *New York Times* v. *Sullivan* was the belief that citizen critics of government officials needed more freedom than the common law provided. But the court also expressed a more general concern to protect 'debate on public issues', which might well involve defamation of persons other than public officials. Thus, it seemed likely from the outset that at least some of the *New York Times* restrictions would be applied eventually to plaintiffs other than public officials.

The opportunity first presented itself in two libel cases that the Supreme Court decided jointly in 1967.[38] One plaintiff, Wally Butts, was athletics director at a state university but was paid by a private alumni organisation. The other, General Edwin Walker, had retired from the army and was defamed in the course of activities he undertook as a private citizen after retirement. All members of the Court agreed that, although neither was a public official, both were 'public figures', criticism of who should receive some constitutional protection. Warren CJ wrote:

> although they are not subject to the restraints of the political process, 'public figures,' like 'public officials,' often play an influential role in ordering society... Our citizenry has a legitimate and substantial interest in the conduct of such persons, and freedom of the press to engage in uninhibited debate about their involvement in public issues and events is as crucial as it is in the case of 'public officials'.[39]

Although four members of the court would have adopted a somewhat lower constitutional barrier for public figures, the majority voted to apply the same standards as in public official cases. The court voted five to four to affirm Butts' $460,000 judgment on the ground that he had met the constitutional burden, but unanimously reversed Walker's $500,000 award because he had not.

Determining whether a plaintiff is a public figure is not always easy. The lower courts generally have treated sports and entertainment celebrities as public figures, without much regard to their involvement in public issues.[40] Even the faintest of luminaries often fail to challenge their classification as public figures, so the applicability to celebrities of Warren CJ's rationale for extending the *New York Times* rules to public figures has not been thoroughly explored.

The Supreme Court has not decided a celebrity case, but has tended to describe the public figure category somewhat more narrowly than the lower courts.[41]

That designation may rest on either of two bases. In some instances an individual may achieve such pervasive fame or notoriety that he becomes a public figure for all purposes and in all contexts. More commonly, an individual voluntarily injects himself

[38] *Butts* v. *Curtis Pub. Co.* and *Walker* v. *Associated Press*, decided together at 388 US 130, 87 SCt. 1975 (1967).

[39] *Ibid.*, at 164 (US).

[40] E.g. *Carson* v. *Allied News Co.*, 529 F 2d 206 (7th Cir. 1976) (television entertainer); *Maule* v. *NYM Corp.*, 54 NY 2d 880 (1981) (sports writer).

[41] *Gertz* v. *Robert Welch Inc.*, 418 US 323, 351, 94 SCt. 2997, 3012–13 (1974).

or is drawn into a particular public controversy and thereby becomes a public figure for a limited range of issues. In either case such persons assume special prominence in the resolution of public questions.

The Supreme Court has refused to treat as a public figure a prominent civil-liberties lawyer,[42] a socialite involved in a notorious divorce case[43] and a scientist who had received more than $500,000 in federal research funds.[44] The public-figure classification has both a geographical and a contextual dimension. A person who is well known locally may be treated as a public figure for purposes of a publication circulating primarily in that locale, even though he is unknown nationally.[45] And a person may be a public figure in connection with discussion of her role in one activity but not another.[46] A person need not seek the limelight to become a public figure; one of the first two women to become combat pilots in the Navy was held to be a public figure on the ground that she

> attained a position of special prominence in the controversy [over women in combat roles] when she 'suited up' as an F-14 combat pilot.[47]

As a result of the broad interpretations given to both the public-official and public-figure categories, the *New York Times* restrictions apply to a very large number—perhaps a majority—of American defamation cases. For these plaintiffs, success is very unlikely. One study showed that plaintiffs ultimately prevailed in only about 10 per cent of the media defamation cases in which the *New York Times* rules applied.[48]

4. PRIVATE PLAINTIFFS

In the United States as in England, there has been disagreement as to the kinds of information that are of sufficient public importance to require protection from the operation of defamation law. For a time it appeared that the Supreme Court would apply the *New York Times* rules to all plaintiffs defamed in connection with public affairs, even if they were neither public officials nor public figures. A number of lower courts had reasoned that 'uninhibited, robust, and wide-open' debate on public issues was certain to produce defamation of private persons as well as public and that libel suits by the former were just as likely to cause self-censorship as those by the latter.[49] But the Supreme Court has declined to give the highest level of constitutional protection to all such speech.

42 *Ibid.*

43 *Time, Inc.* v. *Firestone*, 424 US 448, 96 SCt. 958 (1976).

44 *Hutchinson* v. *Proxmire*, 443 US 111, 99 SCt. 2675 (1979).

45 E.g. *Williams* v. *Pasma*, 656 P 2d 212 (1982) (Montana), *cert. denied* 461 US 945, 103 SCt. 2122 (1983).

46 E.g. *Vitale* v. *National Lampoon*, 449 F Supp. 442 (1978).

47 *Lohrenz* v. *Donnelly*, 350 F 3d 1272, 1274 (DC Cir. 2003).

48 See M. A. Franklin, 'Winners, Losers, and Why? A Study of Defamation Litigation' (1980) *Am. Bar Found. Res. J* 455.

49 See e.g. *Time, Inc.* v. *McLaney*, 406 F 2d 565 (5th Cir. 1969), *cert. denied* 395 US 922, 89 SCt. 1769 (1969).

The court did apply the *New York Times* rules to a private plaintiff in one case, disallowing a $275,000 judgment won by a magazine distributor defamed in reporting about his arrest on obscenity charges. The case was *Rosenbloom* v. *Metromedia, Inc.*[50] Three justices agreed with lower courts that:

Drawing a distinction between 'public' and 'private' figures makes no sense in terms of the First Amendment guarantees.[51]

But no majority of the court ever fully embraced that view and three years later the court decided to draw precisely that distinction.

The case was *Gertz* v. *Robert Welch, Inc.*,[52] the second most important case in the American law of defamation after *New York Times* v. *Sullivan*. The plaintiff was a lawyer who had been called a 'Communist-fronter' by a right-wing political group. His case had been decided by the trial court on the theory that since he was not a public figure, he need not meet the *New York Times* requirements. The United States Court of Appeals held that this was erroneous in the light of *Rosenbloom*. Gertz clearly had been defamed in the course of debate on a public issue; the article claimed Communists were plotting to discredit American police and that Gertz was involved. The Supreme Court, however, repudiated *Rosenbloom*. The majority decided that applying *New York Times* to all those defamed in discussion of public issues would entail too great a sacrifice of the reputations of private persons. The latter deserve more protection from the law, the court asserted, because (*a*) private individuals have not voluntarily assumed a risk of public criticism by engaging in politics or achieving prominence in a particular field and (*b*) they are less likely than public plaintiffs to have access to media to rebut false charges.[53] Thus, while the free-speech interest in encouraging robust debate might be the same whether the individuals affected were public or private, the countervailing reputational interest was higher in the case of the latter and a different balance was therefore required.

This did not mean, however, that private plaintiff cases were to be free from constitutional restraints. The court believed that the common law, with its principles of strict liability tempered by numerous privileges and defences, gives too little protection to speech, even in private plaintiff cases, so it promulgated a different set of constitutional rules for cases where the discussion is about a matter of public concern but the person defamed is private.

First, the states may no longer impose strict liability in such cases. There must be some showing of fault (presumably negligence) on the part of the publisher; this spares private plaintiffs the difficulty of meeting the *New York Times* test, 'yet shields the press and broadcast media from the rigors of strict liability for defamation'.[54]

Second, such plaintiffs may recover only if they can show they have suffered actual injury. Unlike the common-law concept of special damages, which is limited to pecuniary

50 403 US 29, 91 SCt. 1811 (1971).
51 *Ibid.*, 45.
52 18 US 323 (1974).
53 *Ibid.*, 344.
54 *Ibid.*, 348.

losses, 'actual injury' may include humiliation and mental anguish. But it may not include presumed damages or punitive damages. The rationale is that the minimal fault requirement of *Gertz* strikes the proper balance between free-speech interests and the legitimate interest in redressing a private plaintiff 's actual injury; a private plaintiff who wishes to recover more than that (i.e. presumed or punitive damages) must meet the higher constitutional requirement of actual malice.[55]

Under *New York Times* and *Gertz*, the American law of defamation is subject to two different sets of constitutional restrictions. Suits by public officials and public figures are subject to the 'actual malice' requirement, the 'clear and convincing' proof requirement and aggressive judicial review of jury verdicts. Private plaintiffs face none of these requirements, but must show fault and actual injury and are denied presumed and punitive damages unless they opt to proceed under the public plaintiff rules and prove actual malice.

These divergent rules tend to make litigation quite complex, especially where the appropriate classification of the plaintiff is itself an issue. Most states have eased this difficulty somewhat by holding that whether the plaintiff is public or private is a question of law; it therefore can be decided by the judge before trial.[56] Where it is treated as a question of fact, the jury must be given alternative sets of instructions, the controlling set to be determined by the jury's decision on the public–private issue.[57]

The foregoing applies to defamation arising from discussion of matters of public concern. Subsequently the Supreme Court made matters more complicated by holding that private plaintiffs who are defamed in discussion about matters *not* of public concern need not meet all of the *Gertz* restrictions.[58]

The case involved a credit-reporting agency that falsely reported to its private subscribers that the plaintiff corporation was bankrupt. The Vermont courts held that such purely private libels were not affected by *Gertz* and allowed the plaintiff to recover presumed and punitive damages without a showing of actual malice. The Supreme Court affirmed. The *Gertz* restrictions on damages were appropriate, the court said, where speech on issues of public concern might be chilled by the prospect of punitive and presumed damages. But in the case at hand, such damages properly could be awarded even without a showing of actual malice, 'in light of the reduced constitutional value of speech involving no matters of public concern'.[59] Since the private circulation of a credit report involved no subject of public concern, the *Gertz* rules on damages were not applicable. The court did not decide whether the *Gertz* rule on fault also would be inapplicable, because the Vermont courts had found the defendant negligent and the question therefore was not before the Supreme Court.

A similar result has been reached in cases involving defamation that occurs in advertising. The Supreme Court has held in other contexts that 'commercial speech' requires

[55] *Ibid.*, 349–50.

[56] See e.g. *Waldbaum* v. *Fairchild Publications, Inc.*, 627 F 2d 1287 (2d Cir. 1980), *cert. denied* 449 US 898, 101 SCt. 266 (1980).

[57] Cf. *Nash* v. *Keene Pub. Corp.*, 214 NH 127, 498 A 2d 348 (1985).

[58] *Dun & Bradstreet, Inc.*, v. *Greenmoss Builders, Inc.*, 472 US 749, 105 SCt. 2939 (1985).

[59] 472 US at 761, 105 SCt. at 2946 (1985).

less protection than non-commercial speech.[60] Some courts have reasoned that this distinction, developed in cases involving governmental regulation of advertising, should apply to private suits for defamation as well. This rationale may mean that a person defamed in an advertisement need not show either actual malice or negligence and does not bear the burden of proving falsity.[61]

Thus, the two tiers of constitutional limitations that existed after *New York Times* and *Gertz* are now three tiers: one for public plaintiffs, one for private plaintiffs defamed in connection with public issues, and one for plaintiffs defamed in purely private contexts and/or in advertising. The Supreme Court may ultimately decide that plaintiffs in this third tier must meet some constitutional minimum less than the full *Gertz* regime, but unless and until that happens, it appears that these cases may be controlled entirely by the common law.

The second complicating factor is the Supreme Court's limited power in the American federal system. The court has no power to promulgate rules of tort law. That is the exclusive province of the state courts and state legislatures and (within limited imposed by the concept of state sovereignty) the federal Congress. The Supreme Court's power is only negative. If a state permits liability to be imposed on a basis inconsistent with the constitutional rules announced by the Supreme Court, the court can invalidate the judgment but the effect of the court's decision is only to impose a set of constitutional restrictions on the existing body of state law, not to create a new federal law of defamation. This has far-reaching consequences. Instead of supplanting contrary state law, the court's rules become a constitutional floor, defining a level of protection for defendants below which the states may not go.

For example, in public plaintiff cases (and other cases in which actual malice is shown) the federal constitutional rules do not prohibit punitive damages.[62] A number of state courts prohibit them in all defamation cases, however, as a matter of interpretation of their own state free-speech guarantees or as a result of their own more stringent interpretations of the federal constitution.[63] In private plaintiff cases *Gertz* requires only a minimal level of fault, but some of the states require more. *New York Times* requires a showing of 'gross irresponsibility'.[64] A few states require the same level of fault as would be required in a public plaintiff case: reckless or knowing falsehood.[65] Most states require the minimum permitted under *Gertz*: negligence.[66] Though the federal constitutional restrictions do not necessarily apply to purely private libels, some states apply the *Gertz* rules to all defamation cases.[67] Before the Supreme Court

60 See *Central Hudson Gas & Elec. Corp. v. Public Serv. Comm'n*, 447 US 557, 100 SCt. 2343 (1980).

61 See *Procter & Gamble Co. v. Amway, Inc.*, 242 F 3d 539 (5th Cir. 2001).

62 See *Curtis Pub. Co. v. Butts*, 388 US 130, 87 SCt. 1975 (1967).

63 See e.g. *Wheeler v. Green*, 286 Or. 99, 593 P 2d 777 (1979); *Stone v. Essex County Newspapers*, 367 Mass. 849, 330 NE 2d 161 (1975).

64 *Chapadeau v. Utica Observer-Dispatch, Inc.*, 38 NY 2d 196, 379 NYS 2d 61, 341 NE 2d 569 571 (1975).

65 See e.g. *Aafco Heating & Air Conditioning Co. v. Northwest Publications, Inc.*, 321 NE 2d 580 (1974) (Indiana App.), *cert. denied* 424 US 913, 96 SCt. 1112 (1976).

66 See e.g. *Miami Herald v. Ane*, 458 So. 2d 239, 242 (1984) (Florida).

67 E.g. *Jacron Sales, Inc. v. Sindorf*, 276 Md. 580; 350 A 2d 688 (1976).

intervened in 1964, the 'American' law of defamation consisted of fifty different bodies of law, derived from the English common law but each with its own variations. It is probably safe to say that, despite the imposition of a complex set of federal constitutional rules, there is less uniformity today than ever before.

5. TRUTH AND FALSITY

No principle of the English common law was more fully accepted in the United States than the rule that the defendant had the burden of pleading and proving truth. The implication of the rule—that a statement is presumed to be false merely because it is alleged to be defamatory—might seem anathema to American ideas about free speech. But American courts, like the English, believed the risk of unprovability ought to fall on the party who, by putting the defamatory words in circulation, purports to know the facts. Despite its universal acceptance, however, the common law rule probably was doomed from the day *New York Times* v. *Sullivan* was decided. Though that decision spoke of 'the defence of truth' and said nothing about shifting that burden, by requiring proof of knowledge of falsity or reckless disregard for truth the court made it a virtual necessity for public plaintiffs to prove falsity also. A theoretical possibility of proving reckless disregard of falsity without proving the statement actually *was* false remained, but as a practical matter proof of the latter was usually a prerequisite to proving the former. After *Gertz* the same practical necessity faced private plaintiffs; one who could not show the defamation was false would have little hope of proving the defendant was negligent with respect to its falsity. Nevertheless, it was not until 1986 that the Supreme Court explicitly shifted the burden of proving falsity to plaintiffs, and then only by a five–four vote.

The case was *Philadelphia Newspapers, Inc.* v. *Hepps*.[68] Hepps was a private businessman accused by a newspaper of being connected with organised crime. The Pennsylvania Supreme Court had applied the traditional common law rule that truth was a defence to be pleaded and proved by the defendant. The US Supreme Court found that rule insufficiently protective of free speech.

> To ensure that true speech on matters of public concern is not deterred, we hold that the common law presumption that defamatory speech is false cannot stand when a plaintiff seeks damages against a media defendant for speech of public concern.[69]

The decision appears to apply to both public and private plaintiffs, but only if the defamation occurs in relation to matters of public concern.[70] It is in terms limited to media defendants, but two members of the majority disavowed that limitation. The

[68] 475 US 767, 106 SCt. 1558 (1986).

[69] *Ibid.*, 776–7. The court declined to decide whether falsity must be established with 'convincing clarity'.

[70] If the defamation occurs in advertising, the plaintiff may be relieved of the burden of proving falsity even if the speech touches on matters of public concern. See *Fanelle* v. *LoJack, Corp.*, 2000 WL 1801270 (ED Pa. 7 Dec. 2000).

court has consistently refused to give media protection not enjoyed by other litigants, however, so it is not likely to deny non-media defendants the benefit of the *Hepps* rule.

Despite the narrow vote, *Hepps* is a formidable precedent. Had the case been one where the plaintiff could prove falsity as easily as the defendant could prove truth, the decision might have left open a possibility that the burden would not be placed on plaintiffs for whom it would be onerous. But the facts of *Hepps* presented precisely the kind of case where the burden on the plaintiff is most difficult to meet. How is Hepps to prove that he does *not* have ties with organised crime? The defendant presumably has access to proof of the facts upon which its accusation is based. The plaintiff must undertake either to exonerate his associates or to exonerate himself from being associated with whomever the defendant believed to be criminals. For Hepps himself, the difficulty was compounded by the defendant's refusal to reveal the identity of confidential sources upon whose information the allegation was based. That the court was willing to shift the burden to a plaintiff who seemed to have so little chance of meeting it extinguished any thought that the *Hepps* rule might be limited to cases in which it imposes no insuperable burden on the plaintiff.

6. OPINION AND RHETORIC

The constitutional requirements also have implications for defamatory statements couched as opinion or hyperbole. The result is that some rhetorical excesses that would be actionable in England are absolutely protected in the United States.

As noted in the preceding sub-section, the First Amendment requires libel plaintiffs to prove falsity. This implies that the statement complained of must be one that by its nature is capable of being proved true or false. In *Milkovich* v. *Lorain Journal*,[71] the Supreme Court rejected an argument that this necessarily means no statement of opinion can be actionable, but suggested that it does protect some statements of opinion that would be actionable at common law. The requirement that plaintiffs prove falsity 'ensures that a statement of opinion relating to matters of public concern which does not contain a provably false factual connotation will receive full constitutional protection'.[72]

A similar implication protects rhetorical hyperbole. If a statement cannot be reasonably interpreted as stating actual facts about the plaintiff, it is not capable of being proved false and therefore cannot sustain liability. The court held that a pornographic magazine could not be held liable for publishing a parody that portrayed evangelist Jerry Falwell as a drunk who committed incest with his mother in an outhouse, because readers could not reasonably understand the publication to be an account of actual facts.[73] For similar

[71] 497 US 1, 110 SCt. 2695 (1990). [72] *Ibid.*, 20.

[73] *Hustler Magazine, Inc.* v. *Falwell*, 485 US 46, 108 SCt. 876 (1988). This was not a defamation case, but the Sup. Ct. has subsequently held that its principle is applicable to defamation. See *Masson* v. *New Yorker Magazine, Inc.*, 501 US 496, 111 SCt. 2419 (1991).

reasons, a statement describing the plaintiff as a 'blackmailer' cannot be actionable if the context makes clear that the term is meant rhetorically rather than literally.[74]

Some American lower courts have been willing to go even further, holding that all statements of opinion are absolutely protected. Among the statements held to be constitutionally protected opinion are: an allegation that a university professor 'has no status within the profession'[75] and an assertion that a state official's criminal prosecution of an American Indian leader was motivated by personal revenge.[76]

These courts reject the common law proposition that a statement in the form of an opinion may be actionable if it implies the existence of undisclosed defamatory facts.[77] Ultimately the classification of the statement as 'fact' or 'opinion' seems to turn on an assessment of the likelihood that a reasonable reader would understand that the statement should not be taken as an assertion of literal fact. Statements that occur in political argument are likely to be treated as opinion even though on their face they appear to be factual assertions. The same is true of statements that appear in recognised forums for expression of opinion, such as newspaper editorials and letters-to-the-editor columns.[78] The Supreme Court has now made clear that the First Amendment does not support such a sweeping rule, but some lower courts still interpret the rule broadly.[79] Moreover, the states are free to protect opinion more broadly than the federal constitution requires, and the highest court of New York has chosen to do so. That court held that the New York state constitution requires the contextual analysis rejected by the Supreme Court in *Milkovich*.[80]

The 'opinion defence' enjoyed extraordinary success in the years preceding *Milkovich* and it has not disappeared despite that decision. One reason for its popularity may be that it gives courts a way of disposing of unmeritorious cases before trial. Whether a statement is to be characterised as opinion is a question of law.[81] The issue usually requires little development of a factual record, so defendants may move for dismissal or summary judgment at an early stage in the litigation. The doctrine is thus one of the few mechanisms in American defamation law that invites a speedy and inexpensive disposition before trial.

74 *Greenbelt Cooperative Publishing Ass'n.* v. *Bressler*, 398 US 6, 90 SCt. 1537 (1970).

75 *Ollman* v. *Evans*, 750 F 2d 970 (1984) (DC Cir.) (*en banc*), *cert. denied* 471 US 1127, 105 SCt. 2662 (1985).

76 *Janklow* v. *Newsweek, Inc.*, 788 F 2d 1300 (1986) (9th Cir.) (*en banc*).

77 Instead of focusing on the implications of such a statement these courts engage in a contextual analysis, looking at (*a*) the common usage of the language, (*b*) the verifiability of the statement, (*c*) the journalistic context in which the statement occurs (e.g. news report or commentary) and (*d*) the nature of the subject being discussed (e.g. political controversy). See *Ollman* v. *Evans*, n. 75 above.

78 E.g. *Kotlikoff* v. *Community News*, 89 NJ 62, 444 A 2d 1086 (1982); *Miskovsky* v. *Oklahoma Pub. Co.*, 654 P 2d 587 (1982) (Oklahoma) *cert. denied* 459 US 923, 103 SCt. 235.

79 See, e.g., *Dilworth* v. *Dudley*, 75 F 3d 307 (7th Cir. 1996); *Moldea* v. *New York Times Co.*, 22 F 3d 310 (2d Cir. 1994) *cert. denied* 513 US 875, 115 SCt. 202.

80 *Immuno AG* v. *Moor-Jankowski*, 77 NY 2d 235, 567 NE 2d 1270 (1991), 566 NYS 2d 906 (1991), *cert. denied* 500 US 954, 111 SCt. 2261 (1991).

81 E.g. *Lewis* v. *Time, Inc.*, 710 F 2d 549 (9th Cir. 1983).

7. THE LAW IN PRACTICE

The intricacy of the constitutional rules tends to make American defamation litigation complex and protracted and the possibility of high stakes encourages both sides to spare no effort. A major case generates many thousands of pages of depositions, motions and briefs before it ever reaches trial. Pre-trial battles, trial, post-trial motions, and appeals invariably last for years. As a result, costs often run into seven figures. General William Westmoreland is reported to have spent more than $3 million before abandoning his libel suit against the Columbia Broadcasting System and CBS reportedly spent $10 million on its defence. Although American libel defendants are less likely than their English counterparts ultimately to lose, the combination of expensive and protracted litigation and possible multi-million-dollar judgments in the United States make libel a matter of some concern to the media nonetheless.

In addition to the financial costs, libel defendants sometimes face intrusive pre-trial discovery procedures. A plaintiff is entitled to scrutinise a defendant's records and question its employees, not only to find admissible evidence, but also to search for anything that might lead to the discovery of admissible evidence. In the case of media defendants, that gives their adversaries opportunities to probe newsroom practices and editing decisions and tie up media personnel in protracted depositions and record searches. It is even possible in some cases for plaintiffs to compel disclosures of confidential news sources.[82] All of these factors tend to make libel suits a greater threat to the media than doctrine alone would lead one to suppose.

In an attempt to reduce the costs and other burdens that libel litigation imposes on defendants, many state legislatures have enacted special procedural protections. A number of states have 'anti-SLAPP'[83] statutes, which permit defendants to move before trial for dismissal (and in some circumstances an award of attorneys' fees) upon a judicial determination that the suit is without merit. The statutes were passed initially to protect citizen activists from retaliation by polluters, developers and other targets of their activism, but media soon persuaded the courts to give them the benefit of the statutes also.[84] A Texas statute gives a libel defendant an automatic right of interlocutory appeal from denial of any motion for summary judgment based on a constitutional argument.[85]

The purpose of all these measures is to spare defendants the costs and burdens of fully litigating defamation claims. Of course, they may also have the effect of discouraging legitimate claims. Where they are in effect, any plaintiff must be prepared to finance these additional proceedings before obtaining a jury trial.

[82] See e.g. *Miller* v. *Transamerican Press, Inc.*, 621 F 2d 721 (5th Cir. 1980), *cert. denied* 450 US 1041, 101 SCt. 1759 (1981). In *Hepps* (475 US 767, 106 SCt. 1558 (1986)) a state statute prevented disclosure of the source.

[83] See, e.g., Cal.Code Civ.Proc. §425.16. The acronym stands for 'Strategic Lawsuit Against Public Policy'. The premise is that defamation suits are sometimes brought to silence whistleblowers and other critics, in violation of public policy.

[84] See, e.g., *Braun* v. *Chronicle Pub. Co.*, 5 Cal. App. 4th 1036 (1997).

[85] Tex. Civ. Prac. & Rem. Code Ann. §51.04(A)(6) (1997).

In both England and America, courts are quite aggressive in controlling the size of libel judgments. The Court of Appeal in England has power to control damages by substituting its own judgment for that of the jury in cases in which the court finds the jury's award excessive[86] and does so quite frequently.[87] Courts in America have no such power, but through the device of *remittitur* they may require a plaintiff to choose between a reduced award and a new trial; as a result defendants on average pay less than half as much as the jury awards.[88]

In England the media and other defendants enjoy several advantages not available to defendants in the United States. For unintentional defamation, English law gives a defendant an opportunity seek an early resolution of the claim by making an 'offer of amends'—a correction and apology and an offer to pay the claimant some compensation.[89] The American law of retraction typically allows defendants to mitigate damages but does not spare them the expense of a full trial. The libel claimant under 'the English rule' must be prepared, if he loses, to pay the opponent's legal costs in addition to his own. The American plaintiff normally need not be concerned with any costs other than his own, although media lawyers have become increasingly aggressive in seeking sanctions against libel plaintiffs on the ground that their suits were frivolous.[90] Under some circumstances defendants in England can bring an early end to the proceedings by demanding that the claimant post security for costs. English defendants have a significant advantage in persuading claimant to accept settlement. A defendant can make a 'payment in' to the court as a settlement offer. A claimant who rejects the offer may be required to pay all of the defendant's costs from the time of the payment onward, unless the claimant secures a judgment larger than the amount paid in.[91] This can be a potent weapon against a claimant who has unrealistic monetary expectations.

Up to now, potential defendants in England have not needed to worry much about being sued for libel by ordinary citizens. Legal aid is not available to defamation claimant[92] and until recently England did not permit the contingency fee system by which American lawyers agree to represent tort plaintiffs for a percentage of the recovery. In 2000, however, the Lord Chancellor put into place new regulations that permit conditional fee agreements under specified circumstances.[93] The Press had predicted

[86] Courts and Legal Services Act 1990, s. 8(2).

[87] See, e.g., *John* v. *MGN Ltd* [1996] All ER 35 (CA) (reducing compensatory damages from £75,000 to £25,000 and exemplary damages from £275,000 to £50,000), *Rantzen* v. *Mirror Group Newspapers Ltd.* [1993] 4 All ER 975 (CA) (compensatory damage award reduced from £250,000 to £110,000).

[88] From 1980 to 2005, the median jury award in libel cases against media was $275,000 and the median final result after appeals was $90,500. See Media Law Resource Center, *MLRC 2006 Report on Trials and Damages* (Feb. 2006).

[89] Defamation Act 1996, s. 2(4). This provision has become more useful because of a decision allowing the defendant to make use of it even if he has been negligent, as long as he did not know or have reason to believe the statement referred to the plaintiff and was false and defamatory. See *Milne v. Express Newspapers* [2003] 1 WLR 927.

[90] See, e.g., *Project Creation, Inc.* v. *Neal*, 2001 Tenn. App. Lexis 624 (21 Aug. 2001) (approving award of $9,262 as sanction for filing meritless libel suit).

[91] RSC Ord. 22, r. 1.

[92] Legal Aid Act 1971, s. 7, Sch. 1, Part II(1).

[93] Legal Services, England and Wales, Conditional Fee Agreements Regulations 2000 (SI No. 2000/692).

that this would unleash a wave of unwarranted libel litigation,[94] but its actual effect remains to be seen; libel suits are comparatively few in the United States despite the universal acceptance of contingency fee arrangements.

Because of the globalisation of media operations and the growth of the Internet, the possibility of being sued for libel abroad has become a very real one for many defendants in the United States and elsewhere. Although a great deal of rhetoric has been expended decrying the absence of First Amendment protections in foreign jurisdictions, American defendants have had little success in persuading foreign courts either to decline jurisdiction or to apply US law.

The leading case is *Dow Jones & Co.* v. *Gutnick*,[95] in which an Australian businessman sued the publisher of Barron's magazine for damages he suffered in his home state of Victoria. The publisher had no physical presence in Victoria but the entire contents of the magazine were published on its website, which had several hundred paid subscribers in Victoria. Under local law, Victorian courts have jurisdiction if the material is communicated there and causes harm there. Dow Jones argued that in Internet cases, publication should be deemed to have occurred where the material was uploaded onto the server (in New Jersey, in this case). The Australian High Court noted that because a disproportionate number of servers are located in the United States, this rule would make US courts and law dominant. It declined to adopt a special jurisdictional rule for internet defamation, rejected the defendant's *forum non conveniens* argument, and held that Victorian law would govern the case under the usual place-of-wrong standard. The decision produced much hand-wringing among US media but it employed conventional jurisdictional and choice of law reasoning that seems likely to be followed elsewhere unless a different solution is reached by international agreement.

A few American courts have refused to enforce English defamation judgments. By statute, courts are obliged to honour foreign judgments when the winners seek to collect their judgments from assets located in the United States, but an exception allows them to refuse when the 'cause of action upon which the judgment is based is repugnant to the public policy of the state'. Some judgment debtors have argued that English defamation law is so unprotective of speech that it falls within the exception. The leading precedent holds that English law is inconsistent with Maryland public policy because it allows defamatory statements to be presumed false, allows qualified privileges to be overcome by proof of improper motive and does not recognise the US constitutional limits relating to fault, opinion and punitive damages.[96] The majority seemed to take no note of other differences that make English law more protective of defendants. A dissenting justice said this decision 'seems inclined to make Maryland libel law applicable to the rest of the world by providing a safe haven for foreign libel judgment debtors'. It cannot be doubted that American law gives defendants in

[94] See, e.g., A. Brett, 'No Win, No Fee: No Free Press', *The Times*, 28 Apr. 1998. (The author was the company solicitor of Times Newspapers.)

[95] [2002] HCA 56, 194 ALR 433.

[96] *Telnikoff* v. *Matusevitch*, 347 Md. 561, 702 A 2d 230 (1997). See also *Bachchan* v. *India Abroad Publications*, 154 Misc. 2d 228, 585 NYS 2d 661 (1992) (NYS).

defamation cases more protection than English law. But it hardly follows that the English resolution of the conflict between speech and reputation interests is wrong, let alone repugnant.

8. INVASION OF PRIVACY

In defamation, English law has moved closer to American law by becoming more protective of speech. In privacy, the opposite is true: the differences have widened, primarily because the English courts have become more protective of privacy. This is more than a little ironic, because while the English courts have yet to explicitly recognise any tort for invasion of privacy, United States law recognises four distinct privacy torts. Rarely do we see stronger proof of the principle that what matters is what the law does, not what it says. Chapter 22 demonstrates how English judges have found ways to protect privacy without elaborating much of a tort framework; in the United States, the law rarely protects privacy despite an elaborate doctrinal framework. The breakthrough cases in the UK, such as *Campbell* v. *MGN Ltd.*[97] and *A* v. *B plc*,[98] would be decided against the claimants in the United States.[99]

To some extent privacy law is an outgrowth of changes in the law of defamation. At one time a truthful statement made without adequate justification might have been actionable as defamation in either the United States or England, but as truth became an absolute defence, at least in the United States, the need for some other remedy became apparent. In America, the remedy is a civil action for 'invasion of privacy', an umbrella term encompassing four distinct torts. American law recognises other 'rights of privacy' that are not torts and are beyond the scope of this discussion. For example, a constitutional 'right of privacy' protects against governmental interference in such personal matters as abortion and contraception,[100] while 'privacy' statutes restrict governmental acquisition and use of certain types of personal information.[101] The issue of horizontality—the possibility that rights against the state might also create rights against third parties—which is mentioned in the preceding chapter in connection with the Human Rights Act does not exist in the United States. Privacy rights created by the US Constitution are protections against state action only, and create no remedies against nongovernmental invasions. On the other hand, remedies against private actors become state action when they are imposed by the courts, so they must comport with constitutional free-speech limitations.[102] As a result,

97 [2004] 2 AC 457.

98 [2002] WLR 542; [2002] EWCA 337.

99 With *Campbell*, compare *Shulman* v. *Group W Productions*, 18 Cal. 4th 200, 74 Cal. Rptr. 2d 843 (1998) (denying recovery for television broadcast of cries and images of highway accident victim trapped in overturned vehicle). With *A v. B plc*, compare *Bonome* v. *Kaysen*, 17 Mass. 695, 32 Media L Rep. 1520 (Mass. Super. Ct. Mar. 3, 2004) (holding that memoirist had constitutional right to tell details of her sexual relationship with plaintiff).

100 *Roe* v. *Wade*, 410 US 113, 93 SCt. 705 (1973) *Griswold* v. *Connecticut*, 381 US 479, 85 SCt. 1678 (1965).

101 E.g. Privacy Act of 1974, 5 USC, s. 552a (1992).

102 See *The Florida Star* v. *BJF*, 491 US 524, 109 SCt. 2603 (1993).

the constitution plays an entirely one-sided role in the tort law of privacy: it creates no tort rights, but it can limit them in the interest of free speech.

Of the four privacy torts, the one closest to the core of the privacy concept is the cause of action for public disclosure of embarrassing private facts. A person may recover damages for a disclosure that would be highly offensive to a reasonable person and is not of legitimate public concern.[103] Sexual activities and medical abnormalities are among the kinds of disclosures that are most often litigated. The matter need not have been completely secret before the defendant's disclosure. Even the most intimate secrets usually are known to one's closest friends and family, so it is enough that the defendant has disclosed publicly a matter that previously was known only to such a limited circle.[104] On the other hand, matters of official record may be disclosed with impunity, even if they were previously unknown by the public.[105]

The central issue is what facts are 'private' and the law has defined that term so narrowly—and the concept of legitimate public concern so broadly—that very few disclosures are actionable. Courts look to contemporary *mores* to determine what reasonable people would find highly offensive. From that point of reference, disclosure of such matters as one's income or net worth,[106] personal idiosyncrasies,[107] illegitimacy[108] or medical diagnosis[109] usually are held not to be sufficiently offensive. Rigorous application of this requirement sometimes produces results that seem hard to justify. For example, one court held that disclosure in a national magazine that a private person had bizarre but harmless personal habits and had never learned to read or write was not highly offensive because he 'comes across as the tough, aggressive maverick, an archetypal character occupying a respected place in the American consciousness'.[110] So far the English courts have declined to limit their remedy to disclosures that are highly offensive,[111] and perhaps wisely so. The alternative that is evolving there seems to be 'reasonable objective expectation of privacy'.[112] The purpose of the American 'highly offensive' standard is to exclude claims for disclosures that some people may find distasteful but that are commonplace in a society that values openness. Whether the English alternative will be a satisfactory means of maintaining that line remains to be seen.

The concept of legitimate public concern is inspired by First Amendment values and therefore is interpreted expansively. The public usually is held to have a legitimate

[103] *Restatement (Second) of Torts*, s. 652D (1977).

[104] *Sipple* v. *Chronicle Publishing Co.*, 154 Cal. App. 3d 1040, 201 Cal. Rptr. 665 (1984), *Dias* v. *Oakland Tribune, Inc.*, 139 Cal. App. 3d 118, 188 Cal. Rptr. 762 (1983), *Melvin* v. *Reid*, 112 Cal. App. 285, 297 P 91 (1931).

[105] *Howard* v. *Des Moines Register & Tribune Co.*, 283 NW 2d 289 (1979) (Iowa), *cert. denied* 445 US 904, 100 SCt. 1081 (1980).

[106] *Wolf* v. *Regardie*, 553 A 2d 1213 (1989) (DC App.), *Schoneweis* v. *Dando*, 231 Neb. 180, 435 NW 2d 666 (1989).

[107] *Virgil* v. *Time, Inc.*, 527 F 2d 1122 (9th Cir. 1975), *cert. denied* 425 US 998 (1976), *Sidis* v. *F. R. Publishing Corp.*, 113 F 2d 806 (2nd Cir. 1940), *cert. denied* 311 US 711, 61 SCt. 393 (1940).

[108] *Heath* v. *Playboy Enterprises Inc.*, 732 F Supp. 1145 (1990).

[109] *Davis* v. *Monsanto Co.*, 627 F Supp. 418 (1990), *Child Protection Group* v. *Cline*, 350 SE 2d 541 (1986), *Meetze* v. *Associated Press*, 230 SC 330, 95 SE 2d 606 (1956).

[110] *Virgil v. Sports Illustrated*, 424 F Supp. 1286 (SD. Cal. 1976).

[111] See *Campbell* v. *MGN Ltd.* [2004] 2 AC 457.

[112] See *Campbell*, judgment of Lady Hale, [2004] 2 WLR 1233, [135].

interest in the identity of victims of crimes (including rape and other sex offences),[113] the sexual activities and medical problems of public officials[114] and the marital difficulties of celebrities.[115] This is one respect in which American law may well be less protective of privacy than English law. For example, American law apparently permits the broadcast of purloined videotape of an actress having sex with her boyfriend on the ground that 'romantic relationships of celebrities are a matter of public concern'.[116] Guidelines issued by the Court of Appeal suggest that disclosures about sexual relationships of celebrities could be actionable as breach of confidence even though the public is interested in them.[117] American courts are reluctant to second-guess an editor's judgement that a matter is of legitimate public concern; some judges have gone so far as to say they will defer to the editor's judgement unless it is one no rational editor could have made.[118]

English courts appear to be inclined to protect some zones of privacy even for public officials and public figures, but in the United States those persons have 'virtually no right of privacy insofar as the facts may relate, even remotely, to the plaintiff's public life'.[119] Thus, legitimate public concern over the conduct of a former police chief accused of assault was held to extend even to information from his wife's medical files, precluding recovery by the wife for publication of the information by a newspaper.[120]

In America privacy interests do not stand on an equal footing with speech rights, as they do under the European Convention; free speech is a constitutional right, while privacy of the sort involved in tort actions is not. Because of this, the free flow of information is treated as a paramount value and judges find it difficult to impose liability for disclosing truth. The tort of public disclosure of truthful but embarrassing private facts, therefore, exists more in theory than in practice; claims are numerous, but they almost never succeed.

The second American privacy tort is a cause of action for publications that depict a person in a false light. The falsehood need not be defamatory, but it must place the person in a false light that would be highly offensive to a reasonable person. For example, affixing the plaintiff's by-line to a sensational 'first-person' account that he did not write gave rise to a cause of action for false-light invasion of privacy.[121] The tort is a

113 *The Florida Star* v. *BJF*, 491 US 524, 109 SCt. 2603 (1993), *Cox Broadcasting Corp.* v. *Cohn*, 420 US 469, 95 SCt. 1029 (1975).

114 *Hubert* v. *Harte-Hanks Texas Newspapers Inc.*, 652 SW 2d 546 (1983), *Kapellas* v. *Kofman*, 1 Cal. 3d 20, 81 Cal. Rptr. 360, 459 P 2d 912 (1969).

115 *Carlisle* v. *Fawcett Publications Inc.*, 201 Cal. App. 2d 733, 20 Cal. Rptr. 405 (1962).

116 See *Michaels* v. *Internet Entertainment Group, Inc.*, 1998 US Dist. LEXIS 20786 (CD Cal. 1998). It should be noted that this is a trial court decision not binding on any other court. Nevertheless, it is not a great deviation from the position other courts have taken.

117 See *A* v. *B plc* ([2002] WLR 542; [2002] EWCA 337). The court denied relief in part on the ground that protecting the celebrity's privacy in this case would deny the free speech rights of the other party, who wanted to disclose the matter. In the *Michaels* case, cited above, the disclosure was permitted although both parties objected to it.

118 *Gilbert* v. *Medical Economics Co.*, 665 F 2d 305 (1981) (10th Cir.).

119 Robert W. Sack, *Libel, Slander and Related Problems* (3rd edn., 1999), para. 12.4.5.1.

120 *Irvine v. Akron Beacon Journal*, 30 Media L. Rep. 2008 (Ohio Ct. App. 2002), appeal denied, 2002 Ohio 4534, 774 NE 2d 765 (2002).

121 *Dempsey* v. *National Enquirer*, 702 F Supp. 934 (1989).

cousin to defamation and is subject to many of the same state law restrictions.[122] Similar constitutional restrictions also apply. A plaintiff who is a public official or public figure must show that the defendant published with reckless disregard of the possible falsity.[123] Private plaintiffs probably must prove at least that the defendant was negligent with respect to the falsity and sometimes have been required to meet the same standard as a public plaintiff.[124] Because of these restrictions and the necessity of showing a high degree of offensiveness, false-light cases rarely succeed. Some states have refused to recognise the tort at all[125] and there is considerable scholarly debate about its legitimacy.[126]

The two remaining privacy torts are of more practical significance. One is a cause of action for intentional and highly offensive intrusion into a person's private life. This tort supplements the law of trespass in two principal ways. First, it provides a remedy where the intrusion is physical but does not occur on the plaintiff's premises. Thus, President Kennedy's widow was able to stop the famous paparazzo Ron Galella from shadowing her and her children to photograph them in public parks, restaurants and schools.[127] Second, it provides a remedy where the intrusion is accomplished without physical invasion, for example, by electronic surveillance or telescopic lenses.[128]

The intrusion branch of privacy provides a more effective remedy for media invasions of personal privacy than the other branches. In part, this is because the First Amendment provides less protection for newsgathering activities than for publication. An important California Supreme Court decision illustrates this. A television cameraman accompanied a helicopter rescue crew to the site of a highway accident, outfitted the flight nurse with a microphone and filmed the rescue of a woman who was seriously and permanently injured in the wreck. The woman sued for both the intrusion and the subsequent broadcast of the video showing her begging to be allowed to die. The court held that the First Amendment barred the woman's claims for public disclosure of the sounds and images because those were a matter of legitimate public concern, but did not bar her claim for the television crew's intrusion into a situation in which she had legitimate expectations of privacy. With two dissenting votes, the court rejected the defendants' argument that they had a First Amendment right to intrude to obtain information that was of legitimate public concern.[129]

This decision was based on common law, but the California legislature subsequently created a stronger statutory remedy. The statute makes it a tort to trespass or use a 'visual

[122] *Fellows* v. *National Enquirer Inc.*, 42 Cal. 3d 234, 721 P 2d 97, 228 Cal. Rptr. 215 (1986).

[123] *Cantrell* v. *Forest City Publishing Co.*, 419 US 245, 95 SCt. 465 (1974).

[124] *Lovgren* v. *Citizens First National Bank*, 126 Ill. 2d 411, 534 NE 2d 987 (1989).

[125] *Renwick* v. *The News and Observer Pub. Co.*, 310 NC 312, 312 SE 2d 405 (1984), *cert. denied* 469 US 858, 105 SCt. 187 (1984).

[126] See e.g. D. Zimmerman, 'False Light Invasion of Privacy: The Light that Failed' (1989) 64 *NYULR* 364.

[127] *Galella* v. *Onassis*, 487 F 2d 986 (2nd Cir. 1973).

[128] *Dietemann* v. *Time Inc.*, 449 F 2d 245 (9th Cir. 1971).

[129] See *Shulman* v. *Group W Productions*, 18 Cal. 4th 200, 74 Cal. Rptr. 843, 955 P 2d 469 (1998).

or auditory enhancing device'—e.g., a telephoto lens or a directional microphone—to film or record a person engaging in personal or familial activities under circumstances in which the person had a reasonable expectation of privacy. A person violating the statute is liable for up to three times the amount of special and general damages, plus punitive damages, and also may be enjoined.[130]

Even if privacy-invading information was obtained through intrusion or illegal wire-tapping or eavesdropping, its disclosure by the media may be protected if they did not participate in its illegal acquisition. This is because the First Amendment gives more protection to publication than acquisition, as mentioned above. In the leading case, the Supreme Court held that a radio station could not be held liable for broadcasting a private conversation that was illegally taped by an unknown third party.[131] The station had reason to know the tape had been made illegally, and the state and federal statutes that forbade the taping also forbade disclosure of a tape known to have been recorded illegally, but the court held that the First Amendment protected the station's use of the tape because the conversation it recorded was about a matter of public concern. Whether the First Amendment would protect a recipient who knows who did the illegal recording remains unclear,[132] but it seems clear that a defendant might be held liable if it had authorised or encouraged the illegal taping.[133]

The final privacy tort, which generates more successful claims than the other three branches combined, provide a remedy for commercial exploitation of a person's name or likeness. It arose from the un-consented to use of a person's photograph or testimonial in advertisements,[134] but it now extends to unauthorised use of a person's distinctive nickname,[135] slogan[136] or costume,[137] or to the use of a model that looks like the plaintiff[138] or a singer who imitates the plaintiff's vocal style.[139] This branch of the tort has produced an entire industry based on the value of celebrity endorsements and often seems to have more to do with commerce than with personal privacy. Indeed, the interest it protects is sometimes called a 'right of publicity' rather than a right of privacy. Unlike the other privacy torts, which are personal to the victim and cannot be assigned or enforced after death, the right to control commercial exploitation is assignable

[130] See Cal. Civil Code s. 1708.8. The same remedies are available against a publisher or broadcaster who induces another person to violate the statute and, if the image or recording is published or broadcast, the plaintiff may recover the profits gained thereby.

[131] *Bartnicki* v. *Vopper*, 532 US 514, 121 SCt. 753 (2001).

[132] Such a person could be held liable, according to *Boehner* v. *McDermott*, 441 F 3d 1010 (DC Cir. 2006), but that decision has been vacated pending reconsideration by the full court of appeals.

[133] See *Peavy* v. *WFAA-TV*, Inc., 221 F 3d 158 (5th Cir. 2000). The Supreme Court in the *Bartnicki* decision expressly distinguished this case, in which the media defendant may have participated in the illegal recording.

[134] *Pavesich* v. *New England Life Insurance Co.*, 122 Ga. 190, 50 SE 68 (1905).

[135] *Hirsch* v. *S. C. Johnson & Son Inc.*, 90 Wis. 2d 379, 280 NW 2d 129 (1979).

[136] *Carson* v. *Here's Johnny Portable Toilets Inc.*, 698 F 2d 831 (6th Cir. 1983).

[137] *Motschenbacher* v. *R. J. Reynolds Tobacco Co.*, 498 F 2d 821 (9th Cir. 1974).

[138] *Onassis* v. *Christian Dior-New York Inc.*, 122 Misc. 2d 603, 472 NYS 2d 254 (1984), *aff'd.*, 110 AD 2d 1095, 488 NYS 2d 943 (1985).

[139] *Midler* v. *Ford Motor Co.*, 849 F 2d 460 (9th Cir. 1988), *cert. denied* 503 US 951, 112 SCt. 1513 (1997).

inter vivos[140] and in most jurisdictions is held to be a descendable interest enforceable at least for a number of years after the person's death.[141]

The tort is not conspicuously effective in protecting personal privacy because it covers only exploitation for commercial purposes, and most uses of personality for purposes even tangentially related to journalism or entertainment are not considered commercial. It is not actionable for a television station to use film of a bleeding accident victim to promote a documentary about emergency medical treatment,[142] or for a magazine that had published photographs of a sports hero to republish the photographs in advertisements promoting the magazine.[143]

In summary, despite the existence of four rather elaborate privacy torts, American law rarely provides a remedy for people who believe their privacy has been invaded by media or others, primarily because it has made the determination that privacy is not as important as freedom of speech.

140 *Factors Etc. Inc.* v. *Pro Arts Inc.*, 579 F 2d 215 (2nd Cir. 1978), *cert. denied* 440 US 908, 99 SCt. 1215 (1979).

141 *Martin Luther King Jnr., Centre for Social Change Inc.* v. *American Heritage Products Inc.*, 250 Ga. 135, 296 SE 2d 697 (1982).

142 *Anderson* v. *Fisher Broadcasting Co. Inc.*, 300 Or. 452, 712 P 2d 803 (1986).

143 *Namath* v. *Sports Illustrated.*, 80 Misc. 2d 531, 363 NYS 2d 279 (1975) (SCt.), *aff'd.*, 48 AD 2d 487, 371 NYS 2d 10, 352 NE 2d 584 (1976).

PART VIII

DEFENCES AND REMEDIES

24 Defences
25 Damages
26 Other Remedies and Multiple Liabilities

24

DEFENCES

1. THE ROLE OF DEFENCES IN THE LAW OF TORTS

In Chapter 3 we examined the concept of duty of care in the tort of negligence and the ways in which the courts use it to set the boundaries to tort liability. The general defences that are the subject of this chapter perform a similar function. Historically, the defences of contributory negligence, consent (or assumption of risk), and common employment were of great importance in limiting the availability of personal injury claims to those injured at work or on the highway. The scope of these defences is now much reduced. This has been achieved by legislation which, in its way, has been just as important as the decision of the House of Lords in *Donoghue* v. *Stevenson*[1] in determining the nature of the contemporary tort system. Formerly the contributory negligence of the plaintiff was a complete defence to a claim in negligence. Thanks to the Law Reform (Contributory Negligence) Act 1945, which gave the courts the power to apportion responsibility for damage between claimant and defendant and to adjust the claimant's damages accordingly, it is now a partial defence. The doctrine of common employment, which provided that an employee impliedly took the risk of any injuries at work caused by the negligence of a fellow employee, was also abolished by the Law Reform (Personal Injuries) Act 1948. The defence of consent survived these statutory changes unscathed, but the courts themselves ensured that it would have only a limited application in personal injury cases.[2] Finally, in 1977 a further narrowing of the scope for defences occurred when Parliament enacted the Unfair Contract Terms Act, which restricted the use of contract terms and notices to exclude or limit tortious and contractual liability. These defences are considered below, together with other defences which may be available to a defendant, including necessity and private defence, inevitable accident, authorisation, and limitation of action. The application of the defences in the context of the torts of interference with the person and interference with property have already been considered in earlier chapters. What follows is thus mainly concerned with their application to torts which require proof of damage in order to be actionable, and in particular with the tort of negligence.

[1] [1932] AC 562.

[2] *Smith* v. *Charles Baker & Sons* [1891] AC 325, *Dann* v. *Hamilton* [1939] 1 KB 509.

2. CONTRIBUTORY NEGLIGENCE

Contributory negligence provides a partial defence to a claim in tort in a case where the claimant's own carelessness was a material cause of his loss. Prior to the Law Reform (Contributory Negligence) Act 1945 the defence had the effect of excluding the plaintiff's claim completely. The 1945 Act displaced this common rule in favour of a provision enabling the court to apportion responsibility for the loss between plaintiff and defendant and to adjust the plaintiff's damages accordingly. It is in this sense that the defence now operates as a partial exclusion of liability, as opposed, for example, to the total exclusion that results from the application of the defence of consent. The Act of 1945, as subsequently interpreted by the courts, greatly simplified the law. The common law had produced 'a vast proliferation of case law which added greatly to the hazards of litigation';[3] little of this now survives. Nonetheless, certain conceptual and practical problems continue to surround the modern defence. These principally relate to: the role of causation; the notion of the claimant's 'fault'; the position of certain special claimants, such as children and rescuers; the process of apportionment; and the scope of the defence with regard to breach of contract and to torts other than negligence.

(A) CAUSATION AND CONTRIBUTORY NEGLIGENCE

The nature of the relationship between contributory negligence and causation was briefly considered in an earlier chapter.[4] Although the two areas are closely linked, contributory negligence is a defence in its own right. The general principles of causation underwent substantial modification prior to 1945, to produce the distinctive contributory negligence defence.[5] Since 1945 the approach of the courts to causation questions has been heavily influenced by the possibility of apportionment which the Act opened up. The complete exclusion of liability under the old common law was difficult to explain on straightforward causation grounds. In *Butterfield* v. *Forrester*[6] the plaintiff collided with a pole which the defendant had negligently placed across the highway; the plaintiff was held to have been riding too quickly and to have been the sole cause of his injury. The case subsequently came to be treated as authority for the proposition that 'if there is blame causing the accident on both sides, however small that blame may be on one side, the loss lies where it falls'.[7] In other words, where any causal weight, no matter how small, could be attached to the plaintiff's fault, the defendant's fault ceased to matter. The potential injustice of this approach led the courts to fashion an exception

3 G. L. Williams, *Joint Torts and Contributory Negligence* (Select Bibliography), 236.

4 See ch. 4, Section 2.

5 See Williams, *Joint Torts* (Select Bibliography), chs. 9 and 10, which contain a comprehensive review of the relevant case law.

6 (1809) 11 East 60; 103 ER 926.

7 *Cayzer, Irvine & Co.* v. *Carron Co.* (1884) 9 App. Cas. 873, 881 (Lord Blackburn).

known as the 'last opportunity' rule, according to which the party who had the last chance of avoiding the accident in question was deemed to be solely responsible for the ensuing damage. In *Davies* v. *Mann*[8] the plaintiff carelessly let his donkey roam loose on the highway where it was struck by a cart driven by the defendant; the plaintiff recovered for the damage to the donkey notwithstanding his initial negligence. The last-opportunity rule itself was hedged about with various kinds of exceptions and the area was further complicated by the decision of the Privy Council in *British Columbia Electric Railway* v. *Loach*.[9] This established the principle of 'constructive last opportunity', according to which responsibility would lie on the party who, but for his prior negligence, *would have had* the last chance of avoiding the accident.

There are judicial *dicta* explaining the last opportunity rule in terms of causation and remoteness: thus the failure of the defendant to take due care was regarded as a *nova causa interveniens* which cancelled out the earlier carelessness of the plaintiff.[10] The plaintiff's carelessness was a cause in fact of his loss but it was not sufficiently proximate to the damage to be regarded as a cause in law.[11] Although the rule could therefore be seen as an application of the principles of remoteness, Glanville Williams argued convincingly against this view on the grounds that:

> Except under the obscure doctrine of *Loach's* case,[12] the last opportunity rule in its heyday placed emphasis upon the act of negligence latest in time, whereas in the law generally 'the proximate cause is not necessarily the one that operates last.'[13] According to the one rule, it is the last straw that breaks the camel's back; according to the other, part of the blame is attributed to the weight of straws already lying there, which have placed the animal in such imminent peril.[14] Moreover, the rule was not applied in cases having nothing to do with contributory negligence where the courts, as opposed to distinguishing between the relative fault of plaintiff and defendant, had the task of attaching responsibility to one or more of several co-defendants. In such cases it was acknowledged that joint and several liability could flow from concurrent causes, regardless of which one operated last in time.[15] In truth 'the law of last opportunity was introduced as a palliative for the crude common law rule allowing a wrongdoer's loss to lie where it fell', and was not applied more generally in the law of torts.[16]

The question is of more than just theoretical importance since it now affects the interpretation given to the Contributory Negligence Act 1945. If the last opportunity doctrine could be regarded as simply an illustration of the principles of causation and remoteness, it would be possible for it to survive the changes made by the Act. Under section 1(1):

> Where any person suffers damage as the result partly of his own fault and partly of the fault of any other person or persons, a claim in respect of this damage shall not be defeated by reason

[8] (1842) 10 M & W 546; 152 ER 588.

[9] [1916] 1 AC 719.

[10] *Radley* v. *London and North Western Railway* (1875) LR 10 Ex. 100, 108–9 (Denman J); see also *Swadling* v. *Cooper* [1931] AC 1, 8–9 (Viscount Hailsham) and *Caswell* v. *Powell Duffryn* [1940] AC 152.

[11] For the meaning of 'cause in fact' and 'cause in law' see the discussion in ch. 4, Section 2 above.

[12] [1916] 1 AC 719.

[13] *Yorkshire Dale SS Co.* v. *Minister of War Transport* [1942] AC 691, 698 (Viscount Simon LC).

[14] Williams, *Joint Torts* (Select Bibliography), 244–5.

[15] E.g. *Grant* v. *Sun Shipping Co. Ltd.* [1948] AC 549.

[16] Williams, *Joint Torts* (Select Bibliography), 247.

of the fault of the person suffering the damage, but the damages recoverable in respect thereof shall be reduced to such extent as the court thinks just and equitable having regard to the claimant's share in the responsibility for the damage.

The old rule derived from *Butterfield* v. *Forrester*[17] which let the loss lie where it fell is clearly ousted by the requirement that the claimant's claim 'shall not be defeated' by reason of his own negligence. Could it still be argued, however, that in a case where one party or the other had the last opportunity, he could be held *fully* responsible for the consequences of the accident? This would have the result of either allowing the claimant to recover in full or, in a case where his negligence was last in time, of defeating his claim completely, with no possibility of apportionment.

The Act does not purport to affect the normal common law principles of causation. The retention of the last-opportunity doctrine has, nonetheless, been clearly rejected by the courts. In *Cakebread* v. *Hopping Bros. (Whetstone) Ltd.*[18] the Court of Appeal declined to apply 'last opportunity' to a case of an employer's breach of statutory duty in which the employee had had, on one interpretation, an adequate chance to avoid the danger posed by the employer's breach. The plaintiff's damages were apportioned. There was a similar result in a road traffic case, *Davies* v. *Swan Motor Co. (Swansea) Ltd.*,[19] in which Denning LJ argued that last opportunity 'was dead before the Act, though it remained in use as a practical test. Since the Act, it is no longer a practical test and should disappear from the books.'[20] In *Jones* v. *Livox Quarries Ltd.*[21] he asserted that 'the doctrine of last opportunity is now obsolete'.[22] Since then, no court has seen fit to revive it. This is not surprising given the enormous complexity of the pre-1945 case law and the unsatisfactory distinctions between contemporaneous and successive acts of negligence to which it gave rise. To revive the doctrine would also frustrate the purpose of the Act by preventing apportionment from taking place in a large category of cases. Apportionment under the Act gives the court a degree of flexibility which was not possible under the all-or-nothing approach of the common law. This greater flexibility has altered the approach of the courts to causation, making it unnecessary for them to absolve claimants completely from blame in order to do justice in a particular case.[23] Some strained interpretations of what constitutes an operative cause have thereby been avoided. In *Jones* v. *Livox Quarries* the plaintiff rode on the back bumper of a traxcavator, contrary to his employer's express instructions, and was injured in a collision with a dumper caused by the negligence of the dumper driver (who was employed by a different employer). Lord Denning regarded the case as a 'good illustration of the practical effect of the Act of 1945': prior to the Act, 'the negligence of the dumper driver would have been regarded as the predominant cause. Now, since the Act, we have regard

[17] (1809) 11 East 60; 103 ER 926.
[18] [1947] KB 641.
[19] [1947] 2 KB 291.
[20] *Ibid.*, 321.
[21] [1952] 2 QB 608.
[22] On the possibility that the doctrine was defunct anyway before the Act, see Lord Wright, 'Contributory Negligence' (1950) 13 *MLR* 2.
[23] *Stapley* v. *Gypsum Mines Ltd.* [1953] AC 663, 677 (Lord Porter).

to all the causes, and one of them undoubtedly was the plaintiff's negligence in riding on the tow bar of the traxcavator. His share in the responsibility was not great—the judge assessed it at one-fifth—but, nevertheless, it was his share, and he must bear it himself.'[24]

The flexibility provided by apportionment has not, however, relieved the court of the difficult task of identifying whether a particular act or omission is an operative cause in the first place. The Act refers to the damage being the 'result', in part, of the claimant's fault, and this has been taken to imply that the general principles of causation are relevant.[25] For the defence of contributory negligence to have any application at all, it must be shown, then, that the claimant's carelessness or other fault was a factual cause of his loss—in other words, that on the balance of probabilities the damage would not have occurred 'but for' his fault. But this is not sufficient on its own; as we have seen, it must also be shown that the claimant's fault was a legally proximate cause of his injury.[26] If the claimant's fault was a 'mere condition' of his injury, no defence will arise. In *Jones* v. *Livox Quarries* the plaintiff's carelessness in riding on the back of the traxcavator would have been irrelevant if, instead of being hit by another vehicle, he had been struck in the eye by a shot fired by a negligent sportsman.[27]

Another way of putting this is that there must be a link, then, between the injury suffered and the risk to which the defendant unduly exposed the claimant by virtue of his negligence claimant, through his carelessness, and which, conversely, the claimant failed adequately to guard against. As Sedley LJ put it in *Pride Valley Foods* v. *Hall and Partners*,[28] the question is 'whether [the claimant's] fault lay within the very risk which it was the defendant's duty to guard against'. In *Sahib Foods Ltd. (In Liquidation)* v. *Paskin Kyriakides Sands (A Firm)*[29] Clarke LJ said that this meant that 'in considering an allegation of contributory negligence in a case such as this, where the defendant's duty is to guard against the effects of a fire which might be caused by the fault of the claimant, that fact is relevant to questions which the court must decide'. The causal link runs from fault to damage and not to the accident as such. If the claimant has contributed to the accident he will be taken to have contributed to his injuries as well if these were more likely than not to result from the accident. But he may also be contributorily negligent without having caused an accident in any way by, for example, failing to wear a seat-belt and as a consequence suffering much more extensive injuries than he otherwise would have done. As Lord Denning explained in *Froom* v. *Butcher*[30] in such cases 'the *accident* is caused by the bad driving. The *damage* is caused in part by the bad driving of the defendant, and in part by the failure of the plaintiff to wear a seat belt. If the plaintiff was to blame in not wearing a seat belt, the damage is in part the result of

24 [1952] 2 QB 608, 617.

25 Section 1; *Stapley* v. *Gypsum Mines Ltd.* [1953] AC 663, 677.

26 See ch. 4, above.

27 See the judgment of Denning LJ in *Jones* v. *Livox Quarries Ltd.* [1952] 2 QB 608.

28 [2001] EWCA Civ. 1001, at [69].

29 [2003] EWCA Civ. 1832, at [66].

30 [1976] QB 286, 292.

his own fault.' Similarly, in a case where an employee is exposed to a dangerous substance, such as asbestos, from which he contracts cancer, he can be found to be contributorily negligent for having regularly smoked cigarettes in a way which materially contributed to that condition.[31]

The court's approach to analysing the legal effect of multiple causes in contributory negligence was considered in *The Volute*.[32] Lord Birkenhead's judgment makes it clear that the causal effect of an initial act of negligence will not be lost simply because the immediate cause of the damage occurs after a substantial interval of time. In some cases it would be clear that only the second event had any causative link to the damage. But 'there are cases in which the two acts come so closely together, and the second act of negligence is so much mixed up with the state of things brought about by the first act that the party secondly negligent... might... invoke the prior negligence as being part of the cause of the collision so as to make it a case of contribution'. This *dictum* was applied to the difficult facts of *Stapley* v. *Gypsum Mines Ltd*.[33] Two miners agreed to carry on working in dangerous conditions after failing to take the necessary safety precautions as instructed by their employer. One of them was killed when the roof of the mine collapsed. His widow brought an action against the employer on the basis of its vicarious liability for the negligence and breach of statutory duty committed by the deceased's co-worker. The Court of Appeal held that the deceased had been responsible for his own death, but the House of Lords allowed an appeal by a bare majority. Lord Reid held that the lack of care of each employee had been so bound up with that of the other that it was impossible to absolve the man who survived from all responsibility; damages were reduced by 80 per cent.

Although the possibility of apportionment has made it easier for the courts to avoid the need to find a 'sole cause', there are nevertheless cases in which the plaintiff's carelessness has been held totally to outweigh the negligence of the defendant. Such a case was *McKew* v. *Holland and Hannen and Cubitts (Scotland) Ltd*.[34] The plaintiff, who had earlier been injured by the defendants' negligence and forced to wear a cast on his leg as a result, fell down a flight of stairs when his leg gave way beneath him. His lack of care in venturing on to a steep flight of stairs without a handrail was held to have been a *nova causa interveniens* which broke the chain of causation, absolving the defendants of any responsibility for the further injuries he sustained as a result of his fall. The outcome has overtones of the now discredited 'last opportunity' rule, and the courts' failure to apply contributory negligence and apportion damages goes against the grain of most decisions in this area since the 1945 Act came into force. By contrast, in *Reeves* v. *Commissioner of Police for the Metropolis*[35] the House of Lords, by a majority (Lord

[31] *Badger* v. *Ministry of Defence* [2005] EWHC 2941.

[32] [1922] 1 AC 129. Admiralty law recognised the principle of apportionment for losses caused by maritime collisions before the more general adoption of the principle in the Contributory Negligence Act. See the Maritime Conventions Act 1911, s. 1.

[33] [1953] AC 663.

[34] [1969] 3 All ER 1621. The same approach has been taken in breach of statutory duty cases: see *Rushton* v. *Turner Brothers Asbestos Co. Ltd.* [1960] 1 WLR 96, *Ginty* v. *Belmont Building Supplies Ltd.* [1959] 1 All ER 414, *Jayes* v. *IMI (Kynoch) Ltd.* [1958] ICR 155.

[35] [2000] 1 AC 360.

Hobhouse dissenting), ruled that the chain of causation had not been broken in a case where the deceased committed suicide while in police custody. On the facts, a clear breach of a duty of care was found, since the cell in which the deceased was being held was defectively equipped and created a clear risk of suicide of which the defendants should have been aware. Given the nature of the duty of care in this case, which was to take steps to ensure that the risk of suicide was minimised, it was held to be inappropriate to regard the deceased's act as completely cancelling out the causal responsibility of the defendant: this was 'the very thing at which the duty was directed'.[36]

(B) CLAIMANT'S FAULT

For apportionment to be possible under section 1 of the Contributory Negligence Act, the damage must result partly from the claimant's 'fault' and partly from that of the defendant. Under section 4, 'fault' is defined as 'negligence, breach of statutory duty or other act or omission that gives rise to liability in tort or would, apart from this Act, give rise to the defence of contributory negligence'. It has been suggested that the first part of this definition refers to the defendant's breach of duty and that the second part refers to the claimant's lack of care; otherwise, the definition makes little sense.[37] If this is so, the meaning of contributory negligence from the claimant's point of view is unchanged by the Act.

It is not necessary for the defendant to show that the claimant owed him a duty of care or that the claimant's carelessness caused him, the defendant, damage.[38] Rather than providing a cause of action in its own right, 'contributory negligence is set up as a shield' against the claim.[39] It is possible that the defendant may bring a counter-claim based on damage caused to him by a separate breach of a duty of care by the claimant, but that is a different matter. The standard applied to the claimant in contributory negligence is the same as that of the 'reasonable person' in negligence liability generally. Here, as there, the test is not whether the damage or the accident was foreseeable but whether the claimant acted reasonably, that is to say, with the amount of self-care that a normal person would have exercised in the circumstances. This is clear from *Froom* v. *Butcher*: wearing a seat-belt is a sensible practice for all journeys no matter how short or whatever the conditions.[40] For even if the risk of an accident occurring is thought to be slight, the magnitude of the harm that might result is very great and the costs of preventing it by fastening the seat-belt are minimal. The same approach applies to the failure of motorcyclists to wear crash helmets.[41]

The fact that, in general, legislation makes it compulsory for seat-belts[42] and crash helmets[43] to be worn by road-users is, without doubt, a useful indicator of what is

36 *Ibid.*, 374 (Lord Jauncey of Tullichettle).

37 Williams, *Joint Torts* (Select Bibliography), 318–19.

38 This might be thought to be obvious, but the principle recently had to be reasserted by the Court of Appeal in *Sahib Foods Ltd. (In Liquidation)* v. *Paskin Kyriakides Sands (A Firm)* [2003] EWCA Civ. 1832.

39 *Nance* v. *British Columbia Electric Railway Co. Ltd.* [1951] AC 601, 611 (Viscount Simon).

40 [1976] QB 286, 293 (Lord Denning MR).

41 *O'Connell* v. *Jackson* [1972] 1 QB 270, *Capps* v. *Miller* [1989] 1 WLR 839.

42 Road Traffic Act 1988, s. 15; SI Nos. 1982/1202, 1982/1342 and 1989/1219.

43 Road Traffic Act 1988, s. 15.

'reasonable'. Yet the presence of such a criminal regulation does not conclusively settle the issue as far as the defence of contributory negligence is concerned. Nor do the exceptions to these statutory requirements necessarily coincide with the courts' view of what might be 'reasonable' in a particular case. For example, it is possible that a woman in the advanced stages of pregnancy would be acting reasonably even if she had not fastened her seat-belt if this was physically impossible or highly uncomfortable. The fact that she did not have a medical certificate from her doctor for the purposes of obtaining exemption from the Road Traffic Act may thus be irrelevant.[44] A Sikh wearing a turban is exempted from the requirement to comply with the statutory requirement to wear a crash helmet while driving a motorcycle.[45] Whether he would also be able to escape the application of contributory negligence if his failure to do so resulted in him incurring greater injuries in the course of an accident is an open question. Although it might seem unfair that the defendant should be ordered to pay more because of the claimant's decision not to wear a crash helmet, it should be remembered that damages awards of this kind will nearly always be met by liability insurance rather than from the personal resources of defendants. Whether a driver has kept to a speed limit or otherwise obeyed the rules of the highway is a good indication of whether they have behave reasonably, but is not conclusive either way.[46] Drivers who drive vehicles which they know to be defective[47] and passengers who accept lifts with drivers whom they know to be drunk, or would have known but for their own drunkenness,[48] may be caught by the defence, as will those who go joy-riding.[49] In every case, though, 'whether this principle can be relied on successfully is a question of fact and degree to be determined in the circumstances out of which the issue is said to arise'.[50]

The standard expected of the claimant will be modulated in certain cases, just as it would be for the defendant if the normal standard of care were being applied to his behaviour.[51] Children are held to a lower standard of self-protection than adults in regard to their use of the highway, although again it is a matter of degree in each case. In *Gough* v. *Thorne*[52] Lord Denning expressed the view that very young children 'cannot be guilty of contributory negligence', and that in the case of older children the extent to which they would be held to the same standards as adults was a question of degree. On the other hand, in *Morales* v. *Ecclestone*[53] an eleven-year-old boy who was injured when he ran out into the road without looking was held to be 75 per cent to blame for his injuries. Rescuers and those who are placed in a situation of imminent danger and have

[44] SI No. 1982/1201, reg. 5.

[45] Road Traffic Act 1988, s. 16(2).

[46] See *Grealis* v. *Opuni* [2003] EWCA Civ. 177.

[47] *Gregory* v. *Kelly* [1978] RTR 426.

[48] *Owens* v. *Brimmell* [1977] QB 859, *Ashton* v. *Turner* [1981] QB 137, *Meah* v. *McCreamer (No. 1)* [1985] 1 All ER 637.

[49] In that case, the defence of *ex turpi causa* or illegality may also apply: see *Pitts* v. *Hunt* [1991] 1 QB 24, discussed below.

[50] *Owens* v. *Brimmell* [1977] QB 859, 867 (Tasker Watkins J).

[51] See the discussion in ch. 4, above.

[52] [1966] 1 WLR 1387.

[53] [1991] RTR 151.

to act in the heat of the moment are also unlikely to be held to have been contributorily negligent.[54]

Employees are not, as a group, held to any different standard from other potential claimants. Yet the courts have, on occasion, recognised that long hours and the strain of working in noisy conditions, together with the fatigue caused by repetitive work, may mean that a lower standard is expected of those who regularly work in such conditions.[55] Where the employer is guilty of a breach of statutory duty it may have been the intention of the Act to ensure that a momentary lapse or inattention of the employee did not unduly endanger him. In such a case such a lapse would not amount to contributory negligence. For 'the purpose of imposing the absolute obligation is to protect the workman against those very acts of inattention which are sometimes relied upon as constituting contributory negligence so that too strict a standard would defeat the object of the statute'.[56] Nor, for the same reason, will it normally be possible in a breach of statutory duty case for the defendant to argue that the employee should have anticipated his own employer's carelessness.[57] Cases of statutory duty aside, however, such a failure, if unreasonable in the circumstances, could amount to contributory negligence,[58] just as a defendant's failure to anticipate certain careless behaviour of those to whom he owes a duty of care could, in principle, amount to a breach of that duty.[59]

The term 'fault' in section 4 of the Act is, as we have seen, not confined to negligence, but includes a reference to 'any act or omission' capable of giving rise to liability in tort. In relation to the claimant's fault, this has the result of extending the coverage of the defence to include intentional acts of self-harm, such as the suicide of the claimant's husband in *Reeves* v. *Commissioner of Police for the Metropolis*.[60]

(C) APPORTIONMENT

Once contributory negligence is made out, the court will reduce the claimant's damages 'to such an extent as [it] thinks just and equitable having regard to [his] share in the responsibility for the damage'.[61] Deductions for contributory negligence are extremely common in personal injury cases, but the tendency today is for them to be appealed only rarely. The appellate courts have the power to alter the judge's order but, according

54 *Jones* v. *Boyce* (1816) 1 Starkie 493; 171 ER 540 (passenger jumping from a coach); although cf. *Sayers* v. *Harlow UDC* [1958] 1 WLR 623, where the plaintiff's actions in attempting to escape from a lavatory cubicle in which she had been trapped were held to have amounted to contributory negligence.

55 *Caswell* v. *Powell Duffryn Associated Collieries Ltd.* [1940] AC 152.

56 *Staveley Iron & Coal Co. Ltd.* v. *Jones* [1956] AC 627, 648 (Lord Tucker); although cf. *Caswell* v. *Powell Duffryn Associated Collieries Ltd.* [1940] AC 152, 164–7 (Lord Atkin).

57 *Westwood* v. *Post Office* [1974] AC 1, 16 (Lord Kilbrandon).

58 *Jones* v. *Livox Quarries Ltd.* [1952] 2 QB 608, 615 (Denning LJ).

59 *Grant* v. *Sun Shipping Co. Ltd.* [1948] AC 549, 567, *London Passenger Transport Board* v. *Upson* [1949] AC 155, 173; see ch. 4, above.

60 [2000] 1 AC 360; see in particular the judgment of Lord Hope of Craighead, at 382–5.

61 Law Reform (Contributory Negligence) Act 1945, s. 1.

to Lord Denning, will do so only if the judge has misapplied the law, misapprehended the facts or made a decision which is 'clearly wrong'.[62]

It had been thought prior to the decision of the Court of Appeal in *Pitts* v. *Hunt*[63] that there was nothing to prevent a court using the 1945 Act to make a deduction of 100 per cent in an appropriate case. However, in that decision Beldam LJ pointed out that this was not compatible with the requirement laid down by the Act. For in any case where both parties are 'at fault' (as defined in ss. 1 and 4), the court should not allow the defence of contributory negligence completely to defeat the claim and 'to hold that he is himself entirely responsible for the damage effectively defeats his claim'.[64] It seems to follow as a matter of practice if, perhaps, not of law, that if the Act is to operate on the basis of apportionment as opposed to exclusion of damages the court should strive to avoid awarding a deduction *approaching* 100 per cent. In *Pitts* v. *Hunt* the plaintiff had been a passenger on a motorcycle driven by the defendant and which was involved in a collision the immediate cause of which was the defendant's careless driving. Both were drunk at the time of the accident, the plaintiff knew that the defendant was uninsured and without a driving licence, and the plaintiff had encouraged the defendant to drive in a dangerous manner. The plaintiff's action for damages against the estate of the defendant was defeated on the grounds of illegality. But the members of the Court of Appeal held that, had it been necessary, a deduction of 50 per cent for the plaintiff's contributory negligence in placing himself in danger would have been appropriate, reversing the judge's decision that the plaintiff had been 100 per cent contributorily negligent.

In *Reeves* v. *Commissioner of Police for the Metropolis*[65] a 50 per cent deduction was made to reflect the view of the House of Lords of the deceased's responsibility for his own death. The judge had made a 100 per cent deduction, while the Court of Appeal had held that no deduction at all was appropriate. According to Lord Hoffmann, the court is required under the Act to apportion not merely on the basis of degrees of fault, but, more generally, by reference to the 'responsibility' of each party for the harm. This means taking account of the 'policy of the rule ... by which liability is imposed'. In this case, 'a 100 per cent apportionment of responsibility to [the deceased] gives no weight at all to the policy of the law in imposing a duty of care upon the police ... [t]he apportionment must recognize that a purpose of the duty accepted by the Commissioner in this case is to demonstrate publicly that the police do have a responsibility for taking reasonable care to prevent prisoners from committing suicide'. At the same time, the award should also reflect the court's finding of fact that the deceased was of sound mind a short time before his death.[66]

Both the degree of the claimant's lack of care (fault) and the degree to which the damage can be attributed to his carelessness (causation) should be considered under the statutory formula. In *Froom* v. *Butcher*[67] Lord Denning repeated his view, expressed

[62] *Kerry* v. *Carter* [1969] 1 WLR 1372, 1376; cf. the extensive debate at appellate level in *Stapley* v. *Gypsum Mines Ltd.* [1958] AC 663, in which the Court of Appeal disagreed with the trial judge only to see the House of Lords substitute another ruling by a bare majority of 3–2.

[63] [1991] 1 QB 24. [64] *Ibid.*, 28.

[65] [2000] 1 AC 360. [66] *Ibid.*, 372. [67] [1976] QB 286.

in *Davies* v. *Swan Motor Co.*,[68] that 'consideration should be given not only to the causative potency of a particular factor, but also its blameworthiness'. Where the plaintiff could have avoided his injuries by wearing a seat-belt the reduction should only be 25 per cent, since the negligent driver took most of the blame for the accident. Where some injuries would have been sustained in any event, Lord Denning suggested a 15 per cent deduction. In *Russell* v. *Smith*[69] the judge found that the claimant, a child of ten who was injured in a collision with the defendant's car when he cycled on to the highway without looking properly, was three-quarters to blame for the accident, but made a deduction only 50 per cent in respect of his contributory negligence, in part on the grounds that he was a 'vulnerable road user'.[70]

Percentage reductions of various kinds have been established in a number of contexts and tend to be followed as general guidelines to court practice; they do not produce strictly binding precedents since every case is likely to turn on its own facts. The limited deduction in *Froom* v. *Butcher*, for example, may be contrasted with Lord Reid's apportionment in *Stapley* v. *Gypsum Mines*,[71] where damages awarded to the widow of the deceased were reduced by 80 per cent. In that latter case, not only had the deceased been grossly negligent in the circumstances but his own carelessness was a substantial cause of the roof-fall.

(D) IDENTIFICATION

For certain purposes the claimant is identified with the contributory negligence of another person. This is the case, for example, with the derivative action of dependants of the deceased under the Fatal Accidents Act 1976.[72] The deceased's contributory negligence will reduce any damages the dependants are awarded. Under the Congenital Disabilities (Civil Liability) Act 1976 a child is identified with the contributory negligence of one of its parents, where the parent's carelessness caused the child to be born disabled. The damages are reduced by an amount the court considers appropriate 'having regard to the extent of the parent's responsibility'.[73]

(E) THE SCOPE OF THE DEFENCE AND OF THE CONTRIBUTORY NEGLIGENCE ACT 1945

Section 1 of the Contributory Negligence Act requires the court to apportion damages in any case where the claimant's 'damage' is the result partly of his own 'fault' and partly of the defendant's 'fault'. The first issue to arise here is whether, and to what extent, the Act applies to particular kinds of harm suffered by the claimant. 'Damage' is defined as *including* loss of life and personal injury,[74] and so is not *confined* to these two categories.

[68] [1949] 2 KB 291, 326.

[69] [2003] EWHC 2060. See also *Eagle* v. *Chambers* [2003] EWCA Civ. 1108; *Pankhurst* v. *White* [2006] EWCA Civ. 2093.

[70] [2003] EWHC 2060, at [15].

[71] [1953] AC 633.

[72] Section 5.

[73] Section 1(7).

[74] Section 4.

It is well established that apportionment under the Act can be applied to property damage and there is no reason why it should not apply to cases of pure economic loss either. As far as the principle enunciated in *Hedley Byrne & Co. Ltd.* v. *Heller & Partners Ltd.*[75] is concerned, the plaintiff may fail completely, on the grounds of causation, if it can be shown that he would have incurred the loss in question regardless of the defendant's advice.[76] On the other hand, in a case where the plaintiff succeeded in showing that his reasonable reliance on the misstatement was the cause of his loss, the court was reluctant to allow his failure to make additional inquiries to be regarded as contributory negligence at all.[77]

When issues of apportionment have arisen in cases of negligent misstatement, they have proved to be complex and difficult. In principle, the 'damage' to which apportionment applies is only that part of the claimant's overall loss which is jointly attributable both to his own fault and to that of the defendant. If the claimant suffers part of the loss entirely through his own fault, apportionment should be irrelevant. This is an important consideration in the context of liability for negligent misstatement following the judgment of the House of Lords in the *SAAMCO* case.[78] That decision established that, in a case of a loan made on the basis of a negligent valuation of property, the defendant is not normally liable for the full consequences of the bad loan, but, at least on the face of it, only for the difference between the true market value of the property at the time the loan was made and the inflated value wrongly placed upon it. This means that any greater loss, such as that arising from a diminution in the value of the property in the meantime, falls on the claimant. Yet in *Platform Home Loans Ltd.* v. *Oyston Shipways Ltd.*[79] the House of Lords held that the claimant's 'damage', for this purpose, was the full loss flowing from the transaction in question, and proceeded to make a 20 per cent deduction for contributory negligence (on the grounds that the claimant had pursued an imprudent lending policy) from that amount. There is much to be said here for the dissenting judgment of Lord Cooke of Thorndon, who pointed out that the term 'damage' in section 1 of the Contributory Negligence Act must be taken to refer to loss for which the defendant would (but for the defence of contributory negligence) incur liability to the claimant.[80]

The second issue to determine is which civil wrongs of the defendant the Act applies to. While it is self-evident that contributory negligence operates as a defence to the tort of negligence, its application to other torts and to other forms of civil liability is not

75 [1964] AC 465.

76 *JEB Fasteners Ltd.* v. *Marks, Bloom & Co.* [1983] 1 All ER 583.

77 See *Gran Gelato Ltd.* v. *Richcliff (Group) Ltd.* [1992] 1 All ER 865, 877 (Nicholls V-C); although it should be noted that the authorities cited by the Vice Chancellor for this approach, such as *Redgrave* v. *Hurd* (1881) 20 Ch. D 1, pre-dated the Act of 1945 and were therefore concerned not with apportionment but with the possibility that the plaintiff's carelessness might defeat his claim completely.

78 *South Australia Asset Management Ltd.* v. *York Montague Ltd.* [1997] 1 AC 191; see also *Nykredit Mortgage Bank plc* v. *Edward Erdman Group Ltd. (No. 2)* [1997] 1 WLR 1627.

79 [2000] 2 AC 190; see J. Stapleton, 'Risk-Taking by Commercial Lenders' (1999) 115 *LQR* 527; D. Howarth, 'Complexity Strikes Back: Valuation in the House of Lords' (2000) 8 *Tort LR* 85.

80 [2000] 2 AC 190, 195–7.

always so clear. As we have seen, 'fault' is defined under the Act as meaning 'negligence, breach of statutory duty or other act or omission which gives rise to a liability in tort or would, apart from this Act, give rise to the defence of contributory negligence'.[81] We also noted that this unsatisfactory provision only makes sense if the reference to the potential causes of action in the first limb refers to the defendant's fault and the reference to contributory negligence in the second limb refers to the claimant's. By adopting the common law definition of contributory negligence (the definition established 'apart from this Act'), the Act appears to be confining itself to changing the *remedial* aspects of the defence—substituting apportionment for the total exclusion of damages—without altering the scope of the defence. An alternative view is that apportionment is now applicable to all the causes of action listed in the first limb of the definition—negligence, breach of statutory duty, and all other acts and omissions giving rise to liability in tort. If this is correct, the Act has apparently widened the range of situations in which the defence can apply.

Certain cases are clear. A separate Act excludes the defence in cases of conversion.[82] Under the common law contributory negligence did not operate as a defence to deceit;[83] in *Alliance and Leicester Building Society* v. *Edgestop Ltd.*[84] Mummery J decided that the passage of the 1945 Act had not led to any change in this rule, and his approach won the support of the House of Lords in *Standard Chartered Bank* v. *Pakistan National Shipping Corp. (No. 2)*.[85] Conversely, there are indications from both before and after 1945 that the defence does apply to certain cases of nuisance,[86] and its application to the action for breach of statutory duty is well established.[87]

Its application to strict liability torts is unclear. If the defence does not apply, it could be said that a defendant who has not been at fault would be worse off than if he had been negligent, when the defence would clearly be relevant. To apply the defence, however, would mean that, questions of causation aside, the standard set by law would then be somewhat less than strict. A breach of sections 2–4 of the Animals Act 1971 has, nevertheless, been deemed by statute to constitute 'fault' by the defendant for the purposes of section 4 of the Contributory Negligence Act.[88] This is evidently intended to bring in the contributory negligence defence together with statutory apportionment, although it is not clear that it succeeds, given the uncertainty surrounding the interpretation of the word 'fault' in the 1945 Act. There is no clear authority in English law on the application of the defence to liability under the rule in *Rylands* v. *Fletcher*, and Commonwealth authorities go both ways.[89]

[81] Section 4.

[82] Torts (Interference with Goods) Act 1977, s. 11(1); *Lipkin, Gorman* v. *Karpnale Ltd.* [1989] 1 WLR 1340, 1386 (Nicholls LJ).

[83] *Central Railway Co. of Venezuela* v. *Kisch* (1867) LR 2 HL 99, 120 (Lord Chelmsford).

[84] [1994] 2 All ER 38.

[85] [2002] 3 WLR 1547.

[86] *Butterfield* v. *Forrester* (1809) 11 East 60; 103 ER 926 can be seen as a nuisance case; for more recent authority see *Trevett* v. *Lee* [1955] 1 WLR 122.

[87] *Caswell* v. *Powell Duffryn Collieries Ltd.* [1940] AC 921, *Lewis* v. *Deyne* [1940] AC 921.

[88] Animals Act 1971, s. 10(1).

[89] See J. G. Fleming, *The Law of Torts* (8th edn., 1992), at 344–5.

As far as torts of intention are concerned, one might ask why should mere negligence be a defence to an interference on the part of the defendant which was by definition deliberate and therefore, on the face of it, more blameworthy? This argument has less force than it used to, since whereas the defence would once have excluded the defendant's liability it now serves simply to reduce damages. Moreover, relative blame is only one factor in the equation: the court might also wish to take into account the relative causal weight of the parties' actions. Nonetheless, in *Lane* v. *Holloway*[90] the court rejected an argument that provocation by the victim of a savage blow constituted contributory negligence. In *Murphy* v. *Culhane*,[91] by contrast, where the plaintiff initiated a criminal affray in the course of which the defendant struck him a fatal blow on the head, Lord Denning MR suggested that any damages awarded to the dead man's widow would be reduced for his contributory negligence. In the event the claim failed completely on the grounds of consent and *ex turpi causa*.[92] Although the use of contributory negligence in such cases remains theoretically possible, then, in practice it is likely to remain limited.[93]

A particularly difficult question concerns the application of the Act to actions for breach of contract. It was not applied to such actions prior to the 1945 Act. The reference to 'negligence' in section 4 could, however, be read as covering breach of contract in cases where the relevant duty is expressed in terms of a standard to act with reasonable skill and care. In *Forsikringsaktieselskapet Vesta* v. *Butcher*[94] Hobhouse J distinguished between the following three categories: (1) where the defendant's liability arises from a contractual provision which does not depend upon negligence on the part of the defendant; (2) where the defendant's liability arises from some contractual obligation which is expressed in terms of taking care (or its equivalent) but does not correspond to a common-law duty of care which would exist in the given case independently of contract; (3) where the defendant's liability in contract is the same as his liability in the tort of negligence independently of the existence of any contract. The learned judge then went on to hold that only the third and final category was caught by the 1945 Act. His judgment was upheld by the Court of Appeal on the ground that the reference to 'liability in tort' in section 4 meant that it only applied to actions originating in tort and not to actions for breach of a duty originating in contract. This was confirmed by the Court of Appeal in *Tennant Radiant Heat Ltd.* v. *Warrington Development Corp.*[95] According to Dillon LJ, a breach of covenant under a lease, being an obligation created

90 [1969] 1 QB 379.

91 [1977] QB 94, 98–9.

92 See Section 5, below.

93 This is particularly so in the light of the judgments of Lord Hoffmann and Lord Rodger in the deceit case of *Standard Chartered Bank* v. *Pakistan National Shipping Corp. (No. 2)* [2002] 3 WLR 1547, doubting whether there was any room for the contributory negligence defence in the context of the intentional torts as a whole.

94 [1986] 2 All ER 488, 508. The judgments of the Court of Appeal and House of Lords are reported at [1986] AC 852.

95 [1988] 11 EG 71. See also the judgment of the Court of Appeal in *Barclays Bank plc* v. *Fairclough Building Ltd.* [1995] QB 214.

by contract, 'does not fall within the definition of "fault" in section 4 of the 1945 Act'.[96] In *Barclays Bank plc* v. *Fairclough Building Ltd.* the Court of Appeal again refused to extend the scope of the defence. According to Beldam LJ, 'actions for breach of a strict contractual obligation would become unduly complex if contributory negligence were admitted as a partial defence by introducing an element of uncertainty into many straight forward commercial disputes and increasing the issues to be determined'.[97]

Since a number of decisions on the scope of duty of care in the tort of negligence have reduced the potential overlap between separate and concurrent tort and contract duties,[98] the scope to apply the Contributory Negligence Act to cases involving contractual relationships may now be highly restricted. Both the Scottish and English Law Commissions have recommended reform of the law to enable the defence to be applied generally to contract claims.[99] It is possible to use the doctrines of causation and mitigation of damages to defeat a claim for breach of contract by a plaintiff who was responsible for his own losses. It would, however, produce a 'more just and principled outcome' to allow apportionment by extending the scope of the 1945 Act, rather than by relying on 'all or nothing' outcomes.[100]

In *Gran Gelato Ltd.* v. *Richcliff (Group) Ltd.*[101] the question arose whether the 1945 Act applies to claims for damages under section 2(1) of the Misrepresentation Act 1967. According to Sir Donald Nicholls V-C, section 2(1) is 'essentially founded on negligence',[102] with the result that the 1945 Act does apply to a case of concurrent claims for negligence in tort and under section 2(1). However, he went on to hold that it would not be just and equitable to order apportionment in a case where the plaintiff suffered loss as a result of relying on a misrepresentation which the defendant had intended him to regard as accurate. It was a 'well established principle' in cases of misrepresentation that 'carelessness in not making other inquiries provides no answer to a claim when the plaintiff has done that which the representor intended he should do'.[103]

3. CONSENT

The defence which is known variously as 'consent', 'assumption of risk' and '*volenti non fit injuria*' can operate as a total exclusion in respect of all forms of tort liability. However, the relevant principles operate rather differently in cases of negligence and

[96] See also *Lipkin Gorman* v. *Karpnale Ltd.* [1989] 1 WLR 1340, 1360 (May LJ), *The Good Luck* [1989] 2 Lloyd's Rep. 238; P. Marshall and A. Beltrami, 'Contributory Negligence: A Viable Defence for Auditors?' [1992] *LMCLQ* 416.

[97] [1995] QB 214, 230.

[98] See the discussion of duty of care in ch. 3, above.

[99] Scottish Law Commission, *Report on Civil Liability Contribution*, No. 115 (1988); Law Commission, *Contributory Negligence as a Defence in Contract*, No. 114 (1990).

[100] A. Burrows, 'Contributory Negligence in Contract: Ammunition for the Law Commission' (1993) 93 *LQR* 175, a note on *Schering Agrochemicals Ltd.* v. *Resibel NVSA* (Court of Appeal, 26 Nov. 1992; unreported).

[101] [1992] 1 All ER 865.

[102] *Ibid.*, 875.

[103] *Ibid.*, 876.

strict liability from in respect of the torts of intentional interference. In negligence or strict liability, where the court is asking whether the claimant may be taken to have assumed the risk of damage flowing from the defendant's breach of duty, it is engaged in a process of allocating the risk of loss between the parties. In the intentional torts, where the question is whether the claimant can be said to have consented to the interference in question, the issues raise a set of ethical constitutional questions concerning the validity of such consent.

(A) CONSENT AS A DEFENCE TO NEGLIGENCE AND STRICT LIABILITY

Two senses of consent may usefully be distinguished. According to the first, consent signifies the assumption of a particular risk of injury by the claimant; according to the second, the claimant agrees in advance to waive any claim he might have to compensation arising out of an injury. The classic consent defence refers to the first of these two senses. An assumption of risk, which may be express or implied by conduct, negatives a duty of care that would otherwise arise or, which amounts to the same thing in practice, negatives liability for breach of that duty. In *Dann* v. *Hamilton* Asquith J regarded *volenti* as 'a denial of any duty at all, and, therefore, of any breach of duty'.[104] While it is possible for the consent defence to arise in a case of implied waiver of claim,[105] this rarely occurs; the courts normally insist on finding an express waiver, based on an exclusion or limitation clause contained in a specific contract or notice. The interpretation of exclusion and limitation clauses and the application to such clauses of the Unfair Contract Terms Act 1977 give rise to specialised questions which require to be analysed separately from the general defence of consent.[106]

(i) Consent as Assumption of Risk

The claim will be defeated if the claimant is taken to have consented to run the risk of being injured by the defendant's negligence. The same defence applies to certain strict-liability torts. Lord Diplock clarified the nature of the defence when he said that 'the consent that is relevant is not consent to the risk of injury but consent to the lack of reasonable care that may produce the risk'.[107] It is also the case that mere knowledge of the risk is not enough, and that the claimant's consent will not be inferred from his knowledge alone.[108] These two qualifications have substantially restricted the scope of the defence in modern personal injury cases. A leading example of this trend is *Dann* v. *Hamilton*,[109] in which the plaintiff accepted a lift with the defendant whom she knew to

104 [1939] 1 KB 509, 512.

105 See *Nettleship* v. *Weston* [1971] 2 QB 691, 701.

106 See Section 4, below.

107 *Wooldridge* v. *Sumner* [1963] 2 QB 43, 69–70.

108 Hence it is said that the plaintiff must be *volens* and not merely *sciens* as to the risk: *Thomas* v. *Quartermaine* (1887) 18 QBD 685, 696 (Bowen LJ), *Nettleship* v. *Weston* [1971] 2 QB 691, 701.

109 [1939] 1 KB 509.

be drunk. The defendant caused an accident in which he was killed and the plaintiff injured. Asquith J rejected the application of the *volenti* defence. 'The plaintiff, by embarking in the car, or re-entering it, with knowledge that through drink the driver had materially reduced his capacity for driving safely, did not impliedly consent to, or absolve the driver from liability for, any subsequent negligence on his part whereby the plaintiff might suffer harm.'[110] If *volenti* and exclusion are now best regarded as separate defences, they nevertheless have common roots in the nineteenth-century use of express and implied contract terms to limit the liability of occupiers, employers and others. In this respect they were both linked to a further defence, common employment, which has now been abolished by statute.[111] According to the doctrine of common employment, an employee (or 'servant', to refer to the term used by nineteenth-century judges) impliedly took the risk of any injury caused by the negligence of a fellow worker in the same employment. The employer, who would normally have been vicariously liable for the acts of an employee acting in the course of his employment, would thereby escape liability completely. The employer could only be made liable for a breach of his *personal* duty of care to ensure that there was a safe system and place of work and that the plaintiff's fellow workers were reasonably competent.[112] The basis of 'common employment' was a contract term which the judges regarded as an essential aspect of 'the mutual undertakings between the employer and employed to be implied from the relationship of master and servant constituted between them'.[113] The term was automatically implied into the contract of service on the ground that 'when several workmen engage to serve a master in a common work, they know, or ought to know, the risks to which they are exposing themselves including the risks of carelessness, against which their employer cannot secure them, and they must be supposed to contract with reference to such risks'.[114]

This produced some harsh results. Thus in one case two miners were killed when the cage in which they were travelling from the bottom of the pit failed to stop when it reached the top of the shaft. Claims for compensation against their employer were rejected on the ground that the accident was due entirely to the carelessness of a third employee who was operating the cage at the time of the accident.[115]

The doctrine of common employment was never less than controversial. One judge thought that 'there never was a more useful decision, or one of greater practical and

[110] *Ibid.*, 518.

[111] By the Law Reform (Personal Injuries) Act 1948, s. 1.

[112] The personal duty of care was fully recognised by the House of Lords in *Wilsons & Clyde Coal Co.* v. *English* [1938] AC 57, but there are indications of the doctrine in earlier cases and hints that it constituted an exception to the defence of common employment: see e.g. *Smith* v. *Charles Baker & Sons* [1891] AC 325, 343 (Lord Watson).

[113] *Johnson* v. *Lindsay & Co.* [1891] AC 371, 380 (Lord Herschell).

[114] *Bartonshill Coal Co.* v. *Reid* (1856) 3 Macq. 266, 295 (Lord Cranworth LC). The basis of the doctrine was said to be the judgment of Lord Abinger in *Priestley* v. *Fowler* (1837) 3 M & W 1; 150 ER 1030, but its rationale was first clearly articulated in the Massachusetts decision, *Farwell* v. *Boston Railroad Corporation* (1846) 4 Metcalf 49, and, in England, in *Hutchinson* v. *York, Newcastle and Berwick Railway Co.* (1850) 5 Exch. 343; 155 ER 150. The *Bartonshill* judgment in the House of Lords applied the doctrine to both English and Scots law.

[115] *Bartonshill Coal Co.* v. *Reid* (1856) 3 Macq. 266.

social importance in the whole history of the law'.[116] Not everyone, however took such a view. The Scottish courts thus found it 'a principle as distasteful as it is alien to Scottish jurisprudence'[117] and were persuaded to follow it only by House of Lords authority in the *Bartonshill* cases.[118] Common employment would have no application in a case where the injury to the plaintiff was caused by a person other than a fellow employee, such as the employee of a different employer. However, the same rationale of an assumption of risk could then be applied using the more general defence of *volenti non fit injuria*. In *Woodley* v. *Metropolitan District Railway Co.*[119] the plaintiff, a workman employed by contractors who had been engaged by the defendant railway company, was struck by one of their trains while he was working in an unlit tunnel. He claimed damages for negligence based on the defendants' failure to provide a system to warn of the approach of trains. The Court of Appeal rejected his claim on the grounds that 'a man who enters on a necessarily dangerous employment with his eyes open takes it with its accompanying risks'. Cockburn CJ explained the scope of the *volenti* defence as follows:

> If a man chooses the employment, or to continue in it with a knowledge of the danger, he must abide the consequences, so far as any claim to compensation against the employer is concerned. Morally speaking, those who employ men on dangerous work without doing all in their power to obviate the danger are highly reprehensible, as I certainly think the company were in the present instance. The workman who depends on his employment for the bread of himself and his family is thus tempted to incur risks to which, as a matter of humanity, he ought not to be exposed. But looking at the matter in a legal point of view, if a man, for the sake of the employment, takes it or continues it with a knowledge of its risks, he must trust to himself to keep clear of injury.

The growth in the size and financial stability of industrial undertakings and the greater availability of liability insurance gradually altered the perception that the employer was no better placed than his employees to ensure their safety at work. In 1880 Parliament passed the Employers' Liability Act which excluded the defence in a case where the plaintiff was injured by the negligence of a superior worker with supervisory or managerial responsibilities, as opposed to a fellow servant in general employment. This was only a partial restriction of the defence, but it nevertheless marked a turning-point in the law of employers' liability. A short while later the House of Lords limited the scope of the *volenti* defence in the great case of *Smith* v. *Charles Baker & Sons*,[120] itself an appeal in an action for damages under the 1880 Act. The plaintiff was employed on the construction of a railway and was injured by a stone that fell from a crane that was being used to shift rock from a cutting. He had been aware for several months of the danger posed by the crane being swung, without warning, over his head, but had nevertheless continued in the employment. The House of Lords rejected an argument that consent

[116] Pollock CB in *Vose* v. *Lancashire and Yorkshire Railway Co.* (1858) 2 LJ Ex. 249.

[117] The expression of Lord Macmillan in *Radcliffe* v. *Ribble Motor Services Ltd.* [1939] AC 215, 235.

[118] *Bartonshill Coal Co.* v. *Reid* (1853) 3 Macq. 266, *Bartonshill Coal Co.* v. *Maguire* (1853) 3 Macq. 300.

[119] (1887) 2 Ex. D 384.

[120] [1891] AC 325.

could be inferred either at common law or under the Act from the fact of his staying at work. Lord Watson's formulation continues to be applicable:

In its application to questions between the employer and the employed, the maxim [of *volenti*] as now used generally imports that the workman had either expressly or by implication agreed to take upon himself the risks attendant upon the particular work which he was engaged to perform, and from which he has suffered injury. The question which has most frequently to be considered is not whether he voluntarily and rashly exposed himself to injury, but whether he agreed that, if injury should befall him, the risk was to be his and not his master's. When, as is commonly the case, his acceptance or non-acceptance of the risk is left to implication, the workman cannot reasonably be held to have undertaken it unless he knew of its existence and appreciated or had the means of appreciating its danger. But assuming that he did so, I am unable to accede to the suggestion that the mere fact of his continuing at his work, with such knowledge and appreciation, will in every case necessarily imply his acceptance. Whether it will have that effect or not depends, in my opinion, to a considerable extent upon the nature of the risk, and the workman's connection with it, as well as upon other considerations which must vary according to the circumstances of each case.[121]

Lord Bramwell, dissenting, argued that it was a 'question of bargain. The plaintiff here thought the pay worth the risk and he did not bargain for a compensation if hurt: in effect, he undertook the work, with its risks, for his wages and no more.'[122] It was this wide view of *volenti*, using the continuation of the contract as evidence of implied consent, which the majority ruling in *Smith* v. *Baker* decisively rejected. The implied term theory nevertheless lingered on for a further half-century, since the doctrine of common employment remained in place, albeit in a form that became progressively more confined. In *Radcliffe* v. *Ribble Motor Services Ltd.*[123] an action was brought under the Fatal Accidents Act 1847 by the widow of a bus driver who was killed in an accident which happened to have been caused by another driver employed by the same company. The House of Lords held that for the defence of common employment to apply, the employees in question had to be employed not just by the same employer but also on 'common work', denoting a joint venture which necessarily exposed them to the risk of each other's negligence.

While this strained interpretation of the doctrine enabled the courts to avoid its application in the case in question, the House of Lords nevertheless felt unable to overturn the defence completely on the ground that it had become too well established as a principle of the common law. It was thus left to Parliament to repeal it by section 1(1) of the Law Reform (Personal Injuries) Act 1948. This provided that 'It shall not be a defence to an employer who is sued in respect of personal injuries caused by the negligence of a person employed by him, that that person was at the time the injuries were caused in common employment with the person injured.' Section 1(2) of the Act renders void any contract term for the exclusion of an employer's liability to those employed by him in respect of injuries caused by the negligence of persons in common employment.

[121] *Ibid.*, 355. [122] *Ibid.*, 344. [123] [1939] AC 215.

(ii) The Scope of the Modern Defence

The abolition of common employment and the conversion by statute of contributory negligence into a partial as opposed to a complete defence encouraged the courts further to limit the operation of *volenti*. In *Nettleship* v. *Weston*[124] Lord Denning said:

> Now that contributory negligence is not a complete defence, but only a ground for reducing the damages, the defence of *volenti non fit injuria* has been closely considered and, in consequence, it has been severely limited. Knowledge of the risk of injury is not enough. Nor is a willingness to take the risk of injury. Nothing will suffice short of an agreement to waive any claim for negligence. The plaintiff must agree, expressly or impliedly, to waive any claim for any injury that may befall him due to the lack of reasonable care by the defendant.

In *Nettleship*'s case an amateur driving instructor was held not to have waived any claim which might arise out of the negligence of a learner driver whom he was supervising, since he specifically asked whether he would be protected by the car-owner's liability insurance policy.[125] Lord Denning's *dictum*, however, goes too far in suggesting that nothing short of an express or implied contract will suffice for the defence to apply. A contract or notice as such is not necessary. Nor is the defence confined to the case of an agreement to waive a future claim. Consent in the sense of a general assumption of risk can still prevent liability arising. In *Dann* v. *Hamilton*[126] Asquith J distinguished two situations. In the first the defendant by his negligence creates a risk of physical danger which the plaintiff, in full knowledge of the risk, chooses to accept. In the second, the plaintiff, by his words or conduct, is taken to consent to a subsequent act of negligence. It is more difficult to establish *volenti* in the second situation (as in *Dann*'s case itself) since it is less plausible that the plaintiff would have given his consent to negligence in advance of it occurring. Nevertheless, Asquith J accepted that even then the defence would apply where 'the drunkenness of the driver at the material time is so extreme and so glaring that to accept a lift from him is like engaging in an intrinsically and obviously dangerous occupation, intermeddling with an unexploded bomb or walking on the edge of an unfenced cliff'. However, in holding that the plaintiff had not been *volens* even though she had made the apparently fatalistic remark that 'if anything is going to happen it will happen',[127] Asquith J appeared to have left very little scope for the defence to apply in passenger–driver cases. He later recorded that he would have accepted a plea of contributory negligence (which would then have been a complete defence), but none was made.[128] His approach was not followed in similar road-accident cases in Australia.[129]

More recently, in *Pitts* v. *Hunt*,[130] the plaintiff, who was injured when riding as a pillion passenger on a motorcycle driven by the defendant, actively encouraged the defendant to drive in a dangerous manner and also knew that he was uninsured.

124 [1971] 2 QB 691, 701.

125 Salmon LJ dissented: see [1971] 2 QB 691, 704.

126 [1939] 1 KB 509, 516–17; see also *Morris* v. *Murray* [1991] 2 QB 6, 14–15 (Fox LJ), 19–20 (Stocker LJ).

127 [1939] 1 KB 509, 514.

128 See (1953) 49 *LQR* 317.

129 *Insurance Commissioner* v. *Joyce* (1948) 77 CLR 39, *Rogenkamp* v. *Bennett* (1950) 80 CLR 292.

130 [1991] 1 QB 24. See also *Winnik* v. *Dick* (1984) SLR 185.

Beldam LJ thought that the *volenti* defence would have applied but for the provision which is now section 149 of the Road Traffic Act 1988. This invalidates any agreement to limit or restrict the liability of a vehicle user to a passenger in circumstances where the user is required to be covered by a policy of insurance. It also provides that 'the fact that a person so carried has willingly accepted as his the risk of negligence on the part of the user shall not be treated as negativing any such liability on the part of the user'.[131] The other two members of the Court of Appeal took the same view of the application of the Act, and did not state an opinion on whether *volenti* would have been made out on the facts. The Court of Appeal returned to the question of the application of the *volenti* defence in *Morris* v. *Murray*.[132] Plaintiff and defendant decided, after spending most of the day drinking alcohol, to go for a flight in the defendant's light aircraft. The defendant, who had consumed the equivalent of seventeen measures of whisky, crashed the plane shortly after take-off; he was killed and the plaintiff severely injured. The plaintiff brought an action against the defendant's estate. There was no question here of compulsory liability insurance and no equivalent to section 149 of the Road Traffic Act 1988. Fox LJ held that 'the *volenti* doctrine can apply to the tort of negligence, though it must depend upon the extent of the risk, the passenger's knowledge of it and what can be inferred as to his acceptance of it'. In this case the plaintiff had not been 'blind drunk' but simply 'merry', and hence knew what he was doing when he went on a flight with a pilot who had been drinking all afternoon. Accordingly, 'the wild irresponsibility of the venture is such that the law should not intervene to award damages and should leave the loss where it falls. Flying is inherently dangerous and flying with a drunken pilot is great folly. The situation is very different from what has arisen in motoring cases.'[133] This suggests that the defence could have had a wider application to passenger cases on the highway but for its abrogation by the Road Traffic Act.

In *Morris* v. *Murray* Fox LJ suggested that '*volenti* as a defence has, perhaps, been in retreat during this century—certainly in relation to master and servant cases'.[134] One reason for this is, it seems, an understandable reluctance on the part of the courts to be seen reviving in any form whatsoever the now discredited defence of common employment. The *volenti* defence is only likely to apply in the most extreme of cases, such as *ICI* v. *Shatwell*.[135] Here two shot-firers (who happened to be brothers) decided to circumvent normal safety procedures, contrary to the express orders of their employer, in an attempt to finish a job more quickly. An explosion resulted in which both were injured; one brother then brought an action against the employer on the basis that it was

131 Road Traffic Act 1988, s. 149(3).

132 [1991] 2 QB 6.

133 [1991] 2 QB 6, 17. The need to show that the plaintiff was fully aware of the danger of a course of action led the Court of Appeal to reject a *volenti* plea in *Kirkham* v. *Chief Constable of Greater Manchester* [1990] 2 QB 283, where the plaintiff committed suicide in a police cell while in an unbalanced state of mind. By contrast, in *Reeves* v. *Commissioner of Police of the Metropolis* [2000] 1 AC 360, where the deceased was found to be of sound mind shortly before he took his own life, the House of Lords stressed the limited scope of the *volenti* defence, given the nature of the police's duty of care to minimise the risk of suicides by prisoners in their custody.

134 [1991] 2 QB 6, 17.

135 [1965] AC 656.

vicariously liable for the negligence of the other brother. The House of Lords was unwilling to accept the proposition that if 'two men collaborate in doing what they know is dangerous and is forbidden and as a result both are injured, each has a cause of action against the other'. According to Lord Reid, 'there is a world of difference between two fellow servants collaborating carelessly, so that the acts of both contribute to cause injury to one of them, and two fellow servants combining to disobey an order deliberately, though they know the risk involved'.[136] The plaintiff's claim failed.

By and large, however, the courts adhere to the view that in employment cases the defence should be applied 'with extreme caution'. Thus, 'it can hardly ever be applicable where the act to which the servant is said to be "*volens*" arises out of his ordinary duty, unless the work for which he is engaged is one in which danger is necessarily involved'.[137] Even then it is difficult to conceive of an employee working on a potentially dangerous site such as a North Sea oil rig, for example, consenting in advance to run the risk of *negligence* on the employer's part, which is what the defence requires. As with employment, so with occupiers' liability: although *volenti* is, in principle, available as a defence,[138] in the absence of an express exclusion of liability through contract or notice it is much more likely that the courts will use contributory negligence to apportion the loss.[139]

Care must be taken in applying the *volenti* defence in the context of sporting injuries. The participants in a game involving a high risk of physical contact are normally taken to have consented to touchings which are inherent in the nature of that game; to that extent, consent operates as a defence to most potential battery claims.[140] Consent to a claim in negligence is a different matter. While a boxer may be taken to have consented to receiving certain blows which would otherwise amount to a battery, this does not mean that he will have consented to negligence in the making of medical and related arrangements made by the sport's regulatory body.[141] However, it may be difficult, in a sporting context, to show that a participant has been careless in the first place. In *Wooldridge* v. *Sumner*[142] a press photographer at the Royal International Horse Show was injured by a horse which collided with him in the course of a round. Acording to Diplock LJ, the spectator in such a case accepts the risk of injury 'unless the participant's conduct is such as to evince a reckless disregard of the spectator's safety', but this is not because of *volenti* but because 'such an act involves no breach of the duty of care owed by the participant to him'.[143] A spectator or participant cannot be taken to have assented to an injury caused by an action which has nothing to do

136 [1965] AC 656, at 672.

137 Goddard LJ in *Bowater* v. *Bowley Regis Corporation* [1944] KB 476, 480–1.

138 The Occupiers' Liability Act 1957, s. 2(5), preserves the common law in this regard. See ch. 6, above.

139 See *Slater* v. *Clay Cross Co. Ltd.* [1956] 2 QB 264, 271 (Denning LJ); cf. *McGinlay* v. *British Railways Board* [1983] 1 WLR 1427.

140 *Blake* v. *Galloway* [2004] 1 WLR 2844, 2853.

141 *Watson* v. *British Boxing Board of Control* [2001] QB 1134.

142 [1963] 2 QB 43.

143 *Ibid.*, 69.

with the course of play, such as a golfer carelessly hitting a spectator with his club while demonstrating a stroke.[144]

Volenti was invoked to explain the outcome in *Simms* v. *Leigh Rugby Football Club Ltd.*[145] where a rugby league player, whose leg was injured when he was thrown against a wall in the course of a tackle, was held to have consented to the risk of such an injury occurring. It follows that if a foul is committed in the course of a game, consent can normally be assumed for the purposes of both a battery and a negligence claim, unless the conduct of the defendant is completely beyond normal expectations of the participants in some way: 'a breach of the duty of care will only be established where there has been recklessness or a very high degree of carelessness'.[146] Where there is a foul, the fact that the action is prohibited by the rules of the game will not, in itself, provide conclusive proof of negligence.[147]

In addition to applying to negligence under the circumstances noted above, the defence can also apply to strict liability torts. The defence of 'common benefit' under *Rylands* v. *Fletcher* is essentially an application of consent,[148] and the defence is also preserved by section 5(2) of the Animals Act 1971. The application of the defence to breach of statutory duty is slightly more problematic. In principle, it is said not to be possible for the claimant to give his consent in advance to an act that amounts to a breach of a regulatory (frequently criminal) statute.[149] It does not seem to matter, for this purpose, whether the claimant is alleged to have assumed the risk or to have agreed to waive any future claim: the defence is excluded in either event. One of the principal merits of the action for breach of statutory duty for judges in the late nineteenth century was precisely its potential as a means of avoiding the defences of *volenti* and common employment in personal injury cases. A possible exception was discussed by the House of Lords in *ICI* v. *Shatwell*,[150] namely the situation in which the employer is placed in statutory breach solely by virtue of his vicarious liability for the act of an employee of the same rank as the claimant. The claimant himself must also assent to and participate in the statutory breach. There are difficulties with this approach: it may not always be clear, for example, what is meant by an employee of a rank superior to that of the claimant, nor indeed that there is any useful purpose in drawing such a distinction. It may be that there are good reasons for applying the *volenti* defence to breach of statutory duty in the same way as it is applied to negligence, now that the scope of the defence has been greatly restricted. However, as long as breach of statutory duty is regarded as a tort which, being separate from common law negligence, is based on failure to perform a duty imposed by Parliament, the courts are likely to proceed cautiously.

144 *Gleghorn* v. *Oldham* (1927) 43 TLR 465.

145 [1969] 2 All ER 923.

146 *Blake* v. *Galloway* [2004] 1 WLR 2844, 2853.

147 See *Condon* v. *Basi* [1985] 1 WLR 866; *Blake* v. *Galloway* [2004] 1 WLR 2844.

148 See ch. 16, above.

149 *Baddeley* v. *Earl Granville* (1887) 19 QBD 423, *Wheeler* v. *New Merton Board Mills Ltd.* [1953] 2 KB 669.

150 [1965] AC 656, above.

(B) CONSENT AS A DEFENCE TO TORTS OF INTENTIONAL INTERFERENCE

This question has already been analysed in earlier chapters, to which the reader is referred for a more detailed treatment.[151] Consent is, in principle, effective as a defence to the torts of assault and battery, but this is limited in some cases by an overriding principle of public policy which, for example, may prevent a person validly consenting to a serious battery, or to medical intervention which assists him to commit suicide.[152] A second problematic area concerns consent to medical treatment, where the courts have in effect obviated the need for formal consent in certain cases such as those involving children and patients in certain disabling physical conditions. In general, though, consent to interference with the person must be clearly expressed; the circumstances under which the courts will infer consent from conduct are limited. In relation to false imprisonment, although consent may again be a defence, this runs up against the principle that it is not permissible to confine another simply for a breach of contract. As far as trespass to goods, conversion, and trespass to land are concerned, the defence is well established.[153]

4. EXCLUSION AND LIMITATION OF LIABILITY

(A) THE NATURE OF THE DEFENCE

The defence of exclusion or liability through a contract term or notice raises similar issues to those that arise in relation to the defence of *volenti*, but if the two are 'analogous' they are nevertheless distinct. A formal exclusion may enable the defendant to avoid liability in a case where *volenti* has no application.

In *White* v. *Blackmore*[154] the plaintiff's husband was killed following a freak accident while attending a day of jalopy races organised by the defendants. The cause of the accident was a vehicle becoming entangled with some safety ropes about a third of a mile away from where the plaintiff's husband had been standing; he became caught up in the ropes and sustained the injuries of which he later died. Buckley LJ noted that the deceased was not standing in a particularly dangerous place at the time of the accident and so could not have been said to have assumed a particular risk of injury from the alleged negligence of the course organisers. However, the defendants succeeded by virtue of an exclusion clause contained in a notice posted at the spectators' entrance. The principle that occupiers of land can exclude or limit their liability to those who come on to their land as lawful visitors is well established in the law of occupiers' liability.[155]

151 See ch. 9, above.

152 See *Airedale NHS Trust* v. *Bland* [1993] 1 All ER 821, 895 (Lord Mustill), *Pretty* v. *DPP &* [2002] 1 AC 800.

153 See chs. 11 and 12, above.

154 [1972] 2 QB 651.

155 See ch. 6, Section 2.

In *Ashdown* v. *Samuel Williams & Sons Ltd.*[156] the defendants knew that employees of a neighbouring employer, including the plaintiff, were used to taking a short-cut across their land to get to work. The short-cut crossed a railway track. When the plaintiff was taking the short-cut on her way to work one morning she was struck and injured by a railway wagon being shunted by the first defendants' employees, who were held to have been negligent in not keeping a look-out. It was held that the plaintiff had not been a trespasser—she had an implied licence to cross the defendants' land, based on their knowledge of the short-cut and its use. However, the defendants were absolved by a notice to the effect that those using their land did so at their own risk and were to have no claim for damages for injuries, whether or not it was the result of the defendants' negligence or breach of duty. 'It is not in dispute', said Jenkins LJ, 'that it is competent to an occupier of land to restrict or exclude any liability he might otherwise be under to any licensee of his, including liability for his own or his servants' negligence, by his conditions aptly framed and adequately made known to the licensee.'[157] In the circumstances the notice was deemed adequate and the plaintiff, who had read part of it, was bound by its terms. The decision was confirmed by section 2(1) of the Occupiers' Liability Act 1957, according to which the occupier is free to 'restrict, modify or exclude his duty to any visitor or visitors by agreement or otherwise'. If the occupier has the right to exclude others from his land, he also has the power to set conditions upon their lawful entry.[158]

(B) THE APPLICATION OF THE UNFAIR CONTRACT TERMS ACT 1977

This power is now subject, however, to the provisions of the Unfair Contract Terms Act 1977 (UCTA), which regulates the use of exclusion or limitation clauses for the purposes of liability in both contract and tort.[159] The provisions of the Act have already been considered in the context of occupiers' liability. They apply only to 'business liability', that is to say, liability arising from things done in the course of a business or from the occupation of business premises.[160] Subject to this limitation, section 2(1) of the Act prohibits the exclusion or limitation of liability for personal injury or death caused by negligence. The exclusion or restriction of liability in negligence for other forms of loss (such as property damage or pure economic loss) is subjected to a test of reasonableness.[161] The fact that the plaintiff was aware of or agreed to the terms of any such contract term or notice 'is not to be taken as indicating his voluntary risk'.[162]

156 [1957] 1 QB 409. 157 *Ibid.*

158 This, of course, must now be read in the light of the Unfair Contract Terms Act 1977. For further details see ch. 6, above.

159 Other important examples of the statutory regulation of exclusion clauses and the like are provided by s. 149 of the Road Traffic Act 1988 (discussed above) and s. 7 of the Consumer Protection Act 1987.

160 More precisely, premises 'used for business purposes of the occupier': UCTA, s. 1(3).

161 *Ibid.*, s. 2(2).

162 *Ibid.*, s. 2(3). The Act also regulates exclusion clauses affecting certain contractual obligations, namely those in contracts for the sale or supply of goods (ss. 5–7), contracts between businesses and consumers, and

The orthodox view of exclusion clauses is that they take effect by means of an express or implied agreement between the parties, by which one or the other of them is exempted from liability for breach of a duty arising in contract or tort. To adopt language used by Lord Diplock,[163] they affect the 'secondary' obligations of the parties to pay damages for a breach of duty. But they do not affect the scope of that duty, that is to say the 'primary obligations' of performance in contract or the duty of care in the tort of negligence. A contrary view has been put by Professor Brian Coote, namely that exemption clauses are not always what they appear to be: in a given case, the correct analysis may well be to regard them as defining the nature of the initial obligations between the two parties to a contract.[164] This view could also be extended to certain duties of care in tort which depend upon the consent of one or both of the parties to the creation of a specific, pre-tort relationship. The occupier's common duty of care to lawful visitors is one such example, as is the duty of care under *Hedley Byrne & Co. Ltd.* v. *Heller & Partners Ltd.*,[165] which rests upon the notion of a 'special relationship' between plaintiff and defendant. If this is correct, the effect of a notice or disclaimer is to exclude a duty of care in the sense of preventing one arising in the first place; and if there is no duty, there is no 'exemption clause' on which the Unfair Contract Terms Act can 'bite'.

The question was considered by the House of Lords in two consolidated appeals, *Harris* v. *Wyre Forest District Council* and *Smith* v. *Eric S. Bush*.[166] In each case the plaintiffs had purchased residential properties in reliance on mortgage valuations made by surveyors acting for the potential mortgagee. In *Smith* v. *Bush* the valuation was passed on by the building society to the plaintiff with a disclaimer to the effect that neither the building society nor the surveyors assumed any responsibility for its accuracy. In *Harris* v. *Wyre Forest DC* there was another disclaimer and the report was not even passed on to the plaintiffs. Nevertheless, they assumed, when the local authority proceeded to grant them the loan, that the surveyors had reported that the house was worth at least as much as the intended purchase price. In both cases the surveyors had negligently failed to report serious structural defects, with the result that the plaintiffs incurred serious financial losses of various kinds for which they were awarded damages at first instance.[167] In *Harris* the Court of Appeal overruled the judge's decision on the ground

contracts on the written standard terms of the party claiming the protection of the exclusion (s. 3). On the definition of 'consumer', see s. 12.

[163] In *Photo Production Ltd.* v. *Securicor Transport Ltd.* [1980] AC 827.

[164] B. Coote, *Exception Clauses* (1964). Two critics write: 'the thesis was elegantly formalistic, and ignored both the historical development of the problem, and the realities of the situation': J. Adams and R. Brownsword, 'The Unfair Contract Terms Act: A Decade of Discretion' (1988) 104 *LQR* 94, 95–6. See also E. Macdonald, 'Exclusion Clauses: The Ambit of s. 13(1) of the Unfair Contract Terms Act 1977' (1992) 12 *Leg. Stud.* 277.

[165] [1964] AC 465.

[166] [1990] 1 AC 831.

[167] In *Smith* v. *Bush* [1990] 1 AC 831 the loss—damage to the structure of the house caused by a chimney flue which collapsed—could conceivably be characterised as damage to property according to certain of the *dicta* in *Murphy* v. *Brentwood DC* [1991] 1 AC 398. In *Harris* v. *Wyre Forest DC* [1988] 1 QB 835 (CA) and [1990] 1 AC 831 (HL), by contrast, the loss was undoubtedly economic in the sense of a loss of value in the house once settlement was discovered. As the *Smith* and *Harris* cases preceded *Murphy*, and as they clearly came within the broad *Hedley Byrne* principle, nothing turned on the precise classification of the loss.

that the surveyor's disclaimer prevented any duty of care arising under the principle in *Hedley Byrne* v. *Heller* (the point was not considered by the separate Court of Appeal which heard and rejected the appeal in *Smith* v. *Bush*). Kerr LJ thought that the judge had been wrong to characterise the disclaimer as an exclusion clause:

In order to decide the primary question whether or not the defendant owes any duty of care to the plaintiff it is not relevant to determine, on their true construction, the precise legal effect of the terms of any disclaimer or warning.[168] Considerations of the legal effect of any such provisions only arise if and when the existence of a duty of care has been established. However, in determining whether or not the circumstances warrant the inference that any such duty of care was owed by the defendant to the plaintiff, any disclaimer of responsibility and warning addressed by the defendant to the plaintiff may be of the greatest importance.

In this regard, Kerr LJ distinguished between cases 'where the existence of a duty of care is not open to doubt'—such as the duty of care owed by a driver of a motor vehicle to other users of the highway, which 'he necessarily assumes by driving'—and cases of misstatement in which 'the entirety of the statements made must be considered in order to determine whether or not the maker should be held to have assumed, or for some reason to be subjected to, a duty of care to the person addressed'.[169] There is some authority, albeit rather unclear, for this view in *Hedley Byrne* itself, where the defendants used their disclaimer to escape liability that the House of Lords would otherwise have imposed. Lord Reid said that 'the respondents never undertook any duty to exercise care in making their replies', and Lord Morris said that they 'effectively disclaimed any assumption of a duty of care'.[170]

Such a view, whatever its theoretical merit, would have had the effect of nullifying a large part of the effect of the Unfair Contract Terms Act 1977 (which, of course, could not have been anticipated in *Hedley Byrne* itself). Prior to *Harris* v. *Wyre Forest DC* most courts had taken a wide view of what constituted an exclusion clause: in *Phillips Products Ltd.* v. *T. Hyland and Hamstead Plant Hire Co. Ltd.* Slade LJ said that, in applying section 2(2), 'it is not relevant to consider whether the form of a condition is such that it can aptly be given the label of an "exclusion" or "restriction" clause. There is no mystique about "exclusion" or "restriction" clauses. To decide whether a person "excludes" liability by reference to a contract term, you look at the effect of the term.'[171] A good reason for taking this approach is provided by section 13(1) UCTA.

This provides that to the extent that the Act prevents the exclusion or restriction of any liability, section 2 also prevents 'excluding or restricting liability by reference to terms and notices that exclude or restrict the relevant obligation or duty'. Allowing the appeal in *Harris* v. *Wyre Forest DC*, Lord Templeman noted that Kerr LJ's view of UCTA 'would not give effect to the manifest intention of the Act but would emasculate the Act'.

168 Let alone by the application of the Unfair Contract Terms Act 1977.

169 *Harris* v. *Wyre Forest DC* [1988] 1 QB 835, 853.

170 [1964] AC 465, 483 and 504 respectively, cited by Caulfield J in the Court of Appeal in *Harris* v. *Wyre Forest DC* [1988] 1 QB 835, 849.

171 [1987] 2 All ER 620, 626.

He further argued that the proposed distinction between situations where the duty of care was 'inescapable' and other situations had no authority either under the Act or under the general law. According to his Lordship, the Act applied to 'all exclusion notices which would in common law provide a defence to an action for negligence'.[172] Lord Jauncey of Tullichettle concluded that the words of section 13(1) are unambiguous and are entirely appropriate to cover a disclaimer which prevents a duty coming into existence. It follows that the disclaimers here given are subject to the provisions of the Act and will therefore be effective only if they satisfy the requirement of reasonableness.[173]

It may be, though, that the but-for test adopted by the House of Lords goes too far in drawing into the scope of the Act *all* clauses which potentially modify a *prima facie* duty of care. For this reason it has been suggested that in certain cases the courts should instead apply a test of 'reasonable expectations' according to which 'a clause should be regarded as an exclusion clause "in nature" if it would lead to the required contractual performance being less than that reasonably expected by the parties, when their expectations of performance are ascertained at the factual rather than the legal level'.[174] By extension this same approach could be applied to duties of care arising in tort, thereby offering a compromise between the 'all or nothing' approaches apparently adopted by the courts in the *Harris* v. *Wyre Forest* litigation.

The application of the test of 'reasonableness' is one of the most vexed questions to arise under the Act; it has been suggested that 'judicial development of the statutory discretion in commercial cases is both significant and difficult to predict'.[175] This development is surprising since the principal aim of the Act was to protect consumers in their dealings with businesses, although it is important to stress that the Act does also regulate relations between businesses in cases of negligence liability,[176] written standard-form contracts,[177] and certain specialised exchanges such as contracts for the sale of goods and hire purchase.[178] As far as tort liability is concerned, the application of the Act to commercial cases will be rare. The *Hedley Byrne* duty of care in tort does not *normally* arise between two business parties.[179] The leading authority on the application of the reasonableness test in consumer cases is now the judgment of Lord Griffiths in *Smith* v. *Bush*.[180] Lord Griffiths suggested that four matters, in particular, should be considered. Were the parties of equal bargaining power? In the case of advice, could the advice have been easily obtained elsewhere? How difficult was the task for which liability is being excluded? And what would be the practical consequences—for example, for

[172] [1990] 1 AC 831, 848–9.

[173] *Ibid.*, 873. Lord Griffiths cited Law Com. No. 69, *Exemption Clauses: Second Report by the Two Commissions* (Scot. Law Com. No. 39) (HC 605) (1975) in favour of the same interpretation: [1990] 1 AC 831, 857.

[174] E. Macdonald, 'Exclusion Clauses: The Ambit of s. 13(1) of the Unfair Contract Terms Act 1977' (1992) 12 *Leg. Stud.* 277, 287.

[175] J. Adams and R. Brownsword, 'The Unfair Contract Terms Act: A Decade of Discretion' (1988) 104 *LQR* 94, at 94.

[176] Section 2.

[177] *Ibid.*, s. 3.

[178] *Ibid.*, ss. 5–8.

[179] *Esso Petroleum Co.* v. *Mardon* [1976] QB 801 is a rare exception.

[180] [1990] 1 AC 831, 858 ff.

insurance—of the court's decision on the question of reasonableness? In this particular case, it had to be recognised that the purchasers of 'a dwelling house of modest value' were likely to be far less able to bear the risks attached to the property proving to be defective than the surveyors. For the latter could bear an incremental increase in their insurance premiums and, if necessary, pass part of the costs on to all house purchasers through an increase in fees. This was not a situation in which adequate insurance cover was unavailable, and it was also relevant that the surveyor and house purchaser were not far removed from being in a direct contractual relation, when there would have been no question of the exclusion being reasonable.

In certain situations the interaction between express contract terms, duties of care in tort, and the legislation governing exclusion and limitation may give rise to complex problems which have yet to receive a clear doctrinal treatment. In *Johnstone* v. *Bloomsbury Health Authority*[181] the plaintiff, a junior hospital doctor, was employed under a contract of employment under which his standard working week was forty hours. On top of this he was required to be available for an additional forty-eight hours a week on average. He sought an injunction and declaration to the effect that he should not be required to work any longer than was compatible with maintaining his health and safety, and damages for ill health brought on by the excessive hours which he had been required to work. The defendant argued that the express contract term should prevail and sought to have the claim struck out on the ground of failure to disclose a cause of action. This application failed, but the two judges making up the majority in the Court of Appeal gave different reasons for their decisions. Sir Nicolas Browne-Wilkinson V-C agreed with the dissenting judge, Leggatt LJ, on the relationship between concurrent tort and contract duties. The effect of the express term governing working hours was to cut down the scope of the employer's duty of care in tort to have regard for the employee's health and safety. According to Sir Nicolas:

The approach adopted in the *Tai Hing* case[182] shows that where there is a contractual relationship between the parties their respective rights and duties have to be analysed wholly in contractual terms and not as a mixture of duties in tort and contract. It necessarily follows that the scope of the duties owed by one party to the other will be defined by the terms of the contract between them. Therefore, if there is a term of the contract which is in general terms (e.g. a duty to take reasonable care not to injure the employee's health) and another term which is precise and detailed (e.g. an obligation to work on particular tasks notwithstanding that they involve an obvious health risk expressly referred to in the contract) the ambit of the employer's duty of care for the employee's health will be narrower than it would be were there no such express term . . . The express and implied terms of the contract have to be capable of co-existence without conflict.[183]

Where Sir Nicolas disagreed with Leggatt LJ was in the interpretation of the relevant contract term. Sir Nicolas regarded the employer as having no absolute right to call on

[181] [1992] 1 QB 333; see also the discussion in ch. 18, above.
[182] *Tai Hing Cotton Mill Ltd.* v. *Liu Chong Hing Bank Ltd.* [1986] AC 80.
[183] [1992] 1 QB 333, 350.

the employee to work the additional hours, but instead a right impliedly limited by the need to have regard for the employee's health. Sir Nicolas's view that a contract between parties necessarily excludes or limits the scope of the relevant duty in tort appears to pay no regard to the need to ensure that the precise requirements of the defences of *volenti* or exclusion are made out in the circumstances. As Stuart-Smith LJ pointed out, the contract term in question could not be construed either as an express exclusion clause or as tantamount to an assumption of risk in the sense required by *volenti non fit injuria*. Yet this was the effect of saying that the employee agreed, in effect, to take the risk of illness that arose from working long hours, even though it would foreseeably injure his health.[184] The use in this context of the *dictum* of Lord Scarman in *Tai Hing Cotton Mill Ltd.* v. *Liu Chong Hing Bank Ltd.*,[185] to the effect that the law would not search for liability in tort in a situation where the parties are in contractual relationship, seems misplaced. That latter instance involved a case concerning pure economic loss where the considerations are different. There is no authority for using contract, independently of the defences of *volenti* and exclusion, to cut down on a duty of care in tort which relates to physical health and safety, in particular now that legislation has abrogated the defence of common employment for cases of personal injury.

All three judges agreed that if the effect of the relevant contract term was to modify the employer's duty of care in tort, there was an arguable case that it was nullified by section 2(1) of UCTA.[186] It has not been conclusively established that UCTA applies to contracts of employment. It can be argued that the employer contracts in the course of his business and is therefore bound by section 2. Under paragraph 4 of Schedule 1 it is provided that 'section 2(1) and (2) do not extend to a contract of employment, except in favour of the employee': this appears to indicate that the Act does indeed apply in the employee's favour. In addition, if the employee can only with difficulty be regarded as a consumer for the purposes of the 1977 Act, he may nevertheless be able to invoke section 3 in a case where the contract is concluded on the employer's standard written terms.[187]

(C) EXTENDING THE EFFECT OF EXEMPTION CLAUSES TO THIRD PARTIES

A separate issue arising from the interaction of tort and contract concerns the use of tort to extend the benefit of certain exclusion and limitation clauses to third parties external to the contract containing the clause in question. This issue arises, for example, in a case where the owner of a site enters into a contract with a builder for work to be carried out, part of which is then subcontracted.[188] The main contract may contain an

[184] [1992] 1 QB 333, 343.

[185] T. Weir, 'Physician—Kill Thyself!' [1991] *CLJ* 397.

[186] See the analysis of E. Macdonald, 'Exclusion Clauses: The Ambit of s. 13(1) of the Unfair Contract Terms Act 1977' (1992) 12 *Leg. Stud.* 277, 285. An argument that the term could be struck down on the ground of public policy was rejected, cf. the views of Weir, 'Physician—Kill Thyself!' [1991] *CLJ* 397, at 399.

[187] Although for a contrary view, see *Brigden* v. *American Express Bank Ltd.* [2000] IRLR 94, 95–6.

[188] See e.g. *Norwich City Council* v. *Harvey* [1989] 1 WLR 828.

exclusion or limitation clause that purports to protect both the main contractor and the subcontractor. According to the common-law doctrine of privity of contract, the subcontractor is not in a position to take advantage of an exemption clause in a contract to which he is not a party; he may therefore have to bear the loss of any negligence in full. Another example is that of the liability of a stevedore who damages goods when unloading them at their destination.[189] There is usually an exemption clause in the contract between the carrier and the owner of the goods which limits the carrier's liability for damage to the goods and which purports to do the same for the stevedore. Again, the stevedore has difficulty taking advantage of a clause contained in a contract to which he is not a party. In a commercial context, where all parties know the risks in advance and will have taken out insurance accordingly, this possibility may upset the basis upon which the various risks were allocated when the contracts were drawn up.

There is, accordingly, a strong argument from a practical point of view for ensuring that the subcontractor receives the benefit of the exemption. One possibility would be to apply the defence of *volenti* against the plaintiff. Where he has had notice of the exemption, which he clearly has if it is contained in the main contract to which he is a party, the defence of *volenti* should apply to any claim he brings against the third-party defendant. This possibility was discussed by Lord Denning in *Scruttons Ltd.* v. *Midland Silicones Ltd.*[190] but rejected, for no very good reason, by the remainder of the House of Lords. One difficulty may be the problem of applying *volenti* to a limitation clause: it is normally a total defence to any claim, and not one that has the effect of restricting the plaintiff's damages. On the other hand, the defence appears to be flexible enough in principle to accommodate a situation like this.[191] In *The Eurymedon* the Privy Council came up with a different solution, namely an implied unilateral contract between (in this case) the owner of goods being shipped and the stevedore employed by the carrier to unload them. In the building case of *Southern Water Co.* v. *Carey* this solution was described, with some justice, as 'uncomfortably artificial'.[192] Here various subcontractors were sued for negligence in design and in the supply of equipment in the completion of a sewerage scheme. The main contract contained a clause exempting both the main contractor and his subcontractors from liability in respect of such defects or damage. The judge rejected analyses extending the effect of the clause in contract, on the basis of agency and unilateral contract, in favour of a finding that the clause in question negatived the existence of any duty of care in tort for the damage in question. This finding was, perhaps, acceptable, since the losses in question fell into the category of pure economic loss that, as we have seen, is rarely recoverable in the tort of negligence.[193] In *Norwich City Council* v. *Harvey*[194] the Court of Appeal reached the same outcome in a

[189] See e.g. *Scruttons Ltd.* v. *Midland Silicones Ltd.* [1962] AC 446.

[190] *Ibid.*, 488–9.

[191] See the judgment of Robert Goff LJ in *The Aliakmon* [1985] QB 350. His application of the doctrine of 'transferred loss' was rejected in the House of Lords [1986] AC 785. See ch. 3, Section 3(c) above.

[192] [1985] 2 All ER 1077, 1084.

[193] *Murphy* v. *Brentwood DC* [1991] 1 AC 398; see also the use of the same rationale in *Pacific Associates Inc.* v. *Baxter* [1990] QB 993.

[194] [1989] 1 WLR 828.

case where the subcontractor's negligence caused property damage to the site owner. The difficulty with this outcome is that, in contrast to pure economic loss, property damage is normally within the scope of the general duty of care in the tort of negligence. The negativing of the duty of care via the defence of *volenti* would have provided a better explanation. More generally, one reading of these cases 'is that they are really contract cases solved through tort', a route made necessary by the unduly restricted doctrine of privity of contract in English law.[195]

This criticism has now been addressed by the passage of the Contracts (Rights of Third Parties) Act 1999. This makes it possible for a third party to enforce a term in a contract if the contract either 'expressly provides that he may' or 'the term purports to confer a benefit on him' unless, in the second case, it appears form a 'proper construction of the contract' that the parties did not intend the term to be enforceable by him.[196] The Act makes explicit reference to the possibility of a third party enforcing an exclusion or limitation clause by this route,[197] and, while in other respects exempting many contracts for the carriage of goods from the coverage of the Act, preserves the Act's effect in relation to exclusion or limitation clauses for the benefit of a third party.[198] For present purposes it is particularly important to note that the third party must be identified in the contract by name, class or description for the Act to apply.[199] There are other limitations on the statutory action, which mean that the common law (which still remains in place) may continue to be relevant in cases not covered by the Act, although the existence of the statutory action may make the courts less willing to develop the common law one.[200]

5. ILLEGALITY

Illegality can only rarely succeed as a defence to liability in tort. As Sedley LJ has pointed out:

> in the field of what one can call ordinary personal injury litigation the turpitude doctrine has been consciously eliminated by the courts on policy grounds. In road accident cases, for example, it is common enough to find that the injured claimant has contributed to the accident by speeding or driving with faulty brakes; but I know of no decision that such a claimant cannot sue another driver who has negligently caused his injuries. Nor can I see any justice in so deciding when the criminal law is there to deal his criminality and the power to apportion damages [under the Law Reform (Contributory Negligence) Act 1945] will deal with his own contribution to his injuries.[201]

195 B. S. Markesinis, 'Doctrinal Clarity in Tort Litigation: A Comparative Lawyer's Viewpoint' (1991) 25 *International Lawyer* 953, 963; and see our discussion in ch. 3, Section 3(c), above.

196 Contracts (Rights of Third Parties) Act 1999, s. 1(2).

197 *Ibid.*, s. 1(6), applied in *Precis Ltd.* v. *William M. Mercer Ltd.* [2004] EWCA Civ 114.

198 *Ibid.*, s. 6(5). 199 *Ibid.*, s. 1(3).

200 See J. Beatson, *Anson's Law of Contract* (28th edn., 2002), at 469.

201 In a dissenting judgment in *Vellino* v. *Chief Constable of Greater Manchester* [2001] 1 WLR 218. In this case the majority of the Court of Appeal (Schiemann LJ and Sir Murray Stuart Smith) held that the police owed

In *Pitts* v. *Hunt*[202] Dillon LJ said, 'it is clear for a start that the fact that a plaintiff was engaged in an illegal activity which brought about his injury does not automatically bring it about that his claim for damages for personal injury as a result of the negligence of the defendant must be dismissed'. Something more precise is needed. Two formulations of the defence have, from time to time, found favour with the courts. According to one, the defence is based on an overriding consideration of public policy: to compensate the plaintiff in certain cases would either affront the 'public conscience' or promote criminal acts or other behaviour deemed contrary to the general good. This point of view is expressed in the usage of the maxim *ex turpi causa non oritur actio*, which roughly translated means that no cause of action may be founded upon an immoral or illegal act.[203] According to the other formulation, the defence is based on a negation of liability in a situation where the claimant's participation in illegality makes it impossible for the court to assess the relevant standard of care. An example would be where both plaintiff and defendant were engaged in a joint illegal enterprise, such as robbing a bank or joy-riding in a stolen car.[204] This test is more precise and, in most contexts, easier to apply than the rather open-ended test of public policy.[205] However, it is unlikely that the defence can be confined to this second category. Its use may be uncommon, but the courts appear to treat it as a defence that may be kept in reserve for an appropriate case and have accordingly retained a loose approach to defining its scope and rationale.[206]

Both formulations of the defence were adopted in various judgments of the Court of Appeal in *Pitts* v. *Hunt*.[207] The plaintiff, a passenger on a motorcycle being driven by the defendant, was seriously injured when the latter negligently collided with another vehicle. He was killed and the plaintiff brought an action for damages against his estate. The plaintiff knew when he set off on the journey that the deceased was uninsured and unlicensed. Both had been drinking alcohol for most of the evening; and the plaintiff had encouraged the deceased to drive in a recklessly dangerous manner, to the extent that the lives of other road-users had been put at risk. The court agreed unanimously that the defence was made out, but disagreed on its proper basis. Balcombe LJ and, to a certain extent, Dillon LJ relied on the view of Mason J of the High Court of Australia in *Jackson* v. *Harrison*. There the view was taken that the denial of relief should not be based on the nature of the illegal activity in the sense of the degree of moral turpitude involved, but rather on the 'more secure foundation' that 'the plaintiff must fail when

no duty to effect the arrest of a suspect in such a way as to minimise the risk that he would harm himself in the course of trying to escape. The majority also held, *obiter*, that the illegality defence would have applied on the facts had there been a duty of care. For further discussion of the scope of the illegality defence in this context, see R. Glofcheski, 'Plaintiff's Illegality as a Bar to Recovery of Personal Injury Damages' (Select Bibliography).

202 [1991] 1 QB 24, 53.

203 *Holman* v. *Johnson* (1775) 1 Cowp. 341, 343; 98 ER 1120 (Lord Mansfield).

204 *Jackson* v. *Harrison* (1978) 138 CLR 438.

205 See C. A. Hopkins, 'Two Tales of Topers' [1991] *CLJ* 27, 28.

206 The lack of clarity of the defence has been the subject of discussion by the Law Commission: Law Commission, *The Illegality Defence in Tort*, Consultation Paper No. 160 (2001).

207 [1991] 1 QB 24.

the character of the enterprise in which the parties are engaged is such that it is impossible for the court to determine the standard of care which is appropriate to be observed'. This formulation was 'more limited in its application—and for that reason fairer in its operation'.[208] In applying this test, the High Court of Australia has denied recovery to plaintiffs injured in the course of joy-riding[209] while allowing a claim made by a plaintiff injured by the careless driving of one whom he knew to be disqualified at the time of the accident.[210] In this case, the disqualification had no bearing on the standard of care that the plaintiff could have expected of the defendant. Similarly, in the English case of *Ashton* v. *Turner*[211] a burglar who was injured while in the course of escaping from the scene of the crime in a getaway car was held to have no cause of action in negligence against the driver of the car, whose reckless driving caused the collision. In *Pitts* v. *Hunt* the involvement of the plaintiff in the reckless and dangerous driving of the deceased made it 'impossible to determine the appropriate standard of care', with the consequence, in Balcombe LJ's view, that the deceased owed the plaintiff no duty of care.[212]

Beldam LJ based his judgment, by contrast, on public policy, namely the policy enshrined in various Acts of Parliament of promoting road safety by creating the offences of causing death by reckless driving and driving when under the influence of drink and/or drugs. He rejected an argument to the effect that the law did not recognise the existence of a duty of care between the deceased and the plaintiff. The judge thus said: 'I am not convinced of the wisdom of a policy which might encourage a belief that the duty to behave responsibly in driving motor vehicles is diminished even to the limited extent that they may in certain circumstances not owe a duty to each other, particularly when those circumstances involve conduct which is highly dangerous to others.'[213] One possible response to the last point is that there is no reason why the relevant standard of care should be the same with regard to all road-users.[214]

However, there are numerous other cases in which the courts have taken a similarly broad-brush approach to public policy. Lord Diplock referred on one occasion to a rule 'that the courts will not enforce a right which would otherwise be enforceable if the right arises out of an act committed by the person asserting that right...which is regarded by the court as sufficiently anti-social to justify the court's refusing to enforce that right'.[215] In some recent decisions the courts have taken the view that the public policy basis of the defence is founded on the need to deter illegal acts, rather than the looser notion of disallowing claims which affront the 'public conscience'. In *Clunis* v. *Camden and Islington Health Authority*[216] the plaintiff, who had a history of mental

208 *Jackson* v. *Harrison* (1978) 138 CLR 438, 455–6.

209 *Smith* v. *Jenkins* (1970) 44 ALJR 78, *Bondarenko* v. *Summers* (1969) 69 SR (NSW) 269.

210 *Jackson* v. *Harrison* (1978) 138 CLR 438.

211 [1981] QB 137.

212 [1991] 1 QB 25, 50–1.

213 *Ibid.*, 47.

214 See ch. 4, above, for discussion of this point in the context of breach of duty.

215 *Hardy* v. *Motor Insurers' Bureau* [1964] 2 QB 745, 767.

216 [1998] QB 978, doubting, on this point, *Meah* v. *McCreamer (No. 1)* [1985] 1 All ER 367; see also *Murphy* v. *Culhane* [1977] QB 94, *Tinsley* v. *Milligan* [1994] 1 AC 340. In *Clunis* v. *United Kingdom*, Application No.

illness, was discharged from hospital and placed under the 'after-care' of the defendant health authority, a form of 'care in the community'. While in this situation, he committed an unprovoked attack upon a stranger in the London Underground, killing him. He was then convicted of manslaughter. He sued the defendant in negligence on the ground that the medical staff caring for him should have realised that he was a danger to others, and that had they treated him properly he would not have committed the assault for which he was imprisoned. The case was dismissed on various grounds, one of which was illegality: according to Beldam LJ, a manslaughter conviction ruled out the plaintiff's claim unless it could have been shown that he did not know what he was doing, which was not the case here.

Whichever test is adopted in a particular case, it is necessary to show that there was a causal link between the illegality in which the plaintiff was implicated and the loss of which he is now complaining. The 'cause' to be identified here is not simply the 'but-for' or 'factual cause'; the court may also be required to make a more complex judgment on the degree to which the plaintiff's illegality can be deemed to be a 'legal cause' of his loss. Thus:

> If two burglars, A and B, agree to open a safe by means of explosives, and A so negligently handles the explosive charge as to injure B, B might find some difficulty in maintaining an action for negligence against A. But if A and B are proceeding to the premises which they intend burglariously to enter, and before they enter them B picks A's pocket and steals his watch, I cannot prevail on myself to believe that A could not sue in tort . . . The theft is totally unconnected with the burglary.[217]

A's presence at the scene of the crime is a 'mere condition' of his loss. Similarly, in *Saunders* v. *Edwards*[218] the plaintiff brought an action for fraudulent misrepresentation against the defendant over the sale to him of the defendant's flat. The two of them had previously agreed to undervalue the flat in favour of inflating the value of certain chattels included in the sale, with the aim of avoiding the payment of stamp duty. Since the fraud on the Inland Revenue was wholly unconnected with the fraud perpetrated by the defendant on the plaintiff, the latter's action was allowed to proceed. In *Pitts* v. *Hunt* Dillon LJ considered that the plaintiff was barred from claiming damages since his loss arose 'directly *ex turpi causa*'.[219]

A direct, causal connection in the sense described above is a necessary element of the defence, but it cannot be enough on its own: Dillon LJ's approach begs the question of exactly what is *turpi causa*. In making this assessment the courts can hardly avoid making some difficult value judgements about the degree of 'moral turpitude' of the plaintiff's act and balancing this against the nature and extent of the loss he sustained. In *Pitts* v. *Hunt* all three members of the Court of Appeal considered that the plaintiff's

45049/98, judgment of 11 Sept. 2001, the ECtHR held that the denial of the claim in *Clunis* did not amount to a breach of Art. 6 of the ECHR.

217 *National Coal Board* v. *England* [1954] AC 403, 428–9 (Lord Asquith of Bishopstone).

218 [1987] 1 WLR 1116.

219 [1991] 1 QB 24, 24, 60.

behaviour was indeed morally reprehensible—it had put the lives of other road-users at risk. The fact that the plaintiff himself suffered serious injuries, including permanent partial paralysis, did not weigh greatly in his favour. By contrast, the fraud against the Inland Revenue perpetrated by the plaintiff in *Saunders* v. *Edwards* was not considered sufficiently serious to bar him from suing the defendant for the consequences of *his* fraud; perhaps a rather surprising conclusion. But that decision is a reminder of how limited the defence of illegality is. As Bingham LJ put it, 'it is unacceptable that the court should, on the first indication of unlawfulness affecting any aspect of a transaction, draw up its skirts and refuse all assistance to the plaintiff, no matter how serious his loss nor how disproportionate his loss to the unlawfulness of his conduct'.[220]

6. NECESSITY

Certain applications of the defence of necessity have already been considered. Its principal significance is in relation to the torts of intentional interference or trespass; necessity can rarely justify negligence in the sense of a lack of care.[221] Necessity may be a defence to the tort of trespass to the person in the contexts of medical treatment and emergencies.[222] As far as the torts of trespass to goods and trespass to land are concerned, damage to property may be justified by the presence of an imminent danger to life and limb. 'The necessity for saving life has at all times been considered a proper ground for inflicting such damage as may be necessary upon another's property.'[223] In some cases, a countervailing threat to property will suffice, but here the scope of the defence is strictly limited. In each case the defendant must be shown to have acted reasonably in the circumstances.[224]

7. INEVITABLE ACCIDENT, ACT OF GOD

In the context of the tort of negligence, the plea of 'inevitable accident' is akin to saying that the defendant was not at fault, so this is not so much a defence as a denial of one of the main elements of liability. It operates as a defence only when *res ipsa loquitur* is pleaded and the defendant has to rebut what is akin to a reversal of the normal burden

220 [1987] 1 WLR 1116, 1134, and see *Webb* v. *Chief Constable of Merseyside Police* [2000] QB 427: the illegality defence did not prevent the claimants, who had been acquitted of drug-trafficking charges, suing for the return of money seized by the police on suspicion that it represented the proceeds of drug trafficking, notwithstanding a finding that, on the balance of probabilities (the lower standard of proof required in a civil claim), this was the source of the money.

221 See *Rigby* v. *Chief Constable of Northamptonshire* [1985] 1 WLR 1242, discussed in ch. 16, above.

222 See ch. 9, above.

223 *Southport Corp.* v. *Esso Petroleum Co.* [1954] QB 182 (Devlin J).

224 See the judgment of Lord Goff in *Re F* [1990] 2 AC 1, discussed in ch. 9, above.

of proof. In cases of strict liability, where fault is irrelevant, inevitable accident may also constitute a defence.[225]

'Act of God' amounts to a claim that an accident occurred as a result of natural forces outside the control of the defendant or anyone else; as such it may be a defence to a claim of liability under *Rylands* v. *Fletcher*.[226]

8. AUTHORISATION

Authorisation is not, as such, a defence, but there are a number of instances in which lawful authority exists for persons to commit what would otherwise be torts. For example, police powers of search and arrest which are now largely defined by statute—that is, the Police and Criminal Evidence Act 1984—take priority over the common law in relation to the torts of trespass to the person and trespass to property.[227] Damage to property may be authorised by statute in the case of bodies set up to execute public works or to carry out public functions. Legal issues here concern the notion of negligence in the exercise of a statutory power[228] and the defence of statutory authority in the tort of nuisance.[229] One should also note the existence of the doctrine of 'act of state', according to which authorisation or subsequent endorsement by the Crown acts as a defence to an otherwise tortious act committed against a foreign citizen on foreign soil.[230]

9. LIMITATION OF ACTION

It is a basic principle of the law of civil liability that actions should be barred after the passage of a certain period of time, in order to avoid both the administrative expense of examining 'stale claims' and potential injustice to defendants of reviving old wrongs. Limitation rules may also help to promote a degree of certainty in the allocation of liability, which is of assistance to insurance companies. Limitation Acts, the first dating from 1623, have accordingly required plaintiffs to initiate legal action within a specified time. The present limitation periods are mainly to be found in the Limitation Act 1980, as amended by the Latent Damage Act 1986 and by the Consumer Protection Act 1987. The basic principle is that actions in tort are subject to a limitation period of six years

225 See *Southport Corp.* v. *Esso Petroleum Co. Ltd.* [1954] QB 182 (Devlin J).

226 See *Nicholls* v. *Marsland* (1876) 2 Ex. D 1, *Greenock Corp.* v. *Caledonian Railway Co.* [1917] AC 556; ch. 16, above.

227 The details of police powers lie outside the scope of this book.

228 See ch. 8, above.

229 See ch. 13, above.

230 *Buron* v. *Denman* (1848) 2 Ex. 167, *Johnstone* v. *Pedlar* [1921] 2 AC 262, *Walker* v. *Baird* [1892] AC 491, *Attorney-General* v. *Nissan* [1970] AC 179.

from the date on which the cause of action accrued.[231] But there are some important exceptions. Thus, in actions in tort for damages for personal injury, the relevant period is three years. This starts to run either from the date on which the cause of action accrued or from the date upon which the person injured first had knowledge of his injury, a concept that the Act then develops in greater detail.[232] This extension of the basic period is based on the notion of the 'discoverability' of the damage. A further exception incorporating a version of the discoverability test is provided for in cases of latent damage to property; this is examined in detail below.[233] The normal limitation period for claims under the Consumer Protection Act 1987, whether for personal injuries or for other forms of damage actionable under that Act, is three years,[234] and this period also applies to claims in defamation.[235]

A complete account of the details of limitation of actions lies outside the scope of this book.[236] However, certain features of the defence will be outlined here. The defence has become increasingly important as a source of case law on the nature of the cause of action in tort and on the interrelation of concurrent liabilities in contract and tort. Three issues in particular will be considered: the concept of the accrual of a cause of action; the limited statutory concessions made towards the discoverability test; and the problems raised in this context by two difficult cases of concurrent duties in contract and tort, namely those of defective buildings and professional negligence.

(A) THE ACCRUAL OF THE CAUSE OF ACTION

The basic rule that the limitation period begins to run from the date on which the claimant's cause of action accrued has, since the Limitation Act 1939, been subject to a power of the court to grant relief in certain cases such as deliberate concealment or other fraud by the defendant.[237] These limited provisions notwithstanding, the basic rule is capable of causing injustice in a case where the claimant's cause of action has accrued without him being aware of it. This will not often occur in the case of torts actionable *per se* (such as battery or conversion) because the claimant will normally be aware of the act of interference which constitutes the tort, but it is possible that it will. A large number of cases have been brought recent years by the victims of sexual assaults and related abuse suffered in care homes. In such cases, the nature and extent of the abuse, and their link to psychiatric illness suffered in later years, have only become clear to claimants many years after the assaults in question took place, often as a result of psychiatric treatment received in adulthood. Where psychiatric illness arises, in this way, as a consequence of intentional torts, the case falls under the basic rule in section 2 of the

231 Limitation Act 1980, s. 2.
232 *Ibid.*, ss. 11 and 14.
233 *Ibid.*, ss. 14A, 14B; Latent Damage Act 1986, ss. 1, 3–5.
234 Consumer Protection Act 1987, s. 11A.
235 Administration of Justice Act 1985, s. 57.
236 For a full account, see *Clerk and Lindsell on Torts* (19th revised edn., 2005), ch. 33.
237 Section 26; see now Limitation Act 1980, s. 33.

Act, and is therefore subject to the normal, non-extendable limitation period of six years. The discoverability rules which apply under sections 11–14 of the Act only work in the case of claims of physical injury arising from negligence or related torts.[238] This odd effect of the way in which the Act is structured is capable of causing considerable injustice; claims arising from intentional torts are not entirely defeated, but claimants have to rely on the discretionary powers of the courts under section 33 of the Act, rather than being able to begin litigation by right.

In torts requiring damage, the starting position is that the cause of action accrues when the damage is *first* sustained, regardless of the claimant's knowledge. Although the damage may increase in scale and extent over time, the cause of action accrues when the damage first starts to occur, and there will be no new cause of action unless a fresh causative factor is involved or a different kind of damage is sustained. In *Cartledge* v. *E. Jopling & Sons Ltd.*[239] the plaintiff contracted pneumoconiosis by inhaling noxious dust at his place of work over a number of years. Pneumoconiosis is a disease which gradually destroys tissue in the lungs over a period of time, without the victim being immediately aware that this is happening. The employer had replaced the unsafe system of work which had caused the problem more than six years (then the relevant period) before the plaintiff issued his writ. The House of Lords held that the plaintiff's cause of action had accrued when the initial damage to the lung tissue took place, and that on this basis the claim was out of time. Lord Pearce, with whom the other Lords agreed, said that it was irrelevant that the extent of the damage was revealed only gradually: there can only be one cause of action in respect of a particular injury. Lord Pearce drew a distinction between the initial injury (or in property cases, defect) and the damage flowing from it, adopting the following *dictum* of Lord Halsbury in *Darley Main Colliery Co.* v. *Mitchell*:[240]

> No one will think of disputing the proposition that for one cause of action you must recover all damages incident to it by law once and for ever. A house that has received a shock may not at once show all the damage done to it, but it is damaged none the less to the extent that it is damaged, and the fact that the damage only manifests itself later on by stages does not alter the fact that the damage is there; and so of the more complex mechanism of the human frame, the damage is done in a railway accident, the whole machinery is injured, though it may escape the eye or even the consciousness of the sufferer at the time, the later stages of suffering are but the manifestations of the damage done, and consequent upon the injury originally sustained.

The ruling in *Cartledge* also turned on a point of statutory interpretation: since Parliament had allowed an express exception to the basic rule in the case of fraud or concealment, to discover an implied exception based on the discoverability test would have amounted to judicial legislation. As Lord Reid put it, 'the necessary implication from [s. 26 of the Limitation Act 1939] is that, where fraud or mistake is not involved,

[238] See *KR and Others* v. *Bryn Alyn Community Holdings Ltd. (In Liquidation)* [2003] QB 1441; *A* v. *Hoare* [2006] EWCA Civ. 395 (rejecting an argument that the outcome on this aspect of the *Bryn Alyn* case was contrary to Art. 6 of the European Convention on Human Rights).

[239] [1963] AC 758.

[240] (1886) 11 App. Cas. 127.

time begins to run whether or not the damage could be discovered. So the mischief in the present case can only be prevented by further legislation.'[241]

Parliament duly responded by enacting through the Limitation Act 1963 a limited discoverability test for personal injury claims only,[242] the provisions of which are considered below. The issue of latent damage in non-personal-injury cases—cases of property damage and financial loss—was not addressed at this time. When it came before the House of Lords in *Pirelli General Cable Works Ltd.* v. *Oscar Faber & Partners*,[243] the House felt obliged to follow its earlier decision in *Cartledge*. In *Pirelli* the defendants, consulting engineers, contracted with the plaintiffs in 1969 to advise on the design and construction of a services block on their factory site. The block included a chimney. The defendants recommended as inner lining for the chimney a material, Lytag, which was relatively new and which turned out to be unsuitable for this purpose. The chimney was built in the summer of 1969 and it was found that cracks must have appeared in it not later than April 1970. The damage to the chimney was not, however, discovered until November 1977, whereupon it had to be repaired at the plaintiffs' expense. The plaintiffs sued the defendants for negligence in the design of the chimney and the judge allowed the claim on the basis that the relevant date for the purposes of limitation was the time at which the damage could, with reasonable diligence, have been discovered. He assessed this to have been some time in October 1972, so that the writ was issued within six years of time starting to run. The Court of Appeal, following its own earlier decision in *Sparham-Souter* v. *Town and Country Developments (Essex) Ltd.*[244] upheld this judgment, but it was overturned in the House of Lords. Again, statutory interpretation was important: according to Lord Fraser of Tullybelton, 'it must . . . be taken that [in 1963] Parliament deliberately left the law unchanged'[245] so far as damage other than personal injury was concerned. Lord Fraser thought that in cases of latent defects in property, the cause of action would accrue when the defect in question led to damage to the structure. This 'will commonly consist of cracks coming into existence as a result of the defect even though the cracks or the defect may be undiscovered and undiscoverable'.[246] It could even accrue earlier than this in a case where the 'defect is so gross that the building is doomed from the start', although such cases would be 'exceptional'. He also held that in a case of successive owners of the property, once time began to run against one owner it would start to run against them all: no purchaser could be in a better position than the person he bought from. Once again Parliament had to act to introduce a form of the discoverability test through the Latent Damage Act 1986 which, amongst other things, inserted sections 14A and 14B into the Limitation Act 1980.

241 [1963] AC 758, 772.

242 Limitation Act 1963; see now Limitation Act 1980, ss. 11–14.

243 [1983] 2 AC 1, applied in *Kettelman* v. *Hansel Properties Ltd.* [1987] AC 189 and *Abbott* v. *Will Gannon & Smith Ltd.* [2005] EWCA Civ. 198.

244 [1976] QB 858.

245 [1983] 2 AC 1, 15.

246 *Ibid.*, 17.

(B) THE DISCOVERABILITY TESTS UNDER THE LIMITATION ACT 1980

As far as personal injury caused by negligence, nuisance or other breach of duty (including contractual and statutory duties) is concerned, the 1980 Act now provides that the relevant limitation period is three years from *either* the occurrence of the damage *or* the 'date of knowledge' of the injured party.[247] Should the claimant die without initiating an action within this three-year period, the period is extended by a further three years either from his death or from the 'date of knowledge' of the personal representative.[248] Similarly with claims under the Fatal Accidents Act: there will be no claim if the deceased's own claim would have been time-barred, but if not, the deceased's dependants have three years to bring their Fatal Accidents Act claim either from his death or from their 'date of knowledge'.[249]

The 'date of knowledge' is defined by section 14(1) of the Act as the first date on which the claimant has knowledge of the following facts: (*a*) that the injury in question was significant; (*b*) that the injury was attributable in whole or in part to the act or omission which is alleged to constitute negligence, nuisance or breach of duty; (*c*) the identity of the defendant; and (*d*) if it is alleged that the act or omission was that of a person other than the defendant, the identity of that person and the additional facts supporting the bringing of an action against the defendant. The claimant's knowledge (or lack of it) of his legal position, as opposed to his knowledge of the facts going to make up the cause of action, is irrelevant here. The Act goes on to say in section 14(2) that an injury is significant if the claimant 'would reasonably have considered it sufficiently serious to justify his instituting proceedings for damages against a defendant who did not dispute liability and was able to satisfy a judgment'. In *McCoubrey* v. *Ministry of Defence* the Court of Appeal, overruling a number of earlier authorities, held that the test under this provision is an objective one: the test is 'what a reasonable person who has suffered the particular injury would consider'.[250] The Act specifies that the claimant is deemed to have certain knowledge, namely that which he might reasonably have been expected to acquire 'from facts observable or ascertainable by him' or from 'facts ascertainable by him with the help of medical or other appropriate expert advice which it is reasonable for him to seek'. As far as expert advice is concerned the claimant will have done enough if he has taken reasonable steps to obtain and, if necessary, to act on the advice.[251] In other words, as long as he does this he will not be deemed

247 Limitation Act 1980, s. 11(2). By virtue of s. 11(1), this period applies to claims for personal injury arising from negligence, nuisance, or other breach of duty (including breach of contract and breach of statutory duty). On the meaning of 'damages in respect of personal injuries' in this context, see *Walkin* v. *South Manchester HA* [1995] 1 WLR 1543.

248 See Limitation Act 1980, s. 11(4)-(6).

249 *Ibid.*, ss. 12–13.

250 [2007] EWCA Civ. 17, at [47]. The 'objective' interpretation of s. 14(2) was necessitated, according to the Court, by the earlier decision of the House of Lords in *Adams* v. *Bracknell Forest BC* [2005] 1 AC 76. See also *Catholic Care Diocese of Leeds* v. *Young* [2006] EWCA Civ. 1534.

251 Limitation Act 1980, s. 14(3), on which, see *Adams* v. *Bracknell Forest BC* [2005] 1 AC 76.

to know facts that the expert fails to ascertain or fails to report to him. None of this helps a claimant who receives bad legal advice as opposed to being badly advised on the facts of his claim. In the event of being poorly advised on the law, the claimant's only option is to have the court exercise its discretion to disapply the normal limitation rules[252] or to sue his advisers for negligence.

There is a separate regime for latent damage in cases of negligence leading to property or financial loss. Section 14A(4)(a) of the 1980 Act, as inserted by the Latent Damage Act 1986, begins by preserving the basic rule that the period of limitation starts with the accrual of the cause of action and runs for six years.[253] Paragraph (b) of that sub-section then sets up an exception in the case of latent defects, in respect of which there is a three-year period from the 'earliest date on which the plaintiff or any person in whom the cause of action was vested before him had both the knowledge required for bringing an action for damages in respect of the relevant damage and a right to bring the action'. 'Knowledge' is defined in more or less the same way as it is for personal-injury cases (above)[254]. Section 14B of the 1980 Act then provides for a 'long-stop' according to which the claimant will necessarily be time-barred once fifteen years have elapsed from the defendant's breach of duty. In addition, section 3 of the Latent Damage Act 1986 provides that in the case of successive owners of property with a latent defect which has not yet been discovered, a fresh cause of action accrues each time a new purchaser acquires an interest. Hence the new purchaser will himself be able to take advantage of the discoverability period of three years. Finally, the 1986 Act provides that the provisions of sections 14A and 14B (1980) and section 3 (1986) do not affect causes of action accruing before the 1986 Act came into force (18 September 1986).[255] Actions arising under the Consumer Protection Act 1987 are subject to a basic limitation period of three years and a 'long-stop' of ten years.[256]

(C) LIMITATION AND CONCURRENT DUTIES IN CONTRACT AND TORT

The context in which the courts have had the greatest difficulty in applying the rules of limitation concerns that of concurrent duties in contract and tort. The period of limitation in contract begins to run when the relevant breach of contract takes place and not, as in tort, when the damage is suffered. The problems this poses were explained by Mustill LJ in *Société Commerciale de Réassurance* v. *ERAS (International) Ltd.*:[257]

The different treatment for limitation purposes of claims in contract and in tort is... unsatisfactory because: (1) whatever the legal logic, the fact that claims in contract and in tort

[252] *Ibid.*, s. 33(1); see e.g. *Ramsden* v. *Lee* [1992] 2 All ER 204.

[253] For discussion of these and other aspects of the 1986 Act see N. J. Mullany, 'Reform of the Law of Latent Damage' (1991) 54 *MLR* 349.

[254] For a recent application of the 'knowledge' test under s. 14A, in a case involving financial loss arising from allegedly negligent advice, see *Haward* v. *Fawcetts* [2006] 1 WLR 682.

[255] Latent Damage Act 1986, s. 4.

[256] Limitation Act 1980, s. 11A.

[257] [1992] 2 All ER 82. See also the comments of Mustill LJ in *Bell* v. *Peter Browne & Co.* [1990] 1 QB 495, 511.

between the same parties arising out of the same facts become time-barred on dates which may well be years apart offends common sense; (2) the existence of different rules for what may really be the same claims forces the law into unnatural complications. Whatever the historical justification for holding that there are concurrent rights of action in contract and tort, nobody we believe would trouble nowadays to insist on the difference, but for the fact that one form of claim (usually the one in tort) offers procedural advantages. This is not a sound basis for the development of a practical and self-consistent law of negligence; (3) so far as limitation is concerned, the rules regarding the accrual of the cause of action tend to push the evolution of substantive law in the wrong direction. In most if not all cases a plaintiff will be better off by framing his action in tort whereas, in our judgment, if a contract is in existence this is the natural vehicle for recourse.

The Court of Appeal nevertheless felt obliged to hold that section 14A of the Limitation Act has no application to cases of breach of contract.[258] This is because section 14A simply refers to 'negligence', whereas section 11, which embodies the discoverability rule for personal-injury claims, specifically includes breach of contract within its scope. Under these circumstances the court concluded that the drafter had intended section 14A to be confined to latent damage caused by the *tort of negligence*, but the result is to exacerbate the tendency described by Mustill LJ, namely the divergence between the limitation periods governing contract and tort respectively.

Pirelli General Cable Works Ltd. v. *Oscar Faber & Partners*[259] was itself a case in which the parties had entered into a contractual relationship and in which the plaintiff's sole purpose in formulating the claim in tort was to take advantage of the extended limitation period. The significance of the *Pirelli* ruling and of the Latent Damage Act has been thrown into some doubt, however, by the later decision of the House of Lords in *Murphy* v. *Brentwood District Council.*[260] This is because Lord Fraser's judgment in *Pirelli* was based on the now-discredited theory, derived from *Anns* v. *Merton London Borough Council*,[261] that the loss suffered by the owner of the building is physical or property damage rather than, as *Murphy* decided, pure economic loss. In *Murphy* Lord Keith of Kinkel said of *Pirelli*:

If the plaintiffs had happened to discover the defect before any damage had occurred, there would seem to be no good reason for holding that they would not have had a cause of action in tort at that stage, without having to wait until some damage had occurred. They would have suffered economic loss through having a defective chimney upon which they required to expend money for the purpose of removing the defect. It would seem that in a case such as *Pirelli*, where the tortious liability arose out of a contractual relationship with professional people, the duty extended to take reasonable care not to cause economic loss to the client by the advice given. The plaintiffs built the chimney as they did in reliance on that advice. The case could accordingly fall within the principle of *Hedley Byrne & Co. Ltd.* v. *Heller & Partners Ltd.*[262]

[258] Confirming the approach of Deputy Judge Rokison QC in *Iron Trades Mutual Insurance Co. Ltd.* v. *J. K. Buckenham Ltd.* [1990] 1 All ER 808.

[259] [1983] 2 AC 1.

[260] [1991] 1 AC 398.

[261] [1978] AC 728.

[262] [1991] 1 AC 398, 466.

The implications of *Murphy* for latent damage to buildings were considered by May J in *Nitrigin Eirreann Teoranta* v. *Inco Alloys Ltd*.[263] In June 1981 the defendants manufactured and supplied to the plaintiffs alloy tubing for use as part of a chemical production plant. The tubing was supplied under a contract agreed by the two parties. In July 1983 the tubing was found to be cracked, and on 27 June 1984 it ruptured completely, leading to an explosion which damaged the plant and caused it to be shut down for a period. The writ was issued on 21 June 1990. The judge held that the cause of action did not accrue until the explosion of June 1984, with the result that the action was in time. He rejected the defendant's argument that the cause of action accrued when the cracks first appeared in the tubing. He further concluded that *Pirelli* could no longer be read as authority for liability in negligence based on physical loss in such a case; because the piping was supplied in a defective condition the loss was properly characterised as purely economic. Although *Pirelli* could be explained by *Hedley Byrne*, this was not possible in the *Inco Alloys* case because there was no pre-tort special relationship between the parties: such a relationship, the judge held, cannot arise simply on the basis of a commercial contract of sale between the parties. However, he held that there was a cause of action for the damage caused to the rest of the plant by the explosion: this was physical damage to property other than the product which was supplied, and so fell within the scope of the general duty of care.

If *Pirelli* is to be reclassified as a case of pure economic loss, there are four possibilities for when the cause of action accrues:[264] the date on which the advice was given and relied upon; the date on which the chimney was built; the date of physical damage; and the date on which the economic loss was reasonably discoverable. If the first option is adopted, the implications for limitation are considerable: many claims will be defeated as time will start to run well before the loss is discoverable. This is however one possible interpretation of Lord Keith's remarks in *Murphy*.[265] The second and third possibilities are difficult to reconcile with various *dicta* in *Pirelli* and *Murphy*.[266] The most attractive option, both in conceptual and policy terms, is the fourth: no economic loss is suffered until the claimant becomes aware of the defect and of its financial consequences. This would bring forward the date of the accrual of the cause of action to the point at which most actions of this kind would no longer be caught by the limitation defence. This was the view of Deane J in the Australian case of *Sutherland Shire Council* v. *Heyman*. 'For so long as the inadequacy of the foundations is neither known nor manifest, no identifiable loss has come home; if the purchaser or the tenant sells the freehold or leasehold estate within that time, he or she will sustain no loss by reason of the inadequacy of the foundations.' It is only when the defect becomes known that the loss of market value in the property occurs.[267] Support for this position also comes from *obiter dicta* of Lord Lloyd of Berwick in the Privy Council case of *Invercargill City Council* v. *Hamlin*[268]

263 [1992] 1 All ER 854.

264 See E. McKendrick, '*Pirelli* Re-Examined' (Select Bibliography).

265 R. O'Dair, 'Professional Negligence: Some Limiting Factors' (1992) 55 *MLR* 405, 406.

266 See McKendrick (Select Bibliography), at 333–5.

267 (1985) 157 CLR 424, 505.

268 [1996] AC 624, 648.

and of Tuckey LJ in the recent Court of Appeal decision in *Abbott* v. *Will Gannon & Smith Ltd.*[269]

This approach would have the beneficial (if perhaps rather paradoxical) effect of harmonising the *Pirelli* test, which is based on the *occurrence* of damage, with the test of the *discoverability* of damage which seeks to avoid the situation in which the claim is eliminated before he even knows about it. The Latent Damage Act, however, is clearly based on the assumption that the cause of action in latent-defect cases accrues *before* the economic consequences of the defect are discovered; hence the need for the special statutory test of discoverability in sections 14A and 14B of the Limitation Act. But more generally the decision in *Murphy* and, in particular, Lord Keith's attempt to reclassify *Pirelli* as a *Hedley Byrne* case, have undercut the entire basis of that Act. Now that damage caused by defective buildings is classified as purely financial (unless the defect brings about personal injury or damage to *other* property) and now that *Murphy* has limited very substantially the scope of the duty of care with regard to such pure economic loss, far fewer claimants in building cases will have a good cause of action. With the common law offering decreased protection, the Defective Premises Act 1972 becomes more important; but claims arising under this Act are outside sections 14A and 14B of the Limitation Act, as interpreted by the Court of Appeal in the *ERAS* case.[270] *Murphy* has made it imperative to consider further reform of the Limitation Acts which should involve a more complete reassessment of *Pirelli*. Courts in Canada, New Zealand and Ireland have rejected *Pirelli* in favour of the *Sparham-Souter* test of discoverability, while in Australia its status is in doubt.[271]

Another difficult area concerns liability for economic losses arising from negligent financial advice. In *Forster* v. *Oughtred & Co.*[272] the plaintiff was given negligent advice in reliance on which she mortgaged her property. It was held that she suffered financial loss as soon as the property was encumbered in this way. A similar decision was reached in *Bell* v. *Peter Browne & Co.*[273] In October 1977 the plaintiff consulted the defendants, a firm of solicitors, concerning the division of property between his wife and himself following their divorce. It was agreed that the title to the house, which they then held jointly, would be transferred to his wife, with the plaintiff to receive one-sixth of the sale proceeds in the event of a sale. In September 1978 the solicitors arranged for the

269 [2005] EWCA Civ. 198, at [20]. See also *Hawkins* v. *Clayton* (1988) 164 CLR 539, 587–8 (Deane J), 600–1 (Gaudron J); McKendrick (Select Bibliography), at 335–6; N. J. Mullany, 'Limitations of Actions and Latent Damage' and 'Limitation of Actions: Where Are We Now?' (both: Select Bibliography). See also the judgment of the Court of Appeal in *First National Commercial Bank* v. *Humberts* [1995] 2 All ER 673, in which it was held that the limitation period in an action for damages in respect of a negligent valuation did not begin to run from the point when the loan was advanced, but from a later point when it became clear that the valuation had been negligently made.

270 [1992] 2 All ER 82; see also *Warner* v. *Basildon Development Corp.* (1991) 7 *Const. LJ* 146, 154.

271 *Kamloops* v. *City of Nielsen* [1984] 2 SCR 2 (Canada), *Bowen* v. *Mount Paramount Builders (Hamilton) Ltd.* [1977] 1 NZLR 394, *Mount Albert BC* v. *Johnson* [1979] 2 NZLR 234 (New Zealand), *Brian Morgan* v. *Park Developments Ltd.* [1983] ILRM 156 (Ireland), *Hawkins* v. *Clayton* (1988) 164 CLR 539; see Mullany, 'Limitation of Actions and Latent Damage' (Select Bibliography), at 219–23.

272 [1982] 1 WLR 86.

273 [1990] 1 QB

transfer of title but negligently omitted to protect his continuing interest by a trust deed or mortgage. The plaintiff's wife subsequently sold the house without his knowledge and spent all the proceeds. The plaintiff found out in December 1986 and issued a writ against the solicitors in August 1987. The Court of Appeal held that the action was out of time: the cause of action in tort had accrued when the house was transferred to the plaintiff's wife without steps being taken to protect his interest in the property. According to Nicholls LJ, 'the plaintiff suffered [real] prejudice when the transaction was implemented without his having protection of a formal document'.[274] *Forster* and *Bell* were interpreted as deciding that in a case of contingent losses, damage occurs at the point when the defective transaction is entered into.[275] However, in *Law Society* v. *Sephton* the House of Lords came down firmly in favour of the rule that 'a contingent liability is not as such damage until the contingency occurs'.[276] *Forster* was distinguished as a case in which the contingent liability depressed the value of other property belonging to the plaintiff.[277]

(D) THE DISAPPLICATION OF THE NORMAL LIMITATION RULES

The court can grant relief from the normal limitation rules in a case where the plaintiff was under a disability of some kind at the point when the cause of action accrued,[278] and in cases of fraud, concealment, and mistake.[279] In addition, under section 33 of the 1980 Act the court has a wider power to 'disapply' the normal time-limits on actions in respect of personal injury and death. The Act lays down six guidelines for the exercise of this power. The length of and reasons for the claimant's delay; the extent to which the cogency of evidence adduced by either party might be affected by the delay; the defendant's conduct after the cause of action arose, including his response to requests by the claimant for information or inspection for the purpose of ascertaining relevant facts; the duration of a disability of the claimant after the cause of action arose; and the steps taken by the claimant to obtain expert advice and the nature of the advice he received.[280] The existence of this general power to disapply the limitation period, while no doubt a

274 [1990] 2 QB 495, 502. The court also held that the claim in contract was statute-barred, distinguishing the judgment of Oliver J in *Midland Bank Trust Co. Ltd.* v. *Hett, Stubbs and Kemp* [1979] Ch. 384, in which a continuing breach of contract was found.

275 *Iron Trade Mutual Insurance Co. Ltd.* v. *J. K. Buckenham Ltd* [1990] 1 All ER 808, 813 (Deputy Judge Rokision QC).

276 [2006] UKHL 22, at [30] (Lord Hoffmann).

277 *Ibid.*

278 See ss. 28, 28A and 38(3).

279 *Ibid.*, s. 32. See *Sheldon* v. *R. H. M. Outhwaite (Underwriting Agencies) Ltd.* [1996] AC 102.

280 A substantial body of case law has built up around these provisions, in particular in the areas of liability for sexual assaults against children (see in particular *KR and Others* v. *Bryn Alyn Community Holdings Ltd. (In Liquidation)* [2003] QB 1441; *Adams* v. *Bracknell Forest BC* [2005] 1 AC 76) and liability for failure to diagnose dyslexia in children (see *Rowe* v. *Kingston-upon-Hull CC* [2003] EWCA Civ. 1281; *Smith* v. *Liverpool CC* [2006] EWCA Civ. 743). For a full treatment of this issue, see *Clerk and Lindsell on Torts* (19th revised edn., 2005), ch. 33.

valuable device for overcoming injustices in particular cases, inevitably means that there is little certainty in the application of the limitation periods laid down by statute.

(E) THE EFFECT OF LIMITATION: PROCEDURAL OR SUBSTANTIVE?

The lapse of the limitation period has the effect only of barring the remedy; it does not extinguish the claim as such. Thus 'it is trite law that the English Limitation Acts bar the remedy and not the right, and furthermore, that they do not even have this effect unless and until pleaded';[281] their effects are said to be, accordingly, procedural rather than substantive. In practice not too many consequences follow from this, but one is that the plaintiff cannot recover a payment made in ignorance of his right to invoke the Limitation Act as a defence.[282] Exceptionally, the legislation provides that rights in conversion are extinguished by lapse of time,[283] and the same applies to rights under the Consumer Protection Act 1987 which are barred by the ten-year long-stop under section 11A(3) of the 1980 Act.

(F) REFORM OF THE LAW RELATING TO LIMITATION OF ACTIONS

The Law Commission's *Sixth Programme of Law Reform* took the view that the law on limitation periods was 'uneven, uncertain and unnecessarily complex',[284] and a Consultation Paper published by the Law Commission in 1997[285] made a series of recommendations for reform. The central proposal was that for most civil actions, including the majority of actions in tort, 'there [should] be an initial limitation period of three years that would run from when the plaintiff knows, or ought reasonably to know, that he or she has a cause of action'. This would extend the principle of discoverability beyond its currently limited area of application, and would also aim, in the interests of greater certainty, to supply a general rule which, subject to specified exceptions, would apply to the most common types of civil claim. The Commission also proposed that there should be a general long-stop of thirty years for personal-injury claims and ten years for all other claims, running from the date of the act or omission giving rise to the claim; that the long-stop could be extended by the plaintiff's disability and deliberate concealment by the defendant; and that the courts should cease to have a discretion to disapply the limitation period in particular cases.[286] It remains to be seen whether these proposals will be the subject of legislative action.

281 *Ronex Properties Ltd.* v. *John Laing (Construction) Ltd.* [1983] QB 393, 404 (Sir John Donaldson MR).
282 *Brize* v. *Dickason* (1786) 1 Term Rep. 285.
283 Limitation Act 1980, s. 3.
284 Law Commission, No. 234 (HC 455, 1995), at 28.
285 Law Commission, *Limitation of Actions*, Consultation Paper No. 151 (1998), at para. 1.47.
286 *Ibid.*

SELECT BIBLIOGRAPHY

ATIYAH, P. S., 'Causation, Contributory Negligence and *Volenti Non Fit Injuria*' (1965) 43 *Can. BR* 609.

BATES, F., 'Consenting to the Necessary' (1972) 46 *Aust. LJ* 73.

BOHLEN, F. H., 'Incomplete Privilege to Inflict Intentional Invasions of Interest of Property and Personality' (1926) 39 *Harv. LR* 307.

CRAGO, N. H., 'The Defence of Illegality in Negligence Actions' (1964) 4 *MULR* 534.

DIAS, R. M. W., 'Consent of Parties and *Voluntas Legis*' [1966] *CLJ* 75.

FLEMING, J. G., 'Comparative Negligence at Last by Judicial Choice' (1976) 64 *Cal. LR* 239.

FRIDMAN, G. H. L., 'The Wrongdoing Plaintiff' (1972) 18 *McGill LJ* 275.

GLOFCHESKI, R., 'Plaintiff's Illegality as a Bar to Recovery of Personal Injury Damages' (1999) 19 *Leg. Stud.* 6.

GORDEN, D. M., 'Drunken Drivers and Willing Passengers' (1966) 82 *LQR* 62.

JAFFEY, A. J. E., '*Volenti Non Fit Injuria*' [1985] *CLJ* 87.

LAW COMMISSION, *Limitation of Actions*, Consultation Paper No. 151 (1998).

—*The Illegality Defence in Tort*, Consultation Paper No. 160 (2001).

MCKENDRICK, E., '*Pirelli* Re-Examined' (1991) 11 *Leg. Stud.* 326.

MULLANY, N. J., 'Limitations of Actions and Latent Damage: An Australian Perspective' (1991) 54 *MLR* 216.

—'Reform of the Law of Latent Damage' (1991) 54 *MLR* 349.

—'Limitation of Actions: Where Are We Now?' [1993] *LMCLQ* 34.

PAPE, G. A., 'The Burden of Proof of Inevitable Accident in Actions for Negligence' (1946) 41 *Ill. LR* 151.

WILLIAMS, G. L., *Joint Torts and Contributory Negligence* (1951).

—'The Defence of Necessity' [1953] *CLP* 216.

25

DAMAGES[1]

PRELIMINARY OBSERVATIONS

In this chapter we shall deal with monetary consequences of a proven tort. The separation of liability issues and their consequences—i.e. damages—is not, however, always easy to make; and we shall return to these difficulties later when we shall warn the reader to seek the answers (mainly) in the two main chapters dealing with the tort of negligence. One more preliminary point must be made. In this chapter we shall deal mainly if not exclusively with the damages that will be paid by the tortfeasor (or, more likely, his insurer). But the victim of a tort may also receive his 'compensation' from other sources. The Criminal Injuries Compensation Scheme and the Motor Insurance Bureau provide some recompense in the absence of the tortfeasor. The amounts received under these schemes are not, necessarily the same as the ones received from tort law; if anything they are getting smaller. Nor is the way in which they are calculated the same. Separating them from the tort system is, once again, meant to satisfy government demands for economies (and economies are usually easier to achieve at the expense of poor or needy people). Finally, the amounts received from social security and the interrelationship of such awards with the sums received from tort law also raise difficult issues of principle as well as detail. Once again, however they cannot be dealt with here but only touched upon in different parts of a book if the latter is to avoid attaining gargantuan proportions. For all these reasons, they are dealt with briefly in the introductory chapter under the general rubric of 'alternative systems of compensation', the word 'alternative' here being used to highlight the variations just alluded to from the rules normally applicable to tort compensation.

[1] This chapter naturally updates and recasts the text of the fifth edition. In parts, however, it has also drawn on the contributions of Basil Markesinis and Augustus Ullstein QC in *Compensation for Personal Injury in English, German and Italian Law*, co-authored with Professors Michael Coester and Guido Alpa and published by the Cambridge University Press in 2005. The authors of the present book are grateful to Mr Ullstein, a leading practitioner in this area of the law, for kindly allowing the use of some of this co-authored material.

1. THE NOTIONS OF DAMAGE AND DAMAGES[2]

Though one finds a great deal of case law and literature on *damages*, little effort has been devoted to defining *damage*. The common lawyer, unlike the civil lawyer, rarely asks himself the question 'What damage is redressable in a tort action?' since his system, for a long time, concentrated not on *damnum* but on *injuria*. The reason for this different emphasis is historical: damage awards lay, until comparatively recently, within the exclusive control of juries once the defendant's behaviour had been found to be tortious. Only where damage was an element of tort itself could judges formulate rules in terms of *damage*. So the task of fixing the boundaries of liability had to be achieved through those concepts over which the judge had exclusive control. Causation, remoteness and, later, duty were the obvious devices. This inheritance has still left its mark on modern law with the result that many issues of damages still receive—and have received in this book[3]—their main attention under the general heading of causation.

There are other reasons for the attitude mentioned above. The (English) law of tort has, as we have noted, functions other than that of compensation. In some instances it is used to vindicate private rights and here the award of damages is not related to the claimant's loss (since often there may be none), but merely asserts his right. Thus in torts actionable *per se*, such as trespass to land, assault, false imprisonment and libel, the claimant need not prove damage in order to succeed. The fact that no harm was suffered will not affect liability, though it may affect the quantum of damages. These torts illustrate the two meanings: damage and damages. The damage here is the interference with a legally recognised interest, whereas damages represent the sum awarded for the violation of such an interest.

Not all torts are actionable *per se*. In most torts some damage will have to be proved before there is a tort. Damage here forms the basis of the complaint; but, immediately, difficulties also arise. For we can see how judges could lay down rules about what kind of damage was suitable and the rules they laid down in fact differed according to the type of behaviour in question. Just as the most objectionable forms of behaviour (according to the early way of thinking, at any rate) were made actionable *per se*, we find that the less objectionable the behaviour, the stricter is the definition of the requisite damage. And for the least objectionable forms of damaging behaviour, such as the right to start legal proceedings and the right to speak, this strictness was extended for the definition of that damage to the prescription of the causal link between the behaviour and the damage. Thus, in an action for abuse of legal procedure the claimant fails unless *he* shows that because of the defendant's conduct he has suffered damage in the form of risk of imprisonment, risk to property, actual financial damage or inevitable loss of reputation. Other types of 'injury', like anxiety or a tarnished reputation, will not suffice. Similarly, in all cases of slander, save the four exceptional categories which are

2 This section follows closely the account in P. Catala and J. A. Weir, 'Delict and Torts' (1964) 38 *Tul. LR* 663, 667 ff.

3 Thus, lack of certainty and loss of a chance have been discussed in ch. 4 under the wider notion of causation.

actionable *per se*, the claimant has to show that he suffered special damage in the sense of damage which is capable of pecuniary estimation. Indeed, the cases suggest that a tight causal link will also be required, for it will not suffice to establish that the normal consequence of the words complained of was to make others think worse of the claimant. It will also have to be shown that the words complained of *directly* led others to deny the claimant some economic benefit. Finally, in negligence the claimant must prove damage. Where the harm is physical injury to person or property, the courts' main preoccupation has been with issues of duty and remoteness; and where the claimant's hurt has occurred invisibly in the form of shock or pure financial loss, they have encountered the greatest difficulties. Yet, a few cases apart, the courts have refused to deal with these problems under the rubric of 'damage' and have tried to use the concepts of duty and remoteness with which they are familiar. This brings us back to our opening remarks about the tendency of common law judges to use remoteness or duty terminology where they are really expressing doubts about the compensatability of a particular type of damage.

2. TYPES OF DAMAGES

(A) GENERAL AND SPECIAL DAMAGES

We are not here concerned with special damage, which is what a claimant must prove as part of his cause of action in torts that are not actionable *per se*. Nor are we concerned with the actual awards made by courts. The distinction we have in mind here turns upon whether the losses are precisely quantifiable or not. General damages are awarded in respect of damage which is 'presumed to flow' from the wrong complained of, and include pecuniary losses such as loss of future earnings, as well as non-pecuniary losses, such as damages for pain and suffering incurred before and after the trial. Obviously, general damages such as these must be averred to in the pleadings; but since they refer to inexact or unliquidated losses they need not be specifically pleaded. Special damages, on the other hand, are awarded for damage that the claimant must specify in his pleadings and prove. It is 'particular damage (beyond the general damage), which results from the particular circumstances of the case, and of the plaintiff's claim to be compensated, for which he ought to give warning in his pleadings in order that there may be no surprise at the trial'.[4] They include quantifiable lost earnings up to the trial, damaged property (e.g. clothing), and other out-of-pocket expenses. The distinction is thus of importance for pleading and evidential purposes and also, as we shall see, for the purposes of calculating the rates of interest, but not so much from the point of view of the substantive law.

[4] *Ratcliffe* v. *Evans* [1892] 2 QB 524, 528, per Bowen LJ.

(B) NOMINAL AND SUBSTANTIAL DAMAGES

Where the tort is actionable *per se* the damages awarded will be nominal unless the claimant can prove loss or injury. As stated, the prime purpose of the law of tort is in these cases to vindicate rights that have been invaded.[5] Another reason given in favour of nominal damages is that they provide 'a... peg on which to hang costs'.[6] However, since the award of costs is nowadays left by section 51 of the Supreme Court Act 1981 (together with Order 62 of the Rules of the Supreme Court) to the *discretion* of the court, it is submitted that an undeserving claimant who recovers nominal damages should not be *automatically* regarded as a 'successful' claimant for the purposes of costs. In such cases the court may thus be well justified in refusing such a claimant's claim to unload on the 'losing side' all the costs of the litigation.[7] Substantial, or real, damages may also be awarded for actual loss and their measure is the value of the loss.

(C) CONTEMPTUOUS AND AGGRAVATED DAMAGES

Although a claimant may succeed, the court may indicate its disapproval of his behaviour by awarding him only a derisory amount[8] and, on occasion, he may even be refused costs, which can be a severe punishment for someone who has technically won his action.

Aggravated damages, on the other hand, appear where the damages are general in the sense that they cannot be calculated precisely. Typically, this will occur in the case of certain torts such as defamation (discussed in Chapter 21). But they have also been awarded in cases of false imprisonment and malicious prosecution,[9] assault and battery,[10] deceit[11] and, more recently, in cases of sexual[12] and racial discrimination.[13]

[5] *Constantine* v. *Imperial Hotels Ltd.* [1944] KB 693, a case of unlawful discrimination where 5 guineas were awarded to the successful plaintiff. In *Alexander* v. *Home Office* [1988] 1 WLR 968 the Court of Appeal held that in cases of unlawful racial discrimination 'the prime objective of an award... is restitution.... For the injury to feelings, however, for the humiliation, for the insult, it is impossible to say what is restitution.... Awards should not be minimal.... On the other hand, just because it is impossible to assess the monetary value of injured feelings, awards should be restrained... [nevertheless] even where exemplary or punitive damages are not sought,... compensatory damages may and in some instances should include an element of aggravated damages...', per May LJ at 975.

[6] *Beaumont* v. *Greathead* (1846) 2 CB 494, 499; 135 ER 1039.

[7] Cf. on this the interesting views of Devlin J in *Anglo-Cyprian Trade Agencies Ltd.* v. *Paphos Wine Ltd. Industries* [1951] 1 All ER 873, 874 (a contract case). More recently, see the comments of Jacob J in the copyright infringement case of *Hyde Park Residence* v. *Yelland* [1999] RPC 655, 670: '[i]t seems to me that the whole question of nominal damages is at the end of this century far too legalistic. A [claimant] who recovers only nominal damages has effectively lost and in reality the defendant has established a complete defence.'

[8] *Kelly* v. *Sherlock* (1866) LR 1 QB 686. Such awards are more commonly made in libel actions: see the award of £0.01 made at first instance in *Reynolds* v. *Times Newspapers* [1998] 3 WLR 862, upheld by the Court of Appeal ([2001] 2 AC 127).

[9] *Thompson* v. *Commissioner of Police for the Metropolis* [1998] QB 498.

[10] *Appleton* v. *Garren* [1996] PIQR P1.

[11] *Archer* v. *Brown* [1985] QB 401.

[12] *Zalwalla & Co.* v. *Waila* [2002] IRLR 697.

[13] The statutory wrongs of sex and race discrimination (and related wrongs on other grounds including age, religion or belief, and sexual orientation) are in many respects akin to torts. The relevant legislation provides that, in an appropriate case, compensation may be awarded according to the principles which would apply to a

Factors such as the defendant's behaviour, his intentions and motives, his high-handed, malicious or oppressive manner may be taken into account in assessing the aggravation of the injury to the claimant's *feelings of dignity and pride*,[14] thus producing additional sums that are normally quite moderate but which, in discrimination cases, can amount to several thousand pounds.[15]

Though the general principles applicable to this heading of damages are well established, and they represent a heading of damages which, in theory, is clearly distinct from that of punitive of exemplary damages (discussed below), their application in practice has not been without difficulties. Their award, individually and as part of the total amount given to the claimant must not violate the overall principle of compensation pursued by the law of torts. To avoid or minimise these dangers the Law Commission recommended in its 1997 Report[16] that they should be seen as a species of 'mental distress damages' or 'damages for injured feelings', but the terminological clarification, however welcome, has not yet been implemented in practice.

Courts themselves have made their own effort to move the law in this direction. In *Kralj* v. *McGrath*,[17] for instance, a case of medical negligence involving a plaintiff subjected to a 'horrific' treatment, the Court made no such award, even though it was requested by the claimant. The view taken by Woolf J was that the increased pain and suffering of the plaintiff should be reflected in the plaintiff's *general* damages. This approach was subsequently approved by the Court of Appeal in *AB* v. *South West Water Services*.[18] Yet, it could be argued that clarity and transparency are evaded if the 'aggravated' element of the award is submerged in the general damages, so one must

common-law claim in tort, for the purposes of which it is declared 'for the avoidance of doubt' that damages may include compensation for injury to feelings: see e.g. Sex Discrimination Act 1975, ss. 65–6; Race Relations Act 1976, ss. 56–7. It should be noted that in *R* v. *Secretary of State for Transport, ex parte Factortame (No. 6)* [2001] 1 WLR 942; [2001] 1 CMLR 47, Judge Toulmin QC held that 'Damages to compensate a claimant for distress as a direct consequence of the tort are confined to those torts where the claimant's loss of self-esteem (or loss of enjoyment) is an important part of the damage for which compensation is awarded.' This excluded the possibility of exemplary damages for the government's breach of (what is now) Article 42 of the EC Treaty, concerning the applicants' right to establish themselves freely in the UK (see [227]–[309]).

14 The words are italicised because they appear almost without fail in decisions awarding this kind of damages. That is why cases such as *Messenger Newspaper Group Ltd.* v. *National Graphical Association* [1984] IRLR 397, awarding aggravated damages to a corporation, seem unconvincing.

15 See, for instance, *W* v. *Meah*; *D* v. *Meah* [1986] 1 All ER 935 where £2,500 was awarded in a case of vicious sexual assault. The plea for moderation—it is submitted hardly justified in cases like *W* v. *Meah*—can be found in a number of judgments, e.g. *Archer* v. *Brown* [1985] 1 QB 401 (a case of deceit) and *Alexander* v. *Home Office* [1988] 1 WLR 968 (a case of racial discrimination). In *Appleton* v. *Garrett* [1996] 5 PIQR P1 (discussed briefly below in the text) the judge assessed the 'aggravated' damages at 15 per cent of the amount awarded for pain and suffering. In the racial discrimination case of *Armitage* v. *Johnson* [1997] IRLR 162 aggravated damages of £21,000 were awarded in respect of a systematic campaign of racial harassment directed at the complainant, a prison officer, by his colleagues, for whose conduct his employer was held responsible. In *Smith* v. *Stemler* [2001] CLY 2309 (a malicious-falsehood case concerning an employment reference), just over £37,000 was awarded for loss of past and future earnings (less tax and benefits, plus interest), while £15,000 was awarded in aggravated damages.

16 *Aggravated, Exemplary and Restitutionary Damages*. (Select Bibliography), para. 2.42; Draft Bill, cl. 13.

17 [1986] 1 All ER 54.

18 [1993] QB 507—a case of public nuisance brought against a nationalised corporation for contaminating drinking water and failing to warn the public properly.

note a successful (if limited) attempt of a first instance judge to distinguish the *South West Water* ruling, at least in cases involving intentional torts.[19]

Notwithstanding these difficulties and the fact that matters of detail remain unresolved, it is beyond doubt that aggravated damages, unlike punitive (exemplary) damages, are compensatory in nature,[20] since the emphasis is on the aggravated injury to the claimant which is being compensated. However, the interests affected are so incapable of precise monetary valuation that it is often difficult to say where 'satisfaction' for the claimant ends and punishment of the defendant begins[21]—hence the conceptual confusion with the next heading.

(D) PUNITIVE (OR EXEMPLARY) DAMAGES

The ambiguity that exists between this and the previous heading has, in the past, led some to argue that there were few, if any, cases dealing with punitive damages which could not really be explained as instances of aggravated damages.[22] On the other hand, since the decision in *Rookes* v. *Barnard*,[23] there is little doubt that punitive damages are now acknowledged to form an independent heading of damages.

Rookes was a case of 'intimidation', a trade dispute, and its facts need not concern us here. However, in Lord Devlin's judgment[24] we find some of the clearest statements ever made about punitive damages. There, the learned judge accepted that the prime purpose of damages is to compensate the victim, whereas the purpose of punitive awards is to punish and deter the wrongdoer. In the latter case, therefore, the emphasis is not on the claimant and his hurt but on the defendant and his conduct. Because such awards blur the distinction between the civil and criminal functions of the law,[25] Lord Devlin felt that they should be limited to three kinds of cases.

[19] *Appleton* v. *Garrett* [1996] 5 PIQR P1 where Dyson J awarded aggravated damages against a dentist who deliberately and persistently withheld from young patients information that the treatment he was administering was unnecessary. The same approach would probably be adopted in defamation cases where 'injury to the plaintiff's feelings and self-esteem is an important part of the damage for which compensation is awarded'. See also *Smith* v. *Stemler* [2001] CLY 2309, where the elements of the total sum were carefully separated. Although the judge in *Khodaparast* v. *Shad* [2000] 1 WLR 618 did not break down the award into its component parts, the Court of Appeal refused to overturn his overall assessment.

[20] Most recently stressed by Otton LJ in *Khodaparast* v. *Shad* [2000] 1 WLR 618, 632; [2000] EMLR 265, 282.

[21] Hence, see the remarks of Lawton and Goff LJJ in *Drane* v. *Evangelou* [1978] 1 WLR 455. The most recent (and thorough) discussion of the subject can be found in *Thompson* v. *Commissioner of Police of the Metropolis* and *Hsu* v. *Commissioner of Police of the Metropolis* [1997] 3 WLR 403, yet even this reveals the closeness of the two notions. See also the Law Commission's Consultation Paper on *Aggravated, Exemplary and Restitutionary Damages* (Select Bibliography), which recommended the abolition of aggravated damages as a separate head of damages and their absorption into a 'strict compensatory model' (para. 8.18); see also Law Commission Report No. 247, *Aggravated, Exemplary and Restitutionary Damages* (Select Bibliography).

[22] See e.g. *Merest* v. *Harvey* (1814) 5 Taunt. 442; 128 ER 761; *Emblen* v. *Myers* (1860) 6 H & N 54; 158 ER 23.

[23] [1964] AC 1129.

[24] *Ibid.*, at 1203 ff.

[25] The distinction seems further blurred by the fact that the Court of Appeal recently confirmed that there was, in principle, no argument of public policy prohibiting the defendant—a county council or police authority—from insuring itself against the risk of it being held *vicariously* liable for punitive damages imposed because of the

The *first* category includes oppressive, arbitrary or unconstitutional action by the servants of the government. The law's disapproval is, in these cases, directed against the unconstitutional act rather than focused on the effect it has had on the claimant.[26] It is thus irrelevant that the defendant was unconstitutionally detained for a very short time and, during his detention, treated in a civil manner.[27] The *fons et origo* of this common law category is the famous case of *Wilkes* v. *Wood*[28] in which the legality of general warrants was successfully challenged in court.

Though Lord Devlin's judgment emphasises the exceptional nature of such awards, subsequent courts, in several instances, gave signs of more liberal tendencies. Thus, in *Holden* v. *Chief Constable of Lancashire*[29] exemplary damages were allowed in a case involving an unlawful arrest *without* any 'oppressive' behaviour on the part of the arresting officer. In *Bradford City Metropolitan Council* v. *Arora*[30] a local authority was ordered to pay (modest) punitive damages for practising race and sex discrimination in its hiring policy when filling senior posts in one of its teaching colleges since it was exercising 'a public function' when making these appointments. However, only those defendants who exercise genuine executive functions will be subject to this category.[31]

Such decisions, however, and certainly the *Arora* case, came to be viewed with suspicion after the later judgment of the Court of Appeal in *AB* v. *South West Water Services Ltd.*[32] For it was there said that punitive damages could not/should not be awarded to torts that had not received punitive awards (or, *a fortiori*, had not been recognised as torts) at the time of *Rookes* v. *Barnard*. The result thus seemed to be that no punitive damages could be

conduct of one of its servants (typically, false imprisonment or malicious prosecution committed by one of its constables): *Lancashire CC* v. *Municipal Mutual Insurance Ltd.* [1996] 3 WLR 493. It remains to be decided whether the same is true in the case of *personal* liability to pay punitive damages. It could be argued that insurability in such circumstances would erode further the 'punitive' element of the award. On a more general note, the precise interaction between claims for exemplary damages and principles of vicarious liability seem to be in need of re-examination: see, in particular, Lord Scott's speech in *Kuddus* [2002] 2 AC 122, esp. [123]–[137] and the comments in *McGregor on Damages* (Select Bibliography), paras. 11–044–11–045.

26 Again, *Douglas* v. *Hello!* [2001] 2 WLR 992 provides a helpful illustration: see the judgment of Keene LJ at [171]. The Judgment of the Court of Appeal in *Douglas* v. *Hello! (No.3)* [2006] QB 125, denying *OK!'s* claim for compensation for breach of confidence, suggested greater attention would have to be paid to the grant of interim injunctions in future: if the interest of *OK!* could have been protected by such an injunction pending trial, and yet could legally be vindicated by a damages award, this might suggest that the balance was more strongly in favour of the grant of an interim injunction. However, the judgment of the House of Lords on appeal, overturning the Court of Appeal's ruling and restoring the order of Lindsay J (which had awarded damages to *OK!* as well as the Douglases) has taken some of the tension out of this issue. This suggests that the courts will continue to be unwilling to restrain publication pending trial in such cases.

27 *Huckle* v. *Money* (1763) 2 Wils. KB 205; 95 ER 768.

28 (1763) Lofft. 1; 98 ER 489; see also *A-G of St Christopher, Nevis and Anguilla* v. *Reynolds* [1980] AC 637.

29 [1986] 3 All ER 836; [1987] QB 380 (CA).

30 [1991] 2 QB 507.

31 See *AB* v. *South West Water Services Ltd.* [1993] QB 507: this element of *AB* seems to have survived *Kuddus* v. *Chief Constable of Leicestershire Constabulary* [2002] 2 AC 122. For a recent application, see *Shendish Manor* v. *Coleman* [2001] EWCA Civ. 913, [59]–[63] (per Keene LJ).

32 [1993] QB 507, 518.

awarded for negligence, public nuisance,[33] deceit,[34] sex or race discrimination,[35] patent infringements[36] or for violations of the Consumer Protection Act 1987.

This highly formalistic approach, known as the 'cause of action' test, was the subject of extensive criticism, not least from the Law Commission in its Consultation Paper and Report on *Aggravated, Exemplary and Restitutionary Damages.*[37] And, most recently, the House of Lords in *Kuddus* v. *Chief Constable of Leicestershire*[38] overruled *AB* and has returned us to the use of only Lord Devlin's categories in *Rookes* v. *Barnard*. In *Kuddus*, this allowed their Lordships to hold that it was open to the courts to award punitive damages for misfeasance in public office.[39]

The judgments of their Lordships in *Kuddus* show considerable disagreement over the interpretation of *Rookes* v. *Barnard* in the light of *Broome* v. *Cassell Ltd.*[40] (as, indeed, did the judgments in the Court of Appeal in *Kuddus*). Lord Slynn concluded that *Broome* v. *Cassell Ltd.* disclosed 'no clear or unequivocal decision' in favour of the 'cause of action' test; Lords Mackay and Hutton, after both expressing the difficulty that they had experienced in construing the *dicta* in *Broome* v. *Cassell Ltd.*, inclined to the view that there was nothing in that case which could have constrained the Court of Appeal in *AB* to follow the 'cause of action' test; Lord Nicholls clearly took the view that the result of *Broome* v. *Cassell Ltd.* was precisely as the Court of Appeal had held in *AB*, although he then went on to rule that that position should be rejected; Lord Scott, meanwhile, agreed with Lord Nicholls that *AB* was an accurate representation of the law at the time, before reluctantly concurring in the removal of the 'cause of action' test.

Lord Devlin was also careful *not* to extend this category to oppressive actions by *private* individuals or corporations. The exclusion from the rule of private defendants has not pleased all academic commentators. Yet the distinction is supportable not only because it is compatible with the general more modern trend to limit rather than expand the ambit of punitive damages in civil cases,[41] but also because 'the case of the

[33] *AB* v. *South West Water Services Ltd.* [1993] QB 507. But punitive damages might be appropriate in some instances of private nuisance. See *Guppys (Bridport) Ltd.* v. *Brookling and James* (1984) 14 HLR 1—a case involving tenant harassment.

[34] The views of Sachs LJ in *Mafo* v. *Adams* [1970] 1 QB 548 at 555 have thus come to be preferred over that of Widgery LJ in the same case (*ibid.*, at 558).

[35] *Deane* v. *Ealing LBC* [1993] ICR 329, *Ministry of Defence* v. *Cannock* [1994] IRLR 509. The Law Commission's Report No. 247 on *Aggravated, Exemplary and Restitutionary Damages* (Select Bibliography) recommended that tribunals and courts should be given a power to grant exemplary damages in sex and race discrimination cases.

[36] *Catnic Components* v. *Hill & Smith Ltd.* [1983] FSR 512.

[37] Law Commission Reports Nos. 132 (1993) and 247 (1997) respectively (both Select Bibliography).

[38] [2002] 2 AC 122.

[39] The application of the 'new' approach can be well seen in *Design Progression Ltd.* v. *Thurloe Properties Ltd.* [2005] 1 WLR , where exemplary damages were awarded against a landlord for breach of his statutory duties under s. 1(3) of the Landlord and Tenant Act 1988 (landlord's failure to give a decision to a tenant's application for a licence to assign, motivated by the landlord's desire to force the tenant out of the premises and then re-rent them himself at a higher rent).

[40] [1972] AC 1027.

[41] In *AB* v. *South West Water Services Ltd.* [1993] 2 WLR 507, Stuart-Smith LJ remarked (at 513) that 'this [i.e. the area of punitive damages] is *not* a developing field of the law' (emphasis added). Thus, in that case a nationalised Water Authority was not treated as an emanation of the state for the purposes of being included in Lord

government... is different, for the servants of the government are also the servants of the people and the use of their power must always be subordinated to their duty of service'.[42] In the recent case of *Kuddus*, however, Lord Nicholls doubted whether the exclusion of non-governmental oppression remains appropriate in the modern world, where large corporations and even some individuals can exercise enormous power.[43] This is certainly, something that one encounters in landlord and tenant litigation though, as we have seen, this does not mean that the landlords' rapacious activities are not 'caught' by the second heading of punitive damages—see immediately below—namely 'activity calculated to make him a profit'.

The *second* category includes cases in which the defendant's conduct was 'calculated' to make a profit for himself which could exceed the compensation payable to the claimant. The precise meaning to be attributed to the word 'calculated' has given rise to some judicial discussion. Thus, in *Broome* v. *Cassell* Lord Morris thought that 'the word 'calculated' was [not to be] used to denote some precise balancing process'.[44] And in *Riches* v. *News Group Newspapers*[45]—a defamation case—it was made clear that the judge was entitled to leave the matter to the jury if there was evidence that the newspaper proprietors had felt that the economic benefits of publishing outweighed the risk of paying damages. More recently, the Court of Appeal returned to this issue in *John* v. *Mirror Group Newspapers Ltd.*[46] and repeated the view that no precise mathematical calculation need take place. What, instead, should be investigated is whether the defendant was aware of the fact that what he was planning to do was against the law (or had shown reckless disregard as to whether his proposed conduct was legal or illegal) *and* had, nonetheless, proceeded with his conduct in the belief that the prospect of material advantages outweighed the possibility of material loss. This kind of conduct is particularly likely to happen in libel cases, where Lord Devlin expressly said that 'one man

Devlin's second rule discussed in the text, above. Lord Scott in *Kuddus* [2002] 2 AC 122 also showed strong concern about the possibility of an expansive approach to the availability of exemplary damages: he cited developments in administrative law (to restrain the abuse of public power) and the law of restitution (concerning profits made by the commission of a wrong), as well as the role of vicarious liability and how this dulls any deterrent effect that an award of exemplary damages might have (see, in particular, [108]–[109] and [123] ff).

42 *Rookes* v. *Barnard* [1964] AC 1129, 1226 (per Lord Devlin). McGregor (Select Bibliography), at para. 11–017, provides a third, pragmatic, explanation. It is there suggested that the distinction between public and private sectors may have been 'motivated by the need to retain some scope for exemplary damages in order not to appear to be acting too cavalierly with the doctrine of precedent; in such a search, what better authorities to leave standing than those in which exemplary damages had originated?' These, however, may be academic speculations since in practice punitive damages under this heading are very rare. Thus, see *Holden* v. *Chief Constable of Lancashire* [1987] QB 380 (CA) and *A-G of St Christopher, Nevis and Anguilla* v. *Reynolds* [1980] AC 637. Potentially more significant were Scott J's *obiter dicta* in *Columbia Picture Industries* v. *Robinson* [1987] Ch. 38, 87D-F; and they could be taken to support the view argued in the text that persons acting for the state can wield great and dangerous powers and must thus be subject to stringent controls.

43 [2002] 2 AC 122, para. 66.

44 [1972] AC 1027, 1094.

45 [1986] QB 256 (CA).

46 [1996] 3 WLR 593. The same principles now apply to actions for malicious prosecution and false imprisonment where, according to s. 69(1) of the Supreme Court Act 1981, there is still a right to a jury trial. See *Thompson* v. *Commissioner of Police of the Metropolis* and *Hsu* v. *Commissioner of Police of the Metropolis* [1997] 3 WLR 403 (with a most illuminating judgment from Lord Woolf MR).

should not be allowed to sell another man's reputation for profit'.[47] Thus, where the defendant with cynical disregard for the claimant's rights has calculated that the money to be made out of his wrongdoing will probably exceed the damages at risk, it is necessary for the law to show that it cannot be broken with impunity.[48] This category is not confined to money-making in the strict sense.[49] It extends to cases in which the defendant is seeking to gain at the expense of the claimant some object—perhaps some property that he covets—which he could either not obtain at all or not obtain except at a price greater than he wants to put down. Exemplary damages, in other words, are properly awarded whenever 'it is necessary to teach a wrongdoer that tort does not pay'.[50] The type of cases that gave rise to this litigation involved landlords who in various tortious ways were engineering the eviction of their protected tenants with a view to reletting the premises at an unrestricted rent. Yet the plaintiffs in these cases fared unevenly, in some instances obtaining punitive awards[51] whereas in others failing to do so,[52] thus demonstrating that in practice and for various reasons the success of these claims is by no means assured.

Finally, the *third* category covers cases where exemplary damages are *expressly* authorised by statute, for example (arguably), section 97(2) of the Copyright, Designs and Patents Act 1988.[53] Such statutes are in practice very rare and, since *Rookes* v. *Barnard*, no new statute authorising the award of punitive damages seems to have been enacted.

Though the preceding discussion emphasises the general recent (judicial) trend to bring punitive damages under control, more recently, in the New Zealand case of *A* v. *Bottrill*,[54] Lord Nicholls (in delivering the opinion of the majority of the Judicial Board of the Privy Council) spoke of English law as 'still toiling in the chains of *Rookes* v. *Barnard*', before adopting a rather less restrictive attitude to the availability of punitive damages in New Zealand law than had been taken by the New Zealand Court of Appeal. He held that 'intentional wrongdoing or conscious recklessness is not an essential prerequisite to an order for payment of exemplary damages';[55] rather, 'the basic question is

47 *Rookes* v. *Barnard* [1964] AC 1129, 1227. Yet in practice (and for different reasons) none of the litigated libel cases between *Rookes* and *Broom* yielded any punitive damages. Thus, see *McCarey* v. *Associated Newspapers* [1965] 2 QB 86, *Broadway Approvals* v. *Odhams Press* [1965] 1 WLR 805, *Manson* v. *Associated Newspapers* [1965] 1 WLR 1038.

48 *Rookes* v. *Barnard* [1964] AC 1129, at 1227.

49 Indeed, in *Kuddus* [2002] 2 AC 122 Lord Nicholls expressed doubts that this category is properly confined even to a broad notion of 'profit': '[t]here is no obvious reason why, if exemplary damages are to be available, the profit motive should suffice but a malicious motive should not' ([67]).

50 *Rookes* v. *Barnard* [1964] AC 1129, at 1227.

51 *Drane* v. *Evangelou* [1978] 1 WLR 455 (CA), *Asghar* v. *Ahmed* (1984) 17 HLR 25 (CA), *McMillan* v. *Singh* (1984) 17 HLR 120 (CA)—all trespass cases. Cf. *Guppys (Bridport) Ltd.* v. *Brookling and James* (1983) 14 HLR 1 (CA) where the eviction was effected by means of a private nuisance.

52 *Mafo* v. *Adams* [1970] 1 QB 548, *Millington* v. *Duffy* (1984) 17 HLR 232 (CA).

53 Recent case law discloses no agreement on the availability of punitive damages under s. 97(2) of the 1988 Act: compare *Cala Homes (South) Ltd.* v. *McAlpine Homes East Ltd. (No. 2)* [1996] FSR 36 (where Laddie J held that it did authorise the pursuit of exemplary damages) with *Redrow Homes Ltd.* v. *Bett Brothers plc* 1997 SLT 1125 (where Lord McCluskey held that it did not). The section refers to 'additional damages' and the question is whether this term is better treated as aggravated or exemplary damages.

54 [2003] 1 AC 449 (PC). 55 *Ibid.*, [50].

always whether the defendant's conduct satisfies the outrageous conduct criterion'.[56] This made it possible for certain cases of negligence to lead to an award of punitive damages, although it was stressed that judicial discretion to award such damages would be exercised only in exceptional cases. It should also be noted, however, that Lords Hutton and Millett dissented from Lord Nicholls' exposition of the law on punitive damages, feeling that it focused too strongly upon the court's outrage at the defendant's conduct and did not sufficiently emphasise the function of punitive damages, which is 'to punish the defendant for his outrageous behaviour'. Thus, in the absence of advertent conduct (intent or subjective recklessness), the rationale for any award of punitive damages falls away.[57] Meanwhile, the theoretical debate whether they should be available at all has not abated. The main arguments for and against punitive awards in civil cases already appear in the speeches of Lord Wilberforce and Lord Reid in *Broome* v. *Cassell*[58] and have been further elaborated since.[59]

What can we make from such diametrically opposed views and a rather unclear case law? There is little doubt that for the majority of authors all punitive awards are something of an anomaly since they repeatedly stress that retribution, deterrence[60] and rehabilitation are more appropriately pursued by the criminal law rather than by the law of torts. Yet the rejection of punishment in civil awards, purely on such an abstract and rigid demarcation of crime and tort, is hardly defensible, quite apart from the fact that it ignores existing realities. The true objections, therefore, must be sought elsewhere and Lord Reid's judgment provides some good clues. For example, by allowing punitive awards we may be violating such sacred principles as the *nullum crimen sine lege* rule, especially since such punitive awards can be made for any kind of conduct which can be described as 'high-handed', 'oppressive' or 'malicious'. Then there is no real limit to such punishment, except that these awards must not be unreasonable, which, however, is very vague. Punitive awards in civil actions may also be made by juries, notoriously susceptible to emotional and extra-legal considerations. What is more, the claimant's burden of proof is much lighter in a civil case than it is in a criminal case, so, in this context at least, it is in the defendant's interest to be tried by a criminal court. Finally, since tortious conduct which may result in punitive damages may also be subject to criminal sanctions, defendants may be exposed to both criminal and civil penalties for the same conduct. All these are serious, but not necessarily insurmountable, objections. Take, for example, the danger of excessive punitive awards. This has

[56] *Ibid.*, [40]. [57] *Ibid.*, [72]–[82].

[58] [1972] AC 1027, 1112 and 1083 respectively.

[59] Thus, see, the debates in the House of Lords concerning the Administration of Justice Bill (HL Debs., vol. 429, col. 1293 ff. (6 May 1982). More recently, Professor Peter Birks adopted a more favourable position towards punitive damages in his 'Civil Wrongs: A New World', Butterworths Lectures 1990–1991 (1992), esp. at 77–89. For the reasons given in the text, however, there are no signs that the courts are inclining to that view. See also *Supreme Court Procedure Committee Report on Practice and Procedure in Defamation* (1991), 39–43. One should, perhaps, add that the American experience does not seem to provide much comfort to those who favour punitive awards. See J. G. Fleming, *The American Tort Process* (1989), 214–24.

[60] See also Lord Scott's judgment in *Kuddus* [2002] 2 AC 122 on this matter, where he doubts the impact of any real deterrent effect, in the face of the possibility of vicarious liability for punitive damages ([123] ff.).

certainly materialised in the United States and has contributed to what some describe as a tort crisis (though it has also been pragmatically justified as a means of returning to the claimant part of his compensatory award that he will have to pay to his attorney under the there-prevailing contingency-fee system). But in this country the amounts awarded under this heading have been modest on the whole—about £1,000; though where the facts were particularly exceptional (as they were in *Broome* v. *Cassell*) larger amounts (£25,000) have been awarded. At present, therefore, as far as English law is concerned, this appears to be a theoretical objection.

More serious is the possibility of the same conduct being punished twice by a civil and criminal court. This possibility was avoided in *Archer* v. *Brown*, with the judge refusing to impose additional punitive damages.[61] The principle of prohibiting punitive awards where the defendant has already been subjected to a criminal prosecution has received legislative sanction in some jurisdictions in the United States[62] and is a good one, though a number of details have still to be worked out.

All these correctives to the real or perceived drawbacks of punitive damages in the context of civil suits do not, however, address the real problem presented by this heading of damages. This, quite simply, is that whereas a case can be made for mulcting the bad defendant of the profits he has made from his tortious behaviour, there is no reason why this extra sum should then be given to the claimant, enriching him by a corresponding amount. (Had the punishment been a fine the money would have gone to the state.) In this context, an idea recently developed in some civil law systems may be worth consideration. For in some of these systems the *practice* has developed whereby the additional punitive element of the award is given to charities (designated by the successful claimant) or, alternatively, could be channelled into, say, the legal aid fund.[63] On the whole, therefore, one is left with the impression that much thought still needs to be devoted by our system to this part of the law of damages. Until this is done, our courts are likely to remain hostile to claims for punitive damages when they cannot be brought under one of the (two main) categories identified by Lord Devlin in his judgment in *Rookes* v. *Barnard*. When punitive damages *are* awarded, they are likely to be kept within reasonable bounds.[64] The Law Commission has recommended a rationalisation of the law on exemplary damages, making them available for *any* wrong (whether tortious or equitable, but not breach of contract), where the defendant had 'deliberately and

[61] [1985] QB 401. But not all courts take this view. See *Messenger Newspapers Group Ltd.* v. *National Graphical Association* [1984] IRLR 397 where the judge refused to take into account a £675,000 fine imposed for contempt of court and ordered the defendant to pay an additional £25,000 as punitive damages.

[62] For the American position see C. Morris, 'Punitive Damages in Tort Cases' (1931) 44 *Harv. LR* 1173; 'Criminal Safeguards and the Punitive Damages Defendant' (Note) (1967) 34 *U Chi. LR* 408.

[63] As the Law Commission commented (Report No. 247, *Aggravated, Exemplary and Restitutionary Damages* (Select Bibliography) Part V, para. 5.21(2)), it is interesting to note that, in *Riches* v. *News Group Newspapers Ltd.* [1986] QB 256, the jury asked the judge whether they could award exemplary damages to a charity, rather than to the claimant: the judge was forced to answer in the negative, given the current arrangements in English law.

[64] Thus, see *Thompson* v. *Commissioner of Police for the Metropolis* [1997] 3 WLR 403 as well as the earlier (but important) decision in *John* v. *MGN Ltd.* [1996] 3 WLR 593.

outrageously disregarded the [claimant]'s rights',[65] although the government has not, to date, seemed minded to put forward legislation on the subject.[66]

(E) COMPENSATORY DAMAGES

Compensation being a prime function of tort law, this heading deserves separate and more detailed treatment. The remaining part of this chapter will largely if not exclusively deal with this heading.

3. THE PRINCIPLE OF FULL COMPENSATION

According to classical contract doctrine,[67] 'where a party sustains a loss by reason of a breach of contract, he is, so far as money can do it, to be placed in the same situation, with respect to damages, as if the contract had been performed'. Tort law, by contrast, seeks to put the victim in the position he was in before the tort.[68] This, where the victim's injury has been sustained by replaceable items of his property, the rule will be *restitutio in integrum*.

Where, on the other hand, the damage is to an irreplaceable item of property or consists of personal injury, exact return to the *status quo ante* is impossible. Lawyers then talk not of restitution but of 'fair compensation' (or, better, satisfaction) for harm which by its nature can never be accurately assessed so the aim is to come up with an amount which is 'fair, reasonable and just'.[69] The term is reminiscent of the phrase also invoked to determine whether a duty of care should be discovered in the tort of negligence. Yet in the context of quantification of damages our judges have shown themselves more anxious to strive for certainty and have thus, in recent times, shown not only an obvious (and one might add commendable) tendency to abide by a judicial tariff system in cases of personal injuries but also to guide (in defamation) juries by telling them the prevailing scale of awards for non-pecuniary losses. The same desire can be seen in the judgment of the Court of Appeal in *Thompson* v. *Commissioner of Police for the Metropolis*[70] where guidelines were laid as to the level of damages that should be awarded against the police in false imprisonment and malicious prosecution cases.

[65] Report No. 247, *Aggravated, Exemplary and Restitutionary Damages* (Select Bibliography): a formulation echoed by Lord Nicholls in *Kuddus* [2002] 2 AC 122, when he stated that 'the essence of the conduct constituting the court's discretionary jurisdiction to award exemplary damages is conduct which was an outrageous disregard of the plaintiff's rights' ([68]).

[66] See HC Debs., vol. 337, col. 502 (9 Nov. 1999).

[67] *Robinson* v. *Harman* (1848) 1 Exch. 850, 855; 154 ER 363, 365, per Parke B.

[68] The *locus classicus* can be found in the judgment of Lord Blackburn in *Livingstone* v. *Rawyards Coal Co.* (1880) 5 App. Cas. 25, 39.

[69] *Rowley* v. *London and North Western Ry. Co.* (1873) LR 8 Exch. 221 at 231.

[70] [1998].

In personal injuries cases full compensation is achieved by making tort benefits earnings-related and by insisting that these represent, so far as possible, the full amount of the loss. The difference from social security compensation is thus marked *whenever* the latter tends to work on the basis of flat rates. For the tort system, more tailored as it is to the demands of individual claimants rather than 'average models', such methods of compensation appear unfair. For flat-rate benefits, unlike earnings-related benefits, do not enable victims to maintain their pre-accident standard of living. For example, a man who has taken out a mortgage or entered into a number of hire-purchase agreements on the basis of his earnings will not be able to continue meeting his commitments if after his injury his compensation is unrelated to his pre-accident earnings but is, on the contrary, determined by pre-arranged flat rates. Moreover, flat-rate benefits, depending as they do on some single figure selected from all earners, are likely to lead to under-compensation for most and, perhaps, over-compensation for a few. The inadequacies of social-security flat-rate benefits are, to some extent, avoided whenever certain additional payments are made on an earnings-related basis. But here, too, compensation is unlikely (in all cases) to be full, since ceilings tend to be imposed on earnings-related benefits.

However, the 100 per cent compensation principle, based on the victim's pre-accident earnings, also has its drawbacks, as many of its critics have pointed out.[71] The first is that, insofar as it leads to two people involved in identical accidents being compensated differently, it helps to perpetrate the inequalities of wealth in our society. This argument, however, with all its political and ideological overtones, is unlikely to carry much weight so long as our market-orientated, private wealth system continues to prevail. In any event, it is not the role of tort damages to redress the economic imbalances that exist in life.

The second and (intellectually more interesting) objection is that such earnings-related benefits do not depend on any earnings-related contributions as some social-security benefits do.[72] In the case of a traffic accident, the rich man and the poor man will pay identical premiums if they represent identical risks (live in the same town, drive the same or approximately the same car, and have the same kind of driving experience and accident record). If they are injured, the rich person's compensation for his economic loss will be far greater than the poor person's, even though their injuries and the other conditions of the accident may be identical.[73] It could be said, therefore, that the rich person 'takes out of the system' more than he actually puts in. This objection,

[71] These criticisms are considered by Lord Steyn in *Wells* v. *Wells* [1998] 3 WLR 329, at 350–1. However, his Lordship concludes that '[n]ot only do these arguments contemplate a radical departure from established principle, but controversial issues regarding resources and social policy would be at stake. Such policy arguments are a matter for Parliament and not the judiciary.'

[72] This is true of most social insurance benefits (in particular social insurance benefits in respect of unemployment and invalidity) although not of benefits payable under the industrial injuries system.

[73] As far as non-pecuniary losses are concerned (e.g. pain and suffering, loss of amenity, etc.), if the injuries are identical, so will be their compensation.

rather technical in nature, is valid but is less valid outside the context of road-traffic accidents. In any event, one could again say that a different solution would be unfair to the victim who would have to scale down his standard of living after the commission of the tort.

The third objection to the notion of full compensation that is related to pre-accident earnings is that it can encourage victims and their dependants not to return to work (where this is possible). A young childless widow, for example, who is compensated for her husband's death on the basis of his earnings and her dependency on them can, in theory, end up by being maintained at more or less the same pre-accident standard and need never return to work, even if she is well qualified to do so. This 'incentive argument' has a great deal of force if the full compensation is paid by means of periodic payments which can vary or even be terminated according to changing circumstances. But if the compensation takes the form of a lump sum, as it has for a long time in English law, the full compensation is unlikely to discourage the recipient from returning to work if he is so inclined since, once paid, the compensation cannot be reduced or discontinued.

The fourth objection to the idea of full compensation is, potentially, the most important and, put simply, it is that, in practice, it can lead, not just to full compensation, but to over-compensation. This appears to be widely accepted in the case of minor injuries which are (or could be) almost entirely covered by social-security benefits. But it can also be true in the case of larger awards, which can overlap with social-security and other payments (from private insurance, pension funds, etc.), and may end by actually enriching the victim. That this is an anomaly, given that damages in tort are meant to compensate but not enrich the claimant, is beyond doubt. It will be noticed, however, that the anomaly is due rather to the fact that we lack an effective system of rules to deal with the interrelationships between the various methods of compensation than to the principle of full compensation. We return to this point later, where we shall note that if the relevant proposals of the Pearson Committee were to be implemented (which is unlikely), they would remove some of these problems. Before doing this, however, we should note that this proclaimed aim of full compensation is not always achieved in practice, since three factors seem to have watered it down.

The first is that when awards are made for future economic loss judges tend to 'discount' their awards to take into account a number of contingencies. The fact that our system of awards takes the form of a lump sum makes this inevitable since the court has to try to make an educated guess as to certain contingencies (possible life of the victim and his dependants, his future earnings, etc.) and the tendency, apparently, is to reduce awards too much rather than too little. Empirical studies that substantiate this argument are sadly lacking, though certainly cases can be cited where awards that appeared generous at the time of the trial have, with the passage of time, proved to be inadequate.

The second factor that might lead to less than full compensation is the refusal of judges to calculate damages on systematic actuarial evidence. Though such evidence is admissible in court, the more rough-and-ready method of multiplier and multiplicand, which will be explained below, has always been preferred.[74] There is, however, no conclusive evidence to support this approach. What is more likely, however, is that damages tend to be less adequate in all cases where the period of expected future loss is great. This was clearly in the minds of the members of the Pearson Committee who, by a majority, proposed a 'modified multiplier' system. But Lord Hailsham LC informed the House of Lords[75] that consultations with the members of the legal profession had revealed great hostility to this complicated proposal, so the government was not going to recommend its acceptance.

The third and final factor undermining full compensation has been inflation. Courts tend to ignore it in their calculations except in the most extreme cases, and the reasons they have given, though not entirely convincing, are also not without value. Yet, it is a matter of fact that inflation, especially in the late 1970s and early 1980s when it reached record levels, did eat into awards which at the time that they were made, appeared generous, if not excessive.[76] Inflation has been 'tamed' in recent times so arguments based on the effects it can have on awards are less prominent than they used to be twenty or more years ago. On the other hand one must note that wage inflation has substantially outstripped the Retail Price Index with the result that real costs have and are continuing to erode awards. An example given by Master Lush, the Master of the Court of Protection is *Lim Po Choo*[77] in which care costs at the date of trial were assessed at £8,000. Applying the RPI they should now be £25,000 whereas the actual annual cost is now £69,000.

4. THE INTERRELATIONSHIP OF TORT AND OTHER COMPENSATION SYSTEMS

(A) INTRODUCTORY REMARKS

The Pearson Committee estimated[78] that every year in the United Kingdom some 3,000,000 people are injured and about 21,000 of them die of their injuries. Of these, only about 1,700,000 receive some financial assistance, but not all of them from the tort

[74] For criticism by a leading actuary, see J. H. Prevett, 'Actuarial Assessment of Damages: The Thalidomide Case—I and II' (1972) 35 *MLR* 140 and 257. In *Mitchell* v. *Mulholland (No. 2)* [1972] 1 QB 65, 77, Edmund Davies LJ put it as follows: 'actuary and accountant may to a limited degree provide the judge with a means of cross-checking his calculations, and in arriving at the appropriate multiplier'. In *Auty* v. *National Coal Board* [1985] 1 All ER 930, Oliver LJ used even stronger language when he said: 'As a method of providing a reliable guide to individual behaviour patterns or to future economical and political events, the predictions of an actuary can be only a little more likely to be accurate (and will almost certainly be less interesting) than those of an astrologer' (at 939). See, however, the criticism of the traditional method by Thorpe LJ in *Wells* v. *Wells* [1997] 1 WLR 652.

[75] HL Debs., vol. 426, col. 621 (20 Jan. 1982).

[76] For an earlier recorded instance see *Thurston* v. *Todd* (1966–7) 84 WN Pt. 1.

[77] *Lim Poh Choo* v. *Camden and Islington AHA* [1980] AC 174.

[78] *Royal Commission On Civil Liability and Compensation for Personal Injury* (Select Bibliography), i, para. 35 ff. There is no reason to believe that overall the picture has changed radically in the intervening twenty-odd years.

system. Indeed, only a very small minority, estimated at about 215,000, about 6 per cent of the grand total, received any compensation in the form of tort damages. These figures are over thirty years old; but there is little reason to believe that the general picture has changed significantly. So, for the remaining 94 per cent of injured persons, social security, occupational sick pay or private insurance represent the main, if not sole, source of relief. Yet figures rarely reveal easily the full picture.

Thus, if tort victims represent only a small percentage of accident victims, their share of the aggregate value of compensation payments (estimated at £827 million at 1977 prices) amounted to just over £200 million, so that just over 6 per cent of the accident victims received some 25 per cent of the total compensation paid out. This category certainly includes a substantial percentage of the most serious types of injury, but even allowing for this, it is not disputed that tort victims fare rather better than the victims of other injuries. If these tort victims are allowed to pile on to their tort awards other benefits received from other systems of compensation (such as social security and private insurance), the danger is not only that they may end up by being over-compensated, but also that our overall compensation system may end up by being unduly costly and wasteful as regards some, and rather mean to others. Unfortunately, there is no easy solution to this problem of double compensation. Professor Atiyah, who has written extensively on this subject, has correctly identified its root cause when he wrote that:

> If there [were] any rational pattern to the various compensation systems as a whole, it might have been possible to construct a 'hierarchy' of systems under which a man should be compensated by system A, if that were possible, and if not, he should then be relegated to systems B, C and D in turn. But this is not how things have developed. In fact, each system by and large decides whether it is willing to shoulder a burden, irrespective of other compensation available, or whether it wishes to push the burden on to another system, or whether it is willing to share the burden. But the whole process is one of almost unbelievable complexity.[79]

A victim of an accident may thus find himself receiving financial assistance from a wide variety of sources. He may, for example, have been prudent enough to take out first-party insurance against precisely such a possibility; or he may become entitled to an occupational pension paid by his employer; or he may benefit from the charitable disposition of his fellow human beings made either directly to him or, as is frequently the case these days, as a result of setting up some kind of 'disaster relief fund'. Finally, he may be eligible to receive one or more of a number of social-security benefits from the state. Legislation governs the relationship between tort and social security.[80] In other cases, it is up to the courts to decide whether a particular payment should be deducted from damages starting from the general principle that the purpose of the tort rules is to compensate the claimant and not, directly or indirectly, to allow him to make a gain from the tort.

In principle, the law can take one of three options with regard to collateral benefits:[81] (*a*) cumulation, under which the claimant is allowed to retain the benefit in question

[79] P. S. Atiyah, *Accidents, Compensation and the Law* (4th edn., 1987), 390; see now ch. 15 of the 7th edn. (by P. Cane, 2006).

[80] Social Security (Recovery of Benefits) Act 1997; see below.

[81] See R. Lewis, 'Deducting Collateral Benefits from Damages' (Select Bibliography).

while being paid damages which represent his full loss; (*b*) reduction under which the collateral benefit is fully offset against the damages; and (*c*) recoupment, whereby the third-party provider is given a right to recover the amount of the benefit through an action against the tortfeasor or, in some cases, the victim. At common law, the general approach is, in principle, to allow cumulation, but subject to a highly complex case law which attempts to distinguish (unconvincingly, in the eyes of many commentators) between those benefits which go to reduce the claimant's loss and those which do not. The third option—recoupment—is seemingly barred at common law, but does operate in respect of certain social-security benefits, under a statutory regime which is now provided for by the Social Security (Recovery of Benefits) Act 1997. To analyse this body of law it is therefore necessary to consider separately the common-law rules and those applying to the statutory regime.

(B) BENEFITS NOT COVERED BY THE STATUTORY REGIME

(i) General Observations

The general starting-point against excessive compensation of the claimant has already been mentioned. In theory the compensatory principle thus demands that if the claimant's loss which flows from the tort committed against him is, somehow, diminished as a result of sums received from collateral sources[82] then the tortfeasor's liability should be reduced accordingly. But in its application this theory has given rise to considerable difficulties which flow from countervailing arguments; and our courts have had to grapple with them for decades, not to everyone's satisfaction. Before we discuss the more common cases the following general points may be of use. For deductibility can raise many issues.

Payments made to the claimant by third parties—whether they be insurance companies, charitable organisations or (in the past) the state—will not necessarily be intended as direct replacements for lost earnings. While unemployment benefits and other forms of income replacement have been viewed in this way in the past,[83] charitable donations or insurance moneys may have a separate or a more general purpose. The same is true of certain payments made by the claimant's employer. Disability pensions, for example, become payable after the employment has prematurely come to an end because of the injury and so arguably should not be seen as equivalent to wages or salary, in contrast to sick pay which is paid while the employment is still continuing.[84] It can still be argued

[82] We are, of course, here thinking of benefits *causally related to the loss*. So no one has ever suggested that money won at the lottery a few days after the accident should be deducted from a tort award.

[83] On unemployment benefits, see *Parsons* v. *BNM Laboratories* [1964] 1 QB 95 (a wrongful-dismissal case) and *Nabi* v. *British Leyland (UK) Ltd.* [1980] 1 WLR 529; on supplementary benefit and income support, *Lincoln* v. *Hayman* [1982] 1 WLR 488; on family income supplement and, by extension, family credit, *Gaskill* v. *Preston* [1981] 3 All ER 427; on statutory sick pay, *Palfrey* v. *GLC* [1985] ICR 437; and on redundancy payments, *Colledge* v. *Bass Mitchells and Butlers Ltd.* [1988] ICR 125. The effect of these decisions has now largely been overturned by the legislation discussed in the next sub-section in the text, above.

[84] *Parry* v. *Cleaver* [1970] AC 1 at 16 (per Lord Reid) and 42 (per Lord Wilberforce). The distinction between payments made during and after the end of the employment relationship was deemed to be crucial to the

that all 'collateral benefits' of this kind, which the claimant would not have received but for the accident, should be taken into account (i.e. deducted from the tort award) when calculating his *net* loss. Some support for this view can be found in the House of Lords' decision in *British Transport Commission* v. *Gourley*,[85] which emphasised the importance of establishing the plaintiff's *net* loss by deducting from his claim for lost earnings an amount equivalent to the income tax which he would have paid had he stayed in employment. However, the courts have consistently rejected any general rule of this kind in the area of collateral benefits and decisions following *Gourley* have restricted the ruling of that case to the limited question of the relationship between taxation and lost earnings.[86] So if the formulation of a general rule can be attempted (albeit with great caution) it is that collateral benefits should (and are) deducted from the award except in two broad cases: insurance monies and benevolent payments.

(ii) Insurance Moneys

There was a time when the reason given by the courts for rejecting a general rule of deduction, especially in cases involving insurance payments, were expressed in terms of causation; as Pigott B put it with regard to insurance moneys in *Bradburn* v. *Great Western Railway*:[87]

> [H]e [the plaintiff] does not receive that sum of money because of the accident, but because he had made a contract providing for that contingency; an accident must occur to entitle him to it, but it is not the accident, but his contract, which is the *cause* of his receiving it.

Similarly, in *Parry* v. *Cleaver* Lord Pearson explained the application of tests of causation and remoteness to collateral benefits in the following terms:

> I think the mental picture is this: here on one side is the accident with its train of *direct and natural consequences* happening in the ordinary course of events, and all these consequences are solely or predominantly *caused* by the accident: there on the other side is some completely collateral matter, outside the range of such consequences, having the accident as one of its causes but, on a fair view, *predominantly caused by some extraneous and independent cause*. It is clear from the decided cases that causation is an important factor in determining whether an item is too remote or not, though aspects of fairness and public policy also have a bearing.[88]

decision that a long-term benefit received by the plaintiff was akin to sick pay, and therefore deductible, in *Hussain* v. *New Taplow Paper Mills Ltd.* [1988] 1 AC 514.

85 [1956] AC 185.

86 See *Parry* v. *Cleaver* [1970] AC 1 at 13 (per Lord Reid) and 40 (per Lord Wilberforce); see also the review of the case law by Lord Templeman in *Smoker* v. *London Fire and Civil Defence Authority* [1991] 2 AC 502.

87 (1874) LR 10 Exch. 1, 3 (emphasis added). It should be stressed that this is the rule for *personal* accident insurance. In the case of insurance for *property* damage no double compensation is allowed; so, in practice, the insurer compensates the insured and is then subrogated in his (the insured's) rights against the tortfeasor. The rule in *Bradburn* was approved by both majority and minority in *Parry* v. *Cleaver* [1970] AC 1.

88 [1970] AC 1, 49 (italics supplied). Cf. Lord Pearce's remarks to the effect that: 'Strict causation seems to provide no satisfactory line of demarcation': *ibid.*, at 34.

On the other hand, the limits of the causation approach have frequently been pointed out, as, for example, in the judgment of Windeyer J in the Australian case of *National Insurance Co. of New Zealand* v. *Espagne*:[89]

Causal considerations cannot be decisive of [this] question, unless there be a general rule of law that all benefits, or foreseeable benefits, received by an injured person because of, or as a consequence of, his injury, are to be set off against the damages he can recover from a wrongdoer. In my view, there is no such rule.

An alternative (and more convincing) policy reason for the non-deductibility of insurance payments is thus that the victim has 'paid for' the benefits which he now receives, whether through the payment of insurance premiums or occupational pension contributions, or simply through past service for his employer. At the very least, then, the benefit should not go to the tortfeasor (or his insurer) in the form of a reduced damages award. A broader policy justification (and one with much force) is that such a rule encourages potential accident victims to take out first-party insurance, or at least avoids discouraging them.[90] Similarly, by disregarding charitable or voluntary donations the courts simultaneously respect the benevolent intentions of the donors who, clearly, must have intended their generosity to benefit the victim and not the tortfeasor, at the same time as preserving the incentives of donors to make such payments. As Lord Reid put it in *Parry* v. *Cleaver*:[91]

It would be revolting to the ordinary man's sense of justice, and therefore contrary to public policy, that the sufferer should have his damages reduced so that he would gain nothing from the benevolence of his friends or relations or of the public at large, and that the only gainer would be the wrongdoer.

It is on these grounds that the courts have held that the only occasion upon which a voluntary or *ex gratia* payment will be set off against damages is when it is made by the tortfeasor himself, a topic to be discussed in the following sub-section.

Public policy featured strongly in the majority judgments in the House of Lords in the leading case of *Parry* v. *Cleaver*. In that case a policeman was injured by the negligence of a motorist and was obliged to leave the police force and take up less physically exacting employment elsewhere as a clerical worker. Upon his discharge from the police he became entitled, under his conditions of service, to an occupational disability pension, to which both he and his employer had contributed while he was employed. According to Lord Reid, there was 'no relevant difference between this and any other form of insurance',[92]

89 (1961) 106 CLR 569, 597. See also *Graham* v. *Baker* (1961) 106 CLR 340. In *Parry* v. *Cleaver* [1970] AC 1, four out of five judges involved in the House of Lords rejected the use of causation. One should, however, note that in all these cases our judges are thinking of cause in law. Cause in fact, in the sense of 'would the plaintiff have received the benefit but for the accident', is relevant in deciding whether to deduct the benefit from the tort award.

90 See D. R. Harris, L. D. Campbell, and R. Halson, *Remedies in Contract and Tort* (Select Bibliography), 384.

91 [1970] AC 1, 14. By parity of reasoning the same is true of free board and lodging, etc., received for relatives or friends: *Liffen* v. *Watson* [1940] 1 KB 556. See also *McCamley* v. *Cammell Laird Shipbuilders* [1990] 1 WLR 563.

92 [1970] AC 1, 16.

with the result that it would not be taken into account when assessing the plaintiff's loss of earnings.[93]

Lords Morris and Pearson dissented from the main ruling on assessment on the ground that a disability pension of this kind was a form of deferred pay and therefore analogous to wages or salary. In addition, Lord Morris drew a distinction between an insurance policy taken out by the plaintiff of his own accord, which was purely 'personal and private' to him, and a pension to which he was required to contribute as a condition of his employment. However, as already indicated, in *Smoker* v. *London Fire and Civil Defence Authority*[94] the House of Lords reaffirmed *Parry* v. *Cleaver* in a case where the employer paying a disability pension was also the defendant in the tort claim.

It is arguable that it should make no difference for this purpose whether the pension scheme under which the payment is made is a contributory one or not; even if the employee has not made individual contributions to the pension fund, he can be said to have earned the pension by his past service for the employer.[95] However, in *Hussain* v. *New Taplow Paper Mills*[96] the House of Lords held that payments akin to long-term sick pay were deductible from damages partly because the plaintiff had made no insurance contributions towards the scheme in question. The single greatest difficulty in applying the law as it currently stands lies in distinguishing between sick pay, which is deductible on the ground that it directly offsets the claimant's lost earnings, and disablement and invalidity pensions, which are not deductible under the rule in *Parry* v. *Cleaver*. In practice, it may be highly artificial to draw a clear distinction between these two categories. The Law Commission, in its Consultation Paper on *Damages for Personal Injury: Collateral Benefits*,[97] expressed the view that a 'disablement pension is compensation for lost earnings' and should therefore be deductible.

93 A complicated issue which *Parry* v. *Cleaver* left unclear concerned the relationship between a disability pension paid in respect of premature retirement and loss of the retirement pension which the plaintiff would have expected to receive upon reaching pensionable age. In *Longden* v. *British Coal Corporation* [1998] AC 653; [1998] IRLR 29 the House of Lords held that where the disability pension took the form of a lump sum, that part of the sum which represented payments which the plaintiff would have received post-retirement should be deducted from his damages. See R. Lewis, 'The Overlap between Damages for Personal Injury and Work Related Benefits' (1998) 27 *ILJ* 1, at 18. In the recent Scottish case of *Cantwell* v. *Criminal Injuries Compensation Board* (2001) SLT 966, Lord Hope adopted the same approach in interpreting s. 10 of the Administration of Justice Act 1982 (which concerns the assessment of damages for personal injury claims in Scots law): 'The periods before and after the normal retirement age require to be considered separately. Prior to the retirement age the claim is for loss of earnings. Pension benefits received during that period cannot be set off against the claim for loss of earnings ... After the retirement date the claim is for loss of pension. In order to compare like with like, pension benefits received and to be received after that date must be brought into account.'

94 [1991] 2 All ER 449.

95 Per Cohen LJ in *Payne* v. *Railway Executive* [1952] 1 KB 26, 35–6.

96 [1988] AC 514, 532 (Lord Bridge); see Lewis, n. 93 above, at 13.

97 Consultation Paper No. 147 (Select Bibliography), at para. 4.67; see also paras. 4.5–4.60, where the arguments traditionally put in favour of non-deduction of collateral benefits are subjected to a rigorous (and largely critical) analysis. In its final report on this issue. In its Report No. 262, *Damages for Personal Injury: Medical, Nursing and Other Expenses – Collateral Benefits* (Select Bibliography), the Law Commission came to the conclusion (after consultation showed no firm support for any particular option for reform) that it should not recommend any legislative changes to the current regime for deductions for such 'collateral benefits'. One of the key elements which led it to this conclusion was the difficulty of distinguishing between the different types of

The courts have also considered the rights of the third-party provider of the collateral benefit to recover the sums in question from either the tortfeasor or the victim. At common law the third-party provider has no general right of recoupment, by virtue of the decision of the Court of Appeal in *Metropolitan Police District Receiver* v. *Croydon Corp.*[98] This decision has been criticised by the Law Commission on the grounds that 'a tortfeasor is unjustly enriched at the expense of providers of collateral benefits who act under legal compulsion',[99] although the Law Commission also recognised that third-party providers could protect themselves contractually, by stipulating that the claimant should make the repayment in the event of a damages claim being successful.[100]

(iii) Benevolent Donations

We alluded to this group of cases in the previous sub-section but now we must proceed with a distinction.

If an injured person continues to receive part of his wages or salary from his employer during a period away from work his loss is that much less than it would have been if he had not received these payments. If he is *entitled* to such payment, then this amount must be deducted from the award for, as Lord Morris put it, 'if he receives part of his pay, he cannot assert that he has lost *all* his pay'.[101]

By extension, the same rule in favour of deduction applies to payments made by the employer in substitution for wages, such as sick pay. For, as Lord Templeman put it, 'payments which correspond to wages must be taken into account when assessing loss of wages'.[102] In *Hussain* v. *New Taplow Paper Mills Ltd.*[103] the House of Lords held that the payment by the employer of a long-term sickness benefit fell into the same category as sick pay and had to be deducted from the employee's claim for loss of earnings.

On the other hand, payments made *gratuitously* to the claimant will *not* be deducted from the award since it reasonable to assume that the 'benefactor' who pays these

payments at issue: e.g., many pensions may be payable out of types of insurance fund or contract, meaning that '[l]egislation . . . would therefore need to spell out very clearly when a payment was to be regarded as a disablement pension. This would inevitably lead to complexity. It is also quite likely that however carefully the provision was drafted, there would still be uncertainty about how some payments should be categorised' (para. 11.51). However, it did comment that the most commonly noted inconsistency in the current law is the different treatment accorded to pre-retirement disability pensions (not deductible) and contractual sick pay (deductible) (para. 11.41 ff.).

98 [1957] 1 QB 154.

99 Consultation Paper No. 147, *Damages for Personal Injury: Collateral Benefits* (Select Bibliography) para. 5.6. In its final report on the matter (Report No. 262, *Damages for Personal Injury: Medical, Nursing and Other Expenses – Collateral Benefits* (Select Bibliography)), the Law Commission was still of this view, although it stressed that care should be taken in establishing whether or not the enrichment in question actually was 'unjust' in any given case (para. 12.31).

100 Consultation Paper No. 147, *Damages for Personal Injury: Collateral Benefits* (Select Bibliography), para. 5.13. The Law Commission also considered whether there should be a general right of third parties to recover collateral benefits from the victim; such a matter should, in its view, be left up to the development of the common law rather than be made the subject of statutory intervention (*ibid.*, para. 5.26; see also Report No. 262, *Damages for Personal Injury: Medical, Nursing and Other Expenses—Collateral Benefits* (Select Bibliography) paras. 12.27 and 12.32 for a confirmation of this approach).

101 *Parry* v. *Cleaver* [1970] AC 1 at 34.

102 *Smoker* v. *London Fire Authority* [1991] 2 All ER 449.

103 [1988] AC 514.

amounts is not intending to assist the tortfeasor (by lessening his obligation to make amends) but the victim.[104]

But if the person making the gratuitous payment is also the tortfeasor, then a deduction should normally be made[105] In practice the courts thus try to distinguish between true benevolent payments, from schemes set up by the employers (and paid by them) in order to promote good relations between them and their employees. So, payments made to a seriously injured employee by the employer's group personal accident insurance policy was not a 'true' benevolence payment (made out of sympathy or charity) to the employee and should therefore be deducted from the tort award.[106]

(iv) Payments Made by Local Authorities

Pursuant to the provisions of Section 26 of the National Assistance Act 1948 a local authority has a duty to provide, and pay for, the care of a disabled person. It is also required to recover those costs from the individual concerned unless he satisfies them that he is unable to make a full refund. However, damages paid into the Court of Protection on behalf of a patient, and the income derived from that capital, is to be ignored for the purposes of recoupment by a local authority.[107] These two decisions have led some defendants to argue that they should not have to pay for costs of care since the same will be met by the local authority

In *Sowden* v. *Lodge*[108] the Court of Appeal held that the correct question to be addressed in relation to the care element was what was required to meet the reasonable needs of the claimant and whether those needs would in fact be met by the local authority. The court stressed that it was for the defendants to prove that the relevant local or public authority was under a duty to make provision for the claimant's needs and that they were meeting them at the time of trial and would continue to do so in the future. In two subsequent cases[109] the courts have rejected submissions from the defendants that it was for the claimants to put evidence before the court as to what assistance was available from the local authority and why it was insufficient to meet the claimant's reasonable needs. In the former case the judge went further and declined to hold that a claimant who had not availed herself of provision available from a local authority was guilty of a failure to mitigate her loss. We thus think that it will be a rare case in which a court finds that the assistance available from a local authority is sufficient not least because there can rarely, if ever, be a guarantee that such assistance will continue indefinitely.

104 *Redpath* v. *Belfast and County Down Railway* [1947] NI 167, approved by the House of Lords in *Parry* v. *Cleaver* [1970] AC 1. Moreover, no deduction will be made in respect of payments made to the claimant which are intended to be in the nature of a loan, to be returned in the event of damages being awarded against the tortfeasor: *Browning* v. *War Office* [1963] 1 QB 750, 770 (Diplock LJ).

105 *Williams* v. *BOC Gases* [2000] PIQR Q253, approved by the Court of Appeal in *Gaca* v. *Pirelli General plc* [2004] 1 WLR 2683.

106 *Gaca* v. *Pirelli General plc* [2004] 1 WLR 2683.

107 *Bell* v. *Todd* [2002] Lloyd's Rep. Med. 12 and *Ryan* v. *Liverpool Health Authority* [2002] Lloyd's Rep. Med. 23. Neither decision has been appealed.

108 [2004] EWCA Civ. 1370

109 *Freeman* v. *Lockett* [2006] EWHC 102 and *Walton* v. *Calderdale Healthcare NHS Trust* [2005] EWHC 1053 QB.

(c) BENEFITS SUBJECT TO THE STATUTORY REGIME

The modern welfare state[110] has established many types of benefits that are made to those whose earnings or other sources of income have been interrupted by injury or disease; these include unemployment benefits and benefits in respect of both short-term and long-term illness and disability. In practice, these benefits provide the bulk of financial support received by those without regular income or earnings, including those who are injured in tortious incidents. Only some of the victims of tortious events may also be lucky enough to obtain tort damages.[111] Over the years, opinion has hardened in favour of the view that claimants should not be allowed to cumulate such damages with social-security benefits in such a way as to receive double compensation.[112] But that is as far as agreement seems to have gone. How much deduction should be made, how and by whom have been subjects that have divided 'official' as well as academic opinion. The resulting legislation reflects this uncertainty; and coupled as it is with the usual verbosity favoured by English drafters, it has produced a regime that is as complex as it is intellectually contradictory. Moreover, legislative fine-tuning is still continuing. All attempts to simplify it, even for the purposes of presenting it to law students, are thus bound to produce fuzziness at the fringes. The reader has, accordingly, been warned!

One reason for the complexity is that we now have not one but several statutory regimes dealing with the question of deductibility of state-paid benefits, according to the date on which the cause of action accrued and the claim was made. This is the result of successive statutory changes to the system that was initially established by legislation in 1948. This 'old' regime was more fully described in the earlier editions of this book (especially the third).[113]

The Social Security Act 1989 replaced the 'old' regime with a new scheme of state 'recoupment' of social-security benefits from damages awards which exceed a threshold of £2,500. This scheme, which we may call the 'new' regime, was further amended with effect from 6 October 1997 by the Social Security (Recovery of Benefits) Act 1997. The basic principle is now that the court must disregard receipts of certain specified social-security benefits when making its assessment of damages. However, the *tortfeasor* must then pay to the Department of Social Security the full amount of any of the relevant benefits that the claimant has received in respect of his injury or accident.[114] The

110 The best account on the growth of the welfare protection against accident and disease can be found in W. R. Cornish and G. de N. Clark, *Law and Society in England 1750–1950* (1989), a rare combination of scholarship and readability. A shorter and clear account (though still too detailed for most university tort courses) is found in P. Cane, *Atiyah's Accidents Compensation and the Law* (7th edn., 2006), ch. 13.

111 See our discussion in ch. 1, above.

112 Although, as we have seen, a different view is taken with regard to private and/or employer-based insurance.

113 At its core lay s. 2(1) of the Law Reform (Personal Injuries) Act 1948 which provided that in the case of certain specified benefits there should be a *partial* deduction from damages for personal injury, amounting to *half* the social-security payments made to the plaintiff up to a maximum period of five years from the cause of the action. Benefits both paid and likely to be paid after the judgment were deductible, but in calculating future benefit entitlement no account was taken of likely increases in the levels of payment.

114 The courts have had to consider the complex situation which arises where the claimant was, prior to the accident, in receipt of non-recoupable social security benefits. In such a situation, the claimant may not be able

Department of Social Security is not formally subrogated to the claimant's claim, but the effect is similar. Hence the tortfeasor must now pay in full, but the claimant is worse off than he was (when the 1948 Act applied) since a *complete* (and not 50 per cent) deduction of benefits takes place. The justification for recoupment is the argument that the previous system had the effect of 'subsidising' the activities of tortfeasors, as well as giving rise to double compensation of claimants. Although a full account of the scheme is outside the scope of this book, a number of points concerning its operation may be noted.

First, the deduction is made only against certain heads of damages: these are compensation for lost earnings, for cost of care and for loss of mobility.[115] This is a change made by the 1997 Act. For claims in respect of torts committed between 1989 and 1997, the deduction could be made in respect of all heads of loss. The thinking behind the change made in 1997 is that social-security benefits do not provide compensation for heads of loss such as pain and suffering and loss of amenities;[116] therefore, recoupment is inappropriate in these cases. This marks a partial return to the Act of 1948. However, it is still the case, under the new regime, that no account is taken of contributory negligence. Recoupment of benefits and reductions for contributory negligence will therefore have a cumulative impact in diminishing the plaintiff's award.[117]

Second, the range of social-security benefits in respect of which deduction must be made is now reasonably comprehensive; the drafter appears to have sought to include all benefits which could be payable in respect of one of the heads of damage to which the deduction rule applies. Hence there is little scope for the common law rules to apply as they did to certain social-security payments under the 1948 Act.[118]

Third, there are certain exemptions.[119] These include payments made under specified statutory schemes (such as the Criminal Injuries Compensation Scheme,

to prevent the recoupment of benefits received after the accident (see *Hassall* v. *Secretary of State for Social Security* [1995] 1 WLR 812), but in so far as he is thereby left financially worse off than he would have been had he continued to receive the non-recoupable benefit, he may have a claim for the difference, as special damages, against the tortfeasor: *Neal* v. *Bingle* [1998] 2 WLR 57.

115 See Social Security (Recovery of Benefits) Act 1997, ss. 1(1)(a), 1(4)(b) and 29, and Sch. 2, Col. 1.

116 See, e.g., the decision of the Inner House in *Mitchell* v. *Laing*, (1998) SLT 203, where it was held that 'loss of mobility' under the Act relates to loss of actual mobility as a result of the injury (such as bus or taxi fares which would otherwise have been unnecessary), but not to the annoyance, irritation or frustration of not being as mobile as prior to the injury (at 210C-D).

117 And the operation of contributory negligence will have no effect upon the amount payable by the tortfeasor to the DSS either: it seems that the DSS may still recoup the full cost of all the benefits covered.

118 The 'listed benefits' are those contained in Sch. 2, Col. 2 to the 1997 Act. Should a court be required to consider a benefit falling outside this list, it seems most likely that the residual common law rule of reduction of damages in respect of social security benefits would be applied (*Hodgson* v. *Trapp* [1989] AC 807). This has been confirmed by *Ballantine* v. *Newalls Insulation Co. Ltd.* [2000] PIQR Q327 and *Rand* v. *East Dorset Health Authority* [2001] PIQR Q1. *Rand* concerned a successful claim of a negligent misrepresentation, in the form of the Health Authority's failure to warn the claimant parents of the risk of their child being born with Down's syndrome: Newman J refused to hold that such claims for economic loss (suffered in consequence of the child's disability) fell within the term 'injury' in s. 1(1)(a) of the 1997 Act. He then proceeded to deal with the case under the common-law principles, holding that no deduction should be made, since the benefits had been received on behalf of their child and not with reference to any reduction of the cost of the wrong done to the parents ([13]–[18]).

119 Social Security (Recovery of Benefits) Act 1997, Sch. 1, Part I, and SI No. 1997/2205 (as amended by SI No. 2001/1118), reg. 2.

which has its own rules relating to recoupment) and charitable trusts. Claims made under the Fatal Accidents Act 1976 are also excluded.[120] The Act also grants the Secretary of State the power to adopt regulations exempting payments below a certain amount,[121] but at the time of writing this power has not been exercised. By contrast, between 1989 and 1997, the relevant legislation provided for 'small payments' of below £2,500 to be subject to a modified version of the 'old' regime under the Act of 1948 and this system still applies to compensation payments made in the period between the entry into force of the 1989 Act (which was later consolidated in the Social Security Administration Act 1992) and the entry into force of the 1997 Act.

Fourth, the maximum period for which benefits may be taken into account remains five years, but it may now be shortened to less than that if the payment is made before the five years have expired. In that case no account will then be taken of benefit paid or payable after receipt of the compensation. This appears to be an attempt to encourage early settlements.[122]

Fifth, the introduction of compulsory recoupment has made it necessary to institute a complex and potentially intrusive scheme of state administration of the process of making personal injury payments. The compensator (who would normally be the tortfeasor's insurance company) must not make any payment to the victim until he has applied for and has received a certificate of recoverable benefits from the Secretary of State, specifying the amount to be deducted. The Compensation Recovery Unit of the Department of Social Security has the task of processing these applications. In the last resort the Secretary of State can initiate proceedings against a compensator who fails to apply for a certificate. Both alleged tortfeasors and recipients of state benefits are under a duty to provide the Compensation Recovery Unit with information concerning the claim.[123] So it is the defendant (or his insurer) and not the claimant who has to obtain the relevant certificate from the Unit and to pay what is due.

Whatever its other merits, the recoupment scheme has done little to clarify the law of collateral benefits. The distinctions between different types of benefits are as arbitrary as they were before. For example, the rationale for the exclusion from the scheme of Fatal Accidents Act cases is unclear. The new regime has in effect achieved a partial levelling down of the compensation of tort victims so that they are now at less of an advantage compared to accident victims who are wholly dependent on social security. However, the savings made do not appear to be substantial enough to produce significant improvements in the levels of social security benefits paid to all accident victims, in particular when account is taken of the cost of administering the recoupment scheme. Moreover, accident victims with the benefit of private or occupational insurance continue to receive full compensation without deduction. This preferential treatment of private, as opposed to social, insurance has no clear rationale.[124]

[120] SI No. 1997/200, reg. 2(2)(a). [121] Social Security (Recovery of Benefits) Act 1997, Sch. 1, Part 2.

[122] *Ibid.*, s. 3. [123] See SI No. 1997/2205, regs. 3–6.

[124] It should also be noted in this regard that under the common law, private insurers are not subrogated to the personal-injury claims of claimants taking out first-party life and accident insurance: J. G. Fleming, *The Law of Torts* (8th edn., 1992) at 367.

5. MISCELLANEOUS MATTERS

(A) LUMP SUMS (AND ALTERNATIVE OPTIONS): THE THEORETICAL OPTIONS

The first thing to note is that in tort actions the traditional common law rule has been that damages must be awarded[125] once only in respect of each cause of action and they take the form of a lump sum.[126] The great merit of such an approach was meant to be the idea that with the award of damages a 'closure' was achieved to the incident that caused the harm that tort law normally deals with. Victims and tortfeasors, to the extent that was possible, could now turn the page and begin a new phase in their life. Thus, during their long history, English courts never had (nor sought) any power to order the payment of damages in periodic sums unless the parties agreed to such a method of settling the dispute.[127]

The main consequence of such a philosophy was that they often had to include compensation for future damage that was likely to accrue, in addition to compensation for damage that has already done so. This is easier to decide in theory than to apply in practice. The problems become apparent in personal injury cases, where the judge has to try to guess not only what would have happened to the victim if he had not been injured, but also what is now likely to happen to him as a result of the accident. This 'guessing game' is further aggravated by the fact that it takes place against a number of imponderables, some of which are related to the victim (e.g. the nature of his injury, its likely complications and pre-trial anxiety—known as 'compensation neurosis'—which can postpone complete recovery and complicate the task of assessment of the loss); while others are linked with wider economic factors (e.g. inflation, rates of taxation, etc.) but may affect particularly harshly a victim who, because of the tort, may have reduced earning capacity. The great disadvantage of lump-sum awards is not only that they make such estimates of future developments little more than educated guesses, but also that they are not open to subsequent correction.

[125] *Miliangos* v. *George Frank (Textiles) Ltd.* [1976] AC 443 abolished the old rule that damages must be expressed in sterling. Thus, see *The Despina R* [1979] AC 685. But the sterling rule still applies to non-pecuniary damages such as damages for pain and suffering and loss amenity: *Hoffman* v. *Sofaer* [1982] 1 WLR 1350.

[126] This rule against successive actions has to be qualified in at least two major respects. First, it does not apply to continuing torts (e.g. continuing trespass) and, second, it does not apply whenever two different rights have been violated: *Brunsden* v. *Humphrey* (1884) 14 QBD 141. For a more recent illustration see *Barrow* v. *Bankside Agency Ltd.* [1996] 1 WLR 257 and note that the doctrine of *res judicata* may be relevant in such cases.

[127] *Fournier* v. *Canadian National Railway* [1927] AC 167. At common law it was not clear whether the courts would have the power even if the arrangement was agreed to by the parties themselves (see *Metcalfe* v. *London Passenger Transport Board* [1938] 2 All ER 352 at 355); however, the Damages Act 1996, s. 2, now provides that '[a] court awarding damages in an action for personal injury may, with the consent of the parties, make an order under which the damages are wholly or partly to take the form of periodical payments'.

In *Lim* v. *Camden and Islington Area Health Authority*[128] Lord Scarman was frank about this danger when he said:

Sooner or later . . . if the parties do not settle, a court (once liability is admitted or proved) has to make an award of damages. The award, which covers past, present and future injury and loss, must under our law be a lump sum assessed at the conclusion of the legal process. The award is final; it is not susceptible to review as the future unfolds, substituting fact for estimate. Knowledge of the future being denied to mankind, so much of the award as is to be attributed to future loss and suffering—in many cases the major part of the award—will almost surely be wrong. *There is really only one certainty: the future will prove the award to be either too high or too low.*

These remarks were prompted by Lord Denning MR's attempt in the Court of Appeal[129] to change or, at least, adapt the existing practice and to enable an award of damages in cases such as the one before the court to be regarded as an interim award, allowing the court to make further adjustments in the future. Lord Denning was, as always, restless and prophetic. But prophets rarely meet with approval. Lord Scarman, not surprisingly, thus retorted that the idea was

an attractive, ingenious suggestion—but . . . unsound. For so radical a reform can be made neither by judges nor by modification of rules of court. It raises issues of social, economic and financial policy not amenable to judicial reform which will almost certainly prove to be controversial and can be resolved by the legislature only after full consideration of factors which cannot be brought into clear focus, or be weighed and assessed, in the course of the forensic process.[130]

Lord Scarman certainly had a point when he implied that such a major reform could only come from the legislature as he was also right when he suggested that reform could only come after a variety of factors (which cannot easily be weighed in the forensic context) had been carefully weighed. As we shall note at the end of this section this is, indeed, what happened before periodical payments were introduced into our system in 2003 (but with effect as of 1 April 2005), though it still remains unclear to what extent the insurance position was adequately factored in the thinking of the government.[131]

The alternative to the lump-sum method of payment of damages is the annuity system which has for a long time been adopted (in theory, though not rigidly in practice) by a number of European systems such as, for instance, the French and the German. Its main advantage is its ability to adapt the award downwards or upwards depending on whether the victim's condition and other circumstances become better or worse. In a number of instances—for example, in cases of fatal accidents where the chances of remarriage of the surviving spouse have to be considered—this method of payment of the damages award helps avoid awkward or embarrassing guessing exercises.[132]

128 [1980] AC 174, 182–3 (emphasis added). 129 [1979] QB 196, 214 ff.

130 [1980] AC 174, 183. See also Lord Steyn's highly critical comments on the present system of lump sum payments in *Wells* v. *Wells* [1998] 3 WLR 329, 351.

131 A point made among others by Professor Richard Lewis in 'The Politics and Economic of Tort Law: Judicially Imposed Periodical Payments of Damages' (2006) 69 *MLR* 418.

132 We shall return to this point in our treatment of fatal accidents.

Annuities, however, are not without their problems. For example, they require that the files on cases are 'kept open' and insurance companies, which meet most of the claims, understandably prefer to pay (if they have to pay) and 'close their books'. A mechanism must also be devised to allow for the adjustment of the sums paid and this can involve costs and delays. Who will make the adjustment? When and how often, are all questions which must be addressed; and they can receive different answers. We shall return to this point at the end of this section when we shall describe the position adopted by the Courts Act 2003 (amending the Damages Act 1996).

Annuities present other problems. For instance, what if the entity (legal or physical) who has to pay damages goes bankrupt? Is this a real risk when the payor/defendant is the National Health Service, i.e. typically a local authority? Is this a reason why a plaintiff could insist in being paid in a lump sum? Victims also tend to prefer to receive their compensation in one large amount even though the unexpected receipt of large sums may lead them to spend their awards in a very short time and then leave them without adequate financial resources to maintain themselves. The reason why they may need a lump sum can be understandable and legitimate, for instance the need to make structural adjustments to their homes in order to help them cope with any resulting permanent disability. Alternatively, they may be tempted to profit from a sudden windfall and have 'a good time'. Should the state, by means of a law, protect such victims against their own profligacy? Last but by no means least, lawyers are, in some cases and in some systems, likelier to receive their remuneration without complaints and expeditiously if the client/victim receives a large sum rather than modest, periodic payments. For a variety of practical reasons, therefore, the lump sum method of payment of the damages award has had supporters which extend beyond the force of a long history.

Though the respective strengths and weakness of the two systems of compensation—lump sums versus annuities—were first thoroughly discussed in this country in the mid-1970s, the debate gained momentum with the passage of time, the increase in the size of awards (and the economic consequences this entailed), as well as with a growing feeling of dissatisfaction with the administration of civil (as well as criminal) justice. The search for better solutions was, inevitably, turning towards mixed systems which, so far as possible, would attempt to combine the advantages of the two extreme solutions—namely, the lump sum versus the system of annuity payments. The emerging practice of 'structured settlements', described in sub-section (iv), above, partially addressed these problems in the case of damages for serious injuries; and this helped supplement the three further ways available to the common law to alleviate the underlying problems. These are (*i*) postponed or split trials; (*ii*) interim awards; and (*iii*) provisional damages. But all these proved inadequate and the revolution, as stated, came in 2005 with the introduction of reviewable periodic payments which will form the last sub-section of this part of the chapter.

(i) Postponed or Split Trials

It has already been noted why the lump sum method of payment of damages raises serious difficulties in the calculation of the right level of the award, especially where the extent of the injury is not yet fully determined. One way around this difficulty is to postpone the trial or settlement of the claim until a clearer picture about the victim's position has emerged. Unfortunately, such a solution presupposes that such a delay will make the prognosis of the future easier, which is not always the case. Moreover, this way of proceeding adds to the delays of the tort process, which has always been one of the major weaknesses of the system. Finally, such delays may trigger off in susceptible claimants the so-called problem of 'compensation neurosis' and thus further delay their rehabilitation.

As a result of these limitations the different corrective device of 'split trials' was proposed by the Court of Appeal in 1974 in *Coenen* v. *Payne*.[133] This, as the name suggests, entails separating 'liability' which can be resolved (or admitted) as soon as possible after the accident (when recollections of witnesses are still (relatively) clear), from the 'quantum' of damages, which in most serious cases could be postponed until a clear prognosis could be attempted. Once again, however, there is no certainty that postponement makes prognosis easier; and, under existing law (and subject to what is said below), when the award is made it is final. In any event, this method of proceeding can only have its full effect if it is combined with the possibility of interim damages. Both these ideas, however, have met with little enthusiasm in practice and are mentioned here for the sake of completeness rather than as oft-used procedures in the compensation process.

(ii) Interim Damages

The idea of awarding interim damages is even older. It can be traced back to the Winn Committee report of 1968 and is nowadays regulated by Part II of Order 29 of the Rules of the Supreme Court, rule 11. Such an order can be made at the discretion of the court where 'need' can be shown by the claimant.[134] The money is meant to cover the claimant's interim pecuniary losses (such as loss of earnings, medical expenses and the like) and cannot include a percentage of his (possible) general damages. For a variety of reasons this procedure, too, seems to be underused in practice. Some of the reasons for this seem to be purely technical;[135] and, nowadays, the operation of the Social Security (Recovery of Benefits) Act 1997 (described above in Section 4) may also have an adverse effect in so far as there is the danger that the new scheme might swallow up all interim payments, especially in those cases involving smaller sums. So this device, too, has been of limited use to claimants.

(iii) Provisional Damages

Provisional damages provide the third, comparatively recent, innovation that aims to improve the position of the deserving victim of personal injury. They were made possible by section 6 of the Administration of Justice Act 1982 which empowers the courts 'to make a provisional award in cases where the medical prognosis is particularly

133 [1974] 1 WLR 984, now covered by the Civil Procedure Rules Part 3(2)(1).

134 *Schott Kem Ltd.* v. *Bentley* [1991] 1 QB 61.

135 They are discussed in the Law Commission Consultation Paper No. 125, *Structured Settlements and Interim and Provisional Damages* (Select Bibliography), 71–2.

uncertain and where there is a *chance*,[136] falling short of probability, that some *serious* disease or *serious* deterioration in the plaintiff's condition will accrue at a later date'.[137]

In the debates in the House of Lords the Lord Chancellor, Lord Hailsham, did not envisage that frequent use would be made of this provision;[138] and events have proved him right. The example he gave of a case suitable to be brought under this heading was of a young child whose skull was fractured in an accident and who, at the trial, may appear to have made full recovery. Yet in cases of cranial injuries there is always a chance of subsequent epilepsy. Section 6 will now enable the court to award nothing in respect of the feared event but to give damages later if the feared event materialises. This procedure will avoid trying to evaluate the possibility of the feared event materialising and then awarding for this 'chance' a smaller sum that may end by being too low or too high. Unlike the Pearson proposals on this point, it is not obligatory for the court to adopt this procedure on its own; it will be for the claimant to claim that a provisional damages award be made; and the interests of the defendant will also have to be given due weight. The case of *Willson* v. *Ministry of Defence*[139] has, as already stated, revealed how conservative the approach of the courts has been.

The provision of section 6 of the Administration of Justice Act 1982 was brought into force in July 1985.[140] Under the new regime, as it was judicially explained in *Willson*'s case, three requirements will have to be fulfilled before use of this procedure can be sanctioned. First, there must be a *chance* of the feared event materialising at some later date. The chance may be slim but, as stated, it must be measurable. Second, there must be a serious deterioration of the claimant's physical (and, presumably, also mental) condition and not just an ordinary deterioration or progression of the injury or illness. This is a matter of fact and degree but the facts of *Willson*'s case suggest that the courts are taking a conservative (arguably over-conservative) attitude towards this requirement. Finally, the judge must be persuaded that the case before him justifies the exercise of his discretion to give the claimant the right to return at a later date for more; or, on the contrary, that it is one that is best resolved by a once-and-for-all award of damages. In his decision, the judge will also, normally, specify the period within which the application for further damages must be made, though nowadays there seems to be a preference for not setting a limit at all.[141]

The tort victim may not just get worse as a result of his injuries; he may also die. If a provisional award has been made to him prior to the death, how will this affect the legal position of his dependants? The answer is now to be found in section 3 of the Damages Act 1996 which does not preclude his dependants from bringing a lost-dependency claim. Wisely, however, the Act adds that any part of the provisional award that was 'intended to compensate him for pecuniary loss in a period that in the event falls after his death shall be taken into account in assessing the amount of any loss of support' suffered by the dependants.

[136] In *Willson* v. *Ministry of Defence* [1991] 1 All ER 638 the trial judge was of the view that s. 32A of the Supreme Court Act 1981 was concerned with measurable, not fanciful, chances, thus further limiting the opportunity of using this procedure.

[137] It will be noticed that this section applies to contingencies due to medical reasons.

[138] HL Debs., vol. 428, col. 28 (8 Mar. 1982). [139] [1991] 1 All ER 638, 641.

[140] RSC, Ord. 37, rr. 7–12. [141] See R. J. Bragg, 'Provisional Damages' (1992) 136 *SJ* 654, 655.

For most commentators the regime described above seems to be unduly restrictive. Their arguments can be found in the specialised literature; and they are also conveniently summarised and discussed critically in Law Commission Consultation Paper No. 125.[142] Here it is enough to note two of the most doubtful limitations and, also, add an observation of wider import.

First, one must recall that the feared event must be specified by the claimant's lawyers in the original action in considerable detail. As we have seen, the courts seem to take an overly narrow view on the question whether the subsequent event is a serious deterioration or an ordinary deterioration or development of the injury or illness.

Second, the right to return to the court and have the award adjusted arises only once and this may cause injustice in some cases. For example, suppose that the claimant is injured in his legs and runs the risk of subsequently developing arthritis. Since it is the disease that must be specified by the claimant's application and not the parts of his body that are susceptible to it, what will happen to the claimant who develops arthritis in one of the injured legs? It would be unfair to suggest that he would have to wait until the other leg was also affected by the disease; but it would be equally unfair to limit his subsequent increase of damages to include the arthritis in the one leg.

Finally, one may use this opportunity to ask a wider question concerning the attitudes of our (conservatively inclined) legislators. For, having identified an area of the law that needs reform, why do they then feel such an irresistible urge to circumscribe the reforming rules to such an extent as to make them almost useless? The tendency is obvious in other parts of the law of torts;[143] and readers inclined towards speculating about more general matters might wish to ponder over this question. In the meantime, however, and as far as this particular topic is concerned, all one can say is that the institution of provisional damages is, over ten years after its introduction, still in its formative stages. One must, therefore, hope that the courts will be responsive to calls to liberalise their present position on this issue before judicial accretions (such as *Willson*)[144] make this task truly impossible.

(iv) Structured Settlements[145]

To cure some of the defects of the lump sum which, as we have noted, tend to be aggravated in cases of serious physical injuries, the practice of 'structured settlements'

[142] At 76–84.

[143] For instance, the old s. 4 of the Defamation Act 1952 dealing with 'unintentional defamation'.

[144] A case law search has disclosed only one recent case in which *Willson* was considered and the judge in *Fashade* v. *North Middlesex Hospital NHS Trust* [2001] 4 QB 13 refused to grant provisional damages for the claimant's respiratory disability, on the ground that the risk was not 'clear and severable' as opposed to 'a continuing deterioration'. This continues to suggest a highly restrictive approach on the part of the courts to provisional damages claims, although some commentators have justified this due to the need to prevent the introduction of a 'serious measure of uncertainty into the system' (W. V. H. Rogers, *Winfield and Jolowicz on Tort* (16th edn., 2002), 772–3; the passage no longer finds a place in the 17th edn. (2006)).

[145] A thorough discussion of the practice and its weak points can be found in R. Lewis, *Structured Settlements: The Law and Practice* (Select Bibliography), in the Law Commission's Consultation Paper No. 125, *Structured Settlements and Interim and Provisional Damages* and in its Report No. 224 of the same name (both:

emerged in the late 1980s, following roughly the model established earlier in the United States and Canada. To the extent that they form part of 'an out of court settlement' process they have nothing to do with court awards which are the subject of this chapter. Yet even a book such as this cannot fail to give an account of their existence for two main reasons.

First, because structured settlements from part of the evolutionary regime which our law of damages has followed, from its original preference for lump sums via a systems of periodical payments giving effect to the will of the parties, to the recently introduced system of periodical forms of payment. The latter, however, differ from the structured settlements because they do not derive from the will of the parties (which receives the blessing of the courts) but by a decision of the court itself (though, of course, this is taken after consultation with the parties).

Second, because the emergence of structured settlements constitutes one of those fascinating examples of 'bargains in the shadow of the law' in the sense that structured settlements represent a 'corrective' to existing practices, worked out by practitioners (lawyers, actuaries and insurers), rather than being introduced by legislation[146] or the courts, and finally made viable through the active co-operation of the Inland Revenue.

The latter's intervention was crucial and came in the form of a 1987 interpretation of an earlier court judgment[147] in a way that allows payments to be made to the claimant in the form of an annuity to be treated, in certain circumstances, as payments of capital (and thus not subject to tax) rather than payments of income. This led to four 'model agreements' being reached between the Inland Revenue and the Association of British Insurers which make the new method of payment of awards attractive to all the parties in the dispute. For, by treating the periodic payments as non-taxable capital, liability insurers who adopt one of the four model agreements can pay out less and yet end up by funding payments to the injured claimant that are greater than if he had received from them a lump sum and then invested it directly producing taxable, annual income.

So what were structured settlements?

A structured settlement is the purchase, by the parties at the time of settlement, of an annuity for the injured individual. The structured settlement is based on a lump sum

Select Bibliography). For shorter but just as interesting discussions see: D. Allen, 'Structured Settlements' (1988) 104 *LQR* 448; M. Edwards, 'Structured Settlements' [1989] *LSG* 32; D. Hulls, 'Structuring Personal Injury Awards' [1990] *LSG* 27; R. Lewis, 'Pensions Replace Lump Sum Damages: Are Structured Settlements the Most Important Reform of Tort in Modern Times?' (1988) 15 *J Law Soc.* 392; *idem*, 'Structured Settlements in Practice' [1991] *Civil Justice Quarterly* 212; *idem*, 'Legal Limits on the Structure of Settlement of Damages' [1993] *CLJ* 470; G. Rifkind, 'The Nuts and Bolts of Structured Settlements' [1992] *The Lawyer* 6; E.G. Upenicks, 'Structured Settlements: Are They Here to Stay?' (1982) 3 *Advocates' Quarterly* 393; A. Whitfield, 'The Basics and Tactics of Structured Settlements' (1992) 142 *NLJ* 135.

146 Though now the subject is to some extent covered by the Damages Act 1996—especially ss. 2 and 4—which came into force on 24 Sept. 1996. Before that Act, certain amendments to tax legislation had been made to encourage structured settlements (see Finance Act 1995, s. 142, and further changes made by the Finance Act 1996).

147 *Dott* v. *Brown* [1936] 1 All ER 543. It has been argued by C. Francis, 'Taxation of Structured Settlements' [1991] *British Tax Review* 56, that this interpretation may be, partially at least, wrong. Since it is unlikely, however, that anyone other than the Revenue has *locus standi* to challenge this interpretation, the practical significance of this doubt may be nil, as the author of the article readily admits.

which is calculated using the multiplier and multiplicand method and involves making the usual guesses and estimates about the duration of the claimant's life. The annuity so purchased can either be at a level rate or index-linked. The annual sum payable will then continue for as long as the claimant lives, the risk of the claimant living longer than estimated being borne by the insurers. If the beneficiary survives for only a short period then the annuity dies with him subject only to one proviso. The proviso is that structured settlements will generally have a guaranteed period which may be five or more years. But if the annuity is fixed for a period of time and the beneficiary dies before the expiry of this period, then it will continue for the benefit of his dependants. If, on the other hand, the beneficiary lives for far longer than was expected at the date of trial, he will continue to receive the income from the annuity throughout his life.

A structured settlement can only be entered into by agreement between the parties. The court is unable to impose one. In practice, it is the claimant who decides whether to structure part or all of his damages. For it is of little moment or interest to a defendant since he either pays the lump sum to the claimant or his representatives or pays part or all of it to a financial institution for the purchase of the annuity. But, as stated, it makes a great difference for the claimant to receive his damages in this manner. For not only it relieves him of all the hassle (and expense) of making investment choices; he also receives this income tax-free. To our knowledge, however, it has never been fully explained why the *income*[148] that derives from an investment made by the recipient himself of his lump-sum award should not receive it tax-free as he will if it is derived from an investment made by the defendant insurer in a structured settlement situation.

In the case of structured settlements, the income from the annuity so purchased is thus tax-free in the hands of the claimant or his representative. The Inland Revenue treats the money as if it were the return of capital and not as income. That has substantial advantages. Take a working example: if £100,000 purchases an annuity at 4 per cent per annum the claimant's net income will be £4,000. In order to achieve the same figure from the investment of a conventional award an annual return of £6,000 gross would be required.

As hinted already, the disadvantage of the structured settlement is that the claimant has no access to the capital which has been used for the purchase of the annuity. He does not, therefore, have lump sums available to deal with major emergencies. In times when annuity rates are low, as now, an investment adviser may well be able to achieve a better overall return if he is free to invest partly for capital growth and partly for income. That is why claimants often chose to 'structure' only part of the award and receive the remainder in the form of a lump sum.

Specialist advice is invariably needed before a party decides whether to structure part or all of his damages. The current practice verily entails structuring part of the award whilst leaving another part to be paid and invested in the conventional manner. Structured settlements have become rare over the last two or three years because of the

148 It is important to remind the reader that we are here talking only of income since the lump sum itself is not subject to tax.

collapse of annuity rates in the market which make them far less attractive when compared with the returns which should be available from a prudently invested lump sum. It is now unusual for independent financial advisers to support the use of a structured settlement. The Court has also used its case management powers to adjourn part of a damages claim and direct that the claimant could return for a further award of both special and general damages if they underwent additional treatment in the future.[149] The power to take that step has not been challenged in the Court of Appeal. It is likely to be used sparingly.

(v) Periodic (and Reviewable) Payments

The Courts Act 2003 (ss. 100–101) came into force on 1 April 2005 and amended the Damages Act 1996. At the same time so did another piece of legislation, the Damages (Variation of Periodical Payments) Order 2006 and both were accompanied by related amendments to the Civil Procedure Rules.[150] Their combined effect is a silent—though it is submitted an as yet unfathomable in its extent—revolution in our system of payment of damages since, together, they now give our courts the power to order periodical payments for *future economic losses* resulting from personal injury or death. Section 2 of the Damages Act 1996 provides that the Court can order that the damages should wholly or in part take the form of periodical payments.[151]

This power extends to all existing personal injury claims, whether proceedings have been issued or not and *dealt with by* the courts. We stress 'dealt with by the courts' for settlements reached by the parties out of court will escape the judicial duty to consider imposing compensation in the form of periodical payment. Because the cost of this new scheme, especially on private insurers, is, as we shall note, likely to be high, we would not be surprised if the number of cases ending through settlement rather than judicial decision went up; and if this occurred, the number of cases 'caught' by the new Act might be small. If that proved to be the case, the effect of this legal 'revolution' would be decreased. In the same vein we note that this legislation revolutionises the method used to pay compensation but, in theory, has nothing to do with the principles of quantification of damages discussed above and below. Yet this may only be the theory, practice forcing the parties and their advisers to handle cases in a manner quite different to what we have experienced hitherto.[152]

Though this legislation gives the courts the *power* to award these damages in the form of periodical payments it places them under a *duty* to consider, after giving due

149 *A* v. *National Blood Authority* [2002] Lloyd's Rep. Med. 487.

150 CPR, r. 41.4–41.10. All references to structured settlements have now been removed from our legislation.

151 The likelihood is that damages for future care and/or future loss of earnings will be the subject of periodical payments particularly since the courts have ruled in two cases that indexation should be by reference to the Average Earnings Index rather than the Retail Price Index. *Flora* v. *Wakom Ltd* [2006] EWCA Civ. 1103 and *Thompstone* v. *Tameside and Glossop Acute Services NHS Trust* [2006] EWHC 2904 QB.

152 The point is stressed in Professor Richard Lewis's excellent 'The Politics and Economics of Tort Law: Judicially Imposed Periodical Payments of Damages' (Select Bibliography), an excellent piece which, in our view, is justly critical of the excessively academic account of tort law found in student textbooks.

consideration to the representations of the opposing parties, whether this is, given all the circumstances of the case, the most appropriate form of paying damages.. It must thus be noted that this innovation will not apply to damages for pain and suffering nor will it govern past pecuniary losses. Indeed, for various reasons it will not be always the best way of taking care of the claimants' *future* pecuniary losses. Thus, it is unlikely that this method of payment will be chosen where the value of future loss is small, or seriously reduced by the claimant's contributory negligence, or, finally, the (old) age of the claimant (and the likely duration of his future needs) might make a lump sum a more appropriate way of taking care of these needs. In practice, therefore, the more likely heading of future pecuniary loss that will be dealt with in this manner will be future medical expenses.[153] Moreover, the final awards made by our courts may thus in most cases consist of a mixture of lump sum and periodical payments.

Where such awards are made, the courts will determine the amount payable, the frequency of payments (weekly, monthly, annually) and the total duration of the payments (which may continue after the death of the claimant for the benefit of his dependants).

Unlike structured settlements which, with the help of the multiplier and multiplicand method, proceeded to work out the amount needed to produce an annuity that would meet the claimants' needs, here the starting-point is the working out the current (and future) needs of the claimant without attempting to work out the issue of his longevity.[154] The compensating insurer then has to decide himself how to satisfy the order in the future, for instance whether by obtaining an annuity (through a process similar to that used in structured settlements) or by acting as self-insurer and paying these amounts from his own profits or assets. The legislation provides for a number of ways to ensure that the claimants are protected against the risk of impecuniosity of the debtor or his insurer,[155] a risk which is assumed to be smaller (if non-existent) where the payor is the National Health Service.[156] The overall risk of future inability to meet such claims is one of the factors which the court is entitled to consider when deciding whether to make such an order.

The periodical payment can, further, be made to be variable in the future, though for this to happen some very strict rules have to be observed. Thus one notes, *inter alia*, that *(a)* the variability of the order must be included in the original settlement or order; *(b)* it is allowed if there is a *chance* (not a certainty) that an anticipated disease, deterioration or improvement in the health of the claimant is anticipated to occur; *(c)* these contingencies are specified clearly in the original order; *(d)* a time period (which can be short or extended) within which an application for variation can be made has been fixed; *(e)* the set out procedure for variation has been observed by the person claiming

153 Though the periodical payments ordered to be paid will be index-linked, future medical expenses are notoriously susceptible to increase with the passage of time in a manner that exceeds, often substantially, the rate of inflation. This means that lawyers advising their clients will have to take this risk seriously into account when advising them what system of payment to *try* to secure from the court. We stress 'try' for, as stated, the interests of the defendant will also be weighed by the judge when deciding this issue. See n. 145 above.

154 This is commonly described as the 'bottom-up' approach.

155 See, for instance, the Damages Act 1996, ss. 4 and 6 as amended by the above-mentioned Courts Act 2003.

156 For more details see Lewis, 'The Politics and Economics of Tort Law' (Select Bibliography), 422 ff.

the increase or decrease of the periodical payment. Finally, *(f)* it would seem that only one application only for variation can be made per disease or deterioration mentioned in the varying order.

The regime sketched above is innovative and for seriously injured claimants beneficial. It avoids some of the drawbacks of structured settlements (such as the need to calculate a lump sum which, in turn, requires an informed guess being made about his longevity) and also has the advantage of giving these sums to the claimant free of tax. However, how well this new legislation will work out in practice remains to be seen. Equally, we must suspend judgment on the question whether the insurance industry is able, at present, to cope with this new regime which looks as if it is going to be more costly than the *status quo*.[157] So here suffice it to note that the arguments against annuities, so long propping up the lump-sum awards, have suddenly been swept away, making the common law veer, dare one admit it, once again towards solutions which for centuries have been associated with the civil law systems of contemporary Europe.

Yet, the imitation, be it conscious or subconscious, has not been slavish. This is because the transplantation of a foreign legal institution invariably requires that it be adapted first to being in with local conditions. Costs form one such contextual factor: indeed, only a moment's reflections will shows us how vital English institutions—such the magistracy for instance—though born of history have survived largely because they are, essentially, cheap to run. Money may have thus prompted the NHS (and the government behind it) to favour this switch since periodic payments involve—to begin with—smaller disbursements than the huge amounts needed to set up lump sums. This financial factor is made clear in the explanatory notes to the Act so we need not labour it further.

Second, one is inclined to question the wisdom of the restrictions imposed upon the right to vary the award. Certainly, in the modern civilian systems, variation is much easier and thus retains the essential feature of the annuity system of payment of damages namely its flexibility to adapt to changing circumstances. Whether the restrictions of English law were thus prompted because the legislator found it easy to imitate in this respect the regime already known to him and found in the 'provisional damages' rules a ready-made answer or whether it was done in order to avoid keeping insurers' files 'open' or 'in a state of perpetual uncertainty' is not entirely clear. So it might not be inappropriate to hazard the guess that if the system is to work, the relaxation of the right to vary awards may have to be faced at some time in the future. But this will not come, if indeed it ever does, until its costs for insurers have been worked out in practice.

(B) DUTY TO MITIGATE

The principle of compensation means that the claimant can claim damages only for losses that he has actually sustained.[158] So, damages for lost income resulting from a

[157] See *ibid.*, 436 ff.

[158] Since *Roper* v. *Johnson* (1873) LR 8 CP 167. See, also, *Steele* v. *Robert George and Co. Ltd.* [1942] AC 497, at 501, 503, 506 and 508, *Richardson* v. *Redpath, Brown and Co. Ltd.* [1944] AC 62, at 72, 73 and 75, *Garnac Grain Co. Inc.* v. *H. M. F. Faure and Fairclough Ltd.* [1968] AC 1130. The contrary view, therefore, of the Privy Council

tortiously inflicted injury which resulted in the claimant losing his job will be reduced by any amount earned from alternative employment. If the claimant's loss could have been minimised by accepting an alternative employment then he will, normally, be expected to do this; and he must also undergo 'reasonable' medical treatment, made necessary by his injuries, if this is likely to improve his employment chances or decrease his loss.[159] But the courts will not ask the claimant to undergo a surgical operation that involves a substantial risk;[160] nor will a mother's wrongful birth claim be affected by her failure to have an abortion (as a way of mitigating her loss).[161] What is 'reasonable' will, obviously, depend largely on the circumstances of each case; and most authorities leave it to the defendant to prove that the claimant has failed to mitigate his loss.[162] But courts, especially modern ones, are slow to make unusual demands of claimants. Thus, as Stephenson LJ put it, the claimant's 'conduct in not taking steps to reduce the loss will not be weighed in nice scales at the instance of the party who has occasioned the loss'.[163]

Finally, and contrary to the old authority of *The Liesbosch*[164] (which will be discussed in the section on property damage below), if the plaintiff's impecuniosities lead him to an expenditure which is necessary to hire a substitute vehicle (because his own was damaged) but is one which a wealthy claimant would not have had to make, he will be able to recover it and he will not be deemed to be in breach of his duty to mitigate.[165]

(C) ITEMISATION OF AWARDS

In most cases of personal injury a victim suffers two distinct kinds of damage which are always discussed under two headings. The first includes such items as are capable of direct translation into money terms: for example, loss of earnings, medical expenses and other out-of-pocket expenses. For these items, as stated, the rule is *restitutio in integrum*. Non-pecuniary losses, on the other hand, include all such immeasurable elements as pain and suffering, or loss of an eye or a limb, which clearly cannot be valued accurately in money terms; and for these the guiding principle is 'fair compensation'. This not only indicates the inability to value these losses precisely, but only approximately; it also suggests the underlying idea that there should be some measure of uniformity in the sum awarded for such losses, otherwise great injustice could result.

In this context three major changes in the practice of the courts must be mentioned. Growing realisation of the need for consistency and comparability in awards led the

in *Selvanayagam* v. *University of the West Indies* [1983] 1 WLR 585 (criticised by H. McGregor in (1983) 46 *MLR* 758) placing on the claimant the burden of proof that he acted reasonably, must be regarded as *per incuriam* and, in any event, as not binding on English courts.

159 *Bellingham* v. *Dhillon and Another* [1973] 1 QB 304. But see *Gardner* v. *Marsh & Parsons* [1997] 3 All ER 871 (where the court had to consider whether a benefit which accrued after the tort/breach of contract and benefited the plaintiff should be taken into account in assessing his damages).

160 *McAuley* v. *London Transport Executive* [1957] 2 Lloyd's Rep. 500, *Morgan* v. *T. Wallis* [1974] 1 Lloyd's Rep. 165.

161 *Savage* v. *Wallis* [1966] 1 Lloyd's Rep. 357.

162 *Emeh* v. *Kensington AHA* [1985] QB 1012.

163 *London and South of England Building Society* v. *Stone* [1983 1 WLR 1242 at 1263. See, also, *Morris* v. *Richards* [2003] EWCA Civ. 232.

164 [1933] AC 449.

165 *Lagden* v. *O'Connor* [2004] 1 AC 1067.

Court of Appeal in *Ward* v. *James*[166] to rule that juries should no longer be used for the assessment of damages save in very exceptional cases.[167] Lord Denning MR, delivering the judgment of the full Court of Appeal, justified this as follows:

> recent cases show the desirability of three things. First, *assessability*: In cases of grave injury, where the body is wrecked or the brain destroyed, it is very difficult to assess a fair compensation in money, so difficult that the award must basically be a conventional figure, derived from experience or from awards in comparable cases. Secondly, *uniformity*: There should be some measure of uniformity in awards so that similar decisions are given in similar cases; otherwise there will be great dissatisfaction in the community, and much criticism of the administration of justice. Thirdly, *predictability*: Parties should be able to predict with some measure of accuracy the sum which is likely to be awarded in a particular case, for by this means cases can be settled peaceably and not brought to court, a thing very much to the public good. None of these three is achieved when the damages are left at large to the jury.

It will be noticed that while the first two reasons given for the change are related to what could be called the 'fairness' of the awards, the last is a purely 'administrative' argument, though no less important for that. For it is this consistency which makes it possible to proceed to settlement out of court and thus expedites the administration of justice.

The second change came with *Jefford* v. *Gee*,[168] where it was held that judges must assess separately damages payable: (*i*) for accrued pecuniary loss; (*ii*) for non-pecuniary damages; and (*iii*) for damages for loss of future earnings. This threefold division was largely dictated by the passing of the Administration of Justice Act 1969, which made it obligatory for courts to award interest in any case in which judgment[169] was given for more than £200, all or part of which consisted of damages in respect of personal injury or the death of a person. *Jefford* v. *Gee* was, therefore, the case that elaborated the principles of the award of interest and it did so by dividing the damages headings as above. After some hesitation, these principles were confirmed in *Pickett* v. *British Rail Engineering Ltd.*,[170] and the position is as follows: (*i*) special damages (i.e. pre-trial losses) carry interest at half the usual short-term rate; (*ii*) for non-pecuniary

166 [1966] 1 QB 273, 299–300.

167 There is, according to s. 69(1) of the Supreme Court Act 1981 a *prima facie* right to a jury trial in cases of fraud, malicious prosecution, false imprisonment and, of course, defamation. But s. 69(3) has been seen as strengthening further this presumption against jury trial, since it gives a judge the right to deny a jury trial if the case will require a 'prolonged examination of documents or accounts or any scientific . . . investigation which cannot be made with a jury'. See *H* v. *Ministry of Defence* [1991] 2 QB 103. Recent decisions of the Court of Appeal to intervene in jury awards have struck a further blow to the unfettered powers which juries enjoyed in the past. See, in particular, Lord Woolf's judgment in *Thompson* v. *Commissioner of Police of the Metropolis* and *Hsu* v. *Commissioner of the Police of the Metropolis* [1997] 2 All ER 762, where clear and thorough guidelines where given on the matter of jury instruction.

168 [1970] 2 QB 130.

169 This power of the court to award interest on a judgment meant that if the defendant paid his debt any time between the commencement of the proceedings and the giving of judgment he escaped having to pay interest at all. Now, however, as a result of s. 15 of and Sch. 1 to the Administration of Justice Act 1982 the courts are given power to award interest on any debt outstanding when the writ is issued.

170 [1980] AC 136. Although see the recent, and potentially highly significant judgment of the House of Lords in *Sempra Metals Ltd.* v. *Her Majesty's Commissioners of Inland Revenue* [2007] UKHL 34, which seems to suggest that *compound* interest is also available at common law: see, e.g., [74] ff (per Lord Nicholls).

damages the interest on damages is on a more modest rate—currently 2 per cent;[171] finally (*iii*) future pecuniary losses carry no interest since they have not materialised at the time of the trial.

The final change was firmly established in *George* v. *Pinnock*,[172] where it was accepted that the parties themselves had a right to know how the judge arrived at his final figure. The older practice, therefore, of allowing an appeal only where the total figure was erroneous was deemed to be incorrect. Nowadays, therefore, the most common ground for overturning an award is if there is an error in one of its component parts; and this, typically, consists in the trial judge having failed to consider whether there is an overlap between different headings of damages with the result that the claimant has been enriched.[173]

6. PECUNIARY LOSSES

(A) MEDICAL AND OTHER EXPENSES UP TO THE DATE OF THE TRIAL[174]

(i) Generally

In English law the expression 'special damages' can, as we noted earlier on, have several meanings. In this section we are using it to refer to the amounts payable by a tortfeasor to his victim for the pecuniary losses *actually* suffered between the date of the accident and the date of trial or, in the case of less serious injury, the date of recovery. Thus the basic principle is that the claimant must prove, on the balance of probabilities, either what he has lost in financial terms (as for example in loss of earnings), or what sums he has had to pay, or become liable to pay, in order to meet expenditure directly incurred as a consequence of his injuries.

171 *Birkett* v. *Hayes* [1982] 1 WLR 816, *Wright* v. *British Railways Board* [1983] 2 AC 773.

172 [1973] 1 WLR 118.

173 Thus, see, *Harris* v. *Harris* [1973] 1 Lloyd's Rep. 445 (CA) (future loss of earnings and loss of marriage prospects), *Clarke* v. *Rotax Aircraft Equipment Ltd.* [1975] 1 WLR 1570 (loss of earning capacity and loss of future earnings). It is doubtful, but probably not finally settled, whether there can be an overlap between pecuniary and non-pecuniary losses. See Lord Scarman's *obiter dicta* in *Lim Poh Choo* v. *Camden and Islington AHA* [1980] AC 174 at 192.

174 In some cases the claimant may, despite his injury, retain his employment. His injuries, however, make it unlikely that he will be able to keep his job and in that case one often refers to a reduction (or loss) of his earning capacity. In *Moeliker* v. *A. Reyrolle Ltd.* [1977] 1 All ER 9, the court took the view that an award could be made under this heading where there was a real and substantial risk that the plaintiff would lose his job prematurely. The term 'loss of earning capacity' may also be more appropriate where the injured person is young and has no earnings yet-for instance *Joyce* v. *Yeomans* [1981] 1 WLR 549 and, most recently, *Dhaliwal* v. *Personal Representatives of Hunt* [1995] 4 PIQR Q56. However, in the subsequent case of *Foster* v. *Tyne and Wear CC* [1986] 1 All ER 567 the court took the view that loss of earning capacity was not really a heading of damages different from that of loss of future earnings. So no substantive point turns on the different terminology. The discussion in the text proceeds on this basis which, incidentally, was also shared by the Pearson Committee (Select Bibliography), para. 338.

It is not, of course, every penny expended which is recoverable as damages. The court will look to see whether those payments were reasonably necessary. The principle was explained by Megaw LJ in *Donnelly* v. *Joyce*.[175] While the claimant may say, and believe, that it would aid his recovery to travel in the style and comfort of a Rolls-Royce motor car and to spend an extended holiday in a five-star hotel in the Caribbean, the court is most unlikely to accept that it was reasonably necessary for him to do so. However, judges are disinclined, where the matter is marginal, to say that it was unreasonable for the claimant to have taken a certain course if he has actually expended the money. Past losses are likely to be viewed less strictly than claims for future losses where the money has not yet been expended and where the sums are likely to be greater. But the size of the expenditure is not, of itself, necessarily going to make it unreasonable. Thus, receiving treatment in New York rather than London has been held to be reasonable,[176] as has treatment at home even if it would have been cheaper to treat the victim at an institution.[177]

(ii) Loss of Earnings

First a point of terminology: are loss of earnings and earning capacity different notions? In some cases the claimant may, despite his injury, retain his employment. His injuries, however, make it unlikely that he will be able to keep his job and in that case one often refers to a reduction (or loss) of his earning capacity. In *Moeliker* v. *A. Reyrolle Ltd.*[178] the court took the view that an award could be made under this heading where there was a real and substantial risk that the plaintiff would lose his job prematurely. The term 'loss of earning capacity' may also be more appropriate where the injured person is young and has no earnings yet—for instance *Joyce* v. *Yeomans*.[179] However, in the subsequent case of *Foster* v. *Tyne and Wear County Council*[180] the court took the view that loss of earning capacity was not really a heading of damages different from that of loss of future earnings. So no substantive point seems to turn on the different terminology.[181]

Turning now to the principles of calculation we note that they are precisely the same for past as for future loss of earnings. Because this subject presents greater interest (and difficulty) in the case of future earnings, it will be covered extensively in section (c), below, so the reader is referred to the discussion found therein. One must, however, note here that in this instance the exercise is much easier in so far as (*a*) the multiplier is clearly known and is fixed by reference to the time that has lapsed between injury and trial and (*b*) the same is (approximately) true of the multiplicand in so far as it can be

175 [1974] QB 454 at the text: '[t]he Plaintiff's loss is not the expenditure of money to buy the special boots or to pay for nursing attention. His loss is the existence of the need for those special boots or for those nursing services, the value of which for purposes of damages—for the purpose of the ascertainment of the amount of his loss—is the proper and reasonable cost of supplying these needs.'

176 *Winkworth* v. *Hubbard* [1960] 1 Lloyd's Rep. 150.

177 *Rialas* v. *Mitchel* (1984) 128 *SJ* 704 CA.

178 [1977] 1 All ER 9.

179 [1981] 1 WLR 549 and, most recently, *Dhaliwal* v. *Personal Representatives of Hunt* [1995] 4 PIQR Q56.

180 [1986] 1 All ER 567

181 The discussion in the text proceeds on this basis which, incidentally, was also shared by the Pearson Committee (Select Bibliography), para. 338.

ascertained what the injured person/claimant would have been earning at the time of the trial. But one must remember that what is given to the claimant is his net loss, i.e. his gross lost earning minus taxation[182] and social-security contributions.[183]

Where the actual loss of earnings can be proved, then, whatever the class of earnings in question, the claimant is entitled to recover them. So, damages may be awarded for loss of wages, loss of salary and, in the case of professional men and women, loss of fees. Financial losses accruing down to the date of the trial are part of 'special damages' so they must be specifically pleaded and proved. Their calculation will normally cause little difficulty and they will be made by reference to the claimant's pre-accident earnings and the period of disability and proceed on the assumption that, but for the accident, the claimant would have continued to earn at the same rate.

(iii) Past Medical Care

Different items have to be considered here so we shall look at them under different sub-headings.

(a) Medical Treatment and Therapies An injured claimant is entitled to recover the costs incurred by him in obtaining appropriate treatment and therapy for his injuries and disabilities. The question is whether the expenses were reasonably incurred. This crucial question is implied by section 2(4) of the Law Reform (Personal Injuries) Act 1968.[184] The availability of treatment on the National Health Service is to be ignored.[185] A claimant is not obliged to use the service even though he could be treated free of charge.

The one exception to that rule is that if the injury occurred in a motor accident on the highway or other public place the defendant's insurer is liable to reimburse the National Health Service, up to a maximum of £2,856 for inpatient treatment and £286 for outpatient treatment.[186] The insurer must, however, have already made some payment in respect of the injury and know of the hospital treatment.[187]

(b) House Care Etc. Individuals who suffer personal injury may require nursing care or, at a lower level, assistance at home with the ordinary tasks of daily living such as personal hygiene, cooking, laundry, housework, shopping and the like.

English courts approach this head of loss by considering evidence of how many hours of care have been required for each day that has passed between the time when the individual concerned was discharged from hospital and the date of trial or the date of recovery. The amount of care frequently varies as the individual makes a partial or

[182] *British Transport Commission* v. *Gourley* [1956] AC 185.

[183] *Cooper* v. *Firth Brown Ltd.* [1963] 1 WLR 418. This includes the employee's own contributions to whatever pension scheme he belongs: *Dews* v. *National Coal Board* [1988] AC 1.

[184] See, also, *Winkworth* v. *Hubbard* [1960] 1 Lloyd's Rep. 150; *Cunningham* v. *Harrison* [1973] QB 942.

[185] Law Reform (Personal Injuries) Act 1948, s. 2(4). In relation to future treatment it is for the claimant to prove that he will undergo private treatment rather than availing himself of the National Health Service. *Woodrup* v. *Nicol* [1993] PIQR Q 104.

[186] Road Traffic Act 1988, s. 157.

[187] *Barnet Group Hospital Management Committee* v. *Eagle Star Insurance Co. Ltd.* [1960] 1 QB 107.

complete recovery. It is normal for expert evidence to be obtained as to precisely what level of care has been necessary from the beginning.

The expert witness will produce for the court a schedule of how much care has been required during that period. The level of expertise required of the carer will also be considered. So, for example, an individual with a broken leg may very well need assistance with simple household tasks for which a home help is sufficient. On the other hand an individual who is bedridden, but capable of living at home, may require nursing assistance at least for part of the time. The victim of a catastrophic injury may require more than one carer in order to enable him to be turned, lifted or put into the bath. In those circumstances it may be reasonably necessary to employ someone with nursing training.

In the cases of brain injury it is often reasonably necessary to employ someone with special training to cope with the particular needs and difficulties of the victim.

The recoverable damages will be the amount which the court accepts was reasonable to expend on paying for the appropriate level of assistance for the appropriate number of hours.

The support needed may take other forms. Thus, there is also much authority to support the view that an injured housewife is entitled to claim the cost of employing domestic help;[188] indeed, a Canadian decision recently awarded such a claimant the cost of her husband doing some of this work (even though the minority objected that the tasks performed by the husband were not, really, performed for his wife but for the household which they shared).[189] The Law Commission has proposed that in these circumstances of 'loss of . . . ability to do work in the home', the claimant should be able to recover for the costs of work done in the past by friends or relatives and the claimant should then have a personal liability to account to those helpers for that work done. Where the claimant has 'soldiered on' and done the work himself, the Law Commission prefer to treat such damages as non-pecuniary loss, in line with pain, suffering and loss of amenity.[190]

In many cases care has not actually been provided by paid third parties but by members of the claimant's family who provided it through their natural concern, love and affection for the victim. In those circumstances the court calculates the commercial cost of the care which has been provided and then applies a discount. which will normally be 25 per cent.[191] The cost of care is recoverable by a claimant irrespective of whether he or she is under any legal liability to make recompense to the person or persons who have provided the care. Most spouses or family members would provide the care without any consideration of whether they have a legal entitlement to be paid for it. Nevertheless the claimant is entitled to recover under this head subject only to the discount. Any money received is, technically, held in trust for those who provided the

[188] *Daly* v. *General Steam Navigation Co. Ltd.* [1981] 1 WLR 120; *Shaw* v. *Wirral HA* [1993] 4 Med. LR 275.

[189] *Kroeker* v. *Jansen* (1995) 123 DLR (4th) 652.

[190] See Law Commission, Report No. 262 (Select Bibliography), paras. 3.87–3.93.

[191] *Evans* v. *Pontypridd Roofing Ltd* [2001] EWCA Civ. 1657.

care.[192] In the vast majority of cases, however, that principle is honoured more in the breach than the observance. Most family members decide that they do not want the money for themselves and that it is better used providing a fund for the future of the injured person. That is their decision. It is not open to a defendant to say, after judgment, that the money should be paid back to them because the claimant is in breach of trust. That accords with the principle that it is no business of the defendant how a claimant actually spends the general damages which he recovers.[193]

The above rules do not apply to compensate a spouse who gives her services to the claimant's business in consequence of the injury.[194] The reason for the distinction is that in such a case it is the business and not the individual who has suffered the loss. The word 'business' is, perhaps, insufficiently precise. If the spouse is trading as a sole trader, the loss is recoverable but not if the business is a partnership or a company.

In the case of family members there may be an alternative method of calculating the loss. If the carer has given up paid employment to care for the claimant there is an entitlement to the net loss of earnings of that individual rather than the discounted cost of care. The overriding principle is one of reasonableness. The question for which the court requires an answer is whether it was reasonably necessary for the family member concerned to give up work in order to care for the victim. Plainly, in some cases it may appear disproportionate for the individual concerned to have given up an extremely well-paid job in order to provide the level of care actually required. The court may well be sympathetic to the fact that, for example, the mother of a young child has stopped work in the immediate aftermath of the accident and not returned for a period of months, or in some cases even years. That will depend upon the nature of the injury, the level of care required and the strength of the evidence generally. The court is far more likely to be sympathetic in the case of a mother–child or husband–wife relationship than in others. It is impossible to provide any hard-and-fast rule.[195]

In normal circumstances the loss of earnings will be capped at the level of the cost of commercial care had it been provided. Now, for example, the court will have to assess the level of care required and what it would have cost had it been provided by an outsider. That figure will then be the ceiling of the claim for loss of earnings by the member of the family.[196] It does not follow that because a family member gives up work that would have occupied him or her for eight hours but actually provides twenty-four-hour care that she should be paid more than the amount which he/she would have received in employment. On the other hand, in one case the trial judge reached the

[192] *Hunt* v. *Severs* [1994] 2 AC 350, vindicating twenty years later the position first advanced by Lord Denning in *Cunningham* v. *Harrison* [1973] QB 942, 952, but rejected by a differently constituted Court of Appeal in *Donnelly* v. *Joyce* [1974] QB 454.

[193] This position in 'practice' comes closer to the current state of the law in Australia which has refused to follow *Hunt* v. *Severs*. Thus, see: *Kars* v. *Kars* (1996) 141 ALR 37, *Fitzgerald* v. *Ford* [1996] PIQR Q72

[194] *Hardwick* v. *Hudson* [1999] 1 WLR 1770.

[195] As to the number of hours which fall to be compensated see *Iqbal* v. *Whipps Cross University Hospital NHS Trust* [2006] EWHC 3111 (QB).

[196] *Housecroft* v. *Burnett* [1986] All ER 332; *Fish* v. *Wilcox and Gwent Health Authority* [1994] 5 Med. LR 230.

conclusion that the claimant's wife, who was a nurse, had probably being doing the equivalent of the work of two full-time nurses. He awarded one-and-a-half times the net amount that she would have earned in employment as a nurse.[197]

(c) Personal Expenses This category covers claims for such items as additional heating costs where an injured individual feels the cold[198] or spends more time at home; the provision of special clothing, and extra costs of holidays. That list is not intended to be exclusive.

The principle is precisely the same as it is in other areas, namely whether there is, on all the evidence, a reasonable requirement for the additional expenditure and whether the costs actually expended are themselves reasonable.

In cases of more serious injury special clothing may be required. It may also be necessary to wash clothes or bedclothes far more often than before as a result of incontinence or sweating.[199] In such case the household is likely to use more electricity and soap powder and have to replace the washing machine with greater frequency than normal.

Equally, a seriously injured individual may need to be accompanied on holiday by a carer who will inevitably incur extra fares and additional accommodation costs. Furthermore the type of holiday undertaken may well be more expensive. A younger person may have been used to going camping or sharing a cheap apartment with others. That may well, as a result of his disabilities, no longer be feasible for the injured person. It must be remembered that in accordance with general principles it is only the additional costs incurred that are recoverable.

In relation to clothing, one of the arguments, in the case of younger individuals, that is frequently put forward by a defendant is that the young person would, but for the accident, have spent a lot of money on fashion clothes which he no longer does and that that is to be offset against the claim under this head. Whether that argument succeeds depends upon the judge's impression of the evidence.[200]

(d) Travel Costs In the case of past losses this heading falls to be discussed under three sections.

First, costs incurred by the claimant himself in travelling to and from hospital, medical appointments with his treating doctor and the like.

Second, the claimant is entitled to recover moneys expended by immediate relatives in travelling to visit him in hospital or, where reasonably necessary, accompanying him to hospital and medical appointments. In both cases it is a matter of evidence as to how much has been expended. Although some evidence is required, a court does not, necessarily, expect to see a written receipt for every single journey by taxi or every single bus ticket. It applies its common sense in assessing what is reasonable.

197 *Hogg* v. *Doyle*, CA Judgment of 6 Mar. 1991 (unreported).

198 *Hodgson* v. *Trapp* [1989] AC 807.

199 *Leong San Tan* 1986 (unreported).

200 *Donnelly* v. *Joyce* [1974] QB 454.

Third, the claimant can recover moneys expended on his own travel if they are more than he would have expended had he not been injured. At the lower end of the scale that may be the cost of taxis used to go shopping or get to and from work because the claimant is unable to utilise public transport as a result of his injuries. Whether they were necessarily incurred will depend very largely upon whether the medical experts accept that it was reasonably necessary for the claimant to utilise the more expensive form of travel.

Moving higher up the scale it may be necessary for a claimant to purchase a larger motor car than that which he previously owned or even to adapt a vehicle. Those costs are calculated by looking, first, at whether, on the medical evidence, a larger or adapted vehicle was actually required. The costs of that type of vehicle or the adaptations will then be assessed but there must be offset against them what the claimant would, but for the accident, have spent on buying and/or replacing a motor vehicle.

As with other heads of damages it is for the judge to decide what is reasonable. One matter which is frequently taken into account is that it is generally necessary for an injured individual to have as reliable a car as possible. Thus, the student using an elderly motor car prior to the accident may reasonably require a newer, more comfortable and more reliable vehicle as a result of his disabilities.

If the replacement vehicle costs more to insure and run than that used by the claimant prior to the accident those additional costs will also be recoverable on the same principles.

There exists a government scheme called the Motability Scheme whereby government assistance is given for the purchase and running of a motor vehicle. Such costs can and will be taken into account in accessing what the claimant is reasonably entitled to recover. We consider this issue further in the chapter which deals with benefits.

(e) Aids and Equipment An injured individual may require all manner of aids and equipment to assist him to get about; to help with day-to-day living in the home; or even to amuse himself. The overriding principle is the same here as in what was said before: has a reasonable need been demonstrated on the evidence for purchasing, maintaining and replacing these items?

Expert evidence is almost invariably required to deal with these items. The range is enormous, proceeding from major items such as special baths and hoists to incontinence pads. The evidence will have to provide answers to these questions:

(i) Was it reasonably necessary for the claimant to purchase or hire the various aids and items of equipment claimed in his schedule?

(ii) If so, was the type and model of each item reasonable or ought he to have purchased something cheaper?

(iii) Even if a particular item of equipment was purchased as a result of the accident was that item something which the claimant would probably have acquired in any event? So, for example, in modern times the court will be dubious about a claim that an individual has purchased a mobile telephone—or cordless telephone—purely as a result of the accident. The same might be said of a claim for subscriptions to one of the multi-channel television companies or the purchase of a computer. However, each case must be looked at on its own particular facts and the surrounding evidence.

(f) Accommodation There is, inevitably, an overlap between past and future costs of accommodation. In those cases in which all that is required are minor adaptations to a property the expenditure may well already have been incurred. However, where it is necessary to purchase a property and/or carry out major alterations the injured individual is unlikely to have been able to afford to meet such expenditure out of his own pocket. In generally, therefore, the accommodation is likely to have been provided out of interim payments which are advances against the total sum of damages which he is likely to recover at trial.

Thus those costs are more properly considered when looking at the damages recoverable for long-term losses. One must restate the general suspicion against allowing the total cost of new accommodation.[201]

It is, however, appropriate to consider the type of case in which the claimant resides in rented accommodation and has moved to a larger or better property since the accident. As with all the other categories the court has to consider whether the move has been justified. That will require looking at the medical evidence about the nature of his disabilities; whether a resident carer has had to be engaged (be it a member of the family or an outsider employed at commercial rates); orwhether there were deficiencies in the property in which the claimant originally lived. For example, if it was on the third floor of a block of flats without a lift and the claimant has difficulty in walking the move will be justified.

The amount recoverable in such a case is the difference between the rent which the claimant was paying prior to the accident and the rent which he is paying at the date of trial.

(g) Other Possible Headings In these days of greater numbers of cases of brain damage leading to mental disability, one can claim fees payable to the Court of Protection which often manages the sums awarded as damages.[202] The Court of Appeal, however, has recently been unwilling to treat as allowable expenses the sums that the victim was ordered to pay in matrimonial proceedings that followed the breakdown of her marriage as a result of her injury.[203] The decision, apparently based on considerations of public policy, is not, however, convincing; and the earlier contrary decision of *Jones* v. *Jones*[204] seems preferable.

[201] Cf. *Cunningham* v. *Harrison* [1973] QB 942 and *Moriarty* v. *McCarthy* [1978] 1 WLR 155,163.

[202] Substantial sums can be awarded under this heading. See e.g. *Jones* v. *Jones* [1985] QB 704 (CA) (£28,000 including the Official Solicitor's administration costs).

[203] *Pritchard* v. *J. H. Cobden Ltd.* [1987] 2 WLR 627.

[204] [1985] QB 704 (where, however, the defendant had conceded the point).

(B) PROSPECTIVE LOSSES[205]

(i) Introductory Remarks

Compensation may also be given for failure to realise other gains such as company profits[206] or prize money.[207] In *Moriarty* v. *McCarthy*[208] a twenty-four year-old woman was seriously injured in a car accident. The court took the view that as a result of the accident her chances of marriage were 'grossly reduced' and, in economic terms, that also meant a reduction in her 'chances of finding a man who is prepared to take her on and support her'. This was a perfectly legitimate heading of future economic loss that should be compensated by the courts—a result which subsequent decisions have effected in a somewhat odd manner.[209] In similar vein, a man who was disfigured and suffered a severe personality change which led to his abandonment by his wife, was awarded the costs of home help for the care of his children.[210]

The assessment of general damages for the loss of future (prospective) earnings is, inevitably, less precise and fraught with difficulties to which we have already alluded.

These are largely due to the number of imponderables, such as: how long would the claimant live? How long would he continue working and at what rate? Would he be promoted to get a rise? Conversely, might he lose his job? What will the rate of inflation be in the future? Would there be any significant change in his personal tax status? Though actuarial techniques can be used to assist courts in their task and, apparently, 'figure more prominently [these days] in the evidence on which courts rely',[211] judges have shown a consistent preference[212] for the multiplicand and multiplier method.[213] This tries to discover so far as possible the net annual loss suffered by the victim (the

205 For a discussion of the American approach to the calculation of loss of future earnings, focusing on matters such as wage growth, length of expected working life and the impact of possible residual disability on both of these, see R. Lewis, 'Methods of Calculating Damages for Loss of Future Earnings' or (with R. McNabb, H. Robinson and V. Wass) 'Court Awards of Damages for Loss of Future Earnings' (both: Select Bibliography). His interesting conclusion is that, on these methods, the tort system in the UK regularly under-compensates claimants due to the methods it uses to assess the loss of future earnings.

206 *Lee* v. *Sheard* [1956] 1 QB 192.

207 *Mulvane* v. *Joseph* (1968) 112 SJ 927.

208 [1978] 1 WLR 155, 161.

209 I.e. by not reducing, as they would otherwise have done, the multiplier they would have used if the victim had been a man: see *Hughes* v. *McKeown* [1965] 1 WLR 963, *Housecroft* v. *Burnett* [1986] 1 All ER 332. A number of reasons, it is submitted not all very convincing, have been given for reducing the multiplier for female victims: *viz.* the likelihood of marriage and the possibility of the woman giving up her work, at least for a period of time, in order to bring up children.

210 *Oakley* v. *Walker* (1977) 121 SJ 619.

211 Per Lord Bridge in *Hunt* v. *Severs* [1994] 2 All ER 385 at 396.

212 Thus *ibid.*, at 396, Lord Bridge stated: 'before a judge's assessment of the appropriate multiplier for future loss, which he has arrived at by the conventional method of assessment and which is not attacked as being wrong in principle, can properly be adjusted by an appellate court by reference to actuarial calculations, it is essential, in my judgment, that the particular calculation relied on should be precisely in point and should be seen as demonstrably giving a more accurate assessment than the figure used by the judge'.

213 An excellent illustration of how this is used by judges can be found in Lord Pearson's judgment in *Taylor* v. *O'Connor* [1971] AC 115, 144.

'multiplicand')[214] and arrive at a figure for the award of lump-sum damages by applying to this a 'multiplier', which must reflect not only the predicted number of years for which the loss will last but also the elements of uncertainty contained in that prediction and the fact that the claimant will receive a lump sum immediately, which he is expected to invest. Two factors above all are liable to complicate this process: inflation and taxation. The trend of recent decisions has been strongly in the direction of ignoring the effects of both when computing damages awards.

The guiding principle is that the damages must be assessed on the basis that the total sum awarded will be exhausted at the end of the period contemplated and that during that period the claimant will be expected to draw upon both the income derived from the investment of the sum awarded *and* upon part of the capital itself. Any other calculation which did not require the simultaneous use of income plus capital would result in part of the capital remaining intact at the end of the contemplated period and, consequently, in over-compensation of the claimant. This method of calculation, however, also means that the chosen multiplier will be considerably less than the number of years taken as the period of the loss. So let us turn to these concepts now and see what the courts make of them.

(ii) The Multiplicand

The multiplicand is the annual figure representing each head of loss. So, for example, if the injured individual requires care in the medium to long term evidence will be received of the current annual cost at the date of trial. That is the multiplicand. In certain circumstances there may be more than one multiplicand for a particular head of loss. Staying with future care as an example, the evidence may well be that the claimant will require a certain level of care for a number of years but, when he gets to say, sixty-five, more will be required and the cost will be greater. In those circumstances the court will consider two multiplicands, one for the period immediately following trial and one for a much later date. The number of multiplicands is not limited. There may be any number. However, that approach is only adopted in circumstances, such as care, where there is a degree of probability that by or at a certain date a specific state of affairs will exist. In relation to future loss of earnings the court may be persuaded to adopt a number of different multiplicands to account of the prospect that the claimant would have progressed upwards in his career.[215]

(iii) The Multiplier

As already stated, the guiding principle is that the damages must be assessed on the basis that the total sum awarded will be exhausted at the end of the period contemplated and that during that period the plaintiff will be expected to draw upon *both* the income

[214] Note the comments of Lord Lloyd in *Wells* v. *Wells* [1998] 3 WLR 329; [1999] 1 AC 345, at 377F, that careful scrutiny is needed of the elements which go to make up the multiplicand, especially since 'the effect of reducing the rate of discount is to increase the multiplier in every case'.

[215] This is discussed further in Section 6(b)(iv) below.

derived from the investment of the sum awarded *and* upon part of the capital itself. Any other calculation which did not require the *simultaneous* use of income plus capital would result in part of the capital remaining intact at the end of the contemplated period and, consequently, in over-compensation of the plaintiff. This method of calculation, however, also means that the chosen multiplier may be less than the number of years taken as the period of the loss.

For many years the courts assumed that the lump sum would be invested in equities which, on average, yield a rate of return of around 4–5 per cent per annum, and reduced the multiplier accordingly. In *Wells* v. *Wells*[216] the House of Lords, in a decision which one expert commentator described as 'the most important decision in personal injury litigation since the Second World war',[217] overturned this approach. The former practice had been based on the assumption that the victim should be taken to be in the same position as any other ordinary prudent investor. However, as Lord Lloyd explained:

> Granted that a substantial proportion of equities is the best long-term investment for the ordinary prudent investor, the question is whether the same is true for these plaintiffs. The ordinary investor may be assumed to have enough to live on. He can meet his day-to-day requirements. If the equity market suffers a catastrophic fall, as it did in 1972, he has no immediate need to sell. He can abide his time and wait until the equity market recovers.
>
> The plaintiffs are not in the same happy position. They are not 'ordinary' investors in the sense that they can wait for long-term recovery, remembering that it was not until 1989 that equity prices regained their old pre-1972 level in real terms. For they need the income, and a portion of the capital, every year to meet their current care.[218]

His Lordship concluded that it was more appropriate for the court to assume that the victim would invest most of the lump sum in index-linked government stocks (ILGS). These offer a guarantee of protection against future inflation but, in part because of this protection against inflation, also offer a lower rate of return than equities. On this basis, he said that the multiplier should be calculated on the assumption of a rate of return of 3 per cent per annum instead of the hitherto 4 or 4.5 per cent.

The change has led to inflation in the size of awards. Section 1 of the Damages Act 1996 confers a power upon the Lord Chancellor to set by order the expected rate of return which the courts should follow in such cases, in the interests of achieving greater certainty and consistency of practice; on 25 June 2001, the decision was taken by the Lord Chancellor to set the discount rate at 2.5 per cent,[219] which has inevitably further

[216] [1999] 1 AC 345 (reversing the Court of Appeal [1997] 1 WLR 652).

[217] David Kemp, 'Damages for Personal Injury: A Sea Change' (1998) 114 *LQR* 571 and which the Press of the time thought would bring an unprecedented increase in the level of awards (*The Times*, 17 July 1998).

[218] [1999] 1 AC 345, at 366.

[219] Damages (Personal Injury) Order 2001, SI 2001/2301. It is, nevertheless, possible for the courts to take a 'different rate of return into account if any party to the proceedings shows that it is more appropriate in the case in question' (s. 1(2) of the Damages Act 1996). However, early evidence suggests that the courts are extremely reluctant even to hear arguments that a different rate is more appropriate: see *Warriner* v. *Warriner* [2002] EWCA Civ. 81; [2003] 3 All ER 447, where accountancy evidence as to the correct rate was refused.

increased the level of awards. The Lord Chancellor also has the power to alter the discount rate in the future if he deems it appropriate to do so. But this is unlikely to occur for a number of years.

The Ogden Tables are now updated on an annual basis by the Professional Negligence Bar Association. This confirmed the trend towards a growth in the size of damages awards, heralded by the *Wells* v. *Wells* decision.[220] There are a number of different tables setting out the appropriate multipliers for the whole of the individual's life; for working life to age sixty; for working life to age sixty five; for a term certain or for future loss of pension. Different tables exist for men and women.

The court is not entitled to deviate from those tables although it may, in certain cases, apply a further discount for certain eventualities.[221] That is, however, really only applicable to loss of future earnings. The rationale for that approach is that the court will already have received and taken into account evidence about what is likely to happen in the future in setting both the multiplier and the multiplicand.

The multiplier will also be affected by the age of the victim at the time of the tort. Clearly, the older the victim the smaller the multiplier, the younger the victim the greater the multiplier. It is equally obvious that this method of calculation, despite the tendency to itemise awards, will in the end only lead to approximate compensation for future pecuniary loss. In fact, the number of imponderables in the calculation makes it likely that, the longer the period of the expected future loss, the less adequate the damages. Of the many imponderables, inflation is probably most to blame, though in these days of reduced inflation levels this is not likely to be as great a concern as it was in the late 1970s.

It is now clear that inflation beyond the date of the trial is not taken into account when determining the multiplicand. In *Cookson* v. *Knowles*[221a] the Court of Appeal held, and the House of Lords subsequently agreed, that for the purposes of calculating the dependency in fatal accident cases, as well as for the purposes of calculating loss of earnings in non-fatal cases, the loss should be divided into two parts, the first from the date of the death (or injury) to the date of trial, and the second from the date of trial into the future. In determining the rate of earnings of the deceased (or plaintiff) for the assessment of the first part of the loss, any increase in earnings due to inflation, which he would have received but for the death (or injury), should be taken into account. As to the second part of the loss, i.e. from the trial onwards, this should be assessed on the

220 The escalation of damages awards was subjected to criticism in H. McGregor, *McGregor on Damages* (16th edn., 1997, updated by 3rd Suppl. 2001): see paras. 1601A–1601H, esp. 1601E–1601G, where it is argued that the 2.5 per cent rate would lead to escalation 'to a degree that is far higher than proper compensation'. The main argument seemed to be that investment advice would be accepted by claimants recovering substantial damages, who would 'end up with a portfolio largely of equities, thereby leading to over-compensation as history shows that in the long term the total return on equities has always outstripped that on gilts, index-linked or otherwise'. See now the 17th edn. (Select Bibliography), at para. 35–105: 'Probably not fully compensated in the past, the injured victim, certainly the very severely injured one, is to be over-compensated in the future.' One will have to wait to see whether the more recent volatility of the stock markets will return to the lessons of 'history' before assessing whether these consequences will be the result of the new discount rate. Current evidence suggests that they are not.

221 *Page* v. *Sheerness Steel Co. Plc.*, sub nom. *Wells* v. *Wells* (see n. 216 above).

221a [1979] AC 556.

basis of the assumed rate of earnings at the time of the trial (in our example, £5,000), with no addition for further inflationary increases in the future.

In certain circumstances the court may decline to adopt the multiplier–multiplicand approach at all. That is limited to the circumstance in which the head of loss is undoubtedly genuine but is too speculative to be susceptible to the usual method of calculation. In those circumstances the court awards a lump sum which is more to do with instinct and experience than any mathematical or scientific approach.[222]

(iv) Future Loss of Earnings

This is a head of damage which probably causes more difficulty and debate than any other in the field of future pecuniary losses.

The essential basic principle is easily stated, namely that an injured claimant is entitled to recover the net sum which he would have earned but for the accident. In this context the word 'net' means after deduction of income tax and national insurance.[223] The court does not speculate as to changes in the levels for incidents of tax or national insurance after the date of trial. Earnings which have not been declared to the Inland Revenue are, nevertheless, recoverable but tax and national insurance at the appropriate rate must be deducted from the sums that the claimant would have received.[224] If, however, the earnings were derived from some unlawful act they will not be recoverable at all. The distinction is that in the former case the money came lawfully into the hands of the claimant and his unlawful act occurred subsequently when he failed to declare it to the Inland Revenue. In the latter case he never received the money lawfully at all.[225]

At the lowest level this will involve an investigation of the length of the period for which the claimant, on the balance of probabilities, would be unable to return to his pre-accident employment. It may be that his injury is comparatively minor, in which case he will simply be absent from work, post-trial, for a matter of months. It may be necessary, however, for him to have a gradual return to work, first undertaking light duties at a lower wage than before. In those circumstances his loss is the difference between what he is actually able to earn and what he would have earned had he been fully fit. That includes the loss of opportunity to work overtime. It matters not that the claimant has no absolute contractual right to overtime payments. It is sufficient if, on the evidence, he would have been likely to earn overtime. That is, quite simply, a matter of evidence.

In the case of the more seriously injured individual the question is likely to be far more complicated although the overriding principle remains the same.

In the case of a claimant who will never be able to return to work the loss is his annual net earnings, including overtime and pecuniary benefits, at the date of trial times the appropriate multiplier. That figure will depend upon the age of the claimant at the date

222 *Blamire* v. *South Cumbria HA* [1993] PIQR Q1.

223 *British Transport Commission* v. *Gourley* [1956] AC 185; *Cooper* v. *Firth Brown Ltd.* [1963] 1 WLR 418.

224 *Duller* v. *South East Lincs Engineers* [1981] CLY 585.

225 *Burns* v. *Edman* [1970] 2 QB 541; *Hunter* v. *Butler* [1996] RTR 396.

of trial and the date on which he would probably have retired.[226] That depends on the evidence. A date may be specified in the claimant's contract of employment. The court is, nevertheless, entitled to receive evidence that the particular employer generally permits employees to work beyond that date.

If the claimant is unable to return to his pre-accident employment but is, nevertheless, capable of undertaking some work it will be a question for the judge to decide what he is capable of undertaking and how much he is likely to earn in such a post. In those circumstances the loss of earnings will be the difference between what he is capable of earning and what he would have earned but for the accident. The claimant is not, of course, compelled to undertake employment. But he does have a duty to mitigate his loss. In those circumstances he is not entitled to say that the jobs which he is capable of doing are beneath him. Plainly, however, it may not be realistic for someone with a high-flying career pre-accident to undertake the most menial of tasks in the sense that no one will actually employ him. It is always worthwhile a claimant making job applications, and being turned down, in order to provide the court with evidence as to what is actually available to him. The court will also take account of such matters as the level of unemployment in the area in which the claimant resides. Mitigation of loss does not involve his having to move from one end of the country to the other in order to obtain low-paid employment.

Difficulties arise in this area in the case of individuals who are on a career ladder or who contend that they have lost a chance of promotion. In the case of an individual on a career ladder the court is likely to adopt different multiplicands, and reduced multipliers for each stage of his likely career. Thus, the multiplier will be divided into a number of different periods during each of which the claimant may be earning substantially higher figures.[227]

In the case of promotion the court will have to evaluate the percentage chance of the promotion having been achieved. It will then recalculate the multiplicand for the relevant period subject to a discount for the prospect off the lost chance.

A defendant is entitled to provide evidence, or to argue, on the basis of the claimant's own evidence, that his employment record is poor and that he would have been unlikely to have remained in employment for the whole of his working life. If such evidence is accepted by the court then the multiplier may be reduced.

Females, even in 2007, present a further problem in relation to the likelihood of career breaks to have and/or bring up children. There is not and cannot be any hard and fast rule. The matter must be looked at upon the available evidence in each case. Would she have returned to work immediately? Would she have sought to work part-time or become a full-time mother? In either of the latter events would that have impinged on the progression within her career? Those are all factors which fall to be taken into account by the court.

[226] Ogden Tables 3–10.

[227] *Brittain* v. *Garner*, *The Times* 18 Feb. 1989, but see for an alternative approach where the court used an average figure, *Housecroft* v. *Burnett* [1986] 1 All ER 332.

What is the situation in the case of a young person who has not yet embarked upon a career at all? In such a case the court will need to look at his educational attainment prior to the accident and any stated intention as to likely employment. It will also look, where appropriate, at the type of employment in which his parents and siblings have engaged in order to try and ascertain what type of work the claimant would, on the balance of probabilities, have done.

The younger the claimant, the more uncertain the position. In such a case it may be necessary for the court to abandon the multiplier/multiplicand approach altogether and simply award a lump sum on the basis that anything else is pure guesswork.[228] It is, however, more usual these days for the court to take an average figure for the general type of employment which the claimant's family has undertaken as the multiplicand and to use an appropriate multiplier.

In addition to loss of future earnings the court is entitled, in an appropriate case, to award an additional lump sum for the fact that the claimant is handicapped in the labour market. This head of damage only applies to an individual who is capable of returning to some form of employment but who, because of his disability, may find it more difficult than the average person to obtain further employment on his losing his job.[229]

This head of damage is not calculated in a scientific fashion. The court makes a broad assessment of how long it is likely to take the claimant to obtain further employment. It then awards net earnings for that period. Awards vary between three to six months and three years.[230]

(v) Medical Treatment and Therapies

The principle in relation to recovery of the costs of medical treatment or therapies is the same for the future as for expenditure prior to trial. The guiding principle, as always, is that of reasonable need. The claimant must also establish that he will, or probably will, require or undergo the treatment for which he claims.[231] He may be entitled to the cost of alternative therapies provided that he proves that he will undergo them.[232]

The mere fact that a particular type of therapy (for example hydrotherapy) may be desirable does not make it reasonably necessary. Furthermore, the mere fact that the claimant would benefit from regular swimming does not make the cost recoverable if either he would have been likely to go swimming in any event or the cost replaces another sporting or athletic activity in which he might have taken part had it not been for the accident.[233]

On the other hand the court is prepared to accept, for example, a claim for IVF in the case of the claimant who is in an established relationship but is no longer able to procreate.

228 *Blamire* v. *South Cumbria HA* [1993] PIQR Q1.

229 *Moeliker* v. *A. Reyrolle & Co. Ltd.* [1977] 1 WLR 132; *Smith* v. *Manchester Corporation* [1974] 17 KIR 1.

230 A helpful table of awards and reasons is to be found in Butterworths personal injury litigation service Vol. I Part I.

231 *Woodrup* v. *Nicol* [1993] PIQR Q104.

232 *George* v. *Stagecoach* [2003] EWHC 2042.

233 *Cassell* v. *Riverside HA* [1992] PIQR Q168.

As with other future losses the court will utilise the multiplier–multiplicand method of calculation for future medical expenses. In the case of surgical procedures which do not require to be undertaken annually the calculation is similar to that used for aids and equipment.

Prospective medical expenses will be estimated as accurately as possible[234] and will be awarded as part of the damages. Moreover, in accordance with section 2(4) of the Law Reform (Personal Injuries) Act 1948, failure to use the facilities of the National Health Service will not affect the 'reasonableness' of the plaintiff's expenses. As Slade J put it in *Harris* v. *Brights Asphalt Contractors Ltd.*,[235] 'when an injured plaintiff in fact incurs expenses which are reasonable, that expenditure is not to be impeached on the ground that, if he had taken advantage of the facilities under the NHS Act, 1946, these reasonable expenses might have been avoided'. But if advantage is in fact taken of the NHS, then the plaintiff will not be allowed to claim what he would have had to pay if he had contracted for such services or facilities.[236] In a society like ours the victim's right to be compensated for private hospitalisation is understandable, though some feel that this should not be allowed since even private hospitalisation is nowadays subsidised by the state.[237] What is less easy to justify, however, is the victim's right to claim such compensation, take advantage of free NHS facilities, and use the award for other purposes. This point, however, rarely arises in practice as far as the pre-trial medical expenses are concerned since at this stage plaintiffs are never sure that defendant's insurers will pay and, therefore, rarely risk incurring the expenses themselves.

The Law Commission's Consultation Paper on *Damages for Personal Injury: Medical, Nursing and other Expenses*[238] recommended the retention of section 2(4) of the 1948 Act, and also proposed that the NHS should be able to bring a claim against tortfeasors for the costs of caring for their victims.[239] In its final report on this issue,[240] the Law Commission stood by this provisional view,[241] although no concrete proposals on the recoupment issue were put forward. It should be noted, however, that, during the consultation period prior to the final report, the Road Traffic (NHS Charges) Act 1999 was passed, which provides a working example of how such recoupment might operate on a broader basis (including tariffs determining costs to be recouped and an appeals procedure). It is understood that the discussions surrounding the Law Commission's work in this area contributed to the formulation of the 1999 Act.[242] Most recently, the

234 *Lim Poh Choo* v. *Camden and Islington AHA* [1980] AC 174.

235 [1953] 1 QB 617, 635.

236 *Woodrup* v. *Nicol* [1993] PIQR Q104.

237 The Pearson Committee (Select Bibliography) paras. 339–42, felt that such expenses should be recoverable only if private treatment was reasonable on medical grounds. Note, also, s. 5 of the Administration of Justice Act 1982, discussed below.

238 Consultation Paper No. 144 (Select Bibliography).

239 See *ibid.*, paras. 4.2 and 4.3.

240 *Damages for Personal Injury: Medical, Nursing and Other Expenses–Collateral Benefits*, Report No. 262 (Select Bibliography).

241 See, *ibid.*, paras. 3.18 (on the retention of s. 2(4) of the 1948 Act) and 3.43 (on recoupment by the NHS).

242 *Ibid.*, para. 342.

Department of Health has issued 'The Recovery of National Health Service Costs in Cases involving Personal Injury Compensation: A Consultation'.[243] This draws heavily on Law Commission Report No. 262, especially in using the Road Traffic (NHS Charges) Act 1999 as a basis and poses a number of questions for consultation (covering the types of costs to be recovered,[244] whether industrial illness should be included, how to take account (if at all) of any findings or compromises on contributory negligence and whether the proposed scheme should apply to all relevant compensation payments or only to cases covered by insurance). This suggests a relatively strong political will to adopt this scheme and may be seen to fit in with the current government's priorities in achieving a more stable financial base for the public provision of health services. Equally, the impact on insurance companies and, ultimately, the customers who must pay their premiums, must be recognised as the source of this finance for the NHS. The progress of these proposals is to be awaited with interest.

(C) THIRD PARTIES TAKING CARE OF CLAIMANT'S NEEDS

Not infrequently, relatives or friends come to the assistance of a victim and thereby incur *financial* loss (e.g. of wages) or expenses. The usual reason for this is to ensure that the claimant/victim receives proper medical and nursing care. To do this, the third party may have to give up his or her paid job. In such cases these third parties cannot claim these losses in their own name, for as against them the tortfeasor has committed no tort. The question thus arises whether the 'primary' or 'direct' victim[245] can recover these sums and, if so, is he under a legal or (merely) moral duty to reimburse his benefactor (the third party)? In *Roach* v. *Yates*[246] the Court of Appeal had no difficulty in awarding such compensation to the 'primary' victim, since 'he would naturally feel he ought to compensate [in that case his wife and sister-in-law, who had given up their employment in order to nurse him] for what *they* had lost'. The italicised words could be taken to suggest that the loss in question was, in fact, the third party's (benefactor's) though, for technical reasons, it was claimed by what we have called the 'primary' or 'direct' victim of the tort. Indeed, this position was adopted by Lord Denning in *Cunningham* v. *Harrison*[247] where he also added the rider that the sum thus collected (by the 'primary' victim/claimant) would then be held on trust for the third party (benefactor). By a strange coincidence, however, one day later, in *Donnelly* v. *Joyce*,[248]

243 September 2002, available on the Internet at www.doh.gov.uk/nhscosts.

244 NHS and ambulance costs only or also those incurred by GPs, etc.

245 In what follows, we refer to the injured person/claimant as the 'primary' or 'indirect' victim to distinguish him from the volunteer who comes to his aid (usually giving up his job in order to nurse him) since, in a sense, he too is a victim (albeit indirect) of the tort.

246 [1953] 1 QB 617, 635.

247 [1973] QB 942.

248 [1974] QB 454. In *Donnelly* v. *Joyce* the young plaintiff claimed the cost of special boots, which he needed as a result of the accident and which had been bought for him by his parents, and for his mother's lost earnings as a result of her giving up her job to look after him. The defendant conceded the first claim but contested the second on the ground that the plaintiff was under no legal obligation to reimburse his mother.

a differently constituted Court of Appeal reached the same final result (i.e. that the tortfeasor should pay the loss of the third party/benefactor) but via a different route. This was, quite simply, that the loss was that of *the primary (direct) victim* and it consisted not of the expenditure, itself, but of the *need* for the nursing services.

The *Donnelly* v. *Joyce* ruling, which held sway for the next twenty years, was probably prompted by the desire to put an end to uncertainties which had crept into the practice of the law and concerned how the award thus gained by the 'primary' victim should be handled (i.e. kept by him or held in trust in the name of the benefactor, and should the latter course be open only when there was a formal agreement to such effect between the 'primary' victim and the third party). These difficulties were, apparently, avoided by making it clear that the claim for the award was that of the 'primary' victim and not the third party/benefactor and it was then entirely for him to decide how, in fact, the money would be used. But as Lord Bridge put it in *Hunt* v. *Severs*,[249] the decision which terminated the reign of the *Donnelly* judgment:

> By concentrating on the plaintiff's [primary victim's] need and the plaintiff's loss as the basis of an award... the reasoning in *Donnelly* diverts attention from the award's central objective of compensating the voluntary carer. Once this is recognised it becomes evident that there can be no ground in public policy or otherwise for requiring the tortfeasor to pay to the plaintiff, in respect of services which he himself has rendered, a sum of money which the plaintiff must then repay to him.

One reason why the House of Lords felt obliged to return to the Denning rationale (that what is at issue here is the benefactor's and not the 'primary' victim's loss, so that the primary victim held the damages recovered under this heading on trust for the carer[250]) was that the unusual facts of the case revealed a basic flaw in the *Donnelly* approach and this clarifies the last sentence of Lord Bridge's statement. For in the *Hunt* case the volunteer offering the services (and suffering the loss) was the plaintiff's husband who was also the defendant tortfeasor in the action! So, if the *Donnelly* reasoning had applied, the plaintiff (wife) would have claimed the loss suffered by her husband who gave up his job to look after her. But the husband, it will be recalled, was also the tortfeasor who had injured her in the first place so, on this kind of reasoning, he would be paying damages for his own loss. The House of Lords was able to avoid this result in the instant case while preserving intact the basic principle that in the more run-of-the-mill kind of case plaintiffs would still be able to recover for the gratuitous provision of services by third parties.

The logic of *Hunt* v. *Severs* is clear enough, but the House of Lords' decision gives rise to numerous problems in the case where the defendant is also the provider of care for

249 [1994] 2 All ER 385 at 394.

250 This is similar to the approach taken in Scotland: see Administration of Justice Act 1982, s. 8, although this section involves only a *personal* liability on the claimant to account to the carer. For a discussion of the 'trust' or 'personal liability' issue, see Law Commission, Report No. 262 (Select Bibliography), paras. 3.55 ff. (esp. 3.62), where the Law Commission recommends legislation to make this a personal liability only (and then only for past, not future, care).

the plaintiff.[251] One is that the ruling apparently does not apply if the victim and the carer enter into a contract under which the latter becomes obliged to render the services in question, in return for agreed remuneration. The courts have consistently taken the view that it would be undesirable to place the victim and carer in the position of being required to make a contract of this kind,[252] yet that is precisely the effect of *Hunt* v. *Severs*. The ruling also provides a disincentive for accident victims to accept gratuitous care from close relatives who may be in the best (and most cost-effective) position to provide it for them.[253] These were among the considerations that led the Law Commission, in its Consultation Paper on *Damages for Personal Injury: Medical, Nursing and other Expenses*,[254] to recommend that *Hunt* v. *Severs* should be reversed by statute, in favour of a rule to the effect that the defendant's liability for the claimant's nursing care should be unaffected by any liability which the claimant might incur to pay those damages back to the defendant and the final report on this issue stood by this recommendation.[255]

It could also be said that there is an air of artificiality to the reasoning in *Hunt* v. *Severs*: in practice, it is not the defendant who would have to pay the damages in question (and then have them repaid by the claimant), but the defendant's insurance company. The effect of the House of Lords' judgment, then, was that 'plaintiff and defendant were unable collectively to call upon the proceeds of the defendant's indemnity insurance to cover the cost of caring for the plaintiff.'[256] Both the House of Lords[257] and the Law Commission[258] rejected this line of argument, on the traditional ground that the courts should not be influenced in setting the extent of the defendant's liability by the fact that the defendant was carrying third-party insurance in respect of the loss in question. While this approach may be correct in principle, in a case like *Hunt* v. *Severs* it runs the risk of producing a result that is both unjust to the parties immediately concerned and perverse in the incentives it creates for future parties in the same position. Consideration of a number of these factors led to the Law Commission's proposal to reverse the result in *Hunt* v. *Severs*, as discussed above.

251 See D. Kemp, 'Voluntary Services Provided by Tortfeasor to his Victim' (1994) 110 *LQR* 524; A. Reed, 'A Commentary on *Hunt* v. *Severs*' (1995) 15 *OJLS* 133.

252 See, in particular, *Donnelly* v. *Joyce* [1974] QB 454, at 463–4 (Megaw LJ), *Hunt* v. *Severs* [1993] QB 815, at 831 (Sir Thomas Bingham MR).

253 In support of the need to promote such voluntary care, see Colman J's observation in *Hardwick* v. *Hudson* [1999] 3 All ER 426, 435–6, that 'personal physical care can often be most effectively and economically provided by a family member or close friend'.

254 Law Commission Consultation Paper No. 144 (Select Bibliography), at para. 3.68.

255 Law Commission Report No. 262, (Select Bibliography), para. 3.76, which should be read with the earlier recommendation that the claimant should be under a personal obligation (laid down by statute) to account to the carer for past care which has been provided gratuitously (see para. 3.62). The 'carer' would have to be a 'relative or friend', which is wider than the current position in Scotland (which includes only 'relatives').

256 Law Commission Consultation Paper No. 144 (Select Bibliography), at para. 3.65.

257 [1994] 2 AC 350, at 363 (Lord Bridge).

258 See, e.g., Law Commission Report No. 262 (Select Bibliography), para. 3.74.

The assessment of the award for the services given to the claimant by these third parties has also posed a difficult dilemma. The dilemma is this: should these services (of the third party) be valued at nil (which is what happened prior to *Donnelly*) or at their full—and hence high—commercial rate? The Court of Appeal's compromise suggestion can be found in *Housecroft* v. *Burnett*.[259] There the measure of the loss was said to be 'the proper and reasonable cost' of taking care of the plaintiff's needs. In practice this means the relative's lost earnings (where he or she is engaged in gainful employment), with the commercial rate applicable to such services serving as an upper limit. But where this 'caring' relative does not give up paid employment, the commercial rate will be inappropriate.[260] In its recent report, the Law Commission refused to propose the setting of any limits or thresholds on such damages and did not suggest any legislative changes to the assessment of such damages. However, it did stress that the commercial rate for such caring services represented a 'good starting point' and that the courts should be wary of discounting from this too extensively (to take into account tax and other commercial expenses). Also, the courts were encouraged to 'be more willing to award damages to compensate carers for their lost earnings even though these exceed the commercial cost of care'.[261] In practice in cases where the carer has not given up paid employment the Courts have adopted the *Housecroft* v. *Burnett*[262] approach of taking the commercial rate and discounting the amount by 25 per cent or 30 per cent depending on whether the care provided is in the nature of nursing or specialist care or whether it is no more than domestic assistance.

Finally, in this context, section 5 of the Administration of Justice Act 1982 should be noted. This provides that any saving to the injured person which is the result of his being wholly or partly maintained at public expense in a hospital or nursing home or other institution should be set off against any income lost by him as a result of his injuries.

American, Canadian and German courts have also been called to address a complicated variation of the *Donnelly* problem where what is in issue is not financial loss but physical injury sustained by the third party/volunteer in the interests of the 'primary' victim. Typically, in these cases a person has had a kidney negligently removed in hospital. Unfortunately (for everyone concerned) this 'primary' victim turns out to have one kidney only—apparently something that occurs in one out of 100 people—and thus is in need of an immediate transplant or else he will die. So a close relative (e.g. father/the benefactor) is asked and agrees to donate one of his kidneys in order to save the life of the 'primary' victim. Can the 'primary' victim claim for such harm suffered by the third party/volunteer? The fact that the volunteer's (relative's) loss was the result of his own voluntary act can present legal difficulties; and the decision to donate an organ, coming after due deliberation, distinguishes these cases from the typical rescue cases (where the intervention is on the spur of the moment and unaccompanied by the

259 [1986] 1 All ER 332, at 343, per O'Connor LJ.

260 *McCamley* v. *Cammell Laird Shipbuilders* [1990] 1 WLR 963, 966–7.

261 Law Commission Report No. 262 (Select Bibliography) paras. 3.77–3.86.

262 [1986] 1 All ER 332.

certainty of hurt) which, otherwise, would appear the closest legal concept which could be used as a starting-point in the reasoning process. Yet despite these difficulties, the Canadian and German courts have allowed for the compensation of the donors—a much better solution (it is submitted) than by channelling the claim through the child/primary victim.[263] It must be hoped that if, or rather when, such a case comes before our courts they will be willing to take note of the rich foreign case law on this topic.

(D) REDUCTION OF EXPECTATION OF LIFE

There may be instances where the claimant's injuries are such that he can no longer expect to survive for the span of his pre-accident anticipated working life. In that case, will the claimant's 'lost years' be taken into account when calculating his damages for lost future earnings? In 1962 the Court of Appeal in *Oliver* v. *Ashman*[264] unanimously held that damages for future loss of earnings could be awarded only in respect of the period during which it was anticipated that the plaintiff would survive his accident; nothing was thus recoverable for the 'lost years'. The decision was seriously criticised,[265] yet the result on the facts was not, it is submitted, wrong. For there the plaintiff who was claiming compensation, about two years old at the time of the accident and not quite five at the time of the trial, would normally have lived until the age of sixty-six, but was now expected to die at around thirty-six. He claimed what he would have earned during the thirty years of which the defendant had deprived him, but his claim was rejected. As stated, on these facts, the decision was right. For it is ludicrous to award a child the money he might have *saved* sixty years later. And we are talking of the money he might have saved and not the money he would have used for his living expenses since, *ex hypothesi*, there would be none during the 'lost years'. Furthermore, the same rule operates correctly in the case of an adult without dependants. For surely if we replaced his lost earnings by an annuity, which would cease on his death, we would not increase its annual amount on the ground that his earning life has been shortened. Not to apply the rule in *Oliver* v. *Ashman* to the adult without dependants would really give him more to spend than he would have earned during the spending period of his life. Alternatively, it would swell the bonus which his estate would confer on persons financially unharmed by his death. Though *Oliver* v. *Ashman* produced no injustice in the case of a child or adult *without dependants*, it operated harshly in the case of a victim with dependants, who was kept alive for long enough to deprive his dependants of their dependency. For, as we shall see,[266] under the Fatal Accidents Acts they cannot sue if the

263 Thus, *Urbanski* v. *Patel* (1978) 84 DLR (3d) 650 (Canada); BGH JZ 1988, 150 (Germany) (English translation in B. S. Markesinis and H. Unberath, *The German Law of Torts: A Comparative Treatise* (4th edn., 2001), 60); cf. *Sirianni* v. *Anna*, 285 NYS (2d) 709 (1967), *Moore* v. *Shah*, 458 NYS (2d) 33, *Ornelas* v. *Fry*, 727 P 2d 810.

264 [1962] 2 QB 210.

265 But also defended by J. A. Weir, *Compensation for Personal Injuries and Death* (Select Bibliography), 15–16. On the whole question of lost years, see J. G. Fleming, 'The Lost Years: A Problem in the Computation and Distribution of Damages' (1962) 50 *Cal. LR* 598.

266 Below, Section 8.

victim's action has been satisfied, settled or statute-barred; and he, as a result of *Oliver* v. *Ashman*, could not claim (while still alive) for his lost years and then pass on these sums to his dependants via his estate.[267] The pressure to change the law thus grew and various ways were proposed to achieve this end. In the event the House of Lords in *Pickett* v. *British Rail Engineering Ltd.*[268] overruled *Oliver* v. *Ashman* and allowed a *living* plaintiff to recover the value of his lost earnings during his lost years, minus his living and other expenses during that period.[269] This right, however, is now limited to living claimants and does not survive under the Law Reform Act 1934 for the benefit of his estate.[270]

7. NON-PECUNIARY LOSSES

We now come to the kinds of damages that are particularly vague and difficult to quantify. There is also some controversy as to what function these damages aim to achieve and whether, as in some states in the United Sates, they should be subject to 'caps', i.e. upper limits. Moreover, though different headings do exist, and we shall try to present the law under them, it is evident that clear distinctions between them cannot be maintained. It is thus not always easy to keep strictly separate headings such as pain and suffering and loss of amenities, which is why one must always guard against the risk of 'double compensation'. These definitional overlaps have also been one reason why the various legislative proposals for reform have not, in the case of non-pecuniary damages, recommended the type of elaborate itemisation which they felt was necessary in the case of damages for pecuniary losses.

Before we look at the various heading of recoverable damages we should, however, say about the notion of 'assessement' of damages.

(A) THE 'ASSESSMENT' CONCEPT OF DAMAGES

The figures we shall provide in the next few sections should not be taken to represent anything more than illustrations. Clearly, with the passage of time, they change, on the whole the tend to go up, not least to follow the cost of living. But this is not the point we

[267] *Murray* v. *Shuter* [1976] QB 972 is a case which reveals the potential injustice of the rule and the measures the courts had to take to avoid it.

[268] [1980] AC 136.

[269] For judicial elaborations on the meaning of 'living expenses' and the problems to which this may give rise in the context of the interrelationship between the Fatal Accidents Act 1976 and the Law Reform (Miscellaneous Provisions) Act 1934, see *Benson* v. *Biggs Wall & Co. Ltd.* [1983] 1 WLR 72, 75 ff., *Harris* v. *Empress Motors Ltd.* [1983] 1 WLR 65, *Clay* v. *Pooler* [1982] 3 All ER 570.

[270] Administration of Justice Act 1982, s. 4, overruling *Gammell* v. *Wilson* [1982] AC 27, where the House of Lords had reluctantly decided that a claim for the income which would have accrued to the plaintiff during the 'lost years' survived for the benefit of his estate. This led to potential double compensation as explained and criticised by B. S. Markesinis and A. M. Tettenborn, 'Fatal Accident Damages: How Not to Reform the Law' (1981) 131 *NLJ* 869. Happily, all these complications now belong to history.

wish to warn about here. Rather, we wish to stress in this subsection that the word *assessment* of damage must be and, indeed, is used advisedly. To put it in different words, there is no mathematical or scientific calculation involved in arriving at the appropriate figure.[271] As will be explained there exist tariffs which were recently reviewed by the Court of Appeal in *Heil* v *Rankin*.[272]

The guidelines set a bracket for general damages for all types of injury. What they do not, and could not do, is to provide a bracket for every conceivable combination of injuries. How, therefore, does the trial judge approach his assessment? The answer is through a broad assessment of all the evidence. A useful checklist might be:

(a) What were the circumstances of the accident?

(b) What was the degree of pain and suffering undergone by the claimant in the accident itself?

(c) What was the length and nature of the treatment undergone by the claimant?

(d) What is the most serious injury suffered by the claimant?

(e) What other injuries did the claimant suffer?

(f) What are the residual disabilities of the claimant?

(g) To what extent, if at all, has the claimant been unable to lead a normal life as a result of those disabilities up to the date of trial?

(h) What is the extent to which, if at all, the claimant will be unable to lead a normal life as a result of those disabilities in the future?

The judge then has to make his assessment taking all these matters into account. As has already been said the exercise is neither an exact science nor a mathematical calculation. The judge does not, for example, say that an individual should have £5,000 for a broken leg and £3,000 for an injury to his arm making, £8,000 in all. He will consider all the factors on the checklist and arrive at a final figure.

Despite appearing remote, judges, even in England, are human beings. It would be idle to deny that, inevitably, some claimants make a good impression upon them while others do not. Likewise, while some judges are parsimonious, others are inclined to greater generosity. Practitioners in the subject would subscribe to these views and would deny a too rigid differentiation between the judges' aloofness and the jury's proclivity towards deserving claimants. The Court of Appeal will not interfere with an award of general damages unless it is plainly outside the bracket of what is reasonable, having regard to the broad tariff in the Judicial Studies Board guidelines.[273] As a result, it is rarely possible in England to give an exact figure for what a particular claimant is likely to recover in any given case. The best any practitioner can do is to provide a bracket.

[271] *Fuhri* v. *Jones* 1979 CA No. 199 30 Mar. 1979.

[272] [2001] QB 272.

[273] *Judicial Studies Board Guidelines* (8th edn., 2006).

(B) PAIN AND SUFFERING

A claimant is entitled to recover for his pain and suffering—the two terms have never been clearly distinguished by the courts—actual and prospective, resulting from the tortfeasor's conduct or from medical or surgical treatment made necessary as a result of the tortious conduct. This will include his nervous shock[274] and any other recognised psychiatric symptoms,[275] but not sorrow or grief.[276] The point was affirmed in *Hinz* v. *Berry*;[277] but, in practice, the distinction is not always easy to draw, leaving room for some creative advocacy (and judgments). No award for this type of damage is, however, made if the claimant is permanently unconscious and thus not in any pain.[278] Despite some earlier doubts it is now accepted that the claimant's economic and social position is irrelevant as far as this heading of damages is concerned.[279] Nor may damages for pain and suffering be awarded in a case where death occurs instantaneously.[280]

(C) LOSS OF AMENITIES

The expression 'loss of amenity' is less easy to define. In *H. West & Son Ltd* v. *Shephard*,[281] Lord Reid said:

> There are two views about the true basis for this kind of compensation. One is that the man is simply being compensated for the loss of his leg or the impairment of his digestion. The other is that his real loss is not so much his physical injury as the loss of those opportunities to lead a full and normal life which are now denied to him by his physical condition—for the multitude of deprivations and even petty annoyances which he must tolerate.

It is important in each case to consider precisely what has been lost. All the personal circumstances of the injured individual must be taken into account. That includes age, lifestyle, hopes and expectations, and disabilities existing before accident. Thus, a fit, athletic, active individual, who in consequence of an injury is unable to participate in sport or an outdoor lifestyle and who can no longer play with his young children in the manner that he did before the accident has lost more than a seventy-year-old with a sedentary lifestyle who engages in gentler pursuits.

If the claimant's injuries thus deprive the claimant of the capacity to engage in sport or other pastimes, which he enjoyed before his injury, then this must be compensated.

274 E.g. *Hinz* v. *Berry* [1970] 2 QB 40.

275 Such as 'compensation neurosis'. See *James* v. *Woodall Duckham Construction Co. Ltd.* [1969] 1 WLR 903.

276 Though sometimes the courts can ingeniously link the two and provide some (monetary) solace to the claimant. See *Kralj* v. *McGrath* [1986] 1 All ER 54 and contrast *Kerby* v. *Redbridge HA* [1994] PIQR Q1.

277 [1970] 2 QB 40.

278 *Wise* v. *Kaye* [1962] 1 QB 638. This is so even if the result of lack of consciousness or pain is due to drugs or anaesthetics: *West* v. *Shephard* [1964] AC 326. The greater availability of painkilling drugs may well reduce further these awards and, perhaps, lead the courts into making larger awards under the heading of loss of amenity.

279 *Fletcher* v. *Autocar and Transporters* [1968] 2 QB 322, 340–1 (per Diplock LJ) and 364 (per Salmon LJ).

280 See *Hicks* v. *Chief Constable of South Yorkshire* [1992] 2 All ER 65.

281 [1964] AC 326 at page 341. See also *Lim Poh Choo* v. *Camden and Islington AHA* [1980] AC 174, per Lord Scarman at 183.

Other losses compensated under this heading include: impairment of one of the five senses;[282] loss or impairment of sexual life;[283] diminution of marriage prospects (an item which is additional to the pecuniary loss that may result from such an event); destroyed holiday;[284] inability to play with one's children;[285] and many others.

Until fairly recently, it was uncertain whether this heading of damage was separate from or merely part of any award for pain and suffering. In other words, what was unclear was whether the damages are awarded in respect of the *objective loss of amenities*, or in respect of the subjective mental suffering which comes with the appreciation of such loss. In *Wise* v. *Kaye*[286] the claimant was rendered immediately unconscious and remained so at the time of the trial three-and-a-half years later. Though she had suffered an almost complete loss of her faculties, she had no knowledge whatever of this loss. For Diplock LJ this was a good reason for awarding her a comparatively small sum under this heading. However, the majority of the Court of Appeal thought otherwise, and two years later in *H. West & Son Ltd.* v. *Shephard*[287] the House of Lords agreed with this view. As Lord Morris put it,

> the fact of unconsciousness is . . . relevant in respect of and will eliminate those heads or elements of damage which can exist only by being felt or thought or experienced. The fact of unconsciousness does not, however, eliminate the actuality of the deprivation of the ordinary experiences and amenities of life which may be the inevitable result of some physical injury.

This majority view was reaffirmed in *Lim Poh Choo* v. *Camden & Islington Area Health Authority*,[288] where Lord Scarman said that the cases draw a clear distinction between damages for pain and suffering and damages for loss of amenities. The former depend upon the claimant's personal awareness of pain, her capacity for suffering. But the latter are awarded for the fact of deprivation—a substantial loss, whether the claimant is aware of it or not. Nevertheless, his judgment leaves one with the impression that an important reason for accepting this view was his desire not to disturb what had become an established rule, since it has influenced both judicial awards and extra-judicial settlements for many years.[289]

The levels of awards for pain and suffering *and* loss of amenities have become an increasingly important issue over the past twenty years. In 1999, we noted that the highest awards for pain and suffering and loss of amenities were around the £100,000 mark.[290]

282 E.g. taste and smell: *Cook* v. *J. L. Kier and Co.* [1970] 1 WLR 774.

283 *Ibid.* 284 *Ichard* v. *Frangoulis* [1977] 1 WLR 556.

285 *Hoffman* v. *Sofaer* [1982] 1 WLR 1350. 286 [1962] 1 QB 638.

287 [1964] AC 326. The vigorous dissents of Lords Reid and Devlin repay careful study.

288 [1980] AC 174.

289 [1980] AC 174, 189. A second reason given was that this reform would be best effected by means of comprehensive legislation. Other jurisdictions have not adopted this rule; and the Pearson Committee recommended its abolition (Select Bibliography), i, para. 398. The Law Commission recently recommended that no change should be made to the position established since *H. West & Son Ltd.* v. *Shephard* and confirmed in *Lim* (Report No. 257 (Select Bibliography), esp. paras. 2.19 and 2.24).

290 For instance, £95,000 was awarded in *Brightman* v. *Johnson* (quoted by D. Kemp, *Kemp and Kemp: The Quantum of Damages*, ii, para. 1–010) whereas in *Housecroft* v. *Burnett* [1986] 1 All ER 332, O'Connor LJ thought £75,000 was an appropriate guideline for the average incident of tetraplegia.

Faced with similar (and, often, much larger) awards, various systems (e.g. Canada, Eire, and a number of jurisdictions in the United States) have opted for judicially or legislatively imposed maxima for non-pecuniary losses. The idea—known as 'capping'—has much to commend it, especially in the case of unconscious claimants (who still receive substantial awards for loss of amenities). On the other hand, the Law Commission has, on more than one occasion, suggested that current levels may be insufficient.[291] Now, the Court of Appeal, in the case of *Heil* v. *Rankin*,[292] has ruled that certain increases should be made for more serious injuries where awards are over the £10,000 mark. The increases to be made are not uniform, but range from around a one-third increase for awards at the highest levels (i.e. very serious injuries, e.g. quadriplegia and severe brain damage) tapering down to no increase for awards of £10,000 and below.[293] The Court examined the reasoning which the Law Commission had used in making its 1999 proposals, expressing particular appreciation for the role played by increased life expectancy in such assessments, both in general and in terms of those suffering serious injury, who may often live to a 'normal' average age in spite of their injuries. However, doubts were also expressed about placing too much reliance on evidence found in various surveys since the material collected might well be susceptible to a number of interpretations and explanations, rather than just dissatisfaction with the level of damages for pain and suffering and loss of amenities.[294] The very highest award available in England is thus £235,000 for quadriplegia.[295] No individual, however seriously injured, can receive more under the heading of general damages.

291 See Law Commission, Report No. 225, *Personal Injury Compensation: How Much Is Enough?* (1994) and Report No. 257, *Damages for Personal Injury: Non-Pecuniary Loss* (Select Bibliography) for detailed discussion, including the results of extensive surveys and consultation responses. The 1999 Report proposed that awards up to £2,000 should see no increase, awards between £2,000 and £3,000 should be increased by up to 150 per cent of present levels and awards over £3,000 should see at least an increase of 150 per cent (and, indeed, possibly 200 per cent) of present levels.

292 [2001] QB 272. A five-judge Court of Appeal was convened to hear the appeal, indicating the importance attached to the issue, and Lord Woolf MR delivered the Court's judgment.

293 The judgment states that it 'is our view that between those awards at the highest level, which require an upwards adjustment of one-third, and those awards where no adjustment is required, the extent of the adjustment should taper downwards, as illustrated by our decisions on the individual appeals which are before us'. On closer inspection, this taper does not appear to descend evenly: *Warren* v. *Northern General Hospital NHS Trust* and *Annable* v. *Southern Derbyshire HA* (conjoined appeals with *Heil* v. *Rankin*) saw the Court of Appeal increase the award from £135,000 to £175,000 (the new figure amounting to ~130 per cent of the old), the *Ramsay* v. *Rivers* case saw an increase of approximately 25 per cent (£110,270 to £138,000), *Kent* v. *Griffiths (No. 2)* an increase of around 20 per cent (£80,000 to £95,000), *Rees* v. *Mabco (102) Ltd.* around 10 per cent (£45,000 to £50,000), *Schofield* v. *Saunders & Taylor Ltd.* 10 per cent (£40,000 to £44,000) and in *Connolly* v. *Tasker*, the court reassessed damages on the conventional basis but made no increase in the level available (the sum being only £4,000 after the Court of Appeal's amendment). In *Heil* v. *Rankin* itself, no order was made due to other complications yet to be dealt with in the case, although the Court stressed that it would recommend no increase in the level of damages, since the sum fell below the £10,000 threshold laid down earlier in the judgment. Appended to the judgment is a diagram showing the levels of increases made, which may aid the reader in placing these various increases into context.

294 See [2001] QB 272, 302–13.

295 Judicial Studies Board Guidelines (8th edn. 2006).

(D) DAMAGES FOR BEREAVEMENT

When the claimant's life expectancy is reduced by an injury and this causes him mental suffering this will be taken into account when assessing his damages for pain and suffering and loss of amenity. This was always so and is now embodied in section 1(*b*) of the Administration of Justice Act 1982. In 1935, however, the Court of Appeal in *Flint* v. *Lovell*[296] held that there existed an independent heading of damages for loss of expectation of life and the House of Lords, two years later in *Rose* v. *Ford*,[297] held that this right also survived for the benefit of the deceased's estate. Four years later, however, the House of Lords, in a judgment[298] that often touched on the metaphysical, decided that the sums to be awarded under this heading should be modest conventional figures.[299] As the Pearson Committee observed, such damages were of little significance for living plaintiffs, for where the injuries were serious enough to reduce life expectancy these damages formed only a small part of the total award. In the case of death the only real function these damages performed was to give the parents of young children killed in accidents a small sum which they would otherwise not have obtained under the fatal accidents legislation.[300]

Loss of expectation of life was abolished by section 1(*a*) of the Administration of Justice Act 1982 and was replaced by a new claim, 'bereavement', which gives a fixed sum by way of damages to a spouse for the loss of the other spouse and to parents for the loss of a child. The amount was fixed by the Act at £3,500, but is capable of being increased by order. Since April 1991, the figure had stood at £7,500, until it was increased to £10,000 for actions which accrue on or after 1 April 2002.[301]

As the parliamentary debates show, the acceptance of this new right raises many problems, philosophical as well as legal. In the first place, the very principle of paying a sum for bereavement is doubtful. As the Lord Chancellor put it: 'there is no sum of money at all that one can nominate which is not an insult to the bereaved person, whether it is £10 million or £10'. Having said this, he also accepted that others, perhaps the majority, might think otherwise, hence his willingness to propose this heading. But the sum should, he felt, be fixed. It would be unattractive, if not invidious, for courts to have to calculate a person's grief in money terms. This may explain why the sum is a conventional one, but it does not explain why a similar right was not given to children for the loss of one or both

296 [1935] 1 KB 354. 297 [1937] AC 826.

298 *Benham* v. *Gambling* [1941] AC 157.

299 By 1982, when this heading of damages was abolished, the sum was about £1,250.

300 This is because soon after the first Fatal Accidents Act in 1846 the court held in *Blake* v. *The Midland Railway Co.* (1852) 18 QB 93; 118 ER 35, that only financial loss (and not bereavement) was compensatable under the new statute. In the case of the death of a young child, therefore, its parents could recover nothing. Since it could not earn anything its 'value' to its parents was 'nil'. Like Oscar Wilde's cynic, English law knew the 'price' of everything but the 'value' of nothing. Through the medium of damages for loss of expectation of life 'the meanness of refusing parents damages for their grief was neutralized by the absurdity of giving the dead child a claim for being killed' (Weir (Select Bibliography), 12).

301 Bereavement (Variation of Sum) (England and Wales) Order 2002 (SI No. 2002/644), amending s. 1A of the Fatal Accidents Act 1976 (itself inserted by s. 3 of the Administration of Justice Act 1982).

parents. Awards by way of *solatium* are disapproved of by many lawyers, but to award them in one case and not in another will only strengthen the belief that these awards are arbitrary and, therefore, objectionable on this score as well. The Lord Chancellor's reason for denying children damages for the loss of a parent was more technical. He felt that a minor child's dependency damages would already be substantial and the bereavement damages would add little or nothing. Certainly, as we shall see, courts are conscious of the problem involved here and have in recent years tried to increase dependency damages by awarding children something more than just the cost of hiring 'substitute service'. It is therefore tempting to suggest that bereavement damages should have been either avoided altogether or awarded to both these types of claimants.

(E) LOSS OF MARRIAGE PROSPECTS

Unsurprisingly, in the modern world this is not formally recognised as a separate and distinct head of damage.[302] Various brackets for the type of injury which may adversely affect the ability of an individual to form a relationship with another person already encompass that fact as part of his or her loss of amenity.

Physical injury to sexual or reproductive organs is, however, a recognised, and separate, physical injury and features as such within the JSB guidelines.

Scarring may attract a greater award if the injured individual is a young female. That is not upon the basis of diminution of marriage prospects but rather general loss of amenity and embarrassment.[303]

(F) LOSS OF CONGENIAL EMPLOYMENT

English law recognises, as a separate head of loss, that an individual may well, in consequence of his injuries, lose employment which he found fulfilling and satisfying. A separate sum, in addition to general damages for pain and suffering, and loss of amenity may be awarded for such loss.

It is not necessary that the employment which has been lost should be glamorous or even particularly extraordinary. In *Hale* v. *London Underground Ltd.*,[304] Otton J said:

> There can be no doubt that there is a considerable feeling of fulfilment and satisfaction to attend a fire, to extinguish it quickly and safely, and to rescue any persons inside the building before they suffer fatal or other terrible injuries. I consider this a real loss to Mr Hale and it is not mitigated by any enjoyment from his present work.

The evidence required to establish this head of loss is, as appears from that passage, fulfilment and satisfaction in the job and an obvious commitment to it.

302 *Moriarty* v. *McCarthy* [1978] 1 WLR 155.

303 This is recognised in the *JSB Guidelines* in relation to facial disfigurement where the introduction says, in terms, that the distinction between male and female under subjective approach are of particular significance.

304 [1993] PIQR Q30.

As with general damages awards are not calculated on any mathematical or scientific basis. In *Hale* v. *London Underground* the award was £5,000. That is probably the middle of the bracket for the average case although it is capable of being considerably more in the case of a glamorous occupation. In 2001 the claimant received £7,500 for loss of congenial employment as a kick-boxer and instructor![305] A similar sum was awarded to a twenty-five-year-old woman who lost her career as a professional woman. She was said to have been an exceptionally gifted double-bass player, having studied at the Royal Academy of Music under some of the foremost double-bass players in the world. Had she not succeeded as a soloist, she would have obtained a post in a leading orchestra.[306] The highest award which we have been able to find, to date, is £8,750 for the loss of an executive position.[307]

As will be apparent from the foregoing, the amounts awarded under this head are not large.

(G) PSYCHIATRIC INJURY

This heading has been discussed in great detail in the main chapter on the tort of negligence so here suffice it to point the tendency, where it is recognised as actionable to compensate on the basis of standardised and, if possible, modest figures. The same goes for damages awarded in those difficult cases where parents are forcefully separated from their children on the basis of erroneous and negligent assessments by local authorities about the dangers they—the parents—may pose to their children. As we noted in the chapter on breach of statutory duties, the English courts are currently in a 'conservative' mode that leads them deny the 'deprived' parents any damages; and one way of explaining this decision (mainly supported by policy arguments about the economic consequences of a liability rule) is to invoke the restrictive nervous shock (psychiatric injury) rules. One way around this might be to argue that these are not true 'psychiatric injury' cases (as the term is understood in English law) but human-rights violations—in this case resulting from the violation of Article 8 of the European Convention on Human Rights—and can thus lead to an award of damages under such a heading. Indeed, this has occurred by the Court of Human Rights in Strasbourg; but the validity of the suggested distinction has yet to gain wider support among out own courts.

8. DEATH IN RELATION TO TORT

(A) SURVIVAL OF CAUSES OF ACTION

The death of a person can have effects on tortious liability in two ways: (*a*) it may affect an existing right of action or liability or (*b*) it can create a new liability towards

305 *Langford* v. *Hebran* [2001] EWCA Civ. 361; [2001] PIQR Q160.

306 *Byers* v. *London Borough of Brent*, QBD, judgment of 24 Apr. 1998 (unreported).

307 *Pratt* v. *Smith* 19 Dec. 2002, unreported (transcript available on Westlaw UK: 2002 WL 31676426 (QBD)).

the dependants of the victim. In this section we are concerned with the former, i.e. transmissibility of the cause of action after death.

If a tort has been committed and the claimant or the defendant dies, does the action survive? At common law personal actions died with the party, which was expressed in the maxim *actio personalis moritur cum persona*. The result was not altogether unfair, at any rate after 1846. For a right to sue was of little use to the dead victim. And since the Fatal Accidents Act of 1846, enacted as a result of increased numbers of deaths in the wake of the railway revolution, the victim's surviving spouse and children were given an *independent* right to sue for their lost dependency.[308] The railway revolution was itself overtaken by the car revolution, one consequence of which was that often the tortfeasor, too, was killed along with his victim. It therefore became necessary not only to provide for the victim's dependants, as the 1846 Act had done, but to make sure that this right survived against the estate of the tortfeasor. The Law Reform (Miscellaneous Provisions) Act of 1934 ensured that the tortfeasor's insurance[309] company *remained* liable to the victim's dependents. Having removed half of the common-law rule, and having thereby made the tortfeasor's liability transmissible to his estate, the Act went on to remove the rest of the common law rule and allowed the deceased victim's estate to carry on his action. So *vested* rights against the tortfeasor *survived* against and for the benefit of his estate.[310] Such rights include not only what one could term the traditional claims for personal injury but also claims for compensation arising out of modern legislation such as the Race Relations Act 1970, the Sex Discrimination Act 1975 and the Disability Discrimination Act 1995.[311] The only exceptions to this 'survival rule' are causes of action for defamation (which still die with the wrongdoer or the wronged person) and the more recently created claim for bereavement.[312] The disappearance of the cause of action with the death of the *defamed* person is understandable once it is accepted that the tort action in defamation *primarily* protects a non-pecuniary interest (the defamed person's reputation); but that of the bereavement claim has proved more controversial though it still stands.[313] But the 1934 legislator seems to have been carried away in his reforming zeal and, it is submitted, unconsciously and wrongly excluded the reverse right: the living victim's right to claim against the *defamer's* estate.[314] The period of limitation runs from the accrual of the cause of action.

Where the prospective defendant (wrongdoer) dies, the normal rules apply to the measure of damages and the ordinary periods of limitation also apply by virtue of

308 The law in force until then was embodied in the rule of *Baker* v. *Bolton* (1808) 1 Camp. 493; 170 ER 1033.

309 Compulsory third-party insurance for road accidents was introduced in 1930. If the 1934 Act had not been passed the victim's insurers would have earned an undeserved windfall.

310 Section 1(1). Section 1(4), however, also created one exception: if the tortfeasor died at the same time as his victim, the right of action is 'deemed' to have subsisted before the death and thus the victim can still sue the tortfeasor's estate.

311 *Harris* v. *Lewisham and Guy's Mental Health Trust* [2000] 3 All ER 769.

312 Law Reform (Miscellaneous Provisions) Act 1934, s. 1 (1A), as amended by s. 4(1) of the Administration of Justice Act 1982.

313 See Law Commission, Report No. 263, *Claims for Wrongful Death* (Select Bibliography), paras. 6.63–6.65

314 The Faulks Committee Report, Cmnd. 5909 (1975) proposed that such claims should survive against the estate of the deceased defamer (see ch. 15 of the Report); however, the Supreme Court Procedure Committee's *Report on Practice and Procedure in Defamation* (1991) rejected any need for such a change (see ch. VI of the Report).

section 1 of the Proceedings against Estates Act 1970.[315] Where the prospective claimant (wronged person) dies, the damages recovered for the benefit of the deceased's estate will include all the normal headings discussed above, except that exemplary damages cannot be recovered for the benefit of the deceased's estate even if he himself would have been entitled to them.[316] On the other hand, funeral expenses, which of course would not have been recoverable had the victim lived, are recoverable by the estate.[317] Though section 1(2)(c) of the 1934 Act does not expressly state this, the case law clearly implies that only reasonable funeral expenses will be allowed.[318] In the case of instant deaths, this will, in practice, be the only claim that will be maintained.

It should also be noted that according to section 1(2)(c) of the 1934 Act damages recoverable for the benefit of the estate should be calculated without reference to any loss or gain to the estate consequent on his death. The kind of typical gain that could ensue would come from the proceeds of an insurance policy and these amounts will thus not be taken into account when calculating the amount of damages. The same goes for losses consequent upon death. Thus, if the deceased was a tenant for life of a valuable property the loss of the life interest would be excluded from any calculation of damages awarded to his estate. Similarly, this provision would exclude the loss of an annuity ceasing on death. On the other hand, section 1(5) of the Act states that the rights conferred by it are in addition to and not in derogation from any rights conferred by the Fatal Accidents Act which, as we shall see, provides a remedy where death is caused by the wrongful act, neglect, or default of another person.

Finally, according to section 1(5) of the 1934 Act the rights conferred by it are in addition to and not in derogation of any rights conferred by the Fatal Accidents Acts 1976 to which we now turn our attention.

(B) DEATH AS CREATING A CAUSE OF ACTION

(i) Introduction

The rule in *Baker* v. *Bolton*[319] denied any claim by the dependants of the deceased victim of a tort. As already stated, this rule was altered in 1846 by the Fatal Accidents Act, which

315 And, at present, claims will still lie against the wrongdoer's estate. The Law Commission is in favour of preventing this transmissibility of the claim: see Law Commission, Report No. 247, *Aggravated, Exemplary and Restitutionary Damages* (Select Bibliography), paras. 5.276–5.278.

316 Section 1(2)(a). The Law Commission has proposed that this rule be amended to allow actions to survive for the benefit of the victim's estate: 'wrongdoers ought to be punished whether or not their victims are alive: a wrongdoer should not escape punishment as a result of a fortuity' (*ibid.*, para. 5.275).

317 Section 1(2)(c). Since *Morgan* v. *Scoulding* [1938] 1 KB 786, it has been accepted that the cause of action is completed by the injuries and is vested in the deceased at the moment of the death. In practice this means that in such cases the estate will be able to claim only the funeral expenses. If there is an interval between accident and death, then the estate will be able to claim all pecuniary and (appropriate) non-pecuniary items of damage for that period.

318 See e.g. *Hart* v. *Griffiths-Jones* [1948] 2 All ER 729 and *Gammell* v. *Wilson* [1982] AC 27 where it was suggested that the cost of a headstone is allowable but the cost of a memorial monument is not.

319 (1808) 1 Camp. 493; 170 ER 1033, reinforced in a different context in *Admiralty Commissioners* v. *SS America* [1917] AC 38.

granted a remedy mainly to widows and orphans.[320] In the years that followed, subsequent Acts and decisions widened the categories of possible claimants.[321] The law, consolidated in the Fatal Accidents Act of 1976, was again substantially amended by the Administration of Justice Act 1982. Section 1(1) runs:

If death is caused by any wrongful act, neglect or default which is such as would (if death had not ensued) have entitled the person injured to maintain an action and recover damages in respect thereof, the person who would have been liable if death had not ensued shall be liable to an action for damages, notwithstanding the death of the person injured.

A hypothetical question has to be asked: at the time of his death could the deceased have maintained action against the tortfeasor? If he could not, because either the action had been statute-barred,[322] or there had been accord and satisfaction[323] or there had been judgment,[324] then the dependants cannot bring an action either. That is so even if the action brought by the deceased was against only one of a number of joint tortfeasors.[325] If the deceased could have brought an action himself then, and only then, does the cause of action come into existence. In *Pigney* v. *Pointer's Transport Services Ltd.*[326] the deceased committed suicide while in a condition of acute neurotic depression induced by the accident. It was held that in the circumstances his death did not amount to a *novus actus* and thus his widow was successful in her action. The date of the decision is important because it is clear that it was decided under the influence of the *Re Polemis* rule.[327] Whether the same result would nowadays be reached under the *Wagon Mound* rule has been doubted.[328] Whatever the answer, the case illustrates the role of causation under the Fatal Accidents Act and the Law Reform Act. For under the former, what had

320 The full list of possible claimants, given in ss. 2 and 5, included wives, husbands, parents, grandparents, step-parents, children, grandchildren and stepchildren.

321 Further extensions took place in 1934, 1959, and 1982. McGregor (Select Bibliography), at para. 36–008, rightly draws attention to the more liberal position that prevails in France, Belgium, Switzerland and the Scandinavian countries, where elaborate lists are replaced by the requirement that a relationship of dependency upon the deceased be shown and concludes that these systems have experienced no real difficulties in 'casting the ambit of recovery as widely as this and dispensing with lists'. Some judicial support for this now appears in *Shepherd* v. *The Post Office*, *The Times*, 15 June 1995. The statement, however, was made in the context of cohabitees, discussed below, and was probably not intended to be as broad as Dr McGregor's.

322 *Williams* v. *Mersey Docks* [1905] 1 KB 804.

323 *Read* v. *The Great Eastern Railway Co.* (1868) LR 3 QB 555.

324 *Murray* v. *Shuter* [1972] 1 Lloyd's Rep. 6.

325 *Jameson* v *Central Electricity Generating Board* [2000] AC 455.

326 [1957] 1 WLR 1121.

327 The result of this remarkable case must, surely, represent one of the high-water marks in the application of the *Polemis* rule; but it may also embody some sympathy on the part of the court for the plaintiff and for the dependant of the victim of the original tort. While there is no evidence to support this view and, indeed, a subsequent case (see next note) has shown that such sympathy will not always be shown for dependants, the supposition advanced herein could be tested by asking what would have happened if Mr Pigney had tried unsuccessfully to kill himself and, in the process, increased his original injuries and the cost of their treatment. Would the court have still refused to treat the attempted suicide as a *novus actus* and made the original tortfeasor liable for such extra medical and other costs?

328 *Farmer* v. *Rash* [1969] 1 WLR 160, which is post-*Wagon Mound (No. 1)*, went the other way, but in his short judgment the judge did not go into the problems of causation.

to be shown was that the defendant caused the death of the breadwinner, whereas under the latter, death is only a factor which makes a pre-existing action transmissible to the deceased's estate. In *Pigney*'s case, therefore, the point whether the suicide was a *novus actus* was relevant to the widow's claim under the Fatal Accidents Act, but was not relevant for the Law Reform Act claim of his own estate. For such claims, how the death has come about is irrelevant.[329] The only point one might arguably make is that it is against public policy to allow the deceased's estate to recover from an act of self-destruction. In *Beresford* v. *Royal Insurance Co.*[330] this point was successfully argued and money due under a life-insurance policy was withheld when the death of the insured was caused by his own act. But *Beresford* and *Pigney* are distinguishable, since liability to pay under a life-insurance policy is *created* by the death of the insured and *Beresford* held that it is against public policy for such liability to be *created* by an act of self-destruction; whereas in the claim under the Law Reform Act, Pigney's suicide did not create liability, but only made pre-existing liability *transmissible* to the estate.

Related to the above is the question of contributory negligence on the part of the *deceased*. Section 5 of the Fatal Accidents Act 1976 (as amended by s. 3(2) of the Administration of Justice Act 1982) decrees that:

> where any person dies as the result partly of his own fault and partly of the fault of any other person or persons, and accordingly if an action were brought for the benefit of the estate under the Law Reform Act 1934 the damages recoverable would be reduced under section 1(1) of the Law Reform (Contributory Negligence) Act 1945, and damages recoverable in an action under this Act shall be reduced to a proportionate extent.

Dodds v. *Dodds*[331] clarified a related problem. The father was killed in a car accident caused not by his own negligence, but by that of his wife. An action was brought under the Fatal Accidents Acts with the wife and child as dependants and it was held that, though the widow herself had no claim, the child did and that there should be no reduction of *his* award. The remedy given under the Acts is given to dependants *individually* and not as a group and, therefore, each dependant is regarded as a separate claimant. However, it should be made clear that the reduction or elimination of the dependant's claim in such circumstances is not the result of the Acts, but of his own contributory negligence.

This interrelationship of the dependant's claim with the possible action that the deceased could have brought should not conceal the fact that the cause of action given to the dependants is a completely new one. In Lord Blackburn's words,[332] it is 'new in its species, new in its quality, new in its principle, in every way new'.

(ii) Who Brings the Action

Although the right of action under the Acts exists for the benefit of the dependants, the action must be brought by and in the name of the executor or administrator. If, however,

329 Except with regard to the claim for funeral expenses. 330 [1938] AC 586.
331 [1978] QB 543. 332 *The Vera Cruz* (1884) 10 App. Cas. 59, 70–1.

the executor or administrator does not bring the action six months after the death, or if there is no executor or administrator, all or any of the dependants may bring the action. Section 2 of the 1976 Act, which ordains the above, goes on to say in sub-section 3 that not more than *one* action shall lie for and in respect of the same subject-matter or complaint, so there is no room for consideration of a dependant not named in the proceedings. Such a dependant may, therefore, apply before judgment to be brought into the proceedings. There can be only one claimant who brings the action in the name of all the dependants. Joinder of a second claimant will only be permitted in exceptional circumstances.[333] After judgment, dependants excluded from the action have no claim against the defendant, nor against the dependant(s) party to the original action, though they may have some legal or equitable remedy against the representative. According to section 2B(3) of the Limitation Act 1975 the action must be brought within three years of the deceased's death (or, in certain cases, from the moment the dependants knew they had a cause of action). That is assuming, of course, that the deceased died possessed of this right of action. In principle, he will have lost his right of action if three years have lapsed from the moment the cause of action accrued or he acquired relevant knowledge, whichever is the later. According to section 3(2) of the 1976 Act the damages 'shall be divided among the dependants in such shares as may be directed' which, in the typical case of the death of a breadwinner leaving behind a widow and children, will mean the bulk of the award going to the mother in the confidence that she will look after the children in an appropriate manner.

Section 1(2) stated that the action shall be for the benefit of the dependants of the deceased. This, first, means that a person must a be a *dependant in law*, i.e. one included in the list given in section 1(3) of the 1976 Act, as amended by the Administration of Justice Act 1982, as well as a *dependant in fact*, a requirement discussed below. By the mid-1980s dependants in law were thus the following: the wife or husband (or former wife or husband) of the deceased; *any* of his ascendants or descendants; any person *treated* by the deceased as his parent or child or other descendant; any person who is, or is the issue of, a brother, sister, uncle, or aunt of the deceased. Sub-section 4 adds that, for the purposes of the previous sub-section,

> any relationship of affinity shall be treated as a relationship of consanguinity, any relationship of the half blood as a relationship of the whole blood, and the stepchild of any person as his child, and an illegitimate person shall be treated as the legitimate child of his mother and reputed father.

Adopted children are also entitled to claim following paragraph 3(1) of Schedule 1 to the Children Act 1975. The same is true of a child *en ventre sa mère* at the time of the injury but born after the death of the victim.[334]

333 *Cooper* v *Williams* [1963] 2 All ER 282. As to what happens if there is a conflict between dependants see Augustus Ullstein QC and John Wilson, 'Fatal Accident Act Claims and Beddoe Summons: When Dependants Fall Out', *Butterworths Personal Injury Litigation Service*, Bulletin No. 56, May 2000.

334 *The George and Richard* (1871) LR 3 A & E 466.

This list now includes *all* ascendants (and not, as previously, only parents or grandparents) and former spouses, which, section 1(4) states, includes persons whose marriage with the deceased has been annulled or declared void, as well as those whose marriage with the deceased has been dissolved.

After some hesitation expressed in the debates in the House of Lords,[335] the Administration of Justice Act 1982, section 3, has enlarged the categories of dependants in law by including 'any person living with the deceased as husband (or wife)'. Most commonly this will refer to the deceased's partner,[336] who will now be given a Fatal Accidents Act claim if the following (fairly stringent) requirements are satisfied. *First*, the claimant was living in the same household before the death; *second*, had been so living for at *least* two years before that date; and *third* had been living during the whole[337] of that period *as* the husband or wife of the deceased.

A more radical widening was recommended by the Law Commission, in its Consultation Paper on *Claims for Wrongful Death*, which suggested that 'the statutory list should be abolished and replaced by a test whereby *any* individual has a right of recovery who had a reasonable expectation of a non-business benefit from continuation of the deceased's life, or a test whereby any individual has a right of recovery who was or, but for the death, would have been dependent, wholly or partly, on the deceased'.[338] In its Final Report on *Claims for Wrongful Death*,[339] however, the Law Commission's view was that the list should be retained,[340] but supplemented by a generally worded class of claimant 'whereby any other individual who "was being wholly or partly maintained by the deceased immediately before the death or who would, but for the death, have been so maintained at a time beginning after the death" shall be able to bring an action under the Fatal Accidents Act'.[341]

The only significant change made in this area of the law results from the Civil Partnership Act 2004 and will take effect when section 83 of that Act comes into force. It will include in the list of Fatal Accident dependants homosexual cohabitees, provided

335 HL Debs., vol. 428, col. 42 ff. (8 Mar. 1982).

336 'Mistress' has been the most commonly used term to refer to the partner of a male breadwinner, but English law has experienced as much embarrassment with the terminology as it has with the institution. See A. Allot, *The Limits of the Law* (1980), ch. 8. The increase in the number of extra-marital cohabitations may alter such coy attitudes.

337 Though see *Pounder* v. *London Underground Ltd.* [1995] PIQR P217 where it was held that in the context of a ten-year relationship a brief absence during the two-year period did not affect the claim.

338 Law Commission, Consultation Paper No. 148 (Select Bibliography), para. 4.6.

339 Law Commission, Report No. 263 (Select Bibliography): see paras. 3.14–3.46 for the full discussion of possible alternatives, difficulties and reasons for the eventual proposals.

340 Largely, it seems, because of the danger that any generally worded criteria might serve either to make the class of claimants too wide-ranging (with the 'expectation of a non-business benefit' criterion) (see *ibid.*, paras. 3.25–3.30) or to reduce the class of persons able to sue (under the 'wholly or partly dependent' test) and such a reduction was never the Law Commission's intention (see, *ibid.*, paras. 3.31–3.34).

341 *Ibid.*, para. 3.46, unless that maintenance had been provided only in return for full valuable consideration. The Law Commission's focus on 'maintenance' as the basis for this new general class of claimant is taken from the Inheritance (Provision for Family and Dependants) Act 1975 and the intention is to rely upon the existing case law under those provisions to clarify the operation of 'maintenance' as a qualifying criterion for claimants under these proposals.

they have registered as civil partners. The change must be welcomed as keeping with the changing mores of our times; but it still leaves unprotected the heterosexual cohabitees if they have not been legally married and are not covered by the (somewhat restrictive) condition of the Administration of Justice Act 1982—another reason for favouring the wider phraseology of the Law Commission proposal.[342] Finally, not apparently tested in our courts[343] is the situation involving multiple cohabitees (whether in the context of a polygamous marriage or not).

Second, a claimant need not only be a dependant in law; he must also be a *dependant in fact*. This typically means that he must have been financially dependent on the deceased at the time of the latter's death. Thus, if no pecuniary dependency is proved, the defendant will succeed. Section 3(1) of the 1976 Act contains the basic rule. It states:[344] 'In the action such damages may be awarded as are proportioned to the injury resulting from the death to the dependants respectively.' No further statutory guidance on the damages recoverable is given, save that a sum may be awarded for the funeral expenses of the deceased if they were in fact borne by those for whose benefit the action is brought (but see s. 3(4)).

The Administration of Justice Act 1982 has now added a new section (1A) to the Fatal Accidents Act, creating a claim for damages for bereavement in favour of one spouse for the death of another, or of parents for the death of a minor, unmarried child. The damages here are not at large but are fixed at £10,000[345] and are to be shared equally whenever the claim is made by both parents for the death of their child.

Apart from the claim for bereavement, either the lost pecuniary advantage must have actually been derived from the deceased prior to his death or, alternatively, there must have been a reasonable expectation of pecuniary benefit as of right or otherwise.[346] But the expected pecuniary benefit, however, must not result from crime.[347]

In *Taff Vale Railway* v. *Jenkins*[348] the deceased was an intelligent girl of sixteen, who had almost completed her apprenticeship as a dressmaker. The jury's verdict was in favour of her parents, notwithstanding that she had not as yet earned anything and had so far conferred upon them no pecuniary benefit. There was a clear inference that she would have done so in the future and that was sufficient. Likewise, in *Kandalla* v. *British Airways Board*[349] the plaintiffs who were planning to flee from Iraq and come to the UK where they expected to be maintained by their two daughters who practised as doctors. When the daughters were killed in an air accident the claim against British Airways for

[342] A solution roughly in keeping with that adopted by the French-inspired systems but which has been kept within workable bounds by a variety of causative devices.

[343] Though it has in others such as the French.

[344] Section 3(2) provides that such damages shall be divided among the dependants in such shares as may be directed. This is an important power given to the court and likely to be exercised whenever there are doubts about the mother's ability to look after dependent children.

[345] This sum was set by the Bereavement (Variation of Sum) (England and Wales) Order 2002 (SI No. 2002/644), amending s. 1A of the Fatal Accidents Act 1976 (itself inserted by s. 3 of the Administration of Justice Act 1982).

[346] *Kassam* v. *Kampala Aerated Water* [1965] 1 WLR 668

[347] *Burns* v. *Edman* [1970] 2 QB 541. Will this result be applied to all types of immoral or illegal transactions?

[348] [1913] AC 1.

[349] [1981] QB 158.

loss of this support was accepted by the court. In another case,[350] however, a woman who deserted her husband claimed for loss of support made when he was subsequently killed in an accident. Since deserting her husband the plaintiff had repeatedly committed adultery with the result that her spouse had commenced divorce proceedings. The above events, plus the fact that the *woman* (who had lost the right of maintenance) had failed to prove there was a real chance of reconciliation between them, defeated her claim for loss of support.

It is also essential to show that the benefit that the dependant has lost was derived from the familial relationship subsisting between the deceased and the dependant. But if that is done, it need not be money that has been lost. In *Berry* v. *Humm*[351] a widower was held to have an expectation of pecuniary benefit from the continued performance of domestic services by his wife for which he would otherwise have to pay. But the loss must derive from the family relationship of claimant and deceased. Thus, in *Burgess* v. *Florence Nightingale Hospital for Gentlewomen*[352] a husband claimed in respect of his wife's death, who was also his professional dancing partner, but Devlin J held that, though he was entitled to recover damages for pecuniary loss due to the death of his wife, he could not recover for the loss of earnings caused from the interruption of the professional relationship.

The claim for bereavement has another aspect. What happens when a young child is deprived of the care of its parents, particularly its mother? The Administration of Justice Act 1982 has given no claim for bereavement in this case and the result appears harsh. The reason is that the dependency award for the child will usually be substantial. But in the past the courts have not felt so and have striven to find ways to increase children's dependency awards. One was by recognising that the services of a wife or mother have a pecuniary value for the loss of which damages may be recovered even if no actual expenditure is incurred in replacing them. In *Hay* v. *Hughes*,[353] for example, substantial damages were awarded under this head to two young boys whose parents had been killed, even though the boys' grandmother was looking after them and was prepared to continue doing so indefinitely without expecting any financial reward. The damages were, in fact, assessed on the basis of evidence of the cost of employing a nanny housekeeper. In *Mehmet* v. *Perry*[354] the children's health justified their father giving up

350 *Davies* v. *Taylor* [1974] AC 207.

351 [1915] 1 KB 627.

352 [1955] 1 QB 349; cf. *Malyon* v. *Plummer* [1964] 1 QB 330 and *Cox* v. *Hockenhull* [2000] 1 WLR 750.

353 [1975] QB 790. In *Spittle* v. *Bunney* [1988] 1 WLR 847 the Court of Appeal watered down somewhat the effect of *Hay* v. *Hughes* by taking the view that in assessing damages for the loss of a mother's services the court should take into account the decreasing level of dependency as the child grew older and he became less in need of looking after. The court gave as an example the need to be taken to school which, after a certain age had been reached, would disappear. But though this type of commercial service may change, the level of emotional dependency could well increase. The courts' emphasis on the former aspect must surely be the result of their inability to fix a 'price' on the latter.

354 [1977] 2 All ER 529. See also *Regan* v. *Williamson* [1976] 1 WLR 305 where the court spoke of a special 'qualitative factor', recognising the extra value of maternal (over nanny) care and justifying a modest increase in the award. In *Creswell* v. *Eaton* [1991] 1 WLR 1113, the deceased mother was employed prior to her death, and

his employment after the death of their mother, in order to look after them. It was there held that his actual loss of wages, not the hypothetical cost of employing a housekeeper, provided the correct measure of damages payable.

K v. *JMP Co. Ltd.*[355] presented a different and more acute problem. The children in that case were illegitimate, so their mother herself had no claim under the Fatal Accidents Act. Her union, however, with the deceased was very stable and he had looked after all of them in an exemplary manner, providing, *inter alia*, for their holiday expenses, etc. The Court of Appeal took the view that the children should be compensated not only for the amounts that the father spent on them (which were taken to include the rent, washing-machine instalments and electricity bills), but also for any diminution in the value of their mother's services resulting from their father's death. Thus, though no award was made for the mother's loss, it was held that her expenses for holiday travel could be claimed since this was an item the father would have paid in order to enable his children to enjoy their holidays. By holding it to be a loss to the children it was thus held to be recoverable. These methods of increasing the dependency awards of minors must, on the whole, be encouraged in the interests of proper compensation; and they are likely to be continued by the courts in the face of Parliament's refusal to extend to them the new right of damages for bereavement.[356]

(iii) The Assessment of the Award

The loss here being the loss of an expectation of a future *pecuniary*[357] advantage, it follows that in trying to calculate the award a court must take into account a number of imponderable factors referring to both the dependants and the deceased. As far as the former are concerned, the dependants' own expectation of life is a material factor. In the case of a widow, for example, this may be very material, and evidence of her own expectation of life as well as the state of her health will be admissible in court. If she has actually died before the trial the damages awarded to her estate must be for the period

so was only a 'part-time carer'. By contrast, the children's aunt, who commendably (in the opinion of the court) gave up her job in order to look after them, became a 'full-time carer'. Simon Brown J took the view (*ibid.*, at 1121) that where 'a claim is based in large part upon a relative's actual loss of earning reasonably incurred, modest discount [in the instant case calculated at 15 per cent] only should be made to reflect the part-time nature of the deceased mother's care'.

355 [1976] QB 85.

356 The Law Commission has proposed that there should be an extension of the class of those eligible to claim bereavement damages: see Law Commission, Report No. 263, *Claims for Wrongful Death* (Select Bibliography), para. 6.31, which would add a child of the deceased, a brother or sister of the deceased (including by adoption), a person engaged to be married to the deceased and a cohabitee who had lived with the deceased as husband or wife for at least two years immediately prior to the accident. See, generally, *ibid.*, Part VI 'Reform: Bereavement Damages' for a fuller discussion. While the recommendation to increase the level of the fixed award of bereavement damages to £10,000 has been accepted (see SI No. 2002/644, noted above) there has been no sign of similar movement from the government to extend the class of claimants.

357 Non-pecuniary losses—e.g. for mental suffering—were, despite the neutral wording of the 1846 Act, excluded almost from the start: see *Blake* v. *Midland Ry.* (1852) 18 QB 93. American jurisdictions, though they initially followed the English rule, have, in recent years, moved in a more liberal direction. Megaw J in *Perec* v. *Brown* (1964) 108 SJ 219, however, felt that this was not possible under the Fatal Accidents Act. The claim for bereavement thus is the only (statutory) exception.

of her survival only and should not be calculated on the basis of her life expectancy as it was at the time of her husband's death.[358]

Remarriage raises problems of the assessment both of the widow's dependency and of that of her children. If the widow remarries and her new husband accepts her children as members of his household, he is under a legal obligation to support them. This means that their damages should not be calculated on the basis that they have lost the support of a father, but only so as to compensate them for the risk of loss in the future. Thus, in assessing the damages payable to a child for his father's death, the court is bound to take into account the fact or the prospects of the mother's remarriage;[359] and the same is true when assessing the damages of a widower in respect of his wife's death. In 1971, however, the Law Reform (Miscellaneous Provisions) Act enacted that, in assessing the damages payable to a *widow* in respect of the death of her husband, 'there shall not be taken into account the remarriage of the widow or her prospect of remarriage' and this rule has now been embodied in section 3(3) of the 1976 Act. This reversal of the common law rule (which conformed with the basic principle that damages under the Fatal Accidents Act were awarded for actual pecuniary loss) was accepted because women's organisations resented as much as judges the evaluation of the widow's remarriage prospects. However well-intentioned the reform may have been, it has nonetheless created an anomaly in the law in so far as it allows a widow who has actually remarried and who is supported by her second husband to receive damages for the continuing loss of support of the first husband; and it has also resulted in the second anomaly that claims of widows and widowers are no longer treated alike. Indeed, even a widow's prospects of remarriage must still be considered when the claims of the children are in issue. So, this basic anomaly should either be abolished or, perhaps, be extended to cover widowers and children as well.[360]

In assessing the lost dependency, by far the most difficult part of the calculation is that referring to the deceased. The basic aim is to provide dependants with a sum of money that will afford them material benefits of the same standard and for the same period of time as would have been provided by the deceased, had he not been killed. This means that the total value of the dependency must be assessed and a capital sum arrived at that will enable the dependants to spend each year, free of tax, a sum equal to the pre-accident dependency. More specifically, the starting-point for the assessment of

358 *Williamson* v. *Thornycroft* [1940] 2 KB 658. Likewise in the event of remarriage: *Lloyds Bank and Mellows* v. *Railway Executive* [1952] 1 TLR 1207, *Mead* v. *Clarke Chapman* [1956] 1 WLR 76. The same is true if remarriage has taken place after adjudication but before an appeal is heard: *Curwen* v. *James* [1963] 1 WLR 748. The wider implications of these cases are not affected by the Law Reform (Miscellaneous Provisions) 1971 Act.

359 *Thompson* v. *Price* [1973] QB 838.

360 It seems that the Law Commission is of the view that exclusion of consideration of prospects of remarriage should be extended to any person whose marriage prospects might be assessed under the Act (Law Commission, Report No. 263, *Claims for Wrongful Death* (Select Bibliography), para. 4.44), but that the *fact* of a marriage *should* be taken into account in a relevant case, 'whether the married person is the claimant or not' (*ibid.*, para. 4.48). The proposal is thus to repeal s. 3(3) of the Fatal Accidents Act 1976 (cl. 6(5) of the Draft Bill) and to replace it with a new set of rules in the proposed s. 3(3A) (see cl. 4 of the Draft Bill), which include (*inter alia*) provisions to cover non-married cohabitees (including same-gender couples).

damages will be the amount of the dependency, which in straightforward situations will be ascertained by deducting from the earnings of the deceased the estimated amount of his own personal and living expenses. The deceased's earnings will be calculated not just on the basis of a single figure, but on the basis of all the surrounding circumstances, including the possibility of a variation in his rate of earnings. This approach, however, cannot be used where the pecuniary benefit was in kind rather than in money; where the deceased had not yet started to earn any money; and where the deceased was not the breadwinner of the family but, say, the wife. In these cases different and, perhaps, more speculative methods will be adopted, but here we shall restrict our comments to the most typical case, the death of the breadwinner.

Once the dependency figure is reached it will be capitalised by the application of an appropriate multiplier which, in fatal accident cases (unlike personal injury cases), will be determined at the time of the death.[361] This is for the court to fix on the basis of innumerable vague calculations connected with the likely duration of the dependency, the deceased's pre-accident life expectancy, his rate of earnings, and so on. As in the case of the future lost earnings of a living claimant, here too the multiplier must be such that the capital sum awarded, together with the income it generates, will be exhausted at the end of the period intended to be covered.[362] The calculation is thus made on the assumption, not always supported in real life, that the dependants will spend each year part of the capital as well as the whole of the income which they receive from so much of the capital as remains. Once again, therefore, the multiplier will be considerably lower than the expected duration of the dependency.

The period of dependency, and thus the multiplier, must of course be reckoned from the date of the death. But in *Cookson* v. *Knowles*[363] the House of Lords introduced the following more precise method of calculation. In place of a single lump sum, the damages should be divided into two main parts, the first covering the loss to the dependants from the date of the death until the date of the trial and the second their loss from the date of the trial for the future. The first part of the damages should be calculated like the special damages for loss of earnings in an action for personal injury and should be based on an average of the deceased's rate of earning as it was at his death and the rate as it would have been at the date of the trial. The second part of the damages should be based upon the latter rate, using as a multiplier a figure equivalent to the period of dependency as estimated at the date of the death, less the period which has already elapsed between the death and the trial.

(iv) Pecuniary Gains and Other Deductions and the Question of Duplication of Damages

During the nineteenth century judges restricted the scope of the application of the fatal accidents legislation in any way they could. One was by interpreting the word 'injury' to

361 *Cookson* v. *Knowles* [1979] AC 556, *Graham* v. *Dodds* [1983] 1 WLR 808.

362 *Taylor* v. *O'Connor* [1971] AC 345.

363 [1979] AC 556, approved by the House of Lords in *Graham* v. *Dodds* [1983] 1 WLR 808, 815.

mean financial loss only; another was by insisting that the dependants should set against their award any pecuniary advantage accruing to them as a result of the death of the victim. Pensions and insurance moneys were the two most usual benefits received by dependants and, until the Fatal Accidents Act 1959, they had to be accounted for. The move away from that direction has since gained pace. The law now is in section 4 of the Fatal Accidents Act 1976, as amended by the Administration of Justice Act 1982, which states: 'In assessing damages in respect of a person's death in an action under this Act, benefits which have accrued or will or may accrue to any person from his estate or otherwise as a result of his death shall be disregarded.' Compensation payments made under the Fatal Accidents Act are also excluded from the statutory recoupment provisions of the Social Security (Recovery of Benefits) Act 1997.[364]

The formula adopted in the 1976 Act excludes from the assessment of damages all the pecuniary gains a dependant is likely to receive as a result of the death, including insurance money, return of premiums, gratuities, as well as all benefits from the estate which accrue to the dependants. Thus, in *Pidduck* v. *Eastern Scottish Omnibuses Ltd.*[365] the Court of Appeal held that a widow's allowance, which became payable to her upon her husband's death and which was a pension entitlement of his, should be disregarded from the assessment of her lost dependency. The reason for this was section 4 which, in the words of one of the judges,[366] was meant 'to produce an exception to the common law rules for calculating quantum of damages, namely to prevent the deduction of a benefit which would otherwise have to be deducted in order to arrive at the true loss on a common law basis'. In the later case of *Stanley* v. *Saddique (Mohammed)*,[367] the same judge gave the word 'benefit' in section 4 a wider meaning. For in that case, one of the defendant's contentions was that section 4 excludes, for the purposes of assessing damages for lost dependency, only direct *pecuniary* benefits. In that case, however, the plaintiff had benefited from exceptional services from his stepmother, which he would not have received from his own (unreliable) mother. This, according to the defendants, was not a *pecuniary* benefit and should thus be taken into account and reduce his claim for lost dependency. The court, however, refused to adopt such a view and held that 'the benefits accruing to the plaintiff as a result of his absorption into the family unit consisting of his father and stepmother and sibling should be wholly disregarded for the purposes of assessing damages'.[368] On the other hand, it has been held that the adoption of an infant who has lost his parents in an accident will affect the quantification of his 'lost dependency'. So in *Watson* v. *Willmott*[369] Garland J held that *vis-à-vis* the deceased

[364] See SI No. 1997/2205, reg. 2(2)(a).

[365] [1990] 1 WLR 993.

[366] *Ibid.*, at 998, per Purchas LJ.

[367] [1991] 2 WLR 459; [1992] QB 1, containing an excellent summary of the legislative history of s. 4.

[368] *Ibid.*, at 468–9; cf. *Hayden* v. *Hayden* [1992] 1 WLR 986 and the discussion of *Hayden* in *R* v. *Criminal Injuries Compensation Board, ex parte K* [1999] QB 1131. *Ex parte K* seems to underline the approach of Purchas LJ in *Stanley* v. *Saddique*, discussed in the text, although the Law Commission feels that it is a further indication 'that the interpretation of section 4 continues to cause difficulty' (Report No. 263, *Claims for Wrongful Death* (Select Bibliography), para. 5.21).

[369] [1990] 3 WLR 1103.

father, the infant's lost dependency would be worked out by awarding him the difference (if any) between the lost dependency of his (deceased) *natural* father minus his dependency on his *adoptive* father. *Vis-à-vis* the mother, the court took the view that the adoption replaced the non-pecuniary dependency on the deceased mother and thus the non-pecuniary dependency on the natural, deceased mother would be assessed only up to the date of the adoption.

The above suggests that the wording of the Fatal Accidents Act 1976 may still give some grounds for doubt (and litigation);[370] but the trend towards *not* deducting from awards made under the 1976 Act sums received as a result of the death is still continuing.[371] This may, indirectly, lead towards over-compensation of claimants; but to the extent that this is considered as a disadvantage *in the kind of circumstances that tend to be litigated under this heading* it is, arguably, counterbalanced by the simplification that it is bringing into the law.[372]

9. DAMAGE TO PROPERTY

Generally speaking, property damage receives similar treatment to personal injuries, though assessment of loss in the former is easier when compared with the problems that arise in the latter. For exposition purposes it might be helpful to deal with loss (destruction) and damage separately adding, perhaps, that the bulk of the relevant case law comes from the area of negligence and is concerned mainly with damage or loss of ships and motor vehicles.

With regard to loss, the principal heads under which damages are awarded are found in *Liesbosch Dredger* v. *SS Edison*,[373] which was discussed earlier in Chapter 3. These are the market value[374] of the property (at the place and time of destruction); cost, if any, of

370 A complicated example, concerning the relationship between s. 4 of the 1976 Act and possible claims against concurrent tortfeasors, is the House of Lords' decision in *Jameson* v. *Central Electricity Generating Board* [1999] 2 WLR 141. A further point is the question (as yet unaddressed by the courts) how the reasoning in *Hunt* v. *Severs* [1994] 2 AC 350 might apply to the Fatal Accidents Act. See, generally, Law Commission, Report No. 263, *Claims for Wrongful Death* (Select Bibliography), paras. 2.37–2.64.

371 Although it should be noted that courts have sometimes taken benefits into account, on the ground that they prevented the claimant from suffering any loss: see, e.g., *Auty* v. *National Coal Board* [1985] 1 WLR 784 and *Wood* v. *Bentall Simplex Ltd.* [1992] PIQR P332.

372 The Law Commission has proposed (Report No. 263, *Claims for Wrongful Death* (Select Bibliography)) the repeal of s. 4 of the Fatal Accidents Act and its replacement with a statutory list of the types of benefit to be disregarded in the assessment of damages. Its proposal is that 'the law on collateral benefits in Fatal Accidents Act cases should be rendered as consistent as possible with the common law on collateral benefits in personal injury cases, through listing charity, insurance, survivors' pensions and inheritance as non-deductible' (*ibid.*, para. 5.22, discussed in paras. 5.22–5.39).

373 [1933] AC 449; above, ch. 4, Section 3(e).

374 Itself a concept capable of causing dispute as to its precise meaning in any given context: see, for a complex illustration of the difficulties which may arise, *Kuwait Airways Corp.* v. *Iraqi Airways Co. (Nos. 4 and 5)* [2001] 3 WLR 1117; [2001] 1 Lloyd's Rep. 161 (CA), [559]–[561] and [599] ff., which discusses the concepts of 'fair market value' and 'current market price' in the context of a dispute over aircraft seized from Kuwait by

transporting a substitute to the place in question; loss of profit to a foreseeable extent; and to these should be added loss of use before replacement or other expenses made necessary as a result of the tort.[375] With regard to the market value of the thing destroyed, the estimate is of loss, not the cost of restoration.

In *The Maersk Colombo*[376] the Court of Appeal refused to allow recovery of the cost of replacing the destroyed crane, since larger replacement cranes had already been ordered prior to the accident and the reinstatement costs claimed would never in fact be incurred. Thus, the claimant was limited to recovery of the resale value of the crane, before the accident, since the restoration cost was not an accurate reflection of the claimant's true loss. The judgment of Clark LJ (as he then was) contains an interesting analysis of the criteria applicable when a decision has to be made in asking the defendant to pay the claimant's loss of value or cost of repair. 'Reasonableness' and 'intention' would appear to be a crucial role.

In *Moss* v. *Christchurch Rural District Council*[377] the plaintiff's cottage, which was let, was destroyed by a spark from the defendant's steamroller. The measure of damages was the difference between his interest before and after the fire. Sometimes the loss is equivalent to the cost of restoration;[378] and it can also happen that loss exceeds the cost of restoration, as with the destruction of a historic mansion. The loss to a claimant who has only a limited interest in a thing is the value of his interest.[379] Loss of profit may be actual or estimated.[380] If the market value of the thing in question is calculated so as to include its profitable use, no further loss of profit is recoverable.[381]

Where property is damaged and not destroyed, the broad rule is that a claimant's loss is the reduction in its value. Where land has been damaged, its reduction in value has to be estimated according to the facts. If part of it has been severed, a distinction is drawn between the defendant's intentional and unintentional wrongdoing. If the severance was intentional, the claimant may choose between claiming in respect of the lessened value of his land and the value of the part severed.[382] If it was unintentional, only the lessened value is recoverable.[383]

When a chattel is damaged, the reduction in value is often the reasonable cost of repair.[384] Sometimes the depreciation in value of a thing because of the very fact that it

Iraq during the Gulf War period. It is important to remember the extent to which the determination of a 'market value' takes into account the ability to use the property to earn a profit, lest this profit element leads to double recovery by the claimant (see, e.g., Lord Wright in *The Liesbosch Dredger* [1933] AC 449 for this warning).

[375] E.g. hiring a car, equivalent to the one destroyed, until the delivery of a new one: *Moore* v. *DER Ltd.* [1971] 1 WLR 1476.

[376] [2001] 2 Lloyd's Rep. 275.

[377] [1925] 2 KB 750. See also *Nor-Video Services Ltd.* v. *Ontario Hydro* (1978) 84 DLR (3d) 221, where electrical interference forced the plaintiffs to stop a whole television channel, but they did not lose subscribers or income. The cost of restoring the channel was about $200,000. It was held that the measure of damages was the loss, not restoration.

[378] *J. & E. Hall Ltd.* v. *Barclay* [1937] 3 All ER 620.

[379] Torts (Interference with Goods) Act 1977, ss. 7 and 8.

[380] *The Fortunity* [1961] 1 WLR 351.

[381] *The Llanover* [1947] P 80.

[382] *Peruvian Guano Co. Ltd.* v. *Dreyfus Brothers & Co.* [1892] AC 166.

[383] *Townend* v. *Askern Coal and Iron Co.* [1934] Ch. 463.

[384] *The London Corporation* [1935] P 70, 77 (per Greer LJ).

has had to be repaired exceeds the cost of repair; in which case the claimant recovers his loss.[385] The cost of repair is normally calculated as at the time of the damage, except where the damage was not discoverable until later, or where it was reasonable for the claimant to have postponed repair.[386] Repair means reasonable repair, not meticulous restoration.[387] The cost of unreasonable repair is not recoverable, but it is not always easy to determine what is reasonable. At one end of the spectrum stands a case which decided that a plaintiff who was sentimentally attached to his car could not recover the cost of repair, which far exceeded its market value, and the technical reason given for this was the rule about the need to take reasonable steps to mitigate the damage.[388] At the other end stand cases dealing with damage to unique items where the courts are prepared to sanction the recovery of high repair costs.[389] What of cases falling between these two extremes? The owner of a damaged vintage car has been held entitled to recover the higher repair costs because of the 'legitimately sentimental value'[390] of the damaged article. If so, should not the owner of a treasured but valueless pet, which has been injured through the defendant's negligence, be able to claim the higher cost of cure than the market value, which is nil, or the cost of acquiring a substitute? These are interesting questions, which, however, cannot receive a universal answer beyond restating that a claimant's right to be restored to the *status quo ante* has always to be weighed against the duty to do what is reasonable to mitigate the cost to the defendant. It is of interest to note that in a case where a plaintiff was induced to pay more for a house than it was worth because of a negligent report by the defendant surveyor, damages for vexation and inconvenience were included in the award.[391]

The cost of repair can also include what could be called the 'commercial inferiority' of the repaired vehicle. This occurs whenever the damaged vehicle, though fully repaired, becomes 'marked' as a 'repaired' vehicle and thereby loses some of its resale value. It is not material in this context whether the plaintiff intends to sell the car or whether he intends to go on using it. In *Payton v. Brooks*[392] the plaintiff alleged, but failed to prove, that the value of the damaged new car was diminished even though repairs were well done. Roskill LJ, as he then was, elegantly summarised the applicable principles in the following passage:

There are many cases which arise, whether in the field of contract law or of tort, where the cost of repairs is a prima facie method of ascertaining the diminution in value. But it is not the only method of measuring the loss. In a case where the evidence justifies a finding that there has been, on top of the cost of repairs, some diminution in market value—or, to put the point another way, justifies the conclusion that the loss to the plaintiff has not been fully compensated by the receipt of the cost of complete and adequate repairs, because of a resultant

385 *Payton* v. *Brooks* [1974] RTR 169.
386 *Martindale* v. *Duncan* [1973] 1 WLR 574, *Dodd Properties Ltd.* v. *Canterbury City Council* [1980] 1 WLR 433.
387 *Ibid.* 388 *Darbishire* v. *Warran* [1963] 1 WLR 1067.
389 *O'Grady* v. *Westminster Scaffolding* [1962] 2 Lloyd's Rep. 238.
390 Fleming's expression: J. G. Fleming, *The Law of Torts* (8th edn., 1992), 250.
391 *Perry* v. *Sidney Phillips & Son* [1982] 1 WLR 1297.
392 [1974] 1 Lloyd's Rep. 241

diminution in market value—I can see no reason why the plaintiff should be deprived of recovery under that head of damage also. I would only add one word of caution. This conclusion is not a charter under which infuriated plaintiffs, who have the misfortune to have their cars damaged by careless drivers, acquire an unfettered right to recover diminution of value in every case in addition to the cost of repairs. It is essential in such a case, in my judgment, for appropriate evidence to be called to prove diminution in value.

The reverse situation arises where repairing the car has actually (and substantially) increased its value compared to the *status quo ante*. In principle it would be unfair to allow this to stand, for the defendant cannot be required to improve the plaintiff's overall financial position. A pragmatic approach may be the best one. So, if the replaced part would have normally lasted for the car's 'lifetime' then damages are not reduced. On the other hand, if the part is already worn and is replaced by a new part then the 'betterment' must be taken into account. Thus, suppose that the defendants burn down the claimant's house. If the house is rebuilt can the defendants argue that it should be taken into account that now the claimant now has a new house and therefore more than he would had but for the tort. A leading decision of the German Supreme Court accepted this in principle and made a reduction.[393] However, the court sensibly added that one must weigh all the surrounding circumstances and decide if it makes sense to make a reduction in each case. So, for instance, if the plaintiff is not capable of paying for rebuilding the house himself it would be unfair to take the betterment into account and award him a lower amount of cost of repair than that which will be actually necessary to rebuild. It would appear that a similar approach was adopted in *British Westinghouse Co. Ltd.* v. *Underground Electric Railways Co. of London Ltd.*[394] The defendant there supplied defective turbines. The plaintiff after having used them for a time replaced them by the other turbines which proved very efficient. Even if the original turbines had complied with the contract, it would still have been to the pecuniary advantage of the railway company at their own cost to have replaced them by other turbines. Damages were accordingly reduced. A more cautious note, however, has been struck in other cases. In *Harbutt's Plasticine Ltd.* v. *Wayne Tank and Pump Co. Ltd.*[395] for instance the betterment caused by rebuilding a factory according to a new design was not deducted (though it may have been relevant that the plaintiffs apparently were not allowed to rebuild following the old design).

A claimant may also recover in respect of the loss of use of his thing during repair.[396] But unlike some foreign systems (e.g. German) a claim for the cost of a substitute hire cannot be made if no such hiring has taken place. Thus, in our system, the cost of actual hiring must be strictly pleaded and proved as special damage;[397] and, of course, it must

393 BGHZ 30, 29. For fuller comparative details on all these issues see B.S. Markesinis and H. Unberath, *The German Law of Torts: A Comparative Treatise* (4th edn., 2002), pp. 931 ff. German law is unbelievably rich on all the points here discussed and could thus be a great source of inspiration to potential litigants.

394 [1912] AC 673, 690 (Viscount Haldane)—a contract case. Cf. BGH NJW 1996, 584 (in contract).

395 [1970] 1 QB 447.

396 *Macrae* v. *Swindells* [1954] 1 WLR 597, *The Hebridean Coast* [1961] AC 545.

397 *SS Strathfillan* v. *SS Ikala* [1929] AC 196.

be reasonable.[398] If the profit that would have been earned by the chattel is lower than the cost of hiring the substitute, only the former amount can be claimed. And, conversely, the claimant must account for any extra profit that the hired chattel enabled him to make.[399] The fact that he had a substitute ready to hand, so that his activities were not impaired, is irrelevant; what is estimated is the loss of use of the damaged thing.[400] Loss of use can be measured with reference to the hire of a substitute, which is special damage and, as such, has to be pleaded and proved.[401] Damages may also be claimed for the damage of a non-profit earning chattel.[402] As Earl Halsbury LC memorably put it: 'Supposing a person took away a chair out of my room and kept it for twelve months, could anybody say you had a right to diminish the damages by showing that I did not usually sit in that chair, or that there were plenty of other chairs in the room?'[403]

In recent times negligent valuations of property have given rise to differences of opinion as to how the claimant's loss should be estimated. Typically, the claimant will be a lender of money who lent money to the borrower on the basis of a valuation of the property carried out by a professional valuer. It is important to realise that in these cases two things can go wrong. First, the valuer may (because of his negligence) produce a wrong valuation (typically, an over-valuation), in which case the lender has a diminished security for his loan. In the second case, the value of the property may go down, for instance because of changed market conditions. These two events (which may be combined in practice) may produce widely differing figures; and the problem faced by our courts was to determine the extent of the liability of the valuer where the borrower defaults and the value of the security is insufficient to satisfy the lender's demands. The leading decision is now found in three consolidated appeals reported under the name of *South Australia Asset Management Corp.* v. *York Montague Ltd.* [404]

Lord Hoffmann's leading judgment in that case is notable for its clarity and perceptiveness. This is largely because he commenced his inquiry by making a fundamental distinction: in some cases a professional was hired to provide information (in this case

398 *Moore* v. *DER Ltd.* [1971] 1 WLR 1476. Thus, the owner of a damaged Rolls-Royce can claim the cost of hire of a substitute Rolls-Royce while his car is being repaired: *HL Motorworks (Willesden) Ltd.* v. *Alwahbi* [1977] RTR 276. See also *Giles* v. *Thompson* [1994] 1 AC 142 on the need for it to be reasonable to have hired the replacement for the time in question; the case is also one major landmark in the development of case law on the practice whereby a car hire company takes on the claimant's case against the defendant and provides a hire car in the meantime. This raises difficult issues under the Consumer Credit Act 1974: see *Dimond* v. *Lovell* [2000] 2 WLR 1121; [2002] 1 AC 384 (noted by J. K. Macleod, 'Credit Hire in the House of Lords' [2001] *JBL* 14) and, most recently, *Clark* v. *Ardington Electrical Services (No. 2)* [2003] QB 36 for further details.

399 *The World Beauty* [1969] P 12. 400 *The Mediana* [1900] AC 113.

401 *The Hebridean Coast* [1961] AC 545.

402 Though the calculation here will vary according to the circumstances, and the courts have refused to adopt a single method of assessment.

403 *The Mediana* [1900] AC 113, 117.

404 [1996] 3 All ER 365. See also *Nykredit Mortgage Bank plc* v. *Edward Erdman Group Ltd. (No. 2)* [1997] 1 WLR 1627, *Platform Home Loans Ltd.* v. *Oyston Shipways Ltd.* [1998] Ch 466; [2000] 2 AC 190, and, most recently, *Aneco Insurance Underwriting* v. *Johnson & Higgins* [2002] 1 Lloyd's Rep. 157. *Aneco* illustrates that our most senior judges can disagree over the determination of the scope of the defendant's duty in the particular case (compare Lord Millett's dissent with the leading majority judgment of Lord Steyn), even if they agree that the correct general approach is indeed to determine the scope of that duty.

on the value of the land in question) leaving it to someone else (in this case the lender) to decide upon a course of action—a decision that will be taken on the basis of multiple commercial and financial factors available to the lender. In other cases, however, the professional is hired to advise someone on what to do. The crucial question was thus to determine the precise scope and ambit of the valuer's duty. The best way to do this was to give effect to the express obligations assumed by the valuer, neither cutting them down so that the lender obtains less than he was reasonably entitled to expect, nor extending them so as to impose upon the valuer a liability greater than he could reasonably have thought that he was undertaking.[405]

In the instant case, the valuers were hired to provide information which, along with other factors, would enable the lenders to decide whether to make the loan. He was not asked to advise about the financial merits of entering into the deal or the borrower's creditworthiness. The correct principle as far their liability was concerned was thus, for such cases, generalised as follows:

> It is that a person under a duty to take reasonable care to provide information on which someone else will decide upon a course of action is, if negligent,[406] not generally regarded as responsible for all the consequences of that course of action. He is responsible only for the consequences of the information being wrong. A duty of care which imposes upon the informant responsibility for losses which would have occurred even if the information which he gave had been correct is not in my view fair and reasonable as between the parties. It is therefore inappropriate either as an implied term of a contract or as a tortious duty arising from the relationship between them.[407]

In the *South Australia* case the property in question was valued at £15 million and the lender advanced £11 million. In fact the property was worth only £5 million; and because of a market drop, it was sold at £2.5 million. The lender could thus claim his full loss, i.e. £11 million (loan) minus £2.5 million (price realised from the sale of property).

We may conclude this (very) brief description of a complex area of the law of damages by saying a few words about 'consequential' though, perhaps, inevitable losses of the kind that may arise because of car hire agreements are phrased. The (divided) decision of the House of Lords in *Dimond* v. *Lowell*[408] offers a good glimpse of the difficulties the reader should be aware of.

In the above case, Mrs Dimond's car was negligently damaged in an accident caused by Mr Lovell. While the car was in a garage for repairs she needed a replacement vehicle to go to work. She hired a car from a car accident hire company called 1st Automotive at a rate that *exceeded* the usual rate of hiring an equivalent car. The only issue relevant here, namely whether the increased cost of hiring a car from an accident car hire company could be recovered (or whether the normal cost of hiring a replacement car was the maximum amount allowable) did not arise for decision. Yet Lord Hoffmann

405 [1996] 3 All ER 365, at 371.

406 *Ibid.* Lord Hoffmann carefully limited his comments to negligent valuations and said nothing about fraudulent valuations. In this latter type of case, however, the 'advisee' might be able to claim his full losses.

407 *Ibid.*, at 372.

408 [2000] 2 WLR 1121.

invited their Lordships to express an opinion on this point given its importance in daily life. The majority stated *obiter* that such damages cannot be recovered since the victim fails to mitigate his loss.

Lord Nicholls of Birkenhead dissented.[409] Lord Nicholls based his argument[410] mainly on the interests involved in the former type of situation. Normal insurance, he explained, does not provide for a replacement car; and there are a number of factors that deter victims from making themselves arrangements for hire of a replacement car. Thus, they may be required to produce the hire charge up-front; or they may hesitate to rent a car because they are put off by the prospect of having to sue the negligent driver for the relatively small amount of hire. So accident hire companies fulfil a real need. The hirer does not have to produce any money; the hire company pursues the allegedly negligent driver's insurers. For these additional service they charge more than the usual hiring rate (in the present case double the normal amount).

As suggested, this consideration does not apply with equal force to the German case mentioned in n. 393. But since in Germany most hire companies charge a higher 'accident tariff', the victim will find it difficult to avoid the higher tariff and would be in the end burdened with the costs of the doubtful trading practice. However, there are also schemes in operation which are similar to that used by 1st Automotive: the victim does not need to pay for hiring a replacement car but merely assigns his claim against the insurance to the care hire company.

Lord Nicholls also pointed out the Achilles' heel of such a scheme (regardless whether the hire company offers the additional service of pursuing the claim or not). It is this aspect, also, which these cases raise, and it is one of general interest. Does tort law provide rules which can deal satisfactorily with situations where there is no market mechanism to control the adequacy of the bargain? Since the victim does not have to bear the cost of the hire he will, in the end, be much less critical towards the price of such hiring arrangements. It lies in the nature of such a scheme (someone else, the insurance company, is paying for the service) that there is *no market mechanism* to contain the price of the service. Lord Nicholls sought to accommodate this fear by limiting the damages recoverable to 'a reasonable charge'.

A similar approach was adopted in *Giles* v. *Thompson*,[411] where the question was whether the accident hire contract was champertous. Lord Mustill held that this was not so provided that the charge did not exceed the market rate for car hire companies.[412] It follows also from the German case law that once such extended liability is accepted the only realistic control factor is whether the rate is a reasonable one compared to the average *accident* tariffs which will be at an inflated level already. Hence, Lord Hoffmann was justified in warning of the danger of inflated claims.[413]

409 *Ibid.*, at 1124–5.

410 Much of Lord Nicholls' reasoning reminds one of the line taken by the German Supreme Federal Court in BGHZ 132, 373 (reproduced in translated form in Markesinis and Unberath, *The Germen Law of Torts* (4th edn., 2002), at 1032–6), even though the two cases differ in one important respect. For unlike *Dimond v. Lovell*, the plaintiff in the German case had actually already paid for the cost of the hire.

411 [1994] 1 AC 142.

412 *Ibid.*, at 165.

413 [2000] 2 WLR 1121, at 1126.

SELECT BIBLIOGRAPHY

Atiyah, P. S., 'Collateral Benefits Again' (1969) 32 *MLR* 397.

Bevan, N., and Gregory, H., 'Structured Settlements' (2004) 154 *NLJ* 1280, 1388, 1658.

—'Periodical Payments' (2005) 155 *NLJ* 565, 907, 980.

Bishop, W., and Kay, J., 'Taxation of Damages: The Rule in Gourley's Case' (1987) 104 *LQR* 211.

Burrows, A., *Remedies for Torts and Breach of Contract* (3rd edn., 2004).

Cane, P., *Atiyah's Accidents, Compensation and the Law* (7th edn., 2006), esp. ch. 6, and, to a lesser extent, chs. 13, 14 and 15.

Department For Constitutional Affairs, *The Law on Damages.*, Consultation Paper CP9/07 (4 May 2007). Available on the Internet at http://www.dca.gov.uk/consult/damages/ cp0907.pdf.

—*The Damages Lottery* (1997).

Fleming, J. G., 'The Collateral Source Rule and Loss Allocation in Tort' (1966) 54 *Cal. LR* 1478.

—'Damages: Capital or Rent?' (1969) 19 *UTLJ* 295.

—'Impact of Inflation on Tort Compensation' (1978) 26 *Am. J Comp. L* 51.

Harris, D., Campbell, L. D., and Halson, R., *Remedies in Contract and Tort* (2nd edn., 2002).

Kemp, D. A. (ed.), *Damages for Personal Injury and Death* (7th edn., 1999).

—'The Overlap between Damages for Personal Injury and Work Related Benefits' (1998) 27 *ILJ* 1.

Law Commission, *Structured Settlements and Interim and Provisional Damages*, Consultation Paper No. 125 (1992).

—*Aggravated, Exemplary and Restitutionary Damages*, Consultation Paper No. 132 (1993).

—*Structured Settlements and Interim and Provisional Damages*, Report No. 224 (Cm 2646, 1994).

—*Damages for Personal Injury: Non-Pecuniary Loss*, Consultation Paper No. 140 (1996).

—*Damages for Personal Injury: Medical, Nursing and Other Expenses*, Consultation Paper No. 144 (1996).

—*Aggravated, Exemplary and Restitutionary Damages*, Report No. 247 (HC 346, 1997).

—*Damages for Personal Injury: Collateral Benefits*, Consultation Paper No. 147 (1997).

—*Claims for Wrongful Death*, Consultation Paper No. 148 (1997).

—*Damages for Personal Injury: Non-Pecuniary Loss*, Report No. 257 (HC 344, 1999).

—*Damages for Personal Injury: Medical, Nursing and Other Expenses—Collateral Benefits*, Report No. 262 (HC 806, 1999).

—*Claims for Wrongful Death*, Report No. 263 (HC 807, 1999).

Lewis, R., *Structured Settlements: The Law and Practice* (1993).

—'Deducting Collateral Benefits from Damages: Principle and Policy' (1998) 18 *Leg. Stud.* 15.

—*Deducting Benefits from Damages for Personal Injury* (2000).

—'Methods for Calculating Damages for Loss of Future Earnings' [2002] *JPIL* 151.

—'The Politics and Economics of Tort Law: Judicially Imposed Periodical Payment of Damages' (2006) 69 *MLR* 418.

LEWIS, R., MCNABB, R., ROBINSON, H., and WASS, V., 'Court Awards of Damages for Loss of Future Earnings: An Empirical Study and an Alternative Method of Calculation' (2002) 29 *J of Law and Society* 406.

MCGREGOR, H., *McGregor on Damages* (17th edn., 2003).

MUNKMAN, J., *Damages for Personal Injuries and Death* (10th edn., 1996).

Pearson Committee, *Royal Commission on Civil Liability and Compensation for Personal Injury* (Cmnd. 7054–1 (1978)).

STAPLETON, J., *Disease and the Compensation Debate* (1986).

WEIR, J. A., *Compensation for Personal Injury and Death: Recent Proposals for Reform*, The Cambridge–Tilburg Lectures (1978).

26

OTHER REMEDIES AND MULTIPLE LIABILITIES

Actions for the recovery of land and chattels have been explained earlier.[1] Apart from processes at law, certain forms of self-help are allowed, although they are not actively encouraged by the law; these too have been analysed earlier.[2]

1. INJUNCTIONS

An action for damages lies after a tort has been committed. An injunction is sought to prevent the continuance of a tort or in anticipation of a threatened tort. It is an order commanding the discontinuance of some activity or forbidding the causing of damage. In the nature of things it applies to intentional or continuing acts, so it has no application to negligence.[3] The injunction historically arose in equity and the grant of this remedy is still governed by equitable principles and is hence discretionary, unlike damages that are awarded as of right. In principle an injunction cannot be granted unless it is based on some actual or potential cause of action in tort, contract, breach of trust or otherwise.[4] Courts have on occasion granted injunctions in defence of 'property rights',[5] broadly defined, and to prevent certain breaches of the criminal law in circumstances where it is not clear that any civil-law action for damages would have been available.[6] If these cases are evidence of a wider principle of liability for illicit interference with trade or livelihood that spans existing categories of civil wrong, such a principle has yet to be adequately rationalised.[7]

[1] See chs. 12 and 11 respectively.

[2] Recovery of chattels, above, ch. 11; expulsion of trespassers and re-entry on land, above, ch. 12; distress damage feasant, above, ch. 17; abatement of nuisance, above, ch. 13, Section 6(b); self-defence, above, ch. 9, Section 3(b).

[3] *Miller* v. *Jackson* [1977] QB 966, 980 (per Lord Denning MR).

[4] *White* v. *Mellin* [1895] AC 154, 163–4.

[5] *Springhead Spinning Co.* v. *Riley* (1868) LR 6 Eq. 551 (damage to business), *Gee* v. *Pritchard* (1818) 2 Swans. 402; 36 ER 670 (privacy).

[6] *Ex parte Island Records* [1978] Ch. 122; see above, ch. 15, Section 3(a)(iv).

[7] See previous note.

(A) PROHIBITORY INJUNCTIONS

An injunction may be issued to restrain a threatened act that, unless restrained, is likely to be repeated, with the result that the claimant will then have an action based on a civil law wrong. The court will nearly always grant the claimant such an injunction, unless he has acquiesced in some way in the activity or has misled the defendant or the court.[8] If the harm is trivial an injunction may not be granted.[9] On the other hand, the defendant is not to be allowed to 'buy' the right to continue his infringement of the claimant's interest at the cost of paying nominal damages each time an interference occurs.[10] Nor, in principle, should a court refuse to grant an injunction and award damages instead simply because the injunction will affect the public at large, since this would be to dilute the content of the private rights which it is the role of the court to protect.[11] An injunction may be refused if compliance with it would be impossible or illegal (although a mere breach of contract will not normally prevent the order being made). A court may postpone the coming into force of an injunction in order to give the defendant time to rectify the situation.[12]

(B) MANDATORY INJUNCTIONS

The court may order the defendant to perform some act, for example, to abate a nuisance.[13] Such injunctions are issued only rarely and even then only in cases where the defendant has acted deliberately or unreasonably.[14] In *Redland Bricks Ltd.* v. *Morris*[15] the defendant's excavations withdrew support from the plaintiff's land, making further subsidence likely. The House of Lords refused an interlocutory injunction, partly on the ground that the trial judge's order had been too imprecise and partly on the ground that the cost of restoration far exceeded the market value of the land in question. Lord Upjohn stated the following principles governing the grant of an injunction:[16] (*a*) there must be a very strong probability of grave damage; (*b*) the nature of the injury must be such that damages would be inadequate; (*c*) the cost to the defendant must be taken into account, as should his behaviour in the sense that the court should determine whether he had tried to 'steal a march' on his neighbour or whether his behaviour had been reasonable; and (*d*) it must be possible for the defendant to know exactly what he has to do.[17]

8 *Armstrong* v. *Sheppard and Short Ltd.* [1959] 1 QB 384.

9 *Ibid.*, 396–7 (per Lord Evershed MR).

10 *Woollerton and Wilson Ltd.* v. *R. Costain Ltd.* [1970] 1 WLR 411, 413 (Stamp LJ); cf. *Charrington* v. *Simons & Co. Ltd.* [1971] 1 WLR 598, 603.

11 See *Shelfer* v. *City of London Electric Lighting Co.* [1895] 1 Ch. 287, *Miller* v. *Jackson* [1977] QB 966, *Kennaway* v. *Thompson* [1981] QB 88; ch. 13, Section 6(a) above.

12 *Pride of Derby and Derbyshire Angling Association Ltd.* v. *British Celanese Ltd.* [1953] Ch. 149.

13 *Kelsen* v. *Imperial Tobacco Co. Ltd.* [1957] 2 QB 334. Or to remove a trespass to land: *Nelson* v. *Nicholson*, *The Independent*, 22 Jan. 2001.

14 *Daniel* v. *Ferguson* [1981] 2 Ch. 27.

15 [1970] AC 652, 665–6.

16 For a recent example, see *Daniells* v. *Mendonca* (1999) 78 P & CR 401 (CA).

17 This may often be a key point in the burgeoning privacy case law: if a claimant successfully prevents disclosure of the 'private' information, then at trial the claimant is likely to want to prevent its publication altogether. It will

(C) *QUIA TIMET* INJUNCTIONS

Normally an injunction is sought in order to prevent the continuance or repetition of a tort. Where damage has been done, a prohibitory injunction may be issued with reference to the future, ordering the defendant to cease carrying on the activity, or a mandatory injunction may be issued ordering him to put matters right. Where damage is only threatened, or the cause of action is not yet complete, the injunction sought is known as a *quia timet* action, alleging that the claimant fears that a tort will be committed. He has to show a high probability of substantial damage and that damages will be insufficient or inadequate. In *Redland Bricks Ltd.* v. *Morris*[18] Lord Upjohn said that a *quia timet* injunction will lie (*i*) where the defendant is threatening and intending to do acts which will cause irreparable harm to the claimant and (*ii*) in cases where the claimant has received compensation for his loss but alleges that earlier acts of the defendant will lead to future actionable damage.

(D) INTERLOCUTORY (OR INTERIM) INJUNCTIONS

An interlocutory or interim or provisional injunction is designed to restrain the commission or continuance of an activity pending the settlement of either the legal or factual basis of the claimant's claim, thereby enabling the *status quo* to be preserved. Since a defendant may suffer through being restrained in this way, the claimant is usually required to give an undertaking to pay damages to the defendant in the event of the injunction being discharged at a full trial of the action. It was held in *Patel* v. *W. H. Smith (Eziot) Ltd.*[19] that an interlocutory injunction could be issued to restrain a trespass on land even though there was no special damage.

Prior to the decision of the House of Lords in *American Cyanamid Co.* v. *Ethicon Ltd.*[20] it was generally understood that the plaintiff had to show a *prima facie* case that he would succeed at the full trial of the action if he was to succeed at the interlocutory stage. However, in that case Lord Diplock laid down a new, two-stage test. At the first stage the plaintiff need show, not a *prima facie* case, but simply that there is a serious issue to be tried. At the second stage the court will then decide whether an injunction should be granted on the balance of convenience between the parties. This test greatly favours the *status quo* and has given rise to considerable controversy,[21] not least in the context of the economic torts, where Parliament has intervened to modify its effect on the trade-dispute immunities.[22] Interlocutory injunctions are hardly ever granted in

then be vital for the defendant to know exactly what can and cannot be published in future. Of course, this possibility will only arise if an interim injunction has been awarded, to prevent disclosure until trial: see below.

[18] [1970] AC 692, at 665. [19] [1987] 1 WLR 853. [20] [1975] AC 396.

[21] Compare also the position taken by some judges in breach of confidence claims (esp. Laddie J in *Series 5 Software* v. *Clarke* [1996] 1 All ER 853; [1996] FSR 273, who favoured at least some consideration of the merits at the interim injunction stage—this may be particularly important in such privacy-driven breach of confidence cases where the interim application may well dispose of the matter altogether, as time is often of the essence in such circumstances: see, e.g., *GFI Group* v. *Eaglestone* [1994] FSR 535).

[22] Trade Union and Labour Relations (Consolidation) Act 1992, s. 221. See ch. 15, Section 5 above.

defamation cases, *Cyanamid* notwithstanding.[23] An interlocutory injunction may be issued in the context of an action for nuisance, as in *Burris* v. *Azadani*,[24] where the purpose of the order was to restrain threats of violence and harassment of the plaintiff by the defendant. Such injunctions are also of particular relevance in the privacy cases based upon breach of confidence: if no interim injunction can be secured then the secret will be out and the claimant will be left to pursue a remedy in damages, under an inquisitive media spotlight. However, in this privacy context, section 12 of the Human Rights Act 1998 (which provides in s. 12(3) that '[n]o such relief is to be granted so as to restrain publication before trial unless the court is satisfied that the applicant is likely to establish that publication should not be allowed') may well prove influential, especially because section 12(4) requires the court to 'have particular regard to the importance of the Convention right to freedom of expression'.[25] Early indications are that the courts will be unwilling to grant such injunctions to restrain publication, especially if damages (for any breach of the claimant's rights later established at trial) would prove an adequate remedy.[26]

2. DAMAGES IN LIEU OF AN INJUNCTION

Where a court could issue an injunction, but decides against doing so,[27] it may award damages in lieu. This power was originally conferred by section 2 of the Chancery Amendment Act 1858 (Lord Cairns' Act) and has been continued by later legislation.[28] In *Shelfer* v. *City of London Electric Lighting Co.*[29] A. L. Smith LJ suggested that the power to grant damages could be exercised where (*i*) the injury to the plaintiff is small, (*ii*) it can be expressed in monetary terms, (*iii*) monetary compensation would be adequate in the circumstances and (*iv*) it would be oppressive to the defendant to issue the injunction. The defendant must put forward the case for awarding damages as opposed to an injunction. In later cases courts have interpreted the *Shelfer* guidelines flexibly and have taken into account other considerations, such as the seriousness and persistence of the interference, the behaviour of the two parties and the wider public interest. The matter is very

[23] *Bestobell Paints Ltd.* v. *Gigg* (1975) 119 SJ 678. This suggests that the impact of s. 12(3) and (4) of the Human Rights Act 1998 is unlikely to prove influential in defamation cases.

[24] [1995] 1 WLR 1372.

[25] See, e.g., *Douglas* v. *Hello!* [2001] 2 WLR 992 and *A* v. *B and C* [2002] 2 All ER 545.

[26] Again, *Douglas* v. *Hello!* provides a helpful illustration: see the judgment of Keene LJ (at [171]) The judgment of the Court of Appeal in *Douglas* v. *Hello! (No. 3)* [2006] QB 125, denying *OK!*'s claim for compensation for breach of confidence, suggested that greater attention would have to be paid to the grant of interim injunctions in future: if the interest of *OK!* could have been protected by such an injunction pending trial, and yet could not legally be indicated by a damages award, this might suggest that the balance was more strongly in favour of the grant of an interim injunction. However, the judgment of the House of Lords on appeal ([2007]) UKHL 21), overturning the Court of Appeal's ruling and restoring the order of Lindsay J (which had awarded damages to *OK!* as well as the Douglases), has taken some of the tension out of this issue. This suggests that the courts in such cases will continue to be unwilling to restrain publication pending trial.

[27] *Hooper* v. *Rogers* [1975] Ch. 43, 48 (Russell LJ).

[28] Supreme Court Act 1980, s. 50.

[29] [1895] 1 Ch. 287, 322–33.

much one for the judge's discretion.[30] It has been said that damages awarded in this way should represent a 'proper and fair price' for the continuation of the activity.[31]

SELECT BIBLIOGRAPHY

GRAY, C., 'Interlocutory Injunctions since *Cyanamid*' [1981] *CLJ* 307.

JOLOWICZ, J. A., 'Damages in Equity: A Study of Lord Cairns's Act' [1975] *CLJ* 224.

3. JOINT AND CONCURRENT LIABILITY

(A) JOINT AND CONCURRENT LIABILITY DISTINGUISHED

Where several tortfeasors cause different damage to one claimant, the torts are independent and each person is liable for the damage he inflicts. Where tortfeasors cause the *same* damage they may either be *joint tortfeasors* or *several concurrent tortfeasors*. Tortfeasors are 'joint' in cases of express authorisation or instigation; principal and agent; vicarious liability; the liability of an employer and an independent contractor (where the former is under a personal, non-delegable duty of care); the liability of tortfeasors who act in breach of a joint duty; and tortfeasors who act in pursuance of a common design.[32] Several concurrent tortfeasors are those who, acting independently of each other, combine in their actions to cause damage to the claimant, for example, when two careless motorists collide and injure a pedestrian.[33] In joint liability each tortfeasor is liable for the full amount of the claimant's loss, but there is only one tort and so the cause of action against each one is the same and is supported by the same evidence. The common law took the view that since there is only one tort, judgment against one tortfeasor, even if unsatisfied, bars further action against the other or others.[34] Only if judgment against one defendant only partially satisfies the claimant will successive actions lie.[35] This rule was changed by statute in 1935[36] and the relevant provisions are now found in section 3 of the Civil Liability (Contribution) Act 1978.

(B) SUCCESSIVE ACTIONS

Section 3 of the 1978 Act states that judgment against any one person shall not be a bar to an action, or its continuance, against any other person jointly liable in respect of

30 See e.g. *Sampson* v. *Hodson-Pressinger* [1981] 3 All ER 710, 715 (Eveleigh LJ).

31 *Bracewell* v. *Appleby* [1975] Ch. 408, 419–20. This means that in an appropriate case, damages in lieu of an injunction may compensate the claimant for loss of a bargaining opportunity in respect of the activity: see *Wrotham Park Estates Co. Ltd.* v. *Parkside Homes Ltd.* [1974] 1 WLR 798, *Jaggard* v. *Sawyer* [1995] 1 WLR 269.

32 On the latter, see *Brooke* v. *Bool* [1928] 2 KB 578, *CBS Songs Ltd.* v. *Amstrad Consumer Electronics plc* [1988] AC 1013.

33 *Drinkwater* v. *Kimber* [1952] 2 QB 281, *Thompson* v. *London County Council* [1899] 2 QB 840.

34 *Brinsmead* v. *Harrison* (1872) LR 7 CP 547.

35 *The Koursk* [1924] P 140.

36 The Law Reform (Married Women and Joint Tortfeasors) Act 1935.

the same damage.[37] This provision applies both to joint and to several concurrent tortfeasors. It is possible that a claimant may recover damages in a second action over and above those which he was awarded in the first, for example, if he had underestimated his damage. Section 4, however, states that a claimant who brings another action against a joint or concurrent tortfeasor shall be refused costs in the later action unless he satisfied the court that there was a reasonable ground for bringing it. If joint or concurrent tortfeasors are sued at the same time there will be judgment for a single sum, which they will share between them; the claimant must not be over-compensated for his loss. A controversial rule is that the claimant will be awarded the lowest sum for which any one defendant could be held liable.[38] This can create unfairness to the claimant in the event of exemplary, punitive or aggravated damages being awardable against one defendant. Although the rule is designed to protect the innocent defendant from being made to pay a greater amount than he could personally be held responsible for, it is arguable that he could shift his loss by seeking contribution from the guilty defendant.

Following the abolition of the bar against successive actions, the only remaining distinction between joint and several liability concerns the effect of release of tortfeasors. In joint torts the release of one tortfeasor, whether by accord and satisfaction or under seal, automatically releases the other or others;[39] this is because there is only one obligation resting on all of them, and if this is extinguished with regard to one it is extinguished for all.[40] In contrast, the liabilities of concurrent tortfeasors are separate, with the result that a release of one does not necessarily release the others. An agreement not to sue is not the same as a release for this purpose, in the sense that it does not extinguish the obligation; it merely gives the other party to the agreement a defence should a claim be brought.[41] Such an agreement does not therefore extinguish the cause of action against the rest. This distinction has been called arid, technical and without any merits;[42] accordingly, a court has held that even a release will not extinguish the claim against the others if there is an express or implied reservation of the right of action against them.[43] Nor will it release the other tortfeasors in a case where the settlement does not meet the full value of the claimants claim for damages.[44]

(c) CONTRIBUTION AND APPORTIONMENT

The common law did not provide for contribution between joint or concurrent tortfeasors,[45] unless the tort was clearly illegal in itself and the party claiming contribution acted in the belief that it was lawful or, if the tort was clearly illegal, the party claiming

[37] See *Wah Tat Bank Ltd.* v. *Chan* [1975] AC 507, *Bryanston Finance Ltd.* v. *de Vries* [1975] 1 QB 703, *Birse Construction Ltd.* v. *Haite Ltd. (Watson and Others, Third Parties)* [1996] 1 WLR 675.

[38] *Cassell & Co. Ltd.* v. *Broome* [1972] AC 1027.

[39] *Thurman* v. *Wild* (1840) 11 A & E 453; 113 ER 487.

[40] *Duck* v. *Mayeu* [1892] 2 QB 511, 513.

[41] *Apley Estates Co. Ltd.* v. *de Bernales* [1947] Ch. 217.

[42] *Bryanston Finance Ltd.* v. *de Vries* [1975] QB 703, 723 (Lord Denning MR).

[43] *Gardiner* v. *Moore* [1969] 1 QB 55.

[44] *Jameson* v. *Central Electricity Generating Board (Babcock Energy Ltd., Third Party)* [1997] 3 WLR 151.

[45] *Merryweather* v. *Nian* (1799) 8 Term Rep. 186; 101 ER 1337.

contribution was held vicariously liable for the wrongdoing of another which he had not authorised.[46] Provision for contribution again had to be made by statute. Section 1(1) of the Civil Liability (Contribution) Act 1978 now states that 'any person liable in respect of any damage suffered by another person may recover contribution from any other person liable in respect of the same damage (whether jointly with him or otherwise)'. The Act is not limited to actions in tort; it extends to all forms of civil liability, whether based on tort, breach of contract, breach of trust, or otherwise.[47] The party seeking contribution must be liable, actually or hypothetically: section 1(6) refers to 'liability which has been or could be established in an action'. The wording used here rules out a claim for contribution by a defendant whose liability cannot be established because the period of limitation has elapsed. A contribution may, however, be claimed from a defendant against whom an action has simply been stayed, for example, because, thanks to an exclusive jurisdiction clause, he must be sued in another jurisdiction.[48]

Where, on the other hand, the claimant has paid the original victim of the tort, section 1(2) preserves the right to contribution against a joint or concurrent tortfeasor, even though the claimant is no longer liable to the original victim 'since the time when the damage occurred, provided that he was so liable immediately before he made or was ordered or agreed to make the payment in respect of which the contribution is sought'. At the time contribution is sought the claimant may no longer be liable because of settlement or compromise. Under section 1(4) a party who made a payment under a *bona fide* settlement or compromise may claim contribution 'without regard to whether or not he himself is or ever was liable in respect of the damage, provided, however, that he would have been liable assuming that the factual basis of the claim against him could be established'. The provision is oddly phrased: would a defendant motivated to enter into a compromise as a result of legal as opposed to factual doubts about liability be covered by it?[49] Section 1(4) was enacted in order to clarify this area in the light of *Stott* v. *West Yorkshire Road Car Co. Ltd. and Another, Home Bakeries Ltd. and Another, Third Parties*.[50] Here, one defendant made an out-of-court settlement with the plaintiff without admitting liability, and then sought contribution. It was held that he could recover, provided that the other defendant was liable and provided that the claimant would have been liable had he been sued to judgment.

With regard to the person from whom contribution is claimed, section 1(3) of the 1978 Act provides that 'a person shall be liable to make contribution . . . notwithstanding that he has ceased to be liable in respect of the damage in question since the time when the damage occurred, unless he ceased to be liable by virtue of the expiry of a period of limitation or prescription which extinguished the right on which the claim against him in respect of the damage was based'.

46 *Adamson* v. *Jarvis* (1827) 4 Bing. 66; 130 ER 693, *Lister* v. *Romford Ice and Cold Storage Co. Ltd.* [1957] AC 555.
47 Section 6(1).
48 See *R. A. Lister & Co. Ltd.* v. *E. G. Thomson (Shipping) Ltd. and Another (No. 2)* [1987] 1 WLR 1614.
49 See A. M. Dugdale, 'Civil Liability (Contribution) Act 1978' (1979) 42 *MLR* 182, 184, and cf. the position of the builder who compromised in *Dutton* v. *Bognor Regis UDC* [1972] 1 QB 373.
50 [1971] 2 QB 651.

Limitation does not normally extinguish the action as such[51]—conversion is an exception in this regard.[52] Let D1 signify the defendant seeking contribution and D2 the defendant from whom the contribution is sought. By virtue of section 1(3), the fact that the claimant's claim may be statute-barred against D2 will not now prevent D1 from bringing a claim for contribution against D2 (as long as the limitation rules do not protect D1 himself from an action by the claimant, in which case s. 1(6) rules out his claim for contribution). The problem used to arise where certain classes of defendants were protected by special limitation rules which placed them at an advantage as compared to others: as in the case of *George Wimpey & Co. Ltd.* v. *British Overseas Airways Corporation*;[53] or in a case where the plaintiff initiated an action against D1 within the period of limitation but, by the time D1 sought contribution against D2, this period had elapsed, meaning that D2 would have had a defence against any claim brought by the plaintiff.[54] Section 1(5) provides that judgment in an action by the original claimant against the party from whom contribution is sought 'shall be conclusive in the proceedings for contribution as to any issue determined by that judgment in favour of the person from whom contribution is sought'. This should be read as meaning 'any issue on the merits'; otherwise it might cancel out the effect of section 1(3) by reintroducing the possibility that a limitation defence available to D2 in an action brought by the claimant would indeed prevent D1 from seeking contribution.[55]

The question of the effect upon the right of contribution of a limitation defence available in an action brought by the claimant must be distinguished from the limitation of the period within which the contribution claim itself must be brought. This period is two years from the date when the right of contribution accrues,[56] which is either the date of judgment against the defendant seeking contribution or, in the event of a compromise, the date of the agreement to pay the sum in question.

Under section 2(1) of the Act, the amount of contribution which a party will have to make depends on what the court considers is 'just and equitable having regard to the extent of that person's responsibility for the damage in question'. The court has power to exempt a party completely or, conversely, to order him to pay a complete indemnity.[57] Contribution can only be assessed between parties before the court; no account is to be taken of the possible responsibility of other persons.[58] With regard to the phrase 'responsibility for the damage', here, as under the Law Reform (Contributory Negligence) Act 1945, 'responsibility' implies both causal responsibility and the relative degree of fault of the parties: 'the investigation is concerned with "fault", which includes blameworthiness as well as causation. And no true apportionment can be reached unless both these factors are borne in mind.'[59]

51 See above, ch. 24, Section 9.

52 Limitation Act 1980, s. 3.

53 [1955] AC 169. Section 1(3) effectively reverses the outcome in this case.

54 As in *Ronex Properties Ltd.* v. *John Laing Construction Ltd.* [1983] QB 398.

55 *Nottingham Health Authority* v. *City of Nottingham* [1988] 1 WLR 903, 908 (Balcombe LJ).

56 Limitation Act 1980, s. 10.

57 Civil Liability (Contribution) Act 1978, s. 2(2). For a case of complete indemnity, see *Williams* v. *Trimm Rock Quarries* (1965) 109 SJ 454.

58 *Miraflores* v. *George Livanos* [1967] 1 AC 826, 845 (Lord Pearce).

59 *Ibid*.

The relationship between contribution and contributory negligence was clarified by the House of Lords in *Fitzgerald* v. *Lane*.[60] The plaintiff was seriously injured when he tried to cross a pedestrian crossing against the lights. He was struck by the car of the first defendant and thrown into the path of the car of the second. Both defendants had been driving too quickly and were held liable in negligence. The trial judge assessed the responsibility of the plaintiff and the two defendants as a third each. On this basis he made a deduction of one-third of the plaintiff's damages (under the Contributory Negligence Act) and then held (under the Contribution Act) that each defendant, being equally to blame with the other, should pay half of the resulting sum. The Court of Appeal overturned this judgment on the basis that since the plaintiff was equally to blame with the defendants considered *as a group*, he should recover only *half* of his damages. The House of Lords overruled the Court of Appeal on the law, pointing out that the correct procedure was that adopted by the judge: the court should first of all assess the extent of the plaintiff's responsibility under the Contributory Negligence Act, and only then consider the apportionment of responsibility between the defendants. However, the order of the Court of Appeal was upheld as the House of Lords came to a different conclusion on the extent of the plaintiff's responsibility for the accident, assessing this at 50 per cent and not just a third.

Under section 2(3) the amount of contribution assessed by the court against D2 must not exceed the amount which a court either has or might have awarded the claimant in an action against him for the loss in question, if that amount has been limited either by an enactment or a prior agreement or by virtue of section 1 of the Contributory Negligence Act. As far as prior agreement is concerned, it should be borne in mind that a limitation clause or notice that has this effect will be subject to the Unfair Contract Terms Act 1977.[61] The reference to the Contributory Negligence Act can produce some odd effects, given that the Act does not apply to claims for breach of contract (other than those overlapping with the tort of negligence).[62] Consider, for example, the common situation in which liability for damage caused by a defective product is passed back up the chain of supply. If the retailer is sued for breach of contract, any contributory negligence on the part of the claimant will not be taken into account. Should the retailer then seek contribution from the manufacturer, he will find that the manufacturer's responsibility will be limited. For any action by the claimant against the manufacturer would have been in tort and not contract, the latter could have invoked the defence of contributory negligence to limit his liability, and this reduced sum will set the limit to any contribution he will be required to pay under the Contribution Act.

In practice, difficult issues of causation and attribution of responsibility may arise in cases involving multiple tortfeasors. The principle of contribution may be applied only to that part of the claimant's loss which forms a 'single and indivisible injury'.[63] As we have seen, in respect of such damage, the claimant may go against any one of the

[60] [1989] AC 328. [61] See above, ch. 24, section 2.

[62] *Forsikringsaktieselskapet Vesta* v. *Butcher* [1989] AC 852 (CA).

[63] *Dingle* v. *Associated Newspapers Ltd.* [1961] 2 QB 162, 188–9 (Diplock LJ); *Rahman* v. *Arearose Ltd.* [2001] QB 351, 361 (Laws LJ).

tortfeasors for the full extent of the loss. This is not permissible if the claimant's losses can be broken down into individual parts, each of which can be shown to have been caused by an independent tort. It follows that where only some of the potential tortfeasors are before the court, the way in which the court approaches the issue of causation will significantly affect the extent to which the claimant can recover.

A recent example of the complexity of the apportionment process in cases where multiple tortfeasors are before the court is *Rahman* v. *Arearose Ltd.*[64] The claimant, the manager of a fast-food chain run by D1, was assaulted at work by two youths, as a result of which he sustained an injury to one of his eyes. As a result of medical negligence committed by D2 in the course of an operation, he subsequently lost the sight in his eye entirely. He suffered post-traumatic stress disorder and depression. The judge held that D1 was not liable for the complete loss of the eye but that D2's negligence did not completely break the chain of causation, so that D1 was liable on a continuing basis for part of the claimant's loss. After assessing the damages for which each defendant was separately liable, the judge held D2 was three-quarters to blame for the claimant's psychiatric condition and consequent inability to work and D1 one-quarter; he then increased D1's contribution to one-third to reflect its greater blameworthiness. The Court of Appeal reversed the decision of the judge on this final point, on the ground that D1's continuing responsibility had already been adequately taken into account by the ruling that D2's tort did not break the chain of causation. However, this seems to confuse the issue of causation (did both D1 and D2 contribute to the damage?) with the separate issue of the allocation of responsibility between concurrent tortfeasors, based on the degree to which they were each at fault.

Considerable complications have also arisen recently in cases involving liability for occupational diseases caused by exposure to asbestos. In *Holtby* v. *Brigham & Cowan (Hull) Ltd.*[65] the claimant contracted asbestosis while working as a fitter for the defendant employer. Liability was admitted. However, the court reduced the damages by 25 per cent on the basis of medical evidence to the effect that only part of the claimant's condition was attributable to the defendant's tort. The claimant had inhaled asbestos dust while working for other employers in the same industry prior to being employed by the defendant. The decision is explicable only on the basis that the claimant's condition was not 'single and indivisible'. Asbestosis is a cumulative condition, which is made worse by prolonged and repeated exposure. As a result, the defendant was liable only for the *additional* damage which he caused.

What is not completely clear from the judgment of the Court of Appeal in *Holtby* is where the burden of proof should lie when only one of a number of potential defendants is before the court. The majority (Stuart Smith and Mummery LJJ) thought that the burden of showing causation rests on the claimant throughout; Clarke LJ thought that once the claimant has shown that the defendant's breach has made 'a material contribution to his condition, he is entitled to judgment unless the defendant proves that

[64] [2001] QB 351. [65] [2000] 3 All ER 421.

a definable part of his condition was caused either by "innocent" asbestos or by "guilty" asbestos caused by others'.[66] This view seems correct: once an initial causal link is made out, the burden of showing that the damage is not 'single and indivisible' should rest with the defendant. On its particular facts, *Holtby* can be understood as a case in which the medical evidence led by the defendant prevented the claimant from establishing causation in respect of the whole of his loss.

In contrast to asbestosis, mesothelioma is not a cumulative condition; it can be contracted by exposure to a single fibre of asbestos. In *Fairchild* v. *Glenhaven Funeral Services Ltd.*[67] the House of Lords held that where the claimant had been negligently exposed to asbestos dust by several successive employers, liability could be established where it could be shown that each one had materially increased the risk of him contracting mesothelioma, even if, on the balance of probabilities, it could not be shown which of the employers had been responsible for the particular exposure or exposures which had caused the disease. The issue of apportionment between employers held liable under Fairchild came before the House in *Barker* v. *Corus UK Ltd.*[68] Lord Hoffmann, giving the leading judgment, accepted that where damage was indivisible, the normal principle of joint liability applied. However, he argued that the damage in this case was not indivisible. *Fairchild* had, he said, established a novel principle of liability not for physical harm as such, but for increased exposure to risk, under circumstances where fairness dictated a departure from normal principles of causation. However, fairness also dictated that, where apportionment was concerned, the liability of the employers should be proportionate, that is, linked to the intensity and duration of the exposure for which they were responsible:

> The justification for the joint and several liability rule is that if you caused harm, there is no reason why your liability should be reduced because someone else also caused the same harm. But when liability is exceptionally imposed because you may have caused harm, the same considerations do not apply and fairness suggests that if more than one person may have been responsible, liability should be divided according to the probability that one or other caused the harm.[69]

Lord Hoffmann's reading of *Fairchild* is highly contentious, as Lord Rodger pointed out in his dissent.[70] The implications of the majority position in *Barker* were also highly onerous for claimants. In cases where some of the defendants were insolvent, they would be unable to obtain full compensation. In addition, and most tellingly, before the liability of any single employer could be established, they would have to track down all potential tortfeasors, and ascertain the extent of the exposure for which they were responsible. These considerations led Parliament to enact section 3 of the Compensation Act 2006, almost immediately restoring the rule of joint liability in mesothelioma cases. This curtailed the effect of *Barker* in the one area—liability for mesothelioma under the

66 *Ibid.*, at 432. As in other contexts within tort law, much turns here on the precise meaning of the claimant's 'damage'.

67 [2003] 1 AC 32.

68 [2006] 2 WLR 1027.

69 [2006] 2 WLR 1027, 1042.

70 See, in particular, his judgment *ibid.*, 1050–8.

so-called *Fairchild* exception—where it clearly applied. Whether it will have any more extensive application remains to be seen. There is much to be said for the normal rule, even in cases where, as in *Fairchild*, the normal 'but-for' test of causation is modified. It is not clear that 'fairness', as Lord Hoffmann put it, dictates a rule of proportionate liability here; on the contrary, this rule would have the effect of chilling large numbers of potential claims, for the reasons just discussed.

(D) INDEMNITY

It remains possible to obtain an indemnity separately from the Contribution Act. Agreements for indemnity, such as liability insurance, are common. Such contracts are lawful if the aim is to indemnify the wrongdoer against the consequences of his own carelessness,[71] although not if they seek to indemnify him against intentional wrongdoing unless this was induced by the fraud of another or the act was not obviously wrong.[72] An example of an implied right to indemnity arises in the context of the employment relationship. In *Lister* v. *Romford Ice and Cold Storage Co. Ltd.*[73] the House of Lords held that an employer who is made vicariously liable for a tort committed by an employee in the course of his employment can recover an indemnity from the employee by virtue of a term implied into the contract of employment. The decision flatly contradicts most of the purported justifications for imposing vicarious liability on the employer—for example, the arguments that the employer's 'deep pockets' enable it to bear the costs and spread the risk of liability more effectively and that the employer, as the party who takes the profits from the enterprise, should also bear liability for certain risks arising from its operation. In practice the pressure to recover this indemnity will come, if at all, from the employer's liability insurer who will be subrogated to any claim the employer will have against the employee. As a result of a 'gentlemen's agreement' the insurance companies almost invariably do not pursue their subrogation rights to an indemnity against the employee, as *Lister* would allow them to do.

(E) SECONDARY CIVIL LIABILITY

The English law of tort apparently does not contain a general principle of secondary civil liability, that is to say liability as an accessory to the commission of a civil wrong on a par with the equivalent and well-recognised principle in the criminal law. The existence of such liability, separate from the established categories of joint tortfeasors and liability for the active inducement or procurement of wrongful acts such as is found in the economic torts,[74] has been viewed with scepticism by both the Court of

[71] See *Hardy* v. *Motor Insurers' Bureau* [1964] 2 QB 745, *Gardner* v. *Moore* [1984] AC 548. Intention was stretched to include gross negligence in *Askey* v. *Golden Wine Co. Ltd.* [1948] 2 All ER 35, but in *Tiline* v. *White Cross Insurance Association Ltd.* [1921] 3 KB 327 a motorist found guilty of manslaughter on the basis of 'criminal negligence' was able to recover an indemnity under his liability insurance policy.

[72] *W. H. Smith & Son* v. *Clinton* (1908) 99 LT 840, 841.

[73] [1957] AC 555, *Morris* v. *Ford Motor Co. Ltd.* [1973] QB 792; see above, ch. 18.

[74] See ch. 15, above.

Appeal[75] and the House of Lords.[76] Glanville Williams considered that the criminal-law definition of an accessory could be 'used in tort to indicate a joint tortfeasor';[77] by contrast, Lord Woolf MR has said that 'to seek to draw analogy between the criminal and civil law in this area is unhelpful'.[78]

There is nevertheless some academic support for the existence of a wider principle of secondary civil liability, distinct from the concept of joint torts which has tended to be obscured by the modern-day division of obligations law between contract, tort and equity. Philip Sales has argued that there are two main principles that emerge from the cases. First, liability may be imposed on a person who induces or procures the commission of a civil wrong against the claimant by a third party. Second, liability may be imposed on a person who assists a third party to commit a civil wrong against the claimant. There is a substantial body of authority in support of the first of these principles, and in support of its general applicability throughout the civil law. The second principle is less well recognised, but is also supported by authority in particular areas and should be accepted as a principle of general application along with the first.[79] The first category of cases referred to by Sales contains examples of liability which are familiar and not particularly controversial: these consist of the economic torts of inducing breach of contract;[80] inducing breach of fiduciary duty;[81] and inducing breach of statutory duty;[82] and the principle of liability as a joint tortfeasor for authorising or joining in the tortious act of another.[83]

The second category is much more contentious. Here Sales refers to the well-established liability for knowing assistance in a dishonest breach of trust[84] and to cases in which the notion of joint torts has been extended to cover assistance in the commission of a tort.[85] There is no clear authority, however, for a tort of assisting in a breach of contract (or a breach of statutory duty); nevertheless, it is argued that the dividing line between inducing a third party to commit a wrong and assisting in its commission is so fine as to be non-existent. Often the offering of assistance is itself an inducement to the third party to act wrongfully. Moreover, the connection between the loss suffered by the claimant and the assistance provided to the third-party wrongdoer by the defendant may be as strong as that between the loss and the wrong committed by the third party.[86]

75 *CBS Songs Ltd.* v. *Amstrad Consumer Electronics plc* [1986] FSR 159, 212 (Slade LJ).

76 *Crédit Lyonnais Bank Nederland NV* v. *Export Credit Guarantee Department* [2000] 1 AC 486.

77 *Joint Torts and Contributory Negligence* (1951), at 11.

78 *Crédit Lyonnais Bank Nederland NV* v. *Export Credit Guarantee Department* [2000] 1 AC 486, 500.

79 'The Tort of Conspiracy and Civil Secondary Liability' (Select Bibliography), 503.

80 *Lumley* v. *Gye* (1853) 2 El. & Bl. 216; 118 ER 749.

81 *Midgley* v. *Midgley* [1893] 3 Ch. 282.

82 *Meade* v. *Haringey LBC* [1979] 1 WLR 637.

83 See Williams, *Joint Torts and Contributory Negligence* (Select Bibliography), at 9–16. Sales adds a third category of procuring a contempt of court: *Seaward* v. *Paterson* [1897] 1 Ch. 545. As he says, this could be regarded as quasi-criminal in nature, although he is prepared to argue that 'such secondary liability is a product of the common law which arises out of the civil obligations of the principal contemnor, which are reinforced but are not extended by the order of the court': 'The Tort of Conspiracy' (Select Bibliography), at 505.

84 *Barnes* v. *Addy* (1874) LR 9 Ch. App. 244.

85 [1990] *CLJ* 491, 508.

86 *Ibid.*, 507–8.

What is proposed here is a unifying principle of liability[87] which, in the context of the law of tort, would involve at the very least a clarification and more probably an extension of the category of joint tortfeasors; it would also involve taking another look at the economic torts.[88] A contrary view is taken by Tony Weir and stresses the limits of the economic torts. The correct distinction in the tort of inducing breach of contract is 'between getting a man not to perform his contract and causing him not to',[89] there being no liability in the second case unless unlawful means are used and the defendant aimed to injure the claimant. It seems likely that this difficult area will continue to receive the attention of the courts and that academic writings will inform the approach of the practising Bar and of the Bench.

SELECT BIBLIOGRAPHY

Atiyah, P. S., 'Causation, Contributory Negligence and *Volenti Non Fit Injuria*' (1965) 43 *Can. BR* 609.

Gregory, C. O., 'Contribution among Joint Tortfeasors: A Defence' (1941) 54 *Harv. LR* 1170.

James, F., 'Contribution among Joint Tortfeasors: A Pragmatic Criticism' (1941) 54 *Harv. LR* 1156.

—'Replication' (1941) 54 *Harv. LR* 1178.

Sales, P., 'The Tort of Conspiracy and Secondary Civil Liability' [1990] *CLJ* 491.

Williams, G. L., *Joint Torts and Contributory Negligence* (1951).

[87] The case for the existence of this principle is made by D. Cooper, 'Secondary Liability in Civil Wrongs', Ph.D. Thesis, University of Cambridge, 1995.

[88] See above, ch. 15.

[89] *Casebook on Tort* (8th edn., 1996), at 609. See also the 10th edn. (2004), at 591 ('to cause an involuntary breach of contract is not wrongful in itself') and T. Weir, *Economic Torts* (1997), at 38. Weir's view on this question has since been vindicated by the ruling of the House of Lords in the recent trilogy of economic tort cases (*OBG Ltd.* v. *Allan*; *Douglas* v. *Hello! Ltd.*; *Mainstream Properties Ltd.* v. *Young* [2007] UKHL 21).

INDEX

abatement
  private nuisance 548–50
  statutory nuisance 563
accidents
  access to the law 98–100
  alternative compensation systems 6, 58–71
  Coase Theorem 38–40
  economic analysis of tort 41–2
  witnesses 146–50
accountants
  duty of care 215
acts
  conceptual elements 117–18
  duty of care 199–204
  occupier's liability 351
  role of policy 30–5
  US approach to x-crimes litigation 314–23
acts of God
  meaning 926
  Rylands v. *Fletcher* 620
affirmative duties
  acts and omissions 199–204
  employer's liability 698–9
  tort and contract compared 20
aggravated damages 942–4
airspace 496
alternative systems of compensation
  compensation orders 66–8
  Criminal Injuries Compensation Scheme 62–6
  insurance 62, 70–1, 954–6
  methods of compensation 58–61
  Motor Insurers' Bureau 68–9
  role of State 62
  special *ex gratia* payment schemes 69
  tort claims 62
ambulance service
  duty to rescue 201
amenities
  compensation for loss 1001–3
anaesthetists
  standard of care 232
animals
  dangerous species 636–8
  dogs 644–5, 646–7
  duty of care 632
  non-dangerous 638–44
  origins of special rules 631–4
  straying livestock 634–6
  trespass to land 496
apportionment
  contributory negligence 899–901
  multiple defendants 1034–40
arbitrators
  immunity 213–15
architects
  duty of care 184
armed forces
  duty of care 216–17
assault
  development of liability in tort 397–9
  growing influence of human rights 100–7
  meaning 453
  vicarious liability 690–2
assumption of risk. *see* consent
assumption of responsibility
  negligent misstatements 160–72
  secondary victims 150–2
auditors
  negligent misstatements 165–8

battery
  consent 455–7, 914
  development of liability in tort 397–9
  growing influence of human rights 100–7
  meaning 454–5
  necessity for medical treatment 457–9
  self-defence 462
bereavement
  compensation 1004–5
  secondary victims 142–3
  standing of dependants 1010–15
Bolam test
  professional standard of care 232–5
breach of statutory duty
  availability of civil remedy 383–8
  'but-for' test 391–3
  causation 391–3
  Community law 395
  contributory negligence 391–2, 901–3
  damage contemplated by Statute 389–91
  economic loss 393–5
  employers 662
  exclusion clauses 393
  nature and scope 377–83
  protected persons 389–91
  public authorities 412–14, 426
  restrictions on civil liability 393–5
  standard of care 389–91
bright line rule
  relational economic loss to property 185–6
  US approach 300–2
brokers. *see* insurance brokers
builders
  escape 'into' tort from contract 22–7
  occupier's liability 371–4
  occupier's liability for independent contractors 359–62
  product liability 730–1
buildings
  economic loss 180–5
  US approach to economic loss 298–300
burden of proof
  access to the law 98–100
  alternative explanations of events 249–52
  'but-for' test 246–7
  contributions and apportionment 1040
  defamation 774, 783–4
  misfeasance in public office 427–9
  multiple defendants 252–4
  negligence generally 241–3
  product liability 718–9, 727, 730–1

burden of proof (*cont.*)
public nuisance 555–6
punitive damages 949–51
res ipsa loquitur 241–4
US approach to defamation 877–8
'but-for' test
alternative explanations of events 249–52
breach of statutory duty 391–3
burden of proof 246–7
causation 244–9
exclusion clauses 918
exposure to risk as causal link basis 254–7
indeterminate cause 252–4
loss of chance 261–5
multiple defendants 252–4
probabilistic cause 249–52
product liability 740–1
relaxation 323–4
standard of proof 249
supervening or overtaking events 257–61
US approach 324–5

carelessness
contributory negligence 897–9
deceit 567–8
negligence distinguished 114
carers' expenses 994–8
carriage of goods
relational economic loss to property 185–6
causation
academic importance 82–7
acts of the claimant 268–71
alternative explanations of events 249–52
alternative systems of compensation 58–71
breach of statutory duty 391–3
conceptual elements 120–22
contributions and apportionment 1040
contributory negligence 892–7
death as cause of action 1008–10
deceit 568–9
deduction of non-statutory benefits from compensation 956–61
economic loss 277–9
'eggshell skull' rule 276–7
extent of damage 274–6
foreseeability 247–8
illegality 922–6
multiple defendants 252–4
product liability 740–1
role of policy 30–5
sequence of events 274–6
supervening or overtaking events 257–61
third-party interventions 266–8
two-stage analysis 244–9
US problems with compensation 324–7
US quest for conceptual clarity 286–90
x-crimes litigation 311–13
chattels
assessment of compensation 1019–25
conversion of goods 486–91
negligence 492
Rylands v. *Fletcher* 621
trespass to goods 483–5
children
see also unborn children
contributory negligence 901
duty of care 205
occupiers duty of care 351
occupiers standard of care 351–4
standard of care 229–30
standing for death claims 1010–11
class actions 99
Coase Theorem
economic analysis of tort 38–40
coastguards
duty to rescue 201
common employment doctrine
assumption of risk 907
breach of statutory duty 382
employer's liability 652
compensation
see also measure of damages
access to the law 98–100
alternative compensation systems 954–6
alternative systems 58–71
apportionment 899–901
assessment concept of damages 999–1000, 1015–17
benefits not covered by statutory scheme 956–61
benefits subject to statutory scheme 962–4
benevolent donations 960–1
bereavement damages 1004–5
carers' expenses 994–8
classification by duty of care 116–17
contemptuous and aggravated damages 942–4
conversion of goods 490–1
culture 6–10
death 1006–19
deceit 568–9
deduction of non-statutory benefits 956–61
defamation 784–5, 806–10
dependants' claims 1008–19
disfigurement 1005
duty to mitigate 975–6
economic analysis of tort 41–2
fault-based liability 55–7
functions of tort 49–54
general and special damages 941
general principles 951–4
in lieu of injunctions 1032
insurance moneys 957–60
interim damages 968
itemisation of awards 976–8
life expectancy, reduction of 998–9
local authority payments 961
loss of amenities 1001–3
loss of chance 261–5
loss of congenial employment 1005–6
loss of earnings 979, 990–2
loss of marriage prospects 1005
lump sums 965–6
market share approach in US 324
medical expenses 978–85, 992–4
mitigation of loss 975–6
modern trends 3–16
nominal and substantial damages 942
non-pecuniary losses 999–1006
orders 66–8, 566–8
pain and suffering 1001
payments made by local authorities 961
periodic and reviewable payments 973–5
postponed or split trials 967–8
problems of approach 93–7
product liability 720
property damage 1019–25
prospective losses 986–94

provisional damages 968–70
psychiatric injury 1006
punitive damages 944–51
reduction of expectation of life 998–9
schemes 62–6, 69
scope 939–40
social security benefits 962–4
structured settlements 970–3
supervening or overtaking events 257–61
third party assistance to claimant 980–3, 994–8
third party payments 956–64
ultra vires acts 426
unjust enrichment 956
US problems with causation 323–33
complex structure theory
defective buildings 180–5
concepts
causation 120–3
conduct 117–18
damage 120–3
duty of care 116–18, 118–20
foreseeability 118–20
limitations 123–4
negligence 113–16
privacy 836–52
US quest for clarity 286–90
concurrent liability. *see* multiple defendants
confidentiality agreements 840–1
consent
assumption of risk 906–9
battery 455–7, 914
breach of statutory duty 382
defamation 782–3
dogs 646–7
exclusion clauses distinguished 914–5
false imprisonment 466–7
negligence 905–14
non-dangerous animals 644
occupier's liability 355
private nuisance 542
Rylands v. *Fletcher* 619
scope 910–14
straying livestock 636
strict liability 913
tort and contract compared 17–18
trespass to land 504, 505
consideration
escape 'into' tort from contract 22–7
conspiracy
industrial action 598–601
to injure 596–7
unlawful means 597–8
consulting engineers
duty of care 184
'consumer expectation' test
product liability 712–4, 716, 719–20, 732–6
consumer protection. *see* product liability
contempt of court
interference with trade or business 594–5
contemptuous damages 942–4
contingency fees 6
contraceptives
compensation culture 6–7, 9
duty of care to third parties 177–80
contracts
'bare' interference with performance 582–5
concurrent limitations 932–9
contributory negligence 904–5
emphasis on privity 14–15
escape 'into' tort from contract 22–7
escape 'out of' contract into tort 27–9
indirect interference 581–2
inducing breach 576–80
interference with trade or business 590–1
overlapping duties in tort 189–95
product liability 704–8
reducing value of contractual rights 585
remoteness in tort compared 279–80
tort compared 17–22
contributions
employees 693–5
multiple defendants 1034–40
contributory negligence
acts of the claimant 268–71
apportionment 899–901
breach of statutory duty 391–2, 901–3
causation 892–7
claimant's fault 897–9
contributions distinguished 1037–8
deceit 568–9
derivative actions 901
dogs 646–7
non-dangerous animals 644
private nuisance 542
product liability 740–1
public policy 248
Rylands v. *Fletcher* 621–2
scope 892, 901–5
straying livestock 636
control test
employees and independent contractors distinguished 668–70
conversion of goods
contributory negligence 902–3
scope 486–92
strict liability 487
Criminal Injuries Compensation Board
alternative systems of compensation 62–6
criminality
see also illegality
breaches of statutory duty 386–7
conspiracy 597–8
double process for battery 454–5
economic torts 573–4
interference with trade or business 592–3
intrusions of privacy 834–5
public nuisance 550–3
slander actionable *per se* 758–9
US comparisons between negligence and intentional torts 333–4
Crown
development of liability in tort 397–8
liability in tort 434–5
Crown Prosecution Service
immunity 214–5

damage
breach of confidence 836–42, 861
conceptual elements 120–3
contemplated by Statute for breach of duty 389–91
contributory negligence 901–5
deceit 568–9
economic loss 157–99
foreseeability as the main test 271–4
product liability 727
property 138

damage (*cont.*)
remoteness 276–8
remoteness in contract and tort compared 279–80
role of policy 30–5
scope of physical harm 138–57
US approach to economic loss 293–300
damages. *see* compensation
dangerous species 636–8
data protection 825
death
assessment of award 1015–17
as cause of action 1008–19
deductions from compensation 1017–19
standing of dependants 1008–15
survival of cause of action 1006–8
deceit
carelessness 567–8
causation 568–9
compensation 569–70
damage 569
defences 595–6
defendant's state of mind 567–8
economic duress 595
false statement 565–6
interference with trade or business 586–8
limitations 929–30
requirements 565
statements of fact 566–7
vicarious liability 688–90
defamation
absolute privilege 791–4
apologies 811
claimant's bad reputation 811–13
compensation 806–10
conclusions 813–16
consent 782–3
damages, level of 806–10
defamatory allegations 759–66
executive privilege 794
fair comment 785–90
judicial privilege 792–3
jury awards 806–10
justification 783–5
libel actionable *per se* 758
libel and slander distinguished 756–9
meaning 753–6
mitigation of damage 811–13
offer of amends 779–82
parliamentary privilege 791–2
publication 772–9
qualified privilege 794–806
references to claimant 766–72
slander actionable *per se* 758–9
unintentional 779–82
US approach to burden of proof 877–8
US approach to fair comment 878–9
US comparisons 865–9
US law in practice 880–3
US public figures 872–3
US public officials 869–71
US restraints on private claimants 873–7
defective premises
builders 371–4
liability for nuisance 539
limitations on duty of care 197
occupier's liability 369–70
product liability 730–1
statutory nuisance 562–3
defences
see also under specific headings
act of God 996
animals 644–5
consent 455–8, 461, 505, 906–14
contributory negligence 892–905
in defamation 779–90
dogs 646–7
exclusion clauses 914–22
ignorance 539
illegality 922–6
inevitable accident 539, 926–7
jus tertii 490, 500–1
limitations 927–37
necessity 458, 459–60, 461, 505–6, 926
prescription 539
in private nuisance 539–44
in product liability 738–40
in public law 431–4
right of distress 490
role in tort 891
Rylands v Fletcher 619–20
statutory authority 458–9, 927
to trespass to goods 486–7
to trespass to land 504–6
degrading treatment
duty of care 136–7
dependants
deductions from compensation 1017–19
standing for death claims 1008–15
deterrence
deceit 568–9
functions of tort 49–54
product liability 720, 722–3
punitive damages 944
'development risks' defence
product liability 738–40
distress
conversion of goods 490
distress damage feasant
trespass to land 503
distributors
product liability 723–30
doctors 219–20
dogs
duty of care 644–5, 646–7
livestock 646–7
duty of care
see also standard of care
accountants 215
acts and omissions 199–204
acts of the claimant 268–71
alternative systems of compensation 58–71
animals 632
architects 184
armed forces 216–7
children 205
conceptual elements 117–18, 120–3
conceptual structure 116–118, 118–20
contributory negligence 892–7
dogs 644–5, 646–7
economic loss 157–98
escape 'into' tort from contract 22–7
exclusion clauses 918
government negligence 399–405
Hand formula 235–6
human rights impact 132–87
insurance considerations 195–7
judges and arbitrators 213–5
landowners 206–7
nuisance 513–20
occupier's liability 351
overlapping duties in tort 189–95
parents 205
precautions 204
prisons 205–6
product liability 180–5, 736–8
proof 241–3

psychiatric harm 138–57
public authorities 208–13
public law limitations 414–15
regulatory bodies 215–16
relationship between risk and foreseeability 236–8
rescuers 219–220
revision of the traditional US model 290–3
role of policy 305
schools 205
scope 125–7, 223–6
service performance 172–80
solicitors 214, 215
statutory framework for public authorities 415–8
statutory protection for economic loss 197–8
surveyors 184, 215
third-party acts 205–7
third-party property 185–9
three-stage test 127–32
tort and contract compared 20
trespassers 366–8
unborn children 217–19
US quest for conceptual clarity 286–90
warnings 203–4
dyslexia
failure to diagnose 422–3

economic loss
academic importance 82–4
assumption of responsibility 150–2, 160–72
breaches of statutory duty 393–5
buildings 180–5
causation 277–9
concurrent limitations in tort and contract 932–6
damages 157–99
employer's liability 656–7
escape 'into' tort from contract 22–7
exclusionary rule 157–60
formulation of duty of care 127–32
government negligence 399–405
insurance considerations 195–7
loss of earnings 979–80
negligent misstatements 160–172
overlapping duties in contract and tort 189–95
product liability 180–5, 742–4
remoteness 277–9
remoteness in contract and tort compared 279–80
scope of the duty of care 116–18
service performance 172–80
statutory protection 197–8
summary and conclusion 198–9
third-party property 185–9
tort and contract compared 17–22
trespass to land 501–3
US approach 293–302
economic torts
'bare' interference with performance 582–5
conspiracy 596–8
defences 595
duress 595
framework 571–5
future developments 602–3
indirect interference with contacts 581–2
inducing breach of contract 575–80
inducing breach of fiduciary duty 585
inducing breach of statutory duty 585–6
interference with contracts 580–5
interference with trade or business 586–95
trade dispute immunity 598–601
educational malpractice 422–3
efficiency
economic analysis of tort 42–4
'eggshell skull' rule
remoteness 276–7
ejectment
trespass to land 500–1
emotional harm. *see* psychiatric harm
employees
see also vicarious liability
contributions 693–5
exclusion clauses 919–20
harassment 692–3
independent contractors 574–6
inducing breach of contract 575–6
occupier's liability 346–51
overlapping duties in contract 189–95
public policy 248
secondary victims 155–7
US approach to psychiatric harm 302–7
employer's liability
see also vicarious liability
additional affirmative duties 698–9
adequate materials 659–60, 653
assumption of risk 906–9
common employment doctrine 652
competent staff 653, 659
defective equipment 657–8
delegation to third parties 657
economic loss 656–7
employment defined 649
expansion of non-delegable duties 697
extension of employee status 698
extension of liability 698–9
harassment 692–3
independent contractors 657, 695–6
integration of personal duties 700–1
physical harm 653–4
proper systems 661–2, 653
psychiatric harm 653–6
safe place of work 660–1, 653
scope 649
social security benefits 650–1
statutory duties 662
tort liability 651–2
engineers, consulting 184
environmental protection
private nuisance 559–62
public nuisance 559–60
statutory nuisance 562–3
European Community
breaches of statutory duty 395
environmental protection 561–2
obligations, breach of 586
product liability 714–9, 727–8, 738–40
public authority liability 435–8
exclusion clauses
borrowed employees 674–7
breach of statutory duty 393
'but-for' test 918
consent distinguished 914–5
deceit 568–9
defences 914–22

exclusion clauses (*cont.*)
escape 'into' tort from contract 22–7
negligent misstatements 169–70
occupier's liability 356–9
overlapping duties in contract and tort 192–3
product liability 724, 744–5
subcontractors 920–2
third parties 920–2
unfair contracts 915–22
exclusionary rule
economic loss 157–60
relational economic loss to property 185–9
executive privilege 794
exemplary damages. *see* punitive damages
externalities
economic analysis of tort 41–2

fair comment 785–90
fair just and reasonable
negligent service performance 172–80
three-stage test of duty of care 127–32
fair trial
duty of care 132–7
false imprisonment
confinement 463–6
consent 466–7
defences 468
development of liability in tort 395–6
growing influence of human rights 107–8, 463–4, 468
justification and necessity 467–71
lawful arrest 467–9
meaning 462–6
necessity 468
false statements 565–6
family
carers' expenses 994–8
defamation 773
secondary victims of psychiatric harm 150–2
standing for death claims 1008–15
US approach to psychiatric harm 302–7
fault. *see* intention; malice; negligence; recklessness

fencing
straying livestock 634–6
fiduciary relationships
inducing breach of duty 585
fire services
duty to rescue 152, 201–3
foetuses. *see* unborn children
foreseeability
causation 247–8
conceptual elements 118–20
deceit 569
extent of damage 271–4
misfeasance in public office 427–9
private nuisance 526–8
product liability 738–40
relationship with risk 236–8
rescuers 267–8
Rylands v. *Fletcher* 617–8
secondary victims of psychiatric harm 150–2
sequence of events 274–6
third-party interventions 266–8
three-stage test of duty of care 127–32
fraud. *see* deceit
freedom of expression
compensation for defamation 814
conflict with privacy 855–9
publication in public interest 795–6
US approach 869, 883
US comparisons 869–71

general damages 941
governing law
product liability 744–5
government
Crown proceedings 434–5
development of liability in tort 397–8
human rights 438–45
liability issues 216, 445–7
punitive damages 944–51
special treatment for negligence 399–405
guard dogs 644–5

Hand formula
breach of duty of care 235–6
economic analysis of tort 42–4
standard of care 224–5
harassment 471–4

health and safety at work
see also employer's liability
breaches of statutory duty 383–8
Community law 438–45
fault-based liability 55–7
health authorities
duty of care 207
highways
public nuisance 554–6
straying livestock 634–6
trespass to land 497–8
human rights
cultural influences 6–10
data protection 825
defamation 795–6
duty of care 132–7
false imprisonment 463–4, 468–9
government negligence 399–405
growing influence 107–8
horizontality 101–2
impact on duty of care 132–7
medical treatment withdrawn 461
nuisance 518–20
privacy 820, 855–9
public authority liability 438–45
qualified protection from liability for public authorities 411–12
Rylands v. *Fletcher* 623
standing to sue for nuisance 530–5
statutory authority for nuisance 540–1
statutory regimes and Convention rights 519–20
trespass to land 498
vicarious liability 682–5
withdrawal of medical treatment 461

ignorance
private nuisance 539
illegality 922–6
immunities
see also statutory authority
arbitrators 213–15
armed forces 216–17
barristers 33, 213–14
Crown proceedings 33, 434–5
Crown Prosecution Service 214–15
diplomats 33

government liability 399–405
industrial action 598–601
judicial review 432–4
limitations 431–2
occupier's liability 361–10
Parliamentary privilege 791–2
police 213
public authorities 397–9
regulatory bodies 215–6
solicitors 213–15
trade dispute 598–601
trade unions 33
vicarious liability 677–8
impact rule
US approach to psychiatric harm 302–7
indemnities 1040
independent contractors
employees distinguished 666–77
employer's liability 657, 695–6
occupier's liability 359–62
indirect interference with contacts 581–2
inducement
breach of contract 575–80
breach of fiduciary duty 585
breach of statutory duty 585–6
secondary liability 1040–2
industrial action
conspiracy 598–601
inducing breach of contract 577–9
inducing breach of statutory duty 585–6
inevitable accident
meaning 926
private nuisance 539
injunctions
damages in lieu 1032
freedom of expression 855–9
interim 1031–2
mandatory 1030
private nuisance 544–8
prohibitory 1030
quia timet 1031
injure, conspiracy to 596–7
injurious falsehood 816–17
intrusions of privacy 852–4
US approach to privacy 883–8
innuendo
defamatory allegations 760–6
insurance
alternative systems of compensation 62, 70–1, 954–6
economic analysis of tort 45–9
effect on economic loss 195–7
functions of tort 50
indemnities 1040
occupier's liability for independent contractors 359–62
response to compensation culture 6–10
vicarious liability 694–5
insurance brokers
escape 'out of' contract into tort 28–9
intention
assault 453
battery 454–5
deceit 568–9
defamation 783–5
defences 455–62
false imprisonment 462–6
inducing breach of contract 577–9
interference with trade or business 586–8
physical harm 451–2
private nuisance 556–7
residuary trespass and harassment 471–3
role of policy 30–5
trespass to land 499
intentional interference 451–2
interference with chattels. *see* conversion; trespass to goods
interference with trade or business by unlawful means
breaches of contract 590–1
contempt of court 594–5
criminality 592–3
economic duress 594–5
fraud and misrepresentation 586–8
intention 586–8
justification 594–5
physical threats 586
statutory duty 593–4
unlawful means 588–90, 591, 593
interference with use or enjoyment of land. *see under* private nuisance
interim damages 968
interim injunctions 1031–2
internalisation
economic analysis of tort 41–2
joint liability. *see* multiple defendants
journalistic privilege 798–806
judges
immunity 213–5
outlook influencing judgment 75–82
judicial privilege 792–3
judicial review
procedural immunity for public authorities 432–4
juries
awards 806–10
compensation 977–8
defamation 806–8
defamatory allegations 766–8
differences in US culture 283–5
revision of the traditional US model 290–3
US quest for conceptual clarity 286–90
jurisdiction
tort and contract compared 20–1
jus tertii
conversion of goods 490
defence trespass to goods 485
justiciability
public authorities 418–5
schools 422–5
justification
defamation 783–5
false imprisonment 467–8
inducing breach of contract 580
interference with trade or business 594–5
Kaldor-Hicks efficiency
economic analysis of tort 42–4

land. *see* trespass to land
landlords
liability for nuisance 538
occupier's liability 368–71
landowners
see also occupier's liability
duty of care 206–7
product liability 730–1
latent damage
concurrent limitations in tort and contract 933–5
discoverability test 931–2
limitations 932–6
lawful visitors
occupier's liability 346–51

lawyers
  differences in US culture 284
liability
  role of policy 30–5
  tort and contract compared 17–22
  US approach to causation 324–7
libel
  intrusions of privacy 849–51
  slander distinguished 756–9
  US comparisons 851, 865–7
life expectancy 998
limitation clauses. *see* exclusion clauses
limitations
  accrual of cause of action 929–30
  conceptual elements 123–4
  concurrent duties in contract 932–6
  contributions and apportionment 1034–40
  defences 927–37
  discoverability test 931–2
  discretionary relief from normal rules 936–7
  duty of care 197
  general principles 926–7
  law reform 937
  private nuisance 539
  procedural effects 937
  procedural immunity for public authorities 431–4
  product liability 744–5
  public law 414–15
  tort and contract compared 20–1
  trespass to land 504–6
livestock
  dogs 646–7
  straying 634–6
  strict liability 634–6
local authorities
  breaches of statutory duty 384–5, 388, 391
  development of liability in tort 395–6
  duty of care 132–7, 207
  occupier's liability 374–5
  payments to disabled persons 961
  public policy and justiciability 418–25
  statutory nuisance 562–3
loss. *see* damage
loss of amenities 1001–3
loss of chance
  negligence generally 261–5
loss of earnings 979–80, 990–2
malice
  defamation 805–6
  defeating qualified privilege 805–6
  economic torts 571–5
  fair comment 790
  nuisance 528–9
  role of policy 30–5
malicious falsehood 816–7
  intrusions of privacy 849–51
  US approach to privacy 883–8
malicious prosecution
  failed prosecution 477–8
  malice 479
  reasonable and probable cause 478
  requirements 475
  scope of prosecution 476–7
mandatory injunctions 1030
manufacturers
  product liability 723–30
margin of appreciation
  duty of care 135
measure of damages
  loss of chance 262–5
  problems of approach 97–8
medical expenses
  accommodation 985
  aids and equipment 984–5
  housecare 980–3, 994–8
  management fees 985
  personal expenses 983
  travel costs 983–4
  treatment and therapies 980, 992–4
medical practitioners
  consent to treatment by 455–62
  withdrawal of treatment by 461
mental patients
  consent to medical treatment 458–9
  false imprisonment 463–4
mesne profits
  trespass to land 501–2
misfeasance. *see* acts
misfeasance in public office
  Community law 435–8
  public law remedies 427–9
misrepresentation
  concurrent limitations in tort and contract 935–6
  interference with trade or business 586–8
  product liability 725–6
mistakes
  immaterial in trespass 499
  negligence distinguished 227–9
mistreatment
  false imprisonment 470
mitigation of loss 975–6
Motor Insurers' Bureau 68–9
motor vehicles
  consent 910–11, 914–15
  damage repairs 1021–2
  standard of care 229–31
  vicarious liability 685–7
multiple defendants
  accessories 1040–2
  apportionment 1034–40
  burden of proof 252–4
  'but-for' test 252–4
  contributions 1034–40
  indemnities 1040
  joint and concurrent liability distinguished 1033
  occupiers 344–6
  private nuisance 542–3
  product liability 729–30
  successive actions 1033–4
  US approach to causation 327–33
  vicarious liability 693–5

necessity
  defence to medical treatment without consent 456–7
  scope 926
  trespass to land 504–6
negligence
  see also causation; contributory negligence; occupier's liability
  breach of statutory duty distinguished 377–83
  burden of proof 241–3
  carelessness 114
  chattels 492
  conceptual structure 113–6
  consent 905–14
  development of liability for public bodies 397–8
  functions of tort 47–9
  government 401–2
  growing influence of human rights 107–8
  human rights impact 445–7

mistakes distinguished 227–9
need for conceptual clarity 123–4
nuisance compared 517–19, 557–8
overlap with private nuisance 557–8
overlapping duties in contract 189–95
problems of approach 93–7
recognition of liability for public authorities 405–7
revision of the traditional US model 290–3
role of policy 30–5
special treatment for government 399–405
summary and conclusion 281–8
US controls on expansion 355–7
US quest for conceptual clarity 286–90

negligent misstatements
auditors 165–8
concurrent limitations in tort and contract 935–6
contributory negligence 901–3
economic loss 106–72
exclusion clauses 169–70
overlapping duties in contract 192
product liability 725–6, 742–3
reputation 123–4
secondary victims of psychiatric harm 155

neighbour principle
defined 118–20
negligent service performance 173
qualified protection from liability for public bodies 410

nervous shock. *see* psychiatric harm

no-duty-to-act rule
US approach to x-crimes litigation 314–23

noise
statutory nuisance 563

nominal damages 942

non dangerous animals 644

non-feasance. *see* omissions

Norsk decision
economic analysis 45–9
proximity 188–9
role of policy 36–7

novus actus interveniens
acts of the claimant 268–71
repeated defamation 775–7
third-party interventions 266–8

nuisance. *see* private nuisance; public nuisance
intrusions of privacy 834–5

occupiers
multiple defendants 344–6
standing to sue for nuisance 530–1

occupier's liability
see also Rylands v. *Fletcher*
builders 371–4
children 351–4
consent 355
exclusion clauses 356–9
independent contractors 359–62
landlords 346–71
lawful visitors 346–51
local authorities 374–5
nuisance 535–8
occupier defined 344–6
ramblers 363, 365–8
rights of way 363, 365–8
scope 343–4
standard of care 351–9
statutory negligence 341–3
trespassers 358–9, 363–8
unfair contracts 356–9
vendors 368–71
warnings 355–6

offensive trades
statutory nuisance 562–3

offer of amends
defamation 799–82

omissions
affirmative duties 199–204
conceptual elements 117–18
conversion of goods 487
defective premises 370
duty of care 199–204
formulation of duty of care 126–7
negligent misstatements 165
neighbouring land owners 558
nonfeasance 313–23
occupier's liability 351
US approach to x-crimes litigation 314–23

pain and suffering 1001

parents
see also children
duty of care 205

Pareto efficiency
economic analysis of tort 42–4

Parliamentary privilege 791–2

passing off 816
intrusions of privacy 835–6
US approach to privacy 883–8

periodic and reviewable payments 973–5

personal injury. *see* physical harm

physical harm
see also death
compensation for loss of amenities 1001–3
compensation for pain and suffering 1001
employer's liability 653–4
foreseeability as main test 271–4
intention 451–2
product liability 712–4, 742–3
provisional damages 968–70
psychiatric 138–57
residuary trespass and harassment 471–4
Rylands v. *Fletcher* 621–2
structured settlements 970–3

planning permission
no defence to nuisance 543–4
statutory nuisance 562–3

police
duty of care 133–4
false imprisonment 463, 464, 465
malicious prosecution 476–7
occupier's liability 348
public policy 213–15
secondary victims 156–7
secondary victims of psychiatric harm 151–2

policy. *see* public policy

Posner, R. A.
economic analysis of tort 42–4

postponed trials and settlement 967

pre-existing conditions
supervening or overtaking events 257–61
US approach to causation 331–3

precautions
duty of care 204

pregnancy. *see* unborn children

prerogative orders
government negligence 402

prescription
 private nuisance 539
prevention
 assessing risk and foreseeability 236–7
 compensation for defective buildings 180–5
 cost as a function of the standard of care 237–41
primary victims
 psychiatric harm 140–2
prisons
 duty of care 205–6
privacy
 appropriation of personality 835–6
 breach of, causing damage 840–1
 breach of, statutory duty 380–1
 compensation levels 837
 conceptual problems 836–52, 859–62
 confidence, breach of 841–2, 843
 confidentiality agreements 840
 confidentiality imposed 840–1
 definitional difficulties 820–5, 859–62
 detriment 844–5
 disclosure of private facts 836–42
 duty of care 136
 freedom of expression 850–1
 growing influence of human rights 107–8
 human rights 820, 824, 827, 840–1, 847, 848, 851, 855–9
 information in public domain 845–8
 intrusions 833–5
 nuisance 834
 obligations of confidence 839–40
 photography in public 847–8, 852–4
 public figures, officials and functions 849–52, 852–4
 public interest defences 849–50
 public places 847–8, 852
 scope 820–5
 sexual offences 826–7
 US approach 883–8
private nuisance
 abatement 548–50
 basis of liability 509–12
 character of neighbourhood 525–6
 Coase Theorem 38–40
 consent 542
 contributory negligence 542
 defences 539–44
 defined 509
 duration of interference with use or enjoyment 522–3
 environmental protection 559–62
 fault 526–8
 functions of tort 49–54
 growing influence of human rights 107–8
 injunctions 544–8
 interference with use or enjoyment of land 520–9
 intrusions of privacy 834–5
 malice 528–9
 material damage to property 512, 513–20
 overlap with trespass and negligence 556–8
 parties liable 535–8
 'principle of reasonable user' 509–12
 remedies 544–50
 Rylands v. *Fletcher* distinguished 623
 self-help 548–50
 sensitivity of claimant 524–5
 standing 530–5
 use or enjoyment of land 520–2
privity rule
 importance 14–15
 overlapping duties in contract and tort 193–4
 product liability 704–8, 723–30
producers
 product liability 728
product liability
 builders 730–1
 burden of proof 718–19, 727, 730–1
 'but-for' test 740–1
 causation 740–1
 Community law 714–19, 727–8, 738–40
 compensation 720
 conclusions 746–8
 'consumer expectation' test 712–4, 719–20, 732–6
 'consumers' 723–30
 contracts 704–8
 contributory negligence 740–1
 damage 727
 defences 738–40
 economic loss 180–5, 742–4
 employers 657–8
 escape 'into' tort from contract 22–7
 exclusion clauses 744–5
 foreseeability 740–1
 governing law 746
 limitations 745–6
 market share approach in US 324–5
 negligent misstatements 725–6, 742–3
 overlapping duties in contract 189
 parties to action 723–30
 physical harm 712–4, 742–3
 policy changes away from strict liability 719–23
 'products' covered 730–1
 psychiatric harm 744
 rejection of privity of contract 704–8
 remoteness 740–1
 sources 703–4
 standard of care 719–23, 732–6
 strict liability 710–13
 unfair contracts 744–5
 US approach to economic loss 298–300
 warnings 736–8
 warranties 708–10
professional persons
 standard of care 232–5
prohibitory injunctions 1030
proof. *see* burden of proof; duty of care; standard of proof
property damage
 assessment 1019–25
 defective buildings 180–5
 remoteness 276–7
 scope 138
proportionality
 duty of care 135
prospective losses
 future loss of earnings 990–2
 medical treatment and therapies 992–4
 multiplicand 987
 multiplier 987–90
 third parties assisting claimant's needs 994–8
protected claimants
 rescuers 219–20
 unborn children 217–19

protected persons 389–91
provisional damages 968–70
proximity
acts of the claimant 270
causation 245
negligent service performance 177–8
relational economic loss to property 188–9
secondary victims of psychiatric harm 145–52
three-stage test of duty of care 127–32
psychiatric harm
defined 139–40
duty of care 138–57
employer's liability 653–6
primary victims 140–2
product liability 744
secondary victims 140–1
US approach 302–7
public authorities
see also government; local authorities
breach of statutory duty 412–14, 426
Community law breaches 435–8
Crown proceedings 434–5
defences 431–4
development of liability in tort 397–8
duty of care 132–4, 208–13
duty to rescue 201
human rights 438–45, 519–20
immunity 431–4
justiciability 418–25
liability issues 445–7
misfeasance in public office 427–30
nuisance and statutory regimes 517–8
policy-operation distinction 407–12
prisons 205–6
privacy 856–7
procedural immunity 432–4
public policy 418–25, 519
recognition of common law liability 405–7
regulatory bodies 215–16, 519
statutory sources of liability 412–18
ultra vires acts 426
US defamation comparisons 869–71
public health
statutory nuisance 562–3
public law
defences 431–4
limitations on duty of care 414–15
policy-operation distinctions for public authority liability 407–12
public nuisance
abuses of the highway 550–4
breaches of statutory duty 385
burden of proof 555–6
criminality 550–3
defined 550
environmental protection 559–60, 562–3
functions of tort 49–54
growing influence of human rights 107
highways 554–6
negligence distinguished 551
private nuisance distinguished 550–4
reasonableness 554–5
statutory nuisances 562–3
public policy
causation 30–5, 248
compensation 958–9
consent to assisted suicide 461
consent to battery 914
consent to medical treatment 455–62
contributions from employees 693–5
contributory negligence 248
deceit 568–9
deduction of non-statutory benefits from compensation 956–61
duty of care 208–17
fair comment 785–90
government negligence 399–405
illegality 922–6
injunctions for nuisance 544–8
nuisance 513–20
occupier's liability for trespassers 363–8
police duty of care 212–13
public authorities 418–25
role in the law of tort 30–5
scope of duty of care 178–9
three-stage test of duty of care 127–32
United States 333–7
vicarious liability 679
punitive damages
burden of proof 949–51
defamation 806–10
defendant's profit motive 947–8
deterrence 944
double jeopardy 950
government servants 944–6
statutory authority 948
unjust enrichment 950–1
purchasers
product liability 723–30
putting people in fear of violence 473

qualified privilege 794–806
quia timet injunctions 1031

ramblers
occupier's liability 363, 365–8
reasonableness
exclusion clauses 917–18
hire costs 1022–3
medical expenses 980
negligent service performance 172
private nuisance 509–12
standard of care 227
three-stage test of duty of care 127–32
recklessness
role of policy 30–5
references
negligent misstatements 171–2
regulatory bodies
duty of care 215–16
relational economic los 185–6
relationships
exclusion clauses 919–20
occupiers 344–6
secondary victims 150–2
US approach to x-crimes litigation 314–23
reliance
negligent misstatements 160–72
product liability 184–5
rescue services 209
remoteness
contract and tort compared 279–80
conversion of goods 490
deceit 568–9
economic loss 277–9

remoteness (*cont.*)
'eggshell skull' rule 276–7
foreseeability as the main test 271–4
loss of chance 261–5
product liability 740–1
property damage 276–7
third-party interventions 266–8
replevin
conversion of goods 492
reputation
claimant's bad 811–13
defamation 753–816
injurious falsehood 816
negligent misstatements 171–2
passing off 816
res ipsa loquitur
burden of proof 241–2
product liability 707–8, 731–2
rescuers
ambulance service 201
coastguards 201
doctors 219–20
duty of care 201–3, 219–20
fire service 152, 201–2
foreseeability 267–8
occupiers standard of care 355
US approach to x-crimes litigation 314–23
residuary trespass and harassment 471–4
restitutio in integrum
functions of tort 49–54
general principle of compensation 951–4
retailers
parties to action 723–30
product liability 723–30
rights of way
occupier's liability 363, 365–8
trespass to land 497–8
risk
consent to 906–9
relationship with foreseeability 236–8
'risk-utility' test
product liability 719–23
rivers
trespass to land 498
Rylands v. *Fletcher*
acts of God 620
chattels 621
claimant's act or default 620–2
consent 619
contributory negligence 621–2
developments in the modern environment 624–9
escape 611–13
foreseeability 617–8
human rights 623
'non-natural' use of land 614–7
observations on the general rule 607–10
physical harm 621–2
private nuisance distinguished 623
standing 623
statutory authority 619
third-party acts 619–20
voluntary accumulation 611–13
schools
duty of care 205, 422–3
overlapping duties in contract 191–2
public policy and justiciability 422–4
secondary liability 1040–2
secondary victims
see also protected claimants
bereavement 142–3
employees 155–7
known to claimant 150–5
liability generally 1040–2
psychiatric harm 139–57
relationship with primary victim 150–2
self-help and defence
battery 462
conversion of goods 491–2
private nuisance 548–50
trespass to land 502–4
services
economic loss 172–80
US approach to economic loss 293–6
sexual offences
privacy 826–7
vicarious liability 690–3
shock. *see* psychiatric harm
slander
actionable *per se* 758–9
libel distinguished 756–9
US comparisons 865–9
social security benefits
alternative systems of compensation 62
deduction from compensation 962–4
general principle of compensation 952
solicitors
duty of care to third parties 172–5
escape 'into' tort from contract 22–7
escape 'out of' contract into tort 27–9
immunity 214–215
overlapping duties in contract 189–95
special damages 941
standard of care
assessing the cost of prevention 238–41
breach of statutory duty 389–91
children 229–30
contributory negligence 897–91
inexperienced defendants 229–31
negligence 223–7
negligence distinguished from 'mere errors' 227–9
occupier's liability 351–9
private nuisance 526–8
product liability 719–23, 732–6
professional persons 232–5
reasonable man 227
scope 223–7
standard of proof
'but-for test' 249
loss of chance 261–5
negligence generally 241–3
supervening or overtaking events 257–61
standing
death as cause of action 1008–15
human rights 623
private nuisance 530–5
Rylands v. *Fletcher* 623
'state of the art' defence
product liability 738–40
statutory authorities. *see* local authorities; public authorities
statutory authority
false imprisonment 469–71
private nuisance 540–2
punitive damages 945
Rylands v. *Fletcher* 619
scope 927
statutory benefits 962–4
statutory duty
see also breach of statutory duty
inducing breach 525–6

interference with trade or business 593–4
product liability 738
statutory nuisance
defective premises 562–3
environmental protection 562–3
straying livestock 634–6
strict liability
see also Rylands v. *Fletcher*
consent 913
contributory negligence 903
conversion 487
dangerous animals 636–8
duty of care 225–6
private nuisance 526–8
product liability 710–13
straying livestock 634–6
strikes
conspiracy 598–601
inducing breach of contract 579–80
inducing breach of statutory duty 585–6
structured settlements 970–3
subcontractors
exclusion clauses 920–2
overlapping duties in contract 190–1
substantial damages 942
supervening or overtaking events
causation 257–61
compensation 257–61
pre-existing conditions 259–60
standard of proof 261
US approach to causation 259–60, 331–3
surveyors
see also valuers
duty of care 184, 215
susceptibility
secondary victims of psychiatric harm 145

theft
vicarious liability 687–8
third parties
carers' expenses 994–8
deduction of non-statutory benefits from compensation 960
defence to *Rylands* v. *Fletcher* 619–20
duty of care 205–7
employer's liability 654
escape 'into' tort from contract 22–7
exclusion clauses 920–2
interventions in causation 266–8
negligent service performance 172–80
relational economic loss to property 185–9
remoteness 266–8
Rylands v Fletcher 619–20
straying livestock 634–6
US approach to economic loss 296–7
x-crimes litigation 310
three stage test 127–32
tort
academic importance 82–7
access to the law 98–100
alternative compensation systems 6, 58–71
assault, liability developed in 397–9
battery, liability developed in 397–9
contract distinguished 17–22
Crown liability 397–8, 434–5
defences 891
difficulties of categorization 82–7
economic analysis 36–49
escape 'into' tort from contract 22–7
escape 'out of' contract into tort 27–9
fault-based liability 55–7
functions 49–54
general observations 107–8
growing influence of human rights 100–7
need for reform 93–7
old tools for new social needs 91–3
overlapping duties in contract 189–95
problems of approach 93–7
remoteness in contract compared 279–80
role of defences 891
role of policy 30–5
scope 1–16
transaction costs
Coase Theorem 38–40
trespass
development of liability in tort 397–9
trespass to goods or chattels 483–5
trespass to land
ab initio 499
animals, by 496
defences 500, 504–6
direct interference 495–8
distress damage feasant 503
ejectment 500
human rights 498
intention 499
mesne profits 501
mistake immaterial 499
overlap with private nuisance 556–8
self-help 502
US approach to privacy 883–8
trespass to person 471–4
intrusions of privacy 834–5, 835–6, 836–52
trespassers
occupier's liability 358–9, 363–8
private nuisance 539

ultra vires acts
Community law 435
government negligence 399–40
procedural immunity for public authorities 431–4
public law defences 431–4
public law remedies 426–7
unborn children
see also children
duty of care 217–19
unfair contracts
borrowed employees 674–7
exclusion clauses 915–22
occupier's liability 356–9
product liability 744–5
uninjured bystander rule
US approach to psychiatric harm 302–7
United States
breach of statutory duty 379
burden of proof in defamation 877–8
'but-for' test 324–5
causation and compensation 324–33
compensation culture 6–7, 9
conceptual clarity 286–90
contingency fees 6
controls on expansion of negligence 335–7
cost as a function of the standard of care 238

United States (*cont.*)
crimes and intentional harms 307–23
defamation and burden of proof 877–8
defamation and fair comment 878–9
defamation by public figures 872–3
defamation by public officials 869–71
defamation compared 865–9
defamation law in practice 880–3
defamation restraints on private claimants 873–7
differences in legal culture 283–5
drink-driving and social hosts 207
economic analysis of tort 36–71
economic loss 293–302
foreseeability 274–6
freedom of expression compared 869, 883, 865
juries 283–5, 290–3, 286–90
multiple defendants 252–4
need for conceptual clarity in negligence 123–4
negligence and intentional torts compared 333–4
pre-existing conditions 331–3
privacy 883–8
product liability 298–300, 704–9, 712–14, 716, 719–23, 732, 746–8
psychiatric harm 302–7
public policy 333–7
qualified protection from liability for public bodies 408
revision of the traditional duty of care model 290–3
Rylands v. *Fletcher* 609, 626, 628
standard of care 229–31
strict product liability 710–12
supervening or overtaking events 257–61
x-crimes litigation 314–23
unjust enrichment
general principle of compensation 953
punitive damages 950–1
users
product liability 723–30

valuers
assessment of compensation 1022–5
negligent misstatements 168–70
vendors
occupier's liability 368–71
product liability 723–30
vicarious liability
assault 690–2
borrowed employees 674–7
contributions from employee 693–5
deceit 688–90
drivers 685–7
effect on individual responsibility 14
employee defined 666–77
escape 'out of ' contract into tort 28
harassment 692–3
human rights 679
implied authority 680–2
'in the course of employment' 678–9
insurance 694–5
public policy 679
requirement for employee's tort 677–8
scope of employment 682–5
sexual assaults 690–3
sources 665–6
theft 687–8
victims
see also secondary victims
psychiatric harm 138–57
visitors
occupier's liability 346–51
standing to sue for nuisance 530–1
volenti non fit injuria. see consent

warnings
duty of care 203–4
occupier's liability 355–6
product liability 736–8
warranties
product liability 708–10
wills
duty of care to beneficiaries 173–4
escape 'into' tort from contract 24–5
witnesses
secondary victims of psychiatric harm 146–50
US approach to psychiatric harm 305

x-crimes litigation
causation 311–13
duty to mitigate risk 310
meaning 310–11
US approach 314–23

zone-of-danger rule
US approach to psychiatric harm 304